Com

MW00757503

Compact Oxford Russian Dictionary

Edited by
Della Thompson

OXFORD
UNIVERSITY PRESS

OXFORD
UNIVERSITY PRESS

Great Clarendon Street, Oxford, OX2 6DP,
United Kingdom

Oxford University Press is a department of the University of Oxford.
It furthers the University's objective of excellence in research, scholarship,
and education by publishing worldwide. Oxford is a registered trade mark of
Oxford University Press in the UK and in certain other countries

© Oxford University Press 2013

Database right Oxford University Press (makers)

First Edition published in 2013

Impression: 2

All rights reserved. No part of this publication may be reproduced, stored in
a retrieval system, or transmitted, in any form or by any means, without the
prior permission in writing of Oxford University Press, or as expressly permitted
by law, by licence or under terms agreed with the appropriate reprographics
rights organization. Enquiries concerning reproduction outside the scope of the
above should be sent to the Rights Department, Oxford University Press, at the
address above

You must not circulate this work in any other form
and you must impose this same condition on any acquirer

British Library Cataloguing in Publication Data

Data available

ISBN 978–0–19–957617–3
ISBN 978–0–19–966628–7 (special edition)
ISBN 978–0–19–968549–3 (special edition)

Printed in Great Britain by Clays Ltd, St Ives plc

Contents

Editors and contributors

Managing Editor
Della Thompson

Editors/Proofreaders
Alison Curr
Oksana King
Anne McConnell
Viktor Pekar

Supplementary material
Alexander Levtov
Albina Ozieva
Mikhaïl Pirozhok
Lucy Popova
Terence Wade

Preface

This first edition of the *Compact Oxford Russian Dictionary* is based on the larger *Oxford Russian Dictionary*. It provides comprehensive coverage of the core vocabulary of Russian and English, and reflects the most recent changes to both languages.

Essential information on grammar, style, and pronunciation is provided in a convenient and accessible format, making the dictionary an ideal reference tool. Clear indicators and examples guide you to the appropriate translation, and British and American spelling and usage are differentiated.

All grammatical terms used are explained in a glossary at the back of the dictionary, and there are guides to Russian and English grammar and pronunciation.

This dictionary also includes an A–Z of Russian and British/US life and culture, providing information on contemporary society, traditions, festivals, and holidays, and a practical guide to writing letters and emails. A *Phrasefinder* section enables you to communicate in everyday situations such as travel, shopping, eating out, and organizing leisure activities.

Designed to meet the needs of a wide range of users, from the student at intermediate level and above to the enthusiastic traveller or business professional, the *Compact Oxford Russian Dictionary* is an invaluable practical resource for learners of contemporary, idiomatic Russian or English.

Visit the Oxford Dictionaries site (www.oxforddictionaries.com) today to find free current English definitions and translations in French, German, Spanish, and Italian, as well as grammar guidance, puzzles and games, and our popular blog about words and language.

Oxford Language Dictionaries Online is our subscription site, which you can access for one year with the purchase of this book (details on the back cover).

Предисловие

Настоящее первое издание *Compact Oxford Russian Dictionary* было разработано на основе более крупного *Oxford Russian Dictionary*. Оно посвящено базисной, наиболее употребимой части лексики русского и английского языков и отражает самые последние изменения в обоих языках.

Ключевая информация по грамматике, стилистике и произношению изложена в удобной и доступной форме, благодаря чему этот словарь является отличным инструментом поиска лексикографической информации. Он позволяет пользователю выбрать наиболее подходящий перевод с помощью чётких указателей и иллюстративных примеров употребления слов. В словаре даются отметки о словоупотреблениях, характерных для британского и американского вариантов английского языка.

Все грамматические термины поясняются в глоссарии, приводимом в конце словаря, словарь также снабжён объяснительными статьями по грамматике и произношению русского и английского языков.

Кроме того, словарь содержит краткие заметки о культурных реалиях как России, так и Великобритании и США, включая информацию о современной общественной жизни, традициях, праздниках, а также рекомендации по написанию писем и электронных сообщений. Раздел «Разговорник» поможет пользователю вести общение в стандартных коммуникативных ситуациях, таких как поездка на транспорте, покупки в магазине, посещение ресторана, проведение досуга.

Будучи предназначенным для широкого круга пользователей – от изучающих язык на среднем или продвинутом уровне до посещающих страну во время туристических или деловых поездок, *Compact Oxford Russian Dictionary* является ценным практическим ресурсом для желающих изучить современный русский или английский язык.

Предлагаем Вам посетить наш сайт *Oxford Dictionaries* (www.oxforddictionaries.com), на котором в бесплатном доступе находятся статьи из английских толковых словарей, переводные статьи на французском, немецком, испанском и итальянском языках, а также краткие пособия по грамматике, игры и головоломки, и наш популярный блог о словах и языке.

Доступ на сайт **Oxford Language Dictionaries Online** открыт по платной подписке. Приобретя это издание, Вы получите годовую подписку на этот сайт. С подробностями можно познакомиться на задней обложке.

Guide to the use of the Dictionary

Russian–English Section

Presentation

1 The following devices are used to save space:

(i) The first letter of the headword, followed by a full point, represents the whole headword, e.g.

> **автомоби́л|ь** ... води́ть **а.** (= води́ть автомоби́ль)

(ii) The swung dash, in conjunction with a vertical stroke, represents that part of the headword which is to the left of the vertical stroke, e.g.

> **ава́ри|я** ... потерпе́ть ∼ю (= потерпе́ть ава́рию)

Exceptions: the swung dash is not used in indicating the genitive singular of nouns or the 1st and 2nd persons singular of the present tense of verbs with unchanged stress (for examples, see below: *Grammatical Information: Nouns* and *Verbs*).

Pronunciation

2 With the general exception of monosyllables, stress is indicated for every Russian word. A stress mark above the swung dash, where this sign represents two or more syllables, indicates shift of stress to the syllables immediately preceding the vertical stroke dividing the headword, e.g.

> **запи|са́ть, шу́,** ∼́шешь ... (= запишу́, запи́шешь)

3 Conversely, a stress mark above a syllable to the right of the swung dash indicates shift of stress away from the syllables(s) represented by the swung dash, e.g.

> **а́дрес, а,** *pl.* ∼а́ ... (= адреса́)

4 Where a variant stress is permissible, both variants are shown, e.g.

> **зап|ере́ться** ... ∼́ерся́ ... (= за́перся *or* заперся́)

Meaning

5 Separate meanings of a word are indicated by means of Arabic numerals. Shades of meaning, represented by translations not considered strictly synonymous, are indicated by the means of a semicolon, whereas translations considered synonymous are indicated by a comma, e.g.

> **ава́нс** ...**1** (*де́ньги*) advance
> **2** (*pl. only*; fig.) advances, overtures
> **авантю́ра** ...**1** (*приключе́ние*) adventure; escapade
> **2** (infml) shady enterprise

6 Homonyms are indicated by repetition of the headword as a separate entry, followed by a superscript Arabic numeral, e.g.

> **блок**[1] ... (tech.) block, pulley
> **блок**[2] ... (pol.) bloc

Explanation

7 Where necessary for the avoidance of ambiguity, explanatory glosses are given in brackets in italic type. This device is used in particular in the case of words denoting specifically Russian or Soviet concepts (e.g. **ка́ша, микрорайо́н**) and makes it possible to use one-word transliterations rather than clumsy paraphrases as a substitute for translation.

8 Indications of style or usage are given, where appropriate, in brackets, e.g.

(infml), (fig.), (joc.), (agric.), (pol.), etc.

Grammatical Information

9 The following grammatical information is given:

Nouns

The genitive singular ending and gender of all nouns are shown, e.g.

мо́лот, а *m.* hammer
мо́лни|я, и *f.* lightning
блю́д|о, а *nt.* dish
пья́ниц|а, ы *c.g.* drunkard

Other case endings are shown where declension or stress is, in relation to generally accepted systems of classification, irregular, e.g.

англича́н|ин, ина, *pl.* ~е, ~ *m.* Englishman
бор|ода́, оды́, *a.* ~оду, *pl.* ~оды, ~о́д, ~ода́м *f.* beard

(But the inserted vowel in the genitive plural ending of numerous feminine nouns with nominative singular ending **-ка** is *not* regarded as irregular, e.g. **англича́нка,** *g. pl.* **англича́нок.**)

Adjectives

Only the masculine nominative singular of the full form of the adjective is shown. Endings of the short forms, where these are found, are shown in brackets in most cases, e.g.

глу́|пый, ~, ~á, ~о, ~ы́

The neuter and plural short form endings are omitted where stress is as for the feminine, e.g.

нау́ч|ный, ~ен, ~на

Verbs

Endings are shown of the 1st and 2nd persons singular of the present tense (or of the 1st person only of verbs with infinitive ending **-ать, -овать, -ять, -еть** which retain stem and stress unchanged throughout the present tense), e.g.

говор|и́ть, ю́, и́шь ...
чита́|ть, ю ...

Other endings of the present tense and endings of the past tense are shown where formation or stress is irregular, e.g.

ид|ти́, у́, ёшь, *past* шёл, шла ...
бер|е́чь, егу́, ежёшь, егу́т, *past* ~ёг, ~егла́ ...

Participles and gerunds, and forms of the passive voice, are not shown unless they have special semantic or syntactical features.

If a past participle passive has an adjectival homonym with the same or similar
meaning (as a rule, a participle has a word or words syntactically related to it,
whereas an adjective does not), these homonyms are given as a single entry. In such
cases, if the endings of the short forms of the participle and adjective differ, this is
shown, e.g.

> запу́тан|ный (∼, ∼а) *p.p.p. of* запу́тать *and* (∼, ∼на) *adj.* ...

Verbal aspects: the imperfective aspect is normally treated as the basic form of the
simple verb, a cross reference to the relevant form being shown in brackets, e.g.

> чита́|ть, ю *impf.* (*of* прочита́ть, проче́сть) ...

The corresponding entries are:

> прочита́|ть, ю *pf. of* чита́ть
> про|че́сть, чту́, чтёшь, *past* ∼чёл, ∼чла́ = прочита́ть

In the case, however, of compound verbs formed by means of a prefix, the perfective
aspect is treated as the basic form, e g.

> заш|и́ть, ью́, ьёшь *pf.* (*of* ∼ива́ть) ...

Prefixes and Combining Forms

A number of prefixes and combining forms are shown as separate entries, e.g.

> без... *pref.* in-, un-, -less
> гидро... *comb. form* hydro-

English–Russian Section

Orthography

1 English spelling follows British usage, with American variations also noted, e.g.
honour... (AmE **honor**).

Pronunciation

2 For the convenience of readers whose native language is not English, the
pronunciation of headwords is given, using the International Phonetic Alphabet.
A key to the phonetic symbols used is given on p. xxiii.

Presentation

3 Headwords are printed in **bold roman** type.

Alternative spellings (including American variants) are presented alongside the
preferred spelling; these variants appear again in alphabetical sequence (unless
adjacent to the main entry), as cross references, e.g.

> **cosy** (AmE **cozy**)   **cozy** (AmE) = **cosy**
> **curtsy, curtsey**

Similar treatment is applied to words in which an alternative termination can be
used without affecting the sense, e.g.

> **cyclic, cyclical**

4 Separate headword entries with superscript numerals are created for words
which, though identical in spelling, differ in basic meaning and origin (**fine** as
noun and verb; **fine** as adjective and adverb), or in pronunciation and/or stress
(**house** and **supplement** as nouns and as verbs), or both (**tear** meaning 'teardrop'
and **tear** meaning 'rip').

5 Separate entries for adverbs in '-ly' are made only when they have meanings or usage (idiom, compounds, etc.) which cannot conveniently be treated under the corresponding adjective. Examples are **hardly**, **really**, and **surely**. When there is no separate entry, and no instance of the adverb in the adjectival entry, it can be assumed that the corresponding Russian adverb is also formed regularly from the adjective. Thus, **clumsy** неуклюжий, неловкий implies that the Russian for 'clumsily' is неуклюже and неловко; **critical** критический implies that 'critically' can be translated критически, and so on.

6 Gerundial and participial forms of English verbs, used as nouns or adjectives, are often accommodated within the verb entry (transitive or intransitive as appropriate), e.g.

> **revolving doors** is found under **revolve** *v.i.*
> **become accustomed** is found under **accustom** *v.t.*

but in certain cases, for the sake of clarity, such forms have been treated as independent headwords, e.g.

> **barbed** *adj.*; **flying** *n.* and *adj.*

7 Some headwords are divided by a vertical stroke in order that the unchanging letters preceding the stroke may subsequently be replaced, in inflected forms, by a swung dash. Where there is no divider, the swung dash represents the whole headword, e.g.

> **house** ... ∼**boat**

8 The vertical divider is also used in both English and Russian to separate the main part of a word from its termination when it is necessary to show modifications or alternative forms of the latter: e.g. paragraphs 22(c) and 23.

9 Within the headword entry each grammatical function has its own paragraph, introduced by a part-of-speech indicator: *n., pron., adj., adv., v.t., v.i., prep., conj., int.* A combined heading, e.g. **adagio** *n., adj., & adv.*, may sometimes be used for convenience; the most common instance is *v.t. & i.* when the two uses are not clearly distinguishable, or when the Russian intransitive is expressed by means of the suffix -ся.

10 Verb-adverb combinations forming phrasal verbs normally appear in a separate paragraph headed '*with advs.*', immediately following simple verb usage; they are given in alphabetical order of the adverb.

11 There are also a few verbs (e.g. **go**) where idiomatic usage with prepositions is extensive and complex enough to call for a separate paragraph headed '*with preps.*'.

12 Compounds in which the headword forms the first element (including those that are written as two words rather than being hyphenated or written as one word), are mostly brought together or 'nested' under the headword in a final paragraph.

13 Adjective-noun expressions generally appear under the adjective unless this has relatively little weight, as in '**good riddance**'.

14 Within an entry, differences of meaning or application are defined by a synonym, context, or other means. Major differences may be distinguished by numerals in bold type, e.g.

> **gag** *n.* **1** (to prevent speech etc.) ... **2** (joke) ...

15 A second type of label indicates status or level of usage, e.g.: *archaic*, *sl*(ang), *vulg*(ar). It may apply to the headword as a whole or to one of its functions or meanings, e.g.

> **advert** *n.* (infml) ...
> **bung** ... *v.t.* ... **2** (BrE, sl., throw) ...

16 Russian expressions, especially idioms or proverbs, which parallel rather than translate their English equivalents are preceded by the symbol ≈.

17 The use of the comma or the semicolon to separate Russian words offered as translations of the same English word reflects a greater or lesser degree of equivalence; in the latter case an auxiliary English gloss is often used to express the nuance of difference, e.g.

> **ineligible** *adj.* (for office) ...; (for a benefit) ...

18 To avoid ambiguity the semicolon is used when the alternatives are complete phrases or sentences, and also in most cases between synonymous verbs, e.g.

> **what is he getting at?** что он хо́чет сказа́ть?; куда́ он кло́нит?
> **allow** *v.t.* ... позв|оля́ть, -о́лить; разреш|а́ть, -и́ть ...

Idiom and Illustration

19 In both English and Russian there are many instances when one word in a phrase or sentence may be replaced by a synonymous alternative. This is shown by means of a comma or oblique stroke in English, and an oblique stroke in Russian, e.g.

> **I'll knock a pound off the price**   я сбро́шу/ски́ну/сба́влю фунт с цены́.

20 Non-synonymous alternatives are linked by the oblique stroke in both languages, e.g.

> **carry on a conversation/business**   вести́ разгово́р/де́ло.

21 In most cases the oblique stroke expresses an alternative regarding only one word on either side of it. Other alternatives are generally shown in the form (*or ...*), e.g.

> **I could do with a drink**   я охо́тно (*or* с удово́льствием) вы́пил бы.

Grammatical Information

22 The following grammatical information is given in respect of words offered as translations of headwords:

a) the gender of *masculine* nouns ending in -ь, except when this is made clear by an accompanying adjective (e.g. **polar bear** ·бе́лый медве́дь) or by the existence of a corresponding female form (see (*d*) below).

b) the gender of nouns (e.g. neuters in -мя, masculines in -a and -я, foreign borrowings in -и and -y) whose final letter does not serve as an indicator of gender. Nouns of common gender are designated (*c.g.*). Indeclinable nouns are designated (*indecl.*), preceded by a gender indicator if required. The many adjectives used as nouns (e.g. портно́й) are not specially marked.

c) the gender (or, for *pluralia tantum*, the genitive plural termination) and number (*pl.*) of all plural nouns which translate a headword or compound, e.g.

> **timpani, tympani** *n.* лита́вры (*f. pl.*)
> **pliers** *n.* кле́щ|и (*pl., g.* -е́й)

This information, however, is not given if the singular form has already appeared in the same entry, nor in the case of neuter plurals with an accompanying adjective, where the number and gender are self-evident from the terminations. Plurals of adjectives used substantively are shown as (*pl.*).

d) the forms of nouns used where Russian differs from English in making a verbal distinction between male and female, e.g.

> **teacher** учи́тель (-ница)

e) aspectual information: see paragraphs 23–25 below.

f) case usage with prepositions, e.g. **before** до + *g.*

g) the case, with or without preposition, required to provide an equivalent to an English transitive verb, e.g.

> **attack** *v.t.* нап|ада́ть, -а́сть на + *a.*

If no case is indicated, it is to be taken that the Russian verb is transitive.

h) Use is also made of oblique cases of the Russian pronouns кто and что (in brackets and italics) to indicate case/preposition usage after a verb, e.g.

> **agree** *v.t.* согласо́в|ывать, -а́ть (*что с кем*)

Aspects

23 Aspectual information is given on all verbs (except быть) offered as renderings in infinitive form (except when they are subordinate to the finite verb in a sentence). If the verb is mono-aspectual, or used in a phrase to which only one aspect applies, it is designated either imperfective (*impf.*) or perfective (*pf.*) as the case may be.

With verbs of motion a distinction is made between determinate (*det.*) and indeterminate (*indet.*) forms, the imperfective aspect being assumed unless otherwise stated. Bi-aspectual infinitives are shown as (*impf., pf.*). In all other cases both aspects are indicated (the imperfective always preceding the perfective) as in the following examples:

> (i) получ|а́ть, -и́ть; возвра|жа́ть, -зи́ть; сн|оси́ть, -ести́.
>
> (ii) позв|оля́ть, -о́лить; встр|еча́ть, -е́тить.
>
> (iii) пока́з|ывать, -а́ть (i.e. *pf.* показа́ть); очаро́в|ывать, -а́ть.
>
> (iv) гоня́ть, гнать; брать, взять; вынужда́ть, вы́нудить.
>
> (v) смотре́ть, по-; звать, по- (i.e. *pf.* позва́ть); мости́ть, вы́- (i.e. *pf.* вы́мостить); жа́рить, за-/из-/по-.
>
> (vi) и|мити́ровать, сы-.

24 It will be seen from the above that

i) when the first two or more letters of both aspects are identical, a vertical divider in the imperfective separates these letters from those which undergo change in the perfective. The perfective is then represented by the changed letters, preceded by a hyphen.

ii) a 'change' includes change of stress only if the stress shifts *back* in the perfective to the previous vowel: the divider then precedes this vowel in the imperfective.

iii) if it shifts *forward*, only the stressed syllable of the perfective is shown.

iv) when the two aspects have only their first letter in common, or are in fact different verbs, or both begin with вы- (which is always accented in the perfective), both are given in full.

v) perfectives of the type prefix + imperfective are shown by giving the prefix only, followed by a hyphen. Prefixes are unstressed except for вы́-.

Alternative prefixes are separated by an oblique stroke.

25 When two or three verbs separated by an oblique stroke are followed by the indication (*pf.*) or (*impf.*) this applies to both or all of them.

26 The following grammatical information is given in respect of English headwords.

a) Irregular or difficult plural forms of nouns, e.g.

> **child** ... (*pl.* **children**) ...
>
> **leaf** ... (*pl.* **leaves**) ...
>
> **monkey** ... (*pl.* ~**s**) ...
>
> **referend|um** ... (*pl.* ~**ums** *or* ~**a**) ...

b) Irregular or difficult comparative and superlative forms of adjectives which take
-er, -est, e.g.

> chic ... (chicer, chicest) ...
> glib ... (glibber, glibbest) ...
> tatty ... (tattier, tattiest) ...

c) Irregular or difficult forms of verbs, e.g.

> eat ... (*past* ate; *p.p.* eaten) ...
> go ... (*3rd pers. sg. pres.* goes; *past* went; *p.p.* gone) ...
> hold ... (*past and p.p.* held) ...
> run ... (running; *past* ran; *p.p.* run) ...
> tattoo ... (tattoos, tattooed) ...
> taxi ... (taxis, taxied, taxiing) ...
> tip ... (tipped, tipping) ...

In the case of compound verbs, e.g. **undo**, irregular or difficult forms follow those
of the base verb, in this case **do**.

О пользовании словарём

Русско-английская часть

Заглавное слово

1 В целях экономии места в отношении заглавного слова, повторяющегося в тексте словарной статьи, используются следующие приёмы:

1) начальная буква заглавного слова с последующей точкой заменяет всё слово целиком в его неизменной форме. Например:

> **автомоби́л|ь** ... **води́ть а.** (= **води́ть автомоби́ль**)

2) т. н. тильда (знак ~) заменяет часть заглавного слова, расположенную до сплошной вертикальной черты. Например:

> **ава́ри|я** ... **потерпе́ть ~ю** (= **потерпе́ть ава́рию**)

Исключения. Тильда не применяется для обозначения форм родительного падежа единственного числа существительных и форм 1-го и 2-го лица единственного числа глаголов настоящего времени с неподвижным ударением (см. об этом ниже: *Грамматический комментарий*: *Существительные* и *Глаголы*).

Ударение

2 Ударение последовательно отмечается во всех русских словах за исключением односложных. Знак ударения над тильдой (если та обозначает часть слова, состоящую из двух или более слогов) показывает перенос ударения на слог, ближайший к сплошной вертикальной черте в заглавном слове. Например:

> **запи|са́ть, шу́, ~́шешь** ... (= **запишу́, запи́шешь**)

3 Напротив, знак ударения над слогом правее тильды показывает перенос ударения на этот слог со слога или слогов, заменяемых этим знаком. Например:

> **а́дрес, а,** *pl.* **~а́** ... (= **адреса́**)

4 Допустимые вариантные (в отношении постановки ударения) формы приводятся. Например:

> **зап|ере́ться** ... **~́ерся́** ... (= **за́перся** *или* **заперся́**)

Значения слова

5 Самостоятельные значения слова обозначаются арабскими цифрами. Оттенки значения, представленные переводами, которые не являются близкими синонимами, отделяются точкой с запятой, в то время как тождественные или близкие по значению переводы отделяются запятой. Например:

> **ава́нс** ...**1** (*деньги*) advance
> **2** (*pl. only*; fig.) advances, overtures
> **авантю́ра** ...**1** (*приключение*) adventure; escapade
> **2** (infml) shady enterprise

6 Каждый омоним выделяется в отдельную статью и нумеруется при помощи надстрочной цифры, которая помещается сразу после заглавного слова. Например:

> **блок**[1] ... (tech.) block, pulley
> **блок**[2] ... (pol.) bloc

Пометы и пояснения

7 Во избежание неясности, в скобках приводятся пояснения, набранные курсивом. В особенности этот приём применяется в отношении слов, обозначающих типично русские или советские понятия (как, например, **ка́ша**, **микрорайо́н**), что позволяет использовать транслитерацию в качестве замены неудачным описательным переводам.

8 В необходимых случаях в скобках приводятся стилистические, а также отраслевые и некоторые другие пометы, которые могут относиться как ко всему слову, так и к отдельным его значениям. Примеры таких помет: (infml), (fig.), (joc.), (agric.), (pol.) и т. п.

Грамматический комментарий

9 Грамматический комментарий включает в себя следующее:

Существительные

У всех существительных отмечается форма родительного падежа единственного числа, например:

>   **мо́лот, а** *m.* hammer
>   **мо́лни|я, и** *f.* lightning
>   **блю́д|о, а** *nt.* dish
>   **пья́ниц|а, ы** *c.g.* drunkard

Окончания других падежей приводятся только у существительных, которые имеют особенности в склонении или постановке ударения, и эти особенности не определяются общими правилами. Например:

>   **англича́н|ин, ина,** *pl.* ~е, ~ *m.* Englishman
>   **бор|ода́, оды́,** *a.* ~́оду *pl.* ~́оды, ~́од, ~ода́м *f.* beard

Прилагательные

Прилагательные даются в форме именительного падежа единственного числа мужского рода. Окончания большинства кратких форм, если такие имеются, приводятся в скобках. Например:

>   **глу́|пый,** ~, ~а́, ~о, ~́ы

Окончания кратких прилагательных среднего рода и множественного числа не указываются, если постановка ударения в этих формах не отличается от формы женского рода. Например:

>   **нау́ч|ный,** ~ен, ~на

Глаголы

У глаголов приводятся формы 1-го и 2-го лица единственного числа настоящего времени (исключение составляют глаголы, оканчивающиеся в инфинитиве на **-ать**, **-ова́ть**, **-ять**, **-еть**, у которых приводится только форма 1-го лица единственного числа настоящего времени, так как основа этих глаголов и место постановки ударения не меняются во всех формах настоящего времени). Например:

>   **говор|и́ть, ю́, и́шь ...**
>   **чита́|ть, ю ...**

Другие формы настоящего времени, а также формы прошедшего времени даются только у глаголов, имеющих особенности в спряжении или постановке ударения. Например:

> **ид|ти́, у́, ёшь,** *past* **шёл, шла** ...
>
> **бер|е́чь, егу́, ежёшь, егу́т,** *past* **~ёг, ~егла́** ...

Формы причастий (в т. ч. страдательных) и деепричастий опускаются, если они не обладают особыми семантическими или морфологическими чертами.

Если страдательное причастие прошедшего времени совпадает в полной форме с близким или тождественным по значению прилагательным, оба омонима даются в одной словарной статье, причём, если их краткие формы отличаются, это отмечается в статье. Например:

> **запу́тан|ный (~, ~а)** *p.p.p. of* **запу́тать (~, ~на)** *and adj.* ...

При подаче глаголов, образующих пары глагол несовершенного вида – глагол совершенного вида, используются следующие принципы:

1) если в названной паре глагол несовершенного вида — бесприставочный, то основной *словарной* формой глагола признаётся форма инфинитива несовершенного вида, возле которой и помещается перевод, а в скобках помещается ссылка на соответствующий глагол совершенного вида. При этом словарные статьи глаголов совершенного вида, в случае тождественности значений/переводов глаголов в видовой паре, представляют собой перекрёстные ссылки на статьи о соответствующих глаголах несовершенного вида. Например:

> **чита́|ть, ю** *impf.* (*of* **прочита́ть, прочесть**) ...
>
> **прочита́|ть, ю** *pf. of* **чита́ть**
>
> **про|че́сть, чту́, чтёшь,** *past* **~чёл, ~чла́** = **прочита́ть**

2) если же в видовой паре глагол несовершенного вида – приставочный глагол, то основной *словарной* формой считается форма инфинитива совершенного вида, и перевод следует искать в статье о глаголе совершенного вида. Например:

> **заш|и́ть, ью́, ьёшь** *pf.* (*of* **~ива́ть**) ...

Приставки и составные части сложных слов

Ряд приставок и составных частей сложных слов выделяется в отдельные статьи, например:

> **без** ... *pref.* in-, un-, -less
>
> **гидро** ... *comb. form* hydro-

Англо-русская часть

Орфография

1 Слова английского языка даются в соответствии с британскими правилами орфографии. Американский вариант правописания, в случае расхождения с британским, указывается в скобках, например **honour**… (AmE **honor**).

Произношение

2 В Словаре рассматривается произношение, характерное для жителей южной Англии и известное как *Received Pronunciation* или *RP* (буквально «общепринятое/нормативное произношение»). Для удобства русскоязычной читательской аудитории все заглавные слова приводятся в фонетической транскрипции. Исключение составляют аббревиатуры типа **BBC**, которые произносятся по буквам: отдельно каждая буква в соответствии с её названием.

Названия букв английского алфавита см. на с. 880. У сложных слов, у которых вторая составная часть слова представлена в Словаре в качестве отдельной статьи, приводится транскрипция только первой части.

Перечень используемых транскрипционных символов с примерами слов, содержащих тот или иной звук, см. на с. xxiii.

Заглавное слово и подача информации в словарной статье

3 Заглавные слова печатаются **полужирным** шрифтом.

Вариантные орфографические формы (включая те, которые свойственны американскому английскому) фиксируются наряду с нормативным/преобладающим правописанием слова. Такие формы даются повторно, согласно их положению в алфавитном порядке, с обязательной отсылкой к основному варианту (кроме тех случаев, когда альтернативный вариант примыкает по алфавиту непосредственно к основному). Например:

> **cosy** (ΛmE **cozy**)   **cozy = cosy**
> **curtsy, curtsey**

4 В отдельные словарные статьи, нумерующиеся надстрочными цифрами после заглавного слова, выделяются слова, которые, хотя и имеют одинаковое написание, но отличаются:

1) значением и происхождением (например, **fine** существительное и глагол и **fine** прилагательное и наречие);

2) произношением и/или ударением (например, **house** существительное и **house** глагол);

3) всем вышеперечисленным (например, **tear** в значении «слеза» и **tear** в значении «разрывать, рвать»).

5 Отдельные словарные статьи о наречиях на -ly приводятся только для слов, значение которых не может быть безошибочно определено исходя из значения соответствующего прилагательного. Примеры: **hardly**, **really** и **surely**.

6 Формы герундия и причастий английских глаголов, перешедшие в разряд существительных или прилагательных, нередко помещаются внутри статьи о глаголе (переходном или непереходном, в зависимости от значения). Например:

> **revolving doors** следует искать в статье **revolve** *v.i.*
> **become accustomed** следует искать в статье **accustom** *v.t.*

Но в некоторых случаях, во избежание неясности, подобные существительные и прилагательные выделяются в самостоятельные статьи. Например:

> **barbed** *adj.*; **flying** *n.* и *adj.*

7 Некоторые заглавные слова делит сплошная вертикальная черта. Это указывает на то, что неизменяемая часть слова, находящаяся до вертикальной черты, в изменяемых формах этого слова может заменяться тильдой. При отсутствии разделительной вертикальной линии в заглавном слове, тильда обозначает всё заглавное слово целиком, например:

> **house** ... ∼**boat**

8 Сплошная вертикальная черта, отделяющая неизменяемую часть слова от изменяемой, используется также в английских и русских словах, когда необходимо отобразить словоизменение или привести вариантные формы. См. примеры в пункте 24.

9 Внутри словарной статьи, для каждого лексико-грамматического разряда (части речи) отводится отдельный параграф, начинающийся с указателя части речи:

n., *pron.*, *adj.*, *adv.*, *v.t.*, *v.i.*, *prep.*, *conj.*, *int.* При необходимости такие указатели объединяются в одну запись, например: **adagio** *n.*, *adj.*, *& adv.* Наиболее часто встречается объединение указателей переходного и непереходного глаголов: *v.t. & i.* Последнее наблюдается, когда отличие переходного глагола от непереходного не усматривается явно и когда в переводе русский непереходный глагол образуется при помощи постфикса -ся.

10 Сочетания типа «глагол-наречие», образующие фразовые глаголы, обыкновенно даются отдельным параграфом под заголовком *with advs.*, непосредственно вслед за примерами простого употребления глагола, и размещаются внутри параграфа в алфавитном порядке входящих в эти сочетания наречий.

11 У некоторых глаголов (например **go**), образующих многочисленные идиоматические выражения с предлогами, устойчивые сочетания «глагол-предлог» выделяются в отдельный параграф под заголовком *with preps.*

12 Сложные слова, первая составная часть которых образует заглавное слово словарной статьи, объединяются в заключительном параграфе этой статьи (включая те, которые по правилам английского языка пишутся раздельно).

13 Сочетания типа «прилагательное-существительное» приводятся преимущественно в статье о прилагательном, за исключением случаев, когда прилагательное не оказывает определяющего влияния на значение всего выражения, как например в идиоме **good riddance**.

14 Различия в значении или употреблении слова помечаются пояснительными комментариями в виде синонимов или контекстного окружения слова. Такие пояснения даются в скобках. Для обозначения существенных различий в значении или употреблении слова используются набранные полужирным шрифтом цифры, которые нумеруют самостоятельные значения слова. Например:

> **gag** *n.* **1** (to prevent speech etc.) ... **2** (joke) ...

15 Другой тип пояснений в скобках — стилистические пометы, а также пометы, определяющие или ограничивающие область (географический ареал, профессиональную сферу и пр.) употребления слова. Такие пометы, в зависимости от их местоположения в статье, могут относиться как ко всему слову, так и к отдельным его значениям и случаям употребления в конкретном словосочетании или предложении. Например:

> **advert** *n.* (infml) ...
> **bung** ... *v.t.* ... **2** (BrE, sl., throw) ...

16 Выражения русского языка, в особенности идиомы и пословицы, которые являются скорее переводными аналогами, нежели точными эквивалентами, помечаются предшествующим знаком приблизительного равенства ≈ .

17 Употребление запятой либо точки с запятой для разграничения переводов одного и того же слова указывает на степень тождественности/синонимичности этих переводов: большую для переводов, разделяемых запятой, и меньшую для разделяемых точкой с запятой. В последнем случае для уточнения оттенка значения нередко используется вспомогательный комментарий на английском языке, например:

> **ineligible** *adj.* (for office) ...; (for a benefit) ...

18 Во избежание неясности, точка с запятой применяется для разграничения альтернативных переводов словосочетаний или предложений и большинства видовых пар синонимичных глаголов. Например:

> **what is he getting at?** что он хо́чет сказа́ть?; куда́ он кло́нит?
> **allow** *v.t.* ... позво|ля́ть, -о́лить; разреш|а́ть, -и́ть ...

Устойчивые выражения и примеры употребления слова

19 И в английском, и в русском языках существует немало примеров того, как то или иное слово в словосочетании или предложении может быть заменено синонимом без ущерба для смысла высказывания. Такие синонимы отделяются друг от друга при помощи запятой или косой черты в английских примерах, и посредством косой черты в примерах на русском языке. Например:

I'll knock a pound off the price   я сброшу/скину/сбавлю фунт с цены.

20 Переводные варианты, не являющиеся синонимами, отделяются косой чертой в примерах на обоих языках, например:

carry on a conversation/business   вести разговор/дело.

21 Косая черта, как правило, не применяется, если один из переводов, примыкающий непосредственно к косой черте, состоит из двух и более слов. В таком случае вариант(ы) перевода даются в скобках после слова *or* («или»), например:

I could do with a drink   я охотно (*or* с удовольствием) выпил бы.

Грамматический комментарий

22 В грамматическом комментарии к заглавным словам содержится следующая информация:

а) образуемые не по общим правилам либо вызывающие затруднения в образовании формы множественного числа существительных, например:

child ... (*pl.* **children**) ...
leaf ... (*pl.* **leaves**) ...
monkey ... (*pl.* **~s**) ...
referend|um ... (*pl.* **~ums** *or* **~a**) ...

б) сравнительная и превосходная степень прилагательных, образующих указанные формы путём прибавления -er, -est и вызывающие затруднения в образовании, например:

chic ... (**chicer, chicest**) ...
glib ... (**glibber, glibbest**) ...
tatty ... (**tattier, tattiest**) ...

в) формы неправильных глаголов и сложные случаи образования основных форм у прочих глаголов, например:

eat ... (*past* **ate**; *p.p.* **eaten**) ...
go ... (*3rd pers. sg. pres.* **goes**; *past* **went**; *p.p.* **gone**) ...
hold ... (*past and p.p.* **held**) ...
run ... (**running**; *past* **ran**; *p.p.* **run**) ...
tattoo ... (**tattoos, tattooed**) ...
taxi ... (**taxis, taxied, taxiing**) ...
tip ... (**tipped, tipping**) ...

Неправильные и трудные формы сложных глаголов, таких как **undo**, образуются по модели основного в смысловом отношении глагола, в нашем случае **do**. Иными словами, если известно, что глагол **do** образует неправильные формы **did, done**, то формами простого прошедшего времени и причастия прошедшего времени глагола **undo** будут **undid, undone**.

23 Русскоязычным пользователям следует обратить внимание на следующие основные моменты в грамматическом комментарии к русским переводам заглавных слов:

а) у предлогов приводится управление, например **before** до + *g*.

б) для более точного перевода английских переходных глаголов, в необходимых случаях, у русских глаголов даётся предложное (или беспредложное) управление, например:

> **attack** *v.t.* нап|ада́ть, -а́сть на + *a*.

Если русский глагол не имеет при себе уточнения в виде падежа с предлогом или без, то этот глагол — переходный.

г) управление также может объясняться при помощи местоимений «кто» и «что», приводимых в скобках в соответствующих падежных формах с предлогами или без и выделяемых курсивом, например:

> **agree** *v.t.* извин|я́ться, -и́ться согласо́в|ывать, -а́ть (*что с кем*)

Вид глагола

24 Информация о виде даётся последовательно у всех глаголов в форме инфинитива (за исключением глагола «быть»). У одновидовых глаголов (глаголов, не имеющих соотносительной пары другого вида) категория вида отмечается соответствующей пометой: (*impf.*) или (*pf.*).

Т. н. глаголы движения, подразделяющиеся на глаголы *определённого* (однонаправленного) движения и глаголы *неопределённого* (разнонаправленного) движения, снабжаются пометами, соответственно, (*det.*) и (*indet.*). При этом, если категория вида этих глаголов не указывается, предполагается, что они несовершенного вида.

Инфинитивы двувидовых глаголов помечаются (*impf., pf.*). Во всех остальных случаях указываются оба вида (форма несовершенного вида всегда предшествует форме совершенного вида), что можно проследить на следующих примерах:

(1) получ|а́ть, -и́ть; возра|жа́ть, -зи́ть; сн|оси́ть, -ести́.

(2) позв|оля́ть, -о́лить; встр|еча́ть, -е́тить.

(3) пока́з|ывать, -а́ть (т. е. *pf.* показа́ть); очаро́в|ывать, -а́ть.

(4) гоня́ть, гнать; брать, взять; вынужда́ть, вы́нудить.

(5) смотре́ть, по-; звать, по-; (т. е. *pf.* позва́ть); мости́ть, вы́- (т. е. *pf.* вы́мостить); жа́рить, за-/из-/по-.

(6) и|мити́ровать, сы-.

Символы фонетической транскрипции, используемые в Словаре

Согласные

b	*b*ut	s	*s*it
d	*d*og	t	*t*op
f	*f*ew	v	*v*oice
g	*g*et	w	*w*e
h	*h*e	z	*z*oo
j	*y*es	ʃ	*sh*e
k	*c*at	ʒ	deci*s*ion
l	*l*eg	θ	*th*in
m	*m*an	ð	*th*is
n	*n*o	ŋ	ri*ng*
p	*p*en	tʃ	*ch*ip
r	*r*ed	dʒ	*j*ar

Гласные

æ	c*a*t	aɪ	m*y*
ɑ:	*ar*m	aʊ	h*ow*
e	b*e*d	eɪ	d*ay*
ə:	h*er*	əʊ	n*o*
ɪ	s*i*t	eə	h*air*
i:	s*ee*	ɪə	n*ear*
ɒ	h*o*t	ɔɪ	b*oy*
ɔ:	s*aw*	ʊə	p*oor*
ʌ	r*u*n	aɪə	f*ire*
ʊ	p*u*t	aʊə	s*our*
u:	t*oo*		
ə	*a*go		

(ə) обозначает безударный беглый гласный, который слышится в таких словах, как gard*e*n, carn*a*l и rhyth*m*.

(r) в конце слова обозначает согласный r, который произносится в случае, если следующее слово начинается с гласного звука, как, например, в *clutter up* и *an acre of land*.

Тильда ˜ обозначает носовой гласный звук, как в некоторых заимствованиях из французского языка, например ɑ̃ (*en* masse).

Основное ударение в слове отмечается знаком ' перед ударным слогом.

О произношении звуков английского языка

Произношение английских слов, приводимое в Словаре в транскрипции, соответствует британской норме. Именно о звуках британского английского и пойдёт речь ниже.

Гласные звуки

Среди *гласных звуков* современного английского языка выделяют три основные группы: **монофтонги** (гласные, состоящие из одного звука), **дифтонги** (гласные, состоящие из двух звуков, которые произносятся в пределах одного слога) и **трифтонги** (гласные, состоящие из трёх звуков, произносимых в пределах одного слога).

В современном английском языке 12 монофтонгов, 8 дифтонгов и 2 трифтонга. Особенности их произношения (артикуляции) будут рассмотрены по группам: в отдельности для каждого звука.

Монофтонги

Исторически английские *монофтонги* подразделяются на **краткие** (ɪ, e, æ, ʌ, ɒ, ʊ, ə) и **долгие** (iː, ɑː, ɔː, uː, əː). Долгота последних обозначается в транскрипции двоеточием (ː) после символа соответствующего гласного.

/ɪ/   Краткий гласный звук, произносится без напряжения. Качественно (по месту и способу артикуляции) и количественно (по долготе) противопоставляется долгому /iː/ (см. ниже). Английский /ɪ/ слегка напоминает безударный русский /и/ в слове *игра* и ударный русский /и/ после шипящих. Для правильной артикуляции /ɪ/ язык следует располагать во рту ниже, чем при произношении русского /и/. Согласные перед /ɪ/ не смягчаются, на что нужно обращать особое внимание. В то же время английский /ɪ/ не должен походить на русский /ы/.

      Примеры: sɪt, hɪs, ɪn.

/e/   Краткий гласный звук, произносится без напряжения. Английский /e/ отчасти напоминает русский звук /э/ в словах *свет* и *эти*, если его произносить очень кратко. Следует, однако, помнить о том, что согласные перед английским /e/ не смягчаются. При произнесении английского /e/ средняя часть языка поднята к нёбу выше, чем при произнесении русского /э/, а расстояние между челюстями уже.

      Примеры: dress, bed, men.

/æ/   Краткий гласный звук, произносится с ощутимым напряжением. Качественно противопоставляется звуку /æ/. Во избежание ошибочного произношения русского /э/ вместо /æ/ язык следует располагать низко во рту, как при произнесении русского /а/. Нижняя челюсть должна быть заметно опущена. При этом основная масса языка должна оставаться в передней части рта, а его кончик должен быть прижат к нижним зубам.

      Примеры: cat, bad, man.

/ʌ/   Краткий гласный звук, произносится напряжённо. Положение языка во рту, как при молчании. Английский /ʌ/ похож на русский /а/, произносимый в первом предударном слоге после твёрдых согласных на месте русских букв *а* и *о*, как, например, в словах *скала* и *кора*. По сравнению с русским ударным /a/ при произнесении английского /ʌ/ язык отодвинут назад, а задняя его часть приподнята. Чрезмерно отодвинутый назад язык приведёт к образованию звука, близкого к английскому /ɑ:/, что будет являться грубой фонематической ошибкой, так как данные звуки нередко выполняют смыслоразличительную функцию (duck и dark, lust и last).

Примеры: but, cup, run.

/ɒ/ Краткий гласный звук, произносится без напряжения. Английский /ɒ/ отчасти похож на русский /о/ в слове *конь*, если его произносить не округляя и не выпячивая губы. При произнесении /ɒ/ необходимо максимально отодвинуть назад язык, как при произнесении /ɑ:/ (см. ниже), и, широко раскрывая рот, попытаться добиться минимального округления губ.

Примеры: hot, what, want.

/ʊ/ Краткий гласный звук, произносится без напряжения. Качественно и количественно противопоставляется долгому /u:/ (см. ниже). Основное отличие от русского /у/ в том, что при произнесении /ʊ/ губы почти не округляются и не выпячиваются.

Примеры: put, good, book.

/ə/ Краткий нейтральный (образуемый языком в нейтральном положении) гласный звук, произносится без напряжения. Как и русский язык, английский язык характеризуется сильной качественной редукцией (ослабленным произношением гласных в безударных слогах). Так, звук, близкий английскому /ə/, можно встретить во втором предударном и в двух заударных слогах в русских словах на месте гласных букв *о*, *а* и *е* после твёрдых согласных, например: *садовод*, *даром*, *целиком*.

Ошибка при артикуляции английского /ə/ возникает вследствие смешения парадигм редукции в английском и русском языках. Нейтральный гласный звук /ə/ в английском встречается преимущественно в первом предударном и первом заударном слогах. Носители русского языка в первом и втором предударных слогах и втором заударном нередко произносят гласные, по степени качественной редукции близкие к русским. Частой ошибкой является произношение в первом предударном слоге английских слов русского /э/ вместо /ə/. Для устранения этой ошибки необходимо не смещать язык в переднюю часть рта, сохраняя его в нейтральном срединном положении.

Примеры: ago, father, common.

/i:/ Долгий гласный звук, произносится напряжённо. Качественно и количественно противопоставляется краткому /ɪ/ (см. выше). Английский /i:/ несколько напоминает русский /и/ в слове *ива*, если произнести его напряжённо и протяжно. Согласные перед /i:/ не смягчаются. Помимо долготы английский /i:/ отличается неоднородностью звучания на всем протяжении. При произнесении /i:/ язык движется в полости рта вперёд и вверх.

Примеры: see, cheese, meat.

/ɑ:/ Долгий гласный звук, произносится напряжённо. Своей протяжностью, характерной придавленностью корня языка во рту и низким тембром английский /ɑ:/ напоминает звук, издаваемый при показе горла врачу. Для того чтобы правильно произносить английский /ɑ:/, не делая его похожим на русский /а/, следует как можно дальше отводить корень языка назад и вниз.

Примеры: arm, car, park.

/ɔ:/   Долгий гласный звук. Английский /ɔ:/ произносится напряжённо, при оттянутом назад языке и сильно округлённых губах. Следует избегать характерного для артикуляции русского /о/ выпячивания губ, которое приводит к образованию несвойственного английскому /ɔ:/ призвука /у/.

Примеры: saw, all, sort.

/u:/   Долгий гласный звук, произносится напряжённо. Качественно и количественно противопоставляется краткому /ʊ/ (см. выше). Помимо долготы, английский /u:/, как и /i:/, отличается неоднородностью звучания на всем протяжении. При произнесении /u:/ язык движется в полости рта назад и вверх. Губы в начальный момент заметно округлены и, по мере движения языка, округляются ещё сильнее. Во избежание замены английского /u:/ русским /у/ при округлении губ не следует их выпячивать.

Примеры: too, food, blue.

/ə:/   Долгий гласный звук, произносится напряжённо. Губы при произнесении /ə:/ растянуты, зубы слегка обнажены. Согласные перед /ə:/ не смягчаются. Английский /ə:/ не должен напоминать русские /о/ и /э/. Именно звук /ə:/, как правило, произносится носителями английского языка при обдумывании ответа или подборе нужного слова.

Примеры: her, first, work.

Дифтонги

Дифтонги — это особые гласные звуки, произносимые без паузы в пределах одного слога. У английских дифтонгов основным, ударным элементом — **ядром** — всегда является первый из двух его составляющих. Второй элемент — **скольжение** или **глайд** — всегда безударный, произносится без напряжения.

Интонационно все английские дифтонги — нисходящие, т. е. их произношение сопровождается понижением интонации к конечному элементу.

/eɪ/   Сочетание сильного первого элемента /е/ и ослабленного второго /ɪ/ (см. выше). Следует избегать превращения глайда дифтонга /ɪ/ в английский согласный /j/ или русский /й/.

Примеры: day, they, break.

/aɪ/   Сочетание сильного первого элемента /а/ и ослабленного второго /ɪ/. Английский звук /а/ — ядро дифтонга /aɪ/ — отличается от русского /а/ передним положением языка при его артикуляции. К тому же в начальной стадии звучания английского /а/ язык располагается ниже. Глайд дифтонга /ɪ/ не должен заменяться английским согласным /j/ или русским /й/.

Примеры: my, side, high.

/ɔɪ/   Сочетание сильного первого элемента /ɔ/ и ослабленного второго /ɪ/. Английский звук /ɔ/ — ядро дифтонга /ɔɪ/ — представляет собой нечто среднее между английскими звуками /ɔ:/ и /ɒ/ (см. выше). Превращение глайда дифтонга /ɪ/ в английский согласный /j/ или русский /й/ является ошибкой.

Примеры: boy, soil, noise.

/əʊ/   Сочетание сильного первого элемента /ə/ и незначительно ослабленного второго /ʊ/. Ядро дифтонга /əʊ/ — звук /ə/ — произносится как английский /ə:/ (см. выше), но с раскрытым шире, чем для /ə:/, ртом, и с округлёнными (но не выпяченными) губами. Дифтонг /əʊ/ — единственный английский дифтонг, второй элемент которого произносится отчётливо, без заметного расслабления органов речи.

Примеры: no, show, home.

/aʊ/   Сочетание сильного первого элемента /a/ и ослабленного второго /ʊ/. При произнесении ядра дифтонга /aʊ/ — звука /a/ — язык не настолько продвигается вперёд, как при произнесении ядра /aɪ/, и первый элемент /aʊ/ во многом схож с русским /а/. В отличие от глайда /əʊ/ второй элемент дифтонга /aʊ/ звучит неясно. Следует помнить об этом и не превращать неясный глайд /ʊ/ в самостоятельный гласный /ʊ/ или /u:/, а также русский /у/, который произносится с характерным выпячиванием губ, не свойственным гласным звукам английского языка в целом.

Примеры: how, town, mouth.

/ɪə/   Сочетание сильного первого элемента /ɪ/ и ослабленного второго /ə/ (см. выше). В открытом конечном положении (на конце слова) глайд /ə/ может переходить в звук, близкий к английскому /ʌ/ (см. выше).

Примеры: beer, near, here.

/eə/   Сочетание сильного первого элемента /e/ и ослабленного второго /ə/. Рот при произнесении ядра дифтонга /eə/ — звука /e/ — раскрыт намного шире, чем при произнесении самостоятельного английского гласного /e/, что делает похожим ядро дифтонга /eə/ на русский /э/ в слове этот (но не эти).

Примеры: hair, care, there.

/ʊə/   Сочетание сильного первого элемента /ʊ/ и ослабленного второго /ə/ (см. выше).

Примеры: poor, sure, tour.

Трифтонги

В английском языке сочетания дифтонгов /aɪ/ и /aʊ/ с безударным нейтральным неслоговым гласным /ə/ называются *трифтонгами*. Как и дифтонги, английские трифтонги имеют в своём составе **ядро** — сильный ударный элемент — и **глайд** или **скольжение**, которое включает в себя два безударных элемента.

/aɪə/   Сочетание дифтонга /aɪ/ и нейтрального гласного /ə/. Элемент /ɪ/ не должен превращаться в согласный /j/.

Примеры: fire, liar, iron.

/aʊə/   Сочетание дифтонга /aʊ/ и нейтрального гласного /ə/. Элемент /ʊ/ не должен превращаться в согласный /w/.

Примеры: sour, flower, towel.

Согласные звуки

Английские *согласные* имеют следующие характерные отличительные черты по сравнению с согласными русского языка:

1) «звонкость-глухость» не является основным различительным признаком английских согласных, напротив, применительно к английскому согласному важно знать: является ли он **сильным** или **слабым**, а не звонким или глухим. В русском языке глухие согласные, как правило, слабые, а звонкие — сильные. В английском языке, наоборот, звонкие /b/, /d/, /g/, /j/, /l/, /m/, /n/, /r/, /v/, /w/, /z/, /ʒ/, /ð/, /ŋ/ и /dʒ/ — в большинстве случаев слабые, а глухие /f/, /h/, /k/, /p/, /s/, /t/, /ʃ/, /θ/ и /tʃ/ — сильные;

2) сильные глухие /k/, /p/ и /t/ отличаются от соответствующих русских согласных тем, что они произносятся с сильным **придыханием**, — промежуток между одним из этих согласных и следующим за ним гласным заполняется порцией резко выдыхаемого воздуха, причём воздух этот выходит не из ротовой полости, как в случае с русскими /к/, /п/ и /т/, а непосредственно из лёгких;

3) отличительной чертой системы русских согласных является наличие палатализации (смягчения). За исключением всегда мягких /ч/ и /щ/ и всегда твёрдых /ц/, /ш/ и /ж/ (не путать с двойным «долгим» мягким /жʲжʲ/, как в слове *вожжи*), остальные русские согласные встречаются как в мягкой, так и в твёрдой разновидностях. Согласные английского языка полностью лишены такой артикуляционной особенности, поэтому следует уделять особое внимание тому, чтобы английские согласные не смягчались перед гласными /e/, /ɪ/, /iː/;

4) английские звонкие согласные на конце слов не оглушаются, как русские;

5) удвоенные английские согласные читаются как один звук.

В современном английском языке 24 согласных звука. Особенности их произношения (артикуляции) будут рассмотрены отдельно для каждого звука.

/b/ Произносится как ослабленный русский /б/. Перед гласными /e/, /ɪ/, /iː/, /əː/ и согласным /j/ не смягчается.
     Примеры: *b*ut, *b*ig, *b*est.

/d/ Произносится как ослабленный русский /д/. Перед гласными /e/, /ɪ/, /iː/, /əː/ и согласным /j/ не смягчается. Следует избегать призвука /ə/ перед сочетаниями с /n/ и /l/, для чего образующейся между /d/ и /n/ мгновенной паузе надлежит придавать носовую артикуляцию, а мгновенной паузе между /d/ и /l/ соответственно боковую (по месту образования — между опущенным в одну сторону боковым краем языка и щекой).
     Примеры: *d*og, *d*ay, *d*oor.

/f/ Произносится как русский /ф/, но энергичнее и без участия верхней губы. Перед гласными /e/, /ɪ/, /iː/, /əː/ и согласным /j/ не смягчается.
     Примеры: *f*ew, *f*it, *f*eel.

/g/ Произносится как ослабленный русский /г/. Перед гласными /e/, /ɪ/, /iː/, /əː/ и согласным /j/ не смягчается.
     Примеры: *g*et, *g*o, *g*ive.

/h/ Аналогов этому звуку в русском языке нет. Согласный /h/ представляет собой простой выдох без участия языка и округления губ — как при дуновении на стекло с целью почистить его. Звук /h/ не является шумным и ни в коем случае не должен напоминать русский /х/.
     Примеры: *h*e, *h*ill, *h*air.

/j/ Произносится как заметно ослабленный русский /й/.
     Примеры: *y*es, *y*ou, *y*ear.

/k/   Произносится как русский /к/, но энергичнее и с придыханием перед
      гласными. Перед гласными /e/, /ı/, /i:/, /ə:/ и согласным /j/ не смягчается.
      Примеры: cat, kind, quick.

/l/   В отличие от русского /л/ английский /l/ произносится с участием кончика
      языка, который касается тканей непосредственно за передними верхними
      зубами. Перед гласными звучит несколько мягче, но не так, как русский
      мягкий /лʲ/. В то же время в положении не перед гласными английский /l/
      никогда не звучит так твёрдо, как русский /л/.
      Примеры: leg, like, look.

/m/   Произносится как ослабленный русский /м/. Перед гласными /e/, /ı/, /i:/, /ə:/
      и согласным /j/ не смягчается.
      Примеры: man, me, milk.

/n/   В отличие от русского /н/, который произносится при помощи языка,
      упирающегося в передние верхние зубы, английский /n/ произносится с
      участием кончика языка, который касается тканей за передними верхними
      зубами, но не самих зубов. Английский /n/ звучит менее энергично, чем
      русский /н/. Перед гласными /e/, /ı/, /i:/, /ə:/ и согласным /j/ не смягчается.
      Примеры: no, new, niece.

/p/   Произносится как русский /п/, но энергичнее и с придыханием перед
      гласными. Перед гласными /e/, /ı/, /i:/, /ə:/ и согласным /j/ не смягчается.
      Примеры: pen, put, please.

/r/   Очень слабый согласный звук, лишь условно сравниваемый с русским
      /р/. Произносится он с положением органов речи, как для русского /ж/,
      но щель, образуемая между поднятым кончиком языка и передней частью
      твёрдого нёба, несколько шире, чем для /ж/. Кончик языка загнут назад и не
      должен вибрировать. Вибрируют при произнесении английского /r/ только
      голосовые связки. Средняя и задняя части языка остаются плоскими. Во
      избежание замены английского /r/ русским /р/ следует помнить о том, что
      при образовании английского /r/ язык не ударяется ни о зубы, ни о верхние
      ткани полости рта, оставаясь неподвижным.
      Примеры: red, real, root.

/s/   Напоминает русский /с/, но произносится энергичнее. Язык, по сравнению
      с русским /с/, при произнесении английского /s/ поднят кверху, и струя
      воздуха проходит между кончиком языка и тканями позади передних
      верхних зубов, а не между языком и самими зубами. Перед гласными /e/, /ı/,
      /i:/, /ə:/ и согласным /j/ не смягчается.
      Примеры: sit, same, so.

/t/   Напоминает русский /т/, но произносится энергичнее и с придыханием перед
      гласными. По сравнению с русским /т/ при произнесении английского /t/
      кончик языка приподнят к тканям, расположенным позади передних верхних
      зубов. Перед гласными /e/, /ı/, /i:/, /ə:/ и согласным /j/ не смягчается. Следует
      избегать призвука /ə/ перед сочетаниями с /n/ и /l/, для чего образующейся
      между /t/ и /n/ мгновенной паузе надлежит придавать носовую
      артикуляцию, а мгновенной паузе между /t/ и /l/ соответственно боковую
      (по месту образования — между опущенным в одну сторону боковым краем
      языка и щекой).
      Примеры: top, tea, time.

/v/   Произносится как ослабленный русский /в/, но без участия верхней губы. Перед гласными /e/, /ı/, /i:/, /ə:/ и согласным /j/ не смягчается.

Примеры: *v*oice, *v*ery, *v*iew.

/w/   Аналогов этому звуку в русском языке нет. Английский /w/ получается мгновенным пропусканием струи воздуха через щель, образуемую сильно округлёнными и слегка выпяченными губами. Зубы не касаются нижней губы. Звук /w/ произносится очень кратко и слабо, губы совершают движение, как при задувании свечи.

Примеры: *w*e, *w*hat, *w*ill.

/z/   Произносится как ослабленный русский /з/. Отличается от русского /з/ тем же, чем английский /s/ от русского /с/ (см. выше). Перед гласными /e/, /ı/, /i:/, /ə:/ и согласным /j/ не смягчается.

Примеры: *z*oo, ea*s*y, ro*s*e.

/ʃ/   Произносится как смягчённый русский /ш/, но не настолько мягкий, как /щ/. Положение кончика языка, как при произнесении английского /s/ (см. выше), но щель, в которую пропускается воздух, более широкая, а органы речи напряжены меньше.

Примеры: *sh*e, *sh*all, *sh*op.

/ʒ/   Произносится как смягчённый русский /ж/, но не настолько мягкий, как в слове *вожжи*. Отличается от /ʃ/ только использованием голоса при его произнесении.

Примеры: deci*s*ion, plea*s*ure, u*s*ual.

/θ/   Аналогов этому звуку в русском языке нет. При произнесении сильного английского согласного /θ/ язык лежит плоско во рту, и его кончик находится между передними верхними и нижними зубами. В образуемую таким образом между краем верхних зубов и кончиком языка щель выдыхается воздух. Во избежание образования звука /f/ зубы должны быть обнажены так, чтобы нижняя губа не касалась верхних зубов. Во избежание образования звука /s/ кончик языка должен находиться между зубами, а сам язык оставаться плоским, особенно его передняя часть.

Примеры: *th*in, *th*ree, *th*rough.

/ð/   Аналогов этому звуку в русском языке нет. Произносится так же, как /θ/, но с голосом и менее энергично. Во избежание образования звука /v/ зубы должны быть обнажены так, чтобы нижняя губа не касалась верхних зубов. Во избежание образования звука /z/ кончик языка должен находиться между зубами, а сам язык оставаться плоским, особенно его передняя часть.

Примеры: *th*is, *th*ere, *th*at.

/ŋ/   Аналогов этому звуку в русском языке нет. Упрощённо, английский /ŋ/ представляет собой /g/, если произносить его через нос при полностью опущенном мягком нёбе. Так же, как и для /g/, для произношения /ŋ/ задняя часть языка смыкается с мягким нёбом, но последнее при артикуляции /ŋ/ полностью опущено, и воздух проходит не через рот, а через нос. Кончик языка при произнесении /ŋ/ обязательно должен находиться у нижних зубов, а передняя и средняя части языка не касаться нёба. Следует избегать призвука /g/ после /ŋ/ и не подменять /ŋ/ звуком /n/.

Примеры: ri*ng*, so*ng*, wro*ng*.

/tʃ/   Произносится как русский /ч/, но энергично и твёрдо, без какого бы то ни было смягчения. Для правильной артикуляции английского /tʃ/ второй элемент /ʃ/ следует произносить так же твёрдо, как русский /ш/.

Примеры: *ch*ip, *ch*eese, *ch*ild.

/dʒ/   Произносится так же, как /tʃ/, но с голосом, менее энергично и всегда со вторым мягким элементом /ʒ/.

Примеры: *j*ar, *j*am, *g*in.

Russian pronunciation guide

The pronunciation of Russian headwords is not given in the dictionary because, with the help of the additional information given below, it can be worked out from the spelling.

Russian letter	Approximate English sound and phonetic transcription	
а	like the English *a* in calm, but slightly shorter, as in French *la* or German *Mann*, e.g. **ра́дио**, **мать**; transcribed /a/	❶ See Note 5 below
б	like an English *b*, but with the expulsion of less breath, e.g. **ба́бушка**, **буты́лка**; transcribed /b/	❶ See Note 4 below
в	like an English *v*, e.g. **вино́**, **вот**; transcribed /v/	❶ See Note 4 below
г	like the English *g* in go, but with the expulsion of less breath, e.g. **газе́та**, **гара́ж**; transcribed /g/	❶ See Notes 4, 6 below
д	like an English *d*, but with the expulsion of less breath, e.g. **да**, **дом**; transcribed /d/	❶ See Note 4 below
е	like the English *ye* in yes, e.g. **е́сли**, **обе́д**; transcribed /je/	❶ See Notes 2, 3 below
ё	like the English *yo* in yonder, e.g. **её**, **ёлка**; transcribed /jo/	❶ See Note 2 below
ж	like the English *s* in measure, e.g. **ждать**, **жена́**; transcribed /zh/	❶ See Notes 3, 4 below
з	like an English *z*, e.g. **за́пад**, **зо́нтик**; transcribed /z/	❶ See Note 4 below
и	like the English *ee* in see, e.g. **игра́ть**, **йли**; transcribed /i/	❶ See Notes 2, 3 below
й	like the English *y* in boy, e.g. **мой**, **трамва́й**; transcribed /j/	
к	like an English *k*, but with the expulsion of less breath, e.g. **кто**, **ма́рка**; transcribed /k/	❶ See Note 4 below
л	like an English *l*, but harder, pronounced with the tongue behind the front teeth, e.g. **ла́мпа**, **луна́**; transcribed /l/	
м	like an English *m*, e.g. **ма́ма**, **молоко́**; transcribed /m/	
н	like an English *n*, but harder, pronounced with the tongue behind the front teeth, e.g. **на́до**, **нога́**; transcribed /n/	
о	like the English *o* in for, but pronounced with more rounded lips, e.g. **о́чень**, **мо́ре**; transcribed /o/	❶ See Note 5 below
п	like an English *p*, but with the expulsion of less breath, e.g. **па́па**, **по́сле**; transcribed /p/	❶ See Note 4 below

Russian letter	Approximate English sound and phonetic transcription	
р	like an English *r*, but rolled at the front of the mouth, e.g. **рыба, пора**; transcribed /r/	
с	like an English *s*, e.g. **салат, собака**; transcribed /s/	❶ See Note 4 below
т	like an English *t*, but with the expulsion of less breath, e.g. **тарелка, только**; transcribed /t/	❶ See Note 4 below
у	like the English *oo* in p**oo**l, but pronounced with more rounded lips, e.g. **муж, улица**; transcribed /u/	
ф	like an English *f*, e.g. **футбол, флейта**; transcribed /f/	❶ See Note 4 below
х	like the Scottish *ch* in lo**ch**, e.g. **хлеб, холодно**; transcribed /kh/	
ц	like the English *ts* in nu**ts**, e.g. **центр, цирк**; transcribed /ts/	❶ See Note 3 below
ч	like the English *ch* in **ch**urch, e.g. **чай, час**; transcribed /ch/	❶ See Notes 3, 7 below
ш	like the English *sh* in **sh**op, but harder, pronounced with the tongue lower, e.g. **школа, наш**; transcribed /sh/	❶ See Notes 3, 4 below
щ	either like a long soft English *sh*, similar to the *sh* in **sh**ould, or like an English *shch*, as in fre**sh ch**eese, e.g. **щи, ещё**; transcribed /shch/	❶ See Note 3 below
ъ	hard sign (hardens the preceding consonant), e.g. **объяснять**; transcribed /"/	
ы	like the English *i* in b**i**t, but with the tongue further back in the mouth, e.g. **вы, ты**; transcribed /y/	
ь	soft sign (softens the preceding consonant), e.g. **мать, говорить**; transcribed /'/	
э	like the English *e* in th**e**re, e.g. **это, этаж**; transcribed /e/	
ю	like the English *u* in **u**nit, but pronounced with more rounded lips, e.g. **юбка, юг**; transcribed /ju:/	❶ See Note 2 below
я	like the English *ya* in **ya**rd, but slightly shorter, e.g. **яблоко, моя**; transcribed /ja/	❶ See Notes 2, 5 below

Notes

1. Stress

Russian words have one main stress. In this dictionary this is indicated by an acute accent placed over the vowel of the stressed syllable. The vowel ё is never marked as it is almost always stressed.

2. Hard and soft consonants

An important feature of Russian consonants is that they may be hard or soft. At the end of a word or before a consonant, the soft sign (ь) indicates that the preceding consonant is soft, e.g. день, брать, деньги. In addition, the vowels е, ё, и, ю, and я coming after a consonant indicate that the consonant is soft, e.g. нет, нёс, лить, тюрьма, ряд. A soft consonant is pronounced by placing the tongue closer to the roof of the mouth than in the pronunciation of the equivalent hard consonant. Soft consonants are particularly discernible in the case of the sounds /d, t, n, l/. In British English they can be heard in the words due, tune, new, and illuminate.

In the transcriptions below, a soft consonant is indicated by a /j/ immediately after the consonant, e.g. нет /njet/, except when represented by a soft sign which is transcribed /'/, e.g. лить /ljit'/.

3. Consonants that are always hard or always soft

The consonants ж, ш, and ц are always hard.

If the letter и follows one of these consonants, it is pronounced as if it were ы, e.g. жир /zhyr/, машина /mashýnə/, цирк /tsyrk/.

If a stressed е follows one of these consonants, it is pronounced as if it were э, e.g. жечь /zhech'/, шесть /shest'/, целый /tsélyj/.

If ё follows ж or ш, it is pronounced /o/, e.g. жёлтый /zhóltyj/, шёл /shol/.

The consonants ч and щ are always soft.

This means that following these consonants the vowels а, о, and у are pronounced /ja/, /jo/, and /ju/, e.g. часто /chjástə/, чулок /chjulók/.

4. Unvoicing of voiced consonants and voicing of unvoiced consonants

Voiced consonant sounds (/b, v, g, d, zh, z/) become unvoiced (/p, f, k, t, sh, s/) when they occur

a) at the end of a word, e.g.

хлеб	/khljep/
рукав	/rukáf/
снег	/snjek/
муж	/mush/
мороз	/marós/

or

b) before an unvoiced consonant, e.g.

водка	/vótkə/
автобус	/aftóbus/

Conversely, unvoiced consonant sounds (/p, f, k, t, sh, s/) become voiced (/b, v, g, d, zh, z/) when they occur before another voiced consonant, except before в, e.g.

| сдать | /zdat'/ |
| отда́ть | /addát'/ |

but

| отве́т | /atvjét/ (no voicing before в) |

5. Unstressed vowels

The Russian vowels о, е, а, and я change their pronunciation when they are not stressed:

о is pronounced like the stressed Russian a, transcribed /a/, when it appears in the syllable before the stressed syllable, and like the indeterminate vowel in the first syllable of *amaze*, transcribed as /ə/, when it appears after the stressed syllable or more than one syllable before the stressed syllable, e.g.

окно́	/aknó/
нога́	/nagá/
мно́го	/mnógə/
хорошо́	/khərashó/

е is pronounced like the Russian и, transcribed /i/, when it is unstressed, unless it follows a hard consonant (ж, ц, ш) when it is pronounced like ы, e.g.

пе́рец	/pjérjits/
стена́	/stjiná/
жена́	/zhyná/
на у́лице	/na úljitsy/

а is pronounced like a stressed Russian a, transcribed /a/, when it appears in the syllable before the stressed syllable, but like the indeterminate vowel in the first syllable of *amaze*, transcribed /ə/, when it appears after the stressed syllable or more than one syllable before the stressed syllable, e.g.

маши́на	/mashýnə/
кассе́та	/kasjétə/
магнитофо́н	/məgnjitafón/

я is pronounced like the Russian и, transcribed /i/, when it occurs in the syllable before the stressed syllable, and like the indeterminate vowel in the first syllable of *amaze*, transcribed /ə/, when it appears after the stressed syllable or more than one syllable before the stressed syllable, e.g.

пяти́	/pjitjí/
язы́к	/jizýk/
языка́	/jəzyká/
тётя	/tjótjə/

6.

г is pronounced as if it were в in the words его́, сего́дня, and other words with the genitive ending -ого, -его, e.g. ма́ленького, си́него, ,всего́, ничего́.

7.

ч is pronounced as if it were ш in the words что, что́бы, and коне́чно.

Abbreviations used in the Dictionary
Список условных сокращений

a.	accusative (case)	винительный падеж
abbr.	abbreviat|ion, -ed (to)	сокращение, сокращённо
act.	active (voice)	действительный (залог)
adj., adjs.	adjectiv|e, -al, -es	имя прилагательное, адъективное, имена прилагательные
adv., advs.	adverb, -ial, -s	наречие, наречное, наречия
aeron.	aeronautics	авиация
agric.	agriculture	сельское хозяйство
AmE	American usage	употребительно в Америке
anat.	anatomy	анатомия
archaeol.	archaeology	археология
archit.	architecture	архитектура
astrol.	astrology	астрология
astron.	astronomy	астрономия
attr.	attributive	определительное, атрибутивное
aux.	auxiliary	вспомогательный глагол
bibl.	biblical	библейский термин
biol.	biology	биология
bot.	botany	ботаника
BrE	British usage	употребительно в Великобритании
c.g.	common gender	общий род
chem.	chemistry	химия
cin.	cinema(tography)	кинематография
collect.	collective	собирательное (существительное)
comb.	combin|ation, -ing	сочетание
comm.	commerc|e, -ial	коммерческий термин
comp.	comparative	сравнительная степень
comput.	computing	вычислительная техника
concr.	concrete	конкретный
conj., conjs.	conjunction, -s	союз, -ы
cul.	culinary	кулинария
d.	dative (case)	дательный падеж
det.	determinate	определённый
dim.	diminutive	уменьшительное
eccl.	ecclesiastical	церковный термин
econ.	economics	экономика
elec.	electric|al, -ity	электротехника

emph.	empha|size(s), -sizing; -tic	подчёркива|ть, -ет, -ющее; усилительное
esp.	especially	особенно
euph.	euphemis|m, -tic	эвфеми|зм, -стическое
expr.	express|ed, -es, -ing; -ion	выраж|енный, -ает, -ающее; выражение
f.	feminine	женский род
fem.	female	форма женского рода
fig.	figurative(ly)	в переносном смысле
fin.	financ|e, -ial	финансы, финансовый термин
fut.	future (tense)	будущее время
g.	genitive (case)	родительный падеж
geog.	geography	география
geol.	geology	геология
geom.	geometry	геометрия
gram.	grammar	грамматика
hist.	histor|y, -ical	история
hort.	horticulture	садоводство
i.	instrumental (case); intransitive in *v.i.*	творительный падеж; непереходный глагол
imper.	imperative	повелительное наклонение
impers.	impersonal	безличное
impf.	imperfective	несовершенный вид
indecl.	indeclinable	несклоняемое
indet.	indeterminate	неопределённый
inf.	infinitive	инфинитив
infml	informal	разговорное
inst.	instantaneous	однократный (глагол)
int.	interjection	междометие
interrog.	interrogative	вопросительный
intrans.	intransitive	непереходный глагол
iron.	ironical	ироническое
joc.	jocular	шутливое
ling.	linguistics	лингвистика
lit.	literal(ly)	буквально
liter.	literary	книжное
m.	masculine	мужской род
math.	mathematics	математика
med.	medic|ine, -al	медицин|а, -ский термин
meteor.	meteorology	метеорология
mil.	military	военное дело
min.	mineralogy	минералогия
mus.	music(al)	музыка, -льный термин
myth.	mythology	мифология

n.	noun	имя существительное
naut.	nautical	морское дело
neg.	negative	отрицательный
nn.	nouns	имена существительные
nom.	nominative (case)	именительный падеж
nt.	neuter	средний род
num., nums.	numeral(s)	числительное, числовой, числительные
obj.	object	дополнение
obs.	obsolete	устаревшее слово/выражение
offens.	offensive	оскорбительное
opp.	opposite (to); as opposed to	противоположное
p.	prepositional (case). *See also p.p. and p.p.p.*	предложный падеж
part.	participle	причастие
pass.	passive (voice)	страдательный (залог)
pej.	pejorative	пренебрежительное
pers.	person(s); personal	лиц|о, -а; личный
pert.	pertaining	относительно
pf.	perfective	совершенный вид
phil.	philosophy	философия
philol.	philology	языкознание
phot.	photography	фотография
phr., phrr.	phrase, -s	фраз|а, -ы
physiol.	physiology	физиология
pl.	plural	множественное число
poet.	poet|ical, -ry	поэтическое, поэзия
pol.	political	политический термин
poss.	possessive	притяжательное
p.p.	past participle	причастие второе, причастие прошедшего времени
p.p.p.	past participle passive	страдательное причастие прошедшего времени
pred.	predicate; predicative	сказуемое; предикативный
pref.	prefix	префикс
prep., preps.	preposition, -s	предлог, -и
pres.	present (tense)	настоящее время
pres. part.	present participle	причастие первое, действительное причастие настоящего времени
pron., prons.	pronoun, -s	местоимени|е, -я
pronunc.	pronunciation	произношение
propr.	proprietary term	фирменное название
prov.	proverb	пословица
psych.	psychology	психология
rail.	railway	железнодорожный термин
refl.	reflexive (verb)	возвратный (глагол)
rel.	relative (pronoun)	относительное (местоимение)

relig.	religion	религия
rhet.	rhetorical	высокого стиля
sb	somebody	кто-нибудь
Sc.	Scottish	шотландский (английский) язык
sc.	scilicet	а именно
sg.	singular	единственное число
sl.	slang	сленг
sth	something	что-нибудь
subj.	subject	подлежащее
suff.	suffix	суффикс
superl.	superlative	превосходная степень
t.	transitive in *v.t.*	переходный (глагол)
tech.	technical	техника
teleph.	telephony	телефония
text.	textiles	текстильный термин
theatr.	theatr|e, -ical	театр, театральный термин
trans.	transitive	переходный глагол
TV	television	телевидение
typ.	typography	типографский термин
univ.	university	университетский жаргон
usu.	usually	обычно
v.	verb	глагол
var.	various	разные
v. aux.	auxiliary verb	вспомогательный глагол
vbl.	verbal	отглагольное
v.i.	intransitive verb	непереходный глагол
voc.	vocative (case)	звательный падеж
v.t.	transitive verb	переходный глагол
vulg.	vulgar(ism)	грубое
vv.	verbs	глаголы
zool.	zoology	зоология

The Russian -н. or -л. in illustrative phrases within entries stands for -нибудь or -либо (in the words кто-нибудь, что-нибудь, что-либо, etc.).

This dictionary includes some words which are, or are asserted to be, proprietary names or trademarks. These words are labelled ® or (*propr.*). The presence or absence of this label should not be regarded as affecting the legal status of any proprietary name or trademark.

Аа

а¹ *conj.* **1** (*и*) and; **вот ма́рки, а вот три рубля́ сда́чи** here are the stamps and here's three roubles change **2** (*но*) but (*or not translated*); **я иду́ не в кино́, а в теа́тр** I am not going to the cinema, but to the theatre (BrE), theater (AmE); **пиши́ карандашо́м, а не ру́чкой** write in pencil, not pen **3**: **а как же!** (*infml*) of course!; **а то** or (else), otherwise; **дава́й быстре́е, а то мы опозда́ем!** hurry up or (else) we'll be late!

а² *interrog. particle* (*infml*) eh?; what('s that)?; huh?

а³ *int.* (*infml*) ah, oh

абажу́р, **а** *m.* lampshade

абба́тств|о, **а** *nt.* abbey

аббревиату́р|а, **ы** *f.* abbreviation

абза́ц, **а** *m.* **1** (*typ.*) indention; **сде́лать а.** to indent; **нача́ть с но́вого ~а** to begin a new line, new paragraph **2** (*часть текста*) paragraph

абитурие́нт, **а** *m.* (university/college) entrant

абитурие́нт|ка, **ки** *f. of* ▶ **абитурие́нт**

абонеме́нт, **а** *m.* (*право пользования чем-н.*) subscription; (*многоразовый билет*) season ticket

абоне́нт, **а** *m.* (*телефона*) subscriber; (*библиотеки*) borrower, reader; (*театра*) season-ticket holder

абоне́нтск|ий *adj.* subscription; **~ая пла́та** subscription fee

аборите́н, **а** *m.* aboriginal

або́рт, **а** *m.* abortion; **сде́лать а.** (*о пациентке*) to have an abortion

абрико́с, **а** *m.* apricot

абсолю́тно *adv.* absolutely

абсолю́т|ный, **~ен**, **~на** *adj.* absolute

абстра́кт|ный, **~ен**, **~на** *adj.* abstract

абстра́кци|я, **и** *f.* abstraction

абсу́рд, **а** *m.* absurdity; **довести́ до ~а** to carry to the point of absurdity

абсу́рд|ный, **~ен**, **~на** *adj.* absurd

абха́з, **а** *m.* Abkhaz(ian)

абха́з|ка, **ки** *f. of* ▶ **абха́з**

абха́зский *adj.* Abkhazian

аванга́рд, **а** *m.* the avant-garde

аванга́рдный *adj. of* ▶ **аванга́рд**

ава́нс, **а** *m.* **1** (*деньги*) advance **2** (*in pl.*) (fig.) advances, overtures

ава́нсом *adv.* in advance, on account

авантю́р|а, **ы** *f.* **1** (*приключение*) adventure; escapade **2** (*infml*) shady enterprise

авантю́р|ный, **~ен**, **~на** *adj.* adventurous; **а. рома́н** adventure story

авари́йно-спаса́тельный *adj.* (emergency-)rescue, life-saving

авари́йн|ый *adj.* **1** *adj. of* ▶ **ава́рия**; **~ая поса́дка** crash landing; **а. сигна́л** distress signal **2** (*запасной*) emergency, spare

ава́ри|я, **и** *f.* **1** (*несчастный случай*) crash, accident **2** (*поломка*) breakdown; **потерпе́ть ~ю** to crash, have an accident

а́вгуст, **а** *m.* August

а́вгустовский *adj. of* ▶ **а́вгуст**

а́виа (*abbr. of* **авиапо́чтой**) '(by) airmail'

авиа… *comb. form*, *abbr. of* ▶ **авиацио́нный**

авиаба́з|а, **ы** *f.* air base

авиабиле́т, **а** *m.* airline ticket

авиадиспе́тчер, **а** *m.* air traffic controller

авиака́сс|а, **ы** *f.* air tickets booking office

авиакатастро́ф|а, **ы** *f.* air crash

авиакомпа́ни|я, **и** *f.* airline

авиаконстру́ктор, **а** *m.* aircraft designer

авиала́йнер, **а** *m.* airliner

авиали́ни|я, **и** *f.* airway, air route

авиано́с|ец, **ца** *m.* aircraft carrier

авиапо́чт|а, **ы** *f.* airmail

авиасало́н, **а** *m.* air show

авиацио́нно-косми́ческ|ий *adj.* aerospace; **~ая промы́шленность** the aerospace industry

авиацио́нный *adj. of* ▶ **авиа́ция**

авиа́ци|я, **и** *f.* **1** aviation **2** (*collect.*) aircraft

ави́зо *nt. indecl.* (fin.) advice note

аво́сь *particle*: **на а.** on the off chance

аво́ськ|а, **и** *f.* (*infml*) string bag

австрали́|ец, **йца** *m.* Australian

австрали́й|ка, **ки** *f. of* ▶ **австрали́ец**

австрали́йский *adj.* Australian

Австра́ли|я, **и** *f.* Australia

австри́|ец, **йца** *m.* Austrian

австри́й|ка, **ки** *f. of* ▶ **австри́ец**

австри́йский *adj.* Austrian

А́встри|я, **и** *f.* Austria

авто… *comb. form* **1** self-, auto- **2** *abbr. of* ▶ **автомати́ческий**, ▶ **автомоби́льный**

автоба́з|а, **ы** *f.* motor-transport depot

автобиографи́ческий *adj.* autobiographical

автобиогра́фи|я, **и** *f.* **1** (*описание своей жизни*) autobiography **2** (*описание своей карьеры*) curriculum vitae, CV

авто́бус, **а** *m.* bus; (*междугородный*) coach (BrE), bus (AmE)

авто́бусн|ый *adj.* bus; **~ая остано́вка** bus stop; **~ая ста́нция** bus station

автовокза́л, **а** *m.* bus terminal; coach station (BrE)

a

автого́л, а *m.* (sport) own goal

автого́нк|а, и *f.* car race; (*in pl.*) motor racing (BrE), automobile racing (AmE)

автого́нщик, а *m.* racing driver

авто́граф, а *m.* autograph

автодоро́г|а, и *f.* road; highway

автозаво́д, а *m.* car factory

автозапра́вочн|ый *adj.* filling, refuelling; ~ая ста́нция petrol *or* filling station

автоинспе́ктор, а *m.* traffic inspector

автоинспе́кци|я, и *f.* traffic inspectorate

автокатастро́ф|а, ы *f.* road accident

автоколо́нн|а, ы *f.* motorcade; (mil.) convoy

автолюби́тел|ь, я *m.* (private) motorist

автомагистра́л|ь, и *f.* motorway (BrE), interstate (highway) (AmE)

автомастерск|а́я, о́й *f.* car repair garage

автома́т, а *m.* **1** automatic machine, slot machine; биле́тный а. ticket machine; игрово́й а. fruit machine, slot machine; телефо́н-а. payphone; (fig.) automaton, robot **2** (mil.) submachine gun

автоматиза́ци|я, и *f.* automation

автоматизи́рованн|ый *adj.* computer-aided; ~ое проекти́рование CAD, computer-aided design

автоматизи́р|овать, ую *impf. and pf.* to automate

автома́тик|а, и *f.* **1** (*отрасль науки*) automation **2** (*автоматические механизмы*) automatic equipment

⚹ **автомати́ческий** *adj.* **1** (tech.) automatic **2** (fig.) automatic, involuntary

автома́тчик, а *m.* (mil.) soldier armed with a submachine gun

автомаши́н|а, ы *f.* motor vehicle

автомеха́ник, а *m.* car mechanic

автомобили́ст, а *m.* motorist

⚹ **автомоби́л|ь**, я *m.* motor vehicle; (motor)car; легково́й а. car; грузово́й а. lorry; води́ть а. to drive a car

⚹ **автомоби́льный** *adj.* of ▶ автомоби́ль

автоно́ми|я, и *f.* autonomy

автоно́м|ный, ~ен, ~на *adj.* autonomous; (comput.) stand-alone

автоотве́тчик, а *m.* answering machine

автопило́т, а *m.* autopilot

автопортре́т, а *m.* self-portrait

автоприце́п, а *m.* trailer; жило́й а. caravan (BrE), mobile home; тури́стский а. caravan (BrE), camper (AmE)

⚹ **а́втор**, а *m.* author

авторизо́ванный *adj.* (*издание, перевод*) authorized

авторита́р|ный, ~ен, ~на *adj.* authoritarian

авторите́т, а *m.* authority; по́льзоваться ~ом to enjoy authority, command respect

авторите́т|ный, ~ен, ~на *adj.* authoritative

а́втор|ский *adj.* of ▶ а́втор; а. гонора́р royalty, royalties; ~ское пра́во copyright

а́вторств|о, а *nt.* authorship

авторучк|а, и *f.* fountain pen

автосало́н, а *m.* **1** (*магазин*) car showroom **2** (*выставка*) motor show

автосе́рвис, а *m.* garage (*usu. one that repairs cars, but sometimes one that sells petrol, etc.*)

автосто́п, а *m.* (*способ путешествия*) hitch-hiking; путеше́ствовать (*impf.*) ~ом to hitch-hike

автостоя́нк|а, и *f.* car park

автостра́д|а, ы *f.* motorway (BrE), interstate (highway) (AmE)

автотра́нспорт, а *m.* motor transport

автошко́л|а, ы *f.* driving school; преподава́тель (*m.*) ~ы driving instructor

ага́ *int.* (infml) (*выражает злорадство*) aha!; (*выражает согласие*) uh-huh

аге́нт, а *m.* agent (*in var. senses*)

⚹ **аге́нтств|о**, а *nt.* agency; а. печа́ти news agency, press agency; информацио́нное/ телегра́фное а. news agency

агенту́р|а, ы *f.* **1** (*служба*) secret service **2** (*collect.*) agents

агита́тор, а *m.* (pol.) agitator; campaigner

агитацио́н|ный *adj.* (pol.) agitation; ~ая речь campaign speech

агита́ци|я, и *f.* (pol.) agitation; campaign; вести́ ~ю to campaign; предвы́борная а. electioneering

агити́р|овать, ую *impf.* (pol.) (за + *a.*) to agitate, campaign (for)

аго́ни|я, и *f.* (med., also fig.) death throes

агорафо́бия, и *f.* agoraphobia

агра́рный *adj.* agrarian

агрега́т, а *m.* **1** (*часть машины*) unit **2** (*соединение нескольких машин*) assembly

агресси́в|ный, ~ен, ~на *adj.* aggressive

агре́сси|я, и *f.* (pol.) aggression

агре́ссор, а *m.* aggressor

агро... *comb. form* agro-, agricultural, farm

агроно́м, а *m.* agronomist

агроно́ми|я, и *f.* agronomy; agricultural science

агропромы́шленный *adj.* agro-industrial

ад, а *m.* hell

адапта́ци|я, и *f.* adaptation (*in var. senses*)

ада́птер, а *m.* (tech.) adapter

адапти́р|овать, ую *impf. and pf.* to adapt

адапти́р|оваться, уюсь *impf. and pf.* to adapt; to get used to sth

адвока́т, а *m.* (*поверенный*) solicitor, lawyer; (*выступающий в суде*) barrister (BrE), attorney (AmE); (fig.) advocate

адвокату́р|а, ы *f.* **1** (*деятельность адвоката*) the legal profession; practising law **2** (*collect.*) lawyers; the Bar (BrE)

адеква́т|ный, ~ен, ~на *adj.* appropriate

⚹ **администрати́в|ный** *adj.* administrative; в ~ом поря́дке by administrative order

администра́тор, а *m.* administrator; manager (*of hotel, theatre, etc.*)

⚹ key word

администра́ци|я, и *f.* administration; management

адмира́л, а *m.* admiral

адренали́н, а *m.* adrenalin

а́дрес, а, *pl.* **∼а́, ∼óв** *m.* address; **в а.** (+ *g.*) addressed to; (fig.) directed at; **не по ∼у** (fig.) to the wrong quarter

адреса́т, а *m.* addressee; **в слу́чае ненахожде́ния ∼а** 'if undelivered'; **за ненахожде́нием ∼а** 'not known' (*on letters*)

а́дрес|ный *adj. of* ▶ **а́дрес; ∼ная кни́га** directory; **а. стол** address bureau

адрес|ова́ть, у́ю *impf. and pf.* (*письмо́*) to address; (*кри́тику, вопро́с*) to direct

Адриати́ческ|ое мо́ре, ∼ого мо́ря *nt.* the Adriatic (Sea)

а́дский *adj.* infernal, diabolical; (fig.) hellish, intolerable

адъюта́нт, а *m.* (mil.) aide-de-camp

аза́рт|ный, ∼ен, ∼на *adj.* excited, ardent; **∼ная игра́** game of chance

а́збук|а, и *f.* alphabet; the ABC (also fig.)

Азербайджа́н, а *m.* Azerbaijan

азербайджа́н|ец, ца *m.* Azerbaijani

азербайджа́н|ка, ки *f. of* ▶ **азербайджа́нец**

азербайджа́нский *adj.* Azerbaijani

азиа́т, а *m.* Asian

азиа́т|ка, ки *f. of* ▶ **азиа́т**

азиа́тский *adj.* Asian

А́зи|я, и *f.* Asia

Азо́вск|ое мо́ре, ∼ого мо́ря *nt.* the Sea of Azov

азо́т, а *m.* (chem.) nitrogen

а́ист, а *m.* (zool.) stork

ай *int.* (*выража́ет страх, испу́г*) oh!; (*выража́ет боль*) ow!, ouch!; **ай, бо́льно!** ow, that hurts!; **ай да …!** (*выража́ет одобре́ние*) what a …!; **ай да молоде́ц!** well done!

а́йсберг, а *m.* iceberg

акаде́мик, а *m.* academician (*member of a specific academy*)

академи́ческий *adj.* academic; **а. о́тпуск** sabbatical (leave) (*for undergraduates or postgraduates*)

академи́ч|ный, ∼ен, ∼на *adj.* academic, theoretical

акаде́ми|я, и *f.* academy

аквала́нг, а *m.* aqualung

акваланги́ст, а *m.* (skin *or* scuba) diver

акваланги́ст|ка, ки *f. of* ▶ **акваланги́ст**

акваре́л|ь, и *f.* (*кра́ски*) watercolours (BrE), watercolors (AmE); **писа́ть ∼ью** to paint in watercolours; (*карти́на*) watercolour (BrE), watercolor (AmE)

аква́риум, а *m.* fish tank, aquarium

акклиматиза́ци|я, и *f.* acclimatization

акклиматизи́р|овать, ую *impf. and pf.* to acclimatize

акклиматизи́р|оваться, уюсь *impf. and pf.* to become acclimatized, acclimatize

аккомпанеме́нт, а *m.* (mus.) accompaniment (also fig.); **под а.** (+ *g.*) to the accompaniment of

аккомпани́р|овать, ую *impf.* (+ *d.*) (mus.) to accompany; **а. певцу́ на роя́ле** to accompany a singer on the piano

акко́рд, а *m.* (mus.) chord

аккордео́н, а *m.* accordion

аккордеони́ст, а *m.* accordionist

аккордеони́ст|ка, ки *f. of* ▶ **аккордеони́ст**

аккумули́р|овать, ую *impf. and pf.* to accumulate

аккумуля́тор, а *m.* (tech.) accumulator; (elec.) accumulator (BrE), storage battery (AmE)

аккура́тност|ь, и *f.* **1** (*тща́тельность*) exactness, thoroughness **2** (*опря́тность*) tidiness, neatness

аккура́т|ный, ∼ен, ∼на *adj.* **1** (*тща́тельный*) exact, thorough **2** (*опря́тный*) tidy, neat **3** (*регуля́рный*) regular, punctual

акри́л, а *m.* acrylic

акри́ловый *adj. of* ▶ **акри́л**

акроба́т, а *m.* acrobat

акселера́тор, а *m.* accelerator

аксессуа́р, а *m.* **1** accessory **2** (*in pl.*) (theatr.) props

аксио́м|а, ы *f.* axiom

акт, а *m.* **1** act; **полово́й а.** sexual intercourse **2** (theatr.) act **3** (law) deed, document; **обвини́тельный а.** indictment

акт|ёр, а *m.* actor

актёрский *adj. of* ▶ **актёр**

акти́в, а *m.* (fin.) assets

активизи́р|овать, ую *impf. and pf.* (*приводи́ть в де́йствие*) to activate; (*оживля́ть*) to stimulate, enliven

активи́ст, а *m.* (pol.) activist

активи́ст|ка, ки *f. of* ▶ **активи́ст**

акти́вност|ь, и *f.* activity (*being active*)

акти́в|ный, ∼ен, ∼на *adj.* active, energetic

актри́с|а, ы *f.* actress

актуа́л|ьный, ∼ен, ∼ьна *adj.* topical, current

аку́л|а, ы *f.* (zool.) shark (also fig.)

аку́стик|а, и *f.* acoustics

акусти́ческий *adj.* acoustic

акуше́р, а *m.* obstetrician

акуше́рк|а, и *f.* midwife

акуше́рский *adj.* obstetric(al)

акце́нт, а *m.* accent

акценти́р|овать, ую *impf. and pf.* to accentuate

акционе́р, а *m.* shareholder, stockholder

акционе́р|ный *adj. of* ▶ **акционе́р; ∼ное о́бщество** joint-stock company

а́кци|я¹, и *f.* (fin.) share

а́кци|я², и *f.* action

алба́н|ец, ца *m.* Albanian

Алба́ни|я, и *f.* Albania

алба́н|ка, ки *f. of* ▶ **алба́нец**

алба́нский *adj.* Albanian

а́лгебр|а, ы *f.* algebra

a

алгори́тм, a *m.* algorithm
алеба́стр, a *m.* alabaster
Алжи́р, a *m.* **1** (*страна*) Algeria **2** (*столица*) Algiers
алжи́р|ец, ца *m.* Algerian
алжи́р|ка, ки *f. of* ▶ алжи́рец
алжи́рский *adj.* Algerian
а́либи *nt. indecl.* (law) alibi
алиме́нт|ы, ов (*no sg.*) (law) alimony
алкоголи́зм, a *m.* alcoholism
алкого́лик, a *m.* alcoholic; (infml) drunkard
алкого́л|ь, я *m.* alcohol; **прове́рить на а.** to breathalyse (BrE), breathalyze (AmE)
алкого́льный *adj.* alcoholic
Алла́х, a *m.* Allah
аллего́ри|я, и *f.* allegory
аллерги́ческий *adj.* allergic
аллерги́|я, и *f.* allergy; **а. на клубни́ку** an allergy to strawberries
алле́|я, и *f.* tree-lined path, avenue
аллига́тор, a *m.* alligator
алло́ *int.* hello!
алма́з, a *m.* (uncut) diamond
алта́р|ь, я́ *m.* **1** (*жертвенник*) altar **2** (*восточная часть церкви*) chancel
алфави́т, a *m.* alphabet; (comput., typ.) character set
алфави́тный *adj.* alphabetical; **а. указа́тель** index
алхи́мик, a *m.* alchemist
алхи́ми|я, и *f.* alchemy
а́лч|ный, ∼ен, ∼на *adj.* greedy, grasping
а́л|ый, ∼, ∼а *adj.* scarlet
альбо́м, a *m.* (*книга; пластинка, диск*) album
альмана́х, a *m.* anthology
альпи́йский *adj.* alpine
альпини́зм, a *m.* mountaineering
альпини́ст, a *m.* mountain-climber, mountaineer
альпини́ст|ка, ки *f. of* ▶ альпини́ст
А́льп|ы, ∼ (*no sg.*) the Alps
альт, а́ *m.* (mus.) **1** (*певец, голос*) alto **2** (*инструмент*) viola
альтернати́в|а, ы *f.* alternative
альтернати́в|ный, ∼ен, ∼на *adj.* alternative
альти́ст, a *m.* viola player
альти́ст|ка, ки *f. of* ▶ альти́ст
альт|о́вый *adj. of* ▶ альт; **∼о́вая па́ртия** alto part; **а. конце́рт** viola concerto
альтруи́зм, a *m.* altruism
альтруисти́ческий *adj.* altruistic
алья́нс, a *m.* alliance
алюми́ниевый *adj.* aluminium (BrE), aluminum (AmE)
алюми́ни|й, я *m.* aluminium (BrE), aluminum (AmE)
Аля́ск|а, и *f.* Alaska

амбицио́з|ный, ∼ен, ∼на *adj.* arrogant, conceited
амби́ци|я, и *f.* **1** arrogance **2** (*in pl.*) (**на** + *a.*) claims (to)
амбулато́ри|я, и *f.* (med.) (*в больнице*) outpatient department; (*кабинет врача*) doctor's surgery (BrE), doctor's office (AmE)
амбулато́рный *adj. of* ▶ амбулато́рия; **а. больно́й** outpatient; **а. приём** outpatient reception hours; surgery hours
Аме́рик|а, и *f.* America
америка́н|ец, ца *m.* American
америка́н|ка, ки *f. of* ▶ америка́нец
⚷ **америка́нский** *adj.* American
аммиа́к, a *m.* (chem.) ammonia
амнисти́р|овать, ую *impf. and pf.* to amnesty
амни́сти|я, и *f.* amnesty
амора́л|ьный, ∼ен, ∼ьна *adj.* (*нейтральный в отношении морали*) amoral; (*безнравственный*) immoral
амортиза́тор, a *m.* (tech.) shock absorber
амортиза́ци|я, и *f.* (econ.) amortization, depreciation
амортизи́р|овать, ую *impf. and pf.* (econ.) to amortize
амо́рф|ный, ∼ен, ∼на *adj.* amorphous
ампе́р, a, *g. pl.* а, *m.* (phys.) ampere
ампи́р, a *m.* Empire style (*of furniture, etc.*)
амплиту́д|а, ы *f.* amplitude
амплуа́ *nt. indecl.* (theatr.) type; (fig.) role
а́мпул|а, ы *f.* ampoule (BrE), ampule (AmE)
ампута́ци|я, и *f.* amputation
ампути́р|овать, ую *impf. and pf.* to amputate
Амстерда́м, a *m.* Amsterdam
амуле́т, a *m.* amulet
амуни́ци|я, и *f.* (collect.) (mil., hist.) accoutrements (BrE), accouterments (AmE)
амфи́би|я, и *f.* amphibian
амфитеа́тр, a *m.* (hist.) amphitheatre (BrE), amphitheater (AmE); (theatr.) circle
⚷ **ана́лиз**, a *m.* analysis; **а. кро́ви** blood test
анализи́р|овать, ую *impf. and pf.* (*pf. also* ▶ проанализи́ровать) to analyse (BrE), analyze (AmE)
анали́тик, a *m.* analyst
аналити́ческий *adj.* analytic(al)
ана́лог, a *m.* analogue
⚷ **аналоги́ч|ный**, ∼ен, ∼на *adj.* analogous
аналоги|я, и *f.* analogy; **по ∼и** (**с** + *i.*) by analogy (with), on the analogy (of); **проводи́ть ∼ю** to draw an analogy
анана́с, a *m.* pineapple
анархи́ст, a *m.* anarchist
анархи́ческий *adj.* anarchic(al)
ана́рхи|я, и *f.* anarchy
анатоми́ческий *adj.* anatomical
анато́ми|я, и *f.* anatomy
анахрони́зм, a *m.* anachronism
анаша́, й *f.* (sl.) pot, hash
анга́р, a *m.* (aeron.) hangar

áнгел, а *m.* angel; **а.-храни́тель** guardian angel; **день** ∼а name day

áнгельский *adj.* angelic

анги́н|а, ы *f.* (med.) quinsy; tonsillitis

♂ **англи́йск|ий** *adj.* English; ∼**ая була́вка** safety pin

англика́н|ец, ца *m.* Anglican

англика́н|ка, ки *f. of* ▶ **англика́нец**

англика́нский *adj.* (eccl.) Anglican

англича́н|ин, ина, *pl.* ∼**е,** ∼ *m.* Englishman

англича́нк|а, и *f.* Englishwoman

А́нгли|я, и *f.* England

англоса́кс, а *m.* Anglo-Saxon

англосаксо́нский *adj.* Anglo-Saxon

англоязы́чный *adj.* **1** (*англоговорящий*) English-speaking, anglophone **2** (*на английском языке*) English-language

Анго́л|а, ы *f.* Angola

анго́л|ец, ьца *m.* Angolan

анго́л|ка, ки *f. of* ▶ **анго́лец**

анго́льский *adj.* Angolan

андегра́унд, а *m.* (sl.) underground

А́нд|ы, ∼ (*no sg.*) the Andes

анекдо́т, а *m.* **1** (*рассказ*) anecdote, story **2** (*шутка*) joke

анеми́|я, и *f.* anaemia (BrE), anemia (AmE)

анестезио́лог, а *m.* anaesthetist (BrE), anesthetist (AmE)

анестези́р|овать, ую *impf. and pf.* to anaesthetize (BrE), anesthetize (AmE)

анестези́|я, и *f.* (med.) anaesthesia (BrE), anesthesia (AmE)

ани́с, а *m.* **1** (*растение*) anise **2** (*семя*) aniseed

Анкара́|á, ы́ *m.* Ankara

анке́т|а, ы *f.* (*опросный лист*) questionnaire; (*бланк*) form

анке́т|ный *adj. of* ▶ **анке́та;** ∼**ные да́нные** biographical details

аннекси́р|овать, ую *impf. and pf.* (pol.) to annex

аннота́ци|я, и *f.* abstract, precis

аннули́р|овать, ую *impf. and pf.* (*договор*) to annul, nullify; (*долг*) to cancel; (*закон*) to abrogate

анома́ли|я, и *f.* anomaly

аноним́к|а, и *f.* (infml, *письмо*) poison pen letter

анони́м|ный, ∼**ен,** ∼**на** *adj.* anonymous

ано́нс, а *m.* announcement, notice; (cin.) trailer

анса́мбл|ь, я *m.* ensemble

Антаркти́д|а, ы *f.* Antarctica

Анта́рктик|а, и *f.* the Antarctic

антаркти́ческий *adj.* Antarctic

анте́нн|а, ы *f.* aerial, antenna

анти… *pref.* anti-

антиалкого́льный *adj.* anti-alcohol

антибио́тик, а *m.* (med.) antibiotic

антивое́нный *adj.* anti-war

антидепресса́нт, а *m.* (med.) antidepressant

антикапиталисти́ческий *adj.* anticapitalist

антиква́р, а *m.* (*любитель антикварных предметов*) antiquary; (*дилер*) antique dealer

антиквариа́т, а *m.* (*collect.*) antiques

антиква́рный *adj.* (*книга*) antiquarian; (*ваза; магазин*) antique

антило́п|а, ы *f.* (zool.) antelope

антипа́ти|я, и *f.* antipathy

антисеми́т, а *m.* anti-Semite

антисемити́зм, а *m.* anti-Semitism

антисеми́т|ка, ки *f. of* ▶ **антисеми́т**

антисеми́тский *adj.* anti-Semitic

антисе́птик, а *m.* antiseptic

антитеррористи́ческий *adj.* antiterrorist

антицикло́н, а *m.* (meteor.) anticyclone

анти́чный *adj.* ancient; classical

антра́кт, а *m.* (theatr.) interval

антраци́т, а *m.* (min.) anthracite

антреко́т, а *m.* entrecôte, steak

антрепри́з|а, ы *f.* (theatr.) private theatrical company

антресо́л|ь, и *f.* (*usu. in pl.*) **1** (*полуэтаж*) mezzanine **2** (*полка*) shelf

антропо́лог, а *m.* anthropologist

антропологи́ческий *adj.* anthropological

антрополо́ги|я, и *f.* anthropology

антура́ж, а *m.* environment; (*collect.*) entourage, associates

анчо́ус, а *m.* anchovy

аншла́г, а *m.* (theatr.) sell-out notice; **спекта́кль идёт с** ∼**ом** the show is sold out

АО (*abbr. of* **акционе́рное о́бщество**) joint-stock company

апартаме́нт|ы, ов *m. pl.* (*sg.* ∼, ∼**а**) large apartment

апартеи́д, а *m.* apartheid

апа́ти|я, и *f.* apathy

апгре́йд, а *m.* (comput., infml) upgrade

апелли́р|овать, ую *impf. and pf.* (**к** + *d.*) to appeal (to)

апелляцио́нный *adj. of* ▶ **апелля́ция; а. суд** Court of Appeal (*in England and Wales*); court of appeals (AmE)

апелля́ци|я, и *f.* **1** (*обращение*) (**к** + *d.*) appeal (to) **2** (*обжалование*) (**на** + *a.*) appeal (against)

апельси́н, а *m.* orange

апельси́новый *adj.* orange

Апенни́н|ы, ∼ (*no sg.*) the Apennines

аперити́в, а *m.* aperitif

аплоди́р|овать, ую *impf.* (+ *d.*) to applaud

аплодисме́нт|ы, ов *m. pl.* applause

апоге́|й, я *m.* (astron.) apogee; (fig.) climax

апока́липсис, а *m.* apocalypse

апокалипти́ческий *adj.* apocalyptic

аполити́ч|ный, ∼**ен,** ∼**на** *adj.* apolitical; politically indifferent

апо́стол, а *m.* apostle (also fig.)

апостро́ф, а *m.* apostrophe

a

апофео́з, а *m.* apotheosis

Аппала́ч|и, ей (*no sg.*) the Appalachians

🗝 **аппара́т, а** *m.* **1** (*прибор*) apparatus; appliance; **копирова́льный а.** photocopier; **косми́ческий аппара́т** spacecraft; **ка́ссовый а.** cash register; **слухово́й а.** hearing aid; **телефо́нный а.** telephone **2** (*учреждения*): **госуда́рственный а.** machinery of state **3** (*штат*) staff, personnel

аппара́тн|ый *adj.* (comput.) hardware; **~ые сре́дства** hardware

аппарату́р|а, ы *f.* (tech.) (*collect.*) apparatus, equipment; (comput.) hardware

аппе́ндикс, а *m.* appendix

аппендици́т, а *m.* appendicitis

аппети́т, а *m.* appetite; **прия́тного ~a!** bon appétit!

аппети́т|ный, ~ен, ~на *adj.* appetizing, mouth-watering

апплика́ци|я, и *f.* appliqué

🗝 **апре́л|ь, я** *m.* April

апре́льский *adj. of* ▸ **апре́ль**

апте́к|а, и *f.* chemist's (shop) (BrE), pharmacy

апте́кар|ь, я *m.* chemist (BrE); pharmacist

апте́чк|а, и *f.* (*первой помощи*) first-aid kit; (*коробка*) medicine chest

ара́б, а *m.* Arab

ара́б|ка, ки *f. of* ▸ **ара́б**

ара́бск|ий *adj.* Arab; Arabian; Arabic; **А~ая весна́** Arab spring; **~ие ци́фры** Arabic numerals; **а. язы́к** Arabic

арави́йский *adj.* Arabian

аранжиро́вк|а, и *f.* arrangement

ара́хис, а *m.* peanut, groundnut

арбале́т, а *m.* crossbow

арби́тр, а *m.* (*в споре*) arbiter, arbitrator; (*в спорте*) umpire, referee

арбитра́ж, а *m.* arbitration

арбитра́жный *adj.*: **а. суд** court of arbitration

арбу́з, а *m.* watermelon

Аргенти́н|а, ы *f.* Argentina

аргенти́н|ец, ца *m.* Argentinian

аргенти́н|ка, ки *f. of* ▸ **аргенти́нец**

аргенти́нский *adj.* Argentinian, Argentine

аргуме́нт, а *m.* argument

аргумента́ци|я, и *f.* reasoning, argumentation

аргументи́р|овать, ую *impf. and pf.* to argue; (*pf. only*) to prove

ареа́л, а *m.* (bot. and zool.) natural habitat; (fig.) region

аре́н|а, ы *f.* arena, ring; (fig.) arena

🗝 **аре́нд|а, ы** *f.* lease; **сдать в ~у** to rent, lease (*of owner, landlord*); **взять в ~у** to rent, lease (*of tenant*)

аренда́тор, а *m.* tenant, lessee

аре́нд|ный *adj. of* ▸ **аре́нда**; **~ная пла́та** rent; **а. подря́д** contract for lease (*of land*)

аренд|ова́ть, у́ю *impf. and pf.* to rent, lease (*of tenant*)

аре́ст, а *m.* (*человека*) arrest; (*имущества*) seizure, sequestration; **взять под а.** to place under arrest; **сиде́ть, находи́ться под ~ом** to be under arrest, in custody; **наложи́ть а. на** (+ *a.*) to sequestrate

ареста́нт, а *m.* prisoner

арест|ова́ть, у́ю *pf.* (*of* ▸ **аресто́вывать**) (*человека*) to arrest; (*имущество*) to sequestrate

аресто́выва|ть, ю *impf. of* ▸ **арестова́ть**

аристокра́т, а *m.* aristocrat

аристократи́ческий *adj.* aristocratic

аристокра́ти|я, и *f.* aristocracy

арифме́тик|а, и *f.* arithmetic

арифмети́ческий *adj.* arithmetical

а́ри|я, и *f.* aria

а́рк|а, и *f.* arch

арка́н, а *m.* lasso

А́рктик|а, и *f.* the Arctic

аркти́ческий *adj.* arctic

арме́йский *adj. of* ▸ **а́рмия**

Арме́ни|я, и *f.* Armenia

🗝 **а́рми|я, и** *f.* army; **А. спасе́ния** Salvation Army; **де́йствующая а.** front-line forces

армяни́н, ина́, *pl.* **~e, ~ и́н** *m.* Armenian

армя́н|ка, ки *f. of* ▸ **армяни́н**

армя́нский *adj.* Armenian

арома́т, а *m.* (*цветов*) scent, fragrance; (*пищи*) aroma

ароматиза́тор, а *m.* (cul.) flavouring (BrE), flavoring (AmE)

арома́т|ный, ~ен, ~на *adj.* aromatic, fragrant

арсена́л, а *m.* arsenal

арт... *comb. form* 1 (*abbr. of* **артиллери́йский**) artillery **2** (*искусство*) art

арте́ри|я, и *f.* artery

арти́кл|ь, я *m.* (gram.) article

артиллери́йский *adj.* (mil.) artillery; **а. обстре́л** bombardment, shelling; **а. склад** ordnance depot

артилле́ри|я, и *f.* artillery

арти́ст, а *m.* artist(e); **а. бале́та** ballet dancer; **а. кино́** film actor

артисти́ческ|ий *adj.* artistic; (*as f. n.* **~ая, ~ой**) (theatr.) dressing room

арти́ст|ка, ки *f. of* ▸ **арти́ст**

артри́т, а *m.* arthritis

а́рф|а, ы *f.* harp

арфи́ст, а *m.* harpist

арфи́ст|ка, ки *f. of* ▸ **арфи́ст**

архаи́ч|ный, ~ен, ~на *adj.* archaic

архео́лог, а *m.* archaeologist (BrE), archeologist (AmE)

археологи́ческий *adj.* archaeological (BrE), archeological (AmE)

археоло́ги|я, и *f.* archaeology (BrE), archeology (AmE)

🗝 **архи́в, а** *m.* archive; (*collect.*) archives; **сдать в а.** (infml, fig.) to shelve, leave out of account

архи́вный *adj. of* ▸ **архи́в**

архиепи́скоп, а *m.* archbishop

архиере́|й, я *m.* member of higher orders of clergy (*bishop, archbishop, or metropolitan*)

архипела́г, а *m.* archipelago

архите́ктор, а *m.* architect

архитекту́р|а, ы *f.* architecture

архитекту́рный *adj.* architectural

арьерга́рд, а *m.* (mil.) rearguard

асбе́ст, а *m.* asbestos

асоциа́льный *adj.* antisocial

аспе́кт, а *m.* (*сторона*) aspect; (*точка зрения*) viewpoint, perspective

аспира́нт, а *m.* postgraduate student

аспира́нт|ка, ки *f. of* ▶ аспира́нт

аспиранту́р|а, ы *f.* postgraduate study

аспири́н, а *m.* (med.) aspirin; табле́тка ~а an aspirin

ассамбле́|я, и *f.* assembly

ассениза́тор, а *m.* sewage worker

ассигн|ова́ть, у́ю *impf. and pf.* (fin.) to assign, allocate

ассимиля́ци|я, и *f.* assimilation

ассисте́нт, а *m.* **1** (*помощник*) assistant **2** (*в вузе*) junior member of teaching or research staff

ассисти́р|овать, ую *impf.* (med.) (+ *d.*) to assist

ассортиме́нт, а *m.* assortment; range (*of goods*)

✐ **ассоциа́ци|я**, и *f.* association

ассоции́р|овать, ую *impf. and pf.* (с + *i.*) to associate (with)

астеро́ид, а *m.* asteroid

а́стм|а, ы *f.* asthma

астма́тик, а *m.* asthmatic

а́стр|а, ы *f.* aster

астро́лог, а *m.* astrologer

астрологи́ческий *f.* astrological

астроло́ги|я, и *f.* astrology

астрона́вт, а *m.* astronaut

астроно́м, а *m.* astronomer

астрономи́ческий *adj.* astronomic(al) (*also fig.*)

астроно́ми|я, и *f.* astronomy

астрофи́зик|а, и *f.* astrophysics

асфа́льт, а *m.* asphalt

ата́к|а, и *f.* attack

атак|ова́ть, у́ю *impf. and pf.* (mil., sport) to attack

атама́н, а *m.* ataman (*Cossack chieftain*)

атеи́зм, а *m.* atheism

атеи́ст, а *m.* atheist

атеи́ст|ка, ки *f. of* ▶ атеи́ст

ателье́ *nt. indecl.* studio; а. мод tailor's shop

Атланти́ческ|ий океа́н, ~ого океа́на *m.* the Atlantic Ocean; the Atlantic

а́тлас, а *m.* atlas

атла́с, а *m.* satin

атле́т, а *m.* (*спортсмен*) athlete; (*в цирке*) strongman

атле́тик|а, и *f.* athletics; лёгкая а. (track and field) athletics; тяжёлая а. weightlifting

атлети́ческ|ий *adj.* athletic; ~ое телосложе́ние athletic build

✐ **атмосфе́р|а**, ы *f.* atmosphere

атмосфе́рн|ый *adj.* atmospheric; ~ые оса́дки atmospheric precipitation, rainfall

а́том, а *m.* atom

а́томн|ый *adj.* atomic; nuclear; ~ая бо́мба atomic bomb; ~ая электроста́нция nuclear power station

атрибу́т, а *m.* attribute

атрибу́тик|а, и *f.* **1** (collect.) (*атрибуты*) attributes **2** merchandise (*e.g. of a football club*)

АТС *f. indecl.* (*abbr. of* автомати́ческая телефо́нная ста́нция) automatic telephone exchange

атташе́ *m. indecl.* (pol.) attaché

аттеста́т, а *m.* certificate

аттестацио́нн|ый *adj.*: ~ая коми́ссия examination board

аттеста́ци|я, и *f.* (*действие*) certification; (*отзыв*) reference

аттест|ова́ть, у́ю *impf. and pf.* (*присвоить звание*) to certify; (*оценить знания*) to grade, give a mark

аттракцио́н, а *m.* (theatr.) attraction; sideshow, ride (*at fairground*); парк ~ов amusement park

аудие́нци|я, и *f.* audience (*official interview*)

ауди́т, а *m.* audit

ауди́тор, а *m.* auditor

аудито́ри|я, и *f.* **1** auditorium; lecture hall **2** (collect.) audience

аукцио́н, а *m.* auction, auction sale; продава́ть с ~а to auction

а́ут, а *m.* (sport) out (*also as int.*)

аутенти́ч|ный, ~ен, ~на *adj.* authentic

аути́зм, а *m.* autism

афга́н|ец, ца *m.* Afghan; «а.» Afghan war vet(eran)

Афганиста́н, а *m.* Afghanistan

афга́н|ка, ки *f. of* ▶ афга́нец

афе́р|а, ы *f.* swindle, trickery

афери́ст, а *m.* swindler, trickster

афери́ст|ка, ки *f. of* ▶ афери́ст

Афи́н|ы, ~ (*no sg.*) Athens

афи́ш|а, и *f.* poster, placard; театра́льная а. playbill

афори́зм, а *m.* aphorism

А́фрик|а, и *f.* Africa

африка́н|ец, ца *m.* African

африка́н|ка, ки *f. of* ▶ африка́нец

африка́нский *adj.* African

афроамерика́н|ец, ца *m.* African American

афроамерика́н|ка, ки *f. of* ▶ афроамерика́нец

афроамерика́нский *adj.* African-American

ах *int.* ah! oh!

а́эро... *comb. form* aero-; air-, aerial

a
б

аэро́бик|а, и *f.* aerobics

аэровокза́л, а *m.* air terminal

аэродина́мик|а, и *f.* aerodynamics

аэродинами́ческий *adj.* aerodynamic

аэродро́м, а *m.* aerodrome

аэрозо́л|ь, я *m.* aerosol, spray

аэрона́втик|а, и *f.* aeronautics

⚡ аэропо́рт, а, об ~е, в ~у́ *m.* airport

АЭС *f. indecl.* (*abbr. of* а́томная электроста́нция) atomic power station

а/я *m. indecl.* (*abbr. of* абоне́нтский я́щик) PO (*abbr. of post office*) Box

Бб

⚡ б *particle* = бы (*after words ending in vowel*)

ба́б|а, ы *f.* (infml, also pej.) woman; сне́жная б. snowman

ба́бк|а, и *f.* = ба́бушка

ба́б|ки, ок *f. pl.* (infml) money

ба́бочк|а, и *f.* **1** butterfly; ночна́я б. moth; (*проститутка*) prostitute **2** (*галстук*) bow tie

ба́бушк|а, и *f.* grandmother; (infml) old woman; gran(ny) (*as mode of address*)

бага́ж, á *m.* luggage; сдать свои́ ве́щи в б. to register one's luggage, to check in one's luggage

бага́жник, а *m.* (*в автомобиле*) boot (BrE), trunk (AmE); (*на крыше*) roof rack; (*велосипеда*) carrier

бага́жный *adj. of* ▶ бага́ж; б. ваго́н luggage van (BrE), baggage car (AmE)

Багда́д, а *m.* Baghdad

багро́в|ый, ~, ~а *adj.* crimson, purple

бадминто́н, а *m.* badminton

бадминтони́ст, а *m.* badminton player

бадминтони́ст|ка, ки *f. of* ▶ бадминтони́ст

бад|ья́, ьи́, *g. pl.* ~е́й *f.* tub

⚡ ба́з|а, ы *f.* **1** (mil., archit.) base; (*склад*) depot; (*туристов*) centre (BrE), center (AmE); б. да́нных database **2** (*основание*) basis; на ~е (+ *g.*) on the basis (of)

база́р, а *m.* (infml) market

база́рный *adj. of* ▶ база́р; (infml) of the marketplace, rough, crude

бази́р|оваться, уюсь *impf.* (на + *p.*) **1** to be based (on) **2** (mil.) to be based (at)

ба́зис, а *m.* (archit.) base; (*основание*) basis

⚡ ба́зовый *adj.* **1** basic; б. курс foundation course **2**: б. ла́герь base camp

базу́к|а, и *f.* bazooka

байда́рк|а, и *f.* (*брус*) kayak; canoe

ба́йт, а *m.* (comput.) byte

бак, а *m.* cistern; tank; му́сорный б. dustbin (BrE), garbage can (AmE)

бакала́вр, а *m.* bachelor (*holder of degree*)

бакале́йный *adj.* grocery; б. магази́н grocer's shop (BrE), grocery store (AmE)

бакале́|я, и *f.* **1** (*collect.*) dry goods, groceries **2** (*в магазине*) grocery section; (*магазин*) grocer's (shop)

ба́кен, а *m.* (*буй*) buoy

бакенба́рд|ы, ~ *f. pl.* (*sg.* ~а, ~ы) side whiskers

баклажа́н, а *m.* aubergine (BrE), eggplant (AmE)

бакла́н, а *m.* cormorant

ба́кс|ы, ов *m. pl.* (sl.) bucks, American dollars

бактериологи́ческ|ий *adj.* bacteriological; ~ая война́ germ warfare

бактериоло́ги|я, и *f.* bacteriology

бакте́ри|я, и *f.* bacterium

Баку́ *m. indecl.* Baku

бал, а, о ~е, на ~у́, *pl.* ~ы́ *m.* ball, dance

балала́йк|а, и *f.* balalaika

бала́нс, а *m.* (econ., tech.) balance; платёжный б. balance of payments

баланси́р|овать, ую *impf.* (*сохранять равнове́сие*) to balance

балери́н|а, ы *f.* ballerina

бале́т, а *m.* ballet; б. на льду́ ice show

бале́тный *adj. of* ▶ бале́т

ба́лк|а, и *f.* (*брус*) beam, girder

балка́нский *adj.* Balkan

Балка́н|ы, ~ (*no sg.*) the Balkans

балко́н, а *m.* balcony

балл, а *m.* **1** (meteor.) number; ве́тер в пять ~ов wind force 5 **2** (*в школе*) mark; вы́сший б. an 'A'; проходно́й б. pass mark **3** (sport) point; score

балла́д|а, ы *f.* ballad

балли́стик|а, и *f.* ballistics

баллисти́ческий *adj.* ballistic

балло́н, а *m.* **1** (*сосуд*) container (*of glass, metal, or rubber*); carboy; аэрозо́льный б. spray can; кислоро́дный б. oxygen cylinder **2** (*шина*) balloon tyre (BrE), balloon tire (AmE)

баллоти́р|оваться, уюсь *impf.* (в + *a. or* на + *a.*) to stand (BrE), run (AmE) (for), be a candidate (for)

бал|ова́ть, у́ю *impf. (of* ▶ избалова́ть*)* to spoil; to pamper

бал|ова́ться, у́юсь *impf.* (infml) **1** (*шали́ть*) to get up to mischief **2** (*с + i.*) (*со спи́чками*) to play, fool about (with) **3** (*позволя́ть себе́ что́-л.*) to indulge (in)

баловств|о́, а́ *nt.* **1** (*ша́лости*) mischief **2** (*причу́да*) folly, extravagance

балти́йский *adj.* Baltic; **Балти́йское мо́ре** the Baltic Sea

Ба́лтик|а, и *f.* (*мо́ре*) the Baltic (Sea); (*райо́н*) the Baltic coast

бальза́м, а *m.* balsam; (fig.) balm; **б. для воло́с** hair conditioner

ба́л|ьный *adj. of* ▶ бал; **~ьные та́нцы** ballroom dancing

бамбу́к, а *m.* bamboo

ба́мпер, а *m.* bumper

бана́льность|, и *f.* **1** (*сво́йство*) banality **2** (*замеча́ние*) banal remark; platitude

бана́л|ьный, ~ен, ~ьна *adj.* banal, trite

бана́н, а *m.* banana

Бангко́к, а *m.* Bangkok

Бангладе́ш, а *m.* Bangladesh

бангладе́ш|ец, ца *m.* Bangladeshi

бангладе́ш|ка, ки *f. of* ▶ бангладе́шец

бангладе́шский *adj.* Bangladeshi

ба́нд|а, ы *f.* band, gang

бандеро́л|ь, и *f.* (*почто́вое отправле́ние*) small package

банди́т, а *m.* bandit; thug; armed robber

бандити́зм, а *m.* banditry; thuggery

банди́тский *adj. of* ▶ банди́т

✐ **банк, а** *m.* bank (also fig.); **б. да́нных** databank

ба́нк|а, и *f.* (*стекля́нная*) jar; (*жестяна́я*) tin (BrE), can (AmE)

банке́т, а *m.* banquet

банки́р, а *m.* banker

банкно́т|а, ы *f.* banknote

✐ **ба́нк|овский** *adj. of* ▶ банк; **б. биле́т** banknote; **~овская кни́жка** passbook, bank book

банкома́т, а *m.* cash machine

банкро́т, а *m.* bankrupt; **объявля́ть кого́-л. ~ом** to declare sb bankrupt

банкро́тств|о, а *nt.* bankruptcy

бант, а *m.* bow

ба́н|я, и *f.* (Russian) baths; bathhouse; **фи́нская б.** sauna

бапти́ст, а *m.* Baptist

бапти́ст|ка, ки *f. of* ▶ бапти́ст

бар, а *m.* bar; **пивно́й б.** pub

бараба́н, а *m.* drum

бараба́н|ить, ю, ишь *impf.* to drum

бараба́н|ный *adj. of* ▶ бараба́н; **~ная дробь** drum roll; **~ная перепо́нка** (anat.) ear drum, tympanum

бараба́нщик, а *m.* drummer

бараба́нщи|ца, цы *f. of* ▶ бараба́нщик

бара́к, а *m.* hut

бара́н, а *m.* ram; (wild) sheep

бара́н|ий *adj.* **1** sheep's; ram's **2** (*из ко́жи бара́на*) sheepskin **3** (*о еде́*) mutton; **~ья котле́та** mutton chop

бара́нин|а, ы *f.* mutton; (*молода́я*) lamb

барахл|о́, а́ *nt.* (collect.) (infml) trash, junk

барда́к, а́ *m.* (infml) chaos

бардачо́к, ка́ *m.* (infml) glove compartment (*in car*)

Ба́ренцев|о мо́ре, ~а мо́ря *nt.* the Barents Sea

ба́рж|а, и *f.* barge

барито́н, а *m.* baritone

ба́рмен, а *m.* barman, bartender

баро́кко *nt. indecl.* baroque

баро́метр, а *m.* barometer

баро́н, а *m.* baron

бароне́сс|а, ы *f.* baroness

баррика́д|а, ы *f.* barricade

барс, а *m.* (zool.) snow leopard (*Uncia uncia*)

барсу́к, а́ *m.* badger

ба́ртер, а *m.* barter

ба́рхат, а *m.* velvet

ба́рхатный *adj.* **1** velvet; **б. сезо́н** autumn season, autumn months (*in the south of Russia*) **2** (fig.) velvety

ба́рхат|цы, цев *m. pl.* (*sg.* **~ец, ~ца**) (French/African) marigold (*genus Tagetes*)

барье́р, а *m.* **1** barrier (also fig.); **звуково́й б.** sound barrier; **языково́й б.** language barrier **2** (sport) hurdle; **взять б.** to clear a hurdle

бас, а, *pl.* **~ы́** *m.* (mus.) bass

бас-гита́р|а, ы *f.* bass guitar

баск, а *m.* Basque

баскетбо́л, а *m.* basketball (*the sport*)

баскетболи́ст, а *m.* basketball player

баскетболи́ст|ка, ки *f. of* ▶ баскетболи́ст

баско́н|ка, ки *f. of* ▶ баск

ба́скский *adj.* Basque

баснослóв|ный, ~ен, ~на *adj.* (fig., infml) fabulous

ба́с|ня, ни, *g. pl.* **~ен** *f.* **1** fable **2** (fig., infml) fable, fabrication

✐ **бассе́йн, а** *m.* **1** (man-made) pool; **пла́вательный б.** swimming pool **2** (geog.) basin; **каменноу́гольный б.** coalfield

бастио́н, а *m.* (mil., also fig.) bastion

баст|ова́ть, у́ю *impf.* to strike, go on strike; to be on strike

баталь́он, а *m.* battalion

батаре́йк|а, и *f.* (elec.) battery

батаре́|я, и *f.* (mil. and tech.) battery; (*отопи́тельная*) radiator

бато́н, а *m.* French loaf

бату́т, а *m.* trampoline; **прыжки́ на ~е** trampolining

ба́тюшк|а, и *m.* (*свяще́нник*) father

бахром|а́, ы́ *f.* fringe

башк|а́, и́ (*no g. pl.*) *f.* (infml) head

башма́к, а́ *m.* (*боти́нок*) boot; (*ту́фля*) shoe

ба́ш|ня, ни, *g. pl.* **~ен** *f.* tower; turret

бая́н, а *m.* (mus.) bayan (*a kind of accordion*)

б

б

бди́тельность, и *f.* vigilance, watchfulness

бди́тел|ьный, ~ен, ~ьна *adj.* vigilant, watchful

бег, а, о ~е, на ~у́, *pl.* ~á, ~óв *m.* **1** run, running; jogging; ~óм, на ~у́ running; at the double; **на всём ~у́** at full speed; **б. на ме́сте** running on the spot; marking time (also fig.) **2** (sport, *состяза́ние*) race **3** (*in pl.*) (*го́нки упря́жных лошаде́й*) harness races; trotting races **4**: **быть в ~áх** to be on the run

бе́га|ть, ю *impf.* (*indet. of* ► бежа́ть) **1** to run (about); (*за + i.*) (infml) to run (after), chase (after) **2** (*о глаза́х*) to rove, roam

бегемо́т, а *m.* hippopotamus

бегле́ц, á *m.* fugitive

бе́глый *adj.* **1** (*убежа́вший*) fugitive, runaway **2** (*свобо́дный*) fluent, quick

бегля́нк|а, и *f. of* ► бегле́ц

бег|ово́й *adj. of* ► бег; ~ова́я доро́жка racetrack, running track; (*in gym*) treadmill; ~ова́я ло́шадь racehorse

беготн|я́, и́ *f.* (infml) running about; bustle

бе́гств|о, а *nt.* flight; escape; **обрати́ть в б.** to put to flight; **обрати́ться в б., спаса́ться ~ом** to take to flight

бе|гу́, ~жи́шь *see* ► бежа́ть

бегу́н, á *m.* runner

бед|á, ы́, *pl.* ~ы *f.* **1** (*несча́стье*) misfortune; calamity; (*infml*) to one's cost **2** (*as pred.*) it is awful!; it is a problem!; **б. в том, что** the trouble is (that); **не б.!** it doesn't matter!

бе́дность, и *f.* poverty (also fig.)

бе́д|ный, ~ен, ~на́, ~но, ~ны́ *adj.* poor; meagre (BrE), meager (AmE); (fig.) barren

бедня́г|а, и *m.* (infml) poor devil, poor thing

бедня́к, á *m.* pauper

бедр|о́, á, *pl.* ~а, ~ер, ~рам *nt.* (*ве́рхняя часть ноги́*) thigh; (*таз*) hip

бе́дстви|е, я *nt.* calamity, disaster; **райо́н ~я** disaster area; **сигна́л ~я** distress signal

бе́дствова|ть, ую *impf.* to live in poverty

бе|жа́ть, гу́, жи́шь, гу́т *impf.* (*det. of* ► бе́гать) **1** to run; (fig., *о воде́*) to run; (*о кро́ви*) to flow **2** (*impf. and pf.*) (*спаса́ться*) to escape

бе́жевый *adj.* beige

бе́жен|ец, ца *m.* refugee

бе́жен|ка, ки *f. of* ► бе́женец

✒ **без** *prep. + g.* without; in the absence of; minus, less; **не б.** not without; **б. вас** in your absence; **б. пяти́ (мину́т) три** five (minutes) to three; **б. че́тверти час** a quarter to one; **б. ма́лого** (infml) almost, all but; **быть б. ума́** (*от + g.*) to be crazy (about)

без... *pref.* in-, un-, -less

безалкого́льный *adj.* non-alcoholic; **б. напи́ток** non-alcoholic drink, soft drink

безапелляцио́н|ный, ~ен, ~на *adj.* peremptory, categorical

безбиле́тный *adj.* ticketless; **б. пассажи́р** fare dodger; (*на су́дне, самолёте*) stowaway

безбо́жный *adj.* **1** irreligious, anti-religious **2** (infml, *бессо́вестный*) outrageous

безболе́зненный, ~, ~на *adj.* painless

безбра́чный *adj.* celibate

безбре́ж|ный, ~ен, ~на *adj.* boundless

безве́трен|ный, ~, ~на *adj.* calm, windless

безве́три|е, я *nt.* calm

безвку́с|ный, ~ен, ~на *adj.* tasteless

безво́д|ный, ~ен, ~на *adj.* arid

безвозвра́т|ный, ~ен, ~на *adj.* irrevocable; irretrievable; ~ная ссу́да permanent loan

безвозме́здный *adj.* free (of charge); **б. труд** unpaid work

безво́ли|е, я *nt.* lack of will; weak will

безво́л|ьный, ~ен, ~ьна *adj.* weak-willed

безвре́д|ный, ~ен, ~на *adj.* harmless

безвре́менн|ый *adj.* untimely, premature; ~ая кончи́на untimely end, untimely death

безвы́ездно *adv.* uninterruptedly, without a break

безвы́езд|ный, ~ен, ~на *adj.* uninterrupted; ~ое пребыва́ние continuous residence

безвы́ход|ный, ~ен, ~на *adj.* hopeless, desperate

безгра́мот|ный, ~ен, ~на *adj.* illiterate (also fig.); ignorant

безграни́ч|ный, ~ен, ~на *adj.* infinite, limitless, boundless

безгре́ш|ный, ~ен, ~на *adj.* innocent, without sin

безда́рность, и *f.* **1** (*сво́йство*) lack of talent **2** (*челове́к*) person without talent

безда́р|ный, ~ен, ~на *adj.* (*челове́к*) talentless, undistinguished; (*произведе́ние*) third-rate

безде́йстви|е, я *nt.* inaction, idleness; (law) (criminal) negligence

безделу́шк|а, и *f.* knick-knack

безде́ль|е, я *nt.* idleness

безде́льник, а *m.* idler, loafer

безде́льнича|ть, ю *impf.* to idle, loaf about

безде́т|ный, ~ен, ~на *adj.* childless

бе́здн|а, ы *f.* abyss, chasm

бездоказа́тель|ный, ~ен, ~ьна *adj.* unsubstantiated

бездо́м|ный, ~ен, ~на *adj.* homeless; (*о ко́шке, соба́ке*) stray

бездоро́жь|е, я *nt.* **1** (*отсу́тствие доро́г*) absence of roads **2** (*распу́тица*) bad condition of roads; season when roads are impassable

безду́м|ный, ~ен, ~на *adj.* unthinking; feckless

безе́ *nt. indecl.* meringue

безжа́лост|ный, ~ен, ~на *adj.* ruthless, pitiless

безжи́знен|ный, ~, ~на *adj.* lifeless, inanimate; (fig.) spiritless

беззабо́т|ный, ~ен, ~на *adj.* carefree, light-hearted; (*безду́мный*) careless

беззако́ни|е, я *nt.* **1** (*отсу́тствие зако́нности*) lawlessness **2** (*посту́пок*)

✒ key word

unlawful act

беззащи́т|ный, ∼ен, ∼на *adj.* defenceless (BrE), defensive (AmE), unprotected

беззву́ч|ный, ∼ен, ∼на *adj.* soundless, noiseless

беззло́б|ный, ∼ен, ∼на *adj.* good-natured

беззу́б|ый, ∼, ∼а *adj.* toothless; (fig.) weak, feeble

безли́кий *adj.* featureless; faceless, impersonal

безли́ч|ный, ∼ен, ∼на *adj.* **1** without personality, characterless, impersonal **2** (gram.) impersonal

безлю́д|ный, ∼ен, ∼на *adj.* (*малонаселённый*) uninhabited; sparsely populated; (*улица*) empty, deserted

безмо́згл|ый, ∼, ∼а *adj.* (infml) brainless

безмо́лви|е, я *nt.* silence; **цари́т б.** silence reigns

безмо́лв|ный, ∼ен, ∼на *adj.* silent, mute; ∼ное согла́сие tacit consent

безмяте́ж|ный, ∼ен, ∼на *adj.* serene, placid

безнадёж|ный, ∼ен, ∼на *adj.* hopeless; despairing

безнака́занно *adv.* with impunity; э́то ему́ не пройдёт б. he won't get away with this

безнака́занность, и *f.* impunity

безнали́чный *adj.* (fin.) cashless

безно́г|ий, ∼, ∼а *adj.* (*без ног*) legless; (*без ноги*) one-legged

безнра́вственность, и *f.* immorality

безнра́вствен|ный, ∼, ∼на *adj.* immoral

безоби́д|ный, ∼ен, ∼на *adj.* inoffensive

безо́блач|ный, ∼ен, ∼на *adj.* cloudless; (fig.) serene, unclouded

безобра́зи|е, я *nt.* **1** (*уродство*) ugliness **2** (*поступок*) outrage **3** (*as pred.*) (infml) it is disgraceful!

безобра́знича|ть, ю *impf.* (infml) to behave disgracefully; to make a nuisance of oneself

безобра́з|ный, ∼ен, ∼на *adj.* **1** (*уродливый*) ugly **2** (*поступок*) disgraceful, outrageous

безогово́роч|ный, ∼ен, ∼на *adj.* unconditional, unreserved, absolute

⚡ **безопа́сность**, и *f.* safety, security; по́яс/ реме́нь ∼и seat belt; Сове́т Б∼и Security Council

безопа́с|ный, ∼ен, ∼на *adj.* safe, secure; б. секс safe sex

безору́ж|ный, ∼ен, ∼на *adj.* unarmed; (fig.) defenceless (BrE), defenseless (AmE)

безоснова́тел|ьный, ∼ен, ∼ьна *adj.* groundless

безотве́тствен|ный, ∼, ∼на *adj.* irresponsible

безотка́з|ный, ∼ен, ∼на *adj.* **1** (*человек*) dependable, reliable **2** (*прибор, машина*) trouble-free, reliable

безотноси́тельно *adv.* (к + *d.*) irrespective (of)

безотчёт|ный, ∼ен, ∼на *adj.* **1** (*бесконтрольный*) not subject to control

2 (*бессознательный*) unconscious, instinctive

безоши́боч|ный, ∼ен, ∼на *adj.* correct

безрабо́тиц|а, ы *f.* unemployment

безрабо́т|ный *adj.* unemployed; (*as n. pl.* ∼ые, ∼ых) the unemployed

безра́дост|ный, ∼ен, ∼на *adj.* joyless; dismal

безразде́л|ьный, ∼ен, ∼ьна *adj.* (*внимание*) undivided; ∼ьная власть complete sway

безразли́чи|е, я *nt.* indifference

безразли́чно *adv.* indifferently; относи́ться б. (к + *d.*) to be indifferent (to)

безразли́ч|ный, ∼ен, ∼на *adj.* indifferent; мне ∼но it's all the same to me

безрассу́д|ный, ∼ен, ∼на *adj.* reckless; foolhardy

безрезульта́т|ный, ∼ен, ∼на *adj.* futile; unsuccessful

безру́к|ий, ∼, ∼а *adj.* **1** (*без рук*) armless **2** (*без руки*) one-armed **3** (fig.) clumsy

безуда́р|ный, ∼ен, ∼на *adj.* (ling.) unstressed

безукори́знен|ный, ∼, ∼на *adj.* irreproachable; impeccable

безу́м|ец, ца *m.* madman

безу́ми|е, я *nt.* madness; довести́ до ∼я to drive crazy; люби́ть до ∼я to love to distraction

безу́м|ный, ∼ен, ∼на *adj.* **1** (*план*) mad, crazy **2** (fig., infml, *страсть*) wild; ∼ные це́ны absurd, crazy prices

безупре́ч|ный, ∼ен, ∼на *adj.* (*человек*) irreproachable; (*работа*) flawless

безусло́вно *adv.* **1** (*повиноваться, доверять*) unconditionally, absolutely **2** (infml, *несомненно*) of course, it goes without saying, undoubtedly

безусло́в|ный, ∼ен, ∼на *adj.* **1** (*повиновение, доверие*) unconditional, absolute **2** (*успех*) undoubted, indisputable

безуспе́ш|ный, ∼ен, ∼на *adj.* unsuccessful

безуте́ш|ный, ∼ен, ∼на *adj.* inconsolable

безуча́ст|ный, ∼ен, ∼на *adj.* apathetic, indifferent

безъя́дерный *adj.* nuclear-free

безымя́нный *adj.* (*не имеющий названия*) nameless; (*анонимный*) anonymous; б. па́лец third finger, ring finger

бей and **бе́йте** *imper. of* ▶ бить

Бейру́т, а *m.* Beirut

бейсбо́л, а *m.* baseball

бейсболи́ст, а *m.* baseball player

бейсболи́ст|ка, ки *f. of* ▶ бейсболи́ст

беко́н, а *m.* bacon

Белару́с|ь, и *f.* Belarus

Белгра́д, а *m.* Belgrade

беле́|ть, ю *impf.* (*of* ▶ побеле́ть) **1** (*становиться белым*) to grow white **2** (*no pf.*) (*виднеться*) to show up white

белизн|а́, ы́ *f.* whiteness

бели́л|а, ∼ (*no sg.*) whitewash

б

бел|и́ть, ю́, ~йшь *impf.* (*pf.* по~) to whitewash

бе́лк|а, и *f.* squirrel; **верте́ться, крути́ться как б. в колесе́** to run round in circles

беллетри́ст, а *m.* fiction writer

беллетри́стик|а, и *f.* (liter.) fiction

бело... *comb. form* white-

белогварде́|ец, йца *m.* (pol.) White Guard

бел|о́к[1], ка́ *m.* (chem.) protein

бел|о́к[2], ка́ *m.* (*яйца́*) white (of egg)

бел|о́к[3], ка́ *m.* (*глаза́*) white (of the eye)

белоку́р|ый, ~, ~а *adj.* blond(e), fair(-haired)

белору́с, а *m.* Belarusian, Belorussian

белору́с|ка, ки *f. of* ▶ белору́с

белору́сский *adj.* Belarusian, Belorussian

белосне́ж|ный, ~ен, ~на *adj.* snow-white

белу́г|а, и *f.* beluga, white sturgeon (*Huso huso*)

▸ **бе́л|ый, ~, ~а́** *adj.* [1] white; **~ая берёза** silver birch; **Б. дом** White House (*in Washington and Moscow*); **б. медве́дь** polar bear [2] (*све́тлый*) white; fair; **б. биле́т** 'white chit' (*certificate of exemption from military service*); **~ое вино́** white wine; **б. хлеб** white bread; **на ~ом све́те** in all the world; **средь ~а дня** in broad daylight; (*as n. pl.* **~ые, ~ых**) white(-skinned) people [3] (*чи́стый*) clean; blank; **б. лист** clean sheet (*of paper*) [4]: **б. гриб** cep (*wild mushroom, Boletus edulis*)

бельги́|ец, йца *m.* Belgian

бельги́й|ка, ки *f. of* ▶ бельги́ец

бельги́йский *adj.* Belgian

Бе́льги|я, и *f.* Belgium

бель|ё, я́ *nt.* (collect.) linen; **да́мское б.** lingerie; **ни́жнее б.** underwear; **посте́льное б.** bedlinen

бемо́л|ь, я *m.* (*also as indecl. adj.*) (mus.) flat

бензи́н, а *m.* benzine; (*для автомоби́ля*) petrol (BrE), gas(oline) (AmE)

бензи́новый *adj. of* ▶ бензи́н; petrol (BrE), gas (AmE)

бензо... *comb. form, abbr. of* ▶ бензи́новый

бензоба́к, а *m.* petrol tank (BrE), gas tank (AmE)

бензово́з, а *m.* petrol tanker (BrE), gasoline truck (AmE)

бензоколо́нк|а, и *f.* petrol pump (BrE), gas(oline) pump (AmE)

▸ **бе́рег, а, о ~е, на ~у́, pl. ~а́** *m.* (*реки́*) bank; (*мо́ря, о́зера*) shore; (*су́ша*) land (*opp.* sea); **на ~у́ мо́ря** at the seaside; **вы́броситься на б.** to run aground; **вы́йти из ~о́в** to burst its banks; **сойти́ на б.** to go ashore

бер|ёг, ~егла́ *see* ▶ бере́чь

берегов|о́й *adj.* coastal; waterside; **~а́я оборо́на** coastal defence (BrE), defense (AmE)

бере|гу́, ~жёшь, ~гу́т *see* ▶ бере́чь

бережли́в|ый, ~, ~а *adj.* thrifty, economical

бе́реж|ный, ~ен, ~на *adj.* (*осторо́жный*) careful; cautious; (*забо́тливый*) solicitous

берёз|а, ы *f.* birch

бере́мене|ть, ю, ешь *impf.* (*of* ▶ забере́менеть) to become pregnant

бере́менн|ая, ~а *adj.* (+ *i.*) pregnant (with)

▸ **бере́менность, и** *f.* (*состоя́ние*) pregnancy; (*проце́сс*) gestation

бере́т, а *m.* beret

бер|е́чь, егу́, ежёшь, егу́т, *past* ~ёг, ~егла́ *impf.* [1] (*челове́ка, здоро́вье, предме́т*) to take care (of), look after [2] (*не тра́тить*) to be careful with; **б. ка́ждую копе́йку** to count every penny

бер|е́чься, егу́сь, ежёшься, егу́тся, *past* ~ёгся, ~егла́сь *impf.* [1] (*быть осторо́жным*) to be careful, take care [2] (+ *g. or + inf.*) (*остерега́ться*) to beware (of)

Бе́рингов|о мо́ре, ~а мо́ря *nt.* the Bering Sea

Берли́н, а *m.* Berlin

берло́г|а, и *f.* den, lair

Берму́дск|ие острова́, ~их острово́в (*no sg.*) the Bermudas (*islands*), Bermuda

бер|у́, ёшь *see* ▶ брать

бес, а *m.* demon, devil, evil spirit

бесе́д|а, ы *f.* [1] talk, conversation [2] (*диску́ссия*) discussion; **провести́ ~у** to give a talk

бесе́дк|а, и *f.* summer house

бесе́д|овать, ую *impf.* (*с* + *i.*) to talk, converse (with)

бе|си́ть, шу́, ~сишь *impf.* (*of* ▶ взбеси́ть) (infml) to enrage, madden, infuriate

бе|си́ться, шу́сь, ~сишься *impf.* (*of* ▶ взбеси́ться) [1] to go mad (*of animals*) [2] (fig.) to rage, be furious; **с жи́ру б.** (infml) to grow fastidious, fussy; to be too well off

бескомпроми́сс|ный, ~ен, ~на *adj.* uncompromising

бесконе́чно *adv.* infinitely, endlessly; (infml) extremely

бесконе́чность, и *f.* endlessness; infinity; **до ~и** endlessly

бесконе́ч|ный, ~ен, ~на *adj.* (*доро́га*) endless; (*вре́мя, удово́льствие*) infinite; (*сли́шком дли́нный*) interminable

бескоры́ст|ный, ~ен, ~на *adj.* disinterested, impartial; (*альтруисти́ческий*) unselfish

бескра́йний *adj.* boundless

бескро́в|ный, ~ен, ~на *adj.* (*без кровопроли́тия*) bloodless

бесперебо́йный *adj.* uninterrupted; (*регуля́рный*) regular

беспереса́дочный *adj.* direct; **б. по́езд** through train

бесперспекти́в|ный, ~ен, ~на *adj.* having no prospects; (*безнадёжный*) hopeless

беспе́чность, и *f.* carelessness, unconcern

беспе́ч|ный, ~ен, ~на *adj.* carefree

беспило́тный *adj.* unmanned

▸ **беспла́тно** *adv.* free of charge, gratis

▸ **беспла́т|ный, ~ен, ~на** *adj.* free, gratuitous

беспло́ди|е, я *nt.* (*по́чвы*) barrenness; (*же́нщины*) infertility

бесплóд|ный, ∼ен, ∼на *adj.* **1** (*почва*) barren; (*женщина*) infertile; (*брак*) childless **2** (fig.) fruitless, futile

бесподóб|ный, ∼ен, ∼на *adj.* matchless; incomparable

беспозвонóчно|е, го *nt.* (zool.) invertebrate

беспокó|ить, ю, ишь *impf.* **1** (*волновать*) to concern, worry **2** (*pf.* по∼) (*мешать*) to disturb, worry

беспокó|иться, юсь, ишься *impf.* **1** (о + *p.*) to worry, be worried *or* anxious (about) **2** (*pf.* по∼) to trouble oneself, put oneself out; не ∼йтесь! don't worry!

беспокó|йный, ∼ен, ∼йна *adj.* **1** (*человек, вид, состояние*) agitated, disturbed; anxious; uneasy; (*ребёнок*) fidgety **2** (*сон*) restless, disturbed; (*поездка*) uncomfortable

беспокóйств|о, а *nt.* **1** (*волнение*) agitation; anxiety; unrest; с ∼ом anxiously **2** (*нарушение покоя*) disturbance

бесполéз|ный, ∼ен, ∼на *adj.* useless

беспóмощ|ный, ∼ен, ∼на *adj.* helpless, powerless; (fig.) feeble

беспорядд|ок, ка *m.* disorder, confusion; (*pl. only*) (pol.) disturbances, riots

беспорядочный, ∼ен, ∼на *adj.* disorderly; untidy

беспосáдочный *adj.*: б. перелёт non-stop flight

беспóчвен|ный, ∼, ∼на *adj.* groundless; unfounded

беспóшлинн|ый *adj.* (econ.) duty-free; ∼ая торгóвля free trade

беспощáд|ный, ∼ен, ∼на *adj.* merciless, relentless

беспрáви|е, я *nt.* **1** (*отсутствие законности*) lawlessness; arbitrariness **2** (*отсутствие прав*) lack of rights

беспрáв|ный, ∼ен, ∼на *adj.* without rights

беспредéл, а *m.* (infml) lawlessness, scandalous practices; chaos, mayhem

беспредéл|ьный, ∼ен, ∼ьна *adj.* boundless, infinite

беспрепя́тствен|ный, ∼, ∼на *adj.* free, clear, unimpeded

беспрецедéнт|ный, ∼ен, ∼на *adj.* unprecedented

беспризóрн|ый *adj.* (*бездомный*) homeless; (*as m. n.* б., ∼ого) waif, street urchin

беспринцúп|ный, ∼ен, ∼на *adj.* unscrupulous, unprincipled

беспристрáсти|е, я *nt.* impartiality

беспристрáст|ный, ∼ен, ∼на *adj.* impartial, unbias(s)ed

беспроводнóй *adj.*: б. телефóн cordless telephone; б. (дóступ в) Интернéт wireless Internet (access), Wi-Fi®

беспрóигрыш|ный, ∼ен, ∼на *adj.* safe; risk-free

беспросвéт|ный, ∼ен, ∼на *adj.* **1** pitch-dark; ∼ная тьма thick darkness **2** (fig.) hopeless; unrelieved

беспроцéнтный *adj.* (fin.) interest-free

бессердéч|ный, ∼ен, ∼на *adj.* heartless; callous

бессúли|е, я *nt.* (*слабость*) weakness; debility; (fig.) impotence

бессúль|ный, ∼ен, ∼ьна *adj.* (*слабый*) weak; (fig.) impotent, powerless

бессистéм|ный, ∼ен, ∼на *adj.* unsystematic

бесслáв|ный, ∼ен, ∼на *adj.* ignominious; inglorious

бесслéдно *adv.* without leaving a trace; completely

бесслéд|ный, ∼ен, ∼на *adj.* without leaving a trace; ∼ное исчезновéние complete disappearance

бессловéс|ный, ∼ен, ∼на *adj.* dumb, speechless; (fig.) silent

бессмéн|ный, ∼ен, ∼на *adj.* permanent; continuous

бессмéрти|е, я *nt.* immortality

бессмéрт|ный, ∼ен, ∼на *adj.* immortal; undying

бессмы́слен|ный, ∼, ∼на *adj.* (*поступок*) senseless; foolish; (*слова*) meaningless, nonsensical; (*взгляд*) vacant, inane

бессóвест|ный, ∼ен, ∼на *adj.* **1** (*нечестный*) unscrupulous, dishonest **2** (*бесстыдный*) shameless, brazen

бессодержáтель|ный, ∼ен, ∼ьна *adj.* (*жизнь*) empty; (*слова*) tame; dull

бессознáтель|ный, ∼ен, ∼ьна *adj.* **1** unconscious **2** (*непроизвольный*) involuntary

бессóнниц|а, ы *f.* insomnia, sleeplessness

бессóнный *adj.* sleepless

бесспóрно *adv.* indisputably; undoubtedly

бесспóр|ный, ∼ен, ∼на *adj.* indisputable, incontrovertible

бессрóчный *adj.* without time limit; б. óтпуск indefinite leave

бесстрáст|ный, ∼ен, ∼на *adj.* impassive

бесстрáш|ный, ∼ен, ∼на *adj.* fearless, intrepid

бесстыд|ный, ∼ен, ∼на *adj.* shameless

бессчёт|ный, ∼ен, ∼на *adj.* innumerable

бестáктность|, и *f.* **1 (*свойство*) tactlessness **2** (*поступок*) tactless action, faux pas

бестáкт|ный, ∼ен, ∼на *adj.* tactless

бестолкóв|ый, ∼, ∼а *adj.* **1** (*человек*) slow-witted, muddle-headed **2** (*объяснение*) disconnected, incoherent

бестсéллер, а *m.* bestseller (*book*)

бесфóрмен|ный, ∼, ∼на *adj.* shapeless, formless

бесхарáктер|ный, ∼ен, ∼на *adj.* weak-willed; spineless

бесхúтрост|ный, ∼ен, ∼на *adj.* (*человек*) artless; (*слова*) ingenuous

бесцвéт|ный, ∼ен, ∼на *adj.* colourless (BrE), colorless (AmE)

бесцéл|ьный, ∼ен, ∼ьна *adj.* aimless; idle

бесцéн|ный, ∼ен, ∼на *adj.* **1** (*сокровища*) priceless **2** (*опыт, совет*) invaluable

б

бесцеремо́н|ный, ~ен, ~на *adj.* unceremonious; familiar; cavalier

бесчелове́ч|ный, ~ен, ~на *adj.* inhuman

бесче́ст|ный, ~ен, ~на *adj.* dishonourable (BrE), dishonorable (AmE); disgraceful

бесче́сть|е, я *nt.* dishonour (BrE), dishonor (AmE); disgrace

бесчи́слен|ный, ~, ~на *adj.* innumerable

бесчу́вствен|ный, ~, ~на *adj.* **1** (*лишённый сознания*) insensible **2** (*равнодушный*) insensitive, unfeeling

бесшу́м|ный, ~ен, ~на *adj.* noiseless

бето́н, а *m.* concrete

бето́нный *adj.* concrete

бе́шенств|о, а *nt.* **1** (*med.*) hydrophobia; rabies; **коро́вье б.** mad cow disease **2** (*fig.*) fury, rage; **довести́ до ~а** to enrage

бе́шен|ый *adj.* **1** (*med.*) rabid, mad; **~ая соба́ка** mad dog **2** (*fig.*) furious; violent; **~ая ско́рость** furious pace; **~ые це́ны** (*infml*) exorbitant prices

биатло́н, а *m.* biathlon

библе́йский *adj.* biblical

библио́граф, а *m.* bibliographer

библиографи́ческий *adj.* bibliographical

библиогра́фи|я, и *f.* bibliography

✍ **библиоте́к|а, и** *f.* library

библиоте́кар|ь, я *m.* librarian

би́бли|я, и *f.* bible; (**Б.**) the Bible

бигуд|и́, е́й (*no sg.*) (*also indecl.*) (hair) curlers

биде́ *nt. indecl.* bidet

бидо́н, а *m.* can; **б. для молока́** milk can, milk churn (BrE)

бие́ни|е, я *nt.* beating; throb; **б. се́рдца** heartbeat; **б. пу́льса** pulse

бижуте́ри|я, и *f.* costume jewellery

✍ **би́знес, а** *m.* business; **рекла́мный б.** advertising

бизнесме́н, а *m.* businessman

бики́ни *nt. indecl.* bikini

✍ **биле́т, а** *m.* ticket; (*удостоверение*) card; **входно́й б.** entrance ticket, permit; **еди́ный б.** rover ticket; **обра́тный б.** return ticket; **экзаменацио́нный б.** examination question(-paper) (*at oral examination*)

биллио́н, а *m.* (*10^{12}*) trillion (*one million million*)

билья́рд, а *m.* **1** (*стол*) billiard table **2** (*игра*) billiards

бино́кл|ь, я *m.* binoculars; **полево́й б.** field glasses

бинт, á *m.* bandage

бинт|ова́ть, у́ю *impf.* to bandage

био... *comb. form* bio-

био́граф, а *m.* biographer

биографи́ческий *adj.* biographical

биогра́фи|я, и *f.* biography; (*жизнь*) life story

био́лог, а *m.* biologist

биологи́ческий *adj.* biological

биоло́ги|я, и *f.* biology

биометри́ческий *adj.* biometric

биосфе́р|а, ы *f.* biosphere

биохи́мик, а *m.* biochemist

биохи́ми|я, и *f.* biochemistry

би́рж|а, и *f.* exchange; **фо́ндовая б.** stock exchange; **б. труда́** jobcentre

биржеви́к, á *m.* (fin., infml) stockbroker

биржево́й *adj.* of ▶ **би́ржа**; **б. ма́клер** stockbroker

би́рк|а, и *f.* tag, label

Би́рм|а, ы *f.* Burma

бирюз|á, и́ (*no pl.*) *f.* turquoise

бирюзо́вый *adj.* turquoise

бисексуа́льный *adj.* bisexual

бискви́т, а *m.* sponge cake

бит, а *m.* (comput.) bit

би́т|а, ы *f.* (sport) bat

би́тв|а, ы *f.* battle

бить, бью, бьёшь *impf.* **1** (*pf.* **по~**) (*избивать*) to beat (*a person, an animal, etc.*) **2** (*for pf. use* **уда́рить**) (*ударять*) to strike, hit; **б. в лицо́** to strike, hit in the face (*also fig.*) **3** (*impf. only*) (*убивать*) to kill, slaughter (*animals*) **4** (*pf.* **раз~**) (*ломать*) to break, smash (*crockery, etc.*) **5** (*pf.* **про~**) (*издавать звуки*) to strike, sound; **б. отбо́й** to beat a retreat (*also fig.*); **часы́ бьют пять** the clock is striking five **6** (*impf. only*) (*вытекать*) to spurt, gush; **б. ключо́м** to gush out, well up; (*fig.*) to be in full swing **7** (*impf. only*) (*стрелять*) to shoot, fire; (*достигать на какое-л. расстояние, also fig.*) to hit; to have a range (of); **б. в цель** to hit the target (*also fig.*); **б. наверняка́** (fig.) to take no chances

би́ться, бьюсь, бьёшься *impf.* **1** (с + *i.*) (*драться*) to fight (with, against) **2** (*о сердце*) to beat; **се́рдце его́ переста́ло б.** his heart stopped beating **3** (о + *a.*) (*ударяться*) to knock (against), hit (against); **б. голово́й об сте́ну** to bang one's head against a brick wall **4** (*метаться*) to writhe, struggle; **б. в исте́рике** to writhe in hysterics **5** (над + *i.*) (fig., *стараться изо всех сил*) to struggle (with); **б. над зада́чей** to rack one's brains over a problem **6** (*о стекле*) to break, smash; **легко́ б.** to be very fragile **7**: **б. об закла́д** to bet, wager

бифште́кс, а *m.* beefsteak

би́цепс, а *m.* (anat.) biceps

бич, á *m.* whip; (fig.) scourge

бла́г|о¹, а *nt.* good, the good; blessing; **о́бщее б.** the common weal; **всех благ!** (infml) all the best!

бла́го² *conj.* (infml) since; seeing that; **скажи́те ему́ сейча́с, б. он здесь** tell him now since he is here

благови́д|ный, ~ен, ~на *adj.* plausible

благодар|и́ть, ю́, и́шь *impf.* (of ▶ **поблагодари́ть**) to thank; **~ю́ вас (за** + *a.*)** thank you (for)

б

благода́рност|ь, и *f.* **1** gratitude; **не сто́ит** ∼**и** don't mention it **2** (*usu. in pl.*) (*выраже́ние благода́рности*) thanks

благода́р|ный, ∼ен, ∼на *adj.* **1** grateful **2** (*стоя́щий*) rewarding; worthwhile

благода́рственн|ый *adj.* expressing thanks; ∼ое письмо́ letter of thanks

⚡ **благодаря́** *prep.* + *d.* thanks to, owing to, because of; **б. тому́, что** owing to the fact that

благоде́тел|ь, я *m.* benefactor

благоде́тельниц|а, ы *f.* benefactress

благоду́ш|ный, ∼ен, ∼на *adj.* (*споко́йный*) placid, equable; (*доброду́шный*) good-humoured (BrE), -humored (AmE)

благожела́тельност|ь, и *f.* goodwill; benevolence

благожела́тель|ный, ∼ен, ∼ьна *adj.* (*челове́к*) kind; well disposed; (*приём, улы́бка*) friendly, cordial; (*реце́нзия*) favourable (BrE), favorable (AmE)

благозву́ч|ный, ∼ен, ∼на *adj.* euphonious; (*го́лос*) melodious

благ|о́й *adj.* good; ∼**и́е наме́рения** good intentions

благонадёжност|ь, и *f.* reliability, trustworthiness

благонадёж|ный, ∼ен, ∼на *adj.* reliable, trustworthy

благополу́чи|е, я *nt.* well-being; prosperity

благополу́чно *adv.* well, all right; happily; (*в це́лости и сохра́нности*) safely

благополу́ч|ный, ∼ен, ∼на *adj.* (*уда́чный*) successful; (*прибы́тие*) safe; **б. коне́ц** happy ending

благоприя́т|ный, ∼ен, ∼на *adj.* favourable (BrE), favorable (AmE); ∼**ные ве́сти** good news

благоприя́тств|овать, ую *impf.* (+ *d.*) to favour (BrE), favor (AmE)

благоразу́ми|е, я *nt.* prudence; sense

благоразу́м|ный, ∼ен, ∼на *adj.* prudent; sensible

благоро́д|ный, ∼ен, ∼на *adj.* noble; **б. мета́лл** precious metal

благоро́дств|о, а *nt.* nobleness; nobility

благоскло́нност|ь, и *f.* favour (BrE), favor (AmE); **по́льзоваться чьей-н. ∼ью** to be in sb's good graces

благоскло́н|ный, ∼ен, ∼на *adj.* favourable (BrE), favorable (AmE); gracious

благослове́ни|е, я *nt.* (eccl., fig.) blessing; **с ∼я** (+ *g.*) with the blessing (of)

благослов|и́ть, лю́, и́шь *pf.* (*of* ▶ **благословля́ть**) **1** (*перекрести́ть*) to bless; (*вы́разить одобре́ние*) to give one's blessing (to) **2** (*возда́ть благода́рность*) to be grateful to; **б. свою́ судьбу́** to thank one's stars

благослов|ля́ть, ля́ю *impf. of* ▶ **благослови́ть**

благосостоя́ни|е, я *nt.* well-being, welfare

благотвори́тель, я *m.* (*лицо́*) philanthropist; (*организа́ция*) charity

благотвори́тельниц|а, ы *f. of* ▶ **благотвори́тель**

благотвори́тельност|ь, и *f.* charity, philanthropy

благотвори́тельный *adj.* charitable, philanthropic; **б. спекта́кль** charity performance

благотво́р|ный, ∼ен, ∼на *adj.* beneficial; wholesome, salutary

благоустра́ива|ть, ю *impf. of* ▶ **благоустро́ить**

благоустро́ен|ный, ∼, ∼а *p.p.p. of* ▶ **благоустро́ить** *and* (∼, ∼на) *adj.* well equipped; comfortable; **б. дом** house with all modern conveniences

благоустро́|ить, ю, ишь *pf.* (*of* ▶ **благоустра́ивать**) to equip with services and utilities

благоустро́йств|о, а *nt.* equipping with services and utilities

благочести́в|ый, ∼, ∼а *adj.* pious, devout

благоче́сти|е, я *nt.* piety

блаже́нств|о, а *nt.* bliss

бланк, а *m.* form; **анке́тный б.** questionnaire; **фи́рменный б.** sheet of headed notepaper; **запо́лнить б.** to fill in a form

блат, а *m.* (infml) pull, string-pulling; **получи́ть по ∼у** to obtain through connections

блатн|о́й *adj.* (infml) (*достаю́щийся по бла́ту*) obtained through string-pulling; (*челове́к*) string-pulling; (*язы́к, му́зыка*) criminal, thieves'; (*as n.* **б.**, ∼**о́го**) (*по́льзующийся бла́том*) string-puller; (*свя́занный с престу́пным ми́ром*) criminal

бл|ева́ть, юю́, юёшь *impf.* (sl.) to puke, spew (both infml)

бледне́|ть, ю, ешь *impf.* (*of* ▶ **побледне́ть**) to grow pale; to pale

бле́дност|ь, и *f.* paleness, pallor; (fig.) dullness

бле́д|ный, ∼ен, ∼на́, ∼но *adj.* pale, pallid; **б. как полотно́** white as a sheet; (fig.) colourless (BrE), colorless (AmE), insipid, dull

блеск, а *m.* brightness, brilliance, shine; (fig.) splendour (BrE), splendor (AmE), magnificence; (*as int.*) (sl.): **б.!** brilliant!; great!; super!; **во всём ∼е** in all (one's) glory

блесн|у́ть, у́, ёшь *pf.* to flash; **в мое́й голове́ ∼у́ла мысль** a thought flashed across my mind

бле|сте́ть, щу́, сти́шь *and* ∼**щешь** *impf.* to shine; to glitter; to sparkle; **её глаза́ ∼сте́ли ра́достью** her eyes shone with joy; **он не ∼щет умо́м** he's no genius

блестя́щ|ий, ∼, ∼а, ∼е *pres. part. of* ▶ **блесте́ть** *and adj.* shining, bright; (fig.) brilliant

бле|щу́, ∼**щешь** *see* ▶ **блесте́ть**

бле́|ять, ю, ешь *impf.* to bleat

ближа́йш|ий *superl. of* ▶ **бли́зкий**; (*го́род, по́чта*) nearest; (*день, год*) next; (*зада́ча*) immediate; **в ∼ем бу́дущем** in the near future; **б. друг** closest friend; **б. ро́дственник** next of kin; **при ∼ем**

б

рассмотре́нии on closer examination

бли́же *comp. of* ▶ **бли́зкий**; nearer; (fig.) closer

ближневосто́чный *adj.* Middle East; Middle Eastern

бли́жн|ий *adj.* **1** (*близкий*) near; (*сосе́дний*) neighbouring (BrE), neighboring (AmE); **Б. Восто́к** Middle East **2** (mil.) short range, close range **3** (*родственник*) close; (*as m. n.* **б.**, **∼его**) (fig.) one's neighbour (BrE), neighbor (AmE) **4** (*путь*) shortest

бли́з|иться, ится *impf.* to approach, draw near

⚐ **бли́з|кий**, **∼ок**, **∼ка́**, **∼ко**, **∼ки́** *adj.* **1** (*место*) nearby, close; **на ∼ком расстоя́нии** a short way off; at close range **2** (*конец*) near; imminent **3** (*в те́сных отноше́ниях*) intimate, close; **б. друг** close friend; **быть ∼ким с кем-н.** to be on intimate terms with sb; **быть ∼ким** (+ *d.*) to be dear (to); (*as n.* **∼кие**, **∼ких**) one's nearest and dearest **4** (*похо́жий*) (**к** + *d.*) like; similar (to); close (to); **б. нам по ду́ху челове́к** kindred spirit

бли́зко *adv.* **1** (*от* + *g.*) near, close (to) **2** (*as pred.*) it is not far

близлежа́щий *adj.* neighbouring (BrE), neighboring (AmE), nearby

близне́ц, **á** *m.* twin (*also triplet, etc.*); **Б∼ы́** (*созве́здие*) Gemini

близору́к|ий, **∼**, **∼а** *adj.* short-sighted (BrE), nearsighted (AmE) (also fig.)

бли́зост|ь, **и** *f.* nearness, proximity; (*бли́зкие отноше́ния*) intimacy

блик, **а** *m.* spot/speck/patch of light; **со́лнечный б.** patch of sunlight

блин, **á** *m.* pancake; **пе́рвый б. ко́мом** (*proverb*) practice makes perfect; (*as int.*) (sl.) damn!; shit! (vulg.)

блиста́тел|ьный, **∼ен**, **∼ьна** *adj.* brilliant, splendid

блиста́|ть, **ю** *impf.* to shine

блог, **а** *m.* (comput.) blog, weblog

бло́ггер and **бло́гер а** *m.* (comput.) blogger, weblogger

бло́гер, **а** *m.* = **бло́ггер**

блогосфе́р|а, **ы** *f.* (comput.) blogosphere

блок[1], **а** *m.* (tech.) block, pulley

блок[2], **а** *m.* (pol.) bloc

блок[3], **а** *m.* carton (of cigarettes); unit; **б. пита́ния** power supply (unit)

блока́д|а, **ы** *f.* blockade; **снять ∼у** to raise the blockade

блоки́р|овать, **ую** *impf. and pf.* **1** to blockade **2** (sport) to block

блокно́т, **а** *m.* notebook, notepad

блокпо́ст, **á** or **∼é**, **на ∼ý** *m.* checkpoint

блонди́н, **а** *m.* fair-haired man

блонди́нк|а, **и** *f.* blonde (woman)

блох|á, **и́**, *a.* **∼ý**, **d.** **∼а́м** *and* **∼ам** *f.* flea; **иска́ть ∼** to nitpick (fig.)

бло́чный *adj.* modular

⚐ key word

блужда́|ть, **ю** *impf.* to roam, wander; to rove; **б. по у́лицам** to roam the streets

блужда́ющий *pres. part. of* ▶ **блужда́ть**; **б. огонёк** will-o'-the-wisp

блу́зк|а, **и** *f.* blouse

⚐ **блю́д|о**, **а** *nt.* dish; **обе́д из трёх ∼** three-course dinner; **вку́сное б.** a tasty dish

блю́д|це, **ца**, *g. pl.* **∼ец** *nt.* saucer

блюз, **а** *m.* (mus.) the blues

блю|сти́, **ду́**, **дёшь**, *past* **∼л**, **∼ла́** *impf.* to guard, watch over; **б. поря́док** to keep order

блюсти́тел|ь, **я** *m.* keeper, guardian; **б. поря́дка** (infml, iron.) arm of the law

бляд|ь, **и**, *g. pl.* **∼е́й** *n.* (vulg.) (*же́нщина*) whore; (*мужчина*) bastard; (*as int.*) fuck!

боб, **á** *m.* bean

боб|ёр, **рá** *m.* (*мех*) beaver (fur)

бобр, **á** *m.* beaver

⚐ **Бог**, **а**, *voc. sg.* **Бо́же** *m.* God; god; **Бо́же мой!** good God!, my God!; **Б. зна́ет!**, **Б. весть!** God knows!; **Б. его́ зна́ет!** who knows!; **не дай Б.!** God forbid!; **ра́ди ∼а!** for God's sake!; **Б. с ним!** blow it; **сла́ва ∼у!** thank God!

богате́|ть, **ю**, **ешь** *impf.* (*of* ▶ **разбогате́ть**) to grow rich

бога́тств|о, **а** *nt.* **1** riches, wealth; **есте́ственные ∼а** natural resources **2** (fig.) richness, wealth

⚐ **бога́т|ый**, **∼**, **∼а** *adj.* (+ *i.*) rich (in), wealthy; **∼ая расти́тельность** luxuriant vegetation; **б. о́пыт** wide experience; (*as m. n.* **б.**, **∼ого**) rich man

богаты́р|ь, **я́** *m.* **1** bogatyr (*hero in Russian folklore*) **2** (fig.) Hercules; hero

бога́ч, **á** *m.* rich man; **∼и́** (*collect.*) the rich

боге́м|а, **ы** *f.* (*collect.*) Bohemians; (*о́браз жи́зни*) Bohemianism

боге́мный *adj.* Bohemian

боги́н|я, **и** *f.* goddess (also fig.)

Богоро́диц|а, **ы** *f.* the Virgin, Our Lady

богосло́ви|е, **я** *nt.* theology

богосло́вский *adj.* theological

богослуже́ни|е, **я** *nt.* divine service, worship; liturgy

боготвор|и́ть, **ю́**, **и́шь** *impf.* to worship, idolize

богоху́льств|о, **а** *nt.* blasphemy

бо́дрост|ь, **и** *f.* cheerfulness; good spirits; (*му́жество*) courage

бо́дрствовани|е, **я** *nt.* keeping awake; vigilance

бо́дрств|овать, **ую** *impf.* to stay awake; to keep vigil

бо́др|ый, **∼**, **∼á**, **∼о**, **∼ы́** *adj.* cheerful, bright; (*стари́к*) hale and hearty

боеви́к, **á** *m.* **1** (*солда́т*) fighter; militant **2** (infml, *остросюже́тный фильм*) action movie, thriller

⚐ **боев|о́й** *adj.* **1** military, fighting, battle; **∼ы́е де́йствия** operations; **б. дух** fighting spirit; **∼о́е креще́ние** baptism of fire; **б. патро́н** live cartridge **2** (infml, *вои́нственный*)

militant; energetic

боеголо́вк|а, и *f.* (mil.) warhead

боеприпа́с|ы, ов (*no sg.*) ammunition

боеспосо́б|ный, ~ен, ~на *adj.* (mil.) battle-worthy

бо|е́ц, йца́ *m.* (*участник боя*) fighter; (*солдат*) private soldier

Бо́же *see* ▶ Бог

боже́ствен|ный, ~, ~на *adj.* divine (also fig.)

божеств|о́, а́ *nt.* deity, divine being

бо́ж|ий, ья, ье *adj.* God's; **я́сно как б. день** it is as clear as could be; **~ья коро́вка** (zool.) ladybird

бо|й, я, pl. ~й, ~ёв *m.* **1** (*сражение*) battle, fight, action, combat; **~й fighting; в ~ю** in action **2** (*часов*) striking, strike; **бараба́нный б.** drumbeat **3** (*убой*) killing, slaughtering; **б. кито́в** whaling

бо́йкий, ~ек, ~йка́, ~йко *adj.* **1** (*дерзкий*) bold, spry, smart; **б. ум** ready wit; **б. язы́к** glib tongue **2** (*живой*) lively, animated; **~йкая торго́вля** brisk trade; **~йкая у́лица** busy street

бойко́т, а *m.* boycott; **объяви́ть б.** (+ *d.*) to declare a boycott (of)

бойкоти́р|овать, ую *impf.* to boycott

бо́йн|я, и, g. pl. бо́ен *f.* slaughterhouse, abattoir; (fig.) slaughter, butchery, carnage

бо́йче *comp. of* ▶ бо́йкий

бойче́е = бо́йче

бок, а, о ~е, на ~у́, pl. ~а́ *m.* side; flank; **в б.** sideways; **схвати́ться за ~а́ (от сме́ха)** to split one's sides (with laughter); **на́ б.** sideways, to the side; **на ~у́** on one side; **б. о́ б.** side by side; **под ~ом** nearby, close at hand; **с ~у** from the side, from the flank

бока́л, а *m.* (wine)glass, goblet; **подня́ть б.** (**за** + *a.*) to drink the health (of), raise one's glass (to)

боков|о́й *adj.* side, flank, lateral, sidelong; **~а́я у́лица** side street

бо́ком *adv.* sideways; **ходи́ть б.** to sidle

бокс¹, а *m.* (sport) boxing

бокс², а *m.* (*в больни́це*) cubicle

боксёр, а *m.* (*спортсме́н; соба́ка*) boxer

болва́нк|а, и *f.* **1** (tech.) pig (*of iron, etc.*) **2** (*компа́ктный диск*) blank CD, DVD

болга́р|ин, ина, pl. ~ы, ~ *m.* Bulgarian

Болга́ри|я, и *f.* Bulgaria

болга́р|ка, ки *f. of* ▶ болга́рин

болга́рский *adj.* Bulgarian

болев|о́й *adj. of* ▶ боль; **~о́е ощуще́ние** sensation of pain

бо́лее *adv.* more; **б. то́лстый** thicker; **б. того́** and what is more; **б. и́ли ме́нее** more or less; **не б. и не ме́нее, как** neither more nor less than; **б. всего́** most of all; **тем б., что** especially as

болезнен|ный, ~, ~на *adj.* **1** (*нездоро́вый*) sickly; unhealthy; (fig.) abnormal, morbid; **~ное любопы́тство** morbid curiosity **2** (*вызыва́ющий боль*) painful

боле́зн|ь, и *f.* illness; disease; (fig.) abnormality; **б. Да́уна** Down's syndrome; **б. Паркинсо́на** Parkinson's disease; **морска́я б.** seasickness

боле́льщик, а *m.* (infml) fan, supporter

боле́льщи|ца, цы *f. of* ▶ боле́льщик

боле́|ть¹, ю, ешь *impf.* **1** (+ *i.*) to be ill, be down (with); to ail (*intrans.*); **она́ с де́тства ~ет а́стмой** she has suffered from asthma since childhood; **б. душо́й (за** + *a.*) to be worried (about) **2** (**за** + *a.*) (infml) to be a fan (of), support

боле́|ть², йт, я́т *impf.* to ache, hurt; **у меня́ зу́бы ~я́т** I have toothache

болеутоля́ющ|ий *adj.* soothing, analgesic; **~ее сре́дство** (med.) painkiller, analgesic

боливи́|ец, йца *m.* Bolivian

боливи́й|ка, ки *f. of* ▶ боливи́ец

боливи́йский *adj.* Bolivian

Боли́ви|я, и *f.* Bolivia

боло́тист|ый, ~, ~а *adj.* marshy, boggy, swampy

боло́тн|ый *adj.* marsh; **~ая лихора́дка** marsh fever, malaria

боло́т|о, а *nt.* marsh, bog, swamp; **торфяно́е б.** peat bog; (fig.) mire, slough

болт, а́ *m.* (tech.) bolt

болта́|ть¹, ю *impf.* **1** (*меша́ть*) to stir; (*взба́лтывать*) to shake **2** (+ *i.*) (*нога́ми*) to dangle

болта́|ть², ю *impf.* (infml) to chatter, jabber (away); **б. глу́пости** to talk nonsense; **б. по-францу́зски** to jabber away in French

болта́|ться, юсь *impf.* (infml) **1** (*кача́ться*) to dangle, swing; to hang loosely **2** (*слоня́ться*) to hang about, loaf

болтли́в|ый, ~, ~а *adj.* garrulous, talkative; (*бестакт ный*) indiscreet

болтовн|я́, и́ *f.* (infml) chatter; (*спле́тня*) gossip

болту́н, а́ *m.* (infml) **1** (*пустосло́в*) chatterbox; gasbag **2** (*спле́тник*) gossip

бол|ь, и *f.* pain; ache; **б. в боку́** stitch; **зубна́я б.** toothache; **душе́вная б.** mental anguish

больни́ц|а, ы *f.* hospital; **лечь в ~у** to go to hospital; **лежа́ть в ~е** to be in hospital

больни́чный *adj. of* ▶ больни́ца; **б. лист** medical certificate

бо́льно *adv.* **1** painfully, badly; **б. уши́биться** to be badly bruised **2** (*as pred.*) it is painful (also fig.); **мне б. дыша́ть** it hurts me to breathe **3** (infml) very, too; **э́то б. далеко́** it's too far

бол|ьно́й, ~ен, ~ьна́ *adj.* (*челове́к*) ill, sick; (*о́рган*) diseased; (*часть те́ла*) sore (also fig.); **~ьные дёсны** sore gums; **б. зуб** bad tooth; **он тяжело́ ~ен** he is seriously ill; **б. вопро́с** sore subject; **~ьно́е ме́сто** sore spot; (*as n.* **б., ~ьно́го, f. ~ьна́я, ~ьно́й**) patient, invalid; **амбулато́рный б.** outpatient; **стациона́рный б.** inpatient

бо́льше 1 (*comp. of* ▶ большо́й, ▶ вели́кий)

bigger, larger; (*об отвлечённых понятиях*) greater; **Пари́жа б. Ло́ндон** London is larger than Paris **2** (*compr. of* ▸ **мно́го**) more; **чем б. …, тем б.** the more … the more; **б. не** no more, no longer; **он б. не живёт на той у́лице** he does not live in that street any longer, he no longer lives in that street; **б. не бу́ду!** I won't do it again!; **б. нет вопро́сов?** any more questions?; **б. у** (+ *g.*) (tennis) advantage

большеви́к, а́ *m.* Bolshevik

♂ **бо́льш|ий** *compr. of* ▸ **большо́й**, ▸ **вели́кий**; greater, larger; **по ~ей ча́сти** for the most part; **са́мое ~ee** at most

♂ **большинств|о́, а́** *nt.* majority; most (of); **в ~é слу́чаев** in most cases; **б. голосо́в** a majority vote

♂ **больш|о́й** *adj.* (*по величине*) big, large; (*значительный; важный*) great; (*infml, взрослый*) grown-up; **~а́я бу́ква** capital (letter); **~а́я доро́га** high road; **б. па́лец** thumb; **б. па́лец ноги́** big toe; **б. свет** haut monde, society; **когда́ я бу́ду б.** when I grow up

боля́чк|а, и *f.* sore; scab; (*fig.*) defect

бо́мб|а, ы *f.* bomb; **кассе́тная б.** cluster bomb

бомбардиро́вк|а, и *f.* bombardment; bombing; **ковро́вая б.** carpet bombing

бомбардиро́вщик, а *m.* **1** (*самолёт*) bomber; **пики́рующий б.** dive-bomber **2** (infml, *лётчик*) bomber pilot

бомб|и́ть, лю́, и́шь *impf.* to bomb

бомбоубе́жищ|е, а *nt.* air-raid shelter, bomb shelter

бомж, а *m.* (*abbr. of* **без определённого ме́ста жи́тельства**) homeless person, vagrant

бор, а, о ~е, в ~у́, pl. ~ы́, ~о́в *m.* coniferous forest (*usu. pine*)

борде́л|ь, я *m.* (infml) brothel

бордо́вый *adj.* claret-coloured (BrE), -colored (AmE)

бордю́р, а *m.* border; (*тротуара*) kerb (BrE), curb (AmE)

бор|е́ц, ца́ *m.* **1** (**за** + *a.*) fighter (for); campaigner; activist; **б. за права́ же́нщин** women's liberationist **2** (sport) wrestler

борз|а́я, о́й *f.*: **англи́йская б.** greyhound; **ру́сская б.** borzoi, Russian wolfhound

бормаши́н|а, ы *f.* (dentist's) drill

бормота́ни|е, я *nt.* muttering

бормо|та́ть, чу́, чешь *impf.* (*of* ▸ **пробормота́ть**) to mutter

Борне́о *nt. indecl.* Borneo

бо́ров, а *m.* hog

бор|ода́, оды́, а. ~оду, pl. ~оды, ~о́д, ~ода́м *f.* beard

борода́вк|а, и *f.* wart

борода́т|ый, ~, ~а *adj.* bearded

бор|озда́, озды́, а. ~озду and ~озду́, pl. ~озды, ~о́зд, ~озда́м *f.* furrow

♂ *key word*

бороз|ди́ть, жу́, ди́шь *impf.* (*of* ▸ **избороздить**) to furrow

♂ **бор|о́ться, ю́сь, ~ешься** *impf.* (**с** + *i.*) to wrestle (with) (also fig.); (fig.) (**за** + *a. or* **про́тив** + *g.*) to struggle, fight (for; against)

борт, а, о ~е, на ~у́, pl. ~á, ~о́в *m.* (*судна, грузовика*) side; **на ~у́** on board (*ship or aircraft*); **вы́бросить за́ б.** to throw overboard (also fig.)

бортово́й *adj. of* ▸ **борт**; **б. журна́л** (ship's) logbook

бортпроводни́к, а́ *m.* air steward

бортпроводни́ц|а, ы *f.* stewardess; air hostess (BrE)

борщ, а́ *m.* (cul.) bor(t)sch

♂ **борьб|а́, ы́** *f.* **1** (sport) wrestling **2** (fig.) (**с** + *i. or* **про́тив** + *g.*) struggle, fight (with, against); (**за** + *a.*) struggle, fight (for); **душе́вная б.** mental strife; **кампа́ния по ~é с престу́пностью** crime-prevention campaign

босано́в|а, ы *f.* (*танец, музыка*) bossa nova

босико́м *adv.* barefoot; **ходи́ть б.** to go barefoot

Бо́сния и Герцегови́на, Бо́снии и Герцегови́ны *f.* Bosnia-Herzegovina, Bosnia and Herzegovina

бос|о́й, ~, ~á, ~о *adj.* barefooted; **на ~у́ ногу** with bare feet, barefoot

босоно́ж|ки, ек *f. pl.* (*sg.* ~а, ~и) sandals

босс, а *m.* boss

Босфо́р, а *m.* the Bosporus

бота́ник, а *m.* botanist

бота́ник|а, и *f.* botany

ботани́ческий *adj.* botanical; **б. сад** botanical gardens

боти́н|ок, а, g. pl. б. *m.* boot (*ankle-high*)

бо́цман, а *m.* (naut.) boatswain

бо́чк|а, и *f.* barrel, cask

бочо́н|ок, ка *m.* small barrel, keg

боязли́в|ый, ~, ~а *adj.* timid, timorous

боя́зн|ь, и *f.* (+ *g.*) fear (of), dread of; **б. темноты́** fear of the dark; **из ~и** for fear of, lest

боя́рышник, а *m.* (bot.) hawthorn

♂ **бо|я́ться, ю́сь, и́шься** *impf.* (+ *g.*) **1** (*испытывать страх*) to fear, be afraid (of); **она́ ~и́тся темноты́** she is afraid of the dark; **он ~и́тся пойти́ к врачу́** he is afraid to go to the doctor; **~ю́сь, что он (не) прие́дет** I am afraid that he will (not) come; **~ю́сь, как бы он не прие́хал** I am afraid that he may come **2** (*не переносить*) to be afraid of, suffer from; **э́ти расте́ния ~ятся хо́лода** these plants do not like the cold

бра́вый *adj.* gallant; manly

брази́л|ец, ьца *m.* Brazilian

Брази́ли|я, и *f.* Brazil

брази́льский *adj.* Brazilian

брazilья́нк|а, и *f. of* ▸ **брази́лец**

♂ **брак¹, а** *m.* (*супружество*) marriage; matrimony; **свиде́тельство о ~e** certificate of marriage

брак², а *m.* (*продукция*) rejects; (*изъян*) defect

брако́ван|ный, ∼, ∼а *p.p.p. of* ▶ бракова́ть *and adj.* rejected; defective

брак|ова́ть, у́ю *impf.* (*of* ▶ забракова́ть) to reject

браконье́р, а *m.* poacher

браконье́рств|о, а *nt.* poaching

бракоразво́дный *adj.* divorce; б. **проце́сс** divorce suit

бракосочета́ни|е, я *nt.* wedding, wedding ceremony

бра́нн|ый *adj.* abusive; ∼ое сло́во swear word

бран|ь, и *f.* swearing; abuse; bad language

брасле́т, а *m.* bracelet

брасс, а *m.* (sport) breast stroke

⸎ **брат**, а, *pl.* ∼ья, ∼ьев *m.* **1** brother; сво́дный б. stepbrother; единокро́вный б. half-brother (*by father*); единоутро́бный б. half-brother (*by mother*); двою́родный б. cousin **2** (fig.) brother; comrade; ∼ья-писа́тели fellow-writers

бра́тск|ий *adj.* brotherly, fraternal; ∼ая моги́ла communal grave (*esp. of war dead*)

бра́тств|о, а *nt.* brotherhood, fraternity

⸎ **бра|ть**, беру́, берёшь, *past* ∼л, ∼ла́, ∼ло *impf.* (*of* ▶ взять) **1** to take (*in var. senses*); б. наза́д to take back; б. курс (на + *a.*) to make (for), head (for); б. нача́ло (в + *p.*) to originate (in); б. но́ту to sing, play a note; б. приме́р (с + *g.*) to follow the example (of); б. сло́во (*выступать*) to take the floor; б. в плен to take prisoner; б. на себя́ to take upon oneself; б. под аре́ст to put under arrest **2** (*получить*) to get, obtain; (*принимать*) to take on; б. верх to get the upper hand; б. такси́ to take a taxi; б. своё to get one's way; to make itself felt; беру́т своё age tells; б. взаймы́ to borrow; б. в аре́нду to rent; б. напрока́т to hire **3** (в + *nom.-a.*) to take (as); to marry **4** (*захватить*) to seize; to grip; б. власть to seize power **5** (*требовать*) to exact; to take (= *to demand, require*); б. штраф to exact a fine **6** (*преодолевать*) to take; to surmount; б. барье́р to clear a hurdle **7** (+ *adv. of place*) (infml) to bear; б. вле́во to bear left

бра́|ться, беру́сь, берёшься, *past* ∼лся, ∼ла́сь, ∼ло́сь *impf.* (*of* ▶ взя́ться) **1** *pass. of* ▶ брать **2** (за + *a.*) (*трогать*) to touch, lay hands (upon); б. за́ руки to link arms **3** (за + *a.*) (*приниматься*) to take up; to get down (to); б. за де́ло to get down to business **4** (за + *a. or* + *inf.*) (*принимать на себя*) to undertake; to take upon oneself; б. за поруче́ние to undertake a commission; б. вы́полнить рабо́ту to undertake a job; не беру́сь суди́ть I do not presume to judge **5** (3rd *person only*) (infml, *появляться*) to appear, arise; не зна́ю, отку́да у них де́ньги беру́тся I don't know where they get their money from **6**: б. за ум (infml) to come to one's senses

бра́тья *see* ▶ брат

бра́узер, а *m.* (comput.) browser

бра́чн|ый *adj.* marriage; conjugal; б. во́зраст marriageable age; ∼ая конто́ра marriage bureau; ∼ое свиде́тельство marriage certificate

брев|но́, на́, *pl.* ∼на, ∼ен, ∼нам *nt.* log, beam; (sport) caber; (fig., *тупой человек*) dullard, insensitive person

бред, а, о ∼е, в ∼у́ *m.* delirium; ravings; (fig.) gibberish; быть в ∼у́ to be delirious

бре́|дить, жу, дишь *impf.* to be delirious, rave

бредо́вый *adj.* crackpot, crazy

бре́|жу, дишь *see* ▶ бре́дить

брезгли́в|ый, ∼, ∼а *adj.* squeamish, fastidious; ∼ое чу́вство feeling of disgust

брезе́нт, а *m.* tarpaulin

брело́к, а *m.* charm (*on bracelet*); б. для ключе́й key ring

бре́м|я, ∼ени, *i.* ∼енем, о ∼ени *nt.* burden; load

бре́нд, а *m.* (comm.) brand

бре́ндинг, а *m.* (comm.) branding

бренча́|ть, у́, и́шь *impf.* **1** (+ *i.*) to jingle **2** (infml, *играть*) to strum

бре́|ю, ешь *see* ▶ брить

брига́д|а, ы *f.* **1** (mil.) brigade; (naut.) subdivision **2** (*группа рабочих*), brigade, (work) team

бригади́р, а *m.* team leader; foreman

брига́дный *adj. of* ▶ брига́да

бридж, а *m.* bridge (*card game*)

брике́т, а *m.* briquette

бриллиа́нт, а *m.* (cut) diamond

бриллиа́нтовый *adj. of* ▶ бриллиа́нт

брита́н|ец, ца *m.* Briton; ∼цы the British

Брита́ни|я, и *f.* Britain

брита́н|ка, ки *f. of* ▶ брита́нец

Брита́нск|ие острова́, ∼их острово́в (*no sg.*) the British Isles

брита́нский *adj.* British

бри́тв|а, ы *f.* razor

бри́твенн|ый *adj.* shaving; ∼ые принадле́жности shaving things

бритоголо́в|ый *adj.* shaven-headed; (*as m. n.* б., ∼ого) skinhead

бри́т|ый, ∼, ∼а *p.p.p. of* ▶ брить *and adj.* clean-shaven

бр|ить, е́ю, е́ешь *impf.* (*of* ▶ побри́ть) to shave

брить|ё, я́ *nt.* shave; (*процесс*) shaving; лосьо́н по́сле ∼я́ aftershave

бр|и́ться, е́юсь, е́ешься *impf.* (*of* ▶ побри́ться) to shave, have a shave

бров|ь, и, *pl.* ∼и, ∼е́й *f.* eyebrow; brow; хму́рить ∼и to knit one's brows, frown

брод, а *m.* ford

бро|ди́ть¹, жу́, ∼дишь *impf.* (*гулять*) to wander, roam

бро|ди́ть², ∼дит *impf.* (*о пиве*) to ferment

бродя́г|а, и *c.g.* tramp, vagrant; down-and-out

б

броди́ч|ий *adj.* vagrant; wandering, roving; (fig.) restless; **∼ая соба́ка** stray dog

брожéни|е, я *nt.* fermentation

бро|жу́, ∼дишь *see* ▶ **броди́ть¹**

брóкер, а *m.* broker; **биржево́й б.** stockbroker

брóкколи *f. indecl.* broccoli

бронe... *comb. form* (mil.) armoured (BrE), armored (AmE)

броневи́к, á *m.* armoured car (BrE), armored car (AmE)

бронев|о́й *adj.* armoured (BrE), armored (AmE); **∼ые пли́ты** (mil.) armour plating (BrE), armor plating (AmE)

бронежилéт, а *m.* bulletproof vest

броненóс|ец, ца *m.* (naut.) battleship

бронетранспортёр, а *m.* armoured (BrE), armored (AmE) personnel carrier

брóнз|а, ы *f.* bronze

брóнзовый *adj.* bronze; (*загоре́лый*) tanned; **б. век** the Bronze Age; **б. зага́р** sunburn, suntan

брони́рованный *p.p.p. of* ▶ **брони́ровать** *and adj.* reserved

брониро́ванный *p.p.p. of* ▶ **брони́ровать** *and adj.* armoured (BrE), armored (AmE)

брони́р|овать, ую *impf.* (*of* ▶ **заброни́ровать**) to reserve, book

бронир|ова́ть, у́ю *impf. and pf.* to armour (BrE), armor (AmE)

бронхи́т, а *m.* bronchitis

брон|ь, и *f.* (infml) reservation

брон|я́, и́ *f.* armour (BrE), armor (AmE); (*та́нка, су́дна*) armour plate (BrE), armor plate (AmE)

броса́|ть, ю *impf.* (*of* ▶ **брóсить**) **1** (*мета́ть*) to throw, cast, fling; **б. взгляд** to dart a glance; **б. обвинéния** to hurl accusations; **б. тень** to cast a shadow; **б. на вéтер** to throw away, waste **2** (*покинуть*) to leave, abandon, desert; **б. му́жа** to desert one's husband; **б. рабóту** to give up, chuck in one's job **3** (+ *inf.*) (*перестава́ть*) to give up, leave off; **он брóсил кури́ть** he gave up smoking

брос|а́ться, а́юсь *impf.* **1** (*impf. only*) (+ *i.*) to throw at one another, pelt one another (with) **2** (*impf. only*) (+ *i.*) to throw away; **б. деньга́ми** to throw away, squander one's money **3** (*pf.* **∼иться**) (**на**, в + *a.*) to throw oneself (on, upon), rush (to); **б. на колéни** to fall on one's knees; **б. в объя́тия** (+ *d.*) to fall into the arms (of); **б. на пóмощь** to rush to assistance **4** (*pf.* **∼иться**): **б. в глаза́** to be striking, arrest attention **5** (*pf.* **∼иться**) (+ *inf.*) to begin, start

брó|сить, шу, сишь *pf.* (*of* ▶ **броса́ть**): **∼сь(те)!** stop it!

брó|ситься, шусь, сишься *pf. of* ▶ **броса́ться**

бросóк, ка́ *m.* **1** (*взмах руки́*) throw; **штрафнóй б.** (sport) free throw **2** (*скачок*) bound; spurt

брó|шу, сишь *see* ▶ **брóсить**

брош|ь, и *f.* brooch

брошю́р|а, ы *f.* pamphlet; (*рекла́мная*) brochure

брус, а, *pl.* **∼ья, ∼ьев** *m.* beam; **паралле́льные ∼ья** (sport) parallel bars

брусни́к|а, и *f.* cowberry (*Vaccinium vitis-idaea*)

брус|óк, ка́ *m.* bar; ingot; **точи́льный б.** whetstone

брýтто *adj. indecl.* gross; **вес б.** gross weight

бры́з|гать, жу, жешь *impf.* (*of* ▶ **бры́знуть**) (*чем*) **1** to splash, spatter; (*заби́ть струёй*) to gush, spurt **2** (*pres.* **∼жу** *or* **∼гаю**) (*окропля́ть*) to sprinkle

бры́зга|ться, юсь *impf.* (infml) to splash; to splash oneself, one another

бры́зг|и, ∼ (*no sg.*) spray, splashes

бры́з|жу, жешь *see* ▶ **брызгать**

брыз|ну́ть, ну, нешь *inst. pf. of* ▶ **брызгать**

брыка́|ться, юсь *impf.* (*ребёнок*) to kick; (*лошадь*) to buck; (fig.) to kick, rebel

брюзж|а́ть, у́, и́шь *impf.* to grumble

брю́к|и, ∼ (*no sg.*) trousers; **б.-ю́бка** culottes

брюне́т, а *m.* dark-haired man

брюне́тк|а, и *f.* brunette

Брюссе́л|ь, я *m.* Brussels

брюссе́льск|ий *adj.* Brussels; **∼ая капу́ста** Brussels sprouts

брю́х|о, а, *pl.* **∼и** *nt.* (infml) belly; (*большой живо́т*) paunch

брюшн|о́й *adj.* abdominal; **б. тиф** typhoid (fever)

БТР *m. indecl.* (*abbr. of* **бронетранспортёр**) APC (*armoured personnel carrier*)

бу́б|ен, на *m.* tambourine

бу́бны¹ *pl. of* ▶ **бу́бен**

бу́б|ны², ен *f. pl.* (*sg.* infml **∼на, ∼ны**) (*в ка́ртах*) **1** diamonds; **дво́йка ∼ен** the two of diamonds **2** (*sg.*) a diamond

бу́ги-ву́ги *nt. indecl.* boogie-woogie

Будапе́шт, а *m.* Budapest

будди́зм, а *m.* Buddhism

будди́йский *adj.* Buddhist

будди́ст, а *m.* Buddhist

будди́ст|ка, ки *f. of* ▶ **будди́ст**

бу́дет 1 *3rd person sg. fut. of* ▶ **быть**; **б. ему́ за э́то!** he'll catch it! **2** (*as pred.*) (infml) that's enough!; that'll do!; **б. вам писа́ть!** it's time you stopped writing!

буди́льник, а *m.* alarm clock

бу|ди́ть, жу́, ∼дишь *impf.* **1** (*pf.* **раз∼**) to wake, awaken, call **2** (*pf.* **про∼**) (fig., *возбужда́ть*) to rouse, arouse; to stir up; **б. мысль** to set (one) thinking

бу́дк|а, и *f.* (*сторожа́*) box, booth; (*ларёк*) stall; **карау́льная б.** sentry box; **соба́чья б.** dog kennel; **телефóнная б.** telephone booth

бу́дн|и, ей *pl.* **1** weekdays; working days, workdays; **по ∼ям** on weekdays **2** (*однообразная жизнь*) humdrum life; colourless existence

бу́дний *adj.*: **б. день** weekday

⚲ key word

ⵏ **бу́дто** **1** *conj.* as if, as though **2** *conj.* that (*implying doubt as to the truth of a statement*); **он утвержда́ет, б. свобо́дно говори́т на десяти́ языка́х** he claims that he speaks ten languages fluently **3** (*also* **б. бы, как б.**) *particle* (infml, *кажется*) apparently

бу́д|у, ешь *fut. of* ▶ **быть**

бу́дучи *pres. gerund of* ▶ **быть**; being

ⵏ **бу́дущ|ий** *adj.* future; next; ... to be; ∼ee **вре́мя** (gram.) future tense; **в ∼ем году́** next year; ∼**ая мать** expectant mother; (*as nt. n.* ∼**ee, ∼его**) the future; (gram.) future tense; **в ближа́йшем ∼ем** in the near future

будь and **бу́дьте** *imper. of* ▶ **быть**; **бу́дьте добры́, бу́дьте любе́зны** (+ *inf. or imper.*) please; would you be good enough (to), kind enough (to); **будь, что бу́дет** come what may; **будь он бога́т, будь он бе́ден, мне всё равно́** be he rich or be he poor, it is all one to me; (*sg. also used in place of 'if' clause in conditional sentences*) **не будь вас, всё бы пропа́ло** but for you, all would have been lost

бужени́н|а, ы *f.* boiled salted pork

бу|жу́, ∼дишь *see* ▶ **буди́ть**

бузин|а́, ы́ *f.* (bot., *красная; чёрная*) elder

бу́|йный, ∼ен, ∼йна́, ∼йно *adj.* **1** (*непокорный*) wild; tempestuous; **б. сумасше́дший** violent, dangerous lunatic **2** (*обильный*) luxuriant, lush; **б. рост** luxuriant growth

бу́йств|о, а *nt.* unruly conduct

бук, а *m.* beech

бу́кв|а, ы, *g. pl.* ∼ *f.* letter (*of the alphabet*); **б. зако́на** the letter of the law

буква́льно *adv.* literally; (*дословно*) word for word

буква́льн|ый *adj.* literal; ∼**ое значе́ние** literal meaning; **б. перево́д** literal translation

буква́р|ь, я́ *m.* ABC; primer

буке́т, а *m.* **1** bouquet; bunch of flowers **2** (*аромат*) aroma

букинисти́ческий *adj.*: **б. магази́н** second-hand bookshop

букле́т, а *m.* (fold-out) leaflet

букме́кер, а *m.* bookmaker, bookie (infml)

букси́р, а *m.* **1** (*судно*) tug, tugboat **2** (*канат*) tow rope; **взять на б.** to take in tow; (fig.) to give a helping hand

букси́р|овать, ую *impf.* to tow, have in tow

букс|ова́ть, у́ю *impf.* to skid

була́вк|а, и *f.* pin; **англи́йская б.** safety pin

бу́лк|а, и *f.* (*булочка*) roll; (*белый хлеб*) white bread; **сдо́бная б.** bun

бу́лочн|ая, ой *f.* bakery; baker's shop

булы́жник, а *m.* cobblestone (*also collect.*)

бульва́р, а *m.* avenue; boulevard

бульва́р|ный *adj. of* ▶ **бульва́р**; ∼**ная литерату́ра** pulp fiction; ∼**ная пре́сса** the tabloids; the gutter press

бульдо́г, а *m.* bulldog

бульдо́зер, а *m.* bulldozer

бульо́н, а *m.* broth; stock

бум, а *m.* (econ.) boom

ⵏ **бума́г|а, и** *f.* **1** (*материал*) paper; **газе́тная б.** newsprint **2** (*документ*) document; (*in pl.*) (official) papers; **це́нные ∼и** (fin.) securities

бума́жк|а, и *f.* piece of paper

бума́жник, а *m.* wallet

бума́|жный *adj. of* ▶ **бума́га**; (fig.) (existing only on) paper; ∼**жная волоки́та** red tape; ∼**жные де́ньги** paper money; **б. змей** kite; ∼**жная фа́брика** paper mill

бумера́нг, а *m.* boomerang

бу́нгало *nt. indecl.* bungalow (*in tropical countries*)

бу́нкер, а *m.* bunker

бунт, а *m.* revolt; riot

бунта́рский *adj.* **1** seditious; mutinous **2** (fig.) rebellious; turbulent; **б. дух** rebellious spirit

бунта́р|ь, я́ *m.* rebel (also fig.); insurgent; mutineer; rioter

бунт|ова́ть, у́ю *impf.* (*pf.* **взбунтова́ться**) to revolt, rebel; to mutiny; to riot; (fig.) to rage, go berserk

бунтовщи́к, а́ *m.* rebel, insurgent; mutineer; rioter

буреве́стник, а *m.* stormy petrel

буре́ни|е, я *nt.* (tech.) boring, drilling

буржуази́|я, и *f.* bourgeoisie; **ме́лкая б.** petty bourgeoisie

буржуа́з|ный, ∼ен, ∼на *adj.* bourgeois

бур|и́ть, ю́, и́шь *impf.* (*of* ▶ **пробури́ть**) (tech.) to bore; to drill

бурл|и́ть, ю́, и́шь *impf.* to seethe, boil up (also fig.)

бу́р|ный, ∼ен, ∼на́, ∼но *adj.* **1** (*погода, море*) stormy, rough; (*спор*) heated; (*жизнь, восторг, аплодисменты*) wild **2** (*рост*) rapid

буров|о́й *adj.* boring; ∼**а́я вы́шка** derrick; ∼**а́я сква́жина** bore, borehole, well

бу́р|ый, ∼, ∼а́, ∼о *adj.* brown; **б. медве́дь** brown bear

бу́р|я, и *f.* storm (also fig.); **б. в стака́не воды́** storm in a teacup

буря́т, а, *g. pl.* **б.** *m.* Buryat

буря́т|ка, ки *f. of* ▶ **буря́т**

буря́тский *adj.* Buryat

бу́с|ы, ∼ (*no sg.*) beads

бутербро́д, а *m.* slice of bread and butter; sandwich; (fig.) **зако́н ∼а** Sod's Law, Murphy's Law

бути́к, а *m.* boutique

буто́н, а *m.* bud

бу́тс|ы, ∼ *f. pl.* (*sg.* ∼**а, ∼ы**) football boots

буты́лк|а, и *f.* bottle

бу́фер, а, *pl.* ∼**а́** *m.* (rail., comput.) (also fig.) buffer

буфе́т, а *m.* **1** (*шкаф*) sideboard **2** (*закусочная*) buffet, snack bar; (*стойка*) (refreshment) bar, counter

буха́нк|а, и *f.* loaf

Бухаре́ст, а *m.* Bucharest

б

б

бу́х|ать, аю impf. (of ▸ бу́хнуть¹) **1** (ударять) to thump, bang **2** (о выстреле) to thud, thunder

бух|а́ть, а́ю impf. (of ▸ бу́хнуть²) (infml, пить) to drink heavily, binge-drink

бухга́лтер, а m. bookkeeper, accountant

бухгалте́ри|я, и f. **1** bookkeeping, accountancy **2** (отдел) counting house

бухга́лтерск|ий adj. bookkeeping, account; ∼ая кни́га account book

бу́х|нуть¹, ну, нешь, past ∼нул pf. of ▸ бу́хать

бу́х|нуть², ну, нешь, past ∼нул pf. of ▸ буха́ть

бу́хт|а, ы f. (geog.) bay

буш|ева́ть, у́ю impf. to rage; (fig.) to rage, storm

Буэ́нос-А́йрес, а m. Buenos Aires

бы (abbr. б) particle **1** (выражает предположительную возможность) (see also ▸ е́сли) я мог бы об э́том догада́ться I might have guessed it; **бы́ло бы о́чень прия́тно вас ви́деть** it would be very nice to see you **2**: (+ ни) (forms indefinite prons.) **кто бы ни** whoever; **что бы ни** whatever; **как бы ни** however; **кто бы ни пришёл** whoever comes; **что бы ни случи́лось** whatever happens; **как бы то ни́ было** however that may be; be that as it may **3** (выражает пожелание): **я бы вы́пил пи́ва** I should like a drink of beer **4** (выражает предложение): **вы бы отдохну́ли** you should take a rest

быва́ло see ▸ быва́ть

быва́лый adj. experienced; worldly-wise

быва́|ть, ю impf. **1** (случаться) to happen; (происходить) to take place; ∼ет, что **поезда́ с се́вера опа́здывают** trains from the north are sometimes late **2** (быть) to be; (находиться) to be present; (посещать) to frequent; **они́ ре́дко** ∼**ют в теа́тре** they seldom go to the theatre **3** (быть склонным) to be inclined to be, tend to be; **он** ∼**ет раздражи́тельным** he is inclined to be irritable **4**: **как ни в чём не** ∼**ло** (infml) as if nothing had happened; **как не** ∼**ло** (+ g.) to have completely disappeared; **головно́й бо́ли у меня́ как не** ∼**ло** my headache has completely gone

бы́вший p.p. of ▸ быть and adj. former, ex-; one-time; **б. президе́нт** former president, ex-president

бык, á m. bull; ox; **здоро́в как б.** as strong as an ox

бы́ло particle (indicates that an action was impending or had just begun, but was not completed): **он отпра́вился б. с ни́ми, но верну́лся** he started out with them but turned back; **чуть б.** very nearly; **они́ чуть б. не уби́ли его́** they all but killed him

был|ь, и f. fact, true story

быстроде́йстви|е, я nt. (tech.) speed, response time

быстрот|á, ы́ f. rapidity, quickness; (скорость) speed

быстрохо́д|ный, ∼**ен,** ∼**на** adj. fast, high-speed

бы́стр|ый, ∼, ∼**á,** ∼**o** adj. rapid, fast, quick; (немедленный) prompt

быт, а, о ∼**е, в** ∼**ý** (no pl.) m. way of life; life; **солда́тский б.** army life

быти|é, я́ nt. (phil.) being, existence, objective reality; **кни́га Б**∼**я** (bibl.) Genesis

быт|ово́й adj. of ▸ быт; social; ∼**овы́е прибо́ры** domestic appliances; ∼**ово́е обслу́живание населе́ния** consumer services; ∼**ово́е явле́ние** everyday occurrence

быть, pres. only used in 3rd person sg. **есть,** fut. **бу́ду, бу́дешь,** past **был, была́, бы́ло,** neg. **не́ был, не была́, не́ было,** imper. **бу́дь(те)** (see also ▸ бу́дет, ▸ будь, ▸ бы́ло, ▸ есть²) impf. **1** (существовать) to be; **есть таки́е лю́ди** there are such people, such people do exist **2**: **б. у** (see also ▸ есть¹) (иметь) to be in the possession (of); **у них была́ прекра́сная да́ча** they had a lovely dacha **3** (находиться) to be; **где вы бы́ли вчера́?** where were you yesterday?; **он тут был не при чём** he had nothing to do with it; **на ней была́ ро́зовая ко́фточка** she had on a pink blouse **4** (случаться) to be, happen, take place; **э́того не мо́жет б.!** it cannot be!; **так и б.** so be it, all right, very well, have it your own way • (as v. aux.) to be

бычо́к¹, ká m. (бык) steer

бычо́к², ká m. (рыба) goby

бью, бьёшь see ▸ бить

бюдже́т, а m. budget

бюдже́тник, а m. (infml) person who is paid from the state budget (e.g. a teacher)

бюдже́тный adj. budgetary; **б. год** fiscal year

бюллете́н|ь, я m. **1** bulletin; **информацио́нный б.** newsletter **2**: (избира́тельный) б. ballot paper **3**: (больни́чный) б. medical certificate

бюро́ nt. indecl. **1** (конто́ра) bureau, office; **б. нахо́док** lost property office; **б. по трудоустро́йству** employment agency; **спра́вочное б.** inquiry office, information office; **туристи́ческое б.** travel agency **2** (стол) bureau, writing desk

бюрокра́т, а m. bureaucrat

бюрократи́ческий adj. bureaucratic

бюрокра́ти|я, и f. bureaucracy (also collect.)

бюст, а m. (скульптура) bust; (же́нский) bust, bosom

бюстга́льтер, а m. bra(ssiere)

Вв

в *prep.*

• **I.** (+ *a. and p.*) **1** (+ *a.*) (*указывает на направление*) into, to; (+ *p.*) (*указывает на место*) in, at; **пое́хать в Москву́** to go to Moscow; **роди́ться в Москве́** to be born in Moscow; **сесть в ваго́н** to get into the carriage; **сиде́ть в ваго́не** to be in the carriage; **смотре́ть в окно́** to look out of the window **2** (*указывает на вид*): **руба́шка в кле́тку** check(ed) shirt; **ходи́ть в шу́бе** to wear a fur coat **3** (+ *nom.-a. pl. and p. pl.*) (*указывает на профессию*): **пойти́ в учителя́** to become a teacher **4** (*обозначает время*): **в понеде́льник** on Monday; **в январе́** in January; **в 1899 году́** in 1899; **в двадца́том ве́ке** in the twentieth century; **в четы́ре часа́** at four o'clock; **в четвёртом часу́** between three and four; **в на́ши дни** in our day; **в тече́ние** (+ *g.*) during, in the course (of)
• **II.** (+ *a.*) **1** (*указывает на сходство*): **быть в кого́-н.** to take after sb; to be like sb; **она́ вся в тётю** she is just like her aunt **2** (*указывает на цель*) for, as; **сказа́ть в шу́тку** to say for a joke **3** (+ *раз and comp. adv.*) (*указывает на сравнение*): **в два ра́за бо́льше** twice as big, twice the size; **в два ра́за ме́ньше** half as big, half the size **4** (*указывает на игру, спорт*): **игра́ть в ка́рты, ша́хматы, футбо́л** to play cards, chess, football
• **III.** (+ *p.*) **1** at a distance of; **в трёх киломе́трах от го́рода** three kilometres from the town; **они́ живу́т в десяти́ мину́тах ходьбы́ отсю́да** they live ten minutes' walk from here **2** in; of (= *consisting of, amounting to*); **пье́са в трёх де́йствиях** play in three acts

в. (*abbr. of* **век**) c., century

ваго́н, а *m.* **1** carriage (BrE), coach (BrE), car (AmE); **мя́гкий, жёсткий в.** soft-seated, hard-seated carriage (BrE), car (AmE); **бага́жный в.** luggage van; **в.-рестора́н** dining car, restaurant car; **спа́льный в.** sleeping car **2** (*груз*) wagonload; (fig., infml) loads, lots

вагоне́тк|а, и *f.* truck; trolley

ва́жност|ь, и *f.* **1** importance; significance **2** (*надменность*) pomposity, pretentiousness

ва́ж|ный, ~ен, ~на́, ~но, ~ны́ *adj.* **1** (*short form pl.* ~ны́) important; weighty, consequential; **са́мое ~ное** the (important) thing (is); **~ная пти́ца/ши́шка** (infml) bigwig **2** (*short form pl.* ~ны́) (*гордый*) pompous, pretentious

ва́з|а, ы *f.* vase, bowl

вай-фа́й *m. indecl.* (*in full* **техноло́гия в.**) (comput.) Wi-Fi (technology)®

вака́нси|я, и *f.* vacancy; **я́рмарка ~й** jobs fair

вака́нт|ный, ~ен, ~на *adj.* vacant, unfilled; **~ная до́лжность** vacancy

ва́кс|а, ы *f.* black (shoe) polish

ва́куум, а *m.* vacuum

вакци́н|а, ы *f.* vaccine

вал¹, а, *pl.* **~ы́** *m.* (*волна́*) billow, roller

вал², а, *pl.* **~ы́** *m.* (*на́сыпь*) bank, earthen wall; (mil.) rampart

вал³, а, *pl.* **~ы́** *m.* (tech.) shaft

вале́жник, а (*no pl.*) *m.* (*collect.*) brushwood

ва́лен|ки, ок *m. pl.* (*sg.* ~ок, ~ка) valenki (*felt boots*)

вале́т, а *m.* (cards) jack

вал|и́ть¹, ю́, ~ишь *impf.* **1** (*pf.* по~ *and* с~) (*заставля́ть па́дать*) to throw down, bring down; to overthrow; **в. кого́-н. с ног** to knock sb off his feet; **в. дере́вья** to fell trees **2** (*pf.* с~) (*в ку́чу*) to heap up, pile up **3** (*pf.* с~) (infml): **в. вину́** (**на** + *a.*) to lump the blame (on)

вал|и́ть², и́т *impf.* (infml, *дви́гаться ма́ссой*) to flock, throng, pour; **снег ~и́т кру́пными хло́пьями** the snow is coming down in large flakes

вал|и́ться, ю́сь, ~ишься *impf.* (*of* ▸ **повали́ться,** ▸ **свали́ться**) to fall, collapse; to topple over; **в. от уста́лости** to drop from tiredness

валли́|ец, йца *m.* Welshman

валли́йк|а, и *f.* Welshwoman

валли́йский *adj.* Welsh

валово́й *adj.* (econ.) gross; wholesale; **в. вну́тренний проду́кт** gross domestic product; **в. национа́льный проду́кт** gross national product

валто́рн|а, ы *f.* (mus.) French horn

валторни́ст, а *m.* hornist, (French) horn player

валторни́ст|ка, ки *f. of* ▸ **валторни́ст**

валу́н, а́ *m.* boulder

вальс, а *m.* waltz

валю́т|а, ы *f.* (fin., econ.) **1** (*де́нежная систе́ма*) currency; **курс ~ы** rate of exchange **2** (*collect.*) (*иностра́нные де́ньги*) foreign currency; **твёрдая/свобо́дно конверти́руемая в.** hard currency

валю́тно-фина́нсов|ый *adj.*: **~ая би́ржа** foreign exchange market

валю́тный *adj. of* ▸ **валю́та**; currency; **в. фонд** monetary fund

валя́|ть, ю *impf.* **1** (*pf.* вы́~) (*валя́я, покры́ть чем-н.*) to roll, drag; **в. в грязи́** to drag in the mire **2**: **в. дурака́** (infml) to play the fool

В

валя́|ться, юсь *impf.* **1** (*ката́ться*) to roll **2** (infml, *безде́льничать*) to lie about

вам *d. of* ▸ **вы**

ва́ми *i. of* ▸ **вы**

вампи́р, а *m.* vampire

ванда́л, а *m.* vandal

вандали́зм, а *m.* vandalism

вани́л|ь, и *f.* vanilla

вани́льный *adj. of* ▸ **вани́ль**

ва́нн|а, ы *f.* bath; **приня́ть ~у** to take a bath

ва́нн|ая, ой *f.* bathroom

ва́рварский *adj.* barbaric

ва́рварств|о, а *nt.* barbarity

ва́режк|а, и *f.* mitten

варе́ник, а *m.* varenik (*curd or fruit dumpling*)

варёный *adj.* boiled

варе́нь|е, я *nt.* preserve(s) (*containing whole fruit*); jam (BrE)

⚘ **вариа́нт, а** *m.* (*разнови́дность*) variant; version; (*возмо́жность*) option; (*сцена́рий*) scenario; model

вар|и́ть, ю́, ~ишь *impf.* (*of* ▸ **свари́ть** 1) **1** to boil; to cook; **в. карто́фель** to boil potatoes; **в. обе́д** to cook dinner; **в. пи́во** to brew beer **2** (*о голове́*): **голова́/башка́ у него́ ва́рит** (infml) he's quick on the uptake

вар|и́ться, ~ится *impf.* (*of* ▸ **свари́ться**) **1** (*в кипятке́*) to boil; (*пригото́вляться на огне́*) to cook **2** *pass. of* ▸ **вари́ть**

Варша́в|а, ы *f.* Warsaw

варьи́р|овать, ую *impf.* to vary, modify

вас *g., a., and p. of* ▸ **вы**

василёк, ька́ *m.* (bot.) cornflower

ва́т|а, ы *f.* cotton wool (BrE), absorbent cotton (AmE); (*для подкла́дки*) wadding

Ватика́н, а *m.* the Vatican

ва́тник, а *m.* quilted jacket

ва́тн|ый *adj.* wadded, quilted; **~ое одея́ло** quilt

ватру́шк|а, и *f.* curd tart

ватт, а, *g. pl.* **в.** *m.* watt

ва́учер, а *m.* voucher

ва́фл|я, и, *g. pl.* **~ель** *f.* waffle; wafer

ва́хт|а, ы *f.* (*сме́нная рабо́та*) shift; **нести́ ~у** to be on duty; (naut.) watch; **стоя́ть на ~е** to keep watch

вахтёр, а *m.* janitor, porter

ва́хтовый *adj.* shift-based

⚘ **ваш, ~его,** *f.* **~а, ~ей,** *nt.* **~е, ~его,** *pl.* **~и, ~их** *poss. pron.* (*при существи́тельном*) your; (*без существи́тельного*) yours; **э́то в. каранда́ш** this is your pencil; **э́тот каранда́ш в.** this pencil is yours; (*as pl. n.* **~и, ~их**) your people, your folk

Вашингто́н, а *m.* Washington

вая́|ть, ю *impf.* (*of* ▸ **изва́ять**) to sculpt; (*из ка́мня, де́рева*) to carve, chisel

вбега́|ть, ю *impf.* (**в** + *a.*) to run (into)

вбе|жа́ть, гу́, жи́шь, гу́т *pf. of* ▸ **вбега́ть**

вбива́|ть, ю *impf. of* ▸ **вбить**

вбить, вобью́, вобьёшь *pf.* (*of* ▸ **вбива́ть**) to drive in, hammer in

вблизи́ *adv.* (**от** + *g.*) close by; not far (from); **рассма́тривать в.** to examine closely

вбок *adv.* sideways, to one side

вбра́сывани|е, я *nt.:* **в.** (*мяча́*) throw-in (*in football*); **в. (ша́йбы)** face-off (*in ice hockey*)

вбра́сыва|ть, ю *impf. of* ▸ **вбро́сить**

вбро́|сить, шу, сишь *pf.* (*of* ▸ **вбра́сывать**) to throw in(to)

вва́лива|ться, юсь *impf. of* ▸ **ввали́ться**

ввал|и́ться, ю́сь, ~ишься *pf.* **1** (fig., infml, *входи́ть*) to burst into **2** (*стать впа́лым*) to become hollow, sunken; **с ~и́вшимися щека́ми** hollow-cheeked

⚘ **введе́ни|е, я** *nt.* introduction

вве|ду́, дёшь *see* ▸ **ввести́**

ввез|ти́, у́, ёшь, *past* **~, ~ла́** *pf.* (*of* ▸ **ввози́ть**) to import

вверх *adv.* up, upward(s); **идти́ в. по ле́стнице** to go upstairs; **в. по тече́нию** upstream; **в. дном** upside down; **в. нога́ми** head over heels

вверху́ *adv. and prep.* + *g.* above, overhead; **в. страни́цы** at the top of the page

вве|сти́, ду́, дёшь, *past* **~л, ~ла́** *pf.* (*of* ▸ **вводи́ть**) (*челове́ка, живо́тное*) to lead in, bring in, take in; (*зако́н, по́шлины*) to introduce, bring in; (*помести́ть внутрь*) to introduce, put into; (*да́нные*) to enter, key in; **в. в заблужде́ние** to mislead; **в. в курс чего́-н.** to acquaint with (the facts of) sth

ввиду́ *prep.* + *g.* in view (of); **в. того́, что** as

ввин|ти́ть, чу́, ти́шь *pf.* (*of* ▸ **вви́нчивать**) (**в** + *a.*) to screw (in)

вви́нчива|ть, ю *impf. of* ▸ **ввинти́ть**

⚘ **вво|ди́ть, жу́, ~дишь** *impf. of* ▸ **ввести́**

вво́дн|ый *adj.* introductory; (gram.): **~ое сло́во** parenthetic word, parenthesis

вво|жу́[1], ~дишь *see* ▸ **вводи́ть**

вво|жу́[2], ~зишь *see* ▸ **ввози́ть**

ввоз, а (*no pl.*) *m.* **1** (*де́йствие*) importation **2** (*и́мпорт*) import

вво|зи́ть, жу́, ~зишь *impf. of* ▸ **ввезти́**

ввозн|о́й *adj.* (*това́р*) imported; (*attr.*) import; **~а́я по́шлина** import duty

ВВП *m. indecl.* (*abbr. of* **валово́й вну́тренний проду́кт**) GDP (*gross domestic product*)

ВВС *pl. indecl.* (*abbr. of* **вое́нно-возду́шные си́лы**) Air Force

ввя|за́ться, жу́сь, ~жешься *pf.* (*of* ▸ **ввя́зываться**) (infml) (**в** + *a.*) (*вмеша́ться*) to meddle (in); (*впу́таться*) to get involved (in), mixed up (in)

ввя́зыва|ться, юсь *impf. of* ▸ **ввяза́ться**

вглубь *adv. and prep.* + *g.* deep down; deep into, into the depths

вдалеке́ *adv.* in the distance; **в. от** (+ *g.*) a long way from

вдали́ *adv.* in the distance, far off; **в. от го́рода** a long way from the city; **исчеза́ть в.** to vanish into the distance

вдаль *adv.* afar, at a distance; **гляде́ть в.** to look into the distance

вдво́е *adv.* twice; double; **в. лу́чше** twice as good; **сложи́ть в.** to fold double

вдвоём *adv.* the two together; **они́ написа́ли статью́ в.** the two of them together wrote the article

вдвойне́ *adv.* twice, double; doubly (also fig.); **плати́ть в.** to pay double; **он в. винова́т** he is doubly to blame

вдева́|ть, ю *impf. of* ▶ **вдеть**

вде|ть, ~ну, ~нешь *pf.* (*of* ▶ **вдева́ть**) (**в** + *a.*) to put in(to); **в. ни́тку в иго́лку** to thread a needle

вдоба́вок *adv.* (infml) in addition; moreover; into the bargain; **в. к** (+ *d.*) in addition to

вдов|а́, ы́, *pl.* **~ы** *f.* widow

вдов|е́ц, ца́ *m.* widower

вдо́воль *adv.* **1** (*в изоби́лии*) in abundance **2** (*вполне доста́точно*) enough; **он нае́лся в.** he ate his fill

вдого́нку *adv.* (infml) after, in pursuit of; **бро́ситься в.** (**за** + *i.*) to rush (after)

вдоль 1 *prep.* (+ *g. or* **по** + *d.*) along; **в. бе́рега** along the bank **2** *adv.* lengthwise, longways; **в. и поперёк** (*повсю́ду*) in all directions, far and wide

вдох, а *m.* breath; **сде́лать глубо́кий в.** to take a deep breath

вдохнове́ни|е, я *nt.* inspiration

вдохнов|и́ть, лю́, и́шь *pf.* (*of* ▶ **вдохновля́ть**) (+ *a. or* **на** + *a.*) to inspire (to)

вдохновля́|ть, ю *impf. of* ▶ **вдохнови́ть**

вдохн|у́ть, у́, ёшь *pf.* (*of* ▶ **вдыха́ть**) **1** (*во́здух*) to breathe in; (*дым*) inhale **2** (*настрое́ние*) (**в** + *a.*) to instil (into); **в. му́жество в кого́-н.** to instil courage into sb

вдре́безги *adv.* (*на ме́лкие ча́сти*) to pieces, to smithereens

◆ **вдруг** *adv.* **1** (*неожи́данно*) suddenly, all of a sudden **2** (*as interrog. particle*) (infml, *а что е́сли*) what if, suppose; **(a) в. они́ узна́ют?** but suppose they find out?

вду́м|аться, аюсь *pf.* (*of* ▶ **вду́мываться**) (**в** + *a.*) to think over, ponder, meditate (on)

вду́мыва|ться, юсь *impf. of* ▶ **вду́маться**

вдыха́ни|е, я *nt.* inhalation

вдыха́|ть, ю *impf. of* ▶ **вдохну́ть**

веб-са́йт, а *m.* (comput.) website

веб-страни́ц|а, ы *f.* (comput.) web page

вегетариа́н|ец, ца *m.* vegetarian; **стро́гий в.** vegan

вегетариа́н|ка, ки *f. of* ▶ **вегетариа́нец**

вегетариа́нский *adj.* vegetarian

веда́|ть, ю *impf.* **1** (*знать*) to know **2** (+ *i.*) (*заве́довать*) to manage, be in charge of

◆ **ве́дени|е, я** *nt.* authority; jurisdiction; **э́ти дела́ в моём ~и** I am in charge of these things

◆ **веде́ни|е, я** *nt.* conducting, conduct; **в. хозя́йства** the running of a household

ве́дома (*only in phrr.*): **без в., с в.; без моего́ в.** unknown to me; **с моего́ в.** with my knowledge, with my consent

ве́домост|ь, и *f.* list, register; **платёжная в.** payroll

ве́домственный *adj.* departmental

ве́домств|о, а *nt.* department

вед|ро́, ра́, *pl.* **~ра, ~ер** *nt.* bucket, pail

веду́, ёшь *see* ▶ **вести́**

◆ **веду́щ|ий** *pres. part. act. of* ▶ **вести́** *and adj.* leading; (tech.): **~ее колесо́** driving wheel; (*as m. n.* **в., ~его**) presenter; compère

◆ **ведь** *conj.* **1** (*де́ло в том, что*) you see, you know (*but often requires no translation*); **она́ всё вре́мя покупа́ет но́вые пла́тья: в. она́ о́чень бога́та** she is always buying new dresses — she is very rich, you know **2** (*particle*) (*не пра́вда ли?*) is it not?; is it?; **в. э́то пра́вда?** it's the truth, isn't it?

ве́дьм|а, ы *f.* witch

ве́ер, а, *pl.* **~а́** *m.* fan

ве́жливост|ь, и *f.* politeness, courtesy

ве́жлив|ый, ~, ~а *adj.* polite, courteous

везде́ *adv.* everywhere; **в. и всю́ду** here, there, and everywhere

вездесу́щ|ий, ~, ~а *adj.* (*челове́к*) ubiquitous; (*Бог*) omnipresent

вездехо́д, а *m.* four-wheel drive (vehicle)

везе́ни|е, я *nt.* luck

вез|ти́, у́, ёшь, *past* **~, ~ла́** *impf.* (*of* ▶ **повезти́,** *det. of* ▶ **вози́ть**) **1** (*перемеща́ть*) to take, convey, carry (*of beasts of burden, mechanical transport, or people when on transport*) **2** (infml) (*impers.* + *d.*) (*об уда́че*) to have luck; **ему́ не ~ёт в ка́рты** he has no luck at cards

везу́чий *adj.* (infml) lucky

◆ **век, а, о ~е, на ~у́,** *pl.* **~а́** (obs. **~и́**) *m.* **1** (*столе́тие*) century **2** (*эпо́ха*) age; **ка́менный в.** Stone Age; **Сре́дние ~а́** the Middle Ages; **испоко́н ~о́в** from time immemorial; **в ко́и-то ~и** once in a blue moon **3** (*жизнь*) life, lifetime; **на моём ~у́** in my lifetime

ве́к|о, а, *pl.* **~и, ~** *nt.* eyelid

вексо́й *adj.* ancient, age-old

вёл, вела́ *see* ▶ **вести́**

вел|е́ть, ю́, и́шь *impf. and pf.* (+ *d. and inf. or* **что́бы**) to order; **я ~е́л ему́ сде́лать э́то** *or* **что́бы он сде́лал э́то** I ordered him to do this

велика́н, а *m.* giant

◆ **вели́к|ий, ~, ~а́** *adj.* **1** (*short form* **~а, ~о,** *pl.* **~и**) (*выдаю́щийся*) great; **~ие держа́вы** the Great Powers **2** (*short form* **~а́, ~о́,** *pl.* **~й**) (*большо́й*) big, large; **~ое мно́жество** a lot, a great deal **3** (*short form only* **~а́, ~о́,** *pl.* **~й**) (+ *d. or* **для** + *g.*) (*сли́шком большо́й*) too big; **э́ти брю́ки мне ~й** these trousers are too big for me

Великобрита́ни|я, и *f.* Great Britain

великоду́ши|е, я *nt.* magnanimity, generosity

великоду́ш|ный, ~ен, ~на *adj.* magnanimous, generous

великоле́пи|е, я *nt.* magnificence

B

великоле́п|ный, ~ен, ~на *adj.*
1 (*роскошный*) splendid, magnificent
2 (*отличный*) excellent; **~но!** (*int.*)
splendid!; excellent!
великосве́тский *adj.* high-society (*attr.*)
велича́йший *adj.* (*superl. of* ▸ **вели́кий**)
greatest, extreme, supreme
вели́чественност|ь, и *f.* majesty, grandeur
вели́чествен|ный, ~, ~на *adj.* majestic,
grand
вели́честв|о, а *nt.* majesty; **Ва́ше В.** Your
Majesty
вели́чи|е, я *nt.* greatness; grandeur; **ма́ния
~я** megalomania
▸ **вели́ч|ина́, ины́, pl. ~и́ны, ~и́н, ~и́нам** *f.*
1 size **2** (math.) quantity, magnitude;
(*значение*) value
вело... comb. form bicycle-, cycle-
велого́нк|а, и *f.* cycle race
велого́нщик, а *m.* racing cyclist
велосипе́д, а *m.* bicycle
велосипеди́ст, а *m.* cyclist
велоспо́рт, а *m.* cycling
велотренажёр, а *m.* exercise bicycle
вельве́т, а *m.* corduroy
вельве́товый *adj.* corduroy
велю́р, а *m.* velour
Ве́н|а, ы *f.* Vienna
ве́н|а, ы *f.* (anat.) vein
венге́р|ка, ки *f. of* ▸ **венгр**
венге́рский *adj.* Hungarian
венгр, а *m.* Hungarian
Ве́нгри|я, и *f.* Hungary
венери́ческий *adj.* (med.) venereal
Венесуэ́л|а, ы *f.* Venezuela
венесуэ́л|ец, ца *m.* Venezuelan
венесуэ́л|ка, ки *f. of* ▸ **венесуэ́лец**
венесуэ́льский *adj.* Venezuelan
вен|е́ц, ца́ *m.* (*корона*) crown
венециа́нский *adj.* Venetian
Вене́ци|я, и *f.* Venice
ве́ник, а *m.* **1** (*из прутьев*) besom, broom
2 (*в бане*) birch twigs (*used in Russian baths*)
вен|о́к, ка́ *m.* wreath
ве́нский *adj.* Viennese
ве́нтил|ь, я *m.* valve
вентиля́тор, а *m.* extractor (fan)
вентиля́ци|я, и *f.* ventilation
венча́ни|е, я *nt.* (*бракосочетание*) wedding
ceremony
венча́|ть, ю *impf.* **1** (*pf.* **в.** *and* **у~**)
(*находиться наверху*) to crown **2** (*pf.*
у~) (fig.) to crown **3** (*pf.* **об~** *and* **по~**)
(*соединять браком*) to marry (*of officiating
priest*)
венча́|ться, юсь *impf.* (*pf.* **об~** *and* **по~**)
to be married, marry
ве́нчурный *adj.* (fin.) venture; **в. капита́л**
venture capital

▸ **ве́р|а, ы** *f.* (**в** + *a.*) faith, belief (in);
(*уверенность*) trust, confidence; **приня́ть
на ~у** to take on trust
вера́нд|а, ы *f.* veranda
ве́рб|а, ы *f.* willow
верблю́д, а *m.* camel
ве́рб|ный *adj. of* ▸ **ве́рба**; (eccl.): **В~ное
воскресе́нье** Palm Sunday; **В~ная неде́ля**
Holy Week
верб|ова́ть, у́ю *impf.* (*of* ▸ **завербова́ть**)
to recruit, enlist
верди́кт, а *m.* verdict
верёвк|а, и *f.* cord, rope; string
верени́ц|а, ы *f.* file, line
ве́реск, а *m.* (bot.) heather
веретен|о́, а́, pl. верете́на, верете́н *nt.*
spindle
▸ **ве́р|ить, ю, ишь** *impf.* (*of* ▸ **пове́рить**) (+ *d.
or* **в** + *a.*) to believe, have faith (in); (+ *d.*)
(*доверять*) to trust (in), rely (upon); **в. в
Бо́га** to believe in God; **в. на́ слово** to take
on trust; **я не ~ил свои́м уша́м, свои́м
глаза́м** I could not believe my ears, eyes
ве́р|иться, ится *impf.* (impers. + *d.*): (**мне**)
~ится с трудо́м I find it hard to believe
вермише́л|ь, и *f.* vermicelli
верне́е *adv.* (*comp. of* ▸ **ве́рно**) rather; **в.
(сказа́ть)** to be more exact
верниса́ж, а *m.* (art) **1** (*закрытый просмотр*)
private viewing, preview **2** (*день открытия*)
opening day (*of an exhibition*)
ве́рно *adv. of* ▸ **ве́рный**
ве́рност|ь, и *f.* **1** (*преданность*) faithfulness,
loyalty **2** (*правильность*) truth, correctness
верн|у́ть, у́, ёшь *pf.* (*of* ▸ **возвраща́ть**)
1 (*отдать обратно*) to give back, return
2 (*получить обратно*) to get back, recover,
retrieve
▸ **верн|у́ться, у́сь, ёшься** *pf.* (*of*
▸ **возвраща́ться**) to return (also fig.);
в. домо́й to return home
▸ **ве́р|ный, ~ен, ~на́, ~но, ~ны́** *adj.*
1 (*правильный*) true, correct **2** (*преданный*)
faithful, loyal, true; **в. свои́м убежде́ниям**
true to one's convictions **3** (*надёжный*)
sure, reliable; **в. при́знак** sure sign
4 (*несомненный*) certain, sure; **~ная
смерть** certain death
ве́рование, я *nt.* belief, creed
ве́р|овать, ую *impf.* (**в** + *a.*) to believe (in)
вероиспове́дани|е, я *nt.* creed,
denomination; **свобо́да ~я** freedom of
religion
вероло́м|ный, ~ен, ~на *adj.* treacherous,
perfidious
вероуче́ни|е, я *nt.* (relig.) dogma, teachings
вероя́тно *adv.* probably
вероя́тност|ь, и *f.* probability; **по всей ~и**
in all probability
вероя́т|ный, ~ен, ~на *adj.* probable, likely;
~нее всего́ most probably

▸ key word

ве́рси|я, и f. version

верста́к, а́ *m.* (tech.) (work)bench

ве́ртел, а, *pl.* ~á *m.* spit; skewer

вер|те́ть, чу́, ~тишь *impf.* (+ *a.* or *i.*) (*рукоятку, колесо*) to turn; (*быстро*) to twirl; **в. голово́й** to shake one's head; **в. что-н. в рука́х** to fiddle with sth

вер|те́ться, чу́сь, ~тишься *impf.*
1 (*вращаться*) to rotate, turn (round), revolve (also fig.); **его́ фами́лия весь день ~те́лась у меня́ на языке́** his name was on the tip of my tongue all day; **в. под нога́ми, пе́ред глаза́ми** (infml) to be under one's feet, in the way **2** (infml, *ёрзать*) to fidget

вертика́л|ь, и *f.* (*линия*) vertical line; (*в кроссворде*) down

вертика́л|ьный, ~ен, ~ьна *adj.* vertical

вертолёт, а *m.* helicopter

вертолётчик, а *m.* helicopter pilot

ве́рующ|ий *adj.* religious; (*as m. n.* **в., ~его**) believer

верф|ь, и *f.* dockyard; shipyard

верх, а, *pl.* ~и́ *m.* **1** (*верхняя часть*) top; (*горы*) summit (also fig.); **встре́ча в ~а́х** (pol.) summit conference; (*крайняя степень*) height; **в. глу́пости** the height of folly **2** (*автомашины*) hood (BrE), folding top (AmE); **«верх!»** 'this side up!' (*sign on package, etc.*); **взять в. (над +** *i.*) to gain the upper hand (over) **3** (*лицевая сторона*) outside, top; right side (*of material*)

ве́рхн|ий *adj.* upper; **~яя оде́жда** outer clothing; **~яя пала́та** (pol.) upper chamber

верхо́вн|ый *adj.* supreme; **~ое кома́ндование** high command; **В. Сове́т** (hist.) Supreme Soviet; **В. суд** Supreme Court

верх|ово́й *adj.*: **~ова́я езда́** riding (BrE), horseback riding (AmE); **~ова́я ло́шадь** mount; (*as m. n.* **в., ~ово́го**) rider

верхо́вь|е, я, *g. pl.* ~ев *nt.* upper reaches

верхо́м *adv.* astride; on horseback; **е́здить в.** to ride

верху́шк|а, и *f.* **1** top; **в. а́йсберга** (fig.) tip of the iceberg **2** (fig., infml, *организации*) elite, top

вер|чу́, ~тишь *see* ▸ **верте́ть**

верши́н|а, ы *f.* **1** (*дерева, холма*) top; (*горы*) summit, peak; (fig.) peak, acme **2** (math.) vertex; apex

вес, а (*pl., specialist use only,* ~á) *m.* weight; **ли́шний в.** excess weight; (*багаж*) excess baggage; (fig., *значение*) weight, authority; **на в.** by weight; **на ~у́** balanced, hanging, suspended; **приба́вить, уба́вить в ~е** to put on, lose weight

весел|и́ть, ю́, и́шь *impf.* (*of* ▸ **развесели́ть**) to amuse

весел|и́ться, ю́сь, и́шься *impf.* to enjoy oneself; to have fun

ве́село *adv.* gaily, merrily; (*as pred.*) (+ *d.*) to enjoy oneself; **бы́ло в.** it was fun

вес|ёлый, ~ел, ~ела́, ~ело *adj.* **1** cheerful, merry **2** (*no short forms*) (*фильм, рассказ*)

cheerful, feel-good; (*краски, обои*) bright, cheerful

весе́нний *adj.* of ▸ **весна́**

ве́|сить, шу, сишь *impf.* (иметь тот или иной *вес*) to weigh; **груз ~сит три то́нны** the cargo weighs three tons

ве́с|кий, ~ок, ~ка *adj.* weighty

весл|о́, а́, *pl.* ~а, ~ел, ~ам *nt.* oar

вес|на́, ны́, *pl.* ~ны, ~ен, ~нам *f.* spring (*season*)

весно́й *adv.* in the spring

весну́шк|и, ек *f. pl.* (*sg.* ~ка, ~ки) freckles

весну́шчатый *adj.* freckled

вес|ово́й *adj.* **1** *of* ▸ **вес**; **~ова́я катего́рия** (sport) weight category **2** (*продаваемый на вес*) sold by weight

весо́м|ый, ~, ~а *adj.* (fig.) weighty; substantial

ве́стерн, а *m.* western (*film*)

ве|сти́, ду́, дёшь, *past* ~л, ~ла́ *impf.* (*det. of* ▸ **води́ть**) **1** (*pf.* ~) (*сопровождать*) to lead; to take; (*войска*) to lead **2** (*pf.* про~) (+ *i. and* по + *d.*) to run (over), pass (over, across) **3** (*pf.* про~) (*осуществлять, делать*) to conduct; to carry on; **в. войну́** to wage war; **в. ого́нь** (по + *d.*) (*impf. only*) to fire (on); **в. перегово́ры** to carry on negotiations; **в. перепи́ску** (с + *i.*) (*impf. only*) to correspond (with); **в. проце́сс** to carry on a lawsuit **4** (*impf. only*) (*машину*) to drive; **в. кора́бль** to navigate a ship; **в. самолёт** to pilot an aircraft **5** (*impf. only*) (*руководить*) to conduct, direct, run; (*передачу*) to present; (*собрание*) to chair; **в. де́ло** to run a business; **в. хозя́йство** to keep house **6** (*impf. only*) (*учёт*) to keep; **в. дневни́к** to keep a diary; **в. протоко́л** to keep minutes **7** (*impf. only*) **в. себя́** to behave **8** (*pf.* при~) (*служить путём куда-нибудь*) to lead (also fig.); **куда́ ~дёт э́та доро́га?** where does this road lead (to)?

вестибю́л|ь, я *m.* entrance hall, lobby

Вест-И́нди|я, и *f.* the West Indies

ве́стник, а *m.* messenger, herald

ве́стни|ца, цы *f. of* ▸ **ве́стник**

вест|ь, и, *pl.* ~и, ~е́й *f.* news; piece of news; **пропа́сть бе́з ~и** (mil.) to be missing

вес|ы́, о́в (*no sg.*) **1** scales, balance **2** (**В.**) (astron., astrol.) the Scales, Libra

весь, вся, всё, *g.* всего́, всей, всего́, *pl.* все, всех *pron.* all; **весь день** all day; **вся страна́** the whole country; **вся Фра́нция** the whole of France; **по всему́ го́роду** all over the town; **он весь в отца́** he is the (very) image of his father; **во весь го́лос** at the top of one's voice; **от всего́ се́рдца** from the bottom of one's heart; **пре́жде всего́** before all, first and foremost; **вот и всё** that's all; there's nothing more to it; **всего́ хоро́шего!** goodbye!, all the best!; (*as nt. n.* **всё, всего́**) everything; **все, всех** (*no sg.*) all, everyone

весьма́ *adv.* very, highly

ветви́ст|ый, ~, ~а *adj.* branchy, spreading

ветв|ь, и, *pl.* ~и, ~е́й *f.* branch; (fig.) branch

В

✔ **ве́т|ер, ра** *m.* wind; (fig.): **у него́ в. в голове́** he is a thoughtless fellow

ветера́н, а *m.* veteran

ветерина́р, а *m.* veterinary surgeon (BrE), veterinarian (AmE)

ветерина́рный *adj.* veterinary

ве́тк|а, и *f.* branch; (*ме́лкая*) twig; **железнодоро́жная в.** branch line

ветл|а́, ы́, *pl.* **~лы, ~ел** *f.* (bot., *бе́лая/ сере́бристая ива*) white willow

ве́то *nt. indecl.* veto; **наложи́ть в. (на + a.)** to veto

ве́тошь, и *f.* old clothes, rags

ве́трен|ый, ~, ~а *adj.* **1** windy **2** (fig., *челове́к*) empty-headed

ветров|о́й *adj. of* ▶ **ве́тер; ~о́е стекло́** windscreen (BrE), windshield (AmE)

ветря́нк|а, и *f.* (med.) chickenpox

ветрян|о́й *adj.* wind(-powered); **~а́я ме́льница** windmill

ве́тх|ий, ~, ~а́, ~о *adj.* (*о́чень ста́рый*) old, ancient; (*зда́ние*) dilapidated, tumbledown, decrepit; **В. Заве́т** the Old Testament

ветчин|а́, ы́ (*no pl.*) *f.* ham

ветша́|ть, ю *impf.* (*of* ▶ **обветша́ть**) to decay; to become dilapidated

ве́х|а, и *f.* landmark (also fig.); milestone

✔ **ве́чер, а,** *pl.* **~а́** *m.* **1** (*вре́мя*) evening; **по ~а́м** in the evenings; **под в., к ~у** towards evening **2** (*собра́ние*) party; evening, soirée

вечере́|ть, ет *impf.* (*impers.*) to grow dark; **~ет** night is falling

вечери́нк|а, и *f.* party

вече́рн|ий *adj. of* ▶ **ве́чер; ~яя заря́** twilight, dusk; **~ие ку́рсы** evening classes; **~ее пла́тье** evening dress

ве́чером *adv.* in the evening

ве́чно *adv.* (*всегда́*) for ever, eternally; (infml, *постоя́нно*) always; **они́ в. ссо́рятся** they are always quarrelling

вечнозелёный *adj.* (bot.) evergreen

ве́чность, и *f.* eternity; **це́лую в.** (infml) for ages

ве́чн|ый, ~ен, ~на *adj.* **1** (*льды, сла́ва*) eternal, everlasting; **~ная мерзлота́** permafrost **2** (*бессро́чный*) indefinite, perpetual **3** (infml, *постоя́нный*) perpetual, continual

ве́шалк|а, и *f.* **1** (*крючо́к*) peg; (*пла́нка*) rack; (*сто́йка*) stand **2** (*пе́тля*) tab (*on clothes for hanging on pegs*) **3** (*пле́чики*) (coat) hanger

ве́ша|ть¹, ю *impf.* (*of* ▶ **пове́сить**) to hang; **в. бельё на верёвку** to hang washing on a line; **в. уби́йцу** to hang a murderer

ве́ша|ть², ю *impf.* (*of* ▶ **взве́сить**) to weigh, weigh out

ве́ша|ться, юсь *impf.* (*of* ▶ **пове́ситься**) **1** *pass. of* ▶ **ве́шать¹** (*карти́на*) to be hung **2** (*конча́ть свою́ жизнь*) to hang oneself

ве́|шу, сишь *see* ▶ **ве́сить**

веща́ни|е, я *nt.* broadcasting

веща́|ть, ю *impf.* **1** (*по ра́дио, телеви́дению*) to broadcast **2** (*говори́ть высокопа́рно*) to pontificate, lay down the law

вещев|о́й *adj. of* ▶ **вещь; в. мешо́к** holdall; kitbag; **в. ры́нок** merchandise market; **в. склад** storage warehouse, store; (mil.) stores

веще́ственн|ый *adj.* substantial, material; **~ые доказа́тельства** material evidence

✔ **вещество́, а́** *nt.* substance

✔ **вещь, и,** *pl.* **~и, ~е́й** *f.* **1** thing (*in var. senses*) **2** (*in pl.*) things (= *belongings; baggage; clothes*); **э́то ва́ши ~и?** are these things yours? **3** (*произведе́ние*) work; piece, thing

ве́яни|е, я *nt.* (fig., *тенде́нция*) current, tendency, trend; **в. вре́мени** spirit of the times

ве́|ять, ю, ешь *impf.* (*о ве́тре*) to blow; **~ял прохла́дный ветеро́к** a cool breeze was blowing; (*impers. + i.*) **~ет весно́й** spring is in the air

взаи́мность, и *f.* reciprocity; return (*of affection*); **отвеча́ть кому́-н. ~ью** to reciprocate sb's feelings, return sb's love; **любо́вь без ~и** unrequited love

взаи́мн|ый, ~ен, ~на *adj.* mutual, reciprocal

взаи́мовы́год|ный, ~ен, ~на *adj.* mutually beneficial

✔ **взаимоде́йстви|е, я** *nt.* (*связь*) interaction; (mil.) cooperation, coordination

взаимоде́йств|овать, ую *impf.* to interact; (mil.) to cooperate

взаимозачёт, а *m.* (fin.) offsetting of debts

взаимоотноше́ни|е, я *nt.* (*usu. in pl.*) relationship(s), relation(s)

взаимопо́мощь, и *f.* mutual aid; mutual assistance

взаиморасчёт|ы, ов *m. pl.* (fin.) mutual settlement of accounts

взаимосвя́зь, и *f.* interrelationship

взаймы́ *adv.*: **взять в.** to borrow; **дать в.** to lend, loan

взаме́н *prep. + g.* (*вме́сто*) instead (of); (*в обме́н на что-н.*) in return (for), in exchange (for)

взаперти́ *adv.* **1** (*под замко́м*) under lock and key **2** (infml, *в уедине́нии*) in seclusion

взба́лтыва|ть, ю *impf. of* ▶ **взболта́ть**

взбега́|ть, ю *impf.* (*of* ▶ **взбежа́ть**) to run up; **в. на́ гору** to run up a hill; **в. по ле́стнице** to run upstairs

взбе|жа́ть, гу́, жи́шь, гу́т *pf. of* ▶ **взбега́ть**

взбе|си́ть, шу́, ~сишь *pf. of* ▶ **беси́ть**

взбе|си́ться, шу́сь, ~сишься *pf. of* ▶ **беси́ться**

взбива́|ть, ю *impf. of* ▶ **взбить**

взбира́|ться, юсь *impf. of* ▶ **взобра́ться**

вз|бить, обью́, обьёшь *pf.* (*of* ▶ **взбива́ть**) **1** (*я́йца*) to beat (up); **в. сли́вки** to whip cream **2** (*поду́шку*) to fluff up

взболта́|ть, ю *pf.* (*of* ▶ **взба́лтывать**) to shake (up) (*liquids*)

взбунт|ова́ться, у́юсь *pf. of* ▸ бунтова́ть

взбу́чк|а, и *f.* (infml) **1** (*побои*) thrashing, beating **2** (*выговор*) dressing-down

взва́лива|ть, ю *impf. of* ▸ взвали́ть

взвал|и́ть, ю́, ~ишь *pf.* (*of* ▸ взва́ливать) to load, lift (onto); **в. мешо́к на́ спину** to hoist a pack onto one's back; **всю вину́ ~и́ли на него́** he was made to shoulder all the blame

взве́|сить, шу, сишь *pf.* (*of* ▸ взве́шивать, ▸ ве́шать²) (*груз*) to weigh; (fig., *варианты*) to weigh, consider

взве́шен|ный, ~, ~на *adj.* (*реше́ние, отве́т*) carefully thought out, balanced

взве́шива|ть, ю *impf. of* ▸ взве́сить

взвива́|ться, юсь *impf. of* ▸ взви́ться

взви́згива|ть, ю *impf. of* ▸ взви́згнуть

взви́згн|уть, у, ешь *pf.* to scream, cry out; (*собака*) to yelp

взви́ться, взовью́сь, взовьёшься *pf.* (*of* ▸ взвива́ться) to fly up, soar; (*о флагах*) to be raised, go up

взвод, а *m.* (mil.) platoon

взволно́ван|ный, ~, ~на *adj.* anxious, worried; (*от счастья*) excited

взволн|ова́ть, у́ю *pf. of* ▸ волнова́ть

ꝑ **взгляд, а** *m.* **1** (*выражение глаз*) look; (*быстрый*) glance; (*пристальный*) gaze, stare; **бро́сить в.** (**на** + *a.*) to glance (at); **на пе́рвый в., с пе́рвого ~a** at first sight **2** (*мнение*) view; opinion; **на мой в.** in my opinion, as I see it

взгля́н|уть, у́, ~ешь *pf.* (**на** + *a.*) to look (at); (*быстро*) to cast a glance (at)

вздор, а (*no pl.*) *m.* (infml) nonsense; **говори́ть, нести́ в.** to talk nonsense

вздо́р|ный, ~ен, ~на *adj.* **1** (*нелепый*) foolish, stupid **2** (infml, *сварливый*) cantankerous, quarrelsome

вздох, а *m.* sigh; deep breath; **испусти́ть после́дний в.** to breathe one's last

вздохн|у́ть, у́, ёшь *pf.* (*of* ▸ вздыха́ть) **1** to sigh **2**: **в. свобо́дно** to breathe freely; to relax (*after having been frightened or after exertion*)

вздра́гива|ть, ю *impf. of* ▸ вздро́гнуть

вздремн|у́ть, у́, ёшь *pf.* (infml) to have a nap, doze

вздро́гн|уть, у, ешь *pf.* (*of* ▸ вздра́гивать) (*от неожиданности*) to start; (*от боли*) to wince, flinch; (*дрожать*) to tremble, shudder

вздыха́|ть, ю *impf.* (*of* ▸ вздохну́ть) **1** to breathe; to sigh **2** (*тосковать*) (**о** + *p. or* **по** + *d.*) to pine, yearn (for); (*по девушке*) to be in love (with)

взима́|ть, ю *impf.* (*налог, штраф*) to levy, collect, raise

взла́мыва|ть, ю *impf. of* ▸ взлома́ть

взлёт, а *m.* (*самолёта*) take-off

взлета́|ть, ю *impf. of* ▸ взлете́ть

взле|те́ть, чу́, ти́шь *pf.* (*of* ▸ взлета́ть) (*птица*) to fly up; (*самолёт*) to take off; **в. на во́здух** to explode, blow up

взлёт|ный *adj. of* ▸ взлёт; (aeron.): **~ная доро́жка** runway; **~но-поса́дочная полоса́** landing strip

взлом, а *m.* (*сейфа*) breaking (into); (*двери*) forcing; **кра́жа со ~ом** housebreaking; (*в ночное время*) burglary

взлома́|ть, ю *pf.* (*of* ▸ взла́мывать) to break open, force; (*разворотить*) to smash; **в. замо́к** to force a lock; (comput.) to hack into

взло́мщик, а *m.* burglar; **компью́терный в.** hacker

взмах, а *m.* (*руки*) wave; (*крыльев*) flap, flapping; (*весла*) stroke; **одни́м ~ом** at one stroke

взма́хива|ть, ю *impf. of* ▸ взмахну́ть

взмахн|у́ть, у́, ёшь *pf.* (+ *i.*) (*рукой*) to wave; (*крылом*) flap

взметн|у́ть, у́, ёшь *pf.* (+ *i.*) to throw up, fling up; **в. рука́ми** to throw up one's hands

взметн|у́ться, у́сь, ёшься *pf.* to leap up, fly up

взмо́рь|е, я *nt.* seashore; seaside

взмыва́|ть, ю *impf. of* ▸ взмыть

взм|ыть, о́ю, о́ешь *pf.* (*of* ▸ взмыва́ть) to soar (up)

взнос, а *m.* (*платёж*) payment; (*членский*) fee, dues; **вступи́тельный в.** membership fee; **очередно́й в.** instalment

взобра́|ться, взберу́сь, взберёшься, *past* **~лся, ~ла́сь** *pf.* (*of* ▸ взбира́ться) (**на** + *a.*) to climb (up)

взобью́, ёшь *see* ▸ взбить

взо|йти́, йду́, йдёшь, *past* **~шёл, ~шла́,** *p.p.* **~ше́дший** *pf.* (*of* ▸ всходи́ть, ▸ восходи́ть 1) **1** (**на** + *a.*) to ascend, mount **2** (*солнце; тесто*) to rise **3** (*семена*) to come up

взор, а *m.* look; glance

взорв|а́ть, у́, ёшь *pf.* (*of* ▸ взрыва́ть) (*здание*) to blow up; (*бомбу*) to detonate

взорв|а́ться, у́сь, ёшься, *past* **~а́лся, ~ала́сь** *pf.* (*of* ▸ взрыва́ться) (*о бомбе, газе*) to explode; (*о здании*) to blow up; (fig., *о человеке*) to blow up, explode

взо|шёл, шла́ *see* ▸ взойти́

взрев|е́ть, у́, ёшь *pf.* to let out a roar

ꝑ **взро́сл|ый** *adj.* grown-up, adult; (*also as n.* **в., ~ого**, *f.* **~ая, ~ой**) grown-up (person), adult

взрыв, а *m.* explosion; (fig.) burst, outburst; **«Большо́й в.»** the Big Bang

взрыва́тел|ь, я *m.* detonator

взрыва́|ть, ю *impf. of* ▸ взорва́ть

взрыва́|ться, юсь *impf. of* ▸ взорва́ться

взрывни́к, а́ *m.* explosives expert; shot-firer

взрывн|о́й *adj.* explosive; **~а́я волна́** blast

взрывоопа́с|ный, ~ен, ~на *adj.* explosive (also fig.)

взрывча́тк|а, и *f.* (infml) explosive

взры́вчат|ый *adj.* explosive; **~ое вещество́** explosive

взыска́ни|е, я *nt.* **1** (*выговор*) reprimand; (*наказание*) penalty; punishment

B

2 (*штрафа*) exaction; (*долга*) recovery

взы|ска́ть, щу́, ~́шешь *pf.* (*of* ▸ **взы́скивать**) **1** (*штраф*) to exact; (*долг*) to recover **2** (*c + g.*) to call to account

взы́скива|ть, ю *impf. of* ▸ **взыска́ть**

взыщу́, ~́щешь *see* ▸ **взыска́ть**

взя́ти|е, я *nt.* taking; (*крепости*) capture; (*власти*) seizure

взя́тк|а, и *f.* **1** bribe; backhander **2** (cards) trick; **с него́ ~и гла́дки** (infml) he isn't going to take responsibility

взя́точник, а *m.* bribe-taker

взя́точни|ца, цы *f. of* ▸ **взя́точник**

взя́точничеств|о, а *nt.* bribery, bribe-taking

◦ **взя|ть, возьму́, возьмёшь**, *past* ~л, ~ла́, ~ло *pf.* (*of* ▸ **брать**) **1** *see* ▸ **брать 2** (infml, *думать*): **с чего́ ты взял?** what makes you think so? **3**: **в. да, в. и, в. да и...** (infml) to do sth suddenly; **он ~л да убежа́л** he upped and ran off **4**: **чёрт возьми́!** (infml) damn it!

взя́|ться, возьму́сь, возьмёшься, *past* ~лся, ~ла́сь *pf.* (*of* ▸ **бра́ться**): **отку́да ни возьми́сь** (infml) from nowhere, out of the blue

вибрафо́н, а *m.* (mus.) vibraphone

вибра́ци|я, и *f.* vibration

вибри́р|овать, ую *impf.* to vibrate

вигва́м, а *m.* wigwam

◦ **вид¹, а** *m.* **1** (*внешность*) air, look; appearance; aspect; **у него́ был мра́чный в.** he looked gloomy; **сде́лать в., бу́дто** to make it appear that, pretend that; **для ~а** for the sake of appearances; **под ~ом** (*+ g.*) under the guise (of) **2** (*состояние*) shape, form; condition **3** (*панорама*) view; **ко́мната с ~ом на го́ры** room with a view of the mountains **4** (*in pl.*) (*перспективы*) prospect; **~ы на бу́дущее** prospects for the future; **име́ть ~ы на** (*+ a.*) to have designs on **5** (*поле зрения*) sight; **упусти́ть из ~у** to lose sight (of); **на ~у у** (*+ g.*) within sight of; **быть на ~у** to be in the public eye; **при ~е** (*+ g.*) at the sight (of); **име́ть в ~у** (*намереваться*) to plan, intend; (*подразумевать*) to mean; (*не забывать*) to bear in mind; **что вы име́ли в ~у, говоря́ э́то?** what did you mean when you said that?; **име́й(те) в ~у** bear in mind, don't forget; **име́ться в ~у** to be intended, be envisaged; to be meant

◦ **вид², а** *m.* **1** (biol.) species; **исчеза́ющий в.** endangered *or* threatened species **2** (*тип*) type, kind **3** (gram.) aspect; **соверше́нный, несоверше́нный в.** perfective, imperfective aspect

ви́дени|е, я *nt.* (*способность видеть*) vision; (*восприятие, подход*) vision, outlook

виде́ни|е, я *nt.* (*призрак*) vision, apparition

◦ **ви́део** *nt. indecl.* video (recorder, film, cassette)

видео... *comb. form* video-

видеоза́пис|ь, и *f.* video recording

видеоигр|а́, ы́, *pl.* ~ы *f.* video game

◦ *key word*

видеока́мер|а, ы *f.* video camera, camcorder

видеокассе́т|а, ы *f.* video cassette

видеокли́п, а *m.* video clip, music video

видеомагнитофо́н, а *m.* video recorder

видеонаблюде́ни|е, я *nt.* (*оборудование*) CCTV

видеофи́льм, а *m.* video (film)

◦ **ви́|деть, жу, дишь** *impf.* (*of* ▸ **уви́деть 1**) to see; **в. кого́-н. наскво́зь** to see through sb; **в. во сне** to dream (of); **~дишь (ли)** you see; **вот уви́дишь** (infml) you'll see

ви́|деться, жусь, дишься *impf.* **1** (*встречаться*) to see one another; (*c + i.*) to meet with **2** (*pf.* **при~**) to appear; **ему́ ~дился стра́шный сон** he had a terrifying dream

ви́димо *adv.* evidently, apparently

ви́димост|ь, и *f.* **1** (*различаемость*) visibility **2** (*внешность*) outward appearance; **для ~и** (infml) for show **3**: **по всей ~и** to all appearances

ви́дим|ый, ~, ~а *adj.* **1** visible **2** (*очевидный*) apparent, evident; **без ~ой причи́ны** for no apparent reason **3** (*кажущийся*) apparent, seeming

видне́|ться, ется, ются *impf.* to be visible

◦ **ви́дно** *adv.* **1** obviously, evidently; (*as pred.*) it is obvious, it is apparent; **в. бы́ло, как она́ расстро́илась** you could see how upset she was; **там в. бу́дет** (infml) we'll see **2** (*as pred.*) visible; in sight; **берега́ ещё не́ было в.** the coast was not yet visible

ви́д|ный *adj.* **1** (~ен, ~на́, ~но, ~ны́) (*заметный*) visible; conspicuous **2** (*важный*) distinguished, prominent

видово́й *adj.* (*of* ▸ **вид²**) **1** (biol.) species **2** (gram.) aspectual

видоизмен|и́ть, ю́, и́шь *pf.* (*of* ▸ **видоизменя́ть**) to modify, alter

видоизмен|и́ться, ю́сь, и́шься *pf.* (*of* ▸ **видоизменя́ться**) to alter

видоизмен|я́ть, я́ю *impf. of* ▸ **видоизмени́ть**

видоизмен|я́ться, я́юсь *impf. of* ▸ **видоизмени́ться**

ви́з|а, ы *f.* **1** visa **2** (*пометка*) official signature

визажи́ст, а *m.* make-up artist

Виза́нти|й, я *m.* (hist.) Byzantium

византи́йский *adj.* Byzantine

Византи́|я, и *f.* (hist.) Byzantine Empire

визг, а *m.* (*человека*) scream; (*поросёнка*) squeal; (*собаки*) yelp; (*тормозов*) screech

визгли́в|ый, ~, ~а *adj.* **1** (*голос*) shrill **2** (*крикливый*) given to screaming, squealing, yelping

визж|а́ть, у́, и́шь *impf.* to scream; to squeal; to yelp

визи́т, а *m.* visit; call; **нанести́ в.** to make an (official) visit; **прийти́ с ~ом к кому́-н.** to visit sb, pay sb a call

визи́тк|а, и *f.* (*карточка*) (business) card

визи́т|ный *adj. of* ▸ **визи́т**; **~ная ка́рточка** (business) card

визуа́л|ьный, ~ен, ~ьна *adj.* visual
вика́ри|й, я *m.* (eccl.) vicar
ви́ки *f. indecl.* (comput.) wiki; **техноло́гия в.**
   wiki technology
виктори́н|а, ы *f.* quiz
ви́лк|а, и *f.* **1** fork **2** (elec.) plug
ви́лл|а, ы *f.* villa
вильн|у́ть, у́, ёшь *pf. of* ▸ виля́ть
Ви́льнюс, а *m.* Vilnius
виля́|ть, ю *impf. of* ▸ **вильну́ть 1: в. хвосто́м**
   to wag one's tail **2** (infml, *доро́га*) to wind,
   turn sharply
вин|а́, ы́, *pl.* ~ы *f.* fault, guilt; (*причи́на*)
   blame; **моя́ в.** it is my fault; **не по их ~е́**
   through no fault of theirs; **поста́вить
   кому́-н. в ~у́** to accuse sb of, blame sb for;
   свали́ть ~у́ (на + *a.*) to lay the blame (on);
   по ~е́ (+ *g.*) because of
виндсёрф, а and **виндсёрфер, а** *m.* (infml)
   sailboard
виндсёрфинг, а *m.* windsurfing
винегре́т, а *m.* ≈ beetroot salad (*of diced
   cooked beetroot, potato, and carrot, pickled
   cucumber, and vegetable oil dressing*); (fig.,
   смесь) mishmash
вини́л, а *m.* vinyl
вини́тельный *adj.* (gram.): **в. паде́ж**
   accusative case
вин|и́ть, ю́, и́шь *impf.* (**в** + *p.*) (*обвиня́ть*)
   to accuse (of); (*счита́ть винова́тым*) to
   blame; **я ~ю́ его́ за наш прова́л** I blame him
   for our failure
ви́нный *adj.* wine; winey; **в. спирт** alcohol
⚥ **вин|о́, а́,** *pl.* ~а *nt.* wine
винова́т|ый, ~, ~а *adj.* **1** (*взгляд*) guilty;
   (*челове́к*) guilty; to blame; **мы все ~ы
   в э́том** we are all to blame for this **2**: ~**!**
   sorry!, my fault!
вино́вник, а *m.* culprit; (*торжества́,
   пра́здника*) cause, reason
вино́вност|ь, и *f.* guilt
вино́в|ный, ~ен, ~на *adj.* (**в** + *p.*) guilty
   (of); **призна́ть себя́** ~**ным** to plead guilty
виногра́д, а *m.* **1** (*расте́ние*) vine **2** (collect.)
   (*я́годы*) grapes
виногра́дник, а *m.* vineyard
винт, а́ *m.* **1** (*сте́ржень*) screw **2** (*самолёта*)
   propeller **3** (*спира́ль*) spiral
винто́вк|а, и *f.* rifle
винт|ово́й *adj. of* ▸ винт; spiral; ~**ова́я
   ле́стница** spiral staircase
виолончели́ст, а *m.* cellist
виолончели́ст|ка, ки *f. of* ▸ виолончели́ст
виолонче́л|ь, и *f.* cello
вира́ж, а́ *m.* (*поворо́т*) turn; **круто́й в.** steep
   turn
виртуа́л|ьный, ~ен, ~ьна *adj.* virtual;
   ~**ьная реа́льность** (comput.) virtual reality
виртуо́з, а *m.* virtuoso
виртуо́з|ный, ~ен, ~на *adj.* masterly,
   virtuosic

ви́рус, а *m.* (med.) virus, bug (infml); (comput.)
   virus
ви́русный *adj. of* ▸ ви́рус
ви́селиц|а, ы *f.* gallows, gibbet
ви|се́ть, шу́, си́шь *impf.* to hang; to be
   suspended; **в. над** (+ *i.*) (fig.) to hang over; **в.
   на телефо́не** (infml) to talk a lot on the phone
ви́ски *nt. indecl.* whisky (BrE), whiskey (AmE)
ви́сн|уть, ет *impf.* (comput.) to crash
вис|о́к, ка́ *m.* (anat.) temple
високо́сный *adj.*: **в. год** leap year
вися́чий *adj.* hanging; **в. замо́к** padlock; **в.
   мост** suspension bridge
⚥ **витами́н, а** *m.* vitamin
витами́н|ный *adj.* **1** *adj. of* ▸ витами́н;
   ~**ная недоста́точность** vitamin deficiency
   2 vitamin-rich *or* -packed
вит|о́к, ка́ *m.* **1** (*спира́ли*) turn, twist
   2 (*про́волоки*) coil **3** (*при полёте*) orbit
   4 (fig., *цикл*) round
витра́ж, а́ *m.* stained-glass window
витри́н|а, ы *f.* **1** (*в магази́не*) (shop) window
   2 (*в музе́е*) showcase
ви|ть, вью, вьёшь, *past* ~л, ~ла́, ~ло
   impf. (▸ свить) to weave
ви́|ться, вьётся, *past* ~лся, ~ла́сь *impf.*
   (*of* ▸ сви́ться) **1** (*расте́ние*) to wind, twine
   2 (*во́лосы*) to curl, wave **3** (*пти́ца*) to hover,
   circle **4** (*змея́*) to writhe, twist **5** (*пыль, дым*)
   to spiral up
вихр|ь, я *m.* whirlwind; **снежный в.** blizzard;
   (fig.) whirlwind, maelstrom
ви́це-... *comb. form* vice-
ви́це-президе́нт, а *m.* vice-president
ВИЧ *m. indecl.* (*abbr. of* ви́рус
   иммунодефици́та челове́ка) (med.)
   HIV (*human immunodeficiency virus*);
   ВИЧ-инфици́рованный HIV-positive
вишнёвый *adj.* **1** cherry; **в. сад** cherry
   orchard **2** (*о цве́те*) cherry-coloured,
   burgundy
ви́ш|ня, ни, *g. pl.* ~ен *f.* **1** (*де́рево*) cherry
   tree **2** (*плод*) cherry; (*collect.*) cherries
вка́лыва|ть, ю *impf. of* ▸ вколо́ть
вка́пыва|ть, ю *impf. of* ▸ вкопа́ть
вка|ти́ть, чу́, ~**тишь** *pf.* (*of* ▸ вка́тывать) to
   roll into, onto; (*на колёсах*) to wheel in, into
вка́тыва|ть, ю *impf. of* ▸ вкати́ть
вклад, а *m.* **1** (*в ба́нке*) deposit **2** (*де́йствие*)
   investment **3** (fig.) contribution
вкла́дк|а, и *f.* supplementary sheet, insert
вкла́дчик, а *m.* depositor, investor
вкла́дчи|ца, цы *f. of* ▸ вкла́дчик
вкла́дыва|ть, ю *impf. of* ▸ вложи́ть
вкла́дыш, а *m.* = вкла́дка
⚥ **включа́|ть, а́ю** *impf. of* ▸ включи́ть
включа́|ться, а́юсь *impf. of* ▸ включи́ться
⚥ **включа́я** *pres. gerund of* ▸ включа́ть; (*as
   prep.* + *a.*) including
включе́ни|е, я *nt.* **1** (**в** + *a.*) inclusion (in)
   2 (*ла́мпы, станка́*) switching on, turning on

B

включи́тельно *adv.* inclusive; **с пя́того по девя́тое в.** from the 5th to the 9th inclusive

включи́|ть, у́, и́шь *pf.* (*of* ▸ **включа́ть**) **1** (в + *a.*) to include (in); **в. в себя́** to include, comprise, take in; **в. в спи́сок** to include on a list **2** (tech.) to switch on, turn on; (*в розетку*) to plug in; **в. ра́дио** to switch on the radio; **в. ско́рость** to engage a gear

включи́|ться, у́сь, и́шься *pf.* (*of* ▸ **включа́ться**) **1** (в + *a.*) to join (in), enter (into) **2** (*о свете, радио*) to come on

вкола́чива|ть, ю *impf. of* ▸ **вколоти́ть**

вкол|оти́ть, очу́, о́тишь *pf.* (*of* ▸ **вкола́чивать**) to knock in, hammer in (also fig.)

вкол|о́ть, ю́, ~ешь *pf.* (*of* ▸ **вка́лывать**) (в + *a.*) to stick (in, into)

вкопа́|ть, ю *pf.* (*of* ▸ **вка́пывать**) to dig in

вкра́дчив|ый, ~, ~а *adj.* insinuating, ingratiating

вкра́тце *adv.* briefly; succinctly

вкру|ти́ть, чу́, ~тишь *pf.* (*of* ▸ **вкру́чивать**) to screw in

вкру́чива|ть, ю *impf. of* ▸ **вкрути́ть**

вкру|чу́, ~тишь *see* ▸ **вкрути́ть**

⚘ **вкус, а** *m.* taste (also fig.); **в чьём-н. ~е** to sb's taste; **э́то де́ло ~а** it is a matter of taste; **челове́к со ~ом** a man of taste; **одева́ться со ~ом** to dress tastefully

вку́с|ный, ~ен, ~на́, ~но *adj.* tasty, delicious, good

вла́г|а, и (*no pl.*) *f.* moisture

влага́лищ|е, а *nt.* vagina

⚘ **владе́л|ец, ьца** *m.* owner

владе́л|ица, ицы *f. of* ▸ **владе́лец**

владе́ни|е, я *nt.* **1** ownership; possession **2** (*территория в собственности*) estate

владе́|ть, ю, ешь *impf.* (+ *i.*) **1** (*иметь*) to own, possess **2** (*подчинять себе*) to control; to be in possession (of); **в. собо́й** to control oneself **3** (fig., *уметь пользоваться*) to have (a) command (of); to have the use (of); **она́ ~ет шестью́ языка́ми** she has a command of six languages

вла́жност|ь, и *f.* (*воздуха*) humidity; (*почвы*) dampness

вла́ж|ный, ~ен, ~на́, ~но *adj.* (*воздух, климат*) humid, damp; (*простыня*) damp; (*глаза, лоб*) moist

вла́мыва|ться, юсь *impf. of* ▸ **вломи́ться**

вла́ст|ный, ~ен, ~на *adj.* **1** (*характер, жест*) imperious, commanding; **~ные структу́ры** authorities **2** (над + *i.*, *or inf.*) authoritative, competent; **он не ~ен над собо́й** he can't control himself; **он не ~ен измени́ть что́-нибудь** he is powerless to change anything

⚘ **власт|ь, и**, *pl.* **~и, ~е́й** *f.* **1** (*политическая*) power; (*in pl.*) authorities; **прийти́ к ~и** to come to power; **у ~и** in power **2** (*родительская*) power, authority; **во ~и** (+ *g.*) at the mercy (of), in the power (of);

(*над чувствами*) control

вле́во *adv.* to the left (also fig., pol.)

влеза́|ть, ю *impf. of* ▸ **влезть**

влез|ть, у, ешь, *past* ~, ~ла *pf.* (*of* ▸ **влеза́ть**) **1** (*в окно*) to climb in(to); (*на дерево*) to climb (up); (*на крышу*) to climb onto; **в. в долги́** (fig.) to get into debt **2** (infml, *уместиться*) to fit in, go in, go on; **все э́ти ве́щи не ~ут в мою́ су́мку** these things will not all go into my bag

влет|а́ть, а́ю *impf. of* ▸ **влете́ть**

вле|те́ть, чу́, ти́шь *pf.* (*of* ▸ **влета́ть**) to fly in, into; (fig., infml) to rush in, into; (*impers.*) **ему́ опя́ть ~те́ло** he is in trouble again

влече́ни|е, я *nt.* (к + *d.*) attraction (to)

вле|чь, ку́, чёшь, ку́т, *past* влёк, ~кла́ *impf.* (*тащить*) to draw, drag; (*привлекать*) to attract; **в. за собо́й** to involve, entail

влива́ни|я, й *nt. pl.* (econ.) investment, (financial) aid

влива́|ть, ю *impf. of* ▸ **влить**

вли|ть, волью́, вольёшь, *past* ~л, ~ла́, ~ло *pf.* (*of* ▸ **влива́ть**) to pour in; (med.) to infuse

⚘ **влия́ни|е, я** *nt.* influence; **под ~ем** (+ *g.*) under the influence of; **оказа́ть в. на** (+ *a.*) to influence; **по́льзоваться ~ем** to have influence, be influential

влия́тел|ьный, ~ен, ~ьна *adj.* influential

⚘ **влия́|ть, ю** *impf.* (*of* ▸ **повлия́ть**) (на + *a.*) to influence, have an influence on; (*действовать*) to affect

вложе́ни|е, я *nt.* **1** enclosure **2** (fin.) investment

влож|и́ть, у́, ~ишь *pf.* (*of* ▸ **вкла́дывать**) **1** to put in, insert; (*в письмо*) to enclose (*with a letter*) **2** (fin.) to invest

влом|и́ться, лю́сь, ~ишься *pf.* (*of* ▸ **вла́мываться**) to break in, into

влюб|и́ться, лю́сь, ~ишься *pf.* (*of* ▸ **влюбля́ться**) (в + *a.*) to fall in love (with)

влюблённый, ~ён, ~ена́ *adj.* (*человек*) in love; (*no short forms*) (*взгляд*) loving; tender

влюбля́|ться, юсь *impf. of* ▸ **влюби́ться**

вмен|и́ть, ю́, и́шь *pf.* (*of* ▸ **вменя́ть**) **в. (что́-н.) в вину́** (+ *d.*) to blame (sth) on (sb); **в. в обя́занность кому́-н.** to impose as a duty on (sb)

вменя́ем|ый, ~, ~а *adj.* (law) sane, of sound mind

вменя́|ть, ю *impf. of* ▸ **вмени́ть**

⚘ **вме́сте** *adv.* together; at the same time; **в. с** (+ *i.*) together with; **в. с тем** at the same time, also; **но в. с тем** but; **а в. с тем and also**

вмести́мост|ь, и *f.* capacity

вмести́тел|ьный, ~ен, ~ьна *adj.* capacious; roomy

вме|сти́ть, щу́, сти́шь *pf. of* ▸ **вмеща́ть**

вме|сти́ться, щу́сь, сти́шься *pf. of* ▸ **вмеща́ться**

⚘ **вме́сто** *prep.* + *g.* instead of; in place of

⚘ **вмеша́тельств|о, а** *nt.* interference; (pol., mil., med.) intervention

---
⚘ key word

вмеш|а́ться, а́юсь *pf.* (*of* ▶ **вме́шиваться**) (в + *a.*) (*вторгнуться*) to interfere (in), meddle (with); (*для пресечения нежелательных последствий*) to intervene (in)

вме́шива|ться, юсь *impf. of* ▶ **вмеша́ться**

вмеща́|ть, ю *impf.* (*of* ▶ **вмести́ть**)
1 (*контейнер*) to contain; to hold; (*дом, зал*) to accommodate; **э́та бо́чка ∼ет пятьдеся́т ли́тров** this barrel holds fifty litres **2** (в + *a.*) to put, place (in, into)

вмеща́|ться, юсь *impf.* (*of* ▶ **вмести́ться**)
1 to fit, go in **2** *pass. of* ▶ **вмеща́ть 2**

вмиг *adv.* in an instant; in a flash

ВМФ *m. indecl.* (*abbr. of* **вое́нно-морско́й флот**) Navy

вмя́тин|а, ы *f.* dent

внаём, внаймы́ *adv.*: **отда́ть в.** to let, hire out, rent; **взять в.** to hire, rent; **сдаётся в.** 'to let'

внача́ле *adv.* at first, in the beginning

   вне *prep.* + *g.* outside; out of; **объяви́ть в. зако́на** to outlaw; **в. о́череди** out of turn; **в. себя́** beside oneself; **в. вся́ких сомне́ний** beyond any doubt

**вне... ** *comb. form* extra-

внебра́чный *adj.* extramarital; **в. ребёнок** illegitimate child

внедоро́жник, а *m.* four-wheel drive (vehicle)

   внедре́ни|е, я *nt.* (*методов*) introduction; (*идей*) inculcation

внедр|и́ть, ю́, и́шь *pf.* (*of* ▶ **внедря́ть**)
1 (*методы*) to introduce **2** (*идеи*) to inculcate, instil (BrE), instill (AmE)

внедр|и́ться, ю́сь, и́шься *pf.* (*of* ▶ **внедря́ться**) to take root

внедря́|ть, ю *impf. of* ▶ **внедри́ть**

внедря́|ться, юсь *impf. of* ▶ **внедри́ться**

внеза́пно *adv.* suddenly, all of a sudden

внеза́пный *adj.* sudden

внеочередно́й *adj.* **1** out of turn; **зада́ть в. вопро́с** to ask a question out of turn **2** (*заседание*) extraordinary; (*рейс*) extra

внепла́новый *adj.* (econ.) not provided for by the plan; extraordinary

внесе́ни|е, я *nt.* **1** (*денег*) paying in, deposit **2** (*предложения*) moving, submission

внес|ти́, у́, ёшь, *past* **∼, ∼ла́** *pf.* (*of* ▶ **вноси́ть**)
1 (*принести внутрь*) to bring in, carry in **2** (fig.) to introduce, put in; **в. я́сность в де́ло** to clarify a matter; **в. свой вклад в де́ло** to do one's bit; to make one's contribution **3** (*деньги*) to pay in, deposit **4** (*предложение*) to make, move, table **5** (*вписать*) to insert, enter

вне́шне *adv.* outwardly

внешнеторго́вый *adj.* foreign-trade (*attr.*)

   вне́шн|ий *adj.* **1** outer, exterior; outward, external; outside; **в. вид** appearance **2** (*иностранный*) foreign; **∼яя поли́тика** foreign policy

вне́шност|ь, и *f.* appearance; exterior

внешта́тный *adj.* freelance; casual

вниз *adv.* down, downwards; **в. голово́й** head first; **идти́ в. по ле́стнице** to go downstairs; **в. по тече́нию** downstream; **в. по Во́лге** down the Volga

внизу́ *adv.* below; downstairs; *prep.* + *g.* **в. страни́цы** at the foot of the page

вник|а́ть, а́ю *impf. of* ▶ **вни́кнуть**

вни́к|нуть, ну, нешь, *past* **∼, ∼ла** *pf.* (*of* ▶ **вника́ть**) (в + *a.*) (*изучить*) to go carefully (into), investigate thoroughly; (*понять*) to understand, penetrate

   внима́ни|е, я *nt.* **1** (*сосредоточенность*) attention; heed; notice, note; **обраща́ть в.** (на + *a.*) to pay attention (to); to draw attention (to); **удели́ть в. кому́-н.** to give sb attention; **принима́я во в.** taking into account **2** (*забота*) kindness, consideration **3** (*int.*): **в.!** attention!

внима́тельност|ь, и *f.* attentiveness

внима́тел|ьный, ∼ен, ∼ьна *adj.*
1 attentive **2** (к + *d.*) (*заботливый*) thoughtful, considerate (towards)

вничью́ *adv.* (sport): **па́ртия око́нчилась в.** the game ended in a draw; **на́ша кома́нда сыгра́ла сего́дня в.** our team drew today

   вновь *adv.* **1** (*опять*) afresh, anew; again **2** (*недавно*) newly; **в. прибы́вший** newcomer

   вно|си́ть, шу́, ∼сишь *impf. of* ▶ **внести́**

ВНП *m. indecl.* (*abbr. of* **валово́й национа́льный проду́кт**) GNP (*gross national product*)

внук, а *m.* grandson; grandchild

   вну́тренн|ий *adj.* **1** inner, interior; internal; intrinsic; **в. мир** inner life, inner world **2** (*в государстве*) domestic, inland; **∼ие дохо́ды** inland revenue; **∼яя поли́тика** internal politics; **Министе́рство ∼их дел** Ministry of Internal Affairs

вну́тренност|ь, и *f.* interior; (*pl. only*) entrails, intestines; internal organs

   внутри́ *adv. and prep.* + *g.* inside, within; **в. до́ма** inside the house

**внутри́... ** *comb. form* intra-

внутриве́нный *adj.* (med.) intravenous

внутрь *adv. and prep.* + *g.* within, inside; inwards; **открыва́ться в.** to open inwards; **войти́ в. до́ма** to go inside the house

вну́чк|а, и *f.* granddaughter

внуш|а́ть, а́ю *impf. of* ▶ **внуши́ть**

внуше́ни|е, я *nt.* **1** (*выговор*) reprimand **2** (psych.) suggestion

внуши́тел|ьный, ∼ен, ∼ьна *adj.* imposing, impressive

внуш|и́ть, у́, и́шь *pf.* (*of* ▶ **внуша́ть**) (+ *a. and d.*) to inspire (with); to instil (BrE), instill (AmE); to suggest; **его́ вид ∼и́л мне страх** the sight of him inspired me with fear

вня́т|ный, ∼ен, ∼на *adj.* distinct

   во *prep.* = **в**

вовлека́|ть, ю *impf. of* ▶ **вовле́чь**

вовл|е́чь, еку́, ечёшь, еку́т, *past* **∼ёк, ∼екла́** *pf.* to draw in, involve

вовну́трь *adv. and prep.* + *g.* (infml) inside

В

вóвремя *adv.* in time, on time; **не в.** at the wrong time

✓ **вóвсе** *adv.* (infml) completely; (+ *neg.*) at all; **он в. не бога́тый челове́к** he is not at all a rich man

во-вторы́х *adv.* secondly, in the second place

✓ **во́гнут|ый**, ~, ~а *adj.* concave

✓ **вод|а́**, *а.* ~у, *pl.* ~ы, ~, ~ам *f.* **1** water; **выводи́ть на чи́стую** ~у to show up, unmask; **похо́жи как две ка́пли** ~ы as like as two peas **2** (in *pl.*) (минера́льные) the waters; (куро́рт) spa

✓ **води́тел|ь, я** *m.* driver

води́тельск|ий *adj.:* ~ие права́ driving licence (BrE), driver's license (AmE)

во|ди́ть, жу́, ~дишь *impf.* (indet. of ▸ вести́) **1** (see also ▸ вести́) (сопровожда́ть) to take; to conduct; (маши́ну) to drive **2** (infml) (see also ▸ вести́): **в. дру́жбу** (с + *i.*) to be friends with; **в. знако́мство** (с + *i.*) to keep up an acquaintance (with) **3** (+ *i.; see also* ▸ вести́) to pass (по + *d.* over, across)

во|ди́ться, жу́сь, ~дишься *impf.* **1** (с + *i.*) to associate (with); (о де́тях) to play (with) **2** (обита́ть) to be, be found; **львы́ не** ~дятся в Евро́пе lions are not found in Europe **3** (быть при́нятым) to be the custom; to happen; **как** ~дится as usually happens **4** (infml, быть в нали́чии, име́ться) be abundant; **де́ньги у него́** ~дятся he's always in the money

во́дк|а, и *f.* vodka

во́дн|ый *adj.* water; ~ые лы́жи (вид спо́рта) waterskiing; (экипиро́вка) waterskis

водоворо́т, а *m.* whirlpool; (fig.) maelstrom

водоём, а *m.* reservoir

водола́з, а *m.* diver; (ныря́льщик с аквала́нгом) frogman

водола́зк|а, и *f.* thin polo-necked sweater

водола́зный *adj. of* ▸ водола́з; **в. костю́м** diving suit

Водоле́|й, я *m.* (созве́здие) Aquarius

водонепроница́ем|ый, ~, ~а *adj.* watertight; waterproof

водопа́д, а *m.* waterfall

водопрово́д, а *m.* water supply system; plumbing

водопрово́дчик, а *m.* plumber

водоро́д, а *m.* (chem.) hydrogen

водоросл|ь, и *f.* (bot.) water plant; **морска́я в.** seaweed

водосто́к, а *m.* drain; (на у́лице, кры́ше) gutter

водосто́|чный *adj. of* ▸ водосто́к; ~чная труба́ drainpipe

водохрани́лищ|е, а *nt.* reservoir

во́дочный *adj. of* ▸ во́дка

водяно́й *adj.* **1** *adj. of* ▸ вода́ **2** (живу́щий, расту́щий в воде́) water, aquatic **3** (приводи́мый в движе́ние водо́й) water-driven

во|ева́ть, ю́ю, ю́ешь *impf.* (с + *i.*) to wage war (with), make war (upon); to be at war

воен... *comb. form, abbr. of* ▸ вое́нный

военача́льник, а *m.* commander

военкома́т, а *m.* (abbr. of вое́нный комиссариа́т) military recruitment office

вое́нно-... *comb. form, abbr. of* ▸ вое́нный

вое́нно-возду́шн|ый *adj.:* ~ые си́лы Air Force(s)

вое́нно-морско́й *adj.* naval; **в. флот** the Navy

военнообя́занн|ый, ого *m.* man liable for call-up (including reservists)

военнопле́нн|ый, ого *m.* prisoner of war

вое́нно-полево́й *adj.* (mil.) field; **в. суд** court martial

вое́нно-промы́шленный *adj.* military-industrial

военнослу́жащ|ий, его *m.* serviceman

✓ **вое́нн|ый** *adj.* military; war; (фо́рма) army; **в. врач** (army) medical officer; ~ое вре́мя wartime; ~ое положе́ние martial law; ~ое учи́лище military college; (as *m. n.* **в.,** ~ого) soldier, serviceman; ~ые (collect.) the military

вожделе́ни|е, я *nt.* desire, lust (also fig.)

вожд|ь, я́ *m.* (организа́ции) leader; (пле́мени) chief

во́жж|и, е́й *f. pl.* (sg. ~а́, ~и́) reins

во|жу́[1], ~дишь *see* ▸ води́ть

во|жу́[2], ~зишь *see* ▸ вози́ть

воз, а, о ~е, **на** ~у́, *pl.* ~ы́ *m.* cart, wagon

возбуди́м|ый, ~, ~а *adj.* excitable

возбуди́|ть, жу́, ди́шь *pf.* (of ▸ возбужда́ть) **1** to excite, rouse, arouse; **в. аппети́т** to whet the appetite **2** (law) to institute; **в. де́ло** (про́тив + *g.*) to institute proceedings (against), bring an action (against); **в. иск** (про́тив + *g.*) to bring a suit (against)

возбуди́|ться, жу́сь, ди́шься *pf.* (of ▸ возбужда́ться) (о челове́ке) to get excited

возбужда́|ть, ю *impf. of* ▸ возбуди́ть

возбужда́|ться, юсь *impf. of* ▸ возбуди́ться

возбужде́ни|е, я *nt.* excitement

возбуждённый *p.p.p. of* ▸ возбуди́ть *and adj.* excited

возбу|жу́, ди́шь *see* ▸ возбуди́ть

возбу|жу́сь, ди́шься *see* ▸ возбуди́ться

возве|сти́, ду́, дёшь, *past* ~л, ~ла́ *pf.* (of ▸ возводи́ть) **1** (возвы́сить) to elevate; **в. в сан патриа́рха** to elect to the patriarchate **2** (стро́ить) to erect, put up **3** (math.) to raise; **в. в куб** to cube

возво|ди́ть, жу́, ~дишь *impf. of* ▸ возвести́

возвра́т, а *m.* return; repayment, reimbursement; **без** ~а irrevocably

возвра|ти́ть, щу́, ти́шь *pf.* (of ▸ возвраща́ть) **1** (отда́ть обра́тно) to return, give back; (де́ньги) to pay back **2** (получи́ть обра́тно) to recover, retrieve; **в. де́ньги, о́тданные взаймы́** to recover a loan

возвра|ти́ться, щу́сь, ти́шься *pf.* (of ▸ возвраща́ться) to return; (fig.) to revert

✓ **key word**

возвраща|ть, ю *impf. of* ▶ **возврати́ть,**
▶ **верну́ть**

возвраща|ться, юсь *impf. of*
▶ **возврати́ться,** ▶ **верну́ться**

возвраще́ни|е, я *nt.* return; **в. домо́й**
homecoming

возвра|щу́, ти́шь *see* ▶ **возврати́ть**

возвы́|ситься, шусь, сишься *pf.* (*of*
▶ **возвыша́ться**) to rise, go up

возвыша́|ться, юсь *impf.* **1** *impf. of*
▶ **возвы́ситься** **2** (*impf. only*) (**над** + *i.*)
to tower (above) (also fig.)

возвыше́ни|е, я *nt.* **1** (*де́йствие*) rise;
raising **2** (*ме́сто*) elevation; raised place

возвы́шенност|ь, и *f.* (geog.) height;
elevation

возвы́шен|ный, ~, ~на *adj.* **1** (*высо́кий*)
high; elevated **2** (*благоро́дный*) lofty,
sublime, elevated; **~ные иде́алы** lofty ideals

возгла́в|ить, лю, ишь *pf.* (*of* ▶ **возглавля́ть**)
to head, be at the head of

возглавля́|ть, ю *impf. of* ▶ **возгла́вить**

во́зглас, а *m.* cry, exclamation

воздвига́|ть, ю (*of* ▶ **воздви́гнуть**) to
raise, erect

воздви́г|нуть, ну, нешь, *past* ~, ~ла *pf. of*
▶ **воздвига́ть**

ᵔ **возде́йстви|е, я** *nt.* influence; **он э́то
сде́лал под физи́ческим ~ем** he did it
under coercion

возде́йств|овать, ую *impf. and pf.* (**на** + *a.*)
to influence, affect; to exert influence

возде́ла|ть, аю *pf.* (*of* ▶ **возде́лывать**) to
cultivate, till

возде́лыва|ть, ю *impf. of* ▶ **возде́лать**

воздержа́вш|ийся *p.p. of* ▶ **воздержа́ться**;
(*as n.* **в.**, **~егося**) *m.* abstainer; **предложе́ние
бы́ло при́нято при трёх ~ихся** the motion
was carried with three abstentions

воздержа́ни|е, я *nt.* **1** abstinence **2** (**от** + *g.*)
abstention (from)

возд|ержа́ться, держу́сь, де́ржишься
pf. (*of* ▶ **возде́рживаться**) (**от** + *g.*) **1** (*от
замеча́ния, куре́ния*) to refrain (from);
(*от алкого́ля, куре́ния, мя́са*) to abstain
(from) **2** (*от голосова́ния*) to abstain

возде́ржива|ться, юсь *impf. of*
▶ **воздержа́ться**

ᵔ **во́здух, а** *m.* **1** (*no pl.*) *m.* air; **на (откры́том)
~е** out of doors; **вы́йти на в.** to go out of
doors; **в ~е** (fig.) in the air **2** (*атмосфе́ра*)
atmosphere

возду́ш|ный *adj.* **1** air, aerial; **в. змей**
kite; **~ная трево́га** air-raid warning; **в.
шар** balloon **2** (*приводи́мый в движе́ние
во́здухом*) air-driven **3** (~**ен**, ~**на**) (*о́чень
лёгкий*) airy, light; flimsy

воззва́ни|е, я *nt.* appeal

во|зи́ть, жу́, ~зишь *impf.* (*indet. of* ▶ **везти́**)
to take, convey; to carry; (*мяну́ть*) to draw

во|зи́ться, жу́сь, ~зишься *impf.* (**с** + *i.*)
(*с чем-н. тру́дным*) to take trouble (over);
(*с детьми́*) to spend time, busy oneself

(with); (infml, *копа́ться*) to potter; **он лю́бит
в. в саду́** he likes pottering about in the
garden

возлага́|ть, ю *impf. of* ▶ **возложи́ть**

во́зле *prep.* + *g.* by, near; *adv.* nearby

возлож|и́ть, у́, ~ишь *pf.* (*of* ▶ **возлага́ть**)
1 (*положи́ть*) to lay; **в. вено́к на моги́лу** to
lay a wreath on a grave **2** (*поручи́ть*) (**на** +
a.) to entrust (to); **в. вину́/отве́тственность
на** (+ *a.*) to lay the blame/responsibility on

возлю́бленн|ый, ого *m.* (*n. declined as
an adj.; f.* ~**ая**, ~**ой**) beloved, sweetheart;
(*любо́вник*) lover; (*любо́вница*) mistress

возме́зди|е, я *nt.* retribution

возме|сти́ть, щу́, сти́шь *pf.* (*of* ▶ **возмеща́ть**)
to compensate (for), make up (for); **в.
расхо́ды** to refund expenses

возмеща́|ть, ю *impf. of* ▶ **возмести́ть**

возмеще́ни|е, я *nt.* **1** (*су́мма*) compensation;
(law) damages **2** (*расхо́дов*) reimbursement

возме|щу́, сти́шь *see* ▶ **возмести́ть**

ᵔ **возмо́жно** *adv.* **1** possibly **2** (*as pred.*) it is
possible; **в., что мы за́втра уе́дем** we may
possibly go away tomorrow

ᵔ **возмо́жност|ь, и** *f.* **1** possibility; **по (ме́ре)
~и** as far as possible **2** (*удо́бный слу́чай*)
opportunity; **при пе́рвой ~и** at the first
opportunity **3** (*in pl.*) (*сре́дства*) means,
resources

ᵔ **возмо́ж|ный, ~ен, ~на** *adj.* **1** possible;
врач сде́лал для неё всё ~ное the doctor
did all in his power for her **2** (*наибо́льший*)
the greatest possible

возмути́тел|ьный, ~ен, ~ьна *adj.*
disgraceful, outrageous, scandalous

возму|ти́ть, щу́, ти́шь *pf.* to anger, outrage

возму|ти́ться, щу́сь, ти́шься *pf.* (+ *i.*) to be
indignant (at); to be outraged (at)

возмуща́|ть, ю *impf. of* ▶ **возмути́ть**

возмуща́|ться, юсь *impf. of* ▶ **возмути́ться**

возмуще́ни|е, я *nt.* indignation, outrage

возму|щу́, ти́шь *see* ▶ **возмути́ть**

вознагражде́ни|е, я *nt.* **1** (*за труд, за
по́двиг*) reward, recompense; (*компенса́ция*)
compensation **2** (*опла́та*) fee, remuneration

ᵔ **возник|а́ть, а́ю** *impf. of* ▶ **возни́кнуть**
1 (*тру́дности, подозре́ние*) to arise, spring
up; **у меня́ ~ла мысль** the thought occurred
to me **2** (infml, *появля́ться*) to appear, pop up
3 (*начина́ться*) to begin

ᵔ **возникнове́ни|е, я** *nt.* rise, beginning,
origin

ᵔ **возни́к|нуть, ну, нешь,** *past* ~, ~ла *pf. of*
▶ **возника́ть**

возн|я́, и́ (*no pl.*) *f.* (infml) **1** (*шум*) row, noise
2 (*хло́поты*) bother, trouble

возоблада́|ть, ю *pf.* (**над** + *i.*) to prevail
(over)

возобнов|и́ть, лю́, и́шь *pf.* (*of*
▶ **возобновля́ть**) (*перегово́ры, отноше́ния*)
to resume; (*абонеме́нт, контра́кт*) to renew

возобновле́ни|е, я *nt.* resumption, renewal

возобновля́|ть, ю *impf. of* ▶ **возобнови́ть**

В

возража́|ть, ю *impf.* (*of* ▶ возрази́ть): не ∼ю I have no objection

возраже́ни|е, я *nt.* objection; (*резкий ответ*) retort

возра|зи́ть, жу́, зи́шь *pf.* (*of* ▶ возража́ть) **1** (про́тив + *g. or* на + *a.*) to object (to); to take exception (to); про́тив э́того не́чего в. nothing can be said against it **2** (*pf. only*) (*ответить резко*) to retort

✓ **во́зраст, а** *m.* age; в ∼е два́дцати лет at the age of twenty; ребёнок в ∼е двена́дцати лет a twelve-year-old child

возраста́ни|е, я *nt.* growth, increase

возраста́|ть, а́ю *impf. of* ▶ возрасти́

возраст|и́, у́, ёшь, *past* возро́с, возросла́ *pf.* (*of* ▶ возраста́ть) to grow, increase

возрастно́й *adj. of* ▶ во́зраст; ∼на́я гру́ппа age group

возро|ди́ть, жу́, ди́шь *pf.* (*of* ▶ возрожда́ть) (*хозяйство, город*) to regenerate; (*надежду, культуру*) to revive

возро|ди́ться, жу́сь, ди́шься *pf.* (*of* ▶ возрожда́ться) to revive

возрожда́|ть, ю *impf. of* ▶ возроди́ть

возрожда́|ться, юсь *impf. of* ▶ возроди́ться

возрожде́ни|е, я *nt.* regeneration; revival; эпо́ха В∼я Renaissance

возьм|у́, ёшь *see* ▶ взять

возьм|у́сь, ёшься *see* ▶ взя́ться

во́ин, а *m.* warrior; fighter

во́инск|ий *adj.* **1** military; ∼ая пови́нность conscription **2** (*свойственный военному*) martial, warlike

во́инствен|ный, ∼, ∼на *adj.* **1** (*народ*) warlike **2** (*вид, тон*) bellicose

во́й, я (*no pl.*) *m.* howl, howling; wail, wailing

во́й|ду́, дёшь *see* ▶ войти́

во́йлок, а *m.* felt

✓ **войн|а́, ы́,** *pl.* ∼ы *f.* war; (*ведение войны*) warfare; вести́ ∼у́ to wage war; объяви́ть ∼у́ to declare war

✓ **войск|а́, ∼** *nt. pl.* (*sg.* ∼о, ∼а) troops; forces; наёмные в. mercenaries

войсково́й *adj.* military

✓ **во|йти́, йду́, йдёшь,** *past* ∼шёл, ∼шла́ *pf.* (*of* ▶ входи́ть) (в. + *a.*) (*вступить*) to enter; (*из данного места внутрь*) to go in(to); (*извне в данное место*) to come in(to); (*уместиться*) to go in, fit in; (*в состав чего-н.*) to enter; в. в исто́рию to go down in history; в. в мо́ду to become fashionable; в. в систе́му (comput.) to log on

вока́лист, а *m.* (mus.) vocalist

вокали́ст|ка, ки *f. of* ▶ вокали́ст

вока́льный *adj.* vocal

вокза́л, а *m.* (large) station; железнодоро́жный в. railway (esp. main or terminus) station; морско́й в. port arrival and departure building

✓ **вокру́г** *adv. and prep.* + *g.* round, around; (*по поводу*) about; в. све́та round the world;

✓ **key word**

ходи́ть в. да о́коло (infml) to beat about the bush

вол, а́ *m.* ox, bullock

Во́лг|а, и *f.* the Volga (*river*)

волды́р|ь, я́ *m.* (*пузырь*) blister

волево́й *adj.* (*человек, натура*) strong-willed; (*лицо, голос*) determined

волейбо́л, а *m.* volleyball

волейболи́ст, а *m.* volleyball player

волейболи́ст|ка, ки *f. of* ▶ волейболи́ст

волк, а, *pl.* ∼и, ∼о́в *m.* wolf

волкода́в, а *m.* wolfhound

✓ **волн|а́, ы́,** *pl.* ∼ы, ∼, ∼а́м *f.* wave

волне́ни|е, я *nt.* **1** (*на воде*) choppiness **2** (fig.) (*нервное*) agitation; (*радостное*) excitement; (*душевное*) emotion; прийти́ в в. to become agitated, excited **3** (*usu. in pl.*) (pol.) disturbance(s); unrest

волни́ст|ый, ∼, ∼а *adj.* wavy

волн|ова́ть, у́ю *impf.* (*of* ▶ взволнова́ть) (*возбуждать*) to excite; (*беспокоить*) to worry; (*воду*) to disturb, agitate (also fig.)

волн|ова́ться, у́юсь *impf.* **1** (*нервно*) to worry, be nervous; (*радостно*) to be excited; она́ ∼у́ется о де́тях/за дете́й she worries about her children **2** (*вода*) to be agitated, choppy

волноре́з, а *m.* breakwater

волну́ющий *pres. part. act. of* ▶ волнова́ть *and adj.* (*беспокоящий*) disturbing, worrying; (*захватывающий*) exciting, thrilling

волоки́т|а¹, ы *f.* (infml, *бюрократизм*) red tape

волоки́т|а², ы *m.* (infml, *мужчина*) philanderer

волок|но́, на́, *pl.* ∼на, ∼он, ∼нам *nt.* fibre (BrE), fiber (AmE)

волонтёр, а *m.* volunteer

✓ **во́лос, а,** *pl.* ∼ы, воло́с, ∼а́м *m.* hair; (*in pl.*) hair (*of the head*); рвать на себе́ ∼ы to tear one's hair

волоса́т|ый, ∼, ∼а *adj.* hairy

волос|о́к, ка́ *m. dim. of* ▶ во́лос; на в. (*от* + *g.*) within a hair's breadth (of); висе́ть на ∼ке́ to hang by a thread

волоч|и́ть, у́, ∼ишь *impf.* to drag; в. но́ги to shuffle one's feet

вол|о́чь, оку́, очёшь, оку́т, *past* ∼о́к, ∼окла́ *impf.* (infml) to drag

волше́бник, а *m.* magician; wizard

волше́бниц|а, ы *f.* enchantress

волше́б|ный, ∼ен, ∼на *adj.* **1** magic (*attr.*); magical; ∼ная па́лочка magic wand **2** (fig.) magical, bewitching; enchanting

волшебств|о́, а́ *nt.* magic

волы́нк|а, и *f.* bagpipes

вольер, а *m.* cage; enclosure

вольер|а, ы *f.* = вольер

вольнонаёмный *adj.* (*рабочий, труд*) hired; freelance

✓ **во́льност|ь, и** *f.* freedom; liberty; поэти́ческая в. poetic licence (BrE), poetic license (AmE)

во́ль|ный *adj.* **1** free **2** (sport) free, freestyle; ∼ьная борьба́ freestyle wrestling **3** (∼ен,

~ьна́, ~ьно, *pl.* ~ьны́) (*short forms only*) free, at liberty; вы ~ьны́ де́лать, что хоти́те you are at liberty to do as you wish

вольт, а, *g. pl.* в. *m.* (elec.) volt

волью́, ёшь *see* ▸ влить

◆ **во́л|я**, и (*no pl.*) *f.* **1** will; после́дняя в. last will; си́ла ~и willpower; по до́брой ~е of one's own free will; не по своей ~е against one's will **2** (*свобода*) freedom, liberty; на ~е at liberty; дать ~ю (+ *d.*) to give free rein (to)

вон[1] *adv.* out; off, away; вы́йти в. to go away; в. отсю́да! get out!

вон[2] *particle* (*на отдалении*) there, over there; в. он идёт there he goes

вон|жу́, зи́шь *see* ▸ вонзи́ть

вонза́|ть, ю *impf. of* ▸ вонзи́ть

вонза́|ться, юсь **1** *impf. of* ▸ вонзи́ться **2** *pass. of* ▸ вонза́ть

вон|зи́ть, жу́, зи́шь *pf.* (*of* ▸ вонза́ть) (в + *a.*) to plunge, thrust (into)

вон|зи́ться, жу́сь, зи́шься *pf.* (*of* ▸ вонза́ться 1) to pierce, penetrate; стрела́ ~зи́лась ему́ в се́рдце the arrow pierced his heart

вон|ь, и (*no pl.*) *f.* stink, stench

воня́|ть, ю *impf.* (infml) (+ *i.*) to stink, reek (of)

вообража́емый *pres. part. pass. of* ▸ вообража́ть *and adj.* imaginary; fictitious

вообража́|ть, ю (*of* ▸ вообрази́ть) to imagine

воображе́ни|е, я *nt.* imagination

вообра|зи́ть, жу́, зи́шь *pf.* (*of* ▸ вообража́ть): ~зи́(те)! (just) imagine!

◆ **вообще́** *adv.* **1** (*в общем*) in general; on the whole; в. говоря́ generally speaking **2** (*всегда*) always **3** (*with neg.*) at all

воодушеви́|ть, лю́, и́шь *pf.* (*of* ▸ воодушевля́ть) (кого́-н. на + *a.*) to inspire (to), rouse (to)

воодушевле́ни|е, я *nt.* **1** (*действие*) rousing **2** (*увлечение*) enthusiasm, fervour (BrE), fervor (AmE)

воодушевля́|ть, ю *impf. of* ▸ воодушеви́ть

вооружа́|ть, а́ю *impf. of* ▸ вооружи́ть

вооружа́|ться, а́юсь *impf. of* ▸ вооружи́ться

вооруже́ни|е, я *nt.* **1** (*действие*) arming **2** (*оружие*) arms, armament; быть на ~и to be deployed **3** (*принадлежности*) equipment

вооруж|ённый, ~ён, ~ена́ *p.p.p. of* ▸ вооружи́ть *and adj.* armed; ~ённые си́лы armed forces

вооруж|и́ть, у́, и́шь *pf.* (*of* ▸ вооружа́ть) (+ *i.*) to arm; to equip (with) (also fig.)

вооруж|и́ться, у́сь, и́шься *pf.* (*of* ▸ вооружа́ться) to arm oneself; (fig.) to equip oneself

◆ **во-пе́рвых** *adv.* first, first of all, in the first place

вопло|ти́ть, щу́, ти́шь *pf.* (*of* ▸ воплоща́ть) to embody, personify; в. в себе́ to be the embodiment (of); в. в жизнь (*планы*) to realize

вопло|ти́ться, щу́сь, ти́шься *pf.* (*of* ▸ воплоща́ться) to be realized; to be fulfilled

воплоща́|ть, ю *impf. of* ▸ воплоти́ть

воплоща́|ться, юсь *impf. of* ▸ воплоти́ться

воплоще́ни|е, я *nt.* embodiment

вопл|ь, я *m.* cry, wail; wailing, howling

вопреки́ *prep.* + *d.* (*несмотря на*) despite, in spite of; (*наперекор*) against, contrary to

◆ **вопро́с**, а *m.* **1** question; зада́ть в. to ask, put a question; отве́тить на в. to answer a question **2** (*проблема*) question, problem; (*дело*) matter; подня́ть, поста́вить в. (о + *p.*) to raise the question (of); в. жи́зни и сме́рти matter of life and death; спо́рный в. moot point

вопроси́тельный *adj.* interrogative; в. знак question mark; в. взгляд inquiring look

вор, а, *pl.* ~ы́, ~о́в *m.* thief

ворв|а́ться, у́сь, ёшься, *past* ~а́лся, ~ала́сь *pf.* (*of* ▸ врыва́ться) to burst (into)

вороб|е́й, ья́ *m.* sparrow

воро́ванный *adj.* stolen

вор|ова́ть, у́ю *impf.* (infml *pf.* с~) to steal; в. де́ньги у кого́-н. to steal money from sb

воро́вк|а, и *f. of* ▸ вор

воровств|о́, а́ *nt.* stealing; theft

во́рон, а *m.* raven

воро́н|а, ы *f.* crow

воро́нк|а и *f.* **1** (*для переливания*) funnel (*for pouring liquids*) **2** (mil., *яма*) crater

воро́т|а, ~ (*no sg.*) **1** gate, gates; (*вход*) gateway **2** (sport) goal

вороти́л|а, ы *m.* (infml) big shot

воротни́к, а́ *m.* collar

во́рох, а, *pl.* ~а́ *m.* heap, pile

воро́ча|ться, юсь *impf.* (infml) to turn, move; в. с бо́ку на бок to toss and turn

ворч|а́ть, у́, и́шь *impf.* (на + *a.*) to grumble (at); (*о собаке*) to growl (at)

ворчли́в|ый, ~, ~а *adj.* querulous

восемна́дцатый *adj.* eighteenth

восемна́дцат|ь, и *num.* eighteen

во́с|емь, ьми́, *i.* емью́ *and* ьмью́ *num.* eight

во́с|емьдесят, ьми́десяти *num.* eighty

вос|емьсо́т, ьмисо́т, *i.* емьюста́ми *and* ьмьюста́ми *num.* eight hundred

воск, а *m.* wax

восклик|ну́ть, у, ешь *pf. of* ▸ восклица́ть

восклица́ни|е, я *nt.* exclamation

восклица́тельный *adj.* exclamatory; в. знак exclamation mark

восклица́|ть, ю *impf.* (*of* ▸ воскли́кнуть) to exclaim

восково́й *adj.* wax; (*цвет*) waxen

воскреса́|ть, а́ю *impf.* (*of* ▸ воскре́снуть) to rise again, rise from the dead; (fig.) to revive

воскресе́ни|е, я *nt.* resurrection

воскресе́нь|е, я *nt.* Sunday

воскре|си́ть, шу́, си́шь *pf.* (*of* ▸ воскреша́ть) to raise from the dead, resurrect; (fig.) to revive

В

B

воскре́с|нуть, ну, нешь, *past* ~, ~**ла** *pf. of*
▶ **воскреса́ть**

воскре́сный *adj.* Sunday

воскреша́|ть, ю *impf. of* ▶ **воскреси́ть**

воскреше́ни|е, я *nt.* resurrection; (fig.)
revival

воспале́ни|е, я *nt.* (med.) inflammation;
в. лёгких pneumonia

воспал|ённый, ~**ён,** ~**ена́** *adj.* sore;
inflamed

воспал|и́ться, ю́сь, и́шься *pf.* (*of*
▶ **воспаля́ться**) to become inflamed

воспаля́ться, я́юсь *impf. of* ▶ **воспали́ться**

⚔ **воспита́ни|е, я** *nt.* **1** upbringing; (*образование*)
education **2** (*воспитанность*) (good)
breeding

воспи́танник, а *m.* **1** (*школьник*) pupil
2 (*приёмыш*) ward

воспи́танный *p.p.p. of* ▶ **воспита́ть** *and adj.*
well brought up

воспита́тел|ь, я *m.* teacher; (*приёмыша*)
guardian

воспита́тель|ница, ницы *f. of*
▶ **воспита́тель**

воспит|а́ть, а́ю *pf.* (*of* ▶ **воспи́тывать**)
(*вырастить*) to bring up; (*дать*
образование) to educate

воспи́тыва|ть, ю *impf. of* ▶ **воспита́ть**

воспламен|и́ть, ю́, и́шь *pf.* (*of*
▶ **воспламеня́ть**) to kindle, ignite; (fig.)
to inflame

воспламен|и́ться, ю́сь, и́шься *pf.* (*of*
▶ **воспламеня́ться**) to catch fire, ignite; (fig.)
to flare up

воспламеня́|ть, ю *impf. of* ▶ **воспламени́ть**

воспламеня́|ться, юсь *impf. of*
▶ **воспламени́ться**

воспо́лн|ить, ю, ишь *pf.* to fill in

восполня́|ть, ю *impf. of* ▶ **воспо́лнить**

⚔ **воспо́льз|оваться, уюсь** *pf. of*
▶ **по́льзоваться 2**

воспомина́ни|е, я *nt.* **1** recollection,
memory **2** (*in pl.*) (*мемуары*) memoirs;
reminiscences

воспрепя́тств|овать, ую *pf. of*
▶ **препя́тствовать**

воспреща́|ться, ется *impf.* to be prohibited

восприи́мчив|ый, ~, ~**а** *adj.* **1** (*ум,
натура*) receptive; impressionable
2 (*подверженный*) susceptible

восприм|у́, ~**ешь** *see* ▶ **восприня́ть**

воспринима́|ть, ю *impf. of* ▶ **восприня́ть**

воспри|ня́ть, му́, ~**мешь,** *past* ~**нял,**
~**няла́,** ~**няло** *pf.* (*of* ▶ **воспринима́ть**)
1 (*ощутить*) to perceive, apprehend;
(*понять*) to grasp, take in **2** (*понять как*)
to take (for), interpret

восприя́ти|е, я *nt.* (phil., psych.) perception

воспроизведе́ни|е, я *nt.* **1** reproduction;
в. челове́ческого ро́да reproduction of
the human species; **ве́рное в. карти́ны**

Ру́бенса faithful reproduction of a painting
by Rubens **2** (electronics) playback, replay;
заме́дленное/уско́ренное в. slow-motion/
high-speed playback

воспроизве|сти́, ду́, дёшь, *past* ~**л,** ~**ла́**
pf. (*of* ▶ **воспроизводи́ть**) to reproduce; **в. в**
па́мяти to recall

воспроизво|ди́ть, жу́, ~**дишь** *impf. of*
▶ **воспроизвести́**

воссоедине́ни|е, я *nt.* reunification

воссоедин|и́ть, ю́, и́шь *pf.* (*of*
▶ **воссоединя́ть**) to reunite

воссоединя́|ть, ю *impf. of* ▶ **воссоедини́ть**

воссозда|ва́ть, ю́, ёшь *impf. of* ▶ **воссозда́ть**

воссозда́ни|е, я *nt.* reconstruction

воссоз|да́ть, да́м, да́шь, да́ст, дади́м,
дади́те, даду́т, *past* ~**да́л,** ~**дала́,** ~**да́ло**
pf. (*of* ▶ **воссоздава́ть**) to reconstruct,
reconstitute

восста|ва́ть, ю́, ёшь *impf. of* ▶ **восста́ть**

восстана́влива|ть, ю *impf. of*
▶ **восстанови́ть**

восста́ни|е, я *nt.* uprising, insurrection

восстанови́тельн|ый *adj.* restorative;
в. пери́од period of reconstruction; ~**ые**
рабо́ты restoration work

восстанов|и́ть, лю́, ~**ишь** *pf.* (*of*
▶ **восстана́вливать**) **1** to restore; **в. в**
па́мяти to recall, recollect **2** (**про́тив** + *g.*)
to set (against), antagonize

⚔ **восстановле́ни|е, я** *nt.* restoration,
renewal; **в. в до́лжности** reinstatement

восста́|ть, ну, нешь, *imper.* ~**нь** *pf.*
(*of* ▶ **восстава́ть**) (**про́тив** + *g.*) to rise
(against); (fig.) to be up in arms (against),
revolt (against)

⚔ **восто́к, а** *m.* **1** east; **на в., с** ~**а** to, from the
east **2** (**В.**) the East; the Orient; **Бли́жний**
В~ the Middle East; **Да́льний В.** the Far
East

восто́рг, а *m.* delight; rapture; **быть в** ~**е** (**от**
+ *g.*) to be delighted (with); **приходи́ть в в.**
от (+ *g.*) to go into raptures (over)

восто́ржен|ный, ~, ~**на** *adj.* (*поклонник*)
enthusiastic; (*приём, отзыв*) rapturous

восторжеств|ова́ть, у́ю *pf. of*
▶ **торжествова́ть**

⚔ **восто́чный** *adj.* east, eastern; (*направление,
ветер*) easterly; (*культура*) oriental

востре́бовани|е, я *nt.* claiming, demand; **до**
~**я** poste restante

восхити́тельн|ый, ~**ен,** ~**ьна** *adj.*
(*женщина, красота*) ravishing; (*вечер,
музыка*) delightful; (*вкус, запах*) delicious

восхи|ти́ть, щу́, ти́шь *pf.* to delight, captivate

восхи|ти́ться, щу́сь, ти́шься *pf.* (+ *i.*) to
be delighted (by); to be carried away (by);
to admire

восхища́|ть, ю *impf. of* ▶ **восхити́ть**

восхища́|ться, юсь *impf. of* ▶ **восхити́ться**

восхище́ни|е, я *nt.* admiration; (*восторг*)
delight, rapture; **прийти́ в в. от** (+ *g.*) to be
delighted with

⚔ key word

восхи|щу́, ти́шь *see* ▸ восхити́ть

восхи|щу́сь, ти́шься *see* ▸ восхити́ться

восхо́д, а *m.* rising; **в. со́лнца** sunrise

восхо|ди́ть, жу́, ~дишь *impf.* **1** *impf. of* ▸ взойти́ **2** (*impf. only*) (к + *d.*) to go back (to), date (from); **в. к дре́вности** to go back to antiquity

восходя́щий *pres. part. of* ▸ восходи́ть *and adj.*: **~я́щая звезда́** (fig.) rising star

восхожде́ни|е, я *nt.* ascent; **в. на Монбла́н** the ascent of Mont Blanc

восьма́я *see* ▸ восьмо́й

восьмёрк|а, и *f.* **1** (*цифра, игра́льная ка́рта*) eight **2** (infml, *авто́бус, трамва́й*) No. 8 (*bus, tram, etc.*) **3** (*гру́ппа из восьмеры́х*) (group of) eight **4** (*фигу́ра*) (figure of) eight

восьми́... *comb. form* eight-, octo-

восьмиуго́льный *adj.* octagonal

восьмичасово́й *adj.* eight-hour; **в. рабо́чий день** eight-hour (working) day

восьм|о́й *adj.* eighth; (*as f. n.* **~а́я, ~о́й**) an eighth

вот *particle* **1** (*здесь*) here (is); (*там*) there (is); (*это*) this is; **в. мой дом** here is my house, this is my house; **в. идёт авто́бус** here comes the bus; **в. мы пришли́** here we are; **в. где я живу́** this is where I live **2** (*emphasizing prons.; unstressed*): **в. э́ти ту́фли ей нра́вились** these are the shoes she liked **3** (*in int.*) here's a ..., there's a ... (for you); **вот тебе́ исто́рия!** here's a pretty kettle of fish!; **в. и всё** I've said it all, that's that; (*expr. surprise*) **вот как!, вот (оно́) что!** really? you don't mean to say so!; **в. тебе́ на́!** well!; well, I never!; (*expr. surprise and disapproval*) **в. ещё!** no way!; what(ever) next!; (*expr. approval and/or encouragement*) **в. так!, в.-в.!** that's right!; that's it!; **в. так и что's that; вот тебе́ и...** so much for ...; **вот тебе́ и пое́здка в Пари́ж!** so much for the trip to Paris!; **в.** (*ука́зывает на заверше́ние чего́-н.*): **в. и пришли́** here we are

вот-во́т *adv.* (infml) just, on the point of, any minute; **по́езд в.-в. придёт** the train is just coming

воткн|у́ть, у́, ёшь *pf.* (*of* ▸ втыка́ть) (в + *a.*) to stick (into); (*с больши́м уси́лием*) to drive (into)

вотр|у́, ёшь *see* ▸ втере́ть

во́тум, а (*no pl.*) *m.* vote; **в. (не)дове́рия** (+ *d.*) vote of (no) confidence (in)

воцар|и́ться, ю́сь, и́шься *pf.* (*of* ▸ воцаря́ться) **1** to come to power **2** (fig.) to set in; to be established

воцаря́|ться, юсь *impf. of* ▸ воцари́ться

вошёл, ла́ *see* ▸ войти́

вошь, вши, *i.* **~ю, pl. вши, вшей** *f.* louse

во́|ю, ешь *see* ▸ выть

вою́|ю, ешь *see* ▸ воева́ть

впада́|ть, ю *impf.* **1** *impf. of* ▸ впасть **2** (*impf. only*) (*о реке́*) (в + *a.*) flow (into)

впа́дин|а, ы *f.* cavity, hollow

впад|у́, ёшь *see* ▸ впасть

впа|сть, ду́, дёшь, *past* **~л, ~ла** *pf.* (*of* ▸ впада́ть 1) (в + *a.*) to fall (into), lapse (into), sink (into)

впервы́е *adv.* for the first time, first; **в. слы́шу об э́том** it's the first I've heard of it

вперёд *adv.* **1** forward(s), ahead; **взад и в.** (infml) back and forth **2** (*ава́нсом*) in advance

впереди́ **1** *adv.* in front, ahead **2** *adv.* (*в бу́дущем*) in (the) future; ahead; **у него́ всё в.** he has his whole life in front of him **3** *prep. + g.* in front of, before

впечатле́ни|е, я *nt.* impression; **произвести́ в.** (на + *a.*) to make an impression (upon)

впечатли́тел|ьный, ~ен, ~ьна *adj.* impressionable

впечатля́|ть, ю *impf.* to impress

впечатля́ющий *adj.* impressive

впива́|ться, юсь *impf. of* ▸ впи́ться

впи|са́ть, шу́, ~шешь *pf.* (*of* ▸ впи́сывать) to enter; to insert; **в. своё и́мя в спи́сок** to enter one's name on a list

впи|са́ться, шу́сь, ~шешься *pf.* (*of* ▸ впи́сываться) (*гармони́ровать*) to fit in, blend in

впи́сыва|ть, ю *impf. of* ▸ вписа́ть

впи́сыва|ться, юсь *impf. of* ▸ вписа́ться

впит|а́ть, а́ю *pf.* (*of* ▸ впи́тывать) to absorb; (fig.) to absorb, take in

впит|а́ться, а́юсь *pf.* (*of* ▸ впи́тываться) (в + *a.*) to soak (into)

впи́тыва|ть, ю *impf. of* ▸ впита́ть

впи́тыва|ться, юсь *impf. of* ▸ впита́ться

впи|ться, вопью́сь, вопьёшься, *past* **~лся, ~ла́сь** *pf.* (*of* ▸ впива́ться) (в + *a.*) (*вонзи́ться*) to stick (into); (*укуси́ть*) to bite; (*ужа́лить*) to sting; **гвоздь ~лся мне в но́гу** a nail stuck into my foot

ВПК *m. indecl.* (*abbr. of* вое́нно-промы́шленный ко́мплекс) military-industrial complex

вплавь *adv.* by swimming

вплотну́ю *adv.* close; (fig.) in earnest; **в. к стене́** right up against the wall

вплоть *adv.*: **в. до** (+ *g.*) (*до преде́ла*) (right) up to; until; (*включа́я*) including

вплыва́|ть, ю *impf. of* ▸ вплыть

вплы|ть, ву́, вёшь, *past* **~л, ~ла́, ~ло** *pf.* (*of* ▸ вплыва́ть) (*о челове́ке*) to swim in; (*о корабле́*) to sail in

вполго́лоса *adv.* in an undertone, under one's breath

вполза́|ть, а́ю *impf. of* ▸ вползти́

вполз|ти́, у́, ёшь, *past* **~, ~ла́** *pf.* (*of* ▸ вполза́ть) to creep in, crawl in; (*подня́ться вверх*) to creep up, crawl up

вполне́ *adv.* fully, entirely; quite

впосле́дствии *adv.* subsequently; afterwards

впра́ве *as pred.*: **быть в.** (+ *inf.*) to have a right (to)

впра́в|ить, лю, ишь *pf.* (*of* ▸ вправля́ть) (med., *кость*) to set

B

вправля|ть, ю *impf. of* ▶ **вправить**

вправо *adv.* (от + *g.*) to the right (of)

впредь *adv.* in future, henceforth; **в. до** until

впрок *adv.* **1** (*про запас*) for future use; **заготовить в.** to stock up on **2** (*as pred.*) (*на пользу*) to advantage; **это не пойдёт ему в.** it will do him no good

✍ **впрочем** *adv. and conj.* **1** (*однако, но*) however, but **2** (*выражает нерешимость*) or rather; but then again; **приезжайте завтра, в., лучше даже послезавтра** come tomorrow, or, even better, the day after

впряга|ть, ю *impf. of* ▶ **впрячь**

впряга|ться, юсь *impf. of* ▶ **впрячься**

впря|чь, гу́, жёшь, гу́т, *past* впряг, ∼гла́ *pf.* (*of* ▶ **впрягать**) (в + *a.*) to harness (to)

впря|чься, гу́сь, жёшься, гу́тся, *past* впря́гся, ∼гла́сь *pf.* (*of* ▶ **впрягаться**) (в + *a.*) to harness oneself (to)

впуска|ть, ю *impf. of* ▶ **впустить**

впу|стить, щу́, ∼стишь *pf.* (*of* ▶ **впускать**) to admit, let in

впустую *adv.* (infml) for nothing, to no purpose

впу|щу, ∼стишь *see* ▶ **впустить**

впятером *adv.* five (together)

✍ **враг**, а́ *m.* enemy; (*collect.*) the enemy

вражд|а́, ы́ *f.* enmity, hostility

враждеб|ный, ∼ен, ∼на *adj.* hostile

вражд|овать, у́ю *impf.* (с + *i.*) to be at enmity (with), at odds (with)

вра́жеский *adj.* (mil.) enemy; hostile

врань|е́, я́ *nt.* (infml) (*ложь*) lies; (*вздор*) nonsense

врасплох *adv.* (infml): **застать, захватить, застигнуть в.** to take unawares; to catch off guard

враст|а́ть, а́ю *impf.* (*of* ▶ **врасти**) to grow in(to); **∼а́ющий ноготь** ingrowing nail

врас|ти́, у́, ёшь, *past* врос, вросла́ *pf. of* ▶ **врастать**

врата́р|ь, я́ *m.* (sport) goalkeeper

вр|ать, у, ёшь, *past* ∼ал, ∼ала́, ∼а́ло *impf.* (*of* ▶ **наврать**, ▶ **соврать**) (infml) **1** (*лгать*) to lie, tell lies **2** (*говорить вздор*) to talk nonsense **3** (*быть неточным*) to be wrong (*of inanimate objects only*)

✍ **врач**, а́ *m.* doctor, physician; **детский в.** paediatrician (BrE), pediatrician (AmE); **зубной в.** dentist

враче́бный *adj.* medical

враща́|ть, ю *impf.* to revolve, rotate; **в. глаза́ми** to roll one's eyes

враща́|ться, юсь *impf.* to revolve, rotate; **он ∼ется в худо́жественных круга́х** he moves in artistic circles

враще́ни|е, я *nt.* rotation; revolution

вред, а́ *m.* (no pl.) **1** (*человеку*) harm, injury; (*здоровью, зданию*) damage; **без ∼а́ (для + *g.*) without detriment (to); **во ∼** (+ *d.*) to the detriment of

вреди́тел|ь, я *m.* (agric.) pest

вре|ди́ть, жу́, ди́шь *impf.* (*of* ▶ **навредить**, ▶ **повредить 1**) (+ *d.*) (*человеку*) to injure, harm, hurt; (*здоровью, зданию*) to damage

вредно *adv.* as pred. it is harmful; **в. для здоровья** it is bad for one's health

вред|ный, ∼ен, ∼на, ∼но, ∼ны́ *adj.* harmful, unhealthy; (*производство*) hazardous; (*no short forms*) (infml, *человек*) nasty

вре́|жу, жешь *see* ▶ **врезать**

вре|жу́, ди́шь *see* ▶ **вредить**

вре́|жусь, жешься *see* ▶ **врезаться**

вре́|зать, жу, жешь *pf.* (*of* ▶ **врезать**) **1** to cut in; (*вставить*) to set in **2** (*pf. only*) (infml) (+ *d.*) (*ударить*) to whack (sb)

вреза́|ть, а́ю *impf. of* ▶ **врезать 1**

вре́|заться, жусь, жешься *pf.* (*of* ▶ **врезаться**) (*удариться*) (в + *a.*) to smash (into)

вреза́|ться, а́юсь *impf. of* ▶ **врезаться**

времена́ми *adv.* at times, now and then, now and again

вре́менный *adj.* temporary; provisional

✍ **врем|я, ени**, *i.* ∼енем, о ∼ени, *pl.* ∼ена́, ∼ён, ∼ена́м *nt.* **1** time; **в. от ∼ени** from time to time; **в да́нное в.** at the present moment; **(в) пе́рвое в.** at first; **(в) после́днее в.** lately, of late; **в своё в.** (*о прошлом*) in one's time, once, at one time; (*о будущем*) in due course; in one's own time; **за после́днее в.** lately; **на в.** for a while; **на пе́рвое в.** for the time being; **одно́ в.** once (*in the past*); **с тече́нием ∼ени** in the course of time; **всё в.** all the time, continually; **ско́лько ∼ени?** what is the time?; **тем ∼енем** meanwhile **2**: **в. го́да** season **3** (gram.) tense **4**: **в то в. как** while, whereas **5**: **во в.** (+ *g.*) during, in

времяпрепровожде́ни|е, я *and* **времяпровожде́ни|е, я** *nt.* pastime; way of spending one's time

вро́вень *adv.* (с + *i.*) level (with); **в. с края́ми** to the brim

✍ **вро́де 1** *prep.* + *g.* like; **не́что в.** (infml) a sort of, a kind of **2** *particle* (infml, *кажется*) it looks as if

врождён|ный, ∼, ∼на *adj.* (*способность*) innate; (*недостаток*) congenital

врозь *adv.* separately, apart

врун, а́ *m.* (infml) liar

вруча́|ть, а́ю *impf. of* ▶ **вручить**

вруч|и́ть, у́, и́шь *pf.* (*of* ▶ **вручать**) (*письмо, посылку*) to hand, deliver; (*медаль*) to present

вручну́ю *adv.* by hand

врыва́|ться, юсь *impf. of* ▶ **ворваться**

✍ **вряд, ли** *adv.* (infml) hardly, it is unlikely; **в. ли сто́ит** it is hardly worth it; **они́ в. ли приду́т** they are unlikely to come

вса́дник, а *m.* rider, horseman

вса́дниц|а, ы *f.* rider, horsewoman

✍ **все** *see* ▶ **весь**

всё 1 *pron. see* ▶ **весь 2** *adv.* (infml) always; all the time **3**: в. (ещё) still; **дождь в. (ещё) идёт** it is still raining; **в. же** after all, nevertheless **4** (infml) only, all; **э́то в. из-за тебя́!** it is all because of you! **5** (*as conj.*) (*всё равно*) however, nevertheless **6** (*as particle, strengthening comp.*): **в. бо́лее и бо́лее** more and more; **он в. толсте́ет** he is getting fatter and fatter **7** (*pred.*) (infml, *кончено*) that's it!

все... *comb. form* all-, omni-, pan-; most (*gracious, etc.*)

всевозмо́жн|ый *adj.* all kinds of; every possible; **~ые това́ры** goods of all kinds

Всевы́шн|ий, ~его *n.* (relig.) the Almighty

всегда́ *adv.* always

всего́ 1 *pron. see* ▶ **весь; бо́льше в.** (the) most; **лу́чше в.** (the) best; **ча́ще в.** most often **2** *adv.* (*итого*) in all, all told; (*лишь*) only; **в. лишь** (infml) only; **в.-на́всего** only, all in all; **то́лько и в.** (infml) that's all

вседозво́ленност|ь, и *f.* permissiveness

Вселе́нн|ая, ой (*no pl.*) *f.* (*космос*) the universe

вселе́нский *adj.* universal; (eccl.) ecumenical; **в. собо́р** ecumenical council

всел|и́ть, ю́, и́шь *pf.* (*of* ▶ **вселя́ть**) **1** (*жильца*) to move (sb) in; to install **2** (fig., rhet.) to breed; instill (BrE), instill (AmE) (in); **в. страх** (в + *a.*) to strike fear (into)

всел|и́ться, ю́сь, и́шься *pf.* (*of* ▶ **вселя́ться**) (в + *a.*) **1** (*в дом*) to move in(to) **2** (fig.) to be implanted (in)

вселя́|ть, ю *impf. of* ▶ **всели́ть**

вселя́|ться, юсь *impf. of* ▶ **всели́ться**

всем *see* ▶ **весь**

всеме́рный *adj.* all possible

всеми́рный *adj.* world (attr.); worldwide

всемогу́щ|ий, ~, ~а *adj.* omnipotent, all-powerful; **В.** (*о Боге*) Almighty

всенаро́дно *adv.* publicly

всенаро́дный *adj.* national; nationwide

всено́щн|ая, ой *f.* (eccl.) vespers

всео́бщ|ий *adj.* universal; general; **~ая во́инская пови́нность** universal military service; **~ая забасто́вка** general strike; **~ие вы́боры** general election

всеобъе́млющ|ий, ~, ~а *adj.* all-embracing, comprehensive

всеросси́йский *adj.* all-Russian

всерьёз *adv.* seriously, in earnest

всеси́льн|ый, ~ен, ~ьна *adj.* all-powerful

всесторо́нний *adj.* (*образование*) all-round; (*анализ*) thorough, detailed

всё-таки *conj. and particle* still, all the same

всех *see* ▶ **весь**

всеце́ло *adv.* completely

всея́дный *adj.* omnivorous

вска́кива|ть, ю *impf. of* ▶ **вскочи́ть**

вска́пыва|ть, ю *impf. of* ▶ **вскопа́ть**

вскара́бка|ться, аюсь *pf. of* ▶ **кара́бкаться**

вски́дыва|ть, ю *impf. of* ▶ **вски́нуть**

вски́|нуть, ну, нешь *pf.* (*of* ▶ **вски́дывать**) (*кинуть*) to throw up; **в. на плечи** to shoulder; (*поднять*) to raise (*suddenly*); **в. глаза́** to look up suddenly

вскипа́|ть, ю *impf. of* ▶ **вскипе́ть**

вскип|е́ть, лю́, и́шь *pf.* (*of* ▶ **вскипа́ть**) **1** (*вода*) to boil up **2** (fig.) to flare up, fly into a rage

вскипяти́ть, чу́, ти́шь *pf. of* ▶ **кипяти́ть**

вскользь *adv.* slightly; in passing; **упомяну́ть в.** to mention in passing

вскопа́|ть, ю *pf.* (*of* ▶ **вска́пывать**, ▶ **копа́ть 1**) to dig over

вско́ре *adv.* soon, shortly after

вско́ч|ить, у́, ~ишь *pf.* (*of* ▶ **вска́кивать**) **1** (в/на + *a.* or с + *g.*) to leap up (into/on to; from) **2** (infml, *шишка*) to come up (of bumps, boils, etc.)

вскро́|ю, ешь *see* ▶ **вскрыть**

вскрыва́|ть, ю *impf. of* ▶ **вскрыть**

вскрыва́|ться, юсь *impf. of* ▶ **вскры́ться**

вскры́ти|е, я *nt.* **1** (*письма*) opening, unsealing; (*сейфа*) unlocking **2** (med., *нарыва*) lancing **3** (med., *трупа*) autopsy, post-mortem

вскр|ы́ть, о́ю, о́ешь *pf.* (*of* ▶ **вскрыва́ть**) **1** (*письмо*) to open, unseal; (*сейф*) to unlock **2** (med., *нарыв*) to lance

вскры́|ться, о́юсь, о́ешься *pf.* (*of* ▶ **вскрыва́ться**) **1** (*река*) to become clear (of ice); to become open **2** (med.) to break, burst

вслед 1 *adv.* (за + *i.*) after **2** *prep. + d.* after; **смотре́ть в.** to follow with one's eyes

всле́дствие *prep. + g.* in consequence of, owing to, due to

вслух *adv.* aloud, out loud

вслу́ш|аться, аюсь *pf.* (*of* ▶ **вслу́шиваться**) (в + *a.*) to listen attentively (to)

вслу́шива|ться, юсь *impf. of* ▶ **вслу́шаться**

всмя́тку *adv.*: **яйцо́ в.** soft-boiled, lightly-boiled egg

вспа|ха́ть, шу́, ~шешь *pf.* (*of* ▶ **вспа́хивать**, ▶ **паха́ть 1**) to plough up (BrE), plow up (AmE)

вспа́хива|ть, ю *impf. of* ▶ **вспаха́ть**

всплеск, а *m.* splash

всплыва́|ть, ю *impf.* (*of* ▶ **всплыть**): **всплыва́ющее окно́** (comput.) pop-up (window)

всплы́|ть, ву́, вёшь, *past* ~л, ~ла́, ~ло *pf.* (*of* ▶ **всплыва́ть**) to rise to the surface, surface; (fig., *факт*) to come to light; (*вопрос*) to arise

вспомина́|ть, ю *impf. of* ▶ **вспо́мнить**

вспо́м|нить, ню, нишь *pf.* (*of* ▶ **вспомина́ть**) (*детство*) to remember, recall, recollect; (о + *p.*, *что*) to remember

вспомога́тельный *adj.* auxiliary; subsidiary; (gram.) auxiliary

вспоте́|ть, ю *pf.* (*of* ▶ **поте́ть**) to come out in a sweat

вспу́гива|ть, ю *impf. of* ▶ **вспугну́ть**

вспуг|ну́ть, ну́, нёшь *pf.* (*of* ▶ вспу́гивать)
to scare away; (*дичь*) to put up

вспыл|и́ть, ю́, и́шь *pf.* to flare up; **в.** (**на** + *a.*)
to fly into a rage (with)

вспы́льчив|ый, ~, ~a *adj.* hot-tempered;
irascible

вспы́хива|ть, ю *impf. of* ▶ вспы́хнуть

вспы́х|нуть, ну, нешь *pf.* (*of* ▶ вспы́хивать)
(*огонь, свет*) to flash; (*бумага*) to burst
into flames, blaze up; (*пожар*) to break out;
(fig., *ссора, конфликт*) to flare up; (*паника,
война*) to break out

вспы́шк|а, и *f.* flash; (phot.) flash (attachment);
(*гнева*) outburst; (*энергии*) burst; (*болезни*)
outbreak

вста|ва́ть, ю́, ёшь *impf. of* ▶ встать

вста́в|ить, лю, ишь *pf.* (*of* ▶ вставля́ть) to
put in, insert; **в ра́му** to frame; **в. себе́
зу́бы** to have false teeth, dentures made

вста́вк|а, и *f.* **1** (*действие*) fixing, insertion
2 (*в одежде*) inset **3** (*в тексте*) insertion

вставля́|ть, ю *impf. of* ▶ вста́вить

вставн|о́й *adj.* inserted; ~ы́е зу́бы false
teeth, dentures; ~ы́е ра́мы removable
window frames

вста|ть, ну, нешь *pf.* (*of* ▶ встава́ть)
1 (*с постели*) to get up, rise; (*на ноги*) to
stand up, rise, get up; (*солнце*) to rise
2 (**в** + *a.*) (infml) to go (into), fit (into);
большо́й шкаф не ~нет в э́ту ко́мнату
the large cupboard will not go into this
room **3** (*вопрос, образ*) to appear, arise
4 (*impf. only*) (*часы*) to stop (working)

встрево́жен|ный *adj.* (*выражающий
тревогу*) (~, ~на) anxious; (*испытывающий
тревогу*) (~, ~a) anxious

встре́|тить, чу, тишь *pf.* (*of* ▶ встреча́ть)
1 (*запланированно*) to meet; (*случайно*) to
meet, come across; (*сопротивление*) to meet
with, encounter; (*обнаружить*) to come
across **2** (*оказать приём*) to receive, greet;
(*Новый год, Пасху*) to celebrate

встре́|титься, чусь, тишься *pf.* (*of
* ▶ встреча́ться 1) **1** (**с** + *i.*) to meet (with),
encounter, come across; **в. с затрудне́ниями**
to encounter difficulties **2** (*на пути*) to
be found, occur **3** (*собраться*) to gather,
congregate

✐ **встре́ч|а, и** *f.* **1** meeting; (*приём*) reception;
в. в верха́х (pol.) summit; **в. Но́вого го́да** New
Year's Eve party **2** (sport) match, meeting

✐ **встреча́|ть, ю** *impf. of* ▶ встре́тить

✐ **встреча́|ться, юсь** *impf.* **1** *impf. of
* ▶ встре́титься **2** (*impf. only*) (*ареал
распространения*) to be found; **в Шотла́ндии
ещё ~ются ди́кие ко́шки** wild cats are still
found in Scotland

встре́чный *adj.* **1** (*поезд, машина*)
proceeding from opposite direction;
oncoming; (*as n.* **пе́рвый в.**) the first person
you meet, anyone **2** (*предложение*) counter;
в. иск (law) counterclaim

✐ **key word**

встро́енный *adj.* built-in

встря́хива|ть, ю *impf. of* ▶ встряхну́ть

встря́х|нуть, ну́, нёшь *pf.* (*of* ▶ встря́хивать)
to shake; (fig.) to shake up, rouse

вступа́|ть, ю *impf. of* ▶ вступи́ть

вступа́|ться, юсь *impf. of* ▶ вступи́ться

вступи́тельный *adj.* introductory; **в. взнос**
entrance fee; **в. экза́мен** entrance exam

вступ|и́ть, лю́, ~ишь *pf.* (*of* ▶ вступа́ть)
1 (**в** + *a.*) (*войти, въехать*) to enter; (*стать
членом*) to join; (*в спор, переговоры*) to enter
into; **в. в бой** to join battle; **в. в де́йствие**
(*договор, закон*) to come into force; **в. в брак**
to marry **2** (**на** + *a.*) to mount, go up; **в. на
престо́л** to ascend the throne

вступ|и́ться, лю́сь, ~ишься *pf.* (*of
* ▶ вступа́ться) (**за** + *a.*) to stand up (for)

вступле́ни|е, я *nt.* **1** (*в клуб*) joining; (*в
должность*) assumption (of) **2** (*в музыке*)
prelude; (*в книге*) introduction

всхли́п|нуть, ну, нешь *pf.* (*of* ▶ всхли́пывать)
to sob

всхли́пывани|е, я *nt.* (*действие*) sobbing;
(*звуки*) sobs

всхли́пыва|ть, ю *impf. of* ▶ всхли́пнуть

всхо|ди́ть, жу́, ~дишь *impf. of* ▶ взойти́

всхо́д|ы, ов (*no sg.*) shoots

всю́ду *adv.* everywhere

вся *see* ▶ весь

✐ **вся́к|ий** *pron.* **1** any; **во ~ом слу́чае** in
any case, at any rate; (*as n.*) anyone
2 (*разнообразный*) all sorts of; every; **на в.
слу́чай** just in case

Вт (*abbr. of* ватт) W, watt

вта́йне *adv.* secretly, in secret

вта́лкива|ть, ю *impf. of* ▶ втолкну́ть

втека́|ть, ет, ют *impf. of* ▶ втечь

втер|е́ть, вотру́, вотрёшь, *past* ~, ~ла́ *pf.*
(*of* ▶ втира́ть) (**в** + *a.*) to rub in(to)

вте|чь, чёт, ку́т, *past* ~к, ~кла́ *pf.* (*of
* ▶ втека́ть) to flow in(to)

втира́|ть, ю *impf. of* ▶ втере́ть

втолкн|у́ть, у́, ёшь *pf.* (*of* ▶ вта́лкивать)
(**в** + *a.*) to push in(to), shove in(to)

вторг|а́ться, а́юсь *impf. of* ▶ вто́ргнуться

вто́рг|нуться, нусь, нешься, *past* ~ся,
~лась *pf.* (*of* ▶ вторга́ться) (**в** + *a.*)
(*в страну*) to invade; (*в чужие дела*) to
interfere (in)

вторже́ни|е, я *nt.* invasion; interference

втори́чн|ый *adj.* **1** (*второй*) second
2 (*второстепенный*) secondary **3**: ~oe
сырьё recyclable material

вто́рник, а *m.* Tuesday; **во в.** on Tuesday; **на
в.** for Tuesday; **в сле́дующий/про́шлый в.**
next/last Tuesday

✐ **втор|о́й** *adj.* **1** second; **в. час** (it is) past one;
(*не главный*) secondary; **на ~о́м пла́не** (fig.)
in the background **2** (*as nt. n.* ~о́е, ~о́го)
main course (*of meal*)

второсо́ртный *adj.* of the second-best
quality; second-rate

второстепе́н|ный, ~ен, ~на adj. secondary; minor

в-тре́тьих adv. thirdly, in the third place

втро́е adv. three times; **в. бо́льше** three times as big; **увели́чить в.** to triple

втроём adv. three (together); **мы в.** the three of us

втройне́ adv. three times as much, treble

втыка́|ть, ю impf. of ▶ воткну́ть

втя́гива|ть, ю impf. of ▶ втяну́ть

втя́гива|ться, юсь impf. of ▶ втяну́ться

втя|ну́ть, ну́, ~нешь pf. (of ▶ втя́гивать) **1** (ло́дку; щёки, живо́т) to draw (in, into, up), pull (in, into, up); (во́здух, жи́дкость) to absorb, take in **2** (fig.) (в + a.) to draw (into), involve (in); **в. в спор** to draw into an argument

втя|ну́ться, ну́сь, ~нешься pf. (of ▶ втя́гиваться) (в + a.) **1** (постепе́нно войти́) to draw (into), enter **2** (щёки) to sag, fall in **3** (infml, привы́кнуть) to get accustomed (to), used (to)

вуа́л|ь, и f. veil

вуз, а m. (abbr. of **вы́сшее уче́бное заведе́ние**) institution of higher education

вулка́н, а m. volcano

вульга́р|ный, ~ен, ~на adj. vulgar

вход, а m. **1** (де́йствие) entry **2** (ме́сто) entrance

вхо|ди́ть, жу́, ~дишь impf. of ▶ войти́

входн|о́й adj. of ▶ вход; **в. биле́т** entrance ticket; **~а́я пла́та** entrance fee

входя́щий pres. part. of ▶ входи́ть and adj. (по́чта, звоно́к) incoming

вцеп|и́ться, лю́сь, ~ишься impf. (of ▶ вцепля́ться) (в + a.) to seize hold of

вцепля́|ться, юсь impf. of ▶ вцепи́ться

вчера́ adv. yesterday

вчера́шн|ий adj. (дождь, суп) yesterday's; **в. день** yesterday; (fig.) yesterday, the past; **жить ~им днём** to live in the past

вче́тверо adv. four times

въезд, а m. **1** (де́йствие) entry; «**В. запрещён**» 'No entry' (official notice and road sign) **2** (ме́сто) entrance

въездн|о́й adj. of ▶ въезд; **~а́я ви́за** entry visa

въезжа́|ть, ю impf. of ▶ въе́хать

въе́|хать, ду, дешь pf. (of ▶ въезжа́ть) **1** (в + a.) to enter, ride in(to), drive in(to); (на + a.) (наве́рх) to ride up, drive up **2** (в дом) to move in **3** (sl.) to understand

вы, вас, вам, ва́ми, вас pers. pron. (pl. and formal or respectful mode of address to one person) you; **быть на в.** (с + i.) to be on formal terms (with)

вы... pref. indicating **1** motion outwards **2** action directed outwards **3** acquisition (as outcome of a series of actions) **4** completion of a process

выбега́|ть, ю impf. of ▶ вы́бежать

вы́бе|жать, гу, жишь, гут pf. (of ▶ выбега́ть) to run out

вы́бер|у, ешь see ▶ вы́брать

выбива́|ть, ю impf. of ▶ вы́бить

выбива́|ться, юсь impf. of ▶ вы́биться

выбира́|ть, ю impf. of ▶ вы́брать

выбира́|ться, юсь impf. of ▶ вы́браться

вы́|бить, ью, ьешь pf. (of ▶ выбива́ть) **1** (заста́вить вы́пасть) to knock out; (врага́) to drive out; to dislodge **2** (очи́стить) to beat (clean); **в. ковёр** to beat a carpet

вы́|биться, ьюсь, ьешься pf. (of ▶ выбива́ться) **в. в лю́ди** to make one's way in the world; **в. из сил** to wear oneself out; to be exhausted

вы́бор, а m. **1** choice; option **2** (ассортиме́нт) selection; assortment; **по своему́ ~у** of one's choice **3** (pl. only) (pol.) election(s); **дополни́тельные ~ы** by-election

вы́борк|а, и f. **1** (статисти́ческая) selection; sample **2** (usu. in pl.) (цита́та) excerpt

вы́борный adj. **1** (кампа́ния) election (attr.); **в. бюллете́нь** ballot paper **2** (о́рган, до́лжность) elective

вы́борочный adj. selective

вы́борщик, а m. (pol.) elector (in indirect elections); **колле́гия ~ов** electoral college

вы́бор|ы, ов see ▶ вы́бор 3

выбра́сыва|ть, ю impf. of ▶ вы́бросить

вы́|брать, еру, ерешь pf. (of ▶ выбира́ть) **1** to choose, select, pick out **2** (голосова́нием) to elect

вы́|браться, ерусь, ерешься pf. (of ▶ выбира́ться) **1** (из + g.) to get out (of) **2** (infml, найти́ возмо́жность) to (find time to) get to; **в. в о́перу** to manage to get to the opera

вы́брос, а m. discharge, emission; spillage; (in pl.) emissions

вы́бро|сить, шу, сишь pf. (of ▶ выбра́сывать) **1** (за преде́лы чего́-н., нару́жу) to throw out **2** (ста́рые ве́щи) to discard, throw away; (отхо́ды) to discharge

выбыва́|ть, ю impf. of ▶ вы́быть

вы́|быть, уду, удешь pf. (of ▶ выбыва́ть) (из + g.) (из го́рода) to leave; (из соревнова́ния) to be eliminated

выва́лива|ть, ю impf. of ▶ вы́валить

выва́лива|ться, юсь impf. of ▶ вы́валиться

вы́вал|ить, ю, ишь pf. (of ▶ выва́ливать) (из + g.) **1** to empty out (of) **2** (infml, толпа́) to pour out (of)

вы́вал|иться, юсь, ишься pf. (of ▶ выва́ливаться) (из + g.) to fall out (of), tumble out (of)

вывали́ва|ть, ю pf. of ▶ валя́ть 1

вы́веде|ни|е, я nt. **1** leading out, bringing out **2** (фо́рмулы) deduction, conclusion **3** (цыпля́т) hatching (out); (расте́ний) growing; (живо́тных) breeding, raising **4** (пя́тен) removal (of stains); (вреди́телей) extermination (of pests)

B

вы́вез|ти, у, ешь, past **~, ~ла** pf. (of ▶ вывози́ть) **1** (везя, удалить) to take out, remove; (везя, отправить) to take; (привезти с собой) to bring **2** (econ., за границу) to export

вы́вер|нуть, ну, нешь pf. (of ▶ вывора́чивать) **1** (винт) to unscrew; (пробку) to pull out **2** (infml, ногу) to twist, wrench **3** (карман) to turn (inside) out

вы́ве|сить, шу, сишь pf. (of ▶ выве́шивать) **1** (объявление) to put up; to post up **2** (бельё, флаг) to hang out

вы́веск|а, и f. **1** sign, signboard **2** (fig.) screen, pretext; **под ~ой** (+ g.) under the guise of

вы́ве|сти, ду, дешь, past **~л, ~ла** pf. (of ▶ выводи́ть) **1** to lead out, bring out; (войска) to withdraw; **в. кого́-н. в лю́ди** to help sb on in life; **в. кого́-н. из себя́** to drive sb out of his wits; **в. из стро́я** to disable, put out of action; (also fig.): **в. из терпе́ния** to exasperate **2** (исключить) to force out, expel **3** (пятна) to remove; (вредителей) to exterminate **4** (заключить) to deduce, conclude **5** (птенцов) to hatch (out); (растения) to grow; (животных) to breed, raise

вы́ве|стись, детя, дется, past **~лся, ~лась** pf. (of ▶ выводи́ться) (цыплята) to hatch out

выве́шива|ть, ю impf. of ▶ вы́весить

вы́вин|тить, чу, тишь pf. (of ▶ вывинчивать) to unscrew

выви́нчива|ть, ю impf. of ▶ вы́винтить

вы́вих, а m. dislocation

выви́хива|ть, ю impf. of ▶ вы́вихнуть

вы́вих|нуть, ну, нешь pf. (of ▶ выви́хивать) to dislocate, put out (of joint)

✍ **вы́вод, а** m. **1** (заключение) deduction, conclusion **2** (выведение) leading out, bringing out; **в. войск** withdrawal of troops; **в. да́нных** (comput.) output

выво|ди́ть, жу́, ~дит impf. of ▶ вы́вести

выво|ди́ться, ~дится impf. of ▶ вы́вести

выво|жу́[1], ~дишь see ▶ выводи́ть

выво|жу́[2], ~зишь see ▶ вывози́ть

вы́воз, а m. **1** (отправление) sending, dispatch **2** (экспорт) export

выво|зи́ть, жу́, ~зишь impf. of ▶ вы́везти

вывозн|о́й adj. (товар) exported; (attr.) export; **~а́я по́шлина** export duty

вывора́чива|ть, ю impf. of ▶ вы́вернуть

выгиба́|ть, ю impf. of ▶ вы́гнуть

выгиба́|ться, юсь impf. of ▶ вы́гнуться

выгла|дить, жу, дишь pf. of ▶ гла́дить 1

✍ **выгля|деть, жу, дишь** impf. (человек) to look (like); **он ~дит о́чень мо́лодо** he looks very young; **она́ пло́хо ~дит** she does not look well; (показания) to appear (to be)

выгля́дыва|ть, ю impf. of ▶ вы́глянуть

вы́гля|нуть, ну, нешь pf. (of ▶ выгля́дывать) **1** (из окна) to look out **2** (показаться) to

peep out, emerge

вы́г|нать, оню, онишь pf. (of ▶ выгоня́ть) **1** (удалить) to drive out; to expel; **в. с рабо́ты** (infml) to sack (BrE), fire (AmE) **2** (скот) to send out to pasture

вы́гнут|ый, ~, ~а adj. curved; convex

вы́гн|уть, у, ешь pf. (of ▶ выгиба́ть) to bend

вы́гн|уться, усь, ешься pf. (of ▶ выгиба́ться) to bend

выгова́рива|ть, ю impf. of ▶ вы́говорить

вы́говор, а m. **1** (произношение) accent; pronunciation **2** (порицание) reprimand; rebuke

вы́говор|ить, ю, ишь pf. (of ▶ выгова́ривать) to articulate, speak

вы́год|а, ы f. (польза) advantage, benefit; (прибыль) profit, gain

вы́годно adv. **1** advantageously **2** (as pred.) it is profitable, it pays

вы́год|ный, ~ен, ~на adj. (дающий пользу) advantageous, beneficial; (прибыльный) profitable

выгоня́|ть, ю impf. of ▶ вы́гнать

вы́гравир|овать, ую pf. of ▶ гравирова́ть

выгружа́|ть, ю impf. of ▶ вы́грузить

выгружа́|ться, юсь impf. of ▶ вы́грузиться

вы́гру|зить, жу, зишь pf. (of ▶ выгружа́ть) to unload

вы́гру|зиться, жусь, зишься pf. (of ▶ выгружа́ться) (люди) to disembark; (корабль) to unload

вы́грузк|а, и f. unloading; (людей) disembarkation

выгу́лива|ть, аю impf. of ▶ вы́гулять

выгуля́|ть, ю pf. (of ▶ выгу́ливать) to walk (a dog, etc.)

✍ **выда|ва́ть, ю́, ёшь** impf. of ▶ вы́дать

выда|ва́ться, ю́сь, ёшься impf. of ▶ вы́даться

вы́дав|ить, лю, ишь pf. (of ▶ выда́вливать) **1** (выжать) to press out, squeeze out (also fig.); **в. улы́бку** to force a smile **2** (выломать) to break, knock out

выда́влива|ть, ю impf. of ▶ вы́давить

вы́да|ть, м, шь, ст, дим, дите, дут pf. (of ▶ выдава́ть) **1** (дать) to give (out), issue; (изготовить) to produce; **в. зарпла́ту** to pay out wages; **в. про́пуск** to issue a pass; **в. кого́-н. за́муж (за** + a.) to give sb in marriage (to) **2** (предать) to give away, betray; (в чужую страну) to extradite **3** (за** + a.) to pass off (as), give out to be; **в. (себя́)** to pose (as)

вы́да|ться, мся, шься, стся, димся, дитесь, дутся pf. (of ▶ выдава́ться) **1** to protrude, project, jut out **2** (infml, случиться) to happen

вы́дач|а, и f. **1** (предоставление) giving, issuing; (изготовление) production **2** (преступника) extradition

выдаю́щийся pres. part. of ▶ выдава́ться and adj. prominent, salient; (fig., замечательный) outstanding, eminent; prominent

выдвига́|ть, ю *impf. of* ▸ вы́двинуть

выдвига́|ться, юсь *impf. of* ▸ вы́двинуться

вы́дви|нуть, ну, нешь *pf.* (*of* ▸ **выдвига́ть**) **1** (*стол, шкаф*) to move out, pull out; (*ящик*) to pull open **2** (fig., *предложить*) to put forward, advance; **в. обвине́ние** to bring an accusation **3** (*по рабо́те*) to promote **4** (*кандида́та*) to nominate, propose

вы́дви|нуться, нусь, нешься *pf.* (*of* ▸ **выдвига́ться**) **1** (*вперёд*) to move forward; (*нару́жу*) to move, move out; (*ящик*) to slide in and out **2** (*рабо́тник*) to rise, get on (in the world)

выделе́ни|е, я *nt.* **1** (*средств*) allocation, assignment **2** (physiol.) secretion; (*обрабо́танных веще́ств*) excretion

вы́дел|ить, ю, ишь *pf.* (*of* ▸ **выделя́ть**) **1** (*сре́дства*) to allocate, assign, earmark; (*вре́мя*) to allot **2** (*отобра́ть*) to pick out, single out; (mil.) to detach, detail; (comput.) to highlight; (typ.): **в. курси́вом** to italicize

вы́дел|иться, юсь, ишься *pf.* (*of* ▸ **выделя́ться**) **1** (*отдели́ться от це́лого*) to split off, separate **2** (+ *i.*) to stand out (on account of) **3** (*пот*) to ooze out, exude; (*газ*) to be emitted

вы́делк|а, и *f.* **1** (*ка́чество*) workmanship **2** (*ко́жи*) dressing, currying

☞ **выделя́|ть**, ю *impf. of* ▸ вы́делить

выделя́|ться, юсь *impf. of* ▸ вы́делиться

выдёргива|ть, ю *impf. of* ▸ вы́дернуть

вы́держа|нный, ~н, ~на *p.p.p. of* ▸ вы́держать *and* (~н, ~нна) *adj.* **1** (*после́довательный*) consistent **2** (*владе́ющий собо́й*) self-possessed; (*сто́йкий*) firm **3** (*сыр, вино́*) mature; (*де́рево*) seasoned

вы́держ|ать, у, ишь *pf.* (*of* ▸ **выде́рживать**) **1** (*под тя́жестью, давле́нием*) to bear, hold; (**э́тот**) лёд вас не ~ит the ice will not hold you **2** (fig., *вы́терпеть*) to bear, stand (up to) endure; **не в.** to give in, break down; **я не мог э́того бо́льше в.** I could not stand it no longer **3**: **в. не́сколько изда́ний** to run into several editions **4** (*сыр, вино́*) to mature; (*де́рево*) to season **5** (*соблюсти́*) to maintain, sustain; **в. па́узу** to pause

выде́ржива|ть, ю *impf. of* ▸ вы́держать

вы́держк|а¹, и *f.* **1** (*самооблада́ние*) self-possession; (*терпе́ние*) endurance **2** (phot.) exposure **3** (*ви́на, сы́ра*) maturation; **вино́ 8-ле́тней ~и** eight-year-old wine

вы́держк|а², и *f.* (*цита́та*) excerpt, quotation

вы́дер|нуть, ну, нешь *pf.* (*of* ▸ **выдёргивать**) to pull out

вы́дох, а *m.* exhalation

вы́дохн|уть, у, ешь *pf.* (*of* ▸ выдыха́ть) to breathe out

вы́дрессир|овать, ую *pf. of* ▸ дрессирова́ть

вы́думан|ный, ~, ~а *p.p.p. of* ▸ вы́думать *and* (~, ~на) *adj.* made-up, fabricated; ~ная исто́рия fabrication, fiction

вы́дум|ать, аю *pf.* (*of* ▸ **выду́мывать**) to invent; to make up, fabricate

вы́думк|а, и *f.* **1** invention **2** (*изобрета́тельность*) inventiveness **3** (*вы́мысел*) invention, fabrication (lie)

выду́мыва|ть, ю *impf. of* ▸ вы́думать

выдыха́|ть, ю *impf. of* ▸ вы́дохнуть

вы́еб|ать, у, ешь *pf. of* ▸ еба́ть

вы́езд, а *m.* **1** (*отъе́зд*) departure **2** (*ме́сто*) exit

выезжа́|ть, ю *impf. of* ▸ вы́ехать

вы́е|хать, ду, дешь *pf.* (*of* ▸ **выезжа́ть**) **1** (*уе́хать*) to depart, leave (in or on a vehicle or on an animal); (*из го́рода, из воро́т*) (*на маши́не*) to drive out; (*на ло́шади*) to ride out **2** (*из кварти́ры*) to leave, move (out)

вы́ж|ать, му, мешь *pf.* (*of* ▸ **выжима́ть**) (*бельё*) to wring (out); (*лимо́н*) to squeeze; (*сок*) to squeeze out; **как ~атый лимо́н** a has-been; **как ~атый лимо́н** absolutely exhausted; (fig., *извле́чь*) to wring (out), squeeze (out)

вы́жд|ать, у, ешь *pf.* (*of* ▸ **выжида́ть**) to wait (for); to bide one's time

вы́ж|ечь, гу, жешь *pf.* (*of* ▸ **выжига́ть**) **1** (*сжечь целико́м*) to burn down; to burn out; (*со́лнце*) to scorch **2** (*сде́лать знак*) to make a mark *etc.*, by burning; **в. клеймо́** (на + *p.*) to brand

выжива́ни|е, я *nt.* survival

выжива́|ть, ю *impf. of* ▸ вы́жить

выжига́|ть, ю *impf. of* ▸ вы́жечь

выжида́|ть, ю *impf. of* ▸ вы́ждать

выжима́|ть, ю *impf. of* ▸ вы́жать

вы́жи|ть, ву, вешь *pf.* (*of* ▸ **выжива́ть**) **1** (*оста́ться в живы́х*) to survive **2**: **в. из ума́** to lose possession of one's faculties

вы́з|вать, ову, овешь *pf.* (*of* ▸ **вызыва́ть**) **1** (*пригласи́ть*) to call (out); to send for; (*потре́бовать яви́ться*) to summon; **в. врача́** to send for a doctor **2** (*гнев, любопы́тство*) to provoke, arouse; (*пожа́р, боле́знь*) to cause; (*интере́с*) to stimulate; (*спор*) to provoke

выздора́влива|ть, ю *impf. of* ▸ вы́здороветь

вы́здорове|ть, ю, ешь *pf.* (▸ **выздора́вливать**) to recover, get better

выздоровле́ни|е, я *nt.* recovery; convalescence

вы́зов, а *m.* **1** (*приглаше́ние*) call **2** (*тре́бование яви́ться*) summons **3** (*предложе́ние вступи́ть в борьбу́*) challenge; **бро́сить в. кому́-н.** to throw down a challenge to sb

☞ **вызыва́|ть**, ю *impf. of* ▸ вы́звать

вызыва́ющий *pres. part. act. of* ▸ вызыва́ть *and adj.* defiant; provocative

выи́гр|ать, аю *pf.* (*of* ▸ **выи́грывать**) (*войну́, па́ртию; мно́го де́нег*) to win; (*получи́ть по́льзу*) to gain; **в. вре́мя** to gain time

выи́грыва|ть, ю *impf. of* ▸ вы́играть

вы́игрыш, а *m.* **1** (*побе́да*) win; winning **2** (*де́ньги*) winnings; (*пре́мия*) prize; (*вы́года*) gain; **быть в ~е** (*в игре́*) to be the winner; (fig.) to stand to gain

вы́игрышный adj. **1** winning; **в. ход** winning move **2** (выгодный) advantageous

ꙮ **вы́|йти, йду, йдешь,** past ~шел, ~шла pf. (of ▶ **выходи́ть 1**) **1** to go out; to come out; **она́** ~шла из ко́мнаты she went out of/ left the room; **в. в отста́вку** to retire; **в. в фина́л** (sport) to reach the final; **в. из грани́ц/ преде́лов** (+ g.) (fig.) to exceed the bounds (of); **в. из себя́** to lose one's temper; **в. из систе́мы** (comput.) to log off; **в. из терпе́ния** to lose patience; **в. на прогу́лку** to go out for a walk **2**: **в. (в свет)** (быть изданным) to come out, appear **3**: **в. (за́муж)** (за + a.) (о женщине) to marry **4** (получаться) to come (out); to turn out (also impers.); to ensue; (произойти) to happen, occur; **в. победи́телем** to come out victor; **из э́того ничего́ не** ~йдет nothing will come of it; ~шло, что он винова́т it turned out that he was to blame **5** (быть родом) to be by origin; **она́** ~шла из крестья́н she is of peasant stock **6** (израсходоваться) to be used up; (о сроке) to have expired; **срок уже́** ~шел time is up

выка́лыва|ть, ю impf. of ▶ **вы́колоть**

выка́пыва|ть, ю impf. of ▶ **вы́копать**

выки́дыва|ть, ю impf. of ▶ **вы́кинуть**

вы́кидыш, а m. (med.) miscarriage

вы́ки|нуть, ну, нешь pf. (of ▶ **выки́дывать**) **1** (выбросить) to throw out **2** (вывесить) to put out; **в. флаг** to hoist a flag **3** (infml, pej.): **в. фо́кус** to play a trick

выкипа́|ть, ет impf. of ▶ **вы́кипеть**

вы́кип|еть, ит pf. (of ▶ **выкипа́ть**) to boil away

выкла́дыва|ть, ю impf. of ▶ **вы́ложить**

выключа́тел|ь, я m. switch

выключа́|ть, ю impf. of ▶ **вы́ключить**

выключа́|ться, юсь impf. of ▶ **вы́ключиться**

вы́ключ|ить, у, ишь pf. (of ▶ **выключа́ть**) **1** (свет, радио) to turn off, switch off **2** (исключить) to remove, exclude

вы́ключ|иться, усь, ишься pf. (of ▶ **выключа́ться**) **1** (о свете) to go off **2** (о человеке) to switch off

вы́к|овать, ую, уешь pf. of ▶ **кова́ть 1**

вы́кол|оть, ю, ешь pf. (of ▶ **выка́лывать**) to poke out

вы́копа|ть, ю pf. (of ▶ **выка́пывать**, ▶ **копа́ть 2**) (яму) to dig; (картофель) to dig up; (труп) to exhume

выкра́ива|ть, ю impf. of ▶ **вы́кроить**

вы́кра|сить, шу, сишь pf. (of ▶ **выкра́шивать**) (стену) to paint; (ткань, волосы) to dye

выкра́шива|ть, ю impf. of ▶ **вы́красить**

вы́кро|ить, ю, ишь pf. (of ▶ **выкра́ивать**) **1** (вырезать) to cut out **2** (fig., уделить) to find; **в. вре́мя** to find time

вы́кройк|а, и f. pattern

вы́кру|тить, чу, тишь pf. (of ▶ **выкру́чивать**) **1** (лампочку, винт) to unscrew **2** (руку) to

twist, wrench

вы́кру|титься, чусь, тишься pf. (of ▶ **выкру́чиваться**) **1** (винт) to come unscrewed **2** (fig., infml, выпутаться) to extricate oneself, get oneself out (of)

выкру́чива|ть, ю impf. of ▶ **вы́крутить**

выкру́чива|ться, юсь impf. of ▶ **вы́крутиться**

вы́куп, а m. **1** (law) redemption **2** (плата) ransom

выкупа́|ть, ю pf. of ▶ **купа́ть**

выкуп|а́ть, а́ю impf. of ▶ **вы́купить**

выкупа́|ться, юсь pf. of ▶ **купа́ться**

вы́куп|ить, лю, ишь pf. (of ▶ **выкупа́ть**) **1** (заложника) to ransom **2** (вещи) to redeem

вы́лазк|а, и f. (mil.) sortie (also fig.)

выла́мыва|ть, ю impf. of ▶ **вы́ломать**

вылеза́|ть, ю impf. of ▶ **вы́лезти**

вы́лез|ти, у, ешь, past ~, ~ла pf. (of ▶ **вылеза́ть**) **1** (ползком) to crawl out; (карабкаясь) to climb out; (infml, выйти) to get out, alight **2** (infml, выпасть) to fall out, come out

вы́лет, а m. (самолёта) take-off; **зал** ~а departure lounge

вылета́|ть, ю impf. of ▶ **вы́лететь**

вы́ле|теть, чу, тишь pf. (of ▶ **вылета́ть**) (птица) to fly out; (самолёт) to take off; (fig., infml) to rush out; **в. из головы́** to slip one's mind

вылле́чива|ть, ю impf. of ▶ **вы́лечить**

выле́чива|ться, юсь impf. of ▶ **вы́лечиться**

вы́леч|ить, у, ишь pf. (of ▶ **выле́чивать**) (от + g.) to cure (of) (also fig.)

вы́леч|иться, усь, ишься pf. (of ▶ **выле́чиваться**) (от + g.) to be cured (of); to get over (also fig.)

вы́леч|у[1], ишь see ▶ **вы́лечить**

вы́ле|чу[2], тишь see ▶ **вы́лететь**

вылива́|ть, ю, ет impf. of ▶ **вы́лить**

вылива́|ться, ется impf. of ▶ **вы́литься**

вы́л|ить, ью, ешь pf. (of ▶ **вылива́ть**) to pour out; (ведро) to empty (out)

вы́л|иться, ьется pf. (of ▶ **вылива́ться**) (жидкость) to run out, flow out; (fig.) to flow (from), spring (from)

вы́лож|ить, у, ишь pf. (of ▶ **выкла́дывать**) **1** (товар, вещи) to lay out, spread out; (fig., infml, сказать) to tell; to reveal **2** (+ i.) (покрыть) to cover, lay (with); **в. дёрном** to turf; **в. ка́мнем** to face with masonry

вы́лома|ть, ю pf. (of ▶ **выла́мывать**) (замок) to break open; (дверь) to break down

вылуп|и́ться, ится pf. (of ▶ **вылупля́ться**) to hatch (out)

вылупля́|ться, ется impf. of ▶ **вы́лупиться**

вы́л|ью, ьешь see ▶ **вы́лить**

выма́нива|ть, ю impf. of ▶ **вы́манить**

вы́ман|ить, ю, ишь pf. (of ▶ **выма́нивать**) **1** (что-н. у кого-н.) (получить обманом) to cheat sb out of sth; (получить лестью) to wheedle (out of) **2** (из + *g.*) to lure (out of, from)

вы́м|ереть, рет, рут, *past* ~ер, ~ерла *pf.* (*of* ▶ **вымира́ть**) **1** (*исчезнуть*) to die out, become extinct **2** (*опустеть*) to become desolate, deserted

вы́мерший *p.p. act. of* ▶ **вы́мереть** *and adj.* extinct

вымира́ни|е, я *nt.* dying out, extinction

вымира́|ть, ю *impf. of* ▶ **вы́мереть**

вымога́тел|ь, я *m.* extortionist

вымога́тельств|о, а *nt.* extortion

вымога́|ть, ю *impf.* to extort; **в. де́ньги у кого́-н.** to extort money from sb

вымока́|ть, ю *impf. of* ▶ **вы́мокнуть**

вы́мок|нуть, ну, нешь, *past* ~, ~ла *pf.* (*of* ▶ **вымока́ть**) to be drenched, be soaked; **мы ~ли до ни́тки** we are soaked to the skin

вы́м|ою, оешь *see* ▶ **вы́мыть**

вы́мпел, а *m.* pennant

вы́мр|ет, ут *see* ▶ **вы́мереть**

вымыва́|ть, ю *impf. of* ▶ **вы́мыть**

вы́мыс|ел, ла *m.* **1** (*ложь*) invention, fabrication **2** (*фантазия*) fantasy

вы́м|ыть, ою, оешь *pf.* (*of* ▶ **мыть**, ▶ **вымыва́ть**) **1** (*сделать чистым*) to wash; **в. посу́ду** to wash up **2** (*размыть*) to wash away

вы́м|ыться, оюсь, оешься *pf.* (*of* ▶ **мы́ться**) to wash oneself

вы́мышлен|ный, ~, ~а *adj.* fictitious, imaginary, invented

вына́шива|ть, ю *impf. of* ▶ **вы́носить**

вынесе́ни|е, я *nt.* **1** (*решения*) taking **2** (*благодарности*) giving, expressing **3** (*на рассмотрение*) submitting **4** (*приговора*) pronouncement

вы́нес|ти, у, ешь, *past* ~, ~ла *pf.* (*of* ▶ **выноси́ть** 1) **1** (*удалить за пределы*) to carry out, take out; (*to take away*; (*убрать*) to carry away; (*доставить*) to bring; **в. на бе́рег** to wash ashore **2** (fig., *получить*) to take away, receive, derive; **в. прия́тное впечатле́ние** to be favourably impressed **3**: **в. вопро́с (на собра́ние, на обсужде́ние)** to put, submit a question (on a meeting, for discussion) **4** (*вытерпеть*) to bear, stand, endure; **в. на свои́х плеча́х** (fig.) to shoulder, take the full weight (of), bear the full brunt (of) **5**: **в. благода́рность** to express gratitude; **в. пригово́р** (+ *d.*) to pass sentence (on), pronounce sentence (on); **в. реше́ние** to decide; (law) to pronounce judgement

вынима́|ть, ю *impf. of* ▶ **вы́нуть**

вы́нос, а *m.* (*покойника*) bearing-out; **на в.** (*о еде*) to take away (BrE), to take out (AmE)

вы́но|сить, шу, сишь *pf.* (*of* ▶ **вына́шивать**) (*ребёнка*) to bear, bring forth (*a child at full term*); (*план, мысль*) to nurture

выно|си́ть, шу, ~сишь *impf. of* ▶ **вы́нести 1** (*impf. only*) (+ *neg.*) to be unable to bear/stand; **я его́ не ~шу́** I can't

stand him

выно́сливост|ь, и *f.* (power of) endurance; staying power

выно́слив|ый, ~, ~а *adj.* (*человек, растение*) hardy

вы́но|шу, сишь *see* ▶ **выноси́ть**

вы́но|шу, ~сишь *see* ▶ **выноси́ть**

вы́ну|дить, жу, дишь *pf.* (*of* ▶ **вынужда́ть**) (+ *inf.*) to force, compel

вынужда́|ть, ю *impf. of* ▶ **вы́нудить**

вы́нужден|ный, ~, ~а *p.p.p. of* ▶ **вы́нудить** *and* (~, ~на) *adj.* forced; ~ная поса́дка (aeron.) forced landing

вы́н|уть, у, ешь *pf.* (*of* ▶ **вынима́ть**) to take out; to pull out, extract

вы́пад, а *m.* (*враждебное выступление*) attack

выпада́|ть, ю *impf. of* ▶ **вы́пасть**

вы́па|сть, ду, дешь, *past* ~л *pf.* (*of* ▶ **выпада́ть**) **1** (*упасть наружу*) to fall out **2** (*дождь, снег*) to fall **3** (+ *d.*) (*задача*) to befall, fall (to); **мне ~ло сча́стье** (+ *inf.*) I had the luck (to) **4** (*случиться*) to occur, turn out; **ночь ~ла звёздная** it turned out a starry night

вы́пек *see* ▶ **вы́печь**

выпека́|ть, ю *impf. of* ▶ **вы́печь**

вы́печк|а, и *f.* baking

вы́пе|чь, ку, чешь, кут, *past* ~к, ~кла *pf.* (*of* ▶ **выпека́ть**) to bake

выпива́|ть, ю *impf.* **1** *impf. of* ▶ **вы́пить** **2** (*impf. only*) (infml) to be fond of the bottle

вы́пивк|а, и *f.* (infml, collect.) drinks

вы́пи|сать, шу, шешь *pf.* (*of* ▶ **выпи́сывать**) **1** (*переписать*) to copy out; to excerpt **2** (*документ*) to write out; **в. квита́нцию** to write out a receipt **3** (*сделать заказ*) to send for (*in writing*) **4** (*из больницы*) to discharge **5** (*газету, журнал*) to subscribe to

вы́пи|саться, шусь, шешься *pf.* (*of* ▶ **выпи́сываться**) (*из больницы*) to be discharged; **он уже́ ~сался из больни́цы** he is already out of hospital; (*из квартиры*) to officially change one's place of residence

вы́писк|а, и *f.* **1** (*списывание*) copying, excerpting **2** (*цитата*) extract, excerpt **3** (*книг, газет*) subscription **4** (*из больницы*) discharge

выпи́сыва|ть, ю *impf. of* ▶ **вы́писать**

выпи́сыва|ться, юсь *impf. of* ▶ **вы́писаться**

вы́п|ить, ью, ьешь *pf.* (*of* ▶ **выпива́ть 1**, ▶ **пить**) to drink

вы́пи|шу, шешь *see* ▶ **вы́писать**

✎ **вы́плат|а, ы** *f.* payment

вы́пла|тить, чу, тишь *pf.* (*of* ▶ **выпла́чивать**) **1** to pay (out) **2** (*долг*) to pay off

выпла́чива|ть, ю *impf. of* ▶ **вы́платить**

вы́пла|чу, тишь *see* ▶ **вы́платить**

выплёвыва|ть, ю *impf. of* ▶ **вы́плюнуть**

выплёскива|ть, ю *impf. of* ▶ **вы́плеснуть**

вы́плес|нуть, ну, нешь *pf.* (*of* ▶ **выплёскивать**) to pour out

B

вы́плюн|уть, у, ешь pf. (of ▶ выплёвывать) to spit out

выполза́|ть, ю impf. of ▶ вы́ползти

вы́ползти, у, ешь, past ~, ~ла pf. (of ▶ выполза́ть) (из + g.) to crawl out, creep out (from); (змея) to slither out

♂ **выполне́ни|е, я** nt. (работы, приказа) execution, carrying-out; (желания) fulfilment (BrE), fulfillment (AmE)

выполни́м|ый, ~, ~a adj. practicable, feasible

вы́полн|ить, ю, ишь pf. (of ▶ выполня́ть) (приказание, работу) to carry out; (обязанность, желание, план) to fulfil (BrE), fulfill (AmE); (рисунок) to execute

♂ **выполня́|ть, ю** impf. of ▶ вы́полнить

вы́прав|ить, лю, ишь pf. (of ▶ выправля́ть) **1** (сделать прямым) to straighten (out) **2** (исправить) to correct; (улучшить) to improve

вы́прав|иться, люсь, ишься pf. (of ▶ выправля́ться) **1** (выпрямиться) to become straight **2** (стать лучше) to improve

выправля́|ть, ю impf. of ▶ вы́править

выправля́|ться, юсь impf. of ▶ вы́правиться

выпра́шива|ть, ю impf. **1** impf. of ▶ вы́просить **2** (impf. only) to try to get, beg for

вы́про|сить, шу, сишь pf. (of ▶ выпра́шивать **1**) (у + g.) to get (out of sb), obtain, elicit (by begging sb)

вы́про|шу, сишь see ▶ вы́просить

выпры́гива|ть, ю impf. of ▶ вы́прыгнуть

вы́прыг|нуть, ну, нешь pf. (of ▶ выпры́гивать) to jump out, spring out

вы́прям|ить, лю, ишь pf. (of ▶ выпрямля́ть) to straighten (out)

вы́прям|иться, люсь, ишься pf. (of ▶ выпрямля́ться) to become straight; **в. во весь рост** to draw oneself up to one's full height

выпрямля́|ть, ю impf. of ▶ вы́прямить

выпрямля́|ться, юсь impf. of ▶ вы́прямиться

вы́пуклост|ь, и f. (неровность) protuberance; bulge

вы́пукл|ый, ~, ~a adj. (неровный) protuberant; prominent, bulging

♂ **вы́пуск, a** m. **1** (товаров) output; (денег, акций) issue; **в. новостей** newscast; **срочный в. новостей** newsflash **2** (романа) part, instalment (BrE), installment (AmE) **3** (в школе, институте) leavers; graduates

♂ **выпуска́|ть, ю** impf. of ▶ вы́пустить

выпускни́к, á m. **1** (окончивший учебное заведение) graduate; **бы́вший в.** old boy **2** (на последнем курсе) final-year student

выпускни́|ца, цы f. of ▶ выпускни́к

выпускн|о́й adj. **1** of ▶ вы́пуск; **в. экза́мен** final examination, finals **2** (as m. n. **в.,**
~о́го) school leaving party, prom (AmE)

вы́пу|стить, щу, стишь pf. (of ▶ выпуска́ть) **1** (дать выйти) to let out; (заключённого, фильм) to release; (из учебного заведения) to turn out; **в. из рук** to let go of; **в. из тюрьмы́** to release from prison **2** (деньги, акции) to issue; (продукцию) to turn out, produce; **в. в прода́жу** to put on the market; **в. (в свет)** to publish

вы́пя|тить, чу, тишь pf. (of ▶ выпя́чивать) (infml) to stick out; **в. грудь** to stick out one's chest

выпя́чива|ть, ю impf. of ▶ вы́пятить

выраба́тыва|ть, ю impf. of ▶ вы́работать

вы́работа|ть, ю pf. (of ▶ выраба́тывать) **1** (произвести) to manufacture; to produce, make **2** (план) to work out, draw up; (привычку) to develop

вы́работк|а, и f. (производство) manufacture; production, making

выра́внива|ть, ю impf. of ▶ вы́ровнять

выра́внива|ться, юсь impf. of ▶ вы́ровняться

♂ **выража́|ть, ю** impf. of ▶ вы́разить

выража́|ться, юсь impf. of ▶ вы́разиться); **мя́гко ~ясь** to put it mildly

♂ **выраже́ни|е, я** nt. expression

вы́ражен|ный, ~, ~a p.p.p. of ▶ вы́разить and (~, ~на) adj. pronounced, marked

вырази́тел|ьный, ~ен, ~ьна adj. expressive

вы́ра|зить, жу, зишь pf. (of ▶ выража́ть) to express

вы́ра|зиться, жусь, зишься pf. (of ▶ выража́ться) **1** (сказать словами) to express oneself **2** (обнаружиться) (в + p.) to manifest itself (in) **3** (произносить неприличные слова) to swear, use swear words

выраста́|ть, ю impf. of ▶ вы́расти

♂ **вы́р|асти, асту, астешь,** past ~ос, ~осла pf. (of ▶ выраста́ть, ▶ расти́) **1** to grow (up) **2** (в + a. or i.) (стать) to grow (into), develop (into), become **3** (из + g.) to grow (out of) (clothing) **4** (увеличиться) to increase **5** (появиться) to appear, rise up

вы́ра|стить, щу, стишь pf. (of ▶ выра́щивать) (детей) to bring up; (животных) to rear, breed; (растения) to grow, cultivate

выра́щива|ть, ю impf. of ▶ вы́растить

вы́рв|ать¹, у, ешь pf. (of ▶ вырыва́ть¹) **1** to pull out, tear out; **в. зуб** to pull out a tooth; (отнять) to snatch **2** (fig., добиться) to extort, wring; **в. призна́ние у кого́-н.** to wring a confession out of sb

вы́рв|ать², у, ешь pf. of ▶ рвать²

вы́рв|аться, усь, ешься pf. (of ▶ вырыва́ться) **1** (из + g.) (освободиться) to tear oneself away (from); to break out (from), break loose (from), break free (from); **в. из чьих-н. объя́тий** to tear oneself away from sb's embrace; (уехать) to get away (from) **2** (стон, замечание) to burst (from), escape **3** (3rd pers. only)

♂ key word

(*стремительно устремиться наружу*) to
shoot up, shoot out

вы́рез, а *m.* (*выемка*) cut; notch; (*в одежде*)
neck; **пла́тье с больши́м ~ом** low-necked
dress

вы́ре|зать, жу, жешь *pf.* (*of* ▸ **выреза́ть**)
1 (*опухоль; заметку из газеты*) to cut out;
(comput.) to cut **2** (*из дерева*) to cut, carve;
(*на металле, на камне*) to engrave **3** (fig.,
infml, *убить*) to slaughter, butcher

выреза́|ть, ю *impf. of* ▸ **вы́резать**

вы́резк|а, и *f.* **1**: **газе́тная в.** press cutting
2 (*говяжья*) sirloin steak; (*свиная, баранья
и т. д.*) fillet steak

вы́рис|ова́ться, уется *pf.* (*of*
▸ **вырисо́вываться**) to appear (in outline);
to stand out; (fig., *ситуация*) to emerge

вырисо́выва|ться, ется *impf. of*
▸ **вы́рисоваться**

вы́ровня|ть, ю *pf.* (*of* ▸ **выра́внивать**)
1 (*шероховатое*) to smooth (out), level;
(*шаг, дыхание*) to regulate **2** (*по прямой
линии*) to align

вы́ровня|ться, юсь *pf.* (*of* ▸ **выра́вниваться**)
to become level; to become even

вы́род|иться, ится *pf.* (*of* ▸ **вырожда́ться**)
to degenerate

вырожда́|ться, ется *impf. of* ▸ **вы́родиться**

вырожде́ни|е, я *nt.* degeneration

вы́рон|ить, ю, ишь *pf.* to drop

вы́р|ою, оешь *see* ▸ **вы́рыть**

вы́рубк|а, и *f.* **1** cutting down, felling; **в. ле́са**
(*or* ле́со́в) deforestation **2** (*вырубленное
место*) clearing

вы́руга|ть, ю *pf. of* ▸ **руга́ть 1**

вы́руга|ться, юсь *pf. of* ▸ **руга́ться**

выруча́|ть, ю *impf. of* ▸ **вы́ручить**

вы́руч|ить, у, ишь *pf.* (*of* ▸ **выруча́ть**)
(*помочь*) to help out; to come to the help,
aid (of)

вы́ручк|а, и *f.* **1** help, assistance; **прийти́
на ~у** to come to the rescue **2** (*деньги*)
takings; earnings

вырыва́|ть¹, ю *impf. of* ▸ **вы́рвать¹**

вырыва́|ть², ю *impf. of* ▸ **вы́рвать**

вырыва́|ться, юсь *impf. of* ▸ **вы́рваться**

вы́р|ыть, ою, оешь *pf.* (*of* ▸ **вырыва́ть²**)
(*землю, яму*) to dig; (*предмет*) to dig up,
dig out

вы́са|дить, жу, дишь *pf.* (*of* ▸ **выса́живать**)
1 (*пассажира*) to drop off, set down; **в. на
бе́рег** to put ashore; (*заставить выйти*) to
throw off, out **2** (*растение*) to plant out

вы́са|диться, жусь, дишься *pf.* (*of*
▸ **выса́живаться**) (*из, с* + *g.*) to alight
(from), get off; (*с судна, самолёта*) to
disembark

вы́садк|а, и *f.* **1** (*с судна*) debarkation,
disembarkation; (*из автобуса*) alighting,
getting off **2** (*растения*) planting out

выса́жива|ть, ю *impf. of* ▸ **вы́садить**

выса́жива|ться, юсь *impf. of* ▸ **вы́садиться**

вы́са|жу, дишь *see* ▸ **вы́садить**

вы́свобо|дить, жу, дишь *pf.* (*of*
▸ **высвобожда́ть**) **1** (*вынуть, освободить*)
to free **2** (*средства, рабочих*) to free up,
release

высвобожда́|ть, ю *impf. of* ▸ **вы́свободить**

выселе́ни|е, я *nt.* eviction

вы́сел|ить, ю, ишь *pf.* (*of* ▸ **выселя́ть**)
1 (*из квартиры*) to evict **2** (*переселить*)
to evacuate, move

вы́сел|иться, юсь, ишься *pf.* (*of*
▸ **выселя́ться**) to move

выселя́|ть, ю *impf. of* ▸ **вы́селить**

выселя́|ться, юсь *impf. of* ▸ **вы́селиться**

вы́с|иться, ится *impf.* to tower (up), rise

вы́ска|зать, жу, жешь *pf.* (*of* ▸ **выска́зывать**)
to express; to state; **в. предположе́ние** to come
out with a suggestion

вы́ска|заться, жусь, жешься *pf.* (*of*
▸ **выска́зываться**) **1** to speak out; to speak
one's mind; to have one's say **2** (*за* + *a.* or
про́тив + *g.*) to speak (for *or* against)

выска́зывани|е, я *nt.* (*суждение*)
pronouncement; (*мнение*) opinion

выска́зыва|ть, ю *impf. of* ▸ **вы́сказать**

выска́зыва|ться, юсь *impf. of* ▸ **вы́сказаться**

выска́кива|ть, ю *impf. of* ▸ **вы́скочить**

выска́льзыва|ть, ю *impf. of* ▸ **вы́скользнуть**

вы́скользн|уть, у, ешь *pf.* (*of*
▸ **выска́льзывать**) to slip out (also fig.)

вы́скоч|ить, у, ишь *pf.* (*of* ▸ **выска́кивать**)
(*выпрыгнуть*) to jump out; to leap out,
spring out; (*выбежать*) to run out

вы́слать, шлю, шлешь *pf.* (*of* ▸ **высыла́ть**)
1 (*посылку, помощь*) to send, send out,
dispatch **2** (pol.) to exile; (*иностранца*) to
deport

вы́сле|дить, жу, дишь *pf.* (*of*
▸ **выслеживать 1**) to trace; to track down

выслеживать|ть, ю **1** *impf. of*
▸ **вы́следить 2** (*impf. only*) to be on the
track of; to shadow

вы́сле|жу, дишь *see* ▸ **вы́следить**

выслуша|ть, ю *pf.* (*of* ▸ **выслу́шивать**) to
hear out

выслу́шива|ть, ю *impf. of* ▸ **вы́слушать**

высма́трива|ть, ю *impf. of* ▸ **вы́смотреть**

высме́ива|ть, ю *impf. of* ▸ **вы́смеять**

вы́сме|ять, ю, ешь *pf.* (*of* ▸ **высме́ивать**)
to ridicule

вы́сморка|ть, ю *pf. of* ▸ **сморка́ть**

вы́сморка|ться, юсь *pf. of* ▸ **сморка́ться**

вы́смотр|еть, ю, ишь *pf.* (*of* ▸ **высма́тривать**)
(*найти*) to spy out; to locate (*by eye*)

высо́выва|ть, ю *impf. of* ▸ **вы́сунуть**

высо́выва|ться, юсь *impf. of* ▸ **вы́сунуться**

◦ **высо́к|ий, ~, ~а́** *adj.* (*дом, гора; цена,
температура; качество, мнение*) high;
(*человек*) tall; (*мысль, стиль*) lofty; (*гость*)
distinguished; (*честь*) great; **в ~ой сте́пени**
highly

высоко́ *adv.* **1** (*располагаться*) high (up)
2 (*as pred.*) it is high (up); it is a long way

B

up; **окно было в. от земли** the window was high up off the ground **3**: **оценить в.** to value highly

высоко... *comb. form* high-, highly-

высокогорный *adj.* alpine, mountain

высококачественный *adj.* high-quality

высококвалифицированный *adj.* highly qualified

высокомери|е, я *nt.* haughtiness, arrogance

высокомер|ный, ~ен, ~на *adj.* haughty, arrogant

высокооплачиваемый *adj.* highly-paid

высокопоставленный *adj.* high-ranking

⚬ **высот|а́, ы́,** *pl.* **~ы, ~** *f.* **1** (*здания, столба*) height; (*над земной поверхностью*) altitude; (*температуры, давления*) level; (*mus.*) pitch; **набрать ~у** (aeron.) to gain altitude **2** (*возвышенность*) height; **командные ~ы** commanding heights (also fig.) **3** (*искусства, мастерства*) high level; **достигнуть новых высот** to reach new heights **4** (fig.): **оказаться на ~é положения** to rise to the occasion

высотк|а, и *f.* (infml) tower block

высотн|ый *adj.* **1** high-altitude **2**: **~ое здание** high-rise building, tower block

высох|нуть, ну, нешь, *past* **~, ~ла** *pf.* (*of* ▶ **высыхать**) **1** (*бельё*) to dry (out); (*река*) to dry up **2** (*растение*) to wither, fade; (fig., *исхудать*) to waste away, fade away

высохший *p.p. act. of* ▶ **высохнуть** *and adj.* dried-up; shrivelled; wizened

Высочеств|о, а *nt.*: (**Ваше**) **В.** (Your) Highness

высп|аться, люсь, ишься *pf.* (*of* ▶ **высыпаться²**) to have a good sleep

выстав|ить, лю, ишь *pf.* (*of* ▶ **выставлять**) **1** (*поставить наружу*) to put out, move out; (*картины, товары*) to exhibit, display; **в. на продажу** to put on sale; **в. напоказ** to show off, parade **2** (*часовых*) to post **3** (+ *i.*) (*представить*) to represent (as), make out (as); **в. в плохом свете** to represent in an unfavourable light; **его ~или трусом** he was made out to be a coward **4** (*предложить*) to put forward; **в. свою кандидатуру** to come forward as a candidate

выстав|иться, люсь, ишься *pf.* (*of* ▶ **выставляться**) (*о художнике*) to exhibit

⚬ **выставк|а, и** *f.* exhibition, show

выставля́|ть, ю *impf. of* ▶ **выставить**

выставля́|ться, юсь *impf. of* ▶ **выставиться**

выставочный *adj. of* ▶ **выставка**

выста́ива|ть, ю, ешь *impf. of* ▶ **выстоять 1**

выст|елю, елешь *see* ▶ **выстлать**

выстила́|ть, ю *impf. of* ▶ **выстлать**

выстира́|ть, ю *pf. of* ▶ **стирать²**

выст|лать, елю, елешь *pf.* (*покрыть*) to cover; (*вымостить*) to pave

высто́|ять, ю, ишь *pf.* (*of* ▶ **выстаивать**) **1** (*долго простоять*) to stand **2** (*pf. only*)

(*не сдаться*) to stand one's ground

выстрада|ть, ю *pf.* **1** (*пережить много страданий*) to suffer; to go through **2** (*достигнуть страданиями*) to gain, achieve through suffering

выстраива|ть, ю *impf. of* ▶ **выстроить**

выстраива|ться, юсь *impf. of* ▶ **выстроиться**

выстрел, а *m.* shot; **произвести в.** to fire a shot; **раздался в.** a shot rang out

выстрел|ить, ю, ишь *pf.* to shoot, fire; **я ~ил в него три раза** I fired three shots at him

выстро|ить, ю, ишь *pf.* (*of* ▶ **выстраивать**) **1** to build **2** (mil.) to draw up, form up

выстро|иться, юсь, ишься *pf.* (*of* ▶ **выстраиваться**) **1** (mil.) to form up **2** (*стоять рядами*) to stand in rows

выступ, а *m.* projection, ledge

⚬ **выступа́|ть, ю** *impf.* **1** *impf. of* ▶ **выступить** **2** (*impf. only*) to project, jut out, stick out

⚬ **выступ|ить, лю, ишь** *pf.* (*of* ▶ **выступать 1**) **1** (*выйти вперёд*) to come forward; to come out **2** (*публично*) to appear (*publicly*); **в. за** + *a.* to come out in favour of; **в. против** + *g.* to come out against; **в. в печати** to appear in print; **в. с речью** to make a speech; **в. по телевидению** to appear on television

⚬ **выступлени|е, я** *nt.* (*публичное*) appearance; (*речь*) speech; (*актёра*) performance

высун|уть, у, ешь *pf.* (*of* ▶ **высовывать**) to put out, thrust out, stick out; **в. язык** to put/stick one's tongue out

высун|уться, усь, ешься *pf.* (*of* ▶ **высовываться**) **1** (*о человеке*) to show oneself, thrust oneself forward; **в. из окна** to lean out of the window **2** (*о ноге, руке*) to stick out

высушива|ть, ю *impf. of* ▶ **высушить**

высуш|ить, у, ишь *pf. of* ▶ **сушить**

высуш|иться, усь, ишься *pf. of* ▶ **сушиться**

высчита|ть, ю *pf.* (*of* ▶ **высчитывать**) to calculate

высчитыва|ть, ю *impf. of* ▶ **высчитать**

высш|ий *adj.* (*comp. and superl. of* ▶ **высокий**) (*самый высокий*) highest; (*самый главный*) supreme; (*более высокий*) higher; **~шего качества** of the highest quality; **~шая мера наказания** capital punishment; **~шее образование** higher education; **~шее учебное заведение** *see* ▶ **вуз**; **в ~шей степени** in the highest degree

высыла́|ть, ю *impf. of* ▶ **выслать**

высып|ать, лю, лешь *pf.* (*of* ▶ **высыпать**) **1** to pour out (*trans.*); (*нечаянно*) to spill **2** (infml) to pour out (*intrans.*)

высыпа́|ть, ю *impf. of* ▶ **высыпать**

высып|аться, лется, лются *pf.* (*of* ▶ **высыпаться¹**) to pour out (*intrans.*); (*нечаянно*) to spill (*intrans.*)

высыпа́|ться¹, ется *impf. of* ▶ **высыпаться**

высыпа́|ться², юсь *impf. of* ▶ **выспаться**

высыха́|ть, ю *impf. of* ▶ **высохнуть**

⚬ key word

вытáлкива|ть, ю *impf. of* ▸ **вы́толкнуть**

вытáскива|ть, ю *impf. of* ▸ **вы́тащить**

вытáщ|ить, у, ишь *pf.* (*of* ▸ **вытáскивать**) (*из кармана, из сумки*) to pull out, extract

вытекá|ть, ю *impf.* **1** *impf. of* ▸ **вы́течь** **2** (*impf. only*) (*река*) to flow (from, out of) **3** (*impf. only*) (fig., *вывод*) to result, follow (from)

вы́текут *see* ▸ **вы́течь**

вы́т|ереть, ру, решь, *past* ~**ер,** ~**ерла** *pf.* (*of* ▸ **вытирáть**) (*руки, глаза, посуду, стол*) to wipe; (*грязь*) to wipe up; **в. пыль** to dust

вы́терп|еть, лю, ишь *pf.* to bear, endure

вытеснéни|е, я *nt.* ousting; (*замена собой*) displacing, supplanting

вы́тесн|ить, ю, ишь *pf.* (*of* ▸ **вытеснять**) (*врага*) to force out; to oust; (*заменить собой*) to displace, supplant

вытесня́|ть, ю *impf. of* ▸ **вы́теснить**

вы́те|чь, чет, кут, *past* ~**к,** ~**кла** *pf.* (*of* ▸ **вытекáть 1**) to flow out, run out

вытирá|ть, ю *impf. of* ▸ **вы́тереть**

вы́толкн|уть, у, ешь *pf.* (*of* ▸ **вытáлкивать**) **1** to throw out **2** (*пробку*) to push out, force out

вы́торг|овать, ую *pf.* (*of* ▸ **выторгóвывать**) (infml) (*получить уступку*) to get a reduction (of); (fig.) to manage to get

выторгóвыва|ть, ю *impf.* (infml) **1** *impf. of* ▸ **вы́торговать** **2** to try to get (*by bargaining*); to haggle over

вы́трав|ить, лю, ишь *pf. of* ▸ **трави́ть**

вы́т|ру, решь *see* ▸ **вы́тереть**

вытряса́|ть, ю *impf. of* ▸ **вы́трясти**

вы́тряс|ти, у, ешь, *past* ~, ~**ла** *pf.* (*песок, мусор*) to shake out

вытря́хива|ть, ю *impf. of* ▸ **вы́тряхнуть**

вы́тряхн|уть, у, ешь *pf.* (*of* ▸ **вытря́хивать**) (*песок, мусор; скатерть*) to shake out

выть, вóю, вóешь *impf.* (*собака, волк, ветер*) to howl; (*сирена*) to wail

вытя́гива|ть, ю *impf. of* ▸ **вы́тянуть**

вытя́гива|ться, юсь *impf. of* ▸ **вы́тянуться**

вы́тян|уть, у, ешь *pf.* (*of* ▸ **вытя́гивать**) **1** (*вытащить*) to pull out **2** (*ноги, руки*) to stretch (out); (*сделать длиннее*) to extend **3** (*дым, гной*) to draw out, extract (also fig.); (*impers.*) **газ** ~**уло в окнó** the gas had escaped through the window

вы́тян|уться, усь, ешься *pf.* (*of* ▸ **вытя́гиваться**) **1** (*растянуться*) to stretch (*intrans.*); (*вдоль реки; на полу*) to stretch out; **лицо́ у неё** ~**улось** (infml) her face fell **2** (*выпрямиться*) to stand erect

вы́учива|ть, ю *impf. of* ▸ **вы́учить**

вы́уч|ить, у, ишь *pf.* (*of* ▸ **учи́ть 4,** ▸ **вы́учивать**) **1** to learn **2** (+ *a. and d. or* + *inf.*) to teach; **он** ~**ил нас испáнскому языкý** he taught us Spanish

вы́уч|иться, усь, ишься *pf.* (*of* ▸ **учи́ться 3**) (+ *d. or inf.*) to learn; (infml, *на кого-н.*) to learn (to be)

вы́хва|тить, чу, тишь *pf.* **1** (*отнять*) to snatch out; to grab **2** (*вытащить*) to pull out, draw; **в. нож** to draw a knife

выхвáтыва|ть, ю *impf. of* ▸ **вы́хватить**

вы́хва|чу, тишь *see* ▸ **вы́хватить**

выхлопн|óй *adj.* (tech.) exhaust; ~**áя трубá** exhaust pipe; ~**ы́е гáзы** exhaust (fumes)

вы́ход, а *m.* **1** (*на улицу*) going out; (*с целью уйти*) leaving, departure; (*из партии*) leaving; (*поезда, корабля*) departure; **в. в отстáвку** retirement **2** (*место выхода*) way out, exit; (*трубки*) outlet; (*способ*) way out; **дать в.** (+ *d.*) to give vent (to) **3** (*издания*) appearance; (*фильма*) release; (theatr.) entrance **4** (comput.) exit; logoff

вы́ход|ец, ца *m.* **1** (*из другой страны*) immigrant **2** (*из другой социальной среды*) person moving from one social group to another; **он — в. из крестья́н** he is of peasant origin

выхо|ди́ть, жý, ~**дишь** *impf. of* ▸ **вы́йти** **1** *impf. of* ▸ **вы́йти** (*impf. only*) to look out (on), give (on), face; **егó кóмната** ~**дит óкнами на у́лицу** his room looks onto the street **3**: **не в. из головы́,** не **в.** из ума́ to be unforgettable, stick in one's mind **4** (*as pred.*): ~**дит(, что)** (infml) it turns out that

вы́ходк|а, и *f.* (pej.) trick; escapade

выходн|óй *adj.* **1** exit; ~**áя дверь** street door **2**: **в. день** day off; ~**áя одéжда** 'best' clothes
● *n.* **1** (**в.,** ~**óго**) (*день*) day off **2** (**в.,** ~**óго,** *f.* ~**áя,** ~**óй**) (infml, *человек*) person having day off; **он сегóдня в.** it is his day off today **3** (*in pl.*) (~**ые,** ~**ы́х**) severance pay

выхо|жý, ~**дишь** *see* ▸ **выходи́ть**

вы́ч|ел, ла *see* ▸ **вы́честь**

вычёркива|ть, ю *impf. of* ▸ **вы́черкнуть**

вы́черкн|уть, у, ешь *pf.* (*слова*) to cross out; (*из списка*) to cross off; **в. из пáмяти** to erase from one's memory

вы́черпа|ть, ю *pf.* (*of* ▸ **вычéрпывать**) (*из* + *g.*) (*содержимое*) to take out; (*из лодки*) to bail (out); **в. вóду из лóдки** to bail out a boat

вычéрпыва|ть, ю *impf. of* ▸ **вы́черпать**

вы́ч|есть, ту, тешь, *past* ~**ел,** ~**ла,** *pres. gerund* ~**тя** *pf.* (*of* ▸ **вычита́ть**) **1** (math.) to subtract **2** (*удержать*) to deduct, keep back

вычислéни|е, я *nt.* calculation

вычисли́тельн|ый *adj.* calculating, computing; ~**ая тéхника** computers

вы́числ|ить, ю, ишь *pf.* (*of* ▸ **вычисля́ть**) to calculate, compute

вычисля́|ть, ю *impf. of* ▸ **вы́числить**

вы́чи|стить, щу, стишь *pf.* (*of* ▸ **чи́стить 2,** ▸ **вычища́ть**) to clean (up, out)

вычита́ни|е, я *nt.* (math.) subtraction

вычита́|ть, ю *impf. of* ▸ **вы́честь**

вычища́|ть, ю *impf. of* ▸ **вы́чистить**

вы́чи|щу, стишь *see* ▸ **вы́чистить**

вы́ч|ту, тешь *see* ▸ **вы́честь**

В

вы́ше **1** *comp. of* ▶ высо́кий, ▶ высоко́; higher, taller **2** *prep. + g.* (*вверх от*) above, beyond; (*больше*) over; **в. нуля́** above zero; (*за преде́лами*) beyond; **э́то в. моего́ понима́ния** it is beyond my comprehension **3** *adv.* (liter.) above; **смотри́ в.** see above

вы́ше... *comb. form* above-, afore-

вы́|шел, шла *see* ▶ вы́йти

вышеска́занный *adj.* aforesaid

вышестоя́щий *adj.* higher

вышеука́занный *adj.* foregoing

вышеупомя́нутый *adj.* aforementioned

вышива́ни|е, я *nt.* embroidery, needlework

вышива́|ть, ю *impf. of* ▶ вы́шить

вы́шивк|а, и *f.* embroidery, needlework

вы́ш|ить, ью, ьешь, *imper.* ∼ей *pf.* (*of* ▶ вышива́ть) to embroider

вы́шк|а, и *f.* (*ба́шня*) (watch)tower; **сторожева́я в.** watchtower; **бурова́я в.** derrick

вы́|шлю, шлешь *see* ▶ вы́слать

вы́щип|ать, лю, лешь *pf.* (*of* ▶ выщи́пывать) to pull out, pluck; **в. пе́рья у ку́рицы** to pluck a chicken

выщи́пыва|ть, ю *impf. of* ▶ вы́щипать

вы́яв|ить, лю, ишь *pf.* (*of* ▶ выявля́ть) **1** (*преда́ть гла́сности*) to bring out; to make known **2** (*недоста́тки*) to expose

вы́яв|иться, люсь, ишься *pf.* (*of* ▶ выявля́ться) (*недоста́тки*) to come to light, be revealed, be exposed

⚷ выявля́|ть, ю *impf. of* ▶ вы́явить

выявля́|ться, юсь *impf. of* ▶ вы́явиться

выясне́ни|е, я *nt.* clarification; explanation

вы́ясн|ить, ю, ишь *pf.* (*of* ▶ выясня́ть) (*сде́лать поня́тным*) to clarify, clear up, explain; (*установи́ть*) to find out, ascertain

вы́ясн|иться, ится *pf.* (*of* ▶ выясня́ться) (*объясни́ться*) to become clear; (*стать*

я́вным*) to turn out, prove

выясн|я́ть, я́ю, я́ет *impf. of* ▶ вы́яснить

выясн|я́ться, я́ется *impf. of* ▶ вы́ясниться

Вьетна́м, а *m.* Vietnam

вьетна́м|ец, ца *m.* Vietnamese

вьетна́м|ка, ки *f.* **1** *of* ▶ вьетна́мец **2** (*usu. in pl.*) (infml, *о́бувь*) flip-flop

вьетна́мский *adj.* Vietnamese

вью, вьёшь *see* ▶ вить

вью́г|а, и *f.* snowstorm, blizzard

вью́щ|ийся *pres. part. of* ▶ ви́ться *and adj.*: ∼**иеся во́лосы** curly hair; ∼**ееся расте́ние** (bot.) creeper, climber

вя́|жу́, ∼жешь *see* ▶ вяза́ть

вяз, а *m.* elm (tree)

вяза́ни|е, я *nt.* knitting, crocheting

вяза́нк|а, и *f.* bundle

вя́заный *adj.* knitted

вя|за́ть, жу́, ∼жешь *impf.* **1** (*pf.* с∼) to tie, bind **2** (*pf.* с∼) (*спи́цами*) to knit; (*крючко́м*) to crochet **3** (*impf. only*) to be astringent; (*impers.*) **у меня́** ∼**жет во рту** my mouth feels constricted

вя|за́ться, жу́сь, ∼жешься *impf.* (infml) (c + i.) to agree, tally (with)

вя́з|кий, ∼ок, ∼ка́, ∼ко *adj.* **1** (*кле́йкий*) viscous, sticky **2** (*то́пкий*) boggy

вя́з|нуть, ну, нешь, *past* ∼, ∼ла *impf.* (в + p.) to get stuck (in)

вя́лост|ь, и *f.* (*ко́жи, мышц*) flabbiness; limpness; (fig.) sluggishness; inertia; slackness

вя́л|ый *adj.* **1** (*расте́ние*) faded **2** (∼, ∼а) (*ко́жа, те́ло*) flabby; limp; (fig.) sluggish, inert; slack

вя́н|уть, у, ешь, *past* вял/вя́нул, вя́ла, вя́ло, вя́ли *impf.* (*of* ▶ завя́нуть) (*расте́ние*) to fade, wither; (fig., *красота́, спосо́бности*) to fade

Гг

⚷ **г.** *abbr. of* **1** (**год**) yr (year) **2** (**го́род**) city, town **3** (**гора́**) Mt (Mount)

габари́т, а *m.* (*usu. in pl.*) (tech.) size, dimensions

габари́т|ный *adj. of* ▶ габари́т; ∼**ные огни́** sidelights (BrE), sidemarker lights (AmE)

Гава́й|и, ев *m. pl.* Hawaii

га́ван|ь, и *f.* harbour (BrE), harbor (AmE)

га́вка|ть, ю *impf.* (infml) to bark

гага́р|а, ы *f.* (zool.) diver (BrE), loon (AmE)

гад, а *m.* (fig., infml) louse, rat, skunk

гада́лк|а, и *f.* fortune teller

гада́ни|е, я *nt.* (*дога́дка*) guesswork

гада́|ть, ю *impf.* **1** (*pf.* по∼) (на + *p. or* по + *d.*) (*предска́зывать*) to tell fortunes (by) **2** (*impf. only*) (о + *p.*) (*предполага́ть*) to guess

га́дин|а, ы *f.* = гад

га́|дить, жу, дишь *impf.* (*of* ▶ нага́дить) (infml) **1** (*о живо́тных*) to defecate **2** (+ *d.*)

(*вредить*) to play dirty tricks (on)

гáд|кий, ∼ок, ∼кá, ∼ко *adj.* nasty, vile, repulsive; **г. утёнок** ugly duckling

гáдост|ь, и *f.* **1** (infml, *дрянь*) filth, muck **2** (*поступок*) dirty trick; **говорúть** ∼и to say foul things

гадю́к|а, и *f.* adder, viper

гáечный *adj. of* ▶ **гáйка**; **г. ключ** spanner, wrench

гáже *comp. of* ▶ **гáдкий**

♂ **газ**, а *m.* **1** gas **2** (infml): **педáль** ∼а accelerator, gas pedal; **дáть** ∼у to step on the gas; **сбáвить г.** to reduce speed **3** (*in pl.*) (*в кишечнике*) wind

♂ **газéт|а**, ы *f.* newspaper

газирóванный *adj.* carbonated

газирóвк|а, и *f.* (infml) carbonated water, soda (water)

газовщи́к, á *m.* gasman

гáзов|ый *adj. of* ▶ **газ**; ∼ая плитá gas cooker, gas stove; **г. счётчик** gas meter; ∼ая кáмера gas chamber

газóн, а *m.* grassed area, lawn

газонокоси́лк|а, и *f.* lawnmower

газопровóд, а *m.* gas pipeline; gas main

ГАЙ *f. indecl.* (*abbr. of* **Госудáрственная автомоби́льная инспéкция**) State Motor Vehicle Inspectorate; traffic police

Гаи́ти *indecl.* (*госудáрство*) Haiti; (*m.*) (*остров*) Hispaniola

гаитя́н|ин, ина, *pl.* ∼е, ∼ *m.* Haitian

гаитя́н|ка, ки *f. of* ▶ **гаитя́нин**

гаитя́нский *adj.* Haitian

гаи́шник, а *m.* (infml) traffic cop

Гайáн|а, ы *f.* Guyana

гайáн|ец, ца *m.* Guyanese

гайáн|ка, ки *f. of* ▶ **гайáнец**

гайáнский *adj.* Guyanese

гáйк|а, и *f.* nut; **закрути́ть** ∼и (fig.) to put the screws on

гайморúт, а *m.* (med.) sinusitis

галáктик|а, и *f.* (astron.) galaxy

галантерéйный *adj. of* ▶ **галантерéя**; **г. магазúн** haberdashery, fancy goods shop

галантерé|я, и *f.* haberdashery, fancy goods

галáнт|ный, ∼ен, ∼на *adj.* chivalrous

галéр|а, ы *f.* galley

♂ **галерé|я**, и *f.* gallery

гáлк|а, и *f.* jackdaw

галлóн, а *m.* gallon

галлюцинáци|я, и *f.* hallucination

галлюциногéн, а *m.* hallucinogen

гáлочк|а, и *f.* tick, check (AmE)

гáлстук, а *m.* tie; **г.-бáбочка** bow tie

гáл|ька, ьки *f.* (*g. pl.* ∼ек) pebble; (*collect.*) pebbles, shingle

гам, а *m.* (infml) din, uproar

гамáк, á *m.* hammock

Гáмби|я, и *f.* Gambia

гáмбургер, а *m.* (ham)burger

гáмм|а, ы *f.* (mus.) scale; (fig.) gamut

Гáн|а, ы *f.* Ghana

гáнгстер, а *m.* gangster

гандбóл, а *m.* handball

гандболи́ст, а *m.* handball player

гандболи́ст|ка, ки *f. of* ▶ **гандболи́ст**

гáн|ец, ца *m.* Ghanaian

гáнк|а, и *f. of* ▶ **гáнец**

гáнский *adj.* Ghanaian

гарáж, á *m.* garage

гарáнт, а *m.* guarantor

гаранти́йный *adj.* guarantee

гаранти́р|овать, ую *impf. and pf.* to guarantee, vouch for

♂ **гарáнти|я**, и *f.* guarantee; (*охрана*) safeguard

гардерóб, а *m.* **1** (*шкаф*) wardrobe **2** (*помещение*) cloakroom **3** (*collect.*) (*одежда*) wardrobe

гардерóбщик, а *m.* cloakroom attendant

гардерóбщи|ца, цы *f. of* ▶ **гардерóбщик**

гарéм, а *m.* harem

гармони́р|овать, ую *impf.* (**с** + *i.*) to be in harmony (with); (*о красках*) to tone (with), go (with)

гармони́ст, а *m.* accordion player

гармони́ч|ный, ∼ен, ∼на *adj.* harmonious

гармóни|я, и *f.* **1** (mus.) harmony **2** (fig.) harmony, concord

гармóн|ь, и *f.* accordion, concertina

гарнизóн, а *m.* garrison

гарни́р, а *m.* (cul.) garnish; (*из овощей*) vegetables; **на г.** as a side dish

гарниту́р, а *m.* set; (*мебели*) suite

гарпу́н, á *m.* harpoon

га|си́ть, шу́, ∼сишь *impf.* (*of* ▶ **погаси́ть**) **1** (*pf. also* **за**∼) (*пожар, свет*) to put out, extinguish; **г. свет** to put out the light **2** (*погашать*) to cancel; **г. задóлженность** to liquidate a debt

гáс|нуть, ну, нешь, *past* ∼, ∼ла *impf.* (*of* ▶ **погáснуть**) (*переставать гореть*) to be extinguished, go out; (*слабеть*) to grow feeble; (*о чувствах*) to fade, weaken

гастри́т, а *m.* gastritis

гастроли́р|овать, ую *impf.* to tour, be on tour (*of an artiste*)

гастрóл|ь, и *f.* (*usu. in pl.*) tour; engagement (*of touring artiste*)

гастронóм, а *m.* grocer's (shop) (BrE), grocery store (AmE)

гастронóми|я, и *f.* **1** (*продукты*) high-quality cooked meats, fish, cheeses, *etc.* **2** (*гастрономический отдел*) delicatessen counter

гаши́ш, а *m.* hashish

ГБ (*abbr. of* **óрганы госудáрственной безопáсности**) (organs of) state security

гвалт, а *m.* (infml) row, uproar, rumpus

гвардéец, йца *m.* (mil.) guardsman

гвáрди|я, и *f.* (mil.) Guards (*pl.*); ∼и капитáн *и т. п.* (*в званиях*) Captain, *etc.*, of the Guards

Гватемáл|а, ы *f.* Guatemala

гватема́л|ец, ьца *m.* Guatemalan
гватема́л|ка, ки *f. of* ▶ гватема́лец
гватема́льский *adj.* Guatemalan
гвине́|ец, йца *m.* Guinean
гвине́й|ка, ки *f. of* ▶ гвине́ец
гвине́йский *adj.* Guinean
Гвине́|я, и *f.* Guinea
гвозди́к|а[1], и *f.* (bot.) pink(s); carnation(s)
гвозди́к|а[2], и *f.* (collect.) (пряность) cloves
гвозд|ь, я́, *pl.* ~и, ~е́й *m.* **1** nail **2** (+ *g.*)
(fig., infml) (самое главное) crux; highlight;
(программы) highlight, main attraction
◊ гг. *abbr. of* **1** (го́ды) yrs (years) **2** (города́)
cities, towns
◊ где *adv.* **1** (interrog. and rel.) where; г. бы
ни wherever; г. бы то ни́ было no matter
where **2** (infml, где-нибудь) somewhere;
anywhere
где́-либо *adv.* anywhere
где́-нибудь *adv.* somewhere; anywhere
◊ где́-то *adv.* somewhere
ге́|й, я *m.* (sl.) gay (homosexual); г.-клуб gay
club
гекта́р, а *m.* hectare (10,000 square metres)
гел|ь, я *m.* gel
геморро́|й, я *m.* (med.) haemorrhoids (BrE),
hemorrhoids (AmE), piles
гемофи́лик, а *m.* (med.) haemophiliac (BrE),
hemophiliac (AmE)
гемофили́|я, и *f.* (med.) haemophilia (BrE),
hemophilia (AmE)
ген, а *m.* (physiol.) gene
ген... *comb. form, abbr. of* ▶ генера́льный
генеалоги́ческий *adj.* genealogical
генеало́ги|я, и *f.* genealogy
генера́л, а *m.* general; г.-майо́р major
general; г.-губерна́тор governor general
◊ генера́льн|ый *adv.* general; г. констру́ктор
chief designer; г.-ая репети́ция dress
rehearsal; г. секрета́рь general secretary;
~ая убо́рка spring-clean; г. штаб general
staff
генера́льский *adj.* general's; г. чин rank of
general
генера́тор, а *m.* (tech.) generator
гене́тик|а, и *f.* genetics
генети́ческий *adj.* genetic
гениа́л|ьный, ~ен, ~ьна *adj.* (поэт,
произведение) brilliant; (решение) ingenious
ге́ни|й, я *m.* (талант, способность) genius;
(человек) a genius
генита́ли|и, й (no sg.) (med.) genitalia,
genitals
ге́н|ный *adj. of* ▶ ген; ~ная инжене́рия
genetic engineering
гено́м, а *m.* genome; ~ челове́ка human
genome
генофо́нд, а *m.* gene pool
геноци́д, а *m.* genocide

◊ key word

генсе́к, а *m.* (abbr. of генера́льный
секрета́рь) (infml) general secretary
гео... *comb. form, abbr. of* ▶ географи́ческий
гео́граф, а *m.* geographer
географи́ческий *adj.* geographical
геогра́фи|я, и *f.* geography
геодези́ст, а *m.* land surveyor
геоде́зи|я, и *f.* geodesy, (land) surveying
гео́лог, а *m.* geologist
геологи́ческий *adj.* geological
геоло́ги|я, и *f.* geology
геометри́ческий *adj.* geometric(al)
геоме́три|я, и *f.* geometry
геополити́ческий *adj.* geopolitical
георги́н, а *m.* dahlia
гепати́т, а *m.* hepatitis
гера́н|ь, и *f.* geranium
герб, а́ *m.* arms, coat of arms
геркуле́с, а *m.* (sg. only) (крупа) rolled oats;
porridge
Герма́ни|я, и *f.* Germany
герма́нский *adj.* Germanic
геро́изм, а *m.* heroism
герои́н, а *m.* heroin
герои́н|я, и *f.* heroine
герои́ческий *adj.* heroic
◊ геро́|й, я *m.* hero; (liter., де́йствующее лицо́)
character; гла́вный г. protagonist
геро́йский *adj.* heroic
ге́рпес, а *m.* herpes
герц, а, *g. pl.* г. *m.* (phys.) hertz
ге́рцог, а *m.* duke; г. Эдинбу́ргский the Duke
of Edinburgh
герцоги́н|я, и *f.* duchess
гетеросексуа́льный *adj.* heterosexual
ге́тр|ы, гетр *f. pl.* (sg. ~а, ~ы) **1** gaiters
2 (sport) football socks **3** (балетные) leg
warmers
ге́тто *nt. indecl.* ghetto
г-жа́ (abbr. of госпожа́) (замужняя) Mrs;
(незамужняя) Miss; (без указания на
семейное положение) Ms
гиаци́нт, а *m.* hyacinth
ГИБДД (abbr. of Госуда́рственная
инспе́кция безопа́сности доро́жного
движе́ния) State Road Safety Inspectorate
ги́бел|ь, и *f.* (смерть) death; (уничтожение)
destruction, ruin; (потеря) loss;
(государства) downfall
ги́б|кий, ~ок, ~ка́ ~ко *adj.* **1** flexible;
(тело) supple; г. диск (comput.) floppy (disk)
2 (ум) adaptable, versatile
ги́бкост|ь, и *f.* **1** flexibility; (тела) suppleness
2 (ума) versatility, resourcefulness
ги́блый *adj.* (infml) (место) godforsaken;
(безнадёжный) hopeless
ги́б|нуть, ну, нешь, *past* ~ *and* ~нул, ~ла
impf. (of ▶ поги́бнуть) to perish
Гибралта́р, а *m.* Gibraltar
гибри́д, а *m.* hybrid
гига... *comb. form* giga-

гигаба́йт, а *m.* (comput.) gigabyte

гига́нт, а *m.* giant

гига́нтский *adj.* gigantic

гигие́н|а, ы *f.* hygiene

гигиени́ческ|ий *adj.* hygienic, sanitary; ∼ая прокла́дка sanitary towel (BrE), napkin (AmE)

гид, а *m.* guide

гидро... *comb. form* hydro-

гидроста́нци|я, и *f.* hydroelectric (power) station

гидроэлектроста́нци|я, и *f.* hydroelectric power station

ги́льз|а, ы *f.* cartridge case

Гимала́|и, ев (*no sg.*) the Himalayas

гимн, а *m.* hymn; госуда́рственный г. national anthem

гимна́зи|я, и *f.* grammar school (BrE), high school

гимна́ст, а *m.* gymnast

гимна́стик|а, и *f.* gymnastics; спорти́вная г. artistic gymnastics; худо́жественная г. rhythmic gymnastics

гимнасти́ческий *adj.* gymnastic; г. зал gymnasium

гимна́ст|ка, ки *f. of* ▸ гимна́ст

гинеко́лог, а *m.* gynaecologist (BrE), gynecologist (AmE)

гинекологи́ческий *adj.* gynaecological (BrE), gynecological (AmE)

гинеколо́ги|я, и *f.* gynaecology (BrE), gynecology (AmE)

гиперма́ркет, а *m.* hypermarket (BrE)

гиперссы́лк|а, и *f.* (comput.) hyperlink

гипертони́|я, и *f.* (med.) hypertension, high blood pressure

гипно́з, а *m.* hypnosis

гипнотизёр, а *m.* hypnotist

гипнотизи́р|овать, ую *impf.* (*of* ▸ загипнотизи́ровать) to hypnotize

гипноти́ческий *adj.* hypnotic

гипо́тез|а, ы *f.* hypothesis

гипотети́ческий *adj.* hypothetical

гипс, а *m.* **1** (min.) gypsum **2** (art, материал) plaster of Paris **3** (хирургическая повязка) plaster cast, plaster

гирля́нд|а, ы *f.* garland

ги́р|я, и *f.* (для весов) weight; (sport) weight, dumb-bell

гита́р|а, ы *f.* guitar

гитари́ст, а *m.* guitarist

гитари́ст|ка, ки *f. of* ▸ гитари́ст

глав... *comb. form, abbr. of* ▸ гла́вный

глав|а́¹, ы́, *pl.* ∼ы *c.g.* (начальник) head, chief; г. делега́ции head of a delegation; быть/стоя́ть во ∼е́ (+ g.) to be at the head (of), lead; во ∼е́ (с + i.) under the leadership (of), led (by)

глав|а́², ы́, *pl.* ∼ы *f.* (раздел книги) chapter

главнокома́ндующий, его *m.* commander-in-chief; Верхо́вный г. Supreme Commander

гла́вн|ый *adj.* (самый важный) chief, main, principal; (старший) head, senior; г. врач head physician; г. инжене́р chief engineer; ∼ое управле́ние central directorate; ∼ым о́бразом chiefly, mainly, for the most part; (as nt. n. ∼ое, ∼ого) the chief thing, the main thing; the essentials

глаго́л, а *m.* verb

глади́льн|ый *adj.* ironing; ∼ая доска́ ironing board

гладио́лус, а *m.* gladiolus

гла́|дить, жу, дишь *impf.* (*of* ▸ погла́дить) **1** (*pf. also* вы∼) (выравнивать утюгом) to iron, press **2** (ласково проводить рукой по чему-н.) to stroke

гла́д|кий, ∼ок, ∼ка́, ∼ко *adj.* (дорога) smooth; (волосы) straight; (ткань) plain

гла́дко *adv. of* ▸ гла́дкий; smoothly

гла́же *comp. of* ▸ гла́дкий

гла́женье, я *nt.* ironing

глаз, а, о ∼е, в ∼у́, *pl.* ∼а́, ∼, ∼а́м *m.* (орган зрения) eye; (зрение) eyesight; в ∼а́ to one's face; в ∼а́х (+ g.) in the eyes (of); я его́ в ∼а́ не ви́дел I have never seen him; руга́ть кого́-н. за ∼а́ to abuse sb behind his back; на ∼а́х before one's eyes; не попада́йся мне на ∼а́! keep out of my sight!; на г. approximately, by eye; с ∼у на́ г. tête-à-tête, cheek by jowl; с г. доло́й out of sight; смотре́ть во все ∼а́ to be all eyes; закрыва́ть ∼а́ (на + a.) to close one's eyes (to); открыва́ть кому́-н. ∼а́ (на + a.) to open sb's eyes (to); идти́ куда́ ∼а́ глядя́т to follow one's nose

глазн|о́й *adj. of* ▸ глаз; г. врач ophthalmologist; ∼о́е я́блоко eyeball

глаз|о́к, ка́, *pl.* ∼ки, ∼ок *and* ∼ки́, ∼ко́в *m.* **1** (*pl.* ∼ки) *dim. of* ▸ глаз; стро́ить ∼ки кому́-н. to make eyes at sb **2** (*pl.* ∼ки́) (infml) peephole

глазу́нь|я, ьи, *g. pl.* ∼ий *f.* fried eggs (*with yolk and white unmixed*)

глазу́р|ь, и *f.* **1** (на посуде) glaze **2** (cul.) icing

гламу́р|ный, ∼ен, ∼на *adj.* (infml) glamorous, glitzy

гла́нд|а, ы *f.* (anat.) tonsil; удали́ть ∼ы to take out tonsils; воспале́ние гланд glandular fever

гла|си́ть, шу́, си́шь *impf.* to say, run; докуме́нт ∼си́т сле́дующее the paper runs as follows; как ∼си́т погово́рка as the saying goes

гла́сно *adv.* openly, publicly

гла́сность, и *f.* **1** (известность) publicity; преда́ть ∼и to make public, make known, publish **2** (pol.) openness, glasnost

гла́сный¹ *adj.* (открытый) open, public; г. суд public trial

гла́сн|ый² *adj.* (ling.) vowel, vocalic; (as m. n. г., ∼ого) vowel

глауко́м|а, ы *f.* glaucoma

гли́н|а, ы *f.* clay

глиноби́тный *adj.* adobe; mud

глинтве́йн, а *m.* mulled wine

гли́нян|ый *adj.* (*сделанный из глины*) clay; earthenware; ∼ая посу́да earthenware crockery

глобализа́ци|я, и *f.* globalization

глоба́льный *adj.* global; (*fig.*) extensive

гло́бус, а *m.* globe

гло|да́ть, жу́, ∼жешь *impf.* to gnaw (at) (*also fig.*)

глота́|ть, ю *impf.* (*of* ▸ проглоти́ть) to swallow

гло́тк|а, и *f.* **1** (anat.) gullet **2** (infml, *горло*) throat

глот|о́к, ка́ *m.* gulp, mouthful; (*небольшое количество*) drop

гло́х|нуть, ну, нешь, *past* ∼нул *and* ∼, ∼ла *impf.* **1** (*pf.* о∼) (*становиться глухим*) to become deaf **2** (*pf.* за∼) (*о звуках*) to die away, subside; (*о моторе*) to stall

глу́бже *comp. of* ▸ глубо́кий, ▸ глубоко́[1]

⚹ **глубин|а́, ы́,** *pl.* ∼ы *f.* **1** depth; **на** ∼е́ трёхсо́т ме́тров at a depth of 300 metres **2** (*in pl.*) (the) depths **3** (+ *g.*) heart, interior (also fig.); **в** ∼е́ ле́са in the heart of the forest; **в** ∼е́ души́ at heart, in one's heart of hearts

глуби́нный *adj.* deep

⚹ **глубо́к|ий,** ∼, ∼а́ *adj.* **1** deep; **г. сон** deep sleep; ∼ая таре́лка soup plate **2** (*основательный*) profound; thorough; (*серьёзный*) serious **3** (*время, возраст*) late; advanced; extreme; **до** ∼ой но́чи (until) far into the night; ∼ая ста́рость extreme old age **4** (*очень сильный*) deep, profound, intense; **с** ∼им приско́рбием with deep regret (*in obituary formula*)

глубоко́[1] *adv.* deep; (*fig.*) deeply, profoundly

глубоко́[2] *as pred.* it is deep

глубоково́д|ный, ∼ен, ∼на *adj.* deepwater

глубокоуважа́емый *adj.* (*в письмах*) dear

глубоча́йший *superl. of* ▸ глубо́кий

глум|и́ться, лю́сь, и́шься *impf.* (над + *i.*) to mock (at)

глу́пост|ь, и *f.* **1** (*свойство*) foolishness, stupidity **2** (*поступок*) foolish, stupid action; foolish, stupid thing **3** (*usu. in pl.*) (*вздор*) nonsense; ∼и! nonsense!

глу́п|ый, ∼, ∼а́, ∼о, ∼ы́ *adj.* foolish, stupid; silly

глуха́р|ь, я́ *m.* (zool.) capercaillie, woodgrouse

глух|о́й, ∼, ∼а́, ∼о *adj.* **1** (*лишённый слуха*) deaf (also fig.); (*as m. n. г.,* ∼о́го) deaf person **2** (*звук*) muffled, indistinct **3** (*густо заросший*) thick, dense; **г. лес** dense forest **4** (*отдалённый*) remote; godforsaken (*затаённый, скрытый*) concealed, hidden **6** (*закрытый*) sealed; blank, blind; ∼а́я стена́ blind wall **7** (*время, сезон*) quiet, dead; ∼а́я ночь dead of night

глухонем|о́й *adj.* deaf and mute (often offens.), profoundly deaf; (*as m. n.* г., ∼о́го) deaf mute (often offens.), profoundly deaf person

глухота́, ы́ *f.* deafness

глу́ше *comp. of* ▸ глухо́й

глуши́тел|ь, я *m.* (tech.) silencer, muffler (AmE)

глуш|и́ть, у́, ∼и́шь *impf.* **1** (*pf.* о∼) (*рыбу*) to stun, stupefy **2** (*pf.* за∼) (*звуки*) to muffle; **г. боль** to dull pain; **г. мото́р** to stop the engine **3** (*pf.* за∼) (*растения*) to choke, stifle

глуш|ь, и́ *f.* (*заросшая часть*) overgrown part; (*пустынное место*) backwoods (also fig.); **жить в** ∼и́ to live in the back of beyond

глюк, а *m.* (sl.) **1** (*often in pl.*) (*галлюцинация*) trip (*effect of drugs*) (infml) **2** (comput.) glitch, bug (infml)

глюко́з|а, ы *f.* glucose

гля|де́ть, жу́, ди́шь *impf.* (*of* ▸ погляде́ть 1) (на + *a.*) to look (at); to peer (at); to gaze (upon)

гля́н|ец, ца *m.* gloss, lustre (BrE), luster (AmE)

гля́|нуть, ну, нешь *pf.* (на + *a.*) glance (at)

гля́нцев|ый *adj.* glossy, lustrous; ∼ая кра́ска gloss paint; **г. журна́л** glossy magazine, glossy (infml)

г-н (*abbr. of* господи́н) Mr

гна|ть, гоню́, го́нишь, *past* ∼л, ∼ла́, ∼ло *impf.* (*det. of* ▸ гоня́ть) **1** (*стадо*) to drive **2** (*торопить*) to urge (on); (infml, *автомобиль*) to drive hard **3** (infml, *быстро ехать*) to dash, tear **4** (*преследовать*) to hunt, chase **5** (*выгонять*) to throw out, turf out **6** (*водку*) to distil (BrE), distill (AmE)

гна́|ться, гоню́сь, го́нишься, *past* ∼лся, ∼ла́сь *impf.* (*det. of* ▸ гоня́ться) (за + *i.*) (*преследовать*) to pursue; (*стремиться*) to strive (for, after); (fig., *стараться быть не хуже*) to (try to) keep up with

гнев, а *m.* anger, rage, wrath

гне́в|ный, ∼ен, ∼на́, ∼но *adj.* angry, irate

гнезди́ться, ди́тся *impf.* to nest

гнезд|о́, а́, *pl.* гнёзда *nt.* **1** (*птицы*) nest; оси́ное г. wasps' nest (fig.), hornets' nest **2** (*животного*) den, lair (also fig.) **3** (tech.) socket; seat; housing

гнёт, а *m.* oppression, yoke; **г. ра́бства** the yoke of slavery

гние́ни|е, я *nt.* decay, putrefaction, rot

гнил|о́й, ∼, ∼а́, ∼о *adj.* rotten (also fig.)

гнил|ь, и *f.* **1** (*что-н. гнилое*) rotten stuff **2** (*плесень*) mould

гни|ть, ю́, ёшь *impf.* (*of* ▸ сгнить) to rot, decay

гно|и́ться, ю́сь, и́шься *impf.* to suppurate, fester

гно|й, я, в ∼е́ *or* **в** ∼ю́ *m.* pus

гнойни́к, а́ *m.* (*нарыв*) abscess; (*язва*) ulcer

гно́йный *adj.* purulent

гну́с|ный, ∼ен, ∼на́, ∼но *adj.* vile, foul

гнуть, гну, гнёшь *impf.* (*of* ▸ согну́ть) (*проволоку*) to bend; (*деревья*) to bow;

⚹ key word

г. спи́ну, ше́ю (пе́ред + *i.*) (infml) to cringe (before), kowtow (to)

гну́ться, гнусь, гнёшься *impf.* (*of* ▶ согну́ться) (*о материале, палке*) to bend; (*о деревьях*) to be bowed

гобеле́н, а *m.* tapestry

гобо́ист, а *m.* oboist

гобо́ист|ка, ки *f. of* ▶ гобо́ист

гобо́|й, я *m.* oboe

говн|о́, а́ *nt.* (vulg.) shit

⚭ **говор|и́ть**, ю́, и́шь *impf.* **1** (*impf. only*) (*владеть устной речью*) to speak, talk; он ещё не ∼и́т he can't speak yet; г. по-францу́зски to speak French **2** (*pf.* ▶ сказа́ть) (*выражать, сообщать*) to say; to tell; to speak, talk; г. пра́вду to tell the truth; ∼я́т they say, it is said; стро́го ∼я́ strictly speaking; не ∼я́ уже́ (о + *p.*) not to mention **3** (*pf.* ▶ поговори́ть 1) (о + *p.*) (*беседовать*) to talk (about), discuss **4** (*impf. only*) (*значить*) to mean, convey, signify; э́то и́мя мне ничего́ не ∼и́т this name means nothing to me **5** (*impf. only*) (о + *p.*) (*свидетельствовать*) to point (to), indicate, testify (to); всё ∼и́т о том, что он поко́нчил с собо́й everything points to his having committed suicide

⚭ **говор|и́ться**, и́тся *impf.* (*pass. of* ▶ говори́ть): как ∼и́тся as they say, as the saying goes

говя́дин|а, ы *f.* beef

говя́жий *adj.* beef

го́гот, а *m.* (*крик гусей*) cackle; (infml, *хохот*) loud laughter

гого|та́ть, чу́, ∼чешь *impf.* to cackle

⚭ **год**, а, о ∼е, в ∼у́, *pl.* ∼ы and ∼а́, *g.* ∼о́в and лет *m.* **1** (*g. pl.* лет) year; високо́сный г. leap year; кру́глый г. (*as adv.*) the whole year round; в бу́дущем, про́шлом ∼у́ next, last year; в г. a year, per annum; спустя́ три ∼а three years later; че́рез три ∼а in three years' time; ей пошёл пятна́дцатый г. she is in her fifteenth year **2**: двадца́тые, тридца́тые *и т. п.*∼ы (*g.* ∼о́в) (*pl. only*) the twenties, the thirties, *etc.* **3** (∼а́ and ∼ы, ∼о́в) (*pl. only*) years, age, time; в ∼ы (+ *g.*) in the days (of); during; в те ∼ы in those days; не по ∼а́м beyond one's years, precocious(ly)

года́ми *adv.* for years (on end)

го|ди́ться, жу́сь, ди́шься *impf.* **1** (на + *a.* or для + *g.*, *or* + *d.*) (*быть полезным*) to be fit (for), be suited (for), do (for), serve (for) **2** (в + *nom.-a.*) (*быть впору*) to serve (as), be suited to be **3** (в + *nom.-a.*) (*подходить по возрасту*) to be old enough to be; она́ ∼ди́тся тебе́ в ма́тери she is old enough to be your mother **4**: не ∼ди́тся (+ *inf.*) it does not do (to), one should not

го́дност|ь, и *f.* fitness, suitability; (*билета*) validity; срок ∼и expiry date

го́д|ный, ∼ен, ∼на́, ∼но, ∼ны́ *adj.* fit, suitable; (*о билете*) valid; г. к вое́нной слу́жбе fit for military service

годова́лый *adj.* one-year-old, yearling

годово́й *adj.* annual, yearly

годовщи́н|а, ы *f.* anniversary

гол, а *m.* (sport) goal; заби́ть г. to score a goal

голени́щ|е, а *nt.* top (*of a boot*)

го́лен|ь, и *f.* shin

голки́пер, а *m.* (sport) goalkeeper

голла́нд|ец, ца *m.* Dutchman

Голла́нди|я, и *f.* Holland

голла́ндк|а, и *f.* Dutchwoman

голла́ндский *adj.* Dutch

⚭ **голов|а́**, ы́, *a.* го́лову, *pl.* го́ловы, голо́в, ∼а́м *f.* **1** head (also fig.); на све́жую го́лову while one is fresh; быть на́ голову вы́ше кого́-н. (fig.) to be head and shoulders above sb; с ∼ы́ до ног from head to foot; у неё г. шла кру́гом her head was going round and round; у меня́ г. кру́жится I feel giddy **2** (*единица счёта скота*) head (*of cattle*) **3** (fig., *ум*) head; brain, mind; wits; ей пришла́ в го́лову мысль it occurred to her, it struck her **4** (fig., *человек, как носитель каких-либо свойств*) head (= *person*); горя́чая г. hothead **5** (fig., *жизнь*) head, life; на свою́ го́лову to one's cost; отвеча́ть ∼о́й за что-н. to stake one's life on sth

голова́стик, а *m.* tadpole

голо́вк|а, и *f.* (*булавки, спички, цветка*) head; г. лу́ка an onion, onion bulb; г. чеснока́ head of garlic

головн|о́й *adj.* **1** *adj. of* ▶ голова́; ∼а́я боль headache; г. платóк headscarf; г. убо́р headgear, headdress **2** (anat.): г. мозг brain, cerebrum **3** (fig.) head, leading

головокруже́ни|е, я *nt.* giddiness

головокружи́тельн|ый *adj.* dizzy, giddy (also fig.); ∼ая высота́ dizzy height

головоло́мк|а, и *f.* puzzle, conundrum

го́лод, а (у) *m.* **1** hunger; (*длительное недоедание*) starvation; умира́ть с ∼у to die of starvation; мори́ть ∼ом to starve (*trans.*) **2** (*народное бедствие*) famine **3** (*недостаток продуктов питания*) dearth, acute shortage

голода́ни|е, я *nt.* **1** (*недоедание*) starvation **2** (*воздержание*) fasting

голод|а́ть, а́ю *impf.* **1** (*скудно питаться*) to starve **2** (*воздерживаться от пищи*) to fast, go without food **3** (*быть на диете*) to diet

голода́ющ|ий *pres. part. act. of* ▶ голода́ть *and adj.* starving, hungry; (*as n.* г., ∼его, *f.* ∼ая, ∼ей) starving person

голо́дн|ый, ∼оден, ∼одна́, ∼одно, ∼одны́ *adj.* **1** (*желающий есть*) hungry **2** (*вызванный голодом*) hunger, starvation **3** (*скудный*) meagre, scanty, poor; г. год lean year

голодо́вк|а, и *f.* (*в знак протеста*) hunger strike

гололёд, а *m.* = гололе́дица

гололе́диц|а, ы *f.* black ice

⚭ **го́лос**, а, *pl.* ∼а́ *m.* **1** voice; во весь г. at the top of one's voice **2** (mus.) voice, part

3 (fig., *мнение*) voice, word, opinion **4** (pol.) vote; **пра́во** ~a the vote, suffrage; **пода́ть г.** to answer; (**за** + a.) to vote (for)

голосло́в|ный, ~ен, ~на adj. unsubstantiated

голосова́ни|е, я nt. voting; poll

голос|ова́ть, у́ю impf. (of ▶ **проголосова́ть**) **1** (**за** + a. or **про́тив** + g.) to vote (for; against) **2** (*ставить на голосование*) to put to the vote, vote on

голосов|о́й adj. vocal; (anat.): ~ы́е свя́зки vocal chords; ~а́я по́чта voice mail

голуби́к|а, и f. great bilberry, bog whortleberry (*Vaccinium uliginosum*)

голу́бк|а, и f. (*самка голубя*) female pigeon, dove

голуб|о́й adj. pale blue, sky blue; ~а́я кровь (fig.) blue blood; (*as m. n.* **голуб|о́й, о́го**) (sl.) gay (= *homosexual*)

го́лубь, я, g. pl. ~е́й m. pigeon, dove

голубя́т|ня, ни, g. pl. ~ен f. dovecot(e), pigeon loft

го́л|ый, ~, ~а́, ~о adj. naked, bare (also fig.); ~ыми рука́ми with one's bare hands

гольф, а m. golf; игро́к в г. golfer

го́льф|ы, ов (*sg.* ~, ~a) m. pl. (infml) knee-length socks

гомеопа́т, а f. homeopath(ist)

гомеопати́ческий adj. homeopathic

гомеопа́ти|я, и f. homeopathy

го́мик, а m. (infml, pej.) queer, poof(ter) (infml, pej.), gay

гомосексуали́зм, а m. homosexuality

гомосексуали́ст, а m. homosexual; gay

гомосексуа́льный adj. homosexual; gay

гонг, а m. gong

гондо́л|а, ы f. **1** (*лодка*) gondola **2** (aeron.) car (*of balloon*)

Гондура́с, а m. Honduras

гондура́с|ец, ца m. Honduran

гондура́с|ка, ки f. of ▶ **гондура́сец**

гондура́сский adj. Honduran

гоне́ни|е, я nt. persecution

го́нк|а, и f. (sport) (*usu. in pl.*) race; **г. вооруже́ний** arms race

Гонко́нг, а m. Hong Kong

гонора́р, а m. fee; **а́вторский г.** royalties

гоноре́|я, и f. gonorrhoea (BrE), gonorrhea (AmE)

го́ночный adj. of ▶ **го́нка**; **г. автомоби́ль** racing car

гонча́р, а́ m. potter

го́нщик, а m. racing driver

гоню́, го́нишь see ▶ **гнать**

гоню́сь, го́нишься see ▶ **гна́ться**

гоня́|ть, ю impf. (indet. of ▶ **гнать**) (*стада*) to drive; (*птиц*) to chase off

гоня́|ться, юсь impf. (indet. of ▶ **гна́ться**) (**за** + i.) to chase, pursue; (*на охоте*) to hunt

♂ **key word**

гор... comb. form, abbr. of **1** ▶ **городско́й 2** ▶ **го́рный**

♂ **гор|а́, ы́**, a. ~у, pl. ~ы, d. ~а́м f. mountain; hill; **г. Эвере́ст** Mount Everest; **в** ~у uphill (also fig.); **по́д** ~у downhill (also fig.)

♂ **гора́здо** adv. (+ comp. adjs. and advs.) much, far, by far; г. лу́чше far better

горб, а́, о ~е́, на ~у́ m. hump

горба́т|ый, ~, ~a adj. hunchbacked; **г. нос** hooked nose

горб|иться, люсь, ишься impf. (of ▶ **сго́рбиться**) (*о человеке*) to stoop; (*о спине*) to become bent

горбу́ш|а, и f. humpback salmon

горд|и́ться, жу́сь, ди́шься impf. (+ i.) to be proud (of), pride oneself (on)

го́рдост|ь, и f. pride

го́рд|ый, ~, ~а́, ~о, ~ы́ adj. proud

го́р|е, я nt. **1** (*печаль*) grief, sorrow, woe; **на своё г.** to one's sorrow **2** (*беда*) misfortune, trouble **3** (*as pred.*) (+ d.) (infml) woe (unto), woe betide

гор|ева́ть, юю, юешь impf. (о + p.) to grieve (for)

горе́лк|а, и f. burner; **при́мусная г.** Primus stove®

горе́ни|е, я nt. burning, combustion; (fig.) enthusiasm

гор|е́ть, ю́, и́шь impf. **1** (*о доме*) to burn, be on fire **2** (*о дровах, свете*) to burn, be alight; **в ку́хне у них** ~е́л свет the lights were on in their kitchen **3** (+ i.) (fig.) to burn (with); **г. жела́нием** (+ inf.) to be itching (to), be impatient (to)

го́р|ец, ца m. mountain-dweller

го́реч|ь, и f. **1** (*вкус*) bitter taste **2** (*горькое чувство*) bitterness

горизо́нт, а m. horizon (also fig.); skyline

горизонта́л|ь, и f. **1** horizontal; **по** ~и across (*in crossword*) **2** (geog.) contour line

горизонта́л|ьный, ~ен, ~ьна adj. horizontal

гори́лл|а, ы f. gorilla

гори́ст|ый, ~, ~а adj. mountainous, hilly

го́рк|а, и f. **1** hill, hillock **2** (*для детей*) slide

го́рлиц|а, ы f. turtle dove

го́рл|о, а nt. **1** throat; **дыха́тельное г.** windpipe; **во всё г.** at the top of one's voice; **сыт по г.** full up; (fig.) fed up **2** (*сосуда*) neck

горлови́н|а, ы f. mouth, orifice; **г. вулка́на** crater

гормо́н, а m. hormone

гормона́льный adj. hormone, hormonal

горн, а m. (*печь*) furnace, forge

го́рничн|ая, ой f. (*в гостинице*) chambermaid; (*в доме*) maid

горнолы́жник, а m. Alpine skier

горнолы́жн|ый adj.: **г. спорт** Alpine skiing; ~ая тра́сса piste

горноста́|й, я m. ermine

го́рн|ый adj. **1** adj. of ▶ **ropá**; mountain; (*гористый*) mountainous; ~ые лы́жи downhill skis; ∼ая цепь mountain range **2** (*минера́льный*) mineral; ∼ая поро́да rock; г. хруста́ль rock crystal **3** (*относя́щийся к разрабо́тке недр*) mining; ∼ое де́ло mining

♂ **го́род**, а, *pl.* ∼а́ *m.* town; city; вы́ехать за́ г. to go out of town; жить за́ ∼ом to live out of town

горо́д|о́к, ка́ *m.* small town; университе́тский г. campus

♂ **городско́|й** *adj.* urban; city; municipal; (*as m. n.* г., ∼о́го) city-dweller, town-dweller

горожа́н|ин, ина, *pl.* ∼е, ∼ *m.* city-dweller, town-dweller; townsman

горожа́н|ка, ки *f. of* ▶ горожа́нин; townswoman

гороско́п, а *m.* horoscope

горо́х, а (*no pl.*) *m.* **1** pea **2** (*collect.*) peas

горо́ш|ек, ка *m.* **1** *dim. of* ▶ горо́х; души́стый г. (bot.) sweet peas **2** (*collect.*) polka dots; пла́тье в г. polka-dot dress

горо́шин|а, ы *f.* a pea

горст|ь, и, *g. pl.* ∼е́й *f.* **1** (*ладо́нь с со́гнутыми па́льцами*) cupped hand **2** (*находя́щееся на/в ладо́ни*) handful (also fig.)

го́рче *comp. of* ▶ го́рький 1

горч|и́ть, и́т *impf.* (*impers.*) to have a bitter taste

горчи́ц|а, ы *f.* mustard

го́рше *comp. of* ▶ го́рький 2

горш|о́к, ка́ *m.* pot; ночно́й г. chamber pot; (*ребёнка*) potty

го́р|ький, ∼ек, ∼ька́, ∼ько, ∼ький *adj.* **1** (*comp.* ∼че) bitter **2** (*comp.* ∼ше) (fig.) bitter; hard; ∼ькие слёзы bitter tears

го́рько[1] *adv.* bitterly

го́рько[2] *as pred.* **1**: у меня́ г. во рту I have a bitter taste in my mouth **2** it is bitter; мне г. I am very disappointed **3**: г.! ≈ kiss the bride! (*shouted by wedding guests, asking the bride and groom to kiss*)

горю́ч|ее, его *nt.* fuel

горю́чий *adj.* combustible, inflammable

♂ **горя́ч|ий**, ∼, ∼а́ *adj.* **1** hot (also fig.); ∼ая ли́ния hotline **2** (*любо́вь, жела́ние*) passionate **3** (*челове́к*) hot-tempered **4** (*спор*) heated; (*речь*) impassioned **5** (*вре́мя*) busy, hectic

горячо́[1] *adv.* hot

горячо́[2] *as pred.* it is hot

гос… *comb. form, abbr. of* ▶ госуда́рственный

Госду́м|а, ы *f.* State Duma (*lower house of the Russian parliament*)

го́спел, а *m.* (*жанр му́зыки*) gospel music

госпитализи́р|овать, ую *impf. and pf.* to hospitalize

го́спитал|ь, я *m.* hospital (esp. mil.)

госпита́льный *adj. of* ▶ го́спиталь

Го́споди *int.* good heavens!; good Lord!

♂ **господ|и́н**, и́на, *pl.* ∼а́, ∼, ∼ам *m.* (*при фами́лии*) Mr; ∼а́ (*при обраще́нии*) gentlemen; (*мужчи́ны и же́нщины*) ladies and gentlemen

госпо́дств|о, а *nt.* **1** (*власть*) supremacy **2** (*преоблада́ние*) predominance

госпо́дств|овать, ую *impf.* **1** (*облада́ть вла́стью*) to hold sway **2** (*преоблада́ть*) to predominate, prevail **3** (*над* + *i.*) (*возвыша́ться*) to command, dominate; to tower (above)

госпо́дствующий *pres. part. act. of* ▶ госпо́дствовать *and adj.* **1** (*вла́ствующий*) ruling **2** (*преоблада́ющий*) prevailing **3** (*возвыша́ющийся*) commanding

Госпо́дь, Го́спода, *voc.* Го́споди *m.* God, the Lord

госпож|а́, и́ *f.* (*при фами́лии; заму́жняя*) Mrs, Ms; (*незаму́жняя*) Miss, Ms

гостеприи́м|ный, ∼ен, ∼на *adj.* hospitable

гостеприи́мств|о, а *nt.* hospitality

гости́н|ая, ой *f.* living room, sitting room

гости́н|ец, ца *m.* (infml) present

♂ **гости́ниц|а**, ы *f.* hotel

гост|и́ть, гощу́, гости́шь *impf.* (у + *g.*) to stay (with), be on a visit (to)

♂ **гост|ь**, я, *g. pl.* ∼е́й *m.* guest, visitor; пойти́ в ∼и (к + *d.*) to visit; быть в гостя́х (у + *g.*) to be a guest (at, of); to be visiting

го́ст|ья, ьи, *g. pl.* ∼ий *f. of* ▶ гость

госуда́рственник, а *m.* supporter of a powerful state

♂ **госуда́рственн|ый** *adj.* state, public; г. переворо́т coup d'état; ∼ая изме́на high treason; ∼ая слу́жба public service; г. слу́жащий civil servant

♂ **госуда́рств|о**, а *nt.* state

госуда́р|ь, я *m.* sovereign; (Г.) Your Majesty, Sire (*as form of address*)

го́тик|а, и *f.* Gothic (style)

готи́ческий *adj.* Gothic

♂ **гото́в|ить**, лю, ишь *impf.* **1** to prepare, make ready; (*обуча́ть*) to train **2** (*пи́щу*) to cook

гото́в|иться, люсь, ишься *impf.* **1** (к + *d.* or + *inf.*) to get ready (for, to); to prepare (oneself) (for) **2** (*предстоя́ть*) to be at hand, in the offing

гото́вност|ь, и *f.* **1** readiness, preparedness; в боево́й ∼и ready for action **2** (*согла́сие*) readiness, willingness

♂ **гото́в|ый**, ∼, ∼а *adj.* **1** (к + *d.*) ready (for), prepared (for) **2** (на + *a.* or + *inf.*) (*согла́сный*) ready (for, to), prepared (for, to); willing (to); мы ∼ы на всё we are prepared for anything; она́ не ∼а идти́ she is not willing to go **3** (+ *inf.*) (*находя́щийся в состоя́нии бли́зком к чему́-либо*) on the point (of), on the verge (of), ready (to) **4** (*оконча́тельно сде́ланный*) ready-made, finished; ready-to-wear; ∼ые изде́лия finished articles, the finished product

граб, а *m.* (bot.) hornbeam

грабёж, а́ *m.* robbery (also fig., infml)

граби́тел|ь, я *m.* robber; (*до́ма*) burglar

гра́б|ить, лю, ишь *impf.* **1** (*pf.* о∼) (*челове́ка*) to rob; (*дом*) to burgle; (fig.) to rob

2 (*pf.* **раз~**) (*город*) to loot, pillage

гра́б|ли, лей *or* **~ель** (*no sg.*) rake

гра́ви|й, я *m.* gravel

гравир|ова́ть, у́ю, у́ешь *impf.* (*of* ▶ **вы́гравировать**) to engrave

гравиро́вк|а, и *f.* engraving

гравита́ци|я, и *f.* (phys.) gravitation

гравю́р|а, ы *f.* engraving, print; (*офорт*) etching

град, а *m.* **1** hail **2** (fig., *поток*) hail, shower, torrent

града́ци|я, и *f.* gradation, scale

гра́дус, а *m.* degree; **у́гол в 40 ~ов** angle of 40 degrees; **сего́дня 20 ~ов тепла́, моро́за** it is twenty degrees above, below zero today

гра́дусник, а *m.* thermometer

☛ **граждани́н, а,** *pl.* **гра́ждане, гра́ждан** *m.* citizen

гражда́н|ка, ки *f. of* ▶ **граждани́н**

☛ **гражда́нск|ий** *adj.* **1** (law, etc.) civil; citizen's; civic; **г. иск** civil suit; **~ое пра́во** civil law **2** (*нецерковный, светский*) civil, secular; **г. брак** civil marriage **3** (*невоенный*) civilian; **~ое пла́тье** civilian clothes **4** (*подобающий гражданину*) civic, befitting a citizen **5**: **~ая война́** civil war

гражда́нств|о, а *nt.* citizenship, nationality; **права́ ~a** civic rights

грамм, а *m.* gramme, gram

грамма́тик|а, и *f.* **1** (*раздел языкознания*) grammar **2** (*учебник*) grammar (book)

граммати́ческий *adj.* grammatical

граммофо́н, а *m.* gramophone

гра́мотнос|ть, и *f.* **1** (*умение читать и писать*) literacy (also fig.) **2** (*отсутствие грамматических ошибок*) grammatical correctness **3** (*умелость*) competence

гра́мот|ный, ~ен, ~на *adj.* **1** (*умеющий читать и писать*) literate; able to read and write **2** (*без ошибок*) grammatically correct **3** (*умелый*) competent

грампласти́нк|а, и *f.* gramophone record (BrE), phonograph record (AmE)

грана́т, а *m.* pomegranate

грана́т|а, ы *f.* (mil.) shell, grenade; **ручна́я г.** hand grenade

гранатомёт, а *m.* (mil.) grenade launcher

грандио́з|ный, ~ен, ~на *adj.* grandiose; mighty; vast

гранё|ный *adj.* (*алмаз*) cut, faceted; (*стакан*) cut-glass; **~ое стекло́** cut glass

грани́т, а *m.* granite

грани́тный *adj.* granite

☛ **грани́ц|а, ы** *f.* **1** frontier, border; **за ~ей** abroad; **е́хать за ~у** to go abroad **2** (fig.) boundary, limit

грани́ч|ить, у, ишь *impf.* (**с** + *i.*) **1** to border (on) **2** (fig.) to border (on), verge (on)

грант, а *m.* grant

гран|ь, и *f.* **1** border, verge, brink; **на ~и безу́мия** on the verge of insanity **2** (geom.) face; (*алмаза*) facet

граф, а *m.* count

граф|а́, ы́ *f.* (*столбец*) column; (*раздел*) section

☛ **гра́фик, а** *m.* **1** (*диаграмма*) graph, chart **2** (*расписание*) schedule; **пло́тный г.** packed schedule; **ско́льзящий г.** flexible working hours; flexitime

гра́фик|а, и *f.* (art) graphic art; (comput.) graphics

графи́н, а *m.* carafe; (*с про́бкой*) decanter

графи́н|я, и *f.* countess

графи́т, а *m.* **1** (min.) graphite **2** (*карандаша*) pencil lead

графи́ческий *adj.* graphic; **г. паке́т** (comput.) graphics package

гра́фств|о, а *nt.* county

грацио́з|ный, ~ен, ~на *adj.* graceful

гра́ци|я, и *f.* grace, gracefulness

грач, а́ *m.* (zool.) rook

гре́б|ень, ня *m.* **1** (*для расчёсывания волос*) comb **2** (*птицы*) comb, crest **3** (*волны, горы*) crest

гребл|я, и *f.* rowing

грейпфру́т, а *m.* grapefruit

грек, а *m.* Greek

гре́лк|а, и *f.* hot-water bottle

грем|е́ть, лю́, и́шь *impf.* (of ▶ **прогреме́ть**) to thunder, roar; (*о колоколах*) to peal; (*посу́дой*) to clatter; (*ключами*) to jangle; (fig.) to resound, ring out

гре́нк|а, и *f.* toast; (*для супа, салата*) crouton

Гренла́нди|я, и *f.* Greenland

гре|сти́, бу́, бёшь, *past* **~б, ~бла́** *impf.* **1** to row; (*веслом, руками*) to paddle **2** (*граблями*) to rake

греть, гре́ю, гре́ешь *impf.* **1** (*intrans.*) to give out warmth **2** (*trans.*) to warm, heat (up); (*предохранять от холода*) to keep warm

гре́|ться, юсь, ешься *impf.* (*о человеке*) to warm oneself; (*о воде*) to warm, heat (up)

грех, а́ *m.* **1** (relig.) (also fig.) sin **2** (*as pred.* + *inf.*) it is a sin, it is sinful; **не г.** (+ *inf.*) there is no harm (in) **3**: **с ~о́м попола́м** (only) just

Гре́ци|я, и *f.* Greece

гре́цкий *adj.*: **г. оре́х** walnut

греча́нк|а, и *f. of* ▶ **грек**

гре́ческий *adj.* Greek

гречи́х|а, и *f.* buckwheat

гре́чк|а, и *f.* (infml) buckwheat

гре́чнев|ый *adj.* buckwheat; **~ая ка́ша** buckwheat porridge

греш|и́ть, у́, и́шь *impf.* **1** (*pf.* **со~**) to sin **2** (*pf.* **по~**) (*против* + *g.*) (*допускать ошибку*) to sin (against)

гре́шник, а *m.* sinner

гре́шни|ца, цы *f. of* ▶ **гре́шник**

гре́ш|ный, ~ен, ~на́, ~но, ~ны́ *adj.* sinful

☛ key word

гриб, á *m.* fungus; (*съедобный*) mushroom; (*поганка*) toadstool

грибно́й *adj. of* ▶ **гриб**; mushroom; **г. дождь** rain while the sun is shining

гриб|о́к, ка́ *m.* **1** *dim. of* ▶ **гриб 2** (biol.) fungus, microorganism

гри́в|а, ы *f.* mane

гри́зли *m. indecl.* grizzly (bear)

грил|ь, я *m.* grill (BrE), broiler (AmE)

грим, а *m.* (theatr.) make-up; greasepaint

грима́с|а, ы *f.* grimace; **стро́ить ~ы** to make *or* pull faces

гримёр, а *m.* (theatr.) make-up artist

гримёрн|ая, ой *f.* (theatr.) make-up (room)

гримир|ова́ть, у́ю *impf.* (*of* ▶ **загримирова́ть**) (theatr.) to make up

гримир|ова́ться, у́юсь *impf.* (*of* ▶ **загримирова́ться**) (theatr.) to make up (*intrans.*); (+ *i. под* + *a.*) (fig.) to make oneself out

грипп, а *m.* influenza; flu

гриф¹, а *m.* (zool.) vulture

гриф², а *m.* (mus.) fingerboard

гриф³, а *m.* (*штемпель*) seal, stamp

гри́фел|ь, я *m.* (*карандаша*) lead

гроб, а, о/на ~е, в ~у́, *pl.* ~ы́ *m.* **1** coffin **2** (fig.) the grave; **вогна́ть в г.** to drive to the grave; **до ~а, по г. жи́зни** (infml) until the end of one's days

гробни́ц|а, ы *f.* tomb

гробов|о́й *adj.* **1** *adj. of* ▶ **гроб**; ~**ая доска́** (fig.) the grave; **ве́рный до ~ой доски́** faithful unto death **2** (*мрачный*) sepulchral, deathly; ~**ая тишина́** deathly silence

гроз|а́, ы́, *pl.* ~ы́ *f.* **1** (thunder)storm **2** (fig.) (+ *g.*) threat (to)

грозд|ь, и, *pl.* ~**и**, ~**е́й** *and* ~**ья**, ~**ьев** *f.* cluster, bunch (*of fruit or flowers*)

гро|зи́ть, жу́, зи́шь *impf.* **1** (*pf.* **при~**) (+ *d. and i. or* + *inf.*) (*предупреждать с угрозой*) to make threatening gestures **2** (*pf.* **по~**) (*делать угрожающий жест*) to make threatening gestures **3** (*no pf.*) (*предстоять*) to threaten; **ему́ ~зи́т банкро́тство** he is threatened with bankruptcy

гро́з|ный, ~**ен**, ~**на́**, ~**но** *adj.* **1** (*угрожающий*) menacing, threatening **2** (*ужасный*) terrible; formidable

гроз|ово́й *adj. of* ▶ **гроза́**; ~**ова́я ту́ча** storm cloud, thundercloud

гром, а, *pl.* ~ы́, ~о́в *m.* thunder (also fig.); **уда́р ~а** thunderclap

грома́д|ный, ~**ен**, ~**на** *adj.* huge, vast, enormous

гром|и́ть, лю́, и́шь *impf.* (*of* ▶ **разгроми́ть**) to destroy; (mil.) to smash, rout

гро́м|кий, ~**ок**, ~**ка́**, ~**ко** *adj.* **1** loud **2** (*известный*) famous; (*пресловутый*) notorious **3** (*напыщенный*) fine-sounding; ~**кие слова́** (iron.) big words

гро́мко *adv.* loud(ly); (*вслух*) aloud

громкоговори́тел|ь, я *m.* loudspeaker

гро́мкост|ь, и *f.* (*звука*) loudness, volume

громов|о́й *adj.* **1** *adj. of* ▶ **гром**; ~**ые раска́ты** peals of thunder **2** (*громкий*) thunderous, deafening

громогла́с|ный, ~**ен**, ~**на** *adj.* **1** (*громкий*) loud; (*о человеке*) loud-voiced **2** (*открытый*) public, open

громо́зд|кий, ~**ок**, ~**ка** *adj.* cumbersome, unwieldy

гро́мче *comp. of* ▶ **гро́мкий**, ▶ **гро́мко**

гроссме́йстер, а *m.* grandmaster (*at chess*)

гроте́ск, а *m.* (art) grotesque

гро́хот, а *m.* crash, din

грох|ота́ть, очу́, о́чешь *impf.* to crash; roll, rumble; roar

грош, á, *pl.* ~**и́**, ~**е́й** *m.* (fig., infml) penny, cent; **рабо́тать за ~и́** to work for peanuts

груб|и́ть, лю́, и́шь *impf.* (*of* ▶ **нагруби́ть**) (+ *d.*) to be rude (to)

гру́бо *adv.* **1** (*неискусно*) crudely **2** (*невежливо*) rudely **3** (*приблизительно*) roughly; **г. говоря́** roughly speaking

гру́бост|ь, и *f.* **1** (*невежливость*) rudeness **2** (*замечание*) rude remark; **говори́ть ~и** to be rude

гру́б|ый, ~, ~**á**, ~**о**, ~**ы́** *adj.* **1** (*без изящества*) coarse, rough **2** (*недопустимый*) gross, flagrant; **г. обма́н** gross deception **3** (*человек, слово*) rude; coarse, crude **4** (*приблизительный*) rough

грудн|о́й *adj. of* ▶ **грудь**; ~**áя кле́тка** (anat.) thorax; **г. ребёнок** baby

ơ **груд|ь**, и́, *i.* ~**ью**, в/на/о ~**и́**, *pl.* ~**и**, ~**е́й** *f.* **1** (anat.) chest **2** (*женщины*) breast; bosom; bust; **корми́ть ~ью** to breastfeed

ơ **груз**, а *m.* **1** (*тяжесть*) weight; (*кладь*) load, cargo, freight **2** (fig.) weight, burden

грузи́н, а, *g. pl.* **г.** *m.* Georgian

грузи́н|ка, ки *f. of* ▶ **грузи́н**

грузи́нский *adj.* Georgian

гру|зи́ть, жу́, ~**зишь** *impf.* **1** (*pf.* **за~** *and* **на~**) (*судно*) to load **2** (*pf.* **по~**) (*товар*) to load

гру|зи́ться, жу́сь, ~**зишься** *impf.* (*of* ▶ **погрузи́ться 2**) (*о судне*) to load (*intrans.*), take on cargo; (*о людях*) to board

Гру́зи|я, и *f.* Georgia

грузови́к, á *m.* lorry (BrE), truck

грузов|о́й *adj.* goods, cargo, freight; ~**о́е су́дно** cargo boat, freighter

грузоподъёмност|ь, и *f.* payload capacity; freight-carrying capacity

гру́зчик, а *m.* loader; (*в порту*) docker (BrE), stevedore

грунт, а *m.* (*почва*) soil, earth; (*дно*) bottom

грунтов|о́й *adj. of* ▶ **грунт**; ~**ые во́ды** subsoil waters; ~**áя доро́га** dirt road

ơ **гру́пп|а**, ы *f.* group; **г. кро́ви** (med.) blood group; **операти́вная г.** task force; **рабо́чая г.** working party

группир|ова́ть, у́ю *impf.* (*of* ▶ **сгруппирова́ть**) to group;

(*классифицировать*) to classify

группиро́вк|а, и *f.* **1** grouping; (*классификация*) classification; **г. сил** (mil.) distribution of forces **2** (*совокупность лиц*) group, grouping **3** (*бандитская*) (criminal) gang

группово́|й *adj.* group; **~ые заня́тия** group study, group work

гру|сти́ть, щу́, сти́шь *impf.* to grieve, mourn; (**о** + *p. or* **по** + *d.*) to pine (for)

гру́стно[1] *adv.* sadly, sorrowfully

гру́стно[2] *as pred.* it is sad; **ей г.** she feels sad

гру́ст|ный, ~ен, ~на́, ~но *adj.* sad, melancholy

грусть, и *f.* sadness, melancholy

гру́ш|а, и *f.* **1** pear **2** : **боксёрская г.** punchball

гры́ж|а, и *f.* (med.) hernia

грыз|ть, у́, ёшь, *past* **~, ~ла** *impf.* to gnaw; to nibble; **г. но́гти** to bite one's nails

грызу́н, а́ *m.* rodent

гряд|а́, ы́, *pl.* **~ы́, ~, ~а́м** *f.* **1** (*pl.* **~ы́, ~, ~а́м**) (*гор*) ridge **2** (*pl.* **~ы́, ~, ~а́м**) (*в огоро́де*) bed **3** (*pl.* **~ы́, ~, ~а́м**) (*ряд*) row, series

гря́дк|а, и *f. dim. of* ▸ **гряда́** 2

гряду́щ|ий *adj.* coming, future; **~ие го́ды** years to come; (*as nt. n.* **~ее, ~его**) the future

гря́зно[1] *adv. of* ▸ **гря́зный**

гря́зно[2] *as pred.* it is dirty

гря́з|ный, ~ен, ~на́, ~но, ~ны́ *adj.* **1** (*покрытый гря́зью*) muddy **2** (*нечистый*) dirty; **~ное бельё** dirty washing (also fig.) **3** (*неопрятный*) untidy **4** (fig., *непристойный*) dirty, filthy; **~ное де́ло** dirty business

гряз|ь, и, о ~и, в ~и́ *f.* **1** mud (also fig.) **2** (*in pl.*) (*лечебное средство*) mud baths **3** (*отсутствие чистоты*) dirt, filth (also fig.)

губ|а́, ы́, *pl.* **~ы, ~, ~а́м** *f.* lip; **наду́ть ~ы** to pout

⚬ **губерна́тор, а** *m.* governor

губ|и́ть, лю́, ~ишь *impf.* (*of* ▸ **погуби́ть**) (*разрушать*) to destroy; (*портить*) to ruin, spoil

гу́бк|а, и *f.* sponge; **мыть ~ой** to sponge

губн|о́й *adj.* lip; **~ая пома́да** lipstick

гуверна́нтк|а, и *f.* governess

гуверне́р, а *m.* tutor

гуде́ни|е, я *nt.* drone; hum; (*об автомобильном гудке*) honk

гу|де́ть, жу́, ди́шь *impf.* **1** to drone; to hum; (*impers.*) **у меня́ ~де́ло в уша́х** there was a buzzing in my ears **2** (*о гудке*) to hoot; to honk

гуд|о́к, ка́ *m.* **1** (*устройство*) (*автомобиля*) horn; (*фабрики*) siren **2** (*звук*) hoot(ing); honk; toot **3** (teleph.) tone

гул, а *m.* (*машин, голосов*) drone, hum; (*орудий*) rumble

гуля́н|ье, ья, *g. pl.* **~ий** *nt.* (*празднество*) outdoor party

гуля́|ть, ю *impf.* (*of* ▸ **погуля́ть**) **1** to walk, stroll; **го go for a walk 2** (infml, *веселиться*) to make merry, have a good time

гуля́ш, а́ *m.* (cul.) goulash

гумани́зм, а *m.* humanism

гуманита́р|ный *adj.* **1** pertaining to the humanities; **~ые нау́ки** the humanities, the liberal arts; **~ое образова́ние** liberal education **2** (*гуманный*) humane; **~ая по́мощь** humanitarian aid

гума́нност|ь, и *f.* humanity, humaneness

гума́н|ный, ~ен, ~на *adj.* humane

гурма́н, а *m.* gourmet

гу́ру *m. indecl.* guru

гуса́р, а *m.* hussar

гу́сениц|а, ы *f.* **1** (zool.) caterpillar **2** (*трактора*) (caterpillar) track

гус|ёнок, ёнка, *pl.* **~я́та** *m.* gosling

гу́сто *adv.* thickly, dense

густ|о́й, ~, ~а́, ~о, ~ы́ *adj.* **1** thick, dense; **~ые бро́ви** bushy eyebrows **2** (*о цвете*) deep, rich

густонаселённый *adj.* densely populated

густот|а́, ы́ *f.* **1** thickness, density **2** (*цвета*) deepness, richness

гус|ь, я, *pl.* **~и, ~е́й** *m.* goose

гу́щ|а, и *f.* **1** (*осадок*) sediment; **кофе́йная г.** coffee grounds **2** (*чаща*) thicket; (fig.) thick, centre; **в са́мой ~е собы́тий** in the thick of things

гу́ще *comp. of* ▸ **густо́й**

Гц (*abbr. of* **герц**) Hz (= hertz)

гэ́льский *adj.* Gaelic

ГЭС *f. indecl.* (*abbr. of* **гидроэлектроста́нция**) hydroelectric power station

Дд

⚹ **да¹** *particle* **1** yes **2** (*interrog.*) yes?, is that so?, really? **3** (*emph.*) why; well; **да нет!** of course not!; not likely! **4** (*emph. pred.*): **когда́-н. э́то да ко́нчится** it must end some time **5**: **вот э́то да!** (infml) splendid!

да² *particle* (+ *3rd pers. pres. or fut. of v.*) (*пусть*) may, let; **да здра́вствует Росси́я!** long live Russia!

⚹ **да³** *conj.* **1** *mainly in conventional phrr.* (*и*) and; **ко́жа да ко́сти** skin and bone **2**: **да ещё** (*к тому же*) and (besides); and what is more **3**: **да и то́лько** and that's all **4** but; **я охо́тно проводи́л бы тебя́, да вре́мени нет** I would gladly come with you, but I haven't the time

дава́й and **дава́йте** *imper.* **1** (+ *inf. or 1st pers. pl. of fut.*) let's **2** (+ *imper.*) (infml) come on; **дава́й, расскажи́ что-н.!** come on, tell us a story!

⚹ **да|ва́ть, ю́, ёшь** *impf. of* ▸ **дать**

да|ва́ться, ю́сь, ёшься *impf.* (*of* ▸ **да́ться**) **1** *pass. of* ▸ **дава́ть 2**: **легко́ д.** to come easily, naturally; **ру́сский язы́к ему́ даётся легко́** Russian comes easily to him

дав|и́ть, лю́, ⌒ишь *impf.* **1** (+ *a. or* на + *a.*) to press (upon); (*о сапоге*) to pinch; (fig., *угнетать*) to oppress, weigh (upon) **2** (*насекомых*) to crush; to trample; (*о машине*) to run over **3** (*лимон, сок*) to squeeze

дав|и́ться, лю́сь, ⌒ишься *impf.* (*of* ▸ **подави́ться**) (+ *i. or* от + *g.*) to choke (with)

да́вк|а, и *f.* (infml) throng, crush

⚹ **давле́ни|е, я** *nt.* pressure

да́вн|ий *adj.* **1** ancient **2** (*существующий издавна*) of long standing; **с ⌒их пор, времён** for a long time

⚹ **давно́** *adv.* **1** (*много времени тому назад*) long ago; **2** (*в течение долгого времени*) for a long time

давны́м-давно́ *adv.* (infml) ages ago

Дагеста́н, а *m.* Dagestan

дагеста́н|ец, ца *m.* Dagestani

дагеста́н|ка, ки *f. of* ▸ **дагеста́нец**

дагеста́нский *adj.* Dagestani

⚹ **да́же** *particle* even; **е́сли д.** even if; **о́чень д. пло́хо** extremely bad

дактилоскопи́|я, и *f.* identification by means of fingerprints; **ге́нная д.** genetic fingerprinting

далай-ла́м|а, ы *m.* Dalai Lama

⚹ **да́лее** *adv.* further; **и так д.** (*abbr.* **и т. д.**) and so on, et cetera

⚹ **дал|ёкий, ⌒ёк, ⌒ека́, ⌒еко́** and **⌒ёко** *adj.*

(*страна, выстрел*) distant; **д. путь** long journey; **⌒ёкое про́шлое** distant past

⚹ **далеко́¹** *adv.* **1** (*о расстоянии*) far, far off; (от + *g.*) far (from) **2** (fig.) far, by a long way, by much; (*of time*): **бы́ло д. за по́лночь** it was long after midnight; **д. не** far from

далеко́² *as pred.* it is far, it is a long way; (+ *d. and* до + *g.*) (fig.) to be far (from), be much inferior (to); **ему́ д. до соверше́нства** he is far from perfect

дал|ь, и, о ⌒и, в ⌒и́ *f.* **1** (*далёкое пространство*) distance; distant prospect **2** (infml, *далёкое место*) distant spot

дальневосто́чный *adj.* Far Eastern

⚹ **дальне́йш|ий** *adj.* further, furthest; **в ⌒ем** (*в будущем*) in future, henceforth

да́льн|ий *adj.* (*далёкий*) distant, remote; **Д. Восто́к** the Far East; **⌒ее пла́вание** long voyage; **⌒его де́йствия** long-range; **⌒его сле́дования** (*о поезде*) long-distance **2** (*о родстве*) distant

дальнови́д|ный, ⌒ен, ⌒на *adj.* far-sighted

дальнозо́р|кий, ⌒ок, ⌒ка *adj.* long-sighted (BrE), far-sighted (AmE); (fig.) far-sighted

да́льност|ь, и *f.* distance; range

дальто́ник, а *m.* colour-blind (BrE), color-blind (AmE) person

да́льше 1 *comp. of* ▸ **далёкий 2** *adv.* further; **д. не́куда** (infml) that's the limit; **ти́ше е́дешь, д. бу́дешь** (*proverb*) more haste, less speed **3** *adv.* (*продолжая начатое*) further; **д.!** go on! **4** *adv.* (*затем*) then, next **5** *adv.* (*долее*) longer

да́м|а, ы *f.* **1** (*женщина*) lady **2** (*игральная карта*) queen

да́мб|а, ы *f.* dike

да́м|ский *adj. of* ▸ **да́ма**; **⌒ская су́мка** ladies' handbag

Да́ни|я, и *f.* Denmark

⚹ **да́нн|ые, ых** (*no sg.*) **1** (also comput.) data; (*факты*) facts, information **2** (*свойства*) qualities, gifts

⚹ **да́нн|ый** *p.p.p. of* ▸ **дать** and *adj.* given; present; in question; **в д. моме́нт** at present; **в ⌒ом слу́чае** in this case

дан|ь, и *f.* (fig., *моде, традиции*) tribute; debt; **отда́ть д.** (+ *d.*) to pay tribute to, recognize

дар, а, *pl.* **⌒ы́** *m.* **1** (*подарок*) gift, donation **2** (+ *g.*) (*талант, способность*) gift (of)

дари́тел|ь, я *m.* donor

дар|и́ть, ю́, ⌒ишь *impf.* (*of* ▸ **подари́ть**) (+ *d. and a.*) (*давать*) to give

дарова́ни|е, я *nt.* gift, talent

дарово́й *adj.* free (of charge), gratuitous

да́ром adv. **1** (бесплатно) free (of charge), gratis **2** (напрасно) in vain, to no purpose; **пропа́сть д.** to be wasted

✔ **да́т|а, ы** f. date

да́тельный adj. (gram.) dative

дати́р|овать, ую impf. and pf. to date

да́тский adj. Danish

да́тчик, а m. sensor

✔ **дать, дам, дашь, даст, дади́м, дади́те, даду́т,** past **дал, дала́, да́ло́, да́ли** pf. (of ▶ **дава́ть**) **1** to give; **д. взаймы́** to lend (money); **на чай** to tip; **д. конце́рт** to give a concert **2** to give, administer; **д. лека́рство** to give medicine **3** (по + d. or в + a.) (infml, ударить) to give (it); to hit (on; in) **4** (fig.) to give; **д. сло́во** to give one's word **5** (fig.) to give, grant; **д. во́лю** (+ d.) to give (free) rein (to), give vent (to); **д. доро́гу** (+ d.) to make way (for) **6** (with certain nn. expr. action related to meaning of n.): **д. звоно́к** to ring (a bell); **д. тре́щину** to crack **7** (+ inf.) (позволить) to let; **д. поня́ть** to give to understand; **да́йте ему́ сказа́ть** let him speak

да́ться, да́мся, да́шься etc., past **да́лся, дала́сь** pf. of ▶ **дава́ться**

да́ч|а, и f. **1** (загородный дом) dacha **2**: **быть на ∼е** to be in the country; **пое́хать на ∼у** to go to the country

да́чник, а m. (holiday) visitor (in the country)

дБ (abbr. of **децибе́л**) dB, decibel(s)

✔ **два,** f. **две,** m., f., nt. **двух, двум, двумя́, о двух** num. two; **в двух слова́х** briefly, in short; **в д. счёта** in no time; **в двух шага́х** a short step away; **ка́ждые д. дня** every other day

двадцати́… comb. form twenty-

двадцатиле́тний adj. **1** (срок) twenty-year, of twenty years **2** (человек) twenty-year-old

двадца́т|ый adj. twentieth; **одна́ ∼ая** a twentieth; **∼ое января́** the twentieth of January; **∼ые го́ды** the twenties

два́дцат|ь, и, i. **ью** num. twenty; **д. оди́н** и т. n. twenty-one, etc.

два́жды adv. twice; **д. два — четы́ре** twice two is four

двена́дцатый adj. twelfth

двена́дцат|ь, и num. twelve

дверно́й adj. of ▶ **дверь**

две́р|ца, ы, g. pl. **∼ец** f. door (of car, cupboard, etc.)

✔ **двер|ь, и, о ∼и, в ∼й,** pl. **∼и, ∼ей,** i. **∼я́ми** and **∼ьми́** f. door; **в ∼я́х** in the doorway

две́сти, двухсо́т, двумста́м, двумяста́ми, о двухста́х num. two hundred

✔ **дви́гател|ь, я** m. motor, engine; (fig.) motive force

дви́га|ть, ю and **дви́жу** impf. (of ▶ **дви́нуть**) **1** (∼ю) to move **2** (∼ю) (+ i.) (шевелить) to move (part of the body); to make a movement (of) **3** (дви́жу) (приводить в движение) to set in motion, get going (also fig.)

дви́га|ться, юсь and **дви́жусь** impf. (of ▶ **дви́нуться**) **1** to move; **д. вперёд** to advance (also fig.) **2** (отправляться) to start, get going **3** pass. of ▶ **дви́гать**

✔ **движе́ни|е, я** nt. **1** movement; motion; **привести́ в д.** to set in motion; **д. «зелёных»** the green movement **2** (физическое) movement, exercise **3** (дорожное) traffic; **односторо́ннее д.** one-way traffic

дви́н|уть, ну, нешь pf. of ▶ **дви́гать**

дви́н|уться, нусь, нешься pf. of ▶ **дви́гаться**

дво́е, двои́х num. **1** (collect.) two; **нас бы́ло д.** there were two of us; **д. су́ток** forty-eight hours **2** (+ nn. denoting objects usu. found in pairs) two pairs; **д. чуло́к** two pairs of stockings

двоето́чи|е, я nt. (gram.) colon

дво́|иться, ю́сь, и́шься impf. (казаться двойным) to appear double; **у него́ ∼и́лось в глаза́х** he saw (objects) double

дво́ичный adj. (math.) binary

дво́йк|а, и f. **1** (цифра, игральная карта) two **2** (отметка) 'two' (out of five) **3** (infml, автобус, трамвай) No. 2 (bus, tram, etc.)

двойни́к, а́ m. (кого-н.) double

двойн|о́й adj. double; **∼а́я фами́лия** double-barrelled (BrE), double-barreled (AmE) surname

дво́|йня, йни, g. pl. **∼ен** f. twins

✔ **двор, а́** m. **1** (при одном доме) yard; (между домами) courtyard **2**: **ско́тный д.** farmyard **3**: **на ∼е́** out of doors, outside **4** (королевский) court; **при ∼е́** at court

двор|е́ц, ца́ m. palace

дворе́цк|ий, ого m. butler

дво́рник, а m. **1** (работник) caretaker **2** (infml, в машине) windscreen wiper (BrE), windshield wiper (AmE)

дворян|и́н, и́на, pl. **∼е, ∼** m. nobleman

дворя́н|ка, ки f. of ▶ **дворяни́н**

дворя́нский adj. of the nobility

дворя́нств|о, а nt. (collect.) nobility

двою́родный adj. related through grandparent; **д. брат** (first) cousin (male); **д. дя́дя** (first) cousin once removed

дву́…, двух… comb. form bi-, di-, two-, double-

двузна́чный adj. two-digit

двули́ч|ный, ∼ен, ∼на adj. (fig.) two-faced

двуро́г|ий adj. two-horned; **∼ая луна́** crescent moon

двуру́чный adj. two-handled

двусмы́слен|ный, ∼, ∼на adj. ambiguous

двуспа́льный adj. double (of beds)

двуство́лк|а, и f. double-barrelled (BrE), double-barreled gun (AmE)

двусторо́н|ний, ∼ен, ∼ня adj. **1** double-sided; **∼нее воспале́ние лёгких** double pneumonia **2** (движение) two-way **3** (соглашение) bilateral

двухдне́вный adj. two-day

двухколёсный *adj.* two-wheeled

двухме́стный *adj.* two-seater; **д. но́мер** double room

двухмото́рный *adj.* twin-engined

двухсо́тый *adj.* two-hundredth

двухчасово́й *adj.* **1** (*фильм*) two-hour **2** (*поезд*) two o'clock

двухэта́жный *adj.* two-storey (BrE), two-story (AmE); (*автобус*) double-decker

двуязы́чный, ~ен, ~на *adj.* bilingual

деба́т|ы, ов (*no sg.*) debate

де́бет, а *m.* debit

дебет|ова́ть, у́ю *impf. and pf.* to debit

дебето́в|ый *adj. of* ▶ де́бет; ~ая ка́рточка debit card

деби́л, а *m.* **1** learning-disabled person **2** (*infml, pej.*) moron

де́бр|и, ей (*no sg.*) **1** jungle; thickets **2** (*fig.*) maze, labyrinth

дебю́т, а *m.* debut

дебюта́нт, а *m.* debutant

дебюта́нтк|а, и *f.* debutante

дебюти́р|овать, ую *impf. and pf.* to make one's debut

де́в|а, ы *f.* **1** (*obs.*) girl, maiden; **ста́рая д.** (*infml*) old maid **2** (**Д.**) (*созвездие*) Virgo

девальва́ци|я, и *f.* devaluation

дева́|ть, ю *impf. of* ▶ деть

дева́|ться, юсь *impf. of* ▶ де́ться

де́вер|ь, я, *pl.* ~ья́, ~е́й *m.* brother-in-law (*husband's brother*)

деви́з, а *m.* motto

деви́ц|а, ы *f.* girl, maiden

деви́честв|о, а *nt.* girlhood; **в ~е Ивано́ва** née Ivanova

де́вич|ий *adj.* girlish; ~ья фами́лия maiden name

◆ **де́вочк|а**, и *f.* (little) girl

де́вственник, а *m.* virgin

де́вственниц|а, ы *f.* virgin

де́вственност|ь, и *f.* virginity; chastity

де́вствен|ный, ~, ~на *adj.* **1** (*целомудренный*) virgin **2** (*невинный*) virginal; innocent **3** (*fig.*) virgin; **д. лес** virgin forest

◆ **де́вушк|а**, и *f.* **1** (*unmarried*) girl **2** (*infml, обращение*) miss

девчо́нк|а, и *f.* (*infml*) (little) girl

девяно́ст|о, а *g., d., i., and p.* а *num.* ninety

девяно́стый *adj.* ninetieth

де́вятер|о, ы́х *num.* (*collect.*) nine; **нас д.** there are nine of us

девятисо́тый *adj.* nine-hundredth

девя́тк|а, и *f.* **1** (*цифра, игральная карта*) nine **2** (*infml, автобус, трамвай*) No. 9 (*bus, tram, etc.*) **3** (*группа из девятерых*) (group of) nine

девятна́дцатый *adj.* nineteenth

девятна́дцат|ь, и *num.* nineteen

девя́тый *adj.* ninth

де́вят|ь, и́, *i.* ью *num.* nine

девятьсо́т, девятисо́т, девятиста́м, девятьюста́ми, о девятиста́х *num.* nine hundred

дёг|оть, тя (*no pl.*) *m.* tar

деграда́ци|я, и *f.* degradation

дегради́р|овать, ую *impf. and pf.* to become degraded

дегуста́ци|я, и *f.* tasting; **д. вин** wine tasting

дед, а *m.* **1** grandfather; (*in pl.*) (*fig.*) grandfathers, forefathers **2** (*infml, старик*) grandad, grandpa **3**: **Д. Моро́з** Father Christmas, Santa Claus

дедовщи́н|а, ы *f.* (mil., sl.) bullying, harassment (*of subordinates*)

деду́кци|я, и *f.* deduction

де́душк|а, и *m.* grandfather, grandpa

дееприча́сти|е, я *nt.* (gram.) gerund (*e.g. читая, прочитав*)

дееспосо́б|ный, ~ен, ~на *adj.* **1** able to function, active **2** (law) capable

дежу́р|ить, ю, ишь *impf.* **1** (*быть дежурным*) to be on duty **2** (*неотлучно находиться*) to be in constant attendance

дежу́рн|ый *adj.* **1** duty; on duty; **д. офице́р** (mil.) orderly officer; ~ая апте́ка chemist's shop open outside normal opening hours **2** (*as m. n.* д., ~ого, *f.* ~ая, ~ой) man, woman on duty; **кто д.?** who is on duty?

дежу́рств|о, а *nt.* (being on) duty; **гра́фик ~** rota; (mil.) roster

дезерти́р, а *m.* deserter

дезерти́р|овать, ую *impf. and pf.* to desert

дезинфе́кци|я, и *f.* disinfection

дезинфици́р|овать, ую *impf. and pf.* to disinfect

дезинформа́ци|я, и *f.* misinformation; (*намеренная*) disinformation

дезинформи́р|овать, ую *impf. and pf.* to misinform

дезодора́нт, а *m.* deodorant

дезоргани́з|ова́ть, у́ю *impf. and pf.* to disrupt

дезориенти́р|овать, ую *impf. and pf.* to disorient

◆ **де́йстви|е**, я *nt.* **1** (*деятельность*) action, operation; activity; **ввести́ в д.** to bring into operation, bring into force **2** (*функционирование*) functioning (*of a machine, etc.*) **3** (*влияние*) effect; action; **под ~ем** (+ *g.*) under the influence (of) **4** (*события, о которых идёт речь*) action (*of a story, etc.*) **5** (*часть пьесы*) act **6** (*in pl.*) (*поступки*) actions; (mil.) operations

◆ **действи́тельно** *adv.* really; indeed

действи́тельност|ь, и *f.* reality; **в ~и** in reality, in fact

действи́тел|ьный, ~ен, ~на *adj.* **1** (*настоящий*) real, actual; true, authentic; ~ьное положе́ние веще́й the true state of affairs; ~ьная слу́жба (mil.) active service **2** (*имеющий силу*) valid

◆ **де́йств|овать**, ую *impf.* **1** (*impf. only*)

Д

(*совершать действия*) to act; (*функционировать*) to work, function; to operate **2** (*pf.* по~) (на + *i.*) (*влиять*) to affect, have an effect (upon), act (upon); **лека́рство** ~**ует** the medicine is taking effect

✓ **де́йствующ|ий** *pres. part. act. of* ▶ **де́йствовать** *and adj.*: ~**ая а́рмия** army in the field; **д. вулка́н** active volcano; ~**ие ли́ца** (theatr.) characters

✓ **декабр|ь, я́** *m.* December

дека́брьский *adj. of* ▶ **дека́брь**

дека́д|а, ы *f.* (*срок*) ten-day period

деклара́ци|я, и *f.* declaration; **нало́говая д.** tax return

деклари́р|овать, ую *impf. and pf.* to declare, proclaim

декоди́р|овать, ую *impf. and pf.* to decode

декольте́ *nt. indecl.* décolleté (*also as adj.*); décolletage

декорати́в|ный, ~ен, ~на *adj.* decorative, ornamental

декора́тор, а *m.* (*помещения*) interior decorator; (theatr.) scene painter

декора́ци|я, и *f.* (theatr.) set, scenery

декре́тный *adj.*: **д. о́тпуск** maternity leave

де́ланный *adj.* artificial, forced, affected

✓ **де́ла|ть, ю** *impf.* (*of* ▶ **сде́лать**) **1** (*производить*) to make **2** (*приводить в какое-н. состояние*) to make; **д. кого́-н. несча́стным** to make sb unhappy **3** (*поступать*) to do; **д. не́чего** it can't be helped **4** (+ *var. nn.*) to make, do, give; **д. вид** to pretend, feign; **д. вы́воды** to draw conclusions

де́ла|ться, юсь *impf.* (*of* ▶ **сде́латься**) **1** (*становиться*) to become, get, grow **2** (*происходить*) to happen; **что там** ~**ется?** what is going on?

делега́т, а *m.* delegate

делега́ци|я, и *f.* delegation; group

делеги́р|овать, ую *impf. and pf.* to delegate

деле́ни|е, я *nt.* **1** division **2** (*на шкале*) point, degree, unit

Де́ли *m. indecl.* Delhi

деликате́с, а *m.* delicacy; **магази́н** ~**ов** delicatessen

делика́тность|ь, и *f.* delicacy

делика́т|ный, ~ен, ~на *adj.* delicate

дел|и́ть, ю́, ~ишь *impf.* **1** (*pf.* раз~) to divide; **д. шесть на́ три** to divide six by three **2** (*pf.* по~) (с + *i.*) to share (with); **д. с кем-н. го́ре и ра́дость** to share sb's sorrows and joys

дел|и́ться, ю́сь, ~ишься *impf.* **1** (*pf.* раз~) (на + *a.*) to divide (into) **2** (*pf.* по~) (+ *i. and* с + *i.*) to share (with); to communicate (to); (+ *i.*) **д. куско́м хле́ба с кем-н.** to share a crust of bread with sb **3** (*impf. only*) (на + *a.*) to be divisible (by); **число́ со́рок де́вять** ~**ится на семь** forty-nine is divisible by seven

✓ **де́л|о, а,** *pl.* ~**а́,** ~**,** ~**а́м** *nt.* **1** (*работа, занятие*) business, affair(s); **по** ~**у, по** ~**а́м** on business; **э́то моё д.** that is my affair; **име́ть д.** (с + *i.*) to have to do (with), deal (with); **не вме́шивайтесь не в своё д.** mind your own business; **как (ва́ши)** ~**а́?** how are things going (with you)?, how are you getting on?; **привести́ свои́** ~**а́ в поря́док** to put one's affairs in order; **како́е мне до э́того д.?** what has this to do with me?; **пе́рвым** ~**ом** in the first instance, first of all **2** (*идеи*) cause; **д. ми́ра** the cause of peace **3** (+ *adj.*) (*специальность*) occupation; (*предприятие*) business, concern; **го́рное д.** mining **4** matter, point; **д. вку́са** matter of taste; **д. че́сти** point of honour; **д. в том, что…** the point is that …; **в то́м-то и д.** that's (just) the point; **не в э́том д.** that's not the point **5** (*факт*) fact, deed; thing; **на са́мом** ~**е** in actual fact, as a matter of fact; **в са́мом** ~**е** really, indeed **6** (*поступок*) act, deed **7** (law, *судебное*) case; cause; **возбуди́ть д.** to plead a cause; **возбуди́ть д.** (про́тив + *g.*) to bring an action (against), institute proceedings (against) **8** (*досье*) file, dossier; **ли́чное д.** personal file

делови́т|ый, ~, ~**а** *adj.* businesslike, efficient

✓ **делов|о́й** *adj.* **1** business; work; ~**о́е письмо́** business letter; ~**а́я пое́здка** business trip **2** (*человек, тон*) businesslike

де́льт|а, ы *f.* delta

дельтапла́н, а *m.* hang-glider (*craft*)

дельтапланери́ст, а *m.* hang-glider (*person*)

дельтапланери́ст|ка, ки *f. of* ▶ **дельтапланери́ст**

дельфи́н, а *m.* dolphin

демаго́г, а *m.* demagogue

демаго́ги|я, и *f.* demagogy

демилитариз|ова́ть, у́ю *impf. and pf.* to demilitarize

демисезо́нн|ый *adj.*: ~**ое пальто́** light coat (*for spring and autumn wear*)

демобилиз|ова́ть, у́ю *impf. and pf.* to demobilize

демобилиз|ова́ться, у́юсь *impf. and pf.* to be demobilized

демографи́ческий *adj.* demographic; **д. взрыв** population explosion

демокра́т, а *m.* democrat

демократи́ческий *adj.* democratic

демокра́ти|я, и *f.* democracy

де́мон, а *m.* demon

демонстра́нт, а *m.* (pol.) demonstrator

демонстра́нт|ка, ки *f. of* ▶ **демонстра́нт**

демонстрати́в|ный, ~ен, ~на *adj.* (*вызывающий*) demonstrative, done for effect

демонстра́ци|я, и *f.* **1** demonstration **2** (*публичный показ*) showing (*of a film, etc.*)

демонстри́р|овать, ую *impf. and pf.* (*pf. also* про~) to show, display; to give a demonstration (of)

д

демонти́р|овать, **ую** *impf. and pf.* (tech.) to dismantle

деморализ|ова́ть, **у́ю** *impf. and pf.* to demoralize

⚬ **де́нежный** *adj.* **1** monetary; money; **д. автома́т** cash dispenser; **д. знак** banknote; **д. перево́д** money order **2** (infml, *богатый*) rich; **д. мешо́к** moneybags

⚬ **де́нь, дня** *m.* **1** day; afternoon; **в 4 ч дня** at 4 p.m.; **днём** in the afternoon; **д. рожде́ния** birthday; **д. ото дня** with every passing day, day by day; **в оди́н прекра́сный д.** one fine day; **изо дня в д.** day after day; **на друго́й, сле́дующий д.** next day; **на днях** (*недавно*) the other day; (*скоро*) one of these days, any day now; **со дня на́ д.** daily, from day to day; **че́рез д.** every other day **2** (*in pl.*) (*время; жизнь*) days; **его́ дни сочтены́** his days are numbered

⚬ **де́н|ьги, ег, ьга́м** *pl.* money; **ме́лкие д.** small change; **нали́чные д.** cash, ready money

⚬ **департа́мент, а** *m.* department

депе́ш|а, и *f.* dispatch

депо́ *nt. indecl.* (rail.) depot

депози́т, а *m.* (fin.) deposit

депорта́ци|я, и *f.* deportation

депорти́р|овать, ую *impf. and pf.* to deport

депресси́вный *adj. of* ▶ **депре́ссия**

депре́сси|я, и *f.* (econ., psych.) depression

⚬ **депута́т, а** *m.* deputy; delegate

депута́тский *adj. of* ▶ **депута́т**

дёрга|ть, ю *impf.* (*of* ▶ **дёрнуть**) (*тянуть*) to pull, tug

дёрга|ться, юсь *impf.* (*of* ▶ **дёрнуться**) **1** *pass. of* ▶ **дёргать 2** to twitch

дереве́нский *adj.* **1** (*магазин*) village **2** (*тишина, пейзаж*) rural; (*житель, воздух*) country

⚬ **дере́в|ня, ни**, *g. pl.* ~**е́нь** *f.* **1** (*селение*) village **2** (*местность*) (the) country (*opp. the town*)

⚬ **де́рев|о, а**, *pl.* ~**ья**, ~**ьев** *nt.* **1** (*растение*) tree **2** (*sg. only*) (*древесина*) wood (*as material*)

деревообрабо́тк|а, и *f.* woodworking

дереву́шк|а, и *f.* hamlet

⚬ **деревя́нный** *adj.* wood; wooden

держа́в|а, ы *f.* (pol.) power

⚬ **держа́тел|ь, я** *m.* **1** (fin.) holder **2** (*приспособление*) holder

⚬ **держ|а́ть, у́, ~ишь** *impf.* **1** (*в руках*) to hold; (*не отпускать*) to hold on to; ~**и́те во́ра!** stop thief! **2** (*поддерживать*) to hold up, support **3** (*заставлять находиться в каком-н. состоянии*) to keep, hold; **д. путь** (**к** + *d. or* **на** + *a.*) to head (for), make (for); **д. пари́** to bet; **д. чью-н. сто́рону** to take sb's side **4** (*животных*) to keep; **д. лошаде́й** to keep horses **5** (+ *certain nouns*) to carry out; **д. речь** to make a speech

держ|а́ться, у́сь, ~ишься *impf.* **1** (**за** + *a.*) to hold (on to); ~**и́тесь за пери́ла** hold on to the banister **2** (**на** + *p.*) to be held up (by),

be supported (by) **3** (*находиться где-либо*) to keep, stay, be; **д. вме́сте** to stick together; **д. в стороне́** to hold aloof **4** (*стоять*) to hold oneself; (fig., *вести себя*) to behave **5** (*сохраняться*) to last **6** (*не сдаваться*) to hold out, stand firm **7** (+ *g.*) (*придерживаться определённого направления*) to keep (to); **д. ле́вой стороны́** to keep to the left **8** (+ *g.*) (*следовать чему-либо*) to adhere (to), stick (to)

де́рз|кий, ~ок, ~ка́, ~ко *adj.* **1** (*грубый*) impertinent, cheeky **2** (*смелый*) audacious

де́рзост|ь, и *f.* **1** (*грубость*) impertinence; cheek; **говори́ть ~и** to be impertinent **2** (*смелость*) audacity

дермати́н, а *m.* leatherette

дермати́т, а *m.* dermatitis

дермато́лог, а *m.* dermatologist

дерматоло́ги|я, и *f.* dermatology

дёрн, а *m.* turf

дёрн|уть, у, ешь *pf. of* ▶ **дёргать**

дёрн|уться, усь, ешься *pf.* (*of* ▶ **дёргаться**) to start up (with a jerk); to dart

деру́, ёшь *see* ▶ **драть**

дерьм|о́, а́ *nt.* (vulg.) (*животных*) dung; (*человека*) crap; (fig.) crap

деса́нт, а *m.* (mil.) **1** (*высадка войск*) landing **2** (*войска*) landing force; **вы́садить, вы́бросить д.** to make a landing

деса́нтник, а *m.* paratrooper

десе́рт, а *m.* dessert

десн|а́, ы́, *pl.* ~**ы, дёсен** *f.* (anat.) gum

де́сятер|о, ых *пит.* (collect.) ten

десятибо́рь|е, я *nt.* (sport) decathlon

десятикра́тный *adj.* tenfold

десятиле́ти|е, я *nt.* **1** (*срок*) decade **2** (*годовщина*) tenth anniversary

десяти́чн|ый *adj.* decimal; ~**ая дробь** decimal fraction

деся́тк|а, и *f.* **1** (*цифра, игральная карта*) ten **2** (infml, *автобус, трамвай*) No. 10 (*bus, tram, etc.*) **3** (*группа из десятерых*) (group of) ten **4** (infml, *десять рублей*) ten-rouble note, tenner

⚬ **деся́т|ок, ка** *m.* **1** (*десять*) ten **2** (*десять лет*) ten years, decade (*of life*) **3** (*in pl.*) (math.) tens **4** (*in pl.*) (*множество*) dozens, scores; ~**ки люде́й** scores of people

деся́тый *пит.* tenth

⚬ **де́сят|ь, и,** *i.* **ью** *пит.* ten

⚬ **дета́л|ь, и** *f.* **1** (*подробность*) detail **2** (*часть машины*) part, component

детдо́м, а *m.* children's home

детекти́в, а *m.* **1** (*человек*) detective **2** (*роман*) detective story **3** (*фильм*) detective film

детекти́вный *adj.* detective (*attr.*)

детёныш, а *m.* young (*of animals*)

де́т|и, ~е́й, ~ям, ~ьми́, о ~ях *nt. pl.* (*sg.* **дитя́**, oblique cases in *sg.* not used) children

детса́д, а *m.* kindergarten, nursery school

де́тск|ая, ой *f.* playroom; nursery

Д

◦ **де́тский** *adj.* **1** child's, children's; **д. дом** children's home; **д. сад** kindergarten, nursery school; **д. церебра́льный парали́ч** (*med.*) cerebral palsy **2** (*ребя́ческий*) childish; **д. язы́к** baby talk

◦ **де́тств|о, а** *nt.* childhood

деть, де́ну, де́нешь *pf.* (*of* ▶ **дева́ть**) (*infml*) to put, do (with); **куда́ ты дел мою́ ру́чку?** what have you done with my pen?

де́|ться, нусь, нешься *pf.* (*of* ▶ **дева́ться**) to get to, disappear; **куда́ ~лись мои́ часы́?** where has my watch got to?

дефе́кт, а *m.* defect

дефи́с, а *m.* hyphen

дефици́т, а *m.* **1** (*econ.*) deficit **2** (*нехва́тка*) shortage, deficiency

дефици́т|ный, ~ен, ~на *adj.* in short supply; scarce

дефо́лт, а *m.* (*fin.*) default (in payment)

деформа́ци|я, и *f.* deformation

деформи́р|овать, ую *impf. and pf.* (*исказить*) to deform; (*изменить форму чего-н.*) to change the form of

деформи́р|оваться, уюсь *impf. and pf.* to change shape; to become deformed

**деци... ** *comb. form* deci-

децибе́л, а, g. pl. д. *m.* decibel

дециме́тр, а *m.* decimetre (*BrE*), decimeter (*AmE*)

дешеве́|ть, ю *impf.* (*of* ▶ **подешеве́ть**) to fall in price, become cheaper

дешеви́зн|а, ы *f.* cheapness; low price

деше́вле *comp. of* ▶ **дешёвый**, ▶ **дёшево**

дёшево *adv.* cheap, cheaply; (*fig.*) cheaply, lightly

◦ **дешёвый, дёшев, дешева́, дёшево** *adj.* cheap; (*fig.*) cheap; empty, worthless

дешифр|ова́ть, у́ю *impf. and pf.* to decipher, decode

де́ятел|ь, я *m.* agent; **госуда́рственный д.** statesman; **обще́ственный д.** public figure

◦ **де́ятельност|ь, и** *f.* **1** activity, activities; work; **обще́ственная д.** public work **2** (*physiol., psych., etc.*) activity, operation

де́ятел|ьный, ~ен, ~ьна *adj.* active, energetic

джаз, а *m.* jazz

джаз-ба́нд, а *m.* jazz band

джази́ст, а *m.* jazzman, jazz musician

джазме́н, а *m.* = **джази́ст**

джем, а *m.* jam (*BrE*), jelly (*AmE*)

дже́мпер, а *m.* jumper

джентльме́н, а *m.* gentleman

джентльме́нский *adj.* gentlemanly

джин, а *m.* gin (*liquor*); **д.-то́ник** gin and tonic

джинсо́вый *adj.* denim

джинс|ы, ов (*no sg.*) jeans

джип, а *m.* jeep®

джиха́д, а *m.* (*relig.*) jihad

джо́йстик, а *m.* (*comput.*) joystick

◦ **key word**

джо́кер, а *m.* (*cards*) joker

джу́нгл|и, ей (*no sg.*) jungle

джут, а *m.* (*bot.*) jute

дзюдо́ *nt. indecl.* judo

дзюдои́ст, а *m.* judoist, judoka

дзюдои́ст|ка, ки *f. of* ▶ **дзюдои́ст**

диабе́т, а *m.* diabetes

диабе́тик, а *m.* diabetic

диа́гноз, а *m.* diagnosis

диагности́р|овать, ую *impf. and pf.* to diagnose; (*tech.*) to check

диагона́л|ь, и *f.* diagonal; **по ~и** diagonally

диагра́мм|а, ы *f.* diagram; chart

диаде́м|а, ы *f.* diadem, tiara

диале́кт, а *m.* dialect

диало́г, а *m.* dialogue (*BrE*), dialog (*AmE*)

диало́гов|ый *adj.* (*comput.*) interactive; **~ое окно́** dialog box

диа́метр, а *m.* diameter

диапазо́н, а *m.* **1** (*mus.*) diapason, range **2** (*fig.*) range, compass **3** (*tech., fig.*) range; **д. волн** (*radio*) waveband

диа́спор|а, ы *f.* diaspora

дива́н, а *m.* divan (*couch*); sofa; **д.-крова́ть** sofa bed

диверса́нт, а *m.* saboteur

диверсифика́ци|я, и *f.* diversification

диве́рси|я, и *f.* **1** (*mil.*) diversion **2** sabotage

дивиде́нд, а *m.* dividend

Ди-ви-ди́ (*usu. spelt* **DVD**) *m. indecl.* DVD

диви́зи|я, и *f.* (*mil.*) division

дие́з, а *m.* (*also as indecl. adj.*) (*mus.*) sharp

◦ **дие́т|а, ы** *f.* diet; **сиде́ть на ~е** to be on a diet; **соблюда́ть ~у** to keep to a diet

диети́ческий *adj.* dietetic

◦ **диза́йн, а** *m.* design

диза́йнер, а *m.* designer

ди́зел|ь, я *m.* diesel engine

ди́зельный *adj.* diesel

дизентери́|я, и *f.* dysentery

дика́р|ь, я *m.* savage; (*некульту́рный челове́к*) barbarian

ди́к|ий, ~, ~а́, ~о *adj.* **1** (*живо́тное, расте́ние*) wild; **~ая ко́шка** wild cat **2** (*пле́мя*) savage **3** (*необу́зданный*) wild; **~ие кри́ки** wild cries; **д. восто́рг** wild delight **4** (*абсу́рдный*) ridiculous **5** (*засте́нчивый*) shy; unsociable **6** (*стра́шный*) terrible, awful

ди́ко¹ *adv.* **1** *adv. of* ▶ **ди́кий 2** (*в испу́ге*) in fright; startled; **д. озира́ться** to look around wildly

ди́ко² *as pred.* it is ridiculous

дикобра́з, а *m.* porcupine

дикорасту́щий *adj.* wild

ди́кост|ь, и *f.* absurdity; **э́то соверше́нная д.** it is quite absurd

дикта́нт, а *m.* dictation

дикта́тор, а *m.* dictator

диктату́р|а, ы *f.* dictatorship

дикт|ова́ть, у́ю, у́ешь *impf.* (*of* ▶ **продиктова́ть**) to dictate

ди́ктор, а *m.* announcer; (*программы новостей*) newscaster

диктофо́н, а *m.* Dictaphone®

ди́кци|я, и *f.* diction; enunciation

ди́лер, а *m.* dealer

дилета́нт, а *m.* amateur, dilettante, dabbler

дина́мик, а *m.* loudspeaker

дина́мик|а, и *f.* dynamics

динами́т, а *m.* dynamite

динами́ческий *adj.* dynamic

динами́чный *adj.* dynamic

дина́сти|я, и *f.* dynasty

ди́нго *m. indecl.* (zool.) dingo

диноза́вр, а *m.* dinosaur

дио́д, а *m.*: светоизлуча́ющий д. light-emitting diode, LED

дипло́м, а *m.* **1** (*документ*) diploma, certificate; degree **2** (infml, *работа*) degree work, research

диплома́т, а *m.* **1** diplomat **2** (infml) attaché case, (rigid) briefcase

дипломати́ческий *adj.* diplomatic

дипломати́ч|ный, ∼ен, ∼на *adj.* (fig.) diplomatic

диплома́ти|я, и *f.* diplomacy

дипло́м|ный *adj. of* ▸ **дипло́м**; ∼ная рабо́та degree work, degree thesis

директи́в|а, ы *f.* directive

✧ **дире́ктор**, а, *pl.* ∼а́ *m.* director, manager; д. шко́лы head (master, mistress); principal

дире́кци|я, и *f.* management; board (of directors)

дирижа́бл|ь, я *m.* airship, dirigible

дирижёр, а *m.* (mus.) conductor

дирижи́р|овать, ую *impf.* (+ *i.*) (mus.) to conduct

✧ **диск**, а *m.* **1** disk; (*телефонный*) telephone dial **2** (sport) discus **3** (*грампластинка*) disc, record **4** (*компьютерный, музыкальный*) disk, CD, DVD

дисквалифика́ци|я, и *f.* disqualification

диске́т|а, ы *f.* (comput.) diskette

ди́ско *nt. indecl.* disco music

дисково́д, а *m.* (comput.) disk drive

дискомфо́рт, а *m.* discomfort

диско́нтн|ый *adj.*: ∼ая ка́рта discount card

дискоте́к|а, и *f.* disco(theque)

дискредити́р|овать, ую *impf. and pf.* to discredit

дискримина́ци|я, и *f.* discrimination; д. же́нщин sexism; д. по во́зрасту ageism

дискримини́р|овать, ую *impf. and pf.* to discriminate against

дискусси|я, и *f.* discussion

дискути́р|овать, ую *impf. and pf.* (+ *a.* or o + *p.*) to discuss

дислока́ци|я, и *f.* (mil.) deployment, distribution (*of troops*)

диспансе́р, а *m.* (med.) clinic, (health) centre

диспе́тчер, а *m.* controller (*of movement of transport, etc.*); (comput.) manager

диспе́тчер|ский *adj.* of ▸ **диспе́тчер**; (aeron.): ∼ская слу́жба flying control organization; (*as f. n.* ∼ская, ∼ской) controller's office; (aeron.) control tower

дисппле́|й, я *m.* (comput.) display, VDU (*visual display unit*)

диспропо́рци|я, и *f.* disproportion

ди́спут, а *m.* (public) debate

диссерта́ци|я, и *f.* dissertation, thesis

диссиде́нт, а *m.* dissident

диссона́нс, а *m.* (mus., also fig.) dissonance, discord

дистанцио́нн|ый *adj.*: ∼ое управле́ние remote control

диста́нци|я, и *f.* **1** distance; на большо́й, ма́лой ∼и at a great, short distance **2** (sport) distance; сойти́ с ∼и to withdraw **3** (mil.) range

дистрибью́тор, а *m.* distributor, supplier

дисципли́н|а, ы *f.* discipline

дисциплини́рованный *adj.* disciplined

дитя́, *pl.* де́ти (*oblique cases not used in sg.*) *nt.* child; baby

дифтери́|я, и *f.* diphtheria

дифференциа́л, а *m.* **1** (math.) differential **2** (tech.) differential gear

дифференциа́льн|ый *adj.* differential; ∼ое исчисле́ние (math.) differential calculus

дича́|ть, ю *impf.* (*of* ▸ одича́ть) to run wild, become wild; (fig.) to become unsociable

дичь|, и *f.* (collect.) game; wildfowl

✧ **длин|а́**, ы́ *f.* length; в ∼у́ longways, lengthwise; во всю ∼у́ at full length; ∼о́й (в) шесть ме́тров six metres long (BrE), six meters long (AmE)

длинно... *comb. form* long-

✧ **дли́н|ный**, ∼ен, ∼на́, ∼но *adj.* long; lengthy

✧ **дли́тельность|**, и *f.* duration

✧ **дли́тельн|ый**, ∼ен, ∼ьна *adj.* long, protracted

дли́|ться, ится *impf.* (*of* ▸ продли́ться) to last

✧ **для** *prep.* + *g.* **1** (*в пользу кого, чего*) for (the sake of); э́то д. тебя́ this is for you **2** (*выражает цель*) for; д. того́, что́бы... in order to ... **3** (*по отношению к*) for, to; вре́дно д. дете́й bad for children **4** (*по отношению к норме*) for, of; он о́чень высо́к д. свои́х лет he is very tall for his age

дневни́к, а́ *m.* diary, journal; вести́ д. to keep a diary

дневн|о́й *adj.* **1** day; в ∼о́е вре́мя during daylight hours; д. свет daylight **2** (*одного дня*) day's, daily

днём *adv.* **1** in the daytime, by day **2** (*после обеда*) in the afternoon; сего́дня д. this afternoon

дни́щ|е, а *nt.* bottom (*of vessel or barrel*)

ДНК *f. indecl.* (*abbr. of* дезоксирибонуклеи́новая кислота́) (chem.) DNA (*deoxyribonucleic acid*)

дно, дна, *pl.* до́нья, до́ньев *nt.* **1** (*сосуда*) bottom; вверх дном upside down; (пей)

д

до дна! bottoms up! **2** (*no pl.*) (*моря, реки*) bottom, bed

◆ **до¹** *prep.* + *g.* **1** (*о пределе, границе*) to, up to; as far as; **от Ло́ндона до Москвы́** from London to Moscow **2** (*о временно́м пределе*) to, up to; until, till; **до сих пор** up to now, till now, hitherto; **до тех пор** till then, before; **до тех пор, пока́** until; **до свида́ния!** goodbye! **3** (*перед*) before; **до войны́** before the war; **до на́шей э́ры** (*до н. э.*) before Christ (*abbr.* BC); **до того́ как** before **4** (*о пределе состояния*) to, up to, to the point of; **до бо́ли** until it hurt(s); **до того́..., что** to the point where **5** (*о количественном пределе*) under, up to (= *not over, not more than*); **де́ти до пяти́ лет** children under five; **до ты́сячи рубле́й** up to a thousand roubles **6** (*приблизительно*) about, approximately **7** (*относительно*) with regard to, concerning; **что до меня́** as far as I am concerned; **до** *и т. п.* **не до** (*infml*) I don't *etc.* feel like, am not in the mood for; **мне не до разгово́ра** I don't feel like talking

до² *nt. indecl.* C (mus.)

до...¹ *vbl. pref.* **1** (*expr. completion of action*): **дочита́ть кни́гу** to finish (reading) a book **2** (*indicates that action is carried to a certain point*): **дочита́ть до страни́цы 270** to read as far as page 270 **3** (*expr. supplementary action*): **докупи́ть** to buy in addition **4** (+ *refl. vv., expr. eventual attainment of goal*): **дозвони́ться** to ring until one gets an answer

до...² *pref.* (*of nn. and adjs., used to indicate priority in chronological sequence*) pre-

◆ **доба́в|ить, лю, ишь** *pf.* (*of* ▶ **добавля́ть**) (+ *a.* or *g.*) to add

доба́вк|а, и *f.* **1** (*пищевая*) additive **2** (*дополнительная порция*) second helping

добавле́ни|е, я *nt.* addition

◆ **добавля́|ть, ю** *impf. of* ▶ **доба́вить**

доба́вочн|ый *adj.* **1** additional, extra; **~ое вре́мя** (sport) extra time **2** (teleph.) extension; **д. три́дцать** extension 30

добега́|ть, ю *impf. of* ▶ **добежа́ть**

добе|жа́ть, гу́, жи́шь, гу́т *pf.* (*of* ▶ **добега́ть**) (**до** + *g.*) to run (to, as far as); (*достигнуть*) to reach (also fig.)

доберма́н, а and **доберма́н-пи́нчер, доберма́на-пи́нчера** *m.* Dobermann (pinscher)

добива́|ть, ю *impf. of* ▶ **доби́ть**

◆ **добива́|ться, юсь** *impf.* **1** *impf. of* ▶ **доби́ться 2** (+ *g.*) to try to get, strive (for), aim (at)

добира́|ться, юсь *impf. of* ▶ **добра́ться**

до|би́ть, бью, бьёшь *pf.* (*of* ▶ **добива́ть**) to finish off, do for

до|би́ться, бью́сь, бьёшься *pf.* (*of* ▶ **добива́ться**) (+ *g.*) to get, obtain, secure; **д. своего́** to get one's way

до́блест|ь, и *f.* valour (BrE), valor (AmE), gallantry

◆ key word

до|бра́ться, беру́сь, берёшься, *past* **~бра́лся, ~брала́сь** *pf.* (*of* ▶ **добира́ться**) **1** (**до** + *g.*) to get (to), reach **2** (infml) to get (one's hands on); **я до тебя́ ~беру́сь!** I'll get you!

добр|о́, а́ *nt.* **1** good; (*поступок*) good deed; **не к ~у́ э́то** it is a bad omen **2** (collect.) (infml, *имущество*) goods, property **3**: **д. пожа́ловать!** welcome!

доброво́л|ец, ьца *m.* volunteer

доброво́льно *adv.* voluntarily

доброво́л|ьный, ~ен, ~ьна *adj.* voluntary

доброде́тел|ь, и *f.* virtue

добро́душ|ный, ~ен, ~на *adj.* good-natured

доброжела́тел|ьный, ~ен, ~ьна *adj.* benevolent

доброка́чествен|ный, ~, ~на *adj.* **1** of good quality **2** (med.) benign

добросо́вест|ный, ~ен, ~на *adj.* conscientious

доброт|а́, ы́ *f.* goodness, kindness

добро́т|ный, ~ен, ~на *adj.* of good, high quality; durable

◆ **до́бр|ый, ~, ~а́, ~о, ~ы́** *adj.* **1** (*хороший*) good; **~ое и́мя** good name; **~ое у́тро!** good morning!; **всего́ ~ого!** goodbye!; all the best!; **по ~ой во́ле** of one's own free will **2** (*отзывчивый*) kind, good; **бу́дьте ~ы** (+ *imper.*) please, would you be so kind as to **3** (infml, *не ме́ньше чем*) a good; **д. час** a good hour

добыва́|ть, ю *impf. of* ▶ **добы́ть**

до|бы́ть, бу́ду, бу́дешь, *past* **~бы́л, ~была́, ~было** *pf.* (*of* ▶ **добыва́ть**) **1** (*достать*) to get, obtain, procure **2** (*из земли́*) to extract, mine, quarry

добы́ч|а, и *f.* **1** (*действие*) extraction (*of minerals*); mining, quarrying **2** (*захва́ченное*) booty, spoils, loot **3** (*охотника*) bag; (*рыболова*) catch **4** (*добытое из недр земли́*) mineral products; output

довез|ти́, у́, ёшь, *past* **~, ~ла́** *pf.* (*of* ▶ **довози́ть**) to take (to)

дове́ренност|ь, и *f.* warrant, power of attorney; **по ~и** by proxy

дове́р|енный *p.p.p. of* ▶ **дове́рить** and *adj.* trusted; **~енное лицо́** (*as m. n.* **д., ~енного**) agent, proxy

дове́ри|е, я *nt.* trust, confidence; **слу́жба/телефо́н ~я** helpline

довери́тельный *adj.* confiding, trusting

дове́р|ить, ю, ишь *pf.* (*of* ▶ **доверя́ть 1**) (+ *d.*) to entrust (to)

дове́р|иться, юсь, ишься *pf.* (*of* ▶ **доверя́ться**) (+ *d.*) to trust (in), confide (in)

до́верху *adv.* to the top; to the brim

дове́рчив|ый, ~, ~а *adj.* trustful, credulous

доверя́|ть, ю *impf.* **1** *impf. of* ▶ **дове́рить 2** (*impf. only*) (+ *d.*) to trust, confide (in)

доверя́|ться, юсь *impf. of* ▶ **дове́риться**

дове́с|ок, ка *m.* makeweight

дове|сти́, ду́, дёшь, *past* **~л, ~ла́** *pf.* (*of* ▶ **доводи́ть**) **1** (*до како́го-то ме́ста*) to lead (to), take (to), accompany (to) **2** (*до како́го-то состоя́ния*) to bring (to); to drive (to), reduce (to); **д. до соверше́нства** to perfect; **д. до све́дения** (+ *g.*) to inform, let know

до́вод, а *m.* argument

дово|ди́ть, жу́, ~дишь *impf. of* ▶ **довести́**

довое́нный *adj.* pre-war

дово|зи́ть, жу́, ~зишь *impf. of* ▶ **довезти́**

◦ **дово́льно¹** *adv.* (*доста́точно*) quite, fairly; rather, pretty; **д. хоро́ший фильм** quite a good film

◦ **дово́льно²** *adv.* (*с удовлетворе́нием*) contentedly

дово́л|ьный, ~ен, ~ьна *adj.* **1** contented, satisfied; **д. вид** contented expression **2** (+ *i.*) contented (with), satisfied (with), pleased (with); **д. собо́й** pleased with oneself, self-satisfied

дово́льств|овать, уюсь *impf.* (+ *i.*) to be content (with), be satisfied (with)

дог, а *m.* mastiff; **далма́тский д.** Dalmatian

догад|а́ться, а́юсь *pf.* (*of* ▶ **дога́дываться 1**) to guess

дога́дк|а, и *f.* surmise, conjecture; (*in pl.*) guesswork; **теря́ться в ~ах** to be lost in conjecture

дога́длив|ый, ~, ~а *adj.* quick-witted, bright

дога́дыва|ться, юсь *impf.* **1** *impf. of* ▶ **догада́ться 2** (*impf. only*) to suspect

до́гм|а, ы *f.* dogma

до́гмат, а *m.* **1** (*relig.*) doctrine, dogma **2** (*принцип*) tenet, foundation

до|гна́ть, гоню́, го́нишь, *past* **~гна́л, ~гнала́, ~гна́ло** *pf.* (*of* ▶ **догоня́ть**) to catch up (with) (also fig.)

догова́рива|ть, ю *impf. of* ▶ **договори́ть**

догова́рива|ться, юсь *impf.* **1** *impf. of* ▶ **договори́ться 2** (*impf. only*) (о + *p.*) to negotiate (about)

◦ **догово́р, а** *m.* agreement; (*pol.*) treaty, pact

договорённост|ь, и *f.* agreement, understanding; (*pol.*) accord

договор|и́ть, ю́, и́шь *pf.* (*of* ▶ **догова́ривать**) to finish saying; to finish telling

договор|и́ться, ю́сь, и́шься *pf.* (*of* ▶ **догова́риваться 1**) **1** (о + *p.*) to come to an agreement, understanding (about); to arrange; **~и́лись!** agreed!; it's a deal! **2** (**до** + *g.*) to come (to); to talk (to the point of)

догово́рн|ый *adj.* agreed; contractual; **~ая цена́** agreed price

догола́ *adv.* stark naked; **разде́ться д.** to strip naked

догоня́|ть, ю *impf. of* ▶ **догна́ть**

догора́|ть, а́ю *impf. of* ▶ **догоре́ть**

догор|е́ть, ю́, и́шь *pf.* (*of* ▶ **догора́ть**) (*сгоре́ть до како́го-либо преде́ла*) to burn down; (*сгоре́ть до конца́*) to burn out

дода|ва́ть, ю́, ёшь *impf. of* ▶ **дода́ть**

дода́|ть, м, шь, ст, ди́м, ди́те, ду́т, *past* **до́дал, ~ла́, до́дало** *pf.* (*of* ▶ **додава́ть**) to make up (the rest of); to pay up

доде́л|ать, аю *pf.* (*of* ▶ **доде́лывать**) to finish

доде́лыва|ть, ю *impf. of* ▶ **доде́лать**

доду́м|аться, аюсь *pf.* (*of* ▶ **доду́мываться**) (**до** + *g.*) to hit (upon) (*afterthought*)

доду́мыва|ться, юсь *impf. of* ▶ **доду́маться**

доеда́|ть, ю *impf. of* ▶ **дое́сть**

доезжа́|ть, ю *impf. of* ▶ **дое́хать**

до|е́сть, е́м, е́шь, е́ст, еди́м, еди́те, едя́т *pf.* (*of* ▶ **доеда́ть**) to eat up, finish eating

до|е́хать, е́ду, е́дешь *pf.* (*of* ▶ **доезжа́ть**) (**до** + *g.*) to reach, arrive (at)

дожд|а́ться, у́сь, ёшься, *past* **~а́лся, ~ала́сь, ~ало́сь** *pf.* **1** (+ *g.*) to wait (for); **д. конца́ спекта́кля** to wait until the end of the show **2**: **д. того́, что** to end up (by); **он ~а́лся того́, что ему́ указа́ли на дверь** he ended up by being shown the door

дождеви́к, а́ *m.* (infml) raincoat

дождево́й *adj. of* ▶ **дождь**

до́ждик, а *m.* shower

дождли́в|ый, ~, ~а *adj.* rainy

дожд|ь, я́ *m.* **1** rain (also fig.); **под ~ём** in the rain; **ме́лкий д.** drizzle; **проливно́й д.** downpour; **идёт д.** it is raining **2** (fig.) cascade

дожива́|ть, ю *impf.* **1** *impf. of* ▶ **дожи́ть 2** (*impf. only*) to live out; **д. свой век** to live out one's days

дожида́|ться, юсь *impf.* (*of* ▶ **дожда́ться**) (+ *g.*) to wait (for)

до|жи́ть, живу́, живёшь, *past* **~жи́л, ~жила́, ~жи́ло** *pf.* (*of* ▶ **дожива́ть 1**) **1** (**до** + *g.*) (*прожи́ть*) to live (until); to attain the age (of); **она́ ~жила́ до конца́ войны́** she lived to see the end of the war **2** (**до** + *g.*) (*дойти́ до како́го-л. состоя́ния*) to come (to), be reduced (to); **до чего́ мы ~жи́ли!** what have we come to!

до́з|а, ы *f.* dose

дозапра́вк|а, и *f.* refuelling (BrE), refueling (AmE)

дозвон|и́ться, ю́сь, и́шься *pf.* (**до** + *g.* or **к** + *d.* or **в** + *a.*) to ring until one gets an answer; to get through (to) (*on telephone*); **я не мог д. к тебе́/до тебя́** I could not get through (to you); **в институ́т не дозвони́ться** it's impossible to get through to the institute

дозиро́вк|а, и *f.* dosage

дозна́ни|е, я *nt.* (law) inquiry; inquest

дозо́р, а *m.* patrol

дозо́р|ный *adj. of* ▶ **дозо́р**; (*as m. n.* **д., ~ного**) (mil.) scout

дозрева́|ть, ю *impf. of* ▶ **дозре́ть**

дозр|е́ть, е́ю *pf.* (*of* ▶ **дозрева́ть**) to ripen

дои́гр|ать, а́ю *pf.* (*of* ▶ **дои́грывать**) to finish (playing)

дои́грыва|ть, ю *impf. of* ▶ **доигра́ть**

д

доисторический *adj.* prehistoric

до|и́ть, ю́, ~йшь *impf.* (*of* ▸ **подои́ть**) to milk

до|йти́, йду́, йдёшь, *past* ~шёл, ~шла́ *pf.* (*of* ▸ **доходи́ть**) **1** (до + *g.*) to reach; **д.** до того́, что... to reach a point where ...; ру́ки не ~шли́ (до + *g.*) I, *etc.*, had no time (for) **2** (*infml*) (до + *g.*) (*произвести впечатление*) to make an impression (upon); (*стать поня́тным в хо́де объясне́ния*) to get through [**3**] (*impers.; also* де́ло ~йдёт, ~шло́ до + *g.*) to come (to); (де́ло чуть не ~шло́ до дра́ки it nearly came to blows

док, а *m.* dock

доказа́тельств|о, а *nt.* proof, evidence

док|аза́ть, ажу́, а́жешь *pf.* (*of* ▸ **дока́зывать** 1) to demonstrate, prove; счита́ть ~а́занным to take for granted

✓ **дока́зыва|ть, ю** *impf. of* ▸ **доказа́ть** [**2**] (*impf. only*) to argue, try to prove

дока́пыва|ться, юсь *impf. of* ▸ **докопа́ться**

док|ати́ться, ачу́сь, а́тишься *pf.* (*of* ▸ **дока́тываться**) **1** (до + *g.*) to roll (to) **2** (*о звука́х*) to roll, thunder, boom

дока́тыва|ться, юсь *impf. of* ▸ **докати́ться**

до́кер, а *m.* docker

✓ **докла́д, а** *m.* report; lecture; paper; talk; чита́ть **д.** to give a report; to read a paper

докла́дчик, а *m.* speaker

докла́дчи|ца, цы *f. of* ▸ **докла́дчик**

докла́дыва|ть, ю *impf. of* ▸ **доложи́ть**[1]

докопа́|ться, юсь *pf.* (*of* ▸ **дока́пываться**) (до + *g.*) **1** to dig down (to) **2** (*fig.*) to get to the bottom (of); to find out, discover

✓ **до́ктор, а,** *pl.* ~а́ *m.* doctor

до́ктор|ский *adj. of* ▸ **до́ктор**; ~ская диссерта́ция doctoral thesis

доктри́н|а, ы *f.* doctrine

✓ **докуме́нт, а** *m.* document

документа́льный *adj.* documentary; **д.** фильм documentary (film)

документа́ци|я, и *f.* (*collect.*) documentation

долб|и́ть, лю́, и́шь *impf.* to hollow out; to gouge

✓ **долг, а, о ~е, в ~у́,** *pl.* ~и́ *m.* **1** (*обя́занность*) duty **2** (*одо́лженное*) debt; в **д.** on credit; быть у кого́-н. в ~у́ to be indebted to sb

✓ **до́л|гий, ~ог, ~га́, ~го** *adj.* long

✓ **до́лго** *adv.* long, (for) a long time

долгове́чн|ый, ~ен, ~на *adj.* lasting; durable

долгов|о́й *adj. of* ▸ **долг** 2; ~о́е обяза́тельство promissory note

долговре́мен|ный, ~, ~на *adj.* of long duration, prolonged

долговя́з|ый, ~, ~а *adj.* (*infml*) lanky

долгожда́нный *adj.* long-awaited

долгожи́тел|ь, я *m.* long-lived person

долгожи́тель|ница, ницы *f. of* ▸ **долгожи́тель**

✓ key word

долголе́ти|е, я *nt.* longevity

долголе́тний *adj.* of many years; long-standing

долгосро́чн|ый, ~ен, ~а *adj.* (*креди́т*) long-term; (*о́тпуск*) of long duration

долгот|а́, ы́, *pl.* ~ы *f.* **1** (*sg. only*) (*дня*) duration **2** (*geog.*) longitude

долет|а́ть, а́ю *impf. of* ▸ **долете́ть**

доле|те́ть, чу́, ти́шь *pf.* (*of* ▸ **долета́ть**) (до + *g.*) to fly (to, as far as); to reach

до́лж|ен, ~на́, ~но́ *pred. adj.* **1** owing; он **д.** мне три рубля́ he owes me three roubles **2** (+ *inf.*) (*обя́зан, вы́нужден*): я **д.** идти́ I must go, I have to go [**3**] (+ *inf.*) (*вероя́тно*): она́ ~на́ ско́ро прийти́ she should be here soon; ~но́ быть probably

должни́к, а́ *m.* debtor

должностн|о́й *adj.* official; ~о́е лицо́ official, functionary, public servant

✓ **до́лжност|ь, и,** *g. pl.* ~е́й *f.* post, office

✓ **до́лжн|ый** *adj.* due, fitting, proper; ~ым о́бразом properly; (*as n.* ~ое, ~ого) due

долива́|ть, ю *impf. of* ▸ **доли́ть**

доли́н|а, ы *f.* valley

дол|и́ть, ью́, ьёшь, *past* ~и́л, ~ила́, ~и́ло *pf.* (*of* ▸ **долива́ть**) **1** (*жи́дкость*) to add; to pour in addition **2** (*сосу́д*) to fill (up); to refill

✓ **до́ллар, а** *m.* dollar

доло́ж|ить[1], у́, ~ишь *pf.* (*of* ▸ **докла́дывать**) **1** (+ *a.* or о + *p.*) (*сде́лать докла́д*) to report; to give a report (on) **2** (о + *p.*) (*сообщи́ть о прихо́де посети́теля*) to announce (*a guest, etc.*)

доло́ж|ить[2], у́, ~ишь *pf.* (*of* ▸ **докла́дывать**) (*доба́вить*) to add

доло́й *adv.* (+ *a.*) (*infml*) down (with), away (with); **д.** изме́нников! down with the traitors!

доло́т|о́, а́, *pl.* ~а́, ~ *nt.* chisel

до́льше *adv.* longer

✓ **до́л|я, и,** *g. pl.* ~е́й *f.* **1** (*часть*) part, portion; share; quota; войти́ в ~ю (с + *i.*) to go shares (with) **2** (*судьба́*) lot, fate; вы́пасть на чью-н. ~ю to fall to sb's lot

✓ **дом, а (у),** *pl.* ~а́ *m.* **1** (*жило́е зда́ние*) house; (*многокварти́рный*) block (of flats) (BrE); apartment block (AmE); (*зда́ние учрежде́ния*) building; **д.** культу́ры palace of culture; ≈ arts (and leisure) centre; **д.** о́тдыха holiday home; **д.-музе́й**... ... House; **Д.-музе́й** Пу́шкина Pushkin House **2** (*своё жильё*) home; (*семья́*) household

дом... *comb. form, abbr. of* ▸ **дома́шний**

до́ма *adv.* at home, in; быть как **д.** to feel at home; бу́дьте как **д.** make yourself at home; у него́ не все **д.** he's not all there

✓ **дома́шн|ий** *adj.* **1** house; home; domestic; **д.** а́дрес home address; ~яя страни́ца (*comput.*) home page; под ~им аре́стом under house arrest **2** (*самоде́льный*) home-made [**3**] (*не ди́кий*) domestic; ~ие живо́тные domestic animals; ~яя пти́ца (*collect.*) poultry

доме́н *m.* (*comput.*) domain

до́мик, а *m. dim. of* ▶ **дом**

Доминика́нск|ая Респу́блика, ~ой Респу́блики *f.* the Dominican Republic

домини́р|овать, ую *impf.* to dominate, prevail (fig.)

домино́ *nt. indecl.* (*игра*) dominoes

домкра́т, а *m.* (tech.) jack

домо... comb. form 1 home- **2** abbr. of ▶ **дома́шний**

домовладе́л|ец, ьца *m.* house-owner; (*по отношению к нанимателю*) landlord

домога́тельств|о, а *nt.* solicitation, demand, bid; **сексуа́льное д.** sexual harassment

домо́й *adv.* home, homewards; **нам пора́ д.** it's time for us to go home

домофо́н, а *m.* electronic security system (*at entrance to building*); entryphone® (BrE)

домохозя́йк|а, и *f.* housewife

домрабо́тниц|а, ы *f.* domestic (servant), maid; **приходя́щая д.** home help

до́мысел, ла *m.* conjecture

дона́шива|ть, ю *impf. of* ▶ **доноси́ть¹**

донесе́ни|е, я *nt.* report, message

донес|ти́¹, у́, ёшь, *past* ~, ~ла́ *pf.* (*of* ▶ **доноси́ть²**) (*до + g.*) to carry (to, as far as); (*звук, запах*) to carry, bear

донес|ти́², у́, ёшь, *past* ~, ~ла́ *pf.* (*of* ▶ **доноси́ть³**) **1** to report, announce; (*+ d.*) to inform **2** (*на + a.*) (*сделать донос*) to inform (on, against), denounce

донес|ти́сь, у́сь, ёшься, *past* ~ся, ~ла́сь *pf.* (*of* ▶ **доноси́ться²**) **1** (*о звуках, запахах, новостях*) to reach **2** (infml, *быстро доехать, добежать*) to reach quickly

до́низу *adv.* to the bottom

до́нор, а *m.* donor

доно́с, а *m.* denunciation

дон|оси́ть¹, ошу́, ~о́сишь *pf.* (*of* ▶ **дона́шивать**) **1** to wear out **2** to wear sth handed down **3** (*usu. with neg.*): **д. ребёнка** to carry to full term

дон|оси́ть², ошу́, ~о́сишь *impf. of* ▶ **донести́¹**

дон|оси́ть³, ошу́, ~о́сишь *impf. of* ▶ **донести́²**

дон|оси́ться¹, ~о́сится *pf.* to wear out, be worn out

дон|оси́ться², ~о́сится *impf. of* ▶ **донести́сь**

доно́счик, а *m.* informer

доно́счи|ца, цы *f. of* ▶ **доно́счик**

допива́|ть, ю *impf. of* ▶ **допи́ть**

до́пинг, а *m.* drugs, dope

допи|са́ть, шу́, ~шешь *pf.* (*of* ▶ **допи́сывать**) **1** (*письмо*) to finish writing; (*картину*) to finish painting **2** (*приписать*) to add

допи́сыва|ть, ю *impf. of* ▶ **дописа́ть**

доп|и́ть, ью́, ьёшь, *past* ~и́л, ~ила́, ~и́ло *pf.* (*of* ▶ **допива́ть**) to drink (up)

допла́т|а, ы *f.* additional payment; surcharge

допла|ти́ть, ачу́, ~а́тишь *pf.* (*of* ▶ **допла́чивать**) to pay in addition, pay

the remainder

допла́чива|ть, ю *impf. of* ▶ **доплати́ть**

доплыва́|ть, ю *impf. of* ▶ **доплы́ть**

доплы́|ть, ву́, вёшь, *past* ~л, ~ла́, ~ло *pf.* (*of* ▶ **доплыва́ть**) (*до + g.*) (*вплавь*) to swim (to, as far as); (*на корабле*) to sail (to, as far as); (fig.) to reach

допоздна́ *adv.* (infml) till late

дополне́ни|е, я *nt.* supplement, addition; addendum

дополни́тельно *adv.* in addition

дополни́тельн|ый *adj.* supplementary, additional, extra; **~ое вре́мя** (sport) extra time

допо́лн|ить, ю, ишь *pf.* (*of* ▶ **дополня́ть**) to supplement, add to

дополн|я́ть, я́ю *impf. of* ▶ **допо́лнить**

допото́пный *adj.* antediluvian

допра́шива|ть, ю *impf. of* ▶ **допроси́ть**

допро́с, а *m.* (law) interrogation

допр|оси́ть, ошу́, о́сишь *pf.* (*of* ▶ **допра́шивать**) (law) to interrogate, question

до́пуск, а *m.* (*к + d.*) access (to); (*в + a.*) right of entry, admittance

допуска́|ть, ю *impf. of* ▶ **допусти́ть**

допусти́м|ый, ~, ~а *adj.* permissible, admissible

допу|сти́ть, щу́, ~стишь *pf.* (*of* ▶ **допуска́ть**) **1** (*до + g. or к + d.*) to admit, to give access (to); **д. к ко́нкурсу** to allow to compete **2** (*позволить*) to allow, permit **3** (*предположить*) to grant, assume; **~стим** let us assume **4** (*сделать*): **д. оши́бку** to make a mistake

допуще́ни|е, я *nt.* (*предположение*) assumption

допыт|а́ться, а́юсь *pf.* (*of* ▶ **допы́тываться**) to find out

допы́тыва|ться, юсь *impf.* (*of* ▶ **допыта́ться**) (*impf. only*) to try to find out, try to elicit

дораба́тыва|ть, ю *impf. of* ▶ **дорабо́тать**

дорабо́та|ть, ю *pf.* (*of* ▶ **дораба́тывать**) **1** (*усовершенствовать*) to refine **2** (*до + g.*) to work (until)

дораст|а́ть, а́ю *impf. of* ▶ **дорасти́**

дораст|и́, у́, ёшь, *past* доро́с, доросла́ *pf.* (*of* ▶ **дораста́ть**) (*до + g.*) to grow (to); (fig.) to attain (to), come up (to)

дорв|а́ться, у́сь, ёшься, *past* ~а́лся, ~ала́сь, ~а́лось *pf.* (*до + g.*) (infml) to fall upon, seize upon

дореволюцио́нный *adj.* pre-revolutionary

доро́г|а, и *f.* **1** (*путь сообщения*) road; (*путь следования*) way (also fig.); **желе́зная д.** railway (BrE), railroad (AmE); **дать, уступи́ть кому́-н. ~у** to make way for sb (also fig.) **2** (*путешествие*) journey; **отпра́виться в ~у** to set out; **в ~е** on the journey, en route **3** (*направление пути, маршрут*) (the) way, route; **показа́ть ~у** to show the way; **сби́ться**

с ~и to lose one's way

до́рого *adv.* dear, dearly; **д. обойти́сь** (+ *d.*) to cost one dear

дорогови́зн|а, ы *f.* high prices

доро́гой *adv.* on the way, en route

✓ **дорог|о́й, до́рог, дорога́, до́рого** *adj.* **1** dear, expensive **2** (*близкий се́рдцу*) dear; precious; (*as n.* **д.**, ~о́го, *f.* ~а́я, ~о́й) (my) dear

дорожа́|ть, ет *impf.* (*of* ▶ **подорожа́ть**) to rise (in price), go up

доро́же *comp. of* ▶ **дорого́й,** ▶ **до́рого**

дорож|и́ть, у́, и́шь *impf.* (+ *i.*) to value

доро́жк|а, и *f.* **1** path **2** (*sport*) track; lane **3** (*коврик*) runner **4** (*магнитофо́на*) track

✓ **доро́жн|ый** *adj.* **1** *adj. of* ▶ **доро́га; д. знак** road sign; ~ая поли́ция traffic police **2** (*для путеше́ствия*) travel, travelling (BrE), traveling (AmE); **д. чек** traveller's cheque (BrE), traveler's check (AmE)

доса́д|а, ы *f.* annoyance; кака́я **д.!** what a nuisance!

доса|ди́ть, жу́, ди́шь *pf.* (*of* ▶ **досажда́ть**) (+ *d.*) (*раздражи́ть*) to annoy, vex

доса́д|ный, ~ен, ~на *adj.* annoying

досажда́|ть, ю *impf. of* ▶ **досади́ть**

доск|а́, и́, *a.* ~у, *pl.* ~и, досо́к, ~а́м *f.* **1** board, plank; **д. объявле́ний** noticeboard **2** (*мра́морная*) slab; (*металли́ческая*) plaque, plate **3** (*для сёрфинга, скейтбо́рдинга и т. п.*) board

доскона́л|ьный, ~ен, ~ьна *adj.* thorough

до|сла́ть, шлю́, шлёшь *pf.* (*of* ▶ **досыла́ть**) to send in addition; to send the remainder

досло́вно *adv.* verbatim, word for word

досло́вный *adj.* literal, verbatim; **д. перево́д** literal translation

дослу́ша|ть, ю *pf.* (*of* ▶ **дослу́шивать**) to listen to (sth) till the end

дослу́шива|ть, ю *impf. of* ▶ **дослу́шать**

досма́трива|ть, ю *impf. of* ▶ **досмотре́ть**

досмо́тр, а *m.* examination; inspection

досмотр|е́ть, ю́, ~ишь *pf.* (*of* ▶ **досма́тривать**) (*до* + *g.*) to watch, look at (to, as far as); мы ~е́ли пье́су до тре́тьего а́кта we saw the play as far as the third act

доспе́х|и, ов *m. pl.* (*sg.* ~, ~а) armour (BrE), armor (AmE)

досро́ч|ный, ~ен, ~на *adj.* ahead of schedule, early

доста|ва́ть, ю́, ёшь *impf. of* ▶ **доста́ть**

доста|ва́ться, ю́сь, ёшься *impf. of* ▶ **доста́ться**

доста́в|ить, лю, ишь *pf.* (*of* ▶ **доставля́ть**) **1** (*груз, посы́лку*) to deliver; (*пассажи́ров*) to transport, convey **2** (*удово́льствие*) to give; (*тру́дности*) to cause

✓ **доста́вк|а, и** *f.* delivery

доставля́|ть, ю *impf. of* ▶ **доста́вить**

доста́т|ок, ка *m.* prosperity

✓ **key word**

✓ **доста́точно¹** *adv.* sufficiently, enough; (*значи́тельно*) considerably

доста́точно² *as pred.* it is enough; **д. сказа́ть** suffice it to say

доста́точ|ный, ~ен, ~на *adj.* sufficient

доста́|ть, ну, нешь *pf.* (*of* ▶ **доставáть**) **1** (*взять*) to fetch; to take out; **д. плато́к из карма́на** to take a handkerchief out of one's pocket **2** (+ *g. or* до + *g.*) (*косну́ться*) to touch; to reach **3** (*получи́ть*) to get, obtain

доста́|ться, нусь, нешься *pf.* (*of* ▶ **доставáться**) (+ *d.*) **1** (*перейти́ в со́бственность*) to pass (to) (by inheritance) **2** (*вы́пасть на до́лю*) to fall to one's lot

✓ **достига́|ть, ю** *impf. of* ▶ **дости́гнуть,** ▶ **дости́чь**

✓ **дости́г|нуть, ну, нешь,** *past* ~, ~ла *pf.* (*of* ▶ **достига́ть**) (+ *g.*) **1** (*дойти́, дое́хать*) to reach **2** (*доби́ться*) to attain, achieve

✓ **достиже́ни|е, я** *nt.* achievement, attainment

достижи́м|ый, ~, ~а *adj.* achievable, attainable

дости́чь = **дости́гнуть**

достове́рност|ь, и *f.* (*правди́вость*) trustworthiness, reliability; (*о докуме́нте*) authenticity

достове́р|ный, ~ен, ~на *adj.* (*правди́вый*) reliable, trustworthy; (*о докуме́нте*) authentic

✓ **досто́инств|о, а** *nt.* **1** (*хоро́шее ка́чество*) merit, virtue **2** (*sg. only*) (*уваже́ние*) dignity; чу́вство со́бственного ~а self-respect **3** (*сто́имость*) value; моне́та ~ом в пять рубле́й, моне́та пятирублёвого ~а a five-rouble coin

досто́йно *adv.* suitably, fittingly

✓ **досто́|йный, ~ин, ~йна** *adj.* **1** (+ *g.*) (*стоя́щий*) worthy (of), deserving; **д. внима́ния** worthy of note **2** (*заслу́женный*) deserved; fitting, adequate **3** (*соотве́тствующий*) suitable, fit

достопримеча́тельност|ь, и *f.* sight; place, object of note; осма́тривать ~и to see the sights

✓ **до́ступ, а** *m.* access, admittance

✓ **досту́п|ный, ~ен, ~на** *adj.* **1** (*ме́сто*) accessible; (*для* + *g.*) open (to); available (to) **3** (*кни́га*) easily understood; intelligible **4** (*це́ны*) moderate, reasonable

досу́г, а *m.* leisure, leisure time; **на ~е** at leisure, in one's spare time

до́суха *adv.* (until) dry; вы́тереть **д.** to rub dry

досчита́|ть, ю *pf.* (*of* ▶ **досчи́тывать**) **1** to finish counting **2** (*до* + *g.*) to count (up to); **д. до ста** to count up to a hundred

досчи́тыва|ть, ю *impf. of* ▶ **досчита́ть**

досыла́|ть, ю *impf. of* ▶ **досла́ть**

досье́ *nt. indecl.* dossier, file

досяга́емост|ь, и *f.* reach; (*mil.*) range; вне преде́лов ~и beyond reach

дота́скива|ть, ю *impf. of* ▶ **дотащи́ть**

дота́ци|я, и *f.* grant, subsidy

дотащ|и́ть, у́, ~ишь *pf.* (*of* ▶ **дота́скивать**) (infml) (**до** + *g.*) to carry, drag (to)

дотла́ *adv.* utterly, completely; **сгоре́ть д.** to burn to the ground

дотра́гива|ться, юсь *impf. of* ▶ **дотро́нуться**

дотро́н|уться, усь, ешься *pf.* (*of* ▶ **дотра́гиваться**) (**до** + *g.*) to touch

дотя́гива|ть, ю, ешь *impf. of* ▶ **дотяну́ть**

дотя́гива|ться, юсь, ешься *impf. of* ▶ **дотяну́ться**

дотян|у́ть, у́, ~ешь *pf.* (*of* ▶ **дотя́гивать**) (**до** + *g.*) **1** to draw, drag (to, as far as) **2** (infml, *дойти, доехать*) to reach, make **3** (infml, *выдержать*) to hold out (till); (*дожить*) to live (till)

дотян|у́ться, у́сь, ~ешься *pf.* (*of* ▶ **дотя́гиваться**) (**до** + *g.*) to reach; to touch

до́хл|ый, ~а, ~о *adj.* (*мёртвый*) dead (*of animals*)

до́х|нуть, ну, нешь, *past* ~, ~ла *impf.* (*of* ▶ **издо́хнуть**, ▶ **подо́хнуть**, ▶ **сдо́хнуть**) **1** (*о животных*) to die **2** (infml, pej., *о людях*) to peg out, kick the bucket

⚡ **дохо́д, а** *m.* income; receipts; revenue

дохо|ди́ть, жу́, ~дишь *impf. of* ▶ **дойти́**

дохо́д|ный, ~ен, ~на *adj.* **1** profitable, lucrative, paying **2** *adj. of* ▶ **дохо́д**

дохо́дчив|ый, ~, ~а *adj.* intelligible, easy to understand

доце́нт, а *m.* reader (BrE), associate professor (AmE)

до́чери, до́черью *see* ▶ **дочь**

доче́рний *adj.* (*о компании, предприятии*) daughter; branch

дочит|а́ть, а́ю *pf.* (*of* ▶ **дочи́тывать**) **1** (*окончить чтение чего-н.*) to finish reading **2** (**до** + *g.*) to read (to, as far as)

дочи́тыва|ть, ю *impf. of* ▶ **дочита́ть**

до́чк|а, и *f.* (infml) = **дочь**

⚡ **доч|ь, ~ери**, *i.* ~ерью, *pl.* ~ери, ~ере́й, ~еря́м, ~ерьми́, *o* ~еря́х *f.* daughter

дошко́льник, а *m.* preschooler

дошко́льни|ца, цы *f. of* ▶ **дошко́льник**

дошко́льный *adj.* preschool

доща́тый *adj.* made of planks, boards; **д. насти́л** duckboards

до́йрк|а, и *f.* milkmaid

⚡ **др.** (*abbr. of* **други́е**) **и ~** & co.; (*при опускании фамилий авторов в научных изданиях*) et al.

д-р (*abbr. of* **до́ктор**) Dr, Doctor

драгоце́нность|, и *f.* jewel; gem; (*in pl.*) jewellery

драгоце́н|ный, ~ен, ~на *adj.* precious

дразн|и́ть, ю́, ~ишь *impf.* **1** (*собаку*) to tease **2** (*аппетит, любопытство*) to stimulate

дра́йвер, а *m.* (comput.) driver

дра́к|а, и *f.* fight

драко́н, а *m.* dragon

дра́м|а, ы *f.* **1** drama **2** (fig.) crisis, calamity

драматизи́р|овать, ую *impf. and pf.* to dramatize

драмати́ческий *adj.* **1** dramatic; drama; **д. теа́тр** theatre (BrE), theater (AmE) **2** (*напыщенный*) dramatic, theatrical

драмати́ч|ный, ~ен, ~на *adj.* (fig.) dramatic

драмату́рг, а *m.* playwright, dramatist

драп, а *m.* thick woollen cloth

дра|ть, деру́, дерёшь, *past* ~л, ~ла́, ~ло *impf.* **1** (*impf. only*) (*рвать*) to tear (up, to pieces) **2** (*pf.* **со~**) (*снимать*) to tear off

дра́|ться, деру́сь, дерёшься, *past* ~лся, ~ла́сь, ~ло́сь *impf.* **1** (*pf.* **по~**) (**с** + *i.*) to fight (with) **2** (fig.) (**за** + *a.*) to fight, struggle (for)

дребезж|а́ть, и́т *impf.* to jingle, tinkle

древеси́н|а, ы *f.* **1** (*плотная часть дерева*) wood **2** (*лесоматериалы*) timber

древнегре́ческий *adj.* ancient, classical Greek

древнееврейский *adj.* ancient, classical Hebrew

древнеру́сский *adj.* Old Russian

⚡ **дре́в|ний, ~ен, ~няя** *adj.* ancient; ~няя исто́рия ancient history

дре́вность|, и *f.* **1** (*sg. only*) (*далёкое прошлое*) antiquity **2** (*in pl.*) antiquities

дрези́н|а, ы *f.* (rail.) trolley (BrE), handcar (AmE)

дрейф|ова́ть, у́ю *impf.* (naut.) to drift

дрел|ь, и *f.* (tech.) drill

дрем|а́ть, лю́, ~лешь *impf.* to doze; **не д.** (also fig.) to be watchful; to be wide awake

дрена́ж, а *and* а́ *m.* drainage

дрена́ж|ный *adj. of* ▶ **дрена́ж**; ~ная труба́ drainpipe

дрессиро́ванн|ый *p.p.p. of* ▶ **дрессирова́ть** *and adj.*: ~ые живо́тные performing animals

дрессир|ова́ть, у́ю *impf.* (*of* ▶ **вы́дрессировать**) to train

дрессиро́вщик, а *m.* trainer

дресс-ко́д, а *m.* dress code

⚡ **дро́б|ный, ~ен, ~на** *adj.* **1** (math.) fractional **2** (*частый и мелкий*) staccato, abrupt; **д. стук** staccato knocking; **д. дождь** pattering rain

дробови́к, а́ *m.* shotgun

дроб|ь, и, *pl.* ~и, ~е́й *f.* **1** (collect.) (*для стрельбы*) small shot **2** (*звуки*) drumming; tapping; patter; **бараба́нная ~** drum roll **3** (math.) fraction **4** (*черта*) slash

дров|а́, ~, ~а́м (*no sg.*) firewood

дровосе́к, а *m.* woodcutter

дро́гн|уть, у, ешь, *past* ~ул, ~ула *pf.* **1** to shake, move; (*о свете*) to flicker **2** (*о человеке*) to waver, falter

дрож|а́ть, у́, и́шь *impf.* **1** to tremble; to shiver, shake; to quiver; to vibrate; (*о свете*) to flicker **2** (**за** + *a. or* **пе́ред** + *i.*) (fig.) to tremble (for; before) **3** (**над** + *i.*) to grudge; **д. над ка́ждой копе́йкой** to count every penny

дро́жж|и, е́й (*no sg.*) yeast, leaven

дрож|ь, и *f.* shivering, trembling; (*в голосе*) tremor, quaver

дрозд, á *m.* thrush; **чёрный д.** blackbird

дро́тик, а *m.* **1** (*оружие*) spear, javelin **2** (*в игре*) dart

✐ **друг[1], а,** *pl.* **друзья́, друзе́й** *m.* friend

друг[2] (*short form of* ▸ **друго́й**) **д.** ~а each other, one another; **д. за** ~ом one after another; **д. с** ~ом with each other

✐ **друг|о́й** *adj.* **1** other, another; different; **и тот и д.** both; **ни тот ни д.** neither; (**э́то**) **совсе́м** ~**о́е де́ло** (that is) quite another matter; ~**и́ми слова́ми** in other words; **с** ~**о́й стороны́** on the other hand; **на д. день** the next day; (*as n. pl.* ~**и́е,** ~**и́х**) others **2** (*второй*) second

дру́жб|а, ы *f.* friendship

дружелю́б|ный, ~**ен,** ~**на** *adj.* friendly, amicable

дру́жеский *adj.* friendly

дру́жественный *adj.* friendly, amicable; (*comput.*) user-friendly

дру́ж|ить, у́, ~**ишь** *impf.* (**с** + *i.*) to be friends (with)

дру́жно *adv.* **1** harmoniously, in concord **2** (*вместе*) (all) together, in concert

дру́ж|ный, ~**ен,** ~**на́,** ~**но,** ~**ны́** *adj.* **1** (*единодушный*) amicable; harmonious **2** (*одновременный*) simultaneous, concerted

друзья́ *see* ▸ **друг[1]**

дря́бл|ый, ~, ~**á,** ~**о** *adj.* flabby

дрян|но́й, ~**ен,** ~**на́,** ~**но,** ~**ны́** *adj.* (*infml*) worthless, rotten; good-for-nothing

дрян|ь, и *f.* (*infml*) trash, rubbish

дря́хл|ый, ~, ~**á,** ~**о** *adj.* decrepit, senile

ДТП *nt. indecl.* (*abbr. of* **доро́жно-тра́нспортное происше́ствие**) road accident

дуб, а, *pl.* ~**ы́** *m.* oak

дуби́нк|а, и *f.* cudgel, truncheon

дублёнк|а, и *f.* (*infml*) sheepskin coat

дублёр, а *m.* (*theatr.*) understudy; (*cin.*) stand-in

Ду́блин, а *m.* Dublin

дубли́р|овать, ую *impf.* to duplicate; **д. роль** (*theatr.*) to understudy a part

дубо́вый *adj.* **1** oak **2** (*fig., infml, глупый*) thick

дуг|á, и́, *pl.* ~**и** *f.* arc

ду́дк|а, и *f.* pipe, fife; **пляса́ть под чью-н.** ~**у** (*fig.*) to dance to sb's tune

ду́л|о, а *nt.* (*отверстие ствола*) muzzle; (*ствол*) barrel

✐ **Ду́м|а, ы** *f.* Duma (*lower house of the Russian parliament*)

✐ **ду́ма|ть, ю** *impf.* (*of* ▸ **поду́мать 1**) **1** (**о** + *p. or* **над** + *i.*) to think (about); to be concerned (about) **2** (*impf. only*): **д. что...** to think, suppose that ... **3** (+ *inf.*) to think of, plan to; **он** ~**ет пое́хать в Ло́ндон** he is thinking of

going to London

ду́ма|ться, ется *impf.* (*impers., +* *d.*) to seem; **мне** ~**ется** I think, I fancy; ~**ется** it seems

ду́м|ец, ца *m.* (*infml*) member of Duma

ду́мский *adj. of* ▸ **Ду́ма**

ду́н|уть, у, ешь *pf.* to blow

дупл|о́, á, *pl.* ~**а, ду́пел** *nt.* **1** (*в стволе дерева*) hollow **2** (*в зубе*) cavity

ду́р|а, ы *f. of* **дура́к**

дура́к, á *m.* fool, ass; **оста́вить в** ~**áх** to make a fool of

дура́цкий *adj.* (*infml*) stupid, foolish, idiotic

дура́ч|ить, у, ишь *impf.* (*of* ▸ **одура́чить**) to fool, dupe

дура́ч|иться, усь, ишься *impf.* to play the fool

дурдо́м, а *m.* (*infml*) madhouse

ду́рно *as pred.* (*impers.+* *d.*): **мне** *и т. п.* **д.** I feel, *etc.*, faint, bad

дур|но́й, ~**ён,** ~**на́,** ~**но,** ~**ны́** *adj.* **1** (*плохой*) bad, evil; nasty; **д. вкус** nasty taste; ~**ные мы́сли** evil thoughts; ~**ные привы́чки** bad habits **2**: **д.** (*собо́ю*) (*некрасивый*) ugly

дуршла́г, а *m.* (*cul.*) colander

дуть, ду́ю, ду́ешь *impf.* (*of* ▸ **поду́ть 1**) to blow; **сего́дня ду́ет за́падный ве́тер** there is a west wind today

✐ **дух, а** *m.* **1** (*relig., phil., fig. also*) spirit; **Свято́й Д.** the Holy Spirit **2** (*моральное состояние*) spirit(s); heart; mind; **быть в** ~**е** to be in good (high) spirits; **не в** ~**е** in low spirits **3** (*дыхание*) breath; (*infml*) air; **перевести́ д.** to take breath **4** (*призрак*) spectre (BrE), specter (AmE), ghost

дух|и́, о́в (*no sg.*) perfume, scent

духове́нств|о, а *nt.* (*collect.*) clergy, priesthood

духо́вк|а, и *f.* oven

духовни́к, á *m.* (*eccl.*) confessor

духо́вность|ь, и *f.* spirituality

✐ **духо́вный** *adj.* **1** spiritual; inner; **д. мир** inner world **2** (*церковный*) ecclesiastical, church; religious; **д. сан** holy orders

духово́й *adj.* (*mus.*) wind; **д. инструме́нт** wind instrument; **д. орке́стр** brass band

духот|á, ы́ *f.* stuffiness, closeness

душ, а *m.* shower; **приня́ть д.** to take a shower

✐ **душ|á, и́,** *a.* ~**у,** *pl.* ~**и** *f.* **1** soul; (*fig.*) heart; **д. в** ~**у** at one, in harmony; **в** ~**е́** inwardly, secretly; at heart **2** (*чувства*) feelings, spirit **3** (*человек, при указании количества*) soul; **на** ~**у** per head

душев|áя, о́й *f.* shower room

душевнобольн|о́й *adj.* insane; mentally ill; (*as n. д.,* ~**о́го,** *f.* ~**áя,** ~**о́й**) insane person; psychiatric patient

душе́вн|ый *adj.* **1** mental; ~**ая боле́знь** mental illness **2** (*искренний*) sincere, heartfelt; **д. челове́к** understanding person

души́ст|ый, ~, ~**а** *adj.* fragrant, sweet-scented

души́|ть¹, ý, ~ишь *impf.* (*of* ▶ задуши́ть) **1** (*убивать*) to strangle; to stifle, smother, suffocate; (fig., *угнетать*) to stifle, suppress **2** (*impf. only*) (*лишать возможности дышать*) to choke; его́ ~и́л гне́в he choked with rage

души́|ть², ý, ~ишь *impf.* (*of* ▶ надуши́ть) to scent, perfume

души́|ться¹, ýсь, ~ишься *impf., pass. of* ▶ души́ть¹

души́|ться², ýсь, ~ишься *impf.* (*of* ▶ надуши́ться) (+ *i.*) to perfume oneself (with)

ду́шно *as pred.* it is stuffy; it is stifling, suffocating; мне ста́ло д. I felt suffocated

ду́ш|ный, ~ен, ~на́, ~но *adj.* stuffy, close, sultry; stifling

дуэ́л|ь, и *f.* duel

дуэ́т, а *m.* duet

ДЦП *m. indecl.* (*abbr. of* де́тский церебра́льный парали́ч) (med.) cerebral palsy

ды́бом *adv.* on end; во́лосы у него́ вста́ли д. his hair stood on end

дым, а (у), о ~е, в ~ý, *pl.* ~ы́ *m.* smoke

дыми́|ться, и́тся *impf.* to smoke; (*о тумане*) to billow

ды́мк|а, и *f.* haze (also fig.)

дымово́й *adj. of* ▶ дым

дымохо́д, а *m.* flue

ды́мчат|ый, ~, ~а *adj.* smoke-coloured (BrE), smoke-colored (AmE); (*очки*) tinted

ды́н|я, и *f.* melon

дыр|а́, ы́, *pl.* ~ы́ *f.* hole (also fig., infml)

ды́рк|а, и *f.* hole

дыроко́л, а *m.* hole puncher, hole punch

дыря́в|ый, ~, ~а *adj.* full of holes, holey

дыха́ни|е, я *nt.* breathing; breath; иску́сственное д. artificial respiration

дыха́тельн|ый *adj.* respiratory; ~ые пути́ respiratory tract

дыша́|ть, ý, ~ишь *impf.* (+ *i.*) to breathe; (*быть проникнутым чем-либо*) to exude

дья́вол, а *m.* devil

дья́вольск|ий *adj.* devilish, diabolical

дья́кон, а *m.* (eccl.) deacon

дю́жин|а, ы *f.* dozen

дюйм, а *m.* inch

дю́н|а, ы *f.* dune

дюра́л|ь, я *m.* = дюралюми́ний

дюралюми́ни|й, я *m.* (tech.) Duralumin®

дя́д|я, и, *g. pl.* ~ей *m.* **1** (*родственник*) uncle **2** (infml, *обращение*) mister (*as term of address*) **3** (infml, *мужчина*) guy

дя́т|ел, ла *m.* woodpecker

Ee

ёбаный *adj.* (vulg.) fucking

еб|а́ть, ý, ёшь *impf.* (*of* ▶ вы́ебать) (vulg.) to fuck; (*as int.*) (*чёрт возьми!*) fuck!; fucking hell!; ёб твою́ мать! fuck you!

Ева́нгели|е, я *nt.* (collect.) the Gospels; gospel (also fig.)

евразийский *adj.* Eurasian

Евра́зи|я, и *f.* Eurasia

евре́|й, я *m.* Jew; (*древний*) Hebrew

евре́йк|а, и *f.* Jewish woman, girl

евре́йский *adj.* Jewish; ~ язы́к (*иврит*) Hebrew

◆ е́вро *m. indecl.* euro (*currency unit*)

е́вро... *comb. form* Euro-

еврозо́н|а, ы *f.* eurozone

Евро́п|а, ы *f.* Europe

Европарла́мент, а *m.* European Parliament

европе́|ец, йца *m.* European

европе́йк|а, ки *f. of* ▶ европе́ец

◆ европе́йский *adj.* European

евроремо́нт, а *m.* restoration carried out to Western standards

Евросою́з, а *m.* European Union

Еги́п|ет, та *m.* Egypt

еги́петский *adj.* Egyptian

египтя́н|ин, ина, *pl.* ~е, ~ *m.* Egyptian

египтя́н|ка, ки *f. of* ▶ египтя́нин

его́ **1** *g. and a. sg. of* ▶ он **2** *poss. pron.* (*относящийся к человеку*) his; (*относящийся к предмету*) its

◆ ед|а́, ы́ *f.* **1** (*пища*) food **2** (*трапеза*) meal; во вре́мя ~ы́ at mealtimes, while eating

едва́ *adv. and conj.* **1** *adv.* (*с трудом*) hardly, barely **2** *adv.* (*чуть*) hardly, scarcely **3**: е. ли *adv.* hardly, scarcely (*in judgements of probability*) **4**: е. (ли) не *adv.* nearly, almost, all but; я е. не по́мер со́ смеху I nearly died laughing **5** *conj.* hardly, scarcely, barely; е. ..., как scarcely ... when; no sooner ... than; е. самолёт взлете́л, как отказа́л оди́н из дви́гателей no sooner had the plane taken off than one of the engines seized up

еди́м *see* ▶ есть¹

◆ едини́ц|а, ы *f.* **1** (*цифра*) one; figure 1; (math.) unity **2** unit; е. мо́щности unit of power; **боевы́е ~ы фло́та** naval units; **15 ~ боево́й те́хники** 15 military vehicles **3** (*отме́тка*) 'one' (*lowest mark in Russian school marking system*)

едини́чный *adj.* single; **е. слу́чай** isolated case

единобо́жи|е, я *nt.* monotheism

единобо́рств|о, а *nt.* single combat

единовла́сти|е, я *nt.* autocracy, absolute rule

единовре́мен|ный, ~ен, ~на *adj.* extraordinary, unique; **~ное посо́бие** extraordinary grant

единогла́сно *adv.* unanimously

единогла́с|ный, ~ен, ~на *adj.* unanimous

единоду́ши|е, я *nt.* unanimity

единоду́ш|ный, ~ен, ~на *adj.* unanimous

единомы́шленник, а *m.* person who holds the same views; like-minded person

единообра́з|ный, ~ен, ~на *adj.* uniform

единоро́г, а *m.* (myth.) unicorn

еди́нственно *adv.* only, solely; **е. возмо́жный ход** the only possible move

✍ **еди́нствен|ный, ~ and ~ен, ~на** *adj.* only, sole; **е. сын** only son; **он е. оста́лся в живы́х** he was the sole survivor; **~ное число́** (gram.) singular (number)

еди́нств|о, а *nt.* unity

✍ **еди́н|ый, ~, ~а** *adj.* **1** (*еди́нственный*) one; single, sole; **там не́ было ни ~ой души́** there was not a soul there; **все до ~ого** to a man **2** (*оди́н*) united, unified **3** (*о́бщий*) common, single; **~ая во́ля** single will/purpose

еди́те *see* ▶ **есть¹**

е́д|кий, ~ок, ~ка́, ~ко *adj.* **1** caustic; acrid, pungent **2** (fig.) caustic, sarcastic

е́д|у, ешь *see* ▶ **е́хать**

едя́т *see* ▶ **есть¹**

✍ **её 1** *g. and a. of* ▶ **она́ 2** *poss. pron.* (*относя́щийся к челове́ку*) (*при существи́тельном*) her; (*без существи́тельного*) hers; (*относя́щийся к предме́ту*) its

ёж, ежа́ *m.* hedgehog

ежеви́к|а, и *f.* **1** (*collect.*) blackberries **2** (*куста́рник*) bramble, blackberry bush

ежего́дный *adj.* annual, yearly

ежедне́в|ный, ~ен, ~на *adj.* daily; everyday

ежеме́сячный *adj.* monthly

ежемину́т|ный, ~ен, ~на *adj.* **1** occurring every minute, at intervals of a minute **2** (*непреры́вный*) incessant, continual

еженеде́льный *adj.* weekly

ежеча́сный *adj.* hourly

ездá, ы́ *f.* **1** ride, riding; (*на маши́не*) drive **2** (*in phrr. indicating distance from one point to another*) journey, drive; **отсю́да до о́зера — до́брых три часá ~ы́** from here to the lake is a good three hours' journey

éз|дить, жу, дишь *impf.* (*indet. of* ▶ **е́хать**) **1** to go (*in or on a vehicle or on an animal*); to

✍ **key word**

ride, drive; **е. верхо́м** to ride (on horseback) **2** (*уме́ть е́здить*) to (be able to) ride, drive **3** (к + d.) (*посеща́ть*) to visit

езжа́|ть (infml): **~й(те)!** (*as imper. of* ▶ **е́хать**) go!; get going!

ей *d. and i. of* ▶ **она́**

ел, е́ла *see* ▶ **есть¹**

éле *adv.* **1** (*с трудо́м*) hardly, barely, only just **2** (*почти́ не*) hardly, scarcely, barely, only just; **по́езд е. дви́гался** the train was scarcely moving

ёлк|а, и *f.* **1** fir (tree), spruce; **нового́дняя ё.** Christmas tree **2** (infml, *пра́здник*) Christmas, New Year's party

ёлочн|ый *adj. of* ▶ **ёлка**; **~ые украше́ния** Christmas tree decorations

ель, и *f.* spruce (*Picea*); fir (tree)

ем *see* ▶ **есть¹**

ём|кий, ~ок, ~ка *adj.* capacious

ёмкост|ь, и *f.* (*вмести́мость*) capacity, cubic content; (*вмести́лище*) container

ему́ *d. of* ▶ **он**

ено́т *m.* raccoon

епа́рхи|я, и *f.* (eccl.) diocese

епи́скоп, а *m.* bishop

ерала́ш, а *m.* (infml) jumble, muddle

éрес|ь, и, *pl.* **~и, ~ей** *f.* heresy

ёрза|ть, ю *impf.* (infml) to fidget

ерунд|а́, ы́ *f.* (infml) **1** (*чепуха́*) nonsense, rubbish; **говори́ть ~у́** to talk nonsense **2** (*пустя́к*) trifle, trifling matter; child's play

ЕС *m. indecl.* (*abbr. of* **Европе́йский сою́з**) EU (*European Union*)

✍ **е́сли** *conj.* if; **е. не** unless; **е. то́лько** provided; **е. бы не** but for, if it were not for; **е. бы** (*в восклица́ниях*) if only; **что е. …?** what if …?

ест *see* ▶ **есть¹**

есте́ственно *adv.* **1** naturally **2** (*as particle*) naturally, of course

есте́ственно² *as pred.* it is natural

✍ **есте́ствен|ный, ~, ~на** *adj.* natural; **~ные нау́ки** natural sciences; **е. отбо́р** (biol.) natural selection

естествозна́ни|е, я *nt.* (natural) science

есть¹, ем, ешь, ест, еди́м, еди́те, едя́т, *past* **ел, е́ла,** *imper.* **ешь,** *impf.* (*of* ▶ **съесть**) **1** (*принима́ть пи́щу*) to eat **2** (*impf. only*) (*мета́лл*) to corrode, eat away **3** (*impf. only*) (*о ды́ме*) to sting, cause to smart

есть² 1 *3rd pers. sg.* (*also, rarely, substituted for all persons*) *pres. of* ▶ **быть 2** there is; there are; **у меня́, него́ и т. п. е.** I have, he has, *etc.*

✍ **е́хать, е́ду, е́дешь** *impf.* (*of* ▶ **пое́хать,** *det. of* ▶ **е́здить**) to go (*in or on a vehicle or on an animal*); to ride, drive; **е. верхо́м** to ride (*on horseback*); **е. по́ездом, на по́езде** to go by train

ехи́д|ный, ~ен, ~на *adj.* (infml) malicious, spiteful; **~ные замеча́ния** snide remarks, taunts

ешь *see* ▶ **есть¹**

✵ **ещё** *adv.* **1** (*по-пре́жнему*) still; yet; **е. не, нет е.** not yet; **всё е.** still **2** (*бо́льше*) some more; any more; yet, further; again; **вам нали́ть е. (вина́** *и т. п.*)? may I pour you some more (wine, *etc.*)?; **е. оди́н** one more, yet another; **е. раз** once more, again **3** (*уже́*) already; as long ago as, as far back as; **е. в 1900 году́** in 1900 already; as long ago as 1900 **4** (*дополни́тельно*) else; **кто е. хо́чет ко́фе?** who else wants coffee?; **вы хоти́те е. что-нибудь?** do you want anything else? **5** (+ *comp.*) still, yet, even; **е. гро́мче** even louder; **е. и е.** more and more **6** (+ *prons. and advs., as emph. particle*): **ты не ви́дел кота́? — како́го е. кота́?** have you seen the cat? — what cat, for heaven's sake? **7**: **е. бы!** (infml, *коне́чно, безусло́вно*) yes, rather!; you bet!, of course!

ЕЭС *nt. indecl.* (*abbr. of* **Европе́йское экономи́ческое соо́бщество**) EEC (*European Economic Community*)

е́ю *i. of* ▶ **она́**

Жж

✵ **Ж = же**[1]**, же**[2]

жа́б|а, ы *f.* (zool.) toad

жа́ворон|ок, ка *m.* (zool.) lark; (fig.) early riser

жа́дност|ь, и *f.* **1** (*к деньга́м, еде́, де́йствию*) greed (for); greediness **2** (*ску́пость*) avarice, meanness

жа́д|ный, ~ен, ~на́, ~но *adj.* **1** (*к + d.*) greedy (for); avid (for) **2** (*скупо́й*) avaricious, mean

жа́жд|а, ы (*no pl.*) *f.* thirst; (+ *g.*) (fig.) thirst, craving (for); **ж. зна́ний** thirst for knowledge

жа́жд|ать, у *impf.* (+ *g. or inf.*) (fig.) to thirst (for, after), crave

жаке́т, а *m.* jacket (*ladies'*)

жале́|ть, ю *impf.* (*of* ▶ **пожале́ть**) **1** (*чу́вствовать жа́лость*) to pity, feel sorry (for) **2** (*о + p. or g. or что*) (*сожале́ть*) to regret, be sorry (for, about) **3** (+ *a. or g.*) (*скупи́ться*) to spare; to grudge; **не ~я сил** not sparing oneself, unsparingly

жа́л|ить, ю, ишь *impf.* (*of* ▶ **ужа́лить**) to sting; to bite

жа́л|кий, ~ок, ~ка́, ~ко *adj.* pitiful, pathetic, wretched; **име́ть ж. вид** to be a sorry sight

жа́лко[1] *adv. of* ▶ **жа́лкий**

жа́лко[2] *as pred.* (*impers.*) **1** (+ *d. and a.*) (*о чу́встве сострада́ния*) to pity, feel sorry (for); **мне ж. бра́та** I feel sorry for my brother **2** (*о чу́встве гру́сти*) (it is) a pity, a shame; (+ *d. and g. or a.*) it grieves me, *etc.*; to regret **3** (+ *g. or + inf.*) (*скупи́ться*) to grudge

жа́л|о, а *nt.* (*пчелы́*) sting (also fig.)

жа́лоб|а, ы *f.* complaint; **пода́ть ~у (на + a.)** to make, lodge a complaint (about)

жа́лоб|ный, ~ен, ~на *adj.* plaintive; mournful

жа́лованье, я *nt.* salary

жа́л|оваться, уюсь *impf.* (*of* ▶ **пожа́ловаться**) (**на** + *a.*) to complain (of, about)

жа́лост|ь, и *f.* pity, compassion; **из ~и (к** + *d.*) out of pity (for); **кака́я ж.!** what a pity!

жаль *as pred.* (*impers.*) **1** (+ *d. and a.*) (*о чу́встве сострада́ния*) to pity, feel sorry (for); **мне ж. тебя́** I pity you **2** (*о чу́встве гру́сти*) (it is) a pity, a shame; (+ *d.*) it grieves (*me, etc.*); to regret, feel sorry **3** (+ *g. or + inf.*) (*скупи́ться*) to grudge; (**мне**) **ж. де́нег** I begrudge the money

жалюзи́ *pl. indecl.* Venetian blind

жанда́рм, а *m.* gendarme

жанр, а *m.* genre

жар, а (у), о ~е, в ~у́ (*no pl.*) *m.* **1** heat; heat of the day; hot place **2** (*лихора́дка*) fever; (high) temperature

жар|а́, ы́ *f.* heat; hot weather; **в са́мую ~у́** in the heat of the day

жарго́н, а *m.* jargon; slang

жа́реный *adj.* (*на сковороде́*) fried; (*в духо́вке*) roast; (*на решётке*) grilled (BrE), broiled (AmE)

жа́р|ить, ю, ишь *impf.* (*pf.* **за~** or **из~** or **по~**) (*на сковороде́*) to fry; (*в духо́вке*) to roast; (*на решётке*) to grill (BrE), broil (AmE)

жа́р|иться, юсь, ишься *impf.* **1** (*pf.* **за~** or **из~**) to roast, fry **2**: **ж. на со́лнце** (infml) to bask in the sun, sun oneself **3** *pass. of* ▶ **жа́рить**

жа́р|кий, ~ок, ~ка́, ~ко *adj.* **1** hot; (*тропи́ческий*) tropical **2** (fig.) hot, heated; ardent; passionate; **ж. спор** heated argument

жа́рко[1] *adv. of* ▶ **жа́ркий**

жа́рко[2] *as pred.* it is hot; **мне** *и т. п.* **ж.** I am, *etc.*, hot

жарко́|е, о́го *nt.* (fried) meat

жаропро́ч|ный, ~ен, ~на *adj.* ovenproof; **~ная кастрю́ля** casserole (dish)

жар-пти́ц|а, ы *f.* the Firebird (*in folklore*)

жа́рче *comp. of* ▸ жа́ркий, ▸ жа́рко¹

жасми́н, а *m.* jasmine

жа́тв|а, ы (*no pl.*) *f.* reaping, harvesting; harvest (also fig.)

жа́тк|а, и *f.* harvester, reaping machine

жать¹, жму, жмёшь *impf.* (*no pf.*) **1** (*руку*) to press, squeeze; **ж. ру́ку** to shake (sb) by the hand **2** (*о платье, обуви*) to pinch, be tight; (*impers.*) **в плеча́х жмёт** it is tight on the shoulders

жать², жну, жнёшь *impf.* (*of* ▸ сжать²) to reap, cut, mow

жва́чк|а, и *f.* (infml) chewing gum

жва́чн|ый *adj.* (zool.) ruminant; (*as nt. n.* ∼ое, ∼ого) ruminant

жгу, жжёшь, жгут *see* ▸ жечь

жгут, а́ *m.* **1** plait (BrE); braid **2** (med.) tourniquet

жгу́ч|ий, ∼, ∼а, ∼е *adj.* burning hot (also fig.); ∼ая боль smart, smarting pain; ж. брюне́т person with jet-black hair and eyes

ж. д. (*abbr. of* желе́зная доро́га) railway (BrE); railroad (AmE)

ждать, жду, ждёшь, *past* ждал, ждала́, жда́ло *impf.* (+ *g.*) **1** to wait (for); to await; заста́вить ж. to keep waiting; не заста́вить себя́ ж. to come quickly; что нас ждёт? what is in store for us? **2** (*надеяться на, предполагать*) to expect

же¹ *conj.* **1** (*при противопоставлении*) but; иди́, е́сли тебе́ охо́та, я же оста́нусь здесь you go, if you feel like it, but I shall stay here **2** (*для присоединения*) and; Ока́ впада́ет в Во́лгу, Во́лга же в Каспи́йское мо́ре the Oka flows into the Volga, and the Volga flows into the Caspian Sea **3** (*ведь*) after all; расскажи́ ей: она́ же твоя́ мать tell her — she's your mother, after all

же² *emph. particle*: что же ты де́лаешь? whatever are you doing, what *are* you doing?

же³ *particle* (*подчёркивает значение слова, после которого ставится*): тот же, тако́й же the same; тогда́ же at the same time

жева́тельн|ый *adj.*: ∼ая рези́нка chewing gum

жева́ть, жую́, жуёшь *impf.* to chew

жёг, жгла *see* ▸ жечь

жезл, а́ *m.* (*символ власти*) rod, staff (of office); (*милиционера*) baton

жела́ни|е, я *nt.* **1** (+ *g.*) wish (for), desire (for); при всём ∼и with the best will in the world **2** (*просьба*) request **3** (*вожделение*) desire, lust

жела́нный *p.p.p. of* ▸ жела́ть *and adj.* wished for, longed for, desired, beloved; ж. гость welcome visitor

жела́тельно¹ *adv.* preferably

жела́тельно² *as pred.* it is desirable; it is advisable, preferable

жела́тел|ьный, ∼ен, ∼ьна *adj.* desirable; advisable

жела́|ть, ю *impf.* (*of* ▸ пожела́ть) **1** (+ *g.*) to wish (for), desire **2** (*чтобы or + inf.*) to wish, want **3** (+ *d. and g. or inf.*) to wish (*sb sth*); ∼ю вам успе́ха/уда́чи! good luck!; это оставля́ет ж. лу́чшего it leaves much to be desired

жела́|ющий *pres. part. act. of* ▸ жела́ть; ∼ющие persons interested, those who so desire

желе́ *nt. indecl.* jelly

железа́|, ы́, *pl.* же́лезы, желёз, ∼а́м *f.* (anat.) gland; *pl.* (infml) tonsils

железнодоро́жник, а *m.* railway worker

железнодоро́жный *adj.* rail, railway, railroad (AmE); ж. путь (railway) track; ж. у́зел (railway) junction

желе́зн|ый *adj.* **1** iron (also fig.); (chem.) ferric, ferrous; ж. век the Iron Age; ж. за́навес the 'Iron Curtain' **2**: ∼ая доро́га railway (BrE), railroad (AmE); по ∼ой доро́ге by rail

желе́з|о, а *nt.* iron

железобето́н, а *m.* (tech.) reinforced concrete, ferroconcrete

жёлоб, а, *pl.* желоба́, желебо́в *m.* (*водосточный*) gutter; (*для ссыпания чего-л.*) chute

желте́|ть, ю *impf.* (*pf.* ▸ пожелте́ть) (*становиться жёлтым*) to turn yellow

желт|о́к, ка́ *m.* yolk

желту́х|а, и *f.* (med.) jaundice

жёлтый, жёлт, желта́, желто́ *and* жёлто *adj.* yellow; жёлтая пре́сса the yellow press, the tabloids; Жёлтые страни́цы Yellow Pages®

желу́д|ок, ка *m.* stomach; несваре́ние ∼ка indigestion

желу́дочный *adj.* stomach; gastric; ж. сок gastric juice

жёлуд|ь, я, *g. pl.* желуде́й *m.* acorn

жёлч|ь, и *and* (infml) желч|ь, и (*no pl.*) *f.* bile, gall (also fig.)

жема́н|ный, ∼ен, ∼на *adj.* affected

жемчуг, а, *pl.* ∼а́ *m.* (collect.) pearl(s)

жемчу́жин|а, ы *f.* pearl (also fig.)

жемчу́жн|ый *adj. of* ▸ же́мчуг; (fig.) pearly(-white); ∼ое ожере́лье pearl necklace

жен|а́, ы́, *pl.* ∼ы, ∼, ∼а́м *f.* wife; быть у ∼ы́ под каблуко́м to be henpecked

жена́т|ый, ∼ married; ж. (на + *p.*) (*о мужчине*) married (to)

жени́тьб|а, ы *f.* marriage

жен|и́ться, ю́сь, ∼ишься *impf. and pf.* (на + *p.*) (*о мужчине*) to marry, get married (to)

жени́х, а́ *m.* **1** fiancé **2** (*на свадьбе*) bridegroom

женоподо́б|ный, ∼ен, ∼на *adj.* effeminate

же́нский *adj.* woman's; female; feminine

же́нствен|ный, ∼ *and* ∼ен, ∼на *adj.* feminine, womanly

же́нщин|а, ы *f.* woman

женьше́н|ь, я *m.* (bot., med.) ginseng

▸ key word

жереб|ёнок, ёнка, pl. **~я́та, ~я́т** m. foal, colt

жереб|е́ц, ца́ m. stallion

жеребьёвк|а, и f. casting of lots; (sport) draw (for play-off)

жёрнов, а, pl. **жернова́, жерново́в** m. millstone

⚥ **же́ртв|а, ы** f. **1** sacrifice (also fig.); **принести́ ~у** (+ d.) to make a sacrifice (to); **принести́ в ~у** to sacrifice **2** (пострада́вший) victim; **пасть ~ой** (+ g.) to fall victim (to)

же́ртв|овать, ую impf. (of ▶ **поже́ртвовать**) **1** (дари́ть) to make a donation (of), present **2** (+ i.) (подверга́ть опа́сности) to sacrifice, give up

жертвоприноше́ни|е, я nt. sacrifice

жест, а m. gesture (also fig.)

жестикули́р|овать, ую impf. to gesticulate

жестикуля́ци|я, и f. gesticulation

⚥ **жёсткий, жёсток, жестка́, жёстко** adj. hard; tough; (fig.) rigid, strict; **ж. диск** (comput.) hard disk

жёстко[1] adv. of ▶ **жёсткий**

жёстко[2] as pred. it is hard

жесто́к|ий, ~, ~а adj. cruel; brutal; (fig.) severe, sharp

жесто́кост|ь, и f. cruelty, brutality

жёстче comp. of ▶ **жёсткий**, ▶ **жёстко**[1]

жест|ь, и f. tinplate

жест|яно́й adj. of ▶ **жесть**; **~яна́я посу́да** tinware

жестя́|нщик, а m. tinsmith

жето́н, а m. **1** (награ́да) medal; (опознава́тельный знак) badge (of police officer, porter, etc.) **2** (сре́дство опла́ты) token

жечь, жгу, жжёшь, жгут, past **жёг, жгла** impf. **1** (pf. **с~**) to burn; (дотла́) to burn down **2** (impf. only) to burn, sting; (impers.) **от э́того ликёра жжёт в го́рле** this liqueur burns one's throat

же́чься, жгусь, жжёшься, жгу́тся, past **жёгся, жглась** impf. to burn, sting

жжёшь see ▶ **жечь**

жи́во adv. **1** (я́рко) vividly **2** (оживлённо) with animation **3** (о́стро) keenly **4** (infml, бы́стро) quickly, promptly

⚥ **жив|о́й, ~, ~а́, ~о** adj. **1** (облада́ющий жи́знью) living, live, alive; **оста́ться в ~ы́х** to survive **2** (энерги́чный) lively; keen; active **3** (вырази́тельный) lively, vivacious; bright; **~ы́е глаза́** bright eyes **4** (без предвари́тельной за́писи) live; **~а́я му́зыка** live music

живопи́с|ец, ца m. painter

живопи́с|ный, ~ен, ~на adj. **1** (относя́щийся к жи́вописи) pictorial **2** (краси́вый) picturesque (also fig.); **~ное ме́сто** beauty spot

жи́вопис|ь, и f. **1** painting **2** (collect.) paintings

жи́вост|ь, и f. liveliness, vivacity; animation

⚥ **живо́т, а́** m. abdomen, belly; stomach; (infml) tummy

животново́дств|о, а nt. stockbreeding, animal husbandry

⚥ **живо́тно|е, го** nt. animal; **дома́шнее ж.** pet

живо́тный adj. **1** animal **2** (гру́бый) bestial, brute

живу́ч|ий, ~, ~а adj. **1** tenacious of life; (bot.) hardy; **он ~ как ко́шка** he has nine lives like a cat **2** (fig., обы́чай) deep-rooted, enduring

живьём adv. (infml) alive; **петь ж.** to sing live; **постара́йтесь взять его́ ж.** try to catch him alive

жи́голо m. indecl. gigolo

жи́дкий, ~ок, ~ка́, ~ко adj. **1** (име́ющий сво́йство течь) liquid; fluid **2** (водяни́стый) watery; weak, thin; **ж. суп** thin soup **3** (о волоса́х) sparse, scanty; **~кая борода́** straggly beard

жидкокристалли́ческий adj.: **ж. диспле́й** liquid crystal display (abbr. LCD)

жи́дкост|ь, и f. liquid; fluid

жи́ж|а, и f. (no pl.) f. liquid; swill; slush

жи́же comp. of ▶ **жи́дкий**

жизнедея́тельност|ь, и f. (biol.) vital activity

⚥ **жи́знен|ный, ~, ~на** adj. **1** (of) life; (biol.) vital; **ж. у́ровень** standard of living **2** (бли́зкий к жи́зни, реа́льный) close to life; lifelike **3** (fig.) vital, vitally important

жизнеобеспе́чени|е, я nt.: **систе́ма ~я** life-support system

жизнеописа́ни|е, я nt. biography

жизнера́дост|ный, ~ен, ~на adj. cheerful; vivacious

жизнеспосо́б|ный, ~ен, ~на adj. capable of living; (biol.) viable; (fig.) vigorous, flourishing

⚥ **жизн|ь, и** f. life; (существова́ние) existence; **зараба́тывать на ж.** to earn one's living; **как ж.?** (infml) how is life?; **лиши́ть себя́ ~и** to take one's life; **о́браз ~и** way of life; lifestyle

жи́л|а, ы f. **1** (сухожи́лие) tendon, sinew; (infml, кровено́сный сосу́д) vein **2** (min.) vein

жиле́т, а m. waistcoat (BrE), vest (AmE); **спаса́тельный ж.** life jacket

жиле́|ц, льца́ m. tenant

жи́лист|ый, ~, ~а adj. **1** (ру́ки) having prominent veins **2** (те́ло) sinewy; (стари́к) wiry; **~ое мя́со** stringy meat

жили́щ|е, а nt. dwelling, abode, (living) quarters

жили́щ|ный adj. of ▶ **жили́ще**; **~ные усло́вия** housing conditions

⚥ **жил|о́й** adj. **1** dwelling; residential; **ж. дом** dwelling house, block of flats; **ж. кварта́л** residential area; **~ая пло́щадь** = **жилпло́щадь 2** (обита́емый) inhabited

жилпло́щад|ь, и f. housing, accommodation

⚥ **жиль|ё, я́** nt. **1** (селе́ние) habitation; dwelling **2** (жили́ще) lodging; (living) accommodation

жи́молост|ь, и f. (bot.) honeysuckle

жир, а (у), о ~**е, в** ~**у́,** pl. ~**ы́** m. fat; grease

жира́ф, а m. giraffe

жи́р|ный, ~**ен,** ~**на́,** ~**но** adj. **1** (*пища, мясо*) fatty; (*руки, волосы*) greasy **2** (*человек*) fat, plump **3** (*земля*) rich **4** (typ.) bold

жиров|о́й adj. fatty, aliphatic; (anat.) adipose; ~**а́я ткань** adipose tissue

жите́йск|ий adj. **1** worldly; of life; ~**ая му́дрость** worldly wisdom **2** (*обыденный*) everyday

✍ **жи́тел|ь, я** m. inhabitant; dweller; **ми́рные** ~**и** civilians

жи́тель|ница, ницы f. of ▶ **жи́тель**

жи́тельств|о, а nt. residence; **вид на ж.** residence permit

✍ **жить, живу́, живёшь,** past **жил, жила́, жи́ло,** neg. **не́ жил, не жила́, не́ жило** impf. **1** to live; **ж. в Москве́** to live in Moscow **2** (+ i. or **на** + a.) to live (on); (+ i.) (fig.) to live (in, for); **нам не́ на что ж.** we have nothing to live on

жи́ться, живётся, past **жило́сь** impf. (impers., + d.) (infml) to live, get on; **ей ве́село живётся** she enjoys her life

ЖК-дисплле́|й, я m. (abbr. of **жидкокристалли́ческий дисппле́й**) liquid crystal display

жму, жмёшь see ▶ **жать¹**

жму́р|ки, ок (no sg.) blind man's buff

жнец, а́ m. reaper

жни́ц|а, ы f. of ▶ **жнец**

жну, жнёшь see ▶ **жать²**

жоке́|й, я m. jockey

жонгли́р|овать, ую impf. (+ i.) to juggle (with) (also fig.)

жо́п|а, ы f. (vulg.) arse (BrE), ass (AmE); **иди/ пошёл (ты) в** ~**у!** piss off!; **пья́ный в** ~**у** very drunk

жр|ать, у́, ёшь, past ~**а́л,** ~**ала́,** ~**а́ло** impf. (of ▶ **сожра́ть**) **1** (*о животных*) to eat

2 (sl., *о человеке*) to guzzle, gobble

жре́би|й, я m. **1** lot; **броса́ть ж.** to cast lots; **тяну́ть ж.** to draw lots **2** (fig.) lot, fate, destiny; **ж. бро́шен** the die is cast

жрец, а́ m. (pagan) priest; (fig.) devotee

жри́ц|а, ы f. priestess

жу́желиц|а, ы f. (zool.) ground beetle

жужжа́ни|е, я nt. hum, buzz, drone; humming, buzzing, droning

жужж|а́ть, у́, и́шь impf. to hum, buzz, drone; (*о пулях*) to whizz

жук, а́ m. **1** beetle; **ма́йский ж.** May bug, cockchafer **2** (infml, *плут*) rogue, swindler

жу́лик, а m. petty thief; cheat, swindler

жура́вл|ь, я m. (zool.) crane

✍ **журна́л, а** m. **1** (*периодическое издание*) magazine; periodical; journal **2** (*книга для записи*) journal, diary; (*классный*) register

✍ **журнали́ст, а** m. journalist

журнали́стик|а, и f. journalism

журч|а́ть, и́т impf. to babble, murmur (*of water*) (also fig., poet.)

жу́т|кий, ~**ок,** ~**ка́,** ~**ко** adj. terrible, terrifying; awe-inspiring, eerie

жу́тко¹ adv. terrifyingly; (infml) terribly, awfully

жу́тко² as pred.: **ж. поду́мать об э́том** it's terrible to think about it; (impers. + d.) **мне** и т. п. **ж.** I am, etc., terrified, feel awestruck

жут|ь, и f. (infml) **1** (*страх*) terror; awe **2** (as pred.): **ж.!** it is terrible!

жучо́к, ка́ m. **1** dim. of ▶ **жук 1 2** (infml, *пробка*) makeshift fuse **3** (infml, *подслушивающее устройство*) bug

жу|ю́, ёшь see ▶ **жева́ть**

ЖЭК, а and **жэк, а** m. (abbr. of **жили́щно-эксплуатацио́нная конто́ра**) housing office

жюри́ nt. indecl. (collect.) judges (*of competition, etc.*)

Зз

✍ **за** prep. **I.** (+ a. and i.; + a.: *indicates motion or action*; + i.: *indicates rest or state*) **1** (*позади*) behind; **за крова́ть, за крова́тью** behind the bed **2** (*вне*) beyond; across, the other side of; **за́ борт, за бо́ртом** overboard; **за́ угол, за угло́м** round the corner; **за го́родом** out of town **3** (*у*) at; **сесть за роя́ль** to sit down at the piano **4** (*занимаясь данным предметом*) at, to (*or translated by part.*);

приня́ться за рабо́ту to get down to work; **заста́ть кого́-н. за рабо́той** to find sb at work, working; **проводи́ть всё своё вре́мя за чте́нием** to spend all one's time reading **5**: **вы́йти за́муж за** (+ a.) to marry (*of a woman*); (быть) **за́мужем за** (+ i.) (to be) married (to)

● **II.** (+ a.) **1** (*свыше*) after (*of time*); over (*of age*); **далеко́ за по́лночь** long after midnight; **ему́ уже́ за со́рок** he is already over forty **2** (*на расстоянии*): **самолёт** разби́лся за ми́лю от дере́вни the aeroplane crashed a mile from the village; **за час** an hour before, an hour early **3** (*в тече́ние*) during, in the space of; **за́ ночь** during the night, overnight; **за су́тки** in (the space of) twenty-four hours **4** (*ука́зывает на предме́т, кото́рый охва́тывается*) by; **вести́ за́ руку** to lead by the hand **5** for (*in var. senses*); **плати́ть за биле́т** to pay for a ticket; **подписа́ть за дире́ктора** to sign for the director; **боя́ться, ра́доваться за кого́-н.** to fear, be glad for sb

• **III.** (+ *i.*) **1** (*по́сле*) after; **друг за дру́гом** one after another; **год за го́дом** year after year; **сле́довать за кем-н.** to follow sb **2** (*забо́тясь*) after; **следи́ть за детьми́** to look after children (*что́бы доста́ть, получи́ть*) for; **идти́ за молоко́м** to go for milk; **зайти́ за кем-н.** to call for sb **4** (*во вре́мя*) at, during; **за за́втраком** at breakfast **5** (*по причи́не*) for, on account of, because of; **за неиме́нием** (+ *g.*) for want of **6** (+ *prons.*) (*ука́зывает на отве́тственного должника́*): **за тобо́й пять рубле́й** you are owing five roubles

• **IV.** (*as pred.*) (*согла́сен*) for, in favour (BrE), favor (AmE)

за… *pref.* **I.** (*of vv.*) **1** (*indicates commencement of action*): **зала́ять** to start barking **2** (*indicates direction of action beyond given point*): **заверну́ть за́ угол** to turn a corner **3** (*indicates continuation of action to excess*): **закорми́ть** to overfeed **4** forms *pf.* aspect of *some vv.*

• **II.** (*of nn. and adjs.*) trans-; **Закавка́зье** Transcaucasia

заба́в|а, ы *f.* **1** (*игра́*) game; (*развлече́ние*) pastime **2** (*поте́ха*) amusement, fun; **он э́то сде́лал для ~ы** he did it for fun

заба́вно¹ *adv. of* ▸ **заба́вный**

заба́вно² *as pred.* it is amusing, funny; **(мне) з.** I find it amusing, funny; **з.!** how funny!

заба́в|ный, ~ен, ~на *adj.* amusing; funny

забасто́вк|а, и *f.* strike; **всео́бщая з.** general strike; **голо́дная з.** hunger strike

забасто́вщик, а *m.* striker

забасто́вщи|ца, цы *f. of* ▸ **забасто́вщик**

забве́ни|е, я *nt.* oblivion; **преда́ть ~ю** to consign to oblivion

забе́г, а *m.* (sport) race

забега́ловк|а, и *f.* (infml) snack bar

забега́|ть, ю *pf.* **1** (*нача́ть бе́гать*) to start running **2** (*о глаза́х*) to become shifty

забега́|ть, ю *impf. of* ▸ **забежа́ть**

забе|жа́ть, гу́, жи́шь, гу́т *pf.* (*of* ▸ **забега́ть**) **1** (*в* + *a.*) to run (in(to)) **2** (*к* + *d.*) (infml) to drop in (to see) **3** (*далеко́*) to run off; (*неизве́стно куда́*) to stray **4**; **з. вперёд** to run ahead; (fig., infml) to rush ahead

забеле́|ть, ет *pf.* **1** (*нача́ть беле́ть*) to begin to turn white **2** (*показа́ться*) to appear white (in the distance)

забере́мене|ть, ю *pf.* (*of* ▸ **бере́менеть**) to become pregnant

забеспоко́|иться, юсь, ишься *pf.* to begin to worry

забива́|ть, ю *impf. of* ▸ **заби́ть¹**

забива́|ться, юсь *impf. of* ▸ **заби́ться**

забинт|ова́ть, у́ю *pf.* (*of* ▸ **забинто́вывать**) to bandage

забинто́выва|ть, ю *impf. of* ▸ **забинтова́ть**

забира́|ть, ю *impf. of* ▸ **забра́ть**

забира́|ться, юсь *impf. of* ▸ **забра́ться**

заби́|ть¹, ью́, ьёшь *pf.* (*of* ▸ **забива́ть**) **1** (*вбить*) to drive in, hammer in, ram in **2** (sport) to score; **з. мяч** to kick the ball into the goal **3** (*заде́лать*) to seal, block up **4** (*закры́ть прохо́д*) to obstruct **5** (+ *i.*) (infml, *напо́лнить*) to cram, stuff (with) **6** (*изби́ть*) to beat up; **з. до́ сме́рти** to beat to death; (fig.) to render defenceless (BrE), defenseless (AmE) **7** (*уби́ть*) to slaughter (*cattle*)

заби́|ть², ью́, ьёшь *pf.* to begin to beat (*trans. and intrans.*) (*in some cases forms pf. aspect of* ▸ **бить**)

заби́|ться, ью́сь, ьёшься *pf.* (*of* ▸ **забива́ться**) **1** (*в* + *a.*) (*спря́таться*) to hide (in), take refuge (in) **2** (*в* + *a.*) (*прони́кнуть*) to get (into), penetrate **3** (+ *i.*) (*засоря́ться*) to become cluttered (with), clogged (with)

заблаговре́менно *adv.* in good time; well in advance

забле|сте́ть, щу́, сти́шь *pf.* to begin to shine, glitter, glow

заблуди́ться, жу́сь, ~дишься *pf.* to lose one's way, get lost

заблужда́|ться, юсь *impf.* to be mistaken

заблужде́ни|е, я *nt.* error; delusion; **ввести́ в з.** to delude, mislead

забо́й, я *m.* (*убо́й*) slaughter

заболева́ни|е, я *nt.* sickness, illness

заболева́|ть¹, ю *impf. of* ▸ **заболе́ть¹**

заболева́|ть², ет *impf. of* ▸ **заболе́ть²**

заболе́|ть¹, ю, ешь *pf.* (*of* ▸ **заболева́ть¹**) (*зарази́ться*) to fall ill, fall sick; (+ *i.*) to be taken ill (with), go down (with)

заболе́|ть², и́т *pf.* (*of* ▸ **заболева́ть²**) (*о появи́вшейся бо́ли*) to (begin to) ache, hurt; **у меня́ ~е́л зуб** my tooth has started to ache

забо́р, а *m.* fence

забо́т|а, ы *f.* **1** (*беспоко́йство*) care(s), trouble(s); **без ~** carefree **2** (*ухо́д*) care, attention(s); concern

забо́|титься, чусь, тишься *impf.* (*of* ▸ **позабо́титься**) (о + *p.*) **1** (*беспоко́иться*) to worry, be troubled (about) **2** (*уха́живать*) to take care (of); to take trouble (about); to care (about)

забо́тлив|ый, ~, ~а *adj.* solicitous, thoughtful; caring

забрако́ванный *p.p.p. of* ▸ **забракова́ть**; **з. това́р** rejects

забрак|ова́ть, у́ю *pf. of* ▸ **бракова́ть**

забра́л|о, а *nt.* visor

забра́сыва|ть, ю *impf. of* ▶ **заброса́ть,** ▶ **забро́сить**

забра́|ть, заберу́, заберёшь, *past* ∼**л,** ∼**ла́,** ∼**ло** *pf. (of* ▶ **забира́ть)** **1** *(взять)* to take (*in one's hands*); *(человека)* to take (with one); **з. с собо́й ве́щи** to take one's things with one **2** *(арестова́ть)* to arrest; *(отня́ть)* to take away; to seize, appropriate

забра́|ться, заберу́сь, заберёшься, *past* ∼**лся,** ∼**ла́сь,** ∼**ло́сь** *(of* ▶ **забра́ться)** **1** *(в + a.)* to get (into); *(в, на + a.)* to climb (into, on to) **2** *(уйти́, уе́хать)* to get to; *(спря́таться)* to hide out, go into hiding

заброни́р|овать, ую *pf. (of* ▶ **брони́ровать)** to reserve

заброса́|ть, ю *pf. (of* ▶ **забра́сывать)** *(+ a. and i.) (запо́лнить)* to fill (up) (with)

забро́|сить, шу, сишь *pf. (of* ▶ **забра́сывать)** **1** *(метну́ть)* to throw (*with force or to a distance*) **2** *(оста́вить)* to throw up, give up, abandon; to neglect, let go; **з. дете́й** to neglect children **3** *(доста́вить в определённое ме́сто)* to take, bring

забро́шенный *p.p.p. of* ▶ **забро́сить** *and adj.* **1** *(сад, челове́к)* neglected **2** *(ме́сто)* deserted, desolate

забры́зг|ать, аю *pf. (+ i.)* to splash (with)

заб|у́ду, у́дешь *see* ▶ **забы́ть**

⚡ **забыва́|ть, ю** *impf. of* ▶ **забы́ть**

забыва́|ться, юсь *impf. of* ▶ **забы́ться**

забы́вчив|ый, ∼**,** ∼**а** *adj.* forgetful; absent-minded

⚡ **заб|ы́ть, у́ду, у́дешь** *pf. (of* ▶ **забыва́ть)** **1** *(+ a. or o + p. or inf.)* to forget **2** *(случа́йно оста́вить)* to leave behind, forget (to bring)

заб|ы́ться, у́дусь, у́дешься *pf. (of* ▶ **забыва́ться)** **1** *(задрема́ть)* to doze off, drop off **2** *(замечта́ться)* to sink into a reverie **3** *(infml, вы́йти из грани́ц прили́чия)* to forget oneself

зава́л, а *m.* obstruction, blockage

зава́лива|ть, ю *impf. of* ▶ **завали́ть**

зава́лива|ться, юсь *impf. of* ▶ **завали́ться**

завал|и́ть, ю́, ∼**ишь** *pf. (of* ▶ **зава́ливать)** **1** *(загромозди́ть)* to block up, obstruct; to fill (*so as to block up*); **з. вход мешка́ми с песко́м** to block up the entrance with sandbags **2** *(+ i.) (infml, запо́лнить)* to pile (with); to fill cram-full (with); (fig., *переобремени́ть*) to overload with; **реда́кция** ∼**ена рабо́той** the editors are snowed under with work

завал|и́ться, ю́сь, ∼**ишься** *pf. (of* ▶ **зава́ливаться)** **1** *(упа́сть)* to fall; to collapse; **нож** ∼**и́лся за шкаф** the knife has fallen behind the cupboard **2** *(infml, лечь)* to lie down; **з. спать** to fall into bed **3** *(infml, опроки́нуться)* to overturn, tip up

зава́рива|ть, ет *impf. of* ▶ **завари́ть**

зава́рива|ться, ется *impf. of* ▶ **завари́ться**

завар|и́ть, ю́, ∼**ишь** *pf. (of* ▶ **зава́ривать)** to make (*drinks, etc., by pouring on boiling*

water); **з. чай** to brew tea

завар|и́ться, ю, ∼**ится** *pf. (of* ▶ **зава́риваться)** *(о напи́тках)* to brew

зава́рк|а, и *f.* **1** *(де́йствие)* brewing (*of tea, etc.*) **2** *(infml) (сухо́й чай)* enough tea for one brew; *(зава́ренный чай)* brew

⚡ **заведе́ни|е, я** *nt.* establishment, institution

заве́д|овать, ую *impf. (+ i.)* to manage, superintend; to be in charge (of)

заве́домо *adv.* wittingly; *(+ adj.)* known to be; **з. зна́я** being fully aware

заве|ду́, дёшь *see* ▶ **завести́**

заве́дующ|ий, его *m. (+ i.)* manager (of); head (of); person in charge (of); **з. отде́лом** head of a department

завез|ти́, у́, ёшь, *past* ∼**,** ∼**ла́** *pf. (of* ▶ **завози́ть)** **1** *(привезти́)* to deliver, drop off; **з. запи́ску по доро́ге домо́й** to deliver a note on the way home **2** *(увезти́)* to take (to a distance *or* out of one's way); **з. далеко́ в лес** to take deep into the forest

заверб|ова́ть, у́ю *pf. of* ▶ **вербова́ть**

заве́р|ить, ю, ишь *pf. (of* ▶ **заверя́ть)** **1** *(в + p.) (убеди́ть)* to assure (of) **2** *(удостове́рить)* to certify; **з. по́дпись** to witness a signature

заверн|у́ть, у́, ёшь *pf. (of* ▶ **завора́чивать)** **1** *(в + a.) (оберну́ть)* to wrap (in) **2** *(загну́ть)* to tuck up, roll up (*sleeve, etc.*) **3** *(сверну́ть в сто́рону)* to turn; **з. напра́во** to turn to the right **4** *(завинти́ть)* to screw tight; *(закры́ть)* to turn off (*by screwing*); **з. кран** to turn off a tap

заверн|у́ться, у́сь, ёшься *pf. (of* ▶ **завора́чиваться)** **1** *(в + a.)* to wrap oneself up (in), muffle oneself (in) **2** *pass. of* ▶ **заверну́ть**

заверша́|ть, а́ю *impf. of* ▶ **заверши́ть**

заверше́ни|е, я *nt.* completion; end; **в з.** in conclusion

заверш|и́ть, у́, и́шь *pf. (of* ▶ **заверша́ть)** to complete, conclude, crown

заверя́|ть, я́ю *impf. of* ▶ **заве́рить**

заве́с|а, ы *f.* (fig.) veil, screen; **дымова́я з.** (mil.) smokescreen

заве́|сить, шу, сишь *pf. (of* ▶ **заве́шивать)** to curtain (off)

заве|сти́, ду́, дёшь, *past* ∼**л,** ∼**ла́** *pf. (of* ▶ **заводи́ть)** **1** *(привести́)* to take, bring (*to a place*); to leave, drop off (*at a place*) **2** *(увести́)* to take (to a distance *or* out of one's way) **3** *(основа́ть)* to set up; to start; **з. семью́** to start a family **4** *(приобрести́)* to acquire **5** *(ввести́)* to institute, introduce (*as a custom*); **з. привы́чку** *(+ inf.)* to get into the habit (of) **6** *(часы́)* to wind (up); *(маши́ну)* to start; **з. мото́р** to start an engine

заве|сти́сь, ду́сь, дёшься, *past* ∼**лся,** ∼**ла́сь** *pf. (of* ▶ **заводи́ться)** **1** *(появи́ться)* to be; to appear; **в по́гребе** ∼**ли́сь кры́сы** there are rats in the cellar **2** *(о механи́зме)* to start

Заве́т, а *m.*: **Ве́тхий, Но́вый З.** the Old, the New Testament

заве́тный *adj.* (*мечты*) cherished

заве́шива|ть, ю *impf. of* ▶ **заве́сить**

завеща́ни|е, я *nt.* will, testament

завеща́|ть, ю *impf. and pf.* (+ *a. and d.*) to leave (to), bequeath (to); (+ *d.* + *inf.*) (*поручить*) to instruct

завива́|ть, ю *impf. of* ▶ **зави́ть**

завива́|ться, юсь *impf. of* ▶ **зави́ться**

зави́дно *as pred.* (*impers.* + *d.*) to feel envious; **мне з.** I feel envious

зави́д|ный, ~ен, ~на *adj.* enviable

зави́д|овать, ую *impf.* (*of* ▶ **позави́довать**) (+ *d.*) to envy; to be jealous of

завизж|а́ть, у́, и́шь *pf.* to begin to scream, squeal

завин|ти́ть, чу́, ти́шь *pf.* (*of* ▶ **зави́нчивать**) to screw up

зави́нчива|ть, ю *impf. of* ▶ **завинти́ть**

зави́са|ть, ю *impf. of* ▶ **зави́снуть**

зависа́ть, иса́ет *impf. of* ▶ **зави́снуть**

⚇ **зави́|сеть, шу, сишь** *impf.* (**от** + *g.*) to depend (on)

⚇ **зави́симост|ь, и** *f.* dependence; **з. от нарко́тиков** dependence on drugs, drug dependence; **в ~и** (**от** + *g.*) depending (on), subject (to)

зави́сим|ый, ~, ~а *adj.* (**от** + *g.*) dependent (on)

зави́с|нуть, ну, нешь, *past* **~, ~ла** *pf.* (*of* ▶ **зависа́ть**) **1** (*о вертолёте и т. д.*) to hover, hang (in the air) **2** (comput.) to crash **3** (infml, *о вопросе, ситуации*) to be in limbo, unresolved, up in the air

зави́сн|уть, ет *pf.* (*of* ▶ **зависа́ть**) (comput.) to crash

зави́стлив|ый, ~, ~а *adj.* envious

за́вист|ь, и *f.* envy; jealousy

завит|о́к, ка́ *m.* **1** (*локон*) curl, lock **2** (*почерка*) flourish

зави́|ть, ью́, ьёшь, *past* **~и́л, ~ила́, ~и́ло** *pf.* (*of* ▶ **завива́ть**) to curl, wave, twist, wind

зави́|ться, ью́сь, ьёшься, *past* **~и́лся, ~ила́сь, ~и́ло́сь** *pf.* (*of* ▶ **завива́ться**) **1** (*виться*) to curl, wave, twine **2** (*завить себе́ во́лосы*) to curl, wave one's hair; (*у парикма́хера*) to have one's hair curled, waved

завладева́|ть, ю *impf. of* ▶ **завладе́ть**

завладе́|ть, ю *pf.* (*of* ▶ **завладева́ть**) (+ *i.*) to take possession (of); to seize, capture (also fig.); **он ~л внима́нием слу́шателей** he captured the audience's attention

завлека́|ть, ю *impf. of* ▶ **завле́чь**

завле́|чь, ку́, чёшь, ку́т, *past* **~к, ~кла́** *pf.* (*of* ▶ **завлека́ть**) **1** (*замани́ть*) to lure, entice **2** (*соблазни́ть*) to fascinate, captivate

⚇ **заво́д¹, а** *m.* **1** factory, mill; works **2**: (**ко́нный**) **з.** stud (farm)

заво́д², а *m.* (*у часо́в*) winding mechanism; **игру́шка с ~ом** clockwork toy

заво|ди́ть, жу́, ~дишь *impf. of* ▶ **завести́**

заво|ди́ться, ~ится *impf. of* ▶ **завести́сь**

заводско́й *adj. of* ▶ **заво́д¹**

завоева́ни|е, я *nt.* **1** (*де́йствие*) conquest; winning **2** (*захва́ченная террито́рия*) conquest; (fig., *достиже́ние*) achievement

завоева́тел|ь, я *m.* conqueror

заво|ева́ть, ю́ю, ю́ешь *pf.* (*of* ▶ **завоёвывать**) to conquer; (fig.) to win, gain; **з. симпа́тии** to gain sympathy

завоёвыва|ть, ю *impf.* (*of* ▶ **завоева́ть**) to try to get

заво|зи́ть, жу́, ~зишь *impf. of* ▶ **завезти́**

завола́кива|ть, ю, ет *impf. of* ▶ **заволо́чь**

завола́кива|ться, ется *impf. of* ▶ **заволо́чься**

заволн|ова́ться, у́юсь *pf.* to become agitated

заволо́|чь, ку́, чёшь, ку́т, *past* **~к, ~кла́** *pf.* (*of* ▶ **завола́кивать**) to cloud; to obscure; **тума́н ~к со́лнце** the sun was obscured by fog; **её глаза́ ~кло слеза́ми** her eyes were clouded with tears

заволо́|чься, чётся, ку́тся, *past* **~кся, ~кла́сь** *pf.* (*of* ▶ **завола́киваться**) to cloud over, become clouded

завоп|и́ть, лю́, и́шь *pf.* (infml) to cry out, yell; to give a cry

завора́чива|ть, ю *impf. of* ▶ **заверну́ть**

завора́чива|ться, юсь *impf. of* ▶ **заверну́ться**

за́втра *adv.* tomorrow; **до з.!** see you tomorrow!

за́втрак, а *m.* breakfast; **второ́й з.** elevenses, mid-morning snack

за́втрака|ть, ю *impf.* (*of* ▶ **поза́втракать**) to (have) breakfast; (*среди́ дня*) to (have) lunch

за́втрашний *adj.* tomorrow's; **з. день** tomorrow

за́вуч, а *m.* (*abbr. of* **заве́дующий/ заве́дующая уче́бной ча́стью**) director of studies

завхо́з, а *m.* (*abbr. of* **заве́дующий/ заве́дующая хозя́йством**) bursar, steward

завыва́|ть, ю *impf.* to howl

завы́|сить, шу, сишь *pf.* (*of* ▶ **завыша́ть**) to raise too high; **з. отме́тку на экза́мене** to give too high a mark in an examination

зав|ы́ть, о́ю, о́ешь *pf.* to begin to howl

завыша́|ть, ю *impf. of* ▶ **завы́сить**

завя|за́ть¹, жу́, ~жешь *pf.* (*of* ▶ **завя́зывать**) **1** (*у́зел, шнурки́*) to tie; to tie up; (*паке́т*) to knot **2** (*па́лец*) to bind (up) **3** (fig., *нача́ть*) to start; **з. разгово́р** to strike up a conversation

завя|за́ть², ю *impf. of* ▶ **завя́знуть**

завя|за́ться, ~жется *pf.* (*of* ▶ **завя́зываться**) **1** *pass. of* ▶ **завяза́ть¹** **2** (*нача́ться*) to start; to arise

завя́з|нуть, ну, нешь, *past* **~, ~ла** *pf.* (*of* ▶ **завяза́ть²**) to stick, get stuck

завя́зыва|ть, ет *impf. of* ▶ **завяза́ть¹**

завя́зыва|ться, ется *impf. of* ▶ завяза́ться

завя́|нуть, ну, нешь, *past* ∼л *pf. of* ▶ вя́нуть

загада́|ть, а́ю *pf.* (*of* ▶ зага́дывать) **1**: з. зага́дки to ask riddles **2** (*задумать*) to think of; ∼а́йте число́ think of a number

зага́дк|а, и *f.* riddle; (*fig.*) enigma; mystery

зага́доч|ный, ∼ен, ∼на *adj.* enigmatic; mysterious

зага́дыва|ть, ю *impf. of* ▶ загада́ть

загазо́ванност|ь, и *f.* pollution (*with gases*)

загазо́ван|ный, ∼, ∼а *adj.* polluted (*with gases*)

зага́р, а *m.* sunburn, (sun)tan

зага́|си́ть, шу́, ∼си́шь *pf. of* ▶ гаси́ть 1

загиба́|ть, ю *impf. of* ▶ загну́ть

загиба́|ться, юсь *impf. of* ▶ загну́ться

загипнотизи́р|овать, ую *pf. of* ▶ гипнотизи́ровать

загла́ви|е, я *nt.* title; heading; под ∼ем entitled, headed

загла́в|ный *adj. of* ▶ загла́вие; ∼ная бу́ква capital letter

загла́|дить, жу, дишь *pf.* (*of* ▶ загла́живать) **1** (*сделать гладким*) to iron (out), press **2** (fig., *смягчить*) to make up (for), make amends (for)

загла́жива|ть, ю *impf. of* ▶ загла́дить

загла́тыва|ть, ю *impf. of* ▶ заглота́ть

заглота́|ть, ю *pf.* (*of* ▶ загла́тывать) to swallow

заглу́хн|уть, у, ешь *pf. of* ▶ гло́хнуть 2

заглуша́|ть, а́ю *impf. of* ▶ заглуши́ть

заглуш|и́ть, у́, и́шь *pf.* (*of* ▶ глуши́ть 3, ▶ заглуша́ть) **1** (*звуки*) to drown, deaden, muffle **2** (*передачи*) to jam **3** (*растения*) to choke

загля|де́ться, жу́сь, ди́шься *pf.* (*of* ▶ загля́дываться) (на + *a.*) (infml) to stare (at); to stare (at); to be lost in admiration (of)

загля́дыва|ть, ю *impf. of* ▶ загляну́ть

загля́дыва|ться, юсь *impf. of* ▶ загляде́ться

загля|ну́ть, у́, ∼ешь *pf.* (*of* ▶ загля́дывать) **1** (*взглянуть*) to peep; to glance **2** (infml, *зайти*) to look in, drop in

загна́ива|ться, ется *impf. of* ▶ загнои́ться

загна́|ть, загоню́, заго́нишь, *past* ∼л, ∼ла́, ∼ло *pf.* (*of* ▶ загоня́ть) **1** to drive in; з. коро́в в хлев to drive the cows into the shed, get the cows in **2** (infml, *вбить*) to drive home **3** (infml, *продать*) to sell, flog (BrE)

загнива́|ть, ю *impf. of* ▶ загни́ть

загни́|ть, ю́, ёшь, *past* ∼л, ∼ла́, ∼ло *pf.* (*of* ▶ загнива́ть) to begin to rot; to rot, decay (also fig.)

загно|и́ться, и́тся *pf.* (*of* ▶ загна́иваться) to fester

загн|у́ть, у́, ёшь *pf.* (*of* ▶ загиба́ть) (*вверх*) to turn up; (*вниз*) to turn down; (*сгибать*) to bend, fold; to crease

загн|у́ться, у́сь, ёшься *pf. of* ▶ загиба́ться) **1** (*вверх*) to turn up, stick up; (*вниз*) to turn down **2** (sl., *умереть*) to turn up one's toes

загова́рива|ться, юсь *impf.* (*of* ▶ заговори́ться) **1** (*увлечься разговором*) to be carried away by a conversation **2** (*impf. only*) (*говорить бессмыслицу*) to rave; to ramble (*in speech*)

за́говор[1], а *m.* plot, conspiracy

за́говор[2], а *m.* (*заклинание*) charm, spell

заговор|и́ть, ю́, и́шь *pf.* (*начать говорить*) to begin to speak

заговор|и́ться, ю́сь, и́шься *pf. of* ▶ загова́риваться

загово́рщик, а *m.* conspirator, plotter

загово́рщи|ца, цы *f. of* ▶ загово́рщик

заголо́в|ок, ка *m.* **1** (*заглавие*) title; heading **2** (*газетный*) headline

заго́н, а *m.* (*для скота*) enclosure; (*для овец*) pen

за|гоню́, го́нишь *see* ▶ загна́ть

загоня́|ть, ю *impf. of* ▶ загна́ть

загора́жива|ть, ю *impf. of* ▶ загороди́ть

загора́|ть, ю *impf. of* ▶ загоре́ть

загора́|ться, юсь *impf. of* ▶ загоре́ться

загоре́лый *adj.* sunburnt; brown, bronzed

загор|е́ть, ю́, и́шь *pf.* (*of* ▶ загора́ть) to become sunburnt; to acquire a tan

загор|е́ться, ю́сь, и́шься *pf.* (*of* ▶ загора́ться) (*начать гореть*) to catch fire; to begin to burn

загоро|ди́ть, жу́, ∼ди́шь *pf.* (*of* ▶ загора́живать) **1** (*огородить*) to enclose, fence in **2** (*преградить*) to barricade; to obstruct; з. кому́-н. свет to stand in sb's light

загоро́дк|а, и *f.* (infml) fence

за́городный *adj.* out-of-town; country

загота́влива|ть, ю *impf. of* ▶ загото́вить

загото́в|ить, лю, ишь *pf.* (*of* ▶ загота́вливать, ▶ заготовля́ть) (*создать запас чего-либо*) to lay in; to stockpile

загото́вк|а, и *f.* **1** (*зерна, корма*) laying in; stockpiling **2** (*закупка государством*) procurement

заготовля́|ть, ю *impf. of* ▶ загото́вить

загражде́ни|е, я *nt.* obstacle, barrier, obstruction

заграни́ц|а, ы *f.* (infml) foreign countries (*see also* ▶ грани́ца)

заграни́чный *adj.* foreign

За́греб, а *n.* Zagreb

загреба́|ть, ю *impf. of* ▶ загрести́

загре|сти́, бу́, бёшь, *past* ∼б, ∼бла́ *pf.* (*of* ▶ загреба́ть) (infml) to rake up; (fig.) to rake in

загримир|ова́ть, у́ю *pf. of* ▶ гримирова́ть

загримир|ова́ться, у́юсь *pf. of* ▶ гримирова́ться

загро́бн|ый *adj.* beyond the grave; ∼ая жизнь life after death

загружа́|ть, ю *impf. of* ▶ загрузи́ть 3

загр|узи́ть, ужу́, у́зишь *pf.* **1** (*impf.* **грузи́ть**) to load **2** (*impf.* **~ужа́ть**) (tech.) to feed, charge, prime; (comput., *компьютер*) to boot; (*программу, данные*) to load; (*скопировать, откуда*) to download; (*куда*) to upload **3** (*impf.* **~ужа́ть**) (infml, *занять рабо́той*) to keep fully occupied

загру́зк|а, и *f.* **1** (*де́йствие*) loading **2** (*объём рабо́ты*) capacity, workload

загру|сти́ть, щу́, сти́шь *pf.* to grow sad

загрыза́|ть, ю *impf. of* ▶ **загры́зть**

загры́з|ть, у́, ёшь, *past* **~, ~ла** *pf.* (*of* ▶ **загрыза́ть**) (*уби́ть*) to kill

загрязне́ни|е, я *nt.* soiling; (*приро́ды*) pollution

загрязн|и́ть, ю́, и́шь *pf.* (*of* ▶ **загрязня́ть**) to soil, make dirty; (*приро́ду*) to pollute

загрязня́|ть, ю *impf. of* ▶ **загрязни́ть**

ЗАГС, а and **загс, а** *m.* (*abbr. of* **отде́л за́писи а́ктов гражда́нского состоя́ния**) registry office

загуб|и́ть, лю́, ~ишь *pf.* (*погуби́ть*) to ruin; **з. чью-н. жизнь** to make sb's life a misery

зад, а, о ~е, на/в ~у́, *pl.* **~ы́** *m.* **1** (*маши́ны, до́ма*) back; **~ом напере́д** back to front **2** (*живо́тного*) hind quarters; rump; (*челове́ка*) behind, buttocks

◢ **зада|ва́ть, ю́, ёшь** *impf. of* ▶ **зада́ть**

задав|и́ть, лю́, ~ишь *pf.* to crush; (*о маши́не*) to run over, knock down

◢ **зада́ни|е, я** *nt.* task, job

зада́ром *adv.* (infml, *беспла́тно*) for nothing; very cheaply; **купи́ть з.** to buy for a song

зада́т|ок, ка *m.* deposit

за|да́ть, да́м, да́шь, да́ст, дади́м, дади́те, даду́т, *past* **~да́л, ~дала́, ~да́ло** *pf.* (*of* ▶ **задава́ть**) to set; to give; **з. вопро́с** to put a question

◢ **зада́ч|а, и** *f.* **1** (math., etc.) problem **2** (*цель*) task; mission

зада́чник, а *m.* book of (mathematical) problems

задвига́|ть, ю *pf.* to begin to move

задвига́|ть, ю *impf. of* ▶ **задви́нуть**

задви́н|уть, у, ешь *pf.* (*of* ▶ **задвига́ть**) **1** (*перемести́ть*) to push **2**: **з. за́навески** to draw the curtains

задво́р|ки, ок (*no sg.*) backyard; (fig.) out-of-the-way place, backwoods

задева́|ть, ю *impf. of* ▶ **заде́ть**

заде́л|ать, аю *pf.* (*of* ▶ **заде́лывать**) (*ды́ру, щель*) to block up, close up; **з. течь** to stop up a leak

заде́лыва|ть, ю *impf. of* ▶ **заде́лать**

задёргива|ть, ю *impf. of* ▶ **задёрнуть**

задержа́ни|е, я *nt.* (*престу́пника*) detention, arrest

заде́ржанн|ый, ого *m.* detainee

задерж|а́ть, у́, ~ишь *pf.* (*of* ▶ **заде́рживать**) **1** (*останови́ть*) to stop, hold back, delay; detain; (*отсро́чить*) to delay **2** (*удержа́ть*) to withhold, keep back; **з. зарпла́ту** to stop wages; **з. дыха́ние** to hold one's breath

3 (*арестова́ть*) to detain, arrest

задерж|а́ться, у́сь, ~ишься *pf.* (*of* ▶ **заде́рживаться**) **1** (*на рабо́те, в гостя́х*) to be held up, delayed; to stay too long **2** (*у вхо́да, перед магази́ном*) to linger **3** (*не сде́лать во́время*) to be late

заде́ржива|ть, ю *impf. of* ▶ **задержа́ть**

заде́ржива|ться, юсь *impf. of* ▶ **задержа́ться**

заде́ржк|а, и *f.* delay; hold-up

задёрн|уть, у, ешь *pf.* (*of* ▶ **задёргивать**) to pull; to draw; **з. занаве́ски** to draw the curtains

заде́|ть, ну, нешь *pf.* (*of* ▶ **задева́ть**) (*косну́ться*) to touch, brush (against); (fig., *оби́деть*) to offend, wound; **его́ ~ло за живо́е** he was stung to the quick

задира́|ть, ю, ет *impf. of* ▶ **задра́ть**

задира́|ться, ется *impf. of* ▶ **задра́ться**

◢ **за́дн|ий** *adj.* (*сиде́нье*) back, rear; (*ноги*) hind; **~яя мысль** ulterior motive; **з. прохо́д** (anat.) anus; **дать з. ход** to go into reverse; to back up; **~им число́м** later, with hindsight

за́дник, а *m.* **1** back, counter (*of shoe*) **2** (theatr.) backdrop

за́дниц|а, ы *f.* (infml) backside, butt (AmE)

задо́лго *adv.* long before

задо́лженност|ь, и *f.* debts; **погаси́ть з.** to pay off one's debts

за́дом *adv.* backwards

задо́р, а *m.* fervour (BrE), fervor (AmE), ardour (BrE); ardor (AmE); passion

задо́р|ный, ~ен, ~на *adj.* fervent, ardent; impassioned

задох|ну́ться, ну́сь, нёшься *pf.* (*of* ▶ **задыха́ться**) **1** (*умере́ть*) to suffocate; to choke **2** (*тяжело́ дыша́ть*) to pant; to gasp for breath

зад|ра́ть, еру́, ерёшь, *past* **~ра́л, ~рала́, ~ра́ло** *pf.* (*of* ▶ **задира́ть**) (infml, *подня́ть кве́рху*) to lift up; to pull up; **з. го́лову** to crane one's neck; **з. нос** (fig.) to cock one's nose

зад|ра́ться, ерётся, *past* **~ра́лся, ~рала́сь** *pf.* (*of* ▶ **задира́ться**) (infml, *о пла́тье*) to ride up

задрем|а́ть, лю́, ~лешь *pf.* to doze off, begin to nod

задрож|а́ть, у́, и́шь *pf.* to begin to tremble; (*от хо́лода*) to begin to shiver

задува́|ть, ю *impf. of* ▶ **заду́ть**

заду́ма|ть, ю *pf.* (*of* ▶ **заду́мывать**) **1** (+ *a.* or *inf.*) (*реши́ть*) to plan; to intend; to conceive the idea (of) **2** (*число́*) to think of

заду́ма|ться, юсь *pf.* to become thoughtful, pensive; to fall to thinking

заду́мчив|ый, ~, ~а *adj.* thoughtful, pensive

заду́мыва|ть, ю *impf. of* ▶ **заду́мать**

заду́мыва|ться, юсь *impf.* (*погружа́ться в свои́ мы́сли*) to be thoughtful, be pensive; (*размышля́ть*) to meditate; to ponder; **з. о** (+ *p.*) to think about

заду́|ть, ю, ешь *pf.* (*of* ▶ задува́ть)
  1 (*погаси́ть*) to blow out **2** (*нача́ть дуть*) to begin to blow

задуш|и́ть, ý, ∼ишь *pf. of* ▶ души́ть¹

задыха́|ться, юсь *impf. of* ▶ задохну́ться

заеда́|ть, ю *impf. of* ▶ зае́сть¹, ▶ зае́сть²

заезжа́|ть, ю *impf. of* ▶ зае́хать

заём, за́йма *m.* loan

заёмщик, a *m.* borrower, debtor

зае́|сть¹, м, шь, ст, ди́м, ди́те, дя́т, *past*
  ∼л *pf.* (*of* ▶ заеда́ть) **1** (*уку́сами*) to bite to death; (*загры́зть*) to kill; (fig., infml, *измучить*) to torment, oppress; **его́ ∼ла тоска́** he fell prey to melancholy **2** (*impers.*) (tech.) to jam; (naut.) to foul; **кана́т ∼ло the cable has fouled**

зае́|сть², м, шь, ст, ди́м, ди́те, дя́т, *past* **∼л** *pf.* (*of* ▶ заеда́ть) (+ *a. and i.*) to take (with); **он ∼л лека́рство са́харом** he took the medicine with sugar

зае́|хать, ду, дешь *pf.* (*of* ▶ заезжа́ть)
  1 (к + *d.*) to call in (at); to drop in (on); (в + *a.*) to enter, ride into, drive into; (за + *a.*) to go beyond, past; (за + *i.*) to call for; to fetch, pick up **2** (*уе́хать или попа́сть куда́-н. далеко́ или куда́ не сле́дует*) to get (to); to go; **он ∼хал в кана́ву** he landed in the ditch

зажа́р|ить, ю, ит *pf. of* ▶ жа́рить

зажа́р|иться, ится *pf. of* ▶ жа́риться

зажа́т|ый, ∼, ∼а *p.p.p. of* ▶ зажа́ть *and adj.*
  (infml, *о челове́ке*) tense, uptight

зажа́|ть, мý, мёшь *pf.* (*of* ▶ зажима́ть)
  (*сти́снуть*) to squeeze; to press; to clutch; (*заткну́ть*) to stop up; **з. в руке́** to grip; **з. рот кому́-н.** (fig.) to stop sb's mouth

зажг|ý, жёшь, гýт *see* ▶ заже́чь

заж|е́чь, гý, жёшь, гýт, *past* **∼ёг, ∼гла́** *pf.* (*of* ▶ зажига́ть) (*ого́нь, ла́мпу*) to light; (*свет*) to turn on; **з. спи́чку** to strike a match

заж|е́чься, гýсь, жёшься, гýтся, *past* **зажёгся, зажгла́сь** *pf.* (*of* ▶ зажига́ться) (*об огне́*) to begin to burn; (*о фона́рях*) to go on, light up

зажива́|ть, ю *impf. of* ▶ зажи́ть

зажига́лк|а, и *f.* (cigarette) lighter

зажига́ни|е, я *nt.* (*в маши́не*) ignition

зажига́|ть, ю *impf. of* ▶ заже́чь

зажига́|ться, юсь *impf. of* ▶ заже́чься

зажи́м, a *m.* **1** (tech.) clamp; clip **2** (elec.) terminal

зажима́|ть, ю *impf. of* ▶ зажа́ть

зажи́точ|ный, ∼ен, ∼на *adj.* well-to-do; prosperous; affluent

зажи́|ть, вý, вёшь, *past* **за́жил, ∼ла́, за́жило** *pf.* (*of* ▶ зажива́ть) **1** (*о ра́не*) to heal; to close up **2** (*нача́ть жить*) to begin to live; **з. по-но́вому** to begin a new life

зазвен|е́ть, ю́, и́шь *pf.* to begin to ring

зазвон|и́ть, ю́, и́шь *pf.* to begin to ring

зазвуч|а́ть, ý, и́шь *pf.* to begin to sound; to begin to resound

заземле́ни|е, я *nt.* (elec.) **1** (*де́йствие*) earthing (BrE), grounding (AmE) **2** (*устро́йство*) earth (BrE), ground (AmE)

заземл|и́ть, ю́, и́шь *pf.* (elec.) to earth

зазим|ова́ть, ýю *pf.* to winter; to pass the winter

зазна|ва́ться, ю́сь, ёшься *impf. of* ▶ зазна́ться

зазна́|ться, юсь *pf.* (*of* ▶ зазнава́ться) (infml) to give oneself airs, become conceited

зазо́р, a *m.* gap

зазо́р|ный, ∼ен, ∼на *adj.* (infml) shameful, disgraceful

заигра́|ть, ю *pf.* (*нача́ть игра́ть*) to begin to play

заигра́|ться, юсь *pf.* (*of* ▶ заи́грываться) to become absorbed in playing

заи́грыва|ть, ю *impf.* (с + *i.*) (infml) to flirt (with); to make advances (to) (also fig.)

заи́грыва|ться, юсь *impf. of* ▶ заигра́ться

заика́ни|е, я *nt.* stammer(ing), stutter(ing)

заика́|ться, юсь *impf.* to stammer, stutter; (*нереши́тельно говори́ть*) to falter (*in speech*)

займств|овать, ую *impf.* (*of* ▶ позаимствовать) to borrow

заинтересо́ван|ный, ∼, ∼a *p.p.p. of* ▶ заинтересова́ть *and* (∼, ∼на) *adj.* (в + *p.*) interested (in); **∼ная сторона́** interested party

заинтерес|ова́ть, ýю *pf.* to interest; to excite the curiosity (of)

заинтерес|ова́ться, ýюсь *pf.* (+ *i.*) to become interested; to take an interest (in)

заи́скива|ть, ю *impf.* (**пе́ред** + *i.*) to try to ingratiate oneself (with)

зайд|ý, дёшь *see* ▶ зайти́

за́йма *see* ▶ заём

займ|ý, ёшь *see* ▶ заня́ть

за|йти́, йдý, йдёшь, *past* **∼шёл, ∼шла́** *pf.* (*of* ▶ заходи́ть) **1** (*посети́ть*) to call (on); to look in; to drop in (at) **2** (за + *i.*) (*что́бы взять*) to call for, fetch **3** (в + *a.*) (*войти́*) to go into, get into; (*попа́сть*) to get to (*a place*); to find oneself (*in a place*) **4** (*о разгово́ре*) to turn to **5** (за + *a.*) (*скры́ться за чем-н.*) to go behind; (*продолжа́ться*) to go on, continue (after); (*зака́тываться*) to set (*of sun, etc.*); **з. за́ угол** to turn a corner; **з. сли́шком далеко́** (fig.) to go too far

Закавка́зь|е, я *nt.* Transcaucasia

зака́дровый *adj.*: **з. коммента́рий** (TV, cin.) voice-over

⚡ **зака́з, a** *m.* order; (*биле́тов, стола́*) reservation; (*портре́та*) commission; **на з.** to order; **как по ∼у** as if to order

зака|за́ть, жý, ∼жешь *pf.* (*of* ▶ зака́зывать) to order; (*биле́ты, стол*) to reserve; (*портре́т*) to commission

зака́зник, a *m.* (game) reserve

заказн|о́й *adj.* **1** done or made to order; ~а́я статья́ article written to order; ~а́я журнали́стика chequebook journalism; ~о́е уби́йство contract killing **2**: ~о́е письмо́ registered letter

⚡ **зака́зчик, а** *m.* customer, client

⚡ **зака́зыва|ть, ю** *impf. of* ▶ заказа́ть

закал|ённый, ~ён, ~ена́ *p.p.p. of* ▶ закали́ть *and* (~ён, ~енна́) *adj.* hardened, hard

закал|и́ть, ю́, и́шь *pf.* (*of* ▶ закаля́ть) (tech.) to temper; to case-harden; (fig.) to temper, harden; to make hard, hardy

зака́лк|а, и *f.* tempering; hardening; (sport) conditioning

зака́лыва|ть, ю *impf. of* ▶ заколо́ть

закаля́|ть, ю *impf. of* ▶ закали́ть

⚡ **зака́нчива|ть, ю, ет** *impf. of* ▶ зако́нчить

зака́нчива|ться, ется *impf. of* ▶ зако́нчиться

зака́п|ать, аю *pf.* (*impf.* ~ывать) to spot, stain

зака́пыва|ть, ю *impf. of* ▶ закопа́ть, ▶ зака́пать

зака́рмлива|ть, ю *impf. of* ▶ закорми́ть

зака́т, а *m.* setting; з. (со́лнца) sunset; (fig.) decline

заката́|ть, ю *pf.* (*of* ▶ зака́тывать) **1** (infml, *рукава́*) to roll up **2** (*ба́нку, кры́шку*) to close, hermetically seal

зака|ти́ть, чу́, ~тишь *pf.* (*of* ▶ зака́тывать) (*мяч*) to roll; з. исте́рику (infml) to go off into hysterics; з. глаза́ to roll one's eyes

зака|ти́ться, чу́сь, ~тишься *pf.* (*of* ▶ зака́титься) **1** (*о мяче*) to roll **2** (*о солнце*) to set (*of heavenly bodies*); (fig., *о славе*) to wane; to vanish

зака́тыва|ть, ю *impf. of* ▶ закати́ть, ▶ закати́ть

зака́тыва|ться, юсь *impf. of* ▶ закати́ться

зака́шля|ться, юсь *pf.* to have a fit of coughing

заква́ск|а, и *f.* (*для теста*) leaven; (*для кефира*) culture

закида́|ть, ю *pf.* (*of* ▶ заки́дывать) (+ *a. and i.*) **1** (*осыпать*) to bespatter (with); to shower (with); з. камня́ми to stone **2** (*заполнить*) to fill up (with); (*сверху*) to cover (with)

заки́дыва|ть, ю *impf. of* ▶ закида́ть, ▶ заки́нуть

заки́н|уть, у, ешь *pf.* (*мяч в сетку, майку под кровать*) to throw; (*невод, удочку*) to cast

закипа́|ть, ет *impf. of* ▶ закипе́ть

закип|е́ть, и́т *pf.* (*of* ▶ закипа́ть) (*начать кипеть*) to begin to boil; (*кипеть*) to be on the boil; (fig., *о работе*) to be in full swing

закла́д, а *m.* (*залог*) pawning; (*недвижимости*) mortgaging

закла́дк|а, и *f.* (*в книге*) bookmark (also comput.)

закла́дыва|ть, ю *impf. of* ▶ заложи́ть

закле́ива|ть, ю, ет *impf. of* ▶ закле́ить

закле́|ить, ю, ишь *pf.* (*of* ▶ закле́ивать) to glue up; to stick up; з. конве́рт to seal an envelope

заклина́ни|е, я *nt.* **1** (*магические слова*) incantation; spell **2** (*мольба*) entreaty

заклина́тел|ь, я *m.* exorcist; з. змей snake charmer

заклина́тель|ница, ницы *f. of* ▶ заклина́тель

заклина́|ть, ю *impf. of* ▶ закли́нить

закли́н|ить, ю, ишь *pf.* (*of* ▶ закли́нивать) **1** (*закрепить*) to wedge, fasten with a wedge **2** (*лишить возможности вращаться*) to jam; (*also. impers.*) дверь ~ило the door jammed

⚡ **заключа́|ть, ю** *impf. of* ▶ заключи́ть

⚡ **заключа́|ться, а́ется** *impf.* **1** *pass. of* ▶ заключа́ть **2** (*impf. only*) (в + *p.*) to consist (of); to lie (in)

⚡ **заключе́ни|е, я** *nt.* **1** (*конец*) conclusion, end; (*завершение*) conclusion, ending; в з. in conclusion **2** (*вывод*) conclusion, inference **3** (*договора, сделки*) conclusion, signing **4** (*лишение свободы*) confinement, detention; тюре́мное з. imprisonment

заключ|ённый, ~ён, ~ена́ *p.p.p. of* ▶ заключи́ть; (*as n.* з., ~ённого, *f.* ~ённая, ~ённой) (law) prisoner, convict

заключи́тельный *adj.* final, concluding

заключ|и́ть, у́, и́шь *pf.* (*of* ▶ заключа́ть) **1** (*сделать вывод*) to conclude, infer **2** (*принять*) to conclude, enter into; з. брак to contract marriage; з. догово́р to conclude a treaty; з. сде́лку to strike a bargain **3**: з. в себе́ to contain, enclose; to comprise; з. в ско́бки to enclose in brackets **4** (*лишить свободы*) to confine; з. в тюрьму́ to imprison

зак|ова́ть, ую́, уёшь *pf.* (*of* ▶ зако́вывать) to chain; з. в канда́лы to shackle, put in irons

зако́выва|ть, ю *impf. of* ▶ закова́ть

закола́чива|ть, ю *impf. of* ▶ заколоти́ть

заколдо́ванный *p.p.p. of* ▶ заколдова́ть *and adj.* enchanted; spellbound; (fig.): з. круг vicious circle

заколд|ова́ть, у́ю *pf.* (*of* ▶ заколдо́вывать) to bewitch, enchant; to lay a spell (on)

заколдо́выва|ть, ю *impf. of* ▶ заколдова́ть

заколеб|а́ться, ~лю́сь, ~лешься *pf.* to begin to shake; (fig.) to begin to waver, to vacillate

зако́лк|а, и *f.* hairgrip (BrE), bobby pin (AmE)

заколо|ти́ть, чу́, ~тишь *pf.* (*of* ▶ закола́чивать) (*досками*) to board up; (*гвоздями*) to nail up

закол|о́ть, ю́, ~ешь *pf.* (*of* ▶ зака́лывать, ▶ коло́ть² 2, ▶ коло́ть² 3) **1** (*убить*) to stab (to death); (*животное*) to slaughter **2** (*прикрепить*) to pin (up) **3** (*impers.*): у меня́ и *т. п.* ~о́ло в боку́ I have, *etc.*, a stitch in my side

⚡ **зако́н, а** *m.* law; свод ~ов code, statute book; объяви́ть вне ~а to outlaw

зако́нност|ь, и *f.* **1** (*документа, постановления*) lawfulness, legality **2** (*соблюдение законов*) law and order

зако́н|ный, ~ен, ~на *adj.* **1** *(де́йствия)* lawful, legal; *(докуме́нт, до́говор)* legal; **з. брак** lawful wedlock; **з. владе́лец** rightful owner **2** *(fig., возмуще́ние)* legitimate, understandable, natural

законода́тел|ь, я *m.* legislator; lawgiver; **з. мод/мо́ды** trendsetter

законода́тельный *adj.* legislative

⚲ **законода́тельств|о, а** *nt.* legislation

закономе́рност|ь, и *f.* regularity; conformity with a law; normality

закономе́р|ный, ~ен, ~на *adj.* **1** *(разви́тие, успе́х)* natural, logical **2** *(fig., поня́тный)* legitimate, understandable, natural

законопослу́ш|ный, ~ен, ~на *adj.* law-abiding

законопрое́кт, а *m.* (pol., law) bill

законсерви́р|овать, ую *pf. of* ▶ **консерви́ровать**

зако́нчен|ный, ~, ~а *p.p.p. of* ▶ **зако́нчить** *and* **(~, ~на)** *adj.* *(де́ло)* finished; *(мысль, фра́за)* complete; *(негодя́й)* consummate; **з. лгун** consummate liar

зако́нч|ить, у, ишь *pf.* *(of* ▶ **зака́нчивать)** to end, finish

зако́нч|иться, у, ится *pf.* *(of* ▶ **зака́нчиваться)** to end, finish

закопа́|ть, ю *pf.* *(of* ▶ **зака́пывать)** *(спря́тать в земле́)* to bury

закоп|ти́ть, чу́, ти́шь *pf.* *(of* ▶ **копти́ть)** **1** *(ры́бу, око́рок)* to smoke **2** *(покры́ть копо́тью)* to blacken with smoke

закоп|ти́ться, чу́сь, ти́шься *pf.* *(покры́ться копо́тью)* to become covered with soot

закорм|и́ть, лю́, ~ишь *pf.* *(of* ▶ **зака́рмливать)** to overfeed; to stuff

закра́|сить, шу, сишь *pf.* *(of* ▶ **закра́шивать)** to paint over, paint out

закра́шива|ть, ю *impf. of* ▶ **закра́сить**

закреп|и́ть, лю́, и́шь *pf.* *(of* ▶ **закрепля́ть)** **1** to fasten, secure; (naut.) to make fast; (phot.) to fix **2** (fig.) to consolidate **3** *(+ a. and* **за** *+ i.)* *(помеще́ние)* to allot, assign (to); *(челове́ка)* to appoint, attach (to); **з. за собо́й** to secure

закреп|и́ться, лю́сь, и́шься *pf.* *(of* ▶ **закрепля́ться)** **1** *(о войска́х)* **(на** *+ a.)* to consolidate one's hold (on) **2** *(о сло́ве, привы́чке)* to establish itself

закрепля́|ть, ю *impf. of* ▶ **закрепи́ть**

закрепля́|ться, юсь *impf. of* ▶ **закрепи́ться**

закрича́|ть, у́, и́шь *pf.* **1** *(нача́ть крича́ть)* to begin to shout **2** *(однокра́тно)* to give a shout, cry out

закро́йщик, а *m.* cutter

закро́йщи|ца, цы *f. of* ▶ **закро́йщик**

закругл|и́ть, ю́, и́шь *pf.* *(of* ▶ **закругля́ть)** to make round; to round off

закругл|и́ться, ю́сь, и́шься *pf.* *(of* ▶ **закругля́ться)** (infml) to round off, conclude

закругля́|ть, ю *impf. of* ▶ **закругли́ть**

закругля́|ться, юсь *impf. of* ▶ **закругли́ться**

закруж|и́ться, у́сь, ~и́шься *pf. of* ▶ **кружи́ться**

закру|ти́ть, чу́, ~тишь *pf.* *(of* ▶ **закру́чивать,** ▶ **крути́ть 2) 1** *(верёвку)* to twist; *(усы́)* to twirl; *(вокру́г)* to wind round **2** *(кран)* to turn; *(га́йку)* to screw in

закру|ти́ться, чу́сь, ~ти́шься *pf.* *(of* ▶ **закру́чиваться)** to twist; to twirl; to wind round

закру́чива|ть, ю *impf. of* ▶ **закрути́ть**

закру́чива|ться, юсь *impf. of* ▶ **закрути́ться**

⚲ **закрыва́|ть, ю** *impf. of* ▶ **закры́ть**

закрыва́|ться, юсь *impf. of* ▶ **закры́ться**

закры́ти|е, я *nt.* closing; shutting; *(коне́ц)* close

закры́т|ый, ~, ~а *p.p.p. of* ▶ **закры́ть** *and adj.* closed, shut; *(не для всех)* private; **с ~ыми глаза́ми** (fig.) blindly; **в ~ом помеще́нии** indoors

закр|ы́ть, о́ю, о́ешь *pf.* *(of* ▶ **закрыва́ть)** **1** *(сде́лать недосту́пным)* to close, shut; **з. глаза́ (на** *+ a.)* to shut one's eyes (to); **з. счёт** to close an account **2** *(вы́ключить)* to shut off, turn off **3** *(ликвиди́ровать)* to close down, shut down **4** *(покры́ть)* to cover

закр|ы́ться, о́юсь, о́ешься *pf.* *(of* ▶ **закрыва́ться)** **1** *(стать недосту́пным)* to close, shut; *(око́нчиться)* to end; *(переста́ть существова́ть)* to close down **2** *(покры́ть себя́)* to cover oneself; to take cover

закули́сный *adj.* (fig.) secret; underhand, undercover

закупа́|ть, ю *impf. of* ▶ **закупи́ть**

закуп|и́ть, лю́, ~ишь *pf.* *(of* ▶ **закупа́ть)** **1** *(скупи́ть)* to buy up (wholesale) **2** *(запасти́сь)* to lay in; to stock up with

заку́порива|ть, ю *impf. of* ▶ **заку́порить**

заку́пор|ить, ю, ишь *pf.* *(of* ▶ **заку́поривать)** to cork; to stop up

заку́рива|ть, ю *impf. of* ▶ **закури́ть**

закур|и́ть, ю́, ~ишь *pf.* *(of* ▶ **заку́ривать)** **1** *(сигаре́ту)* to light up **2** *(стать кури́льщиком)* to begin to smoke

заку|си́ть, шу́, ~сишь *pf.* *(of* ▶ **заку́сывать)** **1** *(пое́сть)* to have a snack, have a bite **2** *(+ a. and i.)* to take (with); **з. во́дку ры́бой** to drink vodka with fish hors d'oeuvres

заку́ск|а, и *f.* *(usu. in pl.)* hors d'oeuvre; snack; **на ~у** for a titbit; (fig., infml) as a special treat

заку́сыва|ть, ю *impf. of* ▶ **закуси́ть**

заку́та|ть, ю *pf.* *(of* ▶ **заку́тывать)** to wrap up, muffle; **з. в одея́ло** to tuck up (in bed)

заку́та|ться, юсь *pf.* *(of* ▶ **заку́тываться)** to wrap oneself up, muffle oneself

заку́тыва|ть, ю *impf. of* ▶ **заку́тать**

заку́тыва|ться, юсь *impf. of* ▶ **заку́таться**

⚲ **зал, а** *m.* hall; **з. ожида́ния** waiting room; **з. вы́лета** departure lounge *(in airport)*

залега́|ть, ю *impf. of* ▶ **зале́чь**

залеза́|ть, ю *impf. of* ▶ **зале́зть**

⚲ key word

зале́з|ть, у, ешь, *past* ~, ~ла *pf.* **1** (на + *a.*) (*на де́реве, кры́шу*) to climb (up, on to) **2** (в + *a.*) (infml, *в ко́мнату*) to get (into); to break into

залета́|ть, ю *impf. of* ▶ залете́ть

зале́|те́ть, чу́, ти́шь *pf.* **1** (в + *a.*) to fly (into); (за + *a.*) to fly (over, beyond) **2** (в + *a.*) to make a stopover (at), call in (at)

зал|е́чь, я́гу, я́жешь, я́гут, *past* ~ёг, ~егла́ *pf.* (*of* ▶ залега́ть) **1** (*лечь*) to lie down; (*притаи́ться*) to lie low **2** (geol.) to lie, be deposited

зали́в, а *m.* bay; (*дли́нный*) gulf; (*ма́ленький*) cove

залива́|ть, ю *impf. of* ▶ зали́ть

залива́|ться, юсь *impf. of* ▶ зали́ться

заливн|о́е, о́го *nt.* fish or meat in aspic

зал|и́ть, ью, ьёшь, *past* ~и́л, ~ила́, ~и́ло *pf.* (*of* ▶ залива́ть) **1** (*покры́ть жи́дкостью*) to flood, inundate **2** (*испа́чкать жи́дким*) (+ *a. and i.*) to pour (over); to spill (on) **3** (*потуши́ть водо́й*) to quench, extinguish (*with water*); з. пожа́р to put out a fire **4** (*напо́лнить, покры́ть жи́дким*) to fill, cover with **5** (*нали́ть, напо́лнив что-н.*): з. бензи́н в бак to fill up with petrol (BrE), gas (AmE)

зал|и́ться, ью́сь, ьёшься, *past* ~и́лся, ~ила́сь *pf.* (*of* ▶ зали́ться) **1** (*попа́сть*) to pour; to spill; водá ~ила́сь мне за воротни́к water has gone down my neck **2** (+ *i.*) (*зазвуча́ть*) to break into, burst out (into); соба́ка ~ила́сь ла́ем the dog began to bark furiously

зало́г, а *m.* **1** deposit; pledge; security; (law) bail; под з. (+ *g.*) on the security of; отда́ть в з. (*в ломба́рде*) to pawn; (*дом*) to mortgage; вы́купить из ~а to redeem; to pay off mortgage (on); з. успе́ха guarantee of success **2** (fig., *доказа́тельство*) pledge, token

залож|и́ть, у́, ~ишь *pf.* (*of* ▶ закла́дывать) **1** (*положи́ть за что-н.*) to put (behind); он ~и́л ру́ки за́ спину he put his hands behind his back **2** (*положи́ть основа́ние чему-л.*) to lay (the foundation of) **3** (+ *i.*) (*загромозди́ть*) to pile up, heap up (with); to block up (with); (*impers. + d.*) мне ~и́ло нос my nose is blocked up **4** (*ме́сто в кни́ге*) to mark, put a marker in **5** (*для хране́ния*) to lay in, store, put by **6** (*часы́*) to pawn; (*дом*) to mortgage

зало́жник, а *m.* hostage

зало́жни|ца, цы *f. of* ▶ зало́жник

залп, а *m.* volley; salvo; ~ом (fig., infml) without pausing for breath; вы́пить ~ом to drain at one draught

зама́з|ать, жу, жешь *pf.* (*of* ▶ ма́зать 3, ▶ зама́зывать) **1** (*покры́ть кра́ской*) to paint over; (*зачеркну́ть*) to efface; (fig.) to slur over **2** (*залепи́ть*) to putty **3** (*запа́чкать*) to daub, smear, to soil

зама́|заться, жусь, жешься *pf.* (*of* ▶ ма́заться 1, ▶ зама́зываться) to smear oneself; to get dirty

зама́зк|а, и *f.* **1** (*вещество́*) putty **2** (*де́йствие*) puttying

зама́зыва|ть, ю *impf. of* ▶ зама́зать

зама́зыва|ться, юсь *impf. of* ▶ зама́заться

зама́нива|ть, ю *impf. of* ▶ замани́ть

заман|и́ть, ю́, ~ишь *pf.* (*of* ▶ зама́нивать) to entice, lure; (*обма́ном*) to decoy

зама́нчив|ый, ~, ~а *adj.* tempting, alluring

замарин|ова́ть, у́ю *pf. of* ▶ маринова́ть

замаскир|ова́ть, у́ю *pf. of* ▶ маскирова́ть

замаскир|ова́ться, у́юсь *pf. of* ▶ маскирова́ться

зама́тыва|ть, ю *impf. of* ▶ замота́ть

зама́|ха́ть, шу́, ~шешь *pf.* to begin to wave

зама́хива|ться, юсь *impf. of* ▶ замахну́ться

замахн|у́ться, у́сь, ёшься *pf.* **1** (+ *i. and* на + *a.*) to raise (sth) threateningly (at sb) **2** (*подня́ть ру́ку*) (на + *a.*) to raise a hand against **3** (на + *a.*) (fig., infml) to set one's sights on

зама́чива|ть, ю *impf. of* ▶ замочи́ть 1

замби́|ец, йца *m.* Zambian

замби́йк|а, и *f.* Zambian

замби́йский *adj.* Zambian

За́мби|я, и *f.* Zambia

заме́дленн|ый *p.p.p. of* ▶ заме́длить *and adj.* delayed; бо́мба ~ого де́йствия delayed-action bomb, time bomb; (fig.) time bomb; ~ое воспроизведе́ние slow-motion replay

заме́дл|ить, ю, ишь *pf.* (*of* ▶ замедля́ть) to slow down, delay; з. шаг to slacken one's pace; з. ход to reduce speed

заме́дл|иться, юсь, ишься *pf.* (*of* ▶ замедля́ться) to slow down; to slacken, become slower

замедля́|ть, ю *impf. of* ▶ заме́длить

замедля́|ться, юсь *impf. of* ▶ заме́длиться

✎ **заме́н|а**, ы *f.* **1** (*де́йствие*) substitution; replacement **2** (*тот, кто* (*и́ли то, что*) *заменя́ет*) substitute

замени́тел|ь, я *m.* (+ *g.*) substitute; з. са́хара sweetener

замен|и́ть, ю́, ~ишь *pf.* (*of* ▶ заменя́ть) **1** (+ *a. and i.*) to replace (by), substitute (for); з. ма́сло маргари́ном to use margarine instead of butter **2** (*заня́ть ме́сто кого́-то, чего́-то*) to take the place of; тру́дно бу́дет з. его́ it will be hard to replace him

✎ **замен|я́ть**, я́ю *impf. of* ▶ замени́ть

зам|ере́ть, ру́, рёшь, *past* ~ер, ~ерла́, ~ерло́ *pf.* (*of* ▶ замира́ть) **1** (*стать неподви́жным*) to stand still; to freeze, be rooted to the spot; to die (fig.) **2** (*о зву́ках*) to die down, die away

замерза́|ть, ю *impf. of* ▶ замёрзнуть

замёрз|нуть, ну, нешь, *past* ~, ~ла *pf.* (*of* ▶ замерза́ть) (*о реке́, окне́*) to freeze (up); (*умере́ть от моро́за*) to freeze to death; (*о расте́ниях*) to be killed by frost; я ~ I'm frozen

за́мертво *adv.* like one dead; она́ упа́ла з. she collapsed in a dead faint

зам|еси́ть, ешу́, е́сишь *pf. of* ▸ **меси́ть**

заме|сти́, ту́, тёшь, *past* ∼л, ∼ла́ *pf.* (*of* ▸ **замета́ть**) **1** (*подмести*) to sweep up **2** (*покрыть*) to cover (up); (*impers.*) **доро́гу** ∼ло́ сне́гом the road is covered with snow

✧ **замести́тел|ь, я** *m.* substitute; deputy; з. **дире́ктора** deputy director

заме|сти́ть, щу́, сти́шь (*of* ▸ **замеща́ть**) **1** (+ *a. and i.*) (*заменить*) to replace (by); to substitute (for) **2** (*должность*) to fill **3** (*заменить собой*) to deputize for, act for

замета́|ть, ю *impf. of* ▸ **замести́**

заме|та́ться, чу́сь, ∼че́шься *pf.* to begin to rush about; (*в постели*) to begin to toss

✧ **заме́|тить, чу, тишь** *pf.* (*of* ▸ **замеча́ть**) **1** (*увидеть*) to notice **2** (*обратить внимание (на)*) to take notice (of); (*пометить*) to make a note (of) **3** (*сказать*) to remark, observe

заме́тк|а, и *f.* **1** (*запись*) note **2** (*краткое сообщение*) notice; paragraph

заме́т|ный, ∼ен, ∼на *adj.* (*видимый*) noticeable; (*ощутимый*) appreciable; ∼но (*as pred.*) it is noticeable

замеча́ни|е, я *nt.* **1** remark, observation **2** (*упрёк*) reprimand; reproof

замеча́тельно *adv.* **1** (*with verbs*) splendidly, brilliantly, wonderfully **2** (*with adjectives, adverbs*) remarkably **3** (*pred.*): з.! (it's) splendid!, wonderful!

✧ **замеча́тель|ный, ∼ен, ∼ьна** *adj.* remarkable; splendid, wonderful

✧ **замеча́|ть, ю** *impf. of* ▸ **заме́тить**

замеша́тельств|о, а *nt.* confusion; embarrassment; **привести́ в з.** to throw into confusion; **прийти́ в з.** to be confused, be embarrassed

заме́шка|ться, юсь *pf.* (*infml*) to linger, dawdle

замеща́|ть, ю *impf. of* ▸ **замести́ть**

заминир|овать, ую *pf. of* ▸ **мини́ровать**

замира́|ть, ю *impf. of* ▸ **замере́ть**

за́мкнут|ый, ∼, ∼а *adj.* **1** (*no short forms*) (*среда, жизнь*) isolated, secluded **2** (*человек*) reserved, withdrawn

замкн|у́ть, у́, ёшь *pf.* (*of* ▸ **замыка́ть**) to lock; to close; **з. ше́ствие, з. коло́нну** to bring up the rear

замкн|у́ться, у́сь, ёшься *pf.* (*of* ▸ **замыка́ться**) **1** (*цепь*) to be joined at the ends; **круг** ∼у́лся (fig.) everything fell into place **2** to shut oneself up; (fig.): **з. в себе́** to become reserved, retire into oneself

✧ **за́м|ок, ка** *m.* castle

✧ **зам|о́к, ка́** *m.* **1** lock; **вися́чий з.** padlock **2** (*браслета*) clasp; (*серьги*) clip

замолча́|ть, у́, и́шь *pf.* (fig.) to fall silent; (fig.) to cease corresponding

замора́жива|ть, ю *impf. of* ▸ **заморо́зить**

заморо́|женный *p.p.p. of* ▸ **заморо́зить** *and adj.* frozen; iced; ∼женное мя́со frozen meat

заморо́|зить, жу, зишь *pf.* (*of* ▸ **замора́живать**) to freeze

за́мороз|ок, ка *m.* (*usu. in pl.*) (light) frost

заморо́ч|ить, у, ишь *pf. of* ▸ **моро́чить**

замо́тан|ный, ∼, ∼а *adj.* (infml) worn out, shattered

замота́|ть, ю *pf.* (*of* ▸ **зама́тывать**) **1** to wind, twist; (+ *i.*) (*обмотать*) to wrap (in, with) **2** (fig., infml, *утомить*) to tire out

замоч|и́ть, у́, ∼ишь 1 *pf.* (*of* ▸ **зама́чивать**) (*слегка*) to wet; (*погрузить в воду*) to soak **2** *pf. of* ▸ **мочи́ть 2**

за́муж *adv.*: **вы́йти з. за кого́-н.** to marry sb (*of woman*); **вы́дать кого́-н. з.** (за + *a.*) to give sb in marriage (to); to marry off (to)

за́мужем *adv.*: **быть з.** (за + *i.*) to be married (to) (*of woman*)

замур|ова́ть, у́ю *pf.* to brick up; (*человека*) to immure

замуро́выва|ть, ю *impf. of* ▸ **замурова́ть**

замуч|ить, у, ишь *pf.* (*of* ▸ **му́чить**) to torment; (*утомить*) to wear out; (*разговорами*) to bore to tears; (*убить*) to torture to death

замуч|иться, усь, ишься *pf.* (*of* ▸ **му́читься**) to be worn out

за́мш|а, и *f.* chamois (leather); suede

замыка́ни|е, я *nt.* locking; **коро́ткое з.** (elec.) short circuit

замыка́|ть, ю *impf. of* ▸ **замкну́ть**

замыка́|ться, юсь *impf. of* ▸ **замкну́ться**

за́мыс|ел, ла *m.* (*план*) project, plan; design, scheme; (*смысл*) idea

замы́сл|ить, ю, ишь *pf.* (*of* ▸ **замышля́ть**) (+ *a. or inf.*) to plan; to contemplate; **он** ∼ил **самоуби́йство** he contemplated suicide

замылова́т|ый, ∼, ∼а *adj.* intricate, complicated

замышля́|ть, ю *impf. of* ▸ **замы́слить**

за́навес, а *m.* curtain

занаве́|сить, шу, сишь *pf.* (*of* ▸ **занаве́шивать**) to curtain; to cover

занаве́ск|а, и *f.* curtain

занаве́шива|ть, ю *impf. of* ▸ **занаве́сить**

занес|ти́, у́, ёшь, *past* ∼, ∼ла́ *pf.* (*of* ▸ **заноси́ть**) **1** (*принести*) to bring; (*доставить мимоходом*) to drop off **2** (*поднять*) to raise, lift **3** (*записать*) to note down; **з. в протоко́л/спи́сок** to enter in the minutes/list **4** (*impers.*): **з. сне́гом** to cover with snow; **доро́гу** ∼ло́ сне́гом the road is snowed up

занима́тел|ьный, ∼ен, ∼ьна *adj.* entertaining; diverting; absorbing

✧ **занима́|ть¹, ю** *impf.* (*of* ▸ **заня́ть**) **1** (*город, квартиру*) to оссupy; **крова́ть** ∼ет **мно́го ме́ста** the bed takes up a lot of room; **он** ∼ет **высо́кое положе́ние** (fig.) he occupies a high post **2** (*увлекать*) to occupy; to interest; **бо́льше всего́ его́** ∼ют **вопро́сы филосо́фии** his chief interest is in philosophy **3** (*время*) to take; **э́то** ∼ет **мно́го вре́мени** this takes a lot of time

4 (*пост, должность*) to take up **5**: з. ме́сто кому́-н./для кого́-н. to reserve a seat for sb; з. пе́рвое ме́сто to take first place

⚹ **занима́ть²**, ю *impf.* (*of* ▸ заня́ть) (*де́ньги*) to borrow

⚹ **занима́ться**, юсь *impf.* (*of* ▸ заня́ться) (+ *i.*) **1** to be occupied (with), be engaged (in); (*рабо́тать*) to work (at, on); (*учи́ться*) to study; to practise; чем он ∼ется? what does he do? (*for a living*) **2** (*посвяща́ть себя́*) to devote oneself (to); з. есте́ственными нау́ками to devote oneself to the natural sciences; з. собо́й to devote time to oneself **3** (с + *i.*) (*помога́ть в уче́нии*) to assist with (*study*)

за́ново *adv.* anew

зано́з|**а**, ы *f.* splinter

зано|**зи́ть**, жу́, зи́шь *pf.* to get a splinter into

зано́с, а *m.* drift; сне́жные ∼ы snowdrifts; песча́ный з. sand drift

зано|**си́ть**, шу́, ∼сишь *impf. of* ▸ занести́

зано́счив|**ый**, ∼, ∼а *adj.* arrogant, haughty

зану́д|**а**, ы *c.g.* (infml) tiresome person, pain in the neck

зану́д|**ный**, ∼ен, ∼на *adj.* (infml) tiresome

⚹ **заня́ти**|**е**, я *nt.* **1** (*де́ло*) occupation; pursuit **2** (*in pl.*) studies; (*usu. in pl.*) (*уро́к*) lesson, class

заня́т|**ный**, ∼ен, ∼на *adj.* (infml) entertaining, amusing

занято́й *adj.* busy

за́нятост|**ь**, и *f.* **1** busyness, lack of time **2** (econ.) employment; по́лная з. full employment; центр ∼и jobcentre (BrE), employment agency

за́нят|**ый**, ∼, ∼а́, ∼о *p.p.p. of* ▸ заня́ть *and adj.* **1** occupied; ∼о (*телефо́н, туале́т*) engaged **2** (*only short forms*) (*челове́к*) busy; он сейча́с ∼ he is busy at the moment

⚹ **заня́**|**ть**, займу́, займёшь, *past* ∼я́л, ∼яла́, ∼я́ло *pf. of* ▸ занима́ть¹

заня́|**ться**, займу́сь, займёшься, *past* ∼я́лся, ∼яла́сь *pf. of* ▸ занима́ться

заодно́ *adv.* in concert, at one; де́йствовать з. to act in concert

заокеа́нский *adj.* transoceanic

заор|**а́ть**, у́, ёшь *pf.* (infml) to begin to bawl, begin to yell

заострённый *adj.* pointed, sharp

зао́чно *adv.* **1** (*в отсу́тствие кого́-н.*) in one's absence **2** (*об обуче́нии*) by correspondence course, externally

зао́чн|**ый** *adj.*: з. курс correspondence course; ∼ое обуче́ние distance learning

⚹ **за́пад**, а *m.* **1** west **2** (З.) (pol.) the West

⚹ **за́падный** *adj.* west, western; (*направле́ние, ве́тер*) westerly

западн|**я́**, и́, *g. pl.* ∼е́й *f.* trap, snare; попа́сть в ∼ю́ to fall into a trap (also fig.)

запак|**ова́ть**, у́ю *pf.* (*of* ▸ запако́вывать) to pack (up); to wrap up, do up

запако́выва|**ть**, ю *impf. of* ▸ запакова́ть

запа́л, а *m.* fuse

⚹ **запа́с**, а *m.* **1** supply, stock; reserve; про з. for an emergency; отложи́ть про з. to put by; слова́рный з. vocabulary; у меня́ день в ∼е I have one day in reserve, to spare **2** (mil.) reserve; его́ уво́лили в з. he has been transferred to the reserve

запаса́|**ть**, ю *impf. of* ▸ запасти́

запаса́|**ться**, юсь *impf. of* ▸ запасти́сь

запасно́й *adj.* spare; (*игро́к*) reserve; з. вы́ход emergency exit; (*as m. n.* з., ∼о́го) (mil.) reservist; (sport) reserve

запас|**ти́**, у́, ёшь, *past* ∼́, ∼ла́ *pf.* (*of* ▸ запаса́ть) (+ *a. or g.*) to stock, store; to lay in a stock of

запас|**ти́сь**, у́сь, ёшься, *past* ∼ся́, ∼ла́сь *pf.* (*of* ▸ запаса́ться) (+ *i.*) to provide oneself (with); to stock up (on, with); з. терпе́нием (fig.) to arm oneself with patience

запатентова́ть *pf. of* ▸ патентова́ть

за́пах, а *m.* smell

запа́чка|**ть**, ю *pf. of* ▸ па́чкать

запа́чка|**ться**, юсь *pf. of* ▸ па́чкаться

запева́|**ть**, ю *impf. of* ▸ запе́ть

запека́|**ть**, ю *impf. of* ▸ запе́чь

зап|**ере́ть**, ру́, рёшь, *past* ∼́ер, ерла́, ∼́ерло *pf.* (*of* ▸ запира́ть) **1** (*дверь*) to lock; з. на засо́в to bolt **2** (*челове́ка*) to lock in; to shut up **3** (*прегради́ть до́ступ*) to bar; to block up

зап|**ере́ться**, ру́сь, рёшься, *past* ∼́ерся́, ∼́ерла́сь, ∼́ерло́сь *pf.* (*of* ▸ запира́ться) **1** to lock oneself in **2** (*дверь*) to lock

запе́|**ть**, ою́, оёшь *pf.* (*of* ▸ запева́ть) (*нача́ть петь*) to begin to sing; з. пе́сню to break into a song

запеча́т|**ать**, аю *pf.* (*of* ▸ запеча́тывать) to seal

запеча́тыва|**ть**, ю *impf. of* ▸ запеча́тать

запе́|**чь**, ку́, чёшь, ку́т, *past* ∼́к, ∼кла́ *pf.* (*of* ▸ запека́ть) to bake

запива́|**ть**, ю *impf. of* ▸ запи́ть

запина́|**ться**, юсь *impf.* (*of* ▸ запну́ться) to stumble

запира́|**ть**, ю *impf. of* ▸ запере́ть

запира́|**ться**, юсь *impf. of* ▸ запере́ться

запи́с|**ать**, шу́, ∼шешь *pf.* (*of* ▸ запи́сывать) **1** (*занести́ на бума́гу*) to note, make a note (of); to take down (in writing); (*конце́рт, фильм*) to record (*with apparatus*); з. (на плёнку) to tape; з. (на ви́део) to video **2** (*включи́ть в соста́в чего́-либо*) to enter, register, enrol

запи́с|**аться**, шу́сь, ∼шешься *pf.* (*of* ▸ запи́сываться) to register, enter one's name, enrol; з. в клуб to join a club; з. к врачу́ to make an appointment with the doctor

запи́ск|**а**, и *f.* note; делова́я з. memorandum, minute

записн|**о́й** *adj.*: ∼а́я кни́жка notebook

запи́сыва|**ть**, ю *impf. of* ▸ записа́ть

запи́сыва|**ться**, юсь *impf. of* ▸ записа́ться

⚹ **за́пис**|**ь**, и *f.* **1** (*де́йствие*) writing down;

3

recording; registration **2** (*в дневнике*) entry; (comput.) record; (*заметка*) note; (*на плёнку*) recording; (law) deed

зап|и́ть, ью́, ьёшь *pf.* (*of* ▶ запива́ть) **1** (*past* ~и́л, ~ила́, ~и́ло) (+ *a. and i.*) to wash down (with); to take (with, after); з. табле́тку водо́й to take a tablet with water **2** (*past* ~и́л, ~ила́, ~и́ло) to begin to drink heavily

запи́|шу́, ~шешь *see* ▶ записа́ть

запла́кан|ный, ~, ~a *adj.* tear-stained; in tears

запла́|кать, чу, чешь *pf.* to begin to cry

заплани́р|овать, ую *pf. of* ▶ плани́ровать

заплáт|а, ы *f.* patch (*in garments*); наложи́ть ~у (на + *a.*) to patch

заплати́ть, чу́, ~тишь *pf. of* ▶ плати́ть

запла́|чу, чешь *see* ▶ запла́кать

заплачу́, ~тишь *see* ▶ заплати́ть

запле|сти́, ту́, тёшь, *past* ~л, ~ла́ *pf.* (*of* ▶ заплета́ть) (*волосы*) to braid, plait

заплета́|ть, ю *impf. of* ▶ заплести́

запломбир|ова́ть, у́ю *pf.* (*of* ▶ пломбирова́ть) **1** (*зуб*) to fill **2** (*вагон, избирательную урну*) to seal

заплыва́|ть, ю *impf. of* ▶ заплы́ть¹, ▶ заплы́ть²

заплы́|ть¹, ву́, вёшь, *past* ~л, ~ла́, ~ло *pf.* (*of* ▶ заплыва́ть) (*о пловце*) to swim far out; (*о судне*) to sail away

заплы́|ть², ву́, вёшь, *past* ~л, ~ла́, ~ло *pf.* (*of* ▶ заплыва́ть) to be swollen; to be bloated; ~вшие жи́ром глаза́ bloated eyes

запн|у́ться, у́сь, ёшься *pf. of* ▶ запина́ться

запове́дник, a *m.* reserve; preserve; sanctuary; госуда́рственный з. national park

за́повед|ь, и *f.* precept; (relig., fig. also) commandment; де́сять ~ей the Ten Commandments

запода́зрива|ть, ю *impf. of* ▶ заподо́зрить

заподо́зр|ить, ю, ишь *pf.* (*of* ▶ запода́зривать) (+ *a. and* в + *p.*) to suspect (of)

запозда́лый *adj.* belated

заполза́|ть, ю *impf. of* ▶ заползти́

заполз|ти́, у́, ёшь, *past* ~, ~ла́ *pf.* (*of* ▶ заполза́ть) (в, под + *a.*) to creep, crawl (into, under)

запо́лн|ить, ю *pf.* (*of* ▶ заполня́ть) to fill in, fill up; з. бланк to fill in (BrE), fill out (AmE) a form

запо́лн|иться, ится *pf.* (*of* ▶ заполня́ться) to fill up

заполня́|ть, ю, ет *impf. of* ▶ запо́лнить

заполня́|ться, ется *impf. of* ▶ запо́лниться

заполя́рье, я *nt.* (geog.) polar regions

запомина́|ть, ю *impf. of* ▶ запо́мнить

запомина́|ться, юсь *impf. of* ▶ запо́мниться

запо́мн|ить, ю, ишь *pf.* (*of* ▶ запомина́ть) **1** (*текст, номер*) to memorize **2** (*человека,*

картину, событие) to remember

запо́мн|иться, юсь, ишься *pf.* (*of* ▶ запомина́ться) to stick, remain in one's memory

за́понк|а, и *f.* cufflink; stud

запо́р, a *m.* (med.) constipation

запотева́|ть, ю *impf. of* ▶ запоте́ть

запоте́|ть, ю *pf.* (*of* ▶ поте́ть, ▶ запотева́ть) to mist over

зап|ою́, оёшь *see* ▶ запе́ть

заправ|ить, лю, ишь *pf.* (*of* ▶ заправля́ть) **1** (*вставить*) to insert; з. брюки в сапоги́ to tuck one's trousers into one's boots **2** (*приготовить*) to prepare; з. автомоби́ль бензи́ном to fill a car up with petrol **3** (+ *i.*) (*добавить*) to mix in; (*сдобрить*) to season (with)

заправ|иться, люсь, ишься *pf.* (*of* ▶ заправля́ться) (*горючим*) to refuel

запра́вк|а, и *f.* **1** (*приправа*) seasoning; з. для сала́та salad dressing **2** (*машины*) refuelling (BrE), refueling (AmE) **3** (infml, заправочная станция) filling station

заправля́|ть, ю *impf.* (*of* ▶ запра́вить) (+ *i.*) (infml) to be in charge (of)

заправля́|ться, юсь *impf. of* ▶ запра́виться

запра́вочн|ый *adj.*: ~ая ста́нция filling station

запра́шива|ть, ю *impf. of* ▶ запроси́ть

запре́т, a *m.* prohibition, ban; быть под ~ом to be banned; наложи́ть з. (на + *a.*) to place a ban (on)

запре|ти́ть, щу́, ти́шь *pf. of* ▶ запреща́ть (*не позволять*) to prohibit, forbid; «въезд запрещён» 'No Entry'; (*книгу, наркотики, оружие*) to ban

запре́тн|ый *adj.* forbidden; ~ая те́ма taboo subject

▸ **запреща́|ть, ю** *impf. of* ▶ запрети́ть

запреща́|ться, ется *impf.* to be forbidden, to be prohibited

запрограмми́р|овать, ую *pf. of* ▶ программи́ровать

запроки́дыва|ть, ю *impf. of* ▶ запроки́нуть

запроки́н|уть, у, ешь *pf. of* ▶ запроки́дывать

▸ **запро́с, a** *m.* **1** inquiry; (pol.) question **2** (*pl. only*) (*потребности*) needs, requirements

запро|си́ть, шу́, ~сишь *pf.* (*of* ▶ запра́шивать) **1** (*o* + *p.*) to inquire (about); (+ *a.*) (*попросить*) to request **2**: з. сли́шком высо́кую це́ну (infml) to ask an exorbitant price

за́просто *adv.* (infml) (*без формальностей*) without ceremony, without formality; (*легко*) without any problem, easily

зап|ру́, рёшь *see* ▶ запере́ть

запры́гива|ть, ю *impf. of* ▶ запры́гнуть

запры́гн|уть, у, ешь *pf.* (*of* ▶ запры́гивать) (за + *a.*) to leap (over); (на + *a.*) to jump (onto)

запряга́|ть, ю *impf. of* ▶ запря́чь

запря́|чь, гу́, жёшь, гу́т, *past* ~г, ~гла́ *pf.* (*of* ▶ запряга́ть) to harness (also fig.)

3

запу́ганный *p.p.p. of* ▶ **запуга́ть** *and adj.*
broken-spirited; frightened

запуга́|ть, ю *pf.* (*of* ▶ **запу́гивать**) to
intimidate, cow; to frighten

запу́гива|ть, ю *impf. of* ▶ **запуга́ть**

за́пуск, а *m.* (*мотора*) starting; (*ракеты*)
launch, launching; (*comput.*) running

запус|ка́ть, ка́ю *impf. of* ▶ **запусти́ть**[1],
▶ **запусти́ть**[2]

запусте́ни|е, я *nt.* neglect; desolation

запу|сти́ть[1], **щу́, ~сти́шь** *pf.* (*of* ▶ **запуска́ть**)
1 (+ *i.* and **в** + *a.*) (infml, *бросить*) to throw
(at), fling (at) **2** (**в** + *a.*) (*засунуть*) to
thrust (hands, *etc.*) (into); з. **ко́гти, ла́пы,
ру́ки** (**в** + *a.*) (fig.) to get one's hands on
3 (*привести в действие*) to start (up);
(*comput.*) to run; з. **мото́р** to start up the
engine; з. **раке́ту** to launch a rocket

запу|сти́ть[2], **щу́, ~сти́шь** *pf.* (*of* ▶ **запуска́ть**)
1 (*оставить без ухода*) to neglect, allow
to fall into neglect; з. **дела́** to neglect one's
affairs; з. **сад** to neglect a garden **2** (*дать
развиться*) to allow to develop unchecked

запу́тан|ный, ~, ~а *p.p.p. of* ▶ **запу́тать**
and (~, ~на) *adj.* tangled; (fig.) intricate,
involved; з. **вопро́с** knotty question

запу́та|ть, ю *pf.* (*of* ▶ **запу́тывать**, ▶ **пу́тать**)
1 (*нитки, волосы*) to tangle (up) **2** (fig.)
(*человека*) to confuse; (*дело*) to complicate;
to muddle

запу́та|ться, юсь *pf.* (*of* ▶ **запу́тываться**,
▶ **пу́таться**) **1** (*нитки, волосы*) to become
entangled; to foul; (**в** + *p.*) (*в сетях*) to
entangle oneself (in), be caught (in)
2 (**в** + *p.*) (fig., *в деле*) to become entangled
(in); become involved (in); (*дело, речь*) to
become confused, complicated; (*сбиться
с толку*) to get in a muddle

запу́тыва|ть, ю *impf. of* ▶ **запу́тать**

запу́тыва|ться, юсь *impf. of* ▶ **запу́таться**

запу́щен|ный, ~, ~а *p.p.p. of* ▶ **запусти́ть**[2]
and (~, ~на) *adj.* neglected

запча́ст|и, е́й *f. pl.* (*sg.* ~ь, ~и) (*abbr. of*
запасна́я ча́сть) spare parts; spares

запыха́|ться, юсь *pf.* (infml) to be out of
breath

запя́сть|е, я *nt.* wrist

запят|а́я, о́й *f.* comma

✎ **зараба́тыва|ть, ю** *impf. of* ▶ **зарабо́тать** 1

зарабо́та|ть, ю *pf.* (*of* ▶ **зараба́тывать**)
1 (*приобрести работой*) to earn **2** (*no
impf.*) (*начать работать*) to begin to work;
to start (up)

за́работн|ый *adj.*: ~ая **пла́та** wages, pay,
salary

за́работ|ок, ка *m.* earnings; **лёгкий** з. easy
money

зара́внива|ть, ю *impf. of* ▶ **заровня́ть**

заража́|ть, ю *impf. of* ▶ **зарази́ть**

заража́|ться, юсь *impf. of* ▶ **зарази́ться**

зараже́ни|е, я *nt.* infection; (*местности*)
contamination

зара|жу́, зи́шь *see* ▶ **зарази́ть**

зара́з|а, ы *f.* **1** infection, contagion **2** (fig.,
infml, *негодяй*) pest

зарази́тел|ьный, ~ен, ~ьна *adj.* infectious;
catching; з. **смех** infectious laughter

зара|зи́ть, жу́, зи́шь *pf.* (*of* ▶ **заража́ть**)
(+ *i.*) to infect (with) (also fig.); (*местность*)
to contaminate

зара|зи́ться, жу́сь, зи́шься *pf.* (*of*
▶ **заража́ться**) (+ *i.*) to be infected (with);
catch (also fig.)

зара́з|ный, ~ен, ~на *adj.* infectious;
contagious; з. **больно́й** infectious case; (*as n.*
з., ~ного, *f.* ~ная, ~ной) infectious case

✎ **зара́нее** *adv.* beforehand; in good time;
заплати́ть з. to pay in advance

зараста́|ть, ю *impf. of* ▶ **зарасти́**

зараст|и́, у́, ёшь, *past* **заро́с, заросла́** *pf.*
(*of* ▶ **зараста́ть**) **1** (+ *i.*) to be overgrown
(with); **тропа́ заросла́ мхом** the path was
overgrown with moss **2** (*о ране*) to heal

✎ **зарегистри́р|овать, ую** *pf.* (*of*
▶ **регистри́ровать**) to register

зарегистри́р|оваться, уюсь *pf.* (*of*
▶ **регистри́роваться**) to register oneself

заре́|зать, жу, жешь *pf.* (*of* ▶ **ре́зать** 3)
(*человека*) to murder; to knife; (*животное*)
to slaughter; (infml, *о волке*) to devour, kill

зарезерви́р|овать, ую *pf. of*
▶ **резерви́ровать**

зарекоменд|ова́ть, у́ю *pf.*: з. **себя́** (+ *i.*) to
prove oneself, show oneself (to be); **хорошо́**
з. **себя́** to show oneself to advantage

заржаве́|ть, ет *pf.* (*of* ▶ **ржаве́ть**) to rust; to
have got rusty

зарис|ова́ть, у́ю *pf.* (*of* ▶ **зарисо́вывать**)
to sketch

зарисо́вк|а, и *f.* sketch

зарисо́выва|ть, ю *impf. of* ▶ **зарисова́ть**

заровня́|ть, ю *pf.* (*of* ▶ **зара́внивать**) to
level, even up; з. **я́му** to fill up a hole

заро|ди́ться, жу́сь, ди́шься *pf.* (*of*
▶ **зарожда́ться**) (*возникнуть*) to arise, come
into being; **у него́** ~**ди́лось сомне́ние** a
doubt arose in his mind

заро́дыш, а *m.* (biol.) embryo; (fig.) embryo,
germ; **подави́ть в** ~**е** to nip in the bud

заро́дышевый *adj.* embryonic

зарожда́|ться, юсь *impf. of* ▶ **зароди́ться**

за́росл|ь, и *f.* (*usu. in pl.*) thicket

зар|о́ю, о́ешь *see* ▶ **зары́ть**

✎ **зарпла́т|а, ы** *f.* (*abbr. of* **за́работная пла́та**)
wages, pay, salary; **сего́дня** з. today is pay day

заруба́|ть, ю *impf. of* ▶ **заруби́ть**

✎ **зарубе́жный** *adj.* foreign

зарубе́жь|е, я *nt.* foreign countries; **бли́жнее**
з. the countries of the former Soviet Union;
да́льнее з. abroad (*excluding the countries of
the former Soviet Union*)

заруб|и́ть, лю́, ~ишь *pf.* (*of* ▶ **заруба́ть**)
1 (*убить*) to hack to death **2** (*сделать
зарубку*) to notch, make an incision (on)

зарыва́|ть, ю *impf. of* ▶ **зары́ть**

3

зарыва́|ться, юсь *impf. of* ▶ зары́ться

зар|ы́ть, о́ю, о́ешь *pf.* (*of* ▶ зарыва́ть) to bury

зар|ы́ться, о́юсь, о́ешься *pf.* (*of* ▶ зарыва́ться) to bury oneself

зар|я́, й, *pl.* зо́ри, зорь, зо́рям *f.* daybreak, dawn (also fig.)

заря|ди́ть, жу́, ~ди́шь *pf.* (*of* ▶ заряжа́ть) **1** (*оружие, фотоаппарат*) to load **2** (elec., *батарею*) to charge

заря́дк|а, и *f.* **1** (*ружья*) loading; (elec.) charging **2** (*упражнения*) exercises; drill

заря́дн|ый *adj.*: ~ое устро́йство charger, charging unit (*for battery*)

заряжа́|ть, ю *impf. of* ▶ заряди́ть

заря|жу́, ~ди́шь *see* ▶ заряди́ть

заса́д|а, ы *f.* ambush

заса́лива|ть, ю *impf. of* ▶ засоли́ть

заса́сыва|ть, ю *impf. of* ▶ засоса́ть

засверка́|ть, ю *pf.* to begin to sparkle, begin to twinkle

засве|ти́ться, ~ти́тся *pf.* to light up (also fig.)

заседа́ни|е, я *nt.* (*собрание*) meeting; (*совещание*) conference; (*суда*) session, sitting

заседа́|ть, ю *impf.* to sit; to meet

засе́ива|ть, ю *impf. of* ▶ засе́ять

засекре́|тить, чу, тишь *pf.* (*of* ▶ засекре́чивать) to place on secret list; to classify as secret, restrict

засекре́ченный *p.p.p. of* ▶ засекре́тить *and adj.* secret; (*документы, сведения*) classified

засекре́чива|ть, ю *impf. of* ▶ засекре́тить

засел|и́ть, ю́, и́шь *pf.* (*of* ▶ засели́ть) (*землю*) to settle; to colonize; з. но́вый дом to occupy a new house

засел|я́ть, я́ю *impf. of* ▶ засели́ть

засе́|ять, ю, ешь *pf.* (*of* ▶ засе́ивать) to sow

заска́кива|ть, ю *impf. of* ▶ заскочи́ть

заскоч|и́ть, у́, ~ишь *pf.* (*of* ▶ заска́кивать) **1** (за + *a. or* на + *a.*) to jump, spring (behind, onto) **2** (в + *a.*) (fig.) to drop in (to, at)

заскуча́|ть, ю *pf.* **1** to get bored **2** (по + *d.*) to begin to miss

за|сла́ть, шлю́, шлёшь *pf.* (*of* ▶ засыла́ть) to send, dispatch; з. шпио́на to send out a spy

заслон|и́ть, ю́, и́шь *pf.* (*of* ▶ заслоня́ть) (*закрыть*) to hide, cover; (*защитить*) to shield, screen

заслон|и́ться, ю́сь, и́шься *pf.* (*of* ▶ заслоня́ться) (от + *g.*) to shield oneself, screen oneself (from)

засло́нк|а, и *f.* oven door; (*регулятор тяги*) damper

заслон|я́ть, я́ю *impf. of* ▶ заслони́ть

заслон|я́ться, я́юсь *impf. of* ▶ заслони́ться

заслу́г|а, и *f.* service; contribution; они́ получи́ли по ~ам they got what they deserved

заслу́жива|ть, ю *impf.* (*of* ▶ заслужи́ть) (+ *g.*) to deserve, merit

заслуж|и́ть, у́, ~ишь *pf.* (*of* ▶ заслу́живать) (+ *a.*) to deserve, merit; (*выслужить*) to win, earn

засме|я́ться, ю́сь, ёшься *pf.* to begin to laugh

засне́жен|ный, ~, ~а *adj.* snow-covered

засн|у́ть, у́, ёшь *pf.* (*of* ▶ засыпа́ть¹) to go to sleep, fall asleep

засо́в, а *m.* bolt, bar

засо́выва|ть, ю *impf. of* ▶ засу́нуть

засол|и́ть, ю́, ~и́шь *pf.* (*of* ▶ заса́ливать) to salt; to pickle

засор|и́ть, ю́, и́шь *pf.* (*of* ▶ засоря́ть) **1** (*трубу*) to clog, block up, stop **2** (*глаза*) to get dirt into

засор|и́ться, и́тся *pf.* (*of* ▶ засоря́ться) to become obstructed, blocked up

засоря́|ть, ю, ет *impf. of* ▶ засори́ть

засоря́|ться, ется *impf. of* ▶ засори́ться

засос|а́ть, у́, ёшь *pf.* (*of* ▶ заса́сывать) to suck in, engulf, swallow up (also fig.)

засо́х|нуть, ну, нешь, *past* ~, ~ла *pf.* (*of* ▶ засыха́ть) **1** (*о булке, красках*) to dry (up) **2** (*о траве*) to wither

заста́в|а, ы *f.* **1** (*пограничная застава*) border post **2** (mil.) picket; outpost

заста|ва́ть, ю́, ёшь *impf. of* ▶ заста́ть

заста́в|ить, лю, ишь *pf.* (*of* ▶ заставля́ть¹) **1** (*загромоздить*) to cram, fill; з. ко́мнату ме́белью to cram a room with furniture **2** (*загородить*) to block up, obstruct

заста́в|ить², лю, ишь *pf.* (*of* ▶ заставля́ть²) (+ *a. and inf.*) (*принудить*) to compel, force, make

заста́вк|а, и *f.* (TV) repeated image at the start of TV programme; logo; музыка́льная з. signature tune

заставля́|ть¹, ю *impf. of* ▶ заста́вить¹

заставля́|ть², ю *impf. of* ▶ заста́вить²

заста́|ну, нешь *see* ▶ заста́ть

заста́|ть, ну, нешь *pf.* (*of* ▶ застава́ть) to find; вы ~ли его́ до́ма? did you find him in?; з. враспло́х to catch napping; з. на ме́сте преступле́ния to catch red-handed

заста|ю́, ёшь *see* ▶ застава́ть

застёгива|ть, ю *impf. of* ▶ застегну́ть

застёгива|ться, юсь *impf.* (*of* ▶ застегну́ться) **1** to fasten, do up; воротни́к ~ется на пу́говицу the collar does up with a button **2** to button oneself up; з. на все пу́говицы to do up all one's buttons

застег|ну́ть, ну́, нёшь *pf.* (*of* ▶ застёгивать) to fasten, do up; з. (на пу́говицы) to button up

застег|ну́ться, ну́сь, нёшься *pf. of* ▶ застёгиваться

застёжк|а, и *f.* fastening; clasp

застекл|и́ть, ю́, и́шь *pf. of* ▶ застекля́ть, ▶ стекли́ть to glaze, fit with glass; з. портре́т to frame a portrait

застекл|я́ть, я́ю *impf. of* ▶ застекли́ть

застел|и́ть, ю́, ~ешь *pf.* = застла́ть 1

засте́нчив|ый, ~, ~а *adj.* shy; bashful

⚘ key word

засти|г, гла *see* ▶ застичь

засти|гать, гаю *impf. of* ▶ застигнуть, ▶ застичь

застигнуть = застичь

застила|ть, ю *impf. of* ▶ застлать

застичь, гну, гнешь, *past* ~г, ~гла *pf. (of* ▶ застигать) to catch; to take unawares; нас ~гла гроза we were caught by the storm

заст|лать, елю, е́лешь *pf. (of* ▶ застилать) **1** (+ *i.*) to cover (with); з. ковром to carpet, lay a carpet (over) **2** (fig.) to hide from view; to cloud; слёзы ~ла́ли её глаза́ tears dimmed her eyes **3** (*кровать*) to make

засто́|й, я *m.* stagnation (fig.); в ~е at a standstill; (econ.) depression

засто́ль|е, я *nt.* (infml) celebratory meal

засто́льн|ый *adj.* table-, occurring at table; ~ая бесе́да table talk; ~ая пе́сня drinking song

застра́ива|ть, ю *impf. of* ▶ застро́ить

застрахо́ван|ный *p.p.p. of* ▶ застрахова́ть *and adj.* insured; (*as m. n.* з., ~ного) insured person

застрах|ова́ть, у́ю *pf. (of* ▶ страхова́ть) (от + *g.*) to insure (against)

застрах|ова́ться, у́юсь *pf. (of* ▶ страхова́ться) to insure oneself

застрева́|ть, ю *impf. of* ▶ застря́ть

застре́лива|ть, ю *impf. of* ▶ застрели́ть

застре́лива|ться, юсь *impf. of* ▶ застрели́ться

застрел|и́ть, ю́, ~ишь *pf. (of* ▶ застре́ливать) to shoot (dead)

застрел|и́ться, ю́сь, ~ишься *pf. (of* ▶ застре́ливаться) to shoot oneself; to blow one's brains out

застро́енный *p.p.p. of* ▶ застро́ить *and adj.* built-up

застро́|ить, ю, ишь *pf. (of* ▶ застра́ивать) to build on, develop

застро́йк|а, и *f.* building; development; пра́во ~и building permit

застря́|ну, нешь *see* ▶ застря́ть

застря́|ть, ну, нешь *pf. (of* ▶ застрева́ть) **1** to stick; з. в грязи́ to get stuck in the mud; слова́ ~ли у него́ в го́рле the words stuck in his throat **2** (fig., infml, *задержаться*) to be held up; to become bogged down

за́ступ, а *m.* spade

заступа́|ться, юсь *impf. of* ▶ заступи́ться

заступ|и́ться, лю́сь, ~ишься *pf.* (за + *a.*) to stand up for; to plead (for)

застыва́|ть, ю *impf. of* ▶ засты́ть

засты́|ну, нешь *see* ▶ засты́ть

засты́ть *pf. (of* ▶ застыва́ть) **1** (*о желе, цементе*) to set; (*о лаве*) to harden **2** (infml, *о руках*) to become stiff; (fig.): з. от у́жаса to be paralysed with fright **3** (infml, *о воде*) to freeze (also fig.)

засу́н|уть, у, ешь *pf. (of* ▶ засо́вывать) to stick in, thrust in; з. ру́ки в карма́ны to thrust one's hands into one's pockets

за́сух|а, и *f.* drought

засу́чива|ть, ю *impf. of* ▶ засучи́ть

засуч|и́ть, у́, ~ишь *pf. (of* ▶ засу́чивать): ~ рукава́ *и т. п.* to roll up sleeves, *etc.*

засу́шива|ть, ю, ет *impf. of* ▶ засуши́ть

засу́шива|ться, ется *impf. of* ▶ засуши́ться

засуш|и́ть, у́, ~ишь *pf. (of* ▶ засу́шивать) to dry up (*plants*) (also fig.)

засуш|и́ться, ~ится *pf. (of* ▶ засу́шиваться) to dry up (*intrans.*), shrivel

засу́шлив|ый, ~, ~а *adj.* dry, droughty

засчит|а́ть, а́ю *pf. (of* ▶ засчи́тывать) to take into consideration; з. в упла́ту до́лга to reckon towards payment of a debt

засчи́тыва|ть, ю *impf. of* ▶ засчита́ть

засыла́|ть, ю *impf. of* ▶ засла́ть

засы́п|ать, лю, лешь *pf. (of* ▶ засыпа́ть²) **1** (*яму*) to fill up **2** (+ *i.*) (*покры́ть*) to cover (with), strew (with) **3** (+ *i.*) (fig., infml): з. вопро́сами to bombard with questions **4** (в + *a.*) (infml) to put (into)

засыпа́|ть¹, ю *impf. of* ▶ засну́ть

засыпа́|ть², ю *impf. of* ▶ засы́пать

засыха́|ть, ю *impf. of* ▶ засо́хнуть

зата́ива|ть, ю *impf. of* ▶ затаи́ть

зата́ива|ться, юсь *impf. of* ▶ затаи́ться

зата|и́ть, ю́, и́шь *pf. (of* ▶ зата́ивать) (*мечту, злобу*) to harbour (BrE), harbor (AmE), cherish; з. оби́ду (на + *a.*) to nurse a grievance (against); з. дыха́ние to hold one's breath

зата|и́ться, ю́сь, и́шься *pf. (of* ▶ зата́иваться) (infml) to hide

зата́лкива|ть, ю *impf. of* ▶ затолка́ть, ▶ затолкну́ть

зата́плива|ть, ю *impf. of* ▶ затопи́ть¹

зата́птыва|ть, ю *impf. of* ▶ затопта́ть

зата́скива|ть, ю *impf. of* ▶ затащи́ть

зата́чива|ть, ю *impf. of* ▶ заточи́ть

затащ|и́ть, у́, ~ишь *pf. (of* ▶ зата́скивать) (infml) to drag off, drag away (also fig.)

затвердева́|ть, ет *impf. of* ▶ затверде́ть

затверде́|ть, ет *pf. (of* ▶ затвердева́ть, ▶ тверде́ть) (*о земле, цементе*) to harden, become hard; (*о жидкости*) to set

затво́р, а *m.* **1** (*винто́вки*) bolt; breechblock; (*плоти́ны*) floodgate **2** (phot.) shutter

затева́|ть, ю *impf. of* ▶ зате́ять

затека́|ть, ю *impf. of* ▶ зате́чь

зате́м *adv.* **1** (*после этого*) after that, then; next **2** (*для этого*) for that reason; з. что because, since, as; она́ прие́хала з., что́бы уха́живать за тобо́й she has come (in order) to look after you

зате́|чь, чёт, ку́т, *past* ~к, ~кла́ *pf. (of* ▶ затека́ть) (*онеме́ть*) to become numb; у меня́ нога́ ~кла́ my foot's gone numb

зате́|я, и *f.* undertaking, enterprise, venture

зате́|ять, ю *pf. (of* ▶ затева́ть) (infml) (*путеше́ствие*) to undertake; (*игру*) to organize; (*разгово́р, дра́ку, спор*) to start

затих|а́ть, а́ю *impf. of* ▶ зати́хнуть

3

зати́х|нуть, ну, нешь, past ~, ~ла pf. (of
▶ затиха́ть) (о звуке, ветре, буре) to die
down, abate; (BrE) to quieten down
(BrE), quiet down (AmE)

зати́шь|е, я nt. calm; lull

заткн|у́ть, у́, ёшь pf. (of ▶ затыка́ть) **1** (+ a.
and i.) to stop up; to plug; з. буты́лку
про́бкой to cork a bottle; з. рот, гло́тку
кому́-н. (infml) to shut sb up **2** (засу́нуть)
to stick, thrust; з. кого́-н. за по́яс (fig., infml)
to outdo sb

заткн|у́ться, у́сь, ёшься pf. (infml) to shut
up; ~и́сь! shut up!

затмева́|ть, ю impf. of ▶ затми́ть

затме́ни|е, я nt. **1** (astron.) eclipse **2** (fig.,
infml) blackout

затм|и́ть, и́шь pf. (of ▶ затмева́ть) **1** to
obscure **2** (fig.) to eclipse; to overshadow

◆ зато́ conj. (infml) but then, but on the other
hand; but to make up for it; до́рого, з.
хоро́шая вещь it is expensive, but then it is
good stuff

затолка́|ть, ю pf. (of ▶ зата́лкивать) to jostle

затолкн|у́ть, у́, ёшь pf. (of ▶ зата́лкивать)
(infml) to shove in

затон|у́ть, у́, ~ешь pf. of ▶ тону́ть 1

затоп|и́ть¹, лю́, ~ишь pf. (of ▶ зата́пливать)
(печь) to light; (включи́ть отопле́ние) to
turn on the heating

затоп|и́ть², лю́, ~ишь pf. (of ▶ затопля́ть)
1 (о́стров, окре́стности) to flood; to
submerge **2** (су́дно) to sink; з. кора́бль to
scuttle a ship

затопля́|ть, ю impf. of ▶ затопи́ть²

затоп|та́ть, чу́, ~чешь pf. (of ▶ зата́птывать)
(траву́, цветы́) to trample down; (костёр,
папиро́су) to stamp out

затоп|чу́, ~чешь see ▶ затопта́ть

зато́р, а m. blocking, obstruction; з. у́личного
движе́ния traffic jam, congestion

затормо|зи́ть, жу́, зи́шь pf. of ▶ тормози́ть

заточ|и́ть, у́, ~ишь pf. (of ▶ зата́чивать) to
sharpen

затра́гива|ть, ю impf. of ▶ затро́нуть

◆ затра́т|а, ы f. **1** (де́йствие) expenditure
2 (usu. in pl.) (расхо́ды) expenses, outlay

затра́|тить, чу, тишь pf. (of ▶ затра́чивать)
to expend, spend

затра́чива|ть, ю impf. of ▶ затра́тить

затре́щин|а, ы f. (infml) box on the ears

затро́н|уть, у, ешь pf. (of ▶ затра́гивать)
1 to affect **2** (fig.) to touch (on); з. вопро́с
to broach a question

затрудне́ни|е, я nt. difficulty

затруднённый p.p.p. of ▶ затрудни́ть and
adj. laboured (BrE), labored (AmE)

затрудни́тел|ьный, ~ен, ~ьна adj.
difficult; embarrassing

затрудн|и́ть, ю́, и́шь pf. (of ▶ затрудня́ть)
1 (кого́-н.) to trouble; to cause trouble (to);
to embarrass **2** (что́-н.) to make difficult;

to hamper

затрудн|я́ть, я́ю impf. of ▶ затрудни́ть

затуп|и́ть, лю́, ~ишь pf. (of ▶ затупля́ть) to
blunt; to dull

затуп|и́ться, ~ится pf. (of ▶ затупля́ться)
to become blunt(ed)

затупля́|ть, ю, ет impf. of ▶ затупи́ть

затупля́|ться, ется impf. of ▶ затупи́ться

затух|а́ть, а́ет impf. of ▶ зату́хнуть

зату́х|нуть, нет, past ~, ~ла pf. (of
▶ затуха́ть) **1** (переста́ть горе́ть) to go
out, be extinguished **2** (fig., infml, о зву́ке) to
die away

затуш|и́ть, у́, ~ишь pf. to put out,
extinguish; (fig.) to suppress

за́тхл|ый, ~а adj. (за́пах) musty; (во́здух)
stale, stuffy; (fig.) stagnant

затыка́|ть, ю impf. of ▶ заткну́ть

заты́л|ок, ка m. **1** back of the head
2: в з. in single file

заты́чк|а, и f. (infml) stopper; plug; з. для
уше́й earplug

затя́гива|ть, ю impf. of ▶ затяну́ть

затя́гива|ться, юсь impf. of ▶ затяну́ться

затяжн|о́й adj. long drawn-out, protracted;
~а́я боле́знь protracted, lingering illness;
~ы́е дожди́ long periods of rain

затя́|нуть, ну́, ~нешь pf. (of ▶ затя́гивать)
1 (у́зел, по́яс) to tighten; (naut.) to haul taut
2 (покры́ть) to cover; to close; (impers.)
не́бо ~ну́ло ту́чами it has clouded over
3 (засоса́ть) to drag down, drag in; (fig.,
infml, вовле́чь) to inveigle **4** (infml, продли́ть)
to drag out, spin out

затя́|нуться, ну́сь, ~нешься pf. (of
▶ затя́гиваться) **1** (затяну́ть на себе́)
to lace oneself up; (ту́го завяза́ться) to
tighten; у́зел ~ну́лся the knot tightened
2 (покры́ться) to be covered; (of a wound)
to close, heal over **3** (infml, продли́ться) to
drag on **4** (при куре́нии) to inhale

зау́м|ный, ~ен, ~на adj. abstruse, esoteric,
unintelligible

заун|ы́вный, ~ен, ~на adj. doleful,
plaintive

заупоко́й|ный adj. for the repose of the
soul; ~ая слу́жба requiem

заур|я́дный, ~ен, ~на adj. (обыкнове́нный)
ordinary, commonplace; (посре́дственный)
mediocre

зау́ченный p.p.p. of ▶ заучи́ть and adj.
studied

зау́чива|ть, ю impf. of ▶ заучи́ть

зау|чи́ть, чу́, ~чишь pf. (of ▶ зау́чивать)
(твёрдо вы́учить) to learn by heart

зафарши́р|ова́ть, у́ю pf. of ▶ фарширова́ть

зафикси́р|овать, ую pf. of ▶ фикси́ровать

зафрахт|ова́ть, у́ю pf. of ▶ фрахтова́ть

захва́т, а m. seizure, capture; (вла́сти)
seizure; з. зало́жников hostage-taking

захва|ти́ть, чу́, ~тишь pf. (of ▶ захва́тывать)
1 (взять) to take; они́ ~ти́ли с собо́й
дете́й they have taken the children with

them **2** (*завладеть*) to seize; to capture; з. власть to seize power; мы ~ти́ли три́ста пле́нных we took three hundred prisoners **3** (fig., *увлечь*) to carry away; to thrill, excite

захва́тчик, a *m*. invader; aggressor

захва́тыва|ть, ю *impf. of* ▸ захвати́ть

захва́тывающий *pres. part. act. of* ▸ захва́тывать *and adj.* (fig.) gripping

захлеб|ну́ться, ну́сь, нёшься *pf.* (*of* ▸ захлёбываться) **1** to choke; to swallow the wrong way **2** (fig., *infml*): з. от восто́рга to be breathless with delight; ата́ка ~ну́лась (mil.) the attack misfired

захлёбыва|ться, юсь *impf.* (*of* ▸ захлебну́ться) to choke

захло́п|нуть, ну, нешь *pf.* (*of* ▸ захло́пывать) (*дверь*) to slam

захло́п|нуться, нется *pf.* (*of* ▸ захло́пываться) to slam to; to close with a bang

захло́пыва|ть, ю, ет *impf. of* ▸ захло́пнуть

захло́пыва|ться, ется *impf. of* ▸ захло́пнуться

захо́д, a *m*. **1** (*also* з. со́лнца) sunset **2** (*куда-н.*) stopping (at), putting in (at); без ~а в Ло́ндон without calling at London

захо|ди́ть, жу́, ~дишь *impf. of* ▸ зайти́

захороне́ни|е, я *nt.* burial

захорон|и́ть, ю́, ~ишь *pf. of* ▸ хорони́ть

захо|те́ть, чу́, ~чешь, ~чет, ти́м, ти́те, тя́т *pf. of* ▸ хоте́ть

захо|те́ться, ~чется *pf. of* ▸ хоте́ться

зацве|сти́, ту́, тёшь, *past* ~л, ~ла́ *pf.* (*of* ▸ зацвета́ть) to break into blossom

зацвета́|ть, ю *impf. of* ▸ зацвести́

зацве|ту́, тёшь *see* ▸ зацвести́

зацеп|и́ть, лю́, ~ишь *pf.* (*of* ▸ зацепля́ть) to hook

зацеп|и́ться, лю́сь, ~ишься *pf.* (*of* ▸ зацепля́ться) (за + *a*.) **1** to catch (on); чуло́к у неё ~и́лся за гвоздь her stocking caught on a nail **2** (infml, *ухватиться*) to catch hold (of)

зацепля́|ть, ю *impf. of* ▸ зацепи́ть

зацепля́|ться, юсь *impf. of* ▸ зацепи́ться

заци́клива|ться, юсь *impf. of* ▸ заци́клиться

заци́кл|иться, юсь, ишься *pf.* (*of* ▸ заци́кливаться) (на + *p*.) (infml) to become obsessed (with)

зачаро́ванный *p.p.p. of* ▸ зачарова́ть *and adj.* spellbound

зачар|ова́ть, у́ю *pf.* (*of* ▸ зачаро́вывать) to bewitch, enchant, captivate

зачаро́выва|ть, ю *impf. of* ▸ зачарова́ть

зачасту́ю *adv.* (infml) often, frequently

зача́ти|е, я *nt.* (physiol.) conception

зач|а́ть, ну́, нёшь, *past* ~а́л, ~ала́, ~а́ло *pf.* (*of* ▸ зачина́ть) to conceive (*trans. and intrans.*)

зача́х|нуть, ну, нешь, *past* ~, ~ла *pf. of* ▸ ча́хнуть

⚜ **заче́м** *interrog. and rel. adv.* why; what for; з. ты пришла́? why did you come?; так *вот* ты з. пришла́ so that's why you came

заче́м-то *adv.* for some reason or other

заче́ркива|ть, ю *impf. of* ▸ зачеркну́ть

зачерк|ну́ть, ну́, нёшь *pf.* (*of* ▸ заче́ркивать) to cross out, strike out

зачерп|ну́ть, ну́, нёшь *pf.* (*of* ▸ заче́рпывать) to scoop up; (*ложкой*) to ladle out

заче́рпыва|ть, ю *impf. of* ▸ зачерпну́ть

зачёт, a *m*. **1** reckoning; в з. пла́ты in payment **2** (*экзамен*) test; получи́ть з., сдать з. (по + *d*.) to pass a test (in); поста́вить (*кому*) з. по (+ *d*.) to pass (a person) (in); мне поста́вили з. по исто́рии they have passed me in history

зачина́|ть, ю *impf. of* ▸ зача́ть

зачи́нщик, a *m*. (pej.) instigator, ringleader

зачисле́ни|е, я *nt.* enrolment

зачи́сл|ить, ю, ишь *pf.* (*of* ▸ зачисля́ть) **1** (*записать*) to include; з. на счёт to enter in an account **2** (*включить в состав*) to enrol, enlist; з. в штат to take on

зачи́сл|иться, юсь, ишься *pf.* (*of* ▸ зачисля́ться) (в + *a*.) to join, enter

зачисл|я́ть, я́ю *impf. of* ▸ зачи́слить

зачисл|я́ться, я́юсь *impf. of* ▸ зачи́слиться

зашива́|ть, ю *impf. of* ▸ заши́ть

заш|и́ть, ью́, ьёшь *pf.* (*of* ▸ зашива́ть) **1** (*дыру, пальто*) to mend **2** (med.) to stitch (up)

зашифр|ова́ть, у́ю *pf.* (*of* ▸ шифрова́ть, ▸ зашифро́вывать) to encipher, put into code

зашифро́выва|ть, ю *impf. of* ▸ зашифрова́ть

за|шлю́, шлёшь *see* ▸ засла́ть

зашнур|ова́ть, у́ю *pf.* (*of* ▸ шнурова́ть)

зашто́па|ть, ю *pf.* (*of* ▸ што́пать) to darn

защёлк|а, и *f.* (*в двери*) latch; (*в механизме*) catch

защёлкива|ть, ю *impf. of* ▸ защёлкнуть

защёлк|нуть, ну, нешь *pf.* (*of* ▸ защёлкивать) (infml) to latch

⚜ **защи́т|а**, ы (*no pl.*) *f.* defence (BrE), defense (AmE); (от, про́тив + *g*.) protection (from, against); (*collect.*) the defence (BrE), defense (AmE) (law and sport); в ~у (+ *g*.) in defence (BrE), defense (AmE) (of); под ~ой (+ *g*.) under the protection (of); з. окружа́ющей среды́ *or* приро́ды environmentalism, conservation

защи|ти́ть, щу́, ти́шь *pf. of* ▸ защища́ть

защи|ти́ться, щу́сь, ти́шься *pf. of* ▸ защища́ться

защи́тник, a *m*. **1** defender, protector; (law) counsel for the defence (BrE), defense attorney (AmE) **2** (sport) (full)back; ле́вый, пра́вый з. left, right back

защи́тн|ый *adj.* protective; ~ые очки́ goggles; з. цвет khaki

⚜ **защища́|ть**, ю *impf. of* (*impf. of* ▸ защити́ть) **1** to defend, protect **2** (law) to defend;

з. диссерта́цию to defend a thesis (*before examiners*)

защища́|ться, юсь *impf.* (*of ▶* **защити́ться**) **1** to defend oneself, protect oneself **2** *pass. of ▶* **защища́ть**

защищённост|ь, и *f.* protection

⚹ **заяв|и́ть, лю́, ~ишь** *pf.* (*of ▶* **заявля́ть**) (+ *a. or* о + *p. or* что) to announce, declare; **з. свои́ права́** (**на** + *a.*) to claim one's rights (to); **з. об ухо́де со слу́жбы** to announce one's resignation

⚹ **зая́вк|а, и** *f.* (**на** + *a.*) (*про́сьба*) application (for); (*о своих права́х*) claim (for); demand (for); (*зака́з*) order (for); **з. на изобрете́ние** patent application; **бланк ~и** application form

⚹ **заявле́ни|е, я** *nt.* **1** (*сообще́ние*) statement, declaration **2** (*про́сьба*) application; **пода́ть з.** to put in an application

⚹ **заявля́|ть, ю** *impf. of ▶* **заяви́ть**

за́|яц, йца *m.* **1** hare; **одни́м уда́ром уби́ть двух ~йцев** (*proverb*) to kill two birds with one stone **2** (*infml, пассажи́р*) stowaway; fare-dodger; **е́хать ~йцем** to travel without paying for a ticket

зва́ни|е, я *nt.* rank; title; **ры́царское з.** knighthood

зва|ть, зову́, зовёшь, *past* **~л, ~ла́, ~ло** *impf.* (*of ▶* **позва́ть**) **1** to call; **з. на по́мощь** to call for help **2** (*приглаша́ть*) to ask, invite **3** (*impf. only*) (*называ́ть*) to call; **как вас зову́т?** what is your name?; **меня́ зову́т Влади́мир** my name is Vladimir

⚹ **звезда́, ы́,** *pl.* **~ы, ~,** **~ам** *f.* **1** star; **но́вая з.** (astron.) nova; (fig.): **з. экра́на** film star **2** (zool.): **морска́я з.** starfish

звёздн|ый *adj. of ▶* **звезда́**; **з. дождь** meteor shower; **shooting stars; ~ая ночь** starlit night; **з. час** finest hour

звёздочк|а, и *f.* **1** *dim. of ▶* **звезда́ 2** (typ.) asterisk

звен|е́ть, ю́, и́шь *impf.* **1** to ring; **у неё ~е́ло в уша́х** there was a ringing in her ears **2** (+ *i.*): **з. моне́тами** to jingle coins

звен|о́, а́, *pl.* **~ья, ~ьев** *nt.* **1** (*це́пи*) link (also fig.) **2** (fig.) (*на предприя́тии*) team, section; (aeron.) flight

звере́|ть, ю, ешь *impf.* (*of ▶* **озвере́ть**) to become brutalized

звери́н|ец, ца *m.* menagerie

звери́ный *adj. of ▶* **зверь**; animal; savage

зве́рски *adv.* **1** brutally, bestially **2** (infml) terribly, awfully

зве́рский *adj.* **1** brutal, bestial **2** (infml, *чрезвыча́йный*) terrific, tremendous; **у него́ з. аппети́т** he has a tremendous appetite

зве́рств|о, а *nt.* brutality; atrocity; **~а** atrocities (*in war, etc.*)

звер|ь, я, *pl.* **~и, ~е́й** *m.* **1** wild animal, wild beast; **пушно́й з.** fur-bearing animal **2** (fig., *челове́к*) brute, beast

звон, а *m.* (ringing) sound, peal

звон|и́ть, ю́, и́шь *impf.* (*pf. of ▶* **позвони́ть**) (в + *a.*) to ring; **з. кому́-н.** (*по телефо́ну*) to phone sb, call sb; **вы не туда́ ~и́те** you've got the wrong number; **~я́т** sb is ringing

зво́н|кий, ~ок, ~ка́, ~ко *adj.* ringing, clear; **~кая моне́та** hard cash, coin

звон|о́к, ка́ *m.* bell; **дать з.** to ring; **з. (по телефо́ну)** (phone) call

зво́нче *comp. of ▶* **зво́нкий**

⚹ **звук, а** *m.* sound; **пусто́й звук** (fig.) (mere) name, empty phrase; (ling.): **гла́сный з.** vowel; **согла́сный з.** consonant

звук|ово́й *adj. of ▶* **звук**; **з. барье́р** sound barrier; **~ова́я ка́рта** (comput.) sound card

звукоза́пис|ь, и *f.* sound recording

звукоизоля́ци|я, и *f.* soundproofing

звуконепроница́ем|ый, ~, ~а *adj.* soundproof

звукорежиссёр, а *m.* sound engineer

звуча́|ть, у́, и́шь *impf.* (*of ▶* **прозвуча́ть**) **1** (*раздава́ться*) to be heard; to sound; **вдали́ ~а́ли голоса́** voices could be heard in the distance **2** (+ *adv. or i.*) (fig., *выража́ться*) to sound; to express, convey; **з. и́скренно** to ring true

зву́ч|ный, ~ен, ~на́, ~но *adj.* sonorous

звя́к|ать, аю *impf. of ▶* **звя́кнуть 1**

звя́к|нуть, ну, нешь *pf.* (*of ▶* **звя́кать**) **1** (+ *i.*) to jingle; to tinkle **2** (*pf. only*): (+ *d.*) **з. (по телефо́ну)** (infml) to ring up; to give sb a buzz

⚹ **зда́ни|е, я** *nt.* building

⚹ **здесь** *adv.* **1** here **2** (infml) here, at this point (*of time*); in this; **з. мы засмея́лись** here we burst out laughing; **з. нет ничего́ смешно́го** there is nothing funny in this

зде́шний *adj.* local; of this place; **вы з.? — нет, я не з.** are you a local? — no, I am a stranger here

здоро́ва|ться, юсь *impf.* (*of ▶* **поздоро́ваться**) (с + *i.*) to greet; to say hello (to); **з. за́ руку** to shake hands (*in greeting*)

здо́рово (infml) *adv.* **1** (*отли́чно*) splendidly, magnificently; **ты з. порабо́тал** you have worked splendidly **2** (*о́чень си́льно*) very, very much; **вчера́ они́ з. вы́пили** they had a great deal to drink yesterday **3** (*as int.*) great!; well done!

здоро́во *int.* (infml) hello!, hi!

⚹ **здоро́в|ый[1], ~, ~а** *adj.* **1** healthy; **бу́дь(те) ~ы)!** take care! (*said on parting*); (*to sb sneezing*) bless you! **2** (*поле́зный*) health-giving, wholesome; (fig.) sound, healthy; **з. кли́мат** healthy climate

⚹ **здоро́в|ый[2], ~, ~а, ~о** *adj.* (infml) **1** (*большо́й, си́льный: о челове́ке*) robust, sturdy **2** (*большо́й, си́льный: о предме́тах, явле́ниях*) strong, powerful; sound

⚹ **здоро́вь|е, я** (*no pl.*) *nt.* health; **пить за чьё-н. з.** to drink sb's health; **(за) ва́ше з.!** your health!; **как ва́ше з.?** how are you?; **на з.** to your heart's content, as you please

здравоохране́ни|е, я *nt.* health care; public health; **Министе́рство ~я** Ministry of Health

здра́вств|овать, ую *impf.* to be healthy; (*процвета́ть*) to thrive, prosper; ~уй(те)! how do you do?; how are you?; да ~ует Росси́я! long live Russia!

здра́в|ый, ~, ~а *adj.* sensible; з. смысл common sense; **быть в ~ом уме́** to be in one's right mind

зе́бр|а, ы *f.* (zool.) zebra ② (*ме́сто перехо́да*) zebra crossing (BrE)

зев|а́ть, а́ю *impf.* ① (*pf.* ~ну́ть) to yawn ② (*no pf.*) (infml) to gape, stand gaping; **не ~а́й!** keep your wits about you! ③ (*pf.* про~) (infml) to miss opportunities

зев|ну́ть, ну́, нёшь *pf. of* ▶ зева́ть 1

зелене́|ть, ю *impf.* ① (*pf.* по~) (*станови́ться зелёным*) to turn green, come out green ② (*видне́ться*) to show green

зеленогла́з|ый, ~, ~а *adj.* green-eyed

зелёный, зе́лен, зелена́, зе́лено, зе́лены *and* зелены́ *adj.* green (also fig.); з. горо́шек green peas; з. лук spring onions (BrE), green onions (AmE)

зе́лен|ь, и (*no pl.*) *f.* ① (*зелёный цвет*) green colour (BrE), color (AmE) ② (*collect.*) (*расти́тельность*) greenery ③ (*collect.*) (*о́вощи*) greens

земе́льн|ый *adj.* land; з. наде́л plot of land; ~ая ре́нта ground rent

землевладе́л|ец, ьца *m.* landowner

земледе́л|ец, ьца *m.* arable farmer

земледе́ли|е, я *nt.* arable farming

земледе́льческий *adj.* agricultural

землеко́п, а *m.* navvy

землеме́р, а *m.* land surveyor

землеро́йк|а, и *f.* (zool.) shrew

землетрясе́ни|е, я *nt.* earthquake

землечерпа́лк|а, и *f.* (tech.) dredger, excavator

зем|ля́, ли́, *a.* ~лю, *pl.* ~ли, ~е́ль, ~ля́м *f.* ① (З.) (*плане́та*) Earth ② (*су́ша*) (dry) land; уви́деть ~лю to sight land; упа́сть на ~лю to fall to the ground ③ (*владе́ние*) land; soil (fig.) ④ (*по́чва*) earth, soil

земля́к, а́ *m.* fellow countryman, compatriot

земляни́к|а, и (*no pl.*) *f.* (collect.) wild strawberries

земля́н|ин, ина, *pl.* ~е, ~ *m.* earth-dweller, earthling

земля́нк|а, и *f.* dugout

земля́н|о́й *adj.* ① earthen, of earth; ~ые рабо́ты excavations ② earth-; з. оре́х peanut

земля́чк|а, и *f.* fellow countrywoman, compatriot

земново́дн|ый *adj.* amphibious; (zool.) (*as pl. n.* ~ые, ~ых) amphibia; (*as nt. sg. n.* ~ое, ~ого) amphibian

земн|о́й *adj.* ① earthly; terrestrial; ~а́я кора́ (earth's) crust; з. шар the globe ② (*мирско́й*) mundane

зени́т, а *m.* zenith (also fig.)

зе́ркал|о, а, *pl.* ~а́, зерка́л, ~а́м *nt.* mirror (also fig.); **криво́е з.** distorting mirror

зерка́льн|ый *adj.* of ▶ зе́ркало; (fig.) smooth; ~ое стекло́ plate glass; ~ое окно́ plate-glass window; ~ая пове́рхность smooth surface

зер|но́, на́, *pl.* ~на, ~ен, ~нам *nt.* ① (*пшени́цы*) grain; (*ма́ка*) seed; (fig.) grain; (*ядро́*) kernel, core; ко́фе в ~нах coffee beans ② (collect., *sg. only*) grain, cereal

зернов|о́й *adj.* grain, cereal; ~ые зла́ки cereals

зернохрани́лищ|е, а *nt.* granary

зигза́г, а *m.* zigzag

зим|а́, ы́, *a.* ~у, *pl.* ~ы, *d.* ~ам *f.* winter; на́ ~у for the winter; всю ~у all winter

зи́мний *adj.* of ▶ зима́; winter; (*пого́да*) wintry

зим|ова́ть, у́ю *impf.* (of ▶ перезимова́ть) to winter, pass the winter

зимо́й *adv.* in winter

злак, а *m.* (bot.) grass; хле́бные ~и cereals

зле́йший *superl. of* ▶ злой

зл|ить, ю, ишь *impf.* (of ▶ разозли́ть) to anger; to vex; to irritate

зл|и́ться, юсь, и́шься *impf.* (of ▶ разозли́ться) (на + *a.*) to be in a bad temper; to be angry (with)

зло¹, зла, *no pl. except g.* зол *nt.* ① (*не́что дурно́е*) evil; harm; отплати́ть ~м за добро́ to repay good with evil ② (*беда́*) evil, misfortune, disaster; жела́ть кому́-н. зла to bear sb malice ③ (*sg. only*) (*доса́да*) malice, spite; vexation; меня́ з. берёт it annoys me, I feel annoyed

зло² *adv. of* ▶ злой

зло́б|а, ы *f.* malice; spite; anger; по ~е out of spite; со ~ой maliciously

зло́б|ный, ~ен, ~на *adj.* malicious, spiteful; bad-tempered

злове́щ|ий, ~, ~а *adj.* ominous, ill-omened; sinister

злово́н|ный, ~ен, ~на *adj.* fetid, stinking

зловре́д|ный, ~ен, ~на *adj.* harmful, pernicious

злоде́|й, я *m.* villain, scoundrel (also joc.)

злоде́йк|а, ки *f. of* ▶ злоде́й

злодея́ни|е, я *nt.* crime, evil deed

злой, зол, зла, зло *adj.* ① (*о челове́ке*) evil; bad; з. ге́ний evil genius ② (*выража́ющий зло́бу*) wicked; malicious; malevolent; vicious; зла́я улы́бка malevolent smile; со злым у́мыслом with malicious intent; (law) of malice prepense ③ (*short form only*) (на + *a.*) (*серди́т*) angry; она́ зла на всех she is angry with everybody ④ (*о живо́тных*) fierce, savage; «осторо́жно, зла́я соба́ка!» 'beware of the dog!'

злока́чествен|ный, ~, ~на *adj.* (med.) malignant; ~ная о́пухоль malignant tumour (BrE), tumor (AmE)

злопа́мят|ный, ~ен, ~на *adj.* rancorous, unforgiving

злора́д|ный, ~ен, ~на *adj.* gloating

зло́ст|ный, ~ен, ~на *adj.* ① (*созна́тельно недобросо́вестный*) conscious, intentional; ~ное банкро́тство fraudulent bankruptcy;

з. неплате́льщик persistent defaulter (*in payment of debt*) **2** (*закоренелый*) inveterate, hardened

зло́ст|ь, и *f.* malice, fury

злоумы́шленник, а *m.* plotter; criminal

злоупотреб|и́ть, лю́, и́шь *pf.* (*of* ▸ злоупотребля́ть) (+ *i.*) to abuse; (*сладким*) to indulge in to excess; з. вла́стью to abuse power; з. чьим-н. внима́нием to take up too much of sb's time

злоупотребле́ни|е, я *nt.* (+ *i.*) abuse (of); з. дове́рием breach of confidence

злоупотреб|ля́ть, ля́ю *impf. of* ▸ злоупотреби́ть

змей, зме́я *m.*: (бума́жный) з. kite; запусти́ть зме́я to fly a kite

зме|я́, и́, *pl.* ∼и, ∼й *f.* snake (also fig.)

⚡ знак, а *m.* **1** sign; (*след*) mark; (*символ*) token, symbol; (*comput.*) character; номерно́й з. number plate (BrE), license plate (AmE); ∼и препина́ния punctuation marks; ∼и отли́чия decorations (and medals); в з. (+ *g.*) as a mark (of), as a token (of), to show **2** (*предзнаменование*) omen **3** (*сигнал*) signal; пода́ть з. to give a signal

знако́м|ить, лю, ишь *impf.* (*of* ▸ познако́мить) (+ *a. and* с + *i.*) to acquaint sb (with); to introduce sb (to)

знако́м|иться, люсь, ишься *impf.* (*of* ▸ познако́миться) (с + *i.*) **1** (*с человеком*) to meet, make the acquaintance (*of a person*) **2** (*представляться*) to introduce oneself; ∼тесь! (informal mode of introduction) may I introduce you? **3** (*с вещью*) to become acquainted (with), familiarize oneself (with); to study, investigate

⚡ знако́мств|о, а *nt.* **1** (с + *i.*) (*между людьми*) acquaintance (with); слу́жба ∼ dating service **2** (*collect.*) (circle of) acquaintances; по ∼у by exploiting one's personal connections, by pulling strings **3** (с + *i.*) (*знание*) familiarity (with), knowledge (of)

⚡ знако́м|ый, ∼, ∼а *adj.* **1** familiar; его́ лицо́ мне ∼о his face is familiar (to me) **2** (с + *i.*) familiar (with); быть ∼ым (с + *i.*) to be acquainted (with), know **3** (*as n.* з., ∼ого, *f.* ∼ая, ∼ой) acquaintance, friend

зна́м|ени, енем *etc., see* ▸ зна́мя

знамени́тост|ь, и *f.* celebrity

⚡ знамени́т|ый, ∼, ∼а *adj.* celebrated, famous, renowned; печа́льно з. infamous, notorious

знамёнос|ец, ца *m.* standard-bearer (also fig.)

зна́м|я, *g., d., and p.* ∼ени, *i.* ∼енем, *pl.* ∼ёна, ∼ён *nt.* banner; standard; под ∼енем (+ *g.*) (fig., rhet.) in the name of

⚡ зна́ни|е, я *nt.* **1** knowledge; со ∼ем де́ла capably, competently **2** (*in pl.*) learning; accomplishments

зна́т|ный, ∼ен, ∼а́, ∼но *adj.* (*аристократический*) noble

знато́к, а́ *m.* expert; connoisseur

⚡ зна|ть¹, ∼ю *impf.* to know, have a knowledge of; вы ∼ете Алекса́ндрова? do you know Alexandrov?; з. в лицо́ to know by sight; з. ме́ру to know when to stop; не з. поко́я to know no peace; дать кому́-н. з. to let sb know; кто/Бог/чёрт его́ ∼ет! (infml) goodness knows!; God knows!; the devil (only) knows!; вам лу́чше з. you know best; ∼ешь (ли), ∼ете (ли) (infml) you know, do you know what

знат|ь², и (*no pl.*) *f.* (*collect.*) the nobility, the aristocracy

⚡ значе́ни|е, я *nt.* **1** (*смысл*) meaning, significance **2** (*важность*) importance, significance; придава́ть большо́е з. (+ *d.*) to attach great importance (to); э́то не име́ет ∼я it is of no importance **3** (math.) value

зна́чимост|ь, и *f.* significance

зна́чит (infml) so, then; well then; он у́мер до войны́? з., вы не́ были с ним знако́мы he died before the war? then you didn't know him

⚡ значи́тельно *adv.* considerably, significantly

⚡ значи́тель|ный, ∼ен, ∼ьна *adj.* **1** (*большо́й*) considerable, sizeable; в ∼ьной сте́пени to a considerable extent **2** (*важный*) important **3** (*выразительный*) significant, meaningful

⚡ зна́ч|ить, у, ишь *impf.* **1** (*иметь смысл*) to mean, signify **2** (*иметь значе́ние*) to mean, have significance, be of importance; ничего́ не ∼ит it is of no importance; э́то о́чень мно́го ∼ит для неё it means a great deal to her

значо́к, ка́ *m.* **1** badge **2** (*пометка*) mark

зна́ющий *pres. part. act. of* ▸ знать¹ *and adj.* expert; learned, erudite

зно|й, я *m.* intense heat; sultriness

зно́й|ный, ∼ен, ∼йна *adj.* hot, sultry; torrid; burning (also fig.)

зоб, а, *pl.* ∼ы́, ∼о́в *m.* **1** (*птицы*) crop, craw **2** (med.) goitre (BrE), goiter (AmE)

зов, а *m.* call, summons

зов|у́, ёшь *see* ▸ звать

зодиа́к, а *m.* (astron.) zodiac; зна́ки ∼a signs of the zodiac

зол¹ *see* ▸ злой

зол² *g. pl. of* ▸ зло¹

зол|а́, ы́ (*no pl.*) *f.* ashes, cinders

золо́вк|а, и *f.* sister-in-law (*husband's sister*)

золоти́ст|ый, ∼, ∼а *adj.* golden (*of colour*)

зо́лот|о, а (*no pl.*) *nt.* gold; (*collect.*) gold (*coins, ware*) (fig.); она́ — настоя́щее з. she is pure gold, a treasure; на вес ∼a worth its weight in gold

⚡ золот|о́й *adj.* gold; golden (also fig.); ∼ы́х дел ма́стер goldsmith; з. песо́к gold dust; з. запа́с (econ.) gold reserves; ∼а́я ры́бка goldfish; з. век the Golden Age; ∼а́я молодёжь gilded youth; ∼а́я середи́на golden mean

золочёный *adj.* gilded, gilt

⚡ зо́н|а, ы *f.* **1** zone; area **2** (geol.) stratum, layer **3** (sl.) (*тюрьма́*) prison; (*ла́герь*) prison camp

зонд, а *m.* **1** (med.) probe **2** (meteor.) weather balloon

зонт, а́ *m.* **1** umbrella **2** (*навес*) awning

зо́нтик, а *m.* umbrella; (*от солнца*) sunshade, parasol

зоо… *comb. form, abbr. of* ▸ зоологи́ческий

зоо́лог, а *m.* zoologist

зоологи́ческий *adj.* zoological; **з. парк, з. сад** zoological garden(s)

зооло́ги|я, и *f.* zoology

зоомагази́н, а *m.* pet shop

зоопа́рк, а *m.* zoo

зо́ри *see* ▸ заря́

зо́р|кий, ∼ок, ∼ка́, ∼ко *adj.* **1** sharp-sighted **2** (fig.) (*проницательный*) perspicacious, penetrating; (*бдительный*) vigilant

зрачо́к, ка́ *m.* pupil (*of the eye*)

зре́лищ|е, а *nt.* **1** (*предмет наблюдения*) sight **2** (*представление*) spectacle; show; pageant

зре́лост|ь, и *f.* (*винограда*) ripeness; (*человека*) maturity (also fig.); **полова́я з.** puberty

зре́л|ый, ∼, ∼а́, ∼о *adj.* (*виноград*) ripe; (*человек*) mature (also fig.); **дости́гнуть ∼ого во́зраста** to reach maturity; **з. ум** mature mind

⚥ **зре́ни|е, я** *nt.* (eye)sight; **по́ле ∼я** (phys.) field of vision; **обма́н ∼я** optical illusion; **то́чка ∼я** point of view

зре|ть, ю, ешь *impf. of* ▸ созре́ть

⚥ **зри́тел|ь, я** *m.* spectator, observer; **быть ∼ем**
to look on

зри́тельный *adj.* **1** visual; optic; **з. нерв** optic nerve **2**; **з. зал** hall, auditorium

зря *adv.* (infml) to no purpose, for nothing; **болта́ть з.** to chatter idly; **рабо́тать з.** to work in vain

⚥ **зуб, а** *m.* **1** (*pl.* ∼ы, ∼о́в) (*во рту*) tooth; **з. му́дрости** wisdom tooth; **вооружённый до ∼о́в** armed to the teeth; **не по ∼а́м** beyond one's capacity **2** (*pl.* ∼ья, ∼ьев) (*зубец*) tooth, cog

зуба́ст|ый, ∼, ∼а *adj.* (infml) sharp-toothed; (fig.) sharp-tongued

зуб|е́ц, ца́ *m.* tooth, cog

зуби́л|о, а *nt.* (tech.) chisel

зубн|о́й *adj.* dental; **∼а́я боль** toothache; **з. врач** dentist; **∼а́я па́ста** toothpaste; **∼а́я щётка** toothbrush

зубочи́стк|а, и *f.* toothpick

зубр, а *m.* (zool.) (European) bison

зуд, а *m.* itch; (fig.) itch, urge

зы́б|кий, ∼ок, ∼ка́, ∼ко *adj.* (*поверхность*) rippling; (*почва*) unsteady, shaky; (fig.) unstable, vacillating

зэк, а *m.* (sl.) prisoner, convict

зя́блик, а *m.* chaffinch

зят|ь, я, *pl.* ∼ья́, ∼ьёв *m.* (*муж дочери*) son-in-law; (*муж сестры, муж сестры мужа*) brother-in-law

Ии

и *conj.* **1** and **2**: **и… и** both … and; **и тот и друго́й** both **3** (*тоже*) too; (with neg.) either; **она́ сказа́ла, что и муж придёт** she said that her husband would come too **4** (*даже*) even; **и знатоки́ ошиба́ются** even experts may be mistaken

⚥ **и́бо** *conj.* for

и́в|а, ы *f.* willow

иври́т, а *m.* (modern) Hebrew

игл|а́, ы́, *pl.* ∼ы, ∼ *f.* **1** (*для шитья*) needle **2** (bot.) (*у хвойных деревьев*) needle; (*у растения*) thorn, prickle **3** (*ежа*) quill, spine **4** (*проигрывателя*) needle, stylus

иглоука́лывани|е, я *nt.* acupuncture

игнори́р|овать, ую *impf. and pf.* to ignore; to disregard

иго́лк|а, и *f.* needle; **сиде́ть как на ∼ах** to be on tenterhooks

иго́рный *adj.* gambling, gaming; **и. дом** casino

⚥ **игр|а́, ы́,** *pl.* ∼ы *f.* **1** (*действие*) play, playing;
и. слов play on words **2** (*занятие*) game

игра́льн|ый *adj.* playing; **∼ые ка́рты** playing cards

⚥ **игра́|ть, ю** *impf.* (*of* ▸ сыгра́ть) **1** to play; **и. пье́су** to put on a play; **и. роль** to play a part; **э́то не ∼ет ро́ли** it is of no importance; **и. в ка́рты, те́ннис, футбо́л, ша́хматы** to play cards, tennis, football, chess; **и. на роя́ле, скри́пке** to play the piano, the violin **2** (*impf. only*) (+ *i. or* с + *i.*) (*относиться несерьёзно*) to play with, toy with, trifle with (also fig.); **и. с огнём** (fig.) to play with fire **3** (*impf. only*) (*сверкать*) to play; to sparkle (*of wine, jewellery, etc.*); **улы́бка ∼ла на её лице́** a smile played on her face

игри́в|ый, ∼, ∼а *adj.* playful; (infml) naughty, ribald

игри́ст|ый, ∼, ∼а *adj.* sparkling (*of wine*)

⚥ **игр|ово́й** *adj. of* ▸ игра́; **и. автома́т** one-armed bandit, fruit machine (BrE); **∼ова́я приста́вка** (comput.) game(s) console

⚥ **игро́к, а́** *m.* **1** (в + *a. or* на + *p.*) player (of)

2 (*в азартные игры*) gambler

игру́шечный *adj.* toy; **и. парово́з** toy engine

игру́шк|а, и *f.* toy; (fig.) plaything; **ёлочные ~и** Christmas tree decorations

идеа́л, а *m.* ideal

идеализи́р|овать, ую *impf. and pf.* to idealize

идеали́зм, а *m.* idealism

идеали́ст, а *m.* idealist

идеалисти́ческий *adj.* idealistic

✓ **идеа́л|ьный, ~ен, ~ьна** *adj.* ideal (*also phil.*); perfect; **~ьное состоя́ние** perfect condition

иде́йный, ~ен, ~йна *adj.* **1** (*идеологический*) ideological **2** (*преданный какой-н. идее*) expressing an idea *or* ideas; committed, engagé **3** (*принципиальный*) high-principled, acting on principle

идентифика́ци|я, и *f.* identification

идентифици́р|овать, ую *impf. and pf.* to identify

иденти́чност|ь, и *f.* identity

иденти́ч|ный, ~ен, ~на *adj.* identical

идео́лог, а *m.* ideologist

идеологи́ческий *adj.* ideological

идеоло́ги|я, и *f.* ideology

✓ **иде́|я, и** *f.* **1** idea (also infml); notion, concept **2** (*главная мысль*) point, purport (*of a work of art*); **по ~е** (infml) in principle

идио́м|а, ы *f.* idiom

идиосинкрази́|я, и *f.* (med.) allergy

идио́т, а *m.* idiot, imbecile

идио́тский *adj.* idiotic, imbecile

идио́тств|о, а *nt.* idiocy, stupidity

и́диш *m. indecl.* Yiddish (*language*)

и́дол, а *m.* idol (also fig.)

✓ **ид|ти́, у́, ёшь,** *past* **шёл, шла** *impf.* (*of* ▶ **пойти́ 1,** *det. of* ▶ **ходи́ть**) **1** to go; (*impf. only*) (*приближаться*) to come; **и. в го́ру** to go uphill; **авто́бус ~ёт** the bus is coming **2** (**на** + *a.*) (*поступать*) to enter; (**в** + *nom.-a.*) to become; **и. на госуда́рственную слу́жбу** to enter government service **3** (**в** + *a.*) (*использоваться*) to be used (for); (**на** + *a.*) to go to make; **и. в корм** to be used for fodder; **и. в лом** to go for scrap; **и. на ю́бку** to go to make a skirt **4** (**из, от** + *g.*) (*о дыме, воде*) to come (from), proceed (from); **из трубы́ шёл чёрный дым** black smoke was coming from the chimney **5** (infml, *находить сбыт*) to sell, be sold; **хорошо́ и.** to be selling well **6** (*о механизме*) to go, run, work **7** (*о дожде, снеге*) to fall; **дождь, снег ~ёт** it is raining, snowing **8** (*о времени*) to pass; **шли го́ды** years passed; **ей пошёл тридца́тый год** she is in her thirtieth year **9** (*происходить*) to go on, be in progress; (*о спектакле*) to be on, be showing; (*о переговоры* etc. are in progress; **сего́дня ~ёт «Дя́дя Ва́ня»** 'Uncle Vanya' is on today **10** (+ *d. or* **к** + *d.*) (*быть к лицу*) to suit, become; **э́та шля́па ей**

не ~ёт this hat does not suit her **11** (о + *p.*) (*о разговоре*) to be (about); **речь ~ёт о том, что...** the point is that ..., it is a matter of ...

иезуи́т, а *m.* (eccl.) Jesuit

ие́н|а, ы *f.* yen (*Japanese currency*)

иерархи́ческий *adj.* hierarchical

иера́рхи|я, и *f.* hierarchy

иеро́глиф, а *m.* (*египетский*) hieroglyph; (*китайский, японский*) character

Иерусали́м, а *m.* Jerusalem

иждиве́н|ец, ца *m.* dependant; (*нахлебник*) sponger

иждиве́ни|е, я *nt.* maintenance; **на чьём-н. ~и** at sb's expense ▶

иждиве́н|ка, ки *f. of* ▶ **иждиве́нец**

✓ **из, изо** *prep.* + *g.* **1** (*обозначает источник действия*) from, out of; of; **прие́хать из Ло́ндона** to come from London; **пить из ча́шки** to drink out of a cup **2** (*обозначает часть целого*): **оди́н из её покло́нников** one of her admirers; (**ни**) **оди́н из ста** (not) one in a hundred **3** (*обозначает состав, компоненты*): **из чего́ э́то сде́лано?** what is it made of?; **варе́нье из абрико́сов** apricot jam; **обе́д из трёх блюд** a three-course dinner **4** (*обозначает средство*): **изо всех сил** with all one's might **5** (*обозначает причину*): **из благода́рности** in/out of gratitude

из..., *also* **изо..., изъ..., ис...** *vbl. pref. indicating* **1** motion outwards **2** action over entire surface of object, in all directions **3** expenditure of instrument *or* object in course of action; continuation *or* repetition of action to extreme point; exhaustiveness of action

изб|а́, ы́, *pl.* **~ы** *f.* izba (*peasant's hut or cottage*)

изба́в|ить, лю, ишь *pf.* (*of* ▶ **избавля́ть**) (**от** + *g.*) to save, deliver (from); **~ьте меня́ от ва́ших замеча́ний** spare me your remarks

изба́в|иться, люсь, ишься *pf.* (*of* ▶ **избавля́ться**) (**от** + *g.*) to be saved (from), escape; to get out (of); to get rid (of); **и. от привы́чки** to get out of a habit

избавля́|ть, ю *impf. of* ▶ **изба́вить**

избавля́|ться, юсь *impf. of* ▶ **изба́виться**

избало́ванный *p.p.p. of* ▶ **избалова́ть** *and adj.* spoilt

избал|ова́ть, у́ю *pf.* (*of* ▶ **балова́ть,** ▶ **избало́вывать**) to spoil (*a child, etc.*)

избало́outва|ть, ю *impf. of* ▶ **избалова́ть**

✓ **избега́|ть, аю** *impf.* (*of* ▶ **избегну́ть,** ▶ **избежа́ть**) (+ *g. or inf.*) (*сторониться*) to avoid; (*избавиться*) to escape, evade

избе́г|нуть, ну, нешь, *past* **~нул** *and* **~, ~ла** *pf. of* ▶ **избега́ть**

избе|жа́ть, гу́, жи́шь, гу́т *pf. of* ▶ **избега́ть**

избива́|ть, ю *impf. of* ▶ **изби́ть**

избие́ни|е, я *nt.* (*убийство*) slaughter, massacre

избира́тел|ь, я *m.* elector, voter

избира́тельн|ый *adj.* **1** electoral; **и. бюллете́нь** voting paper; **~ая кампа́ния**

election campaign **2** (tech.) selective

избира́|ть, ю *impf. of* ▸ **избра́ть**

изби́тый *p.p.p. of* ▸ **изби́ть** *and adj.* (fig.) hackneyed, trite

из|би́ть, обью́, обьёшь *pf.* (*of* ▸ **избива́ть**) (*человека*) to beat up

изборозд|ди́ть, жу́, ди́шь *pf.* ▸ **борозди́ть**

избра́ни|е, я *nt.* election

и́збран|ный *p.p.p. of* ▸ **избра́ть** *and adj.* **1** (*отобранный*) selected; ~ные сочине́ния Пу́шкина selected works of Pushkin **2** (*лучший*) select; (*as pl. n.* ~ные, ~ных) elite

из|бра́ть, беру́, берёшь, *past* ~бра́л, ~брала́, ~бра́ло *pf.* (*of* ▸ **избира́ть**) (+ *a. and i.*) to elect (as, for); to choose; его́ ~бра́ли чле́ном парла́мента he has been elected a Member of Parliament

избы́т|ок, ка *m.* (*излишек*) surplus, excess; (*обилие*) abundance, plenty; в ~ке in plenty; от ~ка чувств from a fullness of heart

избы́точ|ный, ~ен, ~на *adj.* surplus

изва́ни|е, я *nt.* statue, sculpture; graven image

изва́я|ть, ю *pf. of* ▸ **вая́ть**

и́зверг, а *m.* monster, fiend

изверг|а́ться, а́ется *impf.* to erupt (*of volcanoes*)

изверже́ни|е, я *nt.* **1** (*вулкана*) eruption **2** (fig.) ejection, expulsion

изверн|у́ться, у́сь, ёшься *pf.* (*of* ▸ **изворачиваться**) (infml) to dodge, take evasive action (also fig.)

изве́сти|е, я *nt.* (о + *p.*) news (of); после́дние ~я the latest news

изве|сти́ть, щу́, сти́шь *pf.* (*of* ▸ **извеща́ть**) to inform, notify

изве́стк|а, и *f.* (slaked) lime

⵿ **изве́стно** *as pred.* it is (well) known; **как и.** as is well known; **наско́лько мне и.** as far as I know

изве́стность, и *f.* (*слава*) fame, reputation; (*лгуна, преступника*) notoriety; **приноси́ть и.** (+ *d.*) to bring fame (to); **поста́вить кого́-н. в и.** to inform, notify

⵿ **изве́ст|ный, ~ен, ~на** *adj.* **1** (+ *d.*) well known (to); (+ *i.*) (well) known (for); (за + *a.*) (well) known (as) **2** (*лгун, преступник*) infamous, notorious **3** (*некоторый*) (a) certain; **до ~ной сте́пени, в ~ной ме́ре** to a certain extent

известня́к, á *m.* limestone

и́звесть, и *f.* lime

извеща́|ть, ю *impf. of* ▸ **извести́ть**

извеще́ни|е, я *nt.* notification, notice; (comm.) advice

извива́|ться, юсь *impf.* **1** (*о змее, канате*) to coil; (*о черве*) to wriggle **2** (impf. only) (*о дороге, реке*) to twist, wind; to meander

изви́лист|ый, ~, ~а *adj.* winding, twisting, tortuous

извине́ни|е, я *nt.* **1** (*оправдание*) excuse **2** (*просьба о прощении*) apology; **приня́ть**

~я to accept an apology **3** (*прощение*) pardon

извин|и́ть, ю́, и́шь *pf.* (*of* ▸ **извиня́ть**) **1** (*простить*) to excuse; ~и́те (меня́)! I beg your pardon; excuse me!; (I'm) sorry!; ~и́те, что я опозда́л sorry I'm late; **прошу́ и. меня́ за беста́ктное замеча́ние** I apologize for my tactless remark **2** (*оправдать*) to excuse; **э́то ниче́м нельзя́ и.** this is inexcusable

извин|и́ться, ю́сь, и́шься *pf.* (*of* ▸ **извиня́ться**) **1** (*перед* + *i.*) (*попросить проще́ния*) to apologize (to); ~и́тесь за меня́ present my apologies, make my excuses **2** (+ *i.*) (*оправда́ться*) to excuse oneself (on account of, on the ground of); to make excuses

извин|я́ть, я́ю *impf. of* ▸ **извини́ть**

извин|я́ться, я́юсь *impf.* (*of* ▸ **извини́ться**): ~я́юсь! (infml) I apologize!; (I'm) sorry!

извлека́|ть, ю *impf. of* ▸ **извле́чь**

извле́|чь, ку́, чёшь, ку́т, *past* ~к, ~кла́ *pf.* (*of* ▸ **извлека́ть**) to extract; (fig.) to derive, elicit; **и. уро́к** (*из* + *g.*) to learn a lesson (from); **и. по́льзу** (*из* + *g.*) to derive benefit (from); **и. ко́рень** (math.) to find the root

извне́ *adv.* from without

извора́чива|ться, юсь *impf. of* ▸ **извернуться**

изворо́тлив|ый, ~, ~а *adj.* (*спорщик, ум*) versatile, resourceful; (*человек*) wily, shrewd

извра|ти́ть, щу́, ти́шь *pf.* (*of* ▸ **извраща́ть**) **1** (*испортить*) to pervert **2** (*ложно истолкова́ть*) to misinterpret, misconstrue; **и. и́стину** to distort the truth; **и. чью-н. мысль** to misinterpret sb

извраща́|ть, ю *impf. of* ▸ **изврати́ть**

извраще́н|ец, ца *m.* pervert

извраще́ни|е, я *nt.* **1** (*ненормальность*) perversion **2** (*искажение*) misinterpretation, distortion (fig.)

изги́б, а *m.* bend, twist

изгиба́|ть, ю *impf. of* ▸ **изогну́ть**

изгиба́|ться, юсь *impf. of* ▸ **изогну́ться**

изгна́ни|е, я *nt.* **1** (*действие*) banishment; expulsion **2** (*ссылка*) exile

изгна́нник, а *m.* exile (*person*)

из|гна́ть, гоню́, го́нишь, *past* ~гна́л, ~гнала́, ~гна́ло *pf.* (*of* ▸ **изгоня́ть**) to banish, expel; (*сослать*) to exile

из|гоню́, го́нишь *see* ▸ **изгна́ть**

изгоня́|ть, ю *impf. of* ▸ **изгна́ть**

и́згород|ь, и *f.* fence; **живая и.** hedge

изгота́влива|ть, ю *impf.* = **изготовля́ть**

изготови́тел|ь, я *m.* manufacturer, producer

изгото́в|ить, лю, ишь *pf.* (*of* ▸ **изготовля́ть**) to manufacture

⵿ **изготовле́ни|е, я** *nt.* manufacture

изготовля́|ть, ю *impf. of* ▸ **изгото́вить**

изда|ва́ть, ю́, ёшь *impf. of* ▸ **изда́ть**

изда|ва́ться, ю́сь, ёшься *impf. of* ▸ **изда́ться**

И

и́здавна *adv.* for a long time; from time immemorial

издалека́ *adv.* from afar; from a distance; **го́род ви́ден и.** the town is visible from afar; **прие́хать и.** to come from a distance

и́здали *adv.* = **издалека́**

✓ **изда́ни|е, я** *nt.* **1** (*книг*) publication; (*закона*) promulgation **2** (*то, что издано*) edition

изда́тел|ь, я *m.* publisher

изда́тель|ский *adj.* of ▶ **изда́тель**, ▶ **изда́тельство**; **~ское де́ло** publishing

изда́тельств|о, а *nt.* publishing house, publisher

изда|ть, м, шь, ст, ди́м, ди́те, ду́т, *past* **~л, ~ла́, ~ло** *pf.* (*of* ▶ **издава́ть**) **1** (*опубликовать*) to publish; **и. ука́з** to issue an edict **2** (*запах*) to produce, emit; (*звук*) to let out; **и. крик** to let out a cry

изда|ться, мся, шься, стся, ди́мся, ди́тесь, ду́тся, *past* **~лся, ~ла́сь, ~лось** *pf.* to be published

издева́тельский *adj.* mocking

издева́тельств|о, а *nt.* (*действие*) mockery; (*насмешка*) taunt, insult; (*оскорбительное поведение*) ill-treatment

издева́|ться, юсь *impf.* (**над** + *i.*) to mock (at), scoff (at)

✓ **изде́ли|е, я** *nt.* (manufactured) article; (*in pl.*) wares

изде́рж|ки, ек *f. pl.* (*sg.* **~ка, ~ки**) expenses; costs; **суде́бные и.** (law) costs; **и. произво́дства** production costs

издо́х|нуть, ну, нешь, ~ла, *past* **~, ~ла** *pf.* (*of* ▶ **до́хнуть,** ▶ **издыха́ть**) to die (*of animals*)

издыха́|ть, ю *impf. of* ▶ **издо́хнуть**

изжа́р|ить, ю, ишь *pf. of* ▶ **жа́рить**

изжа́р|иться, юсь, ишься *pf. of* ▶ **жа́риться**

изжива́|ть, ю *impf. of* ▶ **изжи́ть**

изжи|ть, ву́, вёшь, *past* **~л, ~ла́, ~ло** *pf.* (*of* ▶ **изжива́ть**) **1** (*искоренить*) to eliminate **2**: **и. себя́** to become obsolete

✓ **из-за** *prep.* + *g.* **1** from behind; **из-за две́ри** from behind the door; **встать из-за стола́** to rise from the table **2** (*по причине*) because of, through **3** (*ради*) for; **жени́ться из-за де́нег** to marry for money

излага́|ть, ю *impf. of* ▶ **изложи́ть**

излече́ни|е, я *nt.* **1** (*лечение*) medical treatment **2** (*выздоровление*) recovery

изле́чива|ть, ю *impf. of* ▶ **излечи́ть**

изле́чива|ться, юсь *impf. of* ▶ **излечи́ться**

излечи́м|ый, ~, ~а *adj.* curable

излеч|и́ть, у́, ~ишь *pf.* (*of* ▶ **изле́чивать**) to cure

излеч|и́ться, у́сь, ~ишься *pf.* (*of* ▶ **изле́чиваться**) (**от** + *g.*) to make a complete recovery (from); to be cured (of); (fig.) to rid oneself (of), shake off

изли́ш|ек, ка *m.* surplus; remainder

изли́шеств|о, а *nt.* excess; overindulgence

изли́ш|ний, ~ен, ~ня, ~не *adj.* (*чрезмерный*) excessive; (*ненужный*) unnecessary, superfluous

изложе́ни|е, я *nt.* exposition, account; **кра́ткое и.** synopsis, outline

излож|и́ть, у́, ~ишь *pf.* (*of* ▶ **излага́ть**) to expound, state; to set forth; **и. на бума́ге** to commit to paper

изло́м, а *m.* **1** (*место перелома*) break, fracture **2** (*изгиб*) sharp bend

излуч|а́ть, а́ю *impf.* to radiate (also fig.); **её глаза́ ~а́ли не́жность** her eyes radiated tenderness

излуч|а́ться, а́ется *impf.* **1** (**из** + *g.*) to emanate (from) **2** *pass. of* ▶ **излуча́ть**

излуче́ни|е, я *nt.* radiation; emanation

излю́бленный *adj.* favourite (BrE), favorite (AmE)

изма́|зать, жу, жешь *pf.* (*of* ▶ **ма́зать 3,** ▶ **изма́зывать**) (infml) to make dirty, smear; **и. пальто́ кра́ской** to get paint all over one's coat

изма́|заться, жусь, жешься *pf.* (*of* ▶ **ма́заться 1,** ▶ **изма́зываться**) (infml) to get dirty; **он весь ~зался в кра́ске** he has got paint all over himself

изма́зыва|ть, ю *impf. of* ▶ **изма́зать**

изма́зыва|ться, юсь *impf. of* ▶ **изма́заться**

изма́тыва|ть, ю *impf. of* ▶ **измота́ть**

изме́н|а, ы *f.* betrayal; treachery; **госуда́рственная и.** high treason; **супру́жеская и.** unfaithfulness, (conjugal) infidelity

✓ **измене́ни|е, я** *nt.* change, alteration

измен|и́ть¹, ю́, ~ишь *pf.* (*of* ▶ **изменя́ть**) to change, alter; (pol.): **и. законопрое́кт** to amend a bill

измен|и́ть², ю́, ~ишь *pf.* (*of* ▶ **изменя́ть**) (+ *d.*) (*родине, другу*) to betray; (*мужу*) to be unfaithful (to); (fig.): **зре́ние ~и́ло ему́** his eyesight had failed him

✓ **измен|и́ться, ю́сь, ~ишься** *pf.* (*of* ▶ **изменя́ться**) to change, alter; **и. к лу́чшему, к ху́дшему** to change for the better, for the worse

изме́нник, а *m.* traitor

изме́нни|ца, цы *f. of* ▶ **изме́нник**

изме́нчивост|ь, и *f.* changeableness; (*непостоянство*) inconstancy, fickleness

✓ **изменя́|ть, я́ю** *impf. of* ▶ **измени́ть¹,** ▶ **измени́ть²**

изменя́|ться, я́юсь *impf. of* ▶ **измени́ться**

✓ **измере́ни|е, я** *nt.* **1** measurement, measuring; (*глубины́ моря*) sounding, fathoming; (*температу́ры*) taking **2** (math.) dimension

измери́тельный *adj.* (for) measuring

изме́р|ить, ю, ишь *pf.* (*of* ▶ **измеря́ть**) to measure; **и. кому́-н. температу́ру** to take sb's temperature

измеря́|ть, я́ю *impf. of* ▶ **изме́рить**

и́зморозь, и *f.* hoar frost

и́зморос|ь, и *f.* drizzle

измота́|ть, ю *pf.* (*of* ▶ изма́тывать) (*infml*) to exhaust, wear out

изму́ч|аться, аюсь *pf.* = изму́читься

изму́ченный *adj.* worn out, tired out

изму́чива|ть, ю *impf. of* ▶ изму́чить

изму́чива|ться, юсь *impf. of* ▶ изму́читься

изму́ч|ить, у, ишь *pf.* (*of* ▶ изму́чивать) to torment; to tire out, exhaust

изму́ч|иться, усь, ишься *pf.* (*of* ▶ изму́чиваться) to be tired out, be exhausted

измышле́ни|е, я *nt.* fabrication, invention

изм|я́ть, омну́, омнёт *pf. of* ▶ мять 2

из|мя́ться, омнётся *pf. of* ▶ мя́ться

изна́нк|а, и *f.* the wrong side (*of material, clothing*); с ~и on the inner side; и. жи́зни the seamy side of life

изнаси́лование|е, я *nt.* rape

изнаси́л|овать, ую *pf.* (*of* ▶ наси́ловать 2) to rape

изна́шива|ть, ю *impf. of* ▶ износи́ть

изна́шива|ться, юсь *impf. of* ▶ износи́ться

изне́женный *adj.* pampered; soft, effete

изнеможе́ни|е, я *nt.* exhaustion; рабо́тать до ~я to work to the point of exhaustion

изно́с, а (у) *m.* (*infml*) wear; wear and tear

изно|си́ть, шу́, ~сишь *pf. of* ▶ изна́шивать) to wear out

изно|си́ться, шу́сь, ~сишься *pf.* (*of* ▶ изна́шиваться) to wear out; (*fig., infml*) to be used up, be played out

изно́шенный *p.p.p. of* ▶ износи́ть *and adj.* worn out

изнури́тел|ьный, ~ен, ~ьна *adj.* exhausting; gruelling; ~ьная боле́знь wasting disease

изнутри́ *adv.* from within; дверь запира́ется и. the door fastens on the inside

изо *prep.* = из

изо...¹ *pref.* = из...

изо...² *comb. form* **1** iso- **2** *abbr. of* ▶ изобрази́тельный

изоби́ли|е, я *nt.* abundance, plenty

изоби́л|овать, ует *impf.* (+ *i.*) to abound (in), be rich (in)

изоблич|а́ть, а́ю *impf.* **1** *impf. of* ▶ изобличи́ть **2** (*no pf.*) (в + *p. and a.*) to show (to be), point to (as being); все его́ посту́пки ~а́ли в нём моше́нника his every action pointed to his being a swindler

изоблич|и́ть, у́, и́шь *pf.* (*of* ▶ изоблича́ть 1) (+ *a. and* в + *p.*) to expose (as); to unmask; его́ ~и́ли во лжи he stands exposed as a liar

изобража́|ть, ю *impf. of* ▶ изобрази́ть

✐ изображе́ни|е, я *nt.* representation, portrayal; image

изобрази́тельный *adj.* graphic; decorative

изобра|зи́ть, жу́, зи́шь *pf.* (*of* ▶ изобража́ть) **1** (+ *i.*) to depict, portray, represent (as); и. из себя́ (+ *a.*) to make oneself out (to be), represent oneself (as) **2** (*имити́ровать*) to imitate, take off **3** (*вы́разить*) to express, show

изобре|сти́, ту́, тёшь, *past* ~̈л, ~ла́ *pf.* (*of* ▶ изобрета́ть) (*созда́ть что-либо но́вое*) to invent; (*приду́мать*) to devise, contrive

изобрета́тел|ь, я *m.* inventor

изобрета́тел|ьный, ~ен, ~ьна *adj.* inventive; resourceful

изобрета́|ть, ю *impf. of* ▶ изобрести́

изобрете́ни|е, я *nt.* invention

изо́гнутый *p.p.p. of* ▶ изогну́ть *and adj.* bent, curved, winding

изогн|у́ть, у́, ёшь *pf.* (*of* ▶ изгиба́ть) to bend, curve

изогн|у́ться, у́сь, ёшься *pf.* (*of* ▶ изгиба́ться) to bend, curve

изойти́, йду, йдёшь, *past* ~шёл, ~шла́ *pf. of* ▶ исходи́ть 3

изоли́рованный *p.p.p. of* ▶ изоли́ровать *and adj.* isolated; separate

изоли́р|овать, ую *impf. and pf.* to isolate

изоля́тор, а *m.* **1** (*med.*) isolation ward **2** (*в тюрьме́*) solitary confinement cell

изорв|а́ть, у́, ёшь, *past* ~а́л, ~ала́, ~а́ло *pf.* (*of* ▶ изрыва́ть¹) to tear (to shreds)

изощрённый *adj.* (*ум, вкус*) refined; (*слух*) keen, acute

из-под *prep.* + *g.* **1** from under **2** (*го́рода*) from near **3** (*о вмести́лище*) for (*or not translated*); ба́нка из-под варе́нья jam jar

Изра́ил|ь, я *m.* Israel

изра́ильский *adj.* Israeli

израильтя́н|ин, ина, *pl.* ~е, ~ *m.* Israeli

израильтя́н|ка, ки *f. of* ▶ израильтя́нин

изра́н|ить, ю, ишь *pf.* to cover with wounds

израсхо́д|овать, ую *pf. of* ▶ расхо́довать

и́зредка *adv.* now and then; from time to time

изре́|зать, жу, жешь *pf.* (*of* ▶ изре́зывать, ▶ изреза́ть) **1** (*на мно́го часте́й*) to cut into pieces; to cut up; (*сде́лать на чём-н. мно́го надре́зов*) to make cuts in **2** (*geog.*) to cut across

изреза́|ть, а́ю *impf.* (*infml*) *of* ▶ изре́зать

изре́зыва|ть, ю *impf. of* ▶ изре́зать

изрис|ова́ть, у́ю *pf.* (*of* ▶ изрисо́вывать) to cover with drawings

изрисо́выва|ть, ю *impf. of* ▶ изрисова́ть

изрыва́|ть¹, ю *impf. of* ▶ изорва́ть

изрыва́|ть², ю *impf. of* ▶ изры́ть

изр|ы́ть, о́ю, о́ешь *pf.* (*of* ▶ изрыва́ть²) to dig up; to dig through

изря́д|ный, ~ен, ~на *adj.* (*infml*) fair, handsome; fairly large, tolerable; ~ное коли́чество a fair amount

изуве́чива|ть, ю *impf. of* ▶ изуве́чить

изуве́ч|ить, у, ишь *pf.* (*of* ▶ изуве́чивать) to maim, mutilate

изуми́тел|ьный, ~ен, ~ьна *adj.* amazing, astounding

изум|и́ть, лю́, и́шь *pf.* (*of* ▶ изумля́ть) to amaze, astound

изум|и́ться, лю́сь, и́шься *pf.* (*of* ▶ изумля́ться) to be amazed, astounded

и

изумле́ни|е, я *nt.* amazement

изумлённый *p.p.p. of ▶* изуми́ть *and adj.* amazed, astounded; dumbfounded

изумля́|ть, ю *impf. of ▶* изуми́ть

изумля́|ться, юсь *impf. of ▶* изуми́ться

изумру́д, а *m.* emerald

изумру́дный *adj.* **1** emerald **2** (*цвет*) emerald(-green)

изуро́д|овать, ую *pf. of ▶* уро́довать

✎ **изуч|а́ть, а́ю** *impf.* (*of ▶* изучи́ть) to learn; (*impf. only*) to study

✎ **изуче́ни|е, я** *nt.* study, studying

изуч|и́ть, у́, ∼ишь *pf.* (*of ▶* изуча́ть) **1** to learn **2** (*понять*) to come to know (very well), come to understand

**изъ... ** *pref.* = из...

изъе́з|дить, жу, дишь *pf.* (*of ▶* изъе́зживать) to travel all over, round; **мы ∼дили весь свет** we have been all round the world

изъе́зжива|ть, ю *impf. of ▶* изъе́здить

изъяв|и́ть, лю́, ∼ишь *pf.* (*of ▶* изъявля́ть) to indicate, express; **и. своё согла́сие** to give one's consent

изъявля́|ть, ю *impf. of ▶* изъяви́ть

изъя́н, а *m.* defect, flaw

изъя́ти|е, я *nt.* withdrawal; removal

изъя́ть, изыму́, изы́мешь *pf.* (*of ▶* изыма́ть) to withdraw; to remove; **и. из обраще́ния** to withdraw from circulation; **и. в по́льзу госуда́рства** to confiscate

изыма́|ть, ю *impf. of ▶* изъя́ть

изыму́, изы́мешь *see ▶* изъя́ть

изы́скан|ный, ∼, ∼на *adj.* refined

изы|ска́ть, щу́, ∼щешь *pf.* (*of ▶* изы́скивать) to find; to search out; **и. сре́дства на постро́йку домо́в** to find funds for house-building

изы́скива|ть, ю *impf.* (*of ▶* изыска́ть) to search out; to try to find

изю́м, а (у) (*no pl.*) *m.* raisins

изя́ществ|о, а *nt.* elegance, grace

изя́щ|ный, ∼ен, ∼на *adj.* elegant, graceful

Иису́с, а *m.* (*bibl.*): **И. (Христо́с)** Jesus Christ

ик|а́ть, а́ю *impf.* (*of ▶* икну́ть) to hiccup

ик|ну́ть, ну́, нёшь *pf. of ▶* ика́ть

ико́н|а, ы *f.* (*relig., comput.*) icon

ико́нк|а, и *f.* (*comput.*) icon

ико́т|а, ы *f.* hiccups

икр|а́¹, ы́ (*no pl.*) *f.* **1** (hard) roe; spawn; **мета́ть ∼у́** to spawn; (*fig., infml*) to rage **2** (*рыбный деликатес*) caviar; (*из овоще́й*) pâté; **баклажа́нная и.** aubergine pâté

икр|а́², ы́, *pl.* **∼ы** *f.* (*anat.*) calf

икри́нк|а, и *f.* grain of caviar

ил, а *m.* silt

✎ **и́ли** *conj.* or; **и. ... и.** either ... or

иллю́зи|я, и *f.* illusion

иллюзо́р|ный, ∼ен, ∼на *adj.* illusory

иллюмина́тор, а *m.* (*naut., aeron.*) porthole

иллюмина́ци|я, и *f.* illuminations

иллюстра́тор, а *m.* illustrator

иллюстра́ци|я, и *f.* illustration

иллюстри́рованный *p.p.p. of ▶* иллюстри́ровать *and adj.* illustrated

иллюстри́р|овать, ую *impf. and pf.* (*pf. also ▶* проиллюстри́ровать) to illustrate (also fig.)

им **1** *i. of prons.* ▶ он, ▶ оно́ **2** *d. of pron.* ▶ они́

им. (*abbr. of* и́мени) named after; **музе́й им. Пу́шкина** Pushkin Museum

има́м, а *nt.* imam (*Muslim priest or leader*)

имби́р|ь, я *m.* ginger

и́м|ени, енем *see ▶* и́мя

име́ни|е, я *nt.* estate

имени́нник, а *m.* person whose birthday it is; birthday boy; (*relig.*) person whose name day it is

имени́нни|ца, цы *f. of ▶* имени́нник

имени́т|ый, ∼, ∼а *adj.* distinguished

✎ **и́менно** *adv.* **1**: (а) *(перед перечислением)* namely; to wit **2** (*как раз, точно*) just, exactly; to be exact; **где и. она́ живёт?** where exactly does she live?; **вот и.!** exactly!; precisely!

имен|ова́ть, у́ю *impf.* (*of ▶* наименова́ть) to name

имен|ова́ться, у́юсь *impf.* (+ *i.*) to be called; to be termed

✎ **име́|ть, ю, ешь** *impf.* to have (*of abstract possession*); **и. возмо́жность** (+ *inf.*) to have an opportunity (to), be in a position (to); **и. де́ло** (**c** + *i.*) to have dealings (with), have to do (with); **и. значе́ние** (**для** + *g.*) to matter (to), be important (to); **и. ме́сто** to take place; **и. в виду́** (*не забыва́ть*) to bear in mind, think of; (*подразумева́ть*) mean

✎ **име́|ться, ется** *impf.* **1** to be; to be present, be available; **в на́шем го́роде ∼ется два кинотеа́тра** there are two cinemas in our town **2**: **∼ется у, ∼ются у = есть² 2**

име́ющийся *pres. part. of ▶* име́ться *and adj.* available; present

и́ми *i. of ▶* они́

и́мидж, а *m.* image

имиджме́йкер, а *m.* image-maker

имита́ци|я, и *f.* mimicry; mimicking; imitation

имити́р|овать, ую *impf.* (*of ▶* сымити́ровать) to mimic, imitate

имми́гра́нт, а *m.* immigrant

имми́гра́нт|ка, ки *f. of ▶* иммигра́нт

иммигра́ци|я, и *f.* **1** immigration **2** (*collect.*) (*иммигра́нты*) immigrants

иммигри́р|овать, ую *impf. and pf.* to immigrate

иммуните́т, а *m.* (*med., law*) immunity

импера́тор, а *m.* emperor

императри́ц|а, ы *f.* empress

империали́зм, а *m.* imperialism

импе́ри|я, и *f.* empire

импе́рский *adj.* imperial

импи́чмент *m.* (*pol.*) impeachment

✎ key word

и́мпорт, а *m.* **1** (*ввоз товаров*) import **2** (*collect.*) (*infml, товары*) foreign goods

импорти́р|овать, ую *impf. and pf.* (econ.) to import

и́мпорт|ный *adj. of* ▶ и́мпорт; ~ные по́шлины import duties

импрессиони́зм, а *m.* (art) impressionism

импрессиони́ст, а *m.* (art) impressionist

импровиза́ци|я, и *f.* improvisation

импровизи́р|овать, ую *impf.* (*of* ▶ сымпровизи́ровать) to improvise; to extemporize

и́мпульс, а *m.* (к + *d.*) impulse, impetus (for)

⚘ **иму́щество|о**, а *nt.* property, belongings; **дви́жимое и.** (law) personalty, personal estate; **недви́жимое и.** (law) realty, real estate

⚘ **и́м|я**, *g., d., and p.* ~ени, *i.* ~енем, *pl.* ~ена́, ~ён, ~ена́м *nt.* **1** name; (*личное название*) first, Christian name; **вы́мышленное и.** alias, false name; **во и.** (+ *g.*) in the name of; **от** ~ени (+ *g.*) on behalf of **2** (fig., *репутация*) name, reputation **3** (gram.): **и. прилага́тельное** adjective; **и. существи́тельное** noun, substantive; **и. числи́тельное** numeral

ин... and **ино...** *comb. form, abbr. of* ▶ иностра́нный

инакомы́сли|е, я *nt.* dissidence; nonconformism

инакомы́слящ|ий *adj.* dissident; nonconformist; (*as m. n.* **и.**, ~его) dissident

⚘ **ина́че** **1** *adv.* differently, otherwise; **так и́ли и.** in either event, at all events **2** *conj.* otherwise, or (else); **поторопи́тесь, и. вы опозда́ете** hurry up, or you will be late

инвали́д, а *m.* invalid; disabled person

инвали́дност|ь, и *f.* disablement; disability; invalidity (BrE); **посо́бие по** ~и disability/ invalidity benefit

инвентариза́ци|я, и *f.* inventory making, stocktaking

инвента́р|ь, я́ *m.* stock; equipment, appliances; **сельскохозя́йственный и.** agricultural implements

инвести́р|овать, ую *impf. and pf.* to invest

⚘ **инвестицио́нный** *adj.* investment

⚘ **инвести́ци|я**, и *f.* investment

⚘ **инве́стор**, а *m.* (fin.) investor

ингаля́ци|я, и *f.* (med.) inhaling

ингредие́нт, а *m.* ingredient

ингу́ш, а́, *g. pl.* ~е́й *m.* Ingush

Ингуше́ти|я, и *f.* Ingushetia

ингу́ш|ка, ки *f. of* ▶ ингу́ш

ингу́шский *adj.* Ingush

инде́|ец, йца, *pl.* ~йцы, ~йцев *m.* American Indian, Native American

инде́йк|а, и *f.* turkey (hen)

инде́йский *adj. of* ▶ инде́ец

и́ндекс, а *m.* index; **и. цен** (econ.) price index; **почто́вый и.** postcode (BrE), zip code (AmE)

индекса́ци|я, и *f.* (econ.) indexation

индиа́н|ка, ки *f. of* ▶ инде́ец, ▶ инди́ец

индивидуа́льност|ь, и *f.* individuality

⚘ **индивидуа́л|ьный**, ~ен, ~ьна *adj.* individual

индиви́дуум, а *m.* individual

инди́го *nt. indecl.* indigo; **пла́тье цве́та и.** indigo dress

инди́|ец, йца, *pl.* ~йцы, ~йцев *m.* Indian

инди́йский *adj.* Indian

Инди́йск|ий океа́н, ~ого океа́на *m.* the Indian Ocean

индика́тор, а *m.* (tech.) indicator

И́нди|я, и *f.* India

индонези́|ец, йца, *pl.* ~йцы, ~йцев *m.* Indonesian

индонези́й|ка, ки *f. of* ▶ индонези́ец

индонези́йский *adj.* Indonesian

Индоне́зи|я, и *f.* Indonesia

индуи́зм, а *m.* Hinduism

инду́кци|я, и *f.* (phil., phys.) induction

инду́с, а *m.* Hindu

инду́с|ка, ки *f. of* ▶ инду́с

инду́сский *adj.* Hindu

индустриализа́ци|я, и *f.* industrialization

индустриа́льный *adj.* industrial

индустри́|я, и *f.* industry

индю́к, а́ *m.* turkey (cock)

и́не|й, я (*no pl.*) *m.* hoar frost

ине́рт|ный, ~ен, ~на *adj.* (phys.) inert; (fig.) sluggish, inactive

ине́рци|я, и *f.* (phys., also fig.) inertia; momentum; **дви́гаться по** ~и to move under its own momentum; (fig.): **де́лать что-н. по** ~и to do sth from force of inertia, mechanically

инжене́р, а *m.* engineer; **и.-меха́ник** mechanical engineer

инжене́р|ный *adj.* engineering; ~ое де́ло engineering

инжи́р, а (*no pl.*) *m.* (*дерево; плод*) fig

инициа́л|ы, ов *m. pl.* (*sg.* ~, ~а) initials

⚘ **инициати́в|а**, ы *f.* initiative; **по со́бственной** ~е on one's own initiative

инициати́в|ный, ~ен, ~на *adj.* full of initiative, enterprising; dynamic, go-getting

инициа́тор, а *m.* initiator

инкасса́тор, а *m.* (fin.) security guard (*delivering money to a bank*)

инквизи́ци|я, и *f.* inquisition

инко́гнито **1** *adv.* incognito **2** *n.; c.g. indecl.* incognito (*person*)

инкримини́р|овать, ую *impf. and pf.* (+ *d. and a.*) to charge (with); **ему́** ~уют поджо́г he is being charged with arson

инкруста́ци|я, и *f.* inlaid work, inlay

инкуба́тор, а *m.* incubator

инкубацио́нный *adj.* incubative, incubatory; **и. пери́од** (med.) incubation

ино... *see* ▶ ин...

инове́р|ец, ца *m.* (relig.) adherent of different faith, creed

и

✓ **иногда́** *adv.* sometimes
иногоро́дний *adj.* of, from another town
иноземный *adj.* foreign
✓ **ин|о́й** *adj.* **1** (*другой*) different; other; ~ыми слова́ми in other words; не кто и., как; не что ~о́е, как none other than **2** (*некоторый*) some; и. раз sometimes
инома́рк|а, и *f.* foreign car, foreign make of car
инопланетный *adj.* alien, extraterrestrial
инопланетя́н|ин, ина, *pl.* ~е, ~ *m.* alien, extraterrestrial
иноро́д|ный, ~ен, ~на *adj.* alien; ~ное те́ло (med., also fig.) foreign body
иностра́н|ец, ца *m.* foreigner
иностра́н|ка, ки *f. of* ▸ **иностранец**
✓ **иностра́нный** *adj.* foreign
иноязы́чный *adj.* **1** (*население*) speaking another language **2** (*слово*) belonging to another language
инсектици́д, а *m.* insecticide
инсинуа́ци|я, и *f.* insinuation
инспе́ктор, а *m.* inspector; (mil.) inspecting officer
инспе́кци|я, и *f.* **1** (*действие*) inspection; и. на ме́сте (mil.) on-site inspection **2** (*организация*) inspectorate
инсти́нкт, а *m.* instinct
инстинкти́в|ный, ~ен, ~на *adj.* instinctive
✓ **институ́т, а** *m.* **1** (*общественное установление*) institution; и. бра́ка the institution of marriage **2** (*учебное или научное заведение*) institute; school; медици́нский и. medical school
инструкта́ж, а *m.* instructing; (mil., aeron.) briefing
инструкти́р|овать, ую *impf. and pf.* (*pf. also* ▸ **проинструкти́ровать**) to instruct, brief
инстру́ктор, а *m.* instructor
✓ **инстру́кци|я, и** *f.* instructions, directions; (instructions) manual
✓ **инструме́нт, а** *m.* (mus.; tech.) instrument; (tech.) tool, implement; (*sg.; collect.*) tools
инсули́н, а *m.* insulin
инсу́льт, а *m.* (med.) stroke
инсцени́р|овать, ую *impf. and pf.* **1** (*роман*) to dramatize, adapt (for stage *or* screen) **2** (fig.) to feign, stage; и. о́бморок to stage a faint
интегра́ци|я, и *f.* integration
интелле́кт, а *m.* intellect; иску́сственный и. (comput.) artificial intelligence
интеллектуа́л, а *m.* intellectual
интеллектуа́л|ьный, ~ен, ~ьна *adj.* intellectual
интеллиге́нт, а *m.* member of the intelligentsia, intellectual
интеллиге́нт|ный, ~ен, ~на *adj.* cultured, educated

интеллиге́нци|я, и *f.* (collect.) intelligentsia
интенси́в|ный, ~ен, ~на *adj.* intensive
интеракти́вный *adj.* interactive
интерва́л, а *m.* interval
интерве́нци|я, и *f.* (pol.) intervention
интервью́ *nt. indecl.* interview; взять ~ у (+ g.) to interview (a person)
✓ **интере́с, а** *m.* **1** interest; представля́ть и. to be of interest; прояви́ть и. (к + d.) to show interest (in) **2** (*выгода*) interest; (*in pl.*) interests; в ва́ших ~ах пое́хать it is in your interest to go
✓ **интере́сно** *as pred.* it is, would be interesting; и., что из него́ вы́йдет I wonder how he will turn out
✓ **интере́с|ный, ~ен, ~на** *adj.* interesting
✓ **интерес|ова́ть, у́ю** *impf.* to interest
интерес|ова́ться, у́юсь *impf.* (+ i.) to be interested (in); (infml, *осведомля́ться*) to enquire
интерна́т, а *m.* **1** (*школа*) boarding school **2** (*общежитие*) boarding house (*at private school*)
интернациона́льный *adj.* international
✓ **Интерне́т, а** *m.* the Internet; путеше́ствовать по ~у to surf the Internet
Интерне́т-са́йт, а *m.* website
интерпрета́ци|я, и *f.* interpretation
интерпрети́р|овать, ую *impf. and pf.* to interpret
интерфе́йс, а *m.* (comput.) interface
интерфере́нци|я, и *f.* (phys.) interference
✓ **интерье́р, а** *m.* (art) interior
инти́м|ный, ~ен, ~на *adj.* intimate; ~ные места́ private parts
интоксика́ци|я, и *f.* (med.) intoxication; алкого́льная и. alcoholic poisoning
интона́ци|я, и *f.* intonation
интри́г|а, и *f.* intrigue
интрове́рт, а *m.* introvert
интуити́в|ный, ~ен, ~на *adj.* intuitive
интуи́ци|я, и *f.* intuition
инфанти́л|ьный, ~ен, ~ьна *adj.* infantile
инфа́ркт, а *m.* (med.) heart attack; infarction
инфекцио́нный *adj.* infectious; ~ая больни́ца isolation hospital
инфе́кци|я, и *f.* infection
инфля́ци|я, и *f.* (econ.) inflation
информати́в|ный, ~ен, ~на *adj.* informative
информа́тик|а, и *f.* information science, information technology
информа́тор, а *m.* informant
✓ **информацио́нный** *adj. of* ▸ **информа́ция**
✓ **информа́ци|я, и** *f.* information
информи́р|овать, ую *impf. and pf.* (*pf. also* ▸ **проинформи́ровать**) to inform
инфраструкту́р|а, ы *f.* infrastructure
инциде́нт, а *m.* incident; пограни́чный и. frontier incident
инъе́кци|я, и *f.* injection

и. о. (*abbr. of* **исполня́ющий обя́занности**) (+ *g.*) acting ...

Иорда́н, а *m.* Jordan (*river*)

иорда́н|ец, ца *m.* Jordanian

Иорда́ни|я, и *f.* Jordan (*country*)

иорда́н|ка, ки *f. of* ▶ иорда́нец

иорда́нский *adj.* Jordanian

ипоте́к|а, и *f.* mortgage

ипоте́чный *adj. of* ▶ ипоте́ка; **и. банк** mortgage bank; ≈ building society

ипподро́м, а *m.* racecourse

Ира́к, а *m.* Iraq

ира́к|ец, ца *m.* Iraqi

ира́кский *adj.* Iraqi

Ира́н, а *m.* Iran

ира́н|ец, ца *m.* Iranian

ира́н|ка, ки *f. of* ▶ ира́нец

ира́нский *adj.* Iranian

йрис, а *m.* (bot.) iris

ири́с, а *m.* toffee

ирла́нд|ец, ца *m.* Irishman

Ирла́нди|я, и *f.* Ireland

ирла́нд|ка, ки *f. of* ▶ ирла́ндец

ирла́ндский *adj.* Irish

иронизи́р|овать, ую *impf.* (над + *i.*) to speak ironically (about)

ирони́ческий *adj.* ironic(al)

ирони́ч|ный, ~ен, ~на *adj.* = ирони́ческий

иро́ни|я, и *f.* irony

иррациона́л|ьный, ~ен, ~ьна *adj.* irrational

иррига́ци|я, и *f.* (agric. and med.) irrigation

ис... *pref.* = из...

иск, а *m.* (law) suit, action; **предъяви́ть и. (к) кому́-н.** to sue, prosecute sb, bring an action against sb

искажа́|ть, ю *impf. of* ▶ искази́ть

искаже́ни|е, я *nt.* distortion, perversion

искажённый *p.p.p. of* ▶ искази́ть *and adj.* distorted, perverted

иска|зи́ть, жу́, зи́шь *pf.* (*of* ▶ искажа́ть) to distort, pervert, twist; to misrepresent; **и. чьи́-н. слова́** to twist sb's words; **и. фа́кты** to misrepresent the facts

искале́ченный *p.p.p. of* ▶ искале́чить *and adj.* (*человек, живо́тное*) maimed, disabled; (*машина, стол*) damaged; (fig.) perverted, corrupt

искале́ч|ить, у, ишь *pf.* (*человека, живо́тного*) to maim, disable; (*машину, стол*) to damage; (fig.) to pervert, corrupt

иска́тел|ь, я *m.* seeker, searcher; **и. жемчуга** pearl diver

ⱷ **иска́ть**, ищу́, и́щешь *impf.* **1** (+ *a.*) to look for, search for; to seek (*sth concrete*) **2** (+ *g.*) to seek, look for, try to obtain (*sth abstract*); **и. слу́чая, сове́та** to seek an opportunity, seek advice

ⱷ **исключа́|ть**, ́аю *impf. of* ▶ исключи́ть

исключа́я *pres. gerund of* ▶ исключа́ть; (*as prep. + g.*) excepting, with the exception

of; **и. прису́тствующих** present company excepted

ⱷ **исключе́ни|е**, я *nt.* **1** (*отклоне́ние от но́рмы*) exception; **за ~ем** (+ *g.*) with the exception (of) **2** (*из спи́ска*) exclusion; (*из организа́ции*) expulsion; **ме́тодом ~я** by process of elimination

ⱷ **исключи́тельно** *adv.* **1** (*необыкнове́нно*) exceptionally **2** (*то́лько*) exclusively, solely

исключи́тел|ьный, ~ен, ~ьна *adj.* **1** (*необыкнове́нный*) exceptional **2** (*не для всех*) exclusive; **~ьное пра́во** exclusive right, sole right

исключ|и́ть, у́, и́шь *pf.* (*of* ▶ исключа́ть) **1** (*удали́ть*) to exclude; to eliminate; **и. из спи́ска** to strike off a list **2** (*из организа́ции*) to expel; to dismiss **3** (*не допусти́ть*) to rule out; **не ~ено́, что на́ши проигра́ют** our side could conceivably lose

иско́нный *adj.* (*права́*) immemorial, age-old; (*населе́ние*) native, indigenous

ископа́ем|ое, ого *nt.* **1** fossil (also fig., iron.) **2** (*also* поле́зное ~) (*usu. in pl.*) mineral

искорен|и́ть, ю́, и́шь *pf.* (*of* ▶ искореня́ть) to eradicate

искорен|я́ть, я́ю *impf. of* ▶ искорени́ть

йскр|а, ы *f.* spark; (fig.) flash

йскренне *adv.* sincerely, candidly; **и. Ваш** Yours sincerely; Yours faithfully (*in letters, etc.*)

йскрен|ний, ~ен, ~на, ~не *and* ~но, *pl.* ~ни *and* ~ны *adj.* sincere, candid

йскренность|ь, и *f.* sincerity, candour

искрив|и́ть, лю́, и́шь *pf.* (*of* ▶ искривля́ть) to bend; (fig.) to distort

искривля́|ть, ю *impf. of* ▶ искриви́ть

йскр|и́ться, ~и́тся *impf.* to sparkle; to scintillate (also fig.)

искупа́|ть[1], ю *pf.* to bath

искупа́|ть[2], ́аю *impf. of* ▶ искупи́ть

искупа́|ться, юсь *pf.* (*of* ▶ купа́ться) to bathe; to take a bath

искуп|и́ть, лю́, ~ишь *pf.* (*of* ▶ искупа́ть[2]) (relig., also fig., *вину́, грех*) to expiate, atone for

искупле́ни|е, я *nt.* redemption, expiation, atonement

искуса́|ть, ́аю *pf.* (*of* ▶ иску́сывать) (*о комара́х*) to bite badly, all over; (*о пчёлах*) to sting badly, all over

иску́с|ить, шу́, си́шь *pf. of* ▶ искуша́ть

иску́с|ный, ~ен, ~на *adj.* skilful (BrE), skillful (AmE); expert

иску́ствен|ный *adj.* **1** artificial; (*ткань, волокно́*) synthetic, man-made; **~ное дыха́ние** artificial respiration **2** (fig., *смех*) artificial, feigned

ⱷ **иску́сств|о**, а *nt.* **1** art; **изобрази́тельные, изя́щные ~а** fine arts **2** (*уме́ние*) craftsmanship, skill; **и. верхово́й езды́** horsemanship

искусство́вед, а *m.* art historian

искусствове́дени|е, я *nt.* history of art, art history

искýсыва|ть, ю impf. of ▸ **искусáть**

искуша|ть, ю impf. (of ▸ **искусúть**) to tempt; to seduce; **и. судьбý** to tempt fate

искушéни|е, я nt. temptation; seduction; **поддáться ~ю, впасть в и.** to yield to temptation

искушённый p.p.p. of ▸ **искусúть** and adj. (политик) experienced; (публика) sophisticated

ислáм, а m. Islam

ислáмский adj. Islamic

Ислáнди|я, и f. Iceland

испáн|ец, ца m. Spaniard, Spanish man

Испáни|я, и f. Spain

испáнк|а, и f. Spaniard, Spanish woman

испáнский adj. Spanish

испарéни|е, я nt. **1** (действие) evaporation **2** (usu. in pl.) (пар) fumes

испар|úться, юсь, úшься pf. (of ▸ **испаря́ться**) to evaporate; (fig., joc., исчезнуть) to vanish into thin air

испар|я́ться, я́юсь impf. of ▸ **испарúться**

испáчка|ть, ю pf. of ▸ **пáчкать**

испáчка|ться, юсь pf. of ▸ **пáчкаться**

испепел|úть, ю́, úшь pf. (of ▸ **испепеля́ть**) to reduce to ashes, incinerate

испепел|я́ть, я́ю impf. of ▸ **испепелúть**

испе́|чь, кý, чёшь, кýт, past **~к, ~клá** pf. of ▸ **печь**[1]

испе́|чься, чётся, кýтся, past **~кся, ~клáсь** pf. of ▸ **печь́ся**

испещр|úть, ю́, úшь pf. (of ▸ **испещря́ть**) (+ a. and i.) to spot (with); to mark all over (with)

испещр|я́ть, я́ю impf. of ▸ **испещрúть**

исписá|ть, шý, ~шешь pf. (of ▸ **испúсывать**) **1** (тетрадь) to cover with writing; **он ужé ~сáл двáдцать тетрáдей** he has already filled up twenty exercise books **2** (карандаш, бумагу) to use up (in writing)

испúсыва|ть, ю impf. of ▸ **исписáть**

исповéд|ать, аю pf. (infml) = **исповéдовать**[1]

исповéд|аться, аюсь pf. (infml) = **исповéдоваться**

исповéд|овать[1], **ую** impf. and pf. (eccl.) to hear the confession (of)

исповéд|овать[2], **ую** impf. (веру) to profess

исповéд|оваться, уюсь impf. and pf. **1** (+ d. or y + g.) to confess, make one's confession (to) **2** (+ d. or перед + i.) (fig., infml) to confess; to unburden oneself of; **он ~овался мне в своих сомнéниях** he confessed his doubts to me

úсповед|ь, и f. (eccl.) confession

исподлóбья adv. from under the brows (distrustfully, sullenly)

исподтишкá adv. (infml) in an underhand way; on the quiet, on the sly; **смеяться и.** to laugh in one's sleeve

⚔ **исполнéни|е, я** nt. **1** (желания) fulfilment

⚔ key word

(BrE), fulfillment (AmE); (приказа) execution; (долгов) discharge; **привести́ в и.** to carry out, execute **2** (роли, музыки) performance; (theatr., mus.): **в ~и** (+ g.) (as) played (by), (as) performed (by)

исполнúтел|ь, я m. **1** executor; **судéбный и.** bailiff **2** (theatr., mus., etc.) performer; **состáв ~ей** cast

исполнúтель|ница, ницы f. of ▸ **исполнúтель**

⚔ **исполнúтель|ный** adj. **1** (власть, директор, комитет) executive **2** (~ен, ~ьна) (человек) efficient and dependable

исполн|ить, ю, ишь pf. (of ▸ **исполня́ть**) **1** (заказ) to carry out, execute; (желание) to fulfil (BrE), fulfill (AmE); **и. обещáние** to keep a promise; **и. прóсьбу** to grant a request **2** (роль, танец) to perform; **и. роль** (+ g.) to take the part (of)

исполн|иться, юсь, ишься pf. (of ▸ **исполня́ться**) **1** (осуществиться) to be fulfilled **2** (impers.) (о возрасте, сроке): **емý ~илось семь лет** he is seven, was seven last birthday

⚔ **исполн|я́ть, я́ю** impf. (of ▸ **испóлнить**): **~я́ющий обя́занности** (+ g.) acting

исполн|я́ться, я́юсь impf. of ▸ **испóлниться**

⚔ **использовани|е, я** nt. use; (сырья) utilization

⚔ **использ|овать, ую** impf. and pf. to use, make use of, utilize

испóр|тить, чу, тишь pf. of ▸ **пóртить**

испóр|титься, чусь, тишься pf. of ▸ **пóртиться**

испóрченн|ый p.p.p. of ▸ **испóртить** and adj. **1** (человек) depraved; corrupted **2** (настроение, день) ruined; (товары) spoiled; bad, rotten; **~ое мя́со** tainted meat **3** (infml, ребёнок) spoiled **4** (comput.) corrupt

испрáв|ить, лю, ишь pf. (of ▸ **исправля́ть**) **1** (ошибку) to rectify, correct, emend **2** (починить) to repair, mend

испрáв|иться, люсь, ишься pf. (of ▸ **исправля́ться**) to improve; to reform

исправлéни|е, я nt. correcting; repairing; correction

исправля́|ть, ю impf. of ▸ **испрáвить**

исправля́|ться, юсь impf. of ▸ **испрáвиться**

испрáв|ный, ~ен, ~на adj. (механизм) in good order

испражнéни|е, я nt. **1** (действие) defecation **2** (in pl.) (экскременты) faeces

испражн|úться, ю́сь, úшься pf. of ▸ **испражня́ться**

испражн|я́ться, я́юсь impf. (of ▸ **испражнúться**) to defecate

испýг, а (у) m. fright; alarm; **с ~у/~а** from fright

испýганный p.p.p. of ▸ **испугáть** and adj. frightened, scared, startled

испугá|ть, ю pf. of ▸ **пугáть**

испуга́|ться, юсь *pf. of* ▶ **пуга́ться**

испуска́|ть, ю *impf. of* ▶ **испусти́ть**

испу|сти́ть, щу́, ~стишь *pf.* (*of* ▶ **испуска́ть**) (*свет, лучи*) to emit; (*стон*) to let out; **и. дух** to breathe one's last

✔ **испыта́ни|е, я** *nt.* test, trial; (fig.) ordeal

испы́танный *p.p.p. of* ▶ **испыта́ть** *and adj.* tried, well tried

испыта́тел|ь, я *m.* tester; **лётчик-и.** test pilot

испыт|а́ть, а́ю *pf.* (*of* ▶ **испы́тывать**) **1** (*проверить*) to test, put to the test **2** (*ощутить*) to feel, experience

✔ **испы́тыва|ть, ю** *impf. of* ▶ **испыта́ть**

✔ **иссле́довани|е, я** *nt.* **1** (*темы*) research; (*местности*) exploration; (*проблемы*) examination; (*крови, состава*) analysis **2** (*научный труд*) paper; study

иссле́довател|ь, я *m.* researcher; (*страны*) explorer

иссле́дователь|ница, ницы *f. of* ▶ **иссле́дователь**

иссле́довательский *adj.* research

иссле́д|овать, ую *impf. and pf.* (*ситуацию, проблему*) to investigate; (*тему*) to research into; (*страну*) to explore; (*кровь*) to analyse (BrE), analyze (AmE)

иссяка́|ть, а́ю *impf. of* ▶ **иссякнуть**

исся́к|нуть, ну, нешь, *past* ~, ~**ла** *pf.* (*of* ▶ **иссяка́ть**) to run dry, dry up; (fig., *терпение, силы*) to run out

истека́|ть, ю *impf. of* ▶ **истечь**

исте́к|ший *p.p.p. of* ▶ **исте́чь** 1 *and adj.* past, preceding; **в тече́ние ~кшего го́да** during the past year

истерза́|ть, ю *pf.* **1** (*разорвать на части*) to tear in pieces; to mutilate **2** (*измучить*) to torment

исте́рик|а, и *f.* hysterics

истери́ческий *adj.* hysterical; **и. припа́док** fit of hysterics

истери́|я, и *f.* (med.) hysteria; (fig.): **ма́ссовая и.** mass hysteria

ист|е́ц, ца́ *m.* (law) plaintiff

истече́ни|е, я *nt.* **1** outflow; **и. кро́ви** haemorrhage (BrE), hemorrhage (AmE) **2** (*окончание*) expiry, expiration; **по ~и сро́ка гара́нтии** on the expiry of the guarantee period

исте́|чь, ку́, чёшь, ку́т, *past* ~к, ~кла́ *pf.* (*of* ▶ **истека́ть**) **1**: **и. кро́вью** to bleed profusely **2** (*окончиться*) to expire, elapse; **вре́мя ~кло́** time is up

йстин|а, ы *f.* truth; **избитая и.** truism

йстин|ный, ~ен, ~на *adj.* true, veritable

ист|и́ца, и́цы *f. of* ▶ **исте́ц**

исто́к, а *m.* source (also fig.)

истолк|ова́ть, у́ю *pf.* (*of* ▶ **истолко́вывать**) (*смысл, слово*) to interpret; (*письменный памятник*) to comment upon; **и. замеча́ние в дурну́ю сто́рону** to put a nasty construction on a remark

истолко́выва|ть, ю *impf. of* ▶ **истолкова́ть**

исто́м|а, ы *f.* languor

истопни́к, а́ *m.* stoker; (*котлов*) boilerman

исто́рик, а *m.* historian

✔ **истори́ческ|ий** *adj.* **1** historical; **~ое лицо́** historical figure **2** (*важный*) historic; **~ое реше́ние** historic decision

✔ **исто́ри|я, и** *f.* **1** history; **и. боле́зни** case history **2** (infml, *рассказ*) story **3** (infml, *событие*) incident, event; scene; **вчера́ со мной произошла́ заба́вная и.** a funny thing happened to me yesterday

✔ **исто́чник, а** *m.* **1** spring **2** (fig.) source; **и. информа́ции** source of information; **и. све́та** source of light; **служи́ть ~ом** (+ *g.*) to be a source (of)

истоще́ни|е, я *nt.* exhaustion

истощённый *adj.* exhausted; (*исхудалый*) emaciated

истра́|тить, чу, тишь *pf. of* ▶ **тра́тить**

истреби́тел|ь, я *m.* **1** (*человек*) destroyer **2** (*самолёт*) fighter **3** (*лётчик*) fighter pilot

истреб|и́ть, лю́, и́шь *pf.* (*of* ▶ **истребля́ть**) (*посевы*) to destroy; (*крыс*) to exterminate

истребле́ни|е, я *nt.* (*посевов*) destruction; (*крыс*) extermination

истребля́|ть, ю *impf. of* ▶ **истреби́ть**

истука́н, а *m.* idol, statue

истяза́ни|е, я *nt.* torture

истяза́|ть, ю *impf.* to torture

исхо́д, а *m.* (*итог*) outcome; (*конец*) end; **быть на ~е** to be nearing the end, be coming to an end; **на ~е дня** towards evening

✔ **исхо|ди́ть, жу́, ~дишь** *impf.* (*of* ▶ **изойти́**) **1** (*impf. only*) (*из* + *g.*) (*происходить*) to come (from); to emanate (from); **отку́да исхо́дит э́тот слух?** where does this rumour (BrE), rumor (AmE) come from? **2** (*impf. only*) (*из* + *g.*) (*основываться*) to proceed (from), base oneself (on) **3**: **и. кро́вью** to become weak through loss of blood

исхо́дн|ый *adj.* initial; **~ое положе́ние** point of departure

исходя́щий *adj.* outgoing

исхуда́|ть, ю *pf.* to become emaciated, become wasted

✔ **исцеле́ни|е, я** *nt.* **1** (*действие*) healing, cure **2** (*выздоровление*) recovery

исцел|и́ть, ю́, и́шь *pf.* (*of* ▶ **исцеля́ть**) to heal, cure

исцеля́|ть, я́ю *impf. of* ▶ **исцели́ть**

исчеза́|ть, а́ю *impf. of* ▶ **исче́знуть** to disappear, vanish

исчезнове́ни|е, я *nt.* disappearance

исче́з|нуть, ну, нешь, *past* ~, ~**ла** *pf. of* ▶ **исчеза́ть**

исче́рп|ать, аю *pf.* (*of* ▶ **исче́рпывать**) **1** to exhaust, drain **2** (*довести до конца*) to settle, conclude; **и. вопро́с** to settle a question

исче́рпыва|ть, ю *impf. of* ▶ **исче́рпать**

исче́рпывающий *pres. part. act. of* ▶ **исче́рпывать** *and adj.* exhaustive

исчисле́ни|**е, я** *nt.* calculation; (math.) calculus

☞ **ита́к** *conj.* thus; so then

Ита́ли|**я, и** *f.* Italy

италья́н|**ец, ца** *nt.* Italian

италья́н|**ка, ки** *f. of* ▸ италья́нец

италья́нский *adj.* Italian

☞ **и т. д.** (*abbr. of* **и так да́лее**) etc., et cetera, and so on

☞ **ито́г, а** *m.* **1** (*о́бщая су́мма*) sum, total; **о́бщий и.** grand total **2** (fig., *результа́т*) result; **подвести́ и.** to sum up; **в ~е** (*в конце концо́в*) in the end; (*в результа́те*) as a result

итого́ *adv.* in all, altogether; (sub)total

ито́говый *adj.* (*су́мма*) total; (*заверша́ющий*) final, concluding

☞ **и т. п.** (*abbr. of* **и тому́ подо́бное**) etc., et cetera, and so on

иудаи́зм, а *m.* Judaism

иуде́|**й, я** *m.* (liter.) Jew

иуде́й|**ка, ки** *f. of* ▸ иуде́й

иуде́йский *adj.* (hist., relig.) Judaic

их¹ *a. and g. of* ▸ они́

их² *poss. pron.* (*при существи́тельном*) their; (*без существи́тельного*) theirs; **их маши́на ме́ньше, чем на́ша** their car is smaller than ours

иша́к, а́ *m.* donkey, ass; (fig., infml) dogsbody (BrE), gofer

ишь *int.* (infml, *выража́ет удивле́ние, отвраще́ние, возраже́ние*) look!; just look!; well I never!; **и. ты!** fancy that!

ище́йк|**а, и** *f.* bloodhound

и́щущий *pres. part. act. of* ▸ иска́ть *and adj.*: **и. взгляд** searching look

☞ **ию́л**|**ь, я** *m.* July

ию́льский *adj. of* ▸ ию́ль

☞ **ию́н**|**ь, я** *m.* June

ию́ньский *adj. of* ▸ ию́нь

И

Й

К

Йй

Йе́мен, а *m.* Yemen

йе́мен|**ец, ца** *m.* Yemeni

йе́мен|**ка, ки** *f. of* ▸ йе́менец

йе́менский *adj.* Yemeni

йо́г|**а, и** *f.* yoga

йо́гурт, а *m.* yog(h)urt

йод, а *m.* iodine

Кк

☞ **к, ко** *prep. + d.* **1** (*при обозначе́нии ме́ста*) to, towards; **мы подъезжа́ли к Москве́** we were nearing Moscow; **прислони́те ле́стницу к стене́** place the ladder against the wall; (fig.): **лицо́м к лицу́** face to face; **к лу́чшему** for the better; **к (не)сча́стью** (un)fortunately; **к тому́ же** besides, moreover **2** (*при обозначе́нии преде́льного сро́ка*) to, towards; by; **зима́ подходи́ла к концу́** winter was drawing to a close; **к пе́рвому января́** by the first of January; **к тому́ вре́мени** by then, by that time; **к сро́ку** on time **3** (*при указа́нии назначе́ния*) for; **к чему́?** what for?;

э́то ни к чему́ it is no use

-ка *particle* (infml) **1** (*modifying force of imper.*): **скажи́-ка мне** come on now, tell me; **дай-ка мне посмотре́ть** come on, let me take a look; **ну́-ка** well; **ну́-ка, спо́йте что-н.!** come on, give us a song! **2** (*with 1st pers. sg. of fut.*) (*выража́ет неуве́ренное реше́ние*): **напишу́-ка ей письмо́** I think I'll write to her; **куплю́-ка тот га́лстук** maybe I'll buy that tie

каба́к, а́ *m.* tavern; (infml, fig.) noisy place

кабал|**а́, ы́** *f.* servitude, bondage

каба́н, а́ *m.* (wild) boar

кабаре́ *nt. indecl.* cabaret

кабачо́к, ка́ *m.* (*расте́ние*) (vegetable) marrow (BrE), squash (AmE)

☞ **key word**

ка́бел|**ь, я** *m.* cable; **о́птико-волоко́нный к.** (*or* волоко́нно-опти́ческий к.) fibre-optic cable (BrE), fiber-optic cable (AmE)

ка́бель|**ный** *adj. of* ▶ ка́бель; ~**ное телеви́дение** cable television

каби́н|**а, ы** *f.* (*в самолёте, для пассажиров*) cabin; (*в самолёте, для лётчика*) cockpit; (*грузовика*) cab; (*в туале́те*) cubicle; (*телефонная; для голосования*) booth; (*для купальщиков*) bathing hut; (*лифта*) cage

✐ **кабине́т**[1], **а** *m.* **1** (*в доме*) study; (*на работе*) office; (*врача*) surgery (BrE), office (AmE) **2** (*комплект ме́бели*) suite

✐ **кабине́т**[2], **а** *m.* (*also* **к. мини́стров**, *often* **К.**) (pol.) cabinet

каблу́к, á *m.* heel (*of footwear*)

кабриоле́т, а *m.* cabriolet

Кабу́л, а *m.* Kabul

кавале́р[1], **а** *m.* **1** (*в танце*) partner; (*мужчина*) (gentle)man **2** (infml, *поклонник*) admirer, suitor

кавале́р[2], **а** *m.*: **к.** (**о́рдена**) knight, holder (of an order)

кавалери́ст, а *m.* cavalryman

кавале́ри|**я, и** *f.* cavalry

ка́вер-ве́рси|**я, и** *f.* cover version (*of a song*)

Кавка́з, а *m.* the Caucasus

кавка́з|**ец, ца** *m.* Caucasian

кавка́з|**ка, ки** *f. of* ▶ кавка́зец

кавка́зский *adj.* Caucasian

кавы́чки *f. pl.* (*sg.* ~**ка**, ~**ки**) inverted commas, quotation marks; **в** ~**ках** in inverted commas, in quotes; (fig., iron.) so-called

каде́т, а *m.* cadet

ка́дк|**а, и** *f.* tub, vat

✐ **кадр, а** *m.* (cin.) (*снимок*) frame; (*эпизод*) shot; **го́лос за** ~**ом** voice-over

кадри́л|**ь, и** *f.* quadrille (*dance*)

ка́дровый *adj.* **1** (mil., *офице́р*) regular **2** (*рабочий*) skilled; best

ка́др|**ы, ов** *pl.* (*collect.*) **1** (mil.) (regular, peacetime) establishment **2** (*работники*) personnel; **отде́л** ~**ов** HR department **3** (pol.) cadres

кады́к, á *m.* (infml) Adam's apple

каждодне́вный *adj.* daily

✐ **ка́ждый** *adj.* **1** every, each; **к. день** every day; **к. из них получи́л по пять фу́нтов** they received five pounds each **2** (*as n.*) everyone

ка́жущийся *adj.* apparent

каза́к, á, *pl.* ~**й** *m.* Cossack

каза́рм|**а, ы** *f.* barracks

✐ **ка**|**за́ться, жу́сь,** ~**жешься** *impf.* (*of* ▶ показа́ться 1) **1** to seem, appear; **она́** ~**жется ста́рше свои́х лет** she looks older than she is (*impers.*): **мне** *и т. п.* ~**жется,** ~**за́лось** it seems, seemed (to me, *etc.*); apparently; **мне** ~**жется, что он был прав** I think he was right; **вы,** ~**жется, из Москвы́?** you are from Moscow, I believe?; ~**за́лось бы** it would seem, one would think

каза́х, а *m.* Kazakh

каза́хский *adj.* Kazakh

Казахста́н, а *m.* Kazakhstan

каза́честв|**о, а** *nt.* (collect.) the Cossacks

каза́чий *adj.* Cossack

каза́ч|**ка, ки** *f. of* ▶ каза́к

каза́ш|**ка, ки** *f. of* ▶ каза́х

каземáт, а *m.* casemate; (*камера*) (prison) cell (*for one person*)

казённ|**ый** *adj.* **1** (*государственный*) state, public; ~**ое иму́щество** state property; **на к. счёт** at public cost **2** (fig., *бюрократи́ческий*) bureaucratic, formal; **к. язы́к** language of officialdom, official jargon

казино́ *nt. indecl.* casino

казн|**á, ы́** (*no pl.*) *f.* (*государственное иму́щество*) Exchequer, Treasury

казначе́|**й, я** *m.* **1** (*кассир*) treasurer, bursar (BrE) **2** (mil.) paymaster; (naut.) purser

казначе́йств|**о, а** *nt.* Treasury, Exchequer

казн|**и́ть, ю́, и́шь** *impf. and pf.* to execute, put to death

казнокра́дств|**о, а** *nt.* embezzlement of public funds

казн|**ь, и** *f.* execution, capital punishment; **сме́ртная к.** death penalty

Каи́р, а *m.* Cairo

ка|**йма́, йми́,** *pl.* ~**йми́,** ~**ём,** ~**йма́м** *f.* edging, border

кайма́н, а *m.* (zool.) cayman

кайф, а *m.* (infml) kicks, 'high'; turn-on; buzz; **быть под** ~**ом** to be high *or* spaced out

✐ **как**[1] *adv. and particle* **1** how; **к. вам нра́вится Москва́?** how do you like Moscow?; **к. (ва́ши) дела́?** how are you getting on?; **забы́л, к. э́то де́лается** I have forgotten how to do this; **к. вам не сты́дно!** you ought to be ashamed!; **к. его́ фами́лия?, к. его́ зову́т?** what is his name?, what is he called?; **к. называ́ется э́тот цвето́к?** what is this flower called?; **к. вы ду́маете?** what do you think?; (*выража́ет удивле́ние, неудово́льствие*): **к.! ты опя́ть здесь?** what! are you here again?; **к. же так?** how is that?; (infml): **к. сказа́ть** it all depends; **кому́ к.** it depends on the person **2** (infml, *о внеза́пном де́йствии*): **она́ к. закричи́т!** she suddenly cried out **3**: **к. ни, к. … ни** however; **к. ни стара́йтесь** however hard you may try, try as you may

✐ **как**[2] *conj.* **1** (*выража́ет сравне́ние*) as; like; **бе́лый к. снег** white as snow; **бу́дьте к. до́ма** make yourself at home; **к. мо́жно, к. нельзя́** as … as possible; **к. мо́жно скоре́е** as soon as possible **2**: **к. …, так и** both … and; **к. ма́льчики, так и де́вочки** both the boys and the girls **3** (*что*) (following vv. *of perceiving, not translated*): **я ви́дел, к. она́ ушла́** I saw her go out **4** (*когда*) when; (*с тех пор, как*) since; **прошло́ два го́да, к. мы встре́тились** it is two years since we met; **к. то́лько** as soon as, when **5** (+ *neg.*) but, except, than; **что ему́ остава́лось де́лать, к. не созна́ться** what could he do but confess?; **кому́, к. не мне знать э́то!** if anyone knows, I do! **6**: **в то вре́мя к.;**

К

до того́ к.; ме́жду тем к.; тогда́ к. *see* ▶ **вре́мя**

какаду́ *m. indecl.* (zool.) cockatoo

кака́о *nt. indecl.* cocoa

ка́к|ать, аю *impf.* (baby talk) to (do a) poo

как бу́дто, бы **1** *conj.* as if, as though; **к. б. вы не зна́ете!** as if you didn't know! **2** *particle* (infml, *кажется*) it would seem

как бы **1** (+ *inf.*) how; **к. б. э́то сде́лать?** how is it to be done, I wonder **2**: **к. б. ни** however; **к. б. то ни́ было** however that may be, be that as it may **3** as if, as though **4**: **к. б. не** (*выража́ет опасе́ние*) what if, supposing; (*following v.*) that, lest; **к. б. он не опозда́л!** what if he is late!

ка́к-либо *adv.* somehow

ка́к-нибудь *adv.* **1** (*так или ина́че*) somehow (or other) **2** (infml, *когда́-нибудь*) some time; **загляни́те к.-н.** look in some time

как-ника́к *adv.* (infml) nevertheless, for all that

како́в, ~а́, ~о́, ~ы́ *pron.* (*interrog., and in exclamations expr. strong feeling*) what; of what sort; **к. результа́т?** what is the result?; **к. он?** what is he like?; **к. он собо́й?** what does he look like?; **а пого́да-то ~а́!** what (*splendid, filthy*) weather!

◆ **как|о́й** *pron.* **1** (*interrog. and rel.; and in exclamations*) what; **~о́е сего́дня число́?** what is today's date?; **~и́м о́бразом?** how? **2**: (*тако́й*) **к.** such as; **гнев, ~о́го он никогда́ не испы́тывал** anger such as he had never felt **3**: **к. ни** whatever, whichever

◆ **како́й-либо** *pron.* = **како́й-нибудь**

◆ **како́й-нибудь** *pron.* some; any

◆ **как|о́й-то** *pron.* **1** (*неизве́стно како́й*) some, a **2** (*напомина́ющий*) a kind of; **э́то ~а́я-то боле́знь** it is a kind of disease

как раз *adv.* just, exactly; **к. р. то, что мне ну́жно** just what I need; (*as pred.*) **э́ти ту́фли мне к. р.** these shoes are just right

◆ **ка́к-то** *adv.* **1** somehow; **он к.-то ухитри́лся сде́лать э́то** he managed to do it somehow **2** (infml): **к.-то (раз)** once

ка́ктус, а *m.* (bot.) cactus

кал, а *m.* faeces, excrement

каламбу́р, а *m.* pun

каланч|а́, и́, *g. pl.* **~е́й** *f.* watchtower; **пожа́рная к.** fire observation tower; (infml, pej., *о челове́ке*) beanpole

калейдоско́п, а *m.* kaleidoscope

кале́к|а, и *c.g.* disabled person (*who has difficulty walking*)

календа́р|ь, я́ *m.* calendar

кале́ч|ить, у, ишь *impf.* to maim, mutilate; (fig.) to twist, pervert; to ruin

кали́бр, а *m.* **1** calibre (BrE), caliber (AmE) **2** (tech.) gauge

ка́ли|й, я *m.* (chem.) potassium

кали́н|а, ы (*no pl.*) *f.* (bot.) guelder rose, viburnum

кали́тк|а, и *f.* (wicket) gate

кали́ф, а *m.* caliph; **к. на час** (iron.) king for a day

Калифо́рни|я, и *f.* California

ка́лл|а, ы *f.* (bot.) arum lily (BrE), calla lily (AmE)

каллигра́фи|я, и *f.* calligraphy

калмы́к, а *m.* Kalmyk

калмы́цкий *adj.* Kalmyk

калмы́ч|ка, ки *f. of* ▶ **калмы́к**

калори́йност|ь, и *f.* **1** (*пи́щи*) calorie content **2** (phys.) calorific value

калори́|йный, ~ен, ~йна *adj.* high-calorie; fattening

кало́ри|я, и *f.* calorie

ка́л|ька, ьки, *g. pl.* **~ек** *f.* **1** (*бума́га*) tracing paper **2** (*ко́пия*) (tracing paper) copy **3** (ling.) loan translation, calque

калькуля́тор, а *m.* calculator

Калькутт|а, ы *f.* Calcutta, Kolkata

кальма́р, а *m.* (zool.) squid

кальсо́н|ы, ~ (*no sg.*) long johns

ка́льци|й, я *m.* (chem.) calcium

кальн|а́н, а *m.* hookah, shisha

ка́мбал|а, ы *f.* plaice; flounder

Камбо́дж|а, и *f.* Cambodia

камбоджи́|ец, йца *m.* Cambodian

камбоджи́й|ка, ки *f. of* ▶ **камбоджи́ец**

камбоджи́йский *adj.* Cambodian

каме́ли|я, и *f.* (bot.) camellia

камене́|ть, ю *impf.* (*of* ▶ **окамене́ть**) (*станови́ться твёрдым*) to become petrified, turn to stone; (fig., *о се́рдце*) to harden; (*от стра́ха*) to be petrified

камени́ст|ый, ~, ~а *adj.* stony

ка́менн|ый, ~ **1** stone-; stony; **к. век** the Stone Age; **~ая кла́дка** stonework **2** (fig.) stony; **~ое се́рдце** stony heart

каменоло́мн|я, ни, *g. pl.* **~ен** *f.* quarry

ка́менщик, а *m.* bricklayer

◆ **ка́м|ень, ня,** *pl.* **~ни, ~не́й** *m.* stone; (*зубно́й*) tartar; **драгоце́нный к.** precious stone, gem

◆ **ка́мер|а, ы** *f.* **1** chamber (*in var. senses*); (*в тюрьме́*) cell; **моро́зильная к.** freezer compartment (*of refrigerator*); **к. хране́ния** (*багажа́*) left-luggage office (BrE), baggage room (AmE) **2** (*фо́то*) camera; (*ви́део*) camcorder **3** (*ши́ны*) inner tube; (*мяча́*) bladder

ка́мерн|ый *adj.* (mus.): **~ая му́зыка** chamber music

камерто́н, а *m.* tuning fork

каме́|я, и *f.* cameo

камика́дзе *m. indecl.* kamikaze pilot

ками́н, а *m.* fireplace

камнепа́д, а *m.* rockfall

камо́рк|а, и *f.* (infml) closet, tiny room; box room

кампа́ни|я, и *f.* campaign

камуфля́ж, а (*no pl.*) *m.* camouflage

Камча́тк|а, и *f.* Kamchatka

камы́ш, а́ *m.* reed, rush (*also collect.*)

◆ key word

кана́в|а, ы *f.* ditch; **сто́чная к.** gutter

Кана́д|а, ы *f.* Canada

кана́д|ец, ца, *g. pl.* **~цев** *m.* Canadian

кана́д|ка, ки *f. of* ▶ **кана́дец**

кана́дский *adj.* Canadian

☞ **кана́л, а** *m.* **1** (*искусственное русло*) canal; (*морской*) channel; **2** (fig., *путь*) channel; **дипломати́ческие ~ы** diplomatic channels **3** (anat.) duct, canal **4** (*телевизионный*) channel

канализа|цио́нный *adj. of* ▶ **канализа́ция**; **~цио́нная труба́** sewer (pipe)

канализа́ци|я, и *f.* sewerage system

канаре́йк|а, и *f.* canary

Кана́рск|ие острова́, ~их острово́в (*no sg.*) Canary Islands

кана́т, а *m.* rope; cable

кандал|ы́, о́в (*no sg.*) shackles, fetters; **ручны́е к.** manacles; **закова́ть в к.** to put into irons

☞ **кандида́т, а** *m.* candidate; **~ нау́к** (*учёная степень*) Doctor

кандидату́р|а, ы *f.* candidature; **вы́ставить чью-н. ~у** to nominate sb for election; (*кандидат*) candidate

кани́кул|ы, ~ (*no sg.*) (*школьные*) holidays (BrE), vacation (AmE); (*университетские*) vacation

кани́стр|а, ы *f.* jerrycan

канифо́л|ь, и *f.* rosin

ка́нн|а, ы *f.* (bot.) canna (lily)

канниба́л, а *m.* cannibal

каннибали́зм, а *m.* cannibalism

кано́н, а *m.* canon

канона́д|а, ы *f.* cannonade

канониза́ци|я, и *f.* (eccl.) canonization

канонизи́р|овать, ую *impf. and pf.* (eccl., also fig.) to canonize

кано́э *nt. indecl.* canoe

кану́н, а *m.* eve; **к. Но́вого го́да** New Year's Eve; **к. Рождества́** Christmas Eve

канцеля́ри|я, и *f.* clerical office

канцеля́р|ский *adj. of* ▶ **канцеля́рия**; **~ские принадле́жности/това́ры** stationery, office supplies

канцероге́нный *adj.* carcinogenic

ка́нцлер, а *m.* chancellor

каньо́н, а *m.* (geog.) canyon

ка́п|ать, аю *impf.* (*of* ▶ **нака́пать**) **1** (*no pf., 3rd pers. only*) (*падать каплями*) to drip, drop; to trickle; to dribble; to fall (in drops); **слёзы ~али у неё из глаз** teardrops were falling from her eyes **2** (*наливать каплями*) to pour out (*in drops*); **к. лека́рство в рю́мку** (+ *i.*) (*проливать*) to spill; **ты ~аешь водо́й на ска́терть** you are spilling water on the cloth

капе́лл|а, ы *f.* **1** (*хор*) choir **2** (*часовня*) chapel

капелла́н, а *m.* chaplain

ка́пельниц|а, ы *f.* (med.) drip

ка́перс|ы, ов *m. pl.* (cul.) capers

☞ **капита́л, а** *m.* (fin.) capital; (fig.): **полити́ческий к.** political capital

капитали́зм, а *m.* capitalism

капитали́ст, а *m.* capitalist

капиталисти́ческий *adj.* capitalist

капиталовложе́ни|е, я *nt.* capital investment

капита́льный *adj.* (fin.) capital; (*основной*) main, fundamental; (*самый важный*) most important; **к. ремо́нт** major repairs, refurbishment

капита́н, а *m.* captain

капитуля́ци|я, и *f.* capitulation

капка́н, а *m.* trap; **попа́сться в к.** to fall into a trap (also fig.)

ка́п|ля, ли, *g. pl.* **~ель** *f.* **1** drop; **похо́жи как две ~ли воды́** as like as two peas; (fig.): **к. в мо́ре** a drop in the ocean (BrE), bucket (AmE) **2** (*in pl.*) (med.) drops **3** (fig., infml) drop, bit; **в нём (нет) ни ~ли благоразу́мия** he hasn't a drop of sense

ка́п|нуть, ну, нешь *pf.* to drop, let fall a drop

капо́т, а *m.* (*машины*) bonnet (BrE), hood (AmE)

капри́з, а *m.* caprice, whim; **к. судьбы́** twist of fate

капри́знича|ть, ю *impf.* to behave capriciously; (*о ребёнке*) to play up

капри́з|ный, ~ен, ~на *adj.* capricious

капро́н, а *m.* kapron (*synthetic fibre, similar to nylon*)

ка́псул|а, ы *f.* capsule

капу́ст|а, ы *f.* cabbage; **брюссе́льская к.** Brussels sprouts; **цветна́я к.** cauliflower

капу́стный *adj. of* ▶ **капу́ста**

капюшо́н, а *m.* hood

ка́р|а, ы *f.* (rhet.) punishment, retribution

караби́н, а *m.* (*винтовка*) carbine

кара́бка|ться, юсь *impf.* (*of* ▶ **вскара́бкаться**) to clamber

карава́|й, я *m.* cottage loaf

карава́н, а *m.* **1** (*верблюдов*) caravan **2** (*судов*) convoy

карака́тиц|а, ы *f.* (zool.) cuttlefish

кара́кул|ь, я (*no pl.*) *m.* Persian lamb; astrakhan

кара́кул|я, и, *g. pl.* **~ей** *and* **~ь** *f.* scrawl, scribble

караме́л|ь, и (*no pl.*) *f.* **1** (collect.) (*конфеты*) caramels **2** (*жжёный сахар*) caramel

каранда́ш, á *m.* pencil

каранти́н, а *m.* quarantine

карао́ке *nt. indecl.* karaoke

кара́т, а *m.* carat

карате́ *nt. indecl.* karate

кара́тельный *adj.* punitive; **к. отря́д** death squad

кара́|ть, ю *impf.* (*of* ▶ **покара́ть**) to punish

карау́л, а *m.* guard; watch; **нести́ к.** to be on guard duty; **смени́ть к.** to relieve the guard

карау́л|ить, ю, ишь *impf.* to guard

карбюра́тор, а *m.* (tech., chem.) carburettor (BrE), carburetor (AmE)

К

кардина́л, а *m.* (eccl.) cardinal

кардина́л|ьный, ~ен, ~ьна *adj.* cardinal; fundamental

кардиогра́мм|а, ы *f.* cardiogram

кардио́лог, а *m.* cardiologist

кардиоло́ги|я, и *f.* cardiology

кардиохиру́рг, а *m.* heart surgeon

каре́т|а, ы *f.* carriage, coach

кари́бский *adj.* Caribbean

Кари́бск|ое мо́ре, ~ого мо́ря *nt.* the Caribbean Sea; the Caribbean

ка́риес, а *m.* (med.) caries

ка́рий *adj.* (*глаза*) brown, hazel

карикату́р|а, ы *f.* caricature, cartoon; (fig.) caricature

карка́с, а *m.* (tech.) frame; (fig.) framework

ка́рк|ать, аю *impf.* to caw

ка́рк|нуть, ну, нешь *pf.* to give a caw

ка́рлик, а *m.* dwarf (offens.), abnormally small person

ка́рликовый *adj.* dwarf

ка́рли|ца, цы *f. of* ▶ **ка́рлик**

карма́н, а *m.* pocket; (fig., infml): **э́то мне не по ~у** I can't afford it

карма́нник, а *m.* pickpocket

карма́н|ный *adj. of* ▶ **карма́н**; **к. вор** pickpocket; **~ные де́ньги** pocket money

карнава́л, а *m.* carnival

карни́з, а *m.* (archit., mountaineering) cornice

карп, а *m.* carp (*fish*)

ка́рри *nt. indecl.* curry

◆ **ка́рт|а, ы** *f.* **1** (geog.) map **2** (*игра́льная*) (playing) card; **игра́ть в ~ы** to play cards; **поста́вить на ~у** to stake, risk **3** (*бланк*) form **4** = **ка́рточка 1; магни́тная к.** swipe card

карт-бла́нш *m. indecl.* carte blanche

◆ **карти́н|а, ы** *f.* **1** picture **2** (theatr.) scene

◆ **карти́нк|а, ы** *f.* (small) picture

карти́н|ный, ~ен, ~на *adj.* **1** *adj. of* ▶ **карти́на**; **~ная галере́я** art gallery, picture gallery **2** (*жест, поза*) theatrical, mannered

карто́граф, а *m.* cartographer

картогра́фи|я, и *f.* cartography

карто́н, а *m.* card, cardboard

картоте́к|а, и *f.* card index

картофели́н|а, ы *f.* (infml) potato

карто́фель, я (*no pl.*) *m.* **1** (collect.) potatoes; **жа́реный к.** fried potatoes; **молодо́й к.** new potatoes **2** (*расте́ние*) potato plant

карто́фель|ный *adj. of* ▶ **карто́фель**; **~ное пюре́** mashed potatoes

ка́рточк|а, и *f.* **1** card; **визи́тная к.** visiting card, business card; **креди́тная к.** credit card **2** (*проездно́й биле́т*) season ticket

ка́рточ|ный *adj.* **1** *adj. of* ▶ **ка́рта**; **к. долг** gambling debt; (infml): **к. до́мик** house of cards (also fig.); **к. фо́кус** card trick **2** *adj. of* ▶ **ка́рточка**; **~ная систе́ма** rationing system

карто́шк|а, и *f.* (infml) **1** (collect.) (*карто́фель*) potatoes **2** (*карто́фелина*) potato

ка́ртридж, а *m.* cartridge

карусе́л|ь, и *f.* merry-go-round, carousel

ка́рцер, а *m.* isolation cell

карье́р¹, а *m.* (*гало́п*) career, full gallop; (fig.): **с ме́ста в к.** straight away, without more ado

карье́р², а *m.* (*каменоло́мня*) quarry; (*песо́чный*) sandpit; **у́гольный к.** open-cast mine

карье́р|а, ы *f.* career; **сде́лать ~у** to make good, get on

карьери́ст, а *m.* careerist

каса́ни|е, я *nt.* contact

каса́тельно *prep. + g.* touching, concerning

◆ **каса́|ться, юсь** *impf.* (*of* ▶ **косну́ться**) **1** (+ g.) to touch **2** (+ g.) (fig., *вопро́са, те́мы*) to touch (on, upon) **3** (+ g.) (fig., *име́ть отноше́ние*) to concern, relate (to); **э́то тебя́ не ~ется** it is no concern of yours; **что ~ется** as to, as regards, with regard to

ка́ск|а, и *f.* helmet

каска́д, а *m.* cascade

каскадёр, а *m.* stunt man

Каспи́йск|ое мо́ре, ~ого мо́ря *nt.* the Caspian Sea

ка́сс|а, ы *f.* **1** (*я́щик*) cash box; (*аппара́т в магази́не*) till, cash register; (*ме́сто в магази́не*) cash desk **2** (*де́ньги*) cash **3** (*железнодоро́жная*) booking office; (*театра́льная*) box office; **сберега́тельная к.** savings bank

касса|цио́нный *adj.*: **~цио́нная жа́лоба** appeal; **к. суд** Court of Appeal

кассе́т|а, ы *f.* cassette

кассе́тный *adj. of* ▶ **кассе́та**; **к. магнитофо́н** cassette recorder

касси́р, а *m.* cashier

ка́сс|овый *adj.* **1** *adj. of* ▶ **ка́сса**; **~овая кни́га** cash book **2**: **к. спекта́кль, фильм** a box office success

касте́т, а *m.* knuckleduster

кастри́р|овать, ую *impf. and pf.* to castrate

кастрю́л|я, и *f.* saucepan

◆ **катало́г, а** *m.* catalogue (BrE), catalog (AmE)

катамара́н, а *m.* catamaran

ката́ни|е, я *nt.* **1** (*мяча́*) rolling **2**: **к. в экипа́же** driving; **к. верхо́м** riding; **к. на ло́дке** boating; **к. на конька́х** skating; **к. на ро́ликах** roller skating

катапу́льт|а, ы *f.* catapult

катапульти́р|оваться, уюсь *impf. and pf.* (*о лётчике*) to eject

Ка́тар, а *m.* Qatar

ката́р, а *m.* (med.) catarrh

катара́кт|а, ы *f.* (med.) cataract

катастро́ф|а, ы *f.* catastrophe, disaster; (*ава́рия*) accident

катастрофи́ческий *adj.* catastrophic

К

ката́|ть, а́ю *impf.* (*indet. of* ▶ **кати́ть**) **1** (*мяч*) to roll; (*велосипед, та́чку*) to wheel, trundle **2** (*челове́ка*) to drive, take for a drive; (*на санка́х*) to take for a ride **3** (*pf.* **с~**) (*из гли́ны, те́ста*) to roll

ката́|ться, а́юсь *impf.* (*indet. of* ▶ **кати́ться**) **1** (*о мяче́*) to roll; **к. с горы́** to slide down a hill **2** (*на маши́не*) to go for a drive; **к. верхо́м** to ride, go riding; **к. на велосипе́де** to cycle, go cycling; **к. на конька́х** to skate, go skating; **к. на ло́дке** to go boating

катафа́лк, а *m.* hearse

категори́чески *adv.* categorically; **к. отказа́ться** to flatly refuse

✧ **катего́ри|я, и** *f.* category

ка́тер, а, *pl.* **~á** *m.* (naut.) boat; **сторожево́й к.** patrol boat

кате́тер, а *m.* (med.) catheter

ка|ти́ть, чу́, ~тишь *impf.* (*of* ▶ **покати́ть** 1) **1** *det. of* ▶ **ката́ть 2** (infml, *бы́стро е́хать*) to bowl along, tear

ка|ти́ться, чу́сь, ~тишься *impf.* (*of* ▶ **покати́ться** 1) **1** *det. of* ▶ **ката́ться**; **к. под го́ру** (fig.) to go downhill **2** (*течь*) to flow, stream; (fig.) to roll; **слёзы ~ти́лись по её щека́м** tears were rolling down her cheeks **3** (infml): **~ти́сь; ~ти́сь отсю́да!** get out!; clear off!

кат|о́к¹, ка́ *m.* (*ледяна́я площа́дка*) skating rink

кат|о́к², ка́ *m.* (*маши́на*) roller

като́лик, а *m.* (Roman) Catholic

католици́зм, а *m.* (Roman) Catholicism

католи́ческий *adj.* (Roman) Catholic

католи́чество, а *nt.* (Roman) Catholicism

католи́чк|а, и *f. of* ▶ **като́лик**

ка́торг|а, и (*no pl.*) *f.* penal servitude, hard labour (BrE), labor (AmE)

ка́торжник, а *m.* convict

кату́шк|а, и *f.* **1** reel, spool **2** (elec.) coil

каучу́к, а *m.* (India) rubber, caoutchouc

каучу́ковый *adj. of* ▶ **каучу́к**; rubber

кафе́ *nt. indecl.* cafe; **к.-моро́женое** ice-cream parlour (BrE), parlor (AmE)

✧ **ка́федр|а, ы** *f.* **1** (*в це́ркви*) pulpit; (*для ора́тора*) rostrum, platform **2** (*профе́ссорство*) chair; **получи́ть ~у** to obtain a chair **3** (*в университе́те*) department

кафедра́льный *adj.*: **к. собо́р** cathedral

ка́фел|ь, я *m.* (collect.) Dutch tiles

ка́фель|ный *adj. of* ▶ **ка́фель**; **~ная печь** tiled stove; **~ная пли́тка** Dutch tile

кафете́ри|й, я *m.* cafeteria

кача́|ть, а́ю *impf.* (*of* ▶ **качну́ть**) **1** (+ *a.*) (*ребёнка, колыбе́ль*) to rock; (+ *i.*) (*голово́й, ного́й*) to shake; (*impers.*) **ло́дку ~ает** the boat is rolling **2** (*подбра́сывать вверх*) (infml) to lift up, chair (*as mark of esteem or congratulation*) **3** (*pf.* **накача́ть**) (*насо́сом*) to pump **4** (*pf.* **накача́ть**) (infml): **к. му́скулы** to do bodybuilding exercises; to work out; to pump iron

кача́|ться, а́юсь *impf.* (*of* ▶ **качну́ться**) **1** to rock, swing; (*о ло́дке*) to roll, pitch **2** (*при ходьбе́*) to reel, stagger **3** (*pf.* ▶ **накача́ться**) (infml) to practise bodybuilding; to work out; to pump iron

каче́л|и, ей (*no sg.*) swing (*child's*); (*доска-каче́ли*) see-saw

✧ **ка́чествен|ный, ~, ~на** *adj.* **1** (*разли́чие, измене́ние*) qualitative **2** (*това́р*) quality

✧ **ка́честв|о, а** *nt.* **1** quality; **ни́зкого ~а** poor quality; low-grade; **в ~е** (+ *g.*) in the capacity (of); **в ~е исключе́ния** as a special concession

кач|ну́ть, ну́, нёшь *pf. of* ▶ **кача́ть**

кач|ну́ться, ну́сь, нёшься *pf. of* ▶ **кача́ться**

ка|чу́, ~тишь *see* ▶ **кати́ть**

ка́ш|а, и *f.* **1** kasha (*dish of cooked grain or groats*); porridge; **ма́нная к.** semolina; **ри́совая к.** boiled rice **2** (fig., infml) (*ме́сиво*) jumble; (*пу́таница*) muddle; **расхлёбывать ~у** to put things right

кашало́т, а *m.* (zool.) sperm whale

ка́ш|ель, ля *m.* cough

ка́шлян|уть, у, ешь *pf.* to give a cough

ка́шля|ть, ю *impf.* **1** to cough **2** (*как боле́знь*) to have a cough

кашне́ *nt. indecl.* scarf, muffler

кашпо́ *nt. indecl.* decorative flowerpot holder

кашта́н, а *m.* **1** (*оре́х*) chestnut **2** (*де́рево*) chestnut tree; **ко́нский к.** horse chestnut

кашта́новый *adj.* **1** *adj. of* ▶ **кашта́н 2** (*цвет*) chestnut(-coloured)

каю́т|а, ы *f.* cabin

кая́к, а *m.* kayak

ка|я́ться, юсь, ешься *impf.* (*of* ▶ **пока́яться**) (в + *p.*) **1** (*сожале́ть*) to repent (of); **он сам тепе́рь ~ется** he is sorry himself now **2** (*призна́ться*) to confess

КБ (*abbr. of* **констру́кторское бюро́**) construction office

✧ **кв.** (*abbr. of* **кварти́ра**) flat (BrE), apartment (AmE)

квадра́т, а *m.* (math.) square; **возвести́ в к.** to square; **в ~е** squared

квадра́тный *adj.* square; **к. ко́рень** square root; **к. метр** square metre (BrE), meter (AmE)

ква́ка|ть, ю *impf.* to croak

ква́кн|уть, у, ешь *pf.* to give a croak

квалифика́ци|я, и *f.* qualification; (*профе́ссия*) profession

квалифици́рова|нный, ~н, ~на *p.p.p. of* ▶ **квалифици́ровать** *and* (**~н, ~нна**) *adj.* **1** (*рабо́тник*) qualified, skilled **2** (*труд*) skilled

квалифици́р|овать, ую *impf. and pf.* **1** (*специали́ста, спортсме́на*) to rank, test **2** (*оцени́ть*) to categorize; **как к. тако́е поведе́ние?** how should one describe such conduct?

квант, а *m.* (phys.) quantum

ква́нт|овый *adj. of* ▶ **квант**; (phys.): **~овая меха́ника** quantum theory; **~овая тео́рия** quantum theory

К

К

кварта́л, а *m.* **1** (*домов*) block **2** (*часть города*) quarter; **кита́йский к.** Chinatown **3** (*года*) quarter

кварте́т, а *m.* (mus.) quartet

кварти́р|а, ы *f.* **1** flat (BrE), apartment (AmE) **2** (*снимаемое жильё*) lodgings; **жить на ~е** to live in lodgings

квартира́нт, а *m.* lodger, tenant

квартира́нт|ка, ки *f. of* ▶ квартира́нт

кварти́р|ный *adj. of* ▶ кварти́ра; **~ная пла́та** rent

квартпла́т|а, ы *f.* (*abbr. of* кварти́рная пла́та) rent

кварц, а *m.* (min.) quartz

ква́рцевый *adj. of* ▶ кварц

квас, а, *pl.* ~ы́ *m.* kvass (*drink made from fermented rye bread*)

кве́рху *adv.* up, upwards

квита́нци|я, и *f.* receipt; **бага́жная к.** luggage ticket (BrE), baggage check (AmE)

кво́т|а, ы *f.* quota

кВт (*abbr. of* килова́тт) kW, kilowatt(s)

кг (*abbr of* килогра́мм) k, kg, kilo(s), kilogram(s)

КГБ *m. indecl.* (*abbr. of* Комите́т госуда́рственной безопа́сности*) (hist.) KGB, State Security Committee

ке́гл|и, ей *f. pl.* (*sg* ~я, ~и) **1** skittles, ninepins; **спорти́вные к.** bowls **2** (*in sg.*) skittle; pin

кедр, а *m.* cedar; **сиби́рский к.** Siberian pine

ке́дровый *adj. of* ▶ кедр

ке́д|ы, ов *or* ~ *m. pl.* (*sg.* кед, а) trainers (BrE), sneakers (AmE)

кекс, а *m.* fruit cake

кельт, а *m.* Celt

ке́льтский *adj.* Celtic

кем *i. of* ▶ кто

Ке́мбридж, а *m.* Cambridge

ке́мпинг, а *m.* campsite

кенгуру́ *m. indecl.* kangaroo

кени́|ец, йца *m.* Kenyan

кени́йк|а, и *f.* Kenyan

кени́йский *adj.* Kenyan

Ке́ни|я, и *f.* Kenya

ке́пк|а, и *f.* cloth cap

кера́мик|а, и *f.* ceramics

керами́ческий *adj.* ceramic

кероси́н, а *m.* paraffin (BrE), kerosene (AmE)

ке́тчуп, а *m.* ketchup

кефа́л|ь, и *f.* grey mullet

кефи́р, а *m.* kefir (*thin yoghurt drink*)

киберата́к|а, и *f.* (comput.) cyberattack

киберне́тик|а, и *f.* cybernetics

киберпреступле́ни|е, я *nt.* (comput.) cybercrime (*single offence*)

киберпресту́пност|ь, и *f.* (comput.) cybercrime (*collect.*)

кив|а́ть, а́ю *impf.* (*of* ▶ кивну́ть): **к. (голово́й)** to nod (one's head); (*в знак согла́сия*) to nod assent

ки́ви *m. & nt. indecl.* **1** *m.* (zool.) kiwi **2** *m. & nt.* kiwi fruit

кив|ну́ть, ну́, нёшь *pf. of* ▶ кива́ть

киво́к, ка́ *m.* nod

ки|да́ть, да́ю *impf.* (*of* ▶ ки́нуть) **1** to throw, fling, cast (*usage as for броса́ть*); **куда́ ни кинь** whichever way you turn **2** (sl., *обма́нывать*) to cheat, con

ки|да́ться, да́юсь *impf.* (*of* ▶ ки́нуться) **1** to throw oneself, fling oneself; (*устреми́ться куда-н.*) to rush **2** (+ *i.*) to throw, fling **3** *pass. of* ▶ кида́ть

Ки́ев, а *m.* Kiev

киевля́н|ин, ина, *pl.* ~е, ~ *m.* Kievan

киевля́н|ка, ки *f. of* ▶ киевля́нин

ки́|й, я́, *pl.* ~й, ~ёв *m.* (sport) cue

ки́ллер, а *m.* contract killer, hit man

килоба́йт, а *m.* (comput.) kilobyte

килова́тт, а, *g. pl.* ~ *m.* (elec.) kilowatt

килогра́мм, а *m.* kilogram

киломе́тр, а *m.* kilometre (BrE), kilometer (AmE)

кил|ь, я *m.* (naut.) keel

ки́льк|а, и *f.* sprat

кимоно́ *nt. indecl.* kimono

кинемато́граф, а *m.* cinematography

кинематографи́ст, а *m.* cinematographer, film-maker

кинематогра́фи|я, и *f.* cinematography

кинжа́л, а *m.* dagger

кино́ *nt. indecl.* **1** (*как иску́сство*) the cinema **2** (infml, *зда́ние*) cinema (BrE), movie theater (AmE) **3** (infml, *фильм*) film, movie

кино... *comb. form* cinema, film

киноактёр, а *m.* film actor (BrE), movie actor (AmE)

киноактри́с|а, ы *f.* film actress (BrE), movie actress (AmE)

кинозáл, а *m.* **1** (*зда́ние*) cinema (BrE), movie theater (AmE) **2** (*зал*) auditorium

кинозвезд|а́, ы́, *pl.* ~ы, ~, ~ам *f.* film star (BrE), movie star (AmE)

кинозри́тел|ь, я *m.* filmgoer, moviegoer

кинока́мер|а, ы *f.* cine camera (BrE), movie camera

кинокоме́ди|я, и *f.* comedy film, movie

кинокри́тик, а *m.* film critic

кинооперáтор, а *m.* cameraman

киноплёнк|а, и *f.* cine film (BrE), movie film (AmE)

кинорежиссёр, а *m.* film director

киносеа́нс, а *m.* (cinema) performance, showing

киносту́ди|я, и *f.* film studio (BrE), movie studio (AmE)

киносцена́ри|й, я *m.* screenplay

киносъёмк|а, и *f.* filming, shooting

кинотеа́тр, а *m.* cinema (BrE), movie theater (AmE)

кинофи́льм, а *m.* film, movie

✧ key word

кинохро́ник|а, и *f.* newsreel

ки́|нуть, ну, нешь *pf. of* ▶ **кида́ть**

ки́|нуться, нусь, нешься *pf. of* ▶ **кида́ться**

кио́ск, а *m.* kiosk, stall; **газе́тный к.** news stand

ки́п|а, ы *f.* pile, stack

кипари́с, а *m.* (bot.) cypress

кипе́ни|е, я *nt.* boiling; **то́чка ~я** boiling point

кип|е́ть, лю́, и́шь *impf.* to boil, seethe; **рабо́та ~е́ла** work was in full swing

Кипр, а *m.* Cyprus

киприо́т, а *m.* Cypriot

киприо́т|ка, ки *f. of* ▶ **киприо́т**

ки́прский *adj.* Cypriot

кипяти́льник, а *m.* kettle, boiler

кипя|ти́ть, чу́, ти́шь *impf.* (*of* ▶ **вскипяти́ть**) to boil

кипят|о́к, ка́ *m.* boiling water

кипячёный *adj.* boiled

кирги́з, а *m.* Kyrgyz

Кирги́зи|я, и *f.* Kyrgyzstan

кирги́з|ка, ки *f. of* ▶ **кирги́з**

кирги́зский *adj.* Kyrgyz

кири́ллиц|а, ы *f.* Cyrillic alphabet

кирилли́ческий *adj.* Cyrillic

кирк|а́, и́ *f.* pick(axe)

кирпи́ч, а́ *m.* **1** brick **2** (*collect.*) bricks **3** (infml, *дорожный знак*) no-entry sign

кисе́л|ь, я́ *m.* kissel (*a kind of blancmange*)

кислоро́д, а *m.* oxygen

ки́сло-сла́д|кий, ~ок, ~ка *adj.* sweet-and-sour

кислот|а́, ы́, *pl.* **~ы** *f.* **1** sourness; acidity **2** (chem.) acid

кисло́тный *adj.* (chem.) acid; **к. дождь** acid rain

ки́с|лый, ~ел, ~ла́, ~ло *adj.* **1** (*яблоко*) sour; (fig.): **~лое настрое́ние** sour mood **2** (*закисший*) sour, fermented; **~лая капу́ста** sauerkraut **3** (chem.) acid

кист|ь¹, и, *pl.* **~и, ~ей** *f.* **1** (bot.) cluster, bunch; **к. виногра́да** bunch of grapes **2** (*для рисования*) brush; **маля́рная к.** paintbrush **3** (*на скатерти*) tassel

кист|ь², и, *pl.* **~и, ~ей** *f.* hand

кит, а́ *m.* whale

кита́|ец, йца, *pl.* **~йцы, ~йцев** *m.* Chinese

Кита́|й, я *m.* China

кита́йск|ий *adj.* Chinese; **~ая гра́мота** double Dutch

китая́нк|а, и *f. of* ▶ **кита́ец**

китч, а *m.* kitsch

киш|е́ть, и́т *impf.* (+ *i.*) to swarm (with), teem (with)

кише́чник, а *m.* (anat.) bowels, intestines

киш|ка́, ки́, *g. pl.* **~о́к** *f.* (anat.) gut, intestine

клавеси́н, а *m.* (mus.) harpsichord

клавиату́р|а, ы *f.* keyboard

кла́виш|а, и *f.* key (*of piano, computer, etc.*)

кла́вишны|е, х *m. pl.* keyboard(s) (*musical instrument*)

клад, а *m.* treasure; (fig., infml) treasure

кла́дбищ|е, а *nt.* cemetery, graveyard; (*при церкви*) churchyard

кладова́|я, о́й *f.* (*для провизии*) pantry, larder; (*для товаров*) storeroom

кла|ду́, дёшь *see* ▶ **класть**

клад|ь, и *f.* (*sg. only*) load; **ручна́я к.** hand luggage (BrE), baggage (AmE)

клан, а *m.* clan

кла́ня|ться, юсь *impf.* (*of* ▶ **поклони́ться**) **1** (+ *d.* or *с* + *i.*) to bow (to); (*приветствовать*) to greet **2** (*передавать привет*) to send, convey greetings; **~йтесь ему́ от меня́** give him my regards **3** (+ *d.* or *пе́ред* + *i.*) (infml, *униженно просить*) to cringe (before); to humiliate oneself (before)

кла́пан, а *m.* valve

кларне́т, а *m.* clarinet

кларнети́ст, а *m.* clarinettist

кларнети́ст|ка, ки *f. of* ▶ **кларнети́ст**

⚥ **класс, а** *m.* **1** class **2** (*комната*) classroom

кла́ссик|а, и *f.* the classics

классифика́ци|я, и *f.* classification

классифици́р|овать, ую *impf. and pf.* to classify

классици́зм, а *m.* classicism

⚥ **класси́ческий** *adj.* (*музыка, образование, язык*) classical; (*работа, пример, одежда*) classic

кла́сс|ный *adj.* (*of* ▶ **класс**) **1**: **~ная рабо́та** class work **2** (infml, *отличный*) excellent, great

кла́ссов|ый *adj.* (pol.) class; **~ая борьба́** class struggle

кла|сть, ду́, дёшь, *past* **~л, ~ла** *impf.* **1** (*pf.* **положи́ть**) (*помещать*) to lay; to put; to place **2** (*pf.* **сложи́ть**) (*строить*) to build

клаустрофо́би|я, и *f.* claustrophobia

клёв, а *m.* biting, bite; **сего́дня хоро́ший к.** the fish are biting well today

кл|ева́ть, юю, юёшь *impf.* (*of* ▶ **клю́нуть**) **1** (*о птице*) to peck **2** (*о рыбе*) to bite

кле́вер, а *m.* (bot.) clover

клевет|а́, ы́ *f.* slander; (*в печати*) libel

клеве|та́ть, щу́, ~щешь *impf.* (*of* ▶ **оклевета́ть** (*кого*), ▶ **наклевета́ть** (*на кого* + *d.*)) to slander, malign; (*в печати*) to libel; **он оклевета́л меня́/он наклевета́л на меня́** he slandered me; **он клевета́л нача́льнику на всех сотру́дников в тече́ние двух лет** he made slanderous remarks/complained to the boss about all the staff over a period of two years; **он наклевета́л мне на вас** he made slanderous remarks/complained to me about you

клеве|щу́, ~щешь *see* ▶ **клевета́ть**

клёвый *adj.* (sl.) brill, knockout, fantastic

клеёнк|а, и *f.* oilcloth

кле́|ить, ю, ишь *impf.* (*of* ▶ **скле́ить**) to glue; to gum; to paste

кле|**й, я, о ~е, в ~е/~ю, на ~ю** *m.* glue

кле́йк|**ий** *adj.* sticky; **~ая ле́нта** adhesive tape

клейм|**о́, а́,** *pl.* **~а** *nt.* brand, stamp

кле́йстер, а *m.* paste

клён, а *m.* maple

клено́вый *adj. of* ▶ **клён**

⚬ **кле́тк**|**а, и** *f.* **1** cage; (*для кур*) coop; (*для кроликов*) hutch **2** (*на бумаге*) square; (*на ткани*) check **3** (anat.): **грудна́я к.** thorax **4** (biol.) cell

кле́тчатый *adj.* checked; **к. плато́к** checked headscarf

клёш, а *m. and indecl. adj.* flare; **брю́ки к.** flared trousers

клещ, а́ *m.* (zool.) tick

кле́щ|**и, е́й** (*no sg.*) pincers, pliers, tongs

⚬ **клие́нт, а** *m.* client

клие́нт|**ка, ки** *f. of* ▶ **клие́нт**

клиенту́р|**а, ы** *f.* (*collect.*) clientele

кли́зм|**а, ы** *f.* (med.) enema

кли́макс, а *m.* menopause

кли́мат, а *m.* climate

климати́ческий *adj.* climatic

клин, а, *pl.* **~ья, ~ьев** *m.* wedge

кли́ник|**а, и** *f.* clinic

клини́ческий *adj.* clinical

клин|**о́к, ка́** *m.* blade

клип, а *m.* video clip

клипс|**ы, ~** *f. pl.* (*sg.* **~а, ~ы**) clip-on earrings; clip-ons

клич, а *m.* (rhet.) call; **боево́й к.** war cry

кли́чк|**а, и** *f.* **1** (*животного*) name **2** (*человека*) nickname

клише́ *nt. indecl.* (typ., *also fig.*) cliché

клозе́т, а *m.* (infml) water closet, W.C.

клок, а́, *pl.* **кло́чья, кло́чьев** *and* **~й, ~о́в** *m.* rag, shred; **разорва́ть в кло́чья** to tear to shreds

клоко|**та́ть, чу́, ~чешь** *impf.* to bubble; to gurgle; (*кипеть*) to boil up (*also fig.*)

клон, а *m.* (biol., etc.) clone

клони́р|**овать, ую** *impf. and pf.* (biol., etc.) to clone

клон|**и́ть, ю́, ~ишь** *impf.* **1** to bend; to incline; (*impers.*) **старика́ уже́ ~и́ло ко сну́** the old man was already nodding off **2** (fig., infml) to lead (*conversation*); **куда́ ты ~ишь?** what are you driving at?

клон|**и́ться, ю́сь, ~ишься** *impf.* **1** to bow, bend **2** (**к** + *d.*) (fig.) to be nearing; to be leading up (to)

клоп, а́ *m.* bedbug

кло́ун, а *m.* clown

⚬ **клуб**[1], **а** *m.* **1** (*общество*) club **2** (*здание*) clubhouse

клуб[2], **а,** *pl.* **~ы́, ~о́в** *m.* (*дыма*) puff; **~ы́ пы́ли** clouds of dust

клуб|**и́ться, и́тся** *impf.* to swirl; to curl, wreathe

⚬ *key word*

клубни́к|**а, и** *f.* (cultivated) strawberry

клуб|**о́к, ка́** *m.* **1** ball; **сверну́ться ~ко́м, в к.** to roll oneself up into a ball **2** (fig., *запутанное сцепление чего-н.*) tangle, mass; **к. противоре́чий** a mass of contradictions

клу́мб|**а, ы** *f.* (flower) bed

клык, а́ *m.* **1** (*у человека*) canine (tooth) **2** (*у животного*) fang; (*бивень*) tusk

клюв, а *m.* beak; bill

клю́кв|**а, ы** *f.* cranberry

клю́н|**уть, у, ешь** *pf. of* ▶ **клева́ть**

⚬ **ключ**[1], **а́** *m.* **1** key; **запере́ть на к.** to lock; **га́ечный к.** spanner, wrench

⚬ **ключ**[2], **а́** *m.* (*источник*) spring; source; **бить ~о́м** to spout, jet; (fig.) to be in full swing

⚬ **ключ**|**ево́й** *adj. of* ▶ **ключ**[1]; **~евы́е о́трасли промы́шленности** key industries

ключи́ц|**а, ы** *f.* (anat.) collarbone

клю́шк|**а, и** *f.* (*гольф*) (golf) club; (*хоккей*) (hockey) stick

кл|**ю́ю, юёшь** *see* ▶ **клева́ть**

кля́кс|**а, ы** *f.* blot, smudge

кля́нч|**ить, у, ишь** *impf.* (infml) (**у** + *g.*) to pester, nag (*sb for*); **к. де́ньги у кого́-н.** to pester sb for money

кляп, а *m.* gag; **засу́нуть к. в рот** (+ *d.*) to gag

кля|**сться, ну́сь, нёшься,** *past* **~лся, ~ла́сь** *impf.* (*of* ▶ **покля́сться**) (**в** + *p. or* + *inf. or* + **что**) to swear, vow; **к. отомсти́ть** to vow vengeance; **к. че́стью** to swear on one's honour (BrE), honor (AmE)

кля́тв|**а, ы** *f.* oath, vow; **дать ~у** to take an oath

кля́уз|**а, ы** *f.* (infml) petty slander, malicious gossip

⚬ **км** (*abbr. of* **киломе́тр**) km, kilometre(s) (BrE), kilometer(s) (AmE)

КНДР *f. indecl.* (*abbr. of* **Коре́йская Наро́дно-Демократи́ческая Респу́блика**) Democratic People's Republic of Korea

⚬ **кни́г**|**а, и** *f.* book

книгоизда́тел|**ь, я** *m.* publisher

книготорго́в|**ец, ца** *m.* bookseller

книготорго́вл|**я, и** *f.* book trade

кни́жк|**а, и** *f.* **1** *dim. of* ▶ **кни́га**; **записна́я к.** notebook **2** (*документ*) book, card; **че́ковая к.** chequebook (BrE), checkbook (AmE)

кни́жн|**ый** *adj.* **1** *adj. of* ▶ **кни́га**; **~ая по́лка** bookshelf; **к. шкаф** bookcase **2** (*отвлечённый*) bookish; **к. червь** bookworm

кни́зу *adv.* downwards

⚬ **кно́пк**|**а, и** *f.* **1** (*гвоздик*) drawing pin (BrE), thumbtack (AmE); **прикрепи́ть ~ой** to pin **2** (*застёжка*) press stud, popper (BrE), snap (AmE) **3** (elec.) button; knob

КНР *f. indecl.* (*abbr. of* **Кита́йская Наро́дная Респу́блика**) PRC (People's Republic of China)

кнут, а́ *m.* whip

княги́н|**я, и** *f.* princess (*wife of prince*)

княз|**ь, я,** *pl.* **~ья́, ~е́й** *m.* prince; **вели́кий к.** grand duke

ко see ▸ **к**

коали́ци|я, и *f.* (pol.) coalition

ко́бр|а, ы *f.* cobra

кобур|а́, ы́ *f.* holster

кобы́л|а, ы *f.* (*лошадь*) mare

ко́ваный *adj.* **1** forged; hammered **2** (fig.) terse

кова́р|ный, ∼ен, ∼на *adj.* crafty; treacherous

кова́ть, кую, куёшь *impf.* **1** (*pf.* вы∼) to forge (also fig.); (*железо*) to hammer **2** (*pf.* под∼) to shoe (*horses*)

ковбо́|й, я *m.* cowboy

ков|ёр, ра́ *m.* carpet; (*маленький*) rug; mat

ко́врик, а *m.* rug; mat; **к. для мы́ши** mouse mat (BrE), mouse pad (AmE)

ковче́г, а *m.* ark; **Но́ев к.** Noah's ark

ковш, а́ *m.* **1** scoop, ladle **2** (tech.) bucket

ковыля́|ть, ю *impf.* (infml) to hobble

ковыр|ну́ть, ну́, нёшь *pf. of* ▸ **ковыря́ть**

ковыр|я́ть, я́ю *impf.* (*of* ▸ **ковырну́ть**) to dig into; (в + *p.*) to pick (at); **к. в зуба́х/носу́** to pick one's teeth/nose

когда́[1] *adv.* **1** interrog. and rel. when **2** : **к. (бы) ни** whenever; **к. бы вы ни пришли́** whenever you come **3** (infml): **к. ..., к.** sometimes ..., sometimes; **я занима́юсь к. у́тром, к. ве́чером** sometimes I work in the morning, sometimes in the evening **4** (infml): **к. как** it depends

  когда́[2] *conj.* when; while; as; **я встре́тил её, к. шёл домо́й** I met her as I was going home

когда́-либо *adv.* = когда́-нибудь

когда́-нибудь *adv.* **1** (*в бу́дущем*) some time, some day **2** (*в вопро́сах*) ever; **вы бы́ли к.-н. в Кита́е?** have you ever been to China?

когда́-то *adv.* once; some time; formerly

кого́ *a. and g. of* ▸ **кто**

ко́г|оть, тя, *pl.* ∼ти, ∼те́й *m.* claw

  код, а *m.* code

  ко́декс, а *m.* (law, also fig.) code; **гражда́нский к.** civil code; **уголо́вный к.** criminal code

ко́дов|ый *adj. of* ▸ **код**; **∼ое назва́ние** code name

ко́е-где́ *adv.* here and there, in places

ко́е-ка́к *adv.* **1** (*пло́хо, небре́жно*) anyhow **2** (*с трудо́м*) somehow (or other), just; **мы доплы́ли до того́ бе́рега** somehow we managed to swim to the other side

ко́е-како́й, ко́е-како́го *pron.* some

ко́е-кто́, ко́е-кого́ *pron.* somebody; some people

ко́е-что́, ко́е-чего́ *pron.* something; (*немно́го*) a little

  ко́ж|а, и *f.* **1** (*у челове́ка и живо́тных*) skin; (*у кру́пных живо́тных*) hide **2** (*материа́л*) leather

ко́жаный *adj.* leather

кожур|а́, ы́ *f.* rind, peel, skin

коз|а́, ы́, *pl.* ∼ы *f.* **1** (*вид*) goat **2** (*са́мка козла́*) nanny goat

коз|ёл, ла́ *m.* (*живо́тное*) billy goat

Козеро́г, а *m.* (*созве́здие*) Capricorn; **тро́пик ∼а** (geog.) Tropic of Capricorn

ко́з|ий *adj. of* ▸ **коза́**; **∼ье молоко́** goat's milk

козл|ёнок, ёнка, *pl.* ∼я́та, ∼я́т *m.* kid

козл|и́ный *adj. of* ▸ **козёл**; **∼и́ная боро́дка** goatee

козл|я́та, я́т *see* ▸ **козлёнок**

козыр|ёк, ька́ *m.* (cap) peak; **взять под к.** (+ *d.*) to salute

ко́зыр|ь, я, *pl.* ∼и, ∼е́й *m.* (cards, also fig.) trump

ко́йк|а, и *f.* **1** (*на судне*) berth, bunk **2** (*в больни́це*) bed

койо́т, а *m.* coyote

кока́ин, а *m.* cocaine

кока́рд|а, ы *f.* cockade

ко́кер-спание́л|ь, я *m.* cocker spaniel

коке́тк|а, и *f.* coquette, flirt

коке́тлив|ый, ∼, ∼а *adj.* coquettish, flirtatious

коклю́ш, а *m.* whooping cough

ко́кон, а *m.* cocoon

коко́с, а *m.* **1** (*де́рево*) coconut palm **2** (*плод*) coconut

кокте́йл|ь, я *m.* cocktail; (*встре́ча*) cocktail party; **моло́чный к.** milk shake

кол, а *m.* **1** (*pl.* ∼ья, ∼ьев) stake, picket **2** (*pl.* ∼ы́, ∼о́в) (infml, *ни́зшая шко́льная отме́тка*) a 'very poor' (*mark*)

ко́лб|а, ы *f.* (chem.) flask

колбас|а́, ы́, *pl.* ∼ы *f.* sausage

колго́т|ки, ок (*no sg.*) tights

колд|ова́ть, у́ю *impf.* to practise witchcraft

колдовств|о́, а́ *nt.* witchcraft, sorcery, magic

колду́н, а́ *m.* sorcerer, magician, wizard

колду́нь|я, и, *g. pl.* ∼ий *f.* witch, sorceress

колеба́ни|е, я *nt.* **1** (phys.) oscillation, vibration; **к. ма́ятника** swing of the pendulum **2** (*измене́ние*) fluctuation, variation **3** (fig., *сомне́ние*) hesitation, wavering, vacillation

колеб|а́ть, ∼лю, ∼лешь *impf.* (*of* ▸ **поколеба́ть**) to shake

колеб|а́ться, ∼люсь, ∼лешься *impf.* (*of* ▸ **поколеба́ться** 1) **1** to shake to and fro, sway; (phys.) to oscillate **2** (*изменя́ться*) to fluctuate, vary **3** (fig., *не реша́ться*) to hesitate; to waver, vacillate

коле́н|о, а *nt.* **1** (*pl.* ∼и, ∼ей, ∼ям) knee; **стать на ∼и (пе́ред)** to kneel (to); **по к., по ∼и** knee-deep, up to one's knees **2** (*pl. only:* ∼и, ∼ей, ∼ям) lap; **сиде́ть у кого́-н. на ∼ях** to sit on sb's lap **3** (*pl.* ∼ья, ∼ьев) (tech.) knee, joint

колесни́ц|а, ы *f.* chariot

  колес|о́, а́, *pl.* ∼а *nt.* wheel; **запасно́е к.** spare wheel; **рулево́е к.** driving wheel

коле|я́, и́ *f.* **1** rut; (fig.): **войти́ в ∼ю́** to settle down (again); **вы́битый из ∼й** unsettled **2** (rail.) track; gauge

коли́бри *f. and m. indecl.* (zool.) hummingbird

коли́т, а *m.* (med.) colitis

коли́чественн|ый *adj.* quantitative; ~ое **числи́тельное** cardinal number; ~ое **смягче́ние** (econ.) quantitative easing

✓ **коли́честв|о**, а *nt.* quantity, amount; number

коллаборациони́ст, а *m.* (pol., pej.) collaborator

колла́ж, а *m.* collage

колла́пс, а *m.* collapse

✓ **колле́г|а**, а *c.g.* colleague

колле́ги|я, и *f.* board; **к. адвока́тов** the Bar; **к. вы́борщиков** electoral college

ко́лледж, а *m.* college

✓ **коллекти́в**, а *m.* collective, team; (*in many phrr. does not require separate translation*) **нау́чный к.** (the) scientists

коллекти́в|ный, ~ен, ~на *adj.* collective; joint; ~ное владе́ние joint ownership

коллекционе́р, а *m.* collector

коллекциони́р|овать, ую *impf.* to collect

✓ **колле́кци|я**, и *f.* collection

ко́лли *f. indecl.* collie (*dog*)

коло́д|а¹, ы *f.* block, log

коло́д|а², ы *f.* (*карт*) pack (*of cards*)

коло́д|ец, ца *m.* **1** well **2** (tech.) shaft

ко́локол, а, *pl.* ~а́, ~о́в *m.* bell

колоко́ль|ня, ьни, *g. pl.* ~ен *f.* bell tower

колоко́льчик, а *m.* **1** small bell **2** (bot.) campanula

колониа́льный *adj.* colonial

колониза́ци|я, и *f.* colonization

колонизи́р|овать, ую *impf. and pf.* to colonize

коло́ни|я, и *f.* colony; settlement

коло́нк|а, и *f.* **1** *dim. of* ▶ **коло́нна** **2** (*для нагре́ва воды*) geyser (BrE), water heater **3** (*на у́лице*) standpipe; water pump **4**: **бензи́новая к.** petrol pump (BrE), gas pump (AmE) **5** (*столбец*) column (*in a table, in a newspaper*) **6** (infml, *громкоговори́тель*) (loud)speaker

коло́нн|а, ы *f.* column; (mil.): **та́нковая к.** tank column

колори́т, а *m.* colouring, colour (BrE); coloring, color (AmE); (fig.): **ме́стный к.** local colour (BrE), color (AmE)

колори́т|ный, ~ен, ~на *adj.* colourful (BrE), colorful (AmE); colour (*also fig.*)

ко́лос, а, *pl.* ~ья, ~ьев *m.* (agric.) ear, spike

коло́сс, а *m.* colossus

колосса́л|ьный, ~ен, ~ьна *adj.* colossal; (infml) terrific, great

коло́|ти́ть, чу́, ~ти́шь *impf.* (*of* ▶ **поколоти́ть**) **1** (*impf. only*) (**по** + *d. or* **в** + *a.*) to strike (on); to batter (on), pound (on); **к. в дверь** to bang on the door **2** (infml, *бить*) to thrash, beat

коло́|ть¹, ~ю, ~ешь *impf.* (*of* ▶ **расколо́ть** 1) to break, chop, split; **к. дрова́** to chop wood; **к. оре́хи** to crack nuts

✓ **key word**

кол|о́ть², ю́, ~ешь *impf.* **1** (*pf.* у~) (*була́вкой*) to prick **2** (*pf.* за~) (*рани́ть, убива́ть чем-нибудь о́стрым*) to stab; (*impers.*) **у меня́ ~ет в боку́** I've got a stitch in my side **3** (*pf.* за~) (*живо́тных*) to slaughter

коло́|ться¹, ю́сь, ~ешься *impf., pass. of* ▶ **коло́ть¹**

коло́|ться², ю́сь, ~ешься *impf.* **1** (*причиня́ть уко́л*) to be prickly **2** (*pf.* у~ 2) (infml, *о наркома́не*) to inject oneself; to be on drugs

колпа́к, а́ *m.* **1** cap **2** (*ла́мпы*) lampshade; (tech.) cowl

колумби́|ец, йца *m.* Colombian

колумби́й|ка, ки *f. of* ▶ **колумби́ец**

колумби́йский *adj.* Colombian

Колу́мби|я, и *f.* Colombia

колу́н, а́ *m.* chopper, hatchet

колхо́з, а *m.* (*abbr. of* **коллекти́вное хозя́йство**) collective farm

колхо́зник, а *m.* member of collective farm

колхо́зн|ица, ицы *f. of* ▶ **колхо́зник**

колыбе́л|ь, и *f.* cradle; (fig.): **с ~и** from the cradle

колыбе́ль|ный *adj. of* ▶ **колыбе́ль**; ~ная (**пе́сня**) lullaby

колы́|ха́ться, ~шется *impf.* (*of* ▶ **колыхну́ться**) (*о ве́тках*) to sway; (*о мо́ре*) to heave; (*о фла́гах*) to flutter

колых|ну́ться, ну́сь, нёшься *pf. of* ▶ **колыха́ться**

колье́ *nt. indecl.* necklace

кол|ьну́ть, ьну́, ьнёшь *inst. pf. of* ▶ **коло́ть²**

кольра́би *f. indecl.* (bot.) kohlrabi

кольцев|о́й *adj.* annular; circular; ~а́я **доро́га** ring road; ~а́я **развя́зка** roundabout

кол|ьцо́, ~ьца́, *pl.* ~ьца, ~е́ц, ~ьцам *nt.* ring; обруча́льное к. wedding ring

колю́ч|ий, ~, ~а *adj.* prickly; thorny; (fig.) sharp, biting; ~ая **про́волока** barbed wire

колю́чк|а, и *f.* (infml) prickle; thorn; (*у ежа́*) quill

коля́ск|а, и *f.* **1** (*экипа́ж*) carriage **2** (*де́тская*) к. pram (BrE), baby carriage (AmE); (*раскладна́я*) pushchair (BrE), stroller (AmE); **инвали́дная к.** wheelchair **3** (*у мотоци́кла*) sidecar

ком¹, а, *pl.* ~ья, ~ьев *m.* lump; ball; (fig.): **к. в го́рле** lump in the throat

ком² *p. of* ▶ **кто**

ком... *comb. form, abbr. of* **1** **коммунисти́ческий** **2** ▶ **команди́р**

ко́м|а, ы *f.* (med.) coma

✓ **кома́нд|а**, ы *f.* **1** (*прика́з*) command, order; **дать ~у** to give a command **2** (mil., *отря́д*) party, detachment, crew; (naut.) crew; **пожа́рная к.** fire brigade **3** (sport) team

команди́р, а *m.* (mil.) commander, commanding officer

командиро́вк|а, и *f.* business trip; **е́хать в ~у** to go on a business trip; **он в ~е** he is away on business

кома́нд|ный *adj.*: ~ная игра́ team game

кома́ндовани|е, я *nt.* **1** commanding, command; **приня́ть к. (над +** *i.*) to take command (of, over) **2** (*collect.*) command

кома́нд|овать, ую *impf.* (*pf.* ▶ **скома́ндовать**) **1** to give orders **2** (*no pf.*) (*+ i.*) (*быть команди́ром*) to command, be in command (of)

кома́ндующ|ий, его *m.* commander

кома́р, а́ *m.* mosquito

комба́йн, а *m.* (tech.) combine; **зерново́й к.** combine harvester; **ку́хонный к.** food processor

комбина́т, а *m.* industrial complex; plant

комбина́ци|я¹, и *f.* **1** combination **2** (fig.) scheme, system; (pol., sport) manoeuvre (BrE), maneuver (AmE)

комбина́ци|я², и *f.* (*же́нское бельё*) slip

комбинезо́н, а *m.* overalls; dungarees

комбини́р|овать, ую *impf.* (*of* ▶ **скомбини́ровать**) to combine, arrange

коме́ди|я, и *f.* **1** comedy **2** (fig.) farce; **лома́ть ~ю** to put on an act

коменда́нт, а *m.* **1** (mil.) commandant **2** (*обще́ственного зда́ния*) manager; warden; **к. общежи́тия** warden of a hostel

коменда́нтский *adj. of* ▶ **коменда́нт**; **к. час** (mil.) curfew

коме́т|а, ы *f.* comet

ко́мик, а *m.* **1** comic actor **2** (fig.) comedian

ко́микс, а *m.* (*кни́жка*) comic (book); (*се́рия рису́нков*) comic strip

комисса́р, а *m.* commissar, commissioner; **верхо́вный к.** high commissioner

комиссариа́т, а *m.* commissariat

комисс|ио́нный *adj.*: **к. магази́н** second-hand shop (*where goods are sold on commission*); (*as pl. n.* ~**ио́нные,** ~**ио́нных**) (comm.) commission

✍ **коми́сси|я, и** *f.* commission, committee

✍ **комите́т, а** *m.* committee

коми́ческий *adj.* **1** comic **2** (*смешно́й*) comical, funny

ко́мка|ть, ю *impf.* (*of* ▶ **ско́мкать**) to crumple

✍ **коммента́ри|й, я** *m.* **1** (*разъясни́тельные замеча́ния*) commentary **2** (*in pl.*) (*рассужде́ния*) comment; ~**и изли́шни** comment is superfluous; **без ~ев!** no comment!

коммента́тор, а *m.* commentator

коммент́и́р|овать, ую *impf. and pf.* to comment (upon)

коммерса́нт, а *m.* businessman

комме́рци|я, и *f.* commerce, trade

✍ **комме́рческий** *adj.* **1** commercial; **к. флот** merchant navy **2** (*негосуда́рственный*) private

коммивояжёр, а *m.* commercial traveller (BrE), travelling salesman (BrE), traveling salesman (AmE)

комму́н|а, ы *f.* commune

коммуна́лк|а, и *f.* (infml) 'communal' flat (BrE), apartment (AmE)

коммуна́льн|ый *adj.* **1** communal; municipal; ~**ая кварти́ра** 'communal' flat (*in which kitchen, bathroom, and toilet are shared by several tenants*); ~**ые услу́ги** public utilities **2** *adj. of* ▶ **комму́на**

коммуни́зм, а *m.* communism

коммуника́бельн|ый, ~**ен,** ~**ьна** *adj.* sociable, communicative

коммуника́ци|я, и *f.* communication; (mil.) line of communication

коммуни́ст, а *m.* communist

коммунисти́ческий *adj.* communist

коммуни́ст|ка, ки *f. of* ▶ **коммуни́ст**

коммута́тор, а *m.* **1** (elec.) commutator **2** (teleph.) switchboard

коммюнике́ *nt. indecl.* communiqué

✍ **ко́мнат|а, ы** *f.* room

ко́мнатн|ый *adj.* **1** *adj. of* ▶ **ко́мната** **2** (*дома́шний*) indoor; ~**ые расте́ния** house plants; ~**ая температу́ра** room temperature

компа́кт-ди́ск, а *m.* compact disc, CD; **прои́грыватель** (*m.*) ~**ов** compact disc *or* CD player

компа́ктн|ый, ~**ен,** ~**на** *adj.* compact; (fig.) concise

✍ **компа́ни|я, и** *f.* company; **соста́вить кому́-н.** ~**ю** to keep sb company; **за** ~**ю** for company

компаньо́н, а *m.* **1** (comm.) partner **2** (*това́рищ*) companion

компаньо́н|ка, ки *f.* **1** *f. of* ▶ **компаньо́н** **2** (lady's) companion; chaperone

компа́рти|я, и *f.* Communist Party

компенса́ци|я, и *f.* compensation

компенси́р|овать, ую *impf. and pf.* to compensate

компете́нт|ный, ~**ен,** ~**на** *adj.* competent; **к. исто́чник** reliable source

компете́нци|я, и *f.* (*о́бласть зна́ния*) competence; (*круг полномо́чий*) jurisdiction; **э́то не в мое́й** ~**и** it is beyond my scope

✍ **ко́мплекс, а** *m.* complex; (*набо́р*) set; **к. неполноце́нности** inferiority complex; **к. мероприя́тий** package of measures

✍ **ко́мплексный** *adj.* all-embracing, all-in; **к. обе́д** table d'hôte dinner

комплекс|ова́ть, у́ю *impf.* (infml) to suffer from complexes; to feel inadequate, insecure

✍ **компле́кт, а** *m.* set; kit; **к. белья́** bedding, bedclothes

компле́кци|я, и *f.* build

комплиме́нт, а *m.* compliment; **сде́лать к.** (*+ d.*) to pay a compliment (to)

компози́тор, а *m.* (mus.) composer

компози́ци|я, и *f.* composition

✍ **компоне́нт, а** *m.* component

компо́т, а *m.* compote, stewed fruit

компре́сс, а *m.* (med.) compress; **поста́вить к.** to apply a compress

компре́ссор, а *m.* (tech., med.) compressor

K

компрома́т, а *m.* (*abbr. of* **компромети́рующий материа́л**) compromising material

компромети́р|овать, **ую** *impf.* (*of* ▶ **скомпромети́ровать**) to compromise

компроми́сс, а *m.* compromise; **идти́ на к.** to make a compromise, meet halfway

✓ **компью́тер**, а *m.* computer; **портати́вный к.** laptop (computer); **со зна́нием ~а** computer literate

✓ **компью́тер|ный** *adj. of* ▶ **компью́тер**; **~ная игра́** computer game

компью́терщик, а *m.* (infml) computer specialist; computer buff

кому́ *d. of* ▶ **кто**

комфо́рт, а *m.* comfort

комфорта́бел|ьный, **~ен**, **~ьна** *adj.* comfortable

конве́йер, а *m.* (tech.) conveyor (*belt*); **сбо́рочный к.** assembly line

конве́рси|я, и *f.* (econ., fin.) conversion

конве́рт, а *m.* **1** (*для писем*) envelope **2** (*для грампласти́нки*) sleeve

конверти́р|овать, **ую** *impf. and pf.* (fin.) to convert

конверти́руемый *adj.* (fin.) convertible

конво́й, а *m.* escort

конво́|й, я *m.* escort

конву́льси|я, и *f.* (med.) convulsion

Ко́нго *nt. indecl.* Congo; **Демократи́ческая Респу́блика Ко́нго** Democratic Republic of the Congo (*formerly Zaire*)

конголе́з|ец, ца *m.* Congolese

конголе́з|ка, ки *f. of* ▶ **конголе́зец**

конголе́зский *adj.* Congolese

конгре́сс, а *m.* congress; (*в США*) Congress

конгрессме́н, а *m.* congressman

конденса́т, а *m.* condensation

конденса́ци|я, и *f.* condensation

конди́тер, а *m.* confectioner, pastry cook

конди́терск|ая, ой *f.* (*продаю́щая конфе́ты*) confectioner's, sweet shop (BrE), candy store (AmE); (*продаю́щая то́рты*) cake shop, pastry shop

кондиционе́р, а *m.* air conditioner

ко́ндор, а *m.* (zool.) condor

конду́ктор, а, *pl.* **~а́**, **~о́в** *m.* (*челове́к*) conductor (*of bus, tram*); (rail.) guard

кон|ёк, ька́ *m.* **1** *dim. of* ▶ **конь**; **морско́й к.** (zool.) sea horse **2** (fig., infml) hobby horse; hobby; **сесть на своего́ ~ька́** to mount one's hobby horse **3** *see* ▶ **конько́й**

✓ **кон|е́ц**, ца́ *m.* **1** end; **в ~це́ ~цо́в** in the end, after all; **положи́ть к.** (+ *d.*) to put an end to; **своди́ть ~цы́ с ~ца́ми** (infml) to make both ends meet **2** (infml, *расстоя́ние, путь*) distance, way; **в оди́н к.** one way; **в о́ба ~ца́** there and back, return; **биле́т в о́ба ~ца́** return ticket

✓ **коне́чно** *adv.* of course, certainly

коне́чност|ь, и *f.* (anat.) extremity

✓ **коне́ч|ный**, **~ен**, **~на** *adj.* **1** final, last; ultimate; **~ная ста́нция** terminus; **~ная цель** ultimate aim; **в ~ном ито́ге**, **счёте** ultimately, in the last analysis **2** (*име́ющий коне́ц*) finite

кони́н|а, ы (*no pl.*) *f.* horseflesh

✓ **конкре́т|ный**, **~ен**, **~на** *adj.* concrete; specific

конкуре́нт, а *m.* competitor; rival

конкуре́нт|ка, ки *f. of* ▶ **конкуре́нт**

конкурентоспосо́бност|ь, и *f.* competitiveness

конкурентоспосо́б|ный, **~ен**, **~на** *adj.* competitive

конкуре́нци|я, и *f.* competition; **вне ~и** unrivalled

конкури́р|овать, **ую** *impf.* (**с** + *i.*) to compete (with)

✓ **ко́нкурс**, а *m.* competition; contest

конкурса́нт, а *m.* competitor; contestant

конкурса́нт|ка, ки *f. of* ▶ **конкурса́нт**

ко́нкурсный *adj. of* ▶ **ко́нкурс**; **к.** экза́мен competitive examination

ко́нник, а *m.* cavalryman

ко́нниц|а, ы *f.* cavalry

ко́нный *adj. of* ▶ **конь**; horse; mounted; equestrian; **к.** спорт equestrianism

конопл|я́, и́ *f.* (bot.) hemp; (*нарко́тик*) cannabis

консерва́нт, а *m.* preservative

консервати́в|ный, **~ен**, **~на** *adj.* conservative

консервати́зм, а *m.* conservatism

консерва́тор, а *m.* (esp. pol.) conservative

консервато́ри|я, и *f.* conservatoire, music college

консерви́рован|ный, **~**, **~а** *p.p.p. of* ▶ **консерви́ровать** *and adj.*: **~ные фру́кты** bottled fruit, canned fruit

консерви́р|овать, **ую** *impf. and pf.* (*pf. also* **за~**) to preserve; to can; to bottle

консе́рв|ный *adj. of* ▶ **консе́рвы**; **~ная ба́нка** tin can; **к.** нож can opener

консе́рв|ы, ов (*no sg.*) canned food

консолида́ци|я, и *f.* consolidation

консо́л|ь, и *f.* (comput.) console

конспе́кт, а *m.* outline, summary

конспирати́в|ный, **~ен**, **~на** *adj.* secret, clandestine

конспира́тор, а *m.* conspirator

констати́р|овать, **ую** *impf. and pf.* to ascertain; to establish; **к.** смерть to certify death; **к.** факт to establish a fact

конституцио́нный *adj.* (pol.) constitutional

конститу́ци|я, и *f.* (pol., med.) constitution

констру́ир|овать, **ую** *impf. and pf.* (*pf. also* **с~**) (*стро́ить*) to construct; (*проекти́ровать*) to design

конструктиви́зм, а *m.* (art) constructivism

✓ key word

конструкти́в|ный, ~ен, ~на *adj.*
1 structural; construction **2** (*критика*) constructive

констру́ктор, а *m.* designer

констру́ктор|ский *adj. of* ▶ констру́ктор; ~ское бюро́ design office

⚶ **констру́кци|я**, и *f.* **1** (*состав*) construction; design **2** (*сооружение*) structure

ко́нсул, а *m.* consul

ко́нсульств|о, а *nt.* consulate

консульта́нт, а *m.* consultant, adviser; (*в вузе*) tutor

⚶ **консульта́ци|я**, и *f.* **1** consultation; specialist advice **2** (*учреждение*) advice bureau; же́нская к. antenatal (BrE), prenatal (AmE) clinic; gynaecological (BrE), gynecological (AmE) clinic; юриди́ческиая к. legal advice office

консульти́р|овать, ую *impf.* (*pf.* про~) to advise; (*в вузе*) to act as tutor (to)

консульти́р|оваться, уюсь *impf.* (*of* ▶ проконсульти́роваться) (с + *i.*) to consult

⚶ **конта́кт**, а *m.* contact; вступи́ть в к. с кем-н. to come into contact, get in touch with sb

конта́кт|ный, ~ен, ~на *adj.* **1** contact; к. телефо́н contact number; ~ные ли́нзы (med.) contact lenses **2** (infml, *о человеке*) sociable

конте́йнер, а *m.* container

конте́кст, а *m.* context

континге́нт, а *m.* contingent; batch; к. во́йск a military force; к. новобра́нцев batch, squad of recruits

контине́нт, а *m.* continent

континента́льный *adj.* continental

конто́р|а, ы *f.* office, bureau

контраба́нд|а, ы *f.* **1** (*действие*) contraband, smuggling; занима́ться ~ой to smuggle **2** (*товары*) contraband

контрабанди́ст, а *m.* smuggler

контрабанди́ст|ка, ки *f. of* ▶ контрабанди́ст

контраба́с, а *m.* (mus.) double bass

контрабаси́ст, а *m.* double bass player

контрабаси́ст|ка, ки *f. of* ▶ контрабаси́ст

⚶ **контра́кт**, а *m.* contract

контра́ктник, а *m.* (infml) contract worker

контра́льто *nt. indecl.* (mus.) (*голос*) contralto; (*f. indecl.*) (infml, *певица*) contralto

контра́ст, а *m.* contrast; по ~у (с + *i.*) by contrast (with)

контра́ст|ный, ~ен, ~на *adj.* contrasting

контрата́к|а, и *f.* (mil., sport) counter-attack

контрацепти́в, а *m.* contraceptive

контролёр, а *m.* inspector; (*билетов*) ticket collector

контроли́р|овать, ую *impf.* (*of* ▶ проконтроли́ровать) (*проверять*) to check; (*держать под своим контролем*) to control

⚶ **контро́л|ь**, я *m.* **1** control **2** (*проверка*) check(ing); inspection; (tech., mil.) monitoring; (mil.) verification

контро́льно-пропускно́й *adj.*: к. пункт checkpoint

контро́ль|ный *adj. of* ▶ контро́ль; ~ная рабо́та test

контрразве́дк|а, и *f.* counter-espionage; counter-intelligence

контрреволю́ци|я, и *f.* counter-revolution

конту́зи|я, и *f.* contusion, bruising; (*при разрыве снаряда*) shell shock

ко́нтур, а *m.* **1** contour **2** (elec.) circuit

конур|а́, ы́ *f.* kennel; (fig.) hovel, dump

ко́нус, а *m.* cone

конфедера́ци|я, и *f.* confederation

конферансье́ *m. indecl.* (theatr.) compère, master of ceremonies (*abbr.* MC)

конфере́нц-за́л, а *m.* conference hall

⚶ **конфере́нци|я**, и *f.* conference

конфе́сси|я, и *f.* confession, faith

конфе́т|а, ы *f.* sweet; шокола́дная к. chocolate

конфигура́ци|я, и *f.* configuration

конфиденциа́льность, и *f.* confidentiality

конфиденциа́ль|ный, ~ен, ~ьна *adj.* confidential

конфиска́ци|я, и *f.* confiscation, seizure

конфиск|ова́ть, у́ю *impf. and pf.* to confiscate

⚶ **конфли́кт**, а *m.* conflict

конфликт|ова́ть, у́ю *impf.* (с + *i.*) (infml) to clash (with), come up (against)

конфо́рк|а, и *f.* ring (*on cooker*)

конфронта́ци|я, и *f.* confrontation, showdown

конфу́з, а *m.* (infml) discomfiture, embarrassment

концентра́т, а *m.* concentrate

концентрацио́нный *adj.*: к. ла́герь concentration camp

концентра́ци|я, и *f.* concentration

концентри́рованный *p.p.p. of* ▶ концентри́ровать *and adj.* concentrated

концентри́р|овать, ую *impf.* (*of* ▶ сконцентри́ровать) to concentrate; (mil.) to mass

концентри́р|оваться, уюсь *impf.* (*of* ▶ сконцентри́роваться) **1** to mass, collect **2** (fig.) (на + *p.*) to concentrate

концептуа́ль|ный, ~ен, ~ьна *adj.* conceptual

⚶ **конце́пци|я**, и *f.* conception, idea

конце́рн, а *m.* (econ.) concern

⚶ **конце́рт**, а *m.* (mus.) **1** concert; recital; симфони́ческий к. symphony concert; быть на ~е to be at a concert **2** (*произведение*) concerto

конце́сси|я, и *f.* (econ.) concession

концла́гер|ь, я *m.* (*abbr. of* концентрацио́нный ла́герь) concentration camp

концо́вк|а, и *f.* ending

конч|а́ть, а́ю *impf. of* ▶ ко́нчить

К

конч|а́ться, а́юсь *impf. of* ▸ ко́нчиться

ко́нч|енный *p.p.p. of* ▸ ко́нчить; (*as int.*)
⁓ено! enough!; всё ⁓ено! it's all over!

ко́нчик, а *m.* tip; point; на ⁓е языка́ on the
tip of one's tongue

кончи́н|а, ы *f.* (rhet.) decease, demise

ко́нч|ить, у, ишь *pf.* (*of* ▸ конча́ть) **1** to
finish, end; на э́том он ⁓ил here he
stopped; к. шко́лу to finish/leave school;
к. университе́т to graduate; к. (жизнь)
самоуби́йством to commit suicide; пло́хо к.
to come to a bad end **2** (с + *i.*) to be finished
(with), give up **3** (+ *inf.*) to stop **4** (infml) to
come (= *have an orgasm*)

ко́нч|иться, усь, ишься *pf.* (*of* ▸ конча́ться)
(+ *i.*) to end (in), finish (by); to come to an
end; де́ло ⁓илось ниче́м it came to nothing

конъюнкту́р|а, ы *f.* **1** state of affairs,
juncture; междунаро́дная к. international
situation **2** (econ.) state of the market

конъюнкту́р|ный **1** *adj. of* ▸ конъюнкту́ра
2; ⁓ные це́ны (free) market prices **2** (pej.,
поведение, человек) ready to compromise;
opportunistic

кон|ь, я́, *pl.* ⁓и, ⁓е́й *m.* **1** horse **2** (*шахматы*)
knight

конь|ки́, ько́в *m. pl.* (*sg.* ⁓ёк, ⁓ка́) skates;
ро́ликовые к. roller skates; ката́ться на
⁓ка́х to skate

конькобе́ж|ец, ца *m.* skater

конькобе́жный *adj.* skating; к. спорт
skating

конья́к, á ý *m.* brandy

ко́нюх, а *m.* groom, stableman

коню́ш|ня, ни, *g. pl.* ⁓ен *f.* stable

кооперати́в, а *m.* **1** (*организация*)
cooperative society **2** (infml) (*магазин*)
cooperative store; (*квартира*) flat in
housing cooperative

кооперати́вный *adj.* cooperative

координа́т|а, ы *f.* (math.) coordinate; (*in pl.*)
(infml) contact details (*address, telephone
number, etc.*)

координа́ци|я, и *f.* coordination

коп|а́ть, а́ю *impf.* **1** (*pf.* вс⁓) to dig **2** (*pf.*
вы⁓) to dig up, dig out

копа́|ться, юсь *impf.* **1** (в + *p.*) (*в сундуке*)
to rummage (in); (*в песке*) to root around
(in); (fig.): к. в душе́ to be given to soul-
searching **2** (infml) (с + *i.*) (*канителиться*)
to dawdle (over) **3** *pass. of* ▸ копа́ть

копе́йк|а, и, *g. pl.* копе́ек *f.* kopek

Копенга́ген, а *m.* Copenhagen

ко́п|и, ей *f. pl.* (*sg.* ⁓ь, ⁓и) mines

копи́лк|а, и *f.* money box

копира́йт, а *m.* copyright

копи́р|овать, ую *impf.* (*of* ▸ скопи́ровать)
to copy; to imitate, mimic

коп|и́ть, лю́, ⁓ишь *impf.* (*of* ▸ накопи́ть) to
accumulate, amass; to store up; к. де́ньги to
save up; (fig.): к. си́лы to save one's strength

коп|и́ться, ⁓ится *impf.* (*of* ▸ накопи́ться)
to accumulate

ко́пи|я, и *f.* copy; печа́тная к. (comput.) hard
copy; резе́рвная к. (comput.) backup; снять
⁓ю (с + *g.*) to copy, make a copy (of)

коп|на́, ны́, *pl.* ⁓ны, ⁓ён, ⁓на́м *f.* shock,
stook (*of corn*); к. се́на haycock; к. воло́с
shock of hair

ко́пот|ь, и *f.* soot; lampblack

копош|и́ться, у́сь, и́шься *impf.* **1** (*о
насекомых*) to swarm **2** (fig., infml, *о мыслях*)
to stir, creep in **3** (infml, *возиться*) to potter
about

коп|ти́ть, чу́, ти́шь *impf. of* ▸ закопти́ть

копчёный *adj.* smoked

коп|чу́, ти́шь *see* ▸ копти́ть

копы́тн|ый *adj.* (zool.) hoofed, ungulate; (*as
pl. n.* ⁓ые, ⁓ых) ungulates

копы́т|о, а *nt.* hoof

копь *see* ▸ ко́пи

копь|ё, я́, *pl.* ⁓я, ⁓ий, ⁓ьям *nt.* spear,
lance

кор|а́, ы́ *f.* **1** (bot.) bark **2** (anat.): к. головно́го
мо́зга cerebral cortex **3** (*Земли*) crust;
земна́я к. the earth's crust

кораблекруше́ни|е, я *nt.* shipwreck;
потерпе́ть к. to be shipwrecked

кораблестрое́ни|е, я *nt.* shipbuilding

⚓ кора́бл|ь, я́ *m.* ship, vessel; лине́йный к.
battleship; косми́ческий к. spaceship;
сади́ться на к. to go on board (ship), to
embark

кора́лл, а *m.* coral

Кора́н, а *m.* the Koran

коре́|ец, йца *m.* Korean

коре́йк|а, и *f.* smoked back bacon

коре́йский *adj.* Korean

корена́ст|ый, ⁓, ⁓а *adj.* thickset, stocky

коренн|о́й *adj.* radical, fundamental; к.
зуб molar (tooth); к. жи́тель native; ⁓о́е
населе́ние indigenous population

⚓ ко́р|ень, ня, *pl.* ⁓ни, ⁓не́й *m.* (*in var. senses*)
root; вы́рвать с ⁓нем to uproot (also fig.)

Коре́|я, и *f.* Korea

коре́ян|ка, ки *f. of* ▸ коре́ец

корзи́н|а, ы *f.* basket

кориа́ндр, а *m.* coriander

коридо́р, а *m.* corridor, passage

кори́ц|а, ы *f.* cinnamon

кори́чневый *adj.* brown

ко́рк|а, и *f.* **1** (*хлеба*) crust **2** (*апельсина*)
peel, rind

корм, а, о ⁓е, на ⁓е and на ⁓у́, *pl.* ⁓а́,
⁓о́в *m.* **1** (*пища*) food, fodder; пти́чий к.
birdseed **2** (*действие*) feeding

корм|а́, ы́ *f.* (naut.) stern

корм|и́ть, лю́, ⁓ишь *impf.* **1** (*pf.* на⁓ and
по⁓) (*давать корм*) to feed; к. гру́дью
to nurse, (breast)feed **2** (*pf.* про⁓)
(*содержать*) to keep, maintain

корм|и́ться, лю́сь, ∼́ишься *impf.* (*of*
  ▶ **прокорми́ться**) (+ *i.*) (*содержать себя*)
to live (on); **к. уро́ками** to make a living by
giving tuition

кормле́ни|е, я *nt.* feeding

корму́шк|а, и *f.* (agric.) (feeding) trough; (*для
птиц*) bird table, bird feeder

корнепло́д, а *m.* root vegetable

корнишо́н, а *m.* (cul.) gherkin

коро́бк|а, и *f.* box, case; **к. скоросте́й** (tech.)
gearbox; **черепна́я к.** (anat.) cranium

коро́б|о́к, ка́ *m.* (small) box

коро́в|а, ы *f.* cow

коро́в|ий *adj. of* ∼ **коро́ва**; ∼**ье ма́сло** butter

коро́в|ка, ки *f.* affectionate dim. of ▶ **коро́ва**;
бо́жья к. ladybird

коро́вник, а *m.* cowshed

короле́в|а, ы *f.* queen

короле́вский *adj.* royal

короле́вств|о, а *nt.* kingdom

коро́л|ь, я́ *m.* king; (fig.) baron

коро́н|а, ы *f.* crown (also fig.)

корона́ци|я, и *f.* coronation

коро́нк|а, и *f.* crown (*of tooth*)

корон|ова́ть, у́ю *impf. and pf.* to crown

коро́ст|а, ы *f.* scab

  ♂ **коро́т|кий, коро́ток, коротка́, ко́ротко,** *pl.*
ко́ротки́ *adj.* short; **э́то пальто́ тебе́ ко́ротко**
this coat is too short for you

ко́ротко¹ *see* ▶ **коро́ткий**

ко́ротко² *adv.* briefly

короткометра́жный *adj.*: **к. фильм** short
(film)

коро́че *comp. of* ▶ **коро́ткий,** ▶ **ко́ротко¹**;
shorter; **к. говоря́** in short, to cut a long
story short

  ♂ **корпорати́в|ный, ∼ен, ∼на** *adj.* corporate

корпора́ци|я, и *f.* corporation

ко́рпус¹, а, *pl.* ∼**ы** *m.* **1** (*туловище*) body
2 (*мера*) length (*of animal, as unit of
measurement*)

  ♂ **ко́рпус², а,** *pl.* ∼**а́,** ∼**о́в** *m.* **1** (mil.) corps;
каде́тский, морско́й к. military school, naval
college; **дипломати́ческий к.** diplomatic corps
2 (*здание*) building; block **3** (*корабля́*) hull;
(tech.) frame, body, case

корректи́р|овать, ую *impf.* (*of*
  ▶ **скорректи́ровать**) to correct

корре́кт|ный, ∼ен, ∼на *adj.* correct, proper

корре́ктор, а *m.* proofreader

корре́кци|я, и *f.* correction

корреспонде́нт, а *m.* correspondent

корреспонде́нт|ка, ки *f. of* ▶ **корреспонде́нт**

корреспонде́нци|я, и *f.* **1** (*переписка;
письма*) correspondence **2** (*сообщение*)
dispatch, report

корри́д|а, ы *f.* bullfight

корро́зи|я, и *f.* (chem.) corrosion

коррумпи́рован|ный, ∼, ∼а *adj.* corrupt

корру́пци|я, и *f.* (pol.) corruption

корса́ж, а *m.* bodice

корсе́т, а *m.* corset

корт, а *m.* (tennis) court

корте́ж, а *m.* procession, cortège;
(*автомоби́лей*) motorcade

ко́ртик, а *m.* dagger

ко́рточ|ки, ек (*no sg.*) **сиде́ть на** ∼**ках, сесть
на к.** to squat

корч|ева́ть, у́ю *impf.* to uproot, root out

ко́ршун, а *m.* (zool.) kite

коры́ст|ный, ∼ен, ∼на *adj.* mercenary,
selfish

коры́т|о, а *nt.* tub; trough

кор|ь, и *f.* measles

коря́в|ый, ∼, ∼а *adj.* (infml) **1** (*дуб, па́льцы*)
gnarled **2** (*по́черк, речь, стиль*) clumsy

коря́г|а, и *f.* (*ве́твь*) dead branch; (*пень*) dead
tree stump (*often submerged under water*)

кос|а́¹, ы́, *a.* ∼́**у́,** *pl.* ∼́**ы** *f.* (*во́лосы*) plait,
pigtail, braid

кос|а́², ы́, *pl.* ∼́**ы** *f.* (*ору́дие*) scythe

коса́тк|а, и *f.* killer whale

ко́свенн|ый *adj.* indirect, oblique; ∼**ые
ули́ки** circumstantial evidence; (gram.): ∼**ая
речь** indirect speech

коси́лк|а, и *f.* mowing machine, mower;
газо́нная к. lawn mower

ко|си́ть¹, шу́, ∼**́сишь** *impf.* (*of* ▶ **скоси́ть¹**)
(*траву́*) to mow; to cut

ко|си́ть², шу́, си́шь *impf.* (*of* ▶ **скоси́ть²**)
1 (*глаза́ при косогла́зии*) to squint **2** (*рот,
глаза́*) to twist, slant **3** (*no pf.*) (*быть
косогла́зым*) to have a squint

ко|си́ться, шу́сь, си́шься *impf.* (*of*
  ▶ **покоси́ться**) **1** (*о до́ме*) to slant **2** (infml)
(**на** + *a.*) to cast a sidelong look (at); (fig.) to
look askance (at)

коси́чк|а, и *f. dim. of* ▶ **коса́¹**

косма́т|ый, ∼, ∼а *adj.* shaggy

косме́тик|а, и *f.* cosmetics, make-up

космети́ческ|ий *adj.* cosmetic; **к. кабине́т**
beauty salon; ∼**ая ма́ска** face pack; **к.
ремо́нт** redecoration

космети́чк|а, и *f.* (infml) make-up bag

космето́лог, а *m.* **1** (*врач в кли́нике*)
cosmetic surgeon **2** (*специали́ст в сало́не*)
beautician

косми́ческий *adj.* **1** space (*attr.*) **2** (*пыль,
радиа́ция*) cosmic; **к. кора́бль** spaceship

космодро́м, а *m.* cosmodrome, space centre
(BrE), center (AmE)

космона́вт, а *m.* astronaut, cosmonaut,
spaceman

космона́втик|а, и *f.* astronautics, space
exploration

космополи́т, а *m.* cosmopolitan

космополити́ческий *adj.* cosmopolitan

ко́смос, а *m.* cosmos; outer space

косноязы́ч|ный, ∼ен, ∼на *adj.* speaking
thickly

косн|у́ться, у́сь, ёшься *pf. of* ▶ **каса́ться**

ко́с|ный, ∼ен, ∼на *adj.* (*ум*) inert, sluggish;
(*о́браз жи́зни, о́бщество*) stagnant

К

ко́со *adv.* slantwise, askew; obliquely; смотре́ть к. to look askance, scowl

Ко́сово, а *nt.* Kosovo

косогла́зие, я *nt.* squint, cast in the eye

косогла́з|ый, ~, ~a *adj.* cross-eyed, squint-eyed

кос|о́й, ~, ~á, ~́o *adj.* **1** slanting; oblique **2** (*косогла́зый*) squinting; cross-eyed

косола́п|ый, ~, ~a *adj.* pigeon-toed; (fig.) clumsy

костёл, а *m.* (Roman Catholic) church

кост|ёр, ра́ *m.* bonfire; (*похо́дный*) campfire; заже́чь/развести́ к. to make a fire

костля́в|ый, ~, ~a *adj.* bony

ко́стный *adj.* osseous; (anat.): к. мозг marrow

ко́сточк|а, и *f.* **1** *dim. of* ▶ кость **2** (*сли́вы, абрико́са*) stone; (*лимо́на, виногра́да*) pip

косты́л|ь, я́ *m.* crutch; ходи́ть на ~я́х to walk on crutches

кост|ь, и, *pl.* ~и, ~е́й *f.* **1** bone; слоно́вая к. ivory **2** (*in pl.*) (*в игре́*) dice

костю́м, а *m.* **1** (*оде́жда*) dress, clothes; маскара́дный к. fancy dress **2** (*пиджа́к и брю́ки; жаке́т и ю́бка*) suit; вече́рний к. dress suit; купа́льный к. swimsuit **3** (theatr.) costume

костюме́р, а *m.* (theatr.) wardrobe master

костя́к, а́ *m.* (fig.) (+ *g.*) backbone (of)

косу́л|я, и *f.* roe deer

косы́нк|а, и *f.* (triangular) kerchief, scarf

кося́к¹, а́ *m.* (*дверно́й*) (door)post; jamb

кося́к², а́ *m.* **1** (*лошаде́й*) herd **2** (*рыб*) shoal, school; (*птиц*) flock

кося́к³, а́ *m.* (sl., *с марихуа́ной*) joint

кот, а́ *m.* tomcat

Кот-д'Ивуа́р, а *m.* the Ivory Coast

кот|ёл, ла́ *m.* **1** pot, cauldron; о́бщий к. communal pot **2** (tech.) boiler

котел|о́к, ка́ *m.* **1** pot **2** (mil.) mess tin **3** (*шля́па*) bowler (hat)

коте́льн|ая, ой *f.* boiler house

кот|ёнок, ёнка, *pl.* ~я́та, ~я́т *m.* kitten

ко́тик, а *m.* **1** (*тюле́нь*) fur seal **2** (*мех*) sealskin

коти́р|овать, ую *impf. and pf.* (fin.) to quote

коти́р|оваться, уюсь *impf. and pf.* **1** (fin.) to be quoted **2** (fig.) to be rated

котле́т|а, ы *f.* burger; rissole; (отбивна́я) к. chop

котлова́н, а *m.* (tech.) foundation pit

кото́мк|а, и *f.* knapsack

☞ **кото́рый** *pron.* **1** *interrog. and rel.* (*о предме́тах*) which; к. час? what time is it? **2** (infml, *не оди́н*) some, quite a few; к. год он не пи́шет he hasn't been writing for some years **3** *rel.* (*о лю́дях*) who

котте́дж, а *m.* cottage

кот|я́та, я́т *see* ▶ котёнок

ко́фе *m. indecl.* coffee; раствори́мый к. instant coffee; к. в зёрнах coffee beans

кофева́рк|а, и *f.* coffee maker

кофеи́н, а *m.* caffeine

кофе́йник, а *m.* coffee pot

кофе́йный *adj. of* ▶ ко́фе

кофе́|йня, йни, *g. pl.* ~ен *f.* coffee house

кофемо́лк|а, и *f.* coffee grinder

ко́фт|а, ы *f.* jacket, cardigan (*woman's*)

ко́фточк|а, и *f.* blouse

коча́н, а́ *m.*: к. капу́сты head of cabbage

коч|ева́ть, у́ю *impf.* **1** (*о племена́х*) to be a nomad, to roam from place to place; (fig., *передвига́ться*) to wander **2** (*о живо́тных*) to migrate

коче́вник, а *m.* nomad

кочево́й *adj.* **1** (*лю́ди*) nomadic **2** (*живо́тные*) migratory

кочега́р, а *m.* stoker, fireman

кочер|га́, ги́, *g. pl.* ~ёг *f.* poker

ко́чк|а, и *f.* hummock; tussock

кошел|ёк, ька́ *m.* purse

коше́лк|а, и *f.* (infml) small basket

ко́шк|а, и *f.* cat; (fig., infml) игра́ть в ~и-мы́шки to play cat-and-mouse; жить как к. с соба́кой to lead a cat-and-dog life

кошма́р, а *m.* **1** nightmare (also fig.) **2** (*as pred.*) (infml) it is a nightmare

кошма́р|ный, ~ен, ~на *adj.* nightmarish; (fig.) horrible, awful

ко|шу́, ~си́шь *see* ▶ коси́ть¹, ▶ коси́ть²

кощу́нств|о, а *nt.* blasphemy

коэффицие́нт, а *m.* (math.) coefficient; (tech.): к. поле́зного де́йствия efficiency (also fig.); к. у́мственных спосо́бностей intelligence quotient, IQ

КПП *m. indecl.* (*abbr. of* контро́льно-пропускно́й пункт) checkpoint

краб, а *m.* (zool.) crab

кра́ден|ый *adj.* stolen; ~ое (*collect.*) stolen goods

кра|ду́, дёшь *see* ▶ красть

кра́ж|а, и *f.* theft; к. со взло́мом burglary; магази́нная к. shoplifting

☞ **кра|й, я, о ~е, в ~ю́,** *pl.* ~я́, ~ёв *m.* **1** (*поля́, оде́жды*) edge; (*сосу́да*) brim; (*про́пасти*) brink (also fig.); на ~ю́ све́та at the world's end **2** (*страна́, о́бласть*) land, country; в на́ших ~я́х in our part of the world; в чужи́х ~я́х in foreign parts

☞ **кра́йне** *adv.* extremely

☞ **кра́йн|ий** *adj.* **1** extreme; (*после́дний*) last; К. Се́вер the Far North; в ~ем слу́чае in the last resort; к. срок deadline; по ~ей ме́ре at least **2** (sport) outside, wing

кра́йност|ь, и *f.* (*кра́йняя сте́пень*) extreme; (*тяжёлое положе́ние*) (no *pl.*) extremity

крал, а *see* ▶ красть

кран¹, а *m.* (*водопрово́дный*) tap, faucet (AmE); (*на трубопрово́дах*) valve

кран², а *m.* (*маши́на*) crane

крапи́в|а, ы *f.* (stinging) nettle; (*collect.*) nettles

☞ **key word**

краса́в|ец, ца *m.* handsome man; good-looker (*male*)

краса́виц|а, ы *f.* beauty; good-looker (*female*)

✔ **краси́в|ый, ~, ~а** *adj.* beautiful; (*мужчина*) handsome; (*поступок, слова*) fine

краси́тел|ь, я *m.* dye(-stuff); пищево́й к. food colouring

кра́|сить, шу, сишь *impf.* (*of* ▶ покра́сить) **1** (*стену, губы*) to paint **2** (*ткань, волосы*) to dye; (*дерево, стекло*) to stain

кра́|ситься, шусь, сишься *impf.* **1** (*pf.* на~) to make up one's face **2** (*pf.* по~) to dye one's hair **3** (*no pf.*) (*пачкать собой*) to run **4** *pass. of* ▶ кра́сить

✔ **кра́ск|а, и** *f.* **1** (*материал*) paint; (*для ткани*) dye; акваре́льная к. watercolour (BrE), watercolor (AmE); ма́сляная к. oil paint **2** (*in pl.*) (fig., *колорит*) colours (BrE), colors (AmE); сгуща́ть ~и (infml) to lay it on thick

красне́|ть, ю *impf.* (*of* ▶ покрасне́ть) **1** (*становиться красным*) to redden, become red **2** (*от стыда*) to blush; (fig.): к. за (+ *a.*) to blush for

красноречи́в|ый, ~, ~а *adj.* eloquent

красноре́чи|е, я *nt.* eloquence

красну́х|а, и *f.* (med.) German measles

✔ **кра́с|ный, ~ен, ~на́, ~но** *adj.* red (also fig., pol.); ~ное де́рево mahogany; К. Крест Red Cross; ~ная строка́ (first line of) new paragraph

✔ **красот|а́, ы́, *pl.* ~ы** *f.* beauty

красо́тк|а, и *f.* (infml) good-looking girl; beauty

кра́с|очный *adj.* **1** *adj. of* ▶ кра́ска **2** (~очен, ~очна) colourful (BrE), colorful (AmE)

кра|сть, ду́, дёшь, *past* ~л, ~ла *impf.* (*of* ▶ укра́сть) to steal

кра́|сться, ду́сь, дёшься, *past* ~лся, ~лась *impf.* to steal, creep, sneak

кра́тер, а *m.* crater

кра́т|кий, ~ок, ~ка́, ~ко *adj.* short; brief; я бу́ду ~ок I'll be brief; (*сжатый*) concise; «и» ~кое the Russian letter «й»

кра́тко *adv.* briefly

кратковре́мен|ный, ~ and ~ен, ~на *adj.* of short duration, brief; к. дождь shower

краткосро́ч|ный, ~ен, ~на *adj.* (*ссуда*) short-term; (*отпуск*) short

кратча́йший *superl. of* ▶ кра́ткий

краудсо́рсинг, а *m.* crowdsourcing (*carrying out a piece of work by recruiting a number of people, esp. via the Internet*)

крах, а *m.* (fin., also fig.) crash, collapse; (fig., *провал*) failure; потерпе́ть к. to fail

крахма́л, а *m.* starch

кра́шен|ый *adj.* **1** (*стена*) painted; ~ое яйцо́ (decorated) Easter egg **2** (*ткань*) dyed

креве́тк|а, и *f.* (zool.) (*мелкая*) shrimp; (*крупная*) prawn

✔ **креди́т, а** *m.* credit; в к. on credit

креди́тк|а, и *f.* (infml) credit card

✔ **креди́т|ный** *adj. of* ▶ креди́т; к. биле́т banknote; ~ная ка́рточка/ка́рта credit card; ~ный кри́зис credit crisis

кредито́р, а *m.* creditor

кредитоспосо́бность, и *f.* creditworthiness, credit rating

кредитоспосо́б|ный, ~ен, ~на *adj.* creditworthy

кре́йсер, а, *pl.* ~ы and ~а́ (mil.) *m.* cruiser; лине́йный к. battle cruiser

кре́кер, а *m.* cracker

крем, а *m.* cream; к. для о́буви shoe polish

кремато́ри|й, я *m.* crematorium

крема́ци|я, и *f.* cremation

крем|ень, ня *m.* flint

кремлёвский *adj. of* ▶ кремль

кремл|ь, я́ *m.* citadel; (моско́вский) К. the Kremlin

кре́мни|й, я *m.* (chem.) silicon

кре́мовый *adj.* cream(-coloured)

креп|и́ть, лю́, и́шь *impf.* **1** (*прочно прикреплять*) to fasten **2** (*усиливать*) to strengthen

креп|и́ться, лю́сь, и́шься *impf.* **1** to hold out **2** *pass. of* ▶ крепи́ть

кре́п|кий, ~ок, ~ка́, ~ко, ~ки́ *adj.* (*чай, кофе; запах; ветер; организм; ткань*) strong; (*сон*) sound; (*забор*) sturdy, robust; (*мороз, удар*) hard; (fig., *стойкий*) firm; ~кие напи́тки spirits; ~кое словцо́ (infml) swear word, strong language

кре́пко *adv.* (*держать; завя́зать*) tight; (*построенный*) strongly; (*спать*) soundly

крепле́ни|е, я *nt.* **1** (naut.) lashing; furling **2** (*лыжное*) binding

креп|ну́ть, у, ешь *impf.* (*of* ▶ окре́пнуть) to get stronger

кре́пост|ь[1], и *f.* (*свойство*) strength

кре́пост|ь[2], и *f.* (mil.) fortress

кре́пче *comp. of* ▶ кре́пкий, ▶ кре́пко

кре́с|ло, ла, *g. pl.* ~ел *nt.* armchair, easy chair; (fig., *должность*) post, office; инвали́дное к. wheelchair; к.-кача́лка rocking chair; к.-крова́ть sofa bed; (theatr.) seat

крест, а́ *m.* **1** cross; поста́вить к. (на + *p.*) to give up for lost **2** (*жест*) the sign of the cross

кре|сти́ть, щу́, ~стишь *impf.* **1** (*pf.* к. or о~) to baptize, christen **2** (+ *a.* and у + *gen.*) to be godfather, godmother (*to the child of*); я у них ~сти́ла дочь I was godmother to their daughter **3** (*pf.* пере~) to make the sign of the cross over

кре|сти́ться, щу́сь, ~стишься *impf.* **1** (*pf.* к.) to be baptized, be christened **2** (*pf.* пере~) to cross oneself

крест-на́крест *adv.* crosswise

кре́стник, а *m.* godson, godchild

кре́стниц|а, ы *f.* goddaughter, godchild

крёст|ный *adj.*: к. оте́ц (*also as m. n. к.,* ~ого) godfather; ~ая мать (*also as f. n.* ~ая, ~ой) godmother; ~ые де́ти godchildren

К

крестоно́с|ец, ца *m.* crusader

крестья́н|ин, ина, *pl.* **~е, ~** *m.* peasant

крестья́нк|а, и *f.* peasant (woman)

крестья́нский *adj.* peasant

крестья́нств|о, а *nt.* (*collect.*) the peasants, peasantry

крети́н, а *m.* (med.) cretin (*person with learning difficulties and physical deformities because of congenital thyroid deficiency*); (fig., infml) idiot, imbecile

креще́ни|е, я *nt.* baptism, christening; **боево́е к.** (fig.) baptism of fire

кре|щу́, ~стишь *see* ▶ **крести́ть**

крив|а́я, о́й *f.* (math., econ., etc.) curve

кривля́|ться, юсь *impf.* to behave affectedly; to show off

крив|о́й, ~, ~а́, ~о *adj.* crooked; **~о́е зе́ркало** (also fig.) distorting mirror

кривоно́г|ий, ~, ~а *adj.* bandy-legged, bow-legged

☞ **кри́зис, а** *m.* crisis

кри́зис|ный *adj. of* ▶ **кри́зис; ~ная ситуа́ция** crisis situation, crisis

крик, а *m.* cry, shout; (*in pl.*) clamour (BrE), clamor (AmE), outcry; **к. души́** emotional outpouring

кри́кет, а *m.* cricket; **игро́к в к.** cricketer

крикли́в|ый, ~, ~а *adj.* **1** (*ребёнок*) clamorous, bawling **2** (*голос*) loud, penetrating

кри́кн|уть, у, ешь *inst. pf. of* ▶ **крича́ть**

кримина́л, а *m.* (infml) **1** (*плохое поведение*) foul play **2** (*преступление*) crime

криминали́ст, а *m.* (law) specialist in crime detection

криминали́стик|а, и *f.* (science of) crime detection

кримина́л|ьный, ~ен, ~ьна *adj.* criminal

криминоге́н|ный, ~ен, ~на *adj.* criminogenic, conducive to crime

криста́лл, а *m.* crystal

☞ **крите́ри|й, я** *m.* criterion

кри́тик, а *m.* critic

кри́тик|а, и *f.* **1** criticism **2** (*отрицательное суждение*) critique

критик|ова́ть, у́ю *impf.* to criticize

крити́ческий *adj.* critical; **к. моме́нт** (fig.) crucial moment

кри|ча́ть, чу́, чи́шь *impf.* (*of* ▶ **кри́кнуть**) **1** to cry, shout; to yell, scream; **к. (на + *a.*)** to shout (at); **к. о по́мощи** to call for help **2** (**о** + *p.*) (infml) to make a song and dance (about), talk a lot (about)

крича́щий *pres. part. act. of* ▶ **крича́ть** *and adj.* (fig.) loud; blatant

крова́вый *adj.* (*режим, события*) bloody

крова́тк|а, и *f.*: **де́тская к.** cot (BrE), crib (AmE)

крова́т|ь, и *f.* bed; **двухъя́русная к.** bunk bed

кро́в|ля, ли, *g. pl.* **~ель** *f.* roof

кро́вн|ый *adj.* blood; **~ая месть** blood feud

кровожа́д|ный, ~ен, ~на *adj.* bloodthirsty

кровоизлия́ни|е, я *nt.* (med.) haemorrhage (BrE), hemorrhage (AmE)

кровообраще́ни|е, я *nt.* circulation of the blood

кровопроли́ти|е, я *nt.* bloodshed

кровотече́ни|е, я *nt.* bleeding; (*сильное*) haemorrhage (BrE), hemorrhage (AmE)

кровоточ|и́ть, ~и́т *impf.* to bleed

☞ **кров|ь, и, о ~и, в ~и́,** *g. pl.* **~е́й** *f.* blood (also fig.); **в к., до ~и** till it bleeds; **пусти́ть к.** (+ *d.*) to bleed; (fig.): **по ~и** by birth

кровяно́й *adj. of* ▶ **кровь**

кро|и́ть, ю́, и́шь *impf.* (*of* ▶ **скрои́ть**) to cut (out)

кро|й, я *m.* **1** cutting (out) **2** (*фасон*) cut (*of dress, etc.*)

кро́йк|а, и *f.* cutting (out)

кроке́т, а *m.* (*игра*) croquet

крокоди́л, а *m.* crocodile

кро́кус, а *m.* (bot.) crocus

кро́лик, а *m.* **1** (*животное*) rabbit **2** (*мех*) rabbit fur

☞ **кро́ме** *prep.* + *g.* **1** (*за исключением*) except **2** (*в добавление*) besides, in addition to; **к. того́** besides, moreover, furthermore; (infml): **к. шу́ток** joking apart

кро́мк|а, и *f.* edge; (*ткани*) selvage; **к. тротуа́ра** kerb (BrE), curb (AmE)

кро́н|а, ы *f.* (*дерева*) crown

кронште́йн, а *m.* (tech.) (*полки*) bracket; (*балкона*) corbel

кропотли́в|ый, ~, ~а *adj.* painstaking, precise

кроссво́рд, а *m.* crossword

кроссо́вк|и, ок *f. pl.* (*sg.* **~ка, ~ки**) trainers (BrE), sneakers (AmE)

крот, а́ *m.* mole

кро́т|кий, ~ок, ~ка́, ~ко *adj.* meek, mild

кро́хотный *adj.* (infml) tiny, minute

кро́шеч|ный, ~ен, ~на *adj.* (infml) tiny, minute

крош|и́ть, у́, ~ишь *impf.* **1** (*pf.* **на~** *or* **рас~**) (*хлеб*) to crumb, crumble; (*нарезать*) to dice; (fig.) to hack to pieces **2** (*pf.* **на~**) (+ *i.*) (*сорить*) to drop, spill crumbs (of)

крош|и́ться, ~ится *impf.* (*of* ▶ **раскроши́ться**) to crumble

кро́шк|а, и *f.* (*хлеба*) crumb

круасса́н, а *m.* (cul.) croissant

☞ **круг, а,** *pl.* **~и́** *m.* **1** (= *circular area, p. sg.* **в, на ~у́,** = *circumference, p. sg.* **в, на ~е**) circle; **движе́ние по ~у** movement in a circle **2** (*круглый предмет*) ring; **спаса́тельный к.** lifebelt; **~и́ под глаза́ми** rings round the eyes **3** (sport) (*p. sg.* **на ~е**) беговой **к.** racecourse, ring; **к. почёта** lap of honour (BrE), honor (AmE) **4** (fig.) (*p. sg.* **в ~у́**) (*сфера, область*) sphere, range; compass; **к. вопро́сов** range of questions **5** (fig.) (*p. sg.* **в ~у́**) (*группа людей*) circle (*of persons*); **официа́льные**

~й official quarters; **в семе́йном** ~**ý** in the family circle

круглогоди́чный *adj.* year-round

круглоли́ц|ый, ~, ~**a** *adj.* round-faced

круглосу́точный *adj.* round-the-clock, twenty-four-hour

◆ **кру́гл|ый**, ~, ~**á**, ~**о**, ~**ы́** *adj.* **1** round; **к. год** all the year round; ~**ая да́та** 10th, 20th, 30th, etc. anniversary; ~**ые ско́бки** round brackets; ~**ые су́тки** day and night; ~**ая су́мма** round sum **2** (*no short forms*) (infml) complete, utter, perfect; **к. дура́к** utter fool; **к.**, ~**ая сирота́** orphan (*having neither father nor mother*)

круговоро́т, а *m.* (*цикличность*) cycle; (*событий*) flow

кругозо́р, а *m.* **1** prospect **2** (fig.) horizon, range of interests

круго́м¹ *adv.* **1** round, around **2** (*вокруг*) (all) round, round about; **к. всё бы́ло ти́хо** all around was still **3** (infml, *совершенно*) completely, entirely; **вы к. винова́ты** you are entirely to blame

круго́м² *prep.* + *g.* round, around

кругообра́з|ный, ~**ен**, ~**на** *adj.* circular

кругосве́тный *adj.* round-the-world

круж|ева́, ~**ев**, ~**ева́м** = **кру́жево**

кружевно́й *adj.* of ▶ **кружева́**, ▶ **кру́жево**

кру́жев|о, **а** *nt.* lace

круж|и́ть, у́, ~**и́шь** *impf.* **1** (*заставлять двигаться по кругу*) to whirl, spin round **2** (*кружиться*) to circle

круж|и́ться, у́сь, ~**и́шься** *impf.* (of ▶ **закружи́ться**) to whirl, spin round; (*о птицах*) to circle; **у меня́** ~**ится голова́** my head is going round, I feel giddy

кру́жк|а, и *f.* mug

круж|о́к, ка́ *m.* **1** *dim. of* ▶ **круг 2** (*группа*) circle, club; (*учебный*) study group

круи́з, а *m.* cruise

круп|а́, ы́, *pl.* ~**ы** *f.* (collect.) groats; **гре́чневая к.** buckwheat; **ма́нная к.** semolina; **овся́ная к.** oatmeal

крупномасшта́б|ный, ~**ен**, ~**на** *adj.* large-scale; (fig.) ambitious

◆ **кру́п|ный**, ~**ен**, ~**на́**, ~**но**, ~**ны́** *adj.* **1** (*большой*) large, big; (*крупномасштабный*) large-scale; (fig., *значительный*) prominent, outstanding; **к. рога́тый скот** cattle; ~**ный план** (cin.) close-up **2** (*песок*) coarse **3** (*важный*) important; (*серьёзный*) serious; ~**ная неприя́тность** serious trouble

крупье́ *m. indecl.* croupier

кру|ти́ть, чу́, ~**тишь** *impf.* **1** (*pf.* **с**~) to twist; to twirl **2** (*pf.* **за**~) (*кран, ручку*) to turn, wind

кру|ти́ться, чу́сь, ~**тишься** *impf.* **1** (*вращаться*) to turn, spin, revolve **2** (*кружиться*) to whirl **3** (fig., infml, *быть в хлопотах*) to be in a whirl

кру́то *adv.* **1** (*вверх, вниз*) steeply **2** (*внезапно*) suddenly; abruptly, sharply; **к. поверну́ть** to turn round sharply **3** (infml) harshly; **к.**

распра́виться с кем-н. to give sb short shrift **4** (*туго*) tightly

крут|о́й, ~, ~**á**, ~**о** *adj.* **1** (*подъём*) steep **2** (*внезапный*) sudden; abrupt, sharp **3** (infml) (*характер*) severe; (*меры*) drastic **4** (cul., *каша*) thick; ~**о́е яйцо́** hard-boiled egg **5** (sl.) (*отличный*) cool; ~**о!** cool!; (*сильный и властный*) tough; (*влиятельный*) influential; (*богатый*) well off

кру́че *comp. of* ▶ **круто́й**, ▶ **кру́то**

кру|чу́, ~**тишь** *see* ▶ **крути́ть**

круше́ни|е, я *nt.* **1** (*авария*) crash; (*судна*) wreck; **потерпе́ть к.** (*поезд, самолёт*) to crash; (*корабль*) to be wrecked **2** (fig., *надежд; коммунизма*) collapse

круш|и́ть, у́, и́шь *impf.* to destroy (also fig.)

крыжо́вник, а *m.* gooseberry

крыла́т|ый *adj.* winged (also fig.); ~**ые слова́** pithy saying(s); ~**ая раке́та** cruise missile

крыл|о́, á, *pl.* ~**ья**, ~**ьев** *nt.* (*птицы, самолёта, дома*) wing; (*мельницы*) sail, vane; (*автомобиля*) wing, mudguard (BrE), fender (AmE)

крыль|цо́, ца́, *pl.* ~**ца**, ~**éц**, ~**ца́м** *nt.* porch

Крым, а, о ~**е, в** ~**ý** *m.* the Crimea

крыс|а, ы *f.* rat

кры́тый *adj.* covered; sheltered; **к. ры́нок** covered market

кры́ш|а, и *f.* roof; (infml, *преступная группировка, охранное предприятие и т. п., обеспечивающие защиту или покровительство*) protection, front

кры́шк|а, и *f.* **1** (*кастрюли, банки, чемодана*) lid; (*люка*) cover **2** (infml) death, end; **ему́ к.** he's done for; he's finished

крю|к, ка́ *m.* (*pl.* ~**ки́**, ~**ко́в**) hook

крюч|о́к, ка́ *m.* hook; **спусково́й к.** trigger

кря́ду *adv.* (infml) running; in a row

кряж, а *m.* **1** (*горный*) (mountain) ridge **2** (*дубовый*) block, log

кря́к|ать, аю *impf.* to quack

кря́к|нуть, ну, нешь *pf.* to give a quack

кряхт|éть, чу́, ти́шь *impf.* to groan

ксенофо́би|я, и *f.* xenophobia

ксероко́пи|я, и *f.* Xerox®, photocopy

ксе́рокс, а *m.* **1** (*ксерография*) xerography **2** (*устройство*) Xerox (machine)®, photocopier **3** (infml, *копия*) Xerox®, photocopy

ксилофо́н, а *m.* (mus.) xylophone

◆ **кста́ти** *adv.* **1** (*уместно*) to the point, apropos **2** (*своевременно*) opportunely; **э́тот пода́рок оказа́лся о́чень к.** the present has proved most welcome **3** (infml, *заодно*) at the same time, incidentally; **к., зайди́те, пожа́луйста, в апте́ку** will you please call at the chemist's at the same time **4**: **к. (сказа́ть)** by the way

к/т (*abbr. of* **кинотеа́тр**) cinema

◆ **кто, кого́, кому́, кем, о ком** *pron.* **1** (interrog.) (*какой человек?*) who; **к. э́то тако́й?** who is that? **2** (rel.) (*в придаточных*) who (*normally after pron. antecedent*); **тот, к.**

he who; **те, к.** those who **3** (*indefinite*): **к. (бы) ни** who(so)ever; **к. бы то ни́ был** whoever it may be **4** (*indefinite*): **к. ... к.** some ... others; (+ *adv.*) **разбежа́лись к. куда́** they scattered in all directions; **как они́ устро́ились? — к. как** how did they settle in? — in all sorts of ways

кто́-либо, кого́-либо *pron.* = кто́-нибудь

кто́-нибудь, кого́-нибудь *pron.* (*в вопросах*) anyone, anybody; (*в утвержде́ниях*) someone, somebody

⚲ **кто́-то, кого́-то** *pron.* someone, somebody

куб, а, *pl.* ∼ы́ *m.* **1** (math.) cube; **два в** ∼**е** two cubed **2** (*infml, куби́ческий метр*) cubic metre (BrE), meter (AmE)

Ку́б|а, ы *f.* Cuba

куби́зм, а, *m.* (art) cubism

ку́бик, а *m.* (*in pl.*) (*игру́шка*) blocks, bricks

куби́н|ец, ца *m.* Cuban

куби́н|ка, ки *f. of* ▸ **куби́нец**

куби́нский *adj.* Cuban

ку́б|ок, ка *m.* **1** (*бока́л*) goblet **2** (sport) cup

кубоме́тр, а *m.* cubic metre (BrE), meter (AmE)

кува́лд|а, ы *f.* sledgehammer

Куве́йт, а *m.* Kuwait

куве́йт|ец, ца *m.* Kuwaiti

куве́йт|ка, ки *f. of* ▸ **куве́йтец**

куве́йтский *adj.* Kuwaiti

кувши́н, а *m.* jug; pitcher

кувши́нк|а, и *f.* (bot.) water lily

кувырк|а́ться, а́юсь *impf.* (*of* ▸ **кувыркну́ться**) to turn somersaults, go head over heels

кувырк|ну́ться, ну́сь, нёшься *inst. pf. of* ▸ **кувырка́ться**

кувырко́м *adv.* (infml) head over heels; topsy-turvy; **полете́ть к.** to go head over heels; **всё пошло́ к.** everything went haywire

кугуа́р, а *m.* (zool.) puma, cougar

⚲ **куда́** *adv.* **1** (*interrog. and rel.*) where, whither; **к. ты идёшь?** where are you going? **2**: **к. (бы) ни** wherever **3** (infml, *для чего*) what for; **к. вам сто́лько багажа́?** what do you want so much luggage for? **4** (+ *comp.*) (infml, *гора́здо*) much, far; **сего́дня мне к. лу́чше** I am much better today

куда́-либо *adv.* = куда́-нибудь

куда́-нибудь *adv.* anywhere; somewhere

куда́-то *adv.* somewhere

куда́х|тать, чу, чешь *impf.* to cackle, cluck

ку́др|и, е́й (*no sg.*) curls

кудря́в|ый, ∼, ∼**а** *adj.* (*во́лосы*) curly; (*челове́к*) curly-headed

кузе́н, а *m.* cousin

кузи́н|а, ы *f.* cousin

кузне́ц, а́ *m.* (black)smith; farrier

кузне́чик, а *m.* grasshopper

ку́зниц|а, ы *f.* forge, smithy

ку́зов, а, *pl.* ∼а́ *and* ∼ы *m.* (*автомоби́ля*) body

кукаре́ка|ть, ю *impf.* to crow

⚲ key word

ку́киш, а *m.* (infml) fig (*gesture of derision or contempt, consisting of thumb placed between index and middle fingers*); **показа́ть кому́-н. к.** to make this gesture, ≈ to cock a snook, give the V-sign

ку́кл|а, лы, *g. pl.* ∼**ол** *f.* doll; (*в теа́тре*) puppet

ку́колк|а, и *f.* (zool.) chrysalis, pupa

ку́кольный *adj.* doll's; **к. теа́тр** puppet theatre (BrE), theater (AmE)

кукуру́з|а, ы *f.* maize, (sweet)corn; **возду́шная к.** popcorn

кукуру́зный *adj. of* ▸ **кукуру́за**

куку́шк|а, и *f.* cuckoo; **часы́ с** ∼**ой** cuckoo clock

кула́к, а́ *m.* fist

кул|ёк, ька́ *m.* (paper) bag

кули́к, а́ *m.* (zool.) stint; sandpiper (*Calidris*)

кулинари́|я, и *f.* **1** (*иску́сство*) cookery **2** (*магази́н*) delicatessen

кулина́р|ный *adj.* culinary; ∼**ая кни́га** cookery book (BrE), cookbook (AmE); **к. отде́л** delicatessen counter

кули́с|ы, ∼ *f. pl.* (*sg.* ∼**а,** ∼**ы**) (theatr.) wings; **за** ∼**ами** behind the scenes (also fig.)

кули́ч, а́ *m.* Easter cake

куло́н, а *m.* pendant

кульби́т, а *m.* somersault

ку́льман, а *m.* drawing board

кульмина́ци|я, и *f.* culmination

культ, а *m.* cult; **к. ли́чности** personality cult; cult of personality

культ... *comb. form, abbr. of* ▸ **культу́рный**

культиви́р|овать, ую *impf.* to cultivate (also fig.)

ку́льт|овый *adj. of* ▸ **культ**; ∼**овый режиссёр** cult filmmaker

⚲ **культу́р|а, ы** *f.* **1** culture; **Министе́рство** ∼**ы** Ministry of Culture **2** (*у́ровень*) standard, level; **к. ре́чи** standard of speech **3** (*usu. in pl.*) (agric., *расте́ние*) crop; **зерновы́е** ∼**ы** cereals; **кормовы́е** ∼**ы** forage crops **4**: **физи́ческая к.** physical education

культури́зм, а *m.* bodybuilding

⚲ **культу́р|ный,** ∼**ен,** ∼**на** *adj.* **1** (*челове́к, о́бщество*) cultured, cultivated **2** (*у́ровень, свя́зи, обме́н*) cultural **3** (agric., hort., *не ди́кий*) cultivated

кум, а, *pl.* ∼**овья́,** ∼**овьёв** *m.* godfather of one's child; father of one's godchild

кум|а́, ы́ *f.* godmother of one's child; mother of one's godchild

куми́р, а *m.* idol (also fig.)

кунжу́т, а *m.* (bot.) sesame

куни́ц|а, ы *f.* (zool.) marten

купа́льник, а *m.* bathing costume (BrE), bathing suit (AmE), swimsuit

купа́льный *adj.* bathing, swimming; **к. костю́м** bathing costume (BrE), bathing suit (AmE), swimsuit

купа́|ть, ю *impf.* (*of* ▸ **вы́купать,** ▸ **искупа́ть¹**) to bathe; to bath

купа́|ться, юсь *impf.* (*of* ▸ **вы́купаться,** ▸ **искупа́ться**) (*пла́вать*) to swim, bathe;

(*в ванне*) to have, take a bath; **к. в луча́х
сла́вы** to bask in glory
купе́ *nt. indecl.* compartment (*of railway
carriage*)
куп|е́ц, ца́ *m.* merchant
куп|и́ть, лю́, ~ишь *pf.* (*of* ▶ **покупа́ть**) to
buy, purchase
купле́т, а *m.* **1** (*строфа*) stanza, strophe,
verse **2** (*in pl.*) (*сатирические песенки*)
satirical ballad(s), song(s)
ку́пол, а, *pl.* **~а́** *m.* cupola, dome
купо́н, а *m.* coupon
купю́р|а, ы *f.* **1** (*сокращение*) cut **2** (fin.)
(*деньги*) banknote, bill (AmE); (*облигация*)
bond
кураг|а́, и́ *f.* (*collect.*) dried apricots
кура́нт|ы, ов (*no sg.*) chiming clock; chimes
кура́тор, а *m.* **1** (*попечитель*) curator
2 (*студента*) (academic) supervisor
курга́н, а *m.* burial mound
курд, а *m.* Kurd
ку́рдский *adj.* Kurdish
курдя́нк|а, и *f. of* ▶ **курд**
куре́ни|е, я *nt.* **1** (*действие*) smoking
2 (*ладан*) incense
кури́льщик, а *m.* smoker
кури́льщи|ца, цы *f. of* ▶ **кури́льщик**
кури́ный *adj.* (*яйцо*) hen's; (*бульон*) chicken
кури́р|овать, ую *impf.* to supervise
кури́тельн|ый *adj.* smoking; **~ая (ко́мната)**
smoking room
кур|и́ть, ю́, ~ишь *impf.* (*of* ▶ **покури́ть 1**)
1 to smoke; **к. тру́бку** to smoke a pipe
2 (+ *a. or i.*) to burn
ку́р|ица, ицы, *pl.* **~ы, ~** *f.* hen
курно́с|ый, ~, ~а *adj.* snub-nosed
кур|о́к, ка́ *m.* hammer; **взвести́ к.** to cock;
спусти́ть к. to pull the trigger
куропа́тк|а, и *f.* (zool.): (*серая*) **к.** partridge;
бе́лая к. willow grouse
куро́рт, а *m.* holiday resort; **водолече́бный
к.** spa
куро́ртный *adj. of* ▶ **куро́рт**
курс, а *m.* **1** course; **взять к. на се́вер** to
steer northwards; (pol.) policy; **к. ле́кций/
обуче́ния** course of lectures/instruction;
быть на тре́тьем ~е to be in the third year
(*of a course of studies*); **держа́ть к. (на** + *a.*)
to head (for); **быть в ~е (де́ла)** to be au
courant, be in the know **2** (fin.) exchange
rate; **ра́зница ~ов (валю́т)** difference in
exchange rates
курса́нт, а *m.* (mil.) cadet
курси́в, а *m.* italic type, italics; **~ом** in italics
курс|ово́й *adj. of* ▶ **курс; ~ова́я рабо́та**
project; short dissertation

курсо́р, а *m.* (comput.) cursor
ку́ртк|а, и *f.* jacket; anorak
курча́в|ый, ~, ~а *adj.* (*волосы*) curly;
(*человек*) curly-haired
ку́ры *see* ▶ **ку́рица**
курьёз|ный, ~ен, ~на *adj.* curious; funny
курье́р, а *m.* (*в учреждении*) messenger;
(*дипломатический*) courier
курье́рский *adj.* **1** *adj. of* ▶ **курье́р 2** fast; **к.
по́езд** express
куря́тин|а, ы *f.* (infml) chicken (*as meat*)
куря́тник, а *m.* henhouse
кур|я́щий *pres. part. act. of* ▶ **кури́ть**; (*as n.* **к.,
~я́щего**) smoker
куса́|ть, ю *impf.* (*о собаке, о человеке*) to
bite; (*о пчеле*) to sting
куса́|ться, юсь *impf.* **1** (*о собаке*) to bite;
(*о крапиве, о пчеле*) to sting **2** (*кусать друг
друга*) to bite one another
куса́ч|ки, ек (*no sg.*) pliers; wire cutters
кус|о́к, ка́ *m.* piece, bit; (*хлеба*) slice; (*сахара*)
lump; (*мыла*) cake
кусо́ч|ек, ка *m.* bit
куст, а́ *m.* bush, shrub; **спря́таться в ~ы́** (fig.)
to scarper, make oneself scarce
куста́рник, а *m.* (*collect.*) bushes, shrubs;
shrubbery
куста́рн|ый *adj.* **1** handicraft; **~ые изде́лия**
craftwork **2** (fig., pej.) amateurish, primitive
куста́р|ь, я́ *m.* craftsman
ку|ти́ть, чу́, ~тишь *impf.* (*of* ▶ **кутну́ть**) to
carouse; to go on the booze
кут|ну́ть, ну́, нёшь *inst. pf. of* ▶ **кути́ть**
кухáрк|а, и *f.* cook
ку́х|ня, ни, *g. pl.* **~онь** *f.* **1** (*помещение*)
kitchen **2** (*кушанья*) cooking, cuisine
ку́хонн|ый *adj.* kitchen; **~ая плита́** kitchen
range
ку́ц|ый, ~, ~а, ~е *adj.* **1** (*животное*)
tailless; bobtailed **2** (*одежда*) skimpy; (fig.)
limited, abbreviated
ку́ч|а, и *f.* **1** heap, pile; (*людей*) group; (infml):
вали́ть всё в одну́ ~у to lump everything
together **2** (infml) (+ *g.*) heaps (of), piles
(of); **у него́ к. де́нег** he has heaps of money
ку́чер, а, *pl.* **~а́, ~о́в** *m.* coachman
куша́|ть, ю *impf.* (*of* ▶ **поку́шать**, ▶ **ску́шать**)
to eat (*esp. in polite invitation*); **ку́шайте,
пожа́луйста** please help yourself/yourselves
куше́тк|а, и *f.* couch
ку|ю́, ёшь *see* ▶ **кова́ть**
к/ф (*abbr. of* **кинофи́льм**) (cinema) film,
movie
Кыргызста́н, а *m.* Kyrgyzstan
кюве́т, а *m.* ditch (*at side of road*)

к

Лл

⚷ **л** (*abbr. of* **литр**) l, litre(s) (BrE), liter(s) (AmE)
лабири́нт, а *m.* labyrinth, maze
лабора́нт, а *m.* laboratory assistant
лабора́нт|ка, ки *f. of* ▶ **лабора́нт**
лаборато́ри|я, и *f.* laboratory
лабрадо́р, а *m.* labrador (*dog*)
ла́в|а, ы *f.* (*вулканическая*) lava
лава́нд|а, ы *f.* (bot.) lavender
лава́ш, а *m.* lavash (*flat white loaf*)
лави́н|а, ы *f.* avalanche (also fig.)
лави́р|овать, ую *impf.* **1** (naut.) to tack
2 (fig.) to manoeuvre (BrE), maneuver (AmE)
ла́вк|а¹, и *f.* (*скамья*) bench
ла́вк|а², и *f.* (*магазин*) small shop
лавр, а *m.* **1** (bot.) laurel; bay (tree) **2** (*in pl.*) (fig.) laurels
ла́вр|о́вый *adj. of* ▶ **лавр**; ~о́вый вено́к laurel wreath; (fig.) laurels; ~о́вый лист bay leaf
ла́герный *adj. of* ▶ **ла́герь**
⚷ **ла́гер|ь**, я *m.* **1** (*pl.* ~я́, ~е́й) camp; (mil.): располага́ться, стоя́ть ~ем to camp, be encamped **2** (*pl.* ~и, ~ей) (fig.) camp
лагу́н|а, ы *f.* lagoon
лад, а, о ~е, в ~у́, *pl.* ~ы́, ~о́в *m.* **1** (mus., also fig.) (*согласие*) harmony, concord; жить в ~у́ (с + *i.*) to live in harmony (with); быть не в ~а́х (с + *i.*) to be at odds (with); (infml): идти́, пойти́ на л. to go well, be successful **2** (*способ*) manner, way; на свой л. in one's own way
ла́дан, а *m.* incense; дыша́ть на л. (fig., infml) to have one foot in the grave
ла́|дить, жу, дишь *impf.* (с + *i.*) to get on (with), be on good terms (with); они́ не ~дят they don't get on
ла́дно *particle* (infml) all right!, OK!
ладо́н|ь, и *f.* palm (*of hand*); быть (ви́дным) как на ~и to be clearly visible
лазаре́т, а *m.* (mil.) field hospital; (naut.) sickbay
ла́з|ать, аю *impf.* (infml) = **ла́зить**
лазе́йк|а, и *f.* hole, gap; (fig., infml) loophole
ла́зер, а *m.* (phys., tech.) laser
ла́зерный *adj. of* ▶ **ла́зер**; л. при́нтер laser printer
ла́|зить, жу, зишь *impf.* (*indet. of* ▶ **лезть**) **1** (на + *a. or* по + *d.*) to climb, clamber (on to, up); л. по дере́вьям to climb trees **2** (в + *a.*) to climb (into), get (into)
лазу́р|ный, ~ен, ~на *adj.* sky blue, azure; Л. Бе́рег French Riviera

ла|й, я *m.* bark(ing)
ла́йк|а¹, и *f.* (*собака*) husky
ла́йк|а², и *f.* (*кожа*) kidskin
ла́йнер, а *m.* (naut., aeron.) liner
лак, а *m.* varnish, lacquer; л. для воло́с hair spray
лаке́|й, я *m.* footman; lackey, flunkey (also fig., pej.)
лакиро́в|анный *p.p.p. of* ▶ **лакирова́ть** *and adj.* varnished, lacquered; ~анная ко́жа patent leather
лакир|ова́ть, у́ю *impf.* (*of* ▶ **отлакирова́ть**) to varnish, lacquer; (fig., pej.) to varnish
ла́к|овый *adj. of* ▶ **лак**; varnished, lacquered; ~овые ту́фли patent leather shoes
ла́ком|ый ~, ~а *adj.* tasty, delicious; л. кусо́(че)к tasty morsel (also fig.)
лакони́ч|ный, ~ен, ~на *adj.* laconic
лакри́ц|а, ы *f.* (bot.) liquorice (BrE), licorice (AmE)
ла́м|а, ы *m.* llama
Ла-Ма́нш, а *m.* the (English) Channel
ла́мп|а, ы *f.* **1** lamp; л. дневно́го све́та fluorescent lamp **2** (radio) valve; tube
лампа́д|а, ы *f.* icon lamp
лампа́с, а *m.* stripe (*down side of trousers*)
ла́мпочк|а, и *f.* **1** *dim. of* ▶ **ла́мпа** **2** (electric light) bulb; стова́ттная л. 100-watt bulb **3**: мне э́то до ~и (sl.) I couldn't care less about it
лангу́ст, а *m.* spiny lobster, langouste
ландша́фт, а *m.* landscape
ла́ндыш, а *m.* lily of the valley
ланце́т, а *m.* (med.) lancet; вскры́ть ~ом to lance
ланч, а *m.* lunch
Лао́с, а *m.* Laos
лао́с|ец, ца *m.* Laotian
лао́с|ка, ки *f. of* ▶ **лао́сец**
лао́сский *adj.* Laotian
ла́п|а, ы *f.* (*животного*) paw; (*птицы*) foot; (fig., infml, *нога*) big foot; (fig., infml, *рука*) big hand; попа́сть в ~ы к кому́-н. to fall into sb's clutches
ла́п|оть, тя, *pl.* ~ти, ~те́й *m.* **1** (*обувь*) bast shoe **2** (infml, *о человеке*) oaf, bumpkin
лапш|а́, и́ *f.* **1** noodles **2** (*суп*) noodle soup **3**: ве́шать кому́-н. ~у́ на у́ши (infml) to deceive sb
лар|ёк, ька́ *m.* stall
лар|е́ц, ца́ *m.* casket
ларинги́т, а *m.* laryngitis
ла́ск|а, и *f.* **1** caress, endearment; (*in pl.*) petting **2** (*доброе отношение*) kindness

ласка́|ть, ю *impf.* to caress, fondle, pet; (*о ветре, о воде*) to caress

ласка́|ться, юсь *impf.* (к + *d.*) to show affection (towards); (*о собаке*) to fawn (on)

ла́сков|ый, ~, ~а *adj.* affectionate, tender; (fig.) gentle; **л. ве́тер** gentle wind

лассо́ *nt. indecl.* lasso

ласт, а *m.* flipper

ла́стик, а *m.* (infml, *для стирания написанного*) rubber (BrE), eraser

ла́сточк|а, и *f.* swallow; **берегова́я л.** sand martin; **городска́я л.** (house) martin

латви́|ец, йца *m.* Latvian

латви́й|ка, ки *f. of* ▶ **латви́ец**

латви́йский *adj.* Latvian

Ла́тви|я, и *f.* Latvia

ла́текс, а *m.* latex

лати́ниц|а, ы *f.* Roman alphabet, Roman letters

латиноамерика́н|ец, ца *m.* Latin American

латиноамерика́н|ка, ки *f. of*
▶ **латиноамерика́нец**

латиноамерика́нский *adj.* Latin American

лати́нск|ий *adj.* Latin; **Л~ая Аме́рика** Latin America

лату́к, а *m.* (bot.) lettuce

лату́н|ь, и *f.* brass

латы́н|ь, и *f.* Latin (*language*)

латы́ш, á, *pl.* **~и́,** *d.* **~а́м** *m.* Latvian

латы́ш|ка, ки *f. of* ▶ **латы́ш**

латы́шский *adj.* Latvian

лауреа́т, а *m.* prizewinner; laureate; **л. Но́белевской пре́мии** Nobel prizewinner

ла́цкан, а, *pl.* **~ы, ~ов** *m.* lapel

лачу́г|а, и *f.* (infml) hovel, shack

ла́|ять, ю, ешь *impf.* to bark; (*о гончих*) to bay

лба, лбу *etc., see* ▶ **лоб**

лгать, лгу, лжёшь, лгут, *past* **лгал, лгала́, лга́ло** *impf.* (*of* ▶ **солга́ть**) to lie; to tell lies

лгун, á *m.* liar

лгу́н|ья, ьи, *g. pl.* **~ий** *f. of* ▶ **лгун**

лебёдк|а, и *f.* (tech.) winch, windlass

ле́бед|ь, я, *pl.* **~и, ~е́й** *m.* swan

лев, льва *m.* **1** (*животное*) lion; **морско́й л.** sea lion **2** (**Л.**) (astron., astrol.) Leo

левита́ци|я, и *f.* levitation

левобере́жный *adj.* left-bank

левш|а́, и́, *i.* **~о́й,** *g. pl.* **~е́й** *c.g.* left-hander

◌ **ле́в|ый** *adj.* **1** left; (*со стороны левой руки*) left-hand; (naut.) port; **л. борт** port side; **~ая сторона́** left-hand side **2** (infml, *незаконный*) illegal, unofficial; **~ая рабо́та** work on the side **3** (pol.) left-wing; (*as m. n.* **л., ~ого**) left-winger; (*pl.; collect.*) the left

лега́в|ая, ой *f.* (*in full* **длинношёрстная л.**) setter; (*in full* **короткошёрстная л.**) pointer

легализа́ци|я, и *f.* legalization

легализ|ова́ть, у́ю *impf. and pf.* to legalize

лега́л|ьный, ~ен, ~ьна *adj.* legal

леге́нд|а, ы *f.* legend; (*на карте*) key, legend

легенда́р|ный, ~ен, ~на *adj.* legendary

легио́н, а *m.* legion; (fig., *очень много*) plethora

легионе́р, а *m.* **1** (hist.) legionary **2** (sport, *игрок-иностранец*) foreign player

легити́м|ный, ~ен, ~на *adj.* (*власть*) legitimate

◌ **лёг|кий, ~ок, легка́** *adj.* **1** (*на вес*) light; **л. за́втрак** light breakfast; **~ая промы́шленность** light industry **2** (*нетрудный*) easy; **у него́ л. хара́ктер** he is easy to get on with; **~кая атле́тика** (sport) athletics (BrE), track and field (AmE) **3** (*незначительный*) light; slight; **~кая просту́да** slight cold

◌ **легко́** *adv.* (*несильно*) lightly; (*без труда*) easily; (*слегка*) slightly; **э́то ему́ л. даётся** it comes easily to him; (*as pred.*) it is easy; **л. сказа́ть!** easier said than done!

легкоатле́т, а *m.* (track and field) athlete

легкове́р|ный, ~ен, ~на *adj.* credulous, gullible

легково́й *adj.* passenger (*conveyance*); **л. автомоби́ль** (motor) car

лёгк|ое, ого *nt.* (anat.) lung; **односторо́ннее, двусторо́ннее воспале́ние ~их** single, double pneumonia

легкомы́слен|ный, ~, ~на *adj.* thoughtless; flippant, frivolous

лёгкост|ь, и *f.* **1** (*веса*) lightness **2** (*нетрудность*) easiness **3** (*свобода*) ease; **с ~ью** with ease

ле́гче *comp. of* ▶ **лёгкий,** ▶ **легко́;** (*as pred.*) **больно́му л.** the patient is feeling better; **мне от э́того не л.** I am none the better for it

лёд, льда, о льде́, во/на льду́ *m.* ice; **л. сло́ман** (fig.) the ice is broken

ледене́|ть, ю *impf.* (*of* ▶ **оледене́ть**) to freeze

леден|е́ц, ца́ *m.* fruit drop

ледни́к, á *m.* glacier

леднико́вый *adj.* glacial; **л. пери́од** ice age

ледо́в|ый *adj.* ice; **~ое пла́вание** Arctic voyage

ледоко́л, а *m.* ice-breaker

ледору́б, а *m.* ice axe

ледохо́д, а *m.* drifting of ice

лед|яно́й *adj.* **1** *adj. of* ▶ **лёд;** **~яна́я гора́/ го́рка** ice slope (*for tobogganing*) **2** (*ветер; взгляд*) icy; ice-cold

лёжа *adv.* lying down, in lying position

◌ **леж|а́ть, у́, и́шь** *impf.* to lie; (*о предметах*) to be (situated); **л. в больни́це** to be in hospital; **на нём ~и́т отве́тственность за э́то** it is his responsibility

лежа́чий *adj.* lying, recumbent; **л. больно́й** bed patient

ле́зви|е, я *nt.* blade

лез|ть, у, ешь, *past* **~, ~ла** *impf.* (*of* ▶ **поле́зть 1,** *det. of* ▶ **ла́зить**) **1** (*на* + *a.* or *по* + *d.*) (*взбираться вверх*) to climb (up, on to); **л. на де́рево** to climb a tree **2** (*в* + *a.* or *под* + *a.*) (*проникать*) to climb, clamber, crawl (through, into, under) **3** (*тайком*) to sneak **4** (**в** + *a.*) (*проникать рукой*) to thrust the hand (into) **5** (infml, *вмешиваться*) to interfere; **л. не в своё дело** to poke one's nose into sb else's affairs

лейбл, а *m.* (comm., mus.) label

лейбори́ст, а *m.* (pol.) Labourite (BrE), Laborite (AmE); labour supporter (BrE), labor supporter (AmE)

лейбори́стск|ий *adj.* (pol.) Labour (BrE), Labor (AmE); ~**ая па́ртия** Labour Party (BrE), Labor Party (AmE)

ле́йк|а, и *f.* **1** (*для поливки*) watering can **2** (infml, *воронка*) funnel

лейкеми́|я, и *f.* (med.) leukaemia (BrE), leukemia (AmE)

лейкопла́стыр|ь, я *m.* sticking plaster (BrE), adhesive tape (AmE), Band-Aid® (AmE)

лейкоци́т, а *m.* (physiol.) leucocyte

лейтена́нт, а *m.* lieutenant

лека́рственный *adj.* (*растение, настой*) medicinal; **л. препара́т** medicine, drug

лека́рств|о, а *nt.* medicine; **л. от ка́шля** cough medicine

ле́ксик|а, и *f.* vocabulary; (*всего языка*) lexis

ле́ктор, а *m.* (*в учебном заведении*) lecturer; (*выступающий*) speaker

ле́кци|я, и *f.* lecture; **чита́ть** ~**ю** to lecture, deliver a lecture

леле́|ять, ю *impf.* **1** to coddle, pamper **2** (fig.) to cherish, foster; **л. мечту́** to cherish a hope

ле́мминг, а *m.* (zool.) lemming

лён, льна *m.* (bot.) flax; (*ткань*) linen

лени́в|ец, ца *m.* (zool.) sloth

лени́в|ый, ~, ~а *adj.* lazy, idle; (*походка, вид*) sluggish

Ленингра́д, а *m.* (hist.) Leningrad

лен|и́ться, ю́сь, ~**ишься** *impf.* **1** to be lazy, idle **2** (+ *inf.*) to be too lazy (to)

ле́нт|а, ы *f.* (*украшение; орденская*) ribbon; (*магнитная*) tape; (*фильм*) film

лентя́|й, я *m.* lazybones

лен|ь, и *f.* **1** laziness **2** (*as pred.*) (+ *d. and inf.*) (infml) to feel too lazy (to), to not feel like; **ему́ бы́ло л. вы́ключить ра́дио** he was too lazy to turn the radio off

леопа́рд, а *m.* leopard

лепест|о́к, ка́ *m.* petal

лепе|та́ть, чу́, ~**чешь** *impf.* to babble

лепёшк|а, и *f.* flat cake, unleavened bread, flatbread

леп|и́ть, лю́, ~**ишь** *impf.* **1** (*pf.* **с**~) to model, fashion; to mould **2** (*pf.* **на**~) (infml, *наклеить*) to stick (on)

ле́пк|а, и *f.* modelling (BrE), modeling (AmE)

лепни́н|а, ы *f.* (collect.) moulding(s) (BrE), molding(s) (AmE)

✒ **лес, а (у),** *pl.* ~**а́** *m.* **1** (**в** ~**у́**) (*большой*) forest; (*небольшой*) wood(s); **вы́йти из**

~**а (из** ~**у)** to come out of the wood; **тропи́ческий л.** rainforest **2** (**в** ~**е**) (*sg. only; collect.*) timber (BrE), lumber (AmE)

лес|а́[1] *pl. of* ▶ **лес**

лес|а́[2]**, о́в** *m. pl.* (*строительные*) scaffolding

лесбия́нк|а, и *f.* lesbian

ле́ск|а, и *f.* fishing line

лесни́ч|ий, его *m.* forestry officer; forest warden

лес|но́й *adj. of* ▶ **лес; л. двор, склад** timber yard; ~**но́е хозя́йство** forestry

лесопа́рк, а *m.* wooded park

лесопи́лк|а, и *f.* sawmill

лесопова́л, а *m.* tree felling

лесору́б, а *m.* lumberjack

ле́стниц|а, ы *f.* stairs, staircase; (*приставная*) ladder; **пожа́рная л.** fire escape; **складна́я л.** steps, stepladder; **служе́бная л.** career ladder

ле́стни|чный *adj. of* ▶ **ле́стница;** ~**чная кле́тка** stairwell; ~**чная площа́дка** landing

ле́ст|ный, ~ен, ~**на** *adj.* flattering

лест|ь, и *f.* flattery

лет|а́, ~ *pl.* **1** years; age; **с де́тских** ~ from childhood; **сре́дних** ~ middle-aged **2** (*in g.*) (*as g. pl. of* ▶ **год**) years; **ско́лько вам** ~? how old are you?; **ему́ бо́льше, ме́ньше сорока́** ~ he is over, under forty

лет|а́ть, а́ю *indet. of* ▶ **лете́ть**

лета́ющ|ий *adj.:* ~**ая таре́лка** (infml) flying saucer

ле|те́ть, чу́, ти́шь *impf. of* ▶ **полете́ть 1,** *det. of* ▶ **лета́ть 1** to fly **2** (fig., *мчаться*) to fly; to rush, tear **3** (fig., infml, *падать*) to fall, drop

✒ **ле́тний** *adj.* summer; **л. сад** pleasure garden(s)

-ле́тний *comb. form* -year-old; **пятиле́тняя де́вочка** five-year-old girl

✒ **ле́т|о, а** *nt.* summer; **ба́бье л.** Indian summer; **ско́лько** ~, **ско́лько зим!** it's been ages!

летоисчисле́ни|е, я *nt.* chronology

ле́том *adv.* in summer

ле́топис|ь, и *f.* chronicle, annals

летуч|ий *adj.* **1** flying; ~**ая мышь** bat **2** (chem.) volatile

лётчик, а *m.* pilot; **л.-испыта́тель** test pilot; **л.-истреби́тель** fighter pilot

лече́бниц|а, ы *f.* clinic (*usu. psychiatric or veterinary*)

лече́бный *adj.* **1** (*учреждение; средства*) medical **2** (*свойства; мазь*) medicinal; **л. препара́т** medicine, drug

✒ **лече́ни|е, я** *nt.* (medical) treatment; **амбулато́рное л.** outpatient treatment

леч|и́ть, у́, ~**ишь** *impf.* to treat (*medically*)

леч|и́ться, у́сь, ~**ишься** *impf.* **1** (**от** + *g.*) to receive, undergo (medical) treatment (for) **2** (**у** + *g.*) to be sb's patient

ле|чу́[1]**, ти́шь** *see* ▶ **лете́ть**

ле|чу́[2]**,** ~**ишь** *see* ▶ **лечи́ть**

лечь, ля́гу, ля́жешь, ля́гут, *past* **лёг, легла́,** *imper.* **ляг, ля́гте** *pf.* (*of* ▶ **ложи́ться**) to lie (down); **л. в посте́ль, л. спать** to go to bed; **л. в больни́цу** to go into hospital

ле́ш|ий, его *m.* wood goblin

лещ, á *m.* bream (*fish*)

лжец, á *m.* liar

лжёшь *see* ▶ лгать

лжи́в|ый, ∼, ∼а *adj.* **1** (*челове́к*) lying; mendacious **2** (*улы́бка*) false, deceitful

♂ **ли, ль 1** (*interrog. particle*): **возмо́жно ли?** is it possible? **2** (*conj.*) whether, if; **не зна́ю, придёт ли он** I don't know whether he is coming **3**: **ли... ли** whether ... or; **сего́дня ли, за́втра ли** whether today or tomorrow

либера́л, а *m.* liberal; **л.-демокра́т** Liberal Democrat

либерализа́ци|я, и *n.* liberalization

либерали́зм, а *m.* liberalism

либерализ|ова́ть, у́ю *impf. and pf.* to liberalize

либера́л|ьный, ∼ен, ∼ьна *adj.* liberal

либери́|ец, йца *m.* Liberian

либери́й|ка, ки *f. of* ▶ либери́ец

либери́йский *adj.* Liberian

Либе́ри|я, и *f.* Liberia

♂ **ли́бо** *conj.* or; **л. ... л.** (either) ... or

либре́тто *nt. indecl.* libretto

Лива́н, а *m.* (the) Lebanon

лива́н|ец, ца *m.* Lebanese

лива́н|ка, ки *f. of* ▶ лива́нец

лива́нский *adj.* Lebanese

ли́в|ень, ня *m.* heavy shower, downpour

ли́вер, а *m.* (cul.) offal

ли́вер|ный *adj. of* ▶ ли́вер; **∼ная колбаса́** offal sausage

ливи́|ец, йца *m.* Libyan

ливи́й|ка, ки *f. of* ▶ ливи́ец

ливи́йский *adj.* Libyan

Ли́ви|я, и *f.* Libya

ли́г|а, и *f.* league

♂ **ли́дер, а** *m.* leader

лиди́р|овать, ую *impf.* to lead, be in the lead

ли|за́ть, жу́, ∼жешь *impf.* (*of* ▶ лизну́ть) to lick

ли́зинг, а *m.* (econ.) leasing

лиз|ну́ть, ну́, нёшь *inst. pf. of* ▶ лиза́ть

лизоблю́д, а *m.* (infml, pej.) lickspittle, bootlicker

ликвида́ци|я, и *f.* **1** (comm.) liquidation **2** (pol., etc., *отме́на*) liquidation; elimination, abolition

ликвиди́р|овать, ую *impf. and pf.* **1** (comm.) to liquidate, wind up **2** (*отменя́ть*) to eliminate, abolish

ликви́д|ный, ∼ен, ∼на *adj.* (fin.) liquid; **∼ные акти́вы, сре́дства** liquid assets

ликёр, а *m.* liqueur

ликёрово́дочный *adj.*: **∼ заво́д** distillery

лик|ова́ть, у́ю *impf.* to rejoice, exult

лилипу́т, а *m.* (*челове́к*) dwarf (offens.) (*person affected by dwarfism*)

ли́ли|я, и *f.* lily

лило́вый *adj.* purple

лима́н, а *m.* estuary; (*солёное о́зеро*) salt marshes

лими́т, а *m.* (*но́рма*) quota; (**на** + *a.*) (*ограниче́ние*) limit (on)

лимо́н, а *m.* lemon

лимона́д, а *m.* **1** lemonade; lemon squash **2** (*любо́й газиро́ванный напи́ток*) fizzy drink

лимузи́н, а *m.* limousine

ли́мф|а, ы *f.* (physiol.) lymph

лингви́ст, а *m.* linguist

лингви́стик|а, и *f.* linguistics

лингвисти́ческий *adj.* linguistic

лине́йк|а, и *f.* **1** (*на бума́ге*) (ruled) line **2** (*инструме́нт*) ruler **3** (*строй в шере́нгу*) line; parade

ли́нз|а, ы *f.* lens

♂ **ли́ни|я, и** *f.* line; (fig.) policy

лино́леум, а *m.* linoleum

линя́|ть, ет *impf.* (*of* ▶ полиня́ть) **1** (*о мате́рии*) to fade; (*о кра́ске*) to run **2** (*о живо́тных*) to moult (BrE), molt (AmE)

ли́п|а, ы *f.* lime (tree)

ли́п|кий, ∼ок, ∼ка́, ∼ко *adj.* sticky, adhesive

ли́р|а, ы *f.* lyre

ли́рик|а, и *f.* lyric poetry

лири́ческий *adj.* **1** (*поэ́зия, сопра́но*) lyric **2** (*настрое́ние*) lyrical

лис|á, ы́, *pl.* **∼ы** *f.* fox; **чернобу́рая л.** silver fox

лис|ёнок, ёнка, *pl.* **∼я́та, ∼я́т** *m.* fox cub

ли́сий *adj. of* ▶ лиса́

лиси́ц|а, ы *f.* fox; vixen

Лиссабо́н, а *m.* Lisbon

♂ **лист[1], á,** *pl.* **∼ья, ∼ьев** *m.* (*расте́ния*) leaf

♂ **лист[2], á,** *pl.* **∼ы́, ∼о́в** *m.* **1** (*бума́ги*) sheet **2**: **опро́сный л.** questionnaire; **охра́нный л.** safe conduct

листа́|ть, ю *impf.* (infml) to leaf through

листв|á, ы́ *f.* (collect.) leaves, foliage

ли́ственниц|а, ы *f.* (bot.) larch

ли́ственный *adj.* (bot.) deciduous

листо́вк|а, и *f.* leaflet

лист|о́к, ка́ *m.* **1** *dim. of* ▶ лист[1], ▶ лист[2] **2** (*листо́вка*) leaflet **3** (*бланк*) form

листопа́д, а *m.* fall of the leaves

лита́вр|ы, ∼ *f. pl.* (*sg.* **∼а, ∼ы**) kettledrum

Литв|á, ы́ *f.* Lithuania

лите́йный *adj.* founding, casting

литера́тор, а *m.* man of letters

♂ **литерату́р|а, ы** *f.* literature; **худо́жественная л.** fiction

литерату́р|ный, ∼ен, ∼на *adj.* literary

литературове́д, а *m.* literary critic

лито́в|ец, ца *m.* Lithuanian

лито́в|ка, ки *f. of* ▶ лито́вец

лито́вский *adj.* Lithuanian

литогра́фи|я, и *f.* **1** (*о́ттиск*) lithograph **2** (*иску́сство*) lithography

л

лит|ой *adj.* cast; ~**ая сталь** cast steel

литр, а *m.* litre (BrE), liter (AmE)

литурги|я, и *f.* liturgy

лить, лью, льёшь, *past* **лил, лила́, ли́ло,**
imper. **лей** *impf.* ▮ to pour (*trans. and
intrans.*); **л. слёзы** to shed tears; **дождь льёт
как из ведра́** it is raining cats and dogs
▮ (tech.) to found, cast, mould (BrE), mold
(AmE)

ли́|ться, льётся, *past* ~**лся,** ~**ла́сь** *impf.*
▮ to flow; to stream, pour ▮ *pass. of* ▶ **лить**

лифт, а *m.* lift, elevator

лифтёр, а *m.* lift operator

ли́фчик, а *m.* bra

лих|о́й, ~, ~**а́,** ~**о,** ~**и́** *adj.* (infml) dashing,
spirited; jaunty

лихора́дк|а, и *f.* ▮ fever (also fig.); **сенна́я л.**
hay fever ▮ (*на губа́х*) cold sore

лицев|о́й *adj.* ▮ (anat.) facial; ~**ая
сторона́** (*зда́ния*) facade, front; (*мате́рии*)
right side; (*моне́ты*) obverse ▮ (bookkeeping):
л. счёт personal account

лице́|й, я *m.* lycée

лицеме́р, а *m.* hypocrite

лицеме́ри|е, я *nt.* hypocrisy

лицеме́р|ный, ~**ен,** ~**на** *adj.* hypocritical

лицензио́нный *adj.* (econ.) (*сде́лка*)
licensing; (*произведённый по лице́нзии*)
licensed

лицензи́р|овать, ую *impf. and pf.* (econ.)
to license

лице́нзи|я, и *f.* (econ.) licence (BrE), license
(AmE)

☞ **лиц|о́, а́,** *pl.* ~**а** *nt.* ▮ face; **черты́** ~**а́** features;
сказа́ть в л. кому́-н. to say to sb's face; **знать
кого́-н. в л.** to know sb by sight; **быть к** ~**у́**
(+ *d.*) to suit, become; (fig.) to become, befit;
~**о́м к** ~**у́** face to face; **пе́ред** ~**о́м** (+ *g.*) in
the face (of) ▮ (*нару́жная сторона́*) exterior;
(*мате́рии*) right side; (fig.): **показа́ть това́р**
~**о́м** to show sth to advantage; to make the
best of sth ▮ (*челове́к*) person; **гражда́нское
л.** civilian; **должностно́е л.** official; **духо́вное
л.** clergyman; **в** ~**е́** (+ *g.*) in the person (of);
от ~**а́** (+ *g.*) in the name (of), on behalf (of)
▮ (*индивидуа́льный о́блик*) identity

личи́нк|а, и *f.* larva, grub; maggot

☞ **ли́чно** *adv.* personally, in person

☞ **ли́чност|ь, и** *f.* ▮ (*индивидуа́льность*)
personality ▮ (*челове́к*) person, individual;
удостовере́ние ~**и** identity card;
установи́ть чью-н. л. to establish sb's
identity

☞ **ли́чн|ый** *adj.* personal; (*ча́стный*) private;
~**ая охра́на** bodyguard; ~**ая со́бственность**
personal property; **л. соста́в** staff

лиша́йник, а *m.* (bot.) lichen

лиш|а́ть, а́ю *impf. of* ▶ **лиши́ть**

лиш|а́ться, а́юсь *impf. of* ▶ **лиши́ться**

лише́ни|е, я *nt.* ▮ (*де́йствие*) deprivation; **л.
гражда́нских прав** (law) disenfranchisement

▮ (*usu. in pl.*) (*недоста́ток*) privation,
hardship

лиш|ённый, ~**ён,** ~**ена́,** ~**ено́** *p.p.p. of*
▶ **лиши́ть** *and adj.* (+ *g.*) lacking (in), devoid
(of)

лиш|и́ть, у́, и́шь *pf.* (*of* ▶ **лиша́ть**) (+ *g.*)
to deprive (of); **л. кого́-н. насле́дства** to
disinherit sb; **л. себя́ жи́зни** to take one's life

лиш|и́ться, у́сь, и́шься *pf.* (*of* ▶ **лиша́ться**)
(+ *g.*) to lose, be deprived (of); **л. зре́ния** to
lose one's sight

☞ **ли́шн|ий** *adj.* ▮ (*избы́точный*) superfluous;
unnecessary; unwanted ▮ (*запасно́й*) spare,
odd; **л. раз** once more; **с** ~**им** (infml) and
more, odd

☞ **лишь** *adj. and conj.* only; **не хвата́ет л. одного́**
one thing only is lacking; **л. то́лько** as soon
as; **л. бы** if only, provided that; **л. бы он мог
прие́хать** provided that he can come

лоб, лба, о лбе́, во на лбу́, *pl.* **лбы, лбов**
m. forehead, brow

ло́бби *nt. indecl.* (pol.) lobby

лобби́р|овать, ую *impf. and pf.* (pol.)
▮ (*кого́*) to lobby (*sb*) ▮ (*что*) to lobby
for (*sth*)

ло́бзик, а *m.* fretsaw

лобов|о́й *adj.* frontal; ~**ая ата́ка** (mil.)
frontal attack; ~**о́е стекло́** windscreen (BrE),
windshield (AmE)

лов|и́ть, лю́, ~**ишь** *impf.* (*of* ▶ **пойма́ть**) to
(try to) catch; (fig.): **л. (удо́бный) моме́нт**
to (try to) seize an opportunity; to look for
an opportunity; **л. себя́ на чём-н.** to catch
oneself at sth; **л. ста́нцию** (radio) to try to
pick up a station

ло́в|кий, ~**ок,** ~**ка́,** ~**ко** *adj.* ▮ (*иску́сный*)
adroit, dexterous, deft; **л. ход** master stroke
▮ (*хи́трый*) cunning, smart

ло́вко *adv.* (*иску́сно*) adroitly; **он л. устро́ился**
he fixed himself up with a good job

ло́вкост|ь, и *f.* ▮ (*иску́сность*) adroitness,
dexterity, deftness; **л. рук** sleight of hand
▮ (*хи́трость*) cunning, smartness

ло́в|ля, ли, *g. pl.* ~**ель** *f.* catching, hunting;
рыбная л. fishing

лову́шк|а, и *f.* snare, trap (also fig.)

ло́в|че and ~**чее** *comp. of* ▶ **ло́вкий,** ▶ **ло́вко**

логари́фм, а *m.* (math.) logarithm

ло́гик|а, и *f.* logic

логи́ческий *adj.* logical

логи́ч|ный, ~**ен,** ~**на** *adj.* = **логи́ческий**

ло́гов|о, а *nt.* den, lair

логопе́д, а *m.* speech therapist

логоти́п, а *m.* (*эмбле́ма*) logo

ло́дк|а, и *f.* boat; **подво́дная л.** submarine;
спаса́тельная л. lifeboat; **ката́ться на** ~**е** to
go boating

ло́дочник, а *m.* boatman

лоды́жк|а, и *f.* (anat.) ankle bone

ло́ж|а, и *f.* ▮ (theatr.) box ▮ (*масо́нская*) lodge

ложби́н|а, ы *f.* (geog.) hollow, dip

лож|и́ться, у́сь, и́шься *impf. of* ▶ **лечь**

☞ (margin) **Л**

ло́жк|а, и *f.* **1** spoon; **столо́вая л.** tablespoon; **ча́йная л.** teaspoon **2** (*количество*) spoonful

ло́ж|ный, ~ен, ~на *adj.* false; **~ная тревога** false alarm

ложь, лжи *f.* lie

лоз|а́, ы́, *pl.* **~ы** *f.* vine

ло́зунг, а *m.* **1** (*призыв*) slogan **2** (*плакат*) banner

лока́л|ьный, ~ен, ~ьна *adj.* local; **~ьная сеть** (comput.) local area network

лока́тор, а *m.* locator

локомоти́в, а *m.* locomotive

ло́кон, а *m.* lock, curl, ringlet

ло́к|оть, тя, *pl.* **~ти, ~те́й** *m.* elbow

лом, а, *pl.* **~ы́, ~о́в** *m.* **1** (*инструмент*) crowbar **2** (*sg. only; collect.*) scrap, waste; (*ломаные предметы*) scrap, waste; **желе́зный л.** scrap iron

ло́маный *adj.* broken; **л. англи́йский язы́к** broken English

лома́|ть, ю *impf.* (*of* ▶ **слома́ть**) **1** to break **2** (*no pf.*) (fig.): **л. себе́ го́лову** (**над** + *i.*) to rack one's brains (over); **л. ру́ки** to wring one's hands

лома́|ться, юсь *impf.* **1** (*pf.* **с~**) to break **2** (*pf.* **с~**) (*о голосе*) to crack, break **3** (*pf.* **по~**) (infml, *кривляться*) to pose, put on airs

ломба́рд, а *m.* pawnshop; **заложи́ть в л.** to pawn

лом|и́ть, лю́, ~ишь *impf.* **1** (*impers.*) to cause to ache; **у меня́ ~ит спи́ну** my back aches **2** (infml, *пробиваться*) to break through, rush

лом|и́ться, ~лю́сь, ~ишься *impf.* **1** (*быть переполненным*) to be (near to) breaking; (**от** + *g.*) to burst (with), be crammed (with); **ве́тви ~ятся от плодо́в** the boughs are groaning with fruit **2** (infml) (*стремиться проникнуть*) to force one's way; (*идти толпами*) (**на** + *a.*) to flock (to)

ло́м|кий, ~ок, ~ка́, ~ко *adj.* fragile, brittle

ло́мтик, а *m.* slice; **ре́зать ~ами** to slice

Ло́ндон, а *m.* London

ло́ндон|ец, ца *m.* Londoner

ло́ндон|ка, ки *f. of* ▶ **ло́ндонец**

ло́ндонский *adj.* London

лопа́т|а, ы *f.* spade, shovel

лопа́тк|а, и *f.* **1** (*лопата*) shovel; (*садовника*) trowel; (cul.) spatula; blade (*of turbine*) **2** (anat.) shoulder blade; (*часть туши*) shoulder

ло́п|аться, аюсь *impf. of* ▶ **ло́пнуть**

ло́п|нуть, ну, нешь *pf.* (*of* ▶ **ло́паться**) **1** (*о пузыре, шине, почке*) burst; (*о стекле*) to break, crack; (*о верёвке, струне*) to snap, break; (fig., infml) **чуть не л. от сме́ха** to split one's sides with laughter, burst with laughter; **моё терпе́ние ~нуло** my patience is exhausted **2** (fig., infml) (*потерпеть неудачу*) to fail, be a failure; (fin.) to go bankrupt, crash

лопу́х, а́ *m.* **1** (bot.) burdock **2** (sl.) fool

лорд, а *m.* lord; **пала́та ~ов** House of Lords

Лос-А́нджелес, а *m.* Los Angeles

лоск, а *m.* lustre (BrE), luster (AmE), gloss, shine (also fig.)

лоску́т, а́, *pl.* **~ы́, ~о́в** *and* **~ья, ~ьев** *m.* rag, shred, scrap

лосн|и́ться, ю́сь, и́шься *impf.* to be glossy, shine

лосо́с|ь, я, *pl.* **~и, ~ей** *m.* salmon

лос|ь, я, *pl.* **~и, ~е́й** *m.* elk (BrE), moose (AmE)

лосьо́н, а *m.* lotion; (*после бритья*) aftershave

лот, а *m.* (*на аукционе*) lot

лоте́рейный *adj. of* ▶ **лотере́я**; **л. биле́т** lottery ticket

лотере́|я, и *f.* lottery, raffle

лот|о́к, ка́ *m.* **1** (*прилавок*) hawker's stand; (*ящик для торговли*) hawker's tray **2** (*для ссыпания*) chute; (*для стока*) gutter

ло́тос, а *m.* (bot.) lotus

лото́чник, а *m.* hawker

лох, а *m.* (sl.) simpleton, halfwit

лохма́т|ый, ~, ~а *adj.* **1** (*животное*) shaggy(-haired) **2** (*человек, волосы*) dishevelled (BrE), disheveled (AmE), tousled

лохмо́ть|я, ев (*no sg.*) rags; **в ~ях** in rags, ragged

лошади́н|ый *adj.* of horses; equine; **~ая си́ла** horsepower

ло́шад|ь, и, *pl.* **~и, ~е́й, ~я́м, ~ьми́, о ~я́х** *f.* horse; **бегова́я, скакова́я л.** racehorse; **чистокро́вная л.** thoroughbred; **сади́ться на л.** to mount

лоя́льность, и *f.* loyalty

лоя́л|ьный, ~ен, ~ьна *adj.* loyal (*to the State authorities*)

ЛСД *m. indecl.* (*abbr. of* **диэтиламид лизерги́новой кислоты́**) LSD

луг, а, о ~е, на ~у́, *pl.* **~а́, ~о́в** *m.* meadow; **заливно́й л.** water meadow

лу́ж|а, и *f.* puddle, pool; **сесть в ~у** (fig., infml) to get into a mess; to slip up

лужа́йк|а, и *f.* (*полянка*) (forest) glade; (*газон*) lawn

лу́з|а, ы *f.* (billiard) pocket

лук¹, а *m.* (collect.) (*растение*) onions; **голо́вка ~а** (a single) onion; **зелёный л.** spring onion(s) (BrE), scallion(s); **л.-поре́й** leek(s)

лук², а *m.* (*оружие*) bow

лука́в|ый, ~, ~а *adj.* **1** (*хитрый*) crafty, sly, cunning **2** (*игривый*) arch

лу́ковиц|а, ы *f.* **1** (*головка лука*) onion **2** (bot.) bulb

лун|а́, ы́, *pl.* **~ы** *f.* moon; **Л.** the Moon

луна́тик, а *m.* sleepwalker, somnambulist

лу́нк|а, и *f.* hole

лу́н|ный *adj.* of ▶ **луна́**; (astron.) lunar; **~ое затме́ние** lunar eclipse; **~ная ночь** moonlit night; **л. свет** moonlight

лу́п|а, ы *f.* magnifying glass

луч, а́ *m.* ray; beam; **рентге́новские ~и́** X-rays

лучев|о́й *adj. of* ▶ **луч 2** radial **3** (med.): **~а́я боле́знь** radiation sickness

лу́чник, а *m.* archer

Л

лу́чше **1** (*comp. of* ▶ хоро́ший, ▶ хорошо́¹) better; **тем л.** so much the better; **л. всего́, л. всех** best of all; **как мо́жно л.** as well as possible; **нам л. верну́ться** we had better go back **2** (*as particle*) (*предпочти́тельнее*) rather, instead; **дава́йте л. поговори́м об э́том** let's talk it over instead

лу́чш|ий *adj.* (*comp. and superl. of* ▶ хоро́ший) better; best; **к ~ему** for the better; **в ~ем слу́чае** at best

лы́ж|а, и *f.* ski; **го́рные ~и** alpine skis; **бе́гать, ходи́ть на ~ах** to ski

лы́жник, а *m.* skier

лы́жни|ца, цы *f. of* ▶ лы́жник

лыжн|я́, и́ *f.* ski track

лысе́|ть, ю *impf.* (*of* ▶ облысе́ть, ▶ полысе́ть) to go bald

лы́син|а, ы *f.* bald patch

лы́с|ый, ~, ~а́, ~о *adj.* bald; (*гора́*) bare

ль = ли

льв|ёнок, ёнка, *pl.* **~я́та, ~я́т** *m.* lion cub

льви́н|ый *adj. of* ▶ лев; **~ая до́ля** (fig.) the lion's share

льви́ца, ы *f.* lioness

львя́та *see* ▶ львёнок

льго́т|а, ы *f.* (*блока́дникам, инвали́дам*) privilege; advantage; benefit; (*при опла́те*) discount

льго́тный *adj.* privileged; favourable (BrE), favorable (AmE); **л. биле́т** concessionary ticket

льда *g. sg. of* ▶ лёд

льди́н|а, ы *f.* block of ice, ice floe

льна, льну *see* ▶ лён

льня́н|о́й *adj.* of flax; **~о́го цве́та** flaxen **2** (*пла́тье*) linen

льстец, а́ *m.* flatterer

льсти́в|ый, ~, ~а *adj.* (*слова́*) flattering; (*челове́к*) smooth-tongued

льстить, льщу, льстишь *impf.* (*of* ▶ польсти́ть) **1** (+ *d.*) to flatter; to gratify; **э́то льстит его́ самолю́бию** it flatters his self-esteem **2** (+ *a.*, *with refl. pron. only*) to delude; **л. себя́ наде́ждой** to flatter oneself with the hope

лью, льёшь *see* ▶ лить

лэпто́п, а *m.* laptop (computer)

любе́зност|ь, и *f.* **1** (*сво́йство*) courtesy; politeness, civility **2** (*услу́га*) kindness; **оказа́ть, сде́лать кому́-н. л.** to do sb a kindness

любе́зн|ый, ~ен, ~на *adj.* **1** (*ве́жливый*) courteous; polite; obliging **2** (*ми́лый*) kind, amiable; **бу́дьте ~ны...** (polite form of request) be so kind as ...

люби́м|ец, ца *m.* favourite (BrE), favorite (AmE), darling

люби́м|ица, ицы *f. of* ▶ люби́мец

люби́мчик, а *m.* (pej.) pet, blue-eyed boy

⚷ **люби́м|ый, ~, ~а** *adj.* **1** (*дорого́й*) beloved, loved; (*as n. m.*, **~ого,** *f.* **~ая, ~ой**) (my)

beloved **2** (*предпочита́емый*) favourite (BrE), favorite (AmE)

люби́тел|ь, я *m.* **1** (+ *g. or* + *inf.*) lover; **л. му́зыки** music lover; **л. соба́к** dog lover; **он л. спле́тничать** he loves gossiping **2** (*непрофессиона́л*) amateur

люби́тель|ница, ницы *f. of* ▶ люби́тель

люби́тельский *adj.* **1** amateur; **л. спекта́кль** amateur performance **2** (pej.) amateurish

⚷ **люб|и́ть, лю́, ~ишь** *impf.* **1** (*мать, ро́дину*) to love **2** (*чита́ть, му́зыку*) to like, be fond (of) **3** (infml, *о расте́ниях*) to like; **фиа́лки ~ят тень** violets like shade

люб|ова́ться, у́юсь *impf.* (*of* ▶ полюбова́ться) (+ *i. or* **на** + *a.*) to admire

любо́вник, а *m.* lover

любо́вниц|а, ы *f.* lover, mistress

любо́вн|ый *adj.* **1** love-; **~ая исто́рия** love affair **2** (*отноше́ние*) loving

⚷ **люб|о́вь, ви́,** *i.* **~о́вью** *f.* (**к** + *d.*) love (for, of); **занима́ться ~о́вью** to make love

любозна́тел|ьный, ~ен, ~ьна *adj.* inquisitive

⚷ **любо́й** **1** *adj.* any; (*из двои́х*) either; **л. цено́й** at any price **2** (*as n.*) anyone; (*из двои́х*) either

любопы́т|ный, ~ен, ~на *adj.* curious; interesting; (*impers.* + *d. and inf.*) **~но, придёт ли она́** I wonder if she will come

любопы́тств|о, а *nt.* curiosity

лю́д|и, е́й, ~ям, ~ьми, о ~ях (*no sg.*) **1** (*pl. of* ▶ челове́к) people **2** (mil.) men **3** (*ка́дры*) staff, people

людое́д, а *m.* **1** (*челове́к*) cannibal; (*живо́тное*) maneater; **тигр-л.** man-eating tiger **2** (*в ска́зках*) ogre

люк, а *m.* **1** (naut., aeron.) hatch, hatchway **2** (theatr.) trap **3**: **светово́й л.** skylight

люкс *adj. indecl.* de luxe, luxury

Люксембу́рг, а *m.* Luxembourg

люксембу́ргский *adj.* Luxembourg

люксембу́рж|енка and **люксембу́рж|ка, (ен)ки** *f. of* ▶ люксембу́ржец

люксембу́рж|ец, ца *m.* Luxembourger

лю́тик, а *m.* (bot.) buttercup

лю́т|ня, ни, *g. pl.* **~ен** and **~ней** *f.* (mus.) lute

лю́т|ый, ~, ~а́, ~о *adj.* ferocious, fierce, cruel; (*моро́з*) sharp; (*не́нависть*) intense

ля *nt. indecl.* (mus.) A; **л. бемо́ль** A flat

ляг and **ля́гте** *imper. of* ▶ лечь

ляга́|ть, а́ю *impf.* (*of* ▶ лягну́ть) to kick

ляга́|ться, юсь *impf.* to kick (intrans); (*друг дру́га*) to kick one another

лягн|у́ть, у́, нёшь *inst. pf. of* ▶ ляга́ть

ля́|гу, жешь, гут *see* ▶ лечь

лягу́шк|а, и *f.* frog

ля́жк|а, и *f.* (infml) thigh, haunch

лязг, а (*no pl.*) *m.* clank, clang

ля́зга|ть, ю *impf.* (+ *i.*) to clank, clang; **он ~л зуба́ми** his teeth were chattering

ля́мк|а, и *f.* strap

ля́п|нуть, ну, нешь *pf.* (infml) to blurt out

Мм

м (*abbr. of* **метр**) m, metre(s) (BrE), meter(s) (AmE)

мавзоле́|й, я *m.* mausoleum

Маврита́ни|я, и *f.* Mauritania

маг, а *m.* magician, wizard

магази́н, а *m.* **1** shop; **гастрономи́ческий/ продово́льственный м.** grocer's (shop) (BrE), grocery store (AmE); **универса́льный м.** department store **2** (*у стрелкового оружия*) magazine

МАГАТЭ́ *nt. indecl.* (*abbr. of* **Междунаро́дное аге́нтство по а́томной эне́ргии**) IAEA (*International Atomic Energy Agency*)

маги́стр, а *m.* **1** (*лицо*) holder of a master's degree **2** (*учёная степень*) master's degree

магистра́л|ь, и *f.* **1** (*водная, газовая*) main; (*железнодорожная*) main line **2** (*улица*) arterial road, main road

маги́ческий *adj.* magic(al)

ма́ги|я, и *f.* magic

магна́т, а *m.* magnate, tycoon

магнети́зм, а *m.* magnetism

магнети́ческий *adj.* magnetic

ма́гни|й, я *m.* (chem.) magnesium

магни́т, а *m.* magnet

магни́тн|ый *adj.* magnetic; **~ая ка́рточка** smart card, swipe card

магнито́л|а, ы *f.* radio cassette player

магнитофо́н, а *m.* tape recorder; **ви́део~** video (cassette) recorder, VCR

магно́ли|я, и *f.* (bot.) magnolia

маде́р|а, ы *f.* Madeira (wine)

мадо́нн|а, ы *f.* madonna

Мадри́д, а *m.* Madrid

мажо́р, а *m.* (mus.) major key

ма́|зать, жу, жешь *impf.* **1** (*pf.* **на~**, **по~**) (*смазывать*) to oil, grease, lubricate **2** (*pf.* **на~**, **по~**) (*намазывать*) to smear (with); **м. хлеб ма́слом** to spread butter on bread, butter bread **3** (*pf.* **из~**, **за~**) (infml, *пачкать*) to soil, stain **4** (*pf.* **про~**) (*не попадать*, infml) to miss

ма́|заться, жусь, жешься *impf.* **1** (*pf.* **из~**, **за~**) (*пачкаться*) to soil oneself, stain oneself **2** (*pf.* **на~**) to make up **3** (*pf.* **на~**) (+ *i.*) to apply (*ointment, cream, etc.*)

мазохи́ст, а *m.* masochist

мазохи́ст|ка, ки *f. of* ▸ **мазохи́ст**

мазу́т, а *m.* (tech.) fuel oil

маз|ь, и *f.* **1** (*лекарство*) ointment **2** (*для смазки*) grease

ма́|й, я *m.* May

ма́йк|а, и *f.* sleeveless top; (*нижняя*) vest (BrE), undershirt (AmE)

майоне́з, а *m.* (cul.) mayonnaise

майо́р, а *m.* major (*military rank*)

майора́н, а *m.* (bot.) marjoram

ма́йский *adj.* of ▸ **май**; **м. жук** cockchafer

мак, а *m.* (*растение*) poppy; (*семена*) poppy seed(s)

мака́к|а, и *f.* (zool.) macaque

макаро́н|ы, ~ *pl.* pasta

мак|а́ть, а́ю *impf.* (*of* ▸ **макну́ть**) to dip

македо́нец Macedonian

Македо́ни|я, и *f.* Macedonia

македо́н|ка, ки *f. of* ▸ **македо́нец**

македо́нский *adj.* Macedonian; **Алекса́ндр М.** Alexander the Great

маке́т, а *m.* model; (*книги*) dummy

макия́ж, а *m.* make-up

ма́клер, а *m.* (comm.) broker

мак|ну́ть, ну́, нёшь *inst. pf. of* ▸ **мака́ть**

максимали́зм, а *m.* uncompromisingness

максимали́ст, а *m.* uncompromising person

максима́л|ьный, ~ен, ~ьна *adj.* maximum

ма́ксимум, а *m.* **1** maximum **2** (*as adv.*) at most; **м. сто рубле́й** a hundred roubles at most

макулату́р|а, ы *f.* paper for recycling

маку́шк|а, и *f.* **1** (*дерева*) top **2** (*головы*) crown

мала́|ец, йца *m.* Malay

Мала́йзи|я, и *f.* Malaysia

мала́й|ка, ки *f. of* ▸ **мала́ец**

мала́йский *adj.* Malay, Malayan

Мала́й|я, и *f.* Malaya

малахи́т, а *m.* (min.) malachite

мале́йший *adj.* (*superl. of* ▸ **ма́лый**) least, slightest

мал|ёк, ька́ *m.* young fish; (*collect.*) fry

ма́леньк|ий *adj.* **1** little, small **2** (*незначительный*) slight **3** (*малолетний*) young; (*as n.* **м.**, **~ого**, *f.* **~ая**, **~ой**) the baby, the child; **~ие** the young

мали́н|а, ы (*по pl.*) *f.* (*кустарник*) raspberry bush; (*ягоды*) raspberries

мали́новый *adj.* **1** (*варенье*) raspberry **2** (*цвет*) crimson

ма́ло *adv.* (*времени, денег*) little, not much; (*книг, людей*) few; (*недостаточно*) not enough; (*читать*) not much; **э́того ма́ло** this is not enough; **я м. где быва́л** I have hardly been anywhere; **м. того́** moreover; **м. того́, что...** not only ..., it is not enough that ...; **м. того́ он сам прие́хал, он привёз всех това́рищей** it was not enough that he came himself, but he had to bring

M

all his friends

маловáж|ный, ~ен, ~на *adj.* of little importance, insignificant

маловáт, ~а, ~о *adj.* (infml) on the small side

малодýш|ный, ~ен, ~на *adj.* faint-hearted

маложи́рный *adj.* low-fat

малоиму́щ|ий, ~, ~а *adj.* needy, indigent

малокалори́й|ный, ~ен, ~йна *adj.* low-calorie

малокро́ви|е, я *nt.* anaemia (BrE), anemia (AmE)

малоле́тн|ий *adj.* **1** young; juvenile **2** (*as n.* м., ~его, *f.* ~яя, ~ей) (*ребёнок*) infant; (*подросток*) juvenile, minor

малолитрáж|ка, и *f.* (infml) compact (car); mini

малому́щ|ный, ~ен, ~на *adj.* low-powered; weak

малоподви́ж|ный, ~ен, ~на *adj.* not mobile, slow-moving

малоро́сл|ый, ~, ~а *adj.* undersized, stunted

малоупотреби́тел|ьный, ~ен, ~ьна *adj.* infrequent, rarely used

малочи́слен|ный, ~, ~на *adj.* small (in numbers); scanty

М ✍ **мá|лый**, ~, ~á, ~ó *adj.* little, (too) small; э́ти сапоги́ мне ~ы́ these boots are too small for me; (*as nt. n.* ~ое, ~ого) little; сáмое ~ое (infml) at the least; без ~ого almost, all but

✍ **малы́ш**, á *m.* (infml) child, kid; little boy

мáльв|а, ы *f.* (bot.) mallow

Мальо́рк|а, и *f.* Majorca

Мáльт|а, ы *f.* Malta

мальти́|ец, йца *m.* Maltese

мальти́й|ка, ки *f. of* ▶ **мальти́ец**

мальти́йский *adj.* Maltese

✍ **мáльчик**, а *m.* boy

мальчи́шеский *adj.* boyish

мальчи́шк|а, и *m.* (infml) (little) boy

маля́р, á *m.* (house) painter, decorator

маляри́|я, и *f.* (med.) malaria

маля́р|ный *adj. of* ▶ **маля́р**; ~ная кисть paintbrush

✍ **мáм|а**, ы *f.* mum, mummy (BrE), mom, mommy (AmE)

мáмин *adj.* mother's

мáмонт, а *m.* mammoth

мáнго *nt. indecl.* (bot.) mango

мангу́ст, а *m.* (zool.) mongoose

мандари́н, а *m.* (*дерево, плод*) mandarin, tangerine

мандáт, а *m.* mandate

мандоли́н|а, ы *f.* (mus.) mandolin

манёвр, а *m.* **1** manoeuvre (BrE), maneuver (AmE); manoeuvres (BrE), maneuvers (AmE) **2** (*in pl.*) (rail.) shunting

маневри́р|овать, ую *impf.* (*of* ▶ сманеври́ровать) to manoeuvre (BrE),

✍ key word

maneuver (AmE)

манéж, а *m.* **1** riding school, manège **2** (*цирка*) ring **3**: спорти́вный м. sports hall **4**: (дéтский) м. playpen

манекéн, а *m.* mannequin; dummy

манекéнщик, а *m.* male model

манекéнщиц|а, ы *f.* model

манéр|а, ы *f.* **1** manner, style; м. вести́ себя́ way of behaving; м. держáть себя́ bearing, carriage; петь в ~е Карýзо to sing in the style of Caruso **2** (*in pl.*) manners; у негó плохи́е ~ы he has no manners

манéр|ный, ~ен, ~на *adj.* affected

манжéт|а, ы *f.* cuff

маникю́р, а *m.* manicure

маникю́рш|а, и *f.* manicurist

манипули́р|овать, ую *impf.* (+ *i.*) to manipulate

манипуля́ци|я, и *f.* **1** manipulation **2** (fig.) machination, intrigue

мани́|ть, ю́, ~ишь *impf.* (*of* ▶ помани́ть) to beckon

манифéст, а *m.* manifesto; proclamation

манифестáци|я, и *f.* (street) demonstration

мани́шк|а, и *f.* (false) shirt front, dicky

мáни|я, и *f.* **1** mania; м. вели́чия megalomania **2** (fig.) passion, craze

мáнк|а, и *f.* (infml) semolina

мансáрд|а, ы *f.* attic, garret

мáнти|я, и *f.* cloak, mantle; robe, gown

мантó *nt. indecl.* fur coat (*lady's*)

манускри́пт, а *m.* manuscript

манья́к, а *m.* maniac

марáзм, а *m.* (med.) marasmus; стáрческий м. senility; (fig.) decay

марафóн, а *m.* marathon

маргари́н, а *m.* margarine

маргари́тк|а, и *f.* (bot.) daisy

маргинáл, а *m.* person living on the fringes of society

маргинáл|ьный, ~ен, ~ьна *adj.* marginal

маринáд, а *m.* marinade

марини́ст, а *m.* painter of seascapes

марино́ванный *p.p.p. of* ▶ маринова́ть *and adj.* (cul.) pickled

марин|овáть, у́ю *impf.* (*pf.* за~) to pickle

марионéт|ка, ки *f.* marionette; puppet (also fig.)

марионéт|очный *adj. of* ▶ марионéтка; ~очное госудáрство puppet state

марихуáн|а, ы *f.* marijuana

✍ **мáрк|а**, и *f.* **1** (*почтóвая*) (postage) stamp **2** (*сорт*) brand, make; фабри́чная м. trademark

мáркер, а *m.* (*фломáстер*) marker (pen)

мáркéтинг, а *m.* marketing

марки́з|а, ы *f.* marchioness

маркси́зм, а *m.* Marxism

мáрл|я, и *f.* gauze

мармелáд, а *m.* (*конфéты*) fruit jellies

мародёр, а *m.* marauder, pillager

мародёрств|о, а *nt.* pillage, looting

марокка́н|ец, ца *m.* Moroccan

марокка́н|ка, ки *f. of* ▶ **марокка́нец**

марокка́нский *adj.* Moroccan

Маро́кко *nt. indecl.* Morocco

Марс, а *m.* (astron., myth.) Mars

марсиа́н|ин, ина, *pl.* **~е, ~** *m.* Martian

✐ **март, а** *m.* March

ма́ртовский *adj. of* ▶ **март**

марты́шк|а, и *f.* marmoset; (fig., infml) monkey

марципа́н, а *m.* (кондитерское изделие) (из теста) marzipan sweet; (начинка, глазурь) marzipan

марш, а *m.* march; **м. проте́ста** protest march

ма́ршал, а *m.* marshal

маршир|ова́ть, у́ю *impf.* (of ▶ **промарширова́ть**) to march

✐ **маршру́т, а** *m.* route

ма́ск|а, и *f.* mask; (fig.): **сбро́сить с себя́ ~у** to throw off the mask

маскара́д, а *m.* masked ball; (fig.) masquerade

маскара́дный *adj. of* ▶ **маскара́д**; **м. костю́м** fancy dress

маскир|ова́ть, у́ю *impf.* (of ▶ **замаскирова́ть**) to mask, disguise; (mil.) to camouflage

маскир|ова́ться, у́юсь *impf.* (of ▶ **замаскирова́ться**) to disguise oneself; (mil.) to camouflage oneself

Ма́слениц|а, ы *f.* Shrovetide; carnival

маслёнк|а, и *f.* **1** (посуда для сливочного масла) butter dish **2** (tech.) oilcan

масли́н|а, ы *f.* **1** (дерево) olive tree **2** (плод) olive

✐ **ма́с|ло, ла,** *pl.* **~ла́, ~ел, ~ла́м** *nt.* **1** (in full сли́вочное м.) butter **2** (растительное) oil; **как по ~лу** (fig., infml) swimmingly **3** (краски) oil (paints); **писа́ть ~лом** to paint in oils

масляни́ст|ый, ~, ~а *adj.* oily

масо́н, а *m.* Freemason, Mason

масо́нский *adj.* Masonic

✐ **ма́сс|а, ы** *f.* **1** mass; (in pl.) (pol.) the masses; **в (о́бщей) ~е** on the whole **2** (infml, множество) a lot, lots

масса́ж, а *m.* massage; **то́чечный м.** shiatsu, acupressure

массажи́ст, а *m.* masseur

массажи́стк|а, и *f.* masseuse

масси́в, а *m.* (geog.) massif; (fig.) expanse; **жило́й м.** housing development

масси́в|ный, ~ен, ~на *adj.* massive

масси́рование, я *nt.* massing, concentration

масси́рованный *adj.* intensive

масс-ме́диа *pl. indecl.* mass media

✐ **ма́ссов|ый** *adj.* mass; **~ое произво́дство** mass production; **м. чита́тель** general reader

✐ **ма́стер, а,** *pl.* **~а́** *m.* **1** (цеха) foreman **2** (ремесленник) craftsman, skilled workman **3** (на + a. or + g.) (знаток) expert, master (at, of); (sport) vet(eran); **м. (по ремо́нту)** repairman; **телевизио́нный м.**

TV repairman; **м. на все ру́ки** person able to turn his hand to anything, jack of all trades

ма́стер-кла́сс, а *m.* masterclass

мастерск|а́я, о́й *f.* (столяра) workshop; (художника) studio; (на заводе) shop; **авторемо́нтная м.** car repair garage

ма́стерски *adv.* skilfully; in masterly fashion

мастерств|о́, а́ *nt.* **1** (ремесло) trade, craft **2** (умение) skill, craftsmanship

масти́к|а, и *f.* **1** (смола) mastic **2** (замазка) putty **3** (для натирания полов) floor polish

мастурба́ци|я, и *f.* masturbation

мастурби́р|овать, ую *impf.* to masturbate

маст|ь, и, *pl.* **~и, ~е́й** *f.* **1** (цвет шерсти) colour (BrE), color (AmE) **2** (cards) suit; **ходи́ть в м.** to follow suit

масшта́б, а *m.* scale; **конфли́кт большо́го ~а** large-scale conflict

масшта́б|ный, ~ен, ~на *adj.* **1** scale; **~ная моде́ль** scale model **2** (большой) large-scale

мат[1]**, а** *m.* (chess) checkmate, mate; **объяви́ть м.** (+ d.) to mate

мат[2]**, а** *m.* (половик, тюфяк) mat

мат[3]**, а** *m.* (брань) foul language, abuse; **руга́ться ~ом** to use foul language

матема́тик, а *m.* mathematician

матема́тик|а, и *f.* mathematics

математи́ческий *adj.* mathematical

✐ **материа́л, а** *m.* material; (для публикации в прессе) copy

материали́зм, а *m.* materialism

материализ|ова́ться, у́юсь *impf. and pf.* to materialize

материали́ст, а *m.* materialist

✐ **материа́л|ьный, ~ен, ~ьна** *adj.* material; **~ные затрудне́ния** financial difficulties; **~ное положе́ние** economic conditions

матери́к, а́ *m.* **1** (континент) continent **2** (суша) mainland

материко́вый *adj.* continental

матери́нск|ий *adj.* maternal, motherly; **~ая пла́та** (comput.) motherboard

матер|и́ться, ю́сь, и́шься *impf.* (infml) to swear

мате́ри|я[1]**, и** *f.* (phil.) matter

мате́ри|я[2]**, и** *f.* (text.) material, cloth

матёрчатый *adj.* made of cloth, cloth

матёр|ый, ~, ~а *adj.* **1** (достигший полной зрелости) full-grown, mature (of animal) **2** (опытный) experienced, practised **3** (неисправимый) inveterate, out-and-out

ма́тк|а, и *f.* **1** (anat.) uterus, womb **2** (самка) female; (пчелиная) queen (bee)

ма́тов|ый *adj.* matt; **~ое стекло́** frosted glass

матра́с, а *m.* mattress; **надувно́й м.** air bed, inflatable mattress

матра́|ц, ца = **матра́с**

матрёшк|а, и *f.* matryoshka, (set of) nested Russian dolls

ма́триц|а, ы *f.* **1** (typ.) matrix **2** (tech.) die, mould (BrE), mold (AmE)

М

матро́с, а *m.* sailor, seaman

✍ матч, а *m.* (sport) match; **междунаро́дный м.** Test (match)

✍ мат|ь, *g., d., p.* ~ери, ~ерью, *pl.* ~ери, ~ере́й *f.* **1** mother; **бу́дущая м.** expectant mother, mother-to-be; **м.-одино́чка** single mother **2** (infml) *familiar form of address to a woman*

мафио́зи *m. indecl.* Mafioso

мафио́зный *adj. of* ▶ **ма́фия**

ма́фи|я, и *f.* Mafia

мах, а (у) *m.* (*руко́й*) swing, stroke; (*крыла́*) flap; **одни́м ~ом** at one stroke, in a trice; **с ~у** (infml) rashly, without thinking

ма|ха́ть, шу́, ~шешь *impf.* (*of* ▶ **махну́ть 1**) (+ *i.*) (*руко́й*) to wave; (*ве́ткой*) to brandish; (*хвосто́м*) to wag; (*кры́льями*) to flap

махи́н|а, ы *f.* (infml) bulky and cumbersome object

махина́ци|я, и *f.* machination, intrigue

мах|ну́ть, ну́, нёшь *pf.* **1** *pf. of* ▶ **маха́ть**; **м. руко́й** (**на** + *a.*) (fig., infml) to give up as a bad job **2** (infml, *поеха́ть*) to go, travel

махови́к, а́ *m.* flywheel

махро́вый *adj.* (*ткань*) terry

мац|а́, ы́ (*no pl.*) *f.* matzos (*Jewish biscuits for Passover*)

маче́те *nt. indecl.* machete

ма́чех|а, и *f.* stepmother

ма́чт|а, ы *f.* mast

✍ маши́н|а, ы *f.* **1** (*механи́ческое устро́йство*) machine (also fig.); **посудомо́ечная м.** dishwasher **2** (*автомоби́ль*) car; vehicle; **м. «ско́рой по́мощи»** ambulance

машина́л|ьный, ~ен, ~ьна *adj.* automatic (fig.); **м. отве́т** an automatic response

маши́ни́ст, а *m.* **1** (*комба́йна*) driver, operator (*workman in charge of machinery*) **2** (*локомоти́ва*) engine driver (BrE), engineer (AmE)

машини́стк|а, и *f.* typist

маши́н|ка, ки *f. dim. of* ▶ **маши́на**; (**пи́шущая**) **м.** typewriter

машинопи́сный *adj.* typewritten; **м. текст** typescript

машинострое́ни|е, я *nt.* mechanical engineering, machinery construction

машинострои́тельный *adj. of* ▶ **машинострое́ние**

мая́к, а́ *m.* lighthouse; beacon (also fig.)

ма́ятник, а *m.* pendulum

ма́|яться, юсь, ешься *impf.* (infml) **1** (**с** + *i.*) (*труди́ться*) to toil (with, over) **2** (*томи́ться*) to pine, suffer

мая́ч|ить, у, ишь *impf.* (infml) to loom (up), appear indistinctly

МВД *nt. indecl.* (*abbr. of* **Министе́рство вну́тренних дел**) Ministry of Internal Affairs; ≈ Home Office

МВФ *m. indecl.* (*abbr. of* **Междунаро́дный валю́тный фонд**) IMF (*International Monetary Fund*)

мг (*abbr of* **миллигра́мм**) mg, milligram(s)

мгл|а, ы *f.* **1** (*тума́н*) haze; mist **2** (*темнота́*) gloom, darkness

мгнове́ни|е, я *nt.* instant, moment; **в м. о́ка** in the twinkling of an eye

мгнове́нно *adv.* instantly, in a flash

мгнове́н|ный, ~ен, ~на *adj.* **1** (*сра́зу возника́ющий*) instantaneous **2** (*бы́стро проходя́щий*) momentary

МГУ *m. indecl.* (*abbr. of* **Моско́вский госуда́рственный университе́т**) Moscow State University

✍ ме́бел|ь, и *f.* furniture

ме́бельщик, а *m.* furniture maker

меблир|ова́ть, у́ю *impf. and pf.* to furnish

мегаба́йт, а *m.* (comput.) megabyte

мегафо́н, а *m.* megaphone

мёд, а, о ~е, в меду́/~е, на меду́, *pl.* меды́, медо́в *m.* **1** honey **2** (*стари́нный напи́ток*) mead

мед... *comb. form, abbr. of* ▶ **медици́нский**

медали́ст, а *m.* medallist (BrE), medalist (AmE); medal winner

медали́ст|ка, и *f. of* ▶ **медали́ст**

меда́л|ь, и *f.* medal

медальо́н, а *m.* medallion, locket

медве́диц|а, ы *f.* she-bear; (astron.): **Больша́я М.** the Great Bear (Ursa Major)

медве́д|ь, я *m.* bear (also fig.); **бе́лый м.** polar bear

медвежа́та *pl. of* ▶ **медвежо́нок**

медве́ж|ий *adj. of* ▶ **медве́дь**; **~ья услу́га** well-meant action having opposite effect

медвеж|о́нок, о́нка, *pl.* ~а́та, ~а́т *m.* bear cub

меди́йный *adj.* media

ме́дик, а *m.* **1** (*врач*) physician, doctor **2** (*студе́нт*) medical student

медикаме́нт, а *m.* (*usu. in pl.*) medicine

медита́ци|я, и *f.* meditation

медити́р|овать, ую *impf.* to meditate

ме́диум, а *m.* medium, spiritualist

медици́н|а, ы *f.* medicine

✍ медици́нский *adj.* medical

ме́дленно *adv.* slowly

ме́длен|ный, ~/~ен, ~на *adj.* slow

медли́тел|ьный, ~ен, ~ьна *adj.* sluggish; slow

ме́дл|ить, ю, ишь *impf.* to linger; to tarry; (**с** + *i.*) to be slow (in); **он ~ит с отве́том** he takes a long time to reply, he is slow in replying

ме́дный *adj.* **1** copper **2** (chem.) cupric, cuprous; **м. купоро́с** copper sulphate, bluestone **3** (mus.) brass

медо́вый *adj. of* ▶ **мёд**; **м. ме́сяц** honeymoon

медосмо́тр, а *m.* medical (examination), checkup; **пройти́ м.** to have a checkup

медпу́нкт, а *m.* first-aid station

медсестр|а́, ы́ *f.* (med.) nurse

меду́з|а, ы f. (zool.) jellyfish

мед|ь, и f. **1** copper; жёлтая м. brass **2** (collect.) (*монеты*) coppers

меж (infml) = ме́жду

меж... *comb. form* inter-

межгосуда́рственный *adj.* interstate

междоме́ти|е, я *nt.* (gram.) interjection

междоусо́бный *adj.* internecine

⚹ ме́жду *prep.* (+ i.) or (obs.) (+ g. pl.) **1** between; м. про́чим incidentally; м. тем meanwhile; м. тем как while, whereas **2** (*среди*) among, amongst

междугоро́дний *adj.* = междугоро́дный

междугоро́дный *adj.* intercity; long-distance

⚹ междунаро́дный *adj.* international; М. валю́тный фонд International Monetary Fund

межконтинента́льн|ый *adj.* intercontinental; ~ая баллисти́ческая раке́та intercontinental ballistic missile

межправи́тельственный *adj.* intergovernmental

межрегиона́льный *adj.* inter-regional

межэтни́ческий *adj.* interethnic

мейнстри́м, а *m.* (infml) the mainstream (*of culture, music*)

Ме́кк|а, и f. Mecca

Ме́ксик|а, и f. Mexico

мексика́н|ец, ца *m.* Mexican

мексика́н|ка, ки f. of ▶ мексика́нец

мексика́нский *adj.* Mexican

мел, а, о ~е, в ~у́ *m.* chalk

меланхо́ли|я, и f. melancholy

мелиора́ци|я, и f. (agric.) land improvement, reclamation

⚹ ме́л|кий, ~ок, ~ка́, ~ко *adj.* **1** (*небольшой*) small **2** (*неглубокий*) shallow **3** (*дождь; песок*) fine **4** (fig., *человек*) petty, small-minded; ~кая со́шка small fry

ме́лко *adv.* **1** (*некрупно*) fine, into small particles **2** (*неглубоко*) not deep

мелково́д|ный, ~ен, ~на *adj.* shallow

мелоди́ч|ный, ~ен, ~на *adj.* melodious, melodic

мело́ди|я, и f. melody, tune

мелодра́м|а, ы f. melodrama

мелома́н, а *m.* music lover

ме́лоч|ный, ~ен, ~на *adj.* **1** petty, trifling **2** (pej., *человек*) petty, small-minded

ме́лоч|ь, и, pl. ~и, ~е́й f. **1** (collect.) (*мелкие предметы*) small items; small fry **2** (collect.) (*монеты*) (small) change **3** (in pl.) (*пустяки*) trifles, trivialities

мел|ь, и, о ~и, на ~и́ f. shoal; bank; песча́ная м. sandbank; на ~и́ aground; (fig.) on the rocks, high and dry; сесть на м. to run aground

мельк|а́ть, а́ю impf. (of ▶ мелькну́ть) **1** (*являться и исчезать*) to flash (past) **2** (*мерцать*) to twinkle **3** (*о мыслях*) to flash

мельк|ну́ть, ну́, нёшь inst. pf. (of ▶ мелька́ть): у меня́ ~ну́ла мысль I had a sudden idea

ме́льком *adv.* in passing, cursorily

ме́льник, а *m.* miller

ме́льниц|а, ы f. mill

мельхио́р, а *m.* cupro-nickel

мельча́йший superl. of ▶ ме́лкий

ме́льче comp. of ▶ ме́лкий, ▶ ме́лко

мелю́, ме́лешь see ▶ моло́ть

мембра́н|а, ы f. (tech.) diaphragm; (biol.) membrane

мемора́ндум, а *m.* memorandum

мемориа́л, а *m.* memorial

мемориа́льный *adj.* memorial

мемуа́р|ы, ов (no sg.) memoirs

⚹ ме́неджер, а *m.* manager; м. по сбы́ту sales manager

ме́неджмент, а *m.* management

⚹ ме́нее *adv.* (comp. of ▶ ма́ло) less; тем не м. none the less

менестре́л|ь, я *m.* (hist.) minstrel

мензу́рк|а, и f. (chem.) measuring glass

менинги́т, а *m.* (med.) meningitis

менструа́льный *adj.* menstrual

менструа́ци|я, и f. menstruation

мент, а́ *m.* (sl.) police officer, cop

менталите́т, а *m.* mentality

менто́л, а *m.* (chem.) menthol

менуэ́т, а *m.* minuet

ме́ньше comp. of ▶ ма́ленький, ▶ ма́ло; smaller; less

⚹ ме́ньш|ий *adj.* (comp. of ▶ ма́ленький) lesser, smaller; younger; по ~ей ме́ре at least; са́мое ~ее at the least

меньшинств|о́, á *nt.* minority

меню́ *nt. indecl.* menu

меня́ a. and g. of ▶ я

⚹ меня́|ть, ю impf. **1** (no pf.) to change **2** (pf. об~, по~) (+ a. and на + a.) to exchange (for)

меня́|ться, юсь impf. **1** (no pf.) to change; м. в лице́ to change countenance **2** (+ i.) (pf. об~, по~) to exchange; м. с кем-н. ко́мнатами to exchange rooms with sb

⚹ ме́р|а, ы f. measure; вы́сшая м. наказа́ния capital punishment; по ~е возмо́жности, по ~е сил as far as possible; по ~е того́, как as, (in proportion) as; по кра́йней, ме́ньшей ~е at least; в ~у fairly; сверх ~ы excessively, immoderately; знать ~у see ▶ знать[1]

мерза́в|ец, ца *m.* (infml) swine, bastard

ме́рз|кий, ~ок, ~ка́, ~ко *adj.* disgusting, loathsome; abominable, foul

мерзлот|а́, ы́ f. frozen condition of ground; ве́чная м. permafrost

мёрз|нуть, ну, нешь, past ~, ~ла impf. (of ▶ замёрзнуть) to freeze

ме́рзост|ь, и f. **1** (*свойство*) vileness, loathsomeness **2** (*мерзкая вещь*) abomination

меридиа́н, а *m.* meridian; Гри́нвичский м. Greenwich meridian

М

ме́рин, а *m.* gelding

ме́р|ить, ю, ишь *impf.* **1** (*pf.* с~) to measure; **м. взгля́дом** to look up and down **2** (*pf.* по~, при~) (*примерять*) to try on (*clothing, footwear*)

ме́р|иться, юсь, ишься *impf.* (*of* ▸ поме́риться) to measure (against); **м. ро́стом с кем-н.** to compare heights with sb

ме́рк|а, и *f.* **1** (*определённый размер*) measurements **2** (*предмет для измерения*) measure; (fig.) yardstick

меркантил|ьный, ~ен, ~ьна *adj.* (fig., pej.) mercenary

ме́рк|нуть, нет, *past* ~нул *and* ~, ~ла *impf.* (*of* ▸ поме́ркнуть) to grow dark, grow dim; (fig.) to fade

Мерку́ри|й, я *m.* (myth., astron.) Mercury

мероприя́ти|е, я *nt.* **1** (*мера*) measure **2** (*событие*) event, function

мертве́ц, а́ *m.* corpse, dead person

мёртв|ый, ~, мертва́, ~о *and* **мертво́** *adj.* dead; **спать ~ым сном** (infml) to sleep like the dead; **~ая хва́тка** mortal grip

мерца́|ть, ю *impf.* to twinkle, glimmer, flicker

ме́сив|о, а *nt.* (*мешанина*) medley, jumble, mishmash; (*корм*) mash; (*на дороге*) slush

ме|си́ть, шу́, ~сишь *impf.* (*of* ▸ замеси́ть) to knead

ме́сс|а, ы *f.* (relig., mus.) Mass

месси́|я, и *m.* Messiah

места́ми *adv.* here and there, in places

ме|сти́, ту́, тёшь, *past* мёл, ~ла́ *impf.* **1** (*пол, двор*) to sweep; (*сор*) to sweep up **2** (*развевать*) to whirl; (*impers.*) ~тёт there is a snowstorm

ме́стност|ь, и *f.* **1** (*дачная, сельская*) locality, district; area **2** (mil., *гористая, открытая*) ground, country, terrain

ме́стный *adj.* local

-ме́стный *comb. form* -seated, -seater

ме́ст|о, а, *pl.* ~а́, ~, ~а́м *nt.* **1** place; site; **больно́е м.** (fig.) tender spot, sensitive point; **име́ть м.** to take place; **не к ~у** (fig.) out of place; **ни с ~а!** don't move!; stay put! **2** (*в театре*) seat; (*на пароходе, поезде*) berth, seat **3** (*свободное пространство*) space; room; **нет ~а** there is no room **4** (*должность*) post, situation; job **5** (*часть текста*) passage **6** (*о багаже*) piece (*of luggage*)

местоиме́ни|е, я *nt.* (gram.) pronoun

местонахожде́ни|е, я *nt.* location, the whereabouts

месторожде́ни|е, я *nt.* (geol.) deposit

мест|ь, и *f.* vengeance, revenge

ме́сяц, а *m.* **1** month; **медо́вый м.** honeymoon **2** (*луна*) moon; **молодо́й м.** new moon

ме́сячн|ый *adj.* monthly; (*as pl. n.* ~ые, ~ых) (infml) (menstrual) period

метаболи́зм, а *m.* metabolism

мета́лл, а *m.* metal

металли́ческий *adj.* metal; (*звук, привкус*) metallic

металлоиска́тел|ь, я *m.* metal detector

металлу́рг, а *m.* metallurgist

металлурги́ческий *adj.* metallurgical; **м. заво́д** metal works, iron and steel works

металлурги́|я, и *f.* metallurgy

мета́н, а *m.* (chem.) methane

ме|та́ть, чу́, ~чешь *impf.* (*of* ▸ метну́ть) (*бросать*) to throw, cast, fling

ме|та́ться, чу́сь, ~чешься *impf.* (*по комнате*) to rush about; (*в постели*) to toss

метафи́зик|а, и *f.* metaphysics

мета́фор|а, ы *f.* metaphor

мете́л|ь, и *f.* snowstorm; blizzard

метеори́т, а *m.* (astron.) meteorite

метеоро́лог, а *m.* meteorologist; weather forecaster; (infml) weatherman

метеорологи́ческ|ий *adj.* meteorological; **~ая ста́нция** weather station

метеороло́ги|я, и *f.* meteorology

метеосво́дк|а, и *f.* weather report

ме|тить¹, чу, тишь *impf.* (*of* ▸ поме́тить) (*ставить знак на*) to mark

ме|тить², чу, тишь *impf.* (**в** + *a.*) (*стараться попасть*) to aim at; (fig., infml) (**в** + *nom.-a. pl.*) to aim (at), aspire (to)

ме́тк|а, и *f.* mark

ме́тк|ий, ~ок, ~ка́, ~ко *adj.* well aimed, accurate; **м. стрело́к** a good shot; (fig.): **~кое замеча́ние** apt remark

ме́ткост|ь, и *f.* marksmanship; accuracy; (fig.) aptness

мет|ла́, лы́, *pl.* ~лы, ~ел, ~лам *f.* broom

мет|ну́ть, ну́, нёшь *inst. pf. of* ▸ мета́ть

ме́тод, а *m.* method

мето́дик|а, и *f.* method(s), system; principles; **м. преподава́ния ру́сского языка́** methods of teaching Russian

методи́чн|ый, ~ен, ~на *adj.* methodical, orderly

метр, а *m.* **1** (*единица длины; в стихе*) metre (BrE), meter (AmE) **2** (*линейка такой длины*) metre (BrE), meter (AmE), rule

метра́ж, а́ *m.* (*квартиры*) metric area; (*ткани*) length in metres (BrE), meters (AmE)

метрдоте́л|ь, я *m.* head waiter

ме́трик|а, и *f.* birth certificate

метри́ческий *adj.* metric

метро́ *nt. indecl.* (*abbr. of* **метрополите́н**) **1** (*железная дорога*) underground (railway system) (BrE); the tube (BrE), subway (AmE) **2** (infml, *станция*) metro station; tube station (BrE), subway station (AmE)

метрополите́н, а *m.* underground (railway) (BrE), subway (AmE)

метропо́ли|я, и *f.* mother country, centre (*of empire*)

ме|ту́, тёшь *see* ▸ мести́

ме́тче *comp. of* ▸ ме́ткий

мех, а, о ~е, в ~у́/~е, на ~у́, *pl.* ~а́, ~о́в *m.* fur; **на ~у́** fur-lined

⚹ **механи́зм**, а *m.* mechanism, gear(ing); (*pl.; collect.*) machinery (also fig.)

меха́ник, а *m.* mechanic

меха́ник|а, и *f.* mechanics

механи́ческий *adj.* mechanical; **м. цех** machine shop

мехи́, ~о́в *m. pl.* bellows

Ме́хико *m. indecl.* Mexico City

мехово́й *adj. of* ▸ **мех; м. магази́н** furrier's

мецена́т, а *m.* patron

ме́ццо-сопра́но *nt. indecl.* (mus.) (*голос*) mezzo-soprano; (*f. indecl.*) (infml, *певица*) mezzo-soprano

меч, а́ *m.* sword

мече́т|ь, и *f.* mosque

меч-ры́б|а, ы *f.* swordfish

мечт|а́, ы́ (*g. pl. not used*) *f.* **1** dream, daydream **2** (*предмет желаний*) dream, ambition

мечта́тел|ь, я *m.* dreamer; daydreamer

мечта́тел|ьница, ницы *f. of* ▸ **мечта́тель**

мечта́тел|ьный, ~ен, ~ьна *adj.* dreamy

мечта́|ть, ю *impf.* (о + *p.*) to dream (of, about)

ме́|чу, тишь *see* ▸ **ме́тить¹**, ▸ **ме́тить²**

ме|чу́, ~чешь *see* ▸ **мета́ть**

⚹ **меша́|ть¹**, ю *impf.* (*pf.* ▸ **помеша́ть¹**) **1** (+ *d.* + *inf.*) (*препятствовать*) to prevent (from); to hinder, impede, hamper; **что ~ет вам прие́хать в Москву́?** what prevents you from coming to Moscow? **2** (+ *d.*) (*беспокоить*) to disturb; **не ~ло бы** (+ *inf.*) (infml) it would not hurt (to)

⚹ **меша́|ть²**, ю *impf.* **1** (*pf.* **по~**) (*чай, кашу*) to stir; **м. в котле́** to stir the pot **2** (*pf.* **с~**) (*с* + *i.*) (*вино с водой*) to mix (with), blend (with) **3** (*pf.* **с~**) (*путать*) to confuse, mix up

ме́шка|ть, ю *impf.* (infml) (*с* + *i.*) to linger, dawdle, be slow (with)

мешкови́н|а, ы *f.* sacking, hessian

меш|о́к, ка́ *m.* bag; sack

меща|ни́н, и́на, *pl.* ~е, ~ *m.* **1 (hist.) petty bourgeois **2** (fig.) Philistine

меща́нский *adj. of* ▸ **меща́нин**; (fig.) Philistine; bourgeois, narrow-minded

ми *nt. indecl.* (mus.) E

миг, а *m.* moment, instant

миг|а́ть, а́ю *impf.* (*of* ▸ **мигну́ть**) **1** (*непроизвольно*) to blink **2** (+ *d.*) (*подавать знак*) to wink (at); (fig., *мерцать*) to wink, twinkle

миг|ну́ть, ну́, нёшь *inst. pf. of* ▸ **мига́ть**

мигра́нт, а *m.* migrant

миграцио́нный *adj. of* ▸ **мигра́ция**

мигра́ци|я, и *f.* migration

мигре́н|ь, и *f.* migraine

мигри́р|овать, ую *impf.* to migrate

МИД, а *m.* (*abbr. of* **Министе́рство иностра́нных дел**) Ministry of Foreign Affairs; Foreign Office (BrE), State Department (AmE)

ми́ди|я, и *f.* mussel

мизантро́п, а *m.* misanthrope

мизи́н|ец, ца *m.* (*на руке*) little finger; (*на ноге*) little toe

микро... *comb. form* micro-

микроавто́бус, а *m.* minibus

микро́б, а *m.* microbe

микробио́лог, а *m.* microbiologist

микробиоло́ги|я, и *f.* microbiology

микробло́г, а *m.* (comput.) microblog

микроволно́в|ый *adj.:* ~ая пе́чь microwave (oven)

микрокли́мат, а *m.* microclimate

микро́н, а *m.* (phys.) micron

микроорганизм, а *m.* (biol.) micro-organism; разлага́емый ~ами biodegradable

микроплёнк|а, и *f.* microfilm

микропроце́ссор, а *m.* microprocessor

микрорайо́н, а *m.* neighbourhood (*administrative subdivision of urban area*)

микроско́п, а *m.* microscope

микросхе́м|а, ы *f.* microcircuit, microchip

микрофо́н, а *m.* microphone

микрохирурги́|я, и *f.* microsurgery

микрочи́п, а *m.* microchip

ми́ксер, а *m.* (cul.) mixer, blender, liquidizer

миксту́р|а, ы *f.* (liquid) medicine, mixture

милитари́зм, а *m.* militarism

милице́йский *adj. of* ▸ **мили́ция**

милиционе́р, а *m.* policeman (*in Russia*)

мили́ци|я, и *f.* police (*in Russia*)

миллиа́рд, а *m.* (*10⁹*) billion (= *thousand million*)

миллиарде́р, а *m.* billionaire

миллиа́рдный *adj.* billionth

миллигра́мм, а *m.* milligram(me)

миллили́тр, а *m.* millilitre (BrE), milliliter (AmE)

миллиме́тр, а *m.* millimetre (BrE), millimeter (AmE)

⚹ **миллио́н**, а *m.* million

миллионе́р, а *m.* millionaire

миллио́нный *adj.* millionth

ми́л|овать, ую *impf.* (*of* ▸ **поми́ловать**) to pardon, spare

милови́д|ный, ~ен, ~на *adj.* pretty, nice-looking

милосе́рди|е, я *nt.* mercy, charity

милосе́рд|ный, ~ен, ~на *adj.* merciful, charitable

ми́лостын|я, и *f.* alms

ми́лост|ь, и *f.* **1** (*благодеяние*) favour (BrE), favor (AmE) **2** (*доброта*) kindness; charity; **из ~и** out of charity

ми́л|ый, ~, ~а́, ~о, ~лы *adj.* **1** nice, sweet; lovable; **э́то о́чень ~о с ва́шей стороны́** it is very nice of you **2** dear; (*as n.* **м.**, ~ого, **f.** ~ая, ~ой) dear, darling

ми́л|я, и *f.* mile

ми́мик|а, и *f.* facial expressions

ми́мо *adv. and prep.* + *g.* by, past; **пройти́, прое́хать м.** to pass by, pass; **м.!** miss(ed)!

мимо́з|а, ы *f.* (bot.) mimosa

М

мимолёт|ный, ∼ен, ∼на *adj.* fleeting, transient

мимохо́дом *adv.* in passing; **м. упомяну́ть** (fig., infml) to mention in passing

мин. (*abbr of* **мину́та**) min., minute(s)

ᴓ ми́н|а¹, ы *f.* **1** (mil., naut.) mine **2** (mil., *снаряд миномёта*) mortar shell, mortar bomb

ми́н|а², ы *f.* (*выражение лица*) expression, mien

минаре́т, а *m.* minaret

минда́л|ь, я *m.* **1** (*дерево*) almond tree **2** (collect.) (*орехи*) almonds

минера́л, а *m.* mineral

минера́лк|а, и *f.* (infml) mineral water

Минздра́в, а *m.* (*abbr. of* **Министе́рство здравоохране́ния**) Ministry of Health

ми́ни *nt. indecl.* mini (*garment*)

миниатю́р|а, ы *f.* (art, mus.) miniature; (theatr.) short piece, play

миниатю́р|ный, ∼ен, ∼на *adj.* **1** *adj. of* ▶ **миниатю́ра 2** (fig.) diminutive, tiny, dainty

ми́ни-ди́ск, а *m.* minidisc

ᴓ минима́льный, ∼ен, ∼ьна *adj.* minimum

ᴓ ми́нимум, а *m.* **1** minimum; **прожи́точный м.** living wage **2** (*as adv.*) at the least, at the minimum

мини́р|овать, ую *impf. and pf.* (*pf. also* **за**∼) (mil., naut.) to mine

министе́рский *adj.* ministerial

ᴓ министе́рств|о, а *nt.* (pol.) ministry

ᴓ мини́стр, а *m.* (pol.) minister; **премье́р-м.** Prime Minister, premier

мин|ова́ть, у́ю *impf. and pf.* **1** (*пройти/ проехать мимо*) to pass (by); ∼у́я подро́бности omitting details **2** (*pf. only*) (*окончиться*) to be over, be past; **опа́сность** ∼ова́ла the danger is past **3** (*only with* **не** + *g.*) (*избежать*) to escape, avoid; **не м. тебе́ тюрьмы́** you cannot escape being sent to prison

миноме́т, а *m.* (mil.) mortar

миноно́с|ец, ца *m.* (naut.) torpedo boat; **эска́дренный м.** destroyer

мино́р, а *m.* (mus.) minor key

Минск, а *m.* Minsk

мину́вш|ий *adj.* past; (*as nt. n.* ∼ее, ∼его) the past

ми́нус, а *m.* **1** (math.) minus **2** (fig., infml, *недостаток*) shortcoming, drawback

ᴓ мину́т|а, ы *f.* minute

мину́т|ный *adj.* **1** *adj. of* ▶ **мину́та**; ∼ная стре́лка minute hand **2** momentary; ∼ная встре́ча brief encounter

ᴓ мир¹, а *m.* (*согласие*) peace; **заключи́ть м. то** make peace

ᴓ мир², а *pl.* ∼ы́ *m.* (*вселенная*) world; universe; **живо́тный м.** fauna; **расти́тельный м.** flora

мира́ж, а́ *m.* mirage; optical illusion

мир|и́ть, ю́, и́шь *impf.* **1** (*pf.* **по**∼) (*враждующих*) to reconcile **2** (*pf.* **при**∼)

(*с* + *i.*) (*заставлять терпимо относиться*) to reconcile (to)

мир|и́ться, ю́сь, и́шься *impf.* (*с* + *i.*) **1** (*pf.* **по**∼) (*прекращать вражду*) to be reconciled (with), make it up (with) **2** (*pf.* **при**∼) (*терпимо относиться*) to reconcile oneself (to); **м. со свои́м положе́нием** to accept the situation

ми́р|ный, ∼ен, ∼на *adj.* **1** *adj. of* ▶ **мир¹ 2** peaceful; peaceable

мировоззре́ни|е, я *nt.* (world) outlook, Weltanschauung; (one's) philosophy (of life)

ᴓ мир|ово́й *adj. of* ▶ **мир²**; ∼ова́я война́ world war

мирозда́ни|е, я *nt.* the universe

миролюби́в|ый, ∼, ∼а *adj.* peaceable

миротво́р|ец, ца *m.* peacemaker

мирско́й *adj.* secular, lay; mundane, worldly

мирт, а *m.* (bot.) myrtle

ми́ск|а, и *f.* basin, bowl

мисс *f. indecl.* Miss

миссионе́р, а *m.* missionary

ми́ссис *nt. indecl.* Mrs

ми́сси|я, и *f.* mission

ми́стер, а *m.* mister, Mr

ми́стик|а, и *f.* mysticism; (infml) mystery

мистифика́ци|я, и *f.* hoax, leg-pull

мистифици́р|овать, ую *impf. and pf.* to hoax, mystify

мисти́ческий *adj.* mystic(al)

ми́тинг, а *m.* (political) mass meeting; rally

митрополи́т, а *m.* (eccl.) metropolitan

миф, а *m.* myth (also fig.)

мифи́ческий *adj.* mythical

мифологи́ческий *adj.* mythological

мифоло́ги|я, и *f.* mythology

мише́н|ь, и *f.* target

ми́шка, и *m.* (infml) **плю́шевый м.** teddy (bear)

мл (*abbr. of* **миллили́тр**) ml, millilitre(s)

младе́н|ец, ца *m.* baby, infant

младе́нческий *adj.* infantile

мла́дший *adj.* (*comp. and superl. of* ▶ **молодо́й**) **1** (*более молодой*) younger **2** (*самый молодо́й*) the youngest **3** (*по служебному положению*) junior; **м. лейтена́нт** second lieutenant

млекопита́ющ|ее, его *nt.* (zool.) mammal

мле|ть, ю *impf.* (**от** + *g.*) to be overcome (*with delight, fright, etc.*)

ᴓ млн. (*abbr. of* **миллио́н**) m, million(s)

ᴓ млрд. (*abbr. of* **миллиа́рд**) b., billion(s) (= *thousand million*)

ᴓ мм (*abbr. of* **миллиме́тр**) mm, millimetre(s) (BrE), millimeter(s) (AmE)

мне *d. and p. of* ▶ **я**

ᴓ мне́ни|е, я *nt.* opinion

мни́мый *adj.* **1** (*воображаемый*) imaginary **2** (*притворный*) sham, pretended; **м. больно́й** hypochondriac

мни́тел|ьный, ∼ен, ∼ьна *adj.* **1** (*ипохондрический*) hypochondriac

---

ᴓ key word

М

2 (*подозрительный*) mistrustful, suspicious

мно́г|ие, их *adj. and n.* many; **во ~их отноше́ниях** in many respects

мно́го *adv.* (+ *g.*) much; many; a lot (of); **м. вре́мени** much time; **м. лет** many years

мно́го... *comb. form* many-, poly-, multi-

многобо́р|ец, ца *m.* all-round athlete, multi-eventer

многобо́рь|е, я *nt.* multi-discipline event *or* competition

многогра́н|ный, ~ен, ~на *adj.* (math.) polyhedral; (fig.) many-sided; multi-faceted

многоде́т|ный, ~ен, ~на *adj.* having many children

многодне́вный *adj.*: **м. путь** a journey lasting several days

мно́г|ое, ого *nt.* much, a great deal; **во ~ом** in many respects

многожёнств|о, а *nt.* polygamy

многозначи́тель|ный, ~ен, ~ьна *adj.* significant

многозна́ч|ный, ~ен, ~на *adj.* **1** (math.) multi-digit **2** (ling.) polysemantic

многокра́т|ный, ~ен, ~на *adj.* repeated; frequent

многоле́тний *adj.* **1** lasting *or* living many years; of many years' standing **2** (bot.) perennial

многоли́к|ий, ~, ~а *adj.* many-sided

многолю́д|ный, ~ен, ~на *adj.* (*район*) populous; (*улица*) crowded

многонациона́л|ьный, ~ен, ~ьна *adj.* multinational

многообеща́ющий *adj.* **1** (*ученик*) promising, hopeful **2** (*взгляд*) significant

многообра́зи|е, я *nt.* variety, diversity

многопарти́йный *adj.* multiparty

многосери́йный *adj.* serial

многосло́в|ный, ~ен, ~на *adj.* verbose

многосторо́н|ний, ~ен, ~ня *adj.* **1** (*no short forms*) (math.) polygonal **2** (*договор*) multilateral **3** (*человек*) many-sided; versatile

многострада́л|ьный, ~ен, ~ьна *adj.* long-suffering

многоуго́льник, а *m.* (math.) polygon

многоцелево́й *adj.* multipurpose

многочи́слен|ный, ~, ~на *adj.* numerous

многоэта́жный *adj.* multistorey (BrE), multistory (AmE), high-rise

мно́жествен|ный *adj.* plural; **~ое число́** (gram.) plural (number)

мно́жеств|о, а *nt.* a great number, a quantity; multitude; (math.) set

мно́ж|ить, у, ишь *impf.* (*of* ▶ помно́жить, ▶ умно́жить) (math.) to multiply

мной, мно́ю *i. of* ▶ я

мобилиза́ци|я, и *f.* mobilization

мобилиз|ова́ть, у́ю *impf. and pf.* (**на** + *a.*) to mobilize (for)

моби́льник, а *m.* (infml) mobile (phone) (BrE), cellphone

моби́л|ьный, ~ен, ~ьна *adj.* mobile; (*as in* infml **м., ~ьного**) (*also* **м. телефо́н**) mobile (phone) (BrE), cellphone

моги́л|а, ы *f.* grave

моги́льщик, а *m.* gravedigger

мо|гу́, ~́гут *see* ▶ мочь

могу́ч|ий, ~, ~а *adj.* mighty, powerful

могу́ществен|ный, ~, ~на *adj.* powerful; potent

могу́ществ|о, а *nt.* power, might

мо́д|а, ы *f.* fashion, vogue; **выходи́ть из ~ы** to go out of fashion

моде́л|ь, и *f.* model; (*платья*) design; (*для отливки*) pattern

моделье́р, а *m.* fashion designer, couturier

моде́м, а *m.* (comput.) modem

моде́рн, а *m.* modernist style, art nouveau

модерниза́ци|я, и *f.* modernization; updating; (comput., *of hardware*) upgrade

модернизи́р|овать, ую *impf. and pf.* to modernize; to update; (comput., *hardware*) to upgrade

модерни́зм, а *m.* (art) modernism

модифика́ци|я, и *f.* modification

модифици́р|овать, ую *impf. and pf.* to modify

мо́д|ный, ~ен, ~на́, ~но *adj.* **1** fashionable, stylish **2** *adj. of* ▶ мо́да; **м. журна́л** fashion magazine

мо́дул|ь, я *m.* (math.) modulus; (tech.) module

мо́жет *see* ▶ мочь

можже́вельник, а *m.* (bot.) juniper

мо́жно *pred.* (*impers.* + *inf.*) **1** (*возможно*) it is possible; **м. бы́ло э́то предви́деть** it could have been foreseen; **как м.** (+ *comp.*) as ... as possible; **как м. скоре́е** as soon as possible **2** (*разрешается*) it is permissible, one may; **м. (мне/нам) идти́?** may I/we go?

моза́ик|а, и *f.* mosaic; (*искусство*) mosaic work

Мозамби́к, а *m.* Mozambique

мозамби́к|ец, ца *m.* Mozambican

мозамби́кский *adj.* Mozambican

мозг, а, в ~у́, *pl.* ~и́, ~о́в *m.* **1** brain (also fig.); (fig.) nerve centre (BrE), center (AmE); **головно́й м.** brain, cerebrum; **спинно́й м.** spinal cord **2** (anat.) marrow; **до ~а косте́й** (fig., infml) to the core

мозо́л|ь, и *f.* corn; callus; **ру́ки в ~ях** calloused hands

мой *poss. pron.* (*при существительном*) my; (*без существительного*) mine; (*as pl. n.* **мой, мои́х**) my people; **по моему́ мне́нию** in my opinion; (*так, как я счита́ю пра́вильным*) as I think right

мо́йк|а, и *f.* **1** (*действие*) washing **2** (*машина*) washer **2** (*раковина*) sink

мо́йщик, а *m.* washer; cleaner

мокри́ц|а, ы *f.* **1** (zool.) woodlouse **2** (bot.) chickweed (*Stellaria media*)

мо́кр|ый, ~, ~а́, ~о *adj.* wet; **м. снег** sleet; (*impers., pred.*) **~о** it is wet

мол¹, а *m.* mole, pier

мол² *abbr.* (*of obs.* мо́лвить) (*infml*) he says (said), they say (said), *etc.*; (*indicating reported speech*): он, м., никогда́ там не́ был he said he had never been there

молдава́н|ин, ина, *pl.* ∼е, ∼ *m.* Moldovan

молдава́н|ка, ки *f. of* ▶ молдава́нин

молда́вский *adj.* Moldovan; (*язык*) Moldavian

Молдо́в|а, ы *f.* Moldova

моле́кул|а, ы *f.* (phys.) molecule

моли́тв|а, ы *f.* prayer

мол|и́ть, ю́, ∼ишь *impf.* (*a. and* о + *p.*) to pray (for), implore (for), beseech; ∼ю́ вас о по́мощи I beg you to help me

мол|и́ться, ю́сь, ∼ишься *impf.* **1** (*pf.* по∼) (+ *d.*) to pray (to) **2** (fig.) (на + *a.*) to idolize

моллю́ск, а *m.* mollusc; shellfish

молниено́с|ный, ∼ен, ∼на *adj.* (quick as) lightning; ∼ная война́ blitzkrieg

мо́лни|я, и *f.* **1** lightning **2**: (застёжка-)м. zip (BrE), zipper (AmE)

молодёжный *adj. of* ▶ молодёжь

✐ **молодёж|ь**, и *f.* (*collect.*) youth; young people

молод|е́ц, ца́ *m.* fine fellow; (*о женщине*) fine girl; (*as int.*) м.! well done!

молодожён|ы, ов *m. pl.* (*sg.* ∼, ∼а) newly married couple, newly-weds

✐ **молод|о́й**, мо́лод, ∼а́, мо́лодо *adj.* **1** young; (*свойственный молодости*) youthful **2** (*as n.*) (infml) (м., ∼о́го) bridegroom; (∼а́я, ∼о́й) bride; (∼ые, ∼ы́х) newly married couple, newly-weds

мо́лодост|ь, и *f.* youth; youthfulness

моложа́в|ый, ∼, ∼а *adj.* (*человек*) young-looking; (*вид*) youthful

моло́же *comp. of* ▶ молодо́й

✐ **молок|о́**, а́ (*no pl.*) *nt.* milk

мо́лот, а *m.* hammer; кузне́чный м. sledgehammer

молот|о́к, ка́ *m.* hammer; отбо́йный м. pneumatic drill; прода́ть с ∼ка́ to sell by auction, auction

мо́лот|ый, ∼, ∼а *p.p.p. of* ▶ моло́ть *and adj.* ground

моло́ть, мелю́, ме́лешь *impf.* (*of* ▶ смоло́ть) to grind; м. вздор (*no pf.*) (fig., infml) to talk nonsense

моло́чн|ый *adj.* **1** *adj. of* ▶ молоко́; м. брат foster-brother; ∼ые проду́кты dairy products; ∼ое хозя́йство dairy farm(ing) **2** milky; lactic

мо́лча *adv.* silently, in silence

молчали́в|ый, ∼, ∼а *adj.* **1** (*человек*) taciturn, silent **2** (*одобрение*) tacit, unspoken

молча́ни|е, я *nt.* silence

молч|а́ть, у́, и́шь *impf.* to be silent; (о + *p.*) to keep silent (about)

мол|ь, и *f.* (clothes) moth

мольб|а́, ы́ *f.* entreaty, supplication

мольбе́рт, а *m.* easel

✐ **моме́нт**, а *m.* **1** (*миг*) moment; instant; в да́нный м. at the present time; at the moment **2** (*черта*) feature, element, factor

момента́льно *adv.* in a moment, instantly

момента́л|ьный, ∼ен, ∼ьна *adj.* instantaneous; м. сни́мок snapshot

мона́рх, а *m.* monarch

монархи́зм, а *m.* monarchism

мона́рхи|я, и *f.* monarchy

монасты́р|ь, я́ *m.* monastery; (же́нский) м. convent, nunnery

мона́х, а *m.* monk

мона́хин|я, и *f.* nun

монго́л, а *m.* Mongol, Mongolian

Монго́ли|я, и *f.* Mongolia

монго́л|ка, ки *f. of* ▶ монго́л

монго́льский *adj.* Mongolian

моне́т|а, ы *f.* coin; разме́нная м. change; приня́ть за чи́стую ∼у (fig., infml) to take at face value, take in good faith

монито́р, а *m.* (TV, comput.) monitor

мо́но *nt. indecl.* mono

монографи|я, и *f.* monograph

моноли́т, а *m.* monolith

моноли́т|ный, ∼ен, ∼на *adj.* (pol., also fig.) monolithic; (fig.) solid

моноло́г, а *m.* monologue, soliloquy

монопо́ли|я, и *f.* (econ., also fig.) monopoly

монотеи́зм, а *m.* monotheism

моното́н|ный, ∼ен, ∼на *adj.* monotonous

монстр, а *m.* monster

✐ **монта́ж**, а́ *m.* **1** (tech., *действие*) assembling, mounting, installation **2** (cin.) editing, montage; (art, mus., liter.) arrangement

монта́жник, а *m.* (*на стройке*) rigger; (*на заводе*) fitter

монтёр, а *m.* **1** fitter **2** (*электромонтёр*) electrician

монти́р|овать, ую *impf.* (*of* ▶ смонти́ровать) **1** (tech.) to assemble, mount, fit **2** (cin.) to edit; (art, mus., liter.) to arrange

монуме́нт, а *m.* monument

монумента́л|ьный, ∼ен, ∼ьна *adj.* monumental (also fig.)

мопе́д, а *m.* moped

мора́л|ь, и *f.* **1** (*нормы поведения*) (code of) morals, ethics **2** (infml, *нравоучение*) moralizing; чита́ть м. to moralize, preach

мора́льный, ∼ен, ∼ьна *adj.* moral; ethical

морато́ри|й, я *m.* (law, comm.) moratorium

морг, а *m.* morgue, mortuary

морг|а́ть, а́ю *impf.* (*of* ▶ моргну́ть) to blink; to wink

морг|ну́ть, ну́, нёшь *pf.* (*of* ▶ морга́ть): гла́зом не ∼ну́в (infml) without batting an eyelid

мо́рд|а, ы *f.* **1** snout, muzzle **2** (infml, *лицо*) mug

мордв|а́, ы́ *f.* (*collect.*) the Mordva, the Mordvins

М

мордви́н, а *m.* Mordvin

мордви́н|ка, ки *f.* of ▶ **мордви́н**

Мордо́ви|я, и *f.* Mordvinia

мордо́вский *adj.* Mordvinian

⚥ **мо́р|е**, я, *pl.* ∼я́, ∼е́й *nt.* sea; **у** ∼я́ by the sea; **на́ м./на** ∼е at sea; **за́** ∼**ем** overseas; **из-за** ∼я́ from overseas; **пое́хать на м.** to go to the seaside

морепла́вани|е, я *nt.* navigation, seafaring

морж, а́ *m.* walrus; (infml) (open-air) winter bather

морко́вк|а, и *f.* (infml) a carrot

морко́в|ь, и *f.* carrot; (collect.) carrot(s)

моро́жен|ое, ого *nt.* ice (cream)

моро́женый *adj.* frozen; (карто́фель) frost-damaged

моро́з, а *m.* **1** frost; **у меня́ м. по ко́же** (or **пошёл**) it makes (made) my flesh creep **2** (usu. in pl.) intensely cold weather

морози́лк|а, и *f.* (infml) freezer compartment; freezer

морози́льник, а *m.* freezer

моро́зн|ый *adj.* frosty; (impers., pred.) ∼о it is freezing

морозосто́|йкий, ∼ек, ∼йка *adj.* (bot.) frost-resistant

морос|и́ть, и́т *impf.* to drizzle

моро́ч|ить, у, ишь *impf.* (of ▶ **заморо́чить**) (infml) to fool; **м. го́лову кому́-н.** to take sb in

морс, а *m.* fruit drink

⚥ **морск|о́й** *adj.* **1** sea; maritime; marine, nautical; **м. волк** (infml) old salt; ∼**а́я звезда́** starfish; **м. конёк** (zool.) sea horse; ∼**а́я сви́нка** guinea pig **2** naval; ∼**а́я пехо́та** marines; **м. флот** navy, fleet

мо́рфи|й, я *m.* (chem.) morphine

морфоло́ги|я, и *f.* morphology

морщи́н|а, ы *f.* wrinkle

морщи́нист|ый, ∼, ∼а *adj.* wrinkled

мо́рщ|иться, усь, ишься *impf.* (of ▶ **смо́рщиться**) **1** (де́лать грима́сы) to make a wry face, wince **2** (об оде́жде) to crease, wrinkle

моря́к, а́ *m.* sailor

Москв|а́, ы́ *f.* **1** (го́род) Moscow **2** (река́) the Moskva

москви́ч, а́ *m.* Muscovite

москви́чк|а, ки *f.* of ▶ **москви́ч**

моски́т, а *m.* mosquito

моски́т|ный *adj.* of ▶ **моски́т**; ∼**ная се́тка** mosquito net

⚥ **моско́вский** *adj.* (of) Moscow

⚥ **мост**, ∼а́, о ∼е́, на ∼у́, *pl.* ∼ы́ *m.* **1** (че́рез ре́ку) bridge **2** (автомоби́ля) axle

мо́стик, а *m.* **1** *dim.* of ▶ **мост 2**: **капита́нский м.** (naut.) bridge (on a ship)

мостк|и́, о́в (no sg.) **1** (для перехо́да) planked walkway **2** (площа́дка) wooden platform

мостов|а́я, о́й *f.* road(way), carriageway

мот|а́ть, а́ю *impf.* **1** (pf. на∼) (ни́тки, шерсть) to wind, reel **2** (pf. ∼ну́ть) (+ i.)

(infml, голово́й) to shake (head, etc.)

мота́|ться[1], ется *impf.* (infml) to dangle

мота́|ться[2], юсь *impf.* (infml) to rush about

моте́л|ь, я *m.* motel

моти́в[1], а *m.* **1** (по́вод) motive **2** (до́вод) reason

моти́в[2], а *m.* **1** (mus.) tune, motif **2** (fig.) motif

мотиви́р|овать, ую *impf. and pf.* to give reasons (for), justify

мот|ну́ть, ну́, нёшь *inst. pf.* of ▶ **мота́ть**

мотого́н|ки, ок (no sg.) motorcycle races

мотого́нщик, а *m.* motorcycle racer

мотого́нщи|ца, цы *f.* of ▶ **мотого́нщик**

мот|о́к, ка́ *m.* skein, hank

мото́р, а *m.* motor; (автомоби́ля, самолёта) engine

моторо́ллер, а *m.* (motor) scooter

мотоспо́рт, а *m.* motorcycle racing

мотоци́кл, а *m.* motorcycle

мотоцикли́ст, а *m.* motorcyclist; biker

мотоцикли́ст|ка, ки *f.* of ▶ **мотоцикли́ст**

мотыг|а, и *f.* hoe

мотыл|ёк, ька́ *m.* moth

мох, мха *and* мо́ха, о мхе *and* о мо́хе, во (на) мху́, *pl.* мхи, мхов *m.* moss

мохе́р, а *m.* mohair

мохна́т|ый, ∼, ∼а *adj.* hairy, shaggy

моч|а́, и́ *f.* urine

моча́лк|а, и *f.* bath sponge, loofah

мочево́й *adj.* urinary, uric; **м. пузы́рь** (anat.) bladder

моч|и́ть, у́, ∼ишь *impf.* **1** *impf.* of ▶ **намочи́ть 1 2** (pf. за∼) (sl., убива́ть) to kill

⚥ **мочь**, могу́, мо́жешь, мо́гут, past мог, могла́ *impf.* (of ▶ **смочь**) to be able; **мо́жет быть, быть мо́жет** perhaps, maybe; **мо́жет** (infml): = **мо́жет быть**; **не мо́жет быть!** impossible!

моше́нник, а *m.* swindler, crook

моше́ннича|ть, ю *impf.* (of ▶ **смоше́нничать**) to swindle

моше́нничеств|о, а *nt.* swindling; cheating

мо́шк|а, и *f.* midge

мощёный *adj.* paved

мо́щ|и, е́й (no sg.) (relig.) relics

⚥ **мо́щност|ь**, и *f.* power; (tech.) capacity, rating; output; **дви́гатель** ∼**ью в сто лошади́ных сил** hundred horsepower engine

⚥ **мо́щ|ный**, ∼ен, ∼на́, ∼но *adj.* powerful, mighty; (рост) vigorous

мощ|ь, и *f.* power, might

мо́|ю, ешь *see* ▶ **мыть**

мо́ющ|ий *pres. part. act.* of ▶ **мыть** *and adj.* detergent; ∼**ие сре́дства** detergents

мо́ющ|ийся *adj.* washable; ∼**иеся обо́и** washable wallpaper

мраз|ь, и (no pl.) *f.* (infml) dregs, scum

мрак, а *m.* darkness, gloom (also fig., rhet.)

мра́мор, а *m.* marble

мра́морный adj. marble; (fig.) (white as) marble; (бумага) marbled

мра́ч|ный, ∼ен, ∼на́, ∼но, ∼ны́ adj. **1** dark, sombre (BrE), somber (AmE) **2** (fig.) gloomy, dismal

мсти́ть, мщу, мсти́шь impf. (of ▶ отомсти́ть) **1** (+ d.) to take revenge/vengeance (on sb) **2** (за + a.) to avenge; **м. за дру́га** to avenge one's friend **3** (+ d. and за + a.) to take revenge on sb for sth; to avenge oneself on sb for sth

мудре́ц, а́ m. (rhet.) sage, wise man

му́дрост|ь, и f. wisdom

му́др|ый, ∼, ∼а́, ∼о, ∼ы́ adj. wise

✓ **муж**, а m. **1** (pl. ∼ья́, ∼е́й, ∼ья́м) husband **2** (pl. ∼и́, ∼е́й, ∼а́м) (rhet., мужчи́на) man; **госуда́рственный м.** statesman; **учёный м.** scholar

мужа́|ться, юсь impf. to take heart, take courage; ∼йтесь! courage!

му́жествен|ный, ∼, ∼на adj. manly, steadfast

му́жеств|о, а nt. courage, fortitude

мужи́к, а́ m. **1** (крестья́нин) muzhik (Russian peasant) **2** (infml, мужчи́на) bloke, guy

✓ **мужско́й** adj. (го́лос, рукопожа́тие) masculine; (пол, кле́тка) male; (туале́т, пла́тье) men's; **м. род** (gram.) masculine gender

✓ **мужчи́н|а**, ы m. man

му́з|а, ы f. muse

✓ **музе́|й**, я m. museum

✓ **му́зык|а**, и f. music

✓ **музыка́л|ьный**, ∼ен, ∼ьна adj. music (attr.); musical

музыка́нт, а m. musician

музыкове́д, а m. musicologist

му́к|а, и f. torment; torture; (in pl.) pangs, throes; **родовы́е ∼и** labour (BrE), labor (AmE) pains

мук|а́, и́ f. (пшени́чная, кукуру́зная) flour; (костяна́я, ры́бная) meal

мулл|а́, ы́ m. mullah

мультиме́диа pl. indecl. multimedia

мультимеди́йный adj. multimedia

мультиплика́ци|я, и f. (film) animation

мультфи́льм, а m. cartoon, animation

му́ми|я, и f. mummy (corpse)

мунди́р, а m. full dress uniform

мундшту́к, а́ m. **1** (сигаре́ты, тру́бки) mouthpiece; (тру́бочка, в кото́рую вставля́ют сигаре́ту) cigarette holder **2** (mus.) mouthpiece

муниципалите́т, а m. municipality; town council; **зда́ние ∼а** town hall

✓ **муниципа́льный** adj. municipal; **∼ая кварти́ра** council flat

мураве́|й, ья́ m. ant

мураве́йник, а m. anthill

мураве́д, а m. (zool.) anteater

мурлы́|кать, чу, чешь impf. **1** (о ко́шке) to purr **2** (infml, о челове́ке) to hum

муска́т, а m. **1** (оре́х) nutmeg **2** (виногра́д) muscadine, muscat **3** (вино́) muscatel, muscat

му́скул, а m. muscle

мускулату́р|а, ы f. (collect.) muscular system, musculature

мускули́ст|ый, ∼, ∼а adj. muscular, brawny

му́сор, а m. rubbish (BrE), garbage (AmE)

му́сорный adj. of ▶ му́сор; **м. я́щик** dustbin (BrE), garbage can (AmE)

мусорово́з, а m. dustcart (BrE), garbage truck (AmE)

мусоропрово́д, а m. refuse chute

му́сорщик, а m. dustman (BrE), garbage collector (AmE)

мусульма́н|ин, ина, pl. ∼е, ∼ m. Muslim

мусульма́н|ка, ки f. of ▶ мусульма́нин

мусульма́нский adj. Muslim

мусульма́нств|о, а nt. Islam

мута́нт, а m. (biol.) mutant

мута́ци|я, и f. (biol.) mutation

мути́р|овать, ую impf. and pf. (biol.) to mutate

му́т|ный, ∼ен, ∼на́, ∼но, ∼ны́ adj. **1** cloudy, turbid **2** (fig.) dull(ed); confused

му́фт|а, ы f. **1** (для рук) muff **2** (tech.) coupling; (elec.) connecting box; **м. сцепле́ния** clutch

му́фти|й, я m. (relig.) mufti

му́х|а, и f. fly; **де́лать из ∼и слона́** (fig.) to make a mountain out of a molehill

мухомо́р, а m. (гриб) fly agaric (mushroom)

муче́ни|е, я nt. torment, torture

му́ченик, а m. martyr

му́чени|ца, цы f. of ▶ му́ченик

мучи́тел|ьный, ∼ен, ∼ьна adj. excruciating; agonizing

му́ч|ить, у, ишь impf. (of ▶ заму́чить) to torment; to worry, harass

му́ч|иться, усь, ишься impf. (of ▶ заму́читься) **1** (от + g. or + i.) passive of ▶ му́чить; **м. от бо́ли** to be racked with pain; **м. сомне́ниями** to be tormented by doubts **2** (из-за + g.) to worry (about), feel unhappy **3** (над + i.) to torment oneself (over, about)

мха, мху see ▶ мох

мч|а́ться, усь, и́шься impf. to rush, race, tear along; **м. во весь опо́р** to go at full speed; **вре́мя ∼и́тся** time flies

МЧС m. (abbr. of **Министе́рство по чрезвыча́йным ситуа́циям**) Ministry of Emergency Situations

✓ **мы**, а., g., p. **нас**, d. **нам**, i. **на́ми** pers. pron. we; **мы с ва́ми** you and I

мы́л|о, а nt. **1** soap **2** (у ло́шади) foam, lather

мы́льни|ца, ы f. soap dish

мы́л|ьный adj. of ▶ мы́ло; **∼ьная о́пера** soap opera

мыс, а m. (geog.) cape, promontory

мы́сленный *adj.* mental; **м. о́браз** mental image

мысли́м|ый, **∼**, **∼a** *adj.* conceivable, thinkable

мысли́тел|ь, **я** *m.* thinker

мысли́тельный *adj.* intellectual, of thought; **м. проце́сс** thought process

мы́сл|ить, **ю**, **ишь** *impf.* **1** (*ду́мать*) to think; to reason **2** (*представля́ть себе́*) to conceive, imagine

ℐ **мы́сл|ь**, **и** *f.* (**o** + *p.*) thought (of, about); (*иде́я*) idea; **о́браз ∼ей** way of thinking, views; **собира́ться с ∼ями** to collect one's thoughts

мыть, **мо́ю**, **мо́ешь** *impf.* (*of* ▶ **вы́мыть**) to wash

мы́ться, **мо́юсь**, **мо́ешься** *impf.* (*of* ▶ **вы́мыться**) **1** to wash (oneself) **2** *pass. of* ▶ **мыть**

мыч|а́ть, **у́**, **и́шь** *impf.* **1** (*о коро́ве*) to moo; (*о быке́*) to bellow **2** (fig., infml, *о челове́ке*) to mumble

мышело́вк|а, **и** *f.* mousetrap

мыши́|ный *adj. of* ▶ **мышь**; **∼йная возня́** pointless fussing over trifles

мы́шк|а¹, **и** *f. dim. of* ▶ **мышь**

мы́шк|а², **и** *f.* armpit; **под ∼у**, **под ∼ой** under one's arm; **нести́ под ∼ой** to carry under one's arm

мышле́ни|е, **я** *nt.* thinking, thought

мы́шц|а, **ы** *f.* muscle

мыш|ь, **и**, *pl.* **∼и**, **∼е́й** *f.* **1** (also comput.) mouse **2**: **лету́чая м.** bat

мышья́к, **а́** *m.* (chem.) arsenic

Мья́нм|а, **ы** *f.* Myanmar

мэр, **а** *m.* mayor

мэ́ри|я, **и** *f.* **1** (*управле́ние*) town council **2** (*зда́ние*) town hall

мю́зикл, **а** *m.* musical

мю́зик-хо́лл, **а** *m.* music hall

мю́сли *pl. and nt. indecl.* muesli

ℐ **мя́г|кий**, **∼ок**, **∼ка́**, **∼ко** *adj.* soft; (fig.) mild, gentle; (*о пригово́ре*) lenient; **м. ваго́н** (rail.) soft(-seated) carriage (BrE), sleeping car; **м. знак** (ling.) soft sign (*name of Russian letter «ь»*); **∼кое кре́сло** easy chair

мя́гко *adv.* softly; (fig.) mildly, gently

мя́гче *comp. of* ▶ **мя́гкий**, ▶ **мя́гко**

мя́кот|ь, **и** *f.* **1** (*мя́са*) flesh **2** (*пло́да*) pulp (*of fruit*)

мяси́ст|ый, **∼**, **∼a** *adj.* fleshy; meaty

мясни́к, **а́** *m.* butcher

мясно́й *adj. of* ▶ **мя́со**; **∼ны́е консе́рвы** tinned meat

ℐ **мя́с|о**, **а** *nt.* meat; **пу́шечное м.** (fig.) cannon fodder

мясору́бк|а, **и** *f.* mincer

мя́т|а, **ы** *f.* (bot.) mint; **пе́речная м.** peppermint

мяте́ж, **а́** *m.* mutiny, revolt

мяте́жник, **а** *m.* mutineer, rebel

мяте́ж|ный, **∼ен**, **∼на** *adj.* **1** rebellious, mutinous **2** (fig.) restless; stormy

мя́тн|ый *adj.* mint; **∼ые леденцы́** peppermints

мя́тый *p.p.p. of* ▶ **мять** *and adj.* creased

мять, **мну**, **мнёшь** *impf.* **1** (*pf.* **раз∼**) (*гли́ну*) to work up, knead **2** (*pf.* **из∼** *and* **с∼**) (*бума́гу*, *пла́тье*) to crumple; **м. траву́** to trample grass

мя́ться, **мнётся** *impf.* (*of* ▶ **измя́ться**, ▶ **смя́ться**) to become crumpled; to crease easily

мяу́ка|ть, **ю** *impf.* to mew, miaow

мяч, **а́** *m.* ball

M

Н

Нн

ℐ **на** *prep.* **I.** (+ *a.*) **1** on (to); to; into; over, through; **положи́те кни́гу на стол** put the book on the table; **сесть на авто́бус**, **по́езд** to board a bus, a train; **на се́вер** to the north; **на заво́д** to the factory; **перевести́ на англи́йский** to translate into English **2** (*о вре́мени де́ятельности*) at; on; until; to (*or untranslated*); **на друго́й день**, **на сле́дующий день** (the) next day; **на э́тот раз** this time, for this once **3** (*при обозначе́нии сро́ка*) for; **на два дня** for two days; **собра́ние назна́чено на понеде́льник** the meeting is fixed for Monday; (*при обозначе́нии це́ли, назначе́ния*) for; **на́ зиму**

for the winter; **ко́мната на двои́х** a room for two **4** (*при обозначе́нии ме́ры*) by (*or untranslated*); **коро́че на дюйм** shorter by an inch; **опозда́ть на час** to be an hour late; **ста́рше на три го́да** three years older; **четы́ре ме́тра (в длину́) на два (в ширину́)** four metres (long) by two (broad); (*при умноже́нии, деле́нии*): **помно́жить пять на́ три** to multiply five by three; **дели́ть на́ два** to divide into two **5** (*при обозначе́нии сто́имости*) worth (*of sth*); **ма́рок на рубль** a rouble's worth of stamps

● **II.** (+ *p.*) **1** on, upon; in; at; **на столе́** on the table; **на бума́ге** on paper; (also fig.):

на се́вере in the north; на заво́де at the factory; на со́лнце in the sun; на во́здухе in the open air; на дворе́, на у́лице out of doors; на рабо́те at work; игра́ть на роя́ле to play the piano; писа́ть на неме́цком языке́ to write in German **2** (во время чего-н.) in (or untranslated); during; на э́той неде́ле this week **3** (при помощи чего-н.) on (or untranslated); на ва́те padded; э́тот дви́гатель рабо́тает на не́фти this engine runs on oil **4** (о транспорте) by; е́хать на по́езде/авто́бусе to go by train/bus

на́ int. (infml) here; here you are; here, take it; на́ кни́гу! here, take the book!

на... vbl. pref. **1** forms pf. aspect **2** indicates action continued to sufficiency, to point of satisfaction or exhaustion **3** indicates action relating to determinate quantity or number of objects

набалда́шник, а m. knob

набе́г, а m. raid; foray

набега́|ть, ю impf. of ▶ набежа́ть

набе|гу́, жи́шь, гу́т see ▶ набежа́ть

набе|жа́ть, гу́, жи́шь, гу́т pf. (of ▶ набега́ть) **1** (натолкнуться) (на + a.) to run into, smash into; (о волнах) to lap against **2** (сбежаться) to come running (together)

на́бережн|ая, ой f. embankment

набива́|ть, ю impf. of ▶ наби́ть

набира́|ть, ю impf. of ▶ набра́ть

набира́|ться, юсь impf. of ▶ набра́ться

наб|и́ть, ью, ьёшь pf. (of ▶ набива́ть) (+ a. and i.) to stuff (with), pack (with), fill (with); н. тру́бку to fill one's pipe

наблюда́тел|ь, я m. observer

наблюда́тел|ьный adj. **1** (∼ен, ∼ьна) (внимательный) observant **2** (для наблюдения) observation (attr.); н. пункт (mil.) observation post

✎ наблюда́|ть, ю impf. **1** (следить глазами; изучать) to observe; to watch **2** (за + i.) (за детьми) to take care (of), look after **3** (за + i.) to supervise, superintend; н. за у́личным движе́нием to control traffic

✎ наблюде́ни|е, я nt. **1** observation **2** (надзор) supervision, superintendence

на́бок adv. on one side, awry

✎ набо́р, а m. **1** (рабочих) recruitment; (скорости, высоты) gaining, gathering **2** (typ.) composition, typesetting **3** (комплект) set, collection

набра́сыва|ть, ю impf. of ▶ наброса́ть¹, ▶ набро́сить

набра́сыва|ться, юсь impf. of ▶ набро́ситься

набра́|ть, наберу́, наберёшь, past ∼л, ∼ла́, ∼ло pf. (of ▶ набира́ть) **1** (+ g. or a.) (собрать) to gather; to collect, assemble; н. угля́ to take on coal; н. но́мер to dial a (telephone) number; н. ско́рость to pick up, gather speed; н. высоту́ (aeron.) to gain height; to climb **2** (рабочих) to recruit,

enrol, engage **3** (typ.) to compose, set up

набра́|ться, наберу́сь, наберёшься, past ∼лся, ∼ла́сь, ∼ло́сь pf. (of ▶ набира́ться) **1** (usu. impers.) (скопиться) (о людях) to assemble, gather, collect; (о пыли, деньгах, работе) to accumulate **2** (+ g.) (храбрости, сил) to find, muster; (знаний) to acquire

наброса́|ть¹, ю pf. (of ▶ набра́сывать) (рисунок и т. п.) to sketch, outline

наброса́|ть², ю pf. (накидать) to throw about; to throw (in successive instalments)

набро́|сить, шу, сишь pf. (of ▶ набра́сывать) to throw (on, over)

набро́|ситься, шусь, сишься pf. (of ▶ набра́сываться) (на + a.) to fall upon; to go for; соба́ка ∼силась на меня́ the dog went for me; (infml, на работу, на еду) to attack, get stuck into

набро́с|ок, ка m. (рисунок) sketch; (статьи) draft

набух|а́ть, а́ю impf. of ▶ набу́хнуть

набу́х|нуть, ну, нешь, past ∼, ∼ла pf. (of ▶ набуха́ть) to swell

наб|ью́, ьёшь see ▶ наби́ть

наважде́ни|е, я nt. delusion; (призрак) hallucination

нава́лива|ть, ю impf. of ▶ навали́ть

нава́лива|ться, юсь impf. of ▶ навали́ться

навал|и́ть, ю́, ∼ишь pf. (of ▶ нава́ливать) (наложить наверх) to heap, pile; (возложить) to load (also fig.); (impers.) сне́гу ∼и́ло по коле́но the snow had piled up knee deep

навал|и́ться, ю́сь, ∼ишься pf. (of ▶ нава́ливаться) (на + a.) **1** (infml, на еду, на работу) to attack, get stuck into **2** (на дверь, на человека) to lean (on, upon); to bring all one's weight to bear (on) **3** (насыпаться) to pile up (on)

наве|ду́, дёшь see ▶ навести́

наве́к adv. for ever

наве́ки = наве́к

✎ наве́рно and наве́рное adv. (вводное слово) probably, most likely; он, н., не позвони́т he probably won't phone

наверняка́ adv. (infml) **1** (несомненно) for sure, certainly **2** (безошибочно) safely, without taking risks; бить н. to take no chances

наверста́|ть, ю pf. (of ▶ навёрстывать) to make up (for); н. поте́рянное вре́мя to make up for lost time; н. упу́щенное to repair an omission; to catch up

навёрстыва|ть, ю impf. of ▶ наверста́ть

наве́рх adv. (вверх) up, upward; (по лестнице) upstairs; (на поверхность) to the top

наверху́ adv. above; (в верхнем этаже) upstairs; (fig., в руководстве) at the top

наве́с, а m. **1** (крыша) roof; (тент) awning **2** (скалы) overhang **3** (sport) lob

наве́|сить, шу, сишь pf. (of ▶ наве́шивать¹) **1** (+ a. or g.) (дверь, замок) to hang; (повесить много) to hang (a number of)

н

pictures **2** (sport) to lob

наве|сти́, ду́, дёшь, *past* ~**л**, ~**ла́** *pf.* (*of* ▶ **наводи́ть**) **1** (**на** + *a.*) (*указать направление*) to direct (at); (*орудие, прожектор*) to aim (at); **н. кого́-н. на мысль** to suggest an idea to sb; **н. на след** to put on the track **2** (*устро́ить, сде́лать*) to lay, put, make; **н. поря́док** to introduce order, establish order; **н. спра́вку** to make an inquiry

наве|сти́ть, щу́, сти́шь *pf.* (*of* ▶ **навеща́ть**) to visit, call on

наве́тренный *adj.* windward

наве́чно *adv.* for ever

наве́ш|ать, аю *pf.* (*of* ▶ **наве́шивать²**) (+ *a. or g.*) to hang (up), suspend

наве́шива|ть¹, ю *impf. of* ▶ **наве́сить**

наве́шива|ть², ю *impf. of* ▶ **наве́шать**

навеща́|ть, ю *impf. of* ▶ **навести́ть**

на́взничь *adv.* backwards, on one's back

навига́ци|я, и *f.* navigation

навис|а́ть, а́ю *impf.* (*of* ▶ **нави́снуть**) (**на** + *a. or* **над** + *i.*) to hang (over), overhang; (fig.) to impend, threaten; **над на́ми** ~**ла опа́сность** danger threatened us

нави́с|нуть, ну, нешь, *past* ~, ~**ла** *pf. of* ▶ **нависа́ть**

навлека́|ть, ю *impf. of* ▶ **навле́чь**

навле|ку́, чёшь, ку́т *see* ▶ **навле́чь**

навле́|чь, ку́, чёшь, ку́т, *past* ~**к**, ~**кла́** *pf.* (*of* ▶ **навлека́ть**) (**на** + *a.*) to bring (on); **н. на себя́ гнев** to incur anger

наво|ди́ть, жу́, ~дишь *impf. of* ▶ **навести́**

наводне́ни|е, я *nt.* flood, flooding; (*това́рами*) flooding, inundation

наводн|и́ть, ю́, и́шь *pf.* (*of* ▶ **наводня́ть**) (+ *a. and i.*) to flood (with), inundate (with); (fig.): **н. ры́нок дешёвыми това́рами** to flood the market with cheap goods

наводня́|ть, я́ю *impf. of* ▶ **наводни́ть**

наво|жу́, ~дишь *see* ▶ **наводи́ть**

наво́з, а *m.* manure

на́волочк|а, и *f.* pillowcase, pillowslip

навор|ова́ть, у́ю *pf.* (infml) to steal (*a quantity of*)

наворо́чен|ный, ~, ~а *adj.* (infml) fancy

навр|а́ть, у́, ёшь, *past* ~**а́л**, ~**ала́**, ~**а́ло** *pf.* (*of* ▶ **врать**) (infml) **1** to tell lies **2** (**в** + *p.*) to make mistakes (in); **н. в расска́зе** to get the story wrong

навре|ди́ть, жу́, ди́шь *pf. of* ▶ **вреди́ть**

навря́д ли *adv.* scarcely, hardly

навсегда́ *adv.* for ever, for good; **раз и н.** once (and) for all

навстре́чу *adv. and prep.* (+ *d.*) to meet; towards; **он вы́шел н. гостя́м** he went out to meet the guests; (fig.) to help, show sympathy towards; **идти́ н. чьим-н. пожела́ниям** to meet sb's wishes

⚲ **на́вык, а** *m.* skill

на́вынос *adv.* to take away (BrE), to go (AmE); for consumption off the premises

навя|за́ть, жу́, ~жешь *pf.* (*of* ▶ **навя́зывать**) **1** (**на** + *a.*) (*привязать*) to tie on (to), fasten (to) **2** (fig.) (+ *d. and a.*) (*заста́вить приня́ть*) to thrust (on); to foist (on); **н. кому́-н. сове́т** to thrust advice on sb

навя|за́ться, жу́сь, ~жешься *pf.* (*of* ▶ **навя́зываться**) (infml) (+ *d.*) to thrust oneself (upon), intrude (upon)

навя́зчив|ый, ~, ~а *adj.* **1** (*челове́к*) importunate; annoying **2** (*мысль*) persistent; ~**ая иде́я** idée fixe, obsession

навя́зыва|ть, ю *impf. of* ▶ **навяза́ть**

навя́зыва|ться, юсь *impf. of* ▶ **навяза́ться**

нага́|дить, жу, дишь *pf. of* ▶ **га́дить**

нагиба́|ть, ю *impf. of* ▶ **нагну́ть**

нагиба́|ться, юсь *impf. of* ▶ **нагну́ться**

нагишо́м *adv.* (infml) stark naked

нагле́ц, а́ *m.* impudent fellow, insolent fellow

на́глост|ь, и *f.* impudence, insolence, impertinence

на́гл|ый, ~, ~а́, ~о *adj.* impudent, insolent, impertinent

нагля́д|ный, ~ен, ~на *adj.* **1** (*очеви́дный*) clear; graphic, obvious **2** (*no short forms*) (*в обуче́нии*) visual

наг|на́ть, оню́, о́нишь, *past* ~**на́л**, ~**нала́**, ~**на́ло** *pf.* (*of* ▶ **нагоня́ть**) **1** (*догна́ть*) to overtake, catch up (with) **2** (*наверста́ть*) to make up (for) **3** (+ *a. or g.*) to herd together (*a number of*) **4** (fig., infml, *внуши́ть*) to inspire, arouse, occasion

нагн|у́ть, у́, ёшь *pf.* (*of* ▶ **нагиба́ть**) to bend

нагн|у́ться, у́сь, ёшься *pf.* (*of* ▶ **нагиба́ться**) to bend (down), stoop

нагова́рива|ть, ю *impf. of* ▶ **наговори́ть¹**

наговор|и́ть¹, ю́, и́шь *pf.* (*of* ▶ **нагова́ривать**) (infml) (**на** + *a.*) to slander, calumniate

наговор|и́ть², ю́, и́шь *pf.* (+ *a. or g.*) to talk, say a lot (of); **н. чепухи́** to talk a lot of nonsense

наг|о́й, ~, ~а́, ~о *adj.* (*о челове́ке*) naked, nude; (*о части тела*) bare

нагоня́|ть, ю *impf. of* ▶ **нагна́ть**

наго́рь|е, я *nt.* tableland, plateau

нагот|а́, ы́ *f.* nakedness, nudity

нагото́ве *adv.* in readiness; ready to hand; **быть н.** to hold oneself in readiness, be on call

награб|ить, лю, ишь *pf.* (+ *a. or g.*) to amass by robbery

награ́д|а, ы *f.* **1** reward, recompense; **в** ~**у** as a reward **2** (*почётный знак, орден*) award; decoration; (*в шко́ле*) prize

награ|ди́ть, жу́, ди́шь *pf.* (*of* ▶ **награжда́ть**) (+ *a. and i.*) **1** to reward (with) **2** (*о́рденом, меда́лью*) to decorate (with); to award, confer; (fig.) to endow (with)

награжда́|ть, ю *impf. of* ▶ **награди́ть**

награждён|ный *p.p.p. of* ▶ **награди́ть**; (*as n.* **н.**, ~**ого**) *m.* recipient (*of an award*)

нагрева́ни|е, я *nt.* heating

нагрева́тел|ь, я *m.* (tech.) heater

нагрева́|ть, ю *impf. of* ▶ **нагре́ть**

нагрева́|ться, юсь *impf. of* ▶ **нагре́ться**

нагре́|ть, ю *pf.* (*of* ▶ **нагрева́ть**) to warm, heat

нагре́|ться, юсь *pf.* (*of* ▶ **нагрева́ться**) (*стать тёплым*) to become warm; (*стать горячим*) to become hot; to warm up, heat up

нагроможде́ни|е, я *nt.* pile, heap

нагруб|и́ть, лю́, и́шь *pf. of* ▶ **груби́ть**

нагру́дник, а *m.* (*детский*) bib

нагружа́|ть, ю *impf. of* ▶ **нагрузи́ть**

нагру|зи́ть, жу́, ~зишь *pf.* (*of* ▶ **грузи́ть** 1, ▶ **нагружа́ть**) (+ *a. and i.*) to load (with)

◆ **нагру́зк|а, и** *f.* **1** (*груз*) load **2** (*fig.*) work; commitments

нагря́н|уть, у, ешь *pf.* (*вдруг появиться*) to appear unexpectedly; (**на** + *a.*) to descend (on)

◆ **над** *prep.* + *i.* **1** (*выше*) over, above **2** (*при обозначении предмета труда*) on; at; **рабо́тать над диссерта́цией** to be working on a dissertation; **смея́ться над** to laugh at

над... *comb. form* super-, over-

нада|ва́ть, ю́, ёшь *pf.* (infml) **1** (+ *a., and a. or g.*) to give (*a large quantity of*) **2** (*побить*) (+ *d.*) to thrash

надав|и́ть, лю́, ~ишь *pf.* (*of* ▶ **нада́вливать**) (**на** + *a.*) (*кнопку*) to press (on)

нада́влива|ть, ю *impf. of* ▶ **надави́ть**

надба́вк|а, и *f.* (*повышение*) addition, increase; (*о цене*) extra charge; **н. к зарпла́те** rise (BrE), raise (AmE) (*in wages*)

надвига́|ть, ю *impf. of* ▶ **надви́нуть**

надвига́|ться, юсь *impf. of* ▶ **надви́нуться**

надви́н|уть, у, ешь *pf.* (*of* ▶ **надвига́ть**) to move, pull (up to, over)

надви́н|уться, усь, ешься *pf.* (*of* ▶ **надвига́ться**) to approach, draw near

на́двое *adv.* in two

надева́|ть, ю *impf. of* ▶ **наде́ть**

◆ **наде́жд|а, ы** *f.* hope; **в ~е на** (+ *a.*) in the hope of; **подава́ть ~ы** to promise well

◆ **надёж|ный, ~ен, ~на** *adj.* (*человек*) reliable, trustworthy; (*замок, фундамент*) solid, secure; (*средство*) safe

наде́ла|ть, ю *pf.* (+ *a. or g.*) **1** (*пельменей*) to make (*a quantity of*) **2** (infml) (+ *g.*) (*неприятностей*) to cause (*a lot of*); (*ошибок*) to make (*a lot of*) **3** (infml, *сделать что-то плохое*) to do (*sth wrong*); **что ты ~л?** what have you done?

надел|и́ть, ю́, и́шь *pf.* (*of* ▶ **наделя́ть**) (+ *a. and i.*) to provide (with); (fig.) to endow (with)

наделя́|ть, ю *impf. of* ▶ **надели́ть**

наде́|ну, нешь *see* ▶ **наде́ть**

наде́|ть, ну, нешь *pf.* (*of* ▶ **надева́ть**) to put on (*clothes, etc.*)

◆ **наде́|яться, юсь, ешься** *impf.* (*of* ▶ **понаде́яться**) **1** (**на** + *a.*) (*успех*) to hope (for); **н. на лу́чшее** to hope for the best **2** (**на** + *a.*) (*друга, помощь*) to rely (on),

count on **3** (+ *inf.*) to hope to

надзе́мный *adj.* (*над поверхностью*) overground; (*на поверхности*) surface

надзира́тел|ь, я *m.* overseer, supervisor; **тюре́мный н.** prison guard

надзира́|ть, ю *impf.* (**за** + *i.*) to oversee, supervise

надзо́р, а *m.* **1** supervision; (*за подозреваемым*) surveillance **2** (*collect.*) (*орган*) inspectorate

надлежа́щий *adj.* appropriate; fitting, proper

надме́н|ный, ~ен, ~на *adj.* haughty, arrogant

◆ **на́до**[1] = **над**

◆ **на́до**[2] (+ *d. and inf.*) it is necessary; one must; one ought to; (+ *a. or g.*) there is need of; **не н.** (*не нужно*) one need not; (*нельзя*) one must not; **мне н. идти́** I must go, I ought to go; **так ему́ и н.!** serves him right!; **н. же!** well, I never!

надоеда́|ть, ю *impf. of* ▶ **надое́сть**

надое́длив|ый, ~, ~а *adj.* annoying, boring, tiresome

надое́|сть, м, шь, ст, ди́м, ди́те, дя́т *pf.* (*of* ▶ **надоеда́ть**) **1** (+ *d. and i.*) to get on the nerves (of); (*просьбами*) to pester (with), plague (with) **2** (*impers.* + *d. and inf.*): **мне** *и т. п.* **~ло** I am, *etc.*, tired (of), sick (of); **нам ~ло гуля́ть** we are tired of walking

надо́лго *adv.* for a long time

надорв|а́ться, у́сь, ёшься, *past* ~а́лся, ~ала́сь, ~а́ло́сь *pf.* (*of* ▶ **надрыва́ться** 1) to (over)strain oneself; (*переутомиться*) to tire oneself out

надпи|са́ть, шу́, ~шешь *pf.* (*of* ▶ **надпи́сывать**) (*книгу*) to inscribe

надпи́сыва|ть, ю *impf. of* ▶ **надписа́ть**

на́дпис|ь, и *f.* inscription

надре́з, а *m.* cut, incision; (*зарубка*) notch

надре́|зать, жу, жешь *pf.* (*of* ▶ **надреза́ть**) to make an incision (in)

надреза́|ть, а́ю *impf. of* ▶ **надре́з**

надруга́|ться, юсь *pf.* (**над** + *i.*) to commit an outrage (against)

надры́в, а *m.* **1** (*надорванное место*) slight tear, rent **2** (*физический*) strain **3** (fig., *нервный*) breakdown **4** (*возбуждённость*) hysteria

надрыва́|ться, юсь *impf.* **1** *impf. of* ▶ **надорва́ться 2** (*no pf.*) (*стараться*) to exert oneself; to break one's neck **3** (*no pf.*) (*кричать*) to yell, bellow

надсмо́трщик, а *m.* overseer, supervisor; (*тюремный*) jailer

надстра́ива|ть, ю *impf. of* ▶ **надстро́ить**

надстро́|ить, ю, ишь *pf.* (*of* ▶ **надстра́ивать**) **1** (*этаж*) to build on **2** (*здание*) to raise the height (of)

надстро́йк|а, и *f.* **1** (*действие*) building on; raising **2** (*надстроенная часть*) superstructure (*also phil.*)

надува́|ть, ю *impf. of* ▶ **наду́ть**

надува́|ться, юсь *impf. of* ▶ **наду́ться**

◆ key word

н

надувн|о́й *adj.* pneumatic; **н. матра́с** air bed; **~а́я/рези́новая ло́дка** inflatable/rubber dinghy

наду́ман|ный, ~, ~на *adj.* far-fetched, forced

наду́|ть, ю, ешь *pf.* (*of* ▶ **надува́ть**) **1** (*шар, мяч, колесо*) to puff out; **н. велосипе́дную ка́меру** to inflate, blow up a bicycle tyre (BrE), tire (AmE); **н. гу́бы** (infml) to pout one's lips **2** (infml, *обмануть*) to dupe; to swindle

наду́|ться, юсь, ешься *pf.* (*of* ▶ **надува́ться**) (*шар, мяч, колесо*) to inflate; (*паруса*) to fill out, swell out; (*вена, почка*) to swell

надуш|и́ть, у́, ~ишь *pf. of* ▶ **души́ть²**

надуш|и́ться, у́сь, ~ишься *pf. of* ▶ **души́ться²**

наеда́|ться, юсь *impf. of* ▶ **нае́сться**

наедине́ *adv.* privately, in private; **н. с** (+ *i.*) alone (with); **н. с собо́й** alone, by oneself

нае́|ду, дешь *see* ▶ **нае́хать**

нае́зд, а *m.* **1** (*столкновение*) collision; **маши́на соверши́ла н. на пешехо́да** the car hit a pedestrian **2** (*визит*) flying visit; **быва́ть ~ом/~ами** to pay short, infrequent visits

нае́здник, а *m.* horseman, rider

нае́здни|ца, цы *f. of* ▶ **нае́здник**

наезжа́|ть, ю *impf. of* ▶ **нае́хать**

на|ём, ~йма *m.* (*на короткий период, рабочих*) hire; (*в длительное пользование, квартиры, мебели*) renting; **взять в н.** to rent; **сдать в н.** to let

наёмник, а *m.* **1** (mil.) mercenary **2** (*наёмный работник*) hireling; (fig.) mercenary

наёмный *adj.* hired; rented; **н. уби́йца** hit man

нае́|сться, мся, шься, стся, ди́мся, ди́тесь, дя́тся, *past* **~лся, ~лась** *pf.* (*of* ▶ **наеда́ться**) **1** to eat one's fill **2** (+ *g.* or *i.*) to eat (a large quantity of), stuff oneself (with)

нае́|хать, ду, дешь *pf.* (*of* ▶ **наезжа́ть**) **1** (на + *a.*) to run (into, over), collide (with); **на нас ~хал авто́бус** a bus ran into us, hit us **2** (infml, *приехать*) to come, arrive (*unexpectedly or in numbers*) **3** (sl.) (на + *a.*) (*придраться; выругать*) to go on (at), give (sb) a hard time; (*о рэкете*) to try to blackmail (sb)

наж|а́ть, му́, мёшь *pf.* (*of* ▶ **нажима́ть**) **1** (+ *a.* or на + *a.*) to press (on); **н. (на) кно́пку** to press the button **2** (fig., infml) (на + *a.*) (*понудить*) to put pressure (upon)

нажи́в|а, ы *f.* gain, profit

нажива́|ть, ю *impf. of* ▶ **нажи́ть**

нажива́|ться, юсь *impf. of* ▶ **нажи́ться**

нажи́вк|а, и *f.* bait

нажи|ву́, вёшь *see* ▶ **нажи́ть**

нажи́м, а *m.* pressure (also fig.); **сде́лать что-н. под ~ом** to do sth under pressure

нажима́|ть, ю *impf. of* ▶ **нажа́ть**

нажи́|ть, иву́, ивёшь, *past* **~ил, ~ила́, ~ило** *pf.* (*of* ▶ **нажива́ть**) (*богатство*) to acquire, gain; (fig., infml, *болезнь*) to contract, get

нажи́|ться, иву́сь, ивёшься, *past* **~и́лся, ~ила́сь** *pf.* (*of* ▶ **нажива́ться**) (на + *p.*) to become rich (from), make a fortune (from)

наж|му́, мёшь *see* ▶ **нажа́ть**

✍ **наза́д** *adv.* **1** (*оглянуться*) back; (*катиться*) backwards; (*на прежнее место*) back; **н.!** back!; stand back! **2**: **(тому́) н.** ago

✍ **назва́ни|е, я** *nt.* name; **под ~ем** named

✍ **наз|ва́ть, ову́, овёшь,** *past* **~ва́л, ~вала́, ~ва́ло** *pf.* (*of* ▶ **называ́ть**) (+ *a. and i.*) to call; to name

наз|ва́ться, ову́сь, овёшься, *past* **~ва́лся, ~вала́сь** *pf.* (*of* ▶ **называ́ться**) (+ *i.*) **1** (*получить какое-н. имя*) to call oneself; to be named **2** (*представиться*) to give one's name **3** (*журналистом*) to claim to be

назём|ный *adj.* ground, surface; **~ые войска́** (mil.) ground troops; **~ая по́чта** surface mail

назида́тель|ный, ~ен, ~ьна *adj.* edifying

назло́ 1 *adv.* (*сделать*) out of spite **2** *prep.* (+ *d.*) (*родителям*) to spite

✍ **назнача́|ть, а́ю** *impf. of* ▶ **назна́чить**

✍ **назначе́ни|е, я** *nt.* **1** (*на работу*) appointment **2** (med.) prescription **3** (*цель*) purpose; **испо́льзовать что́-н. по ~ю** to use sth properly, appropriately; **отря́д осо́бого ~я** special task force **4**: **ме́сто ~я** destination

назна́ч|ить, у, ишь *pf.* (*of* ▶ **назнача́ть**) **1** (*дату, место, размер*) to fix, set, appoint; **н. день встре́чи** to fix, appoint a day for a meeting; **н. кому́-н. свида́ние** to make a date with sb **2** (+ *a. and i.*) to appoint, nominate; **его́ ~или дире́ктором** he has been appointed director **3** (med.) to prescribe

назо́йлив|ый, ~, ~а *adj.* importunate, troublesome

назрева́|ть, ю *impf.* (*of* ▶ **назре́ть**) to become imminent; **кри́зис ~л** a crisis was brewing

назре́|ть, ю, ешь *pf. of* ▶ **назрева́ть**

называ́емый *pres. part. pass. of* ▶ **называ́ть**; **так н.** so-called

✍ **называ́|ть, ю** *impf.* (*of* ▶ **назва́ть**): **н. ве́щи свои́ми имена́ми** to call a spade a spade

✍ **называ́|ться, юсь** *impf.* (*of* ▶ **назва́ться**) (*носить какое-н. наименование, имя*) to be called; **как ~ется э́то село́?** what is this village called?

✍ **наибо́лее** *adv.* (the) most

наибо́льший *adj.* the greatest; (*по величине*) the largest

наи́вность|, и *f.* naivety

наи́в|ный, ~ен, ~на *adj.* naive; (*простой*) artless

наивы́сш|ий *adj.* the highest; **в ~ей сте́пени** to the utmost

наизна́нку *adv.* inside out; **вы́вернуть н.** to turn inside out

✍ **наизу́сть** *adv.* by heart; from memory

наилу́чший *adj.* (the) best

наиме́нее *adv.* (the) least

наимен|ова́ть, у́ю *pf. of* ▸ именова́ть

наиме́ньший *adj.* (the) least; (*по величине́*) the smallest

наискосо́к *adv.* = на́искось

на́искось *adv.* obliquely, slantwise

наиху́дший *adj.* (the) worst

⚡ **на|йти́**[1], **йду́, йдёшь,** *past* ～шёл, ～шла́ *pf.* (*of* ▸ находи́ть) to find; **н. иде́ю интере́сной** to find the idea interesting

на|йти́[2], **йду́, йдёшь,** *past* ～шёл, ～шла́ *pf.* (*of* ▸ находи́ть) (**на** + *a.*) (*натолкну́ться*) to come (across, upon); (*о чу́вствах*) to come over; **что э́то на неё ～шло́?** what has come over her?; (*закры́ть собо́й*) to cover

на|йти́сь, йду́сь, йдёшься, *past* ～шёлся, ～шла́сь *pf.* (*of* ▸ находи́ться[1])
1 (*обнару́житься*) (*по́сле по́исков*) to be found; to turn up; (*вы́зваться*) to volunteer **2** (*не растеря́ться*) to not be at a loss; **я не ～шёлся, что сказа́ть** I was at a loss for what to say

наказа́ни|е, я *nt.* punishment

нака|за́ть, жу́, ～жешь *pf.* (*of* ▸ нака́зывать) to punish

нака́зыва|ть, ю *impf. of* ▸ наказа́ть

нака́лива|ть, ю *impf. of* ▸ накали́ть

нака́лива|ться, юсь *impf. of* ▸ накали́ться

накал|и́ть, ю́, и́шь *pf.* (*of* ▸ нака́ливать) to heat, incandesce; (fig., *ситуа́цию*) to inflame

накал|и́ться, ю́сь, и́шься *pf.* (*of* ▸ нака́ливаться, ▸ накаля́ться) to glow, incandesce; (fig., *обстано́вка*) to become inflamed; **стра́сти ～и́лись** passions were running high

накаля́|ть, ю *impf. of* ▸ накали́ть

накаля́|ться, юсь *impf. of* ▸ накали́ться

накану́не **1** *adv.* the day before **2** (*prep.*) (+ *g.*) on the eve (of); **н. Рождества́** on Christmas Eve

нака́п|ать, аю *pf. of* ▸ ка́пать

нака́пливать *impf. of* ▸ накопи́ть

нака́пливаться *impf. of* ▸ накопи́ться

накач|а́ть[1], **а́ю** *pf.* (*of* ▸ нака́чивать) (*ши́ну, ка́меру*) to pump up, pump full

накач|а́ть[2], **а́ю** *pf.* (*of* ▸ нака́чивать, ▸ кача́ть 3) (*воды́*) to pump (*a quantity of*)

накач|а́ть[3], **а́ю** *pf.* (*of* ▸ кача́ть 4, ▸ нака́чивать) (infml) to be muscly from pumping iron

накача́|ться, юсь *pf. of* ▸ кача́ться 3

нака́чива|ть, ю *impf. of* ▸ накача́ть[1], ▸ накача́ть[2], ▸ накача́ть[3]

наки́дк|а, и *f.* cloak, mantle; wrap

наки́дыва|ться, юсь *impf. of* ▸ наки́нуться

наки|́нуться, нусь, нешься *pf.* (*of* ▸ наки́дываться) (**на** + *a.*) to fall (on, upon); (*на еду́, на рабо́ту*) to attack, get stuck into

накладн|а́я, о́й *f.* invoice, waybill

⚡ key word

накладн|о́й *adj.* **1** (*прикреплённый пове́рх чего́-н.*) superimposed; **н. карма́н** patch pocket; **～ые расхо́ды** overheads **2** (*иску́сственный*) false; **～ая борода́** false beard

накла́дыва|ть, ю *impf. of* ▸ наложи́ть[1], ▸ наложи́ть[2]

наклеве|та́ть, щу́, ～щешь *pf. of* ▸ клевета́ть

накле́ива|ть, ю *impf. of* ▸ накле́ить

накле́|ить, ю, ишь *pf.* (*of* ▸ накле́ивать) to stick on, paste on

накле́йк|а, и *f.* sticker

накло́н, а *m.* (*головы́*) inclination; (*по́черка*) slope, slant; (*пока́тая пове́рхность*) slope, incline

наклон|и́ть, ю́, ～ишь *pf.* (*of* ▸ наклоня́ть) to incline, bend

наклон|и́ться, ю́сь, ～ишься *pf.* (*of* ▸ наклоня́ться) to stoop, bend

накло́нност|ь, и *f.* (к + *d.*) inclination (towards), tendency (towards), propensity (for)

накло́нн|ый *adj.* inclined, sloping; **～ая пло́скость** inclined plane

наклоня́|ть, я́ю *impf. of* ▸ наклони́ть

наклоня́|ться, я́юсь *impf. of* ▸ наклони́ться

накова́льн|я, ни, *g. pl.* ～ен *f.* anvil

⚡ **наконе́ц** *adv.* at last, finally, in the end; **н.-то!** at last!, about time too!; (*ещё, кро́ме всего́*) after all; (*выража́ет недово́льство*) ever; **переста́ньте, н., спо́рить!** will you ever stop arguing!

наконе́чник, а *m.* tip, point

накоп|и́ть, лю́, ～ишь *pf.* (*of* ▸ копи́ть, ▸ нака́пливать) (+ *a. or g.*) to accumulate, amass

накоп|и́ться, ～ится *pf.* (*of* ▸ нака́пливаться, ▸ копи́ться) to accumulate

накопле́ни|е, я *nt.* **1** accumulation **2** (*in pl.*) (*сбереже́ния*) savings

накорм|и́ть, лю́, ～ишь *pf. of* ▸ корми́ть 1

накра́|сить, шу, сишь *pf.* (*of* ▸ накра́шивать) **1** (*но́гти, гу́бы*) to paint **2** (*лицо́*) to make up

накра́|ситься, шусь, сишься *pf. of* ▸ кра́ситься 1

накра́шива|ть, ю *impf. of* ▸ накра́сить

накро|и́ть, ю́, ～ишь *pf.* (*of* ▸ кроши́ть) **1** to crumble, shred (*a quantity of*) **2** (*насо́рить кро́шками*) to spill crumbs

накро́|ю, ёшь *see* ▸ накры́ть

накру|ти́ть, чу́, ～тишь *pf.* (*of* ▸ накру́чивать) **1** (*намота́ть*) (**на** + *a.*) to wind (around, on to) **2** (*верёвок*) to twist (*a quantity of*)

накру́чива|ть, ю *impf. of* ▸ накрути́ть

накрыва́|ть, ю *impf. of* ▸ накры́ть

накрыва́|ться, юсь *impf. of* ▸ накры́ться

накр|ы́ть, о́ю, о́ешь *pf.* (*of* ▸ накрыва́ть) to cover; **н. (на) стол** to lay the table; **н. к у́жину** to lay supper

накр|ы́ться, о́юсь, о́ешься *pf.* (*of* ▸ накрыва́ться) (+ *i.*) to cover oneself (with)

накуп|а́ть, а́ю *impf. of* ▸ накупи́ть

накуп|и́ть, лю́, ∼ишь *pf.* (*of* ▶ **накупа́ть**) (+ *a. or g.*) to buy up (*a number or quantity of*)

нал, а *m.* (*infml*) cash

налага́|ть, ю *impf. of* ▶ **наложи́ть¹** 2, ▶ **наложи́ть¹** 4

нала́|дить, жу, дишь *pf.* (*of* ▶ **нала́живать**) **1** (*отрегулировать*) to regulate, adjust; (*исправить*) to repair, put right **2** (*организовать*) to set going, arrange; **н. дела́** to get things going

нала́|диться, дится *pf.* (*of* ▶ **нала́живаться**) to go right; **рабо́та ∼дилась** the work is well in hand

нала́жива|ть, ю, ет *impf. of* ▶ **нала́дить**

нала́жива|ться, ется *impf. of* ▶ **нала́диться**

нале́во *adv.* **1** (*от* + *g.*) to the left (of); **н.!** (*mil.*) left turn! **2** (*infml*, *продавать*) on the side (= *illicitly*); **рабо́тать н.** to moonlight

налеп|и́ть¹, лю́, ∼ишь *pf.* (*of* ▶ **лепи́ть** 2) to stick on

налеп|и́ть², лю́, ∼ишь *pf.* (+ *a. or g.*) to model (*a number of*)

налёт¹, а *m.* (*нападение*) raid; (*на кварти́ру, на магази́н*) robbery, burglary; **возду́шный н.** air raid

налёт², а *m.* (*тонкий слой*) deposit; thin coating; (*на бро́нзе*) patina; **зубно́й н.** dental plaque; (*fig.*) touch, soupçon; **с ∼ом иро́нии** with a touch of irony

налет|а́ть, а́ю *impf. of* ▶ **налете́ть¹**, ▶ **налете́ть²**

нале|те́ть¹, чу́, ти́шь *pf.* (*of* ▶ **налета́ть**) **1** (*на* + *a.*) (*наброситься*) to fall (upon); (*о пти́це*) to swoop down (on); to fly (upon, against); (*натолкну́ться*) to run (into) **2** (*о ве́тре, бу́ре*) to spring up

нале|те́ть², чу́, ти́шь *pf.* (*of* ▶ **налета́ть**) (*прилете́ть*) to fly in, drift in (*in quantities, in large numbers*)

налива́|ть, ю *impf. of* ▶ **нали́ть**

нал|и́ть, ью́, ьёшь, *past* ∼и́л, ∼ила́, ∼и́ло *pf.* (*of* ▶ **налива́ть**) **1** (*влить*) to pour out; (*напо́лнить*) (+ *i.*) to fill (with) **2** (*проли́ть*) to spill

налицо́ *adv.* present, available, on hand

⚹ **нали́чи|е, я** *nt.* presence; **быть, оказа́ться в ∼и** to be present, be available

нали́чник, а *m.* (*двери, окна́*) casing

нали́чн|ый *adj.* on hand, available; **∼ые (де́ньги)** ready money, cash; **плати́ть ∼ыми** to pay in cash

налов|и́ть, лю́, ∼ишь *pf.* (+ *a. or g.*) to catch (*a number of*)

⚹ **нало́г, а** *m.* tax; **подохо́дный н.** income tax; **н. на доба́вленную сто́имость** value added tax, VAT; **н. на при́быль** profits tax

⚹ **нало́г|овый** *adj. of* ▶ **нало́г**; **∼овая деклара́ция** tax return; **н. инспе́ктор** tax inspector

налогообложе́ни|е, я *nt.* taxation

налогоплате́льщик, а *m.* taxpayer

налож|и́ть¹, у́, ∼ишь *pf.* **1** (*impf.* **накла́дывать**) (*повя́зку; лак*) to apply;

(*положи́ть све́рху*) to put on, over **2** (*impf.* **накла́дывать, налага́ть**) (*печа́ть, визу́*) to affix; **н. отпеча́ток на** (+ *a.*) (*fig.*) to have a great influence (on) **3** (*impf.* **накла́дывать**) (*навали́ть*) to load, pack **4** (*impf.* **налага́ть**) (*на* + *a.*) (*подве́ргнуть*) to lay (on), impose; **н. штраф** to impose a fine; **н. аре́ст на чьё-н. иму́щество** (*law*) to seize sb's property

налож|и́ть², у́, ∼ишь *pf.* (*of* ▶ **накла́дывать**) (+ *a. or g.*) to put, lay (*a quantity of*)

нал|ью́, ьёшь *see* ▶ **нали́ть**

нам *d. of* ▶ **мы**

нама́з, а *m.* Muslim prayer

нама́|зать, жу, жешь *pf. of* ▶ **ма́зать** 2, ▶ **нама́зывать**

нама́|заться, жусь, жешься *pf.* **1** (*impf.* **∼зываться**) (+ *i.*) to rub oneself (with) **2** *pf. of* ▶ **ма́заться** 2, ▶ **ма́заться** 3

нама́зыва|ть, ю *impf. of* ▶ **нама́зать**

нама́зыва|ться, юсь *impf. of* ▶ **нама́заться**

нама́тыва|ть, ю *impf.* (*of* ▶ **намота́ть**) to wind, reel

нама́чива|ть, ю *impf. of* ▶ **намочи́ть** 1

намёк, а *m.* hint; **сде́лать н.** to drop a hint

намек|а́ть, а́ю *impf.* (*of* ▶ **намекну́ть**) (**на** + *a. or* **о** + *p.*) to hint (at), allude (to)

намек|ну́ть, ну́, нёшь *pf. of* ▶ **намека́ть**

намерева́|ться, юсь *impf.* (+ *inf.*) to intend (to), mean (to)

наме́рен, ∼а, ∼о *adj. as pred.* (+ *inf.*) intending; **я н. за́втра е́хать** I intend to go tomorrow; **что вы ∼ы де́лать?** what do you intend to do?

наме́рени|е, я *nt.* intention; purpose; **без вся́кого ∼я** unintentionally

наме́ренно *adv.* intentionally, deliberately

наме́ренн|ый, ∼, ∼на *adj.* intentional, deliberate

наме́|тить¹, чу, тишь *pf.* (*of* ▶ **намеча́ть¹**) (*изобрази́ть*) to sketch, outline

наме́|тить², чу, тишь *pf.* (*of* ▶ **намеча́ть²**) **1** (*плани́ровать*) to plan, project; to have in view; **н. пое́здку в Росси́ю** to plan a visit to Russia **2** (*предположи́ть*) to nominate; (*назна́чить*) to select; **н. зда́ние к разруше́нию** to designate a building for demolition

наме́|титься, тится *pf.* (*of* ▶ **намеча́ться**) to begin to appear; to take shape

намеча́|ть¹, ю *impf. of* ▶ **наме́тить¹**

намеча́|ть², ю *impf. of* ▶ **наме́тить²**

намеча́|ться, ется *impf. of* ▶ **наме́титься**

на́ми *i. of* ▶ **мы**

намиби́|ец, йца *m.* Namibian

намиби́й|ка, ки *f. of* ▶ **намиби́ец**

намиби́йский *adj.* Namibian

Нами́би|я, и *f.* Namibia

намно́го *adv.* much, far (*with comparatives*); **н. лу́чше** much, far better; greatly, considerably (*with verbs*)

намок|а́ть, а́ю *impf.* (*of* ▶ **намо́кнуть**) to become wet, get wet

намо́к|нуть, ну, нешь, *past* ∼, ∼ла *pf. of*
▶ **намока́ть**

намо́рдник, а *m.* muzzle

намота́|ть, ю *pf. of* ▶ **мота́ть 1,** ▶ **нама́тывать**

намочи́|ть, у́, ∼ишь *pf.* **1** (*of* ▶ **нама́чивать,**
▶ **мочи́ть 2**) (*делать мокрым*) to wet,
moisten; (*бельё*) to soak **2** (*пол*) to splash,
spill water on

нанес|ти́, у́, ёшь, *past* ∼, ∼ла́ *pf.* (*of*
▶ **наноси́ть**) **1** (+ *a. or g.*) to bring (*a
quantity of*); to pile up (*a quantity of*);
(*о снеге, песке*) (*usu. impers.*) to drift
2 (*начертить*) (**на** + *a.*) to draw, plot (*on a
map, etc.*) **3** (*причинить*) to cause; to inflict;
н. оскорбле́ние to insult; **н. уще́рб** to inflict
damage **4** (*лак, краску*) to apply

нани|за́ть, жу́, ∼жешь *pf. of* ▶ **нани́зывать**

нани́зыва|ть, ю *impf.* to string, thread

нанима́тель|, я *m.* **1** (*квартиры*) tenant
2 (*рабочей силы*) employer

нанима́тель|ница, ницы *f. of* ▶ **нанима́тель**

нанима́|ть, ю *impf. of* ▶ **наня́ть**

нанима́|ться, юсь *impf. of* ▶ **наня́ться**

нано|си́ть, шу́, ∼сишь *impf. of* ▶ **нанести́**

нан|я́ть, найму́, наймёшь, *past* ∼я́л, ∼яла́,
∼я́ло *pf.* (*of* ▶ **нанима́ть**) (*квартиру*)
to rent; (*машину, рабочих*) to hire; **н. на
рабо́ту** to engage, take on

нан|я́ться, найму́сь, наймёшься, *past*
∼я́лся, ∼яла́сь *pf.* (*of* ▶ **нанима́ться**) to
get a job

✓ **наоборо́т** *adv.* **1** (*обратной стороной*)
back to front; **прочте́сь сло́во н.** to read
a word backwards **2** (*не так*) the other
way round; the wrong way (round) **3** (*при
противопоставлении*) on the contrary; **как
раз н.** quite the contrary; **и н.** and vice versa

наобу́м *adv.* (*не подумав*) without thinking;
(*наудачу*) at random

наор|а́ть, у́, ёшь *pf.* (**на** + *a.*) (*infml*) to shout
(at)

наотре́з *adv.* flatly, point-blank

напада́|ть, ю *impf. of* ▶ **напа́сть**

напада́ющий, его *m.* (*sport*) forward

нападе́ни|е, я *nt.* attack, assault; (*sport*)
(*collect.*) forwards, forward line

напа|ду́, дёшь *see* ▶ **напа́сть**

напа́рник, а *m.* fellow worker, mate

напа́|сть, ду́, дёшь, *past* ∼л *pf.* (*of*
▶ **напада́ть**) (**на** + *a.*) **1** to attack; to descend
(on) **2** (*о чувстве*) to come (over); to grip,
seize; **на нас** ∼**л страх** fear seized us

напева́|ть, ю *impf.* **1** *impf. of* ▶ **напе́ть**
2 (*тихо, вполголоса*) to hum; to croon

наперере́з *adv. and prep.* (+ *d.*) so as to cross
one's path; **бежа́ть кому́-н. н.** to run to head
sb off

напёрст|ок, ка *m.* thimble

нап|е́ть, ою́, оёшь *pf.* (*of* ▶ **напева́ть 1**) to
hum, sing sketchily

напеча́та|ть, ю *pf. of* ▶ **печа́тать**

напеча́та|ться, юсь *pf. of* ▶ **печа́таться**

напива́|ться, юсь *impf. of* ▶ **напи́ться**

напи́льник, а *m.* (*tech.*) file

✓ **напи|са́ть, шу́, ∼шешь** *pf. of* ▶ **писа́ть**

напи́т|ок, ка *m.* drink, beverage

нап|и́ться, ью́сь, ьёшься, *past* ∼и́лся,
∼ила́сь, ∼ило́сь *pf.* (*of* ▶ **напива́ться**)
1 (+ *g.*) (*утолить жажду*) to slake one's
thirst (with, on); (*выпить*) to have a drink
(of) **2** (*infml, стать пьяным*) to get drunk

напих|а́ть, а́ю *pf.* (*of* ▶ **напи́хивать**) (**в** + *a.*)
to cram (into), stuff (into)

напи́хива|ть, ю *impf. of* ▶ **напиха́ть**

напишу́, ∼шешь *see* ▶ **написа́ть**

напл|ева́ть, юю́, юёшь *pf.* **1** (+ *g.*) to spit
(out) **2** (*fig., infml*) (**на** + *a.*) to wash one's
hands (of); **н.!** to hell with it!, who cares!;
мне н.! I couldn't care less!

нап|ои́ть, ою́, ои́шь *pf.* (*of* ▶ **пои́ть**)
1 (*дать попить*) to give to drink; to water
(*an animal*) **2** (*довести до опьянения*) to
make drunk

напока́з *adv.* for show; **вы́ставить н.** to show
off (also fig.)

напо́лн|ить, ю, ишь *pf.* (*of* ▶ **наполня́ть**)
(+ *i.*) to fill (with)

напо́лн|иться, юсь, ишься *pf.* (*of*
▶ **наполня́ться**) (+ *i.*) to fill (with)

наполн|я́ть, я́ю *impf. of* ▶ **напо́лнить**

наполн|я́ться, я́юсь *impf. of* ▶ **напо́лниться**

наполови́ну *adv.* half; **зал ещё н. пуст** the
hall is still half empty

напомина́ни|е, я *nt.* **1** (*действие*) reminding
2 (*что-н. напоминающее*) reminder

✓ **напомина́|ть, ю** *impf. of* ▶ **напо́мнить**

✓ **напо́мн|ить, ю, ишь** *pf.* (*of* ▶ **напомина́ть**)
1 (+ *d. and o* + *p., or* + *d. and a.*) (*заставить
вспомнить*) to remind (of); **портре́т** ∼**ил
мне о про́шлом** the portrait reminded
me of the past **2** (*иметь сходство*) to
remind (of), recall (= *to resemble*); **он** ∼**ил
мне моего́ де́да** he reminded me of my
grandfather

напо́р, а *m.* (*воздуха, воды*) pressure (also
fig.); **под** ∼**ом** under pressure

напо́рист|ый, ∼, ∼a *adj.* energetic; pushy

напосле́док *adv.* (*infml*) in the end, finally,
after all

напо|ю́[1], оёшь *see* ▶ **напе́ть**

напо|ю́[2], и́шь *see* ▶ **напои́ть**

✓ **напра́в|ить, лю, ишь** *pf.* (*of* ▶ **направля́ть**)
1 (**на** + *a.*) (*устремить*) to direct (to,
at); **н. внима́ние** (**на** + *a.*) to direct one's
attention (to); **н. уда́р** to aim a blow (at)
2 (*отправить*) to send; **н. заявле́ние** to
send in an application; (*к врачу, к юристу*)
to refer

напра́в|иться, люсь, ишься *pf.* (*of*
▶ **направля́ться**) (**к** + *d. or* **в** + *a. or* **на** +
a.) (*двинуться куда-н.*) to make (for);
(*двинуться куда-н.*) to make (for)

✓ **направле́ни|е, я** *nt.* **1** (*линия, путь*)
direction; **по** ∼**ю** (**к** + *d.*) in the direction (of),
towards **2** (*fig., в экономике, в политике*)

trend, tendency; **либера́льное** н. liberal tendency; (*группиро́вка*) movement **3** (*докуме́нт*) order, warrant

напра́вленност|ь, и *f.* direction, focus, purposefulness

◌ **направля́|ть, ю** *impf. of* ▶ напра́вить

направля́|ться, юсь *impf.* (*of* ▶ напра́виться): ~емся в Му́рманск we are bound for Murmansk

направля́ющ|ая, ей *f.* (tech.) guide

напра́во *adv.* (от + *g.*) to the right (of)

напра́сно *adv.* **1** (*бесполе́зно*) vainly, in vain; to no purpose **2** (*несправедли́во*) wrong, unjustly, mistakenly

напра́с|ный, ~ен, ~на *adj.* **1** (*бесполе́зный*) vain, idle; ~ная наде́жда vain hope **2** (*нену́жный*) needless

напра́шива|ться, юсь *impf.* (*of* ▶ напроси́ться) (*impf. only*) to arise, suggest itself; ~ется вопро́с the question arises

◌ **наприме́р** for example, for instance

напрока́т *adv.* for hire, on hire; **взять** н. to hire, rent; **дать** н. to hire out, let

напроло́м *adv.* straight, regardless of obstacles (also fig.)

напроро́ч|ить, у, ишь *pf. of* ▶ проро́чить

напро|си́ться, шу́сь, ~сишься *pf.* (*of* ▶ напра́шиваться) (infml) to thrust oneself upon; (на + *a.*) to provoke; н. на комплиме́нты to fish for compliments

напро́тив *adv. and prep.* + *g.* **1** opposite; **он живёт** н. (**на́шего до́ма**) he lives opposite (our house) **2** (*при противопоставле́нии*) on the contrary

на́прочь *adv.* (infml) completely

напря́г, а *m.* (sl.) pressure, difficulties; **у меня́ сейча́с ~ с деньга́ми** I don't have much money at the moment

напряга́|ть, ю *impf. of* ▶ напря́чь

напряга́|ться, юсь *impf. of* ▶ напря́чься

напря|гу́, жёшь *see* ▶ напря́чь

◌ **напряже́ни|е, я** *nt.* **1** (*затра́та уси́лий*) effort, exertion; **рабо́тать с ~ем** to exert oneself; (*тру́дное положе́ние*) strain, tension **2** (phys., tech.) strain; stress; (elec.) voltage

напряжённост|ь, и *f.* tension, strain

напряжён|ный, ~, ~на *adj.* tense, strained; ~ные отноше́ния strained relations; ~ная рабо́та intensive work

напрями́к *adv.* **1** (*пойти́*) straight **2** (fig., *сказа́ть*) straight out, bluntly

напря́|чь, гу́, жёшь, гу́т, *past* ~г, ~гла́ *pf.* (*of* ▶ напряга́ть) (*му́скулы*) to strain; (*го́лос, слух, внима́ние*) to strain (also fig.)

напря́|чься, гу́сь, жёшься, гу́тся, *past* ~гся, ~гла́сь *pf.* (*of* ▶ напряга́ться) **1** (*о му́скулах*) to become tense **2** (*о челове́ке*) to exert oneself, strain oneself **3** (*о взгля́де, си́лах*) to be concentrated

напуга́|ть, ю *pf. of* ▶ пуга́ть

напу́др|ить, ю, ишь *pf. of* ▶ пу́дрить

напу́др|иться, юсь, ишься *pf. of* ▶ пу́дриться

напуска́|ть, ю *impf. of* ▶ напусти́ть

напускно́й *adj.* assumed, put on

напу|сти́ть, щу́, ~стишь *pf.* (*of* ▶ напуска́ть) **1** (+ *g.*) (*ды́ма, мух*) to let in; **н. воды́ в ва́нну** to fill a bath **2** (*напра́вить для нападе́ния*) (на + *a.*) to let loose on, set on **3** (на себя́ + *a.*) to affect, put on; **н. на себя́ ва́жность** to assume an air of importance

напу́та|ть, ю *pf.* (infml) (в + *p.*) to make a mess (of), make a hash (of); (*ошиби́ться*) to confuse, get wrong

напу|щу́, ~стишь *see* ▶ напусти́ть

наравне́ *adv.* (с + *i.*) equally (with); on an equal footing (with); together (with)

нараст|а́ть, а́ю *impf. of* ▶ нарасти́

нарас|ти́, ту́, тёшь, *past* **наро́с, наросла́** *pf.* (*of* ▶ нараста́ть) **1** (на + *p.*) to grow (on), form (on); **мох наро́с на камня́х** moss has grown on the stones **2** (*увели́читься*) to increase; (*о зву́ке*) to swell **3** (*накопи́ться*) to accumulate

нара|сти́ть, щу́, сти́шь *pf.* (*of* ▶ нара́щивать) **1** (*му́скулы*) to develop **2** (*удлини́ть*) to lengthen; (fig., *увели́чить*) to increase, augment

нара́щивани|е, я *nt.* increase; build-up; **н. вооруже́ний** arms build-up; **н. воло́с** hair extension

нара́щива|ть, ю *impf. of* ▶ нарасти́ть

на́рд|ы, ов *pl.* backgammon

наре́|жу, жешь *see* ▶ нареза́ть

наре́|зать, жу, жешь *pf.* (*of* ▶ нареза́ть) **1** (+ *a.* or *g.*) (*хле́ба, сыр*) to cut; to slice **2** (tech.) to thread

нареза́|ть, а́ю *impf. of* ▶ наре́зать

нарека́ни|е, я *nt.* censure; reprimand

наре́чи|е, я *nt.* (gram.) adverb

нарис|ова́ть, у́ю *pf. of* ▶ рисова́ть

наркоби́знес, а *m.* drug trafficking

нарко́з, а *m.* anaesthetic (BrE), anesthetic (AmE); **ме́стный** н. local anaesthetic; **о́бщий** н. general anaesthetic

нарко́лог, а *m.* expert in drug and alcohol abuse

наркома́н, а *m.* drug addict

наркома́ни|я, и *f.* drug addiction

наркома́н|ка, ки *f. of* ▶ наркома́н

нарко́тик, а *m.* narcotic; drug; **торго́вля ~ами** drug trafficking

наркоти́ческ|ий *adj.* narcotic; ~ие сре́дства narcotics, drugs

наркоторго́в|ец, ца *m.* drug dealer

◌ **наро́д, а (у)** *m.* (*все жи́тели*) people; (*на́ция*) nation; ~ы ми́ра nations of the world; **англи́йский** н. the English people, the people of England; **челове́к из ~а** a man of the people; **на ми́тинге бы́ло ма́ло ~у** there were not many people at the meeting

наро́дност|ь, и *f.* **1** (*наро́д*) nationality **2** (*sg. only*) (*иску́сства*) national character; national traits

◌ **наро́дн|ый** *adj.* **1** (*национа́льный*) national; ~ое хозя́йство national economy **2** (*пе́сня,*

Н

искусство) folk **3** (*восстание, движение*) of the (*sc. common, working*) people, popular **4** (*в составе почётных званий, названий некоторых учреждений, коммунистических штатов, и т. п.*): **н. арти́ст Росси́и** National Artist of Russia; **н. суд** the People's Court; **Кита́йская Н~ая Респу́блика** the People's Republic of China

наро́ст, а *m.* **1** (*грязи*) layer **2** (*на растении*) excrescence, growth

наро́чно *adv.* **1** (*намеренно*) on purpose, purposely; **как н.** (infml) to make things worse; **н. не приду́маешь** it is quite something **2** (infml, *в шутку*) for fun, pretending

наруб|и́ть, лю́, ~ишь *pf.* (+ *a.* or *g.*) to chop (*a quantity of*)

нару́жность|ь, и *f.* exterior; (outward) appearance; **н. обма́нчива** appearances are deceptive

нару́жн|ый *adj.* (*стена, дверь*) external, exterior; (*изменение*) external; (*спокойствие*) outward; (tech.) male (*of screw thread*); **~ое (лека́рство)** medicine for external application

нару́жу *adv.* outside, on the outside; **вы́йти н.** to come out; (fig.) to come to light, transpire

нарука́вник, а *m.* oversleeve; armlet

нарука́вн|ый *adj.* (worn on the) sleeve; **~ая повя́зка** armband

нару́чник, а *m.* (*usu. in pl.*) handcuff, manacle

нару́чн|ый *adj.* worn on the arm; **~ые часы́** wristwatch

наруша́|ть, ю, ет *impf. of* ▶ **нару́шить**

наруша́|ться, ется *impf. of* ▶ **нару́шиться**

☞ **наруше́ние, я** *nt.* **1** (*закона, дисциплины*) breach; violation; (*обещания*) breaking **2** (*покоя*) disturbance

наруши́тел|ь, я *m.* (*правила, закона*) transgressor, infringer

наруши́тель|ница, ницы *f. of* ▶ **наруши́тель**

нару́ш|ить, у, ишь *pf.* (*of* ▶ **наруша́ть**) **1** (*сон, покой*) to break, disturb **2** (*закон, обещание*) to break; **н. грани́цу** to cross a border illegally

нару́ш|иться, ится *pf.* (*of* ▶ **наруша́ться**) (*сон, покой, связь*) to be broken

нарци́сс, а *m.* narcissus; (*жёлтый*) daffodil

на́р|ы, ~ (*no sg.*) plank bed; bunk

нары́в, а *m.* abscess; boil

наря́д, а *m.* (*одежда*) attire, apparel, costume

наря|ди́ть, жу́, ~дишь *pf.* (*of* ▶ **наряжа́ть**) **1** (в + *a.*) to dress (in), array (in); **н. ёлку** to decorate a Christmas tree **2** (+ *i.*) to dress up (as)

наря|ди́ться, жу́сь, ~дишься *pf.* (*of* ▶ **наряжа́ться**) **1** (в + *a.*) to array oneself (in) **2** (+ *i.*) to dress up (as)

наря́д|ный, ~ен, ~на *adj.* (*человек*) well dressed; elegant; (*одежда*) smart; (*комната*) well decorated

наряду́ *adv.* (с + *i.*) side by side (with), equally (with); together (with); **н. с э́тим** at the same time

наряжа́|ть, ю *impf. of* ▶ **наряди́ть**

наряжа́|ться, юсь *impf. of* ▶ **наряди́ться**

нас *a., g., and p. of* ▶ **мы**

наса|ди́ть¹, жу́, ~дишь *pf.* (*of* ▶ **наса́живать**) (*надеть*) to put; to stick, pin; **н. червяка́ на крючо́к** to fix a worm on to a hook

наса|ди́ть², жу́, ~дишь *pf.* (*of* ▶ **насажда́ть**) (fig.) to inculcate; to propagate

насажда́|ть, ю *impf. of* ▶ **насади́ть²**

насажде́ни|е, я *nt.* **1** (*действие*) planting; (fig.) propagation, dissemination **2** (*деревья*) plantation

наса́жива|ть, ю *impf. of* ▶ **насади́ть¹**

наса́лива|ть, ю *impf. of* ▶ **насоли́ть**

насви́стыва|ть, ю *impf.* to whistle (*a tune*)

наседа́|ть, ю *impf.* (*of* ▶ **насе́сть**) (на + *a.*) to press

насе́дк|а, и *f.* sitting hen

насеко́м|ое, ого *nt.* insect

☞ **населе́ни|е, я** *nt.* population; (*города, деревни*) inhabitants

населённый *p.p.p. of* ▶ **насели́ть** *and adj.* (*район*) densely populated; **н. пункт** (official designation) locality, place

насел|и́ть, ю́, и́шь *pf.* (*of* ▶ **населя́ть**) to people, settle

населя́|ть, ю *impf. of* ▶ **насели́ть**

нас|е́сть, я́ду, я́дешь, *past* **~е́л** *pf. of* ▶ **наседа́ть**

наси́ли|е, я *nt.* (*физическое*) violence; (*принуждение*) force

наси́л|овать, ую *impf.* **1** (*принуждать*) to coerce, constrain **2** (*pf.* **из~**) (*принуждать к половому акту*) to rape

наси́льник, а *m.* **1** tyrant; aggressor **2** (*сексуальный*) rapist

наси́льно *adv.* by force, forcibly

наси́льственн|ый *adj.* (*меры*) violent; (*выселение*) forcible; **~ая смерть** murder

наска́кива|ть, ю *impf. of* ▶ **наскочи́ть**

наскво́зь *adv.* (*полностью*) through (and through); throughout; **промо́кнуть н.** to get wet through; (*пробить, прострелить*) through

☞ **наско́лько** *adv.* **1** (interrog.) how?; **н. э́то серьёзно?** how serious is it?; (in clauses) **я не зна́ю, н. э́то сро́чно** I don't know how urgent it is **2** (rel.) (*помню, знаю*) as far as; **н. мне изве́стно** as far as I know **3** (*в такой степени*) so; **н. э́то трудне́е!** it is so much more difficult!

наскоч|и́ть, у́, ~ишь *pf.* (*of* ▶ **наска́кивать**) (на + *a.*) **1** (*столкнуться*) to run (against), collide (with) **2** (fig., infml, *с упрёками*) to fly (at)

наску́ч|ить, у, ишь *pf.* (+ *d.*) to bore; **мне э́то ~ило** I am sick of it

насла|ди́ться, жу́сь, ди́шься *pf.* (*of* ▶ **наслажда́ться**) (+ *i.*) to enjoy; to take pleasure (in), delight (in)

наслажда́|ться, юсь *impf. of* ▶ **наслади́ться**

Н

наслажде́ни|е, я *nt.* enjoyment, delight

насле́ди|е, я *nt.* legacy; (*культурное*) heritage

насле́дник, а *m.* heir; (fig.) successor, inheritor

насле́дниц|а, ы *f.* heiress

насле́д|овать, ую *impf. and pf.* **1** (*pf. also* **у~**) to inherit **2** (+ *d.*) to succeed (to)

насле́дственность|ь, и *f.* heredity

насле́дств|о, а *nt.* **1** inheritance, legacy; **получи́ть в н., по ~у** to inherit **2** (fig.) heritage

наслу́ша|ться, юсь *pf.* (+ *g.*) **1** (*услышать много*) to hear (a lot of) **2** (*вдоволь послушать*) to hear enough, listen to long enough

на́смерть *adv.* to death; **испуга́ть н.** (fig.) to frighten to death

насмеха́|ться, юсь *impf.* (**над** + *i.*) to mock, ridicule

насме́ш|ить, у́, и́шь *pf. of* ▸ **смеши́ть**

насме́шк|а, и *f.* jibe, taunt; (*in pl.*) mockery; **сказа́ть что-н. в ~у** to say sth to hurt sb

насме́шлив|ый, ~, ~а *adj.* mocking

на́сморк, а *m.* cold (*in the head*); **схвати́ть, получи́ть н.** to catch a cold

насмотр|е́ться, ю́сь, ~ишься *pf.* **1** (+ *g.*) (*увидеть много*) to see a lot (of) **2** (**на** + *a.*) to have looked enough (at), to see enough (of); **не н.** to not tire of looking (at)

насол|и́ть, ю́, ~и́шь *pf.* (*of* ▸ **наса́ливать**) **1** (*usu.* ~и́шь) (+ *a. or g.*) (*огурцов, грибов*) to salt, pickle (*a quantity of*) **2** (*usu.* ~и́шь) (fig.) (+ *d.*) (*сделать неприятность*) to spite; to do a bad turn (to)

насор|и́ть, ю́, и́шь *pf. of* ▸ **сори́ть**

насо́с, а *m.* pump

на́спех *adv.* hastily; carelessly

насра́|ть, у́, ёшь *pf. of* ▸ **срать**

наста|ва́ть, ёт, ю́т *impf. of* ▸ **наста́ть**

наста́в|ить¹, лю, ишь *pf.* (*of* ▸ **наставля́ть**) **1** (*платье*) to lengthen; (*кусок ткани*) to put on, add on **2** (**на** + *a.*) (*нацелить*) to aim (at), point (at); **н. револьве́р на кого́-н.** to point a revolver at sb

наста́в|ить², лю, ишь *pf.* (*of* ▸ **наставля́ть**) (*научить*) to edify; to exhort, admonish; **н. на путь и́стинный** to set on the right path

наста́в|ить³, лю, ишь *pf.* (+ *a. or g.*) (*стульев*) to set up, place (*a quantity of*); (*синяков*) to cause

наставля́|ть, ю *impf. of* ▸ **наста́вить¹**, ▸ **наста́вить²**

наста́вник, а *m.* (*воспитатель*) mentor; (*преподаватель*) teacher, instructor

настаёт *see* ▸ **наставать**

наста́ива|ть, ю *impf. of* ▸ **настоя́ть**

наста́ива|ться, ется *impf. of* ▸ **настоя́ться**

наста́|ть, нет, нут *pf.* (*of* ▸ **настава́ть**) (*наступить*) to come, begin

на́стежь *adv.* wide open; **откры́ть н.** to open wide

насте́нный *adj.* wall (*attr.*)

настига́|ть, аю *impf. of* ▸ **насти́гнуть**, ▸ **насти́чь**

насти́гн|уть, у, ешь *pf.* = **насти́чь**

насти́л, а *m.* flooring; planking

насти́|чь, гну, гнешь, *past.* ~г, ~гла *pf.* (*of* ▸ **настига́ть**) to overtake (also fig.)

насто́йк|а, и *f.* **1** (*спиртной напиток*) liqueur **2** (med.) tincture

насто́йчив|ый, ~, ~а *adj.* **1** (*человек*) persistent **2** (*просьба, тон*) urgent, insistent

насто́лько *adv.* so; so much; **н., наско́лько** as much as

насто́льн|ый *adj.* **1** table, desk; desktop; **~ая игра́** board game; **~ая изда́тельская систе́ма** desktop publishing system; **н. те́ннис** table tennis **2** (fig.) for constant reference, in constant use; **~ая кни́га** bible

настора́жива|ться, юсь *impf. of* ▸ **насторожи́ться**

насторож|и́ться, у́сь, и́шься *pf.* (*of* ▸ **настора́живаться**) to prick up one's ears

настоя́тел|ь, я *m.* (eccl.) **1** (*монастыря*) prior, superior **2** (*церкви*) senior priest

настоя́тельниц|а, ы *f.* (eccl.) prioress, mother superior

настоя́тельн|ый, ~ен, ~ьна *adj.* **1** (*требование*) persistent; insistent; **~ьная про́сьба** urgent request **2** (*необходимость*) urgent, pressing

насто|я́ть, ю́, и́шь *pf.* (*of* ▸ **наста́ивать**) (**на** + *p.*) to insist (on); **н. на своём** to insist on having it one's own way; **он ~я́л на том, что́бы пойти́ самому́** he insisted on going himself

насто|я́ться, и́тся, я́тся *pf.* (*of* ▸ **наста́иваться**) (*о чае, травах*) to infuse, draw, brew

настоя́щ|ий *adj.* **1** (*теперешний*) present; this; **в ~ее вре́мя** at present, now; (*as nt. n.* ~ее, ~его) the present (time); **жить ~им** to live in the present **2** (*подлинный*) real, genuine; **н. друг** real friend **3** (infml, *совершенный*) complete, utter, absolute; **он н. дура́к** he is an absolute fool

настрада́|ться, юсь *pf.* (infml) to suffer much

настра́ива|ть, ю *impf. of* ▸ **настро́ить**

настрое́ни|е, я *nt.* **1** (*душевное состояние*) mood, temper, humour (BrE), humor (AmE); **припо́днятое/пода́вленное н.** high/low spirits; **быть в плохо́м** *и т. п.* **~и** to be in a bad, *etc.*, mood; **не в ~и** in a bad mood **2** (+ *inf.*) mood (for); **у меня́ нет ~я танцева́ть** I don't feel like dancing

настро́|ить, ю, ишь *pf.* (*of* ▸ **настра́ивать**) **1** (mus.) (*пианино, рояль*) to tune; (*скрипку, флейту*) to tune up, tune **2** (*приёмник*) to tune **3** (*механизм*) to tune, adjust **4** (fig.) (**на** + *a.*) to dispose (to), incline (to); to incite; **н. кого́-н.** (**про́тив** + *g.*) to incite sb (against)

настро́йк|а, и *f.* (mus., radio) tuning

настро́йщик, а *m.* tuner

наступ|а́ть[1], **а́ю** *impf. of* ▸ наступи́ть[1], ▸ наступи́ть[2]

наступа́|ть[2], **ю** *impf.* (mil.) to advance, be on the offensive

наступа́ющий *pres. part. act. of* ▸ наступа́ть[1] *and adj.* coming; **с ~им днём рожде́ния!** have a great birthday!

наступ|и́ть[1], **лю́, ~ишь** *pf.* (*of* ▸ наступа́ть[1]) (**на** + *a.*) to tread (on)

наступ|и́ть[2], **~ит** *pf.* (*of* ▸ наступа́ть[1]) (*о времени, состоянии*) to come, begin; (*о молчании, тишине*) to ensue; to set in; **~ит вре́мя, когда́...** there will come a time, when ...

наступле́ни|е[1], **я** *nt.* (mil.) offensive; attack; **перейти́ в н.** to assume the offensive

наступле́ни|е[2], **я** *nt.* (*зимы*) coming, approach; onset

настуч|а́ть, у́, и́шь *pf. of* ▸ стуча́ть 3

насу́щ|ный, ~ен, ~на *adj.* vital, urgent; **хлеб н.** daily bread (also fig.)

насчёт *prep.* + *g.* about; as regards, concerning

насы́п|ать, лю, лешь *pf.* (*of* ▸ насыпа́ть) **1** (+ *a. or g.*) to pour (in, into); to fill (with); **н. муки́ в мешо́к** to pour flour into a bag **2** (+ *a. or g. and* **на** + *a.*) (*посыпать*) to spread (on) **3** (*холм*) to raise (*a heap or pile of sand, etc.*)

насыпа́|ть, а́ю *impf. of* ▸ насы́пать

на́сып|ь, и *f.* embankment

насы́|титься, щусь, тишься *pf.* (*of* ▸ насыща́ться) **1** (*наесться*) to be full; to be sated **2** (chem.) to become saturated

насыща́|ться, юсь *impf. of* ▸ насы́титься

насы́щен|ный *adj.* **1** (**~, ~а**) saturated **2** (**~, ~на**) (fig., *содержательный*) rich

ната́лкива|ть, ю, ет *impf. of* ▸ натолкну́ться

ната́плива|ть, ю *impf. of* ▸ натопи́ть

натвор|и́ть, ю́, и́шь *pf.* (+ *g.*) (infml, pej.) to do, get up to; **н. вся́ких глу́постей** to get up to every sort of stupid trick; **что ты ~и́л!** whatever have you done?

на|тере́ть, тру́, трёшь, *past* **~тёр, ~тёрла** *pf.* (*of* ▸ натира́ть) **1** (*намазать*) to rub (in, on) **2** (*пол*) to polish **3** (*повредить*) to rub sore; to chafe; **н. себе́ мозо́ль** to get a corn **4** (+ *a. or g.*) (*сыр(у)*) to grate (*a quantity of*)

на|тере́ться, тру́сь, трёшься, *past* **~тёрся, ~тёрлась** *pf.* (*of* ▸ натира́ться) (+ *i.*) to rub oneself (with)

натира́|ть, ю *impf. of* ▸ натере́ть

натира́|ться, юсь *impf. of* ▸ натере́ться

наткн|у́ться, у́сь, ёшься *pf.* (*of* ▸ натыка́ться) (**на** + *a.*) **1** to run (against), strike; to stumble (upon); **н. на гвоздь** to run against a nail **2** (fig.) to stumble (upon, across), come (across); **н. на интере́сную мысль** to stumble across an interesting idea

HА́ТО *nt. indecl.* NATO (*abbr. of North Atlantic Treaty Organization — Организа́ция Североатланти́ческого догово́ра*)

на́товский *adj. of* ▸ НА́ТО

натолкн|у́ться, у́сь, ёшься *pf.* (*of* ▸ ната́лкиваться) (**на** + *a.*) to run (against); (fig.) to run across

натоп|и́ть, лю́, ~ишь *pf.* (*of* ▸ ната́пливать) to heat well, heat up

наточ|и́ть, у́, ~ишь *pf. of* ▸ точи́ть 1

натрав|и́ть, лю́, ~ишь *pf.* (*of* ▸ натра́вливать) (**на** + *a.*) (*собаку*) to set (on); (fig.) to set (against)

натра́влива|ть, ю *impf. of* ▸ натрави́ть

на́три|й, я *m.* (chem.) sodium

на́трое *adv.* in three

нат|ру́, рёшь *see* ▸ натере́ть

нату́р|а, ы *f.* **1** (*характер*) nature **2** (*натурщик*) (artist's) model, sitter **3** (econ.) kind; **плати́ть ~ой** to pay in kind **4** (*естественная обстановка*) natural setting; **рисова́ть с ~ы** to paint from life

натурализа́ци|я, и *f.* naturalization

натурализ|ова́ть, у́ю *impf. and pf.* to naturalize

натурализ|ова́ться, у́юсь *impf. and pf.* to become naturalized

натурали́ст, а *m.* naturalist

натура́ль|ный, ~ен, ~ьна *adj.* **1** natural; **в ~ьную величину́** life-size **2** (*настоящий*) (*мех, кожа, кофе*) real; (*смех*) genuine **3** (econ.) in kind; **н. обме́н** barter

нату́рщик, а *m.* (artist's) model, sitter

нату́рщи|ца, цы *f. of* ▸ нату́рщик

натыка́|ться, юсь *impf. of* ▸ наткну́ться

натюрмо́рт, а *m.* (art) still life

натя́гива|ть, ю, ет *impf. of* ▸ натяну́ть

натя́гива|ться, ется *impf. of* ▸ натяну́ться

натя́жк|а, и *f.* strained interpretation; **с ~ой** (fig.) at a stretch

натя́н|утый *p.p.p. of* ▸ натяну́ть *and adj.* **1** tight **2** (fig.) strained; forced; **~утые отноше́ния** strained relations

натя|ну́ть, ну́, ~нешь *pf.* (*of* ▸ натя́гивать) **1** (*сделать тугим*) to stretch; to draw (tight); **н. лук** to draw a bow **2** (*надеть*) to pull on; **н. ша́пку на́ уши** to pull a cap over one's ears

натя|ну́ться, ~нется, ~нутся *pf.* (*of* ▸ натя́гиваться) to stretch

наугра́д *adv.* at random, by guesswork

науда́чу *adv.* at random, by guesswork

⚲ **нау́к|а, и** *f.* (*система знаний*) science; (*учение*) learning; scholarship; **есте́ственные ~и** science

наукоём|кий, ~ок, ~ка *adj.* high-technology, high-tech

нау́тро *adv.* next morning

науч|и́ть, у́, ~ишь *pf.* (*of* ▸ учи́ть 1) (+ *a. and d. or* + *inf.*) to teach; **н. кого́-н. ру́сскому языку́** to teach sb Russian; **н. кого́-н. води́ть маши́ну** to teach sb to drive (a car)

⚲ key word

научи́|ться, у́сь, ∼ишься *pf.* (*of* ▸ **учи́ться 1**) (*+ d. or inf.*) to learn

нау́чно-иссле́довательск|ий *adj.* scientific research; ∼ая рабо́та (scientific) research work

нау́чно-фантасти́ческий *adj.* science fiction

♂ **нау́ч|ный, ∼ен, ∼на** *adj.* scientific; **н. рабо́тник** researcher; ∼ная фанта́стика science fiction

нау́шник, а *m.* (*in pl.*) headphones

наха́л, а *m.* (*infml*) impudent fellow, cheeky fellow

наха́лк|а, и *f.* (*infml*) impudent woman, cheeky woman

наха́л|ьный, ∼ен, ∼ьна *adj.* impudent, cheeky

нахам|и́ть, лю́, и́шь *pf. of* ▸ **хами́ть**

нахват|а́ть, а́ю *pf.* (*of* ▸ **нахва́тывать**) (*infml*) (*+ a. or g.*) to pick up, get hold (of); (*fig.*, *зна́ний*) to pick up, come by

нахват|а́ться, а́юсь *pf.* (*of* ▸ **нахва́тываться**) (*infml, fig.*) (*+ g.*) (*слов, привы́чек, зна́ний*) to pick up

нахва́тыва|ть, ю *impf. of* ▸ **нахвата́ть**

нахва́тыва|ться, юсь *impf. of* ▸ **нахвата́ться**

нахле́бник, а *m.* parasite, hanger-on

нахлобу́чива|ть, ю *impf. of* ▸ **нахлобу́чить**

нахлобу́ч|ить, у, ишь *pf.* (*of* ▸ **нахлобу́чивать**) (*infml*) to pull down (over one's head *or* eyes)

нахму́р|ить, ю, ишь *pf. of* ▸ **хму́рить**

нахму́р|иться, юсь, ишься *pf. of* ▸ **хму́риться**

♂ **нахо|ди́ть, жу́, ∼дишь** *impf. of* ▸ **найти́¹**, ▸ **найти́²**

нахо|ди́ться¹, жу́сь, ∼дишься *impf. of* ▸ **найти́сь**

♂ **нахо|ди́ться², жу́сь, ∼дишься** *impf.* to be (situated); **где ∼дится ста́нция?** where is the station?; (*под наблюде́нием, стре́ссом*) to be

нахо́дк|а, и *f.* **1** find **2** (*fig.*) (*подходя́щее*) godsend; (*приём*) device

нахо́дчив|ый, ∼, ∼а *adj.* **1** (*челове́к*) resourceful **2** (*отве́т*) quick-witted

наце|ди́ть, жу́, ∼дишь *pf.* (*+ a. or g.*) to strain

наце́лива|ть, ю *impf. of* ▸ **наце́лить**

наце́лива|ться, юсь *impf. of* ▸ **наце́литься**

наце́л|ить, ю, ишь *pf.* **1** (*impf.* **це́лить** *and* ∼ивать) (*ору́жие*) to aim, level **2** (*impf.* ∼ивать) (*fig.*) (**на** *+ a.*) (*на выполне́ние*) to aim, direct

наце́л|иться, юсь, ишься *pf.* (*of* ▸ **наце́ливаться**) **1** (**в** *+ a.*) to aim (at), take aim (at) **2** (*fig.*) (**на** *+ a.*) to aim (at, for), strive (for) **3** (*fig.*) (*+ inf.*) to aim, strive (to do)

наце́нк|а, и *f.* markup

нацеп|и́ть, лю́, ∼ишь *pf.* (*of* ▸ **нацепля́ть**) **1** to fasten on; to attach (*by means of hook or pin*) **2** (*infml, наде́ть*) to put on

нацеп|ля́ть, ля́ю *impf. of* ▸ **нацепи́ть**

наци́зм, а *m.* Nazism

национализа́ци|я, и *f.* nationalization

национализи́р|овать, ую *impf. and pf.* to nationalize

национали́зм, а *m.* nationalism

национали́ст, а *m.* nationalist

националисти́ческий *adj.* nationalist(ic)

национали́ст|ка, ки *f. of* ▸ **национали́ст**

национа́льност|ь, и *f.* **1** (*принадле́жность к на́ции*) nationality **2** (*на́ция*) nation

♂ **национа́льн|ый** *adj.* national; ∼ое меньшинство́ national minority

наци́ст, а *m.* Nazi

наци́ст|ка, ки *f. of* ▸ **наци́ст**

наци́стский *adj.* Nazi

на́ци|я, и *f.* nation

♂ **нача́л|о, а** *nt.* **1** beginning; start; **в** ∼е **четвёртого** soon after three (o'clock); **по** ∼у at first; **положи́ть, дать н.** (*+ d.*) to begin, commence; (*тради́ции, па́ртии*) to establish **2** (*исто́чник*) origin, source; **брать н.** (**в** *+ p.*) to originate (from, in)

♂ **нача́льник, а** *m.* head, chief; superior; **н. отде́ла** head of a department, section

нача́льн|ый *adj.* **1** (*находя́щийся в нача́ле*) initial, first **2** (*первонача́льный*) primary, elementary; ∼ая шко́ла primary school (BrE), elementary school (AmE)

нача́льств|о, а *nt.* **1** (*collect.*) (the) authorities, management **2** (*infml, нача́льник*) chief, boss

♂ **нача́|ть, ну́, нёшь,** *past* ∼л, ∼ла́, ∼ло *pf.* (*of* ▸ **начина́ть**) **1** to begin, start, commence; **н. с нача́ла** to begin at the beginning; **н. всё снача́ла** to start all over again, start afresh **2** (*но́вую па́чку, тетра́дь*) to start

♂ **нача́|ться, нётся,** *past* ∼лся́, ∼ла́сь *pf.* (*of* ▸ **начина́ться**) to begin, start

начеку́ *adv.* on the alert, on one's guard

наче́р|ти́ть, чу́, ∼тишь *pf. of* ▸ **черти́ть**

начина́ни|е, я *nt.* undertaking, initiative

♂ **начина́|ть, ю, ет** *impf. of* ▸ **нача́ть**

♂ **начина́|ться, ется** *impf. of* ▸ **нача́ться**

начина́|ющий *pres. part. act. of* ▸ **начина́ть** *and adj.* (*писа́тель*) fledgling; (*as m. n.* **н.,** ∼ющего) beginner

начина́я *as prep.* **1** (**с** *+ g.*) (*о вре́мени*) as from, starting from; (*в том числе́*) starting with, including **2** (**от** *+ g.*) starting with, including

начи́нк|а, и *f.* (*cul.*) (*ку́рицы, у́тки*) stuffing; (*пиро́жка*) filling

начи́|стить, щу, стишь *pf.* (*of* ▸ **начища́ть**) (*сапоги́, кастрю́лю*) to polish, shine

на́чисто *adv.* **1** clean, fair; **переписа́ть н.** to make a fair copy (of) **2** (*infml, совсе́м*) completely, thoroughly

начи́тан|ный, ∼, ∼на *adj.* well read, widely read

начита́|ться, юсь *pf.* **1** (*+ g.*) (*прочита́ть мно́го*) to have read (*a lot of*) **2** (*почита́ть* *вдово́ль)* to have read one's fill

начища́|ть, ю *impf. of* ▶ **начи́стить**

начн|у́, нёшь *see* ▶ **нача́ть**

✐ **наш, ~его,** *f.* **~а, ~ей,** *nt.* **~е, ~его,** *pl.* **~и, ~их** *poss. pron. & adj.* (*при существительном*) our; (*без существительного*) ours; (*as pl. n.* **~и, ~их**) our people, people on our side; **его́ счита́ют одни́м из ~их** they regard him as one of us

наше́ствие, я *nt.* (also fig.) invasion, descent

наши́вк|а, и *f.* stripe, chevron

нашинк|ова́ть, у́ю *pf. of* ▶ **шинкова́ть**

нащу́п|ать, аю *pf.* (*of* ▶ **нащу́пывать**) to find, discover (*by groping*)

нащу́пыва|ть, ю *impf.* (*of* ▶ **нащу́пать**) to grope (for, after); to fumble (for, after); to feel about (for) (also fig.)

наяву́ *adv.* waking; in reality

НДС *m. indecl.* (*abbr. of* **нало́г на доба́вленную сто́имость**) VAT (*Value Added Tax*)

✐ **не¹** not; **я не зна́ю** I do not know; **я не могу́ не сказа́ть** I can't but say; I must say; **не без волне́ния** with some excitement; **не до** (+ *g.*) not time for; **мне не до шу́ток** I have no time for jokes; **не..., не** neither ... nor; **не то** otherwise, or else

✐ **не²** *separable component of prons.* ▶ **не́кого,** ▶ **не́чего; не́ о чем бы́ло говори́ть** there was nothing to talk about

не... *pref.* un-, in-, non-, mis-, dis-

неаккура́т|ный, ~ен, ~на *adj.*
1 (*небрежный*) careless; inaccurate
2 (*неопрятный*) untidy

неаппети́т|ный, ~ен, ~на *adj.* unappetizing (also fig.)

небезопа́с|ный, ~ен, ~на *adj.* unsafe, insecure

небезоснова́тел|ьный, ~ен, ~ьна *adj.* not unfounded

небезразли́ч|ный, ~ен, ~на *adj.* not indifferent

небезуспе́ш|ный, ~ен, ~на *adj.* not unsuccessful

небезызве́ст|ный, ~ен, ~на *adj.* not unknown; (iron.) notorious; **~но, что...** it is no secret that ...

небезынтере́с|ный, ~ен, ~на *adj.* not without interest

небеса́ *pl. of* ▶ **не́бо**

небе́сн|ый *adj.* heavenly, celestial; **~ые свети́ла** heavenly bodies; **Ца́рство Н~ое** the Kingdom of Heaven; **~ого цве́та** sky blue

неблагови́д|ный, ~ен, ~на *adj.* unseemly, improper

неблагода́рност|ь, и *f.* ingratitude

неблагода́р|ный, ~ен, ~на *adj.* **1** (*человек*) ungrateful **2** (*задача*) thankless

неблагозву́ч|ный, ~ен, ~на *adj.* disharmonious

неблагополу́ч|ный, ~ен, ~на *adj.* unfavourable (BrE), unfavorable (AmE), bad; unsuccessful

неблагоприя́т|ный, ~ен, ~на *adj.* unfavourable (BrE), unfavorable (AmE), inauspicious

неблагоскло́н|ный, ~ен, ~на *adj.* unfavourable (BrE), unfavorable (AmE); (к + *d.*) ill-disposed (towards)

✐ **не́б|о, а,** *pl.* **~еса́, ~е́с, ~еса́м** *nt.* sky; (relig.) heaven; **под откры́тым ~ом** in the open (air)

не́б|о, а *nt.* (anat.) palate

✐ **небольш|о́й** *adj.* small; not great; **о́чень ~о́е расстоя́ние** a very short distance; **ты́сяча с ~им** a thousand odd

небосво́д, а *m.* firmament; the vault of heaven

небоскло́н, а *m.* horizon (*strictly, sky immediately over the horizon*)

небоскрёб, а *m.* skyscraper

небре́жност|ь, и *f.* carelessness, negligence

небре́ж|ный, ~ен, ~на *adj.* (*человек, работа*) careless; (*одежда, почерк*) untidy; (*тон, манера*) offhand

небри́т|ый, ~, ~а *adj.* unshaven

небыва́л|ый, ~, ~а *adj.* unprecedented

небыли́ц|а, ы *f.* (*сказка*) fable; (*выдумка*) cock-and-bull story

небыти́е́, я́ *nt.* non-existence

небью́щийся *adj.* unbreakable

Нев|а́, ы́ *f.* the Neva (*river*)

нева́жно *adv.* not too well, indifferently; **дела́ иду́т н.** things are not going too well

нева́ж|ный, ~ен, ~на́, ~но *adj.*
1 (*незначительный*) unimportant **2** (infml, *посредственный*) poor, indifferent

невдалеке́ *adv.* not far away, not far off

неве́дени|е, я *nt.* ignorance; **пребыва́ть в блаже́нном ~и** (iron.) to be in a state of blissful ignorance

неве́домо *adv.* (infml) **+ что, как, когда́, куда́** *и т. п.* God knows, no one knows; **он так и появи́лся, н. отку́да** he just turned up, God knows where from

неве́дом|ый, ~, ~а *adj.* **1** unknown **2** (fig., *таинственный*) mysterious

неве́ж|а, и *c.g.* boor, lout

неве́жд|а, ы *c.g.* ignoramus

неве́жествен|ный, ~, ~на *adj.* ignorant

неве́жеств|о, а *nt.* ignorance

неве́жлив|ый, ~, ~а *adj.* rude, impolite

невезе́ни|е, я *nt.* (infml) bad luck

неве́ри|е, я *nt.* unbelief; lack of faith

неве́рност|ь, и *f.* **1** (*неправильность*) incorrectness **2** (*друга*) disloyalty; (*супруга*) infidelity, unfaithfulness

неве́р|ный, ~ен, ~на́, ~но *adj.*
1 (*ошибочный*) incorrect; **~ная но́та** false note **2** (*друг*) faithless, disloyal; (*муж, жена*) unfaithful

невероя́тно *adv.* incredibly, unbelievably

невероя́т|ный, ~ен, ~на *adj.*
1 (*неправдоподобный*) improbable,
unlikely **2** (*чрезвычайный*) incredible,
unbelievable (also *fig.*); (*impers., as pred.*)
~но it is incredible, it is unbelievable; it is
beyond belief
неве́рующ|ий *adj.* (*relig.*) unbelieving; (*as n.*
н., ~его, *f.* ~ая, ~ей) unbeliever
невес|ёлый, ~ёл, ~ела́, ~ело *adj.* sad,
gloomy, melancholy
невесо́мост|ь, и *f.* weightlessness
невест|а, ы *f.* fiancée; (*в день свадьбы*) bride
неве́стк|а, и *f.* **1** (*жена сына*) daughter-in-
law **2** (*жена брата*) sister-in-law
невзира́я *prep.* (на + *a.*) in spite of,
regardless of
невзра́ч|ный, ~ен, ~на *adj.*
unprepossessing, unattractive; plain
неви́дан|ный, ~, ~на *adj.* unprecedented
неви́дим|ый, ~, ~а *adj.* invisible
неви́нност|ь, и *f.* innocence; (*девственность*)
virginity
неви́н|ный, ~ен, ~на *adj.* innocent;
(*девственный*) virgin(al); ~ная же́ртва
innocent victim
невино́в|ный, ~ен, ~на *adj.* (в + *p.*)
innocent (of); (*law*) not guilty; призна́ть
~ным to acquit
невку́с|ный, ~ен, ~на́, ~но *adj.*
unpalatable
невменя́ем|ый, ~, ~а *adj.* **1** (law)
irresponsible **2** (*infml*) beside oneself
невмеша́тельств|о, а *m.* (pol.) non-
intervention, non-interference
невнима́ни|е, я *nt.* **1** (*рассеянность*)
inattention; carelessness **2** (к + *d.*)
(*пренебрежение*) lack of consideration (for)
невнима́тельност|ь, и *f.* inattention;
(*небрежность*) thoughtlessness
невнима́тел|ьный, ~ен, ~ьна *adj.*
(*рассеянный*) inattentive; (*незаботливый*)
thoughtless
невня́т|ный, ~ен, ~на *adj.* indistinct,
incomprehensible
не́вод, а, *pl.* ~а́, ~о́в *m.* seine, sweep net
невозмо́ж|ный, ~ен, ~на *adj.* impossible;
(*impers., pred.*) ~но it is impossible; (*as nt.*
n. ~ное, ~ного) the impossible
невозмути́м|ый, ~, ~а *adj.* **1** (*человек*)
imperturbable **2** (*тон*) calm, unruffled
невозобновля́емый *adj.* non-renewable
нево́льно *adv.* involuntarily;
unintentionally, unwittingly
нево́льный *adj.* **1** (*вздох, трепет*)
involuntary; (*ложь, обида*) unintentional
2 (*вынужденный*) forced
нево́л|я, и *f.* bondage; captivity
невообрази́м|ый, ~, ~а *adj.* unimaginable,
inconceivable; **н. шум** (*fig.*) unimaginable din
невооружён|ный *adj.* unarmed; ~ым
гла́зом with the naked eye
невоспи́тан|ный, ~, ~на *adj.* ill-bred;
bad-mannered

невосполни́м|ый, ~, ~а *adj.* irreplaceable
невоспри́имчив|ый, ~, ~а *adj.* **1** (к
зна́ниям) unreceptive **2** (med.) (к + *d.*)
immune (to)
невразуми́тел|ьный, ~ен, ~ьна *adj.*
unintelligible, incomprehensible
невралги́|я, и *f.* neuralgia
неврасте́ник, а *m.* neurasthenic
неврастени́|я, и *f.* neurasthenia
невреди́м|ый, ~, ~а *adj.* unharmed, intact;
цел и ~ safe and sound
невро́з, а *m.* neurosis
невропато́лог, а *m.* neuropathologist
невы́год|ный, ~ен, ~на *adj.* **1** (*положение*)
disadvantageous, unfavourable (BrE),
unfavorable (AmE); показа́ть себя́ с ~ной
стороны́ to show oneself at a disadvantage
2 (*сделка*) unprofitable, unremunerative;
(*impers., pred.*) ~но it does not pay
невыноси́м|ый, ~, ~а *adj.* unbearable,
insufferable, intolerable
невыполни́м|ый, ~, ~а *adj.* impracticable;
unrealizable
невырази́м|ый, ~, ~а *adj.* inexpressible,
beyond expression
невырази́тел|ьный, ~ен, ~ьна *adj.*
inexpressive, expressionless
невысо́к|ий, ~, ~а́, ~о and ~о́, ~и and
~и́ *adj.* (*забор, потолок, голос*) rather low;
(*человек*) rather short; ~ого ка́чества of
poor quality; быть ~ого мне́ния (о + *p.*) to
have a low opinion (of)
негати́в, а *m.* (phot.) negative
негати́в|ный, ~ен, ~на *adj.* negative
не́где *adv.* (+ *inf.*) there is nowhere; **н. доста́ть**
э́ту кни́гу this book is nowhere to be had
негла́с|ный, ~ен, ~на *adj.* secret
неглу́п|ый, ~, ~а́, ~о *adj.* quite intelligent;
он о́чень ~ he is no fool
него́ *a.* and *g.* of ▶ **он** *after preps.*
него́д|ный, ~ен, ~на *adj.* unfit, unsuitable
негодова́ни|е, я *nt.* indignation
негодо|ва́ть, у́ю *impf.* (на + *a.* or про́тив + *g.*)
to be indignant (with)
негра́мотност|ь, и *f.* illiteracy (also *fig.*)
негра́мот|ный, ~ен, ~на *adj.* illiterate
(also *fig.*); (*as n.* ~ного, *f.* ~ная, ~ной)
illiterate (*person*)
негро́мк|ий, ~ок, ~ка́, ~ко *adj.* quiet, low
негума́н|ный, ~ен, ~на *adj.* inhumane
неда́вний *adj.* recent
неда́вно *adv.* recently
недал|ёкий *adj.* **1** (~ёк, ~ека́, ~ёко and
~еко́) (*место*) nearby, not far off, near;
(*путешествие, прогулка, расстояние*) short
2 (~ёк, ~ёка) (fig., *глуповатый*) not bright,
dull-witted
недалеко́ *adv.* not far, near
недальнови́д|ный, ~ен, ~на *adj.* short-
sighted (fig.)
неда́ром *adv.* not for nothing; for good
reason

✓ **недви́жимост|ь, и** *f.* (law) (immovable) property, real estate

недви́жим|ый *adj.*: ∼ое иму́щество = недви́жимость

недееспосо́бност|ь, и *f.* (law) incapacity

недееспосо́б|ный, ∼ен, ∼на *adj.* (law, *человек*) incapacitated

недействи́тел|ьный, ∼ен, ∼ьна *adj.* (law) invalid

недели́м|ый, ∼, ∼а *adj.* indivisible

неде́льный *adj.* of a week's duration

✓ **неде́л|я, и** *f.* week; на э́той ∼е this week

недоброжела́тел|ь, я *m.* ill-wisher

недоброжела́тел|ьный, ∼ен, ∼ьна *adj.* malevolent, ill-disposed

недобросо́вест|ный, ∼ен, ∼на *adj.* **1** (*нечестный*) unscrupulous **2** (*небрежный*) lacking in conscientiousness; careless

недо́бр|ый *adj.* **1** (*человек, взгляд*) unkind; unfriendly **2** (*намерение, чувство*) evil; ∼ая весть bad news

недове́ри|е, я *nt.* distrust; mistrust; во́тум ∼я vote of no confidence

недове́рчив|ый, ∼, ∼а *adj.* distrustful; mistrustful

недово́л|ьный, ∼ен, ∼ьна *adj.* (+ *i.*) dissatisfied, discontented, displeased (with); (*as n.* н., ∼ьного, *f.* ∼ьная, ∼ьной) malcontent

недово́льств|о, а *nt.* dissatisfaction, discontent, displeasure

недога́длив|ый, ∼, ∼а *adj.* slow(-witted)

недогля|де́ть, жу́, ди́шь *pf.* to overlook, miss

недода|ва́ть, ю́, ёшь *impf. of* ▶ недода́ть

недо|да́ть, да́м, да́шь, да́ст, дади́м, дади́те, даду́т, *past* ∼да́л, ∼дала́, ∼да́ло *pf.* (*of* ▶ недодава́ть) to give short; to deliver short; он мне ∼да́л пятьдеся́т рубле́й he gave me fifty roubles short

недоеда́|ть, ю *impf.* to be undernourished, be underfed

недозво́лен|ный, ∼, ∼а *adj.* illicit, unlawful

недозре́лый *adj.* (*яблоко*) unripe; (fig., *человек*) immature

недо́л|гий, ∼ог, ∼га́, ∼го *adj.* short, brief

недо́лго *adv.* **1** not long; н. ду́мая without hesitation **2** (infml, *легко*): н. и (+ *inf.*) one can easily; it is easy (to)

недолгове́ч|ный, ∼ен, ∼на *adj.* short-lived, ephemeral

недолю́блива|ть, ю *impf.* (+ *a.* or *g.*) (infml) to be not overfond of; они́ ∼ли друг дру́га there was no love lost between them

недомога́ни|е, я *nt.* indisposition

недоно́шен|ный, ∼, ∼а *adj.* (med.) premature

недооце́нива|ть, ю *impf. of* ▶ недооцени́ть

недооцен|и́ть, ю́, ∼ишь *pf.* (*of* ▶ недооце́нивать) to underestimate,

underrate

недополуч|а́ть, а́ю *impf. of* ▶ недополучи́ть

недополуч|и́ть, у́, ∼ишь *pf.* (*of* ▶ недополуча́ть) to receive less (than one's due)

недопусти́м|ый, ∼, ∼а *adj.* inadmissible, intolerable

недора́звит|ый, ∼, ∼а *adj.* underdeveloped, backward

недоразуме́ни|е, я *nt.* misunderstanding

недо́рого *adv.* not dear, cheaply

недор|ого́й, ∼ог, ∼ога́, ∼ого *adj.* inexpensive; reasonable (*of price*)

недоса́лива|ть, ю *impf. of* ▶ недосоли́ть

недосмотр|е́ть, ю́, ∼ишь *pf.* **1** (+ *g.*) to overlook, miss **2** (за + *i.*) not to look after properly

недосол|и́ть, ю́, ∼ишь *pf.* (*of* ▶ недоса́ливать) to put too little salt in

недос|па́ть, плю́, пи́шь *pf.* (*of* ▶ недосыпа́ть) to not get enough sleep

недоста|ва́ть, ёт *impf.* (*of* ▶ недоста́ть) (*impers.* + *g.*) to be missing, be lacking, be wanting; ему́ ∼ёт о́пыта he lacks experience

✓ **недоста́т|ок, ка** *m.* **1** (+ *g.* or в + *p.*) shortage (of), lack (of); име́ть н. в рабо́чей си́ле to be short-handed **2** (*несовершенство*) shortcoming, imperfection; defect; н. зре́ния defective eyesight

недоста́точно *adv.* **1** insufficiently **2** (*pred.* + *g.*) (*не хватает*) not enough

недоста́точ|ный, ∼ен, ∼на *adj.* insufficient; inadequate

недоста́|ть, нет *pf. of* ▶ недостава́ть

недостижи́м|ый, ∼, ∼а *adj.* unattainable

недостове́р|ный, ∼ен, ∼на *adj.* unreliable, apocryphal

недосто́|йный, ∼ин, ∼йна *adj.* unworthy

недосту́п|ный, ∼ен, ∼на *adj.* inaccessible (also fig.); э́то по моему́ понима́нию it is beyond my comprehension

недосчит|а́ться, а́юсь *pf.* (*of* ▶ недосчи́тываться) (+ *g.*) to find missing, miss; to be out (in one's accounts); он ∼а́лся десяти́ рубле́й he found he was ten roubles short

недосчи́тыва|ться, юсь *impf. of* ▶ недосчита́ться

недосыпа́|ть, ю *impf. of* ▶ недоспа́ть

недосяга́ем|ый, ∼, ∼а *adj.* unattainable

недоумева́|ть, ю *impf.* to be perplexed, be at a loss

недоуме́ни|е, я *nt.* perplexity, bewilderment; быть в ∼и to be in a quandary

недочёт, а *m.* (*usu. in pl.*) defect, shortcoming

не́др|а (*no sg.*) **1** depths (*of the earth*); н. земли́ bowels of the earth; разве́дка ∼ prospecting of mineral wealth **2** (fig.) depths, heart

не́друг, а *m.* enemy, foe

недружелю́б|ный, ∼ен, ∼на *adj.* unfriendly

неду́г, а *m.* ailment, disease

✓ key word

неё *a. and g. of* ▸ **она** *after preps.*

неесте́ственный, ~, ~на *adj.* unnatural

нежда́нный *adj.* unexpected

нежела́тельный, ~ен, ~ьна *adj.* undesirable

нежена́тый, ~ *adj.* unmarried (*of a man*)

неживо́й *adj.* **1** (*мёртвый*) lifeless, dead **2** (*неорганический*) inanimate, inorganic **3** (fig., *вялый*) dull, lifeless

нежило́й *adj.* **1** (*необитаемый*) uninhabited **2** (*негодный для жилья*) not fit for habitation; uninhabitable

не́житься, усь, ишься *impf.* to luxuriate; **н. на со́лнце** to bask in the sun

не́жность, и *f.* **1** (*ласковость*) tenderness **2** (*тонкость*) delicacy

не́жный, ~ен, ~на́, ~но *adj.* **1** tender; affectionate; **~ный во́зраст** tender age **2** (*тонкий*) delicate (= *soft, fine; of colours, taste, skin, etc.*) **3** (*хрупкий*) delicate

незабу́дка, и *f.* (bot.) forget-me-not

незабыва́емый, ~, ~а *adj.* unforgettable

незави́симо *adv.* independently; **н. от** irrespective of

незави́симость, и *f.* independence

незави́симый, ~, ~а *adj.* independent

незадо́лго *adv.* (*до + g. or* **пе́ред** + *i.*) shortly (before), not long (before)

незако́нный, ~ен, ~на *adj.* illegal, unlawful

незако́нченный, ~, ~на *adj.* incomplete, unfinished

незамедли́тельно *adv.* without delay

незамени́мый, ~, ~а *adj.* **1** irreplaceable **2** (*очень нужный*) indispensable

незаме́тно *adv.* imperceptibly; **н., чтобы ...** you cannot tell that ...

незаме́тный, ~ен, ~на *adj.* **1** (*следы*) imperceptible **2** (*человек*) unremarkable

незаму́жняя *adj.* unmarried, single

незаслу́женный, ~, ~на *adj.* undeserved, unmerited

незауря́дный, ~ен, ~на *adj.* outstanding, exceptional

не́зачем *adv.* (+ *inf.*) there is no point (in), it is pointless; there is no need (to)

незде́шний *adj.* (infml) not of these parts; **я н.** I am a stranger here

нездоро́виться, ~ся *impf.* (*impers. + d.*) to feel unwell

нездоро́вый, ~, ~а *adj.* **1** unhealthy (also fig.) **2** (*as pred.*) unwell, poorly

незе́мной *adj.* unearthly

незнако́мец, ца *m.* stranger

незнако́мка, ки *f. of* ▸ **незнако́мец**

незнако́мый, ~, ~а *adj.* **1** unknown, unfamiliar **2** (*с + i.*) unacquainted (with)

незна́ние, я *nt.* ignorance

незначи́тельный, ~ен, ~ьна *adj.* insignificant, negligible, trivial

незре́лость, и *f.* unripeness, (fig.) immaturity

незре́лый, ~, ~а *adj.* unripe (also fig.); (fig.) immature

незри́мый, ~, ~а *adj.* invisible

незы́блемый, ~, ~а *adj.* unshakeable, stable

неизбе́жный, ~ен, ~на *adj.* inevitable, unavoidable; inescapable

неизве́стность, и *f.* **1** (*отсутствие сведений*) uncertainty; **быть в ~и** (*о + p.*) to be uncertain (about), be in the dark (about) **2** (*незаметное существование*) obscurity; **жить в ~и** to live in obscurity

неизве́стный, ~ен, ~на *adj.* unknown; **~но где, когда́** *и т. n.* no one knows where, when, *etc.* (= *somewhere, at some time, etc.*); (*as n. н.,* **~ного,** *f.* **~ная, ~ной**) unknown person; (*as nt. н.* **~ное, ~ного**) (math.) unknown (quantity)

неизлечи́мый, ~, ~а *adj.* incurable

неизме́нный, ~ен, ~на *adj.* (*постоянный*) invariable, immutable

неиме́ние, я *nt.* lack, want; **за ~ем лу́чшего** for want of sth better

неимове́рный, ~ен, ~на *adj.* incredible, unbelievable

неиму́щий *adj.* indigent, poor

неинтере́сный, ~ен, ~на *adj.* uninteresting

нейскре́нний, ~ен, ~на *adj.* insincere

неисправи́мый, ~, ~а *adj.* **1** (*человек*) incorrigible **2** (*недостаток, ошибка*) irremediable, irreparable

неиспра́вность, и *f.* (*машины*) disrepair; fault, defect

неиспра́вный, ~ен, ~на *adj.* (*машина*) out of order; faulty, defective

неиссяка́емый, ~, ~а *adj.* inexhaustible

нейстовый, ~, ~а *adj.* furious, frenzied

неистощи́мый, ~, ~а *adj.* inexhaustible

неистреби́мый, ~, ~а *adj.* ineradicable; undying

неисчерпа́емый, ~, ~а *adj.* inexhaustible

неисчисли́мый, ~, ~а *adj.* innumerable; incalculable

ней *d., i., and p. of* ▸ **она** *after preps.*

нейло́н, а *m.* nylon

нейло́новый *adj.* nylon, made of nylon

нейрохиру́рг, а *m.* neurosurgeon

нейтрализа́ция, и *f.* neutralization

нейтрализова́ть, у́ю *impf. and pf.* to neutralize

нейтралите́т, а *m.* (pol.) neutrality

нейтра́льный, ~ен, ~ьна *adj.* neutral

нейтро́н, а *m.* (phys.) neutron

нека́чественный, ~, ~а *adj.* poor-quality

неквалифици́рованный, ~, ~на *adj.* unqualified; **н. рабо́чий** unskilled labourer (BrE), laborer (AmE)

⚜ **не́кий** *pron.* a certain; a kind of; **вас спра́шивал н. господи́н Па́влов** a (certain) Mr Pavlov was asking for you

не́когда[1] *adv.* once, formerly; in the old days

H

не́когда² *adv.* there is no time; **мне сего́дня н. разгова́ривать** I have no time to chat today

не́кого, не́кому, не́кем, не́ о ком *pron.* (+ *inf.*) there is nobody (to); **н. вини́ть** nobody is to blame; **ей не́ с кем пойти́** she has nobody to go with (her)

некомпете́нт|ный, ~ен, ~на *adj.* incompetent, unqualified

неконкурентоспосо́б|ный, ~ен, ~на *adj.* uncompetitive

неконституцио́н|ный, ~ен, ~на *adj.* unconstitutional

некорре́кт|ный, ~ен, ~на *adj.* discourteous, impolite

♂ **не́котор|ый** *pron.* some; **мы с ~ых пор живём здесь** we have been living here for some time; **~ым о́бразом** somehow, in some way; **в, до ~ой сте́пени** to some extent, to a certain extent; (*as pl. n.* **~ые, ~ых**) (infml) some; some people

некраси́в|ый, ~, ~а *adj.* **1** ugly, unattractive **2** (infml, *поведение*) unseemly, not nice

некредитоспосо́б|ный, ~ен, ~на *adj.* insolvent

некроло́г, а *m.* obituary (notice)

некста́ти *adv.* (*прийти, сказать*) at the wrong moment, inopportunely; (*о замечании*) inopportune, inappropriate

некта́р, а *m.* nectar

не́кто *pron.* someone; **н. Петро́в** one Petrov, a certain Petrov

не́куда *adv.* (+ *inf.*) there is nowhere (to); **мне н. пойти́** I have nowhere to go

некульту́р|ный, ~ен, ~на *adj.* **1** (*нецивилизованный*) uncivilized; backward **2** (*грубый*) rough(-mannered), boorish

некуря́щ|ий *adj.* non-smoking; (*as m. n.* **н., ~его**) non-smoker; **ваго́н для ~их** non-smoking carriage

нелега́л, а *m.* (infml) illegal person (*person living somewhere illegally or doing sth illegally*)

нелега́л|ьный, ~ен, ~ьна *adj.* illegal

нелёг|кий, ~ок, нелегка́ *adj.* **1** (*трудный*) difficult, not easy **2** (*тяжёлый*) heavy, not light (also fig.)

неле́п|ый, ~, ~а *adj.* absurd, ridiculous

нело́в|кий, ~ок, ~ка́, ~ко *adj.* **1** (*неуклюжий*) awkward; clumsy **2** (fig.) awkward; embarrassing; **~кое молча́ние** awkward silence

нело́вко *adv.* awkwardly; uncomfortably; **чу́вствовать себя́ н.** to feel ill at ease, feel awkward, feel uncomfortable

нело́вкост|ь, и *f.* **1** (*свойство*) awkwardness, clumsiness (also fig.) **2** (*поступок*) blunder, gaffe

нелоги́ч|ный, ~ен, ~на *adj.* illogical

♂ **нельзя́** *adv.* (+ *inf.*) **1** (*нет возможности*)

it is impossible; **н. не призна́ть** it is impossible not to admit, one cannot but admit **2** (*запреща́ется*) it is not allowed; **здесь н. кури́ть** smoking is not allowed here **3** (*нехорошо*) one ought not, one should not; **н. ложи́ться (спать) так по́здно** you ought not to go to bed so late

нём *p. of* ▸ **он** *after preps.*

нема́ло *adv.* **1** (*времени, денег*) not a little; a good deal of; (*людей*) quite a few **2** (*читать, гордиться*) a good deal, quite a lot

немалова́ж|ный, ~ен, ~на *adj.* of no small importance

нема́л|ый, ~, ~а́ *adj.* considerable

неме́дленно *adv.* immediately

неме́|ть, ю *impf.* (*of* ▸ **онеме́ть**) **1** (*становиться немым*) to become dumb, grow dumb **2** (*цепенеть*) to become numb, grow numb

не́м|ец, ца *m.* German

♂ **неме́цк|ий** *adj.* German; **~ая овча́рка** Alsatian (dog) (BrE), German shepherd

неминуе́м|ый, ~, ~а *adj.* inevitable, unavoidable

не́м|ка, ки *f. of* ▸ **не́мец**

немно́г|ие *adj.* few, a few; (*as pl. n.* **н., ~их**) few

♂ **немно́го** *adv.* **1** (+ *g.*) (*времени, денег*) a little, some, not much; (*людей*) a few, not many **2** (*слегка*) a little, somewhat, slightly; **я н. уста́л** I am a little tired

немно́г|ое, ого *nt.* few things, little

немно́жко *adv.* (infml) a little; a bit

нем|о́й, ~, ~а́, ~о *adj.* **1** mute (often offens.), profoundly deaf; (*as m. n.* **н., ~о́го**) mute (often offens.), profoundly deaf person **2** (fig.) silent; **н. фильм** silent film

не|молодо́й, ~мо́лод, ~молода́, ~мо́лодо *adj.* not young, elderly

немот|а́, ы́ *f.* muteness (often offens.), profound deafness

нему́ *d. of* ▸ **он** *after preps.*

немы́слим|ый, ~, ~а *adj.* unthinkable, inconceivable

ненави́|деть, жу, дишь *impf.* to hate, detest, loathe

ненави́ст|ный, ~ен, ~на *adj.* hated; hateful

не́навист|ь, и *f.* hatred, detestation

ненавя́зчив|ый, ~, ~а *adj.* unobtrusive

ненадёж|ный, ~ен, ~на *adj.* (*человек; сведение*) unreliable, untrustworthy; (*защита; лёд*) insecure

ненадо́лго *adv.* for a short while, not for long

ненаме́ренно *adv.* unintentionally, unwittingly, accidentally

ненаме́рен|ный, ~, ~на *adj.* unintentional, accidental

ненаст|ный, ~ен, ~на *adj.* (*погода*) bad, foul

ненастоя́щий *adj.* (*мех*) artificial; (*деньги*) counterfeit

нена́сть|е, я *nt.* bad, foul weather

ненормáл|ьный, ~ен, ~ьна *adj.*
1 abnormal **2** (*сумасшедший*) mad

ненýж|ный, ~ен, ~нá, ~но *adj.* (*мягкость*) unnecessary; (*книга, человек*) superfluous

необдýман|ный, ~, ~на *adj.* thoughtless, precipitate

необитáем|ый, ~, ~а *adj.* uninhabited; **н. óстров** desert island

необозрúм|ый, ~, ~а *adj.* boundless, immense

необоснóван|ный, ~, ~на *adj.* unfounded, groundless

необрабóтан|ный, ~, ~а *adj.* **1** (*земля*) uncultivated, untilled **2** (*минерал*) raw, crude

необразóван|ный, ~, ~на *adj.* uneducated

необратúм|ый, ~, ~а *adj.* irreversible

необýздан|ный, ~, ~на *adj.* (*фантазия*) unbridled; (*нрав*) ungovernable

✓ **необходúмост|ь**, и *f.* necessity; **по ~и** out of necessity; **при ~и** if necessary

✓ **необходúм|ый**, ~, ~а *adj.* necessary, essential; (*impers., as pred.*) ~**о** it is necessary *or* imperative

необщúтел|ьный, ~ен, ~ьна *adj.* unsociable

необъектúв|ный, ~ен, ~на *adj.* not objective; biased

необъяснúм|ый, ~, ~а *adj.* inexplicable, unaccountable

необъя́т|ный, ~ен, ~на *adj.* immense, unbounded

необыкновéн|ный, ~ен, ~на *adj.* unusual, uncommon

необыча́|йный, ~ен, ~йна *adj.* extraordinary, exceptional

необы́ч|ный, ~ен, ~на *adj.* unusual

необяза́тел|ьный, ~ен, ~ьна *adj.*
1 (*предмет, курс*) not obligatory, optional **2** (*человек*) unreliable

неограни́чен|ный, ~, ~на *adj.* unlimited, unbounded

неоднозна́ч|ный, ~ен, ~на *adj.*
1 ambiguous, equivocal **2** (*сложный*) complex, complicated

неоднокра́тно *adv.* repeatedly

неоднокра́т|ный, ~ен, ~на *adj.* repeated

неоднорóд|ный, ~ен, ~на *adj.* heterogeneous; dissimilar

неодобрéни|е, я *nt.* disapproval

неодолúм|ый, ~, ~а *adj.* insuperable

неодушевлённый *adj.* inanimate

неожúданност|ь, и *f.* **1** unexpectedness, suddenness **2** (*событие*) surprise

неожúдан|ный, ~, ~на *adj.* unexpected, sudden

неокóнченный *adj.* unfinished

неóн, а *m.* (chem.) neon

неонацúст, а *m.* neo-Nazi

неонацúст|ка, ки *f. of* ▶ **неонацúст**

неóновый *adj.*: ~ **свет** neon light

неопáс|ный, ~ен, ~на *adj.* (*место, путешествие*) safe; (*болезнь, собака*)
harmless

неописýем|ый, ~, ~а *adj.* indescribable

неопóзнан|ный, ~, ~а *adj.* unidentified

неопрáвдан|ный, ~, ~на *adj.* unjustified, unwarranted

неопределённост|ь, и *f.* vagueness, uncertainty

неопределён|ный, ~ен, ~на *adj.*
1 indefinite; ~**ная фóрма глагóла** (gram.) infinitive **2** indeterminate; vague, uncertain

неопровержúм|ый, ~, ~а *adj.* irrefutable

неопря́т|ный, ~ен, ~на *adj.* slovenly; untidy, sloppy

неóпыт|ный, ~ен, ~на *adj.* inexperienced

неосмотрúтел|ьный, ~ен, ~ьна *adj.* imprudent, incautious

неоспорúм|ый, ~, ~а *adj.* unquestionable, incontestable, indisputable

неосторóжност|ь, и *f.* carelessness; imprudence

неосторóж|ный, ~ен, ~на *adj.* careless; imprudent, incautious

неотвратúм|ый, ~, ~а *adj.* inevitable

неóткуда *adv.* there is nowhere; **мне н. э́то получúть** there is nowhere I can get it from

неотлóж|ный, ~ен, ~на *adj.* urgent, pressing; ~**ная медицúнская пóмощь** emergency medical service

неотразúм|ый, ~, ~а *adj.* irresistible (also fig.)

неотъéмлем|ый, ~, ~а *adj.* inalienable; ~**ое прáво** inalienable right; ~**ая часть** integral part

неофашúзм, а *m.* neo-fascism

неофашúст, а *m.* neo-fascist

неофашúст|ка, ки *f. of* ▶ **неофашúст**

неофашúстский *adj.* neo-fascist

неофициáл|ьный, ~ен, ~ьна *adj.* unofficial

неохóт|а, ы *f.* **1** reluctance **2** (+ *d., as pred.*) (infml): **мне** *и т. п.* **н. идтú** I have, *etc.*, no wish to go, don't feel like going

неохóтно *adv.* reluctantly; unwillingly

неоценúм|ый, ~, ~а *adj.* inestimable; priceless, invaluable

Непáл, а *m.* Nepal

непáл|ец, ьца *m.* Nepalese

непáл|ка, ки *fem. of* ▶ **непáлец**

непáльский *adj.* Nepalese

непереводúм|ый, ~, ~а *adj.* untranslatable

непередавáем|ый, ~, ~а *adj.* inexpressible, indescribable

непереходный *adj.* (gram.) intransitive

неплатёжеспосóб|ный, ~ен, ~на *adj.* (fin.) insolvent

неплатéльщик, а *m.* defaulter; person in arrears with payment (*of taxes, etc.*)

неплóхо *adv.* not badly, quite well

неплох|óй, ~, ~á, ~о *adj.* not bad, quite good

непобедúм|ый, ~, ~а *adj.* invincible

неповорóтлив|ый, ~, ~а *adj.* (*неуклюжий*) clumsy, awkward; (*медлительный*) sluggish, slow

Н

неповтори́м|ый, ~, ~а *adj.* unique

непого́д|а, ы *f.* bad weather

неподалёку *adv.* not far off

неподви́жность|ь, и *f.* immobility

неподви́ж|ный, ~ен, ~на *adj.* motionless, immobile, immovable (also fig.); fixed, stationary

неподде́л|ьный, ~ен, ~ьна *adj.* genuine; unfeigned, sincere

неподку́п|ный, ~ен, ~на *adj.* incorruptible

неподража́ем|ый, ~, ~а *adj.* inimitable

непозволи́тел|ьный, ~ен, ~ьна *adj.* inadmissible, impermissible

непоколеби́м|ый, ~, ~а *adj.* steadfast, unshakeable

непоко́р|ный, ~ен, ~на *adj.* recalcitrant; unruly

непола́дк|а, и *f.* defect, fault

неполноце́нность|ь, и *f.* inferiority; ко́мплекс ~и inferiority complex

неполноце́н|ный, ~ен, ~на *adj.* inferior; substandard; **у́мственно** н. learning-disabled; **физи́чески** н. disabled

непо́л|ный, ~он, ~на́, ~но, ~ны́ *adj.* (*ведро́, корзи́на*) not full; (*зна́ния, пере́чень*) incomplete; ~ная семья́ single-parent family; рабо́тать ~ную неде́лю to work part-time

непонима́ни|е, я *nt.* incomprehension

непоня́тлив|ый, ~, ~а *adj.* slow (to grasp things), dim

непоня́т|ный, ~ен, ~на *adj.* unintelligible, incomprehensible; (*impers., as pred.*) ~но it is incomprehensible; **мне** ~но, **как он мог э́то сде́лать** I cannot understand how he could do it

непоправи́м|ый, ~, ~а *adj.* irreparable, irremediable; irretrievable

непоря́доч|ный, ~ен, ~на *adj.* dishonourable (BrE), dishonorable (AmE)

непосе́длив|ый, ~, ~а *adj.* fidgety, restless

непосле́довательность|ь, и *f.* inconsistency; inconsequence

непосле́довател|ьный, ~ен, ~ьна *adj.* inconsistent; inconsequent

непослу́ш|ный, ~ен, ~на *adj.* disobedient, naughty

непосре́дственность|ь, и *f.* spontaneity, ingenuousness

⚤ **непосре́дствен|ный**, ~, ~на *adj.*
1 (*результа́т*) immediate, direct; **в** ~ной бли́зости (**от** + *g.*) in the immediate vicinity (of) **2** (*fig., нату́ра*) direct; spontaneous, ingenuous

непостижи́м|ый, ~, ~а *adj.* incomprehensible, inscrutable; **уму́** ~о it passes understanding

непостоя́н|ный, ~ен, ~на *adj.* inconstant, changeable

непостоя́нств|о, а *nt.* inconstancy

непра́вд|а, ы *f.* untruth, lie

⚤ key word

неправдоподо́б|ный, ~ен, ~на *adj.* improbable, unlikely; implausible

непра́вильно *adv.* incorrectly, erroneously; (*in conjunction with vv. frequently*) mis-; **н. истолкова́ть** to misinterpret

непра́виль|ный, ~ен, ~ьна *adj.*
1 (*разви́тие, черты́, фо́рма*) irregular; **н. глаго́л** irregular verb **2** (*расчёт, сужде́ние*) incorrect, erroneous, wrong, mistaken

неправоме́р|ный, ~ен, ~на *adj.* illegal

непра́в|ый, ~, ~а́, ~о *adj.*
1 (*заблужда́ющийся*) wrong, mistaken **2** (*несправедли́вый*) unjust

непредвзя́т|ый, ~, ~а *adj.* unbiased

непредви́денный *adj.* unforeseen

непреднаме́рен|ный, ~, ~на *adj.* unpremeditated

непредсказу́ем|ый, ~, ~а *adj.* unpredictable

непредумы́шленн|ый *adj.* unpremeditated; ~ое уби́йство manslaughter

непрекло́н|ный, ~ен, ~на *adj.* inflexible, unbending; inexorable, adamant

непреме́нно *adv.* **1** (*обяза́тельно*) without fail; certainly; **они́ н. приду́т за́втра** they are sure to come tomorrow **2** (*о́чень*) absolutely; **мне н. ну́жно поговори́ть с ним** it is absolutely essential that I speak to him

непреме́н|ный, ~ен, ~на *adj.* (*усло́вие*) necessary; (*сле́дствие*) unavoidable; (*черта́*) indispensable

непреодоли́м|ый, ~, ~а *adj.* insuperable, insurmountable; (*жела́ние*) irresistible; ~ая си́ла (law) force majeure

непреры́вно *adv.* uninterruptedly, continuously

непреры́вность|ь, и *f.* continuity

непреры́в|ный, ~ен, ~на *adj.* uninterrupted, unbroken; continuous

непреста́нно *adv.* incessantly, continually

неприве́тлив|ый, ~, ~а *adj.* (*челове́к, взгляд*) unfriendly, ungracious; (*ме́стность*) bleak, forbidding

непривлека́тел|ьный, ~ен, ~ьна *adj.* unattractive

непривы́ч|ный, ~ен, ~на *adj.* unaccustomed, unwonted; unusual

непригля́д|ный, ~ен, ~на *adj.* unattractive, unsightly

неприго́д|ный, ~ен, ~на *adj.* unfit, useless; unserviceable; (*для вое́нной слу́жбы*) ineligible

неприе́млем|ый, ~, ~а *adj.* unacceptable

непри́знан|ный, ~, ~а *adj.* unrecognized, unacknowledged

неприкоснове́нность|ь, и *f.* inviolability; **дипломати́ческая** н. diplomatic immunity

неприкоснове́н|ный, ~ен, ~на *adj.* inviolable; **н. запа́с** (mil.) emergency ration, iron ration

неприли́ч|ный, ~ен, ~на *adj.* indecent, improper; unseemly, unbecoming

неприме́т|ный, ~ен, ~на *adj.* **1** (*ра́зница*) imperceptible **2** (*fig., челове́к*) unremarkable, undistinguished

непримири́м|ый, ~, ~а *adj.* (*противоречия*) irreconcilable; (*характер*) intransigent, uncompromising

непринуждён|ный, ~, ~на *adj.* natural, relaxed; laid-back

непристо́йность|ь, и *f.* obscenity; indecency

непристо́|йный, ~ен, ~йна *adj.* obscene; indecent

непристу́п|ный, ~ен, ~на *adj.* **1** (*скала*) inaccessible; (*крепость*) unassailable, impregnable **2** (fig., *начальник*) inaccessible, unapproachable

неприхотли́в|ый, ~, ~а *adj.* **1** (*человек*) unpretentious; modest; (*растение, животное*) undemanding **2** (*рисунок*) simple, plain; ~ая пи́ща frugal meal

неприча́ст|ный, ~ен, ~на *adj.* (к + *d.*) not implicated (in), not involved (in)

неприя́тел|ь, я *m.* enemy; (mil.) the enemy

неприя́тность|ь, и *f.* unpleasantness; trouble

неприя́т|ный, ~ен, ~на *adj.* unpleasant, disagreeable

непродолжи́тел|ьный, ~ен, ~ьна *adj.* of short duration, short-lived

непроду́ман|ный, ~, ~на *adj.* ill-considered

непрозра́ч|ный, ~ен, ~на *adj.* opaque

непроизво́л|ьный, ~ен, ~ьна *adj.* involuntary

непромока́ем|ый, ~, ~а *adj.* waterproof; **н. плащ** waterproof (coat), raincoat

непроница́ем|ый, ~, ~а *adj.* (*мрак, ночь; тайна*) impenetrable; (*для жидкостей, газов*) impermeable; **н. для зву́ка** soundproof

непрости́тел|ьный, ~ен, ~ьна *adj.* unforgivable, unpardonable, inexcusable

непроходи́м|ый, ~, ~а *adj.* impassable

непро́ч|ный, ~ен, ~на́, ~но *adj.* fragile, flimsy; (fig.) precarious, unstable

нераб|отоспосо́б|ный, ~ен, ~на *adj.* unable to work, disabled

нерабо́ч|ий *adj.* non-working; ~ее вре́мя time off, free time

нера́венств|о, а *nt.* inequality, disparity

неравноду́ш|ный, ~ен, ~на *adj.* (к + *d.*) not indifferent (to)

неравноме́р|ный, ~ен, ~на *adj.* uneven, irregular

нера́в|ный, ~ен, ~на́ *adj.* unequal

неради́в|ый, ~, ~а *adj.* negligent, careless

неразбо́рчив|ый, ~, ~а *adj.* **1** (*почерк*) illegible, indecipherable **2** (fig., *читатель, вкус*) undiscriminating; not fastidious; **н. в сре́дствах** unscrupulous; **сексуа́льно н.** promiscuous

неразгово́рчив|ый, ~, ~а *adj.* taciturn, not talkative

неразличи́м|ый, ~, ~а *adj.* indistinguishable; indiscernible

неразлу́ч|ный, ~ен, ~на *adj.* inseparable

неразреши́м|ый, ~, ~а *adj.* insoluble

неразу́м|ный, ~ен, ~на *adj.* unreasonable; unwise; foolish

нерасторо́п|ный, ~ен, ~на *adj.* sluggish, slow

нерв, а *m.* nerve; **де́йствовать кому́-н. на ~ы** to get on sb's nerves

не́рвнича|ть, ю *impf.* to be *or* become fidgety; to fret; to be *or* become irritable

не́рв|ный, ~ен, ~на́, ~но *adj.* **1** (*болезнь, тик; походка, жест; состояние*) nervous; ~ная систе́ма the nervous system; **н. центр** (fig.) nerve centre (BrE), center (AmE) **2** (*человек*) nervous, highly strung **3** (*работа*) nerve-racking

нерво́з|ный, ~ен, ~на *adj.* nervy, irritable

нереа́л|ьный, ~ен, ~ьна *adj.* **1** (*местность*) unreal **2** (*предложение*) impracticable

нере́дко *adv.* not infrequently, quite often

нерезиде́нт, а *m.* non-resident

нерента́бел|ьный, ~ен, ~ьна *adj.* unprofitable

не́рест, а *m.* (zool.) spawning

нереши́тельность|ь, и *f.* indecision; indecisiveness; **быть в ~и** to be undecided

нереши́тел|ьный, ~ен, ~ьна *adj.* indecisive, irresolute

нержаве́ющ|ий *adj.* non-rusting; ~ая сталь stainless steel

неро́в|ный, ~ен, ~на́, ~но *adj.* **1** (*поверхность*) uneven, rough **2** (*пульс, дыхание*) irregular **3** (*линия*) crooked

не́рп|а, ы *f.* (zool.) ringed seal

несве́дущ|ий, ~, ~а *adj.* (в + *p.*) ignorant (about), not well informed (about)

несве́ж|ий, ~, ~а́, ~е *adj.* **1** (*еда*) not fresh, stale **2** (*бельё; воздух*) dirty

несвоевре́мен|ный, ~, ~на *adj.* inopportune, untimely, unseasonable

несгиба́ем|ый, ~, ~а *adj.* unbending, inflexible

несгово́рчив|ый, ~, ~а *adj.* intractable

несде́ржан|ный, ~, ~на *adj.* unrestrained

несерьёз|ный, ~ен, ~на *adj.* **1** (*человек*) frivolous **2** (*замечание*) flippant **3** (*дело, рана*) trivial

нескла́д|ный, ~ен, ~на *adj.* ungainly, awkward; absurd

несклоня́ем|ый, ~, ~а *adj.* (gram.) indeclinable

✧ **не́скольк|о¹, их** *num.* some, several; a few; **в ~их слова́х** in a few words; **н. челове́к** several people

✧ **не́сколько²** *adv.* somewhat, rather, slightly; **они́ н. разочаро́ваны** they are rather disillusioned

нескро́м|ный, ~ен, ~на́, ~но *adj.* **1** (*человек*) immodest; vain **2** (*вопрос*) indiscreet **3** (*жест*) indecent

нескрыва́ем|ый, ~, ~а *adj.* undisguised

несло́ж|ный, ~ен, ~на́, ~но *adj.* simple, uncomplicated

Н

неслыхан|ный, ~, ~на *adj.* unheard-of, unprecedented

неслыш|ный, ~ен, ~на *adj.* inaudible

несмолка́ем|ый, ~, ~a *adj.* ceaseless, unremitting

✍ **несмотря́** *prep.* (на + *a.*) in spite of, despite; **н. ни на что** in spite of everything

несовершеннолетн|ий *adj.* under-age; (*as n.* н., ~его, *f.* ~яя, ~ей) minor

несоверше́н|ный, ~ен, ~на *adj.* imperfect, incomplete

несовмести́м|ый, ~, ~a *adj.* incompatible

несогла́си|е, я *nt.* **1** disagreement **2** (*разлад*) discord **3** (*sg. only*) (*отказ*) refusal

несоизмери́м|ый, ~, ~a *adj.* incommensurable, incommensurate

несокруши́м|ый, ~, ~a *adj.* unshakeable

несомне́нно *adv.* undoubtedly, doubtless

несомне́н|ный, ~ен, ~на *adj.* undoubted, indubitable, unquestionable

несостоя́тельн|ый, ~ен, ~ьна *adj.* **1** (*обанкротившийся*) insolvent, bankrupt; (*бедный*) poor **2** (*необоснованный*) groundless, unsupported

неспе́л|ый, ~, ~á, ~о *adj.* unripe

неспе́ш|ный, ~ен, ~на *adj.* unhurried

неспоко́|йный, ~ен, ~йна *adj.* (*сон, характер*) restless; (*жизнь*) troubled; (*море, погода*) rough

неспосо́бность|, и *f.* incapacity, inability

неспосо́б|ный, ~ен, ~на *adj.* dull, not able; (к + *d. or* на + *a.*) incapable (of); **она́ ~на к языка́м** she has no aptitude for languages; **н. на ложь** incapable of a lie

несправедли́вость|, и *f.* injustice, unfairness

несправедли́в|ый, ~, ~a *adj.* **1** (*человек, суд*) unjust, unfair **2** (*мнение*) incorrect, unfounded

неспроста́ *adv.* (*infml*) not without purpose; with an ulterior motive

несравне́нно *adv.* **1** incomparably **2** (+ *compr.*) far, by far; **н. лу́чше** far better

несравне́н|ный, ~ен, ~на *adj.* incomparable

нестаби́льность|, и *f.* instability

нестаби́л|ьный, ~ен, ~ьна *adj.* unstable

нестерпи́м|ый, ~, ~a *adj.* unbearable, intolerable

✍ **нес|ти́**[1], у́, ёшь, *past* ~, ~ла́ *impf.* (*of* ▸ **понести́** 1, *det. of* ▸ **носи́ть** 1) **1** (*перемещать на себе*) to carry **2** (*поддерживать*) to support **3** (*fig., терпеть*) to bear; to suffer; to incur; **н. убы́тки** (fin.) to incur losses **4** (*выполнять*) to perform; **н. дежу́рство** to be on duty **5** (*fig., причинять*) to bear, bring; **н. ги́бель** to bring destruction **6** (*infml*) ~ти вздор, чепуху́ *и т. п.* to talk (nonsense)

✍ **нес|ти́**[2], ёт, *past* ~, ~ла́ *impf.* (*of* ▸ **снести́**[2])

✍ key word

(*яйца*) to lay

нес|ти́сь, у́сь, ёшься, *past* нёсся, ~ла́сь *impf.* (*of* ▸ **понести́сь** 1) (*det.*) **1** (*о человеке, машине*) to rush, tear, fly; (*по воздуху, воде*) to float, drift; (**по** + *d. or* **вдоль** + *g. or* **над** + *i.*) to skim (along, over) **2** (*о звуке, запахе*) to spread, be diffused

несура́з|ный, ~ен, ~на *adj.* **1** (*глупый*) absurd, senseless **2** (*неуклюжий*) awkward

несуще́ствен|ный, ~, ~на *adj.* inessential, immaterial

несча́ст|ный, ~ен, ~на *adj.* **1** unhappy; unfortunate, unlucky; **н. слу́чай** accident **2** (*as m. n.* н., ~ного) wretch; an unfortunate

несча́сть|е, я *nt.* **1** (*беда*) misfortune; **к ~ю** unfortunately **2** (*несчастный случай*) accident

несъедо́б|ный, ~ен, ~на *adj.* inedible

✍ **нет**[1] **1** (*при отрицании*) no; not; **вы его́ ви́дели? — н.** You saw him? — No; **вы не ви́дели его́? — н., ви́дел** You didn't see him? — Yes, I did **2** nothing, naught; **свести́ на н.** to bring to naught; **свести́сь (сойти́) на н.** to come to naught

✍ **нет**[2] (+ *g.*) (*не имеется*) (there) is no, (there) are no; **у меня́ н. вре́мени** I have no time

нетакти́ч|ный, ~ен, ~на *adj.* tactless

нетвёрдо *adv.* **1** (*ходить*) unsteadily, not firmly **2** (fig.) not definitely; **знать н.** to have a shaky knowledge of

нетерпели́в|ый, ~, ~a *adj.* impatient

нетерпе́ни|е, я *nt.* impatience

нетерпи́мость|, и *f.* intolerance

нетерпи́м|ый, ~, ~a *adj.* **1** (*поступок*) intolerable **2** (*человек*) intolerant

нетороплив|ый, ~, ~a *adj.* leisurely, unhurried

нето́чность|, и *f.* **1** (*свойство*) inaccuracy, inexactitude **2** (*ошибка*) error, slip

нето́ч|ный, ~ен, ~на́, ~но, ~ны́ *adj.* inaccurate, inexact

нетрадицио́н|ный, ~ен, ~на *adj.* unconventional

нетре́зв|ый, ~, ~á, ~о *adj.* not sober, drunk; **в ~ом ви́де** in a state of intoxication

нетривиа́л|ьный, ~ен, ~ьна *adj.* not trivial; outstanding, exceptional

нетро́нут|ый, ~, ~a *adj.* (*почва, снег*) virgin; (*обед*) untouched; (fig., *целомудренный*) unsullied, virginal

нетрудоспосо́б|ный, ~ен, ~на *adj.* disabled; invalid

не́ту (*infml*) = **нет**[2]

неубеди́тельн|ый, ~ен, ~ьна *adj.* unconvincing

неуваже́ни|е, я *nt.* disrespect, lack of respect; (law): **н. к суду́** contempt of court

неуважи́тельн|ый, ~ен, ~ьна *adj.* **1** (*причина*) inadequate; not acceptable **2** (infml, *непочтительный*) disrespectful

неуве́ренность|, и *f.* uncertainty; **н. в себе́** lack of self-confidence

неуве́рен|ный, ~, ~на and (with syntactically related word(s)) ~а adj. **1** (человек) lacking confidence, unsure; **н. в себе́** lacking self-confidence, unsure of oneself **2** (походка, движение) uncertain

неувя́зк|а, и f. (infml) (в расчётах) discrepancy; (недоразумение) misunderstanding

неуда́ч|а, и f. failure

неуда́чник, а m. unlucky person, failure, loser

неуда́чни|ца, цы f. of ▶ **неуда́чник**

неуда́ч|ный, ~ен, ~на adj. unsuccessful; (несчастливый) unfortunate; (плохой) bad; ~ное нача́ло bad start

неудержи́м|ый, ~, ~а adj. irrepressible

неудо́б|ный, ~ен, ~на adj. **1** (одежда, постель) uncomfortable **2** (fig.) (время) inconvenient; (положение) awkward; embarrassing

неудо́бств|о, а nt. **1** (постели) discomfort **2** (положения) awkwardness; embarrassment

неудовлетвори́тел|ьный, ~ен, ~ьна adj. unsatisfactory

неудово́льстви|е, я nt. dissatisfaction, displeasure

неуже́ли interrog. particle really? is it possible?; **н. он так ду́мает?** does he really think that?; **н. ты не знал, что мы здесь?** did you really not know that we were here?; surely you knew that we were here!

неузнава́ем|ый, ~, ~а adj. unrecognizable

неуклю́ж|ий, ~, ~а, ~е adj. clumsy, awkward

неулови́м|ый, ~, ~а adj. **1** (человек) elusive, difficult to catch **2** (fig., звук) imperceptible

неуме́л|ый, ~, ~а adj. clumsy; unskilful (BrE), unskillful (AmE)

неуме́рен|ный, ~, ~на adj. (аппетит, восторг) immoderate; excessive

неуме́ст|ный, ~ен, ~на adj. **1** (шутка) inappropriate **2** (факт, информация) irrelevant

неу́м|ный, ~ён, ~на́ adj. foolish; (решение) unwise

неумоли́м|ый, ~, ~а adj. implacable; inexorable

неуравнове́шен|ный, ~, ~на adj. (psych.) unbalanced

неурожа́|й, я m. bad harvest, crop failure

неусто́йчив|ый, ~, ~а adj. unstable, unsteady

неустраши́м|ый, ~, ~а adj. fearless, intrepid

неутеши́тел|ьный, ~ен, ~ьна adj. not comforting, depressing; ~ьные ве́сти distressing news

неутоми́м|ый, ~, ~а adj. tireless, indefatigable

неучти́в|ый, ~, ~а adj. discourteous, impolite, uncivil

неую́т|ный, ~ен, ~на adj. bleak, comfortless

неуязви́м|ый, ~, ~а adj. **1** (пози́ция, человек, подво́дная ло́дка) invulnerable **2** (доказа́тельство) unassailable

неформа́л, а m. (infml) member of an unofficial organization

неформа́л|ьный, ~ен, ~ьна adj. unofficial; informal

нефтедо́ллар, а m. petrodollar

нефтеперераба́тывающий adj. oil-refining; **н. заво́д** oil refinery

нефтепрово́д, а m. oil pipeline

нефт|ь, и f. oil, petroleum; **сыра́я н.** crude oil

нефтя́ник, а m. oil (industry) worker

нефтян|о́й adj. oil; ~а́я вы́шка derrick

нехва́тк|а, и f. (infml) shortage

нехоро́ш|ий, ~, ~а́ adj. bad

не́хотя adv. reluctantly, unwillingly

нецелесообра́з|ный, ~ен, ~на adj. inexpedient; pointless

нецензу́р|ный, ~ен, ~на adj. unprintable; ~ные слова́ swear words, obscenities

неча́янный adj. accidental; unintentional

не́чего, не́чему, не́чем, не́ о чем 1 pron. (+ inf) there is nothing (to); **мне н. чита́ть** I have nothing to read; **не́ о чём бы́ло говори́ть** there was nothing to talk about; **от н. де́лать** for want of sth better to do, to while away the time **2** (as pred.) (impers. + inf.) (незачем) it's no good, it's no use; there is no need; **н. жа́ловаться** it's no use complaining

нечелове́ческий adj. **1** (уси́лия) superhuman **2** (отноше́ния) inhuman

нече́стност|ь, и f. dishonesty

нече́ст|ный, ~ен, ~на́, ~но, ~ны́ adj. **1** (человек) dishonest **2** (посту́пок) dishonourable (BrE), dishonorable (AmE); ~ная игра́ (sport) foul play

нечёт|кий, ~ок, ~ка adj. illegible; (рису́нок) indistinct; (изложе́ние) unclear

нечётный adj. odd

нечистопло́т|ный, ~ен, ~на adj. **1** (гря́зный) dirty; (неопря́тный) untidy, slovenly **2** (fig., нече́стный) unscrupulous

нечистот|а́, ы́, pl. ~ы, ~ f. **1** (sg. only) dirtiness **2** (pl. only) (отбро́сы) sewage, garbage

нечи́ст|ый, ~, ~а́, ~о, ~ы́ adj. **1** (гря́зный) unclean, dirty (also fig.); ~ое де́ло suspicious affair **2** (с при́месью чего́-л.) impure, adulterated **3** (неаккура́тный) careless, inaccurate **4** (нече́стный) dishonourable (BrE), dishonorable (AmE); dishonest; **быть ~ым на́ руку** to be light-fingered **5**: ~ая си́ла evil spirits

не́что pron. (nom. and a. cases only) something

нечувстви́тел|ьный, ~ен, ~ьна adj. (к + d.) insensitive (to)

нешу́точ|ный, ~ен, ~на adj. grave, serious; **де́ло ~ное** it is no joke; it is no laughing matter

неэффекти́в|ный, ~ен, ~на adj. ineffective; inefficient

нея́с|ный, ~ен, ~на́, ~но adj. vague, obscure

✓ **ни 1** (correlative conj.): **ни... ни** neither ... nor; **ни тот ни друго́й** neither (the one nor the other) **2** (particle) not a; **ни оди́н, ни одна́, ни одно́** not a, not one, not a single; **на у́лице не́ было ни души́** there was not a soul about **3** (separable component of prons. **никако́й, никто́, ничто́,** following preps.): **ни в како́м (ни в ко́ем)** слу́чае on no account; **ни за что (на све́те!)** in no circumstances; not for the world! **4** (particle, in comb. with **как, кто, куда́,** etc.) -ever; **как бы мы ни стара́лись** however hard we tried; **что бы он ни говори́л** whatever he might say

нигде́ adv. nowhere

Ни́гер, а m. **1** (страна) Niger **2** (река) the Niger

нигери́|ец, йца m. Nigerian

нигери́й|ка, ки f. of ▶ **нигери́ец**

нигери́йский adj. Nigerian

Ниге́ри|я, и f. Nigeria

нидерла́ндский adj. Dutch, Netherlands; (язык) Dutch

Нидерла́нд|ы, ов (no sg.) the Netherlands

ни́же 1 comp. of ▶ **ни́зкий 2** prep. (+ g.) and adv. below, beneath

✓ **ни́жн|ий** adj. lower; ~ее бельё underclothes, underwear; ~яя пала́та Lower Chamber, Lower House; ~яя ю́бка slip

низ, а, pl. ~ы́ m. **1** bottom **2** (in pl.) (о́бщества) lower classes

низи́н|а, ы f. low-lying area

✓ **ни́з|кий**, ~ок, ~ка́, ~ко adj. **1** low; ~кого происхожде́ния of humble origin; **быть** ~кого мне́ния о (+ p.) to have a low opinion of **2** (по́длый) base, mean; **н. посту́пок** shabby act

низокача́ествен|ный, ~, ~на adj. low-quality

низкоопла́чиваем|ый, ~, ~а adj. poorly-paid

низкоро́сл|ый, ~, ~а adj. (челове́к) short; (де́рево) undersized, stunted

низкоуглево́д|ный, ~ен, ~на adj. low-carb

низкоуглеро́дистый adj. low-carbon

ни́зменност|ь, и f. (geog.) lowland (not exceeding 200 m above sea level)

ни́змен|ный, ~, ~на adj. **1** low-lying **2** (по́длый) low; base, vile; ~ные инсти́нкты basic instincts

низо́в|ье, ья, g. pl. ~ьев nt. the lower reaches (of a river)

ни́зост|ь, и f. lowness; (по́длость) baseness, meanness

ни́зший superl. of ▶ **ни́зкий**; lowest

НИИ m. indecl. (abbr. of **нау́чно-иссле́довательский институ́т**) research institute

✓ **key word**

✓ **ника́к** adv. (никаки́м о́бразом) by no means, in no way; **он н. не мог узна́ть её а́дрес** in no way could he discover her address

✓ **никак|о́й** pron. no; **не... ~о́го, ~о́й, ~их** no ... whatever; **я не име́ю ~о́го представле́ния (поня́тия)** I have no idea, no conception; ~их возраже́ний! no objections!

Никара́гуа nt. & f. indecl. Nicaragua

никарагуа́н|ец, ца m. Nicaraguan

никарагуа́н|ка, ки f. of ▶ **никарагуа́нец**

никарагуа́нский adj. Nicaraguan

ни́кел|ь, я m. nickel

✓ **никогда́** adv. never; **как н.** as never before

ник|о́й pron.: ~им о́бразом by no means, in no way; **ни в ко́ем слу́чае** on no account, in no circumstances

никоти́н, а m. nicotine

никоти́новый adj. of ▶ **никоти́н**

✓ **никто́, никого́, никому́, нике́м, ни о ком** pron. nobody, no one; **ни у кого́ нет э́того** no one has it

никуда́ adv. nowhere; **э́то н. не годи́тся** (fig.) this won't do; it is no good at all

никче́м|ный, ~ен, ~на adj. (infml) useless, good-for-nothing

Нил, а m. the Nile (river)

ним i. of ▶ **он**, d. of ▶ **они́** after preps.

нима́ло adv. not in the least, not at all

ни́ми i. of ▶ **они́** after preps.

ни́мф|а, ы f. nymph

ниотку́да adv. from nowhere; **н. не сле́дует, что...** it in no way follows that ...

нирва́н|а, ы f. nirvana

ниско́лько adv. not at all, not in the least; **ей от э́того бы́ло н. не лу́чше** she was none the better for it

ни́тк|а, и f. thread; **н. же́мчуга** string of pearls; **промо́кнуть до ~и** (fig.) to get soaked to the skin

нитра́т, а m. (chem.) nitrate

нитроглицери́н, а m. (chem.) nitroglycerine

нит|ь, и f. **1** thread **2** (bot., elec.) filament **3** (med.) suture

них a., g., and p. of ▶ **они́** after preps.

ничего́[1] g. of ▶ **ничто́**

ничего́[2] adv. (infml) **1** (also **н. себе́**) so-so; passably, not (too) badly; all right; **как вы чу́вствуете себя́? — н.** how do you feel? — all right **2** (as indecl. adj.) not (too) bad, passable, tolerable; **па́рень он н.** he is not a bad chap

нич|е́й, ~ья́, ~ье́ pron. nobody's, no one's; ~ья́ земля́ no man's land; (as f. n. ~ья́, g., d., i., p. ~ье́й) (sport) draw, drawn game

ничко́м adv. prone, face downwards

✓ **ничто́, ничего́, ничему́, ниче́м, ни о чём** pron. nothing; **э́то ничего́ не зна́чит** it means nothing; **ничего́ подо́бного!** nothing of the kind!; **ничего́!** (infml) that's all right!; never mind!

ничто́жеств|о, а nt. **1** (убо́жество) poverty **2** (челове́к) a nonentity, a nobody

ничто́ж|ный, ~ен, ~на *adj.* (*незначительный*) insignificant; (*человек*) paltry, worthless

ничу́ть *adv.* (*infml*) not at all, not in the least, not a bit; **н. не быва́ло** not at all

ничь|я́, е́й *f. see* ▸ **ниче́й**

ни́ш|а, и *f.* niche, recess; (*archit.*) alcove, bay

ни́щенский *adj.* beggarly

ни́щенств|овать, ую *impf.* **1** (*занима́ться ни́щенством*) to beg, go begging **2** (*жить в нищете́*) to be destitute

нищет|а́, ы́ *f.* poverty (*also* fig.)

ни́щ|ий *adj.* **1** destitute; poverty-stricken **2** (*as m. n. н.*, ~его) beggar; pauper

НЛО *m. indecl.* (*abbr. of* **неопо́знанный лета́ющий объе́кт**) UFO (*unidentified flying object*)

но *conj.* but; (*after concessive clause not translated or*) still, nevertheless; **хотя́ он и бо́лен, но наме́рен прийти́** although he is ill, he (still) intends to come

Но́в|ая Зела́ндия, ~ой Зела́ндии *f.* New Zealand

нове́йший *superl. of* ▸ **но́вый**; newest; (*после́дний*) latest

нове́лл|а, ы *f.* novella

новизн|а́, ы́ *f.* novelty; newness

нови́нк|а, и *f.* new thing, novelty; **кни́жные ~и** new books

новичо́к, ка́ *m.* **1** (в + *p.*) novice (at), beginner (at) **2** (*в шко́ле*) new boy; new girl

новобра́н|ец, ца *m.* recruit

новобра́чн|ые, ых *pl.* newly-weds

нововведе́ни|е, я *nt.* innovation

нового́дн|ий *adj.* New Year's; **~яя ночь** New Year's Eve

новозела́нд|ец, ца *m.* New Zealander

новозела́нд|ка, ки *f. of* ▸ **новозела́ндец**

новозела́ндский *adj.* New Zealand

новолу́ни|е, я *nt.* new moon

новорождён|ный, ~ (*as* **н. н.**, ~ого, *f.* ~ая, ~ой) the baby; (*med.*) neonate

новосе́ль|е, я *nt.* house-warming; **справля́ть н.** to give a house-warming party

новостно́й *adj.* news (*attr.*)

новостро́йк|а, и *f.* (*зда́ние*) newly erected building

но́вост|ь, и, *g. pl.* ~е́й *f.* news

но́вшеств|о, а *nt.* innovation, novelty

но́в|ый, ~, ~а́, ~о, ~ы́ *adj.* **1** new; **соверше́нно н.** brand new; **Н. год** New Year's Day; **Н. Заве́т** the New Testament; **что ~ого?** what's the news?; what's new? **2** (*совреме́нный*) modern; recent; **~ая исто́рия** modern history

ног|а́, и́, *a.* ~у, *pl.* ~и, ~, ~а́м *f.* (*ступня́*) foot; (*до ступни́*) leg; **вверх ~а́ми** head over heels; **положи́ть ~у на ~у** to cross one's legs

ноготк|и́, о́в *m. pl.* (common *or* pot) marigold (*genus Calendula*)

но́г|оть, тя, *pl.* ~ти, ~те́й *m.* (finger/toe)nail

нож, а́ *m.* knife; **перочи́нный н.** penknife; **садо́вый н.** pruning knife; **н. в спи́ну** (fig.)

stab in the back

но́жик, а *m.* (small) knife

но́жк|а, и *f.* **1** *dim. of* ▸ **нога́**; **подста́вить ~у** (+ *d.*) to trip up **2** (*ме́бели, у́твари*) leg; (*рю́мки*) stem **3** (bot.) stalk; (*гриба́*) stem

но́жниц|ы, ~ *pl.* **1** scissors, pair of scissors; (*больши́е*) shears **2** (econ., *расхожде́ние*) discrepancy

ножно́й *adj. of* ▸ **нога́**; **н. то́рмоз** foot brake

но́ж|ны, ~ен, ~нам *pl.* sheath; scabbard

ножо́вк|а, и *f.* hacksaw

ноздр|я́, и́, *pl.* ~и, ~е́й *f.* nostril

нол|ь, я́ *m.* = **нуль**

но́мер, а, *pl.* ~а́ *m.* **1** (*телефо́на, маши́ны, до́ма*) number; (*газе́ты, журна́ла*) number, issue **2** (*разме́р*) size **3** (*в гости́нице*) room **4** (*конце́рта*) item on the programme (BrE); program (AmE); number, turn; **со́льный н.** solo (number)

номеро́к, ка́ *m.* (*в гардеро́бе*) ticket

номина́льн|ый *adj.* nominal; **~ая цена́** face value

номина́нт, а *m.* nominee

номина́нт|ка, ки *f. of* ▸ **номина́нт**

номина́ци|я, и *f.* nomination

номини́р|овать, ую *impf. and pf.* to nominate

нор|а́, ы́, *pl.* ~ы, ~, ~а́м *f.* (*за́йца*) burrow, hole; (*лисы́*) lair

Норве́ги|я, и *f.* Norway

норве́ж|ец, ца *m.* Norwegian

норве́ж|ка, ки *f. of* ▸ **норве́жец**

норве́жский *adj.* Norwegian

но́рк|а, и *f.* mink

но́рм|а, ы *f.* **1** (*поведе́ния*) standard, norm **2** (*величина́*) rate; **н. вы́работки** rate of output

норма́льно *as pred.* (*infml*) it is all right, fine, OK

норма́льн|ый, ~ен, ~ьна *adj.* normal

нормати́вн|ый, ~ен, ~на *adj.* standard

нос, а, о ~е, **в/на** ~у́, *pl.* ~ы́ *m.* **1** nose; **оста́ться с ~ом** (infml) to be duped; be left looking a fool; **сова́ть н. не в своё де́ло** (infml) to poke one's nose into other people's affairs **2** (*пти́цы*) beak **3** (naut.) bow, head; prow

носа́т|ый, ~, ~а *adj.* big-nosed

но́сик, а *m.* (*ча́йника*) spout

носи́л|ки, ок (*no sg.*) stretcher

носи́льщик, а *m.* porter

носи́тел|ь, я *m.* **1** (fig., *иде́й*) bearer; repository **2** (*инфе́кции, гри́ппа*) carrier

но|си́ть, шу́, ~сишь *impf.* **1** *indet. of* ▸ **нести́**[1] **2** (*indet. only*) (*ве́щи; ребёнка*) to carry; (*большу́ю тя́жесть*) to bear (*also* fig.); **н. свою́ деви́чью фами́лию** to use one's maiden name **3** (*indet. only*) (*оде́жду, украше́ния*) to wear **4** (*indet. only*) (*хара́ктер*) to have (*a certain character*); to be of (*a certain nature*)

но|си́ться, шу́сь, ~сишься *impf.* **1** *indet. of* ▸ **нести́сь**; **э́то ~сится в во́здухе** (fig.)

it is in the air, it is rumoured (BrE), rumored (AmE) **2** (с + i.) (с человеком) to make a fuss (of); **н. с мы́слью** to be obsessed with an idea **3** intr. (одежда) to wear; **э́та мате́рия хорошо́ ~ситься** this material wears well

носово́й adj. of ▸ **нос**; **н. плато́к** (pocket) handkerchief

нос|о́к¹, **ка́** m. (ботинка, чулка) toe

нос|о́к², **ка́**, pl. **~ки́**, **~ко́в** or **~о́к** m. (чулок) sock

носоро́г, **а** m. rhinoceros

ностальги́|я, **и** f. homesickness; (о прошлом) nostalgia

но́т|а¹, **ы** f. (mus.) **1** note **2** (in pl.) (текст) (sheet) music; **игра́ть по ~ам (без нот)** to play from music (without music)

но́т|а², **ы** f. (diplomatic) note

нота́риус, **а** m. notary

ноутбу́к, **а** m. notebook (computer)

но́у-ха́у nt. indecl. know-how

ноч|ева́ть, **у́ю** impf. (of ▸ **переночева́ть**) to spend, pass the night

ночни́к, **а́** m. night light

ночн|о́й adj. night; **н. по́езд** overnight train; **~а́я руба́шка** (мужская) nightshirt; (женская) nightdress

⚲ **ноч|ь**, **и**, **о ~и**, **в ~и́**, pl. **~и**, **~е́й** f. night; **споко́йной ~и!** goodnight!; **по ~а́м** by night, at night

но́чью adv. by night

но́ш|а, **и** f. burden

но́шеный adj. second-hand

но́|ю, **ешь** see ▸ **ныть**

⚲ **ноя́бр|ь**, **я́** m. November

ноя́брьский adj. of ▸ **ноя́брь**

нрав, **а** m. **1** (характер) disposition, temper; **быть (+ d.) по ~у** to please **2** (in pl.) (обычаи) customs, ways

⚲ **нра́в|иться**, **люсь**, **ишься** impf. (of ▸ **понра́виться**) (+ d.) to please; **мне, ему́ и** m. n. **~ится** I like, he likes, etc.; **мне о́чень ~ится э́та пье́са** I like this play very much; (impers.) **ей не ~ится ката́ться на ло́дке** she does not like going in boats

нра́вственность, **и** f. morality; morals

нра́вственн|ый, **~**, **~на** adj. moral

⚲ **ну** int. and particle (infml) **1** well!; well ... then!; come on!; **ну, ну!** come, come!; come now! **2**; **да ну!** really?; you don't say (so)! **3** (выражает удивление, восхищение, негодование, иронию) well; **ну и...!** what (a) ...!; here's ... (for you)!; there's ... (for you)!; **ну вот и..!** there you are,

you see ...! **4** (выражает согласие, уступку, примирение, облегчение) well; **ну вот** (в повествовании) well, well then; **ну что ж, ну так** well then; **ну хорошо́** all right then

нуди́ст, **а** m. nudist, naturist

нуди́ст|ка, **ки** f. of ▸ **нуди́ст**

ну́дн|ый, **~ен**, **~на́**, **~но**, **~ны́** adj. (infml) tedious

нужд|а́, **ы́**, pl. **~ы** f. **1** (sg. only) (бедность) want, poverty **2** (необходимость) need; necessity

⚲ **нужда́|ться**, **юсь** impf. **1** (жить в бедности) to be in want; to be needy, hard up **2** (в + p.) to need, require; to be in need (of)

⚲ **ну́жно** (+ d.) **1** (impers.; + inf. or + чтобы) it is necessary; (one) ought, (one) should, (one) must, (one) need(s); **н. бы́ло (бы) взять такси́** you should have taken a taxi; **н., чтобы она́ реши́лась** she ought to make up her mind **2** (impers.; + a. or g.) (infml) I need, etc.; **мне н. пять рубле́й** I need five roubles **3** see ▸ **ну́жный**

⚲ **ну́жн|ый**, **~ен**, **~на́**, **~но**, **~ны́** adj. necessary; requisite; (pred. forms + d.) I need, etc.; **что вам ~но?** what do you need?, what do you want?

ну́-ка int. (infml) now then!; come on!

нулево́й adj. of ▸ **нуль**; (math.) zero; **н. вариа́нт** zero option

нул|ь, **я́** m. nought; (о температуре) zero; (в играх) nil

ны́не adv. now, currently, at present

⚲ **ны́нешний** adj. (infml) present; present-day; **н. президе́нт** the incumbent president

ны́нче adv. (infml) **1** (сегодня) today **2** (теперь) nowadays

ныр|ну́ть, **ну́**, **нёшь** pf. of ▸ **ныря́ть**

ныря́льщик, **а** m. diver

ныря́льщи|ца, **цы** f. of ▸ **ныря́льщик**

ныр|я́ть, **я́ю** impf. (of ▸ **нырну́ть**) to dive

ныть, **но́ю**, **но́ешь** impf. **1** (болеть) to ache **2** (infml, жаловаться) to moan

Нью-Йо́рк, **а** m. New York

н. э. (abbr. of на́шей э́ры) AD; **до н. э.** (abbr. of до на́шей э́ры) BC

нюа́нс, **а** m. nuance

нюх, **а** m. scent; (fig.) (на + a.) a nose (for)

нюха|ть, **ю** impf. (of ▸ **поню́хать**) (цветок) to smell; (воздух; наркотик) to sniff

ня́нчить, **у**, **ишь** impf. to look after, mind

ня́н|я, **и** f. **1** nanny; childminder; **приходя́щая н.** babysitter **2** (infml, в больнице) auxiliary nurse

Oo

о, об, обо *prep.* **1** (+ *p.*) (*указывает на предмет речи, мысли*) of, about, concerning; on; **о чём вы ду́маете?** what are you thinking about? **2** (+ *a.*) (*указывает на соприкосновение, столкновение*) against; on, upon; over; **опере́ться о сте́ну** to lean against the wall; **споткну́ться о ка́мень** to stumble on, over a stone; **бок ó бок** side by side; **рука́ об руку** hand in hand

оа́зис, а *m.* oasis (also *fig.*)

об *prep. see* ▶ о

о́ба, *m. and nt.* **обо́их**, *f.* **о́бе, обе́их** *пит.* both; **обе́ими рука́ми** (*fig., infml*) zealously; very willingly, readily

обанкро́|титься, чусь, тишься *pf.* to go bankrupt

обая́ни|е, я *nt.* fascination, charm

обая́тел|ьный, ~ен, ~ьна *adj.* fascinating, charming

обва́л, а *m.* (*стены*) collapse; caving-in; (*камней*) rockfall; (*снежный*) avalanche; (econ.) collapse, dive

обва́лива|ться, ется *impf. of* ▶ обвали́ться

обвал|и́ться, ~ится *pf.* (*of* ▶ обва́ливаться) to fall, collapse, cave in

обве|ду́, дёшь *see* ▶ обвести́

обвенча́|ть, ю *pf. of* ▶ венча́ть

обвенча́|ться, юсь *pf. of* ▶ венча́ться

обве|сти́, ду́, дёшь, *past* ~̃л, ~ла́ *pf.* (*of* ▶ обводи́ть) **1** (*провести вокруг*) to lead round, take round; **о. вокру́г па́льца** (*fig., infml*) to twist round one's little finger **2** (*очертить*) to outline; **о. чертёж ту́шью** to outline a sketch in ink

обве́тренный *adj.* (*скалы, лицо*) weather-beaten; (*губы*) chapped

обветша́|ть, ю *pf. of* ▶ ветша́ть

обвива́|ть, ю *impf. of* ▶ обви́ть

обвива́|ться, юсь *impf. of* ▶ обви́ться

обвине́ни|е, я *nt.* **1** charge, accusation; **по ~ю (в** + *p.*) on a charge (of) **2** (law) (*collect.*) the prosecution

обвини́тел|ь, я *m.* accuser; (law) prosecutor

обвини́тельный *adj.*: **о. пригово́р** verdict of 'guilty'

обвин|и́ть, ю́, и́шь *pf.* (*of* ▶ обвиня́ть) **1** (в + *p.*) to accuse (of), charge (with) **2** (law) to prosecute, indict

обвиня́ем|ый, ого *m.* (law) the accused; defendant

обвиня́|ть, я́ю *impf. of* ▶ обвини́ть

обви́|ть, обовью́, обовьёшь, *past* ~л, ~ла́, ~ло *pf.* (*of* ▶ обвива́ть) to wind (round), entwine; **о. ше́ю рука́ми** to throw one's arms round sb's neck

обви́|ться, обовью́сь, обовьёшься, *past* ~лся, ~ла́сь *pf.* (*of* ▶ обвива́ться) to wind round, twine round

обво|ди́ть, жу́, ~дишь *impf. of* ▶ обвести́

обвола́кива|ть, ю *impf. of* ▶ обволо́чь

обволо́|чь, ку́, чёшь, ку́т, *past* ~к, ~кла́ *pf.* (*of* ▶ обвола́кивать) to cover; to envelop (also *fig.*)

обворо́в|овать, у́ю *pf.* (*of* ▶ обворо́вывать) (infml) to rob

обворо́выва|ть, ю *impf. of* ▶ обворова́ть

обворожи́тел|ьный, ~ен, ~ьна *adj.* fascinating, charming, enchanting

обвя|за́ться, жу́сь, ~жешься *pf.* (*of* ▶ обвя́зываться) (+ *i.*) to tie round oneself; **о. верёвкой** to tie a rope round oneself

обвя́зыва|ться, юсь *impf. of* ▶ обвяза́ться

обгла́дыва|ть, ю *impf. of* ▶ обглода́ть

обгло|да́ть, жу́, ~жешь *pf.* (*of* ▶ обгла́дывать) to pick, gnaw round

обгова́рива|ть, ю *impf. of* ▶ обговори́ть

обговор|и́ть, ю́, и́шь *pf.* (*of* ▶ обгова́ривать) (infml) to discuss

обго́н, а *m.* passing, overtaking

обгоню́|ю, ~ишь *see* ▶ обогна́ть

обгоня́|ть, ю *impf. of* ▶ обогна́ть

обгор|а́ть, а́ю *impf. of* ▶ обгоре́ть

обгор|е́ть, ю́, и́шь *pf.* (*of* ▶ обгора́ть) to be burnt; (*на солнце*) to get burnt

обда|ва́ть, ю́, ёшь *impf. of* ▶ обда́ть

обд|а́ть, а́м, а́шь, а́ст, ади́м, ади́те, аду́т, *past* ~ал, ~ала́, ~ало *pf.* (*of* ▶ обдава́ть) (+ *i.*) **1** to pour over; **о. кого́-н. кипятко́м** to pour boiling water over sb **2** (*fig.*) to seize, cover; **меня́ ~ало хо́лодом** (*impers.*) I came over cold

обде́л|ать, аю *pf.* (*of* ▶ обде́лывать) (infml) **1** to finish; to dress (*leather, stone, etc.*); **о. драгоце́нные ка́мни** to set precious stones **2** (*fig.*) to manage, arrange; **о. свои́ дели́шки** to manage one's affairs with profit

обдел|и́ть, ю́, ~ишь *pf.* (*of* ▶ обделя́ть) (+ *a. and i.*) to do out of one's (fair) share (of); **он ~и́л сестёр насле́дством** he did his sisters out of their share of the legacy

обде́лыва|ть, ю *impf. of* ▶ обде́лать

обделя́|ть, я́ю *impf. of* ▶ обдели́ть

обдер|у́, ёшь *see* ▶ ободра́ть

обдира́|ть, ю *impf. of* ▶ ободра́ть

обду́ман|ный 1 (~, ~а) *p.p.p. of* ▶ обду́мать **2** (~, ~на) *adj.* well considered, carefully thought out обду́м|ать, аю *pf.* (*of* ▶ обду́мывать) to consider, think over

обду́мыва|ть, ю *impf. of* ▶ обду́мать

о́бе *see* ▶ о́ба

обега́|ть, ю *impf. of* ▶ обежа́ть

обе́д, а *m.* **1** lunch, dinner **2** (*время*) lunchtime, dinner time (= *midday*); пе́ред ∼ом before lunch, dinner; in the morning; по́сле ∼а after lunch, dinner; in the afternoon

обе́да|ть, ю *impf.* (*of* ▶ пообе́дать) to have lunch, dinner

обе́д|енный *adj. of* ▶ обе́д; ∼енное вре́мя lunch, dinner time; о. переры́в lunch hour, lunch break; о. стол dinner table

обе|жа́ть, гу́, жи́шь, гу́т *pf.* (*of* ▶ обега́ть) to run round

обезбо́ливание, я *nt.* anaesthetization (BrE), anesthetization (AmE)

обезбо́лива|ть, ю *impf. of* ▶ обезбо́лить

обезбо́лива|ющий *pres. part. act. of* ▶ обезбо́ливать; ∼ющее сре́дство anaesthetic (BrE), anesthetic (AmE)

обезбо́л|ить, ю, ишь *pf.* (*of* ▶ обезбо́ливать) to anaesthetize (BrE), anesthetize (AmE)

обезво́жен|ный, ∼, ∼а *adj.* dehydrated

обезвре́|дить, жу, дишь *pf.* (*of* ▶ обезвре́живать) (*человека*) to render harmless; (*бомбу*) to defuse; (*мину*) to deactivate

обезвре́жива|ть, ю *impf. of* ▶ обезвре́дить

обезгла́в|ить, лю, ишь *pf.* (*of* ▶ обезгла́вливать) **1** to behead, decapitate **2** (fig., *лишить главы*) to deprive of a head, of a leader

обезгла́влива|ть, ю *impf. of* ▶ обезгла́вить

обездо́лен|ный, ∼, ∼а *adj.* unfortunate, hapless

обезжи́ренный *adj.* fat-free; skimmed

обезопа́|сить, шу, сишь *pf.* (от + *g.*) to protect (against)

обезопа́|ситься, шусь, сишься *pf.* (от + *g.*) to secure oneself, protect oneself (against)

обезору́жива|ть, ю *impf. of* ▶ обезору́жить

обезору́ж|ить, у, ишь *pf.* (*of* ▶ обезору́живать) to disarm (also fig.)

обезу́ме|ть, ю *pf.* to lose one's senses, lose one's head; о. от испу́га to become panic-stricken

обезья́н|а, ы *f.* monkey; (*бесхвостая*) ape

обели́ск, а *m.* obelisk

оберега́|ться, юсь *impf. of* ▶ оберечься

обере́|чься, гу́сь, жёшься, гу́тся, *past* ∼гся, ∼гла́сь *pf.* (*of* ▶ оберега́ться) (от + *g.*) to guard oneself (from, against), protect oneself (from)

оберн|у́ть, у́, ёшь *pf.* (*of* ▶ обора́чивать) **1** (*шарф вокруг шеи*) to wind (round), twist (round) **2** (*посылки*) to wrap up

оберн|у́ться, у́сь, ёшься *pf.* (*of* ▶ обора́чиваться) **1** (*повернуться*) to turn; о. лицо́м to turn one's head **2** (*о делах*) to turn out; собы́тия ∼у́лись ина́че, чем мы ожида́ли events turned out otherwise than we expected **3** (infml, *сходить, съездить туда и обратно*) to (go and) come back; я ∼у́сь за два часа́ I shall be back in two hours

обёртк|а, и *f.* wrapper; (*книги*) dust jacket, dust cover

✎ обеспече́ни|е, я *nt.* **1** (*мира, успеха*) securing, guaranteeing; ensuring **2** (+ *i.*) (*углём*) providing (with), provision (of, with), supplying (of, with) **3** (*гарантия*) guarantee; security (= *pledge*) **4** (*материальные средства к жизни*) security; safeguard(s); социа́льное о. social security **5** (comput.): аппара́тное о. hardware; програ́ммное о. software

обеспе́ч|енный, ∼ен, ∼ена *p.p.p. of* ▶ обеспе́чить *and* (∼, ∼на) *adj.* well-to-do; well provided for

✎ обеспе́чива|ть, ю *impf. of* ▶ обеспе́чить

обеспе́ч|ить, у, ишь *pf.* (*of* ▶ обеспе́чивать) **1** (*семью; старость*) to provide for **2** (+ *i.*) (*снабдить чем-н.*) to provide (with), guarantee supply (of) **3** (*успех*) to secure, guarantee; to ensure

обеспоко́енный *adj.* worried, concerned

обесси́ле|ть, ю *pf.* to grow weak, lose one's strength

обесси́лива|ть, ю *impf. of* ▶ обесси́лить

обесси́л|ить, ю, ишь *pf.* (*of* ▶ обесси́ливать) to weaken

обесце́ненный *p.p.p. of* ▶ обесце́нить *and adj.* depreciated

обесце́нива|ть, ю, ет *impf. of* ▶ обесце́нить

обесце́нива|ться, ется *impf. of* ▶ обесце́ниться

обесце́н|ить, ю, ишь *pf.* (*of* ▶ обесце́нивать) to depreciate, cheapen

обесце́н|иться, ится *pf.* (*of* ▶ обесце́ниваться) to depreciate

обеща́ни|е, я *nt.* promise; дать, сдержа́ть, нару́шить о. to give, keep, break a promise (*or* one's word)

✎ обеща́|ть, ю *impf. and pf.* (*pf. also* ▶ пообеща́ть) to promise

обжа́л|овать, ую *pf.* (law) to appeal (against)

обжа́рива|ть, ю *impf. of* ▶ обжа́рить

обжа́р|ить, ю, ишь *pf.* (*of* ▶ обжа́ривать) (cul.) to fry on both sides, to brown all over

обжечь, обожгу́, обожжёшь, обожгу́т, *past* обжёг, обожгла́ *pf.* (*of* ▶ обжига́ть) **1** to burn, scorch; о. себе́ па́льцы to burn one's fingers (also fig.) **2** (*кирпич*) to fire, bake **3** (*о крапиве*) to sting

обже́чься, обожгу́сь, обожжёшься, обожгу́тся, *past* обжёгся, обожгла́сь *pf.* (*of* ▶ обжига́ться) (+ *i.* *or* на + *p.*) to burn oneself (on, with); о. горя́чим ча́ем to scald oneself with hot tea

обжига́|ть, ю *impf. of* ▶ обже́чь

обжига́|ться, юсь *impf. of* ▶ обже́чься

обжо́р|а, ы *c.g.* (infml) glutton

обжо́рств|о, а *nt.* gluttony

обзаве|сти́сь, ду́сь, дёшься, *past* ∼лся, ∼ла́сь *pf.* (*of* ▶ обзаводи́ться) (+ *i.*) (infml) to get oneself; to set up; **о. семьёй** to start a family; **о. хозя́йством** to set up home

обзаво|ди́ться, жу́сь, ∼дишься *impf. of* ▶ обзавести́сь

обзо́р, а *m.* **1** (*сжатое сообщение*) survey, review, overview **2** (mil.) field of view

обзо́р|ный *adj.* giving an overall view; ∼ная ле́кция, ∼ная статья́ survey

обзыва́|ть, ю *impf. of* ▶ обозва́ть

обива́|ть, ю *impf. of* ▶ оби́ть

оби́вк|а, и *f.* upholstery

оби́д|а, ы *f.* insult; (*чувство*) offence, (sense of) grievance, resentment; **затаи́ть** ∼у to nurse a grievance; **не дава́ть себя́ в** ∼у to (be able to) stick up for oneself

оби́|деть, жу, дишь *pf.* (*of* ▶ обижа́ть) **1** to offend; to hurt (the feelings of), wound **2** (*причинить ущерб*) to hurt; to do damage (to); **му́хи не** ∼дит (fig.) he would not harm a fly **3** (+ *i.*) (*наделить чем-л. недостаточно*) to stint, begrudge; **приро́да не** ∼**дела его́ тала́нтом** he has plenty of natural ability

оби́|деться, жусь, дишься *pf.* (*of* ▶ обижа́ться) (на + *a.*) to take offence (at); to feel hurt (by), resent

оби́д|ный, ∼ен, ∼на *adj.* **1** offensive; **мне** ∼но I feel hurt, it pains me **2** (*досадный*) annoying; ∼но (*impers.*) it is a pity, it is a nuisance; ∼но, что мы опозда́ли it is a pity that we are late

оби́дчив|ый, ∼, ∼а *adj.* touchy, sensitive

оби́дчик, а *m.* offender

обижа́|ть, ю *impf. of* ▶ оби́деть

обижа́|ться, юсь *impf.* (*of* ▶ оби́деться): **не** ∼**йтесь** don't be offended

оби́|женный *p.p.p of* ▶ оби́деть *and adj.* offended, aggrieved; **быть** ∼**женным (на** + *a.*) to have a grudge (against); **о. Бо́гом, о. приро́дой** (joc.) not over-blessed (with talents); ill-starred

оби́ли|е, я *nt.* abundance, plenty

оби́л|ьный, ∼ен, ∼ьна *adj.* abundant, plentiful; (+ *i.*) rich (in); ∼**ьное угоще́ние** lavish entertainment

обира́|ть, ю *impf. of* ▶ обобра́ть

обита́ем|ый, ∼, ∼а *adj.* inhabited

обита́тел|ь, я *m.* inhabitant

обита́|ть, ю *impf.* (в + *p.*) to live (in)

оби́|ть, обобью́, обобьёшь *pf.* (*of* ▶ обива́ть) (+ *i.*) to cover (with); **о. гвоздя́ми** to stud; **о. желе́зом** to bind with iron

обихо́д, а *m.* (*употребление*) use; **войти́ в о.** to come into (general) use; **вы́йти из** ∼а to go out of use, fall into disuse

обихо́д|ный, ∼ен, ∼на *adj.* everyday; ∼ное выраже́ние colloquial expression

обкла́дыва|ть, ю *impf. of* ▶ обложи́ть 1, ▶ обложи́ть 2, ▶ обложи́ть 3

обкра́дыва|ть, ю *impf. of* ▶ обокра́сть

обку́рен|ный, ∼, ∼а *adj.* (sl.) stoned (*from smoking marijuana, etc.*)

обла́в|а, ы *f.* (*на преступников*) raid; round-up

облага́|ть, ю *impf. of* ▶ обложи́ть 4

облада́тел|ь, я *m.* possessor

✍ **облада́|ть, ю** *impf.* (+ *i.*) to possess, have; **о. пра́вом** to have the right

о́блак|о, а, *pl.* ∼á, ∼óв *nt.* cloud; **вита́ть в** ∼áх (fig.) to be in the clouds

обла́мыва|ть, ю *impf. of* ▶ обломá́ть

обла́мыва|ться, юсь *impf. of* ▶ обломá́ться

✍ **областно́й** *adj.* regional

✍ **о́бласт|ь, и,** *g. pl.* ∼éй *f.* **1** (*административная единица*) oblast; province **2** (*часть страны*) region, district; belt **3** (fig., *отрасль*) field, sphere, realm, domain

о́блачность, и *f.* cloudiness; **переме́нная о.** overcast with sunny periods

о́блач|ный, ∼ен, ∼на *adj.* cloudy

облега́|ть, ю *impf.* (*об одежде*) to fit tightly; to cling to

облега́|ющий *adj.* tight-fitting

облегч|а́ть, а́ю *impf. of* ▶ облегчи́ть

облегч|а́ться, а́юсь *impf. of* ▶ облегчи́ться

облегче́ни|е, я *nt.* **1** (*действие*) facilitation, lightening, easing **2** (*чувство успокоения*) relief; **вздохну́ть с** ∼ем to heave a sigh of relief

облегч|и́ть, у́, и́шь *pf.* (*of* ▶ облегча́ть) **1** (*груз, вес*) to lighten **2** (*сделать менее трудным*) to make easier **3** (*упростить*) to simplify

облегч|и́ться, у́сь, и́шься *pf.* (*of* ▶ облегча́ться) (*стать более лёгким*) to become easier; to become lighter

обледене́|ть, ю *pf.* to ice over, become covered with ice

обле́зл|ый, ∼, ∼а *adj.* (infml) shabby, bare; ∼ая ко́шка mangy cat

облени́ва|ться, юсь *impf. of* ▶ облени́ться

облени́|ться, ю́сь, ∼ишься *pf.* (*of* ▶ обле́ниваться) to grow lazy

облеп|и́ть, лю́, ∼ишь *pf.* (*of* ▶ облепля́ть) **1** (*прилипнуть*) to stick (to); (fig.) to cling (to); (*окружить*) to surround, throng; **нас** ∼**и́ла ку́ча мальчи́шек** we were surrounded by a swarm of small boys **2** (+ *a. and i.*) (*заклеить*) to paste all over (with), plaster (with)

облепля́|ть, ю *impf. of* ▶ облепи́ть

облет|а́ть, а́ю *impf. of* ▶ облете́ть

обле|те́ть, чу́, ти́шь *pf.* (*of* ▶ облета́ть) **1** (+ *a. or* вокру́г + *g.*) to fly (round) **2** (*о новостях*) to spread (round, all over); **за полчаса́ весть о побе́де** ∼**те́ла весь го́род** in half an hour the news of the victory had spread round the town **3** (*о листьях*) to fall

облива́|ть, ю *impf. of* ▶ обли́ть

облива́|ться, юсь *impf.* (*of* ▶ обли́ться): **се́рдце у меня́ кро́вью** ∼**ется** my heart bleeds

O

облига́ци|я, и *f.* (fin.) bond, debenture

обли|за́ть, жу́, ∼жешь *pf.* (*of* ▶ обли́зывать) to lick (all over); to lick clean

обли|за́ться, жу́сь, ∼жешься *pf.* (*of* ▶ обли́зываться) **1** (*о человеке*) to smack one's lips (also fig.) **2** (*о животном*) to lick itself

обли́зыва|ть, ю *impf.* (*of* ▶ облиза́ть): о. гу́бы (fig., infml) to smack one's lips

обли́зыва|ться, юсь *impf. of* ▶ облиза́ться

о́блик, а *m.* look, appearance

обл|и́ть, оболью́, обольёшь, *past* ∼и́л, ∼ила́, ∼и́ло *and* ∼и́л, ∼ила́, ∼и́ло *pf.* (*of* ▶ облива́ть) (*намеренно*) to pour (over); (*случайно*) to spill (over); о. гря́зью (fig., infml) to vilify

обли́|ться, оболью́сь, обольёшься, *past* ∼лся, ∼ла́сь, ∼ло́сь *pf.* (*of* ▶ облива́ться) (+ *i.*) **1** to have a shower; to sponge down; о. холо́дной водо́й to have a cold shower **2** (*случайно*) to spill over oneself

облицо́вк|а, и *f.* facing, cladding

облич|а́ть, а́ю *impf.* (*of* ▶ обличи́ть) **1** (*разоблачать*) to expose, unmask, denounce **2** (*impf. only*) (*показывать*) to reveal, display, manifest; to point (to)

облич|и́ть, у́, и́шь *pf. of* ▶ облича́ть

облож|и́ть, у́, ∼ишь *pf.* **1** (*impf.* обкла́дывать) (*положить вокруг*) to put (round); to edge; о. больно́го поду́шками to surround a patient with pillows **2** (*impf.* обкла́дывать) (*покрыть*) to cover **3** (*impf.* обкла́дывать) (*окружить*) to surround **4** (*impf.* облага́ть) to assess; о. нало́гом to tax

обло́жк|а, и *f.* (dust) cover; (*для бумаг*) folder

облока́чива|ться, юсь *impf. of* ▶ облокоти́ться

облоко|ти́ться, чу́сь, ти́шься *pf.* (*of* ▶ облока́чиваться) (на + *a.*) to lean one's elbow(s) (on, against)

обло́м, а *m.* **1** (*действие*) breaking off **2** (*место*) break **3** (sl., *неудача*) failure, misfortune

облома́|ть, ю *pf.* (*of* ▶ обла́мывать) to break off, snap

облома́|ться, юсь *pf.* (*of* ▶ обла́мываться) **1** (*ветка*) to break off, snap **2** (sl.) to fail

облом|и́ть, лю́, ∼ишь *pf.* to break off

облом|и́ться, лю́сь, ∼ишься *pf.* = облом́аться

обло́м|ок, ка *m.* **1** fragment **2** (*in pl.*) debris, wreckage

облуче́ни|е, я *nt.* (med.) irradiation

облысе́|ть, ю, ешь *pf. of* ▶ лысе́ть

облюб|ова́ть, у́ю *pf.* (*of* ▶ облюбо́вывать) to pick, choose

облюбо́выва|ть, ю *impf. of* ▶ облюбова́ть

обма́|зать, жу, жешь *pf.* (*of* ▶ обма́зывать) to coat (with)

обма́зыва|ть, ю *impf. of* ▶ обма́зать

обма́кива|ть, ю *impf. of* ▶ обмакну́ть

обмак|ну́ть, ну́, нёшь, *past* ∼ну́л *pf.* (*of* ▶ обма́кивать) to dip

обма́н, а *m.* fraud, deception; о. зре́ния optical illusion

обман|у́ть, у́, ∼ешь *pf.* (*of* ▶ обма́нывать) to deceive; (*мошеннически*) to cheat, swindle; (*нарушить обещание*) to fail; to let sb down; о. чьи-н. наде́жды to disappoint sb's hopes

обман|у́ться, у́сь, ∼ешься *pf.* (*of* ▶ обма́нываться) to be deceived; о. в свои́х ожида́ниях to be disappointed in one's expectations

обма́нчив|ый, ∼, ∼а *adj.* deceptive, delusive; вне́шность ∼а appearances are deceptive

обма́нщик, а *m.* deceiver; cheat, fraud

обма́нщи|ца, цы *f. of* ▶ обма́нщик

обма́нрыва|ть, ю *impf. of* ▶ обмануть

обма́нрыва|ться, юсь *impf. of* ▶ обману́ться

обма́тыва|ть, ю *impf. of* ▶ обмота́ть

обма́тыва|ться, юсь *impf. of* ▶ обмота́ться

♂ обме́н, а *m.* (+ *i.*) exchange (of); о. мне́ниями exchange of opinions; о. веще́ств (biol.) metabolism; в о. (на + *a.*) in exchange (for)

обме́нива|ть, ю *impf. of* ▶ обменя́ть

обме́нива|ться, юсь *impf. of* ▶ обменя́ться

обме́нный *adj. of* ▶ обме́н

обмен|я́ть, я́ю *pf.* (*of* ▶ меня́ть 2, ▶ обме́нивать) (+ *a. and* на + *a.*) to exchange (sth for sth)

обмен|я́ться, я́юсь *pf.* (*of* ▶ меня́ться 2, ▶ обме́ниваться) (+ *i.*) to exchange; to swap; о. впечатле́ниями to compare notes

обме́рива|ть, ю *impf. of* ▶ обме́рить

обме́р|ить, ю, ишь *pf.* (*of* ▶ обме́ривать) (*измерить*) to measure

обмо́лв|иться, люсь, ишься *pf.* (infml) **1** (*оговориться*) to make a slip in speaking **2** (+ *i.*) (*сказать*) to say; to utter; не о. ни сло́вом (о + *p.*) to say not a word (about)

обмороже́ни|е, я *nt.* frostbite

обморо́|зить, жу, зишь *pf.*: я ∼зил себе́ нос, ру́ки my nose is, hands are, frostbitten

о́бморок, а *m.* fainting fit; упа́сть в о. to faint

обмота́|ть, ю *pf.* (*of* ▶ обма́тывать) (+ *a. and i., or* + *a. and* вокру́г + *g.*) to wind (round); о. ше́ю ша́рфом to wind a scarf round one's neck

обмота́|ться, юсь *pf.* (*of* ▶ обма́тываться) **1** (+ *i.*) to wrap oneself (in) **2** *pass. of* ▶ обмота́ть

обмундирова́ни|е, я *nt.* uniform

обнадёжива|ть, ю *impf. of* ▶ обнадёжить

обнадёж|ить, у, ишь *pf.* (*of* ▶ обнадёживать) to reassure

обнаж|а́ть, а́ю *impf. of* ▶ обнажи́ть

обнаж|а́ться, а́юсь *impf. of* ▶ обнажи́ться

обнажённый *p.p.p. of* ▶ обнажи́ть *and adj.* naked, bare; nude

обнаж|и́ть, у́, и́шь *pf.* (*of* ▶ обнажа́ть) **1** to bare, uncover; о. го́лову to bare one's head; о. шпа́гу to draw the sword **2** (fig., *раскры́ть*) to lay bare, reveal

обнаж|и́ться, у́сь, и́шься *pf. (of*
▶ **обнажа́ться*) **1** to bare oneself, uncover
oneself **2** (fig., *стать я́вным*) to be revealed

обнаро́д|овать, ую *impf. and pf.* (liter.) to
publish, promulgate (*esp. official documents*)

обнаруже́ни|е, я *nt.* **1** displaying, revealing
2 discovery; detection

♂ **обнару́жива|ть, ю** *impf. of* ▶ **обнару́жить**

обнару́жива|ться, юсь *impf. of*
▶ **обнару́житься**

обнару́ж|ить, у, ишь *pf. (of* ▶ **обнару́живать**)
1 (*показа́ть*) to display, reveal; **о. свою́
ра́дость** to betray one's joy **2** (*найти́*) to
discover; to detect

обнару́ж|иться, усь, ишься *pf. (of*
▶ **обнару́живаться**) **1** (*оказа́ться*) to be
revealed; to come to light **2** (*найти́сь*) to
turn up, be found

обнес|ти́, у́, ёшь, *past* **~́, ~ла́** *pf. (of*
▶ **обноси́ть**) (+ *i.*) to enclose (with); **о.
и́згородью** to fence (in)

обнима́|ть, ю *impf. of* ▶ **обня́ть**

обнима́|ться, юсь *impf. of* ▶ **обня́ться**

обнов|и́ть, лю́, и́шь *pf. (of* ▶ **обновля́ть**)
1 (*па́мятник*) to renovate; (*жизнь, ду́шу*)
to revitalize; (*го́речь*) to renew; (*гардеро́б,
репертуа́р,* also comput.) to update; to
replenish **2** (fig.) **о. свои́ зна́ния** (fig.) to refresh
one's knowledge

обнов|и́ться, лю́сь, и́шься *pf. (of*
▶ **обновля́ться**) to revive, be restored

обновле́ни|е, я *nt.* renovation; revitalization;
renewal; replenishment; (comput., *of software*)
upgrade, update; **вне́шнее о.** facelift

обновля́|ть, ю *impf. of* ▶ **обнови́ть**

обновля́|ться, юсь *impf. of* ▶ **обнови́ться**

обно|си́ть, шу́, ~́сишь *impf. of* ▶ **обнести́**

обню́х|ать, аю *pf. (of* ▶ **обню́хивать**) to
sniff (around)

обню́хива|ть, ю *impf. of* ▶ **обню́хать**

обн|я́ть, иму́, и́мешь, *past* **~я́л, ~яла́,
~я́ло** *pf. (of* ▶ **обнима́ть**) to embrace; to
clasp in one's arms; (fig.) to envelop; **он шёл,
~я́в её за та́лию** he was walking with his
arm round her waist

обн|я́ться, иму́сь, и́мешься, *past* **~я́лся,
~яла́сь, ~яло́сь** *pf. (of* ▶ **обнима́ться**) to
embrace; to hug (one another)

обо *prep.* = **о**

обобра́|ть, оберу́, оберёшь, *past* **~л, ~ла́,
~ло** *pf. (of* ▶ **обира́ть**) (infml) to rob, clean
out (infml)

обобща́|ть, áю *impf. of* ▶ **обобщи́ть**

обобще́ни|е, я *nt.* generalization

обобщ|и́ть, у́, и́шь *pf. (of* ▶ **обобща́ть**) to
generalize (from)

обога|ти́ть, щу́, ти́шь *pf. (of* ▶ **обогаща́ть**)
to enrich

обога|ти́ться, щу́сь, ти́шься *pf. (of*
▶ **обогаща́ться**) to become rich; (+ *i.*) to
enrich oneself (with)

обогаща́|ть, ю *impf. of* ▶ **обогати́ть**

обогаща́|ться, юсь *impf. of* ▶ **обогати́ться**

обогаще́ни|е, я *nt.* enrichment

обогн|а́ть, обгоню́, обго́нишь, *past* **~л,
~ла́, ~ло** *pf. (of* ▶ **обгоня́ть**) to pass,
overtake; (fig.) to outstrip, outdistance

обогн|у́ть, у́, ёшь *pf. (of* ▶ **огиба́ть**) to
round; to skirt

обогрева́тел|ь, я *m.* (tech.) heater

обогрева́|ть, ю *impf. of* ▶ **обогре́ть**

обогрева́|ться, юсь *impf. of* ▶ **обогре́ться**

обогре́|ть, ю, ешь *pf. (of* ▶ **обогрева́ть**)
(*помеще́ние*) to heat; (*челове́ка*) to warm

обогре́|ться, юсь, ешься *pf. (of*
▶ **обогрева́ться**) to warm oneself; (*о
помеще́нии*) to warm up

о́бод, а, *pl.* **~́ья, ~́ьев** *m.* (*колеса́*) rim;
(*бо́чки*) hoop

ободра́|ть, обдеру́, обдерёшь, *past*
обобра́л, обобрала́, обобра́ло *pf. (of*
▶ **обдира́ть**) **1** (*сте́ну, пру́тик*) to strip;
(*уби́того зве́ря*) to skin; (infml, *лицо́, ру́ку*)
to scratch; **о. ко́ру с де́рева** to bark a tree
2 (fig., infml) to fleece

ободр|и́ть, ю́, и́шь *pf. (of* ▶ **ободря́ть**) to
cheer up; to encourage, reassure

ободр|я́ть, я́ю *impf. of* ▶ **ободри́ть**

обожа́|ть, ю *impf.* to adore, worship

обож|гу́, жёшь, гу́т *see* ▶ **обже́чь**

обожжённый *p.p.p. of* ▶ **обже́чь**

обо́з, а *m.* convoy

обзва́|ть, обзову́, обзовёшь, *past* **~л,
~ла́, ~ло** *pf. (of* ▶ **обзыва́ть**) (+ *a. and i.*) to
call; **о. кого́-н. дурако́м** to call sb a fool

обознава́|ться, юсь, ёшься *impf. of*
▶ **обозна́ться**

обозна́|ться, юсь, ешься *pf. (of*
▶ **обознава́ться**) (infml) to take sb for sb else;
to be mistaken

обознача́|ть, а́ю *impf.* **1** (*no pf.*) (*зна́чить*)
to mean **2** (*pf.* **~и́ть**) (*отмеча́ть*) to mark
3 (*pf.* **~и́ть**) (*де́лать заме́тным*) to reveal;
to emphasize

обозначе́ни|е, я *nt.* **1** (*де́йствие*) marking
2 (*знак*) sign, symbol; **усло́вные ~я**
conventional signs, legend (*on maps, etc.*)

обознач|и́ть, у, ишь *pf. of* ▶ **обознача́ть** 3

обозрева́тел|ь, я *m.* commentator;
columnist

обозре́ни|е, я *nt.* **1** (*де́йствие*) surveying,
viewing; looking round **2** (*обзо́р*) survey;
overview

обо́|и, ев (*no sg.*) (also comput.) wallpaper;
окле́ить ~ями to paper

обо́йм|а, ы, *g. pl.* **~** *f.* (mil.) cartridge clip

обо|йти́, йду́, йдёшь, *past* **~шёл, ~шла́**
pf. (of ▶ **обходи́ть¹**) **1** (*пройти́, окружа́я,
минуя́*) to go round **2** (*пройти́ по всему́
простра́нству чего-л.*) to make the round
(of), go (all) round; (*о враче́*) to make
one's round(s); **слух ~шёл весь го́род**
the rumour spread all over the town
3 (*избежа́ть*) to avoid; to leave out; to pass
over; **о. зако́н** to get round (evade) a law

обо|йти́сь, йду́сь, йдёшься, *past* ~шёлся, ~шла́сь *pf.* (*of* ▸ обходи́ться) **1** (с + *i.*) to treat; пло́хо о. с ке́м-н. to treat sb badly **2** (infml) to cost, come to **3** (+ *i.*) to manage (with, on), make do (with, on) **4** (*закончиться*) to turn out, end; всё ~шло́сь everything worked out; всё ~шло́сь благополу́чно everything turned out all right

обокра́|сть, обкраду́, обкрадёшь, *past* ~л, ~ла *pf.* (*of* ▸ обкра́дывать) to rob

обо|лга́ть, лгу, лжёшь, *past* ~лга́л, ~лгала́, ~лга́ло *pf.* to slander

оболо́чк|а, и *f.* **1** (*скорлупа*) shell; (tech.) casing **2** (anat.) membrane; ра́дужная о. iris

оболь|сти́ться, щу́сь, сти́шься *pf.* (*of* ▸ обольща́ться) to be *or* labour (BrE), labor (AmE) under a delusion; (+ *i.*) to flatter oneself (with)

обольща́|ться, юсь *impf. of* ▸ обольсти́ться

оболью́, ёшь *see* ▸ обли́ть

обоня́ни|е, я *nt.* sense of smell; име́ть то́нкое о. to have a fine sense of smell

обора́чива|ть, ю *impf. of* ▸ оберну́ть

обора́чива|ться, юсь *impf. of* ▸ оберну́ться

оборв|а́ть, у́, ёшь, *past* ~а́л, ~ала́, ~а́ло *pf.* (*of* ▸ обрыва́ть) **1** (*цветы, яблоки*) to tear off, pluck **2** (*нитку*) to break; to snap **3** (fig., *разговор; человека*) to cut short, interrupt

оборв|а́ться, у́сь, ёшься, *past* ~а́лся, ~ала́сь, ~ало́сь *pf.* (*of* ▸ обрыва́ться) **1** (*о верёвке*) to break; to snap **2** (*о человеке*) to fall; (*о вещах*) to come away **3** (*о жизни, песне*) to be cut short, come abruptly to an end

обо́рк|а, и *f.* frill, flounce

оборо́н|а, ы (*no pl.*) *f.* defence (BrE), defense (AmE)

оборони́тельный *adj.* defensive

оборон|и́ть, ю́, и́шь *pf.* (*of* ▸ обороня́ть) to defend

оборон|и́ться, ю́сь, и́шься *pf.* (*of* ▸ обороня́ться) (от + *g.*) to defend oneself (from)

оборон|я́ть, я́ю *impf. of* ▸ оборони́ть

оборон|я́ться, я́юсь *impf. of* ▸ оборони́ться

◢ оборо́т, а *m.* **1** turn **2** (*употребление*) circulation; (fin., comm.) turnover; ввести́ в о. to put into circulation **3** (*обратная сторона*) back; смотри́ на ~е please turn over

оборо́т|ень, ня *m.* werewolf

оборо́т|ный *adj.* *of* ▸ оборо́т; о. капита́л (fin., comm.) working capital; ~ная сторона́ verso; reverse side (also fig.)

◢ обору́довани|е, я *nt.* **1** (*действие*) equipping **2** (*приборы*) equipment

обору́д|овать, ую *impf. and pf.* to equip, fit out

обоснова́ни|е, я *nt.* **1** (*действие*) substantiation **2** (*довод*) basis, ground

◢ key word

обосно́ванный *p.p.p. of* ▸ обоснова́ть *and adj.* well founded, well grounded

обосн|ова́ть, ую́, уёшь *pf.* (*of* ▸ обосно́вывать) to substantiate

обосн|ова́ться, ую́сь, уёшься *pf.* (*of* ▸ обосно́вываться) to settle

обосно́выва|ть, ю *impf. of* ▸ обоснова́ть

обосно́выва|ться, юсь *impf. of* ▸ обоснова́ться

обосо́бленный *adj.* isolated, solitary

обостре́ни|е, я *nt.* **1** (*чувств*) sharpening, intensification **2** (*боли*) aggravation, exacerbation; (*отношений*) straining; (*кризиса, конфликта*) worsening, deepening

обостр|и́ться, ю́сь, и́шься *pf.* (*of* ▸ обостря́ться) **1** (*об ощущениях*) to become more sensitive, become keener **2** (*о боли*) to become aggravated, become exacerbated; (*об отношениях*) to become strained; (*о кризисе, конфликте*) to worsen, deepen

обостр|я́ться, я́юсь *impf. of* ▸ обостри́ться

обо́чин|а, ы *f.* (*дороги*) edge, side; (*тротуара*) kerb (BrE), curb (AmE)

обою́д|ный, ~ен, ~на *adj.* mutual, reciprocal; по ~ному согла́сию by mutual consent

обраба́тыва|ть, ю *impf. of* ▸ обрабо́тать

обрабо́та|ть, ю *pf.* (*of* ▸ обраба́тывать) **1** (*кожу*) to treat, process; о. зе́млю to work the land; о. ра́ну to dress a wound **2** (*статью; голос*) to polish, perfect

◢ обрабо́тк|а, и *f.* **1** (*кожи*) treatment, processing; о. земли́ cultivation of land **2** (*статьи*) polishing

обра́д|овать, ую *pf. of* ▸ ра́довать

обра́д|оваться, уюсь *pf. of* ▸ ра́доваться

◢ о́браз, а *m.* **1** (*вид*) shape, form; appearance **2** (*представление*) image; мы́слить ~ами to think in images **3** (liter., *тип*) type; figure; о. Га́млета the Hamlet type **4** (*порядок*) mode, manner; way; о. жи́зни way of life, lifestyle; каки́м ~ом? how?; таки́м ~ом thus; гла́вным ~ом mainly, chiefly, largely

◢ образ|е́ц, ца́ *nt.* **1** model, pattern **2** (*товарный*) specimen, sample; (*материи*) pattern

о́браз|ный, ~ен, ~на *adj.* picturesque, vivid; (liter.) figurative; employing images

◢ образова́ни|е[1], я *nt.* (*действие*) formation

◢ образова́ни|е[2], я *nt.* (*обучение*) education

образо́ванный *p.p.p. of* ▸ образова́ть *and adj.*: о. челове́к educated person

◢ образова́тельный *adj.* educational

образ|ова́ть, у́ю *impf.* (*in pres. tense*), *and pf.* (*of* ▸ образо́вывать) to form; to make up

образ|ова́ться, у́ется *pf.* (*of* ▸ образо́вываться) to form; to arise

образо́выва|ть, ю, ет *impf. of* ▸ образова́ть

образо́выва|ться, ется *impf. of* ▸ образова́ться

образцо́вый *adj.* model; exemplary

обраст|а́ть, а́ю *impf. of* ▸ обрасти́

обраст|и́, у́, ёшь, *past* **обро́с, обросла́** *pf.* (*of* ▸ **обраста́ть**) (+ *i.*) **1** (*покрыться растительностью*) to become/be overgrown (with) **2** (fig., *создать вокруг себя*) to become/be surrounded (by); to acquire, accumulate

обрати́м|ый, ~, ~a *adj.* reversible

обра|ти́ть, щу́, ти́шь *pf.* (*of* ▸ **обраща́ть**) to turn; (**в** + *a.*) to turn (into); **о. внима́ние** (**на** + *a.*) to pay attention (to), take notice (of); **о. чьё-н. внима́ние** (**на** + *a.*) to call, draw sb's attention (to); **о. на себя́ внима́ние** to attract attention (to oneself)

ᐟ **обра|ти́ться, щу́сь, ти́шься** *pf.* (*of* ▸ **обраща́ться 1**) **1** to turn; **о. в бе́гство** to take to flight **2** (**к** + *d.*) to turn (to), appeal (to); to apply (to); to accost; **она́ не зна́ла, к кому́ о. за по́мощью** she did not know to whom to turn for help

обра́тно *adv.* **1** back; **туда́ и о.** there and back; **пое́здка туда́ и о.** round trip **2** (*наоборот*) conversely; inversely

ᐟ **обра́тн|ый** *adj.* **1** reverse; **о. а́дрес** sender's address; **о. биле́т** (BrE), round trip (AmE) ticket; **о. путь** return journey; **на ~ом пути́** on the way back **2** (*противоположный*) opposite; **в ~ую сто́рону** in the opposite direction **3** (math.) inverse; **~ое отноше́ние** inverse ratio

ᐟ **обраща́|ть, ю** *impf. of* ▸ **обрати́ть**

ᐟ **обраща́|ться, юсь** *impf.* **1** *impf. of* ▸ **обрати́ться 2** (physiol., econ., etc.) to circulate **3** (**с** + *i.*) to treat; **пло́хо о. с кем-н.** to treat sb badly, maltreat sb **4** (**с** + *i.*) (*пользоваться*) to handle, manage (*an inanimate object*)

ᐟ **обраще́ни|е, я** *nt.* **1** (**к** + *d.*) appeal (to), address (to) **2** (**в** + *a.*) conversion (to, into) **3** (econ.) circulation **4** (**с** + *i.*) treatment (of); **плохо́е о.** ill-treatment **5** (**с** + *i.*) (*пользование*) handling (of), use (of)

обреза́ни|е, я *nt.* (relig.) circumcision

обре́|зать, жу, жешь *pf.* (*of* ▸ **обреза́ть**) to clip, trim; to cut

обрез|а́ть, а́ю *impf. of* ▸ **обре́зать**

обре́|заться, жусь, жешься *pf.* (*of* ▸ **обреза́ться**) (*поранить себя*) to cut oneself

обрез|а́ться, а́юсь *impf. of* ▸ **обре́заться**

обрека́|ть, ю *impf. of* ▸ **обре́чь**

обре|ку́, чёшь, ку́т *see* ▸ **обре́чь**

обремени́тельный, ~ен, ~ьна *adj.* burdensome, onerous

обречённый *adj.* doomed

обре́|чь, ку́, чёшь, ку́т, *past* **~к, ~кла́** *pf.* (*of* ▸ **обрека́ть**) (**на** + *a.*) to condemn, doom (to)

обрис|ова́ть, у́ю *pf.* (*of* ▸ **обрисо́вывать**) to outline, delineate, depict (also fig.)

обрисо́выва|ть, ю *impf. of* ▸ **обрисова́ть**

обр|и́ть, е́ю, е́ешь *pf.* (*голову*) to shave; (*усы*) to shave off

обр|и́ться, е́юсь, е́ешься *pf.* to shave one's head

обруга́|ть, ю *pf. of* ▸ **руга́ть 2,** ▸ **руга́ть 3**

обрусе́|ть, ю *pf.* to become Russified, become Russianized

о́бруч, а, *pl.* **~и, ~е́й** *m.* (*на бочке; гимнастический*) hoop; (*для волос*) hairband

обруча́льн|ый *adj.*: **~ое кольцо́** wedding ring

обруч|а́ться, а́юсь *impf. of* ▸ **обручи́ться**

обруч|и́ться, у́сь, и́шься *pf.* (*of* ▸ **обруча́ться**) (**с** + *i.*) to become engaged (to)

обру́шива|ть, ю *impf. of* ▸ **обру́шить**

обру́шива|ться, юсь *impf. of* ▸ **обру́шиться**

обру́ш|ить, у, ишь *pf.* (*of* ▸ **обру́шивать**) to bring down, rain down

обру́ш|иться, усь, ишься *pf.* (*of* ▸ **обру́шиваться**) **1** (*о здании, крыше*) to come down, collapse, cave in **2** (fig.) (**на** + *a.*) to come down (upon), fall (upon)

обры́в, а *m.* **1** precipice **2** (tech.) break, rupture

обрыва́|ть, ю *impf. of* ▸ **оборва́ть**

обрыва́|ться, юсь *impf. of* ▸ **оборва́ться**

обры́в|ок, ка *m.* (*бумаги; разговора*) scrap; (*верёвки*) piece; (*песни, мелодии*) snatch

обры́зг|ать, аю *pf.* (*of* ▸ **обры́згивать**) (+ *i.*) (*водой*) to besprinkle (with); (*грязью*) to splash; to bespatter (with)

обры́згива|ть, ю *impf. of* ▸ **обры́згать**

обря́д, а *m.* rite, ceremony

обса|ди́ть, жу́, ~дишь *pf.* (*of* ▸ **обса́живать**) to plant round

обса́жива|ть, ю *impf. of* ▸ **обсади́ть**

обсервато́ри|я, и *f.* observatory

обсле́довани|е, я *nt.* (+ *g.*) (*осмотр*) inspection (of); (*в больнице*) observation, tests

обсле́д|овать, ую *impf. and pf.* (*произвести осмотр*) to inspect; (*исследовать*) to investigate; **о. больно́го** to examine a patient

ᐟ **обслу́живани|е, я** *nt.* service; (tech.) servicing, maintenance; **медици́нское о.** health service

обслу́жива|ть, ю *impf. of* ▸ **обслужи́ть**

обслуж|и́ть, у́, ~ишь *pf.* (*of* ▸ **обслу́живать**) to serve; **о. потреби́теля** to serve a customer

обсо́х|нуть, ну, нешь, *past* **~, ~ла** *pf.* (*of* ▸ **обсыха́ть**) to dry (off)

ᐟ **обстано́вк|а, и** *f.* **1** (*квартиры*) furniture; decor **2** (theatr.) set **3** (*положение*) situation **4** (*атмосфера*) atmosphere, environment

обстоя́тельный, ~ен, ~ьна *adj.* thorough, detailed

ᐟ **обстоя́тельств|о, а** *nt.* circumstance; **по незави́сящим от меня́ ~ам** for reasons beyond my control; **ни при каки́х ~ах** in no circumstances

обсто|я́ть, и́т *impf.* to be; to get on; **как ~и́т де́ло?** how is it going?; **вот как ~я́т дела́** that is the way it is; that's how matters stand

обстре́л, а *m.* firing, fire; **артилле́рийский о.** bombardment, shelling; **попа́сть под о.** to come under fire

О

обстре́лива|ть, ю *impf. of* ▸ обстреля́ть

обстрел|я́ть, я́ю *pf.* (*of* ▸ обстре́ливать) to fire (at, on); to bombard

обступ|а́ть, а́ю *impf. of* ▸ обступи́ть

обступ|и́ть, лю́, ~ишь *pf.* (*of* ▸ обступа́ть) to surround; to cluster (round)

обсу|ди́ть, жу́, ~дишь *pf.* (*of* ▸ обсужда́ть) to discuss; to consider

⚲ обсужда́|ть, ю *impf. of* ▸ обсуди́ть

⚲ обсужде́ни|е, я *nt.* discussion

обсу́шива|ть, ю *impf. of* ▸ обсуши́ть

обсу́шива|ться, юсь *impf. of* ▸ обсуши́ться

обсуш|и́ть, у́, ~ишь *pf.* (*of* ▸ обсу́шивать) to dry (out)

обсуш|и́ться, у́сь, ~ишься *pf.* (*of* ▸ обсу́шиваться) to dry oneself, get dry

обсчит|а́ть, а́ю *pf.* (*of* ▸ обсчи́тывать) to shortchange

обсчит|а́ться, а́юсь *pf.* (*of* ▸ обсчи́тываться) to make a mistake (*in counting*)

обсчи́тыва|ть, ю *impf. of* ▸ обсчита́ть

обсчи́тыва|ться, юсь *impf. of* ▸ обсчита́ться

обсыха́|ть, ю *impf. of* ▸ обсо́хнуть

обта́чива|ть, ю *impf. of* ▸ обточи́ть

обтека́ем|ый, ~, ~а *adj.* **1** (tech.) streamlined **2** (fig., infml) evasive

обтека́|ть, ю *impf. of* ▸ обте́чь

обтер|е́ть, оботру́, оботрёшь, *past* ~, ~ла *pf.* (*of* ▸ обтира́ть) **1** (*высушить*) to wipe; to wipe dry **2** (+ *i.*) (*натереть*) to rub all over (with)

обтер|е́ться, оботру́сь, оботрёшься, *past* ~ся, ~лась *pf.* (*of* ▸ обтира́ться) **1** (*обтереть себя*) to wipe oneself dry, dry oneself **2** (*водой*) to sponge down

обте́|чь, ку́, чёшь, ку́т, *past* ~к, ~кла́ *pf.* (*of* ▸ обтека́ть) **1** to flow round **2** (mil.) to bypass

обтира́ни|е, я *nt.* **1** sponge-down **2** (infml, *жидкость*) lotion

обтира́|ть, ю *impf. of* ▸ обтере́ть

обтира́|ться, юсь *impf. of* ▸ обтере́ться

обточ|и́ть, у́, ~ишь *pf.* (*of* ▸ обта́чивать) to grind smooth; (*на станке*) to turn

обтя́гивающий *adj.* skin-tight, figure-hugging

обува́|ть, ю *impf. of* ▸ обу́ть

обува́|ться, юсь *impf. of* ▸ обу́ться

обувно́й *adj. of* ▸ о́бувь; о. магази́н shoe shop

о́був|ь, и (*no pl.*) *f.* footwear; shoes

обу́глива|ться, юсь *impf. of* ▸ обу́глиться

обу́гл|иться, юсь, ишься *pf.* (*of* ▸ обу́гливаться) to become charred, char

обусло́влива|ться, ется *impf.* (+ *i.*) to be conditional (upon); to depend (on); разме́р ~ется тре́бованиями the size is conditioned by the requirements

обу́|ть, ю, ешь *pf.* (*of* ▸ обува́ть) **1**: о. кого́-н. to put sb's boots/shoes on for him/her

2 (infml, *снабдить обувью*) to provide with boots/shoes **3** (*сапоги*) to put on

обу́|ться, юсь, ешься *pf.* (*of* ▸ обува́ться) **1** (*надеть обувь*) to put on one's boots/shoes **2** (infml, *снабдить себя обувью*) to provide oneself with boots/shoes

обуча́|ть, а́ю *impf. of* ▸ обучи́ть

обуча́|ться, а́юсь *impf. of* ▸ обучи́ться

⚲ обуче́ни|е, я *nt.* teaching; instruction, training

обуч|и́ть, у́, ~ишь *pf.* (*of* ▸ учи́ть 1, ▸ обуча́ть) (*кого-н. чему-н.*) to teach (sb sth); to instruct, train (sb in)

обуч|и́ться, у́сь, ~ишься *pf.* (*of* ▸ учи́ться 1, ▸ обуча́ться) (+ *d.* or + *inf.*) to learn

обхо́д, а *m.* **1** (*врача, почтальона*) round **2** (*кружной путь*) roundabout way; bypass **3** (*уклонение*) evasion, circumvention (*of law, etc.*); в о. (+ *g.*) round, bypassing; (*минуя*) evading

обхо|ди́ть¹, жу́, ~дишь *impf. of* ▸ обойти́

обхо|ди́ть², жу́, ~дишь *pf.* (*город, друзей*) to go all round

обхо|ди́ться, жу́сь, ~дишься *impf. of* ▸ обойти́сь

обша́рива|ть, ю *impf. of* ▸ обша́рить

обша́р|ить, ю, ишь *pf.* (*of* ▸ обша́ривать) (infml) to ransack

обшива́|ть, ю *impf. of* ▸ обши́ть

обши́вк|а, и *f.* **1** (*воротника*) trim **2** (*корабля*) plating **3** (*дома*) cladding; (*стен*) panelling (BrE), paneling (AmE)

обши́р|ный, ~ен, ~на *adj.* extensive (also fig.); (*комната*) spacious; (*пространство*) vast

об|ши́ть, ошью́, ошьёшь *pf.* (*of* ▸ обшива́ть) **1** (*одежду*) to edge, trim **2** (*корабль*) to plate; (*дом*) to clad; (*стены*) to panel

обща́|ться, юсь *impf.* (с + *i.*) to associate (with), mix (with)

общедосту́п|ный, ~ен, ~на *adj.* **1** available to all **2** (*цены*) moderate **3** (*книга, лекция*) accessible, popular

общежи́ти|е, я *nt.* (*рабочее*) hostel; (*студенческое*) hall of residence (BrE), dormitory (AmE)

общеизве́ст|ный, ~ен, ~на *adj.* well known, generally known; (*преступник*) notorious

общенаро́д|ный, ~ен, ~на *adj.* national; public; о. пра́здник public holiday

⚲ обще́ни|е, я *nt.* relations, links; ли́чное о. personal contact

общеобразова́тельный *adj.* of general education

общепри́знан|ный, ~, ~а *adj.* universally recognized

общепри́нят|ый, ~, ~а *adj.* generally accepted

обще́ственност|ь, и *f.* (collect.) (the) public, the community; англи́йская о. the British public; нау́чная о. the scientific community

⚲ key word

ꙅ **обще́ственн|ый** *adj.* **1** social, public; ~ая жизнь public life; ~ое мне́ние public opinion **2** (*доброво́льный*) voluntary, unpaid; ~ые организа́ции voluntary organizations

ꙅ **о́бществ|о, а** *nt.* **1** society **2** (*компа́ния*) company; в ~е кого́-н. in sb's company; попа́сть в дурно́е о. to fall into bad company

обществове́дени|е, я *nt.* social science

общеупотреби́тел|ьный, ~ен, ~ьна *adj.* in general use

общечелове́ческий *adj.* common to all mankind

ꙅ **о́бщ|ий** *adj.* general; common; о. знако́мый mutual acquaintance; ~ее собра́ние general meeting; ~ая су́мма sum total

общи́н|а, ы *f.* (*о́бщество*) community; (*комму́на*) commune

общи́тел|ьный, ~ен, ~ьна *adj.* sociable

объеда́|ться, юсь *impf. of* ▸ объе́сться

ꙅ **объедине́ни|е, я** *nt.* **1** (*де́йствие*) unification; amalgamation **2** (*сою́з*) union, association

объединённый *p.p.p. of* ▸ объедини́ть *and adj.* united; Организа́ция Объединённых На́ций United Nations (Organization)

объедин|и́ть, ю́, и́шь *pf.* (*of* ▸ объединя́ть) (*люде́й*) to unite; (*организа́ции*) to amalgamate; о. уси́лия to combine efforts

объедин|и́ться, ю́сь, и́шься *pf.* (*of* ▸ объединя́ться) (с + *i.*) to unite (with); to amalgamate (with)

ꙅ **объедин|я́ть, я́ю** *impf. of* ▸ объедини́ть

объедин|я́ться, я́юсь *impf. of* ▸ объедини́ться

объе́д|ки, ков *m. pl.* (*sg.* ~ок, ~ка) (infml) leftovers, scraps

объе́зд, а *m.* **1** (*де́йствие*) travelling (BrE), traveling (AmE) round, riding round, going round **2** (*ме́сто*) detour, diversion (BrE); пое́хать в о. to make a detour

объе́з|дить¹, жу, дишь *pf.* (*of* ▸ объезжа́ть¹) (*страну́*) to travel all over; (*друзе́й*) to go round visiting

объе́з|дить², жу, дишь *pf.* (*of* ▸ объезжа́ть²) (*лошаде́й*) to break in

объезжа́|ть¹, ю *impf. of* ▸ объе́здить¹, ▸ объе́хать

объезжа́|ть², ю *impf. of* ▸ объе́здить²

ꙅ **объе́кт, а** *m.* **1** object **2** (mil.) objective **3** (*предприя́тие*) establishment; строи́тельный о. building site

объекти́в, а *m.* (optics) lens

объекти́вност|ь, и *f.* objectivity

объекти́в|ный, ~ен, ~на *adj.* objective

ꙅ **объём, а** *m.* volume (also fig.); (*величина́*) size

объём|ный, ~ен, ~на *adj.* **1** by volume, volumetric; (*изображе́ние*) three-dimensional **2** (*большо́й по объёму*) voluminous, bulky

объе́|сться, мся, шься, стся, ди́мся, ди́тесь, дя́тся, *past* ~лся *pf.* (*of* ▸ объеда́ться) to overeat

объе́|хать, ду, дешь *pf.* (*of* ▸ объезжа́ть¹) **1** (*боло́то*) to go round, skirt **2** (*всю*

страну́) to travel over

объяв|и́ть, лю́, ~ишь *pf.* (*of* ▸ объявля́ть) to declare, announce; о. войну́ to declare war

ꙅ **объявле́ни|е, я** *nt.* **1** declaration, announcement; (*вы́веска*) notice **2** (*рекла́мное*) advertisement; дать о. в газе́ту, помести́ть о. в газе́те to put an advertisement in a paper

объявля́|ть, ю *impf. of* ▸ объяви́ть

объясне́ни|е, я *nt.* explanation

объясн|и́ть, ю́, и́шь *pf.* (*of* ▸ объясня́ть) to explain

объясн|и́ться, ю́сь, и́шься *pf.* (*of* ▸ объясня́ться) **1** to explain oneself; (с + *i.*) to have a talk (with); to have it out (with); о. в любви́ (+ *d.*) to make a declaration of love (to) **2** (*найти́ себе́ объясне́ние*) to become clear, be explained

ꙅ **объясн|я́ть, я́ю** *impf. of* ▸ объясни́ть

объясн|я́ться, я́юсь *impf.* **1** *impf. of* ▸ объясни́ться **2** to speak; to make oneself understood; о. же́стами и зна́ками to use sign language **3** (+ *i.*) to be explained (by), be accounted for (by); э́тим ~я́ется его́ стра́нное поведе́ние that accounts for his strange behaviour

объя́ти|е, я *nt.* embrace; с распростёртыми ~ями with open arms

обыва́тел|ь, я *m.* philistine

обыва́тельский *adj.* philistine; narrow-minded

обыгр|а́ть, а́ю *pf.* (*of* ▸ обы́грывать) **1** (*сопе́рника*) to beat (*at a game*) **2** (theatr.) to use with (good) effect, play up; (fig., *оши́бку*) to turn to advantage, turn to account

обы́грыва|ть, ю *impf. of* ▸ обыгра́ть

обы́ден|ный, ~, ~на *adj.* ordinary; commonplace, everyday

обыкнове́нно *adv.* usually, as a rule

обыкнове́н|ный, ~ен, ~на *adj.* usual; ordinary; commonplace; ~ная исто́рия everyday occurrence

о́быск, а *m.* search; о́рдер на о. search warrant

обы́ска́ть, щу́, ~щешь *pf.* (*of* ▸ обы́скивать) to search

обы́скива|ть, ю *impf. of* ▸ обыска́ть

обы́ча|й, я *m.* custom

ꙅ **обы́чно** *adv.* usually; as a rule; как о. as usual

ꙅ **обы́ч|ный, ~ен, ~на** *adj.* usual; ordinary

ꙅ **обя́занност|ь, и** *f.* duty; responsibility; во́инская о. military service; исполня́ть ~и дире́ктора to act as director; исполня́ющий ~и дире́ктора acting director

ꙅ **обя́зан|ный, ~, ~а** *adj.* **1** (+ *inf.*) obliged, bound; он ~ верну́ться he is obliged to go back; it is his duty to go back **2** (+ *d.*) obliged, indebted (to); она́ вам ~а свое́й жи́знью she owes her life to you

ꙅ **обяза́тельно** *adv.* without fail; definitely; он о. там бу́дет he is sure to be there, he is bound to be there; не о. not necessarily

О

✎ **обязáтел|ьный, ~ен, ~ьна** *adj.* **1** obligatory; compulsory; binding; **~ное обучéние** compulsory education **2** (*человек*) reliable

✎ **обязáтельств|о, а** *nt.* **1** obligation; **взять на себя́ о.** (+ *inf.*) to commit oneself (to), undertake (to) **2** (*in pl.*) (law) liabilities

обя|зáться, жу́сь, ~жешься *pf.* (*of* ▶ **обя́зываться**) to bind oneself, pledge oneself, undertake

обя́зыва|ться, юсь *impf. of* ▶ **обязáться**

овáл, а *m.* oval

овáл|ьный, ~ен, ~ьна *adj.* oval

овáци|я, и *f.* ovation

Óве́н, Óвнá *m.* (astron., astrol.) Aries

ов|ёс, сá *m.* oats

овладевá|ть, ю *impf. of* ▶ **овладéть**

овладé|ть, ю *pf.* (*of* ▶ **овладевáть**) (+ *i.*) **1** (*взять*) to seize; to take possession (of); **о. собóй** to get control of oneself, regain self-control **2** (fig., *усвоить*) master

óвод, а, *pl.* **~ы, ~ов** (*and* **~á, ~óв**) *m.* gadfly

óвощ|и, éй *m. pl.* (*sg.* **~, ~а**) vegetables

овощнóй *adj.* vegetable; **о. магази́н** greengrocer's (shop)

оврáг, а *m.* ravine, gully

овся́нк|а, и *f.* (infml) **1** (*крупа*) oatmeal **2** (*каша*) porridge (BrE), oatmeal (AmE)

овся́н|ый *adj.* made of oats; oatmeal; **~ая кáша** (oatmeal) porridge (BrE), oatmeal (AmE); **~ая крупá** oatmeal

овц|á, ы́, *pl.* **~ы, овéц, ~áм** *f.* sheep; (*самка*) ewe

овчáрк|а, и *f.* sheepdog; **немéцкая о.** Alsatian (BrE), German shepherd (*dog*)

огибá|ть, ю *impf. of* ▶ **обогну́ть**

оглавлéни|е, я *nt.* table of contents

огла|си́ть, шу́, си́шь *pf.* (*of* ▶ **оглашáть**) (*объявить*) to proclaim, announce; **о. резолю́цию** to read out a resolution

оглáск|а, и *f.* publicity; **избегáть ~и** to shun publicity; **предáть ~е** to make public, make known

оглашá|ть, ю *impf. of* ▶ **огласи́ть**

оглóх|нуть, ну, нешь, *past* **~, ~ла** *pf. of* ▶ **глóхнуть 1**

оглуш|áть, áю *impf. of* ▶ **оглуши́ть 2**

оглуши́тел|ьный, ~ен, ~ьна *adj.* deafening

оглуш|и́ть, у́, и́шь *pf.* **1** *pf. of* ▶ **глуши́ть 1** **2** (*impf.* **~áть**) to deafen; (*ударом*) to stun (also fig.)

огля́дыва|ться, юсь *impf. of* ▶ **огляну́ться**

огля|ну́ться, ну́сь, ~нешься *pf.* (*of* ▶ **огля́дываться**) to turn (back) to look at sth; to glance back

óгнен|ный, ~, ~на *adj.* fiery (also fig.)

огнеопáс|ный, ~ен, ~на *adj.* inflammable

огнетуши́тел|ь, я *m.* fire extinguisher

огнеупóр|ный, ~ен, ~на *adj.* fire-resistant, fireproof

оговáрива|ть, ю *impf. of* ▶ **оговори́ть[1]**

оговáрива|ться, юсь *impf. of* ▶ **оговори́ться**

оговор|и́ть[1], ю́, и́шь *pf.* (*of* ▶ **оговáривать**) (*оклеветать*) to slander

оговор|и́ть[2], ю́, и́шь *pf.* (*of* ▶ **оговáривать**) **1** (*заранее условиться о чём-л.*) to stipulate (for); to fix, agree (on); **мы ~и́ли усло́вия рабо́ты** we have fixed the conditions of work **2** (*сделать оговорку*) to spell out; to specify

оговор|и́ться, ю́сь, и́шься *pf.* (*of* ▶ **оговáриваться**) **1** (*сделать оговорку*) to make a reservation, make a proviso **2** (*в речи*) to make a slip in speaking

оговóр|ка, ки *f.* **1** reservation, proviso; **он согласи́лся, но с не́которыми ~ками** he agreed but made certain reservations **2** (*в речи*) slip of the tongue

огол|и́ть, ю́, и́шь *pf.* (*of* ▶ **оголя́ть**) to bare; (*провод*) to strip; (*шашку*) to draw; **о. фланг** (mil.) to expose one's flank

огол|и́ться, ю́сь, и́шься *pf.* (*of* ▶ **оголя́ться**) **1** to strip (oneself) **2** (*о проводе*) to become exposed; (*о дереве*) to become bare

оголя́|ть, я́ю *impf. of* ▶ **оголи́ть**

оголя́|ться, я́юсь *impf. of* ▶ **оголи́ться**

✎ **ог|óнь, ня́** *m.* **1** (*пламя*) fire (also fig.) **2** (*свет*) light

огорáжива|ть, ю *impf. of* ▶ **огороди́ть**

огорóд, а *m.* kitchen garden, vegetable garden

огоро|ди́ть, жу́, ~ди́шь *pf.* (*of* ▶ **огорáживать**) to fence in, enclose

огорчá|ть, áю *impf. of* ▶ **огорчи́ть**

огорчá|ться, áюсь *impf. of* ▶ **огорчи́ться**

огорчéни|е, я *nt.* distress; chagrin

огорч|и́ть, у́, и́шь *pf.* (*of* ▶ **огорчáть**) to distress, upset

огорч|и́ться, у́сь, и́шься *pf.* (*of* ▶ **огорчáться**) to be distressed; **не ~áйтесь!** cheer up!

ограб|ить, лю, ишь *pf. of* ▶ **грáбить**

ограблéни|е, я *nt.* robbery; (*дома*) burglary

огра́д|а, ы *f.* (*забор*) fence; (*решётка*) railings

огра|ди́ть, жу́, ди́шь *pf.* (*of* ▶ **ограждáть**) (*от* + *g.*) to guard (against, from), protect (against)

огра|ди́ться, жу́сь, ди́шься *pf.* (*of* ▶ **ограждáться**) (*от* + *g.*) to defend oneself (against); to protect oneself (against)

ограждá|ть, ю *impf. of* ▶ **огради́ть**

ограждá|ться, юсь *impf. of* ▶ **огради́ться**

ограждéни|е, я *nt.* barrier

✎ **ограничéни|е, я** *nt.* limitation, restriction

ограни́ченный *p.p.p. of* ▶ **ограни́чить** *and adj.* limited; **о. человéк** (fig.) narrow(-minded) person

ограни́чива|ть, ю *impf. of* ▶ **ограни́чить**

ограни́чива|ться, юсь *impf. of* ▶ **ограни́читься**

ограничи́тельный *adj.* restrictive, limiting

ограни́ч|ить, у, ишь *pf.* (*of* ▶ **ограни́чивать**) to limit, restrict, cut down; **о. себя́ в**

о

расхо́дах to cut down one's expenditure

ограни́ч|иться, усь, ишься pf.
(of ▸ ограни́чиваться) (+ i.)
1 (удовлетвори́ться) to limit oneself (to), confine oneself (to) **2** (оста́ться в каки́х-л. преде́лах) to be limited (to), be confined (to)

⚘ **огро́м|ный, ~ен, ~на** adj. huge; vast; enormous

огрыза́|ться, а́юсь impf. (of ▸ огрызну́ться) (infml) (на + a.) to snap (at)

огрыз|ну́ться, ну́сь, нёшься pf. of ▸ огрыза́ться

огры́з|ок, ка m. (infml) (я́блока, соси́ски) leftover bit; (каранда́ша) stub

огур|е́ц, ца́ m. cucumber

о́д|а, ы f. ode

ода́лжива|ть, ю impf. of ▸ одолжи́ть

одарённый adj. gifted, talented

одева́|ть, ю impf. of ▸ оде́ть

одева́|ться, юсь impf. of ▸ оде́ться

⚘ **оде́жд|а, ы** f. clothes; clothing; ве́рхняя о. outer clothing, overcoat; мужска́я о. menswear; фо́рменная о. uniform

одеколо́н, а m. eau de cologne

одёргива|ть, ю impf. of ▸ одёрнуть

одержи́м|ый, ~, ~а adj. (+ i.) possessed (by); afflicted (by); о. стра́хом consumed with fear

одёр|нуть, ну, нешь pf. (of ▸ одёргивать)
1 (руба́шку, ю́бку) to pull down, straighten **2** (fig., infml, челове́ка) to call to order; to silence; to snub

оде́тый p.p.p. of ▸ оде́ть and adj. (+ i. or в + a.) dressed (in), clothed (in); with one's clothes on; хорошо́ о. well dressed

оде́|ть, ну, нешь pf. (of ▸ одева́ть) **1** (в + a.) to dress (in), clothe (in); о. ребёнка в брю́ки to dress a child in trousers; (+ i.) (покры́ть) to cover (with), wrap (in) **2** (снабди́ть оде́ждой) to clothe

оде́|ться, нусь, нешься pf. (of ▸ одева́ться) **1** to dress (oneself); to clothe oneself; о. в вече́рнее пла́тье to put on an evening dress **2** (покры́ться) (+ i.) to be covered with

одея́л|о, а nt. blanket

⚘ **оди́н, одного́,** f. **одна́, одно́й,** nt. **одно́, одного́,** pl. **одни́, одни́х** num. and pron.
1 (число́) one; одно́ one thing; о. за други́м one after the other, one by one; одни́... други́е some ..., (while) others; с одно́й стороны́... с друго́й (стороны́) on the one hand ... on the other hand; одно́ вре́мя at one time; о. раз once; одни́м сло́вом in a word **2** (не́кий) a, an; a certain; я встре́тил одного́ моего́ бы́вшего колле́гу I met an old colleague of mine **3** (без други́х) alone; by oneself; я живу́ о. I live alone **4** (без супру́ги) single **5** (infml, то́лько) only; она́ чита́ет одни́ детекти́вные рома́ны she reads nothing but detective stories **6** о., о. и тот же the same, one and the same; мы с ней одного́ во́зраста she and I are the same age

одина́ково adv. equally, alike

одина́ков|ый, ~, ~а adj. (с + i.) identical (with), the same (as)

оди́ннадцатый adj. eleventh

оди́ннадцат|ь, и num. eleven

одино́к|ий, ~, ~а adj. **1** solitary; lonely; lone **2** (as n. о., ~ого) single man, bachelor; (~ая, ~ой) single woman

одино́ко adv. lonely; чу́вствовать себя́ о. to feel lonely

одино́честв|о, а nt. solitude; loneliness

одино́чк|а, и c.g. lone person; мать-о. single mother; оте́ц-о. single father

одино́чн|ый adj. **1** (одного́ челове́ка) individual; one-man; ~ое заключе́ние solitary confinement **2** (отде́льный) solitary; single

одича́|ть, ю pf. of ▸ дича́ть

одна́жды adv. once; one day; о. у́тром (ве́чером, но́чью) one morning (evening, night)

⚘ **одна́ко** adv. and conj. however; but; though

⚘ **одновре́ме́нно** adv. simultaneously, at the same time

одновр|е́ме́нный, ~е́ме́нен, ~е́ме́нна adj. simultaneous

одногла́зый adj. one-eyed

однодне́вный adj. one-day

однозна́ч|ный, ~ен, ~на adj.
1 (тожде́ственный) synonymous **2** (fig., недвусмы́сленный) unambiguous; simple; straightforward

одноимён|ный, ~ен, ~на adj. of the same name

однокла́ссник, а m. classmate

однокла́ссни|ца, цы f. of ▸ однокла́ссник

одноку́рсник, а m. person in the same year of study

одноку́рсни|ца, цы f. of ▸ одноку́рсник

одноме́стный adj. single-seated, single-seater

одноно́гий adj. one-legged

однообра́з|ный, ~ен, ~на adj. monotonous

однопо́лый adj. of the same sex; о. брак same-sex marriage, gay marriage

однора́зовый adj. (шприц) disposable; (про́пуск) temporary, valid only once

однор́од|ный, ~ен, ~на adj. (одина́ковый во всех частя́х) homogeneous

однору́кий adj. one-armed

односельча́н|ин, ина, pl. **~е, ~** m. fellow villager

односельча́н|ка, ки f. of ▸ односельча́нин

односло́ж|ный adj. **1** monosyllabic **2** (ток) (fig.) terse, abrupt

односторо́нн|ий adj. **1** (ткань) one-sided (also fig.); (разоруже́ние, догово́р) unilateral **2** (ток) one-way; ~ее движе́ние one-way traffic; о. ум (fig.) one-track mind

одноти́п|ный, ~ен, ~на adj. of the same type, of the same kind; о. кора́бль sister ship

однофами́л|ец, ьца m. (с + i.) person having the same surname (as), namesake

однофами́л|ица, ицы f. of ▸ однофами́лец

о

одноцве́т|ный, ~ен, ~на *adj.* (*ткань*)
plain; (fig.) monochrome

одноэта́жный *adj.* single-storey (BrE),
single-story (AmE)

одобре́ни|е, я *nt.* approval

одобри́тел|ьный, ~ен, ~ьна *adj.*
approving; (*отзыв*) favourable (BrE),
favorable (AmE)

одо́бр|ить, ю, ишь *pf.* (*of* ▶ одобря́ть) to
approve (of); не о. to disapprove (of)

одобря́|ть, я́ю *impf. of* ▶ одо́брить

одолева́|ть, ю *impf. of* ▶ одоле́ть

одоле́|ть, ю *pf.* (*of* ▶ одолева́ть) **1** to
overcome, conquer; его́ ~л сон he was
overcome by sleepiness **2** (fig.) to master;
to cope (with); to get through

одолже́ни|е, я *nt.* favour (BrE), favor (AmE),
service; сде́лайте мне о. do me a favour
(BrE), favor (AmE)

одолж|и́ть, у́, и́шь *pf.* (*of* ▶ ода́лживать)
1 (+ *d.*) to lend **2** (infml) (у + *g.*) to borrow
(from)

одува́нчик, а *m.* (bot.) dandelion

оду́м|аться, аюсь *pf.* (*of* ▶ оду́мываться)
to change one's mind; to think better of it

оду́мыва|ться, юсь *impf. of* ▶ оду́маться

одура́чива|ть, ю *impf. of* ▶ одура́чить

одура́ч|ить, у, ишь *pf.* (*of* ▶ дура́чить,
▶ одура́чивать) (infml) to make a fool (of),
fool

одухотворённый *adj.* inspired; (*лицо́*)
spiritual

оды́шк|а, и *f.* short breath; страда́ть ~ой to
be short-winded

ожере́ль|е, я *nt.* necklace

ожесточа́|ть, а́ю *impf. of* ▶ ожесточи́ть

ожесточа́|ться, а́юсь *impf. of*
▶ ожесточи́ться

ожесточе́ни|е, я *nt.* bitterness

ожесточённый *p.p.p. of* ▶ ожесточи́ть *and*
adj. (*бой, спор*) bitter; (*челове́к*) embittered;
hardened

ожесточ|и́ть, у́, и́шь *pf.* (*of* ▶ ожесточа́ть)
to embitter; to harden

ожесточ|и́ться, у́сь, и́шься *pf.* (*of*
▶ ожесточа́ться) to become embittered; to
become hardened

ожива́|ть, ю *impf. of* ▶ ожи́ть

ожив|и́ть, лю́, и́шь *pf.* (*of* ▶ оживля́ть)
1 (*челове́ка*) to revive **2** (fig.) (*о́бщество, ве́чер*) to liven up,
enliven; (*торго́влю*) to revitalize; (*лицо́,
карти́ну*) to brighten up

ожив|и́ться, лю́сь, и́шься *pf.* (*of*
▶ оживля́ться) **1** (*челове́к, разгово́р*) to
become animated, liven (up); (*взгляд*) to
brighten up **2** (*у́лица*) to come to life

оживле́ни|е, я *nt.* **1** (*состоя́ние*) animation,
gusto **2** (*де́йствие*) reviving; enlivening

оживлённый *p.p.p. of* ▶ ожи́вить *and adj.*
animated; lively

оживля́|ть, ю *impf. of* ▶ оживи́ть

оживля́|ться, юсь *impf. of* ▶ оживи́ться

ожида́ни|е, я *nt.* expectation; waiting;
обману́ть ~я to disappoint; в ~и (+ *g.*)
pending; сверх ~я beyond expectation

◆ **ожида́|ть**, ю *impf.* (+ *g.*) to wait (for);
(*предви́деть*) to expect, anticipate; как я и
~л just as I expected

ожире́ни|е, я *nt.* obesity

ож|и́ть, иву́, иве́шь, *past* ~ил, ~ила́, ~ило
pf. (*of* ▶ ожива́ть) to come to life, revive
(also fig.)

ожо́г, а *m.* burn; (*жи́дкостью, па́ром*) scald

озабо́|тить, чу, тишь *pf.* to trouble, worry

озабо́ченност|ь, и *f.* anxiety

озабо́чен|ный, ~, ~а *p.p.p. of* ▶ озабо́тить
and (~, ~на) *adj.* anxious, worried

озагла́в|ить, лю, ишь *pf.* (*of*
▶ озагла́вливать) to entitle; (*гла́ву, разде́л*)
to head

озагла́влива|ть, ю *impf. of* ▶ озагла́вить

озада́ченный, ~ен, ~ена *p.p.p. of*
▶ озада́чить *and* (~ен, ~енна) *adj.*
perplexed, puzzled

озада́чива|ть, ю *impf. of* ▶ озада́чить

озада́ч|ить, у, ишь *pf.* (*of* ▶ озада́чивать) to
perplex, puzzle, take aback

озвере́|ть, ю *impf. of* ▶ звере́ть

озву́чива|ть, ю *impf. of* ▶ озву́чить

озву́ч|ить, у, ишь *pf.* (*of* ▶ озву́чивать)
1 (cin.) to add a soundtrack to **2** (infml,
выска́зать) to state, formulate

◆ **о́зер|о**, а, *pl.* озёра, озёр *nt.* lake

ози́м|ый *adj.* winter; (*as pl. n.* ~ые, ~ых)
winter crops

◆ **означа́|ть**, ет *impf.* to mean, signify, stand
for; что ~ют э́ти бу́квы? what do these
letters stand for?

озно́б, а *m.* shivering; chill; почу́вствовать о.
to feel shivery

озо́н, а *m.* ozone

озо́н|овый *adj. of* ▶ озо́н; ~овая дыра́
ozone hole; о. слой ozone layer

озорно́й *adj.* (infml) mischievous

озорств|о́, а́ *nt.* (infml) mischief

озя́б|нуть, ну, нешь, *past* ~, ~ла *pf.* (infml)
to be cold; я ~! I am frozen!

ой *and* **ой-ой-о́й** *int* (*выража́ет удивле́ние,
удово́льствие*) oh; (*выража́ет боль*) ow,
ouch!; (*выража́ет удивле́ние со́бственной
оши́бки*) oops!

оказа́ни|е, я *nt.* rendering (*of first aid, etc.*)

ока|за́ть, жу́, ~жешь *pf.* (*of* ▶ ока́зывать)
to render, show; о. влия́ние (на + *a.*)
to influence, exert influence (upon); о.
де́йствие (на + *a.*) to have an effect (upon);
to take effect; о. по́мощь (+ *d.*) to help, give
(sb) help; о. услу́гу (+ *d.*) to do, render (sb) a
service; to do (sb) a good turn

◆ **ока|за́ться**, жу́сь, ~жешься *pf.* (*of*
▶ ока́зываться) **1** to turn out (to be), prove
(to be) **2** (*очути́ться*) to find oneself; to be

found; **я ~за́лся в больни́це** I found myself in hospital

ꟷ **ока́зыва|ть, ю** *impf. of* ▶ **оказа́ть**

ꟷ **ока́зыва|ться, юсь** *impf. of* ▶ **оказа́ться**

окайм|и́ть, лю́, и́шь *pf.* (*of* ▶ **окаймля́ть**) (+ *i.*) to border (with), edge (with)

окаймля́|ть, ю *impf. of* ▶ **окайми́ть**

окамене́|ть, ю *pf. of* ▶ **камене́ть**

ока́нчива|ть, ю, ет *impf. of* ▶ **око́нчить**

ока́нчива|ться, ется *impf. of* ▶ **око́нчиться**

ока|ти́ть, чу́, ~́тишь *pf.* (*of* ▶ **ока́чивать**) to pour (over); **о.** **холо́дной водо́й** to pour cold water (over) (also fig.)

ока|ти́ться, чу́сь, ~́тишься *pf.* (*of* ▶ **ока́чиваться**) to pour over oneself

ока́чива|ть, ю *impf. of* ▶ **окати́ть**

ока́чива|ться, юсь *impf. of* ▶ **окати́ться**

ока́янный *adj.* damned, cursed

океа́н, а *m.* ocean

Океа́ни|я, и *f.* Oceania (*the islands of the Pacific and adjacent seas*)

океа́нский *adj.* ocean; oceanic; **о. парохо́д** ocean(-going) liner

о́кис|ь, и *f.* (chem.) oxide

оккупа́ци|я, и *f.* (mil.) occupation

оккупи́р|овать, ую *impf. and pf.* (mil.) to occupy

окла́д, а *m.* salary

оклеве|та́ть, щу́, ~́щешь *pf. of* ▶ **клевета́ть**

окле́ива|ть, ю *impf. of* ▶ **окле́ить**

окле́|ить, ю, ишь *pf.* (*of* ▶ **окле́ивать**) (+ *i.*) to cover (with); to paste over (with); **о. ко́мнату обо́ями** to paper a room

оклика́|ть, а́ю *impf. of* ▶ **окли́кнуть**

окли́к|нуть, ну, нешь *pf.* (*of* ▶ **оклика́ть**) to hail, call (to)

ꟷ **окн|о́, а́, о́кон, ~а** *nt.* **1** (also comput.) window; **диало́говое о.** (comput.) dialog box **2** (fig., *отверстие*) gap, break

око́в|ы, ~ (*no sg.*) fetters (also fig.)

ꟷ **о́коло** *prep.* + *g. and adv.* **1** (*рядом, возле*) by; (*вблизи*) close (to), near; (*вокруг*) around, about **2** (*приблизительно*) about; **о. полу́ночи** about midnight

око́нн|ый *adj. of* ▶ **окно́**; **~ая ра́ма** window frame; **~ое стекло́** windowpane

ꟷ **оконча́ни|е, я** *nt.* (*завершение*) completion, conclusion; (*конец*) end; **о. сро́ка** expiration; **по ~и университе́та** on graduating; (gram.) ending

оконча́тельно *adv.* (*бесповоротно*) finally, definitively; (*совершенно*) completely

оконча́тел|ьный, ~ен, ~ьна *adj.* (*бесповоротный*) final, definitive; (*совершенный*) complete

око́нч|ить, у, ишь *pf.* (*of* ▶ **ока́нчивать**) to finish, end; **о. шко́лу** to leave school (BrE), to graduate from high school (AmE); **о. университе́т** to graduate

око́нч|иться, ится *pf.* (*of* ▶ **ока́нчиваться**) to finish, end; to be over

око́п, а *m.* (mil.) trench; entrenchment

о́коро|к, ка, *pl.* **~ка́** *m.* ham; (*баранины, телятины*) leg

око́шко, ка, ка, *pl.* **~ки, ~ек, ~кам** *nt.* window

ОКР (*abbr. of* **обсесси́вно-компульси́вное расстро́йство**) (med.) OCD (*obsessive-compulsive disorder*)

окра́ин|а, ы *f.* **1** (*города*) outskirts; outlying districts; (*леса, деревни*) edge **2** (*in pl.*) (*страны*) border areas

окра́|сить, шу, сишь *pf.* (*of* ▶ **окра́шивать**) (*стену, крышу*) to paint; (*ткань, волосы*) to dye; (*жизнь*) to colour (BrE), color (AmE); **слегка́ о.** to tinge, tint

окра́ск|а, и *f.* **1** (*действие*) painting; dyeing **2** (*цвет*) colouring (BrE), coloring (AmE), coloration; **защи́тная о.** (zool.) protective coloration **3** (fig.) tinge, tint; (pol.) slant

окра́шива|ть, ю *impf. of* ▶ **окра́сить**

окре́п|нуть, ну, нешь, *past* **~, ~ла** *pf. of* ▶ **кре́пнуть**

окре|сти́ть, щу́, ~́стишь *pf. of* ▶ **крести́ть 1**

окре́стност|ь, и *f.* (*usu. in pl.*) **1** (*столицы, деревни*) environs **2** (*окружающее пространство*) neighbourhood (BrE), neighborhood (AmE), vicinity

о́крик, а *m.* shout, cry

окрова́влен|ный, ~, ~а *adj.* bloodstained; bloody

ꟷ **о́круг, а,** *pl.* **~а́** *m.* region, district; circuit; **избира́тельный о.** electoral district

окру́г|а, и *f.* (infml) neighbourhood (BrE), neighborhood (AmE)

округл|и́ть, ю́, и́шь *pf.* (*of* ▶ **округля́ть**) (*счёт, цифры*) to express in round numbers

окру́гл|ый, ~, ~а *adj.* rounded; (*лицо*) round

округля́|ть, я́ю *impf. of* ▶ **округли́ть**

окружа́|ть, а́ю *impf. of* ▶ **окружи́ть**

ꟷ **окружа́|ющий** *pres. part. act. of* ▶ **окружа́ть** *and adj.* surrounding; (*as nt. n.* **~ющее, ~ющего**) environment; (**~ющие, ~ющих**) the people around/surrounding one

окруже́ни|е, я *nt.* **1** (*действие*) encirclement **2** (*среда*) surroundings; environment; milieu; **в ~и** (+ *g.*) surrounded (by), in the midst (of); (*люди*) the people around/surrounding one

окруж|и́ть, у́, и́шь *pf.* (*of* ▶ **окружа́ть**) to surround; to encircle; **о. кого́-н. забо́тами** to lavish attentions on sb

окружн|о́й *adj.* **1** *adj. of* ▶ **о́круг**; **о. суд** circuit court **2** operating (situated) about a circle; **~а́я желе́зная доро́га** circle line

окру́жност|ь, и *f.* circumference; (*замкнутая кривая*) circle

О́ксфорд, а *m.* Oxford

окта́в|а, ы *f.* (mus.) octave

ꟷ **октя́бр|ь, я́** *m.* October (fig.) (= *Russian revolution of October 1917*)

октя́брьский *adj. of* ▶ **октя́брь**

окули́ст, а *m.* ophthalmic optician

окуля́р, а *m.* eyepiece

окуна́|ть, а́ю *impf. of* ▶ **окуну́ть**

окун|а́ться, а́юсь *impf. of* ▶ окну́ться

окну́|ть, у́, ёшь *pf.* (*of* ▶ окуна́ть) to dip

окну́|ться, у́сь, ёшься *pf.* (*of* ▶ окуна́ться) **1** to dip (oneself) **2** (*fig.*) (в + *a.*) to plunge (into), become (utterly) absorbed (in), engrossed (in)

о́кун|ь, я, *pl.* ∼и, ∼ей *m.* (zool.) perch; морско́й о. redfish, North Atlantic rockfish

окуп|а́ть, а́ю *impf. of* ▶ окупи́ть

окуп|а́ться, а́юсь *impf. of* ▶ окупи́ться

окуп|и́ть, лю́, ∼ишь *pf.* (*of* ▶ окупа́ть) to compensate, repay, make up (for); о. расхо́ды to cover one's outlay

окуп|и́ться, лю́сь, ∼ишься *pf.* (*of* ▶ окупа́ться) to be compensated, be repaid; (*fig.*) to pay; to be justified, be requited, be rewarded; затра́ченные на́ми уси́лия ∼и́лись our efforts were rewarded

оку́р|ок, ка *m.* (*сигаре́ты*) butt

оку́т|ать, аю *pf.* (*of* ▶ оку́тывать) (+ *i.*) **1** to wrap up (in) **2** (*fig.*) to shroud, cloak (in)

оку́т|аться, аюсь *pf.* (*of* ▶ оку́тываться) (+ *i.*) **1** to wrap oneself up (in) **2** (*fig.*) to shroud, cloak oneself (in); о. та́йной to shroud oneself in mystery

оку́тыва|ть, ю *impf. of* ▶ оку́тать

оку́тыва|ться, юсь *impf. of* ▶ оку́таться

ола́д|ья, ьи, *pl.* ∼ьи, ∼ий *f.* fritter; карто́фельная о. potato cake

оледене́|ть, ю *pf. of* ▶ ледене́ть

олени́н|а, ы *f.* venison

оле́н|ь, я *m.* deer; благоро́дный о. stag, red deer; се́верный о. reindeer

оли́вк|а, и *f.* olive

оли́вков|ый *adj.* **1** olive; ∼ое ма́сло olive oil **2** (*цвет*) olive-green

олига́рх, а *m.* oligarch

олимпиа́д|а, ы *f.* **1** (**О.**) (*олимпи́йские и́гры*) Olympics **2** (*соревнова́ния*) Olympiad

олимпи́йский *adj.* Olympic; О∼е и́гры Olympic Games, Olympics

олицетворе́ни|е, я *nt.* personification

олицетвор|и́ть, ю́, и́шь *pf.* (*of* ▶ олицетворя́ть) to personify

олицетвор|я́ть, я́ю *impf. of* ▶ олицетвори́ть

о́лов|о, а *nt.* tin

оловя́нн|ый *adj.* tin; ∼ая фо́льга tin foil

О́льстер, а *m.* Ulster

ольх|а́, и́, *pl.* ∼и *f.* alder (tree)

ома́р, а *m.* lobster

омерзи́тел|ьный, ∼ен, ∼ьна *adj.* loathsome, disgusting

омле́т, а *m.* omelette (BrE), omelet (AmE)

ОМО́Н *m. indecl.* (*abbr. of* отря́д мили́ции осо́бого назначе́ния) special forces unit; riot squad

омо́нов|ец, ца *m.* member of the special force

ОМП (*abbr. of* ору́жие ма́ссового пораже́ния) WMD (*weapons of mass destruction*)

⚔ key word

омрач|а́ть, а́ю *impf. of* ▶ омрачи́ть

омрач|а́ться, а́юсь *impf. of* ▶ омрачи́ться

омрач|и́ть, у́, и́шь *pf.* (*of* ▶ омрача́ть) to darken, cloud

омрач|и́ться, у́сь, и́шься *pf.* (*of* ▶ омрача́ться) to darken, become clouded (also *fig.*)

о́мут, а *m.* **1** (*водоворо́т*) whirlpool; (*fig.*) maelstrom **2** (*глубо́кое ме́сто*) deep place (*in river or lake*)

⚔ он, его́, ему́, им, о нём *pers. pron.* he

⚔ она́, её, ей, ей (е́ю), о ней *pers. pron.* she

онани́зм, а *m.* masturbation

онда́тр|а, ы *f.* muskrat, musquash

онеме́|ть, ю *pf. of* ▶ неме́ть

⚔ они́, их, им, и́ми, о них *pers. pron.* they

о́никс, а *m.* (min.) onyx

онко́лог, а *m.* oncologist

онкологи́ческий *adj.* oncological

онколо́ги|я, и *f.* oncology

⚔ онла́йн, а *m.*, *adv.*, *adj. indecl.* (comput.): в ∼е (*or* (в режи́ме) о.) online; ба́нковские опера́ции в режи́ме о. online banking; о.-кинотеа́тр online cinema

онла́йновый *adj.* (comput.) online

⚔ оно́, его́, ему́, им, о нём *pers. pron.* **1** it **2** (*э́то*) this, that; о. и ви́дно that is evident **3** (*as emph. particle*): вот о. что! oh, I see!

ООН *f. indecl.* (*abbr. of* Организа́ция Объединённых На́ций) UN (*United Nations Organization*)

⚔ ООО (*abbr. of* о́бщество с ограни́ченной отве́тственностью) Ltd

опада́|ть, ет *impf. of* ▶ опа́сть

опа́здыва|ть, ю *impf. of* **1** *impf. of* ▶ опозда́ть **2** (*impf. only*) (infml, *о часа́х*) to be slow

опа́л, а *m.* opal

опа́лива|ть, ю *impf. of* ▶ опали́ть

опал|и́ть, ю́, и́шь *pf.* (*of* ▶ опа́ливать) to singe

опаса́|ться, юсь *impf.* **1** (+ *g.*) (*боя́ться*) to fear, be afraid (of) **2** (+ *g. or inf.*) (*избега́ть*) to beware (of); to avoid, keep off

опасе́ни|е, я *nt.* fear; apprehension

⚔ опа́сность, и *f.* danger; peril; вне ∼и out of danger

⚔ опа́с|ный, ∼ен, ∼на *adj.* dangerous, perilous

опа́|сть, дёт *pf.* (*of* ▶ опада́ть) **1** (*о ли́стьях*) to fall (off) **2** (*об о́пухоли*) to go down; (*о суфле́*) to sink

ОПЕ́К *f. indecl.* OPEC (*abbr. of Organization of Petroleum Exporting Countries* — *Организа́ция стран - экспортёров не́фти*)

опе́к|а, и *f.* guardianship (also *fig.*); (*над иму́ществом*) trusteeship; взять под ∼у to take into one's care; (*fig.*) to take charge (of)

опека́|ть, ю *impf.* **1** (*сиро́т*) to be guardian (to) **2** (*fig.*, *мла́дших*) to take care of

опеку́н, а́ *m.* (law) guardian; (*над иму́ществом*) trustee

опеку́н|ша, ши *f.* (infml) *of* ▶ опеку́н

о́пер|а, ы *f.* opera; **«мы́льная о.»** soap (opera)

операти́вник, а *m.* detective

операти́в|ный *adj.* **1** (~ен, ~на)
(*руководство*) efficient **2** (*штаб, работа*)
executive **3** (med.) surgical **4** (comput.): ~ная
па́мять random-access memory

⚹ **опера́тор, а** *m.* **1** (*оборудования*) operator
2 (*кинооператор*) cameraman **3** (comput.)
computer operator

опера|цио́нный *adj.* of ▶ **опера́ция**;
~цио́нная систе́ма (comput.) operating
system; **о. стол** operating table; **о. зал**
(**на би́рже**) (fin.) trading floor; (*as f. n.*
~цио́нная, ~цио́нной) operating theatre
(BrE), operating room (AmE)

⚹ **опера́ци|я, и** *f.* (med., mil., etc.) operation;
перенести́ ~ю to have an operation; to be
operated (upon); **сде́лать** ~ю to perform
an operation

опере|ди́ть, жу́, ди́шь *pf.* (*of* ▶ **опережа́ть**)
1 (*в беге, в развитии*) to outstrip, leave
behind **2** (*успеть раньше*) to forestall

опережа́|ть, ю *impf.* of ▶ **опереди́ть**

опере́ни|е, я *nt.* plumage

опере́тт|а, ы *f.* musical comedy, operetta

опере́|ться, обопру́сь, обопрёшься, *past*
опёрся, оперла́сь *pf.* (*of* ▶ **опира́ться**)
1 (**на** + *a.* or **о** + *a.*) to lean (on; against); **о.
о подоко́нник** to lean against the window
sill **2** (fig.) to rely on; to depend on

опери́р|овать, ую *impf. and pf.* **1** (med.) to
operate (upon) **2** (mil.) to operate, act
3 (+ *i.*) (fin.) to deal (in); (fig.) to use, handle;
о. недоста́точными да́нными to operate
with inadequate data

опеча́т|ка, ки *f.* misprint; **спи́сок** ~ок (list
of) errata

опира́|ться, юсь *impf.* of ▶ **опере́ться**

⚹ **описа́ни|е, я** *nt.* description; account; **э́то не
поддаётся** ~ю it is beyond description

опи|са́ть, шу́, ~**шешь** *pf.* (*of* ▶ **опи́сывать**)
1 to describe **2** (*сделать опись*) to list,
inventory

опи́ск|а, и *f.* slip of the pen

⚹ **опи́сыва|ть, ю** *impf.* of ▶ **описа́ть**

о́пис|ь, и *f.* list; inventory; **о. иму́щества** (law)
distraint

о́пиум, а *m.* opium

опла́|кать, чу, чешь *pf.* (*of* ▶ **опла́кивать**) to
mourn (over); to bewail, bemoan

опла́кива|ть, ю *impf.* of ▶ **опла́кать**

⚹ **опла́т|а, ы** *f.* pay, payment

опла|ти́ть, чу́, ~**тишь** *pf.* to pay (for); **о.
счёт** to settle the account, the bill; **о.
убы́тки** to pay damages

опла́чива|ть, ю *impf.* of ▶ **оплати́ть**

опла́|чу, чешь *see* ▶ **опла́кать**

опла|чу́, ~**тишь** *see* ▶ **оплати́ть**

оплеу́х|а, и *f.* (infml) slap in the face

оплодотворе́ни|е, я *nt.* fertilization

оплодотвор|и́ть, ю́, и́шь *pf.* (*of*
▶ **оплодотворя́ть**) to fertilize

оплодотвор|я́ть, я́ю *impf. of*
▶ **оплодотвори́ть**

опломбир|ова́ть, у́ю *pf.*
▶ **пломбирова́ть 1**

опло́шност|ь, и *f.* blunder

опове|сти́ть, щу́, сти́шь *pf.* (*of* ▶ **оповеща́ть**)
to notify, inform

оповеща́|ть, ю *impf.* of ▶ **оповести́ть**

опозда́ни|е, я *nt.* lateness; delay; **без** ~я on
time; **с** ~ем **на де́сять мину́т** ten minutes
late

опозда́|ть, ю *pf.* (*of* ▶ **опа́здывать 1**) to be
late; **о. на ле́кцию** to be late for the lecture;
о. на полчаса́ to be half an hour late

опозна|ва́ть, ю́, ~**ёшь** *impf.* of ▶ **опозна́ть**

опозна́ни|е, я *nt.* (law) identification

опозна́|ть, ю *pf.* (*of* ▶ **опознава́ть**) to identify

опозо́р|ить, ю, ишь *pf.* of ▶ **позо́рить**

опозо́р|иться, юсь, ишься *pf.* of
▶ **позо́риться**

ополо́скива|ть, ю *impf.* of ▶ **ополосну́ть**

о́ползе|нь, ня *m.* landslide, landslip

ополосн|у́ть, у́, ёшь *pf.* (*of* ▶ **ополо́скивать**)
to rinse

ополче́н|ец, ца *m.* militiaman; home guard

ополче́ни|е, я *nt.* **1** militia; home guard
2 (*collect.*) (hist.) irregulars; levies

опо́мн|иться, юсь, ишься *pf.* (*прийти в
созна́ние*) to come round; (*одуматься*) to
come to one's senses

опо́р|а, ы *f.* support (also fig.); (*моста*) pier

опорожн|и́ть, ю́, и́шь *pf.* (*of* ▶ **опорожня́ть**)
to empty

опорожн|я́ть, ю *impf.* of ▶ **опорожни́ть**

оппози́ци|я, и *f.* opposition

оппоне́нт, а *m.* opponent

опра́в|а, ы *f.* frame; (*очков*) frames

оправда́ни|е, я *nt.* **1** justification
2 (*извинение*) excuse **3** (law) acquittal,
discharge

оправда́тельный *adj.*: **о. пригово́р** verdict
of 'not guilty'

оправда́|ть, а́ю *pf.* (*of* ▶ **опра́вдывать**)
1 (*показать себя достойным*) to justify,
warrant; **о. ожида́ния** to come up to
expectations **2** (*извинить*) to excuse
3 (law) to acquit, discharge

оправда́|ться, а́юсь *pf.* (*of* ▶ **опра́вдываться
1**) **1** to justify oneself **2** to be justified;
на́ши опасе́ния ~а́лись our fears have been
confirmed

опра́вдыва|ть, ю *impf.* (*of* ▶ **оправда́ть**):
о. незна́нием (law) to plead ignorance

опра́вдыва|ться, юсь *impf.* **1** *impf.*
of ▶ **оправда́ться 2** to try to justify *or*
vindicate oneself

опра́шива|ть, ю *impf.* of ▶ **опроси́ть**

⚹ **определе́ни|е, я** *nt.* (*понятия*) definition;
(chem., phys., etc.) determination

⚹ **определён|ный,** ~**ен,** ~**на** *adj.* **1** (*точно
установленный*) definite; fixed **2** (*некоторый*)

О

certain; **в ~ных слу́чаях** in certain cases

определ|и́ть, ю́, и́шь *pf.* (*of* ▶ **определя́ть**) (*поня́тие*) to define; (*установи́ть*) to determine; (*назна́чить*) to fix, appoint

определ|и́ться, ю́сь, и́шься *pf.* (*of* ▶ **определя́ться**) to be formed; to take shape; to be determined

✓ **определ|я́ть, я́ю** *impf. of* ▶ **определи́ть**

✓ **определ|я́ться, я́юсь** *impf. of* ▶ **определи́ться**

опро́б|овать, ую *pf.* to test

опроверг|а́ть, а́ю *impf. of* ▶ **опрове́ргнуть**

опрове́рг|нуть, ну, нешь, *past* ~ *and* ~**нул,** ~**ла** *pf.* (*of* ▶ **опроверга́ть**) to refute, disprove

опроверже́ни|е, я *nt.* refutation; disproof; denial

опроки́дыва|ть, ю *impf. of* ▶ **опроки́нуть**

опроки́дыва|ться, юсь *impf. of* ▶ **опроки́нуться**

опроки́|нуть, ну, нешь *pf.* (*of* ▶ **опроки́дывать**) (*ча́шку*) to knock over; (*ло́дку*) to overturn

опроки́|нуться, нусь, нешься *pf.* (*of* ▶ **опроки́дываться**) (*о стака́не*) to fall over, topple over; (*о ло́дке*) to capsize

опроме́тчив|ый, ~, ~**а** *adj.* precipitate, hasty

опро́с, а *m.* (*свиде́телей*) questioning; **о. обще́ственного мне́ния** opinion poll

опро|си́ть, шу́, ~**сишь** *pf.* (*of* ▶ **опра́шивать**) (*свиде́телей*) to question; (*обще́ственное мне́ние*) to canvass, survey

опроти́ве|ть, ю *pf.* to become loathsome, become repulsive

опры́ск|ать, ю *pf.* (*of* ▶ **опры́скивать**) (+ *i.*) to sprinkle (with); to spray (with)

опры́ск|аться, аюсь *pf.* (*of* ▶ **опры́скиваться**) (+ *i.*) to sprinkle oneself (with); to spray oneself (with)

опры́скива|ть, ю *impf. of* ▶ **опры́скать**

опры́скива|ться, юсь *impf. of* ▶ **опры́скаться**

опря́т|ный, ~**ен,** ~**на** *adj.* neat, tidy

о́птик|а, и *f.* **1** (*разде́л фи́зики*) optics **2** (*collect.*) optical instruments

✓ **оптима́л|ьный,** ~**ен,** ~**ьна** *adj.* optimum, optimal

оптими́зм, а *m.* optimism

оптими́ст, а *m.* optimist

оптимисти́ч|ный, ~**ен,** ~**на** *adj.* optimistic

оптими́ст|ка, ки *f. of* ▶ **оптими́ст**

опти́ческ|ий, ~**ая** optic, optical; ~**ое волокно́** optical fibre (BrE), fiber (AmE); **о. обма́н** optical illusion

оптови́к, а́ *m.* wholesaler

опто́вый *adj.* wholesale

о́птом *adv.* wholesale; **о. и в ро́зницу** wholesale and retail

опублик|ова́ть, у́ю *pf.* (*of* ▶ **публикова́ть,** ▶ **опублико́вывать**) to publish; **о. зако́н to**

promulgate a law

✓ **опублико́outlinewa|ть, ю** *impf. of* ▶ **опубликова́ть**

опуска́|ть, ю *impf. of* ▶ **опусти́ть**

опуска́|ться, юсь *impf. of* ▶ **опусти́ться**

опусте́|ть, ет *pf. of* ▶ **пусте́ть**

опу|сти́ть, щу́, ~**стишь** *pf.* (*of* ▶ **опуска́ть**) **1** (*што́ры*) to lower; to let down; **о. глаза́** to look down; **о. ру́ки** (fig.) to lose heart **2** (*воротни́к*) to turn down

опу|сти́ться, щу́сь, ~**стишься** *pf.* (*of* ▶ **опуска́ться**) **1** to lower oneself; **о. в кре́сло** to sink into a chair; **о. на коле́ни** to go down on one's knees **2** (*о со́лнце*) to sink, go down **3** (fig., *вне́шне, мора́льно*) to let oneself go; to go to pieces

опустош|а́ть, а́ю *impf. of* ▶ **опустоши́ть**

опустош|и́ть, у́, и́шь *pf.* (*of* ▶ **опустоша́ть**) to devastate, lay waste, ravage

опу́т|ать, аю *pf.* (*of* ▶ **опу́тывать**) to enmesh, entangle (also fig.); (fig.) to ensnare

опу́тыва|ть, ю *impf. of* ▶ **опу́тать**

опух|а́ть, а́ю *impf. of* ▶ **опу́хнуть**

опу́х|нуть, ну, нешь, *past* ~, ~**ла** *pf.* (*of* ▶ **опуха́ть**) to swell (up)

о́пухол|ь, и *f.* swelling; (med.) tumour (BrE), tumor (AmE); **о. мо́зга** brain tumour (BrE), tumor (AmE)

✓ **о́пыт, а** *m.* **1** experience; **на ~е, по ~у** by experience **2** (*экспериме́нт*) experiment; test, trial; (*попы́тка*) attempt

о́пытность, и *f.* experience

о́пыт|ный *adj.* **1** (~**ен,** ~**на**) (*челове́к*) experienced **2** (*эксперимента́льный*) experimental; **узна́ть ~ным путём** to learn by means of experiment

опьяне́ни|е, я *nt.* intoxication

опьяне́|ть, ю *pf. of* ▶ **пьяне́ть**

✓ **опя́ть** *adv.* again

ора́кул, а *m.* oracle

орангута́н, а and **орангута́нг, а** *m.* orang-utan

ора́нжевый *adj.* orange (*colour*)

оранжере́|я, и *f.* hothouse, greenhouse, conservatory

ора́тор, а *m.* orator, (public) speaker

ор|а́ть, у́, ёшь *impf.* (infml) to bawl, yell

орби́т|а, ы *f.* (astron., also fig.) orbit; **вы́вести на ~у** to put into orbit

орга́зм, а *m.* orgasm, climax

✓ **о́рган, а** *m.* (biol., pol., etc.) organ; ~**ы вла́сти** organs of government; **половы́е ~ы** genitals

орга́н, а *m.* (mus.) organ

✓ **организа́тор, а** *m.* organizer

✓ **организа́ци|я, и** *f.* organization; **О. Объединённых На́ций** United Nations Organization

✓ **органи́зм, а** *m.* organism

организо́ван|ный adj., ~**а** *p.p.p. of* ▶ **организова́ть** and (~, ~**на**) adj. organized; ~**ная престу́пность** organized crime

организ|ова́ть, у́ю *impf. and pf.* to organize

✔ организо́выва|ть, ю *impf. of* ▸ организова́ть
органи́ст, а *m.* organist
органи́ст|ка, ки *f. of* ▸ органи́ст
органи́ч|ный, ~ен, ~на *adj.* organic
о́рги|я, и *f.* orgy
оргте́хник|а, и *f. (abbr. of* организацио́нная
те́хника) office equipment
о́рден¹, а, *pl.* ~а́, ~о́в *m.* (*знак отличия*)
order; decoration
о́рден², а, *pl.* ~ы, ~ов *m.* (*организация*)
order; иезуи́тский о. Society of Jesus
о́рдер, а, *pl.* ~а́, ~о́в *m.* order, warrant; (law)
writ; о. на о́быск search warrant
ор|ёл, ла́ *m.* eagle; о. и́ли ре́шка? heads or
tails?
орео́л, а *m.* halo, aureole
оре́х, а *m.* **1** (*плод*) nut; гре́цкий о. walnut;
коко́совый о. coconut; лесно́й о. hazelnut
2 (*дерево*) nut tree **3** (*древесина*) walnut
оригина́льность|ь, и *f.* originality
✔ оригина́л|ьный, ~ен, ~ьна *adj.* original
ориента́ци|я, и *f.* (на + *a.*) orientation
(towards)
ориенти́р, а *m.* reference point; guiding line;
(есте́ственный) о. landmark
ориенти́р|овать, ую *impf. and pf.* (*pf. also*
▸ сориенти́ровать) to orient, orientate
ориенти́р|оваться, уюсь *impf. and pf.* (*pf.
also* ▸ сориенти́роваться) to orient oneself;
to find one's bearings (also fig.)
ориентиро́вочно *adv.* tentatively;
approximately
орке́стр, а *m.* orchestra; (*духовой,
джазовый*) band
оркестро́вк|а, и *f.* orchestration
оркестро́вый *adj.* orchestral
орна́мент, а *m.* ornament
орнито́лог, а *m.* ornithologist
орнитоло́ги|я, и *f.* ornithology
ороше́ни|е, я *nt.* irrigation; поля́ ~я sewage
farm (BrE), sewage plant (AmE)
ортодокса́л|ьный, ~ен, ~ьна *adj.* orthodox
ортопе́д, а *m.* orthopaedist (BrE), orthopedist
(AmE)
ортопеди́ческий *adj.* orthopaedic (BrE),
orthopedic (AmE)
ору́ди|е, я *nt.* **1** instrument; implement; tool
(also fig.) **2** (*артиллери́йское*) gun
оружено́с|ец, ца *m.* armour-bearer, sword-
bearer; (fig.) henchman
✔ ору́жи|е, я *nt.* weapon; (*collect.*) arms,
weapons
орфогра́фи|я, и *f.* orthography, spelling
орхиде́|я, и *f.* (bot.) orchid
ос|а́, ы́, *pl.* ~ы f. wasp
оса́д|а, ы f. siege; снять ~у to raise a siege
оса́д|и́ть, жу́, ди́шь *pf.* (*of* ▸ осажда́ть)
to besiege, lay siege to; to beleaguer; о.
про́сьбами to bombard with requests
оса́д|ок, ка *m.* **1** (*in pl.*) (*атмосфе́рные*)
precipitation **2** (*частицы*) sediment,
deposit

осажда́|ть, ю *impf. of* ▸ осади́ть
оса́нк|а, и *f.* carriage, bearing
осва́ива|ть, ю *impf. of* ▸ осво́ить
осва́ива|ться, юсь *impf. of* ▸ осво́иться
осве́дом|ить, лю, ишь *pf.* (*of* ▸ осведомля́ть)
to inform
осве́дом|иться, люсь, ишься *pf.* (*of*
▸ осведомля́ться) (о + *a.*) to inquire (about)
осведом|ля́ть, ля́ю *impf. of* ▸ осве́домить
осведом|ля́ться, ля́юсь *impf. of*
▸ осве́домиться
осве́ж|а́ть, а́ю *impf. of* ▸ освежи́ть
освежи́тел|ьный, ~ен, ~ьна *adj.* refreshing
освеж|и́ть, у́, и́шь *pf.* (*of* ▸ освежа́ть) to
refresh, revive
освети́тел|ь, я *m.* lighting technician
освети́тельный *adj.* lighting, illuminating;
о. прибо́р light
осве|ти́ть, щу́, ти́шь *pf.* (*of* ▸ освеща́ть) to
light up; to illuminate; (fig.) to throw light
on; (*в пре́ссе*) to cover, report
осве|ти́ться, щу́сь, ти́шься *pf.* (*of*
▸ освеща́ться) to light up; to brighten
освеща́|ть, ю *impf. of* ▸ освети́ть
освеща́|ться, юсь *impf. of* ▸ освети́ться
освеще́ни|е, я *nt.* light, lighting,
illumination; (*в пре́ссе*) coverage;
электри́ческое о. electric light
освещённый *p.p.p. of* ▸ освети́ть; о. луно́й
moonlit
освободи́тел|ь, я *m.* liberator
освобо|ди́ть, жу́, ди́шь *pf.* (*of*
▸ освобожда́ть) **1** (*город, страну,
человека*) to free, liberate; (*заключённого;
животное*) to release, set free **2** (*от
должности*) to dismiss **3** (*кварти́ру*) to
vacate; (*место; полку от книг*) to clear,
empty
освобо|ди́ться, жу́сь, ди́шься *pf.* (*of*
▸ освобожда́ться) **1** (от + *g.*) to free
oneself (of, from); to become free **2** *pass. of*
▸ освободи́ть
освобожда́|ть, ю *impf. of* ▸ освободи́ть
освобожда́|ться, юсь *impf. of*
▸ освободи́ться
освобожде́ни|е, я *nt.* (*города*) liberation;
(*заключённого*) release
освобождённый *p.p.p. of* ▸ освободи́ть; о.
от нало́га tax-free, exempt from tax
осво́|ить, ю, ишь *pf.* (*of* ▸ осва́ивать) to
assimilate, master; to cope (with); to become
familiar (with)
осво́|иться, юсь, ишься *pf.* (*of*
▸ осва́иваться) **1** (с + *i.*) to familiarize
oneself (with) **2** to feel at home; о. в но́вой
среде́ to get the feel of new surroundings
освя|ти́ть, щу́, ти́шь *pf.* (*of* ▸ освяща́ть)
(eccl.) to bless
освяща́|ть, ю *impf. of* ▸ освяти́ть
оседа́|ть, ю *impf. of* ▸ осе́сть
ос|ёл, ла́ *m.* donkey; ass (also fig.)
осе́нний *adj. of* ▸ о́сень; autumnal

O

ꙮ **о́сен|ь, и** *f.* autumn

о́сенью *adv.* in autumn

ос|е́сть, я́ду, я́дешь, *past* ~**е́л,** ~**е́ла** *pf.*
(*of* ▶ оседа́ть) **1** (*о зда́нии*) to subside; (*о
пыли, оса́дке*) to settle **2** (*о лю́дях*) to settle

осети́н, а, *g. pl.* **о.** *m.* Ossetian

осети́н|ка, ки *f. of* ▶ осети́н

осети́нский *adj.* Ossetian

осётр, á *m.* sturgeon

осетри́н|а, ы *f.* (flesh of) sturgeon

осе́чк|а, и *f.* misfire; **дать** ~**у** to misfire
(also fig.)

оси́н|а, ы *f.* aspen

оска́лива|ть, ю *impf. of* ▶ оска́лить

оска́лива|ться, юсь *impf. of* ▶ оска́литься

оска́л|ить, ю, ишь *pf.* (*of* ▶ оска́ливать): **о.**
зу́бы to bare one's teeth

оска́л|иться, юсь, ишься *pf.* (*of*
▶ оска́ливаться) to bare one's teeth

оскверн|и́ть, ю́, и́шь *pf.* (*of* ▶ оскверня́ть)
to defile; to profane

оскверн|я́ть, я́ю *impf. of* ▶ оскверни́ть

оско́л|ок, ка *m.* splinter; fragment

оскорби́тел|ьный, ~**ен,** ~**ьна** *adj.*
insulting, abusive

оскорб|и́ть, лю́, и́шь *pf.* (*of* ▶ оскорбля́ть)
to insult, offend

оскорбле́ни|е, я *nt.* insult

оскорбля́|ть, ю *impf. of* ▶ оскорби́ть

ослабева́|ть, ю *impf. of* ▶ ослабе́ть

ослабе́|ть, ю *pf.* (*of* ▶ слабе́ть, ▶ ослабева́ть)
(*о челове́ке, стране́, реши́тельности*)
to weaken, grow weak, become weak;
(*о внима́нии, кана́те, напряже́нии*) to
slacken; (*о шу́ме, ве́тре*) to abate

осла́б|ить, лю, ишь *pf.* (*of* ▶ ослабля́ть)
1 to weaken **2** (*сде́лать ме́нее натя́нутым*)
to slacken, relax; to loosen; **о. внима́ние** to
relax one's attention; **о. по́яс** to loosen a belt

ослабля́|ть, ю *impf. of* ▶ осла́бить

осла́б|нуть, ну, нешь, *past* ~, ~**ла** *pf.*
= ослабе́ть

ослепи́тел|ьный, ~**ен,** ~**ьна** *adj.* blinding,
dazzling

ослеп|и́ть, лю́, и́шь *pf.* (*of* ▶ ослепля́ть) to
blind, dazzle (also fig.)

ослепле́ни|е, я *nt.* **1** blinding, dazzling
2 (fig.) blindness

ослепля́|ть, ю *impf. of* ▶ ослепи́ть

осле́п|нуть, ну, нешь, *past* ~, ~**ла** *pf. of*
▶ сле́пнуть

О́сло *m. indecl.* Oslo

осложне́ни|е, я *nt.* complication

осложн|и́ть, ю́, и́шь *pf.* (*of* ▶ осложня́ть) to
complicate

осложн|и́ться, и́тся *pf.* (*of* ▶ осложня́ться)
to become complicated; (*о боле́зни*) to
develop complications

осложн|я́ть, я́ю *impf. of* ▶ осложни́ть

осложн|я́ться, я́ется *impf. of* ▶ осложни́ться

ꙮ key word

ослу́ш|аться, аюсь *pf.* (*of* ▶ ослу́шиваться)
to disobey

ослу́шива|ться, юсь *impf. of* ▶ ослу́шаться

ослы́ш|аться, усь, ишься *pf.* to mishear

осма́трива|ть, ю *impf. of* ▶ осмотре́ть

осма́трива|ться, юсь *impf. of* ▶ осмотре́ться

осме́ива|ть, ю *impf. of* ▶ осмея́ть

осме́лива|ться, юсь *impf. of* ▶ осме́литься

осме́л|иться, юсь, ишься *pf.* (*of*
▶ осме́ливаться) (+ *inf.*) to dare; to take the
liberty (of)

осме|я́ть, ю́, ёшь *pf.* (*of* ▶ осме́ивать) to
mock, ridicule

осмо́тр, а *m.* (*багажа́*) examination,
inspection; (*шко́лы*) inspection; **медици́нский
о.** medical (examination); check-up

осмотр|е́ть, ю́, ~**ишь** *pf.* (*of* ▶ осма́тривать)
(*бага́ж, больно́го*) to examine; (*шко́лу*) to
inspect; (*вы́ставку*) to look round, look over

осмотр|е́ться, ю́сь, ~**ишься** *pf.* (*of*
▶ осма́триваться) **1** to look round **2** (fig.)
to take one's bearings, see how the land lies

осмотри́тел|ьный, ~**ен,** ~**ьна** *adj.*
circumspect, cautious

осмы́слен|ный, ~, ~**а** *p.p.p. of*
▶ осмы́слить *and* (~, ~**на**) *adj.* intelligent,
sensible

осмы́слива|ть, ю *impf. of* ▶ осмы́слить

осмы́сл|ить, ю, ишь *pf.* (*of* ▶ осмы́сливать,
▶ осмысля́ть) (*истолкова́ть*) to interpret;
(*поня́ть*) to comprehend

осмысл|я́ть, я́ю *impf.* = осмы́сливать

осна|сти́ть, щу́, сти́шь *pf.* (*of* ▶ оснаща́ть)
(naut.) to rig; (fig.) to fit out, equip

оснаща́|ть, ю *impf. of* ▶ оснасти́ть

оснаще́ни|е, я *nt.* **1** (*де́йствие*) rigging;
fitting out **2** (*обору́дование*) equipment

ꙮ **осно́в|а, ы** *f.* (*зда́ния*) foundation; (fig.) basis,
foundation; (*in pl.*) fundamentals; **лежа́ть в**
~**е** (+ *g.*) to be the basis (of)

ꙮ **основа́ни|е, я** *nt.* **1** (*де́йствие*) founding,
foundation **2** (chem., math., etc.) base; (*зда́ния*)
foundation; **о. горы́** foot of a mountain;
разру́шить до ~**я** to raze to the ground
3 (fig.) foundation, basis; ground, reason;
на како́м ~**и вы э́то утвержда́ете?** on
what grounds do you assert this?; **име́ть о.
предполага́ть** to have reason to suppose

основа́тел|ь, я *m.* founder

основа́тель|ница, ницы *f. of* ▶ основа́тель

основа́тел|ьный, ~**ен,** ~**ьна** *adj.*
1 (*сове́т, причи́на*) well founded; just
2 (*постро́йка*) solid, sound; (*челове́к*) solid;
(*осмо́тр*) thorough; ~**ьные до́воды** sound
arguments

осн|ова́ть, ую́, уёшь *pf.* (*of* ▶ осно́вывать)
1 (*учреди́ть*) to found **2** (**на** + *p.*) to base
(on)

ꙮ **основн|о́й** *adj.* (*причи́на, цель*) main;
(*при́нцип*) fundamental, basic; ~**а́я мысль**
keynote; ~**ы́е цвета́** primary colours; **в** ~**о́м**
on the whole; basically

основополо́жник, а *m.* founder, initiator

◆ осно́выва|ть, ю *impf. of* ▸ основа́ть

осно́выва|ться, юсь *impf.* (на + *p.*) to base oneself (on); to be based, founded (on)

осо́б|а, ы *f.* person, individual, personage; ва́жная о. (iron.) bigwig

◆ осо́бенно *adv.* especially; particularly; unusually; не о. not very, not particularly

◆ осо́бенност|ь, и *f.* peculiarity; в ~и especially, in particular, (more) particularly

осо́бенн|ый *adj.* (e)special, particular, peculiar; ничего́ ~ого nothing in particular; nothing much

особня́|к, á *m.* private residence; mansion, manor house

◆ осо́бо *adv.* especially, particularly

◆ осо́б|ый *adj.* special; particular; peculiar; удели́ть ~ое внима́ние (+ *d.*) to give special attention (to)

осозна|ва́ть, ю, ёшь *impf. of* ▸ осозна́ть

осо́знанный *adj.* deliberate; conscious

осозна́|ть, ю *pf.* (*of* ▸ осознава́ть) to realize

осо́к|а, и *f.* (bot.) sedge

о́сп|а, ы *f.* smallpox; ве́тряная о. chicken pox

оспа́рива|ть, ю *impf.* ◼1 *impf. of* ▸ оспо́рить ◼2 (*impf. only*) to contend (for)

оспо́р|ить, ю, ишь *pf.* (*of* ▸ оспа́ривать 1) to dispute, question; о. завеща́ние to dispute a will

◆ оста|ва́ться, ю́сь, ёшься *impf. of* ▸ оста́ться

◆ оста́в|ить, лю, ишь *pf.* (*of* ▸ оставля́ть) ◼1 to leave; (*покинуть*) to abandon; (*надежду*) to give up; (*перестать, бросить*) to stop, give up; о. в поко́е to leave alone, let alone; о. госте́й ночева́ть/ обе́дать to ask guests to stay the night/stay to dinner ◼2 (*сохранить*) to reserve; to keep; о. за собо́й пра́во to reserve the right

◆ оставля́|ть, ю *impf.* (*of* ▸ оста́вить): ~ет жела́ть лу́чшего it leaves much to be desired

◆ остальн|о́й *adj.* the rest of; в ~о́м in other respects; (*as pl. n.* ~ы́е) the others; (*as nt. n.* ~о́е) the rest; всё ~о́е everything else

остана́влива|ть, ю *impf. of* ▸ останови́ть

остана́влива|ться, юсь *impf. of* ▸ останови́ться

оста́нк|и, ов (*no sg.*) remains

останов|и́ть, лю́, ~ишь *pf.* (*of* ▸ остана́вливать) ◼1 to stop ◼2 (*сдержать*) to stop short, restrain ◼3 (на + *p.*) (*направить*) to direct (to), concentrate (on); о. взгляд to rest one's gaze (on)

останов|и́ться, лю́сь, ~ишься *pf.* (*of* ▸ остана́вливаться) ◼1 to stop; to come to a stop, come to a halt ◼2 (*переночевать*) to stay, put up; stop (infml); о. у знако́мых to stay with friends ◼3 (на + *p.*) (fig., *в речи, докладе*) to dwell (on); (*о взгляде*) to settle (on), rest (on)

остано́вк|а, и *f.* ◼1 (*в пути, работе*) stop; (*задержка*) stoppage ◼2 (*автобусная*) stop; коне́чная о. terminus; мне на́до прое́хать ещё одну́ ~у I have to go one stop further

оста́т|ок, ка *m.* ◼1 remainder; rest; (*ткани*) remnant; (*in pl.*) remains; (*еды*) leftovers ◼2 (fin., comm.) rest, balance

◆ оста́|ться, нусь, нешься *pf.* (*of* ▸ остава́ться) to remain; to stay; to be left (over); о. в живы́х to survive, come through; о. на́ ночь to stay the night; от обе́да ничего́ не ~лось there is nothing left over from dinner; (*impers.*) ~ётся, ~лось (+ *d.*) it remains (remained), it is (was) necessary; ~лось то́лько заплати́ть it remained only to pay

остекл|и́ть, ю́, и́шь *pf.* (*of* ▸ остекля́ть) to glaze

остекл|я́ть, я́ю *impf. of* ▸ остекли́ть

остерега́|ться, ю́сь *impf.* (*of* ▸ остере́чься) (+ *g. or inf.*) to beware (of); to be careful (of); ~йтесь соба́ки! beware of the dog!

остере|чься, гу́сь, жёшься, гу́тся, *past* ~гся, ~гла́сь *pf. of* ▸ остерега́ться

о́стов, а *m.* frame, framework (also fig.)

осторо́жно *adv.* carefully; cautiously; о.! look out!

осторо́жност|ь, и *f.* care; caution

осторо́ж|ный, ~ен, ~на *adj.* careful; cautious; бу́дьте ~ны! take care!

остри|ё, я́ *nt.* ◼1 (*иголки, штыка*) point ◼2 (*ножа, бритвы*) (cutting) edge

остр|и́ть, ю́, и́шь *impf.* (*of* ▸ состри́ть) (*говорить остроты*) to be witty; to make witticisms, crack jokes

остри|чь, гу́, жёшь, гу́т, *past* ~г, ~гла *pf. of* ▸ стричь 1, ▸ стричь 2

◆ о́стров, а, *pl.* ~а́ *m.* island; isle

островитя́н|ин, ина, *pl.* ~е, ~ *m.* islander

островитя́н|ка, ки *f. of* ▸ островитя́нин

остроконе́ч|ный, ~ен, ~на *adj.* pointed

остро́т|а, ы *f.* witticism, joke; пло́ская о. stupid joke; то́нкая о. subtle crack

острот|а́, ы́ *f.* (*ножа, ума*) sharpness; (*зрения, слуха*) keenness; (*ситуации; боли*) acuteness; (*запаха*) pungency; (*чувства*) poignancy

остроу́ми|е, я *nt.* ◼1 wit; wittiness ◼2 (*изобретательность*) ingenuity

остроу́м|ный, ~ен, ~на *adj.* ◼1 witty ◼2 (*изобретательный*) ingenious

◆ о́стр|ый, остёр *and* ~, ~á, ~о, (*in fig. sense*) ~ó, ~ы, (*in fig. sense*) ~ы́ *adj.* (*нож, ум*) sharp; (*нос*) pointed (also fig.); (*ситуация; боль*) acute; (*зрение, слух*) keen; ~ое зре́ние keen eyesight; о. интере́с (к + *d.*) keen interest (in); о. у́гол (math.) acute angle

остря́к, á *m.* wit

осту|ди́ть, жу́, ~дишь *pf.* (*of* ▸ остужа́ть) to cool

остужа́|ть, ю *impf. of* ▸ остуди́ть

оступ|а́ться, а́юсь *impf. of* ▸ оступи́ться

оступ|и́ться, лю́сь, ~ишься *pf.* (*of* ▸ оступа́ться) to stumble

остыва́|ть, ю *impf. of* ▸ осты́ть

осты́|ть, ну, нешь *pf.* (*of* ▸ остыва́ть) to get cold; (fig.) to cool (down); у вас чай ~л your tea is cold

о

осу|ди́ть, жу́, ~дишь pf. (of ▶ осужда́ть) **1** (*порицать*) to censure, condemn **2** (law) (*на смерть*) to condemn, sentence; (*за* + *a.*) to convict (of) **3** (**на** + *a.*) (fig., *обречь*) to condemn

осужда́|ть, ю impf. of ▶ осуди́ть

осужде́ни|е, я nt. **1** censure, condemnation **2** (law) conviction

осуждённ|ый p.p.p. of ▶ осуди́ть and adj. condemned; convicted; (*as n.* **о.**, **~ого**, f. **~ая**, **~ой**) convict

осу́н|уться, усь, ешься pf. (*о лице*) to grow thin, get pinched(-looking)

осуш|а́ть, а́ю impf. of ▶ осуши́ть

осуш|и́ть, у́, ~ишь pf. (of ▶ осуша́ть) (*болото, луга, стакан*) to drain; (*помещение*) to dry

осуществи́м|ый, ~, ~а adj. practicable, feasible

осуществ|и́ть, лю́, и́шь pf. (of ▶ осуществля́ть) (*мечту*) to realize, bring about; (*намерение*) to carry out; (*решение*) to implement; (*контроль, руководство*) to exercise

осуществ|и́ться, и́тся pf. (of ▶ осуществля́ться) to be fulfilled, come true

✎ **осуществле́ни|е, я** nt. realization; accomplishment; implementation

✎ **осуществля́|ть, ю, ет** impf. of ▶ осуществи́ть

✎ **осуществля́|ться, ется** impf. of ▶ осуществи́ться

осчастли́в|ить, лю, ишь pf. (of ▶ осчастли́вливать) to make happy

осчастли́влива|ть, ю impf. of ▶ осчастли́вить

осы́п|ать, лю, лешь pf. (of ▶ осыпа́ть) (+ *a.* and *i.*) (*покрыть*) to strew (with); to shower (on); (fig.) to heap (on); **о. поцелу́ями** to smother with kisses

осып|а́ть, а́ю impf. of ▶ осы́пать

осы́п|аться, люсь, лешься pf. (of ▶ осыпа́ться) (*о насыпи*) to crumble; (*о листьях*) to fall

осып|а́ться, а́юсь impf. of ▶ осы́паться

ос|ь, и, pl. **~и, ~е́й** f. **1** (geom.) axis; **земна́я о.** axis of the equator **2** (*колеса*) axle

осьмино́г, а m. (zool.) octopus

осяза́ем|ый, ~, ~а adj. tangible; **~ые результа́ты** tangible results

осяза́ни|е, я nt. touch; **чу́вство ~я** a sense of touch

✎ **от, ото** prep. + *g.* **1** from; of; for; (*указывает на исходную точку, источник чего-н.*): **от це́нтра го́рода** from the centre of the town; **от нача́ла до конца́** from beginning to end; **де́ти от пяти́ до десяти́ лет** children from five to ten (years); **бли́зко от го́рода** near the town; **на се́вер от Москвы́** to the north of Moscow; **от всей души́** with all one's heart; **от и́мени** (+ *g.*) on behalf

(of); **я получи́л письмо́ от до́чери** I have received a letter from my daughter; **сын от пре́жнего бра́ка** a son by a previous marriage **2** (*указывает на причину чего-н.*): **вскри́кнуть от ра́дости** to cry out for joy; **дрожа́ть от стра́ха** to tremble with fear; **умере́ть от го́лода** to die of hunger; **глаза́, кра́сные от слёз** eyes red with weeping **3** (*указывает на дату документа*): **ва́ше письмо́ от пе́рвого а́вгуста** your letter of the first of August **4** (*указывает на целое, которому принадлежит часть*): **ключ от две́ри** door key; **пу́говица от пиджака́** coat button **5** (*против*) for; against; **микстура от ка́шля** cough mixture; **защища́ть глаза́ от со́лнца** to shield one's eyes from the sun; **застрахова́ть от огня́** to insure against fire

ота́плива|ть, ю impf. of ▶ отопи́ть

ота́р|а, ы f. large flock (*of sheep*)

отбега́|ть, ю impf. of ▶ отбежа́ть

отбе|жа́ть, гу́, жи́шь, гу́т pf. (of ▶ отбега́ть) to run off

отбе́ливател|ь, я m. bleach

отбе́лива|ть, ю impf. of ▶ отбели́ть

отбел|и́ть, ю́, ~ишь pf. (of ▶ отбе́ливать) to bleach

отбива́|ть, ю impf. of ▶ отби́ть

отбива́|ться, юсь impf. of ▶ отби́ться

отбивн|о́й adj.: **~а́я котле́та** (cul.) chop

отбира́|ть, ю impf. of ▶ отобра́ть

отби́|ть, отобью́, отобьёшь pf. (of ▶ отбива́ть) **1** to beat off, repel; **о. ата́ку** to beat off an attack; **о. уда́р** to parry a blow **2** (*вернуть себе силой*) to retake, recapture; (*привлечь к себе*) to win over; (infml) **о. кого́/что у кого́-н.** to take sb/sth off sb, do sb out of sb/sth **3** (*удалить*) to remove, dispel; **о. у кого́-н. охо́ту к чему́-н.** to discourage sb from sth, take away sb's inclination for sth **4** (*отколоть*) to break off, knock off; **о. но́сик у ча́йника** to knock the spout off a teapot **5**: **о. такт** to beat (out) time **6** (*повредить ударами*) to damage by blows, by knocks; **о. ру́ку нело́вким уда́ром** to hurt one's hand with a clumsy blow

отби́|ться, отобью́сь, отобьёшься pf. (of ▶ отбива́ться) **1** (**от** + *g.*) to defend oneself (against); to repel, beat off **2** (*отстать*) to drop behind, straggle; **о. от ста́да** to stray from the herd

отблагодар|и́ть, ю́, и́шь pf. to show one's gratitude (to)

отбо́р, а m. selection; **есте́ственный о.** (biol.) natural selection

отбо́рный adj. choice, select(ed)

отбра́сыва|ть, ю impf. of ▶ отбро́сить

отбро́|сить, шу, сишь pf. (of ▶ отбра́сывать) **1** to throw off; to cast away; **о. тень** to cast a shadow **2** (mil.) to repel **3** (*отвергнуть*) to give up, reject, discard; **о. мысль** to give up an idea

отбро́с|ы, ов m. pl. (sg. **~, ~а**) garbage, refuse; **о. произво́дства** industrial waste;

о. о́бщества (fig.) dregs of society

отва́г|а, и f. courage, bravery

отва́ж|ный, ~ен, ~на adj. courageous, brave

отва́лива|ться, юсь impf. of ▶ отвали́ться

отвал|и́ться, ю́сь, ~ишься pf. (of ▶ отва́ливаться) to fall off

отва́рива|ть, ю impf. of ▶ отвари́ть

отвар|и́ть, ю́, ~ишь pf. (of ▶ отва́ривать) to boil

отвез|ти́, у́, ёшь, past ~, ~ла́ pf. (of ▶ отвози́ть) (везя, доставить) to take; (везя, убрать) to take away

отверг|а́ть, а́ю impf. of ▶ отве́ргнуть

отве́рг|нуть, ну, нешь, past ~/~нул, ~ла pf. (of ▶ отверга́ть) to reject, turn down

отверн|у́ться, у́сь, нёшься pf. (of ▶ отвора́чиваться) to turn away, turn aside; о. от кого́-н. (fig.) to turn one's back upon sb

отве́рсти|е, я nt. opening; (дыра) hole; (в торговом/игровом автомате) slot

отвёртк|а, и f. screwdriver

отве́с|ный, ~ен, ~на adj. (линия) perpendicular; (скала) steep

отве|сти́, ду́, дёшь, past ~л, ~ла́ pf. (of ▶ отводи́ть) **1** (ведя, доставить) to lead, take, conduct **2** (ведя, направить в сторону) to draw aside, take aside **3** (изменить направление движения чего-либо) to deflect; он не мог о. от неё глаз he could not take his eyes off her **4** (выделить) to allot, assign

♂ **отве́т, а** m. **1** answer, reply, response; в о. (на + a.) in reply (to), in response (to) **2**: быть в ~е to be answerable (for); призва́ть к ~у to call to account

ответвле́ни|е, я nt. branch, offshoot (also fig.)

♂ **отве́|тить, чу, тишь** pf. (of ▶ отвеча́ть 1) **1** (на + a.) to answer, reply (to); о. на письмо́ to answer a letter; о. уро́к to repeat one's lesson **2** (на + a. and i.) to answer (with), return; о. на чьё-н. чу́вство to return sb's feelings **3** (за + a.) to answer (for), pay (for); вы ~тите за э́ти слова́! you will pay for these words!

отве́тный adj. given in reply; (визит) return; (меры) retaliatory

♂ **отве́тственност|ь, и** f. responsibility; привле́чь к ~и (за + a.) to call to account, bring to book

отве́тственн|ый, ~, ~на adj. **1** (человек; работа) responsible **2** (решающий) crucial; о. моме́нт crucial point

отве́тчик, а m. (law) defendant

отве́тчи|ца, цы f. of ▶ отве́тчик

♂ **отвеча́|ть, ю** impf. **1** impf. of ▶ отве́тить **2** (за + a.) to answer (for), be answerable (for) **3** (+ d.) to answer (to), meet, be up (to); о. тре́бованиям to meet requirements

отвин|ти́ть, чу́, ти́шь pf. (of ▶ отви́нчивать) to unscrew

отвин|ти́ться, ти́тся pf. (of ▶ отви́нчиваться) to unscrew, come unscrewed

отви́нчива|ть, ю, ет impf. of ▶ отвинти́ть

отви́нчива|ться, ется impf. of ▶ отвинти́ться

отвлека́|ть, ю impf. of ▶ отвле́чь

отвлека́|ться, юсь impf. of ▶ отвле́чься

отвлечён|ный, ~, ~на adj. abstract

отвле́|чь, ку́, чёшь, ку́т, past ~к, ~кла́ pf. (of ▶ отвлека́ть) to distract, divert; о. чьё-н. внима́ние to divert sb's attention

отвле́|чься, ку́сь, чёшься, ку́тся, past ~кся, ~кла́сь pf. (of ▶ отвлека́ться) **1** to be distracted; о. от те́мы to digress **2** (от + g.) (абстрагироваться) to abstract oneself (from)

отво|ди́ть, жу́, ~дишь impf. of ▶ отвести́

отвое|ва́ть¹, ю́ю, ю́ешь pf. (of ▶ отвоёвывать) (у + a.) (вернуть войной) to win back (from), retake (from)

отвое|ва́ть², ю́ю, ю́ешь pf. (infml) **1** (какое-н. время) to fight, spend in fighting; мы де́сять лет ~ева́ли we have fought for ten years **2** (кончить воевать) to finish fighting

отвоёвыва|ть, ю impf. of ▶ отвоева́ть¹

отво|зи́ть, жу́, ~зишь impf. of ▶ отвезти́

отвора́чива|ться, юсь impf. of ▶ отверну́ться

отвор|и́ть, ю́, ~ишь pf. (of ▶ отворя́ть) to open

отвор|и́ться, ~ится pf. (of ▶ отворя́ться) to open

отворо́т, а m. (на пиджаке) lapel; (на брюках) turn-up (BrE), cuff (AmE); (сапога, рукава) cuff

отвор|я́ть, я́ю, я́ет impf. of ▶ отвори́ть

отвор|я́ться, я́ется impf. of ▶ отвори́ться

отврати́тель|ный, ~ен, ~ьна adj. repulsive, disgusting

отвраще́ни|е, я nt. disgust, repugnance; пита́ть о. (к + d.) to have an aversion (for), loathe

отвыка́|ть, ю impf. of ▶ отвы́кнуть

отвы́к|нуть, ну, нешь, past ~, ~ла pf. (of ▶ отвыка́ть) (от + g. or + inf.) (от плохой привычки) to break oneself (of the habit of), give up; (от работы, ходьбы) to get out of the habit of, become unaccustomed to; (от друзей, своей страны) to become estranged from

отвя|за́ть, жу́, ~жешь pf. (of ▶ отвя́зывать) to untie, unfasten

отвя|за́ться, жу́сь, ~жешься pf. (of ▶ отвя́зываться) **1** (освободиться от привязи) to come untied, come loose **2** (fig., infml) (от + g.) (отделаться) to get rid (of), shake off, get shot (of) **3** (fig., infml) (перестать надоедать) to leave alone, leave in peace; to stop nagging; ~жи́сь от меня́! leave me alone!

отвя́зыва|ть, ю impf. of ▶ отвяза́ть

отвя́зыва|ться, юсь impf. of ▶ отвяза́ться

отгад|а́ть, а́ю pf. (of ▶ отга́дывать) to guess

отга́дк|а, и f. answer, solution (to a riddle)

отга́дыва|ть, ю impf. of ▶ отгада́ть

отгиба́|ть, ю, ет impf. of ▶ отогну́ть

отгиба́|ться, ется impf. of ▶ отогну́ться

отговáрива|ть, ю *impf. of* ▶ отговори́ть
отговор|и́ть, ю́, и́шь *pf.* (*of* ▶ отговáривать)
(от + *g. or* + *inf.*) to dissuade (from); я ∼и́л
егó éхать I have talked him out of going
отговóрк|а, и *f.* excuse
отгоня́|ть, ю *impf. of* ▶ отогнáть
отгорáжива|ть, ю *impf. of* ▶ отгороди́ть
отгорáжива|ться, юсь *impf. of*
▶ отгороди́ться
отгоро|ди́ть, жý, ∼ди́шь *pf.* (*of*
▶ отгорáживать) to fence off, partition off
отгоро|ди́ться, жýсь, ∼ди́шься *pf.* (*of*
▶ отгорáживаться) to fence oneself off;
(fig., infml) (от + *g.*) to shut *or* cut oneself off
(from)
отгрыз|áть, áю *impf. of* ▶ отгры́зть
отгры́з|ть, ý, ёшь, *past* ∼, ∼ла *pf.* (*of*
▶ отгрызáть) to bite off, gnaw off
⚡ отда|вáть, ю́, ёшь *impf. of* ▶ отдáть
отда|вáться, ю́сь, ёшься *impf. of*
▶ отдáться
отдав|и́ть, лю́, ∼ишь *pf.* to crush; о. комý-н.
нóгу to tread on sb's foot
отдалён|ный, ∼, ∼на *adj.* distant, remote
отд|áть, áм, áшь, áст, ади́м, ади́те, адýт,
past ∼áл, ∼алá, ∼áло *pf.* (*of* ▶ отдавáть)
1 (*дать обрáтно*) to give back, return; о.
себé отчёт (в + *p.*) to be aware (of), realize
2 (*посвяти́ть*) to devote; о. жизнь наýке
to devote one's life to scholarship **3** (+ *a.*
and d., or + *a.* and за + *a.*) (*вы́дать зáмуж*)
to give in marriage (to), give away **4** (в + *a.*
or под + *a.*) (*вручи́ть*) to give, put, place
(= hand over for certain purpose); о. кни́гу в
переплёт to send a book to be bound; о. под
суд to prosecute **5** (*in comb. with certain
nn.*) to give; to make (*or not requiring
separate translation*); о. прикáз (+ *d.*) to
issue an order (to)
отд|áться, áмся, áшься, áстся, ади́мся,
ади́тесь, адýтся, *past* ∼áлся, ∼алáсь *pf.*
(*of* ▶ отдавáться) **1** (+ *d.*) (*победи́телю*)
to give oneself up (to); (*наýке*) to devote
oneself (to); (*о жéнщине*) to give oneself
(to) **2** (*о гóлосе, об эхе*) to resound; to
reverberate; to ring
отдáч|а, и *f.* **1** (*от влóженного*) return
2 (*эффекти́вность*) efficiency, performance
3 (*при вы́стреле*) recoil
⚡ отдéл, а *m.* department; о. кáдров personnel
department
отдéл|ать, аю *pf.* (*of* ▶ отдéлывать) to finish,
put the finishing touches (to); to decorate
отдéл|аться, аюсь *pf.* (*of* ▶ отдéлываться)
(infml) **1** (от + *g.*) to get rid (of), get shot (of)
2 (+ *i.*) to escape (with); легкó о. to have a
lucky escape
⚡ отделéни|е, я *nt.* **1** (*дéйствие*) separation;
о. цéркви от госудáрства separation
of church and state, secularization;
(*с обретéнием незави́симости*) secession
2 (*учреждéние*) department, branch; о.

мили́ции local police station
3 (*вмести́лища*) compartment, section;
(*представлéния*) part **4** (mil.) section
отдел|и́ть, ю́, ∼ишь *pf.* (*of* ▶ отделя́ть)
1 (*отня́ть*) to separate **2** (*отграни́чить*)
to separate off; о. перегорóдкой to partition
off
отдел|и́ться, ю́сь, ∼ишься *pf.* (*of*
▶ отделя́ться) (*отодви́нуться*) to
move away, separate; (*оторвáться*)
to get detached; to come off; (*быть
отграни́ченным от чегó-л.*) to be separated
отдéлк|а, и *f.* **1** (*дéйствие*) finishing;
trimming **2** (*украшéние*) finish, decoration;
(*в кóмнате*) decor
отдéлыва|ть, ю *impf. of* ▶ отдéлать
отдéлыва|ться, юсь *impf. of* ▶ отдéлаться
отдéльно *adv.* separately
⚡ отдéльн|ый *adj.* **1** separate; (*нéкоторый*)
individual; (*еди́ничный*) isolated **2** (mil.)
independent
отдел|я́ть, я́ю *impf. of* ▶ отдели́ть
отдел|я́ться, я́юсь *impf. of* ▶ отдели́ться
отдёргива|ть, ю *impf. of* ▶ отдёрнуть
отдёр|нуть, ну, нешь *pf.* (*of* ▶ отдёргивать)
1 (*в стóрону*) to draw aside, pull aside
2 (*рýку*) to pull back, withdraw
отдирá|ть, ю *impf. of* ▶ отодрáть
отдохн|ýть, ý, ёшь *pf.* (*of* ▶ отдыхáть) to
rest; to have a rest
отдýшин|а, ы *f.* air hole, (air) vent; (fig.)
outlet
⚡ óтдых, а *m.* rest; relaxation; (*óтпуск*)
holiday (BrE), vacation (AmE)
⚡ отдыхá|ть, ю *impf.* (*of* ▶ отдохнýть) to be
resting; (*быть в óтпуске*) to be on holiday
(BrE), vacation (AmE); (*проводи́ть óтпуск*) to
holiday (BrE), vacation (AmE)
отдыхá|ющий *pres. part. of* ▶ отдыхáть;
(*as n.* о., ∼ющего, *f.* ∼ющая, ∼ющей)
holidaymaker (BrE), vacationer (AmE)
отдыш|áться, ýсь, ∼ишься *pf.* to recover
one's breath
отёк, а *m.* (med.) oedema (BrE), edema (AmE);
о. лёгких emphysema
⚡ отéл|ь, я *m.* hotel
⚡ от|éц, цá *m.* father (also fig.); О. Небéсный
(relig.) the heavenly Father
⚡ отéчественн|ый *adj. of* ▶ отéчество;
Вели́кая О∼ая войнá the Great Patriotic
War (1941-45)
отéчеств|о, а *nt.* native land, fatherland,
homeland
отжáть, отожмý, отожмёшь *pf.* (*of*
▶ отжимáть) to wring out
отжимá|ть, ю *impf. of* ▶ отжáть
óтзвук, а *m.* echo (also fig.)
⚡ óтзыв, а *m.* **1** (*мнéние*) opinion, judgement
2 (*рекомендáция*) reference; testimonial;
дать хорóший о. о кóм-н. to give sb a good
reference **3** (*рецéнзия*) review
отзывá|ться, юсь *impf. of* ▶ отозвáться
отзы́вчив|ый, ∼, ∼а *adj.* responsive

⚡ key word

ОТИ́Т, а *m.* (med.) otitis (*inflammation of the ear*)

✵ **ОТКА́З, а** *m.* **1** refusal; получи́ть о. to be refused, be turned down; до ∼а to the maximum; стака́н напо́лнен до ∼а the glass is full to overflowing; поверни́те ру́чку до ∼а turn the handle to the maximum **2** (от + *g.*) renunciation (of), giving up (of) **3** (*механизма*) failure

ОТКА|ЗА́ТЬ, жу́, ∼жешь *pf.* (*of* ▶ отка́зывать) **1** (+ *d. and* в + *p.*) to refuse, deny; она́ ∼за́ла ему́ в про́сьбе she refused his request; ему́ нельзя́ о. в тала́нте there is no denying that he has talent **2** (*о механизме*) to fail, break down

ОТКА|ЗА́ТЬСЯ, жу́сь, ∼жешься *pf.* (*of* ▶ отка́зываться) **1** (от + *g. or* + *inf.*) to refuse, decline; о. от предложе́ния to turn down a proposal; о. от свои́х слов to retract one's words **2** (*отре́чься*) to renounce, give up; (*от пра́ва*) to relinquish; (*от вла́сти*) to abdicate; о. от борьбы́ to give up the struggle

ОТКА́ЗЫВА|ТЬ, ю *impf. of* ▶ отказа́ть

✵ **ОТКА́ЗЫВА|ТЬСЯ, юсь** *impf. of* ▶ отказа́ться

ОТКА́ЛЫВА|ТЬ, ю *impf. of* ▶ отколо́ть

ОТКА́ЛЫВА|ТЬСЯ, юсь *impf. of* ▶ отколо́ться

ОТКА́ПЫВА|ТЬ, ю *impf. of* ▶ откопа́ть

ОТКА́РМЛИВА|ТЬ, ю *impf. of* ▶ откорми́ть

ОТКА|ТИ́ТЬ, чу́, ∼тишь *pf.* (*of* ▶ отка́тывать) (*бревно́*) to roll away

ОТКА|ТИ́ТЬСЯ, чу́сь, ∼тишься *pf.* (*of* ▶ отка́тываться) to roll away

ОТКА́ТЫВА|ТЬ, ю *impf. of* ▶ откати́ть

ОТКА́ТЫВА|ТЬСЯ, юсь *impf. of* ▶ откати́ться

ОТКАЧА́|ТЬ, а́ю *pf.* (*of* ▶ отка́чивать) **1** (*во́здух, во́ду*) to pump out **2** (*челове́ка*) to resuscitate

ОТКА́ЧИВА|ТЬ, ю *impf. of* ▶ откача́ть

ОТКА́ШЛ|ИВАТЬСЯ, иваюсь *impf. of* ▶ отка́шляться

ОТКА́ШЛ|ЯТЬСЯ, яюсь *pf.* (*of* ▶ отка́шливаться) to clear one's throat

ОТКИ́ДЫВА|ТЬСЯ, юсь *impf. of* ▶ отки́нуться

ОТКИ́|НУТЬСЯ, нусь, нешься *pf.* (*of* ▶ отки́дываться) to lean back; to recline, settle back

ОТКЛА́ДЫВА|ТЬ, ю *impf. of* ▶ отложи́ть

ОТКЛЕ́ИВА|ТЬ, ю, ет *impf. of* ▶ откле́ить

ОТКЛЕ́ИВА|ТЬСЯ, ется *impf. of* ▶ откле́иться

ОТКЛЕ́|ИТЬ, ю, ишь *pf.* (*of* ▶ откле́ивать) to peel off

ОТКЛЕ́|ИТЬСЯ, ится *pf.* (*of* ▶ откле́иваться) to come unstuck

О́ТКЛИК, а *m.* (*отве́т на зов*) response; (fig., *в печа́ти*) comment

ОТКЛИКА́|ТЬСЯ, а́юсь *impf.* (*of* ▶ откли́кнуться) (на + *a.*) to answer, respond (to) (also fig.)

ОТКЛИ́К|НУТЬСЯ, нусь, нешься *pf. of* ▶ откликаться

ОТКЛОНЕ́НИ|е, я *nt.* **1** (*отхо́д в сто́рону; от но́рмы*) deviation; divergence **2** (*отка́з*) declining, refusal

ОТКЛОН|И́ТЬ, ю́, ∼ишь *pf.* (*of* ▶ отклоня́ть) **1** (*в сто́рону*) to deflect **2** (*отказа́ть*) to decline; о. предложе́ние to decline an offer

ОТКЛОН|И́ТЬСЯ, ю́сь, ∼ишься *pf.* (*of* ▶ отклоня́ться) (*от ку́рса*) to deviate; (*от уда́ра*) to dodge; (*отодви́нуться*) to move aside; о. от те́мы to digress

ОТКЛОНЯ́|ТЬ, ю *impf. of* ▶ отклони́ть

ОТКЛОНЯ́|ТЬСЯ, юсь *impf. of* ▶ отклони́ться

ОТКЛЮЧА́|ТЬ, а́ю *impf. of* ▶ отключи́ть

ОТКЛЮЧА́|ТЬСЯ, а́юсь *impf. of* ▶ отключи́ться

ОТКЛЮЧ|И́ТЬ, у́, и́шь *pf.* (*of* ▶ отключа́ть) (elec.) to cut off, disconnect

ОТКЛЮЧ|И́ТЬСЯ, у́сь, и́шься *pf.* (*of* ▶ отключа́ться) **1** to become disconnected **2** (infml, *о челове́ке*) to switch off

ОТКОЛ|О́ТЬ, ю́, ∼ешь *pf.* (*of* ▶ отка́лывать) **1** (*отлома́ть*) to break off; (*отби́ть*) to chop off; (*от семьи́*) to cut off **2** (*була́вку, чепе́ц*) to unpin

ОТКОЛ|О́ТЬСЯ, ю́сь, ∼ешься *pf.* (*of* ▶ отка́лываться) **1** (*отлома́ться*) to break off **2** (*о була́вке, чепце́*) to come unpinned *or* undone **3** (fig., *от семьи́*) to break away; to cut oneself off

ОТКОПА́|ТЬ, ю *pf.* (*of* ▶ отка́пывать) **1** to dig out; (*труп*) to exhume, disinter **2** (fig., infml, *найти́*) to dig up, unearth

ОТКОРМ|И́ТЬ, лю́, ∼ишь *pf.* (*of* ▶ отка́рмливать) to fatten (up)

ОТКО́С, а *m.* **1** (*пока́тый спуск*) slope, side (*of embankment, etc.*); о. холма́ hillside **2** (rail.) embankment; пусти́ть по́езд под о. to derail a train

ОТКРОВЕ́НИ|е, я *nt.* revelation

ОТКРОВЕ́ННОСТ|Ь, и *f.* candour (BrE), candor (AmE), frankness; (*in pl.*) (infml) candid revelations

ОТКРОВЕ́Н|НЫЙ, ∼ен, ∼на *adj.* **1** (*и́скренний*) candid, frank **2** (*нескрыва́емый*) open, unconcealed; ∼ная неприя́знь unconcealed hostility **3** (infml, *о пла́тье*) revealing

ОТКРУ|ТИ́ТЬ, чу́, ∼тишь *pf.* (*of* ▶ откру́чивать) to untwist; о. кран to turn off a tap

ОТКРУ́ЧИВА|ТЬ, ю *impf. of* ▶ открути́ть

ОТКРЫВА́ЛК|а, и *f.* (infml) **1** (*для ба́нок*) can opener **2** (*для буты́лок*) bottle opener

✵ **ОТКРЫВА́|ТЬ, ю** *impf. of* ▶ откры́ть

ОТКРЫВА́|ТЬСЯ, юсь *impf. of* ▶ откры́ться

✵ **ОТКРЫ́ТИ|е, я** *nt.* **1** (*де́йствие*) opening **2** (*нау́чное*) discovery

ОТКРЫ́ТК|а, и *f.* postcard

ОТКРЫ́ТО *adv.* openly

✵ **ОТКРЫ́Т|ЫЙ** *p.p.p. of* ▶ откры́ть *and adj.* open; на ∼ом во́здухе, под ∼ым не́бом out of doors, in the open (air); ∼ое мо́ре the open sea; ∼ое пла́тье low-necked dress

✵ **ОТКР|Ы́ТЬ, о́ю, о́ешь** *pf.* (*of* ▶ открыва́ть) **1** to open; о. кому́-н. глаза́ на что-н. (fig.) to open sb's eyes to sth; о. ого́нь (mil.) to open fire; о. счёт to open an account **2** (*обнажи́ть*) to uncover, reveal (also fig.); о. секре́т to reveal a secret **3** (*обнару́жить*) to discover; о.

Аме́рику (fig., iron.) to retail stale news **4** (во́ду, газ) to turn on

откр|ы́ться, о́юсь, о́ешься pf. (of ▶ открыва́ться) **1** (дверь, глаза́) to open **2** (обнаружиться) to come to light, be revealed; пе́ред на́ми ∼ы́лся великоле́пный вид a magnificent view unfolded before us

◆ отку́да adv. interrog. where from; rel. whence, from which; о. вы? where are you from?; о. вы об э́том зна́ете? how come you know about it?

отку́да-нибудь adv. from somewhere or other

отку́да-то adv. from somewhere

откуп|а́ться, а́юсь impf. of ▶ откупи́ться

откуп|и́ться, лю́сь, ∼ишься pf. (of ▶ откупа́ться) (от + g.) to pay off

отку́порива|ть, ю impf. of ▶ отку́порить

отку́пор|ить, ю, ишь pf. (of ▶ отку́поривать) (буты́лку) to uncork; (ба́нку) to open

отку|си́ть, шу́, ∼сишь pf. (of ▶ отку́сывать) to bite off; (щипца́ми) to cut off

отку́сыва|ть, ю impf. of ▶ откуси́ть

отла́дчик, а m. (comput., программа) debugger

отлакир|ова́ть, у́ю pf. of ▶ лакирова́ть

отла́мыва|ть, ю, ет impf. of ▶ отломи́ть, ▶ отломи́ть

отла́мыва|ться, ется impf. of ▶ отломи́ться, ▶ отломи́ться

отлет|а́ть, а́ю impf. of ▶ отлете́ть

отле|те́ть, чу́, ти́шь pf. (of ▶ отлета́ть) **1** (улете́ть) to fly (away, off); (fig., исчезнуть) to fly, vanish **2** (о мяче́) to rebound, bounce back **3** (infml, о пу́говице) to come off

отли́в, а m. ebb, ebb tide

отлива́|ть, ю impf. of ▶ отли́ть

отли́ть, отолью́, отольёшь, past о́тли́л, отлила́, о́тли́ло pf. (of ▶ отлива́ть) **1** (+ a. or g.) (молока́) to pour off; (отхлынуть) to flood back **2** (tech.) to cast, found

отлич|а́ть, а́ю impf. of ▶ отличи́ть

◆ отлич|а́ться, а́юсь impf. **1** (pf. ∼и́ться) to distinguish oneself, excel (also joc., iron.) **2** (impf. only) (от + g.) to differ (from) **3** (impf. only) (+ i.) to be notable (for)

◆ отли́чи|е, я nt. **1** difference, distinction; в о. от (+ g.) unlike, in contrast to **2** (оце́нка) distinction; (заслу́га) distinguished services

отличи́тельный adj. distinctive; distinguishing; о. при́знак distinguishing feature

отлич|и́ть, у́, и́шь pf. (of ▶ отлича́ть) **1** to distinguish; о. одно́ от друго́го to tell one thing from another **2** (вы́делить из числа́ други́х) to single out

отлич|и́ться, у́сь, и́шься pf. of ▶ отлича́ться 1

отли́чно **1** adv. excellently; perfectly; extremely well; о. знать to know perfectly

well **2** n., nt. indecl. 'excellent' mark (in school, etc.)

◆ отли́ч|ный, ∼ен, ∼на adj. **1** (от + g.) (ино́й) different (from) **2** (превосхо́дный) excellent; perfect; extremely good; ∼но! excellent!

отло́г|ий, ∼, ∼а adj. sloping

отлож|и́ть, у́, ∼ишь pf. (of ▶ откла́дывать) **1** (положи́ть в сто́рону) to put aside, set aside; (сохрани́ть) to put away, put by; о. на чёрный день to put by for a rainy day **2** (отсро́чить) to put off, postpone **3** (о пти́цах) to lay

отлома́|ть, ю pf. (of ▶ отла́мывать) to break off

отлома́|ться, ю, ет, ется pf. (of ▶ отла́мываться) to break off

отлом|и́ть, лю́, ∼ит pf. (of ▶ отла́мывать) = отлома́ть

отлом|и́ться, ∼ится pf. = отлома́ться

отлуч|а́ться, а́юсь impf. of ▶ отлучи́ться

отлуч|и́ться, у́сь, и́шься pf. (of ▶ отлуча́ться) to absent oneself

отма́хива|ть, ю impf. of ▶ отмахну́ть

отма́хива|ться, юсь impf. of ▶ отмахну́ться

отмах|ну́ть, ну́, нёшь pf. (of ▶ отма́хивать) to wave away, brush off (with one's hand)

отмах|ну́ться, ну́сь, нёшься pf. (of ▶ отма́хиваться) (от + g.) **1** = отмахну́ть; о. от комаро́в to brush mosquitoes off **2** (fig.) to brush aside

о́тмел|ь, и f. sandbank

отме́н|а, ы f. abolition; repeal; cancellation

отмен|и́ть, ю́, ∼ишь pf. (of ▶ отменя́ть) (нало́г) to abolish; (зако́н) to repeal; (реше́ние, приказа́ние) to revoke; (заседа́ние) to cancel

отме́н|ный, ∼ен, ∼на adj. excellent

отмен|я́ть, я́ю impf. of ▶ отмени́ть

отмер|е́ть, отомрёт, past о́тмер, ∼ла́, о́тмерло pf. (of ▶ отмира́ть) to die off; (fig.) to die out, die away

отмерз|а́ть, а́ет impf. of ▶ отмёрзнуть

отмёрз|нуть, нет, past ∼, ∼ла pf. (of ▶ отмерза́ть) (infml) to freeze; ру́ки у меня́ ∼ли my hands are frozen

отме́рива|ть, ю impf. of ▶ отме́рить

отме́р|ить, ю, ишь pf. (of ▶ отме́ривать, ▶ отмеря́ть) to measure off

отмер|я́ть, я́ю impf. = отме́ривать

отме|сти́, ту́, тёшь, past ∼л, ∼ла́ pf. (of ▶ отмета́ть) to sweep aside (also fig.)

отмета́|ть, ю impf. of ▶ отмести́

◆ отме́|тить, чу, тишь pf. (of ▶ отмеча́ть) **1** (ме́сто в кни́ге) to mark, note; (прису́тствующих; высоту́) to make a note (of); о. га́лочкой to tick off **2** (досто́инства) to point to, mention, record; о. чьи-н. по́двиги to point to sb's feats **3** (день рожде́ния) to celebrate

отме́тк|а, и f. **1** (знак) mark; (за́пись) note **2** (оце́нка) mark

◆ отмеча́|ть, ю impf. of ▶ отме́тить

отмира́|ть, ет impf. of ▶ отмере́ть

О

отмора́жива|ть, ю *impf. of* ▶ отморо́зить

отморо́|зить, жу, зишь *pf.* (*of*
▶ отмора́живать) to injure by frostbite;
я ∼зил себе́ у́ши my ears are frostbitten

отмыва́ни|е, я *nt.*: о. де́нег money
laundering

отмыва́|ть, ю *impf. of* ▶ отмы́ть

отмыва́|ться, юсь *impf. of* ▶ отмы́ться

отм|ы́ть, о́ю, о́ешь *pf.* (*of* ▶ отмыва́ть)
1 (*руки*) to wash clean **2** (*грязь*) to wash
off, wash away **3** (fig., infml): о. де́ньги to
launder money

отм|ы́ться, о́юсь, о́ешься *pf.* (*of*
▶ отмыва́ться) **1** (*о челове́ке*) to wash
oneself clean **2** (*о рука́х*) to become/get
clean **3** (*о грязи́*) to come out, come off

отнес|ти́, у́, ёшь, *past* ∼, ∼ла́ *pf.* (*of*
▶ относи́ть) **1** (*доста́вить*)
to take (to) **2** to carry away, carry off;
(*impers.*) ло́дку ∼ло́ тече́нием the
boat was carried away by the current;
(*перемести́ть*) to move **3** (к + *d.*) to ascribe
(to), attribute (to), refer (to); мы ∼ли его́
раздражи́тельность на счёт глухоты́ we put
his irritability down to his deafness

отнес|ти́сь, у́сь, ёшься, *past* ∼ся, ∼ла́сь
pf. (*of* ▶ относи́ться 1) (к + *d.*) to treat; to
regard; хорошо́ о. к кому́-н. to treat sb well,
be nice to sb; как вы ∼ли́сь к его́ слова́м?
what did you think of what he said?

отнима́|ть, ю *impf. of* ▶ отня́ть

⚡ **относи́тельно 1** *adv.* relatively **2** *prep.*
(+ *g.*) concerning, about, with regard to

относи́тельност|ь, и *f.* relativity; тео́рия
∼и Эйнште́йна Einstein's Theory of
Relativity

относи́тель|ный, ∼ен, ∼ьна *adj.* relative

⚡ **отно|си́ть**, шу́, ∼сишь *impf. of* ▶ отнести́

⚡ **отно|си́ться**, шу́сь, ∼сишься *impf.*
1 *impf. of* ▶ отнести́сь **2** (*impf. only*)
(к + *d.*) to concern, have to do (with), relate
(to); э́то к де́лу не ∼сится that's beside
the point, that is irrelevant **3** (*impf. only*)
(к + *d.*) to date (from); э́тот храм ∼сится к
двена́дцатому ве́ку this church dates from
the twelfth century

⚡ **отноше́ни|е**, я *nt.* **1** (к + *d.*) attitude (to);
treatment (of) **2** (*связь*) relation; respect;
име́ть о. к чему́-н. to bear a relation to sth,
have a bearing on sth; не име́ть ∼я (к + *d.*)
to bear no relation (to), have nothing to do
(with); в ∼и (+ *g.*) *or* по ∼ю (к + *d.*) with
respect (to), with regard (to) **3** (*in pl.*) (*свя́зи
между людьми́*) relations; terms; быть в
дру́жеских ∼ях (с + *i.*) to be on friendly
terms (with); вы́яснить ∼я (с + *i.*) to have
it out (with) **4** (math.) ratio; в прямо́м
(обра́тном) ∼и in direct (inverse) ratio

отны́не *adv.* (rhet.) henceforth

отню́дь *adv.* by no means, not at all

от|ня́ть, ниму́, ни́мешь, *past* ∼ня́л, ∼няла́,
∼ня́ло *pf.* (*of* ▶ отнима́ть) to take (away);
о. жизнь у кого́-н. to take sb's life; от шести́
о. три to take away three from six

ото *prep.* = от

отобража́|ть, ю *impf. of* ▶ отобрази́ть

отобра|зи́ть, жу́, зи́шь *pf.* (*of* ▶ отобража́ть)
to reflect; to represent

от|обра́ть, беру́, берёшь, *past* ∼обра́л,
∼обрала́, ∼обра́ло *pf.* (*of* ▶ отбира́ть)
1 (*отня́ть*) to take (away) **2** (*вы́брать*) to
select, pick out

отовсю́ду *adv.* from everywhere, from every
quarter

от|огна́ть, гоню́, го́нишь, *past* ∼огна́л,
∼огнала́, ∼огна́ло *pf.* (*of* ▶ отгоня́ть) to
drive away, chase away

отогн|у́ть, у́, ёшь *pf.* (*of* ▶ отгиба́ть) to bend
back

отогн|у́ться, ётся *pf.* (*of* ▶ отгиба́ться) to
bend back

отогрева́|ть, ю *impf. of* ▶ отогре́ть

отогрева́|ться, юсь *impf. of* ▶ отогре́ться

отогре́|ть, ю *pf.* (*of* ▶ отогрева́ть) to warm

отогре́|ться, юсь *pf.* (*of* ▶ отогрева́ться) to
warm oneself

отодвига́|ть, ю *impf. of* ▶ отодви́нуть

отодвига́|ться, юсь *impf. of* ▶ отодви́нуться

отодви́|нуть, ну, нешь *pf.* (*of* ▶ отодвига́ть)
1 to move aside **2** (fig., infml, *отсро́чить*) to
put off, put back

отодви́|нуться, нусь, нешься *pf.* (*of*
▶ отодвига́ться) **1** to move aside **2** (infml,
о сро́ке) to be postponed

от|одра́ть, деру́, дерёшь, *past* ∼одра́л,
∼одрала́, ∼одра́ло *pf.* (*of* ▶ отдира́ть) to
tear off, rip off

от|озва́ться, зову́сь, зовёшься,
past ∼озва́лся, ∼озвала́сь *pf.* (*of*
▶ отзыва́ться) **1** (на + *a.*) to answer; to
respond (to) **2** (о + *p.*) to speak (of)
3 (*сказа́ться*) (на + *a.*) to tell (on, upon)

ото|йти́, йду́, йдёшь, *past* ∼шёл, ∼шла́ *pf.*
(*of* ▶ отходи́ть) **1** to move away; to move
off; (*о по́езде*) to leave, depart **2** (*оста́вить
свою́ пре́жнюю пози́цию*) to withdraw; to
recede; (mil.) to withdraw, fall back; (fig.) (от
+ *g.*) to move away (from); to digress (from),
diverge (from) **3** (*о пя́тнах*) to come out;
(от + *g.*) to come away (from), come off; обо́и
∼шли́ от стены́ the paper has come off (the
wall) **4** (*прийти́ в обы́чное состоя́ние*) to
recover (normal state) **5** (к + *d.*) (*перейти́ в
чью́-л. со́бственность*) to pass (to), go (to)

отом|сти́ть, щу́, сти́шь *pf. of* ▶ мсти́ть

отоп|и́ть, лю́, ∼ишь *pf.* (*of* ▶ ота́пливать) to
heat

отопле́ни|е, я *nt.* heating

оторв|а́ть, у́, ёшь, *past* ∼а́л, ∼ала́, ∼а́ло
pf. (*of* ▶ отрыва́ть) (*пу́говицу*) to tear off;
(*отвле́чь*) to tear away (fig.); о. кого́-н. от
рабо́ты to tear sb away from his work

оторв|а́ться, у́сь, ёшься, *past* ∼а́лся,
∼ала́сь *pf.* (*of* ▶ отрыва́ться) **1** (*о пу́говице*)
to come off, be torn off **2** (aeron.): о. от
земли́ to take off **3** (fig.) (от + *g.*) (*от
друзе́й*) to be cut off (from), lose touch

(with); (*от сопе́рников; от отря́да*) to break away (from) **4** (fig.) (*от + g.*) to tear oneself away (from); **я не мог о. от э́той кни́ги** I could not tear myself away from this book

ото|сла́ть, шлю́, шлёшь *pf.* (*of* ▶ отсыла́ть) **1** to send off, dispatch **2** (**к** + *d.*) to refer (to)

ото|шёл, шла́ *see* ▶ отойти́

ото|шлю́, шлёшь *see* ▶ отосла́ть

отпада́|ть, ю *impf. of* ▶ отпа́сть

отпа́рыва|ть, ю *impf. of* ▶ отпоро́ть

отпа́|сть, ду́, дёшь, *past* ∼л *pf.* (*of* ▶ отпада́ть) **1** (*отдели́ться*) to fall off, drop off **2** (fig.) (**от** + *g.*) to drop out (of) **3** (fig., *утра́тить си́лу*) to pass, fade; **вопро́с об э́том** ∼**л** the question no longer arises

отпере́ть, отопру́, отопрёшь, *past* **о́тпер, отперла́, о́тперло** *pf.* (*of* ▶ отпира́ть) to unlock; to open

отпере́ться, отопрётся, *past* **отперся́, отперла́сь** *pf.* (*of* ▶ отпира́ться) to open

отпеча́т|ать, аю *pf.* **1** (*impf.* печа́тать) to print (off) **2** (*impf.* ∼ывать) to imprint **3** (*impf.* ∼ывать) (*помеще́ние*) to open (up)

отпеча́т|аться, ается *pf.* to leave an imprint; to be imprinted

отпеча́т|ок, ка *m.* imprint (also fig.); **о. па́льца** fingerprint

отпеча́тыва|ть, ю, ет *impf. of* ▶ отпеча́тать

отпеча́тыва|ться, ется *impf. of* ▶ отпеча́таться

отпива́|ть, ю *impf. of* ▶ отпи́ть

отпи́лива|ть, ю *impf. of* ▶ отпили́ть

отпил|и́ть, ю́, ∼ишь *pf.* (*of* ▶ отпи́ливать) to saw off

отпира́|ть, ю, ет *impf. of* ▶ отпере́ть

отпира́|ться, ется *impf. of* ▶ отпере́ться

от|пи́ть, опью́, опьёшь, *past* ∼пи́л, ∼пила́, ∼пи́ло *pf.* (*of* ▶ отпива́ть) (+ *a. or g.*) to take a sip (of)

отплат|и́ть, чу́, ∼тишь *pf.* (*of* ▶ отпла́чивать) (+ *d.*) to pay back (to); to repay; **о. кому́-н. той же моне́той** to pay sb in his own coin

отпла́чива|ть, ю *impf. of* ▶ отплати́ть

отплыва́|ть, ю *impf. of* ▶ отплы́ть

отплы́ти|е, я *nt.* sailing, departure

отплы́|ть, ву́, вёшь, *past* ∼л, ∼ла́, ∼ло *pf.* (*of* ▶ отплыва́ть) (*о корабле́*) to sail, set sail; (*о плыву́щих лю́дях*) to swim off

отполза́|ть, а́ю *impf. of* ▶ отползти́

отполз|ти́, у́, ёшь, *past* ∼, ∼ла́ *pf.* (*of* ▶ отполза́ть) to crawl away

отполир|ова́ть, у́ю *pf. of* ▶ полирова́ть

отпо́р, а *m.* repulse; rebuff; **дать о.** (+ *d.*) to repulse; **встре́тить о.** to be repulsed; to meet with a rebuff

отпор|о́ть, ю́, ∼ешь *pf.* (*of* ▶ отпа́рывать) to rip off

отпра́в|ить, лю, ишь *pf.* (*of* ▶ отправля́ть) to send; (*по по́чте*) to post (BrE), mail

(AmE); to send off; **о. на тот свет** to send to kingdom come

отпра́в|иться, люсь, ишься *pf.* (*of* ▶ отправля́ться) to set out, set off, start; (*о по́езде*) to leave, depart

отправле́ни|е, я *nt.* **1** (*де́йствие*) sending **2** (*почто́вое, заказно́е*) item **3** (*по́езда*) departure

⚹ **отправля́|ть, ю** *impf. of* ▶ отпра́вить

отправля́|ться, юсь *impf. of* ▶ отпра́виться

отпра́здн|овать, ую *pf. of* ▶ пра́здновать

отпра́шива|ться, юсь *impf.* (*of* ▶ отпроси́ться) (*проси́ть разреше́ния*) to ask (for) leave

отпро|си́ться, шу́сь, ∼сишься *pf.* (*of* ▶ отпра́шиваться) (*получи́ть разреше́ние*) to obtain leave

отпры́гива|ть, ю *impf. of* ▶ отпры́гнуть

отпры́г|нуть, ну, нешь *pf.* (*of* ▶ отпры́гивать) (*наза́д*) to jump back; (*в сто́рону*) to jump aside

отпу́гива|ть, ю *impf. of* ▶ отпугну́ть

отпуг|ну́ть, ну́, нёшь *pf.* (*of* ▶ отпу́гивать) to frighten off, scare away

о́тпуск, а, в ∼**е,** *pl.* ∼**а́,** ∼**о́в** *m.* leave, holiday(s) (BrE), vacation (AmE); (mil.) leave, furlough; **в** ∼**е** on leave

отпуска́|ть, ю *impf. of* ▶ отпусти́ть

отпу|сти́ть, щу́, ∼стишь *pf.* (*of* ▶ отпуска́ть) **1** (*позво́лить кому́-н. уйти́; переста́ть держа́ть*) to let go; (*в сад, во двор*) to let out; (*освободи́ть*) to set free; to release; (*дать о́тпуск*) to give leave (of absence) **2** (*осла́бить*) to relax, slacken **3** (*бо́роду*) to (let) grow; (*пла́тье*) to let down **4** (*вы́дать*) to issue, give out; (*прода́ть*) to sell

отраба́тыва|ть, ю *impf. of* ▶ отрабо́тать

отрабо́танный *p.p.p. of* ▶ отрабо́тать *and adj.* (tech.) worked out; spent; **о. газ** waste gas

отрабо́та|ть, ю *pf.* (*of* ▶ отраба́тывать) **1** (*долг*) to work off **2** (*како́е-н. вре́мя*) to work **3** (*прида́ть оконча́тельный вид*) to put the finishing touches to **4** (*упражне́ние, приём*) to work through, give a workout to

отра́в|а, ы *f.* poison

отра́в|ить, лю́, ∼ишь *pf.* (*of* ▶ отравля́ть) to poison (also fig.)

отра́в|иться, лю́сь, ∼ишься *pf.* (*of* ▶ отравля́ться) to poison oneself

отравле́ни|е, я *nt.* poisoning

отравля́|ть, ю *impf. of* ▶ отрави́ть

отравля́|ться, юсь *impf. of* ▶ отрави́ться

отра́д|ный, ∼ен, ∼на *adj.* gratifying, pleasing; comforting

⚹ **отража́|ть, ю** *impf. of* ▶ отрази́ть

отража́|ться, юсь *impf. of* ▶ отрази́ться

отраже́ни|е, я *nt.* **1** reflection **2** (*нападе́ния*) repelling; warding off

отра|зи́ть, жу́, зи́шь *pf.* (*of* ▶ отража́ть) **1** to reflect (also fig.) **2** (*нападе́ние*) to repel; to ward off

отра|зи́ться, жу́сь, зи́шься *pf.* (*of* ▶ отража́ться) **1** to be reflected **2** (fig.)

⚹ key word

(на + *p.*) to affect; to tell (on); **пое́здка в го́ры благоприя́тно ∼зи́лась на его́ рабо́те** the mountain trip had a beneficial effect on his work

о́трасл|ь, и *f.* branch; **о. промы́шленности** branch of industry

отраст|а́ть, а́ю *impf. of* ▸ отрасти́

отраст|и́, у́, ёшь, *past* **отро́с, отросла́** *pf.* (*of* ▸ отраста́ть) to grow

отра|сти́ть, щу́, сти́шь *pf.* (*of* ▸ отра́щивать) to (let) grow; **о. во́лосы** to grow one's hair long

отра́щива|ть, ю *impf. of* ▸ отрасти́ть

отреаги́р|овать, ую *pf.* (infml) *of* ▸ реаги́ровать 2

отрегули́р|овать, ую *pf. of* ▸ регули́ровать 3

отредакти́р|овать, ую *pf. of* ▸ редакти́ровать 1

отре́|зать, жу, жешь *pf.* (*of* ▸ отреза́ть) **1** to cut off (also fig.) **2** (infml, *резко ответить*) to snap back

отрез|а́ть, а́ю *impf. of* ▸ отре́зать

отре́з|ок, ка *m.* (*ткани*) piece, cut; (*пути*) section; (math.) segment; **о. вре́мени** stretch of time

отрека́|ться, юсь *impf. of* ▸ отре́чься

отремонти́р|овать, ую *pf. of* ▸ ремонти́ровать

отрепети́р|овать, ую *pf. of* ▸ репети́ровать

отреставри́р|овать, ую *pf. of* ▸ реставри́ровать

отре́|чься, ку́сь, чёшься, ку́тся, *past* **∼кся, ∼кла́сь** *pf.* (*of* ▸ отрека́ться) (от + *g.*) to renounce, disavow, give up; **о. от престо́ла** to abdicate

отрица́ни|е, я *nt.* denial; negation

отрица́тел|ьный, ∼ен, ∼ьна *adj.* negative

отрица́|ть, ю *impf.* to deny; to disclaim; **о. вино́вность** (law) to plead not guilty

отруб|а́ть, а́ю *impf. of* ▸ отруби́ть

отруб|и́ть, лю́, ∼ишь *pf.* (*of* ▸ отруба́ть) (*сук*) to chop off

отруга́|ть, ю *pf. of* ▸ руга́ть 1, ▸ руга́ть 2

отры́в, а *m.* **1** tearing off **2** (fig.) alienation, isolation; loss of contact; **в ∼е (от** + *g.*) out of touch (with)

отрыва́|ть, ю *impf. of* ▸ оторва́ть

отрыва́|ться, юсь *impf. of* ▸ оторва́ться

отры́вист|ый, ∼, ∼а *adj.* jerky, abrupt; (*речь*) curt

отры́в|ок, ка *m.* (*разговора*) fragment; (*книги*) excerpt; passage; **о. из фи́льма** film clip

отры́жк|а, и *f.* belch

отря́д, а *m.* (mil.) detachment; (*группа*) group, party, brigade; **передово́й о.** (fig.) vanguard

отря́хива|ть, ю *impf. of* ▸ отряхну́ть

отря́хива|ться, юсь *impf. of* ▸ отряхну́ться

отрях|ну́ть, ну́, нёшь *pf.* (*of* ▸ отря́хивать) to shake down, shake off

отрях|ну́ться, ну́сь, нёшься *pf.* (*of* ▸ отря́хиваться) to shake oneself down

о́тсвет, а *m.* reflection; reflected light

отсе́ива|ть, ю *impf. of* ▸ отсе́ять

отсе́ива|ться, юсь *impf. of* ▸ отсе́яться

отсе́к, а *m.* **1** (naut., etc.) compartment **2** (astronautics) module

отсека́|ть, ю *impf. of* ▸ отсе́чь

отсе́|чь, ку́, чёшь, ку́т, *past* **∼к, ∼кла́** *pf.* (*of* ▸ отсека́ть) to cut off, chop off

отсе́|ять, ю, ешь *pf.* (*of* ▸ отсе́ивать) **1** to sift, screen **2** (fig.) to eliminate, screen out

отсе́|яться, юсь, ешься *pf.* (*of* ▸ отсе́иваться) **1** to be separated **2** (fig.) to fall off, fall away

отси|де́ть, жу́, ди́шь *pf.* (*of* ▸ отси́живать) **1** (*просидеть*) to stay (for); to sit out; **он ∼де́л де́сять лет в тюрьме́** he has done ten years (in prison) **2** (*вызвать онемение части тела*) to make numb by sitting; **я ∼де́л себе́ но́гу** I have pins and needles in my leg

отси|де́ться, жу́сь, ди́шься *pf.* (*of* ▸ отси́живаться) (infml) to sit tight

отси́жива|ть, ю *impf. of* ▸ отсиде́ть

отси́жива|ться, юсь *impf. of* ▸ отсиде́ться

отска́кива|ть, ю *impf. of* ▸ отскочи́ть

отскоч|и́ть, у́, ∼ишь *pf.* (*of* ▸ отска́кивать) **1** (*отпрыгнуть*) to jump (aside, away); (*о мяче*) to rebound, bounce back **2** (infml, *отделиться*) to come off, break off

отскреба́|ть, ю *impf. of* ▸ отскрести́

отскре|сти́, бу́, бёшь, *past* **∼б, ∼бла́** *pf.* (*of* ▸ отскреба́ть) to scrape off

отслуж|и́ть, у́, ∼ишь *pf.* ▸ служи́ть 5

отсоедин|и́ть, ю́, и́шь *pf.* ▸ отсоединя́ть to disconnect

отсоединя́|ть, ю *impf. of* ▸ отсоедини́ть

отсортир|ова́ть, у́ю *pf.* (*of* ▸ отсортиро́вывать) to sort (out)

отсортиро́выва|ть, ю *impf. of* ▸ отсортирова́ть

отсро́чива|ть, ю *impf. of* ▸ отсро́чить

отсро́ч|ить, у, ишь *pf.* (*of* ▸ отсро́чивать) to postpone, defer

отсро́чк|а, и *f.* postponement, deferment

отстава́ни|е, я *nt.* lag

отста|ва́ть, ю́, ёшь *impf. of* ▸ отста́ть

отста́вк|а, и *f.* (mil.) retirement; (hist., *с государственной службы*) resignation; **вы́йти в ∼у** to retire; to resign

отставно́й *adj.* (mil.) retired

отста́ива|ть, ю *impf. of* ▸ отстоя́ть

отста́лый *adj.* (fig.) backward; **у́мственно о.** learning-disabled

отста́|ть, ну, нешь *pf.* (*of* ▸ отстава́ть) **1** (от + *g.*) (*оказаться позади*) to fall behind; to lag behind; (*умственно*) to be learning-disabled **2** (от + *g.*) (*отделиться*) to become detached (from); **о. от по́езда** to be left behind by the train (sc., *at a station en route*); **обо́и ∼ли от стены́** the wallpaper came off **3** (*о часах*) to be slow; **о. на полчаса́** to be half an hour slow **4** (infml) (от + *g.*)

(*перестать надоедать*) to leave alone; ~нь от меня́! leave me alone!

отстёгива|ть, ю *impf. of* ▶ отстегну́ть

отстег|ну́ть, ну́, нёшь *pf.* (*of* ▶ отстёгивать) (*крючок*) to unfasten, undo; (*пуговицы*) to unbutton

отстир|а́ть, а́ю *pf.* (*of* ▶ отсти́рывать) to wash off

отстир|а́ться, а́ется *pf.* (*of* ▶ отсти́рываться) to wash off, come out in the wash

отсти́рыва|ть, ю, ет *impf. of* ▶ отстира́ть

отсти́рыва|ться, ется *impf. of* ▶ отстира́ться

отсто|я́ть, ю́, и́шь *pf.* (*of* ▶ отста́ивать) to defend

отстра́ива|ть, ю *impf. of* ▶ отстро́ить

отстран|и́ть, ю́, и́шь *pf.* (*of* ▶ отстраня́ть) **1** (*отодвинуть*) to push aside **2** (*уволить*) to dismiss, discharge

отстран|я́ть, я́ю *impf. of* ▶ отстрани́ть

отстре́лива|ться, юсь *impf. of* ▶ отстреля́ться

отстрел|я́ться, я́юсь *pf.* (*of* ▶ отстре́ливаться) **1** (от + *g.*) to defend oneself (by shooting) (against) **2** (*ответить стрельбой на стрельбу*) to return fire, fire back

отстрига́|ть, ю *impf. of* ▶ отстри́чь

отстри́|чь, гу́, жёшь, гу́т, *past* ~г, ~гла *pf.* (*of* ▶ отстрига́ть) to cut off, clip

отстро́|ить, ю, оишь *pf.* (*of* ▶ отстра́ивать) to complete the construction of, finish building

о́тступ, а *m.* (*typ.*) indentation

отступ|а́ть, а́ю *impf. of* ▶ отступи́ть

отступ|а́ться, а́юсь *impf. of* ▶ отступи́ться

отступ|и́ть, лю́, ~ишь *pf.* (*of* ▶ отступа́ть) **1** (*отойти назад*) to step back; to recede **2** (mil.) to retreat, fall back **3** (fig.) (от + *g.*) (*от чего-н. установленного*) to deviate (from); о. от те́мы to digress

отступ|и́ться, лю́сь, ~ишься *pf.* (*of* ▶ отступа́ться) (infml) (от + *g.*) to give up, renounce; о. от своего́ сло́ва to go back on one's word

отступле́ни|е, я *nt.* **1** (mil., also fig.) retreat **2** (*от темы*) deviation; digression

⚐ отсу́тстви|е, я *nt.* absence; (+ *g.*) lack (of); в его́ о. in his absence; за ~ем (+ *g.*) (*кого-н.*) in the absence (of); (*чего-н.*) for lack (of), for want (of)

⚐ отсу́тств|овать, ую *impf.* (*о человеке*) to be absent; (*о доказательстве*) to be lacking

отсу́тств|ующий *pres. part. of* ▶ отсу́тствовать *and adj.* absent (also fig.); о. вид blank expression; (*as m. n. o., ~ующего*) absentee

отсчит|а́ть, а́ю *pf.* (*of* ▶ отсчи́тывать) to count out, count off; о. кому́-н. пятьсо́т рубле́й to count out five hundred roubles to sb

отсчи́тыва|ть, ю *impf. of* ▶ отсчита́ть

отсыла́|ть, ю *impf. of* ▶ отосла́ть

отсы́п|ать, лю, лешь *pf.* (*of* ▶ отсыпа́ть) (+ *a. or g.*) to pour off; to measure off

отсып|а́ть, а́ю *impf. of* ▶ отсы́пать

отсыре́|ть, ю *pf. of* ▶ сыре́ть

отсю́да *adv.* from here; hence (also fig.); (fig.) from this; о. сле́дует, что... from this it follows that ...

Отта́в|а, ы *f.* Ottawa

отта́ива|ть, ю *impf. of* ▶ отта́ять

отта́лкива|ть, ю *impf. of* ▶ оттолкну́ть

отта́лкива|ться, юсь *impf. of* ▶ оттолкну́ться

отта́скива|ть, ю *impf. of* ▶ оттащи́ть

оттащ|и́ть, у́, ~ишь *pf.* (*of* ▶ отта́скивать) to drag aside (away), pull aside (away)

отта́|ять, ю, ешь *pf.* (*of* ▶ отта́ивать) to thaw out (*trans. and intrans.*)

оттён|ок, ка *m.* (*цвета*) shade, hue; (fig.) shade, nuance; он говори́л с ~ком иро́нии there was a note of irony in his voice

о́ттепел|ь, и *f.* thaw

оттер|е́ть, ототру́, ототрёшь, *past* ~, ~ла *pf.* (*of* ▶ оттира́ть) (*грязь*) to rub off, rub out

оттесн|и́ть, ю́, и́шь *pf.* (*of* ▶ оттесня́ть) to drive back; to press back; to push aside, shove aside (also fig.); о. проти́вника (mil.) to force the enemy back

оттесн|я́ть, я́ю *impf. of* ▶ оттесни́ть

оттира́|ть, ю *impf. of* ▶ оттере́ть

оттого́ *adv.* = потому́

отто́к, а *m.* mass departure, haemorrhage (BrE), hemorrhage (AmE) (*of specialists, sportsmen, etc.*)

оттолкн|у́ть, у́, ёшь *pf.* (*of* ▶ отта́лкивать) **1** (*стул*) to push away, push aside **2** (fig., *друзей*) to antagonize, alienate

оттолкн|у́ться, у́сь, ёшься *pf.* (*of* ▶ отта́лкиваться) **1** (от + *g.*) to push off (from) **2** (fig.) (от + *g.*) to take as a starting point

оттопы́рен|ный, ~, ~а *adj.* (infml) protruding, sticking out; (*карманы*) bulging

отторже́ни|е, я *nt.* tearing away, seizure; (med.) rejection (*of a transplanted organ*)

отту́да *adv.* from there

оття́гива|ть, ю *impf. of* ▶ оттяну́ть

оття|ну́ть, ну́, ~нешь *pf.* (*of* ▶ оття́гивать) **1** to pull, drag (away) **2** (mil., *отряд*) to draw off **3** (*карман*) to stretch, weigh down

отупе́ни|е, я *nt.* stupefaction, dullness, torpor

отуч|а́ть, а́ю *impf. of* ▶ отучи́ть

отуч|а́ться, а́юсь *impf. of* ▶ отучи́ть, ▶ отучи́ться[1]

оту́чива|ться, юсь *impf. of* ▶ отучи́ться[2]

отуч|и́ть, у́, ~ишь *pf.* (*of* ▶ отуча́ть) (от + *g.* or + *inf.*) to break (of); о. от груди́ to wean

отуч|и́ться[1], у́сь, ~ишься *pf.* (*of* ▶ отуча́ться) (от + *g. or inf.*) (*отвыкнуть*) to break oneself (of)

отуч|и́ться[2], у́сь, ~ишься *pf.* (*of* ▶ оту́чиваться) (*кончить учиться*) to have finished one's lessons; to finish learning

отфильтр|ова́ть, у́ю *pf.* (*of* ▸ фильтрова́ть)

отформати́р|овать, ую *pf.* (*of* ▸ формати́ровать)

отхва|ти́ть, чу́, ~тишь *pf.* (*of* ▸ отхва́тывать) (infml) **1** (*отрезать*) to snip off; (*отрубить*) to chop off **2** (*достать*) to get hold of

отхва́тыва|ть, ю *impf. of* ▸ отхвати́ть

отхлеб|ну́ть, ну́, нёшь *pf.* (*of* ▸ отхлёбывать) (infml) (+ *a.* or *g.*) to take a sip (of); to take a mouthful (of)

отхлёбыва|ть, ю *impf. of* ▸ отхлебну́ть

отхлы́н|уть, у, ешь *pf.* to rush back, flood back (also fig.)

отхо́д, a *m.* **1** departure **2** (mil.) withdrawal **3** (от + *g.*) (*отклонение*) deviation (from); (*разрыв*) break (with) **4** *see* ▸ отхо́ды

отхо|ди́ть, жу́, ~дишь *impf. of* ▸ отойти́

отхо́д|ы, ов (tech.) waste (products)

отцеп|и́ть, лю́, ~ишь *pf.* (*of* ▸ отцепля́ть) to unhook; to uncouple

отцеп|и́ться, лю́сь, ~ишься *pf.* (*of* ▸ отцепля́ться) to come unhooked; to come uncoupled

отцепля́|ть, ю *impf. of* ▸ отцепи́ть

отцепля́|ться, юсь *impf. of* ▸ отцепи́ться

отцо́вский *adj.* one's father's; paternal

отча́ива|ться, юсь *impf. of* ▸ отча́яться

отча́сти *adv.* partly

отча́яни|е, я *nt.* despair

отча́ян|ный, ~, ~на *adj.* (*положение, взор, крик*) desperate; (*смелый до безрассудности*) daring, reckless; (infml, *ужасный*) terrible, awful

отча́|яться, юсь, ешься *pf.* (*of* ▸ отча́иваться) (в + *p.* or + *inf.*) to despair (of)

отчего́ *adv.* why; **вот о.** that's why

отчего́-нибудь *adv.* for some reason or other

отчего́-то *adv.* for some reason

о́тчеств|о, а *nt.* patronymic; **как его́ по ~у?** what is his patronymic?

✍ **отчёт, a** *m.* account; **дать о.** (в + *p.*) to give an account (of), report (on); **отдава́ть себе́ о.** (в + *p.*) to be aware (of), realize

отчётлив|ый, ~, ~a *adj.* intelligible, clear, distinct

отчётный *adj. of* ▸ отчёт; **о. год** financial year, current year; **о. докла́д** report

о́тчим, a *m.* stepfather

отчи́|стить, щу, стишь *pf.* (*of* ▸ отчища́ть) **1** (*пятно*) to clean off; to brush off **2** (*одежду*) to clean

отчи́|ститься, щусь, стишься *pf.* (*of* ▸ отчища́ться) **1** (*о грязи*) to come off, come out **2** (*об одежде*) to become clean

отчит|а́ться, а́юсь *pf.* (*of* ▸ отчи́тываться) (в + *p.*) to give an account (of), report (on); **о. пе́ред избира́телями** to report back to the electors

отчи́тыва|ться, юсь *impf. of* ▸ отчита́ться

отчища́|ть, ю *impf. of* ▸ отчи́стить

отчища́|ться, юсь *impf. of* ▸ отчи́ститься

отшатн|у́ться, у́сь, ёшься *pf.* (*of* ▸ отша́тываться) (от + *g.*) (*от удара*) to start back (from); to recoil (from) **2** (fig., *прекратить общение*) to give up; to break (with)

отша́тыва|ться, юсь *impf. of* ▸ отшатну́ться

отшвы́рива|ть, ю *impf. of* ▸ отшвырну́ть

отшвыр|ну́ть, ну́, нёшь *pf.* (*of* ▸ отшвы́ривать) to fling away; to throw off

отше́льник, a *m.* hermit; recluse

отшлёпа|ть, ю *pf. of* ▸ шлёпать

отшлиф|ова́ть, у́ю *pf.* (*of* ▸ отшлифо́вывать, ▸ шлифова́ть) **1** (tech.) to polish; to grind **2** (fig., *совершенствовать*) to polish, perfect

отшлифо́выва|ть, ю *impf. of* ▸ отшлифова́ть

отъеда́|ть, ю *impf. of* ▸ отъе́сть

отъеда́|ться, юсь *impf. of* ▸ отъе́сться

отъе́зд, a *m.* departure; **быть в ~е** to be away

отъезжа́|ть, ю *impf. of* ▸ отъе́хать

отъе́|сть, м, шь, ст, ди́м, ди́те, дя́т, *past* **~л, ~ла** *pf.* (*of* ▸ отъеда́ть) to bite off and eat

отъе́|сться, мся, шься, стся, ди́мся, ди́тесь, дя́тся, *past* **~лся, ~лась** *pf.* (*of* ▸ отъеда́ться) to put on weight; to feed well

отъе́|хать, ду, дешь *pf.* (*of* ▸ отъезжа́ть) to depart

отъя́вленный *adj.* (infml, pej.) thorough, inveterate, out-and-out

отыгр|а́ться, а́юсь *pf.* (*of* ▸ оты́грываться) to win (having lost); to get back what one has lost

оты́грыва|ться, юсь *impf. of* ▸ отыгра́ться

оты́ска|ть, щу́, ~щешь *pf.* (*of* ▸ оты́скивать 1) to find; to track down, run to earth

оты́ска́|ться, щу́сь, ~щешься *pf.* (*of* ▸ оты́скиваться) to turn up, appear

оты́скива|ть, ю *impf.* **1** *impf. of* ▸ отыска́ть **2** (*impf. only*) to look for, try to find

оты́скива|ться, юсь *impf. of* ▸ отыска́ться

отяжеле́|ть, ю *pf.* to become heavy

✍ **о́фис, a** *m.* office

о́фисный *adj.* office (*attr.*)

офице́р, a *m.* officer

офице́р|ский *adj. of* ▸ офице́р; **~ское собра́ние** officers' mess

✍ **официа́льн|ый** *adj.* official; **~ое лицо́** an official

официа́нт, a *m.* waiter

официа́нтк|a, и *f.* waitress

офла́йновый *adj.* (comput.) offline

оформи́тел|ь, я *m.* designer; **о. спекта́кля** set designer

оформи́тел|ьница, ницы *f. of* ▸ оформи́тель

офо́рм|ить, лю, ишь *pf.* (*of* ▸ оформля́ть) **1** to design; **о. витри́ну** to dress a window **2** (*узаконить*) to register officially, legalize; **о. догово́р** to draw up an agreement **3** (*на работу*) to enrol, take on

О

офо́рм|иться, люсь, ишься *pf.* (*of*
▶ оформля́ться) **1** (*об идеях*) to take shape
2 (*узако́ниться*) to be registered; to legalize
one's position **3** (*на рабо́ту*) to be taken on,
join the staff

ꝏ оформле́ни|е, я *nt.* **1** design; сцени́ческое
о. staging **2** (*узаконе́ние*) registration,
legalization

ꝏ оформля́|ть, ю *impf. of* ▶ офо́рмить

оформля́|ться, юсь *impf. of* ▶ офо́рмиться

офо́рт, а *m.* (*вид гравю́ры на мета́лле*) etching

офтальмо́лог, а *m.* ophthalmologist

офтальмоло́ги|я, и *f.* ophthalmology

офшо́рный *adj.* (fin.) offshore

о́х|ать, аю *impf.* (*of* ▶ о́хнуть) (*от бо́ли*) to
moan, groan; (*от печа́ли*) to sigh

охва|ти́ть, чу́, ~тишь *pf.* (*of* ▶ охва́тывать)
1 (*обхвати́ть*) to envelop; to enclose; дом
~ти́ло пла́менем the house was enveloped
in flames **2** (*о чу́встве*) to grip, seize; их
~ти́л у́жас they were seized with panic

охва́тыва|ть, ю *impf. of* ▶ охвати́ть

охва́ченный *p.p.p. of* ▶ охвати́ть; о. у́жасом
terror-stricken

охла|ди́ть, жу́, ди́шь *pf.* (*of* ▶ охлажда́ть) to
cool, cool off (also fig.)

охла|ди́ться, жу́сь, ди́шься *pf.* (*of*
▶ охлажда́ться) to become cool, cool down
(also fig.)

охлажда́|ть, ю *impf. of* ▶ охлади́ть

охлажда́|ться, юсь *impf. of* ▶ охлади́ться

охлажда́|ющий *pres. part. act. of* ▶ охлажда́ть
and adj. cooling, refrigerating; ~ющая
жи́дкость coolant

охлажде́ни|е, я *nt.* **1** cooling (off); с
возду́шным ~ем air-cooled **2** (fig.) coolness

о́х|нуть, ну, нешь *pf. of* ▶ о́хать

охо́т|а¹, ы *f.* hunt, hunting; chase

охо́т|а², ы *f.* (к + *d. or* + *inf.*) desire, wish,
inclination; о. тебе́ спо́рить с ним! (infml)
what makes you argue with him!

охо́|титься, чусь, тишься *impf.* to hunt;
(fig.) (за + *i.*) to hunt for

охо́тник, а *m.* hunter

охо́тничий *adj.* hunting

охо́тно *adv.* willingly, gladly, readily

о́хр|а, ы *f.* ochre (BrE), ocher (AmE)

ꝏ охра́н|а, ы *f.* **1** (*помеще́ния*) guarding;
(*приро́ды*) protection; (*по труда́*) health and
safety measures **2** (*гру́ппа люде́й*) guard;
ли́чная о. bodyguard; пограни́чная о.
frontier guard

охран|и́ть, ю́, и́шь *pf.* (*of* ▶ охраня́ть)
(*грани́цу, помеще́ние*) to guard; (*приро́ду;
интере́сы*) to protect

охра́нник, а *m.* guard

охран|я́ть, я́ю *impf. of* ▶ охрани́ть

охри́п|нуть, ну, нешь, *past* ~, ~ла *pf.* (*of*
▶ хри́пнуть) to become hoarse

оцара́па|ть, ю *pf.* (*of* ▶ цара́пать) to scratch

ꝏ key word

ꝏ оце́нива|ть, ю *impf. of* ▶ оцени́ть

оцен|и́ть, ю́, ~ишь *pf.* (*of* ▶ оце́нивать)
1 (*определи́ть це́ну чего́-н.*) to estimate
the value of, value; (*назна́чить це́ну
чему́-н.*) to price; (*определи́ть це́нность,
значи́тельность чего́-н.*) to evaluate,
appraise **2** (*призна́ть досто́инства
чего́-н.*) to appreciate; о. что-н. по
досто́инству to appreciate sth at its true
value

ꝏ оце́нк|а, и *f.* **1** (*иму́щества*) valuation;
(*рабо́ты*) evaluation, appraisal **2** (*мне́ние
о це́нности*) appreciation **3** (*отме́тка*)
mark, grade

оцепене́ни|е, я *nt.* stupor

оцеп|и́ть, лю́, ~ишь *pf.* (*of* ▶ оцепля́ть) to
surround; to cordon off

оцепле́ни|е, я *nt.* **1** (*де́йствие*) surrounding;
cordoning off **2** (*лю́ди*) cordon

оцепля́|ть, ю *impf. of* ▶ оцепи́ть

оча́г, а́ *m.* **1** hearth (also fig.); дома́шний о.
(fig.) hearth, home **2** (fig.) centre, seat

очарова́тел|ьный, ~ен, ~ьна *adj.*
charming, fascinating

очар|ова́ть, у́ю *pf.* (*of* ▶ очаро́вывать) to
charm, fascinate

очаро́выва|ть, ю *impf. of* ▶ очарова́ть

очеви́д|ец, ца *m.* eyewitness

ꝏ очеви́дно *adv.* obviously, evidently; вы, о.,
не согла́сны you obviously do not agree

очеви́д|ный, ~ен, ~на *adj.* obvious, evident

ꝏ о́чень *adv.* (*при прилага́тельных и наре́чиях*)
very; (*при глаго́лах*) very much

ꝏ очередно́й *adj.* **1** next; next in turn; о.
вопро́с the next question; о. вы́пуск latest
issue (*of a journal, etc.*) **2** usual; regular; о.
о́тпуск regular holidays

ꝏ о́черед|ь, и, *pl.* ~и, ~е́й *f.* **1** turn; о. за
ва́ми it is your turn; в свою́ о. in one's turn;
по ~и in turn, in order; в пе́рвую о. in the
first place/instance **2** (*ряд*) queue (BrE),
line (AmE); стоя́ть в ~и (за + *i.*) to queue
(for) (BrE), stand in line (for) (AmE); стать
в о́чередь to queue (up) (BrE), stand in line
(AmE) **3** (mil.): (*пулемётная*) о. burst

о́черк, а *m.* essay, sketch, study; (*ко́нтур*)
outline; ~и ру́сской исто́рии studies in
Russian history

очерта́ни|е, я *nt.* (*usu. in pl.*) outline

очи́|стить, щу, стишь *pf.* (*of* ▶ очища́ть,
▶ чи́стить 3) **1** (*таре́лку, о́бувь*) to clean;
(*во́ду, спирт*) to purify; (*со́весть*) to salve,
clear; (*ду́шу*) to cleanse, purify **2** (от + *g.*)
(*стол*) to clear (of); о. кише́чник to open
bowels **3** (*карто́фелину, я́блоко*) to peel

очи́|ститься, щусь, стишься *pf.* (*of*
▶ очища́ться) (от + *g.*) to become clear (of)

очи́стк|а, и *f.* **1** (*о́буви*) cleaning; (*души́*)
cleansing, purification; (*во́ды*) purification;
(*овоще́й*) peeling **2** (от + *g.*) clearing,
clearance (of); freeing (of)

очи́стк|и, ов (*no sg.*) peelings

ꝏ очища́|ть, ю *impf. of* ▶ очи́стить

очища́|ться, юсь *impf. of* ▶ очи́ститься

очк|и́, **о́в** (*no sg.*) glasses, spectacles (BrE), eyeglasses (AmE); (*защи́тные*) goggles

✓ **очк|о́**, **а́**, *pl.* ~**и́**, ~**о́в** *nt.* (sport) point

очн|у́ться, **у́сь**, **ёшься** *pf.* **1** (*по́сле сна*) to wake **2** (*по́сле о́бморока*) to come to, regain consciousness

о́чн|ый *adj.* **1** (*opp.* зао́чный) internal (*instruction, student, etc., as opposed to external, extra-mural*) **2**: ~**ая ста́вка** (law) confrontation

очу́т|и́ться, ~**и́шься** *pf.* to find oneself; to come to be; **как вы здесь** ~**и́лись?** how did you come to be here?

оше́йник, **а** *m.* collar (*animal's*)

ошелом|и́ть, **лю́**, **и́шь** *pf.* (*of* ▶ ошеломля́ть) to stun

ошеломля́|ть, **ю** *impf. of* ▶ ошеломи́ть

ошиб|а́ться, **а́юсь** *impf. of* ▶ ошиби́ться

ошиб|и́ться, **у́сь**, **ёшься**, *past* ~**ся**, ~**ла́сь** *pf.* (*of* ▶ ошиба́ться) to be mistaken, make a mistake, make mistakes

✓ **оши́бк|а**, **и** *f.* mistake; error; **по** ~**е** by mistake

оши́боч|ный, ~**ен**, ~**на** *adj.* erroneous, mistaken

ошпа́рива|ть, **ю** *impf. of* ▶ ошпа́рить

ошпа́р|ить, **ю**, **ишь** *pf.* (*of* ▶ ошпа́ривать, ▶ шпа́рить 1) (infml) to scald

оштраф|ова́ть, **у́ю** *pf. of* ▶ штрафова́ть

оштукату́р|ить, **ю**, **ишь** *pf. of* ▶ штукату́рить

ощети́нива|ться, **юсь** *impf. of* ▶ ощети́ниться

ощети́н|иться, **юсь**, **ишься** *pf.* (*of* ▶ ощети́ниваться, ▶ щети́ниться) to bristle (also fig.)

ощип|а́ть, **лю́**, ~**лешь** *pf.* (*of* ▶ щипа́ть 3, ▶ ощи́пывать) to pluck

ощи́пыва|ть, **ю** *impf. of* ▶ ощипа́ть

ощу́п|ать, **аю** *pf.* (*of* ▶ ощу́пывать) to feel

ощу́пыва|ть, **ю** *impf. of* ▶ ощу́пать

о́щуп|ь, **и** *f.*: **на о.** to the touch; by touch; **идти́ на о.** to grope one's way

ощути́м|ый, ~, ~**а** *adj.* **1** (*за́пах, похолода́ние*) perceptible, noticeable **2** (fig., *недоста́тки, расхо́ды*) appreciable

ощу|ти́ть, **щу́**, **ти́шь** *pf.* (*of* ▶ ощуща́ть) to feel, sense; **о. го́лод** to feel hunger

ощуща́|ть, **ю** *impf. of* ▶ ощути́ть

✓ **ощуще́ни|е**, **я** *nt.* **1** (physiol.) sensation **2** (*стра́ха, ра́дости*) feeling, sense

Пп

о
п

павильо́н, **а** *m.* **1** pavilion **2** (cin.) film studio

павли́н, **а** *m.* peacock

па́вод|ок, **ка** *m.* flood (*esp. resulting from melting of snow*)

па́год|а, **ы** *f.* pagoda

па́дал|ь, **и** *f.* (*usu. collect.*) carrion

па́да|ть, **ю** *impf.* **1** (*pf.* пасть *and* упа́сть) to fall; (*о настрое́нии*) to sink; (*о нра́вах*) to decline; **п. в о́бморок** to faint **2** (*pf.* пасть) (fig.) (**на** + *a.*) to fall (on, to); **отве́тственность** ~**ет на вас** the responsibility falls on you

паде́ж, **а́** *m.* (gram.) case

паде́ни|е, **я** *nt.* fall; (*нра́вов*) decline

па́дчериц|а, **ы** *f.* stepdaughter

па|ёк, **йка́** *m.* ration

пазл, **а** *m.* jigsaw puzzle

па́зух|а, **и** *f.* bosom; **за** ~**ой** in one's bosom

✓ **паке́т**, **а** *m.* **1** (*свёрток*) parcel, package **2** (*письмо́*) (official) letter **3** (*мешо́к*) (paper) bag **4** (comput.) package

Пакиста́н, **а** *m.* Pakistan

пакиста́н|ец, **ца** *m.* Pakistani

пакиста́н|ка, **ки** *f. of* ▶ пакиста́нец

пакиста́нский *adj.* Pakistani

пак|ова́ть, **у́ю** *impf.* (*of* ▶ упакова́ть) to pack

па́кост|ь, **и** *f.* **1** (*о посту́пке*) dirty trick; **де́лать** ~**и** (+ *d.*) to play dirty tricks (on) **2** (*дрянь*) filth

пакт, **а** *m.* pact; **п. о нападе́нии** non-aggression pact

✓ **пала́т|а**, **ы** *f.* **1** (*в больни́це*) ward **2** (pol.) chamber, house; **ве́рхняя, ни́жняя п.** Upper, Lower Chamber; **п. ло́рдов** House of Lords; **п. общи́н** House of Commons **3** (*назва́ние не́которых госуда́рственных учрежде́ний*): **Торго́вая п.** Chamber of Commerce

пала́тк|а, **и** *f.* **1** tent; (*больша́я*) marquee **2** (*ларёк*) stall, booth

пала́ч, **а́** *m.* executioner; (fig.) butcher

палеонто́лог, **а** *m.* palaeontologist (BrE), paleontologist (AmE)

палеонтоло́ги|я, **и** *f.* palaeontology (BrE), paleontology (AmE)

Палести́н|а, **ы** *f.* Palestine

палести́н|ец, **ца** *m.* Palestinian

палести́н|ка, **ки** *f. of* ▶ палести́нец

палести́нский *adj.* Palestinian

✓ **па́л|ец**, **ьца** *m.* finger; **п. ноги́** toe; **большо́й п.** thumb; **смотре́ть сквозь** ~**ьцы на что-н.**

(infml) to shut one's eyes to sth
палиса́дник, а *m.* small front garden
пали́тр|а, ы *f.* palette
пал|и́ть, ю́, и́шь *impf.* (infml, *стреля́ть*) to fire (*from gun*)
па́лк|а, и *f.* stick; **вставля́ть кому́-н. ~и в колёса** to put a spoke in sb's wheel
пало́мник, а *m.* pilgrim (also fig.)
па́лочк|а, и *f. dim. of* ▶ па́лка; **бараба́нная п.** drumstick; **волше́бная п.** magic wand; **дирижёрская п.** conductor's baton
па́лтус, а *m.* halibut; (*также в рыболо́встве*) turbot
па́луб|а, ы *f.* deck
па́льм|а, ы *f.* palm (tree)
пал|ьну́ть, ьну́, ьнёшь *inst. pf.* (*of* ▶ пали́ть) (infml) to fire a shot
пальто́ *nt. indecl.* (over)coat
пампа́с|ы, ов (*no sg.*) (geog.) pampas
памфле́т, а *m.* lampoon
па́мятк|а, и *f.* (list of) instructions, guidelines
✒ **па́мятник**, а *m.* monument; (*на моги́ле*) tombstone; (*ста́туя*) statue; (*археологи́ческий*) relic
па́мят|ный, ~ен, ~на *adj.* memorable
✒ **па́мят|ь**, и *f.* **1** (also comput.) memory; **на мое́й ~и** within my memory; **по ~и** from memory **2** (*воспомина́ние*) memory, recollection, remembrance; **в п.** (+ *g.*) in memory (of); **подари́ть на п.** to give as a keepsake **3** (*созна́ние*) mind, consciousness; **быть без ~и** to be unconscious; **быть от кого́-н. без ~и** (infml) be crazy about sb
Пана́м|а, ы *f.* Panama
пана́м|а, ы *f.* panama (hat)
па́нд|а, ы *f.* panda
✒ **пане́л|ь**, и *f.* **1** (*тротуа́р*) pavement (BrE), sidewalk (AmE) **2** (*обши́вка*) panel, panelling (BrE), paneling (AmE) **3**: **прибо́рная п.** instrument panel; dashboard
па́ник|а, и *f.* panic
паник|ова́ть, у́ю *impf.* (*no pf.*) (infml) to panic
панихи́д|а, ы *f.* funeral service; requiem; **гражда́нская п.** civil funeral
пани́ческий *adj.* panic-stricken; **п. страх** utter terror
панк, а *m.* (*also as indecl. adj.*) punk
панно́ *nt. indecl.* panel
панора́м|а, ы *f.* panorama
панора́мный *adj.* panoramic
пансио́н, а *m.*: **по́лный ~** (full) board and lodging
пансиона́т, а *m.* boarding house, guest house
пантеи́зм, а *m.* pantheism
пантео́н, а *m.* pantheon
панте́р|а, ы *f.* panther
пантоми́м|а, ы *f.* mime
па́нцир|ь, я *m.* (zool.) shell
па́п|а¹, ы *m.* (infml) dad, daddy, papa (AmE)

па́п|а², ы *m.*: **П. Ри́мский** pope; the Pope
папа́й|я, и *f.* papaya, pawpaw
папара́цци *c.g. indecl.* paparazzo
па́перт|ь, и *f.* church porch, parvis
папиро́с|а, ы *f.* cigarette (*of Russian type, with cardboard mouthpiece*)
папи́рус, а *m.* papyrus
па́пк|а, и *f.* folder, file; (comput.) folder
па́поротник, а *m.* fern
па́прик|а, и *f.* paprika
Па́пуа — Но́вая Гвине́я, Па́пуа — Но́вой Гвине́и *f.* Papua New Guinea
папуа́с, а *m.* Papuan
папуа́с|ка, ки *f. of* ▶ папуа́с
папуа́сский *adj.* Papuan
папье́-маше́ *nt. indecl.* papier mâché
✒ **па́р|а**, ы *f.* (*сапо́г, чуло́к, но́жниц*) pair; (*два предме́та, дво́е люде́й*) couple; **супру́жеская п.** married couple; **она́ ему́ не п.** she is no match for him
Парагва́|й, я *m.* Paraguay
пара́граф, а *m.* paragraph
пара́д, а *m.* (*ше́ствие*) parade; (mil.) review
паради́гм|а, ы *f.* paradigm
пара́д|ный, ~ен, ~на *adj.* **1** (*торже́ственный*) ceremonial; ~ная фо́рма full dress (uniform) **2** (*пы́шный*) gala **3** (*гла́вный*) main, front; **п. подъе́зд** main entrance; (*as f. n.* ~ная, ~ной) front door
парадо́кс, а *m.* paradox
парази́т, а *m.* (biol., also fig.) parasite
парализо́ванный *p.p.p. of* ▶ парализова́ть *and adj.* paralysed (also fig.)
парализ|ова́ть, у́ю *impf. and pf.* to paralyse (also fig.)
парали́ч, а́ *m.* paralysis; **он разби́т ~о́м** he is completely paralysed
паралле́л|ь, и *f.* parallel; **провести́ п.** (**ме́жду** + *i.*) to draw a parallel (between)
паралле́льно *adv.* **1** (+ *d. or* с + *i.*) parallel (to, with) **2** (*одновреме́нно*) simultaneously (with), at the same time (as)
паралле́л|ьный, ~ен, ~ьна *adj.* parallel
✒ **пара́метр**, а *m.* parameter
парано́ик, а *m.* (med.) paranoid
парано́й|я, и *f.* (med.) paranoia
паранорма́льный *adj.* paranormal
параолимпи́йск|ий *adj.* Paralympic; **П~е и́гры** Paralympics
парапе́т, а *m.* parapet
парафи́н, а *m.* paraffin (wax)
парашю́т, а *m.* parachute
парашюти́ст, а *m.* parachutist; skydiver
✒ **па́р|ень**, ня, *pl.* ~ни, ~не́й *m.* **1** (*ю́ноша*) boy, lad **2** (infml, *мужчи́на*) chap (BrE), fellow, guy; **свой п.** a good guy
пари́ *nt. indecl.* bet; **держа́ть п.** to bet, lay a bet; **держу́ п., что...** I bet that ...

✒ key word

Пари́ж, а *m.* Paris

парижа́н|ин, ина, *pl.* ~**е,** ~ *m.* Parisian

парижа́н|ка, ки *f. of* ▶ **парижа́нин** Parisienne

пари́жский *adj.* Parisian

пари́к, á *m.* wig

парикма́хер, а *m.* hairdresser; (*мужской*) barber

парикма́херск|ая, ой *f.* hairdresser's; hairdressing salon; (*мужская*) barber's (shop)

парите́т, а *m.* parity

пар|и́ть, ю́, и́шь *impf.* (*no pf.*) to soar, swoop, hover; **п. в облака́х** (fig.) to live in the clouds

па́р|иться, юсь, ишься *impf. of* ▶ **попа́риться**

парк, а *m.* **1** (*сад*) park; **разби́ть п.** to lay out a park **2** (*место стоянки*) yard, depot **3** (*подвижной состав*) fleet; stock; pool

парке́т, а *m.* parquet; parquetry

парк|ова́ть, у́ю *impf. of* ▶ **припаркова́ть**

парк|ова́ться, у́юсь *impf. of* ▶ **припаркова́ться**

парко́вк|а, и *f.* parking

парла́мент, а *m.* parliament

парламента́ри|й, я *m.* parliamentarian

парла́ментский *adj.* parliamentary; **п. запро́с** interpellation

парни́к, á *m.* hotbed, polytunnel; (*из стекла*) greenhouse

парн|о́й *adj.* fresh; ~**о́е мя́со** fresh meat

па́рн|ый *adj.* pair; forming a pair; twin; **п. носо́к, п. сапо́г** *и т. п.* pair, fellow (*other one of pair of socks, boots, etc.*); ~**ое ката́ние** (*на конька́х*) pair skating

парово́з, а *m.* (steam) engine, locomotive

паров|о́й *adj.* **1** *adj. of* ▶ **пар;** ~**ая маши́на** steam engine **2** (*cul.*) steamed

пароди́ст, а *m.* impressionist, mimic

паро́ди|я, и *f.* **1** (*произведение*) parody **2** (**на** + *a.*) (*на справедливость*) travesty, caricature

паро́л|ь, я *m.* password

паро́м, а *m.* ferry (boat); **перепра́вить на** ~**е** to ferry

парохо́д, а *m.* steamship

па́рт|а, ы *f.* (school) desk

парте́р, а *m.* (theatr.) the stalls

партиза́н, а, *g. pl.* ~ *m.* (*на войне*) partisan; (*против режима*) guerrilla

парти́йн|ый *adj.* (pol.) party; **п. биле́т** party-membership card

партиту́р|а, ы *f.* (mus.) score

⚥ **па́рти|я¹, и** *f.* (pol.) party

⚥ **па́рти|я², и** *f.* **1** (*группа лиц*) party, group **2** (*в производстве*) batch; lot; (*груза*) consignment; (*отправленных товаров*) shipment **3** (sport) game; set **4** (mus.) part

⚥ **партнёр, а** *m.* partner

па́рус, а, *pl.* ~**á** *m.* sail; **на всех** ~**áх** in full sail (also fig.)

паруси́н|а, ы *f.* canvas, sailcloth

па́русник, а *m.* sailing vessel

па́русный *adj. of* ▶ **па́рус; п. спорт** sailing

парфюме́р, а *m.* perfumer

парфюме́ри|я, и *f.* (*промышленность*) perfumery; (*духи*) perfumes; (*косметика*) cosmetics; (*отдел духов*) perfume department; (*отдел косметики*) cosmetics department

парфюме́рный *adj. of* ▶ **парфюме́рия; п. магази́н** (*только духи*) perfumery, perfumer's shop; (*косметика*) cosmetics shop

парч|á, и́, *g. pl.* ~**е́й** *f.* brocade

парши́в|ый, ~, ~**а** *adj.* (infml, fig.) rotten, lousy

пас, а *m.* (sport) pass

па́смур|ный, ~**ен,** ~**на** *adj.* **1** (*день*) dull, cloudy; overcast **2** (fig., *лицо*) gloomy, sullen

пас|ова́ть, у́ю *impf. and pf.* (sport) to pass

па́спорт, а, *pl.* ~**á** *m.* **1** passport **2** (*машины, аппарата*) registration certificate

пасса́ж, а *m.* **1** (*галерея*) arcade **2** (mus.) passage

пассажи́р, а *m.* passenger

пассажи́р|ка, ки *f. of* ▶ **пассажи́р**

пассажи́рский *adj. of* ▶ **пассажи́р**

пасса́т, а *m.* (meteor.) trade wind

пасси́в|ный, ~**ен,** ~**на** *adj.* passive

па́ст|а, ы *f.* paste; **зубна́я п.** toothpaste; **тома́тная п.** tomato purée

па́стбищ|е, а *nt.* pasture

па́ств|а, ы *f.* (eccl.) flock, congregation

пасте́л|ь, и *f.* **1** (collect.) (*карандаши*) pastel(s) **2** (*in full* **рису́нок** ~**ью**) pastel (drawing)

пастеризова́ть, у́ю *impf. and pf.* to pasteurize

пастерна́к, а *m.* parsnip

пас|ти́, у́, ёшь, *past* ~, ~**ла́** *impf.* (*no pf.*) (*скот*) to graze, pasture; (*гусей*) to tend

пас|ти́сь, ётся, *past* ~**ся,** ~**ла́сь** *impf.* (*no pf.*) to graze; to browse; (infml, fig.) to hang about

па́стор, а *m.* (Protestant) minister, pastor

пасту́х, á *m.* (*коров*) herdsman; (*овец*) shepherd

пасту́шк|а, и *f.* shepherdess

па́стыр|ь, я *m.* (eccl.) pastor

па|сть¹, ду́, дёшь, *past* ~**л,** ~**ла́ 1** *pf. of* ▶ **па́дать 2** (*pf. only*) (*погибнуть*) to die, fall; **п. же́ртвой чего́-н.** to fall victim to **3** (*pf. only*) (*о крепости, о городе*) to fall, surrender; **п. ду́хом** to despair

пас|ть², и *f.* (*зверя*) mouth; jaws

Па́сх|а, и *f.* **1** (*в иудаизме*) Passover **2** (*в христианстве*) Easter **3** **п.** (cul.) paskha (*sweet cream cheese dish eaten at Easter*)

па́сын|ок, ка *m.* stepson, stepchild

пате́нт, а *m.* (**на** + *a.*) (*на изобретение*) patent (for); (*торговый*) licence (BrE), license (AmE) (for)

патент|ова́ть, у́ю *impf.* (*of* ▶ **запатентова́ть**) to patent; to take out a patent for

патети́ческий *adj.* passionate; emotional

патóлог, а *m.* pathologist
патологи́ческ|ий *adj.* pathological; ~ая анатóмия (anatomical) pathology
патолóги|я, и *f.* pathology
патологоанатóм, а *m.* (anatomical) pathologist
патриáрх, а *m.* patriarch
патриархáл|ьный, ~ен, ~ьна *adj.* patriarchal
патриархи́|я, и *f.* (eccl.) patriarchate
патриóт, а *m.* patriot
патриоти́зм, а *m.* patriotism
патриоти́ческий *adj.* patriotic
патриóт|ка, ки *f. of* ▶ патриóт
патрóн[1], а *m.* **1** (*покровитель*) patron **2** (*хозяин*, infml) boss
патрóн[2], а *m.* **1** (mil.) cartridge **2** (tech.) chuck (*of drill, lathe*), holder **3** (*лампочки*) socket
патрули́р|овать, ую *impf.* (*no pf.*) (mil.) to patrol
патрýл|ь, я́ *m.* patrol
патч, а *m.* (comput.) patch
пáуз|а, ы *f.* pause; interval; (mus.) rest
пáук, á *m.* spider
паути́н|а, ы *f.* cobweb, spider's web; (fig.) web; Всеми́рная п. (comput.) the Web
пáфос, а *m.* **1** (+ *g.*) enthusiasm (for), zeal (for) **2** (*сущность*) spirit; emotional content
пах, а, о ~е, в ~ý *m.* (anat.) groin
пáхар|ь, я *m.* ploughman (BrE), plowman (AmE)
па|хáть, шý, ~шешь *impf.* **1** (*pf.* вс~) to plough (BrE), plow (AmE), till **2** (infml, *работать*) to slave (away)
пáх|нуть, ну, нешь, *past* ~ *or* ~нул, ~ла *impf.* (*no pf.*) (+ *i.*) to smell (of); ~нет лýком there is a smell of onions; (fig.) (*usu. impers.*) to savour (BrE), savor (AmE) (of), smack (of); ~ло ссóрой a quarrel was in the air
пахýч|ий, ~, ~а *adj.* strong-smelling
пацáн, á *m.* (infml) boy, lad
✎ **пациéнт**, а *m.* patient
пациéнт|ка, ки *f. of* ▶ пациéнт
пацифи́зм, а *m.* pacifism
пацифи́ст, а *m.* pacifist
пáчк|а, и *f.* **1** (*писем, газет*) bundle; (*сигарет, чая, печенья*) packet (BrE), pack **2** (*балерины*) tutu
пáчка|ть, ю *impf.* (*of* ▶ запáчкать, ▶ испáчкать) to dirty, soil, stain, sully (also fig.); п. рýки (fig.) to soil one's hands
пáчка|ться, юсь *impf.* (*of* ▶ запáчкаться, ▶ испáчкаться) **1** (*человек*) to make oneself dirty; to soil oneself **2** (*вещь*) to become dirty
пáш|ня, ни, *g. pl.* ~ен *f.* arable land; ploughland (BrE), plowland (AmE)
паштéт, а *m.* pâté
пая́льник, а *m.* soldering iron
пая́снича|ть, ю *impf.* (*no pf.*) (infml) to clown, play the fool
пая́|ть, ю *impf.* (*no pf.*) to solder

пая́ц, а *m.* (fig., pej.) clown
пев|éц, цá *m.* singer
певи́ц|а, ы *f. of* ▶ певéц
пéвч|ий **1** *adj.* singing; ~ая пти́ца songbird **2** (*as m. n.* п., ~его) chorister
педагóг, а *m.* teacher
педагоги́ческий *adj.* pedagogic(al); educational; п. институ́т college of education (BrE), teachers' college (AmE)
педáл|ь, и *f.* pedal
педáнт, а *m.* pedant
педанти́ч|ный, ~ен, ~на *adj.* pedantic
педиáтр, а *m.* paediatrician (BrE), pediatrician (AmE)
педиатри́ческий *adj.* paediatric (BrE), pediatric (AmE)
педиатри́|я, и *f.* paediatrics (BrE), pediatrics (AmE)
пéдик, а *m.* (infml, pej.) queer, poof (BrE)
педикю́р, а *m.* pedicure
педофи́л, а *m.* paedophile (BrE), pedophile (AmE)
педофили́|я, и *f.* paedophilia (BrE), pedophilia (AmE)
пéйджер, а *m.* pager
пейзáж, а *m.* **1** landscape; scenery **2** (*картина*) landscape
пёк, пеклá *see* ▶ печь[1]
пекáр|ня, ни, *g. pl.* ~ен *f.* bakery, bakehouse
пéкар|ь, я, *pl.* ~и, ~ей *m.* baker
Пеки́н, а *m.* Beijing
пéкл|о, а *nt.* **1** (*сильный жар*) scorching heat **2** (*ад*) hell, hellfire
пекý, пекýт *see* ▶ печь[1]
пелен|á, ы́, *pl.* ~ы́, ~, ~ám *f.* shroud; у негó слóвно п. с глаз упáла the scales fell from his eyes
пелён|ка, ки *f.* (*usu. in pl.*) swaddling clothes; с пелёнок (fig.) from the cradle
пеликáн, а *m.* pelican
пельмéн|и, ей *m. pl.* (*sg.* ~ь, ~я) (cul.) pelmeni (*a kind of ravioli*)
пéн|а, ы *f.* (*на море*) foam; (*на бульóне*) scum; (*на пиве*) froth
пенáл, а *m.* pencil case
пéни|е, я *nt.* singing
пéнист|ый, ~, ~а *adj.* foamy; frothy
пéн|иться, ится *impf.* to foam; to froth (up)
пеницилли́н, а *m.* penicillin
пéнный *adj.* = пéнистый
пеноплáст, а *m.* foam plastic
пенс, а *m.* penny
пенсионéр, а *m.* pensioner
пенсионéр|ка, ки *f. of* ▶ пенсионéр
пенсиóнный *adj. of* ▶ пéнсия; п. вóзраст retirement age; п. фонд pension fund
пéнси|я, и *f.* pension; он на ~и he is retired; вы́йти на ~ю to retire
пенснé *nt. indecl.* pince-nez
пентхáус, а *m.* penthouse
пень, пня *m.* stump

пенько́|а, й *f.* hemp

пенько́вый *adj.* hempen

пенью́ар, а *m.* peignoir, negligee

пе́н|я, и *f.* fine

пе́п|ел, ла *m.* ash(es)

пе́пельниц|а, ы *f.* ashtray

пе́пельн|ый *adj.* ashy; **~ого цве́та** ash-grey

пе́рвенств|о, а *nt.* first place; (sport) championship

перви́чный *adj.* (*главный*) primary; (*первоначальный*) initial

первобы́т|ный, ~ен, ~на *adj.* primitive; primordial; primeval (also *fig.*)

ℰ **пе́рв|ое, ого** *nt.* first course (*of a meal*)

первозда́нный *adj.* primordial; (geol.) primitive, primary; **п. ха́ос** primordial chaos (also *fig.*, *iron.*)

первоисто́чник, а *m.* (*сведений*) primary source; (*основа*) origin

первокла́сс|ный, ~ен, ~на *adj.* first-class, first-rate

первонача́л|ьный, ~ен, ~ьна *adj.* **1** (*самый первый*) original **2** (*являющийся началом*) initial

первооткрыва́тел|ь, я *m.* discoverer

первоочередн|о́й *adj.* immediate; **~а́я зада́ча** immediate task

первопрохо́д|ец, ца *m.* (also *fig.*, *rhet.*) pioneer; trailblazer

первосо́рт|ный, ~ен, ~на *adj.* **1** top-quality **2** (infml, *превосходный*) first-class, first-rate

ℰ **пе́рв|ый** *adj.* **1** first; (*по времени*) earliest, first; **~ого января́** on the first of January; **быть ~ым, идти́ ~ым** to come first, lead; **~ое вре́мя** at first; **~ая скри́пка** first violin; **п. эта́ж** ground floor (BrE), first floor (AmE); **в ~ую о́чередь** in the first place; **на п. взгляд, с ~ого взгля́да** at first sight **2** (*лучший*) best

перга́мент, а *m.* parchment

пер|де́ть, ди́шь *impf.* (vulg.) to fart

пере... *vbl. pref. indicating* **1** (*action across or through sth*) trans- **2** (*repetition of action*) re- **3** (*superiority, excess, etc.*) over-, out- **4** (*extension of action to encompass many or all objects or cases of a given kind*) **5** (*division into two or more parts*) **6** (*reflexives*) reciprocity of action

переадрес|ова́ть, у́ю *pf.* (*of* ▸ **переадресо́вывать**) to re-address; to forward

переадресо́выва|ть, ю *impf. of* ▸ **переадресова́ть**

перебази́р|оваться, уюсь *pf.* to relocate

переба́рщива|ть, ю *impf. of* ▸ **переборщи́ть**

перебега́|ть, ю *impf. of* ▸ **перебежа́ть**

перебе|жа́ть, гу́, жи́шь, гу́т *pf.* (*of* ▸ **перебега́ть**) **1** (*через + a.*) to cross (running); **п. (че́рез) у́лицу** to run across the street **2** (*fig.*, infml) (**к + d.**) (*к противнику*) to go over (to), desert **1**

перебе́жчик, а *m.* deserter; (fig.) turncoat

перебе́жчи|ца, цы *f. of* ▸ **перебе́жчик**

перебива́|ть, ю *impf. of* ▸ **переби́ть**

перебинт|ова́ть, у́ю *pf.* (*of* ▸ **перебинто́вывать**) (*поменять повязку*) to change the dressing (on), put a new dressing (on)

перебинто́выва|ть, ю *impf. of* ▸ **перебинтова́ть**

перебира́|ть¹, ю *impf. of* ▸ **перебра́ть**

перебира́|ть², ю *impf. of* **1** (*касаться пальцами*) to finger; **п. стру́ны** to run one's fingers over the strings **2** (*+ i.*) (*ногами, пальцами*) to move (*in turn or in a regular manner*)

перебира́|ться, ~юсь *impf. of* ▸ **перебра́ться**

переб|и́ть, ью́, ьёшь *pf.* (*of* ▸ **перебива́ть**) (*говорящего*) to interrupt

перебо́|й, я *m.* (*перерыв*) interruption; (*задержка*) hold-up; (*двигателя*) misfire; (*сердца*) irregularity; **пульс с ~ями** irregular pulse

переболе́|ть, ю *pf.* (*+ i.*) to have had, have been down (*with an illness*); **де́ти все ~ли ветря́нкой** the children have all been down with chickenpox

перебо́рк|а, и *f.* (*перегородка*) partition; (naut.) bulkhead

перебор|о́ть, ю́, ~ешь *pf.* (*no impf.*) to overcome

перебор|щи́ть, у́, и́шь *pf.* (*of* ▸ **переба́рщивать**) (**в + p.**) (infml) to go too far; to overdo it; to go over the top

переба́сыва|ть, ю *impf. of* ▸ **перебро́сить**

пере|бра́ть, беру́, берёшь, *past* **~бра́л, ~брала́, ~бра́ло** *pf.* (*of* ▸ **перебира́ть¹**) **1** (*сортировать*) to sort; (*пересмотреть*) to look through **2** (*fig.*, *в уме*) to turn over (in one's mind) **3** (*взять слишком много*) to take too much

пере|бра́ться, беру́сь, берёшься, *past* **~бра́лся, ~брала́сь, ~бра́ло́сь** *pf.* (*of* ▸ **перебира́ться**) (infml) **1** (*перейти*) to get over, cross **2** (*переселиться*) to move

перебро́|сить, шу, сишь *pf.* (*of* ▸ **переба́сывать**) **1** (*мяч*) to throw over **2** (*переместить*) to transfer (*troops, etc.*)

перева́л, а *m.* (geog.) pass

перева́лива|ть, ю *impf. of* ▸ **перевали́ть**

перева́лива|ться¹, юсь *impf. of* ▸ **перевали́ться**

перева́лива|ться², юсь *impf.* (*no pf.*) to waddle

перевал|и́ть, ю́, ~ишь *pf.* (*of* ▸ **перева́ливать**) **1** (*переместить*) to transfer, shift **2** (*перейти*) to cross; (*impers.*) (infml, *о пределе*) to be past; **~и́ло за́ полночь** it is past midnight

перевал|и́ться, ю́сь, ~ишься *pf.* (*of* ▸ **перева́ливаться¹**) to roll over

перева́рива|ть, ю *impf. of* ▸ **перевари́ть**

перевар|и́ть, ю́, ~ишь *pf.* (*of* ▸ **перева́ривать**) to digest

перевез|ти́, у́, ёшь, *past* ~, ~ла́ *pf.* (*of*
▸ **перевози́ть**) **1** (*переместить, людей
через реку*) to take across, transport across
2 (*везя, доставить, детей на дачу*) to
transport, take (*from A to B*)

переверн|у́ть, у́, ёшь *pf.* (*of*
▸ **перевора́чивать**) **1** (*с одной стороны
на другую*) to turn over; (*вверх дном*) to
turn upside down **2** (*изменить*) to change
radically, transform **3** (*потрясти*) to
shake, stun

переверн|у́ться, у́сь, ёшься *pf.* (*of*
▸ **перевора́чиваться**) to turn over

переве́|сить¹, шу, сишь *pf.* (*of
▸ **переве́шивать**) (*пальто*) to hang
somewhere else; **п. карти́ну с одно́й стены́
на другу́ю** to move a picture from one wall
to another

переве́|сить², шу, сишь *pf.* (*of
▸ **переве́шивать**) to outweigh, outbalance
(also fig.); (fig., *оказаться более весомым*) to
tip the scales

переве|сти́, ду́, дёшь, *past* ~л, ~ла́ *pf.* (*of
▸ **переводи́ть**) **1** (*ведя, переместить*) to
take across; **п. дете́й че́рез у́лицу** to take
children across the road **2** (*в другое место*)
to transfer, move, switch, shift; **п. на другу́ю
рабо́ту** to transfer to another post; **п. де́ньги**
to transfer money **3** (*с + g. and на + a.*) to
translate (from, into); (**в, на** + *a.*) (*в другие
единицы*) to convert (to), express (as, in); **п.
с ру́сского языка́ на англи́йский** to translate
from Russian into English; **п. в метри́ческие
ме́ры** to convert to metric units **4** (*взгляд,
разговор*) to shift; **п. разгово́р на другу́ю
те́му** to change the subject

переве́шива|ть, ю *impf. of* ▸ **переве́сить¹**,
▸ **переве́сить²**

перевива́|ть, ю *impf. of* ▸ **переви́ть**

перевира́|ть, ю *impf. of* ▸ **переврáть**

переви́|ть, ью, ьёшь, *past* ~л, ~ила́,
~ило *pf.* (*of* ▸ **перевива́ть**) (+ *i.*) to
interweave (with), intertwine (with)

📌 **перево́д, а** *m.* **1** (*в другое место*) transfer,
move, switch, shift; **де́нежный п.** remittance;
почто́вый п. postal order **2** (*с одного языка
на другой*) translation; (*в другие единицы*)
conversion

перево|ди́ть, жу́, ~дишь *impf. of*
▸ **перевести́**

перево́дчик, а *m.* translator; (*устный*)
interpreter

перево́дчи|ца, цы *f. of* ▸ **перево́дчик**

перево|зи́ть, жу́, ~зишь *impf. of* ▸ **перевезти́**

перево́з|ка, и *f.* transportation, conveyance

перевоплоще́ни|е, я *nt.* reincarnation; (fig.)
transformation

перевора́чива|ть, ю *impf. of* ▸ **переверну́ть**

перевора́чива|ться, юсь *impf. of*
▸ **переверну́ться**

переворо́т, а *m.* revolution;
госуда́рственный п. coup d'état

перевоспита́ни|е, я *nt.* re-education;
rehabilitation

перевр|а́ть, у́, ёшь, *past* ~а́л, ~ала́, ~а́ло
pf. (*of* ▸ **перевира́ть**) (infml) to garble, confuse;
to misinterpret; **п. цита́ту** to misquote

перевы́бор|ы, ов (*no sg.*) re-election

перевя|за́ть, жу́, ~жешь *pf.* (*of
▸ **перевя́зывать**) **1** (*рану*) to dress, bandage
2 (*коробку*) to tie up, cord

перевя́з|ка, и *f.* dressing, bandage

перевя́зочный *adj. of* ▸ **перевя́зка; п.
материа́л** dressing; **п. пункт** dressing station

перевя́зыва|ть, ю *impf. of* ▸ **перевяза́ть**

переги́б, а *m.* **1** bend, twist; (*линия*) fold
2 (fig., *преувеличение*) exaggeration;
(*в политике, в руководстве*): **допусти́ть п. в
чём-н.** to carry sth too far

перегиба́|ть, ю *impf. of* ▸ **перегну́ть**

перегиба́|ться, юсь *impf. of* ▸ **перегну́ться**

перегля́дыва|ться, юсь *impf. of*
▸ **перегляну́ться**

перегля|ну́ться, ну́сь, ~нешься *pf.* (*of
▸ **перегля́дываться**) (с + *i.*) to exchange
glances (with)

пере|гна́ть, гоню́, го́нишь, *past* ~гна́л,
~гнала́, ~гна́ло *pf.* (*of* ▸ **перегоня́ть**)
1 (*обогнать*) to outdistance, leave behind;
(fig.) to overtake, surpass **2** (*скот*) to drive
(*somewhere else; from A to B*) **3** (chem.) to
distil (BrE), distill (AmE)

перегно́|й, я *m.* humus

перег|ну́ть, ну́, нёшь *pf.* (*of* ▸ **перегиба́ть**)
to bend; (fig., infml) to go too far; **п. па́лку** (fig.)
to go too far

перег|ну́ться, ну́сь, нёшься *pf.* (*of
▸ **перегиба́ться**) **1** (*о человеке*) to lean
over, bend over **2** (*о ветви*) to bend

перегова́рива|ться, юсь *impf.* (с + *i.*) to
exchange remarks (with)

📌 **перегово́р|ы, ов** (*no sg.*) negotiations, talks;
вести́ п. (с + *i.*) to negotiate, hold talks (with)

перегоня́|ть, ю *impf. of* ▸ **перегна́ть**

перегора́жива|ть, ю *impf. of* ▸ **перегороди́ть**

перегора́|ть, а́ю *impf. of* ▸ **перегоре́ть**

перегор|е́ть, и́т *pf.* (*of* ▸ **перегора́ть**)
1 (*о лампочке*) to burn out **2** (*о балке*)
to burn through

перегоро|ди́ть, жу́, ~ди́шь *pf.* (*of
▸ **перегора́живать**) to partition off

перегоро́д|ка, и *f.* **1** partition **2** (fig.) barrier

перегре́в, а *m.* overheating

перегрева́|ть, ю *impf. of* ▸ **перегре́ть**

перегрева́|ться, юсь *impf. of* ▸ **перегре́ться**

перегре́|ть, ю *pf.* (*of* ▸ **перегрева́ть**) to
overheat

перегре́|ться, юсь *pf.* (*of* ▸ **перегрева́ться**)
to overheat; (*на солнце*) to spend too long
in the sun

перегружа́|ть, ю *impf. of* ▸ **перегрузи́ть¹**

перегру́|зи́ть, жу́, ~зишь *pf.* (*of
▸ **перегружа́ть**) to overload; **п. рабо́той** to
overwork

перегру|зи́ть², жу́, ∼зишь *pf.* (*of*
▶ **перегружа́ть**) to load (*somewhere else;
from A to B*); to trans-ship; **п. с по́езда на
парохо́д** to load from a train on to a ship

перегру́зк|а, и *f.* overloading; (*usu. in pl.*)
strain, stress

перегрыза́|ть, ю *impf. of* ▶ **перегры́зть**

перегры́з|ть, у́, ёшь, *past* ∼, ∼ла *pf.* (*of*
▶ **перегрыза́ть**) to gnaw through, bite
through

перегры́з|ться, у́сь, ёшься, *past* ∼ся,
∼лась *pf.* (*no impf.*) (из-за + *g.*) (infml,
о собаках) to fight (over); (fig.) to quarrel
(over), wrangle (about)

⚲ **пе́ред** and **пе́редо** *prep.* + *i.* **1** (*при
обозначении места*) in front of; before;
п. до́мом in front of the house; (also fig.):
п. опа́сностью/тру́дностями in the face of
danger/difficulties **2** (*раньше*) before; **п.
обе́дом** before dinner; **п. тем, как** (*conj.*)
before **3** (*в присутствии*) in the presence
of, in front of; **п. учи́телем** in front of the
teacher **4** (*в отношении; по сравнению*) to;
извини́ться п. кем-н. to apologize to sb

⚲ **переда|ва́ть**, ю́, ёшь *impf. of* ▶ **переда́ть**

переда|ва́ться, ю́сь, ёшься *impf. of*
▶ **переда́ться**

переда́тчик, а *m.* transmitter

переда́|ть, м, шь, ст, ди́м, ди́те, ду́т,
past пе́редал, ∼ла́, пе́редало *pf.* (*of*
▶ **передава́ть**) **1** (*отдать через кого-н.*)
to pass; (*вручить*) to hand; (*свои права,
коллекцию*) to hand over; to transfer
2 (*сообщить*) to tell; to communicate;
переда́йте ему́, что я приезжа́ю за́втра
tell him I shall be arriving tomorrow;
(*распространить*) to transmit, convey;
п. по ра́дио/телеви́дению to broadcast (on
the radio/television); **п. приве́т** to send one's
regards **3** (*воспроизвести*) to reproduce
(*a sound, a thought, etc.*)

переда́|ться, стся, ду́тся, *past* ∼лся,
∼ла́сь *pf.* (*of* ▶ **передава́ться**) to pass;
(*о тревоге, болезни*) to be transmitted,
be communicated; (*по наследству*) to be
inherited; **корь ∼ла́сь ему́ от сосе́дских
дете́й** he picked up measles from the
children next door

⚲ **переда́ч|а**, и *f.* **1** (*действие*) passing;
transmission; communication; transfer,
transference **2** (*больному, заключённому*)
parcel **3** (*по телевидению, по радио*)
broadcast; **пряма́я п.** live broadcast;
(*программа*) programme (BrE), program
(AmE) **4** (tech.) drive; gear(ing);
transmission; **ремённая п.** belt drive

передвига́|ть, ю *impf. of* ▶ **передви́нуть**

передвига́|ться, юсь *impf. of*
▶ **передви́нуться**

передвижно́й *adj.* **1** (*перегородка*)
movable **2** (*библиотека*) mobile, travelling
(BrE), traveling (AmE)

передви́|нуть, ну, нешь *pf.* (*of*
▶ **передвига́ть**) to move, shift (also fig.);
п. сро́ки экза́менов to alter the date of
examinations

передви́|нуться, нусь, нешься *pf.* (*of*
▶ **передвига́ться**) to move, shift

переде́л|ать, аю *pf.* (*of* ▶ **переде́лывать**)
(*сделать заново*) to redo; (*сделать по-
иному*) to alter; (fig.) to refashion, recast; **п.
пла́тье** to alter a dress

переде́лыва|ть, ю *impf. of* ▶ **переде́лать**

передержа́|ть, у́, ∼ишь *pf.* (*of*
▶ **переде́рживать**) **1** (*кушанье*) to overdo;
to overcook **2** (phot.) to overexpose

переде́ржива|ть, ю *impf. of* ▶ **передержа́ть**

⚲ **пере́дн|ий** *adj.* front; ∼ие коне́чности
forelegs; **п. план** foreground

пере́дник, а *m.* apron

пере́дн|яя, ей *f.* (entrance) hall, lobby

пе́редо = **пе́ред**

передово́й *adj.* (*отряд*) forward;
(*технология*) advanced; (*взгляды*)
progressive

передозиро́вк|а, и *f.* (med.) overdose

передохн|у́ть, у́, ёшь *pf.* (*of* ▶ **передыха́ть**)
(infml) to pause for breath, take a short rest

передра́знива|ть, ю *impf. of*
▶ **передразни́ть**

передразн|и́ть, ю́, ∼ишь *pf.* (*of*
▶ **передра́знивать**) to take off, mimic

пере|дра́ться, деру́сь, дерёшься, *past*
∼дра́лся, ∼драла́сь, ∼драло́сь *pf.*
(*no impf.*) (infml) to fight, brawl (*of many
people, etc.*)

переду́м|ать, аю *pf.* (*of* ▶ **переду́мывать**)
to change one's mind

переду́мыва|ть, ю *impf. of* ▶ **переду́мать**

передыха́|ть, ю *impf. of* ▶ **передохну́ть**

переда́|ть, ю *impf. of* ▶ **пере́сть**

перее́зд¹, а *m.* (*место*) crossing

перее́зд², а *m.* (*переселение*) move

переезжа́|ть, ю *impf. of* ▶ **перее́хать**

перее́|сть, м, шь, ст, ди́м, ди́те, дя́т, *past*
∼л *pf.* (*of* ▶ **переда́ть**) to overeat

перее́|хать, ду, дешь *pf.* (*of* ▶ **переезжа́ть**)
1 (+ *a. or* чéрез + *a.*) (*дорогу*) to cross
2 (*задавить*) to run over, knock down
3 (*переселиться*) to move

переждá|ть, у́, ёшь, *past* ∼áл, ∼ала́, ∼áло
pf. (*of* ▶ **пережида́ть**) to wait through; **мы
∼а́ли грозу́** we waited till the storm was over

переже́|вáть, ую́, уёшь *pf.* (*of*
▶ **пережёвывать**) to masticate, chew

пережёвыва|ть, ю *impf. of* ▶ **пережевáть**

пережива́ни|е, я *nt.* (*события*) experience;
(*душевное состояние*) feeling

пережива́|ть, ю *impf.* **1** *impf. of* ▶ **пережи́ть**
2 (*impf. only*) (за + *a.*) (infml) to be upset,
worry (for, on behalf of)

пережида́|ть, ю *impf. of* ▶ **переждáть**

пережи́т|ок, ка *m.* relic, vestige, survival

пережи́|ть, ву́, вёшь, *past* пе́режил, ∼лá,
пе́режило *pf.* (*of* ▶ **пережива́ть 1**)
1 (*испытать*) to experience; to go/live
through; (*выдержать*) to endure, suffer;

П

тяжело́ п. что-н. to take sth hard; (*оста́ться в живы́х*) to survive **2** (*прожи́ть до́льше*) to outlive, survive

перезагру|жа́ть, жа́ю *impf. of* ▸ **перезагрузи́ть**

перезагру|зи́ть, ужу́, у́зишь *pf.* (*of* ▸ **перезагружа́ть**) (comput.) to reboot

перезаря|ди́ть, жу́, ~ди́шь *pf.* (*of* ▸ **перезаряжа́ть**) **1** (*аккумуля́тор*) to recharge **2** (*револьве́р, фотоаппара́т*) to reload

перезаряжа́|ть, ю *impf. of* ▸ **перезаряди́ть**

перезва́нива|ть, ю *impf. of* ▸ **перезвони́ть**

перезвон|и́ть, ю́, и́шь *pf.* (*of* ▸ **перезва́нивать**) to ring back (BrE), call back (AmE)

перезим|ова́ть, у́ю *pf.* (*of* ▸ **зимова́ть**) to winter, pass the winter

перезрева́|ть, ю *impf. of* ▸ **перезре́ть**

перезре́лый *adj.* overripe; (fig.) passé, past one's prime

перезре́|ть, ю *pf.* (*of* ▸ **перезрева́ть**) **1** to become overripe **2** (fig.) to be past one's prime

переигр|а́ть, а́ю *pf.* (*of* ▸ **переи́грывать**) **1** (*па́ртию*) to play again **2** (*сыгра́ть мно́гое или многокра́тно или повто́рно*) to play (*a lot, or many times, or repeatedly*); to play (*all, a number of*) **3** (infml, sport) to outplay; to beat **4** (theatr., infml) to overact, overdo

переи́грыва|ть, ю *impf. of* ▸ **переигра́ть**

переизбира́|ть, ю *impf. of* ▸ **переизбра́ть**

переиз|бра́ть, беру́, берёшь, *past* ~бра́л, ~брала́, ~бра́ло *pf.* (*of* ▸ **переизбира́ть**) to re-elect

переизда|ва́ть, ю́, ёшь *impf. of* ▸ **переизда́ть**

переизда́|ть, м, шь, ст, ди́м, ди́те, ду́т, *past* ~л, ~ла́, ~ло *pf.* (*of* ▸ **переиздава́ть**) to republish, reprint

переимен|ова́ть, у́ю *pf.* (*of* ▸ **переимено́вывать**) (в + *a.*) to rename

переимено́выва|ть, ю *impf. of* ▸ **переименова́ть**

пере|йти́, йду́, йдёшь, *past* ~шёл, ~шла́ *pf.* (*of* ▸ **переходи́ть**) **1** (+ *a. or* че́рез + *a.*) (*перепра́виться*) to cross; to get across, get over, go over; п. грани́цу to cross the frontier; п. че́рез мост to go across a bridge **2** (в, на + *a. or* к + *d.*) (*в друго́е ме́сто*) to pass (to); п. в сосе́днюю ко́мнату to go into the next room; п. на другу́ю рабо́ту to change one's job **3** (в + *a.*) (*преврати́ться*) to turn (into); их ссо́ра ~шла́ в дра́ку their quarrel turned into a fight

перека́пыва|ть, ю *impf. of* ▸ **перекопа́ть**

перека́рмлива|ть, ю *impf. of* ▸ **перекорми́ть**

перека|ти́ть, чу́, ~тишь *pf.* (*of* ▸ **перека́тывать**) (*бо́чку*) to roll; (*велосипе́д*) to wheel

перека|ти́ться, чу́сь, ~тишься *pf.* (*of* ▸ **перека́тываться**) to roll

перека́тыва|ть, ю *impf. of* ▸ **перекати́ть**

перека́тыва|ться, юсь *impf. of* ▸ **перекати́ться**

перекач|а́ть, а́ю *pf.* (*of* ▸ **перека́чивать**) to pump over, pump across

перека́чива|ть, ю *impf. of* ▸ **перекача́ть**

перекид|а́ть, а́ю *pf.* (*of* ▸ **переки́дывать**) to throw (one after another)

переки́дыва|ть, ю *impf. of* ▸ **перекида́ть**, ▸ **переки́нуть**

переки́дыва|ться, юсь *impf. of* ▸ **переки́нуться**

переки́|нуть, ну, нешь *pf.* (*of* ▸ **переки́дывать**) to throw (over)

переки́|нуться, нусь, нешься *pf.* (*of* ▸ **переки́дываться**) **1** (*бы́стро перемести́ться*) to leap (over) **2** (*ого́нь*) to spread **3** (+ *i.*) (*мячо́м*) to throw (one to another); (*слова́ми*) to bandy, exchange

перекла́дин|а, ы *f.* **1** (*брус*) cross-beam, crosspiece, transom **2** (sport) horizontal bar

перекла́дыва|ть, ю *impf. of* ▸ **переложи́ть**

переклик|а́ться, а́юсь *impf.* (с + *i.*) **1** (*pf.* ~нуться) to call to one another **2** (*no pf.*) (fig., *быть подо́бным*) to have sth in common (with)

перекли́к|нуться, нусь, нешься *pf.* ▸ **перекликаться 1**

перекли́чк|а, и *f.* roll-call; де́лать ~у to call the roll

переключа́тел|ь, я *m.* (tech.) switch

переключ|а́ть, а́ю *impf. of* ▸ **переключи́ть**

переключ|а́ться, а́юсь *impf. of* ▸ **переключи́ться**

переключ|и́ть, у́, и́шь *pf.* (*of* ▸ **переключа́ть**) (tech., also fig.) (на + *a.*) to switch (over to); п. ско́рость to change gear (BrE), shift gears (AmE); п. телеви́зор/ра́дио на другу́ю програ́мму to switch over, change channels (*on the TV/radio*)

переключ|и́ться, у́сь, и́шься *pf.* (*of* ▸ **переключа́ться**) (tech, also fig.) (на + *a.*) to switch (over to); внима́ние пу́блики ~и́лось на говоря́щего attention switched to the speaker

перекопа́|ть, ю *pf.* (*of* ▸ **перека́пывать**) **1** (*карто́фель; огоро́д*) to dig up **2** (*чемода́н*) to rummage through **3** (*доро́гу*) to dig a ditch across

перекорм|и́ть, лю́, ~ишь *pf.* (*of* ▸ **перека́рмливать**) to overfeed

переко́с, а *m.* **1** (*искривле́ние*) warping **2** (fig., *тенденцио́зность*) slant

переко́шен|ный, ~, ~a *adj.* distorted, twisted

перекра́ива|ть, ю *impf. of* ▸ **перекро́ить**

перекра́|сить, шу, сишь *pf.* (*of* ▸ **перекра́шивать**) (*сте́ну*) to repaint; (*в друго́й цвет*) to paint another colour (BrE), color (AmE); (*во́лосы*) to re-dye

перекра́шива|ть, ю *impf. of* ▸ **перекра́сить**

перекре|сти́ть, щу́, ~стишь *pf.* (*of* ▸ **крести́ть 3**) to make the sign of the cross over

перекре|сти́ться, щу́сь, ~сти́шься *pf.*
(*of* ▶ крести́ться 2) (*о человеке*) to cross
oneself

перекрёстн|ый *adj.* cross; **п. ого́нь** (mil.)
crossfire; **~ая ссы́лка** cross reference

перекрёст|ок, ка *m.* crossroads, crossing

перекри́кива|ть, ю *impf. of* ▶ перекрича́ть

перекри|ча́ть, чу́, чи́шь *pf.* (*of*
▶ перекри́кивать) (*шум*) to shout above;
(*человека*) to shout down

перекро|и́ть, ю́, и́шь *pf.* (*of*
▶ перекра́ивать) to cut out again; (fig.,
статью, план) to rehash; to re-shape

перекрыва́|ть, ю *impf. of* ▶ перекры́ть¹,
▶ перекры́ть²

перекр|ы́ть¹, о́ю, о́ешь *pf.* (*of*
▶ перекрыва́ть) (*покры́ть за́ново*) to
re-cover

перекр|ы́ть², о́ю, о́ешь *pf.* (*of*
▶ перекрыва́ть) (*доро́гу*) to close; (*во́ду,
до́ступ*) to cut off; (*ре́ку*) to dam

перекувы́ркива|ться, юсь *impf. of*
▶ перекувырну́ться

перекувыр|ну́ться, ну́сь, нёшься *pf.* (*of*
▶ перекувы́ркиваться) (infml) **1** (*упа́сть*)
to topple over **2** (*переверну́ться кувырко́м*)
to turn a somersault

перекур, а *m.* (infml) smoking break; (*переры́в
вообще́*) break; **пойдём на п.** let's take five

переку|си́ть, шу́, ~сишь *pf.* (*of*
▶ переку́сывать) (infml, *поесть*) to have a
bite, have a snack

переку́сыва|ть, ю *impf. of* ▶ перекуси́ть

перела́мыва|ть, ю, ет *impf. of* ▶ переломи́ть

перела́мыва|ться, ется *impf. of*
▶ переломи́ться

перелеза́|ть, а́ю *impf. of* ▶ переле́зть

переле́з|ть, у, ешь, *past* ~, **~ла** *pf.* (*of*
▶ перелеза́ть) to climb over, get over

переле́с|ок, ка *m.* copse, coppice

перелёт, а *m.* **1** (*самолёта*) flight **2** (*птиц*)
migration

перелет|а́ть, а́ю *impf. of* ▶ перелете́ть

переле|те́ть, чу́, ти́шь *pf.* (*of* ▶ перелета́ть)
1 (+ *a.* or **че́рез** + *a.*) to fly over **2** (*да́льше
ну́жного*) to fly too far; to overshoot (the
mark)

перелётн|ый *adj.*: **~ая пти́ца** bird of
passage (also fig.); migratory bird

пере|ле́чь, ля́гу, ля́жешь, ля́гут, *past*
~лёг, **~легла́** *pf.* (*no impf.*) to lie
somewhere else; to move; **п. с дива́на на
крова́ть** to move from the sofa to the bed

перели́в, а *m.* (*цвета*) tint, tinge; (*цветов*)
play (of colours (BrE), colors (AmE)); (*голоса*)
modulation

перелива́ни|е, я *nt.* **1** decanting, pouring
2 (med.) transfusion

перелива́|ть, ю *impf. of* ▶ перели́ть

перелива́|ться, ется *impf. of* ▶ перели́ться

перелист|а́ть, а́ю *pf.* (*of* ▶ перели́стывать)
1 to leaf through **2** (*бегло просмотре́ть*)

to look through, flick through

перели́стыва|ть, ю *impf. of* ▶ перелиста́ть

перели́|ть, ью, ьёшь, *past* ~**йл, ~ила́,
~и́ло** *pf.* (*of* ▶ перелива́ть) **1** to pour
(*somewhere else; from A into B*); to decant;
п. молоко́ из кастрю́ли в кувши́н to pour
milk from a saucepan into a jug **2** (med.) to
transfuse; **п. кровь** (+ *d.*) to administer a
blood transfusion (to) **3** (*через край*) to let
overflow

перели́|ться, ьётся, *past* ~**и́лся, ~ила́сь**
pf. (*of* ▶ перелива́ться) **1** (*ли́ться в друго́е
ме́сто*) to flow **2** (*вы́литься*) to overflow,
run over

переложи́|ть, у́, ~ишь *pf.* (*of*
▶ перекла́дывать) **1** to put somewhere
else; to shift, move; (fig.) to shift, transfer;
п. отве́тственность на кого́-н. to shift
the responsibility on to sb **2** (+ *a. and i.*)
to interlay (with); **п. посу́ду соло́мой** to
interlay crockery with straw

перело́м, а *m.* break, breaking; (*кости*)
fracture

перелом|и́ть, лю́, ~ишь *pf.* (*of*
▶ перела́мывать) **1** to break in two **2** (fig.)
to break, master; **п. ход собы́тий** to turn
events around

перелом|и́ться, ~ится *pf.* (*of*
▶ перела́мываться) to break in two; to be
fractured

перело́мный *adj. of* ▶ перело́м; **п. моме́нт**
critical moment, crucial moment

перема́лыва|ть, ю, ет *impf. of* ▶ перемоло́ть

перема́лыва|ться, ется *impf. of*
▶ перемоло́ться

перема́нива|ть, ю *impf. of* ▶ перемани́ть

переман|и́ть, ю́, ~ишь *pf.* (*of*
▶ перема́нивать) (infml) to entice; **п. на свою́
сто́рону** to win over

перема́тыва|ть, ю *impf. of* ▶ перемота́ть

перемежа́|ть, ю *impf.* (*no pf.*) (+ *a. and
i.* or **с** + *i.*) to alternate; **он ~л угро́зы (с)
обеща́ниями** he alternated threats and
promises

перемежа́|ться, ется *impf.* (*no pf.*) (+ *i.* or
с + *i.*) to alternate; **снег ~лся (с) дождём**
snow alternated with rain, it snowed and
rained by turns

переме́н|а, ы *f.* **1** change **2** (*в шко́ле*) break
(BrE), recess (AmE)

перемен|и́ть, ю́, ~ишь *pf.* (*of* ▶ переменя́ть)
to change; **п. пози́цию** to shift one's ground
(also fig.); **п. тон** (fig.) to change one's tune

перемен|и́ться, ю́сь, ~и́шься *pf.* (*of*
▶ переменя́ться) to change; **п. в лице́** to
change countenance; **п. к кому́-н.** to change
(one's attitude) towards sb

переме́нн|ый *adj.* variable; **~ая величина́**
(math.) variable (quantity); **п. ток** (elec.)
alternating current; **с ~ым успе́хом** with
varying success

перемен|я́ть, я́ю *impf. of* ▶ перемени́ть

перемен|я́ться, я́юсь *impf. of*
▶ перемени́ться

переме|сти́ть, щу́, сти́шь *pf.* (*of*
▶ перемеща́ть) to move (*somewhere else*);
(*на другую работу*) to transfer

переме|сти́ться, щу́сь, сти́шься *pf.* (*of*
▶ перемеща́ться) to move

перемеш|а́ть, а́ю *pf.* (*of* ▶ переме́шивать)
to (inter)mix, intermingle; **п. у́гли в пе́чке**
to poke the fire

перемеш|а́ться, а́юсь *pf.* (*of*
▶ переме́шиваться) to get mixed (up); **всё у
него́ в голове́ ~а́лось** he has got everything
mixed up

переме́шива|ть, ю *impf. of* ▶ перемеша́ть

переме́шива|ться, юсь *impf. of*
▶ перемеша́ться

перемеща́|ть, ю *impf. of* ▶ перемести́ть

перемеща́|ться, юсь *impf. of*
▶ перемести́ться

перемеще́ни|е, я *nt.* (*изменение положения*)
transference, shift; (*движение*) movement;
(*по службе*) transfer

переми́ри|е, я *nt.* armistice, truce

перемнож|а́ть, а́ю *impf. of* ▶ перемно́жить

перемно́ж|ить, у, ишь *pf.* (*of*
▶ перемножа́ть) to multiply

перем|оло́ть, елю́, е́лешь *pf.* (*of*
▶ перема́лывать) (*кофе, зерно*) to grind,
mill; (fig., *разрушить*) to pulverize

перем|оло́ться, е́лется *pf.* (*of*
▶ перема́лываться): **~е́лется — мука́ бу́дет**
(*proverb*) it will all come right in the end

перемота́|ть, ю *pf.* (*of* ▶ перема́тывать)
1 (*на что-н. другое*) to wind; to reel; **п.
наза́д** to rewind; **п. вперёд** to fast forward
2 (*намотать заново*) to rewind

перемыва́|ть, ю *impf. of* ▶ перемы́ть

перем|ы́ть, о́ю, о́ешь *pf.* (*of* ▶ перемыва́ть)
1 (*вымыть заново*) to wash up again
2 (*вымыть многое*) to wash (up) (*all or a
quantity of*)

перемы́чк|а, и *f.* (tech.) **1** (*соединение*)
crosspiece **2** (*заграждение*) cofferdam

перенапряга́|ться, юсь *impf. of*
▶ перенапря́чься

перенапря́|чься, гу́сь, жёшься, *past
~гся, ~гла́сь pf.* (*of* ▶ перенапряга́ться)
to overstrain oneself

перенес|ти́¹, у́, ёшь, *past ~, ~ла́ pf.* (*of*
▶ переноси́ть) **1** (*через пространство*)
to carry (*somewhere else*); (*поместить в
другое место*) to move, transfer **2**: **п. сло́во**
(typ.) to carry over (*part of word*) to the next
line **3** (*отсрочить*) to put off, postpone; to
carry over

перенес|ти́², у́, ёшь, *past ~, ~ла́ pf.* (*of*
▶ переноси́ть) (*выдержать*) to endure,
bear, stand; **п. боле́знь** to have an illness;
я э́того не мог п. I couldn't stand that

перенес|ти́сь, у́сь, ёшься, *past ~ся,
~ла́сь pf.* (*of* ▶ переноси́ться) to be
carried, be borne

перено́с, а *m.* **1** transfer; moving **2** (typ.)
hyphenation at the end of a line; word
division; (*знак*) hyphen (*at the end of
a line*); **знак ~а** hyphen **3** (*заседания*)
postponement

перено|си́ть, шу́, ~сишь *impf. of*
▶ перенести́¹

перено|си́ться, шу́сь, ~сишься *impf. of*
▶ перенести́сь

перено́сиц|а, ы *f.* bridge of the nose

переносно́й *adj.* (*приёмник*) portable

перено́сный *adj.* (ling.) figurative

переноч|ева́ть, у́ю *pf.* (*of* ▶ ночева́ть) to
spend the night

переобува́|ть, ю *impf. of* ▶ переобу́ть

переобува́|ться, юсь *impf. of* ▶ переобу́ться

переобу́|ть, ю, ешь *pf.* (*of* ▶ переобува́ть)
to change sb's shoes; **п. ту́фли** to change
one's shoes

переобу́|ться, юсь, ешься *pf.* (*of*
▶ переобува́ться) to change one's shoes,
boots, *etc.*

переобуча́|ть, ю *impf. of* ▶ переобучи́ть

переобуче́ни|е, я *nt.* retraining

переобу́|чи́ть, чу́, ~чишь *pf.* (*of*
▶ переобуча́ть) to retrain

переодева́|ть, ю *impf. of* ▶ переоде́ть

переодева́|ться, юсь *impf. of* ▶ переоде́ться

переоде́тый *adj.* disguised

переоде́|ть, ну, нешь *pf.* (*of* ▶ переодева́ть)
1 (*платье, свитер*) to change; (*ребёнка,
больного*) to change sb's clothes; **п. пла́тье**
to change one's dress **2** (+ *i. or* в + *a.*) to
dress up, disguise (as, in)

переоде́|ться, нусь, нешься *pf.* (*of*
▶ переодева́ться) **1** to change (one's
clothes) **2** (+ *i. or* в + *a.*) to disguise oneself
or dress up (as, in); **она́ ~лась в ма́льчика**
she disguised herself as a boy

переосмы́сл|ить, ю, ишь *pf.* (*of*
▶ переосмысля́ть) to re-examine

переосмысля́|ть, ю *impf. of*
▶ переосмы́слить

переоце́нива|ть, ю *impf. of* ▶ переоцени́ть

переоцен|и́ть, ю́, ~ишь *pf.* (*of*
▶ переоце́нивать) to overestimate, overrate

перепа́д, а *m.* (*температур, давления*)
differential, difference

перепа́чка|ть, ю *pf.* to make all dirty

перепа́чка|ться, юсь *pf.* to make oneself
dirty (all over)

пе́репел, а, *pl.* ~á *m.* (zool.) quail

перепелен|а́ть, а́ю *pf.* (*of*
▶ перепелёнывать): **п. ребёнка** to change
a baby

перепелёныва|ть, ю *impf. of*
▶ перепелена́ть

перепи́лива|ть, ю *impf. of* ▶ перепили́ть

перепил|и́ть, ю́, ~ишь *pf.* (*of*
▶ перепи́ливать) to saw in two

перепи|са́ть¹, шу́, ~шешь *pf.* (*of*
▶ перепи́сывать) **1** (*заново*) to rewrite; **п.**

п

на́бело to make a fair copy (of) **2** (*списа́ть*) to copy

перепи|са́ть², шу́, ~шешь *pf.* (*of* ▸ **перепи́сывать**) (*сде́лать спи́сок*) to make a list (of), list; **п. всех прису́тствующих** to take the names of all those present

перепи́ск|а, и *f.* **1** (*де́йствие*) copying **2** (*корреспонде́нция*) correspondence; **быть в ~е (с + i.)** to be in correspondence (with) **3** (*collect.*) (*все пи́сьма*) correspondence, letters

перепи́сыва|ть, ю *impf. of* ▸ **переписа́ть¹**

перепи́сыва|ться, юсь *impf.* (**с** + i.) to correspond (with)

пе́репис|ь, и *f.* census

перепла́в|ить, лю, ишь *pf.* (*of* ▸ **переплавля́ть**) (*руду́*) to smelt

переплавля́|ть, ю *impf. of* ▸ **перепла́вить**

переплани́ро́вк|а, и *f.* replanning

перепла́т|а, ы *f.* overpayment

перепле|сти́, ту́, тёшь, *past* ~л, ~ла́ *pf.* (*of* ▸ **переплета́ть**) **1** (*кни́гу*) to bind **2** (+ *i.*) (*ни́ти, верёвки*) to interlace (with), interknit (with)

перепле|сти́сь, тётся, *past* ~лся, ~ла́сь *pf.* (*of* ▸ **переплета́ться**) **1** (*сте́бли, верёвки*) to interlace, interweave **2** (fig., *собы́тия*) to be interwoven

переплёт, а *m.* **1** (*де́йствие*) binding; **отда́ть кни́гу в п.** to have a book bound **2** (*обло́жка*) binding, book cover

переплета́|ть, ю, ет *impf. of* ▸ **переплести́сь**

переплета́|ться, ется *impf. of* ▸ **переплести́сь**

переплете́ни|е, я *nt.* **1** (*ни́тей*) weave **2** (*собы́тий*) interweaving

переплыва́|ть, ю *impf. of* ▸ **переплы́ть**

переплы́|ть, ву́, вёшь, *past* ~л, ~ла́, ~ло *pf.* (*of* ▸ **переплыва́ть**) (*вплавь*) to swim (across); (*на парохо́де*) to sail (across)

переподгото́вк|а, и *f.* retraining

перепол|за́ть, а́ю *impf. of* ▸ **переползти́**

перепол|зти́, у́, ёшь, *past* ~, ~ла́ *pf.* (*of* ▸ **переполза́ть**) to crawl across

перепо́лн|ить, ю, ишь *pf.* (*of* ▸ **переполня́ть**) (*сосу́д*) to overfill; (*авто́бус*) to overcrowd

перепо́лн|иться, юсь *pf.* (*of* ▸ **переполня́ться**) (*о сосу́де*) to be overfilled; (*о се́рдце, душе́*) to overflow; (*об авто́бусе*) to be overcrowded; **её се́рдце ~илось ра́достью** her heart overflowed with joy

переполн|я́ть, я́ю *impf. of* ▸ **переполни́ть**

переполн|я́ться, я́юсь *impf. of* ▸ **переполни́ться**

перепо́нк|а, и *f.* membrane; **бараба́нная п.** (anat.) eardrum, tympanum

перепоруча́|ть, а́ю *impf. of* ▸ **перепоручи́ть**

перепоруч|и́ть, у́, ~ишь *pf.* (*of* ▸ **перепоруча́ть**) (+ *d.*) to turn over (to), reassign (to)

перепра́в|а, ы *f.* (*де́йствие*) crossing; (*ме́сто*) crossing (place); (*брод*) ford

перепра́в|ить¹, лю, ишь *pf.* (*of* ▸ **переправля́ть**) **1** (*перевезти́*) to convey, transport; to take across **2** (*письмо́*) to forward (*mail*)

перепра́в|ить², лю, ишь *pf.* (*of* ▸ **переправля́ть**) (*испра́вить*) to correct

перепра́в|иться, люсь, ишься *pf.* (*of* ▸ **переправля́ться**) to cross, get across; (*вплавь*) to swim across; (*на парохо́де*) to sail across

переправля́|ть, ю *impf. of* ▸ **перепра́вить¹**, ▸ **перепра́вить²**

переправля́|ться, юсь *impf. of* ▸ **перепра́виться**

перепро́б|овать, ую *pf.* (*еду́*) to taste (*all or a quantity of*); (fig., *сре́дства*) to try

перепрода|ва́ть, ю́, ёшь *impf. of* ▸ **перепрода́ть**

перепрода|ть, м, шь, ст, ди́м, ди́те, ду́т, *past* **перепро́дал**, ~ла́, **перепро́дало** *pf.* (*of* ▸ **перепродава́ть**) to resell

перепроизво́дств|о, а *nt.* overproduction

перепры́гива|ть, ю *impf. of* ▸ **перепры́гнуть**

перепры́г|нуть, ну, нешь *pf.* (*of* ▸ **перепры́гивать**) (+ *a. or* **че́рез** + *a.*) to jump (over)

перепуга́|ть, ю *pf.* (*no impf.*) to frighten, give a fright

перепуга́|ться, юсь *pf.* (*no impf.*) to get a fright

перепу́т|ать, аю *pf.* (*of* ▸ **перепу́тывать**) **1** (*ни́ти*) to entangle **2** (fig., *имена́, фа́кты*) to confuse, mix up, muddle up

перепу́т|аться, ается *pf.* (*of* ▸ **перепу́тываться**) **1** (*ни́ти*) to get entangled **2** (fig., *мы́сли*) to get confused, get mixed up

перепу́тыва|ть, ю, ет *impf. of* ▸ **перепу́тать**

перепу́тыва|ться, ется *impf. of* ▸ **перепу́таться**

перераба́тыва|ть, ю *impf. of* ▸ **перерабо́тать¹**

перерабо́та|ть¹, ю *pf.* (*of* ▸ **перераба́тывать**) **1** (*сырьё*) to process; (*преобразова́ть*) to convert (to); to treat; **п. свёклу в са́хар** to convert beet to sugar **2** (*переде́лать*) to remake; (fig., *статью́*) to revise, recast, reshape

перерабо́та|ть², ю *pf.* (*of* ▸ **перераба́тывать**) to exceed fixed hours of work, work overtime; (infml, *переутоми́ться*) to overwork

перерабо́тк|а¹, и *f.* **1** (*сырья́*) processing, treatment **2** (*переде́лка*) remaking; (*втори́чное испо́льзование*) recycling

перерабо́тк|а², и *f.* (*вре́мя*) overtime work

перераспределе́ни|е, я *nt.* redistribution

перераспредел|и́ть, ю́, и́шь *pf.* (*of* ▸ **перераспределя́ть**) to redistribute

перераспредел|я́ть, я́ю *impf. of* ▸ **перераспредели́ть**

перераст|а́ть, а́ю *impf. of* ▸ **перерасти́**

п

перераст|и́, у́, ёшь, *past* **переро́с, переросла́** *pf.* (*of* ▶ **перераста́ть**) **1** (*стать выше*) to outgrow, (over)top; (*превзойти*) to outstrip (*in height, also fig.*); **п. своего́ учи́теля** to outstrip one's teacher **2** (fig.) (**в** + *a.*) (*превратиться*) to grow (into), develop (into), turn (into) **3** (*оказаться по возрасту старше, чем нужно*) to be too old (for)

перерасхо́д, а *m.* **1** (*денег, энергии*) overspending, over-expenditure **2** (fin., *в банковском счёте*) overdraft

перерасхо́д|овать, ую *pf.* (*no impf.*) **1** (*деньги, энергию*) to overspend, spend to excess **2** (fin., *в банковском счёте*) to overdraw

перерасчёт, а *m.* recalculation; (*в другие еди́ницы*) conversion

переpé|зать, жу, жешь *pf.* (*of* ▶ **перереза́ть**) **1** (*верёвку*) to cut (in two) **2** (fig., *путь*) to cut off

перере́з|а́ть, а́ю *impf. of* ▶ **переpé́зать**

переруб|а́ть, а́ю *impf. of* ▶ **переруби́ть**

переруб|и́ть, лю́, ~ишь *pf.* (*of* ▶ **переруба́ть**) to chop in two

переры́в, а *m.* break; **обе́денный п.** lunch break; **без ~а** without a break; **с ~ами** off and on

перерыва́|ть, ю *impf. of* ▶ **перерыть**

переры́|ть, о́ю, о́ешь *pf.* (*of* ▶ **перерыва́ть**) (fig., infml) to rummage (*through*)

пересади́ть, жу́, ~дишь *pf.* (*of* ▶ **переса́живать**) **1** (*заставить пересесть*) to move, make sb change his seat; (*на другой поезд*) to transfer **2** (bot.) to transplant **3** (med.) (*сердце*) to transplant; (*кожу*) to graft

пересадк|а, и *f.* **1** (bot.) transplantation **2** (med.) transplant; grafting; **опера́ция по ~е се́рдца** heart transplant operation **3** (*переход на другой поезд, автобус*) change; **сде́лать ~у** to change (*trains, buses, etc.*)

переса́жива|ть, ю *impf. of* ▶ **пересади́ть**

переса́жива|ться, юсь *impf. of* ▶ **пересе́сть**

переса́лива|ть, ю *impf. of* ▶ **пересоли́ть**

пересда|ва́ть, ю́, ёшь *impf. of* ▶ **пересда́ть**

пересда́|ть, м, шь, ст, ди́м, ди́те, ду́т, *past* **~л, ~ла́, ~ло** *pf.* (*of* ▶ **пересдава́ть**) **1** (*помещение*) to relet; to sublet **2** (cards) to redeal **3** (*экзамен*) to resit (BrE), retake

пересека́|ть, ю, ет *impf. of* ▶ **пересе́чь**

пересека́|ться, ется *impf. of* ▶ **пересе́чься**

переселе́н|ец, ца *m.* settler

переселе́ни|е, я *nt.* migration; resettlement

пересел|и́ть, ю́, и́шь *pf.* (*of* ▶ **переселя́ть**) to move; (*на новую террито́рию*) to resettle

пересел|и́ться, ю́сь, и́шься *pf.* (*of* ▶ **переселя́ться**) to move; (*на новую террито́рию*) to migrate

пересел|я́ть, я́ю *impf. of* ▶ **переселить**

пересел|я́ться, я́юсь *impf. of* ▶ **переселиться**

перес|е́сть, я́ду, я́дешь *pf.* (*of* ▶ **переса́живаться**) **1** (*на другое место*) to change one's seat **2** (*сделать пересадку*) to change (*trains, etc.*)

пересече́ни|е, я *nt.* crossing, intersection

пересе́|чь, ку́, чёшь, ку́т, *past* **~к, ~кла́** *pf.* (*of* ▶ **пересека́ть**) **1** (*перейти*) to cross; to traverse; **п. у́лицу** to cross the road **2** (*город, местность*) to cross, cut across

пересе́|чься, чётся, ку́тся, *past* **~кся, ~кла́сь** *pf.* (*of* ▶ **пересека́ться**) to cross, intersect

переси́лива|ть, ю *impf. of* ▶ **переси́лить**

переси́л|ить, ю, ишь *pf.* (*of* ▶ **переси́ливать**) to overcome, master

переска́з, а *m.* **1** (*содержания романа*) retelling, narration **2** (*изложение*) exposition

переска|за́ть, жу́, ~жешь *pf.* (*of* ▶ **переска́зывать**) **1** to retell, narrate **2** (*рассказать подробно*) to retail, relate; **п. слу́хи** to retail rumours (BrE), rumors (AmE)

переска́зыва|ть, ю *impf. of* ▶ **пересказа́ть**

переска́кива|ть, ю *impf. of* ▶ **перескочи́ть**

перескоч|и́ть, у́, ~ишь *pf.* (*of* ▶ **переска́кивать**) **1** (+ *a.* or **че́рез** + *a.*) to jump (over); (fig., *пропустить*) to skip (over) **2** (fig.) to skip; **п. с одно́й те́мы на другу́ю** to skip from one topic to another

пере|сла́ть, шлю́, шлёшь *pf.* (*of* ▶ **пересыла́ть**) (*отправить*) to send; (*деньги*) to remit; (*по другому адресу*) to forward

пересма́трива|ть, ю *impf. of* ▶ **пересмотре́ть**

пересмотр|е́ть, ю́, ~ишь *pf.* (*of* ▶ **пересма́тривать**) **1** (*книгу, документ*) to look through; to go over again **2** (*решение*) to reconsider; (law) to review **3** (*ища что-л.*) to go through (*in search of sth*)

пересним|а́ть, ю *impf. of* ▶ **пересня́ть**

пересн|я́ть, иму́, и́мешь, *past* **~я́л, ~яла́, ~я́ло** *pf.* (*of* ▶ **переснима́ть**) **1** (*фотографи́ровать заново*) to photograph/film again **2** (*копировать*, infml) to make a copy of

пересол|и́ть, ю́, ~ишь *pf.* (*of* ▶ **переса́ливать**) to put too much salt (into)

пересо́х|нуть, нет, *past* **~, ~ла** *pf.* (*of* ▶ **пересыха́ть**) (*о белье́*) to dry out; (*о земле, речке*) to dry up, become parched

пересп|а́ть, лю́, и́шь, *past* **~а́л, ~ала́, ~а́ло** *pf.* (infml) **1** (*проспать слишком долго*) to oversleep **2** (**с** + *i.*) (euph.) to sleep (with)

переспо́р|ить, ю, ишь *pf.* to defeat in argument

переспра́шива|ть, ю *impf. of* ▶ **переспроси́ть**

переспро|си́ть, шу́, ~сишь *pf.* (*of* ▶ **переспра́шивать**) (*повторить вопрос*) to ask again; (*просить повторить*) to ask to repeat

переста|ва́ть, ю́, ёшь *impf. of* ▶ **переста́ть**

переста́в|ить, лю, ишь *pf.* (*of* ▶ **переставля́ть**) to move, shift; **п. ме́бель**

п

to rearrange the furniture

переставля́|ть, ю *impf. of* ▶ **переста́вить**

перестано́вк|а, и *f.* **1** rearrangement, transposition **2** (math.) permutation

переста́|ть, ну, нешь *pf.* (*of* ▶ **переставать**) (+ *inf.*) to stop, cease; **они́ ~ли разгова́ривать** they stopped talking; **~ньте!** stop it!

перестел|и́ть, ю́, ~ешь *pf.* (*of* ▶ **перестила́ть**) to relay; **п. посте́ль** to remake a bed

перестила́|ть, ю *impf. of* ▶ **перестели́ть**

перестра́ива|ть, ю *impf. of* ▶ **перестро́ить**

перестра́ива|ться, юсь *impf. of* ▶ **перестро́иться**

перестрах|ова́ться, у́юсь *pf.* (*of* ▶ **перестрахо́вываться**) **1** to reinsure oneself **2** (fig., pej.) to play safe

перестрахо́выва|ться, юсь *impf. of* ▶ **перестрахова́ться**

перестре́лк|а, и *f.* exchange of fire, shoot-out

перестро́|ить, ю, ишь *pf.* (*of* ▶ **перестра́ивать**) **1** (*дом*) to rebuild, reconstruct **2** (*план, работу*) to redesign, refashion, reshape; to reorganize; **п. фра́зу** to reshape a sentence

перестро́|иться, юсь, ишься *pf.* (*of* ▶ **перестра́иваться**) to re-form; to reorganize oneself; to restructure

перестро́йк|а, и *f.* **1** (*здания*) rebuilding, reconstruction; (pol., econ.) perestroika **2** (*реорганизация*) reorganization

переступ|а́ть, а́ю *impf. of* ▶ **переступи́ть**

переступ|и́ть, лю́, ~ишь *pf.* (*of* ▶ **переступа́ть**) (+ *a. or* че́рез + *a.*) to step over; (fig.) to overstep; **п. поро́г** to cross the threshold; **п. зако́н** to break the law

пересу́шива|ть, ю *impf. of* ▶ **пересуши́ть**

пересуш|и́ть, у́, ~ишь *pf.* (*of* ▶ **пересу́шивать**) to overdry

пересчит|а́ть¹, а́ю *pf.* (*of* ▶ **пересчи́тывать**) **1** to recount **2** (в + *p.*) to convert (to), express (in terms of)

пересчит|а́ть², а́ю *pf.* (*no impf.*) (*многое*) to count

пересчи́тыва|ть, ю *impf. of* ▶ **пересчита́ть¹**

пересыла́|ть, ю *impf. of* ▶ **пересла́ть**

пересы́п|ать, лю, лешь *pf.* (*of* ▶ **пересыпа́ть**) to pour (*dry substance*) into another container; **п. зерно́ в мешки́** to pour off grain into bags

пересып|а́ть, а́ю *impf. of* ▶ **пересы́пать**

пересы́ха|ть, ет *impf. of* ▶ **пересо́хнуть**

перета́скива|ть, ю *impf. of* ▶ **перетащи́ть**

перетас|ова́ть, у́ю *pf. of* ▶ **тасова́ть**

перетащ|и́ть, у́, ~ишь *pf.* (*of* ▶ **перета́скивать**) (*волоча*) to drag over; (*неся*) to carry over; (*переместить*) to move, shift; **п. сунду́к на черда́к** to move a trunk into the attic

перетека́|ть, ю *impf. of* ▶ **перете́чь**

перете́|чь, чь, чёшь, кут, past ~к, ~кла́ *pf.* (*of* ▶ **перетека́ть**) to overflow

перетя́гива|ть, ю *impf. of* ▶ **перетяну́ть**

перетя́|ну́ть, ну́, ~нешь *pf.* (*of* ▶ **перетя́гивать**) **1** to pull, draw (*somewhere else; from A to B*); **п. ло́дку от одного́ бе́рега к друго́му** to pull the boat from one bank to the other **2** (fig., infml) to pull over, attract; **п. на свою́ сто́рону** to win over, gain support of **3** (*крепко стяну́ть*) to tighten

переубе|ди́ть, ди́шь *pf.* (*of* ▶ **переубежда́ть**) to make *sb* change his, her, *etc.* mind

переубежда́|ть, ю *impf. of* ▶ **переубеди́ть**

переу́л|ок, ка *m.* lane, side street

переутом|и́ть, лю́, и́шь *pf.* (*of* ▶ **переутомля́ть**) to tire out; to overwork

переутом|и́ться, лю́сь, и́шься *pf.* (*of* ▶ **переутомля́ться**) to tire oneself out; to overwork; (*pf. only*) to be run down

переутомле́ни|е, я *nt.* exhaustion; overwork

переутомля́|ть, ю *impf. of* ▶ **переутоми́ть**

переутомля́|ться, юсь *impf. of* ▶ **переутоми́ться**

перефрази́р|овать, ую *impf. and pf.* to paraphrase

перехва|ти́ть, чу́, ~тишь *pf.* (*of* ▶ **перехва́тывать**) to intercept, catch; **я ~ти́л его́ по доро́ге на рабо́ту** I caught him on the way to work

перехва́тыва|ть, ю *impf. of* ▶ **перехвати́ть**

перехитр|и́ть, ю́, и́шь *pf.* to outwit

⚔ **перехо́д, а** *m.* **1** (*действие; место*) crossing; (*к другому состоянию, к другой системе*) transition, switch(-over); **подзе́мный п.** underpass, subway **2** (mil.) (day's) march

⚔ **перехо|ди́ть, жу́, ~дишь** *impf. of* ▶ **перейти́**

переходни́к, а́ *m.* adaptor

перехо́дный *adj.* **1** (*период*) transitional **2** (gram.) transitive

пе́р|ец, ца *m.* pepper

пе́реч|ень, ня *m.* (*список*) list; (*перечисление*) enumeration

перечёркива|ть, ю *impf. of* ▶ **перечеркну́ть**

перечер|кну́ть, ну́, нёшь *pf.* (*of* ▶ **перечёркивать**) to cross (out); (fig., *уничтожить*) to cancel

перечи́сл|ить, ю, ишь *pf.* (*of* ▶ **перечисля́ть**) **1** to enumerate **2** (*перевести*) to transfer; **п. на теку́щий счёт** (fin.) to transfer to one's current account

перечисля́|ть, я́ю *impf. of* ▶ **перечи́слить**

перечи́т|ать¹, а́ю *pf.* (*of* ▶ **перечи́тывать**) (*заново*) to reread

перечит|а́ть², а́ю *pf.* (*всё или многое*) to read (*all or a quantity of*); **он ~а́л все кни́ги в библиоте́ке** he has read all the books in the library

перечи́тыва|ть, ю *impf. of* ▶ **перечита́ть¹**

пе́речниц|а, ы *f.* (*для молотого перца*) pepper pot

переша́гива|ть, ю *impf. of* ▶ **перешагну́ть**

переша́г|ну́ть, ну́, нёшь *pf.* (*of* ▶ **переша́гивать**) to step over; **п. (че́рез) поро́г** to cross the threshold

п

переше́е|ек, йка *m.* isthmus

перешива́|ть, ю *impf. of* ▶ **переши́ть**

переши́|ть, ью, ьёшь *pf. (of* ▶ **перешива́ть)**
to alter; to have altered

пери́л|а, ~ *(no sg.)* rail(ing); handrail;
(лестницы) banisters

пери́метр, а *m.* (math.) perimeter

пери́н|а, ы *f.* feather bed

✓ **пери́од, а** *m.* period; **леднико́вый п.** (geol.)
ice age

периоди́к|а, и *f.* (collect.) periodicals

периоди́ческ|ий *adj.* periodic(al);
recurring; **п. журна́л** periodical, magazine;
~ое явле́ние recurrent phenomenon

периско́п, а *m.* periscope

перифери́|я, и *f.* **1** periphery **2** (collect.)
(ме́стность, удалённая от центра) the
provinces; the outlying districts **3** (comput.)
peripherals, peripheral devices

перламу́тр, а *m.* mother-of-pearl

перламу́тровый *adj. of* ▶ **перламу́тр**

перма́нент|ный, ~ен, ~на *adj.* permanent

перна́т|ый, ~, ~а *adj.* feathered; *(as n. pl.*
~ые, ~ых) birds

пёр|нуть, ну, нешь *inst. pf. of* ▶ **перде́ть**
(vulg.) to fart

пер|о́, а́, *pl.* **~ья, ~ьев** *nt.* **1** *(птицы)*
feather **2** (hist.) quill; *(стально́е)* nib

перочи́нный *adj.*: **п. нож** penknife

перпендикуля́р|ный, ~ен, ~на *adj.*
perpendicular

перро́н, а *m.* platform *(at railway station)*

перси́дский *adj.*: **П. зали́в** the Persian Gulf

пе́рсик, а *m.* **1** *(плод)* peach **2** *(де́рево)*
peach tree

персо́н|а, ы *f.* person; **обе́д на́ шесть ~**
dinner for six

персона́ж, а *m.* (liter.) character; (fig.) personage

✓ **персона́л, а** *m.* personnel, staff

персона́льный *adj.* personal; individual; **п.**
компью́тер personal computer

✓ **перспекти́в|а, ы** *f.* **1** (art) perspective
2 (fig.) prospect, outlook; **име́ть ~у** to have
prospects, have a future *(before one)*

перспекти́в|ный *adj.* **1** (art) perspective
2 *(план)* long-term **3** **(~ен, ~на)**
(многообеща́ющий) having prospects;
promising

пёрст|ень, ня *m.* ring

Перу́ *nt. & f. indecl.* Peru

перуа́н|ец, ца *m.* Peruvian

перуа́н|ка, ки *f. of* ▶ **перуа́нец**

перуа́нский *adj.* Peruvian

перфе́кт, а *m.* (gram.) perfect (tense)

пе́рхот|ь, и *f.* dandruff

перча́тк|а, и *f.* glove; **бро́сить ~у** (fig.) to
throw down the gauntlet

пе́рч|ить, ~у, ~ишь *impf. (of* ▶ **попе́рчить)**
to pepper

✓ key word

пёс, пса *m.* dog

пес|е́ц, ца́ *m.* Arctic fox

✓ **пе́с|ня, ни,** *g. pl.* **~ен** *f.* song

пес|о́к, ка́ *m.* **1** sand; **са́харный п.** granulated
sugar **2** *(in pl.)* sands

песо́чн|ый *adj.* **1** *adj. of* ▶ **песо́к**; sandy;
~ые часы́ sandglass, hourglass **2** (cul.)
short; **~ое пече́нье** shortbread

пессими́зм, а *m.* pessimism

пессими́ст, а *m.* pessimist

пессимисти́ческий *adj.* pessimistic

пессимисти́ч|ный, ~ен, ~на *adj.*
= **пессимисти́ческий**

пессими́ст|ка, ки *f. of* ▶ **пессими́ст**

пёстр|ый, ~, пестра́, ~о and пестро́ *adj.*
1 variegated, multicoloured (BrE), -colored
(AmE) **2** (fig., infml) mixed; **п. соста́в**
населе́ния mixed population

песча́н|ый *adj.* sandy; **~ая коса́** sandbar; **п.**
холм dune

песчи́нк|а, и *f.* grain of sand

петáрд|а, ы *f.* banger (BrE), firecracker

петербу́ргский *adj.* St Petersburg

петербу́рж|ец, ца *m.* St Petersburger

пети́ци|я, и *f.* petition

петли́ц|а, ы *f.* buttonhole; tab

петл|я́, ли́, *pl.* **~ли, ~ель** *f.* **1** loop **2** (fig.)
noose **3** *(для пу́говицы)* buttonhole
4 *(в вяза́нии)* stitch **5** *(две́ри)* hinge

петля́|ть, ю *impf.* (infml) to dodge

петру́шк|а, и *f.* parsley

пету́х, а́ *m.* cock; **встава́ть с ~а́ми** to rise
with the lark

петь, пою́, поёшь *impf. (of* ▶ **спеть²)** to sing;
п. ба́сом to have a bass voice; **п. вполго́лоса**
to hum

пехо́т|а, ы *f.* infantry; **морска́я п.** (the) marines

пехоти́н|ец, ца *m.* infantryman

печа́л|ь, и *f.* grief, sorrow

печа́л|ьный, ~ен, ~ьна *adj.* **1** sad, doleful
2 *(приско́рбный)* bad, regrettable; **п. коне́ц**
bad end

печа́та|ть, ю *impf. (of* ▶ **напеча́тать,**
▶ **отпеча́тать** 1) to print; *(на маши́нке)* to
type

печа́та|ться, юсь *impf. (of* ▶ **напеча́таться,**
1 to have *(literary compositions, etc.)*
published; **в три́дцать лет он ещё нигде́ не**
~лся at thirty he had not yet had anything
published **2** *(находи́ться в печа́ти)* to be at
the printer's

печа́т|ный *adj.* **1** printing; **п. лист** quire,
printer's sheet **2** *(напеча́танный)* printed;
in the press; **~ая кни́га** printed book *(opp.*
manuscript) **3**: **писа́ть ~ыми бу́квами** to
(write in) print; to write in block capitals

✓ **печа́т|ь¹, и** *f. (для получе́ния отти́ска)* seal,
stamp (also fig.); **на мои́х уста́х п. молча́ния**
my lips are sealed

✓ **печа́т|ь², и** *f.* **1** *(печа́тание)* print(ing);
вы́йти из ~и to come out, be published
2 *(вид напеча́танного)* print, type; **ме́лкая**

п. small print; **кру́пная п.** large print
3 (*пресса*) (the) press; **свобо́да ~и** freedom of the press
печёнк|а, и *f.* liver (*of animal, as food*)
печёный *adj.* (cul.) baked
пе́чен|ь, и *f.* liver
пече́нь|е, я *nt.* biscuit (BrE), cookie (AmE)
пе́чк|а, и *f.* stove
печь[1]**, пеку́, печёшь, пеку́т,** *past* **пёк, пекла́** *impf.* (*of* ▸ **испе́чь**) to bake; **со́лнце пекло́** there was a scorching sun
печ|ь[2]**, и, о ~и, в ~й,** *pl.* **~и, ~е́й** *f.*
1 stove; (*духовка*) oven **2** (tech.) furnace; (*обжиговая*) kiln
пе́чься, печётся, пеку́тся, *past* **пёкся, пекла́сь** *impf.* (*of* ▸ **испе́чься**) to bake
пешехо́д, а *m.* pedestrian
пешехо́дный *adj.* pedestrian; **п. мост** footbridge
пе́ший *adj.* **1** pedestrian **2** (mil.) unmounted, foot
пе́шк|а, и *f.* (chess, also fig.) pawn
пешко́м *adv.* on foot
пеще́р|а, ы *f.* cave
пиани́но *nt. indecl.* (upright) piano
пиани́ст, а *m.* pianist
пиани́ст|ка, ки *f. of* ▸ **пиани́ст**
пиа́р, а *m.* PR (*public relations*)
пивн|а́я, о́й *f.* pub
пи́в|о, а *nt.* beer
пивова́р, а *m.* brewer
пивоваре́ни|е, я *nt.* brewing
пивова́ренн|ый *adj.*: **п. заво́д** brewery; **~ая промы́шленность** brewing
пигме́нт, а *m.* pigment
пиджа́к, а́ *m.* jacket, coat
пижа́м|а, ы *f.* pyjamas (BrE), pajamas (AmE)
пижо́н, а *m.* (infml) fop
пизд|а́, ы́ (*pl. not generally used*) *f.* (vulg.) cunt
пик[1]**, а** *m.* (geog.) peak; (fig.) pinnacle
пик[2]**, а** *m.* **1** peak (*of work, traffic, etc.*); **п. нагру́зки** (elec.) peak load **2** (*adj. indecl.*): **часы́ пик** rush hour
пи́к|а[1]**, и** *f.* (*оружие*) pike, lance
пи́к|а[2]**, и** *f.* (cards) spade
пика́п, а *m.* pickup (truck)
пике́т, а *m.* (*группа бастующих*) picket
пикети́р|овать, ую *impf.* to picket
пи́кколо *nt. indecl.* piccolo
пикни́к, а́ *m.* picnic
пи́ксел|ь, я *m.* (comput.) pixel
пиктогра́мм|а, ы *f.* pictogram; (comput.) icon
пил|а́, ы́, *pl.* **~ы, ~** *f.* saw
пила́-ры́ба, пилы́-ры́бы *f.* sawfish
пилигри́м, а *m.* pilgrim
пил|и́ть, ю́, ~ишь *impf.* to saw
пило́т, а *m.* pilot
пило́тк|а, и *f.* (mil.) forage cap
пилю́л|я, и *f.* pill (also fig.)
пина́|ть, ю *impf. of* ▸ **пнуть**

пингви́н, а *m.* penguin
пинг-по́нг, а *m.* ping-pong
пинце́т, а *m.* (tech.) pincers; (med.) tweezers
пи́нчер, а *m.* (*собака*) pinscher
пио́н, а *m.* (bot.) peony
пионе́р, а *m.* pioneer
пипе́тк|а, и *f.* pipette; medicine dropper
пир, а, о ~е, на ~у́, *pl.* **~ы́** *m.* feast, banquet
пирами́д|а, ы *f.* (also fin.) pyramid
пира́т, а *m.* pirate
пира́тский *adj.* (*судно*) pirate; (*обычаи*) piratical; (*издание*) pirated
пира́тств|о, а *nt.* piracy
Пирене́|и, ев (*no sg.*) the Pyrenees
пиро́г, а́ *m.* pie; **п. с мя́сом** meat pie
пиро́г|а, и *f.* pirogue, canoe
пиро́жн|ое, ого *nt.* (fancy) cake, pastry
пирож|о́к, ка́ *m.* pasty (BrE), patty, pie
пи́рсинг, а *m.* body piercing
пи́ршеств|о, а *nt.* feast, banquet
◆ **писа́тел|ь, я** *m.* writer, author
писа́тель|ница, ницы *f. of* ▸ **писа́тель**
пи́са|ть, ю *impf.* (*of* ▸ **попи́сать**) (infml) to pee, have a pee
◆ **пи|са́ть, шу́, ~шешь** *impf.* (*of* ▸ **написа́ть**) **1** to write; (*на маши́нке*) to type **2** (+ *i.*) (*кра́сками*) to paint (in)
писк, а *m.* (*ребёнка, мы́ши*) squeak; (*цыпля́т*) cheep
пи́скн|уть, у, ешь *inst. pf.* (*of* ▸ **пища́ть**) (infml) to give a squeak, cheep
пистоле́т, а *m.* pistol
пи́сьменност|ь, и *f.* **1** (*литерату́рные па́мятники*) literature; (*collect.*) literary texts **2** (*сре́дства пи́сьменного обще́ния*) the written language
пи́сьменн|ый *adj.* **1** (*для письма́*) writing; **п. стол** writing table, bureau **2** (*напи́санный*) written; **в ~ом ви́де, в ~ой фо́рме** in writing, in written form; **п. экза́мен** written examination
◆ **письм|о́, а́,** *pl.* **~а, пи́сем, ~ам** *nt.* **1** letter; **заказно́е п.** registered letter **2** (*систе́ма графи́ческих зна́ков*) script; **ара́бское п.** Arabic script
◆ **пита́ни|е, я** *nt.* **1** (*де́йствие*) feeding, nutrition; (*хара́ктер пи́щи*) diet; **недоста́точное п.** malnutrition; (*пи́ща*) food **2** (tech.) feed, supply **3** (elec.) power supply
пита́тел|ьный, ~ен, ~ьна *adj.* nourishing, nutritious; **~ьная среда́** (biol.) culture medium; (fig.) breeding ground
пита́|ться, юсь *impf.* (+ *i.*) to feed (on), live (on); **хорошо́ п.** to be well fed, eat well
Пи́тер, а *m.* (infml) St Petersburg
пи́терский *adj.* of ▸ **Пи́тер**
пито́мник, а *m.* nursery (*for plants or animals*) (also fig.)
пито́н, а *m.* python
◆ **пить, пью, пьёшь,** *past* **пил, пила́, пи́ло** *impf.* (*of* ▸ **вы́пить**) to drink; **мне хо́чется п.**

I am thirsty; п. за (+ a.), за здоро́вье (+ g.) to drink to, to the health (of)

пить|ё, я́ nt. drink

пих|а́ть, а́ю impf. (of ▶ **пихну́ть**) (infml) ▌**1** (толка́ть) to push; shove, jostle ▌**2** (запи́хивать) to shove, cram

пих|ну́ть, ну́, нёшь pf. of ▶ **пиха́ть**

пи́хт|а, ы f. fir (tree)

пи́цц|а, ы f. pizza

◆ **пи́щ|а, и** (no pl.) f. food

пищ|а́ть, у́, и́шь impf. (of ▶ **пи́скнуть**) (о мы́ши, о две́ри) to squeak; (о цыпля́тах) to cheep

пищеваре́ни|е, я nt. digestion; **расстро́йство ~я** indigestion

пищ|ево́й adj. of ▶ **пи́ща**; **~евы́е проду́кты** foodstuffs

пия́вк|а, и f. leech

ПК m. indecl. (abbr. of **персона́льный компью́тер**) PC (personal computer)

пла́вани|е, я nt. ▌**1** swimming ▌**2** (на судне) sailing; navigation; **отпра́виться в п.** to put out to sea

пла́вательный adj. swimming; **п. бассе́йн** swimming pool

пла́ва|ть, ю impf. ▌**1** indet. of ▶ **плыть** ▌**2** (держа́ться на воде) to float

пла́в|ить, лю, ишь impf. to smelt

пла́в|иться, ится impf. to melt

пла́вк|а, и f. fusing; fusion

пла́в|ки, ок (no sg.) swimming trunks

плавни́к, а́ m. (ры́бы) fin; (дельфи́на, тюле́ня) flipper

пла́в|ный, ~ен, ~на adj. smooth; **~ная речь** flowing speech

плаву́чий adj. floating

плагиа́т, а m. plagiarism

пла́зм|а, ы f. (biol., phys.) plasma

пла́зменный adj.: **~ экра́н** (TV, comput.) plasma screen

плака́т, а m. poster

пла́|кать, чу, чешь impf. to cry, weep; **п. навзры́д** to sob

плакси́в|ый, ~, ~а adj. (infml) (ребёнок) given to crying; whining; (го́лос, лицо́, улы́бка) pathetic

пла́мен|ный, ~ен, ~на adj. ardent, burning

пла́м|я, ени nt. flame; (я́ркое) blaze

◆ **план, а** m. ▌**1** (наме́рение; чертёж, ка́рта) plan; **по ~у** according to plan ▌**2** (ме́сто): **пере́дний п.** foreground; **за́дний п.** background); **кру́пный п.** close-up (in filming)

пла́нер, а m. (aeron.) glider

◆ **плане́т|а, ы** f. ▌**1** planet ▌**2** (Земля́) (the) planet (= Earth)

плани́рование, я nt. planning

◆ **плани́р|овать, ую** impf. (of ▶ **заплани́ровать**) to plan

планиро́вк|а, и f. layout

пла́нк|а, и f. lath, slat

планкто́н, а m. (biol.) plankton

пла́нов|ый adj. planned, systematic; **~ое хозя́йство** planned economy

планоме́р|ный, ~ен, ~на adj. systematic, planned

планта́ци|я, и f. plantation

планше́т, а m. (comput.) tablet (computer)

планше́тный adj.: **п. компью́тер** tablet (computer); **п. ска́нер** flatbed scanner

пласт, а́ m. layer; sheet; (archit.) course; (geol.) stratum, bed

пла́стик, а m. plastic (material)

пла́стиковый adj. plastic

пластили́н, а m. plasticine®

пласти́н|а, ы f. plate (thin flat sheet)

пласти́нк|а, и f. ▌**1** plate; (вини́ловая) п. (vinyl) record ▌**2** (infml, зубно́й проте́з) plate

пласти́ческ|ий adj. plastic; **~ая хирурги́я** plastic surgery

пласти́ч|ный, ~ен, ~на adj. ▌**1** (материа́л, вещество́) plastic; pliant ▌**2** (пла́вный) rhythmical; fluent, flowing; (изя́щный) graceful; (гармони́чный) harmonious

пластма́сс|а, ы f. plastic

пластма́ссовый adj. of ▶ **пластма́сса**

пла́стыр|ь, я m. (med.) plaster

◆ **пла́т|а¹, ы** f. ▌**1** (за труд) pay; salary; **зарабо́тная п.** wages ▌**2** (за получе́ние, испо́льзование чего́-н.) payment, charge; fee; **входна́я п.** entrance fee; **кварти́рная п.** rent; **п. за прое́зд** fare

пла́т|а², ы f. (comput.) card, board; **монта́жная п.** circuit board

плата́н, а m. plane (tree)

◆ **платёж, ежа́** m. payment

платёжеспосо́б|ный, ~ен, ~на adj. solvent

платёж|ный adj. of ▶ **платёж**; **~ная ве́домость** payroll; **~ное поруче́ние** payment order

пла́тин|а, ы f. (min.) platinum

◆ **пла|ти́ть, чу́, ~тишь** impf. (of ▶ **заплати́ть**) ▌**1** to pay; **п. нали́чными** to pay in cash, pay in ready money ▌**2** (fig.) (+ i. and за + a.) to pay back, return; **п. кому́-н. услу́гой за услу́гу** to make it up to sb, return a favour (BrE), favor (AmE)

пла́т|ный adj. ▌**1** paid; requiring payment, chargeable; **~ая доро́га** toll road ▌**2** paying; (шко́ла) fee-paying; (больни́ца) private

плато́ nt. indecl. (geog.) plateau

плато́к, ка́ m. (на пле́чи) shawl; (на го́лову) headscarf; **носово́й п.** (pocket) handkerchief

платфо́рм|а, ы f. ▌**1** (перро́н) platform ▌**2** (ваго́н) (open) goods truck (BrE), flatcar (AmE) ▌**3** (fig., pol.) platform

пла́ть|е, я, g. pl. **~ев** nt. ▌**1** (же́нское) dress; (дли́нное) gown; **вече́рнее п.** evening dress ▌**2** (оде́жда) clothes, clothing

плач, а m. weeping, crying

плаче́в|ный, ~ен, ~на adj. lamentable, deplorable, sorry; **в ~ном состоя́нии** in a

◆ key word

sorry state

плашмя́ *adv.* flat; flatways; prone

плащ, á *m.* **1** (*непромокаемое пальто*) raincoat **2** (*накидка*) cloak

плева́ть, плюю́, плюёшь *impf.* (*of* ▶ **плю́нуть**) **1** to spit **2** (**на** + *a.*) (infml) to spit (upon); **им п. на всё** they don't give a damn about anything

плев|о́к, ка́ *m.* spit(tle)

плед, а *m.* travelling rug (BrE), lap robe (AmE)

пле́ер, а *m.* (*аудиокассет, аудиодисков*) personal stereo, Walkman®; MP3, DVD, *etc.*, player

пле́м|я, ени, *pl.* ~ена́, ~ён, ~ена́ми *nt.* tribe

племя́нник, а *m.* nephew

племя́нниц|а, ы *f.* niece

плен, а, о ~е, в ~у́ *m.* captivity; **попа́сть в п.** (**к** + *d.*) to be taken prisoner (by)

плени́тел|ьный, ~ен, ~ьна *adj.* captivating, charming

плёнк|а, и *f.* (*тонкий слой*) film (also phot.); (*магнитофонная*) tape

пле́нник, а *m.* prisoner, captive

пле́нни|ца, цы *f. of* ▶ **пле́нник**

пле́нн|ый *adj.* captive; (*as m. n.* **п.**, **~ого**) captive, prisoner

пле́нум, а *m.* plenum, plenary session

пле́сен|ь, и *f.* mould (BrE), mold (AmE)

плеск, а *m.* splash; **п. волн** lapping of waves

пле|ска́ть, щу́, ~щешь *impf.* (*of* ▶ **плесну́ть**) to splash; **п. на кого́-н. водо́й** to splash sb (with water)

пле|ска́ться, щу́сь, ~щешься *impf.* to splash; (*о волнах*) to lap

плес|ну́ть, ну́, нёшь *inst. pf. of* ▶ **плеска́ть**

пле|сти́, ту́, тёшь, *past* **~л, ~ла́ 1** *impf. of* ▶ **сплести́ 2** (*pf.* ▶ **заплести́**) (*волосы*) to braid, plait

пле|сти́сь, ту́сь, тёшься, *past* **~лся, ~ла́сь** *impf.* (infml) to trudge, plod (along)

плет|ь, и, *pl.* ~и, ~е́й *f.* lash

плечи́ст|ый, ~, ~а *adj.* broad-shouldered

⚔ **плеч|о́, á, *pl.* ~и, ~, ~а́м** *nt.* shoulder; **име́ть го́лову на ~а́х** to have a good head on one's shoulders; **э́то ему́ не по ~у́** he is not up to it; **пожа́ть ~а́ми** to shrug one's shoulders

плеши́в|ый, ~, ~а *adj.* bald

плеш|ь, и *f.* bald patch

пли́нтус, а *m.* **1** (archit.) plinth **2** (*между стеной и полом*) skirting board (BrE), baseboard (AmE)

плит|á, ы́, *pl.* ~ы *f.* **1** (*металлическая*) plate; (*каменная*) slab; (*для настилки полов*) flag(stone); **моги́льная п.** gravestone, tombstone; **мра́морная п.** marble slab **2** (*печь*) stove; cooker

пли́тк|а, и *f.* **1** *dim. of* ▶ **плита́**; (*облицовочная*) tile, (thin) slab; **п. шокола́да** bar of chocolate **2** (*печь*) small stove

плов, а *m.* (cul.) pilaf

плов|е́ц, ца́ *m.* swimmer

плов|чи́ха, чи́хи *f. of* ▶ **плове́ц**

плод, á *m.* **1** fruit (also fig.); **приноси́ть ~ы́** to bear fruit; **запре́тный п.** (fig.) forbidden fruit **2** (biol.) fetus

плодо́в|ый *adj. of* ▶ **плод**; **~ое де́рево** fruit tree

плодоро́ди|е, я *nt.* fertility

плодоро́д|ный, ~ен, ~на *adj.* fertile

плодотво́р|ный, ~ен, ~на *adj.* fruitful

пло́мб|а, ы *f.* **1** (*на вагоне*) seal **2** (*в зубе*) filling; **ста́вить ~у** to fill a tooth

пломбир|ова́ть, у́ю *impf.* **1** (*pf.* **о~**, **за~**) (*вагон, избирательную урну*) to seal **2** (*pf.* **за~**) (*зуб*) to fill

пло́с|кий, ~ок, ~ка́, ~ко *adj.* **1** flat; plane; **~кая пове́рхность** plane surface; **~кий экра́н** flat screen **2** (fig., *пошлый*) trivial, tame; **~кая шу́тка** feeble joke

плоского́р|ье, я *nt.* plateau; tableland

плоскогу́бцы, ев (*no sg.*) pliers

пло́скост|ь, и, *pl.* ~и, ~е́й *f.* (*поверхность*) plane (also fig.); **накло́нная п.** inclined plane

плот, á, о ~е́, на ~у́ *m.* raft

плотв|á, ы́ *f.* roach (*fish*)

плоти́н|а, ы *f.* dam

пло́тник, а *m.* carpenter

пло́тно *adv.* **1** close(ly), tightly; **п. заколоти́ть дверь** to board up a door **2**: **п. пое́сть** to eat heartily

пло́тност|ь, и *f.* **1** (*тумана, населения*) density (also phys.) **2** (*человека*) solidity

пло́т|ный, ~ен, ~на́, ~но, ~ны́ *adj.* **1** (*туман, население*) dense (also phys.) **2** (*бумага*) thick, solid, strong; (*человек*) thickset, solidly built **3** (*папка*) tightly-filled **4** (infml, *завтрак*) hearty

плотоя́д|ный, ~ен, ~на *adj.* **1** carnivorous **2** (fig., *сладострастный*) lustful; voluptuous

плот|ь, и *f.* flesh; **во ~и** in the flesh

⚔ **пло́хо** *adv.* bad(ly); ill; **чу́вствовать себя́ п.** to feel unwell; **п. па́хнуть** to smell bad

⚔ **плох|о́й, ~, ~á, ~о** *adj.* bad; poor; **~ое настрое́ние** bad mood; (*as pred.*) **ему́ о́чень ~о** he is in a very bad way

⚔ **площа́дк|а, и** *f.* **1** ground, area; **де́тская п.** children's playground; **спорти́вная п.** sports ground; **строи́тельная п.** building site; **те́ннисная п.** tennis court; **киносъёмочная п.** (film) set; **п. для игры́ в го́льф** golf course **2** (*лестничная*) landing (*on staircase*) **3** (*в вагоне*) platform; **пускова́я п.** launch pad (*of rocket*)

⚔ **пло́щад|ь, и, *pl.* ~и, ~е́й** *f.* **1** (*в городе*) square **2** (*пространство*) area; space; **жила́я п.** living space **3** (math.) area

плуг, а, *pl.* ~и́ *m.* plough (BrE), plow (AmE)

плут, á *m.* cheat; rogue

плы|ть, ву́, вёшь, *past* **~л, ~ла́, ~ло** *impf.* (*det. of* ▶ **пла́вать** 1) **1** (*о человеке, о животном*) to swim; (*об облаках, о звуках*) to float **2** (*ехать на судне*) to sail; **п. на вёслах** to row; **п. под паруса́ми** to sail

плю́н|уть, у, ешь *pf. of* ▶ **плева́ть**

плюрали́зм, а *m.* (phil. & pol.) pluralism

✧ **плюс, а** *m.* **1** plus; (*math.*): **два п. два равно́ четырём** two plus two equals four **2** (*fig., infml, преиму́щество*) advantage

плю́х|аться, аюсь *impf. of* ▸ **плю́хнуться**

плю́х|нуться, нусь, нешься *pf. (of* ▸ **плю́хаться**) (infml) to flop (down)

плюш, а *m.* plush

плю́шевый *adj. of* ▸ **плюш**

плющ, á *m.* ivy

пляж, а *m.* beach

пля|са́ть, шу́, ~шешь *impf. (of* ▸ **спляса́ть**) to dance

пля́ск|а, и *f.* (*де́йствие*) dancing; (*танец*) dance (*esp. folk dance*)

пневмати́ческий *adj.* pneumatic

пневмони́|я, и *f.* pneumonia; **атипи́чная п.** SARS (*severe acute respiratory syndrome*)

пнуть, пну, пнёшь *inst. pf. (of* ▸ **пина́ть**) (infml) to kick

✧ **по** *prep.* **I.** (+ *d.*) **1** (*на пове́рхности*) on; (*вдоль*) along; **идти́ по траве́** to walk on the grass; **éхать по у́лице** to go along the street; **идти́ по следа́м** (+ *g.*) to follow in the tracks (of); **по всему́, по всей** all over **2** (*в ра́зные места́*) round, about; **ходи́ть по магази́нам** to go round the shops **3** (*посре́дством*) by, on, over; **по желе́зной доро́ге** by rail; **по по́чте** by post; **по ра́дио** on/over the radio; **по телефо́ну** on/over the telephone **4** (*в соотве́тствии, согла́сно*) according to; by; in accordance with; **по пра́ву** by right(s); **по расписа́нию** according to schedule; **звать по и́мени** to call by first name **5** (*в отноше́нии*) by, in (= *in respect of*); **по профе́ссии** by profession; **по происхожде́нию он армяни́н** he is of Armenian origin; **лу́чший по ка́честву** better in quality; **това́рищ по шко́ле** schoolmate **6** (*в о́бласти*) at, on, in (= *in the field of*); **лéкции по европе́йской исто́рии** lectures on European history; **специали́ст по я́дерной фи́зике** specialist in nuclear physics **7** (*из-за*) by (reason of); on account of; from; **по боле́зни** on account of sickness; **по рассе́янности** from absent-mindedness **8** (*ука́зывает на предме́т де́йствия*) at, for (*or not translated*); **скуча́ть по де́тям** to miss one's children **9** (*ука́зывает время*) on; in; **по пра́здникам** on holidays

● **II.** (*в распредели́тельном значе́нии*): **по одному́(одно́й)/по ты́сяче/по миллио́ну/ по миллиа́рду** one thousand/a million/a billion each; (*with other numerals + a.*) **по́ два (две)/по три/по четы́ре/по две́сти/по три́ста/по четы́реста** two/three/four/two hundred/three hundred/four hundred each; **да́йте им по** (*sc. одному́*) **я́блоку** give them an apple each; **мы получи́ли по три фу́нта** we received three pounds each; **по рублю́ шту́ка** one rouble each

● **III.** (+ *a.*) (*до*) to, up to; **по по́яс в воде́** up to the waist in water

● **IV.** (+ *p.*) (*по́сле*) on, after; **по прибы́тии** on arrival

по...¹ *vbl. pref.* **1** *forms pf. aspect* **2** (*indicates action of short duration or of incomplete character*): **порабо́тать** to do a little work; **поспа́ть** to have a sleep **3** (*with ...ыва..., ...ива...*) (*indicates action repeated at intervals or of indet. duration*): **позва́нивать** to keep ringing

по...² *pref. modifying comp. adj. or adv., as:* **погро́мче** a little louder

по- + *d. of adj. or in names of languages, forms adv. indicating* **1** (*manner of action, conduct, etc.*): **жить по-ста́рому** to live in the old manner **2** (*use of given language*): **говори́ть по-ру́сски** to speak Russian **3** (*accordance with opinion or wish*): **по-мо́ему** in my opinion

поба́ива|ться, юсь *impf.* (+ *g. or inf.*) (infml) to be rather afraid

поба́лива|ть, ю *impf.* (infml) (*немно́го*) to ache a little; (*иногда́*) to ache on and off

побе́г, а *m.* flight; escape

✧ **побе́д|а, ы** *f.* victory; **одержа́ть ~у** to gain a victory

✧ **победи́тел|ь, я** *m.* victor; (sport) winner

победи́тель|ница, ницы *f. of* ▸ **победи́тель**

победи́|ть, и́шь *pf. (of* ▸ **побежда́ть**) (*врага́*) to conquer; (*сопе́рника*) to defeat, beat; **на́ша кома́нда победи́ла** our team won; (*fig.*) to master, overcome

побе́дный *adj.* victorious, triumphant; **п. гол** winning goal

побе|жа́ть, гу́, жи́шь, гу́т *pf.* **1** *pf. of* ▸ **бежа́ть 1 2** to break into a run

побежда́|ть, ю *impf. of* ▸ **победи́ть**

побеле́|ть, ю *pf. of* ▸ **беле́ть 1**

побел|и́ть, ю́, ~и́шь *pf. of* ▸ **бели́ть**

побе́лк|а, и *f.* whitewashing

побере́жь|е, я *nt.* coast, seaboard

побесе́д|овать, ую *pf.* to have a (little) talk, have a chat

побеспоко́|ить, ю, ишь *pf. (of* ▸ **беспоко́ить 2**): **позво́льте вас п.!** may I trouble you?

побеспоко́|иться, юсь, ишься *pf. of* ▸ **беспоко́иться 2**

побива́|ть, ю *impf. (of* ▸ **поби́ть 2**) (*проти́вника*) to beat; (*реко́рд*) to break

поб|и́ть, ью́, ьёшь 1 *pf. of* ▸ **бить 1 2** *pf. of* ▸ **побива́ть 3** (*pf. only*) (*расте́ния*) to beat down, damage; (*о моро́зе*) to nip **4** (*pf. only*) (*посу́ду*) to break, smash

поб|и́ться, ью́сь, ьёшься *pf.* (infml) **1** (*used only in 3rd pers.*) (*получи́ть повреждéния*) to get damaged; (*о фру́ктах и овоща́х*) to bruise; (*о посу́де, я́йцах*) to break, smash **2** (*над* + *i.*) (fig.) to struggle (with) (for some time)

поблагодар|и́ть, ю́, и́шь *pf. of* ▸ **благодари́ть**

побледне́|ть, ю *pf. of* ▸ **бледне́ть**

поблёскива|ть, ю *impf.* to gleam

побли́зости *adv.* nearby; **п.** (*от* + *g.*) near (to)

поболта́|ть, ю *pf.* (infml) to have a chat

побор|о́ть, ю́, ~ешь *pf.* to overcome

п

побо́чный *adj.* secondary; **п. эффе́кт** side effect; **п. проду́кт** by-product

побо|я́ться, ю́сь, и́шься *pf.* (+ *g. or inf.*) to be afraid

побри́ть, е́ю *pf. of* ▸ **брить**

побри́ться, е́юсь *pf. of* ▸ **бри́ться**

поброса́ть, ю **1** (*бросить как попало*) to throw **2** (*покинуть*) to desert, abandon

побыва́|ть, ю *pf.* **1** (*посетить*) to have been, have visited; **в про́шлом году́ мы ~ли в Норве́гии и Шве́ции** last year we were in Norway and Sweden **2** (*зайти*) to drop in, call in; **он ~л у друзе́й** he dropped in to see some friends

по|бы́ть, бу́ду, бу́дешь, *past* **~был, ~была́, ~было** *pf.* to stay (*for a short time*); **мы ~были в Ло́ндоне два дня** we stayed in London for two days

пова́дк|а, и *f.* (infml) habit

повал|и́ть¹, ю́, ~ишь *pf. of* ▸ **вали́ть¹ 1**

повал|и́ть², ю́, ~ишь *pf.* to begin to throng, begin to pour; **дым ~и́л из трубы́** smoke began to pour from the chimney

повал|и́ться, ю́сь, ~ишься *pf. of* ▸ **вали́ться**

пова́льный *adj.* general, mass

по́вар, а, *pl.* **~а́** *m.* cook

по-ва́шему *adv.* **1** (*по вашему мнению*) in your opinion **2** (*как вы хотите*) as you wish

⚘ **поведе́ни|е, я** *nt.* behaviour (BrE), behavior (AmE)

повез|ти́, у́, ёшь, *past* **~, ~ла́** *pf. of* ▸ **везти́**

повели́тельн|ый *adj.*: **~ое наклоне́ние** (gram.) imperative mood, the imperative

повенча́|ть, ю *pf. of* ▸ **венча́ть**

повенча́|ться, юсь *pf. of* ▸ **венча́ться**

поверг|а́ть, а́ю *impf. of* ▸ **пове́ргнуть**

пове́рг|нуть, ну, нешь, *past* **~ and ~нул, ~ла** *pf.* (*of* ▸ **поверга́ть**) (**в** + *a.*) to plunge (into); **п. в отча́яние** to plunge into despair

пове́р|ить, ю, ишь *pf. of* ▸ **ве́рить**

поверн|у́ть, у́, нёшь *pf.* (*of* ▸ **повора́чивать**) to turn; (fig.) to change

поверн|у́ться, у́сь, нёшься *pf.* (*of* ▸ **повора́чиваться**) to turn; **кругóм** to turn round, turn about; **п. спино́й** (**к** + *d.*) to turn one's back (upon)

пове́рх *prep.* + *g.* over, above; on top of; **смотре́ть п. очко́в** to look over the top of one's spectacles

пове́рхностн|ый *adj.* **1** surface, superficial; **~ное натяже́ние** (tech.) surface tension **2** (**~ен, ~на**) (fig.) superficial

⚘ **пове́рхност|ь, и** *f.* surface

по́верху *adv.* on the surface, on top

повеселе́|ть, ю *pf.* to cheer up, become cheerful

по-весе́ннему *adv.* as in spring

пове́|сить, шу, сишь *pf. of* ▸ **ве́шать¹**

пове́|ситься, шусь, сишься *pf. of* ▸ **ве́шаться 2**

повествова́ни|е, я *nt.* narrative, narration

повеств|ова́ть, у́ю *impf.* (**о** + *p.*) to narrate, recount, relate

пове|сти́, ду́, дёшь, *past* **~л, ~ла́** *pf. of* ▸ **вести́ 1**

пове́стк|а, и *f.* notice, notification; **п. в суд** summons, writ, subpoena; **на ~е дня** on the agenda (also fig.)

по́вест|ь, и, *pl.* **~и, ~е́й** *f.* story, tale

повзросле́|ть, ю *pf.* to grow up

повида́|ть, ю *pf.* (infml) to see

повида́|ться, юсь *pf.* (infml) (**с** + *i.*) to meet; to see one another

по-ви́димому *adv.* apparently, seemingly

пови́дл|о, а *nt.* jam

повинност|ь, и *f.* duty, obligation; **во́инская п.** compulsory military service, conscription

повин|ова́ться, у́юсь *impf.* (*in past tense also pf.*) (+ *d.*) to obey

повинове́ни|е, я *nt.* obedience

повис|а́ть, а́ю *impf. of* ▸ **пови́снуть**

пови́с|нуть, ну, нешь, *past* **~, ~ла** *pf.* (*of* ▸ **повиса́ть**) **1** (**на** + *p.*) to hang (by) **2** (*склониться*) to hang down, droop; **п. в во́здухе** (fig.) to hang in mid-air; (*о шутке*) to fall flat

повле́|чь, ку́, чёшь, ку́т, *past* **~к, ~кла́** *pf.*: (**за собо́й**) to entail, bring in one's train; **п. за собо́й неприя́тные после́дствия** to have unpleasant consequences

повлия́|ть, ю *pf. of* ▸ **влия́ть**

⚘ **по́вод, а,** *pl.* **~ы** *m.* (**к** + *d.*) occasion, cause, ground (for, of); **дать п.** (+ *d.*) to give occasion (to), give cause (for); **без вся́кого ~а** without cause; **по ~у** (+ *g.*) apropos (of), as regards, concerning

пово́д|о́к, ка́ *m.* lead (BrE), leash (AmE)

пово́зк|а, и *f.* cart

повора́чива|ть, ю *impf.* (*of* ▸ **поверну́ть**)

повора́чива|ться, юсь *impf.* (*of* ▸ **поверну́ться**): **~йся!, ~йтесь!** (infml) get a move on!, look sharp!

поворо́т, а *m.* turn(ing); **указа́тели ~а** (direction) indicator lamps/lights (*of car*); (fig.) turning point; **на ~е доро́ги** at the turn of the road

повре|ди́ть, жу́, ди́шь *pf.* **1** *pf. of* ▸ **вреди́ть** **2** (*pf.* ▸ **поврежда́ть**) (*испортить*) to damage; (*поранить*) to injure, hurt

повреди́ться, жу́сь, ди́шься *pf.* (*of* ▸ **поврежда́ться**) (*испортиться*) to be damaged

поврежда́|ть, ю *impf. of* ▸ **повреди́ть**

поврежда́|ться, юсь *impf. of* ▸ **повреди́ться**

поврежде́ни|е, я *nt.* damage; injury

повседне́вный *adj.* daily; everyday

повсеме́стно *adv.* everywhere

повста́н|ец, ца *m.* rebel, insurgent

повстреча́|ть, ю *pf.* (infml) to meet, run into

повстреча́|ться, юсь *pf.* (infml) (+ *d. or* **с** + *i.*) to meet, run into; **я ~лся со знако́мым**

п

I met an acquaintance

повсю́ду *adv.* everywhere

повто́р, а *m.* replay

повторе́ни|е, я *nt.* **1** (*действия*) repetition **2** (*события*) recurrence **3** (*урока*) revision

повтор|и́ть, ю́, и́шь *pf.* (*of* ▶ **повторя́ть**) **1** to repeat **2** (*уроки*) to revise

повтор|и́ться, ю́сь, и́шься *pf.* (*of* ▶ **повторя́ться**) **1** (*повторить сказанное*) to repeat oneself **2** (*о событиях*) to reoccur; (*о болезни*) to recur

повто́р|ный, ~ен, ~на *adj.* (*визит*) second, repeated; (*заболевание*) recurring

✔ **повтор|я́ть, я́ю** *impf. of* ▶ **повтори́ть**

повтор|я́ться, я́юсь *impf. of* ▶ **повтори́ться**

повы́|сить, шу, сишь *pf.* (*of* ▶ **повыша́ть**) **1** to raise, heighten; **п. вдво́е, втро́е** to double, treble; **п. в пять раз** *и т. п.* to raise fivefold, *etc.*; **п. давле́ние** to increase pressure; **п. го́лос** to raise one's voice; (*улучшить*) to improve **2** (*работника*) to promote, advance; **п. кого́-н. по слу́жбе** to give sb promotion

повы́|ситься, шусь, сишься *pf.* (*of* ▶ **повыша́ться**) to rise; (*увеличиться*) to increase; (*улучшиться*) to improve; **на́ши а́кции ~сились** our shares have gone up; (*fig.*) our stock has risen

✔ **повыша́|ть, ю** *impf. of* ▶ **повы́сить**

повыша́|ться, юсь *impf. of* ▶ **повы́ситься**

повы́ше *comp. adj. and adv.* a little higher (up); (*о росте человека*) a little taller

✔ **повыше́ни|е, я** *nt.* rise, increase; **п. по слу́жбе** advancement, promotion

п ✔ **повы́шенный** *p.p.p. of* ▶ **повы́сить** *and adj.* increased, heightened

повя|за́ть, жу́, ~жешь *pf.* (*of* ▶ **повя́зывать**) to tie; **п. га́лстук** to tie a tie

повя́зк|а, и *f.* **1** (*лента*) band **2** (*бинт*) bandage

повя́зыва|ть, ю *impf. of* ▶ **повяза́ть**

погада́|ть, ю *pf. of* ▶ **гада́ть 1**

пога́нк|а, и *f.* (*гриб*) toadstool

пога|си́ть, шу́, ~сишь *pf.* (*of* ▶ **гаси́ть**, ▶ **погаша́ть**) to liquidate, cancel; **п. долг** to clear a debt

пога́с|нуть, ну, нешь, *past* ~, ~ла *pf. of* ▶ **га́снуть**

погаша́|ть, ю *impf. of* ▶ **погаси́ть**

погиба́|ть, а́ю *impf. of* ▶ **поги́бнуть**

поги́б|нуть, ну, нешь, *past* ~, ~ла *pf.* (▶ **ги́бнуть**, ▶ **погиба́ть**) to perish; (*naut.* also *fig.*) to be lost; **кора́бль ~ со всей кома́ндой** the ship was lost with all hands

поги́бший *p.p. of* ▶ **поги́бнуть** *and adj.* lost, ruined

погла́|дить, жу, дишь *pf. of* ▶ **гла́дить**

погла́жива|ть, ю *impf.* to stroke (*every so often*)

поглоти́ть, щу́, ~тишь *pf.* (*of* ▶ **поглоща́ть**) to soak up, absorb (also *fig.*); **п. во́ду** to absorb water

поглоща́|ть, ю *impf. of* ▶ **поглоти́ть**

погля|де́ть, жу́, ди́шь *pf.* **1** *pf. of* ▶ **гляде́ть 2** (*взглянуть*) to have a look **3** (*некоторое время*) to look for a while

погля́дыва|ть, ю *impf.* **1** (**на** + *a.*) to glance from time to time (at) **2** (**за** + *i.*) (*infml*) to keep an eye (on)

по|гна́ть, гоню́, го́нишь, *past* ~гна́л, ~гнала́, ~гна́ло *pf.* to drive; (*начать гнать*) to begin to drive

по|гна́ться, гоню́сь, го́нишься, *past* ~гна́лся, ~гнала́сь, ~гнало́сь *pf.* (**за** + *i.*) to run (after); to give chase; (*fig.*) to strive (after, for)

погн|у́ть, у́, ёшь *pf.* to bend

погн|у́ться, ётся *pf.* to bend

погова́рива|ть, ю *impf.* (**о** + *p.*) to talk (of); ~**ют** there is talk (of)

поговор|и́ть, ю́, и́шь 1 *pf. of* ▶ **говори́ть 3 2** (*pf. only*) to have a talk

погово́рк|а, и *f.* saying

пого́д|а, ы *f.* weather

погол́овный *adj.* general, universal

пого́н, а, *g. pl.* ~ *m.* (mil.) shoulder strap

пого́н|я, и *f.* pursuit, chase

погоня́|ть, ю *impf.* (*торопить*) to urge on, drive (also fig.)

пого|сти́ть, щу́, сти́шь *pf.*: (**у** + *g.*) to stay for a while (at, with)

пограни́чник, а *m.* border guard, frontier guard

пограни́чн|ый *adj.* (*страны*) border, frontier; (*участки*) boundary; ~**ая стра́жа** border guards

по́греб, а, *pl.* ~**á** *m.* cellar (also fig.); **ви́нный п.** wine cellar

погребе́ни|е, я *nt.* burial, interment

погрему́шк|а, и *f.* rattle

погре́|ть, ю *pf.* to warm

погре́|ться, юсь *pf.* to warm oneself

погреш|и́ть, у́, и́шь *pf. of* ▶ **греши́ть 2**

погре́шност|ь, и *f.* error, mistake

погро|зи́ть, жу́, зи́шь *pf. of* ▶ **грози́ть 2**

погро́м, а *m.* pogrom; (infml) chaos

погружа́|ть, ю *impf. of* ▶ **погрузи́ть**

погружа́|ться, юсь *impf. of* ▶ **погрузи́ться**

погруже́ни|е, я *nt.* submergence; immersion; (*подводной лодки*) dive, diving

погру|зи́ть, жу́, ~зи́шь, ~зишь 1 (*pf. of* ▶ **погружа́ть**) (**в** + *a.*) to immerse; (*в темноту*) to plunge **2** (~**зишь**) *pf. of* ▶ **грузи́ть 2**

погру|зи́ться, жу́сь, ~зи́шься, ~зишься *pf.* **1** (~**зи́шься**) (*pf. of* ▶ **погружа́ться**) (**в** + *a.*) to sink (into), plunge (into); (*о подводной лодке*) to submerge, dive; (fig.) to be plunged (in); to be absorbed (in), buried (in), be lost (in); **п. в темноту́** to be plunged into darkness; **п. в размышле́ния** to be deep in thought **2** (~**зишься**) *pf. of* ▶ **грузи́ться**

погру́зк|а, и *f.* loading

✔ key word

погряз|áть, áю *impf. of* ▸ **погря́знуть**

погря́з|нуть, ну, нешь, *past* ~, ~**ла** *pf.* (*of* ▸ **погрязáть**) (в + *p.*) to be stuck (in); to be bogged down (in); (*в разврáте*) to wallow (in); **п. в долгáх** to be up to one's eyes in debt

погуб|и́ть, лю́, ~ишь *pf. of* ▸ **губи́ть**

погуля́|ть, ю *pf. of* ▸ **гуля́ть**

⚆ **под,** *also* **подо** *prep.* **1** (+ *a.* and *i.*) (*ниже*) under; **постáвить п. стол** to put under the table; **п. ви́дом** (+ *g.*) in the guise (of); **п. влия́нием** (+ *g.*) under the influence (of); **п. вопрóсом** open to question; **п. землёй** underground; **взять когó-н. пóд руку** to take sb's arm; **п. рукóй** (close) at hand, to hand; **отдáть п. суд** to prosecute **2** (+ *a.* and *i.*) (*óколо*) in the environs of, near; **жить п. Москвóй** to live near Moscow **3** (+ *a.*) (*для*) for; (to serve) as; **отвести́ помещéние п. шкóлу** to earmark premises for a school **4** (+ *a.*) (*о времени*) towards; on the eve of; **п. вéчер** towards evening; **п. Нóвый год** on New Year's Eve; **емý п. пятьдеся́т (лет)** he is getting on for fifty **5** (+ *a.*) (*в сопровождéнии*) to (the accompaniment of); **танцевáть п. мýзыку** to dance to music **6** (+ *i.*) (*при обозначéнии понятия*) by; **что нáдо понимáть п. э́тим выражéнием?** what is meant by this expression?; **что п. э́тим подразумевáется?** what is implied by this? **7** (+ *a.*) (*в обмéн*) on (= *in exchange for*); **п. залóг** on security (of); **п. распи́ску** on receipt

под...[1] and **подо..., подъ...** *vbl. pref.* indicating **1** (*action from beneath or affecting lower part of sth*): **подчеркнýть** to underline **2** (*motion upwards*): **поднять** to raise **3** (*motion towards*): **подъéхать** to approach

под...[2] and **подо..., подъ...** *as pref. of nn. and adjs.* under-, sub-

⚆ **подá|вáть, ю́, ёшь** *impf. of* ▸ **подáть**

подав|и́ть, лю́, ~ишь *pf.* (*of* ▸ **подавля́ть**) **1** (*восстáние; стон*) to suppress; to repress **2** (fig., *ослáбить, угнетáть*) to depress; to crush, overwhelm

под|ави́ться, авлю́сь, áвишься *pf. of* ▸ **дави́ться**

подáвленный *p.p.p. of* ▸ **подави́ть** *and adj.* **1** (*стон, смех*) suppressed, stifled **2** (*человéк, настроéние*) depressed, dispirited

подавля́|ть, ю *impf. of* ▸ **подави́ть**

подавля́|ющий *pres. part. act. of* ▸ **подавля́ть** *and adj.* overwhelming

подáгр|а, ы *f.* gout

подáльше *adv.* (infml) a little further

подар|и́ть, ю́, ~ишь *pf. of* ▸ **дари́ть**

⚆ **подáр|ок, ка** *m.* present, gift; **получи́ть в п.** to receive as a present

подáтлив|ый, ~, ~а *adj.* **1** pliant, pliable **2** (fig., *уступчивый*) complaisant

по|дáть, дáм, дáшь, дáст, дади́м, дади́те, дадýт, *past* ~**дáл,** ~**далá,** ~**дáло** *pf.* (*of* ▸ **подавáть**) **1** to give; **п. примéр** to set an example; **п. рýку** (+ *d.*) to offer one's hand;

п. сигнáл to give the signal **2** (*еду*) to serve; **обéд ~дáн** dinner is served **3** (sport): **п. мяч** to serve **4** (*заявлéние, жáлобу*) to serve, present, hand in; **п. заявлéние** to hand in an application; **п. в отстáвку** to tender one's resignation; **п. в суд** (**на** + *a.*) to bring an action (against)

подáч|а, и *f.* **1** giving, presenting; **п. заявлéния** sending in of application **2** (*в тéннисе, волейбóле*) service, serve; (*в футбóле*) pass

подбегá|ть, ю *impf. of* ▸ **подбежáть**

подбе|жáть, гý, жи́шь, гýт *pf.* (*of* ▸ **подбегáть**) (к + *d.*) to run up (to), come running up (to)

подбивá|ть, ю *impf. of* ▸ **подби́ть**

⚆ **подбирá|ть, ю** *impf. of* ▸ **подобрáть**

подбирá|ться, юсь *impf. of* ▸ **подобрáться**

под|би́ть, обью́, обьёшь *pf.* (*of* ▸ **подбивáть**) **1** (+ *i.*) (*пальтó*) to line (with) **2** (*обувь*) to resole **3** (*ушиби́ть*) to injure; **п. комý-н. глаз** to give sb a black eye **4** (*самолёт, утку*) to shoot down **5** (**на** + *a.* or + *inf.*) (infml, *подстрекáть*) to incite (to)

подбодр|и́ть, ю́, и́шь *pf.* (*of* ▸ **подбодря́ть**) to cheer up

подбодр|я́ть, я́ю *impf. of* ▸ **подбодри́ть**

подбóр, а *m.* selection, assortment

подбóрк|а, и *f.* set, selection

подборóд|ок, ка *m.* chin

подбрáсыва|ть, ю *impf. of* ▸ **подбрóсить**

подбрó|сить, шу, сишь *pf.* (*of* ▸ **подбрáсывать**) **1** to throw up, toss up; (**под** + *a.*) to throw (under); **п. монéту** to toss up **2** (+ *a.* or *g.*) to throw in, throw on; **п. дров в печь** to throw more wood on the fire **3** (*положи́ть скры́тно*) to place surreptitiously

подвáл, а *m.* cellar; basement

подвез|ти́, ý, ёшь, *past* ~, ~**лá** *pf.* (*of* ▸ **подвози́ть**) **1** (*довезти́*) to bring, take (with one); to give a lift (*on the road*) **2** (+ *a.* or *g.*) (*достáвить*) to bring up, transport

подверг|áть, áю *impf. of* ▸ **подвéргнуть**

подверг|áться, áюсь *impf. of* ▸ **подвéргнуться**

подвéрг|нуть, ну, нешь, *past* ~ *and* ~**нул,** ~**ла** *pf.* (*of* ▸ **подвергáть**) (+ *d.*) to subject (to); to expose (to); **п. испытáнию** to put to the test; **п. опáсности** to expose to danger, endanger

подвéрг|нуться, нусь, нешься, *past* ~**ся** *and* ~**нулся,** ~**лась** *pf.* (*of* ▸ **подвергáться**) (+ *d.*) to undergo, be subjected to

подвéрж|енный, ~, ~а *adj.* (+ *d.*) (*влия́нию ветрóв*) subject (to); (*прости́де*) prone (to), susceptible (to)

подвер|нýть, нý, нёшь *pf.* (*of* ▸ **подвёртывать**) **1** (*подвинти́ть*) to screw up a little **2** (*подоткнýть*) to tuck in, tuck up; **п. брю́ки** to tuck up one's trousers **3** (*повреди́ть*) to twist, sprain; **п. нóгу** to sprain one's ankle

подвер|нýться, нýсь, нёшься *pf.* (*of* ▸ **подвёртываться**) **1** to be twisted,

п

sprained **2** (fig., infml, *попасться*) to turn up, show up; **он кста́ти** ∼**ну́лся** he turned up just at the right moment

подвёртыва|ть, ю *impf. of* ▶ **подверну́ть**

подвёртыва|ться, юсь *impf. of*
▶ **подверну́ться**

подве́|сить, шу, сишь *pf.* (*of* ▶ **подве́шивать**) to hang up, suspend

подве́ск|а, и *f.* **1** (*действие*) hanging up, suspension **2** (*украшение*) pendant

подве|сти́, ду́, дёшь, *past* ∼́л, ∼ла́ *pf.* (*of* ▶ **подводи́ть**) **1** (к + *d.*) (*человека*) to lead up (to); (*поезд*) to bring up (to); (*дорогу*) to extend (to) **2** (под + *a.*) to place (under) **3** (infml, *поставить в трудное положение*) to let down; to put in a spot

подве́тренный *adj.* leeward

подве́шива|ть, ю *impf. of* ▶ **подве́сить**

по́двиг, а *m.* exploit, feat; heroic deed

подвига́|ть, ю *impf. of* ▶ **подви́нуть**

подвига́|ться, юсь *impf. of* ▶ **подви́нуться**

по́двид, а *m.* (biol.) subspecies

подви́ж|ный, ∼ен, ∼на *adj.* **1** (*группа войск*) mobile **2** (*ребёнок*) lively; ∼ное **лицо́** mobile features

подви́|нуть, ну, нешь *pf.* (*of* ▶ **подвига́ть**) to move; to push; ∼ньте стул! pull up a chair!

подви́|нуться, нусь, нешься *pf.* (*of* ▶ **подвига́ться**) to move; ∼ньтесь и да́йте **мне сесть!** move up and let me sit down!

подвла́ст|ный, ∼ен, ∼на *adj.* (+ *d.*) subject to, under the control of

подво|ди́ть, жу́, ∼́дишь *impf. of* ▶ **подвести́**

подво́дн|ый *adj.* submarine; underwater; ∼ая ло́дка submarine

подво|зи́ть, жу́, ∼зишь *impf. of* ▶ **подвезти́**

подгиба́|ть, ю *impf. of* ▶ **подогну́ть**

подгля|де́ть, жу́, ди́шь *pf.* (*of* ▶ **подгля́дывать**) (за + *i.*) (infml) to peep (at); to spy (on), watch furtively

подгля́дыва|ть, ю *impf. of* ▶ **подгляде́ть**

подгова́рива|ть, ю *impf. of* ▶ **подговори́ть**

подговор|и́ть, ю́, и́шь *pf.* (*of* ▶ **подгова́ривать**) (на + *a. or* + *inf.*) to put up (to), incite (to)

подголо́вник, а *m.* headrest

подгоня́|ть, ю *impf. of* ▶ **подогна́ть**

подгор|а́ть, а́ет *impf. of* ▶ **подгоре́ть**

подгор|е́ть, и́т *pf.* (*of* ▶ **подгора́ть**) to burn slightly

✐ **подгота́влива|ть**, ю *impf. of* ▶ **подгото́вить**

подгота́влива|ться, юсь *impf. of*
▶ **подгото́виться**

подготови́тельный *adj.* preparatory

подгото́в|ить, лю, ишь *pf.* (*of*
▶ **подгота́вливать**) (для + *g. or* к + *d.*) to prepare (for); **п. по́чву** (fig.) to pave the way

подгото́в|иться, люсь, ишься *pf.* (*of*
▶ **подгота́вливаться**) (к + *d.*) to prepare (for), get ready (for)

✐ **key word**

✐ **подгото́вк|а**, и *f.* **1** (к + *d.*) preparation (for), training (for) **2** (в + *p. or* по + *d.*) grounding (in), schooling (in)

подгру́пп|а, ы *f.* subgroup

подгу́зник, а *m.* nappy (BrE), diaper (AmE)

подда|ва́ться, ю́сь, ёшься *impf. of*
▶ **подда́ться**

по́дданн|ый, ∼ого, *f.* ∼ая, ∼ой *n.* subject, national

по́дданств|о, а *nt.* citizenship, nationality

под|да́ться, да́мся, да́шься, да́стся, дади́мся, дади́тесь, даду́тся, *past* ∼да́лся, ∼дала́сь *pf.* (*of* ▶ **поддава́ться**) (+ *d.*) to yield (to), give way (to), give in (to); **дверь не** ∼дала́сь the door would not give; **п. искуше́нию** to yield to temptation; **не** ∼дава́ться описа́нию to beggar description

поддева́|ть, ю *impf. of* ▶ **подде́ть**

подде́л|ать, аю *pf.* (*of* ▶ **подде́лывать**) to forge; to counterfeit

подде́лк|а, и *f.* forgery; counterfeit, fake; **п. под же́мчуг** imitation pearls

подде́лыва|ть, ю *impf. of* ▶ **подде́лать**

подде́льн|ый *adj.* forged, counterfeit; (*неискренний*) sham; **п. па́спорт** forged passport

поддерж|а́ть, у́, ∼́ишь *pf.* (*of*
▶ **подде́рживать**) **1** to support (also fig.); to back, second; **п. резолю́цию** to second a resolution **2** (*не дать прекрати́ться*) to keep up, maintain; **п. разгово́р** to keep up a conversation

✐ **подде́ржива|ть**, ю *impf. of* **1** *impf. of*
▶ **поддержа́ть; подде́рживать отноше́ния** (с + *i.*) to keep in touch (with) **2** (*impf. only*) to bear, support

✐ **подде́ржк|а**, и *f.* support; backing; seconding

подде́|ть, ну, нешь *pf.* (*of* ▶ **поддева́ть**) **1** (под + *a.*) (infml) to put on under, wear under; ∼нь(те) сви́тер под ку́ртку put a sweater on under your jacket **2** (*зацепить*) to hook; to catch up **3** (fig., infml, *человека*) to catch out; to have a dig at sb

поддо́н, а *m.* (*для кирпичей*) pallet; (*подставка*) stand, tray

подде́йств|овать, ую *pf. of* ▶ **де́йствовать 2**

поде́ла|ть, ю *pf.* (*no impf.*) (infml) to do; **ничего́ не** ∼ешь it can't be helped

подел|и́ть, ю́, ∼́ишь *pf. of* ▶ **дели́ть 2**

подел|и́ться, ю́сь, ∼́ишься *pf. of*
▶ **дели́ться 2**

поде́лк|а, и *f.* handmade article; ∼и из **де́рева** handmade wooden articles

поде́ржанный *adj.* second-hand

подерж|а́ть, у́, ∼́ишь *pf.* (*в рука́х*) to hold for some time; (*у себя́*) to keep for some time

под|ержа́ться, ержу́сь, е́ржишься *pf.* **1** (за + *a.*) to hold (on to) for some time **2** (*сохрани́ться*) to hold (out), last

подешеве́|ть, ет *pf. of* ▶ **дешеве́ть**

поджа́рива|ть, ю *impf. of* ▶ **поджа́рить**

поджа́р|ить, ю, ишь *pf.* (*of* ▶ поджа́ривать) (*на сковороде*) to fry; (*в духовке*) to roast; п. хлеб to toast bread

под|жа́ть, ожму́, ожмёшь *pf.* (*of* ▶ поджима́ть) to draw in; п. гу́бы to purse one's lips

под|же́чь, ожгу́, ожжёшь, ожгу́т, *past* ∼жёг, ∼ожгла́ *pf.* (*of* ▶ поджига́ть) to set fire (to), set on fire

поджига́|ть, ю *impf. of* ▶ подже́чь

поджида́|ть, ю *impf.* to wait (for)

поджима́|ть, ю *impf. of* ▶ поджа́ть

поджо́г, а *m.* arson; arson attack

подзаголо́в|ок, ка *m.* subtitle, subheading

подзаты́льник, а *m.* (infml) clip round the ear

подзащи́тн|ый, ого *m.* (law) client

подземе́л|ье, ья, *g. pl.* ∼ий *nt.* cave; (*тюрьма*) dungeon

подзе́мк|а, и *f.* (infml) underground (railway), tube

подзе́мный *adj.* underground, subterranean

подзыва́|ть, ю *impf. of* ▶ подозва́ть

подка́лыва|ть, ю *impf. of* ▶ подколо́ть

подка́пыва|ться, юсь *impf. of* ▶ подкопа́ться

подка́рмлива|ть, ю *impf. of* ▶ подкорми́ть

подка|ти́ть, чу́, ∼тишь *pf.* (*of* ▶ подка́тывать) **1** (*мяч*) to roll; (*велосипед*) to wheel **2** (infml, *об автомобиле, экипаже*) to roll up, drive up

подка|ти́ться, чу́сь, ∼тишься *pf.* (*of* ▶ подка́тываться) (*под* + *a.*) to roll (under)

подка́тыва|ть, ю *impf. of* ▶ подкати́ть

подка́тыва|ться, юсь *impf. of* ▶ подкати́ться

подки́дыва|ть, ю *impf. of* ▶ подки́нуть

подки́|нуть, ну, нешь *pf.* (*of* ▶ подки́дывать) = подбро́сить

подкла́дк|а, и *f.* lining

подкла́дыва|ть, ю *impf. of* ▶ подложи́ть

подкле́ива|ть, ю *impf. of* ▶ подкле́ить

подкле́|ить, ю, ишь *pf.* (*of* ▶ подкле́ивать) to glue up, paste up

подключа́|ть, а́ю *impf. of* ▶ подключи́ть

подключа́|ться, а́юсь *impf. of* ▶ подключи́ться

подключ|и́ть, у́, и́шь *pf.* (*of* ▶ подключа́ть) (*к* + *d.*) **1** (tech.) to link up (to), connect up (to) **2** (fig.) to attach (to); to involve; к рабо́те ∼и́ли специали́стов specialists were involved in the work

подключ|и́ться, у́сь, и́шься *pf.* (*of* ▶ подключа́ться) **1** (tech.) to be connected up **2** (fig.) to get involved, become a participant

подко́в|а, ы *f.* (horse)shoe

подко|ва́ть, у́ю, у́ёшь *pf.* (*of* ▶ подко́вывать) to shoe

подко́выва|ть, ю *impf. of* ▶ подкова́ть

подкол|о́ть, ю́, ∼ешь *pf.* (*of* ▶ подка́лывать) **1** (*волосы*) to pin up **2** (*документ к делу*) to attach, append

подкопа́|ться, юсь *pf.* (*of* ▶ подка́пываться) (*под* + *a.*) **1** (*о животных*) to burrow (under) **2** (fig., infml) to undermine

подкорм|и́ть, лю́, ∼ишь *pf.* (*of* ▶ подка́рмливать) to feed up; to fatten (up)

подкра́дыва|ться, юсь *impf. of* ▶ подкра́сться

подкра́|сить, шу, сишь *pf.* (*of* ▶ подкра́шивать) (*стену*) to tint, colour (BrE), color (AmE); (*губы*) to touch up

подкра́|сться, ду́сь, дёшься *pf.* (*of* ▶ подкра́дываться) (*к* + *d.*) to steal up (to), sneak up (to)

подкра́шива|ть, ю *impf. of* ▶ подкра́сить

подкреп|и́ться, лю́сь, и́шься *pf.* (*of* ▶ подкрепля́ться) to fortify oneself (*with food and/or drink*)

подкрепля́|ться, юсь *impf. of* ▶ подкрепи́ться

по́дкуп, а *m.* bribery; corruption

подкуп|а́ть, а́ю *impf. of* ▶ подкупи́ть

подкуп|и́ть, лю́, ∼ишь *pf.* (*of* ▶ подкупа́ть) **1** (*деньгами*) to bribe **2** (fig., *добротой*) to win over

подла́мыва|ться, ется *impf. of* ▶ подломи́ться

по́дле *prep.* + *g.* by the side of, beside

подлеж|а́ть, у́, и́шь *impf.* (+ *d.*) to be liable (to), be subject (to); э́тот дом ∼и́т сно́су this house is to be pulled down

подлежа́щее, его *nt.* (gram.) subject

подлеза́|ть, а́ю *impf. of* ▶ подле́зть

подле́з|ть, у, ешь *pf.* (*of* ▶ подлеза́ть) (*под* + *a.*) to crawl (under), creep (under)

подлета́|ть, а́ю *impf. of* ▶ подлете́ть

подле|те́ть, чу́, ти́шь *pf.* (*of* ▶ подлета́ть) (*к* + *d.*) to fly up (to); (fig.) to rush up (to)

подле́ц, а́ *m.* scoundrel, villain, rascal

подле́чива|ть, ю *impf. of* ▶ подлечи́ть

подле́чива|ться, юсь *impf. of* ▶ подлечи́ться

подлеч|и́ть, у́, ∼ишь *pf.* (*of* ▶ подле́чивать) (infml) to treat

подлеч|и́ться, у́сь, ∼ишься *pf.* (*of* ▶ подле́чиваться) (infml) to take medical treatment

подлива́|ть, ю *impf. of* ▶ подли́ть

подли́вк|а, и *f.* sauce; (*салатная*) dressing; (*мясная*) gravy

по́длинник, а *m.* original (*opp. copy*)

по́длин|ный, ∼ен, ∼на *adj.* **1** (*не поддельный*) genuine; authentic; (*не копия*) original **2** (*истинный*) true, real; п. учёный a true scholar

под|ли́ть, олью́, ольёшь, *past* ∼ли́л, ∼лила́, ∼ли́ло *pf.* (*of* ▶ подлива́ть) (+ *a. or g. and* в + *a.*) to add (to); п. ма́сла в ого́нь (fig.) to add fuel to the fire

подлож|и́ть, у́, ∼ишь *pf.* (*of* ▶ подкла́дывать) **1** (*под* + *a.*) to lay under **2** (+ *a. or g.*) (*добавить*) to add; ∼и́те дров put some more wood on **3** (*скрытно*) to put furtively;

п. кому́-н. свинью́ to play a dirty trick on sb

подлоко́тник, а *m.* elbow rest; arm (*of chair*)

подлом|и́ться, ∼ится *pf.* (*of*
▸ **подла́мываться**) (**под** + *i.*) to break
(under)

по́длост|ь, и *f.* **1** (*свойство*) meanness,
baseness **2** (*поступок*) mean trick, low-
down trick

по́дл|ый, ∼, ∼а́, ∼о *adj.* mean, base,
despicable

подма́нива|ть, ю *impf. of* ▸ **подмани́ть**

подман|и́ть, ю́, ∼ишь *pf.* (*of*
▸ **подма́нивать**) to call (to); to beckon

подме́н|а, ы *f.* substitution (*of sth false for
sth real*)

подмен|и́ть, ю́, ∼ишь *pf.* (*of* ▸ **подменя́ть**)
(+ *a. and i.*) to substitute (for) (*intentionally*);
кто́-то на вечери́нке ∼и́л мне шля́пу sb at
the party took my hat (and left his instead)

подменя́|ть, я́ю *impf. of* ▸ **подмени́ть**

подме|сти́, ту́, тёшь, *past* ∼л, ∼ла́ *pf.* (*of*
▸ **подмета́ть**) **1** (*место*) to sweep **2** (*мусор*)
to sweep up

подмета́|ть, ю *impf. of* ▸ **подмести́**

подмётк|а, и *f.* sole

подмеш|а́ть, а́ю *pf.* (*of* ▸ **подме́шивать**) to
stir in, mix in

подме́шива|ть, ю *impf. of* ▸ **подмеша́ть**

подми́гива|ть, ю *impf. of* ▸ **подмигну́ть**

подмиг|ну́ть, ну́, нёшь *pf.* (*of*
▸ **подми́гивать**) (+ *d.*) to wink (at)

подмина́|ть, ю *impf. of* ▸ **подмя́ть**

подмоско́вный *adj.* (situated) near
Moscow

подмыва́|ть, ю *impf. of* ▸ **подмы́ть**

подм|ы́ть, о́ю, о́ешь *pf.* (*of* ▸ **подмыва́ть**)
1 (*ребёнка*) to wash sb's bottom **2** (*берег*)
to wash away, undermine

подмы́шк|а, и *f.* armpit

под|мя́ть, омну́, омнёшь *pf.* (*of*
▸ **подмина́ть**) to crush

поднес|ти́, у́, ёшь, *past* ∼, ∼ла́ *pf.* (*of*
▸ **подноси́ть**) **1** (**к** + *d.*) to take
(to), bring (to) **2** (+ *d. and a.*) (*подарить*)
to present (with); to take (as a present);
(*угостить*) to treat (to); **п. кому́-н. буке́т
цвето́в** to present sb with a bouquet

✎ **поднима́|ть**, ю *impf. of* ▸ **подня́ть**

поднима́|ться, юсь *impf. of* ▸ **подня́ться**

поднов|и́ть, лю́, и́шь *pf.* (*of* ▸ **подновля́ть**)
(*краску*) to freshen up, touch up; (*мебель*)
to renovate

подновля́|ть, ю *impf. of* ▸ **поднови́ть**

подно́жи|е, я *nt.* **1** (*горы, башни*) foot
2 (*пьедестал*) pedestal

подно́жк|а¹, и *f.* (*автобуса*) step, footboard

подно́жк|а², и *f.* (*в борьбе*) backheel; **дать
кому́-н. ∼у** to trip sb up

подно́с, а *m.* tray

подно|си́ть, шу́, ∼сишь *impf. of* ▸ **поднести́**

под|ня́ть, ниму́, ни́мешь, *past* ∼ня́л,
∼няла́, ∼ня́ло *pf.* (*of* ▸ **поднима́ть**) **1** to
raise; to lift; **п. настрое́ние** (+ *g. or d.*) to cheer
up, raise the spirits (of); **п. паруса́** to set
sail; **п. флаг** to hoist a flag **2** (*подобрать*)
to pick up **3** (*возбудить*) to rouse, stir up;
п. восста́ние to stir up rebellion; **п. ссо́ру** to
pick a quarrel; **п. на́ ноги** to rouse

под|ня́ться, ниму́сь, ни́мешься, *past*
∼ня́лся, ∼няла́сь *pf.* (*of* ▸ **поднима́ться**)
1 (*о температуре, ценах, солнце*) to rise; (*по
лестнице*) to go up; (*встать*) to get up; **п. на
ноги** to rise to one's feet **2** (**на** + *a.*) (*гору*) to
climb, ascend, go up **3** (*возникнуть*) to arise;
to break out, develop; **∼ня́лся ве́тер** a wind
got up **4** (econ., fig., *улучшиться*) to improve;
to recover

подо́ *prep.* = **под**

подо…¹ *vbl. pref.* = **под…¹**

подо…² *as pref. of nn. and adjs.* = **под…²**

подо́би|е, я *nt.* **1** likeness; **по своему́
о́бразу и ∼ю** in one's own image **2** (math.)
similarity

подо́бно *adv.* + *d.* like; **п. тому́, как** just as

✎ **подо́б|ный**, ∼ен, ∼на *adj.* like; similar;
∼ное поведе́ние such behaviour (BrE),
behavior (AmE); **ничего́ ∼ного!** (infml)
nothing of the kind!; **и тому́ ∼ное** (*abbr* **и т.
п.**) and so on, and such like

под|обра́ть, беру́, берёшь, *past* ∼обра́л,
∼обра́ла, ∼обра́ло *pf.* (*of* ▸ **подбира́ть**)
1 (*поднять*) to pick up **2** (*ноги*) to tuck
up; (*вожжи*) to take up **3** (*выбрать*) to
select, pick; **п. дже́мпер под цвет костю́ма**
to choose a jumper to match a suit

под|обра́ться, беру́сь, берёшься, *past*
∼обра́лся, ∼обрала́сь, ∼обра́ло́сь
pf. (*of* ▸ **подбира́ться**) **1** (*составиться,
образоваться*) to get together, be formed
2 (**к** + *d.*) (*незаметно подойти*) to steal up
(to), approach stealthily

под|огна́ть, гоню́, го́нишь, *past* ∼огна́л,
∼огнала́, ∼огна́ло *pf.* (*of* ▸ **подгоня́ть**)
1 (**к** + *d.*) (*приблизить*) to drive (to)
2 (infml, *заставить идти быстрее*) to drive
on, urge on, hurry **3** (**к** + *d.*) (*приспособить*)
to adjust (to), fit (to)

под|огну́ть, огну́, огнёшь *pf.* (*of*
▸ **подгиба́ть**) to tuck in; to bend under

подогрева́|ть, ю *impf. of* ▸ **подогре́ть**

подогре́|ть, ю *pf.* (*of* ▸ **подогрева́ть**) to
warm up, heat up

пододвига́|ть, ю *impf. of* ▸ **пододви́нуть**

пододви́|нуть, ну, нешь *pf.* (*of*
▸ **пододвига́ть**) (**к** + *d.*) to move up (to),
push up (to)

пододея́льник, а *m.* blanket cover, duvet
cover

подожд|а́ть, у́, ёшь, *past* ∼а́л, ∼ала́, ∼а́ло
pf. (+ *a. or g.*) to wait (for)

под|озва́ть, зову́, зовёшь, *past* ∼озва́л,
∼озвала́, ∼озва́ло *pf.* (*of* ▸ **подзыва́ть**)
to call over; (*жестом*) to beckon

подозрева́|ть, ю *impf.* (*no pf.*) to suspect (*sb or that sth is the case*); я ~ю его́ в преступле́нии I suspect him of a crime

подозре́ни|е, я *nt.* suspicion; по ~ю (в + *p.*) on suspicion (of); быть под ~ем, на ~и to be under suspicion

подозри́тел|ьный, ~ен, ~ьна *adj.* suspicious

подо|йти́, ю́, ~йшь *pf. of* ▶ дойти́

подо|йти́, йду́, йдёшь, *past* ~шёл, ~шла́ *pf.* (*of* ▶ подходи́ть) **1** (к + *d.*) (*приблизиться*) to approach (also *fig.*); to come up (to), go up (to); по́езд ~шёл к ста́нции the train pulled in to the station **2** (*годиться*) (+ *d.*) to do (for); to suit; (*по размеру*) to fit

подоко́нник, а *m.* window sill

подо́лгу *adv.* for a long time; for ages; for long periods of time; они́ п. не разгова́ривали друг с дру́гом they had long periods of not speaking to each other

подо́н|ки *m. pl.* (*sg.* ~ок, ~ка) dregs (also fig.); (*fig.*) scum; riff-raff

подорв|а́ть, у́, ёшь, *past* ~а́л, ~ала́, ~а́ло *pf.* (*of* ▶ подрыва́ть) **1** to blow up **2** (*fig.*) to undermine; to damage severely; п. здоро́вье to damage one's health

подорожа́|ть, ю *pf. of* ▶ дорожа́ть

подо|сла́ть, шлю́, шлёшь *pf.* (*of* ▶ подсыла́ть) to send, dispatch (*secretly*)

под|остла́ть, стелю́, сте́лешь *pf.* (*of* ▶ подстила́ть) (под + *a.*) to lay (under), stretch (under)

подоткн|у́ть, у́, ёшь *pf.* (*of* ▶ подтыка́ть) (infml) to tuck in, tuck up; п. ю́бку to tuck up one's skirt

подо́х|нуть, ну, нешь, *past* ~, ~ла *pf.* (*of* ▶ до́хнуть) **1** (*о животных*) to die **2** (sl., pej., *о людях*) to peg out, kick the bucket

подохо́дный *adj.*: п. нало́г income tax

подо́шв|а, ы *f.* sole

подпада́|ть, ю *impf. of* ▶ подпа́сть

подпа́|сть, ду́, дёшь, *past* ~л *pf.* (*of* ▶ подпада́ть) (под + *a.*) to fall (under); п. под чьё-н. влия́ние to fall under sb's influence

подпева́|ть, ю *impf.* (+ *d.*) to join (in singing); (fig.) to echo

под|пере́ть, опру́, опрёшь, *past* ~пёр, ~пёрла *pf.* (*of* ▶ подпира́ть) to prop up

подпи́лива|ть, ю *impf. of* ▶ подпили́ть

подпил|и́ть, ю́, ~ишь *pf.* (*of* ▶ подпи́ливать) **1** (*подрезать пилой*) to saw; (*напильником*) to file **2** (*укоротить пилой*) to saw a little off; (*напильником*) to file down

подпира́|ть, ю *impf. of* ▶ подпере́ть

подпи|са́ть, шу́, ~шешь *pf.* (*of* ▶ подпи́сывать) **1** (*поставить подпись (на)*) to sign **2** (*включить в число подписчиков*) to subscribe

подпи|са́ться, шу́сь, ~шешься *pf.* (*of* ▶ подпи́сываться) **1** (под + *i.*) to sign; (fig., *согласиться*) to subscribe (to) **2** (на + *a.*) to

subscribe (to, for); п. на журна́л to subscribe to a magazine

подпи́ск|а, и *f.* **1** (*на журнал*) subscription **2** (*письменное обязательство*) written undertaking; signed statement

подпи́счик, а *m.* (+ *g.*) subscriber (to)

подпи́сыва|ть, ю *impf. of* ▶ подписа́ть

подпи́сыва|ться, юсь *impf. of* ▶ подписа́ться

по́дпис|ь, и *f.* **1** signature; поста́вить свою́ п. to put one's signature (to) **2** (*надпись*) caption; inscription

подплыва́|ть, ю *impf. of* ▶ подплы́ть

подплы́|ть, ву́, вёшь, *past* ~л, ~ла́, ~ло *pf.* (*of* ▶ подплыва́ть) **1** (к + *d.*) (*вплавь*) to swim up (to); (*на лодке*) to sail up (to) **2** (под + *a.*) to swim under

подполза́|ть, а́ю *impf. of* ▶ подползти́

подполз|ти́, у́, ёшь, *past* ~, ~ла́ *pf.* (*of* ▶ подполза́ть) (к + *d.*) to creep up (to); to crawl up (to); (под + *a.*) to creep (under); to crawl (under)

подполко́вник, а *m.* lieutenant colonel

подпо́ль|е, я *nt.* (fig.) underground (*organization, activities*); уйти́ в п. to go underground

подпо́льный *adj.* underground (also fig.)

подпо́рк|а, и *f.* prop, support

подпо́р|тить, чу, тишь *pf.* (infml) to spoil slightly

подпоя́|саться, шусь, шешься *pf.* (*of* ▶ подпоя́сываться) to belt oneself; to put on a belt

подпоя́сыва|ться, юсь *impf. of* ▶ подпоя́саться

подпра́в|ить, лю, ишь *pf.* (*of* ▶ подправля́ть) to touch up

подправля́|ть, ю *impf. of* ▶ подпра́вить

подпры́гива|ть, ю *impf. of* ▶ подпры́гнуть

подпры́г|нуть, ну, нешь *pf.* (*of* ▶ подпры́гивать) to leap up, jump up

подпуска́|ть, ю *impf. of* ▶ подпусти́ть

подпу|сти́ть, щу́, ~стишь *pf.* (*of* ▶ подпуска́ть) to allow to approach; п. на расстоя́ние вы́стрела to allow to come within range

подраба́тыва|ть, ю *impf. of* ▶ подрабо́тать

подрабо́та|ть, ю *pf.* (*of* ▶ подраба́тывать) (infml, *ради дополнительного заработка*) to earn additionally

подра́внива|ть, ю *impf. of* ▶ подровня́ть

подража́|ть, ю *impf.* (*no pf.*) (+ *d.*) to imitate

подразде́л, а *m.* subsection

подразделе́ни|е, я *nt.* **1** subdivision **2** (mil.) subunit

подраздел|и́ть, ю́, и́шь *pf.* (*of* ▶ подразделя́ть) to subdivide

подразделя́|ть, ю, я́ю *impf. of* ▶ подраздели́ть

подразумева́|ть, ю *impf.* to mean

подразумева́|ться, ется *impf.* to be implied, be meant

п

подраст|а́ть, а́ю impf. (of ▶ подрасти́): ~а́ющее поколе́ние the rising generation

подраст|и́, у́, ёшь, past **подро́с, подросла́** pf. to grow (a little)

по|дра́ться, деру́сь, дерёшься, past ~дра́лся, ~драла́сь, ~дра́ло́сь pf. of ▶ дра́ться 1

подре́|зать, жу, жешь pf. (of ▶ подреза́ть) (*во́лосы*) to cut; (*но́гти, куст*) to clip, trim; (*дере́вья*) to prune, lop

подреза́|ть, ю impf. of ▶ подре́зать

подрис|ова́ть, у́ю pf. (of ▶ подрисо́вывать) **1** (*подпра́вить*) to touch up **2** (*доба́вить*) to add, put in (on a painting, etc.)

подрисо́выва|ть, ю impf. of ▶ подрисова́ть

подро́бно adv. minutely, in detail; at (great) length

подро́бност|ь, и f. detail; вда́ться в ~и to go into detail; во всех ~ях in every detail

подро́б|ный, ~ен, ~на adj. detailed, minute

подровня́|ть, ю pf. (of ▶ подра́внивать) (*сде́лать бо́лее ро́вным*) to level; (*бо́роду, во́лосы*) to trim

подро́ст|ок, ка m. adolescent, teenager

подру́г|а, и f. (female) friend, girlfriend; п. по шко́ле school friend

по-дру́жески adv. in a friendly way; as a friend

подр|ужи́ться, ужу́сь, у́жишься pf. (с + i.) to make friends (with)

подру́жк|а, и f. affectionate dim. of ▶ подру́га; п. неве́сты bridesmaid

подру́чн|ый adj. **1** (*инструме́нт*) at hand, to hand; (*сре́дства*) improvised, makeshift **2** (as m. n. п., ~ого) assistant, mate

подрыва́|ть, ю impf. of ▶ подорва́ть

подря́д[1] adv. in succession; running; on end; три го́да п. three years running; не́сколько дней п. шёл дождь it rained for days on end

подря́д[2], **а** m. contract; взять п. на постро́йку плоти́ны to contract to build a dam

подря́дчик, а m. contractor

подса|ди́ть, жу́, ~дишь pf. (of ▶ подса́живать) **1** (в, на + a.) to help (into, on to); п. кого́-н. на ло́шадь to help sb on to a horse **2** (к + d.) to place next (to)

подса́жива|ть, ю impf. of ▶ подсади́ть

подса́жива|ться, юсь impf. of ▶ подсе́сть

подсве́чник, а m. candlestick

под|се́сть, ся́ду, ся́дешь, past ~се́л pf. (of ▶ подса́живаться) (к + d.) to sit down (near, next to), take a seat (near, next to)

подска|за́ть, жу́, ~жешь pf. (of ▶ подска́зывать) (+ d. and a.) **1** (*напо́мнить*) to prompt (sb with sth) (also fig.) **2** (*реше́ние*) to suggest

подска́зк|а, и f. prompt(ing)

подска́зыва|ть, ю impf. of ▶ подсказа́ть

подска́кива|ть, ю impf. of ▶ подскочи́ть

подскоч|и́ть, у́, ~ишь pf. (of ▶ подска́кивать) **1** (к + d.) to run up (to), come running (to)

2 to jump up, leap up; п. от ра́дости to jump with joy; це́ны ~и́ли (infml) prices soared

подслу́ш|ать, аю pf. (of ▶ подслу́шивать) to overhear; to eavesdrop (on)

подслу́шива|ть, ю impf. of ▶ подслу́шать

подсма́трива|ть, ю impf. of ▶ подсмотре́ть

подсме́ива|ться, юсь impf. (над + i.) to laugh (at), make fun (of)

подсмотр|е́ть, ю́, ~ишь pf. (of ▶ подсма́тривать) to spy

подсне́жник, а m. (bot.) snowdrop

подсо́выва|ть, ю impf. of ▶ подсу́нуть

подсоедин|и́ть, ю́, и́шь pf. (of ▶ подсоединя́ть) (*телефо́н*) to connect up; (*стира́льную маши́ну*) to plumb in

подсоедин|я́ть, я́ю impf. of ▶ подсоедини́ть

подсозна́ни|е, я nt. the subconscious

подсозна́тел|ьный, ~ен, ~ьна adj. subconscious

подсо́лнечник, а m. sunflower

подсо́лнечн|ый adj. of ▶ подсо́лнечник; ~ое ма́сло sunflower oil

подсо́лнух, а m. (infml) **1** (*цвето́к*) sunflower **2** (*семена́*) sunflower seeds

подста́в|ить, лю, ишь pf. (of ▶ подставля́ть) **1** (под + a.) to put (under), place (under); п. го́лову под струю́ воды́ из кра́на to put one's head under a tap **2** (fig.) to expose; (infml, *поста́вить кого́-л. в неприя́тное положе́ние*) to leave sb holding the baby (BrE), bag (AmE)

подста́вк|а, и f. stand; (*для буты́лки, стака́на*) coaster

подставля́|ть, ю impf. of ▶ подста́вить

подстерега́|ть, ю impf. of ▶ подстере́чь

подстере́|чь, гу́, жёшь, гу́т, past ~г, ~гла́ pf. (of ▶ подстерега́ть) to be on the watch (for), lie in wait (for)

подстила́|ть, ю impf. of ▶ подостла́ть

подсти́лк|а, и f. bedding

подстра́ива|ть, ю impf. of ▶ подстро́ить

подстрах|ова́ть, у́ю pf. (of ▶ подстрахо́вывать) **1** (*гимна́ста*) to stand by ready to help **2** (fig.) to (take measures to) protect; to provide with additional insurance

подстрахо́выва|ть, ю impf. of ▶ подстрахова́ть

подстрек|а́ть, а́ю impf. (к + d. or на + a.) to incite (to)

подстре́лива|ть, ю impf. of ▶ подстрели́ть

подстрел|и́ть, ю́, ~ишь pf. (of ▶ подстре́ливать) to wound (by a shot); to wing

подстрига́|ть, ю impf. of ▶ подстри́чь

подстрига́|ться, юсь impf. of ▶ подстри́чься

подстри́|чь, гу́, жёшь, гу́т, past ~г, ~гла pf. (of ▶ подстрига́ть) (*во́лосы, но́гти, газо́н*) to cut, trim; (*де́рево*) to prune

подстри́|чься, гу́сь, жёшься, гу́тся, past ~гся, ~гла́сь pf. (of ▶ подстрига́ться) to trim one's hair; to have a haircut

✂ key word

п

подстро́|ить, ю, ишь *pf.* (*of* ▶ подстра́ивать) (infml) to contrive; (pej.) to arrange; э́то де́ло ~ено it's a put-up job

подступ|а́ть, а́ю *impf. of* ▶ подступи́ть

подступ|а́ться, а́юсь *impf. of* ▶ подступи́ться

подступ|и́ть, лю́, ~ишь *pf.* (*of* ▶ подступа́ть) (к + *d.*) to approach, come up (to), come near; слёзы ~и́ли к её глаза́м tears came to her eyes

подступ|и́ться, лю́сь, ~ишься *pf.* (*of* ▶ подступа́ться) (к + *d.*) to approach

подсуди́м|ый, ого *m.* (law) defendant; the accused

подсу́н|уть, у, ешь *pf.* (*of* ▶ подсо́вывать) **1** (под + *a.*) to shove (under) **2** (+ *d. and a.*) (infml) to slip (into); to palm off (on, upon); они́ мне ~ули не ту кни́гу they palmed off the wrong book on me

подсу́шива|ть, ю *impf. of* ▶ подсуши́ть

подсуш|и́ть, у́, ~ишь *pf.* (*of* ▶ подсу́шивать) to dry a little

подсчёт, а *m.* calculation; count

подсыла́|ть, ю *impf. of* ▶ подосла́ть

подсы́п|ать, лю, лешь *pf.* (*of* ▶ подсыпа́ть) (+ *a. or g.*) to add, pour in

подсып|а́ть, а́ю *impf. of* ▶ подсы́пать

подта́скива|ть, ю *impf. of* ▶ подтащи́ть

подтащ|и́ть, у́, ~ишь *pf.* (*of* ▶ подта́скивать) (к + *d.*) to drag up (to)

подтвер|ди́ть, жу́, ди́шь *pf.* (*of* ▶ подтвержда́ть) to confirm; to corroborate, bear out; п. получе́ние чего́-н. to acknowledge receipt of sth

подтвер|ди́ться, ди́тся *pf.* (*of* ▶ подтвержда́ться) to be confirmed

подтвержда́|ть, ю, ет *impf. of* ▶ подтверди́ть

подтвержда́|ться, ется *impf. of* ▶ подтверди́ться

подтвержде́ни|е, я *nt.* confirmation; corroboration

подтыка́|ть, ю *impf. of* ▶ подоткну́ть

подтя́гива|ть, ю *impf. of* ▶ подтяну́ть

подтя́гива|ться, юсь *impf. of* ▶ подтяну́ться

подтя́ж|ки, ек (*no sg.*) braces (BrE), suspenders (AmE)

подтя|ну́ть, ну́, ~нешь *pf.* (*of* ▶ подтя́гивать) **1** (*пояс*) to tighten **2** (к + *d.*) (*подтащить*) to pull up (to), haul up (to); п. ло́дку к бе́регу to haul up a boat on shore **3** (mil.) to bring up, move up **4** (fig., infml, *ученика*) to take in hand, pull up, chase up

подтя|ну́ться, ну́сь, ~нешься *pf.* (*of* ▶ подтя́гиваться) **1** to gird oneself more tightly; п. по́ясом to tighten one's belt **2** (*на перекладине*) to pull oneself up (*on gymnastic apparatus, etc.*) **3** (mil.) to move up, move in **4** (fig., infml, *об ученике*) to pull oneself together, take oneself in hand

поду́ма|ть, ю *pf.* **1** *pf. of* ▶ ду́мать; п. (то́лько)! just think!; ~ешь! (*as int.*) (infml, iron.) I say!; what do you know?; мо́жно п. one might think **2** (*немного*) to think a little, for a while

по-дура́цки *adv.* (infml) foolishly, like a fool

поду́|ть, ю, ешь *pf.* **1** *pf. of* ▶ дуть **2** (*начать дуть*) to begin to blow

подуш|и́ться, у́сь, ~ишься *pf.* to put some perfume on

поду́шк|а, и *f.* (*в постели*) pillow; (*диванная*) cushion

подхали́м, а *m.* toady

подхва|ти́ть, чу́, ~тишь *pf.* (*of* ▶ подхва́тывать) to catch (up); to pick up; to take up; п. на́сморк to catch, pick up a cold; п. пе́сню to catch up a melody, join in a song

подхва́тыва|ть, ю *impf. of* ▶ подхвати́ть

подхлест|ну́ть, ну́, нёшь *pf.* (*of* ▶ подхлёстывать) to whip up (also fig., infml)

подхлёстыва|ть, ю *impf. of* ▶ подхлестну́ть

⚔ **подхо́д, а** *m.* approach

⚔ **подхо|ди́ть, жу́, ~дишь** *impf. of* ▶ подойти́

подходя́щий *pres. part. of* ▶ подходи́ть *and adj.* suitable, appropriate; п. моме́нт the right moment

подцеп|и́ть, лю́, ~ишь *pf.* (*of* ▶ подцепля́ть) (infml) to hook on, couple on; (fig., joc., *девушку*) to pick up; п. на́сморк to pick up a cold

подцепля́|ть, ю *impf. of* ▶ подцепи́ть

подча́с *adv.* sometimes, at times

⚔ **подчёркива|ть, ю** *impf. of* ▶ подчеркну́ть

подчерк|ну́ть, ну́, нёшь *pf.* (*of* ▶ подчёркивать) **1** to underline **2** (fig.) to emphasize, stress

подчине́ни|е, я *nt.* subordination; submission, subjection; быть в ~и (у + *g.*) to be subordinate (to)

подчин|ённый **1** *p.p.p. of* ▶ подчини́ть; (+ *d.*) under, under the command (of) **2** *adj.* subordinate; (*as m. n.* п., ~ённого) subordinate

подчин|и́ть, ю́, и́шь *pf.* (*of* ▶ подчиня́ть) (+ *d.*) to subordinate (to), subject (to); to place under the command (of); п. свое́й во́ле to bend to one's will

подчин|и́ться, ю́сь, и́шься *pf.* (*of* ▶ подчиня́ться) (+ *d.*) to submit (to); п. прика́зу to obey an order

подчин|я́ть, я́ю *impf. of* ▶ подчини́ть

подчин|я́ться, я́юсь *impf. of* ▶ подчини́ться

подшива́|ть, ю *impf. of* ▶ подши́ть

подши́пник, а *m.* (tech.) bearing

под|ши́ть, ошью́, ошьёшь *pf.* (*of* ▶ подшива́ть) **1** (*пришить*) to sew on, in; (*платье, платок*) to hem; (*с изнанки*) to line; (*обувь*) to sole **2** (*бумаги*) to file

подшу|ти́ть, чу́, ~тишь *pf.* (*of* ▶ подшу́чивать) (над + *i.*) to make fun of; to mock; to play a trick (on)

подшу́чива|ть, ю *impf. of* ▶ подшути́ть

подъ...¹ *vbl. pref.* = под...¹

подъ...² *as pref. of nn. and adjs.* = под...²

подъе́зд, а *m.* **1** (*вход*) entrance, doorway **2** (*к реке*) approach(es)

подъезжа́|ть, ю *impf. of* ▶ **подъе́хать**
подъём, а *m.* **1** (*груза*) lifting; (*флага*) raising **2** (*в го́ру*) ascent **3** (aeron.) climb **4** (fig., *рост, разви́тие*) development; rise; **промы́шленный п.** boom, upsurge **5** (fig.) elan; enthusiasm, animation; **говори́ть с больши́м ~ом** to speak with great animation
подъёмник, а *m.* lift (BrE), elevator (AmE); hoist
подъёмн|ый *adj.* **1** lifting; **п. кран** crane; **~ое окно́** sash window **2**: **п. мост** drawbridge
подъе́|хать, ду, дешь *pf.* (*of* ▶ **подъезжа́ть**) (**к** + *d.*) to drive up (to), draw up (to)
подыгра́|ть, а́ю *pf.* (*of* ▶ **поды́грывать**) (+ *d.*) (infml) **1** (mus.) to accompany **2** (theatr.) to play up (to)
поды́грыва|ть, ю *impf. of* ▶ **подыгра́ть**
поды́|скать, щу́, ~щешь *pf.* (*of* ▶ **поды́скивать**) to find
поды́скива|ть, ю *impf.* (*of* ▶ **подыска́ть**) to seek, try to find
подыха́|ть, ю *impf. of* ▶ **подо́хнуть**
подыш|а́ть, у́, ~ишь *pf.* to breathe; **вы́йти п. све́жим во́здухом** to go out for a breath of fresh air
поеда́|ть, ю *impf. of* ▶ **пое́сть 3**
поеди́н|ок, ка *m.* duel
по́езд, а, *pl.* **~а́** *m.* train; **~ом** by train; **п. да́льнего сле́дования** long-distance train
⚹ **пое́здк|а, и** *f.* trip, excursion, outing, tour
по|е́сть, е́м, е́шь, е́ст, еди́м, еди́те, едя́т, *past* **~е́л** *pf.* **1** (*pf. only*) to eat (up) **2** (*pf. only*) (*немно́го*) to eat a little; to take some food, have a bite **3** (*impf.* **~еда́ть**) (*о кро́ликах, насеко́мых*) to eat, devour
пое́|хать, ду, дешь *pf.* (*of* ▶ **е́хать**) to go (*in or on a vehicle or on an animal*); (*отпра́виться*) to set off, depart; **~хали!** (infml) let's go!
пожале́|ть, ю *pf. of* ▶ **жале́ть**
пожа́л|оваться, уюсь *pf. of* ▶ **жа́ловаться**
пожа́луй *adv.* perhaps; very likely; it may be
⚹ **пожа́луйста** *particle* **1** (*при про́сьбе*) please; **сади́тесь, п.!** please sit down! **2** (*при согла́сии*) certainly!, by all means!, with pleasure! (*or not translated*); **переда́йте мне, п., кни́гу!** — n. would you mind passing me the book? — there you are **3** (*в отве́т на «спаси́бо»*) don't mention it; not at all
пожа́р, а *m.* fire
пожа́рить *pf. of* ▶ **жа́рить**
пожа́рник, а *m.* (infml) fireman, firefighter
пожа́рн|ый *adj. of* ▶ **пожа́р;** **~ная кома́нда** fire brigade; **~ная ле́стница** fire escape; **~ная маши́на** fire engine; (*as m. n.* **п., ~ного**) fireman, firefighter
по|жа́ть, жму, жмёшь *pf.* (*of* ▶ **пожима́ть**) to press, squeeze; **п. ру́ку** (+ *d.*) to shake hands (with); **п. плеча́ми** to shrug one's shoulders

пожела́ни|е, я *nt.* wish, desire
пожела́|ть, ю *pf. of* ▶ **жела́ть**
пожелте́|ть, ю *pf. of* ▶ **желте́ть**
пожен|и́ться, ~имся *pf.* (*pl. used only*) to get married (*of two people*)
поже́ртвовани|е, я *nt.* donation
поже́ртв|овать, ую *pf. of* ▶ **же́ртвовать**
пожива́|ть, ю *impf.*: **как (вы) ~ете?** how are you (getting on)?
пожи́знен|ный, ~, ~на *adj.* life(long); for life; **~ное заключе́ние** life imprisonment
пожило́й *adj.* elderly
пожима́|ть, ю *impf. of* ▶ **пожа́ть**
пожира́|ть, ю *impf. of* ▶ **пожра́ть**
пожи́тк|и, ов (*no sg.*) (infml) belongings; (one's) things
по|жи́ть, живу́, живёшь, *past* **~жи́л, ~жила́, ~жи́ло** *pf.* to live (*for a time*); to stay; **мы ~жи́ли три го́да в Ки́еве** we lived for three years in Kiev
пожму́, ёшь *see* ▶ **пожа́ть**
пожра́|ть, у́, ёшь, *past* **~а́л, ~ала́, ~а́ло** *pf.* (*of* ▶ **пожира́ть**) to devour
по́з|а, ы *f.* pose, attitude, posture; (fig.) pose; **приня́ть каку́ю-н. ~у** to strike an attitude, adopt a pose
позаба́в|ить, лю, ишь *pf.* to amuse a little
позаба́в|иться, люсь, ишься *pf.* to amuse oneself a little
позабо́|титься, чусь, тишься *pf. of* ▶ **забо́титься**
позабыва́|ть, ю *impf. of* ▶ **позабы́ть**
позаб|ы́ть, у́ду, у́дешь (*of* ▶ **позабыва́ть**) (+ *a.* or о + *p.*) (infml) to forget (about)
позави́д|овать, ую *pf. of* ▶ **зави́довать**
поза́втрака|ть, ю *pf. of* ▶ **за́втракать**
позавчера́ *adv.* the day before yesterday
позади́[1] *adv.* behind; **оста́вить п.** to leave behind; **все пробле́мы п.** all our/your problems are in the past; all our/your problems are behind us/you
позади́[2] *prep.* + *g.* behind
позаи́мств|овать, ую *pf. of* ▶ **заи́мствовать**
позапро́шлый *adj.* before last; **п. год** the year before last
по|зва́ть, зову́, зовёшь, *past* **~зва́л, ~звала́, ~зва́ло** *pf. of* ▶ **звать 2**
⚹ **позво́л|ить, ю, ишь** *pf.* (*of* ▶ **позволя́ть**) (+ *d.* of person and inf., + *a.* of inanimate object) to allow, permit; **п. себе́** (+ *inf.*) to venture, take the liberty (of); (+ *a.*) to be able to afford; **п. себе́ сде́лать замеча́ние** to venture a remark; **~ь(те)** (*ве́жливая фо́рма обраще́ния с про́сьбой*): **~ьте предста́вить до́ктора Х.** allow me to introduce Doctor X.; (*выраже́ния несогла́сия, возраже́ния*): **~ьте, что э́то зна́чит?** excuse me, what does that mean?
⚹ **позвол|я́ть, я́ю** *impf. of* ▶ **позво́лить**
позвон|и́ть, ю́, и́шь *pf. of* ▶ **звони́ть**
позвоно́чник, а *m.* (anat.) spine, backbone
позвоно́чно|е, го *nt.* (zool.) vertebrate

поздне́е *comp. of* ▶ по́здний, ▶ по́здно; later

поздне́йший *adj.* (*бо́лее по́здний*) later; (*са́мый по́здний*) latest

◆ **по́здн|ий** *adj.* late; до ~ей но́чи until late at night, late into the night; ~о it is late

по́здно *adv.* late

поздоро́ва|ться, юсь *pf. of* ▶ здоро́ваться

поздра́в|ить, лю, ишь *pf.* (*of* ▶ поздравля́ть) (с + *i.*) to congratulate (on, upon); п. кого́-н. с Но́вым го́дом to wish sb a happy New Year

поздравле́ни|е, я *nt.* congratulation, greeting(s)

поздравля́|ть, ю *impf. of* ▶ поздра́вить

позелене́|ть, ю *pf. of* ▶ зелене́ть 1

по́зже *comp. of* ▶ по́здний, ▶ по́здно; later (on)

пози́р|овать, ую *impf.* (+ *d.*) to pose (for)

позити́в|ный, ~ен, ~на *adj.* positive

◆ **пози́ци|я**, и *f.* position

познако́м|ить, лю, ишь *pf. of* ▶ знако́мить

познако́м|иться, люсь, ишься *pf. of* ▶ знако́миться

позна́ни|е, я *nt.* **1** (phil.) cognition; тео́рия ~я epistemology **2** (*in pl.*) knowledge

позоло́т|а, ы *f.* gilding, gilt

позо́р, а *m.* shame, disgrace

позо́р|ить, ю, ишь *impf.* (*of* ▶ опозо́рить) to disgrace

позо́р|иться, юсь, ишься *impf.* (*of* ▶ опозо́риться) to disgrace oneself

позо́р|ный, ~ен, ~на *adj.* shameful, disgraceful; ignominious

поигра́|ть, ю *pf.* to have a game, play a little

пойм|ка, и *f.* capture

по-ино́му *adv.* differently, in a different way

поинтерес|ова́ться, у́юсь *pf.* (+ *i.*) to be curious (about); to display interest (in); он ~ова́лся узна́ть, кто вы he was curious to find out who you are

◆ **по́иск**, а *m.* (comput.) search; (*in pl.*) search; в ~ах (+ *g.*) in search (of), in quest (of)

пои́с|кать, щу́, ~щешь *pf.* to look for, search for; ~щи́те хороше́нько have a good look

поиско́в|ый *adj.*: ~ая систе́ма/маши́на (comput.) search engine

пои́стине *adv.* indeed, in truth

по|и́ть, ю́, ~и́шь *impf.* (*of* ▶ напои́ть) to give to drink; (*скот*) to water; п. вино́м to treat to wine

пои́щу, и́щешь *see* ▶ поиска́ть

пойд|у́, дёшь *see* ▶ пойти́

пойма́|ть, ю *pf. of* ▶ лови́ть

пойм|у́, ёшь *see* ▶ поня́ть

◆ **пойти́**, ду́, дёшь, *past* пошёл, пошла́ *pf.* **1** *pf. of* ▶ идти́, ▶ ходи́ть; пошёл вон! be off!; off with you! **2** (*нача́ть ходи́ть*) to begin to (be able to) walk **3** (в + *a.*) to take after; он пошёл в отца́ he takes after his father

◆ **пока́**[1] *adv.* for the present, for the time being; п. что (infml) in the meanwhile; п.! (infml) bye!

◆ **пока́**[2] *conj.* **1** while; нам на́до попроси́ть его́, п. он тут we must ask him while he is here **2**: п. не until, till, before; п. (ещё) не по́здно before it's too late

◆ **показа́тель**, я *m.* **1** indicator; index **2** (math.) exponent, index

показа́тел|ьный, ~ен, ~ьна *adj.* **1** (*характе́рный*) significant; instructive, revealing **2** (*образцо́вый*) model; demonstration; п. проце́сс show trial; п. уро́к object lesson **3** (math.) exponential

◆ **пока|за́ть**, жу́, ~жешь *pf.* (*of* ▶ пока́зывать) **1** to show; to display, reveal; п. свои́ зна́ния to display one's knowledge **2** (*о прибо́ре*) to show, register, read **3** (на + *a.*) to point (at, to)

пока|за́ться, жу́сь, ~жешься *pf.* **1** *pf. of* ▶ каза́ться **2** (*pf. of* ▶ пока́зываться) to show oneself; to appear; to come in sight; из-за облако́в ~за́лась луна́ the moon appeared from behind the clouds; п. врачу́ to see a doctor **3** *pass. of* ▶ показа́ть

показно́й *adj.* (*сочу́вствие*) affected; (*ро́скошь*) ostentatious

◆ **пока́зыва|ть**, ю *impf. of* ▶ показа́ть

◆ **пока́зыва|ться**, юсь *impf. of* ▶ показа́ться

покара́|ть, ю *pf. of* ▶ кара́ть

поката́|ть[1], ю *pf.* to roll

поката́|ть[2], ю *pf.* to take for a drive; п. дете́й на са́нках to take children tobogganing

поката́|ться, юсь *pf.* to go for a drive; п. на ло́дке to go out boating

пока|ти́ть, чу́, ~тишь *pf.* **1** *pf. of* ▶ кати́ть **2** (*мяч*) to start (rolling), set rolling

пока|ти́ться, чу́сь, ~тишься *pf.* **1** *pf. of* ▶ кати́ться **2** (*нача́ть кати́ться*) to start rolling

пока́чива|ть, ю *impf.* to rock slightly; идти́ ~ясь to walk unsteadily

пока́шлива|ть, ю *impf.* to have a slight cough; to cough intermittently

пока́яни|е, я *nt.* **1** (eccl., *испове́дь*) confession **2** (*раска́яние*) penitence, repentance; принести́ п. (в + *p.*) to repent (of)

пока́|яться, юсь, ешься *pf. of* ▶ ка́яться

по́кер, а *m.* poker (*card game*)

покида́|ть, ю *impf. of* ▶ поки́нуть

поки́нутый *p.p.p. of* ▶ поки́нуть *and adj.* deserted, abandoned

поки́|нуть, ну, нешь *pf.* (*of* ▶ покида́ть) to leave; to desert, abandon, forsake

покла́дист|ый, ~, ~а *adj.* complaisant, obliging

покло́н, а *m.* bow

поклон|и́ться, ю́сь, ~ишься *pf. of* ▶ кла́няться

покло́нник, а *m.* admirer; fan

покло́нни|ца, цы *f. of* ▶ покло́нник

поклоня́|ться, юсь *impf.* (+ *d.*) to worship

покля́|сться, ну́сь, нёшься *pf. of* ▶ кля́сться

поко́|й, я *m.* rest, peace; оста́вить в ~е to leave in peace; уйти́ на п., удали́ться на п. to retire

поко́йник, а *m.* the deceased

П

покойни|ца, цы *f. of* ▶ **покойник**

покойн|ый *adj.* (*умерший*) (the) late; (*as n.* **п.**, **~ого**, *f.* **~ая**, **~ой**) the deceased

поколеб|áть, ~лю, ~лешь *pf. of* ▶ **колебáть**

поколеб|áться, ~люсь, ~лешься *pf.* **1** *pf. of* ▶ **колебáться 2** to waver (for a time), hesitate (for a time)

✓ **поколéни|е, я** *nt.* generation

поколо|тить, чý, ~тишь *pf. of* ▶ **колотить 2**

поконч|ить, у, ишь *pf.* (**с** + *i.*) **1** (*завершить*) to finish off; to finish (with), be through (with), have done (with); **с э́тим ~ено** that's done with **2** (*уничтожить*) to put an end (to); to do away (with); **п. жизнь самоуби́йством** to commit suicide

покорéни|е, я *nt.* conquest

покорúтел|ь, я *m.* conqueror

покор|úть, ю́, úшь *pf.* (*of* ▶ **покоря́ть**) to conquer, subdue

покор|úться, ю́сь, úшься *pf.* (*of* ▶ **покоря́ться**) (+ *d.*) to submit (to); to resign oneself (to); **п. свое́й ýчасти** to resign oneself to one's lot

покорм|и́ть, лю́, ~ишь *pf. of* ▶ **корми́ть 1**

покóрн|ый, ~ен, ~на *adj.* (+ *d.*) submissive (to), obedient; **п. судьбе́** resigned to one's fate

покоря́|ть, я́ю *impf. of* ▶ **покори́ть**

покоря́|ться, я́юсь *impf. of* ▶ **покори́ться**

поко|си́ться, шýсь, си́шься *pf. of* ▶ **коси́ться**

покрá|сить, шу, сишь *pf. of* ▶ **крáсить**

покрá|ситься, шусь, сишься *pf. of* ▶ **крáситься**

покраснé|ть, ю *pf. of* ▶ **краснéть**

покрови́тел|ь, я *m.* patron, protector

покрови́тельниц|а, ы *f.* patroness, protectress

покрови́тельствен|ный, ~, ~на *adj.* **1** protective; **~ная окрáска** (zool.) protective colouring **2** (*снисходительный*) condescending, patronizing

покрови́тельств|о, а *nt.* protection, patronage; **под ~ом** (+ *g.*) under the patronage (of), under the auspices (of)

покрывá|ло, а *nt.* **1** (*кусок ткани*) cover; (*на кровать*) bedspread, counterpane **2** shawl; (*вуаль*) veil

покрывá|ть, ю *impf. of* ▶ **покры́ть**

покрывá|ться, юсь *impf. of* ▶ **покры́ться**

✓ **покры́ти|е, я** *nt.* **1** covering; **п. доро́ги** road surfacing; **п. кры́ши** roofing **2** (*возмещение*) covering, discharge, payment; **п. расхо́дов** defrayment of expenses

покр|ы́ть, о́ю, о́ешь *pf.* (*of* ▶ **покрывáть**) **1** to cover; **п. крáской** to coat with paint; **п. лáком** to varnish, lacquer; **п. позо́ром** to cover with shame **2** (*возместить*) to meet, pay off; **п. расхо́ды** to cover expenses, defray expenses **3** (*расстояние*) to cover

покр|ы́ться, о́юсь, о́ешься *pf.* (*of* ▶ **покрывáться**) (+ *i.*) **1** (*накрыть себя*) to cover sb **2** (*заполниться, усеяться*) to be, get covered (with)

покры́шк|а, и *f.* tyre (BrE), tire (AmE)

✓ **покупáтел|ь, я** *m.* (*дома, машины*) buyer, purchaser; (*в магазине*) customer

✓ **покупáтель|ница, ницы** *f. of* ▶ **покупáтель**

✓ **покупá|ть, ю** *impf. of* ▶ **купи́ть**

✓ **покýпк|а, и** *f.* **1** (*действие*) buying; purchasing, purchase **2** (*вещь*) purchase; **вы́годная п.** bargain; **дéлать ~и** to go shopping

покур|и́ть, ю́, ~ишь *pf.* **1** *pf. of* ▶ **кури́ть 2** to have a smoke; **давáй ~им** let's have a smoke

покусá|ть, ю *pf.* to bite; (*о пчёлах*) to sting

поку|си́ться, шýсь, си́шься *pf.* (*of* ▶ **покушáться**) (**на** + *a.*) **1** (*попытаться сделать что-н.*) to attempt, make an attempt (upon) **2** (*попытаться завладеть чем-н.*) to encroach (on, upon)

покýша|ть, ю *pf. of* ▶ **кýшать**

покушá|ться, юсь *impf. of* ▶ **покуси́ться**

покушéни|е, я *nt.* attempt; **п. на жизнь** (+ *g.*) *or* **п. на** (+ *a.*) attempt upon the life (of)

✓ **пол¹, а, о ~е, на/в ~ý,** *pl.* **~ы́** *m.* floor

✓ **пол², а,** *pl.* **~ы́, ~óв** *m.* sex; **обóего ~а** of both sexes

пол... *comb. form, abbr. of* ▶ **полови́на**; half; **полчасá** half an hour; **полдеся́того** half past nine

✓ **полагá|ть, ю** *impf.* to suppose, think; **нáдо п.** it is to be supposed; one must suppose

полагá|ться, юсь *impf.* **1** *impf. of* ▶ **положи́ться 2** (*impers.*): **~ется** one is supposed (to) **3**: **~ется** (+ *d.*) to be due (to)

полá|дить, жу, дишь *pf.* (**с** + *i.*) to come to an understanding (with); to get on (with)

полвéка, полувéка *m.* half a century

полгóда, полугóда *m.* half a year, six months

пóлдень, полýдня *and* **пóлдня** *m.* noon, midday; **зá полдень** past noon; **к полýдню** towards noon

пóлдник, а *m.* (afternoon) snack

полдорóг|и *f.* halfway; **останови́ться на ~е** to stop halfway (also fig.)

✓ **пóл|е, я,** *pl.* **~я́, ~éй** *nt.* **1** field; **п. би́твы, п. сражéния** battlefield; **п. зрéния** field of vision **2** (art) ground; (heraldry) field **3** (*in pl.*) (*чистая полоса*) margin **4** (*in pl.*) (*шляпы*) brim

полев|óй *adj.* (bot., mil.) field; **п. команди́р** warlord; **~ы́е услóвия** field conditions; **~ы́е цветы́** wild flowers

✓ **полéз|ный, ~ен, ~на** *adj.* useful; helpful; (*пища*) wholesome, health-giving; **чем могý быть ~ен?** can I help you?

полéз|ть, у, ешь, *past* **~, ~ла** *pf.* **1** *pf. of* ▶ **лезть 2** (*начать лезть*) to start to climb

полéмик|а, и *f.* polemic(s); dispute, controversy

✓ key word

п

полен|и́ться, ю́сь, ∼ишься *pf.* (+ *inf.*)
to be too lazy to

поле́н|о, а, *pl.* **∼ья, ∼ьев** *nt.* log

полёт, а *m.* flight; flying; **вид с высоты́ пти́чьего ∼а** bird's-eye view; **п. фанта́зии** flight of fancy

поле|те́ть, чу́, ти́шь *pf.* **1** *pf. of* ▶ **лете́ть 2** (*начать лете́ть*) to start to fly; to fly off

по-ле́тнему *adv.* as in summer, as for summer; **оде́т п.** (dressed) in summer clothes

полеч|и́ть, у́, ∼ишь *pf.* to treat (*for a while*)

полеч|и́ться, у́сь, ∼ишься *pf.* to undergo treatment (*for a while*)

пол|е́чь, я́гу, я́жешь, я́гут, *past* **∼ёг, ∼егла́** *pf.* **1** to lie down (*in numbers*) **2** (fig., *погибнуть*) to fall, be killed (*in numbers*)

по́лз|ать, аю *impf., indet. of* ▶ **ползти́**

полз|ти́, у́, ёшь, *past* **∼, ∼ла́** *impf.* **1** to crawl, creep (along); **по́езд ∼** the train was crawling **2** (*о жидкости*) to ooze (out)

полиартри́т, а *m.* (med.) polyarthritis

полива́|ть, ю *impf. of* ▶ **поли́ть**

полива́|ться, юсь *impf. of* ▶ **поли́ться**

поли́вк|а, и *f.* watering

полигло́т, а *m.* polyglot

полиго́н, а *m.* (mil.) (artillery *or* bombing) range; **испыта́тельный п.** proving ground, testing area

полиграфи́|я, и *f.* printing

поликли́ник|а, и *f.* clinic; health centre (BrE), center (AmE)

полинези́|ец, йца *m.* Polynesian

полинези́й|ка, ки *f. of* ▶ **полинези́ец**

полинези́йский *adj.* Polynesian

Полине́зи|я, и *f.* Polynesia

полиня́|ть, ет *pf. of* ▶ **линя́ть**

поли́п, а *m.* (zool., med.) polyp

полир|ова́ть, у́ю *impf.* (*of* ▶ **отполирова́ть**) to polish

по́лис, а *m.* policy; **страхово́й п.** insurance policy

полистиро́л, а *m.* polystyrene

политехни́ческий *adj.*: **п. институ́т** polytechnic

политзаключённ|ый, ого *m.* political prisoner

поли́тик, а *m.* politician

⚔ **поли́тик|а, и** *f.* **1** policy; **проводи́ть ∼у** to carry out a policy **2** (*наука*) politics; **п. си́лы** power politics

⚔ **полити́ческ|ий** *adj.* political; **п. де́ятель** political figure, politician; **∼ая корре́ктность** political correctness; **∼ое убе́жище** political asylum

полито́лог, а *m.* political scientist

политоло́ги|я, и *f.* political science

политтехно́лог, а *m.* spin doctor

пол|и́ть, ью́, ьёшь, *past* **∼и́л, ∼ила́, ∼и́ло** *pf.* (impf. ▶ **полива́ть**) **1** (+ *a. and i.*) (*смочить*) to pour (on, upon); **п. цветы́** to water the flowers **2** (*no impf.*) (*начать*

лить) to begin to pour

пол|и́ться, ью́сь, ьёшься, *past* **∼и́лся, ∼ила́сь** *pf.* (*of* ▶ **полива́ться**) **1** (+ *i.*) (*полить себя́*) to pour over oneself **2** (*начать литься*) to begin to flow

полице́йск|ий *adj.* police; **п. уча́сток** police station; (*as m. n.* **п., ∼ого**) policeman, police officer

поли́ци|я, и *f.* police

полиэтиле́н, а *m.* polythene

полк, а́, о ∼е́, в ∼у́ *m.* regiment

по́лк|а, и *f.* **1** shelf; **кни́жная п.** bookshelf **2** (*в по́езде*) berth

полко́вник, а *m.* colonel

полково́д|ец, ца *m.* commander; military leader

поллино́з, а *m.* hay fever

пол-ли́тра, полули́тра *m.* half a litre (BrE), liter (AmE)

полне́йший *adj.* sheer, utter(most)

полне́|ть, ю *impf.* (*of* ▶ **пополне́ть**) to grow stout, put on weight

полно́ *adv.* (+ *g.*) (infml) lots; **в ко́мнате полно́ наро́ду** the room is packed with people

полнолу́ни|е, я *nt.* full moon

полномо́чи|е, я *nt.* authority, power; (law) proxy; **превыше́ние ∼й** exceeding one's commission; **дать ∼я** (+ *d.*) to empower

полнопра́в|ный, ∼ен, ∼на *adj.* enjoying full rights; **п. член** full member

⚔ **по́лностью** *adv.* fully, in full; completely

полнот|а́, ы́ (*no pl.*) *f.* **1** fullness, completeness; **п. вла́сти** absolute power **2** (*тучность*) stoutness, corpulence

полноце́н|ный, ∼ен, ∼на *adj.* proper; fully fledged (BrE), full fledged (AmE)

по́лночь, полу́ночи *and* **по́лночи** *f.* midnight; **за́ п.** after midnight

⚔ **по́л|ный, ∼он, ∼на́, ∼но́** *adj.* **1** (+ *g. or i.*) (*наполненный*) full (of); (*совершенный*) complete, entire, total; absolute; **п. карма́н** (+ *g.*) a pocketful (of); **∼ное собра́ние сочине́ний** complete works; **в ∼ной ме́ре** fully, in full measure; **на ∼ном ходу́** at full speed **2** (*толстый*) stout, portly; plump

по́ло *nt. indecl.* (sport) polo; **во́дное п.** water polo

полови́к, а́ *m.* mat; long narrow carpet, runner

⚔ **полови́н|а, ы** *f.* half; **два с ∼ой** two and a half; **п. шесто́го** half past five; **во второ́й ∼е дня** in the afternoon

поло́вник, а *m.* ladle

полово́дь|е, я *nt.* flood, high water (*at time of spring thaw*)

полов|о́й *adj.* sexual; **∼а́я зре́лость** puberty; **∼ы́е о́рганы** genitals, sexual organs; **∼а́я связь** sexual intercourse

поло́г|ий, ∼, ∼а *adj.* gently sloping

⚔ **положе́ни|е, я** *nt.* **1** (*местонахожде́ние*) position; whereabouts **2** (*тела*) position; posture; attitude; **в сидя́чем ∼и** in a sitting position **3** (*состояние*) position; condition; state; situation; (*социальное*) status;

п

(*обстоя́тельство*) circumstances; **семе́йное п.** marital status; **вое́нное п.** martial law; **чрезвыча́йное п.** state of emergency; **веще́й** state of affairs; **выходи́ть из ∼я** to find a way out

поло́женный *adj.* agreed, appointed; **в п. час** at the appointed hour

поло́жено *pred.* (infml) (impers.) one is supposed to, it is customary; **э́того де́лать не п.** one is not supposed to do that

поло́жим let us assume; **п., что вы пра́вы** let us assume that you are right

✗ **положи́тель|ный, ∼ен, ∼ьна** *adj.* **1** positive **2** (*утверди́тельный*) affirmative; **п. отве́т** affirmative reply **3** (*благоприя́тный*) favourable (BrE), favorable (AmE)

полож|и́ть, у́, ∼ишь *pf. of* ▶ **класть 1**

полож|и́ться, у́сь, ∼ишься *pf.* (*of* ▶ **полага́ться 1**) (**на** + *a.*) to rely (upon), count (upon)

полома́|ть, ю *pf.* (infml) to break, put out of action

полома́|ться, юсь *pf. of* ▶ **лома́ться 3**

поло́мк|а, и *f.* **1** (*маши́ны*) breakdown **2** (*ме́сто*) damaged part; damage

полоне́з, а *m.* polonaise

полос|а́, ы́, *a.* **по́лосу,** *pl.* **по́лосы, поло́с, ∼а́м** *f.* **1** (*како́го-н. цве́та*) stripe; streak **2** (*воды́, бума́ги*) strip **3** (*пери́од*) period; phase **4** (*газе́ты*) page

полоса́т|ый, ∼, ∼а *adj.* striped

поло́ск|а, и *f. dim. of* ▶ **полоса́; в ∼у** striped

поло|ска́ть, щу́, ∼щешь *impf. of* ▶ **прополоска́ть**

полоте́н|це, ца, *g. pl.* **∼ец** *nt.* towel

полоте́р, а *m.* floor polisher

полот|но́, на́, *pl.* **∼на, ∼ен, ∼нам** *nt.* **1** (*ткань*) linen; **бле́дный как п.** white as a sheet **2** (*карти́на*) canvas **3** (*доро́ги*) roadbed **4** (tech., *пилы́*) blade

полотня́ный *adj.* linen

полоу́м|ный, ∼ен, ∼на *adj.* (infml) crazy

полпути́ *m. indecl.:* **на п.** halfway; **останови́ться на п.** (fig.) to stop halfway

полста́вки *pl. indecl.:* **на п.** part-time

полтора́, полу́тора (*used with m. and nt. nouns*) one and a half; **в п. ра́за бо́льше** half as much again

полтора́ста, полу́тораста *num.* a hundred and fifty

полторы́ *num.* (*used with f. nouns*) = **полтора́; п. ты́сячи** one and a half thousand

полу… *comb. form* half-, semi-, demi-

полуго́ди|е, я *nt.* half-year, six months

полугодова́лый *adj.* six-month-old

полужив|о́й, ∼, ∼а́, ∼о *adj.* half dead; more dead than alive

полузащи́тник, а *m.* (sport) halfback, midfield player; **центра́льный п.** centre half (BrE), center half (AmE)

полукру́г, а *m.* semicircle

полукру́глый *adj.* semicircular

полулеж|а́ть, у́, и́шь *impf.* to recline

полуме́сяц, а *m.* half moon; crescent

полумра́к, а *m.* semi-darkness

полуоде́т|ый, ∼, ∼а *adj.* half-dressed, half-clothed

полуо́стров, а *m.* peninsula

полуоткры́т|ый, ∼, ∼а *adj.* half-open; (*дверь, окно́*) ajar (*pred.*)

полупроводни́к, а́ *m.* (phys.) semiconductor

полуразру́шен|ный, ∼, ∼а *adj.* tumbledown, dilapidated

полуфабрика́т, а *m.* (*изде́лие*) semi-finished product; (*пищево́й*) semi-prepared foodstuff, convenience food

полуфина́л, а *m.* semi-final

✗ **получ|а́ть, а́ю, ет** *impf. of* ▶ **получи́ть**

✗ **получ|а́ться, ется** *impf. of* ▶ **получи́ться**

✗ **получе́ни|е, я** *nt.* receipt; obtaining; **распи́ска в ∼и** receipt

✗ **получ|и́ть, у́, ∼ишь** *pf.* (*of* ▶ **получа́ть**) to get, receive, obtain; **п. на́сморк** to catch a cold; **п. удово́льствие** to derive pleasure

✗ **получ|и́ться, ∼ится** *pf.* (*of* ▶ **получа́ться**) **1** (*оказа́ться*) to turn out, prove, be; **∼и́лось, что он был прав** it turned out that he was right, he proved right **2** (infml) (*оказа́ться уда́чным*) to work out; (*о сни́мке*) to come out

полу́чше *adv.* (infml) a little better

полуша́ри|е, я *nt.* hemisphere

полушу́б|ок, ка *m.* (knee-length) sheepskin coat

полцены́ *f. indecl.:* **за п.** at half price; for half its value

получаса́, получа́са *pl.* half an hour; **ка́ждые п.** every half-hour

по́лый *adj.* hollow

полы́н|ь, и *f.* wormwood

полысе́|ть, ю *pf. of* ▶ **лысе́ть**

✗ **по́льз|а, ы** *f.* use; advantage, benefit, profit; **извлека́ть из чего́-н. ∼у** to benefit from sth; to profit by sth; **принести́ ∼у** (+ *d.*) to be of benefit (to); **в ∼у** (+ *g.*) in favour (BrE), favor (AmE) (of), on behalf (of); **два-ноль в ∼у Дина́мо** (sport) 2-0 to Dynamo; **пойти́ на ∼у кому́-н.** to be of benefit to sb

по́льзовани|е, я *nt.* (+ *i.*) use (of)

✗ **по́льзовател|ь, я** *m.* user

✗ **по́льз|оваться, уюсь** *impf.* (+ *i.*) **1** (*pf.* **вос∼**) to make use (of), use, utilize **2** (*pf.* **вос∼**) (*извлека́ть вы́году*) to profit (by); **п. слу́чаем** to take an opportunity **3** (*облада́ть*) to enjoy; **п. успе́хом** to enjoy success, be a success

по́льк|а¹, и *f.* (*же́нщина*) Pole, Polish woman

по́льк|а², и *f.* (*та́нец*) polka

по́льский *adj.* Polish

польс|ти́ть, щу́, ти́шь *pf. of* ▶ **льстить**

По́льш|а, и *f.* Poland

п

полюб|и́ть, лю́, ~ишь *pf.* to come to like, grow fond (of); (*влюби́ться*) to fall in love (with)

полюб|ова́ться, у́юсь *pf.* (*of* ▶ **любова́ться**): ~у́йся, ~у́йтесь (**на** + *a.*) (*infml, iron.*) just look; ~у́йся на э́того дурака́! just look at that fool!

по́люс, а *m.* (*geog., phys., also fig.*) pole; Се́верный п. North Pole

поля́к, а *m.* Pole

поля́н|а, ы *f.* glade, clearing

поля́рн|ый *adj.* **1** polar, arctic; П~ая звезда́ Pole star, North Star; Се́верный п. круг Arctic Circle **2** (*fig.*) polar, diametrically opposed

пома́д|а, ы *f.* pomade; губна́я п. lipstick

пома́|зать, жу, жешь *pf. of* ▶ **ма́зать 1**, ▶ **ма́зать 2**

пома́з|ок, ка́ *m.* (small) brush

пома́лкива|ть, ю *impf.* (*infml*) to hold one's tongue, keep quiet

поман|и́ть, ю́, ~ишь *pf. of* ▶ **мани́ть**

пома́рк|а, и *f.* (*исправление*) correction (*by hand*); (*вычеркнутое место*) crossing-out

пома|ха́ть, шу́, ~шешь *pf.* (+ *i.*) to wave (*for a while, a few times*)

пома́хива|ть, ю *impf.* (+ *i.*) to wave, brandish, swing (*from time to time*); соба́ка ~ла хвосто́м the dog would wag his tail

поме́ньше *compar. of* ▶ **ма́ленький**, ▶ **ма́ло** (*infml*) (*по размеру*) somewhat smaller, a little smaller; (*по количеству*) somewhat less, a little less

поменя́|ть, ю *pf. of* ▶ **меня́ть 2**

поменя́|ться, юсь *pf. of* ▶ **меня́ться 2**

по|мере́ть, мру́, мрёшь, *past* ~мер, ~мерла́, ~мерло** *pf.* (*of* ▶ **помира́ть**) (*infml*) to die; п. со́ смеху to split one's sides (with laughing)

поме́р|ить, ю, ишь *pf. of* ▶ **ме́рить**

поме́р|иться, юсь, ишься *pf. of* ▶ **ме́риться**

поме́рк|нуть, ну, нешь, *past* ~, ~ла** *pf. of* ▶ **ме́ркнуть**

поме|сти́ть, щу́, сти́шь *pf.* (*of* ▶ **помеща́ть**) **1** (*поселить*) to lodge, accommodate; to put up **2** (*поставить*) to put, place; (*fin.*) to invest; п. объявле́ние в газе́те to put an advertisement in a paper

поме|сти́ться, щу́сь, сти́шься *pf.* (*of* ▶ **помеща́ться 3**) **1** (*жить*) to find room; to put up; (*о вещах*) to go in; в э́тот я́щик мои́ ве́щи не ~стя́тся my things will not go into this drawer **2** *pass. of* ▶ **помести́ть**

поме́ст|ье, ья, *g. pl.* ~ий** *nt.* estate

по́мес|ь, и *f.* **1** hybrid; cross; п. терье́ра и овча́рки, п. терье́ра с овча́ркой a cross between a terrier and a sheepdog **2** (*fig.*) mixture, hotchpotch

поме́|тить, чу, тишь *pf.* (▶ **помеча́ть**, ▶ **ме́тить¹**) to mark; to date; п. га́лочкой to tick

поме́х|а, и *f.* **1** hindrance; obstacle; быть ~ой (+ *d.*) to hinder, impede **2** (*usu. in pl.*) (radio, TV) interference

помеча́|ть, ю *impf. of* ▶ **поме́тить**

поме́шан|ный, ~, ~а *adj.* **1** mad, crazy; insane; (*as n.* п., ~ного) madman; (~ная, ~ной) madwoman **2** (на + *p.*) (*fig., infml*) mad (on, about), crazy (about)

помеша́|ть¹, ю *pf. of* ▶ **меша́ть¹**

помеша́|ть², ю *pf. of* ▶ **меша́ть² 1**

помеща́|ть, ю *impf. of* ▶ **помести́ть**

помеща́|ться, юсь *impf.* **1** (*impf. only*) (*находиться*) to be; to be located, be situated; (*храниться*) to be housed **2** (*impf. only*): на э́том стадио́не ~ется се́мьдесят ты́сяч челове́к this stadium holds seventy thousand people **3** *impf. of* ▶ **помести́ться**

помеще́ни|е, я *nt.* **1** (*действие*) placing, location; (*капитала*) investment **2** (*жильё*) room, lodging, apartment; (*для учреждения*) premises; жило́е п. housing

поме́щик, а *m.* landowner

помидо́р, а, *g. pl.* ~ов** *m.* tomato

поми́ловани|е, я *nt.* (*law*) pardon, forgiveness; про́сьба/проше́ние о ~и appeal (for pardon)

поми́л|овать, ую *pf.* (*of* ▶ **ми́ловать**) to pardon, forgive

поми́мо *prep.* + *g.* **1** (*кроме*) apart from; besides; п. всего́ про́чего apart from anything else **2** (*минуя*) without the knowledge (of), unbeknown (to); всё э́то реши́лось п. меня́ all this was decided without my knowledge

поми́н|ки, ок (*no sg.*) funeral repast, wake

помину́т|ный, ~ен, ~на *adj.* **1** occurring every minute; (*fig., infml, очень частый*) continual, constant **2** (*оплата*) by the minute

помира́|ть, ю *pf. of* ▶ **помере́ть**

помир|и́ть, ю́, и́шь *pf. of* ▶ **мири́ть 1**

помир|и́ться, ю́сь, и́шься *pf. of* ▶ **мири́ться 1**

по́мн|ить, ю, ишь *impf.* (+ *a. or* о + *p.*) to remember

по́мн|иться, ится *impf.* (*impers.* + *d.*) I remember, *etc.*; наско́лько мне ~ится as far as I can remember

помно́гу *adv.* (*infml*) in plenty, in large quantities; in large numbers

помно́ж|ить, у, ишь *pf. of* ▶ **мно́жить**

помога́|ть, ю *impf. of* ▶ **помо́чь**

пом|огу́, о́жешь, о́гут *see* ▶ **помо́чь**

по-мо́ему *adv.* **1** (*по моему мнению*) in my opinion **2** (*как я хочу*) as I wish

помо́|и, ев (*no sg.*) slops; обли́ть кого́-н. ~ями (*fig., infml*) to fling mud at sb

помо́й|ка, ки, *g. pl.* помо́ек** *f.* rubbish dump (BrE), garbage dump (AmE); (*яма*) cesspit

помо́й|ный *adj.*: ~ное ведро́ slop bucket; ~иная яма cesspit

помо́лвк|а, и *f.* betrothal, engagement

помол|и́ться, ю́сь, ~ишься *pf. of* ▶ **моли́ться 1**

п

помолч|а́ть, у́, и́шь *pf.* to be silent for a while

помо́ст, а *m.* platform, rostrum

помо́|чь, гу́, жешь, гу́т, *past* ∼г, ∼гла́ *pf.* (*of* ▶ помога́ть) **1** (+ *d.*) to help, aid, assist; ∼ги́(те) ей наде́ть пальто́ help her on with her coat **2** (*о лека́рстве*) to relieve, bring relief; уко́л ∼гли́ от бо́ли the injections relieved the pain

помо́щник, а *m.* **1** helper **2** (*замести́тель*) assistant; п. дире́ктора assistant director; п. капита́на (naut.) mate

помо́щни|ца, цы *f. of* ▶ помо́щник 1

по́мощ|ь, и *f.* help, assistance; оказа́ть п. to help, assist; позва́ть на п. to call for help; прийти́ на п. (+ *d.*) to come to the aid (of); на п.! help!; с ∼ью (+ *g.*) *or* при ∼и (+ *g.*) with the help (of), by means (of); ско́рая п. ambulance; пе́рвая п. first aid

по́мп|а, ы *f.* pump

помпе́з|ный, ∼ен, ∼на *adj.* pompous

помуч|ить, у, ишь *pf.* to make suffer, torment (*for a time*)

помуч|иться, усь, ишься *pf.* to suffer (*for a time*)

помч|а́ться, у́сь, и́шься *pf.* to begin to rush, begin to tear along

пом|ы́ть, о́ю, о́ешь *pf. of* ▶ мыть

пом|ы́ться, о́юсь, о́ешься *pf. of* ▶ мы́ться

пом|я́ть, ну́, нёшь *pf.* to rumple slightly; to crumple slightly

пом|я́ться, нётся *pf. of* ▶ мя́ться

понаде́|яться, юсь, ешься *pf. of* ▶ наде́яться

понадо́б|иться, люсь, ишься *pf.* to be, become necessary; е́сли ∼ится if necessary

по-настоя́щему *adv.* properly

понача́лу *adv.* (infml) at first

по-на́шему *adv.* **1** (*по на́шему мне́нию*) in our opinion **2** (*как мы хоти́м*) as we wish

понево́ле *adv.* against one's will

понеде́льник, а *m.* Monday

понемно́гу *adv.* **1** (*немно́го*) little, a little at a time **2** (*постепе́нно*) little by little

понес|ти́, у́, ёшь, *past* ∼, ∼ла́ *pf.* **1** *pf. of* ▶ нести́[1] **2** (*о лошадя́х*) to bolt

понес|ти́сь, у́сь, ёшься, *past* ∼ся, ∼ла́сь *pf.* **1** *pf. of* ▶ нести́сь **2** to rush off, tear off, dash off

по́ни *m. indecl.* pony

понижа́|ть, ю, ет *impf. of* ▶ пони́зить

понижа́|ться, ется *impf. of* ▶ пони́зиться

пониже́ни|е, я *nt.* fall, drop; lowering; reduction; п. цен reduction, fall in prices; п. по слу́жбе demotion

пони́|зить, жу, зишь *pf.* (*of* ▶ понижа́ть) (*го́лос*) to lower; (*це́ны*) to reduce; п. по слу́жбе to demote

пони́|зиться, зится *pf.* (*of* ▶ понижа́ться) to fall, drop, go down, be reduced

по́низу *adv.* (infml) low; along the ground

поника́|ть, ю *impf. of* ▶ пони́кнуть

пони́к|нуть, ну, нешь, *past* ∼, ∼ла *pf.* (*of* ▶ поника́ть) to droop, wilt; п. голово́й to hang one's head

понима́ни|е, я *nt.* **1** understanding, comprehension; э́то вы́ше моего́ ∼я it is beyond me **2** (*толкова́ние*) interpretation, conception

понима́|ть, ю *impf.* (*of* ▶ поня́ть) **1** to understand; to comprehend; to realize; ∼ю! I see! **2** (*толкова́ть*) to interpret; непра́вильно п. to misunderstand; как вы ∼ете э́тот посту́пок? what do you make of this action? **3** (*impf. only*) (+ *a. or* в + *p.*) (*знать толк*) to be a (good) judge (of), know (about); я ничего́ не ∼ю в му́зыке I know nothing about music

по-но́вому *adv.* in a new fashion; нача́ть жить п. to start life afresh, turn over a new leaf

поно́с, а *m.* diarrhoea (BrE), diarrhea (AmE)

поно́|сить, шу́, ∼сишь *pf.* **1** (*ребёнка*) to carry (*for a while*) **2** (*сви́тер*) to wear (*for a while*)

поно́шенный *p.p.p. of* ▶ поноси́ть *and adj.* worn, shabby, threadbare

понра́в|иться, люсь, ишься *pf. of* ▶ нра́виться

понто́н, а *m.* pontoon

пону́р|ый, ∼, ∼а *adj.* downcast

по́нчик, а *m.* doughnut (BrE), donut (AmE)

по́нчо *nt. indecl.* poncho

поню́ха|ть, ю *pf. of* ▶ ню́хать

поня́ти|е, я *nt.* **1** (*о́бщая мысль*) conception **2** (*представле́ние*) notion, idea; ∼я не име́ю! (infml) I've no idea!; I haven't a clue! **3** (*usu. in pl.*) (*понима́ние*) notions; level (of understanding)

поня́тлив|ый, ∼, ∼а *adj.* sharp, quick (on the uptake)

поня́т|ный, ∼ен, ∼на *adj.* **1** (*обосно́ванный*) understandable; ∼но, что... it is understandable that ...; it is natural that ...; ∼ное де́ло (infml) of course, naturally **2** (*я́сный*) clear, intelligible; ∼но? (infml) (do you) see?; is that clear?; ∼но! (infml) I see!; I understand!

поня́|ть, пойму́, поймёшь, *past* ∼л, ∼ла́, ∼ло *pf.* (*of* ▶ понима́ть 2) to understand; to comprehend; (*осозна́ть*) to realize; дать п. to give to understand

пообе́да|ть, ю *pf. of* ▶ обе́дать

пообеща́|ть, ю *pf.* (*of* ▶ обеща́ть) to promise

поочерёдно *adv.* in turn, by turns

поощр|и́ть, ю́, и́шь *pf.* (*of* ▶ поощря́ть) to encourage

поощр|я́ть, я́ю *impf. of* ▶ поощри́ть

попада́ни|е, я *nt.* hit (*on target*); прямо́е п. direct hit

попада́|ть, ю *impf. of* ▶ попа́сть

попада́|ться, юсь *impf. of* ▶ попа́сться

попа́р|иться, юсь, ишься *pf.* (*impf.* па́риться) (*в ба́не*) to steam, sweat

поп-а́рт, а *m.* pop art

⚔ **попа́|сть, ду́, дёшь,** *past* ~**л** *pf.* (*of*
▶ **попада́ть**) **1** (в + *a.*) to hit; **п. в цель**
to hit the target; **не п. в цель** to miss
2 (в + *a.*) (*оказаться*) to get (to), find
oneself (in); (**на** + *a.*) to hit (upon), come
(upon); **п. домо́й** to get home; **п. в плен** to
be taken prisoner; **п. кому́-н. в ру́ки** to fall
into sb's hands; **не туда́ п.** to get the wrong
number (*on telephone*); **п. в беду́** to get into
trouble, come to grief

попа́|сться, ду́сь, дёшься, *past* ~**лся** *pf.*
(*of* ▶ **попада́ться**) **1** (+ *d.*) to come across;
он мне ~**лся навстре́чу на у́лице** I ran into
him in the street; **п. кому́-н. на глаза́** to catch
sb's eye; **пе́рвый** ~**вшийся** the first person
one happens to meet **2** (*быть пойманным*)
to be caught; (в + *a.*) to get (into); **п. с
поли́чным** to be taken red-handed

попа́хива|ть, ет *impf.* (infml) (+ *i.*) to smell
slightly (of)

попере́к *adv. and prep.* + *g.* across; **де́рево
упа́ло п. доро́ги** the tree fell across the road;
стоя́ть у кого́-н. п. доро́ги to be in sb's way;
знать что́-н. вдоль и п. to know sth inside out

попере́чн|ый *adj.* transverse, cross-; ~**ая
ба́лка** cross-beam; **п. разре́з,** ~**ое сече́ние**
cross section

поперхн|у́ться, у́сь, ёшься *pf.* (+ *i.*) to
choke (over)

поп|е́рчить, е́рчу, е́рчишь *pf.* (*of* ▶ **пе́рчить**)

попи́са|ть, ю *pf.* (*of* ▶ **писа́ть**)

по|пи́ть, пью́, пьёшь, *past* ~**пи́л,** ~**пила́,**
~**пи́ло** *pf.* to have a drink

попко́рн, а *m.* popcorn

попла́ва|ть, ю *pf.* to have, take a swim

поплав|о́к, ка́ *m.* float

попла́|кать, чу, чешь *pf.* to cry (*a little, for a
while*); to shed a few tears

попла|ти́ться, чу́сь, ~**тишься** *pf.* (+ *i.
and* **за** + *a.*) to pay (with, for); **она́** ~**ти́лась
жи́знью за свою́ неосторо́жность** she paid
for her carelessness with her life

поплы́|ть, ву́, вёшь, *past* ~**л,** ~**ла́,** ~**ло**
pf. (*о человеке*) to strike out, start swimming;
(*о судне*) to set sail

поп-му́зык|а, и *f.* pop music

попола́м *adv.* in two, in half; half-and-half;
раздели́ть п. to divide in two, divide in half,
halve; **ви́ски п. с водо́й** whisky and water
half-and-half

пополне́|ть, ю *pf. of* ▶ **полне́ть**

попо́лн|ить, ю, ишь *pf.* (*of* ▶ **пополня́ть**)
to replenish, fill up; to restock; (*колле́кцию*)
to enlarge; (*mil.*) to reinforce; **п. горю́чим** to
refuel; **п. свои́ зна́ния** to supplement one's
knowledge

попо́лн|иться, ится *pf.* (*of* ▶ **пополня́ться**)
1 to increase **2** *pass. of* ▶ **пополни́ть**

пополн|я́ть, я́ю, я́ет *impf. of* ▶ **попо́лнить**

пополн|я́ться, я́ется *impf. of* ▶ **попо́лниться**

пополу́дни *adv.* in the afternoon, p.m.; **в два
часа́ п.** at 2 p.m.

пополу́ночи *adv.* after midnight, a.m.; **в два
часа́ п.** at 2 a.m.

попо́н|а, ы *f.* horse blanket/cloth

попра́в|ить, лю, ишь *pf.* (*of* ▶ **поправля́ть**)
1 (*починить*) to mend, repair **2** (*ошибку,
ученика́*) to correct, set right, put right
3 (*шля́пу*) to adjust, set straight; **п. причёску**
to tidy one's hair **4** (*улу́чшить*) to improve,
better

попра́в|иться, люсь, ишься *pf.* (*of*
▶ **поправля́ться**) **1** (*испра́вить свою́
оши́бку*) to correct oneself **2** (*вы́здороветь*)
to get better, recover; **я совсе́м** ~**ился** I am
completely recovered **3** (*пополне́ть*) to put
on weight; to look better; **он о́чень** ~**ился**
he has put on a lot of weight; he looks much
better **4** (*о дела́х*) to improve

попра́вк|а, и *f.* **1** (*почи́нка*) mending,
repairing **2** (*оши́бки*) correction;
amendment; **внести́** ~**и в законопрое́кт** to
amend a bill

поправля́|ть, ю *impf. of* ▶ **попра́вить**

поправля́|ться, юсь *impf. of*
▶ **попра́виться**

по-пре́жнему *adv.* as before; as usual

⚔ **попро́б|овать, ую** *pf. of* ▶ **про́бовать**

⚔ **попро|си́ть, шу́,** ~**сишь** *pf. of* ▶ **проси́ть**

попро|си́ться, шу́сь, ~**сишься** *pf. of*
▶ **проси́ться**

по́просту *adv.* (infml) simply; **п. говоря́** to put
it bluntly

попроща́|ться, юсь *pf.* (с + *i.*) to take leave
(of), say goodbye (to)

попря́|тать, чу, чешь *pf.* (infml) to hide
(*many objects*)

попря́|таться, чемся, чутся *pf.* (infml,
о мно́гих) to hide (oneself)

попс|а́, ы́ *f.* (infml) **1** popular culture; sth
trendy **2** (mus.) pop music

попсо́вый *adj.* (infml) pop

попуга́|й, я *m.* parrot; **волни́стый** ~**й(чик)**
budgie, budgerigar

попу́др|ить, ю, ишь *pf.* to powder

попу́др|иться, юсь, ишься *pf.* to powder
one's face

попули́ст, а *m.* populist

популяризи́р|овать, ую *impf. and pf.* to
popularize

популяриз|ова́ть, у́ю *impf. and pf.*
= **популяризи́ровать**

популя́рность, и *f.* popularity

⚔ **популя́р|ный,** ~**ен,** ~**на** *adj.* popular

попу́тн|ый *adj.* **1** accompanying; (*маши́на*)
passing; **п. ве́тер** fair wind, favourable (BrE),
favorable (AmE) wind; ~**ая струя́** backwash
2 (fig.) passing, incidental; ~**ое замеча́ние**
passing remark

попу́тчик, а *m.* fellow-traveller (BrE),
-traveler (AmE) (also fig., pol.)

попу́тчи|ца, цы *f. of* ▶ **попу́тчик** (lit. only)

попыта́|ться, юсь *pf. of* ▶ **пыта́ться**

⚔ **попы́тк|а, и** *f.* attempt, try; **предприня́ть** ~**у**
to make an attempt; **со второ́й** ~**и** at the

п

second attempt

попя́|титься, чусь, тишься *pf. of* ▶ **пя́титься**

по́р|а, ы *f.* pore

⚷ **пор|а́, ы́,** *a.* ∼у *f.* ◼ time, season; **весе́нняя
п.** springtime; **осе́нняя п.** autumn; **до каки́х
∼? till when?, till what time?; до каки́х ∼
вы пробу́дете здесь?** how long will you
be here?; **до сих ∼** till now, up to now;
с да́вних ∼ long, for a long time, for ages;
с тех ∼, с э́тих ∼ ... (ever) since ...; **с э́тих ∼** since
then, since that time ◼ (*as pred.*) it is time;
давно́ п. it is high time; **п. спать!** (it is)
bedtime!

порабо́та|ть, ю *pf.* to do some work

поравня́|ться, юсь *pf.* (**с** + *i.*) to pull
alongside (of)

пора́д|овать, ую *pf. of* ▶ **ра́довать**

пора́д|оваться, уюсь *pf. of* ▶ **ра́доваться**

поража́|ть, ю *impf. of* ▶ **порази́ть**

поража́|ться, юсь *impf. of* ▶ **порази́ться**

пораже́ни|е, я *nt.* defeat

порази́тел|ьный, ∼ен, ∼ьна *adj.* striking;
staggering, startling

пора|зи́ть, жу́, зи́шь *pf.* (*of* ▶ **поража́ть**)
◼ to hit, strike; **п. кинжа́лом** to stab with a
dagger ◼ (fig., *удивить*) to strike; to stagger;
меня́ ∼зи́л её мра́чный вид I was struck by
her gloomy appearance

пора|зи́ться, жу́сь, зи́шься *pf.* (*of*
▶ **поража́ться**) to be staggered, be astounded

по-ра́зному *adv.* differently, in different
ways

пора́н|ить, ю, ишь *pf.* to wound, injure, hurt
(*slightly*)

пора́н|иться, юсь, ишься *pf.* to injure, hurt
oneself (*slightly*)

порв|а́ть, у́, ёшь, *past* ∼а́л, ∼ала́, ∼а́ло *pf.*
◼ to tear slightly ◼ (*impf.* **порыва́ть**)
(**с** + *i.*) (fig.) to break (with); to break off
(with); **она́ давно́ ∼ала́ с ним** she broke
with him long ago

порв|а́ться, ётся, *past* ∼а́лся, ∼ала́сь,
∼а́лось *pf.* ◼ (*о верёвке*) to break (off),
snap ◼ (*об одежде*) to tear

пореде́|ть, ет *pf. of* ▶ **реде́ть**

поре́з, а *m.* cut

поре́|зать, жу, жешь *pf.* ◼ (*поранить*) to
cut; **п. себе́ па́лец** to cut one's finger ◼ (+ *a.*
or g.) (*нарезать*) to cut (*a quantity of*)

поре́|заться, жусь, жешься *pf.* to cut
oneself

порекоменд|ова́ть, у́ю *pf. of*
▶ **рекомендова́ть**

порица́|ть, ю *impf.* to censure; to reprimand

по́рно *nt. indecl.* (infml) porn

порнографи́ческий *adj.* pornographic

порногра́фи|я, и *f.* pornography

порнофи́льм, а *m.* porno film, blue movie

по́ровну *adv.* equally, in equal parts;
раздели́ть п. to divide equally, into equal
parts

⚷ key word

поро́г, а *m.* ◼ threshold (also fig.); **переступи́ть
п.** to cross the threshold ◼ (geog.) (*usu. in pl.*)
rapids

поро́д|а, ы *f.* ◼ (*животных*) breed;
(*деревьев*) species; (fig., *людей*) kind, sort,
type ◼ (geol.) rock; **го́рная п.** rock; (*пласт*)
layer, stratum

поро́дист|ый, ∼, ∼а *adj.* thoroughbred,
pedigree

поро|ди́ть, жу́, ди́шь *pf.* (*of* ▶ **порожда́ть**)
to give rise (to), spawn, engender

порожда́|ть, ю *impf. of* ▶ **породи́ть**

поро́й and **поро́ю** *adv.* at times, now and then

поро́к, а *m.* ◼ (*человека*) vice ◼ (*вещи*)
defect; flaw, blemish; **п. се́рдца** heart disease

пороло́н, а *m.* foam rubber

порос|ёнок, ёнка, *pl.* ∼я́та, ∼я́т *m.* piglet

по́росл|ь, и *f.* verdure, shoots

по́рох, а (у), *pl.* ∼а́, ∼о́в *m.* gunpowder;
powder

поро́ч|ный, ∼ен, ∼на *adj.*
◼ (*безнравственный*) depraved; wanton
◼ (*неправильный*) faulty; fallacious; **п. круг**
vicious circle

порошо́к, ка́ *m.* powder

порт, а, о ∼е, в ∼у́, *pl.* ∼ы́, ∼о́в *m.* port;
(*гавань*) harbour; (comput.) port; **возду́шный
п.** airport; **морско́й п.** seaport

порта́л, а *m.* (comput.) portal

портати́в|ный, ∼ен, ∼на *adj.* portable

портве́йн, а *m.* port (*wine*)

по́ртик, а *m.* portico

по́р|тить, чу, тишь *impf.* (*of* ▶ **испо́ртить**)
◼ (*аппетит, вечер, настроение, ребёнка*)
to spoil; (*машину, здоровье, зрение*) to
damage ◼ (*развращать*) to corrupt

по́р|титься, чусь, тишься *impf.* (*of*
▶ **испо́ртиться**) ◼ (*о здоровье, погоде,
отношениях*) to deteriorate; (*о продуктах*)
to go off; (*о зубах*) to decay; to rot;
отноше́ния ста́ли п. relations have begun to
deteriorate ◼ (*о механизме*) to get out of
order ◼ (*нравственно*) to become corrupt

портни́х|а, и *f.* dressmaker

портн|о́й, о́го *m.* tailor

портре́т, а *m.* portrait

портсига́р, а *m.* cigarette case

португа́л|ец, ьца *m.* Portuguese

Португа́ли|я, и *f.* Portugal

португа́л|ка, ки *f. of* ▶ **португа́лец**

португа́льский *adj.* Portuguese

портфе́л|ь, я *m.* ◼ briefcase ◼ (pol., comm.)
portfolio

портье́ *m. indecl.* (*in hotel*) porter, doorman

портье́р|а, ы *f.* portière; (*heavy*) curtain

портя́нк|а, и *f.* foot binding; puttee

поруб|и́ть, лю́, ∼ишь *pf.* to chop down (*all
or a large number of*)

поруга́|ться, юсь *pf.* ◼ to swear, curse
◼ (**с** + *i.*) (infml) to fall out (with)

по-ру́сски *adv.* (in) Russian; **говори́ть п.** to
speak Russian

поруча́|ть, а́ю *impf. of* ▸ поручи́ть

поруче́ни|е, я *nt.* (*зада́ние*) errand; (*весо́мое*) mission, assignment; по ~ю (+ *g.*) on the instructions (of); (*от и́мени*) per procurationem (p.p.)

по́руч|ень, ня *m.* handrail

поручи́|ть, у́, ~ишь *pf.* (*of* ▸ поруча́ть) **1** (*возложи́ть на кого́-н. исполне́ние чего́-н.*) to charge, commission; to instruct; **он ~и́л мне переда́ть вам де́ньги** he charged me to hand you the money **2** (*вве́рить кого́-, что́-н. забо́те кого́-н.*) to entrust

поручи́|ться, у́сь, ~ишься *pf. of* ▸ руча́ться

порх|а́ть, а́ю *impf.* (*of* ▸ порхну́ть) to flutter, fly about

порх|ну́ть, ну́, нёшь *pf. of* ▸ порха́ть

по́рци|я, и *f.* portion

по́рш|ень, ня *m.* (tech.) (*дви́гателя*) piston; (*насо́са*) plunger

поры́в, а *m.* **1** (*ве́тра*) gust; rush **2** (fig., *чу́вства*) fit; upsurge; **п. гне́ва** fit of temper

порыва́|ть, ю *impf. of* ▸ порва́ть 2

поры́вист|ый, ~, ~а *adj.* **1** (*ве́тер*) gusty **2** (*движе́ние*) jerky **3** (fig., *хара́ктер*) impetuous, violent

поры́|ться, о́юсь, о́ешься *pf.* (в + *p.*) (infml) to rummage (in, among); **п. в па́мяти** to give one's memory a jog

поря́дков|ый *adj.* ordinal; ~ое числи́тельное ordinal numeral

◆ **поря́д|ок, ка** *m.* **1** order; (*пра́вильное состоя́ние, расположе́ние*): **привести́ в п.** to put in order; **привести́ себя́ в п.** to tidy oneself up; **всё в ~ке!** everything is all right!; **не в ~ке** out of order, not right **2** (*после́довательность*): **алфави́тный п.** alphabetical order; **по ~ку** in order, in succession **3** (*спо́соб*) manner, way; procedure; **в обяза́тельном ~ке** without fail **4** (mil., *построе́ние*): **боево́й п.** battle order **5** (*in pl.*) (*обы́чаи*) customs, usages, observances

поря́доч|ный, ~ен, ~на *adj.* **1** (*че́стный*) decent; honest; ~ные лю́ди decent folk **2** (infml, *значи́тельный*) fair, considerable; **он п. плут** he is pretty much of a rogue

поса́|ди́ть, жу́, ~дишь *pf. of* ▸ сажа́ть

поса́дк|а, и *f.* **1** (*семя́н*) planting **2** (*на су́дно*) embarkation; (*на по́езд, авто́бус*) boarding **3** (aeron.) landing; **вы́нужденная п.** forced landing

поса́дочный *adj.* (aeron.) landing; **п. биле́т/ тало́н** boarding pass

поса́хар|ить, ю, ишь *pf. of* ▸ са́харить

посве|ти́ть, чу́, ~тишь *pf.* **1** to shine for a while **2** (+ *d.*) to hold a light (for)

посви|сте́ть, щу́, сти́шь *pf.* to whistle, give a whistle

посви́стыва|ть, ю *impf.* to whistle (*softly, from time to time*)

по-сво́ему *adv.* in one's own way; **де́лайте п., поступа́йте п.** have it your own way

посвя|ти́ть, щу́, ти́шь *pf.* (*of* ▸ посвяща́ть) **1** (+ *a.* and в + *a.*) to let (into); **мы вас ~ти́м в на́шу та́йну** we will let you into our secret **2** (+ *a.* and *d.*) (*жизнь*) to devote (to), give up (to); (*кни́гу*) to dedicate (to); **п. себя́ нау́ке** to devote oneself to (the cause of) learning; **он ~ти́л пе́рвую кни́гу свое́й ма́тери** he dedicated his first book to his mother **3** (+ *a.* and в + *nom.-a.*) (*в сан*) to ordain, consecrate; **п. в ры́цари** to knight, confer a knighthood (upon)

◆ **посвяща́|ть, ю** *impf. of* ▸ посвяти́ть

посе́в, а *m.* **1** (*де́йствие*) sowing **2** (*то, что посе́яно*) crops; **пло́щадь ~ов** sown area, area under crops

поседе́|ть, ю *pf. of* ▸ седе́ть

поселе́н|ец, ца *m.* **1** settler **2** (*со́сланный*) deportee

поселе́ни|е, я *nt.* settlement

поселе́н|ка, ки *f. of* ▸ поселе́нец

посели́|ть, ю́, и́шь *pf.* (*of* ▸ поселя́ть, ▸ сели́ть) to settle; to lodge

посели́|ться, ю́сь, и́шься *pf.* (*of* ▸ поселя́ться, ▸ сели́ться) to settle, take up residence

◆ **посёл|ок, ка** *m.* village; settlement

посел|я́ть, я́ю *impf. of* ▸ посели́ть

посел|я́ться, я́юсь *impf. of* ▸ посели́ться

посереди́не *adv. and prep.* (+ *g.*) in the middle (of)

◆ **посети́тел|ь, я** *m.* visitor

посети́тель|ница, ницы *f. of* ▸ посети́тель

посе|ти́ть, щу́, ти́шь *pf.* (*of* ▸ посеща́ть) to visit; **п. ле́кции** to attend lectures

◆ **посеща́|ть, ю** *impf. of* ▸ посети́ть

посеще́ни|е, я *nt.* visit; (*ле́кций*) attendance

посе́|ять, ю *pf. of* ▸ се́ять

посиде́|ть, жу́, ди́шь *pf.* to sit (*for a while*)

поска|ка́ть, чу́, ~чешь *pf. of* ▸ скака́ть 1, ▸ скака́ть 2

поскользн|у́ться, у́сь, ёшься *pf.* to slip

◆ **поско́льку** *conj.* **1** as far as; **мы путеше́ствуем посто́льку, п. позволя́ют сре́дства** we travel (just) as much as we can afford **2** (*так как*) in so far as, since; so long as

поскоре́е *adv.* (infml) somewhat quicker; (*int.*) **п.!** quick!

посла́ни|е, я *nt.* **1** (*официа́льное*) dispatch; (*дру́жеское*) message **2** (liter.) epistle; **П~я** (bibl.) the Epistles

посла́нник, а *m.* envoy, minister

по|сла́ть, шлю́, шлёшь *pf.* (*of* ▸ посыла́ть) to send; **п. по по́чте** to post; **п. приве́т** to send one's regards; **п. кого́-н. к чёрту** (fig., infml) to tell sb to go to hell

◆ **по́сле** *adv. and prep.* (+ *g.*) after; afterwards, later (on); (*after a neg.*) since; **п. войны́** after the war; **п. чего́** whereupon; **п. того́, как** after

послевое́нный *adj.* post-war

◆ **после́дн|ий** *adj.* **1** last; (*реше́ние, сло́во*) final; **(в) ~ее вре́мя, за ~ее вре́мя** lately, of late, recently; **(в)** n. **раз** for the last time **2** (*самый новый*) (the) latest; ~ие изве́стия the latest news **3** (*из упомянутых*) the latter **4** (infml, *самый плохой*) worst, lowest; ~яя ка́пля the last straw

после́довател|ь, я *m.* follower

после́довательность|ь, и *f.* succession, sequence

после́довател|ьный, ~ен, ~ьна *adj.* **1** (*следующий один за другим*) successive, consecutive **2** (*логичный*) consistent, logical

после́д|овать, ую *pf. of* ▶ сле́довать[1] 1, ▶ сле́довать[1] 2

✓ после́дстви|е, я *nt.* consequence

✓ после́дующий *adj.* subsequent

послеза́втра *adv.* the day after tomorrow

послеобе́денный *adj.* after-dinner

послеоперацио́нный *adj.* post-operative

послеродово́й *adj.* post-natal

послесло́ви|е, я *nt.* afterword, postface; concluding remarks

посло́виц|а, ы *f.* proverb

послуж|и́ть, у́, ~ишь *pf. of* ▶ служи́ть 4

послу́ша|ть, ю *pf. of* ▶ слу́шать

послу́ша|ться, юсь *pf. of* ▶ слу́шаться

послу́ш|ный, ~ен, ~на *adj.* obedient

послы́ш|аться, ится *pf. of* ▶ слы́шаться

посма́трива|ть, ю *impf.* (на + *a.*) to look (at) from time to time

посме́ива|ться, юсь *impf.* to chuckle, laugh softly; п. в кула́к to laugh up one's sleeve

посме́ртный *adj.* posthumous

посме́|ть, ю *pf. of* ▶ сметь

✓ посмотр|е́ть, ю́, ~ишь *pf. of* ▶ смотре́ть

посмотр|е́ться, ю́сь, ~ишься *pf. of* ▶ смотре́ться 1

посо́би|е, я *nt.* **1** (*денежная помощь*) allowance, benefit; п. по безрабо́тице unemployment benefit; п. на дете́й child benefit **2** (*учебник*) textbook; (*учебный предмет*) (educational) aid; уче́бные ~я educational supplies; school textbooks

посове́т|овать, ую *pf. of* ▶ сове́товать

посове́т|оваться, уюсь *pf. of* ▶ сове́товаться

посо́|л, ла́ *m.* (*дипломатический представитель*) ambassador

посол|и́ть, ю́, ~ишь *pf. of* ▶ соли́ть

посо́льств|о, а *nt.* embassy

по́сох, а *m.* **1** (*пастуха*) staff, crook **2** (*епископа, монарха*) crozier

посп|а́ть, лю́, и́шь, *past* ~а́л, ~ала́, ~а́ло *pf.* to have a sleep, have a nap

поспева́|ть, ет *impf. of* ▶ поспе́ть

поспе́|ть, ет *pf.* (*of* ▶ поспева́ть) (infml) to ripen

поспеш|и́ть, у́, и́шь *pf. of* ▶ спеши́ть 1

поспе́ш|ный, ~ен, ~на *adj.* hasty, hurried

поспо́р|ить, ю, ишь *pf.* **1** *pf. of* ▶ спо́рить **2** (*заключить пари*) to bet, have a bet

посреди́ *adv. and prep.* + *g.* in the middle (of), in the midst (of)

посре́дник, а *m.* **1** mediator, intermediary; go-between **2** (comm.) middleman

посре́дственно *adv.* so-so, mediocrely, not particularly well; он игра́ет в те́ннис п. he is not particularly good at tennis

посре́дственность|ь, и *f.* (*свойство, о человеке*) mediocrity

посре́дствен|ный, ~, ~на *adj.* **1** mediocre, middling **2** (*отметка*) fair, satisfactory

посре́дством *prep.* + *g.* by means of; with the aid of

поссо́р|ить, ю, ишь *pf. of* ▶ ссо́рить

поссо́р|иться, юсь, ишься *pf. of* ▶ ссо́риться

✓ пост[1], а́, о ~е́, на ~у́, *pl.* ~ы́ *m.* post; наблюда́тельный п. observation post; занима́ть высо́кий п. to hold a high post

пост[2], а́, о ~е́ *m.* **1** (в ~е́) (*воздержание от пищи*) fasting; (fig., infml) abstinence **2** (в ~у́) (eccl.) fast; Вели́кий п. Lent

✓ поста́в|ить[1], лю, ишь *pf. of* ▶ ста́вить

поста́в|ить[2], лю, ишь *pf.* (*of* ▶ поставля́ть) (*снабдить*) to supply

✓ поста́вк|а, и *f.* supply; delivery; ма́ссовая п. bulk delivery

✓ поставля́|ть, ю *impf. of* ▶ поста́вить[2]

поставщи́к, а́ *m.* supplier

постаме́нт, а *m.* pedestal, base

постанов|и́ть, лю́, ~ишь *pf.* to decide, resolve; to decree

постано́вк|а, и *f.* **1** (*дела, работы*) arrangement, organization **2** (theatr.) staging, production

✓ постановле́ни|е, я *nt.* **1** (*решение*) decision, resolution; вы́нести п. to pass a resolution **2** (*распоряжение*) decree; изда́ть п. to issue a decree

постара́|ться, юсь *pf. of* ▶ стара́ться

постаре́|ть, ю *pf. of* ▶ старе́ть 1

по-ста́рому *adv.* **1** (*как раньше*) as before **2** (*как в старые времена*) as of old

постел|и́ть, ю́, ~ешь *pf. of* ▶ стели́ть

посте́л|ь, и *f.* bed; лечь в п. to get into bed; встать с ~и to get out of bed

✓ постепе́нно *adv.* gradually, little by little

постепе́н|ный, ~ен, ~на *adj.* gradual

постесня́|ться, юсь *pf. of* ▶ стесня́ться

постига́|ть, а́ю *impf. of* ▶ пости́гнуть, ▶ пости́чь

пости́гнуть = пости́чь

постила́|ть, ю *impf. of* ▶ постла́ть

постимпрессиони́зм, а *m.* post-impressionism

постира́|ть, ю *pf.* to wash

по|сти́ться, щу́сь, сти́шься *impf.* to fast

пости́|чь, гну, гнешь, *past* ~г *pf.* (*of* ▶ постига́ть) **1** (*понять*) to comprehend, grasp **2** (*о горе, о несчастье*) to befall, strike; **их ~гло́ ещё одно́ несча́стье** yet another misfortune has befallen them

пост|ла́ть, елю́, е́лешь *pf.* (*of* ▶ **стла́ть**, ▶ **постила́ть**) to spread, lay; **п. ковёр** to lay a carpet; **п. посте́ль** to make one's bed

постмодерни́зм, а *m.* postmodernism

постмодерни́стский *adj.* postmodern

по́ст|ный, ~ен, ~на́, ~но *adj.* **1** Lenten; **п. день** (eccl.) fast day; **п. обе́д** meatless dinner **2** (infml, *о мя́се*) lean

посто́льку *conj.*: **п., поско́льку** in so far as …

посторо́нн|ий *adj.* **1** (*побо́чный*) extraneous, outside; **без ~ей по́мощи** unaided **2** (*чужо́й*) strange; (*as m. n.* **п., ~его**) stranger; outsider; **«~им вход воспрещён»** 'unauthorized persons not admitted'

&#x26 a; **постоя́нно** *adv.* constantly, continually

&#x26 a; **постоя́н|ный** *adj.* **1** constant, continual; **п. посети́тель** constant visitor **2** (*не вре́менный*) constant; permanent, invariable; **п. а́дрес** permanent address; **~ная рабо́та** a permanent job; **п. ток** (elec.) direct current **3** (**~ен, ~на**) (*не изме́нчивый*) constant, unchanging

посто|я́ть¹, ю́, и́шь *pf.* (*не́которое вре́мя*) to stand (*for a while*)

посто|я́ть², ю́, и́шь *pf.* (**за** + *a.*) (*защити́ть*) to stand up (for)

пострада́|вший *p.p. of* ▶ **пострада́ть**; (*as m. n.* **п., ~вшего**) victim

пострада́|ть, ю *pf. of* ▶ **страда́ть 3**

постре́лива|ть, ю *impf.* to fire intermittently

постреля́|ть, ю *pf.* **1** (*не́которое вре́мя*) to do some shooting **2** (+ *a. or g.*) (infml, *застрели́ть мно́гих*) to shoot, bag (*a number of*)

постри́|чь, гу́, жёшь, гу́т, *past* **~г, ~гла** *pf. of* ▶ **стричь**

постри́|чься, гу́сь, жёшься, гу́тся, *past* **~гся, ~гла́сь** *pf. of* ▶ **стри́чься 1**

постро́е́ни|е, я *nt.* construction

&#x26 a; **постро́|ить, ю, ишь** *pf. of* ▶ **стро́ить**

постро́|иться, юсь, ишься *pf. of* ▶ **стро́иться**

постро́йк|а, и *f.* **1** (*де́йствие*) building, erection, construction **2** (*зда́ние*) building

постскри́птум, а *m.* postscript

&#x26 a; **поступ|а́ть, а́ю** *impf. of* ▶ **поступи́ть**

поступ|а́ться, а́юсь *impf. of* ▶ **поступи́ться**

&#x26 a; **поступ|и́ть, лю́, ~ишь** *pf.* (*of* ▶ **поступа́ть**) **1** to act; **они́ с ним пло́хо ~и́ли** they have treated him badly **2** (**в, на** + *a.*) (*зачи́слиться*) to enter, join; **п. в университе́т** to enter the university; **п. на рабо́ту** to start work **3** (*о по́сланном, дойти́*) to come through; to be received; **~и́ла жа́лоба** a complaint has been received, has come in; **п. в прода́жу** to go on sale, come on the market

поступ|и́ться, лю́сь, ~ишься *pf.* (*of* ▶ **поступа́ться**) (+ *i.*) to waive, forgo; to give up

поступле́ни|е, я *nt.* **1** (*в университе́т*) entering; (*в па́ртию, клуб*) joining; **п. на вое́нную слу́жбу** enlisting, joining up **2** (*де́нежное*) receipt; (*в библиоте́ке*) acquisition

посту́п|ок, ка *m.* action; deed; (*pl., collect.*) behaviour (BrE), behavior (AmE)

постуч|а́ть, у́, и́шь *pf. of* ▶ **стуча́ть**

постуч|а́ться, у́сь, и́шься *pf. of* ▶ **стуча́ться**

посты|ди́ться, жу́сь, ди́шься *pf. of* ▶ **стыди́ться**

посты́д|ный, ~ен, ~на *adj.* shameful

посу́д|а, ы *f.* (collect.) crockery; **гли́няная п., фая́нсовая п.** earthenware; **ку́хонная п.** kitchen utensils

посудомо́ечн|ый *adj.*: **~ая маши́на** dishwasher, dishwashing machine

посчастли́в|иться, ится *pf.* (impers. + *d.*) to have the luck (to); to be lucky enough (to)

посчита́|ть, ю *pf. of* ▶ **счита́ть**

посыла́|ть, ю *impf. of* ▶ **посла́ть**

посы́лк|а, и *f.* parcel

посы́п|ать, лю, лешь *pf.* (*of* ▶ **посыпа́ть**) (+ *i.*) to sprinkle (with)

посып|а́ть, а́ю *impf. of* ▶ **посы́пать**

посы́п|аться, лется *pf.* to begin to fall; (fig.) to rain down

посяг|а́ть, а́ю *impf. of* ▶ **посягну́ть**

посяг|ну́ть, ну́, нёшь *pf.* (*of* ▶ **посяга́ть**) (**на** + *a.*) to encroach (on, upon), infringe (on, upon)

пот, а, о ~е, в ~у́, *pl.* **~ы́, ~о́в** *m.* sweat, perspiration; **весь в ~у́** all of a sweat, bathed in sweat

по-тво́ему *adv.* **1** (*по твоему́ мне́нию*) in your opinion **2** (*как ты хо́чешь*) as you wish

потемне́|ть, ю *pf. of* ▶ **темне́ть 1**

потенциа́л, а *m.* potential

потенциа́л|ьный, ~ен, ~ьна *adj.* potential

потепле́ни|е, я *nt.* warm(er) spell

потепле́|ть, ет *pf. of* ▶ **тепле́ть**

потерп|е́ть, лю́, ~ишь *pf. of* ▶ **терпе́ть 1**

потёрт|ый, ~, ~а *adj.* shabby, threadbare

&#x26 a; **поте́р|я, и** *f.* loss; (*in pl.*) (mil.) losses

&#x26 a; **потеря́|ть, ю** *pf. of* ▶ **теря́ть**

потеря́|ться, юсь *pf. of* ▶ **теря́ться**

&#x26 a; **поте́|ть, ю** *impf.* **1** to sweat, perspire **2** *impf. of* ▶ **запоте́ть**

поте́|чь, ку́, чёшь, ку́т, *past* **~к, ~кла́** *pf.* to begin to flow

потихо́ньку *adv.* (infml) **1** (*ме́дленно*) slowly **2** (*ти́хо*) softly, noiselessly **3** (*та́йно*) on the sly, secretly

по́т|ный, ~ен, ~на́, ~но *adj.* sweaty, damp with perspiration

&#x26 a; **пото́к, а** *m.* stream; flow; **п. слов** flow of words

пото́ков|ый *adj.* streaming; **~ое ви́део** streaming video

потоло́|к, ка́ *m.* ceiling

п

потолсте́|ть, ю *pf. of* ▶ толсте́ть

✍ **пото́м** *adv.* (*после*) afterwards; (*позже*) later (on); (*затем*) then, after that; **мы п. придём** we shall come later

пото́м|ок, ка *m.* descendant; (*in pl.*) offspring, progeny

пото́мств|о, а *nt.* (*collect.*) posterity, descendants

✍ **потому́** **1** (*adv.*) that is why **2** (*conj.*): **п. что; п. ..., что** because, as; **я не знал об э́том, п. что был в о́тпуске** I did not know about it because I was on leave

пото́п, а *m.* flood, deluge; **Всеми́рный п.** (bibl.) the Flood

потоп|и́ть, лю́, **~ишь** *pf.* (*of* ▶ потопля́ть, ▶ топи́ть³ 1) to sink

потопля́|ть, ю *impf. of* ▶ потопи́ть

потороп|и́ть, лю́, **~ишь** *pf. of* ▶ торопи́ть

потороп|и́ться, лю́сь, **~ишься** *pf. of* ▶ торопи́ться

потра́|тить, чу, тишь *pf. of* ▶ тра́тить

✍ **потреби́тель**, я *m.* consumer, user

потреб|и́ть, лю́, йшь *pf.* (*of* ▶ потребля́ть) to consume, use

потребле́ни|е, я *nt.* consumption

потребля́|ть, ю *impf. of* ▶ потреби́ть

✍ **потре́бность**, и *f.* need, requirement; **испы́тывать п. в чём-н.** to feel a need for sth

потре́б|овать, ую *pf. of* ▶ тре́бовать

потре́б|оваться, уюсь *pf. of* ▶ тре́боваться

потрево́ж|ить, у, ишь *pf. of* ▶ трево́жить

потрево́ж|иться, усь, ишься *pf. of* ▶ трево́житься

потрёпанный *p.p.p. of* ▶ потрепа́ть *and adj.* **1** (*рубаха, книга*) shabby; tattered **2** (fig., *вид*) worn, seedy

потреп|а́ть, лю́, **~лешь** *pf. of* ▶ трепа́ть

потреп|а́ться, лю́сь, **~лешься** *pf. of* ▶ трепа́ться

потре́ска|ться, ется *pf. of* ▶ тре́скаться

потро́га|ть, ю *pf.* to touch, run one's hand over; **п. па́льцем** to finger

потроха́, о́в (*no sg.*) giblets

потру|ди́ться, жу́сь, **~дишься** *pf.* to take pains; to do some work

потряса́|ть, ю *impf. of* ▶ потрясти́¹

потряса́ющий *pres. part. act. of* ▶ потряса́ть *and adj.* (infml) staggering, stupendous, tremendous

потрясе́ни|е, я *nt.* shock; (*социальное*) upheaval

потряс|ти́¹, у́, ёшь, *past* **~**, **~ла́** *pf.* (*of* ▶ потряса́ть) **1** (+ *i.*) **п. до основа́ния** to rock its foundations **2** (+ *i.*) (*взмахнуть*) to brandish, shake; **п. кулако́м** to shake one's fist **3** (fig., *удивить*) to shake; to stagger, stun

потряс|ти́², у́, ёшь, *past* **~**, **~ла́** *pf.* to shake (*a little, a few times*)

потускне́|ть, ет *pf. of* ▶ тускне́ть

потуха́|ть, а́ю *impf. of* ▶ поту́хнуть

поту́х|нуть, ну, нешь, *past* **~**, **~ла** *pf.* (of ▶ ту́хнуть¹, ▶ потуха́ть) to go out; (fig.) to be extinguished, die out

потуш|и́ть¹, у́, **~ишь** *pf. of* ▶ туши́ть¹

потуш|и́ть², у́, **~ишь** *pf.* (*мясо*) to stew (*for a while*)

потя́гива|ться, юсь *impf. of* ▶ потяну́ться

потян|у́ть, у́, **~ешь** *pf.* to begin to pull

потян|у́ться, у́сь, **~ешься** *pf.* (of ▶ потя́гиваться) to stretch oneself; (*растянуться*) to stretch out

поу́жина|ть, ю *pf. of* ▶ у́жинать

поумне́|ть, ю *pf. of* ▶ умне́ть

поуча́|ть, ю *impf.* (infml, iron.) to preach (at), lecture

поучи́тел|ьный, **~ен**, **~ьна** *adj.* instructive

поучи́|ться, у́сь, **~ишься** *pf.* to study (*for a while*); to do a bit of studying

похвал|а́, ы́ *f.* praise; **отозва́ться с ~о́й (о + p.)** to praise, speak favourably (BrE), favorably (AmE) (of)

похвал|и́ть, ю́, **~ишь** *pf. of* ▶ хвали́ть

похва́л|ьный, **~ен**, **~ьна** *adj.* **1** (*заслуживающий похвалы*) praiseworthy, commendable **2** (*содержащий похвалу*) laudatory; **~ьная гра́мота** certificate of merit

похва́ста|ть, ю *pf. of* ▶ хва́стать

похва́ста|ться, юсь *pf. of* ▶ хва́статься

похити́тел|ь, я *m.* thief; kidnapper; abductor; hijacker

похити́тел|ьница, ницы *f. of* ▶ похити́тель

похи́|тить, щу, тишь *pf.* (*of* ▶ похища́ть) (*вещь*) to steal; (*человека*) to kidnap; to abduct; (*самолёт*) to hijack

похища́|ть, ю *impf. of* ▶ похи́тить

похище́ни|е, я *nt.* theft; kidnapping; abduction; hijacking

похлёбк|а, и *f.* soup, broth

похло́па|ть, ю *pf.* to slap, clap (a few times)

похме́л|ье, я *nt.* hangover; **быть с ~я** to have a hangover

похо́д, а *m.* **1** (mil.) march; (naut.) cruise **2** (mil., fig.) campaign; **кресто́вый п.** (also fig.) crusade **3** (*прогулка*) walking tour, hike

похо|ди́ть¹, жу́, **~дишь** *impf.* (на + *a.*) to resemble, look like

похо|ди́ть², жу́, **~дишь** *pf.* to walk (*for a while*)

похо́дк|а, и *f.* gait, walk, step

похожде́ни|е, я *nt.* adventure, escapade

✍ **похо́ж|ий**, **~**, **~а** *adj.* **1** resembling, alike; (на + *a.*) like; **он ~ на де́да** he is like his grandfather; **они́ о́чень ~и друг на дру́га** they are very much alike **2** (infml): **~е it** appears, it would appear; **~е на то, что...** it looks as if ...; **он, ~е, бо́лен** it would appear he is ill

похолода́ни|е, я *nt.* fall of temperature, cold spell

похолода́|ть, ет *pf. of* ▶ холода́ть

похолоде́|ть, ю *pf. of* ▶ холоде́ть

✍ key word

П

похорон|и́ть, ю́, ∼ишь *pf. of* ▶ хорони́ть

похоро́нн|ый *adj.* funeral; ∼ое бюро́ undertaker's

по́хор|оны, о́н, она́м (*no sg.*) funeral; burial

по-хоро́шему *adv.* in an amicable way

похотли́в|ый, ∼, ∼а *adj.* lustful, lewd, lascivious

похуде́|ть, ю *pf. of* ▶ худе́ть

поцара́па|ть, ю *pf.* to scratch (slightly)

поцара́па|ться, юсь *pf.* to get slightly scratched

поцел|ова́ть, у́ю *pf. of* ▶ целова́ть

поцел|ова́ться, у́юсь *pf. of* ▶ целова́ться

поцелу́|й, я *m.* kiss

по́чв|а, ы *f.* **1** soil, ground, earth **2** (fig., *основа*) foundation, basis; на ∼е (+ *g.*) owing (to), because (of)

почём *interrog. and rel. adv.* (infml) how much; п. сего́дня я́блоки? how much are apples today?

почему́ **1** *interrog. and rel. adv.* why; п. вы так ду́маете? why do you think that? **2** *as conj.* (and) so; which is why; она́ простуди́лась, п. и оста́лась до́ма she has caught a cold, which is why she has stayed at home

почему́-либо = почему́-нибудь

почему́-нибудь *adv.* for some reason or other

почему́-то *adv.* for some reason

по́черк, а *m.* handwriting; (fig.) hallmark

почерне́|ть, ю *pf. of* ▶ черне́ть 1

поче|са́ть, шу́, ∼шешь *pf. of* ▶ чеса́ть

поче|са́ться, шу́сь, ∼шешься *pf. of* ▶ чеса́ться

почёт, а *m.* honour (BrE), honor (AmE); respect, esteem; быть в ∼е у кого́-н. to stand high in sb's esteem

почёт|ный *adj.* **1** (*пользующийся почётом*) honoured (BrE), honored (AmE); п. гость guest of honour (BrE), honor (AmE) **2** (*избираемый в знак почёта*) honorary; п. член honorary member **3** (∼ен, ∼на) (*являющийся проявлением почёта; доставляющий почёт*) honourable (BrE), honorable (AmE)

почин|и́ть, ю́, ∼ишь *pf.* (*of* ▶ чини́ть) to repair, mend

почи́нк|а, и *f.* repairing, mending; отда́ть что́-н. в ∼у to have sth repaired, mended

почи́|стить, щу, стишь *pf. of* ▶ чи́стить

почита́|ть, ю *pf.* to read (*a little, for a while*)

по́чк|а¹, и *f.* (bot.) bud

по́чк|а², и *f.* (anat.) kidney; иску́сственная п. (med.) kidney machine

по́чт|а, ы *f.* **1** (*система*) post; возду́шная п. airmail; электро́нная п. email; посла́ть по ∼е, ∼ой to send by post, post **2** (*письма*) (the) post, (the) mail; пришла́ ли п.? has the post come? **3** (*учреждение*) post office

почтальо́н, а *m.* postman, postwoman (BrE), letter carrier (AmE)

почтальо́нк|а, и *f.* (infml) postwoman (BrE), letter carrier (AmE)

почта́мт, а *m.* main post office (*of city or town*)

почте́ни|е, я *nt.* respect, esteem; deference

почти́ *adv.* almost, nearly; п. ничего́ next to nothing; п. что (infml) almost, nearly

почти́тел|ьный, ∼ен, ∼ьна *adj.* respectful, deferential

почт|о́вый *adj. of* ▶ по́чта; п. и́ндекс postcode (BrE), zip code (AmE); ∼о́вая ка́рточка postcard; ∼о́вая ма́рка (postage) stamp; ∼о́вое отделе́ние post office; п. я́щик letter box, postbox (BrE), mailbox (AmE); (comput.) mailbox

почу́вств|овать, ую *pf. of* ▶ чу́вствовать

пошатн|у́ться, у́сь, ёшься *pf.* **1** to sway, totter, stagger **2** (fig.) to be shaken; её здоро́вье ∼у́лось her health has suffered

пошевел|и́ть, ю́, ∼и́шь *pf. of* ▶ шевели́ть

пошевел|и́ться, ю́сь, ∼и́шься *pf. of* ▶ шевели́ться

пошевельн|у́ть, у́, ёшь *pf.* (infml) = пошевели́ть

пошевельн|у́ться, у́сь, ёшься *pf.* (infml) = пошевели́ться

пошёл, ла́ *see* ▶ пойти́

по́шлин|а, ы *f.* duty; и́мпортная п. import duty; э́кспортная п. export duty

по́шлост|ь, и *f.* **1** (*свойство*) vulgarity, commonness **2** (*замечание*) trite remark, banality; говори́ть ∼и to utter banalities

по́шл|ый, ∼, ∼а́, ∼о *adj.* **1** (*низкий*) vulgar; у него́ о́чень ∼ые вку́сы he has very vulgar tastes **2** (*банальный*) trite, banal; ∼ая по́весть banal story

пошум|е́ть, лю́, и́шь *pf.* to make a bit of a noise

пошу|ти́ть, чу́, ∼тишь *pf. of* ▶ шути́ть

поща|ди́ть, жу́, ди́шь *pf. of* ▶ щади́ть

пощеко|та́ть, чу́, ∼чешь *pf. of* ▶ щекота́ть

пощёчин|а, ы *f.* slap in the face (also fig.); дать ∼у (+ *d.*) to slap in the face

пощу́па|ть, ю *pf. of* ▶ щу́пать

поэ́зи|я, и *f.* poetry

поэ́м|а, ы *f.* (narrative) poem (*usu. of epic proportions*)

поэ́т, а *m.* poet

поэте́сс|а, ы *f.* poetess

поэти́ческий *adj.* poetic(al)

поэ́тому *adv.* therefore, and so

по|ю́¹, ёшь *see* ▶ петь

по|ю́², ∼и́шь *see* ▶ пои́ть

появ|и́ться, лю́сь, ∼ишься *pf.* (*of* ▶ появля́ться) to appear

появле́ни|е, я *nt.* appearance

появля́|ться, юсь *impf. of* ▶ появи́ться

по́яс, а, *pl.* ∼а́, ∼о́в *m.* **1** belt; спаса́тельный п. lifebelt **2** (*талия*) waist; по п. up to the waist, waist-deep, waist-high **3** (geog., econ.) zone, belt

поясне́ни|е, я *nt.* explanation

поясн|и́ть, ю́, и́шь *pf.* (*of* ▶ **поясня́ть**) to explain, elucidate

поясни́ц|а, ы *f.* small of the back; **боль в** ~**е** lumbago

поясн|я́ть, я́ю *impf. of* ▶ **поясни́ть**

прабабушк|а, и *f.* great-grandmother

✓ **пра́вд|а, ы** *f.* **1** truth; the truth; **су́щая п.** the honest truth; **э́то п.** it is true; it is the truth; **по** ~**е сказа́ть, говоря́** to tell the truth **2** (*справедли́вость*) justice; **иска́ть** ~**ы** to seek justice **3**: **п.?** is that so?; really?; **п. (ли), что он умира́ет?** is it true that he is dying?; **не п. ли?** *in interrog. sentences indicates that affirmative answer is expected;* **вы погаси́ли свет, не п. ли?** you (did) put out the light, didn't you? **4** (*as concessive conj.*) true; **п., я ему́ не написа́л, но я вот-во́т собира́лся позвони́ть** true I had not written to him, but I was on the point of phoning

правди́в|ый, ~, ~**а** *adj.* **1** true; veracious; **п. расска́з** true story **2** (*челове́к*) truthful; upright; **п. отве́т** honest answer

правдоподо́бн|ый, ~**ен,** ~**на** *adj.* probable, likely; plausible

пра́ведн|ый, ~**ен,** ~**на** *adj.* **1** (*благочести́вый*) righteous; upright **2** (*справедли́вый*) just

✓ **пра́вил|о, а** *nt.* **1** rule; regulation; ~**а у́личного движе́ния** traffic regulations; **как п.** as a rule **2** (*при́нцип*) rule, principle; **взять за п.** to make it a rule; **взять себе́ за п.** (+ *inf.*) to make a point (of)

✓ **пра́вильно** *adv.* **1** (*ве́рно*) rightly; correctly; **п. ли иду́т ва́ши часы́?** is your watch right? **2** (*регуля́рно*) regularly

✓ **пра́вил|ьный,** ~**ен,** ~**ьна** *adj.* **1** (*ве́рный*) right, correct; **п. отве́т** the right answer; ~**ьно** (*as pred.*) it is correct; ~**ьно!** that's right! **2** (*регуля́рный*) regular; ~**ьные черты́ лица́** regular features

прави́тел|ь, я *m.* ruler

прави́тельственн|ый *adj.* governmental; government; ~**ое учрежде́ние** government establishment

✓ **прави́тельств|о, а** *nt.* government

пра́в|ить¹, лю, ишь *impf.* (+ *i.*) to rule (over), govern

пра́в|ить², лю, ишь *impf.* to correct; **п. корректу́ру** (*typ.*) to read, correct proofs

пра́вк|а, и *f.* correcting; **п. корректу́ры** (*typ.*) proofreading

правле́ни|е, я *nt.* **1** (*де́йствие*) government; **фо́рма** ~**я** form of government **2** (*о́рган*) board, governing body

пра́внук, а *m.* great-grandson

пра́внучк|а, и *f.* great-granddaughter

✓ **пра́в|о, а,** *pl.* ~**а́** *nt.* **1** (*нау́ка*) law; **гражда́нское п.** civil law; **уголо́вное п.** criminal law **2** (*свобо́да*) right; (**води́тельские**) ~**а́** driving licence (BrE), driver's license (AmE); **п. го́лоса,**

избира́тельное п. the vote, suffrage; ~**а́ челове́ка** human rights; **по** ~**у** by rights; **име́ть п.** (**на** + *a.*) to have the right (to), be entitled (to)

✓ **правове́р|ный,** ~**ен,** ~**на** *adj.* (*relig.*) orthodox

✓ **правов|о́й** *adj.* legal; lawful; ~**о́е госуда́рство** (*pol.*) state based on the rule of law

правозащи́тник, а *m.* human rights activist

правозащи́тни|ца, цы *f. of* ▶ **правозащи́тник**

правоме́р|ный, ~**ен,** ~**на** *adj.* (*де́йствие, посту́пок*) lawful, rightful; (*вопро́с, сомне́ние*) legitimate

правомо́ч|ный, ~**ен,** ~**на** *adj.* competent, authorized

правонаруше́ни|е, я *nt.* infringement of the law, offence

правонаруши́тел|ь, я *m.* offender

правоохрани́тельн|ый *adj.* law enforcement; ~**ые о́рганы** law enforcement agencies

правописа́ни|е, я *nt.* spelling, orthography

правопоря́д|ок, ка *m.* law and order

правосла́ви|е, я *nt.* (*relig.*) Orthodoxy

✓ **правосла́вн|ый** *adj.* (*relig.*) orthodox; ~**ая це́рковь** Orthodox Church; (*as n.* **п.,** ~**ого,** *f.* ~**ая,** ~**ой**) member of the Orthodox Church

правосу́ди|е, я *nt.* justice

правот|а́, ы́ *f.* rightness; (*law*) innocence

✓ **пра́в|ый¹** *adj.* **1** (*по направле́нию*) right; right-hand; (*naut.*) starboard; ~**ая рука́** (*fig.*) right-hand man **2** (*pol.*) right-wing, right; ~**ая па́ртия** party of the right

✓ **пра́в|ый²,** ~, ~**а́,** ~**о** *adj.* right, correct; **вы не совсе́м** ~**ы** you are not quite right

Пра́г|а, и *f.* Prague

прагмати́зм, а *m.* pragmatism

прагмати́ческий *adj.* pragmatic

пра́дед, а *m.* **1** great-grandfather **2** (*in pl.*) ancestors, forefathers

прадеду́шк|а, и *m. dim. of* ▶ **пра́дед 1**

✓ **пра́здник, а** *m.* **1** (public) holiday; (*религио́зный*) (religious) feast, festival; **по** ~**ам** on high days and holidays **2** (*день ра́дости, торжества́*) festive occasion; **по слу́чаю** ~**а** to celebrate the occasion

пра́здничн|ый *adj.* holiday; festive; **п. день** holiday; ~**ое настрое́ние** festive mood

пра́здн|овать, ую *impf.* (*of* ▶ **отпра́здновать**) to celebrate

пра́здн|ый, ~**ен,** ~**на** *adj.* idle, inactive; empty; ~**ное любопы́тство** idle curiosity

✓ **пра́кти|ка, и** *f.* **1** practice; **на** ~**е** in practice; **вам не хвата́ет разгово́рной** ~**и** you need more conversational practice **2** (*фо́рма обуче́ния*) practical work **3** (*рабо́та врача́, юри́ста*) practice

практика́нт, а *m.* trainee

практика́нт|ка, ки *f. of* ▶ **практика́нт**

практик|ова́ть, у́ю *impf.* **1** to practise (BrE), practice (AmE) **2** (*о враче́, юри́сте*) to practise (BrE), practice (AmE)

✓ key word

П

практик|ова́ться, у́юсь *impf.* **1** (в + *p.*) to practise (BrE), practice (AmE); **п. в игре́ на скри́пке** to practise the violin **2** *pass. of* ▶ **практикова́ть**; **э́тот приём бо́льше не ~у́ется** this method is no longer used

⚹ **практи́ческ|ий** *adj.* practical; **~ие заня́тия** practical training

практи́ч|ный, ~ен, ~на *adj.* practical

прах, а (*no pl.*) *m.* **1** (*liter., пыль*) dust, earth; **обрати́ть в п., пове́ргнуть в п.** to reduce to dust/ashes **2** (*rhet., уме́ршего*) ashes, remains; **мир ~у его́** may he rest in peace

пра́чечн|ая, ой *f.* laundry; **п. самообслу́живания** (*автомати́ческая*) launderette

пра́чк|а, и *f.* laundress

пращ|а́, и́, *g. pl.* **~е́й** *f.* sling (*weapon*)

пре... [1] *adj. pref.* (*indicating superl. degree*) very, most, exceedingly

пре... [2] *vbl. pref.* (*indicating action in extreme degree or superior measure*) sur-, over-, out- (*cf.* ▶ **пере...**)

пребыва́ни|е, я *nt.* stay; **ме́сто постоя́нного ~я** permanent residence; **п. в до́лжности, п. на посту́** tenure/period of office

превали́р|овать, ую *impf.* (**над** + *i.*) to prevail (over)

превзо|йти́, йду́, йдёшь, *past* **~шёл, ~шла́** *pf.* (*of* ▶ **превосходи́ть**) (в + *p.* or + *i.*) to surpass (in); to excel (in); **п. все ожида́ния** to exceed all expectations

превозмога́|ть, ю *impf. of* ▶ **превозмо́чь**

превозмо́|чь, гу́, ~жешь, ~гут, *past* **~г, ~гла́** *pf.* (*of* ▶ **превозмога́ть**) to overcome, surmount

превознес|ти́, у́, ёшь, *past* **~, ~ла́** *pf.* (*of* ▶ **превозноси́ть**) to extol

превозно|си́ть, шу́, ~сишь *impf. of* ▶ **превознести́**

превосхо|ди́ть, жу́, ~дишь *impf. of* ▶ **превзойти́**

превосхо́д|ный, ~ен, ~на *adj.* **1** superb, outstanding **2** **~ная сте́пень** (gram.) superlative degree

превосхо́дств|о, а *nt.* superiority

превра|ти́ть, щу́, ти́шь *pf.* (*of* ▶ **превраща́ть**) (в + *a.*) to turn (to, into), convert (into); **п. в ка́мень** to turn to stone

превра|ти́ться, щу́сь, ти́шься *pf.* (*of* ▶ **превраща́ться**) (в + *a.*) to turn (into), change (into)

превра́т|ный, ~ен, ~на *adj.* wrong, false

превраща́|ть, ю *impf. of* ▶ **преврати́ть**

превраща́|ться, юсь *impf. of* ▶ **преврати́ться**

превраще́ни|е, я *nt.* transformation, conversion

превы́|сить, шу, сишь *pf.* (*of* ▶ **превыша́ть**) to exceed; **п. полномо́чия** to exceed one's authority

⚹ **превыша́|ть, ю** *impf. of* ▶ **превы́сить**

превы́ше *adv.* far above; **п. всего́** above all

прегра́д|а, ы *f.* barrier; obstacle

прегра|ди́ть, жу́, ди́шь *pf.* (*of* ▶ **прегражда́ть**) to bar, obstruct, block; **п. путь кому́-н.** to bar sb's way

прегражда́|ть, ю *impf. of* ▶ **прегради́ть**

преда|ва́ть, ю́, ёшь *impf. of* ▶ **преда́ть**

преда|ва́ться, ю́сь, ёшься *impf. of* ▶ **преда́ться**

пре́данност|ь, и *f.* devotion

пре́дан|ный, ~, ~а *p.p.p. of* ▶ **преда́ть** *and* (**~, ~на**) *adj.* (+ *d.*) devoted (to); (*делу*) dedicated (to); **п. друг** staunch friend

преда́тел|ь, я *m.* traitor

преда́тель|ница, ницы *f. of* ▶ **преда́тель**

преда́тельский *adj.* treacherous (also fig.)

преда́тельств|о, а *nt.* treachery, betrayal

пре|да́ть, да́м, да́шь, да́ст, дади́м, дади́те, даду́т, *past* **~дал, ~дала́, ~дало** *pf.* (*of* ▶ **предава́ть**) **1** (+ *d.*) (*отда́ть*) to hand over (to), commit (to); **п. забве́нию** to consign to oblivion; **п. земле́** to commit to the earth **2** (*измени́ть*) to betray

пре|да́ться, да́мся, да́шься, да́стся, дади́мся, дади́тесь, даду́тся, *past* **~да́лся, ~дала́сь** *pf.* (*of* ▶ **предава́ться**) (+ *d.*) to give oneself up (to); **п. отча́янию** to give way to despair

предвари́тельно *adv.* in advance, beforehand

⚹ **предвари́тель|ный, ~ен, ~на** *adj.* (*замеча́ния, рабо́та*) preliminary; (*прода́жа, зака́з*) advance; **п. пока́з** preview; **~ное усло́вие** precondition

предвеща́|ть, ю *impf.* (*no pf.*) herald, presage, portend; **ту́чи ~ли грозу́** the clouds heralded a storm

предвзя́т|ый, ~, ~а *adj.* prejudiced, biased

предви́дени|е, я *nt.* foresight; (*предсказа́ние*) prediction

предви́|деть, жу, дишь *impf.* (*no pf.*) to foresee; (*предсказа́ть*) to predict

предвкуша́|ть, ю *impf.* to look forward (to)

предвкуше́ни|е, я *nt.* anticipation (*of something pleasant*); **в ~и** (+ *g.*) in anticipation (of)

предводи́тел|ь, я *m.* leader

предвое́нный *adj.* pre-war

предвосхи́|тить, щу, тишь *pf.* (*of* ▶ **предвосхища́ть**) to anticipate

предвосхища́|ть, ю *impf. of* ▶ **предвосхи́тить**

предвы́борн|ый *adj.* (pre-)election; **~ая кампа́ния** election campaign

предго́р|ье, ья, *g. pl.* **~ий** *nt.* (*often in pl.*) foothills

⚹ **преде́л, а** *m.* limit; bound; **в ~ах** (+ *g.*) within, within the limits (of), within the bounds (of); **за ~ами** (+ *g.*) outside, beyond; **в ~ах досяга́емости** within reach

преде́л|ьный *adj.* **1** *adj. of* ▶ **преде́л**; **п. во́зраст** age limit; **п. срок** time limit, deadline **2** (*кра́йний*) maximum, utmost; **с ~ьной я́сностью** with the utmost clarity

п

предзнаменова́ни|е, я *nt.* omen, augury

предисло́ви|е, я *nt.* preface, foreword

⚬ **предлага́|ть**, ю *impf. of* ▸ **предложи́ть**

предло́г¹, а *m.* pretext; **под ~ом** (+ *g.*) on the pretext (of)

предло́г², а *m.* (gram.) preposition

⚬ **предложе́ни|е¹**, я *nt.* **1** (*по́мощи*) offer; (*иде́я*) suggestion, proposition; (*бра́ка*) proposal (of marriage); **сде́лать п. кому́-н.** to propose (marriage) to sb **2** (*на заседа́нии*) proposal, motion; **внести́ п.** to introduce a motion; **отклони́ть п.** to turn down a proposal **3** (econ.) supply; **зако́н спро́са и ~я** law of supply and demand

предложе́ни|е², я *nt.* (gram.) sentence

⚬ **предлож|и́ть**, у́, **~ишь** *pf.* (*of* ▸ **предлага́ть**) **1** (*по́мощь, услу́ги*) to offer **2** (*реше́ние, прое́кт*) to propose; to suggest; **мы ~и́ли ей обрати́ться к врачу́** we suggested that she should see a doctor **3** (*зада́ть*) to put, set; **п. зада́чу** to set a problem **4** (*потре́бовать*) to order, require; **им ~и́ли освободи́ть кварти́ру** they have been ordered to vacate their apartment

предме́ст|ье, ья, *g. pl.* **~ий** *nt.* suburb

⚬ **предме́т**, а *m.* **1** object; (*вещь*) article, item; (*in pl.*) goods; **~ы пе́рвой необходи́мости** necessities **2** (*те́ма*) subject, topic, theme; (+ *g.*) object (of); **п. спо́ра** point at issue **3** (*в шко́ле*) subject; (*цель*) object; **на п.** (+ *g.*) with the object (of)

⚬ **предназнача́|ть**, а́ю *impf. of* ▸ **предназна́чить**

предназна́ч|ить, у, ишь *pf.* (*of* ▸ **предназнача́ть**) (**для** + *g. or* **на** + *a.*) to intend (for); **мы ~или э́ти де́ньги для поку́пки автомоби́ля** we set aside this money to buy a car

преднаме́рен|ный, ~, **~на** *adj.* premeditated; deliberate

пре́д|ок, ка *m.* forefather, ancestor; (*in pl.*) forbears

предопределе́ни|е, я *nt.* predestination

предоста́в|ить, лю, ишь *pf.* (*of* ▸ **предоставля́ть**) **1** (+ *d. and inf.*) (*дать пра́во*) to let; to leave; **нам ~или сами́м реши́ть де́ло** we were left to decide the matter for ourselves **2** (*дать*) to give, grant; **п. креди́т** to give credit; **п. пра́во** to concede a right; **п. возмо́жность** to afford an opportunity, give a chance

⚬ **предоставле́ни|е**, я *nt.* granting

⚬ **предоставля́|ть**, ю *impf. of* ▸ **предоста́вить**

предостерега́|ть, ю *impf. of* ▸ **предостере́чь**

предостереже́ни|е, я *nt.* warning, caution

предостере́|чь, гу́, жёшь, гу́т, *past* **~г**, **~гла́** *pf.* (*of* ▸ **предостерега́ть**) (**от** + *g.*) to warn (against), caution (against)

предосторо́жност|ь, и *f.* **1** (*осторо́жное поведе́ние*) caution; **ме́ры ~и** precautionary measures, precautions **2** (*ме́ра*) precaution

предотврати́ть, щу́, ти́шь *pf.* (*of* ▸ **предотвраща́ть**) to prevent, avert; to stave off; **п. войну́** to avert a war; **п. опа́сность** to stave off, avert danger

предотвраща́|ть, ю *impf. of* ▸ **предотврати́ть**

предохрани́тел|ь, я *m.* guard, safety device; (elec.) fuse

предохрани́тельный *adj.* (tech.) safety; protective; **п. кла́пан** safety valve

предохран|и́ть, ю́, и́шь *pf.* (*of* ▸ **предохраня́ть**) (**от** + *g.*) to protect (from, against)

предохран|и́ться, ю́сь, и́шься *pf.* (*of* ▸ **предохраня́ться**) (**от** + *g.*) to protect oneself (from, against)

предохран|я́ть, я́ю *impf. of* ▸ **предохрани́ть**

предохран|я́ться, я́юсь *impf. of* ▸ **предохрани́ться**

предписа́ни|е, я *nt.* order, injunction; (*in pl.*) directions, instructions; (med.) prescription; **по ~ю врача́** on doctor's orders

предпле́ч|ье, ья, *g. pl.* **~ий** *nt.* (anat.) forearm

предполага́емый *pres. part. pass. of* ▸ **предполага́ть** *and adj.* proposed

⚬ **предполага́|ть**, ю *impf.* **1** *impf. of* ▸ **предположи́ть** **2** (*impf. only*) (*намерева́ться*) to intend, propose **3** (*impf. only*) (*име́ть свои́м усло́вием*) to presuppose

предполага́|ться, ется *impf.* **1** to be planned; **сва́дьба ~лась ле́том** the wedding was planned for the summer **2** (*impers.*): **~ется** it is proposed, it is intended

предположе́ни|е, я *nt.* supposition, assumption

предположи́тельно *adv.* **1** hypothetically; supposedly, presumably **2** (*in parenthesis*) (*вероя́тно*) probably

предположи́тельный *adj.* (*да́та, результа́т*) hypothetical; (*дохо́д*) estimated, anticipated

предполож|и́ть, у́, **~ишь** *pf.* (*of* ▸ **предполага́ть** 1) to suppose, assume; **~и́м, что он опозда́л на по́езд** (let us) suppose he missed the train

предпосле́дний *adj.* penultimate, last but one, next to last; one from the bottom (*on list*)

предпосы́лк|а, и *f.* **1** prerequisite, precondition **2** (phil.) premise

предпоч|е́сть, ту́, тёшь, *past* **~ёл**, **~ла́** *pf.* (*of* ▸ **предпочита́ть**) (+ *a. and d.*) to prefer; **п. говя́дину бара́нине** to prefer beef to lamb; **я ~ёл бы идти́ пешко́м** I would rather walk; (+ *inf.*) to choose to; **он ~ёл уйти́** he chose to leave

предпочита́|ть, ю *impf. of* ▸ **предпоче́сть**

предпочте́ни|е, я *nt.* preference; **отда́ть п.** (+ *d.*) to show a preference (for), give preference (to)

предпочти́тель|ный, **~ен**, **~ьна** *adj.* preferable

⚬ key word

предприи́мчивост|ь, и *f.* enterprise

предприи́мчив|ый, ~, ~а *adj.* enterprising

⚲ **предпринима́тел|ь**, я *m.* entrepreneur; businessman

предпринима́тельств|о, а (*no pl.*) *nt.* enterprise; **свобо́дное п.** free enterprise

предпринима́|ть, ю *impf. of* ▶ **предприня́ть**

предпри|ня́ть, му́, ~мешь, *past* ~**ня́л,** ~**няла́,** ~**няло** *pf.* (*of* ▶ **предпринима́ть**) to undertake; (*mil.,* etc.) to launch; **п. шаги́** to take steps

⚲ **предприя́ти|е, я** *nt.* **1** (*предпринятое дело*) undertaking, enterprise; (*инициатива*) venture; **риско́ванное п.** risky undertaking, venture **2** (econ.) enterprise, concern, business; (*завод, фабрика*) works; **совме́стное п.** joint venture

предрасположе́нност|ь, и *f.* (к + *d.*) predisposition (to)

предрассу́д|ок, ка *m.* prejudice

предрека́|ть, ю *impf. of* ▶ **предре́чь**

предре́|чь, ку́, чёшь, ку́т, *past* ~**к,** ~**кла́** *pf.* (*of* ▶ **предрека́ть**) to foretell

предреш|а́ть, а́ю *impf. of* ▶ **предреши́ть**

предреш|и́ть, у́, и́шь *pf.* (*of* ▶ **предреша́ть**) to predetermine

⚲ **председа́тел|ь, я** *m.* (*собрания, правления*) chairman; (*общества*) president

предсказа́ни|е, я *nt.* prediction

предска|за́ть, жу́, ~жешь *pf.* (*of* ▶ **предска́зывать**) to foretell, predict

предска́зыва|ть, ю *impf. of* ▶ **предсказа́ть**

⚲ **представи́тел|ь, я** *m.* **1** representative; (*должностное лицо*) (+ *g.*) spokesman (for); **полномо́чный п.** plenipotentiary **2** (bot., etc.) specimen

представи́тель|ница, ницы *f. of* ▶ **представи́тель** 1

представи́тельств|о, а *nt.* **1** representation, representing **2** (*collect.*) representation, representatives; **торго́вое п.** trade mission

⚲ **предста́в|ить, лю, ишь** *pf.* (*of* ▶ **представля́ть** 1) **1** (*причинить*) to present; **п. интере́с** to be of interest **2** (*предъявить*) to produce, submit; **п. доказа́тельства** to produce evidence **3** (+ *a. and d.*) (*познакомить*) to introduce (to), present (to) **4** : **п. (себе́)** to imagine **5** (*изобразить*) to represent, display

предста́в|иться, люсь, ишься *pf.* (*of* ▶ **представля́ться**) **1** (*возникнуть*) to present itself, arise; ~**ился слу́чай пое́хать в Москву́** a chance arose to go to Moscow **2** (+ *d.*) (*познакомиться*) to introduce oneself (to)

⚲ **представле́ни|е, я** *nt.* **1** introduction; **п. но́вого сотру́дника** introduction of a new colleague **2** (theatr.) performance **3** (psych., math.) representation **4** (*понимание*) idea, notion, conception; **дать п.** (о + *p.*) to give an idea (of); **я не име́ю ни мале́йшего ~я** I have not the faintest idea

⚲ **представля́|ть, ю** *impf.* **1** *impf. of*

▶ **предста́вить 2** (*impf. only*) (*страну, интересы*) to represent **3** (*являться*) to represent, be, constitute; **п. угро́зу** to represent a threat **4**: **п. собо́й** (*являться*) to represent, be; to constitute; **э́то ~ет собо́й исключе́ние** this constitutes an exception

представля́|ться, юсь *impf. of*

▶ **предста́виться**

предсто|я́ть, и́т *impf.* (+ *d.*) to be in prospect (for), lie ahead (of), be at hand; to be in store (for); ~**я́ла суро́вая зима́** a hard winter lay ahead; **нам ~и́т столкну́ться со мно́гими неприя́тностями** we are in for a lot of trouble

предстоя́|щий *pres. part. of* ▶ **предстоя́ть** *and adj.* forthcoming; impending; ~**щие вы́боры** the forthcoming elections

предубежде́ни|е, я *nt.* prejudice, bias

предубежде́нный, ~**ён,** ~**ена́** *adj.* (**про́тив** + *g.*) prejudiced, biased (against)

предупреди́тельный *adj.* (*меры*) preventive, precautionary

предупре|ди́ть, жу́, ди́шь *pf.* (*of* ▶ **предупрежда́ть**) **1** (о + *p.*) to let know beforehand (about), notify in advance (about), warn (about); to give notice (of, about); **п. об увольне́нии за неде́лю** to give a week's notice (of dismissal) **2** (*предотвратить*) to prevent, avert; **п. ава́рию** to prevent an accident

предупрежда́|ть, ю *impf. of* ▶ **предупреди́ть**

предупрежде́ни|е, я *nt.* **1** (*извещение*) notice; notification **2** (*предотвращение*) prevention **3** (*предостережение*) warning; (*взыскание*) caution

⚲ **предусма́трива|ть, ю** *impf. of*

▶ **предусмотре́ть**

предусмотр|е́ть, ю́, ~ишь *pf.* (*of* ▶ **предусма́тривать**) (*предвидеть*) to envisage, foresee; (*обеспечить*) to provide (for), make provision (for)

предусмотри́тел|ьный, ~**ен,** ~**ьна** *adj.* prudent; far-sighted

предчу́встви|е, я *nt.* presentiment; (*дурного*) foreboding, premonition

предчу́вств|овать, ую *impf.* to have a presentiment (of, about), have a premonition (of, about)

предше́ственник, а *m.* predecessor; forerunner, precursor

предше́ственни|ца, цы *f. of*

▶ **предше́ственник**

предше́ств|овать, ую *impf.* (+ *d.*) to go in front (of); to precede; **её сме́рти** ~**овала дли́тельная боле́знь** her death was preceded by a long illness

предъяв|и́ть, лю́, ~ишь *pf.* (*of* ▶ **предъявля́ть**) **1** to show, produce, present; **п. биле́т** to show one's ticket; **п. доказа́тельства** to produce evidence, present proofs **2** (law, etc.) to bring (forward); **ему́ ~и́ли обвине́ние в поджо́ге** he is charged with arson

предъявля́|ть, ю *impf. of* ▶ **предъяви́ть**

п

 предыду́щ|ий *adj.* previous, preceding; (*as nt. n.* ∼ее, ∼его) the foregoing
прее́мник, а *m.* successor
прее́мственност|ь, и *f.* succession; (*тради́ций, культу́ры*) continuity
 пре́жде **1** (*adv.*) (*opp.* ▶ пото́м) (*снача́ла*) before; first; **п. чем** (*as conj.*) before **2** (*adv.*) (*opp.* ▶ тепе́рь) (*ра́ньше*) formerly, in former times; before **3** (*prep. + g.*) before; **они́ пришли́ п. нас** they arrived before us; **п. всего́** first of all, to begin with; (*са́мое ва́жное*) first and foremost
преждевре́менно *adv.* prematurely; (*умере́ть*) before one's time
преждевре́мен|ный, ∼ and ∼ен, ∼на *adj.* premature, untimely; ∼ные ро́ды (*med.*) premature birth
 пре́жний *adj.* previous, former
презента́ци|я, и *f.* presentation; launch; **п. кни́ги** book launch
презервати́в, а *m.* condom
 президе́нт, а *m.* président
президе́нт|ский *adj. of* ▶ президе́нт; ∼ские вы́боры presidential elections
президе́нтств|о, а *nt.* presidency
прези́диум, а *m.* presidium
презира́|ть, ю *impf.* to despise, hold in contempt
презре́ни|е, я *nt.* contempt, scorn
презри́тел|ьный, ∼ен, ∼ьна *adj.* contemptuous, scornful
преиму́щественно *adv.* mainly, chiefly, predominantly
 преиму́ществ|о, а *nt.* advantage; **получи́ть п.** (*пе́ред + i.*) to gain an advantage (over)
прейскура́нт, а *m.* price list
преклони́|ться, ю́сь, и́шься *pf.* (*of* ▶ преклоня́ться) (*пе́ред + i.*) to admire, worship
преклон|я́ться, я́юсь *impf. of* ▶ преклони́ться
 прекра́сно *adv.* **1** excellently; (*знать, понима́ть*) perfectly well; **они́ п. зна́ют, что э́то запрещено́** they know perfectly well that it is forbidden **2** (*as int.*) excellent!; splendid!
 прекра́с|ный, ∼ен, ∼на *adj.* **1** (*краси́вый*) beautiful, fine; **в оди́н п. день** one fine day, once upon a time; (*as nt. n.* ∼ное, ∼ного) the beautiful **2** (*отли́чный*) excellent, capital, first-rate
прекра|ти́ть, щу́, ти́шь *pf.* (*of* ▶ прекраща́ть) to stop; (*положи́ть коне́ц*) to put a stop (to); (*отноше́ния*) to break off; **п. войну́** to end the war
прекра|ти́ться, ти́тся *pf.* (*of* ▶ прекраща́ться) to cease, end
прекраща́|ть, ю, ет *impf. of* ▶ прекрати́ть
прекраща́|ться, ется *impf. of* ▶ прекрати́ться
прекраще́ни|е, я *nt.* stopping, cessation; **п. вое́нных де́йствий** cessation of hostilities;

 п. огня́ ceasefire
преле́ст|ный, ∼ен, ∼на *adj.* charming, delightful, lovely
пре́лест|ь, и *f.* charm, delight; **кака́я п.!** how lovely!
преломле́ни|е, я *nt.* **1** (*phys.*) refraction **2** (*fig.*) interpretation, construction
пре́л|ый, ∼, ∼а *adj.* rotten, fusty
прель|сти́ться, щу́сь, сти́шься *pf.* (*of* ▶ прельща́ться) (*+ i.*) to be attracted (by); to be tempted (by), fall (for)
прельща́|ться, юсь *impf. of* ▶ прельсти́ться
прелюбодея́ни|е, я *nt.* adultery
прелю́ди|я, и *f.* (*mus., also fig.*) prelude
 пре́ми|я, и *f.* **1** (*победи́телю*) prize; (*рабо́тнику*) bonus; **Но́белевская п.** Nobel Prize; **п. О́скар** Oscar **2** (*fin., в страхова́нии*) premium; **страхова́я п.** insurance premium
премье́р|а, ы *f.* (*theatr.*) premiere, opening night
премье́р-мини́стр, а *m.* prime minister, premier
пренебрега́|ть, ю *impf. of* ▶ пренебре́чь
пренебреже́ни|е, я *nt.* **1** (*презре́ние*) scorn, contempt, disdain **2** (*невнима́ние*) neglect, disregard; **п. свои́ми обя́занностями** neglect of one's duties, dereliction of duty
пренебрежи́тел|ьный, ∼ен, ∼ьна *adj.* scornful, disdainful
пренебре́|чь, гу́, жёшь, гу́т, *past* ∼́г, ∼гла́ *pf.* (*of* ▶ пренебрега́ть) (*+ i.*) **1** (*презре́ть*) to scorn, despise; **п. сове́том** to scorn advice **2** (*обя́занностями*) to neglect, disregard
преоблада́|ть, ет *impf.* to predominate; to prevail
преобража́|ть, ю *impf. of* ▶ преобрази́ть
преобража́|ться, юсь *impf. of* ▶ преобрази́ться
преобра|зи́ть, жу́, зи́шь *pf.* (*of* ▶ преобража́ть) to transform
преобра|зи́ться, жу́сь, зи́шься *pf.* (*of* ▶ преобража́ться) to be transformed
преобразова́ни|е, я *nt.* **1** (*в что-н. друго́е*) transformation **2** (*рефо́рма*) reform; reorganization
преобраз|ова́ть, у́ю *pf.* (*of* ▶ преобразо́вывать) **1** to transform (also phys., tech.) **2** (*реформи́ровать*) to reform; (*реорганизова́ть*) to reorganize
преобразо́outwa|ть, ю *impf. of* ▶ преобразова́ть
преодолева́|ть, ю *impf. of* ▶ преодоле́ть
преодоле́|ть, ю *pf.* (*of* ▶ преодолева́ть) to overcome, get over; **п. препя́тствия** to surmount obstacles; **п. тру́дности** to overcome difficulties
 препара́т, а *m.* (*chem., med.*) preparation
препина́ни|е, я *nt.*: **зна́ки** ∼я (*gram.*) punctuation marks
препира́|ться, юсь *impf.* (*с + i.*) to wrangle (with), squabble (with)
 преподава́тел|ь, я *m.* teacher; (*ву́за*)

lecturer, instructor

преподава́тель|ница, ницы *f.* (infml) *of*
▶ **преподава́тель**

препода|ва́ть, ю́, ёшь *impf.* to teach

преподнес|ти́, у́, ёшь, *past* ~, ~ла́ *pf.* (*of*
▶ **преподноси́ть**) (+ *a. and d.*) to present
(with); (*све́дения*) to convey; (*сюрприз*)
to give

преподно|си́ть, шу́, ~сишь *impf. of*
▶ **преподнести́**

препя́тстви|е, я *nt.* **1** obstacle, impediment,
hindrance **2** (sport) obstacle; **бег с ~ями,
ска́чки с ~ями** steeplechase; **взять п.** to
clear an obstacle; (fig.) to clear a hurdle

препя́тств|овать, ую *impf.* (*of*
▶ **воспрепя́тствовать**) (+ *d.*) to hinder,
impede; to stand in the way (of)

прерв|а́ть, у́, ёшь, *past* ~а́л, ~ала́, ~а́ло
pf. (*of* ▶ **прерыва́ть**) (*прекрати́ть*) to
break off, sever; (*переби́ть*) to interrupt,
cut short; **п. молча́ние** to break a silence;
п. ора́тора to interrupt a speaker; **нас
~а́ли** we have been cut off (*while on the
telephone*)

прерв|а́ться, ётся, *past* ~а́лся, ~ала́сь,
~а́ло́сь *pf.* (*of* ▶ **прерыва́ться**)
1 (*приостанови́ться*) to be interrupted;
(*оборва́ться*) to be broken off **2** (*о го́лосе,
от волне́ния*) to break

пререка́|ться, юсь *impf.* (**с** + *i.*) to argue
(with)

прерогати́в|а, ы *f.* prerogative

прерыва́|ть, ю, ет *impf. of* ▶ **прерва́ть**

прерыва́|ться, ется *impf. of* ▶ **прерва́ться**

преры́вист|ый, ~, ~а *adj.* (*дыха́ние, звук*)
intermittent; (*ли́ния*) broken, dotted

пресека́|ть, ю, ешь *impf. of* ▶ **пресе́чь**

пресе́|чь, ку́, чёшь, кут́, *past* ~к, ~кла́
pf. (*of* ▶ **пресека́ть**) to cut short, stop; **п. в
ко́рне** to nip in the bud

пресле́довани|е, я *nt.* **1** (*пого́ня*) pursuit
2 (*притесне́ние*) persecution, victimization;
ма́ния ~я persecution complex **3** (law):
суде́бное п. prosecution

пресле́дователь, я *m.* **1** (*тот, кто
го́нится за кем-н.*) pursuer **2** (*тот, кто
притесня́ет кого́-н.*) persecutor

пресле́д|овать, ую *impf.* **1** (*врага́, зве́ря*)
to pursue; (fig., *о мы́слях, чу́вствах*) to haunt
2 (fig., *интере́сы, за́мысел, же́нщину*)
to pursue; **п. цель** to pursue an end
3 (*притесни́ть*) to persecute **4** (law) to
prosecute

пресмыка́ющ|ееся, егося *nt.* reptile

пресново́дный *adj.* freshwater

пре́с|ный, ~ен, ~на́, ~но *adj.* **1** (*вода́*)
fresh, sweet **2** (*хлеб*) unleavened **3** (*пи́ща*)
flavourless (BrE), flavorless (AmE), tasteless;
(fig.) insipid, vapid

пресс, а *m.* press

пре́сс|а, ы *f.* (collect.) the press; **ло́жа ~ы**
press gallery

пресс-конфере́нци|я, и *f.* press conference

пресс|ова́ть, у́ю *impf.* (*of* ▶ **спрессова́ть**)
to press, compress

пресс-рели́з, а *m.* press release

пресс-секрета́р|ь, я́ *m.* press secretary

пресс-це́нтр, а *m.* press office

престаре́л|ый *adj.* aged, old; **дом ~ых** old
people's home

прести́ж, а *m.* prestige

прести́ж|ный, ~ен, ~на *adj.* prestigious

престо́л, а *m.* **1** throne; **взойти́ на п.** to
come to the throne; **отре́чься от ~а** to
abdicate **2** (eccl.) altar

✎ **преступле́ни|е, я** *nt.* crime, offence

престу́пник, а *m.* criminal; **вое́нный п.** war
criminal

престу́пни|ца, цы *f. of* ▶ **престу́пник**

престу́пност|ь, и *f.* (collect.) crime;
организо́ванная п. organized crime

престу́п|ный, ~ен, ~на *adj.* criminal

претенде́нт, а *m.* (**на** + *a.*)
pretender, claimant (to); (*на насле́дство*)
claimant (to); (*на до́лжность*) candidate
(for); (sport) contender

претенде́нт|ка, ки *f. of* ▶ **претенде́нт**

претенд|ова́ть, у́ю *impf.* (**на** + *a.*) (*на
престо́л, на остроу́мие*) to have pretensions
(to); (*на насле́дство*) to lay claim (to); (*на
до́лжность*) to aspire (to); **он ~у́ет на
пост мини́стра** he aspires to the position of
minister

прете́нзи|я, и *f.* **1** (*заявле́ние прав*) claim;
заявля́ть ~ю (**на** + *a.*) to claim, lay claim
(to), make claims (on) **2** (*на остроу́мие*)
pretension; **быть в ~и на кого́-н.** to have a
grievance against sb **3** (*жа́лоба*) complaint

претенцио́зный, ~ен, ~на *adj.*
pretentious, affected

претерпева́|ть, ю *impf. of* ▶ **претерпе́ть**

претерп|е́ть, лю́, ~ишь *pf.* (*of*
▶ **претерпева́ть**) (*подве́ргнуться*) to
undergo; (*вы́терпеть*) to suffer, endure;
план ~е́л измене́ния the plan has
undergone changes

преувеличе́ни|е, я *nt.* exaggeration;
overstatement

преувели́чива|ть, ю *impf. of* ▶ **преувели́чить**

преувели́ч|ить, у, ишь *pf.* (*of*
▶ **преувели́чивать**) to exaggerate; to
overstate

преуменьш|а́ть, а́ю *impf. of* ▶ **преуме́ньшить**

преуме́ньш|ить, у, ишь *pf.* (*of*
▶ **преуменьша́ть**) (*предста́вить ме́ньшим*)
to underestimate, minimize; (*предста́вить
ме́нее ва́жным*) to belittle; to understate;
п. опа́сность to underestimate the danger

преуспева́|ть, ю *impf.* **1** *impf. of* ▶ **преуспе́ть**
2 (*impf. only*) to thrive, prosper, flourish

преуспева́ющий *pres. part. act. of*
▶ **преуспева́ть** *and adj.* successful,
prosperous

преусп|е́ть, ю *pf.* (*of* ▶ **преуспева́ть** 1)
(**в** + *p.*) to succeed (in), be successful (in);
п. в жи́зни to get on in life

п

прецеде́нт, а *m.* precedent

☞ **при** *prep.* + *p.* **1** (*около*) by, at; (*в присутствии*) in the presence of; **би́тва при Ватерло́о** the Battle of Waterloo; **письмо́ бы́ло подпи́сано при мне** the letter was signed in my presence **2** (*под эги́дой*) attached to, affiliated to, under the auspices of (*usu. not translated*); **при магази́не есть кафе́** there is a cafe attached to the shop **3** (*с собо́й*) by, with; about, on; **у него́ не́ было при себе́ де́нег** he had no money on him **4** (*при нали́чии*) with; (*несмотря́ на*) for, notwithstanding; **при таки́х тала́нтах он далеко́ пойдёт** with such talent he will go far; **при уча́стии** (+ *g.*) with the participation (of); **при всём том** with it all, moreover, for all that; **при чём тут я?** what has it to do with me? **5** (*во вре́мя, в эпо́ху*) in the time of, in the days of; under (*sc. the rule of*); during; **при Ива́не Гро́зном** during the reign of, in the time of Ivan the Terrible **6** (*ука́зывает на обстоя́тельства*) by; **при све́те ла́мпы** by lamplight **7** (*когда́*) when; on; in case of; **при перехо́де че́рез у́лицу** when crossing the street; **при усло́вии(, что)** under the condition (that)

при...¹ *vbl. pref. indicating* **1** completion of action or motion up to given terminal point: **прие́хать** to arrive **2** action of attaching: **пристро́ить** to build on **3** direction of action towards speaker: **пригласи́ть** to invite **4** direction of action from above downward: **придави́ть** to press down **5** incompleteness or tentativeness of action: **приоткры́ть** to open slightly **6** exhaustiveness of action: **приучи́ть** to train

при...² *as pref. of nn. and adjs.* (esp. geog.) indicates juxtaposition or proximity: **приозе́рье** lakeside; **прибре́жный, примо́рский** coastal

приба́в|ить, лю, ишь *pf.* (*of* ► прибавля́ть) **1** (+ *a.* or *g.*) to add; **к пяти́ п. три** to add three to five; **п. (в ве́се)** to put on (weight) **2** (+ *g.*) (*увели́чить*) to increase; **п. ша́гу** to hasten one's steps

приба́в|иться, ится *pf.* (*of* ► прибавля́ться) to increase; (*о воде́*) to rise; (*о луне́*) to wax

прибавле́ни|е, я *nt.* addition; **п. семе́йства** addition to the family; **сказа́ть в п.** to say in addition, add

прибавля́|ть, ю, ет *impf. of* ► приба́вить

прибавля́|ться, ется *impf. of* ► приба́виться

прибалти́йский *adj.* Baltic (= *adjacent to the Baltic Sea, esp. of former Soviet republics*)

Приба́лтик|а, и *f.* the Baltic States (*esp. the former Soviet republics*)

прибега́|ть¹, ю *impf. of* ► прибе́гнуть

прибега́|ть², ю *impf. of* ► прибежа́ть

прибе́г|нуть, ну, нешь, *past* ~(нул), ~ла *pf.* (*of* ► прибега́ть¹) (к + *d.*) to resort (to), have resort (to); **п. к си́ле** to resort to force

прибе|жа́ть, гу́, жи́шь, гу́т *pf.* (*of* ► прибега́ть²) (*бего́м или в спе́шке*) to come running

☞ *key word*

прибе́жищ|е, а *nt.* refuge; **после́днее п.** (fig.) last resort; **найти́ п.** (в + *p.*) to take refuge (in)

прибега́|ть, ю *impf. of* ► прибере́чь

прибере́|чь, гу́, жёшь, гу́т, *past* ~г, ~гла́ *pf.* (*of* ► прибера́ть) to save up

прибива́|ть, ю *impf. of* ► приби́ть

прибира́|ть, ю *impf. of* ► прибра́ть

прибира́|ться, юсь *impf. of* ► прибра́ться

приб|и́ть, ью, ьёшь *pf.* (*of* ► прибива́ть) **1** (*гвоздя́ми*) to nail; **п. до́ску к стене́** to nail a board to a wall **2** (*usu. impers.*) (*волно́й, тече́нием*) to wash up; **труп** ~и́ло **к бе́регу** a body was washed ashore

приближа́|ть, ю *impf. of* ► прибли́зить

приближа́|ться, юсь *impf. of* ► прибли́зиться

приближе́ни|е, я *nt.* approach; approaching, drawing near

приблизи́тельно *adv.* approximately, roughly

приблизи́тел|ьный, ~ен, ~ьна *adj.* approximate, rough

прибли́|зить, жу, зишь *pf.* (*of* ► приближа́ть) **1** (*придви́нуть бли́же*) to bring nearer, move nearer; (*сде́лать бли́зким*) to bring closer **2** (*уско́рить*) to hasten, advance

прибли́|зиться, жусь, зишься *pf.* (*of* ► приближа́ться) (к + *d.*) to approach, draw near; to draw nearer (to), come nearer (to)

прибо́|й, я *m.* surf, breakers

☞ **прибо́р, а** *m.* **1** instrument, device, apparatus, appliance **2** (*компле́кт*) set; **бри́твенный п.** shaving things

при|бра́ть, беру́, берёшь, *past* ~бра́л, ~брала́, ~бра́ло *pf.* (*of* ► прибира́ть) (infml) **1** (*привести́ в поря́док*) to clear up, clean up, tidy (up); **п. ко́мнату, п. в ко́мнате** to do a room; **п. что-н. к рука́м** to lay one's hands on sth **2** (*убра́ть*) to put away

при|бра́ться, беру́сь, берёшься, *past* ~бра́лся, ~брала́сь, ~бра́ло́сь *pf.* (*of* ► прибира́ться) (infml) (*произвести́ убо́рку*) to tidy/clear/clean up; (*привести́ себя́ в поря́док*) to tidy oneself up; to get dressed up

прибре́ж|ный *adj.* **1** (*у бе́рега мо́ря*) coastal; ~**ая полоса́** coastal strip **2** (*у бе́рега реки́*) riverside

прибыва́|ть, ю *impf. of* ► прибы́ть

☞ **при́бы|ль, и** *f.* profit; **чи́стая п.** net profit

при́был|ьный, ~ен, ~ьна *adj.* profitable, lucrative

прибы́ти|е, я *nt.* arrival

при|бы́ть, бу́ду, бу́дешь, *past* ~был, ~была́, ~было *pf.* (*of* ► прибыва́ть) (*прийти́, прие́хать*) to arrive

прива́л, а *m.* **1** (*остано́вка*) halt, stop **2** (*ме́сто остано́вки*) stopping place

прива́рива|ть, ю *impf. of* ► привари́ть

привар|и́ть, ю́, ~ишь *pf.* (*of* ► прива́ривать) (к + *d.*) to weld on (to)

приватиза́ци|я, и *f.* privatization

приватизи́р|овать, ую *impf. and pf.* to privatize

привез|ти́, у́, ёшь, *past* ~, ~ла́ *pf. (of* ▸ **привози́ть**) to bring (*not on foot*); (*товар, почту*) to deliver

привере́длив|ый, ~, ~а *adj.* fussy, finicky

приве́ржен|ный, ~, ~а *adj.* (+ *d.*) attached (to), devoted (to)

ℰ **приве|сти́, ду́, дёшь**, *past* ~л, ~ла́ *pf.* (*of* ▸ **приводи́ть**, ▸ **вести́** 8) **1** to bring; (*о доро́ге*) to lead, take; **он** ~л **с собо́й неве́сту** he has brought his fiancée (with him) **2** (к + *d.*) (fig.) to lead (to), bring (to), result (in); **э́то к добру́ не** ~дёт no good will come of it **3** (в + *a.*) to put, set (*or translated by v. corresponding to n. governed by* в); **п. в бе́шенство** to throw into a rage, drive mad, madden; **п. в движе́ние, в де́йствие** to set in motion, set going; **п. в отча́яние** to reduce to despair; **п. в поря́док** to put in order, tidy (up); to arrange, fix **4** (*слова́, доказа́тельства*) to adduce, cite; **п. приме́р** to give an example

приве́т, а *m.* greeting(s); regards; **п.!** (infml) hi!; **переда́ть п.** to send one's regards

приве́тлив|ый, ~, ~а *adj.* friendly; affable; cordial

приве́тстви|е, я *nt.* **1** greeting, salutation **2** (*речь*) speech of welcome

приве́тств|овать, ую *impf.* **1** (*in past tense also pf.*) to greet; to welcome **2** (fig.) to welcome

привива́|ть, ю, ет *impf. of* ▸ **приви́ть**

привива́|ться, ется *impf. of* ▸ **приви́ться**

приви́вк|а, и *f.* (от, про́тив + *g.*) (med.) inoculation (against); vaccination

привиде́ни|е, я *nt.* ghost, spectre (BrE), specter (AmE); apparition

приви́|деться, дится *pf. of* ▸ **ви́деться** 2

привилегиро́ванный *adj.* privileged

привиле́ги|я, и *f.* privilege; (*для ветера́нов, инвали́дов*) benefit

привин|ти́ть, чу́, ти́шь *pf.* (*of* ▸ **приви́нчивать**) to screw on

приви́нчива|ть, ю *impf. of* ▸ **привинти́ть**

прив|и́ть, ью́, ьёшь, *past* ~и́л, ~ила́, ~и́ло *pf.* (*of* ▸ **привива́ть**) (+ *a. and d.*) (med.) to inoculate (with); **п. кому́-н. о́спу** to vaccinate sb against smallpox

прив|и́ться, ьётся, *past* ~и́лся, ~ила́сь *pf.* (*of* ▸ **привива́ться**) **1** (*о вакци́не, черенке́*) to take **2** (fig.) (*иде́и, тео́рия*) to find acceptance; (*мо́да, интере́с*) to catch on

при́вкус, а *m.* (*посторо́нний вкус*) aftertaste; (*характе́рный вкус*) flavour (BrE), flavor (AmE)

привлека́тел|ьный, ~ен, ~ьна *adj.* attractive

ℰ **привлека́|ть, ю** *impf. of* ▸ **привле́чь**

привле|чь, ку́, чёшь, ку́т, *past* ~к, ~кла́ *pf.* (*of* ▸ **привлека́ть**) **1** to attract; **п. внима́ние** to attract attention **2** (*сде́лать уча́стником*) to draw in, involve; **п. на свою́ сто́рону** to win over (*to one's side*) **3** (law) to have up; **п. к суду́** to take to court; to put on trial; **п. к отве́тственности/отве́ту** (за + *a.*)

to make answer (for), call to account (for)

при́вод, а *m.* (comput., tech.) drive

ℰ **приво|ди́ть, жу́, ~дишь** *impf. of* ▸ **привести́**

приво|жу́[1], ~**дишь** *see* ▸ **приводи́ть**

приво|жу́[2], ~**зишь** *see* ▸ **привози́ть**

приво|зи́ть, жу́, ~зишь *impf. of* ▸ **привезти́**

привра́тник, а *m.* doorman, porter

привста|ва́ть, ю́, ёшь *impf. of* ▸ **привста́ть**

привста́|ть, ну, нешь *pf.* (*of* ▸ **привстава́ть**) to half-rise

привыка́|ть, аю *impf. of* ▸ **привы́кнуть**

ℰ **привы́к|нуть, ну, нешь**, *past* ~, ~ла *pf.* (*of* ▸ **привыка́ть**) (к + *d.* or + *inf.*) **1** (*осво́иться*) to get accustomed (to), get used (to) **2** (*получи́ть привы́чку*) to get into the habit (of); **он** ~ **руга́ться** he has got into the habit of swearing

привы́чк|а, и *f.* habit; **войти́ в** ~у to become a habit; **име́ть** ~у (к + *d.*) to be accustomed (to); to be in the habit (of); **приобрести́** ~у (+ *inf.*) to get into the habit (of); **сде́лать что-н. по** ~е to do sth out of habit

привы́ч|ный, ~ен, ~на *adj.* habitual, usual, customary

привя́занност|ь, и *f.* (к + *d.*) attachment (to); affection (for, towards)

привя|за́ть, жу́, ~жешь *pf.* (*of* ▸ **привя́зывать**) (к + *d.*) to tie (to), fasten (to), attach (to); **п. верёвку/соба́ку к забо́ру** to tie a rope/the dog to the fence

привя|за́ться, жу́сь, ~жешься *pf.* (*of* ▸ **привя́зываться**) (к + *d.*) **1** to become attached (to); **она́ о́чень к вам** ~**за́лась** she has become very attached to you **2** to attach oneself (to); **на доро́ге к нам** ~**за́лся како́й-то ни́щий** a beggar attached himself to us on the road

привя́зыва|ть, ю *impf. of* ▸ **привяза́ть**

привя́зыва|ться, юсь *impf. of* ▸ **привяза́ться**

пригла́|дить, жу, дишь *pf.* (*of* ▸ **пригла́живать**) to smooth

пригла́жива|ть, ю *impf. of* ▸ **пригла́дить**

пригла|си́ть, шу́, си́шь *pf.* (*of* ▸ **приглаша́ть**) **1** to invite; ask; **п. кого́-н. на та́нец** to ask sb to dance, ask sb for a dance; **п. в го́сти** to invite, ask round **2** (*врача́*) to call

ℰ **приглаша́|ть, ю** *impf. of* ▸ **пригласи́ть**

приглаше́ни|е, я *nt.* **1** invitation; **по** ~ю by invitation; **разосла́ть** ~я to send out invitations **2** (*на рабо́ту*) offer (*of employment*)

приглуша́|ть, аю *impf. of* ▸ **приглуши́ть**

приглуш|и́ть, у́, и́шь *pf.* (*of* ▸ **приглуша́ть**) (*звук*) to muffle, deaden; (*го́лос, речь*) to mute; (*свет, ра́дио*) to turn down; (*ого́нь*) to choke, damp; (*тоску́*) to relieve

пригля|де́ть, жу́, ди́шь *pf.* (*of* ▸ **пригля́дывать**) (infml) **1** (*подыска́ть*) to find, look out (BrE) **2** (за + *i.*) to look after; **п. за детьми́** to look after children

пригля|де́ться, жу́сь, ди́шься *pf.* (*of* ▸ **пригля́дываться**) (infml) (к + *d.*)

п

1 (*внимательно посмотреть*) to look closely (at), scrutinize **2** (*привыкнуть*) to get accustomed (to), get used (to); **п. к темноте́** to get accustomed to darkness

пригля́дыва|ть, ю *impf. of* ▶ **пригляде́ть**

пригля́дыва|ться, юсь *impf. of* ▶ **пригляде́ться**

приглян|у́ться, у́сь, ∼ешься *pf.* (+ *d.*) (infml) to take one's fancy, attract; **она́ сра́зу ∼у́лась ему́** he was attracted to her instantly

при|гна́ть¹, гоню́, го́нишь, *past* ∼гна́л, ∼гнала́, ∼гна́ло *pf.* (*of* ▶ **пригоня́ть**) (*гоня, доставить*) to drive

при|гна́ть², гоню́, го́нишь, *past* ∼гна́л, ∼гнала́, ∼гна́ло *pf.* (*of* ▶ **пригоня́ть**) (*приладить*) to fit, adjust

пригов́а́рива|ть, ю *impf. of* ▶ **приговори́ть**

пригово́р, а *m.* (*судьи*) sentence; **вы́нести п.** to pass sentence; **отмени́ть п.** to quash a sentence; (*присяжных*) verdict

приговор|и́ть, ю́, и́шь *pf.* (*of* ▶ **пригова́ривать**) (к + *d.*) to sentence (to), condemn (to)

приго|ди́ться, жу́сь, ди́шься *pf.* (+ *d.*) to prove useful (to), come in handy; to stand in good stead

приго́д|ный, ∼ен, ∼на *adj.* (к + *d.*) fit (for), suitable (for), good (for)

пригоня́|ть, ю *impf. of* ▶ **пригна́ть¹**, ▶ **пригна́ть²**

пригор|а́ть, а́ет *impf. of* ▶ **пригоре́ть**

пригор|е́ть, и́т *pf.* (*of* ▶ **пригора́ть**) to be burnt

при́город, а *m.* suburb

при́городный *adj.* suburban; **п. по́езд** local train

пригота́влива|ть, ю *impf.* = **приготовля́ть**

пригота́влива|ться, юсь *impf.* = **приготовля́ться**

пригото́в|ить, лю, ишь *pf.* (*of* ▶ **пригота́вливать**, ▶ **приготовля́ть**) to prepare; **п. обе́д** to cook, prepare a dinner

пригото́в|иться, люсь, ишься *pf.* (*of* ▶ **пригота́вливаться**, ▶ **приготовля́ться**) (+ *inf.*) to prepare (to); (к + *d.*) to prepare (oneself) (for)

⚘ **приготовле́ни|е, я** *nt.* preparation

приготовля́|ть, ю *impf. of* ▶ **пригото́вить**

приготовля́|ться, юсь *impf. of* ▶ **пригото́виться**

пригро|зи́ть, жу́, зи́шь *pf. of* ▶ **грози́ть 1**

прида|ва́ть, ю́, ёшь *impf. of* ▶ **прида́ть**

прида́|ть, м, шь, ст, ди́м, ди́те, ду́т, *past* ∼л, ∼ла́, ∼ло *pf.* (*of* ▶ **придава́ть**) **1** to add **2** (*усилить*) to increase, strengthen; **п. бо́дрости** (+ *d.*) to hearten, put heart (into) **3** (+ *a. and d.*) (*свойство, состояние*) to give (to), impart (to); (fig.) to attach (to); **п. значе́ние** to attach importance (to); **п. фо́рму** to shape (to)

придвига́|ть, ю *impf. of* ▶ **придви́нуть**

придвига́|ться, юсь *impf. of* ▶ **придви́нуться**

придви́|нуть, ну, нешь *pf.* (*of* ▶ **придвига́ть**) to move (up), draw (up); ∼нь(те) кре́сло к пе́чке draw your chair up to the stove

придви́|нуться, нусь, нешься *pf.* (*of* ▶ **придвига́ться**) (к + *d.*) to move

придво́рн|ый *adj.* court; **п. шут** court jester; (*as m. n.* **п., ∼ого**) courtier

приде́л|ать, аю *pf.* (*of* ▶ **приде́лывать**) (к + *d.*) to fix (to), attach (to)

приде́лыва|ть, ю *impf. of* ▶ **приде́лать**

приде́ржива|ться, юсь *impf.* **1** (за + *a.*) to hold on (to) **2** (+ *g.*) to hold (to), keep (to) (also fig.); (fig.) to stick (to), adhere (to); (*моды, советов*) to follow; **п. пра́вой стороны́** to keep to the right; **п. догово́ра** to adhere to an agreement; **п. мне́ния** to hold the opinion, be of the opinion; **п. пра́вил** to stick to, follow the rules

придира́|ться, юсь *impf. of* ▶ **придра́ться**

при|дра́ться, деру́сь, дерёшься, *past* ∼дра́лся, ∼драла́сь, ∼дра́ло́сь *pf.* (*of* ▶ **придира́ться**) (к + *d.*) to find fault (with), carp (at); to nag (at), pick (on); **п. к кому́-н. из-за пустяко́в/по пустяка́м** to find fault with sb over trifles

приду́ *see* ▶ **прийти́**

приду́м|ать, аю *pf.* (*of* ▶ **приду́мывать**) **1** (*отговорку, выход*) to think of, think up; (*приспособление*) to devise, invent; (*сказку, песню*) to make up; (*музыку*) to compose, make up; **наконе́ц я ∼ал, что де́лать** at last I have thought of what to do **2** (*вообразить*) to imagine

приду́мыва|ть, ю *impf. of* ▶ **приду́мать**

приду́р|ок, ка *m.* (infml) idiot, fool

прие́зд, а *m.* arrival, coming; **с ∼ом!** welcome!

⚘ **приезжа́|ть, ю** *impf. of* ▶ **прие́хать**

прие́зж|ий *adj.* newly arrived; visiting; (*as n.* **п., ∼его,** *f.* **∼ая, ∼ей**) newcomer; (*гость*) visitor

⚘ **прие́м, а** *m.* **1** (*действие*) receiving; reception; **часы́ ∼а** (reception) hours, calling hours; (*врача*) surgery (hours) (BrE), office hours (AmE) **2** (*гостей*) reception, welcome; **оказа́ть кому́-н. раду́шный п.** to accord sb a hearty welcome **3** (*в партию, клуб*) admittance **4** (*собрание приглашённых*) reception **5** (*лекарства*) dose **6** (*отдельное действие*) go; motion, movement; **в оди́н п.** at one go; **испо́лнить кома́нду в три ∼а** to execute a command in three movements **7** (*способ*) method, way, mode; (*уловка*) device, trick (also pej.); (sport) hold, grip; **лече́бный п.** method of treatment **8** (radio, TV) reception

прие́млем|ый, ∼, ∼а *adj.* acceptable; admissible

приёмн|ая, ой *f.* **1** (*для ожидания*) waiting room **2** (*где принимают гостей*) reception room

приёмник, а *m.* (*радиоприёмник*) radio (set); (*для приёма сигналов*) receiver

---

⚘ key word

приёмн|ый *adj.* **1** receiving; reception; **п. день** visiting day; **~ые часы́** (BrE) (reception) hours; (*врача́*) surgery (hours) (BrE), office hours (AmE); **п. поко́й** casualty ward **2** selection; entrance; **~ая коми́ссия** selection committee **3** foster, adoptive; **п. оте́ц** foster-father; **п. сын** adopted son, foster-son

⚡ **прие́|хать, ду, дешь** *pf.* (*of ▶* **приезжа́ть**) to arrive, come (*not on foot*)

прижа́|ть, му́, мёшь *pf.* (*of ▶* **прижима́ть**) (к + *d.*) to press (to), clasp (to); **п. к груди́** to clasp to one's bosom; **п. к стене́** (fig.) to drive into a corner

прижа́|ться, му́сь, мёшься *pf.* (*of ▶* **прижима́ться**) (к + *d.*) (*прислони́ться*) to press oneself (to, against); (*к ма́тери*) to cuddle up (to), snuggle up (to), nestle up (to); **п. к стене́** to flatten oneself against the wall

приже́|чь, жгу, жжёшь, жгу́т, *past* **~жёг, ~жгла́** *pf.* (*of ▶* **прижига́ть**) to cauterize, sear

прижива́|ться, юсь *impf. of ▶* **прижи́ться**

прижига́|ть, ю *impf. of ▶* **приже́чь**

прижима́|ть, ю *impf. of ▶* **прижа́ть**

прижима́|ться, юсь *impf. of ▶* **прижа́ться**

прижи́|ться, иву́сь, ивёшься, *past* **~йлся, ~ила́сь** *pf.* (*of ▶* **прижива́ться**) **1** (*прожи́в, привы́кнуть*) to settle down, get acclimatized (BrE), acclimated (AmE) **2** (*о расте́ниях*) to take root

приз, а, *pl.* **~ы́** *m.* prize; **получи́ть п.** to win a prize; **присуди́ть п.** (+ *d.*) to award a prize (to)

призва́ни|е, я *nt.* (*назначе́ние*) vocation, calling; **сле́довать своему́ ~ю** to follow one's vocation; (*скло́нность*) aptitude; (*му́зыки, теа́тра*) mission, purpose

призва́|ть, зову́, зовёшь, *past* **~зва́л, ~звала́, ~зва́ло** *pf.* (*of ▶* **призыва́ть**) (*позва́ть яви́ться*) to call, summon; (*позва́ть де́лать что-н.*) to call upon, appeal; **п. на вое́нную слу́жбу** to call up (*for military service*); **п. к поря́дку** to call to order

призе́мист|ый, ~, ~а *adj.* stocky, squat; thickset

приземле́ни|е, я *nt.* (aeron.) landing, touchdown

приземл|и́ться, ю́сь, и́шься *pf.* (*of ▶* **приземля́ться**) (aeron.) to land, touch down

приземля́|ться, юсь *impf. of ▶* **приземли́ться**

призёр, а *m.* prizewinner

при́зм|а, ы *f.* prism

⚡ **призна|ва́ть, ю́, ёшь** *impf. of ▶* **призна́ть**

призна|ва́ться, ю́сь, ёшься *impf. of ▶* **призна́ться**

⚡ **при́знак, а** *m.* sign; indication; **служи́ть ~ом** (+ *g.*) to be a sign (of); **обнару́живать ~и** (+ *g.*) to show signs (of); **не подава́ть ~ов**

жи́зни to show no sign of life

призна́ни|е, я *nt.* **1** (*заявле́ние*) confession, declaration; admission, acknowledgement; **п. вины́** (*обвиня́емым*) admission of guilt; **п. вино́вным** (*судо́м*) guilty verdict; **п. в любви́** declaration of love **2** (*оце́нка по досто́инству*) recognition; **получи́ть п.** to obtain, win recognition

при́знанный *p.p.p. of ▶* **призна́ть** *and adj.* acknowledged, recognized

призна́тел|ьный, ~ен, ~ьна *adj.* grateful

призна́|ть, ю *pf.* (*of ▶* **признава́ть**) **1** (law, pol.) to recognize; **п. прави́тельство** to recognize a government **2** (*созна́ть*) to admit, acknowledge; **п. себя́ вино́вным** (law) to plead guilty; **п. свою́ оши́бку** to admit one's mistake **3** (*счита́ть*) to deem; **п. недействи́тельным** to declare invalid; **п. (не)вино́вным** to find (not) guilty

призна́|ться, юсь *pf.* (*of ▶* **признава́ться**) (в + *p.*) to confess (to)

при́зрак, а *m.* spectre (BrE), specter (AmE), ghost, apparition

призы́в, а *m.* **1** (*про́сьба*) call, appeal; **откли́кнуться на чей-н. п.** to respond to sb's call **2** (mil.) call-up, conscription

призыва́|ть, ю *impf. of ▶* **призва́ть**

призывни́к, а́ *m.* conscript

⚡ **при|йти́, ду́, дёшь,** *past* **~шёл, ~шла́** *pf.* (*of ▶* **приходи́ть**) to come; to arrive; **п. пе́рвым** to come first; **п. в восто́рг** (от + *g.*) to go into raptures (over); **п. в у́жас** to be horrified; **п. в я́рость** to fly into a rage; **п. в го́лову кому́-н.** to occur to sb, strike sb, cross sb's mind; **п. в себя́, п. в чу́вство** to come round, regain consciousness; (fig.) to come to one's senses; **п. к соглаше́нию** to come to an agreement

⚡ **при|йти́сь, ду́сь, дёшься,** *past* **~шёлся, ~шла́сь** *pf.* (*of ▶* **приходи́ться** 1) **1** (по + *d.*) to fit; **п. кому́-н. по вку́су, по нра́ву** to be to sb's taste, liking **2** (на + *a.*) (*о да́тах, собы́тиях*) to fall (on); **Па́сха ~шла́сь на 28-е ма́рта** Easter fell on the 28th of March **3** (*impers.* + *d.*) (*оказа́ться ну́жным*) to have (to); **ей ~дётся неме́дленно верну́ться в Москву́** she will have to return to Moscow immediately **4** (*impers.* + *d.*) (*вы́пасть на до́лю*) to happen (to), fall to the lot (of); **мне ~шло́сь быть ря́дом в тот моме́нт, когда́ он упа́л в о́бморок** I happened to be standing by when he fainted; **ему́ ~шло́сь тяжело́** he had a hard time; **как ~дётся** (infml) anyhow; **что ~дётся** anything; **что ~дётся** whatever comes along

⚡ **прика́з, а** *m.* order, command; **вы́полнить п.** to carry out an order; **отда́ть п.** to give an order; **по ~y** by order

прика|за́ть, жу́, ~жешь *pf.* (*of ▶* **прика́зывать**) (+ *d.*) to order; to give orders; **дире́ктор ~за́л соста́вить но́вый гра́фик** the director ordered that a new schedule should be worked out

прика́зыва|ть, ю *impf. of ▶* **приказа́ть**

п

прика́лыва|ть, ю *impf. of* ▶ приколо́ть

прика́нчива|ть, ю *impf. of* ▶ прико́нчить

прикаса́|ться, юсь *impf. of* ▶ прикосну́ться

прики́дыва|ться, юсь *impf. of* ▶ прики́нуться

прики́|нуться, нусь, нешься *pf. (of* ▶ прики́дываться) (+ *i.*) (infml) to pretend (to be), feign; **п. больны́м** to pretend to be ill; to feign illness

прикла́д, а *m.* (*ружья́*) butt

прикладн|о́й *adj.* applied; ~о́е иску́сство applied arts; ~а́я програ́мма (comput.) application (program)

прикла́дыва|ть, ю *impf. of* ▶ приложи́ть 1, ▶ приложи́ть 2

прикле́ива|ть, ю, ет *impf. of* ▶ прикле́ить

прикле́ива|ться, ется *impf. of* ▶ прикле́иться

прикле́|ить, ю, ишь *pf.* (*of* ▶ прикле́ивать) to stick; to glue; **п. ма́рку** to stick on a stamp; **п. афи́шу к стене́** to stick a bill (up) on a wall

прикле́|иться, ится *pf.* (*of* ▶ прикле́иваться) (к + *d.*) to stick (to), adhere (to)

приключа́|ться, а́ется *impf. of* ▶ приключи́ться

приключе́ни|е, я *nt.* adventure

приключ|и́ться, и́тся *pf.* (*of* ▶ приключа́ться) (infml) to happen, occur

прик|ова́ть, ую́, уёшь *pf.* (*of* ▶ прико́вывать) (к + *d.*) **1** to chain (to) **2** (fig.) (*взгляд*) to fix; (*внима́ние*) to rivet; **боле́знь ~ова́ла его́ к посте́ли** illness confined him to his bed

прико́выва|ть, ю *impf. of* ▶ прикова́ть

прикола́чива|ть, ю *impf. of* ▶ приколоти́ть

приколо|ти́ть, чу́, ~тишь *pf.* (*of* ▶ прикола́чивать) to nail, fasten with nails

прикол|о́ть, ю́, ~ешь *pf.* (*of* ▶ прика́лывать) to pin, fasten with a pin

прико́нч|ить, у, ишь *pf.* (*of* ▶ прика́нчивать) (infml) **1** (*израсхо́довать*) to use up **2** (fig., *умертви́ть*) to finish off

прикоснове́ни|е, я *nt.* touch

прикосн|у́ться, у́сь, ёшься *pf.* (*of* ▶ прикаса́ться) (к + *d.*) to touch (lightly)

прикреп|и́ть, лю́, и́шь *pf.* (*of* ▶ прикрепля́ть) (к + *d.*) to fasten (to)

прикрепля́|ть, ю *impf. of* ▶ прикрепи́ть

прикру|ти́ть, чу́, ~тишь *pf.* (*of* ▶ прикру́чивать) (к + *d.*) to tie (to), bind (to), fasten (to)

прикру́чива|ть, ю *impf. of* ▶ прикрути́ть

прикрыва́|ть, ю *impf. of* ▶ прикры́ть

прикрыва́|ться, юсь *impf. of* ▶ прикры́ться

прикр|ы́ть, о́ю, о́ешь *pf.* (*of* ▶ прикрыва́ть) **1** (+ *i.*) (*покры́ть*) to cover (with); to screen **2** (*защити́ть*) to protect, shield; **п. глаза́ руко́й** to shade, shield one's eyes (with one's hand); (*о войска́х*) to cover **3** (infml, *ликвиди́ровать*) to close down, wind up

4 (infml, *закры́ть непло́тно*) to close (*a door, etc.*) to

прикр|ы́ться, о́юсь, о́ешься *pf.* (*of* ▶ прикрыва́ться) **1** (+ *i.*) to cover oneself (with); (fig.) to use as a cover, take refuge (in), shelter (behind); **он ~ы́лся боле́знью** he took refuge in being ill **2** (infml, *ликвиди́роваться*) to close down, go out of business **3** (infml, *закры́ться непло́тно*) to close to

прику́рива|ть, ю *impf. of* ▶ прикури́ть

прикур|и́ть, ю́, ~ишь *pf.* (*of* ▶ прику́ривать): **п. у кого́-н.** to get a light (*from sb's cigarette*)

прила́в|ок, ка *m.* counter; (*на ры́нке*) stall

прилага́тельн|ое *adj.*: **и́мя ~ое** (*or as nt. n.* ~ое, ~ого) adjective

прилага́|ть, ю *impf. of* ▶ приложи́ть 3

приласка́|ть, ю *pf.* to caress, pet; (*отнести́сь хорошо́*) to show kindness to

приласка́|ться, юсь *pf.* (к + *d.*) to snuggle up (to)

приле́ж|ный, ~ен, ~на *adj.* diligent, assiduous

прилеп|и́ть, лю́, ~ишь *pf.* (*of* ▶ прилепля́ть) (к + *d.*) to stick (to, on)

прилеп|и́ться, лю́сь, ~ишься *pf.* (*of* ▶ прилепля́ться) (к + *d.*) to stick (to, on)

прилепля́|ть, ю *impf. of* ▶ прилепи́ть

прилепля́|ться, юсь *impf. of* ▶ прилепи́ться

прилёт, а *m.* arrival (*by air*)

прилет|а́ть, а́ю *impf. of* ▶ прилете́ть

приле|те́ть, чу́, ти́шь *pf.* (*of* ▶ прилета́ть) **1** to arrive (*by air*), fly in **2** (fig., infml, *бы́стро прибы́ть*) to fly, come flying

при|ле́чь, ля́гу, ля́жешь, ля́гут, *past* ~лёг, ~легла́ *pf.* to lie down, have a lie-down (BrE)

прили́в, а *m.* **1** rising tide; (fig., *люде́й, де́нег*) influx; **п. и отли́в** ebb and flow **2** (med.) congestion; (fig.): **п. эне́ргии, негодова́ния** surge of energy, indignation

прилип|а́ть, а́ет *impf. of* ▶ прили́пнуть

прили́п|нуть, нет, *past* ~, ~ла *pf.* (*of* ▶ прилипа́ть) (к + *d.*) to stick (to), adhere (to)

прили́ч|ный, ~ен, ~на *adj.* **1** decent, proper; decorous, seemly **2** (infml, *доста́точно хоро́ший*) decent, fair; ~ная зарпла́та a decent wage; (*доста́точно большо́й*) sizeable

⚜ приложе́ни|е, я *nt.* **1** (*докуме́нтов к письму́*) enclosure; (comput., *к электро́нному письму́*) attachment **2** (*к журна́лу, газе́те*) supplement **3** (*к кни́ге*) appendix; (*к докуме́нту*) addendum **4** (comput.) (*прикладна́я програ́мма*) application; (*небольшо́е*) applet

прилож|и́ть, у́, ~ишь *pf.* **1** (impf. прикла́дывать) (к + *d.*) (*положи́ть*) to put (to), hold (to); **п. ру́ку ко лбу** to put one's hand to one's head **2** (impf. прикла́дывать *and* прилага́ть) (*прибавить*) to add; (*к письму*) to enclose; (*печать*) to affix **3** (*impf.* **прилага́ть** (*использование*) to apply; **п. все уси́лия** to make every effort

прима́нива|ть, ю *impf. of* ▶ **примани́ть**

приман|и́ть, ю́, ∼ишь *pf.* (*of* ▶ **прима́нивать**) (infml) to lure; to entice

прима́нк|а, и *f.* bait; (fig.) enticement, allurement

прима́т, а *m.* (zool.) primate

⚹ **примене́ни|е, я** *nt.* application; (*употребление*) use, employment; **на́ши ме́тоды получи́ли широ́кое п.** our methods have been widely adopted; **непра́вильное п.** misuse; **в ∼и (к +** *d.*) in application (to)

примен|и́ть, ю́, ∼ишь *pf.* (*of* ▶ **применя́ть**) to apply; to employ, use; **п. свои́ зна́ния** to apply one's knowledge; **п. на пра́ктике** to put into practice

примен|и́ться, ю́сь, ∼ишься *pf.* (*of* ▶ **применя́ться**) (**к +** *d.*) to be used; to be applied

⚹ **применя́|ть, ю** *impf. of* ▶ **примени́ть**

⚹ **применя́|ться, юсь** *impf. of* ▶ **примени́ться**

⚹ **приме́р, а** *m.* **1** example, instance; **привести́ п.** to give an example; **к ∼у** for example **2** (*образец*) example; model; **брать п. с кого́-н., сле́довать чьему́-н. ∼у** to follow sb's example; **показа́ть п.** to give an example, give the lead; **по ∼у** (**+** *g.*) after the example (of), on the pattern (of)

приме́р|ить, ю, ишь *pf.* (*of* ▶ **ме́рить 2,** ▶ **примеря́ть**) to try on

⚹ **приме́рно** *adv.* approximately, roughly

приме́р|ный, ∼ен, ∼на *adj.* **1** (*отличный*) exemplary, model **2** (*приблизительный*) approximate, rough

приме́рочн|ая, ой *f.* fitting room

примеря́|ть, я́ю *impf. of* ▶ **приме́рить**

при́мес|ь, и *f.* admixture; dash; (fig.) touch; **без ∼ей** unadulterated

приме́т|а, ы *f.* (*признак*) sign, token; mark; (*суеверие*) omen; **осо́бые ∼ы** distinguishing marks

приме́т|ный, ∼ен, ∼на *adj.* **1** (*след, волнение*) perceptible, noticeable **2** (*человек, внешность*) conspicuous, prominent

примеча́ни|е, я *nt.* note, comment; (*сноска*) footnote

примеча́тельный, ∼ен, ∼ьна *adj.* noteworthy, notable, remarkable

примина́|ть, ю *impf. of* ▶ **примя́ть**

примире́ни|е, я *nt.* reconciliation

примир|и́ть, ю́, и́шь *pf.* (*of* ▶ **примиря́ть,** ▶ **мири́ть 2**) to reconcile; **п. супру́гов** to reconcile a husband and wife

примир|и́ться, ю́сь, и́шься *pf.* (*of* ▶ **примиря́ться,** ▶ **мири́ться 2**) (*с чем-н.*) to reconcile oneself (to); **п. с неудо́бствами** to reconcile oneself to discomforts

примиря́|ть, я́ю *impf. of* ▶ **примири́ть**

примиря́|ться, я́юсь *impf. of* ▶ **примири́ться**

примити́в|ный, ∼ен, ∼на *adj.* primitive

примкн|у́ть, у́, ёшь *pf.* (*of* ▶ **примыка́ть 1**) (**к +** *d.*) **1** (*плотно придвинуть, присоединить*) to fix (to), attach (to) **2** (fig., *присоединиться*) to join, attach oneself (to); to side (with)

примо́рский *adj.* seaside; (*растение, климат*) maritime

примо́чк|а, и *f.* wash, lotion

при́мус, а *m.* Primus (stove)®

примч|а́ться, у́сь, и́шься *pf.* to come tearing along

примыка́|ть, ю *impf.* **1** *impf. of* ▶ **примкну́ть** **2** (*impf. only*) (**к +** *d.*) to adjoin, abut (upon)

при|мя́ть, мну́, мнёшь *pf.* (*of* ▶ **примина́ть**) to crush, flatten; (*ногами*) to trample down, tread down

⚹ **принадлеж|а́ть, у́, и́шь** *impf.* **1** (**+** *d.*) to belong (to) **2** (**к +** *d.*) (*быть членом*) to belong (to), be a member (of); (*входить в состав*) to be among; to be one/some of **3**: **Герма́нии ∼и́т веду́щая роль в хими́ческой промы́шленности** Germany plays a leading role in the chemical industry **4**: **п. ки́сти/перу́** (**+** *g.*) to be the work of

принадле́жност|ь, и *f.* **1** (**к +** *d.*) belonging (to), membership (of) **2** (*in pl.*) accessories; equipment; gear; **канцеля́рские ∼и** stationery

⚹ **принес|ти́, у́, ёшь,** *past* **∼, ∼ла́** *pf.* (*of* ▶ **приноси́ть**) **1** (*неся, доставить*) to bring (also fig.); to fetch; **п. обра́тно** to bring back; **п. в же́ртву** to sacrifice; **п. извине́ния** to apologize **2** (*приплод, урожай*) to bear, yield; **п. результа́т** to yield/give results; (*причинить*) to bring in; **п. большо́й дохо́д** to bring in big revenues, show a large return; **п. по́льзу** to be of use, be of benefit; (*о чём-н. нежелательном*): **отку́да тебя́ ∼ло́ в тако́й час?** where have you come from at this hour?

приник|а́ть, а́ю *impf. of* ▶ **прини́кнуть**

прини́к|нуть, ну, нешь, *past* **∼, ∼ла** *pf.* (*of* ▶ **приника́ть**) (**к +** *d.*) to press oneself (against, to); (*прильнуть*) to nestle up (against, to); **мы ∼ли к земле́** we pressed ourselves to the ground

⚹ **принима́|ть, ю** *impf. of* ▶ **приня́ть**

принима́|ться, юсь *impf. of* ▶ **приня́ться**

приноравлива|ться, юсь *impf. of* ▶ **приноровиться**

принаров|иться, лю́сь, и́шься *pf.* (*of* ▶ **принора́вливаться**) (**к +** *d.*) to adapt oneself (to), accommodate oneself (to)

⚹ **прино|си́ть, шу́, ∼сишь** *impf. of* ▶ **принести́**

при́нтер, а *m.* (comput.) printer

принуди́тель|ный, ∼ен, ∼ьна *adj.* compulsory, forced; **∼ьные рабо́ты** forced labour (BrE), labor (AmE)

прин|уди́ть, у́жу, у́дишь *pf.* (*of* ▶ **принужда́ть**) to force, compel, coerce

принужда́|ть, ю *impf. of* ▶ **принуди́ть**

принужде́ни|е, я *nt.* compulsion, coercion; **по ∼ю** under duress

принц, а *m.* prince

принце́сс|а, ы *f.* princess

◆ **при́нцип**, а *m.* principle; **в ~е** in principle

принципиа́льно *adv.* **1** (*из при́нципа*) on principle; **п. отказа́ться** to refuse on principle **2** (*в при́нципе*) in principle **3**: **п. отлича́ться** to differ fundamentally

принципиа́л|ьный, **~ен**, **~ьна** *adj.* **1** of principle; based on, guided by principle; **п. челове́к** man of principle; **име́ть ~ьное значе́ние** to be a matter of principle **2** (*в основно́м*) in principle; general; **они́ да́ли ~ьное согла́сие** they consented in principle **3** (*коренно́й*): **~ьное разли́чие** fundamental difference

приню́х|аться, аюсь *pf.* (*of* ▶ **приню́хиваться**) (infml) to sniff

приню́хива|ться, юсь *impf. of* ▶ **приню́хаться**

◆ **приня́ти|е**, я *nt.* **1** (*пи́щи, лека́рства, реше́ния, прися́ги*) taking; (*по́ста, по́зы*) taking up **2** (*приглоше́ния, предложе́ния*) acceptance **3** (*госте́й, пацие́нтов*) receiving **4** (*в па́ртию*) admission, admittance; **п. гражда́нства** naturalization

при́нят|ый *p.p.p. of* ▶ **приня́ть**; **~о** (+ *inf.*) it is accepted, it is usual (*to do sth*); **не ~о** it is not done, it is not accepted

◆ **при|ня́ть**, му́, **~мешь**, *past* **~нял**, **~няла́**, **~ня́ло** *pf.* (*of* ▶ **принима́ть**) **1** to take; (*взять как дар; согласи́ться*) to accept; **п. ва́нну/душ** to take, have a bath/shower; **п. лека́рство** to take medicine; **п. ме́ры** to take measures; **п. пода́рок** to accept a present; **п. реше́ние** to take, reach a decision; **п. уча́стие** (**в** + *p.*) to take part (in); to participate (in); **п. во внима́ние** to take into consideration; **не п. во внима́ние** to disregard **2** (*пост*) to take up; **п. дела́** (**от** + *g.*) to take over duties (from) **3** (*че́рез голосова́ние*) to accept; **п. резолю́цию** to pass, adopt, carry a resolution **4** (**в**, **на** + *a.*) (*зачи́слить*) to admit (to); to accept (for); **п. на слу́жбу** to accept for a job **5** (*посети́телей, пацие́нтов, зака́з*) to receive; **они́ ~няли нас раду́шно** they gave us a warm welcome, a cordial reception **6** (*приобрести́*) to assume, take (on); **перегово́ры ~няли благоприя́тный оборо́т** the talks took a favourable (BrE), favorable (AmE) turn **7** (+ *a. and* **за** + *a.*) (*счесть по оши́бке*) to take (for); **я ~нял вас за шотла́ндца** I took you for a Scotsman

при|ня́ться, му́сь, **~мешься**, *past* **~нялся́**, **~няла́сь** *pf.* (*of* ▶ **принима́ться**) **1** (+ *inf.*) (*нача́ть*) to begin; to start **2** (**за** + *a.*) to set (to), get down (to); **п. за рабо́ту** to set to work

приободр|и́ть, ю́, **и́шь** *pf.* (*of* ▶ **приободря́ть**) to cheer up, encourage, hearten

приободр|я́ть, **я́ю** *impf. of* ▶ **приободри́ть**

приобре|сти́, ту́, **тёшь**, *past* **~л**, **~ла́** *pf.* (*of* ▶ **приобрета́ть**) **1** (*дом, друзе́й, маши́ну*) to acquire; (*авторите́т, репута́цию*) to gain; **п. о́пыт** to gain experience **2** (*сво́йство*) to take on, assume; **пробле́ма ~ла́ осо́бое**

◆ **key word**

значе́ние the problem took on a special significance

◆ **приобрета́|ть**, ю *impf. of* ▶ **приобрести́**

◆ **приобрете́ни|е**, я *nt.* acquisition

приобща́|ть, а́ю *impf. of* ▶ **приобщи́ть**

приобща́|ться, а́юсь *impf. of* ▶ **приобщи́ться**

приобщ|и́ть, у́, **и́шь** *pf.* (*of* ▶ **приобща́ть**) **1** (**к** + *d.*) (*познако́мить*) to introduce (to); **п. ребёнка к иску́сству** to introduce a child to art **2** (*присоедини́ть*) to join, attach; **п. к де́лу** to file

приобщ|и́ться, у́сь, **и́шься** *pf.* (*of* ▶ **приобща́ться**) (**к** + *d.*) to join (in), become involved (in)

приоде́|ть, ну, **нешь** *pf.* (infml) to dress up, smarten up

приоде́|ться, нусь, **нешься** *pf.* (infml) to dress up; to get dressed up; to smarten oneself up

приорите́т, а *m.* priority

приоса́нива|ться, юсь *impf. of* ▶ **приоса́ниться**

приоса́н|иться, юсь, **ишься** *pf.* (infml) to assume a dignified air

приостана́влива|ть, ю *impf. of* ▶ **приостанови́ть**

приостана́влива|ться, юсь *impf. of* ▶ **приостанови́ться**

приостанов|и́ть, лю́, **~ишь** *pf.* (*of* ▶ **приостана́вливать**) to halt, suspend

приостанов|и́ться, лю́сь, **~ишься** *pf.* (*of* ▶ **приостана́вливаться**) to halt, come to a halt; (*о челове́ке*) to pause

приоткрыва́|ть, ю *impf. of* ▶ **приоткры́ть**

приоткрыва́|ться, юсь *impf. of* ▶ **приоткры́ться**

приоткр|ы́ть, о́ю, **о́ешь** *pf.* (*of* ▶ **приоткрыва́ть**) to open slightly, half-open; **п. дверь** to half-open the door, set the door ajar

приоткр|ы́ться, о́юсь, **о́ешься** *pf.* (*of* ▶ **приоткрыва́ться**) to open slightly, half-open

припада́|ть, ю *impf. of* ▶ **припа́сть**

припа́д|ок, ка *m.* fit; attack; **не́рвный п.** attack of nerves

припа́ива|ть, ю *impf. of* ▶ **припая́ть**

припарк|ова́ть, у́ю *pf.* (*of* ▶ **паркова́ть**) to park

припарк|ова́ться, у́юсь *pf.* (*of* ▶ **паркова́ться**) to park

припа́|сть, ду́, **дёшь**, *past* **~л** *pf.* (*of* ▶ **припада́ть**) (**к** + *d.*) (*к земле́, к груди́*) to press oneself (to); (*склони́ться*) to fall down (before); **п. у́хом** to press one's ear (to)

припая́|ть, ю *pf.* (*of* ▶ **припа́ивать**) (**к** + *d.*) to solder (to)

припи|са́ть, шу́, **~шешь** *pf.* (*of* ▶ **припи́сывать**) **1** (*написа́ть в добавле́ние*) to add **2** (**к** + *d.*) (*причи́слить, записа́ть*) to register (at) **3** (+ *d.*) to attribute (to); to ascribe (to); to put down (to); **п. стихотворе́ние Пу́шкину** to attribute a poem to Pushkin; **п. неуда́чу ле́ни** to put a failure down to laziness

припи́сыва|ть, ю *impf. of* ▶ **приписа́ть**

приплыва́|ть, ю *impf. of* ▶ **приплы́ть**

приплы́|ть, ву́, вёшь, *past* ∼**л,** ∼**ла́,** ∼**ло** *pf. (of* ▶ **приплыва́ть)** *(вплавь)* to swim up; *(на ло́дке)* to sail up

приплю́снут|ый, ∼**,** ∼**а** *adj.* flattened; **п. нос** flat nose

приподнима́|ть, ю *impf. of* ▶ **приподня́ть**

приподнима́|ться, юсь *impf. of* ▶ **приподня́ться**

припо́днятый *p.p.p. of* ▶ **приподня́ть** *and adj. (оживлённый)* elated; animated; *(торже́ственный)* elevated

приподн|я́ть, иму́, и́мешь, *past* ∼**ял,** ∼**яла́,** ∼**яло** *pf. (of* ▶ **приподнима́ть)** to raise slightly; to lift slightly

приподн|я́ться, иму́сь, и́мешься, *past* ∼**я́лся,** ∼**яла́сь** *pf. (of* ▶ **приподнима́ться)** to raise oneself (a little); **п. на носки́** to rise on one's toes

приполз|а́ть, а́ю *impf. of* ▶ **приползти́**

приполз|ти́, у́, ёшь, *past* ∼**,** ∼**ла́** *pf. (of* ▶ **приполза́ть)** to creep up, crawl up

припомина́|ть, ю *impf. of* ▶ **припо́мнить**

припо́м|нить, ню, нишь *pf. (of* ▶ **припомина́ть)** **1** to remember, recollect, recall **2** to remind; **я э́то тебе́** ∼**ню!** (infml) you won't forget this!; I'll get even with you for this!

приправ|а, ы *f.* flavouring (BrE), flavoring (AmE), seasoning; *(со́ус)* dressing; **п. к сала́ту** salad dressing

приправ|ить, лю, ишь *pf. (of* ▶ **приправля́ть)** *(+ i.)* to season (with), flavour (BrE), flavor (AmE) (with); *(со́усом)* to dress (with)

приправля́|ть, ю *impf. of* ▶ **припра́вить**

припря́|тать, чу, чешь *pf. (of* ▶ **припря́тывать)** (infml) to put by, store up *(for future use)*

припря́тыва|ть, ю *impf. of* ▶ **припря́тать**

припу́гива|ть, ю *impf. of* ▶ **припугну́ть**

припуг|ну́ть, ну́, нёшь *pf. (of* ▶ **припу́гивать)** (infml) to intimidate, scare

прира́внива|ть, ю *impf. of* ▶ **приравня́ть**

приравн|я́ть, я́ю *pf. (of* ▶ **прира́внивать)** *(к + d.)* to equate (with)

прираст|а́ть, а́ю *impf. of* ▶ **прирасти́**

прираст|и́, у́, ёшь, *past* **приро́с, приросла́** *pf. (of* ▶ **прираста́ть)** **1** *(к + d.)* to adhere (to); *(о пересаженной тка́ни, о че́ренке)* to take **2** *(увели́читься)* to increase; *(проце́нты)* to accrue

⚥ **приро́д|а, ы** *f.* **1** nature **2** *(хара́ктер)* nature, character; **от** ∼**ы** by nature, congenitally; **по** ∼**е** by nature, naturally

⚥ **приро́дн|ый** *adj.* **1** *(со́зданный приро́дой)* natural; ∼**ые бога́тства** natural resources; **п. газ** natural gas **2** *(врождённый)* inborn, innate; **п. ум** native wit

природове́дени|е, я *nt.* natural history

прирождённый *adj.* **1** *(о спосо́бностях)* inborn, innate **2** *(о челове́ке)* a born; **п. лгун** a born liar

приро́ст, а *m.* increase, growth

прируч|а́ть, а́ю *impf. of* ▶ **приручи́ть**

прируче́ни|е, я *nt.* taming; domestication

прируч|и́ть, у́, и́шь *pf. (of* ▶ **прируча́ть)** to tame (also fig.); to domesticate

приса́жива|ться, юсь *impf. of* ▶ **присе́сть 1**

приса́сыва|ться, юсь *impf. of* ▶ **присоса́ться**

присва́ива|ть, ю *impf. of* ▶ **присво́ить**

присво́|ить, ю, ишь *pf. (of* ▶ **присва́ивать)** **1** *(завладе́ть)* to appropriate; **незако́нно п. сре́дства** to misappropriate funds **2** *(+ a. and d.) (дать)* to give, award, confer; **ему́** ∼**или сте́пень до́ктора нау́к** he has been given the degree of Doctor

приседа́|ть, ю *impf. of* ▶ **присе́сть 2**

при|се́сть, ся́ду, ся́дешь, *past* ∼**се́л** *pf.* **1** *(impf.* ∼**са́живаться)** *(сесть)* to sit down, take a seat **2** *(impf.* ∼**седа́ть)** *(на ко́рточки)* to squat; *(от стра́ха)* to cower

приска|ка́ть, чу́, ∼**чешь** *pf.* to come galloping, arrive at a gallop; *(fig., infml)* to rush, tear

приско́рб|ный, ∼**ен,** ∼**на** *adj.* regrettable, deplorable

при|сла́ть, шлю́, шлёшь *pf. (of* ▶ **присыла́ть)** to send

прислон|я́ть, ю, ∼**и́шь** *pf. (of* ▶ **прислоня́ть)** *(к + d.)* to lean (against), rest (against)

прислон|и́ться, ю́сь, и́шься *pf. (of* ▶ **прислоня́ться)** *(к + d.)* to lean (against), rest (against)

прислон|я́ть, я́ю *impf. of* ▶ **прислони́ть**

прислон|я́ться, я́юсь *impf. of* ▶ **прислони́ться**

прислу́г|а, и *f.* **1** maid, servant **2** *(collect.)* servants, domestics

прислу́ш|аться, аюсь *pf. (of* ▶ **прислу́шиваться)** *(к + d.)* **1** to listen (to) **2** *(fig., приня́ть во внима́ние)* to listen (to); to heed; **п. к чьему́-н. сове́ту** to listen to sb's advice

прислу́шива|ться, юсь *impf. of* ▶ **прислу́шаться**

присма́трива|ть, ю *impf.* **1** *impf. of* ▶ **присмотре́ть 1 2** *(impf. only)* to seek, try to find

присма́трива|ться, юсь *impf. of* ▶ **присмотре́ться**

присмире́|ть, ю *pf.* to grow quiet, calm down

присмир|и́ть, ю́, и́шь *pf. (of* ▶ **присмиря́ть)** to quieten (BrE), quiet (AmE)

присмир|я́ть, я́ю *impf. of* ▶ **присмири́ть**

присмотр|е́ть, ю́, ∼**ишь** *pf. (of* ▶ **присма́тривать)** **1** *(за + i.)* to look after, keep an eye (on); **п. за ребёнком** to mind the baby **2** *(pf. only)* (infml, подыска́ть) to find; **п. себе́ рабо́ту** to find a job

присмотр|е́ться, ю́сь, ∼**ишься** *pf. (of* ▶ **присма́триваться)** *(к + d.)* to look closely (at); **п. к кому́-н.** to size sb up

п

присн|úться, юсь, úшься *pf. of* ▸ **снúться**

присоединéни|е, я *nt.* **1** addition **2** (pol.) annexation

присоедин|úть, ю, úшь *pf.* (*of* ▸ **присоединя́ть**) **1** to add; to join **2** (pol.) to annex **3** (elec.) to connect

присоедин|úться, ю́сь, úшься *pf.* (*of* ▸ **присоединя́ться**) (к + *d.*) **1** to join; **порá нам п. к остальны́м** it is time we joined the others **2** (*согласи́ться*) to endorse, associate oneself (with); **п. к мнéнию** to subscribe to an opinion

присоедин|я́ть, я́ю *impf. of* ▸ **присоедини́ть**

присоедин|я́ться, я́юсь *impf. of* ▸ **присоединиться**

присос|áться, у́сь, ёшься *pf.* (*of* ▸ **приса́сываться**) (к + *d.*) to stick (to), adhere to (*by suction*)

приспоса́блива|ть, ю *impf. of* ▸ **приспосо́бить**

приспоса́блива|ться, юсь *impf. of* ▸ **приспосо́биться**

приспосо́б|ить, лю, ишь *pf.* (*of* ▸ **приспоса́бливать**) to adapt, convert; **п. шко́лу под больни́цу** to convert a school into a hospital

приспосо́б|иться, люсь, ишься *pf.* (*of* ▸ **приспоса́бливаться**) (к + *d.*) to adapt oneself (to)

приспособлéни|е, я *nt.* device; appliance

приспуска́|ть, ю *impf. of* ▸ **приспусти́ть**

приспу|сти́ть, щу́, ~стишь *pf.* (*of* ▸ **приспуска́ть**) to lower a little; **п. флаг** to lower a flag to half mast

приста|ва́ть, ю́, ёшь *impf. of* ▸ **приста́ть**

приста́в|ить, лю, ишь *pf.* (*of* ▸ **приставля́ть**) (к + *d.*) to put (to, against), lean (against); **п. лéстницу к стенé** to put a ladder against the wall

приста́вк|а, и *f.* attachment; (gram.) prefix

приставля́|ть, ю *impf. of* ▸ **приста́вить**

при́стально *adv.* intently; **п. смотрéть** (**на** + *a.*) to look intently (at); to stare (at), gaze (at)

при́стал|ьный, ~ен, ~ьна *adj.* fixed, intent; **п. взгляд** intent look; stare, gaze

при́стан|ь, и, *pl.* **~и, ~éй** *f.* landing stage, jetty; pier; wharf

приста́|ть, ну, нешь *pf.* (*of* ▸ **приставáть**) (к + *d.*) **1** (*прилипну́ть*) to stick (to), adhere (to) **2** (*присоедини́ться*) to join; to attach oneself (to); **п. к гру́ппе экскурса́нтов** to join a party of tourists **3** (*надоéсть*) to pester, bother; **п. с предложéниями** to pester with suggestions **4** (naut.) to put in (to), come alongside

пристёгива|ть, ю *impf. of* ▸ **пристегну́ть**

пристег|ну́ть, ну́, нёшь *pf.* (*of* ▸ **пристёгивать**) to fasten; to button up

пристра́ива|ть, ю *impf. of* ▸ **пристро́ить**

пристра|сти́ться, щу́сь, сти́шься *pf.* (к + *d.*) to develop a passion (for)

пристра́ст|ный, ~ен, ~на *adj.* partial, biased

пристрéлива|ть, ю *impf. of* ▸ **пристрели́ть**

пристрел|и́ть, ю́, ~́ишь *pf.* (*of* ▸ **пристрéливать**) to shoot (down)

пристро́|ить, ю, ишь *pf.* (*of* ▸ **пристра́ивать**) (к + *d.*) to add (*to a building*), build on (to)

пристро́йк|а, и *f.* annex, extension

при́ступ, а *m.* **1** (mil.) assault, storm; **пойти́ на п.** to go in to the assault **2** (*припа́док*) fit, attack; **п. гнéва/ка́шля** fit of temper/coughing; **сердéчный п.** heart attack

приступ|а́ть, а́ю *impf. of* ▸ **приступи́ть**

приступ|и́ть, лю́, ~́ишь *pf.* (*of* ▸ **приступа́ть**) (к + *d.*) to set about, get down (to), start; **п. к дéлу** to set to work, get down to business

присты|ди́ть, жу́, ди́шь *pf. of* ▸ **стыди́ть**

прису|ди́ть, жу́, ~́дишь *pf.* (*of* ▸ **присужда́ть**) **1** (+ *a.* and к + *d.*, or + *a.* and *d.*) to sentence (to), condemn (to); **п. к штра́фу, п. штраф** (+ *d.*) to fine, impose a fine (on) **2** (+ *d.*) to award; to confer (on); **ему́ ~́ди/ли стéпень до́ктора** a doctorate has been conferred on him

присужда́|ть, ю *impf. of* ▸ **присуди́ть**

прису́тстви|е, я *nt.* presence; **в ~и детéй** in the presence of the children, in front of the children

☞ **прису́тств|овать, ую** *impf.* (**на** + *p.*) to be present (at), attend

прису́тств|ующий *pres. part. act. of* ▸ **прису́тствовать** *and adj.* present; (*as pl. n.* **~ующие, ~ующих**) those present

прису́щ|ий, ~, ~а *adj.* (+ *d.*) inherent (in); characteristic; **~ая ей щéдрость** her characteristic generosity

присыла́|ть, ю *impf. of* ▸ **присла́ть**

прися́г|а, и *f.* oath; **под ~ой** on oath, under oath

прися́жн|ый *adj.*: **п. заседáтель** juror; (*as m. n.* **п., ~ого**) juror; **суд ~ых** jury

притáскива|ть, ю *impf. of* ▸ **притащи́ть**

притащ|и́ть, у́, ~́ишь *pf.* (*of* ▸ **притáскивать**) to bring, drag, haul

притвор|и́ться, ю́сь, и́шься *pf.* (*of* ▸ **притворя́ться**) (+ *i.*) to pretend (to be); to feign; **п. больны́м** to pretend to be ill, feign illness

притвор|я́ться, я́юсь *impf. of* ▸ **притвори́ться**

притеснéни|е, я *nt.* oppression

притесн|и́ть, ю́, и́шь *pf.* (*of* ▸ **притесня́ть**) to oppress, keep down

притесн|я́ть, я́ю *impf. of* ▸ **притесни́ть**

притиха́|ть, а́ю *impf. of* ▸ **притихнуть**

прити́х|нуть, ну, нешь, *past* **~, ~ла** *pf.* (*of* ▸ **притиха́ть**) to quieten (BrE), quiet (AmE) down; to grow quiet

прито́к, а *m.* **1** (geog.) tributary **2** (*воздуха, воды, дéнег*) inflow; (*людéй*) influx

п

притóм *conj.* (and) besides; and what's more

притóн, а *m.* den; **воровскóй п.** den of thieves

притóр|ный, ~ен, ~на *adj.* sickly sweet, cloying (also fig.); **~ная улы́бка** unctuous smile

притрáгива|ться, юсь *impf. of* ▶ притрóнуться

притрóн|уться, усь, ешься *pf.* (*of* ▶ притрáгиваться) (**к** + *d.*) to touch; **они́ не ~улись к ýжину** they have not touched their supper

притуп|и́ть, лю́, ~ишь *pf.* (*of* ▶ притупля́ть) to blunt; (fig.) to dull, deaden

притуп|и́ться, лю́, ~ится *pf.* (*of* ▶ притупля́ться) to become blunt; (fig., *о пáмяти, зрéнии*) to fail

притупля́|ть, ю, ет *impf. of* ▶ притупи́ть

притупля́|ться, ется *impf. of* ▶ притупи́ться

притуш|и́ть, ý, ~ишь *pf.* (infml, *огóнь*) to damp; **п. фáры** to dip lights

при́тч|а, и *f.* parable

притя́гива|ть, ю *impf. of* ▶ притяну́ть

притяжáтельный *adj.* (gram.) possessive

притяжéни|е, я *nt.* (phys.) attraction; **закóн земнóго ~я** law of gravity

притязáни|е, я *nt.* claim, pretension; **имéть ~я** (**на** + *a.*) to have claims (to, on)

притя|ну́ть, ну́, ~нешь *pf.* (*of* ▶ притя́гивать) **1** to drag (up), pull (up) **2** (fig., *привлéчь*) to draw, attract; **п. как магни́т** to attract like a magnet

приукрá|сить, шу, сишь *pf.* (*of* ▶ приукрáшивать) (infml) (*успéхи*) to exaggerate; (*расскáз*) to embellish, embroider

приукрáшива|ть, ю *impf. of* ▶ приукрáсить

приуменьшáть, áю *impf. of* ▶ приумéньшить

приумéньш|ить, у, ишь *pf.* (*of* ▶ приуменьшáть) to diminish, lessen, reduce

приуч|áть, áю *impf. of* ▶ приучи́ть

приуч|áться, áюсь *impf. of* ▶ приучи́ться

приуч|и́ть, ý, ~ишь *pf.* (*of* ▶ приучáть) (**к** + *d. or* + *inf.*) to train (to), school (to, in); **п. когó-н. к дисципли́не** to inculcate discipline in sb

приуч|и́ться, ýсь, ~ишься *pf.* (*of* ▶ приучáться) (+ *inf.*) to train oneself (to); to accustom oneself (to)

прихва|ти́ть, чý, ~тишь *pf.* (*of* ▶ прихвáтывать) (infml) to catch up, seize up

прихвáтыва|ть, ю *impf. of* ▶ прихвати́ть

прихóд¹, а *m.* (*прибы́тие*) coming, arrival

прихóд², а *m.* (eccl.) parish

⚘ **прихо|ди́ть, жý, ~дишь** *impf. of* ▶ прийти́

⚘ **прихо|ди́ться, жýсь, ~дишься** *impf.* **1** *impf. of* ▶ прийти́сь **2** (*impf. only*) (+ *d. and i.*) to be (*in a given degree of relationship to*); **я ей ~жýсь дя́дей** I am her uncle

прихожáн|ин, ина, *pl.* **~е** *m.* parishioner

прихожáн|ка, ки *f. of* ▶ прихожáнин

прихóж|ая, ей *f.* (entrance) hall, lobby

прихотли́в|ый, ~, ~а *adj.* intricate

при́хот|ь, и *f.* whim, caprice, fancy

прицéл, а *m.* (back)sight; **взять на п.** to take aim (at), aim (at); (fig.) to keep a watch on

прицéлива|ться, юсь *impf. of* ▶ прицéлиться

прицéл|иться, юсь, ишься *pf.* (*of* ▶ прицéливаться) to take aim

прицéп, а *m.* trailer

прицеп|и́ть, лю́, ~ишь *pf.* (*of* ▶ прицепля́ть) (**к** + *d.*) **1** to hitch (to), hook on (to); (*вагóны*) to couple (to) **2** (infml, *брóшку, бант*) to pin on (to), fasten (to)

прицеп|и́ться, лю́сь, ~ишься *pf.* (*of* ▶ прицепля́ться) (**к** + *d.*) **1** to stick (to), cling (to) **2** (fig., infml) (*пристáть*) to pester; to nag (at)

прицепля́|ть, ю *impf. of* ▶ прицепи́ть

прицепля́|ться, юсь *impf. of* ▶ прицепи́ться

причáл, а *m.* berth, moorage

причáлива|ть, ю *impf. of* ▶ причáлить

причáл|ить, ю, ишь *pf.* (*of* ▶ причáливать) **1** (**к** + *d.*) to moor (to) **2** to moor up

причáсти|е¹, я *nt.* (gram.) participle

причáсти|е², я *nt.* (eccl.) **1** communion; the Eucharist **2** (*причащéние*) making one's communion, communicating

прича|сти́ться, щýсь, сти́шься *pf.* (*of* ▶ причащáться) (eccl.) to receive communion

причáст|ный, ~ен, ~на *adj.* (**к** + *d.*) connected (with), involved (in); **быть ~ным** (**к** + *d.*) to be connected (with), be involved (in)

причащá|ться, юсь *impf. of* ▶ причасти́ться

⚘ **причём** *conj.* moreover, and; **бы́ло óчень темнó, п. я плóхо ориенти́ровалась на мéстности** it was very dark and I didn't know the area well

приче|сáть, шý, ~шешь *pf.* (*of* ▶ причёсывать) to comb; **п. когó-н.** to brush, comb sb's hair

приче|сáться, шýсь, ~шешься *pf.* (*of* ▶ причёсываться) to brush, comb one's hair

причёск|а, и *f.* hair style, hairdo; **сдéлать причёску** to style one's hair; (*у парикмáхера*) to have one's hair done

причёсыва|ть, ю *impf. of* ▶ причесáть

причёсыва|ться, юсь *impf. of* ▶ причесáться

⚘ **причи́н|а, ы** *f.* (*пожáра, болéзни*) cause; (*основáние*) reason; **по той простóй ~е, что** for the simple reason that; **по ~е** (+ *g.*) by reason (of), on account (of), owing (to), because (of)

причин|и́ть, ю́, и́шь *pf.* (*of* ▶ причиня́ть) to cause

причиня́|ть, я́ю *impf. of* ▶ причини́ть

причитá|ть, ю *impf.* (**по** + *p.*) to lament (for); to bewail

пришварт|овáть, ýю *pf. of* ▶ швартовáть

пришварт|ова́ться, у́юсь *pf. of*
▶ швартова́ться

пришёл|ец, ьца *m.* alien

пришива́|ть, ю *impf. of* ▶ приши́ть

приши́|ть, ью́, ьёшь *pf.* (*of* ▶ пришива́ть)
to sew on

прищем|и́ть, лю́, и́шь *pf.* (*of* ▶ прищемля́ть)
to pinch, catch; **п. себе́ па́лец две́рью** to
pinch one's finger in the door

прищемля́|ть, ю *impf. of* ▶ прищеми́ть

прище́пк|а, и *f.* (clothes) peg (BrE),
clothespin (AmE)

прищу́рива|ться, юсь *impf. of*
▶ прищу́риться

прищу́р|иться, юсь, ишься *pf.* (*of*
▶ прищу́риваться) to screw up one's eyes,
squint

прию́т, а *m.* **1** shelter, refuge **2**: **де́тский п.**
orphanage

прия́тел|ь, я *m.* friend

прия́тельниц|а, ы *f.* (female) friend

⚹ **прия́т|ный, ∼ен, ∼на** *adj.* nice, pleasant,
pleasing; (*impers., pred.*) ∼но it is pleasant;
it is nice; **о́чень** ∼но! pleased to meet you!;
how do you do?

⚹ **про** *prep.* (+ *a.*) **1** (*о*) about **2**: **про себя́** to
oneself; **чита́ть про себя́** to read to oneself

про...[1] *vbl. pref. indicating* **1** *action through,
across or past object:* **простре́ли́ть** to shoot
through; **прое́хать** to pass (by) **2** *overall
or exhaustive action:* **прогре́ть** to warm
thoroughly **3** *duration of action throughout
given period of time:* **просиде́ть всю ночь** to
sit up all night **4** *loss or failure:* **проигра́ть**
to lose (*a game*)

про...[2] *as pref. of nn. and adjs.* pro-

проанализи́р|овать, ую *pf. of*
▶ анализи́ровать

про́б|а, ы *f.* **1** (*маши́ны*) trial, test; try-
out; (*мета́лла*) assay; (*theatr.*) audition;
п. сил trial of strength **2** (*для ана́лиза*)
sample **3** (*драгоце́нного мета́лла*) standard
(*measure of purity of gold*); **зо́лото 96-й**
∼ы pure gold, 24-carat gold **4** (*клеймо́*)
hallmark

проба́лтыва|ться, юсь *impf. of*
▶ проболта́ться

пробега́|ть, ю *impf. of* ▶ пробежа́ть

пробе|жа́ть, гу́, жи́шь, гу́т *pf.* (*of* ▶ пробега́ть)
1 (*ми́мо*) to run past; (*че́рез*) to run
through; (*по*) to run along; **п. па́льцами по
клавиату́ре** to run one's fingers over the
keyboard **2** (fig., *пронести́сь*) to run, flit
(over, down, across); **хо́лод** ∼жа́л по её
спине́ a chill ran down her spine

пробе́жк|а, и *f.* run, jog

пробе́л, а *m.* **1** blank, gap; **запо́лнить**
∼ы to fill in the blanks **2** (*недоста́ток*)
deficiency, gap; ∼ы в зна́ниях gaps in one's
knowledge

пробива́|ть, ю *impf. of* ▶ проби́ть[1]

пробива́|ться, юсь *impf. of* ▶ проби́ться

пробира́|ться, юсь *impf. of* ▶ пробра́ться

проби́рк|а, и *f.* test tube

про|би́ть[1]**, бью́, бьёшь,** *past* ∼би́л,
∼би́ла, ∼би́ло *pf. of* ▶ бить 5

про|би́ть[2]**, бью́, бьёшь** *pf.* (*of* ▶ пробива́ть)
to make a hole (in); to pierce; to punch; **п.
сте́ну** to breach a wall

про|би́ться, бью́сь, бьёшься *pf.* (*of*
▶ пробива́ться) **1** to fight one's way
through; to break, strike through; **п. сквозь
толпу́** to fight one's way through the crowd
2 (*о расте́ниях*) to appear, push up

про́бк|а, и *f.* **1** (*материа́л*) cork (*substance*)
2 (*для буты́лок*) cork; stopper; (*в ра́ковину*)
plug; **глуп как п.** (infml) daft as a brush
3 (elec.) fuse **4** (fig., *на у́лице*) traffic jam;
congestion

⚹ **пробле́м|а, ы** *f.* problem

проблемати́чный *adj.* problematic(al)

про́блеск, а *m.* flash; ray, gleam (also fig.);
п. наде́жды ray of hope

про́бный *adj.* trial, test; **п. ка́мень**
touchstone; **п. полёт** test flight

про́б|овать, ую *impf. of* ▶ попро́бовать)
1 (*проверя́ть*) to test; **п. пи́щу** to taste,
try food **2** (+ *inf.*) (*стара́ться*) to try (to),
attempt (to)

проболта́|ться, юсь *pf.* (*of*
▶ проба́лтываться) (infml) to shoot one's
mouth off, let the cat out of the bag

пробо́р, а *m.* parting (BrE), part (AmE) (*of the
hair*); **прямо́й п.** middle part(ing); **косо́й п.**
side part(ing)

пробормо|та́ть, чу́, ∼чешь *pf. of*
▶ бормота́ть

про|бра́ться, беру́сь, берёшься, *past*
∼бра́лся, ∼брала́сь, ∼брало́сь *pf.* (*of*
▶ пробира́ться) **1** (*с трудо́м*) to fight, force
one's way **2** (*ти́хо*) to steal (through, past);
п. о́щупью to feel one's way; **п. на цы́почках**
to tiptoe (through)

пробу|ди́ть, жу́, ∼дишь *pf.* (*of* ▶ буди́ть 2,
▶ пробужда́ть) to wake; to awaken, rouse,
arouse (also fig.)

пробу|ди́ться, жу́сь, ∼дишься *pf.* (*of*
▶ пробужда́ться) to wake up, awake (also fig.)

пробужда́|ть, ю *impf. of* ▶ пробуди́ть

пробужда́|ться, юсь *impf. of* ▶ пробуди́ться

пробужде́ни|е, я *nt.* waking up, awakening

пробур|и́ть, ю́, и́шь *pf. of* ▶ бури́ть

проб|ы́ть, у́ду, у́дешь, *past* ∼ыл, ∼ыла́,
∼ыло *pf.* to stay, remain; to be (*for a certain
time*); **он** ∼ыл у нас три неде́ли he stayed
with us for three weeks

прова́йдер, а *m.* Internet service provider
(*abbr.* ISP)

прова́л, а *m.* **1** (*де́йствие*) collapse **2** (geog.)
gap; hole **3** (*неуда́ча*) failure; **по́лный п.** a
complete flop

прова́лива|ться, юсь *impf. of*
▶ провали́ться

⚹ **key word**

П

провали́ться, ю́сь, ~ишься *pf.* (*of* ▶ прова́ливаться) **1** to collapse, fall through; **потоло́к** ~и́лся the ceiling has come down **2** (fig., infml) (*потерпе́ть неуда́чу*) to fail, fall through; (*на экза́мене*) to fail

⚡ **проведе́ни|е**, я *nt.* **1** (*челове́ка*) leading, taking; (*су́дна*) piloting **2** (*доро́ги*) construction; (*электри́чества*) installation **3** (*опера́ции*) carrying out, carrying through; (*заседа́ния*) conducting; п. кампа́нии (mil., pol.) conduct of a campaign; п. в жизнь putting into effect, implementation

провез|ти́, у́, ёшь, *past* ~, ~ла́ *pf.* (*of* ▶ провози́ть) **1** (*везя́, доста́вить*) to convey, transport; п. контраба́ндой to smuggle **2** (*перевезти́ с собо́й*) to bring (with one)

прове́р|ить, ю, ишь *pf.* (*of* ▶ проверя́ть) **1** to check; to verify; п. биле́ты to examine tickets **2** (*на пра́ктике*) to test; п. свои́ си́лы to try one's strength

⚡ **прове́рк|а**, и *f.* **1** checking; examination; verification; check-up **2** (*на пра́ктике*) testing

⚡ **проверя́|ть**, я́ю *impf. of* ▶ прове́рить

⚡ **прове|сти́**, ду́, дёшь, *past* ~л, ~ла́ *pf.* (*of* ▶ проводи́ть[1] 1, ▶ вести́ 2, ▶ вести́ 3) **1** (*челове́ка*) to lead, take; (*су́дно*) to pilot; (*доро́гу*) to build; (*электри́чество*) to install **3** (*рефо́рмы, о́пыты*) to carry out; (*кампа́нию*) to carry on; (*уро́к, заседа́ние*) to conduct, hold; п. бесе́ду to give a talk **4** (*черту́*) to draw; п. грани́цу to draw a boundary line **5** (+ *i.*) (*руко́й*) to pass over, run over; она́ ~ла́ руко́й по лбу she passed her hand over her forehead **6** (*вре́мя*) to spend, pass; что́бы п. вре́мя to pass the time **7** (infml, *обману́ть*) to take in, trick, fool

прове́трива|ть, ю *impf. of* ▶ прове́трить

прове́тр|ить, ю, ишь *pf.* (*of* ▶ прове́тривать) to air; to ventilate

прови́зи|я, и (*no pl.*) *f.* provisions

провин|и́ться, ю́сь, и́шься *pf.* (в + *p.*) to be guilty (of); to commit an offence; п. пе́ред кем-н. to wrong sb; в чём мы ~и́лись? what have we done wrong?

провинциа́л|ьный, ~ен, ~ьна *adj.* provincial (also fig.)

прови́нци|я, и *f.* **1** (*о́бласть*) province **2** (*удалённая ме́стность*) the provinces; жить в глухо́й ~и to live in the depths of the country

про́вод, а, *pl.* ~а́ *m.* wire, lead; п. под напряже́нием live wire

⚡ **проводи́ть¹**, жу́, ~дишь *impf.* **1** *impf. of* ▶ провести́ **2** (*impf. only*) (phys., elec.) to conduct

⚡ **прово|ди́ть²**, жу́, ~дишь *pf.* (*of* ▶ провожа́ть) to accompany; to see off; п. кого́-н. домо́й to take, see sb home; п. кого́-н. до двере́й to see sb to the door; п. глаза́ми to follow with one's eyes

прово́дк|а, и *f.* (collect.) (elec.) wiring, wires

проводни́к¹, а́ *m.* **1** (*провожа́тый*) guide **2** (*в по́езде*) conductor; guard (BrE)

проводни́к², а́ *m.* (phys., elec.) conductor

проводни́|ца, цы *f.* of ▶ проводни́к¹

про́вод|ы, ов (*no sg.*) seeing-off; send-off

провожа́|ть, ю *impf. of* ▶ проводи́ть²

прово́з, а *m.* carriage, conveyance, transport; пла́та за п. payment for carriage

провозгла|си́ть, шу́, си́шь *pf.* (*of* ▶ провозглаша́ть) to proclaim; его́ ~си́ли королём he was proclaimed king

провозглаша́|ть, ю *impf. of* ▶ провозгласи́ть

прово|зи́ть, жу́, ~зишь *impf. of* ▶ провезти́

провока́тор, а *m.* **1** agent provocateur **2** (fig.) instigator, provoker

провока́ци|я, и *f.* provocation

про́волок|а, и *f.* wire; колю́чая п. barbed wire

прово́р|ный, ~ен, ~на *adj.* **1** (*бы́стрый*) quick, swift, expeditious **2** (*ло́вкий*) agile, nimble, adroit, dexterous

провоци́р|овать, ую *impf. and pf.* (*pf. also* с~) to provoke

прогиба́|ться, юсь *impf. of* ▶ прогну́ться

прогла́тыва|ть, ю (*impf. of* ▶ проглоти́ть): говори́ть, ~я слова́ to swallow one's words

прогло|ти́ть, чу́, ~тишь *pf.* (*of* ▶ прогла́тывать, ▶ глота́ть) to swallow (also fig.); п. язы́к to lose one's tongue; п. кни́гу to devour a book

прогля|де́ть, жу́, ди́шь *pf.* (*of* ▶ прогля́дывать) **1** (*просмотре́ть*) to look through, skim through **2** (*pf. only*) (*не заме́тить*) to overlook

прогля́дыва|ть, ю *impf. of* ▶ прогляде́ть

про|гна́ть, гоню́, го́нишь, *past* ~гна́л, ~гнала́, ~гна́ло *pf.* (*of* ▶ прогоня́ть) (*заста́вить уйти́*) to drive away (also fig.); (fig.) to banish

прогнива́|ть, ет *impf. of* ▶ прогни́ть

прогни́|ть, ёт, *past* ~л, ~ила́, ~и́ло *pf.* (*of* ▶ прогнива́ть) to rot through

прогно́з, а *m.* prognosis; forecast; п. пого́ды weather forecast

прогн|у́ться, у́сь, ёшься *pf.* (*of* ▶ прогиба́ться) to cave in, sag

прогова́рива|ть, ю *impf. of* ▶ проговори́ть

прогова́рива|ться, юсь *impf. of* ▶ проговори́ться

проговор|и́ть, ю́, и́шь *pf.* (*of* ▶ прогова́ривать) **1** (*сказа́ть*) to say, utter; п. сквозь зу́бы to mutter **2** (*не́которое вре́мя*) to speak, talk

проговор|и́ться, ю́сь, и́шься *pf.* (*of* ▶ прогова́риваться) to shoot one's mouth off, let the cat out of the bag

проголода́|ться, юсь *pf.* to get hungry, grow hungry

проголос|ова́ть, у́ю *pf. of* ▶ голосова́ть

прогоня́|ть, ю *impf. of* ▶ прогна́ть

прогор|а́ть, а́ю *impf. of* ▶ прогоре́ть

п

прогор|е́ть, ю́, и́шь pf. (of ▶ **прогора́ть**) **1** (*сгоре́ть совсе́м*) to burn through; to burn to a cinder **2** (infml, *разори́ться*) to go bankrupt, go bust

◆ **програ́мм|а, ы** f. programme (BrE), program (AmE); (comput.) program, application

программи́р|овать, ую impf. (of ▶ **запрограмми́ровать**) to programme (BrE), program (AmE); (comput.) to program

программи́ст, а m. (computer) programmer

программи́ст|ка, ки f. of ▶ **программи́ст**

◆ **програ́мм|ный** adj. of ▶ **програ́мма**; ∼ное обеспе́чение (comput.) software

прогрева́|ть, ю impf. of ▶ **прогре́ть**

прогрева́|ться, юсь impf. of ▶ **прогре́ться**

прогрем|е́ть, лю́, и́шь pf. of ▶ **греме́ть**

прогре́сс, а m. progress

прогресси́в|ный, ∼ен, ∼на adj. progressive

прогре́|ть, ю pf. (of ▶ **прогрева́ть**) to heat, warm up

прогре́|ться, юсь pf. (of ▶ **прогрева́ться**) to warm up

прогу́л, а m. (*на рабо́те*) absence; (*в шко́ле*) truancy

прогу́лива|ть, ю impf. of ▶ **прогуля́ть**

прогу́лива|ться, юсь impf. **1** impf. of ▶ **прогуля́ться 2** (impf. only) to stroll, saunter

прогу́л|ка, и f. **1** (*хожде́ние*) walk; stroll **2** (*пое́здка*) outing; (*в автомоби́ле*) drive; (*верхо́м*) ride

прогуля́|ть, ю pf. (of ▶ **прогу́ливать**) (*на рабо́те*) to be absent from work; (*шко́лу*) to play truant

прогуля́|ться, юсь pf. (of ▶ **прогу́ливаться 1**) to take a walk, stroll

◆ **прода|ва́ть, ю́, ёшь** impf. of ▶ **прода́ть**

прода|ва́ться, ю́сь, ёшься impf. **1** (impf. only) to be on sale, be for sale; дом ∼ётся the house is for sale; «∼ётся мотоци́кл» 'motorcycle for sale' (*formula of advertisement of sale*) **2** (impf. only) to sell; дёшево п. to sell cheap, go cheap; его́ но́вый рома́н хорошо́ ∼ётся his new novel is selling well **3** impf. of ▶ **прода́ться**

продав|е́ц, ца́ m. **1** seller; vendor **2** (*в магази́не*) salesman, shop assistant

продавщи́ц|а, ы f. **1** seller; vendor **2** (*в магази́не*) saleswoman, shop assistant

◆ **прода́ж|а, и** f. sale; опто́вая п. wholesale; п. в ро́зницу/ро́зничная п. retail; нет в ∼е out of stock; sold out

прода́ж|ный adj. **1** sale; selling; ∼ная цена́ selling price **2** (∼ен, ∼на) (fig.) corrupt; ∼ная же́нщина prostitute

прода́лблива|ть, ю impf. of ▶ **продолби́ть**

прода́|ть, м, шь, ст, ди́м, ди́те, ду́т, past про́дал, ∼ла́, про́дало pf. (of ▶ **продава́ть**) to sell; п. о́птом to sell wholesale; п. в ро́зницу to sell retail

прода́|ться, мся, шься, стся, ди́мся, ди́тесь, ду́тся, past ∼лся, ∼ла́сь pf. (of ▶ **продава́ться 3**) (*о челове́ке*) to sell oneself

продвига́|ться, юсь impf. of ▶ **продви́нуться**

продвиже́ни|е, я nt. **1** advancement **2** (mil., fig.) progress, advance

продви́нут|ый, ∼, ∼а (infml) adj. advanced

продви́|нуться, нусь, нешься pf. (of ▶ **продвига́ться**) **1** to advance (also fig.); to move on, move forward; to push on **2** (*по слу́жбе*) to be promoted

продева́|ть, ю impf. of ▶ **проде́ть**

проде́л|ать, аю pf. (of ▶ **проде́лывать**) **1** (*отве́рстие, прохо́д*) to make **2** (*рабо́ту, упражне́ния*) to do, perform, accomplish

проде́лыва|ть, ю impf. of ▶ **проде́лать**

продемократи́ческий adj. pro-democracy

продемонстри́р|овать, ую pf. of ▶ **демонстри́ровать**

продерж|а́ть, у́, ∼ишь pf. (*чемода́н*) to hold (*for a certain time*); (*челове́ка*) to keep (*for a certain time*); его́ ∼а́ли два ме́сяца в больни́це he was kept in hospital for two months

продерж|а́ться, у́сь, ∼ишься pf. to hold out

проде́|ть, ну, нешь pf. (of ▶ **продева́ть**) to pass, run; п. ни́тку в иго́лку to thread a needle

продикт|ова́ть, у́ю pf. of ▶ **диктова́ть**

продира́|ться, юсь impf. of ▶ **продра́ться**

продлева́|ть, ю impf. of ▶ **продли́ть**

продле́ни|е, я nt. extension, prolongation

продл|и́ть, ю́, и́шь pf. (of ▶ **продлева́ть**) to extend, prolong; п. срок де́йствия ви́зы to extend a visa

продл|и́ться, и́тся pf. of ▶ **дли́ться**

продово́льстве|нный adj. of ▶ **продово́льствие**; п. магази́н grocery (store); п. склад food store; (mil.) ration store, ration dump; ∼нные това́ры foodstuffs

продово́льстви|е, я nt. foodstuffs, provisions; (mil.) rations

продолб|и́ть, лю́, и́шь pf. (of ▶ **прода́лбливать**) to make a hole (in), chisel through

продолгова́т|ый, ∼, ∼а adj. oblong

◆ **продолж|а́ть, а́ю** impf. **1** to continue, go on; п. рабо́тать to continue to work, go on working **2** impf. of ▶ **продо́лжить**

продолж|а́ться, а́ется impf. (of ▶ **продо́лжиться**) to continue, last, go on; восста́ние ∼а́ется уже́ второ́й год the insurrection is now in its second year

продолже́ни|е, я nt. **1** continuation **2** (*расска́за*) continuation; sequel; п. сле́дует to be continued **3**: в п. (+ g.) in the course (of), during, for, throughout; в п. почти́ двух лет я ни ра́зу её не ви́дел for almost two years I did not see her once

продолжи́тельност|ь, и f. duration, length

продолжи́тел|ьный, ~ен, ~ьна *adj.* long; prolonged, protracted

продо́лж|ить, у, ишь *pf.* (*of* ▸ продолжа́ть) to extend, prolong

продо́лж|иться, ится *pf. of* ▸ продолжа́ться

продо́льн|ый *adj.* longitudinal; ~ая ось longitudinal axis

про|дра́ться, деру́сь, дерёшься, *past* ~дра́лся, ~драла́сь, ~дра́ло́сь *pf.* (*of* ▸ продира́ться) (infml) to squeeze through, force one's way through

продрем|а́ть, лю́, ~лешь *pf.* to doze (*for a certain time*)

продро́г|нуть, ну, нешь, *past* ~, ~ла *pf.* to be chilled to the marrow

продува́|ть, ю *impf. of* ▸ проду́ть

☞ **проду́кт**, а *m.* **1** product; побо́чный п. by-product **2** (*in pl.*) produce; provisions, foodstuffs; моло́чные ~ы dairy produce

продукти́в|ный, ~ен, ~на *adj.* productive; (fig.) fruitful

продукто́вый *adj.* food; п. магази́н grocery (store)

☞ **проду́кци|я**, и *f.* production, output

проду́м|ать, аю *pf.* (*of* ▸ проду́мывать) (*вопрос*) to think over; (*план*) to think out

проду́мыва|ть, ю *impf. of* ▸ проду́мать

проду́|ть, ю, ешь *pf.* (*of* ▸ продува́ть) **1** (*прочистить*) to blow through; to clean by blowing **2** (*impers.* + *a.*) to be in a draught (BrE), draft (AmE); меня́ и т. п. ~ло I have, etc., caught a cold from being in a draught (BrE), draft (AmE) **3** (infml, *проиграть*) to lose (*at games*)

продыря́в|ить, лю, ишь *pf.* (*of* ▸ продыря́вливать) to make a hole (in), pierce

продыря́влива|ть, ю *impf. of* ▸ продыря́вить

продю́сер, а *m.* producer

прое́зд, а *m.* **1** (*место*) passage, thoroughfare; «~а нет!» 'no thoroughfare!' **2** (*в транспорте*) trip, journey

проездно́й *adj.* travelling (BrE), traveling (AmE); п. биле́т ticket

проезжа́|ть, ю *impf. of* ▸ прое́хать

☞ **прое́кт**, а *m.* **1** (*здания*) design **2** (*предварительный текст*) draft; п. догово́ра draft treaty **3** (*замысел*) plan, project

проекти́ровани|е, я *nt.* designing; автоматизи́рованное п. CAD, computer-aided design

проекти́р|овать, ую *impf.* (*of* ▸ спроекти́ровать) to design; п. теа́тр to design a theatre (BrE), theater (AmE)

проектиро́вщик, а *m.* designer

прое́ктн|ый *adj.* **1** planning, designing; ~ое бюро́ planning office **2** (*предусмотренный*) planned; ~ая мо́щность (tech.) rated capacity

прое́ктор, а *m.* projector

прое́кци|я, и *f.* projection

проём, а *m.* (archit.) aperture; embrasure; дверно́й п. doorway

прое́|хать, ду, дешь *pf.* (*of* ▸ проезжа́ть) **1** (*на транспорте*) to pass (by, through); to drive (by, through), ride (by, through) **2** (*по ошибке*) to pass, go past **3** (*расстояние*) to go, do, make, cover

проеци́р|овать, ую *impf. and pf.* (*изображение*) to project

прожа́рива|ть, ю, ет *impf. of* ▸ прожа́рить

прожа́рива|ться, ется *impf. of* ▸ прожа́риться

прожа́р|ить, ю, ишь *pf.* (*of* ▸ прожа́ривать) to fry, roast thoroughly

прожа́р|иться, ится *pf.* (*of* ▸ прожа́риваться) to fry, roast thoroughly

прожд|а́ть, у́, ёшь, *past* ~а́л, ~ала́, ~а́ло *pf.* (+ *a. or g.*) to wait (for), spend (*a certain time*) waiting (for)

прож|ева́ть, ую́, уёшь *pf.* (*of* ▸ прожёвывать) to chew well

прожёвыва|ть, ю *impf. of* ▸ прожева́ть

проже́ктор, а, *pl.* ~ы and ~а́ *m.* searchlight, floodlight

про|же́чь, жгу́, жжёшь, жгу́т, *past* ~жёг, ~жгла́ *pf.* (*of* ▸ прожига́ть) to burn a hole in

☞ **прожива́|ть**, ю *impf.* **1** (*иметь жилище*) to live, reside **2** *impf. of* ▸ прожи́ть

прожига́|ть, ю *impf. of* ▸ проже́чь

про|жи́ть, живу́, живёшь, *past* ~жил, ~жила́, ~жило (*of* ▸ прожива́ть 2) **1** (*пробыть живым*) to live; он ~жил сто лет he lived to be a hundred **2** (*провести*) to spend; мы ~жили ме́сяц а́вгуст на берегу́ мо́ря we spent the month of August at the seaside

прожо́рлив|ый, ~, ~а *adj.* voracious, gluttonous

про́з|а, ы *f.* prose

проза́ик, а *m.* prose writer

про|зва́ть, зову́, зовёшь, *past* ~зва́л, ~звала́, ~зва́ло *pf.* (*of* ▸ прозыва́ть) (+ *a. and i.*) to nickname (sb sth)

про́звище, а *nt.* nickname

прозвуч|а́ть, и́т *pf. of* ▸ звуча́ть

прозева́|ть, ю *pf.* (*of* ▸ зева́ть 3) (infml) to miss

прозорли́в|ый, ~, ~а *adj.* sagacious, perspicacious

прозра́чность|, и *f.* transparency

прозра́ч|ный, ~ен, ~на *adj.* transparent (also fig.); (*вода*, *воздух*) clear, pellucid; (*ткань*, *одежда*) see-through, transparent; п. намёк transparent hint

прозрева́|ть, ю *impf. of* ▸ прозре́ть

прозре́ни|е, я *nt.* **1** recovery of sight **2** (fig.) insight

прозре́|ть, ю, ешь *pf.* (*of* ▸ прозрева́ть) **1** to recover one's sight **2** (fig.) to see the light

прозыва́|ть, ю *impf. of* ▸ прозва́ть

п

проигнори́р|овать, ую *pf.* to ignore

проигр|а́ть, а́ю *pf.* (*of* ▶ **прои́грывать**) **1** (*потерпе́ть неуда́чу*) to lose; **п. суде́бный проце́сс** to lose a case **2** (*сыгра́ть*) to play (through, over); **п. конце́рт** to play through a concerto **3** (*pf. only*) (*некоторое время*) to play

прои́грыватель, я *m.* record player; **п. компа́кт-ди́сков** CD player

прои́грыва|ть, ю *impf. of* ▶ **проигра́ть 2**

про́игрыш, а *m.* loss; **оста́ться в ~е** to be the loser, come off loser

◆ **произведе́ни|е, я** *nt.* **1** (*искусства, литерату́ры*) work; **и́збранные ~я Л. Н. Толсто́го** selected works of L. N. Tolstoy **2** (math.) product

произве|сти́, ду́, дёшь, *past* **~л, ~ла́** *pf.* (*of* ▶ **производи́ть**) **1** (*сде́лать*) to make; (*ремонт, опыты*) to carry out; **п. вы́стрел** to fire a shot **2** (*вы́звать*) to cause, produce; **п. впечатле́ние (на + a.)** to create an impression (on, upon); **п. сенса́цию** to cause a sensation

◆ **производи́тел|ь, я** *m.* producer; **ме́лкие ~и** small producers

производи́тельност|ь, и *f.* productivity

◆ **произво|ди́ть, жу́, ~дишь** *impf.* **1** *impf. of* ▶ **произвести́ 2** (*impf. only*) (*изготовля́ть*) to produce

◆ **произво|ди́ться, ~дится** *impf.* to be produced

произво́дн|ый *adj.* derivative, derived; (*as f. n.* **~ая, ~ой**) (math.) derivative

◆ **произво́дственный** *adj. of* ▶ **произво́дство**; production; industrial

◆ **произво́дств|о, а** *nt.* **1** (*това́ров*) production, manufacture; **япо́нского ~а** Japanese-made **2** (*заво́д*) factory, works

произво́л, а *m.* **1** (*необоснова́нность*) arbitrariness **2** (*своево́лие*) arbitrary rule

произво́льно *adv.* **1** (*необосно́ванно*) arbitrarily **2** (*по жела́нию*) at will

произво́льный, ~ен, ~ьна *adj.* arbitrary

произнес|ти́, у́, ёшь, *past* **~, ~ла́** *pf.* (*of* ▶ **произноси́ть**) **1** (*вы́говорить*) to pronounce; to articulate **2** (*сказа́ть*) to pronounce, say, utter; **п. речь** to deliver a speech

произно|си́ть, шу́, ~сишь *impf. of* ▶ **произнести́**

произноше́ни|е, я *nt.* pronunciation

◆ **произо|йти́, йду́, йдёшь,** *past* **~шёл, ~шла́** *pf.* (*of* ▶ **происходи́ть 1**) **1** (*случи́ться*) to happen, occur, take place **2** (*от, из-за + g.*) (*по причи́не*) to arise (from), result (from) **3** (*из, от + g.*) (*роди́ться*) to come (from, of), be descended (from)

произраст|а́ть, а́ет *impf. of* ▶ **произрасти́**

произраст|и́, ёт, *past* **произро́с, произросла́** *pf.* (*of* ▶ **произраста́ть**) to grow, spring up

проиллюстри́р|овать, ую *pf.* (*of* ▶ **иллюстри́ровать**) to illustrate

проинструкти́р|овать, ую *pf.* (*of* ▶ **инструкти́ровать**) to instruct, give instructions (to)

проинформи́р|овать, ую *pf.* (*of* ▶ **информи́ровать**) to inform

про́иск|и, ов (*no sg.*) intrigues; machinations

◆ **происхо|ди́ть, жу́, ~дишь** *impf.* **1** *impf. of* ▶ **произойти́ 2** (*impf. only*) to go on, be going on; **что тут ~дит?** what is going on here?

происхожде́ни|е, я *nt.* origin; (*по рожде́нию*) birth; **по ~ю он армяни́н** he is (an) Armenian by birth

происше́стви|е, я *nt.* event, incident, happening, occurrence; (*ава́рия*) accident

◆ **про|йти́, йду́, йдёшь,** *past* **~шёл, ~шла́** *pf.* (*of* ▶ **проходи́ть¹ 1**) **1** (*передви́нуться*) to pass (by, through); to go (by, through); **п. ми́мо** to pass by, go by, go past **2** (*по оши́бке*) to pass, pass past **3** (*расстоя́ние*) to go, do, cover; **п. две ты́сячи миль за неде́лю** to do two thousand miles in a week **4** (*о новостя́х, слу́хах*) to travel, spread **5** (*о дожде́, снеге*) to fall **6** (*о вре́мени*) to pass, elapse, go, go by; **~шёл це́лый год** a whole year had passed **7** (*минова́ть*) to be over; (*прекрати́ться*) to pass (off), stop, let up; **~шло ле́то** summer was over; **дождь ~шёл** the rain stopped **8** (*+ a. or through*) (*че́рез + a.*) to pass, go through, get through **9** (*заверши́ться*) to go, go off; **заседа́ние ~шло уда́чно** the meeting went off successfully **10** (*ку́рсы*) to do, take; **п. курс лече́ния** to take a course of treatment

про|йти́сь, йду́сь, йдёшься, *past* **~шёлся, ~шла́сь** *pf.* (*of* ▶ **проха́живаться**) to walk, stroll; (*прогуля́ться*) to take a stroll; **п. по ко́мнате** to pace up and down the room

прока́з|а¹, ы *f.* (*боле́знь*) leprosy

прока́з|а², ы *f.* (*ша́лость*) mischief, prank, trick

прока́зник, а *m.* mischief-maker; prankster

прока́зни|ца, цы *f. of* ▶ **прока́зник**

прока́лыва|ть, ю *impf. of* ▶ **проколо́ть**

прока́т, а *m.* (*аре́нда*) hire

прока|ти́ться, чу́сь, ~тишься *pf.* (*of* ▶ **прока́тываться**) **1** (*о мяче́*) to roll; (*о гро́ме*) to roll **2** (*для развлече́ния*) to go for a drive, go for a spin

прока́тыва|ться, юсь *impf. of* ▶ **прокати́ться**

прока́шлива|ться, юсь *impf. of* ▶ **прока́шляться**

прока́шл|яться, яюсь *pf.* (*of* ▶ **прока́шливаться**) to clear one's throat

прокипя|ти́ть, чу́, ти́шь *pf.* to boil thoroughly

прокис|а́ть, а́ет *impf. of* ▶ **проки́снуть**

проки́с|нуть, нет *pf.* (*of* ▶ **прокиса́ть**) to turn (sour)

прокла́дк|а, и *f.* **1** (*де́йствие*) laying; building, construction; **п. трубопрово́да** pipe laying **2** (tech., *дета́ль*) washer, gasket;

◆ key word

packing, padding **3** (infml, *гигиеническая*) sanitary towel

прокла́дыва|ть, ю *impf. of* ▸ проложи́ть

проклина́|ть, ю *impf. of* ▸ прокля́сть

прокл|я́сть, яну́, янёшь, *past* ~я́л, ~яла́, ~я́ло *pf.* (*of* ▸ проклина́ть) to curse, damn

прокля́ти|е, я *nt.* **1** (*осуждение*) damnation **2** (*слово, выражение*) curse

прокля́тый *adj.* damned; cursed

проко́л, а *m.* **1** (*в шине*) puncture **2** (*на билете*) (*неудача*) hole **3** (infml) (*неудача*) failure; (*оплошность*) blunder

проко́л|оть, ю́, ~ешь *pf.* (*of* ▸ прока́лывать) **1** (*шину*) to puncture **2** (*уши*) to pierce **3** (*дыру*) to pierce, prick

проконсульти́р|овать, ую *pf. of* ▸ консульти́ровать

проконсульти́р|оваться, уюсь *pf. of* ▸ консульти́роваться

проконтроли́р|овать, ую *pf. of* ▸ контроли́ровать

прокорм|и́ть, лю́, ~ишь *pf. of* ▸ корми́ть

прокорм|и́ться, лю́сь, ~ишься *pf. of* ▸ корми́ться

прокра́дыва|ться, юсь *impf. of* ▸ прокра́сться

прокра́|сться, ду́сь, дёшься *pf.* (*of* ▸ прокра́дываться) to steal; п. ми́мо to steal by, past

прокрич|а́ть, у́, и́шь **1** to shout, cry; to give a shout, raise a cry **2** (о + *p.*) (infml) to trumpet

прокурату́р|а, ы *f.* office of public prosecutor

прокуро́р, а *m.* public prosecutor

проку|си́ть, шу́, ~сишь *pf.* (*of* ▸ проку́сывать) to bite through

проку́сыва|ть, ю *impf. of* ▸ прокуси́ть

прола́мыва|ть, ю, ет *impf. of* ▸ проломи́ть

прола́мыва|ться, ется *impf. of* ▸ проломи́ться

пролега́|ть, ет *impf.* to lie, run; доро́га ~ла вдоль бе́рега кана́ла the path lay along the canal

пролез|а́ть, а́ю *impf. of* ▸ проле́зть

проле́з|ть, у, ешь, *past* ~, ~ла *pf.* (*of* ▸ пролеза́ть) **1** (*проникнуть куда-н.*) to get through, climb through **2** (в + *a.*) (fig., infml, pej.), to worm oneself (into, on to); он ~ в чле́ны комите́та he has wormed his way on to the committee

пролетариа́т, а *m.* proletariat

пролет|а́ть[1], а́ю *impf. of* ▸ пролете́ть

пролет|а́ть[2], а́ю *pf.* to fly (*for a certain time*)

проле|те́ть, чу́, ти́шь *pf.* (*of* ▸ пролета́ть[1]) **1** (*какое-н. расстояние*) to fly, cover **2** (*мимо*) to fly (by, through, past) (also fig.); кани́кулы ~те́ли the holidays flew by **3** (fig., *мелькнуть*) to flash, flit

проли́в, а *m.* (geog.) strait, sound

пролива́|ть, ю *impf. of* ▸ проли́ть

проливно́й *adj.*: п. дождь pouring rain; шёл п. дождь it was pouring

прол|и́ть, ью́, ьёшь, *past* ~и́л, ~ила́, ~и́ло *pf.* (*of* ▸ пролива́ть) to spill, shed; п. чью-н. кровь to shed sb's blood; п. свет (на + *a.*) (fig.) to shed light (on)

проло́г, а *m.* prologue (BrE), prolog (AmE)

полож|и́ть, у́, ~ишь *pf.* (*of* ▸ прокла́дывать) **1** to lay; to build, construct; п. путь (fig.) to pave the way **2** (ме́жду + *i.* or + *a.* and *i.*) to interlay; to insert (between)

проло́м, а *m.* break; gap

проло́м|ить, лю́, ~ишь *pf.* (*of* ▸ прола́мывать) to break (through); п. че́реп to fracture one's skull

проло́м|иться, ~ится *pf.* (*of* ▸ прола́мываться) to break, give way

прома́|зать, жу, жешь *pf. of* ▸ ма́зать 4

промарширова́ть, у́ю *pf. of* ▸ марширова́ть

про́мах, а *m.* miss; (fig.) slip, blunder

прома́хива|ться, юсь *impf. of* ▸ промахну́ться

промах|ну́ться, ну́сь, нёшься *pf.* (*of* ▸ прома́хиваться) to miss

прома́чива|ть, ю *impf. of* ▸ промочи́ть

промедле́ни|е, я *nt.* delay; procrastination

промежу́т|ок, ка *m.* (*между событий*) interval; (*между предметами*) space; п. вре́мени period, stretch of time

промежу́точный *adj.* (*положение*) intermediate; (*период*) intervening

промельк|ну́ть, у́, ёшь *pf.* **1** to flash; (*о времени*) to fly by **2** (*появиться*) to be faintly perceptible; в его́ слова́х ~у́ло разочарова́ние there was a shade of disappointment in his words

проме́нива|ть, ю *impf. of* ▸ променя́ть

промен|я́ть, я́ю *pf.* (*of* ▸ проме́нивать) (на + *a.*) to exchange, swap (for); to trade (for), barter (for)

промерз|а́ть, а́ю *impf. of* ▸ промёрзнуть

промёрз|нуть, ну, нешь, *past* ~, ~ла *pf.* (*of* ▸ промерза́ть) to freeze through

промо́зглый *adj.* dank

промок|а́ть, а́ю **1** *impf. of* ▸ промо́кнуть **2** (*impf. only*) to let water through, not be waterproof; э́ти боти́нки ~а́ют these boots are not waterproof

промо́к|нуть, ну, нешь *pf.* (*of* ▸ промока́ть 1) to get soaked, get drenched

промолч|а́ть, у́, и́шь *pf.* to keep silent, say nothing

промо́утер, а *m.* promoter

промо́ушен, а *m.* promotion

промоч|и́ть, у́, ~ишь *pf.* (*of* ▸ прома́чивать) to get wet (through); to soak, drench; п. но́ги to get one's feet wet

промч|а́ться, у́сь, и́шься *pf.* **1** to tear (by, past, through); п. стрело́й to dart (by, past), flash (by, past) **2** (*о времени*) to fly (by)

промыва́|ть, ю *impf. of* ▸ промы́ть

про́мыс|ел, ла *m.* **1** (*охота*) hunting, catching; пушно́й п. trapping **2** (*занятие*) trade, business; **го́рный** n. mining **3** (*in pl.*) (*предприятие*) fields, mines; **нефтяны́е ~лы** oilfields

пром|ы́ть, о́ю, о́ешь pf. (*of* ▶ **промыва́ть**) **1** to wash well, thoroughly; **п. мозги́** (+ d.) (fig.) to brainwash **2** (med.) to bathe

промы́шленник, а m. manufacturer, industrialist

✓ **промы́шленност|ь, и** f. industry

✓ **промы́шленный** adj. industrial

пронес|ти́, у́, ёшь, past **~, ~ла́** pf. (*of* ▶ **проноси́ть**) **1** to carry (by, past, through) **2**: **~ло́!** (infml) the danger is over!

пронес|ти́сь, у́сь, ёшься, past **~ся, ~ла́сь** pf. (*of* ▶ **проноси́ться**) **1** to rush (by, past, through); (*об облаках*) to scud (past) **2** (*о времени*) to fly by

пронз|а́ть, а́ю impf. of ▶ **пронзи́ть**

пронзи́тельн|ый, ~ен, ~ьна adj. piercing

прон|зи́ть, жу́, зи́шь pf. (*of* ▶ **пронза́ть**) to pierce

прони|за́ть, жу́, ~жешь pf. (*of* ▶ **прони́зывать**) to pierce; to permeate, penetrate; (fig.) to run through; **свет ~за́л темноту́** the light pierced the darkness; **одна́ иде́я ~за́ла все его́ произведе́ния** one idea ran through all his works

прони́зыва|ть, ю impf. of ▶ **прониза́ть**

прони́зывающий pres. part. act. of ▶ **прони́зывать** and adj. piercing

проник|а́ть, а́ю impf. of ▶ **прони́кнуть**

прони́к|нуть, ну, нешь, past **~, ~ла** pf. (*of* ▶ **проника́ть**) (**в** + a.) to penetrate (also fig.); (**че́рез** + a.) to percolate (through)

проница́тельн|ый, ~ен, ~ьна adj. perspicacious; shrewd; penetrating, piercing

проно|си́ть, шу́, ~сишь impf. of ▶ **пронести́**

проно|си́ться, шу́сь, ~сишься impf. of ▶ **пронести́сь**

прообраз, а m. prototype

пропага́нд|а, ы f. propaganda; promotion, advocacy

пропаганди́р|овать, ую impf. to propagandize; to advocate

пропада́|ть, ю impf. of ▶ **пропа́сть**

пропа́ж|а, и f. loss

пропа́лыва|ть, ю impf. of ▶ **прополо́ть**

пропа́н, а m. propane

про́пасть|ь, и f. precipice (also fig.); abyss; **на краю́ ~и** (fig.) on the brink of disaster

пропа́|сть, ду́, дёшь, past **~л** pf. (*of* ▶ **пропада́ть**) **1** (*потеряться*) to be missing; to be lost; **п. без вести** (mil.) to be missing **2** (*исчезнуть*) to disappear, vanish; **куда́ вы ~ли?** where did you vanish to? **3** (*погибнуть*) to be lost, be done for; (*о цветах*) to die; **тепе́рь мы ~ли!** now we're done for!

пропа́х|нуть, ну, нешь, past **~, ~ла** pf. to become permeated with the smell (of)

пропека́|ть, ю, ет impf. of ▶ **пропе́чь**

✓ key word

пропека́|ться, ется impf. of ▶ **пропе́чься**

пропе́ллер, а m. propeller

пропе|чь, ку́, чёшь, ку́т, past **~к, ~кла́** pf. (*of* ▶ **пропека́ть**) to bake well, thoroughly

пропе́|чься, чётся, ку́тся, past **~кся, ~кла́сь** pf. (*of* ▶ **пропека́ться**) to bake well, get baked through

пропива́|ть, ю impf. of ▶ **пропи́ть**

пропи́лива|ть, ю impf. of ▶ **пропили́ть**

пропил|и́ть, ю́, ~ишь pf. (*of* ▶ **пропи́ливать**) to saw through

пропи|са́ть, шу́, ~шешь pf. (*of* ▶ **пропи́сывать**) **1** (*лекарство*) to prescribe **2** (*жильца*) to register

пропи|са́ться, шу́сь, ~шешься pf. (*of* ▶ **пропи́сываться**) to register

пропи́ск|а, и f. **1** (*регистрация*) registration **2** (*отметка в паспорте*) residence permit

прописно́й adj. (*буква*) capital; **писа́ться с п. бу́квы** to be written with a capital letter

пропи́сыва|ть, ю impf. of ▶ **пропиcа́ть**

пропи́сыва|ться, юсь impf. of ▶ **прописа́ться**

пропит|а́ть, а́ю pf. (*of* ▶ **пропи́тывать**) (+ i.) to impregnate (with), steep (in); **п. ма́слом** to oil

пропит|а́ться, а́юсь pf. (*of* ▶ **пропи́тываться**) (+ i.) to become saturated (with)

пропи́тыва|ть, ю impf. of ▶ **пропита́ть**

пропи́тыва|ться, юсь impf. of ▶ **пропита́ться**

про|пи́ть, пью́, пьёшь, past **~пи́л, ~пила́, ~пи́ло** pf. (*of* ▶ **пропива́ть**) **1** (*деньги*) to spend on drink, squander on drink **2** (infml, *талант*) to ruin (through excessive drinking)

проплава́|ть, ю pf. (*вплавь*) to swim (*for a certain time*); (*на судне*) to sail (*for a certain time*)

проплá|кать, чу, чешь pf. to cry, weep (*for a certain time*)

проплыва́|ть, ю impf. of ▶ **проплы́ть**

проплы́|ть, ву́, вёшь, past **~л, ~ла́, ~ло** pf. (*of* ▶ **проплыва́ть**) **1** (*вплавь*) to swim (by, past, through); (*на судне*) to sail (by, past, through); (*о предмете*) to float, drift (by, past, through) **2** (*расстояние*) to cover (*a certain distance*)

пропове́дник, а m. **1** preacher **2** (+ g.) (fig.) advocate (of)

пропове́д|овать, ую impf. **1** to preach **2** (fig.) to advocate, propagate

про́повед|ь, и f. sermon; homily

проползá|ть, а́ю impf. of ▶ **проползти́**

пропол|зти́, у́, ёшь, past **~, ~ла́** pf. (*of* ▶ **проползáть**) to creep, crawl (by, past, through)

прополо́|скáть, щу́, ~щешь pf. (*of* ▶ **полоскáть**) to rinse, swill; **п. го́рло** to gargle

пропол|о́ть, ю́, ~ешь pf. (*of* ▶ **пропáлывать**) to weed

пропорциона́л|ьный, ∼ен, ∼ьна *adj.*
1 proportional; proportionate
2 (*обладающий правильными пропорциями*) well proportioned

пропо́рци|я, и *f.* proportion

про́пуск, а *m.* **1** (*no pl.*) (*действие*) admission **2** (*pl.* ∼á) (*документ*) pass, permit **3** (*pl.* ∼á) (*mil.*) password **4** (*pl.* ∼и) (+ *g.*) (*непосещение*) non-attendance (at), absence (from) **5** (*pl.* ∼и) (*пустое место*) blank, gap

пропуска́|ть, ю *impf.* **1** *impf. of* ▶ пропусти́ть **2** (*impf. only*) to let pass; п. во́ду to leak; не п. воды́ to be waterproof

пропускн|о́й *adj.*: п. пункт checkpoint; ∼áя спосо́бность capacity; (*comput.*) bandwidth

пропу|сти́ть, щу́, ∼стишь *pf.* (*of* ▶ пропуска́ть 1) **1** (*дать пройти*) to let pass, let through; to make way (for); (*впустить*) to let in, admit; (*обслужить*) to put through, deal with; п. на перро́н to let on to the platform **2** (*через* + *a.*) to run (through), pass (through); п. че́рез фильтр to filter **3** (*при чтении, письме*) to omit, leave out; to skip **4** (*не яви́ться*) to miss; п. ле́кцию to miss a lecture

пропылесо́с|ить, ишь *pf. of* ▶ пылесо́сить

прораба́тыва|ть, ю *impf. of* ▶ прорабо́тать[1]

прорабо́та|ть[1], ю *pf.* (*of* ▶ прораба́тывать) (*infml*) **1** (*изучить*) to work (at), study **2** (*критиковать*) to pick holes (in)

прорабо́та|ть[2], ю *pf.* (*некоторое время*) to work (*for a while*)

прораст|а́ть, а́ет *impf. of* ▶ прорасти́

прораст|и́, ёт, *past* проро́с, проросла́ *pf.* (*of* ▶ прораста́ть) (*of plant*) to germinate, sprout, shoot (*of plant*)

прорв|а́ть, у́, ёшь, *past* ∼а́л, ∼ала́, ∼а́ло *pf.* (*of* ▶ прорыва́ть[1]) **1** to break through; to tear, make a hole (in); п. ли́нию оборо́ны проти́вника to break through the enemy's defence line; (*impers.*) плоти́ну ∼а́ло the dam has burst **2** (*impers.*) (*infml*) to lose patience

прорв|а́ться, у́сь, ёшься, *past* ∼а́лся, ∼ала́сь, ∼а́ло́сь *pf.* (*of* ▶ прорыва́ться) **1** (*сломаться*) to break, burst (open) **2** (*разорваться*) to tear **3** (*силой проложить себе путь*) to break (out, through); to force one's way (through)

прореаги́р|овать, ую *pf. of* ▶ реаги́ровать 2

проре́|зать, жу, жешь *pf. of* ▶ проре́зывать, ▶ проре́зать) to cut through (*also fig.*)

проре́за|ть, ю *impf. of* ▶ проре́зать

проре́зыва|ть, ю *impf. of* ▶ проре́зать

про́рез|ь, и *f.* opening, aperture

проржаве́|ть, ет *pf.* to rust through

проро́к, а *m.* prophet

проро́ч|ить, у, ишь *impf.* (*of* ▶ напроро́чить) to prophesy, predict

проруб|а́ть, а́ю *impf. of* ▶ проруби́ть

проруб|и́ть, лю́, ∼ишь *pf.* (*of* ▶ проруба́ть) to hack through, cut through

про́руб|ь, и *f.* ice hole

проры́в, а *m.* break; (*mil.*) breakthrough, breach

прорыва́|ть[1], ю *impf. of* ▶ прорва́ть

прорыва́|ть[2], ю *impf. of* ▶ проры́ть

прорыва́|ться, юсь *impf. of* ▶ прорва́ться

проры́|ть, о́ю, о́ешь *pf.* (*of* ▶ прорыва́ть[2]) to dig through

проса́чива|ться, ется *impf. of* ▶ просочи́ться

просверл|и́ть, ю́, и́шь *pf. of* ▶ сверли́ть

просве́т, а *m.* shaft of light; (*fig.*) ray of hope

просве|ти́ть[1], щу́, ти́шь *pf.* (*of* ▶ просвеща́ть) to educate; to enlighten

просве|ти́ть[2], чу́, ∼тишь *pf.* (*of* ▶ просве́чивать[1]) (*med.*) to X-ray

просве́чива|ть[1], ю *impf. of* ▶ просвети́ть[2]

просве́чива|ть[2], ю *impf.* **1** (*быть прозрачным*) to be translucent; (*одежда, занавески*) to be see-through **2** (*через, сквозь* + *a.*) (*быть видным*) to be visible (through), show (through), appear (through); (*о солнце*) to shine (through)

просвеща́|ть, ю *impf. of* ▶ просвети́ть[1]

просвеще́ни|е, я *nt.* **1** (*образование*) education; наро́дное п. public education **2** enlightenment; эпо́ха П∼я (*hist.*) the Age of the Enlightenment

просвещ|ённый *p.p.p. of* ▶ просвети́ть[1] *and adj.* enlightened; educated, cultured; ∼ённое мне́ние expert opinion; п. челове́к educated person

про́сек|а, и *f.* cutting (*in a forest*)

просиде́ть, жу́, ди́шь *pf.* (*of* ▶ проси́живать) to sit (*for a certain time*); п. ночь у посте́ли больно́го to sit up all night with a patient

проси́жива|ть, ю *impf. of* ▶ просиде́ть

✍ **про|си́ть, шу́, ∼сишь** *impf.* (*of* ▶ попроси́ть) **1** (+ *a. of person asked*; + *a. or g. of thing sought or* о + *p.*) to ask (for), beg; ∼шу́ (вас) please; п. кого́-н. о по́мощи to ask sb for help, ask sb's assistance; п. разреше́ния to ask permission; п. сове́та to ask (for) advice; п. извине́ния у кого́-н. to apologize to sb **2** (*за* + *a.*) (*вступаться*) to intercede (for) **3** (*приглашать*) to invite; вас ∼сят к столу́ please take your places at the table

про|си́ться, шу́сь, ∼сишься *impf.* (*of* ▶ попроси́ться) (+ *inf. or* в + *a. or* на + *a.*) to ask (for); п. в о́тпуск to apply for leave

проска́кива|ть, ю *impf. of* ▶ проскочи́ть

проска́льзыва|ть, ю *impf. of* ▶ проскользну́ть

проскользн|у́ть, у́, ёшь *pf.* (*of* ▶ проска́льзывать) (*infml*) to slip in, creep in (*also fig.*); ∼у́ло мно́го оши́бок many errors have crept in

проскоч|и́ть, у́, ∼ишь *pf.* (*of* ▶ проска́кивать) **1** (*пробежать*) to rush by, tear by **2** (*через* + *a.*) to slip (through) **3** (*сквозь* + *a. or* ме́жду + *i.*) to fall (through, between); п. ме́жду па́льцами to fall through one's fingers **4** (*не остановиться, где нужно*) to overshoot

просла́в|иться, люсь, ишься pf. (of
▶ прославля́ться) (+ i.) to become famous
(for)

прославля́|ться, юсь impf. of
▶ просла́виться

прросле|ди́ть, жу́, ди́шь pf. (of
▶ просле́живать) **1** (вы́следить) to track
(down) **2** (иссле́довать) to trace (through);
to trace back, retrace

просле́жива|ть, ю impf. of ▶ проследи́ть

просло́йк|а, и f. layer, stratum (also fig.)

прослуж|и́ть, у́, ~ишь pf. **1** to work,
serve (for a certain time) **2** (пробы́ть в
употребле́нии) to last (for a certain time);
э́то пальто́ ~ит мне ещё оди́н год this coat
will last me another year

прослу́ш|ать, аю pf. **1** (impf. слу́шать) to
hear (through); п. курс ле́кций to attend a
course of lectures **2** (impf. ~ивать) (med.)
to listen to; п. чьё-н. се́рдце to listen to sb's
heart **3** (impf. ~ивать) (infml) to miss, not
catch; прости́те, я ~ал, что вы сказа́ли I am
sorry, I did not catch what you said

прослу́шивани|е, я nt. audition

прослу́шива|ть, ю impf. of ▶ прослу́шать 2,
▶ прослу́шать 3

просма́трива|ть, ю impf. of ▶ просмотре́ть

✐ просмо́тр, а m. survey; view, viewing;
предвари́тельный п. preview

просмотр|е́ть, ю́, ~ишь pf. (of
▶ просма́тривать) **1** to survey; to view
2 (чита́я) to look over, look through;
(бе́гло) to glance over, glance through; п.
ру́копись to glance through a manuscript
3 (пропусти́ть) to overlook, miss

прос|ну́ться, ну́сь, нёшься pf. (of
▶ просыпа́ться¹) to wake up, awake

просо́выва|ть, ю impf. of ▶ просу́нуть

просо́выва|ться, юсь impf. of
▶ просу́нуться

просо́х|нуть, ну, нешь, past ~, ~ла pf. (of
▶ просыха́ть) to get dry, dry out

просоч|и́ться, и́тся pf. (of ▶ проса́чиваться)
1 to percolate; to filter; to leak; to seep
out **2** (fig.) to filter through; to leak out

проспа́|ть¹, лю́, и́шь, past ~а́л, ~ала́, ~а́ло
pf. (of ▶ просыпа́ть²) **1** (не просну́ться
во́время) to oversleep **2** (пропусти́ть) to
miss, pass (due to being asleep)

проспа́|ть², лю́, и́шь, past ~а́л, ~ала́,
~а́ло pf. (не́которое вре́мя) to sleep (for a
certain time)

проспе́кт¹, а m. (у́лица) avenue

проспе́кт², а m. **1** (спра́вочное изда́ние)
brochure, prospectus **2** (план) outline,
résumé

проспо́рива|ть, ю impf. of ▶ проспо́рить

проспо́р|ить, ю, ишь pf. (of ▶ проспо́ривать)
(де́ньги) to lose (in a bet)

проспряга́|ть, ю pf. of ▶ спряга́ть

просро́ченный p.p.p. of ▶ просро́чить and
adj. overdue

просро́чива|ть, ю impf. of ▶ просро́чить

просро́ч|ить, у, ишь pf. (of ▶ просро́чивать)
to exceed the time limit; п. платёж to fail to
pay in time

проста́ива|ть, ю impf. of ▶ простоя́ть

проста́к, а́ m. simpleton

проста́т|а, ы f. (anat.) prostate (gland)

проститу́тк|а, и f. prostitute

проститу́ци|я, и f. prostitution

про|сти́ть, щу́, сти́шь pf. (of ▶ проща́ть)
1 to forgive, pardon; ~сти́те (меня́)! excuse
me!; I beg your pardon! **2** (долг) to remit; п.
долг кому́-н. to remit sb's debt

про|сти́ться, щу́сь, сти́шься pf. (of
▶ проща́ться) (с + i.) to say goodbye (to),
bid farewell (to)

✐ про́сто adv. simply; п. так for no particular
reason; э́то п. невероя́тно it is simply
incredible

простоду́ш|ный, ~ен, ~на adj. simple-
hearted; ingenuous, artless

✐ прост|о́й, ~, ~а́, ~о, ~ы́ adj. **1** (нетру́дный)
simple; easy; вам ~о́ критикова́ть it is easy
(or all very well) for you to criticize
2 (одноро́дный) simple (= unitary);
~о́е число́ (math.) prime number
3 (обыкнове́нный) simple; ordinary;
п. наро́д the common people **4** (без
прете́нзий) simple, plain; unaffected,
unpretentious; ~ы́е лю́ди ordinary people;
homely people **5** (не бо́лее как) mere;
п. сме́ртный a mere mortal; по той ~о́й
причи́не, что for the simple reason that

простон|а́ть, у́, ~ешь pf. to groan

просто́р, а m. **1** (простра́нство)
spaciousness; space, expanse **2** (свобо́да)
freedom, scope

просто́р|ный, ~ен, ~на adj. spacious,
roomy; (об оде́жде) loose-fitting

простот|а́, ы́ f. simplicity

просто|я́ть, ю́, и́шь pf. (of ▶ проста́ивать)
1 (не́которое вре́мя) to stay, stand; по́езд
~я́л на запа́сном пути́ всю ночь the train
stood on a siding all night **2** (безде́йствовать)
to stand idle, lie idle **3** (о зда́нии) to stand,
last

простра́н|ный, ~ен, ~на adj. verbose

простра́нственный adj. spatial

✐ простра́нств|о, а nt. space; (неограни́ченная
протяжённость) expanse; возду́шное п. air
space; пусто́е п. void

простра́ци|я, и f. prostration

простре́лива|ть, ю impf. of ▶ прострели́ть

прострел|и́ть, ю́, ~ишь pf. (of
▶ простре́ливать) **1** (вы́стрелом проби́ть
наскво́зь) to shoot through **2** (sport) to cross
low

просту́д|а, ы f. (chest) cold; схвати́ть/
подхвати́ть ~у (infml) to catch (a) cold

п

просту|ди́ть, жу́, ~́дишь pf. (of ▸ **простужа́ть**) to let catch cold; **п. себе́ го́рло** to get a sore throat

просту|ди́ться, жу́сь, ~́дишься pf. (of ▸ **простужа́ться**) to catch (a) cold

простужа́|ть, ю impf. of ▸ **простуди́ть**

простужа́|ться, юсь impf. of ▸ **простуди́ться**

проступ|а́ть, а́ет impf. of ▸ **проступи́ть**

проступ|и́ть, ~ит pf. (of ▸ **проступа́ть**) to appear, show through, come through; **сы́рые пя́тна ~и́ли на сте́нах** damp patches have appeared on the walls

просту́п|ок, ка m. misdeed; (law) misdemeanour (BrE), misdemeanor (AmE)

простыва́|ть, ю impf. of ▸ **просты́ть**

простын|я́, и́, pl. ~и, ~е́й/~ь, ~я́м f. sheet

просты́|ть, ну, нешь pf. (of ▸ **простыва́ть**) (infml) to catch cold

просу́н|уть, у, ешь pf. (of ▸ **просо́вывать**) (**в + a.**) to push (through, in), shove (through, in), thrust (through, in)

просу́н|уться, усь, ешься pf. (of ▸ **просо́вываться**) to push through, force one's way through

просу́шива|ть, ю impf. of ▸ **просуши́ть**

просу́шива|ться, юсь impf. of ▸ **просуши́ться**

просуш|и́ть, у́, ~ишь pf. (of ▸ **просу́шивать**) to dry thoroughly, properly

просуш|и́ться, у́сь, ~ишься pf. (of ▸ **просу́шиваться**) to (get) dry

просуществ|ова́ть, у́ю pf. (*прожи́ть*) to exist; (*продли́ться*) to last, endure

просчёт, а m. **1** (*де́йствие*) counting (up), reckoning (up) **2** (*оши́бка*) error (*in counting, reckoning*)

просчит|а́ться, а́юсь pf. (of ▸ **просчи́тываться**) to miscalculate

просчи́тыва|ться, юсь impf. of ▸ **просчита́ться**

просы́п|ать, лю, лешь pf. (of ▸ **просыпа́ть**[1]) to spill

просып|а́ть[1]**, а́ю** impf. of ▸ **просы́пать**

просып|а́ть[2]**, а́ю** impf. of ▸ **проспа́ть**[1]

просы́п|аться, летca pf. (of ▸ **просыпа́ться**[2]) to spill, get spilled

просып|а́ться[1]**, а́юсь** impf. of ▸ **проснуться**

просып|а́ться[2]**, а́ется** impf. of ▸ **просы́паться**

просыха́|ть, ю impf. of ▸ **просо́хнуть**

◌ **про́сьб|а, ы** f. request; **обраща́ться с ~ой** to make a request; **у меня́ к вам п.** I have a favour (BrE), favor (AmE) to ask you; **по мое́й ~е** at my request; **«п. не кури́ть!»** 'no smoking, please!'

прота́лкива|ть, ю impf. of ▸ **протолкну́ть**

прота́птыва|ть, ю impf. of ▸ **протопта́ть**

прота́скива|ть, ю impf. of ▸ **протащи́ть**

протащ|и́ть, у́, ~ишь pf. (of ▸ **прота́скивать**) to pull (through, along), drag (through, along), trail

протеже́ c.g. indecl. protégé (*fem.* protégée)

проте́з, а m. prosthesis; artificial limb; **зубно́й п.** false tooth, denture

протеи́н, а m. (chem.) protein

протека́|ть, ю impf. **1** impf. of ▸ **проте́чь** **2** (impf. only) (*о реке, струе*) to flow, run **3** (impf. only) (*о крыше*) to leak, be leaky

про|тере́ть, тру́, трёшь, past ~тёр, ~тёрла pf. (of ▸ **протира́ть**) **1** (*окна́*) to rub over, wipe over **2**: **п. глаза́** (infml) to rub one's eyes

проте́ст, а m. **1** protest; **заяви́ть п.** to make a protest **2** (law) objection

протеста́нт, а m. (relig.) Protestant

протеста́нт|ка, ки f. of ▸ **протеста́нт**

протеста́нтский adj. (relig.) Protestant

протест|ова́ть, у́ю impf. (**про́тив + g.**) to protest (against)

проте́|чь, чёт, ку́т, past ~к, ~кла́ pf. (of ▸ **протека́ть**) **1** to ooze, seep **2** (*о вре́мени*) to elapse, pass **3** (*о боле́зни*) to take its course

◌ **про́тив** prep. + g. **1** against; **п. тече́ния** against the current; **за и п.** for and against, pro and con; **име́ть что-н. п.** to have sth against; to mind, object; **вы ничего́ не име́ете п. того́, что я курю́?** do you mind my smoking? **2** (*пря́мо пе́ред*) opposite; facing; **друг п. дру́га** facing one another **3** (*вопреки́*) contrary to; **п. на́ших ожида́ний** contrary to our expectations

про́тив|ень, ня m. (*неглубо́кий*) baking sheet, baking tray; (*глубо́кий*) roasting pan

◌ **проти́вник, а** m. **1** opponent, adversary **2** (collect.) (mil.) the enemy

проти́вн|ый[1] adj. opposite; contrary; **в ~ом слу́чае** otherwise; **доказа́тельство от ~ого** the rule of contraries

проти́вн|ый[2]**, ~ен, ~на** adj. (*отврати́тельный*) nasty, disgusting; **п. за́пах** nasty smell; **он мне ~ен** I find him offensive

противове́с, а m. (tech., also fig.) counterbalance, counterpoise

противога́з, а m. gas mask

противоде́йстви|е, я nt. opposition, counteraction

противоде́йств|овать, ую impf. (+ d.) to oppose, counteract

противоесте́ствен|ный, ~, ~на adj. unnatural

противозако́н|ный, ~ен, ~на adj. unlawful; (law) illegal

противозача́точн|ый adj. contraceptive; **~ое сре́дство** contraceptive

противопожа́рн|ый adj. fire-prevention; **~ая дверь** fire door

противополо́жность, и f. **1** (*несхо́дство*) opposition; contrast; **в п. (+ d.)** as opposed (to), by contrast (with) **2** (*что-н. противополо́жное*) opposite, antithesis; **пряма́я п.** exact opposite

противополо́жн|ый, ~ен, ~на adj. **1** (*бе́рег*) opposite **2** (*мне́ние*) opposed, contrary

П

противопоста́в|ить, лю, ишь pf. (of
▶ **противопоставля́ть**) (+ d.) **1** (направить против) to oppose (with), counter (with); **си́ле п. си́лу** to oppose force with force **2** (сравнить) to contrast (with), set off (against)

противопоставля́|ть, ю impf. of
▶ **противопоста́вить**

противопра́в|ный, ~ен, ~на adj.
unlawful, illegal

противоречи́в|ый, ~, ~а adj.
contradictory; conflicting; **~ые сообще́ния** conflicting reports

противоре́чи|е, я nt. **1** (несоответствие) contradiction; inconsistency **2** (возражение) contrariness; defiance **3** (конфликт) conflict, clash; **находи́ться в ~и (с** + i.) to be at variance (with), conflict (with)

противоре́ч|ить, у, ишь impf. (+ d.) **1** (возражать) to contradict **2** (несоответствовать) to be at variance (with), conflict (with), be contrary (to); **их показа́ния ~ат друг дру́гу** their evidence is conflicting

противостоя́ни|е, я nt. **1** (astron.) opposition **2** (pol.) confrontation

противоя́ди|е, я nt. antidote

протира́|ть, ю impf. of ▶ **протере́ть**

проткн|у́ть, у́, ёшь pf. (of ▶ **протыка́ть**) to pierce

прото́к, а m. **1** channel **2** (anat.) duct

протоко́л, а m. **1** (заседания) minutes; report; **вести́ п.** to take the minutes **2** (law) statement; charge sheet; **соста́вить п.** to draw up a report **3** (pol., comput.) protocol

протолкн|у́ть, у́, ёшь pf. (of ▶ **прота́лкивать**) to push through, press through

прото́н, а m. (phys.) proton

протоп|та́ть, чу́, ~чешь pf. (of ▶ **прота́птывать**) to beat, make (by walking); **п. тропи́нку** to make a path

прототи́п, а m. prototype

прото́чн|ый adj. flowing, running; **~ая вода́** running water; **п. пруд** pond fed by springs

протрезве́|ть, ю pf. of ▶ **трезве́ть**

протрезв|и́ться, лю́сь, и́шься pf. (of ▶ **протрезвля́ться**) to sober up

протрезвля́|ться, юсь impf. of
▶ **протрезви́ться**

протух|а́ть, а́ет impf. of ▶ **проту́хнуть**

проту́х|нуть, нет, past **~, ~ла** pf. (of ▶ **протуха́ть**) (мясо, рыба) to go bad

проту́хший p.p. act. of ▶ **проту́хнуть** and adj. rotten; bad

протыка́|ть, ю impf. of ▶ **проткну́ть**

протя́гива|ть, ю impf. of ▶ **протяну́ть**

протя́гива|ться, юсь impf. of ▶ **протяну́ться**

✍ **протяже́ни|е, я** nt. **1** extent; (пространство) expanse, area; **на всём ~и** (+ g.) along the whole length (of), all along **2**; **на ~и** (+ g.) during, for the duration (of)

протя́ж|ный, ~ен, ~на adj. long drawn-out

прот|яну́ть, яну́, ~я́нешь pf. (of ▶ **протя́гивать**) **1** (верёвку) to stretch; (линию связи) to extend **2** (руки, ноги) to stretch out; (газету, книгу) to hold out; **п. ру́ку по́мощи** to extend a helping hand

прот|яну́ться, яну́сь, ~я́нешься pf. (of ▶ **протя́гиваться**) **1** (о дороге, о пространстве) to extend, stretch, reach **2** (pf. only) (продлиться) to last, go on

проу́чива|ть, ю impf. of ▶ **проучи́ть**

проуч|и́ть, у́, ~ишь pf. (of ▶ **проу́чивать**) (infml, наказать) to teach (a lesson)

профа́н, а m. ignoramus; (неспециалист) layman

профессиона́л, а m. professional

профессионали́зм, а m. professionalism

✍ **профессиона́льный** adj. **1** professional, occupational; **п. диплома́т** career diplomat; **п. секре́т** trade secret; **п. сою́з** trade union **2** (компетентный) professional (opp. amateur)

профе́сси|я, и f. profession, occupation, trade; **по ~и** by profession, by trade

✍ **профе́ссор, а,** pl. **~á** m. professor

про́фи c.g. indecl. (infml) professional; pro (infml)

профила́ктик|а, и f. **1** (med.) prophylaxis **2** (collect.) preventive measures, precautions

профилакто́ри|й, я m. sanatorium, health farm

про́фил|ь, я m. **1** (вид сбоку) profile; side view; **в п.** in profile **2** (специфический характер) type; **шко́лы ра́зного ~я** schools of various types

профильтр|ова́ть, у́ю pf. (of ▶ **фильтрова́ть**)

профсою́з, а m. trade union

проха́жива|ться, юсь impf. of ▶ **пройти́сь**

прохла́д|а, ы f. coolness

прохла́д|ный, ~ен, ~на adj. **1** cool; (impers., pred.) **~но** it is cool **2** (fig.) cool

прохо́д, а m. **1** (действие) passage; **не дава́ть ~а** (+ d.) to give no peace, pester **2** (место) passageway; (между рядами) gangway, aisle

проходи́м|ец, ца m. (infml) rogue, rascal

проходи́м|ый, ~, ~а adj. passable

✍ **прохо|ди́ть¹, жу́, ~дишь** impf. **1** impf. of ▶ **пройти́ 2** (impf. only) (че́рез + a.) to lie (through), go (through), pass (through)

прохо|ди́ть², жу́, ~дишь pf. (некоторое время) to walk; **мы ~ди́ли весь день** we have spent the whole day walking

прохо́ж|ий adj. passing, in transit; (as n. **п.**, ~**его,** f. ~**ая,** ~**ей**) passer-by

процвета́ни|е, я nt. prosperity, well-being; flourishing

процвета́|ть, ю impf. to prosper, flourish, thrive

✍ key word

процеди́ть, жу́, ~дишь *pf. (of* ▶ **проце́живать)** **1** to filter, strain **2**: п. сквозь зу́бы to say through clenched teeth

процеду́ра, ы *f.* **1** procedure **2** *(usu. in pl.)* (med.) treatment

проце́жива|ть, ю *impf. of* ▶ **процеди́ть**

проце́нт, а *m.* **1** percentage; per cent; **сто ~ов** one hundred per cent **2** *(дохо́д с капита́ла)* interest

проце́сс, а *m.* **1** process **2** (law) trial; legal proceedings; lawsuit

проце́ссия, и *f.* procession

проце́ссор, а *m.* (comput.) processor; **центра́льный п.** central processing unit

процессуа́льн|ый *adj.* procedural; **~ые но́рмы** legal procedure

процити́р|овать, ую *pf. of* ▶ **цити́ровать**

про́черк, а *m.* dash, line

про|че́сть, чту́, чтёшь, *past* **~чёл, ~чла́** *pf.* = **прочита́ть**

про́ч|ий *adj.* other; **и ~ee** *(abbr.* **и пр.,** **и проч.)** et cetera, and so on; **~ие** (the) others; **ме́жду ~им** by the way; **поми́мо (всего́) ~его** in addition

прочи́|стить, щу, стишь *pf. (of* ▶ **прочища́ть)** to clean out

прочита́|ть, ю *pf. of* ▶ **чита́ть**

прочища́|ть, ю *impf. of* ▶ **прочи́стить**

про́чно *adv.* firmly, soundly, solidly, well

про́чность, и *f.* firmness, soundness, stability, solidity; durability; strength; **запа́с ~и, коэффицие́нт ~и** safety factor, safety margin

про́ч|ный, ~ен, ~на́, ~но, ~ны *adj.* firm, sound, stable, solid; durable, lasting; **~ные зна́ния** sound knowledge; **~ная ткань** durable fabric

прочь *adv.* **1** away, off; **(поди́) п.!** go away!; be off!; **п. с доро́ги!** (get) out of the way!, make way!; **ру́ки п.!** hands off! **2** *(as pred.)* averse (to); **не п.** *(+ inf.)* (infml) to have no objection (to); to be not averse (to)

проше́дш|ий *p.p. act. of* ▶ **пройти́** *and adj.* past; last; **~ee вре́мя** (gram.) past tense; *(as nt. n.* **~ee, ~его)** the past

прошеп|та́ть, чу́, ~чешь *pf. of* ▶ **шепта́ть**

прошива́|ть, ю *impf. of* ▶ **проши́ть**

прош|и́ть, ью́, ьёшь *pf. (of* ▶ **прошива́ть)** to sew, stitch (on)

прошлого́дний *adj.* last year's; of last year

про́шл|ый *adj.* **1** *(происходи́вший ране́е)* past; former; *(as nt. n.* **~ое, ~ого)** the past; **далёкое ~ое** the distant past **2** *(предше́ствовавший настоя́щему)* last; **в ~ом году́** last year; **на ~ой неде́ле** last week

прошмы́гива|ть, ю *impf. of* ▶ **прошмыгну́ть**

прошмыг|ну́ть, ну́, нёшь *pf. (of* ▶ **прошмы́гивать)** (infml) *(челове́к)* to slip (by, past, through); *(живо́тное)* to scurry past

проща́й and **проща́йте** goodbye!; farewell!

проща́ни|е, я *nt.* farewell; parting, leave-taking; **на п.** at parting

проща́|ть, ю *impf. of* ▶ **прости́ть**

проща́|ться, юсь *impf. of* ▶ **прости́ться**

про́ще *comp. of* ▶ **просто́й,** ▶ **про́сто;** simpler; plainer; easier

проще́ни|е, я *nt.* forgiveness; *(преступника)* pardon; *(греха)* absolution; **проси́ть ~я у кого́-н.** to ask sb's pardon; **прошу́ ~я!** I beg your pardon!; (I am) sorry!

проэкзамен|ова́ть, у́ю *pf. of* ▶ **экзаменова́ть**

прояв|и́ть, лю́, ~ишь *pf. (of* ▶ **проявля́ть)** **1** to show, display; **п. интере́с (к** + *d.)* to show interest (in); **п. себя́** (+ *i.*) to show oneself, prove (to be) **2** (phot.) to develop

прояв|и́ться, ~ится *pf. (of* ▶ **проявля́ться)** to show (itself), reveal itself, manifest itself

проявле́ни|е, я *nt.* display, manifestation

проявля́|ть, ю, ет *impf. of* ▶ **прояви́ть**

проявля́|ться, ется *impf. of* ▶ **прояви́ться**

проясн|и́ть, ю́, и́шь *pf. (of* ▶ **проясня́ть)** to clarify

проясн|и́ться, и́тся *pf. (of* ▶ **проясня́ться)** **1** *(о пого́де)* to clear (up); **днём ~и́лось** in the afternoon it cleared up **2** *(о мы́слях, о положе́нии)* to become clear

проясн|я́ть, я́ю *impf. of* ▶ **проясни́ть**

проясн|я́ться, я́ется *impf. of* ▶ **проясни́ться**

пруд, а́, в ~у́, *pl.* **~ы́** *m.* pond

пружи́н|а, ы *f.* spring

Пру́ссия, и *f.* Prussia

прут, а́ *m. (pl.* **~ья, ~ьев)** twig; switch; **и́вовый п.** withe, withy

прыга́л|ка, и *f.* (infml) skipping rope (BrE), jump rope (AmE)

пры́га|ть, аю *impf. (of* ▶ **пры́гнуть)** **1** to jump, leap, spring; to bound; **п. на одно́й ноге́** to hop on one leg; **п. со скака́лкой** to skip **2** *(о мяче́)* to bounce

пры́г|нуть, ну, нешь *inst. pf. of* ▶ **пры́гать**

прыгу́н, а́ *m.* (sport) jumper; **п. в во́ду** diver; **п. в длину́** long jumper

прыгу́н|ья, ьи, *g. pl.* **~ий** *f. of* ▶ **прыгу́н**

прыж|о́к, ка́ *m.* **1** jump, leap, spring **2** (sport) jump; **~ки́** jumping; **п. в во́ду** diving; **п. в высоту́** high jump; **п. в длину́** long jump

пры́ска|ть, ю *impf. of* ▶ **пры́снуть**

пры́с|нуть, ну, нешь *pf. (of* ▶ **пры́скать)** (infml) **1** (+ *i.*) to sprinkle (with); to spray (with) **2** *(поли́ться струёй)* to spurt, gush

пры́т|кий, ~ок, ~ка *adj.* quick, lively, sharp *(often disapproving)*

прыщ, а́ *m.* pimple, spot

прядь, и *f.* lock *(of hair)*

пря́ж|а, и *(no pl.)* *f.* yarn

пря́жк|а, и *f.* buckle

пря́лк|а, и *f.* spinning wheel

прям|а́я, о́й *f.* straight line; **провести́ ~у́ю** to draw a straight line; **расстоя́ние по ~о́й** distance as the crow flies

прямико́м *adv.* (infml) straight

пря́мо *adv.* **1** straight (on); **иди́те п.!** (go) straight on!; **держа́ться п.** to hold oneself straight *or* erect **2** *(непосре́дственно)* straight, directly; **смотре́ть п. в глаза́ кому́-н.** to look sb straight in the face **3** (fig., *откровенно*) straight; frankly, openly; **сказа́ть что-н. кому́-н. п. в лицо́** to say sth to sb's face **4** (infml, *точно*) just, exactly; **он вы́глядит п. как оте́ц** he looks just like his father

✎ **прям|о́й, ~, ~а́, ~о, ~ы́** adj. **1** (*без изгибов*) straight; (*вертикальный*) upright, erect; **п. у́гол** (math.) right angle **2** (*без промежуточных пунктов*) through; direct; **~а́я ли́ния** direct (telephone) line **3** (*непосредственный*) direct; **~ые вы́боры** direct elections; **~ая противополо́жность** direct opposite **4** (*откровенный*) straightforward, frank

прямолине́й|ный, ~ен, ~йна adj. **1** rectilinear **2** (fig.) straightforward; direct

прямоуго́льник, а m. (math.) rectangle

пря́ник, а m. spice cake; gingerbread; **медо́вый п.** honey cake

пря́ност|ь, и f. spice

пря|сть, ду́, дёшь, past **~л, ~ла́, ~ло** impf. (of ▶ **спрясть**) to spin

пря́|тать, чу, чешь impf. (of ▶ **спря́тать**) to hide, conceal

пря́|таться, чусь, чешься impf. (of ▶ **спря́таться**) to hide; to conceal oneself; to take refuge

пря́т|ки, ок (no sg.) hide-and-seek; **игра́ть в п.** to play hide-and-seek

пря́х|а, и f. spinner

псал|о́м, ма́ m. psalm

псевдони́м, а m. pseudonym; (comput.) alias

псих, а m. (infml) loony, nutcase

психиа́тр, а m. psychiatrist

психиатри́ческий adj. psychiatric

психиатри́|я, и f. psychiatry

пси́хик|а, и f. state of mind; psyche; **вре́дно де́йствовать на ~у** to have a harmful effect on the psyche

психи́чески adv. mentally, psychically, psychologically; **п. больно́й** mentally ill; (as m. п. **п. больно́й, п. больно́го**) mental patient

психи́ческ|ий adj. mental; **~ая боле́знь** mental illness

психоана́лиз, а m. psychoanalysis

психоанали́тик, а m. psychoanalyst

психо́з, а m. mental illness; (med.) psychosis

психо́лог, а m. psychologist

✎ **психологи́ческий** adj. psychological

психоло́ги|я, и f. psychology

психопа́т, а m. psychopath; (infml) lunatic

психотерапе́вт, а m. psychotherapist

психотерапи́|я, и f. psychotherapy

псориа́з, а m. (med.) psoriasis

птен|е́ц, ца́ m. chick; fledgling (also fig.)

✎ **пти́ц|а, ы** f. bird; **дома́шняя п.** (collect.) poultry; **хи́щные ~ы** birds of prey; **ва́жная п.**

(fig., infml) big noise

птицефе́рм|а, ы f. poultry farm

ПТУ nt. indecl. (abbr. of **профессиона́льно-техни́ческое учи́лище**) vocational technical school

пу́блик|а, и f. (collect.) (the) public; (*зрители, слушатели*) (the) audience

✎ **публика́ци|я, и** f. **1** (*действие*) publication **2** (*объявление*) advertisement, notice

публик|ова́ть, у́ю impf. (of ▶ **опубликова́ть**) to publish

публици́стик|а, и f. sociopolitical journalism

публи́чно adv. publicly; in public; openly

публи́чн|ый adj. public; **~ая библиоте́ка** public library; **п. дом** brothel

пу́гал|о, а nt. scarecrow

пуга́|ть, ю impf. (of ▶ **испуга́ть,** ▶ **напуга́ть**) **1** to frighten, scare **2** (+ i.) to threaten (with)

пуга́|ться, юсь impf. (of ▶ **испуга́ться**) (+ g.) to be frightened (of), be scared (of); to take fright (at); (*о лошади*) to shy (at)

пугли́в|ый, ~, ~а adj. fearful, timid

пу́говиц|а, ы f. button

пу́дел|ь, я, pl. **~и, ~ей** or **~я, ~е́й** m. poodle

пу́динг, а m. pudding

пу́др|а, ы f. powder

пу́др|ить, ю, ишь impf. (of ▶ **напу́дрить**) to powder

пу́др|иться, юсь, ишься impf. (of ▶ **напу́дриться**) to use powder, powder one's face

пуза́т|ый, ~, ~а adj. (infml) pot-bellied

пу́з|о, а nt. (infml) belly, paunch

пузы́р|ь, я́ m. **1** (*шарик*) bubble; **мы́льный п.** soap bubble **2** (anat.): **мочево́й п.** (urinary) bladder

пулемёт, а m. machine gun

пулемётчик, а m. machine-gunner

пуленепробива́емый adj. bulletproof

пуло́вер, а m. pullover

пульс, а m. pulse

пульси́р|овать, ую impf. to pulsate; (*о боли*) to throb

пульт, а m. **1** (*пюпитр*) desk, stand **2** (*диспетчерский*) control panel; **п. ДУ, п. дистанцио́нного управле́ния** (TV etc.) remote control

пу́л|я, и f. bullet

✎ **пункт, а** m. **1** point; spot; **населённый п.** inhabited area **2** (*организационный центр*) station, centre (BrE), center (AmE); post, point; **медици́нский п.** first-aid station; **наблюда́тельный п.** observation post, point **3** (*документа*) point; paragraph, item; **соглаше́ние из трёх ~ов** a three-point agreement

пункти́р, а m. dotted line

пунктуа́л|ьный, ~ен, ~ьна adj. punctual

пунктуа́ци|я, и f. punctuation

пунцо́в|ый, ~, ~а adj. crimson

пунш, а *m.* punch (*drink*)

пупови́н|а, ы *f.* (anat.) umbilical cord

пуп|о́к, ка́ *m.* navel

пурпу́рный *adj.* purple

пуск, а *m.* starting (up); setting in motion

пуска́й *particle, conj.* (infml) = пусть

пуска́|ть, ю *impf. of* ▶ пусти́ть

пуска́|ться, юсь *impf. of* ▶ пусти́ться

пусте́|ть, ет *impf.* (*of* ▶ опусте́ть) to (become) empty; to become deserted

пу|сти́ть, щу́, ~стишь *pf.* (*of* ▶ пуска́ть) **1** (*дать свободу*) to let go **2** (*разрешить идти*) to let; to allow, permit; нас не ~сти́ли в пала́ту they would not let us into the ward **3** (*разрешить войти*) to let in, allow to enter; не п. to keep out **4** (*привести в движение*) to start, set in motion, set going; to set working; п. во́ду to turn on water; п. слух to start a rumour (BrE), rumor (AmE) **5** (*заставить или дать возможность двигаться*) to set, put; to send; п. в ход to start, launch, set going, set in train; п. кора́бль ко дну to send a ship to the bottom

пу|сти́ться, щу́сь, ~стишься *pf.* (*of* ▶ пуска́ться) (в + *a. or* + *inf.*) (infml) **1** (*отправиться*) to set out; п. в путь to set out, get on the way **2** (*начать*) to begin, start; to set to; п. в пляс to break into a dance

пуст|ова́ть, у́ю *impf.* to be empty, stand empty; (*о земле*) to lie fallow

пуст|о́й, ~, ~а́, ~о, ~ы́ *adj.* **1** empty; п. взгляд vacant look; ~о́е ме́сто blank space **2** (fig., *несерьёзный*) idle; shallow; frivolous; п. челове́к shallow person **3** (fig., *напрасный*) vain, ungrounded; ~ые слова́ mere words; ~ые угро́зы empty threats, bluster

пустот|а́, ы́, *pl.* **~ы** *f.* **1** emptiness; void; (phys.) vacuum **2** (fig.) emptiness, shallowness **3** (*полое место*) cavity

пу́стошь, и *f.* waste (plot of) land, waste ground

пусты́н|ный, ~ен, ~на *adj.* **1** (*необитаемый*) uninhabited; п. о́стров desert island **2** (*безлюдный*) deserted

пусты́н|я, и *f.* desert, wilderness

пусты́р|ь, я́ *m.* wasteland, vacant plot (of land)

пусты́шк|а, и *f.* (infml, *у младенца*) dummy (BrE), pacifier (AmE)

ᵈ пусть 1 (*particle*) let; п. она́ сама́ реши́т let her decide herself **2** (*as conj.*) though, even if; п. им бу́дет проти́вно, но я до́лжен вы́сказать своё мне́ние even if they hate it, I must express my opinion **3** (*particle*) (infml, *ладно*) all right, very well

пустя́к, а́ *m.* (infml) trifle; ~и́! (*ничего*) it's nothing!; never mind!; (*вздор*) nonsense!; rubbish!

пу́таниц|а, ы *f.* muddle, confusion; mess, tangle

пу́та|ть, ю *impf.* (*of* ▶ спу́тать, ▶ запу́тать) **1** (*нитки*) to tangle **2** (*сбивать с толку*) to confuse, muddle **3** (*смешивать*) to confuse,

mix up; ты (всё) ещё ~ешь на́ши имена́ you are still mixing our names up

пу́та|ться, юсь *impf.* (*of* ▶ спу́таться, ▶ запу́таться) **1** (*о нитках*) to get tangled **2** (*о мыслях*) to get confused **3** (*сбиваться с толку*) to get mixed up, get muddled; п. в расска́зе to give a muddled account

путёвк|а, и *f.* **1** (*удостоверение*) pass, authorization; пода́ть зая́вку на ~у в санато́рий to apply for a place in a sanatorium **2** place on a tour, package holiday; я купи́л ~у в Ита́лию I have booked a package holiday to Italy **3** (*водителя транспорта*) schedule of duties

путеводи́тел|ь, я *m.* guide, guidebook

путём¹ *prep.* (+ *g.*) by means of, by dint of

путём² *adv.* (infml, *как следует*) properly; он ничего́ п. не уме́ет объясни́ть he cannot explain anything properly

путепрово́д, а *m.* (*над дорогой*) overpass, flyover; (*под дорогой*) underpass

путеше́ственник, а *m.* traveller (BrE), traveler (AmE)

путеше́ственни|ца, цы *f. of* ▶ путеше́ственник

ᵈ путеше́стви|е, я *nt.* **1** journey; trip; (*морской*) voyage; cruise **2** (*also in pl.*) (*as literary genre*) travels

путеше́ств|овать, ую *impf.* to travel, go on travels; (*по морю*) to voyage

путч, а *m.* (pol.) putsch

ᵈ пут|ь, и́, i. ём, о ~и́, *pl.* **~и́, ~е́й, ~я́м** *m.* **1** (*дорога*) way, track, path; (aeron.) track; (astron.) race; (fig.) road, course; ~й сообще́ния communications; на пра́вильном ~и́ on the right track **2** (rail.) track **3** (*путешествие*) journey; voyage; в ~й on one's way, en route; в четырёх дня́х ~й (от + *g.*) four days' journey (from); на обра́тном ~и́ on the way back; по ~и́ on the way **4** (fig., *средство*) way, means; ми́рным ~ём amicably, peaceably; пойти́ по ~и́ (+ *g.*) to take the path (of)

пух, а, о ~е, в ~у́ *m.* down; fluff; ни ~а ни пера́! (infml) good luck!

пу́хл|ый, ~, ~а́, ~о *adj.* (*человек*) chubby, plump; (*книга, досье*) fat

пу́х|нуть, ну, нешь, *past* ~ *and* ~нул, ~ла *impf.* to swell

пучегла́з|ый, ~, ~а *adj.* (infml) goggle-eyed

пучи́н|а, ы *f.* gulf, abyss (also fig.); (*морская бездна*) the deep

пуши́ст|ый, ~, ~а *adj.* fluffy, downy

пу́шк|а, и *f.* gun, cannon

пуэрторика́н|ец, ца *m.* Puerto Rican

пуэрторика́н|ка, ки *f. of* ▶ пуэрторика́нец

пуэрторика́нский *adj.* Puerto Rican

Пуэ́рто-Ри́ко *nt. indecl.* Puerto Rico

пчел|а́, ы́, *pl.* **~ы** *f.* bee

пшени́ц|а, ы *f.* wheat

пшени́чный *adj.* wheat(en)

пшённый *adj. of* ▶ пшено́

пшен|о́, а́ *nt.* millet

пыла́|ть, ю *impf.* **1** to blaze, flame **2** (*о лице*) to glow **3** (+ *i.*) (fig.) to burn (with); **п. стра́стью** to be burning with passion

пылесо́с, а *m.* vacuum cleaner, Hoover®

пылесо́с|ить, ишь *impf.* (*of* ▶ пропылесо́сить) to vacuum(-clean), hoover

пыли́нк|а, и *f.* speck of dust

пы́л|кий, ~ок, ~ка́, ~ко *adj.* (*желание, речь*) ardent, passionate; (*воображение*) fervid

пыл|ь, и, о ~и, в ~й *f.* dust

пы́л|ьный, ~ен, ~ьна́, ~ьно *adj.* dusty

пыльц|а́, ы́ *f.* (bot.) pollen

пыта́|ть, ю *impf.* to torture (also fig.); (fig.) to torment

✎ пыта́|ться, юсь *impf.* (*of* ▶ попыта́ться) to try, attempt

пы́тк|а, и *f.* torture, torment (also fig.); **ору́дие ~и** instrument of torture

пытли́в|ый, ~, ~а *adj.* inquisitive

пых|те́ть, чу́, ти́шь *impf.* to puff, pant

пы́ш|ный, ~ен, ~на́, ~но *adj.* **1** (*великолепный*) splendid, magnificent **2** (*пушистый*) fluffy; light; luxuriant; ~ные во́лосы fluffy hair

пьедеста́л, а *m.* pedestal (also fig.)

пье́с|а, ы *f.* **1** (theatr.) play **2** (mus.) piece

пьяне́|ть, ю, ешь *impf.* (*of* ▶ опьяне́ть) to get drunk, get intoxicated

пья́ниц|а, ы *c.g.* drunkard

пья́нк|а, и *f.* (infml) drinking bout, binge, booze-up

пья́нств|о, а *nt.* drunkenness

пья́н|ый, ~, ~а́, ~о, ~ы́ *adj.* drunk; drunken; intoxicated; (*as m. n.* п., ~ого) (a) drunk

пюре́ *nt. indecl.* (cul.) purée; **карто́фельное п.** mashed potatoes

пятёрк|а, и *f.* **1** (*цифра, игральная карта*) five **2** (*отметка*) five (*highest mark in Russian educational marking system*) **3** (infml, *автобус, трамвай*) No. 5 (*bus, tram, etc.*) **4** (*группа из пятерых*) (group of) five **5** (infml, *пять рублей*) five-rouble note, fiver

пя́тер|о, ~ых *num.* (*collect.*) five

пятидеся́т|ый *adj.* fiftieth; ~ые го́ды the fifties

пятизвёздочный *adj.* five-star

пятикра́тный *adj.* fivefold

пятисо́тый *adj.* five-hundredth

пя́|титься, чусь, тишься *impf.* (*of* ▶ попя́титься) to back, move backward(s); (*о лошади*) to jib

пя́тк|а, и *f.* heel (*also of sock or stocking*)

пятна́дцатый *adj.* fifteenth

пятна́дцат|ь, и *num.* fifteen

пятни́ст|ый, ~, ~а *adj.* spotted, dappled; **п. оле́нь** spotted deer

пя́тниц|а, ы *f.* Friday

пятн|о́, а́, *pl.* ~а, ~ен, ~ам *nt.* **1** (*место иной окраски*) spot; patch; (*запачканное место*) stain; **роди́мое п.** birthmark **2** (fig.) blot, stain; blemish

пя́т|ый *adj.* fifth; **глава́ ~ая** chapter five; **в ~ом часу́** after four (o'clock)

✎ пят|ь, и́, *i.* ью́ *num.* five

пятьдеся́т, пяти́десяти, *i.* пятью́десятью *num.* fifty

пятьсо́т, пятисо́т, пятиста́м, пятьюста́ми *num.* five hundred

пя́тью *adv.* five times; **п. шесть** five times six

Рр

раб, а́ *m.* slave

✎ рабо́т|а, ы *f.* **1** (*действие*) work, working; (*функционирование*) functioning; running **2** (*занятие, труд*) work; labour (BrE), labor (AmE); **дома́шняя р.** homework; **сельскохозя́йственные ~ы** agricultural work **3** (*как источник заработка*) work, job; **постоя́нная р.** regular work; **случа́йная р.** casual work, odd job(s); **иска́ть ~у** to look for a job

✎ рабо́та|ть, ю *impf.* **1** (над + *i.*) to work (on); **он ~ет над но́вым рома́ном** he is working on a new novel; (на + *a.*) to work (for, on

behalf of); **она́ ~ет на поли́цию** she works for the police **2** (*функциони́ровать*) to work, run, function; **не р.** to not work, to be out of order **3** (*быть откры́тым*) to be open; **галере́я не ~ет по воскресе́ньям** the gallery is not open on Sundays **4** (+ *i.*) (*управля́ть*) to work, operate; **р. вёслами** to ply the oars

✎ рабо́тник, а *m.* worker; (*учреждения*) employee

рабо́тниц|а, ы *f.* (female) worker; (*учреждения*) (female) employee

работода́тел|ь, я *m.* employer

работоспосо́б|ный, ~ен, ~на *adj.* **1** (*могущий рабо́тать*) able to work,

✎ key word

able-bodied **2** (*способный много работать*) able to work hard, hardworking

работя́щий *adj.* (infml) hard-working, industrious

✓ **рабо́ч|ий¹, его** *m.* worker; workman; ~ие (*collect.*) the workers (*as a social class*)

✓ **рабо́ч|ий²** *adj.* **1** (*относящийся к рабочим*) workers', working-class; **р. класс** the working class **2** (*выполняющий работу*) work, working; ~ая си́ла manpower **3** (*предназначенный для работы*) working; ~ее вре́мя working time, working hours; **р. день** working day (BrE), workday (AmE); ~ее ме́сто (*помещение*) working place, workplace; (*пост*) job **4**: **в ~ем поря́дке** while working, without breaking off from work

ра́бский *adj.* **1** *adj. of* ▶ **раб**; **р. труд** slave labour (BrE), labor (AmE) **2** (fig., *раболепный*) servile

ра́бств|о, а *nt.* slavery, servitude

рабы́н|я, и, *g. pl.* ~ь *f.* (female) slave

равви́н, а *m.* rabbi

ра́венств|о, а *nt.* equality; parity; **знак ~а** (math.) equals sign

равио́л|и, ей *m. pl.* ravioli

равни́н|а, ы *f.* plain

равно́ *nt. pred. form of* ▶ **ра́вный 1** (math.) make(s), equals, is; **три плюс три р. шести́** three plus three equals six **2**: **всё р.** it is all the same, it makes no difference; (*as adv.*) all the same; **всё р., что** it is just the same as, it is equivalent to; **мне всё р.** I don't care; it's all the same, all one to me; **я всё р. вам позвоню́** I will ring you all the same

равнове́си|е, я *nt.* equilibrium (also fig.); balance; **душе́вное р.** mental equilibrium; **сохраня́ть р.** to keep one's balance

равноде́нстви|е, я *nt.*: **весе́ннее, осе́ннее р.** spring, autumn equinox

равноду́ши|е, я *nt.* indifference

равноду́ш|ный, ~ен, ~на *adj.* (**к** + *d.*) indifferent (to)

равнозна́ч|ный, ~ен, ~на *adj.* equivalent

равноме́р|ный, ~ен, ~на *adj.* even; uniform

равнопра́ви|е, я *nt.* (possession of) equal rights; equality

равноси́л|ьный, ~ен, ~ьна *adj.* (+ *d.*) equal (to), equivalent (to), tantamount (to); **э́то ~ьно изме́не** it is tantamount to treachery; it amounts to treachery

равноце́н|ный, ~ен, ~на *adj.* of equal value, of equal worth; equivalent

✓ **ра́в|ный, ~ен, ~на́, ~но́** *adj.* equal; **ему́ нет ~ных** he has no equal

равня́|ться, юсь *impf.* **1** (**по** + *d.*) (mil.) to dress; ~йсь! eyes right! (*word of command*) **2** (*impf. only*) (+ *d.*) to equal, be equal (to); (fig.) to be equivalent (to); **два́жды пять ~ется десяти́** twice five is ten

рагу́ *nt. indecl.* (cul.) stew

✓ **рад, ~а, ~о** *pred. adj.* (+ *d. or* + *inf. or* что)

glad (of; to; that); (о́чень) **р. познако́миться с ва́ми!** pleased to meet you!

рада́р, а *m.* radar

✓ **ра́ди** *prep.* (+ *g.*) for the sake of; **чего́ р.?** what for?; **р. бо́га** (infml) for God's sake

радиа́тор, а *m.* radiator

радиа́ци|я, и *f.* radiation

ра́ди|й, я *m.* (chem.) radium

радика́л, а *m.* (pol., chem.) radical

радикализа́ци|я, и *f.* radicalization

радикализи́р|овать, ую *impf. and pf.* to radicalize

радика́л|ьный, ~ен, ~ьна *adj.* **1** (pol.) radical **2** (*решительный*) radical, drastic; ~ьное сре́дство drastic remedy

радикули́т, а *m.* radiculitis; sciatica

ра́дио *nt. indecl.* **1** (*средство связи*) radio; **по р.** by radio, over the air; **переда́ть по р.** to broadcast; **слу́шать р.** to listen in **2** (*радиоприёмник*) radio

радиоакти́вност|ь, и *f.* radioactivity

радиоакти́в|ный, ~ен, ~на *adj.* radioactive

радиовеща́ни|е, я *nt.* (radio) broadcasting

радиолока́тор, а *m.* radar set

радиоприёмник, а *m.* radio (set)

радиоста́нци|я, и *f.* radio station

радиотелефо́н, а *m.* cordless (tele)phone

радиотерапи́|я, и *f.* radiotherapy

ради́ст, а *m.* radio operator

ради́ст|ка, ки *f. of* ▶ **ради́ст**

ра́диус, а *m.* radius; **р. де́йствия** range

ра́д|овать, ую *impf.* (*of* ▶ **обра́довать**, ▶ **пора́довать**) to gladden, make happy

ра́д|оваться, уюсь *impf.* (*of* ▶ **обра́доваться**, ▶ **пора́доваться**) (+ *d.*) to be glad (at), be happy (at), rejoice (in)

ра́дост|ный, ~ен, ~на *adj.* glad, joyous, joyful; ~ное изве́стие glad tidings, good news

✓ **ра́дост|ь, и** *f.* gladness, joy; **к всео́бщей ~и** to everybody's delight; **с ~ью** with pleasure, gladly

ра́дуг|а, и *f.* rainbow

ра́дужн|ый *adj.* **1** (*переливчатый*) iridescent, opalescent; ~ая оболо́чка (гла́за) (anat.) iris **2** (*светлый, радостный*) cheerful; optimistic; ~ые наде́жды high hopes

раду́ш|ный, ~ен, ~на *adj.* cordial

✓ **раз¹, а,** *pl.* **~ы́, ~, ~а́м** *m.* **1** time; occasion; **оди́н р., ка́к-то р.** once; **два ~а** twice; **мно́го р.** many times; **ещё р.** once again, once more; **не р.** more than once; time and again; **ни ~у** not once, never; **р. (и) навсегда́** once (and) for all; **р. в день** once a day; **вся́кий р.** every time, each time; **вся́кий р., когда́** whenever; **в друго́й р.** another time, some other time; **на э́тот р.** this time, on this occasion, for (this) once; **с пе́рвого ~а** from the very first; **как р.** just, exactly **2** (*при счёте, один*) one

раз² *conj.* if; since; **р. вы бу́дете во Фра́нции, не смо́жете ли вы прие́хать и сюда́?** if you are going to be in France, can't you come here too?

раз...¹ and **разо..., разъ..., рас...** *vbl. pref. indicating* **1** *division into parts* (dis-, un-) **2** *distribution, direction of action in different directions* (dis-) **3** *action in reverse* (un-) **4** *termination of action or state* **5** *intensification of action*

раз...² and **разо..., разъ..., рас...** (*infml*) *adjectival pref. indicating high degree of a quality*

разба́в|ить, лю, ишь *pf.* (*of* ▶ **разбавля́ть**) to dilute

разбавля́|ть, ю *impf. of* ▶ **разба́вить**

разба́лива|ться, юсь *impf. of* ▶ **разболе́ться¹**, ▶ **разболе́ться²**

разба́лтыва|ть, ю *impf. of* ▶ **разболта́ть¹**, ▶ **разболта́ть²**

разба́лтыва|ться, юсь *impf. of* ▶ **разболта́ться**

разбе́г, а *m.* run, running start; **пры́гнуть с ∼а** to take a running jump; **р. при взлёте** (*aeron.*) take-off run

разбега́|ться, юсь *impf. of* ▶ **разбежа́ться**

разбе|жа́ться, гу́сь, жи́шься, гу́тся *pf.* (*of* ▶ **разбега́ться**) **1** (*взять разбег*) to take a run, run up **2** (*в разные стороны*) to scatter, disperse **3** (*о мыслях*) to be scattered; **глаза́ у меня́ ∼жа́лись** I was dazzled

разбива́|ть, ю *impf. of* ▶ **разби́ть**

разбива́|ться, юсь *impf. of* ▶ **разби́ться**

разбинт|ова́ть, у́ю *pf.* (*of* ▶ **разбинто́вывать**) to remove a bandage (from)

разбинто́выва|ть, ю *impf. of* ▶ **разбинтова́ть**

разбира́тельств|о, а *nt.* (*law*) examination, investigation; **суде́бное р.** court examination

разбира́|ть, ю *impf. of* ▶ **разобра́ть**

разбира́|ться, юсь *impf. of* ▶ **разобра́ться**

раз|би́ть, обью́, обьёшь *pf.* (*of* ▶ **разбива́ть**) **1** (*impf. also* **бить 4**) (*окно, чашку*) to break, smash **2** (*разделить*) to divide (up); to break up; **р. на гру́ппы** to divide up into groups **3** (*расположить*) to lay out, mark out; **р. ла́герь** to pitch a camp **4** (*повредить*) to damage severely, hurt badly; to fracture; **р. кому́-н. нос в кровь** to make sb's nose bleed **5** (*победить*) to beat, defeat, smash (*also fig.*)

раз|би́ться, обью́сь, обьёшься *pf.* (*of* ▶ **разбива́ться**) **1** (*расколоться*) to break, get broken, get smashed **2** (*разделиться*) to divide; to break up **3** (*пораниться*) to hurt oneself badly; to smash oneself up

разбогате́|ть, ю, ешь *pf. of* ▶ **богате́ть**

разбо́|й, я *m.* robbery; **морско́й р.** piracy

разбо́йник, а *m.* robber; **морско́й р.** pirate

разболе́|ться¹, юсь, ешься *pf.* (*of* ▶ **разба́ливаться**) (*infml*) to become ill; **он**

совсе́м **∼лся** his health has completely cracked

разбол|е́ться², и́тся *pf.* (*of* ▶ **разба́ливаться**) to begin to ache badly

разболта́|ть¹, ю *pf.* (*of* ▶ **разба́лтывать**) (*размешать*) to mix in

разболта́|ть², ю *pf.* (*of* ▶ **разба́лтывать**) (*infml, секрет*) to blab out, give away

разболта́|ться, юсь *pf.* (*of* ▶ **разба́лтываться**) **1** (*о муке*) to mix in (*as result of stirring*) **2** (*о гайке*) to come loose, work loose **3** (*fig., об ученике*) to get out of hand; to come unstuck

разбомб|и́ть, лю́, и́шь *pf.* (*no impf.*) to destroy by bombing

разбо́рк|а, и *f.* **1** (*бумаг*) sorting out **2** (*механизма*) stripping, dismantling **3** (*infml, ссора*) quarrel, fight, argument

разбо́рчив|ый, ∼, ∼а *adj.* **1** (*требовательный*) fastidious, exacting; discriminating; scrupulous **2** (*чёткий*) legible

разбра́сыва|ть, ю *impf. of* ▶ **разброса́ть**

разбреда́|ться, юсь *impf. of* ▶ **разбрести́сь**

разбре|сти́сь, ду́сь, дёшься, *past* **∼лся, ∼ла́сь** *pf.* (*of* ▶ **разбреда́ться**) to disperse; **р. по дома́м** to disperse and go home

разбро́д, а *m.* disorder

разброса́|ть, ю *pf.* (*of* ▶ **разбра́сывать**) to scatter, spread

разбры́зг|ать, аю *pf.* (*of* ▶ **разбры́згивать**) to splash; to spray

разбры́згиватель|, я *m.* sprinkler

разбры́згива|ть, ю *impf. of* ▶ **разбры́згать**

разбу|ди́ть, жу́, ∼дишь *pf. of* ▶ **буди́ть 1**

разбуха́|ть, а́ет *impf. of* ▶ **разбу́хнуть**

разбу́х|нуть, нет, *past* **∼, ∼ла** *pf.* (*of* ▶ **разбуха́ть**) to swell (*also fig.*)

разбуш|ева́ться, у́юсь *pf.* (*о буре*) to rage; to blow up; (*о море*) to run high

разва́л, а *m.* **1** (*распад*) breakdown, disintegration; (*беспорядок*) disorder **2** (*рынок*) flea market

разва́лива|ть, ю *impf. of* ▶ **развали́ть**

разва́лива|ться, юсь *impf. of* ▶ **развали́ться**

развали́н|а, ы *f.* (*in pl.*) ruins; **лежа́ть в ∼ах** to be in ruins; **преврати́ть в ∼ы** to reduce to ruins

развал|и́ть, ю́, ∼ишь *pf.* (*of* ▶ **разва́ливать**) **1** to pull down (*a building, etc.*) **2** (*fig., хозяйство*) to ruin

развал|и́ться, ю́сь, ∼ишься *pf.* (*of* ▶ **разва́ливаться**) **1** (*распасться*) to fall down, collapse **2** (*fig., прийти в упадок*) to go to pieces, fall to pieces, break down **3** (*infml, сидеть, раскинувшись*) to lounge, sprawl

✎ **ра́зве 1** (*interrog. particle, neutral or indicating that neg. answer is expected; + neg. indicates that affirmative answer is expected*): **р. они́ все поместя́тся в э́той маши́не?** will they (really) all get in this car?; **р. ты не знал, что он ру́сский?** didn't you know that he is Russian?; surely you knew that he is Russian! **2**: **р. (что), р. (то́лько)** (*as adv.*) only; perhaps; (*as conj.*) except that, only; **он вы́глядит так же как всегда́, р. что похуде́л** he looks the same as ever, except that he has lost weight

развева́|ться, ется *impf.* (*флаг*) to flutter; (*волосы, плащ*) to blow about

разве́д|ать, аю *pf.* (*of* ▸ **разве́дывать**) **1** (infml) to find out (about) **2** (mil.) to reconnoitre (BrE), reconnoiter (AmE) **3** (geol.) to prospect (for); (*pf. only*) to locate; **р. нефть** to prospect for oil

разведе́ни|е, я *nt.* (*скота*) breeding, rearing; (*сада*) cultivation; (*костра*) making

разведённ|ый *p.p.p. of* ▸ **развести́**[1], ▸ **развести́**[2] *and adj.* divorced; (*as n.* **р.**, ~**ого**, *f.* ~**ая**, ~**ой**) divorcee

разве́дк|а, и *f.* **1** (geol., etc.) prospecting **2** (mil., *для получе́ния све́дений*) reconnaissance **3** (pol.) intelligence service

разве́дчик, а *m.* **1** (mil.) scout **2** (pol.) intelligence officer

разве́дывательный *adj.* **1** (mil.) reconnaissance; **р. бой** probing attack; **р. отря́д** reconnaissance detachment **2** (pol.) intelligence; **р. отде́л** intelligence section

разве́дыва|ть, ю *impf. of* ▸ **разве́дать**

развез|ти́, у́, ёшь, *past* ~, ~**ла́** *pf.* (*of* ▸ **развози́ть**) (*доста́вить*) to deliver

разве́|ять, ю *impf. of* ▸ **разве́ять**

разве́ива|ться, юсь *impf. of* ▸ **разве́яться**

развёрнутый *p.p.p. of* ▸ **разверну́ть** *and adj.* **1** (*предпри́нятый в широ́ких масшта́бах*) extensive **2** (*подро́бный*) detailed

развер|ну́ть, ну́, нёшь *pf.* (*of* ▸ **развора́чивать**) **1** (*бума́гу*) to unfold; (*ковёр*) to unroll; (*свёрток*) to unwrap; (*зна́мя*) to unfurl **2** (mil., *перестро́ить*) to deploy **3** (fig., *прояви́ть*) to show, display **4** (fig., *стро́йку, торго́влю, рабо́ту*) to develop; to expand **5** (*маши́ну*) to turn (around)

развер|ну́ться, ну́сь, нёшься *pf.* (*of* ▸ **развора́чиваться**) **1** (*о бума́ге*) to come unfolded; (*о ковре́*) to come unrolled; (*о свёртке*) to come undone **2** (mil., *перестро́иться*) to deploy **3** (fig., *прояви́ться*) to show *or* display oneself **4** (fig., *о стро́йке, торго́вле, рабо́те*) to develop; to expand **5** (*о маши́не*) to turn (around)

развесел|и́ть, ю́, и́шь *pf. of* ▸ **весели́ть**

развесел|и́ться, ю́сь, и́шься *pf.* to cheer up

разве́|сить[1]**, шу, сишь** *pf.* (*of* ▸ **разве́шивать**) **1** (*карти́ны*) to hang **2** (*ве́тви*) to spread

разве́|сить[2]**, шу, сишь** *pf.* (*of* ▸ **разве́шивать**) (*белья́*) to hang out

разве|сти́[1]**, ду́, дёшь,** *past* ~**л, ~ла́** *pf.* (*of* ▸ **разводи́ть**) **1** (*ведя́, доста́вить*) to take, conduct; **р. дете́й по дома́м** to take the children to their homes **2** (*в ра́зные сто́роны*) to part, separate; **р. мост** to raise

a bridge; **р. рука́ми** to shrug one's shoulders **3** (*сок*) to dilute; (*порошо́к*) to dissolve

разве|сти́[2]**, ду́, дёшь,** *past* ~**л, ~ла́** *pf.* (*of* ▸ **разводи́ть**) **1** (*живо́тных*) to breed, rear; (*сад*) to cultivate; **р. парк** to lay out a park **2** (*разже́чь*) to start; **р. костёр** to make a campfire

разве|сти́сь[1]**, ду́сь, дёшься,** *past* ~**лся́, ~ла́сь** *pf.* (*of* ▸ **разводи́ться**) (с + *i.*) to divorce, get divorced (from)

разве|сти́сь[2]**, дётся,** *past* ~**лся́, ~ла́сь** *pf.* (*of* ▸ **разводи́ться**) (*о живо́тных*) to breed, multiply

разветвле́ни|е, я *nt.* **1** (*де́йствие*) branching; forking **2** (*ме́сто*) branch; fork (*of road, etc.*)

разве́ш|ать, аю *pf.* (*of* ▸ **разве́шивать**) to hang

разве́шива|ть, ю *impf. of* ▸ **разве́сить**[1], ▸ **разве́сить**[2], ▸ **разве́шать**

разве́|ять, ю, ешь *pf.* (*of* ▸ **разве́ивать**) to scatter, disperse; (fig., *грусть, сомне́ния*) to dispel; **р. миф** to shatter a myth

разве́|яться, юсь, ешься *pf.* (*of* ▸ **разве́иваться**) **1** (*о тума́не*) to disperse; (fig., *о тоске́*) to be dispelled **2** (infml, *о челове́ке*) to relax

✎ **развива́|ть, ю** *impf. of* ▸ **разви́ть**

✎ **развива́|ться, юсь** *impf. of* ▸ **разви́ться**

развин|ти́ть, чу́, ти́шь *pf.* (*of* ▸ **разви́нчивать**) to unscrew

развин|ти́ться, чу́сь, ти́шься *pf.* (*of* ▸ **разви́нчиваться**) to come unscrewed

разви́нчива|ть, ю *impf. of* ▸ **развинти́ть**

разви́нчива|ться, юсь *impf. of* ▸ **развинти́ться**

✎ **разви́ти|е, я** *nt.* development; evolution

разви́т|о́й, ра́звит, ~а́, ра́звито *adj.* **1** developed **2** (*у́мственно*) (intellectually) mature; adult

раз|ви́ть, овью́, овьёшь, *past* ~**ви́л, ~вила́, ~ви́ло** *pf.* (*of* ▸ **развива́ть**) to develop; **р. мускулату́ру** to develop one's muscles; **р. ско́рость** to gather speed

раз|ви́ться, овью́сь, овьёшься, *past* ~**ви́лся, ~вила́сь** *pf.* (*of* ▸ **развива́ться**) (*о му́скулах, о тала́нте*) to develop

развлека́тел|ьный, ~ен, ~ьна *adj.* entertaining; ~**ьное чте́ние** light reading

развлека́|ть, ю *impf. of* ▸ **развле́чь**

развлека́|ться, юсь *impf. of* ▸ **развле́чься**

развлече́ни|е, я *nt.* entertainment; amusement

развле́|чь, ку́, чёшь, ку́т, *past* ~**к, ~кла́** *pf.* (*of* ▸ **развлека́ть**) **1** (*повесели́ть*) to entertain, amuse **2** (*отвле́чь*) to divert

развле́|чься, ку́сь, чёшься, ку́тся, *past* ~**кся, ~кла́сь** *pf.* (*of* ▸ **развлека́ться**) **1** (*повесели́ться*) to have a good time; to amuse oneself **2** (*отвле́чься*) to be distracted

развод, а *m.* divorce; **они́ в ~е** they are divorced

р

разво|ди́ть, жу́, ~дишь *impf. of* ▶ **развести́**[1], ▶ **развести́**[2]

разво|ди́ться, жу́сь, ~дишься *impf. of* ▶ **развести́сь**[1], ▶ **развести́сь**[2]

разво|зи́ть, жу́, ~зишь *impf. of* ▶ **развезти́**

разволн|ова́ться, у́юсь *pf.* to get excited, get agitated

развора́чива|ть, ю *impf. of* ▶ **разверну́ть**

развора́чива|ться, юсь *impf. of* ▶ **разверну́ться**

развор|ова́ть, у́ю *pf.* (*of* ▶ **развора́вывать**) to loot, clean out

развора́выва|ть, ю *impf. of* ▶ **разворова́ть**

разворо́т, а *m.* **1** (*машины*) U-turn **2** (*в книге*) double page

разворош|и́ть, у́, и́шь *pf.* to turn upside down, scatter

разврат, а *m.* (*половой*) debauchery; (*духовный*) depravity

разврати́ть, щу́, ти́шь *pf.* (*of* ▶ **развраща́ть**) to corrupt

развра́т|ный, ~ен, ~на *adj.* debauched; corrupt

развраща́|ть, ю *impf. of* ▶ **разврати́ть**

развя|за́ть, жу́, ~жешь *pf.* (*of* ▶ **развя́зывать**) to untie, undo; to unleash; **р. кому́-н. ру́ки** to untie sb's hands; (*also fig.*): **р. войну́** to unleash war

развя|за́ться, жу́сь, ~жешься *pf.* (*of* ▶ **развя́зываться**) to come untied, come undone

развя́зк|а, и *f.* **1** (liter.) denouement **2** (*завершение*) outcome, upshot; **де́ло идёт к ~е** things are coming to a head **3**: (*тра́нспортная*) р. (traffic) roundabout

развя́з|ный, ~ен, ~на *adj.* (unduly) familiar; free and easy

развя́зыва|ть, ю *impf. of* ▶ **развяза́ть**

развя́зыва|ться, юсь *impf. of* ▶ **развяза́ться**

разгада́|ть, а́ю *pf.* (*of* ▶ **разга́дывать**) (*тайну, замысел*) to guess; (*загадку*) to solve; (*сны*) to interpret; (*шифр*) to break; (*человека*) to figure out

разга́дк|а, и *f.* solution (*of a riddle, etc.*)

разга́дыва|ть, ю *impf. of* ▶ **разгада́ть**

разга́р, а *m.*: **в ~е** (+ *g.*) at the height (of); **в по́лном ~е** in full swing; **в ~е бо́я** in the heat of the battle; **р. сезо́на** peak season

разгиба́|ть, ю *impf. of* ▶ **разогну́ть**

разгиба́|ться, юсь *impf. of* ▶ **разогну́ться**

разглаго́льств|овать, ую *impf.* (infml) to hold forth; to talk big

разгла́|дить, жу, дишь *pf.* (*of* ▶ **разгла́живать**) to smooth out; to iron out, press

разгла́|диться, дится *pf.* (*of* ▶ **разгла́живаться**) (*платье*) to become smoothed out; (*морщины*) to drop out

разгла́жива|ть, ю, ет *impf. of* ▶ **разгла́дить**

разгла́жива|ться, ется *impf. of* ▶ **разгла́диться**

разгла|си́ть, шу́, си́шь *pf.* (*of* ▶ **разглаша́ть**) to divulge, give away, let out

разглаша́|ть, ю *impf. of* ▶ **разгласи́ть**

разгля|де́ть, жу́, ди́шь *pf.* to make out, discern

разгля́дыва|ть, ю *impf.* to examine closely, scrutinize

⚹ **разгова́рива|ть, ю** *impf.* (**с** + *i.*) to talk (to, with), speak (to, with); **переста́ньте р.!** stop talking!; **они́ друг с дру́гом не ~ют** they are not on speaking terms

⚹ **разгово́р, а** *m.* **1** talk, conversation; **без ~ов!** and no argument! **2** (*in pl.*) (infml, *толки*) gossip

разговор|и́ть, ю́, и́шь *pf.* (infml) to get (sb) to talk

разговор|и́ться, ю́сь, и́шься *pf.* **1** (**с** + *i.*) to get into conversation (with) **2** (*увлечься разговором*) to warm to one's theme

разгово́рник, а *m.* phrase book

разгово́рный *adj.* colloquial

разгово́рчив|ый, ~, ~а *adj.* talkative

разго́н, а *m.* **1** (*толпы*) dispersal; **р. собра́ния** breaking up of a meeting **2** (sport) running start **3** (*машины*) acceleration

разгоня́|ть, ю *impf. of* ▶ **разогна́ть**

разгоня́|ться, юсь *impf. of* ▶ **разогна́ться**

разгор|а́ться, а́ется *impf. of* ▶ **разгоре́ться**

разгор|е́ться, и́тся *pf.* (*of* ▶ **разгора́ться**) **1** (*об огне*) to flare up **2** (fig., *о битве, о споре*) to flare up

разгра́б|ить, лю, ишь *pf.* to plunder, loot

разграниче́ни|е, я *nt.* **1** (*размежевание*) demarcation, delimitation **2** (*определение*) differentiation

разграни́чива|ть, ю *impf. of* ▶ **разграни́чить**

разграни́ч|ить, у, ишь *pf.* (*of* ▶ **разграни́чивать**) **1** (*размежевать*) to delimit, demarcate **2** (*точно определить*) to differentiate, distinguish

разгреба́|ть, ю *impf. of* ▶ **разгрести́**

разгре|сти́, бу́, бёшь, *past* **~б, ~бла́** *pf.* (*of* ▶ **разгреба́ть**) to rake (aside); to shovel (aside)

разгро́м, а *m.* (*неприятеля*) crushing defeat, rout

разгром|и́ть, лю́, и́шь *pf. of* ▶ **громи́ть**

разгружа́|ть, ю *impf. of* ▶ **разгрузи́ть**

разгружа́|ться, юсь *impf. of* ▶ **разгрузи́ться**

разгру|зи́ть, жу́, ~зишь *pf.* (*of* ▶ **разгружа́ть**) **1** to unload **2** (**от** + *g.*) (fig., infml) to relieve (of)

разгру|зи́ться, жу́сь, ~зишься *pf.* (*of* ▶ **разгружа́ться**) to unload

разгру́зк|а, и *f.* unloading

разгрыза́|ть, ю *impf. of* ▶ **разгры́зть**

разгры́з|ть, у́, ёшь, *past* **~, ~ла** *pf.* (*of* ▶ **разгрыза́ть**) to crack (*with one's teeth*)

разгу́л, а *m.* **1** (*весе́лье*) revelry **2** (+ *g.*) (fig.) wave (of); outburst (of); **р. антисемити́зма** a wave of anti-Semitism

разгу́лива|ть, ю *impf.* to stroll about, walk about

раздя|ва́ть, ю́, ёшь *impf. of* ▸ **разда́ть**

разда|ва́ться, ёшься *impf. of* ▸ **разда́ться**

раздав|и́ть, лю́, ~ишь *pf.* (*of* ▸ **разда́вливать**) (*насеко́мых*) to crush, squash; (*о маши́не*) to run over

разда́влива|ть, ю *impf. of* ▸ **раздави́ть**

разда́|ть, м, шь, ст, ди́м, ди́те, ду́т, *past* ~л, ~ла́, ~ло *pf.* (*of* ▸ **раздава́ть**) to distribute, give out, serve out, dispense; **р. кни́ги** to give out books

разда́|ться, стся, ду́тся, *past* ~лся, ~ла́сь, ~ло́сь *pf.* (*of* ▸ **раздава́ться**) to be heard; to resound; to ring (out); ~лся вы́стрел a shot rang out; ~лся стук (в дверь) a knock at the door was heard

разда́ч|а, и *f.* distribution

раздва́ива|ться, юсь *impf. of* ▸ **раздвои́ться**

раздвига́|ть, ю, ет *impf. of* ▸ **раздви́нуть**

раздвига́|ться, ется *impf. of* ▸ **раздви́нуться**

раздви́|нуть, ну, нешь *pf.* (*of* ▸ **раздвига́ть**) to move apart, slide apart; **р. занаве́ски** to draw back the curtains; **р. стол** to extend a table

раздви́|нуться, нется *pf.* (*of* ▸ **раздвига́ться**) to move apart; **за́навес** ~нулся the curtain was drawn back; (*в теа́тре*) the curtain rose; **толпа́** ~нулась the crowd made way

раздвое́ни|е, я *nt.* division into two; bifurcation; **р. ли́чности** (med.) split personality

раздво|и́ться, ю́сь, и́шься *pf.* (*of* ▸ **раздва́иваться**) to bifurcate, fork, split, become double

раздева́лк|а, и *f.* (infml) **1** (*гардеро́б*) cloakroom **2** (*в ба́нях*) changing room

раздева́ни|е, я *nt.* undressing

раздева́|ть, ю *impf. of* ▸ **разде́ть**

раздева́|ться, юсь *impf. of* ▸ **разде́ться**

⚐ **разде́л**, а *m.* **1** (*иму́щества*) division; (*земли́*) allotment **2** (*часть*) section, part (*of book, etc.*)

разде́л|ать, аю *pf.* (*of* ▸ **разде́лывать**) (*ту́шу*) to dress, prepare

разде́л|аться, аюсь *pf.* (*of* ▸ **разде́лываться**) (с + *i.*) **1** (*с поруче́ниями*) to be through (with); (*с кредито́рами*) to settle (accounts) (with); **р. с долга́ми** to pay off debts **2** (fig., *распра́виться*) to settle accounts (with), get even (with), make short work of

разделе́ни|е, я *nt.* division; **р. труда́** division of labour

раздел|и́ть, ю́, ~ишь *pf.* (*of* ▸ **разделя́ть**, ▸ **дели́ть** 1) **1** (*де́ньги*) to divide **2** (*разъедини́ть*) to separate, part **3** (*мне́ние, убежде́ние*) to share

раздел|и́ться, ю́сь, ~ишься *pf.* (*of* ▸ **разделя́ться**, ▸ **дели́ться** 1) **1** (на + *a.*) to divide (into); to be divided; **мне́ния** ~и́лись

opinions were divided

разде́лыва|ть, ю *impf. of* ▸ **разде́лать**

разде́лыва|ться, юсь *impf. of* ▸ **разде́латься**

разде́льн|ый *adj.* separate; ~ое обуче́ние separate education for boys and girls

разделя́|ть, я́ю *impf. of* ▸ **раздели́ть**

разделя́|ться, я́юсь *impf. of* ▸ **раздели́ться**

разде́|ть, ну, нешь *pf.* (*of* ▸ **раздева́ть**) to undress

разде́|ться, нусь, нешься *pf.* (*of* ▸ **раздева́ться**) to undress, get undressed; (*снять пальто́, ша́пку*) to take off one's things

раздира́|ть, ю *impf.* **1** *impf. of* ▸ **разодра́ть** **2** (*impf. only*) (fig.) to rend, tear, lacerate, harrow

раздобыва́|ть, ю *impf. of* ▸ **раздобы́ть**

раздо|бы́ть, бу́ду, бу́дешь, *past* ~бы́л *pf.* (*of* ▸ **раздобыва́ть**) (infml) get, procure, get hold of

раздраж|а́ть, а́ю *impf. of* ▸ **раздражи́ть**

раздраж|а́ться, а́юсь *impf. of* ▸ **раздражи́ться**

раздража́ющий *pres. part. act. of* ▸ **раздража́ть** *and adj.* irritating, annoying

раздраже́ни|е, я *nt.* irritation

раздражи́тельн|ый, ~ен, ~ьна *adj.* irritable; short-tempered

раздраж|и́ть, у́, и́шь *pf.* (*of* ▸ **раздража́ть**) **1** to irritate, annoy **2** (med.) to irritate

раздраж|и́ться, у́сь, и́шься *pf.* (*of* ▸ **раздража́ться**) **1** to get irritated, get annoyed **2** (med.) to become inflamed

раздува́|ть, ю *impf. of* ▸ **разду́ть**

раздува́|ться, юсь *impf. of* ▸ **разду́ться**

разду́м|ать, аю *pf.* (*of* ▸ **разду́мывать** 1) to change one's mind; (+ *inf.*) to decide not (to); **я** ~ал подава́ть заявле́ние на э́то ме́сто I decided not to apply for that job; I changed my mind about applying for that job

разду́мыва|ть, ю *impf.* **1** *impf. of* ▸ **разду́мать** **2** (*impf. only*) (o + *p.*) to ponder (on, over), consider; **не** ~я without a moment's thought

разду́|ть, ю, ешь *pf.* (*of* ▸ **раздува́ть**) **1** (*разже́чь*) to blow; to fan; **р. пла́мя** (fig.) to fan the flames **2** (*наду́ть*) to blow (out); **р. щёки** to blow out one's cheeks **3** (fig., infml, *преувели́чить*) to exaggerate; to inflate, swell; **р. поте́ри** to exaggerate losses **4** (*разве́ять*) to blow about; (*impers.*) **бума́ги** ~ло́ по́ по́лу the papers had blown all over the floor

разду́|ться, юсь, ешься *pf.* (*of* ▸ **раздува́ться**) to swell

разева́|ть, ю *impf. of* ▸ **рази́нуть**

разжа́лоб|ить, лю, ишь *pf.* to move (to pity)

разжа́л|овать, ую *pf.* (mil.) to demote; **р. в солда́ты** to reduce to the ranks

раз|жа́ть, ожму́, ожмёшь *pf.* (*of* ▸ **разжима́ть**) (*ру́ки*) to unclasp; (*пружи́ну*) to release; (*кула́к, зу́бы*) to unclench

р

разж|а́ться, ожмётся *pf.* (*of* ▶ разжима́ться) (*о пружине*) to come loose; (*о кулаке, губах*) to relax

разж|ева́ть, ую́, уёшь *pf.* (*of* ▶ разжёвывать) **1** to chew **2** (*fig.*, *infml*, *разъяснить*) to spell out

разжёвыва|ть, ю *impf. of* ▶ разжева́ть

раз|же́чь, ожгу́, ожжёшь, ожгу́т, *past* ∼жёг, ∼ожгла́ *pf.* (*of* ▶ разжига́ть) **1** (*заставить гореть*) to kindle **2** (*fig.*) to kindle, rouse, stir up; р. стра́сти to arouse passion

разжига́|ть, ю *impf. of* ▶ разже́чь

разжима́|ть, ю, ет *impf. of* ▶ разжа́ть

разжима́|ться, ется *impf. of* ▶ разжа́ться

рази́н|уть, у, ешь *pf.* (*of* ▶ разева́ть) (*infml*) to open wide (*the mouth*); to gape; слу́шать, ∼ув рот to listen open-mouthed

разлага́|ть, ю *impf. of* ▶ разложи́ть²

разлага́|ться, юсь *impf. of* ▶ разложи́ться²

разла́д, а *m.* discord, dissension

разла́мыва|ть, ю, ет *impf. of* ▶ разлома́ть, ▶ разломи́ть

разла́мыва|ться, ется *impf. of* ▶ разлома́ться, ▶ разломи́ться

разле́нива|ться, юсь *impf. of* ▶ разлени́ться

разлен|и́ться, ю́сь, ∼ишься *pf.* (*of* ▶ разле́ниваться) (*infml*) to become sunk in sloth

разлет|а́ться, а́юсь *impf. of* ▶ разлете́ться

разле|те́ться, чу́сь, ти́шься *pf.* (*of* ▶ разлета́ться) **1** (*о птицах*) to fly away; to scatter (*in the air*); (*о людях*) to scatter **2** (*infml*, *разбиться*) to smash, shatter **3** (*fig.*, *infml*, *о мечтах*) to vanish, be shattered **4** (*о новостях*) to spread

разл|е́чься, я́гусь, я́жешься, *past* ∼ёгся, ∼егла́сь *pf.* (*infml*) to sprawl; to stretch oneself out

разли́в, а *m.* **1** (*вина*) bottling **2** (*реки*) flood; overflow

разлива́|ть, ю, ет *impf. of* ▶ разли́ть

разлива́|ться, ется *impf. of* ▶ разли́ться

разливно́й *adj.* (*пиво*) on tap; draught (BrE), draft (AmE)

раз|ли́ть, олью́, ольёшь, *past* ∼ли́л, ∼лила́, ∼ли́ло *pf.* (*of* ▶ разлива́ть) to pour out; р. по буты́лкам to bottle; р. чай to pour out tea

раз|ли́ться, ольётся, *past* ∼ли́лся, ∼лила́сь *pf.* (*of* ▶ разлива́ться) **1** (*пролиться*) to spill; суп ∼лился по ска́терти the soup has spilled over the tablecloth **2** (*о реке*) to overflow **3** (*fig.*, *распространиться*) to spread; по её лицу́ ∼лила́сь улы́бка a smile spread across her face

различ|а́ть, а́ю *impf. of* ▶ различи́ть

различ|а́ться, юсь *impf.* to differ

разли́чи|е, я *nt.* distinction; difference; де́лать р. (ме́жду + *i.*) to make distinctions (between); без ∼я without distinction

различ|и́ть, у́, и́шь *pf.* (*of* ▶ различа́ть) **1** (*установить различие*) to distinguish; to tell the difference (between) **2** (*воспринять*) to discern, make out

◆ разли́ч|ный, ∼ен, ∼на *adj.* **1** (*несходный*) different; у нас бы́ли ∼ные мне́ния our opinions differed **2** (*разнообразный*) various, diverse; по ∼ным соображе́ниям for various reasons

разложе́ни|е, я *nt.* **1** (*на составные части*) breaking down **2** (*гниение*) decomposition, decay **3** (*fig.*, *деморализация*) demoralization; disintegration

разлож|и́ть¹, у́, ∼ишь *pf.* (*of* ▶ раскла́дывать) **1** (*положить по разным местам*) to put; р. свои́ ве́щи по я́щикам to put one's things in their respective drawers **2** (*в определённом порядке*) to lay out, spread (out)

разлож|и́ть², у́, ∼ишь *pf.* (*of* ▶ разлага́ть) **1** (*на составные части*) to break down; р. вещество́ на составны́е ча́сти to break a substance down into its component parts **2** (*fig.*, *деморализовать*) to break down, demoralize

разлож|и́ться¹, у́сь, ∼ишься *pf.* (*of* ▶ раскла́дываться) (*infml*, *разместить свои вещи*) to lay one's things out

разлож|и́ться², у́сь, ∼ишься *pf.* (*of* ▶ разлага́ться) **1** (*сгнить*) to decompose, rot; труп уже́ ∼и́лся the body has already decomposed **2** (*fig.*, *деморализоваться*) to become demoralized; to go to pieces

разло́м, а *m.* (*место*) break

разлома́|ть, ю *pf.* (*of* ▶ разла́мывать) to break (in pieces)

разлома́|ться, ется *pf.* (*of* ▶ разла́мываться) to break (in pieces); to break up

разлом|и́ть, лю́, ∼ишь *pf.* (*of* ▶ разла́мывать) to break (in pieces)

разлом|и́ться, ∼ится *pf.* (*of* ▶ разла́мываться) to break in pieces

разлу́к|а, и *f.* **1** separation; жить в ∼е (с + *i.*) to live apart (from), be separated (from) **2** (*расставание*) parting; час ∼и hour of parting

разлуч|а́ть, а́ю *impf. of* ▶ разлучи́ть

разлуч|а́ться, а́юсь *impf. of* ▶ разлучи́ться

разлуч|и́ть, у́, и́шь *pf.* (*of* ▶ разлуча́ть) (+ *a. and* с + *i.*) to separate (from), part (from)

разлуч|и́ться, у́сь, и́шься *pf.* (*of* ▶ разлуча́ться) (с + *i.*) to separate, part (from)

разлюб|и́ть, лю́, ∼ишь *pf.* (*человека*) to cease to love, stop loving; (*гулять; Москву*) to cease to like

разма́|зать, жу, жешь *pf.* (*of* ▶ разма́зывать) to spread, smear; р. варе́нье по всему́ лицу́ to get jam all over one's face

разма́|заться, жется *pf.* (*of* ▶ разма́зываться) to spread; to get smeared

разма́зыва|ть, ю, ет *impf. of* ▶ разма́зать

◆ key word

разма́зыва|ться, ется *impf. of*
▶ **разма́заться**

разма́лыва|ть, ю *impf. of* ▶ **размоло́ть**

разма́тыва|ть, ю, ет *impf. of* ▶ **размота́ть**

разма́тыва|ться, ется *impf. of*
▶ **размота́ться**

разма́х, а *m.* (*рук, крыльев*) span; (fig.) scope, range

разма́хива|ть, ю *impf.* (+ *i.*) to swing; to brandish; **р. рука́ми** to gesticulate

разма́хива|ться, юсь *impf. of*
▶ **размахну́ться**

размах|ну́ться, ну́сь, нёшься *pf.* (*of*
▶ **разма́хиваться**) to swing one's arm
(*to strike or as if to strike*)

разма́чива|ть, ю *impf. of* ▶ **размочи́ть**

размельч|а́ть, а́ю *impf. of* ▶ **размельчи́ть**

размельч|и́ть, у́, и́шь *pf.* (*of* ▶ **размельча́ть**)
to divide into particles; to pulverize

разме́н, а *m.* exchange; **р. де́нег** changing of money

разме́нива|ть, ю *impf. of* ▶ **разменя́ть**

разме́нн|ый *adj.*: ∼**ая моне́та** small change

размен|я́ть, я́ю *pf.* (*of* ▶ **разме́нивать**)
to change; **р. сторублёвку** to change a hundred-rouble note

размер, а *m.* **1** (*масштаб*) dimensions; **воро́нка** ∼**ом в де́сять квадра́тных ме́тров** a crater measuring ten square metres **2** (*оде́жды, о́буви*) size (in); (*in pl.*) measurements; **како́й у вас р.?** what size do you take? **3** (*зарпла́ты, проце́нтов*) rate, amount; **получа́ть зарпла́ту в** ∼**е ты́сячи рубле́й в день** to be paid at the rate of a thousand roubles per day **4** (*сте́пень*) scale, extent; (*in pl.*) proportions; **увели́читься до огро́мных** ∼**ов** to assume enormous proportions **5** (*ритм стиха́, му́зыки*) rhythm

разме́ренн|ый *adj.* measured; ∼**ая похо́дка** measured tread

разме|сти́, ту́, тёшь, past ∼**л, ∼ла́** *pf.*
(*of* ▶ **размета́ть¹**) **1** (*доро́жку*) to sweep clean **2** (*снег*) to shovel, sweep away

разме|сти́ть, щу́, сти́шь *pf.* (*of* ▶ **размеща́ть**)
(*помести́ть по места́м*) to place, accommodate; **р. делега́тов по гости́ницам** to accommodate the delegates in hotels

разме|сти́ться, щу́сь, сти́шься *pf.* (*of*
▶ **размеща́ться**) **1** (*заня́ть места́*) to take one's seat **2** (*помести́ться*) to be housed, located

размета́|ть¹, ю *impf. of* ▶ **размести́**

разме|та́ть², чу́, ∼чешь *pf.* (*of*
▶ **размётывать**) to scatter, disperse

разме́|тить, чу, тишь *pf.* (*of* ▶ **размеча́ть**)
to mark

размётыва|ть, ю *impf. of* ▶ **размета́ть²**

размеча́|ть, ю *impf. of* ▶ **разме́тить**

размеш|а́ть, а́ю *pf.* (*of* ▶ **разме́шивать**)
to stir

разме́шива|ть, ю *impf. of* ▶ **размеша́ть**

размеща́|ть, ю *impf. of* ▶ **размести́ть**

размеща́|ться, юсь *impf. of* ▶ **размести́ться**

размеще́ни|е, я *nt.* **1** (*по места́м*) placing, accommodation; **р. промы́шленности** location of industry **2** (fin., *капита́ла*) placing, investment

размина́|ть, ю *impf. of* ▶ **размя́ть**

размина́|ться, юсь *impf. of* ▶ **размя́ться**

размини́р|овать, ую *pf.* to clear of mines

разми́нк|а, и *f.* (sport) limbering-up; warm-up

размин|у́ться, у́сь, ёшься *pf.* (infml)
1 (с + *i.*) to pass (*without meeting*); to miss;
мы, должно́ быть, ∼у́лись с ним на доро́ге
we must have passed one another on the
road **2** (*о пи́сьмах*) to cross

размнож|а́ть, а́ю, ает *impf. of* ▶ **размно́жить**

размнож|а́ться, ается *impf. of*
▶ **размно́житься**

размноже́ни|е, я *nt.* **1** duplicating; photocopying **2** (biol.) reproduction, propagation

размно́ж|ить, у, ишь *pf.* (*of* ▶ **размножа́ть**)
to duplicate; to photocopy

размно́ж|иться, ится *pf.* (*of*
▶ **размножа́ться**) (biol.) to reproduce; to breed

размок|а́ть, а́ет *impf. of* ▶ **размо́кнуть**

размо́к|нуть, нет, past ∼**, ∼ла** *pf.* (*of*
▶ **размока́ть**) to get soaked; to get sodden

размо́лвк|а, и *f.* tiff, disagreement

раз|моло́ть, мелю́, ме́лешь *pf.* (*of*
▶ **разма́лывать**) to grind

размора́жива|ть, ю, ет *impf. of*
▶ **разморо́зить**

размора́жива|ться, ется *impf. of*
▶ **разморо́зиться**

разморо́|зить, жу, зишь *pf.* (*of*
▶ **размора́живать**) to defrost

разморо́|зиться, зится *pf.* (*of*
▶ **размора́живаться**) to defrost

размота́|ть, ю *pf.* (*of* ▶ **разма́тывать**) to
unwind, uncoil, unreel

размота́|ться, ется *pf.* (*of* ▶ **разма́тываться**)
to unwind, uncoil, unreel; to come unwound

размоч|и́ть, у́, ∼ишь *pf.* (*of* ▶ **разма́чивать**)
to soak, steep

размыва́|ть, ю *impf. of* ▶ **размы́ть**

размыка́|ть, ю *impf. of* ▶ **разомкну́ть**

размы́|ть, ю, ́ешь *pf.* (*of* ▶ **размыва́ть**)
to wash away; (geol.) to erode

размышле́ни|е, я *nt.* reflection, meditation,
thought; **быть погруже́нным в** ∼**я** to be lost
in thought

размышля́|ть, ю *impf.* (о + *p.*) to reflect (on,
upon), meditate (on, upon), ponder (over)

размягч|а́ть, а́ю *impf. of* ▶ **размягчи́ть**

размягч|и́ть, у́, и́шь *pf.* (*of* ▶ **размягча́ть**)
to soften

раз|мя́ть, омну́, омнёшь *pf.* (*of* ▶ **мять 1**,
▶ **размина́ть**) (*гли́ну*) to knead; (*карто́шку*)
to mash

раз|мя́ться, омну́сь, омнёшься *pf.* (*of*
▶ **размина́ться**) **1** to grow soft (*as result*

р

of kneading) **2** (infml) to stretch one's legs; (sport) to limber up, loosen up

разне́рвнича|ться, юсь *pf.* (infml) to become very nervous

разнес|ти́, у́, ёшь, *past* ~, ~ла́ *pf.* (*of* ► **разноси́ть**) **1** to carry, convey; to take round; **р.** газе́ты to deliver newspapers; (*слух*) to spread **2** (infml, *разбить*) to smash, break up **3** (*рассеять*) to scatter, disperse

разнес|ти́сь, ётся, *past* ~ся, ~ла́сь *pf.* (*of* ► **разноси́ться**) **1** (*о слухах*) to spread **2** (*о звуках*) to resound

разнима́|ть, ю *impf. of* ► **разня́ть**

✓ **ра́зниц|а, ы** *f.* difference; disparity; кака́я **р.?** (infml) what difference does it make?

разнови́дност|ь, и *f.* variety

разногла́си|е, я *nt.* **1** (*во мнениях*) difference, disagreement; ~я во взгля́дах difference of opinion **2** (*противоречие*) discrepancy; **р. в** показа́ниях conflicting evidence

разнообра́зи|е, я *nt.* variety, diversity; для ~я for a change

✓ **разнообра́з|ный, ~ен, ~на** *adj.* various, varied, diverse

разноро́д|ный, ~ен, ~на *adj.* heterogeneous

разно|си́ть, шу́, ~сишь *impf. of* ► **разнести́**

разно|си́ться, ~сится *impf. of* ► **разнести́сь**

разносторо́н|ний, ~ен, ~ня *adj.* many-sided; versatile

ра́зност|ь, и *f.* difference

разно́счик, а *m.* (*газет, телеграмм*) delivery man; (*новостей*) bearer; (*инфекции*) carrier

разноцве́т|ный, ~ен, ~на *adj.* of different colours (BrE), colors (AmE); multicoloured (BrE), multicolored (AmE)

✓ **ра́зн|ый** *adj.* **1** (*взгляды*) different, differing **2** (*разнообразный*) various, diverse; ~ого ро́да of various kinds; (*as nt. n.* ~ое, ~ого) (*на повестке дня*) miscellaneous

разня́ть, ниму́, ни́мешь, *past* ~ня́л, ~няла́, ~ня́ло *pf.* (*of* ► **разнима́ть**) to part, separate

разо… *vbl. pref.* = раз…¹, раз…²

разоблача́|ть, а́ю *impf. of* ► **разоблачи́ть**

разоблаче́ни|е, я *nt.* exposure, unmasking

разоблач|и́ть, у́, и́шь *pf.* (*of* ► **разоблача́ть**) to expose, unmask

раз|обра́ть, беру́, берёшь, *past* ~обра́л, ~обра́ла, ~обра́ло *pf.* (*of* ► **разбира́ть**) **1** (*механизм*) to take to pieces, dismantle **2** (*раскупить*) to buy up; (*взять*) to take **3** (*привести в порядок*) to sort out **4** (*ссору, дело*) to investigate, look into **5** (*понять*) to make out, understand

раз|обра́ться, беру́сь, берёшься, *past* ~обра́лся, ~обра́лась *pf.* (*of* ► **разбира́ться**) (в + *р.*) (*понимать*) to understand, know about; (infml, *разложить свои вещи*) to unpack, sort out one's things

разобщённо *adv.* apart, separately; де́йствовать **р.** to act independently

ра́зов|ый *adj.* valid for one occasion (only); ~ого по́льзования disposable

раз|огна́ть, гоню́, го́нишь, *past* ~огна́л, ~огнала́, ~огна́ло *pf.* (*of* ► **разгоня́ть**) **1** to drive away; (fig.) to dispel; **р.** демонстра́цию to break up a demonstration **2** (infml, *автомобиль*) to drive at high speed, race

раз|огна́ться, гоню́сь, го́нишься, *past* ~огна́лся, ~огнала́сь, ~огна́лось *pf.* (*of* ► **разгоня́ться**) to gather speed; to gather momentum

разогн|у́ть, у́, ёшь *pf.* (*of* ► **разгиба́ть**) to unbend, straighten; **р.** спи́ну to straighten one's back

разогн|у́ться, у́сь, ёшься *pf.* (*of* ► **разгиба́ться**) to straighten oneself up

разогрева́|ть, ю *impf. of* ► **разогре́ть**

разогрева́|ться, юсь *impf. of* ► **разогре́ться**

разогре́|ть, ю *pf.* (*of* ► **разогрева́ть**) to warm up

разогре́|ться, юсь *pf.* (*of* ► **разогрева́ться**) to warm up, grow warm

разоде́|ть, ну, нешь *pf.* (infml) to dress up

разоде́|ться, нусь, нешься *pf.* (infml) to dress up

раз|одра́ть, деру́, дерёшь, *past* ~одра́л, ~одра́ла, ~одра́ло *pf.* (*of* ► **раздира́ть** 1) to tear up

разозл|и́ть, ю́, и́шь *pf.* (*of* ► **злить**) to make angry, enrage

разозл|и́ться, ю́сь, и́шься *pf.* (*of* ► **злиться**) to get angry, get in a rage

раз|ойти́сь, ойду́сь, ойдёшься, *past* ~оше́лся, ~ошла́сь *pf.* (*of* ► **расходи́ться**) **1** (*уйти*) to go away; (*рассеяться*) to disperse; толпа́ ~ошла́сь the crowd broke up **2** (с + *i.*) (*расстаться*) to part (from); (*о супругах*) to separate (from); он ~оше́лся с жено́й he has separated from his wife **3** (*о линиях, о дорогах*) to branch off, diverge; (*о лучах*) to radiate **4** (*разминуться*) to pass (*without meeting*) **5** (с + *i.*) (*обнаружить разногласие*) to conflict (with); **р.** во мне́нии с кем-н. to disagree with sb **6** (*раствориться*) to dissolve; (*растаять*) to melt **7** (infml, *дать волю себе*) to get going; бу́ря ~ошла́сь the storm raged

разомкн|у́ть, у́, ёшь *pf.* (*of* ► **размыка́ть**) to open, unfasten; (tech.) to break, disconnect

разонра́в|иться, люсь, ишься *pf.* (infml) (+ *d.*) to cease to please, lose its attraction (for)

разор|а́ться, у́сь, ёшься *pf.* (infml) to start shouting

разорв|а́ть, у́, ёшь, *past* ~а́л, ~ала́, ~а́ло *pf.* (*of* ► **разрыва́ть¹**) **1** (*письмо*) to tear up; (*пакет, конверт*) to tear open; (*одежду*) to tear **2** (impers.) (*взорвать*) to blow up, burst; котёл ~а́ло the boiler has blown up

3 (fig., *прекрати́ть*) to break (off), sever; **р. дипломати́ческие отноше́ния** to break off diplomatic relations

разорв|а́ться, у́сь, ёшься, *past* ~а́лся, ~ала́сь, ~а́ло́сь *pf.* (*of* ▶ разрыва́ться) **1** (*о верёвке*) to tear, become torn **2** (*взорваться*) to blow up; to explode **3** (*об отношениях*) to be broken off, severed

разоре́ни|е, я *nt.* (*города*) destruction, ravage; (*народа*) ruin

разор|и́ть, ю́, и́шь *pf.* (*of* ▶ разоря́ть) **1** (*опустошить*) to destroy, ravage **2** (*довести до нищеты*) to ruin, bring to ruin

разор|и́ться, ю́сь, и́шься *pf.* (*of* ▶ разоря́ться) **1** (*прийти в упадок*) to be ruined **2** (*впасть в нищету*) to go broke, ruin oneself

разоруж|а́ть, а́ю *impf. of* ▶ разоружи́ть

разоруж|а́ться, а́юсь *impf. of* ▶ разоружи́ться

разоруже́ни|е, я *nt.* (*действие*) disarming; (*политика*) disarmament

разоруж|и́ть, у́, и́шь *pf.* (*of* ▶ разоружа́ть) to disarm

разоруж|и́ться, у́сь, и́шься *pf.* (*of* ▶ разоружа́ться) to disarm

разор|я́ть, я́ю *impf. of* ▶ разори́ть

разор|я́ться, я́юсь *impf. of* ▶ разори́ться

разо|сла́ть, шлю́, шлёшь *pf.* (*of* ▶ рассыла́ть) to send out

разостла́ть, расстелю́, рассте́лешь *pf.* = расстели́ть

разостла́ться, рассте́лется *pf.* = расстели́ться

разочарова́ни|е, я *nt.* disappointment

разочар|ова́ть, у́ю *pf.* (*of* ▶ разочаро́вывать) to disappoint

разочар|ова́ться, у́юсь *pf.* (*of* ▶ разочаро́вываться) (**в** + *p.*) to be disappointed (in sb, with sth)

разочаро́выва|ть, ю *impf. of* ▶ разочарова́ть

разочаро́выва|ться, юсь *impf. of* ▶ разочарова́ться

☞ **разраба́тыва|ть, ю** *impf. of* ▶ разрабо́тать

☞ **разрабо́та|ть, ю** *pf.* (*of* ▶ разраба́тывать) **1** (*подготовить*) to develop; to elaborate; **р. пла́н** to work out a plan **2** (mining) to work, exploit

☞ **разрабо́тк|а, и** *f.* **1** (*проекта*) working out; development; elaboration **2** (mining) working, exploitation; **откры́тая р.** opencast mining **3** **нефтяна́я р.** oilfield

разра́внива|ть, ю *impf. of* ▶ разровня́ть

разража́|ться, юсь *impf. of* ▶ разрази́ться

разра|зи́ться, жу́сь, зи́шься *pf.* (*of* ▶ разража́ться) (*о грозе, о катастрофе*) to break out, burst out; (**слеза́ми** to burst into tears; **р. сме́хом** to burst out laughing

разраст|а́ться, а́ется *impf. of* ▶ разрасти́сь

разраст|и́сь, ётся, *past* разро́сся, разросла́сь *pf.* (*of* ▶ разраста́ться) to grow; to spread; **де́ло разросло́сь** the business has grown; **сире́нь разросла́сь** the lilac has spread

разре́з, а *m.* **1** (*отверстие*) cut; slit; **ю́бка с ~ом** slit skirt **2** (*сечение*) section; **попере́чный р.** cross section; **р. глаз** shape of one's eyes

разре́|зать, жу, жешь *pf.* (*of* ▶ разреза́ть) to cut; to slit

разреза́|ть, а́ю *impf. of* ▶ разре́зать

разреш|а́ть, а́ю *impf. of* ▶ разреши́ть

разреш|а́ться, а́ется *impf.* **1** *impf. of* ▶ разреши́ться **2** (*impf. only*) to be allowed; **здесь кури́ть не ~а́ется** smoking is not allowed here

☞ **разреше́ни|е, я** *nt.* **1** (*право*) permission; **с ва́шего ~я** with your permission, by your leave **2** (*документ*) permit, authorization; **р. на въезд** entry permit **3** (*проблемы*) solution **4** (*спора*) settlement **5** (tech., *степень детализации*) resolution

разреши́м|ый, ~, ~а *adj.* solvable

разреш|и́ть, у́, и́шь *pf.* (*of* ▶ разреша́ть) **1** (+ *d.*) to allow, permit; ~и́те пройти́! do you mind letting me pass? **2** (*книгу, фильм*) to authorize; **р. кни́гу к печа́ти** to authorize the printing of a book **3** (*проблему*) to solve **4** (*конфликт*) to settle; **р. сомне́ния** to resolve doubts

разреш|и́ться, и́тся *pf.* (*of* ▶ разреша́ться 1) **1** (*о проблеме*) to be solved **2** (*о конфликте*) to be settled

разрис|ова́ть, у́ю *pf.* (*of* ▶ разрисо́вывать) to cover with drawings

разрисо́выва|ть, ю *impf. of* ▶ разрисова́ть

разровня́|ть, ю *pf.* (*of* ▶ разра́внивать) to level

разро́знен|ный, ~, ~на *adj.* **1** (*лишенный единства*) uncoordinated **2**: **р. компле́кт** incomplete set; ~ные тома́ odd volumes

разруб|а́ть, а́ю *impf. of* ▶ разруби́ть

разруб|и́ть, лю́, ~ишь *pf.* (*of* ▶ разруба́ть) to cut, cleave

разру́х|а, и *f.* ruin, collapse

разруш|а́ть, а́ю, а́ет *impf. of* ▶ разру́шить

разруш|а́ться, а́ется *impf. of* ▶ разру́шиться

разруше́ни|е, я *nt.* destruction; (*in pl.*) havoc

разруши́тел|ьный, ~ен, ~ьна *adj.* destructive

разру́ш|ить, у, ишь *pf.* (*of* ▶ разруша́ть) **1** to destroy; to ruin; **р. чьи-н. наде́жды** to ruin sb's hopes

разру́ш|иться, ится *pf.* (*of* ▶ разруша́ться) to go to ruin, be destroyed, collapse

разры́в, а *m.* **1** (*пространство*) break; gap; (*прореха*) tear; (*отношений*) breaking, severance; (**с кем-н.**) break-up; (*несоответствие*) gap; **р. ме́жду поколе́ниями** generation gap **2** (*снаряда*) burst, explosion

разрыва́|ть¹, ю *impf. of* ▶ разорва́ть

р

разрыва́|ть², ю *impf. of* ▸ разры́ть

разрыва́|ться, юсь *impf. of* ▸ разорва́ться

разр|ы́ть, о́ю, о́ешь *pf.* (*of* ▸ разрыва́ть²)
1 to dig up **2** (fig., infml, *раскида́ть*) to turn upside-down, rummage through

разря́д¹, а *m.* (*электричества*) discharge

разря́д², а *m.* (*категория*) category, sort; (*в профессии, в спорте*) rank, class; **пе́рвого** ~а first class

разря|ди́ть, жу́, ди́шь *pf.* (*of* ▸ разряжа́ть)
1 (elec.) to discharge; **р. атмосфе́ру** (fig.) to clear the air **2** (*ружьё*) to unload; (*стреляя*) to discharge

разря|ди́ться, ди́тся *pf.* (*of* ▸ разряжа́ться)
1 (elec.) to run down; (fig.) to clear, ease **2** (*об оружии*) to be unloaded; (*стреляя*) to be discharged

разряжа́|ть, ю, ет *impf. of* ▸ разряди́ть

разряжа́|ться, ется *impf. of* ▸ разряди́ться

разубе|ди́ть, жу́, ди́шь *pf.* (*of* ▸ разубежда́ть) (в + *p.*) to dissuade (from)

разубе|ди́ться, жу́сь, ди́шься *pf.* (*of* ▸ разубежда́ться) (в + *p.*) to change one's mind (about)

разубежда́|ть, ю *impf. of* ▸ разубеди́ть

разубежда́|ться, юсь *impf. of* ▸ разубеди́ться

разува́|ть, ю *impf. of* ▸ разу́ть

разува́|ться, юсь *impf. of* ▸ разу́ться

разуве́р|ить, ю, ишь *pf.* (*of* ▸ разуверя́ть) (в + *p.*) to cause sb to lose faith, stop believing (in); to persuade to the contrary; **он меня́ ~ил в том, что э́того мо́жно доби́ться** he persuaded me that it could not be achieved

разуве́р|иться, юсь, ишься *pf.* (*of* ▸ разуверя́ться) (в + *p.*) to lose faith (in)

разуверя́|ть, ю *impf. of* ▸ разуве́рить

разуверя́|ться, юсь *impf. of* ▸ разуве́риться

разузна|ва́ть, ю́, ёшь *impf.* **1** *impf. of* ▸ разузна́ть **2** (*impf. only*) to make inquiries (about)

разузна́|ть, ю *pf.* (*of* ▸ разузнава́ть 1) to find out

разукра́|сить, шу, сишь *pf.* (*of* ▸ разукра́шивать) to adorn; to decorate; to embellish

разукра́шива|ть, ю *impf. of* ▸ разукра́сить

ра́зум, а *m.* reason; (*интеллект*) intellect

⚘ **разуме́|ться**, ется *impf.* (под + *i.*) to be understood (by), be meant (by); **под э́тим** ~**ется...** by this is meant ...; (**са́мо собо́й**) ~**ется** it goes without saying, of course; **он,** ~**ется, не знал, что вы уже́ пришли́** he, of course, did not know that you were already here

разу́м|ный, ~ен, ~на *adj.* **1** (*существо*) rational, intelligent **2** (*парень*) intelligent, clever **3** (*поступок*) reasonable; **э́то (вполне́)** ~**но** it is (perfectly) reasonable

разу́|ть, ю, ешь *pf.* (*of* ▸ разува́ть): **р. кого́-н.** to take sb's shoes off

разу́|ться, юсь, ешься *pf.* (*of* ▸ разува́ться) to take one's shoes off

разу́чива|ть, ю *impf. of* ▸ разучи́ть

разу́чива|ться, юсь *impf. of* ▸ разучи́ться

разучи́|ть, у́, ~ишь *pf.* (*of* ▸ разу́чивать) to learn (up); **р. роль** to learn, study one's part

разучи́|ться, у́сь, ~ишься *pf.* (*of* ▸ разу́чиваться) (+ *inf.*) to forget (how to); **я** ~**и́лся ходи́ть на лы́жах** I have forgotten how to ski

разъ... *vbl. pref.* = раз...¹, раз...²

разъеда́|ть, ю *impf. of* ▸ разъе́сть

разъедине́ни|е, я *nt.* **1** separation **2** (elec.) disconnection, breaking

разъедин|и́ть, ю́, и́шь *pf.* (*of* ▸ разъединя́ть)
1 (*друзей*) to separate **2** (elec.) to disconnect; **нас** ~**и́ли** we were cut off (*on telephone*)

разъедин|и́ться, и́тся *pf.* (*of* ▸ разъединя́ться) to separate, part; (*о проводах*) to come apart, be disconnected

разъедин|я́ть, я́ет *impf. of* ▸ разъедини́ть

разъедин|я́ться, я́ется *impf. of* ▸ разъедини́ться

разъе́зд, а *m.* **1** (*людей*) departure **2** (*in pl.*) (*поездки*) travels **3** (mil.) mounted patrol **4** (rail.) siding

разъезжа́|ть, ю *impf.* to drive (about, around), ride (about, around); to travel; **р. по дела́м** to travel about on business

разъезжа́|ться, юсь *impf. of* ▸ разъе́хаться

разъе́|сть, ст, дя́т, *past* ~л *pf.* (*of* ▸ разъеда́ть) to eat away; to corrode (*also fig.*)

разъе́|хаться, дусь, дешься *pf.* (*of* ▸ разъезжа́ться) **1** (*уехать*) to depart; to disperse **2** (*о супругах*) to separate, stop living together **3** (*о машинах*) to (be able to) pass **4** (*размину́ться*) to pass one another (*without meeting*); to miss one another

разъяр|и́ться, ю́сь, и́шься *pf.* (*of* ▸ разъяря́ться) to fly into a rage

разъяр|я́ться, я́юсь *impf. of* ▸ разъяри́ться

разъясне́ни|е, я *nt.* explanation

разъясн|и́ть, ю́, и́шь *pf.* (*of* ▸ разъясня́ть) to explain

разъясн|и́ться, и́тся *pf.* (*of* ▸ разъясня́ться) to become clear, be cleared up

разъясн|я́ть, я́ю, я́ет *impf. of* ▸ разъясни́ть

разъясн|я́ться, я́ется *impf. of* ▸ разъясни́ться

разыгра́|ть, а́ю *pf.* (*of* ▸ разы́грывать)
1 (*исполнить*) to play (through); to perform; **р. дурака́** to play the fool **2** (*игру, карту*) to play **3** (*в лотерее*) to raffle **4** (infml, *одура́чить*) to play a trick (on)

разыгра́|ться, а́юсь *pf.* (*of* ▸ разы́грываться)
1 (*увле́чься игро́й*) to be carried away by a game, by play **2** (*о музыка́нте, об актёре*) to warm up **3** (*о ве́тре, бу́ре*) to get up; (*о чу́вствах*) to run high

---

⚘ key word

p

разы́грыва|ть, ю *impf. of* ▶ разыгра́ть
разы́грыва|ться, юсь *impf. of*
▶ разыгра́ться
разы|ска́ть, щу́, ~щешь *pf.* to find (*after searching*)
разы́скива|ть, ю *impf.* to hunt, search for
разы́скива|ться, юсь *impf.* to be searched, hunted for; **р. поли́цией** to be wanted by the police
ра|й, я, о ~е, в ~ю́ *m.* paradise
✧ райо́н, а *m.* **1** region **2** (*административная единица*) district
райо́нный *adj. of* ▶ райо́н
рак, а *m.* **1** (zool.) (*речно́й*) crayfish (BrE), crawfish (AmE); (*морско́й*) spiny lobster **2** (med.) cancer **3** (*P.*) (astrol., astron.) Crab, Cancer
раке́т|а, ы *f.* **1** (*для сигна́лов; фейерве́рк; косми́ческая*) rocket; **пусти́ть ~у** to let off a rocket **2** (mil.) rocket, ballistic missile; **крыла́тая р.** cruise missile
раке́т|ка, ки *f.* (sport) racket
раке́тчик, а *m.* missile specialist
ра́ковин|а, ы *f.* **1** (*моллю́ска*) shell **2** (*для умыва́ния*) sink; washbasin
раку́шк|а, и *f.* shell; seashell
ра́лли *nt. indecl.* rally
ра́м|а, ы *f.* **1** frame; **вста́вить в ~у** to frame **2** (*маши́ны*) chassis
Рамада́н, а *m.* = Рамаза́н
Рамаза́н, а *m.* (relig.) Ramadan
✧ ра́мк|а, и *f.* frame; (*те́кста*) border
ра́м|ки, ок *pl. only*) framework; limits; **в ~ках** (+ *g.*) within the framework (of), within the limits (of); **вы́йти за р.** (+ *g.*) to exceed the limits (of)
ра́мп|а, ы *f.* (theatr.) footlights
ра́н|а, ы *f.* wound
ранг, а *m.* class, rank
✧ ра́нее *adv.* = ра́ньше
ране́ни|е, я *nt.* **1** (*де́йствие*) wounding; injuring **2** (*ра́на*) wound; injury
ра́нен|ый *adj.* wounded; injured; (*as m. n.* **р.**, ~ого) injured man; wounded man; casualty; (*in pl.*) the injured; the wounded
ра́н|ец, ца *m.* (*похо́дный, солда́тский*) knapsack, pack; (*учени́ческий*) satchel
рани́м|ый, ~, а *adj.* vulnerable
ра́н|ить, ю, ишь *impf. and pf.* to wound; to injure
✧ ра́нн|ий *adj.* early; **~им у́тром** early in the morning; **с ~его де́тства** from early childhood
ра́но¹ *pred.* it is early; **ещё р. ложи́ться спать** it is too early for bed
ра́но² *adv.* early; **р. и́ли по́здно** sooner or later
рантье́ *m. indecl.* rentier
ра́нчо *nt. indecl.* ranch
ра́ньше *adv.* **1** earlier; **как мо́жно р.** as early as possible; as soon as possible **2** (+ *g.*)

(*пре́жде*) before; **до Ло́ндона он р. ве́чера не дое́дет** he will not reach London before evening **3** (*пре́жде*) before, formerly; **р. мы жи́ли в дере́вне** we used to live in the country
ра́порт, а *m.* report
рапорт|ова́ть, у́ю *impf. and pf.* to report
рапс, а *m.* (bot.) rape
рарите́т, а *m.* rarity, curiosity
рас... *vbl. pref.* = раз...¹, раз...²
ра́с|а, ы *f.* race
раси́зм, а *m.* racism
раси́ст, а *m.* racist
раси́ст|ка, ки *f. of* ▶ раси́ст
раси́стский *adj.* racist
раска́ива|ться, юсь *impf. of* ▶ раска́яться
раскалённый *p.p.p. of* ▶ раскали́ть *and adj.* scorching, burning hot
раскал|и́ть, ю́, и́шь *pf.* (*of* ▶ раскаля́ть) to bring to a great heat
раскал|и́ться, ю́сь, и́шься *pf.* (*of* ▶ раскаля́ться) to glow, become hot
раска́лыва|ть, ю *impf. of* ▶ расколо́ть
раска́лыва|ться, юсь *impf. of* ▶ расколо́ться
раскал|я́ть, я́ю *impf. of* ▶ раскали́ть
раскал|я́ться, я́юсь *impf. of* ▶ раскали́ться
раска́пыва|ть, ю *impf. of* ▶ раскопа́ть
раска́т, а *m.* roll, peal; **р. гро́ма** peal of thunder
раскат|а́ть, а́ю *pf.* (*of* ▶ раска́тывать) **1** (*ковёр*) to unroll **2** (*те́сто*) to roll (out); (*доро́гу*) to level
раска́тыва|ть, ю *impf. of* ▶ раската́ть
раскач|а́ть, а́ю *pf.* (*of* ▶ раска́чивать) **1** (*каче́ли*) to swing; to rock **2** (*расшата́ть*) to loosen, shake loose
раскач|а́ться, а́юсь *pf.* (*of* ▶ раска́чиваться) **1** (*на каче́лях*) to swing (back and forth); (*о ло́дке*) to rock **2** (*расшата́ться*) to shake loose
раска́чива|ть, ю *impf. of* ▶ раскача́ть
раска́чива|ться, юсь *impf. of* ▶ раскача́ться
раска́яни|е, я *nt.* repentance
раска́|яться, юсь *pf.* (*of* ▶ раска́иваться) (**в** + *p.*) to repent (of)
расквартир|ова́ть, у́ю *pf.* (*of* ▶ расквартиро́вывать) to quarter, billet
расквартиро́выва|ть, ю *impf. of* ▶ расквартирова́ть
раскид|а́ть, а́ю *pf.* (*of* ▶ раски́дывать) to scatter
раски́дыва|ть, ю *impf. of* ▶ раскида́ть, ▶ раски́нуть
раски́дыва|ться, юсь *impf. of* ▶ раски́нуться
раски́|нуть, ну, нешь *pf.* (*of* ▶ раски́дывать) **1** (*ру́ки*) to stretch (out) **2** (*ковёр*) to spread (out); (*ла́герь*) to set up; (*пала́тку*) to pitch
раски́|нуться, нусь, нешься *pf.* (*of* ▶ раски́дываться) **1** to spread out, stretch out **2** (infml) to sprawl

р

расклад, а *m.* (*расположение*) disposition, arrangement; (*сил, средств*) apportionment; (*положение дел*) state of affairs

раскладн|ой *adj.* folding; ~ая кровать camp bed (BrE), cot (AmE)

раскладу́шк|а, и *f.* (infml) camp bed (BrE), cot (AmE)

раскла́дыва|ть, ю *impf. of* ▶ разложи́ть¹

раскла́дыва|ться, юсь *impf. of* ▶ разложи́ться¹

раскла́нива|ться, юсь *impf. of* ▶ раскла́няться

раскла́н|яться, яюсь *pf.* (*of* ▶ раскла́ниваться) **1** to exchange bows (*on meeting or leave-taking*) **2** (*об актёре*) to take a bow

расклеи́ва|ть, ю *impf. of* ▶ расклеи́ть

расклеи́ва|ться, юсь *impf. of* ▶ расклеи́ться

расклеи́|ть, ю, ишь *pf.* (*of* ▶ расклеи́вать) **1** (*конверт*) to unstick **2** (*афиши*) to stick, paste (*in various places*)

расклеи́|ться, юсь, ишься *pf.* (*of* ▶ расклеи́ваться) **1** to come unstuck **2** (fig., infml, *о планах*) to fall through, to come unstuck **3** (fig., infml, *о человеке*) to feel unwell; **он совсе́м ~ился** he has gone to pieces

раско́ванный *adj.* relaxed, uninhibited

раско́л, а *m.* **1** (relig., hist.) schism, dissent **2** (pol., etc.) split, division

раскол|о́ть, ю́, ~ешь *pf.* **1** *pf. of* ▶ коло́ть¹ **2** (*impf.* раска́лывать) (fig.) to disrupt, break up

раскол|о́ться, ю́сь, ~ешься *pf.* (*of* ▶ раска́лываться) to split (also fig.)

раскопа́|ть, ю *pf.* (*of* ▶ раска́пывать) to dig up, unearth (also fig.); (*об археологах*) to excavate

раско́пк|а, и *f.* (*действие*) digging up; (*in pl.*) (*археологические*) excavations

раскра́ива|ть, ю *impf. of* ▶ раскрои́ть

раскра́|сить, шу, сишь *pf.* (*of* ▶ раскра́шивать) to paint, colour (BrE), color (AmE)

раскра́ск|а, и *f.* **1** (*действие*) painting, colouring (BrE), coloring (AmE) **2** (*расцветка*) colours (BrE), colors (AmE), colour scheme (BrE), color scheme (AmE)

раскра́шива|ть, ю *impf. of* ▶ раскра́сить

раскрепо|сти́ться, щу́сь, сти́шься *pf.* (*of* ▶ раскрепоща́ться) to free *or* liberate oneself

раскрепоща́|ться, юсь *impf. of* ▶ раскрепости́ться

раскритик|ова́ть, у́ю *pf.* to criticize severely, slam

раскрич|а́ться, у́сь, и́шься *pf.* **1** to start shouting, start crying **2** (*на + a.*) to shout (at)

раскро|и́ть, ю́, и́шь *pf.* (*of* ▶ раскра́ивать) **1** (*ткань*) to cut out **2** (fig., infml) to cut open; **р. кому́-н. че́реп** to split sb's skull

раскрош|и́ть, у́, ~ит *pf. of* ▶ кроши́ть

раскрош|и́ться, ~ится *pf. of* ▶ кроши́ться

раскру|ти́ть, чу́, ~тишь *pf.* (*of* ▶ раскру́чивать) **1** (*развить*) to untwist, undo **2** (*колесо*) to spin, rotate **3** (infml) (*заставить развиваться*) to develop, establish; (*рекламировать*) to promote, popularize

раскру|ти́ться, чу́сь, ~тишься *pf.* (*of* ▶ раскру́чиваться) **1** (*развиться*) to come untwisted, come undone **2** (*начать крутиться*) to start spinning, rotating **3** (infml) (*начать действовать*) to develop, get established; (*получить известность*) to become famous, popular

раскру́чива|ть, ю *impf. of* ▶ раскрути́ть

раскру́чива|ться, юсь *impf. of* ▶ раскрути́ться

раскрыва́|ть, ю *impf. of* ▶ раскры́ть

раскрыва́|ться, юсь *impf. of* ▶ раскры́ться

раскр|ы́ть, о́ю, о́ешь *pf.* (*of* ▶ раскрыва́ть) **1** (*открыть*) to open (wide); **р. зо́нтик** to put up an umbrella; **р. кни́гу** to open a book **2** (*сделать видным*) to expose, bare **3** (*обнаружить*) to reveal, disclose, lay bare; (*найти*) to discover; **р. секре́т** to disclose a secret

раскр|ы́ться, о́юсь, о́ешься *pf.* (*of* ▶ раскрыва́ться) **1** to open **2** (*раскрыть себя*) to uncover oneself **3** (*обнаружиться*) to come out; to come to light

раскуп|а́ть, а́ю *impf. of* ▶ раскупи́ть

раскуп|и́ть, лю́, ~ишь *pf.* (*of* ▶ раскупа́ть) to buy up

раску́рива|ть, ю, ет *impf. of* ▶ раскури́ть

раскур|и́ть, ю́, ~ишь *pf.* (*of* ▶ раскуривать) **1** (*заставить куриться*) to puff at (*a pipe or cigarette*) **2** (*зажечь*) to light up

раску|си́ть, шу́, ~сишь *pf.* (*of* ▶ раску́сывать) **1** (*конфету*) to bite into **2** (*pf. only*) (infml, *узнать, понять*) to suss out

раску́сыва|ть, ю *impf. of* ▶ раскуси́ть

ра́совый *adj.* racial

распа́д, а *m.* **1** disintegration, break-up; (fig.) collapse **2** (chem.) decomposition

распада́|ться, ется *impf. of* ▶ распа́сться

распак|ова́ть, у́ю *pf.* (*of* ▶ распако́вывать) to unpack

распако́выва|ть, ю *impf. of* ▶ распакова́ть

распа́рыва|ть, ю *impf. of* ▶ распоро́ть

распа|сться, дётся, *past* ~лся *pf.* (*of* ▶ распада́ться) **1** to disintegrate; (fig.) to break up; to collapse; **коали́ция ~лась** the coalition broke up **2** (chem.) to decompose

распа|ха́ть, шу́, ~шешь *pf.* (*of* ▶ распа́хивать) to plough up (BrE), plow up (AmE)

распа́хива|ть, ю *impf. of* ▶ распаха́ть, ▶ распахну́ть

распа́хива|ться, юсь *impf. of* ▶ распахну́ться

распах|ну́ть, ну́, нёшь *pf.* (*of*
▶ **распа́хивать**) to open wide; to throw
open; **широко́ р. две́ри** (+ *d.*) to open wide
the doors (to) (also fig.)

распах|ну́ться, ну́сь, нёшься *pf.* (*of*
▶ **распа́хиваться**) **1** (*о две́ри, об окне́*) to
fly open, swing open **2** (*распахну́ть по́лы
свое́й оде́жды*) to throw open one's coat

распере́ть, разопру́, разопрёшь, *past*
распёр, распёрла *pf.* (*of* ▶ **распира́ть**)
(infml) to burst open, cause to burst

распеча́т|ать, аю *pf.* (*of* ▶ **распеча́тывать**)
1 (*вскрыть*) to unseal; **р. письмо́** to
open a letter **2** (*напеча́тать во мно́гих
экземпля́рах*) to print off **3** (comput.) to
print (out)

распеча́тк|а, и *f.* printout; (*де́йствие*)
printing out

распеча́тыва|ть, ю *impf. of* ▶ **распеча́тать**

распи́лива|ть, ю *impf. of* ▶ **распили́ть**

распил|и́ть, ю́, ~ишь *pf.* (*of*
▶ **распи́ливать**) to saw up

распира́|ть, ю *impf. of* ▶ **распере́ть**

расписа́ни|е, я *nt.* timetable, schedule

распи|са́ть, шу́, ~шешь *pf.* (*of*
▶ **распи́сывать**) **1** (*све́дения*) to enter; to
note down; **р. счета́ по кни́гам** to enter bills
in the account book **2** (*распредели́ть*) to
assign, allot **3** (*разрисова́ть*) to paint

распи|са́ться, шу́сь, ~шешься *pf.* (*of*
▶ **распи́сываться**) **1** to sign (one's name);
(**в** + *p.*) to sign (for); **р. в получе́нии
зака́зного письма́** to sign for a registered
letter **2** (infml, *регистри́ровать брак*)
to register one's marriage **3** (**в** + *p.*)
(fig., *призна́ться*) to acknowledge; **р. в
со́бственном неве́жестве** to acknowledge
one's own ignorance

распи́ск|а, и *f.* receipt; **р. в получе́нии** (+ *g.*)
receipt (for)

распи́сыва|ть, ю *impf. of* ▶ **расписа́ть**

распи́сыва|ться, юсь *impf. of*
▶ **расписа́ться**

распих|а́ть, а́ю *pf.* (*of* ▶ **распи́хивать**) (infml)
1 (*растолка́ть*) to shove; **2** (*рассова́ть*)
to shove; **р. я́блоки по карма́нам** to stuff
apples into one's pockets

распи́хива|ть, ю *impf. of* ▶ **распиха́ть**

распла́в|ить, лю, ишь *pf.* (*of*
▶ **расплавля́ть**) to melt, fuse

распла́в|иться, ится *pf.* (*of*
▶ **расплавля́ться**) to melt, fuse

расплавля́|ть, ю, ет *impf. of* ▶ **распла́вить**

расплавля́|ться, ется *impf. of*
▶ **распла́виться**

распла́|каться, чусь, чешься *pf.* to burst
into tears

распла́т|а, ы *f.* payment; (fig.) retribution;
час ~ы day of reckoning

распла|ти́ться, чу́сь, ~тишься *pf.* (*of*
▶ **распла́чиваться**) **1** (**с** + *i.*) to pay off; to
settle accounts (with), get even (with) (also
fig.); **р. с долга́ми** to pay off one's debts

2 (*за* + *a.*) (fig.) to pay (for)

распла́чива|ться, юсь *impf. of*
▶ **расплати́ться**

распле|ска́ть, щу́, ~щешь *pf.* (*of*
▶ **расплёскивать**) to spill

распле|ска́ться, ~щется *pf.* (*of*
▶ **расплёскиваться**) to spill

расплёскива|ть, ю *impf. of* ▶ **расплеска́ть**

расплёскива|ется, ется *impf. of*
▶ **расплеска́ться**

распле|сти́, ту́, тёшь, *past* **~л, ~ла́** *pf.*
(*of* ▶ **расплета́ть**) (*верёвку*) to untwine,
untwist; (*ко́су*) to undo

распле|сти́сь, тётся, *past* **~лся, ~ла́сь** *pf.*
(*of* ▶ **расплета́ться**) (*о верёвке*) to untwine,
untwist; (*о косе*) to come undone

расплета́|ть, ю, ет *impf. of* ▶ **расплести́**

расплета́|ться, ется *impf. of* ▶ **расплести́сь**

расплыва́|ться, ется *impf. of*
▶ **расплы́ться**

расплы́вчат|ый, ~, ~а *adj.* (*рису́нок*)
blurred; (*отве́т*) vague

расплы́|ться, вётся, *past* **~лся, ~ла́сь**
pf. (*of* ▶ **расплыва́ться**) **1** (*о жи́дкости*)
to run; **черни́ла ~лись** the ink has run;
(*о фигу́рах*) to become blurred; (*о ма́ссе*)
to disperse; (*уплы́ть*) to swim off **2** (infml,
потолсте́ть) to spread; to run to fat; **р. в
улы́бку** to break into a smile

расплю́щива|ть, ю, ет *impf. of*
▶ **расплю́щить**

расплю́щива|ться, ется *impf. of*
▶ **расплю́щиться**

расплю́щ|ить, у, ишь *pf.* (*of*
▶ **расплю́щивать**) to flatten, crush

расплю́щ|иться, ится *pf.* (*of*
▶ **расплю́щиваться**) to become flat

распозна|ва́ть, ю́, ёшь *impf. of* ▶ **распозна́ть**

распозна́|ть, ю, ешь *pf.* (*of* ▶ **распознава́ть**)
to recognize, identify; **р. боле́знь** to diagnose
an illness

располага́|ть¹, ю *impf.* (+ *i.*) to have at one's
disposal, have available; **р. вре́менем** to have
time available

располага́|ть², ю *impf. of* ▶ **расположи́ть**

располага́|ться, юсь *impf. of*
▶ **расположи́ться**

располага́ющий 1 *pres. part. act. of*
▶ **располага́ть¹ 2** *pres. part. act. of*
▶ **располага́ть²** *and adj.* pleasant,
prepossessing

располз|а́ться, а́юсь *impf. of*
▶ **расползти́сь**

располз|ти́сь, у́сь, ёшься, *past* **~ся,
~ла́сь** *pf.* (*of* ▶ **расползаться**) **1** to
crawl (away) **2** (infml, *об оде́жде*) to come
unravelled; to tear, give at the seams

расположе́ни|е, я *nt.* **1** (*предме́тов*)
disposition, arrangement; **р. по кварти́рам**
(mil.) billeting **2** (*местоположе́ние*)
situation, location **3** (*симпа́тия*) favour
(BrE), favor (AmE); sympathies; **по́льзоваться**

чьим-н. ~ем to enjoy sb's favour (BrE), favor (AmE), to be liked by sb **4**: р. (ду́ха) disposition, mood, humour (BrE), humor (AmE); быть в плохо́м ~и ду́ха to be in a bad mood

располо́жен|ный, ~, ~а *p.p.p. of*
▶ **расположи́ть** *and pred. adj.* **1** (к + *d.*) (*питающий чувство симпатии*) well disposed (to, towards) **2** (к + *d. or* + *inf.*) (*склонный*) disposed (to), inclined (to); in the mood (for); **я не о́чень ~ сего́дня рабо́тать** I don't feel much like working today

располож|и́ть, у́, ~ишь *pf.* (*of*
▶ **располага́ть**[2]) **1** (*разместить*) to dispose, arrange, set out **2** (*вызвать симпатию в ком-н.*) to win over, gain; **р. кого́-н. к себе́, в свою́ по́льзу** to gain sb's favour (BrE), favor (AmE)

располож|и́ться, у́сь, ~ишься *pf.* (*of*
▶ **располага́ться**) (*разместиться*) to take up position; to settle *or* compose oneself; to make oneself comfortable

распор|о́ть, ю́, ~ешь *pf.* (*of* ▶ **распа́рывать**) to unstitch, unpick

распоря|ди́ться, жу́сь, ди́шься *pf.* (*of*
▶ **распоряжа́ться** 1) **1** (о + *p. or* + *inf.*) to order; to see (that); **я ~жу́сь, что́бы вам возмести́ли расхо́ды** I will see that you are reimbursed for the expenses **2** (+ *i.*) to manage; to deal (with)

распоря́д|ок, ка *m.* order; routine; **пра́вила вну́треннего ~ка** (*в учреждении, на фабрике и т. д.*) office, factory, *etc.*, regulations

распоряжа́|ться, юсь *impf.* **1** *impf. of*
▶ **распоряди́ться** **2** (*impf. only*) to give orders, be in charge

распоряже́ни|е, я *nt.* **1** (*приказ*) order; instruction, direction; **до осо́бого ~я** until further notice **2**: **име́ть в своём ~и** to have at one's disposal

распоя|са́ться, шусь, шешься *pf.* (*of*
▶ **распоя́сываться**) **1** to take off one's belt; to ungird oneself **2** (*fig., infml, pej., стать распущенным*) to throw aside all restraint; to let oneself go

распоя́сыва|ться, юсь *impf. of*
▶ **распоя́саться**

распра́в|а, ы *f.* harsh punishment; reprisal; **крова́вая р.** massacre

распра́в|ить, лю, ишь *pf.* (*of* ▶ **расправля́ть**) **1** (*выпрямить*) to straighten; to smooth out **2** (*вытянуть*) to spread, stretch; **р. кры́лья** to spread one's wings (also fig.)

распра́в|иться[1], **ится** *pf.* (*of*
▶ **расправля́ться**) (*выпрямиться*) to get smoothed out

распра́в|иться[2], **люсь, ишься** *pf.* (*of*
▶ **расправля́ться**) (с + *i.*) (*произвести расправу*) to deal (with); **р. без суда́** to take the law into one's own hands; (*распорядиться*) to deal with, dispose of

расправля́|ть, ю *impf. of* ▶ **распра́вить**

расправля́|ться, юсь *impf. of*
▶ **распра́виться**[1], ▶ **распра́виться**[2]

распределе́ни|е, я *nt.* distribution; allocation, assignment; **р. нало́гов** assessment of taxes

распредели́тел|ь, я *m.* **1** (*устройство*) regulator; **р. зажига́ния** distributor **2** (*учреждение*) distribution centre (BrE), center (AmE)

распредели́тельн|ый *adj.* distributive, distributing; **~ая доска́, р. щит** (tech.) switchboard; **р. щит(о́к) (с предохрани́телями/ про́бками)** (elec.) fuse box; **р. вал** (tech.) camshaft

распредел|и́ть, ю́, и́шь *pf.* (*of*
▶ **распределя́ть**) to distribute; to allocate, assign; **р. своё вре́мя** to allocate one's time

распределя́|ть, я́ю *impf. of* ▶ **распредели́ть**

распрода|ва́ть, ю́, ёшь *impf. of*
▶ **распрода́ть**

распрода́ж|а, и *f.* sale; clearance sale

распрода́|ть, м, шь, ст, ди́м, ди́те, ду́т, *past* **распро́дал, ~ла́, распро́дало** *pf.* (*of*
▶ **распродава́ть**) (*землю, вещи*) to sell off; (*билеты*) to sell out of; **биле́ты распро́даны** all the tickets are sold

распро|сти́ться, щу́сь, сти́шься *pf.* (с + *i.*) to say goodbye to; **р. с мечто́й** to bid farewell to one's dream(s)

☞ **распростране́ни|е, я** *nt.* (*слухов, заразы*) spreading; (*знания, идей*) dissemination; (*владений*) expansion; (*оружия*) proliferation; (*товаров*) distribution; **име́ть большо́е р.** to be widely practised (BrE), practiced (AmE)

☞ **распространённый** *p.p.p. of*
▶ **распространи́ть** *and adj.* (*мнение*) widespread, prevalent; (*растения*) common

распространи́тел|ь, я *m.* (*слухов, знаний*) spreader, disseminator; (*книг, газет*) distributor

распространи́тель|ница, ницы *f. of*
▶ **распространи́тель**

распростран|и́ть, ю́, и́шь *pf.* (*of*
▶ **распространя́ть**) **1** (*слухи, заразу*) to spread; (*знания, информа́цию*) to disseminate; (*товары, книги*) to distribute; (*письмо, мемора́ндум*) to circulate; (*владения*) to increase **2** (*расширить*) to extend; **р. де́йствие зако́на на всех** to extend the application of a law to all **3** (*запах*) to give off

распростран|и́ться, ю́сь, и́тся *pf.* (*of*
▶ **распространя́ться**) (*огонь, слухи, запах*) to spread; (*стать больше*) to extend; (*о законе*) to apply

распространя́|ть, я́ю, я́ет *impf. of*
▶ **распространи́ть**

распространя́|ться, я́ется *impf. of*
▶ **распространи́ться**

распроща́|ться, юсь *pf.* (с + *i.*)
= **распрости́ться**

распряга́|ть, ю *impf. of* ▶ **распря́чь**

распрям|и́ть, лю́, и́шь *pf.* (*of* ▶ **распрямля́ть**) (*проволоку*) to straighten, unbend; (*спину*) to straighten

распрям|и́ться, лю́сь, и́шься *pf.* (*of* ▶ **распрямля́ться**) to straighten oneself up

распрямля́|ть, ю *impf. of* ▶ **распрями́ть**

распрямля́|ться, юсь *impf. of* ▶ **распрями́ться**

распря|чь, гу́, жёшь, гу́т, *past* ~г, ~гла́ *pf.* (*of* ▶ **распряга́ть**) to unharness

распуг|а́ть, а́ю *pf.* (*of* ▶ **распу́гивать**) (*infml*) to scare away, frighten away

распу́гива|ть, ю *impf. of* ▶ **распуга́ть**

распуска́|ть, ю *impf. of* ▶ **распусти́ть**

распуска́|ться, юсь *impf. of* ▶ **распусти́ться**

распу|сти́ть, щу́, ~**стишь** *pf.* (*of* ▶ **распуска́ть**) **1** (*учеников*) to dismiss; (*расформировать*) to disband; **р. парла́мент** to dissolve parliament **2** (*ремень, узел галстука*) to loosen, let out; **р. во́лосы** to let one's hair down; **р. паруса́** to set sail **3** (*fig., infml, избаловать*) to allow to get out of hand; to spoil **4** (*infml, слухи*) to spread, put out

распу|сти́ться, щу́сь, ~**стишься** *pf.* (*of* ▶ **распуска́ться**) **1** (bot.) to open, come out **2** (*fig., infml, о детях*) to become undisciplined, get out of hand

распу́т|ать, аю *pf.* (*of* ▶ **распу́тывать**) **1** (*узел*) to untangle; to unravel **2** (*животное*) to untie **3** (*fig., сложный вопрос*) to disentangle; to puzzle out

распу́т|аться, аюсь *pf.* (*of* ▶ **распу́тываться**) **1** to get disentangled; to come undone **2** (fig., infml) to get disentangled, be cleared up

распу́т|ный, ~**ен,** ~**на** *adj.* dissolute, dissipated, debauched

распу́тыва|ть, ю *impf. of* ▶ **распу́тать**

распу́тыва|ться, юсь *impf. of* ▶ **распу́таться**

распух|а́ть, а́ю *impf. of* ▶ **распу́хнуть**

распу́х|нуть, ну, нешь, *past* ~, ~ла *pf.* (*of* ▶ **распуха́ть**) to swell up

распу́щенный *p.p.p. of* ▶ **распусти́ть** *and adj.* **1** (*недисциплинированный*) undisciplined; **р. ребёнок** spoiled child **2** (*безнравственный*) dissolute, dissipated

распыли́тел|ь, я *m.* spray(er)

распыл|и́ть, ю́, и́шь *pf.* (*of* ▶ **распыля́ть**) **1** (*краску*) to spray **2** (fig.) to scatter; **р. си́лы** to scatter one's forces

распыл|и́ться, и́тся *pf.* (*of* ▶ **распыля́ться**) to disperse; to get scattered

распыл|я́ть, я́ю, ет *impf. of* ▶ **распыли́ть**

распыл|я́ться, ется *impf. of* ▶ **распыли́ться**

распя́ти|е, я *nt.* cross, crucifix

расса́д|а, ы (*no pl.*) *f.* seedlings

расса|ди́ть, жу́, ~**дишь** *pf.* (*of* ▶ **расса́живать**) **1** (*гостей*) to seat, offer seats **2** (*посадить порознь*) to separate, seat separately **3** (*растения*) to plant out

расса́жива|ть, ю *impf. of* ▶ **рассади́ть**

расса́жива|ться, юсь *impf. of* ▶ **рассе́сться**

расса́сыва|ться, ется *impf. of* ▶ **рассоса́ться**

рассве|сти́, тёт, *past* ~ло́ *pf.* (*of* ▶ **рассвета́ть**) to dawn; **уже́** ~ло́ it was already light

рассве́т, а *m.* dawn, daybreak; (fig., *начало*) dawn

рассвета́|ть, ет *impf.* (*of* ▶ **рассвести́**): ~ет day is breaking

рассе́ива|ть, ю *impf. of* ▶ **рассе́ять**

рассе́ива|ться, ется *impf. of* ▶ **рассе́яться**

рассека́|ть, ю *impf. of* ▶ **рассе́чь**

рассекре́|тить, чу, тишь *pf.* (*of* ▶ **рассекре́чивать**) to declassify

рассекре́чива|ть, ю *impf. of* ▶ **рассекре́тить**

расселе́ни|е, я *nt.* **1** settling (*in a new place*) **2** (*порознь*) separation; settling apart

рассел|и́ть, ю́, и́шь *pf.* (*of* ▶ **расселя́ть**) **1** to settle (*in a new place*) **2** (*порознь*) to separate; to settle apart

рассел|и́ться, ю́сь, и́шься *pf.* (*of* ▶ **расселя́ться**) **1** to settle (*in a new place*) **2** (*порознь*) to separate, settle separately

рассел|я́ть, я́ю *impf. of* ▶ **рассели́ть**

рассел|я́ться, я́юсь *impf. of* ▶ **рассели́ться**

рассер|ди́ть, жу́, ~**дишь** *pf. of* ▶ **серди́ть**

рассер|ди́ться, жу́сь, ~**дишься** *pf.* (*of* ▶ **серди́ться**) (**на** + *a.*) to get, become angry (with, at, about)

рас|се́сться, ся́дусь, ся́дешься, *past* ~се́лся *pf.* (*of* ▶ **расса́живаться**) **1** to take one's seat **2** (infml, *развалиться*) to sprawl

рассе́|чь, ку́, чёшь, ку́т, *past* ~к, ~кла́ *pf.* (*of* ▶ **рассека́ть**) **1** (*разрубить*) to cut through; (*волну, небо*) to cleave **2** (*поранить*) to cut (badly); **я** ~**к себе́ па́лец** I have cut my finger (badly)

рассе́янно *adv.* absent-mindedly; (*смотреть*) vacantly

рассе́янност|ь, и *f.* (*невнимательность*) absent-mindedness

рассе́янный *p.p.p. of* ▶ **рассе́ять** *and adj.* **1** (*свет*) diffused **2** (*население*) scattered, dispersed **3** (*невнимательный*) absent-minded; **р. взгляд** vacant look

рассе́|ять, ю, ешь *pf.* (*of* ▶ **рассе́ивать**) **1** (*население, толпу*) to scatter, disperse **2** (*сомнения*) to dispel

рассе́|яться, ется *pf.* (*of* ▶ **рассе́иваться**) to disperse; (*в беспорядке*) to scatter; (*о неприятном чувстве*) to pass; **толпа́** ~**ялась** the crowd dispersed; **тума́н** ~**ялся** the fog cleared

расси|де́ться, жу́сь, ди́шься *pf.* (*of* ▶ **расси́живаться**) (infml) to sit for a long time; to sit around

расси́жива|ться, юсь *impf. of* ▶ **расси де́ться**

✍ **расска́з, а** *m.* **1** story **2** (*очевидца*) account

✍ **расска|за́ть, жу́,** ~**жешь** *pf.* (*of* ▶ **расска́зывать**) **1** (+ *a. and d.*) to tell, relate (*sth to sb*) **2** (**о** + *p.*) to tell of; **р. о**

р

де́тстве to tell of one's childhood **3**: р., как всё произошло́ to tell how it all happened

расска́зчик, а *m.* storyteller, narrator

расска́зчи|ца, цы *f. of* ▸ **расска́зчик**

⚡ **расска́зыва|ть**, ю *impf. of* ▸ **рассказа́ть**

рассла́б|ить, лю, ишь *pf.* (*of* ▸ **расслабля́ть**) **1** (*пояс, воротничо́к*) to loosen **2** (*мы́шцы*) to relax

рассла́б|иться, люсь, ишься *pf.* (*of* ▸ **расслабля́ться**) to relax

расслабля́|ть, ю *impf. of* ▸ **рассла́бить**

расслабля́|ться, юсь *impf. of* ▸ **рассла́биться**

рассла́ива|ться, ется *impf. of* ▸ **расслои́ться**

расслед́ование, я *nt.* investigation; (law) inquiry; **провести́ р.** (+ *g.*) to hold an inquiry (into)

расслед́|овать, ую *impf. and pf.* to investigate

расслои́|ться, и́тся *pf.* (*of* ▸ **рассла́иваться**) to become stratified (also fig.); (*отслои́ться*) to flake off

рассл́ыш|ать, у, ишь *pf.* to catch; **я не ~ал вас** I didn't catch what you said

⚡ **рассма́трива|ть**, ю *impf.* **1** *impf. of* ▸ **рассмотре́ть 2** (*impf. only*) (*счита́ть*) to regard (as), consider **3** (*impf. only*) (*внима́тельно смотре́ть*) to scrutinize, examine

рассме́ш|ить, у́, и́шь *pf.* to make laugh

рассме|я́ться, ю́сь, ёшься *pf.* to burst out laughing

⚡ **рассмотре́ни|е**, я *nt.* examination, scrutiny; (*обсужде́ние*) consideration; **предста́вить на р.** to submit for consideration; **быть на ~и** to be under consideration

рассмотр|е́ть, ю́, ~ишь *pf.* (*of* ▸ **рассма́тривать 1**) **1** (*различи́ть*) to discern, make out; **мы с трудо́м ~е́ли на́дпись на па́мятнике** we had difficulty in making out the inscription on the monument **2** (*обсуди́ть*) to examine, consider; **р. заявле́ние** to consider an application

расс|ова́ть, ую́, уёшь *pf.* (*of* ▸ **рассо́вывать**) (infml) to shove, stuff; **р. свои́ ве́щи по чемода́нам** to stuff one's things into suitcases

рассо́выва|ть, ю *impf. of* ▸ **рассова́ть**

рассо́л, а *m.* brine

рассо́р|иться, юсь, ишься *pf.* (с + *i.*) to fall out (with)

рассортир|ова́ть, у́ю *pf.* (*of* ▸ **рассортиро́вывать**) to sort out; (*по ассортиме́нту*) to classify; (*по ка́честву*) to grade, sort

рассортиро́выва|ть, ю *impf. of* ▸ **рассортирова́ть**

рассос|а́ться, ётся *pf.* (*of* ▸ **расса́сываться**) (*об о́пухоли*) to go down; (infml, *о толпе́*) to disperse

рассо́х|нуться, нется, *past* ~ся, ~лась *pf.* (*of* ▸ **рассыха́ться**) to crack

расспра́шива|ть, ю *impf. of* ▸ **расспроси́ть**

расспро|си́ть, шу́, ~сишь *pf.* (*of* ▸ **расспра́шивать**) to question; (o + *p.*) (*узна́ть, спра́шивая*) to find out

рассро́чк|а, и *f.* instalment system; **в ~у** by, in instalments

расстава́ни|е, я *nt.* parting; **при ~и** on parting

расста|ва́ться, ю́сь, ёшься *impf. of* ▸ **расста́ться**

расста́в|ить, лю, ишь *pf.* (*of* ▸ **расставля́ть**) **1** (*размести́ть*) (*кни́ги, ме́бель*) to place, arrange; (*ка́дры, рабо́тников*) to place, position; **р. часовы́х** to post sentries; (*запяты́е*) to put, add **2** (*раздви́нуть*) to move apart; **р. но́ги** to stand with one's legs apart

расставля́|ть, ю *impf. of* ▸ **расста́вить**

расстано́вк|а, и *f.* placing, arrangement

расста́|ться, нусь, нешься *pf.* (*of* ▸ **расстава́ться**) (с + *i.*) **1** to part (with); **я ~лся с ней** I parted with her; **~немся друзья́ми** let us part friends **2** (*с мечто́й, с мы́слью*) to give up

расстёгива|ть, ю *impf. of* ▸ **расстегну́ть**

расстёгива|ться, юсь *impf. of* ▸ **расстегну́ться**

расстег|ну́ть, ну́, нёшь *pf.* (*of* ▸ **расстёгивать**) to undo, unfasten

расстег|ну́ться, ну́сь, нёшься *pf.* (*of* ▸ **расстёгиваться**) **1** (*об оде́жде, о предме́те*) to come undone **2** (*о челове́ке*) to undo one's coat, shirt, *etc.*; to undo one's buttons

рассте́л|ить, ю́, ~ешь *pf.* (*of* ▸ **расстила́ть**) to spread (out), lay (out)

рассте́л|иться, ~ется *pf.* (*of* ▸ **расстила́ться**) to spread

расстила́|ть, ю, ет *impf. of* ▸ **расстели́ть**, ▸ **разостла́ть**

расстила́|ться, ется *impf. of* ▸ **расстели́ться**, ▸ **разостла́ться**

⚡ **расстоя́ни|е**, я *nt.* distance; **на ~и** (*ви́деть*) at a distance; (*управля́ть*) from a distance; **на бли́зком ~и** (**от** + *g.*) at a short distance (from); **они́ живу́т на ~и двух миль от ближа́йшего го́рода** they live two miles from the nearest town

расстра́ива|ть, ю *impf. of* ▸ **расстро́ить**

расстра́ива|ться, юсь *impf. of* ▸ **расстро́иться**

расстре́л, а *m.* **1** (*казнь*) execution (*by firing squad*); **приговори́ть к ~у** to sentence to be shot **2** (*обстре́л*) (+ *g.*) shooting at; firing at, on

расстре́лива|ть, ю *impf. of* ▸ **расстреля́ть**

расстрел|я́ть, я́ю *pf.* (*of* ▸ **расстре́ливать**) **1** (*уби́ть*) to shoot, execute by shooting **2** (*та́нки*) to shoot at; (*демонстра́цию*) to open fire on **3** (*снаря́ды*) to use up (*in firing*)

расстро́енный *p.p.p. of* ▸ **расстро́ить** *and adj.* (*здоровье*) damaged, weak; (*нервы*) shattered; (*человек, вид*) upset; (*роя́ль*) out of tune

расстро́|ить, ю, ишь *pf.* (*of* ▸ **расстра́ивать**) **1** (*здоровье, хозя́йство*) to damage; (*пла́ны*) to upset **2** (*челове́ка*) to upset

расстро́|иться, юсь, ишься *pf.* (*of* ▸ **расстра́иваться**) **1** (*о здоро́вье, хозя́йстве*) to be damaged; (*о пла́нах*) to fall through **2** (*из-за* + *g.*) (*о челове́ке*) to be upset (over, about) **3** (mus.) to become out of tune

расстро́йств|о, а *nt.* disorder; confusion; **р. желу́дка** stomach upset; **р. пищеваре́ния** indigestion; **не́рвное р.** nervous breakdown; **р. ре́чи** speech defect; **дела́ пришли́ в р.** things are in disarray

расступ|а́ться, а́ется *impf. of* ▸ **расступи́ться**

расступ|и́ться, ~ится *pf.* (*of* ▸ **расступа́ться**) to part, make way; **толпа́ ~и́лась** the crowd parted

рассуди́тел|ьный, ~ен, ~ьна *adj.* reasonable; sensible

рассу́|ди́ть, жу́, ~дишь *pf.* **1** (*люде́й*) to judge (between), arbitrate (between); **~ди́те нас** be our judge; settle our dispute **2** (*реши́ть*) to decide

рассу́д|ок, ка *m.* **1** (*спосо́бность*) reason; intellect; **лиши́ться ~ка** to lose one's reason **2** (*здра́вый смысл*) good sense

рассужда́|ть, ю *impf.* **1** (*мы́слить*) to reason **2** (*о* + *p. от на* + *a.*) (*обсужда́ть*) to debate; to argue (about); **р. на каку́ю-н. те́му** to discuss a topic

рассужде́ни|е, я *nt.* **1** (*проце́сс*) reasoning **2** (*usu. in pl.*) (*обсужде́ние*) debate; argument; **без ~й** without argument

рассчи́т|анный *p.p.p. of* ▸ **рассчита́ть** *and adj.* **1** calculated, deliberate **2** (**на** + *a.*) intended (for), designed (for); **кни́га, ~анная на широ́кого чита́теля** a book intended for the general public

рассчита́|ть, а́ю *pf.* (*of* ▸ **рассчи́тывать 1**) (*сто́имость, расхо́ды*) to calculate; **он не ~а́л свои́х сил** he miscalculated his strength

рассчита́|ться, а́юсь *pf.* (*of* ▸ **рассчи́тываться**) (**с** + *i.*) to settle accounts (with); (fig.) to settle scores (with)

⟋ **рассчи́тыва|ть, ю** *impf.* **1** *impf. of* ▸ **рассчита́ть 2** (*impf. only*) (**на** + *a.*) (*предполага́ть*) to count (on, upon), reckon (on, upon); (+ *inf.*) to expect (to), hope (to); **мы ~ли зако́нчить рабо́ту в э́том году́** we were hoping to finish the work this year **3** (*impf. only*) (**на** + *a.*) (*полага́ться*) to count (on, upon), rely (on, upon), depend (upon)

рассчи́тыва|ться, юсь *impf. of* ▸ **рассчита́ться**

рассыла́|ть, ю *impf. of* ▸ **разосла́ть**

рассы́лк|а, и *f.* distribution, dispatch; (*по электро́нной по́чте*) mailing

рассы́п|ать, лю, лешь *pf.* (*of* ▸ **рассыпа́ть**) (*нево́льно*) to spill; (*разбро́сать*) to strew, scatter

рассып|а́ть, а́ю *impf. of* ▸ **рассы́пать**

рассы́п|аться, люсь, лешься *pf.* (*of* ▸ **рассыпа́ться**) **1** (*о муке́*) to spill; **моне́ты ~ались по́ полу** the coins spilt onto the floor; (*о толпе́*) to scatter; (*о дома́х*) to be scattered **2** (*о стене́, о хле́бе*) to crumble; to disintegrate (also fig.) **3** (infml) (**в** + *p.*) to be profuse (in); **р. в похвала́х** (+ *d.*) to shower praises (upon)

рассып|а́ться, а́юсь *impf. of* ▸ **рассы́паться**

рассыха́|ться, ется *impf. of* ▸ **рассо́хнуться**

раста́лкива|ть, ю *impf. of* ▸ **растолкну́ть**

растапливa|ть, ю *impf. of* ▸ **растопи́ть**[1]

растáптыва|ть, ю *impf. of* ▸ **растопта́ть**

растаск|а́ть, а́ю *pf.* (*of* ▸ **раста́скивать**) (infml) **1** (*унести́ по частя́м*) to take away, remove (*little by little, bit by bit*) **2** (*укра́сть*) to pilfer, filch (infml)

раста́скива|ть, ю *impf. of* ▸ **растаска́ть**, ▸ **растащи́ть**

растащ|и́ть, у́, ~ишь *pf.* (*of* ▸ **раста́скивать**) **1** (*деру́щихся*) to part, separate, drag apart **2** = **растаска́ть**

раста́|ять, ю, ешь *pf. of* ▸ **та́ять**

раство́р, а *m.* **1** (chem.) solution **2** (tech., строи́тельный) mortar

раствори́м|ый, ~, ~а *adj.* soluble; **р. ко́фе** instant coffee

раствори́тел|ь, я *m.* solvent

раствор|и́ть[1]**, ю́, ~ишь** *pf.* (*of* ▸ **растворя́ть**) (*окно́*) to open

раствор|и́ть[2]**, ю́, ишь** *pf.* (*of* ▸ **растворя́ть**) (*соль*) to dissolve

раствор|и́ться[1]**, ~ится** *pf.* (*of* ▸ **растворя́ться**[1]) (*об окне́*) to open

раствор|и́ться[2]**, ится** *pf.* (*of* ▸ **растворя́ться**[2]) (*о со́ли*) to dissolve; (fig., *исче́знуть*) to vanish

раствор|я́ть, я́ю, я́ет *impf. of* ▸ **раствори́ть**[1], ▸ **раствори́ть**[2]

раствор|я́ться, я́ется *impf. of* ▸ **раствори́ться**[1], ▸ **раствори́ться**[2]

растека́|ться, юсь *impf. of* ▸ **расте́чься**

⟋ **расте́ни|е, я** *nt.* plant

растере́ть, разотру́, разотрёшь, *past* **растёр, растёрла** *pf.* (*of* ▸ **растира́ть**) **1** to grind; **р. в порошо́к** to grind to powder **2** (**по** + *d.*) (*мазь*) to rub (over), spread (over) **3** (*те́ло*) to rub, massage

растере́ться, разотру́сь, разотрёшься, *past* **растёрся, растёрлась** *pf.* (*of* ▸ **растира́ться**) **1** (*о зёрнах*) to become powdered, turn into powder **2** (+ *i.*) (*обтере́ть себя́*) to rub oneself briskly (with)

растерз|а́ть, а́ю *pf.* (*of* ▸ **расте́рзывать**) **1** (*умертви́ть*) to tear to pieces **2** (fig., poet., *изму́чить*) to lacerate; to harrow

расте́рзыва|ть, ю *impf. of* ▸ **растерза́ть**

расте́рянност|ь, и *f.* confusion, bewilderment

расте́рянный *p.p.p. of* ▶ **растеря́ть** *and adj.* confused, bewildered

растер|я́ть, я́ю *pf.* to lose (*little by little*)

растер|я́ться, я́юсь *pf.* (*утратить самообладание*) to lose one's head, nerve; **он не ~я́лся пе́ред лицо́м опа́сности** he kept his head in the face of danger

расте́|чься, чётся, ку́тся, *past* **~кся, ~кла́сь** *pf.* (*of* ▶ **растека́ться**) (*о воде*) to spill; (*о краске*) to run

⚲ **раст|и́, у́, ёшь,** *past* **рос, росла́** *impf.* (*of* ▶ **вы́расти**) **1** (*о детях*) to grow up; **он рос на Украи́не** he grew up in Ukraine **2** (*увеличиваться*) to grow, increase **3** (*совершенствоваться*) to advance, develop

растира́|ть, ю *impf. of* ▶ **растере́ть**

растира́|ться, юсь *impf. of* ▶ **растере́ться**

расти́тельност|ь, и *f.* **1** (*растения*) vegetation **2** (*волосы*) hair (*on face or body*)

расти́тельн|ый *adj.* vegetable; **~ое ма́сло** vegetable oil

ра|сти́ть, щу́, сти́шь *impf.* **1** (*детей*) to raise, bring up; (*кадры*) to nurture **2** (*цветы*) to grow, cultivate; (*животных*) to rear; **р. бо́роду** to grow a beard

растлева́|ть, ю *impf. of* ▶ **растли́ть**

растл|и́ть, ю́, и́шь *pf.* (*of* ▶ **растлева́ть**) **1** (*малолетних*) to sexually abuse (*minors*) **2** (*морально*) to corrupt, deprave

растолка́|ть, ю *pf.* (*of* ▶ **раста́лкивать**) (*infml*) **1** (*толпу*) to push asunder, apart **2** (*спящего*) to shake (*in order to awaken*)

растолсте́|ть, ю *pf.* to put on weight

растоп|и́ть¹, лю́, ~ишь *pf.* (*of* ▶ **раста́пливать**) (*печь*) to light

растоп|и́ть², лю́, ~ишь *pf.* (*of* ▶ **раста́пливать**) (*сало, лёд*) to melt

растоп|та́ть, чу́, ~чешь *pf.* (*of* ▶ **раста́птывать**) to trample, stamp (on), crush (*also fig.*)

растопы́рива|ть, ю *impf. of* ▶ **растопы́рить**

растопы́р|ить, ю, ишь *pf.* (*of* ▶ **растопы́ривать**) (*infml*) to spread wide, open wide

расторг|а́ть, а́ю *impf. of* ▶ **расто́ргнуть**

расто́рг|нуть, ну, нешь, *past* **~, ~ла** *pf.* (*of* ▶ **расторга́ть**) (*контракт, догово́р*) to dissolve, annul; **р. брак** to dissolve a marriage

расточи́тел|ьный, ~ен, ~ьна *adj.* extravagant, wasteful

растра́т|а, ы *f.* **1** (*денег, времени*) waste, squandering **2** (*незаконная*) embezzlement

растра́|тить, чу, тишь *pf.* (*of* ▶ **растра́чивать**) **1** to waste, squander **2** (*незаконно*) to embezzle

растра́чива|ть, ю *impf. of* ▶ **растра́тить**

растрёпанный *p.p.p. of* ▶ **растрепа́ть** *and adj.* (*волосы*) dishevelled; (*книга*) tattered

растреп|а́ть, лю́, ~лешь *pf.* **1** (*волосы*) to mess up, tousle **2** (*книгу*) to reduce to tatters, tear

растрепа́|ться, ~лется *pf.* **1** (*о волосах*) to get messed up, get dishevelled **2** (*о книге*) to get tattered, get torn

растро́га|ть, ю *pf.* to move, touch; **р. кого́-н. до слёз** to move sb to tears

растя́гива|ть, ю *impf. of* ▶ **растяну́ть**

растя́гива|ться, юсь *impf. of* ▶ **растяну́ться**

растяже́ни|е, я *nt.* (*med.*) strain, sprain

растя́|нуть, ну́, ~нешь *pf.* (*of* ▶ **растя́гивать**) **1** (*ковёр, ска́терть*) to stretch, spread (out); (*лишить упру́гости*) to stretch; (*платежи*) to spread **2** (*med.*) to strain, sprain **3** (*сде́лать сли́шком дли́нным*) to stretch out; (*fig.*) to protract, drag out

растя́|нуться, ну́сь, ~нешься *pf.* (*of* ▶ **растя́гиваться**) **1** to stretch (out); (*стать ме́нее упру́гим*) to be stretched **2** (*стать сли́шком дли́нным*) to stretch too far; (*fig., рабо́та, собра́ние*) to drag on; **обсужде́ние его́ докла́да ~ну́лось на полтора́ часа́** discussion of his lecture dragged on for an hour and a half

растя́п|а, ы *c.g.* (*infml*) bungler

расхва́лива|ть, ю *impf. of* ▶ **расхвали́ть**

расхвал|и́ть, ю́, ~ишь *pf.* (*of* ▶ **расхва́ливать**) to lavish, shower praise (on, upon)

расхи́|тить, щу, тишь *pf.* (*of* ▶ **расхища́ть**) to embezzle, misappropriate

расхища́|ть, ю *impf. of* ▶ **расхи́тить**

⚲ **расхо́д, а** *m.* **1** (*затра́та*) expense; (*in pl.*) expenses, outlay, cost; **доро́жные ~ы** travel expenses; **накладны́е ~ы** overheads; **де́ньги на карма́нные ~ы** pocket money **2** (*эне́ргии*) consumption; **р. горю́чего** fuel consumption **3** (*в бухгалте́рии*) expenditure, outlay; **прихо́д и р.** income and expenditure

расхо|ди́ться, жу́сь, ~дишься *impf. of* ▶ **разойти́сь**

расхо́д|овать, ую *impf.* (*of* ▶ **израсхо́довать**) **1** (*де́ньги, вре́мя*) to spend, expend **2** (*ресу́рсы*) to use (up), consume; **маши́на ~ует мно́го бензи́на** the car uses a lot of petrol (*BrE*), gas (*AmE*)

расхожде́ни|е, я *nt.* (*луче́й, доро́г*) divergence; (*иде́йное*) difference; **р. во мне́ниях** difference of opinion; (*в те́ксте*) discrepancy

расхо|те́ть, чу́, ~чешь, ти́м, ти́те, тя́т *pf.* (+ *g. or a. or inf.*) (*infml*) to no longer want; **я ~те́л спать** I am no longer sleepy

расхо|те́ться, ~чется *pf.* (*impers.* + *d.*) (*infml*) to no longer want; **мне ~те́лось есть** I no longer want to eat

расхохо|та́ться, чу́сь, ~чешься *pf.* to burst out laughing

расцве|сти́, ту́, тёшь, *past* **~л, ~ла́** *pf.* (*of* ▶ **расцвета́ть**) (*цвето́к, де́вушка*) to blossom; (*нау́ка, иску́сство*) to flourish; (*повеселе́ть*) to become radiant

р

расцве́т, а *m.* blossoming; (*науки*) flourishing; flowering; **в ~е сил** in one's prime

расцвета́|ть, ю *impf. of* ▶ **расцвести́**

расцве́тк|а, **и** *f.* colour (BrE), color (AmE) scheme, colours (BrE), colors (AmE)

расцел|ова́ть, **у́ю** *pf.* to smother with kisses

расце́нива|ть, ю *impf. of* ▶ **расцени́ть**

расце́нива|ться, ется *impf.* to be regarded

расцен|и́ть, ю́, ~ишь *pf.* (*of* ▶ **расце́нивать**) (*поступок, слова*) to regard; **его́ речь ~и́ли как провока́цию** his speech was regarded as provocation

расце́нк|а, **и** *f.* (*usu. in pl.*) (*цена*) tariff, rates

расчер|ти́ть, чу́, ~тишь *pf.* (*of* ▶ **расче́рчивать**) to rule, line

расче́рчива|ть, ю *impf. of* ▶ **расчерти́ть**

расче|са́ть, шу́, ~шешь *pf.* (*of* ▶ **расчёсывать**) **1** (*волосы*) to comb; (*лён, шерсть*) to card **2** (*руку*) to scratch

расче|са́ться, шу́сь, ~шешься *pf.* (*of* ▶ **расчёсываться**) (infml, *расчесать волосы*) to comb one's hair

расчёск|а, **и** *f.* comb

расчёсыва|ть, ю *impf. of* ▶ **расчеса́ть**

расчёсыва|ться, юсь *impf. of* ▶ **расчеса́ться**

🖉 **расчёт**[1], а *m.* **1** (*стоимости*) calculation; (*смета*) statement; (*приблизительный*) estimate, reckoning; **из ~а** on the basis (of), at a rate (of); **приня́ть в р.** to take into account, consideration; **по мои́м ~ам** by my reckoning; **в ~е на** (+ *a.*) hoping for, reckoning on **2** (*c* + *i.*) settling (with); (*оплата*) payment; **нали́чный р.** cash payment; **быть в ~е** (*c* + *i.*) to be quits (with), be even (with); **производи́ть ~ы** (*c* + *i.*) to settle accounts (with)

расчёт[2], а *m.* (mil.) crew; **оруди́йный р.** gun crew

расчётлив|ый, ~, ~а *adj.* thrifty

расчётн|ый *adj.* **1** calculation; ~ая табли́ца calculation table **2** pay, accounts; **р. день** pay day **3** (tech.) rated; ~ая мо́щность rated capacity

расчи́|стить, щу, стишь *pf.* (*of* ▶ **расчища́ть**) to clear; **р. путь, доро́гу** (fig.) to pave the way

расчи́|ститься, стится *pf.* (*of* ▶ **расчища́ться**) (*о небе*) to clear

расчища́|ть, ю, ет *impf. of* ▶ **расчи́стить**

расчища́|ться, ется *impf. of* ▶ **расчи́ститься**

расчлен|и́ть, ю́, и́шь *pf.* (*of* ▶ **расчленя́ть**) to break up, divide

расчлен|я́ть, я́ю *impf. of* ▶ **расчлени́ть**

расшат|а́ть, а́ю *pf.* (*of* ▶ **расша́тывать**) **1** to shake loose; to make rickety **2** (fig.) (*дисциплину*) to undermine, impair; (*хозяйство*) to cripple; (*нервы, здоровье*) to damage

расшат|а́ться, а́юсь *pf.* (*of* ▶ **расша́тываться**) **1** to get loose; to become rickety **2** (fig.) (*дисциплина*) to be undermined; (*хозяйство*) to be crippled; (*нервы, здоровье*) to go to pieces, crack up

расша́тыва|ть, ю *impf. of* ▶ **расшата́ть**

расша́тыва|ться, юсь *impf. of* ▶ **расшата́ться**

расшеве́лива|ть, ю *impf. of* ▶ **расшевели́ть**

расшевел|и́ть, ю́, и́шь *pf.* (*of* ▶ **расшеве́ливать**) to stir, shake; (fig., *стимули́ровать*) to stir, rouse

расшиб|а́ть, а́ю *impf. of* ▶ **расшиби́ть**

расшиб|а́ться, а́юсь *impf. of* ▶ **расшиби́ться**

расшиб|и́ть, у́, ёшь, *past* ~, ~ла *pf.* (*of* ▶ **расшиба́ть**) **1** (*ушибить*) to hurt; to knock, stub **2** (infml, *разбить*) to break up, smash to pieces

расшиб|и́ться, у́сь, ёшься, *past* ~ся, ~лась *pf.* (*of* ▶ **расшиба́ться**) to hurt oneself, knock oneself

расшива́|ть, ю *impf. of* ▶ **расши́ть**

🖉 **расшире́ни|е**, я *nt.* **1** (*отверстия*) widening; (*кругозора, знаний*) broadening **2** (*производства*) expansion **3** (med.) dilation, dilatation **4** (comput., *файла*) extension; **пла́та ~я** expansion card (*graphics card, sound card, etc.*)

расши́ренный *p.p.p. of* ▶ **расши́рить** *and adj.* (*отверстие*) widened; (*программа*) broadened, more extensive; (*заседание*) expanded; (*зрачки*) dilated

расши́р|ить, ю, ишь *pf.* (*of* ▶ **расширя́ть**) (*отверстие*) to widen; (*производство*) to expand; (*кругозор, знания*) to broaden; (*сферу влияния*) to extend

расши́р|иться, ится *pf.* (*of* ▶ **расширя́ться**) (*об отверстии*) to widen; (*о производстве, о знаниях*) to expand; (*о кругозоре*) to broaden; (*о зрачках*) to dilate

расширя́|ть, я́ю, я́ет *impf. of* ▶ **расши́рить**

расширя́|ться, я́ется *impf. of* ▶ **расши́риться**

расши́|ть, разошью́, разошьёшь *pf.* (*of* ▶ **расшива́ть**) to embroider

расшифр|ова́ть, у́ю *pf.* (*of* ▶ **расшифро́вывать**) to decipher, decode; (fig., *угадать смысл*) to figure out

расшифро́вк|а, **и** *f.* deciphering, decoding; (fig.) interpretation

расшифро́выва|ть, ю *impf. of* ▶ **расшифрова́ть**

расшнур|ова́ть, у́ю *pf.* (*of* ▶ **расшнуро́вывать**) to unlace

расшнур|ова́ться, у́юсь *pf.* (*of* ▶ **расшнуро́вываться**) to come unlaced, come undone

расшнуро́выва|ть, ю *impf. of* ▶ **расшнурова́ть**

расшнуро́выва|ться, юсь *impf. of* ▶ **расшнурова́ться**

расшум|е́ться, лю́сь, и́шься *pf.* (infml) to get noisy, kick up a din

расще́лин|а, ы *f.* cleft, crevice

ратифика́ци|я, и *f.* ratification

ратифици́р|овать, ую *impf. and pf.* to ratify

р

ра́унд, a *m.* (sport) round; (*переговоров*) series, round

ра́ут, a *m.* reception

рафини́рован|ный, ~, ~a *adj.* refined

рацио́н, a *m.* ration

рационализа́ци|я, и *f.* rationalization, improvement

рационализи́р|овать, ую *impf. and pf.* to rationalize, improve

рационали́зм, a *m.* (phil.) rationalism

рациона́льно *adv.* (*мыслить, поступать*) rationally; (*вести хозяйство*) efficiently; **р. испо́льзовать** to make efficient use (of)

рациона́л|ьный, ~ен, ~ьна *adj.* (*поступок*) rational; (*использование средств*) efficient; **~ьное пита́ние** sound nutrition

ра́ци|я, и *f.* (*на корабле, в здании*) radio set; (*небольшая переносная*) walkie-talkie

рван|у́ть, у́, ёшь *pf.* **1** (*дёрнуть резко*) to jerk; to tug (at); **р. кого́-н. за рука́в** to tug sb by the sleeve **2** (*машина*) to start (with a jerk) **3** (infml, *помчаться*) to dash off, shoot off **4** (infml, *взорвать*) to explode, blow up; **в сосе́днем до́ме ~у́ло** there was an explosion in the next house

рван|у́ться, у́сь, ёшься *pf.* to rush, dash

рва́н|ый *adj.* torn; lacerated; **~ые башмаки́** broken shoes; **~ая ра́на** (med.) laceration

рвать¹, рву, рвёшь, *past* **рвал, рвала́, рва́ло** *impf.* **1** (*одежду*) to tear (up); to rip; **р. на ча́сти** (*предмет*) to tear to pieces; (*человека*) to overburden; **р. письмо́** to tear up a letter; **р. на себе́ во́лосы** to pull one's hair **2** (*выдёргивать*) to pull out, tear out; **р. зу́бы** to pull out teeth; **р. с ко́рнем** to uproot **3** (*брать*) to pick, pluck; **р. цветы́** to pick flowers

рвать², рвёт, *past* **рва́ло** *impf.* (*of* ▶ **вы́рвать²**) (*impers.*) (infml) to vomit, throw up, be sick

рва́|ться¹, рвётся, *past* **~лся, ~ла́сь, ~ло́сь** *impf.* **1** (*об одежде*) to break; to tear; (*об отношениях*) to break up, be severed **2** (*взрываться*) to burst, explode

рва́|ться², рвусь, рвёшься, *past* **~лся, ~ла́сь, ~ло́сь** *impf.* (*стремиться*) to strain (to, at); to be bursting (to); **р. в бой/дра́ку** to be spoiling for a fight; **р. к вла́сти** to be hungry for power

рве́ни|е, я *nt.* zeal, enthusiasm

рво́т|а, ы *f.* **1** (*действие*) vomiting **2** (*масса*) vomit

ре *nt. indecl.* (mus.) D

реабилита́ци|я, и *f.* rehabilitation

реабилити́р|овать, ую *impf. and pf.* to rehabilitate

реабилити́р|оваться, уюсь *impf. and pf.* **1** to vindicate oneself **2** *pass. of* ▶ **реабилити́ровать**

реаги́р|овать, ую *impf.* (**на** + *a.*) **1** (*pf.* **от~, с~**) (*на свет*) to react (to) **2** (*pf.* **от~, про~,**

с~) (*на критику*) to react (to), respond (to)

реакти́вный *adj.* **1** (chem., phys.) reactive **2** (tech., aeron.) jet(-propelled); **р. дви́гатель** jet engine; **р. самолёт** jet-propelled aircraft, jet

реа́ктор, a *m.* (tech.) reactor

реакцио́н|ный, ~ен, ~на *adj.* (pol.) reactionary

⚡ **реа́кци|я, и** *f.* reaction

⚡ **реализа́ци|я, и** *f.* (*планов*) realization; (*договора*) implementation; (*товаров*) sale, disposal

реали́зм, a *m.* realism

⚡ **реализ|ова́ть, у́ю** *impf. and pf.* (*pf. also* ▶ **реализо́вывать**) (*планы*) to realize; (*договор*) to implement; (*товар*) to sell, dispose of; **р. це́нные бума́ги** to realize securities

реализо́выва|ть, ю *impf. of* ▶ **реализова́ть**

реали́ст, a *m.* realist

реалисти́ческий *adj.* **1** (*искусство*) realist **2** (*взгляд*) realistic

реалисти́ч|ный, ~ен, ~на *adj.* = **реалисти́ческий 2**

⚡ **реа́льност|ь, и** *f.* **1** (*действительность*) reality **2** (*осуществимость*) practicability, feasibility

⚡ **реа́л|ьный, ~ен, ~ьна** *adj.* **1** (*действительный*) real; **~ьная действи́тельность** reality **2** (*осуществимый*) practicable, feasible, workable; **р. план** workable plan **3** (*практический*) realistic; practical

реанимацио́нн|ый *adj.*: **~ое отделе́ние** intensive care unit

реанима́ци|я, и *f.* resuscitation; **отделе́ние ~и** intensive care unit

реаними́р|овать, ую *impf. and pf.* **1** (*человека*) to resuscitate **2** (fig.) to revive

⚡ **ребён|ок, ка,** *pl.* **ребя́та, ребя́т** *and* **де́ти, дете́й** *m.* child; (*младенец*) infant; **грудно́й р.** baby

ребре́ндинг, a *m.* (comm.) rebranding

ребр|о́, а́, *pl.* **~а, рёбер, ~ам** *nt.* **1** (anat., tech.) rib **2** (*край*) edge; **поста́вить ~о́м** to place edgeways, place on its side

⚡ **ребя́та, ребя́т** *m. pl.* **1** *pl. of* ▶ **ребёнок**; children **2** (infml, *парни*) boys, lads

рёв, a *m.* **1** roar; bellow, howl; **р. ве́тра** the howling of the wind **2** (infml, *плач*) howl (*of a child, etc.*); **подня́ть р.** to raise a howl

рева́нш, a *m.* revenge; (sport) return match

реве́н|ь, я́ *m.* rhubarb

реверанс, a *m.* curtsy

рев|е́ть, у́, ёшь *impf.* **1** to roar; to bellow, howl **2** (infml, *плакать*) to howl

реви́зи|я, и *f.* **1** (*учреждения*) inspection; (*бухгалтерская*) audit **2** (*взглядов*) revision

ревизо́р, a *m.* inspector; (*финансов*) auditor

ревмати́зм, a *m.* rheumatism

ревни́в|ый, ~, ~a *adj.* jealous

ревн|ова́ть, у́ю *impf.* to be jealous; **р. кого́-н.** (**к** + *d.*) to be jealous because of sb's

р

attachment (to), begrudge sb's attachment (to); она́ ∼ова́ла му́жа к его́ рабо́те she was jealous of her husband's work

ре́вност|ный, ∼ен, ∼на *adj.* zealous, fervent

ре́вность, и *f.* jealousy

револьве́р, а *m.* revolver

революционе́р, а *m.* revolutionary

революционе́р|ка, ки *f. of*
▶ **революционе́р**

революцио́н|ный, ∼ен, ∼на *adj.* revolutionary

◆ **револю́ци|я**, и *f.* (pol., *also* fig.) revolution

рега́т|а, ы *f.* regatta

ре́гби *nt. indecl.* rugby (football), rugger

регби́ст, а *m.* rugby player

ре́гги *m. indecl.* reggae

ре́гент, а *m.* **1** regent **2** (mus.) conductor of church choir, precentor

◆ **регио́н**, а *m.* region, area

◆ **региона́льный** *adj.* regional

реги́стр, а *m.* register

регистра́тор, а *m.* registrar; (*в поликлинике, гостинице*) receptionist

регистрату́р|а, ы *f.* records office, registry; (*в поликлинике*) reception desk

◆ **регистра́ци|я**, и *f.* registration; (*в гостинице*) reception desk

регистри́р|овать, ую *impf. and pf.* (*pf. also* за∼) to register, record

регистри́р|оваться, уюсь *impf. and pf.* (*pf. also* за∼) **1** to register (oneself) **2** (*пожениться*) to register one's marriage **3** *pass. of* ▶ **регистри́ровать**

регла́мент, а *m.* **1** (*правила*) regulations; standing orders **2** (*время для речи*) time limit

регули́рование|е, я *nt.* (*движения, цен*) regulation, control

регули́р|овать, ую *impf.* **1** (*движение, цены*) to regulate; to control **2** (*pf.* у∼) (*отношения*) to normalize **3** (*pf.* от∼) to adjust; **р. мото́р** to tune an engine

регуля́р|ный, ∼ен, ∼на *adj.* regular; ∼ные войска́ regular troops

регуля́тор, а *m.* (tech.) regulator; (*in pl.*) controls (*on TV, etc.*)

редакти́р|овать, ую *impf.* **1** (*pf.* от∼) (*рукопись*) to edit **2** (*impf. only*) (*журнал*) to be editor of; to edit

реда́ктор, а *m.* **1** editor; гла́вный р. editor-in-chief, chief editor **2** (comput.): те́кстовый р. (*программа*) word processor

редакцио́н|ный *adj.* editorial, editing; ∼ая колле́гия editorial board; ∼ая статья́ editorial

реда́кци|я, и *f.* **1** (*работники*) editorial staff **2** (*учреждение*) editorial office **3** (*действие*) editing; под ∼ей (+ *g.*) edited (by) **4** (*формулировка*) wording **5** (*вариант текста*) edition

реде́|ть, ю *impf.* (*of* ▶ **пореде́ть**) to thin out; ∼ющие во́лосы thinning hair

реди́с, а (*no pl.*) *m.* (collect.) radish(es)

реди́ск|а, и *f.* (single) radish; (*collect.*) radishes

◆ **ре́д|кий**, ∼ок, ∼ка́, ∼ко *adj.* **1** (*негустой*) thin, sparse; ∼кие во́лосы thin hair; **р. лес** sparse wood **2** (*необычный*) rare; uncommon, unusual; ∼кая кни́га rare book; ∼кая красота́ rare beauty **3** (*гость, письмо*) occasional

ре́дко *adv.* **1** (*не густо*) sparsely; far apart **2** (*не часто*) rarely, seldom

редколле́ги|я, и *f.* editorial board

ре́дкост|ь, и *f.* **1** (*населения*) sparseness **2** (*книги*) rarity; на р. uncommonly; на р. проница́тельный челове́к a person of rare discernment **3** (*редкая вещь*) rarity

рее́стр, а *m.* list, roll, register

ре́же *comp. of* ▶ **ре́дкий**, ▶ **ре́дко**

◆ **режи́м**, а *m.* **1** (pol.) regime **2** (*распорядок*) routine; procedure; (med.) regimen; (*станка*) mode of operation; **р. пита́ния** diet; **р. рабо́ты** mode of operation **3** (*условия*) conditions; (tech.) operating conditions

◆ **режиссёр**, а *m.* (*в театре*) producer; (*в кино*) director

режиссёрский *adj. of* ▶ **режиссёр**

ре́|зать, жу, жешь *impf.* **1** (*impf. only*) to cut; э́ти но́жницы бо́льше не ∼жут these scissors do not cut any longer **2** (*impf. only*) (*хлеб*) to cut; to slice **3** (*pf.* за∼) (*убивать*) to kill; to slaughter **4** (*impf. only*) (*по* + *d.*) (*делать изображения*) to carve (on), engrave (on) **5** (*impf. only*) (*причинять боль*) to cut (into); to cause sharp pain; реме́нь ∼зал ему́ плечо́ the strap was cutting into his shoulder; **р. слух** to grate upon the ears

резви́ться, лю́сь, и́шься *impf.* to gambol, romp

ре́зв|ый, ∼, ∼а́, ∼о *adj.* **1** playful, frisky **2** (*лошадь*) fast

резе́рв, а *m.* (mil., etc.) reserve(s)

резерва́ци|я, и *f.* reservation

резерви́р|овать, ую *impf. and pf.* (*pf. also* за∼) to reserve, book

резе́рвн|ый *adj.* (mil. and fin.) reserve; (comput.) backup; ∼ая ко́пия backup copy

резервуа́р, а *m.* reservoir, tank

резиде́нци|я, и *f.* residence

рези́н|а, ы *f.* (India) rubber

рези́нк|а, и *f.* **1** (*ластик*) rubber (BrE), eraser (AmE) **2** (*тесёмка*) (piece of) elastic **3** (*жвачка*) chewing gum

рези́нов|ый *adj.* rubber; ∼ая тесьма́, ле́нта rubber band, elastic band

ре́з|кий, ∼ок, ∼ка́, ∼ко *adj.* (*ветер, слова, увеличение, движение, черты лица*) sharp; (*голос, свет, критика*) harsh; (*изменение, манера*) abrupt; **р. за́пах** strong smell

резно́й *adj.* carved

резня́, и́ *f.* slaughter

◆ **резолю́ци|я**, и *f.* **1** (*решение*) resolution; вы́нести, приня́ть ∼ю to pass, carry a

р

resolution **2** (*на докуме́нте*) instructions; **наложи́ть** ~**ю** to append instructions

резона́нс, а *m.* **1** (phys.) resonance **2** (fig.) response

резонёрств|овать, ую *impf.* to moralize

резо́н|ный, ~ен, ~на *adj.* reasonable

⚘ **результа́т, а** *m.* result; outcome; **дать** ~**ы** to yield results; **в** ~**е** (*в ито́ге*) in the end; (+ *g.*) (*всле́дствие*) as a result (of)

ре́зче *comp. of* ▶ **ре́зкий**

ре́зчик, а *m.* engraver, carver

резьб|а́, ы́ *f.* carving

резюме́ *nt. indecl.* summary, résumé

рейд, а *m.* raid

рейс, а *m.* (*авто́буса*) trip, run; (*парохо́да*) voyage, passage; (*самолёта*) flight; **но́мер** ~**а** flight number

⚘ **ре́йтинг, а** *m.* rating

рейту́з|ы, ~ (*no sg.*) leggings

⚘ **рек|а́, и́, а.** ~**у́, pl.** ~**и** *f.* river (also fig.)

ре́квием, а *m.* (eccl. and mus.) requiem

реквизи́р|овать, ую *impf. and pf.* to requisition

реквизи́т, а *m.* (theatr.) props

⚘ **рекла́м|а, ы** *f.* **1** (*това́ра, собы́тия*) advertising, publicity **2** (*объявле́ние*) advertisement

реклами́р|овать, ую *impf. and pf.* to advertise, publicize

⚘ **рекла́мный** *adj.* (*аге́нтство, кампа́ния*) advertising; (*оповести́тельный*) publicity

рекламода́тел|ь, я *m.* advertiser

рекоменда́тельн|ый *adj.* recommendatory; ~**ое письмо́** letter of recommendation

⚘ **рекоменда́ци|я, и** *f.* recommendation

⚘ **рекоменд|ова́ть, у́ю** *impf. and pf.* (*pf. also* ▶ **порекомендова́ть**) **1** (*предложи́ть приня́ть*) to recommend **2** (+ *d.* + *inf.*) (*сове́товать*) to recommend, advise; **я вам** ~**у́ю сходи́ть к врачу́** I recommend you to see a doctor

реконструи́р|овать, ую *impf. and pf.* to reconstruct

реконстру́кци|я, и *f.* reconstruction

реко́рд, а *m.* record; **поби́ть р.** to break a record; **установи́ть р.** to set up, establish a record

реко́рдный *adj.* record, record-breaking

рекордсме́н, а *m.* record holder; record breaker; **р. ми́ра** world record holder

рекордсме́н|ка, ки *f. of* ▶ **рекордсме́н**

ре́ктор, а *m.* principal

реле́ *nt. indecl.* (tech.) relay

⚘ **религио́з|ный, ~ен, ~на** *adj.* religious

рели́ги|я, и *f.* religion

рели́кви|я, и *f.* relic; (*семе́йная*) heirloom

релье́ф, а *m.* (art and geol.) relief

релье́ф|ный, ~ен, ~на *adj.* relief, raised; (*ткань, обо́и*) embossed; ~**ная ка́рта** relief map; (fig., *отчётливый*) clear-cut

рельс, а *m.* rail; **сойти́ с** ~**ов** to be derailed, go off the rails

рем|е́нь, ня́ *m.* (*по́яс*) belt; (*для багажа́*) strap; **р. безопа́сности** seat belt

реме́сленник, а *m.* artisan, craftsman

ремесл|о́, ла́, pl. ~**ла,** ~**ел** *nt.* trade

⚘ **реми́сси|я, и** *f.* (med., comm.) remission

⚘ **ремо́нт, а** *m.* repair(s); maintenance; (*зда́ния*) refurbishment; (*ме́лкий*) redecoration; **капита́льный р.** overhaul, refit, major refurbishment, repairs; **в** ~**е** under repair; **р. о́буви** shoe repair

ремонти́р|овать, ую *impf. and pf.* (*pf. also* **от**~) (*чини́ть*) to repair; (*кварти́ру*) to refurbish, redecorate

ремо́нт|ный *adj. of* ▶ **ремо́нт**; ~**ная мастерска́я** repair shop; ~**ные рабо́ты** repair/maintenance work

Ренесса́нс, а *m.* renaissance

ре́нт|а, ы *f.* **1** rent; **земе́льная р.** ground rent **2** (*проце́нты*) income (*from investments, etc.*); **ежего́дная р.** annuity

рента́бел|ьный, ~ен, ~ьна *adj.* profitable

рентге́н, а *m.* X-ray treatment, X-rays

рентгено́лог, а *m.* radiologist

рентгеноло́ги|я, и *f.* radiology

реорганиза́ци|я, и *f.* reorganization

реорганиз|ова́ть, у́ю *impf. and pf.* to reorganize

ре́п|а, ы *f.* turnip

репатриа́ци|я, и *f.* repatriation

репатрии́р|овать, ую *impf. and pf.* to repatriate

репертуа́р, а *m.* (theatr., *also* fig.) repertoire; **он в своём** ~**е** he is in his element

репети́р|овать, ую *impf.* (*pf.* **от**~) (theatr.) to rehearse

репети́тор, а *m.* tutor, coach

репети́ци|я, и *f.* rehearsal; **генера́льная р.** dress rehearsal

ре́плик|а, и *f.* **1** (*возраже́ние*) retort; (*отве́т*) reply; (*вражде́бная*) heckling comment **2** (theatr.) cue; **пода́ть** ~**у** to give the cue

репорта́ж, а *m.* (*де́ятельность*) reporting; (*сообще́ние*) report

репортёр, а *m.* reporter

репресси́р|овать, ую *impf. and pf.* to subject to repression

репре́сси|я, и *f.* (*usu. in pl.*) punitive measure

репроду́ктор, а *m.* loudspeaker

репроду́кци|я, и *f.* reproduction (*of a picture, etc.*)

репти́ли|я, и *f.* reptile

репута́ци|я, и *f.* reputation

ре́пчатый *adj.*: **р. лук** (common) onion

ресни́ц|а, ы *f.* eyelash

респекта́бел|ьный, ~ен, ~ьна *adj.* respectable

респира́тор, а *m.* respirator

⚘ **респу́блик|а, и** *f.* republic

республика́н|ец, ца *m.* republican

⚘ key word

республика́н|ка, ки *f. of* ▶ **республика́нец**
республика́нский *adj.* republican
рессо́р|а, ы *f.* spring (*of vehicle*)
реставра́тор, а *m.* restorer
реставра́ци|я, и *f.* restoration
реставри́р|овать, ую *impf. and pf.* (*pf. also* ▶ **отреставри́ровать**) to restore
⚹ **рестора́н, а** *m.* restaurant; **р. бы́строго обслу́живания** fast-food restaurant
⚹ **ресу́рс, а** *m.* (*usu. in pl.*) resource; **де́нежные ~ы** financial resources; **после́дний р.** the last resort; **приро́дные ~ы** natural resources
рефера́т, а *m.* **1** (*кни́ги, статьи́*) synopsis, abstract **2** (*доклад*) paper, essay
рефере́ндум, а *m.* referendum
ре́фери *m. indecl.* referee
рефле́кс, а *m.* reflex
рефле́кси|я, и *f.* reflection; introspection
рефлексоло́ги|я, и *f.* reflexology
рефо́рм|а, ы *f.* reform; **проводи́ть ~ы** to implement reforms
реформа́тор, а *m.* reformer
Реформа́ци|я, и *f.* (hist.) Reformation
реформи́р|овать, ую *impf. and pf.* to reform
рефрижера́тор, а *m.* (*грузовик*) refrigerated lorry (BrE), truck (AmE); (*судно*) refrigerated ship
рецензе́нт, а *m.* reviewer
реце́нзи|я, и *f.* review; **р. на кни́гу** book review
⚹ **реце́пт, а** *m.* **1** (med.) prescription; **вы́писать р.** to write a prescription **2** (cul.) recipe
рециди́в, а *m.* (med., etc.) recurrence; relapse
ре́чк|а, и *f.* small river; rivulet
речн|о́й *adj.* river; **~ы́е пути́ сообще́ния** inland waterways; **~о́е судохо́дство** river navigation
⚹ **речь, и** *f.* **1** (*спосо́бность*) speech **2** (*произноше́ние*) way of speaking; **отчётливая р.** distinct enunciation **3** (*стиль языка́*) language; **делова́я р.** business language **4** (*разгово́р*) conversation, talk; **о чём шла р.?** what were they/you talking about?, what was it all about?; **р. идёт о том, где/как/когда́** *и т. п.* the question is where/how/when, *etc.*; **об э́том не мо́жет быть и ~и** that is out of the question **5** (*выступле́ние*) speech; address; **вы́ступить с ~ью** to make a speech **6** (gram.) speech; **прямая р.** direct speech; **ко́свенная р.** indirect speech; **ча́сти ~и** parts of speech
⚹ **реш|а́ть, а́ю** *impf. of* ▶ **реши́ть**
реш|а́ться, а́юсь *impf. of* ▶ **реши́ться**
реша́ющий *pres. part. act. of* ▶ **реша́ть** *and adj.* decisive, deciding; **р. го́лос** casting vote; **р. фа́ктор** decisive factor
⚹ **реше́ни|е, я** *nt.* **1** decision; **прийти́ к ~ю** to come to a decision; **приня́ть р.** to take a decision, make up one's mind **2** (*суда́, дире́кции*) judgement; decision, verdict; **вы́нести р.** to deliver a judgement; to pass

a resolution **3** (*зада́чи*) solving; (*к зада́че*) solution; answer; (*пробле́мы*) solution
решётк|а, ы *f.* **1** grating; (*око́нная*) grille; (*огра́да*) railings; (*садо́вая*) trellis; (*перед ками́ном*) fireguard; (*радиа́тора*) grille; **за ~ой** (fig., infml) behind bars (= *in prison*); **посади́ть за ~у** to put behind bars **2** (comput.) (*also* **знак ~и**) hash, hash sign **3** (*в ками́не*) (fire) grate **4** (*в духо́вке*) shelf
решет|о́, а́, pl. ~а *nt.* sieve
реши́мост|ь, и *f.* resolution, resoluteness
реши́тельно *adv.* **1** (*твёрдо*) resolutely **2** (*категори́чески*) decidedly, definitely; **р. отказа́ться** to flatly refuse
реши́тел|ьный, ~ен, ~ьна *adj.* resolute, determined; **~ьные ме́ры** drastic measures
⚹ **реш|и́ть, у́, и́шь** *pf.* (*of* ▶ **реша́ть**) **1** (+ *inf. or* + *a.*) to decide; **он ~и́л уе́хать** he decided to go away **2** (*найти́ отве́т*) to solve; to settle; **р. зада́чу** to solve a problem; to accomplish a task
реш|и́ться, у́сь, и́шься *pf.* (*of* ▶ **реша́ться**) **1** (*на* + *a. or* + *inf.*) to make up one's mind (to), decide (to) **2** (*получи́ть реше́ние*) to be resolved
ре́|ять, ет *impf.* **1** (*о пти́це*) to soar, hover **2** (*о фла́ге*) to flutter
ржаве́|ть, ет *impf.* (*of* ▶ **заржаве́ть**) to rust
ржа́вчин|а, ы *f.* rust
ржа́вый *adj.* rusty
ржано́й *adj.* rye
рж|ать, у, ёшь *impf.* to neigh; (infml) to laugh loudly
Ри́г|а, и *f.* Riga
рикоше́т, а *m.* ricochet, rebound; **~ом** on the rebound (also fig.)
Рим, а *m.* Rome
ри́млян|ин, ина, pl. ~е, ~ *m.* Roman
ри́млян|ка, ки *f. of* ▶ **ри́млянин**
ри́мск|ий *adj.* Roman; **Па́па Р.** the Pope; **~ие ци́фры** Roman numerals
ринг, а *m.* (sport) ring
ри́н|уться, усь, ешься *pf.* to dash, dart
Рио-де-Жане́йро *m. indecl.* Rio de Janeiro
⚹ **рис, а** *m.* rice
⚹ **риск, а** *m.* risk; **на свой (страх и) р.** at one's own risk, at one's peril; **с ~ом (для** + *g.*) at the risk (of); **пойти́ на р.** to run risks, take chances
рискн|у́ть, у́, ёшь *pf.* (+ *inf.*) to take the risk (of), venture (to)
риско́ван|ный, ~, ~на *adj.* **1** risky; **~ное предприя́тие** risky venture **2** (*шу́тка, те́ма*) risqué
риск|ова́ть, у́ю *impf.* **1** to run risks, take chances **2** (+ *i.*) to risk; (+ *inf.*) to risk, take the risk (of); **ничём не р.** to run no risk; **р. опозда́ть на по́езд** to risk missing the train
рисова́ни|е, я *nt.* (*карандашо́м*) drawing; (*кра́сками*) painting
рис|ова́ть, у́ю *impf.* (*of* ▶ **нарисова́ть**) **1** (*карандашо́м*) to draw; (*кра́сками*) to paint; **р. с нату́ры** to draw, paint from life

р

▨ (fig., *описывать*) to depict, paint, portray

ри́сов|ый *adj.* rice; ~**ая ка́ша** rice pudding

❧ **рису́н|ок, ка** *m.* (*изображение*) drawing; (*в книге*) illustration; (*в научной статье*) figure; (*на ткани*) pattern, design; (*контур*) outline; **акваре́льный р.** watercolour (BrE), watercolor (AmE)

ритм, а *m.* (*музыки, сердца*) rhythm; (*работы, жизни*) pace

ритми́ческ|ий *adj.* rhythmic; ~**ая гимна́стика** aerobics

ритми́ч|ный, ~ен, ~на *adj.* rhythmic; ~**ная рабо́та** smooth functioning

рито́рик|а, и *f.* rhetoric

риторический *adj.* rhetorical

ритуа́л, а *m.* ritual

ритуа́льн|ый *adj.* ritual; ~**ые услу́ги** funeral services

риф, а *m.* reef; **кора́лловый р.** coral reef

ри́фм|а, ы *f.* rhyme

рифм|ова́ть, у́ю *impf.* (*слова*) to make rhyme

рифм|ова́ться, у́юсь *impf.* to rhyme

ро́б|а, ы *f.* working clothes, overalls

ро́б|кий, ~ок, ~ка́, ~ко *adj.* timid, shy

ро́бост|ь, и *f.* timidity, shyness

ро́бот, а *m.* robot

ров, рва, о рве, во рву *m.* ditch; **крепостно́й р.** moat

рове́сник, а *m.* person of the same age; peer; **мы с ним ~и** we are of the same age

рове́сни|ца, цы *f. of* ▸ **рове́сник**

ро́вно *adv.* **▨** (*равномерно*) regularly, evenly **▨** (*точно*) exactly; **р. пять рубле́й** five roubles exactly; (*о времени*) sharp; **р. в час** at one o'clock sharp

ро́вн|ый, ~ен, ~на́, ~но *adj.* **▨** (*дорога, поверхность*) flat, even, level; (*линия*) straight **▨** (*пульс*) regular; (*шаг, голос*) even; (*характер*) stable **▨** (*одинаковый*) equal; **для ~ного счёта** to make it even; to bring to a round figure; ~**ным счётом** exactly

ровня́|ть, ю *impf.* (*of* ▸ **сровня́ть**) to even, level

рог, а, *pl.* ~а́, ~о́в *m.* **▨** horn; (*олений*) antler **▨** (*музыкальный инструмент*) bugle, horn; **охо́тничий р.** hunting horn

рога́лик, а *m.* crescent-shaped roll, croissant

рога́тк|а, и *f.* catapult (BrE), slingshot (AmE)

рога́т|ый, ~, ~а *adj.* horned; **кру́пный р. скот** cattle

❧ **род, а, о ~е, в ~у́** *m.* **▨** (*pl.* ~**ы́**, ~**о́в**) family, kin, clan; **челове́ческий р.** mankind, human race **▨** (*pl.* ~**ы́**, ~**о́в**) (*происхождение*) birth, origin, stock; (*поколение*) generation; **он ~ом из Ирла́ндии** he is an Irishman by birth **▨** (*pl.* ~**ы́**, ~**о́в**) (biol.) genus **▨** (*pl.* ~**а́**, ~**о́в**) (*тип*) sort, kind; **р. во́йск** arm of the service; **вся́кого ~а** of all kinds; **тако́го ~а** of such a kind, such; **в не́котором ~е** to

some extent; **в своём ~е** in one's own way

▨ (*pl.* ~**ы́**, ~**о́в**) (gram.) gender; **же́нский р.** feminine (gender)

роддо́м, а *m.* (*abbr. of* **роди́льный дом**) maternity hospital

роде́о *nt. indecl.* rodeo

роди́льн|ый *adj.*: **р. дом** maternity hospital; ~**ое отделе́ние** maternity unit

❧ **ро́дин|а, ы** *f.* native land; home, homeland; **верну́ться на ~у** to return home; **тоска́ по ~е** homesickness

ро́динк|а, и *f.* birthmark

❧ **роди́тел|и, ей** (*no sg.*) parents

роди́тельн|ый *adj.* (gram.) genitive; **в ~ом падеже́** in the genitive (case)

роди́тельский *adj.* parental, parents'; paternal; **р. комите́т** parents' committee

ро|ди́ть, жу́, ди́шь, past impf. ~ди́л, ~дила́, ~ди́ло, past pf. ~ди́л, ~дила́, ~ди́ло *impf. and pf.* **▨** (*impf. also* **рожа́ть**) to bear, give birth (to) **▨** (*impf. also* **рожда́ть**) (fig.) to give birth, rise (to); (*о почве*) to yield

❧ **ро|ди́ться, жу́сь, ди́шься, past ~ди́лся́, ~дила́сь, ~ди́ло́сь** *impf. and pf.* (*impf. also* **рожда́ться**) **▨** to be born; **р. преподава́телем** (**у + g.**) to be born of; **у неё ~дила́сь дочь** she had a daughter; **от пе́рвой жены́ у него́ ~ди́лся сын** he had a son by his first wife **▨** (fig., *мысль, план, город*) to arise, come into being

родни́к, а́ *m.* spring (*where water wells up*)

❧ **родн|о́й** *adj.* **▨** (*мать, брат, дядя*) related by blood; natural; **р. брат** one's brother (*opp.* cousin, etc.); (*as pl. n.* ~**ы́е**, ~**ы́х**) relations, relatives **▨** (*отечественный*) native; home; **р. язы́к** mother tongue

родн|я́, и́ *f.* (collect.) (*родственники*) relatives

родово́й¹ *adj.* **▨** family, tribal, ancestral **▨** (biol.) generic

родов|о́й² *adj.* birth, labour (BrE), labor (AmE); ~**ы́е схва́тки** contractions

родонача́льник, а *m.* ancestor, forefather; (fig., *литературы*) father

ро́дственник, а *m.* relation, relative; **ближа́йший р.** next of kin

ро́дственни|ца, цы *f. of* ▸ **ро́дственник**

ро́дствен|ный, ~ and ~ен, ~на *adj.* **▨** kindred, related; ~**ые свя́зи** kinship ties **▨** (*близкий*) related, allied **▨** (*свойственный родственникам*) familiar, intimate

родств|о́, а́ *nt.* relationship, kinship (also fig.); **быть в ~е́ (с + i.)** to be related (to)

ро́д|ы, ов (*no sg.*) birth; childbirth; **в ~ах** in labour (BrE), labor (AmE)

ро́ж|а, и *f.* (infml) mug (= *face*); **ко́рчить, стро́ить ~и** to make faces

рожа́|ть, ю *impf. of* ▸ **роди́ть 1**

рожда́емост|ь, и *f.* birth rate

рожда́|ть, ю *impf. of* ▸ **роди́ть**

рожда́|ться, юсь *impf. of* ▸ **роди́ться**

р

рожде́ни|е, я *nt.* birth; **день ~я** birthday; **ме́сто ~я** birthplace; **глухо́й от ~я** deaf from birth

рождённый *p.p.p. of* ▶ **роди́ть** (+ *inf.*) born (to), destined (to)

рожде́стvenск|ий *adj.* Christmas; **~ая ёлка** Christmas tree; **~ая пе́сня** carol; **р. соче́льник** Christmas Eve

Рождеств|о́, а́ *nt.* (*праздник*) Christmas; **на Р.** at Christmas (time); **под Р.** on Christmas Eve; (*само рождение*) Nativity

рож|о́к, ка́ *m.* (mus.) horn; bugle; **англи́йский р.** cor anglais

рожь, ржи *f.* rye

ро́з|а, ы *f.* (*цветок*) rose; (*растение*) rose tree, rose bush

розе́тк|а, и *f.* **1** (*украшение*) rosette **2** (elec.) socket; electric outlet **3** (*для варенья*) jam dish

розмари́н, а *m.* (bot.) rosemary

ро́зниц|а, ы *f.* retail; **торгова́ть в ~у** to engage in retail trade; to retail

ро́зничн|ый *adj.* retail; **р. торго́вец** retailer; **~ая цена́** retail price

ро́зов|ый, ~, ~а *adj.* **1** *adj. of* ▶ **ро́за**; **~ое де́рево** rosewood; **р. куст** rose bush **2** (*цвет*) pink, rose-coloured (BrE), -colored (AmE) **3** (fig.) rosy

ро́зыгрыш, а *m.* **1** (*лотереи*) drawing **2** (*шутка*) practical joke

ро́зыск, а *m.* **1** (*разыскивание*) search **2** (law, *дознание*) inquiry; **Уголо́вный р.** Criminal Investigation Department (BrE), Federal Bureau of Investigation (AmE)

рой, ро́я, *pl.* **рои́** *m.* (*пчёл, комаров*) swarm

рок¹, а *m.* (*судьба*) fate

рок², а *m.* (mus.) rock; **тяжёлый р.** hard rock

рок-гру́пп|а, ы *f.* rock band

рок-му́зык|а, и *f.* rock music

рок-музыка́нт, а *m.* rock musician

рок-н-ро́лл, а *m.* rock 'n' roll

роков|о́й *adj.* **1** fateful; fated; **~ая же́нщина** femme fatale **2** (*имеющий тяжёлые последствия*) fatal

ро́кот, а *m.* roar, rumble

ро́лик, а *m.* **1** roller, castor **2** (*in pl.*) (*коньки*) roller skates **3**: **рекла́мный р.** (cin.) advertisement; (*фильма*) trailer **4** (*бумаги, плёнки*) roll

ро́лик|овый *adj. of* ▶ **ро́лик**; **~овые коньки́** roller skates

роль, и, *pl.* **~и, ~е́й** *f.* (theatr.) role (also fig.); (*текст*) part; **в ~и** (+ *g.*) in the role (of); **игра́ть р.** (+ *g.*) to take the part (of), play, act; (fig.) to matter, count, be of importance; **э́то не игра́ет ~и** it is of no importance, it does not count

ром, а *m.* rum

рома́н, а *m.* **1** novel **2** (infml, *любовная связь*) love affair; romance

рома́нс, а *m.* (mus.) romance

рома́нский *adj.* Romance; (archit.) Romanesque

романти́зм, а *m.* romanticism

рома́нтик, а *m.* romantic

рома́нтик|а, и *f.* romance

романти́ческий *adj.* romantic

романти́ч|ный, ~ен, ~на *adj.* = романти́ческий

рома́шк|а, и *f.* camomile

ромб, а *m.* (math.) rhombus

рон|я́ть, ю *impf.* (of ▶ **урони́ть**) **1** (*из рук*) to drop; (*голову, руки*) to let fall; (*книгу с полки*) to knock off; **р. слёзы** to shed tears **2** (*impf. only*) (*лишаться*) to shed **3** (fig., *унижать*) to discredit; **р. себя́ в чьих-н. глаза́х** to discredit oneself in sb's eyes; (*авторитет*) to lose

ро́пот, а *m.* murmur, grumble

рос, ~ла́ *see* ▶ **расти́**

рос|а́, ы́, *pl.* **~ы** *f.* dew

роско́ш|ный, ~ен, ~на *adj.* luxurious

ро́скош|ь, и *f.* **1** (*излишества*) luxury; **жить в ~и** to live in luxury **2** (*великолепие*) splendour (BrE), splendor (AmE)

ро́слый *adj.* tall, strapping

ро́спис|ь, и *f.* painting; **р. стен** wall painting(s), mural(s)

росси́йский *adj.* Russian

Росси́|я, и *f.* Russia

россия́н|ин, а, *pl.* **~е, ~** *m.* (*русский*) Russian; (*житель России*) Russian citizen

россия́н|ка, ки *f. of* ▶ **россия́нин**

рост, а *m.* **1** (*растений, городов, индустрии*) growth; (fig., *цен, преступности*) increase, rise **2** (*вышина*) height, stature; **~ом** in height; **он ~ом с вас** he is (of) your height; **высо́кого ~а** tall; **во весь р.** full length; (fig.) in all its magnitude; **встать во весь р.** to stand upright, stand up straight **3** (*одежды*) length

ростовщи́к, а́ *m.* usurer, moneylender

рост|о́к, ка́ *m.* shoot; **пусти́ть ~ки́** to sprout; (*in pl.*) (+ *g.*) beginnings (of)

рот, рта, о рте́, во рту́ *m.* mouth; **не брать в р.** (+ *g.*) to not touch; **зажа́ть, заткну́ть кому́-н. р.** (infml) to shut sb up

ро́т|а, ы *f.* (mil.) company

рота́ци|я, и *f.* rotation

ротве́йлер, а *m.* Rottweiler

ро́щ|а, и *f.* small wood, grove

роя́л|ь, я *m.* piano; grand piano; **игра́ть на ~e** to play the piano

ртут|ь, и *f.* mercury

руба́н|ок, ка *m.* (tech.) plane

руба́шк|а, и *f.* **1** shirt; **ночна́я р.** nightdress **2** (*игральной карты*) back

рубе́ж, а́ *m.* boundary, border(line); **жить за ~о́м** to live abroad

руб|е́ц, ца́ *m.* **1** (*от ран*) scar **2** (*шов*) hem, seam

руби́н, а *m.* ruby

руби́новый *adj.* ruby

руб|и́ть, лю́, ~ишь *impf.* **1** (*дерево*) to fell **2** (*дрова*) to chop **3** (cul.) to mince, chop up

р

рубл|ь, я́ *m.* rouble; **биле́т сто́ит два ~я́** a ticket costs two roubles

ру́брик|а *и f.* **1** (*заголовок*) rubric, heading **2** (*раздел*) column

ру́ган|ь, и *f.* (*непристойная*) bad language, swearing, abuse

руга́тельств|о, а *nt.* abuse; (*непристойное*) swear word

руга́|ть, ю *impf.* (*pf.* **от~** *or* **вы~**) (*отчитывать*) to scold, tell off **2** (*pf.* **об~** *or* **от~**) (*оскорблять*) to curse, swear (at), abuse **3** (*pf.* **об~**) (*критиковать*) to tear to pieces

руга́|ться, юсь *impf.* **1** to curse, swear, use bad language **2** (**с** + *i.*) (*ссориться*) to quarrel (with), have a row (with)

руд|а́, ы́, *pl.* **~ы** *f.* ore; **желе́зная р.** iron ore

рудиме́нт, а *m.* rudiment

рудни́к, а́ *m.* mine, pit

руж|ьё, ья́, *pl.* **~ья, ~ей, ~ьям** *nt.* (hand)gun, rifle

руи́н|а, ы *f.* (*usu. in pl.*) ruin; **го́род лежа́л в ~ах** the town lay in ruins

рук|а́, и́, а. ~у, *pl.* **~и, ~, ~а́м** *f.* **1** (*кисть*) hand; (*от кисти до плеча*) arm; **пожа́ть ~у** (+ *d.*) to shake hands (with); **вести́ за́ ~у** to lead by the hand; **держа́ть на ~а́х** to hold in one's arms; **р. о́б ~у** hand in hand; **написа́ть от ~и́** to write out by hand; **взять кого́-н. под ~у** to take sb's arm **2** (*почерк*) hand, handwriting **3** (*сторона*) side; **по пра́вую ~у** on the right, to the right **4** (*fig.*) hand; **э́то бу́дет им на́ ~у** that will serve their purpose; it will be playing into their hands; **на ско́рую ~у** offhand; **под ~о́й** at hand, to hand; **махну́ть ~о́й (на** + *a.*) to give up as lost; **наложи́ть на себя́ ~и** (*infml*) to commit suicide

рука́в, а́, *pl.* **~а́** *m.* **1** (*одежды*) sleeve **2** (*tech.,* *шланг*) hose

рукави́ц|а, ы *f.* (*меховая*) mitten; (*рабочая*) gauntlet

руководи́тел|ь, я *m.* **1** (*учреждения, отдела*) head, manager; (*делегации, похода, восстания*) leader; **р. прое́кта** project manager; **кла́ссный р.** (*в школе*) class teacher **2** (*воспитатель*) instructor; guide; **нау́чный р.** supervisor of studies

руководи́тель|ница, ницы *f.* (infml of) ▶ **руководи́тель**

руково|ди́ть, жу́, ди́шь *impf.* (+ *i.*) (*учреждением, отделом*) to be in charge of; to manage; (*походом, восстанием*) to lead; (*кружком, клубом*) to run; (*аспирантами*) to supervise; (*побуждать*) to govern

руково́дств|о, а *nt.* **1** (*действие*) leadership; guidance; management **2** (*то, чему следуют*) guiding principle, guide; **р. к де́йствию** guide to action **3** (*книга*) handbook, guide, manual; **р. по эксплуата́ции** instructions for use; user guide **4** (*collect.*) (*руководители*) (the) leadership, leaders; governing body

руково́дств|оваться, уюсь *impf.* (+ *i.*) to follow; to be guided (by)

рукоде́ли|е, я *nt.* needlework

рукопи́сный *adj.* (*текст*) handwritten; (*фонд*) manuscript

ру́копис|ь, и *f.* manuscript

рукопожа́ти|е, я *nt.* handshake

рукоя́тк|а, и *f.* handle

рулев|о́й *adj. of* ▶ **руль**; **~о́е колесо́** steering wheel; **~а́я коло́нка** steering column; (*as m. n. р.,* **~о́го**) (sport) cox(swain); (*на судне*) helmsman

руле́т, а *m.* (cul.) **1** (*пирог*) roll; **мясно́й р.** meat loaf **2** (*окорок без кости*) boned gammon

руле́тк|а, и *f.* **1** (*для измерения*) tape measure **2** (*игра*) roulette

рул|и́ть, ю́, и́шь *impf.* (*в машине, в лодке*) to steer

руло́н, а *m.* roll

рул|ь, я́ *m.* (*судна*) rudder; helm (also fig.); (*автомобиля*) (steering) wheel; (*велосипеда*) handlebars; **стоя́ть у ~я́** (fig.) to be at the helm

румы́н, а *m.* Romanian

Румы́ни|я, и *f.* Romania

румы́н|ка, ки *f. of* ▶ **румы́н**

румы́нский *adj.* Romanian

румя́н|а, ~ (*no sg.*) rouge; blusher

румя́н|ец, ца *m.* (high) colour (BrE), color (AmE); flush; blush

румя́н|ый, ~, ~а *adj.* rosy, ruddy

ру́н|а, ы *f.* (philol.) rune

ру́пор, а *m.* megaphone; loud hailer; (*fig., партии*) mouthpiece

руса́лк|а, и *f.* mermaid

ру́сл|о, а, g. pl. **ру́сел** *and* **~** *nt.* **1** (*river*) bed, channel; **измени́ть р. реки́** to change the course of a river **2** (*fig., направление*) channel, course; **войти́ в обы́чное р.** to resume the normal course

ру́сск|ая, ой *f. of* ▶ **ру́сский** (*as n.*)

ру́сск|ий *adj.* Russian; (*also as m. n.* **р., ~ого**) Russian (person)

ру́с|ый, ~, ~а *adj.* light brown

рути́н|а, ы *f.* (pej.) routine; rut

ру́хлядь|, и *f.* (collect.) (infml) junk

ру́хн|уть, у, ешь *pf.* to crash down, tumble down, collapse; (fig., *планы, мечты*) to collapse, fall through

руча́|ться, юсь *impf.* (of ▶ **поручи́ться**) (**за** + *a.*) to guarantee; to answer (for), vouch (for); **р. голово́й (за** + *a.*) to stake one's life (on)

руче́|й, ья́ *m.* brook, stream

ру́чк|а, и *f.* **1** *dim. of* ▶ **рука́** **2** (*двери, чайника*) handle; (*кресла, дивана*) arm; **р. две́ри** door handle, doorknob **3** (*для письма*) pen; **ша́риковая р.** ballpoint pen

ручн|о́й *adj.* **1** hand; (*управление*) manual; **~а́я кладь** hand luggage; **~а́я рабо́та**

р

ру́шить, у, ишь *impf.* (*здание*) to pull down; (*семью*) to wreck

ру́ш|иться, ится *impf. and pf.* to fall down, collapse; (fig., *планы, надежды*) to collapse

РФ *f. indecl.* (*abbr. of* **Росси́йская Федера́ция**) Russian Federation

⚡ ры́б|а, ы *f.* fish; (*in pl.* **Р~ы**) (astron., astrol.) Pisces; **ни р. ни мя́со** neither fish nor fowl; **чу́вствовать себя́ как р. в воде́** to feel in one's element

рыба́к, а́ *m.* fisherman

рыба́лк|а, и *f.* fishing; fishing trip; **идти́ на ~у** to go fishing

ры́бн|ый *adj.* fish; **~ые консе́рвы** tinned fish; **~ая ло́вля** fishing; **р. магази́н** fish shop, fishmonger's

рыболо́в, а *m.* fisherman; angler

рыболо́вн|ый *adj.* fishing; **~ые принадле́жности, ~ая снасть** fishing tackle

рыв|о́к, ка́ *m.* **1** (*резкое движение*) jerk **2** (*бегуна*) dash, spurt; (*в тяжёлой атле́тике*) snatch **3** (*в работе*) push, spurt

рыг|а́ть, а́ю *impf.* (*of* ▶ рыгну́ть) to belch, to burp (infml)

рыг|ну́ть, ну́, нёшь *inst. pf. of* ▶ рыга́ть

рыда́ни|е, я *nt.* sobbing

рыда́|ть, ю *impf.* to sob

ры́ж|ий, ~, ~а́, ~е *adj.* (*волосы*) red, ginger; (*человек*) red-haired, ginger-haired; (*лошадь*) chestnut

ры́пл|о, а *nt.* snout (*of pig, etc.*)

⚡ ры́н|ок, ка *m.* **1** market(place) **2** (econ.) market; **вне́шний р.** foreign market; **вну́тренний р.** domestic, internal market; **на ~ке** on the market

ры́но́чный *adj. of* ▶ ры́нок; **~чная эконо́мика** market economy; **по ~чной цене́** at the market price

рыса́к, а́ *m.* trotter (*horse*)

ры́|скать, щу, щешь *impf.* **1** (*по + d.*) (*в поисках*) to scour, ransack; **р. по карма́нам** to ransack one's pockets **2** (*блуждать*) to rove, roam; **р. глаза́ми** to let one's eyes roam

рыс|ь¹, и, о ~и, на ~й *f.* (*бег*) trot

рыс|ь², и *f.* (*животное*) lynx

ры́твин|а, ы *f.* rut, groove

рыть, ро́ю, ро́ешь *impf.* **1** (*яму, окопы*) to dig; (*картошку*) to dig up **2** (*в поисках*) to rummage, root about (in)

ры́ться, ро́юсь, ро́ешься *impf.* (*в + p.*) (*в земле́*) to dig (in); (fig., *в мусоре, в чемода́не*) to rummage (in); (*в книгах*) to root about (in)

ры́хл|ый, ~, ~а́, ~о *adj.* (*почва, камень*) friable, crumbly; (*снег*) loose

ры́цар|ский *adj.* **1** *adj. of* ▶ ры́царь; **р. поеди́нок** joust; **р. рома́н** tale of chivalry **2** (fig.) chivalrous

ры́цар|ь, я *m.* knight

рыча́г, а́ *m.* lever

рыча́ни|е, я *nt.* growl, snarl

рыч|а́ть, у́, и́шь *impf.* to growl, snarl

рья́н|ый, ~, ~а *adj.* zealous

рэ́кет, а *m.* racket

рэкети́р, а *m.* racketeer

рэп, а *m.* rap (music)

рэ́ппер, а *m.* rapper (*performer of rap music*)

рюкза́к, а́ *m.* rucksack; backpack

рю́мк|а, и *f.* (small) glass

ряби́н|а, ы *f.* **1** (*дерево*) rowan tree, mountain ash **2** (*ягода*) rowan berry

ряб|и́ть, и́т *impf.* **1** to ripple **2** (*impers.*): **у меня́ ~и́т в глаза́х** I am dazzled

ряб|о́й, ~, ~а́, ~о, ~и́ *adj.* **1** (*лицо́*) pockmarked **2** (*курица*) speckled

ря́бчик, а *m.* (zool.) hazel grouse

ряб|ь, и *f.* **1** (*на воде́*) ripple(s) **2** (*в глаза́х*) stars

ря́вк|ать, аю *impf.* (*of* ▶ ря́вкнуть) (**на** + *a.*) (infml) to bellow (at), to bark (at)

ря́вк|нуть, ну, нешь *pf. of* ▶ ря́вкать

⚡ ряд, а, в ~е *and* в ~у́, *pl.* ~ы́, ~о́в *m.* **1** (*предметов, лиц*) row; **пе́рвый/после́дний р.** (theatr.) front/back row; **стоя́ть в одно́м ~у́** (**с** + *i.*) to rank (with) **2** (*в а́рмии, в па́ртии*) file, rank; **в пе́рвых ~а́х** in the first ranks; (fig.) in the forefront **3** (*серия*) series (*also math.*); (*совоку́пность*) number; **в це́лом ~е слу́чаев** in a number of cases **4** (*на ры́нке*) stalls (*of one type of goods set out in a row*); **ры́бный ~** the fish stalls

рядов|о́й *adj.* **1** (*член, рабо́тник, случай*) ordinary, common **2** (mil.): **р. соста́в** rank and file; men, other ranks; (*as m. n.* **р., ~о́го**) private (soldier)

⚡ ря́дом *adv.* **1** alongside; (*о двух лю́дях*) side by side; (**с** + *i.*) (*о́коло*) next to; (*в сравне́нии с*) compared with; **он сиди́т р. с премье́р-мини́стром** he is sitting next to the prime minister **2** (*поблизости*) near, close by, next door; **э́то совсе́м р.** it is quite near, close

ря́с|а, ы *f.* cassock

р

Cc

⚹ **с** *prep.*
- **I.** (+ *g.*) **1** from; off; **с ю́го-восто́ка** from the south-east; **перево́д с ру́сского** translation from Russian; **верну́ться с рабо́ты** to return from work **2** (*по причи́не*) for, from, with; **со стыда́** for shame, with shame **3** on, from; **с одно́й, с друго́й стороны́** on the one, on the other hand **4** (*на основа́нии*) with; **с ва́шего согла́сия** with your consent **5** (*посре́дством*) by, with; **писа́ть с большо́й бу́квы** to write with a capital letter **6** (*о вре́мени*) from, since; as from; **с девяти́ (часо́в) до пяти́** from nine (o'clock) till five; **с де́тства** from childhood; **мы с ней не ви́делись с января́** I have not seen her since January
- **II.** (+ *a.*) (*приблизи́тельно*): **с пятиэта́жный дом** the size of a five-storey (BrE), five-story (AmE) house; **на́ша до́чка ро́стом с ва́шу** our daughter is about the same height as yours
- **III.** (+ *i.*) **1** with; and; **с удово́льствием** with pleasure; **мы с ва́ми** you and I **2** (*ука́зывает на нали́чие чего́-л.*): **хлеб с ма́слом** bread and butter; **челове́к со стра́нностями** peculiar person **3** (*посре́дством*) by, on; **получи́ть с пе́рвой по́чтой** to receive by first post **4** (*при наступле́нии чего́-л.*) with; **с года́ми** with the years; **с ка́ждым днём** every day **5** (*относи́тельно*) with (*or not translated*); **как у вас дела́ с рабо́той?** how is the work going?; **что с ва́ми?** what is the matter with you?; what's up?

с..., *also* **со...** *and* **съ...** *vbl. pref. indicating* **1** *unification, movement from various sides to a point:* **свари́ть** (*мета́лл*) to weld **2** *movement or action made in a downward direction:* **спусти́ться** to descend **3** *removal of sth from somewhere:* **сорва́ть** to tear off

са́б|**ля, ли,** *g. pl.* **∼ель** *f.* sabre (BrE), saber (AmE)

сабота́ж, а *m.* sabotage

сабота́жник, а *m.* saboteur

са́ван, а *m.* shroud, cerement; **снежный с.** blanket of snow

сава́нн|**а, ы** *f.* (geog.) savannah

са́г|**а, и** *f.* saga

⚹ **сад, а, о ∼е, в ∼у́,** *pl.* **∼ы́** *m.* garden; **фрукто́вый с.** orchard; **де́тский с.** kindergarten

сади́зм, а *m.* sadism

сади́ст, а *m.* sadist

сади́ст|**ка, ки** *f. of* ▸ **сади́ст**

сади́стский *adj.* sadistic

са|**ди́ться, жу́сь, ди́шься** *impf.* (*of* ▸ **сесть¹**): **∼ди́(те)сь!** (polite request) take a seat!

садо́вник, а *m.* gardener

садово́дств|**о, а** *nt.* (*хо́бби*) gardening; (*нау́ка*) horticulture

садо́вый *adj.* **1** *adj. of* ▸ **сад 2** (*культу́рный*) garden, cultivated

сад|**о́к, ка́** *m.* place for keeping live creatures; **кро́личий с.** rabbit hutch; **ры́бный с.** fish pond

са́ж|**а, и** *f.* soot

сажа́|**ть, ю** *impf.* (*of* ▸ **посади́ть**) **1** (*цветы́*) to plant **2** (*го́стя*) to seat; (*помеща́ть*) to set, put; (*предлага́ть сесть*) to offer a seat; **с. в тюрьму́** to put into prison, imprison, jail; **с. под аре́ст** to put under arrest

са́жен|**ец, ца** *m.* seedling; sapling

саза́н, а *m.* wild carp (*Cyprinus carpio*)

⚹ **сайт, а** *m.* (comput.) (web)site

саквоя́ж, а *m.* travelling bag (BrE), traveling bag (AmE)

саксофо́н, а *m.* saxophone

саксофони́ст, а *m.* saxophonist

саксофони́ст|**ка, ки** *f. of* ▸ **саксофони́ст**

салама́ндр|**а, ы** *f.* salamander

сала́т, а *m.* **1** (*расте́ние*) lettuce **2** (*куша́нье*) salad

сала́тниц|**а, ы** *f.* salad dish, salad bowl

сала́т|**ный** *adj. of* ▸ **сала́т**; **∼ного цве́та** light green

са́л|**ки, ок** *f. pl.* (*sg.* **∼ка, ∼ки**) (*игра́*) tag, touch

са́л|**о, а** *nt.* fat; lard

⚹ **сало́н, а** *m.* **1** (*для вы́ставок; магази́н*) salon; **автомоби́льный с.** car showroom **2** (*самолёта, авто́буса*) passenger section **3** (*в оте́ле*) lounge; (*на парохо́де*) saloon

салфе́тк|**а, и** *f.* napkin, serviette (BrE)

Сальвадо́р, а *m.* El Salvador

сальвадо́р|**ец, ца** *m.* Salvadorean

сальвадо́р|**ка, ки** *f. of* ▸ **сальвадо́рец**

сальвадо́рский *adj.* Salvadorean

са́л|**ьный, ∼ен, ∼ьна** *adj.* greasy

са́льто *nt. indecl.* somersault

салю́т, а *m.* salute; (*фейерве́рк*) fireworks display

саля́ми *f. indecl.* salami

⚹ **сам, самого́,** *f.* **сама́, само́й,** *nt.* **∼о́, самого́,** *pl.* **са́ми, сами́х** *refl. pron.* (*я*) myself; (*ты, вы*) yourself; (*он*) himself, *etc.*; **с. по себе́** in itself, per se; (*без по́мощи*) by oneself, unassisted; **с. собо́й** of itself, of its own accord

са́мб|**а, ы** *f.* samba

сам|**е́ц, ца́** *m.* male (*of species*)

сáмк|а, и *f.* female (*of species*)

сáммит, а *m.* (pol.) summit (meeting)

само... *comb. form* self-, auto-

самобичевáни|е, я *nt.* self-reproach

самобы́т|ный, ~ен, ~на *adj.* original

самовáр, а *m.* samovar

самовлюблённый *adj.* narcissistic

самовóлк|а, и *f.* (infml) absence without leave

самовóл|ьный, ~ен, ~ьна *adj.* **1** (*человек*) wilful, self-willed **2** (*отсутствие*) unauthorized; ~ьная отлýчка (mil.) absence without leave

самогóн, а *m.* home-made vodka, hooch, moonshine (AmE)

самодéльный *adj.* home-made

самодержáви|е, я *nt.* autocracy

самодéятельност|ь, и *f.* **1** (*художественная с.*) amateur activities (*theatricals, music, etc.*) **2** initiative, self-motivation

самодéятель|ный, ~ен, ~ьна *adj.* **1** (*не профессиональный*) amateur **2** self-motivated

самодовóл|ьный, ~ен, ~ьна *adj.* self-satisfied, smug, complacent

самодостáточ|ный, ~ен, ~на *adj.* self-sufficient

самозабвéн|ный, ~ен, ~на *adj.* selfless

самозащи́т|а, ы *f.* self-defence (BrE), self-defense (AmE)

самозвáн|ец, ца *m.* impostor, pretender

самокáт, а *m.* (child's) scooter

самоконтрóл|ь, я *m.* self-control

самокри́тик|а, и *f.* self-criticism

самокрýтк|а, и *f.* (infml) roll-up (BrE), roll-your-own

самолёт, а *m.* (aero)plane (BrE), (air)plane (AmE); aircraft

самолюби́в|ый, ~, ~а *adj.* proud, haughty

самолюби|е, я *nt.* pride, self-esteem; лóжное с. false pride

самомнéни|е, я *nt.* conceit, self-importance

самонадéян|ный, ~, ~на *adj.* conceited, arrogant

самооблада́ни|е, я *nt.* self-control, self-possession, composure

самообмáн, а *m.* self-deception

самооборóн|а, ы *f.* self-defence (BrE), self-defense (AmE)

самообслýживани|е, я *nt.* self-service

самоопределéни|е, я *nt.* self-determination

самоотвéржен|ный, ~, ~на *adj.* selfless, self-sacrificing

самооцéнк|а, и *f.* self-appraisal

самопи́с|ец, ца *m.*: бортовóй с. (aeron.) flight recorder

самопожéртвовани|е, я *nt.* self-sacrifice

самопроизвóл|ьный, ~ен, ~ьна *adj.* spontaneous

самород|ок, ка *m.* (min.) nugget

самосвáл, а *m.* dump truck

самосохранéни|е, я *nt.* self-preservation

самостоя́тельно *adv.* independently; on one's own

самостоя́тельност|ь, и *f.* independence

самостоя́тел|ьный, ~ен, ~ьна *adj.* independent

самосýд, а *m.* lynch law, mob law

самоуби́йственный *adj.* suicidal (also fig.)

самоуби́йств|о, а *nt.* suicide; покóнчить жизнь ~ом to commit suicide

самоуби́йц|а, ы *c.g.* suicide (*victim*)

самоуважéни|е, я *nt.* self-esteem

самоувéрен|ный, ~, ~на *adj.* self-confident, self-assured

самоуправлéни|е, я *nt.* self-government; мéстное с. local government

самоупрáвств|о, а *nt.* arbitrariness

самоучи́тел|ь, я *m.* manual for self-tuition; с. англи́йского языкá teach-yourself English book

самоýчк|а, и *c.g.* self-taught person

самоцвéт, а *m.* semi-precious stone, gem

самоцéл|ь, и *f.* end in itself

самочýвстви|е, я *nt.* general state; у негó плохóе с. he feels bad; как вáше с.? how are you (keeping)?

самши́т, а *m.* box (tree)

сáм|ый *pron.* **1** (*in conjunction with nouns, esp. denoting time or place*) the very, right; с ~ого начáла from the very outset, right from the start; с ~ого утрá ever since the morning, since first thing; в ~ом углý right in the corner; до ~ого Владивостóка right to, all the way to Vladivostok; в ~ом дéле? indeed?, really?; на ~ом дéле actually, in (actual) fact; тот с., этот с. the very, this very; тот с. человéк, котóрый... the very man who ...; на этом сáмом мéсте in this very place **2**: тот же с. (, котóрый/что) the same (as); этот же с. the same **3** (*forms superl. of adjs.; also expr. superl. in conjunction with certain nn. denoting degree of quantity or quality*): с. глýпый the stupidest, the most stupid

сан, а *m.* rank; office; высóкий с. high office; духóвный с. holy orders, the cloth

санатóри|й, я *m.* sanatorium

сандáл, а *m.* (bot.) sandalwood tree

сандáли|я, и *f.* sandal

сáн|и, éй (*no sg.*) sledge (BrE), sled (AmE); sleigh

санитáр, а *m.* hospital orderly; (mil.) medical orderly

санитáр|ка, ки *f. of* ▸ санитáр

санитáр|ный *adj.* **1** (*связанный с медицинской службой*) medical; hospital; ~ая слýжба health service, medical service **2** (*связанный с санитарией*) sanitary; sanitation; с. врач sanitary inspector; ~ые прáвила sanitary regulations

сáн|ки, ок (*no sg.*) **1** = сáни **2** (*детские*) toboggan

✦ **Санкт-Петербу́рг**, а *m.* St Petersburg

санкт-петербу́ргский *adj.* St Petersburg

санкциони́р|овать, ую *impf. and pf.* to sanction

са́нкци|я, и *f.* ◼️1 sanction, approval ◼️2 (*in pl.*) (pol., econ.) sanctions

санскри́т, а *m.* Sanskrit

Са́нта-Кла́ус, **Са́нта-Кла́уса** *m.* Santa Claus

санте́хник, а *m.* plumber

санте́хник|а, и *f.* plumbing equipment

сантиме́тр, а *m.* ◼️1 centimetre (BrE), centimeter (AmE) ◼️2 (infml, *лента*) tape measure

Сан-Франци́ско *m. indecl.* San Francisco

сапёр, а *m.* (mil.) sapper

сапо́г, а́, *g. pl.* сапо́г *m.* boot

сапо́жник, а *m.* shoemaker, cobbler

сапо́жный *adj.* boot, shoe; **с. крем** shoe polish

сапфи́р, а *m.* sapphire

сара́|й, я *m.* (*для дров, животных*) shed; (*для сена*) barn

сарафа́н, а *m.* (*платье*) pinafore dress (BrE), jumper (AmE)

сарде́льк|а, и *f.* sausage (*fat, of frankfurter type*)

сарди́н|а, ы *f.* sardine, pilchard

сарка́зм, а *m.* sarcasm

саркасти́ческий *adj.* sarcastic

сатан|а́, ы́ *m.* Satan

сатани́нский *adj.* satanic

сати́р|а, ы *f.* satire

сати́рик, а *m.* satirist

сатири́ческий *adj.* satirical

сау́дов|ец, ца *m.* Saudi

сау́дов|ка, ки *f. of* ▸ сау́довец

Сау́довск|ая Ара́вия, ∼ой Ара́вии *f.* Saudi Arabia

сау́довский *adj.* Saudi

са́ун|а, ы *f.* sauna

саундтре́к, а *m.* soundtrack

сафа́ри *nt. indecl.* safari; **с.-па́рк** safari park

са́хар, а (у) *m.* sugar

Caxáp|a, ы *f.* the Sahara (*desert*)

сахари́н, а *m.* saccharin

са́хар|ить, ю, ишь *impf.* (*of* ▸ посаха́рить) to sugar, sweeten

са́харниц|а, ы *f.* sugar bowl

са́харный *adj. of* ▸ са́хар; (fig.) sugary; **с. песо́к** granulated sugar

сач|о́к, ка́ *m.* net; **с. для ба́бочек** butterfly net

сба́в|ить, лю, ишь *pf.* (*of* ▸ сбавля́ть) (с + *g.*) to reduce

сбавля́|ть, ю *impf. of* ▸ сба́вить

сбаланси́рован|ный, ∼, ∼а *adj.* well balanced, emotionally stable

сбе́га|ть, ю *pf.* (за + *i.*) (infml) to run (for), run to fetch; ∼**й за до́ктором!** run for a doctor!

сбега́|ть, ю, ет *impf. of* ▸ сбежа́ть

сбега́|ться, ется *impf. of* ▸ сбежа́ться

сбе|жа́ть, гу́, жи́шь, гу́т *pf.* (*of* ▸ сбега́ть) ◼️1 (с + *g.*) (*спуститься*) to run down (from); **с. с ле́стницы** to run downstairs ◼️2 (*убежать*) to run away

сбе|жа́ться, жи́тся, гу́тся *pf.* (*of* ▸ сбега́ться) to come running; to gather, collect

сберба́нк, а *m.* (infml) savings bank

сберега́тельн|ый *adj.*: ∼**ый банк** savings bank; ∼**ая кни́жка** passbook, bank book

сберега́|ть, ю *impf. of* ▸ сбере́чь

сбереже́ни|е, я *nt.* (*in pl.*) (*деньги*) savings

сбере́|чь, гу́, жёшь, гу́т, *past* ∼г, ∼гла́ *pf.* (*of* ▸ сберега́ть) (*время*) to save; (*семью́*) to protect, look after; (*здоро́вье*) to preserve

сберка́сс|а, ы *f.* (infml, hist.) savings bank

сберкни́жк|а, и *f.* (infml) savings book

сбива́|ть, ю *impf. of* ▸ сбить

сбива́|ться, юсь *impf.* ◼️1 *impf. of* ▸ сби́ться ◼️2 (*impf. only*) (на + *a.*) to resemble; to remind one (of)

сби́вчив|ый, ∼, ∼а *adj.* inconsistent, contradictory

сбить, собью́, собьёшь *pf.* (*of* ▸ сбива́ть) ◼️1 (*ударом*) to bring down, knock down; (с чего-л.) to knock off, dislodge; (*птицу, самолёт*) to bring down, shoot down; (*цену, температуру*) to bring down ◼️2 (*запутать*) to distract; to deflect; **с. кого́-н. с то́лку** to confuse sb ◼️3 (*каблуки, туфли*) to wear down ◼️4 (*составить*) to knock together; **с. я́щик из досо́к** to knock together a box out of planks

сби́ться, собью́сь, собьёшься *pf.* (*of* ▸ сбива́ться 1) ◼️1 (*сдвинуться с места*) to be dislodged; to slip; **у тебя́ шля́па сби́лась на́бок** your hat is crooked, skew-whiff ◼️2 (*ошибиться*) to go wrong; **с. с доро́ги, с. с пути́** to lose one's way; (*also* fig.): **с. со счёта** to lose count

сближа́|ть, ю *impf. of* ▸ сбли́зить

сближа́|ться, юсь *impf. of* ▸ сбли́зиться

сближе́ни|е, я *nt.* ◼️1 (pol.) rapprochement ◼️2 (*дружба*) intimacy

сбли́|зить, жу, зишь *pf.* (*of* ▸ сближа́ть) to bring together, draw together

сбли́|зиться, жусь, зишься *pf.* (*of* ▸ сближа́ться) ◼️1 (*об интересах*) to converge ◼️2 (с + *i.*) (*о людях*) to become close friends (with)

сбо|й, я *m.* interruption; malfunction

сбо́ку *adv.* from one side; on one side; **вид с.** side view; **смотре́ть на кого́-н. с.** to look sideways at sb

сболтну́|ть, у́, ёшь *pf.* (infml) to blurt out, let out

✦ **сбор**, а *m.* ◼️1 (*действие*) collection; **с. урожа́я** harvest; **с. нало́гов** tax collection ◼️2 (*деньги*) dues; duty; (*выручка*) takings, returns; **тамо́женный с.** customs duty; **де́лать хоро́шие** ∼**ы** (theatr.) to play to full houses, get good box office returns **3** (*встреча*) assembly, gathering; **быть в ~е** to be assembled, be in session **4** (*in pl.*) (*приготовления*) preparations

сбо́рк|а, и *f.* assembling, assembly, erection

сбо́рник, а *m.* collection; (*литературных произведений*) anthology

сбо́рный *adj.* **1** (*дом*) prefabricated; (*мебель*) in kit form **2** (*из разнородных частей*) mixed, combined; (*as n.*) national team **3** (mil.) assembly; **с. пункт** assembly point

сбра́сыва|ть, ю *impf. of* ▶ **сбро́сить**

сбрива́|ть, ю *impf. of* ▶ **сбрить**

сбрить, сбре́ю, сбре́ешь *pf.* (*of* ▶ **сбрива́ть**) to shave off

сброд, а (*no pl.*) *m.* (collect.) riff-raff, rabble

сбро́|сить, шу, сишь *pf.* (*of* ▶ **сбра́сывать**) **1** (*бросить вниз*) to throw down; to drop; **с. бо́мбы** to drop bombs **2** (*скинуть*) to throw off (also fig.); (*кожу, листья*) to shed; **с. (с себя́) одея́ло** to throw off a blanket; (*свергнуть*) to overthrow **3** (*сбавить*) to reduce

сбру́|я, и *f.* (collect.) harness

сбыва́|ться, юсь *impf. of* ▶ **сбы́ться**

сбыт, а (*no pl.*) *m.* (econ., comm.) sale; **ры́нок ~а** (seller's) market

сбы́ться, сбу́дется, *past* **сбы́лся, сбыла́сь** *pf.* (*of* ▶ **сбыва́ться**) to come true, be realized

св. (*abbr. of* **святой**) St, Saint

свадебный *adj.* wedding; **с. пода́рок** wedding present

сва́д|ьба, ьбы, *g. pl.* **~еб** *f.* wedding; **справля́ть ~ьбу** to celebrate a wedding

сва́лива|ть, ю *impf. of* ▶ **свали́ть**

сва́лива|ться, юсь *impf. of* ▶ **свали́ться**

свал|и́ть, ю́, ~ишь *pf.* (*of* ▶ **вали́ть**[1], ▶ **сва́ливать**) **1** (*ударом*) to throw down, bring down; (infml, *о болезни*) to lay low **2** (*дрова, уголь*) to heap up, pile up; **с. вину́** (**на** + *a.*) to lump the blame (on)

свал|и́ться, ю́сь, ~ишься *pf.* (*of* ▶ **вали́ться**, ▶ **сва́ливаться**) to fall (down), collapse; **с. как снег на́ голову** to come like a bolt from the blue

сва́лк|а, и *f.* dump; scrap heap

сваля́|ться, ется *pf.* to get tangled

сва́рива|ть, ю *impf. of* ▶ **свари́ть**

свар|и́ть, ю́, ~ишь *pf.* **1** *pf. of* ▶ **вари́ть** **2** (*impf.* **~ивать**) (tech.) to weld

свар|и́ться, ~ится *impf. of* ▶ **вари́ться**

сва́рк|а, и *f.* (tech.) welding

сварли́в|ый, ~, ~а *adj.* quarrelsome, shrewish

сва́рщик, а *m.* welder

сва́стик|а, и *f.* swastika

сва́|я, и *f.* pile

✎ **сведе́ни|е, я** *nt.* **1** (*известие*) piece of information; (*in pl.*) information, intelligence **2** (*знание*) knowledge; attention, consideration, notice; **приня́ть**

к ~ю to take into consideration

све́дущ|ий, ~, ~а *adj.* (**в** + *p.*) knowledgeable (about); (well) versed (in)

све́жест|ь, и *f.* freshness; (*прохлада*) coolness

✎ **све́ж|ий, ~, ~á, ~о́, ~и** *adj.* fresh; **~ее бельё** clean underclothes; **с. ве́тер** fresh breeze; **на ~ем во́здухе** in the fresh air; **~ие но́вости** recent news

свёкл|а, ы *f.* beet, beetroot (BrE)

свёк|ор, ра *m.* father-in-law (*husband's father*)

свекро́в|ь, и *f.* mother-in-law (*husband's mother*)

сверг|а́ть, а́ю *impf. of* ▶ **све́ргнуть**

све́рг|нуть, ну, нешь, *past* **~ and ~нул, ~ла** *pf.* (*of* ▶ **сверга́ть**) to throw down, overthrow; **с. с престо́ла** to dethrone

све́р|ить, ю, ишь *pf.* (*of* ▶ **сверя́ть**) (+ *a.* and **с** + *i.*) to check (sth against)

све́рк|а, и *f.* collation

сверка́|ть, ю *impf.* to sparkle; to glitter; to gleam; (*о молнии*) to flash

сверкн|у́ть, у́, ёшь *inst. pf.* to flash (also fig.)

сверл|и́ть, ю́, и́шь *impf.* (*of* ▶ **просверли́ть**) **1** (tech.) to bore, drill; **с. зуб** to drill a tooth **2** (*о насекомых*) to bore through

сверл|о́, а́, *pl.* **~а, ~** *nt.* (tech.) (*инструмент*) drill; (*наконечник*) drill bit

сверн|у́ть, у́, ёшь *pf.* (*of* ▶ **свора́чивать**) **1** to roll (up); **с. ковёр** to roll up the carpet; **с. ше́ю кому́-н.** to wring sb's neck **2** (fig., *сократить*) to reduce, contract, cut down **3** (*повернуть*) to turn; **с. нале́во** to turn to the left; **с. с доро́ги** to turn off the road

сверн|у́ться, у́сь, ёшься *pf.* (*of* ▶ **свора́чиваться**) **1** to roll up, curl up; to coil up; **с. клубко́м** to roll oneself up into a ball **2** (*о молоке*) to curdle; (*о крови*) to coagulate, clot **3** (fig., *сократиться*) to contract

све́рстник, а *m.* person of the same age; contemporary, peer; **они́ ~и** they are the same age

све́рстни|ца, цы *f. of* ▶ **све́рстник**

сверх *prep.* + *g.* (*нормы*) above, beyond; over and above; in excess of; **с. пла́на** in excess of the plan; **с. (вся́кого) ожида́ния** beyond (all) expectation

сверх... *comb. form* super-, supra-, extra-, over-, preter-

сверхдержа́в|а, ы *f.* superpower

сверхзвуково́й *adj.* (phys., aeron.) supersonic

сверхпла́новый *adj.* over and above the plan

све́рху *adv.* **1** from above (also fig.); from the top; **с. до́низу** from top to bottom; **смотре́ть на кого́-н. с. вниз** (fig.) to look down on sb **2** (*на пове́рхности*) on the surface; on the top

сверхуро́чн|ый *adj.* overtime; **~ая рабо́та** overtime; (*as pl. n.* **~ые, ~ых**) overtime pay

сверхчелове́к, а *m.* superman

С

сверхъесте́ствен|ный, ~, ~на *adj.*
supernatural

сверч|о́к, ка́ *m.* (zool.) cricket

свер|я́ть, я́ю *impf. of* ▶ **све́рить**

све́|сить, шу, сишь *pf.* (*of* ▶ **све́шивать**) to
let down, lower; **сиде́ть**, ~сив но́ги to sit
with one's legs dangling

све́|ситься, шусь, сишься *pf.* (*of*
▶ **све́шиваться**) to lean over; to hang over;
(*о ветвях*) to overhang; **с. че́рез пери́ла** to
lean over the banisters

све|сти́, ду́, дёшь, *past* ~л, ~ла́ *pf.* (*of*
▶ **своди́ть¹**) **1** (с + *g.*) (*спустить сверху
вниз*) to take down (from, off); **с. с ума́** to
drive mad **2** (*соединить; собрать*) to bring
together; to put together; to unite; **судьба́**
~ла́ их fate threw them together; **с. концы́
с конца́ми** to make (both) ends meet
3 (к + *d.* or на + *a.*) (*довести*) to reduce
(to), bring (to); **с. на нет** to bring to naught
4 (*о судороге*) to cramp, convulse; **у меня́**
~ло́ но́гу I have cramp in my foot

све|сти́сь, дётся, *past* ~лся, ~ла́сь *pf.* (*of*
▶ **своди́ться**) (к + *d.*) to come (to), reduce (to)

⚹ **свет¹**, а *m.* light (also fig.); **лу́нный с.**
moonlight; **заже́чь с.** to turn the light on;
в ~е (+ *g.*) in the light (of); **на ~у́** in the
light; **при ~е** (+ *g.*) by the light (of)

⚹ **свет²**, а *m.* **1** (*мир*) world (also fig.); **Ста́рый,
Но́вый С.** the Old, the New World; **тот с.**
the next world; **коне́ц ~а** doomsday, the
end of the world; **появи́ться на ~е** to come
into the world; **ни за что на ~е** not for
the world **2** (*высшее общество*) society;
вы́сший с. high society

света́|ть, ет *impf.* (*impers.*): ~ет it is
dawning, it is getting light, day is breaking

свети́л|о, а *nt.* luminary (also fig.); **небе́сные**
~а heavenly bodies

свети́льник, а *m.* lamp

све|ти́ть, чу́, ~тишь *impf.* **1** (*излучать
свет*) to shine **2** (+ *d.*) to light the way
(for) **3** to shine a light (for)

све|ти́ться, чу́сь, ~тишься *impf.* to shine,
gleam

све́тло-... *comb. form* light (*with names of
colours*); **све́тло-зелёный** light green

светволо́с|ый, ~, ~а *adj.* light-haired

све́т|лый, ~ел, ~ла́, ~ло, ~лы *and in
pred. use* ~ло́, ~лы́ *adj.* **1** (*комната,
волосы, краски*) light; (*день*) bright; **на
у́лице ~ло́** it is daylight **2** (fig., *радостный*)
bright, radiant, joyous; pure, unclouded;
~лое бу́дущее bright future **3** (fig.,
проницательный) lucid, clear; **он — ~лая
голова́** he has a lucid mind

светопреставле́ни|е, я *nt.* **1** the end of
the world, doomsday **2** (fig., infml) chaos

светофи́льтр, а *m.* light filter

светофо́р, а *m.* traffic lights

све́тск|ий *adj.* **1** society, fashionable; ~ая
жизнь high life; **с. челове́к** man of the world

2 (*манеры*) refined **3** (*не церковный*)
temporal, lay, secular; worldly

светя́щийся *pres. part. of* ▶ **свети́ться** *and
adj.* luminous, luminescent

свеч|а́, и́, *i.* ~о́й, *pl.* ~и, ~е́й, ~а́м *f.*
1 candle **2**: **с. зажига́ния** spark
plug **3** (med.) suppository

свече́ни|е, я *nt.* luminescence, fluorescence;
phosphorescence

све́шива|ть, ю *impf. of* ▶ **све́сить**

све́шива|ться, юсь *impf. of* ▶ **све́ситься**

свида́ни|е, я *nt.* meeting; (*деловое*)
appointment; (*влюблённых*) date; **назна́чить
с.** (на + *a.*) to arrange a meeting (for), make
an appointment (for), make a date (for); **до
~я!** goodbye!

свиде́тел|ь, я *m.* witness; **с. обвине́ния,
защи́ты** witness for the prosecution, for the
defence (BrE), defense (AmE)

свиде́тель|ница, ницы *f. of* ▶ **свиде́тель**

свиде́тельств|о, а *nt.* **1** evidence
2 (*документ*) certificate; **с. о бра́ке**
marriage certificate

свиде́тельств|овать, ую *impf.* **1** to give
evidence (concerning); to testify; (о + *p.*
or + *a.* or + что) (law) to give evidence
(concerning); to testify **2** (о + *p.*)
(*подтверждать, доказывать*) to show,
attest to, be evidence (of); **э́то письмо́ ~ует
о его́ беста́ктности** this letter is evidence of
his tactlessness

свина́рник, а *m.* pigsty

свин|е́ц, ца́ *m.* lead

свини́н|а, ы *f.* pork

сви́н|ка¹, ки *f. dim. of* ▶ **свинья́**; **морска́я с.**
guinea pig

сви́н|ка², и *f.* (med.) mumps

свин|о́й *adj. of* ▶ **свинья́**; ~а́я ко́жа pigskin;
~а́я котле́та pork chop; ~о́е са́ло lard

сви́нский *adj.* (infml) (*подлый*) swinish;
(*грязный*) filthy

сви́нств|о, а *nt.* (infml) (*подлость*)
swinishness; (*поступок*) swinish trick;
(*грязь*) filth

свин|ти́ть, чу́, ти́шь *pf.* (*of* ▶ **сви́нчивать**)
1 (*соединить*) to screw together **2** (*гайку*)
to unscrew

сви́нчива|ть, ю *impf. of* ▶ **свинти́ть**

свинь|я́, и́, *pl.* ~и, ~е́й, ~ям *f.* **1** pig;
(*самка*) sow **2** (fig., pej., *человек*) swine;
подложи́ть ~ью́ (+ *d.*) (infml) to play a dirty
trick (on)

свире́л|ь, и *f.* (reed) pipe

свире́п|ый, ~, ~а *adj.* fierce, ferocious

свис|а́ть, а́ю *impf.* to hang down

свист, а *m.* whistle; whistling

сви|сте́ть, щу́, сти́шь *impf.* to whistle

сви́стн|уть, у, ешь *pf.* **1** to give a whistle
2 (infml, *украсть*) to steal, snatch

свист|о́к, ка́ *m.* whistle

сви́тер, а *m.* sweater

сви́т|ок, ка *m.* roll, scroll

⚹ key word

свить, совью, совьёшь, *past* **свил, свила́, сви́ло** *pf.* (*of* ▶ **вить**) to twist, wind

сви́ться, совьётся, *past* **свила́сь, свила́сь** *pf.* (*of* ▶ **ви́ться**) to roll up, curl up, coil

свихн|у́ться, у́сь, ёшься *pf.* (infml) to go off one's head

свобо́д|а, ы *f.* freedom, liberty; **с. во́ли** free will; **с. сло́ва** freedom of speech; **на ~е** at large

свобо́дно *adv.* **1** (*без принужде́ния*) freely; (*с лёгкостью*) with ease; **она́ с. говори́т на пяти́ языка́х** she speaks five languages fluently **2** (*просто́рно*) loose, loosely

свобо́д|ный, ~ен, ~на *adj.* **1** free **2** (*без помех*) free; easy; **с. до́ступ** easy access **3** (*не за́нятый*) free; (*но́мер*) vacant; (*ме́сто*) spare; **~ное вре́мя** free time; **~ное ме́сто** vacant seat, spare seat; **вы ~ны сего́дня ве́чером?** are you free this evening? **4** (*поведе́ние*) free (and easy) **5** (*оде́жда*) loose, loose-fitting; flowing

свободолюби́в|ый, ~, ~а *adj.* freedom-loving

свод¹, а *m.* code; (*докуме́нтов*) collection; **с. зако́нов** code of laws

свод², а *m.* (*перекры́тие*) arch, vault; **небе́сный с.** the firmament

сво|ди́ть¹, жу́, ~дишь *impf. of* ▶ **свести́**

сво|ди́ть², жу́, ~дишь *pf.* (*отвести́ и привести́ обра́тно*) to take (*and bring back*); **мы ~ди́ли дете́й в кино́** we took the children to the cinema

сво|ди́ться, ~дится *impf. of* ▶ **свести́сь**

сво́дк|а, и *f.* summary; report; **с. пого́ды** weather forecast, weather report

сво́дн|ый *adj.* **1** combined; collated; **~ая табли́ца** summary table, index **2** step-; **с. брат** stepbrother

сво́дчатый *adj.* arched, vaulted

своево́л|ьный, ~ен, ~ьна *adj.* self-willed, wilful

своевре́мен|ный, ~ and ~ен, ~на *adj.* timely, opportune

своенра́в|ный, ~ен, ~на *adj.* wilful, capricious

своеобра́з|ный, ~ен, ~на *adj.* original; peculiar, distinctive

сво|зи́ть, жу́, ~зишь *pf.* (*отвезти́ и привезти́ обра́тно*) to take (*and bring back*); **мы ~зи́ли дете́й в цирк** we took the children to the circus

свой *poss. adj.* one's (my, your, his, *etc.*, *in accordance with subject of sentence or clause*), one's own; **у них с. дом** they have a house of their own; **умере́ть свое́й сме́ртью** to die a natural death; **в своё вре́мя** at one time, in my, his, *etc.*, time; (*своевре́менно*) in due time, in due course; **он не в своём уме́** he is not right in the head; (*as pl. n.* **свои́**) one's (own) people; **своё** one's own; **доби́ться своего́** to get one's own way

сво́йствен|ный, ~ and ~ен, ~на *adj.* (+ *d.*) characteristic (of)

сво́йств|о, а *nt.* characteristic

сво́лоч|ь, и, *g. pl.* **~е́й** *f.* (infml) scum, swine

свора́чива|ть, ю *impf. of* ▶ **сверну́ть**

свора́чива|ться, юсь *impf. of* ▶ **сверну́ться**

свор|ова́ть, у́ю (infml) *pf. of* ▶ **ворова́ть**

своя́к, á *m.* brother-in-law (*husband of wife's sister*)

своя́чениц|а, ы *f.* sister-in-law (*wife's sister*)

свык|а́ться, а́юсь *impf. of* ▶ **свы́кнуться**

свы́к|нуться, нусь, нешься, *past* **~ся, ~лась** *pf.* (*of* ▶ **свыка́ться**) (с + *i.*) to get used (to)

свысока́ *adv.* condescendingly; **обраща́ться с кем-н. с.** to talk down to, patronize sb

свы́ше 1 *adv.* from above; (relig.) from on high **2** *prep.* (+ *g.*) over, more than; (*вне*) beyond; **с. ты́сячи самолётов уча́ствовало в налёте** over a thousand planes took part in the raid

свя|за́ть, жу́, ~жешь *pf.* (*of* ▶ **вяза́ть** 2, ▶ **свя́зывать**) **1** to tie; to bind (also fig.); **с. свою́ судьбу́** (с + *i.*) to throw in one's lot (with) **2** (fig., *соедини́ть*) to connect, link; **быть (те́сно) ~занным** (с + *i.*) to be (closely) connected (with), be bound up (with) **3** : **быть ~занным** (с + *i.*) (fig., *повле́чь*) to involve, entail; **э́то предприя́тие бу́дет ~зано с огро́мными расхо́дами** this undertaking will involve huge expense **4** (*установи́ть связь*) to link, associate; **не́которые ~за́ли эпиде́мию с плохи́м водоснабже́нием** some connected the epidemic with the bad water supply

свя|за́ться, жу́сь, ~жешься *pf.* (*of* ▶ **свя́зываться** 1) (с + *i.*) **1** to get in touch (with), communicate (with) **2** (infml, pej.) to get involved (with), get mixed up (with)

свя́зк|а, и *f.* **1** (*ключе́й*) bunch; (*книг, бума́г*) bundle **2** (anat.) cord; ligament; **голосовы́е ~и** vocal cords

свя́з|ный, ~ен, ~на *adj.* connected, coherent

свя́зыва|ть, ю *impf. of* ▶ **связа́ть**

свя́зыва|ться, юсь *impf.* **1** *impf. of* ▶ **связа́ться 2** (*impf. only*) (с + *i.*) to have to do (with); **не ~йся с ни́ми** don't have anything to do with them

связ|ь, и, *о* **~и**, **в ~и́** *f.* **1** (*отноше́ние*) connection; **в связи́ с** (+ *i.*) (*всле́дствие*) due to; owing to; (*по по́воду*) in connection with; **в связи́ с э́тим** in this connection **2** (*те́сное обще́ние*) link, tie, bond; **дру́жеские ~и** friendly relations, ties of friendship **3** (*любо́вная*) liaison; relationship **4** (*in pl.*) (*бли́зкое знако́мство*) connections, contacts; **у него́ мно́го ~ей в Москве́** he has many influential connections in Moscow **5** (*сообще́ние*) communication; **с. по ра́дио** radio communication **6** (*sg. only*) (*по́чта, телефо́н*) (post and tele)communications; **отделе́ние ~и** (branch) post office

свят|о́й, ~, ~á, ~о *adj.* **1** (*свяще́нный*) holy; sacred (also fig.); **~áя вода́** holy water; **С. Дух**

the Holy Ghost, the Holy Spirit **2** (*человек*) saintly **3** (*preceding name, or as n.* с., ∼о́го, *f.* ∼а́я, ∼о́й) saint; **причи́слить к ли́ку ∼ы́х** (eccl.) to canonize

свя́тост|ь, и *f.* holiness; sanctity

святота́тств|о, а *nt.* sacrilege

святы́н|я, и *f.* **1** (eccl.) (*предмет*) object of worship; (*место*) sacred place **2** (fig., *предмет*) sacred object

свяще́нник, а *m.* (*православный*) priest (*of Orthodox Church*); clergyman

свяще́н|ный, ∼ен, ∼на *adj.* holy; sacred (also fig.); **С∼ное Писа́ние** Holy Writ, Scripture

сгиб, а *m.* **1** bend **2** (anat.) flexion

сгиба́|ть, ю *impf. of* ▶ согну́ть

сгиба́|ться, юсь *impf. of* ▶ согну́ться

сги́н|уть, у, ешь *pf.* (infml) to disappear, vanish

сгла́|дить, жу, дишь *pf.* (*of* ▶ сгла́живать) **1** (*выровнять*) to smooth out **2** (fig., *смягчить*) to smooth over, soften

сгла́|диться, дится *pf.* (*of* ▶ сгла́живаться) **1** (*выровняться*) to become smooth **2** (fig., *смягчиться*) to be smoothed over, be softened

сгла́жива|ть, ю, ет *impf. of* ▶ сгла́дить

сгла́жива|ться, ется *impf. of* ▶ сгла́диться

сглаз, а *m.* (infml) the evil eye

сгла́|зить, жу, зишь *pf.* to put the evil eye (on, upon); (fig., infml) to jinx

сгни|ть, ю́, ёшь *pf.* (*of* ▶ гнить) to rot, decay

сгова́рива|ться, юсь *impf. of* ▶ сговори́ться

сговор|и́ться, ю́сь, и́шься *pf.* (*of* ▶ сгова́риваться) (с + *i.*) to arrange (with)

сгово́рчив|ый, ∼, ∼а *adj.* compliant, tractable

сгора́ни|е, я *nt.* combustion; **дви́гатель вну́треннего ∼я** internal-combustion engine

сгор|а́ть, а́ю **1** *impf. of* ▶ сгоре́ть **2** (*от + g.*) (fig.) to be dying (of); **с. от стыда́, любопы́тства** to be dying of shame, curiosity

сгорб|иться, люсь, ишься *pf. of* ▶ го́рбиться

сго́рблен|ный, ∼, ∼а *adj.* crooked, bent; hunchbacked

сгор|е́ть, ю́, и́шь *pf.* (*of* ▶ сгора́ть 1) **1** to burn down; to be burnt out, down; **наш дом ∼е́л** our house was burnt down **2** (*о топливе*) to be consumed, be used up

сгоряча́ *adv.* in the heat of the moment; in a fit of temper

сгреба́|ть, ю *impf. of* ▶ сгрести́

сгре|сти́, бу́, бёшь, *past* ∼б, ∼бла́ *pf.* (*of* ▶ сгреба́ть) (*собрать*) to rake up, rake together

сгруд|и́ться, и́тся *pf.* (infml) to crowd, mill, bunch

сгруппир|ова́ть, у́ю *pf. of* ▶ группирова́ть

сгуб|и́ть, лю́, ∼ишь *pf.* (infml) to ruin

сгу|сти́ть, щу́, сти́шь *pf.* (*of* ▶ сгуща́ть) to thicken; (*конденсировать*) to condense; **с. кра́ски** (fig.) to lay it on thick

сгу|сти́ться, сти́тся *pf.* (*of* ▶ сгуща́ться) to thicken; (*конденсироваться*) to condense; (*о крови*) to clot

сгу́ст|ок, ка *m.* clot

сгуща́|ть, ю, ет *impf. of* ▶ сгусти́ть

сгуща́|ться, ется *impf. of* ▶ сгусти́ться

✍ **сда|ва́ть, ю́, ёшь** *impf.* (*of* ▶ сдать): **с. экза́мен** to take, sit an examination

сда|ва́ться, ю́сь, ёшься *impf. of* ▶ сда́ться

сдав|и́ть, лю́, ∼ишь *pf.* (*of* ▶ сда́вливать) to squeeze

сда́влива|ть, ю *impf. of* ▶ сдави́ть

сдать, сдам, сдашь, сдаст, сдади́м, сдади́те, сдаду́т, *past* **сдал, сдала́, сда́ло** *pf.* (*of* ▶ сдава́ть) **1** (*передать*) to hand over, pass; **с. бага́ж на хране́ние** to deposit one's luggage **2** (*отдать внаём*) to let, let out, hire out; **с. в аре́нду** to lease **3** (*возвратить*) to give change **4** (*уступить*) to surrender, yield, give up **5** (*экзамен*) to pass (*an examination, a subject, etc.*); **он сдал то́лько латы́нь** he only passed in Latin **6** (*карты*) to deal (cards) **7** (infml) (*о моторе, сердце*) to give out; (*о старике, здоровье*) to become weaker

сда́|ться, мся, шься, стся, ди́мся, ди́тесь, ду́тся, *past* ∼лся, ∼ла́сь *pf.* (*of* ▶ сдава́ться) to surrender, yield; (chess) to resign

сда́|ча, и *f.* **1** (*квартиры*) letting out, hiring out; **с. в аре́нду** leasing **2** (*города*) surrender **3** (*деньги*) change; **три рубля́ ∼и** three roubles change; **с. с рубля́** change from one rouble; **дать ∼и** (+ *d.*) (fig., infml) to give as good as one gets

сдвиг, а *m.* **1** displacement; (geol.) fault **2** (fig., *улучшение*) change (for the better), improvement

сдвига́|ть, ю *impf. of* ▶ сдви́нуть

сдвига́|ться, юсь *impf. of* ▶ сдви́нуться

сдви́|нуть, ну, нешь *pf.* (*of* ▶ сдвига́ть) **1** to shift, move, displace; **с. с ме́ста** (fig.) to get moving, set in motion **2** (*соединить*) to move together, bring together

сдви́|нуться, нусь, нешься *pf.* (*of* ▶ сдвига́ться) to move, budge; **с. с ме́ста** (fig.) to progress; **де́ло не ∼нулось с ме́ста** no headway has been made

✍ **сде́ла|ть, ю** *pf. of* ▶ де́лать

сде́ла|ться, юсь *pf. of* ▶ де́латься

✍ **сде́лк|а, и** *f.* transaction, deal, bargain

сде́льн|ый *adj.* piecework; **∼ая опла́та** payment by the piece, by the job; **∼ая рабо́та** piecework

сде́ржан|ный, ∼, ∼а *p.p.p. of* ▶ сдержа́ть *and* (∼, ∼на) *adj.* restrained, reserved

сдерж|а́ть, у́, ∼ишь *pf.* (*of* ▶ сде́рживать) **1** to hold (back); (*неприятеля*) to hold

с

in check, contain **2** (fig., *чувства*) to keep back, restrain; **с. слёзы** to suppress tears **3** (*обещание*) to keep; **с. сло́во** to keep one's word

сдерж|а́ться, у́сь, ~ишься *pf.* (*of* ▸ **сде́рживаться**) to restrain oneself, contain oneself; to check oneself

сде́ржива|ть, ю *impf. of* ▸ **сдержа́ть**

сде́ржива|ться, юсь *impf. of* ▸ **сдержа́ться**

сдира́|ть, ю *impf. of* ▸ **содра́ть**

сдо́хн|уть, у, ешь *pf.* (*of* ▸ **сдыха́ть**) **1** (infml, *о животных*) to die **2** (vulg. sl., pej., *о людях*) to peg out, kick the bucket

сдруж|и́ться, у́сь, ~ишься *pf.* (с + *i.*) to become friends (with)

сдува́|ть, ю *impf. of* ▸ **сдуть**

сду|ть, ~ю, ~ешь *pf.* (*of* ▸ **сдува́ть**) to blow away, blow off

сдыха́|ть, ю *impf. of* ▸ **сдо́хнуть**

сеа́нс, а *m.* **1** (*представление*) performance, show **2** (*массажа, гипноза*) session **3** (*портретиста*) sitting **4** (*спиритический*) seance

себе́[1] *see* ▸ **себя́**

себе́[2] *particle* (infml) (*modifying v. or pron. and usu. containing hint of reproach*): **ничего́ с.** not bad; **так с.** so-so

себесто́имост|ь, и *f.* (econ.) cost (*of manufacture*); cost price; **прода́ть по ~и** to sell at cost price

⚜ **себя́, себе́, собо́й** *and* **собо́ю, о себе́** *refl. pron.* oneself; (*я*) myself; (*ты, вы*) yourself; (*он*) himself, *etc.*; **прийти́ в с.** (от + *g.*) to get over; to come to one's senses; **не в себе́** not oneself; **от с.** away from oneself, outwards; (*лично, от своего имени*) for oneself, on one's own behalf; **чита́ть про с.** to read to oneself; **у с.** at home, at one's (own) place

себялюби́в|ый, ~, ~а *adj.* egotistical, selfish

се́вер, а *m.* north

⚜ **се́верн|ый** *adj.* north, northern; (*направление, ветер*) northerly; **с. оле́нь** reindeer; **С. по́люс** North Pole; **С. Ледови́тый океа́н** Arctic Ocean; **С. поля́рный круг** Arctic Circle; **~ое сия́ние** Northern Lights, aurora borealis

североамерика́нский *adj.* North American

се́веро-восто́к, а *m.* north-east

се́веро-восто́чный *adj.* north-east, north-eastern

се́веро-за́пад, а *m.* north-west

се́веро-за́падный *adj.* north-west, north-western

североирла́ндский *adj.* Northern Irish

северя́н|ин, ина, *pl.* **~е, ~** *m.* northerner

севрю́г|а, и *f.* stellate sturgeon (*Acipenser stellatus*)

сегме́нт, а *m.* segment

⚜ **сего́дня** *adv.* today; **с. ве́чером** this evening, tonight

⚜ **сего́дня|шний** *adj. of* ▸ **сего́дня**; **с. день**

today; **~шняя газе́та** today's paper

седе́|ть, ю *impf.* (*of* ▸ **поседе́ть**) to go grey (BrE), gray (AmE)

седин|а́, ы́, *pl.* **~ы, ~** *f.* grey (BrE), gray (AmE) hair(s)

седл|о́, ла́, *pl.* **~ла, ~ел** *nt.* saddle

сед|о́й, ~, ~а́, ~о, ~ы *adj.* (*волосы*) grey (BrE), gray (AmE); (*человек*) grey-haired (BrE), gray-haired (AmE)

седьм|о́й *adj.* seventh; **быть на ~о́м не́бе** to be in seventh heaven

⚜ **сезо́н, а** *m.* season

сезо́нн|ый *adj.* seasonal; **с. биле́т** season ticket; **~ые рабо́ты** seasonal work

⚜ **сей, f. сия́, nt. сие́,** *pl.* **сий** *pron.* this; **сию́ мину́ту** this (very) minute; at once, instantly; **до сих пор** up to now, till now, hitherto; **на с. раз** this time, for this once; **по с. день** to this day

сейсми́ческий *adj.* seismic

сейсмоопа́сн|ый, ~ен, ~на *adj.* earthquake-prone

сейсмосто́й|кий, ~ек, ~йка *adj.* earthquake-proof

сейф, а *m.* safe

⚜ **сейча́с** *adv.* **1** (*тепе́рь*) (right) now, at present, at the (present) moment **2** (*очень ско́ро*) presently, soon; **с. же** at once, immediately; **с.!** in a minute!; half a minute!

секи́р|а, ы *f.* axe (BrE), ax (AmE)

секре́т, а *m.* secret; **по ~у** confidentially, in confidence

секрета́р|ша, ши *f.* (infml) *of* ▸ **секрета́рь**

секрета́р|ь, я́ *m.* secretary; **ли́чный с.** private secretary, personal secretary; **генера́льный с.** secretary general

секре́тно *adv.* secretly, in secret; (*на́дпись*) 'secret', 'confidential'; **соверше́нно с.** 'top secret'

секре́тност|ь, и *f.* secrecy

секре́т|ный, ~ен, ~на *adj.* secret; confidential

секре́ци|я, и *f.* (physiol.) secretion

⚜ **секс, а** *m.* sex

сексо́лог, а *m.* sexologist

сексоло́ги|я, и *f.* sexology

сексуа́льност|ь, и *f.* sexuality

сексуа́л|ьный, ~ен, ~ьна *adj.* sexual; (*эроти́чный*) sexy; **~ьное домога́тельство** sexual harassment; **~ьные отноше́ния** sexual relations

се́кт|а, ы *f.* sect

секта́нт, а *m.* sectarian; member of a sect

⚜ **се́ктор, а,** *pl.* **~ы, ~ов** *and* **~а́, ~о́в** *m.* **1** (math., mil.) sector; **с. Га́за** the Gaza Strip **2** (*отдел*) section, department; (econ.) sector

⚜ **секу́нд|а, ы** *f.* second; **одну́ ~у!** just a moment!

секундоме́р, а *m.* stopwatch

се́кци|я, и *f.* section

селёдк|а, и *f.* herring

селезёнк|а, и *f.* (physiol.) spleen

с

се́лез|ень, ня *m.* drake

селекционе́р, а *m.* **1** (agric.) breeder **2** (sport) scout

селе́кци|я, и *f.* **1** (agric.) selective breeding **2** (sport) selection

селе́ни|е, я *nt.* settlement

сели́тр|а, ы *f.* (chem.) saltpetre (BrE), saltpeter (AmE)

сел|и́ть, ю́, и́шь *impf.* (*of* ▶ посели́ть) to settle

сел|и́ться, ю́сь, и́шься *impf.* (*of* ▶ посели́ться) to settle

ⱷ **сел|о́, а́,** *pl.* **~а** *nt.* village

сел|ь, я *m.* (seasonal) mountain torrent

сельдере́|й, я *m.* celery

сельд|ь, и, *pl.* **~и, ~е́й** *f.* herring

ⱷ **се́льск|ий** *adj.* **1** (*не городско́й*) country, rural; **~ая ме́стность** rural area; countryside; **~ое хозя́йство** agriculture, farming **2** (*шко́ла, у́лица*) village

сельскохозя́йственный *adj.* agricultural, farming

сема́нтик|а, и *f.* **1** (*нау́ка*) semantics **2** (*значе́ние сло́ва*) meanings

семафо́р, а *m.* semaphore

сёмг|а, и *f.* salmon

ⱷ **семе́йн|ый** *adj.* **1** family; domestic; **по ~ым обстоя́тельствам** for domestic reasons **2** (*име́ющий семью́*) having a family; **с. челове́к** family man

семе́йств|о, а *nt.* family

семена́ *see* ▶ **се́мя**

семёрк|а, и *f.* **1** (*ци́фра, игра́льная ка́рта*) seven **2** (infml, *авто́бус, трамва́й*) No. 7 (bus, tram, etc.) **3** (*гру́ппа из семеры́х*) (group of) seven; **Больша́я с.** the seven economically most developed nations

се́мер|о, ы́х *num.* (collect.) seven

семе́стр, а *m.* term (BrE), semester (AmE)

семе́ч|ко, ка, *pl.* **~ки, ~ек** *nt.* **1** *dim. of* ▶ се́мя **2** (*in pl.*) (*подсо́лнечника*) sunflower seeds; (*ты́квенные*) pumpkin seeds

семибо́рь|е, я *nt.* heptathlon

семидеся́т|ый *adj.* seventieth; **~ые го́ды** the seventies

семиле́тний *adj.* **1** (*срок*) seven-year **2** (*ребёнок*) seven-year-old

ⱷ **семина́р, а** *m.* seminar

семина́ри|я, и *f.* seminary, training college; **духо́вная с.** theological college

семисо́тый *adj.* seven-hundredth

семи́т, а *m.* Semite

семна́дцатый *adj.* seventeenth

семна́дцат|ь, и *num.* seventeen

ⱷ **сем|ь, и́,** *i.* **~ью́** *num.* seven

се́м|ьдесят, семи́десяти, *i.* **семью́десятью** *num.* seventy

семьсо́т, семисо́т, семиста́м, семьюста́ми, о семиста́х *num.* seven hundred

ⱷ key word

се́мью *adv.* seven times

ⱷ **сем|ья́, ьи́,** *pl.* **~ьи, ~е́й, ~ьям** *f.* family

се́м|я, ени, *pl.* **~ена́, ~я́н, ~ена́м** *nt.* **1** (bot., *also fig.*) seed **2** (*спе́рма*) semen, sperm

сена́т, а *m.* senate

сена́тор, а *m.* senator

сенберна́р, а *m.* St Bernard (*dog*)

Сенега́л, а *m.* Senegal

сенега́л|ец, ьца *m.* Senegalese

сенега́л|ка, ки *f. of* ▶ сенега́лец

сенега́льский *adj.* Senegalese

сенн|о́й *adj.* hay; **~а́я лихора́дка** hay fever

се́н|о, а *nt.* hay

сеноко́с, а *m.* haymaking; hayfield

сенсацио́н|ный, ~ен, ~на *adj.* sensational

сенса́ци|я, и *f.* sensation

сентимента́л|ьный, ~ен, ~ьна *adj.* sentimental

ⱷ **сентя́бр|ь, я́** *m.* September

сентя́брьский *adj. of* ▶ сентя́брь

сепарати́зм, а *m.* (pol.) separatism

сепарати́ст, а *m.* (pol.) separatist

се́р|а, ы *f.* **1** (chem.) sulphur (BrE), sulfur (AmE) **2** (*в уша́х*) earwax

серб, а *m.* Serb, Serbian

Се́рби|я, и *f.* Serbia

се́рб|ка, ки *f. of* ▶ серб

се́рбский *adj.* Serb, Serbian

серва́нт, а *m.* sideboard

ⱷ **се́рвер, а** *m.* (comput.) server

серви́з, а *m.* service, set; **столо́вый с.** dinner service

сервир|ова́ть, у́ю *impf. and pf.*: **с. стол** to lay a table

ⱷ **се́рвис, а** *m.* (consumer) service

серде́чно-сосу́дистый *adj.* cardiovascular

серде́ч|ный, ~ен, ~на *adj.* **1** of the heart (*also fig.*); (anat.) cardiac; **с. при́ступ** heart attack **2** (*приём*) cordial; (*благода́рность*) heartfelt, sincere **3** (*челове́к*) warm, warm-hearted

серди́т|ый, ~, ~а *adj.* (**на** + *a.*) angry (with, at, about), cross (with, about); irate

серд|и́ть, жу́, ~ишь *impf.* (*of* ▶ рассерди́ть) to anger, make angry

серд|и́ться, жу́сь, ~ишься *impf.* (*of* ▶ рассерди́ться) (**на** + *a.*) to be angry (with, at, about), be cross (with, about)

ⱷ **се́рд|це, ца,** *pl.* **~ца́, ~е́ц** *nt.* heart; **приня́ть (бли́зко) к ~цу** to take to heart; **от всего́ ~ца** from the bottom of one's heart, wholeheartedly

сердцебие́ни|е, я *nt.* palpitation; (med.) tachycardia

сердцеви́н|а, ы *f.* (*плода́, стебля́*) core

серебри́ст|ый, ~, ~а *adj.* silvery

серебр|о́, а́ *nt.* **1** silver **2** (collect.) silver; **столо́вое с.** silver, plate

сере́бряный *adj.* silver

ⱷ **середи́н|а, ы** *f.* middle, midst; **золота́я с.**

the golden mean
серёжк|а, и *f.* **1** earring **2** (bot.) catkin
сержа́нт, а *m.* sergeant
сериа́л, а *m.* (TV/radio) serial
сери́йный *adj.* serial; **сери́йный но́мер** serial number; **сери́йный уби́йца** serial killer
сери|я, и *f.* series; (*часть фильма*) part
се́рн|а, ы *f.* (zool.) chamois
се́рн|ый *adj.* sulphuric (BrE), sulfuric (AmE); **∼ая кислота́** sulphuric acid
сероводоро́д, а *m.* (chem.) hydrogen sulphide (BrE), sulfide (AmE)
серп, а́ *m.* sickle
серпанти́н, а *m.* **1** (*бумажная лента*) paper streamer **2** (*дорога*) winding mountain road
сертифика́т, а *m.* certificate
сёрфинг, а *m.* surfing
сёрфинги́ст, а *m.* surfer
сёрфинги́ст|ка, ки *f. of* ▸ **сёрфинги́ст**
се́р|ый, ∼, ∼а́, ∼о *adj.* **1** grey (BrE), gray (AmE) **2** (fig.) (*бесцветный*) grey (BrE), gray (AmE); dull; drab; **с. день** grey day **3** (fig., infml, *необразованный*) dull, dim
серьг|а́, и́, pl. ∼и, серёг, ∼а́м *f.* earring
серьёзно *adv.* seriously; **с.?** seriously?; really?
серьёз|ный, ∼ен, ∼на *adj.* serious
се́сси|я, и *f.* session, sitting
сестр|а́, ы́, pl. ∼ы, сестёр, ∼а́м *f.* **1** sister; **двою́родная с.** (first) cousin **2**: **медици́нская с.** nurse
сесть¹, ся́ду, ся́дешь, past сел, се́ла *pf.* (*of* ▸ **сади́ться**) **1** to sit down; **с. за стол** to sit down to table; **с. рабо́тать** to get down to work **2** (**в, на** + *a.*) to board, take; **с. на по́езд** to board a train; **с. на ло́шадь** to mount a horse **3** (*о птице*) to alight, settle, perch; (*о самолёте*) to land **4** (*о солнце*) to set **5**: **с. в тюрьму́** to go to prison, jail
сесть², ся́дет, past сел *pf.* (*of* ▸ **сади́ться**) (*о ткани*) to shrink
сетево́й *adj.* net, netting, mesh; (comput.) network; Internet
се́тк|а, и *f.* net; (*для багажа*) (luggage) rack
сет|ь, и, о ∼и, в ∼и and ∼й, pl. ∼и, ∼ей *f.* **1** net (also fig.) **2** (*система*) network; system; **лока́льная с.** (comput.) local area network, LAN **3** (**Сеть**) the Net (*Internet*)
Сеу́л, а *m.* Seoul
сече́ни|е, я *nt.* section; **ке́сарево с.** Caesarean (BrE), Cesarean (AmE) (section); **попере́чное с.** cross section
се́|ять, ю, ешь *impf.* (*of* ▸ **посе́ять**) to sow (also fig.); **с. семена́ раздо́ра** to sow the seeds of dissension
сжа́тый *p.p.p. of* ▸ **сжать¹** *and adj.* **1** compressed (*air, gas*) **2** (fig.) condensed, concise
сжать¹, сожму́, сожмёшь *pf.* (*of* ▸ **сжима́ть**) to squeeze; (*жидкость, газ; изложение*) to compress (also fig.); (*чью-н. руку*) to grip;

с. зу́бы to grit one's teeth; **с. кулаки́** to clench one's fists
сжать², сожну́, сожнёшь *pf. of* ▸ **жать²**
сжа́|ться, сожму́сь, сожмёшься *pf.* (*of* ▸ **сжима́ться**) **1** (*о пальцах, зубах*) to tighten, clench **2** (*о теле*) to contract
сжечь, сожгу́, сожжёшь, сожгу́т, past сжёг, сожгла́ *pf.* (*of* ▸ **жечь 1**, ▸ **сжига́ть**) to burn (up, down); (*в крематории*) to cremate
сжива́|ться, юсь *impf. of* ▸ **сжи́ться**
сжига́|ть, ю *impf. of* ▸ **сжечь**
сжима́|ть, ю *impf. of* ▸ **сжать¹**
сжима́|ться, юсь ся *impf. of* ▸ **сжа́ться**
сжи́|ться, ву́сь, вёшься, past ∼лся, ∼ла́сь *pf.* (*of* ▸ **сжива́ться**) (infml) (**с** + *i.*) to get used (to), get accustomed (to)
сза́ди *adv. and prep.* + *g.* **1** *adv.* from behind; behind; from the end; from the rear; **вид с.** rear view; **тре́тий ваго́н с.** the third coach from the rear **2** *prep.* + *g.* behind
си *nt. indecl.* (mus.) B
сиби́рск|ий *adj.* Siberian; **∼ая я́зва** (med.) anthrax
Сиби́р|ь, и *f.* Siberia
сига́р|а, ы *f.* cigar
сигаре́т|а, ы *f.* cigarette
сигна́л, а *m.* signal; **с. бе́дствия** distress signal
сигнализа́ци|я, и *f.* **1** (*действие*) signalling (BrE), signaling (AmE) **2** (*устройство*) alarm system **3** (*система*) signalling (BrE), signaling (AmE) system
сигнализи́р|овать, ую *impf. and pf.* **1** to signal **2** (+ *a.* or **о** + *p.*) (fig.) to give warning (of)
сиде́лк|а, и *f.* nurse (*looking after sick people*)
сиде́нь|е, я *nt.* seat
сиде́|ть, жу́, ди́шь *impf.* **1** to sit; **с. на ко́рточках** to squat **2** (*находиться*) to be; **с. (в тюрьме́)** to be in prison **3** (**на** + *p.*) (*об одежде*) to fit, set (on)
сиде́|ться, и́тся *impf.* (*impers.* + *d.*) **ему́** *и т. n.* **не ∼и́тся до́ма** he, *etc.*, can't bear staying at home; **ей не ∼и́тся на ме́сте** she can't keep still
Си́дне|й, я *m.* Sydney
си́з|ый, ∼, ∼а́, ∼о *adj.* blue-grey (BrE), blue-gray (AmE)
си́квел, а *m.* (+ *g.* or **к** + *d.*) sequel (to)
сикх, а *m.* Sikh
си́кхский *adj.* Sikh
си́л|а, ы *f.* **1** strength, force; **в ∼у** (+ *g.*) by virtue (of), because (of); **быть в ∼ах** (+ *inf.*) to be able to, have the strength (to); **изо всех ∼, что есть ∼ы** with all one's might; **че́рез ∼у** with the greatest of effort; **∼ой** by force; **свои́ми ∼ами** unaided; **с. во́ли** willpower **2** (phys., tech.) force, power; **лошади́ная с.** horsepower; **с. тя́жести, с. притяже́ния** force of gravity **3** (law, also fig.) force; **име́ющий ∼у** valid; **войти́, вступи́ть в ∼у** to come into force, take effect **4** (*in pl.*) (mil.) forces; **вооружённые ∼ы** armed forces
сила́ч, а́ *m.* strong man

силико́н, а *m.* silicone

си́л|иться, юсь, ишься *impf.* to try very hard, make efforts

силов|о́й *adj.* power; ~а́я устано́вка power plant; ~ы́е структу́ры law enforcement agencies

си́лой *adv.* (infml) by force

сил|о́к, ка́ *m.* snare

силуэ́т, а *m.* silhouette

⚐ си́льно *adv.* **1** strongly; violently **2** (*очень*) very much, greatly; badly

⚐ си́л|ьный, ~ён, ~ьна́, ~ьно, ~ьны́ *adj.* strong; powerful; с. дождь heavy rain; ~ьное жела́ние intense desire; с. за́пах strong smell

симбио́з, а *m.* (biol.) symbiosis

⚐ си́мвол, а *m.* symbol; с. ве́ры (relig.) creed

символизи́р|овать, ую *impf.* to symbolize

символи́зм, а *m.* symbolism

символи́ческий *adj.* symbolic(al)

сим-ка́рт|а, ы *f.* SIM (card)

симметри́ч|ный, ~ен, ~на *adj.* symmetrical

симме́три|я, и *f.* symmetry

симпатизи́р|овать, ую *impf.* (+ *d.*) to like, be fond of

симпати́ч|ный, ~ен, ~на *adj.* (*человек*) nice, pleasant; (*лицо, голос, город*) attractive, pleasant

симпа́ти|я, и *f.* (к + *d.*) liking, fondness (for); чу́вствовать ~ю к кому́-н. to take a liking to sb, be drawn to sb

симпо́зиум, а *m.* symposium

симпто́м, а *m.* symptom

симули́р|овать, ую *impf. and pf.* to simulate, fake, sham

симфони́ческий *adj.* symphonic; с. орке́стр symphony orchestra

симфо́ни|я, и *f.* symphony

синаго́г|а, и *f.* synagogue

Сингапу́р, а *m.* Singapore

сингапу́р|ец, ца *m.* Singaporean

сингапу́р|ка, ки *f. of* ▸ сингапу́рец

сингапу́рский *adj.* Singaporean

синдика́т, а *m.* (econ.) syndicate

синдро́м, а *m.* (med.) syndrome

синев|а́, ы́ *f.* blue

синегла́з|ый, ~, ~а *adj.* blue-eyed

си́н|ий, ~ь, ~я, ~е *adj.* (dark) blue

сини́ц|а, ы *f.* tit (*bird*)

сино́ним, а *m.* synonym

сино́птик, а *m.* weather forecaster

си́нтаксис, а *m.* syntax

си́нтез, а *m.* synthesis

синтеза́тор, а *m.* synthesizer

синтези́р|овать, ую *impf. and pf.* to synthesize

синте́тик|а, и *f.* (collect.) synthetic, synthetics

синтети́ческий *adj.* synthetic

⚐ key word

синхро́нный *adj.* synchronous; (*перевод*) simultaneous

синя́к, а́ *m.* bruise; с. под гла́зом black eye

сиони́зм, а *m.* Zionism

сиони́ст, а *m.* Zionist

сиони́ст|ка, ки *f. of* ▸ сиони́ст

си́пл|ый, ~, ~а *adj.* hoarse, husky

сире́н|а, ы *f.* siren

сире́невый *adj.* lilac; lilac-coloured

сире́н|ь, и *f.* lilac

сири́|ец, йца *m.* Syrian

сири́й|ка, ки *f. of* ▸ сири́ец

сири́йский *adj.* Syrian

Си́ри|я, и *f.* Syria

сиро́п, а *m.* syrup

сирот|а́, ы́, *pl.* ~ы *c.g.* orphan

сиротли́в|ый, ~, ~а *adj.* lonely

⚐ систе́м|а, ы *f.* **1** system **2** (*mun*) type

систематизи́р|овать, ую *impf. and pf.* to systematize, order

системати́ческий *adj.* **1** systematic; methodical **2** (*регулярный*) regular

систе́мный *adj. of* ▸ систе́ма; с. ана́лиз/ анали́тик systems analysis/analyst; с. диск system disk

си́с|ька, ьки, *g. pl.* ~ек *f.* (sl.) (*сосок*) nipple; (*грудь*) tit (vulg.)

си́т|ец, ца *m.* cotton (print); chintz

си́т|о, а *nt.* sieve

⚐ ситуа́ци|я, и *f.* situation

си́филис, а *m.* (med.) syphilis

сифо́н, а *m.* siphon

сия́ни|е, я *nt.* radiance

сия́|ть, ю *impf.* (*о солнце*) to shine; (*о человеке, от радости*) to beam; (*о лице*) to be radiant

сказа́ни|е, я *nt.* story, tale, legend

⚐ ска|за́ть, жу́, ~жешь *pf.* (*of* ▸ говори́ть 2): как с.! it depends; то́чно с. or rather

ска|за́ться, ~жется *pf.* (*of* ▸ ска́зываться) (на + *p.*) to take its toll (on)

ска́зк|а, и *f.* **1** fairy tale **2** (infml, *ложь*) (tall) story, fib

ска́зочник, а *m.* storyteller

ска́зочн|ый *adj.* fairy-tale; (*необычайный*) fabulous, fantastic; ~ое бога́тство fabulous wealth

сказу́ем|ое, ого *nt.* (gram.) predicate

ска́зыва|ться, ется *impf. of* ▸ сказа́ться

скака́лк|а, и *f.* skipping rope (BrE), jump rope (AmE)

ска|ка́ть, чу́, ~чешь *impf.* **1** (*pf.* по~) to skip, jump; с. на одно́й ноге́ to hop **2** (*pf.* по~) (*о лошади, о всаднике*) to gallop **3** (infml, *резко изменяться*) to fluctuate

скаков|о́й *adj.* race, racing; с. круг, ~а́я доро́жка racecourse; ~а́я ло́шадь racehorse

скаку́н, а́ *m.* racehorse

скал|а́, ы́, *pl.* ~ы *f.* rock face, crag; (отве́сная) с. cliff

скали́ст|ый, ~, ~а *adj.* rocky

ска́лк|а, и *f.* (cul.) rolling pin

скалола́з, а *m.* rock climber

скальп, а *m.* scalp

ска́льпел|ь, я *m.* scalpel

скаме́йк|а, и *f.* bench

скам|ья́, ьи́, *pl.* **~ьи́, ~е́й** *f.* bench;
с. подсуди́мых (*law*) the dock

сканда́л, а *m.* **1** scandal **2** (*ссора*) row,
(rowdy) scene

сканда́л|ьный, ~ен, ~ьна *adj.*
1 (*поведение*) scandalous **2** (infml,
человек) rowdy, quarrelsome **3** scandal;
~ьная хро́ника scandal column, page (*of
newspaper*)

скандина́в, а *m.* Scandinavian

Скандина́ви|я, и *f.* Scandinavia

скандина́вк|а, ки *f. of* ▶ **скандина́в**

скандина́вский *adj.* Scandinavian

ска́нер, а *m.* (med., comput.) scanner

скани́р|овать, ую *impf. and pf.* (med., comput.)
to scan

ска́плива|ть, ю, ет *impf. of* ▶ **скопи́ть**

ска́плива|ться, ется *impf. of* ▶ **скопи́ться**

скарлати́н|а, ы *f.* (med.) scarlet fever

ска́рмлива|ть, ю *impf. of* ▶ **скорми́ть**

скат, а *m.* (zool.) ray, skate

скат|а́ть, а́ю *pf.* (*of* ▶ **ска́тывать,** ▶ **ката́ть** 3)
to roll (up)

ска́терт|ь, и, *pl.* **~и, ~е́й** *f.* tablecloth

ска|ти́ть, чу́, ~тишь *pf.* (*of* ▶ **ска́тывать**)
to roll down

ска|ти́ться, чу́сь, ~тишься *pf.* (*of*
▶ **ска́тываться**) to roll down

ска́тыва|ть, ю *impf. of* ▶ **скатать,** ▶ **скати́ть**

ска́тыва|ться, юсь *impf. of* ▶ **скати́ться**

скафа́ндр, а *m.* protective suit; (*водолаза*)
diving suit; (*космонавта*) spacesuit

♂ **скача́|ть, ю** *pf.* (*of* ▶ **ска́чивать**) (comput.)
to download

ска́чива|ть, ю *impf. of* ▶ **скача́ть**

ска́чк|а, и *f.* **1** gallop, galloping **2** (*in pl.*)
(*состязание*) horse race; race meeting, the
races; с. с препя́тствиями steeplechase

скач|о́к, ка́ *m.* **1** jump, leap, bound; ~ка́ми
by leaps **2** (fig., *цен, температуры*) leap

сква́жин|а, ы *f.* slit, chink; замо́чная с.
keyhole; нефтяна́я с. oil well

сквер, а *m.* small public garden

скве́р|ный, ~ен, ~на́, ~но *adj.* (*человек,
поступок*) nasty; (*погода, настроение*)
foul, awful

сквозн|о́й *adj.* **1** through; ~о́е движе́ние
through traffic **2** (*рана, отверстие*)
going right through **3** (*просвечивающий*)
transparent

сквозня́к, á *m.* draught (BrE), draft (AmE)

сквозь *prep.* (+ *a.*) through

скворе́ц, ца́ *m.* starling

сквош, а *m.* (sport) squash

скейтбо́рд, а *m.* skateboard

скейтбо́рдинг, а *m.* skateboarding

скеле́т, а *m.* skeleton

ске́птик, а *m.* sceptic (BrE), skeptic (AmE)

скепти́ческий *adj.* sceptical (BrE), skeptical
(AmE)

ски́дк|а, и *f.* **1** reduction, discount; со ~ой
(в + *a.*) with a reduction (of), at a discount
(of) **2** (на + *a.*) (fig.) allowance(s) (for);
сде́лать ~у на во́зраст to make allowances
for age

ски́дыва|ть, ю *impf. of* ▶ **ски́нуть**

ски́|нуть, ну, нешь *pf.* (*of* ▶ **ски́дывать**)
(infml) **1** (*одежду*) to throw off, cast off;
(*снег с крыши*) to throw down **2** (*с цены*)
to knock off (*from price*)

скинхе́д, а *m.* skinhead

ски́петр, а *m.* sceptre (BrE), scepter (AmE)

скипида́р, а *m.* turpentine

скис|а́ть, а́ю *impf. of* ▶ **ски́снуть**

ски́с|нуть, ну, нешь, *past* **~, ~ла** *pf.* (*of*
▶ **скиса́ть**) to go sour, turn sour; (fig.) to
lose heart

склад[1], а *m.* **1** (*место*) storehouse; (mil.)
depot; това́рный с. warehouse **2** (*запас*)
store; с. боеприпа́сов (mil.) ammunition
dump

склад[2], а *m.* (*образ*) way; с. ума́ cast of mind,
mentality, mindset

скла́дк|а, и *f.* **1** pleat, tuck; crease; ю́бка в
~у pleated skirt; с. на брю́ках trouser crease
2 (*на коже*) wrinkle

складн|о́й *adj.* folding, collapsible; ~а́я
крова́ть camp bed (BrE), cot (AmE); с. нож
penknife

скла́дыва|ть, ю *impf. of* ▶ **сложи́ть**[1]

♂ **скла́дыва|ться, юсь** *impf. of* ▶ **сложи́ться**[1],
▶ **сложи́ться**[2]

скле́ива|ть, ю, ет *impf. of* ▶ **скле́ить**

скле́ива|ться, ется *impf. of* ▶ **скле́иться**

скле́|ить, ю, ишь *pf.* (*of* ▶ **скле́ивать,**
▶ **кле́ить**) to stick together; to glue together

скле́|иться, ится *pf.* (*of* ▶ **скле́иваться**) to
stick together

склеп, а *m.* burial vault, crypt

склеро́з, а *m.* (med.) sclerosis; рассе́янный с.
multiple sclerosis

скло́к|а, и *f.* squabble; row

склон, а *m.* slope

склоне́ни|е, я *nt.* (gram.) declension

склон|и́ть, ю́, ~ишь *pf.* (*of* ▶ **склоня́ть**)
1 to incline, bend, bow; с. го́лову (пе́ред + *i.*)
(fig.) to bow one's head (to, before) **2** (fig.)
(*убедить*) to talk sb over; to win sb over

склон|и́ться, ю́сь, ~ишься *pf.* (*of*
▶ **склоня́ться**) **1** to bend, bow **2** (к + *d.*)
(fig.) to give in (to), yield (to)

скло́нност|ь, и *f.* (к + *d.*) (*к музыке,
живописи*) aptitude (for); (*к полноте,
меланхолии*) susceptibility (to), tendency
(towards); (*к театру, к пиву*) liking,
penchant (for)

скло́н|ный, ~ен, ~на *adj.* (к + *d.*) (*к
болезни*) prone, susceptible (to); (+ *inf.*)
inclined (to)

склоня́|ть, яю *impf. of* ▶ **склони́ть**

с

склон|я́ться, я́юсь *impf. of* ▸ **склони́ться**

скоб|а́, ы́, *pl.* **~ы, ~, ~а́м** *f.* (*зажим*) clamp; (*изогнутая железная полоса*) staple

ско́бк|а, и *f.* **1** *dim. of* ▸ **скоба́ 2** (*знак*) bracket; (*in pl.*) brackets, parentheses; **в ~ах** in brackets; (*fig.*) in parenthesis, by the way, incidentally

скобл|и́ть, ю́, и́шь *impf.* to scrape; (*доску*) to plane

ско́ванный 1 *p.p.p. of* ▸ **скова́ть; с. льда́ми** ice-bound **2** *adj.* (*движения, мысль*) constrained

скова́ть, скую́, скуёшь *pf.* (*of* ▸ **ско́вывать**) **1** (*соединить*) to weld together **2** (*заковать*) to chain; to fetter (also fig.)

сковород|а́, ы́, *pl.* **сково́роды, сковоро́д, ~а́м** *f.* frying pan

сковоро́дк|а, и *f.* (infml) frying pan

ско́выва|ть, ю *impf. of* ▸ **скова́ть**

скола́чива|ть, ю *impf. of* ▸ **сколоти́ть**

сколо|ти́ть, чу́, ~тишь *pf.* (*of* ▸ **скола́чивать**) **1** (*соединить*) to knock together; (*изготовить*) to knock up **2** (fig., infml, *набрать*) to get together; to scrape together

сколь *adv.* how

сколь|зи́ть, жу́, зи́шь *impf.* (*плавно двигаться*) to slide; to glide; (*терять устойчивость*) to slip

ско́льз|кий, ~ок, ~ка́, ~ко *adj.* slippery (also fig.); (fig.) tricky; sensitive, delicate, treacherous

🖋 **ско́лько** *interrog. and rel. adv.* **1** (*денег, хлеба*) how much; (*книг, людей*) how many; **с. сто́ит?** how much does it cost?; **с. вам лет?** how old are you?; **с. вре́мени?** what time is it? **2** = **наско́лько**

ско́лько-нибудь *adv.* any; **у вас при себе́ есть с.-н. де́нег?** have you any money on you?

скома́нд|овать, ую *pf. of* ▸ **кома́ндовать 1**

скомбини́р|овать, ую *pf. of* ▸ **комбини́ровать**

ско́мка|ть, ю *pf. of* ▸ **ко́мкать**

скомпромети́р|овать, ую *pf. of* ▸ **компромети́ровать**

сконструи́р|овать, ую *pf. of* ▸ **конструи́ровать**

сконцентри́р|овать, ую *pf. of* ▸ **концентри́ровать**

сконцентри́р|оваться, уюсь *pf. of* ▸ **концентри́роваться**

сконча́|ться, юсь *pf.* to pass away (= *to die*)

скопи́р|овать, ую *pf. of* ▸ **копи́ровать**

скоп|и́ть, лю́, ~ишь *pf.* (*of* ▸ **ска́пливать**) (+ *a. or g.*) (*накопить*) to save (up); to amass, pile up

скоп|и́ться, ~ится *pf.* (*of* ▸ **ска́пливаться**) **1** to accumulate, pile up **2** (*о людях*) to gather, collect

скопле́ни|е, я *nt.* (*народа*) crowd; (*предметов*) accumulation, mass

скорб|е́ть, лю́, и́шь *impf.* (*о* + *p.*) to grieve (for, over), mourn (for, over), lament

скорб|ь, и, *pl.* **~и, ~е́й** *f.* sorrow, grief

скоре́е and скоре́й 1 *comp. of* ▸ **ско́рый,** ▸ **ско́ро; как мо́жно с.** as soon as possible; **с.!** (be) quick! **2** *adv.* rather, sooner; **с. всего́** most likely, most probably

скорлуп|а́, ы́, *pl.* **~ы** *f.* shell; **с. оре́ха** nutshell; **яи́чная с.** eggshell

скорм|и́ть, лю́, ~ишь *pf.* (*of* ▸ **ска́рмливать**) (+ *d.*) to feed (to)

🖋 **ско́ро** *adv.* **1** (*быстро*) quickly, fast **2** (*вскоре*) soon

скорогово́рк|а, и *f.* **1** (*быстрая речь*) rapid speech, patter **2** (*придуманная фраза*) tongue-twister

скоростно́й *adj.* high-speed

🖋 **ско́рост|ь, и,** *pl.* **~и, ~е́й** *f.* **1** speed; velocity; rate; **со ~ью три́дцать миль в час** at thirty miles per hour **2**: **перейти́ на другу́ю с.** to change gear

скоросшива́тел|ь, я *m.* binder, file; (*на кольцах*) ring binder

скорпио́н, а *m.* scorpion; (**С.**) Scorpio (*sign of zodiac*)

скоррект́и́р|овать, ую *pf. of* ▸ **корректи́ровать**

скорректи́ровать *pf. of* ▸ **корректи́ровать**

🖋 **ско́р|ый, ~, ~а́, ~о** *adj.* **1** (*быстрый*) quick, fast; rapid; **~ая по́мощь** ambulance (service); **на ~ую ру́ку** in rough-and-ready fashion **2** (*близкий по времени*) near, forthcoming, impending; **в ~ом бу́дущем** in the near future

скос, а *m.* **1** (*горы, берега*) slope **2** (*предмета*) slant, bevel

ско|си́ть¹, шу́, ~сишь *pf. of* ▸ **коси́ть¹**

ско|си́ть², шу́, си́шь *pf. of* ▸ **коси́ть² 1, 2**

скот, а́ *m.* (collect.) cattle; livestock

скоти́н|а, ы *f.* **1** (collect.) cattle; livestock **2** (also *m.*) (fig., infml, *грубый человек*) swine, beast

скотобо́|йня, йни, *g. pl.* **~ен** *f.* slaughterhouse

скотово́дств|о, а *nt.* cattle breeding, cattle raising

ско́тский *adj.* (infml) brutal, brutish, bestial

скотч, а *m.* (infml) adhesive tape; Sellotape (BrE); Scotch tape® (AmE)

скра́|сить, шу, сишь *pf.* (*of* ▸ **скра́шивать**) (fig.) to relieve; **он мно́го чита́л, чтобы с. своё одино́чество** he read a lot to relieve his loneliness

скра́шива|ть, ю *impf. of* ▸ **скра́сить**

скребо́к, ка́ *m.* scraper

скре́жет, а *m.* (*металла*) grating, scraping; (*зубов*) gnashing

скреп|и́ть, лю́, и́шь *pf.* (*of* ▸ **скрепля́ть**) **1** (*соединить*) to fasten (together); (tech.) to clamp, brace; (*дружбу*) to cement **2** (*удостоверить*) to countersign, ratify

скре́пк|а, и *f.* paper clip

скрепля́|ть, ю *impf. of* ▸ **скрепи́ть**

скре|сти́, бу́, бёшь, *past* ~б, ~бла́ *impf.* (*о кошке, ногтями*) to scratch, claw; (*дерево*) to sand; (*кастрюлю*) to scour

скре|сти́сь, бу́сь, бёшься, *past* ~бся, ~бла́сь *impf.* to scratch, make a scratching noise

скре|сти́ть, щу́, сти́шь *pf.* (*of* ▸ скре́щивать) **1** to cross; **с. мечи́, с. шпа́ги (с** + *i.*) to cross swords (with) (*also fig.*) **2** (biol.) to cross, interbreed

скрест|и́ться, и́тся *pf.* (*of* ▸ скре́щиваться) **1** to cross; (fig.) to clash **2** (biol.) to cross, interbreed

скре́щива|ть, ю, ет *impf. of* ▸ скрести́ть

скре́щива|ться, ется *impf. of* ▸ скрести́ться

скринсе́йвер, а *m* (comput.) screensaver

скриншо́т, а *m.* (comput.) screenshot, screen grab

скрип, а *m.* (*двери*) squeak, creak; (*снега*) crunch

скрипа́ч, á *m.* violinist

скрипа́ч|ка, ки *f. of* ▸ скрипа́ч

скрип|е́ть, лю́, и́шь *impf.* (*of* ▸ скри́пнуть) (*о двери*) to squeak, creak; (*о снеге*) to crunch

скри́пк|а, и *f.* violin; **пе́рвая с.** first violin; (fig., infml) first fiddle

скри́пн|уть, у, ешь *inst. pf. of* ▸ скрипе́ть

скрипт, а *m.* (comput.) script

скро|и́ть, ю́, и́шь *pf. of* ▸ крои́ть

скро́мност|ь, и *f.* modesty

скро́м|ный, ~ен, ~на́, ~но *adj.* modest

скрупулёз|ный, ~ен, ~на *adj.* scrupulous

скру|ти́ть, чу́, ~тишь *pf.* (*of* ▸ крути́ть 1, ▸ скру́чивать) **1** (*верёвки*) to twist (together); (*папиросу*) to roll **2** (*руки*) to bind, tie up

скру́чива|ть, ю *impf. of* ▸ скрути́ть

скрыва́|ть, ю *impf. of* ▸ скрыть

скрыва́|ться, юсь *impf.* **1** *impf. of* ▸ скры́ться **2** (*impf. only*) to lie in hiding; to lie low

скры́т|ный, ~ен, ~на *adj.* secretive

скры́тый *p.p.p. of* ▸ скрыть *and adj.* secret, concealed; **с. смысл** hidden meaning

скр|ыть, о́ю, о́ешь *pf.* (*of* ▸ скрыва́ть) (*от* + *g.*) to hide (from), conceal (from)

скр|ы́ться, о́юсь, о́ешься *pf.* (*of* ▸ скрыва́ться 1) (*от* + *g.*) (*спря́таться*) to hide (oneself) (from); (*о престу́пнике*) to go into hiding **2** (*удали́ться*) to steal away (from), escape, give the slip **3** (*исче́знуть*) to disappear, vanish

ску́д|ный, ~ен, ~на́, ~но *adj.* (*сре́дства, обе́д*) meagre (BrE), meager (AmE); (*урожа́й*) poor; (*зна́ния, све́дения*) scanty; (*расти́тельность*) sparse

ску́к|а, и *f.* boredom, tedium; **кака́я с.!** what a bore!

скул|á, ы́, *pl.* ~ы *f.* cheekbone

скул|и́ть, ю́, и́шь *impf.* to whine, whimper (*also fig.*)

ску́льптор, а *m.* sculptor

скульпту́р|а, ы *f.* sculpture

ску́мбри|я, и *f.* mackerel

скунс, а *m.* skunk

скуп|а́ть, а́ю *impf. of* ▸ скупи́ть

скуп|и́ть, лю́, ~ишь *pf.* (*of* ▸ скупа́ть) to buy up

скуп|о́й, ~, ~а́, ~о, ~ы́ *adj.* **1** stingy, miserly; **с. на слова́** sparing of words **2** (fig., *недоста́точный*) inadequate

ску́пост|ь, и *f.* stinginess, miserliness

ску́тер, а *m.* (*ка́тер*) outboard motor boat; (*мотороллер*) scooter

скуча́|ть, ю *impf.* **1** to be bored **2** (*по* + *d.*) to miss, yearn (for)

ску́ч|ный, ~ен, ~на́, ~но *adj.* **1** (*кни́га*) boring, tedious, dull **2** (*челове́к, взгляд*) bored; (*as pred.*) **мне** *и т. п.* ~но I am, *etc.*, bored

ску́ша|ть, ю *pf. of* ▸ ку́шать

слабе́|ть, ю *impf. of* ▸ ослабе́ть

слаби́тельн|ый *adj.* (med.) laxative; (*as nt. n.* ~ое, ~ого) laxative

слабоалкого́льный *adj.* low-alcohol

слабоне́рв|ный, ~ен, ~на *adj.* having weak nerves; nervous

сла́бост|ь, и *f.* **1** weakness, feebleness **2** (*к* + *d.*) (*накло́нность*) weakness (for)

слабоу́ми|е, я *nt.* learning disability; **ста́рческое с.** senile dementia

слабоу́м|ный, ~ен, ~на *adj.* learning-disabled

✓ **сла́б|ый, ~, ~á, ~о** *adj.* (*челове́к, хара́ктер, зре́ние, во́ля*) weak; (*го́лос*) feeble; (*верёвка*) slack, loose; (*ве́тер, боль, наде́жда*) slight; (*учени́к, зна́ния*) weak, poor; (*ребёнок, здоро́вье*) delicate; ~ое ме́сто weak point; **с. пол** the weaker sex

✓ **сла́в|а, ы** *f.* **1** glory; fame; **во ~у** (+ *g.*) to the glory (of); **на ~у** (infml) wonderfully well, excellently; (*as int.*, + *d.*) hurrah (for)!; **с. бо́гу** thank God, thank goodness **2** (*репута́ция*) name, reputation; **до́брая с.** good name; **дурна́я с.** infamy **3** (infml, *слу́хи*) rumour (BrE), rumor (AmE)

сла́в|иться, люсь, ишься *impf.* (+ *i.*) to be famous (for), be renowned (for); to have a reputation (for)

сла́в|ный, ~ен, ~на́, ~но *adj.* **1** glorious, famous, renowned **2** (infml) splendid; lovely; **с. ма́лый** nice chap

славян|и́н, и́на, *pl.* ~е, ~ *m.* Slav

славя́н|ка, ки *f. of* ▸ славяни́н

славянофи́л, а *m.* Slavophil(e)

славя́нский *adj.* Slavonic; Slavic; Slav

слага́|ть, ю *impf. of* ▸ сложи́ть[2] 2

сла́д|кий, ~ок, ~ка́, ~ко *adj.* sweet (*also fig.*); (*as nt. n.* ~кое, ~кого) dessert

сладкое́жк|а, и *c.g.* (infml) (person with a) sweet tooth

сладостра́ст|ный, ~ен, ~на *adj.* sensual, voluptuous

С

сла́дост|ь, и *f.* **1** sweetness **2** (*in pl.*) (*кондитерские изделия*) sweets, sweetmeats

сла́|зить, жу, зишь *pf.* (infml) to go, climb; **с. в подва́л за дрова́ми** to go down to the cellar for logs

слайд, а *m.* slide, transparency

сла́лом, а *m.* (sport) slalom

сла́н|ец, ца *m.* **1** (min.) slate **2** (*usu. in pl.*) flip-flop

сласт|ь, и, *pl.* ~и, ~е́й *f.* sweets, sweetmeats

слать, шлю, шлёшь *impf.* to send

сла́ще *comp. of* ▶ сла́дкий

сле́ва *adv.* (от + *g.*) on the left (of), to the left (of); **с. напра́во** from left to right

слегка́ *adv.* lightly, gently; (*немного*) slightly; **с. суту́литься** to stoop slightly

✓ след, а, *pl.* ~ы́ *m.* **1** (*отпечаток*) track; (*ноги*) footprint, footstep; **идти́ по чьим-н. ~а́м** (fig.) to follow in sb's footsteps; **напа́сть на чей-н. с.** to get on sb's trail **2** (fig., *признак*) trace, sign, vestige

✓ сле|ди́ть, жу́, ди́шь *impf.* (за + *i.*) **1** (*смотреть*) to watch; to follow; **с.** (*глаза́ми*) **за полётом мяча́** to follow (with one's eyes) the flight of a ball **2** (fig.) to follow; to keep up (with); **с. за междунаро́дными собы́тиями** to keep up with international affairs **3** (*заботиться*) to look after; to keep an eye (on); **с. за детьми́** to look after children; **с. за поря́дком** to keep order; **с. за тем, что́бы** to see to it that

сле́дователь, я *m.* investigator

сле́довательно *conj.* consequently, therefore, hence

✓ сле́д|овать¹, ую *impf.* (*of* ▶ после́довать) **1** (за + *i.*) to follow, go after **2** (+ *d.*) (*поступать подобно кому-н.*) to follow; (*поступать согласно чему-н.*) to follow; to comply (with); **с. пра́вилам** to conform to the rules **3** (*impf. only*) (до + *g. or* в + *a.*) (*отправляться*) to be bound (for); **э́тот по́езд ~ует в Варша́ву** this train is (bound) for Warsaw **4** (*impf. only*) (*быть следствием*) to follow; to result; **из э́того ~ует, что мы оши́блись** it follows from this that we were mistaken

✓ сле́д|овать², ует *impf.* (impers. + *d. and inf.*) (*нужно, должно*) ought, should; **вам ~ует обрати́ться к ре́ктору** you should approach the rector; **как и ~овало ожида́ть** as was to be expected; **как ~ует** as it should be, properly, well and truly

сле́дом *adv.* (за + *i.*) immediately (after, behind); **идти́ с. за кем-н.** to follow sb close(ly)

следопы́т, а *m.* pathfinder, tracker

сле́дств|енный *adj. of* ▶ сле́дствие²; investigatory; **~енная коми́ссия** committee of inquiry

✓ сле́дстви|е¹, я *nt.* (*результат*) consequence, result; **причи́на и с.** cause and effect

✓ сле́дстви|е², я *nt.* (law, *расследование*) investigation

✓ сле́д|ующий *pres. part. act. of* ▶ сле́довать¹ *and adj.* following, next; **на с. день** next day; **на ~ующей неде́ле** next week

сле́жк|а, и *f.* surveillance; shadowing

слез|а́, ы́, *pl.* ~ы, ~, ~а́м *f.* tear; **довести́ до ~ to reduce to tears**

слеза́|ть, ю *impf. of* ▶ слезть

слез|и́ться, и́тся *impf.* to water; **её глаза́ ~и́лись** her eyes were watering

слез|ть, у, ешь, *past* ~, ~ла *pf.* (*of* ▶ слеза́ть) (с + *g.*) **1** (*с дерева*) to come down (from), get down (from); (*с лошади, велосипеда*) to get off; to dismount (from) **2** (infml, *с автобуса, трамвая*) to get off **3** (infml, *о краске, коже*) to come off, peel

сленг, а *m.* slang

слеп|е́нь, ня́ *m.* gadfly, horsefly

слеп|е́ц, ца́ *m.* blind man

слеп|и́ть¹, лю́, и́шь *impf.* to blind; to dazzle

слеп|и́ть², лю́, ~и́шь *pf. of* ▶ лепи́ть 1

сле́п|нуть, ну, нешь, *past* ~, ~ла *impf.* (*of* ▶ осле́пнуть) to go blind

слеп|о́й, ~, ~а́, ~о *adj.* blind (also fig.); **с. на оди́н глаз** blind in one eye; (*as n.* **с.**, ~о́го, *f.* ~а́я, ~о́й) blind person; (*pl., collect.*) the blind

слепот|а́, ы́ *f.* blindness (also fig.)

сле́сар|ь, я *m.* metal worker; (*специалист по замка́м*) locksmith; (*специалист по почи́нке*) repair man

слета́|ть¹, ю *pf.* to fly (*there and back*)

слета́|ть², ю *impf. of* ▶ слете́ть

слета́|ться, а́юсь *impf. of* ▶ слете́ться

сле|те́ть, чу́, ти́шь *pf.* (*of* ▶ слета́ть²) (с + *g.*) **1** (*вниз*) to fly down (from) **2** (infml, *упасть*) to fall down, fall off; **с. с ло́шади** to fall from a horse **3** (*улететь*) to fly away

слет|е́ться, и́тся *pf.* (*of* ▶ слета́ться) to fly together; (*о птицах*) to congregate

слечь, сля́гу, сля́жешь, *past* слёг, слегла́ *pf.* to take to one's bed

сли́в|а, ы *f.* **1** (*плод*) plum **2** (*дерево*) plum tree

слива́|ть, ю *impf. of* ▶ слить

слива́|ться, юсь *impf. of* ▶ сли́ться

сли́в|ки, ок (*no sg.*) cream (also fig.)

сли́воч|ный *adj.* cream; creamy; **~ое ма́сло** butter

сли|за́ть, жу́, ~жешь *pf.* (*of* ▶ сли́зывать) to lick off

сли́зист|ый, ~, ~а *adj.* **1** slimy **2** (anat.) mucous

слизня́к, а́ *m.* slug

сли́зыва|ть, ю *impf. of* ▶ слиза́ть

слиз|ь, и *f.* **1** slime **2** (anat.) mucus

слип|а́ться, а́ется *impf. of* ▶ сли́пнуться

сли́п|нуться, нется, *past* ~ся, ~лась *pf.* (*of* ▶ слипа́ться) to stick together

сли́тный *adj.* united, continuous

✓ key word

сли́т|ок, ка *m.* ingot, bar; **зо́лото в ~ках** gold bullion

слить, солью́, сольёшь, *past* **слил, слила́, сли́ло** *pf.* (*of* ▶ **слива́ть**) **1** (*вы́лить*) to pour out; (*отли́ть*) to pour off **2** (*вме́сте*) to pour together; (*fig.*) to merge, amalgamate

сли́ться, солью́сь, сольёшься, *past* **сли́лся, слила́сь** *pf.* (*of* ▶ **слива́ться**) **1** (*о ручья́х*) to flow together **2** (*fig.*) (*о голоса́х*) to blend, mingle; (*о конце́рнах*) to merge, amalgamate

слича́|ть, а́ю *impf. of* ▶ **сличи́ть**

сличи́|ть, у́, и́шь *pf.* (*of* ▶ **слича́ть**) (**с** + *i.*) to check (with, against)

сли́шком *adv.* too; (*перед глаго́лами*) too much; **э́то с.!** this is too much!

слия́ни|е, я *nt.* **1** (*рек*) confluence **2** (*fig.*) (*голосо́в*) blending; merging; (*конце́рнов*) amalgamation, merger

словак, а *m.* Slovak

Слова́ки|я, и *f.* Slovakia

слова́р|ь, я́ *m.* **1** (*кни́га*) dictionary; (*глосса́рий*) glossary, vocabulary (*to particular text*) **2** (*collect.*) (*запа́с слов*) vocabulary

слова́цкий *adj.* Slovak, Slovakian

слова́ч|ка, ки *f. of* ▶ **слова́к**

слове́н|ец, ца *m.* Slovene

Слове́ни|я, и *f.* Slovenia

слове́н|ка, ки *f. of* ▶ **слове́нец**

слове́нский *adj.* Slovene, Slovenian

слове́сный *adj.* verbal, oral

сло́вно *conj.* **1** (*как бу́дто*) as if **2** (*как*) like, as

сло́в|о, а, *pl.* **~а́** *nt.* **1** word; **други́ми ~а́ми** in other words; **одни́м ~ом** in a word; **на ~а́х** (*у́стно*) by word of mouth; (*то́лько в разгово́ре*) empty words; **сдержа́ть с.** to keep one's word **2** (*речь*) speech, speaking; **свобо́да ~а** freedom of speech **3** (*выступле́ние*) speech, address; **дать, предоста́вить с.** (+ *d.*) to give the floor, call upon to speak

словоблу́ди|е, я *nt.* (mere) verbiage, phrase-mongering

сло́вом *adv.* in a word, in short

словоохо́тлив|ый, ~, ~а *adj.* talkative, loquacious

словосочета́ни|е, я *nt.* combination of words

слог, а, *pl.* **~и́, ~о́в** *m.* syllable

сло́ган, а *m.* slogan

слоёный *adj.*: **~ое те́сто** puff pastry

сложе́ни|е, я *nt.* (*чи́сел*) adding; (math.) addition

сложи́|ть¹, у́, ~ишь *pf.* (*of* ▶ **скла́дывать**) **1** (*положи́ть вме́сте*) to put (together); (*в ку́чу*) to pile, stack; **с. свои́ ве́щи в чемода́н** to pack one's things in a suitcase **2** (*чи́сла*) to add (up) **3** (*лист, пла́тье*) to fold (up) **4** *pf. of* ▶ **класть 2**

сложи́|ть², у́, ~ишь *pf.* **1** (*impf.* **скла́дывать**) (*сня́в, положи́ть*) to take

off, put down, set down **2** (*impf.* **слага́ть**) (**с** + *g.*) (fig.) to relieve oneself (of); **с. ору́жие** to lay down one's arms; **с. с себя́ обя́занности** to resign

сложи́|ться¹, у́сь, ~ишься *pf.* (*of* ▶ **скла́дываться**) (**с** + *i.*) to club together (with); to pool one's resources

сложи́|ться², ~ится *pf.* (*of* ▶ **скла́дываться**) (*о хара́ктере; об убежде́нии*) to form; (*об обстоя́тельствах*) to turn out; (*о ситуа́ции*) to arise

сло́жно *as pred.* it is difficult; **мне с.** I find it difficult

сло́жност|ь, и *f.* complication; complexity

сло́ж|ный, ~ен, ~на́, ~но, ~ны́ *adj.* **1** (*составно́й*) compound; complex **2** (*тру́дный*) complicated, complex; (*узо́р, компози́ция*) intricate

сло|й, я, *pl.* **~и́** *m.* layer; stratum (also fig.); **все ~и́ населе́ния** all sections of the population

сло́йк|а, и *f.* (*бу́лочка*) puff

слома́|ть, ю *pf. of* ▶ **лома́ть**

слома́|ться, юсь *pf. of* ▶ **лома́ться**

сломи́|ть, лю́, ~ишь *pf.* to break, smash; (fig.) to overcome; **~я́ го́лову** (infml) like mad, at breakneck speed

слон, а́ *m.* **1** elephant **2** (*в ша́хматах*) bishop (chess)

слоня́|ться, юсь *impf.* (infml) to loiter about, mooch about (BrE)

слуг|а́, и́, *pl.* **~и, ~** *m.* servant

служа́нк|а, и *f.* maid

слу́жащий, его *m.* office worker, white-collar worker

слу́жб|а, ы *f.* **1** service; (*рабо́та*) work; employment; **быть на ~е у кого́-н.** to work for sb **2** (*специа́льная о́бласть рабо́ты*) (special) service **3** (eccl., *богослуже́ние*) church service

служе́бн|ый *adj.* **1** *adj. of* ▶ **слу́жба**; office; official; work; **с. автомоби́ль** company car; **~ое вре́мя** office hours; **~ая пое́здка** business trip **2** (*вспомога́тельный*) auxiliary; secondary

служи́|ть, у́, ~ишь *impf.* (*of* ▶ **послужи́ть**) **1** (+ *d.*) to serve, devote oneself (to) **2** (*no pf.*) (+ *i.*) (*рабо́тать*) to serve (as); to work (as), be employed (as), be; **с. в а́рмии** to serve in the army **3** (+ *i. or* для + *g.*) (*функциони́ровать*) to serve (for), do (for), be used (for); **гости́ная ~ит нам и спа́льней** our sitting room serves also as a bedroom; **с. доказа́тельством** (+ *g.*) to serve as evidence (of) **4** (*быть поле́зным*) to be in use, do duty, serve; **мой ста́рый плащ ещё ~ит** my old mac(k)intosh is still in use **5** (*pf.* от**~**) (eccl.) to celebrate; to conduct, officiate (at); **с. обе́дню** to celebrate mass

слух, а *m.* **1** hearing; (mus.) ear; **игра́ть на с., по ~у** to play by ear **2** (*изве́стие*) rumour (BrE), rumor (AmE); **прошёл с., что** it was rumoured (BrE), rumored (AmE) that

слухово́й *adj.* auditory, aural; **с. аппара́т** hearing aid

слу́ча|й, я *m.* **1** case; **во вся́ком ~е** in any case, anyhow, anyway; **ни в ко́ем ~е** in no circumstances; **в лу́чшем, ху́дшем ~е** at best, at worst; **в проти́вном ~е** otherwise; **в тако́м ~е** in that case; **на вся́кий с.** to be on the safe side, just in case; **по ~ю** (+ *g.*) by reason (of), on account (of), on the occasion (of) **2** (*происше́ствие*) event, incident, occurrence; **несча́стный с.** accident **3** (*возмо́жность*) opportunity, occasion, chance; **упусти́ть удо́бный с.** to miss an opportunity; **при ~е** when an opportunity presents itself **4** (*случа́йность*) chance

случа́йно *adv.* **1** by chance, by accident, accidentally; **я с. подслу́шал их разгово́р** I happened to overhear their conversation **2** (*как вво́дное сло́во*) by any chance; **вы, с., не ви́дели моего́ зо́нтика?** have you by any chance seen my umbrella?

случа́йность|, и *f.* chance; **по счастли́вой ~и** by a lucky chance, by sheer luck

случа́|йный, ~ен, ~йна *adj.* **1** (*оши́бка*) accidental; (*встре́ча, разгово́р*) chance; (*гость, уда́ча*) unexpected **2** (*расхо́ды, поруче́ния*) incidental; **с. за́работок** casual earnings

ᵈ **случа́|ться, а́ется** *impf. of* ▶ **случи́ться**

ᵈ **случ|и́ться, и́тся** *pf.* (*of* ▶ **случа́ться**) to happen, come about; **что бы ни ~и́лось** whatever happens, come what may

слу́шани|е, я *nt.* (law) hearing

слу́шатель|, я *m.* **1** listener; (*pl.; collect.*) audience **2** (*студе́нт*) student

слу́шатель|ница, ницы *f. of* ▶ **слу́шатель**

ᵈ **слу́ша|ть, ю** *impf. of* ▶ **послу́шать**, ▶ **прослу́шать** 1) **1** (*му́зыку, ра́дио*) to listen (to); **с. ле́кцию** to attend a lecture; **~й(те)!** (infml) listen!, look here!; **~ю!** at your service!; very good!; (*по телефо́ну*) hello! **2** (*изуча́ть*) to attend lectures (on), go to lectures (on) **3** (*слу́шаться*) to listen (to), obey **4** (law) to hear

слу́ша|ться, юсь *impf.* (*of* ▶ **послу́шаться**) to listen (to), obey; **~юсь!** (mil.) yes, sir! (*indicating readiness to carry out order*)

ᵈ **слы́ш|ать, у, ишь** *impf.* (*of* ▶ **услы́шать**) **1** to hear; **~ишь?, ~ите?** (infml) do you hear? (*emph. command or direction*) **2** (*impf. only*) (*облада́ть слу́хом*) to have the sense of hearing; **не с.** to be hard of hearing

слы́ш|аться, ится *impf.* (*of* ▶ **послы́шаться**) to be heard; to be audible

слы́шно *as pred.* (*impers.*) **1** one can hear; **бы́ло с., как она́ рыда́ла** one could hear her sobbing **2** (infml): **что с.?** what news?, any news?; **о них ничего́ не с.** nothing has been heard of them

слы́ш|ный, ~ен, ~на́, ~но, ~ны́ *adj.* audible

слюд|а́, ы́ *f.* mica

слюн|а́, ы́ *f.* saliva

ᵈ key word

слю́н|и, е́й (*no sg.*) (infml) slobber, spittle; **пусти́ть с.** to dribble

сля́кот|ь, и *f.* slush

ᵈ **см** (*abbr. of* **сантиме́тр**) cm, centimetre(s) (BrE), centimeter(s) (AmE)

см. (*abbr. of* **смотри́**) see (*vide*)

сма́|зать, жу, жешь *pf.* (*of* ▶ **сма́зывать**) **1** to lubricate; to grease; **с. йо́дом** to paint with iodine **2** (*размаза́ть*) to smudge; (*стере́ть*) to rub off **3** (fig., infml, *лиши́ть чёткости*) to slur (over)

сма́зк|а, и *f.* **1** (*де́йствие*) lubrication; greasing **2** (*вещество́*) lubricant; grease

сма́зыва|ть, ю *impf. of* ▶ **сма́зать**

ᵈ **сма́йл** and **сма́йлик** *a m.* (*изображе́ние*) smiley

смак|ова́ть, у́ю *impf.* (infml) to savour (BrE), savor (AmE); to relish (also fig.)

сманеври́р|овать, ую *pf. of* ▶ **маневри́ровать**

смартфо́н, а *m.* smartphone

сма́тыва|ть, ю *impf. of* ▶ **смота́ть**

сма́тыва|ться, юсь *impf. of* ▶ **смота́ться**

сма́хива|ть¹, ю *impf. of* ▶ **смахну́ть**

сма́хива|ть², ю (на + *a.*) (infml) to look like, resemble

смах|ну́ть, ну́, нёшь *pf.* (*of* ▶ **сма́хивать¹**) to brush (away, off), flick (away, off); **с. пыль** (с + *g.*) to dust

сма́чива|ть, ю *impf. of* ▶ **смочи́ть**

сме́ж|ный, ~ен, ~на *adj.* (*ко́мнаты, уча́стки*) adjacent, adjoining; (*профе́ссии, поня́тия*) related

смека́лк|а, и *f.* (infml) native wit; nous; sharpness

смек|а́ть, а́ю *impf.* (*of* ▶ **смекну́ть**) (infml) to see the point (of), grasp

смек|ну́ть, ну́, нёшь *pf. of* ▶ **смека́ть**

сме́ло *adv.* **1** boldly **2** (*с по́лной уве́ренностью*) confidently; **я могу́ с. сказа́ть** I can safely say

сме́лост|ь, и *f.* boldness, audacity; **взять на себя́ с.** (+ *inf.*) to take the liberty (of doing sth); to make so bold (as to do sth)

сме́л|ый, ~, ~а́, ~о, ~ы́ *adj.* bold, audacious, daring

ᵈ **сме́н|а, ы** *f.* **1** (*де́йствие*) changing, change; (*заме́на*) replacement; **с. карау́ла** changing of the guard **2** (*collect.*) replacements; successors; (mil.) relief **3** (*на заво́де*) shift; **у́тренняя, дневна́я, вече́рняя с.** morning, day, night shift **4** (*белья́*) change

смен|и́ть, ю́, ~ишь *pf.* (*of* ▶ **сменя́ть**) **1** to change; (*рабо́тника*) to replace; (mil.) to relieve; **с. бельё** to change linen **2** (*замести́ть*) to replace, relieve, succeed (sb)

смен|и́ться, ю́сь, ~ишься *pf.* (*of* ▶ **сменя́ться**) **1** to hand over; (mil.) to be relieved; **с. с дежу́рства** to go off duty **2** (+ *i.*) to give way (to); **дневно́й зно́й ~и́лся прохла́дой ве́чера** the day's heat gave way to the coolness of evening

сме́нн|ый *adj.* shift; ~ая рабо́та shift work

сменя́|ть, я́ю *impf. of* ▸ смени́ть

сменя́|ться, я́юсь *impf. of* ▸ смени́ться

сме́р|ить, ю, ишь *pf. of* ▸ ме́рить 1

смерк|а́ться, а́ется *impf. (of* ▸ сме́ркнуться) to get dark; ~а́лось it was getting dark, twilight was falling

сме́рк|нуться, нется *pf. of* ▸ смерка́ться

смерте́льно *adv.* **1** mortally; с. ра́ненный mortally wounded **2** (infml, *очень*) extremely, terribly

смерте́л|ьный, ~ен, ~ьна *adj.* **1** (*борьба, враг*) mortal, deadly **2** (infml, fig., *сильный, крайний*) deadly, extreme

сме́ртность, и *f.* mortality, death rate

сме́рт|ный, ~ен, ~на *adj.* **1** mortal; (*as m. n. с., ~ного*) mortal; просто́й с. ordinary mortal **2** deadly, death; ~ная казнь capital punishment, death penalty; с. пригово́р death sentence

смертоно́с|ный, ~ен, ~на *adj.* mortal, fatal, lethal

смерт|ь, и, *pl.* ~и, ~е́й *f.* death; умере́ть свое́й ~ью to die a natural death; до ~и (fig., infml) to death; быть при ~и to be dying

смерч, а *m.* tornado, whirlwind

смеси́тел|ь, я *m.* mixer; (*кран*) mixer tap (BrE), mixing faucet (AmE)

сме|сти́, ту́, тёшь, *past* ~л, ~ла́ *pf. (of* ▸ смета́ть) **1** to sweep off, sweep away; с. кро́шки со стола́ to sweep crumbs off the table **2** (*метя, собрать*) to sweep into, together

сме|сти́ть, щу́, сти́шь *pf. (of* ▸ смеща́ть) **1** to displace, remove; to shift, move **2** (fig., *уволить*) to remove, dismiss

сме|сти́ться, щу́сь, сти́шься *pf. (of* ▸ смеща́ться) to change position, become displaced

смес|ь, и *f.* mixture; (*продукт*) blend

смета́н|а, ы *f.* sour cream

смета́|ть, ю *pf. of* ▸ смести́

сме|ть, ю *impf. (of* ▸ посме́ть) to dare; to make bold; не ~й(те)! don't you dare!

смех, а (у) *m.* laughter; laugh

смехотво́р|ный, ~ен, ~на *adj.* laughable, ludicrous

смеш|а́ть, а́ю *pf. (of* ▸ меша́ть² 2, ▸ меша́ть² 3, ▸ сме́шивать) **1** (с + *i.*) (*соединить*) to mix (with), blend (with) **2** (*перепутать, путать*) to mix up

смеш|а́ться, а́юсь *pf. (of* ▸ сме́шиваться) **1** (*о красках*) to mix, blend; to mingle; с. с толпо́й to mingle in the crowd **2** (*прийти в беспорядок; перепутаться*) to become confused, get mixed up

сме́шива|ть, ю *impf. of* ▸ смеша́ть

сме́шива|ться, юсь *impf. of* ▸ смеша́ться

смеш|и́ть, у́, и́шь *impf. (of* ▸ насмеши́ть) to make (sb) laugh

смеш|но́й, ~о́н, ~на́ *adj.* **1** funny; (*as pred.*) ~но́ it is funny; вам ~но́? do you find it funny? **2** (*нелепый*) absurd, ridiculous, ludicrous

смеш|о́к, ка́ *m.* (infml) chuckle; giggle

смеща́|ть, ю *impf. of* ▸ смести́ть

смеща́|ться, юсь *impf. of* ▸ смести́ться

смеще́ни|е, я *nt.* **1** displacement; shift, removal **2** (*увольнение*) dismissal

сме|я́ться, ю́сь, ёшься *impf.* **1** to laugh; с. шу́тке to laugh at a joke **2** (над + *i.*) to laugh (at), mock, make fun (of) **3** (infml, *говорить в шутку*) to joke, say in jest

⚐ **СМИ** *pl. indecl.* (*abbr. of* сре́дства ма́ссовой информа́ции) mass media

смире́ни|е, я *nt.* humbleness, humility, meekness

смир|и́ться, ю́сь, и́шься *pf. (of* ▸ смиря́ться) to submit; to resign oneself

сми́р|ный, ~ен, ~на́, ~но *adj.* quiet; submissive

смиря́|ться, я́юсь *impf. of* ▸ смири́ться

смо́кинг, а *m.* dinner jacket

смол|а́, ы́, *pl.* ~ы *f.* resin; (*дёготь*) pitch, tar

смоли́ст|ый, ~, ~а *adj.* resinous

смолк|а́ть, а́ю *impf. of* ▸ смо́лкнуть

смо́лк|нуть, ну, нешь, *past* ~, ~ла *pf. (of* ▸ смолка́ть) (*о голосе, о человеке*) to fall silent; (*о шуме*) to cease

смоло́ть, смелю́, сме́лешь *pf. of* ▸ моло́ть

смолч|а́ть, у́, и́шь *pf.* to hold one's tongue

смонти́р|овать, ую *pf. of* ▸ монти́ровать

сморка́|ть, ю *impf. (of* ▸ вы́сморкать): с. нос to blow one's nose

сморка́|ться, юсь *impf. (of* ▸ вы́сморкаться) to blow one's nose

сморо́дин|а, ы (*no pl.*) *f.* **1** (*кустарник*) currant bush **2** (collect.) (*ягоды*) currants; бе́лая, кра́сная, чёрная с. white currants, redcurrants, blackcurrants

смо́рщен|ный, ~, ~а *adj.* wrinkled

смо́рщ|иться, усь, ишься *pf. of* ▸ мо́рщиться

смота́|ть, ю *pf. (of* ▸ сма́тывать) to wind, reel; (infml): с. у́дочки to take to one's heels, make off

смота́|ться, юсь *pf. (of* ▸ сма́тываться) (infml) **1** (*сходить*) to dash (there and back) **2** (*убраться*) to take to one's heels, make off

⚐ **смотр|е́ть, ю́, ~ишь** *impf. (of* ▸ посмотре́ть) **1** (на + *a.* or в + *a.*) to look (at); с. в окно́ to look out of the window; с. в глаза́, в лицо́ (+ *d.*) to look in the face **2** (*фильм, пьесу*) to see; (*фильм, телевидение*) to watch; (*книгу, журнал*) to look through **3** (за + *i.*) to look (after); to be in charge (of), supervise **4**: ~я́ где, как, *и т. n.* it depends (where, how, *etc.*); ~я́ (по + *d.*) depending (on), in accordance (with)

смотр|е́ться, ю́сь, ~ишься *impf. (of* ▸ посмотре́ться) **1** to look at oneself; с. в зе́ркало to look at oneself in the mirror **2** (*no pf.*) (infml, *хорошо выглядеть*) to look good

смоч|и́ть, у́, ~ишь *pf. (of* ▸ сма́чивать) to damp, wet, moisten

⚹ **смо|чь, гу́, ~жешь**, *past* ~г, ~гла́ *pf. of* ▶ **мочь**

смоше́нничаль, ю *pf. of* ▶ **моше́нничать**

смрад, а *m.* stink, stench

сму́гл|ый, ~, ~а́, ~о, ~ы *adj.* swarthy

сму|ти́ть, щу́, ти́шь (*of* ▶ **смуща́ть**) to embarrass, confuse

сму|ти́ться, щу́сь, ти́шься *pf.* (*of* ▶ **смуща́ться**) to be embarrassed, be confused

сму́т|ный, ~ен, ~на́, ~но *adj.* vague; confused; ~ные воспомина́ния dim recollections

смуща́|ть, ю *impf. of* ▶ **смути́ть**

смуща́|ться, юсь *impf. of* ▶ **смути́ться**

смуще́ни|е, я *nt.* embarrassment, confusion

смыва́|ть, ю *impf. of* ▶ **смыть**

смыва́|ться, юсь *impf. of* ▶ **смы́ться**

смыка́|ть, ю, ет *impf. of* ▶ **сомкну́ть**

смыка́|ться, ется *impf. of* ▶ **сомкну́ться**

⚹ **смысл, а** *m.* **1** sense, meaning; прямо́й, переносный с. literal, metaphorical sense; в изве́стном ~е in a sense; в ~е (+ *g.*) as regards **2** (*цель, разумное основание*) sense, point; име́ть с. to make sense; нет никако́го ~а (+ *inf.*) there is no sense (in), there is no point (in) **3** (*разум*) (good) sense; здра́вый с. common sense

смыслов|о́й *adj. of* ▶ **смысл**; ~ые отте́нки shades of meaning

смы|ть, смо́ю, смо́ешь *pf.* (*of* ▶ **смыва́ть**) **1** (*удалить*) to wash off; (fig., *позор*) to clear, wipe out **2** (*снести*) to wash away **3** (*туалет*) to flush

смы́|ться, смо́юсь, смо́ешься *pf.* (*of* ▶ **смыва́ться**) **1** to wash off, come off **2** (fig., infml, *уйти*) to slip away

смыч|о́к, ка́ *m.* (mus.) bow

смягча́|ть, а́ю *impf. of* ▶ **смягчи́ть**

смягча́|ться, а́юсь *impf. of* ▶ **смягчи́ться**

смягч|и́ть, у́, и́шь *pf.* (*of* ▶ **смягча́ть**) **1** (*кожу, тон*) to soften **2** (*боль*) to ease, alleviate; (*наказание*) to mitigate

смягч|и́ться, у́сь, и́шься *pf.* (*of* ▶ **смягча́ться**) **1** (*о коже, тоне, взгляде*) to soften, become softer **2** (*о человеке*) to be mollified; (*о боли, ветре, холоде, ситуации*) to ease (off)

смяте́ни|е, я *nt.* confusion, disarray; commotion

смять, сомну́, сомнёшь *pf.* (*of* ▶ **мять 2**) to crumple; to rumple; с. пла́тье to crush a dress

смя́ться, сомнётся *pf.* (*of* ▶ **мя́ться**) to get creased; to get crumpled

снаб|ди́ть, жу́, ди́шь *pf.* (*of* ▶ **снабжа́ть**) (+ *i.*) to supply (with), furnish (with), provide (with)

снабжа́|ть, ю *impf. of* ▶ **снабди́ть**

снабже́ни|е, я *nt.* supply, supplying, provision

сна́йпер, а *m.* sniper

снару́жи *adv.* on the outside; from (the) outside

снаря́д, а *m.* **1** (mil.) projectile, missile; shell **2** (*прибор*) contrivance, machine, gadget; гимнасти́ческие ~ы gymnastic apparatus

снаря|ди́ть, жу́, ди́шь *pf.* (*of* ▶ **снаряжа́ть**) to equip, fit out

снаря|ди́ться, жу́сь, ди́шься *pf.* (*of* ▶ **снаряжа́ться**) to equip oneself, get ready

снаряжа́|ть, ю *impf. of* ▶ **снаряди́ть**

снаряжа́|ться, юсь *impf. of* ▶ **снаряди́ться**

снаряже́ни|е, я *nt.* equipment, outfit; ко́нское с. harness

снаст|ь, и, *pl.* ~и, ~е́й *f.* **1** (collect.) tackle, gear **2** (*usu. in pl.*) (*на судне*) rigging

⚹ **снача́ла** *adv.* **1** (*прежде*) at first, at the beginning **2** (*снова*) all over again

сна́шива|ть, ю *impf. of* ▶ **сноси́ть¹**

СНГ *nt. indecl.* (abbr. of **Содру́жество Незави́симых Госуда́рств**) CIS (*Commonwealth of Independent States*)

⚹ **снег, а, о ~е, в/на ~у́**, *pl.* ~á *m.* snow; идёт с. it's snowing; мо́крый с. sleet

снеги́р|ь, я́ *m.* bullfinch

снегоочисти́тельн|ый *adj.*: ~ая маши́на snowplough (BrE), snowplow (AmE)

снегопа́д, а *m.* snowfall

снегохо́д, а *m.* snowmobile

снежи́нк|а, и *f.* snowflake

сне́жн|ый *adj.* snow; snowy; ~ая ба́ба snowman; с. зано́с, с. сугро́б snowdrift; ~ая зима́ snowy winter

снеж|о́к, ка́ *m.* **1** light snow **2** (*комок*) snowball; игра́ть в ~ки́ to have a snowball fight

снес|ти́¹, у́, ёшь, *past* ~, ~ла́ *pf.* (*of* ▶ **сноси́ть³**) **1** (*вниз*) to fetch down, bring down **2** (*usu. impers.*) (*о воде*) to carry away; (*о ветре*) to blow off, take off **3** (*разрушить*) to demolish, pull down **4** (*срезать*) to cut off, chop off; с. го́лову кому́-н. to chop sb's head off

снес|ти́², у́, ёшь *pf.* (*of* ▶ **нести́²**) to lay (eggs)

⚹ **снижа́|ть, ю** *impf. of* ▶ **сни́зить**

снижа́|ться, юсь *impf. of* ▶ **сни́зиться**

⚹ **сниже́ни|е, я** *nt.* **1** lowering, reduction; с. зарпла́ты wage cut **2** (aeron.) descent

сни́|зить, жу, зишь *pf.* (*of* ▶ **снижа́ть**) **1** (*спустить ниже*) to bring down, lower **2** (*цены*) to bring down, lower, reduce

сни́|зиться, жусь, зишься *pf.* (*of* ▶ **снижа́ться**) **1** (*спуститься ниже*) to descend, come down **2** (*температура*) to fall, sink, come down

сни́зу *adv.* from below; from the bottom; с. вверх upwards; с. до́верху from top to bottom; (*внизу*) at, on the bottom

⚹ **снима́|ть, ю** *impf. of* ▶ **снять**

снима́|ться, юсь *impf. of* ▶ **сня́ться**

сни́м|ок, ка *m.* photograph, photo

снисходи́тельн|ый, ~ен, ~ьна *adj.* (*не строгий*) indulgent, tolerant, lenient

СНИ́|ТЬСЯ, снюсь, сни́шься *impf.* (*of* ▶ **присни́ться**) (+ *d.*) to dream; **ей ∼лось, что** she dreamed that; **мне ∼лся лев** I dreamed about a lion

СНОБ, а *m.* snob

СНОБИ́ЗМ, а *m.* snobbery

✶ **СНО́ВА** *adv.* again, anew, afresh

СНОВИДЕ́НИ|Е, я *nt.* dream

СНОРО́ВК|А, и *f.* skill, knack

СНОС, а *m.* demolition, pulling down; **дом предназна́чен на с.** the house is to be pulled down

СНО|СИ́ТЬ¹, шу́, ∼сишь *pf.* (*of* ▶ **сна́шивать**) to wear out

СНО|СИ́ТЬ², шу́, ∼сишь *pf.* (infml, *снести и принести́*) to take (*and bring back*)

СНО|СИ́ТЬ³, шу́, ∼сишь *impf. of* ▶ **снести́¹**

СНО́СК|А, и *f.* footnote

СНО́С|НЫЙ, ∼ен, ∼на *adj.* (infml) tolerable; fair, reasonable

СНОТВО́Р|НЫЙ *adj.* soporific (also fig.); **∼ное сре́дство** soporific; (*as nt. n.* **∼ное, ∼ного**) sleeping pill

СНОУБО́РД, а *m.* snowboard

СНОУБО́РДИНГ, а *m.* snowboarding

СНОХ|А́, и́, *pl.* **∼и** *f.* daughter-in-law

СНОШЕ́НИ|Е, я *nt.* (*usu. in pl.*) relations, dealings; (*половой акт*) (sexual) intercourse

СНЯ|ТЬ, сниму́, сни́мешь, *past* **∼л, ∼ла́, ∼ло** *pf.* (*of* ▶ **снима́ть**) **1** (*одежду, крышку,*) to take off; (*вниз*) to take down; **с. карти́ну** to take down a picture; **с. оса́ду** to raise a siege; **с. с себя́ отве́тственность** to decline responsibility **2** (*устранить, отменить*) to remove; to withdraw, cancel; **с. запре́т** to lift a ban; **с. с рабо́ты** to discharge, sack **3** (*изготовить*) to take, make; to photograph, make a photograph (of); **с. ко́пию** (**с** + *g.*) to copy, make a copy (of); **с. фильм** to shoot a film **4** (*взять внаём*) to take, rent (*a house, etc.*) **5** (sl., *девушку*) to pick up, pull

СНЯ|ТЬСЯ, сниму́сь, сни́мешься, *past* **∼лся, ∼ла́сь** *pf.* (*of* ▶ **снима́ться**) **1** (*отделиться*) to come off **2** (*отправиться*) to move off; **с. с я́коря** to weigh anchor; to get under way (also fig.) **3** (*фотографироваться*) to have one's photograph taken **4** (*сыграть роль в фильме*) to play a part in a film

✶ **СО** *prep.* = **с**

СО... *vbl. pref.* = **с...**

СОА́ВТОР, а *m.* co-author

✶ **СОБА́К|А, и** *f.* **1** dog; **охо́тничья с.** gun dog, hound; **с.-поводы́рь** guide dog; **служе́бная с.** guard dog; **уста́ть как с.** (infml) to be dog-tired **2** (comput.) **@** sign (*as used in email addresses, where it is pronounced 'at'*)

СОБА́|ЧИЙ *adj. of* ▶ **соба́ка**; canine; **∼чья жизнь** dog's life; **с. хо́лод** intense cold

СОБЕСЕ́ДНИК, а *m.* interlocutor; **он — забавный с.** he is amusing company

СОБЕСЕ́ДНИ|ЦА, цы *f. of* ▶ **собесе́дник**

СОБЕСЕ́ДОВАНИ|Е, я *nt.* conversation, discussion, interview

✶ **СОБИРА́|ТЬ, ю** *impf. of* ▶ **собра́ть**

✶ **СОБИРА́|ТЬСЯ, юсь** *impf.* **1** *impf. of* ▶ **собра́ться 2** (+ *inf.*) to intend (to), be about (to), be going (to)

СОБЛА́ЗН, а *m.* temptation

СОБЛАЗНИ́ТЕЛЬ|НЫЙ, ∼ен, ∼ьна *adj.* tempting; alluring; (*женщина*) seductive

СОБЛАЗН|И́ТЬ, ю́, и́шь *pf.* (*of* ▶ **соблазня́ть**) **1** (*прельстить*) to tempt **2** (*обольстить*) to seduce

СОБЛАЗН|Я́ТЬ, я́ю *impf. of* ▶ **соблазни́ть**

СОБЛЮДА́|ТЬ, ю *impf. of* ▶ **соблюсти́**

СОБЛЮ|СТИ́, ду́, дёшь, *past* **∼л, ∼ла́** *pf.* (*of* ▶ **соблюда́ть**) (*диету*) to keep (to), stick to; (*порядок*) to maintain; to observe; **с. зако́н** to observe a law; **с. сро́ки** to keep to schedule

СОБО́Й *see* ▶ **себя́**

СОБОЛЕ́ЗНОВАНИ|Е, я *nt.* sympathy; (*in pl.*) condolences

СОБОЛЕ́ЗН|ОВАТЬ, ую *impf.* (+ *d.*) to sympathize (with), commiserate (with)

СО́БОЛ|Ь, я, *pl.* (*furs*) **∼я́, ∼е́й** *and* (*animals*) **∼и, ∼ей** *m.* sable

СОБО́Р, а *m.* **1** (hist., also eccl.) (*съезд*) council, synod, assembly; **вселе́нский с.** ecumenical council **2** (*церковь*) cathedral

СОБО́Ю = **собо́й** *see* ▶ **себя́**

✶ **СОБРА́НИ|Е, я** *nt.* **1** (*заседание*) meeting, gathering; **о́бщее с.** general meeting **2** (*государственный орган*) assembly; **учреди́тельное с.** constituent assembly **3** (*коллекция*) collection; **с. сочине́ний** collected works

СО́БРАННЫЙ *p.p.p. of* ▶ **собра́ть** *and adj.*: **с. челове́к** self-disciplined person

СОБР|А́ТЬ, соберу́, соберёшь, *past* **∼а́л, ∼ала́, ∼а́ло** *pf.* (*of* ▶ **собира́ть**) **1** (*сведения*) to gather; (*книги, деньги*) to collect; (*цветы*) to pick **2** (*людей*) to assemble, muster; to convene; **с. после́дние си́лы** to make a last effort **3** (tech., *радиоприёмник*) to assemble

СОБР|А́ТЬСЯ, соберу́сь, соберёшься, *past* **∼а́лся, ∼ала́сь, ∼а́ло́сь** *pf.* (*of* ▶ **собира́ться**) **1** (*сойтись*) to gather, assemble **2** (**в** + *a.*) (*приготовиться*) to prepare (for); **с. в го́сти** to get ready to go away (*to visit sb*) **3** (+ *inf.*) (*решить*) to intend (to), be about (to), be going (to) **4** (**с** + *i.*) (fig., *сосредоточиться*) to collect; **с. с си́лами** to summon up one's strength

СО́БСТВЕННИК, а *m.* owner, proprietor; **земе́льный с.** landowner

СО́БСТВЕННИ|ЦА, цы *f. of* ▶ **со́бственник**

✶ **СО́БСТВЕННО** *adv.* actually; **с. говоря́** strictly speaking, as a matter of fact

СО́БСТВЕННОРУ́ЧНО *adv.* with one's own hand

✶ **СО́БСТВЕННОСТ|Ь, и** *f.* **1** (*имущество*) property **2** (*владение*) possession, ownership; **приобрести́ в с.** to become the owner (of)

✧ **со́бственн|ый** *adj.* (one's) own; **~ыми глаза́ми** with one's own eyes; **чу́вство ~ого досто́инства** self-respect; **~ой персо́ной** in person; **и́мя ~ое** (*gram.*) proper noun

✧ **собы́ти|е, я** *nt.* event; **теку́щие ~я** current affairs

сов|а́, ы́, *pl.* **~ы** *f.* owl; (*fig.*) night owl

сова́ть, сую́, суёшь *impf.* (*of* ▸ **су́нуть**) to shove, thrust, poke; **с. ру́ки в карма́ны** to stick one's hands in one's pockets; **с. нос** (**в** + *a.*) (*infml*) to poke one's nose (into), pry (into)

сова́ться, сую́сь, суёшься *impf.* (*of* ▸ **су́нуться**) (*infml*) **1** to push, strain **2** (**в** + *a.*) (*fig., в чужи́е дела́*) to butt (in); (*с сове́тами*) to poke one's nose (into)

✧ **соверш|а́ть, а́ю, а́ет** *impf. of* ▸ **соверши́ть**

соверш|а́ться, а́ется *impf. of* ▸ **соверши́ться**

✧ **соверше́нно** *adv.* **1** (*превосхо́дно*) perfectly **2** (*совсе́м*) absolutely, utterly, completely; **с. ве́рно!** quite right!; perfectly true!

совершенноле́ти|е, я *nt.* majority; **дости́гнуть ~я** to come of age, attain one's majority

совершенноле́тний *adj.* of age

соверше́н|ный, ~ен, ~на *adj.* **1** (*превосхо́дный*) perfect **2** (*infml, по́лный*) absolute, complete

соверше́нств|о, а *nt.* perfection; **в ~е** perfectly, to perfection

соверше́нств|овать, ую *impf.* (*of* ▸ **усоверше́нствовать**) to perfect; to develop, improve

соверше́нств|оваться, уюсь *impf.* (*of* ▸ **усоверше́нствоваться**) (**в** + *p.*) to perfect oneself (in); to improve

✧ **соверш|и́ть, у́, и́шь** *pf.* (*of* ▸ **соверша́ть**) **1** (*по́двиг*) to accomplish, carry out; to perform; (*преступле́ние*) to commit **2** (*заключи́ть*) to complete, conclude; **с. сде́лку** to complete a transaction, make a deal

соверш|и́ться, и́тся *pf.* (*of* ▸ **соверша́ться**) (*liter.*) **1** (*о собы́тии*) to happen **2** (*о по́двиге*) to be accomplished; (*о сде́лке*) to be completed

со́вестлив|ый, ~, ~а *adj.* conscientious

со́вест|ь, и *f.* conscience; **чи́стая, нечи́стая с.** clear, guilty conscience; **на ~и** on one's conscience; **со споко́йной ~ью** with a clear conscience

✧ **сове́т, а** *m.* **1** advice; **проси́ть ~а** to ask for advice **2** (*совме́стное обсужде́ние*) discussion; **с. войны́** council of war **3** (*hist., о́рган управле́ния в СССР*) soviet **4** (*администрати́вный о́рган*) council; **С. безопа́сности** Security Council

сове́тник, а *m.* adviser, counsellor

сове́т|овать, ую *impf.* (*of* ▸ **посове́товать**) (+ *d.*) to advise

сове́т|оваться, уюсь *impf.* (*of* ▸ **посове́товаться**) (**с** + *i.*) to consult, ask advice (of), seek advice (from)

✧ **сове́тск|ий** *adj.* (*hist.*) Soviet; **~ая власть** Soviet rule *or* power; **с. наро́д** the Soviet people

Сове́тск|ий Сою́з, ~ого Сою́за *m.* (*hist.*) the Soviet Union

совеща́ни|е, я *nt.* conference, meeting

совеща́|ться, юсь *impf.* **1** (**о** + *p.*) to deliberate (on, about) **2** (**с** + *i.*) to confer (with), consult

совлада́|ть, ю *pf.* (**с** + *i.*) (*infml*) to control; **с. с собо́й** to control oneself

совладе́л|ец, ьца *m.* joint owner

совладе́л|ица, ицы *f. of* ▸ **совладе́лец**

совмести́м|ый, ~, ~а *adj.* compatible

совме|сти́ть, щу́, сти́шь *pf.* (*of* ▸ **совмеща́ть**) to combine

совме́стно *adv.* in common, jointly

✧ **совме́стн|ый** *adj.* joint, combined; **~ые де́йствия** concerted action; **~ое предприя́тие** joint venture

совмеща́|ть, ю *impf. of* ▸ **совмести́ть**

сов|о́к, ка́ *m.* shovel, scoop; **с. для му́сора** dustpan

совокупле́ни|е, я *nt.* copulation

совоку́пност|ь, и *f.* aggregate, sum total; totality; **в ~и** in the aggregate

совпада́|ть, ю *impf. of* ▸ **совпа́сть**

совпаде́ни|е, я *nt.* coincidence

совпа́|сть, ду́, дёшь, *past* **~л** *pf.* (*of* ▸ **совпада́ть**) **1** (**с** + *i.*) (*произойти́ одновре́менно*) to coincide (with); **части́чно с.** to overlap **2** (*оказа́ться о́бщим*) to agree, tally; **их показа́ния не ~да́ли** their evidence did not tally

совра|ти́ть, щу́, ти́шь *pf.* (*of* ▸ **совраща́ть**) (*соблазни́ть*) to lead astray; (*же́нщину*) to seduce; (*ребёнка*) to (sexually) abuse

совр|а́ть, у́, ёшь, *past* **~а́л, ~ала́, ~а́ло** *pf. of* ▸ **врать**

совраща́|ть, ю *impf. of* ▸ **соврати́ть**

совраще́ни|е, я *nt.* corrupting; (*же́нщины*) seducing, seduction; (*ребёнка*) (sexual) abuse; **с. малоле́тних** child (sexual) abuse

совреме́нник, а *m.* contemporary

совреме́нни|ца, цы *f. of* ▸ **совреме́нник**

совреме́нност|ь, и *f.* **1** (*актуа́льность*) contemporaneity **2** (*совреме́нная эпо́ха*) the present (time)

✧ **совреме́н|ный, ~ен, ~на** *adj.* (*относя́щийся к настоя́щему вре́мени*) contemporary, present-day; (*челове́к*) modern; (*те́хника*) up-to-date, state-of-the-art; **~ная англи́йская литерату́ра** modern English literature

✧ **совсе́м** *adv.* quite, entirely, completely; **с. не** not at all, not in the least; **с. не то** nothing of the kind

согла́си|е, я *nt.* **1** (*разреше́ние*) consent; **с ва́шего ~я** with your consent **2** (*единомы́слие*) agreement; **в ~и** (**с** + *i.*)

с

in accordance (with); **прийти́ к ~ю** to come to an agreement **3** (*единоду́шие*) harmony

⚥ **согла|си́ться, шу́сь, си́шься** *pf.* (*of ▸ соглаша́ться*) **1** (**на** + *a.* or + *inf.*) to consent (to), agree (to) **2** (**с** + *i.*) to agree (with)

⚥ **согла́сно** *prep.* (+ *d.* or **с** + *i.*) in accordance (with); according (to); **с. догово́ру** in accordance with the treaty
  ● *adv.* (*жить, петь*) in harmony

согла́с|ный¹, ~ен, ~на *adj.* **1** (**на** + *a.*) agreeable (to); **они́ не́ были ~ны на на́ши усло́вия** they would not agree to our conditions **2** (**с** + *i.*) in agreement (with); **быть ~ным** to agree (with); **~ен, ~на, ~ны?** do you agree?

согла́с|ный², ~ого *adj.* (gram.) consonant(al); (*as m. n.* **с., ~ого**) consonant

соглас|ова́ть, у́ю *pf.* (*of ▸ согласо́вывать*) (**с** + *i.*) **1** to coordinate (with) **2**: **с. что-н. с кем-н.** to agree sth with sb, come to an agreement with sb about sth

согласо́outlet|ть, ю *impf. of ▸ согласова́ть*

соглаша́|ться, юсь *impf. of ▸ согласи́ться*

⚥ **соглаше́ни|е, я** *nt.* agreement; **заключи́ть с.** to conclude an agreement

согн|у́ть, у́, ёшь *pf.* (*of ▸ гнуть, ▸ сгиба́ть*) to bend, curve, crook

согн|у́ться, у́сь, ёшься *pf.* (*of ▸ гну́ться, ▸ сгиба́ться*) to bend, bow (down)

согрева́|ть, ю *impf. of ▸ согре́ть*

согрева́|ться, юсь *impf. of ▸ согре́ться*

согре́|ть, ю *pf.* (*of ▸ согрева́ть*) to warm, heat

согре́|ться, юсь *pf.* (*of ▸ согрева́ться*) to get warm; to warm oneself

согреш|и́ть, у́, и́шь *pf.* (*of ▸ греши́ть* 1) (**про́тив** + *g.*) to sin (against), trespass (against)

со́д|а, ы *f.* soda, sodium carbonate; **питьева́я с.** baking soda

соде́йстви|е, я *nt.* assistance, help

соде́йств|овать, ую *impf. and pf.* (+ *d.*) to assist; to further; to contribute (to)

⚥ **содержа́ни|е, я** *nt.* **1** (*семьи́*) maintenance, upkeep; (**де́нежное**) **с.** allowance, financial support; **с. под аре́стом** custody **2** (*зарпла́та*) pay **3** (*содержи́мое*) content; **с больши́м ~ем** (+ *g.*) rich (in) **4** (*су́щность*) substance; content; **фо́рма и с.** form and content **5** (*кни́ги*) content(s); (*рома́на*) plot **6** (*оглавле́ние*) table of contents

содержа́тель|ный, ~ен, ~ьна *adj.* rich in content

⚥ **содерж|а́ть, у́, ~ишь** *impf.* **1** (*семью́*) to keep, maintain, support **2** (*магази́н*) to keep, have **3** (**в** + *p.*) to keep (*in a given state*); **с. в поря́дке** to keep in order **4** (*име́ть в себе́*) to contain

содерж|а́ться, у́сь, ~ишься *impf.* **1** (*обеспе́чиваться*) to be kept, be maintained **2** (*находи́ться*) to be kept, be **3** (**в** + *p.*) (*заключа́ться*) to be contained (by); **в э́той руде́ ~ится ура́н** this ore contains uranium

содержи́м|ое, ого *nt.* contents

со́дов|ый *adj.* soda; **~ая (вода́)** soda (water)

содра́|ть, сдеру́, сдерёшь, past ~л, ~ла́, ~ло *pf.* (*of ▸ сдира́ть, ▸ драть* 2) to tear off, strip off; **с. ко́жу** (**с** + *g.*) to skin, flay

содрог|а́ться, а́юсь *impf. of ▸ содрогну́ться*

содрог|ну́ться, ну́сь, нёшься *pf.* (*of ▸ содрога́ться*) to shudder, shake, quake

содру́жеств|о, а *nt.* community, commonwealth; **Брита́нское С. на́ций** the British Commonwealth

⚥ **соедине́ни|е, я** *nt.* **1** joining, combination **2** (tech.) joint **3** (chem.) compound **4** (mil.) formation

Соединённое Короле́вство (Великобрита́нии и Се́верной Ирла́ндии), Соединённого Короле́вства (В. и С. И.) *nt.* United Kingdom (of Great Britain and Northern Ireland)

Соединённые Шта́ты (Аме́рики), Соединённых Шта́тов (Аме́рики) (*no sg.*) United States (of America)

соединённый *p.p.p. of ▸ соедини́ть and adj.* united, joint

соедин|и́ть, ю́, и́шь *pf.* (*of ▸ соединя́ть*) **1** (*объедини́ть*) to join, unite **2** (*присоедини́ть*) to connect, link; **с. (по телефо́ну)** to put through

соедин|и́ться, ю́сь, и́шься *pf.* (*of ▸ соединя́ться*) **1** to join, unite **2** (chem.) to combine **3** *pass. of ▸ соедини́ть*

соедин|я́ть, я́ю *impf. of ▸ соедини́ть*

соедин|я́ться, я́юсь *impf. of ▸ соедини́ться*

⚥ **сожале́ни|е, я** *nt.* **1** (**о** + *p.*) regret (for); **к ~ю** unfortunately **2** (**к** + *d.*) pity (for)

сожале́|ть, ю *impf.* (**о** + *p.* or **что**) to regret, deplore

сожи́тел|ь, я *m.* **1** (*по кварти́ре*) flatmate (BrE), room-mate (AmE) **2** (*любо́вник*) lover

сожи́тель|ница, ницы *f. of ▸ сожи́тель*

сожр|а́ть, у́, ёшь, past ~а́л, ~ала́, ~а́ло *pf. of ▸ жрать*

созва́нива|ться, юсь *impf. of ▸ созвони́ться*

созв|а́ть, созову́, созовёшь, past ~л, ~ла́, ~ло *pf.* (*of ▸ созыва́ть*) **1** (*госте́й*) to gather; to invite **2** (*люде́й на сове́т*) to call (together), summon; (*ми́тинг, парла́мент*) to convoke, convene

созве́зди|е, я *nt.* constellation

созвон|и́ться, ю́сь, и́шься *pf.* (*of ▸ созва́ниваться*) (**с** + *i.*) (infml) to speak on the telephone (to)

созву́ч|ный, ~ен, ~на *adj.* (+ *d.*) consonant (with), in keeping (with)

⚥ **созда|ва́ть, ю́, ёт** *impf. of ▸ созда́ть*

созда|ва́ться, ётся *impf. of ▸ созда́ться*

⚥ **созда́ни|е, я** *nt.* **1** (*де́йствие*) creation, making **2** (*произведе́ние*) creation, work

3 (*существо*) creature

созда́тел|ь, я *m.* **1** creator; (*организации*) founder; (*теории*) originator **2** (**С.**) (*Бог*) the Creator

созда́тель|ница, ницы *f. of* ▶ **созда́тель 1**

↙ **созда́|ть, м, шь, ст, ди́м, ди́те, ду́т**, *past* **со́здал, ∼на́, со́здало** *pf.* (*of* ▶ **создава́ть**) to create; (*организацию*) to found; (*теорию*) to originate; **с. впечатле́ние** to give the impression; **с. иллю́зию** to create an illusion

созда́|ться, стся, ду́тся, *past* **∼лся, ∼ла́сь, ∼ло́сь** *and* **со́лось** *pf.* (*of* ▶ **создава́ться**) to be created; to arise; **у нас созда́лось впечатле́ние, что** we gained the impression that

созерца́|ть, ю *impf.* to contemplate

созида́тел|ьный, ∼ен, ∼ьна *adj.* creative, constructive

созна|ва́ть, ю́, ёшь *impf.* **1** *impf. of* ▶ **созна́ть 2** to be conscious (of), realize; **я́сно с.** to be alive (to)

созна|ва́ться, ю́сь, ёшься *impf. of* ▶ **созна́ться**

↙ **созна́ни|е, я** *nt.* **1** consciousness; **потеря́ть с.** to lose consciousness; **прийти́ в с.** to regain, recover consciousness **2** (*ошибки, вины*) recognition, acknowledgement

созна́тел|ьный, ∼ен, ∼ьна *adj.* **1** conscious **2** (*отношение*) intelligent **3** (*намеренный*) deliberate

созна́|ть, ю *pf.* (*of* ▶ **сознава́ть 1**) to recognize, acknowledge

созна́|ться, юсь *pf.* (*of* ▶ **сознава́ться**) (**в** + *p.*) (*в ошибке*) to admit (to); (*в преступлении*) to confess (to); (*law*) to plead guilty

созрева́|ть, ю *impf. of* ▶ **созре́ть**

созре́|ть, ю *pf.* (*of* ▶ **зреть**, ▶ **созрева́ть**) (*о плоде*) to ripen; (*о человеке*) to mature; (*о плане*) to develop, mature

созыва́|ть, ю *impf. of* ▶ **созва́ть**

со|йти́, йду́, йдёшь, *past* **∼шёл, ∼шла́** *pf.* (*of* ▶ **сходи́ть¹**) **1** (*с лестницы, горы*) to go down, come down; (*с автобуса, поезда*) to get off; **с. на нет** to come to naught **2** (*покинуть, уйти*) to leave; **с. с доро́ги** to get out of the way, step aside; **с. с ре́льсов** to come off the rails; **с. с ума́** to go mad, go off one's head **3** (*о краске, о коже*) to come off

со|йти́сь, йду́сь, йдёшься, *past* **∼шёлся, ∼шла́сь** *pf.* (*of* ▶ **сходи́ться**) **1** (*встретиться*) to meet; to come together, gather **2** (**с** + *i.*) (*подружиться*) to meet, take up with, become friends (with); (*вступить в сожительство*) to become (*sexually*) intimate (with) **3** (+ *i. or* **в** + *i.*) (*быть похожим*) to be similar; **они́ не ∼шли́сь хара́ктерами** they could not get on; (**в** + *p. or* **на** + *p.*) (infml, *договориться*) to agree (about); **они́ ∼шли́сь в цене́** they

agreed on a price **4** (*совпасть*) to agree, tally; **счета́ не ∼шли́сь** the figures did not tally

сок, а (у), о ∼е, в ∼е *and* **∼у́** *m.* juice

соковыжима́лк|а, и *f.* juicer

со́кол, а *m.* falcon

сокра|ти́ть, щу́, ти́шь *pf.* (*of* ▶ **сокраща́ть**) **1** (*статью, путь, рабочий день*) to shorten **2** (*расходы, штаты*) to reduce, cut down **3** (*уволить*) (infml) to dismiss, discharge, lay off, make redundant

сокра|ти́ться, ти́тся *pf.* (*of* ▶ **сокраща́ться**) **1** (*о днях*) to grow shorter **2** (*о расходах*) to decrease **3** (*о мышцах*) to contract

сокраща́|ть, ю, ет *impf. of* ▶ **сократи́ть**

сокраща́|ться, ется *impf. of* ▶ **сократи́ться**

сокраще́ни|е, я *nt.* **1** (*рабочего дня*) shortening **2** (*статьи*) abridgement; **с ∼ями** abridged **3** (*слова*) abbreviation **4** (*штатов, вооружений*) reduction, cutting down

сокра|щённый *p.p.p. of* ▶ **сократи́ть** *and adj.* brief; **∼щённое сло́во** abbreviation, contraction

сокрове́н|ный, ∼, ∼на *adj.* secret, concealed; **∼ные мы́сли** innermost thoughts

сокро́вищ|е, а *nt.* treasure

сокруши́тел|ьный, ∼ен, ∼ьна *adj.* shattering; **нанести́ с. уда́р** (+ *d.*) to deal a crippling blow

со|лга́ть, лгу́, лжёшь, лгут, *past* **∼лга́л, ∼лгала́, ∼лга́ло** *pf. of* ▶ **лгать**

солда́т, а, *g. pl.* **∼** *m.* soldier

солда́тик, а *m.* **1** *dim. of* ▶ **солда́т 2** (*игрушка*) toy soldier; **игра́ть в ∼и** to play soldiers

солда́тский *adj. of* ▶ **солда́т**

солё|ный *adj.* **1** salt; **∼ое о́зеро** salt lake **2** (**со́лон, солона́, со́лоно**) (*суп*) salty **3** (*консервированный*) salted; pickled; **с. огуре́ц** pickled cucumber; (*as nt. n.* **∼ое, ∼оро**) salty food

солёнь|е, я *nt.* (*usu. in pl.*) salted food(s); pickles

солида́рност|ь, и *f.* solidarity; **из ∼и** (**с** + *i.*) in sympathy (with)

солида́р|ный, ∼ен, ∼на *adj.* (**с** + *i.*) at one (with), in sympathy (with)

соли́д|ный, ∼ен, ∼на *adj.* **1** (*прочный*) solid, strong, sound; **∼ные зна́ния** sound knowledge **2** (*серьёзный*) solid, sound; (*надёжный*) reliable, respectable; **с. челове́к** a solid man; (*о журнал*) respectable magazine **3** (infml, *значительный*) respectable, sizeable; **∼ная су́мма** tidy sum

соли́ст, а *m.* soloist

соли́ст|ка, ки *f. of* ▶ **соли́ст**

сол|и́ть, ю́, ∼и́шь *impf.* (*of* ▶ **посоли́ть**) **1** (*суп*) to salt **2** (*огурцы*) to pickle; **с. мя́со** to preserve meat in brine

↙ **со́лнечн|ый** *adj.* **1** sun; solar; **∼ое затме́ние** solar eclipse; **с. луч** sunbeam; **с. свет** sunlight, sunshine; **С∼ая систе́ма** solar system; **с. уда́р** (*med.*) sunstroke **2** (*день, пого́да*) sunny

☞ **со́лнц|е, а** *nt.* sun; **на с.** in the sun

солнцезащи́тн|ый *adj.*: **с. крем** suncream; **~ые очки́** sunglasses

со́ло 1 *adv.* solo **2** *n., nt. indecl.* solo

солов|е́й, ья́ *m.* nightingale

со́лод, а *m.* malt

соло́м|а, ы *f.* straw; (*для кры́ши*) thatch

соло́менн|ый *adj.* straw; **~ая кры́ша** thatch, thatched roof; **~ая шля́па** straw hat

соло́минк|а, и *f.* straw; **хвата́ться за ~у** to clutch at straws

солони́н|а, ы *f.* salted beef, corned beef

соло́нк|а, и *f.* salt cellar

сол|ь¹, и, *pl.* **~и, ~е́й** *f.* salt

соль² *nt. indecl.* (*mus.*) G; **с.-дие́з** G sharp; **ключ с.** treble clef

со́л|ьный *adj. of* ▶ **со́ло**; **с. но́мер** solo; **~ьная па́ртия** solo part

соля́нк|а, ~и *f.* solyanka (*a sharp-tasting Russian soup of vegetables and meat or fish*)

Сомали́ *nt. indecl.* Somalia

сомали́ *m. indecl.* Somali (*language*)

сомали́|ец, йца *m.* Somali (*person*)

сомали́й|ка, ки *f. of* ▶ **сомали́ец**

сомали́йский *adj.* Somali

сомкн|у́ть, у́, ёшь *pf.* (*of* ▶ **смыка́ть**) to close; **с. глаза́** to close one's eyes

сомкн|у́ться, ётся *pf.* (*of* ▶ **смыка́ться**) to close (up)

сомнева́|ться, юсь *impf.* **1** (**в** + *p.*) to doubt; to question; **я не ~юсь в его́ че́стности** I do not question his integrity **2** to worry; **мо́жете не с.** you need not worry

☞ **сомне́ни|е, я** *nt.* doubt; uncertainty; **без ~я, вне (вся́кого) ~я** without (any) doubt, beyond doubt

сомни́тел|ьный, ~ен, ~ьна *adj.* **1** (*непрове́ренный*) doubtful, questionable; **~ьно** it is doubtful, it is open to question **2** (*подозри́тельный*) dubious

☞ **сон, сна** *m.* **1** sleep; **во сне, сквозь с.** in one's sleep; **со сна** half awake **2** (*сновиде́ние*) dream; **ви́деть во сне** to dream, have a dream (about)

сона́т|а, ы *f.* (*mus.*) sonata

соне́т, а *m.* sonnet

со́нный *adj.* sleepy, drowsy (*also fig.*)

со́н|я, и *f. and c.g.* **1** *f.* (*грызу́н*) dormouse **2** *c.g.* (*infml, челове́к*) sleepyhead

сообража́|ть, ю *impf.* **1** *impf. of* ▶ **сообрази́ть 2** (*impf. only*): **хорошо́, пло́хо с.** to be quick, slow on the uptake

соображе́ни|е, я *nt.* (*причи́на*) consideration, reason; (*мысль*) notion, idea; **по фина́нсовым ~ям** for financial reasons; **вы́сказать свои́ ~я** to express one's views

сообрази́тел|ьный, ~ен, ~ьна *adj.* quick-witted, sharp, bright

сообра|зи́ть, жу́, зи́шь *pf.* (*of* ▶ **сообража́ть 1**) **1** (*взве́сить*) to consider, ponder; to weigh

(the pros and cons of) **2** (*поня́ть*) to understand, grasp

сообра́зно *adv.* (**с** + *i.*) in conformity (with)

сообща́ *adv.* together, jointly

☞ **сообща́|ть, а́ю, а́ет** *impf. of* ▶ **сообщи́ть**

☞ **сообща́|ться, а́ется** *impf. of* ▶ **сообщи́ться**

☞ **сообще́ни|е, я** *nt.* **1** (*изве́стие*) communication, report; **сро́чное** *or* **экстренное с.** news flash **2** (*связь*) communication; **прямо́е с.** through connection; **пути́ ~я** communications (*rail, road, canal, etc.*)

соо́бществ|о, а *nt.* (*междунаро́дное, мирово́е*) community

☞ **сообщ|и́ть, у́, и́шь** *pf.* (*of* ▶ **сообща́ть**) (+ *a.* or **о** + *p.*) (*уве́домить*) to communicate, report, inform, announce; **с. после́дние изве́стия** to report the latest news

сообщ|и́ться, и́тся *pf.* (*of* ▶ **сообща́ться**) to be communicated

соо́бщник, а *m.* accomplice; partner (*in crime*); (*law*) accessory

соо́бщни|ца, цы *f. of* ▶ **соо́бщник**

сооруди́ть, жу́, ди́шь *pf.* (*of* ▶ **сооружа́ть**) to build, erect

сооружа́|ть, ю *impf. of* ▶ **сооруди́ть**

☞ **сооруже́ни|е, я** *nt.* **1** (*де́йствие*) building, erection **2** (*постро́йка*) building, structure

☞ **соотве́тственно** *adv.* accordingly

☞ **соотве́тстви|е, я** *nt.* accordance, conformity, correspondence; **в ~и** (**с** + *i.*) in accordance (with)

☞ **соотве́тств|овать, ую** *impf.* (+ *d.*) to correspond (to, with), conform (to); **с. действи́тельности** to correspond to the facts; **с. тре́бованиям** to meet the requirements

☞ **соотве́тств|ующий** *pres. part. act. of* ▶ **соотве́тствовать** *and adj.* **1** (+ *d.*) corresponding (to) **2** (*подходя́щий*) proper, appropriate; **поступа́ть ~ующим о́бразом** to act accordingly

соотéчественник, а *m.* compatriot, fellow countryman

соотéчественни|ца, цы *f. of* ▶ **соотéчественник**

соотноше́ни|е, я *nt.* correlation, ratio; **с. сил** correlation of forces, alignment of forces

сопе́рник, а *m.* rival

сопе́рни|ца, цы *f. of* ▶ **сопе́рник**

сопе́рнича|ть, ю *impf.* to be rivals; (**с** + *i.*) to compete (with)

сопе́|ть, лю́, и́шь *impf.* to sniff (heavily and noisily)

сопли́в|ый, ~, ~а *adj.* (*infml*) snotty

сопл|о́, а́, *pl.* **~а, ~ел** *and* **~л** *nt.* nozzle

сопля́к, а́ *m.* (*infml, pej.*) milksop

сопоста́в|ить, лю, ишь *pf.* (*of* ▶ **сопоставля́ть**) (**с** + *i.*) to compare (with)

сопоставля́|ть, ю *impf. of* ▶ **сопоста́вить**

сопра́но *nt. indecl.* (*mus.*) soprano (*voice*); (*f. indecl.*) (*infml*) soprano (*singer*)

С

сопреде́л|ьный, ~ен, ~ьна *adj.*
neighbouring (BrE), neighboring (AmE);
contiguous

соприкаса́|ться, юсь *impf.* (*of*
▶ **соприкосну́ться**) (**с** + *i.*) to adjoin, be
contiguous (to)

соприкосн|у́ться, у́сь, ёшься *pf. of*
▶ **соприкаса́ться**

сопрово|ди́ть, жу́, ди́шь *pf. of*
▶ **сопровожда́ть**

сопровожда́|ть, ю *impf.* (*of*
▶ **сопроводи́ть**) to accompany

сопровожда́|ться, ется *impf.* (+ *i.*) to be
accompanied (by)

сопровожде́ни|е, я *nt.* **1** (*действие*)
accompanying, escort; **в ~и** (+ *g.*)
accompanied (by); escorted (by) **2** (*mus.*)
accompaniment; **звуково́е с.** soundtrack

сопротивле́ни|е, я *nt.* resistance,
opposition; (*phys., tech.*) strength; (*elec.*)
resistance, impedance; **оказа́ть с.** to put up
resistance

сопротивля́|ться, юсь *impf.* (+ *d.*) to
resist, oppose

сопу́тств|овать, ую *impf.* (+ *d.*) to
accompany; **~ующие обстоя́тельства**
attendant circumstances, concomitants

сор, а *m.* litter, rubbish

сора́тник, а *m.* comrade-in-arms

сорван|е́ц, ца́ *m.* (infml) (*ребёнок*) a terror;
(*девочка*) tomboy

сорв|а́ть, у́, ёшь, *past* **~а́л, ~ала́, ~а́ло** *pf.*
(*of* ▶ **срыва́ть**) **1** (*отделить*) to tear off,
break off, tear away, tear down; (*цветок*)
to pick, pluck; **с. ве́тку** to break off a
branch **2** (**на** + *p.*) (*выместить*) to vent
(upon); **с. гнев на ком-н.** to vent one's anger
upon sb **3** (*нарушить*) to wreck, ruin, spoil;
с. забасто́вку to break a strike

сорв|а́ться, у́сь, ёшься, *past* **~а́лся,
~ала́сь, ~а́лось** *pf.* (*of* ▶ **срыва́ться**)
1 (*освободиться*) to break away, break
loose; **с. с пе́тель** to come off its hinges
2 (*упасть*) to fall, come down; **с. с
колоко́льни** to fall from the belfry **3** (infml,
не удаться) to fall through

♂ **соревнова́ни|е, я** *nt.* **1** (sport) competition,
contest; event **2** (*действие*) competition

соревн|ова́ться, у́юсь *impf.* (**с** + *i.*) to
compete (with, against)

сориенти́р|овать, ую *pf. of* ▶ **ориенти́ровать**

сориенти́р|оваться, уюсь *pf. of*
▶ **ориенти́роваться**

сор|и́ть, ю́, и́шь *impf.* (*of* ▶ **насори́ть**)
(+ *a. or i.*) to drop litter; to make a mess;
с. деньга́ми to throw one's money about

сорня́к, а́ *m.* weed

со́рок, *all other cases* **а́** *num.* forty

соро́к|а, и *f.* magpie

сорокови́|ой *adj.* fortieth; **~ые го́ды** the
forties

♂ key word

сороконо́жк|а, и *f.* centipede

соро́чк|а, и *f.* shirt; blouse; (*нижняя*)
camisole; **ночна́я с.** (*мужская*) nightshirt;
(*женская*) nightdress

сорт, а, *pl.* **~а́** *m.* **1** (*качество*) grade, quality;
вы́сший с. best quality; **пе́рвого ~а** first
grade, first-rate **2** (*разновидность*) sort,
kind, variety

сортир|ова́ть, у́ю *impf.* (*товар, уголь*)
to sort, grade; (*корреспонденцию*) to sort;
(comput.) to sort

сортиро́вк|а, и *f.* sorting, grading

сос|а́ть, у́, ёшь *impf.* to suck

сосе́д, а, *pl.* **~и, ~ей** *m.* neighbour (BrE),
neighbor (AmE)

сосе́д|ка, ки *f. of* ▶ **сосе́д**

сосе́дн|ий *adj.* neighbouring (BrE),
neighboring (AmE); adjacent, next; **с. дом**
the house next door; **~яя ко́мната** the next
room

соси́ск|а, и *f.* sausage; (*варёная*) frankfurter

со́ск|а, и *f.* **1** (*пустышка*) dummy (BrE),
pacifier (AmE) **2** (*на бутылке*) teat

соска́блива|ть, ю *impf. of* ▶ **соскобли́ть**

соска́кива|ть, ю *impf. of* ▶ **соскочи́ть**

соска́льзыва|ть, ю *impf. of* ▶ **соскользну́ть**

соскобл|и́ть, ю́, и́шь *pf. of*
▶ **соска́бливать**) to scrape off

соскользн|у́ть, у́, ёшь *pf.* (*of*
▶ **соска́льзывать**) (*упасть*) to slip off, slide
off; (*с горы*) to slide down

соскоч|и́ть, у́, ~ишь *pf.* (*of* ▶ **соска́кивать**)
1 (*с трамвая, коня*) to jump off, leap off;
(*с дерева*) to jump down, leap down; **с. с
крова́ти** to jump out of bed **2** (*упасть*) to
come off; **с. с пе́тель** to come off its hinges

соскреба́|ть, ю *impf. of* ▶ **соскрести́**

соскре|сти́, бу́, бёшь, *past* **~б, ~бла́** *pf.*
(*of* ▶ **соскреба́ть**) to scrape away, off

соску́ч|иться, усь, ишься *pf.*
1 (*почувствовать скуку*) to become bored
2 (**по** + *d.*) to miss, yearn (for); **с. по
друзья́м** to miss one's friends; (*по родине,
городу*) to be homesick (for)

сослага́тельный *adj.* (gram.) subjunctive

со|сла́ть, шлю́, шлёшь *pf.* (*of* ▶ **ссыла́ть**)
to exile, banish

со|сла́ться, шлю́сь, шлёшься *pf.* (*of*
▶ **ссыла́ться**) (**на** + *a.*) **1** (*указать*) to
refer (to), allude (to); (*процитировать*) to
cite, quote **2** (*оправдаться*) to plead; **с. на
недомога́ние** to plead indisposition

сосло́ви|е, я *nt.* (social) class; **дворя́нское с.**
the nobility; **духо́вное с.** the clergy

сослужи́в|ец, ца *m.* colleague, fellow
employee

сослужи́в|ица, ицы *f. of* ▶ **сослужи́вец**

сосн|а́, ы́, *pl.* **~ы, со́сен** *f.* pine (tree)

сос|о́к, ка́ *m.* nipple

сосредото́ченност|ь, и *f.* (degree of)
concentration

сосредото́ченный *p.p.p. of* ▶ **сосредото́чить**
and adj. concentrated; **с. взгляд** fixed stare

сосредото́чива|ть, ю *impf. of*
▶ **сосредото́чить**

сосредото́чива|ться, юсь *impf. of*
▶ **сосредото́читься**

сосредото́ч|ить, у, ишь *pf.* (*of*
▶ **сосредото́чивать**) to concentrate; to
focus; **с. внима́ние (на + *p.*)** to concentrate
one's attention (on, upon)

сосредото́ч|иться, усь, ишься *pf.*
(*of* ▶ **сосредото́чиваться**) **1** (**на + *p.***)
to concentrate (on, upon) **2** *pass. of*
▶ **сосредото́чить**

♂ **соста́в, а** *m.* **1** (*вещества*) composition,
make-up; structure; **входи́ть в с.** (+ *g.*) to
form part (of) **2** (*колле́ктив людей*) staff,
personnel; **ли́чный с.** personnel; **в по́лном
∼е** at full strength; **в ∼е** (+ *g.*) numbering,
consisting (of); **делега́ция в ∼е тридцати́
челове́к** a delegation of thirty (persons);
входи́ть в с. (+ *g.*) to be a member (of)

♂ **соста́в|ить¹, лю, ишь** *pf.* (*of* ▶ **составля́ть**)
1 (*собра́ть, соедини́ть*) to put together;
с. посу́ду to stack crockery **2** (*список,
проект*) to make, draw up; to compile;
to form, construct; **с. мне́ние** to form an
opinion; **с. предложе́ние** to construct a
sentence; **с. слова́рь** to compile a dictionary
3 (*явля́ться*) to be, constitute, make; **э́то не
∼ит большо́го труда́** this will not constitute
a lot of work **4** (*образова́ть*) to form, make,
amount to, total; **с. в сре́днем** to average;
расхо́ды ∼или пятьсо́т фу́нтов expenditure
amounted to five hundred pounds

соста́в|ить², лю, ишь *pf.* (*of* ▶ **составля́ть**)
(*све́рху вниз*) to take down, put down;
с. я́щики на́ пол to put the drawers down
on the floor

соста́в|иться, ится *pf.* (*of* ▶ **составля́ться**)
to form, be formed, be made up

♂ **составля́|ть, ю, ет** *impf. of* ▶ **соста́вить¹**

составля́|ться, ется *impf. of* ▶ **соста́виться**

составн|о́й *adj.* **1** (*составленный из
не́которых частей*) compound, composite
2 (*входящий в состав чего-н.*) component;
∼а́я часть component, constituent

соста́р|ить, ю *pf. of* ▶ **ста́рить**

соста́р|иться, юсь *pf. of* ▶ **ста́риться**

♂ **состоя́ни|е, я** *nt.* **1** state, condition;
position; **в хоро́шем, плохо́м ∼и** in good,
bad condition; **быть в ∼и** (+ *inf.*) to be able
(to), be in a position (to) **2** (*имущество*)
fortune; **нажи́ть с.** to make a fortune

состоя́тельный¹, ∼ен, ∼ьна *adj.*
(*бога́тый*) well off

состоя́тельный², ∼ен, ∼ьна *adj.*
(*обосно́ванный*) well grounded

♂ **состо|я́ть, ю́, и́шь** *impf.* **1** (**из** + *g.*) to
consist (of), comprise, be made up (of);
кварти́ра ∼и́т из трёх ко́мнат the flat
consists of three rooms **2** (**в** + *p.*) to consist
(in), lie (in), be; **ра́зница ∼и́т в том, что…**
the difference is that … **3** (*быть*) to be; **с. в
па́ртии** to be a member of a party

♂ **состо|я́ться, и́тся** *pf.* to take place; **визи́т не**

∼я́лся the visit did not take place

сострада́ни|е, я *nt.* compassion, sympathy

состр|и́ть, ю́, и́шь *pf. of* ▶ **остри́ть**

состяза́ни|е, я *nt.* competition, contest;
match; **с. по фехтова́нию** fencing match

состяза́|ться, юсь *impf.* (**с** + *i.*) to compete
(with)

сосу́д, а *m.* vessel

сосу́льк|а, и *f.* icicle

сосчита́|ть, ю *pf. of* ▶ **счита́ть 1**

сотвор|и́ть, ю́, и́шь *pf. of* ▶ **твори́ть**

со́тк|а, и *f.* (infml) 100 square metres
(= 0.01 hectare)

сотк|а́ть, у́, ёшь, *past* **∼а́л, ∼ала́, ∼а́ло** *pf.
of* ▶ **ткать**

♂ **со́т|ня, ни,** *g. pl.* **∼ен** *f.* (*сто*) a hundred (*esp.
a hundred roubles*)

со́товый *adj.* cellular; **с. телефо́н** cellphone,
mobile phone (BrE)

♂ **сотру́дник, а** *m.* **1** (*колле́га*) colleague
2 (*слу́жащий*) employee, worker; **нау́чный
с.** research assistant; **с. посо́льства** embassy
official **3** (*газеты, журна́ла*) contributor

сотру́дни|ца, цы *f. of* ▶ **сотру́дник**

сотру́днича|ть, ю *impf.* **1** (**с** + *i.*) to work
(with) **2** (**в** + *p.*) to contribute (to); **с. в
газе́те** to contribute to a newspaper; to work
on a newspaper

♂ **сотру́дничеств|о, а** *nt.* collaboration,
cooperation

сотрясе́ни|е, я *nt.* shaking; **с. мо́зга** (med.)
concussion

со́т|ы, ∼ *and* **∼ов** (*no sg.*) honeycombs

со́т|ый *adj.* hundredth; **с. год** the year one
hundred; (*as f. n.* **∼ая, ∼ой**) (a) hundredth

со́ул, а *m.:* (*му́зыка*) **с.** soul music

со́ус, а *m.* sauce; (*мясно́й*) gravy; (*к сала́ту*)
dressing

со́усник, а *m.* sauce boat, gravy boat

соуча́стник, а *m.* accomplice; **с.
преступле́ния** (law) accessory to a crime

соуча́стни|ца, цы *f. of* ▶ **соуча́стник**

соф|а́, ы́, *pl.* **∼ы** *f.* sofa

софи́зм, а *m.* sophism, sophistry

Софи́|я, и *f.* Sofia

со́х|нуть, ну, нешь, *past* **∼, ∼ла** *impf.*
1 (*о белье́*) to dry, get dry; (*о губа́х*) to
become parched **2** (*вя́нуть*) to wither;
(fig., infml, *от любви́*) to pine

♂ **сохране́ни|е, я** *nt.* **1** preservation;
conservation; (*попече́ние*) care, custody
2 (*пра́ва*) retention

сохран|и́ть, ю́, и́шь *pf.* (*of* ▶ **сохраня́ть**)
1 (*бере́чь*) to preserve, keep; to keep safe;
с. ве́рность (+ *d.*) to remain faithful, loyal
(to); **с. на па́мять** to keep as a souvenir
2 (*не теря́ть*) to keep, retain, preserve;
с. хладнокро́вие to keep cool; **с. за собо́й
пра́во** to reserve the right; (comput.) to save

сохран|и́ться, ю́сь, и́шься *pf.* (*of*
▶ **сохраня́ться**) **1** to remain (intact); to last
out, hold out; **он хорошо́ ∼и́лся** he is well

preserved **2** *pass. of* ▶ сохрани́ть

сохра́нност|ь, и *f.* safety, undamaged state; в ∼и safe, intact

⚹ сохран|я́ть, я́ю *impf. of* ▶ сохрани́ть

сохран|я́ться, я́юсь *impf. of* ▶ сохрани́ться

социа́л-демокра́т, а *m.* social democrat

социа́л-демократи́ческий *adj.* social democratic

социали́зм, а *m.* socialism

социали́ст, а *m.* socialist

социалисти́ческий *adj.* socialist

социали́ст|ка, ки *f. of* ▶ социали́ст

⚹ социа́льн|ый *adj.* social; ∼ое обеспе́чение social security; ∼ое положе́ние social status; ∼ая сеть social network

социо́лог, а *m.* sociologist

социологи́ческий *adj.* sociological

социоло́ги|я, и *f.* sociology

⚹ сочета́ни|е, я *nt.* combination

сочета́|ть, ю *impf. and pf.* (с + *i.*) to combine (with)

сочета́|ться, ется *impf. and pf.* **1** to combine; в ней ∼лся ум с красото́й she combined intelligence and good looks **2** (с + *i.*) (*гармони́ровать*) to harmonize (with), go (with); to match

сочине́ни|е, я *nt.* **1** (*де́йствие*) composing **2** (*произведе́ние*) work **3** (*шко́льное*) composition, essay

сочин|и́ть, ю́, и́шь *pf.* (*of* ▶ сочиня́ть) **1** (*созда́ть*) to compose (*a literary or musical work*); to write **2** (*вы́думать*) to make up, fabricate

сочин|я́ть, я́ю *impf. of* ▶ сочини́ть

сочи́|ться, и́тся *impf.* to ooze (out), exude; с. кро́вью to bleed

со́ч|ный, ∼ен, ∼на́, ∼но *adj.* **1** juicy (*also* fig.); succulent **2** (fig.) (*кра́ски*) rich; (*зе́лень*) lush

сочу́встви|е, я *nt.* sympathy; вы́звать с. to gain sympathy

сочу́вств|овать, ую *impf.* (+ *d.*) to sympathize (with), feel (for)

сочу́вств|ующий *pres. part. act. of* ▶ сочу́вствовать *and adj.* sympathetic; (*as m. n.* с., ∼ующего) sympathizer

⚹ сою́з¹, а *m.* **1** (*соглаше́ние*) alliance, union; (*еди́нение*) agreement; заключи́ть с. (с + *i.*) to conclude an alliance (with) **2** (*организа́ция*) union; league; профессиона́льный с. trade union

сою́з², а *m.* (gram.) conjunction

сою́зник, а *m.* ally

сою́зни|ца, цы *f. of* ▶ сою́зник

сою́зн|ый *adj.* allied; ∼ые держа́вы allied powers; (hist.) the Allies

со́|я, и *f.* soya bean

спаге́тти *nt. and pl. indecl.* spaghetti

спад, а *m.* (econ.) slump, recession

спада́|ть, ет *impf. of* ▶ спасть

спазм, а *m.* spasm

спа́ива|ть, ю *impf. of* ▶ споить

спа́льн|ый *adj.* sleeping; с. ваго́н sleeping car; ∼ое ме́сто berth, bunk; с. мешо́к sleeping bag

спа́л|ьня, ьни, g. pl. ∼ен *f.* **1** (*ко́мната*) bedroom **2** (*ме́бель*) bedroom suite

спа́рж|а, и *f.* asparagus

спа́рива|ться, ется *impf. of* ▶ спа́риться

спа́р|иться, ится *pf.* (*of* ▶ спа́риваться) (*о живо́тных*) to mate

спа́рыва|ть, ю *impf. of* ▶ спороть

спаса́тел|ь, я *m.* lifeguard; rescuer; (*in pl.*) rescue party *or* team

спаса́тельн|ый *adj.* rescue, life-saving; с. круг, с. по́яс lifebelt; ∼ая ло́дка lifeboat

спаса́|ть, ю *impf. of* ▶ спасти́

спаса́|ться, юсь *impf. of* ▶ спасти́сь

спасе́ни|е, я *nt.* **1** (*де́йствие*) rescuing, saving **2** (*возмо́жность спасти́сь*) rescue, escape; (relig.) salvation

⚹ спаси́бо *particle* thanks; thank you; (*as n.*) thanks; большо́е вам с. thank you very much, many thanks

спаси́тел|ь, я *m.* **1** rescuer **2** (С.) (relig.) the Saviour (BrE), Savior (AmE)

спас|ти́, у́, ёшь, *past* ∼, ∼ла́ *pf.* (*of* ▶ спаса́ть) to save; to rescue; с. положе́ние to save the situation

спас|ти́сь, у́сь, ёшься, *past* ∼ся, ∼ла́сь *pf.* (*of* ▶ спаса́ться) **1** to save oneself, escape **2** (relig.) to be saved, save one's soul

спа|сть, дёт, *past* ∼л *pf.* (*of* ▶ спада́ть) **1** (с + *i.*) (*упа́сть вниз*) to fall down (from) **2** (*о ве́тре, шу́ме, жаре́*) to abate; (*о температу́ре*) to fall

⚹ спа|ть, сплю, спишь, *past* ∼л, ∼ла́, ∼ло *impf.* to sleep, be asleep; лечь с. to go to bed; пора́ с. it is bedtime; с. с (+ *i.*) to sleep with (euph.)

спа|я́ть, я́ю *pf.* to solder (together)

СПб (*abbr. of* Санкт-Петербу́рг) St Petersburg

спекта́кл|ь, я *m.* (theatr.) performance; show

спектр, а *m.* spectrum

спекули́р|овать, ую *impf.* **1** (+ *i. or* на + *p.*) to speculate (in); to profiteer (in) **2** (на + *p.*) (fig.) to exploit; to profit (by)

спекуля́нт, а *m.* speculator, profiteer

спекуляти́вный *adj.* speculative

спекуля́ци|я, и *f.* **1** (+ *i. or* на + *p.*) speculation (in); profiteering **2** (на + *p.*) (fig.) exploitation (of)

спелеоло́ги|я, и *f.* speleology; potholing

спе́л|ый, ∼, ∼а́, ∼о *adj.* ripe

спе́рва́ *adv.* (infml) at first; first

спе́реди *adv. and prep.* + *g.* in front (of); at the front, from the front

спе́рм|а, ы *f.* sperm

сперматозо́ид, а *m.* (biol.) spermatozoon

⚹ спеси́в|ый, ∼, ∼а *adj.* arrogant, conceited, haughty

с

спе|ть¹, ет *impf.* to ripen

спеть², спою́, спо́ешь *pf. of* ▸ петь

специализа́ци|я, и *f.* specialization

специализи́р|оваться, у́юсь *impf. and pf.* (в + *p.* or по + *d.*) to specialize (in)

ⱷ специали́ст, а *m.* (в + *p.* or по + *d.*) specialist (in), expert (in)

специали́ст|ка, ки *f. of* ▸ специали́ст

ⱷ специа́льно *adv.* specially, especially

специа́льност|ь, и *f.* **1** speciality, special interest **2** (*профессия*) profession

ⱷ специа́л|ьный *adj.* **1** special; с. корреспонде́нт special correspondent **2** (~ен, ~ьна) specialist; ~ьное образова́ние specialist education

специ́фик|а, и *f.* specific character

специфи́ческий *adj.* specific

спе́ци|я, и *f.* (*usu. in pl.*) spice

спецна́з, а *m.* (*abbr. of* отря́д специа́льного назначе́ния) special unit

спецоде́жд|а, ы *f.* working clothes, overalls

спецслу́жб|а, ы *f.* (*usu. in pl.*) special force

спецэффе́кт, а *m.* special effect

спеш|и́ть, у́, и́шь *impf.* (*of* ▸ поспеши́ть) **1** to hurry, be in a hurry; to make haste; (с + *i.*) to hurry up (with); с. домо́й to be in a hurry to get home; де́лать не ~á to do in leisurely style, take one's time over **2** (*no pf.*) (*о часа́х*) to be fast

спе́шк|а, и *f.* (infml) hurry, rush

СПИД, а *m.* (*abbr. of* синдро́м приобретённого иммунодефици́та) (med.) Aids (*acquired immune deficiency syndrome*)

спидо́метр, а *m.* speedometer

спи́кер, а *m.* (pol.) speaker

спи́лива|ть, ю *impf. of* ▸ спили́ть

спил|и́ть, ю́, ~ишь *pf.* (*of* ▸ спи́ливать) (*дерево*) to saw down; (*сук, верхушку*) to saw off

ⱷ спин|á, ы́, *a.* ~у, *pl.* ~ы *f.* back; за ~ой у кого́-н. (fig.) behind sb's back

спи́нк|а, и *f.* **1** *dim. of* ▸ спина́ **2** back (*of article of furniture or clothing*)

спинно́й *adj.* spinal; с. мозг spinal cord

спира́л|ь, и *f.* spiral

спирити́зм, а *m.* spiritualism

спирт, а *m.* alcohol, spirit(s)

спиртн|о́й *adj.* alcoholic, spirituous; ~ые напи́тки alcoholic drinks, spirits; (*as nt. as* ~о́е, ~о́го) alcoholic drinks, spirits

спи|са́ть, шу́, ~шешь *pf.* (*of* ▸ спи́сывать) **1** (с + *i.*) to copy from **2** (у + *g.*) to copy (off), crib (off) **3** (*оборудование, долг*) to write off

ⱷ спи́с|ок, ка *m.* **1** (*рукописная копия*) manuscript copy **2** (*письменный перечень*) list; roll **3**: послужно́й с. service record

спи́сыва|ть, ю *impf. of* ▸ списа́ть

спи́хива|ть, ю *impf. of* ▸ спихну́ть

спих|ну́ть, ну́, нёшь *pf.* (*of* ▸ спи́хивать) to push aside, shove aside; (*вниз*) to push down

спи́ц|а, ы *f.* **1** (*для вяза́ния*) knitting needle **2** (*колеса́*) spoke

спи́чк|а, и *f.* match

сплав, а *m.* (tech.) alloy

спла́чива|ть, ю, ет *impf. of* ▸ сплоти́ть

спла́чива|ться, ется *impf. of* ▸ сплоти́ться

сплёвыва|ть, ю *impf. of* ▸ сплю́нуть

спле|сти́, ту́, тёшь, *past* ~л, ~ла́ *pf.* (*of* ▸ плести́ 1) to weave, plait, interlace

спле́тник, а *m.* gossip, scandalmonger

спле́тниц|а, ы *f. of* ▸ спле́тник

спле́тнича|ть, ю *impf.* to gossip

спле́т|ня, ни, *g. pl.* ~ен *f.* gossip; piece of scandal

спло|ти́ть, чу́, ти́шь *pf.* (*of* ▸ спла́чивать) **1** to join **2** (fig.) to unite, rally; с. ряды́ to close ranks

спло|ти́ться, ти́тся *pf.* (*of* ▸ спла́чиваться) to unite, rally; to close ranks

сплошн|о́й *adj.* **1** unbroken, continuous; ~а́я ма́сса solid mass **2** (*всеобщий*) complete

сплошь *adv.* **1** (*по всей пове́рхности*) all over **2** (infml) (*целиком*) completely, entirely; (*без исключе́ния*) without exception; (*исключи́тельно*) only, exclusively

сплю́н|уть, у, ешь *pf.* (*of* ▸ сплёвывать) **1** (*плюнуть*) to spit **2** (infml, *косточку*) to spit out

сплю́щива|ть, ю, ет *impf. of* ▸ сплю́щить

сплю́щива|ться, ется *impf. of* ▸ сплю́щиться

сплю́щ|ить, у, ишь *pf.* (*of* ▸ сплю́щивать) to flatten

сплю́щ|иться, ится *pf.* (*of* ▸ сплю́щиваться) to become flat

спля|са́ть, шу́, ~шешь *pf. of* ▸ пляса́ть

спо|и́ть, ю́, и́шь *pf.* (*of* ▸ спа́ивать) (infml) to get drunk; to make a drunkard (of)

споко́|йный, ~ен, ~йна *adj.* **1** quiet; calm, tranquil; ~йное мо́ре calm sea; ~йной но́чи! good night! **2** (*человек*) quiet, composed

споко́йстви|е, я *nt.* **1** (*покой*) quiet, tranquillity; calm **2** (*порядок*) order; наруше́ние обще́ственного ~я breach of the peace **3** (*душе́вное*) composure, serenity; с. ду́ха peace of mind

спола́скива|ть, ю *impf. of* ▸ сполосну́ть

сполз|а́ть, а́ю *impf. of* ▸ сползти́

сполз|ти́, у́, ёшь, *past* ~, ~ла́ *pf.* (*of* ▸ сполза́ть) **1** (с + *g.*) to climb down (from) **2** (*о шапке*) to slip down

сполосн|у́ть, у́, ёшь *pf.* (*of* ▸ спола́скивать) to rinse (out)

спонси́р|овать, ую *impf. and pf.* to sponsor

спо́нсор, а *m.* sponsor, backer

спо́нсорств|о, а *nt.* sponsorship

спонта́н|ный, ~ен, ~на *adj.* spontaneous

спор, а *m.* **1** argument; controversy; debate **2** (law) dispute

спо́р|ить, ю, ишь *impf.* (*of* ▸ поспо́рить 1) (о + *p.*) **1** to argue (about); to dispute (about), debate **2** (law) (o + *p.* or за + *a.*) to dispute; **с. о насле́дстве** to dispute a legacy **3** (*держать пари*) to bet (on), have a bet (on)

спо́р|ный, ~ен, ~на *adj.* debatable, questionable; disputed, at issue; **с. вопро́с** moot point

спор|о́ть, ю́, ~ешь *pf.* (*of* ▶ **спа́рывать**) to unstitch, take off (*by cutting stitches*)

✔ **спорт, а** *m.* sport; **ко́нный с.** equestrianism

спортза́л, а *m.* sports hall

✔ **спорти́вн|ый** *adj.* (*инвентарь, комментатор*) sports; (*человек, фигура*) sporty; (*одежда*) casual; **с. зал** gymnasium; **~ая площа́дка** sports ground, playing field

спортко́мплекс, а *m.* sports complex

спортсме́н, а *m.* sportsman

спортсме́нк|а, и *f.* sportswoman

спо́рщик, а *m.* debater, wrangler

спо́рщи|ца, цы *f.* of ▶ **спо́рщик**

✔ **спо́соб, а** *m.* way, method; means; **таки́м ~ом** in this way

✔ **спосо́бност|ь, и** *f.* **1** (*usu. in pl.*) (к + *d.*) (*талант*) ability (for), talent (for), aptitude (for); **челове́к с больши́ми ~ями** person of great abilities; **с. к языка́м** talent for languages, linguistic ability **2** (*возможность*) capacity; **покупа́тельная с.** purchasing power; **пропускна́я с.** capacity

✔ **спосо́б|ный, ~ен, ~на** *adj.* **1** (*талантливый*) able, talented, clever; **с. к матема́тике** good at mathematics **2** (на + *a.* or + *inf.*) capable (of), able (to); **они́ ~ны на всё** they are capable of anything

✔ **спосо́бств|овать, ую** *impf.* (+ *d.*) **1** (*помогать*) to assist **2** (*делать возможным*) to be conducive (to), further, promote

споткн|у́ться, у́сь, ёшься *pf.* (*of* ▶ **спотыка́ться**) **1** (o + *a.*) to stumble (against, over) **2** (на + *p.* or o + *a.*) (fig., infml) to get stuck (on) **3** (infml, *оступиться*) to slip up

спотыка́|ться, юсь *impf. of* ▶ **споткну́ться**

спохва|ти́ться, чу́сь, ~тишься *pf.* (*of* ▶ **спохва́тываться**) (infml) to remember suddenly, think suddenly

спохва́тыва|ться, юсь *impf. of* ▶ **спохвати́ться**

спра́ва *adv.* (от + *g.*) on the right (of), to the right (of)

справедли́вост|ь, и *f.* **1** justice; fairness; **поступа́ть по ~и** to act fairly **2** (*правильность*) truth, correctness

справедли́в|ый, ~, ~а *adj.* **1** just; fair; **с. судья́** impartial judge **2** (*правильный*) justified, true, correct; **на́ши подозре́ния оказа́лись ~ыми** our suspicions proved to be justified

спра́в|ить, лю, ишь *pf.* (*of* ▶ **справля́ть**) (infml, *свадьбу, день рождения*) to celebrate

✔ **key word**

спра́в|иться¹, люсь, ишься *pf.* (*of* ▶ **справля́ться**) (с + *i.*) **1** (*с работой, детьми*) to cope (with), manage **2** (*с противником*) to deal (with), get the better (of); **я с ним ~люсь!** I'll deal with him! **3** (*с волнением, со страхом*) to control

спра́в|иться², люсь, ишься *pf.* (*of* ▶ **справля́ться**) (o + *p.*) to ask (about), inquire (about); **с. в словаре́** to consult a dictionary

спра́вк|а, и *f.* **1** (*сведение*) information; **навести́ ~и** (o + *p.*) to inquire (about) **2** (*документ*) certificate; **с. с ме́ста рабо́ты** document confirming that one works at a place

справля́|ть, ю *impf. of* ▶ **спра́вить**

справля́|ться, юсь *impf. of* ▶ **спра́виться¹**

спра́вочник, а *m.* reference book, handbook, guide; **телефо́нный с.** telephone directory

спра́вочн|ый *adj.* inquiry, information; **~ая** directory enquiries (BrE), directory assistance (AmE); **~ое бюро́, с. стол** inquiries/information office

✔ **спра́шива|ть, ю** *impf. of* ▶ **спроси́ть**

спресс|ова́ть, у́ю *pf. of* ▶ **прессова́ть**

спринт, а *m.* (sport) sprint

спри́нтер, а *m.* (sport) sprinter

спровоци́р|овать, ую *pf. of* ▶ **провоци́ровать**

спроекти́р|овать, ую *pf. of* ▶ **проекти́ровать**

✔ **спрос, а** *m.* (econ.) demand; (на + *a.*) demand (for); **с. и предложе́ние** supply and demand; **по́льзоваться больши́м ~ом** to be much in demand

✔ **спро|си́ть, шу́, ~сишь** *pf.* (*of* ▶ **спра́шивать**) **1** (o + *p.*) (*осведомиться*) to ask (about), inquire (about); **с. доро́гу** to ask the way **2** (+ *a.* or *g.*) (*попросить*) to ask (for); (*пожелать видеть*) to ask to see, desire to speak (to); **~си́те хозя́йку** ask to see the landlady **3** (с + *g.*) (*призвать к ответу*) to make answer (for), make responsible (for)

спрут, а *m.* octopus

спры́гива|ть, ю *impf. of* ▶ **спры́гнуть**

спры́г|нуть, ну, нешь *pf.* (*of* ▶ **спры́гивать**) (с + *g.*) to jump off; to jump down (from)

спряга́|ть, ю *impf.* (*of* ▶ **проспряга́ть**) (gram.) to conjugate

спряже́ни|е, я *nt.* (gram.) conjugation

спря|сть, ду́, дёшь, *past* ~л, ~ла́, ~ло *pf. of* ▶ **прясть**

спря́|тать, чу, чешь *pf. of* ▶ **пря́тать**

спря́|таться, чусь, чешься *pf. of* ▶ **пря́таться**

спу́гива|ть, ю *impf. of* ▶ **спугну́ть**

спуг|ну́ть, ну́, нёшь *pf.* (*of* ▶ **спу́гивать**) to frighten off, scare off

спуск, а *m.* **1** (*флага*) lowering; **с. корабля́** launch(ing) **2** (*с высоты*) descent, descending **3** (*воды*) release; draining **4** (*откос*) slope, descent

спуска|ть, ю *impf. of* ▶ спустить

спуска|ться, юсь *impf. of* ▶ спуститься

спу|стить, щу́, ~стишь *pf.* (*of* ▶ спускать)
1 (*флаг, занавеску*) to let down, lower;
с. корабль (на воду) to launch a ship
2 (*освободить*) to let go, let loose, release;
с. курок to pull, release the trigger; **с. собаку
с привязи** to unleash a dog **3** (*воду, воздух*)
to let out; **с. воду в туалете** to flush a
lavatory **4** (*о шине*) to go down, deflate
5 (infml, *деньги*) to throw away, squander

спу|ститься, щу́сь, ~стишься *pf.* (*of*
▶ спускаться) to descend; to come down, go
down; (*вниз по течению*) to go downstream;
(*о мраке*) to fall; **с. с лестницы** to come
downstairs

спустя *prep.* (+ *a.*) after; later; **с. год** after a
year, a year later

спута|ть, ю *pf. of* ▶ путать

спута|ться, юсь *pf. of* ▶ путаться

спутник, а *m.* **1** (*человек*) (travelling (BrE),
traveling (AmE)) companion; **с. жизни**
husband **2** (*обстоятельство*) concomitant
3 (astron.) satellite; **с. связи** communications
satellite

спутников|ый *adj.*: ~ая связь satellite link;
~ое телевидение satellite television

спутни|ца, цы *f. of* ▶ спутник 1; **с. жизни**
wife

спя|тить, чу, тишь *pf.* (infml) to go nuts, go
off one's rocker

спя́чк|а, и *f.* hibernation

срабатыва|ть, ю *impf. of* ▶ сработать

сработа|ть, ю *pf.* (*of* ▶ срабатывать)
(*машина, сигнализация*) to work

♂ **сравне́ни|е**, я *nt.* comparison; **по ~ю, в ~и**
(с + *i.*) by, in comparison (with), compared
(with)

сра́внива|ть, ю *impf. of* ▶ сравнить,
▶ сравнять

сравни́тельно *adv.* **1** (с + *i.*) by, in
comparison (with) **2**: **с. недорогой/
хороший** comparatively cheap/good

сравни́тельн|ый *adj.* comparative; ~ая
сте́пень (gram.) comparative (degree)

сравн|и́ть, ю́, и́шь *pf.* (*of* ▶ сра́внивать)
(с + *i.*) to compare (to, with)

сравн|и́ться, ю́сь, и́шься *pf.* (с + *i.*) to
compare (with)

сравн|я́ть, я́ю *pf.* (*of* ▶ сра́внивать) to make
even; **с. счёт** (sport) to equalize, bring the
score level

сравня́|ться, юсь *pf.* (с + *i.*) to become
equal (with)

сража́|ть, ю *impf. of* ▶ срази́ть

сража́|ться, юсь *impf. of* ▶ срази́ться
(с + *i.*) to fight; to join battle (with)

сраже́ни|е, я *nt.* battle, engagement

сра|зи́ть, жу́, зи́шь *pf.* (*of* ▶ сража́ть)
1 (*убить*) to slay **2** (fig.) to overwhelm,
crush; **весть о катастрофе ~зи́ла её** she
was crushed by the news of the disaster

сра|зи́ться, жу́сь, зи́шься *pf. of* ▶ сража́ться

♂ **сра́зу** *adv.* **1** (*в один приём*) (all) at once
2 (*немедленно*) straight away, immediately
3 (*рядом*) right, just; **с. за до́мом** right
behind the house

сраст|а́ться, а́ется *impf. of* ▶ срасти́сь

сраст|и́сь, ётся, *past* сро́сся, сросла́сь
pf. (*of* ▶ сраста́ться) **1** (*о костях*) to grow
together; (*о костях*) to knit **2** (fig.) (с + *i.*)
(*соединиться*) to merge (with)

ср|а́ть, у, ёшь *impf.* (*of* ▶ насра́ть) (vulg.)
to shit

среаги́р|овать, ую *pf. of* ▶ реаги́ровать

♂ **сред|а́¹**, ы́, *a.* ~у́, *pl.* ~ы *f.* **1** (*природная*)
environment, surroundings; **окружа́ющая
с.** the environment; (*социальная*)
environment, milieu; (biol.) habitat; **в ~е́**
(+ *g.*) among **2** (phys., chem.) medium

♂ **сред|а́²**, ы́, *a.* ~у, *pl.* ~ы, *d.* ~а́м *f.* (*день
недели*) Wednesday; **в ~у** on Wednesday

♂ **среди́** *prep.* + *g.* **1** (*в числе*) among; amidst; **с.
них** among them, in their midst **2** (*посредине*)
in the middle (of)

Средизе́мн|ое мо́ре, ~ого мо́ря *nt.* the
Mediterranean (Sea)

средиземномо́рский *adj.* Mediterranean

среднеазиа́тский *adj.* central Asian

средневеко́вый *adj.* medieval

Средневеко́вь|е, я *nt.* the Middle Ages

♂ **сре́дн|ий** *adj.* **1** (*комната, ряд*) middle;
(*рост*) medium; **С~ие века́** the Middle
Ages; ~их лет middle-aged; ~его ро́ста
of medium height **2** (*в среднем*) mean,
average; **с. за́работок** average earnings; (*as
nt. n.* ~ее, ~его) mean, average; **в ~ем**
on average **3** (*посредственный*) middling,
average; **ни́же ~его** below average **4** (*школа,
образование*) secondary **5**: **с. род** (gram.)
neuter (gender)

средото́чи|е, я *nt.* focus, centre (BrE), center
(AmE) point

♂ **сре́дств|о**, а *nt.* **1** means; facilities; ~а
ма́ссовой информа́ции mass media;
~а передвиже́ния means of conveyance;
~а к существова́нию livelihood **2** (от + *g.*)
remedy (for); **с. от ка́шля** cough medicine,
sth for a cough **3** (*in pl.*) (*деньги, капитал*)
resources; funds **4** (*in pl.*) (*состояние*)
means; **жить не по ~ам** to live beyond one's
means

срез, а *m.* **1** (*место*) cut **2** (*слой*) section

сре́|зать, жу, жешь *pf.* (*of* ▶ среза́ть)
(*ветку*) to cut off; **с. у́гол** (fig.) to cut off
a corner

среза́|ть, ю *impf. of* ▶ сре́зать

срис|ова́ть, у́ю *pf.* (*of* ▶ срисо́вывать)
to copy

срисо́выва|ть, ю *impf. of* ▶ срисова́ть

сровня́|ть, ю *pf.* (*of* ▶ ровня́ть): **с. с землёй**
to raze to the ground

♂ **срок**, а (у) *m.* **1** (*промежуток времени*)
time, period; term; **ме́сячный с.** period of
one month; **с. де́йствия** period of validity;
с. полномо́чий term of office; ~ом на (+ *a.*)
for a period of **2** (*дата*) date; **кра́йний с.**

С

closing date; **с. хране́ния** shelf life; **в с., к ~у** in time, to time

сро́чно *adv.* urgently; quickly

сро́чност|ь, и *f.* urgency

сро́ч|ный, ~ен, ~на *adj.* **1** (*сообщение, зака́з*) urgent **2** (*ссу́да, вклад*) fixed-term; for a fixed period

сруб|а́ть, а́ю *impf. of* ▸ **сруби́ть**

сруб|и́ть, лю́, ~ишь *pf.* (*of* ▸ **сруба́ть**) to fell, cut down

срыв, а *m.* **1** (*пла́на, рабо́ты*) disruption; **с. рабо́ты** stoppage **2** (*неуда́ча*) failure

срыва́|ть, ю *impf. of* ▸ **сорва́ть**

срыва́|ться, юсь *impf. of* ▸ **сорва́ться**

сса́дин|а, ы *f.* scratch, abrasion

сса|ди́ть, жу́, ~дишь *pf.* (*of* ▸ **сса́живать**) **1** (*помо́чь сойти́*) to help down; **с. кого́-н. с ло́шади** to help sb down from a horse **2** (*заста́вить вы́йти*) to put off, make get off (*from public transport*)

сса́жива|ть, ю *impf. of* ▸ **ссади́ть**

ссо́р|а, ы *f.* quarrel; **она́ в ~е с сестро́й** she's fallen out with her sister

ссо́р|ить, ю, ишь *impf.* (*of* ▸ **поссо́рить**) to cause to quarrel, cause to fall out

ссо́р|иться, юсь, ишься *impf.* (*of* ▸ **поссо́риться**) (**с** + *i.*) to quarrel (with), fall out (with)

☞ **СССР** *m. indecl.* (*abbr. of* **Сою́з Сове́тских Социалисти́ческих Респу́блик**) (hist.) USSR (*Union of Soviet Socialist Republics*)

ссу́д|а, ы *f.* loan; **ба́нковская с.** bank loan

ссуту́л|иться, юсь, ишься *pf. of* ▸ **суту́литься**

ссыла́|ть, ю *impf. of* ▸ **сосла́ть**

ссыла́|ться, юсь *impf. of* ▸ **сосла́ться**

ссы́лк|а¹, и *f.* exile, banishment

☞ **ссы́лк|а², и** *f.* (**на** + *a.*) (*указа́ние*) reference (to); (comput.) link

ссы́п|ать, лю, лешь *pf.* (*of* ▸ **ссыпа́ть**) to pour

ссып|а́ть, а́ю *impf. of* ▸ **ссы́пать**

☞ **ст.** (*abbr. of* **столе́тие**) cent. (century)

стабилизи́р|овать, ую *impf. and pf.* to stabilize

стабилизи́р|оваться, уется *impf. and pf.* to become stable

стаби́льност|ь, и *f.* stability

стаби́л|ьный, ~ен, ~ьна *adj.* stable, firm

ста́в|ень, ня, *g. pl.* **~ней** *m.* shutter (*on window*)

☞ **ста́в|ить, лю, ишь** *impf.* (*of* ▸ **поста́вить¹**) **1** (*помеща́ть*) to put, place, set; (*что-н. вертика́льное*) to stand; **с. цветы́ в ва́зу** to put flowers in a vase; **с. диа́гноз** to diagnose; **с. реко́рд** to set up, create a record; **с. то́чку** to put a full stop; **с. кого́-н. в нело́вкое положе́ние** to put sb in an awkward position **2** (*сооружа́ть*) to put up, erect; (*устана́вливать*) to install; **с. па́мятник** to erect a monument **3** (*назнача́ть*) to put in,

install; **с. но́вого гла́вного инжене́ра** to put in a new chief engineer **4** (*накла́дывать*) to apply, put on; **с. кому́-н. гра́дусник** to take sb's temperature **5** (*вопро́с, пробле́му*) to put, present; (*пье́су*) to put on, stage **6** (*на* + *a.*) (*в игре́*) to place, stake (*money on*); **с. на ло́шадь** to back a horse

☞ **ста́вк|а, и** *f.* **1** (fin.) rate; **проце́нтная с.** interest rate **2** (*в и́грах*) stake; **де́лать ~у** (**на** + *a.*) to stake (on); (fig.) to count (on), gamble (on)

ста́вленник, а *m.* protégé

ста́в|ня, ни, *g. pl.* **~ен** *f.* = **ста́вень**

стадио́н, а *m.* stadium

☞ **ста́ди|я, и** *f.* stage

ста́дный *adj.* (*живо́тное*) gregarious; **с. инсти́нкт** herd instinct

ста́д|о, а, *pl.* **~а́** *nt.* herd; flock

стаж, а *m.* length of service

стажёр, а *m.* **1** (*проходя́щий испыта́тельный срок*) probationer **2** (*студе́нт*) student (*on special practical course*); exchange student

стака́н, а *m.* glass, tumbler

сталева́р, а *m.* steel founder

сталели́тейный *adj.*: **с. заво́д** steelmill, steel works

ста́лкива|ть, ю *impf. of* ▸ **столкну́ть**

ста́лкива|ться, юсь *impf. of* ▸ **столкну́ться**

стал|ь, и *f.* steel; **нержаве́ющая с.** stainless steel

стальн|о́й *adj.* steel; **~а́я во́ля** iron will; **~ы́е не́рвы** nerves of steel

Стамбу́л, а *m.* Istanbul

стаме́ск|а, и *f.* (tech.) chisel

☞ **станда́рт, а** *m.* **1** standard **2** (fig., *шабло́н*) cliché, stereotype

☞ **станда́рт|ный, ~ен, ~на** *adj.* standard

☞ **станов|и́ться, лю́сь, ~ишься** *impf. of* ▸ **стать¹**, ▸ **стать²**

становле́ни|е, я *nt.* (*иде́й, хара́ктера, госуда́рства*) formation; **в проце́ссе ~я** in the making

стан|о́к, ка́ *m.* (tech.) machine tool, machine; **печа́тный с.** printing press; **тка́цкий с.** loom; **тока́рный с.** lathe

☞ **ста́нци|я, и** *f.* station; **авто́бусная с.** bus station; **железнодоро́жная с.** railway (BrE), railroad (AmE) station

ста́птыва|ть, ю *impf. of* ▸ **стопта́ть**

стара́тель|ный, ~ен, ~ьна *adj.* assiduous, diligent

☞ **стара́|ться, юсь** *impf.* (*of* ▸ **постара́ться**) **1** (*усе́рдствовать*) to try; to apply oneself; **с. изо всех сил** to do one's utmost **2** (+ *inf.*) (*стреми́ться*) to try, endeavour; **я ~юсь помо́чь ему́** I'm trying to help him

старе́е *comp. of* ▸ **ста́рый**

старе́ни|е, я *nt.* ageing

старе́|ть, ю *impf.* **1** (*pf.* **по~**) (*челове́к*) to grow old, age **2** (*pf.* **у~**) (*иде́я, маши́на*) to become obsolete

старик, а *m.* old man; **глубокий с.** very old man; **~й** old people

старин|а, ы *f.* antiquity, olden times; **в ~у** in olden days

старинный *adj.* (*книга, обычай*) ancient, old; (*мебель*) antique

стар|ить, ю, ишь *impf.* (*of* ▶ **состарить**) to age

стар|иться, юсь, ишься *impf.* (*of* ▶ **состариться**) to age; to grow old

старомод|ный, ~ен, ~на *adj.* old-fashioned; out-of-date

старост|а, ы *m.* head; **с. класса** (*в школе*) class prefect, monitor

старост|ь, и *f.* old age

старт, а *m.* (sport, fig.) start; **на с.!** on your marks!

старт|овать, ую *impf. and pf.* **1** (sport) to start **2** (aeron.) to take off **3** (*отправляться*) to start out; to depart **4** (*начинаться*) to begin, commence

старух|а, и *f.* old woman, old lady

старушк|а, и *f.* (little) old lady, old woman

старческий *adj.* old person's; **с. возраст** old age; **с. маразм** senility

старше *comp. of* ▶ **старый**; (*взрослее*): **она с. меня на три года** she is three years older than me; (*по служебному положению*): **он с. меня по званию** he is senior to me in rank

старшеклассник, а *m.* senior (pupil)

старшеклассни|ца, цы *f. of* ▶ **старшеклассник**

◆ **старш|ий** *adj.* **1** (*более старый*) elder, older; **с. брат** older brother; (*as pl. n.* **~ие, ~их**) (one's) elders, grown-ups **2** (*самый старый*) oldest, eldest **3** (*по служебному положению*) senior, superior; (*в названиях*) chief, head; **~ая медсестра** senior nurse, sister (BrE); (*as m. n.* **с., ~его**) (mil.) man in charge; chief **4** (*высший*) senior, upper, higher; **с. класс** (*в школе*) higher form (BrE), senior grade (AmE)

старшинств|о, а *nt.* seniority; **по ~у** by seniority

◆ **стар|ый, ~, ~а, ~о** *adj.* old; **с. стиль** the Old Style (*of the Julian calendar*)

стаскива|ть, ю *impf. of* ▶ **стащить 1**

статистик|а, и *f.* statistics

статистический *adj.* statistical

статический *adj.* static

◆ **статус, а** *m.* status

статус-кво *m. & nt. indecl.* status quo

стату|я, и *f.* statue

◆ **стать**¹, **стану, станешь** *pf.* (*of* ▶ **становиться**) **1** (*встать*) to stand; **с. на колени** to kneel; (*поддержать*) to stand up for; **с. на чью-н. сторону** to take sb's side, stand up for sb **2** (*расположиться*) to take up position; **с. на якорь** to anchor **3** (*остановиться*) to stop, come to a halt; **мои часы стали** my watch has stopped

◆ **стать**², **стану, станешь** *pf.* (*of* ▶ **становиться**) **1** (+ *inf.*) (*начать*) to begin (to), start; **она**

стала говорить she began talking **2** (+ *i.*) (*сделаться*) to become, get, grow; **стало темно** it got dark; **ей стало лучше** she was better; she had got better **3** (**с** + *i.*) (*случиться*) to become (of), happen (to); **что с ними стало?** what has become of them? **4**: **не с.** (*impers.* + *g.*) (*умереть*) to die; (*исчезнуть*) to disappear, go

◆ **стат|ья, ьи,** *g. pl.* **~ей** *f.* **1** (*газетная, научная*) article **2** (*закона, договора*) clause; (*финансового документа*) item; (*в словаре*) entry; **расходная с.** debit item

стационар|ный *adj.* **1** (*не изменяющийся*) stationary; **с. объект** (mil.) stationary target **2** (*постоянный*) permanent, fixed **3** (*больничный*) hospital; **с. больной** in-patient; **~ое лечение** hospitalization

стачива|ть, ю *impf. of* ▶ **сточить**

стачк|а, и *f.* (*забастовка*) strike

стащ|ить, у, ~ишь *pf.* (*of* ▶ **стаскивать**) **1** (*сапоги*) to drag off, pull off **2** (*no impf.*) (infml, *украсть*) to nick (BrE), pinch, swipe (infml)

ста|я, и *f.* (*птиц*) flock; (*рыб*) school, shoal; (*волков*) pack

ствол, а *m.* **1** (*дерева*) trunk **2** (*оружия*) barrel; (infml, *само оружие*) gun

ствол|овой *adj. of* ▶ **ствол**; **~овая клетка** (biol.) stem cell

створк|а, и *f.* (*двери, зеркала*) leaf, fold; (*ворот, ставней*) half, side

стеб|ель, ля, *pl.* **~ли, ~лей** *m.* stem, stalk

стеган|ый *adj.* quilted; **~ое одеяло** quilt

стеж|ок, ка *m.* stitch

стека|ть, ет *impf. of* ▶ **стечь**

стекл|ить, ю, ишь *impf.* (*of* ▶ **застеклить**) to glaze

◆ **стек|ло, ла,** *pl.* **~ла, ~ол** *nt.* glass; (*collect.*) glassware

стекловолокн|о, а *nt.* fibreglass (BrE), fiberglass (AmE)

стеклоочистит|ель, я *m.* windscreen (BrE), windshield (AmE) wiper

стеклянный *adj.* **1** glass; **~ые изделия** glassware; (*окно, дверь*) glazed **2** (fig., *взгляд, глаза*) glassy

стекольщик, а *m.* glazier

стел|а, ы *f.* obelisk

стел|ить, ю, ~ешь *impf.* (*of* ▶ **постелить**) to spread; **с. постель** to make a bed; **с. скатерть** to lay a tablecloth

стеллаж, а *m.* shelves

стельк|а, и *f.* insole

стемне|ть *pf. of* ▶ **темнеть 2**

◆ **стен|а, ы,** *a.* **~у,** *pl.* **~ы,** *d.* **~ам** *f.* wall (also fig.); **в ~ах** (+ *g.*) inside, within the precincts (of)

стенд, а *m.* **1** (*на выставке*) stand (BrE), booth (AmE) **2** (*для испытаний*) test bed **3** (*для стрельбы*) rifle range

стенк|а, и *f.* **1** (*стена*) wall; **гимнастическая с.** wall bars **2** (*ящика, кастрюли*) side; (*желудка*) wall **3** (*мебель*) wall unit

С

ꜰ стеногра́фи|я, и *f.* shorthand
стенокарди́|я, и *f.* angina (pectoris)
степе́н|ный, ∼ен, ∼на *adj.* staid
ꜰ сте́пен|ь, и, *g. pl.* ∼е́й *f.* **1** degree, extent; до изве́стной ∼и, до не́которой ∼и to some extent, to a certain extent **2** (math.) power; возвести́ в тре́тью с. to raise to the third power **3** *(звание)* (academic) degree; *(разряд)* class; с. бакала́вра bachelor's degree; учёная с. до́ктора нау́к doctorate
сте́плер, а *m.* stapler
степ|ь, и, о ∼и, в ∼и́, *pl.* ∼и, ∼е́й *f.* steppe
сте́рв|а, ы *f.* (sl.) *(о женщине)* bitch
стервя́тник, а *m.* (zool.) carrion crow
стереосисте́м|а, ы *f.* stereo (system)
стереоти́п, а *m.* stereotype
стер|е́ть, сотру́, сотрёшь, *past* ∼, ∼ла *pf.* *(of* ▸ стира́ть¹) **1** *(рисунок)* to rub out, erase; *(кассету, перезаписываемый диск)* to erase; (comput.) to delete; *(пыль, пот)* to wipe off; с. с лица́ земли́ to wipe off the face of the earth **2** *(ногу)* to rub sore **3** *(в порошок)* to grind (down)
стер|е́ться, сотрётся, *past* ∼ся, ∼лась *pf.* *(of* ▸ стира́ться¹) **1** *(о надписи, краске)* to rub off; (fig., *забыться*) to fade **2** *(о подошвах, пальцах)* to become worn down
стере́|чь, гу́, жёшь, гу́т, *past* ∼г, ∼гла́ *impf.* *(вещи, стадо)* to guard, watch (over)
сте́рж|ень, ня *m.* **1** (tech.) pivot; shank, rod; поршнево́й с. piston rod **2** (fig., *основа*) core
стерилиза́ци|я, и *f.* sterilization
стерилиз|ова́ть, у́ю *impf. and pf.* to sterilize
стери́л|ьный, ∼ен, ∼ьна *adj.* sterile
сте́рлинг, а *m.* (fin.) sterling; фунт ∼ов pound sterling
сте́рляд|ь, и *f.* (zool.) sterlet
стеро́ид, а *m.* steroid
стерп|е́ть, лю́, ∼ишь *pf.* to bear, suffer, endure
стёртый *p.p.p. of* ▸ стере́ть *and adj.* *(надпись, монета)* worn, faded; (fig., *очертание*) faint
стесне́ни|е, я *nt.* *(ограничение)* constraint; *(смущение)* shyness, timidity
стесни́тел|ьный, ∼ен, ∼ьна *adj.* shy; awkward
стесня́|ться, юсь *impf.* *(of* ▸ постесня́ться) *(+ inf.)* to feel too shy (to), be ashamed (to); *(+ g.)* to feel shy (before, of); не ∼йтесь! don't be shy!; не с. в сре́дствах to use any means possible
сте|чь, чёт, ку́т, *past* ∼к, ∼кла́ *pf.* *(of* ▸ стека́ть) to flow down
стилиз|ова́ть, у́ю *impf. and pf.* to stylize
стили́ст, а *m.* **1** *(мастер стиля)* stylist **2** *(гримёр)* make-up artist
стилисти́ческий *adj.* stylistic
ꜰ стил|ь, я *m.* style
сти́л|ьный, ∼ен, ∼ьна *adj.* stylish

сти́мул, а *m.* incentive, stimulus
стимули́р|овать, ую *impf. and pf.* to stimulate, encourage
стимуля́ци|я, и *f.* stimulation; с. ро́дов (med.) induction
стипе́нди|я, и *f.* grant, scholarship
стира́л|ьный *adj.* washing; ∼ая маши́на washing machine; с. порошо́к washing powder
стира́|ть¹, ю *impf. of* ▸ стере́ть
стира́|ть², ю *impf.* *(of* ▸ вы́стирать) to wash, launder
стира́|ться¹, ется *impf. of* ▸ стере́ться
стира́|ться², ется *impf.* to wash; хорошо́ с. to wash well
сти́рк|а, и *f.* washing, laundering; отда́ть в ∼у to send to the laundry
сти́с|нуть, ну, нешь *pf.* to squeeze; с. зу́бы to clench one's teeth
ꜰ стих¹, а́ *m.* verse; (*in pl.*) verses; poetry
стих² *see* ▸ сти́хнуть
стих|а́ть, а́ю *impf. of* ▸ сти́хнуть
стихи́|йный, ∼ен, ∼йна *adj.* **1** elemental; ∼йное бе́дствие natural disaster **2** (fig., *протест*) spontaneous, uncontrolled
стихи́|я, и *f.* element
сти́х|нуть, ну, нешь, *past* ∼, ∼ла *pf.* *(of* ▸ стиха́ть) *(шум, ветер, дождь)* to abate, subside, die down; *(человек)* to calm down
стихотворе́ни|е, я *nt.* poem
стла́ть, стелю́, сте́лешь *impf.* *(of* ▸ постла́ть) = стели́ть
сто, ста, *pl.* *(no nom. & a.)* сот, стам, ста́ми, стах *num.* hundred; не́сколько сот рубле́й several hundred roubles; я сто раз тебе́ говори́л (infml) I've told you a hundred times
стог, а, в/на ∼у́ *and* в/на ∼е, *pl.* ∼а́ *m.* (agric.) stack, rick
ꜰ сто́имост|ь, и *f.* **1** *(цена)* cost; с. прое́зда fare; с. жи́зни cost of living; о́бщей ∼ью в (+ *a.*) to a total value of **2** (econ., *ценность*) value; номина́льная с. face/nominal value
ꜰ сто́|ить, ю, ишь *impf.* **1** to cost (also fig.); ско́лько ∼ит э́то пла́тье? how much is this dress?; до́рого с. to cost dear **2** (+ *g.*) *(заслуживать)* to be worth; to deserve; он её не ∼ит he doesn't deserve her; чего́ ∼ят его́ обеща́ния? his promises are worth nothing; (impers.) ∼ит it is worth while; об э́том ∼ит поду́мать it's worth thinking about **3**: ∼ит то́лько (impers. + *inf.*) one has only (to)
сто́йк|а, и *f.* **1** (sport) stand, stance; с. на рука́х handstand **2** (tech.) support, prop; *(ворот)* bar **3** *(прилавок)* bar, counter
сто́|йкий, ∼ек, ∼йка́, ∼йко *adj.* **1** firm, stable; *(запах)* persistent **2** (fig., *характер*) stable; steadfast, staunch
сто́йл|о, а *nt.* stall
сток, а *m.* **1** *(действие)* flow; drainage, outflow **2** *(место, устройство)* drain, gutter; sewer
Стокго́льм, а *m.* Stockholm

ꜰ key word

стол, а́ m. **1** (*предмет мебели*) table; **пи́сьменный с.** desk; **сесть за с.** to sit down to table; **за ~о́м** at table **2** (*питание*) board; (*кухня*) cooking, cuisine; **ры́бный с.** fish diet; **«шве́дский» с.** smorgasbord **3** (*отделение*) department; office; **с. нахо́док** lost property office

столб, а́ m. post, pole, pillar, column; **телегра́фный с.** telegraph pole

столб|е́ц, ца́ m. (*в газете, словаре*) column

столбня́к, а́ m. **1** (*med.*) tetanus **2** (*infml*) stupor; **на неё нашёл с.** she was in a stupor

столе́ти|е, я *nt.* **1** (*век*) century **2** (*годовщина*) centenary

столе́тн|ий *adj.* **1** hundred-year; **С~яя война́** the Hundred Years' War **2** (*дуб, старец*) hundred-year-old; **~яя годовщи́на** centenary

сто́л|ик, а *m. dim. of* ▶ стол 1; table (*e.g. in a restaurant*); **журна́льный с.** coffee table

столи́ц|а, ы *f.* capital; metropolis

столи́чный *adj. of* ▶ столи́ца; **с. го́род** capital (city)

столкнове́ни|е, я *nt.* (*автомобилей*) collision; (*mil.*, *also fig.*) clash; **вооружённое с.** armed conflict, hostilities; **с. интере́сов** clash of interests

столкн|у́ть, у́, ёшь *pf.* (*of* ▶ ста́лкивать) **1** (*сбросить, сдвинуть*) to push off; **с. ло́дку в во́ду** to push a boat off (into the water) **2** (*сблизить*) to cause to collide; to knock together **3** (*о случае, обстоятельствах*) to bring together

столкн|у́ться, у́сь, ёшься *pf.* (*of* ▶ ста́лкиваться) (с + *i.*) **1** to collide (with) (*also fig.*); (*вступить в конфликт*) to clash (with), conflict (with) **2** (*fig.*) (*встретиться*) to run (into), bump (into); (*с трудностями, равнодушием*) to encounter

столо́в|ая, ой *f.* (*в доме*) dining room; (*в армии*) mess; (*на работе*) canteen, cafeteria; (*общественная*) cafeteria

столо́в|ый *adj.* table; **~ое вино́** table wine; **с. прибо́р** cover

столп|и́ться, и́тся *pf.* to crowd

столь *adv.* so; **э́то не с. ва́жно** it's of no particular importance

сто́лько *adv.* (*с неисчисляемыми*) so much; (*с исчисляемыми*) so many; **с. любви́/де́нег** so much love/money; **нельзя́ с. рабо́тать** you should not work so much; **с. ..., ско́лько** as much ... as; **не с. ..., ско́лько** not so much ... as

столя́р, а́ m. joiner (*BrE*), cabinetmaker

стомато́лог, а *m.* dental surgeon

стоматологи́ческий *adj.* dental

стоматоло́ги|я, и *f.* dentistry

стон, а *m.* moan, groan

стон|а́ть, у́, **~ешь** *impf.* to moan, groan (*also fig.*)

стоп *int.* stop!

стоп|а́, ы́, *pl.* **~ы́** *f.* (*ноги*) foot (*also fig.*)

сто́пк|а, и *f.* (*куча*) pile, heap

стоп-ка́др, а *m.* (*пауза*) freeze-frame; (*снимок*) still (picture/image), snapshot

стоп-кра́н, а *m.* emergency cord (*on train*)

стопроце́нтный *adj.* hundred per cent

стоп|та́ть, чу́, **~чешь** *pf.* (*of* ▶ ста́птывать) (*обувь*) to wear down

сторг|ова́ться, у́юсь *pf. of* ▶ торгова́ться 1

сто́рож, а, *pl.* **~а́**, **~е́й** *m.* watchman, guard

сторожев|о́й *adj.* watch; **~а́я соба́ка** watchdog

сторож|и́ть, у́, и́шь *impf.* (*дом, стадо*) to guard, watch, keep watch (over)

сторо́жк|а, и *f.* lodge

сторон|а́, ы́, *a.* сто́рону, *pl.* сто́роны, сторо́н, **~а́м** *f.* **1** side; (*направление*) direction; **в сто́рону** (+ *g.*) in the direction of; **со ~ы́** (+ *g.*) from the direction of; **в сто́рону, в ~е́** aside; **держа́ться в ~е́** to keep aloof; **по ту сто́рону** (+ *g.*) across, on the other side (of); **пра́вая/ле́вая с.** right/left hand side; **с пра́вой/ле́вой ~ы́** on the right/left side; **с мое́й ~ы́** for my part; **э́то о́чень любе́зно с ва́шей ~ы́** it is very kind of you; **наблюда́ть со ~ы́** to observe from the outside; **со ~ы́** (+ *g.*) on the side of (*indicating line of descent*); **дед со ~ы́ ма́тери** maternal grandfather; **с одно́й ~ы́..., с друго́й ~ы́** on the one hand ..., on the other hand **2** (*в споре*) side, party; **вы на чьей ~е́?** whose side are you on?; **тре́тья с.** third party **3** (*элемент, свойство*) aspect, side

сторо́нник, а *m.* supporter, advocate; **с. ми́ра** peace campaigner

сторо́нни|ца, цы *f. of* ▶ сторо́нник

сточ|и́ть, у́, **~ишь** *pf.* (*of* ▶ ста́чивать) to grind off

сто́чн|ый *adj.* sewage, drainage; **~ые во́ды** sewage

стошн|и́ть, и́т *pf.* (*impers.*) to be sick, vomit; **меня́ ~и́ло** I was sick

сто́я *adv.* standing up

стоя́нк|а, и *f.* **1** (*остановка*) stop; (*автомобилей*) parking; **«с. запрещена́!»** 'no parking!' **2** (*место остановки*) stopping place; (*автомобилей*) parking area; (*судов*) moorage; **автомоби́льная с.** car park (*BrE*), parking lot (*AmE*)

сто|я́ть, ю́, и́шь *impf.* **1** to stand; **с. в о́череди** to stand in a queue; **с. на коле́нях** to kneel **2** (*находиться*) to be, be situated, lie; **кни́ги ~я́т на по́лке** the books are on the shelf; **ча́йник ~и́т на плите́** the kettle is on the stove **3** (*быть*) to be; to continue; **~я́ла хоро́шая пого́да** the weather continued fine **4** (*жить*) to stay, put up; (*mil.*) to be stationed; **с. ла́герем** to be encamped **5** (*за* + *a.*) (*защищать*) to stand up (for); (*на* + *p.*) (*настаивать*) to insist (on); **с. на своём** to refuse to give in **6** (*не двигаться*) to have stopped; to have come to a halt/ standstill; **мои́ часы́ ~я́т** my watch has stopped; ∼й(те)! stop!; halt!

сто́ящий *pres. part. act. of* ▶ **сто́ить** *and adj.* (челове́к) deserving, worthy; (де́ло, предложе́ние) worthwhile

стр. *abbr. of* **1** (страни́ца) p, page **2** (страни́цы) pp., pages

страда́ни|е, я *nt.* suffering

страда́тельный *adj.* (gram.) passive; **с. зало́г** passive voice

страда́|ть, ю *impf.* **1** (*impf. only*) (+ *i.*) to suffer (from); to be subject (to); **с. бессо́нницей** to suffer from insomnia **2** *impf. only* (от + *g.*) to suffer (from), be in pain (with); **с. от зубно́й бо́ли** to have (a) toothache **3** (*pf.* **по∼**) (за + *a.*) to suffer (for, as a result of)

стра́ж|а, и *f.* guard, watch; **под ∼ей** under arrest, in custody; **взять, заключи́ть под ∼у** to take into custody

✓ **стран|а́, ы́,** *pl.* **∼ы** *f.* country; land

✓ **страни́ц|а, ы** *f.* (also comput., fig., rhet.) page

стра́нно *adv.* **1** strangely, in a strange way **2** (*as pred.*) (необы́чно) it is strange; (непоня́тно) funny, odd, queer; **как э́то ни с.** strangely enough; **(мне) с., что** I find it strange that

стра́нность|ь, и *f.* **1** strangeness **2** (стра́нная мане́ра) oddity, eccentricity; **за ним води́лись ∼и** he was an odd person

✓ **стра́н|ный, ∼ен, ∼на́, ∼но** *adj.* (необы́чный) strange; (непоня́тный) funny, odd

стра́нств|овать, ую *impf.* to wander, travel; **с. по све́ту** to wander the earth; to travel the world

Стра́сбург, а *m.* Strasbourg

страстн|о́й *adj.* of Holy Week; **С∼а́я пя́тница** Good Friday

стра́ст|ный, ∼ен, ∼на *adj.* (речь, поцелу́й, челове́к) passionate; (сторо́нник, покло́нник) ardent

страст|ь, и, *g. pl.* **∼е́й** *f.* (к + *d.*) passion (for); **со ∼ью** with passion, fervour (BrE), fervor (AmE)

стратеги́ческий *adj.* strategic

✓ **страте́ги|я, и** *f.* strategy

стратосфе́р|а, ы *f.* stratosphere

стра́ус, а *m.* ostrich

✓ **страх, а** *m.* fear; (си́льный) terror; **со ∼у** from fear; **под ∼ом сме́рти** on pain of death

✓ **страхова́ни|е, я** *nt.* insurance; **с. жи́зни** life insurance

страх|ова́ть, у́ю *impf.* (*of* ▶ **застрахова́ть**) (от + *g.*) to insure (against); **с. себя́** (от + *g.*) (fig.) to insure (against), safeguard oneself (against)

страх|ова́ться, у́юсь *impf.* (*of* ▶ **застрахова́ться**) (от + *g.*) to insure oneself (against) (also fig.)

страхо́вк|а, и *f.* insurance

✓ **страхово́й** *adj.* insurance; **с. по́лис**

✓ key word

insurance policy

страш|и́ть, у́, и́шь *impf.* to frighten, scare

страш|и́ться, у́сь, и́шься *impf.* (+ *g.*) to be afraid (of), fear

стра́шно *adv.* **1** terribly, awfully; **с. испуга́ться** to get a terrible fright; **с. обра́доваться** to be awfully glad **2** (*as pred.*) it is terrible; it is terrifying; **мне с.** I am terrified; **мне с.** (+ *inf.*) I am terrified to do sth

✓ **стра́ш|ный, ∼ен, ∼на́, ∼но** *adj.* (о́чень плохо́й) terrible, awful, dreadful; (вызыва́ющий страх) terrifying, frightening; **с. расска́з** terrifying story; **с. сон** bad dream; **с. шум** (infml) awful din; **С. суд** the Day of Judgement, doomsday; **ничего́ ∼ного** it doesn't matter

стреко́з|а, ы́, *pl.* **∼ы** *f.* dragonfly

стреко|та́ть, чу́, ∼чешь *impf.* (о кузне́чиках) to chirr; (о соро́ках) to chatter; (fig., infml, болта́ть) to rattle, chatter

стрел|а́, ы́, *pl.* **∼ы** *f.* arrow (also fig.)

Стреле́ц, ьца́ *m.* Sagittarius

стре́лк|а, и *f.* **1** pointer, indicator; (часо́в) hand; (ко́мпаса) needle **2** (знак) arrow (on diagram, etc.) **3** (rail.) point(s) (BrE), switch (AmE); **перевести́ ∼у** to change the points; (fig., sl.): **перевести́ ∼и на** (+ *a.*) to lump the blame on

стрел|о́к, ка́ *m.* **1** shot; **отли́чный с.** good shot **2** (mil.) rifleman; (в самолёте, в та́нке) gunner

стрельб|а́, ы́, *pl.* **∼ы** *f.* shooting, firing

стрельн|у́ть, у́, ёшь *inst. pf.* **1** to fire a shot **2** (*impers.*): **у меня́ ∼у́ло в у́хе** I had a stab of pain in my ear **3** (infml, сигаре́ту) to cadge (BrE), bum (AmE)

стреля́|ть, ю *impf.* **1** (в + *a.* or по + *d.*) to shoot (at), fire (at); **с. из револьве́ра, из ружья́** to fire a revolver, a gun; **с. в цель** to shoot at a target; **с. по самолёту** to fire at an aeroplane (BrE), airplane (AmE) **2** (убива́ть) to shoot; **с. куропа́ток** to go partridge shooting **3** (infml, сигаре́ты) to cadge (BrE), bum (AmE) **4** (*impers.*) (о бо́ли) to have a shooting pain

стреля́|ться, юсь *impf.* **1** (самоуби́йца) to shoot oneself **2** (с + *i.*) (на дуэ́ли) to fight a duel (with firearms) (with)

стремгла́в *adv.* headlong

стреми́тель|ный, ∼ен, ∼ьна *adj.* (полёт, бег) swift, headlong; (рост, разви́тие) rapid; (ручей) fast-flowing

✓ **стреми́ться, млю́сь, и́шься** *impf.* **1** (устреми́ться) to rush **2** (к + *d.*) (добива́ться) to strive (for), seek, aspire (to); (+ *inf.*) to strive (to), try (to); **с. к соверше́нству** to strive for perfection **3** (в, на + *a.*) (жела́ть попа́сть) to want to go (to)

стремле́ни|е, я *nt.* (к + *d.*) striving (for), aspiration (to)

стре́м|я, *g., d. and p.* **∼ени,** *i.* **∼енем,** *pl.* **∼ена́, ∼я́н, ∼ена́м** *nt.* stirrup

стремя́нк|а, и *f.* stepladder, steps

стресс, а *m.* (psych.) stress

стре́ссовый *adj.* (*положение*) stressful; (*состояние*) stressed

стриж, а́ *m.* (zool.) swift

стри́жк|а, и *f.* **1** (*действие*) hair cutting; shearing; clipping **2** (*причёска*) haircut, hairstyle

стрипти́з, а *m.* striptease

стриптизёр, а *m.* (male) stripper

стриптизёр|ка, ки *and* ⁓ша, ⁓ши *f.* (female) stripper

стри|чь, гу́, жёшь, гу́т, *past* ⁓г, ⁓гла *impf.* **1** (*pf.* **остри́чь** *and* **постри́чь**) (*волосы, ногти, кусты*) to cut, clip **2** (*pf.* **остри́чь** *and* **постри́чь**) (*овец*) to shear; (*пуделя*) to clip **3** (*pf.* **постри́чь**) (*человека*): **с. кого́-н.** to cut sb's hair; to give sb a haircut

стри́|чься, гу́сь, жёшься, гу́тся, *past* ⁓гся, ⁓глась *impf.* (*pf.* ▶ **постри́чься**) **1** to cut one's hair; to have one's hair cut **2** (*no pf.*) (*носить короткие волосы*) to wear one's hair short

строга́|ть, ю *impf.* (tech.) to plane

стро́г|ий, ⁓, ⁓á, ⁓о *adj.* (*начальник, правила, диета*) strict; (*наказание, причёска*) severe; ⁓ие ме́ры strong measures; **с. пригово́р** severe sentence

стро́го *adv.* strictly; severely; **с. говоря́** strictly speaking

стро́гост|ь, и *f.* strictness; severity

строево́й *adj.* (mil.) **1** combatant, line; ⁓а́я слу́жба (front-)line service, combatant service **2** drill; ⁓а́я подгото́вка drill; **с. шаг** goose-step

строе́ни|е, я *nt.* **1** (*здание*) building, structure **2** (*структура*) structure, composition

строжа́йший *superl. of* ▶ **стро́гий**

стро́же *comp. of* ▶ **стро́гий**, ▶ **стро́го**

стро́ител|ь, я *m.* builder, constructor; (fig.) creator

строи́тельн|ый *adj.* building, construction; ⁓ая площа́дка building site; **с. раство́р** mortar

строи́тельств|о, а *nt.* building, construction (also fig.); **доро́жное с.** road-building; **жили́щное с.** house-building

стро́|ить, ю, ишь *impf.* (*pf.* ▶ **постро́ить**) **1** (*здание, дорогу, мост, плотину*) to build, construct; (*корабль, танк*) to build **2** (*новую жизнь, общество, счастье*) to create, build **3** (*фигуры, фразы, мысли*) to construct; to formulate; **с. фра́зу** to construct a sentence **4** (**на** + *p.*) (*обосновывать*) to base (on); **с. расчёт на** (+ *p.*) to base one's calculations on; **с. отноше́ния на дове́рии** to base relations on trust **5** (*планы, догадки*) to make; **с. гипоте́зу** to advance a hypothesis **6** (*ставить строй*) to draw up, form (up)

стро́|иться, юсь, ишься *impf.* (*of* ▶ **постро́иться**) **1** (*строить себе дом*) to build (a house, etc.) **2** (mil.) to draw up, form up; ⁓йся! (mil.) fall in! **3** *pass. of* ▶ **стро́ить**

стро́й[1], я, о ⁓е, в ⁓е, *pl.* ⁓и, ⁓ев *m.* system, order; structure; **обще́ственный с.** social system

стро́й[2], ⁓я, о ⁓е, в ⁓ю́, *pl.* ⁓й, ⁓ёв *m.* **1** (mil., naut., aeron., *порядок*) formation; **со́мкнутый с.** close order **2** (mil., *шеренга, часть*) unit in formation; **пе́ред ⁓ем** in front of the ranks **3** (mil., also fig., *действующий состав*) service, commission; **вы́вести из ⁓я** to disable; to put out of action; **вступи́ть в с.** to come into service, come into operation; **вы́йти из ⁓я** to be disabled; to become unserviceable; (*машина*) to break down

стро́йк|а, и *f.* **1** (*действие*) building, construction **2** (*место*) building site

стройматериа́л|ы, ов (*no sg.*) building materials

стро́йный, ⁓ен, ⁓йна́, ⁓йно, ⁓йны́ *adj.* **1** (*фигура*) well proportioned; shapely **2** (*пение*) harmonious; (*ряды*) orderly; (*фраза, доклад*) well-constructed

  строк|а́, и́, *pl.* ⁓и, ⁓, ⁓а́м *f.* line; (comput.) string; **нача́ть с кра́сной/но́вой ⁓и́** to begin a new paragraph; **чита́ть ме́жду ⁓** to read between the lines

стропи́л|о, а *nt.* rafter, beam

стропти́вый, ⁓, ⁓а *adj.* obstinate

строф|а́, ы́, *pl.* ⁓ы, ⁓, ⁓а́м *f.* (liter.) stanza, verse

стро́чк|а, и *f.* = **строка́**

стру́|иться, и́тся *impf.* to stream, flow

  структу́р|а, ы *f.* structure

структурали́зм, а *m.* structuralism

структу́рный *adj.* structural

струн|а́, ы́, *pl.* ⁓ы *f.* string

стру́нный *adj.* (mus.): **с. инструме́нт** stringed instrument; **с. кварте́т** string quartet

струп, а, *pl.* ⁓ья, ⁓ьев *m.* scab

стру́|сить, шу, сишь *pf. of* ▶ **тру́сить**

стручо́к, ка́ *m.* pod

стру|я́, и́, *pl.* ⁓и *f.* **1** (*воды*) jet, spurt, stream; (*света, воздуха*) stream; **бить ⁓ёй** to spurt **2** (fig.) spirit; impetus

стряс|ти́сь, ётся, *past* ⁓ся, ⁓ла́сь *pf.* (с + *i.*) (infml) to befall; **беда́ ⁓ла́сь с на́ми** a disaster befell us; **что с тобо́й ⁓ло́сь?** what's the matter with you?

стря́хива|ть, ю *impf. of* ▶ **стряхну́ть**

стря́х|нуть, ну́, нёшь *pf.* (*of* ▶ **стря́хивать**) to shake off

  студе́нт, а *m.* student, undergraduate; **с.-ме́дик** medical student

студе́нт|ка, ки *f. of* ▶ **студе́нт**

студе́нческий *adj. of* ▶ **студе́нт**; **с. биле́т** student card

сту́д|ень, ня *m.* galantine; aspic

сту́ди|я, и *f.* **1** (*живописца; телестудия*) studio; **с. звукоза́писи** recording studio **2** (*школа*) (art, drama, music, etc.) school

сту́ж|а, и *f.* severe cold, hard frost

стук, а *m.* (*в дверь*) knock; (*сердца*) thump; (*пишущей маши́нки*) clatter; (*падающего* *предмета*) thud; **с. в дверь** knock at/on the door; **с. колёс** rumble of wheels

сту́к|ать, аю *impf. of* ▶ **сту́кнуть**

сту́к|аться, аюсь *impf. of* ▶ **сту́кнуться**

стука́ч, а́ *m.* (*sl.*) police informer

сту́к|нуть, ну, нешь *pf.* (*of* ▶ **сту́кать**) **1** (**в** + *a. or* **по** + *d.*) to knock; to bang; **с. в дверь** to knock, bang at/on the door **2** (*ударить*) to bang, hit, strike; **с. кого́-н. по спине́** to slap/clap sb on the back

сту́к|нуться, нусь, нешься *pf.* (*of* ▶ **сту́каться**) (**о** + *a.*) to bang oneself (against), bump oneself (against)

стул, а, *pl.* **~ья, ~ьев** *m.* chair

сту́п|а, ы *f.* mortar

ступ|а́ть, а́ю *impf. of* ▶ **ступи́ть**

ступ|е́нь, е́ни *f.* **1** (*g. pl.* **~ене́й**) (*лестницы*) step; (*стремянки*) rung **2** (*g. pl.* **~ене́й**) (*этап*) stage; (*разряд*) grade; (*уровень*) level

ступе́нь|ка, ки *f.* = **ступе́нь 1**

ступ|и́ть, лю́, ~ишь *pf.* (*of* ▶ **ступа́ть**) to step; to tread

ступн|я́, и́, *pl.* **~и́, ~е́й** *f.* **1** (*стопа*) foot **2** (*подошва*) sole

сту́пор, а *m.* stupor

стуч|а́ть, у́, и́шь *impf.* **1** (*pf.* **по~**) to knock; to bang; to rap; (*о зубах*) to chatter **2** (*no pf.*) (*о сердце*) to thump, pound **3** (*pf.* **на~**) (*sl.*) (**на** + *a.*) (*доносить*) to report (*sb*)

стуч|а́ться, у́сь, и́шься *impf.* (*of* ▶ **постуча́ться**) (**в** + *a.*) to knock (at/on); **с. к сосе́ду** to knock at/on a neighbour's (BrE), neighbor's (AmE) door

стыд, а́ *m.* shame; **к на́шему ~у́** to our shame

стыди́ть, жу́, ди́шь *impf.* (*of* ▶ **пристыди́ть**) to shame, put to shame

стыди́ться, жу́сь, ди́шься *impf.* (*of* ▶ **постыди́ться**) (+ *g.*) to be ashamed (of)

стыдли́в|ый, ~, ~а *adj.* bashful

сты́дно *as pred.* it is a shame; **ему́** *и т. п.* **с.** he is, *etc.*, ashamed

стыко́вк|а, и *f.* docking

стю́ард, а *m.* steward

стюарде́сс|а, ы *f.* stewardess

стя́гива|ть, ю *impf. of* ▶ **стяну́ть 1**

стя́гива|ться, ю *impf. of* ▶ **стяну́ться**

стя|ну́ть, ну́, ~нешь *pf.* (*of* ▶ **стя́гивать**) **1** (*сапоги*) to pull off **2** (*pf. only*) (*infml, украсть*) to pinch (*infml, BrE*), steal

стя|ну́ться, ну́сь, ~нешься *pf.* (*of* ▶ **стя́гиваться**) **1** to tighten **2** (*infml, туго подпоясаться*) to gird oneself tightly **3** (*о войсках, демонстрантах*) to gather, assemble

суахи́ли *m. indecl.* Swahili (*language, people*)

суббо́т|а, ы *f.* Saturday

субмари́н|а, ы *f.* submarine

субподря́д, а *m.* subcontract

субподря́дчик, а *m.* subcontractor

субсиди́р|овать, ую *impf. and pf.* to subsidize

субси́ди|я, и *f.* subsidy

субста́нци|я, и *f.* substance

субти́тр, а *m.* (*usu. in pl.*) subtitle (*in film*)

субтро́пик|и, ов (*no sg.*) subtropics

субтропи́ческий *adj.* subtropical

✍ **субъе́кт, а** *m.* **1** (*phil., gram., med., law*) subject **2** (*infml, человек*) fellow, character, type

субъекти́в|ный, ~ен, ~на *adj.* subjective

сувени́р, а *m.* souvenir

суверените́т, а *m.* (*pol., law*) sovereignty

сувере́нный *adj.* (*pol., law*) sovereign

сугро́б, а *m.* snowdrift

✍ **суд, а́** *m.* **1** court, law court; **зал ~а́** courtroom; **заседа́ние ~а** sitting of the court **2** (*разбирательство*) trial, legal proceedings; **пода́ть в с. на кого́-н.** to bring an action against sb; **отда́ть под с., преда́ть ~у́** to prosecute; **с. прися́жных** jury **3** (*collect.*) (*судьи*) the judges; the bench **4** (*мнение*) judgement, verdict; **с. исто́рии** verdict of history

суда́к, а́ *m.* pikeperch (*fish*)

Суда́н, а *m.* (the) Sudan

суда́н|ец, ца *m.* Sudanese

суда́н|ка, ки *f. of* ▶ **суда́нец**

суда́нский *adj.* Sudanese

✍ **суде́б|ный** *adj.* judicial; legal; (*медицина, психиатрия*) forensic; **с. исполни́тель** bailiff, officer of the court; **~ая оши́бка** miscarriage of justice; **~ое разбира́тельство** legal proceedings, hearing of a case; **~ое реше́ние** court decision, court order

✍ **су|ди́ть, жу́, ~дишь** *impf.* **1** (**о** + *p.*) (*составлять мнение*) to judge; to form an opinion (about, on); **наско́лько мы могли́ с.** as far as we could judge; **~дя** (**по** + *d.*) judging (by), to judge (from); **~дя по всему́** to all appearances **2** (*law*) (**за** + *a.*) (*преступника*) to try (for) **3** (*осуждать*) to judge, pass judgement (upon); **не ~ди́те их стро́го!** don't be hard on them! **4** (*sport*) (*в крикете, теннисе*) to umpire

су|ди́ться, жу́сь, ~дишься *impf.* (**с** + *i.*) to sue

су́д|но, на, *pl.* **~а́, ~о́в** *nt.* vessel

судове́рф|ь, и *f.* shipyard

судовладе́л|ец, ьца *m.* shipowner

судопроизво́дств|о, а *nt.* legal proceedings

су́дорог|а, и *f.* cramp, convulsion, spasm

судостро́ени|е, я *nt.* shipbuilding

судохо́д|ный, ~ен, ~на *adj.* **1** navigable; **с. кана́л** shipping canal **2**: **~ная компа́ния** shipping company

судохо́дств|о, а *nt.* navigation, shipping

✍ **судьб|а́, ьбы́,** *pl.* **~ьбы, ~еб, ~ьбам** *f.* fate, fortune; (*будущее*) destiny; (*история существования*) story; **благодари́ть ~ьбу́** to thank one's lucky stars; **искуша́ть ~ьбу́**

с

суд|ья́, ьи́, pl. **~ьи, ~е́й, ~ьям** m. (also f.) (infml, o женщине) **1** judge; **я вам не с.!** who am I to judge you? **2** (sport) referee; (в крикете, теннисе) umpire; **с. на ли́нии** linesman

су́дя see ▶ **суди́ть**

суеве́ри|е, я nt. superstition

суеве́р|ный, ~ен, ~на adj. superstitious

сует|а́, ы́ f. **1** (тщетность) vanity **2** (хлопоты) bustle, fuss

суе|ти́ться, чу́сь, ти́шься impf. to bustle, fuss

суетли́в|ый, ~, ~а adj. fussy, bustling

сужде́ни|е, я nt. (мнение) opinion; (в логике) judgement

су́жива|ться, ется impf. of ▶ **су́зиться**

су́|зиться, зится pf. (of ▶ **су́живаться**) to narrow (intrans.); get narrow; to taper

суици́д, а m. suicide

сук, а́, о ~е́, на ~у́, pl. **су́чья, су́чьев** m. bough

су́к|а, и f. bitch (also as term of abuse)

сук|но́, на́, pl. **~на, ~он** nt. (heavy, coarse) cloth

сумасбро́д|ный, ~ен, ~на adj. wild, extravagant

сумасше́дш|ий adj. **1** mad; (as m. n. **с.,** ~**его**) madman, lunatic; (~**ая, ~ей**) madwoman, lunatic **2**: **с. дом** (infml) madhouse **3** (fig.) mad, lunatic; ~**ая ско́рость** lunatic speed; **э́то бу́дет сто́ить** ~**их де́нег** it will cost the earth

сумасше́стви|е, я nt. madness, lunacy

сумато́х|а, и f. confusion, chaos

сумбу́р|ный, ~ен, ~на adj. confused, chaotic

суме́|ть, ю pf. (+ inf.) to be able (to), manage (to)

су́мк|а, и f. **1** bag; **хозя́йственная с.** shopping bag **2** (biol.) pouch

су́мм|а, ы f. sum; **о́бщая/по́лная с.** sum total; (количество) amount

сумма́р|ный, ~ен, ~на adj. **1** (количество) total **2** (обзор) summary

сумми́р|овать, ую impf. and pf. **1** (складывать) to add up **2** (обобщить) to summarize; to sum up

су́мочк|а, и f. (дамская) handbag

су́мрак, а m. dusk, twilight

су́мрач|ный, ~ен, ~на adj. gloomy (also fig.)

сунду́к, а́ m. trunk, box, chest

сунни́т, а m. Sunni (Muslim)

су́н|уть, у, ешь pf. of ▶ **сова́ть**

су́н|уться, усь, ешься pf. of ▶ **сова́ться**

суп, а, pl. **~ы́** m. soup

суперзапре́т, а m. superinjunction

суперзвезд|а́, ы́, pl. **~ы, ~, ~ам** f. superstar

суперма́ркет, а m. supermarket

супермоде́л|ь, и f. supermodel

суперобло́жк|а, и f. dust jacket

су́пниц|а, ы f. soup tureen

супру́г, а m. **1** husband, spouse **2** (in pl.) (муж и жена) husband and wife, married couple

супру́г|а, и f. wife, spouse

супру́жеский adj. (чета, жизнь) married; (верность, счастье) marital

супру́жеств|о, а nt. matrimony, wedlock

суро́в|ый, ~, ~а adj. **1** (взгляд, критика) severe, stern; (зима, жизнь, приговор) harsh; (красота, воспитание) austere **2** (ткань) coarse

сур|о́к, ка́ m. marmot; **спать как с.** to sleep like a log

суррога́т, а m. surrogate, substitute

суррога́тн|ый adj. surrogate, substitute; ~**ая мать** surrogate mother

су́слик, а m. (zool.) ground squirrel, gopher (AmE)

суста́в, а m. (anat.) joint

сутенёр, а m. pimp

су́т|ки, ок (no sg.) twenty-four hours; twenty-four-hour period; **це́лые с.** for days and nights

суту́л|иться, юсь, ишься impf. (of ▶ **ссуту́литься**) to stoop

суту́л|ый, ~, ~а adj. round-shouldered, stooping

сут|ь, и f. essence; **с. де́ла** the heart, crux of the matter; **по ~и де́ла** as a matter of fact

су́ффикс, а m. (gram.) suffix

суха́р|ь, я́ m. (хлебный) rusk

су́хо adv. **1** coldly; **нас при́няли с.** we were received coldly **2** (as pred.) it is dry; **на у́лице с.** it is dry out of doors

сухогру́з, а m. bulk carrier

сухожи́ли|е, я nt. (anat.) tendon, sinew

сух|о́й, ~, ~а́, ~о adj. **1** dry; ~**о́е дрова́** dry firewood; ~**о́е ру́сло реки́** dried-up river bed **2** (хлеб) dry; (фру́кты) dried; ~**о́е молоко́** dried milk **3** (кожа) dried-up; (рука) withered; (худоща́вый) lean **4** (без влаги, жидкости) dry; **с. ка́шель** dry cough **5** (fig., холодный) chilly, cold; **с. приём** chilly reception

сухопу́тн|ый adj. land (opp. marine, air); ~**ые си́лы** (mil.) ground forces

сухофру́кт|ы, ов (no sg.) dried fruits

суч|о́к, ка́ m. twig

су́ш|а, и f. (dry) land (opp. sea); **по ~е** by land

су́ше comp. of ▶ **сухо́й,** ▶ **су́хо**

сушён|ый adj. dried

суши́лк|а, и f. **1** (устройство) drying apparatus, dryer; **напо́льная с.** clothes horse **2** (помещение) drying room

суши́|ть, у́, ~ишь impf. (of ▶ **вы́сушить**) to dry (out)

суши́|ться, усь, ~ишься impf. (of ▶ **вы́сушиться**) to dry (out); (человек) to get dry

су́шк|а, и f. **1** drying **2** (cul.) dry (ring-shaped) cracker

С

суще́ствен|ный, ~, ~на *adj.* (*черта, разница*) essential; (*роль, значение*) vital; (*крупный*) substantial; (*вопрос*) important

существи́тельн|ое *adj.*: и́мя **с.** (*or as nt. n.* **с.**, ~ого) noun; **с.** мужско́го/же́нского/сре́днего ро́да masculine/feminine/neuter noun

существ|о́, а́ *nt.* 1 (*сущность*) essence; по ~у́ (*говоря́*) in essence, essentially; говори́ть по ~у́ to speak to the point; не по ~у́ off the point, beside the point 2 (*живая особь*) being, creature; люби́мое **с.** loved one

существова́ни|е, я *nt.* existence; борьба́ за **с.** struggle for survival

существ|ова́ть, у́ю *impf.* to exist

существу́ющий *pres. participle of* ▶ существова́ть *and adj.* existing

су́щ|ий *adj.* (infml, *правда*) absolute; utter; **с.** ад absolute hell; ~ая ерунда́ utter rubbish; э́то/он ~ее наказа́ние it/he is the bane of my life

су́щност|ь, и *f.* essence; в ~и (говоря́) in essence, essentially

сфабрик|ова́ть, у́ю *pf. of* ▶ фабрикова́ть

сфе́р|а, ы *f.* sphere; **с.** влия́ния (pol.) sphere of influence; вы́сшие ~ы highest circles

сфери́ческий *adj.* spherical

сфокуси́р|овать, ую *pf. of* ▶ фокуси́ровать

сфокуси́р|оваться, уюсь *pf. of* ▶ фокуси́роваться

сформир|ова́ть, у́ю *pf. of* ▶ формирова́ть

сформир|ова́ться, у́юсь *pf. of* ▶ формирова́ться

сформули́р|овать, ую *pf. of* ▶ формули́ровать

сфотографи́р|овать, ую *pf. of* ▶ фотографи́ровать

сфотографи́р|оваться, уюсь *pf. of* ▶ фотографи́роваться

схва|ти́ть, чу́, ~тишь *pf.* 1 *pf. of* ▶ хвата́ть¹ 1 2 (*pf. only*) (infml, *простуду*) to catch 3 (*impf.* ~тывать) (infml, *мысль*) to grasp, comprehend; **с.** смысл to grasp the meaning, catch on

схва|ти́ться, чу́сь, ~тишься *pf.* 1 *pf. of* ▶ хвата́ться 2 (*impf.* ~тываться) (с + *i.*) to grapple (with) (also fig.)

схва́тк|а, и *f.* skirmish, fight; (*в спорте*) fight; (*в споре*) clash; рукопа́шная **с.** hand-to-hand fight

схва́т|ки, ок (*no sg.*) (med.) contractions (*of muscles*); spasms; родовы́е **с.** labour (BrE), labor (AmE)

схва́тыва|ть, ю *impf. of* ▶ схвати́ть

схва́тыва|ться, юсь *impf. of* ▶ схвати́ться

схе́м|а, ы *f.* 1 (*чертёж*) diagram, chart; **с.** метро́ metro map 2 (*сочинения*) sketch, outline, plan 3 (elec., radio) circuit

схемати́ч|ный, ~ен, ~на *adj.* sketchy, (over)simplified

схитр|и́ть, ю́, и́шь *pf. of* ▶ хитри́ть

схлы́н|уть, у, ешь *pf.* 1 (*о волнах*) to break and flow back 2 (*о толпе*) to break up; to dwindle 3 (*о чувствах*) to subside

сходи́ть¹, жу́, ~дишь *impf. of* ▶ сойти́

сходи́ть², жу́, ~дишь *pf.* to go (*and come back*); (за + *i.*) to go to fetch; **с.** посмотре́ть to go to see; ~ди за врачо́м! go and fetch a doctor!

сходи́ться, жу́сь, ~дишься *impf. of* ▶ сойти́сь

сходк|а, и *f.* gathering, assembly

схо́дн|и, ей *f. pl.* (*sg.* ~я, ~и) gangway, gangplank

схо́д|ный, ~ен, ~на *adj.* (с + *i.*) similar (to)

схо́дств|о, а *nt.* likeness, resemblance; вне́шнее **с.** similarity in appearance

схо́ж|ий, ~, ~а *adj.* (infml) (с + *i.*) similar (to)

сца́па|ть, ю *pf.* (infml) to grab, catch hold (of)

сце|ди́ть, жу́, ~дишь *pf.* (*of* ▶ сце́живать) to pour off, decant; (*через сито, марлю*) to strain off

сце́жива|ть, ю *impf. of* ▶ сцеди́ть

сце́н|а, ы *f.* 1 (*подмостки*) stage (also fig.) 2 (*эпизод, происшествие*) scene 3 (infml) scene; устро́ить ~у to make a scene

сцена́ри|й, я *m.* 1 (*фильма, передачи*) scenario, script 2 (*детальный план*) plan, programme (BrE), program (AmE) 3 (fig., *вариант*) scenario

сценари́ст, а *m.* scriptwriter

сценари́ст|ка, ки *f. of* ▶ сценари́ст

сцеп|и́ть, лю́, ~ишь *pf.* (*of* ▶ сцепля́ть) 1 (*вагоны, кузова*) to couple 2 (*пальцы*) to clasp

сцеп|и́ться, лю́сь, ~ишься *pf.* (*of* ▶ сцепля́ться) 1 (*вагоны, детали*) to be coupled; (*ветки*) to be intertwined; to intertwine; (*частицы*) to stick together 2 (с + *i.*) (infml, *начать драться*) to grapple (with)

сцепле́ни|е, я *nt.* 1 (*действие*) coupling 2 (tech.) clutch; (*клеток, веществ*) cohesion; выключе́ние ~я clutch release

сцепля́|ть, ю *impf. of* ▶ сцепи́ть

сцепля́|ться, юсь *impf. of* ▶ сцепи́ться

сча́стливо *adv.* (*жить, улыбаться*) happily; **с.** отде́латься (от + *g.*) to have a lucky escape (from); счастли́во (остава́ться)! good luck!

счастли́в|ый, ~лив, ~лива *adj.* 1 (*лицо, детство, человек*) happy; **с.** коне́ц happy end 2 (*игрок, случай, день*) lucky 3: ~ливого пути́! bon voyage!

сча́сть|е, я *nt.* 1 (*чувство*) happiness; жела́ю вам **с.** I wish you happiness 2 (*удача*) luck, good fortune; к ~ю luckily, fortunately; на на́ше **с.** luckily for us; како́е **с.**, что... how fortunate that ...

сче́сть, сочту́, сочтёшь, *past* счёл, сочла́ *pf. of* ▶ счита́ть 3

счёт, а (у), *pl.* ~ы *and* счета́ *m.* 1 (*sg. only*) (*действие*) counting, calculation, reckoning; вести́ **с.** (+ *d.*) to keep count (of); в два

~a in a jiffy, in a trice **2** (*sg. only*) (sport) score; **со** ~**ом** 2:1 with a score of 2-1 **3** (*pl.* **счета́**) (*в рестора́не, за газ, за телефо́н*) bill; (*накладна́я*) invoice; **уплати́ть по** ~**y** to pay the bill **4** (*pl.* **счета́**) (*в ба́нке*) account; **откры́ть с.** to open an account; **за с.** (+ *g.*) at the expense (of) **5** (*sg. only*) (fig.) account, expense; **в с.** (+ *g.*) on the strength (of); **в коне́чном** ~**e** in the end; **за с.** (+ *g.*) at the expense (of); owing (to); **приня́ть на свой с.** to take (sth) personally; **на э́тот с.** in this respect **6** (~**ы**) (fig., *прете́нзии*) accounts, score(s); **ста́рые** ~**ы** old scores; **свести́** ~**ы** (**с** + *i.*) to settle a score (with), get even (with) **7** *see* ▶ **счёты¹**

счётчик, а *m.* meter; counter; **га́зовый с.** gas meter

счёт|ы¹, ов (*no sg.*) abacus

счёты² *see* ▶ **счёт 6**

счи́|стить, щу, стишь *pf.* (*of* ▶ **счища́ть**) to clean off

счи́тан|ый *adj.* a few; **остаю́тся** ~**ые дни** (до + *g.*) one can count the days (until); there are only a few days left (until); ~**ое коли́чество** (*де́нег*) very little; (*предме́тов*) very few

⚡ **счита́|ть**, ю *impf.* (*of* ▶ **посчита́ть**) **1** (*pf. also* **co**~) to count; **с. дни, мину́ты** to count the days, minutes; **не** ~**я** not counting **2** (*pf. also* **счесть**) (+ *i. or* **за** + *a.*) to count, consider, think; to regard (as); **я** ~**ю его́ надёжным челове́ком** I consider him a reliable person; **с. необходи́мым/ну́жным** to consider it necessary **3** (*pf. also* **счесть**): **с. (что)** to consider (that), hold (that)

⚡ **счита́|ться**, юсь *impf.* (*no pf.*) **1** (+ *i.*) to be considered, be thought, be reputed; to be regarded (as); **он** ~**ется первокла́ссным специали́стом** he is considered a first-rate specialist; ~**ется, что...** it is considered that ... **2** (**с** + *i.*) (*принима́ть в расчёт*) to consider, take into consideration; to take into account, reckon (with); **он всегда́** ~**лся с мои́м мне́нием** he always took my opinion into consideration; **он ни с кем не** ~**ется** he has no consideration for anyone

счища́|ть, ю *impf. of* ▶ **счи́стить**

США *pl. indecl.* (*abbr. of* **Соединённые Шта́ты Аме́рики**) US(A) (*United States of America*)

шиб|а́ть, а́ю *impf. of* ▶ **сшиби́ть**

сшиб|и́ть, у́, ёшь, *past* ~, ~**ла** *pf.* (*of* ▶ **сшиба́ть**) (infml) to knock off; **с. с ног** to knock down, knock over

сшива́|ть, ю *impf. of* ▶ **сшить 2**

сшить, сошью́, сошьёшь *pf.* **1** *pf. of* ▶ **шить 2** (*impf.* **сшива́ть**) to sew together; (med.) to suture

съ... *vbl. pref.* = **с...**

съеда́|ть, ю *impf.* (*of* ▶ **съесть**) to eat (up)

съедо́б|ный, ~**ен**, ~**на** *adj.* edible

съёжива|ться, юсь *impf. of* ▶ **съёжиться**

съёж|иться, усь, ишься *pf.* (*of* ▶ **съёживаться**) (*в комо(че)к; от хо́лода*) to huddle up; (*о ли́стьях, лице́*) to shrivel up;

(*о тка́ни*) to shrink

съезд¹, а *m.* (*собра́ние*) congress; conference, convention

съезд², а *m.* (*спуск*) descent

съе́з|дить, жу, дишь *pf.* to go (*and come back*); **как (ты)** ~**дила?** how was your trip?

съезжа́|ть, ю *impf.* ▶ **съе́хать**

съезжа́|ться, юсь *impf. of* ▶ **съе́хаться**

съел *see* ▶ **съесть**

съёмк|а, и *f.* **1** (*ме́стности*) survey, surveying; plotting **2** (*usu. in pl.*) (*фи́льма*) shooting

съёмный *adj.* detachable, removable

съёмщик, а *m.* tenant

съёмщиц|а, ы *f. of* ▶ **съёмщик**

съестн|о́й *adj.* food; ~**ы́е припа́сы** food supplies, provisions; (*as nt. n.* ~**о́е**, ~**о́го**) food

съе|сть, м, шь, ст, ди́м, ди́те, дя́т, *past* ~**л**, ~**ла** *pf.* *of* ▶ **есть¹**, ▶ **съеда́ть**

съе́|хать, ду, дешь *pf.* (*of* ▶ **съезжа́ть**) **1** (*спусти́ться*) to go down, come down **2** (*с кварти́ры*) to move out **3** (fig., infml, *дви́нуться с ме́ста*) to come down, slip; **у тебя́ га́лстук** ~**хал на́бок** your tie is on one side

съе́|хаться, дусь, дешься *pf.* (*of* ▶ **съезжа́ться**) **1** (*встре́титься*) to meet **2** (*собра́ться*) to arrive, gather, assemble

сы́воротк|а, и *f.* serum

сыгра́|ть, ю *pf.* (*of* ▶ **игра́ть**): **с. шу́тку** (**с** + *i.*) to play a practical joke (on)

сымити́р|овать, ую *pf. of* ▶ **имити́ровать**

сымпровизи́р|овать, ую *pf. of* ▶ **импровизи́ровать**

⚡ **сын**, а, *pl.* ~**овья́**, ~**ове́й** *m.* son

сы́п|ать, лю, лешь *impf.* to pour

сы́п|аться, лется *impf.* **1** (*о чём-н. ме́лком*) to fall; (*о сыпуче́м*) to pour out; (*разбега́ться*) to scatter; **мука́** ~**алась из мешка́** flour poured out of the bag **2** (infml, *о зву́ках*) to pour forth (*intrans.*), rain down; **уда́ры** ~**ались гра́дом** blows were raining thick and fast **3** (*о штукату́рке*) to flake off

сып|ь, и *f.* (med.) rash, eruption

сыр, а, *pl.* ~**ы́** *m.* cheese

сыре́|ть, ю *impf.* (*of* ▶ **отсыре́ть**) to become damp

сы́ро *as pred.* it is damp

сыроёжк|а, и *f.* russula (*mushroom*)

сыр|о́й, ~, ~**á**, ~**о** *adj.* **1** (*вла́жный*) damp; (*ле́то, день*) wet **2** (*о́вощи, те́сто*) raw, uncooked; ~**áя вода́** unboiled water; ~**о́е мя́со** raw meat **3** (*незре́лый*) green, unripe **4** (*необрабо́танный*) raw; (*расска́з, план*) unfinished, unrefined

сыр|о́к, ка́ *m.* (*творо́жный*) curd cheese; **пла́вленый с.** processed cheese

сы́рост|ь, и *f.* dampness, humidity

сырь|ё, я́ (*no pl.*) *nt.* raw material(s)

сырьев|о́й *adj. of* **сырьё**; ~**áя ба́за** raw material supply

с

сыск, а *m.* investigation, detection (*of criminals*)

сы́т|ный, ∼ен, ∼на́, ∼но *adj.* (*обед*) substantial, copious; (*пирог*) filling, rich; (*питательный*) nourishing

сы́т|ый, ∼, ∼а́, ∼о *adj.* **1** satisfied, full; **спаси́бо, я ∼** thank you, I am full **2** (*откормленный*) well fed **3** (fig.) (+ *i.*) (*пресыщенный*) fed up with; **я ∼ по го́рло** I'm fed up to the back teeth (with)

сы́щик, а *m.* detective

сэконо́м|ить, лю, ишь *pf. of* ▶ **эконо́мить**

сэр, а *m.* sir

✓ **сюда́** *adv.* here, hither

сюже́т, а *m.* (*картины, симфонии*) subject; (*романа*) plot

сюи́т|а, ы *f.* (mus.) suite

сюрпри́з, а *m.* surprise

сюрреали́зм, а *m.* surrealism

сюрреали́ст, а *m.* surrealist

сюрреалисти́ческий *adj.* surrealist

сюрту́к, а́ *m.* frock coat

сюсю́ка|ть, ю *impf.* (infml) to lisp

Тт

т (*abbr. of* **то́нна**) t, ton(s), tonne(s)

таба́к, а́ у́ *m.* tobacco

табаке́рк|а, и *f.* snuffbox

та́бел|ь, я *m.* **1** (*график*) table, chart **2** (*на заводе*) time board (*for tracking attendance*)

та́бельщик, а *m.* timekeeper

табле́тк|а, и *f.* tablet, pill; **т. аспири́на** aspirin

✓ **табли́ц|а, ы** *f.* table; **электро́нная т.** (comput.) spreadsheet

табло́ *nt. indecl.* (*на вокзале*) information board; (sport) scoreboard

табло́ид, а *m.* tabloid (newspaper)

та́бор, а *m.* **1** (*лагерь*) camp **2** (*группа цыган*) band of gypsies

табу́ *nt. indecl.* taboo

табу́н, а́ *m.* herd (*usu. of horses*)

табуре́т, а *m.* = **табуре́тка**

табуре́т|ка, ки *f.* stool

тавр|о́, а́, *pl.* ∼а, ∼, ∼а́м *nt.* brand (*on cattle, etc.*)

тавтоло́ги|я, и *f.* tautology

тага́н, а́ *m.* trivet

таджи́к, а *m.* Tajik

Таджикиста́н, а *m.* Tajikistan

таджи́кский *adj.* Tajik

таджи́ч|ка, и *f. of* ▶ **таджи́к**

таз¹, а, в ∼у́, *pl.* ∼ы́ *m.* bowl

таз², а, в ∼е *and* **в ∼у́, *pl.* ∼ы́** *m.* (anat.) pelvis

тазобе́дренный *adj.* (anat.) hip; **т. суста́в** hip joint

Таила́нд, а *m.* Thailand

таила́нд|ец, ца *m.* Thai

таила́нд|ка, ки *f. of* ▶ **таила́ндец**

таила́ндский *adj.* Thai

таи́нствен|ный, ∼ *and* **∼ен, ∼на** *adj.* **1** (*место, шорох, взгляд*) mysterious; (*человек*) enigmatic **2** (*цель*) secret **3** (*вид*) secretive

та́инств|о, а *nt.* (relig.) sacrament

Таити *m. indecl.* Tahiti

та|и́ть, ю́, и́шь *impf.* (*горе*) to hide, conceal; (*злобу*) to harbour (BrE), harbor (AmE); **т. зло́бу (про́тив** + *g.*) to harbour a grudge (against); **не́чего/что греха́ т.** it must be admitted, we must admit

та|и́ться, ю́сь, и́шься *impf.* **1** (infml, *скрываться*) to be (in) hiding, lurk **2** (fig., *иметься*) to lurk, be lurking; **что за э́тим ∼и́тся?** what lies behind this?

Тайва́н|ь, я *m.* Taiwan

тайг|а́, и́ *f.* (geog.) taiga

тайко́м *adv.* in secret, surreptitiously; on the quiet

тайм-а́ут, а *m.* (*перерыв в чём-л.*) time off; (sport) timeout

та́йн|а, ы *f.* **1** (*то, что непонятно*) mystery **2** (*секрет*) secret; **храни́ть ∼у** to keep a secret

тайни́к, а́ *m.* hiding place (*for a thing*)

та́йн|ый *adj.* secret; clandestine; **т. аге́нт** undercover agent; **∼ое голосова́ние** secret ballot

та́йский *adj.* Thai

тайфу́н, а *m.* typhoon

тайцзицюа́н|ь *f. indecl.* t'ai chi (chu'an)

✓ **так** *adv.* **1** (*таким образом*) so; thus, in this way, like this; in such a way; **т. мно́го** so many; **мы сде́лали т.** this is what we did, we did as follows; **т. вот** (*выражает продолжение повествования после отступления*) and so, so then; **т. же** in the same way; **т. и́ли ина́че** whatever happens, one way or another; **т. себе́** so-so, middling; **т. сказа́ть** so to speak; **и т. да́лее** (*usu. spelt* **и т. д.**) and so on, and so forth; **(не) т. ли?**

✓ key word

isn't it so? **2** (*как сле́дует*) as it should be; не т. amiss, wrong; не совсе́м т. not quite right **3** (*без специа́льных сре́дств; без после́дствий*) just like that; ему́ э́то т. не пройдёт he won't get away with it like that **4**: т. (то́лько), про́сто т. for no special reason, for no reason in particular; just for fun **5**: т. как (*conj.*) as, since **6**: т. что (*conj.*) so; т. что́бы so that

такела́ж, а *m.* rigging

◦ **та́кже** *adv.* also, too, as well; (*after neg.*) or, nor

-таки *particle* (infml) however, though; опя́ть-таки again

тако́в, *f.* ~а́, *nt.* ~о́, *pl.* ~ы́ *pron.* such; ~ы́ тре́бования зако́на such/these are the legal requirements; и был т. (infml) and that was the last we saw of him

таково́й *adj.*: как т. as such

◦ **тако́|й** *pron.* **1** such; so; т. же the same; он т. до́брый! he is such a kind man!; ~и́м о́бразом thus, in this way; в ~о́м слу́чае in that case **2**: кто он т.? who is he?; что э́то ~о́е? what is this?

тако́й-то *pron.* so-and-so; such-and-such

такси́ *nt. indecl.* taxi

такси́ст, а *m.* taxi driver

таксофо́н, а *m.* payphone

такт[1], а *m.* **1** (mus., *ритм*) time; отбива́ть т. to beat time; (*в нотах*) bar **2** (tech.) stroke (*of engine*)

такт[2], а *m.* (*такти́чность*) tact

та́ктик|а, и *f.* tactics

такти́ческий *adj.* tactical

такти́ч|ный, ~ен, ~на *adj.* tactful

тала́нт, а *m.* **1** (*дар*) talent, gift(s) **2** (*челове́к*) gifted person

тала́нтлив|ый, ~, ~а *adj.* talented, gifted

талисма́н, а *m.* talisman, charm, mascot

та́ли|я, и *f.* waist

Та́ллин, а *m.* Tallinn

тало́н, а *m.* (*на бензи́н*) coupon; поса́дочный т. boarding pass

тальк, а *m.* talcum powder

◦ **там** *adv.* there; т. же in the same place; (*при ссы́лках*) ibid

та́мбур, а *m.* (*железнодоро́жного ваго́на*) platform (*of railway carriage*)

тамбури́н, а *m.* tambourine

тами́л, а *m.* Tamil

тами́л|ка, ки *f. of* ▶ тами́л

тами́льский *adj.* Tamil

тамо́женник, а *m.* customs official

тамо́женный *adj.* customs

тамо́жн|я, и *f.* customs

тампо́н, а *m.* tampon

та́н|ец, ца *m.* **1** (*иску́сство*) dance; dancing; уро́ки ~цев dancing lessons **2** (*in pl.*) (*ве́чер*) a dance, dancing; пойти́ на ~цы to go to a dance, go dancing

танзани́|ец, йца *m.* Tanzanian

танзани́й|ка, ки *f. of* ▶ танзани́ец

танзани́йский *adj.* Tanzanian

Танза́ни|я, и *f.* Tanzania

танк, а *m.* (mil.) tank

та́нкер, а *m.* (naut.) tanker

танки́ст, а *m.* member of tank crew

танц|ева́ть, у́ю *impf.* to dance

танцо́вщик, а *m.* (professional) dancer

танцо́вщиц|а, ы *f. of* ▶ танцо́вщик

танцо́р, а *m.* (professional) dancer

та́почк|а, и *f.* slipper; спорти́вная т. sports shoe, sneaker (AmE)

та́р|а, ы *f.* packing, packaging

тарака́н, а *m.* cockroach

тара́н, а *m.* (mil.) **1** ram; ramming **2** (hist.) battering ram

тара́нтул, а *m.* tarantula

тарато́р|ить, ю, ишь *impf.* (infml) to jabber; to gabble

тарах|те́ть, чу́, ти́шь *impf.* (infml) to rattle, rumble

таре́лк|а, и *f.* **1** plate; глубо́кая т. soup plate **2** (tech.) plate, disc; (infml, *спу́тниковая*) (satellite) dish **3** (*in pl.*) (mus.) cymbals

тари́ф, а *m.* tariff, rate

таска́|ть, ю *impf.* (indet. of ▶ тащи́ть)

таска́|ться, юсь *impf.* (indet. of ▶ тащи́ться)

тас|ова́ть, у́ю *impf.* (of ▶ перетасова́ть) (cards) to shuffle

тата́р|ин, ина, *pl.* ~ы, ~ *m.* Tatar

тата́р|ка, ки *f. of* ▶ тата́рин

татаромонго́л, а *n.* Tartar (hist.)

татаромонго́льский *adj.* Tartar (hist.)

тата́рский *adj.* Tatar

татуи́р|овать, ую *impf. and pf.* to tattoo

татуиро́вк|а, и *f.* tattoo

тахт|а́, ы́ *f.* ottoman

та́чк|а, и *f.* wheelbarrow; (infml, *автомоби́ль*) car

Ташке́нт, а *m.* Tashkent

тащ|и́ть, у́, ~ишь *impf.* (det. of ▶ таска́ть) **1** (*мяну́ть*) to pull; (*что-н. тяжёлое*) to drag, lug; (*нести́*) to carry **2** (infml) (*вести́*) to take; (fig., *заставля́ть пойти́ куда́-н.*) to drag off **3** (*извлека́ть*) to pull out

тащ|и́ться, у́сь, ~ишься *impf.* (det. of ▶ таска́ться) **1** (*идти́ с трудо́м*) to drag oneself along; (*ме́дленно е́хать*) to trundle along; (*за кем-н.*) to trail along **2** (*о подо́ле*) to drag, trail **3** (от + *g.*) (sl.) to be crazy about

та́яни|е, я *nt.* thaw, thawing

та́|ять, ю, ешь *impf.* (of ▶ раста́ять) **1** to melt; to thaw; ~ет it is thawing **2** (fig., *исчеза́ть*) to melt away, dwindle, wane; его́ си́лы ~яли his strength was ebbing **3** (от + *g.*) (fig., *от любви́*) to melt (with), languish (with)

Тбили́си *m. indecl.* Tbilisi

ТВ (*abbr. of* телеви́дение) (*abbr. of* телеви́дение) TV (television)

тва́р|ь, и *f.* creature; (also pej.) (*collect.*) creatures; all creation; (pej., *по́длый челове́к*) swine

Т

тверде́|ть, ет *impf.* to harden, become hard

твер|ди́ть, жу́, ди́шь *impf.* (+ *a.* or *o* + *p.*) to repeat, say over and over again

тве́рдо *adv.* firmly; (*знать, вы́учить*) thoroughly

твердоло́б|ый, ~, ~а *adj.* diehard

твёрдост|ь, и *f.* hardness; (fig.) firmness

твёрд|ый, ~, тверда́, ~о, ~ы and тверды́ *adj.* **1** (*не мя́гкий*) hard **2** (*кре́пкий*) firm; (*не жи́дкий*) solid; **т. переплёт** stiff binding; **~ое те́ло** (phys., chem.) solid **3** (fig.) (*непоколеби́мый*) firm; (*устано́вленный*) stable; (*сто́йкий*) steadfast; **~ое реше́ние** firm decision; **~ые це́ны** stable, fixed prices **4** (ling.) hard; **т. знак** hard sign (*name of Russian letter* «*ъ*»)

тверды́н|я, и *f.* stronghold (also fig.)

твит, а *m.* (comput.) tweet (*a message posted using Twitter* (propr.))

тви́т|ить, ю, ишь *impf.* (comput., *обща́ться в Интерне́те че́рез се́рвис Тви́ттер*) to tweet

Тви́ттер, а *m.* (comput, *се́рвис микробло́гов*) Twitter®

тво|й, его́, *f.* **~я́, ~е́й,** *nt.* **~е, ~его́,** *pl.* **~й, ~и́х** *poss. pron.* (*при существи́тельном*) your; (*без существи́тельного*) yours

творе́ни|е, я *nt.* **1** (*произведе́ние*) creation; work **2** (*существо́*) creature, being

твор|е́ц, ца́ *m.* creator; (**Т.**) (*Бог*) the Creator

твори́тельный *adj.*: **т. паде́ж** (gram.) instrumental case

твор|и́ть, ю́, и́шь *impf.* (*of* ▸ **сотвори́ть**) **1** (*создава́ть*) to create **2** (*де́лать*) to do; to make; **т. чудеса́** to work wonders

твор|и́ться, и́тся *impf.* (infml) to happen, go on

творо́г, а́ and тво́рог, а *m.* curd cheese

тво́рческий *adj.* creative; **т. путь Толсто́го** Tolstoy's career as a writer

тво́рчеств|о, а *nt.* **1** creation; creative work **2** (collect.) works

т. е. (*abbr. of* **то есть**) i.e., that is, viz.

теа́тр, а *m.* **1** theatre (BrE), theater (AmE); **т. и кино́** stage and screen; **т. вое́нных де́йствий** (mil.) theatre of operations

театра́л, а *m.* theatregoer (BrE), theatergoer (AmE)

театра́л|ьный, ~ен, ~ьна *adj.* **1** theatre (BrE), theater (AmE); theatrical; **~ьная ка́сса** box office; **~ьная шко́ла** drama school **2** (fig., *жест, по́за*) theatrical

Тегера́н, а *m.* Teh(e)ran

теза́урус, а *m.* thesaurus

те́зис, а *m.* thesis, proposition

тёзк|а, и *c.g.* namesake

текст, а *m.* **1** text **2** (*пе́сни*) words, lyrics; (*о́перы*) libretto

тексти́льный *adj.* textile

тексти́льщик, а *m.* textile worker

тексти́льщи|ца, цы *f. of* ▸ **тексти́льщик**

те́кстовый *adj. of* ▸ **текст**; **т. реда́ктор** (comput.) word processor

теку́ч|ий, ~, ~а *adj.* **1** (phys.) fluid **2** (*непостоя́нный*) fluctuating, unstable

теку́щ|ий *pres. part. act. of* ▸ **течь²** *and adj.* **1** current; of the present moment; **~ие собы́тия** current events, current affairs; **т. счёт** current account (BrE), checking account (AmE) **2** (*повседне́вный*) routine, ordinary; **т. ремо́нт** routine repairs

тел. (*abbr. of* **телефо́н**) tel., telephone

теле... *comb. form* tele-

телевеща́ни|е, я *nt.* television broadcasting

телеви́дени|е, я *nt.* television, TV

телевизио́нный *adj.* television

телеви́зор, а *m.* television set

теле́г|а, и *f.* cart, wagon

телегра́мм|а, ы *f.* telegram

телегра́ф, а *m.* **1** (*систе́ма*) telegraph **2** (*учрежде́ние*) telegraph office

телеграфи́р|овать, ую *impf. and pf.* to telegraph, wire

телеграфи́ст, а *m.* telegraphist

телеграфи́ст|ка, ки *f. of* ▸ **телеграфи́ст**

телеграфн|ый *adj.* telegraph; telegraphic; **~ое аге́нтство** news agency; **т. столб** telegraph pole (BrE), telephone pole (AmE)

теле́жк|а, и *f.* **1** *dim. of* ▸ **теле́га 2** (*бага́жная; в суперма́ркете*) trolley (BrE), cart (AmE)

телезри́тел|ь, я *m.* (television) viewer

телеигр|а́, ы́ *f.* game show

телека́мер|а, ы *f.* television camera

телекана́л, а *m.* TV channel

телекоммуника́ци|и, й *f. pl.* telecommunications

телекомпа́ни|я, и *f.* TV company

телеконфере́нци|я, и *f.* teleconference, conference call

те́лекс, а *m.* telex

телеметри́|я, и *f.* telemetry

телемо́ст, а and ~а́, pl. ~ы́ *m.* satellite (TV) link-up

телёнок, ёнка, pl. ~я́та, ~я́т *m.* calf

телеопера́тор, а *m.* TV cameraman

телепа́т, а *m.* telepathic person

телепа́ти|я, и *f.* telepathy

телепереда́ч|а, и *f.* TV programme (BrE), program (AmE)

телеско́п, а *m.* telescope

телескопи́ческий *adj.* telescopic

теле́сн|ый *adj.* bodily; corporal; physical; **~ое наказа́ние** corporal punishment; **~ого цве́та** flesh-coloured (BrE), flesh-colored (AmE)

телесту́ди|я, и *f.* television studio

телесуфлёр, а *m.* teleprompter, Autocue®

телете́кст, а *m.* teletext

телефа́кс, а *m.* (tele)fax (machine)

телефо́н, а *m.* **1** telephone; **позвони́ть по ~у** (+ *d.*) to telephone, phone, ring up (BrE); **т.-автома́т** public telephone, call box (BrE)

т

2 (infml, *номер*) telephone number

телефони́ст, а *m.* telephone operator, telephonist

телефони́ст|ка, ки *f. of* ▶ телефони́ст

телефо́н|ный *adj. of* ▶ телефо́н; ~ная кни́га telephone directory

Тел|е́ц, ьца́ *m.* Taurus

те́лик, а *m.* (infml) (the) telly (BrE), (the) TV

те́л|о, а, *pl.* ~а́, ~, ~а́м *nt.* body

телогре́йк|а, и *f.* body warmer

телосложе́ни|е, я *nt.* build, frame

телохрани́тел|ь, я *m.* bodyguard

Тель-Ави́в, а *m.* Tel Aviv

теля́тин|а, ы *f.* veal

теля́ч|ий *adj. of* ▶ телёнок; ~ья ко́жа calf(skin); (cul.) veal

тем 1 *i. sg. m. and nt., d. pl. of* ▶ тот **2** *conj.* (so much) the; **чем вы́ше, т. лу́чше** the taller, the better; **т. лу́чше** so much the better; **т. бо́лее, что** especially as; **т. не ме́нее** nonetheless, nevertheless; **т. са́мым** thus, thereby

те́м|а, ы *f.* **1** subject, topic, theme; **перейти́ к друго́й** ~е to change the subject **2** (mus.) theme

тема́тик|а, и *f.* (*collect.*) subject matter

тембр, а *m.* timbre

Те́мз|а, ы *f.* the Thames (*river*)

те́ми *i. pl. of* ▶ тот

темне́|ть, ю *impf.* **1** (*pf.* по~) to grow *or* become dark; to darken **2** (*pf.* с~): ~ет (*impers.*) it gets dark; it is getting dark **3** (*impf. only*) (*виднеться*) to show up darkly

темн|и́ть, ю́, и́шь *impf.* (infml) to be deliberately obscure

темни́ц|а, ы *f.* dungeon

темно́ *as pred.* it is dark

тёмно-... *comb. form* dark (*with names of colours*); **тёмно-си́ний** dark blue, navy blue

темноволо́с|ый, ~, ~а *adj.* dark-haired

темноко́ж|ий, ~, ~а *adj.* dark-skinned, swarthy

темнот|а́, ы́ *f.* dark, darkness; **в** ~е́ in the dark; **до** ~ы́ before dark

тём|ный, ~ен, темна́ *adj.* **1** dark; ~ное пятно́ (fig., *что-л. позоря́щее*) dark stain, blemish **2** (*нея́сный*) obscure, vague; ~ное пятно́ obscure place **3** (*мра́чный*) gloomy, sombre (BrE), somber (AmE) **4** (*подозри́тельный*) shady, suspicious; ~ное де́ло shady business **5** (*невежественный*) ignorant

темп, а *m.* **1** (mus.) tempo **2** (fig.) tempo; rate, speed, pace; **в** ~е (infml) quickly

темпера́мент, а *m.* temperament

темпера́мент|ный, ~ен, ~на *adj.* energetic; spirited

температу́р|а, ы *f.* **1** temperature; **ме́рить кому́-н.** ~у to take sb's temperature **2** (infml) (heightened) temperature; **у него́ т.** he's got a temperature

те́м|я, ени (*no pl.*) *nt.* crown, top of the head

тенденцио́з|ный, ~ен, ~на *adj.* (pej.) tendentious, biased

тенде́нци|я, и *f.* (к + *d.*) tendency (to, towards)

те́ндер, а *m.* **1** (rail., *ваго́н*) tender **2** (naut., *кора́бль*) cutter **3** (comm.) tender, bid

тенев|о́й *adj.* shady (fig.); ~а́я сторона́ shady side; (fig.) bad side, seamy side; ~а́я эконо́мика shadow economy

те́ннис, а *m.* tennis

тенниси́ст, а *m.* tennis player

тенниси́ст|ка, ки *f. of* ▶ тенниси́ст

те́нниск|а, и *f.* (infml) tennis shirt, polo shirt

те́нлиеи|ый *adj.* tennis; **т. корт**, ~ая площа́дка tennis court

те́нор, а, *pl.* ~а́, ~о́в *m.* (mus.) tenor

тент, а *m.* awning

тен|ь, и, **в** ~и́, *pl.* ~и, ~е́й *f.* **1** (*тени́стое ме́сто*) shade; **сиде́ть в** ~и́ to sit in the shade; **держа́ться в** ~и́ (fig.) to keep in the background **2** (*тёмное отраже́ние*) shadow; **дава́ть т.** to cast a shadow **3** (*при́зрак*) shadow, ghost **4** (fig., *мале́йшая до́ля*) shadow, atom; **нет ни** ~и́ сомне́ния there is not a shadow of doubt **5** (*подозре́ние*) suspicion; **бро́сить т. на кого́-н.** to cast suspicion on sb

теодоли́т, а *m.* (*инструме́нт*) theodolite

теокра́ти|я, и *f.* theocracy

теологи́ческий *adj.* theological

теоло́ги|я, и *f.* theology

теоре́м|а, ы *f.* theorem

теоре́тик, а *m.* theorist

теорети́ческий *adj.* theoretical

тео́ри|я, и *f.* theory

тепе́рь *adv.* now; nowadays, today

тепле́|ть, ет *impf.* (*of* ▶ потепле́ть) to get warm

тепли́ц|а, ы *f.* greenhouse, hothouse

тепло́[1] *adv.* **1** warmly **2** (*as pred.*) it is warm

тепл|о́[2], а́ *nt.* heat; warmth; **де́сять гра́дусов** ~а́ ten degrees (Celsius) above zero

теплово́з, а *m.* diesel locomotive

теплов|о́й *adj.* heat; thermal; **т. уда́р** (med.) heat stroke; ~а́я эне́ргия thermal energy

теплот|а́, ы́ *f.* **1** (phys.) heat; **едини́ца** ~ы́ thermal unit **2** warmth (also fig.); **душе́вная т.** warm-heartedness

теплохо́д, а *m.* motor ship

тёп|лый, ~ел, тепла́ *adj.* **1** (*оде́жда, цве́та*) warm; ~лое месте́чко (infml) cushy job **2** (*да́ча*) warmed, heated **3** (*приём*) warm, cordial **4** (*слова́*) heartfelt

терабайт, а *m.* (comput.) terabyte

тера́кт, а *m.* act of terrorism, terrorist act

терапе́вт, а *m.* therapist

терапевти́ческий *adj.* therapeutic

терапи́|я, и *f.* therapy; **интенси́вная т.** intensive care

тереб|и́ть, лю́, и́шь *impf.* **1** (*дёргать*) to pull (at), tug (at) **2** (fig., infml, *вопро́сами*) to pester, bother

Т

⚬ **тере́ть, тру, трёшь**, *past* **тёр, тёрла** *impf.* **1** (*глаза; грязное место*) to rub **2** (*сыр*) to grate **3** (*ногу, об обуви*) to rub, chafe

тере́ться, трусь, трёшься, *past* **тёрся, тёрлась** *impf.* to rub oneself; (**о, об(о)** + *a.*) to rub (against)

тёрк|а, и *f.* (cul.) grater

те́рмин, а *m.* term

термина́л, а *m.* terminal (*in var. senses*)

терминоло́ги|я, и *f.* terminology

терми́т, а *m.* (zool.) termite

термобельё, я́ *nt.* (collect.) thermal underwear

термо́метр, а *m.* thermometer

те́рмос, а *m.* Thermos (flask)®

термоста́т, а *m.* thermostat

терни́ст|ый, ~, ~а *adj.* (obs.) thorny, prickly; **т. путь** (fig.) difficult path

терно́вник, а *m.* (bot.) blackthorn

терпели́в|ый, ~, ~а *adj.* patient

терпе́ни|е, я *nt.* patience; **вы́вести из ~я** to exasperate

терп|е́ть, лю́, ~ишь *impf.* **1** (*pf.* **по~**) (*испытывать*) to suffer, undergo; **т. пораже́ние** to suffer a defeat **2** (*стойко переносить*) to bear, endure, stand **3** (*запастись терпением*) to have patience **4** (*допускать*) to tolerate, suffer, put up (with); **т. не могу́** I can't stand it; I hate it; **де́ло не ~ит отлага́тельства** the matter won't wait

терп|е́ться, ~ится *impf.* (impers.): **ему́ и т. п. не ~ится** (+ *inf.*) he is, etc., impatient (to)

терпи́мост|ь, и *f.* tolerance; indulgence

терпи́м|ый, ~, ~а *adj.* **1** (*человек, характер*) tolerant; indulgent, forbearing **2** (*условия, боль, жара*) tolerable, bearable

те́рп|кий, ~ок, ~ка́, ~ко *adj.* (*вкус, запах*) astringent; sharp; (*яблоко, виноград*) tart, sharp; (*вино*) sharp, rough

терако́т|а, ы *f.* (*глина; изделие*) terracotta

терра́с|а, ы *f.* terrace

территориа́льный *adj.* territorial

⚬ **террито́ри|я, и** *f.* territory, confines; area

⚬ **терро́р, а** *m.* terror

терроризи́р|овать, ую *impf. and pf.* to terrorize

террори́зм, а *m.* terrorism

террори́ст, а *m.* terrorist

террористи́ческий *adj.* terrorist

террори́ст|ка, ки *f. of* ▶ **террори́ст**

терье́р, а *m.* terrier (*dog*)

теря́|ть, ю *impf.* (*of* ▶ **потеря́ть**) to lose; **т. наде́жду** to lose hope; **т. си́лу** to become invalid; **т. вре́мя на что-н.** to waste time on sth; **т. в ве́се** to lose weight; **не т. из ви́ду/ви́да** to keep in sight; **нам не́чего т.** we have nothing to lose

теря́|ться, юсь *impf.* (*of* ▶ **потеря́ться**) **1** to be lost; to get lost; (*исчезать*) to disappear

2 (*становиться слабее*) to fail, decline, weaken **3** (*лишаться самообладания*) to become flustered **4**: **т. в дога́дках** to be lost in conjecture

те|са́ть, шу́, ~шешь *impf.* to cut, hew

те́сно *adv.* **1** closely (also fig.); tightly; narrowly; **быть т. свя́занным** (**с** + *i.*) to be closely linked (with) **2** (*as pred.*) it is crowded; it is (too) tight; **в трамва́е бы́ло о́чень т.** the tram was very crowded

тесно́т|а́, ы́ *f.* **1** (*свойство*) crowded state; narrowness; tightness; closeness **2** (*недостаток места*) crush, squash; **жить в ~е́** to live cooped up

те́с|ный, ~ен, ~на́, ~но, ~ны́ *adj.* **1** (*непросторный*) crowded, cramped; **мир ~ен!** it's a small world! **2** (*узкий*) narrow **3** (*пиджак*) (too) tight **4** (fig., *близкий*) close, tight; **т. круг друзе́й** close circle of friends

тест, а *m.* test

тести́р|овать, ую *impf.* to test

те́ст|о, а *nt.* dough; pastry

тест|ь, я *m.* father-in-law (*wife's father*)

тесьм|а́, ы́ *f.* tape, ribbon

те́терев, а, *pl.* ~а́, ~о́в *m.* (zool.) black grouse

тетив|а́, ы́ *f.* bowstring

тётк|а, и *f.* **1** aunt **2** (infml, pej., *о немолодой женщине*) woman

тетра́д|ь, и *f.* exercise book (BrE), notebook; **т. для рисова́ния** drawing book; sketchbook

тёт|я, и, *g. pl.* ~ей *f.* **1** aunt **2** (*знакомая немолодая женщина; в сочетании с именем собственным*) auntie **3** (infml, *женщина*) lady

тефте́л|и, ей *f. pl.* (*sg.* infml **~я, ~и**) (cul.) meatballs

тех *g., a., p. pl. of* ▶ **тот**

те́хник, а *m.* technician

⚬ **те́хник|а, и** *f.* **1** technology; **нау́ка и т.** science and technology **2** (*приёмы исполнения*) technique, art **3** (collect.) (*машины*) machinery; technical devices

те́хникум, а *m.* technical college

⚬ **техни́ческий** *adj.* technical; **~ие нау́ки** engineering sciences; **т. те́рмин** technical term; **~ое обслу́живание** maintenance

техно́лог, а *m.* technologist

⚬ **технологи́ческий** *adj.* technological

⚬ **техноло́ги|я, и** *f.* technology

⚬ **тече́ни|е, я** *nt.* **1** (*поток*) flow **2** (fig.) course; **с ~ем вре́мени** in the course of time, in time **3** (*ток, струя*) current, stream (also fig.); **по ~ю, про́тив ~я** with the stream, against the stream (also fig.) **4** (fig., *направление*) trend, tendency **5**: **в т.** (+ *g.*) during, in the course (of)

течь¹, и *f.* leak; **дать т.** to spring a leak; **заде́лать т.** to stop a leak

течь², течёт, теку́т, *past* **тёк, текла́** *impf.* **1** to flow (also fig.); to stream; (fig., *о времени*) to pass; **у тебя́ кровь течёт из но́са** your nose

is bleeding 2 (*иметь течь*) to leak, be leaky
тёщ|а, и *f.* mother-in-law (*wife's mother*)
Тибе́т, а *m.* Tibet
тибе́т|ец, ца *m.* Tibetan
тибе́т|ка, ки *f. of* ▶ тибе́тец
тибе́тский *adj.* Tibetan
тигр, а *m.* tiger
ти́кань|е, я *nt.* tick, ticking (*of a clock*)
ти́ка|ть, ет *impf.* to tick
ти́н|а, ы (*no pl.*) *f.* slime; mire
тине́йджер, а *m.* teenager
✐ **тип, а** *m.* 1 type; model 2 (infml, *человек*) fellow, character; **стра́нный т.** odd character
типи́ч|ный, ~ен, ~на *adj.* typical
типогра́фи|я, и *f.* printing house, press
типогра́фск|ий *adj.* typographical; **~ое де́ло** typography
тир, а *m.* shooting range; shooting gallery
тира́ж, á *m.* 1 drawing (*of loan or lottery*); **вы́йти в т.** to be drawn 2 (*количество экземпляров*) circulation; edition; print run
тира́н, а *m.* tyrant
тирани|я, и *f.* tyranny
тире́ *nt. indecl.* dash
тис, а *m.* yew (tree)
ти́ска|ть, ю *impf.* (*of* ▶ ти́снуть) (infml) to press, squeeze
тиск|и́, óв (*no sg.*) (tech.) vice (BrE), vise (AmE); **в ~áх** (+ *g.*) in the grip (of)
ти́снуть *pf. of* ▶ ти́скать
тита́н¹, а *m.* (myth., also fig.) titan
тита́н², а *m.* (chem.) titanium
титани́ческий *adj.* titanic
титр, а *m.* (*usu. in pl.*) (cin.) title, credit
ти́тул, а *m.* title
ти́тульный *adj. of* ▶ ти́тул; **т. лист** title page
тиф, а *m.* typhus; **брюшно́й т.** typhoid (fever)
ти́х|ий, ~, ~á, ~о *adj.* 1 quiet; (*звук*) low, soft; (*мягкий*) gentle; (*слабый*) faint; **т. го́лос** low voice 2 (*бесшумный*) silent, noiseless; still; **~ая ночь** still night 3 (fig., *спокойный*) quiet, calm; gentle; still; **~ая жизнь** quiet life 4 (*медленный*) slow, slow-moving; **т. ход** slow speed, slow pace
Ти́х|ий океа́н, ~ого океа́на *m.* the Pacific (Ocean)
ти́хо¹ *adv.* 1 (*негромко*) quietly; softly, gently; **т. постуча́ть** to knock gently 2 (*бесшумно*) silently, noiselessly 3 (fig., *спокойно*) quietly, calmly; still; **сиде́ть т.** to sit still; **т.!** gently!, careful! 4 (*медленно*) slowly
ти́хо² *as pred.* it is quiet, there is not a sound; **ста́ло т.** it became quiet
тихо́нько *adv.* (infml) quietly; softly, gently
тихоокеа́нский *adj.* Pacific
ти́ше 1 *comp. of* ▶ ти́хий, ▶ ти́хо¹, ▶ ти́хо² 2: **т.!** (*молчать!*) (be) quiet!, silence!; (*осторожнее!*) gently!; careful!
тишин|á, ы́ *f.* quiet, silence; stillness; **нару́шить ~у́** to break the silence;

соблюда́ть ~у́ to keep quiet
т. к. (*abbr. of* **так как**) as, since
тка́ный *adj.* woven
✐ **ткан|ь, и** *f.* 1 fabric, cloth; **льняны́е ~и** linen(s); **шёлковые ~и** silks 2 (anat.) tissue
ткать, тку, ткёшь, *past* **ткал, ткала́, тка́ло** *impf.* (*of* ▶ сотка́ть) to weave; **т. паути́ну** to spin a web
тка́цкий *adj.* weaver's, weaving; **т. стано́к** loom
ткач, á *m.* weaver
ткачи́х|а, и *f. of* ▶ ткач
ткн|у́ть, у́, ёшь *pf. of* ▶ ты́кать
тле|ть, ет *impf.* 1 (*гнить*) to rot, decay, decompose 2 (*гореть*) to smoulder (BrE), smolder (AmE) (also fig.)
тл|я, и, *g. pl.* **~ей** *f.* aphid
тмин, а *m.* caraway
то¹ *pron.* (*nom. and a. sg. nt. of* ▶ тот) that; **то, что...** the fact that ...; **то есть** that is (to say); **а то** *see* ▶ а¹; **(да) и то** and that, at that
✐ **то²** *conj.* 1 (*in main clause of conditional sentence*) then (*or not translated*) 2: **то..., то...** now ..., now ...; **то тут, то там** now here, now there 3: **не то..., не то...** either ... or ...; whether ... or ...; half ..., half ...; **не то по глу́пости, не то по зло́бе** either through stupidity or through malice 4: **не то, что́бы..., но...** it is not, it was not that ... (but) ...
-то¹ *emphatic particle* (in infml Russian often merely adds familiar tone) just, precisely, exactly (*or not translated*); **в то́м-то и де́ло** that's just it; **вам-то чего́ боя́ться?** what have *you* to be afraid of?
-то² *particle* (*forming indefinite prons. and advs.*): **кто́-то, како́й-то, когда́-то,** *etc.*
тобо́й *i. of* ▶ ты
✐ **това́р, а** *m.* (collect. or in pl.) goods; wares; (*sg.*) article; product, commodity; **~ы широ́кого потребле́ния** consumer goods
това́рищ, а *m.* 1 comrade; (*друг*) friend; (*коллега*) colleague; **т. по несча́стью** fellow sufferer, companion in distress; **т. по рабо́те** colleague; workmate; **т. по шко́ле** school friend 2 (*официальное обращение к гражданину*) comrade
това́рищеск|ий *adj.* 1 comradely; friendly 2 (sport) friendly, unofficial; **~ое состяза́ние, ~ая встре́ча** friendly (match) (BrE)
това́рный *adj.* 1 goods (BrE); freight; **т. знак** trademark; **т. склад** warehouse 2 (rail.) goods (BrE); freight; **т. соста́в** goods train (BrE), freight train 3 (econ.) (*цены, продукция*) commodity; (*вид*) marketable
✐ **тогда́** 1 *adv.* (*в то время*) then, at that time; (*в таком случае*) in that case 2: **когда́..., т. ...** *conj.* when; **когда́ решу́сь, т. напишу́ тебе́** I will write to you when I have decided 3: **т. как** *conj.* whereas, while
тогда́шний *adj.* (infml) of that time; the then
того́ *g. sg. m. and nt. of* ▶ тот
тожде́ствен|ный, ~, ~на *adj.* identical

T

то́же *adv.* also, as well, too

ток, а *m.* (elec.) current

тока́рный *adj.* (tech.) turning; **т. стано́к** lathe

то́кар|ь, я *m.* turner, lathe operator

То́кио *m. indecl.* Tokyo

токсикома́н, а *m.* glue-sniffer, solvent abuser

токсикома́ни|я, и *f.* glue-sniffing, solvent abuse

токси́н, а *m.* (med.) toxin

токси́ческий *adj.* toxic

ток-шо́у *nt. indecl.* talk show

толера́нтност|ь, и *f.* tolerance

толк, а (у) *m.* ◼ (*смысл*) sense; understanding; **бе́з ~у** senselessly ◼ (infml, *польза*) use, profit; **знать т. (в + *p.*)** to know what one is talking about (in)

толк|а́ть, а́ю *impf.* (*of* ▸ толкну́ть) ◼ to push, shove; (*нечаянно*) to jog; **т. ло́ктем** to nudge ◼ (sport): **т. шта́нгу** to lift weights ◼ (**на** + *a.*) (*побуждать*) to push (into), incite (to)

толк|а́ться, а́юсь *impf. only* (*толкать друг друга*) to push (one another)

толк|ну́ть, ну́, нёшь *pf. of* ▸ толка́ть

толкова́ни|е, я *nt.* interpretation

толк|ова́ть, у́ю *impf.* to interpret; **оши́бочно, неве́рно т. чьи-н. слова́** to misinterpret, misconstrue sb's words

толко́в|ый, ~, ~а *adj.* ◼ (*человек*) intelligent, sensible ◼ (*объяснение*) intelligible, clear ◼: **т. слова́рь** defining dictionary

то́лком *adv.* (infml) plainly, clearly

толп|а́, ы́, *pl.* ~ы *f.* crowd; throng; multitude

толпи́|ться, и́тся *impf.* to crowd; to throng

толсте́|ть, ю *impf.* (*of* ▸ потолсте́ть) to grow fat; to put on weight

толсто́вк|а, и *f.* (infml) sweatshirt

толстоко́ж|ий, ~, ~а *adj.* thick-skinned (also fig.)

то́лст|ый, ~, ~а́, ~о, ~ы́ *adj.* ◼ (*человек*) fat ◼ (*книга, бумага, слой*) thick

толстя́к, а́ *m.* (*мужчина*) fat man; (*мальчик*) fat boy

толч|о́к, ка́ *m.* ◼ (*толкающий удар*) push, shove ◼ (*при езде*) jolt, bump; (*при землетрясении*) (earthquake) shock, tremor ◼ (fig., *побуждение*) push, shove; stimulus; **дать т. эконо́мике** to kick-start the economy

то́лщ|а, и *f.* thickness; **т. сне́га** depth of snow

то́лще *comp. of* ▸ то́лстый

толщин|а́, ы́ *f.* ◼ (*человека*) fatness, corpulence ◼ (*бревна, слоя*) thickness

то́лько ◼ (*adv.*) only; solely; alone; just; **не т. ..., но и** not only ..., but also; **подума́й(те) т.!** just think!; **т. и всего́, да и т.** (infml) that's all ◼: **т. что** (*adv. and conj.*) just, only just; **он т. что позвони́л** he has just rung up ◼ (*conj.*): (**+ как, лишь**) as soon

as; one has only to ... ◼ (*conj.*) only, but; **с удово́льствием, т. не сего́дня** with pleasure, only not today ◼: **т. бы** (+ *inf.*) (*particle*) if only

том, а, *pl.* ~а́, ~о́в *m.* volume

тома́т, а *m.* tomato

тома́тный *adj.* tomato; **т. сок** tomato juice

томи́тел|ьный, ~ен, ~ьна *adj.* (*скучный*) tedious; wearing; (*утомительный*) tiring, exhausting; (*гнетущий*) oppressive; (*мучительный*) agonizing, painful

томи́|ться, лю́сь, йшься *impf.* (*голодом, ожиданием*) to be tormented (by); **т. в тюрьме́** to languish in prison

то́м|ный, ~ен, ~на́, ~но *adj.* languid, languorous

томогра́фи|я, и *f.* tomography, CT scanning

тон, а, *pl.* ~ы and ~а́ *m.* ◼ (*pl.* ~ы) (mus., also fig.) tone; **~ом вы́ше, ни́же** a tone higher, lower; **хоро́ший, дурно́й т.** good, bad form ◼ (*pl.* ~а́) (*краски, цвета*) tone, tint

тона́льност|ь, и *f.* (mus.) key

то́нер, а *m.* toner

тонзилли́т, а *m.* tonsillitis

то́ник, а *m.* tonic (water)

то́н|кий, ~ок, ~ка́, ~ко, ~ки́ *adj.* ◼ (*слой*) thin; (*фигура*) slim; **т. ло́мтик** thin slice ◼ (*изысканный*) fine; delicate; refined; **~кое бельё** fine linen; (*не грубый*) subtle, fine; **~кое разли́чие** subtle, fine distinction ◼ (*звук*) high, squeaky ◼ (fig., *проницательный, умный*) shrewd, subtle, penetrating; **т. знато́к** connoisseur ◼ (*зрение, слух*) keen

то́нко *adv.* ◼ (*резать*) thinly ◼ (*чувствовать*) subtly, delicately, finely

то́нкост|ь, и *f.* ◼ thinness; (*фигуры*) slimness ◼ (*ткани, работы*) fineness ◼ (*ума*) subtlety ◼ (*мелкая подробность*) nice point, subtle point; **до ~ей** to a nicety

то́нн|а, ы *f.* metric ton, tonne

тонне́л|ь, я *m.* tunnel; (*пешеходный*) subway

то́нус, а *m.* (physiol., med.) tone; **жи́зненный т.** vitality

тон|у́ть, у́, ~ешь *impf.* ◼ (*pf.* за~) (*о судне*) to sink, go down ◼ (*pf.* у~) (*о человеке*) to drown ◼ (*pf.* у~) (**в** + *p.*) to sink (in); to be lost (in); to be hidden (in, by); **т. в дела́х** to be up to one's eyes in work

то́ньше *comp. of* ▸ то́нкий and ▸ то́нко

топ, а *m.* одежда crop top

то́п|ать, аю *impf.* (*of* ▸ то́пнуть) to stamp; **т. нога́ми** to stamp one's feet

топ|и́ть¹, лю́, ~ишь *impf.* ◼ (*камин*) to stoke (*a boiler, stove, etc.*) ◼ (*помещение*) to heat

топ|и́ть², лю́, ~ишь *impf.* ◼ (*воск*) to melt (down), render ◼: **т. молоко́** to bake milk

топ|и́ть³, лю́, ~ишь *impf.* ◼ (*pf.* по~) (*корабль*) to sink ◼ (*pf.* у~) (*человека*) to drown; (fig., infml) to wreck, ruin

топ|и́ться¹, ~ится *impf.* (*о камине*) to burn, be alight

топи́|ться², ~ится *impf.* **1** (*о воске*) to melt **2** *pass of* ▸ топи́ть²

топи́|ться³, лю́сь, ~ишься *impf.* (*of* ▸ утопи́ться) (*о человеке*) to drown oneself

то́пк|а, и *f.* **1** (*камина*) stoking **2** (*помещения*) heating **3** (*часть печи*) furnace; (rail.) firebox

✍ **то́пливо**, а *nt.* fuel; жи́дкое т. fuel oil; твёрдое т. solid fuel

топ-моде́л|ь, и *f.* top model

то́п|нуть, ну, нешь *pf. of* ▸ то́пать

топографи́ческий *adj.* topographical

то́пол|ь, я, *pl.* ~я́ *m.* poplar

топо́р, а́ *m.* axe (BrE), ax (AmE)

топо́рщ|иться, ится *impf.* (infml) **1** (*о волосах*) to stand on end, bristle **2** (*о еже*) to bristle; (*о птице*) to puff up its feathers **3** (*об одежде*) to stick out, pucker

то́пот, а *m.* tramp; ко́нский т. clatter of horses' hoofs

топ|та́ть, чу́, ~чешь *impf.* **1** (*траву*) to trample (down) **2** (*пол*) to make dirty (*with one's feet*)

топ|та́ться, чу́сь, ~чешься *impf.* to shift from one foot to the other; т. на ме́сте to mark time (also fig.)

топча́н, а́ *m.* trestle bed

топ|ь, и *f.* bog, marsh, swamp

То́р|а, ы *f.* (relig.) Torah

торг, а, о ~е, на ~у́, *pl.* ~и́ *m.* **1** (*действие*) trading **2** (*in pl.*) (*аукцион*) auction; прода́ть с ~о́в to sell by auction

торг|ова́ть, у́ю *impf.* (+ *i.*) to trade (in), deal (in), sell

торг|ова́ться, у́юсь *impf.* **1** (*pf.* с~) (с + *i.*) to bargain (with), haggle (with) **2** (infml, *спорить*) to argue

торго́в|ец, ца *m.* merchant; dealer; tradesman; т. нарко́тиками drug trafficker/pusher

торго́вк|а, и *f.* (infml) (female) stallholder; (woman) street trader

✍ **торго́вл|я**, и *f.* trade, commerce

✍ **торго́в|ый** *adj.* trade, commercial; т. дом firm; ~ая то́чка shop

тореадо́р, а *m.* toreador

тор|е́ц, ца́ *m.* butt end, short side, face; (*здания*) gable end

торже́ствен|ный, ~, ~на *adj.* **1** ceremonial; (*праздничный*) festive; gala; т. день red-letter day **2** (*серьёзный*) solemn

торжеств|о́, а́ *nt.* **1** celebration; (*in pl.*) (*празднество*) festivities, rejoicings **2** (*победа*) triumph (= *victory*) **3** (*радость*) triumph, exultation

торжеств|ова́ть, у́ю *impf.* **1** to celebrate; (fig., *радоваться*) to rejoice **2** (над + *i.*) to triumph (over); to exult (over)

то́ри *m. indecl.* (pol.) Tory

то́рмоз, а *m.* (*pl.* ~а́) brake

тормо|зи́ть, жу́, зи́шь *impf.* (*of* ▸ затормози́ть) **1** (tech.) to brake, apply the brake (to) **2** (fig., *замедлить*) to hamper, impede **3** (psych.) to inhibit

тормош|и́ть, у́, и́шь *impf.* (infml) **1** (*дёргать*) to pull (at), tug (at) **2** (fig., *вопросами*) to pester, plague

тороп|и́ть, лю́, ~ишь (*of* ▸ поторопи́ть) **1** to hurry, hasten; to press; меня́ ~я́т с оконча́нием рабо́ты I am being pressed to finish my work **2** (*события*) to precipitate

тороп|и́ться, лю́сь, ~ишься *impf.* (*of* ▸ поторопи́ться) to hurry, be in a hurry, hasten

торопли́в|ый, ~, ~а *adj.* hurried, hasty

торо́с, а *m.* ice hummock

торпе́д|а, ы *f.* torpedo

торс, а *m.* trunk; torso

торт, а *m.* cake

торф, а *m.* peat

торч|а́ть, у́, и́шь *impf.* **1** (*вверх*) to stick up; (*в сторону*) to stick out; (*о волосах*) to stand on end **2** (infml) (*в каком-л. месте*) to hang about **3** (sl.) (*получать удовольствие*) to feel euphoric (from), get a kick (out of); (*от наркотиков*) to get high (on)

торше́р, а *m.* standard lamp

тоск|а́, и́ *f.* **1** (*уныние*) melancholy; (*тревога*) anguish **2** (*скука*) boredom, ennui; одна́ т., сплошна́я т. a frightful bore **3** (по + *d.*) longing (for); yearning (for), nostalgia (for); т. по ро́дине homesickness

тоскли́в|ый, ~, ~а *adj.* **1** (*настроение*) melancholy; depressed, miserable **2** (*погода, город*) dull, dreary, depressing

тоск|ова́ть, у́ю *impf.* **1** to be melancholy, be depressed, be miserable **2** (по + *d.*) to long (for), yearn (for), pine (for), miss

тост¹, а *m.* toast; провозгласи́ть, предложи́ть т. (за + *a.*) to toast, drink (to); to propose a toast (to)

тост², а *m.* (*ломтик хлеба*) piece of toast

то́стер, а *m.* toaster

✍ **тот**, та, то, те *pron.* **1** (*opp.* э́тот) that; (*in pl.*) those; в то вре́мя then, at that time, in those days **2** (*opp.* э́тот) the former; *replacing 3rd pers. sg. pron.* he; she; it **3** (*opp.* э́тот) (*другой*) the other; the opposite; на той стороне́ on the other side **4** (*opp.* друго́й, *один*) the one; не тот, и друго́й both; ни тот, ни друго́й neither **5**: тот..., (кото́рый) the ... (which); тот, (кто) the one (who), the person (who); тот факт, что the fact that; *see also* ▸ то¹ **6**: тот (же), тот (же) са́мый the same; одно́ и то же one and the same thing, the same thing over again; в то же са́мое вре́мя at the same time, on the other hand **7** (*такой, какой нужен*) the right; не тот the wrong; э́то не та дверь that's the wrong door **8** (+ *preps.* forms the following conjs.): для того́, что́бы in order that, in order to; ме́жду тем, как whereas; несмотря́ на то, что in spite of the fact that; пе́ред тем, как before; по́сле того́, как after; с тем, что́бы in order to, with a view to **9** (*forms part of var. adv. phrr. and* *particles) see also* ▶ **то¹**; **вме́сте с тем** at the same time; **к тому́ же** moreover; **кро́ме того́** besides; **ме́жду тем, тем вре́менем** meanwhile; **тем са́мым** hereby; **тому́ наза́д** ago

тотализа́тор, а *m.* tote, totalizator

тоталита́рный *adj.* (pol.) totalitarian

то́тчас *adv.* at once; immediately (*also of spatial relations*)

точёный *adj.* finely moulded (BrE), finely molded (AmE); (*о чертах лица*) chiselled (BrE), chiseled (AmE)

точи́лк|а, и *f.* (infml) (*для ножей*) steel, knife sharpener; (*для карандашей*) pencil sharpener

точ|и́ть, у́, ∼ишь *impf.* **1** (*pf.* **на∼**) (*нож, карандаш*) to sharpen; **т. зу́бы на кого́-н.** to have a grudge against sb **2** (*impf. only*) (*на токарном станке*) to turn

◊ **то́чк|а, и** *f.* **1** spot, dot; **ста́вить ∼и над «и»** to dot one's i's (and cross one's t's) **2** (gram.) full stop; **т. с запято́й** semicolon **3** (math., phys., tech.) point; **т. замерза́ния, кипе́ния** freezing, boiling point; **т. опо́ры** fulcrum, point of support; (fig.) rallying point **4** (fig.) point; **т. зре́ния** point of view; **горя́чая т.** trouble spot

◊ **то́чно¹** *adv.* **1** exactly, precisely; (*пунктуально*) punctually **2**: **т. так** just so, exactly, precisely; **т. тако́й (же)** just the same **3** (*действительно*) indeed

то́чно² *conj.* as though, as if; like

то́чност|ь, и *f.* exactness; precision; accuracy; punctuality; **в ∼и** exactly, precisely

◊ **то́ч|ный, ∼ен, ∼на́, ∼но, ∼ны́** *adj.* exact, precise; accurate; (*пунктуальный*) punctual; **∼ные нау́ки** exact sciences; **т. перево́д** accurate translation; **т. прибо́р** precision instrument

тошн|и́ть, и́т *impf.* (impers.): **меня́,** *etc.*, **∼и́т** I feel, *etc.*, sick; **меня́ от э́того ∼и́т** (fig.) it makes me sick, it sickens me

тошнот|а́, ы́ *f.* sickness, nausea (also fig.)

тошнотво́р|ный, ∼ен, ∼на *adj.* sickening, nauseating (also fig.)

то́щий, ∼, ∼а́, ∼е *adj.* gaunt, emaciated; skinny

трав|а́, ы́, *pl.* **∼ы** *f.* grass; (*специя, лекарственная*) herb; **со́рная т.** weed

трави́нк|а, и *f.* blade of grass

трав|и́ть, лю́, ∼ишь *impf.* (*of* ▶ **вы́травить**) (*тараканов, крыс*) to exterminate, destroy (*by poisoning*)

тра́вл|я, и *f.* hunting; (fig.) persecution, tormenting

тра́вм|а, ы *f.* (med.) (*психическая*) trauma; (*физическая*) injury

травмати́ческий *adj.* (med., psych.) traumatic

травматологи́ческ|ий *adj.*: **∼ое отделе́ние** casualty department; **т. пункт** first-aid room

травоя́дный *adj.* herbivorous

◊ *key word*

травян|о́й *adj.* **1** grass; herbaceous; **т. покро́в** grass **2**: **∼а́я насто́йка** herb tea

траге́ди|я, и *f.* tragedy

траги́ческ|ий *adj.* tragic; **т. актёр** tragic actor; **∼ое зре́лище** tragic sight

◊ **традицио́н|ный, ∼ен, ∼на** *adj.* traditional

◊ **тради́ци|я, и** *f.* tradition

траекто́ри|я, и *f.* trajectory

тракта́т, а *m.* (*сочинение*) treatise

тракт|ова́ть, у́ю *impf.* **1** (*вопрос*) to treat, discuss **2** (*роль*) to interpret (*a part in a play, etc.*)

тракто́вк|а, и *f.* treatment; interpretation

тра́ктор, а *m.* tractor; **гу́сеничный т., т. на гу́сеничном ходу́** caterpillar tractor

тракторист, а *m.* tractor driver

трактори́ст|ка, ки *f. of* ▶ **тракторист**

трамб|ова́ть, у́ю *impf.* to ram, tamp

трамва́|й, я *m.* tram (BrE), streetcar (AmE); **речно́й т.** river bus

трампли́н, а *m.* (sport, *also* fig.) springboard; (*лыжный*) ski jump

транзи́стор, а *m.* transistor

транзи́т, а *m.* transit

транзи́т|ный *adj. of* ▶ **транзи́т**; **∼ная ви́за** transit visa

транквилиза́тор, а *m.* tranquilliser (BrE), tranquilizer (AmE)

транс, а *m.* trance

трансатланти́ческий *adj.* transatlantic

транскри́пци|я, и *f.* transcription

трансли́р|овать, ую *impf. and pf.* to broadcast; to relay

транслитера́ци|я, и *f.* transliteration

трансля́ци|я, и *f.* (*действие*) transmission, broadcasting; (*передача*) broadcast

трансми́сси|я, и *f.* (tech.) transmission

транснациона́льный *adj.* transnational

транспара́нт, а *m.* banner

транспланта́ци|я, и *f.* (med.) transplantation

◊ **тра́нспорт, а** *m.* **1** (*система перевозки*) transport; **обще́ственный т.** public transport **2** (*перевозка*) transportation, conveyance **3** (mil.) train, transport **4** (naut.) supply ship; troopship

транспорти́р|овать, ую *impf. and pf.* to transport

транспортиро́вк|а, и *f.* transport, transportation

◊ **тра́нспортный** *adj. of* ▶ **тра́нспорт**

транссексуа́л, а *m.* transsexual

транссиби́рск|ий *adj.* Trans-Siberian; **Т∼ая магистра́ль** the Trans-Siberian Railway

трансформа́тор, а *m.* (elec.) transformer

трансформа́ци|я, и *f.* transformation

трансформи́р|овать, ую *impf. and pf.* to transform

транше́|я, и *f.* (mil.) trench

трап, а *m.* (naut., aeron.) gangway

тра́пез|а, ы *f.* **1** (*общий стол*) dining table (*esp. in a monastery*) **2** (*еда*) meal; **дели́ть**

~y (с + i.) to share a meal (with)

трапе́ци|я, и f. **1** (math.) trapezium **2** (циркова́я) trapeze

тра́сс|а, ы f. **1** (трубопровода, метро) route, course; **возду́шная т.** airway **2** (дорога) main road, highway (AmE)

тра́т|а, ы f. expenditure; **пуста́я т. вре́мени** waste of time

тра́|тить, чу, тишь impf. (of ▸ **истра́тить,** ▸ **потра́тить**) to spend, expend, use up; (понапрасну) to waste

тра́улер, а m. trawler

тра́ур, а m. mourning

тра́урн|ый adj. **1** mourning; funeral; **т. марш** funeral march; **~ое ше́ствие** funeral procession **2** (скорбный) mournful, sorrowful; funereal

трафаре́т, а m. stencil

тра́фик, а (comput.) m. traffic

тра́х|ать, аю impf. of ▸ **тра́хнуть**

тра́х|аться, аюсь impf. of ▸ **тра́хнуться**

тра́х|нуть, ну, нешь pf. (of ▸ **тра́хать**) **1** (infml, стукнуть) to bang, crash **2** (vulg., совершить половой акт) to screw, hump

тра́х|нуться, нусь, нешься pf. (of ▸ **тра́хаться**) **1** (infml, стукнуться) to bang, crash **2** (vulg., совершить половой акт) to screw, hump

◦ **тре́бовани|е, я** nt. **1** (действие) demand, request; **по ~ю** on demand, by request; **остано́вка по ~ю** request stop **2** (настоятельная просьба) demand; (притязание) claim; **согласи́ться на чьи-н. ~я** to agree to sb's demands; **вы́двинуть т.** to put in a claim **3** (usu. in pl.) (условие) requirement, condition; **отвеча́ть, соотве́тствовать ~ям** to meet requirements **4** (in pl.) (запросы) aspirations; needs

тре́бователь|ный, ~ен, ~на adj. demanding

◦ **тре́б|овать, ую** impf. (of ▸ **потре́бовать**) **1** (+ g. or чтобы) to demand, require; **они́ ~уют, что́бы мы извини́лись** they demand that we apologize **2** (impf. only) (+ g. and от + g.) to expect (from), ask (of); **вы ~уете сли́шком мно́го от ва́ших ученико́в** you expect too much from your pupils **3** (+ g.) (нуждаться) to require, need, call (for)

◦ **тре́б|оваться, уется** impf. (of ▸ **потре́боваться**) to be needed, be required; **на э́то ~уется мно́го вре́мени** it takes a lot of time; **фи́рме ~уется бухга́лтер** the company seeks an accountant

требух|а́, и́ (no pl.) f. entrails; (cul.) offal, tripe

трево́г|а, и f. **1** (беспокойство) alarm, anxiety **2** (сигнал) alarm; **бить ~y** to sound the alarm (also fig.); **подня́ть ~y** to raise the alarm

трево́ж|ить, у, ишь impf. (of ▸ **потрево́жить**) (мешать) to disturb, interrupt

трево́ж|иться, усь, ишься impf. (of ▸ **потрево́житься**) to trouble oneself,

put oneself out; **не ~ьтесь!** don't bother (yourself)!

трево́ж|ный, ~ен, ~на adj. **1** (полный тревоги) anxious, uneasy, troubled **2** (вызывающий тревогу) alarming, disturbing

трезве́|ть, ю impf. (of ▸ **протрезве́ть**) to sober (up), become sober

тре́звост|ь, и f. **1** sobriety (also fig.); **т. ума́** cool-headedness **2** (воздержание от спиртного) abstinence; temperance

тре́зв|ый, ~, ~а́, ~о, ~ы́ adj. **1** sober (also fig.) **2** (не пьющий) teetotal, abstinent

трезу́б|ец, ца m. trident

тре́йдер, а m. trader (in stocks and shares)

тре́йлер, а m. (передвижной дом-прицеп) caravan (BrE), trailer (AmE)

трек, а m. (sport) track

трелья́ж, а m. **1** (зеркало) three-leaved mirror **2** (для растений) trellis

тренажёр, а m. training apparatus; **лётный т.** flight simulator; (sport) piece of gym equipment

тренажёрный adj.: **т. зал** gym

◦ **тре́нер, а** m. (sport) trainer, coach

тре́ни|е, я nt. **1** friction, rubbing **2** (in pl.) (fig.) friction

тре́нинг, а m. training

трениро́в|ать, ую impf. to train, coach; (память) to train

трениро́в|аться, у́юсь impf. to train oneself, coach oneself; to be in training

трениро́вк|а, и f. training, coaching

трено́г|а, и f. tripod

тре́ньк|ать, ю impf. (infml, на гитаре) to strum

трепл|а́ть, лю́, ~лешь impf. (of ▸ **потрепа́ть**) **1** to pull about; (о ветре) to blow about; **т. языко́м** (infml) to prattle; **т. чьи-н. не́рвы** to get on sb's nerves **2** (одежду) to wear out **3** (по плечу) to pat

трепл|а́ться, лю́сь, ~лешься impf. **1** (pf. по~) (об одежде) to wear out **2** (impf. only) (о флагах) to flutter; (о волосах) to blow about **3** (pf. по~) (infml) to prattle

тре́пет, а m. (дрожь) trembling, quivering; (сердца) palpitation; (страх) trepidation, terror; (волнение) agitation; (уважительность) awe

трепе|та́ть, щу́, ~щешь impf. **1** (дрожать) to tremble, quiver **2** (fig., испытывать волнение) to tremble; to thrill; **т. от восто́рга** to thrill with joy; **т. при мы́сли** (о + p.) to tremble at the thought (of) **3** (перед + i.) (fig., испытывать страх) to tremble (before)

треск, а m. crack; crackle, crackling; **т. огня́** crackling of a fire; **с ~ом провали́ться** (fig., infml) to be a flop

треск|а́, и́ f. cod

тре́ска|ться, ется impf. (of ▸ **потре́скаться**) to crack; to chap

тре́сн|уть, у, ешь pf. **1** (о ветке) to snap **2** (о стакане, коже) to crack; (лопнуть) to burst **3** (+ *i. or a. and* по + *d.*) (*infml*) to bring down with a crash (on); to hit, bang

трест, a *m.* (*econ.*) trust; (*строи́тельный*) company

🗝 **тре́т|ий, ья, ье** *adj.* **1** third; **т. но́мер** number three; **полови́на ∼ьего** half past two; **стра́ны ∼ьего ми́ра** Third World countries **2** (*as nt. n.* **∼ье, ∼ьего**) sweet, dessert

трет|ь, и, *pl.* **∼и, ∼е́й** *f.* third

третьесо́ртный *adj.* third-rate

треуго́льник, a *m.* triangle

треф|ы, ∼ *f. pl.* (*sg.* **∼а, ∼ы**) (cards) clubs; **да́ма ∼** queen of clubs

трёх... *comb. form* three-, tri-

трёхзна́чный *adj.* three-digit

трёхколёсный *adj.* three-wheeled; **т. велосипе́д** tricycle

трёхле́тний *adj.* **1** (*срок*) three-year **2** (*ребёнок*) three-year-old

трёхме́рный *adj.* three-dimensional

трёхме́стный *adj.* three-seater

трёхсо́тый *adj.* three-hundredth

трёхцве́тный *adj.* three-coloured (BrE), three-colored (AmE); tricolour(ed) (BrE), tricolor(ed) (AmE)

трёхчасово́й *adj.* **1** (*экза́мен*) three-hour **2** (*по́езд*) three o'clock

трёхэта́жный *adj.* three-storey (BrE), three-story (AmE)

трещ|а́ть, у́, и́шь *impf.* **1** (*о льде*) to crack; **у меня́ голова́ ∼и́т** I have a splitting headache; **т. по всем швам** (fig.) to go to pieces **2** (*о дрова́х*) to crackle; (*о ме́бели*) to creak; (*о кузне́чиках*) to chirr

тре́щин|а, ы *f.* crack, split (also fig.); **дать ∼у** to crack, split; (fig.) to show signs of cracking

🗝 **три, трёх, трём, тремя́, о трёх** *num.* three

трибу́н|а, ы *f.* **1** platform, rostrum **2** (*на стадио́нах*) stand

трибуна́л, a *m.* tribunal

тривиа́л|ьный, ∼ен, ∼ьна *adj.* trivial, banal; (*по́шлый*) trite

тригономе́три|я, и *f.* trigonometry

тридца́т|ый *adj.* thirtieth; **∼ые го́ды** the thirties

три́дцат|ь, и, *i.* **∼ью** *num.* thirty

три́жды *adv.* three times, thrice

трико́ *nt. indecl.* (*колго́тки*) tights; (*костю́м*) leotard

трикота́ж, a *m.* **1** (*из ше́рсти*) jersey; (*из хло́пка*) cotton jersey **2** (*collect.*) (*изде́лия*) knitwear

трикота́жн|ый *adj.* (*шерстяно́й*) jersey; (*из хло́пка*) knitted; **∼ые изде́лия** knitwear

три́ллер, a *m.* thriller

триллио́н, a *m.* (10^{12}) trillion

трило́ги|я, и *f.* trilogy

трина́дцатый *adj.* thirteenth

трина́дцат|ь, и *num.* thirteen

три́о *nt. indecl.* (*mus.*) trio

три́ста, трёхсо́т, трёмста́м, тремяста́ми, трёхста́х *num.* three hundred

триу́мф, a *m.* triumph; **с ∼ом** triumphantly, in triumph

триумфа́льн|ый *adj.* triumphal; **∼ая а́рка** triumphal arch

тро́гател|ьный, ∼ен, ∼ьна *adj.* touching; moving, affecting

тро́га|ть, ю *impf.* (*of* ▶ **тро́нуть**) **1** (*прикаса́ться*) to touch **2** (*беспоко́ить*) to disturb, trouble; **не ∼й его́!** don't disturb him!; leave him alone! **3** (*волнова́ть*) to touch, move, affect; **т. до слёз** to move to tears

тро́га|ться¹, юсь *impf.* (*of* ▶ **тро́нуться¹** 1) to be touched, be moved, be affected

тро́га|ться², юсь *impf. of* ▶ **тро́нуться²**

тро́е, трои́х *num.* (*collect.*) three; **т. су́ток** seventy-two hours, three days and three nights; **т. друзе́й** three friends

троебо́рь|е, я *nt.* triathlon

троекра́тный *adj.* threefold, treble; (*вы́зов*) thrice-repeated; (*чемпио́н*) three-times; (*штраф*) trebled

тро́ечник, a *m.* mediocre student

Тро́иц|а, ы *f.* (*relig.*) Trinity; (*пра́здник*) Whitsun

Тро́ицын *adj.*: **Т. день** Whit Sunday

тро́йк|а, и *f.* **1** (*ци́фра, игра́льная ка́рта*) three **2** (*отме́тка*) three (*out of five*) **3** (*infml, авто́бус, трамва́й*) No. 3 (*bus, tram, etc.*) **4** (*гру́ппа из трои́х*) (group of) three; (*три челове́ка*) threesome **5** (*упря́жка*) troika **6** (*костю́м*) three-piece suit

тройни́к, а́ *m.* (*elec.*) three-way adaptor

тройн|о́й *adj.* triple, threefold, treble; **т. кана́т** three-ply rope; **т. прыжо́к** triple jump; **в ∼о́м разме́ре** threefold, treble

тролле́йбус, a *m.* trolleybus

тромб, a *m.* (*med.*) blood clot

тромбо́з, a *m.* (*med.*) thrombosis; **т. глубо́ких вен** deep vein thrombosis

тромбо́н, a *m.* trombone

тромбони́ст, a *m.* trombonist

трон, a *m.* throne

тро́|нуть, ну, нешь *pf. of* ▶ **тро́гать**

тро́|нуться¹, нусь, нешься *pf.* **1** *pf. of* ▶ **тро́гаться¹ 2** (*pf. only*) (fig., infml) to be touched (= *to lose one's mind*); **он немно́го ∼нулся** he is a bit touched, he is a bit cracked

тро́|нуться², нусь, нешься *pf.* (*of* ▶ **тро́гаться²**) (*дви́нуться с ме́ста*) to start, set out; **т. с ме́ста** to make a move, get going; **по́езд ∼нулся** the train started

троп|а́, ы́, *pl.* **∼ы, ∼а́м** *f.* path

тро́пик, a *m.* (geog.) **1** tropic; **т. Ра́ка** tropic of Cancer; **т. Козеро́га** tropic of Capricorn **2** (*in pl.*) the tropics

тропи́нк|а, и *f.* path

тропи́ческ|ий *adj.* tropical; **∼ая лихора́дка** jungle fever

трос, а *m.* rope, cable, hawser

тростни́к, á *m.* reed; **са́харный т.** sugar cane

трость, и, *pl.* ~и, ~éй *f.* cane, walking stick

тротуа́р, а *m.* pavement

трофе́й, я *m.* trophy

трою́родн|ый *adj.:* **т. брат**, ~ая сестра́ second cousin; **т. племя́нник** second cousin once removed (*son of second cousin*)

труб|а́, ы́, *pl.* ~ы́ *f.* **1** pipe; **водопрово́дная т.** water pipe; **водосто́чная т.** drainpipe; **канализацио́нная т.** sewage pipe; **подзо́рная т.** telescope **2** (*дымовая, заводская*) chimney; (*парохода*) funnel, smokestack **3** (mus.) trumpet; **игра́ть на ~é** to play the trumpet **4** (anat.) tube; duct

трубаду́р, а *m.* troubadour

труба́ч, á *m.* trumpeter, trumpet player

труб|и́ть, лю́, и́шь *impf.* **1** (**в** + *a.*) (mus.) to blow **2** (*о трубах*) to sound; to blare **3** (*давать сигнал*) to sound (*by blast of trumpet, etc.*); **т. сбор** (mil.) to sound assembly **4** (*о* + *p.*) (infml, *разглашать*) to trumpet, proclaim from the housetops

труб|ка, и *f.* **1** tube; pipe; (*свёрток*) roll; **сверну́ть ~ой** to roll up **2** (*курительная*) (tobacco) pipe; **наби́ть ~у** to fill a pipe **3** (*телефона*) receiver; **взять, подня́ть ~у** to answer the phone

трубопрово́д, а *m.* pipeline

трубочи́ст, а *m.* chimney sweep

труд, á *m.* **1** (*работа*) labour (BrE), labor (AmE), work **2** (*трудность*) difficulty, trouble; **взять на себя́ т.** (+ *inf.*) to take the trouble (to); **с ~о́м** with difficulty; **без ~á** without difficulty **3** (*произведение*) (scholarly) work; (*in pl.*) (*издание*) transactions

труд|и́ться, жу́сь, ~дишься *impf.* (**над** + *i.*) to toil (over), labour (BrE), labor (AmE) (over), work (on)

тру́дно *as pred.* it is hard, it is difficult; **т. сказа́ть** it is hard to say; **мне т.** I find it difficult; **ему́ т. прихо́дится** he has a hard time

труднодосту́п|ный, ~ен, ~на *adj.* difficult to gain access to

тру́дност|ь, и *f.* difficulty; (*препятствие*) obstacle

тру́д|ный, ~ен, ~на́, ~но, ~ны́ *adj.* **1** difficult, hard; (*изнурительный*) arduous; **в ~ную мину́ту** in a time of need **2** (*человек*) difficult, awkward **3** (*случай*) serious, grave

трудов|о́й *adj.* **1** labour (BrE), labor (AmE), work; **~о́е законода́тельство** labour (BrE), labor (AmE) legislation; **~а́я кни́жка** work record book; **т. стаж** length of service **2** (*полученный трудом*) earned; hard-earned

трудого́лик, а *m.* (infml) workaholic

трудоёмк|ий, ~ок, ~ка *adj.* labour-intensive (BrE), labor-intensive (AmE)

трудолюби́в|ый, ~, ~а *adj.* hard-working, industrious

трудоспосо́б|ный, ~ен, ~на *adj.* able-bodied; capable of working

трудоустро́йств|о, а *nt.* placement in a job

труд|я́щийся *pres. part.* of ▸ **труди́ться** *and adj.* working; (*as pl.* n. **~я́щиеся**, **~я́щихся**) working people, the workers

тру́женик, а *m.* (*много работающий*) toiler; (+ *g.*) worker, employee

тру́жени|ца, цы *f.* of ▸ **тру́женик**

труп, а *m.* dead body, corpse; (*животного*) carcass; **то́лько че́рез мой т.** over my dead body

тру́пп|а, ы *f.* company

трус, а *m.* coward

тру́сик|и, ов (*no sg.*) **1** (*шорты*) shorts **2** (*плавки*) swimming trunks **3** (*бельё*) (under)pants; (*женские*) knickers (BrE), panties

тру́|сить, шу, сишь *impf.* (*of* ▸ **стру́сить**) **1** to be a coward; to get cold feet **2** (*перед* + *i.*) to be afraid (of), be frightened (of)

трусли́в|ый, ~, ~а *adj.* cowardly

тру́сост|ь, и *f.* cowardice

трусц|á, ы́ *f.* (infml) **бег ~о́й** (sport) jogging

трус|ы́, о́в (*no sg.*) = **тру́сики**

трут, а *m.* tinder

тру́т|ень, ня *m.* (zool.) drone; (fig.) parasite

трух|á, и́ *f.* dust (*of rotted wood*); (fig., *о чём-н. никчёмном*) rubbish

трущо́б|а, ы *f.* (*often in pl.*) (*жильё, район*) slum

трюк, а *m.* **1** (*акробатический*) feat; (*каскадёра*) stunt; **рекла́мный т.** advertising gimmick **2** (fig., pej., *проделка*) trick

трюм, а *m.* (naut.) hold

трю́фел|ь, я *m.* (*гриб, конфета*) truffle

тря́пк|а, и *f.* **1** rag; (*для пыли*) duster **2** (*in pl.*) (infml, *одежда*) finery, clothes **3** (infml, pej., *человек*) drip

тряси́н|а, ы *f.* quagmire

тряс|ти́, у́, ёшь, past ~, ~ла́ *impf.* **1** to shake **2** (*ковёр; крошки*) to shake out **3** (*о дрожжи*) to cause to shake, cause to shiver (*usu. impers.*); **её ~ло́ от стра́ха** she was trembling with fear **4** (+ *i.*) (*головой, кулаком*) to shake; **т. гри́вой** to toss its mane **5** (*о вагоне*) to jolt, be jolty; (*impers.*) **в авто́бусе ~ёт** the bus is jolting

тряс|ти́сь, у́сь, ёшься, past ~ся, ~ла́сь *impf.* **1** to shake; to tremble, shiver; **т. от хо́лода** to shiver with cold **2** (*за* + *a.*) (*опасаться*) to worry about **3** (*перед* + *i.*) (*бояться*) to tremble before, dread

тряхн|у́ть, у́, ёшь *pf.* to shake; (*в машине*) to give a jolt

туале́т, а *m.* **1** (*уборная*) lavatory, toilet **2** (*наряд*) dress; attire

туале́т|ный *adj.* of ▸ **туале́т**; **~ная бума́га** toilet paper; **~ная вода́** toilet water; **~ные принадле́жности** toiletries; **т. сто́лик** dressing table

ту́б|а¹, ы *f.* (mus.) tuba

ту́б|а², ы *f.* (*большой тюбик*) tube

туберкулёз, а *m.* tuberculosis

ту́го *adv.* **1** tight(ly), taut; **т. наби́ть чемода́н** to pack a suitcase tight **2** (*с трудо́м*) with difficulty

туг|о́й, ~, ~а́, ~о, ~и́ *adj.* **1** (*у́зел, воротничо́к*) tight; (*струна́, пружи́на*) taut **2** (*пло́тно наби́тый*) tightly filled; **т. кошелёк** tightly stuffed purse

⚷ **туда́** *adv.* there; (*в ту сто́рону*) that way; (*куда́ ну́жно*) to the right place; **биле́т т. и обра́тно** return ticket; **не т.!** not that way!; **вы не т. попа́ли** (*по телефо́ну*) you have got the wrong number

ту́же *comp. of* ▸ **туго́й**, ▸ **ту́го**

тужу́рк|а, и *f.* double-breasted jacket (*man's*)

туз, а́ *m.* (cards) ace; **ходи́ть ~о́м** to play an ace

тузе́м|ец, ца *m.* native

тузе́м|ка, ки *f. of* ▸ **тузе́мец**

тузе́мный *adj.* native, indigenous

ту́ловищ|е, а *nt.* trunk; torso

тулу́п, а *m.* sheepskin coat

тума́к, а́ *m.* (infml) cuff, punch

тума́н, а *m.* fog; mist, haze; (*в голове́*) fog, haze; **как в ~е** in a daze

тума́нност|ь, и *f.* **1** (astron.) nebula **2** (*изложе́ния, мы́сли*) haziness, obscurity

тума́н|ный, ~ен, ~на *adj.* **1** foggy; misty; hazy **2** (fig., *ту́склый*) dull, lacklustre (BrE), lackluster (AmE) **3** (fig., *нея́сный*) hazy, obscure, vague

ту́мб|а, ы *f.* **1** (*столб*) bollard **2** (*подста́вка*) pedestal **3** (*афи́шная*) advertisement hoarding (*of cylindrical shape*)

ту́мблер, а *m.* toggle (switch)

ту́мбочк|а, и *f.* bedside table, night table (AmE)

ту́ндр|а, ы *f.* (geog.) tundra

тун|е́ц, ца́ *m.* tuna (fish)

тунея́д|ец, ца *m.* parasite, sponger

тунея́д|ка, ки *f. of* ▸ **тунея́дец**

Туни́с, а *m.* (*страна́*) Tunisia

туни́с|ец, ца *m.* Tunisian

туни́с|ка, ки *f. of* ▸ **туни́сец**

туни́сский *adj.* Tunisian

тунне́л|ь, я *m.* = **тонне́ль**

тупи́к, а́ *m.* **1** blind alley, cul-de-sac **2** (rail.) siding **3** (fig., *безвы́ходное положе́ние*) impasse, deadlock; **зайти́ в т.** to reach a deadlock **4**: **поста́вить в т.** to stump, nonplus

туп|и́ть, лю́, ~ишь *impf.* to blunt

тупи́ц|а, ы *c.g.* (infml) dimwit

туп|о́й, ~, ~а́, ~о, ~ы́ *adj.* **1** (*нож*) blunt **2**: **т. у́гол** (math.) obtuse angle **3** (fig., *боль, чу́вство*) dull **4** (fig., *взгляд, улы́бка*) vacant, stupid **5** (fig., *челове́к; ум*) dim; dull

ту́пост|ь, и *f.* **1** (*ножа́*) bluntness **2** (fig., *взгля́да, ума́*) dullness, slowness

тупоу́м|ный, ~ен, ~на *adj.* dull, obtuse

⚷ **тур, а** *m.* **1** (*турни́ра, вы́боров*) round

2 (*арти́ста*) tour

тураге́нт, а *m.* travel agent

тураге́нтств|о, а *nt.* travel agency

турба́з|а, ы *f.* tourist centre (BrE), center (AmE)

турби́н|а, ы *f.* (tech.) turbine

туре́цкий *adj.* Turkish

тури́зм, а *m.* (*путеше́ствия*) tourism; (*спорт*) hiking; **во́дный т.** boating

⚷ **тури́ст, а** *m.* tourist; (*в похо́дах*) hiker

туристи́ческ|ий *adj.* tourist; **~ое аге́нтство** travel agency; **т. похо́д** hiking tour

тури́ст|ка, ки *f. of* ▸ **тури́ст**

туркме́н, а, *g. pl.* **т.** *m.* Turkmen

Туркмениста́н, а *m.* Turkmenistan

туркме́н|ка, ки *f. of* ▸ **туркме́н**

туркме́нский *adj.* Turkmen

турне́ *nt. indecl.* tour (*esp. of artistes or sportsmen*)

турни́к, а́ *m.* (sport) horizontal bar

турнике́т, а *m.* turnstile

⚷ **турни́р, а** *m.* tournament

ту́р|ок, ка, *g. pl.* **т.** *m.* Turk

Ту́рци|я, и *f.* Turkey

турча́н|ка, ки *f. of* ▸ **ту́рок**

ту́скл|ый, ~, ~а́, ~о, ~ы́ *adj.* **1** (*свет*) dim, dull; (*стекло́*) opaque; (*мета́лл*) tarnished; (*кра́ска, лак*) matt **2** (fig., *взгляд, глаза́; стиль*) dull, lacklustre (BrE), lackluster (AmE)

тускне́|ть, ет *impf.* (*of* ▸ **потускне́ть**) (*о све́те*) to grow dim; (*о кра́сках, тала́нте*) to fade; (*о мета́лле, зе́ркале*) to tarnish

тус|ова́ться, у́юсь *impf.* (infml) to get together, meet, hang out

тусо́вк|а, и *f.* (infml) get-together; (*ме́сто*) meeting place, hang-out

⚷ **тут** *adv.* **1** here; **кто т.?** who's there? **2** (*о вре́мени*) now; **т. же** there and then

ту́ф|ля, ли, *g. pl.* **~ель** *f.* shoe

ту́хл|ый, ~, ~а́, ~о *adj.* rotten, bad

ту́х|нуть¹, нет, *past* **~, ~ла** *impf.* (*of* ▸ **поту́хнуть**) (*ого́нь*) to go out; (*взгляд, глаза́*) to become dull

ту́х|нуть², нет, *past* **~, ~ла** *impf.* (*загнива́ть*) to go bad, become rotten

ту́ч|а, и *f.* **1** (rain) cloud; storm cloud (also fig.); **~и собрали́сь, нави́сли (над + i.)** (fig.) the clouds are gathering (over) **2** (*пы́ли*) cloud; (*мух*) swarm

ту́ч|ный, ~ен, ~на́, ~но *adj.* **1** (*челове́к*) stout, obese, corpulent **2** (*по́чва*) rich, fertile

ту́ш|а, и *f.* carcass

тушёнк|а, и *f.* (infml) tinned meat (BrE), canned meat (AmE)

тушёный *adj.* (cul.) braised, stewed

туш|и́ть¹, у́, ~ишь *impf.* (*of* ▸ **потуши́ть¹**) (*ого́нь, пожа́р*) to extinguish, put out

туш|и́ть², у́, ~ишь *impf.* (cul.) to braise, stew

тушка́нчик, а *m.* jerboa

тушь, и *f.* Indian ink; **т. (для ресни́ц)** mascara

тща́тел|ьный, ~ен, ~ьна *adj.* thorough, careful; painstaking

тщеду́ш|ный, ~ен, ~на *adj.* feeble, frail, weak

тщесла́ви|е, я *nt.* vanity, vainglory

тщесла́в|ный, ~ен, ~на *adj.* vain, vainglorious

тще́тно *adv.* vainly, in vain

тще́т|ный, ~ен, ~на *adj.* vain, futile

⚡ **ты, тебя́, тебе́, тобо́й, о тебе́** *pers. pron.* (*informal mode of address to one person*) you; **быть (с кем-л.) на «ты», говори́ть «ты» (кому́-л.)** to be on familiar terms (with); (*для обобще́ния*) one, you

ты́|кать, чу, чешь *impf.* (*of* ▶ ткну́ть) (+ *i. and* в + *a., or* + *a. and* в + *a.*) to stick (into) (also fig.); to poke (into); to prod; to jab (into); **т. па́лкой** to prod with a stick

ты́кв|а, ы *f.* pumpkin, gourd

тыл, а, о ~е, в ~у́, *pl.* ~ы́ *m.* **1** back, rear **2** (mil.) rear; (*вся страна́*) home front **3** (*in pl.*) (mil., *вспомога́тельные ча́сти*) rear services

ты́льн|ый *adj.* back, rear; ~ая пове́рхность руки́ back of the hand

⚡ **тыс.** (*abbr. of* ты́сяча) thousand(s)

⚡ **ты́сяч|а, и, *i.* ~ей and ~ью** *num. and n., f.* thousand; **в ~у раз** a thousand times (also fig.); ~и людей thousands of people

тысячеле́ти|е, я *nt.* **1** (*срок*) a thousand years; millennium **2** (*годовщина*) thousandth anniversary

тысячеле́тний *adj.* **1** (*период, годовщина*) thousand-year; millennial **2** (*здание*) thousand-year-old

ты́сячн|ый *adj.* **1** thousandth; (*as f. n.* ~ая, ~ой) thousandth **2** (*толпа, стадо*) of many thousands

тьм|а, ы (*no pl.*) *f.* (*мрак*) darkness

тю́бик, а *m.* tube (*of toothpaste, etc.*)

тюк, á *m.* bale, package

тюле́н|ь, я *m.* (zool.) seal

тюл|ь, я *m.* (text.) tulle

тюльпа́н, а *m.* tulip

тюрба́н, а *m.* turban

тюр|е́мный *adj. of* ▶ тюрьма́; ~е́мное заключе́ние imprisonment

тюрьма́, ьмы́, *pl.* ~ьмы, ~ем *f.* prison; jail; **заключи́ть в ~ьму́** to put into prison, jail; **сиде́ть в ~ьме́** to be in prison

тюфя́к, á *m.* mattress (*filled with straw, hay, etc.*)

тя́вк|ать, аю *impf.* (*of* ▶ тя́вкнуть) to yap, yelp

тя́вк|нуть, ну, нешь *inst. pf. of* ▶ тя́вкать

тя́г|а, и *f.* **1** (*действие*) pulling; (*наземного транспорта*) traction; **на ко́нной ~е** horse-drawn **2** (*от воздушного транспорта*) thrust; (*стержень рычага*) rod **3** (*в печи*) draught (BrE), draft (AmE) **4** (к + *d.*) (fig., *влечение*) pull (towards), attraction (towards); (*стремление*) thirst (for), craving (for); (*склонность*) inclination

(to, for); **т. к зна́ниям** thirst for knowledge

тяга́ч, á *m.* tractor (*for pulling train of trailers*)

тя́гост|ный, ~ен, ~на *adj.* painful, distressing; ~ное зре́лище painful spectacle

тяго|ти́ть, щу, ти́шь *impf.* (*обременять*) to burden, be a burden (on, to); (*мысли, обязанности*) to lie heavy (on), oppress

тяго|ти́ться, щу́сь, ти́шься *impf.* (+ *i.*) to be weighed down, oppressed (by)

тягча́йший *superl. of* ▶ тя́жкий

тя́жб|а, ы *f.* (civil) suit, lawsuit; litigation

тяжеле́е *comp. of* ▶ тяжёлый, ▶ тяжело́[1], ▶ тяжело́[2]

тяжеле́|ть, ю *impf.* **1** (*становиться тяжелее*) to become heavier; (*толстеть*) to put on weight **2** (*о глазах*) to become heavy with sleep

тяжело́[1] *adv.* **1** heavily **2** (*серьёзно*) seriously, gravely; **т. больно́й** seriously ill **3** (*с трудом*) with difficulty

тяжело́[2] *as pred.* **1** (*при поднятии*) it is heavy; (*трудно*) it is hard; **мне т. ходи́ть пешко́м** it's hard for me to walk; (*мучительно*) it is painful, it is distressing **2**: **ему́ и т. п. т.** (*о настроении*) he feels, *etc.*, miserable, wretched

тяжелоатле́т, а *m.* (*штангист*) weightlifter

⚡ **тяжёл|ый, ~, тяжела́** *adj.* **1** heavy; **т. чемода́н** heavy suitcase; ~ая атле́тика (sport) weightlifting; ~ое дыха́ние heavy breathing; ~ая промы́шленность heavy industry **2** (*доставляющий беспокойство, неприятность*): **т. за́пах** oppressive, strong smell; ~ая пи́ща heavy, indigestible food **3** (*трудный*) hard, difficult; ~ая зада́ча hard task **4** (*суровый*) heavy, severe; ~ые поте́ри heavy casualties; **т. уда́р** severe blow **5** (*серьёзный*) serious, grave, bad; ~ое ране́ние serious injury **6** (*горестный*) hard, painful; ~ые времена́ hard times; **т. день** bad, hard day **7** (*характер*) difficult **8** (*стиль*) heavy, ponderous, unwieldy

тя́жест|ь, и *f.* **1** (phys.) gravity; **центр ~и** centre of gravity (also fig.) **2** (*тяжёлый предмет*) weight, heavy object **3** (*вес*) weight, heaviness **4** (*трудность*) difficulty

тя́ж|кий, ~ек, ~ка́, ~ко *adj.* **1** (*суровый*) severe; (*серьёзный*) serious, grave; ~кое преступле́ние grave crime, felony **2** (*судьба*) hard, difficult

тян|у́ть, у́, ~ешь *impf.* **1** (*невод*) to pull, draw; to haul; to drag; **т. на букси́ре** to tow; (*руку, шею*) to stretch out; **т. ру́ку к** (+ *d.*) to reach out for, towards **2** (tech., *проволоку*) to draw **3** (*прокладывать*) to lay; **т. телефо́нную ли́нию** to lay a telephone cable **4**: **т. жре́бий** to draw lots **5** (fig., *влечь*) to draw, attract; **меня́** *и т. п.* ~ет I long/want, *etc.*; **его́** ~ет домо́й he wants to go home **6** (*произносить*) to drawl, drag out; **т. но́ту** to sustain a note **7** (*медлить*) to drag out, protract, delay; **т. с отве́том** to delay one's answer **8** (*всасывать*) to draw up; to take in, suck in; **т. че́рез соло́минку** to suck through a straw **9** (**из, с** + *g.*) to extract (from); to extort (from) **10** (*убежда́ть идти́*) to drag; **никто́ тебя́ си́лой не** ⁓**у́л** nobody forced you to go

тяну́ться, у́сь, ⁓**ешься** *impf.* **1** (*о рези́не*) to stretch **2** (*о равни́не*) to stretch, extend; **тайга́** ⁓**ется на со́тни киломе́тров** the taiga stretches for hundreds of kilometres (BrE),

kilometers (AmE) **3** (*о вре́мени*) to drag on; to hang heavy **4** (**к** + *d.*) (*к ма́тери*) to reach (for), reach out (for); (*к сла́ве*) to strive (after) **5** (**за** + *i.*) (fig., infml, *стреми́ться сравня́ться*) to try to keep up (with), try to equal **6** (*дви́гаться оди́н за други́м*) to move one after the other

тяну́чк|а, и *f.* (infml) toffee, caramel

тя́пк|а, и *f.* hoe

Уу

⚔ **у** *prep.* + *g.* **1** (*во́зле*) by; at; **у окна́** by the window; **у воро́т** at the gate; **у руля́** at the wheel; **у мо́ря** by the sea; **у вла́сти** in power **2** (*обознача́ет ме́сто де́йствия*) at; with (*often = French 'chez'*); **у нас** (*в до́ме*) at our place, with us; (*в стране́*) in our country; **у себя́** at one's (own) place, at home; **я был у парикма́хера** I was at the hairdresser's **3** (*обознача́ет принадле́жность*): **у меня́ боли́т зуб** my tooth aches; **у неё больна́ мать** her mother is ill **4** (*ука́зывает на исто́чник*) from, of; **я за́нял де́сять рубле́й у сосе́да** I borrowed ten roubles from a neighbour (BrE), neighbor (AmE) **5** (*обознача́ет владе́льца*): **у меня́** *и т. п.* I have, *etc.*; **у вас есть радиоприёмник?** do you have a radio?; **у меня́ к вам ма́ленькая про́сьба** I have a small favour (BrE), favor (AmE) to ask of you

у... *vbl. pref. indicating* **1** *movement away from a place:* **улете́ть** to fly away **2** *insertion in sth:* **умести́ть** to put in **3** *covering of sth all over:* **усе́ять** to strew **4** *reduction, curtailment, etc.:* **уба́вить** to reduce **5** *achievement of aim sought:* **уговори́ть** to persuade; *with adj. roots, forms vv. expr. comp. degree:* **ускори́ть** to accelerate

уба́в|ить, лю, ишь *pf.* (*of* ▸ **убавля́ть**) **1** (+ *a. or g.*) (*жа́лованье, це́ну*) to reduce, lower; **у. ход** to reduce speed **2**: **у. в ве́се** to lose weight

уба́в|иться, ится *pf.* (*of* ▸ **убавля́ться**) to diminish, decrease; **воды́** ⁓**илось** the water (level) has fallen

убавля́|ть, ю, ет *impf. of* ▸ **уба́вить**

убавля́|ться, ется *impf. of* ▸ **уба́виться**

убаю́к|ать, аю *pf.* (*of* ▸ **убаю́кивать**) to lull (also fig.)

убаю́кива|ть, ю *impf. of* ▸ **убаю́кать**

убега́|ть, ю *impf. of* ▸ **убежа́ть**

⚔ **key word**

убеди́тел|ьный, ⁓**ен,** ⁓**ьна** *adj.* **1** (*доказа́тельный*) convincing, persuasive; **быть** ⁓**ьным** to be convincing, carry conviction **2** (*насто́йчивый*) pressing; earnest; ⁓**ьная про́сьба** pressing request, earnest entreaty

убе|ди́ть (*1st pers. sg. not used*) **ди́шь** *pf.* (*of* ▸ **убежда́ть**) **1** (**в** + *p.*) to convince (of) **2** (+ *inf.*) (*уговори́ть*) to persuade (to), prevail on (to)

убе|ди́ться (*1st pers. sg. not used*) **ди́шься** *pf.* (*of* ▸ **убежда́ться**) (**в** + *p.*) to satisfy oneself (of); to be convinced (of); **мы** ⁓**ди́лись в необходи́мости рефо́рм** we are convinced of the need for reform; **он** ⁓**ди́лся, что э́то тру́дно** he is convinced that it is difficult

убе|жа́ть, гу́, жи́шь, гу́т *pf.* (*of* ▸ **убега́ть**) **1** (*удали́ться бе́гом*) to run away, run off **2** (*спасти́сь бе́гством*) to escape, flee

убежда́|ть, ю *impf. of* ▸ **убеди́ть**

убежда́|ться, юсь *impf. of* ▸ **убеди́ться**

убежде́ни|е, я *nt.* **1** (*де́йствие*) persuasion **2** (*мне́ние*) conviction, belief

убеждённо *adv.* with conviction

убеждённост|ь, и *f.* conviction

убежд|ённый *p.p.p. of* ▸ **убеди́ть** *and adj.* **1** (*p.p.p.*) (⁓**ён,** ⁓**ена́**) (**в** + *p.*) convinced (of) **2** (*adj.*) (⁓**ён,** ⁓**ённа**) (*тон*) assured **3** (*adj., no short forms*) (*непоколеби́мый*) convinced; staunch; **у. сторо́нник** staunch supporter

убе́жищ|е, а *nt.* **1** (*защи́та*) refuge, asylum; **полити́ческое** ⁓**е** political asylum **2** (*укры́тие*) shelter

уберега́|ть, ю *impf. of* ▸ **убере́чь**

уберега́|ться, юсь *impf. of* ▸ **убере́чься**

убере́|чь, гу́, жёшь, гу́т, *past* ⁓**г,** ⁓**гла́** *pf.* (*of* ▸ **уберега́ть**) (**от** + *g.*) to protect (against), guard (against), keep safe (from), preserve (from)

убере́|чься, гу́сь, жёшься, гу́тся, *past*
~гся, ~гла́сь *pf.* (*of* ▸ уберега́ться) (от
+ *g.*) to protect oneself (against), guard
(*intrans.*) (against)

◆ убива́|ть, ю *impf. of* ▸ уби́ть

уби́йствен|ный, ~, ~на *adj.* (*жара, голод*)
unbearable, killing, murderous; (*известие,
результат, взгляд, критика*) devastating

уби́йств|о, а *nt.* killing; (*с заранее
обдуманным злым умыслом*) murder;
(*политическое*) assassination; **заказно́е у.**
contract killing

уби́йц|а, ы *c.g.* killer; murderer; assassin

убира́|ть, ю *impf.* (*of* ▸ убра́ть)

убира́|ться, юсь *impf.* (*of* ▸ убра́ться):
~йся! clear off!, beat it!, hop it!

уби́т|ый, ~, ~а *p.p.p. of* ▸ уби́ть *and adj.*
 1 (*лишённый жизни*): **неприя́тель потеря́л
две ты́сячи** ~**ыми** the enemy lost two
thousand killed; (*as m. n.* **у.**, ~**ого**) dead
man; (*жертва преступления*) murdered
man; (*при аварии*) fatality; **спать как у.**
to sleep like a log **2** (*fig.*, *подавленный*)
crushed, broken

уб|и́ть, ью, ьёшь *pf.* (*of* ▸ убива́ть) **1** to
kill; (*предумышленно*) to murder; (*по
политическим мотивам*) to assassinate
2 (*fig.*, *уничтожить*) to kill, destroy; **её
отка́з** ~**и́л его́** her refusal destroyed him
3 (*infml*, *потратить*) to waste; **у. вре́мя** to
kill time

убо́г|ий, ~, ~а *adj.* (*нищенский*) poverty-
stricken (*also fig.*); (*жилище*) wretched;
(*мысль, работа*) pathetic, dismal

убо́р, а *m.*: **головно́й у./головны́е** ~**ы** headgear

убо́рист|ый, ~, ~а *adj.* close, small (*of
handwriting, etc.*)

убо́рк|а, и *f.* **1** (*урожая*) harvesting; (*хлопка,
ягод*) picking **2** (*помещения*) clearing up,
tidying up

убо́рн|ая, ой *f.* (*туалет*) lavatory; toilet

убо́рщик, а *m.* cleaner

убо́рщи|ца, цы *f. of* ▸ убо́рщик

убра́|ть, уберу́, уберёшь, *past* ~л, ~ла́,
~ло *pf.* (*of* ▸ убира́ть) **1** (*унести*) to
remove, take away; **у. со стола́** to clear the
table **2** (*привести в порядок*) to clear up,
tidy up; **у. посте́ль** to make the bed
3 (*спрятать куда-н.*) to put away; to
store **4** (*урожай*) to harvest **5** (*fig.*, infml)
(*выгнать*) to kick out; (*убить*) to kill, take
out

убра́|ться, уберу́сь, уберёшься, *past*
~лся, ~ла́сь, ~ло́сь *pf.* (*of* ▸ убира́ться)
(infml) **1** (*навести порядок*) to clear up, tidy
up **2** (*уйти*) to clear off

убыва́|ть, ю *impf. of* ▸ убы́ть

убы́т|ок, ка *m.* **1** loss; **терпе́ть, нести́** ~**ки**
to incur losses **2** (*in pl.*) (*возмещение*)
damages; **взыска́ть** ~**ки** to claim damages

убы́точ|ный, ~ен, ~на *adj.* unprofitable

убы́ть, убу́ду, убу́дешь, *past* у́был,
убыла́, у́было *pf.* (*of* ▸ убыва́ть) to
decrease; (*о воде*) to subside, go down;
(*о луне*) to wane (also *fig.*)

◆ уважа́емый *pres. part. pass. of* ▸ уважа́ть
and adj. respected; (*в письме*) dear

уважа́|ть, ю *impf.* to respect, esteem

◆ уваже́ни|е, я *nt.* (к + *d.*) respect, esteem
(for); **внуша́ть у.** to command respect;
из ~**я** (к + *d.*) out of respect (for); **с** ~**ем**
(*в письме*) yours sincerely

уважи́тел|ьный, ~ен, ~на *adj.*
 1 (*достаточный для оправдания*) valid;
~**ьная причи́на** valid cause, good reason
2 (*почтительный*) respectful, deferential

у́вал|ень, ьня *m.* (infml) clumsy oaf,
clodhopper

уве́дом|ить, лю, ишь *pf.* (*of* ▸ уведомля́ть)
to inform, notify

уведомле́ни|е, я *nt.* notification;
(*документ*) letter of advice

уведомля́|ть, ю *impf. of* ▸ уве́домить

увез|ти́, у́, ёшь, *past* ~, ~ла́ *pf.* (*of*
▸ увози́ть) to take (away); (*с собой*) to take
with one

увекове́чива|ть, ю *impf. of* ▸ увекове́чить

увекове́ч|ить, у, ишь *pf.* (*of*
▸ увекове́чивать) **1** (*героев*) to
immortalize **2** (*порядок, систему*)
to perpetuate

◆ увеличе́ни|е, я *nt.* **1** (*зарплаты*) increase;
(*температуры*) rise **2** (*изображения*)
magnification; (*phot.*, *снимка*) enlargement

◆ увели́чива|ть, ю, ет *impf. of* ▸ увели́чить

увели́чива|ться, ется *impf. of*
▸ увели́читься

увеличи́тел|ьный *adj.* magnifying; ~**ое
стекло́** magnifying glass

увели́ч|ить, у, ишь *pf.* (*of* ▸ увели́чивать)
 1 (*в количестве, в объёме*) to increase
2 (*изображение*) to magnify; (*phot.*) to
enlarge

увели́ч|иться, ится *pf.* (*of* ▸ увели́чиваться)
to increase, grow, rise

увенч|а́ть, а́ю *pf.* (*of* ▸ венча́ть 1, ▸ венча́ть
2, ▸ увенчивать) to crown

увенч|а́ться, а́ется *pf.* (*of* ▸ уве́нчиваться)
(+ *i.*) (*fig.*) to be crowned (with); **у. успе́хом**
to be crowned with success

уве́нчива|ть, ю, ет *impf. of* ▸ увенча́ть

уве́нчива|ться, ется *impf. of* ▸ увенча́ться

уве́ренно *adv.* confidently, with confidence

уве́ренност|ь, и *f.* **1** (*шага, голоса*)
confidence; **у. в себе́** self-confidence
2 (*убеждённость*) (в + *p.*) confidence (in),
certainty (of); **мо́жно с** ~**ью сказа́ть** one
can say with confidence, it is safe to say

◆ уве́рен|ный, ~, ~на *adj.* **1** (*твёрдый*)
confident, sure; ~**ная рука́** sure hand
2 (*as pred.* ~, ~**а**) (*убеждённый*) (в + *p.*)
confident (in), sure (of), certain (of); **быть**

у

~ным to be sure, be certain; он ~ в себе́ he is self-confident; я ~а в нём I have confidence in him

уве́р|ить, ю, ишь pf. (of ▶ уверя́ть) to assure; (убеди́ть) to convince, persuade

уве́р|иться, юсь, ишься pf. (of ▶ уверя́ться) to assure oneself, satisfy oneself

увер|ну́ться, ну́сь, нёшься pf. (of ▶ увора́чиваться) (от + g.) to dodge; (also fig.): **у. от прямо́го отве́та** to avoid giving a direct answer

уве́р|овать, ую pf. (в + a.) to come to believe (in)

увер|я́ть, я́ю impf. of ▶ уве́рить

увер|я́ться, я́юсь impf. of ▶ уве́риться

увесели́тельн|ый adj. pleasure, entertainment; ~ая пое́здка pleasure trip, jaunt

уве́сист|ый, ~, ~а adj. (том) weighty; **у. уда́р** (infml) heavy blow

уве|сти́, ду́, дёшь, past ~́л, ~ла́ pf. (of ▶ уводи́ть) to take (away); (с собо́й) to take with one

уве́ч|ить, у, ишь impf. to maim, mutilate

уве́чь|е, я nt. (поврежде́ние) (serious) injury; **нанести́ у. кому́-н.** to maim, injure sb

уве́ш|ать, аю pf. (of ▶ уве́шивать) to cover (with objects suspended); **у. сте́ну карти́нами** to cover a wall with pictures

уве́шива|ть, ю impf. of ▶ уве́шать

☞ **уви́|деть, жу, дишь** pf. **1** pf. of ▶ ви́деть; ~дим we'll see **2** to catch sight of

уви́лива|ть, ю impf. (от + g.) **1** impf. of ▶ увильну́ть **2** (impf. only) to try to get out (of)

увильн|у́ть, у́, ёшь pf. (of ▶ уви́ливать 1) (от + g.) (infml) **1** to dodge **2** (fig., от отве́тственности, от нало́гов) to evade; to get out (of); **у. от отве́та** to get out of replying

увлажн|и́ть, ю́, и́шь pf. (of ▶ увлажня́ть) to moisten, damp, wet

увлажн|и́ться, и́тся pf. (of ▶ увлажня́ться) to become moist, damp, wet

увлажн|я́ть, я́ю, я́ет impf. of ▶ увлажни́ть

увлажн|я́ться, я́ется impf. of ▶ увлажни́ться

увлека́тельн|ый, ~ен, ~ьна adj. fascinating; absorbing

увлека́|ть, ю impf. of ▶ увле́чь

увлека́|ться, юсь impf. of ▶ увле́чься

увлече́ни|е, я nt. **1** (воодушевле́ние) animation **2** (+ i.) (большо́й интере́с) passion (for); enthusiasm (for); (влюблённость) crush (on) **3** (предме́т любви́) (object of) passion

увле́|чь, ку́, чёшь, ку́т, past ~́к, ~кла́ pf. (of ▶ увлека́ть) **1** (увести́) to carry along **2** (fig., о рабо́те) to carry away, distract **3** (восхити́ть) to captivate, fascinate

увле́|чься, ку́сь, чёшься, ку́тся, past ~́кся, ~кла́сь pf. (of ▶ увлека́ться) (+ i.)

1 (забы́ться) to be carried away (by); (заинтересова́ться) to become keen (on); **ора́тор ~кся** the speaker got carried away **2** (влюби́ться) to fall (for)

уво|ди́ть, жу́, ~́дишь impf. of ▶ увести́

уво|зи́ть, жу́, ~́зишь impf. of ▶ увезти́

уво́л|ить, ю, ишь pf. (of ▶ увольня́ть) (с рабо́ты) to dismiss; to sack; (mil.) to discharge

уво́л|иться, юсь, ишься pf. (of ▶ увольня́ться) (уйти́) to resign; (mil.) to get one's discharge; **у. в отста́вку** to retire

увольне́ни|е, я nt. dismissal; (mil.) discharge; (на пе́нсию) retiring, pensioning off

увольня́|ть, ю impf. of ▶ уво́лить

увольня́|ться, юсь impf. of ▶ уво́литься

увора́чива|ться, юсь impf. of ▶ уверну́ться

увы́ int. alas!

увяда́|ть, ю impf. of ▶ увя́нуть

увя|за́ть¹, жу́, ~́жешь pf. (of ▶ увя́зывать) to coordinate

увя|за́ть², а́ю impf. of ▶ увя́знуть

увя|за́ться, жу́сь, ~́жешься pf. (of ▶ увя́зываться) (infml) (за + i.) to tag along (behind), follow closely

увя́з|нуть, ну, нешь, past ~, ~ла pf. (of ▶ увяза́ть²) (в + p.) to get stuck (in); to get bogged down (in) (also fig.)

увя́зыва|ть, ю impf. of ▶ увяза́ть¹

увя́зыва|ться, юсь impf. of ▶ увяза́ться

увя́|нуть, ну, нешь, past ~, ~ла pf. (of ▶ увяда́ть) to fade, wither (also fig.)

угада́|ть, а́ю pf. (of ▶ уга́дывать) to guess (right), divine; (жела́ния) to anticipate

уга́дыва|ть, ю impf. of ▶ угада́ть

Уга́нд|а, ы f. Uganda

уганди́|ец, йца m. Ugandan

уганди́|йка, ки f. of ▶ уганди́ец

уганди́йский adj. Ugandan

уга́рный adj.: **у. газ** carbon monoxide

угаса́|ть, а́ет impf. **1** impf. of ▶ уга́снуть **2** (impf. only) (ого́нь) to die down; **си́лы у него́ ~а́ли** his strength was fading, ebbing

уга́с|нуть, нет, past ~, ~ла pf. (of ▶ угаса́ть 1) (пла́мя, свеча́) to go out; (звук) to die away; (чу́вство) to be extinguished; (челове́к) to die

углево́д, а m. carbohydrate

углеки́слый adj.: **у. газ** carbon dioxide

углеро́д, а m. carbon

углова́т|ый, ~, ~а adj. (infml) awkward

углов|о́й adj. **1** angle; angular **2** (на углу́) corner; **у. дом** corner house; **у. уда́р** (sport) corner; (as m. n. **у.,** ~о́го) (sport) corner

углуб|и́ть, лю́, и́шь pf. (of ▶ углубля́ть) **1** (я́му) to deepen, make deeper **2** (помести́ть глубоко́, глу́бже) to drive in deep, sink deeper **3** (fig.) to deepen, extend

углуб|и́ться, лю́сь, и́шься pf. (of ▶ углубля́ться) **1** (я́ма) to deepen, become deeper **2** (fig.) (о зна́ниях) to deepen, become deeper; (о противоре́чиях) to become intensified **3** (в + *a.*) (*в лес*) to go deep (into); (*в воспоминания*) to become absorbed in, lose oneself in **4** (в + *a.*) (fig., *в чтение*) to become absorbed (in)

углубле́ни|е, я *nt.* **1** deepening **2** (fig.) deepening, extending; intensification **3** (geog.) hollow, depression, dip

углубл|ённый, ~ён, ~ена́ *adj.* intensive; (*интерес*) profound

углубля́|ть, ю *impf. of* ▸ углуби́ть

углубля́|ться, юсь *impf. of* ▸ углуби́ться

угна́|ть, угоню́, уго́нишь, *past* ~л, ~ла́, ~ло *pf.* (*of* ▸ угоня́ть) (*украсть*) to steal; (*самолёт*) to hijack

угнета́|ть, ю *impf.* **1** (*жестоко притеснять*) to oppress **2** (*удручать*) to depress, dispirit

угнете́ни|е, я *nt.* oppression

угнетённ|ый *adj.* **1** (*притесняемый*) oppressed **2** (*удручённый*) depressed; **быть в ~ом состоя́нии** to be depressed, be in low spirits

угова́рива|ть, ю *impf.* **1** *impf. of* ▸ уговори́ть **2** (*impf. only*) to try to persuade, urge

угова́рива|ться, юсь *impf. of* ▸ уговори́ться

уговор|и́ть, ю́, и́шь *pf.* (*of* ▸ угова́ривать 1) (+ *inf.*) to persuade (to); to talk (into)

уговор|и́ться, ю́сь, и́шься *pf.* (*of* ▸ угова́риваться) (infml) (+ *inf.*) to arrange (to), agree (to)

уго|ди́ть¹, жу́, ди́шь *pf.* (*of* ▸ угожда́ть) (+ *d.*) (*удовлетворить*) to please, oblige

уго|ди́ть², жу́, ди́шь *pf.* (infml) (в + *a.*) (*попасть*) to fall (into), get (into); (*при падении*) to bang (against); **у. в западню́** to fall into a trap; **у. в тюрьму́** to land up in prison

уго́длив|ый, ~, ~а *adj.* obsequious

уго́дно **1** (*as pred.*): **там есть всё что у.** there is everything there one could wish for; (+ *d.*) **как вам у.** as you like; please yourself **2** (*particle forming indefinite prons. and advs.*): **кто у.** anyone (you like), whoever you like; **что у.** anything (you like); whatever you like; **ско́лько у.** as much as you like; any amount; **когда́ у.** any time

угожда́|ть, ю *impf. of* ▸ угоди́ть¹

◆ **ýг|ол, ла́, об ~ле́, в ~лу́** *m.* **1** (в ~ле́) (math., phys.) angle; **под ~ло́м** (в + *a.*) at an angle (of); **под прямы́м ~ло́м** at right angles; **у. зре́ния** (fig.) point of view **2** (*улицы, стола, комнаты*) corner; **в ~лу́** in the corner; **на ~лу́** at the corner; **за ~ло́м** round the corner; **из-за ~ла́** (from) round the corner; (fig.) on the sly, behind sb's back; **сре́зать у.** to cut off a corner

уголо́вник, а *m.* (infml) criminal

◆ **уголо́вн|ый** *adj.* criminal; **~ое де́ло** criminal case; **у. ко́декс** criminal code; **~ое пра́во** criminal law; **~ое преступле́ние** crime, felony

угол|о́к, ка́ *m.* corner

ýголь, угля́ *m.* **1** (*pl.* ýгли, ýглей) coal; **ка́менный у.** coal; **древе́сный у.** charcoal **2** (*pl.* ýгли, ýгле́й) (*кусок обгоревшего дерева*) a (piece of) coal **3** (*pl.* ýгли, угле́й) (art) charcoal

угомон|и́ть, ю́, и́шь *pf.* (infml) to calm

угомон|и́ться, ю́сь, и́шься *pf.* (infml) to calm down

уго́н, а *m.* (*велосипеда*) stealing; (*самолёта*) hijacking; **у. маши́ны** car theft

уго́нщик, а *m.* thief; (*самолёта*) hijacker; **у. маши́ны** car thief

угоня́|ть, ю *impf. of* ▸ угна́ть

ýг|орь¹, ря́ *m.* (*рыба*) eel

ýг|орь², ря́ *m.* (often in *pl.*) (*на коже*) blackhead

уго|сти́ть, щу́, сти́шь *pf.* (*of* ▸ угоща́ть) (+ *i.*) to entertain (to), treat (to); **у. кого́-н. обе́дом** to treat sb to dinner

угоща́|ть, ю *impf. of* ▸ угости́ть

угоща́|ться, юсь *impf.*: **угоща́йтесь!** help yourself/yourselves!

угоще́ни|е, я *nt.* **1** (+ *i.*) entertaining (to, with), treating (to) **2** (*то, чем угощают*) refreshments; fare

угро́б|ить, лю, ишь *pf.* (infml) **1** (*убить*) to do in **2** (fig., *загубить*) to ruin, wreck; **у. чью-н. репута́цию** to ruin sb's reputation

угрожа́|ть, ю *impf.* (*кому чем*) to threaten (with); **он ~л ему́ тюрьмо́й** he threatened him with prison; **ему́ ~ет разоре́ние** he is in danger of bankruptcy; **ему́ ~ет опа́сность** he is in danger

угрожа́|ющий *pres. part. act. of* ▸ угрожа́ть *and adj.* threatening, menacing; **~ющее положе́ние** perilous situation

◆ **угро́з|а, ы** *f.* threat

угрызе́ни|е, я *nt.*: **~я со́вести** pangs of conscience

угрю́м|ый, ~, ~а *adj.* gloomy

уда|ва́ться, ётся *impf. of* ▸ уда́ться

удалённый **1** *p.p.p. of* ▸ удали́ть **2** *adj.* (*район, доступ к компьютеру*) remote

удал|и́ть, ю́, и́шь *pf.* (*of* ▸ удаля́ть) **1** (*отдалить*) to take away, move away **2** (*убрать, устранить*) to remove; **у. зуб** to extract a tooth **3** (*заставить уйти*) to remove, send away; (*от дел, обязанностей*) to remove; **у. с по́ля** (sport) to send off (the field)

удал|и́ться, ю́сь, и́шься *pf.* (*of* ▸ удаля́ться) **1** (*отдалиться*) to move off, move away **2** (*уйти*) to leave, withdraw, retire; **у. на поко́й** to retire to a quiet life

удал|о́й, уда́л, ~а́, уда́ло, уда́лы́ *adj.* daring, bold

удал|я́ть, я́ю *impf. of* ▸ удали́ть

удал|я́ться, я́юсь *impf. of* ▸ удали́ться

◆ **уда́р, а** *m.* **1** (*рукой, палкой, топором*) blow; (*ногой*) kick; (*ножом*) stab; **одни́м ~ом** at one stroke; **нанести́ у. кому́-н.** to strike sb a blow; **у. в спи́ну** (fig.) stab in the back; **у. гро́ма** thunderclap; (*неприятность*) blow;

у. судьбы́ a stroke of bad luck **2** (*колокола*) stroke **3** (mil.) blow; attack; thrust; **под ~ом** exposed (to attack) **4** (med.) (*кровоизлияние в мозг*) stroke; (*сердца, пульса*) beat; **со́лнечный у.** sunstroke

ударе́ни|е, я *nt.* **1** (ling.) stress, accent; (fig.) stress, emphasis **2** (*знак*) stress (mark)

уда́р|ить, ю, ишь *pf.* (of ▶**ударя́ть**) **1** (+ *a.* *and* **по** + *d.* *or* **в** + *a.*) (*нанести удар*) to strike; (*нанести удар*): **у. кого́-н. по лицу́** to slap sb's face; **у. кулако́м по́ столу** to bang on the table with one's fist **2** (**в** + *a.* *or* + *a.*) (*дать сигнал*) to strike; to sound; to beat; **у. в бараба́н** to beat a drum; **у. трево́гу** to sound the alarm; **часы́ ~или по́лночь** the clock struck midnight **3** (*раздаться*) to sound; **~ил гром** there was a clap of thunder; (*фонтан, пар*) to gush; (*подействовать резко*): **я́ркий свет ~ил в глаза́** a bright light struck his eyes **4** (**по** + *d.*) (mil.) to attack **5** (**по** + *d.*) to strike (at); to combat; **у. по карма́ну** (infml) to hit one's pocket, set one back

уда́р|иться, юсь, ишься *pf.* (of ▶**ударя́ться**) **1** (**о** + *a.* *or* **в** + *a.*) to strike (against), hit **2** (**в** + *a.* *or* + *inf.*) to break (into)

уда́рник, а *m.* (mus.) percussionist

уда́рн|ый *adj.* **1** (tech. and mil.) percussive; percussion; **~ая си́ла** striking power, force of impact **2** (mus.) percussion **3** (mil.) striking, shock; **~ые ча́сти** shock troops **4** (*гласный*) stressed

ударя́|ть, яю *impf. of* ▶**уда́рить**

ударя́|ться, яюсь *impf. of* ▶**уда́риться**

⚷ **уда́|ться, стся, ду́тся**, *past* **~лся, ~ла́сь** *pf.* (of ▶**удава́ться**) **1** (*получиться*) to be successful, work (well), succeed; **опера́ция ~ла́сь** the operation was a success; **ему́ всё ~ётся** he succeeds in everything he does **2** (*impers.* + *d. and inf.*) to succeed, manage; **мне не ~лось написа́ть статью́ во́время** I did not manage to write the article on time

уда́ч|а, и *f.* success; (*везение*) good luck, good fortune

уда́члив|ый, ~, ~а *adj.* successful, lucky

уда́чн|ый, ~ен, ~на *adj.* **1** (*успешный*) successful **2** (*хороший*) good

удва́ива|ть, ю *impf. of* ▶**удво́ить**

удво́|ить, ю, ишь *pf.* (of ▶**удва́ивать**) (*увеличить вдвое*) to double; (*усилия*) to redouble

уде́л, а *m.* lot, destiny

удел|и́ть, ю́, и́шь *pf.* (of ▶**уделя́ть**) to give, spare, devote; **у. вре́мя чему́-н.** to spare the time for sth

уделя́|ть, яю *impf. of* ▶**удели́ть**

удерж|а́ть, у́, ~ишь *pf.* (of ▶**уде́рживать**) **1** (*не выпустить*) to hold, hold on to, not let go **2** (*сохранить*) to keep, retain; **у. в па́мяти** to retain in one's memory **3** (*не отпустить; не дать сделать*) to hold back, restrain **4** (*вычесть*) to deduct, keep back

удерж|а́ться, у́сь, ~ишься *pf.* (of ▶**уде́рживаться**) **1** (*не отступить*) to hold one's ground, hold out; to stand firm; **у. на нога́х** to remain on one's feet **2** (**от** + *g.*) to keep oneself (from), refrain (from); **у. от собла́зна** to resist a temptation; **мы не могли́ у. от сме́ха** we couldn't help laughing

уде́ржива|ть, ю *impf. of* ▶**удержа́ть**

уде́ржива|ться, юсь *impf. of* ▶**удержа́ться**

удешев|и́ть, лю́, и́шь *pf.* (of ▶**удешевля́ть**) to reduce the price (of)

удешев|и́ться, и́тся *pf.* (of ▶**удешевля́ться**) to become cheaper

удешевля́|ть, ю, ет *impf. of* ▶**удешеви́ть**

удешевля́|ться, ется *impf. of* ▶**удешеви́ться**

удиви́тельно *adv.* **1** amazingly, surprisingly **2** (*чудесно*) wonderfully, marvellously (BrE), marvelously (AmE) **3** (*очень*) very, extremely **4** (*as pred.*) it is amazing, it is surprising; (*странно*) it is funny

удиви́тел|ьный, ~ен, ~ьна *adj.* **1** amazing, surprising **2** (*чудесный*) wonderful, marvellous (BrE), marvelous (AmE)

удив|и́ть, лю́, и́шь *pf.* (of ▶**удивля́ть**) to amaze, surprise

удив|и́ться, лю́сь, и́шься *pf.* (of ▶**удивля́ться**) (+ *d.*) to be amazed (at), be surprised (at); to marvel (at)

удивле́ни|е, я *nt.* surprise, amazement; **к моему́ вели́кому ~ю** to my great surprise

удивля́|ть, ю *impf. of* ▶**удиви́ть**

удивля́|ться, юсь *impf. of* ▶**удиви́ться**

удира́|ть, ю *impf. of* ▶**удра́ть**

уди́ть, ужу́, у́дишь *impf.* (*also* **у. ры́бу**) to fish, angle

удлини́тел|ь, я *m.* extension lead

удлин|и́ть, ю́, и́шь *pf.* (of ▶**удлиня́ть**) to lengthen; (*срок*) to extend, prolong

удлин|и́ться, и́тся *pf.* (of ▶**удлиня́ться**) (*о мехах*) to become longer; (*о сроке*) to be extended, be prolonged

удлин|я́ть, я́ю, я́ет *impf. of* ▶**удлини́ть**

удлин|я́ться, я́ется *impf. of* ▶**удлини́ться**

удму́рт, а *m.* Udmurt

удму́рт|ка, ки *f. of* ▶**удму́рт**

удму́ртский *adj.* Udmurt

удо́бно¹ *adv.* **1** (*сидеть*) comfortably **2** (*расположить*) conveniently

удо́бно² *as pred.* (+ *d.*) **1** (*хорошо*) to feel, be comfortable; to be at one's ease; **нам здесь вполне́ у.** we are very comfortable here **2** (*подходит*) it is convenient (for), it suits; **у. ли вам прие́хать сра́зу?** is it convenient for you to come at once?

⚷ **удо́б|ный, ~ен, ~на** *adj.* **1** (*кресло, туфли*) comfortable; (*уютный*) cosy (BrE), cozy (AmE) **2** (*подходящий*) convenient, suitable; **~ное для вас вре́мя** at your convenience; **по́льзоваться ~ным слу́чаем** (+ *inf.*) to take an opportunity (to do sth)

удобре́ни|е, я *nt.* (agric.) fertilizer; (*навоз*) manure

у

удо́бр|ить, ю, ишь *pf.* (*of* ▸ удобря́ть)
to fertilize

удобр|я́ть, я́ю *impf. of* ▸ удо́брить

удо́бств|о, а *nt.* (*употребления*) convenience;
кварти́ра со все́ми ~ами flat (BrE), apartment
(AmE) with all (modern) conveniences

удовлетворе́ни|е, я *nt.* satisfaction,
gratification

удовлетвори́тельно 1 *adv.* satisfactorily
2 *n., nt. indecl.* (*отметка*) 'satisfactory',
'fair' (*mark*)

удовлетвори́тел|ьный, ~ен, ~ьна *adj.*
satisfactory

удовлетвор|и́ть, ю́, и́шь *pf.* (*of*
▸ удовлетворя́ть) 1 to satisfy; to comply
(with); **у. запро́сы** to satisfy requirements;
у. про́сьбу to comply with a request 2 (+ *d.*)
to answer, meet; **у. тре́бованиям** to answer
requirements

удовлетвор|и́ться, ю́сь, и́шься *pf.* (*of*
▸ удовлетворя́ться) (+ *i.*) to content oneself
(with), be satisfied (with)

удовлетвор|я́ть, я́ю *impf. of*
▸ удовлетвори́ть

удовлетвор|я́ться, я́юсь *impf. of*
▸ удовлетвори́ться

⚓ **удово́льстви|е, я** *nt.* 1 (*sg. only*) pleasure;
доста́вить у. (+ *d.*) to give pleasure; **с ~ем!**
with pleasure! 2 (*забава*) amusement; **жить
в своё у.** to live a life of leisure

удорож|а́ть, а́ю *impf. of* ▸ удорожи́ть

удорож|и́ть, у́, и́шь *pf.* (*of* ▸ удорожа́ть) to
raise the price (of)

удоста́ива|ть, ю *impf. of* ▸ удосто́ить

удоста́ива|ться, юсь *impf. of*
▸ удосто́иться

удостовере́ни|е, я *nt.* (*документ*)
certificate; **у. ли́чности** identity card, ID

удостове́р|ить, ю, ишь *pf.* (*of*
▸ удостоверя́ть) to certify, attest, witness; **у.
по́дпись** to witness a signature

удостове́р|иться, юсь, ишься *pf.* (*of*
▸ удостоверя́ться) (**в** + *p.*) to make sure
(of); to assure oneself (of)

удостовер|я́ть, я́ю *impf. of* ▸ удостове́рить

удостовер|я́ться, я́юсь *impf. of*
▸ удостове́риться

удосто́|ить, ю, ишь *pf.* (*of* ▸ удоста́ивать)
1 (+ *a. and g.*) (*звания, степени*) to award
(to), confer (on); **у. кого́-н. Нобелевской
пре́мии** to award sb a Nobel prize 2 (+ *i.*)
(*usu. iron.*) (*внима́нием*) to favour (BrE), favor
(AmE) (with); **он не ~ил
нас отве́том** he did not deign to give us an
answer

удосто́|иться, юсь, ишься *pf.* (*of*
▸ удоста́иваться) (+ *g.*) 1 (*награды*) to
receive, be awarded 2 (*usu. iron., улыбки*)
to be favoured (BrE), favored (AmE) (with)

удосу́жива|ться, юсь *impf. of*
▸ удосу́житься

удосу́ж|иться, усь, ишься *pf.* (*of*
▸ удосу́живаться) (+ *inf.*) (*infml*) to find time

(to); to manage

удочере́ни|е, я *nt.* adoption (*of daughter*)

удочер|и́ть, ю́, и́шь *pf.* (*of* ▸ удочеря́ть) to
adopt (*as a daughter*)

удочер|я́ть, я́ю *impf. of* ▸ удочери́ть

у́дочк|а, и *f.* (fishing) rod; (*in fig., infml phrr.*)
заки́нуть ~у to cast a line; to put a line out
(= *to try to discover sth*); **попа́сться на ~у** to
swallow the bait

удра́|ть, удеру́, удерёшь, *past* ~л, ~ла́,
~ло́ *pf.* (*of* ▸ удира́ть) (*infml*) to make off;
to do a bunk (BrE)

удруж|и́ть, у́, и́шь *pf.* (+ *d.*) (*infml*) to do sb a
good turn; (*iron.*) to do sb a bad turn

удруч|а́ть, а́ю *impf. of* ▸ удручи́ть

удруч|и́ть, у́, и́шь *pf.* (*of* ▸ удруча́ть) to
depress, dispirit

уду́шлив|ый, ~, ~а *adj.* suffocating; ~ая
жара́ stifling heat

уду́шь|е, я *nt.* breathlessness; suffocation

уедине́ни|е, я *nt.* solitude; seclusion

уединён|ный, ~, ~на *adj.* solitary, secluded

едини́|ться, ю́сь, и́шься *pf.* (*of*
▸ уединя́ться) (**от** + *g.*) to retire (from),
withdraw (from); to go off (by oneself); **у. в
свое́й ко́мнате** to retire to one's room

уедин|я́ться, я́юсь *impf. of* ▸ уедини́ться

уезжа́|ть, ю *impf. of* ▸ уе́хать

УЕФА́ *m. & f. indecl.* UEFA (*Union of
European Football Associations*)

уе́хать, уе́ду, уе́дешь, *imper.* **уезжа́й(те)**
pf. (*of* ▸ уезжа́ть) to go away, leave, depart

уж¹, á *m.* grass snake

⚓ **уж²** 1 *adv.* = уже́ 2 *emph. particle* (*infml,
безусловно*) to be sure, indeed, certainly;
уж он узна́ет he is sure to find out; (*очень*)
very; **э́то не так уж сло́жно** it's not so very
complicated

ужа́л|ить, ю, ишь *pf. of* ▸ жа́лить

у́жас, а *m.* 1 (*чувство страха*) horror,
terror; **прийти́ в у.** to be horrified; **привести́
в у.** to horrify 2 (*usu. in pl.*) (*предмет
страха*) horror; ~ы **го́лода** the horrors of
famine; **фильм ~ов** horror film/movie
3 (*as pred.*) (*infml*) it is awful, it is terrible;
ти́хий у. horror of horrors; **како́й у.!** how
awful!

ужаса́|ть, а́ю *impf. of* ▸ ужасну́ть

ужаса́|ться, а́юсь *impf. of* ▸ ужасну́ться

ужаса́ющий *adj.* awful, terrible

ужа́сно *adv.* 1 horribly, terribly; **у.
себя́ чу́вствовать** to feel awful 2 (*infml,
чрезвыча́йно*) awfully, terribly; **он у. пло́хо
игра́ет** he plays terribly badly

ужа́сно² *as pred.* (*infml*) it is awful, it is terrible

ужас|ну́ть, ну́, нёшь *pf.* (*of* ▸ ужаса́ть) to
horrify, terrify

ужас|ну́ться, ну́сь, нёшься *pf.* (*of*
▸ ужаса́ться) to be horrified, be terrified

ужа́с|ный, ~ен, ~на *adj.* awful, terrible

у́же *comp. of* ▸ у́зкий

⚓ **уже́** 1 *adv.* already; now; by now; **у. не**

no longer; **они́ у. прие́хали** they are here already; **она́ у. не ребёнок** she is no longer a child **2** *emph. particle =* **уж¹**

ужесточа́|ть, ю *impf. of* ▸ **ужесточи́ть**

ужесточ|и́ть, у́, и́шь *pf.* (*of* ▸ **ужесточа́ть**) to make stricter/harsher

ужива́|ться, юсь *impf. of* ▸ **ужи́ться**

у́жин, а *m.* supper

у́жина|ть, ю *impf.* (*of* ▸ **поу́жинать**) to have supper

ужи́|ться, ву́сь, вёшься, *past* ~лся, ~ла́сь *pf.* (*of* ▸ **ужива́ться**) (**с** + *i.*) to get on (with); **мы с ней так и не** ~**ли́сь** she and I simply couldn't get on

узако́нивани|е, я *nt.* legalization

узако́нива|ть, ю *impf. of* ▸ **узако́нить**

узако́н|ить, ю, ишь *pf.* (*of* ▸ **узако́нивать**) (*придать законную силу*) to legalize

узбе́к, а *m.* Uzbek

Узбекиста́н, а *m.* Uzbekistan

узбе́кский *adj.* Uzbek

узбе́ч|ка, ки *f. of* ▸ **узбе́к**

узде́чк|а, и *f.* bridle

у́з|ел, ла́ *m.* **1** (*на верёвке*) knot (also fig.); (*мера скорости*) knot; **завяза́ть у.** to tie a knot **2** (*место пересечения*) junction; (*центр*) centre (BrE), center (AmE); **телефо́нный у.** telephone exchange

узел|о́к, ка́ *m.* **1** small knot (*свёрток*) small bundle

у́з|кий, ~ок, ~ка́, ~ко, ~ки́ *adj.* **1** narrow; ~**кое ме́сто** (fig.) bottleneck **2** (*об одежде*) tight **3** (fig., *ограниченный*) narrow, limited; **у. круг друзе́й** narrow circle of friends

узколо́б|ый, ~, ~а *adj.* (fig.) narrow-minded

✍ **узна|ва́ть**, ю́, ёшь *impf. of* ▸ **узна́ть**

✍ **узна́|ть**, ю *pf.* (*of* ▸ **узнава́ть**) **1** (*старого друга, свою машину*) to recognize **2** (*новости*) to learn, hear; (*обнаружить, выяснить*) to find out **3** (*нужду, любовь*) to get to know; to become familiar with

у́зник, а *m.* (rhet.) prisoner

у́зниц|а, ы *f. of* ▸ **у́зник**

узо́р, а *m.* pattern, design

у́зост|ь, и *f.* narrowness (also fig.); (*одежды*) tightness

уике́нд, а *m.* weekend

уик-э́нд, а *m. =* **уике́нд**

уй|ду́, дёшь *see* ▸ **уйти́**

у́йм|а, ы *f.* (+ *g.*) (infml) lots (of), masses (of)

уйм|у́, ёшь *see* ▸ **уня́ть**

✍ **уй|ти́**, ду́, дёшь, *past* ушёл, ушла́ *pf.* (*of* ▸ **уходи́ть** 1) **1** (*покинуть место*) to go away, go off, leave; (*из, от,* **с** + *g.*) to leave; **у. из ко́мнаты** to leave the room; **у. домо́й** to go (off) home; **мне на́до у.** I must leave **2** (*от, из* + *g.*) (*спастись, избавиться*) to escape (from), get away (from); to evade **3** (*от, из,* **с** + *g.*) (*перестать заниматься чем-н.*) to retire (from), give up; **она́ ушла́ с рабо́ты** she left her job; **у. из поли́тики** to retire

from politics; **у. (из жи́зни)** to pass away (= *to die*) **4** (*от* + *a.*) (*погрузиться*) to sink (into); (fig.) to bury oneself (in); **у. в себя́** to retire into one's shell **5** (**на** + *a.*) (*израсходоваться*) to be spent; **на кни́гу ушёл год** a year was spent on the book **6** (*о времени, об эпохе*) to pass away, slip away

ука́з, а *m.* decree

указа́ни|е, я *nt.* (*инструкция*) instructions, directions

✍ **ука́з|анный** *p.p.p. of* ▸ **указа́ть** *and adj.* fixed, appointed; **на** ~**анном ме́сте** at the place appointed; **как** ~**ано** according to instructions, as instructed

указа́тел|ь, я *m.* **1** (*прибор, стрелка*) indicator; (*надпись*) sign; (comput.) cursor; **доро́жный у.** road sign; **у. у́ровня воды́** water gauge **2** (*справочный список*) index; **у. имён со́бственных** index of proper names **3** (*справочная книга*) guide, directory

указа́тельн|ый *adj.* indicating; ~**ая стре́лка** pointer; **у. па́лец** index finger; **у. знак** road sign

ука|за́ть, жу́, ~жешь *pf.* (*of* ▸ **ука́зывать** 1) **1** (*дорогу*) to show; (*адрес, день*) to indicate **2** (**на** + *a.*) (*жестом*) to point (at, to); (fig., *на ошибку, недостаток*) to point out

ука́зк|а, и *f.* pointer

✍ **ука́зыва|ть**, ю **1** *impf. of* ▸ **указа́ть** **2** (*no pf.*) (*свидетельствовать*) (**на** + *a.*) to indicate

ука|та́ть, а́ю *pf.* (*of* ▸ **ука́тывать¹**) **1** to roll (out); **у. доро́гу** (*катком*) to roll a road; (*ездой*) to make a road smooth **2** (infml, *утомить*) to wear out, tire out

ука|та́ться, а́ется *pf.* (*of* ▸ **ука́тываться¹**) (*о дороге*) to become smooth

ука|ти́ть, чу́, ~тишь *pf.* (*of* ▸ **ука́тывать²**) **1** (*бочку*) to roll away; (*велосипед*) to wheel away **2** (infml, *уехать*) to go off

ука|ти́ться, ~тится *pf.* (*of* ▸ **ука́тываться²**) to roll away

ука́тыва|ть¹, ю *impf. of* ▸ **ука́тать**

ука́тыва|ть², ю *impf. of* ▸ **укати́ть**

ука́тыва|ться¹, ется *impf. of* ▸ **ука́таться**

ука́тыва|ться², ется *impf. of* ▸ **укати́ться**

ука́ч|ать, а́ю *pf.* (*of* ▸ **ука́чивать**) **1** (*до сна*) to rock to sleep **2** (*о море, о езде*) to make sick; (*impers.*) **меня́** ~**а́ло на парохо́де** I was (sea)sick on the boat; **в маши́не её** ука́чивает she gets travel-sick in cars

ука́чива|ть, ю *impf. of* ▸ **укача́ть**

укла́д, а *m.* structure; **у. жи́зни** style of life; **обще́ственно-экономи́ческий у.** social and economic structure

укла́дыва|ть, ю *impf. of* ▸ **уложи́ть**

укла́дыва|ться¹, юсь *impf.* (*of* ▸ **уложи́ться**): **э́то не** ~**ется в голове́** it is hard to take it in

укла́дыва|ться², юсь *impf. of* ▸ **уле́чься** 1, ▸ **уле́чься** 2

укло́н, а *m.* **1** slope; (*градиент*) gradient; **под у.** downhill **2** (fig., *направленность*) bias; **шко́ла с математи́ческим ∼ом** school with a mathematical bias

уклон|и́ться, ю́сь, и́шься pf. (of ▸ **уклоня́ться**) (**от** + g.) (избежать) to avoid; to evade; **у. от отве́тственности** to evade responsibility; **у. от уда́ра** to dodge a blow; **у. от прямо́го отве́та** to avoid giving a direct answer

укло́нчив|ый, ∼, ∼а adj. evasive

уклон|я́ться, я́юсь impf. of ▸ **уклони́ться**

уко́л, а m. **1** (булавкой) prick **2** (med.) injection; jab (BrE, infml) **3** (fig., замечание) jibe

укол|о́ть, ю́, ∼ешь pf. of ▸ **коло́ть**[1]

укол|о́ться, ю́сь, ∼ешься pf. **1** (булавкой) to prick oneself **2** (impf. ▸ **коло́ться**[2] 2) (infml, о наркомане) to inject oneself

укора́чива|ть, ю impf. of ▸ **укороти́ть**

укорен|и́ться, и́тся pf. (of ▸ **укореня́ться**) to take, strike root (also fig.)

укорен|я́ться, я́ется impf. of ▸ **укорени́ться**

укоро|ти́ть, чу́, ти́шь pf. (of ▸ **укора́чивать**) to shorten

укра́дкой adv. stealthily, furtively

Украи́н|а, ы f. Ukraine

украи́н|ец, ца m. Ukrainian

украи́н|ка, ки f. of ▸ **украи́нец**

украи́нский adj. Ukrainian

укра́|сить, шу, сишь pf. (of ▸ **украша́ть**) (дом, комнату) to decorate; (ёлку) to decorate (BrE), trim (AmE); (речь, стиль) to embellish; (жизнь) to enrich

укра́|сть, ду́, дёшь, past ∼л pf. (of ▸ **красть**) to steal

украша́|ть, ю impf. of ▸ **укра́сить**

украше́ни|е, я nt. **1** (действие) decorating, decoration **2** (предмет) decoration, ornament; (ювелирное) jewellery **3** (гордость) pride; (выставки) centrepiece (BrE), centerpiece (AmE)

укреп|и́ть, лю́, и́шь pf. (of ▸ **укрепля́ть**) **1** (стены, ограду, мускулы) to strengthen **2** (mil.) to fortify **3** (fig., убеждение, любовь, власть, положение, семью) to strengthen; **у. дисципли́ну** to tighten up discipline

укреп|и́ться, лю́сь, и́шься pf. (of ▸ **укрепля́ться**) **1** to become stronger **2** (mil.) to fortify one's position **3** (fig., дисциплина, власть) to become firmly established; **у. в убежде́нии** to be confirmed in one's belief

укрепле́ни|е, я nt. **1** strengthening **2** (mil.) fortification

укрепля́|ть, ю impf. of ▸ **укрепи́ть**

укрепля́|ться, юсь impf. of ▸ **укрепи́ться**

укро́м|ный, ∼ен, ∼на adj. secluded; sheltered

укро́п, а m. (bot.) dill

укро|ти́ть, щу́, ти́шь pf. (of ▸ **укроща́ть**) **1** (зверя) to tame **2** (чувство) to curb

укроща́|ть, ю impf. of ▸ **укроти́ть**

укрыва́|ть, ю impf. of ▸ **укры́ть**

укрыва́|ться, юсь impf. of ▸ **укры́ться**

укры́ти|е, я nt. (mil., etc.) cover, concealment; shelter

укры́|ть, о́ю, о́ешь pf. (of ▸ **укрыва́ть**) **1** (ноги, поля) to cover (up) **2** (преступника) to conceal, harbour (BrE), harbor (AmE); (беженца) to (give) shelter

укры́|ться, о́юсь, о́ешься pf. (of ▸ **укрыва́ться**) **1** (одеялом) to cover oneself (up) **2** (от дождя) to take cover; to seek shelter **3** (остаться незаметным) to escape (sb's) notice

у́ксус, а (у) m. vinegar

уку́с, а m. bite; (насекомого) sting

уку|си́ть, шу́, ∼сишь pf. to bite; (о насекомом) to sting

уку́т|ать, аю pf. (of ▸ **уку́тывать**) (+ i. or **в** + a.) to wrap up (in)

уку́т|аться, аюсь pf. (of ▸ **уку́тываться**) (+ i. or **в** + a.) to wrap oneself up (in)

уку́тыва|ть, ю impf. of ▸ **уку́тать**

уку́тыва|ться, юсь impf. of ▸ **уку́таться**

✐ **ул.** (abbr. of **у́лица**) St., Street; Rd, Road

ула́влива|ть, ю impf. of ▸ **улови́ть**

ула́|дить, жу, дишь pf. (of ▸ **ула́живать**) (спорный вопрос, дело, недоразумение) to settle, resolve

ула́|диться, дится pf. (of ▸ **ула́живаться**) to be settled, resolved

ула́жива|ть, ю, ет impf. of ▸ **ула́дить**

ула́жива|ться, ется impf. of ▸ **ула́диться**

ула́мыва|ть, ю impf. of ▸ **уломáть**

Ула́н-Ба́тор, а m. Ulan Bator

у́л|ей, ья m. (bee)hive

улета́|ть, а́ю impf. of ▸ **улете́ть**

улете́|ть, чу́, ти́шь pf. of ▸ **улета́ть** (о птице) to fly (away); (о самолёте, о человеке) to leave (by air)

уле́|чься, я́гусь, я́жешься, я́гутся, past ∼гся, ∼егла́сь pf. **1** (impf. **укла́дываться** (лечь) to lie down **2** (impf. **укла́дываться**) (уместиться) to find room (to lie down) **3** (о пыли) to settle

улизн|у́ть, у́, ёшь pf. (infml) to slip away, steal away

ули́к|а, и f. (piece of) evidence; **ко́свенная у.** circumstantial evidence

ули́тк|а, и f. (zool.) snail

✐ **у́лиц|а, ы** f. street; **на ∼е** in the street; (вне дома) out (of doors), outside

улича́|ть, а́ю impf. of ▸ **уличи́ть**

улич|и́ть, у́, и́шь pf. (of ▸ **улича́ть**) (+ a. and **в** + p.) to expose (as); **его́ ∼и́ли в кра́же/ моше́нничестве** he was exposed as a thief/ fraud

у́личный adj. street

уло́в, а m. catch (of fish)

улов|и́ть, лю́, ∼ишь pf. (of ▸ **ула́вливать**) (заметить) to detect, perceive; (смысл, связь) to grasp, understand

уло́вк|а, и f. trick, ruse

улож|и́ть, у́, ∼ишь pf. (of ▸ **укла́дывать**) **1** (положить) to lay; (положить спать)

у

to put to bed; **у. в посте́ль** to put to bed
2 *(чемода́н, ве́щи)* to pack; *(в гру́ду)* to pile, stack **3** *(+ i.)* *(покры́ть)* to cover (with), lay (with) **4** *(ре́льсы)* to lay **5** *(во́лосы)* to style

уложи́|ться, у́сь, ∼ишься *pf. (of* ▸**укла́дываться¹)** **1** *(упакова́ть ве́щи)* to pack (up) **2** *(в + a.)* *(умести́ться)* to go (in), fit (in) **3** *(в + a.)* *(в преде́лы)* to keep (within), confine oneself (to); **у. в полчаса́** to confine oneself to half an hour **4**; **у. в голове́, в созна́нии** to sink in, go in

улома́|ть, ю *pf. (of* ▸**ула́мывать)** *(infml)* to talk round; *(+ inf.)* to talk into, prevail upon (to)

ᴑ **улучш|а́ть, а́ю, ет** *impf. of* ▸**улу́чшить**

улучш|а́ться, ется *impf. of* ▸**улу́чшиться**

ᴑ **улучше́ни|е, я** *nt.* improvement

улу́чш|ить, у, ишь *pf. (of* ▸**улучша́ть)** to improve

улу́чш|иться, ится *pf. (of* ▸**улучша́ться)** to improve

улыб|а́ться, а́юсь *impf. (of* ▸**улыбну́ться)** **1** *(+ d.)* to smile (at); **она́ мне ∼ну́лась** she smiled at me **2** *(+ d.)* (fig., *о жи́зни, о судьбе́)* to smile (upon)

улы́бк|а, и *f.* smile

улыб|ну́ться, ну́сь, нёшься *pf. of* ▸**улыба́ться**

улы́бчив|ый, ∼, ∼а *adj.* (infml) smiling; happy

ультима́тум, а *m.* ultimatum

ультразву́к, а *m.* ultrasound

ультразвуково́й *adj.* (phys.) ultrasonic

ультрамари́н, а *m.* ultramarine

ультрафиоле́товый *adj.* ultraviolet

ᴑ **ум, а́** *m.* mind, intellect; wits; **склад ∼а́** mentality; **быть без ∼а́ (от + g.)** to be out of one's mind (about); to be crazy (about); **(счита́ть и т. n.)** **в ∼е́** (to count, *etc.*) in one's head; **прийти́ на ум** *(+ d.)* to occur to one, cross one's mind; **быть на ∼е́** (infml) to be on one's mind; **свести́ с ∼а́** to drive mad; (fig., *очарова́ть)* to send wild; **сойти́ с ∼а́** to go mad

умал|и́ть, ю́, и́шь *pf. (of* ▸**умаля́ть)** to belittle, disparage

умалишённ|ый *adj.* mad, mentally ill; *(as n.* **у., ∼ого,** *f.* **∼ая, ∼ой)** madman; madwoman; **дом ∼ых** mental hospital

ума́лчива|ть, ю *impf. of* ▸**умолча́ть**

умал|я́ть, я́ю *impf. of* ▸**умали́ть**

уме́лый *adj.* able, skilful (BrE), skillful (AmE)

уме́ни|е, я *nt.* ability, skill

уменьш|а́ть, а́ю *impf. of* ▸**уме́ньшить**

уменьш|а́ться, а́юсь *impf. of* ▸**уме́ньшиться**

уменьше́ни|е, я *nt.* reduction, diminution, decrease

уменьши́тельн|ый *adj.* (gram.) diminutive; **∼ое и́мя** pet name (*as Kolya for Nikolai*)

уме́ньш|ить, ∼у, ∼ишь *pf. (of* ▸**уменьша́ть)** to reduce, decrease

---

уме́ньш|иться, ∼усь, ∼ишься *pf. (of* ▸**уменьша́ться)** to diminish, decrease; to abate

уме́р|енный *adj.* **1** *(∼ен, ∼енна)* moderate (pol., also fig.); **∼енная поли́тика** moderate policy **2** *(geog., meteor.)* temperate; moderate

ᴑ **умере́ть, умру́, умрёшь,** *past* **у́мер, ∼ла́, у́мерло** *pf. (of* ▸**умира́ть 1)** to die; **у. есте́ственной, наси́льственной сме́ртью** to die a natural, violent death

умер|ить, ю, ишь *pf. (of* ▸**умеря́ть)** *(тре́бования)* to moderate; *(гнев)* to restrain

умер|тви́ть, щвлю́, тви́шь *pf. (of* ▸**умерщвля́ть)** to kill, destroy (also fig.)

умерщвля́|ть, ю *impf. of* ▸**умертви́ть**

умер|я́ть, я́ю *impf. of* ▸**уме́рить**

уме|сти́ть, щу́, сти́шь *pf. (of* ▸**умеща́ть)** to fit, find room (for)

уме|сти́ться, щу́сь, сти́шься *pf. (of* ▸**умеща́ться)** to go in, fit in, find room

уме́ст|ный, ∼ен, ∼на *adj.* appropriate; pertinent; *(сде́ланный во́время)* opportune, timely; **ва́ше предложе́ние вполне́ ∼но** your suggestion is quite in order

ᴑ **уме́|ть, ю** *impf. (+ inf.)* to be able (to), know how (to); **она́ ∼ет ката́ться на конька́х** she can skate; **она́ не ∼ет притворя́ться** she is incapable of pretending

умеща́|ть, ю *impf. of* ▸**умести́ть**

умеща́|ться, юсь *impf. of* ▸**умести́ться**

умил|и́ть, ю́, и́шь *pf. (of* ▸**умиля́ть)** to move, touch

умил|и́ться, ю́сь, и́шься *pf. (of* ▸**умиля́ть)** to be moved, to be touched

умил|я́ть, я́ю *impf. of* ▸**умили́ть**

умил|я́ться, я́юсь *impf. of* ▸**умили́ться**

умира́|ть, ю *impf.* **1** *impf. of* ▸**умере́ть** **2** (fig., *о́чень хоте́ть)* to be dying to; **∼ю, как хочу́ спать** I'm dying to have a sleep; *(от + g.)* to be dying of; **у. от ску́ки** to be dying of boredom; to be bored to death

умиротворён|ный, ∼, ∼на *adj.* tranquil; contented

умне́е *comp. of* ▸**у́мный,** ▸**умно́**

умне́|ть, ю *impf. (of* ▸**поумне́ть)** to grow wiser

у́мник, а *m.* (infml, iron.) know-all, smart alec

у́мниц|а, ы *c.g.* (infml) **1** *(о де́вочке)* good girl; *(о ма́льчике)* good boy **2** *(о челове́ке)* clever person

умно́ *adv.* cleverly, wisely; *(разу́мно)* sensibly

умнож|а́ть, а́ю *impf. of* ▸**умно́жить**

умноже́ни|е, я *nt.* **1** increase, rise **2** (math.) multiplication

умно́ж|ить, у, ишь *pf. (* ▸**мно́жить,** ▸**умножа́ть)** **1** to increase **2** (math.) to multiply

у́м|ный, ∼ён, ∼на́ *adj.* *(челове́к)* clever, wise, intelligent; *(лицо́, глаза́, кни́га)* intelligent; *(разу́мный)* sensible; (*as pred.*) **∼но́** it is wise, it is sensible

умозри́тел|ьный, ∼ен, ∼ьна *adj.* (phil.) speculative; *(отвлечённый)* abstract

---

ᴑ **key word**

умоли́|ть, ю́, ∼ишь *pf.* (*of* ▸ умоля́ть 1) to prevail upon

умолк|а́ть, а́ю *impf.* *of* ▸ умо́лкнуть

умо́лк|нуть, ну, нешь, *past* ∼, ∼ла *pf.* (*of* ▸ умолка́ть) (*о человеке*) to fall silent; (*о звуках*) to cease, stop; (*о славе*) to fade

умолча́ни|е, я *nt.* (comput.): по ∼ю (by) default; шрифт/настро́йки по ∼ю default font/settings

умолча́|ть, ю́ *pf.* (*of* ▸ ума́лчивать) (о + *p.*) to pass over in silence, fail to mention, suppress, hush up; нельзя́ у. о (+ *p.*) one must mention

умоля́|ть, я́ю *impf.* ▮ *impf. of* ▸ умоли́ть ▮ to entreat, implore

умопомрачи́тел|ьный, ∼ен, ∼ьна *adj.* stupendous, tremendous, terrific

умори́тел|ьный, ∼ен, ∼ьна *adj.* (infml) hilarious

у́мственно *adv. of* ▸ у́мственный; у. отста́лый learning-disabled

у́мственный *adj.* mental, intellectual

умч|а́ться, у́сь, и́шься *pf.* ▮ to whirl, hurtle away ▮ (fig., *время, детство*) to fly past

умыва́льник, а *m.* washbasin

умыва́|ть, ю *impf.* *of* ▸ умы́ть

умыва́|ться, юсь *impf.* *of* ▸ умы́ться

у́мыс|ел, ла *m.* design, intent(ion)

ум|ы́ть, о́ю, о́ешь *pf.* (*of* ▸ умыва́ть) to wash; у. ру́ки to wash one's hands (also fig.)

ум|ы́ться, о́юсь, о́ешься *pf.* (*of* ▸ умыва́ться) to wash (oneself)

умы́шленно *adv.* purposely, intentionally

умы́шленный *adj.* intentional, deliberate; (*убийство*) premeditated

унасле́д|овать, ую *pf. of* ▸ насле́довать 1

унес|ти́, у́, ёшь, *past* ∼, ∼ла́ *pf.* (*of* ▸ уноси́ть) ▮ (*уходя, взять с собой*) to take away ▮ (*о воде, ветре*) to carry away, remove; (*impers.*) ло́дку ∼ло́ тече́нием the boat was carried away by the current ▮ (fig., *о мыслях, мечтах*) to carry (*in thought*) ▮ (fig., *жизнь, здоровье*) to claim; война́ ∼ла́ мно́го жи́зней the war claimed many lives

унес|ти́сь, у́сь, ёшься, *past* ∼ся, ∼ла́сь *pf.* (*of* ▸ уноси́ться) ▮ (*поезд, машина*) to speed away; (*тучи*) to be whisked away ▮ (fig., *миновать*) to fly away, fly by ▮ (fig., *в мыслях, мечтах*) to be carried away

универма́г, а *m.* (*abbr. of* универса́льный магази́н) department store

универса́л, а *m.* (infml, *машина*) estate car (BrE), station wagon (AmE)

универса́л|ьный, ∼ен, ∼ьна *adj.* ▮ (*проблема, язык*) universal ▮ (*разносторонний*) many-sided; versatile; ∼ьные зна́ния encyclopedic, knowledge; ∼ьное образова́ние all-round education ▮ (*инструмент*) multi-purpose, all-purpose; у. магази́н department store; у. си́мвол (comput.) wild card

универса́м, а *m.* (*abbr. of* универса́льный магази́н самообслу́живания) supermarket

✍ **университе́т, а** *m.* university; поступи́ть в у. to enter, start university; око́нчить у. to graduate (from a university)

университе́тский *adj. of* ▸ университе́т

унижа́|ть, ю *impf.* *of* ▸ уни́зить

унижа́|ться, юсь *impf.* *of* ▸ уни́зиться

униже́ни|е, я *nt.* humiliation, degradation, abasement

унизи́тел|ьный, ∼ен, ∼ьна *adj.* humiliating, degrading

уни́|зить, жу, зишь *pf.* (*of* ▸ унижа́ть) to humiliate; to degrade

уни́|зиться, жусь, зишься *pf.* (*of* ▸ унижа́ться) to demean oneself; у. до лжи/про́сьбы/шантажа́ to stoop to lying/asking/blackmail

✍ **уника́л|ьный, ∼ен, ∼ьна** *adj.* unique

унима́|ть, ю *impf.* *of* ▸ уня́ть

унима́|ться, юсь *impf.* *of* ▸ уня́ться

унита́з, а *m.* toilet (bowl)

унифо́рм|а, ы *f.* uniform

уничтож|а́ть, а́ю *impf.* *of* ▸ уничто́жить

уничтоже́ни|е, я *nt.* ▮ destruction, annihilation ▮ (*упразднение*) abolition, elimination

уничто́ж|ить, у, ишь *pf.* (*of* ▸ уничтожа́ть) ▮ to destroy; (*врага*) to annihilate; (*насекомых*) to exterminate ▮ (*упразднить*) to abolish; to do away with ▮ (fig., *унизить*) to crush

уно|си́ть, шу́, ∼сишь *impf.* *of* ▸ унести́

уно|си́ться, шу́сь, ∼сишься *impf.* *of* ▸ унести́сь

у́нци|я, и *f.* ounce (*measure*)

уны́л|ый, ∼, ∼а *adj.* ▮ (*человек*) despondent ▮ (*мысль, взгляд*) melancholy, cheerless

уны́ни|е, я *nt.* despondency, dejection

уня́|ть, уйму́, уймёшь, *past* ∼л, ∼ла́, ∼ло *pf.* (*of* ▸ унима́ть) ▮ (*успокоить*) to calm, soothe, pacify ▮ (*боль, кровотечение, слёзы*) to stop; у. пожа́р to stop a fire ▮ (*чувства*) to suppress

уня́|ться, уйму́сь, уймёшься, *past* ∼лся, ∼ла́сь *pf.* (*of* ▸ унима́ться) ▮ (*успокоиться*) to calm down ▮ (*ветер, буря*) to abate, die down; (*боль, обида*) to die down

упа́д|ок, ка *m.* decline; у. ду́ха depression; у. сил breakdown

упа́доч|ный, ∼ен, ∼на *adj.* ▮ (*искусство*) decadent ▮ depressive; ∼ное настрое́ние depression

упак|ова́ть, у́ю *pf.* (*of* ▸ пакова́ть, ▸ упако́вывать) to pack (up)

упако́вк|а, и *f.* ▮ (*действие*) packing, packaging ▮ (*материал*) packaging; (*пакет*) package

упако́выва|ть, ю *impf.* *of* ▸ упакова́ть

упа́|сть, ду́, дёшь, *past* ∼л *pf.* (*of* ▸ па́дать 1) to fall

у

упер|е́ть, упру́, упрёшь, *past* ~, ~ла *pf.*
(*of* ▶ упира́ть 1) (+ *a. and* в + *a.*) to rest
(against), prop (against), lean (against); **у.
ле́стницу в сте́ну** to rest a ladder against
the wall

упер|е́ться, упру́сь, упрёшься, *past* ~ся,
~лась *pf.* (*of* ▶ упира́ться 1) **1** (+ *i. and*
в + *a.*) to rest (against), lean (against);
у. нога́ми в зе́млю to dig one's heels in the
ground **2** (*infml, fig.,* *не согласиться*) to dig
one's heels in

упира́|ть, ю *impf.* **1** *impf. of* ▶ упере́ть
2 (*impf. only*) (**на** + *a.*) (infml) to stress,
insist (on)

упира́|ться, юсь *impf.* **1** *impf. of*
▶ упере́ться **2** (*impf. only*) (**в** + *a.*)
(*сопротивляться*) to come up (against),
be held up (by)

упи́тан|ный, ~, ~на *adj.* well fed;
(*толстый*) plump

упла|ти́ть, чу́, ~тишь *pf.* (*of* ▶ упла́чивать)
to pay; **у. по счёту** to pay a bill, settle an
account

упла́чива|ть, ю *impf. of* ▶ уплати́ть

уплыва́|ть, ю *impf. of* ▶ уплы́ть

уплы́|ть, ву́, вёшь, *past* ~л, ~ла́, ~ло *pf.*
(*of* ▶ уплыва́ть) (*вплавь*) to swim away;
(*о кораблях*) to sail away; (*о вещах*) to float
away

уподо́б|ить, лю, ишь *pf.* (*of* ▶ уподобля́ть)
to liken

уподо́б|иться, люсь, ишься *pf.* (*of*
▶ уподобля́ться) (+ *d.*) to become like

уподобля́|ть, ю *impf. of* ▶ уподо́бить

уподобля́|ться, юсь *impf. of* ▶ уподо́биться

упои́тел|ьный, ~ен, ~ьна *adj.*
intoxicating, ravishing

уполза́|ть, а́ю *impf. of* ▶ уползти́

уполз|ти́, у́, ёшь, *past* ~, ~ла́ *pf.* (*of*
▶ уполза́ть) to creep, crawl away

уполномо́ч|енный *p.p.p. of*
▶ уполномо́чить; (*as m. n.* **у., ~енного**)
representative, authorized person; **у. по
права́м челове́ка** ombudsman

уполномо́чива|ть, ю *impf. of*
▶ уполномо́чить

уполномо́ч|ить, у, ишь *pf.* (*of*
▶ уполномо́чивать) (**на** + *a.*) to authorize

упомина́ни|е, я *nt.* mentioning; (**о** + *p.*)
mention (of)

упомина́|ть, ю *impf. of* ▶ упомяну́ть

упомян|у́ть, у́, ~ешь *pf.* (*of* ▶ упомина́ть)
(+ *a. or* о + *p.*) to mention, refer (to)

упо́р, а *m.* **1** rest, support; (tech.) brace **2**: **в у.**
(mil.) point-blank (also fig.); **сказа́ть кому́-н. в
у.** to tell sb point-blank **3**: **сде́лать у.** (**на** + *a.
or p.*) to lay stress (on)

упо́р|ный, ~ен, ~на *adj.* (*упрямый*)
stubborn; (*настойчивый*) persistent

упо́рств|о, а *nt.* (*упрямство*) stubbornness;
(*настойчивость*) persistence

упорхн|у́ть, у́, ёшь *pf.* to fly, flit away

упоря́дочива|ть, ю *impf. of* ▶ упоря́дочить

упоря́доч|ить, у, ишь *pf.* (*of*
▶ упоря́дочивать) to regulate, put in
(good) order

употреби́тел|ьный, ~ен, ~ьна *adj.*
(widely-)used; common, usual

употреб|и́ть, лю́, и́шь *pf.* (*of*
▶ употребля́ть) to use; to make use (of)

употребле́ни|е, я *nt.* use; (*применение*)
application; **вы́йти из ~я** to fall into disuse

употребля́|ть, ю *impf. of* ▶ употреби́ть

упра́в|иться, люсь, ишься *pf.* (*of*
▶ управля́ться) (**с** + *i.*) (infml) **1** (**с рабо́той**)
to cope (with), manage **2** (**с проти́вником**)
to deal (with) (= *to get the better of*)

☞ **управле́ни|е, я** *nt.* **1** management,
administration; direction; **орке́стр под
~ем Спивако́ва** orchestra conducted by
Spivakov **2** (tech.) control; (*автомоби́лем*)
driving; (*самолётом*) piloting; (*кораблём*)
steering; **дистанцио́нное у.** remote control
3 (*деятельность органов власти*)
government **4** (*учреждение*) office **5** (tech.,
совокупность приборов) controls

управля́|ть, ю *impf.* (+ *i.*) **1** (*учреждением*)
to manage, run; (*оркестром, хором*) to
conduct; (*страной*) to govern **2** (tech.)
(*машиной*) to control, operate;
(*автомоби́лем*) to drive; (*самолётом*) to
pilot; (*кораблём, яхтой*) to steer, navigate

управля́|ться, юсь *impf. of* ▶ упра́виться

управля́ющ|ий, ~его *n.* (*в учреждении*)
manager; (*в имении*) steward

☞ **упражне́ни|е, я** *nt.* (*гимнастическое,
музыкальное*) exercise; (*действие*) (*мышц*)
exercising; (*на рояле*) practice, practising
(BrE), practicing (AmE); **у. па́мяти** memory
training

упражня́|ть, ю *impf.* to exercise, train

упражня́|ться, юсь *impf.* (**в** + *p. or* **на** + *p.
or* **с** + *i.*) to practise (BrE), practice (AmE),
train (at)

упраздн|и́ть, ю́, и́шь *pf.* (*of* ▶ упраздня́ть)
to abolish

упраздн|я́ть, я́ю *impf. of* ▶ упраздни́ть

упра́шива|ть, ю *impf. of* ▶ упроси́ть 1

упре|ди́ть, жу́, ди́шь *pf.* (*of* ▶ упрежда́ть)
to forestall, anticipate

упрежда́|ть, ю *impf. of* ▶ упреди́ть

упрёк, а *m.* reproach; **бро́сить у. кому́-н.** to
reproach sb; **ста́вить кому́-н. что-н. в у.** to
hold sth against sb

упрек|а́ть, а́ю *impf.* (*of* ▶ упрекну́ть) (**в** + *p.*)
to reproach (for)

упрек|ну́ть, ну́, нёшь *inst. pf. of* ▶ упрека́ть

упро|си́ть, шу́, ~сишь *pf.* (*of* ▶ упра́шивать)
1 (*настойчиво просить*) to beg, entreat
2 (*pf. only*) (*убедить сделать что-н.*) to
prevail upon

упро|сти́ть, щу́, сти́шь *pf.* (*of* ▶ упроща́ть)
to simplify; (**до** + *g.*) to reduce (to)

упро|сти́ться, сти́тся pf. (of ▶ упроща́ться) to become simpler, be simplified

упро́чива|ть, ю impf. of ▶ упро́чить

упро́чива|ться, юсь impf. of ▶ упро́читься

упро́ч|ить, у, ишь pf. (of ▶ упро́чивать) to strengthen, consolidate; to establish firmly

упро́ч|иться, усь, ишься pf. (of ▶ упро́чиваться) **1** to be strengthened, consolidated; to be firmly established; на́ше положе́ние ~илось our position is firmly established **2** (упро́чить своё положе́ние) to establish oneself (firmly), settle oneself

упроща́|ть, ю, ет impf. of ▶ упрости́ть

упроща́|ться, ется impf. of ▶ упрости́ться

упроще́ни|е, я nt. simplification

упру́г|ий, ~, ~а adj. elastic, resilient; ~ая похо́дка springy gait

упру́гост|ь, и f. elasticity, resilience; (походки) spring

у́пряж|ь, и f. harness, gear

упря́м|ец, ца m. obstinate person

упря́м|иться, люсь, ишься impf. to be obstinate; (в + p.) to persist (in)

упря́мств|о, а nt. obstinacy, stubbornness

упря́м|ый, ~, ~а adj. **1** (неуступчивый) obstinate, stubborn **2** (настойчивый) persistent

упря́|тать, чу, чешь pf. (of ▶ упря́тывать) **1** (спрятать) to hide, conceal **2** (fig., infml) (убрать) to put away; (услать) to banish; у. в тюрьму́ to lock up

упря́тыва|ть, ю impf. of ▶ упря́тать

упуска́|ть, ю impf. of ▶ упусти́ть

упу|сти́ть, щу́, ~стишь pf. (of ▶ упуска́ть) **1** (из рук) to let go, let slip, let fall; (отпустить) to let go; (не заметить) to miss **2** (fig., пропустить) to let go, let slip; to miss; to lose; у. возмо́жность, слу́чай to miss an opportunity

ура́ int. hurrah!, hurray!

уравне́ни|е, я nt. **1** (в правах) equalization **2** (math.) equation

уравнове́|сить, шу, сишь pf. (of ▶ уравнове́шивать) **1** to balance **2** (fig.) to counterbalance, offset

уравнове́шенный p.p.p. of ▶ уравнове́сить and adj. (fig.) balanced, steady

уравнове́шива|ть, ю impf. of ▶ уравнове́сить

урага́н, а m. hurricane; (fig., событий) storm

Ура́л, а m. (горы) the Urals (pl.)

ура́н, а m. **1** (chem.) uranium **2** (astron.) (У.) Uranus

урв|а́ть, у́, ёшь, past ~а́л, ~ала́, ~а́ло pf. (of ▶ урыва́ть) (infml) to snatch (also fig.), grab; у. мину́ту-две для бесе́ды to snatch a minute or two for a chat

урегули́р|овать, ую pf. (of ▶ регули́ровать 2) (отношения) to normalize; (вопрос, спор) to settle

уре́|зать, жу, жешь pf. (of ▶ урезать) **1** (infml, края) to cut off; to shorten **2** (бюджет) to cut down, reduce; (права) to reduce; у. шта́ты to cut down the staff

уреза́|ть, а́ю impf. of ▶ уре́зать

у́рн|а, ы f. **1** (для праха) urn **2**: избира́тельная у. ballot box **3** (для мусора) refuse bin (BrE), garbage can (AmE)

у́ров|ень, ня m. level; (fig.) standard; у. мо́ря sea level; высота́ над ~нем мо́ря altitude above sea level; у. жи́зни standard of living

уро́д, а m. **1** freak, monster **2** (некрасивый человек) ugly person **3** (оскорбление) bastard (as a term of abuse, usu. of a man)

уро́длив|ый, ~, ~а adj. **1** (с уродством) deformed, misshapen **2** (некрасивый) ugly **3** (fig., плохой, ненормальный) bad; abnormal; faulty; distorted

уро́д|овать, ую impf. (of ▶ изуро́довать) **1** (калечить) to deform, disfigure, mutilate **2** (делать некрасивым) to make ugly **3** (fig., искажать) to distort

уро́дств|о, а nt. **1** (физический недостаток) deformity; disfigurement **2** (некрасивость) ugliness **3** (fig., ненормальность) abnormality

урожа́|й, я m. **1** harvest; crop; собра́ть у. to gather in the harvest **2** (хороший сбор) bumper crop, abundance (also fig., infml)

уроже́н|ец, ца m. (+ g.) native (of)

уроже́н|ка, ки f. of ▶ уроже́нец

уро́к, а m. **1** lesson (also fig.); брать ~и (+ g.) to have, take lessons (in); дава́ть ~и (+ g.) to give lessons (in) **2** (задание) homework; зада́ть у. to set homework; сде́лать ~и to do one's homework

уро́н, а (no pl.) m. (материальный) damages, losses; (о людях) casualties; нанести́ у. (урожаю) to inflict damage (on); (врагу) to inflict casualties (on)

урон|и́ть, ю́, ~ишь pf. of ▶ роня́ть 3

уругва́|ец, йца m. Uruguayan

Уругва́|й, я m. Uruguay

уругва́й|ка, ки f. of ▶ уругва́ец

уругва́йский adj. Uruguayan

урч|а́ть, у́, и́шь impf. to rumble; (о собаке) to growl

урыва́|ть, ю impf. of ▶ урва́ть

ус, а m. **1** (see also ▶ усы́) (человека) moustache hair (BrE), mustache hair (AmE) **2** (животного) whisker

уса|ди́ть, жу́, ~дишь pf. (of ▶ уса́живать) **1** (помочь усесться) to seat, help sit down; (заставить усесться) to make sit down **2** (за + a. or + inf.) to sit (sb) down; у. за уро́ки to sit sb down to his/her lessons

уса́дьб|а, ы, g. pl. уса́деб f. **1** (hist., помещика) country estate **2** (ферма) farmstead

уса́жива|ть, ю impf. of ▶ усади́ть

уса́жива|ться, юсь impf. of ▶ усе́сться

уса́т|ый, ~, ~а adj. **1** (человек) with a moustache (BrE), mustache (AmE) **2** (животное) whiskered

усва́ива|ть, ю impf. of ▶ усво́ить

усво́|ить, ю, ишь pf. (of ▸ усва́ивать) **1** (привычку) to adopt, acquire; to imitate **2** (урок) to master; to assimilate **3** (пищу) to assimilate

усе́ива|ть, ю impf. of ▸ усе́ять

усе́рд|ный, ~ен, ~на adj. diligent, painstaking

усе́|сться, уся́дусь, уся́дешься, past ~лся, ~лась pf. (of ▸ уса́живаться) **1** to take a seat; to settle (down) **2** (за + a. or + inf.) to set (to), settle down (to)

усе́|ять, ю, ешь pf. (of ▸ усе́ивать) (+ i.) **1** (засеять) to sow (with) **2** (покрыть) to cover (with), dot (with), stud (with), strew (with); лицо́, ~янное весну́шками face covered with freckles

уси|де́ть, жу́, ди́шь pf. **1** (остаться сиде́ть) to keep one's place, remain sitting; он так волнова́лся, что е́ле ~де́л he was so excited that he could hardly sit still **2** (infml, удержаться на каком-н. месте) to stay around in a place

у́сик, а m. (zool.) antenna, feeler

усиле́ни|е, я nt. **1** (контроля) strengthening; (охраны, прочности) reinforcement **2** (работы) intensification; (проблем) aggravation; (radio) amplification

уси́л|енный p.p.p. of ▸ уси́лить and adj. **1** (охрана) reinforced; ~енное пита́ние high-calorie diet **2** (внимание, скорость) intensified, increased

уси́лива|ть, ю, ет impf. of ▸ уси́лить

уси́лива|ться, ется impf. of ▸ уси́литься

уси́ли|е, я nt. effort; exertion; приложи́ть все ~я to make every effort, spare no effort

усили́тел|ь, я m. amplifier

уси́л|ить, ю, ишь pf. (of ▸ уси́ливать) **1** (войска, констру́кцию) to strengthen, reinforce **2** (наблюдение, волнение) to intensify, increase; (звук) to amplify

уси́л|иться, ится pf. (of ▸ уси́ливаться) (о ветре, чувстве) to become stronger; (о дожде, боли) to intensify, increase; (звук) to grow louder

уска|ка́ть, чу́, ~чешь pf. **1** (о зайце) to bound away; (infml, о человеке) to run off **2** (о лошади; на лошади) to gallop off

ускольз|а́ть, а́ю impf. of ▸ ускользну́ть

ускольз|ну́ть, ну́, нёшь pf. (of ▸ ускольза́ть) **1** (из рук) to slip out; (из-под ног) to slip away **2** (fig., infml, о человеке) to slip off **3** (fig.) (от + g.) to escape; у. от чьего́-л. внима́ния to escape one's notice

ускоре́ни|е, я nt. acceleration; speeding up

ускори́тел|ь, я m. (tech.) accelerator; у. части́ц particle accelerator

ускор|ить, ю, ишь pf. (of ▸ ускоря́ть) **1** (убыстрить) to quicken; to speed up, accelerate; у. шаг to quicken one's pace **2** (приблизить) to hasten; (смерть, что-н. плохое) to precipitate

ускор|иться, ится pf. (of ▸ ускоря́ться) **1** (шаги) to quicken; (ход механизма) to accelerate **2** (выздоровление, отъезд) to be speeded up

ускор|я́ть, я́ю, я́ет impf. of ▸ ускорить

ускор|я́ться, я́ется impf. of ▸ ускориться

следи́ть, жу́, ди́шь pf. (за + i.) **1** (за ребёнком) to keep an eye (on), mind **2** (за ходом разговора) to follow

✍ **усло́ви|е, я** nt. **1** (требование) condition; stipulation, proviso; поста́вить ~ем to make it a condition, stipulate; при ~и, что; с ~ем, что on condition that, provided that, providing **2** (in pl.) (правила, обстоятельства) conditions; пого́дные ~я weather conditions

усло́в|ный adj. **1** (принятый) conventional; (знак, жест) agreed, prearranged **2** (~ен, ~на) (с условием) conditional; у. пригово́р (law) suspended sentence **3** (~ен, ~на) (относительный) relative **4** (~ен, ~на) (воображаемый) imaginary **5** (gram.) conditional

усложне́ни|е, я nt. complication

усложн|и́ть, ю́, и́шь pf. (of ▸ усложня́ть) to complicate

усложн|и́ться, и́тся pf. (of ▸ усложня́ться) to become complicated

усложн|я́ть, я́ю, я́ет impf. of ▸ усложни́ть

усложн|я́ться, я́ется impf. of ▸ усложни́ться

✍ **услу́г|а, и** f. **1** service; favour (BrE), favor (AmE), good turn; оказа́ть ~у кому́-н. to do sb a service; к ва́шим ~ам at your service **2** (in pl.) service(s); коммуна́льные ~и public utilities

услу́жлив|ый, ~, ~а adj. obliging

✍ **услы́ш|ать, у, ишь** pf. of ▸ слы́шать 1

усмех|а́ться, а́юсь impf. of ▸ усмехну́ться

усмех|ну́ться, ну́сь, нёшься pf. (of ▸ усмеха́ться) to smirk; to grin

усмир|и́ть, ю́, и́шь pf. (of ▸ усмиря́ть) **1** (успокоить) to pacify; to calm, quieten; (укротить) to tame (also fig.) **2** (мятеж) to suppress, put down

усмир|я́ть, я́ю impf. of ▸ усмири́ть

усн|у́ть, у́, ёшь pf. to go to sleep, fall asleep (also fig.)

усоверше́нств|овать, ую pf. of ▸ соверше́нствовать

усоверше́нств|оваться, уюсь pf. of ▸ соверше́нствоваться

усомн|и́ться, ю́сь, и́шься pf. (в + p.) to doubt

усо́х|нуть, ну, нешь, past ~, ~ла pf. (of ▸ усыха́ть) to dry up, dry out; (о человеке) to wither

успева́|ть, ю impf. **1** impf. of ▸ успе́ть **2** (impf. only) (в + p. or по + d.) to make progress (in), get on well (in, at) (studies)

✍ **успе́|ть, ю** pf. (of ▸ успева́ть 1) to have time; to manage; у. написа́ть to have time to write; у. к по́езду to manage to catch the train; не ~л я вы́йти из до́ма, как пошёл

✍ key word

дождь no sooner had I left the house than it started to rain

⚡ успе́х, а *m.* **1** success; **име́ть большо́й** у. to be a great success; **по́льзоваться** ~ом to be a success; **по́льзоваться** ~ом **у кого́-н.** to be successful with sb; **с тем же** ~ом equally well, with the same result; **с** ~ом successfully **2** (*in pl.*) success, progress; **де́лать** ~**и (в + *p.*)** to make progress (in)

⚡ успе́шно *adv.* successfully

⚡ успе́ш|ный, ~ен, ~на *adj.* successful

успока́ива|ть, ю *impf. of* ▶ успоко́ить

успока́ива|ться, юсь *impf. of* ▶ успоко́иться

успокойтел|ьный, ~ен, ~ьна *adj.* calming, soothing; reassuring; (*as nt. n.* ~ьное, ~ьного) sedative

успоко́|ить, ю, ишь *pf.* (*of* ▶ успока́ивать) **1** to calm (down); (*убедить не тревожиться*) to reassure **2** (*боль*) to assuage, deaden

успоко́|иться, юсь, ишься *pf.* (*of* ▶ успока́иваться) **1** (*о человеке*) to calm down; to compose oneself **2** (*быть довольным*) to be satisfied; **у. на дости́гнутом** to be content with what has been achieved **3** (*о боли*) to abate; (*о море*) to become still; (*о ветре*) to drop

уста́в, а *m.* regulations, rules, statutes; (mil.) service regulations; (*в монастыре*) rule; **у. университе́та** university statutes; **У. ООН** UN Charter

уста|ва́ть, ю́, ёшь *impf. of* ▶ уста́ть

уста́лост|ь, и *f.* fatigue, tiredness

уста́лый *adj.* tired, weary

⚡ устана́влива|ть, ю, ет *impf. of* ▶ установи́ть

устана́влива|ться, ется *impf. of* ▶ установи́ться

установ|и́ть, лю́, ~ишь *pf.* (*of* ▶ устана́вливать) **1** (*поставить, поместить*) to place, put, set up; (*оборудование, механизм*) to install, rig up; (*памятник*) to put up; (comput., *программу*) to install **2** (*показание*) to adjust, regulate, set (to, by); **у. часы́ по ра́дио** to set one's watch by the radio **3** (*власть, контакт*) to establish; **у. связь (с + *i.*)** (mil.) to establish communication (with) **4** (*назначить*) to fix, establish; **у. гра́фик** to fix the schedule **5** (*обнаружить, выяснить*) to establish, determine; to ascertain; **у. причи́ну ава́рии** to establish the cause of a crash

установ|и́ться, ~ится *pf.* (*of* ▶ устана́вливаться) to be established; to set in; ~и́лся обы́чай it has become a custom

⚡ устано́вк|а, и *f.* **1** (*действие*) placing, setting up; arrangement; (*оборудования, механизма*) installation, setting up; (*величины*) setting **2** (*часов*) adjustment, setting **3** (comput.) set-up **4** (*цель*) aim, purpose **5** (*директива*) directive

установле́ни|е, я *nt.* establishment; (*определение*) determination

устано́в|ленный *p.p.p. of* ▶ установи́ть *and adj.* established, fixed, prescribed,

regulation; **в** ~ленном поря́дке in prescribed manner

устарева́|ть, ю *impf. of* ▶ устаре́ть

устаре́вший *past. part. act. of* ▶ устаре́ть *and adj.* obsolete

устаре́|ть, ю *pf.* (*of* ▶ устарева́ть, ▶ старе́ть 2) to become obsolete; to become antiquated, out of date

уста́|ть, ну, нешь *pf.* (*of* ▶ устава́ть) to become tired; **я** ~л I am tired; **у. от (+ *g.*)** get tired of (sb, sth); **мы** ~ли **с доро́ги** we're tired from the journey

устила́|ть, ю *impf. of* ▶ устла́ть

устла́ть, устелю́, усте́лешь *pf.* (*of* ▶ устила́ть) (+ *i.*) to cover (with); (*плитами, камнями*) to pave (with)

у́стн|ый *adj.* verbal, oral; ~ая речь spoken language; **у. экза́мен** oral (examination)

усто́йчивост|ь, и *f.* (*опоры*) stability, steadiness; (*веры*) firmness

усто́йчив|ый, ~, ~а *adj.* (*опора, плот*) stable, steady; (*вера, принцип*) firm; ~ая пого́да settled weather

усто|я́ть, ю́, и́шь *pf.* **1** (*не упасть*) to keep one's balance, remain standing; **у. на нога́х** to keep one's balance **2** (fig., *в споре*) to stand one's ground **3** (*не поддаться*) to resist, hold out; **у. пе́ред собла́зном** to resist a temptation

усто|я́ться, и́тся *pf.* (*о взглядах*) to become fixed, become permanent

⚡ устра́ива|ть, ю *impf. of* ▶ устро́ить

устра́ива|ться, юсь *impf. of* ▶ устро́иться

устран|и́ть, ю́, и́шь *pf.* (*of* ▶ устраня́ть) **1** (*убрать в сторону*) to remove; **у. прегра́ды** to remove obstacles; (*уничтожить*) to eliminate **2** (*уволить*) to remove (*from office*); to dismiss

устран|я́ть, я́ю *impf. of* ▶ устрани́ть

устраша́ющий *adj.* frightening, appalling

устрем|и́ться, лю́сь, и́шься *pf.* (*of* ▶ устремля́ться) **1** (*на + *a.*) (*направиться*) to rush (upon, at); to head (for) **2** (**на** + *a.* or **к** + *d.*) (*сосредоточиться*) to be directed (at, towards); to be fixed (upon), be concentrated (on); (*о человеке*) to concentrate (on)

устремля́|ться, юсь *impf. of* ▶ устреми́ться

у́стриц|а, ы *f.* oyster

устро́|ить, ю, ишь *pf.* (*of* ▶ устра́ивать) **1** (*изготовить, соорудить*) to make, construct **2** (*концерт*) to arrange, organize **3** (*вызвать*) to make, cause, create; **у. сканда́л** to make a scene **4** (*наладить*) to settle, put in (good) order; **у. свои́ дела́** to put one's affairs in order **5** (*поместить*) to place, fix up; **у. кого́-н. на рабо́ту** to fix sb up with work **6** (*impers.*) (infml, *оказаться удобным*) to suit, be convenient (to, for)

устро́|иться, юсь, ишься *pf.* (*of* ▶ устра́иваться) **1** (*прийти в порядок*) to work out (well) **2** (*наладить свои дела*) to manage, get by **3** (*расположиться*) to settle down, get settled **4** (*на работу*) to get (*a job*); **он** ~ился **на желе́зную доро́гу**

у

проводнико́м he has got a job on the railway as a conductor

☞ **устро́йств|о, а** *nt.* **1** (*расположе́ние, констру́кция*) construction; layout; (tech.) working principle(s) **2** (*прибо́р*) apparatus, device **3** (*поря́док, строй*) structure, system; **обще́ственное у.** social structure

усту́п, а *m.* (*в стене́, скале́*) shelf, ledge; (agric.) terrace

уступ|а́ть, а́ю *impf. of* ▶ уступи́ть

уступ|и́ть, лю́, ~ишь *pf.* (*of* ▶ уступа́ть) (+ *d.*) **1** (*в по́льзу друго́го*) to let have, give up (to); **у. кому́-н. ме́сто** to give up one's place/seat to sb; **у. доро́гу** (+ *d.*) to make way (for), let pass **2** (*покори́ться*) to yield (to), give in (to); **у. кому́-н. в спо́ре** to give in to sb's argument **3** (*быть ху́же кого́-н., чего́-н.*) to be inferior (to); **как расска́зчик он никому́ не ~ит** as a storyteller he is second to none

усту́пк|а, и *f.* **1** concession, compromise **2** (*в цене́*) reduction, discount

усту́пчив|ый, ~, ~а *adj.* pliant, pliable; compliant

у́сть|е, я, *g. pl.* ~ев *nt.* (*реки́*) mouth, estuary

усугуб|и́ть, ~лю́, ~и́шь *pf.* (*of* ▶ усугубля́ть) to increase; to intensify; to aggravate

усугубля́|ть, ю *impf. of* ▶ усугуби́ть

ус|ы́, о́в *m. pl.* (*sg.* **ус, а**) (*челове́ка*) moustache (BrE), mustache (AmE) (*see also* ▶ ус)

усынов|и́ть, лю́, и́шь *pf.* (*of* ▶ усыновля́ть) to adopt (*as a son*)

усыновле́ни|е, я *nt.* adoption (*of son*)

усыновля́|ть, ю *impf. of* ▶ усынови́ть

усы́п|ать, лю, лешь *pf.* (*of* ▶ усыпа́ть) (+ *i.*) to strew (with), scatter (with); (*покры́ть*) to cover (with)

усып|а́ть, а́ю *impf. of* ▶ усы́пать

усып|и́ть, лю́, и́шь *pf.* (*of* ▶ усыпля́ть) **1** (*перед опера́цией*) to put to sleep; (*пе́нием, чте́нием*) to lull to sleep **2** (fig.) (*подозре́ния*) to lull; (*внима́ние*) to weaken, undermine **3** (*больну́ю соба́ку*) to put to sleep

усыпля́|ть, ю *impf. of* ▶ усыпи́ть

усыха́|ть, ю *impf. of* ▶ усо́хнуть

ута́ива|ть, ю *impf. of* ▶ утаи́ть

ута|и́ть, ю́, и́шь *pf.* (*of* ▶ ута́ивать) **1** (*скрыть*) to conceal; (*умолча́ть*) to keep to oneself, keep secret **2** (*присво́ить*) to appropriate

ута́птыва|ть, ю *impf. of* ▶ утопта́ть

утащ|и́ть, у́, ~ишь *pf.* **1** to drag away, off (*also* fig.) **2** (infml, *укра́сть*) to steal, pinch (BrE)

у́твар|ь, и (*no pl.*) *f.* (*collect.*) utensils, equipment

утверд|и́ть, жу́, ди́шь *pf.* (*of* ▶ утвержда́ть 1) **1** (*диктату́ру, пра́вила*) to establish (*securely, firmly*) **2** (*санкциони́ровать*)

---

to approve; to confirm; (*догово́р*) to ratify; **у. пове́стку дня** to approve an agenda; **у. в до́лжности** to confirm in a job

утверд|и́ться, жу́сь, ди́шься *pf.* (*of* ▶ утвержда́ться) **1** (*укрепи́ться*) to gain a foothold, gain a firm hold (also fig.); (*поря́док, режи́м*) to become firmly established **2** (**в** + *p.*) (*пове́рить*) to be confirmed in (*one's resolve, etc.*); **у. в мы́сли** to become firmly convinced **3** (**за** + *i.*) (*о репута́ции*): **за ним ~ди́лась репута́ция хоро́шего инжене́ра** he gained a reputation for being a good engineer

☞ **утвержда́|ть, ю** *impf.* **1** *impf. of* ▶ утверди́ть **2** (*impf. only*) to assert, maintain; (*без доказа́тельства*) to claim, allege

утвержда́|ться, юсь *impf. of* ▶ утверди́ться

утвержде́ни|е, я *nt.* **1** (*выска́зывание*) claim, allegation **2** (*санкциони́рование*) approval; confirmation; (*догово́ра*) ratification; (law, *завеща́ния*) probate **3** (*диктату́ры, поря́дка*) establishment

утека́|ть, ю *impf. of* ▶ уте́чь

ут|ёнок, ёнка, *pl.* ~я́та, ~я́т *m.* duckling

утепли́тел|ь, я *m.* (tech.) insulating material

утепл|и́ть, ю́, и́шь *pf.* (*of* ▶ утепля́ть) to insulate

утепл|я́ть, я́ю *impf. of* ▶ утепли́ть

утер|е́ть, утру́, утрёшь, *past* ~, ~ла *pf.* (*of* ▶ утира́ть) to wipe (off); to wipe dry; **у. пот со лба** to wipe the sweat off one's brow

утер|е́ться, утру́сь, утрёшься, *past* ~ся, ~лась *pf.* (*of* ▶ утира́ться) to wipe oneself; to dry oneself

утерп|е́ть, лю́, ~ишь *pf.* to restrain oneself

утёс, а *m.* cliff, crag

уте́чк|а, и *f.* (*жи́дкости, информа́ции*) leak, leakage; (*у́быль*) loss, wastage, dissipation; **у. га́за** gas escape; **«у. мозго́в»** brain drain

уте́|чь, ку́, чёшь, ку́т, *past* ~к, ~кла́ *pf.* (*of* ▶ утека́ть) **1** to flow away; to leak; (*о га́зе*) to escape **2** (*о вре́мени*) to pass, go by

утеш|а́ть, а́ю *impf. of* ▶ уте́шить

утеш|а́ться, а́юсь *impf. of* ▶ уте́шиться

утеше́ни|е, я *nt.* comfort, consolation

уте́ш|ить, у, ишь *pf.* (*of* ▶ утеша́ть) to comfort, console

уте́ш|иться, усь, ишься *pf.* (*of* ▶ утеша́ться) **1** to console oneself **2** (+ *i.*) (*мы́слью, собы́тием*) to take comfort (in)

утилиза́ци|я, и *f.* recycling

ути́л|ь, я (*no pl.*) *m.* (*collect.*) scrap, recyclable waste

утира́|ть, ю *impf. of* ▶ утере́ть

утира́|ться, юсь *impf. of* ▶ утере́ться

утих|а́ть, а́ю *impf. of* ▶ ути́хнуть

ути́х|нуть, ну, нешь, *past* ~, ~ла *pf.* (*of* ▶ утиха́ть) **1** (*о ме́сте*) to become quiet, still; (*о зву́ках*) to cease, die away **2** (*о бу́ре, о бо́ли*) to abate, subside; (*о ве́тре*) to drop; (*о спо́ре*) to die down **3** (*о челове́ке*) to become calm, calm down

утихоми́рива|ть, ю *impf. of* ▶ утихоми́рить

☞ key word

утихоми́рива|ться, юсь *impf. of*
▶ **утихоми́риться**

утихоми́р|ить, ю, ишь *pf.* (*of*
▶ **утихоми́ривать**) to calm down; to pacify,
placate

утихоми́р|иться, юсь, ишься *pf.* (*of*
▶ **утихоми́риваться**) to calm down; to abate,
subside

у́тк|а, и *f.* duck

уткн|у́ть, у́, ёшь *pf.* (infml) to bury; to fix; **у.
нос в кни́гу** to bury oneself in a book

уткн|у́ться, у́сь, ёшься *pf.* (**в** + *a.*) (infml)
1 to bury oneself (in), one's head (in); **у. в
газе́ту** to bury one's head in a newspaper
2 (*натолкну́ться*) to bump (into); **ло́дка
~у́лась в бе́рег** the boat bumped into the
bank

утол|и́ть, ю́, и́шь *pf.* (*of* ▶ **утоля́ть**)
1 (*жа́жду*) to quench, slake; (*го́лод,
любопы́тство*) to satisfy **2** (*боль*) to
relieve, alleviate

утол|я́ть, я́ю *impf. of* ▶ **утоли́ть**

утоми́тел|ьный, ~ен, ~ьна *adj.*
1 (*утомля́ющий*) wearisome, tiring
2 (*ску́чный*) tiresome; tedious

утом|и́ть, лю́, и́шь *pf.* (*of* ▶ **утомля́ть**)
to tire, weary, fatigue

утом|и́ться, лю́сь, и́шься *pf.* (*of*
▶ **утомля́ться**) to get tired

утомле́ни|е, я *nt.* tiredness, weariness,
fatigue

утомлённый *p.p.p. of* ▶ **утоми́ть** *and adj.*
tired, weary, fatigued

утомля́|ть, ю *impf. of* ▶ **утоми́ть**

утомля́|ться, юсь *impf. of* ▶ **утоми́ться**

утон|у́ть, у́, ~ешь *pf.* (*of* ▶ **тону́ть** 3,
▶ **утопа́ть** 1) **1** (*погибну́ть*) to drown, be
drowned; (*оказа́ться под водо́й*) to sink
2 (**в** + *p.*) (fig.) to be lost (in)

утончённый *adj.* refined; exquisite, subtle

утопа́|ть, ю *impf.* **1** *impf. of* ▶ **утону́ть**
2 (*impf. only*) (**в** + *p.*) (fig., *в зе́лени*) to be
covered (in); (*в ро́скоши, бога́тстве*) to
wallow (in)

утопа́ющ|ий *pres. part. act. of* ▶ **утопа́ть**
(*as n.* **~ий, ~его**) drowning person

утоп|и́ть, лю́, ~ишь *pf.* (*of* ▶ **топи́ть³** 2)
1 (*челове́ка, живо́тное*) to drown **2** (fig.,
infml, *погуби́ть*) to ruin **3** (*сде́лать едва́
ви́дным*) to bury, embed

утоп|и́ться, лю́сь, ~ишься *pf.* (*of*
▶ **топи́ться³**) to drown oneself

утопи́ческий *adj.* Utopian

уто́пи|я, и *f.* Utopia

уто́пленник, а *m.* drowned man

уто́пленни|ца, цы *f. of* ▶ **уто́пленник**

утоп|та́ть, чу́, ~чешь *pf.* (*of* ▶ **ута́птывать**)
to trample down, pound

уточне́ни|е, я *nt.* clarification; elaboration;
внести́ ~е/~я во что-н. to elaborate on sth

уточн|и́ть, ю́, и́шь *pf.* (*of* ▶ **уточня́ть**) to
make more precise, clarify; to elaborate

уточн|я́ть, я́ю *impf. of* ▶ **уточни́ть**

утра́ива|ть, ю, ет *impf. of* ▶ **утро́ить**

утра́ива|ться, ется *impf. of* ▶ **утро́иться**

утрамб|ова́ть, у́ю *pf.* (*of* ▶ **утрамбо́вывать**)
to ram, tamp (*road material, etc.*)

утрамбо́выва|ть, ю *impf. of* ▶ **утрамбова́ть**

утра́|тить, чу, тишь *pf.* (*of* ▶ **утра́чивать**)
to lose

утра́чива|ю, ю *impf. of* ▶ **утра́тить**

у́тренний *adj.* morning, early

утри́р|овать, ую *impf. and pf.* to exaggerate

✴ **у́тр|о, а, до ~а́, с ~а́, д. ~у (к ~у́),** *pl.* **~а,
~, ~ам,** *in sense 'in the mornings'*: *d.* **по
~а́м,** *i.* **~а́ми** *nt.* morning; **в семь часо́в ~а́**
at 7 a.m.; **на сле́дующее у.** the next morning;
с ~а́ early in the morning; **с ~а́ до ве́чера**
from morning till night; **до́брое у.!** good
morning!

утро́б|а, ы *f.* womb

утро́|ить, ю, ит *pf.* (*of* ▶ **утра́ивать**) to treble

утро́|иться, ится *pf.* (*of* ▶ **утра́иваться**) to
treble

у́тром *adv.* in the morning; **сего́дня у.** this
morning

утружда́|ть, ю *impf.* to trouble; **у. кого́-н.
про́сьбами** to trouble sb with requests

утряса́|ть, а́ю, а́ет *impf. of* ▶ **утрясти́**

утряса́|ться, а́ется *impf. of* ▶ **утрясти́сь**

утряс|ти́, у́, ёшь *pf.* (*of* ▶ **утряса́ть**) (infml)
to settle

утряс|ти́сь, ётся, у́тся *pf.* (*of* ▶ **утряса́ться**)
(infml, *де́ло, пробле́ма*) to sort itself out; **всё
~ётся** everything will be sorted out

уты́к|ать, аю *pf.* (*of* ▶ **утыка́ть**, ▶ **уты́кивать**)
(infml) **1** (*воткну́ть*) to stick (in) all over
2 (*заби́ть*) to stop up, caulk

утык|а́ть, а́ю *impf. of* ▶ **уты́кать**

уты́кива|ть, ю *impf.* = **уты́кать**

утю́г, а́ *m.* iron (*for ironing clothes, etc.*)

уфоло́ги|я, и *f.* ufology

ух|а́, и́ *f.* ukha (*fish soup*)

уха́б, а *m.* pothole (*in road*)

уха́жива|ть, ю *impf.* (**за** + *i.*) **1** (*за больны́м*)
to nurse, tend; (*за живо́тными, расте́ниями*)
to look after **2** (*за же́нщиной*) to court; to
pay court (to), make advances (to)

ухва|ти́ть, чу́, ~тишь *pf.* **1** (*схвати́ть*) to
lay hold (of); (*захвати́ть для себя́*) to seize,
grab **2** (fig., infml, *поня́ть*) to grasp

ухва|ти́ться, чу́сь, ~тишься *pf.* (**за** + *a.*)
1 to grasp, lay hold (of); **у. за ве́тку** to grasp
a branch **2** (fig., infml, *за возмо́жность*) to
seize; to jump (at); **у. за предложе́ние** to
jump at an offer; (*за мысль, за челове́ка*) to
latch on to

ухитр|и́ться, ю́сь, и́шься *pf.* (*of*
▶ **ухитря́ться**) (+ *inf.*) to manage (to),
contrive (to)

ухитр|я́ться, я́юсь *impf. of* ▶ **ухитри́ться**

ухло́п|ать, аю *pf.* (*of* ▶ **ухло́пывать**) (infml)
1 (*уби́ть*) to kill **2** (*истра́тить*) to
squander

ухло́пыва|ть, ю *impf. of* ▶ **ухло́пать**

у

ухмыльн|у́ться, у́сь, ёшься *pf.* (*of*
▶ **ухмыля́ться**) (infml) to smirk, grin

ухмыля́|ться, яюсь *impf. of* ▶ **ухмыльну́ться**

у́х|о, а, *pl.* **у́ши, уше́й** *nt.* ear; **кра́ем ~а**
слу́шать to listen with half an ear; **говори́ть**
кому́-н. на́ у. to have a word in sb's ear, have
a private word with sb

✓ **ухо́д¹, а** *m.* (*из комнаты; с работы*) leaving;
(*с должности*) resignation; (*на пенсию*)
retirement; (*поезда*) departure; (*с собрания;*
в монастырь) withdrawal

✓ **ухо́д², а** *m.* (**за** + *i.*) (*за больным, за садом*)
looking after; care (of); (*за машиной*)
maintenance; (*за зданием*) upkeep

✓ **ухо|ди́ть, жу́, ~дишь** *impf.* **1** *impf. of* ▶ **уйти́**
2 (*impf. only*) (*простираться*) to stretch,
extend

ухо́жен|ный, ~, ~на *adj.* well looked after,
well cared for

ухудш|а́ть, а́ю, а́ет *impf. of* ▶ **уху́дшить**

ухудш|а́ться, а́ется *impf. of* ▶ **ухудшиться**

ухудше́ни|е, я *nt.* worsening, deterioration

уху́дш|ить, у, ишь *pf.* (*of* ▶ **ухудша́ть**) to
make worse, worsen

уху́дш|иться, ится *pf.* (*of* ▶ **ухудша́ться**)
to become worse, worsen, deteriorate

уцеле́|ть, ю *pf.* (*остаться целым*) to remain
intact, escape destruction; (*остаться*
живым) to remain alive, survive

уцеп|и́ться, лю́сь, ~ишься *pf.* (**за** + *a.*)
1 to catch hold (of), seize **2** (fig., infml, *за*
предложение) to jump (at)

✓ **уча́ств|овать, ую** *impf.* (**в** + *p.*) **1** to take part
(in) **2** (*иметь долю*) to have a share (in)

✓ **уча́сти|е, я** *nt.* participation; **у. в**
прибылях profit-sharing; **при ~и, с ~ем**
(+ *g.*) with the participation (of), featuring;
принима́ть у. (**в** + *p.*) to take part (in)
2 (*сочувствие*) sympathy, concern

участ|и́ться, и́тся *pf.* (*of* ▶ **учаща́ться**)
(*удары грома*) to become more frequent;
(*шаг, пульс*) to quicken

✓ **уча́стник, а** *m.* (+ *g.*) participant (in),
member (of); **~и перегово́ров** negotiating
parties; **~и соглаше́ния** parties to the
agreement; **у. состяза́ния** competitor

✓ **уча́ст|ок, ка** *m.* **1** (*земли*) plot; parcel
2 (*площади, стены, дороги*) part, section
3 (*в административном делении*) district,
area; **избира́тельный у.** (*подразделение*)
electoral district, ward; (*здание*) polling
station

у́част|ь, и *f.* lot, fate

учаща́|ться, ется *impf. of* ▶ **участи́ться**

учащённый *adj.* quickened; faster; **у. пульс**
raised pulse/heart rate

✓ **уча́щ|ийся** *pres. part. of* ▶ **учи́ться**; (*as n.*
у., ~егося, *f.* **~аяся, ~ейся**) student;
(*школы*) pupil

учёб|а, ы *f.* **1** studies; studying; learning; **за**
~ой at one's studies **2** (*подготовка*) training

уче́бник, а *m.* textbook

✓ **уче́бн|ый** *adj.* **1** educational; school;
у. год academic year, school year; **~ое**
заведе́ние educational institution; **у. план**
curriculum **2** (mil.) training, practice; **~ая**
стрельба́ practice shoot

уче́ни|е, я *nt.* **1** (mil.) exercise; (*in pl.*) training
2 (*система взглядов*) teaching, doctrine

✓ **учени́к, а́** *m.* **1** (*школы*) pupil **2** (*в ремесле*)
apprentice **3** (*последователь*) disciple,
follower

учени́ц|а, ы *f. of* ▶ **учени́к**

✓ **учён|ый, ~, ~а** *adj.* **1** (*человек*) learned,
erudite; (infml) educated **2** (*научный*)
scholarly; academic; **~ая сте́пень** higher
(university) degree (*PhD or higher*)
3 (*in titles of certain academic posts and*
institutions): **у. сове́т** academic council
4 (*as m. n.* **у., ~ого**) scholar; (*в*
университете) academic; (*в области*
естественных наук) scientist

уч|е́сть, ту́, тёшь, *past* **~ёл, ~ла́** *pf.* (*of*
▶ **учи́тывать**) **1** (*обстоятельства*) to take
into account, consideration **2** (*товары*) to
take stock (of), make an inventory (of)

✓ **учёт, а** *m.* **1** (*действие*) accounting;
бухга́лтерский у. accounting,
bookkeeping; (*товаров*) stocktaking,
inventory-making; (*определение*)
calculation **2** (*обстоятельств*)
taking into account; **без ~а** (+ *g.*)
disregarding **3** (*регистрация*) registration;
взять на у. to register

учи́лищ|е, а *nt.* school, college (*providing*
specialist instruction at secondary level);
вое́нное у. military school

✓ **учи́тел|ь, я** *m.* **1** (*pl.* **~я́**) teacher **2** (*pl.* **~и**)
(fig.) teacher, master (= *authority*)

учи́тельниц|а, ы *f. of* ▶ **учи́тель**

учи́тельск|ая, ой *f.* staff (common) room

✓ **учи́тыва|ть, ю** *impf. of* ▶ **уче́сть**

✓ **уч|и́ть, у́, ~ишь** *impf.* **1** (*pf.* **вы́~, на~** *and*
об~) (+ *a. and d. or* + *inf.*) (*преподавать*) to
teach; **у. кого́-н. неме́цкому языку́** to teach
sb German; **у. игра́ть на скри́пке** to teach to
play the violin **2** (*no pf.*) (*быть учителем*)
to be a teacher **3**: (**что**) (*о теории*) to
teach (that), say (that) **4** (*pf.* **вы́~**) (+ *a.*)
(*усваивать, запоминать*) to learn; to
memorize

✓ **уч|и́ться, у́сь, ~ишься** *impf.* **1** (*pf.* **вы́~,**
на~ *and* **об~**) (+ *d. or* + *inf.*) to learn, study
2 (*быть студентом*) to be a student; **у. в**
шко́ле to go to, be at school **3** (*pf.* **вы́~**) (**на**
кого́-н.) (infml) to study (to be, to become),
learn (to be)

учреди́тел|ь, я *m.* founder

учре|ди́ть, жу́, ди́шь *pf.* (*of* ▶ **учрежда́ть**)
(*основать*) to found, establish, set up;
(*ввести*) to introduce, institute

учрежда́|ть, ю *impf. of* ▶ **учреди́ть**

✓ **учрежде́ни|е, я** *nt.* **1** (*школы, организации*)
founding, establishment, setting up; (*ордена*)
introduction **2** (*заведение*) establishment,

✓ key word

у

institution

учти́в|ый, ~, ~а *adj.* civil, courteous

уша́нк|а, и *f.* (infml) cap with ear flaps

у́ши *see* ▶ **у́хо**

уши́б, а *m.* bruise

ушиб|и́ть, у́, ёшь, *past* ~, ~ла *pf.* to injure (*by knocking*); (*до синяка*) to bruise

ушиб|и́ться, у́сь, ёшься, *past* ~ся, ~лась *pf.* to hurt oneself; to bruise oneself

ушива́|ть, ю *impf. of* ▶ **уши́ть**

уш|и́ть, ью́, ьёшь *pf.* (*of* ▶ **ушива́ть**) (dressmaking) to take in

ушк|о́, а́, *pl.* ~и́, ~о́в *nt.* (*у иголки*) eye

уще́л|ье, ья *g. pl.* ~ий *nt.* ravine, gorge

ущем|и́ть, лю́, и́шь *pf.* (*of* ▶ **ущемля́ть**) **1** (*стеснить*) to limit **2** (*оскорбить*) to wound, hurt; **у. чьё-н. самолю́бие** to hurt sb's pride

ущемле́ни|е, я *nt.* (fig.) **1** (*прав*) limitation **2** (*самолюбия*) wounding, hurting

ущемля́|ть, ю *impf. of* ▶ **ущеми́ть**

уще́рб, а *m.* (*убыток*) detriment; loss; (*вред*) damage, injury; **без** ~а (**для** + *g.*) without prejudice (to); **в у.** (+ *d.*) to the detriment (of)

ущипн|у́ть, у́, ёшь *pf. of* ▶ **щипа́ть 1**

Уэ́льс, а *m.* Wales

уэ́льс|ец, ца *m.* Welshman

уэ́льский *adj.* Welsh

ую́т, а *m.* cosiness (BrE), coziness (AmE)

ую́т|ный, ~ен, ~на *adj.* cosy (BrE), cozy (AmE)

уязви́м|ый, ~, ~а *adj.* vulnerable (also fig.); ~ое ме́сто (fig.) weak spot

уязв|и́ть, лю́, и́шь *pf.* (*of* ▶ **уязвля́ть**) to wound, hurt

уязвля́|ть, ю *impf. of* ▶ **уязви́ть**

уясн|и́ть, ю́, и́шь *pf.* (*of* ▶ **уясня́ть**) (*also* **у. себе́**, *or* **у. для себя́**) to comprehend

уясн|я́ть, я́ю *impf. of* ▶ **уясни́ть**

фа *nt. indecl.* (mus.) F

фа́брик|а, и *f.* factory; (*бумажная*) mill

фабрика́нт, а *m.* manufacturer, factory owner, mill owner

фабрик|ова́ть, у́ю *impf.* (*of* ▶ **сфабрикова́ть**) (fig.) to fabricate

фабри́чн|ый *adj.* **1** factory; manufacturing; ~ое произво́дство manufacturing **2** (*произведённый на фабрике*) factory-made

фа́бул|а, ы *f.* (liter.) plot, story

фавори́т, а *m.* favourite (BrE), favorite (AmE) (also sport)

фавори́т|ка, ки *f. of* ▶ **фавори́т**

фаго́т, а *m.* (mus.) bassoon

фаготи́ст, а *m.* bassoon player

фаготи́ст|ка, ки *f. of* ▶ **фаготи́ст**

фа́з|а, ы *f.* phase; stage

фаза́н, а *m.* pheasant

◆ **файл**, а *m.* (comput.) file

фа́кел, а *m.* torch, flare

факи́р, а *m.* fakir

фа́кс, а *m.* fax; **посла́ть по** ~у to fax

факси́миле *nt. indecl.* facsimile

◆ **факт**, а *m.* fact

◆ **факти́чески** *adv.* in fact, actually

факти́ческ|ий *adj.* actual; real; virtual; ~ие да́нные the facts

◆ **фа́ктор**, а *m.* factor

факту́р|а, ы *f.* **1** (*строение материала*) texture **2** (comm.) (*usu.* счёт-ф.) invoice, bill

факультати́в|ный, ~ен, ~на *adj.* optional

◆ **факульте́т**, а *m.* faculty, department

фала́нг|а, и *f.* (anat.; mil., also hist.) phalanx

фа́ллос, а *m.* phallus

фальсифика́ци|я, и *f.* **1** (*подделывание*) falsification **2** (*поддельный предмет*) forgery, fake, counterfeit

фальсифици́р|овать, ую *impf. and pf.* **1** (*историю*) to falsify **2** (*вино*) to adulterate

фальце́т, а *m.* (mus.) falsetto

фальшивомоне́тчик, а *m.* counterfeiter

фальши́в|ый, ~, ~а *adj.* **1** (*зубы, волосы*) false; (*документ*) forged, fake; (*жемчуг*) artificial, imitation **2** (*неискренний*) false; insincere; **ф. комплиме́нт** insincere compliment **3** (mus.) out of tune, off-key

◆ **фами́ли|я**, и *f.* **1** surname **2** (*род*) family, kin

фами́льный *adj.* family

фамилья́р|ный, ~ен, ~на *adj.* overfamiliar; unceremonious

фана́т, а *m.* (infml) fan

фанати́зм, а *m.* fanaticism

фана́тик, а *m.* fanatic

фанати́ч|ный, ~ен, ~на *adj.* fanatical

у

ф

фана́тк|а, и *f. of* ▶ **фана́т**; (*сопровождающая популярных музыкантов*) groupie

фане́р|а, ы *f.* **1** (*для облицовки*) veneer **2** (*древесный материал*) plywood

фантазёр, а *m.* dreamer, visionary

фантази́р|овать, ую *impf.* **1** (*мечтать*) to dream, indulge in fantasies **2** (*выдумывать*) to make up, dream up

фанта́зи|я, и *f.* **1** (*воображение*) fantasy; imagination; **бога́тая ф.** fertile imagination **2** (*мечта*) fantasy, fancy; **предава́ться ∼ям** to indulge in fantasies **3** (*выдумка*) fabrication

фанта́ст, а *m.* fantasy writer; science fiction writer

фанта́стик|а, и *f.* (*collect.*) (liter.) fantasy; **нау́чная ф.** science fiction; sci-fi

фантасти́ческий *adj.* **1** (*пейзаж, освещение*) fantastic, fabulous, unreal; (*новость, нахал*) fantastic, incredible **2** (*литература*) fantasy

фа́нтик, а *m.* (infml) sweet wrapper

фанто́м, а *m.* phantom

фанфа́р|а, ы *f.* (mus.) **1** (*инструмент*) bugle **2** (*торжественная фраза*) fanfare

фа́р|а, ы *f.* headlight

Фаренге́йт, а *m.* Fahrenheit; **32 гра́дуса/212 гра́дусов по ∼у** 32/212 degrees Fahrenheit (= 0°C/100°C)

фаринги́т, а *m.* (med.) pharyngitis

фарисе́|й, я *m.* Pharisee (also fig.)

фармаколо́ги|я, и *f.* pharmacology

фармаце́вт, а *m.* pharmacist

фармацевти́ческий *adj.* pharmaceutical

фарс, а *m.* (theatr.) farce (also fig.)

фа́ртук, а *m.* apron

фарфо́р, а *m.* **1** (*материал*) porcelain, china **2** (*collect.*) (*посуда*) china

фарш, а *m.* (*начинка*) stuffing; (*мясо*) minced meat

фарши́р|овать, у́ю *impf.* (*of* ▶ **зафарширова́ть**) (cul.) to stuff

фас, а *m.* front

фаса́д, а *m.* facade, front

фасо́л|ь, и *f.* (*растение*) bean plant; (*collect.*) (*плод*) beans

фасо́н, а *m.* cut; style

фаталисти́ческий *adj.* fatalistic

фата́л|ьный, ∼ен, ∼ьна *adj.* (*совпадение*) fateful; (*последствия*) fatal

фа́ун|а, ы *f.* fauna

фаши́зм, а *m.* Fascism

фаши́ст, а *m.* Fascist

фаши́ст|ка, ки *f. of* ▶ **фаши́ст**

фаши́стский *adj.* Fascist

ФБР *nt. indecl.* (*abbr. of* **Федера́льное бюро́ рассле́дований**) FBI (*Federal Bureau of Investigation*)

▸ **февра́л|ь, я́** *m.* February

февра́льский *adj. of* ▶ **февра́ль**

▸ **федера́льный** *adj.* federal

федерати́вный *adj.* federative, federal

▸ **федера́ци|я, и** *f.* federation

фейерве́рк, а *m.* firework(s); (*событие*) firework display

Фейсбу́к, а *m.* Facebook® (*social networking site*)

фека́л|ии, ий *m. pl.* faeces (BrE), feces (AmE)

фе́льдшер, а, *pl.* **∼а́** *and* **∼ы** *m.* medical assistant

фельето́н, а *m.* satirical article

feminíзм, а *m.* feminism

feminíст, а *m.* feminist

feminíст|ка, ки *f. of* ▶ **feminíст**

фен, а *m.* hairdryer

фено́мен, а *m.* (*явление*) phenomenon; (*событие, человек*) marvel

феномена́л|ьный, ∼ен, ∼ьна *adj.* phenomenal

феодали́зм, а *m.* feudalism

феода́л|ьный *adj.* feudal

ферз|ь, я́, *pl.* **∼и́, ∼е́й** *m.* (chess) queen

фе́рм|а, ы *f.* farm

ферме́нт, а *m.* enzyme

фе́рмер, а *m.* farmer

▸ **фестива́л|ь, я** *m.* festival

фети́ш, а *m.* fetish

фетр, а *m.* felt

фехтова́ни|е, я *nt.* fencing

фешене́бел|ьный, ∼ен, ∼ьна *adj.* fashionable

фе́|я, и *f.* fairy

фиа́лк|а, и *f.* viola, violet

фиа́ско *nt. indecl.* fiasco, failure

фибро́м|а, ы *f.* (med.) fibroma

фи́г|а, и *f.* (infml) fig (*gesture of derision or contempt, consisting of thumb placed between index and middle fingers*); **показа́ть кому́-н. ∼у** ≈ to cock a snook, give the V-sign; **получи́ть ∼у** to get nothing

фигн|я́, и́ *f.* (sl.) rubbish

▸ **фигу́р|а, ы** *f.* **1** figure **2** (*в шахматах*) piece, chessman (*excluding pawns*)

фигура́л|ьный, ∼ен, ∼ьна *adj.* figurative, metaphorical

фигури́ст, а *m.* figure skater

фигури́ст|ка, ки *f. of* ▶ **фигури́ст**

фигу́рн|ый *adj.* **1** figured; ornamented **2**: **∼ое ката́ние (на конька́х)** figure skating

Фи́джи *indecl.* Fiji

фи́зик, а *m.* physicist

фи́зик|а, и *f.* physics

физио́лог, а *m.* physiologist

физиологи́ческий *adj.* physiological

физиоло́ги|я, и *f.* physiology

физионо́ми|я, и *f.* (infml) face; physiognomy (also joc.)

физиотерапе́вт, а *m.* physiotherapist

физиотерапи́|я, и *f.* physiotherapy

▸ **физи́ческ|ий** *adj.* **1** physical; **∼ая культу́ра**

ф

physical training, gymnastics; **ф. труд** manual labour (BrE), labor (AmE) **2** *adj. of* ▸ **фи́зика**; **ф. кабине́т** physics laboratory

физкульту́р|а, ы *f.* physical training (*abbr.* PT); physical education (*abbr.* PE); **уро́к ~ы** PE lesson; **лече́бная ф.** exercise therapy

физкульту́рный *adj.* gymnastic; athletic, sports; **ф. зал** gymnasium

фикси́р|овать, ую *impf. and pf.* (*pf. also* **за~**) **1** (*регистрировать*) to record (*in writing, etc.*) **2** (*внимание, взгляд*) to fix, direct

фикти́в|ный, ~ен, ~на *adj.* fictitious; **ф. брак** marriage of convenience, sham marriage

фи́кус, а *m.* (bot.) ficus; rubber plant

филантро́п, а *m.* philanthropist

филармо́ни|я, и *f.* philharmonic society; (*зал*) concert hall

филе́ *nt. indecl.* (cul.) **1** (*мясо высшего сорта*) fillet **2** (*кусок мяса или рыбы без костей*) fillet

✧ **филиа́л, а** *m.* branch (*of an organization*)

филиппи́н|ец, ца *m.* Filipino

филиппи́н|ка, ки *f. of* ▸ **филиппи́нец**

филиппи́нский *adj.* Philippine; (*язык*) Filipino

Филиппи́н|ы, ~ (*no sg.*) the Philippines

фило́лог, а *m.* philologist

филологи́ческий *adj.* philological

филоло́ги|я, и *f.* philology

фило́соф, а *m.* philosopher

филосо́фи|я, и *f.* philosophy

филосо́фский *adj.* philosophic(al)

филосо́фств|овать, ую *impf.* to philosophize

✧ **фильм, а** *m.* (cin.) film, movie

фильтр, а *m.* filter

фильтр|ова́ть, у́ю *impf.* (*of* ▸ **профильтрова́ть**, ▸ **отфильтрова́ть**) to filter

фина́л, а *m.* **1** (*спектакля*) finale **2** (sport) final

финали́ст, а *m.* finalist

финали́ст|ка, ки *f. of* ▸ **финали́ст**

фина́льный *adj.* final; **ф. акко́рд** (mus.) final chord; **ф. матч** (sport) final

✧ **финанси́ровани|е, я** *nt.* financing

финанси́р|овать, ую *impf. and pf.* to finance

финанси́ст, а *m.* **1** (*предприниматель*) financier **2** (*специалист по финансовым наукам*) financial expert

✧ **фина́нсовый** *adj.* financial; **ф. год** fiscal year; **ф. отде́л** finance department

фина́нс|ы, ов (*no sg.*) finance(s)

фи́ник, а *m.* date (*fruit*)

фи́ниш, а *m.* (sport) finish

фи́нк|а, и *f. of* ▸ **финн**

Финля́нди|я, и *f.* Finland

финн, а *m.* Finn

фи́нский *adj.* Finnish; **Ф. зали́в** Gulf of Finland

фиоле́товый *adj.* violet

✧ **фи́рм|а, ы** *f.* (econ.) firm

фи́рм|енный *adj. of* ▸ **фи́рма**; (*хорошего качества*) high-quality; **~енная этике́тка** proprietary label; **ф. бланк** letterhead; **~енное блю́до** speciality dish

фисгармо́ни|я, и *f.* (mus.) harmonium

фиска́льный *adj.* (fin.) fiscal

фити́л|ь, я́ *m.* (*лампы, свечи*) wick; (*для воспламенения зарядов*) fuse

фи́шинг, а *m.* (comput.) phishing (*practice of sending out emails in the name of reputable companies in order to induce people to reveal personal information*)

флаг, а *m.* flag

флагшто́к, а *m.* flagstaff

флако́н, а *m.* (scent) bottle

фламе́нко *nt. indecl.* flamenco

флами́нго *m. indecl.* flamingo

фланг, а *m.* (mil.) flank

фране́л|ь, и *f.* flannel

флегма́тик, а *m.* phlegmatic person

флегмати́ч|ный, ~ен, ~на *adj.* phlegmatic

флейт|а, ы *f.* flute

флейти́ст, а *m.* flautist

флейти́ст|ка, ки *f. of* ▸ **флейти́ст**

флеш-па́мят|ь, и *f.* (comput.) flash memory

фли́гел|ь, я, pl. ~я́, ~ей *m.* **1** (*пристройка*) wing (*of building*) **2** (*отдельное здание*) outbuilding

флирт|ова́ть, у́ю *impf.* (**с** + *i.*) to flirt (with)

флома́стер, а *m.* felt-tip pen, marker

фло́р|а, ы *f.* flora

Флори́д|а, ы *f.* Florida

флот, а *m.* **1** fleet; **вое́нно-морско́й ф.** navy **2**: **возду́шный ф.** (air) fleet

флю́гер, а, pl. ~а́ *m.* weathervane

фля́г|а, и *f.* **1** flask; (mil.) water bottle **2** (*для молока*) churn

фо́би|я, и *f.* phobia

фойе́ *nt. indecl.* foyer

фокстерье́р, а *m.* fox terrier

фо́кус¹, а *m.* (phys.) focus (also fig.)

фо́кус², а *m.* (*трюк*) (conjuring) trick; **пока́зывать ~ы** to do conjuring tricks

фо́кус-гру́пп|а, ы *f.* focus group

фокуси́р|овать, ую *impf.* (*of* ▸ **сфокуси́ровать**) (phys.) to focus; (fig.) (**на** + *p.*) to focus (on)

фокуси́р|оваться, уюсь *impf.* (*of* ▸ **сфокуси́роваться**) (**на** + *p.*) to focus (on), be focussed (on)

фо́кусник, а *m.* conjuror, juggler

фольга́, и́ *f.* foil

фолькло́р, а *m.* folklore

✧ **фон, а** *m.* **1** background (also fig.) **2** (*помехи*) background noise

фона́рик, а *m.* small lamp; torch (BrE), flashlight (AmE)

ф

фона́рный *adj. of* ▶ **фона́рь**; **ф. столб** lamp post

фона́р|ь, я́ *m.* (*с ручкой*) lantern; (*уличный*) lamp; light

▸ **фонд, а** *m.* **1** (fin.) fund; stock, reserves, resources; **валю́тный ф.** currency reserves; **золото́й ф.** gold reserves; **о́бщий ф.** pool **2** (*in pl.*) (fin., *ценные бумаги*) stocks; (fig., obs.) stock **3** (*организация*) fund, foundation **4** (*архив*) archive

фо́нд|овый *adj. of* ▶ **фонд**; **~овая би́ржа** stock exchange

фоне́тик|а, и *f.* phonetics

фонта́н, а *m.* fountain; (fig.) stream; **нефтяно́й ф.** oil gusher; **бить ~ом** to gush forth

форе́л|ь, и *f.* trout

▸ **фо́рм|а, ы** *f.* **1** form; **по ~е, … по содержа́нию** in form, … in content **2** (*для выпечки*) cake tin; shape **3** (tech., *внешнее очертание*) mould (BrE), mold (AmE), cast; **отли́ть в ~у** to mould (BrE), mold (AmE), cast **4** (*одежда*) uniform **5**: **быть в ~е** (infml) to be in (good) form

форма́льност|ь, и *f.* formality

форма́л|ьный, ~ен, ~ьна *adj.* formal

▸ **форма́т, а** *m.* format

формати́р|овать, ую *impf.* (*of* ▶ **отформати́ровать**) (comput.) to format

фо́рменный *adj.* **1** (*платье, фуражка*) uniform **2** (infml, *настоящий*) proper, regular, positive

▸ **формирова́ни|е, я** *nt.* **1** (*действие*) forming; organizing **2** (mil.) unit

формир|ова́ть, у́ю *impf.* (*of* ▶ **сформирова́ть**) to form; to organize; **ф. хара́ктер** to form character; **ф. батальо́н** to raise a battalion

формир|ова́ться, у́юсь *impf.* (*of* ▶ **сформирова́ться**) **1** to form, develop **2** *pass. of* ▶ **формирова́ть**

фо́рмул|а, ы *f.* formula; formulation

формули́р|овать, ую *impf. and pf.* (*pf. also* **с~**) to formulate

формулиро́вк|а, и *f.* **1** formulation **2** (*сформулированная мысль*) wording

форпо́ст, а *m.* (mil.) advanced post; outpost (also fig.)

форс-мажо́р, а *m.* (*also* **~ные обстоя́тельства**) force majeure

форт, а, о ~е, в ~у́, *pl.* **~ы́** *m.* (mil.) fort

форте|пиа́но and **фортепья́но** *nt. indecl.* piano

фо́рточк|а, и *f.* little window (*small hinged pane for ventilation in windows of Russian houses*)

▸ **фо́рум, а** *m.* forum

фосфа́т, а *m.* (chem.) phosphate

фо́сфор, а *m.* phosphorus

▸ **фо́то** *nt. indecl.* (infml) photo

фото… *comb. form* photo-

фотоальбо́м, а *m.* photograph album

фотоаппара́т, а *m.* camera

фотогени́ч|ный, ~ен, ~на *adj.* photogenic

фото́граф, а *m.* photographer

фотографи́р|овать, ую *impf.* (*of* ▶ **сфотографи́ровать**) to photograph

фотографи́р|оваться, уюсь *impf.* (*of* ▶ **сфотографи́роваться**) to be photographed, have one's photo taken

фотографи́ческий *adj.* photographic

▸ **фотогра́фи|я, и** *f.* **1** (*получение изображений*) photography **2** (*снимок*) photograph

фотокопирова́льный *adj.*: **ф. аппара́т** photocopier

фотоко́пи|я, и *f.* photocopy

фоторобо́т, а *m.* identikit (picture)®

фотоси́нтез, а *m.* (bot.) photosynthesis

фотоэлеме́нт, а *m.* (elec.) photoelectric cell

фрагме́нт, а *m.* fragment; detail (*of painting, etc.*); **ф. фи́льма** film clip

фра́з|а, ы *f.* **1** (*предложение*) sentence **2** (*выражение*) phrase

фразеологи́ческий *adj.* phraseological; **ф. оборо́т** idiom; **ф. слова́рь** dictionary of idioms

фрак, а *m.* tailcoat, tails

фра́кци|я, и *f.* (pol.) fraction; faction, group

фраму́г|а, и *f.* transom

франкоязы́чный *adj.* francophone

франт, а *m.* dandy

Фра́нци|я, и *f.* France

францу́женк|а, и *f.* Frenchwoman

францу́з, а *m.* Frenchman

▸ **францу́зский** *adj.* French

фрахт, а *m.* freight

фрахт|ова́ть, у́ю *impf.* (*of* ▶ **зафрахтова́ть**) to charter

фрега́т, а *m.* **1** (naut.) frigate **2** (zool.) frigate bird

фре́зерный *adj.* (tech.) milling; **ф. стано́к** milling machine

фрео́н|ы, ов *m. pl.* (*sg.* **~, ~a**) CFCs (*abbr. of* chlorofluorocarbons)

фре́ск|а, и *f.* fresco

фриво́л|ьный, ~ен, ~ьна *adj.* frivolous

фриги́д|ный, ~ен, ~на *adj.* (med.) frigid

фрикаде́льк|а, и *f.* (*мясная*) meatball; (*рыбная*) fishball (*in soup*)

фронт, а, *pl.* **~ы́** *m.* (mil., meteor., fig.) front; **на два ~а** on two fronts

фрукт, а *m.* fruit; (*in pl.*) fruit (*collect.*)

фрукто́вый *adj.* fruit; **ф. сад** orchard

ФСБ *f. indecl.* (*abbr. of* **Федера́льная слу́жба безопа́сности**) Federal Security Service

фтори́д, а *m.* fluoride

фу́г|а, и *f.* (mus.) fugue

фуга́с, а *m.* (mil.) landmine

фуже́р, а *m.* tall wineglass

фунда́мент, а *m.* foundation, base (also fig.)

фундаментали́зм, а *m.* fundamentalism

фундаментали́ст, а *m.* fundamentalist

фундамента́льн|ый, ~ен, ~ьна *adj.* **1** (*про́чный*) solid, sound; (*основа́тельный*) thorough(going) **2** (*основно́й, гла́вный*) main, basic

фуникулёр, а *m.* funicular (railway)

функциона́льн|ый *adj.* functional; ~ая кла́виша (comput.) function key

функциони́ровани|е, я *nt.* functioning

фу́нкци|я, и *f.* function

фунт¹, а *m.* (*ме́ра ве́са*) pound (*453.6 grams*)

фунт², а *m.* (fin.): ф. (сте́рлингов) pound (sterling)

фунциони́ровать, ую *impf.* to function

фу́р|а, ы *f.* (*фурго́н*) van; (*прице́п*) (truck) trailer

фура́жк|а, и *f.* peak cap; (mil.) service cap

фурго́н, а *m.* van

фурниту́р|а, ы *f.* accessories

фуро́р, а *m.* furore

фут, а *m.* foot (*measure of length,* = 30.48 cm)

футбо́л, а *m.* football (BrE), soccer

футболи́ст, а *m.* football player (BrE), soccer player

футбо́лк|а, и *f.* T-shirt

футбо́л|ьный *adj. of* ▶ футбо́л; ~ьные бу́тсы football boots; ф. мяч football

футля́р, а *m.* case; ф. для очко́в spectacle case; ф. для скри́пки violin case

футури́зм, а *m.* futurism

футури́ст, а *m.* futurist

фы́рк|ать, аю *impf.* (*of* ▶ фы́ркнуть) **1** (*о живо́тном; о маши́не*) to snort **2** (fig., infml, *брюзжа́ть*) to grouse

фы́рк|нуть, ну, нешь *inst. pf. of* ▶ фы́ркать

фэн-шу́й *m. & nt. indecl.* feng shui

фюзеля́ж, а *m.* fuselage

Xx

хаб, а *m.* (comput.) hub

ха́кер, а *m.* (comput.) hacker

ха́ки *nt. indecl. and adj. indecl.* khaki

хала́т, а *m.* **1** (*дома́шний*) dressing gown; (*купа́льный*) bathrobe **2** (*рабо́чий*) overall; до́кторский х. doctor's smock **3** (*восто́чный*) robe

хала́т|ный, ~ен, ~на *adj.* careless, negligent

халту́р|а, ы *f.* (infml) **1** (*небре́жная рабо́та*) poor-quality work **2** (*рабо́та на стороне́*) work done on the side; (*де́ньги*) money earned on the side

халя́в|а, ы *f.*: на ~у (sl.) free of charge; for free

хам, а *m.* (infml) boor, lout

хамелео́н, а *m.* chameleon (also fig.)

хам|и́ть, лю́, и́шь *impf.* (*of* ▶ нахами́ть) (+ *d.*) to be rude (to)

ха́мств|о, а *nt.* (infml) boorishness, loutishness

хандр|а́, ы́ *f.* depression

ханж|а́, и́, *g. pl.* ~е́й *c.g.* sanctimonious person; hypocrite

ха́нжеский *adj.* sanctimonious; hypocritical

Хано́|й, я *m.* Hanoi

ха́ос, а *m.* chaos

хаоти́ческий *adj.* chaotic

хаоти́ч|ный, ~ен, ~на *adj.* = хаоти́ческий

хара́ктер, а *m.* **1** (*челове́ка*) character, personality; они́ не сошли́сь ~ами they could not get on (together) **2** (*твёрдый хара́ктер*) (strong) character; челове́к с ~ом determined person, strong character **3** (*сво́йство*) character, type; х. рабо́ты type of work

характери́стик|а, и *f.* **1** (*описа́ние*) description **2** (*о́тзыв*) reference

хара́ктерно *as pred.* it is characteristic; it is typical

характе́р|ный, ~ен, ~на *adj.* **1** (*сво́йственный*) characteristic; typical; э́то для него́ ~но it is typical of him **2** (*своеобра́зный*) distinctive

хари́зм|а, ы *f.* charisma

харизмати́ческий *adj.* charismatic

ха́рк|ать, аю *impf.* (*of* ▶ ха́ркнуть) (infml) to spit, expectorate; х. кро́вью to spit blood

ха́рк|нуть, ну, нешь *pf. of* ▶ ха́ркать

ха́рти|я, и *f.* charter

харчо́ *nt. indecl.* kharcho (*Caucasian highly seasoned mutton soup*)

ха́р|я, и *f.* (sl.) mug (= *face*)

ха́т|а, ы *f.* **1** peasant house (*in Southern Russia, Ukraine, and Byelorussia*); моя́ х. с кра́ю it's no concern of mine; that's your, their, *etc.,* funeral **2** (sl.) home, 'pad'

хвале́б|ный, ~ен, ~на *adj.* laudatory, eulogistic

хвал|и́ть, ю́, ~ишь *impf.* (*of* ▶ похвали́ть) to praise

хва́ста|ть, ю *impf* = хва́статься

хва́ста|ться, юсь *impf.* (*of* ▶ похва́статься) (+ *i.*) to boast (of)

ф

х

хвастли́в|ый, ∼, ∼а *adj.* boastful

хвастовств|о́, á *nt.* boasting

♂ **хват|а́ть¹**, а́ю *impf.* (*of* ▶ **схвати́ть 1**)
1 to snatch, seize, catch hold (of); to grab,
grasp **2** (*impf. only*) (infml, *вора*) to pick up

♂ **хват|а́ть²**, а́ет *impf.* (*of* ▶ **хвати́ть**) (*impers.*
+ *g.*) (*быть доста́точным*) to suffice, be
enough; to last out; **у меня́** *и т. п.* ∼а́ет
I am, *etc.*, short (of); **у нас не** ∼а́ет **де́нег**
we don't have enough money; **э́того ещё не**
∼а́ло! that's all we need, *etc.*!

хват|а́ться, а́юсь *impf.* (*of* ▶ **схвати́ться 1**)
(за + *a.*) **1** to snatch (at), catch (at); **х. за**
соло́минку to clutch at straws
2 (*принима́ться за де́ло*) to start doing,
take up

хват|и́ть, ∼ит *pf.* (*of* ▶ **хвата́ть²**): ∼ит! that
will do!; that's enough!; **с меня́** ∼ит! I've had
enough!

хва|ти́ться, чу́сь, ∼тишься *pf.* (+ *g.*) (infml)
to miss, notice the absence (of); **по́здно**
∼ти́лись! you thought of it too late!

хва́тк|а, и *f.* grasp, grip

хво́йн|ый *adj.* **1** *adj. of* ▶ **хвоя́ 2** (*де́рево*)
coniferous; (*as pl. n.* ∼ые, ∼ых) (bot.)
conifers

хвора́|ть, ю *impf.* (infml) to be ill (BrE), sick
(AmE)

хво́рост, а *m.* (*collect.*) **1** (*ве́тки*)
brushwood **2** (cul.) (*pastry*) straws, twiglets

хвост, á *m.* **1** tail (also fig.); **маха́ть** ∼о́м to
wag one's tail **2** (fig., *за́дняя часть*) tail,
rear, tail end; **быть, плести́сь в** ∼е́ to get
behind, lag behind

хвоста́т|ый, ∼, ∼а *adj.* **1** (*име́ющий*
хвост) having a tail; caudate **2** (*с больши́м*
хвосто́м) having a large tail

хво́стик, а *m. dim. of* ▶ **хвост**; (*причёска*)
ponytail

хво́|я, и *f.* **1** needle(s) (*of conifer*) **2** (*collect.*)
(*ве́тви*) branches (*of conifer*)

Хе́льсинки *m. indecl.* Helsinki

хеппи-э́нд, а *m.* happy ending

хер, ∼á, ∼у *m.* (sl., euph. of) ▶ **хуй**

хе́рес, а *m.* sherry

хеште́г, а *m.* (comput.) hashtag

хи́жин|а, ы *f.* shack, hut

хи́л|ый, ∼, ∼á, ∼о *adj.* weak, sickly; puny

химе́р|а, ы *f.* chimera

хи́мик, а *m.* chemist

химика́т|ы, ов *m. pl.* chemicals

химиотерапи́|я, и *f.* chemotherapy

♂ **хими́ческ|ий** *adj.* **1** chemical; ∼ие
препара́ты chemicals; ∼ая **чи́стка** (**оде́жды**)
dry-cleaning; **х. элеме́нт** chemical element
2 chemistry; **х. кабине́т** chemistry laboratory

хи́ми|я, и *f.* chemistry

химчи́стк|а, и *f.* dry-cleaner's

хи́нди *m. indecl.* Hindi (*language*)

хи́ппи *c.g. indecl.* hippy

хирома́нти|я, и *f.* palmistry

хиру́рг, а *m.* surgeon

хирурги́ческий *adj.* surgical

хирурги́|я, и *f.* surgery

хит, á *m.* (infml, mus., etc.) hit

хит-пара́д, а *m.* (mus.) the charts

хитре́ц, á *m.* cunning person; (infml) slyboots

хитр|и́ть, ю́, и́шь *impf.* (*of* ▶ **схитри́ть**) to
use cunning, guile; to dissemble

хи́трост|ь, и *f.* **1** (*сво́йство*) cunning,
slyness **2** (*уло́вка*) ruse, stratagem

хитроу́м|ный, ∼ен, ∼на *adj.*
1 (*изобрета́тельный*) cunning; resourceful
2 (*сло́жный*) intricate, complicated

хи́т|рый, ∼ёр, ∼рá, ∼ро́ *adj.* **1** (*лука́вый*)
cunning, sly **2** (infml, *изобрета́тельный*)
cunning, resourceful **3** (infml, *замыслова́тый*)
intricate

хихи́к|ать, аю *impf.* (*of* ▶ **хихи́кнуть**) to
giggle, snigger

хихи́к|нуть, ну, нешь *inst. pf. of* ▶ **хихи́кать**

хище́ни|е, я *nt.* theft; embezzlement,
misappropriation

хи́щник, а *m.* predator; (*живо́тное*) beast of
prey; (*пти́ца*) bird of prey

хи́щный, ∼ен, ∼на *adj.* **1** predatory; ∼ые
зве́ри, пти́цы beasts of prey, birds of prey
2 (fig.) rapacious, grasping

хладнокро́ви|е, я *nt.* composure, sangfroid

хладнокро́в|ный, ∼ен, ∼на *adj.* cool,
composed; (*жесто́кий*) cold-blooded

хлам, а *m.* (*collect.*) rubbish, trash

хлеб, а, *pl.* ∼ы and ∼á *m.* **1** (*sg. only*) bread
(also fig.) **2** (*pl.* ∼ы) (*буха́нка*) loaf **3** (*pl.*
∼á) (*семена́ зла́ков*) bread grain; (*usu. in*
pl.) (*зла́ки*) corn, crops; cereals

хле́б|ец, ца *m.* rusk, dry toast

хле́бниц|а, ы *f.* bread basket

хлебн|у́ть, у́, ёшь *pf.* (infml) **1** (*вы́пить*)
to drink down **2** (+ *g.*) (*перенести́*) to go
through, endure, experience

хле́бн|ый *adj.* **1** *adj. of* ▶ **хлеб 1**; ∼ые
дро́жжи baker's yeast; **х. магази́н** baker's
shop **2** *adj. of* ▶ **хлеб 3**; **х. амба́р** granary
3 (*урожа́йный*) rich (*in grain*); abundant;
grain-producing

хлебозаво́д, а *m.* bread-baking plant, bakery

хлеборо́б, а *m.* peasant (engaged in arable
farming)

хлев, а, в ∼е or в ∼ý, *pl.* ∼á *m.* cowshed;
(fig., infml) pigsty

хле|ста́ть, щу́, ∼щешь *impf.* (*of* ▶ **хлестну́ть**)
1 (+ *a.* or по + *d.*) to lash; to whip **2** (*о*
дожде́) to lash (down), beat (down), pour;
to stream, gush

хлест|ну́ть, ну́, нёшь *inst. pf. of* ▶ **хлеста́ть**

хли́п|кий, ∼ок, ∼кá, ∼ко *adj.* (infml)
1 (*стол, мост*) rickety **2** (fig., *челове́к,*
здоро́вье) weak, fragile

хло́па|ть, ю *impf.* (*of* ▶ **хло́пнуть**) **1** (+ *i.* or
по + *d.*) to bang; to slap; **х. кали́ткой** to bang
the gate; **х. кого́-н. по спине́** to slap sb on the

back **2**: х. (в ладо́ши) (+ d.) to clap, applaud

хлопкоро́б, а m. cotton grower

хло́п|нуть, ну, нешь inst. pf. of ▶ хло́пать

хло́п|ок, ка m. cotton; **х.-сыре́ц** raw cotton

хлоп|о́к, ка́ m. (в ладо́ши) clap; (вы́стрела) bang

хлопот|ы, хлопо́т, ~ам (no sg.) **1** (заня́тия по до́му, по рабо́те) jobs, chores; (забо́ты) trouble **2** (о + p.) (стара́ния доби́ться чего́-н.) efforts (on behalf of, for); pains

хлопу́шк|а, и f. (Christmas) cracker

хлопчатобума́жный adj. cotton

хло́пь|я, ев (no sg.) flakes (of snow, etc., also of certain cereal foods); **кукуру́зные х., пшени́чные х.** cornflakes

хлор, а m. (chem.) chlorine

хлы́н|уть, у, ешь pf. **1** (о кро́ви, дожде́) to gush, pour **2** (fig.) to pour, rush, surge; **толпа́ ~ула на пло́щадь** a crowd poured into the square

хлыст, а́ m. (прут) whip, switch

хлю́па|ть, ю impf. (infml) **1** (гря́зи) to squelch; **х. по гря́зи** to squelch through the mud **2** (пла́ча, всхли́пывать) to snivel; **х. но́сом** to sniff

хля́стик, а m. half belt (on back of coat)

хмел|ь, я m. (bot.) (семена́) hops; (расте́ние) hop plant

хму́р|ить, ю, ишь impf. (of ▶ нахму́рить): **х. бро́ви** to knit one's brows

хму́р|иться, юсь, ишься impf. (of ▶ нахму́риться) **1** (хму́рить бро́ви) to frown **2** (о пого́де, о дне) to become gloomy; (о не́бе) to be overcast, cloudy

хму́р|ый, ~, ~а́, ~о adj. **1** (челове́к) gloomy, sullen **2** (не́бо, день) overcast, cloudy; **х. день** dull day

хмы́ка|ть, ю impf. (infml) to hem (expr. surprise, annoyance, doubt, etc.)

хо́бби nt. indecl. hobby

хо́бот, а m. (zool.) trunk, proboscis

☞ **ход, а (у), о ~е, в/на ~е and ~у́ у́** m. **1** (в ~е, на ~у́) motion, movement, travel, going; speed, pace; **три часа́ ~у** three hours' walk; **за́дний х.** backing, reversing; **дать х.** (+ d.) to set in motion, set going; **пойти́ в х.** to come to be widely used; **пусти́ть в х.** to start, set in motion, set going (also fig.), put into service **2** (в ~е) (fig., разви́тие) course, progress; **х. мы́слей** train of thought; **х. собы́тий** course of events **3** (в ~е, на ~у́) (tech.) work, operation, running; **на холосто́м ~у́** idling **4** (на ~е, pl. ~ы́) (в ша́хматах) move; (в ка́ртах) lead; **х. бе́лых** white's move **5** (в ~е, pl. ~ы́) (fig.) move, gambit; **ло́вкий х.** shrewd move **6** (в, на ~е and ~у́, pl. ~ы́) (путь) passage(way), thoroughfare

хода́тайств|о, а nt. **1** (де́йствие) petitioning; entreaty, pleading **2** (про́сьба) petition; application

☞ **хо|ди́ть, жу́, ~дишь** impf. **1** (передвига́ться, шага́я) (to be able to) walk **2** (indet. of ▶ идти́) to go (on foot); **х. в кино́** to go to

the cinema; **х. под па́русом** to go sailing **3** (о поезда́х) to run **4** (о слу́хах, новостя́х) to pass, go round **5** (в ка́ртах) to lead, play; (в ша́хматах) to move; **х. ферзём** to move one's queen **6** (в + p.) (носи́ть) to wear

ходу́л|и, ей and **~ь** f. pl. (sg. ~я, ~и) stilts

ходьб|а́, ы́ f. walking; **це́рковь нахо́дится в пяти́ мину́тах ~ы́ отсю́да** the church is five minutes' walk from here

ходя́ч|ий adj. walking; able to walk; **~ая энциклопе́дия** walking encyclopedia

☞ **хозя́|ин, ина, pl. ~ева, ~ев** m. **1** (владе́лец) owner, proprietor **2** (свое́й судьбы́; в до́ме) master; (предприя́тия) boss **3** (по отноше́нию к жильцу́) landlord **4** (по отноше́нию к гостя́м) host

хозя́йк|а, и, g. pl. хозя́ек f. **1** (владе́лица) owner, proprietress **2** (свое́й судьбы́; в до́ме) mistress **3** (по отноше́нию к жильцу́) landlady **4** (по отноше́нию к гостя́м) hostess

хозя́йствен|ный, ~, ~на adj. **1** economic, of the economy; **~ная жизнь страны́** the country's economy **2** (това́ры, инвента́рь) household; home management **3** (эконо́мный) economical, thrifty

☞ **хозя́йств|о, а** nt. **1** (эконо́мика) economy; **се́льское х.** agriculture; **дома́шнее х.** housekeeping; **вести́ х.** to manage, carry on management **2** (agric.) farm, holding **3** (рабо́ты по до́му) housekeeping; **хлопота́ть по ~у** to be busy about the house

хоккеи́ст, а m. hockey player

хоккеи́ст|ка, ки f. of ▶ хоккеи́ст

хокке́|й, я m. hockey; **х. с мячо́м, ру́сский х.** bandy; **х. с ша́йбой** ice hockey; **х. на траве́** hockey (BrE), field hockey (AmE)

холе́р|а, ы f. (med.) cholera

холестери́н, а m. cholesterol

холл, а m. hall, vestibule, foyer

холм, а́ m. hill

холми́ст|ый, ~, ~а adj. hilly

хо́лод, а (у), pl. ~а́, ~о́в m. **1** cold; coldness (also fig.); **ди́кий х.** bitter cold **2** (in pl.) cold (spell of) weather

холода́|ть, ет impf. (of ▶ похолода́ть) (impers.) (станови́ться холодне́е) to turn cold

холоде́|ть, ю impf. (of ▶ похолоде́ть) (ру́ки) to get cold

холоде́ц, ца́ m. (cul.) meat in jelly

холоди́льник, а m. refrigerator; **ваго́н-х.** refrigerator van

хо́лодно¹ adv. (fig.) coldly

хо́лодно² as pred. it is cold; **мне, и т. п. х.** I am, etc., cold, feel cold

☞ **холо́д|ный, холо́ден, ~на́, хо́лодно, хо́лодны́** adj. **1** cold; **х. отве́т** cold reply; **х. по́яс** (geog.) frigid zone; **~ная война́** cold war; **~ное ору́жие** side arms, cold steel **2** (оде́жда) light, thin

холост|о́й, хо́лост, ~а́, хо́лосто adj. **1** unmarried, single; bachelor **2** (tech.) idle, free-running; **на ~о́м ходу́** idling **3** (mil.) blank, dummy; **х. патро́н** blank cartridge

холостя́к, á *m.* bachelor

холст, á *m.* **1** (*ткань*) coarse linen, canvas, burlap **2** (art) canvas

холу́|й, я́ *m.* (infml obs. and fig., pej.) lackey

хому́т, á *m.* **1** (*на лошади*) collar **2** (tech.) clamp, ring

хомя́к, á *m.* hamster

хор, **а**, *pl.* **~ы́** *m.* **1** choir **2** (mus., also fig.) chorus; **~ом** all together

хора́л, **а** *m.* chorale

хорва́т, **а** *m.* Croat

Хорва́ти|я, и *f.* Croatia

хорва́т|ка, ки *f. of* ▸ **хорва́т**

хорва́тский *adj.* Croatian, Croat

хор|ёк, ька́ *m.* ferret

хорео́граф, **а** *m.* choreographer

хореогра́фи|я, и *f.* choreography

хорово́д, **а** *m.* round dance (*traditional Slavonic folk dance*)

хорон|и́ть, ю́, ~ишь *impf.* (*of* ▸ **похорони́ть**, ▸ **захорони́ть**) to bury (also fig.)

хоро́шенький *adj.* pretty, nice (also iron.)

хороше́нько *adv.* (infml) properly, thoroughly, well and truly

✍ **хоро́ш|ий, ~, ~á** *adj.* **1** good **2** (*прия́тный*) nice **3** (*only short forms*) (*краси́вый*) pretty, good-looking

✍ **хорошо́[1] 1** *adv.* well; nicely **2** *particle* (*выража́ет согла́сие*) all right!; OK! **3** *n., nt. indecl.* (*отме́тка*) 'good' (*mark*)

✍ **хорошо́[2]** *as pred.* it is good; it is nice; **х., что вы успе́ли прие́хать** it is good that you managed to come

хо́спис, **а** *m.* hospice

хот-до́г, **а** *m.* hot dog

✍ **хоте́|ть, хочу́, хо́чешь, хо́чет, хоти́м, хоти́те, хотя́т** *impf.* (*of* ▸ **захоте́ть**) (+ *g.* or *inf.* or **что́бы** + *past*) to want, desire; **я ~л бы** I would like; **х. пить** to be thirsty; **х. сказа́ть** to mean; **е́сли хоти́те** if you like (*also = perhaps*)

✍ **хоте́|ться, хо́чется** (*no pl.*) *impf.* (*of* ▸ **захоте́ться**) (*impers. + d.*) to want; **мне хо́чется** I want; **мне ~лось бы** I would like

✍ **хоть** *conj.* **1** (*хотя́*) although **2** (*да́же е́сли*) even if (*esp. in set phrr.*) **3** (*as particle*) (*also* **х. бы**) (*по кра́йней ме́ре*) at least, if only **4**: **х. бы** if only

✍ **хотя́** *conj.* **1** although, though **2**: **х. бы** even if **3** (*as particle*): **х. бы** if only; **э́то я́вно ви́дно х. бы из заключи́тельной фра́зы его́ ре́чи** this is evident if only from the final sentence of his speech

хо́хм|а, ы *f.* (infml) joke, quip, gag

хо́хот, **а** *m.* guffaw, loud laugh

хохо|та́ть, чу́, ~чешь *impf.* to guffaw, laugh loudly

храбре́ц, á *m.* brave person

хра́брост|ь, и *f.* bravery, courage

хра́бр|ый, ~, ~á, ~о, ~ы *adj.* brave, courageous

✍ **храм**, **а** *m.* temple, church, place of worship

✍ **хране́ни|е, я** *nt.* keeping, custody; storage, conservation; **ка́мера ~я** left luggage office (BrE), baggage room (AmE)

храни́лищ|е, а *nt.* storehouse, depository

храни́тел|ь, я *m.* **1** keeper, custodian; (fig.) repository **2** (*музе́я*) curator

хран|и́ть, ю́, и́шь *impf.* (*ста́рые пи́сьма, де́ньги в ба́нке*) to keep; (*тради́ции, до́брое и́мя*) to preserve; (*молча́ние, го́рдый вид*) to maintain; **х. в та́йне** to keep secret

хран|и́ться, ~ся *impf.* **1** (*находи́ться*) to be, be kept **2** (*быть в сохра́нности*) to be preserved

храп|е́ть, лю́, и́шь *impf.* **1** to snore **2** (*о лошади*) to snort

хреб|е́т, та́ *m.* **1** (anat.) spine, spinal column; (fig., infml, *спина́*) back **2** (*го́рная цепь*) (mountain) range; ridge; (fig.) crest, peak

хрен, **а (у)** *m.* horseradish; **х. с** (+ *i.*) (infml) to hell (with); **ни ~á** (infml) nothing, bugger all

хрено́вый *adj. of* ▸ **хрен**; (infml) rotten, lousy

хризанте́м|а, ы *f.* chrysanthemum

хрип, **а** *m.* wheeze, wheezing sound

хрип|е́ть, лю́, и́шь *impf.* to wheeze

хри́пл|ый, ~, ~á, ~о *adj.* hoarse; wheezy

хри́п|нуть, ну, нешь, *past* **~, ~ла** *impf.* (*of* ▸ **охри́пнуть**) to become hoarse, lose one's voice

христиа|ни́н, ани́на, *pl.* **~а́не, ~а́н** *m.* Christian

христиа́н|ка, ки *f. of* ▸ **христиани́н**

христиа́нский *adj.* Christian

христиа́нств|о, а *nt.* Christianity

✍ **Христо́с**, á *m.* Christ

хром, **а** *m.* (chem.) chromium, chrome

хрома́|ть, ю *impf.* to limp; (*о живо́тном*) to limp, be lame

хром|о́й, ~, ~á, ~о *adj.* **1** (*о челове́ке*) limping; (*о живо́тном*) limping, lame; **х. на ле́вую но́гу** lame in the left leg; (*as n.* **х., ~о́го**, *f.* **~а́я, ~о́й**) man/woman with walking difficulties **2** (infml, *нога́*) gammy

хромосо́м|а, ы *f.* (biol.) chromosome

хро́ник|а, и *f.* **1** (*ле́топись*) chronicle **2** (*в газе́те*) news items **3** (cin.) newsreel

хрони́ческий *adj.* chronic

хронологи́ческий *adj.* chronological

хроноло́ги|я, и *f.* chronology

хроно́метр, **а** *m.* chronometer

хру́п|кий, ~ок, ~ка́, ~ко *adj.* **1** (*стекло́*) fragile, brittle **2** (fig., *здоро́вье, ребёнок*) fragile, frail; delicate

хруст, **а** *m.* crunch; crunching sound

хруста́л|ь, я́ *m.* cut glass, crystal; **го́рный х.** rock crystal

хруста́льный *adj.* **1** cut glass, crystal **2** (fig.) crystal clear

---
✍ key word

хру|стеть, щу, стишь *impf.* (*of* ▶ **хрустнуть**) to crunch

хруст|нуть, ну, нешь *inst. pf. of* ▶ **хрустеть**

хрустящий *pres. part. of* ▶ **хрустеть** *and adj.*: **х. картофель** potato crisps (BrE), chips (AmE)

хрю́к|ать, аю *impf.* (*of* ▶ **хрюкнуть**) to grunt

хрю́к|нуть, ну, нешь *inst. pf.* (*of* ▶ **хрюкать**) to give a grunt

хряк, á *m.* hog

хрящ, á *m.* (anat.) cartilage, gristle

худе́е *comp. of* ▶ **худой**[1], ▶ **худой**[2]

худе́|ть, ю *impf.* (*of* ▶ **похуде́ть**) to grow thin, lose weight

◆ **худо́жествен|ный, ~, ~на** *adj.* **1** of art, of the arts; **~ная литерату́ра** fiction; **х. фильм** feature film; **~ная шко́ла** art school **2** (*красивый*) artistic; tasteful

◆ **худо́жник, а** *m.* artist; **х. по костю́мам/све́ту** costume/lighting designer

худо́жни|ца, цы *f. of* ▶ **худо́жник**

◆ **худ|о́й**[1], **~, ~á, ~о, ~ы́** *adj.* (*не толстый*) thin, lean

◆ **худ|о́й**[2], **~, ~á, ~о** *adj.* (*плохой*) bad; **на х. коне́ц** if the worst comes to the worst

худоща́в|ый, ~, ~а *adj.* thin, lean

ху́дший *superl. of* ▶ **худой**[2], ▶ **плохо́й**; (the) worst

хуёвый *adj.* (vulg.) shitty, crap(py)

ху́же *comp. of* ▶ **худой**[2], ▶ **плохо́й**, ▶ **пло́хо**; worse

хуй, ху́я, pl. хуи́, хуёв *m.* (vulg.) prick, cock (= penis); **ни хуя́** nothing, fuck all; **пошёл/иди́ на х.!** fuck off!

хуйн|я́, и́ *f.* (vulg.) (*бессмыслица*) (a load of) bollocks, crap; (*что-л. некачественное, ненужное*) crap

хулига́н, а *m.* hooligan

хулига́нств|о, а *nt.* hooliganism

ху́нт|а, ы *f.* (pol.) junta

хурм|á, ы́ *f.* persimmon, sharon fruit (*Diospyros*)

Цц

ца́п|ать, аю *impf.* (*of* ▶ **ца́пнуть**) (infml) to snatch, grab

ца́п|ля, ли, g. pl. ~ель *f.* heron

ца́п|нуть, ну, нешь *pf. of* ▶ **ца́пать**

цара́п|ать, аю *impf.* (*of* ▶ **оцара́пать**) to scratch

цара́па|ться, юсь *impf.* to scratch (oneself); (*друг друга*) to scratch one another

цара́пин|а, ы *f.* scratch

цар|и́ть, ю́, и́шь *impf.* **1** (*первенствовать*) to hold sway, reign supreme **2** (fig., *господствовать*) to reign, prevail; **~и́ла тишина́** silence reigned

цари́ц|а, ы *f.* **1** (*жена царя*) tsarina **2** (fig.) queen

ца́рск|ий *adj.* **1** tsar's, of the tsar; royal **2** (pol.) tsarist **3** (fig.) regal, kingly; **~ая ро́скошь** regal splendour

ца́рств|о, а *nt.* **1** (*государство*) kingdom, realm **2** (*царствование*) reign **3** (fig., *область деятельности*) realm, domain; **живо́тное ц.** animal kingdom

ца́рствовани|е, я *nt.* reign; **в ц.** (+ *g.*) during the reign (of)

ца́рств|овать, ую *impf.* to reign (also fig.)

◆ **цар|ь, я́** *m.* **1** tsar **2** (fig.) king, ruler

цве|сти́, ту́, тёшь, past ~л, ~ла́ *impf.* **1** to flower, bloom, blossom (also fig.); **ц.**

здоро́вьем to be radiant with health **2** (fig.) to prosper, flourish

◆ **цвет**[1], **а, pl. ~á** *m.* (*окраска*) colour (BrE), color (AmE); **ц. лица́** complexion

◆ **цвет**[2], **а** *m.* **1** (fig., *лучшая часть*) flower, cream, pick **2** (*расцвет*) blossoming; (fig.) prime; **в ~у́** in blossom **3** (collect.) (*цветы на растении*) blossom

цвете́ни|е, я *nt.* (bot.) flowering, blossoming

цветни́к, á *m.* flower bed

цветн|о́й *adj.* **1** (*не чёрный, не белый*) coloured (BrE), colored (AmE); colour (BrE), color (AmE); (*о людях*) (wholly or partly) of non-white descent; **~о́е стекло́** stained glass; **~áя капу́ста** cauliflower; **~о́е телеви́дение** colour (BrE), color (AmE) television; (*as m. n.* **ц.**, **~о́го**) (offensive) coloured (BrE), colored (AmE) person **2** (*о металлах*) non-ferrous

цветов|о́й *adj. of* ▶ **цвет**[1]; **~áя га́мма** colour (BrE), color (AmE) spectrum

◆ **цвет|о́к, ка́, pl. ~ы́, ~о́в** *m.* flower; (*pl. also* **~ки́, ~ко́в**) (*орган размножения*) flower

цвето́чн|ый *adj. of* ▶ **цвето́к**; **~ая клу́мба** flower bed; **ц. магази́н** flower shop, florist's

цвету́щий *pres. part. act. of* ▶ **цвести́** *and adj.* **1** (*растение*) flowering, blossoming, blooming; (*здоровье, юноша*) blooming **2** (fig., *страна*) flourishing

це|ди́ть, жу́, ~дишь *impf.* **1** (*через сито*) to strain, filter **2** (infml, *говорить*) to say (through clenched teeth)

целе́б|ный, ~ен, ~на *adj.* healing, medicinal

цел|ево́й *adj.* **1** *adj. of* ▶ **цель 2** having a special purpose; **~евы́е сбо́ры** funds earmarked/ring-fenced for a special purpose **3** (*постройка*) special

целенапра́влен|ный, ~, ~на *adj.* purposeful, single-minded

целесообра́з|ный, ~ен, ~на *adj.* expedient

целеустремлён|ный, ~, ~на *adj.* purposeful

целико́м *adv.* **1** (*в це́лом ви́де*) whole; **проглоти́ть ц.** to swallow whole **2** (*по́лностью*) wholly, entirely; **ц. и по́лностью** utterly and completely

целин|а́, ы́ *f.* virgin lands

цели́тел|ь, я *m.* healer

це́л|ить, ю, ишь *impf.* (*of* ▶ **наце́лить 1**) to take aim; (**в** + *a.*) to aim (at)

це́л|иться, юсь, ишься *impf.* = **це́лить**

целлофа́н, а *m.* cellophane®

целлофа́новый *adj. of* ▶ **целлофа́н**

целлюло́з|а, ы *f.* cellulose

цел|ова́ть, у́ю *impf.* (*of* ▶ **поцелова́ть**) to kiss

цел|ова́ться, у́юсь *impf.* (*of* ▶ **поцелова́ться**) to kiss (one another)

це́л|ое, ого *nt.* **1** whole **2** (math.) integer

целому́дрен|ный, ~, ~на *adj.* chaste

целому́дри|е, я *nt.* chastity

це́лост|ный, ~ен, ~на *adj.* integrated; complete

це́л|ый *adj.* **1** (*по́лный*) whole, entire; **~ое число́** whole number, integer; **в ~ом** as a whole **2** (**~, ~а́, ~о**) (*неповреждённый*) safe, intact; **~ и невреди́м** safe and sound

цел|ь, и *f.* **1** (*мише́нь*) target; **бить в ц., попа́сть в ц.** to hit the target; **бить ми́мо ~и** to miss **2** (*предме́т стремле́ния*) aim, object, goal, end, purpose; **с ~ью** (+ *inf.*) with the object (of), in order (to); **пресле́довать ц.** to pursue a goal

цел|ьный *adj.* **1** (*из одного́ куска́*) of one piece, solid **2** (**~ен, ~ьна́, ~ьно**) (*це́лостный*) entire, integral; single

Це́льси|й, я *m.* Celsius, centigrade; **10° по ~ю** 10° Celsius

цеме́нт, а *m.* cement

цен|а́, ы́, *a.* **~у**, *pl.* **~ы** *f.* **1** price, cost; **~о́й** (+ *g.*) at the price (of), at the cost (of); **любо́й ~о́й** at any cost; **э́тому ~ы нет** it is invaluable **2** (fig., *значе́ние*) worth, value; **знать ~у** (+ *d.*) to know the value/worth (of); **знать себе́ ~у** to be self-assured, self-possessed, to know one's own value/worth

цензу́р|а, ы *f.* censorship

цени́тел|ь, я *m.* judge, connoisseur, expert

цени́тель|ница, ницы *f. of* ▶ **цени́тель**

цен|и́ть, ю́, ~ишь *impf.* to value, appreciate; **высоко́ ц.** to rate highly

це́нник, а *m.* price tag

це́нност|ь, и *f.* **1** (*цена́, сто́имость*) price, value **2** (fig., *значе́ние*) value, importance **3** (*in pl.*) (*предме́ты*) valuables; (*духо́вные*) values

це́н|ный, ~ен, ~на *adj.* **1** (*с обозна́ченной цено́й*) containing valuables; representing a stated value; **~ные бума́ги** (fin.) securities **2** (*дорого́й*) valuable, costly; **~ная вещь** valuable object **3** (fig., *ва́жный*) valuable; precious; important

цент, а *m.* cent (*unit of currency*)

це́нтнер, а *m.* quintal (= *100 kilograms*)

центр, а *m.* centre (BrE), center (AmE)

централиза́ци|я, и *f.* centralization

централиз|ова́ть, у́ю *impf. and pf.* to centralize

центра́льн|ый *adj.* central; **~ые газе́ты** national newspapers; **~ое отопле́ние** central heating

центри́зм, а *m.* centrism

центри́ст, а *m.* centrist

центрифу́г|а, и *f.* (tech.) centrifuge

це́п|кий, ~ок, ~ка́, ~ко *adj.* **1** (*ру́ки, ко́гти*) tenacious, strong (also fig.) **2** (infml, *упо́рный*) obstinate, persistent, strong-willed

цепля́|ть, ю *impf.* **1** (*за* + *a.*) (infml) to hang on to, cling to **2** (*задева́ть чем-н. загну́тым*) to hook **3** (*прицепля́ть*) to hook on (to); to attach (to)

цепля́|ться, юсь *impf.* **1** (*за* + *a.*) (*зацепля́ться*) to hang on to, cling to **2** (*за* + *a.*) (infml, *стреми́ться удержа́ть, сохрани́ть что-н.*) to cling (to), stick (to) **3** (**к** + *d. or* **за** + *a.*) (infml, *придира́ться*) to pick (on) (*to carp at, complain of*)

цепо́чк|а, и *f.* **1** (small) chain **2** (*ряд*) file, series; **идти́ ~ой** to walk in file

цеп|ь, и, о ~и, на/в ~и́, *pl.* **~и, ~е́й** *f.* **1** chain; (*in pl.*) chains (= *fetters; also fig.*); **посади́ть на ц.** to chain (up), shackle **2** (*гор, острово́в*) chain **3** (mil.) line, file **4** (fig., *ряд*) series, succession; **ц. катастро́ф** succession of disasters **5** (elec.) circuit

церемо́ни|я, и *f.* ceremony

церемо́н|ный, ~ен, ~на *adj.* ceremonious

церко́вник, а *m.* churchman, clergyman

церко́вный *adj.* church; **ц. ста́роста** churchwarden; **ц. сто́рож** sexton

це́рк|овь, ви, i. ~овью, *pl.* **~ви, ~ве́й, ~ва́м** *and* **~вя́м** *f.* church

цех, а, в ~е *and* **в ~у́** *m.* **1** (*pl.* **~а́**) (*на заво́де*) shop, section **2** (*pl.* **~и**) (hist.) guild

цивилиза́ци|я, и *f.* civilization

цивилизо́ван|ный, ~, ~на *adj.* civilized

цика́д|а, ы *f.* cicada

цикл, а *m.* cycle; (*ле́кций, конце́ртов*) series

цикли́ческий *adj.* cyclic(al)

цикло́н, а *m.* (meteor.) cyclone

✓ key word

цили́ндр, а *m.* **1** cylinder **2** (*шляпа*) top hat
цилиндри́ческий *adj.* cylindrical
цини́зм, а *m.* cynicism
ци́ник, а *m.* cynic
цини́ч|ный, ~ен, ~на *adj.* cynical
цинк, а *m.* (chem.) zinc
ци́нковый *adj.* zinc
цирк, а *m.* circus
цирка́ч, а́ *m.* (infml) circus artiste
цирка́ч|ка, ки *f. of* ▶ цирка́ч
цирково́й *adj. of* ▶ цирк
циркули́р|овать, ую *impf.* **1** (*о жидкостях*) to circulate; ~овали слу́хи (infml) rumours (BrE), rumors (AmE) were circulating **2** (infml, *ходить*) to pass, go to and fro
ци́ркул|ь, я *m.* (pair of) compasses; dividers
циркуля́р, а *m.* circular (*official*)
циркуля́ци|я, и *f.* circulation
цирро́з, а *m.* (med.) cirrhosis
цисте́рн|а, ы *f.* (*резервуар*) cistern, tank; (*вагон*) tank car; (*автомобиль*) tanker
цитаде́л|ь, и *f.* citadel; (fig.) bulwark, stronghold
цита́т|а, ы *f.* quotation

цити́р|овать, ую *impf.* (*of* ▶ процити́ровать) to quote
ци́трус|овый *adj.* (as pl. n. ~овые, ~овых) citrus plants
цифербла́т, а *m.* dial; (*часов*) face
✧ **ци́фр|а**, ы *f.* **1** figure; digit, number, numeral **2** (in pl.) (*данные*) figures
✧ **цифров|о́й** *adj.* **1** numerical **2** (electronics, comput.) digital; ~а́я за́пись digital recording
цо́кол|ь, я *m.* **1** (archit.) socle, plinth, pedestal **2** (elec.) cap (*metal extremity of light bulb which is fitted into socket*)
ЦРУ *nt. indecl.* (abbr. of **Центра́льное разве́дывательное управле́ние**) CIA (*Central Intelligence Agency*)
цуна́ми *nt. indecl.* tsunami
цыга́н, а, pl. ~е, ~ *m.* Gypsy
цыга́н|ка, ки *f. of* ▶ цыга́н
цыга́нский *adj.* Gypsy
цы́к|ать, аю *impf.* (*of* ▶ цы́кнуть) (на кого́-н.) (infml) to shout at; to silence
цы́к|нуть, ну *pf. of* ▶ цы́кать
цыпл|ёнок, ёнка, pl. ~я́та, ~я́т *m.* chick(en)
цы́поч|ки, ек (no sg.) tiptoe; на ~ках on tiptoe

Чч

ч (abbr. of **час(ы́)**) hour; o'clock
ч. (abbr. of **часть**) part
чабре́ц, а́ *m.* (bot., cul.) thyme
ча́вк|ать, аю *impf.* to champ; to munch noisily
чаев|ы́е, ы́х (no sg.) tip, gratuity
чаепи́ти|е, я *nt.* tea-drinking
✧ **ча|й**, я ю pl. ~и́, ~ёв *m.* **1** tea **2** (*чаепитие*) tea(-drinking); за ~ем, за ча́шкой ~я over (a cup of) tea **3**: дать (+ d.) на ч. to tip
ча́йк|а, и, g. pl. ча́ек *f.* (sea)gull
ча́йн|ая, ой *f.* tea room, tea shop
ча́йник, а *m.* (*для заварки*) teapot; (*для кипячения воды*) kettle
ча́йн|ый *adj.* tea; ч. куст tea plant; ~ая ло́жка teaspoon; ~ая ча́шка teacup
чалм|а́, ы́ *f.* turban
чан, а, в ~е and в ~у́, pl. ~ы́ *m.* vat, tub, tank
чароде́|й, я *m.* sorcerer, magician (also fig.)
ча́ртер, а *m.* charter
ча́р|ы, ~ (no sg.) (infml) magic, charms (also fig.)
✧ **час**, а, о ~е, в ~у́ and в ~е, pl. ~ы́ *m.* **1** hour (also fig.); че́тверть ~а a quarter of an hour **2** (*время по часам*) (g. sg. after

numerals 2, 3, 4 ~а́) o'clock; час one o'clock; два ~а́ two o'clock; во второ́м ~у́ between one and two (o'clock); кото́рый ч.? what is the time? **3** (usu. in pl.) (*время*) hours, time, period; ч. пик, ~ы́ пик rush hour
часа́ми *adv.* for hours
часо́в|ня, ни, g. pl. ~ен *f.* chapel
часово́й[1], о́го *m.* sentry, guard
часово́й[2] *adj.* (of ▶ час) **1** (*продолжающийся один час*) of one hour's duration; ч. переры́в one hour's interval **2** (*по часам*) (measured) by the hour; ч. по́яс time zone
часово́й[3] *adj. of* ▶ часы́; ч. магази́н watch shop, watchmaker's, watch repair shop; ч. механи́зм clockwork; ~а́я стре́лка clock hand, hour hand; по ~о́й стре́лке clockwise
часовщи́к, а́ *m.* watchmaker
части́ц|а, ы *f.* **1** small part, element **2** (phys.) particle **3** (gram.) particle
части́чно *adv.* partly, partially
части́ч|ный, ~ен, ~на *adj.* partial
✧ **ча́стност|ь**, и *f.* detail; в ~и in particular
✧ **ча́стн|ый** *adj.* **1** (*личный*) private, personal; ~ым о́бразом privately **2** (econ.) private, privately-owned; ~ая со́бственность private property **3** (*отдельный, особый*)

particular, individual; (*as nt. n.* ~ое, ~ого) the particular

✓ ча́сто *adv.* often, frequently

✓ частот|а́, ы́, *pl.* ~ы f. frequency

✓ ча́ст|ый, ~, ~а́, ~о *adj.* **1** frequent; он у нас ч. гость he is a frequent visitor at our house **2** (*густой*) close (together); dense, thick; ч. дождь steady rain **3** (*быстрый*) quick, rapid; ч. ого́нь (*mil.*) rapid fire

✓ част|ь, и, *pl.* ~и, ~е́й f. **1** part; portion; бо́льшая ~ью, по бо́льшей ~и for the most part, mostly **2** (*отдел*) section, department **3** (*infml*, *область*) sphere, field; э́то не по мое́й ~и this is not my province; по ~и (+ *g.*) in connection with) **4** (*mil.*) unit

ча́стью *adv.* partly, in part

час|ы́, о́в (*no sg.*) clock, watch

чат, а *m.* (comput.) IRC (abbr. of *Internet Relay Chat*)

ча́хл|ый, ~, ~а *adj.* stunted; poor

ча́х|нуть, ну, нешь, *past* ~, ~ла *impf.* (of ▶ зача́хнуть) **1** (*о растительности*) to wither away **2** (*о человеке*) to fade away

чахо́тк|а, и f. (infml) consumption

ча́ш|а, и f. cup, bowl (also fig.); (eccl.) chalice; ч. весо́в scale pan

ча́шк|а, и f. (*для питья*) cup

ча́щ|а, и f. thicket

ча́ще *comp. of* ▶ ча́стый, ▶ ча́сто; more often; ч. всего́ most often, mostly

чебуре́к, а *m.* cheburek (*a kind of lamb pasty*)

чего́[2] *interrog. adv.* (infml) why? what for?

чего́ *g. of* ▶ что[1]

чей, чья, чьё, *pl.* чьи *interrog. pron. and rel. pron.* whose

чей-либо *pron.* = чей-нибудь

чей-нибудь *pron.* (*в утверждениях*) someone's, somebody's; (*в вопросах*) anyone's, anybody's

чей-то *pron.* someone's, somebody's

чек, а *m.* **1** (*банковский*) cheque (BrE), check (AmE); вы́писать ч. to write a cheque **2** (*с указанием суммы, которую следует уплатить*); (*удостоверяющий, что товар оплачен*) receipt

чеки́ст, а *m.* (hist.) agent of the Cheka (*state security organ 1918-22*)

че́к|овый *adj. of* ▶ чек; ~овая кни́жка chequebook (BrE), checkbook (AmE)

чёлк|а, и f. fringe (BrE), bangs (AmE); (*лошади*) forelock

челно́к, а́ m. **1** (*лодка*) dugout (canoe) **2** (sl.) small trader (*travelling to buy things to resell at home*)

✓ челове́к, а, *pl.* лю́ди, *in combination with nums., g. pl., etc.* челове́к, ~ам, ~ами, о ~ах m. man, person, human being

человеконенави́стнический *adj.* misanthropic

человекообра́з|ный, ~ен, ~на *adj.* anthropomorphous; (zool.) anthropoid

✓ челове́ческий *adj.* **1** (*относящийся к человеку*) human **2** (*гуманный*) humane

челове́честв|о, а *nt.* humanity, mankind

челове́чность|ь, и f. humaneness, humanity

челове́ч|ный, ~ен, ~на *adj.* humane

че́люст|ь, и f. **1** jaw **2** (*зубной протез*) dentures

✓ чем *conj.* **1** than **2** (+ *comp.*): ч. ..., тем... the more ..., the more ...; ч. скоре́е, тем лу́чше the sooner, the better

чемода́н, а *m.* suitcase

чемпио́н, а *m.* champion

✓ чемпиона́т, а *m.* championship

чемпио́н|ка, ки f. of ▶ чемпио́н

чепух|а́, и́ f. (infml) **1** (*вздор*) nonsense, rubbish **2** (*незначительное дело*) a trifle, trifling matter; (*пустяки*) trivialities **3** (*незначительное количество*) trifling amount

че́рв|и[1], е́й and че́рвы, ~ f. pl. (sg. ~а, ~ы) (*в картах*) hearts; коро́ль ~е́й king of hearts

че́рви[2] *pl. of* ▶ червь

черво́вый *adj. of* ▶ че́рви[1]

черв|ь, я́, *pl.* ~и, ~е́й m. worm; maggot

червя́к, а́ m. **1** = червь **2** (tech.) worm

черда́к, а́ m. attic, loft

чередова́ни|е, я *nt.* alternation, interchange, rotation

черед|ова́ть, у́ю *impf.* (с + *i.*) to alternate (with)

черед|ова́ться, у́юсь *impf.* to alternate; to take turns

✓ че́рез *prep.* (+ *a.*) **1** (*улицу, забор*) across; over; (*лес, окно*) through **2** (*о пунктах следования*) via **3** (*посредством*) through; ч. перево́дчика through an interpreter **4** (*по прошествии*) in; ч. полчаса́ in half an hour's time; я верну́сь ч. год I shall be back in a year's time **5** (*минуя какое-н. пространство*) after; (further) on; ч. три киломе́тра three kilometres (further) on **6** (*повторяя в регуля́рные промежутки*): ч. ка́ждые три страни́цы every three pages; дежу́рить ч. день to be on duty every other day, on alternate days

черен|о́к, ка́ m. **1** (*рукоятка*) handle **2** (hort.) cutting

че́реп, а, *pl.* ~а́ m. skull, cranium

черепа́х|а, и f. **1** tortoise; (*морская*) turtle; ползти́ как ч. to go at a snail's pace **2** (*панцирь в качестве материала*) tortoiseshell

черепи́ц|а, ы f. tile; (collect.) tiles

черепи́чный *adj.* tile; tiled

черепн|о́й *adj. of* ▶ че́реп; ~а́я коро́бка cranium

череп|о́к, ка́ m. broken piece of pottery

чересчу́р *adv.* too; (*перед глаголом*) too much

чере́шн|я, и f. cherry (tree) (*Cerasus avium*)

✓ key word

ч

черкéс, а *m.* Circassian

черкéсский *adj.* Circassian

черкéшенк|а, и *f. of* ▶ черкéс

черне́|ть, ю *impf.* **1** (*pf.* по~) (*становиться чёрным*) to turn black, grow black **2** (*виднеться*) to show up black

черни́к|а, и *f.* bilberry

черни́л|а, ~ (*no sg.*) ink

черни́льниц|а, ы *f.* inkpot, inkwell

чернобýрк|а, и *f.* (infml) silver fox (fur)

черновик, á *m.* rough copy, draft

чернов|о́й *adj.* **1** rough, draft; preparatory **2**: ~áя рабóта (infml) heavy, rough, dirty work

черноволóс|ый, ~, ~а *adj.* black-haired

черногла́з|ый, ~, ~а *adj.* black-eyed

черногóр|ец, ца *m.* Montenegrin

Черногóри|я, и *f.* Montenegro

черногóр|ка, ки *f. of* ▶ черногóрец

черногóрский *adj.* Montenegro

чернокóж|ий, ~, ~а *adj.* black; (*as m. n.* ч., ~его) black (man)

чернорабóч|ий, его *m.* unskilled labourer (BrE), laborer (AmE)

чернослив, а *m.* (*collect.*) prunes

черносóтен|ец, ца *m.* (hist.) member of 'Black Hundred' (*name of armed monarchist anti-Semitic groups in Russia, active 1905-7*); (fig.) extreme reactionary, chauvinist

чернот|á, ы́ *f.* blackness (also fig.); darkness

⚘ чёр|ный, ~ен, черна́ *adj.* **1** black; ч. рынок black market; (отложить на) ч. день (to put by for) a rainy day; ~ное де́рево ebony; Ч~ное мóре Black Sea; ~ная сморóдина blackcurrant; (*чернокожий*) black; (*as m. n.* ч., ~ного) (offensive, esp. when referring to person of Caucasian or Central Asian origin) black (man) **2** (*задний*) back; ч. ход back entrance, back door **3** (fig., *мысли, дни*) gloomy, melancholy

черпáк, á *m.* scoop, ladle

чéрп|ать, аю *impf.* (*of* ▶ черпнýть) **1** to draw (up); to scoop; to ladle **2** (fig., *извлекать*) to extract, derive

черп|нýть, нý, нёшь *inst. pf. of* ▶ чéрпать

чёрств|ый, ~, черства́, ~о *adj.* **1** stale **2** (fig., *бездушный*) hard, callous

чёрт, а, *pl.* чéрти, чертéй *m.* devil; ч. возьми/побери! (infml) damn!; до ~а (infml) hellishly; какóго ~а? (infml) why the hell?

⚘ черт|á, ы́ *f.* **1** (*линия*) line; провести́ ~ý to draw a line **2** (*граница*) boundary **3** (*свойство*) trait, characteristic; ~ы́ лица́ features; в общих ~áх in general outline

черт|ёж, ежá *m.* draft, drawing, sketch

чертёжник, а *m.* draughtsman

чер|ти́ть, чý, ~тишь *impf.* (*of* ▶ начерти́ть) (*карту*) to draw; (*план*) to draw up

чертополóх, а *m.* thistle

черче́ни|е, я *nt.* drawing; sketching

че|сáть, шý, ~шешь *impf.* (*of* ▶ почесáть) to scratch

че|сáться, шýсь, ~шешься *impf.* (*of* ▶ почесáться) **1** to scratch oneself **2** (*impf. only*) (*об ощущении зуда*) to itch; рýки у негó *и т. п.*~шутся (+ *inf.*) he is, *etc.*, itching to …

чеснóк, á ý *m.* garlic

чесóтк|а, и *f.* (med.) scabies

чéств|овать, ую *impf.* to honour (BrE), honor (AmE); to pay tribute to

чéстность, и *f.* honesty, integrity

чéст|ный, ~ен, ~на́, ~но, ~ны́ *adj.* honest; (*справедливый*) fair; ~ное слóво! honestly!, truly!

честолюби́в|ый, ~, ~а *adj.* ambitious

честолюби|е, я *nt.* ambition

⚘ чест|ь, и *f.* honour (BrE), honor (AmE); в ч. (+ *g.*) in honour (BrE), honor (AmE) of

чет|á, ы́ *f.* pair, couple; не ч. комý-н. no match for sb

четвéрг, á *m.* Thursday

четвере́ньк|и (infml) на ч., на ~ах on all fours, on one's hands and knees; стать на ч. to go down on all fours

четвёрк|а, и *f.* **1** (*цифра, игральная карта*) four **2** (*отметка*) four (*out of five*) **3** (infml, *автобус, трамвай*) No. 4 (*bus, tram, etc.*) **4** (*группа из четверых*) (group of) four; (*четыре человека*) foursome

чéтвер|о, ы́х *num.* (*collect.*) four; нас бы́ло ч. there were four of us

четвероног|ий *adj.* four-legged; (*as nt. n.* ~ое, ~ого) quadruped

четвёртый *adj.* fourth

чéтверт|ь, и, *g. pl.* ~éй *f.* **1** (*четвёртая часть целого*) quarter **2** (*четверть часа*) quarter (of an hour); без ~и час a quarter to one; ч. деся́того a quarter past nine **3** (*учебного года*) term **4** (mus.) crotchet (BrE), quarter note (AmE)

четвертьфинáл, а *m.* (sport) quarter-final

чёт|ки, ок (*no sg.*) (eccl.) rosary

чёт|кий, ~ок, ~ка и четкá, ~ко *adj.* **1** (*отчётливый*) precise; clear-cut **2** (*изложение*) clear, well defined; (*почерк*) legible; (*звук*) plain, distinct; (*речь*) articulate

чёткост|ь, и *f.* **1** (*движения*) precision, preciseness **2** (*изложения*) clarity, clearness

чётный *adj.* even (*of numbers*)

⚘ четы́р|е, ёх, ём, ьмя, о ~ёх *num.* four

четы́режды *adv.* four times

четы́р|еста, ёхсóт, ёмстáм, ьмястáми, о ~ёхстáх *num.* four hundred

четырёхле́тний *adj.* **1** (*срок*) four-year **2** (*ребёнок*) four-year-old

четырёхсóтый *adj.* four-hundredth

четырёхугóльник, а *m.* quadrangle

четырёхугóльный *adj.* quadrangular

четы́рнадцатый *adj.* fourteenth

четы́рнадцат|ь, и *num.* fourteen

чех, а *m.* Czech

чехардá, ы́ *f.* (*игра*) leapfrog; (fig.) reshuffle

Че́хи|я, и *f.* Czech Republic

чех|о́л, ла́ *m.* (*подушки, кресла*) cover; (*контрабаса*) case

чечеви́ц|а, ы *f.* lentil; (*collect.*) lentils

чече́н|ец, ца *m.* Chechen

чече́н|ка, ки *f. of* ▶ **чече́нец**

чече́нский *adj.* Chechen

Чечн|я́, и́ *f.* Chechnya

че́шк|а, и *f. of* ▶ **чех**

че́шский *adj.* Czech

чешу|я́, и́ (*no pl.*) *f.* (zool.) scales

чизке́йк, а, *m.* cheesecake

Чи́ли *f. indecl.* Chile

чили́|ец, йца *m.* Chilean

чили́|йка, йки *f. of* ▶ **чили́ец**

чили́йский *adj.* Chilean

чин, а, *pl.* **∼ы** *m.* **1** (*разряд*) rank; **в ∼е/∼áх** high-ranking **2** (*чиновник*) official

чин|и́ть, ю́, ∼ишь *impf.* (*of* ▶ **почини́ть**) (*обувь, велосипед*) to repair, mend

чи́н|ный, ∼ен, ∼на́, ∼но *adj.* decorous, proper, orderly

☞ **чино́вник, а** *m.* official, functionary

чип, а *m.* (micro)chip

чи́пс|ы, ов (*no sg.*) (potato) crisps (BrE), chips (AmE)

чири́ка|ть, ю *impf.* to chirp, twitter

чири́кн|уть, у, ешь *inst. pf.* to give a chirp

чи́рк|ать, аю *impf.* (*of* ▶ **чи́ркнуть**) (+ *i.*) (**по** + *d.*) to strike sharply (against, on); **ч. спи́чкой** to strike a match

чи́ркн|уть, ну, нешь *inst. pf. of* ▶ **чи́ркать**

чи́сленност|ь, и *f.* numbers; **ч. населе́ния** population size; (mil.) strength

чи́сленный *adj.* numerical

числи́тельн|ое, ого *nt.* (gram.) numeral

числ|и́ться, юсь, ишься *impf.* **1** to be (*in context of calculation or official records*); **в на́шей дере́вне ∼ится три́ста жи́телей** there are three hundred inhabitants in our village **2** (+ *i.*) to be officially, be on paper; **он ещё ∼ился заве́дующим отде́лом, а все обя́занности исполня́ли его́ замести́тели** he was still head of the department on paper, but all the duties were being performed by his deputies **3** (**за** + *i.*) to be attributed (to), have; **за ним ∼ится мно́го недоста́тков** he has many failings

☞ **чис|ло́, ла́,** *pl.* **∼ла, ∼ел** *nt.* **1** number; **∼ло́м** in number; **без ∼ла́** without number, in great numbers; **в том ∼ле́** including **2** (*дата*) date, day (*of month*); **како́е сего́дня ч.?** what is the date today? **3** (gram.) number; **еди́нственное, мно́жественное ч.** singular, plural

числово́й *adj.* numerical

чисти́лищ|е, а *nt.* (relig.) purgatory

чи́стильщик, а *m.* cleaner

чи́|стить, щу, стишь *impf.* **1** (*pf.* **по∼, вы́∼**) to clean; (*щёткой*) to brush **2** (*pf.* **по∼, вы́∼**) (*дорожки*) to clear; (*канал*)

to dredge **3** (*pf.* **о∼** *and infml* **по∼**) (*овощи, фрукты*) to peel; (*орехи*) to shell; (*рыбу*) to clean

чи́стк|а, и *f.* **1** cleaning; **отда́ть в ∼у** to have cleaned, send to be cleaned **2** (pol.) purge; **этни́ческая ч.** ethnic cleansing

чи́сто¹ *as pred.* it is clean

чи́сто² *adv.* **1** *adv. of* ▶ **чи́стый**; **ч.-на́чисто** spotlessly clean **2** (*as conj.*) (infml) just like, just as if

чистово́й *adj.* fair, clean; **ч. экземпля́р** fair copy

чистокро́в|ный, ∼ен, ∼на *adj.* thoroughbred

чистописа́ни|е, я *nt.* calligraphy

чистопло́т|ный, ∼ен, ∼на *adj.* clean; neat, tidy

чистот|а́, ы́ *f.* **1** cleanliness; (*опрятность*) neatness, tidiness **2** (*безупречность; отсутствие примесей*) purity

☞ **чи́ст|ый, ∼, ∼а́, ∼о, ∼ы́** *adj.* **1** clean; (*опрятный*) neat, tidy; (*голос, речь*) clear; **экологи́чески ч.** eco-friendly **2** (fig., *безупречный*) pure **3** (*без примесей*) pure **4** (*открытый*) clear; open; **ч. лист** blank sheet **5** (fin., *etc.*) net, clear; **∼ая при́быль** clear profit **6** (infml, *сущий*) pure, utter; sheer; complete; **∼ая случа́йность** pure chance

чита́льный *adj.*: **ч. зал** reading room

☞ **чита́тел|ь, я** *m.* reader

чита́тель|ница, ницы *f. of* ▶ **чита́тель**

☞ **чита́|ть, ю** *impf.* (*of* ▶ **прочита́ть**, ▶ **проче́сть**) **1** to read **2**: **ч. ле́кцию** to give a lecture; **ч. стихи́** to recite poetry

чиха́|ть, а́ю *impf.* (*of* ▶ **чихну́ть**) to sneeze

чих|ну́ть, ну́, нёшь *inst. pf. of* ▶ **чиха́ть**

чи́ще *comp. of* ▶ **чи́стый**, ▶ **чи́сто¹**, ▶ **чи́сто²**

☞ **член, а** *m.* **1** member; (*академик*) Fellow; **ч.-корреспонде́нт** corresponding member (*of an Academy*) **2** (math.) term; (gram.) part (*of sentence*) **3** (*конечность*) limb; (*половой*) penis

членоразде́л|ьный, ∼ен, ∼ьна *adj.* articulate

чле́нств|о, а *nt.* membership

чмо́к|ать, аю *impf.* (*of* ▶ **чмо́кнуть**) (infml) **1** to smack one's lips **2** (*целовать*) to give a smacking kiss **3** (*о грязи*) to squelch

чмо́к|нуть, ну, нешь *pf. of* ▶ **чмо́кать**

чо́к|аться, аюсь *impf.* (*of* ▶ **чо́кнуться**) to clink glasses (*when drinking toasts*)

чо́кнутый *adj.* (infml) odd, crazy

чо́к|нуться, нусь, нешься *pf. of* ▶ **чо́каться**

чо́пор|ный, ∼ен, ∼на *adj.* prim; stuck-up; stand-offish

ЧП *nt. indecl.* (*abbr. of* **чрезвыча́йное происше́ствие**) incident, emergency; (*катастрофа*) disaster

чрева́т|ый, ∼, ∼а *adj.* (+ *i.*) fraught (with)

чрезвыча́йно *adv.* extremely, extraordinarily

чрезвыча́й|ный, ∼ен, ∼йна *adj.* **1** extraordinary **2** (*экстренный*) special, emergency; **∼йные ме́ры** emergency

ч

☞ key word

measures; ∼йное положе́ние state of emergency

чрезме́р|ный, ∼ен, ∼на *adj.* excessive, inordinate

✓ **чте́ни|е**, я *nt.* reading

чти́в|о, а *nt.* (infml, pej.) reading matter

чтить, чту, чтишь, чтят *and* чтут *impf.* to honour (BrE), honor (AmE)

✓ **что¹**, чего́, чему́, чем, о чём *interrog. pron.*
1 what?; что с тобо́й? what's the matter (with you)?; что де́лать, что поде́лаешь? it can't be helped; для чего́? why?, what ... for?; что ты (вы)! (*выражает удивление, страх*) you don't mean to say so! **2** (*почему*) why?; что вы не еди́те? why aren't you eating?

✓ **что²**, (*sometimes printed* что) *rel. pron.*
which, that; (infml, *который*) who; я зна́ю, что вы име́ете в виду́ I know what you mean; па́рень, что стоя́л ря́дом со мной the fellow (who was) standing next to me; он всё молча́л, что для него́ не характе́рно he said nothing the whole time, which is unlike him

что³ as far as; что до, что каса́ется (+ *g.*) as for, with regard (to), as far as ... is concerned

✓ **что⁴** *conj.* that; то, что... the fact that ...

✓ **чтоб** *conj.* = чтобы

✓ **чтобы** *conj.* **1** (*выражает цель*) in order to, in order that; ч. ... не lest **2** (that); он хо́чет, ч. она́ пришла́ в шесть часо́в he wants her to come at 6 o'clock **3** (*as particle*) (*выражает требование, пожелание*): ч. я тебя́ бо́льше не ви́дел! may I never see your face again!

что за (infml) **1** (*interrog.*) what? what sort of ... ?; что э́то за пти́ца? what sort of bird is that? **2** (*as int.*): что за день! what a (marvellous) day!

что́-либо, чего́-либо *indefinite pron.* anything

что́-нибудь, чего́-нибудь *indefinite pron.* anything

✓ **что́-то¹**, чего́-то *indefinite pron.* something

что́-то² *adv.* (infml) **1** (*несколько*) somewhat, slightly **2** (*почему-то*) somehow, for no obvious reason; что́-то мне не хо́чется идти́ I don't feel like going for some reason

чуб, а, *pl.* ∼ы́ *m.* forelock

чува́к, а́ *m.* (sl.) guy, fellow (both infml)

чува́ш, а́, *pl.* ∼и́, ∼е́й *m.* Chuvash

чува́ш|ка, ки *f. of* ▶ чува́ш

чува́шский *adj.* Chuvash

чуви́х|а, и *f.* (sl.) chick (infml) (*girl*)

чу́вствен|ный *adj.* **1** (∼, ∼на) sensual **2** (phil.) perceptible; ∼ное восприя́тие perception

чувстви́тельност|ь, и *f.* **1** (*кожи, прибора, человека*) sensitivity, sensitiveness **2** (*сентиментальность*) sentimentality

чувстви́тель|ный, ∼ен, ∼ьна *adj.* **1** (*прибор, человек*) sensitive **2** (*сентиментальный*) sentimental

3 (*толчок, урон*) perceptible

✓ **чу́вств|о**, а *nt.* **1** (physiol.) sense; ч. вку́са sense of taste; о́рганы ∼ senses, organs of sense **2** (*sg. or pl.*) (*сознание*) senses; лиши́ться ∼, упа́сть без ∼ to faint, lose consciousness; прийти́ в ч. to come round, regain consciousness, come to one's senses **3** (*ощущение*) feeling; sense; ч. ю́мора sense of humour (BrE), humor (AmE); пита́ть к кому́-н. не́жные ∼а to have a soft spot for sb

✓ **чу́вств|овать**, ую *impf.* (*of* ▶ почу́вствовать) **1** to feel, sense; ч. себя́ to feel; как вы себя́ ∼уете? how do you feel? **2** (*уметь воспринимать*) to appreciate, have a feeling (for) (*music, etc.*)

чу́вств|оваться, уется *impf.* **1** to be perceptible; to make itself felt **2** *pass. of* ▶ чу́вствовать

чугу́н, а́ *m.* cast iron

чугу́нный *adj.* cast-iron (also fig.)

чуда́к, а́ *m.* eccentric, crank

чуде́с|ный, ∼ен, ∼на *adj.* **1** (*сверхъестественный*) miraculous; ∼ное исцеле́ние miraculous healing **2** (*чудный*) marvellous (BrE), marvelous (AmE), wonderful

чуд|но́й, ∼ён, ∼на́, ∼но́ *adj.* (*странный*) strange, odd

чу́д|ный, ∼ен, ∼на *adj.* marvellous (BrE), marvelous (AmE), wonderful, lovely

✓ **чу́д|о**, а, *pl.* ∼еса́, ∼е́с *nt.*
1 (*сверхъестественное явление*) miracle **2** (*нечто поразительное*) wonder, marvel

чудо́вищ|е, а *nt.* monster

чудо́вищ|ный, ∼ен, ∼на *adj.* **1** monstrous (also fig., pej.) **2** (*огромный*) enormous

чу́дом *adv.* miraculously; ч. спасти́сь to be saved by a miracle

чудотво́р|ец, ца *m.* miracle-worker

чужда́|ться, юсь *impf.* (+ *g.*) (*друзей*) to shun, avoid; (*славы*) to stand aloof (from), remain unaffected (by)

чу́жд|ый, ∼, ∼а́, ∼о *adj.* **1** (+ *d.*) (*идеология, взгляды*) alien (to); extraneous **2** (+ *g.*) (*лишенный*) free (from), devoid (of); он ∼ зло́бы he is devoid of malice

✓ **чуж|о́й** *adj.* **1** (*не свой*) sb else's, another's, others'; на ч. счёт at sb else's expense; (*as nt. n.* ∼о́е, ∼о́го) sb else's belongings **2** (*посторонний*) strange, alien; foreign; (*as m. n.* ч., ∼о́го) stranger

чула́н, а *m.* (*для вещей*) storeroom, lumber room; (*для продуктов*) larder

чул|о́к, ка́, *g. pl.* ч. *m.* stocking

чум|а́, ы́ *f.* plague

чума́з|ый, ∼, ∼а *adj.* (infml) grubby, dirty

чурба́н, а *m.* **1** block, log **2** (infml, *тупой человек*) blockhead

чу́рк|а, и *f.* block, lump

чу́т|кий, ∼ок, ∼ка́, ∼ко *adj.* **1** keen, sharp; ч. нюх keen sense of smell; ч. сон light sleep **2** (fig., *отзывчивый*) sensitive; sympathetic; tactful

Ч

чуть **1** *adv.* (*едва*) hardly, scarcely; just; ч. (**бы́ло**) не, ч. ли не almost, nearly **2** *adv.* (*немного*) (just) a little, very slightly **3** *conj.* (*как то́лько*) as soon as; ч. что at the slightest provocation

чуть|**ё, я́** *nt.* **1** (*у живо́тных*) scent **2** (к + *d.* or на + *a.*) (fig., *спосо́бность*) flair, feeling (for)

чуть-чу́ть *adv.* (infml) a tiny bit; ч.-ч. не; = чуть не

чу́чел|**о, а** *nt.* **1** (*живо́тное*) stuffed animal **2** (*пу́гало*) scarecrow (also fig.)

чушь, и *f.* (infml) nonsense

чу́|ять, ю, ешь *impf.* to scent, smell; (fig.) to sense, feel

Ш ш

шабло́н, а *m.* **1** (tech.) template, pattern; (*фо́рма*) mould (BrE), mold (AmE) **2** (fig., pej.) cliché; routine

шаг, а (у), *after numerals* 2, 3, 4 ~á, о ~е, в/на ~ý/~е, *pl.* ~й, ~óв *m.* step (also fig.); (*похо́дка*) pace; (*большо́й*) stride; ш. на ме́сте marking time; идти́ бы́стрыми ~áми make rapid strides; заме́длить ш. to slow down; в двух ~áх, в не́скольких ~áх a stone's throw away; на ка́ждом ~ý everywhere, at every turn, continually

шаг|**а́ть, а́ю** *impf.* (*of* ▶ шагну́ть) **1** (*ступа́ть*) to step; (*ходи́ть*) to walk; (*больши́ми шага́ми*) to stride; (*ме́рными шага́ми*) to pace **2** (infml, *идти́*) to go, come

шаг|**ну́ть, ну́, нёшь** *inst. pf.* (*of* ▶ шага́ть) to take a step; (fig.) to make progress

ша́гом *adv.* at a walk, at a walking pace; slowly; ш. марш! (mil.) quick march!

ша́йб|**а, ы** *f.* **1** (tech.) washer **2** (sport) puck; хокке́й с ~ой ice hockey

ша́йк|**а, и,** *g. pl.* ша́ек *f.* gang, band

шака́л, а *m.* jackal

шала́ш, á *m.* (*hunter's or fisherman's*) cabin (*made of branches and straw, etc.*)

шал|**и́ть, ю́, и́шь** *impf.* to be naughty; to play up, play tricks (*also of inanimate objects*)

ша́лост|**ь, и** *f.* prank; (*in pl.*) mischief

шалу́н, á *m.* naughty child

шалу́н|**ья, ьи** *f. of* ▶ шалу́н

шалфе́|**й, я** *m.* (bot.) sage

шаль, и *f.* shawl

шальн|**о́й** *adj.* mad, crazy; wild; ~ы́е де́ньги easy money; ~áя пу́ля stray bullet

шама́н, а *m.* (relig.) shaman

шампа́нск|**ое, ого** *nt.* champagne

шампиньо́н, а *m.* field mushroom

шампу́нь, я *m.* shampoo

шампу́р, а *m.* skewer

шанс, а *m.* chance; име́ть мно́го ~ов, больши́е ~ы (на + *a.*) to have a good chance (of)

шансо́н, а *m.* ballad (*also as a genre*)

шансонье́ *m. indecl.* balladeer; singer-songwriter

шанта́ж, á *m.* blackmail

шантажи́р|**овать, ую** *impf.* to blackmail

шантажи́ст, а *m.* blackmailer

шантажи́ст|**ка, ки** *f. of* ▶ шантажи́ст

ша́пк|**а, и** *f.* **1** hat, cap **2** (*заголо́вок*) banner headline(s)

шар, а, *after numerals* 2, 3, 4 ~á, *pl.* ~ы́ *m.* **1** (math.) sphere; земно́й ш. the Earth, globe **2** (*шарови́дный предме́т*) spherical object, ball; возду́шный ш. balloon

шара́х|**аться, аюсь** *impf.* (*of* ▶ шара́хнуться) (infml) (*о ло́шади*) to shy; (*о толпе́*) to start (up); (*броса́ться*) to rush, dash

шара́х|**нуться, нусь, нешься** *pf. of* ▶ шара́хаться

шарж, а *m.* caricature, cartoon

шариа́т, а *m.* sharia (*Islamic canonical law*)

ша́риков|**ый** *adj.*: ~ая ру́чка biro®, ballpoint (pen)

ша́р|**ить, ю, ишь** *impf.* (в + *p.* or по + *d.*) (*иска́ть о́щупью*) to grope about, feel, fumble (in, through); (*о проже́кторе*) to sweep (*in order to locate a target*)

ша́рк|**ать, аю** *impf.* (+ *i.*) to shuffle

шарлата́н, а *m.* charlatan, fraud; quack

шарлата́н|**ка, ки** *f. of* ▶ шарлата́н

шарм, а *m.* charm

шарни́р, а *m.* (tech.) hinge, joint

шарф, а *m.* scarf

шасси́ *nt. indecl.* **1** (*автомоби́ля*) chassis **2** (aeron.) undercarriage

ша́ста|**ть, ю** *impf.* (infml) to roam, hang about

шата́|**ть, ю** *impf.* to rock, shake

шата́|**ться, юсь** *impf.* **1** (*о челове́ке, о ваго́не*) to rock, sway, reel **2** (*о гвозде́*) to be, come loose; (*о сту́ле, забо́ре*) to wobble, be unsteady **3** (infml, *броди́ть*) to roam; to loaf, lounge about

шате́н, а *m.* man/boy with auburn/brown/chestnut hair

шатён|ка, ки *f.* woman/girl with auburn/brown/chestnut hair

шат|ёр, ра *m.* tent, marquee

ша́т|кий, ~ок, ~ка́, ~ко *adj.* **1** (*стол*) unsteady; shaky; (*гайка*) loose **2** (fig.) unstable, insecure, shaky

ша́фер, а, *pl.* ~а́ *m.* best man (*at wedding*)

шафра́н, а *m.* (bot.) saffron

шах¹, а *m.* (*монарх*) Shah

шах², а *m.* (chess) check; **ш. и мат** checkmate; **вам ш.** you're in check

шахмати́ст, а *m.* chess player

шахмати́ст|ка, ки *f. of* ▶ **шахмати́ст**

ша́хматн|ый *adj.* **1** chess; ~ая доска́ chessboard; ~ая па́ртия game of chess **2** (*с квадратами клеток*) chequered (BrE), checkered (AmE); **в ~ом поря́дке** staggered

ша́хмат|ы, ~ (*no sg.*) **1** (*игра*) chess **2** (*фигуры*) chessmen

ша́хт|а, ы *f.* **1** (*горная выработка*) mine, pit **2** (tech., *лифта, вентиляционная*) shaft

шахтёр, а *m.* miner

ша́шк|а¹, и *f.* (*взрывчатка*) charge (*of explosive*)

ша́шк|а², и *f.* **1** (*в игре*) draught (BrE), checker (AmE) (*piece in game of draughts*) **2** (*in pl.*) (*игра*) draughts (BrE), checkers (AmE)

шашлы́к, а́ *m.* (cul.) kebab, shashlik

шва *g. sg. of* ▶ **шов**

шва́бр|а, ы *f.* mop, swab

шварт|ова́ть, у́ю *impf.* (*of* ▶ **пришвартова́ть**) (naut.) to moor

шварт|ова́ться, у́юсь *impf.* (*of* ▶ **пришвартова́ться**) (naut.) to moor

швед, а *m.* Swede

шве́д|ка, ки *f. of* ▶ **швед**

шве́дский *adj.* Swedish

швей́н|ый *adj.* sewing; ~ая маши́на sewing machine

швейца́р, а *m.* porter, doorman

швейца́р|ец, ца *m.* Swiss

Швейца́ри|я, и *f.* Switzerland

швейца́р|ка, ки *f. of* ▶ **швейца́рец**

швейца́рский *adj.* Swiss

Шве́ци|я, и *f.* Sweden

швея́, и́ *f.* seamstress

швыр|ну́ть, ну́, нёшь *inst. pf. of* ▶ **швыря́ть**

швыр|я́ть, я́ю *impf.* (*of* ▶ **швырну́ть**) (+ *a. or i.*) to throw, fling, chuck, hurl

швыря́ться, юсь *impf.* (infml) (+ *i.*) **1** (*камнями*) to throw, fling, hurl (at one another) **2** (*деньгами, друзьями*) to make light (of), trifle (with)

шевел|и́ть, ю́, и́шь *impf.* (*of* ▶ **шевельну́ть**, ▶ **пошевели́ть**) **1** (*переворачивать*) to turn over **2** (+ *i.*) (*слегка сдвигать*) to move, stir; **ш. мозга́ми** (infml, joc.) to use one's brains

шевел|и́ться, ю́сь, и́шься *impf.* (*of* ▶ **шевельну́ться**, ▶ **пошевели́ться**)

шевел|ьну́ть, ьну́, ьнёшь *inst. pf.* (*of* ▶ **шевели́ть**): **па́льцем не ш.** to not lift a finger

шевел|ьну́ться, ьну́сь, ьнёшься *inst. pf. of* ▶ **шевели́ться**

шевелю́р|а, ы *f.* (head of) hair

шеде́вр, а *m.* masterpiece

шезло́нг, а *m.* deckchair; lounger

шей́к|а, и, *g. pl.* **ше́ек** *f.* **1** *dim. of* ▶ **ше́я** **2** (anat.) **ш. ма́тки** cervix

шей́ный *adj. of* ▶ **ше́я**; (anat.) cervical

шейх, а *m.* sheikh

шёл *see* ▶ **идти́**

ше́лест, а *m.* rustle, rustling

шелест|е́ть (*1st pers. not used*) **и́шь** *impf.* to rustle

шёлк, а (у), о ~е, на/в шелку́/~е, *pl.* **шелка́** *m.* silk

шёлковый *adj.* silk

шелохн|у́ться, у́сь, ёшься *pf.* to stir, move

шелух|а́, и́ *f.* (*плодов, овощей*) skin; peel; (*гороха*) pod

шелуш|и́ться, и́тся *impf.* to peel (off)

шепеля́в|ить, лю, ишь *impf.* to lisp

шеп|ну́ть, ну́, нёшь *inst. pf. of* ▶ **шепта́ть**

шёпот, а *m.* whisper (also fig.)

шёпотом *adv.* in a whisper

шеп|та́ть, чу́, ~чешь *impf.* (*of* ▶ **шепну́ть**, ▶ **прошепта́ть**) to whisper

шеп|та́ться, чу́сь, ~чешься *impf.* to whisper, converse in whispers

шере́нг|а, и *f.* **1** (mil.) rank; file, column **2** (fig.) line, row

шери́ф, а *m.* sheriff

шерохова́т|ый, ~, ~а *adj.* rough (also fig.); (*неровный*) uneven

шерст|ь, и *f.* **1** (*на животных*) hair **2** (*волокно*) wool

шерстяно́й *adj.* wool, woollen (BrE), woolen (AmE)

шерша́в|ый, ~, ~а *adj.* rough

шест, а́ *m.* pole

ше́стви|е, я *nt.* procession

шестерёнк|а, и *f.* (tech.) gear (wheel), cogwheel, pinion

шестёрк|а, и *f.* **1** (*цифра, игральная карта*) six **2** (infml, *автобус, трамвай*) No. 6 (*bus, tram, etc.*) **3** (*группа из шестерых*) (group of) six **4** (sl., *подчинённый*) slave, dogsbody (BrE), gofer

ше́стер|о, ы́х *num.* (collect.) six

шестидеся́тый *adj.* sixtieth

шестисо́тый *adj.* six-hundredth

шестиуго́льник, а *m.* (math.) hexagon

шестна́дцат|ый *adj.* sixteenth; ~ая но́та (mus.) semiquaver (BrE), sixteenth note (AmE)

шестна́дцат|ь, и *num.* sixteen

шест|ой *adj.* sixth; **одна́ ~ая** one sixth

ш

⚡ **шест|ь, й,** *i.* **~ью** *num.* six

шестьдеся́т, шести́десяти, *i.*
шестью́десятью, о шести́десяти *num.*
sixty

шест|ьсо́т, исо́т, иста́м, ьюста́ми,
о ~иста́х *num.* six hundred

шеф, а *m.* **1** (infml, *нача́льник*) boss, chief
2 (*покрови́тель*) patron, sponsor

шеф-по́вар, а, *pl.* **~а́, ~о́в** *m.* chef

ше́|я, и *f.* neck; **сиде́ть на ~е у кого́-н.** (infml)
to live off sb

ши́ворот, а *m.* (infml): **за ш.** by the collar, by
the scruff of the neck

шизофре́ник, а *m.* (med.) schizophrenic;
(infml, offensive) crazy person

шизофрени́|я, и *f.* (med.) schizophrenia

шии́т, а *m.* Shiite (Muslim)

шик, а (у) *m.* stylishness; style

шика́р|ный, ~ен, ~на *adj.* (infml)
(*роско́шный*) chic, smart, stylish;
(*отли́чный*) gorgeous

ши́к|ать, аю *impf.* (*of* ▸ **ши́кнуть**) (infml)
(**на** + *a.*) to hush (by crying 'sh'); (**в** *знак*
неодобре́ния) to hiss (at), boo, catcall

ши́к|нуть, ну, нешь *pf. of* ▸ **ши́кать**

шимпанзе́ *m. indecl.* chimpanzee

ши́н|а, ы *f.* **1** tyre (BrE), tire (AmE) **2** (med.)
splint

шине́л|ь, и *f.* greatcoat

шинк|ова́ть, у́ю *impf.* (*of* ▸ **нашинкова́ть**)
(cul.) to shred

шинши́лл|а, ы *f.* chinchilla

шип, а́ *m.* **1** (bot.) thorn **2** (*на спорти́вной*
о́буви) spike; (*на боти́нках альпини́ста*)
crampon

шипе́ни|е, я *nt.* hissing; sizzling; sputtering

шип|е́ть, лю́, йшь *impf.* **1** (*о змее́*) to hiss;
(*при жа́рке*) to sizzle; (*о напи́тке*) to fizz
2 (*от зло́сти*) to hiss

шипу́чий *adj.* (*вино́*) sparkling; (*напи́ток,*
пи́во, вода́) fizzy

ши́ре *comp. of* ▸ **широ́кий,** ▸ **широко́**

ширин|а́, ы́ *f.* width, breadth; (*коле́и*) gauge
(*of railway track*)

ши́рин́к|а, и *f.* fly (*of trousers*)

ши́рм|а, ы *f.* screen (also fig.)

⚡ **широ́к|ий, ~, ~а́, ~о́,** *pl.* **~и** *adj.* **1** wide,
broad (also fig.); **в ~ом смы́сле** in a broad
sense **2** (fig.) big, extensive, general; **това́ры**
~ого потребле́ния (econ.) consumer goods;
ш. круг чита́телей the average reader, the
general reading public; **жить на ~ую но́гу**
to live in grand style

широко́ *adv.* **1** wide, widely, broadly (also
fig.); **ш. раскры́ть глаза́** to open one's eyes
wide; **ш. толкова́ть** to interpret loosely
2 (*в широ́ком масшта́бе*) extensively, on a
large scale

широкопле́ч|ий, ~, ~а *adj.* broad-shouldered

широт|а́, ы́, *pl.* **~ы, ~** *f.* **1** width, breadth
2 (geog.) latitude

широча́йший *superl. of* ▸ **широ́кий**

ширпотре́б, а *m.* (collect.) mass-market goods

шить, шью, шьёшь *impf.* (*of* ▸ **сшить 1**)
1 to sew **2** (*изготовля́ть*) to make (by
sewing); **ш. себе́ что-н.** to have sth made

ши́фер, а *m.* slate

шифр, а *m.* **1** cipher; code **2** (*библиоте́чный*)
shelf mark (BrE), call number (AmE)

шифр|ова́ть, у́ю *impf.* (*of* ▸ **зашифрова́ть**)
to encipher

ши́шк|а, и *f.* **1** (bot.) cone **2** (*буго́рок*) bump;
lump

шишкова́т|ый, ~, ~а *adj.* knobbly; bumpy

шкал|а́, ы́, *pl.* **~ы** *f.* (*зарпла́ты,*
термо́метра) scale; (*приёмника*) dial

шкату́лк|а, и *f.* box, casket, case

шкаф, а, о ~е, в/на ~у́, *pl.* **~ы́** *m.* cupboard;
(*платяно́й*) wardrobe; (*ку́хонный*) dresser;
кни́жный ш. bookcase (with doors);
несгора́емый ш. safe

шквал, а *nt.* squall; (fig., *огня́, возмуще́ния*)
burst

⚡ **шко́л|а, ы** *f.* **1** (*учрежде́ние*) school; **ходи́ть**
в ~у to go to school; **око́нчить ~у** to leave
school; **ш.-интерна́т** boarding school
2 (*вы́учка*) schooling, training

шко́льник, а *m.* schoolboy

шко́льниц|а, ы *f.* schoolgirl

шко́льный *adj.* school; **ш. во́зраст** school age

шку́р|а, ы *f.* skin (also fig.), hide, pelt; **быть в**
чьей-н. ~е to be in sb's shoes

шку́рк|а, и *f.* **1** (*шку́ра*) skin **2** (infml, *плода́*)
rind **3** (*бума́га*) emery paper, sandpaper

шла *see* ▸ **идти́**

шлагба́ум, а *m.* barrier (*of swing beam type,*
at road or rail crossing)

шлак, а *m.* slag; clinker

шланг, а *m.* hose

шлем, а *m.* helmet; **защи́тный ш.** hard hat (*on*
building site, etc.)

шлёпан|цы, цев, *pl. m. pl.* (*sg.* **~ец, ~ца**)
(infml) backless shoes/slippers; (*вьетна́мки*)
flip-flops

шлёп|ать, аю *impf.* (*of* ▸ **отшлёпать**,
▸ **шлёпнуть**) to smack, slap, spank

шлёп|аться, аюсь *impf.* (*of* ▸ **шлёпнуться**)
(infml) to fall with a plop, thud

шлёп|нуть, ну, нешь *inst. pf. of* ▸ **шлёпать**

шлёп|нуться, нусь, нешься *inst. pf. of*
▸ **шлёпаться**

шлёшь, шлёт *etc., see* ▸ **слать**

шли¹ *see* ▸ **идти́**

шли² *see* ▸ **слать**

шлиф|ова́ть, у́ю *impf. of* ▸ **отшлифова́ть**

шло *see* ▸ **идти́**

шлю, шлют *see* ▸ **слать**

шлюз, а *m.* lock, sluice, floodgate

шлю́пк|а, и *f.* launch, boat; **спаса́тельная ш.**
lifeboat

шлю́х|а, и *f.* (vulg.) tart

шля́п|а, ы *f.* hat; **де́ло в ~е** (infml) it's in
the bag

Ш

шля́пк|а, и *f.* **1** (*woman's*) hat **2** (*гвоздя*) head (*of nail, etc.*)

шля́|ться, юсь *impf.* (infml) to loaf about

шмел|ь, я́ *m.* bumblebee

шмо́т|ки, ок (*no sg.*) (infml) clothes

шмы́г|ать, аю (*of* ▸ **шмыгну́ть 1**) (infml) **1** (+ *i.*) (*ногами, туфлями*) to scrape; (*щёткой*) to brush; **ш. но́сом** to sniff **2** (*быстро двигаться*) to rush around; to scurry

шмыг|ну́ть, ну́, нёшь *pf.* (infml) **1** *inst. pf. of* ▸ **шмыга́ть 2** (*быстро убежать*) to dart, nip, sneak (*in order to escape notice*)

шни́цел|ь, я *m.* (cul.) schnitzel

шнур, а́ *m.* **1** (*верёвка*) cord; lace **2** (elec.) flex, cable

шнур|ова́ть, у́ю *impf.* (*of* ▸ **зашнурова́ть**) (*ботинки*) to lace up

шнур|о́к, ка́ *m.* lace

шныр|я́ть, я́ю *impf.* (infml) to dart about

шов, шва *m.* **1** (*швейный*) seam; **без шва** seamless **2** (*в вышивании*) stitch **3** (*хирургический*) stitch, suture; **наложи́ть, снять швы** to put in, remove stitches **4** (tech., *место соединения*) joint, seam, junction

шовини́зм, а *m.* chauvinism

шовини́ст, а *m.* chauvinist

шовинисти́ческий *adj.* chauvinistic

шовини́ст|ка, ки *f. of* ▸ **шовини́ст**

шок, а *m.* (med., fig.) shock

шоки́р|овать, ую *impf.* to shock

шокола́д, а *m.* chocolate

шокола́дк|а, и *f.* (infml, *плитка шоколада*) bar of chocolate

шокола́дный *adj. of* ▸ **шокола́д**

шо́рох, а *m.* rustle

шо́рт|ы, ~ and ~ов (*no sg.*) shorts

шоссе́ *nt. indecl.* highway; surfaced road

шотла́нд|ец, ца *m.* Scotsman, Scot

Шотла́нди|я, и *f.* Scotland; **Но́вая Ш.** (*провинция Канады*) Nova Scotia

шотла́нд|ка¹, ки *f. of* ▸ **шотла́ндец**

шотла́нд|ка², ки *f.* (text.) tartan, plaid

шотла́ндский *adj.* Scottish, Scots

шо́у *nt. indecl.* show

шо́у-би́знес, а *m.* show business

шофёр, а *m.* driver; (*персональный*) chauffeur

шпа́г|а, и *f.* sword; (sport) épée; **скрести́ть ~и** to cross swords (also fig.)

шпага́т, а *m.* **1** string, cord; (agric.) binder twine **2** (*в гимнастике*) the splits

шпаклёвк|а, и *f.* **1** (*действие*) filling, puttying **2** (*вещество*) putty, filler

шпа́л|а, ы *f.* (rail.) sleeper (BrE), cross tie (AmE)

шпан|а́, ы́ *f.* (infml) hooligan; (*also collect.*) rabble

шпарга́лк|а, и *f.* (infml) crib (sheet), cheat sheet (AmE) (*in school, university*)

шпа́р|ить, ю, ишь *impf.* (infml) **1** (*pf.* **о~**) (*обливать кипятком*) to scald, pour boiling water on **2** (*делать, говорить быстро, энергично*) to do, say, *etc.*, in a rush, energetically

шпа́тел|ь, я *m.* (tech., art) palette knife

шпик, а *m.* (cul.) lard

шпил|ь, я *m.* spire, steeple

шпи́льк|а, и *f.* **1** (*для волос*) hairpin **2** (*каблук*) stiletto

шпина́т, а *m.* spinach

шпио́н, а *m.* spy

шпиона́ж, а *m.* espionage

шпио́н|ить, ю, ишь *impf.* (за + *i.*) to spy (on)

шпио́н|ка, ки *f. of* ▸ **шпио́н**

шпио́нский *adj. of* ▸ **шпио́н**

шпо́р|а, ы *f.* spur

шприц, а *m.* (med.) syringe

шпро́т|ы, ~ and ~ов *f. and m. pl.* (*sg.* **~а, ~ы** *and* **~, ~а**) sprats

шрам, а *m.* scar

шрапне́л|ь, я *f.* shrapnel

Шри-Ланк|а́, й *f.* Sri Lanka

шрифт, а, *pl.* **~ы́** *m.* type, type face; (comput.) font

штаб, а, *pl.* **~ы́** *m.* (mil.) (*лица*) staff; (*место*) headquarters

шта́бел|ь, я, *pl.* **~я́, ~е́й** *m.* stack, pile

штаб-кварти́р|а, ы *f.* (mil.) headquarters

штамп, а *m.* **1** (tech., *форма*) die, mould **2** (*печать*) stamp **3** (fig., pej., *банальность*) cliché, stock phrase

штамп|ова́ть, у́ю *impf.* **1** (tech., *детали*) to punch, press **2** (*документы*) to stamp **3** (fig.) (*стихи*) to churn out; (*решения*) to rubber-stamp

шта́нг|а, и *f.* **1** (sport, *стержень с тяжестями*) weight **2** (sport, *ворот*) goalpost

штангенци́ркул|ь, я *m.* (tech.) sliding callipers, slide gauge

штанги́ст, а *m.* (sport) weightlifter

штан|ы́, о́в (*no sg.*) trousers

штат¹, а *m.* state; **Соединённые Ш~ы Аме́рики** United States of America

штат², а *m.* (*sg. or pl.*) (*сотрудники*) staff

штати́в, а *m.* tripod, base, support, stand

шта́тск|ий *adj.* civilian; (*as m. n.* **ш.**, **~ого**) civilian

ште́мпел|ь, я, *pl.* **~я́** *m.* stamp; **почто́вый ш.** postmark

штепсел|ь, я, *pl.* **~я́** *m.* (elec., *вилка*) plug

штил|ь, я *m.* (naut.) calm

што́па|ть, ю *impf.* (*of* ▸ **зашто́пать**) to darn

што́пор, а *m.* corkscrew

што́р|а, ы *f.* curtain; (*твёрдого материала или поднимаемая вверх*) blind

шторм, а *m.* (naut.) strong gale (*wind force 9*); (infml) gale

шторм́о́вк|а, и *f.* (infml) anorak; parka

штраф, а *m.* fine; **наложи́ть ш.** to impose a fine

штраф|но́й *adj.* **1** *adj. of* ▸ **штраф 2** penal, penalty; **~на́я площа́дка** (sport) penalty area; **ш. уда́р** (sport) penalty kick

ш

штраф|ова́ть, у́ю *impf.* (*of* ▶ оштрафова́ть) to fine

штрих, а́ *m.* **1** (*черта*) stroke (*in drawing*) **2** (fig., *частность*) feature, trait

штрихко́д, а *m.* bar code

шту́к|а, и *f.* **1** (*отдельный предмет*) item, one of a kind (*often not translated*); **по рублю́ ш.** one rouble each; **я возьму́ шесть ~** I'll have six (*of item in question*) **2** (infml, *вещь*) thing

штукату́р, а *m.* plasterer

штукату́р|ить, ю, ишь *impf.* (*of* ▶ оштукату́рить) to plaster

штукату́рк|а, и *f.* **1** (*действие*) plastering **2** (*раствор, слой раствора*) plaster

штурва́л, а *m.* steering wheel; controls; **стоя́ть за ~ом** to be at the wheel, helm, controls

штурм, а *m.* (mil.) storm, assault

штурман, а *m.* (naut., aeron.) navigator

штурм|ова́ть, у́ю *impf.* to storm, assault

штык, а́ *m.* bayonet; **встре́тить, приня́ть в ~и́** (fig.) to give a hostile reception (to), oppose adamantly

штыр|ь, я́ *m.* (tech.) pin, dowel

шу́б|а, ы *f.* fur coat

шу́лер, а, *pl.* ~а́ *m.* card sharper, cheat

шум, а (у) *m.* **1** (*звуки*) noise **2** (infml, *брань, скандал*) din, uproar, racket; **подня́ть ш.** to kick up a racket **3** (fig., *оживлённое обсуждение*) sensation, stir

шум|е́ть, лю́, и́шь *impf.* **1** (*издавать шум*) to make a noise **2** (infml, *брани́ться*,

крича́ть) to row **3** (fig., *оживлённо обсужда́ть*) to create a stir, fuss, sensation

шу́м|ный, ~ен, ~на́, ~но, ~ны́ *adj.* **1** noisy; loud **2** (fig.) sensational

шумо́вк|а, и *f.* (cul.) perforated spoon, straining ladle

шу́рин, а *m.* brother-in-law (*wife's brother*)

шуру́п, а *m.* (tech.) screw

шурш|а́ть, у́, и́шь *impf.* to rustle (*also + i., trans.*)

шу́ст|рый, ~ёр, ~ра́, ~ро, ~ры́ *adj.* (infml) smart, bright, sharp

шут, а́ *m.* **1** (hist., *при дворе́*) fool, jester **2** (fig., infml, *пая́ц*) fool, buffoon, clown

шу|ти́ть, чу́, ~тишь *impf.* (*of* ▶ пошути́ть) **1** to joke, jest; **я же не ~чу́** but I'm not joking **2** (**с** + *i.*) (*несерьёзно относи́ться*) to play (with), trifle (with); **ш. с огнём** to play with fire **3** (**над** + *i.*) (*смея́ться*) to laugh (at), make fun (of)

шу́тк|а, и *f.* joke, jest; **не ш.** it's no joke; **с ней ~и пло́хи** she is not to be trifled with; **без шу́ток** joking apart; **сказа́ть в ~у** to say as a joke; **не на ~у** in earnest

шутли́в|ый, ~, ~а *adj.* **1** (*челове́к, хара́ктер*) jokey **2** (*тон, замеча́ние*) joking, light-hearted; (*расска́з, пе́сня*) humorous

шутни́к, а́ *m.* joker

шушу́ка|ться, юсь *impf.* (infml) to whisper; (fig.) to gossip

шху́н|а, ы *f.* schooner

Щщ

ща|ди́ть, жу́, ди́шь *impf.* (*of* ▶ пощади́ть) to spare

ще́б|ень, ня *m.* crushed stone, ballast (*as road surfacing*)

щебе|та́ть, чу́, ~чешь *impf.* to twitter, chirp

щегольну́ть, у́, ёшь *inst. pf. of* ▶ щеголя́ть 2

щегол|я́ть, я́ю *impf.* (infml) **1** (**в** + *p.*) (*в но́вом пла́тье*) to strut around in; to sport **2** (*pf.* ~ьну́ть) (+ *i.*) (*свои́ми зна́ниями*) to show off, parade, flaunt

ще́дрост|ь, и *f.* generosity

ще́др|ый, ~, ~а́, ~о, ~ы́ *adj.* generous; (**на** + *a.*) generous/lavish with

щек|а́, и́, *a.* ~у/~у́, *pl.* ~и, ~, ~а́м *f.* cheek; **уда́рить кого́-н. по ~е́** to slap sb's face

щеко́лд|а, ы *f.* latch; catch

щеко|та́ть, чу́, ~чешь *impf.* (*of* ▶ пощекота́ть) **1** to tickle (*also fig.*) **2** (*impers.*): **у меня́ в го́рле** *и т. п.* ~чет I have a tickle in my throat, *etc.*

щеко́тк|а, и *f.* tickling; **боя́ться ~и** to be ticklish

щекотли́в|ый, ~, ~а *adj.* delicate, sensitive; ~ая те́ма delicate subject

щеко́тно *as pred.* (*impers. + d.*) it tickles

щёлк|ать, аю *impf.* (*of* ▶ щёлкнуть) **1** (*челове́ка, по лбу́ и т. п.*) to flick **2** (+ *i.*) (*производи́ть звук*) to click, snap, crack; (comput.) to click; **два́жды щ.** to double-click **3** (*impf. only*) (*оре́хи*) to crack

щёлк|нуть, ну, нешь *inst. pf. of* ▶ щёлкать 1, ▶ щёлкать 2

щелочно́й *adj.* (chem.) alkaline

щёлоч|ь, и, *pl.* ~и, щелоче́й *f.* (chem.) alkali

♂ key word

щелч|о́к, ка́ *m.* flick (of the fingers); (comput., *мышью*) click; **двойно́й щ.** double click

щел|ь, и, *pl.* **~и, ~е́й** *f.* crack; chink; slit; (*в игровом, торговом автомате*) slot

щен|о́к, ка́ *m.* puppy, pup (also fig.); whelp, cub

щепети́л|ьный, ~ен, ~ьна *adj.* **1** (*человек*) punctilious; (over)scrupulous **2** (*вопрос*) delicate

ще́пк|а, и *f.* splinter, chip (*of wood*); (*collect.*) kindling

щепо́т|ка, ки *f.* pinch (*of salt, snuff, etc.*)

щети́н|а, ы *f.* bristle; (infml, *борода*) stubble

щети́н|иться, юсь, ишься *impf. of* ▶ **ощети́ниться**

щётк|а, и *f.* brush; **зубна́я щ.** toothbrush; **щ. для воло́с** hairbrush

щи, щей, щам, ща́ми, о щах (*no sg.*) shchi (*cabbage soup*)

щи́колотк|а, и *f.* ankle

щип|а́ть, лю́, ~лешь *impf.* **1** (*pf.* **ущипну́ть**) (*зацемлять до боли*) to pinch, nip, tweak **2** (*impf. only*) (*о морозе*) to sting, bite; (*о горчице*) to burn **3** (*pf.* **о~**) (*птицу*) to pluck

щипц|ы́, о́в (*no sg.*) (*каминные*) tongs; (tech.) pincers; (*плоскогубцы*) pliers; (*хирургические*) forceps

щи́пчик|и, ов (*no sg.*) tweezers

щит, а́ *m.* **1** shield; **живо́й щ.** human shield **2** (*ограждение*) shield, screen **3** (*рекламный*) (display) board **4** (tech., *пульт*) panel (*see also* ▶ **распредели́тельный**)

щитови́дн|ый *adj.* (anat.): **~ая железа́** thyroid gland

щит|о́к, ка́ *m.* **1** *dim. of* ▶ **щит 2**, ▶ **щит 3**, ▶ **щит 4**; (*у машины*) dashboard **2** (sport) shin pad **3** (elec.) *see* ▶ **распредели́тельный**

щу́к|а, и *f.* pike (*fish*)

щу́пальце, а, *g. pl.* **щу́палец** *nt.* (zool.) tentacle; antenna

щу́па|ть, ю *impf.* (*of* ▶ **пощу́пать**) to feel (for), touch; (fig., infml) to size up, suss out; **щ. пульс** (med.) to feel the pulse

щу́пл|ый, ~, ~а́, ~о *adj.* weak, puny, frail

щу́р|иться, юсь, ишься *impf.* to screw up one's eyes, squint

Ээ

эвакуа́ци|я, и *f.* evacuation

эвакуи́р|овать, ую *impf. and pf.* to evacuate (*trans.*)

эвакуи́р|оваться, уюсь *impf. and pf.* to be evacuated

Эвере́ст, а *m.* (Mt) Everest

эвкали́пт, а *m.* (bot.) eucalyptus

ЭВМ *f. indecl.* (*abbr. of* **электро́нно-вычисли́тельная маши́на**) computer

эволю́ци|я, и *f.* evolution

эвтана́зи|я, и *f.* euthanasia

эвфеми́зм, а *m.* euphemism

эги́д|а, ы *f.* aegis; **под ~ой** (+ *g.*) under the aegis (of)

эгои́зм, а *m.* egoism, selfishness

эгои́ст, а *m.* egoist

эгоисти́ческий *adj.* egoistic, selfish

эгоисти́ч|ный, ~ен, ~на *adj.* = эгоисти́ческий

эгои́ст|ка, ки *f. of* ▶ **эгои́ст**

эгоцентри́ч|ный, ~ен, ~на *adj.* egocentric

Эдинбу́рг, а *m.* Edinburgh

эй *int.* hey!

эйфори́|я, и *f.* euphoria

Эквадо́р, а *m.* Ecuador

эквадо́р|ец, ца *m.* Ecuadorean

эквадо́р|ка, ки *f. of* ▶ **эквадо́рец**

эквадо́рский *adj.* Ecuadorean

эква́тор, а *m.* equator

эквивале́нт, а *m.* equivalent

эквивале́нт|ный, ~ен, ~на *adj.* equivalent

экза́мен, а *m.* examination; **сдава́ть э.** to take, sit an examination; **сдать э.** to pass an examination; **провали́ться на ~е** to fail an examination; **э. на води́тельские права́** driving test

экзамена́тор, а *m.* examiner

экзаменацио́нн|ый *adj. of* ▶ **экза́мен**; **э. биле́т** examination paper; **~ая се́ссия** examination period, exams

экзамен|ова́ть, у́ю *impf.* (*of* ▶ **проэкзаменова́ть**) to examine

экзе́м|а, а *f.* (med.) eczema

экземпля́|р, а *m.* **1** copy; **переписа́ть в двух ~ах** to make two copies **2** (*животного, растения*) specimen, example

экзистенциали́зм, а *m.* existentialism

экзистенциа́льный *adj.* existential

экзо́тик|а, и *f.* exotica, exotic objects

экзоти́ческий *adj.* exotic

экипа́ж[1], а *m.* (*повозка*) carriage

экипа́ж[2], а *m.* (*команда*) crew (*of ship, aircraft, tank*)

экипиро́вк|а, и *f.* **1** (*действие*) equipping **2** (*снаряжение*) equipment

эклекти́ч|ный, ~ен, ~на *adj.* eclectic

эко́лог, а *m.* ecologist

✓ **экологи́ческий** *adj.* ecological

эколо́ги|я, и *f.* ecology

✓ **эконо́мик|а, и** *f.* **1** (*наука*) economics **2** (*страны*) economy; **ры́ночная э.** market economy

экономи́ст, а *m.* economist

эконо́м|ить, лю, ишь *impf.* (*of* ▸ **сэконо́мить**) **1** (*деньги, силы*) to use sparingly; to save **2** (**на** + *p.*) to economize (on), save (on)

✓ **экономи́ческий** *adj.* economic

экономи́ч|ный, ~ен, ~на *adj.* economical

эконо́ми|я, и *f.* **1** economy, saving **2**: **полити́ческая э.** political economy

эконо́м|ный, ~ен, ~на *adj.* economical; careful, thrifty

экосисте́м|а, ы *f.* ecosystem

экотури́зм, а *m.* ecotourism

экотури́ст, а *m.* ecotourist

✓ **экра́н, а** *m.* **1** (cin., TV, comput.) screen **2** (fig., *киноискусство*) screen **3** (phys., tech.) screen, shield, shade

экраниза́ци|я, и *f.* (cin.) filming, screening; (*романа*) film adaptation

экс-... *pref.* ex-

экскава́тор, а *m.* (tech.) excavator, mechanical digger

эксклюзи́в|ный, ~ен, ~на *adj.* exclusive

экскреме́нт|ы, ов (*no sg.*) excrement

экску́рси|я, и *f.* excursion, (conducted) tour, trip

экскурсово́д, а *m.* guide

экспанси́в|ный, ~ен, ~на *adj.* effusive

экспа́нси|я, и *f.* (pol.) expansion

экспатриа́нт, а *m.* expatriate

экспатриа́нт|ка, ки *f. of* ▸ **экспатриа́нт**

экспеди́тор, а *m.* forwarding agent, shipping clerk

экспеди́ци|я, и *f.* **1** (*действие*) dispatch, forwarding **2** (*поездка; участники этой поездки*) expedition

экспериме́нт, а *m.* experiment

эксперимента́льный *adj.* experimental

эксперимента́тор, а *m.* experimenter

эксперименти́р|овать, ую *impf.* (**над, с** + *i.*) to experiment (on, with)

✓ **экспе́рт, а** *m.* expert

эксперти́з|а, ы *f.* (law, med.) (expert) examination, expert opinion; **произвести́ ~у** to make an examination

экспе́рт|ный *adj. of* ▸ **экспе́рт**; **~ная коми́ссия** commission of experts

✓ **эксплуата́ци|я, и** *f.* **1** (pol., pej.) exploitation **2** (*природных богатств*) exploitation; (*средств производства*) utilization; (*машин*) operation, running; **сдать в ~ю**

to commission, put into operation

эксплуати́р|овать, ую *impf.* **1** (pol., pej.) to exploit **2** (*природные богатства*) to exploit; (*машины*) to operate, run, work

экспози́ци|я, и *f.* **1** (*музейная*) display **2** (liter., mus.) exposition **3** (phot.) exposure

экспона́т, а *m.* exhibit

экспони́р|овать, ую *impf. and pf.* (*для обозрения*) to exhibit

э́кспорт, а *m.* export

экспортёр, а *m.* exporter

экспорти́р|овать, ую *impf. and pf.* to export

э́кспортный *adj. of* ▸ **э́кспорт**

экспре́сс, а *m.* express (*train, motor coach, etc.*)

экспресси́в|ный, ~ен, ~на *adj.* expressive

экспрессиони́зм, а *m.* expressionism

экспрессиони́ст, а *m.* expressionist

экспре́сси|я, и *f.* expression

экспро́мт, а *m.* improvisation; (mus.) impromptu

экста́з, а *m.* ecstasy

э́кстези *m. indecl.* (sl.) ecstasy (*the drug*)

экстенси́в|ный, ~ен, ~на *adj.* extensive

экстерн, а *m.* external student; **око́нчить университе́т ~ом** to take an external degree

экстравага́нт|ный, ~ен, ~на *adj.* eccentric, bizarre

экстраве́рт, а *m.* extrovert

экстради́ци|я, и *f.* (law) extradition

экстраордина́р|ный, ~ен, ~на *adj.* extraordinary

экстрасе́нс, а *m.* psychic

экстрема́л|ьный, ~ен, ~ьна *adj.* extreme

экстреми́зм, а *m.* extremism

экстреми́ст, а *m.* extremist

экстреми́стский *adj.* extremist

э́крен|ный, ~, ~на *adj.* **1** (*срочный*) urgent; emergency; **э. вы́зов** urgent summons; **в ~ном слу́чае** in case of emergency **2** (*чрезвычайный*) extra, special; **~ное заседа́ние** extraordinary session

эксцентри́ч|ный, ~ен, ~на *adj.* eccentric

эласти́ч|ный, ~ен, ~на *adj.* elastic (also fig.); **~ные брю́ки** stretch trousers

элева́тор, а *m.* **1** (agric.) grain store (BrE), elevator (AmE) **2** (tech.) hoist

элега́нт|ный, ~ен, ~на *adj.* elegant, smart

электора́т, а *m.* electorate

эле́ктрик, а *m.* electrician

✓ **электри́ческий** *adj.* electric(al)

электри́честв|о, а *nt.* **1** electricity **2** (*освещение*) electric light; **заже́чь э.** to turn on the light

электри́чк|а, и *f.* (infml) (suburban) electric train

электрово́з, а *m.* electric locomotive

электрогита́р|а, ы *f.* electric guitar

электродви́гател|ь, я *m.* electric motor

электромонтёр, а *m.* electrician

электро́н, а *m.* (phys.) electron

✓ key word

электро́ник|а, и *f.* electronics
ℰ **электро́н|ный** *adj.* **1** *adj. of* ▶ **электро́н; э. микроско́п** electron microscope **2** electronic; **∼ная по́чта** electronic mail, email (*the system*); **∼ное письмо́** email (letter); **э. а́дрес** email address; **∼ная табли́ца** spreadsheet
электропо́езд, а *m.* electric train
электроприбо́р, а *m.* electrical appliance
электропрово́дк|а, и *f.* electric wiring
электроста́нци|я, и *f.* power station
электроте́хник, а *m.* electrical engineer
электроэне́рги|я, и *f.* electric power
ℰ **элеме́нт, а** *m.* **1** (*компонент, доля*) element; **э. изображе́ния** (comput.) pixel **2** (chem.) element
элемента́р|ный, ∼ен, ∼на *adj.* elementary
эли́т|а, ы *f.* elite
элита́р|ный, ∼ен, ∼на *adj.* elite; (pej.) elitist
эли́тный *adj.* best-quality
эльф, а *m.* elf
эмалиро́ванн|ый *adj.* enamelled (BrE), enameled (AmE); **∼ая посу́да** enamel ware
эма́л|ь, и *f.* enamel
эмансипа́ци|я, и *f.* (also law) emancipation
эмба́рго *nt. indecl.* (econ.) embargo
эмбле́м|а, ы *f.* emblem; (mil.) insignia
эмбрио́н, а *m.* (biol.) embryo
эмигра́нт, а *m.* émigré, emigrant
эмигра́нт|ка, ки *f. of* ▶ **эмигра́нт**
эмигра́ци|я, и *f.* **1** emigration **2** (*collect.*) emigration, émigrés
эмигри́р|овать, ую *impf. and pf.* to emigrate
эмо́тикон, а *m.* emoticon
эмоциона́л|ьный, ∼ен, ∼ьна *adj.* emotional
эмо́ци|я, и *f.* emotion
эмпири́ческий *adj.* empirical
эму́льси|я, и *f.* emulsion
энерге́тик, а *m.* energy specialist
энерге́тик|а, и *f.* energy sector (of the economy), power industry
энергети́ческий *adj. of* ▶ **энерге́тика; э. напи́ток** energy drink
энерги́ч|ный, ∼ен, ∼на *adj.* energetic, vigorous, forceful
ℰ **эне́рги|я, и** *f.* **1** (phys.) energy; power; **затра́та ∼и** energy consumption **2** (fig.) energy; vigour (BrE), vigor (AmE), effort
энергосисте́м|а, ы *f.* power (supply) system
энтомо́лог, а *m.* entomologist
энтомоло́ги|я, и *f.* entomology
энтузиа́зм, а *m.* enthusiasm
энтузиа́ст, а *m.* (+ *g.*) enthusiast (about, for), devotee (of)
энциклопе́ди|я, и *f.* encyclopedia
эпиде́ми|я, и *f.* epidemic
эпизо́д, а *m.* episode
эпизоди́ческий *adj.* episodic; occasional, sporadic
эпиле́пси|я, и *f.* epilepsy

эпиле́птик, а *m.* epileptic
эпилепти́ческий *adj.* epileptic
эпило́г, а *m.* epilogue (BrE), epilog (AmE)
эпита́фи|я, и *f.* epitaph
эпи́тет, а *m.* epithet
эпопе́|я, и *f.* epic
э́пос, а *m.* epic literature
ℰ **эпо́х|а, и** *f.* epoch, age, era
э́р|а, ы *f.* era; **до на́шей ∼ы** BC (*before Christ*); **на́шей ∼ы** AD (*Anno Domini*)
эргономи́ч|ный, ∼ен, ∼на *adj.* ergonomic
эре́кци|я, и *f.* (physiol.) erection
эрза́ц, а *m.* ersatz, substitute
Эритре́|я, и *f.* Eritrea
эритроци́т, а *m.* (physiol.) erythrocyte, red corpuscle
эро́зи|я, и *f.* erosion
эро́тик|а, и *f.* **1** (*чувственность*) sensuality **2** (*collect.*) (*искусство*) erotica
эроти́ческий *adj.* erotic, sensual
Эр-Рия́д, а *m.* Riyadh
эруди́рован|ный, ∼, ∼на *adj.* erudite
эруди́ци|я, и *f.* erudition
эскадри́л|ья, ьи, *g. pl.* **∼ий** *f.* (aeron.) squadron
эскадро́н, а *m.* (mil.) squadron
эскала́тор, а *m.* escalator
эскало́п, а *m.* (cul.) escalope
эски́з, а *m.* (*к карти́не*) sketch, study; (*чертёж*) draft, outline
эскимо́с, а *m.* Eskimo, Inuit
эскимо́с|ка, ки *f. of* ▶ **эскимо́с**
эскимо́сский *adj.* Eskimo, Inuit
эско́рт, а *m.* (mil.) escort
эссе́ *nt. indecl.* essay
эссе́нци|я, и *f.* essence
эстака́д|а, ы *f.* **1** (*на желе́зной доро́ге*) viaduct **2** (*на шоссе́*) flyover (BrE), overpass
эстафе́т|а, ы *f.* **1** (sport) relay race **2** (*па́лочка*) baton (*in relay race*)
эсте́т, а *m.* aesthete
эсте́тик|а, и *f.* **1** aesthetics **2** (*худо́жественность*) design
эстети́ческий *adj.* aesthetic
эстети́ч|ный, ∼ен, ∼на *adj.* aesthetic
эсто́н|ец, ца *m.* Estonian
Эсто́ни|я, и *f.* Estonia
эсто́н|ка, ки *f. of* ▶ **эсто́нец**
эсто́нский *adj.* Estonian
эстра́д|а, ы *f.* **1** stage, platform; **вы́йти на ∼у** to come on stage **2** (*представле́ние*) variety; **арти́ст ∼ы** variety performer, artiste
эстра́д|ный *adj. of* ▶ **эстра́да; э. конце́рт** variety show; **∼ная му́зыка** popular music
ℰ **эта́ж, а́** *m.* storey (BrE), story (AmE), floor; **пе́рвый, второ́й** *и т. п.* **э.** ground floor, first floor, *etc.* (BrE); first floor, second floor, *etc.* (AmE)
этало́н, а *m.* standard (*of weights and measures*); (fig., *мери́ло*) benchmark

э

⚔ **эта́п**, а *m.* stage, phase
э́тик|а, и *f.* ethics
этике́т, а *m.* etiquette
этике́тк|а, и *f.* label
этимоло́ги|я, и *f.* etymology
эти́ч|ный, ~ен, ~на *adj.* ethical
этни́ческий *adj.* ethnic
этнографи́ческий *adj.* ethnographic(al)
этногра́фи|я, и *f.* ethnography, social anthropology
э́то¹ *see* ▶ э́тот
э́то² *emph. particle* (infml): куда́ э. он де́лся? wherever has he got to?; э. *вы* спра́шивали? was it *you* who was asking?
⚔ **э́то³** *pron.* (*as n.*) this (is), that (is); э. наш дом this is our house; э. ве́рно that is true; не в ~м де́ло that's not the point
⚔ **э́тот, э́та, э́то**, *pl.* **э́ти** *pron.* this (these); (*as n.*) this one; (*после́днее из на́званных лиц*) the latter
этю́д, а *m.* 1 (art, liter.) study, sketch 2 (mus., *произведе́ние*) étude 3 (mus., *упражне́ние*)

exercise
эфе́с, а *m.* hilt, handle (*of sword, sabre, etc.*)
эфио́п, а *m.* Ethiopian
Эфио́пи|я, и *f.* Ethiopia
эфио́п|ка, ки *f. of* ▶ эфио́п
эфио́пский *adj.* Ethiopian
эфи́р, а *m.* 1 ether; (fig.) air; прямо́й э. live broadcast 2 (chem.) ether
⚔ **эффе́кт**, а *m.* 1 effect, impact; произвести́ э. (на + *a.*) to have an effect (on), make an impression (on) 2 (econ.) result, consequences 3 (*in pl.*) (theatr.) effects; шумовы́е ~ы sound effects
⚔ **эффекти́вность**, и *f.* effectiveness
⚔ **эффекти́в|ный**, ~ен, ~на *adj.* effective
эффе́кт|ный, ~ен, ~на *adj.* effective, striking; eye-catching
э́х|о, а *nt.* echo
эшело́н, а *m.* 1 (mil.) echelon 2 (*поезд*) special train
эякуля́ци|я, и *f.* (physiol.) ejaculation

Юю

юа́н|ь, я *m.* yuan (*Chinese currency unit*)
ЮАР *f. indecl.* (*abbr. of* **Ю́жно-Африка́нская Респу́блика**) RSA (Republic of South Africa)
юбиле́|й, я *m.* 1 (*годовщи́на*) anniversary; jubilee 2 (*пра́зднование*) anniversary celebrations
ю́бк|а, и *f.* skirt; шотла́ндская ю. kilt; ю.-брю́ки culottes; держа́ться за чью-н. ~у to cling to sb's apron strings
ювели́р, а *m.* jeweller (BrE), jeweler (AmE)
ювели́р|ный 1 *adj. of* ▶ ювели́р; ~ные изде́лия jewellery (BrE), jewelry (AmE); ю. магази́н jeweller's (BrE), jeweler's (AmE) 2 (fig., *тща́тельный*) fine, intricate
юг, а *m.* south; the South (*of Russia, etc.*); на ю́ге in the south; к ю́гу от to the south of
ю́го-восто́к, а *m.* south-east
ю́го-восто́чный *adj.* south-east(ern)
ю́го-за́пад, а *m.* south-west
ю́го-за́падный *adj.* south-west(ern)
Югосла́ви|я, и *f.* (hist.) Yugoslavia
югосла́вский *adj.* (hist.) Yugoslav(ian)
южа́н|ин, ина, *pl.* ~е, ~ *m.* southerner
южа́н|ка, ки *f. of* ▶ южа́нин
южне́е *comp. of* ▶ ю́жный; ю. Ло́ндона (to the) south of London

южноамерика́н|ец, ца *m.* South American
южноамерика́н|ка, ки *f. of* ▶ южноамерика́нец
южноамерика́нский *adj.* South American
южноафрика́н|ец, ца *m.* South African
южноафрика́н|ка, ки *f. of* ▶ южноафрика́нец
южноафрика́нский *adj.* South African
⚔ **ю́жный** *adj.* south, southern; Ю́жная Аме́рика South America; Ю́жная А́фрика (*госуда́рство*) South Africa; Ю. по́люс South Pole
юл|а́, ы́ top (*child's toy*)
юл|и́ть, ю́, и́шь *impf.* (infml) 1 (*суети́ться*) to fuss, fidget 2 (*пе́ред* + *i.*) (*лебези́ть*) to play up (to)
ю́мор, а *m.* humour (BrE), humor (AmE); чу́вство ~а a sense of humour (BrE), humor (AmE)
юмори́ст, а *m.* humorist
юмористи́ческий *adj.* humorous, comic, funny
юмори́ст|ка, ки *f. of* ▶ юмори́ст
ю́нг|а, и *m.* cabin boy; sea cadet
ЮНЕ́СКО *f. indecl.* UNESCO (*abbr. of United Nations Educational, Scientific and Cultural Organization* — Организа́ция Объединённых На́ций по вопро́сам образова́ния, нау́ки и культу́ры)
юн|е́ц, ца́ *m.* (infml) youth

⚔ key word

юниóр, а *m.* (sport) junior
юниóр|ка, ки *f. of* ▶ **юниóр**
ю́ност|ь, и *f.* youth (*age*)
ю́нош|а, и *m.* youth (*person*)
ю́ношеский *adj.* youthful
ю́н|ый, ~, ~á, ~о *adj.* **1** young **2** (*свойственный молодости*) youthful
юпи́тер, а *m.* (*осветительный прибор*) floodlight
юриди́ческ|ий *adj.* legal; **~ое лицó** corporation
юрисди́кци|я, и *f.* jurisdiction
юриспрудéнци|я, и *f.* jurisprudence, law (*as academic discipline*)
юри́ст, а *m.* legal expert, lawyer
ю́р|кий, ~ок, ~кá, ~ко *adj.* quick-moving, brisk
ю́ркн|у́ть, у, ешь *or* **ý, ёшь** *pf.* to scamper away, dart away, plunge
юрóдив|ый *adj.* **1** crazy, simple, touched **2** (*as m. n.* **ю., ~ого**) holy fool (*person with mental disability, etc., believed to possess divine gift of prophecy*)
ю́рт|а, ы *f.* yurt (*nomad's tent in Central Asia*)
юсти́ци|я, и *f.* justice
ю|ти́ться, чýсь, ти́шься *impf.* to huddle (together); (*иметь пристанище*) to take shelter

Яя

я, меня́, мне, мной мнóю, обо мне 1 *pers. pron.* I (me) **2** *n.; nt. indecl.* the self, the ego; **вторóе я** alter ego
я́бед|а, ы *f. and c.g.* **1** (*f.*) (obs., *клевета*) slander **2** (*c.g.*) (infml) informer, telltale (BrE)
я́блок|о, а, *pl.* **~и, ~** *nt.* apple; **глазнóе я.** eyeball
я́блон|я, и *f.* apple tree
я́блочк|о, а *nt.* **1** *dim. of* ▶ **я́блоко 2** (*на мишени*) bull's eye
я́блочный *adj. of* ▶ **я́блоко**
яв|и́ться, лю́сь, ~ишься *pf.* (*of* ▶ **явля́ться 1**) **1** (*прийти по вызову*) to appear, present oneself; to report; **я. в суд** to appear before the court; **я. на слýжбу** to report for duty **2** (*прибыть*) to turn up, arrive, show up
явлéни|е, я *nt.* **1** phenomenon; (*событие*) occurrence; **прирóдное я.** natural phenomenon **2** (theatr.) scene
явля́|ться, юсь *impf.* **1** *impf. of* ▶ **яви́ться 2** (*impf. only*) (+ *i.*) (*быть*) to be; to represent
я́вно[1] *adv.* manifestly, patently; obviously
я́вно[2] *as pred.* it is manifest, patent; it is obvious
я́в|ный, ~ен, ~на *adj.* **1** (*открытый*) manifest, patent; overt **2** (*очевидный*) obvious
я́вор, а *m.* sycamore (*tree*)
я́面ствен|ный, ~, ~на *adj.* clear, distinct
ягн|ёнок, ёнка, *pl.* **~я́та, ~я́т** *m.* lamb
я́год|а, ы *f.* berry; (*collect.*) soft fruit; **пойти́ по ~ы** to go berry-picking
я́годиц|а, ы *f.* buttock
ягуáр, а *m.* jaguar
яд, а (у) *m.* poison; venom (also fig.)
я́дерный *adj.* (phys.) nuclear; **я. реáктор** nuclear reactor
ядови́т|ый, ~, ~а *adj.* **1** poisonous; toxic; **я. газ** poison gas; **~ая змея́** poisonous snake **2** (fig., *человек, замечание*) venomous
ядр|ó, á, *pl.* **~́а, я́дер, ~́ам** *nt.* **1** (*ореха*) kernel; (*Земли*) core **2** (phys., biol.) nucleus **3** (*основная группа*) main body (*of a unit, group*) **4** (hist., mil.) ball, shot **5** (sport) shot; **толкáние ~á** putting the shot
я́зв|а, ы *f.* **1** ulcer, sore; **я. желýдка** stomach ulcer **2** (fig., *вред*) plague, curse
язви́тел|ьный, ~ен, ~ьна *adj.* caustic, biting, sarcastic
язы́к[1], á, *pl.* **~и́** *m.* **1** (anat.) tongue; **держáть я. за зубáми, придержáть я.** to hold one's tongue **2** (cul.) tongue; **копчёный я.** smoked tongue
язы́к[2], á, *pl.* **~и́,** *m.* (*речь*) language (also fig.); **владéть мнóгими ~áми** to know many languages
языковéд, а *m.* linguist
языковóй *adj.* linguistic
языкознáни|е, я *nt.* linguistics
язы́ческий *adj.* heathen, pagan
язы́чник, а *m.* heathen, pagan
язы́чни|ца, цы *f. of* ▶ **язы́чник**
яи́чк|о, а, *pl.* **~и** *nt.* (anat.) testicle
яи́чник, а *m.* (anat.) ovary
яи́чниц|а, ы and **яи́чница-глазýнья** *f.* (cul.) fried eggs; **я.-болтýнья** scrambled eggs
яи́чный *adj. of* ▶ **яйцó; я. белóк** white of eggs; **я. желтóк** yolk of egg
яйц|ó, á, *pl.* **~́а, яи́ц, ~́ам** *nt.* **1** egg; (biol.) ovum; **нести́ ~́а** to lay eggs; **я. вкрутýю** hard-boiled egg **2** (*in pl.*) (infml, *у мужчины*)

balls, nuts (= *testicles*)

я́кобы 1 *conj.* (*что*) that (*expr. doubt about validity of another's statement*); **говоря́т, я. он у́мер** they say (= *they claim*) that he has died **2** *particle* (*мнимо*) supposedly, allegedly; **мы посмотре́ли э́ту я. стра́шную карти́ну** we have seen this supposedly terrifying film

я́кор|ь, я, *pl.* ∼**я́,** ∼**е́й** *m.* (naut.) anchor; **стать на я.** to anchor; **бро́сить я.** to cast, drop anchor

яку́т, а *m.* Yakut

яку́т|ка, ки *f.* of ▸ **яку́т**

яку́тский *adj.* Yakut

якша́|ться, юсь *impf.* (с + i.) (infml) to consort (with), hobnob (with)

я́лик, а *m.* skiff, dinghy; yawl

я́м|а, ы *f.* **1** pit, hole; **выгребна́я я.** cesspit; **оркестро́вая я.** orchestra pit **2** (infml, *впадина*) hollow

яма́|ец, йца *m.* Jamaican

Яма́йк|а, и *f.* Jamaica; (**я.**) Jamaican woman

яма́йский *adj.* Jamaican; **я. ром** Jamaica rum

я́мк|а, и *f. dim. of* ▸ **я́ма; я. на щека́х** dimple

ямщи́к, а́ *m.* coachman

янва́рский *adj. of* ▸ **янва́рь**

✓ **янва́р|ь, я́** *m.* January

я́нки *m. indecl.* Yank

янта́р|ь, я́ *m.* amber

япо́н|ец, ца *m.* Japanese

Япо́ни|я, и *f.* Japan

япо́н|ка, ки *f. of* ▸ **япо́нец**

✓ **япо́нский** *adj.* Japanese; **я. лак** japan

ярд, а *m.* yard (*measure, = 0.9144 metre*)

✓ **я́р|кий,** ∼**ок,** ∼**ка́,** ∼**ко** *adj.* **1** bright (*of light, colours, etc.*) **2** (fig.) (*впечатляющий*) colourful (BrE), colorful (AmE), striking; (*живой*) vivid, graphic; **я. приме́р** striking example **3** (fig., *блестящий*) brilliant, outstanding; impressive; ∼**кая речь** brilliant speech

я́ркост|ь, и *f.* **1** brightness **2** (fig., *живость*) vividness **3** (*блеск*) brilliance

ярлы́к, а́ *m.* label, tag

я́рмарк|а, и *f.* (trade) fair

ярм|о́, а́, *pl.* ∼**а** *nt.* yoke (also fig.); **сбро́сить с себя́ я.** (fig.) to cast off the yoke

я́рост|ный, ∼**ен,** ∼**на** *adj.* furious, fierce, savage

я́рост|ь, и *f.* fury, rage

я́рус, а *m.* **1** (theatr.) circle **2** (*ряд*) tier

ярча́йший *superl. of* ▸ **я́ркий**

я́рче *comp. of* ▸ **я́ркий**

я́р|ый, ∼, ∼**а** *adj.* **1** furious, raging; violent **2** (*рьяный*) passionate, fervent; **я. сторо́нник/приве́рженец** strong/staunch supporter, stalwart

я́сен|ь, я *m.* ash tree

я́сл|и, ей (*no sg.*) (*детские*) crèche (BrE), day nursery

✓ **я́сно¹** *adv. of* ▸ **я́сный**

я́сно² *as pred.* **1** (*о погоде*) it is fine **2** (fig.) it is clear **3** (*as affirmative particle*) (*да; понял*) yes, of course

яснови́дящ|ий *adj.* (*also as n.* **я.,** *f.* ∼**ая**) clairvoyant

я́сность|ь, и *f.* (*ночи, неба*) clearness; (*солнца, погоды*) brightness; (*звука*) distinctness; (fig., *вопроса*) clarity; (*речи, ума*) lucidity, preciseness; **внести́ я. во что-н.** to clarify sth

я́с|ный, ∼**ен,** ∼**на́,** ∼**но,** ∼**ны** *adj.* **1** (*ночь, небо*) clear; (*солнце, месяц*) bright; (*погода*) fine **2** (*звук, дальний берег*) distinct **3** (*глаза, счастье*) serene **4** (fig., *вопрос, намерение*) clear, plain; ∼**ное де́ло** of course **5** (*ум, изложение*) lucid; precise, logical

я́стреб, а, *pl.* ∼**а́** *and* ∼**ы** *m.* hawk

ятага́н, а *m.* yataghan, scimitar

я́хт|а, ы *f.* yacht

яхтсме́н, а *m.* yachtsman

яхтсме́н|ка, и *f.* yachtswoman

яче́йк|а, и, *g. pl.* **я́чеек** *f.* (biol., pol., comput.) cell

ячме́н|ь¹, я *m.* (*злак*) barley

ячме́н|ь², я *m.* (*на глазу*) sty (*in the eye*)

я́шм|а, ы *f.* (min.) jasper

я́щериц|а, ы *f.* lizard

я́щик, а *m.* **1** box; (*большой*) chest **2** (*выдвижной*) drawer

я́щур, а *m.* (*заболевание скота*) foot-and-mouth disease

✓ key word

Contents

Russian life and culture

автоно́мная о́бласть — autonomous oblast (region) One of the six types of administrative unit into which **Росси́йская Федера́ция** is divided. Of the 83 units, only one is *автоно́мная о́бласть* (the *Jewish Autonomous Oblast*). Like **автоно́мный о́круг, го́род федера́льного значе́ния, край**, and **о́бласть**, this type of unit is not allowed to have its own constitution (Russian *конститу́ция*), unlike the 21 republics. Instead, it has its own charter (Russian *уста́в*). In common with Russia's 82 other constituent units, the single *автоно́мная о́бласть* has its own

legislature. Formerly, there were four more autonomous oblasts on the territory of the modern Russian Federation. In 1991 they all changed their status to that of republic (**респу́блика**).

автоно́мный о́круг — autonomous okrug (district) One of the six types of administrative unit into which **Росси́йская Федера́ция** is divided. Of the 83 units, four are autonomous okrugs (districts). The autonomous okrugs are all located in sparsely populated areas of Siberia and Russia's Far East, where indigenous peoples form a small part of the entire population and Russians usually make up 60–70% of the population.

For more details ▶ **автоно́мная о́бласть**

аттеста́т об основно́м о́бщем образова́нии — basic study course school-leaving certificate A document awarded to students who successfully finish a 9-year course of study at school (without low marks such as 2 (*дво́йка*)) and pass all their final examinations. With this, students can enter any educational institution below the level of a **вуз**.

аттеста́т о сре́днем (по́лном) о́бщем образова́нии — full study course school-leaving certificate A document awarded to students who successfully finish an 11-year course of study at school (without low marks such as 2 (*дво́йка*)) and pass all their final examinations. With this, students can enter a **вуз**.

Бе́лый дом — the White House (*in Moscow*) The generally accepted unofficial name of the seat of the Russian government. *Бе́лый дом* is situated near the centre of Moscow on the left bank of the Moskva River and together with the buildings of the US and UK embassies it forms an equilateral triangle within which the town hall is located.

бли́жнее зарубе́жье (literally 'close foreign countries') — the former Soviet republics The collective unofficial name for all the former Soviet republics, used especially by telephone operators. Outside Russia it is sometimes considered offensive, mainly because translations of the term in European languages are not quite accurate in register.

Вели́кая Оте́чественная война́ (1941–1945) (literally 'the Great Patriotic War') The Soviet name for the Second World War in the context of the Soviet Union's involvement in it.

Восьмо́е ма́рта, 8-е Ма́рта — 8 March Women's day in Russia (men's day is **23-е Февраля́** or **День защи́тника Оте́чества**). It is still sometimes referred to as *Междунаро́дный же́нский день* (since Communist times) but this is much disputed. Men and boys give flowers (especially blossoming branches of mimosa) and other presents to their female relatives and friends of any age.

вуз — institution of higher education Any type of institution of higher education forming part of the Russian educational system, including *университе́т* (university), *акаде́мия* (academy), and *институ́т* (institute/college). The word *вуз* is an abbreviation of *вы́сшее уче́бное заведе́ние*.

Геро́й Росси́йской Федера́ции — Hero of the Russian Federation The highest honorary title in Russia, awarded for heroic deeds. Holders of this title receive a medal *Золота́я звезда́ Геро́я Росси́йской Федера́ции* (Gold Star of the Hero of the Russian Federation), the highest government award of the Russian Federation.

го́род федера́льного значе́ния — city with federal status One of the six types of administrative unit into which **Росси́йская Федера́ция** is divided. Of the 83 units, two are cities with federal status, *Moscow* and *St Petersburg*.

    For more details ▶ **автоно́мная о́бласть**

Госуда́рственная ду́ма — the State Duma The lower house of **Федера́льное Собра́ние Росси́йской Федера́ции** (the bicameral parliament of the Russian Federation). *Госуда́рственная ду́ма* has 450 members serving four-year terms.

Два́дцать тре́тье февраля́, 23-е Февраля́ ▶ **День защи́тника Оте́чества**

День защи́тника Оте́чества, 23-е Февраля́ — Day of the Defender of the Fatherland, 23 February Men's day in Russia, similar to **Восьмо́е ма́рта** for women. It is a national holiday for everyone although, nominally, it is a holiday for military men only. Women and girls give

Culture

presents to their male relatives or friends of any age, whether they serve or have served in the Soviet/Russian forces or not.

День Побе́ды — Victory Day (*in the Second World War*) VE Day as celebrated in Russia and some other former Soviet republics on 9 May. It is a national holiday in Russia. The date of 9 May (one day later than in western Europe) results from difference in time zones between Russia and western Europe. *День Побе́ды* is undoubtedly the most respected date in Russian history.

дипло́м о вы́сшем образова́нии — college/university degree certificate A document verifying that a student has graduated from a university or college. In order to qualify for this, students must pass their final exams (*госуда́рственные экза́мены*) and complete and defend a dissertation (*дипло́мная рабо́та*).

край — krai (territory) One of the six types of administrative unit into which **Росси́йская Федера́ция** is divided. Of the 83 units, nine are krais (territories). They were originally (and now they are once more) border areas of Russia (Russian *окра́ины* (sg. *окра́ина*) and *край* having the same stem).
For more details ▶ **автоно́мная о́бласть**

мат — foul language This includes the words *еба́ть*, *хуй*, *пизда́*, and *блядь* (see the main Dictionary text) and all their numerous derivatives. In informal situations, these taboo words are very common among people of low social status, whereas cultured, well-educated, and well-brought-up people (almost) never use them. Traditionally, it is considered unacceptable to utter any of the four words of *мат* in front of women or children, and using *мат* in public is a violation of the law. Violators are liable to a fine or, in exceptional cases, they can even be prosecuted.

национа́льность — (ethnic) nationality In the countries of the former Soviet Union, this traditionally means a person's ethnicity rather than their legal or political status. So if a Russian native speaker refers to someone as *ру́сский по национа́льности*, they usually mean that the person is Russian by language, culture, ethnicity, and even religion (e.g. Russian Orthodox), but the person could be a citizen of any country (the US, Ukraine, Germany, etc.).

нача́льная шко́ла — elementary school The first three or, now usually, four years of schooling that Russian children undergo. Separate institutions of such a kind are now rare in Russia and children usually continue at the same school after their first four years.

Но́вый год — New Year's Day This is the favourite holiday in Russia and some other former Soviet republics, celebrated on 1 January as elsewhere in Europe. New Year's Day and 2–4 January are national holidays.

о́бласть — oblast (region) One of the six types of administrative unit into which **Росси́йская Федера́ция** is divided. Of the 83 units, 46 are oblasts (regions).

For more details ▶ **автоно́мная о́бласть**

Парла́мент Росси́йской Федера́ции ▶ **Федера́льное Собра́ние Росси́йской Федера́ции**

Председа́тель Прави́тельства Росси́йской Федера́ции — Prime Minister of the Russian Federation The official (and only correct) title of the Prime Minister of the Russian Federation. *Председа́тель Прави́тельства Росси́йской Федера́ции* is appointed by **Президе́нт Росси́йской Федера́ции** with the consent of **Госуда́рственная ду́ма** (the lower house of Russia's national parliament).

Президе́нт Росси́йской Федера́ции — President of the Russian Federation Under the current Russian Constitution of 1993, *Президе́нт Росси́йской Федера́ции* is head of the state and has very extensive powers. He or she is directly elected by the citizens of Russia for a term of four years and cannot serve more than two consecutive terms. *Президе́нт Росси́йской Федера́ции* is also Supreme Commander-in-Chief of the Armed Forces of the Russian Federation.

респу́блика — republic One of the six types of administrative unit into which **Росси́йская Федера́ция** is divided. Of the 83 units, 21 are republics. Unlike **автоно́мная о́бласть, автоно́мный о́круг, го́род федера́льного значе́ния, край,** and **о́бласть,** each of the 21 republics has its own constitution (other constituent units have only charters (Russian *уста́в*)), and is entitled to introduce its own official language(s) (*госуда́рственный язы́к*) in addition to Russian.

For more details ▶ **автоно́мная о́бласть**

Рождество́ — Christmas Members of the Orthodox Church celebrate this festival on 7 January and it is a national holiday in Russia. The Russian Orthodox Church still uses the Julian calendar in which 7 January corresponds to 25 December in the Gregorian calendar.

Росси́йская Федера́ция, Росси́я — the Russian Federation, Russia Russia is a federal state consisting of 83 political (constituent) units (Russian *субъе́кты Федера́ции*). They are (January 2013):

— 21 republics (Russian **респу́блика**) ((*the Republic of*) *Adygea, the Republic of Altai, the Republic of Bashkortostan, the Republic of Buryatia, the Chechen Republic, the Chuvash Republic* (also *Chuvashia*), *the Republic of Dagestan, the Ingush Republic, the Kabarda-Balkar Republic,* the Republic of Kalmykia, the Karachay-Cherkess Republic, the Republic of Karelia, the Republic of Khakassia, the Republic of Komi, the Republic of Mari El, the Republic of Mordovia, the Republic of North Ossetia-Alania, the Republic of Sakha (also Yakutia), the Republic of Tatarstan (also Tatarstan), the Republic of Tuva (Russian Tyva), and the Udmurt Republic;

— 9 krais (Russian **край**) (Altai Krai, Kamchatka Krai, Khabarovsk Krai, Krasnodar Krai, Krasnoyarsk Krai, Perm Krai, Primorskiy Krai, Stavropol Krai, and Zabaikal Krai);

— 46 oblasts (Russian **область**) (Amur Oblast, Arkhangelsk Oblast, Astrakhan Oblast, Belgorod Oblast, Bryansk Oblast, Chelyabinsk Oblast, Irkutsk Oblast, Ivanovo Oblast, Kaliningrad Oblast, Kaluga Oblast, Kemerovo Oblast, Kirov Oblast, Kostroma Oblast, Kurgan Oblast, Kursk Oblast, Leningrad Oblast, Lipetsk Oblast, Magadan Oblast, Moscow Oblast, Murmansk Oblast, Nizhniy Novgorod Oblast, Novgorod Oblast, Novosibirsk Oblast, Omsk Oblast, Orel Oblast, Orenburg Oblast, Penza Oblast, Pskov Oblast, Rostov Oblast, Ryazan Oblast, Sakhalin Oblast, Samara Oblast, Saratov Oblast, Smolensk Oblast, Sverdlovsk Oblast, Tambov Oblast, Tomsk Oblast, Tver Oblast, Tula Oblast, Tyumen Oblast, Ulyanovsk Oblast, Vladimir Oblast, Volgograd Oblast, Vologda Oblast, Voronezh Oblast, and Yaroslavl Oblast);

— 2 cities with federal status (Russian **го́род федера́льного значе́ния**) (Moscow and St Petersburg);

— 1 autonomous oblast (Russian **автоно́мная о́бласть**) (Jewish Autonomous Oblast);

— 4 autonomous okrugs (Russian **автоно́мный о́круг**) (Chukot Autonomous Okrug, Khanty-Mansi Yugra Autonomous Okrug, Nenets Autonomous Okrug, and Yamalo-Nenets Autonomous Okrug).

Under the current Russian Constitution of 1993, both names — *Росси́я* and *Росси́йская Федера́ция* — can be used as an official name of the country.

Росси́я ▶ Росси́йская Федера́ция

СНГ ▶ Содру́жество Незави́симых Госуда́рств

Сове́т Федера́ции — the Council of the Federation The upper house of **Федера́льное Собра́ние Росси́йской Федера́ции** (the bicameral parliament of the Russian Federation). Each of the 83 constituent units of **Росси́йская Федера́ция** has two representatives in *Сове́т Федера́ции*.

Сово́к, сово́к (*often written in inverted commas*) The former Soviet Union in a pejorative or ironical sense. The term *сово́к* can also mean **1.** a typical Soviet citizen; **2.** the Soviet system as a whole; **3.** the Soviet ideology, lifestyle, etc.; **4.** a person of antiquated ideas living in modern Russia or any of the former Soviet republics.

Содру́жество Незави́симых Госуда́рств, СНГ — the Commonwealth of Independent States, CIS The political alliance of 11 former Soviet republics (January 2013: Armenia, Azerbaijan, Belarus, Kazakhstan, Kyrgyzstan, Moldova, Russia, Tajikistan, Turkmenistan, Ukraine, and Uzbekistan).

сре́дняя общеобразова́тельная шко́ла — secondary school Russian children go to this school until they are 15 so as to get *основно́е о́бщее образова́ние* and **аттеста́т об основно́м о́бщем образова́нии** or until they are 17 so as to get *сре́днее (по́лное) о́бщее образова́ние* and **аттеста́т о сре́днем (по́лном) о́бщем образова́нии**.

Culture

суббо́тник — subbotnik A Soviet invention, consisting of a day of unpaid work, originally on Saturdays (its name derives from *суббо́та* 'Saturday'). The first one took place on 12 April 1919 in the locomotive depot of a Moscow railway station called Moskva-Sortirovochnaya, while the first mass *суббо́тник* was held on 10 May 1919 on the Moscow–Kazan railway. They were a quasi-voluntary show of socially useful work. Nowadays the word is still used to denote some kinds of unpaid work such as cleaning areas of communal use, both indoors and outdoors. When performed on Sundays it is also called *воскре́сник*.

триколо́р, росси́йский триколо́р — the Russian tricolour Popular unofficial name of the national flag of the Russian Federation. It has three horizontal bands of red (lower band), blue, and white (upper band). The surest way to memorize order of colours of the Russian tricolour is to remember the name of the Soviet security police *Комите́т госуда́рственной безопа́сности*, usually abbreviated to *КГБ* (*кра́сный* (red), *голубо́й* (blue), *бе́лый* (white)).

Федера́льное Собра́ние Росси́йской Федера́ции — the Federal Assembly of the Russian Federation The official name of the bicameral national legislature of the Russian Federation. The upper house is called **Сове́т Федера́ции** (the Council of the Federation), while the lower house is called **Госуда́рственная ду́ма** (the State Duma).

Британские и американские культурные реалии

ACT — American College Test Экзамен, который сдают школьники в большинстве американских штатов после окончания средней школы. Он включает ряд предметов, в том числе английский язык и математику. Успешная сдача экзамена даёт право на поступление в университет.

African American — афроамериканец В Америке так называют американцев африканского происхождения. Данный термин является более нейтральным, чем слово «чёрный», которое подразумевает цвет кожи.

Afro-Caribbean — афрокариб В Великобритании и Америке так называют людей африканского происхождения, которые живут или ранее проживали на Карибских островах (к последним относятся Большие и Малые Антильские острова, а также Багамы).

A level — advanced level Выпускной экзамен, который сдают школьники в возрасте 18 лет в Англии и Уэльсе. Ученики, планирующие поступать в университет, должны сдать такой экзамен по трём или четырём предметам. За каждый экзамен ставится отдельная оценка. Университеты и другие вузы отбирают студентов на основе оценок, полученных ими за эти экзамены. Предпочтение отдаётся предметам, которые являются профилирующими для избранного абитуриентом факультета.

American dream — американская мечта Основополагающий принцип американской жизни. В соответствии с ним каждый может добиться успеха, особенно материального, если он будет много трудиться. Для иммигрантов американская мечта предполагает также надежду на свободу и равенство.

Asian-American В Америке так принято называть американцев, которые происходят из стран азиатского региона.

AS level — advanced subsidiary level Экзамен, занимающий промежуточное положение между **GCSE** и **A level**. Приёмные комиссии университетов приравнивают его к половине экзамена на **A level**. После окончания средней школы многие учащиеся сдают экзамены и на **AS level**, и на **A level**.

bed and breakfast Весьма распространённая в Великобритании разновидность гостиничного бизнеса. *Bed and breakfasts* функционируют на базе частных домов и маленьких гостиниц. В них можно переночевать и позавтракать за умеренную цену.

The Big Issue Журнал, освещающий серьёзные общественно-политические темы и отличающийся высоким уровнем журналистики. Его можно купить на улицах британских городов. Журнал распространяют бездомные люди, которые покупают его у издательства за установленную цену. Впоследствии они продают журнал с небольшой наценкой. Вырученные средства позволяют им жить, не прося подаяния.

Britannia Так древние римляне называли Великобританию. В наше время это обозначение стало частью национальной символики. Другим важным элементом этой символики является эмблема, на которой Великобритания изображена в виде женщины в шлеме, держащей в руках щит и трезубец. Данная эмблема воспроизводится на монетах достоинством в 50 пенсов. *Rule, Britannia!* («Правь, Британия!») — патриотическая песня, исполняемая обычно на заключительном вечере променадных концертов (**Proms**).

the British Isles — Британские острова В число этих островов входит 2 крупных острова — Великобритания (государство Великобритания) и Ирландия (Ирландская Республика и Северная Ирландия) — и более мелкие острова, располагающиеся вокруг, — Оркнейские, Гебридские, Шетлендские, Нормандские, острова Мэн и Силли.

broadsheet — широкополосная газета В Великобритании газеты, печатающиеся на широких полосах, противопоставляются таблоидам. Различие проводится не только и не столько по формату газеты, сколько по значимости освещаемого материала и по качеству журналистики. Широкополосные газеты, как правило, обсуждают серьёзные общественно-политические вопросы и демонстрируют высокий уровень журналистики.

Cabinet — Кабинет министров Данный правительственный орган Великобритании включает 20 министров, назначаемых премьер-министром. На заседаниях кабинета обсуждаются политика правительства и административные вопросы. Каждый из министров отвечает за одну определённую сферу государственной жизни. Кабинет в целом принимает решения, касающиеся общей политики правительства. Лидер главной оппозиционной партии назначает свой кабинет, называемый теневым кабинетом (**Shadow Cabinet**).

Culture

the Capitol — Капитолий Здание конгресса США. Оно находится на Капитолийском холме в Вашингтоне.

the City — Сити Финансовый и торговый центр Лондона. Он располагается в пределах исторического ядра города. В Сити сосредоточены головные офисы многих банков, страховых компаний, брокерских фирм и других финансовых организаций. В Сити работает около 500 тысяч человек.

city technology college (CTC) Школы, дающие специальное среднее образование. Они явились результатом сотрудничества между правительством и различными компаниями. Учебная программа предполагает углублённое изучение точных наук. Такого рода школы часто находятся в центре города.

cockney — кокни Диалект, на котором говорят уроженцы нескольких восточных районов Лондона. Основная черта данного диалекта — так называемый рифмованный сленг (**rhyming slang**). Кокни означает также носителей этого диалекта.

college of further education (CFE) Учебное заведение аналогичное профессионально-техническому училищу в России. В него можно поступить по достижении 16 лет. Такие училища дают как специальное, так и общее среднее образование. Учащиеся имеют возможность подготовиться к сдаче **GCSE** или **A Levels** или получить профессиональную квалификацию. Учебная программа предполагает как полные, так и сокращённые учебные дни.

colleges — колледжи В Америке слово *college* применяется как к средним специальным, так и к высшим учебным заведениям. Учебные заведения, где можно получить среднее специальное образование, проводят обучение на базе двухгодичной программы. Для получения высшего образования и степени бакалавра необходимо пройти 4-годичный курс в университете или в так называемом 4-годичном колледже. Приём в колледжи всех категорий производится на основе результатов выпускных экзаменов и текущих оценок, полученных в средней школе.

the Commonwealth — Британское Содружество Объединение в составе Великобритании и 52 стран — в основном её бывших колоний. По состоянию на январь 2013 года членами Содружества являлись: Австралия, Антигуа и Барбуда, Багамские Острова, Бангладеш, Барбадос, Белиз, Ботсвана, Бруней, Вануату, Великобритания, Гайана, Гамбия, Гана, Гренада, Доминика, Замбия, Индия, Камерун, Канада, Кения, Кипр, Кирибати, Лесото, Маврикий, Малави, Малайзия, Мальдивские Острова, Мальта, Мозамбик, Намибия, Науру, Нигерия, Новая Зеландия, Пакистан,

Папуа – Новая Гвинея, Руанда, Самоа, Свазиленд, Сейшельские Острова, Сент-Винсент и Гренадины, Сент-Китс и Невис, Сент-Люсия, Сингапур, Соломоновы Острова, Сьерра-Леоне, Танзания, Тонга, Тринидад и Тобаго, Тувалу, Уганда, Шри-Ланка, Южно-Африканская Республика, Ямайка.

Премьер-министры стран Содружества собираются каждые 2 года на конференцию для обсуждения вопросов экономического и культурного сотрудничества и взаимопомощи. Каждые 4 года проводятся спортивные Игры стран Содружества.

Термин *содружество* является также частью официального названия некоторых американских штатов, например, Кентукки, Вирджинии (Виргинии), Пенсильвании, Массачусета.

community college Разновидность американских университетов. Учебная программа таких университетов нацелена на получение специального образования, в наибольшей степени удовлетворяющего нуждам местной экономики. Данный термин иногда используется в Англии в названиях средних школ.

comprehensive school — средняя общеобразовательная школа В Великобритании дети учатся в такой школе с 11 и до 18 лет.

Congress — конгресс Законодательный орган США. Он состоит из двух палат: палаты представителей и сената. В палату представителей входит 435 членов, избираемых на 2 года. В сенат входит 100 сенаторов (по два от каждого штата), избираемых на 6 лет. Одна треть сенаторов переизбирается или замещается каждые два года. Чтобы провести закон, иначе называемый актом, его проект (билль) должен быть рассмотрен и одобрен обеими палатами, а затем ратифицирован президентом. Конгресс заседает в Вашингтоне в Капитолии на Капитолийском холме. Слова **The Capitol** (Капитолий) и *The Hill* (холм) также относятся к конгрессу.

council tax — местный налог Налог, взимаемый районным советом с местных жителей. Размер налогового взноса зависит от стоимости дома, находящегося во владении налогоплательщика, и количества людей, проживающих в нём.

Downing Street — Даунинг-стрит Улица в центре Лондона, в районе Вестминстер. Дом номер 10 по этой улице является официальной резиденцией премьер-министра Великобритании, дом номер 11 — резиденцией канцлера казначейства (министра финансов). Выражения *Downing Street* и *Number 10* часто означают офис премьер-министра.

elementary school Начальная школа в США. Дети учатся в таких школах с 6 до 12 лет. Иногда их также называют *grade school*.

football pool — футбольный тотализатор Популярная в Великобритании азартная игра. Игроки пытаются предугадать результаты футбольных матчей, ставят определённые суммы на свои прогнозы и заносят предполагаемые результаты на специальные бланки. Выигрыши выплачиваются тем игрокам, чьи прогнозы оказались наиболее точными. Размер выигрыша прямо пропорционален ставке игрока.

further education В Великобритании данный термин применяется ко всем видам образования (кроме университетского) для учащихся от 16 лет и старше. Обязательное школьное образование ограничено возрастом 16 лет. Если учащиеся решили не поступать в университет, то они могут продолжать обучение в системе профессионально-технического и среднего специального образования. В Америке, однако, термин *further education* применяется и к университетскому образованию.

GCSE — General Certificate of Secondary Education

Школьный экзамен в Англии и Уэльсе. Все учащиеся сдают эти экзамены после 5 лет обучения в средней школе независимо от их способностей. Большинство сдают экзамены по нескольким предметам. Экзаменационная оценка ставится за каждый предмет в отдельности.

Учащиеся, намеревающиеся продолжать обучение на последней ступени средней школы и сдавать экзамены на **A Level**, должны успешно сдать определённое количество *GCSE*. Школьники могут сочетать *GCSE* с **GNVQ**.

GNVQ — General National Vocational Qualification

Школьный экзамен, альтернативный GCSE. Эти экзамены были введены в 1992 году. Предметы, по которым они сдаются, имеют профессионально-техническую направленность. Цель такого обучения — дать учащимся определённые профессиональные знания, сориентировав их таким образом на рынке труда. Многие школьники сочетают *GNVQ* с **GCSE**.

God Save the Queen/King — Боже, храни королеву/короля

Государственный гимн Великобритании. Песня, сочинённая неизвестным автором и впервые исполненная в 1745 году в Лондоне. В качестве государственного гимна принята в начале 19 века.

GP (General Practitioner) — врач общей практики/семейный врач

Эквивалент участкового врача в России. Такие врачи обслуживают жителей определённого района, зарегистрированных в местной поликлинике. Консультация для пациентов Национальной службы здравоохранения (**National Health Service**) бесплатная. В случае необходимости врач общей практики направляет их на консультацию к врачу-специалисту.

grade school = elementary school

graduate school — аспирантура Этот термин применяется в американском варианте английского языка. Студенты могут поступить в аспирантуру после 3 или 4 лет обучения в университете.

grammar school Тип средней школы в Великобритании, эквивалентный гимназиям в России. В них могут поступать одарённые дети по достижении 11—12 лет при условии успешной сдачи конкурсных экзаменов. На данный момент таких школ осталось очень мало, так как с 1965 года их стали заменять общеобразовательными школами, в которые детей принимают независимо от способностей.

green card — грин-карта, зелёная карта Документ, разрешающий жить и работать в Америке людям, не имеющим американского гражданства. Этот документ обязателен для тех, кто хочет жить и работать в Америке постоянно.

Greyhound Bus Название автобусов самой большой в Америке автобусной компании. Сеть обслуживания данной компании охватывает большинство городов Америки. Наибольшей популярностью этот вид транспорта пользуется у молодёжи и туристов.

high school Средняя школа в Америке. Такие школы имеют две ступени. Первая ступень — так называемая младшая школа (**junior high school**) для детей от 12 до 14 лет. Вторая ступень — так называемая старшая школа (**senior high school**) для детей от 15 до 18 лет. После окончания средней школы учащиеся сдают выпускные экзамены (**ACT**, **SAT®**), по результатам которых они могут поступить в университет.

Данный термин иногда используется и в Великобритании.

the House of Commons — палата общин Нижняя палата британского парламента. Члены парламента, заседающие в этой палате, избираются на всеобщих выборах. В палате общин обсуждают вопросы внутренней и внешней политики и принимают новые законы.

the House of Lords — палата лордов Верхняя палата британского парламента. Члены этой палаты не избираются на выборах, а назначаются от главных политических партий страны. Кроме того, часть мест в палате передаётся по наследству членам аристократических фамилий. В 1999 году количество таких мест было ограничено 92. В функции палаты входит обсуждение и ратификация законов, ранее одобренных палатой общин. Одновременно палата лордов является высшим апелляционным судом страны.

the House of Representatives — палата представителей Нижняя палата конгресса США. В неё входит 435 представителей от американских штатов, которые избираются каждые два года. Число представителей от штатов зависит от численности их населения. Палата представителей принимает новые законы. Все принимаемые законы должны быть одобрены этим органом.

the Houses of Parliament — Британский парламент Двухпалатный орган, состоящий из палаты общин и палаты лордов. Обе палаты заседают в Вестминстерском дворце. Этот дворец представляет собой комплекс зданий в центре Лондона.

independent school — независимая/частная школа В Великобритании так называют школы, которые финансируются не государством, а родителями учеников, вносящими ежегодную плату за их обучение. В эту категорию входят **public school** и **preparatory school**.

infant school Первая ступень начальной школы в Великобритании. Эти школы получили распространение главным образом в Англии. Дети учатся в них три года. Они могут быть самостоятельными или являться частью полной начальной школы, в которой дети учатся до 11 лет.

the Ivy League Это общее название применяется к восьми старейшим и самым престижным университетам США. Все они находятся на восточном побережье страны. В их число входят Гарвардский, Йельский, Колумбийский, Корнеллский, Дартмутский, Браунский, Принстонский и Пенсильванский университеты. Название, принятое для этих университетов — буквально «Лига плюща» — основано на представлении о том, что старые здания этих университетов со временем заросли плющом. Обучение в этих университетах очень дорогое, но некоторые, одарённые студенты получают стипендии.

jobcentre — биржа труда Государственная служба, содействующая людям, ищущим работу. В число услуг, предоставляемых биржами труда, входит реклама вакансий, организация собеседований с работодателями. Биржи труда есть почти во всех городах Великобритании.

junior high school Младшая средняя школа. В Америке так называют первую ступень средней школы. Дети учатся в таких школах после окончания начальной школы (**elementary school**).

Medicaid Тип медицинского страхования, предоставляемого правительством США малоимущим людям моложе 65 лет.

Medicare Тип медицинского страхования, предоставляемого правительством США людям старше 65 лет.

Middle England — средняя Англия Это выражение часто применяется к среднему классу Великобритании. Так как эта группа населения составляет самую большую часть электората, политические партии стремятся получить на выборах их голоса. Выражение *middle income Britain* имеет аналогичное употребление.

MP (Member of Parliament) — член парламента Это выражение применяется только к членам палаты общин. Они представляют 659 избирательных округов Англии, Уэльса, Шотландии и Северной Ирландии.

the National Health Service (NHS) — Национальная служба здравоохранения В Великобритании система здравоохранения финансируется государством и медицинская помощь в основном бесплатная. Однако пациенты должны платить за зубоврачебные услуги и лекарства. Исключение составляют дети до 18 лет и беременные женщины. Им эти услуги предоставляются бесплатно.

National Insurance (NI) — национальное страхование Взносы по этому страхованию обязательны для работающей части населения и для работодателей. Они отчисляются из заработной платы и идут в фонд оплаты различных социальных услуг — медицинского обслуживания, пособий по безработице, пенсий и т. д.

the National Lottery — национальная лотерея В Великобритании доходы, получаемые от розыгрышей лотереи, идут на финансирование культурных и спортивных проектов, на охрану памятников и на разного рода благотворительные цели.

the National Trust Добровольная общественная организация по охране архитектурных, исторических и природных памятников Великобритании. Она функционирует за счёт взносов членов организации и доходов, получаемых от её владений. За годы своего существования эта организация выкупила или получила в дар огромные земельные угодья, целые деревни и большое количество зданий, представляющих архитектурную или историческую ценность. Несколько месяцев в году дома-музеи и другие владения организации открыты для посещения.

Native American — коренной американец В настоящее время в Америке так принято называть коренных жителей Северной и Южной Америки, а также Карибских островов. Этому термину отдаётся предпочтение в официальных контекстах, так как он считается более точным, чем слово «индеец», которое появилось в результате ошибки, сделанной Х. Колумбом. Уверенный в том, что он достиг Индии, он назвал местных жителей индейцами. Тем не менее, слово *индеец* имеет широкое распространение, и коренные жители обеих Америк не считают его оскорбительным.

NBC — National Broadcasting Company Национальная вещательная компания. Первая вещательная компания США. Она была основана в 1926 году. Первый телевизионный канал *NBC* начал свою работу в 1940 году.

the Open University Заочный университет в Великобритании. Обучение на всех факультетах проводится на заочной основе. В этом университете учатся студенты всех возрастов. Они работают самостоятельно и отсылают письменные работы своим преподавателям. Степень, полученная в этом университете, равноценна степени любого другого университета.

Oxbridge Сращение, образованное от названий *Oxford* и *Cambridge*. Оно относится к университетам Оксфорда и Кембриджа и подчёркивает их престиж и особое положение среди других университетов.

Parliament — парламент Британский парламент — высший законодательный орган страны. Он состоит из двух палат: палаты общин и палаты лордов. Парламент собирается в Вестминстерском дворце. Выборы в парламент проходят каждые 5 лет. Все члены палаты общин должны переизбираться. Царствующий монарх открывает новые сессии парламента и подписывает законы.

the Pledge of Allegiance — клятва верности В американских школах каждый учебный день начинается с переклички и с клятвы американскому флагу. Ученики произносят клятву верности и преданности Америке: «Я клянусь в верности флагу Соединённых Штатов Америки и республике, которую он представляет, её народу, единому перед Богом, свободе и справедливости для всех».

   Иммигранты, принимающие американское гражданство приносят такую же клятву.

politically correct, PC — политически корректный, политкорректный Идея политической корректности появилась в 80-х годах двадцатого века. Суть её заключается в выработке и повсеместном закреплении языковых и поведенческих норм, лишённых любых предрассудков: будь то предрассудки расовые, половые, национальные или иные. В процессе замены старых выражений новыми — политически корректными — в языке наметилась тенденция к избавлению от многих спорных терминов. Очевидно, что слова *афроамериканец* и *коренной американец* в большей мере соответствуют исторической правде, нежели употребляемые в тех же значениях, соответственно, *чёрный* (или *негр*) и *индеец*. Однако некоторые эвфемизмы, возникшие на этой почве, грешат неопределённостью. Таким, например, является выражение *involuntarily leisured* (дословно «на вынужденном отдыхе»), используемое вместо слова *unemployed* (безработный).

Poppy Day — День маков В Великобритании так называют день, в который страна отмечает годовщину окончания Первой мировой войны. В этот день, называемый также *Remembrance Sunday* (Памятное воскресенье) или *Armistice Day* (День перемирия), поминают жертв обеих мировых войн. Многие люди вдевают в петлицы красные бумажные маки. Маки символизируют цветочные поля Франции и Бельгии, на которых похоронены солдаты, павшие в Первой и Второй мировых войнах. Бумажные маки продаются благотворительными организациями. Средства, вырученные от их продажи, идут на помощь ветеранам войны.

prep/preparatory school В Великобритании так называют частные начальные школы. Дети учатся в них с 7 и до 13 лет. Некоторые из этих школ являются интернатами. Обучение в них, как правило, раздельное для мальчиков и девочек. Ученики, окончившие такие школы, обычно поступают в частные средние школы.

В Америке данное выражение относится к очень престижным частным средним школам, которые готовят учащихся к поступлению в лучшие университеты страны.

primaries — праймериз В США так называют выборы делегатов, направляемых на партийные съезды, во время которых выдвигаются кандидаты в президенты и в вице-президенты.

prom В Америке так называют школьный бал в конце учебного года.

the Proms — promenade concerts — променадные концерты Ежегодный фестиваль классической музыки, проходящий в королевском Альберт-холле в Лондоне. Заключительный вечер променадных концертов являет собой шумное зрелище. Зрители поют под аккомпанемент оркестра традиционные песни *Land of Hope and Glory* и *Rule Britannia!* Слово *Proms* является сокращением от выражения *promenade concert* — променадные концерты, которые называются так, потому что значительная часть зрителей слушает концерты стоя.

public school — частная школа Несмотря на своё название, эти школы являются частными. Обычно в них учатся дети из привилегированных и богатых семей. Это связано с тем, что плата за обучение в таких школах чрезвычайно высокая. В особенности это относится к наиболее престижным из них: Итону (*Eton*), Хэрроу (Харроу) (*Harrow*), Винчестеру (*Winchester*), Рагби (*Rugby*). Все эти школы предоставляют стипендии одарённым детям из малоимущих семей. Большинство этих школ является интернатами. Кроме того, обучение в них раздельно для мальчиков и девочек.

В Америке выражение *public school* относится к государственным школам.

the Queen's Speech — речь королевы Эта речь готовится для королевы британским правительством. Она произносит её в палате лордов на ежегодной церемонии официального открытия парламента. Речь королевы — важное событие в политическом календаре, так как в ней освещаются планы правительства на ближайший год.

received pronunciation (RP) — нормативное произношение Произношение английского языка, принятое за норму в Великобритании. Это произношение свободно от влияния каких-либо региональных диалектов и часто ассоциируется с речью людей из привилегированных слоёв. Произношение, принятое на радио и телевидении, часто ориентируется на эту норму, хотя в последние годы произносительный диапазон дикторов стал включать и региональные варианты.

rhyming slang — рифмованный сленг Особенность диалекта кокни, которая делает его совершенно непонятным для непосвящённых. Суть его состоит в том, что отдельные слова заменяются выражениями, которые с ними рифмуются. Например, вместо слова *believe* употребляется сочетание *Adam and Eve*, вместо слова *head* употребляется сочетание *loaf of bread*.

Трудность понимания такой речи усугубляется тем обстоятельством, что носители кокни часто сокращают эти сочетания до отдельных слов. Например, выражение *Use your loaf* означает на самом деле *Use your head*.

SAT 1. Scholastic Aptitude Test. Тест, успешная сдача которого необходима для поступления в американские университеты. Обычно его сдают при окончании средней школы. **2. Standard Assessment Test.** Экзамен, который сдают все школьники Англии и Уэльса в возрасте 7, 11 и 14 лет.

the Scottish Parliament — парламент Шотландии Он открылся в 1999 году после всеобщих шотландских выборов. Парламент уполномочен решать многие вопросы экономической, социальной и культурной политики самостоятельно, без вмешательства парламента Великобритании. Члены шотландского парламента заседают в Эдинбурге, в Холирудхаус (*Holyrood House*).

secondary schools — средние школы В Великобритании существует ряд учебных заведений, дающих среднее образование:

общеобразовательные школы (*comprehensive schools*) — бесплатные школы для мальчиков и девочек, в которых дети учатся независимо от способностей. Эти школы составляют 85% всех средних учебных заведений;

гимназии (*grammar schools*) — школы для более одарённых детей. Они могут быть как частными, так и государственными. Обучение в них обычно раздельное для мальчиков и девочек. Для поступления в такие школы необходимо сдавать вступительный экзамен;

частные школы (*public schools*) — в большинстве случаев это школы-интернаты. Обучение в таких школах очень дорогое.

the Senate — сенат Верхняя палата американского конгресса. В нём заседает 100 сенаторов — по два от каждого штата. Они избираются на 6 лет. Все новые законы должны быть утверждены как сенатом, так и палатой представителей.

Однако сенат отвечает за внешнюю политику и уполномочен «оценивать и одобрять» назначения, сделанные президентом.

senior high school В Америке так называют вторую ступень средней школы. Дети учатся в ней по завершении младшей средней школы (**junior high school**).

Shadow Cabinet ▶ Cabinet

Silicon Valley — Силиконовая долина Так называют долину Санта-Клара в Калифорнии, в которой располагается большое количество компьютерных компаний. Данное название связано с тем, что силикон (кремний) широко используется в электронной промышленности.

the Stars and Stripes Флаг США.

the Star-Spangled Banner **1.** Гимн США. **2.** Одно из названий американского флага.

tabloid — таблоид Малоформатная (бульварная) газета. Такие газеты противопоставляются широкоформатным (широкополосным) газетам (**broadsheet**), которые печатаются на больших листах. Таблоиды ассоциируются с жёлтой прессой, в особенности такие, как *The Sun* и *Daily Mirror*. В последнее время таблоидный формат печати, как более удобный, стал использоваться и некоторыми серьёзными газетами, например, *The Independent, The Times*.

Thanksgiving — День благодарения Зима 1620 года в Новом Свете обернулась катастрофой для английских колонистов. Половина колонии, основанной *отцами-пилигримами*, — первыми поселенцами Северной Америки — погибла в результате болезней. Однако осень 1621 года

Culture

была урожайной, и это позволило оставшимся колонистам выжить. Они решили отпраздновать это событие обедом. На обед были приглашены индейцы, научившие их охотиться и выращивать кукурузу. В наши дни День благодарения отмечается ежегодно в четвёртый четверг ноября. На обед готовится индейка со сладким картофелем и клюквенным соусом. На десерт подаётся тыквенный пирог. В Канаде День благодарения отмечается во второй понедельник октября.

the three Rs Так называются главные предметы в начальной школе: чтение, письмо, арифметика. В английском произношении этих слов — *Reading, wRiting, aRithmetic* — первым звуком является *R*.

TOEFL — Test of English as a Foreign Language Экзамен по английскому языку, который должны сдавать иностранцы, поступающие в американские университеты.

the Union Jack Так называется флаг Соединённого Королевства Великобритании и Северной Ирландии. На полотнище флага крест св. Георгия, символизирующего Англию, крест св. Андрея, символизирующего Шотландию, и крест св. Патрика, символизирующего Северную Ирландию, объединены в одном изображении.

Wall Street — Уолл-стрит Улица в Нью-Йорке, являющаяся финансовым и торговым центром США. Здесь находится фондовая биржа, головные офисы многих банков и страховых компаний и других финансовых учреждений.

Washington DC — Вашингтон Столица США, названная так в честь первого президента страны Джорджа Вашингтона. В административно-территориальном отношении этот город полностью совпадает с федеральным округом Колумбия. В Вашингтоне находятся Белый дом, конгресс, Верховный суд, национальные музеи.

welfare Система социальной защиты в США. Эта программа оказывает поддержку людям с низким доходом. Основными элементами программы являются **Medicaid** (оказание бесплатной медицинской помощи), *food stamps* (талоны на продукты питания) и *Head Start* (финансовая поддержка, оказываемая школьникам из бедных семей).

welfare state — государство всеобщего благосостояния В Великобритании данное понятие включает в себя систему социального обеспечения, нацеленную на поддержание высокого уровня жизни всех граждан. Основными элементами данной системы являются бесплатная медицинская помощь (**the National Health Service**), государственное страхование (**National Insurance**) и социальная защита безработных (*Social Security*).

the Welsh Assembly — Ассамблея Уэльса   Так называется парламент Уэльса, учреждённый в 1999 году. Он заседает в столице Уэльса Кардиффе. Парламент даёт Уэльсу значительную автономию от британского правительства.

Westminster — Вестминстер   Район в центре Лондона. Здесь находятся правительственные учреждения, в том числе британский парламент (**Houses of Parliament**), резиденция премьер-министра (**Downing Street**), Букингемский дворец (*Buckingham Palace*) (резиденция правящего монарха), дворец св. Джеймса (*St James's Palace*) (резиденция принца Уэльского) и др. Слово *Westminster* также означает британский парламент.

Whitehall — Уайтхолл   Улица в центре Лондона, на которой расположены многие правительственные учреждения. В средствах массовой информации словом *Whitehall* часто называют британское правительство.

Correspondence

Letters/Письма

1. Запрос вакансии

Начальнику Отдела кадров
Медицинского училища № 2
г. Санкт-Петербурга
Иванову Петру Трофимовичу
от Григорьевой Ольги Николаевны,
проживающей по адресу:
Московский проспект, д. 147, кв. 3
телефон (812) 824-73-54

Уважаемый Пётр Трофимович!

Прошу Вас сообщить о наличии вакансии
преподавателя биологии в Вашем училище. В настоящий
момент я преподаю биологию и химию в средней школе
№ 396 Кировского района Санкт-Петербурга. В связи с
переменой места жительства я ищу работу преподавателя
в новом районе. После окончания Педагогического
института им. Герцена в 1997 году я преподавала химию
и биологию в средней школе. При наличии вакансии
преподавателя в Вашем училище прошу Вас назначить
мне собеседование в удобное для Вас время.

С уважением,   Григорьева О. Н.
14.01.2013

1. Enquiry to an employer about jobs

73 Brighton Road
Eastbourne
East Sussex
BN21 3YR

4 April 2013

Manager
Rose and Crown Hotel
Eastbourne
East Sussex
BN22 7AP

Dear Mr Davis

I am writing to enquire whether you have any vacancies for bar or restaurant staff over the summer.

I have worked at other hotels in the town in my school holidays over the past few years and have quite a lot of experience at serving behind a bar and waiting at table.

My university term ends on 19 June and I shall then be available until the middle of September when I plan to take two weeks' holiday before returning to Leeds in October.

I would prefer work in the bar or restaurant but would also consider any other jobs you can offer.

I enclose references from two previous employers and a character reference from my university tutor. I look forward to hearing from you.

Yours sincerely

Giles Goodall

Correspondence

2. Ответ на объявление о наличии вакансии

Директору фирмы «Заря»
Логинову Борису Аркадьевичу
от Каца Алексея Владиславовича,
проживающего по адресу:
ул. Сергея Потапова, д. 12/4, кв. 264
г. Калуга, 248921
телефон (0842) 93-14-55

Уважаемый господин директор!

В ответ на объявление в газете «Курьер» от 15 января этого года направляю Вам свое резюме, копию свидетельства об окончании курсов повышения квалификации и справку с настоящего места работы. Меня интересует должность инженера по наладке электронной аппаратуры. В случае если моё предложение заинтересует Вас, я бы хотел узнать подробнее об условиях работы.

С уважением,   Кац А. В.
01.02.2012

2. Reply to a job advertisement

23 Church Road
Blundesdon
LOWESTOFT
Norfolk
NR32 3LS

19.6.12

Personnel Manager
The Norfolk Echo
5 High Street
NORWICH
Norfolk
NR3 2HF

Dear Mr Williams

I am writing in response to the advertisement that appeared last week in *The Guardian* for an Assistant Features Editor on the *Norfolk Echo*.

As you will see from my CV, I successfully completed a Media Studies degree at Lancaster University the year before last, since when I have worked in a freelance capacity for my local radio station and my local paper. I am now keen to move on to more permanent employment and believe that the experience I have gained will be relevant to the job advertised.

Apart from my CV, I enclose some examples of my work in the form of articles I have written and a CD of some interviews that I have conducted with people of local interest.

I am available for interview at any time and could take up the post immediately, should I be appointed. Thank you for considering my application.

Yours sincerely

Louise Ashby

3. Просьба о рекомендательном письме

Уважаемый Николай Константинович!

У меня к Вам большая просьба. Не могли бы Вы написать рекомендательное письмо для меня? С тех пор как меня перевели в *СУ-13, я продолжал работать в должности прораба и заочно учился в Петербургском политехническом институте. В июне я наконец получил диплом, а недавно нашёл место инженера на соседнем предприятии. Для поступления на работу в Отделе кадров у меня попросили кроме обычных документов рекомендательное письмо с предыдущего места работы. Поскольку я проработал под Вашим руководством последние шесть лет, я бы хотел попросить написать такое письмо именно Вас. Пожалуйста, направьте письмо на имя начальника Отдела кадров завода «Оптика» Малинина Георгия Сергеевича по адресу: завод «Оптика», ул. Генерала Петрова, д. 1, г. Самара, 443003.

Заранее Вам благодарен,

12.03.2013
                          Андреев Николай Захарович

*СУ = строительное управление 'construction company'

3. Asking for a reference

6 Highworth Cottages
Inhurst
Tadley
Hants RG26 5JP

1 February 2006

Dear Fiona

I'm sorry I haven't been in touch lately. How are you, and how's life at Basingstoke Comprehensive?

The reason I'm writing is that I was wondering if you would be willing to act as a referee with regard to several jobs I'm applying for at the moment.

After spending the past ten years in industry, I've decided to return to teaching, preferably this time in higher education. As you were my most recent Head of Department I thought that you would be the most suitable person to ask for a reference.

I'm hoping that my practical experience in the food industry will make me better qualified now than I was when I left Basingstoke. So far I have applied for posts at the Oxford & Cherwell Valley College and Kingston University, both involving teaching the catering part of the HND leisure industry course.

Please get in touch if you would like further information about what I have been doing or about the requirements for these jobs.

Best wishes

Debbie Brooks

4. Письмо в отдел кадров

Начальнику Отдела кадров

ООО «Огни»

Фокиной Марии Ивановне

Благодарю Вас за письмо от 15 марта с уведомлением о зачислении меня в фирму «Огни» на должность главного механика по наладке оборудования. К сожалению, мои попытки немедленно уволиться с настоящего места работы не привели к успеху, и я вынужден ждать положенные по закону две недели после подачи заявления об увольнении. Таким образом, я смогу приступить к исполнению своих обязанностей на Вашем предприятии не ранее 1 апреля 2012 г. Сожалею о задержке и надеюсь, что это обстоятельство не повлияет на Ваше решение о предоставлении мне рабочего места.

С уважением,

16.03.2012   Григорьев И. П.

4. Accepting a job

19 Ryden Lane
Clevelode
MALVERN
Worcestershire
WR13 8PD

22/3/12

Personnel Department
Warwickshire College
Warwick New Rd
Leamington Spa
CV32 5JE

Dear Ms Elliott

I was extremely pleased to receive your letter offering me the job of Admissions Secretary at Warwickshire College, and am glad to inform you that I accept the offer.

As discussed at my interview, I need to give a month's notice at my present job and would therefore like to start work at the beginning of May. This will give me a few days for the move and allow me to get settled into my new flat before starting.

I would be grateful if you could let me know who I should report to or where I should go when I first arrive. Please could you also send me a copy of the Terms and Conditions of Employment that you mentioned at the interview, and details of the pension scheme.

I look forward to seeing you in the near future.

Yours sincerely

Amanda Walker

CVs

РЕЗЮМЕ

Ф.И.О.	Михайлова Марина Александровна
Дата рождения, возраст	05.04.1985, 25 лет
Адрес	пр. Байрона, д. 66, кв. 6 г. Петрозаводск, 185000, Республика Карелия
Телефон	(домашний) (8242) 82-32-22, (сотовый) +79217003522
E-mail	mariners@mail.ru
Семейное положение, дети	не замужем, детей нет

Претендую на должность	переводчик (полная занятость)
Заработная плата	от 30 000 рублей

Образование

2005—2010	Петрозаводский государственный университет, филологический факультет, специальность «Английский язык и литература» (диплом с отличием)
январь-август 2008	Университет штата Канзас, практика для студентов, обучающихся по обмену, специальность «Английский язык» (почётный лист со средним баллом 3,65 из 4)
июнь-август 2007	Летняя школа Университета Осло, специальность «Норвежский язык»
1995—2005	Средняя школа №17 г. Петрозаводска с углублённым изучением английского и финского языков (серебряная медаль)

Иностранные языки	свободное владение английским языком (навыки синхронного перевода), разговорный финский, базовые знания норвежского (чтение и перевод неспециальных текстов)

Опыт работы

июль-сентябрь 2010	переводчик делегации ЮНЕСКО в Республике Карелия
июнь-август 2009	преподаватель русского языка как иностранного в Летней школе Петрозаводского государственного университета

Дополнительные навыки	компьютер на уровне уверенного пользователя, водительские права категории «В»

CURRICULUM VITAE

Name: John Phillip Hunt

Address: 24 Mulberry Rd
Brixton
LONDON SW14 5HU

Telephone: 020-592284; mobile 07905339242

Email: jp_hunt@compuserve.com

Nationality: British

Date of birth: 22/5/88

Marital Status: Single

Education/Qualifications:

2010–2011 University of Bristol: MSc in Management

2006–2010 King's College, London: BA (hons.) Russian and German, class 2:1

1999–2006 Burford Community College, Oxford Rd, Burford, Oxon.
9 GCSEs (English, Mathematics, Physics, History, Technology, German, Russian, French, Music)
4 A levels: German (A), Russian (B), History (B), English (C)

Work Experience:

September 2008– June 2009 10 months working in Personnel Department of the Max-Planck-Institut für Informatik in Saarbrücken, Germany

July–August 2007 6 weeks teaching English to foreign students at Swan School of English, Oxford

March 2005 1 week's 'shadowing' experience to Assistant Marketing Manager, EAA Technology (Environmental Energy), Didcot

June 2003 2 weeks' work experience at Marks and Spencer, Oxford

Skills: Computer literate; clean driving licence

Referees: Dr Michael Edwards (Arts Faculty)
King's College
London EC12 4HR

Dr Elaine Grigson
(Management Research Centre)
University of Bristol
Bristol BS8 1TH

SMS

SMS (electronic text messaging)

SMS is the English abbreviation for "Short Message/Messaging Service". Sending an English text message is the same procedure as sending a Russian text message, but abbreviations are used far more often. In English there are countless abbreviations which allow a lot of information to be transmitted using few letters and numbers, e.g. 2l8 = 'too late'. For many messages people type only the initial letters of each word, e.g. ttyl = 'talk to you later', or fyi = 'for your information'. Experienced senders of text messages have no problems in understanding a whole range of such abbreviations.

So-called emoticons or smileys, witty symbols created using punctuation marks, brackets, etc., are popular in text messaging. Some of the more established ones are included below.

Обмен SMS-сообщениями

Аббревиатура SMS расшифровывается как Short Message/Messaging Service, что переводится с английского как «служба обмена короткими сообщениями». Отправка текстового сообщения (SMS) на английском языке такая же тривиальная процедура, как и отправка SMS на русском языке с той лишь разницей, что англоязычные пользователи при написании SMS намного чаще прибегают к различного рода сокращениям. Их число, в силу фонетико-морфологических особенностей английского языка, не поддаётся счёту. Использование сокращений позволяет существенно упростить и ускорить набор, а заодно увеличить объём полезной информации, передаваемой в рамках одного сообщения. Нередко ту или иную мысль получается выразить при помощи всего нескольких букв или цифр. Например, 2l8 означает too late «слишком/уже поздно», где цифра 2 (two) заменяет созвучное ей слово too, буква I соответствует самой себе, а цифра 8 (eight) образует слоговой элемент слова late. Другой распространённый приём пользователей SMS — это образование сокращений из первых букв слов, входящих в состав фразы или предложения. Например, ttyl означает talk to you later «увидимся» или «до встречи» (буквально, «поговорим позже»), а fyi — for your information «к твоему/вашему сведению». Опытные отправители SMS без труда понимают всё множество подобных аббревиатур.

Т. н. эмотиконы или смайлики — остроумные обозначения, состоящие из знаков пунктуации, букв и прочих символов, — также широко применяются в языке SMS. Наиболее устоявшиеся из них приводятся ниже.

Glossary of English SMS abbreviations/Английские SMS-сокращения

(Русский перевод даётся только у выражений, значение которых нельзя получить пословным буквальным переводом. Перевод остальных выражений, а также одиночных слов следует искать в статьях к соответствующим словам в основном корпусе Словаря.)

Abbreviation	Meaning	Значение
@	at	
adn	any day now	(в са́мое ближа́йшее вре́мя)
afaik	as far as I know	(наско́лько я зна́ю, наско́лько мне изве́стно)
atb	all the best	
b	be	
b4	before	
b4n	bye for now	(ну, пока́!)
bbl	be back late(r)	
bcnu	be seeing you	(уви́димся!, до встре́чи!)
bfn	bye for now	(ну, пока́!)
brb	be right back	(обяза́тельно верну́сь (но не зна́ю когда́ то́чно))
btw	by the way	(кста́ти, ме́жду про́чим)
bwd	backward	
c	see	
cu	see you	(уви́димся!, до встре́чи!)
cul8r	see you later	(уви́димся!, до встре́чи!)
f2f	face to face	(лицо́м к лицу́)
f2t	free to talk	(есть вре́мя поболта́ть/поговори́ть)
fwd	forward	
fwiw	for what it's worth	(е́сли э́то име́ет (како́е-то) значе́ние)
fyi	for your information	(к твоему́/ва́шему све́дению)
gal	get a life	((1) займи́сь (лу́чше) де́лом!; (2) займи́сь чем-нибудь (бо́лее) интере́сным, ≈ живи́ по́лной жи́знью!)
gr8	great	
h8	hate	
hand	have a nice day	(всего́ до́брого/хоро́шего!, до свида́ния! (традиционная формула прощания))
hth	hope this helps	
ic	I see	((я) по́нял!; (я) ви́жу!)
iluvu, ilu	I love you	
imho	in my humble opinion	(по моему́ скро́мному мне́нию)
imo	in my opinion	(по-мо́ему)
iow	in other words	(други́ми слова́ми)
jic	just in case	(на вся́кий слу́чай)
jk	just kidding	(шучу́)
kit	keep in touch	((не пропада́й! (= звони́!, пиши́! и т. п.))
kwim	know what I mean?	
l8	late	
l8r	later	
lol	lots of luck; laughing out loud; lots of love	(уда́чи!; залива́юсь сме́хом (гро́мко смею́сь); мно́го(-мно́го) любви́! (как пожела́ние))
mob	mobile	
msg	message	
myob	mind your own business	((а) тебе́ како́е де́ло?, ≈ не будь таки́м любопы́тн/ым (-ой -ой)!)
ne	any	
ne1	anyone	

Abbreviation	Meaning	Значение
no1	no one	
oic	oh, I see	((я) по́нял!; (я) ви́жу!)
otoh	on the other hand	(с друго́й стороны́)
pcm	please call me	
pls	please	
ppl	people	
r	are	
rofl	rolling on the floor, laughing	(ката́юсь по́ полу от сме́ха)
ru	are you	
ruok	are you OK?	(с тобо́й/ва́ми всё в поря́дке?)
sit	stay in touch	(не пропада́й! (= звони́!, пиши́! и т. п.))
som1	someone	
spk	speak	
thkq	thank you	
thx	thanks	
ttyl	talk to you later	(уви́димся!, до встре́чи!; поговори́м по́зже)
tx	thanks	
u	you	
ur	you are	
w/	with	
wan2	want to	
wan2tlk	want to talk?	
werv u bin	where have you been?	(где пропада́л(а)/был(а́)?)
wknd	weekend	
wot	what	
wu	what's up?	(как дела́?)
x	kiss	
xlnt	excellent	
xoxoxo	hugs and kisses	((кре́пко) целу́ю и обнима́ю)
yr	your; you're	
1	one	
2	to; too	
2day	today	
2moro	tomorrow	
2nite	tonight	
3sum	threesome	
4	for	

Emoticon	Meaning	Значение
:-)	smiling, happy face	улыба́ющаяся, счастли́вая ро́жица
:-|	frowning; bored	нахму́рил бро́ви; ску́чно
:-e	disappointed	разочаро́ван/огорчён
:-(	unhappy face	несча́стная ро́жица
%-)	confused	смущён, озада́чен
:~(or :'-(	crying	пла́чу
;-)	winking happy face	подми́гивающая дово́льная ро́жица
|-o	tired; asleep	уста́л; сплю/усну́л
:-	sceptical	с недове́рием/сомне́нием

Emoticon	Meaning	Значение
:-D	big smile, laughing face	улы́бка во весь рот, смею́щаяся ро́жица
:-<>	amazed	изумлён/поражён
X=	fingers crossed	скрести́в па́льцы (*наудачу*)
:-p	tongue sticking out	с вы́сунутым языко́м, пока́зывая язы́к
:-O	shouting; surprised	кричу́; удивлён
:-Q	I don't understand	не понима́ю, не по́нял
:-X	my lips are sealed, I won't tell anyone	держу́ рот на замке́, никому́ не скажу́
O:-)	angel	а́нгел
:-* or :-x	big kiss!	кре́пкий поцелу́й
:-o	"Oooh!"; shocked face	ух ты! (*от удивления/восхищения*), ой/уй! (*от боли*); шоки́рованная ро́жица
@}-,-'—	a rose	ро́за (*как знак любви*)

SMS

*NB: the '-' which represents the nose is often omitted or replaced by an 'o', e.g. :) or :o).

*NB Дефис «-», обозначающий нос, часто опускается или заменяется буквой «о», например, :) или :o).

Internet

Email and the Internet
Электронная почта и Интернет

to be on email	иметь до́ступ к электро́нной по́чте (*or* к Интерне́ту)
an email	электро́нное письмо́, e-mail, име́йл
a mailbox	почто́вый я́щик
an 'at' sign (@)	соба́ка (знак @)
an address book	а́дресная кни́га
an email address	электро́нный а́дрес, e-mail, име́йл
a mailing list	спи́сок адреса́тов
to send (*someone*) an email	пос|ыла́ть, -ла́ть электро́нное письмо́ (*кому-н.*)
to send (*something*) by email	пос|ыла́ть, -ла́ть (*что-н.*) по электро́нной по́чте
to receive an email	получ|а́ть, -и́ть электро́нное письмо́
to forward an email	перес|ыла́ть, -ла́ть электро́нное письмо́
to copy somebody in, to cc somebody	отпр|авля́ть, -а́вить ко́пию (*письма́, сообще́ния и т. п.*) кому́-н.
cc (carbon copy)	ко́пия (*письма*) (*отправляемая другому адресату в дополнение к основному, так что всем получателям письма становятся известными адреса друг друга*)
bcc (blind carbon copy)	скры́тая ко́пия (*письма*) (*отправляемая другому адресату в дополнение к основному, так что другие получатели письма не знают, что этому адресату отправлена копия*)
a file	файл
a folder	па́пка
an emoticon, a smiley (:-))	эмо́тикон, сма́йл(ик)
to attach a file	вкла́дывать, вложи́ть (*or* прикреп|ля́ть, -и́ть *or* присоедин|я́ть, -и́ть) файл
to receive an attachment	получ|а́ть, -и́ть вложе́ние (*к письму́*) (*or* ат(т)а́чмент *or* присоединённый/прикреплённый (к письму́) файл)
to open an attachment	откр|ыва́ть, -ы́ть вложе́ние (*к письму́*) (*or* ат(т)а́чмент *or* присоединённый/прикреплённый (к письму́) файл)
to save a message on the desktop, on the hard disk	сохран|я́ть, -и́ть сообще́ние на рабо́чем столе́, на жёстком ди́ске
to delete a message	удал|я́ть, -и́ть сообще́ние
an inbox	входя́щие (сообще́ния)
an outbox	исходя́щие (сообще́ния)
snail mail (*infml*)	обы́чная по́чта, «ме́дленная по́чта», «черепа́шья по́чта» (*в противоположность электронной*)
to get spam	получ|а́ть, -и́ть спам
to send spam	рассыла́ть, разосла́ть спам
a modem	моде́м
an ADSL modem	ADSL-моде́м
toolbar	пане́ль инструме́нтов
to copy	копи́ровать, с-
to cut	выреза́ть, вы́резать
to paste	вст|авля́ть, -а́вить
to print	распеча́т|ывать, -ать

Toolbar menu buttons on emails	Назва́ния кно́пок меню́ в почто́вых програ́ммах
File	Файл
Edit	Пра́вка
View	Вид
Insert	Вста́вка
Format	Форма́т
Tools	Се́рвис
Actions	Де́йствия
Help	Спра́вка

Internet

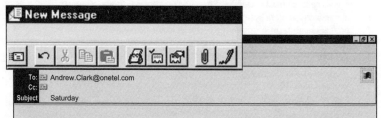

To: Andrew.Clark@onetel.com
Cc:
Subject   Saturday

Hi, Andy!

I spent the afternoon at the Internet cafe on the High Street, and I found this really interesting website: http://www.list.co.uk. You should add it to your favourites. On the home page you can select any town in the UK and it gives you all the bars/restaurants/concert venues etc. in the town you choose. When you double-click on the name of a bar, a map automatically pops up and the place you've selected is highlighted. Mail me when you've had a chance to browse! I'm sure we could find something for Saturday night.

I also attach a joke that Anna sent me this morning. She bought an ADSL modem so she's on email now. It made me laugh. (Don't worry about opening the file: I ran my antivirus over it and got the all-clear.) Speak to you soon!

Tim

PS Can you forward this to Mark? I wanted to copy him in, but I can't find his email address and I deleted his latest email from my inbox. I'm sure he'd be interested as well.

Internet

To: Elizaveta.Gerasimova@yandex.ru
Cc:
Subject: Суббота

Привет, Лиза!

Днём я был в интернет-кафе на Тверской и нашёл один занимательный сайт: http://www.waytorussia.net/destinations.html. Я советую тебе добавить его в «Избранное» твоего браузера. На главной странице ты можешь выбрать из списка российский город, и тебе будут показаны бары, рестораны, концертные площадки, расположенные в нём. Если дважды щёлкнуть на названии заведения, то автоматически во всплывающем окне откроется карта, а искомое место на ней будет выделено цветом. В общем, пиши мне, когда будет возможность. Уверен, мы найдём, где провести время в эту субботу ночью.

Я прикрепляю к письму шутку, которую мне прислал Слава сегодня утром. Он купил ADSL-модем, так что теперь он может переписываться с нами по электронной почте. (Не бойся открывать этот файл: я проверил его антивирусом — вирусов там нет.)

До скорого! Пиши!

Илья

PS Ты не могла бы переслать это письмо Юле? Я хотел отправить ей копию, но не могу найти её электронный адрес, а последнее письмо от неё я удалил из своего почтового ящика. Не сомневаюсь, ей также будет это интересно.

Phrasefinder /
Разгово́рник

Phrasefinder

Useful phrases / Поле́зные фра́зы

yes, please	да, пожа́луйста
no, thank you	нет, спаси́бо
sorry	прости́те
excuse me	извини́те (меня́)
I'm sorry, I don't understand	прости́те, я не понима́ю

Meeting people — Встре́ча

hello/goodbye	здра́вствуйте/до свида́ния
how are you?	как пожива́ете?
nice to meet you	рад/ра́да с ва́ми познако́миться

Asking questions — Вопро́сы

do you speak English/Russian?	вы говори́те по-англи́йски/ по-ру́сски?
what's your name?	как вас зову́т?/как ва́ше и́мя?
where are you from?	отку́да вы?
how much is it?	ско́лько э́то сто́ит?
where is...?	где... ?
can I have...?	мо́жно мне... ?
would you like...?	не хоти́те ли... ?

Statements about yourself	**Немно́го о себе́**
my name is…	меня́ зову́т… , моё и́мя…
I'm American/Russian	я америка́нец/америка́нка/ру́сский/ру́сская
I don't speak Russian/English	я не говорю́ по-ру́сски/по-англи́йски
I live near Chester/Moscow	я живу́ недалеко́ от Че́стера/Москвы́
I'm a student	я студе́нт/студе́нтка
I work in an office	я рабо́таю на фи́рме

Emergencies	**Экстренные слу́чаи**
can you help me, please?	не могли́ бы вы мне помо́чь?
I'm lost	я заблуди́лся/заблуди́лась
I'm ill	я бо́лен/больна́
call an ambulance	вы́зовите ско́рую по́мощь

Reading signs	**Чита́ем на́дписи**
no entry	нет вхо́да
no smoking	не кури́ть
fire exit	запа́сный вы́ход
for sale	продаётся

Going places / Тра́нспорт, пое́здки

On the road　На шоссе́

where's the nearest service station?	где ближа́йшая бензозапра́вочная ста́нция?/где ближа́йший автосе́рвис?
what's the best way to get there?	как быстре́е туда́ добра́ться?
I've got a puncture	у меня́ проко́л ши́ны
I'd like to hire a bike/car	я хоте́л/хоте́ла бы взять напрока́т велосипе́д/автомоби́ль
there's been an accident	произошла́ ава́рия/произошло́ ДТП
my car's broken down	у меня́ слома́лась маши́на
the car won't start	мото́р не заво́дится

By rail — Поезд

where can I buy a ticket?	где я могу купить билет?
what time is the next train to Orel/Oxford?	когда следующий поезд на Орёл/Оксфорд?
do I have to change?	нужно ли мне делать пересадку?
can I take my bike on the train?	меня пустят в вагон с велосипедом?
which platform for the train to Kiev/London?	с какой платформы идёт поезд на Киев/Лондон?
there's a train to London at 10 o'clock	поезд на Лондон отправляется в 10 часов
a single/return to Leeds/Zvenigorod, please	билет в один конец/билет туда и обратно до Лидса/Звенигорода, пожалуйста
I'd like an all-day ticket	мне нужен билет на сутки
I'd like to reserve a seat	я хотел/хотела бы зарезервировать место

At the airport — В аэропорту

when's the next flight to Vladivostok/Manchester?	когда следующий рейс во Владивосток/в Манчестер?
where do I check in?	где регистрация пассажиров?
I'd like to confirm my flight	я хотел/хотела бы подтвердить свой рейс
I'd like a window seat/an aisle seat	мне хотелось бы взять место у окна/у прохода
I want to change/cancel my reservation	я хочу изменить/отменить заказ билета

Getting there — Как проехать?

could you tell me the way to the castle (on foot/by transport)?	не подскажете мне, как пройти/проехать к замку?
how long will it take to get there?	долго ли туда добираться?
how far is it from here?	как далеко это отсюда?
which bus do I take for the cathedral?	какой автобус идёт до собора?
can you tell me where to get off?	вы скажете мне, где выйти?
what time is the last bus?	до какого часа ходит автобус?
how do I get to the airport?	как мне проехать до аэропорта?
where's the nearest underground station, (AmE) subway station?	где ближайшая станция метро?
I'll take a taxi	я возьму такси
can you call me a taxi?	можете мне вызвать такси?

take the first turning on the right	поверни́те на пе́рвом поворо́те напра́во
turn left at the traffic lights/just past the church	поверни́те нале́во у светофо́ра/ сра́зу за це́рковью

Keeping in touch / Сре́дства свя́зи. Отноше́ния

On the phone	Говори́м по телефо́ну
may I use your phone?	мо́жно позвони́ть по ва́шему телефо́ну?
do you have a mobile, (AmE) cell phone?	у вас есть моби́льный телефо́н?
what is the code for St Petersburg/ Edinburgh?	како́й код (телефо́на) в Санкт-Петербу́рг/Эдинбу́рг?
I want to make a phone call	мне ну́жно сде́лать звоно́к
I'd like to reverse the charges, (AmE) call collect	мне ну́жно, что́бы звоно́к оплати́ла вызыва́емая сторона́
I need to top up my mobile, (AmE) cell phone	мне ну́жно доплати́ть за моби́льный телефо́н
the line's engaged, (AmE) busy	ли́ния занята́
there's no answer	отве́та нет
hello, this is John/Igor	алло́, э́то Джон/И́горь
is Oleg/Richard there, please?	пожа́луйста, позови́те Оле́га/Ри́чарда
who's calling?	кто говори́т?
sorry, wrong number	извини́те, не туда́ попа́ли
just a moment, please	одну́ мину́тку, пожа́луйста
please hold the line	не ве́шайте тру́бку, пожа́луйста
please tell him/her I called	пожа́луйста, переда́йте ему́/ей, что я звони́л/звони́ла
I'd like to leave a message for him/her	я хоте́л/хоте́ла бы оста́вить сообще́ние для него́/неё
...I'll try again later	...я ещё поздне́е позвоню́
please tell him/her that Elena called	пожа́луйста, переда́йте ему́/ей, что звони́ла Еле́на
can he/she ring me back?	мо́жет он/она́ мне перезвони́ть?
my home number is...	мой дома́шний телефо́н...
my business number is...	мой рабо́чий телефо́н...
my mobile, (AmE) cell phone number is...	но́мер моего́ моби́льного...
we were cut off	нас прерва́ли

Writing　Пи́шем письмо́

what's your address?	ваш а́дрес?
where is the nearest post office?	где ближа́йшая по́чта?
could I have a stamp for Russia, please?	пожа́луйста, да́йте мне ма́рку для письма́ в Росси́ю
I'd like to send a parcel/a fax	я хоте́л/хоте́ла бы посла́ть посы́лку/факс

Online　Онла́йн

are you on the Internet?	вы подключены́ к Интерне́ту?
what's your email address?	како́й ваш электро́нный а́дрес?
we could send it by email	мы могли́ бы посла́ть э́то по электро́нной по́чте
I'll email it to you on Tuesday	я пошлю́ это вам по электро́нной по́чте во вто́рник
I looked it up on the Internet	я посмотре́л/посмотре́ла э́то по Интерне́ту
the information is on their website	информа́ция есть на их веб-са́йте

Meeting up　Встре́чи

what shall we do this evening?	что мы бу́дем де́лать сего́дня ве́чером?
where shall we meet?	где мы встре́тимся?
I'll see you outside the cafe at 6 o'clock	я вас встре́чу у кафе́ в 6 часо́в
see you later	до встре́чи
I can't today, I'm busy	сего́дня не могу́, я за́нят/занята́

Phrasefinder

Food and drink / Еда́ и напи́тки

Reservations   Зака́з в рестора́не

can you recommend a good restaurant?	мо́жете ли порекомендова́ть хоро́ший рестора́н?
I'd like to reserve a table for four	я хоте́л/хоте́ла бы заказа́ть сто́лик на четверы́х
a reservation for tomorrow evening at eight o'clock	зака́з на за́втра на во́семь часо́в ве́чера

Ordering   Зака́з блюд

could we see the menu/wine list, please?	мо́жно нам меню́/ка́рту вин?
do you have a vegetarian/children's menu?	у вас есть вегетариа́нское/де́тское меню́?
as a starter… and to follow…	на заку́ску… и зате́м…
could we have some more bread/rice?	мо́жно ещё хле́ба/ри́са?
what would you recommend?	что вы порекоменду́ете?
I'd like a	я хоте́л/хоте́ла бы заказа́ть
…white coffee, (AmE) coffee with cream	…ко́фе с молоко́м
…black coffee	…чёрный ко́фе
…decaffeinated coffee	…ко́фе без кофеи́на
…liqueur	…ликёр
could I have the bill, (AmE) check	счёт, пожа́луйста

YOU WILL HEAR	Что вы слы́шите
вы гото́вы зака́зывать?	are you ready to order?
хоти́те заказа́ть апероти́в?	would you like an aperitif?
бу́дете зака́зывать заку́ску?	would you like a starter?
како́е блю́до бу́дете зака́зывать?	what will you have for the main course?
зака́зываете десе́рт?	would you like a dessert?
ко́фе?/ликёр?	would you like coffee/liqueurs?
что ещё зака́жете?	anything else?
прия́тного аппети́та!	enjoy your meal!
обслу́живание (не) включено́	service is (not) included

The menu   Меню́

starters	заку́ски
hors d'oeuvres	заку́ски
omelette	омле́т
soup	суп

заку́ски	starters
заку́ски	hors d'oeuvres
омле́т	omelette
суп	soup

fish	ры́ба
bass	морско́й о́кунь
cod	треска́
eel	у́горь
hake	хек
herring	се́льдь
monkfish	морско́й чёрт
mullet	кефа́ль
mussels	ми́дии
oyster	у́стрица
prawns	короле́вские креве́тки
salmon	лосо́сь, сёмга
sardines	сарди́ны
shrimps	креве́тки
sole	морско́й язык
squid	кальма́р
trout	форе́ль
tuna	туне́ц
turbot	па́лтус

ры́ба	fish
кальма́р	squid
карп	carp
кефа́ль	mullet
креве́тки	prawns, shrimps
лосо́сь	salmon
ми́дии	mussels
морско́й о́кунь	bass
морско́й язы́к	sole
осетри́на	sturgeon
па́лтус	turbot
сарди́ны	sardines
се́льдь	herring
сёмга	salmon
треска́	cod
туне́ц	tuna
хек	hake
у́горь	eel
у́стрица	oyster
форе́ль	trout

meat	мя́со
beef	говя́дина
chicken	цыплёнок
chop	отбивна́я
duck	у́тка
goose	гусь
hare	за́яц
ham	ветчина́
kidneys	по́чки
lamb	(молода́я) бара́нина
liver	печёнка
pork	свини́на
rabbit	крольча́тина
sirloin	филе́
steak	бифште́кс, вы́резка
turkey	инде́йка
veal	теля́тина
venison	олени́на

мя́со	meat
(молода́я) бара́нина	lamb
бифште́кс	steak
ветчина́	ham
вы́резка	steak
говя́дина	beef
гусь	goose
колба́ски	sausages
олени́на	venison
отбивна́я	chop
печёнка	liver
по́чки	kidneys
свини́на	pork
теля́тина	veal
у́тка	duck
филе́	sirloin steak
цыплёнок	chicken

Phrasefinder

Phrasefinder

vegetables	о́вощи
asparagus	спа́ржа
aubergine	баклажа́н
beans	бобы́; фасо́ль
beetroot	свёкла
broccoli	бро́кколи
carrots	морко́вь
cabbage	капу́ста
celery	сельдере́й
courgettes (*BrE*)	цуки́ни
French beans (*BrE*)	стручко́вая фасо́ль
lettuce	сала́т-лату́к
mushrooms	грибы́
peas	горо́шек
(sweet) pepper	сла́дкий пе́рец
potatoes	карто́фель
runner beans	вью́щаяся фасо́ль
tomato	помидо́р
sweet potato	сла́дкий карто́фель, бата́т
zucchini (*AmE*)	цуки́ни

о́вощи	vegetables
баклажа́н	aubergine
бобы́	beans
горо́шек	peas
грибы́	mushrooms
зелёный лук	spring onions
капу́ста	cabbage
карто́фель	potatoes
лук	onions
морко́вь	carrots
огуре́ц	cucumber
(сла́дкий) пе́рец	(sweet) pepper
помидо́р	tomato
реди́с	radish
свёкла	beetroot
сельдере́й	celery
спа́ржа	asparagus
фасо́ль	beans
цветна́я капу́ста	cauliflower

the way it's cooked	как э́то пригото́влено
baked	запечённый
boiled	отварно́й, варёный
fried	жа́реный
griddled	пригото́вленный на пло́ской сковороде́
grilled	(жа́реный) на гри́ле
poached	припу́щенный
pureed	пюре́, пюри́рованный
rare	с кро́вью (*о мясе*)
roast	жа́реный
stewed	тушёный
well done	хорошо́ прожа́ренный

как э́то пригото́влено	the way it's cooked
варёный	boiled
в горшо́чке	casseroled
жа́реный	(*в духовке*) roast; (*на сковороде*) fried
жа́реный на гри́ле	grilled
запечённый	baked
отварно́й	boiled
пригото́вленный на пло́ской сковороде́	griddled
припу́щенный	poached
с кро́вью (*о мясе*)	rare
тушёный	stewed
хорошо́ прожа́ренный	well done

desserts	**десе́рты**
ice cream	моро́женое
fruit	фру́кты
gateau	торт
pie	пиро́г

other	**друго́е**
bread	хлеб
butter	сли́вочное ма́сло
cheese	сыр
cheeseboard	доска́/блю́до с сы́ром
garlic	чесно́к
mayonnaise	майоне́з
mustard	горчи́ца
olive oil	оли́вковое ма́сло
pepper	пе́рец
rice	рис
salt	соль
sauce	со́ус
seasoning	припра́ва
vinegar	у́ксус

drinks	**напи́тки**
beer	пи́во
bottle	буты́лка
carbonated	газиро́ванный
fizzy	шипу́чий
half-bottle	полбуты́лки
liqueur	ликёр
mineral water	минера́льная вода́
red wine	кра́сное вино́
rosé	ро́зовое вино́
soft drink	безалкого́льный напи́ток
still	негазиро́ванный
house wine	дома́шнее вино́
table wine	столо́вое вино́
tap water	водопрово́дная вода́
white wine	бе́лое вино́
wine	вино́

десе́рты	**desserts**
моро́женое	ice cream
пиро́г	pie
торт	gateau
фру́кты	fruit

друго́е	**other**
горчи́ца	mustard
майоне́з	mayonnaise
оли́вковое ма́сло	olive oil
пе́рец	pepper
припра́ва	seasoning
сли́вочное ма́сло	butter
соль	salt
со́ус	sauce
сыр	cheese
у́ксус	vinegar
хлеб	bread
хрен	horseradish
чесно́к	garlic

напи́тки	**drinks**
безалкого́льный напи́ток	soft drink
бе́лое вино́	white wine
буты́лка	bottle
вино́	wine
водопрово́дная вода́	tap water
газиро́ванный	carbonated
дома́шнее вино́	house wine
кра́сное вино́	red wine
ликёр	liqueur
минера́льная вода́	mineral water
негазиро́ванный	still
пи́во	beer
полбуты́лки	half-bottle
ро́зовое вино́	rosé
столо́вое вино́	table wine
шипу́чий	fizzy

Phrasefinder

Phrasefinder

Places to stay / Где останови́ться

Camping · Ке́мпинг

can we pitch our tent here?	мы мо́жем здесь разби́ть пала́тку?
can we park our caravan here?	мо́жем здесь припаркова́ть наш карава́н?
what are the facilities like?	каки́е здесь усло́вия?
how much is it per night?	ско́лько здесь беру́т за су́тки?
where do we park the car?	где мо́жно припаркова́ть маши́ну?
we're looking for a campsite	мы и́щем ке́мпинг
this is a list of local campsites	вот спи́сок ме́стных ке́мпингов
we go on a camping holiday every year	мы ка́ждый год отдыха́ем в ке́мпинге

At the hotel · В гости́нице

I'd like a double/single room with bath	мне ну́жен двухме́стный/ одноме́стный но́мер с ва́нной
we have a reservation in the name of Morris	мы зарезерви́ровали но́мер на фами́лию Мо́ррис
we'll be staying three nights, from Friday to Sunday	мы бу́дем здесь тро́е су́ток, с пя́тницы по воскресе́нье
how much does the room cost?	ско́лько сто́ит но́мер?
I'd like to see the room	я хоте́л/хоте́ла бы посмотре́ть но́мер
what time is breakfast?	когда́ здесь за́втрак?
can I leave this in your safe?	могу́ я э́то оста́вить в ва́шем сейфе́?
bed and breakfast	ночле́г и за́втрак
we'd like to stay another night	мы хоте́ли бы оста́ться ещё на су́тки
please call me at 7.30	пожа́луйста, позвони́те мне в 7.30
are there any messages for me?	есть ли мне сообще́ние?

Hostels · Молодёжные гости́ницы

could you tell me where the youth hostel is?	скажи́те мне, пожа́луйста, где молодёжная гости́ница?
what time does the hostel close?	когда́ молодёжную гости́ницу закрыва́ют?
I'll be staying in a hostel	я остановлю́сь в молодёжной гости́нице
the hostel we're staying in is great value	молодёжная гости́ница, где мы останови́лись, недорога́я и о́чень удо́бная

| I know a really good hostel in Dublin | я зна́ю в Ду́блине весьма́ прили́чную молодёжную гости́ницу |
| I'd like to go backpacking in Australia | я хоте́л/хоте́ла бы попутеше́ствовать с рюкзако́м по Австра́лии |

Rooms to rent / Жильё внаём

I'm looking for a room with a reasonable rent	я ищу́ ко́мнату за уме́ренную це́ну
I'd like to rent an apartment for a few weeks	я хоте́л/хоте́ла бы снять кварти́ру на не́сколько неде́ль
where do I find out about rooms to rent?	где мне узна́ть о ко́мнатах, кото́рые сдаю́тся?
what's the weekly rent?	ско́лько плати́ть за жильё в неде́лю?
I'm staying with friends at the moment	я сейча́с живу́ у друзе́й
I rent an apartment on the outskirts of town	я снима́ю кварти́ру на окра́ине го́рода
the room's fine—I'll take it	ко́мната мне подхо́дит—я сниму́ её
the deposit is one month's rent in advance	зада́ток вперёд в су́мме ме́сячной опла́ты

Shopping and money / Поку́пки и де́ньги

Banking / В ба́нке

I'd like to change some money	я хоте́л/хоте́ла бы поменя́ть де́ньги
I want to change some dollars into euros	я хочу́ поменя́ть до́ллары на е́вро
do you need identification?	вам ну́жно удостовере́ние ли́чности?
what's the exchange rate today?	како́й курс обме́на на сего́дня?
do you accept traveller's cheques, (AmE) traveler's checks?	вы принима́ете доро́жные че́ки?
I'd like to transfer some money from my account	я хоте́л/хоте́ла бы перевести́ не́которую су́мму с моего́ счёта
where is there an ATM/a cash machine?	где здесь банкома́т?
I'd like high denomination notes, (AmE) bills	мне нужны́ кру́пные купю́ры
I'm with another bank	у меня́ счёт в друго́м ба́нке

Finding the right shop

Ну́жный магази́н

where's the main shopping district?	где здесь торго́вый центр?
where can I buy batteries/postcards?	где я могу́ купи́ть батаре́йки/откры́тки?
where's the nearest pharmacy/bookshop?	где ближа́йшая апте́ка/ближа́йший кни́жный магази́н?
is there a good food shop around here?	есть здесь побли́зости хоро́ший продово́льственный магази́н?
what time do the shops open/close?	когда́ магази́ны открыва́ются/закрыва́ются?
where did you get those?	где вы э́то купи́ли?
I'm looking for presents for my family	я ищу́ пода́рки для мои́х родны́х
we'll do our shopping on Saturday	мы пойдём по магази́нам в суббо́ту
I love shopping	я люблю́ ходи́ть по магази́нам

Are you being served?

Вас обслу́живают?

how much does that cost?	ско́лько э́то сто́ит?
can I try it on?	могу́ я э́то приме́рить?
could you wrap it for me, please?	заверни́те, пожа́луйста
can I pay by credit card?	я могу́ плати́ть креди́тной ка́ртой?
do you have this in another colour, (AmE) color?	есть у вас э́то друго́й расцве́тки?
could I have a bag, please?	бу́дьте добры́, да́йте мне паке́т
I'm just looking	я про́сто смотрю́
I'll think about it	я до́лжен/должна́ поду́мать
I'd like a receipt, please	мне нужна́ квита́нция/мне ну́жен чек
I need a bigger/smaller size	мне ну́жен бо́льший/ме́ньший разме́р
I take a size 10/a medium	ношу́ разме́р 10/сре́дний разме́р
it doesn't suit me	мне э́то не подхо́дит
I'm sorry, I don't have any change/anything smaller	прости́те, у меня́ нет ме́лочи/ме́лких де́нег
that's all, thank you	э́то всё, спаси́бо

Changing things

Заме́на това́ра

I'd like to change it, please	я хоте́л/хоте́ла бы э́то поменя́ть
I bought this here yesterday	я купи́л/купи́ла э́то здесь вчера́
can I have a refund?	могу́ я рассчи́тывать на возмеще́ние?/мне верну́т де́ньги?
can you mend it for me?	мо́жете э́то испра́вить/почин$и́ть?
it doesn't work	э́то не рабо́тает
can I speak to the manager?	могу́ я поговори́ть с ме́неджером?

Sport and leisure / Спорт и досýг

Keeping fit	Занятия спóртом
where can we play football/squash?	где мы мóжем поиграть в футбóл/сквош?
where is the local sports centre, (AmE) center?	где здесь мéстный спортивный центр?
what's the charge per day?	скóлько стóит день занятий?
is there a reduction for children/a student discount?	есть ли скидка для детéй/студéнтов?
I'm looking for a swimming pool/tennis court	я ищý бассéйн/тéннисный корт
you have to be a member	вы должны быть члéном (клýба)
I play tennis on Mondays	я играю в тéннис по понедéльникам
I would like to go fishing/riding	я хотéл/хотéла бы заняться рыбной лóвлей/верховóй ездóй
I want to do aerobics	я хочý заняться аэрóбикой
I love swimming/roller skating	я люблю плáвание/катáние на рóликовых конькáх
we want to hire skis/snowboards	мы хотéли бы взять напрокáт лыжи/сноубóрды

Watching sport	Спортивные зрéлища
is there a football match on Saturday?	есть футбóльный матч в воскресéнье?
which teams are playing?	какие комáнды игрáют?
where can I get tickets?	где я могý купить билéты?
I'd like to see a rugby/football match	я хотéл/хотéла бы попáсть на рéгби/футбóл
my favourite, (AmE) favorite team is…	моя любимая комáнда…
let's watch the game on TV	давáйте посмóтрим игрý по телевизору

Going out in the evening	В теáтре, на концéрте
what's on?	что идёт?
when does the box office open/close?	когдá открывáется/закрывáется билéтная кáсса?
what time does the concert/performance start?	когдá начáло концéрта/спектáкля?
when does it finish?	когдá кончáется (спектáкль)?
are there any seats left for tonight?	есть ли свобóдные местá на сегóдня?

how much are the tickets?	ско́лько сто́ят биле́ты?
where can I get a programme, (AmE) program?	где я могу́ купи́ть програ́мму?
I want to book tickets for tonight's performance	я хочу́ заказа́ть биле́ты на сего́дняшний конце́рт/спекта́кль
I'll book seats in the circle	я закажу́ биле́ты на балко́н
I'd rather have seats in the stalls	я бы хоте́л/хоте́ла купи́ть биле́ты на места́ в парте́ре
somewhere in the middle, but not too far back	где-нибу́дь в середи́не, но не о́чень далеко́
four, please	четы́ре биле́та, пожа́луйста
for Saturday	на суббо́ту
we'd like to go to a club	мы бы хоте́ли сходи́ть в ночно́й клуб
I go clubbing every weekend	я хожу́ в ночно́й клуб ка́ждый уи́к-э́нд

Hobbies   Хо́бби

what do you do at the weekend?	что вы де́лаете по суббо́там и воскресе́ньям?
I like yoga/listening to music	мне нра́вится занима́ться йо́гой/слу́шать му́зыку
I spend a lot of time surfing the Net	я мно́го вре́мени провожу́ в Интерне́те/я мно́го брожу́ по Интерне́ту
I read a lot	я мно́го чита́ю
I collect old coins	я собира́ю стари́нные моне́ты

Time / Вре́мя

Telling the time   Ско́лько вре́мени?

what time is it?	ско́лько вре́мени?
it's 2 o'clock	два часа́
at about 8 o'clock	о́коло 8 (восьми́) часо́в
from 10 o'clock onwards	по́сле 10 (десяти́) часо́в
at 5 o'clock in the morning/afternoon	в 5 (пять) (часо́в) утра́/ве́чера
it's five past/quarter past/half past one	пять мину́т/че́тверть/полови́на второ́го
it's twenty-five to/quarter to one	без двадцати́ пяти́/че́тверти час
a quarter/three quarters of an hour	че́тверть часа́/со́рок пять мину́т

Days and dates　　Дни и чи́сла

Sunday, Monday, Tuesday, Wednesday, Thursday, Friday, Saturday	воскресе́нье, понеде́льник, вто́рник, среда́, четве́рг, пя́тница, суббо́та
January, February, March, April, May, June, July, August, September, October, November, December	янва́рь, февра́ль, март, апре́ль, май, ию́нь, ию́ль, а́вгуст, сентя́брь, октя́брь, ноя́брь, дека́брь
what's the date?	како́е сего́дня число́?
it's the second of June	сего́дня второ́е ию́ня
we meet up every Monday	мы ви́димся ка́ждый понеде́льник
we're going away in August	мы уезжа́ем в а́вгусте
on November 8th	восьмо́го ноября́

Public holidays and special days　　Пра́здники, нерабо́чие дни

bank holiday	нерабо́чий день
bank holiday Monday	нерабо́чий понеде́льник
New Year's Day (*1 Jan.*)	Но́вый год (*1-е января́*)
Epiphany (*6 Jan.*)	Креще́ние Госпо́дне, Богоявле́ние (*19-е января́*)
St Valentine's Day (*14 Feb.*)	День свято́го Валенти́на (*14-е февраля́*)
Day of the Defender of the Fatherland	День защи́тника Оте́чества (*23-е февраля́*)
Shrove Tuesday/Pancake Day	вто́рник на ма́сленой неде́ле
Ash Wednesday	пе́рвый день Вели́кого поста́
International Women's Day (*8 March*)	Восьмо́е ма́рта, Междунаро́дный же́нский день (*8-е ма́рта*)
Maundy Thursday	Вели́кий четве́рг (на Страстно́й неде́ле)
Good Friday	Страстна́я пя́тница
Easter	Па́сха
May Day (*1 May*)	Пе́рвое ма́я (*1-е ма́я*)
VE Day (*8 May*)	День Побе́ды (*9-е ма́я*)
Whit Sunday, Pentecost (*7th Sunday after Easter*)	Тро́ица, Тро́ицын день
Russian Defenders' Memorial Day (*marking the beginning of the Great Patriotic War (1941–45)*)	День па́мяти защи́тников Оте́чества (*22-е ию́ня*)
Fourth of July/Independence Day (US)	День незави́симости
Assumption/Dormition of the Virgin Mary (*15 Aug.*)	Успе́ние Пресвято́й Богоро́дицы (*28-е а́вгуста*)

Protecting Veil/Intercession of the Virgin Mary (*people pray for protection from evil and hardships and help in view of the long winter ahead*)	Покро́в Пресвято́й Богоро́дицы (*14-е октября́*)
Halloween (*31 Oct.*)	Ка́нун Дня Всех Святы́х
All Saints' Day (*1 Nov.*)	День Всех Святы́х
Guy Fawkes Day/Bonfire Night (*5 Nov., UK*)	день Га́я Фо́кса, день годовщи́ны раскры́тия «порохово́го за́говора»
National Unity Day	День наро́дного еди́нства (*4-е ноября́*)
Remembrance Sunday (*anniversary of the armistice of 11 November 1918*)	Помина́льное воскресе́нье
Thanksgiving (*4th Thursday in November, US*)	День благодаре́ния
Christmas Eve (*24 Dec.*)	Рожде́ственский соче́льник (*6-е января́*)
Christmas Day (*25 Dec.*)	Рождество́ Христо́во (*7-е января́*)
New Year's Eve (*31 Dec.*)	Нового́дняя ночь (*31-е декабря́*)

Weights and measures / Меры длины, веса, объёма

Length/Длинá

inches/дюймы	0.39	3.9	7.8	11.7	15.6	19.7	39
centimetres/сантимéтры	1	10	20	30	40	50	100

Distance/Расстоя́ние

miles/ми́ли	0.62	6.2	12.4	18.6	24.9	31	62
kilometres/киломéтры	1	10	20	30	40	50	100

Weight/Вес

pounds/фýнты	2.2	22	44	66	88	110	220
kilos/килогрáммы	1	10	20	30	40	50	100

Capacity/Объём

(UK) gallons/галлóны	0.22	2.2	4.4	6.6	8.8	11	22
(US) gallons/галлóны	0.26	2.64	5.28	7.92	10.56	13.2	26.4
litres/ли́тры	1	10	20	30	40	50	100

Temperature/Температýра

°C (Celsius)/ °C (по Цéльсию)	0	5	10	15	20	25	30	37	38	40
°F (Fahrenheit)/ °F (по Фаренгéйту)	32	41	50	59	68	77	86	98.4	100	104

Clothing and shoe sizes/Размéры одéжды и óбуви

Women's clothing sizes/Жéнская одéжда

UK	8	10	12	14	16	18
US	6	8	10	12	14	16
Russia	40	42	44	46	48	50

Men's clothing sizes (chest sizes)/Мужскáя одéжда (костю́мы, пиджакú)

UK/US	36	38	40	42	44	46
Russia	46	48	50	52	54	56

Women's shoes/Жéнская óбувь

UK	2.5	3	3.5	4	4.5	5	5.5	6	6.5	7	7.5	8
US	5	5.5	6	6.5	7	7.5	8	8.5	9	9.5	10	10.5
Russia	35	35.5	36	37	37.5	38	39	39.5	40	40.5	41	42

Men's shoes/Мужскáя óбувь

UK	6	6.5	7	7.5	8	8.5	9	9.5	10	10.5	11	11.5	12
US	6.5	7	7.5	8	8.5	9	9.5	10	10.5	11	11.5	12	12.5
Russia	39.5	40	40.5	41	42	42.5	43	44	44.5	45	46	46.5	47

Phrasefinder

a

Aa

A¹ /eɪ/ *letter*: from ∼ to Z от нача́ла до конца́
■ ∼ **road** *n.* магистра́льная доро́га, (а́вто)магистра́ль

A² /eɪ/ *n.* **1** (mus.) ля (*nt. indecl.*) **2** (academic mark) «отли́чно», пятёрка

✓ **a** /ə, eɪ/, **an** /æn, ən/ *indefinite article* **1** (*not usu. translated*): it's an elephant э́то слон **2** (∼ certain): in ∼ **sense** в како́м-то смы́сле; an old friend of mine оди́н мой ста́рый знако́мый **3** (distributive, in each) в + *a.*; twice ∼ **week** два ра́за в неде́лю; **10 miles an hour** де́сять миль в час; (for each) за + *a.*; **10p** ∼ **pound** 10 пе́нсов за фунт; (from each) с + *g.*; they charged £1 ∼ **head** они́ взя́ли по фу́нту с челове́ка

A & E *n.* (*abbr. of* **Accident and Emergency**) (BrE) отделе́ние неотло́жной по́мощи (*в больни́це*)

aback /ə'bæk/ *adv.*: we were taken ∼ by the news но́вость нас порази́ла

abacus /'æbəkəs/ *n.* (*pl.* ∼**es**) счёт|ы (-ов)

✓ **abandon** /ə'bænd(ə)n/ *v.t.* **1** (forsake, desert) пок|ида́ть, -и́нуть; ост|авля́ть, -а́вить; ∼ **ship!** пок.и́нуть кора́бль! **2** (renounce) отка́з|ываться, -а́ться от + *g.*; we must ∼ the idea мы должны́ отказа́ться от э́той иде́и; they had ∼ed all hope они́ оста́вили вся́кую наде́жду **3** (discontinue) прекра|ща́ть, -ти́ть; the search was ∼ed по́иски бы́ли прекращены́

abandoned /ə'bænd(ə)nd/ *adj.* оста́вленный, поки́нутый

abandonment /ə'bændənmənt/ *n.* **1** (desertion) оставле́ние **2** (of a belief, lawsuit, right) отка́з (of: от + *g.*) **3** (neglect) забро́шенность **4** (of a project) прекраще́ние **5**: ∼ **of a ship** оставле́ние (*or* ухо́д с) корабля́

abase /ə'beɪs/ *v.t.* ун|ижа́ть, -и́зить

abashed /ə'bæʃt/ *adj.* смущённый; she felt ∼ она́ была́ смущена́

abate /ə'beɪt/ *v.i.* (of storm, feelings, pain) ут|иха́ть, -и́хнуть; (of noise) ум|еньша́ться, -е́ньшиться

abattoir /'æbətwɑː(r)/ *n.* скотобо́йня

abbey /'æbɪ/ *n.* (*pl.* ∼**s**) абба́тство

abbot /'æbət/ *n.* абба́т

abbreviate /ə'briːvɪeɪt/ *v.t.* сокра|ща́ть, -ти́ть

abbreviation /əbriːvɪ'eɪʃ(ə)n/ *n.* сокраще́ние, аббревиату́ра

abdicate /'æbdɪkeɪt/ *v.t.* отка́з|ываться, -а́ться от + *g.*

abdication /æbdɪ'keɪʃ(ə)n/ *n.* отка́з (*от чего́*); отрече́ние (от престо́ла)

abdomen /'æbdəmən/ *n.* брюшна́я по́лость; живо́т

abdominal /æb'dɒmɪn(ə)l/ *adj.* брюшно́й; ∼ **pain** боль в животе́; ∼ **wound** ране́ние в живо́т

abduct /əb'dʌkt/ *v.t.* пох|ища́ть, -и́тить

abduction /əb'dʌkʃ(ə)n/ *n.* похище́ние

aberration /æbə'reɪʃ(ə)n/ *n.* **1** (error of judgement or conduct) заблужде́ние; **mental** ∼ помраче́ние рассу́дка, психи́ческое расстро́йство **2** (deviation) отклоне́ние от но́рмы, аберра́ция

abeyance /ə'beɪəns/ *n.*: in ∼ приостано́вленный; the matter is in ∼ де́ло вре́менно приостано́влено

abhor /əb'hɔː(r)/ *v.t.* (**abhorred, abhorring**) испы́т|ывать, -а́ть, отвраще́ние к + *d.*

abhorrent /əb'hɒrənt/ *adj.* омерзи́тельный, отврати́тельный; the very idea is ∼ to me мне проти́вно да́же ду́мать об э́том

abide /ə'baɪd/ *v.i.*: ∼ **by** (comply with) соблю|да́ть, -сти́; приде́рживаться (*impf.*) + *g.*

abiding /ə'baɪdɪŋ/ *adj.* постоя́нный, неизме́нный

✓ **ability** /ə'bɪlɪtɪ/ *n.* **1** (capacity in general) спосо́бность; to the best of one's ∼ по ме́ре спосо́бностей **2** (*in pl.*) (gifts) спосо́бности (*f. pl.*)

abject /'æbdʒekt/ *adj.* (humble) уни́женный; an ∼ **apology** уни́женная мольба́ о проще́нии; (craven): ∼ **fear** малоду́шный страх; (despicable) презре́нный; (pitiful, wretched) жа́лкий; in ∼ **poverty** в кра́йней нищете́

ablaze /ə'bleɪz/ *pred. adj.*: to be ∼ пыла́ть, полыха́ть (*both impf.*); the buildings were ∼ зда́ния полыха́ли *or* пыла́ли в огне́

✓ **able** /'eɪb(ə)l/ *adj.* (**abler, ablest**) **1**: be ∼ to мочь, с-; быть в состоя́нии; (have the strength or power to): he was not ∼ to walk any further он был не в си́лах (*or* не в состоя́нии) идти́ да́льше; (know how to): know how to: **he is** ∼ to swim он уме́ет пла́вать (*impf.*); (skilful) (capable) спосо́бный

■ ∼-**bodied** *adj.* здоро́вый, кре́пкий

ablution /ə'bluːʃ(ə)n/ *n.* (*usu. in pl.*) (act of washing oneself) (also iron.) омове́ние; **perform one's** ∼**s** соверш|а́ть, -и́ть омове́ние

abnormal /æb'nɔːm(ə)l/ *adj.* ненорма́льный

abnormality /æbnɔː'mælɪtɪ/ *n.* ненорма́льность

aboard /ə'bɔːd/ *adv.* **1** (on a ship or aircraft) на борту́; (on a train) в по́езде **2** (on to a ship or aircraft) на́ борт; (on to a train) в по́езд
● *prep.*: ∼ **ship** на борт(у́) корабля́

abode /ə'bəʊd/ *n.* жили́ще; **of no fixed** ∼ без постоя́нного местожи́тельства

abolish /ə'bɒlɪʃ/ *v.t.* отмен|я́ть, -и́ть

abolition /æbə'lɪʃ(ə)n/ *n.* отме́на; **the** ∼ **of capital punishment** отме́на сме́ртной ка́зни

a

abominable /ə'bɒmɪnəb(ə)l/ *adj.*
отврати́тельный, ме́рзкий

abomination /əbɒmɪ'neɪʃ(ə)n/ *n.* (detestation)
отвраще́ние, омерзе́ние; (detestable thing)
ме́рзость; **this hotel is an ~** э́та гости́ница —
ме́рзость

aboriginal /æbə'rɪdʒɪn(ə)l/ *n.* = aborigine
• *adj.* тузе́мный, коренно́й

aborigine /æbə'rɪdʒɪnɪ/ *n.* тузе́м|ец (-ка);
абориге́н; коренно́й жи́тель

abort /ə'bɔːt/ *v.t.* (fig., terminate or cancel
prematurely) приостан|а́вливать, -ови́ть

abortion /ə'bɔːʃ(ə)n/ *n.* (miscarriage) або́рт;
have an ~ де́лать, с- або́рт

abortive /ə'bɔːtɪv/ *adj.* (fig.) неуда́вшийся

abound /ə'baʊnd/ *v.i.* (exist in large numbers or
quantities) быть в изоби́лии; изоби́ловать
(*impf.*)

✓ **about** /ə'baʊt/ *adv.* **1** (in the vicinity; in circulation)
вокру́г, круго́м; **is he anywhere ~?** он где́-то
здесь?; **up and ~** на нога́х **2** (almost) почти́;
it's ~ time we went нам пора́ идти́; **and
~ time too!** давно́ пора́! **3** (approximately)
о́коло + *g.*; приблизи́тельно; **~ 3 o'clock**
о́коло трёх часо́в; **he is ~ your height** он
приблизи́тельно ва́шего ро́ста; **in ~ half
an hour** приме́рно че́рез полчаса́ **4** (~ **to**)
(ready to, just going to): **he was ~ to leave when
I arrived** он собира́лся уходи́ть, когда́ я
пришёл
• *prep.* **1** (at or to var. places in) по + *d.*; **walk ~
the room** ходи́ть (*indet.*) по ко́мнате
2 (concerning) о + *p.*; насчёт + *g.*; относи́тельно
+ *g.*; **what are you talking ~?** о чём вы
говори́те?; **how ~ a game of cards?** не
сыгра́ть ли нам в ка́рты?; **he has called ~ the
rent** он зашёл насчёт квартпла́ты; **she is mad
~ him** она́ без ума́ от него́; **there is no doubt
~ it** в э́том нет сомне́ния
■ **~-face, ~-turn** *nn.* (mil.) поворо́т круго́м;
(fig.) ре́зкий поворо́т

✓ **above** /ə'bʌv/ *prep.* **1** (over; higher than) над + *i.*
2 (more than) свы́ше + *g.*; **~ 30 tons** свы́ше
30 тонн **3** (fig.): **he is getting ~ himself** он
начина́ет зазнава́ться; **~ all** пре́жде всего́;
са́мое гла́вное; **over and ~** вдоба́вок к + *d.*
• *adv.* **1** (overhead; upstairs) наверху́; **we live
in the flat ~** мы живём в кварти́ре этажо́м
вы́ше; (expr. motion) наве́рх; **from ~** све́рху
2 (in text, speech, etc.) вы́ше; ра́нее
• *n.*: **the ~** вышеска́занное; вышепомяну́тое
• *adj.* (~-mentioned) вышепомяну́тый;
(foregoing) предыду́щий
■ **~-board** *adj.* (honourable) че́стный; (open,
frank) откры́тый; **~-mentioned** *adj.*
вышепомяну́тый

abracadabra /æbrəkə'dæbrə/ *n.* абракада́бра

abrasion /ə'breɪʒ(ə)n/ *n.* сса́дина

abrasive /ə'breɪsɪv/ *adj.* абрази́вный; (fig.)
ре́зкий, колю́чий

abreast /ə'brest/ *adv.* в ряд, на одно́й ли́нии;
three ~ по́ трое/три в ряд; (fig.): **~ of events**
в ку́рсе собы́тий

✓ ключева́я ле́ксика

abridge /ə'brɪdʒ/ *v.t.* сокра|ща́ть, -ти́ть

✓ **abroad** /ə'brɔːd/ *adv.* за грани́цей, за
рубежо́м; (motion) за грани́цу, за рубе́ж; **from
~** из-за грани́цы, из-за рубежа́

abrupt /ə'brʌpt/ *adj.* **1** (brusque) ре́зкий
2 (sudden) внеза́пный

abscess /'æbsɪs/ *n.* абсце́сс

abscond /əb'skɒnd/ *v.i.* скр|ыва́ться, -ы́ться;
he ~ed with the takings он скры́лся с
вы́ручкой

abseil /'æbseɪl/ (BrE) *n.* спуск на верёвке
• *v.i.* спус|ка́ться, -ти́ться на верёвке

✓ **absence** /'æbs(ə)ns/ *n.* отсу́тствие; **in his ~** в
его́ отсу́тствие

absent /'æbs(ə)nt/ *adj.* отсу́тствующий; **he
was ~ from school** он отсу́тствовал в шко́ле
■ **~-minded** *adj.* рассе́янный

absentee /æbsən'tiː/ *n.* отсу́тствующий

absenteeism /æbsən'tiːɪz(ə)m/ *n.* (from work,
school) (системати́ческие) прогу́лы (*m. pl.*);
(from voting) абсентеи́зм

absolute /'æbsəluːt/ *adj.* соверше́нный;
абсолю́тный

✓ **absolutely** /'æbsəluːtlɪ/ *adv.* (completely)
абсолю́тно; соверше́нно; (unquestionably)
безусло́вно

absolutism /'æbsəluːtɪz(ə)m/ *n.* абсолюти́зм

absolve /əb'zɒlv/ *v.t.* (of blame) призн|ава́ть,
-а́ть невино́вным; **he was ~d of all blame**
он был при́знан по́лностью невино́вным;
(of sins) отпус|ка́ть, -ти́ть грехи́ + *d.*; **his sins
were ~d** он получи́л отпуще́ние грехо́в;
(of obligation) освобо|жда́ть, -ди́ть

absorb /əb'zɔːb/ *v.t.* **1** (soak up) впи́т|ывать,
-а́ть **2** (engross) погло|ща́ть, -ти́ть

absorbent /əb'zɔːbənt/ *adj.* вса́сывающий,
поглоща́ющий

absorption /əb'zɔːpʃ(ə)n/ *n.* (engrossment):
his ~ in his studies его́ погружённость в
заня́тия

abstain /əb'steɪn/ *v.i.* возде́рж|иваться,
-а́ться; **he ~ed (from drinking) on principle** он
возде́рживался (от спиртно́го) из при́нципа;
the Opposition decided to ~ (from voting)
оппози́ция реши́ла воздержа́ться (от
голосова́ния)

abstainer /əb'steɪnə(r)/ *n.* (from drinking)
тре́звенник, непью́щий; (from voting)
воздержа́вшийся

abstemious /æb'stiːmɪəs/ *adj.* возде́ржанный

abstention /əb'stenʃ(ə)n/ *n.* воздержа́ние
(from: от + *g.*); **the resolution was passed
with three ~s** резолю́ция была́ при́нята при
трёх воздержа́вшихся

abstinence /'æbstɪnəns/ *n.* воздержа́ние
(from: от + *g.*); (moderation) уме́ренность

abstract /'æbstrækt/ *n.*: **in the ~** абстра́ктно,
отвлечённо
• *adj.* абстра́ктный, отвлечённый; **~ art**
абстра́ктное иску́сство

absurd /əb'sɜːd/ *adj.* неле́пый, абсу́рдный

absurdity /əb'sɜːdɪtɪ/ *n.* неле́пость, абсу́рд,
абсу́рдность; **reduce to ~** дов|оди́ть, -ести́

до абсу́рда

abundance /əˈbʌnd(ə)ns/ *n.* (plenty) изоби́лие

abundant /əˈbʌnd(ə)nt/ *adj.* (plentiful) оби́льный; ~ **in** бога́тый, изоби́лующий (*чем*)

✍ **abuse¹** /əˈbjuːs/ *n.* **1** (misuse) злоупотребле́ние; **drug** ~ злоупотребле́ние нарко́тиками; **sexual** ~ сексуа́льное наси́лие; **child** ~ (sexual) совраще́ние малоле́тних; (physical) жесто́кое обраще́ние с детьми́; **human rights** ~ наруше́ние прав челове́ка **2** (reviling) брань; издева́тельство; **term of** ~ оскорбле́ние

abuse² /əˈbjuːz/ *v.t.* **1** (misuse) злоупотреб|ля́ть, -и́ть + *i.* **2** (revile) руга́ть (*impf.*); оскорб|ля́ть, -и́ть

abusive /əˈbjuːsɪv/ *adj.* бра́нный, руга́тельный

abut /əˈbʌt/ *v.i.* (**abutted, abutting**): ~ **on** (border on) прилега́ть (*impf.*) к + *d.*; примыка́ть (*impf.*) к + *d.*; (lean against) уп|ира́ться, -ере́ться в + *a.*

abysmal /əˈbɪzm(ə)l/ *adj.* ужа́сный

abyss /əˈbɪs/ *n.* бе́здна, про́пасть

AC *abbr.* (*of* **alternating current**) переме́нный ток

a/c /əˈkaʊnt/ *n.* (*abbr. of* **account**) счёт

✍ **academic** /ækəˈdemɪk/ *n.* учёный, нау́чный рабо́тник
● *adj.* академи́ческий, нау́чный; (unpractical) академи́чный; теорети́ческий; нереа́льный

academician /əkædəˈmɪʃ(ə)n/ *n.* акаде́мик

academy /əˈkædəmɪ/ *n.* акаде́мия; (police, military, etc.) учи́лище

accede /əkˈsiːd/ *v.i.* **1** (agree, assent) согла|ша́ться, -си́ться (**to:** с + *i.*) **2**: ~ **to** (grant): ~ **to a request** удовлетвор|я́ть, -и́ть про́сьбу; (take up, enter upon) вступ|а́ть, -и́ть в + *a.*; ~ **to the throne** всходи́ть, взойти́ на престо́л

accelerate /əkˈseləreɪt/ *v.t. & i.* уск|оря́ть(ся), -о́рить(ся); (motoring) наб|ира́ть, -ра́ть ско́рость

acceleration /əkseləˈreɪʃ(ə)n/ *n.* ускоре́ние

accelerator /əkˈseləreɪtə(r)/ *n.* **1** (of car) педа́ль га́за; акселера́тор **2** (tech.) ускори́тель (*m.*)

accent /ˈæks(ə)nt/ *n.* **1** (orthographical sign; emphasis) ударе́ние; акце́нт **2** (mode of speech) акце́нт; **he speaks with a slight** ~ он говори́т с лёгким акце́нтом

accentuate /əkˈsentʃʊeɪt/ *v.t.* (fig.) акценти́ровать (*impf.*); подч|ёркивать, -еркну́ть

✍ **accept** /əkˈsept/ *v.t.* **1** (agree to receive) прин|има́ть, -я́ть **2** (recognize, admit) призн|ава́ть, -а́ть; **you must** ~ **this fact** вы должны́ смири́ться с э́тим фа́ктом

acceptable /əkˈseptəb(ə)l/ *adj.* прие́млемый

acceptance /əkˈsept(ə)ns/ *n.* (willing receipt) приня́тие; (approval) одобре́ние

✍ **access** /ˈækses/ *n.* (to person or thing) до́ступ (к + *d.*)
● *v.t.* (comput.): ~ **data** получа́ть, -и́ть до́ступ к да́нным
■ ~ **road** *n.* подъездно́й путь

accessible /əkˈsesɪb(ə)l/ *adj.* досту́пный

accession /əkˈseʃ(ə)n/ *n.* вступле́ние

accessory /əkˈsesərɪ/ *n.* **1** (law) соуча́стник **2** (*in pl.*) (ancillary parts) принадле́жности (*f. pl.*); (of clothing) аксессуа́ры (*m. pl.*)

✍ **accident** /ˈæksɪd(ə)nt/ *n.* **1** (chance) слу́чай, случа́йность; **by** ~ случа́йно **2** (unintentional action): **I'm sorry, it was an** ~ прости́те, я неча́янно **3** (mishap) несча́стный слу́чай; (rail.) круше́ние, ава́рия; **car** ~ автомоби́льная катастро́фа, автокатастро́фа, ава́рия; **he had an** ~ он попа́л в ава́рию

accidental /æksɪˈdent(ə)l/ *adj.* **1** (chance) случа́йный; ~ **death** смерть в результа́те несча́стного слу́чая **2** (incidental) побо́чный

acclaim /əˈkleɪm/ *n.* (public recognition) призна́ние

acclamation /ækləˈmeɪʃ(ə)n/ *n.* (public recognition) призна́ние; (loud approval) шу́мное одобре́ние; (enthusiasm) энтузиа́зм; (*in pl.*) (shouts of welcome or applause) приве́тственные во́згласы (*m. pl.*); **his books won the** ~ **of critics** его́ кни́ги вы́звали шу́мное одобре́ние кри́тиков

acclimate /əˈklaɪmət/ *v.t. & i.* (AmE) = **acclimatize**

acclimatize /əˈklaɪmətaɪz/ *v.t. & i.* акклиматизи́ровать(ся) (*impf., pf.*)

accolade /ˈækəleɪd/ *n.* (praise) похвала́; (reward) награ́да

accommodat|e /əˈkɒmədeɪt/ *v.t.* **1** (house) разме|ща́ть, -сти́ть; (single person) поме|ща́ть, -сти́ть; предост|авля́ть, -а́вить жильё + *d.* **2** (hold, seat) вме|ща́ть, -сти́ть; **the car will** ~**e 6 persons** маши́на вмеща́ет шесть челове́к; **a hall** ~**ing 500** зал на пятьсо́т челове́к

accommodating /əˈkɒmədeɪtɪŋ/ *adj.* сгово́рчивый, услу́жливый

accommodation /əkɒməˈdeɪʃ(ə)n/ *n.* жильё; **can you provide a night's** ~? мо́жно останови́ться у вас на́ ночь?

accompaniment /əˈkʌmpənɪmənt/ *n.* **1** (accompanying) сопровожде́ние **2** (mus.) аккомпанеме́нт

accompanist /əˈkʌmpənɪst/ *n.* (mus.) аккомпаниа́тор

✍ **accompany** /əˈkʌmpənɪ/ *v.t.* **1** (go or be with) сопровожда́ть (*impf.*) **2** (occur with) сопровожда́ть (*impf.*) **3** (mus.) аккомпани́ровать (*impf.*) + *d.*

accomplice /əˈkʌmplɪs/ *n.* соуча́стни|к (-ца); сообщ|и́к (-ца)

accomplish /əˈkʌmplɪʃ/ *v.t.* (complete) заверш|а́ть, -и́ть; (fulfil, perform) выполня́ть, вы́полнить; соверш|а́ть, -и́ть

accomplished /əˈkʌmplɪʃt/ *adj.* соверше́нный, иску́сный

accomplishment /əˈkʌmplɪʃmənt/ *n.* заверше́ние; выполне́ние; (achievement) достиже́ние

accord /əˈkɔːd/ *n.* **1** (agreement) согла́сие, соглаше́ние; **with one** ~ единоду́шно **2** (volition): **of one's own** ~ по со́бственному жела́нию, по со́бственной во́ле

accordance /əˈkɔːd(ə)ns/ *n.* соотве́тствие; **in** ~ **with** в соотве́тствии с + *i.*, согла́сно + *d.*

a

according /ə'kɔːdɪŋ/ *adv*.: ~ **to** (in keeping or conformity with) согла́сно + *d*.; ~ **to the law(s)** в соотве́тствии с законода́тельством; по зако́ну; (on the authority or information of) по + *d*., согла́сно + *d*.; по мне́нию/слова́м/ сообще́нию + *g*.

accordingly /ə'kɔːdɪŋlɪ/ *adv*. **1** (appropriately) соотве́тственно **2** (therefore) поэ́тому; таки́м о́бразом

accordion /ə'kɔːdɪən/ *n*. аккордео́н

accost /ə'kɒst/ *v.t.* пристⱡава́ть, -а́ть к + *d*. (с разгово́рами)

♂ **account** /ə'kaʊnt/ *n*. **1** (comm.) счёт (-а́); **current** ~ теку́щий счёт; **deposit** ~ депози́тный счёт; **joint** ~ о́бщий счёт; **do the** ~**s** провⱡоди́ть, -ести́ счета́; **balance** ~**s** свⱡоди́ть, -ести́ бала́нс **2** (statement, report) отчёт; (description) описа́ние; **by all** ~**s** су́дя по всему́ **3** (estimation, consideration) расчёт; **take into** ~, **take** ~ **of** учⱡи́тывать, -е́сть; принⱡима́ть, -я́ть во внима́ние **4** (reason, cause): **on** ~ **of** (because of) из-за + *g*.; (in consequence of) по причи́не + *g*.; (as a result of) всле́дствие + *g*.; **on no** ~ ни в ко́ем слу́чае
● *v.i.*: ~ **for** (lit., fig., give a reckoning of) отчи́тⱡываться, -а́ться в + *p*.; даⱡва́ть, -ть отчёт в + *p*.; (fig., answer for) отвⱡеча́ть, -е́тить за + *a*.; **is everyone** ~**ed for?** никого́ не забы́ли?; (explain) объясня́ⱡть, -и́ть; (be reason for) явля́ться (*impf.*) причи́ной + *g*.

accountable /ə'kaʊntəb(ə)l/ *adj*. отве́тственный; **he is** ~ **to me** он отчи́тывается пе́редо мной

accountancy /ə'kaʊnt(ə)nsɪ/ *n*. (profession) бухга́лтерское де́ло

accountant /ə'kaʊnt(ə)nt/ *n*. бухга́лтер, счетово́д

accounting /ə'kaʊntɪŋ/ *n*. бухгалте́рия, счетово́дство

accrue /ə'kruː/ *v.i.* (**accrues**, **accrued**, **accruing**) **1** (accumulate) нараст|а́ть, -и́; ~**d interest** наро́сшие проце́нты (*m. pl.*) **2** (come about): **certain advantages will** ~ **from this** э́то даст определённые преиму́щества **3**: ~ **to** (fall to the lot of) достⱡава́ться, -а́ться + *d*.

accumulate /ə'kjuːmjʊleɪt/ *v.t.* накⱡа́пливать, -опи́ть; собⱡира́ть, -ра́ть
● *v.i.* накⱡа́пливаться, -опи́ться; скⱡа́пливаться, -опи́ться

accumulation /əkjuːmjʊ'leɪʃ(ə)n/ *n*. накопле́ние

accuracy /'ækjʊrəsɪ/ *n*. то́чность; (of aim or shot) ме́ткость

accurate /'ækjʊrət/ *adj*. (of persons, statements, instruments, etc.) то́чный; (of aim or shot) ме́ткий

accusation /ækjʊ'zeɪʃ(ə)n/ *n*. обвине́ние

accusative /ə'kjuːzətɪv/ *adj. & n*. вини́тельный (паде́ж)

♂ **accuse** /ə'kjuːz/ *v.t.* обвин|я́ть, -и́ть; **he was** ~**d of stealing** его́ обвини́ли в кра́же

accused /ə'kjuːzd/ *n*.: **the** ~ обвиня́емый, подсуди́мый

accuser /ə'kjuːzə(r)/ *n*. обвини́тель (*m.*)

accustom /ə'kʌstəm/ *v.t.* приуч|а́ть, -и́ть (**to**: к + *d*.); **become** ~**ed** прив|ыка́ть, -ы́кнуть (**to**: к + *d*.)

accustomed /ə'kʌstəmd/ *adj*. (usual) обы́чный, привы́чный

ace /eɪs/ *n*. туз

acerbic /ə'sɜːbɪk/ *adj*. (astringent) те́рпкий; (of speech, manner, etc.) язви́тельный

acetate /'æsɪteɪt/ *n*. ацета́т; уксуснокисла́я соль

ache /eɪk/ *n*. боль
● *v.i.* боле́ть (*impf.*); ныть (*impf.*); **my head** ~**s** у меня́ боли́т голова́

achievable /ə'tʃiːvəb(ə)l/ *adj*. достижи́мый

♂ **achieve** /ə'tʃiːv/ *v.t.* **1** (attain) дост|ига́ть, -и́чь + *g*.; доб|ива́ться, -и́ться + *g*. **2** (carry out) выполня́ть, вы́полнить

♂ **achievement** /ə'tʃiːvmənt/ *n*. (attainment) достиже́ние; (carrying out) выполне́ние; (success) достиже́ние, завоева́ние

acid /'æsɪd/ *n*. кислота́
● *adj*. ки́слый
■ ~ **rain** *n*. кисло́тный дождь; ~ **test** *n*. (fig.) про́бный ка́мень

acidic /ə'sɪdɪk/ *adj*. ки́слый

acidity /ə'sɪdɪtɪ/ *n*. кисло́тность

♂ **acknowledge** /ək'nɒlɪdʒ/ *v.t.* **1** (recognize, admit) призн|ава́ть, -а́ть **2** (confirm receipt of; reply to): ~ **a letter** подтвер|жда́ть, -ди́ть получе́ние письма́ **3** (indicate recognition of): **he did not even** ~ **me as we passed** он прошёл ми́мо и да́же не поздоро́вался

acknowledgement, acknowledgment /ək'nɒlɪdʒmənt/ *n*. **1** (recognition, admission) призна́ние **2** (confirmation) подтвержде́ние

acme /'ækmɪ/ *n*. верх, верши́на

acne /'æknɪ/ *n*. угри́ (*m. pl.*)

acorn /'eɪkɔːn/ *n*. жёлудь (*m.*)

acoustic /ə'kuːstɪk/ *adj*. акусти́ческий; звуково́й; **an** ~ **guitar** класси́ческая гита́ра

acoustics /ə'kuːstɪks/ *n*. (science; acoustic properties) аку́стика

acquaint /ə'kweɪnt/ *v.t.* знако́мить, по-; **I** ~**ed him with the facts** я ознако́мил его́ с фа́ктами; **he soon got** ~**ed with the situation** он бы́стро ознако́мился с положе́нием дел; **be** ~**ed with sb** быть знако́мым с кем-н.

acquaintance /ə'kweɪnt(ə)ns/ *n*. знако́мство; **make the** ~ **of** знако́миться, по- с + *i*.; (person) знако́мый; **an** ~ **of mine** мой знако́мый

acquiescence /ækwɪ'es(ə)ns/ *n*. (agreement) согла́сие; (tractability) усту́пчивость

acquiescent /ækwɪ'es(ə)nt/ *adj*. усту́пчивый

♂ **acquire** /ə'kwaɪə(r)/ *v.t.* приобре|та́ть, -сти́; **asparagus is an** ~**d taste** к спа́рже на́до привы́кнуть

acquisition /ækwɪ'zɪʃ(ə)n/ *n*. приобрете́ние; **the library's new** ~**s** но́вые библиоте́чные поступле́ния

acquisitive /ə'kwɪzɪtɪv/ *adj*. стяжа́тельский; жа́дный

acquisitiveness /ə'kwɪzɪtɪvnɪs/ *n*. стяжа́тельство; жа́дность

♂ ключева́я ле́ксика

acquit /ə'kwɪt/ v.t. (**acquitted, acquitting**)
(declare not guilty) опра́вд|ывать, -а́ть; **he was
~ted of murder** с него́ сня́ли обвине́ние в
уби́йстве

acquittal /ə'kwɪt(ə)l/ n. (in court of law)
оправда́ние

acre /'eɪkə(r)/ n. акр

acreage /'eɪkərɪdʒ/ n. пло́щадь земли́ в а́крах

acrid /'ækrɪd/ adj. е́дкий

acrimonious /ækrɪ'məʊnɪəs/ adj.
ожесточённый, го́рький

acrobat /'ækrəbæt/ n. акроба́т

acrobatic /ækrə'bætɪk/ adj. акробати́ческий

acrobatics /ækrə'bætɪks/ n. акроба́тика

✧ **across** /ə'krɒs/ adv. **1** (crosswise) поперёк;
(in crosswords) по горизонта́ли **2** (on the other
side) на той стороне́ **3** (to the other side) на ту
сто́рону **4** (in width): **the river here is more
than six miles ~** ширина́ реки́ здесь бо́льше
шести́ миль
● prep. **1** (from one side of to the other) че́рез + a.
(sometimes omitted with vv. compounded with
пере…); **he went ~ the street** он перешёл
у́лицу **2** (over the surface of) по + d.; **he hit
me ~ the face** он уда́рил меня́ по лицу́
3 (athwart) поперёк + g.; **she lay ~ the bed**
она́ лежа́ла поперёк крова́ти **4** (on the other
side of) на той стороне́ + g., по ту сто́рону
+ g.

acrylic /ə'krɪlɪk/ n. акри́л
● adj. акри́ловый

✧ **act** /ækt/ n. **1** (action) посту́пок; (feat) по́двиг;
catch in the ~ пойма́ть (pf.) на ме́сте
преступле́ния; **an ~ of kindness** до́брое де́ло
2 (law) акт, зако́н **3** (of drama) де́йствие
4 (performance) но́мер; (fig., infml): **put on an ~**
притвор|я́ться, -и́ться
● v.t. игра́ть (impf.); **~ a part** (lit., fig.) игра́ть
роль; **~ the fool** валя́ть (impf.) дурака́
● v.i. **1** (behave) поступ|а́ть, -и́ть; вести́ (det.)
себя́; (take action, intervene) прин|има́ть, -я́ть
ме́ры **2** (serve, function) де́йствовать (impf.);
~ for sb де́йствовать от и́мени кого́-л.; **he
is ~ing as interpreter** он выступа́ет в ро́ли
перево́дчика **3** (have effect) де́йствовать, по-
(on: на + a.) **4** (theatr.) игра́ть

□ **~ out** v.t. разы́гр|ывать, -а́ть

□ **~ up** v.i. (infml, misbehave) шали́ть (impf.); (give
trouble): **my car has been ~ing up** моя́ маши́на
барахли́т

acting /'æktɪŋ/ n. (theatr.) игра́; (as skill)
актёрское масте́рство
● adj. (doing duty temporarily): **~ manager**
исполня́ющий обя́занности (or и. о.)
заве́дующего

✧ **action** /'ækʃ(ə)n/ n. **1** (acting; activity; effect)
де́йствие; **in ~** в де́йствии; **come into ~**
вступ|а́ть, -и́ть в де́йствие; **put out of
~** выводи́ть, вы́вести из стро́я; **out of
~** него́дный к употребле́нию; **take ~**
прин|има́ть, -я́ть ме́ры **2** (deed) посту́пок;
~s speak louder than words дела́ говоря́т
са́ми за себя́ **3** (physical movement) движе́ние
4 (theatr.): **the ~ takes place in London**
де́йствие происхо́дит в Ло́ндоне **5** (law)

иск, суде́бное де́ло; **bring an ~ against**
предъяв|ля́ть, -и́ть иск к + d. **6** (mil.) бой,
де́йствие; **killed in ~** па́вший, поги́бший
в бою́

activate /'æktɪveɪt/ v.t. (make operative)
прив|оди́ть, -ести́ в де́йствие; активизи́ровать
(impf., pf.)

✧ **active** /'æktɪv/ adj. **1** (lively; energetic; displaying
activity) акти́вный, де́ятельный; **an ~
volcano** де́йствующий вулка́н **2** (gram.)
действи́тельный **3** (mil.): **on ~ service** на
действи́тельной слу́жбе

activism /'æktɪvɪz(ə)m/ n. полити́ческая
акти́вность

✧ **activist** /'æktɪvɪst/ n. активи́ст (-ка)

✧ **activity** /æk'tɪvɪti/ n. **1** (being active; exertion
of energy) акти́вность **2** (usu. in pl.) (pursuit,
sphere of action; doings) де́ятельность

✧ **actor** /'æktə(r)/ n. актёр

actress /'æktrɪs/ n. актри́са

✧ **actual** /'æktʃʊəl/ adj. (real) действи́тельный;
факти́ческий; **in ~ fact** в действи́тельности;
those were his ~ words э́то его́ по́длинные
слова́

✧ **actually** /'æktʃʊəli/ adv. (really; in fact)
действи́тельно; на (са́мом) де́ле; (in sense 'to
tell the truth') со́бственно (говоря́)

actuary /'æktʃʊəri/ n. актуа́рий (сотрудник
компании, производящий страховые
расчёты на основе статистического
анализа)

acumen /'ækjʊmən/ n. (judgement)
сообрази́тельность; (penetration)
проница́тельность; **business ~** делова́я
хва́тка

acupuncture /'ækjuːpʌŋktʃə(r)/ n.
акупункту́ра, иглоука́лывание

acupuncturist /'ækjuːpʌŋktʃərɪst/ n.
иглотерапе́вт

✧ **acute** /ə'kjuːt/ adj. (**acuter, acutest**) (in var.
senses) о́стрый; **~ shortage** о́страя нехва́тка;
~ sense of smell то́нкое обоня́ние
■ **~ accent** n. (ling.) аку́т; **~ angle** n. о́стрый
у́гол

AD abbr. (of **Anno Domini**) н. э. (на́шей э́ры)

✧ **ad** /æd/ n. (infml) = **advertisement**

adage /'ædɪdʒ/ n. погово́рка, посло́вица;
наро́дная му́дрость; **as the old ~ goes:
money talks** как гласи́т дре́вняя му́дрость:
де́ньги реша́ют всё

adagio /ə'dɑːʒɪəʊ/ n., adj. & adv. (pl. **~s**)
(mus.) ада́жио (nt. indecl.)

adamant /'ædəmənt/ adj. (fig.) непрекло́нный

adapt /ə'dæpt/ v.t. **1** приспос|а́бливать, -о́бить
2 (text, book) адапти́ровать (impf., pf.); **~ for
the stage** инсцени́ровать (impf., pf.)
● v.i. приспос|а́бливаться, -о́биться;
адапти́роваться (impf., pf.)

adaptable /ə'dæptəb(ə)l/ adj.
приспособля́емый; (of person) легко́
приспоса́бливающийся

adaptation /ædæp'teɪʃ(ə)n/ n.
приспособле́ние; (of book etc.) адапта́ция;
(for stage) инсцениро́вка

a

adapter, adaptor /ə'dæptə(r)/ *n.* (tech.) адáптер

⚡ **add** /æd/ *v.t.* **1** (make an addition of) прибавля́ть, -а́вить; **you must ~ water** на́до доба́вить воды́; **~ed to this is the fact that …** к э́тому ну́жно приба́вить/доба́вить тот факт, что… **2** (say in addition) доба́вля́ть, -а́вить; **I have nothing to ~** мне не́чего доба́вить **3** (math.) скла́дывать, сложи́ть; **~ two and/to three!** сложи́те два и три!
• *v.i.* **1**: **~ to** (increase, enlarge) увели́чи|вать, -ть; усил|я́ть, -ть; (knowledge etc.) углуб|ля́ть, -и́ть **2** (perform addition) *see* ▶ **add up**
□ **~ on** *v.t.* прибавля́ть, -а́вить; доб|авля́ть, -а́вить; **the tip was ~ed on to the bill** чаевы́е бы́ли включены́ в счёт
□ **~ together** *v.t.* скла́дывать, сложи́ть
□ **~ up** *v.t.* (find sum of) подсчи́т|ывать, -ита́ть; подыто́жи|вать, -ть
• *v.i.* (perform addition): **you can't ~ up!** вы не уме́ете счита́ть!; (total): **it ~s up to 50** э́то в су́мме составля́ет 50
■ **~-ons** *n. pl.* (comput.) дополни́тельный встро́енный/встра́иваемый мо́дуль

addend|um /ə'dendəm/ *n.* (*pl.* ~**a**) приложе́ние, дополне́ние

adder /'ædə(r)/ *n.* (snake) гадю́ка

addict[1] /'ædɪkt/ *n.* (*in full* **drug ~**) наркома́н (-ка)

addict[2] /ə'dɪkt/ *v.t.*: **be, become ~ed to** пристрасти́ться (*pf.*) к + *d.*

addiction /ə'dɪkʃ(ə)n/ *n.* пристра́стие (**to**: к + *d.*); **~ to drugs** наркома́ния

addictive /ə'dɪktɪv/ *adj.* вызыва́ющий привыка́ние

⚡ **addition** /ə'dɪʃ(ə)n/ *n.* **1** (act of adding; thing added) прибавле́ние; добавле́ние; **in ~ to** в дополне́ние к + *d.*; **in ~** (as well) вдоба́вок; (moreover) к тому́ же **2** (math.) сложе́ние

⚡ **additional** /ə'dɪʃən(ə)l/ *adj.* доба́вочный, дополни́тельный

additive /'ædɪtɪv/ *n.* доба́вка, добавле́ние

⚡ **address** /ə'dres/ *n.* а́дрес
• *v.t.* **1** (a letter) адресова́ть (*impf., pf.*) **2** (speak to) обра|ща́ться, -ти́ться к + *d.*
■ **~ book** *n.* (also comput.) записна́я кни́жка

addressee /ædre'si:/ *n.* адреса́т

adenoids /'ædɪnɔɪdz/ *n. pl.* адено́иды (*m. pl.*)

adept /ə'dept/ *adj.* уме́лый; **he is ~ at finding excuses** он ма́стер находи́ть оправда́ния (*or* опра́вдываться)

adequate /'ædɪkwət/ *adj.* **1** (sufficient) доста́точный **2** (suitable) адеква́тный

ADHD *abbr.* (*of* **attention deficit hyperactivity disorder**) СДВГ (синдро́м дефици́та внима́ния и гиперакти́вности)

adhere /əd'hɪə(r)/ *v.i.* прил|ипа́ть, -и́пнуть (**to**: к + *d.*)

adherence /əd'hɪərəns/ *n.* (lit.) прилипа́ние; (fig.) приве́рженность

adherent /əd'hɪərənt/ *n.* приве́рженец

adhesive /əd'hi:sɪv/ *n.* клей; кле́йкое вещество́

• *adj.* ли́пкий; (sticky) кле́йкий
■ **~ tape** *n.* кле́йкая ле́нта, скотч

ad hoc /æd 'hɒk/ *adv.* для да́нного слу́чая; (*attr.*) специа́льный; **~ committee** вре́менный комите́т

ad infinitum /æd ɪnfɪ'naɪtəm/ *adv.* до бесконе́чности

adjacent /ə'dʒeɪs(ə)nt/ *adj.* (neighbouring) сосе́дний; сме́жный; **~ to** примыка́ющий к + *d.*; (geom.): **~ angles** сме́жные углы́

adjectival /ædʒɪk'taɪv(ə)l/ *adj.* (gram.) адъекти́вный

adjective /'ædʒɪktɪv/ *n.* (и́мя) прилага́тельное

adjourn /ə'dʒɜ:n/ *v.t.* (postpone) от|кла́дывать, -ложи́ть; **the meeting was ~ed till Monday** заседа́ние бы́ло отло́жено до понеде́льника

adjournment /ə'dʒɜ:nmənt/ *n.* (postponement) отсро́чка; (break in proceedings) переры́в

adjudicate /ə'dʒu:dɪkeɪt/ *v.t.* (a claim) рассм|а́тривать, -отре́ть

adjudication /ədʒu:dɪ'keɪʃ(ə)n/ *n.* (judgement) суде́бное/арбитра́жное реше́ние

adjudicator /ə'dʒu:dɪkeɪtə(r)/ *n.* арби́тр; (judge) судья́ (*m.*)

adjunct /'ædʒʌŋkt/ *n.* (appendage) приложе́ние; (addition) дополне́ние; (gram.) обстоя́тельство

adjust /ə'dʒʌst/ *v.t.* **1** (arrange; put right or straight) привод|и́ть, -ести́ в поря́док; поп|равля́ть, -а́вить; **he ~ed his tie** он попра́вил га́лстук; (mechanism) регули́ровать, от-; нала́|живать, -дить **2** (fit, adapt) приг|оня́ть, -на́ть; под|гоня́ть, -огна́ть; **well ~ed** (of person) уравнове́шенный

adjustable /ə'dʒʌstəb(ə)l/ *adj.* регули́руемый; подвижно́й

adjustment /ə'dʒʌstmənt/ *n.* (regulation) регули|́рование, -иро́вка; (correction) исправле́ние, попра́вка; (fitting) подго́нка; (adaptation) приспособле́ние

ad-lib /æd 'lɪb/ (infml) *n.* экспро́мт; **his speech was full of ~s** в свое́й ре́чи он мно́го импровизи́ровал
• *v.i.* (**ad-libbed, ad-libbing**) говори́ть (*impf.*) экспро́мтом

administer /əd'mɪnɪstə(r)/ *v.t.* (manage, govern) управля́ть (*impf.*) + *i.*; заве́довать (*impf.*) + *i.*

⚡ **administration** /ədmɪnɪ'streɪʃ(ə)n/ *n.* **1** (management) управле́ние **2** (of public affairs) администра́ция; **the A~** администра́ция, прави́тельство

administrative /əd'mɪnɪstrətɪv/ *adj.* административный, организацио́нный

administrator /əd'mɪnɪstreɪtə(r)/ *n.* администра́тор

admirable /'ædmərəb(ə)l/ *adj.* замеча́тельный, прекра́сный

admiral /'ædmər(ə)l/ *n.* адмира́л

admiration /ædmɪ'reɪʃ(ə)n/ *n.* восхище́ние, восто́рг

⚡ **admire** /əd'maɪə(r)/ *v.t.* (view with pleasure) любова́ться (*impf.*) + *i.*; (respect) восхи|ща́ться, -ти́ться + *i.*; восторга́ться (*impf.*) + *i.*

⚡ ключева́я ле́ксика

admirer /əd'maɪərə(r)/ *n.* поклонни|к (-ца)

admissible /əd'mɪsɪb(ə)l/ *adj.* приемлемый, допустимый

admission /əd'mɪʃ(ə)n/ *n.* **1** (permitted entry or access) вход; доступ **2** (acknowledgement) признание

✓ **admit** /əd'mɪt/ *v.t. & i.* (**admitted, admitting**) **1** (allow, accept) допус|кать, -тить; призн|авать, -ать; **you must ~ he is right** вы должны признать, что он прав (*or* его правоту) **2** (let in) впус|кать, -тить; (to organization) прин|имать, -ять; **the public are not ~ted to the gardens** этот парк закрыт для посещения; **this ticket ~s one (person)** это билет на одно лицо **3** (confess) призн|авать, -ать; **he ~s his guilt** он признаёт свою вину; **~ to feeling ashamed** призн|аваться, -аться, что стыдно

admittance /əd'mɪt(ə)ns/ *n.* (entry) вход; **no ~!** вход воспрещён!

admittedly /əd'mɪtɪdlɪ/ *adv.* правда; признаться

admixture /əd'mɪkstʃə(r)/ *n.* (mixing) смешивание; (addition) примесь

admonish /əd'mɒnɪʃ/ *v.t.* **1** (reprimand) делать, с- внушение/замечание + *d.*; **the boys were ~ed for being late** мальчикам сделали замечание за опоздание **2** (advise, urge) настоятельно советовать, по-; убеди́тельно просить, по-

ad nauseam /æd 'nɔ:zɪæm/ *adv.* до тошноты

ado /ə'du:/ *n.* (fuss) суета; **without further ~** без дальнейших церемоний

adolescence /ædə'les(ə)ns/ *n.* подростковый возраст

adolescent /ædə'les(ə)nt/ *n.* подросток
  ● *adj.* подростковый

✓ **adopt** /ə'dɒpt/ *v.t.* **1** (a son) усыновл|ять, -ить; (a daughter) удочер|ять, -ить **2** (accept) прин|имать, -ять; (take over) перен|имать, -ять; **his methods should be ~ed** следует воспользоваться его методикой

adoption /ə'dɒpʃ(ə)n/ *n.* **1** (of a son) усыновление; (of a daughter) удочерение **2** (acceptance) принятие

adoptive /ə'dɒptɪv/ *adj.* приёмный; **~ parent** усыновитель (-ница)

adorable /ə'dɔ:rəb(ə)l/ *adj.* прелестный, восхитительный

adoration /ædə'reɪʃ(ə)n/ *n.* обожание

ador|e /ə'dɔ:(r)/ *v.t.* (worship) обожать (*impf.*); поклоняться (*impf.*) + *d.*; **her ~ing husband** её любящий муж

adorn /ə'dɔ:n/ *v.t.* укр|ашать, -асить

adornment /ə'dɔ:nmənt/ *n.* украшение

adrenalin /ə'drenəlɪn/ *n.* адреналин

adrift /ə'drɪft/ *pred. adj. & adv.:* **be ~** дрейфова́ть (*impf.*)

adroit /ə'drɔɪt/ *adj.* ловкий

adulation /ædjʊ'leɪʃ(ə)n/ *n.* низкопоклонство, лесть

✓ **adult** /'ædʌlt/ *n. & adj.* **1** взрослый **2** (mature) зрелый
  ■ **~ education** *n.* обучение взрослых

adulterate /ə'dʌltəreɪt/ *v.t.* (debase) портить, ис-; (dilute) разб|авлять, -авить

adulterous /ə'dʌltərəs/ *adj.* неверный

adultery /ə'dʌltərɪ/ *n.* адюльтер, супружеская измена

adulthood /'ædʌlthʊd/ *n.* зрелость; (of men) возмужалость

✓ **advance** /əd'vɑ:ns/ *n.* **1** (forward move) продвижение; (mil. also) наступление; (*in pl.*) (overtures to a person): **make ~s to** заигрывать (*impf.*) с + *i.* **2** (progress) прогресс; (in rank, social position etc.) продвижение **3** (increase) повышение; **an ~ on his original offer** надбавка к первоначальному предложению **4** (loan) ссуда; (payment beforehand) аванс; **an ~ on salary** аванс под зарплату **5**: **in ~** (in front) вперёд; (beforehand) заранее; **in ~ of** впереди + *g.* **6** (*attr.*): **~ booking** предварительный заказ
  ● *v.t.* **1** (move forward) продв|игать, -инуть **2** (fig., put forward): **~ an opinion** выск|азывать, -азать мнение **3** (fig., further): **~ sb's interests** отста|ивать (*impf.*) чьи-н. интересы; служить, по- чьим-н. интересам **4** (of payment) плати́ть, за- авансом; (lend) ссу|жать, -дить
  ● *v.i.* **1** (move forward) продв|игаться, -инуться; **~ on** наступать (*impf.*) на + *a.* **2** (progress) разв|иваться, -иться; делать, с- успехи

advanced /əd'vɑ:nst/ *adj.* **1** (far on): **~ age, years** преклонный возраст **2** (opp. elementary): **an ~ course** курс для продвинутого этапа (обучения) **3** (progressive) передовой

advancement /əd'vɑ:nsmənt/ *n.* (moving forward) продвижение; (promotion) продвижение по службе; (progress) прогресс

✓ **advantage** /əd'vɑ:ntɪdʒ/ *n.* **1** (superiority; more favourable position) преимущество, достоинство **2** (profit, benefit) выгода, польза; **take ~ of sth** воспользоваться (*pf.*) чем-н.; (abuse) злоупотреб|лять, -ить чем-н.; **take ~ of sb** эксплуатировать (*impf.*); **you may learn sth to your ~** вы можете узнать/почерпнуть для себя что́-то полезное **3** (tennis): **~ Henman** больше у Хэнмена

advantageous /ædvən'teɪdʒəs/ *adj.* (favourable) благоприятный; (profitable) выгодный

advent /'ædvent/ *n.* **1** (appearance; occurrence) появление **2** (**A~**) (eccl.) Рождественский пост

adventure /əd'ventʃə(r)/ *n.* приключение
  ■ **~ story** *n.* приключенческий роман

adventurous /əd'ventʃərəs/ *adj.* **1** (of person) смелый; (enterprising) предприимчивый **2** (of actions) рискованный, авантюрный

adverb /'ædvɜ:b/ *n.* наречие

adverbial /əd'vɜ:bɪəl/ *adj.* (gram.) наречный, адвербиальный

adversary /'ædvəsərɪ/ *n.* противник

adverse /'ædvɜ:s/ *adj.* неблагоприятный

adversity /əd'vɜ:sɪtɪ/ *n.* беда, несчастье; **show courage in, under ~** прояв|лять, -ить мужество в беде; **companions in ~** товарищи по несчастью

advert /'ædvɜ:t/ *n.* (BrE, infml) = **advertisement**

a

advertise /'ædvətaɪz/ v.t. (publicize) реклами́ровать (*impf., pf.*); (in newspaper) да|ва́ть, -ть (*or* поме|ща́ть, -сти́ть) объявле́ние о + *p.*
● *v.i.*: she ∼d for a secretary она́ дала́ объявле́ние о вака́нсии секретаря́

advertisement /əd'vɜ:tɪsmənt/ n. рекла́ма; (classified ∼) объявле́ние

advertising /'ædvətaɪzɪŋ/ n. реклами́рование; рекла́мный би́знес
■ ∼ **agent** n. рекла́мный аге́нт

✓ **advice** /əd'vaɪs/ n. (*also* **piece of** ∼) сове́т; **give sb a piece of** ∼ сове́товать, по- кому́-н.

advisable /əd'vaɪzəb(ə)l/ adj. целесообра́зный; **it may be** ∼ **to wait** сто́ит, наве́рное, подожда́ть

✓ **advise** /əd'vaɪz/ v.t. **1** (counsel) сове́товать, по- + *d.*; рекомендова́ть (*impf., pf.*) + *d.*; **what do you** ∼ **(me to do)?** что вы посове́туете мне предприня́ть?; **the doctor** ∼d **complete rest** врач рекомендова́л по́лный поко́й; **I** ∼d **him against going** я посове́товал ему́ не ходи́ть туда́; (give professional advice to) консульти́ровать, про- **2** (comm., notify) изве|ща́ть, -сти́ть (*кого о чём*); **please** ∼ **me of receipt** уве́домите меня́ о получе́нии

adviser, advisor /əd'vaɪzə(r)/ nn. (professional) консульта́нт; (to president etc.) сове́тник (**to:** + *g.*); **legal** ∼ юриско́нсульт; **medical** ∼ врач

advisory /əd'vaɪzərɪ/ adj. совеща́тельный, консультати́вный

advocate¹ /'ædvəkət/ n. **1** (defender) защи́тник; (supporter) сторо́нни|к (-ца) **2** (lawyer) адвока́т; **devil's** ∼ (fig.) «адвока́т дья́вола»

advocate² /'ædvəkeɪt/ v.t. (speak in favour of) выступа́ть, вы́ступить за + *a.*; (advise, recommend) сове́товать, по-; рекомендова́ть (*impf., pf.*)

aegis /'i:dʒɪs/ n.: **under the** ∼ **of** под эги́дой + *g.*

aeration /eə'reɪʃ(ə)n/ n. прове́тривание; (of the soil) аэра́ция

aerial /'eərɪəl/ n. анте́нна
● *adj.* возду́шный
■ ∼ **photography** n. аэрофотосъёмка

aerobatics /eərə'bætɪks/ n. вы́сший пилота́ж; фигу́ры вы́сшего пилота́жа

aerobic /eə'rəʊbɪk/ adj. аэро́бный

aerobics /eə'rəʊbɪks/ n. аэро́бика

aerodrome /'eərədrəʊm/ n. (BrE) аэродро́м

aerodynamic /eərəʊdaɪ'næmɪk/ adj. аэродинами́ческий

aerodynamics /eərəʊdaɪ'næmɪks/ n. аэродина́мика

aeronautics /eərə'nɔ:tɪks/ n. аэрона́втика; воздухопла́вание

aeroplane /'eərəpleɪn/ n. (BrE) самолёт, аэропла́н

aerosol /'eərəsɒl/ n. аэрозо́ль (*m.*)

aerospace /'eərəspeɪs/ n. возду́шно-косми́ческое простра́нство

✓ ключева́я ле́ксика

aesthetic /i:s'θetɪk/ (AmE *also* **esthetic**) adj. эстети́ческий

aesthetics /i:s'θetɪks/ (AmE *also* **esthetics**) n. эсте́тика

afar /ə'fɑ:(r)/ adv. вдалеке́; **from** ∼ и́здали, издалека́

affable /'æfəb(ə)l/ adj. приве́тливый; любе́зный

✓ **affair** /ə'feə(r)/ n. **1** (business, matter) де́ло; **that's my** ∼ э́то моё де́ло; **Ministry of Foreign A∼s** министе́рство иностра́нных дел **2** (*also* **love** ∼) любо́вная связь; рома́н; **they are having an** ∼ у них рома́н
■ ∼s **of state** n. pl. госуда́рственные дела́

✓ **affect** /ə'fekt/ v.t. **1** (act on) де́йствовать, по-на + *a.*; влия́ть, по- на + *a.*; **the climate** ∼ed **his health** кли́мат повлия́л на его́ здоро́вье **2** (concern) каса́ться, косну́ться + *g.*; затр|а́гивать, -о́нуть **3** (touch emotionally) тро́|гать, -нуть; волнова́ть, вз- **4** (of disease): **the lung is** ∼ed лёгкое поражено́

affectation /æfek'teɪʃ(ə)n/ n. **1** (pretence) притво́рство **2** (unnatural behaviour) аффекта́ция **3** (of language or style) иску́сственность

affected /ə'fektɪd/ adj. жема́нный, неесте́ственный

affection /ə'fekʃ(ə)n/ n. привя́занность (**for:** к + *d.*); любо́вь (**for:** к + *d.*)

affectionate /ə'fekʃənət/ adj. не́жный

affidavit /æfɪ'deɪvɪt/ n. (law) пи́сьменное показа́ние под прися́гой, аффиде́вит; **make, swear an** ∼ да|ва́ть, -ть показа́ние под прися́гой

affiliate /ə'fɪlɪeɪt/ v.t. **1** (join, attach) присоедин|я́ть, -и́ть (**to:** к + *d.*); ∼d **company** доче́рняя компа́ния **2** (adopt as member) прин|има́ть, -я́ть в чле́ны
● *v.i.* присоедин|я́ться, -и́ться (**with:** к + *d.*)

affiliation /əfɪlɪ'eɪʃ(ə)n/ n. **1** присоедине́ние **2** приня́тие в чле́ны **3** (connection) связь

affinity /ə'fɪnɪtɪ/ n. **1** (resemblance) схо́дство; (relationship) родство́; (connection) связь; (closeness) бли́зость **2** (liking, attraction) влече́ние, скло́нность

affirm /ə'fɜ:m/ v.t. (assert) утвер|жда́ть, -ди́ть

affirmation /æfə'meɪʃ(ə)n/ n. утвержде́ние

affirmative /ə'fɜ:mətɪv/ n.: **he answered in the** ∼ он отве́тил утверди́тельно
● *adj.* утверди́тельный

afflict /ə'flɪkt/ v.t. **1** (distress: of misfortune etc.) пост|ига́ть, -и́чь (*or* -и́гнуть); **he was** ∼ed **by a great misfortune** его́ пости́гло большо́е несча́стье **2** (*pass.*) (suffer from): **be** ∼ed **with** страда́ть (*impf.*) + *i.*; **he is** ∼ed **with rheumatism** он страда́ет ревмати́змом; **the** ∼ed стра́ждущие (*pl.*)

affliction /ə'flɪkʃ(ə)n/ n. (grief) го́ре; (misfortune) несча́стье; бе́дствие; (illness) боле́знь

affluence /'æfluəns/ n. (wealth) бога́тство; (plenty) изоби́лие

affluent /'æfluənt/ adj. бога́тый

✓ **afford** /ə'fɔ:d/ v.t. (*with* can) (expr. possibility): **I can't** ∼ **all these books** все э́ти кни́ги мне не по карма́ну; **they can** ∼ **a new car** они́ мо́гут позво́лить себе́ но́вую маши́ну; **I can't ～ the time** мне не́когда

affront /ə'frʌnt/ *v.t.* оскорб|ля́ть, -и́ть

Afghan /'æfgæn/ *n.* афга́н|ец (-ка); (*in full* ～ **hound**) афга́нская борза́я
● *adj.* афга́нский

Afghanistan /æf'gænɪstɑːn/ *n.* Афганиста́н

aficionado /əfɪsjə'nɑːdəʊ/ *n.* (*pl.* ～**s**) покло́нни|к (-ца)

afield /ə'fiːld/ *adv.*: **far ～** вдалеке́, вдали́; (expr. motion) вдаль

afloat /ə'fləʊt/ *pred. adj. & adv.* (floating on water) на воде́

afoot /ə'fʊt/ *pred. adj. & adv.*: **there is a plan ～** гото́вится план; **there is sth ～** что́-то затева́ется

aforementioned /ə'fɔːmenʃ(ə)nd/ *adj.* вышеупомя́нутый

aforesaid /ə'fɔːsed/ *adj.* вышеска́занный

◈ **afraid** /ə'freɪd/ *pred. adj.* испу́ганный; **be ～ of** боя́ться (*impf.*) + g.; **don't be ～!** не бо́йтесь!; **I'm ～ he will die** бою́сь, что он умрёт; **I'm ～ he is out** к сожале́нию, его́ нет

afresh /ə'freʃ/ *adv.* за́ново

Africa /'æfrɪkə/ *n.* А́фрика

◈ **African** /'æfrɪkən/ *n.* африка́н|ец (-ка)
● *adj.* африка́нский
■ ～ **American** *n.* афроамерика́н|ец (-ка); ～**-American** *adj.* афроамерика́нский

Afrikaans /æfrɪ'kɑːns/ *n.* (язы́к) африка́анс

Afrikaner /æfrɪ'kɑːnə(r)/ *n.* африка́нер, жи́тель Ю́жно-Африка́нской Респу́блики голла́ндского происхожде́ния

Afro-Caribbean /æfrəʊkærɪ'biːən/ *adj.* афрокари́бский
● *n.* афрокари́б (-ка); уроже́н|ец (-ка) Кари́бских острово́в африка́нского происхожде́ния

◈ **after** /'ɑːftə(r)/ *adv.* **1** (subsequently; then) пото́м, зате́м; **soon ～** вско́ре по́сле э́того **2** (later) поздне́е, по́зже; **3 days ～** спустя́ три дня
● *prep.* **1** (in expressions of time) по́сле + g.; за + i.; че́рез + a.; спустя́ + a.; ～ **dinner** по́сле обе́да; ～ **you!** то́лько по́сле вас!; ～ **that** пото́м, зате́м; **the day ～ tomorrow** послеза́втра; **the week ～ next** (in adv. sense) че́рез две неде́ли; **they met ～ 10 years** они́ встре́тились че́рез де́сять лет; ～ **passing his exams, he …** сдав экза́мены, он…; по́сле того́, как он сдал экза́мены, он…; **it's ～ 6 (o'clock)** уже́ седьмо́й час; (in sequence): **day ～ day** день за днём; **one ～ another** оди́н за други́м; ～ **all** (in the end) в конце́чном счёте; (nevertheless) всё-таки **2** (in expressions of place) за + i.; **run ～ sb** бежа́ть за кем-н. **3** (in search of; trying to get): **the police are ～ him** его́ разы́скивает поли́ция; **what is he ～?** куда́ он ме́тит?; что он замышля́ет? **4** (in accordance with) по + d., согла́сно + d.; **named ～** на́званный по + d. *or* в честь + g.; **he takes ～ his father** он похо́ж на отца́
● *conj.* по́сле того́ как; **I arrived ～ he had left** я пришёл по́сле того́, как он ушёл
■ ～**-effect** *n.* после́дствие; ～**math** *n.* после́дствия (*nt. pl.*); ～**noon** *n.*

послеполу́денное вре́мя; **in the ～noon** днём; по́сле обе́да; во второ́й полови́не дня; **at 3 in the ～noon** в три часа́ дня; **good ～noon!** (in greeting) до́брый день!; (in leave-taking) до свида́ния!; ～**shave** *n.* лосьо́н по́сле бритья́; ～**taste** *n.* при́вкус; ～**thought** *n.* запозда́лая мысль

afterward /'ɑːftəwəd/ *adv.* (AmE) = **afterwards**

afterwards /'ɑːftəwədz/ *adv.* (then) пото́м; (subsequently) впосле́дствии; (later) по́зже

◈ **again** /ə'gen/ *adv.* **1** (expr. repetition) опя́ть, сно́ва; (afresh, anew) вновь; (once more) ещё раз; (with certain vv., by use of pref.) пере…; **read ～** перечи́т|ывать, -а́ть; **say ～** повтор|я́ть, -и́ть; **start ～** нач|ина́ть, -а́ть сно́ва; ～ **and ～** сно́ва и сно́ва; **now and ～** вре́мя от вре́мени; **once ～** ещё раз **2** (*with neg.*) (any more) бо́льше; **never ～** никогда́ бо́льше; **don't do it ～!** бо́льше э́того не де́лай! **3** (expr. return to original state or position): **back ～** обра́тно; **you'll soon be well ～** вы ско́ро попра́витесь

◈ **against** /ə'genst/ *prep.* **1** (in opposition to) про́тив + g.; **I have nothing ～ it** я не име́ю ничего́ про́тив; **I acted ～ my will** я де́йствовал про́тив свое́й во́ли; ～ **the rules** не по пра́вилам **2** (to oppose or combat) на + a.; **march ～ the enemy** наступа́ть (*impf.*) на врага́ **3** (compared with): **3 deaths this year ～ 20 last year** три сме́рти в э́том году́ про́тив двадцати́ в про́шлом **4** (in contrast with): **it shows up ～ a dark background** э́то выделя́ется на тёмном фо́не **5** (in collision with) о + a.; **knock ～ sth** ударя́ться, уда́риться о что-н.

◈ **age** /eɪdʒ/ *n.* **1** (time of life) во́зраст; **he is 40 years of ～** ему́ со́рок лет; **when I was your ～** когда́ я был в ва́шем во́зрасте; **she doesn't look her ～** она́ вы́глядит моло́же свои́х лет; (of inanimate objects): **what is the ～ of this house?** ско́лько лет э́тому до́му? **2** (majority): **he is under ～** он несовершенноле́тний **3** (old ～) ста́рость **4** (period) перио́д; (century) век; **Ice A～** леднико́вый перио́д; **Stone A～** ка́менный век; **the Middle A～s** Сре́дние века́; (*often in pl.*) (infml, long time): **the bus left ～s ago** авто́бус ушёл давны́м-давно́; **we have not seen each other for ～s** мы не ви́делись сто лет (*or* це́лую ве́чность)
● *v.t.* (*pres. part.* **ageing, aging**) ста́рить, со-
● *v.i.* (*pres. part.* **ageing, aging**) (of person) старе́ть, по-; ста́риться, со-; (of thing) старе́ть, у-
■ ～ **group** *n.* возрастна́я гру́ппа; ～ **limit** *n.* преде́льный во́зраст; ～ **of consent** *n.* бра́чный во́зраст

aged¹ /eɪdʒd/ *adj.* (of/at the age of): ～ **six** шести́ лет

aged² /'eɪdʒɪd/ *adj.* (very old) престаре́лый
● *n.*: **the ～** пожилы́е лю́ди, престаре́лые

ageism /'eɪdʒɪz(ə)m/ *n.* дискримина́ция по во́зрасту

ageist /'eɪdʒɪst/ *adj.* дискримини́рующий по во́зрасту

◈ **agency** /'eɪdʒənsɪ/ *n.* аге́нтство;

a

employment ~ аге́нтство по на́йму; **news** ~ информацио́нное аге́нтство; **travel** ~ туристи́ческое аге́нтство, турагентство

⚲ **agenda** /ə'dʒendə/ *n.* пове́стка дня

⚲ **agent** /'eɪdʒ(ə)nt/ *n.* (person acting for others) аге́нт; (representative) представи́тель (*m.*)

agent provocateur /a:ʒɑ̃ prəvɒkə'tə:(r)/ *n.* (*pl.* **agents provocateurs** *pronunc. same*) провока́тор

aggravate /'æɡrəveɪt/ *v.t.* **1** (make worse) усугуб|ля́ть, -и́ть **2** (infml, exasperate) раздраж|а́ть, -и́ть

aggravation /æɡrə'veɪʃ(ə)n/ *n.* **1** (of an illness, situation) усугубле́ние **2** (exasperation) раздраже́ние

aggregate¹ /'æɡrɪɡət/ *n.* **1** (total, mass) совоку́пность; **in the** ~ в совоку́пности **2** (phys.) скопле́ние **3** (ingredient of concrete) заполни́тель (*m.*) (бето́на)
● *adj.* (total) совоку́пный; ~ **membership** о́бщее число́ чле́нов

aggregate² /'æɡrɪɡeɪt/ *v.t.* (collect into a mass) соб|ира́ть, -ра́ть в це́лое

aggression /ə'ɡreʃ(ə)n/ *n.* агре́ссия

aggressive /ə'ɡresɪv/ *adj.* агресси́вный

aggressor /ə'ɡresə(r)/ *n.* агре́ссор

aggrieved /ə'ɡri:vd/ *adj.* оби́женный, огорчённый

aghast /ə'ɡɑ:st/ *pred. adj.* (amazed) потрясённый

agile /'ædʒaɪl/ *adj.* прово́рный; **an** ~ **mind** живо́й ум

agility /ə'dʒɪlɪti/ *n.* прово́рство; ~ **of mind** жи́вость ума́

agitate /'ædʒɪteɪt/ *v.t.* (excite) волнова́ть, вз-; **be** ~**d about sth** волнова́ться (*impf.*) из-за чего́-н.

agitator /'ædʒɪteɪtə(r)/ *n.* **1** (pol.) агита́тор **2** (apparatus) сме́ситель (*m.*); меша́лка (infml)

AGM (BrE) *abbr.* (of **Annual General Meeting**) ежего́дное о́бщее собра́ние

agnostic /æɡ'nɒstɪk/ *n.* агно́стик
● *adj.* агности́ческий

⚲ **ago** /ə'ɡəʊ/ *adv.* тому́ наза́д; **long** ~ давно́; **not long** ~ неда́вно

agonize /'æɡənaɪz/ *v.i.* (fig.): **he** ~**d over his speech** он му́чился над свое́й ре́чью

agony /'æɡənɪ/ *n.* (torment) муче́ние, страда́ние; **I was in** ~ я испы́тывал си́льные страда́ния; я му́чился от бо́ли

agoraphobia /æɡərə'fəʊbɪə/ *n.* агорафо́бия, боя́знь откры́того простра́нства

agoraphobic /æɡərə'fəʊbɪk/ *adj.* страда́ющий агорафо́бией

⚲ **agree** /ə'ɡri:/ *v.t.* (**agrees, agreed, agreeing**) (BrE) согласо́в|ывать, -а́ть (*что с кем*)
● *v.i.* (**agrees, agreed, agreeing**) **1** (concur; be of like opinion) согла|ша́ться, -си́ться (*с кем*) (used mainly for past and future); **I quite** ~ **with you** я соверше́нно с ва́ми согла́сен **2** (reach agreement; make common decision): **we** ~**d to go together** мы

договори́лись е́хать вме́сте; ~ **on a price** догов|а́риваться, -ори́ться о цене́ **3** (consent) согла|ша́ться, -си́ться (*на что*) (used mainly for past and future) **4** (accept): **I** ~ **that it was wrong** согла́сен, что э́то бы́ло непра́вильно **5** ~ **with** (accept as correct or right): **I don't** ~ **with his policy** я не согла́сен с его́ поли́тикой **6** ~ **with** (suit) под|ходи́ть, -ойти́ + *d.*; годи́ться (*impf.*) + *d.*; **fish doesn't** ~ **with me** от ры́бы мне быва́ет пло́хо **7** ~ **with** (conform; tally): **the adjective** ~**s with the noun** прилага́тельное согласу́ется с существи́тельным; **his story** ~**s with mine** его́ расска́з схо́дится с мои́м

agreeable /ə'ɡri:əb(ə)l/ *adj.* прия́тный

⚲ **agreement** /ə'ɡri:mənt/ *n.* **1** (consent) согла́сие; **be in** ~ **with** согла|ша́ться, -си́ться с + *i.* **2** (treaty) соглаше́ние, догово́р; **come to an** ~ при|ходи́ть, -йти́ к соглаше́нию **3** (gram.) согласова́ние

agricultural /æɡrɪ'kʌltʃər(ə)l/ *adj.* сельскохозя́йственный

agriculture /'æɡrɪkʌltʃə(r)/ *n.* се́льское хозя́йство

aground /ə'ɡraʊnd/ *adv.*: **run** ~ *v.i.* сади́ться, сесть на мель

⚲ **ahead** /ə'hed/ *adv.* впереди́; (expr. motion) вперёд; **be, get** ~ **of** опере|жа́ть, -ди́ть; **go** ~! (ну) дава́й(те)!

ahoy /ə'hɔɪ/ *int.*: ~ **there!, ship** ~! эй, на корабле́/су́дне!; **land** ~! земля́!

⚲ **aid** /eɪd/ *n.* **1** (help, assistance) по́мощь; (support) подде́ржка; **first** ~ пе́рвая по́мощь; **with the** ~ **of** при по́мощи + *g.*; **in** ~ **of** в по́мощь + *d.* **2** (appliance) посо́бие; **visual** ~**s** нагля́дные посо́бия
● *v.t.* (help) пом|ога́ть, -о́чь + *d.*; (promote) спосо́бствовать (*impf.*) + *d.*
■ ~ **agency** *n.* организа́ция по оказа́нию по́мощи; ~ **worker** *n.* рабо́тн|ик (-ица) организа́ции по оказа́нию по́мощи

aide /eɪd/ *n.* помо́щни|к (-ца)

Aids, AIDS /eɪdz/ *n.* (*abbr. of* **acquired immune deficiency syndrome**) СПИД (синдро́м приобретённого иммунодефици́та)

ailing /'eɪlɪŋ/ *adj.* больно́й; **an** ~ **economy** больна́я эконо́мика

ailment /'eɪlmənt/ *n.* неду́г, хворь

⚲ **aim** /eɪm/ *n.* **1** (purpose) цель; **with the** ~ **of** с це́лью + *g.* **2** (of a gun, etc.) прице́л; **take** ~ **at** прице́л|иваться, -иться в + *a.*
● *v.t.* нав|оди́ть, -ести́; ~ **a blow at** зама́х|иваться, -ну́ться на + *a.* (fig.): ~ **one's remarks at** предназн|ача́ть, -а́чить свои́ замеча́ния + *d.*
● *v.i.* це́литься (*impf.*); ~ **at** (with rifle) прице́л|иваться, -иться в + *a.*; (fig.): ~ **at** (aspire to) це́литься, на- на + *a.*; стреми́ться (*impf.*) к + *d.*; ~ **for** напр|авля́ться, -а́виться в/на + *a.*

aimless /'eɪmlɪs/ *adj.* бесце́льный

⚲ **air** /eə(r)/ *n.* **1** во́здух; **get some fresh** ~ подыша́ть (*pf.*) све́жим во́здухом; **in the open** ~ на откры́том во́здухе; **travel by** ~ лета́ть (*impf.*) (самолётом) **2** (in fig. phrs.):

⚲ ключева́я ле́ксика

clear the ~ разря|жа́ть, -ди́ть атмосфе́ру;
he vanished into thin ~ его́ и след просты́л;
he was walking on ~ он ног под собо́й
не чу́вствовал **3** (appearance, manner) (of
person) вид; (of place) дух; ~**s and graces**
мане́рность; **put on (or give oneself)** ~**s**
задава́ться, ва́жничать (*both impf.*) **4** (radio,
TV): **go on the** ~ выходи́ть, вы́йти в эфи́р;
go off the ~ (of station) зак|а́нчивать,
-о́нчить переда́чу **5** (*attr.*) (pert. to aviation)
возду́шный; авиацио́нный, авиа…; (mil.)
вое́нно-возду́шный
● *v.t.* **1** (ventilate) прове́три|вать, -ть; (BrE,
dry) суши́ть, вы́- **2** (fig., opinions, feelings)
выска́зывать, вы́сказать
● *v.i.* про|су́шивать, -суши́ть
■ ~ **bag** *n.* авари́йная поду́шка безопа́сности;
~ **bed** *n.* (BrE) надувно́й матра́ц;
~**-conditioned** *adj.* с кондициони́рованным
во́здухом; ~ **conditioning** *n.*
кондициони́рование во́здуха; ~**crew** *n.*
экипа́ж; ~**field** *n.* лётное по́ле; ~ **force** *n.*
вое́нно-возду́шные си́лы; ~ **gun** *n.* духово́е
ружьё; ~ **hostess** *n.* (BrE) бортпроводни́ца,
стюарде́сса; ~ **letter** *n.* авиаписьмо́; ~**lift** *n.*
возду́шная перебро́ска ● *v.t.* перебр|а́сывать,
-о́сить (*or* перев|ози́ть, -езти́) по во́здуху;
~**line** *n.* (company) авиакомпа́ния; ~**mail**
n. авиапо́чта; ~**plane** *n.* (AmE) = **aeroplane**;
~ **raid** *n.* возду́шный налёт; ~**-raid**
warning возду́шная трево́га; ~**-raid shelter**
бомбоубе́жище; ~**-raid warden** ≈ нача́льник
шта́ба гражда́нской оборо́ны; ~ **rifle**
n. пневмати́ческая винто́вка; ~**ship** *n.*
возду́шный кора́бль; дирижа́бль (*m.*);
~**sick** *adj.*: **I was** ~**sick** меня́ укача́ло в
самолёте; ~**strip** *n.* взлётно-поса́дочная
полоса́; ~ **terminal** *n.* аэровокза́л; ~**tight**
adj. гермети́ческий; ~ **traffic control**
n. авиадиспе́тчерская слу́жба; ~ **traffic**
controller *n.* авиадиспе́тчер; ~**waves** *n.*
pl. радиово́лны

aircraft /ˈeəkrɑːft/ *n.* самолёт, (*collect.*)
самолёты, авиа́ция
■ ~**-carrier** *n.* авиано́сец

airing /ˈeərɪŋ/ *n.* прове́тривание
■ ~ **cupboard** *n.* (BrE) суши́льный шкаф

airless /ˈeəlɪs/ *adj.* (stuffy) ду́шный; (still)
безве́тренный

airport /ˈeəpɔːt/ *n.* аэропо́рт

airy /ˈeərɪ/ *adj.* (**airier**, **airiest**) **1** (well ventilated)
све́жий; (spacious) просто́рный **2** (superficial;
light-hearted) ве́треный, беспе́чный

aisle /aɪl/ *n.* прохо́д (*между рядами*)

ajar /əˈdʒɑː(r)/ *pred. adj.* приоткры́тый

aka *abbr.* (*of* **also known as**) изве́стный
та́кже под и́менем

akin /əˈkɪn/ *pred. adj. & adv.* (related)
ро́дственный; ~ **to** сродни́ + *d.*

alarm /əˈlɑːm/ *n.* **1** (warning; warning signal)
трево́га; **false** ~ ло́жная трево́га; **fire** ~
пожа́рная трево́га **2** (~ **clock**) буди́льник
3 (fright): **he ran away in** ~ он убежа́л в
испу́ге
● *v.t.* трево́жить; **to be** ~**ed** трево́житься, вс-

alarmist /əˈlɑːmɪst/ *n.* панике́р (-ша)

alas /əˈlæs/ *int.* увы́!

Albania /ælˈbeɪnɪə/ *n.* Алба́ния

Albanian /ælˈbeɪnɪən/ *n.* **1** (person) алба́н|ец
(-ка) **2** (language) алба́нский язы́к
● *adj.* алба́нский

albeit /ɔːlˈbiːɪt/ *conj.* пусть (и), хотя́ и

✧ **album** /ˈælbəm/ *n.* (book; recordings) альбо́м

alchemist /ˈælkəmɪst/ *n.* алхи́мик

alchemy /ˈælkəmɪ/ *n.* алхи́мия

✧ **alcohol** /ˈælkəhɒl/ *n.* (chem.) алкого́ль (*m.*);
(spirit) спирт
■ ~**-free** *adj.* безалкого́льный

alcoholic /ælkəˈhɒlɪk/ *n.* алкого́лик
● *adj.* алкого́льный; ~ **beverages** спиртно́е;
спиртны́е напи́тки (*m. pl.*)

alcoholism /ˈælkəhɒlɪz(ə)m/ *n.* алкоголи́зм

alcove /ˈælkəʊv/ *n.* алько́в, ни́ша

ale /eɪl/ *n.* эль (*m.*); (beer) пи́во

alert /əˈlɜːt/ *adj.* (vigilant) чу́ткий; (lively) живо́й
● *v.t.* прив|оди́ть, -ести́ в состоя́ние гото́вности;
~ **sb to a situation** предупре|жда́ть, -ди́ть
кого́-н. о созда́вшейся ситуа́ции

A level *n.* (BrE) выпускно́й экза́мен в сре́дней
шко́ле по профили́рующим предме́там
(с повы́шенным у́ровнем сло́жности)

algebra /ˈældʒɪbrə/ *n.* а́лгебра

Algeria /ælˈdʒɪərɪə/ *n.* Алжи́р

Algerian /ælˈdʒɪərɪən/ *n.* алжи́р|ец (-ка)
● *adj.* алжи́рский

alias /ˈeɪlɪəs/ *n.* кли́чка, про́звище;
вы́мышленное и́мя

alibi /ˈælɪbaɪ/ *n.* (*pl.* ~**s**) **1** (plea or proof of being
elsewhere) а́либи (*nt. indecl.*); **establish an** ~
устан|а́вливать, -ови́ть а́либи; **produce an** ~
предст|авля́ть, -а́вить а́либи **2** (infml, excuse)
отгово́рка

alien /ˈeɪlɪən/ *n.* (foreigner) иностра́н|ец
(-ка); (extraterrestrial) инопланетя́н|ин (-ка),
прише́лец (*из космоса*)
● *adj.* **1** (foreign) иностра́нный; (extraterrestrial)
инопланетный **2**; ~ **to** чу́ждый + *d.*

alienate /ˈeɪlɪəneɪt/ *v.t.* (estrange, antagonize)
отвра|ща́ть, -ти́ть; отчужда́ть (*impf.*)

alight[1] /əˈlaɪt/ *pred. adj. & adv.* (on fire)
горя́щий, в огне́; **set** ~ заж|ига́ть, -е́чь

alight[2] /əˈlaɪt/ *v.i.* (**alighted**) **1** (BrE, from
vehicle) сходи́ть, сойти́ (**from:** с + *g.*) **2** (come
to earth) сади́ться, сесть

align /əˈlaɪn/ *v.t.* выра́внивать, вы́ровнять

alignment /əˈlaɪnmənt/ *n.* выра́внивание;
out of ~ неро́вно, не в ряд

alike /əˈlaɪk/ *pred. adj.* (similar) (of people)
похо́жий (на + *a.*); (of objects) схо́жий (с + *i.*)
● *adv.* одина́ково; **treat everyone** ~ обраща́ться
(*impf.*) со все́ми одина́ково; **winter and**
summer ~ как зимо́й, так и ле́том

alimony /ˈælɪmənɪ/ *n.* (law) алиме́нт|ы (-ов)

✧ **alive** /əˈlaɪv/ *pred. adj. & adv.* **1** (living) живо́й;
в живы́х; **buried** ~ похоро́ненный за́живо; ~
and kicking жив-здоро́в (infml) **2** (alert): **look**

a

~! живё! **3** (infested): **the bed was ~ with fleas** кровáть кишéла блóхами

alkali /ˈælkəlaɪ/ *n.* (*pl.* **~s**) щёлочь; (*attr.*) щелочнóй

alkaline /ˈælkəlaɪn/ *adj.* щелочнóй

✐ **all** /ɔːl/ *pron.* (everybody) все; (everything) всё; **~ of us** мы все; **the score is 2 ~** счёт 2:2; **~ but** (almost) почти, чуть не; **~ in ~** (in general) в óбщем и цéлом; **above ~** прéжде всегó; **after ~** в концé концóв; в конéчном счёте; **he came after ~** он всё же пришёл; **not at ~** совсéм/вóвсе не; нискóлько, ничýть; 'Thank you.' — 'Not at ~!' «Спасибо.» — «Нé за что!»; **he has no money at ~** у негó совсéм нет дéнег; **once and for ~** раз и навсегдá

● *adj.* весь; (every) всякий; **~ his life** всю свою жизнь; **~ day long** весь день; **~ the time** всё врéмя; **at ~ times** в любóе врéмя; всегдá; **for ~ that** всё-таки

● *adv.* (quite) совсéм, совершéнно; целикóм; **~ dressed up** наряди́вшись; разряди́вшись в пух и прах; **I got ~ excited** я разволновáлся; **I knew it ~ along** я всегдá э́то знал; **she lived ~ by herself** онá жилá совсéм однá; **she did it ~ by herself** онá сдéлала э́то самá; **I am ~ ears** я весь (*m.*) /вся (*f.*) внимáние; **~ in** (exhausted) выбившийся из сил; (inclusive of everything) включáя всё; **~ over again** (всё) снóва; **~ right!** лáдно!, хорошó!; **'How are you?' — 'A~ right!'** «Как делá?» — «Нормáльно!»; **the film was ~ right** фильм был неплохóй; **are you ~ right?** с вáми всё в порядке?; **~ the same** (however) всё-таки; **he's not ~ there** у негó не все дóма

■ **~-clear** *n.* отбóй (тревóги); **~-important** *adj.* чрезвычáйно вáжный; **~-night** *adj.*: **~-night session** заседáние, продолжáющееся всю ночь; **~-out** *adj.*: **an ~-out effort** максимáльное усилие; **~-star** *adj.*: **with an ~-star cast** с учáстием звёзд; **~-time** *adj.*: **at an ~-time low** на небывáло низком уровне; **~-time record** непревзойдённый рекóрд; **~-weather** *adj.* всепогóдный

Allah /ˈælə/ *n.* Аллáх

allay /əˈleɪ/ *v.t.* (doubts, suspicions) рассé|ивать, -ять; (fears) развé|ивать, -ять; **~ thirst/hunger** утол|ять, -ить жáжду/гóлод

allegation /ælɪˈgeɪʃ(ə)n/ *n.* заявлéние, утверждéние

✐ **allege** /əˈledʒ/ *v.t.* утверждáть (*impf.*); **an ~d murderer** подозревáемый в убийстве

allegedly /əˈledʒɪdlɪ/ *adv.* бýдто бы, якобы

allegiance /əˈliːdʒ(ə)ns/ *n.* (loyalty) вéрность; (devotion) прéданность

allegorical /ælɪˈgɒrɪk(ə)l/ *adj.* аллегори́ческий

allegory /ˈælɪgərɪ/ *n.* аллегóрия

allegro /əˈleɡrəʊ/ *n., adj., & adv.* (*pl.* **~s**) аллéгро (*nt. indecl.*)

alleluia /ælɪˈluːjə/ *n. & int.* аллилýйя

allergic /əˈlɜːdʒɪk/ *adj.* аллерги́ческий; **I'm ~ to strawberries** у меня́ аллерги́я на клубни́ку

allergy /ˈælədʒɪ/ *n.* аллерги́я

alleviate /əˈliːvɪeɪt/ *v.t.* (relieve, lighten) облегч|áть, -и́ть; (mitigate, soften) смягч|áть, -и́ть

alley /ˈælɪ/ *n.* (*pl.* **~s**) переýлок; **blind ~** тупи́к

alliance /əˈlaɪəns/ *n.* соýз; (pol.) альянс

allied /ˈælaɪd/ *adj.* соýзный

allocate /ˈæləkeɪt/ *v.t.* (money) ассигновáть (*impf., pf.*); (distribute) разме|щáть, -сти́ть; (assign) назн|ачáть, -áчить

allocation /æləˈkeɪʃ(ə)n/ *n.* (allocating) выделéние; ассигновáние; размещéние; назначéние; (sum allocated) ассигновáние

allot /əˈlɒt/ *v.t.* (**allotted, allotting**) (distribute) распредел|я́ть, -и́ть; (assign) назн|ачáть, -áчить; **~ a task** да|вáть, -ть задáние

allotment /əˈlɒtmənt/ *n.* (BrE, plot of land) (земéльный) учáсток

✐ **allow** /əˈlaʊ/ *v.t.* **1** (permit) позв|оля́ть, -óлить; разреш|áть, -и́ть; **~ me!** разреши́те!; **he was ~ed to smoke** емý позвóлили кури́ть; **smoking is not ~ed** кури́ть воспрещáется; **no dogs ~ed** вход с собáками воспрещён **2** (grant, provide) да|вáть, -ть; предост|авля́ть, -áвить; допус|кáть, -ти́ть

● *v.i.* **~ for** (take into account) учи́т|ывать, -éсть; **not ~ing for expenses** не принимáя в расчёт издéржек; **~ £50 for emergencies** выделя́ть, выделить 50 фýнтов на непредви́денный слýчай

allowance /əˈlaʊəns/ *n.* **1** (amount provided): **monthly ~** мéсячное посóбие; **make sb an ~** назначáть, назнáчить содержáние комý-н.; (mil.) довóльствие **2** (concession): **we will make an ~ in your case** мы сдéлаем для вас исключéние; **make ~(s) for** учи́т|ывать, -éсть; прин|имáть, -ять во внимáние

alloy /ˈælɔɪ/ *n.* сплав

allude /əˈluːd/ *v.i.*: **~e to** ссылáться, сослáться на + *a.*; упом|инáть, -янýть; (mean): **what are you ~ing to?** на что вы намекáете?

allure /əˈljʊə(r)/ *n.* привлекáтельность, прéлесть

● *v.t.* (entice, attract) заман|ивать, -и́ть; (charm) завлек|áть, -éчь; очарóв|ывать, -áть

allusion /əˈluːʒ(ə)n/ *n.* намёк; ссы́лка

ally¹ /ˈælaɪ/ *n.* соýзник

ally² /əˈlaɪ/ *v.t.* (connect) соедин|я́ть, -и́ть; **~ oneself with** вступ|áть, -и́ть в соýз с + *i.*

almanac /ˈɔːlmənæk/ *n.* альманáх

almighty /ɔːlˈmaɪtɪ/ *n.*: **the A~** Всемогýщий

● *adj.* Всемогýщий; (infml, huge) огрóмный

almond /ˈɑːmənd/ *n.* миндáль (*m.*)

✐ **almost** /ˈɔːlməʊst/ *adv.* почти́; (with vv.) почти́, чуть не, едвá не

✐ **alone** /əˈləʊn/ *adj.* **1** (by oneself, itself) оди́н; еди́нственный **2** (… and no other(s)): **in the month of June ~** тóлько в ию́не мéсяце; **she and I are ~ (together)** мы с ней вдвоём/одни́ **3** **let, leave ~**: **his parents left him ~ all day** роди́тели остáвили егó на цéлый день однóго; (*see also* ▸ **let alone** (▸ **let²**))

✐ **along** /əˈlɒŋ/ *adv.* **1** (on; forward): **move ~** продв|игáться, -и́нуться; **come ~** пошли́!; **a few doors ~ from the station** в нéскольких

✐ ключевáя лéксика

шага́х от вокза́ла **2** (denoting accompaniment): **he brought a book** ~ он принёс с собо́й кни́гу **3** (over there; over here): **he'll be** ~ **in 10 minutes** он бу́дет че́рез де́сять мину́т **4**: **all** ~ (the whole time) всё вре́мя
● *prep.* вдоль + *g.*; **she was walking** ~ **the river** она́ шла вдоль реки́

alongside /əlɒŋˈsaɪd/ *adv.* ря́дом, сбо́ку; **we stopped and the police car drew up** ~ мы останови́лись, и подъе́хавшая полице́йская маши́на вста́ла ря́дом
● *prep.* (*also* ~ **of**) ря́дом с + *i.*; у + *g.*

aloof /əˈluːf/ *adj.* сде́ржанный, отчуждённый

aloofness /əˈluːfnɪs/ *n.* сде́ржанность, отчуждённость

aloud /əˈlaʊd/ *adv.* вслух; **read** ~ чита́ть вслух

alphabet /ˈælfəbet/ *n.* алфави́т, а́збука

alphabetical /ælfəˈbetɪk(ə)l/ *adj.* алфави́тный; **in** ~ **order** в алфави́тном поря́дке

alpine /ˈælpaɪn/ *adj.* альпи́йский

Alps /ælps/ *n. pl.* (*in full* **the** ~) А́льп|ы (*pl., g.* —)

already /ɔːlˈredɪ/ *adv.* уже́

Alsatian /ælˈseɪʃ(ə)n/ *n.* (BrE) неме́цкая овча́рка

also /ˈɔːlsəʊ/ *adv.* то́же; та́кже; (moreover) к тому́ же

altar /ˈɔːltə(r)/ *n.* престо́л, алта́рь

alter /ˈɔːltə(r)/ *v.t. & i.* меня́ть(ся) (*impf.*); измен|я́ть(ся), -и́ть(ся); (remake) переде́л|ывать, -ать; **the dress needs** ~ing э́то пла́тье на́до переде́лать

alteration /ɔːltəˈreɪʃ(ə)n/ *n.* (change) измене́ние; (remaking, e.g. of clothes) переде́лка

altercation /ɔːltəˈkeɪʃ(ə)n/ *n.* ссо́ра, перебра́нка

alternate¹ /ɔːlˈtɜːnət/ *adj.* **1** (taking turns) череду́ющийся; **on** ~ **Saturdays** ка́ждую втору́ю суббо́ту **2** (AmE, alternative) альтернати́вный

alternate² /ˈɔːltəneɪt/ *v.t. & i.* чередова́ть(ся) (*impf.*); перемежа́ть(ся) (*impf.*)

alternative /ɔːlˈtɜːnətɪv/ *n.* альтернати́ва; **there is no** ~ друго́го вы́бора нет
● *adj.* альтернати́вный
■ ~ **medicine** *n.* нетрадицио́нная медици́на; ~ **technology** *n.* техноло́гия безотхо́дного произво́дства

alternatively /ɔːlˈtɜːnətɪvlɪ/ *adv.* (indicating choice): **a £5,000 fine,** ~ **one month's imprisonment** штраф 5000 фу́нтов и́ли оди́н ме́сяц тюре́много заключе́ния

alternator /ˈɔːltəneɪtə(r)/ *n.* (elec.) генера́тор переме́нного то́ка

although /ɔːlˈðəʊ/ *conj.* хотя́; (despite the fact that) несмотря́ на то, что

altitude /ˈæltɪtjuːd/ *n.* (of flight) высота́; (of a place) высота́ над у́ровнем мо́ря

alto /ˈæltəʊ/ *n.* (*pl.* **altos**) альт; (*attr.*) альто́вый

altogether /ɔːltəˈgeðə(r)/ *adv.* **1** (entirely) вполне́; соверше́нно; (completely) совсе́м **2** (in all, in general; as a whole) в о́бщем, в це́лом, в о́бщем; **how much is that** ~? ско́лько всего́?

altruism /ˈæltruːɪz(ə)m/ *n.* альтруи́зм

altruistic /æltruːˈɪstɪk/ *adj.* альтруисти́ческий

aluminium /ˌæljʊˈmɪnɪəm/ (AmE **aluminum** /əˈluːmɪnəm/) *n.* алюми́ний

always /ˈɔːlweɪz/ *adv.* всегда́; (constantly) постоя́нно, всё вре́мя; **he is** ~ **after money** он всегда́/постоя́нно ду́мает о деньга́х

Alzheimer's /ˈæltshaɪməz/ *n.* (*in full* ~ **disease**) боле́знь Альцге́ймера

am /æm/ *1st pers. sing. pres. of* ▶ **be**

a.m. *abbr.* (*of* **ante meridiem**) утра́; (in the morning) у́тром; **6** ~ шесть часо́в утра́

amalgam /əˈmælgəm/ *n.* амальга́ма; (fig.) смесь

amalgamate /əˈmælgəmeɪt/ *v.t. & i.* (companies) слива́ть(ся), сли́ть(ся)

amass /əˈmæs/ *v.t.* накоп|ля́ть, -и́ть

amateur /ˈæmətə(r)/ *n.* люби́тель (*m.*); (*attr.*) люби́тельский

amateurish /ˈæmətərɪʃ/ *adj.* дилета́нтский; непрофессиона́льный

amaze /əˈmeɪz/ *v.t.* изум|ля́ть, -и́ть; **be** ~ed **at** изум|ля́ться, -и́ться + *d.*; ~ing изуми́тельный, удиви́тельный

amazement /əˈmeɪzmənt/ *n.* изумле́ние

Amazon /ˈæməz(ə)n/ *n.* (myth., fig.) амазо́нка; (river) Амазо́нка

ambassador /æmˈbæsədə(r)/ *n.* посо́л; (representative) представи́тель (*m.*)

amber /ˈæmbə(r)/ *n.* **1** (resin) янта́рь (*m.*) **2** (colour) янта́рный цвет, цвет янтаря́

ambidextrous /æmbɪˈdekstrəs/ *adj.* одина́ково владе́ющий обе́ими рука́ми

ambience /ˈæmbɪəns/ *n.* среда́; атмосфе́ра

ambient /ˈæmbɪənt/ *adj.* окружа́ющий; ~ **temperature** температу́ра окружа́ющего во́здуха

ambiguity /æmbɪˈgjuːɪtɪ/ *n.* двусмы́сленность; нея́сность

ambiguous /æmˈbɪgjʊəs/ *adj.* двусмы́сленный; нея́сный

ambition /æmˈbɪʃ(ə)n/ *n.* (desire for distinction) честолю́бие, амби́ция; (aspiration) стремле́ние

ambitious /æmˈbɪʃəs/ *adj.* честолюби́вый; амбицио́зный; **an** ~ **plan** грандио́зный план

ambivalence /æmˈbɪvələns/ *n.* двойственность

ambivalent /æmˈbɪvələnt/ *adj.* двойственный

amble /ˈæmb(ə)l/ *n. v.i.* идти́ (*det.*) лёгкой похо́дкой; прогу́ливаться (*impf.*)

ambulance /ˈæmbjʊləns/ *n.* маши́на ско́рой по́мощи

ambush /ˈæmbʊʃ/ *n.* заса́да
● *v.t.* нап|ада́ть, -а́сть на (*кого*) из заса́ды

ameba /əˈmiːbə/ *n.* (AmE) = **amoeba**

ameliorate /əˈmiːlɪəreɪt/ *v.t. & i.* ул|учша́ть(ся), -у́чшить(ся)

amen /ɑːˈmen/ *int.* ами́нь

amend /əˈmend/ *v.t.* **1** (correct) испр|авля́ть, -а́вить **2** (make changes to) вн|оси́ть, -ести́ попра́вки/измене́ния в + *a.*

amendment /əˈmendmənt/ *n.* **1** (reform) исправле́ние **2** (of document etc.) попра́вка

amends /əˈmendz/ *n. pl.* возмеще́ние; исправле́ние; **make** ~ **to sb** загла́|живать,

a

-дить вину́ пе́ред (+ *i.*) (*за что*); he made ~ for his rudeness он загла́дил свою́ гру́бость

amenity /əˈmiːnɪtɪ/ *n.* (*usu. in pl.*) удо́бства (*nt. pl.*)

America /əˈmerɪkə/ *n.* Аме́рика

♂ **American** /əˈmerɪkən/ *n.* америка́н|ец (-ка) ● *adj.* америка́нский

■ ~ **English** *n.* америка́нский вариа́нт англи́йского языка́; ~ **Indian** *n.* америка́нск|ий инде́ец (-ая индиа́нка)

Americanism /əˈmerɪkənɪz(ə)m/ *n.* американи́зм

amethyst /ˈæmɪθɪst/ *n.* амети́ст; (*attr.*) амети́стовый

amiable /ˈeɪmɪəb(ə)l/ *adj.* приве́тливый; добродушный

amicable /ˈæmɪkəb(ə)l/ *adj.* дружелю́бный; (agreement, separation) дру́жеский; (divorce) ми́рный

amid /əˈmɪd/ *prep.* среди́ + *g.*

amidst /əˈmɪdst/ *prep.* (literary) = **amid**

amino acid /əˈmiːnəʊ/ *n.* аминокислота́

amiss /əˈmɪs/ *pred. adj.* непра́вильный; something is ~ что́-то нела́дно

ammeter /ˈæmɪtə(r)/ *n.* амперме́тр

ammonia /əˈməʊnɪə/ *n.* (gas) аммиа́к; (*attr.*) аммиа́чный

ammunition /æmjʊˈnɪʃ(ə)n/ *n.* боевы́е припа́сы, боеприпа́сы (*m. pl.*)

amnesia /æmˈniːzɪə/ *n.* амнези́я

amnesty /ˈæmnɪstɪ/ *n.* амни́стия

amniocentesis /æmnɪəʊsenˈtiːsɪs/ *n.* (med.) амниоценте́з (*пункция плодного пузыря*)

amoeba /əˈmiːbə/ (AmE *also* **ameba**) *n.* (*pl.* **amoebas** *or* **amoebae** /-biː/) ами́ба

amok /əˈmɒk/ *adv.*: run ~ бу́йствовать (*impf.*); беси́ться (*impf.*)

♂ **among** /əˈmʌŋ/ *prep.* **1** (between) ме́жду + *i.*; conversation ~ friends разгово́р ме́жду друзья́ми **2** (in the midst of) среди́ + *g.*; ме́жду + *g.*; ~ the trees среди́ дере́вьев **3** (expr. one of a number) из + *g.*

amongst /əˈmʌŋst/ *prep.* (BrE) = **among**

amoral /eɪˈmɒr(ə)l/ *adj.* амора́льный

amorphous /əˈmɔːfəs/ *adj.* (shapeless) бесфо́рменный

amortize /əˈmɔːtaɪz/ *v.t.* амортизи́ровать (*impf., pf.*)

♂ **amount** /əˈmaʊnt/ *n.* **1** (sum) су́мма **2** (quantity) коли́чество; he spent a huge ~ of money он истра́тил ку́чу де́нег ● *v.i.*: ~ to (add up to) сост|авля́ть, -а́вить + *g.*; дост|ига́ть, -и́чь + *g.*; the expenses ~ to £600 расхо́ды составля́ют шестьсо́т фу́нтов; (be equivalent to) быть ра́вным/равноси́льным + *d.*; it ~s to the same thing э́то сво́дится всё к тому́ же

amp /æmp/ *n.* (*abbr. of* **ampere**) A (ампе́р)

ampere /ˈæmpeə(r)/ *n.* ампе́р

ampersand /ˈæmpəsænd/ *n.* амперса́нд (*знак* «&»)

amphetamine /æmˈfetəmiːn/ *n.* амфетами́н

amphibian /æmˈfɪbɪən/ *n.* земново́дное; амфи́бия

amphitheatre /ˈæmfɪθɪətə(r)/ (AmE **amphitheater**) *n.* амфитеа́тр

ample /ˈæmp(ə)l/ *adj.* (**ampler**, **amplest**) (sufficient) доста́точный; (abundant) оби́льный

amplifier /ˈæmplɪfaɪə(r)/ *n.* усили́тель (*m.*)

amplify /ˈæmplɪfaɪ/ *v.t.* уси́ли|вать, -ть

amputate /ˈæmpjʊteɪt/ *v.t.* ампути́ровать (*impf., pf.*); отн|има́ть, -я́ть

amuse /əˈmjuːz/ *v.t.* (entertain, divert) развл|ека́ть, -е́чь; (make laugh) смеши́ть (*impf.*); позаба́вить (*pf.*)

amusement /əˈmjuːzmənt/ *n.* **1** (diversion) развлече́ние, заба́ва **2** (tendency to laughter): to everyone's ~ the clown fell over ко всео́бщему удово́льствию кло́ун упа́л

■ ~ **park** *n.* парк с аттракцио́нами; луна́-па́рк

amusing /əˈmjuːzɪŋ/ *adj.* заба́вный; (funny) смешно́й

an /æn, ən/ *see* ▸ **a**

anachronism /əˈnækrənɪz(ə)m/ *n.* анахрони́зм

anaemia /əˈniːmɪə/ (AmE **anemia**) *n.* малокро́вие, анеми́я

anaesthesia /ænɪsˈθiːzɪə/ (AmE **anesthesia**) *n.* анестези́я, обезбо́ливание

anaesthetic /ænɪsˈθetɪk/ (AmE **anesthetic**) *n.* анестези́рующее сре́дство; анесте́тик; general/local ~ о́бщий/ме́стный нарко́з; under ~ под нарко́зом

anaesthetist /əˈniːsθətɪst/ (AmE **anesthetist**) *n.* анестезио́лог

anaesthetize /əˈniːsθətaɪz/ (AmE **anesthetize**) *v.t.* анестези́ровать (*impf., pf.*); обезбо́ли|вать, -ть

anal /ˈeɪn(ə)l/ *adj.* заднепрохо́дный, ана́льный

analgesic /ænəlˈdʒiːzɪk/ *adj.* болеутоля́ющий

analogous /əˈnæləgəs/ *adj.* аналоги́чный

analogy /əˈnælədʒɪ/ *n.* анало́гия; схо́дство

analyse /ˈænəlaɪz/ (AmE **analyze**) *v.t.* анализи́ровать (*impf., pf.*) (*pf. also* про-)

♂ **analysis** /əˈnælɪsɪs/ *n.* (*pl.* **analyses** /-siːz/) ана́лиз; (psycho~) психоана́лиз

♂ **analyst** /ˈænəlɪst/ *n.* анали́тик; (political) коммента́тор; (psych.) психоанали́тик

analytical /ænəˈlɪtɪk(ə)l/, **analytic** /ænəˈlɪtɪk/ *adjs.* аналити́ческий

analyze /ˈænəlaɪz/ *v.t.* (AmE) = **analyse**

anarchic /əˈnɑːkɪk/, **anarchical** /əˈnɑːkɪk(ə)l/ *adjs.* анархи́ческий

anarchist /ˈænəkɪst/ *n.* анархи́ст (-ка)

anarchy /ˈænəkɪ/ *n.* ана́рхия

anathema /əˈnæθəmə/ *n.* (*pl.* ~s) (hated thing): it's ~ to me я непримири́мый/я́рый проти́вник э́того; я органи́чески не прие́млю э́того

♂ ключева́я ле́ксика

anatomical /ænə'tɒmɪk(ə)l/ *adj.* анатоми́ческий

anatomy /ə'nætəmɪ/ *n.* анато́мия

ancestor /'ænsestə(r)/ *n.* пре́док

ancestral /æn'sestr(ə)l/ *adj.* родово́й; ∼ **home** родово́е име́ние

ancestry /'ænsestrɪ/ *n.* (lineage) родосло́вная, происхожде́ние; **he comes of distinguished** ∼ он благоро́дного происхожде́ния

anchor /'æŋkə(r)/ *n.* я́корь (*m.*)

anchovy /'æntʃəvɪ/ *n.* анчо́ус

✓ **ancient** /'eɪnʃ(ə)nt/ *adj.* дре́вний; анти́чный; (very old) стари́нный; веково́й
 ∎ ∼ **history** *n.* дре́вняя исто́рия; ∼ **monument** *n.* (BrE) па́мятник старины́

✓ **and** /ænd/ *conj.* **1** (connecting words or clauses) и; (in addition) и, да; (with certain closely linked pairs, esp. of persons) с + *i.*; **bread** ∼ **butter** хлеб с ма́слом; **you** ∼ **I** мы с ва́ми; (with nums. denoting addition) и; плюс; **2** ∼ **2 are 4** два и/плюс два — четы́ре; (to form compound num., omitted): **260** две́сти шестьдеся́т; (with following fraction) с + *i.* **2** (intensive): **he ran** ∼ **ran** он всё бежа́л и бежа́л; **they talked for hours** ∼ **hours** они́ разгова́ривали часа́ми **3** (in order to, omitted before inf.): **try** ∼ **find out** постара́йтесь узна́ть; **wait** ∼ **see!** погоди́те — ещё уви́дите!

andante /æn'dæntɪ/ *n., adj., and adv.* (mus.) анда́нте (*nt. indecl.*)

androgynous /æn'drɒdʒɪnəs/ *adj.* двупо́лый; (bot.) обоепо́лый

anecdotal /ænɪk'dəʊt(ə)l/ *adj.* анекдоти́ческий

anecdote /'ænɪkdəʊt/ *n.* исто́рия; (joke) анекдо́т

anemia /ə'niːmɪə/ *n.* (AmE) = **anaemia**

anemone /ə'nemənɪ/ *n.* анемо́н; (wood ∼) ве́треница; **sea** ∼ морско́й анемо́н; акти́ния

anesthesia /ænɪs'θiːzɪə/ *n.* (AmE) = **anaesthesia**

anesthetic /ænɪs'θetɪk/ *n.* (AmE) = **anaesthetic**

anesthetist /ə'niːsθətɪst/ *n.* (AmE) = **anaesthetist**

anesthetize /ə'niːsθətaɪz/ *v.t.* (AmE) = **anaesthetize**

anew /ə'njuː/ *adj.* (again) сно́ва; (in a different way) за́ново, по-но́вому

angel /'eɪndʒ(ə)l/ *n.* (lit., fig.) а́нгел

angelic /æn'dʒelɪk/ *adj.* а́нгельский

anger /'æŋgə(r)/ *n.* гнев
 ● *v.t.* серди́ть, рас∼; разгне́вать (*pf.*)

angina /æn'dʒaɪnə/ *n.* (*also* ∼ **pectoris** /'pektərɪs/) стенокарди́я, грудна́я жа́ба

angle[1] /'æŋg(ə)l/ *n.* у́гол; **right** ∼ прямо́й у́гол; **at right** ∼s под прямы́м угло́м; (fig., viewpoint) то́чка зре́ния, подхо́д
 ● *v.t.* ста́вить, по∼ под угло́м; (fig.): **the news was** ∼**d** но́вости бы́ли по́даны тенденцио́зно

angle[2] /'æŋg(ə)l/ *v.i.* (fish) уди́ть (*impf.*) ры́бу; (fig.): ∼ **for compliments** напра́шиваться (*impf.*) на комплиме́нты

angler /'æŋglə(r)/ *n.* рыболо́в

Anglican /'æŋglɪkən/ *n.* англика́н|ец (-ка)
 ● *adj.* англика́нский

Anglo-Saxon /æŋgləʊ'sæks(ə)n/ *n.* англосаксо́нский/древнеангли́йский язы́к
 ● *adj.* англосаксо́нский, древнеангли́йский

Angola /æŋ'gəʊlə/ *n.* Анго́ла

Angolan /æŋ'gəʊlən/ *n.* анго́л|ец (-ка)
 ● *adj.* анго́льский

angora /æŋ'gɔːrə/ *n.* (cloth) анго́рская шерсть
 ● *adj.* анго́рский

✓ **angry** /'æŋgrɪ/ *adj.* (**angrier, angriest**) серди́тый; **be** ∼ **with** серди́ться (*impf.*) на + *a.* (**over, about sth:** за + *a.*); **get** ∼ **with** рассерди́ться (*pf.*) на + *a.*

anguish /'æŋgwɪʃ/ *n.* муче́ние; му́ка

angular /'æŋgjʊlə(r)/ *adj.* углова́тый

✓ **animal** /'ænɪm(ə)l/ *n.* живо́тное
 ● *adj.* живо́тный
 ∎ ∼ **rights** *n. pl.* права́ (*nt. pl.*) живо́тных

animate /'ænɪmeɪt/ *v.t.* оживл|я́ть, -и́ть; **become** ∼**d** оживл|я́ться, -и́ться

animation /ænɪ'meɪʃ(ə)n/ *n.* (enthusiasm) воодушевле́ние; (cin.) мультиплика́ция, анима́ция

animosity /ænɪ'mɒsɪtɪ/ *n.* (hostility) вражде́бность; **feel** ∼ **against** пита́ть (*impf.*) вражду́ к + *d.*

aniseed /'ænɪsiːd/ *n.* ани́с, ани́совое се́мя

ankle /'æŋk(ə)l/ *n.* лоды́жка, щи́колотка
 ∎ ∼ **socks** *n. pl.* носки́ (*m. pl.*)

annex[1] /'æneks/ *n.* (to a building) пристро́йка, фли́гель (*m.*)

annex[2] /æ'neks/ *v.t.* присоедин|я́ть, -и́ть; (territory etc.) аннекси́ровать (*impf., pf.*)

annexation /ænek'seɪʃ(ə)n/ *n.* присоедине́ние; анне́ксия, аннекси́рование

annexe /'æneks/ *n.* (BrE) = **annex**[1]

annihilate /ə'naɪəleɪt/ *v.t.* (destroy) уничт|ожа́ть, -о́жить

anniversary /ænɪ'vɜːsərɪ/ *n.* годовщи́на

annotate /'ænəteɪt/ *v.t.* снаб|жа́ть, -ди́ть коммента́риями *or* примеча́ниями; ∼**d text** текст с коммента́риями *or* примеча́ниями

annotation /ænə'teɪʃ(ə)n/ *n.* (annotating) коммента́рование; (added note) коммента́рий, примеча́ние

✓ **announce** /ə'naʊns/ *v.t.* (state; declare) объявл|я́ть, -и́ть (*что or* о чём); заявл|я́ть, -и́ть (*что or* о чём); (notify, tell) сообщ|а́ть, -и́ть (о чём кому); **he** ∼**d the results of his researches** он огласи́л результа́ты свои́х иссле́дований

announcement /ə'naʊnsmənt/ *n.* объявле́ние, заявле́ние; **put an** ∼ **in the newspaper** поме|ща́ть, -сти́ть объявле́ние в газе́те; (written notification) извеще́ние; (on radio etc.) сообще́ние

announcer /ə'naʊnsə(r)/ *n.* ди́ктор

annoy /ə'nɔɪ/ *v.t.* (vex) доса|жда́ть, -ди́ть + *d.*; (irritate) раздража́ть (*impf.*); де́йствовать (*impf.*) на не́рвы + *d.*; (pester) докуча́ть (*impf.*) + *d.*; **I was** ∼**ed with him** я был серди́т на него́

annoyance /ə'nɔɪəns/ *n.* раздраже́ние

annoying /ə'nɔɪɪŋ/ *adj.* доса́дный; **how** ∼! кака́я доса́да!, вот доса́да!

✓ **annual** /'ænjʊəl/ *n.* **1** (publication) ежего́дник **2** (plant) однолéтнее расте́ние
 ● *adj.* **1** (happening once a year) ежего́дный

a

2 (pert. to whole year) годово́й; ~ **income** годово́й дохо́д

annually /'ænjʊəlɪ/ *adv.* ежего́дно

annul /ə'nʌl/ *v.t.* (**annulled, annulling**) аннули́ровать (*impf., pf.*); отмен|я́ть, -и́ть; **the marriage was ~led** брак был при́знан недействи́тельным

annulment /ə'nʌlmənt/ *n.* аннули́рование, отме́на

anodyne /'ænədaɪn/ *adj.* безоби́дный

anomaly /ə'nɒməlɪ/ *n.* анома́лия

anonymous /ə'nɒnɪməs/ *adj.* анони́мный; безымя́нный

anorak /'ænəræk/ *n.* аля́ска, ку́ртка с капюшо́ном

anorexia /ænə'reksɪə/ *n.* аноре́ксия

anorexic /ænə'reksɪk/ *adj.* страда́ющий аноре́ксией

✤ **another** /ə'nʌðə(r)/ *pron. & adj.* **1** (additional) ещё; ~ **cup of tea?** ещё ча́шку ча́я?; **have** ~ **go!** попыта́йтесь ещё раз!; **in** ~ **10 years** ещё че́рез де́сять лет; **and** ~ **thing** и вот ещё что **2** (similar): ~ **Tolstoy** второ́й Толсто́й **3** (different) друго́й; ~ **time** в друго́й раз

✤ **answer** /'ɑːnsə(r)/ *n.* **1** (reply) отве́т; **what was his** ~**?** что он отве́тил?; **in** ~ **to your letter** в отве́т на Ва́ше письмо́; (retort) возраже́ние **2** (solution) отве́т; реше́ние ● *v.t.* **1** (reply to) отв|еча́ть, -е́тить (*кому, на что*); ~ **the door** откр|ыва́ть, -ы́ть дверь; ~ **the telephone** под|ходи́ть, -ойти́ к телефо́ну; отв|еча́ть, -е́тить на телефо́нные звонки́ **2** (correspond to): **he** ~**s the description exactly** он то́чно соотве́тствует описа́нию **3** (satisfy, grant): **our prayers were** ~**ed** на́ши моли́твы бы́ли услы́шаны ● *v.i.* **1** (reply) отв|еча́ть, -е́тить **2**: ~ **for** руча́ться, поручи́ться за + *a.*; **I will** ~ **for his honesty** я руча́юсь за его́ че́стность **3** (give an account): **I** ~ **to no one** я никому́ не обя́зан отчи́тываться **4**: ~ **back** дерзи́ть, на- ■ ~**phone** *n.* (BrE) автоотве́тчик

answerable /'ɑːnsərəb(ə)l/ *adj.* (responsible) отве́тственный (**to:** пе́ред + *i.*, **for:** за + *a.*)

answering /'ɑːnsərɪŋ/ *adj.*: ~ **machine** автоотве́тчик

ant /ænt/ *n.* мураве́й

antagonism /æn'tæɡənɪz(ə)m/ *n.* антагони́зм

antagonistic /æntæɡə'nɪstɪk/ *adj.* антагонисти́ческий

antagonize /æn'tæɡənaɪz/ *v.t.* вызыва́ть, вы́звать чьё-н. отчужде́ние; отчужда́ть (*impf.*)

Antarctic /æn'tɑːktɪk/ *n.* (**in full the** ~) Анта́рктика ● *adj.* антаркти́ческий

Antarctica /ænt'ɑːktɪkə/ *n.* Антаркти́да

antelope /'æntɪləʊp/ *n.* (*pl.* ~ *or* ~**s**) антило́па

antenatal /æntɪ'neɪt(ə)l/ *adj.* (BrE, of care) дородово́й ■ ~ **clinic** *n.* же́нская консульта́ция

antenna /æn'tenə/ *n.* (*pl.* **antennae** /-niː/) (radio) анте́нна; (of insect) у́сик

anteroom /'æntɪruːm/ *n.* пере́дняя, прихо́жая

anthem /'ænθəm/ *n.* гимн; **national** ~ госуда́рственный гимн

anthology /æn'θɒlədʒɪ/ *n.* антоло́гия

anthrax /'ænθræks/ *n.* сиби́рская я́зва

anthropological /ænθrəpə'lɒdʒɪk(ə)l/ *adj.* антропологи́ческий

anthropologist /ænθrə'pɒlədʒɪst/ *n.* (biological) антропо́лог; **social** ~ этно́граф

anthropology /ænθrə'pɒlədʒɪ/ *n.* (biological) антрополо́гия; **social** (*or* **cultural**) ~ социа́льная антрополо́гия

anti- /'æntɪ/ *pref.* анти…, противо…

antibiotic /æntɪbaɪ'ɒtɪk/ *n.* антибио́тик

antibody /'æntɪbɒdɪ/ *n.* антите́ло

anticapitalist /æntɪ'kæpɪtəlɪst/ *n.* проти́вник капитали́зма ● *adj.* антикапиталисти́ческий

anticipate /æn'tɪsɪpeɪt/ *v.t.* (foresee) предви́деть (*impf.*); предчу́вствовать (*impf.*); (expect) ожида́ть (*impf.*); (with pleasure) предвку|ша́ть, -си́ть

anticipation /æntɪsɪ'peɪʃ(ə)n/ *n.* **1** (looking forward to) ожида́ние **2** (foreseeing) предви́дение, предвосхище́ние; **in** ~ **of a cold winter** предви́дя холо́дную зи́му **3** (foretasting) предвкуше́ние

anticlimax /æntɪ'klaɪmæks/ *n.* (ре́зкий) спад (интере́са *и т. п.*); разочарова́ние

anticlockwise /æntɪ'klɒkwaɪz/ *adj. & adv.* (BrE) про́тив часово́й стре́лки

antics /'æntɪks/ *n. pl.* проде́лки (*f. pl.*)

antidepressant /æntɪdɪ'pres(ə)nt/ *n.* антидепресса́нт

antidote /'æntɪdəʊt/ *n.* противоя́дие, антидо́т

antifreeze /'æntɪfriːz/ *n.* антифри́з

antiglobalization /æntɪɡləʊbəlaɪ'zeɪʃ(ə)n/ *n.* антиглобализа́ция

antihistamine /æntɪ'hɪstəmiːn/ *n.* антигистами́н; (*attr.*) антигистами́нный

antipathy /æn'tɪpəθɪ/ *n.* антипа́тия; **have, feel an** ~ **to, against, for** испы́тывать (*impf.*) антипа́тию к + *d.*

Antipodean /æntɪpə'diːən/ *adj.* (geog.) относя́щийся к Австра́лии и Но́вой Зела́ндии ● *n.* антипо́д, жи́тель Австра́лии и́ли Но́вой Зела́ндии

Antipodes /æn'tɪpədiːz/ *n. pl.* регио́н Австра́лии и Но́вой Зела́ндии

antiquated /'æntɪkweɪtɪd/ *adj.* (obsolete) устаре́лый; (old-fashioned) старомо́дный

antique /æn'tiːk/ *n.* антиква́рная вещь ● *adj.* (vase, table) антиква́рный ■ ~ **dealer** *n.* антиква́р; ~ **shop** *n.* антиква́рный магази́н

antiquity /æn'tɪkwɪtɪ/ *n.* (great age; olden times) дре́вность; (classical times) анти́чность; (*in pl.*) (ancient objects) антиквариа́т

anti-Semitic /æntɪsɪ'mɪtɪk/ *adj.* антисеми́тский

✤ ключева́я ле́ксика

anti-Semitism /ˌæntɪˈsemɪtɪz(ə)m/ *n.* антисемити́зм

antiseptic /ˌæntɪˈseptɪk/ *n.* антисе́птик
● *adj.* антисепти́ческий

antisocial /ˌæntɪˈsəʊʃ(ə)l/ *adj.* антиобще́ственный

antiterrorist /ˌæntɪˈterərɪst/ *adj.* антитеррористи́ческий

antithesis /ænˈtɪθəsɪs/ *n.* (*pl.* **antitheses** /-siːz/) (contrast of opposite ideas) антите́за; (contrast) контра́ст; (opposite) противополо́жность; he is the ~ of his brother он по́лная противополо́жность своему́ бра́ту

anti-war /ˌæntɪˈwɔː(r)/ *adj.* антивое́нный

antlers /ˈæntləz/ *n. pl.* оле́ньи/лоси́ные рога́

anus /ˈeɪnəs/ *n.* за́дний прохо́д, а́нус

anxiety /æŋˈzaɪətɪ/ *n.* **1** (uneasiness) беспоко́йство **2** (desire; keenness) жела́ние/ стремле́ние (+ *inf.*) **3** (*in pl.*) (cares, worries) забо́ты (*f. pl.*)

anxious /ˈæŋkʃəs/ *adj.* **1** (worried, uneasy) озабо́ченный; **be ~ about, over** трево́житься (*impf.*) за + *a.*; беспоко́иться (*impf.*) о + *p.* **2** (causing anxiety) трево́жный, беспоко́йный **3** (keen, desirous): **I am ~ to see him** мне о́чень хо́чется повида́ться с ним

⚔ **any** /ˈenɪ/ *pron.* **1** (in interrog. or conditional sentences, with animates) кто́-нибудь; (with inanimates) что́-нибудь; **if ~ of them should see him** е́сли кто́-нибудь из них уви́дит его́ **2** (in neg. sentences) (with animates) никто́; (with inanimates) ничто́; ни оди́н; **I don't like ~ of these actors** никто́/ни оди́н из э́тих арти́стов мне не нра́вится; **he never spoke to ~ of our friends** ни с кем из на́ших друзе́й он (никогда́) не говори́л **3** (in affirmative sentences) любо́й; **take ~ of these books** возьми́те любу́ю/любы́е из э́тих книг **4**: **he has little money, if ~** де́нег у него́ ма́ло, е́сли (они́) вообще́ есть
● *adj.* **1** (in interrog. or conditional sentences) *untranslated*: **have you ~ children?** у вас есть де́ти?; **have you ~ matches?** (request) у вас не бу́дет спи́чек?; (no matter what) любо́й, како́й уго́дно **2** (in neg. sentences): **we haven't ~ milk** у нас нет молока́; **haven't you ~ cigarettes?** ра́зве у вас нет сигаре́т?; (not ~ at all) никако́й, ни оди́н; **there isn't ~ man who would ...** нет тако́го челове́ка, кото́рый бы ...; (with *hardly*, vv. of prevention etc.): **there is hardly ~ doubt** нет почти́ никако́го сомне́ния; **without ~ doubt** без/безо вся́кого сомне́ния; **they stopped us from scoring ~ goals** они́ не да́ли нам заби́ть ни одного́ го́ла **3** (no matter which) любо́й; **at ~ time** в любо́е вре́мя; (every) любо́й, вся́кий; **in ~ case** во вся́ком слу́чае
● *adv.* **1** (in interrog. or conditional sentences) *untranslated or* ско́лько-нибудь; **do you want ~ more tea?** хоти́те ещё ча́ю?; **if you stay here ~ longer** е́сли вы ещё хоть немно́го заде́ржитесь здесь **2** (in neg. sentences) *untranslated or* ниско́лько; ничу́ть; **I can't go ~ farther** я не могу́ идти́ да́льше; **he doesn't live here ~ more** он здесь бо́льше не живёт

⚔ **anybody** /ˈenɪbɒdɪ/, **anyone** /ˈenɪwʌn/ *nn.* & *prons.* **1** (in interrog. or conditional sentences) кто́-нибудь; кто́-либо; **did you meet ~?** вы кого́-нибудь встре́тили?; **if ~ rings, don't answer** е́сли кто позвони́т, не отвеча́йте; **is this ~'s seat?** э́то ме́сто за́нято? **2** (in neg. sentences) никто́; **I didn't speak to ~** я ни с кем не говори́л **3** (~ at all; no matter who) вся́кий, любо́й; **~ will tell you** любо́й/вся́кий вам ска́жет; **~ who says that is a liar** кто бы э́то ни сказа́л, он лжёц; **~ else** кто́-нибудь ещё; **there was hardly ~ there** там почти́ никого́ не́ было

anyhow /ˈenɪhaʊ/ *adv.* **1** (haphazardly; carelessly) ко́е-ка́к; ка́к-нибудь; **the work was done ~** рабо́та была́ сде́лана ко́е-ка́к **2** (anyway, in any case) во вся́ком слу́чае; так и́ли ина́че; (nevertheless) всё равно́, всё же; **I shall go ~** я всё равно́ пойду́

⚔ **anyone** /ˈenɪwʌn/ *n.* & *pron.* = **anybody**

⚔ **anything** /ˈenɪθɪŋ/ *n.* & *pron.* **1** (in interrog. or conditional sentences) что́-нибудь; что́-либо; что; **is there ~ I can get for you?** вам что́-нибудь принести́?; **have you ~ to say?** у вас (*or* вам) есть, что сказа́ть? **2** (in neg. sentences) ничто́; **I haven't ~ to say to that** мне не́чего сказа́ть на э́то **3** (everything) всё; **I'd give ~ to see him again** я о́тдал бы всё, что́бы опя́ть уви́деть его́; **more, better than ~** бо́льше всего́ **4** (~ at all) что уго́дно **5** (whatever): **I will do ~ you suggest** я сде́лаю всё, что вы ска́жете

⚔ **anyway** /ˈenɪweɪ/ *adv.* = **anyhow** 2

⚔ **anywhere** /ˈenɪweə(r)/ *adv.* **1** (in interrog. and conditional sentences) где́-нибудь; где́-либо; (of motion) куда́-нибудь; куда́-либо; **is there a chemist's ~?** здесь есть апте́ка где́-нибудь?; **have you ~ to stay?** у вас есть где останови́ться? **2** (in neg. sentences) нигде́; (of motion) никуда́; **we haven't been ~ for ages** мы уже́ сто лет нигде́ не́ были **3** (in any place at all; everywhere) где уго́дно; везде́; (по)всю́ду; **it is miles from ~** э́то чёрт-те где (нахо́дится)

AOB (BrE) *abbr.* (*of* **any other business**) ра́зное

⚔ **apart** /əˈpɑːt/ *adv.* **1** (position) в стороне́; (motion) в сто́рону; **joking ~** шу́тки в сто́рону; **~ from** (with the exception of) за исключе́нием + *g.*; кро́ме + *g.*; (other than; besides) кро́ме/поми́мо + *g.* **2** (separate(ly); asunder) отде́льно; **they lived ~ for 2 years** два го́да они́ жи́ли по́рознь; **I could not tell them ~** я не мог их различи́ть/ отличи́ть **3** (distant): **the houses are a mile ~** дома́ нахо́дятся в ми́ле друг от дру́га

apartheid /əˈpɑːteɪt/ *n.* апарте́ид

⚔ **apartment** /əˈpɑːtmənt/ *n.* (AmE) кварти́ра
■ **~ block, ~ house** *nn.* многокварти́рный дом

apathetic /ˌæpəˈθetɪk/ *adj.* равноду́шный, апати́чный

apathy /ˈæpəθɪ/ *n.* апа́тия

ape /eɪp/ *n.* обезья́на

aperitif /əˌperɪˈtiːf/ *n.* аперити́в

apex /ˈeɪpeks/ *n.* (*pl.* **apexes** *or* **apices**) (lit., fig.) верши́на, верх

a

aphid /'eɪfɪd/ *n.* тля

aphorism /'æfərɪz(ə)m/ *n.* афори́зм

aphrodisiac /ˌæfrə'dɪziæk/ *n.* сре́дство, уси́ливающее полово́е влече́ние; афродизиа́к
● *adj.* уси́ливающий полово́е влече́ние

apiary /'eɪpɪərɪ/ *n.* па́сека, пче́льник

apocalypse /ə'pɒkəlɪps/ *n.* апока́липсис

apocalyptic /əˌpɒkə'lɪptɪk/ *adj.* апокалипти́ческий

apocryphal /ə'pɒkrɪf(ə)l/ *adj.* **1** (bibl.) апокрифи́ческий **2** (of doubtful authenticity) недостове́рный

apologetic /əˌpɒlə'dʒetɪk/ *adj.* извиня́ющийся; **he was very ~** он о́чень извиня́лся; **an ~ smile** винова́тая улы́бка

apologize /ə'pɒlədʒaɪz/ *v.i.* извин|я́ться, -и́ться (**to:** пе́ред + *i.*, **for:** за + *a.*)

apolog|y /ə'pɒlədʒɪ/ *n.* извине́ние; **make an ~y to sb for sth** прин|оси́ть, -ести́ извине́ния кому́-н. за что-н.; **please accept my ~ies** прими́те мои́ извине́ния

apostle /ə'pɒs(ə)l/ *n.* апо́стол

apostrophe /ə'pɒstrəfɪ/ *n.* (gram.) апостро́ф

app /æp/ *n.* (comput.) = **application** 5

appal /ə'pɔːl/ (AmE *also* **appall**) *v.t.* (**appalled, appalling**) ужас|а́ть, -ну́ть; устраш|а́ть, -и́ть; **I was ~led at the cost** цена́ меня́ ужасну́ла

appall /ə'pɔːl/ *v.t.* (AmE) = **appal**

appalling /ə'pɔːlɪŋ/ *adj.* ужа́сный, жу́ткий

apparatus /ˌæpə'reɪtəs/ *n.* **1** (instrument; appliance) прибо́р, инструме́нт **2** (in laboratory) аппарату́ра; обору́дование **3** (gymnastic) снаря́ды (*m. pl.*)

apparel /ə'pær(ə)l/ *n.* одея́ние, наря́д

apparent /ə'pærənt/ *adj.* **1** (plain, obvious) очеви́дный; я́вный **2** (seeming) ка́жущийся, мни́мый

apparently /ə'pærəntlɪ/ *adv.* (seemingly) по-ви́димому; вероя́тно; (как) бу́дто

apparition /ˌæpə'rɪʃ(ə)n/ *n.* виде́ние, при́зрак

appeal /ə'piːl/ *n.* **1** (earnest request, plea) обраще́ние (с про́сьбой); (official) воззва́ние; **an ~ on behalf of the Red Cross** обраще́ние от и́мени Кра́сного Креста́; **an ~ for support** про́сьба о по́мощи **2** (reference to higher authority) апелля́ция, обжа́лование; **Court of A~** (in England and Wales) апелляцио́нный суд; **court of ~s** (AmE) апелляцио́нный суд **3** (attraction) привлека́тельность; **this life has little ~ for me** э́та жизнь меня́ ма́ло привлека́ет
● *v.i.* **1** (make earnest request) обра|ща́ться, -ти́ться (**to:** к + *d.*, **for:** за + *i.*); **he ~ed to us for help** он обрати́лся к нам за по́мощью; (address oneself to) апелли́ровать (*impf., pf.*) (**to:** к + *d.*) **2** (law) апелли́ровать (*impf., pf.*); под|ава́ть, -а́ть апелля́цию; обжа́ловать (*pf.*) пригово́р **3:** ~ **to** (attract) привлека́ть (*impf.*); нра́виться (*impf.*) + *d.*

appealing /ə'piːlɪŋ/ *adj.* (attractive) привлека́тельный; (imploring) умоля́ющий

appear /ə'pɪə(r)/ *v.i.* **1** (become visible; arrive) появ|ля́ться, -и́ться **2** (present oneself) выступа́ть, вы́ступить; ~ **in court** предст|ава́ть, -а́ть пе́ред судо́м; (of actor) игра́ть (*impf.*) на сце́не; снима́ться, сня́ться в кино́; (of book) выходи́ть, вы́йти (в свет); быть и́зданным **3** (seem) каза́ться, по-; **he ~s to have left** он, ка́жется, уе́хал **4** (turn out) ока́зываться, -а́ться; **it ~s his wife is a Swede** ока́зывается, его́ жена́ шве́дка

appearance /ə'pɪərəns/ *n.* **1** (act of appearing) появле́ние; (in public) выступле́ние; ~ **in court** я́вка в суд **2** (look, aspect) (of thing) вид; (of person) нару́жность, вне́шность; **judge by ~(s)** суди́ть (*impf.*) по вне́шнему ви́ду; **to, by all ~s** по всем при́знакам; су́дя по всему́

appease /ə'piːz/ *v.t.* (one's conscience) успок|а́ивать, -о́ить; (person) умиротвор|я́ть, -и́ть; (appetites, passions) утол|я́ть, -и́ть

appeasement /ə'piːzmənt/ *n.* **1** успокое́ние; умиротворе́ние **2** (of hunger, desire, etc.) утоле́ние

appendage /ə'pendɪdʒ/ *n.* (anat.) отро́сток, прида́ток; (fig.) прида́ток

appendectomy /ˌæpen'dektəmɪ/ *n.* удале́ние аппе́ндикса

appendices /ə'pendɪsiːz/ *pl. of* ▶ **appendix**

appendicitis /əˌpendɪ'saɪtɪs/ *n.* аппендици́т

appendi|x /ə'pendɪks/ *n.* (*pl.* ~**ces** *or* ~**xes**) **1** (anat.) аппе́ндикс **2** (of a book etc.) приложе́ние

appetite /'æpɪtaɪt/ *n.* аппети́т

appetizer /'æpɪtaɪzə(r)/ *n.* (hors d'oeuvre) заку́ска

appetizing /'æpɪtaɪzɪŋ/ *adj.* аппети́тный

applaud /ə'plɔːd/ *v.t.* (*also v.i.*) (clap) аплоди́ровать (*impf.*) + *d.*

applause /ə'plɔːz/ *n.* аплодисме́нты (*m. pl.*); рукоплеска́ния (*nt. pl.*)

apple /'æp(ə)l/ *n.* я́блоко
■ ~ **sauce** *n.* я́блочное пюре́ (*indecl.*); ~ **tree** *n.* я́блоня

appliance /ə'plaɪəns/ *n.* (instrument) прибо́р, приспособле́ние; **domestic ~** бытово́й прибо́р

applicant /'æplɪk(ə)nt/ *n.* кандида́т, претенде́нт; ~ **for a job** кандида́т, претенде́нт на до́лжность

application /ˌæplɪ'keɪʃ(ə)n/ *n.* **1** (applying) прикла́дывание; наложе́ние **2** (employment; use) примене́ние; приложе́ние **3** (diligence) прилежа́ние; (concentration) сосредото́ченность **4** (request) (for work) зая́вка; (for a grant) зая́вка; (for permission) проше́ние **5** (comput.) (*also* **application program**) приложе́ние
■ ~ **form** *n.* бланк заявле́ния

apply /ə'plaɪ/ *v.t.* **1** (lay, put on) при|кла́дывать, -ложи́ть; (dressing, plaster) накла́дывать, наложи́ть; (paint, cream) нан|оси́ть, -ести́ **2** (bring into action) прил|ага́ть, -ожи́ть; ~ **the brakes** тормози́ть, за- **3** (make use of) примен|я́ть, -и́ть
● *v.i.:* ~ **for** (a job, grant, pass) под|ава́ть, -а́ть заявле́ние на + *a.*; ~ **to** (concern; relate to)

a

относи́ться (*impf.*) к + *d.*

appoint /əˈpɔɪnt/ *v.t.* (nominate) назн|ача́ть, -а́чить; **he was ~ed ambassador** он был назна́чен посло́м

appointment /əˈpɔɪntmənt/ *n.* **1** (act of appointing) назначе́ние **2** (office) до́лжность **3** (at doctor's etc.) за́пи|сываться, -са́ться на приём к + *d.*; полу|ча́ть, -чи́ть назначе́ние к + *d.*; (business) встре́ча

apportion /əˈpɔːʃ(ə)n/ *v.t.* распредел|я́ть, -и́ть; раздел|я́ть, -и́ть

apposite /ˈæpəzɪt/ *adj.* (suitable) подходя́щий; (to the point) уме́стный; уда́чный

appraisal /əˈpreɪz(ə)l/ *n.* оце́нка; (of performance, of a worker) аттеста́ция

appreciable /əˈpriːʃəb(ə)l/ *adj.* (perceptible) заме́тный; (considerable) значи́тельный

appreciate /əˈpriːʃɪeɪt/ *v.t.* **1** (value) оц|е́нивать, -ени́ть; цени́ть (*impf.*); **we ~ your help** мы це́ним ва́шу по́мощь **2** (understand) пон|има́ть, -я́ть **3** (enjoy): **he has learnt to ~ music** он научи́лся понима́ть и цени́ть му́зыку
● *v.i.* (rise in value) пов|ыша́ться, -ы́ситься

appreciation /əpriːʃɪˈeɪʃ(ə)n/ *n.* **1** (estimation, judgement) оце́нка **2** (understanding) понима́ние, призна́ние досто́инств **3** (rise in value) повыше́ние в цене́/сто́имости **4** (gratitude) призна́тельность

appreciative /əˈpriːʃətɪv/ *adj.* **1** (perceptive of merit): **an ~ audience** понима́ющая аудито́рия **2** (grateful) благода́рный, призна́тельный (**of:** за + *a.*)

apprehend /æprɪˈhend/ *v.t.* **1** (understand) уясн|я́ть, -и́ть **2** (arrest) аресто́в|ывать, -а́ть; заде́рж|ивать, -а́ть

apprehension /æprɪˈhenʃ(ə)n/ *n.* **1** (fear) опасе́ние **2** (arrest) аре́ст, задержа́ние **3** (understanding) уясне́ние

apprehensive /æprɪˈhensɪv/ *adj.* озабо́ченный; беспоко́йный; по́лный трево́ги

apprentice /əˈprentɪs/ *n.* подмасте́рье (*m.*)

apprenticeship /əˈprentɪsʃɪp/ *n.* уче́ние, учени́чество

approach /əˈprəʊtʃ/ *n.* **1** (drawing near; advance) приближе́ние; наступле́ние **2** (fig.) подхо́д; **his ~ to the subject** его́ подхо́д к предме́ту **3** (access) по́дступ **4** (fig., overture) предложе́ние; **they made unofficial ~es** они́ де́лали неофициа́льные предложе́ния
● *v.t.* **1** (come near to) прибл|ижа́ться, -и́зиться к + *d.* **2** (make overtures to) обра|ща́ться, -ти́ться к + *d.*
● *v.i.* прибл|ижа́ться, -и́зиться; под|ходи́ть, -ойти́; подъ|езжа́ть, -е́хать

approachable /əˈprəʊtʃəb(ə)l/ *adj.* досту́пный

approbation /æprəˈbeɪʃ(ə)n/ *n.* одобре́ние

appropriate[1] /əˈprəʊprɪət/ *adj.* соотве́тствующий; (suitable) подходя́щий

appropriate[2] /əˈprəʊprɪeɪt/ *v.t.* **1** (funds) ассигнова́ть (*impf., pf.*) **2** (take possession of) присв|а́ивать, -о́ить

approval /əˈpruːv(ə)l/ *n.* одобре́ние; (confirmation) утвержде́ние; (consent) согла́сие;

(sanction) апроба́ция; **on ~** на про́бу

approve /əˈpruːv/ *v.t.* од|обря́ть, -о́брить; (confirm) утвер|жда́ть, -ди́ть
● *v.i.*: **~e of** од|обря́ть, -о́брить; **an ~ing glance** одобри́тельный взгля́д

approximate[1] /əˈprɒksɪmət/ *adj.* приблизи́тельный

approximate[2] /əˈprɒksɪmeɪt/ *v.i.*: **~ to** прибл|ижа́ться, -и́зиться к + *d.*

approximation /əprɒksɪˈmeɪʃ(ə)n/ *n.* приближе́ние; **this is an ~ to the truth** э́то бли́зко к и́стине

apricot /ˈeɪprɪkɒt/ *n.* абрико́с

April /ˈeɪprɪl/ *n.* апре́ль (*m.*); **~ Fool!** пе́рвое апре́ля — никому́ не ве́рю!; **~ Fool's Day** пе́рвое апре́ля

apron /ˈeɪprən/ *n.* (garment) пере́дник; фа́ртук

apt /æpt/ *adj.* **1** (suitable) подходя́щий **2**: **~ to** скло́нный к + *d.*

aptitude /ˈæptɪtjuːd/ *n.* (capacity) спосо́бность
■ **~ test** *n.* прове́рка спосо́бностей

aquaria /əˈkweərɪə/ *pl. of* ▶ aquarium

aquari|um /əˈkweərɪəm/ *n.* (*pl.* **~a** *or* **~ums**) аква́риум

Aquarius /əˈkweərɪəs/ *n.* Водоле́й; **she's (an) Aquarius** она́ — Водоле́й

aquatic /əˈkwætɪk/ *adj.* водяно́й

aqueduct /ˈækwɪdʌkt/ *n.* акведу́к

Arab /ˈærəb/ *n.* (person) ара́б (-ка)
● *adj.* ара́бский
■ **~ Spring** *n.* (pol.) Ара́бская весна́

Arabian /əˈreɪbɪən/ *adj.* арави́йский

Arabic /ˈærəbɪk/ *n.* ара́бский язы́к
● *adj.* ара́бский

arable /ˈærəb(ə)l/ *adj.* па́хотный
■ **~ farming** *n.* земледе́лие

arbitrary /ˈɑːbɪtrərɪ/ *adj.* произво́льный

arbitrate /ˈɑːbɪtreɪt/ *v.i.* (act as arbiter) быть арби́тром; быть трете́йским судьёй

arbitration /ɑːbɪˈtreɪʃ(ə)n/ *n.* арбитра́ж; трете́йский суд

arbor /ˈɑːbə(r)/ *n.* (AmE) = arbour

arboret|um /ɑːbəˈriːtəm/ *n.* (*pl.* **~ums** *or* **~a**) дендра́рий

arbour /ˈɑːbə(r)/ (AmE **arbor**) *n.* бесе́дка

arc /ɑːk/ *n.* дуга́

arcade /ɑːˈkeɪd/ *n.* (covered passage) арка́да; (with shops) пасса́ж

arcane /ɑːˈkeɪn/ *adj.* таи́нственный, та́йный

arch /ɑːtʃ/ *n.* (curved shape) а́рка; (~ed roof; vault) свод
● *v.t.* (part of the body) выгиба́ть, вы́гнуть; **the cat ~ed its back** ко́шка вы́гнула спи́ну

arch- /ɑːtʃ/ *comb. form* архи…; гла́вный

archaeological /ɑːkɪəˈlɒdʒɪk(ə)l/ (AmE *also* **archeological**) *adj.* археологи́ческий

archaeologist /ɑːkɪˈɒlədʒɪst/ (AmE *also* **archeologist**) *n.* архео́лог

archaeology /ɑːkɪˈɒlədʒɪ/ (AmE *also* **archeology**) *n.* археоло́гия

archaic /ɑːˈkeɪɪk/ *adj.* архаи́чный; устаре́вший

archangel /ˈɑːkeɪndʒ(ə)l/ *n.* арха́нгел

a

archbishop /ɑːtʃˈbɪʃəp/ *n.* архиепи́скоп

arch-enemy /ɑːtʃˈenəmi/ *n.* закля́тый враг

archeological /ɑːkɪəˈlɒdʒɪk(ə)l/ *adj.* (AmE) = **archaeological**

archeologist /ɑːkɪˈɒlədʒɪst/ *n.* (AmE) = **archaeologist**

archeology /ɑːkɪˈɒlədʒɪ/ *n.* (AmE) = **archaeology**

archery /ˈɑːtʃərɪ/ *n.* стрельба́ из лу́ка

archetypal /ɑːkɪˈtaɪp(ə)l/ *adj.* (typical) типи́чный

archipelago /ɑːkɪˈpeləgəʊ/ *n.* (*pl.* ~**s** *or* ~**es**) архипела́г

architect /ˈɑːkɪtekt/ *n.* архите́ктор

architectural /ɑːkɪˈtektʃər(ə)l/ *adj.* архитекту́рный; строи́тельный

architecture /ˈɑːkɪtektʃə(r)/ *n.* архитекту́ра

architrave /ˈɑːkɪtreɪv/ *n.* (archit.) архитра́в

archive /ˈɑːkaɪv/ *n.* (*also in pl.*) (also comput.) архи́в
- *v.t.* поме|ща́ть, -сти́ть в архи́в; архиви́ровать (*impf., pf.*)

archivist /ˈɑːkɪvɪst/ *n.* архива́риус

Arctic /ˈɑːktɪk/ *n.* (*in full* **the** ~) А́рктика
- *adj.* Аркти́ческий; (**а**~) (very cold) ледяно́й, студёный
■ ~ **Circle** *n.* Се́верный поля́рный круг; ~ **Ocean** *n.* Се́верный Ледови́тый океа́н

ardent /ˈɑːd(ə)nt/ *adj.* (fervent) горя́чий, пы́лкий; (passionate) стра́стный

ardour /ˈɑːdə(r)/ (AmE **ardor**) *n.* жар, пыл, рве́ние

arduous /ˈɑːdjʊəs/ *adj.* тяжёлый

are /ɑː(r)/ *2nd pers. sing. pres. and pl. pres. of* ▶ **be**

✧ **area** /ˈeərɪə/ *n.* **1** (measurement) пло́щадь; **a room 12 square metres in** ~ ко́мната пло́щадью в 12 м² (= *12 квадра́тных ме́тров*) **2** (defined or designated space) пло́щадь; (expanse) простра́нство; **vast** ~**s of forest** обши́рные лесны́е простра́нства **3** (region) райо́н, край, зо́на; **residential** ~ жило́й райо́н; **wheat-growing** ~ пло́щадь под пшени́цей **4** (sphere) о́бласть, сфе́ра; **in the** ~ **of research** в о́бласти иссле́дования

arena /əˈriːnə/ *n.* (lit., fig.) аре́на

aren't /ɑːnt/ *neg. of* ▶ **are**

Argentina /ɑːdʒənˈtiːnə/ (*also* **the Argentine** /ˈɑːdʒəntaɪn/) *n.* Аргенти́на

Argentine /ˈɑːdʒəntaɪn/, **Argentinian** /ɑːdʒənˈtɪnɪən/ *nn.* аргенти́н|ец (-ка)
- *adjs.* аргенти́нский

✧ **argue** /ˈɑːgjuː/ *v.t.* (**argues**, **argued**, **arguing**) **1** (discuss) обсу|жда́ть, -ди́ть; (debate) дебати́ровать (*impf.*); спо́рить (*impf.*) о + *p.* **2** (contend) дока́зывать (*impf.*)
- *v.i.* **1** (debate; disagree; quarrel) спо́рить (*impf.*); препира́ться (*impf.*); (object) возража́ть (*impf.*); **they** ~**d over who should drive** они́ спо́рили, кому́ вести́ маши́ну **2** (give reasons) прив|оди́ть, -ести́ до́воды, выступа́ть, вы́ступить (**against**: про́тив + *g.*, **for, in favour of**: в защи́ту + *g.*, за + *a.*)

✧ **argument** /ˈɑːgjʊmənt/ *n.* **1** (reason) аргуме́нт; до́вод; **it's an** ~ **for staying at home** э́то до́вод в по́льзу того́, чтобы оста́ться до́ма **2** (discussion, debate) спор; **have an** ~ **over, about** спо́рить (*impf.*) о + *p.*

argumentative /ɑːgjʊˈmentətɪv/ *adj.* сварли́вый

aria /ˈɑːrɪə/ *n.* а́рия

arid /ˈærɪd/ *adj.* (of soil etc.) сухо́й, пересо́хший; (of climate, also fig., dry) сухо́й

Aries /ˈeəriːz/ *n.* (*pl.* ~) (astron., astrol.) Ове́н; **she's (an) Aries** она́ — Ове́н

✧ **arise** /əˈraɪz/ *v.i.* (*past* **arose**, *p.p.* **arisen** /əˈrɪz(ə)n/) (fig., come into being) возн|ика́ть, -и́кнуть; **if the need should** ~ е́сли возни́кнет необходи́мость; **the question arose** возни́к вопро́с

aristocracy /ærɪˈstɒkrəsi/ *n.* аристокра́тия

aristocrat /ˈærɪstəkræt/ *n.* аристокра́т

aristocratic /ærɪstəˈkrætɪk/ *adj.* аристократи́ческий

arithmetic /əˈrɪθmətɪk/ *n.* арифме́тика

arithmetical /ærɪθˈmetɪk(ə)l/ *adj.* арифмети́ческий

✧ **arm¹** /ɑːm/ *n.* **1** (of person) рука́; **he broke his** ~ **on** сломал ру́ку; ~ **in** ~ под руку **2** (of garment) рука́в; (of chair) ру́чка
■ ~**band** *n.* нарука́вная повя́зка; ~**chair** *n.* кре́сло; ~**pit** *n.* подмы́шка

✧ **arm²** /ɑːm/ *n.* (*in pl.*) (weapons) ору́жие
- *v.t.* вооруж|а́ть, -и́ть; (equip) снаб|жа́ть, -ди́ть; ~**ed forces** вооружённые си́лы
■ ~**s race** *n.* го́нка вооруже́ний

armament /ˈɑːməmənt/ *n.* (*also in pl.*) (weapons; military equipment) вооруже́ние

Armenia /ɑːˈmiːnɪə/ *n.* Арме́ния

Armenian /ɑːˈmiːnɪən/ *n.* **1** (person) арм|яни́н (-я́нка) **2** (language) армя́нский язы́к
- *adj.* армя́нский

armistice /ˈɑːmɪstɪs/ *n.* переми́рие

armor /ˈɑːmə(r)/ *n.* (AmE) = **armour**

armored /ˈɑːməd/ *adj.* (AmE) = **armoured**

armory /ˈɑːmərɪ/ *n.* (AmE) = **armoury**

armour /ˈɑːmə(r)/ (AmE **armor**) *n.* (for body) доспе́хи (*m. pl.*)
■ ~-**plated** *adj.* брониро́ванный

armoured /ˈɑːməd/ (AmE **armored**) *adj.* брониро́ванный, бронено́сный

armoury /ˈɑːmərɪ/ (AmE **armory**) *n.* арсена́л

✧ **army** /ˈɑːmɪ/ *n.* а́рмия; **join the** ~ идти́, пойти́ в а́рмию; (*attr.*) арме́йский

aroma /əˈrəʊmə/ *n.* арома́т

aromatherapist /ərəʊməˈθerəpɪst/ *n.* ароматерапе́вт

aromatherapy /ərəʊməˈθerəpɪ/ *n.* ароматерапи́я

aromatic /ærəˈmætɪk/ *adj.* (smell) арома́тный; (substance) арома́тический

arose /əˈrəʊz/ *past of* ▶ **arise**

✧ **around** /əˈraʊnd/ *adv.* (*see also* ▶ **round**) *adv.* вокру́г; круго́м; **all** ~ повсю́ду; **for miles** ~ на ми́ли вокру́г; **they were standing** ~ они́ стоя́ли побли́зости; **this singer has been** ~

for **30 years** э́тот певе́ц уже́ 30 лет поёт ● *prep.* **1** (encircling) вокру́г + *g.*; круго́м + *g.*; **they stood** ∼ **the table** они́ стоя́ли вокру́г стола́; **the path goes** ∼ **the garden** доро́жка огиба́ет сад **2** (over): **he looked** ∼ **the house** он осмотре́л дом **3** (in the vicinity of) о́коло + *g.* **4** (approximately) о́коло + *g.*; приблизи́тельно

arouse /əˈraʊz/ *v.t.* (awaken from sleep) буди́ть, раз-; (fig.) пробу|жда́ть, -ди́ть; (also sexually) возбу|жда́ть, -ди́ть

arrang|e /əˈreɪndʒ/ *v.t.* **1** (put in order) прив|оди́ть, -ести́ в поря́док; **she was** ∼**ing flowers** она́ расставля́ла цветы́ **2** (put in a certain order; group) распол|ага́ть, -ожи́ть; расст|авля́ть, -а́вить **3** (settle) ула́|живать, -дить **4** (organize) устр|а́ивать, -о́ить; (prepare; plan in advance) подгот|а́вливать, -о́вить; организо́в|ывать, -а́ть; нала́|живать, -дить ● *v.i.* догов|а́риваться, -ори́ться; усл|а́вливаться, -о́виться; **I have** ∼**ed for somebody to meet him at the station** я распоряди́лся, что́бы его́ встре́тили на ста́нции

♂ **arrangement** /əˈreɪndʒmənt/ *n.* **1** (setting in order) приведе́ние в поря́док **2** (specific order) расположе́ние **3** (*in pl.*) (planning, preparation) ме́ры (*f. pl.*), приготовле́ния (*nt. pl.*); **make** ∼**s for** организо́в|ывать, -а́ть; устр|а́ивать, -о́ить **4** (agreement, understanding) соглаше́ние, договорённость

array /əˈreɪ/ *n.* **1** (order): **in battle** ∼ в боево́м поря́дке **2** (display) мно́жество **3** (dress, apparel) облаче́ние, одея́ние ● *v.t.* **1** (place in order or line) выстра́ивать, вы́строить; **the troops were** ∼**ed for battle** войска́ бы́ли вы́строены в боево́м поря́дке **2** (set out, display) выставля́ть, вы́ставить **3** (adorn) укр|аша́ть, -а́сить; **she was** ∼**ed in all her finery** она́ облачи́лась в са́мое лу́чшее; (deck out, dress) над|ева́ть, -е́ть

arrears /əˈrɪəz/ *n. pl.* (of payment) задо́лженность; просро́чка; **be in** ∼ просро́чи|вать, -ть платёж

♂ **arrest** /əˈrest/ *n.* аре́ст; **be under** ∼ быть (*impf.*) под аре́стом ● *v.t.* аресто́в|ывать, -а́ть

arrival /əˈraɪv(ə)l/ *n.* прибы́тие; **on his** ∼ по его́ прибы́тии; (of person etc. on foot) прихо́д; (of person by vehicle) прие́зд; (by air) прилёт

♂ **arrive** /əˈraɪv/ *v.i.* **1** (reach destination) приб|ыва́ть, -ы́ть; (of persons on foot, also fig.) при|ходи́ть, -йти́ **2**: ∼ **at a decision/conclusion** приходи́ть, прийти́ к реше́нию/заключе́нию

arrogance /ˈærəg(ə)ns/ *n.* высокоме́рие

arrogant /ˈærəg(ə)nt/ *adj.* высокоме́рный

arrow /ˈærəʊ/ *n.* стрела́; (as symbol or indicator) стре́лка

arse /ɑːs/ (AmE **ass**) *n.* (vulg.) жо́па (vulg.)

arsenal /ˈɑːsən(ə)l/ *n.* (lit., fig.) арсена́л

arsenic /ˈɑːsənɪk/ *n.* мышья́к

arson /ˈɑːs(ə)n/ *n.* поджо́г

♂ **art** /ɑːt/ *n.* **1** (skill, craft) иску́сство; **a work of** ∼ произведе́ние иску́сства **2** (decorative)

иску́сство; **fine** ∼**s** изя́щные/изобрази́тельные иску́сства

■ ∼ **critic** *n.* искусствове́д; ∼ **gallery** *n.* карти́нная галере́я; ∼ **school** *n.* худо́жественное учи́лище

artefact, artifact /ˈɑːtɪfækt/ *n.* худо́жественное изде́лие; (sth small or of little historical/cultural interest) поде́лка

arterial /ɑːˈtɪərɪəl/ *adj.* **1** (anat.) артериа́льный **2**: ∼ **road** магистра́льная доро́га; магистра́ль

artery /ˈɑːtərɪ/ *n.* (anat.) арте́рия

artful /ˈɑːtfʊl/ *adj.* хи́трый

arthritic /ɑːˈθrɪtɪk/ *adj.* (of pain) артри́тный; (of person) страда́ющ|ий (-ая) артри́том; ∼ **joints** артри́т суста́вов

arthritis /ɑːˈθraɪtɪs/ *n.* артри́т

artichoke /ˈɑːtɪtʃəʊk/ *n.* артишо́к

♂ **article** /ˈɑːtɪk(ə)l/ *n.* **1** (item) предме́т; (manufactured) изде́лие; ∼ **of clothing** предме́т оде́жды **2** (piece of writing) статья́ **3** (gram.): **(in)definite** ∼ (не)определённый арти́кль

articulate¹ /ɑːˈtɪkjʊlət/ *adj.* (of speech) членоразде́льный; (of thoughts) отчётливый; (of person) чётко выража́ющий свои́ мы́сли

articulate² /ɑːˈtɪkjʊleɪt/ *v.t.* (ideas) я́сно выража́ть, вы́разить; (words) отчётливо произн|оси́ть, -ести́

articulated /ɑːˈtɪkjʊleɪtɪd/ *adj.*: ∼ **lorry** (BrE) грузови́к с прице́пом; автопо́езд

artifact /ˈɑːtɪfækt/ *n.* = **artefact**

artifice /ˈɑːtɪfɪs/ *n.* хи́трость

artificial /ɑːtɪˈfɪʃ(ə)l/ *adj.* (not natural) иску́сственный; (feigned) притво́рный ■ ∼ **respiration** *n.* иску́сственное дыха́ние

artillery /ɑːˈtɪlərɪ/ *n.* артилле́рия

artisan /ɑːˈtɪzæn, ˈɑːtɪzæn/ *n.* реме́сленн|ик (-ица)

♂ **artist** /ˈɑːtɪst/ *n.* худо́жн|ик (-ица)

artiste /ɑːˈtiːst/ *n.* арти́ст (-ка); профессиона́льный музыка́нт, танцо́р *и т. п.*

artistic /ɑːˈtɪstɪk/ *adj.* (person) худо́жественный; (work) артисти́ческий, артисти́чный

artless /ˈɑːtlɪs/ *adj.* (unskilled) неиску́сный; (ingenuous) простоду́шный; (natural) безыску́сственный

arty /ˈɑːtɪ/ *adj.* (**artier, artiest**) (infml) вычурный; претенцио́зно-боге́мный ■ ∼**-farty** /ˈfɑːtɪ/ *adj.* претенцио́зный

♂ **as** /æz/ *adv. & conj.* **1** (expr. comparison or conformity) как; ∼ **I was saying** как я говори́л; **do** ∼ **follows** де́лайте сле́дующее; **do it** ∼ **follows** де́лайте э́то так/вот как/сле́дующим о́бразом; **such countries** ∼ **Spain** таки́е стра́ны, как Испа́ния; **the same** ∼ … то же са́мое, что…; ∼ **heavy** ∼ **lead** тяжёлый, как свине́ц; **I am** ∼ **tall** ∼ **he** мы с ним одного́ ро́ста; **walk** ∼ **fast** ∼ **you can** иди́те как мо́жно быстре́е; ∼ **quickly** ∼ **possible** как мо́жно скоре́е; **just** ∼ так же, как; ∼ **usual** как всегда́; **he pictured the room** ∼ **it would be** он представля́л себе́, како́й бу́дет ко́мната; **so** ∼ **to** (expr. purpose) что́бы; (expr. manner) так, что́бы **2** (expr. capacity or

a

category) как; **I regard him ~ a fool** я счита́ю его дурако́м; **his appointment ~ colonel** присвое́ние ему́ зва́ния полко́вника; **~ your guardian, I … как** ваш опеку́н, я…; **~ a rule** как пра́вило; **I said it ~ a joke** я сказа́л э́то в шу́тку **3** (concessive): **young ~ I am** хоть я и мо́лод; **much ~ I should like to** как бы мне ни хоте́лось **4** (temporal) когда́; пока́, в то вре́мя как; **(just) ~ I reached the door** когда́ я подошёл к две́ри **5** (causative) так как, поско́льку; **~ you are ready, let us begin** поско́льку вы уже́ гото́вы, дава́йте начнём **6** (var.): **~ far ~ I know** наско́лько мне изве́стно; **~ if** бу́дто (бы); как бу́дто (бы); **it is not ~ if I was poor** не то, что́бы я был бе́ден; **~ much ~ …** сто́лько, ско́лько…; **I thought ~ much!** так я и ду́мал!; **no one so much ~ looked at us** на нас никто́ да́же не посмотре́л; **~ soon ~** как то́лько; **I would just ~ soon go** я предпочёл бы пойти́; **~ though** бу́дто (бы); как бу́дто (бы); **~ well** (in addition) та́кже, то́же; **he came ~ well ~ John** и он, и Джон пришли́; **you might ~ well help me** вы могли́ бы мне помо́чь; **it is just ~ well you came** хорошо́, что вы пришли́

a.s.a.p. abbr. (of **as soon as possible**) как мо́жно скоре́е

asbestos /æz'bestɒs/ n. асбе́ст

ascend /ə'send/ v.t. подн|има́ться, -я́ться по + d. (or на + a.)

ascendancy /ə'send(ə)nsɪ/ n. власть, госпо́дство; **gain, obtain ~ over** доб|ива́ться, -и́ться вла́сти/госпо́дства над + i.

ascent /ə'sent/ n. восхожде́ние, подъём; **~ of a mountain** восхожде́ние на́ гору

ascertain /æsə'teɪn/ v.t. устан|а́вливать, -ови́ть; выясня́ть, вы́яснить

ascribe /ə'skraɪb/ v.t. припи́с|ывать, -а́ть (to: + d.)

asexual /eɪ'seksjʊəl/ adj. беспо́лый

ash¹ /æʃ/ n. (bot.) я́сень (m.)

ash² /æʃ/ n. **1** (also in pl.) зола́; пе́пел **2** (in pl.) (human remains) прах
■ **~tray** n. пе́пельница

ashamed /ə'ʃeɪmd/ adj. пристыжённый; **I am, feel ~ мне** сты́дно; **be ~ of** стыди́ться (impf.) + g.

ashen /æʃ(ə)n/ adj. (pale) ме́ртвенно-бле́дный

ashore /ə'ʃɔː(r)/ adv. (position) на берегу́; (motion) на бе́рег; **go ~** сходи́ть, сойти́ на бе́рег

Asia /'eɪʃə/ n. А́зия
■ **~ Minor** n. (peninsula) Ма́лая А́зия

Asian /'eɪʃ(ə)n/ n. азиа́т (-ка)
● adj. азиа́тский

⚹ **aside** /ə'saɪd/ adv. (place) в стороне́; (motion) в сто́рону; (in reserve) отде́льно, в резе́рве; **take sb ~** отвод|и́ть, -ести́ кого́-н. в сто́рону; **set, put ~** (reserve) от|кла́дывать, -ложи́ть

asinine /'æsɪnaɪn/ adj. (lit., fig.) осли́ный

⚹ **ask** /ɑːsk/ v.t. **1** (enquire) спр|а́шивать, -оси́ть (что у кого or кого о чём); **he ~ed me the**

time он спроси́л меня́, кото́рый час **2** (pose): **~ a question** зад|ава́ть, -а́ть вопро́с **3** (request permission): **he ~ed to leave the room** он попроси́л разреше́ния вы́йти из ко́мнаты **4** (request) проси́ть, по- (что у кого or кого о чём); **I ~ed him to do it** я попроси́л его́ сде́лать э́то **5** (charge) проси́ть, за- **6** (invite) звать, по-; пригла|ша́ть, -си́ть; **~ a girl out** пригла|ша́ть, -си́ть де́вушку на свида́ние
● v.i. **1** (make enquiries) спр|а́шивать, -оси́ть (о + p.); спр|а́шиваться, -а́виться (о + p.); **she ~ed after your health** она́ справля́лась о ва́шем здоро́вье **2** (make a request) проси́ть, по-; **~ for help** проси́ть, по- о по́мощи; **he ~ed him for a pencil** он попроси́л у него́ каранда́ш; **he ~ed for advice** он попроси́л сове́та
■ **~ing price** n. запра́шиваемая цена́

askance /ə'skæns/ adv. ко́со, и́скоса; **he looked at me ~** он посмотре́л на меня́ и́скоса

askew /ə'skjuː/ adv. кри́во, ко́со
● pred. adj. кривой

asleep /ə'sliːp/ pred. adj. спя́щий; **he was sound, fast ~** он спал кре́пким сном; **fall ~** зас|ыпа́ть, -ну́ть

AS level n. (BrE) экза́мен в сре́дней шко́ле (ме́жду GCSE и A level)

asparagus /ə'spærəgəs/ n. спа́ржа

⚹ **aspect** /'æspekt/ n. **1** (look, appearance; expression) вид, выраже́ние **2** (fig., facet) аспе́кт, сторона́; (point of view) то́чка зре́ния **3** (outlook) вид

Asperger's syndrome /'æspə:dʒəz/ n. (med.) синдро́м Аспе́ргера (форма аути́зма)

aspersion /ə'spə:ʃ(ə)n/ n. (slur) клевета́; **cast ~s on** возв|оди́ть, -ести́ клевету́ на + a.; клевета́ть (impf.) на + a.

asphalt /'æsfælt/ n. асфа́льт

asphyxiation /æsfɪksɪ'eɪʃ(ə)n/ n. уду́шье

aspic /'æspɪk/ n. заливно́е; **veal in ~** заливна́я теля́тина

aspiration /æspɪ'reɪʃ(ə)n/ n. стремле́ние

aspire /ə'spaɪə(r)/ v.i. стреми́ться (impf.); **he ~s to be a leader** он стреми́тся стать ли́дером

aspirin /'æsprɪn/ n. (pl. ~ or ~s) аспири́н; (tablet) табле́тка аспири́на

ass¹ /æs/ n. осёл

ass² /æs/ n. (AmE, vulg.) = arse

assail /ə'seɪl/ v.t. (lit., fig.) нап|ада́ть, -а́сть на + a.; атакова́ть (impf., pf.); **I was ~ed by doubts** меня́ одолева́ли сомне́ния; **~ with criticism** обру́ши|ваться, -ться с кри́тикой на + a.; **~ with questions** зас|ыпа́ть, -ы́пать вопро́сами

assailant /ə'seɪlənt/ n. напада́ющ|ий (-ая)

assassin /ə'sæsɪn/ n. уби́йца (c.g.)

assassinate /ə'sæsɪneɪt/ v.t. уб|ива́ть, -и́ть (по полити́ческим моти́вам)

assassination /əsæsɪ'neɪʃ(ə)n/ n. полити́ческое уби́йство

assault /ə'sɒlt/ n. (in general) нападе́ние; (mil.) ата́ка, штурм, при́ступ; (law): **indecent ~** оскорбле́ние де́йствием на сексуа́льной по́чве
● v.t. нап|ада́ть, -а́сть на + a.; (mil.) атакова́ть

⚹ ключева́я ле́ксика

(*impf.*, *pf.*); (law) оскорб|ля́ть, -и́ть де́йствием

assemble /ə'semb(ə)l/ *v.t.* (gather together) соб|ира́ть, -ра́ть; (tech., fit together) монти́ровать, с-
• *v.i.* соб|ира́ться, -ра́ться

assembly /ə'sembli/ *n.* **1** (assembling) собира́ние, сбор **2** (company of persons) собра́ние **3** (of machine parts) сбо́рка
■ ~ **hall** *n.* (in school) а́ктовый зал; ~ **line** *n.* сбо́рочный конве́йер

assent /ə'sent/ *v.i.* согла|ша́ться, -си́ться (**to:** с чем *or* на что)

assert /ə'sə:t/ *v.t.* **1** (declare; affirm) утвер|жда́ть, -ди́ть; заяв|ля́ть, -и́ть **2** (stand up for) отст|а́ивать, -оя́ть; ~ **oneself** самоутвер|жда́ться, -ди́ться

assertion /ə'sə:ʃ(ə)n/ *n.* утвержде́ние

assertive /ə'sə:tɪv/ *adj.* (self-assured) самоуве́ренный

⚔ **assess** /ə'ses/ *v.t.* **1** (estimate value of; appraise) (also fig.) оце́н|ивать, -и́ть **2** (determine amount of) определ|я́ть, -и́ть су́мму/разме́р + g.

⚔ **assessment** /ə'sesmənt/ *n.* (valuation) оце́нка; (for taxation) определе́ние

⚔ **asset** /'æset/ *n.* **1** (advantage; useful quality) це́нность **2** (in pl.) (fin) акти́вы

assiduous /ə'sɪdjʊəs/ *adj.* приле́жный; усе́рдный

assign /ə'saɪn/ *v.t.* **1** (task) возл|ага́ть, -ожи́ть; пору|ча́ть, -чи́ть; (person) назн|ача́ть, -а́чить; (resources) предназн|ача́ть, -а́чить **2** (ascribe) припи́с|ывать, -а́ть **3** (law, transfer) перед|ава́ть, -а́ть

assignation /æsɪg'neɪʃ(ə)n/ *n.* **1** (of person) назначе́ние; (of resources) предназначе́ние; (of task) поруче́ние **2** (illicit meeting) та́йное свида́ние **3** (law, transfer) переда́ча

assignment /ə'saɪnmənt/ *n.* (task, duty) поруче́ние; зада́ние; (schoolwork) зада́ние

assimilate /ə'sɪmɪleɪt/ *v.t.* (absorb by digestion etc., also fig.) ассимили́ровать (*impf.*, *pf.*)

⚔ **assist** /ə'sɪst/ *v.t.* (help) пом|ога́ть, -о́чь + d.; (cooperate with) соде́йствовать (*impf.*, *pf.*) + d.
• *v.i.* (help) пом|ога́ть, -о́чь; прин|има́ть, -я́ть уча́стие

⚔ **assistance** /ə'sɪst(ə)ns/ *n.* по́мощь; соде́йствие

⚔ **assistant** /ə'sɪst(ə)nt/ *n.* помо́щни|к (-ца); ассисте́нт (-ка); (BrE, in shop) продав|е́ц (-щи́ца)
■ ~ **manager** *n.* замести́тель (*m.*) заве́дующего

associate¹ /ə'səʊsɪət/ *n.* **1** (colleague) колле́га (*c.g.*) това́рищ; (in business) партнёр **2** (of a society) член о́бщества

⚔ **associate²** /ə'səʊsɪeɪt/ *v.t.* соедин|я́ть, -и́ть; свя́з|ывать, -а́ть; (esp. psych.) ассоции́ровать (*impf.*, *pf.*); **his name was ~d with the cause of reform** его́ и́мя ассоции́ровалось с реформа́торской де́ятельностью

⚔ **association** /əsəʊsɪ'eɪʃ(ə)n/ *n.* **1** (uniting; joining) объедине́ние; соедине́ние **2** (connection) связь; ассоциа́ция **3** (group) ассоциа́ция, о́бщество

assorted /ə'sɔ:tɪd/ *adj.* (varied) разнообра́зный

assortment /ə'sɔ:tmənt/ *n.* ассортиме́нт

assuage /ə'sweɪdʒ/ *v.t.* (soothe) успок|а́ивать, -о́ить; (alleviate) смягч|а́ть, -и́ть; (appetite etc.) утол|я́ть, -и́ть

⚔ **assume** /ə'sju:m/ *v.t.* **1** (take on) прин|има́ть, -я́ть; ~e **control of** брать, взять на себя́ управле́ние/руково́дство + i. **2** (feign) напус|ка́ть, -ти́ть на себя́; **he went under an ~ed name** он был изве́стен под вы́мышленным и́менем **3** (suppose) предпол|ага́ть, -ожи́ть; допус|ка́ть, -ти́ть; ~**ing that ...** при усло́вии, что...

assumption /ə'sʌmpʃ(ə)n/ *n.* предположе́ние; допуще́ние

assurance /ə'ʃʊərəns/ *n.* завере́ние, увере́ние

assure /ə'ʃʊə(r)/ *v.t.* **1** (ensure) обеспе́чи|вать, -ть **2** (assert confidently) ув|еря́ть, -е́рить; **I can ~ you of this** (я) могу́ вас в э́том уве́рить

asterisk /'æstərɪsk/ *n.* (typ.) звёздочка

asteroid /'æstərɔɪd/ *n.* астеро́ид

asthma /'æsmə/ *n.* а́стма

asthmatic /æs'mætɪk/ *adj.* (pertaining to asthma) астмати́ческий; (suffering from asthma) страда́ющий а́стмой

astigmatism /ə'stɪgmətɪz(ə)m/ *n.* астигмати́зм

astonish /ə'stɒnɪʃ/ *v.t.* пора|жа́ть, -зи́ть; изум|ля́ть, -и́ть; **be ~ed at** пора|жа́ться, -зи́ться + d.; изум|ля́ться, -и́ться + d.; **his success was ~ing** он име́л порази́тельный успе́х

astonishment /ə'stɒnɪʃmənt/ *n.* изумле́ние

astound /ə'staʊnd/ *v.t.* изум|ля́ть, -и́ть; пора|жа́ть, -зи́ть

astray /ə'streɪ/ *pred. adj. & adv.:* **go ~** (lit., miss one's way) заблуди́ться (*pf.*); (fig.) сб|ива́ться, -и́ться с пути́; **lead ~** (fig.) сб|ива́ть, -ить с пути́ (и́стинного)

astride /ə'straɪd/ *adv.* верхо́м
• *prep.:* ~ **a horse** верхо́м на ло́шади

astrologer /ə'strɒlədʒə(r)/ *n.* астро́лог

astrological /æstrə'lɒdʒɪk(ə)l/ *adj.* астрологи́ческий

astrology /ə'strɒlədʒɪ/ *n.* астроло́гия

astronaut /'æstrənɔ:t/ *n.* астрона́вт, космона́вт

astronomer /ə'strɒnəmə(r)/ *n.* астроно́м

astronomical /æstrə'nɒmɪk(ə)l/ *adj.* (lit., fig.) астрономи́ческий

astronomy /ə'strɒnəmɪ/ *n.* астроно́мия

astrophysicist /æstrəʊ'fɪzɪsɪst/ *n.* астрофи́зик

astrophysics /æstrəʊ'fɪzɪks/ *n.* астрофи́зика

astute /ə'stju:t/ *adj.* проница́тельный

asylum /ə'saɪləm/ *n.* прию́т; **political ~** полити́ческое убе́жище
■ ~ **seeker** *n.* претенде́нт (-ка) на получе́ние (полити́ческого) убе́жища

asymmetrical /eɪsɪ'metrɪk(ə)l/ *adj.* асимметри́чный, асимметри́ческий

⚔ **at** /æt/ *prep.* **1** (denoting place) в/на + p.; (near, by) у + g., при + p.; ~ **home** до́ма; ~ **school** в шко́ле; ~ **the station** на вокза́ле/ста́нции; ~ **the concert** на конце́рте; ~ **my aunt's** у мое́й тёти **2** (denoting motion or direction, lit., fig.): **he sat down ~ the table** он сел за стол; **he arrived ~ Moscow** он при́был в Москву́

3 (denoting time or order): ~ **night** но́чью; ~ **2 o'clock** в два часа́; ~ **Easter** на Па́сху; ~ **the beginning** в нача́ле; ~ **first** снача́ла **4** (of activity, state, manner, rate, etc.): ~ **work** на рабо́те; за рабо́той; **good** ~ **languages** спосо́бный к языка́м; ~ **war** в состоя́нии войны́; ~ **60 mph** со ско́ростью шестьдеся́т миль в час; ~ **best** в лу́чшем слу́чае; ~ **least** по кра́йней ме́ре; ~ **most** са́мое бо́льшее; ~ **all** вообще́; (with neg.) совсе́м

ate /et, eɪt/ *past of* ▸ **eat**

atheism /ˈeɪθɪɪz(ə)m/ *n.* атеи́зм

atheist /ˈeɪθɪɪst/ *n.* атеи́ст (-ка)

athlete /ˈæθliːt/ *n.* спортсме́н (-ка)
■ ~'**s foot** *n.* грибко́вое заболева́ние ног

athletic /æθˈletɪk/ *adj.* атлети́ческий

athletics /æθˈletɪks/ *n.* атле́тика

Atlantic /əˈlæntɪk/ *n.* (*in full* **the** ~ (**Ocean**)) Атланти́ческий океа́н
● *adj.* атланти́ческий

atlas /ˈætləs/ *n.* а́тлас

ATM *n.* (*abbr. of* **Automated Teller Machine**) банкома́т

atmosphere /ˈætməsfɪə(r)/ *n.* атмосфе́ра

atmospheric /ætməsˈferɪk/ *adj.* атмосфе́рный

atom /ˈætəm/ *n.* а́том
■ ~ **bomb** *n.* а́томная бо́мба

atomic /əˈtɒmɪk/ *adj.* а́томный

atonal /eɪˈtəʊn(ə)l/ *adj.* (mus.) атона́льный

atone /əˈtəʊn/ *v.i.*: ~ **for** искуп|а́ть, -и́ть

atrocious /əˈtrəʊʃəs/ *adj.* ужа́сный

atrocity /əˈtrɒsɪtɪ/ *n.* зве́рство

✧ **attach** /əˈtætʃ/ *v.t.* **1** (fasten) прикреп|ля́ть, -и́ть; **the** ~**ed document** прилага́емый докуме́нт **2**: ~ **oneself to** присоедин|я́ться, -и́ться к + *d.* **3** (assign) прид|ава́ть, -а́ть **4** (of affection): **she is very** ~**ed to her brother** она́ о́чень привя́зана к своему́ бра́ту

attaché /əˈtæʃeɪ/ *n.* атташе́ (*m. indecl.*)
■ ~ **case** *n.* диплома́т

attachment /əˈtætʃmənt/ *n.* **1** (comput., file) приложе́ние, вло́женный файл **2** (affection) привя́занность

✧ **attack** /əˈtæk/ *n.* **1** нападе́ние; (mil.) ата́ка, нападе́ние; **our troops were under** ~ на́ши войска́ бы́ли атако́ваны **2** (fig., criticism) напа́д|ки (-ок) **3** (of illness) при́ступ; припа́док; **he had a heart** ~ с ним случи́лся серде́чный при́ступ
● *v.t.* **1** (lit., fig.) нап|ада́ть, -а́сть на + *a.*; атакова́ть (*impf., pf.*); обру́ши|ваться, -ться на + *a.* **2** (a task etc.) набр|а́сываться, -о́ситься на + *a.*

attacker /əˈtækə(r)/ *n.* напада́ющий

attain /əˈteɪn/ *v.t.* дост|ига́ть, -и́гнуть (*or* -и́чь) + *g.*; доб|ива́ться, -и́ться + *g.*

attainment /əˈteɪnmənt/ *n.* достиже́ние

✧ **attempt** /əˈtempt/ *n.* **1** (endeavour) попы́тка; **they made no** ~ **to escape** они́ не предприня́ли попы́тки убежа́ть **2** (product of trying to make sth): **her** ~ **at producing a meal** плод её тще́тных

кулина́рных стара́ний **3** (assault): **an** ~ **was made on his life** на его́ жизнь покуша́лись
● *v.t.* (try; try to do) пыта́ться, по-; **he was charged with** ~**ed murder** его́ обвини́ли в покуше́нии на уби́йство

✧ **attend** /əˈtend/ *v.t.* прису́тствовать (*impf.*) на + *p.*; **the concert was well** ~**ed** конце́рт собра́л большо́е коли́чество зри́телей; ~ **school** посеща́ть (*impf.*) шко́лу
● *v.i.* **1** (be present) прису́тствовать (*impf.*) **2** ~ **to** (take care of, look after) следи́ть (*impf.*) за + *i.*; забо́титься, по- о + *p.*; (deal with) зан|има́ться, -я́ться *i*.; **are you being** ~**ed to?** (in shop) вас (уже́) обслу́живают?

attendance /əˈtend(ə)ns/ *n.* **1** (presence) прису́тствие **2**: **in** ~ (present) прису́тствующий

attendant /əˈtend(ə)nt/ *n.* (in museum, car park) служи́тель (*m.*)

✧ **attention** /əˈtenʃ(ə)n/ *n.* **1** (heed) внима́ние; **pay** ~ **to** обра|ща́ть, -ти́ть внима́ние на + *a.*; **draw** ~ **to** привл|ека́ть, -е́чь внима́ние к + *d.* **2** (mil. command) сми́рно!; (posture): **stand to** ~ стоя́ть (*impf.*) сми́рно
■ ~ **deficit disorder** *n.* синдро́м наруше́ния внима́ния

attentive /əˈtentɪv/ *adj.* **1** (heedful) внима́тельный **2** (solicitous) забо́тливый

attest /əˈtest/ *v.t.* (certify) удостов|еря́ть, -е́рить; (bear witness to) свиде́тельствовать, за-; (confirm) подтвер|жда́ть, -ди́ть
● *v.i.*: ~ **to** свиде́тельствовать (*impf.*) о + *p.*

attic /ˈætɪk/ *n.* мансáрда, черда́к

attire /əˈtaɪə(r)/ *n.* облаче́ние, одея́ние; **in night** ~ в ночно́м облаче́нии
● *v.t.* (dress) облач|а́ть, -и́ть; над|ева́ть, -е́ть; **she was** ~**d in white** она́ была́ вся в бе́лом

✧ **attitude** /ˈætɪtjuːd/ *n.* отноше́ние

attorney /əˈtɜːnɪ/ *n.* (*pl.* ~**s**) (AmE, lawyer) адвока́т

✧ **attract** /əˈtrækt/ *v.t.* **1** (of physical forces) притя́|гивать, -ну́ть; (fig.) привл|ека́ть, -е́чь (к себе́) **2** (captivate) влечь (*impf.*), притя́гивать (*impf.*); **he found himself** ~**ed to her** он почу́вствовал, что увлечён е́ю

attraction /əˈtrækʃ(ə)n/ *n.* **1** (phys.) притяже́ние, тяготе́ние **2** (charm) привлека́тельность **3** (thing of interest) достопримеча́тельность; (amusement) аттракцио́н

attractive /əˈtræktɪv/ *adj.* привлека́тельный; притяга́тельный

attribute¹ /ˈætrɪbjuːt/ *n.* сво́йство

attribute² /əˈtrɪbjuːt/ *v.t.*: ~ **sth to** (work of art, quality) припи́с|ывать, -а́ть что-н. + *d.*; (event, result) отн|оси́ть, -ести́ что-н. к + *d.*

attributive /əˈtrɪbjʊtɪv/ *adj.* (gram.) определи́тельный, атрибути́вный

attrition /əˈtrɪʃ(ə)n/ *n.* тре́ние; истира́ние; (fig.) истоще́ние; измо́р; **war of** ~ война́ на истоще́ние

atypical /eɪˈtɪpɪk(ə)l/ *adj.* нетипи́чный

aubergine /ˈəʊbəʒiːn/ *n.* (BrE) баклажа́н

auburn /ˈɔːbən/ *adj.* тёмно-ры́жий

auction /ˈɔːkʃ(ə)n/ *n.* аукцио́н

● *v.t.* (*also* ~ **off**) прод|ава́ть, -а́ть с аукцио́на

■ ~ **room** *n.* аукцио́нный зал

auctioneer /ɔ:kʃə'nɪə(r)/ *n.* аукциони́ст

audacious /ɔ:'deɪʃəs/ *adj.* (bold) сме́лый; (daring) отва́жный; (impudent) де́рзкий

audacity /ɔ:'dæsɪtɪ/ *n.* сме́лость; отва́га; де́рзость

audible /'ɔ:dɪb(ə)l/ *adj.* слы́шимый, слы́шный

ꝺ **audience** /'ɔ:dɪəns/ *n.* (listeners) аудито́рия; слу́шатели (*m. pl.*); (spectators) зри́тели (*m. pl.*); пу́блика

audiobook /'ɔ:dɪəʊbʊk/ *n.* аудиокни́га

audio-visual /ɔ:dɪəʊ'vɪʒʊəl/ *adj.* аудиовизуа́льный

audit /'ɔ:dɪt/ *n.* реви́зия, ауди́т
● *v.t.* (**audited, auditing**) пров|еря́ть, -е́рить отчётность + *g.*; ревизова́ть (*impf., pf.*)

audition /ɔ:'dɪʃ(ə)n/ *n.* прослу́шивание, про́ба
● *v.t.* прослу́ш|ивать, -ать

auditor /'ɔ:dɪtə(r)/ *n.* ауди́тор

auditori|um /ɔ:dɪ'tɔ:rɪəm/ *n.* (*pl.* ~**ums** *or* ~**a**) (where audience sits) зри́тельный зал

augment /ɔ:g'ment/ *v.t.* приумн|ожа́ть, -о́жить; увели́чи|вать, -ть

augur /'ɔ:gə(r)/ *n.* (hist.) авгу́р (*жрец, толкова́вший во́лю бого́в*)
● *v.t.* (portend) предвеща́ть (*impf.*)
● *v.i.* (of things) служи́ть (*impf.*)
предзнаменова́нием + *g.*; **the exam results** ~ **well for his future** результа́ты его́ экза́менов — хоро́шая зая́вка на бу́дущее

ꝺ **August** /'ɔ:gəst/ *n.* а́вгуст

aunt /ɑ:nt/ *n.* тётя, тётка

auntie, aunty /'ɑ:ntɪ/ *n.* тётушка, тётенька

au pair /əʊ 'peə(r)/ *n.* ≈ ня́ня-иностра́нка

aural /'ɔ:r(ə)l/ *adj.* слухово́й

auspices /'ɔ:spɪsɪz/ *n. pl.* (patronage) покрови́тельство; эги́да; **under UN** ~ под эги́дой ООН

auspicious /ɔ:'spɪʃəs/ *adj.* благоприя́тный; **on this** ~ **day** в э́тот знамена́тельный день

austere /ɒ'stɪə(r)/ *adj.* (**austerer, austerest**) стро́гий, суро́вый

austerity /ɒ'sterɪtɪ/ *n.* стро́гость, суро́вость

Australia /ɒ'streɪlɪə/ *n.* Австра́лия

ꝺ **Australian** /ɒ'streɪlɪən/ *n.* австрали́|ец (-йка)
● *adj.* австрали́йский

Austria /'ɒstrɪə/ *n.* А́встрия

Austrian /'ɒstrɪən/ *n.* австри́|ец (-йка)
● *adj.* австри́йский

authentic /ɔ:'θentɪk/ *adj.* по́длинный

authenticate /ɔ:'θentɪkeɪt/ *v.t.* удостов|еря́ть, -е́рить по́длинность + *g.*

authenticity /ɔ:θen'tɪsɪtɪ/ *n.* по́длинность

ꝺ **author** /'ɔ:θə(r)/ *n.* (of specific work) а́втор; (writer in general) писа́тель (*m.*) (-ница)

authoritarian /ɔ:θɒrɪ'teərɪən/ *adj.* авторита́рный

authoritative /ɔ:'θɒrɪtətɪv/ *adj.* авторите́тный

ꝺ **authority** /ɔ:'θɒrɪtɪ/ *n.* **1** (power; right) власть; (legal) полномо́чие; **who is in** ~ **here?** кто

здесь ста́рший/нача́льник?; **who gave you** ~ **over me?** кто вам дал пра́во мне прика́зывать? **2** (*usu. in pl.*) (public bodies) вла́сти (*f. pl.*); о́рганы (*m. pl.*) вла́сти

authorization /ɔ:θəraɪ'zeɪʃ(ə)n/ *n.* (authorizing) уполномо́чивание; санкциони́рование; (sanction) разреше́ние; са́нкция

authorize /'ɔ:θəraɪz/ *v.t.* **1** (give authority to) уполномо́чи|вать, -ть **2** (sanction) разреш|а́ть, -и́ть; дозв|оля́ть, -о́лить; санкциони́ровать (*impf., pf.*)

autism /'ɔ:tɪz(ə)m/ *n.* аути́зм

autistic /ɔ:'tɪstɪk/ *adj.* аутисти́ческий; страда́ющий аути́змом

auto /'ɔ:təʊ/ *n.* (*pl.* ~**s**) (AmE, infml) авто́

autobiographical /ɔ:təbaɪə'græfɪk(ə)l/ *adj.* автобиографи́ческий

autobiography /ɔ:təbaɪ'ɒgrəfɪ/ *n.* автобиогра́фия

autocracy /ɔ:'tɒkrəsɪ/ *n.* самодержа́вие, автокра́тия

autocrat /'ɔ:təkræt/ *n.* самоде́ржец, автокра́т

autocratic /ɔ:tə'krætɪk/ *adj.* самодержа́вный, автократи́ческий; (dictatorial) деспоти́ческий

autocue® /'ɔ:təʊkju:/ *n.* (BrE) автосуфлёр

autograph /'ɔ:təgrɑ:f/ *n.* авто́граф
● *v.t.* надпи́с|ывать, -а́ть

automated /'ɔ:təmeɪtɪd/ *adj.* автоматизи́рованный

ꝺ **automatic** /ɔ:tə'mætɪk/ *n.* (firearm) автомати́ческое ору́жие
● *adj.* автомати́ческий

automation /ɔ:tə'meɪʃ(ə)n/ *n.* автоматиза́ция

automat|on /ɔ:'tɒmət(ə)n/ *n.* (*pl.* ~**a** *or* ~**ons**) автома́т (*робот; челове́к*)

automobile /'ɔ:təməbi:l/ *n.* автомоби́ль (*m.*)

autonomous /ɔ:'tɒnəməs/ *adj.* автоно́мный

autonomy /ɔ:'tɒnəmɪ/ *n.* автоно́мия

autopilot /'ɔ:təʊpaɪlət/ *n.* автопило́т

autopsy /'ɔ:tɒpsɪ/ *n.* вскры́тие тру́па, аутопси́я

ꝺ **autumn** /'ɔ:təm/ *n.* о́сень; (*attr.*) осе́нний

autumnal /ɔ:'tʌmn(ə)l/ *adj.* осе́нний

auxiliary /ɔ:g'zɪljərɪ/ *n.* (assistant) помо́щник; (*in full* ~ **verb**) (gram.) вспомога́тельный глаго́л
● *adj.* доба́вочный

avail /ə'veɪl/ *n.* (use) по́льза; **his entreaties were of no** ~ его́ мольбы́ бы́ли безуспе́шны; **his intervention was of little** ~ от его́ вмеша́тельства бы́ло ма́ло по́льзы; **to no** ~ напра́сно
● *v.t.* **1** (benefit) быть поле́зным/вы́годным + *d.*; **our efforts** ~**ed us nothing** на́ши уси́лия ни к чему́ не привели́ **2**: ~ **oneself of** воспо́льзоваться (*pf.*) + *i.*

availability /əveɪlə'bɪlɪtɪ/ *n.* (presence) нали́чие; (accessibility) досту́пность

ꝺ **available** /ə'veɪləb(ə)l/ *adj.* (product) име́ющийся в прода́же, досту́пный; **it is not** ~ **in your size** ва́шего разме́ра нет; (information): **the information was not** ~ информа́ция была́ недосту́пна; (person)

a

свобо́дный; **she's not** ~ она́ занята́

avalanche /'ævəlɑːntʃ/ *n.* лави́на

avarice /'ævərɪs/ *n.* жа́дность

avaricious /ævə'rɪʃəs/ *adj.* жа́дный

avenge /ə'vendʒ/ *v.t.* мстить, ото- за + *a.*;
she ~d her friend она́ отомсти́ла за дру́га

avenue /'ævənjuː/ *n.* (tree-lined road) алле́я;
(wide street) проспе́кт

✍ **average** /'ævərɪdʒ/ *n.* (mean) сре́днее число́;
(norm) сре́днее; **above/below** ~ вы́ше/ни́же
сре́днего; **on** ~ в сре́днем
● *adj.* сре́дний
● *v.t. & i.*: **my expenses** ~ **£10 a day** мои́
расхо́ды составля́ют в сре́днем де́сять
фу́нтов в день; (do on ~): **he** ~**s 6 hours'
work a day** он рабо́тает в сре́днем шесть
часо́в в день

averse /ə'vɜːs/ *pred. adj.*: ~ **to** не
располо́женный к + *d.*; **I am not** ~ **to a
good dinner** я не прочь хорошо́ пообе́дать

aversion /ə'vɜːʃ(ə)n/ *n.* отвраще́ние,
антипа́тия

avert /ə'vɜːt/ *v.t.*: ~ **one's gaze, eyes** отв|оди́ть,
-ести́ взгляд

aviary /'eɪvɪərɪ/ *n.* пти́чник; вольер(а) для птиц

aviation /eɪvɪ'eɪʃ(ə)n/ *n.* авиа́ция

avid /'ævɪd/ *adj.* жа́дный, а́лчный

avocado /ævə'kɑːdəʊ/ *n.* (*pl.* ~**s**) (*in full* ~
pear) авока́до (*nt. indecl.*)

✍ **avoid** /ə'vɔɪd/ *v.t.* (drive round) объезжа́ть,
объе́хать; (escape, evade) избе|га́ть, -жа́ть + *g.*;
I could not ~ **meeting him** я не мог избежа́ть
встре́чи с ним

avoidable /ə'vɔɪdəb(ə)l/ *adj.*: **delays are** ~
заде́ржек мо́жно избежа́ть; **without** ~ **delay**
без нену́жных/изли́шних заде́ржек

avuncular /ə'vʌŋkjʊlə(r)/ *adj.* (manner, tone)
оте́ческий; (person) дружелю́бный

await /ə'weɪt/ *v.t.* ожида́ть (*impf.*) + *g.*

awake /ə'weɪk/ *pred. adj.*: **are you** ~ **or
asleep?** вы спи́те и́ли нет?; **is he** ~ **yet?** он
просну́лся?; **the baby was wide** ~ у ребёнка
сна не́ было ни в одно́м глазу́
● *v.t.* (*past* **awoke**, *p.p.* **awoken**) буди́ть,
раз-
● *v.i.* (*past* **awoke**, *p.p.* **awoken**)
прос|ыпа́ться, -ну́ться

awaken /ə'weɪkən/ *v.t.* пробу|жда́ть, -ди́ть

✍ **award** /ə'wɔːd/ *n.* награ́да, приз
● *v.t.* прису|жда́ть, -ди́ть (*что кому*)

✍ **aware** /ə'weə(r)/ *pred. adj.*: **be** ~ **of**
сознава́ть (*impf.*); (realize) осозн|ава́ть,
-а́ть; **you are probably** ~ **that …** вам,

вероя́тно, изве́стно, что…

awareness /ə'weənɪs/ *n.* созна́ние

✍ **away** /ə'weɪ/ *adv.* **1** (at a distance): **the shops are
ten minutes' walk** ~ магази́ны нахо́дятся в
десяти́ мину́тах ходьбы́ отсю́да **2** (not present
or near): **he is** ~ он в отъе́зде; **our team are
playing** ~ **(from home)** на́ша кома́нда игра́ет
на вы́езде *or* на чужо́м по́ле *or* в гостя́х
3 (fig., of time or degree): **the wedding is three
weeks** ~ до сва́дьбы (оста́лось) три неде́ли

awe /ɔː/ *n.* благогове́ние, тре́пет
■ ~**-inspiring** *adj.* внуша́ющий благогове́ние

awesome /'ɔːsəm/ *adj.* (impressive)
впечатля́ющий; (AmE, infml, excellent)
потряса́ющий

awful /'ɔːfʊl/ *adj.* ужа́сный, стра́шный

awfully /'ɔːfəlɪ/ *adv.* ужа́сно; ~ **nice** (infml)
ужа́сно ми́лый

awkward /'ɔːkwəd/ *adj.* **1** (clumsy) неуклю́жий
2 (inconvenient, uncomfortable) неудо́бный
3 (difficult): **an** ~ **problem** ка́верзная пробле́ма
4 (embarrassing): **an** ~ **silence** нело́вкое
молча́ние **5** (BrE, of person, hard to manage)
тру́дный; **he's being** ~ **(about it)** он чини́т
препя́тствия

awning /'ɔːnɪŋ/ *n.* наве́с; тент

awoke /ə'wəʊk/ *past of* ▸ **awake**

awoken /ə'wəʊk(ə)n/ *p.p. of* ▸ **awake**

AWOL /'eɪwɒl/ *pred. adj.* (*abbr. of* **absent
without leave**) в самово́льной отлу́чке

awry /ə'raɪ/ *pred. adj.* (distorted)
искажённый
● *adv.* ко́со; (fig.): **things went** ~ дела́ пошли́
скве́рно

axe /æks/ (AmE *also* **ax**) *n.* топо́р
● *v.t.* (**axing**) (fig., staff, budgets) уреза́ть,
уре́зать; (a project) заруб|а́ть, -и́ть

axes /'æksiːz/ *pl. of* ▸ **axis**

axis /'æksɪs/ *n.* (*pl.* **axes**) ось, вал

axle /'æks(ə)l/ *n.* ось

azalea /ə'zeɪlɪə/ *n.* аза́лия

Azerbaijan /æzəbaɪ'dʒɑːn/ *n.* Азербайджа́н

Azerbaijani /æzəbaɪ'dʒɑːnɪ/ *n.* (*pl.* ~**s**)
(person) азербайджа́н|ец (-ка); (language)
азербайджа́нский язы́к
● *adj.* азербайджа́нский

Azov /'æzɒf/ *n.* (*in full* **Sea of** ~) Азо́вское
мо́ре

Aztec /'æztek/ *n.* ацте́к
● *adj.* ацте́кский

azure /'æʒə(r)/ *n.* лазу́рь
● *adj.* лазу́рный, голубо́й

Bb

B /biː/ *n.* **1** (mus.) си (*nt. indecl.*) **2** (academic mark) «хорошо», четвёрка

BA *abbr.* (*of* **Bachelor of Arts**) бакала́вр гуманита́рных нау́к

babble /'bæb(ə)l/ *v.t.* & *i.* болта́ть (*impf.*); лепета́ть (*impf.*); **babbling brook** журча́щий ручей

babe /beɪb/ *n.* (sl.) де́вушка

baboon /bə'buːn/ *n.* бабуи́н, павиа́н

⚥ **baby** /'beɪbɪ/ *n.* **1** младе́нец; (of animals etc.) детёныш **2** (*attr.*): ~ **elephant** слонёнок ■ ~**sit** *v.i.* присма́тривать (*impf.*) за детьми́ в отсу́тствие роди́телей; ~**sitter** *n.* приходя́щая ня́ня; ~**sitting** *n.* присмо́тр за детьми́

babyish /'beɪbɪʃ/ *adj.* де́тский

baccalaureate /bækə'lɔːrɪət/ *n.* сте́пень бакала́вра

bachelor /'bætʃələ(r)/ *n.* **1** холостя́к **2** (academic) бакала́вр

⚥ **back** /bæk/ *n.* **1** (part of body) спина́; ~ **to** ~ спино́й к спине́; **as soon as my** ~ **was turned** не успе́л я отверну́ться **2** (fig.): **behind my** ~ за мое́й спино́й **3** (of chair) спи́нка **4** (other side, rear): ~ **of an envelope** обра́тная сторона́ конве́рта; **at the** ~ **of one's mind** подсозна́тельно; в глубине́ души́ **5** (sport) защи́тник **6** (*attr.*): ~ **door** чёрный ход; ~ **seat** за́днее сиде́нье; ~ **street** глуха́я у́лица
● *adv.* **1** (to or at the rear) наза́д, сза́ди **2** (returning to former position etc.) обра́тно; **he is** ~ **again** он сно́ва здесь; **we shall be** ~ **before dark** мы вернёмся за́светло; **get one's own** ~ отплати́ть (*pf.*) (*кому*)
● *v.t.* **1** (move backwards) дви́|гать, -нуть наза́д (*or* в обра́тном направле́нии); **she** ~**ed the car into the garage** она́ въе́хала за́дним хо́дом в гара́ж **2** (support) (*also* ~ **up**) поддерж|ивать, -а́ть **3** (finance) финанси́ровать (*impf., pf.*) **4**: ~ **up** (comput.) резерви́ровать (*impf., pf.*)
● *v.i.* **1** (of motor vehicle) идти́ (*det.*) за́дним хо́дом **2**: ~ **down (from)** отступ|а́ться, -и́ться (*от чего*); ~ **out (of)** уклон|я́ться, -и́ться (*от чего*)

backache /'bækeɪk/ *n.* боль в спине́/поясни́це

backbencher /bæk'bentʃə(r)/ *n.* (BrE) рядово́й член парла́мента; заднескаме́ечник

backbiting /'bækbaɪtɪŋ/ *n.* злосло́вие

backbone /'bækbəʊn/ *n.* позвоно́чник

backchat /'bæktʃæt/ *n.* (BrE) де́рзкий отве́т, де́рзость

backcloth /'bækklɒθ/ *n.* (BrE, theatr.) за́дник

backdate /bæk'deɪt/ *v.t.* (letter) пом|еча́ть, -е́тить за́дним число́м; (pay) пров|оди́ть, -ести́ за́дним число́м

backdrop /'bækdrɒp/ *n.* **1**: **against the** ~ **of crisis** на фо́не кри́зиса **2** = **backcloth**

backer /'bækə(r)/ *n.* ока́зывающий подде́ржку; субсиди́рующий

backfire /'bækfaɪə(r)/ *v.t.* (of a car, engine) изда|ва́ть, -ть обра́тную вспы́шку; (fig.) прив|оди́ть, -ести́ к обра́тным результа́там

⚥ **background** /'bækɡraʊnd/ *n.* **1** за́дний план, фон; (*attr.*) фо́новый; **in the** ~ **of the picture** на за́днем пла́не карти́ны; **on a dark** ~ на тёмном фо́не; **keep in the** ~ (fig.) держа́ть(ся) (*impf.*) в тени́ **2** (of person) (parentage) происхожде́ние; (education) образова́ние; (experience) о́пыт **3** (to a situation) предысто́рия **4**: ~ **music** музыка́льное сопровожде́ние/оформле́ние

backhand /'bækhænd/ *n.* (sport) уда́р сле́ва

backhanded /bæk'hændɪd/ *adj.* (fig.) сомни́тельный, двусмы́сленный

backhander /'bækhændə(r)/ *n.* (BrE, bribe) взя́тка

backing /'bækɪŋ/ *n.* **1** (assistance) подде́ржка; (subsidy) субсиди́рование **2** (of cloth) подкла́дка

backlash /'bæklæʃ/ *n.* (fig.) реа́кция

backlog /'bæklɒɡ/ *n.* го́ры (*f. pl.*) накопи́вшейся рабо́ты

backpack /'bækpæk/ *n.* рюкза́к

backpacker /'bækpækə(r)/ *n.* челове́к, путеше́ствующий с рюкзако́м

back-pedal /'bækped(ə)l/ *v.i.* (fig.) идти́ (*det.*), пойти́ на попя́тную

backside /bæk'saɪd/ *n.* зад, за́дница

backslash /'bækslæʃ/ *n.* (typ.) обра́тная коса́я черта́

backslide /'bækslaɪd/ *v.t.* вновь подда́ться (*pf.*) искуше́нию; верну́ться (*pf.*) к дурны́м привы́чкам

backstage /bæksteɪdʒ/ *adv.* за кули́сами

backstreet /'bækstriːt/ *adj.* (illicit) подпо́льный

backstroke /'bækstrəʊk/ *n.* пла́вание на спине́

backtrack /'bæktræk/ *v.i.* (fig.) идти́ (*det.*), пойти́ на попя́тную

back-up /'bækʌp/ *n.* (comput.) резе́рвная ко́пия; бэ́кап
● *adj.* (comput.) резе́рвный

backward /'bækwəd/ *adj.* **1** (towards the back) обра́тный; **a** ~ **glance** взгля́д наза́д **2** (lagging) отста́лый

backwardness /'bækwədnɪs/ *n.* отста́лость; (disinclination) неохо́та

backwards /'bækwədz/ *adv.* (in backward direction) назáд; (in reverse order) в обрáтном порядке; **walk** ~ пятиться, по-; ~ **and forwards** взад и вперёд; тудá и обрáтно

backwater /'bækwɔ:tə(r)/ *n.* болóто, тихая зáводь

backyard /bæk'jɑ:d/ *n.* **1** (BrE) зáдний двор **2** (AmE) сáд(ик) за дóмом

bacon /'beɪkən/ *n.* бекóн
■ ~ **and eggs** *n.* яичница с бекóном

bacteria /bæk'tɪərɪə/ *pl. of* ▶ **bacterium**

bacterial /bæk'tɪərɪəl/ *adj.* бактериáльный

bacteriology /bæktɪərɪ'blɒdʒɪ/ *n.* бактериолóгия

bacteri|um /bæk'tɪərɪəm/ *n.* (*pl.* ~**a**) бактéрия

⚹ **bad** /bæd/ *n.* (evil) дурнóе, плохóе
● *adj.* (**worse, worst**) **1** плохóй, дурнóй, сквéрный; **not** ~! неплóхо!; **too** ~! óчень жаль! **2** (morally bad) плохóй, дурнóй; **a** ~ **name** дурнáя репутáция **3** (spoilt) испóрченный; **go** ~ пóртиться, ис- **4** (severe) сильный; **I caught a** ~ **cold** я сильно простудился **5** (harmful) врéдный; **smoking is** ~ **for one** курéние врéдно для здорóвья
■ ~-**mannered** *adj.* невоспитанный; ~-**tempered** *adj.* раздражительный

badge /bædʒ/ *n.* значóк; (fig.) символ

badger /'bædʒə(r)/ *n.* барсýк

badly /'bædlɪ/ *adv.* (**worse, worst**) **1** (not well) плóхо **2** (very much) óчень; сильно **3**: ~ **off** в нуждé

badminton /'bædmɪnt(ə)n/ *n.* бадминтóн

baffle /'bæf(ə)l/ *v.t.* (perplex) сбивáть, -ть с тóлку; озадáчи|вать, -ть

⚹ **bag** /bæg/ *n.* **1** сýмка; (small ~, hand~) сýмочка; (paper ~, plastic ~) пакéт **2** (large ~, sack) мешóк **3** (luggage) чемодáн; **pack one's** ~**s** собрáть (*pf.*) вéщи пéред отъéздом **4** (*var.*): ~**s under the eyes** мешки под глазáми
■ ~**pipe(s)** *n.* (*pl.*) волынка

baggage /'bægɪdʒ/ *n.* багáж
■ ~ **handler** *n.* операáтор на приёме/выдаче багажá; ~ **reclaim** *n.* пункт выдачи багажá

baggy /'bægɪ/ *adj.* (**baggier, baggiest**) мешковáтый

Baghdad /bæg'dæd/ *n.* Багдáд

Bahamas /bə'hɑ:məz/ *n. pl.* (*in full* **the** ~) Багáмские островá (*m. pl.*)

bail¹ /beɪl/ *n.* (pledge) залóг; поручительство; **release on** ~ отпус|кáть, -тить на порýки
● *v.t.*: ~ **sb out** (of detention) брать, взять когó-н. на порýки

bail² /beɪl/ *v.t.* **1** (*also* ~ **out**) вычéрпывать, выχерпать (*воду из лодки*) **2**: ~ **sb out** пом|огáть, -óчь + *d.* (*в трудном положении*)
● *v.i.*: ~ **out** (aeron.) катапультироваться (*impf., pf.*)
■ ~**out** *n.* (econ.) финáнсовая пóмощь

bailiff /'beɪlɪf/ *n.* (law) судéбный пристав; бéйлиф

bait /beɪt/ *n.* (hunting) примáнка; (fishing) насáдка

bake /beɪk/ *v.t.* печь, ис-
● *v.i.* пéчься, ис-

baker /'beɪkə(r)/ *n.* пéкарь (*m.*)

bakery /'beɪkərɪ/ *n.* пекáрня; (shop) бýлочная

Baku /bɑ:'ku:/ *n.* Бакý (*m. indecl.*)

balalaika /bælə'laɪkə/ *n.* балалáйка

⚹ **balance** /'bæləns/ *n.* **1** (machine) вес|ы (-óв) **2** (equilibrium) равновéсие; **lose one's** ~ (fig.) терять, по- душéвное равновéсие; **hang in the** ~ висéть (*impf.*) на волоскé **3** (bookkeeping) балáнс; сáльдо (*indecl.*)
● *v.t.* **1** (lit.): **he** ~**d a pole on his chin** он балансировал шест на подбородке **2** (make equal) уравнове|шивать, -сить **3** (weigh one thing against another) взвé|шивать, -сить; сопоставля́ть, -áвить (*что с чем*)
● *v.i.* (of accounts) сходиться (*impf.*); (be in equilibrium) балансировать (*impf.*)
■ ~ **of payments** *n.* платёжный балáнс; ~ **of trade** *n.* торгóвый балáнс

balanced /'bælənst/ *adj.* (of person) уравновéшенный; ~ **judgement** продýманное суждéние; ~ **diet** сбалансированная/рациональная диéта

balcony /'bælkənɪ/ *n.* балкóн

bald /bɔ:ld/ *adj.* лысый

bale¹ *n.* (of hay) тюк; (of cotton) кипа

bale² /beɪl/ *v.i.* (BrE) = **bail²**

Balkan /'bɔ:lkən/ *n.*: **the** ~**s** Балкáн|ы (*pl., g.* -); Балкáнский полуóстров
● *adj.* балкáнский

ball¹ /bɔ:l/ *n.* (dance) бал
■ ~**room** *n.* танцевáльный зал; ~**room dancing** *n.* бáльные тáнцы (*m. pl.*)

⚹ **ball²** /bɔ:l/ *n.* **1** (sphere) шар **2** (in football, rugby, tennis) мяч; (in golf, table tennis) мячик **3** (of wool) клубóк **4** (*in pl.*) (vulg., testicles) яйца (*nt. pl.*); (BrE, nonsense) чепухá
■ ~**park** *adj.*: **a** ~**park figure** примéрная цифра; ~**point (pen)** *n.* шáриковая рýчка

ballad /'bæləd/ *n.* балláда

ballast /'bæləst/ *n.* баллáст
● *v.t.* грузить, на- баллáстом

ballerina /bælə'ri:nə/ *n.* балерина

ballet /'bæleɪ/ *n.* балéт
■ ~ **dancer** *n.* артист (-ка) балéта

ballistic /bə'lɪstɪk/ *adj.* баллистический

ballistics /bə'lɪstɪks/ *n.* баллистика

balloon /bə'lu:n/ *n.* аэростáт; (also child's) воздýшный шар
● *v.i.* (fly in ~) летáть (*indet.*) на воздýшном шáре

ballot /'bælət/ *n.* (~ paper) избирáтельный бюллетéнь; (vote) голосовáние
● *v.t.* (**balloted, balloting**) пров|одить, -ести голосовáние междý + *i.*
■ ~ **box** *n.* избирáтельная ýрна

Baltic /'bɔ:ltɪk/ *n.* (*in full* **the** ~ (**Sea**)) Балтийское мóре, Бáлтика
● *adj.* балтийский; прибалтийский
■ ~ **States** *n.* (при)балтийские государства, Прибáлтика

balustrade /ˌbæləˈstreɪd/ *n.* балюстра́да
bamboo /bæmˈbuː/ *n.* бамбу́к
bamboozle /bæmˈbuːz(ə)l/ *v.t.* (infml) одура́чи|вать, -ть; над|ува́ть, -у́ть
ⱷ **ban** /bæn/ *n.* (prohibition) запреще́ние, запре́т
● *v.t.* (**banned, banning**) запре|ща́ть, -ти́ть
banal /bəˈnɑːl/ *adj.* бана́льный
banana /bəˈnɑːnə/ *n.* бана́н
ⱷ **band**[1] /bænd/ *n.* **1** (braid) тесьма́; **rubber** ~ рези́нка **2** (strip) полоса́ **3** (radio): **frequency** ~ диапазо́н часто́т
ⱷ **band**[2] /bænd/ *n.* (gang) ба́нда, ша́йка; (mus.) орке́стр; **jazz** ~ джаз-ба́нд, джаз-орке́стр
● *v.i.*: ~ **together** объедин|я́ться, -и́ться
bandage /ˈbændɪdʒ/ *n.* бинт
● *v.t.* бинтова́ть, за-; перевя́з|ывать, -а́ть
bandanna, bandana /bænˈdænə/ *n.* цветно́й плато́к, банда́на
bandit /ˈbændɪt/ *n.* разбо́йник, банди́т
bane /beɪn/ *n.* прокля́тие; **it is the** ~ **of my life** э́то отравля́ет мне жизнь
bang /bæŋ/ *n.* **1** (blow) уда́р **2** (crash) гро́хот; стук **3** (explosion) взрыв
● *v.t.* (strike, thump) уд|аря́ть, -а́рить; ~ **one's fist on the table** сту́кнуть (*pf.*) кулако́м по́ столу; ~ **the door** хло́пнуть (*pf.*) две́рью
● *v.i.* (of door, window, etc.) захло́пнуться (*pf.*); **the door is** ~**ing** дверь хло́пает
● *adv.* (suddenly) вдруг; (BrE, just, exactly) пря́мо; как раз
banger /ˈbæŋə(r)/ *n.* (BrE, infml) (sausage) соси́ска; (car) драндуле́т
Bangkok /bæŋˈkɒk/ *n.* Бангко́к
Bangladesh /ˌbæŋɡləˈdeʃ/ *n.* Бангладе́ш
Bangladeshi /ˌbæŋɡləˈdeʃi/ *n.* (*pl.* ~ *or* ~**s**) бангладе́ш|ец (-ка)
● *adj.* бангладе́шский
bangle /ˈbæŋɡ(ə)l/ *n.* брасле́т
banish /ˈbænɪʃ/ *v.t.* (exile) высыла́ть, вы́слать; (from one's mind) от|гоня́ть, -огна́ть
banisters /ˈbænɪstəz/ *n. pl.* пери́л|а (*pl., g.* —)
banjo /ˈbændʒəʊ/ *n.* (*pl.* ~**s** *or* ~**es**) ба́нджо (*nt. indecl.*)
bank[1] /bæŋk/ *n.* (of river) бе́рег
ⱷ **bank**[2] /bæŋk/ *n.* (fin.) банк
● *v.t.* (put into ~) класть, положи́ть в банк
● *v.i.* (keep money in ~) держа́ть (*impf.*) де́ньги в ба́нке; ~ **on** (fig., rely on) пол|ага́ться, -ожи́ться на + *a.*; де́лать, с- ста́вку на + *a.*
■ ~ **account** *n.* ба́нковский счёт; ~ **card** *n.* ба́нковская креди́тная ка́рта; ~ **clerk** *n.* ба́нковский слу́жащий; ~ **holiday** *n.* ≈ официа́льный нерабо́чий день; ~**note** *n.* банкно́та
banker /ˈbæŋkə(r)/ *n.* банки́р
banking /ˈbæŋkɪŋ/ *n.* (fin.) ба́нковское де́ло
bankroll /ˈbæŋkrəʊl/ *v.t.* финанси́ровать (*impf., pf.*)
bankrupt /ˈbæŋkrʌpt/ *adj.* (also fig.) обанкро́тившийся; несостоя́тельный; **go** ~ обанкро́титься (*pf.*)
bankruptcy /ˈbæŋkrʌptsɪ/ *n.* банкро́тство, несостоя́тельность

banner /ˈbænə(r)/ *n.* (lit., fig.) зна́мя (*nt. pl.*); (with slogan) плака́т
banns /bænz/ *n. pl.* оглаше́ние (предстоя́щего бра́ка); **ask, call, read the** ~ огла|ша́ть, -си́ть имена́ жениха́ и неве́сты
banquet /ˈbæŋkwɪt/ *n.* пир; (formal occasion) банке́т
banter /ˈbæntə(r)/ *n.* подшу́чивание, подтру́нивание
● *v.i.* шути́ть, по-
baptism /ˈbæptɪz(ə)m/ *n.* креще́ние
Baptist /ˈbæptɪst/ *n.* **1**: **St John the** ~ Иоа́нн Крести́тель (*m.*) **2** (member of denomination) бапти́ст (-ка)
baptize /bæpˈtaɪz/ *v.t.* крести́ть, о-; нар|ека́ть, -е́чь
ⱷ **bar**[1] /bɑː(r)/ *n.* **1** (rod) прут; (of chocolate) пли́тка; (of soap) кусо́к; (strip, flat piece) полоса́ **2** (*usu. in pl.*) решётка; **behind** ~**s** за решёткой **3** (mus.) такт
● *v.t.* (**barred, barring**) (bolt) зап|ира́ть, -ере́ть на засо́в; (obstruct) прегра|жда́ть, -ди́ть; (exclude) исключ|а́ть, -и́ть; **soldiers** ~**red the way** солда́ты блоки́ровали доро́гу
■ ~ **code** *n.* штрихко́д
bar[2] /bɑː(r)/ *n.* (legal profession) адвокату́ра
ⱷ **bar**[3] /bɑː(r)/ *n.* (room) бар, буфе́т; (counter) прила́вок
■ ~**maid** *n.* буфе́тчица, ба́рмен; ~**man, ~tender** *nn.* буфе́тчик, ба́рмен
bar[4] /bɑː(r)/ *prep.* (BrE, infml, excluding) исключа́я, не счита́я; ~ **none** без исключе́ния
barbarian /bɑːˈbeərɪən/ *n.* ва́рвар
barbaric /bɑːˈbærɪk/ *adj.* ва́рварский
barbarism /ˈbɑːbərɪz(ə)m/ *n.* ва́рварство; (ling.) варвари́зм
barbarity /bɑːˈbærɪtɪ/ *n.* ва́рварство
barbarous /ˈbɑːbərəs/ *adj.* ва́рварский; (cruel) бесчелове́чный
barbecue /ˈbɑːbɪkjuː/ *n.* (party) барбекю́; пикни́к, где подаю́т мя́со, зажа́ренное на ве́ртеле/жаро́вне
barbed /bɑːbd/ *adj.*: ~ **wire** колю́чая про́волока
barber /ˈbɑːbə(r)/ *n.* парикма́хер (*мужско́й*); ~**'s (shop)** парикма́херская (*мужска́я*)
barbiturate /bɑːˈbɪtjʊrət/ *n.* барбитура́т
bare /beə(r)/ *adj.* **1** (naked, not covered) го́лый, наго́й; обнажённый; **with one's** ~ **hands** го́лыми рука́ми; ~ **feet** босы́е но́ги **2** (empty) пусто́й
● *v.t.*: ~ **one's teeth** ска́лить, о- зу́бы
■ ~**back** *adv.* без седла́; ~**foot** *adj.* босо́й
● *adv.* босико́м
barely /ˈbeəlɪ/ *adv.* едва́
Barents Sea /ˈbærənts/ *n.* Ба́ренцево мо́ре
bargain /ˈbɑːɡɪn/ *n.* **1** (deal) сде́лка, соглаше́ние; **make a** ~ заключ|а́ть, -и́ть сде́лку; **it's a** ~! по рука́м! **2** (thing cheaply acquired) вы́годная поку́пка
● *v.i.* торгова́ться, с-; ~ **for** (expect) ожида́ть (*impf.*); **it was more than I** ~**ed for** на э́то я

b

не рассчи́тывал

barge /bɑːdʒ/ *n.* ба́ржа
• *v.i.* (infml): ~ **in** (intrude) вва́л|иваться, -и́ться

baritone /'bærɪtəʊn/ *n.* (voice, singer) барито́н

barium /'beərɪəm/ *n.* ба́рий

bark¹ /bɑːk/ *n.* (of tree etc.) кора́

bark² /bɑːk/ *n.* (of dog) лай
• *v.i.* (of dog etc.) ла́ять (*impf.*) (**at:** на + *a.*)

barley /'bɑːlɪ/ *n.* ячме́нь (*m.*) (*злак*)

bar mitzvah /bɑː 'mɪtzvə/ *n.* (ceremony and boy undergoing this) бар-ми́цва (*m.*) (*в иудаизме*)

barmy /'bɑːmɪ/ *adj.* (**barmier, barmiest**) (BrE, infml) чо́кнутый, тро́нутый; **go** ~ тро́нуться (*pf.*); спя́тить (*pf.*) (both infml)

barn /bɑːn/ *n.* амба́р, сара́й

barometer /bə'rɒmɪtə(r)/ *n.* баро́метр

baron /'bærən/ *n.* баро́н

baroness /'bærənes/ *n.* бароне́сса

baroque /bə'rɒk/ *n.* баро́кко (*nt. indecl.*)
• *adj.* баро́чный

barrack /'bærək/ *n.* (*usu. in pl.*) каза́рма

barrage /'bærɑːʒ/ *n.* (mil.) загражде́ние; (fig.): a ~ **of questions** град/шквал вопро́сов

barrel /'bær(ə)l/ *n.* **1** бо́чка **2** (of firearm) ствол

barren /'bærən/ *adj.* (**barrener, barrenest**) беспло́дный

barricade /bærɪ'keɪd/ *n.* баррика́да
• *v.t.* баррикади́ровать, за-; ~ **oneself in** баррикади́роваться, за-

barrier /'bærɪə(r)/ *n.* барье́р; (obstacle) поме́ха, прегра́да

barring /'bɑːrɪŋ/ *prep.* за исключе́нием + *g.*

barrister /'bærɪstə(r)/ *n.* (BrE) адвока́т

barrow /'bærəʊ/ *n.* (BrE) (handcart) ручна́я теле́жка; (wheel~) та́чка
■ ~ **boy** *n.* у́личный торго́вец (*с тележкой*)

barter /'bɑːtə(r)/ *v.i.* обме́н|иваться, -я́ться + *i.*; меня́ться (*impf.*) + *i.*

✓ **base¹** /beɪs/ *n.* **1** (of structure) фунда́мент, пьедеста́л, основа́ние, ба́зис **2** (mil. etc.) ба́за
• *v.t.* осно́в|ывать, -а́ть; **the legend is** ~d **on fact** в осно́ве э́той леге́нды лежа́т действи́тельные собы́тия
■ ~**ball** *n.* бейсбо́л; ~ **camp** *n.* ба́за

base² /beɪs/ *adj.* ни́зкий

basement /'beɪsmənt/ *n.* подва́л

bases /'beɪsiːz/ *pl. of* ▶ **basis**

bash /bæʃ/ (infml) *n.* (BrE, attempt) попы́тка; **have a** ~ попыта́ться (*pf.*); (bang): **give sb a** ~ **on the head** дава́ть, дать, кому́-н. по башке́ (infml)
• *v.t.* си́льно ударя́ть, уда́рить

bashful /'bæʃfʊl/ *adj.* засте́нчивый

✓ **basic** /'beɪsɪk/ *adj.* основно́й

✓ **basically** /'beɪsɪkəlɪ/ *adv.* в основно́м

basil /'bæz(ə)l/ *n.* базили́к

basin /'beɪs(ə)n/ *n.* (for food) ми́ска; (washbasin) умыва́льник, ра́ковина

✓ **basis** /'beɪsɪs/ *n.* (*pl.* **bases**) осно́ва, ба́зис; **lay the** ~ **for** заложи́ть (*pf.*) осно́ву + *g.*

bask /bɑːsk/ *v.i.*: ~ **in the sun** гре́ться (*impf.*) на со́лнце; (fig.): ~ **in glory** купа́ться (*impf.*) в луча́х сла́вы

basket /'bɑːskɪt/ *n.* корзи́на, корзи́нка
■ ~**ball** *n.* (the sport) баскетбо́л; (*attr.*) баскетбо́льный; ~ **case** *n.* (infml) (useless person) никчёмный челове́к; (useless thing) бесполе́зная вещь

Basque /bæsk/ *n.* баск (-о́нка)
• *adj.* ба́скский

bass /beɪs/ *n.* (voice, singer) бас; (~ guitar) бас-гита́ра; (double ~) контраба́с

bassoon /bə'suːn/ *n.* фаго́т

bassoonist /bə'suːnɪst/ *n.* фаготи́ст (-ка)

bastard /'bɑːstəd/ *n.* **1** (child) внебра́чный ребёнок **2** (as term of abuse) уро́д

bastion /'bæstɪən/ *n.* бастио́н

bat¹ /bæt/ *n.* (zool.) лету́чая мышь

bat² /bæt/ *n.* (sport) би́та, лапта́
• *v.t.* (**batted, batting**) бить (*impf.*) (*or* удя́ря́ть, -а́рить) би́той/лапто́й

batch /bætʃ/ *n.* **1** (of bread) вы́печка **2** (consignment) па́чка; гру́ппа

bated /'beɪtɪd/ *adj.*: **with** ~ **breath** затаи́в дыха́ние

bath /bɑːθ/ *n.* ва́нна; **take, have a** ~ прин|има́ть, -я́ть ва́нну; купа́ться, ис-
• *v.t. & i.* купа́ть(ся), ис-
■ ~**robe** *n.* купа́льный хала́т; ~**room** *n.* ва́нная (ко́мната); ~**tub** *n.* ва́нна

bathe /beɪð/ *v.t.* **1** (one's face etc.) мыть, по-; обм|ыва́ть, -ы́ть; ~ **one's eyes, a wound** пром|ыва́ть, -ы́ть глаза́/ра́ну **2**: **he was** ~d **in sweat** он облива́лся по́том
• *v.i.* купа́ться, ис-

bather /'beɪðə(r)/ *n.* купа́льщи|к (-ца)

bathing /'beɪðɪŋ/ *n.* купа́ние

baton /'bæt(ə)n/ *n.* **1** (mus.) дирижёрская па́лочка **2** (sport) эстафе́тная па́лочка **3** (BrE, policeman's) дуби́нка

batsman /'bætsmən/ *n.* (sport) бью́щий игро́к, бэ́тсмен

battalion /bə'tælɪən/ *n.* батальо́н

batten /'bæt(ə)n/ *n.* ре́йка, пла́нка
• *v.t.*: ~ **down** (naut.) задра́и|вать, -ть

batter¹ /'bætə(r)/ *n.* (cul.) взби́тое те́сто

batter² /'bætə(r)/ *v.t. & i.* **1** (beat) колоти́ть, по-; дуба́сить, от-; громи́ть, раз- **2** (knock about): **a** ~**ed old car/hat** потрёпанная ста́рая маши́на/шля́па

battery /'bætəri/ *n.* (elec.) (in car) батаре́я; (in torch) батаре́йка

✓ **battle** /'bæt(ə)l/ *n.* би́тва, сраже́ние, бой; (struggle) борьба́
• *v.i.* боро́ться (*impf.*); сража́ться (*impf.*)
■ ~**field**, ~**ground** *nn.* по́ле сраже́ния/бо́я; ~**ship** *n.* лине́йный кора́бль, линко́р

batty /'bætɪ/ *adj.* (**battier, battiest**) (esp. BrE, infml) чо́кнутый, тро́нутый

bauble /'bɔːb(ə)l/ *n.* (on Christmas tree) ёлочный шар; (trinket) безделу́шка

✓ ключева́я ле́ксика

b

bawdy /'bɔːdɪ/ adj. (**bawdier, bawdiest**) непристо́йный, поха́бный

bawl /bɔːl/ v.t. & i. ора́ть (impf.); выкри́кивать, вы́крикнуть; ~ at sb ора́ть на кого́-н.; ~ sb out (infml) наора́ть (pf.) на кого́-н.

bay¹ /beɪ/ n. (bot.) лавр
■ ~ leaf n. лавро́вый лист

bay² /beɪ/ n. (geog.) зали́в, бу́хта

bay³ /beɪ/ n. (fig. uses): **keep sb at** ~ держа́ть (impf.) кого́-н. на расстоя́нии
● v.i. ла́ять (impf.); залива́ться (impf.) ла́ем; выть (impf.)

bayonet /'beɪənet/ n. штык

bazaar /bə'zɑː(r)/ n. база́р

BC abbr. (of **before Christ**) до н. э. (до на́шей э́ры), до рождества́ Христо́ва

↙ **be** /biː/ v.i. (sg. pres. **am, are, is**, pl. pres. **are**, 1st and 3rd pers. sg. past **was**, 2nd pers. sg. past and pl. past **were**, pres. subjunctive **be**, past subjunctive **were**, pres. part. **being**, p.p. **been**) ① быть (impf.); (exist) существова́ть (impf.); (as copula in the pres. tense, usu. omitted or expr. by dash): **the world is round** земля́ кру́глая; **that is a dog** э́то соба́ка ② (more emphatic uses): **an order is an order** прика́з есть прика́з; **there is a God** Бог есть ③ (expr. frequency) быва́ть (impf.); **he is in London every Tuesday** он быва́ет в Ло́ндоне по вто́рникам ④ (more formally, with complement) явля́ться (impf.) + i.; представля́ть (impf.) собо́й ⑤ (expr. present continuous): **she is crying** она́ пла́чет ⑥ (of place, time, cost, etc.): **it is a mile away** э́то в ми́ле отсю́да; **where is the office?** где нахо́дится о́фис?; **he is 21 today** ему́ сего́дня исполня́ется два́дцать оди́н год; **it is 25 pounds a yard** э́то сто́ит два́дцать пять фу́нтов за ярд; (of person or obj. in a certain position) стоя́ть, лежа́ть, сиде́ть (according to sense; all impf.); **the books are on the floor** кни́ги лежа́т на полу́; **Paris is on the Seine** Пари́ж стои́т на Се́не; **he is in hospital** он лежи́т в больни́це; **I was at home all day** я сиде́л до́ма весь день; (of continuing states): **the heat was unbearable** жара́ стоя́ла невыноси́мая ⑦ (expr. motion): **has the postman been?** по́чта уже́ была́? ⑧ (become): **what are you going to** ~ **when you grow up?** кем ты ста́нешь/бу́дешь, когда́ вы́растешь? ⑨ (expr. pass.): **the house is** ~**ing built** дом стро́ится; **I am told** мне сказа́ли ⑩ (behave, act a part): **you are** ~**ing silly** вы ведёте себя́ глу́по; **am I** ~**ing a bore?** я вам надое́л? ⑪ (uses of pres. part. and gerund): ~**ing a doctor, he knew what to do** бу́дучи врачо́м, он знал, что де́лать; **for the time** ~**ing** пока́ что, на вре́мя ⑫ (**be to**): **I am to inform you** я до́лжен сообщи́ть вам; **he is to** ~ **married today** он сего́дня же́нится; **his wife to** ~ его́ бу́дущая жена́ ⑬ (var.): **how are you?** как пожива́ете?; ~ **that as it may** как бы то ни́ было

↙ **beach** /biːtʃ/ n. пляж

beacon /'biːkən/ n. (signal light, fire) сигна́льный ого́нь

bead /biːd/ n. ① бу́син(к)а; **string of** ~**s** бу́с|ы (pl., g. —) ② (drop) ка́пля

beady /'biːdɪ/ adj. (**beadier, beadiest**): ~ **eyes** глаза́-бу́синки

beak /biːk/ n. клюв

beaker /'biːkə(r)/ n. (BrE) (for drinking) пластма́ссовый стака́н (с но́сиком); (in laboratory) мензу́рка

beam¹ /biːm/ n. (of timber etc.) брус, ба́лка

beam² /biːm/ n. (ray) луч
● v.i. (shine) свети́ть (impf.), сия́ть (impf.)

bean /biːn/ n. боб; **French** ~**s** фасо́ль; **string** ~**s** зелёная фасо́ль
■ ~**bag** n. больша́я поду́шка, напо́лненная ша́риками полистиро́ла

bear¹ /beə(r)/ n. медве́дь (m.)

↙ **bear**² /beə(r)/ v.t. (past **bore**, p.p. **borne, born**) ① (carry) носи́ть (indet.), нести́ (det.); ~ **in mind** име́ть (impf.) в виду́ ② (sustain, support): **the ice will** ~ **his weight** лёд вы́держит его́ ③ (endure, tolerate) терпе́ть, с-; выноси́ть, вы́нести; сн|оси́ть, -ести́; **I cannot** ~ **him** я его́ не выношу́ ④ (be capable of): ~ **comparison** выде́рживать (impf.) сравне́ние ⑤ (give birth to): **be born** роди́ться (impf., pf.) ⑥ (yield): **trees/efforts** ~ **fruit** дере́вья/уси́лия прино́сят плоды́
● v.i. (past **bore**, p.p. **borne, born**) ① (of direction): **the road** ~**s to the right** доро́га идёт впра́во ② (exert pressure, affect): **bring one's energy to** ~ **on** напра́вить (pf.) эне́ргию на + a.; ~ **with** терпе́ть (impf.), переноси́ть (impf.)
□ ~ **out** v.t. (confirm) подтвер|жда́ть, -ди́ть
□ ~ **up** v.i. (endure) держа́ться (impf.)

bearable /'beərəb(ə)l/ adj. терпи́мый, сно́сный

beard /bɪəd/ n. борода́

bearer /'beərə(r)/ n. ① (one who carries) несу́щий, нося́щий; ~ **of good news** до́брый ве́стник; (of a cheque) предъяви́тель (m.)

bearing /'beərɪŋ/ n. ① (deportment) мане́ра держа́ться ② (relevance) отноше́ние (on: к + d.) ③ (direction): **get one's** ~**s** определ|я́ть, -и́ть своё местонахожде́ние; ориенти́роваться (impf., pf.)

beast /biːst/ n. ① (animal) живо́тное; (wild animal) зверь (m.) ② (nasty person) скоти́на (c.g.)

beastlier /'biːstlɪ/ adj. (**beastlier, beastliest**) (unpleasant) отврати́тельный; ~ **weather** ужа́сная пого́да; a ~ **headache** ме́рзкая/гну́сная головна́я боль

↙ **beat** /biːt/ n. ① (of drum) бой; (of heart) бие́ние; (rhythm) ритм; (mus.) такт ② (policeman's) райо́н обхо́да
● v.t. (past **beat**, p.p. **beaten**) ① (strike) бить, по-; ~ **eggs** взби|ва́ть, -ть я́йца; ~ **time** отбива́ть (impf.) такт; ~ **about the bush** (fig.) ходи́ть (indet.) вокру́г да о́коло ② (defeat, surpass) поб|ива́ть, -и́ть; побе|жда́ть, -ди́ть; **he** ~ **me at chess** он обыгра́л меня́ в ша́хматы; **he** ~ **the record** он поби́л реко́рд
● v.i. (past **beat**, p.p. **beaten**): **his heart is** ~**ing** его́ се́рдце бьётся; **he heard drums** ~**ing** он слы́шал бараба́нный бой; **the rain** ~ **against the windows** дождь стуча́л в о́кна
□ ~ **back** v.t. отб|ива́ть, -и́ть
□ ~ **down** v.i.: **the sun** ~ **down on us** со́лнце

нещáдно палúло нас

□ **~ off** v.t.: **~ off an attack** отб|ивáть, -úть атáку

□ **~ up** v.t.: **~ sb up** изб|ивáть, -úть когó-н.

beating /'biːtɪŋ/ n. **1** (of heart) биéние **2** (thrashing) пóрка

beautician /bjuː'tɪʃ(ə)n/ n. космéтолог

✓ **beautiful** /'bjuːtɪfʊl/ adj. красú|вый; (excellent) прекрáсный

✓ **beauty** /'bjuːtɪ/ n. (quality) красотá
■ **~ salon** n. космети́ческий кабинéт; **~ spot** n. (BrE, place) живопи́сная мéстность

beaver /'biːvə(r)/ n. (pl. **~** or **~s**) (zool.) бобр

becalm /bɪ'kɑːm/ v.t.: **be ~ed** (naut.) штилевáть (impf.); заштил|евáть, -éть; a **~ed ship** корáбль, попáвший в штиль

became /bɪ'keɪm/ past of ▶ **become**

✓ **because** /bɪ'kɒz/ conj. потомý что; **~ of** из-за + g., (thanks to) благодаря́ + d.

beckon /'bekən/ v.t. & i. манú|ть, по-; заз|ывáть, -вáть; **I ~ed (to) him to approach** я поманúл егó к себé

✓ **become** /bɪ'kʌm/ v.i. (past **became**, p.p. **become**) (come to be) стá|новиться, -ть + i.; (often expr. by v. in ...еть): **~ smaller** умéньшиться (pf.); **what became of him?** что с ним стáлось?; **he became a waiter** он стал официáнтом

✓ **bed** /bed/ n. **1** (esp. bedstead) кровáть; (esp. bedding) постéль; **go to ~** ложúться, лечь спать; (in sexual sense) переспáть (pf.) (**with:** с + i.); **get into ~** ложúться, лечь в постéль/кровáть; **get out of ~** вста|вáть, -ть с постéли/кровáти; **make a ~** уб|ирáть, -рáть, постéль **2** (of the sea) дно; (of a river) рýсло **3**: **~ of flowers** клýмба
■ **~ and breakfast** n. (guest house) мáленькая гостúница; **~ridden** adj. прикóванный к постéли; **~room** n. спáльня; **~side** n.: **keep books at one's ~side** держáть (impf.) кнúги на ночнóм стóлике; **~sit** n. (BrE) однокóмнатная квартúра; **~spread** n. покрывáло; **~time** n. врéмя ложúться/идтú спать

bedevil /bɪ'dev(ə)l/ v.t. (**bedevilled, bedevilling**, AmE **bedeviled, bedeviling**) (cause) спýт|ывать, -ать; вн|осúть, -естú неразберúху в + a.

bedlam /'bedləm/ n. (fig.) бедлáм (infml)

bedraggled /bɪ'dræg(ə)ld/ adj. забрýзганный

bee /biː/ n. пчелá
■ **~hive** n. ýлей

beech /biːtʃ/ n. бук

beef /biːf/ n. говя́дина
■ **~burger** n. рýбленый бифштéкс

beefy /'biːfɪ/ adj. (**beefier, beefiest**) мускулúстый

been /biːn/ p.p. of ▶ **be**

beep /biːp/ n. гудóк
● v.i. гудéть, за-

beer /bɪə(r)/ n. пúво

beet /biːt/ n. свёкла
■ **~root** n. (BrE) свёкла

✓ ключевáя лéксика

beetle /'biːt(ə)l/ n. (zool.) жук

befall /bɪ'fɔːl/ v.t. & i. (past **befell** /bɪ'fel/; p.p. **befallen** /bɪ'fɔːlən/) (liter.) приключ|áться, -úться (с + i.); пост|игáть, -úгнуть (когó/что); **what has ~en him?** что с ним стáло?

befit /bɪ'fɪt/ v.t. (**befitted, befitting**) под|ходúть, -ойтú + d.

✓ **before** /bɪ'fɔː(r)/ adv. рáньше; **six weeks ~** шестью́ недéлями рáньше
● prep. **1** (of time) пéред + i.; (earlier than) до + g.; **~ the war** до войны́; **the week ~ last** позапрóшлая недéля; **don't come ~ I call you** не приходúте, покá я вас не позовý **2** (of place) пéред + i.; впередú + g.; **~ my eyes** на мойх глазáх
● conj. (earlier than) рáньше чем; (immediately ~) прéжде/пéред тем, как; (at a previous time) до тогó как; **do it ~ you forget** сдéлайте э́то, покá не забы́ли; **it will be years ~ we meet** пройдýт гóды, прéжде чем мы встрéтимся; **just ~ you arrived** пéред сáмым вáшим прихóдом
■ **~hand** adv. зарáнее

befriend /bɪ'frend/ v.t. дрýжески отн|осúться, -естúсь к + d.; помогáть (impf.) + d.

befuddle /bɪ'fʌd(ə)l/ v.t. одурмáни|вать, -ть

beg /beg/ v.t. (**begged, begging**) просú|ть, по-; умоля́ть (impf.); **~ sb to do sth** умоля́ть (impf.) когó-н. сдéлать что-н.
● v.i. (**begged, begging**) **1** (ask for charity) просúть мúлостыню, нúщенствовать (both impf.) **2**: **~ for sth** умоля́|ть, -úть о + p.; выпрáшивать, вы́просить что-н.

began /bɪ'gæn/ past of ▶ **begin**

beggar /'begə(r)/ n. нúщий

✓ **begin** /bɪ'gɪn/ v.t. (**beginning**, past **began**, p.p. **begun**) нач|инáть, -áть; **he began the meeting** он откры́л собрáние; (often translated by prefix за-): **~ to sing** запéть (pf.); **he began to cry** он заплáкал
● v.i. нач|инáть(ся), -áть(ся); **the meeting began** собрáние началóсь; **he began as a reporter** он начинáл репортёром; **to ~ with** во-пéрвых

beginner /bɪ'gɪnə(r)/ n. начинáющий

✓ **beginning** /bɪ'gɪnɪŋ/ n. начáло; **at the ~ of April** в начáле (or в пéрвых чúслах) апрéля

begonia /bɪ'gəʊnɪə/ n. бегóния

begrudge /bɪ'grʌdʒ/ v.t. (envy sb for having sth) завúдовать, по- (чему); **I ~ him his success** я завúдую егó успéхам; (give resentfully) **I ~ the time** мне жаль врéмени

beguile /bɪ'gaɪl/ v.t. (charm) очарóв|ывать, -áть

begun /bɪ'gʌn/ p.p. of ▶ **begin**

✓ **behalf** /bɪ'hɑːf/ n.: **on my ~** (as my representative) от моегó úмени/лицá; (for my benefit) в мойх интерéсах, в мою́ пóльзу

behave /bɪ'heɪv/ v.i. вестú (det.) себя́, держáться (impf.); **~ well, ~ oneself** вестú себя́ хорошó; **~ badly** плóхо поступ|áть, -úть

✓ **behaviour** /bɪ'heɪvjə(r)/ (AmE **behavior**) n. поведéние; отношéние (к кому); обращéние (с кем)

behead /bɪ'hed/ v.t. обезглáв|ливать, -ить

beheld /bɪˈheld/ *past and p.p. of* ▶ **behold**

behind /bɪˈhaɪnd/ *n.* (infml) зад, за́дница
● *adv.* сза́ди, позади́; **he is** ~ **in his studies** он отста́л в учёбе; **he is** ~ **with his payments** он запа́здывает с упла́той
● *prep.* (expr. place) за + *i.*; (expr. motion) за + *a.*; (more emphatic) сза́ди, позади́ + *g.*; (after) по́сле + *g.*; **he walked (just)** ~ **me** он шёл сле́дом за мной

behold /bɪˈhəʊld/ *v.t.* (*past and p.p.* **beheld**) (archaic) узре́ть (*pf.*); **lo and** ~! о чу́до!

beige /beɪʒ/ *adj.* бе́жевый

Beijing /beɪˈdʒɪŋ/ *n.* Пеки́н

being /ˈbiːɪŋ/ *n.* **1** (existence) бытие́, существова́ние; **come into** ~ возн|ика́ть, -и́кнуть **2** (creature, person) существо́; **human** ~ челове́к

Beirut /beɪˈruːt/ *n.* Бейру́т

Belarus /belʌˈruːs/ *n.* Белару́сь, Белору́ссия

Belarusian /belʌˈruːsɪən, belʌˈrʌʃ(ə)n/ *n.* (person) белору́с (-ка); (language) белору́сский язы́к
● *adj.* белору́сский

belated /bɪˈleɪtɪd/ *adj.* запозда́лый

belch /beltʃ/ *n.* отры́жка
● *v.t.* (*also* ~ **forth, out**) (smoke etc.) выбра́сывать, вы́бросить
● *v.i.* рыг|а́ть, -ну́ть

beleaguered /bɪˈliːgəd/ *adj.* осаждённый

belfry /ˈbelfrɪ/ *n.* колоко́льня

Belgian /ˈbeldʒ(ə)n/ *n.* бельги́|ец (-йка)
● *adj.* бельги́йский

Belgium /ˈbeldʒəm/ *n.* Бе́льгия

Belgrade /belˈgreɪd/ *n.* Белгра́д

belief /bɪˈliːf/ *n.* **1** (trust) ве́ра (**in:** в + *a.*); дове́рие (**in:** к + *d.*) **2** (acceptance as true; thing believed) ве́ра, ве́рование; **the** ~**s of the Christian church** до́гмы (*nt. pl.*) христиа́нской це́ркви

believe /bɪˈliːv/ *v.t.* ве́рить, по- (*кому, чему*); ду́мать (*impf.*); **I** ~ **so** ду́маю, что э́то так
● *v.i.* ве́рить (*impf.*) (*во что, кого*); ~ **in God** ве́рить (*impf.*) в Бо́га (as a religious believer) ве́ровать (*impf.*); **I** ~ **in taking exercise** я ве́рю в по́льзу заря́дки

believer /bɪˈliːvə(r)/ *n.* **1** (relig.) ве́рующий **2** (advocate) сторо́нни|к (-ца) + *g.*

belittle /bɪˈlɪt(ə)l/ *v.t.* преум|еньша́ть, -е́ньшить; умал|я́ть, -и́ть

bell /bel/ *n.* **1** ко́локол; (smaller) колоко́льчик; (of door, telephone, bicycle, etc.) звоно́к; **ring the** ~ звони́ть (*impf.*) в звоно́к/ко́локол; **that rings a** ~ (fig., infml) э́то мне что́-то припомина́ю

bellicose /ˈbelɪkəʊz/ *adj.* войнственный

belligerent /bɪˈlɪdʒərənt/ *adj.* войнственный

bellow /ˈbeləʊ/ *v.i.* **1** (of animal) мыча́ть, про-; реве́ть (*impf.*) **2** (shout) ора́ть (*impf.*)

bellows /ˈbeləʊz/ *n. pl.* мехи́ (*m. pl.*)

belly /ˈbelɪ/ *n.* живо́т, брю́хо (infml)
■ ~ **button** *n.* (infml) пупо́к

belong /bɪˈlɒŋ/ *v.i.* **1** ~ **to** (be the property of) принадлежа́ть (*impf.*) + *d.*; (be a member of) состоя́ть (*impf.*) в + *p.* **2** (of place): **these**

---

books ~ **here** э́ти кни́ги стоя́т здесь; э́ти кни́ги отсю́да

belongings /bɪˈlɒŋɪŋz/ *n. pl.* ве́щи (*f. pl.*), пожи́тк|и (-ов)

Belorussia /beləʊˈrʌʃə/ *n.* = **Belarus**

Belorussian /beləʊˈrʌʃ(ə)n/ *n., adj.* = **Belarusian**

beloved /bɪˈlʌvɪd/ *n.* возлю́бленн|ый (-ая)
● *adj.* возлю́бленный, люби́мый

below /bɪˈləʊ/ *adv.* (of place) внизу́; (of motion) вниз; (in text etc.) ни́же; **from** ~ сни́зу
● *prep.* (of place) под + *i.*; (of motion) под + *a.*; (lower, downstream) ни́же + *g.*; **he is** ~ **average height** он ни́же сре́днего ро́ста

belt /belt/ *n.* **1** (of leather etc.) реме́нь (*m.*); (of cloth) по́яс (-á) **2** (zone) по́яс, полоса́; **green** ~ зелёный по́яс, зелёная зо́на **3** (tech.) (приводно́й) реме́нь
● *v.t.* **1** (thrash) поро́ть, вы- **2** ~ **out a song** горла́нить (*impf.*) пе́сню

bemuse /bɪˈmjuːz/ *v.t.* ошелом|ля́ть, -и́ть

bench /bentʃ/ *n.* **1** (seat) скамья́, ла́вка **2** (work table) верста́к, стано́к **3** (judges) су́дьи (*m. pl.*), суде́йская колле́гия
■ ~**mark** *n.* этало́н, станда́рт; ~**mark test** эта́лонный тест

bend /bend/ *n.* (curve) изги́б; (in road) поворо́т; (in river) излу́чина
● *v.t.* (*past and p.p.* **bent**) (twist, incline): ~ **an iron bar** изгиба́ть, -огну́ть желе́зный брус; **the axle is bent** ось погну́лась; ~ **one's head over a book** скло́н|я́ться, -и́ться над кни́гой
● *v.i.*: **the trees bent in the wind** дере́вья гну́лись на ветру́; ~ **at the knees** сгиба́ться, согну́ться в коле́нях; ~ **forward** наклон|я́ться, -и́ться (вперёд)
□ ~ **down** *v.t.* наг|иба́ть, -ну́ть; сгиба́ть, согну́ть; преклон|я́ть, -и́ть
● *v.i.* (*also* ~ **over**) наг|иба́ться, -ну́ться; перег|иба́ться, -ну́ться

beneath /bɪˈniːθ/ *adv.* внизу́
● *prep.* (of place) под + *i.*; (of motion) под + *a.*; (lower than) ни́же + *g.*; **it is** ~ **you to complain** жа́ловаться — недосто́йно вас

benefactor /ˈbenɪfæktə(r)/ *n.* благотвори́тель (*m.*) (-ница)

beneficial /benɪˈfɪʃ(ə)l/ *adj.* благотво́рный, поле́зный, вы́годный

beneficiary /benɪˈfɪʃərɪ/ *n.* (law) бенефициа́р(ий) (получа́тель де́нег/дохо́дов от чего-л./кого-л.)

benefit /ˈbenɪfɪt/ *n.* **1** (advantage) по́льза, вы́года, преиму́щество; **give sb the** ~ **of one's advice** помо́чь (*pf.*) кому́-н. сове́том; **I gave him the** ~ **of the doubt** я ему́ пове́рил (на э́тот раз) **2** (grant) посо́бие; **unemployment** ~ посо́бие по безрабо́тице
● *v.t.* (**benefited, benefiting**, AmE **benefitted, benefitting**) прин|оси́ть, -ести́ по́льзу + *d.*, идти́ (*det.*) на по́льзу + *d.*
● *v.i.* (**benefited, benefiting**, AmE **benefitted, benefitting**) извл|ека́ть, -е́чь по́льзу (**from:** из + *g.*)

benevolent /bəˈnevələnt/ *adj.* благожела́тельный

benign /bɪˈnaɪn/ *adj.* (of person) добросердéчный; (med.) доброкáчественный

bent /bent/ *past and p.p. of* ▶ bend

bequeath /bɪˈkwiːð/ *v.t.* завещáть (*impf., pf.*)

bequest /bɪˈkwest/ *n.* (object) вещь, остáвленная в наслéдство; (as part of museum collection) фонд, посмéртный дар; (act) акт завещáния; leave a ~ of завещáть (*impf., pf.*)

berate /bɪˈreɪt/ *v.t.* бранúть (*impf.*)

bereave /bɪˈriːv/ *v.t.*: a ~d husband недáвно овдовéвший муж; the ~d (*as pl.*) рóдственники покóйного

bereavement /bɪˈriːvmənt/ *n.* тяжёлая утрáта/потéря

beret /ˈbereɪ/ *n.* берéт

Bering Sea /ˈbeərɪŋ/ *n.* Бéрингово мóре

Berlin /bəˈlɪn/ *n.* Берлúн

Bermuda /bəˈmjuːdə/ *n.* (*also* (*pl.*) the ~s) Бермýдские островá (*m. pl.*)
■ ~ **shorts** *n. pl.* шóрты-бермýды

berry /ˈberɪ/ *n.* ягода

berserk /bəˈzɜːk/ *n.*: go ~ разъярúться (*pf.*), обезýметь (*pf.*)

berth /bɜːθ/ *n.* **1** (place at wharf) прúстань, причáл **2**: give sb a wide ~ (fig.) обходúть (*impf.*) когó-н. сторонóй (*or* за верстý) **3** (sleeping place on ship) кóйка; (on train) спáльное мéсто
● *v.t.* стáвить (*impf.*) к причáлу
● *v.i.* причáли|вать, -ть

beseech /bɪˈsiːtʃ/ *v.t.* (*past and p.p.* **besought** /bɪˈsɔːt/ *or* **beseeched**) умоля|ть, -́ить; молúть (*impf.*)

beset /bɪˈset/ *v.t.* (**besetting**, *past and p.p.* **beset**) окруж|áть, -úть; осаж|дáть, -дúть

beside /bɪˈsaɪd/ *prep.* **1** (alongside) рядом с + *i.*; (near) óколо + *g.*, у + *g.* **2** (compared with) по сравнéнию с + *i.*; пéред + *i.*; ~ him all novelists are insignificant по сравнéнию с ним все романúсты ничегó не стóят **3**: ~ oneself вне себя

besides /bɪˈsaɪdz/ *adv.* сверх тогó; крóме тогó
● *prep.* крóме + *g.*

besiege /bɪˈsiːdʒ/ *v.t.* осаж|дáть, -дúть

besotted /bɪˈsɒtɪd/ *adj.* одурмáненный; во влáсти (**with**: + *g.*)

besought /bɪˈsɔːt/ *past and p.p. of* ▶ beseech

best /best/ *adj.* лýчший; we are the ~ of friends мы бли́жайшие друзья; at ~ в лýчшем слýчае; do one's ~ сдéлать (*pf.*) всё возмóжное; all the ~! всегó наилýчшего!; hope for the ~ надéяться (*impf.*) на лýчшее
● *adv.* лýчше всегó; I work ~ in the evening мне лýчше всегó рабóтается по вечерáм; you know ~ вам лýчше знать; which town did you like ~? какóй гóрод вам бóльше всегó понрáвился?
■ ~ **man** *n.* (at wedding) шáфер; ~**seller** *n.* (book) бестсéллер; (BrE, author) áвтор бестсéллера; ~**selling** *adj.* ходовóй

bestow /bɪˈstəʊ/ *v.t.*: ~ a title on sb присвá|ивать, -óить комý-н. тúтул

bet /bet/ *n.* парú (*nt. indecl.*), стáвка
● *v.t. & i.* (**betting**, *past and p.p.* **bet** *or* **betted**) держáть (*impf.*) парú; he ~ £5 on a horse он постáвил 5 фýнтов на лóшадь; he ~ me £10 I wouldn't do it он поспóрил со мной на 10 фýнтов, что я не сдéлаю этого
■ ~**ting shop** *n.* (BrE) букмéкерская контóра

betray /bɪˈtreɪ/ *v.t.* измен|я́ть, -ить + *d.*; пред|авáть, -áть

betrayal /bɪˈtreɪəl/ *n.* предáтельство, измéна

better /ˈbetə(r)/ *adj.* лýчший, лýчше; all the ~ тем лýчше; get ~ ул|учшáться, -ýчшиться; (in health) попр|авля́ться, -áвиться; things are getting ~ делá идýт лýчше; get the ~ of sb взять (*pf.*) верх над кем-н.; превзойтú (*pf.*) когó-н.
● *adv.* лýчше; (more) бóльше; you had ~ stay here вам бы лýчше остáться здесь; I thought ~ of it я раздýмал/передýмал; ~ off состоя́тельный
● *v.t.* (improve on) превзойтú (*pf.*)

between /bɪˈtwiːn/ *adv.*: I attended the two lectures and had lunch in ~ я посетúл две лéкции и пообéдал в перерыве
● *prep.* мéжду + *i.*; ~ you and me мéжду нáми; ~ two and three months от двух до трёх мéсяцев; choose ~ the two выбирáть, выбрать однó из двух; we bought a car ~ us мы сообщá купúли машúну

beverage /ˈbevərɪdʒ/ *n.* напúток

bevy /ˈbevɪ/ *n.* грýппа

beware /bɪˈweə(r)/ *v.t. & i.* остер|егáться, -éчься (*impf.*) + *g.*; ~ of the dog осторóжно, злáя собáка

bewilder /bɪˈwɪldə(r)/ *v.t.* сби|вáть, -ть с тóлку; прив|одúть, -естú в замешáтельство; ~ed смущённый, озадáченный

bewilderment /bɪˈwɪldəmənt/ *n.* замешáтельство, озадáченность

bewitch /bɪˈwɪtʃ/ *v.t.* околдóв|ывать, -áть

beyond /bɪˈjɒnd/ *n.*: he lives at the back of ~ он живёт на краю свéта
● *adv.* вдалú; вдаль
● *prep.* (of place) за + *i.*; (of motion) за + *a.*; (later than) пóсле + *g.*; ~ dispute бесспóрно; ~ belief невероя́тно; live ~ one's means жить (*impf.*) не по срéдствам

biannual /baɪˈænjʊəl/ *adj.* выходя́щий двáжды в год; полугодовóй

bias /ˈbaɪəs/ *n.* предрассýдок, предвзя́тое отношéние (к чему)
● *v.t.* (**biased, biasing** *or* **biassed, biassing**) (influence) склон|я́ть, -úть; (prejudice) предубе|ждáть, -дúть; a ~(s)ed opinion предвзя́тое мнéние

bib /bɪb/ *n.* (дéтский) нагрýдник

Bible /ˈbaɪb(ə)l/ *n.* Бúблия; (fig.) бúблия

biblical /ˈbɪblɪk(ə)l/ *adj.* библéйский

bibliographer /bɪblɪˈɒgrəfə(r)/ *n.* библиóграф

bibliographic /bɪblɪəˈgræfɪk/, **bibliographical** /bɪblɪəˈgræfɪk(ə)l/ *adjs.* библиографúческий

bibliography /bɪblɪˈɒgrəfɪ/ *n.* библиогрáфия

bicentenary /baɪsen'tiːnəri/ *n.* двухсотлётие
bicentennial /baɪsen'teniəl/ *n.* двухсотлётие
biceps /'baɪseps/ *n.* (*pl.* ~) би́цепс
bicker /'bɪkə(r)/ *v.t.* (squabble) перебра́ниваться (*impf.*), препира́ться (*impf.*)
bicycle /'baɪsɪk(ə)l/ *n.* велосипе́д
✛ **bid** /bɪd/ *n.* **1** (at auction) зая́вка; предложе́ние цены́ **2** (tender) зая́вка **3** (attempt) ста́вка; попы́тка; **make a** ~ **for power** сде́лать (*pf.*) ста́вку на захва́т вла́сти
• *v.t. & i.* (**bidding**, *past* **bid**, *p.p.* **bid**) **1** (at auction) предлага́ть, -ожи́ть це́ну (*за что*); ~ **against sb** набавля́ть, -а́вить це́ну про́тив кого́-н. **2** (tender): ~ **for a contract** де́лать, с- зая́вку на контра́кт
bidder /'bɪdə(r)/ *n.* (at auction) аукционе́р; **the highest** ~ предложи́вший наивы́сшую це́ну
bide /baɪd/ *v.t.*: ~ **one's time** ждать (*impf.*) благоприя́тного слу́чая
bidet /'biːdeɪ/ *n.* биде́ (*nt. indecl.*)
biennial /baɪ'eniəl/ *n.* (bot.) двуле́тник
• *adj.* двухле́тний
bifocal /baɪ'fəʊk(ə)l/ *adj.*: ~ **spectacles** (*also* ~**s** *pl.*) бифока́льные очки́
✛ **big** /bɪg/ *adj.* (**bigger, biggest**) (in size) большо́й, кру́пный; (great) кру́пный, вели́кий; (magnanimous) великоду́шный; (important) ва́жный; **a** ~ **man** (in stature) кру́пный мужчи́на; (in importance) кру́пная фигу́ра; **as** ~ **as** величино́й в + *a.*; **think** ~ мы́слить (*impf.*) сме́ло/де́рзко; **a** ~ **noise** (person) ши́шка (infml); **my** ~ **brother** мой ста́рший брат; **a** ~ **name** (celebrity) знамени́тость
■ ~**-headed** *adj.* (conceited) зазна́вшийся; возомни́вший о себе́; ~**-hearted** *adj.* великоду́шный; ~ **society** *n.* (pol.) *концепция управления общественной жизни в стране посредством органов добровольного местного самоуправления*; ~**wig** *n.* (infml) ши́шка (*важный человек*)
bigamy /'bɪgəmi/ *n.* бига́мия; (of man) двоежёнство; (of woman) двоему́жие
bigoted /'bɪgətɪd/ *adj.* фанати́ческий, фанати́чный
bike /baɪk/ *n.* **1** (infml) = **bicycle 2** (motorcycle) мотоци́кл
• *v.i.* е́здить (*indet.*) на мотоци́кле
biker /'baɪkə(r)/ *n.* мотоцикли́ст (-ка); (member of a gang) ба́йкер
bikini /bɪ'kiːni/ *n.* (*pl.* ~**s**) бики́ни (*nt. indecl.*)
bilateral /baɪ'lætər(ə)l/ *adj.* двусторо́нний
bilberry /'bɪlbəri/ *n.* черни́ка (*collect.*); (single berry) я́года черни́ки
bilingual /baɪ'lɪŋgw(ə)l/ *adj.* двуязы́чный
bill¹ /bɪl/ *n.* (beak) клюв
✛ **bill²** /bɪl/ *n.* **1** (comm.) счёт **2** (pol.) законопрое́кт, билль (*m.*) **3** (advertisement): **theatre** ~ театра́льная афи́ша **4** (AmE, banknote) банкно́та; **dollar** ~ до́лларовая банкно́та
■ ~**board** *n.* доска́ объявле́ний
billet /'bɪlɪt/ *v.t.* (**billeted, billeting**) (assign to ~) расквартиро́в|ывать, -а́ть; назн|ача́ть,

-а́чить (*or* ста́вить, по-) на посто́й (**on sb:** к + *d.*)
billiards /'bɪljədz/ *n.* билья́рд
✛ **billion** /'bɪljən/ *n.* (*pl.* ~**s** *or* (with numeral or qualifying word) ~) (10⁹, thousand million) миллиа́рд
billionaire /bɪljə'neə(r)/ *n.* миллиарде́р
billow /'bɪləʊ/ *v.i.* (of smoke) вздыма́ться (*impf.*); (of fabric) над|ува́ться, -у́ться
bin /bɪn/ *n.* (BrE) му́сорное ведро́
binary /'baɪnəri/ *adj.* (math.) двои́чный
bind /baɪnd/ *v.t.* (*past and p.p.* **bound**) **1** (tie, fasten) свя́з|ывать, -а́ть; ~ **together** свя́з|ывать, -а́ть **2** (books etc.) перепле|та́ть, -сти́ **3** (oblige, exact promise) обя́з|ывать, -а́ть; **I am bound to say** я до́лжен сказа́ть
binder /'baɪndə(r)/ *n.* па́пка
binding /'baɪndɪŋ/ *n.* переплёт
• *adj.* обя́зывающий; име́ющий обяза́тельную си́лу
binge /bɪndʒ/ *n.* (infml) пья́нка; **go on the** ~ закути́ть, запи́ть (*both pf.*)
■ ~ **drinking** *n.* попо́йка, пья́нка
bingo /'bɪŋgəʊ/ *n.* лото́ (*nt. indecl.*)
binoculars /bɪ'nɒkjʊləz/ *n. pl.* бино́кль (*m.*)
biochemist /baɪəʊ'kemɪst/ *n.* биохи́мик
biochemistry /baɪəʊ'kemɪstri/ *n.* биохи́мия
biodegradable /baɪəʊdɪ'greɪdəb(ə)l/ *adj.* по́ртящийся под де́йствием микрооргани́змов
biodiversity /baɪəʊdaɪ'vɜːsɪti/ *n.* биологи́ческое разнообра́зие
bioengineering /baɪəʊendʒɪ'nɪərɪŋ/ *n.* биоинжене́рия
biographer /baɪ'ɒgrəfə(r)/ *n.* био́граф
biographical /baɪə'græfɪk(ə)l/ *adj.* биографи́ческий
biography /baɪ'ɒgrəfi/ *n.* биогра́фия
biological /baɪə'lɒdʒɪk(ə)l/ *adj.* биологи́ческий
■ ~ **clock** *n.* биологи́ческие часы́; ~ **warfare** *n.* бактериологи́ческая война́
biologist /baɪ'ɒlədʒɪst/ *n.* био́лог
biology /baɪ'ɒlədʒɪ/ *n.* биоло́гия
biometric /baɪəʊ'metrɪk/ *adj.* биометри́ческий
biopsy /'baɪɒpsɪ/ *n.* биопси́я
biotechnology /baɪəʊtek'nɒlədʒɪ/ *n.* биотехноло́гия
bipartisan /baɪpɑː'tɪzæn/ *adj.* двухпарти́йный
bipartite /baɪ'pɑːtaɪt/ *adj.* (divided into two parts) состоя́щий из двух часте́й; (shared by two parties) двусторо́нний
bipolar /baɪ'pəʊlə(r)/ *adj.* (phys.) двухполя́рный, биполя́рный
■ ~ **disorder** *n.* (med.) биполя́рное аффекти́вное расстро́йство
birch /bɜːtʃ/ *n.* берёза
✛ **bird** /bɜːd/ *n.* пти́ца
■ ~ **flu** *n.* пти́чий грипп; ~ **of prey** *n.* хи́щная пти́ца; ~**'s-eye view** *n.* вид с высоты́ пти́чьего полёта; о́бщая перспекти́ва; ~**watcher** *n.* орнито́лог-люби́тель (*m.*)
biro® /'baɪərəʊ/ *n.* (*pl.* ~**s**) (BrE) ша́риковая ру́чка

b

↙ **birth** /bɜ:θ/ n. **1** (being born) рожде́ние; (giving birth) ро́ды (pl.) **2** (descent): **an Englishman by ~** англича́нин по происхожде́нию
■ **~ certificate** n. свиде́тельство о рожде́нии; **~ control** n. регули́рование рожда́емости; (contraception) противозача́точные ме́ры (f. pl.); **~mark** n. роди́мое пятно́; **~place** n. ме́сто рожде́ния; ро́дина; **~ rate** n. рожда́емость

birthday /'bɜ:θdeɪ/ n. день рожде́ния

↙ **biscuit** /'bɪskɪt/ n. (BrE) пече́нье; (AmE) ≈ бу́лочка

bisect /baɪ'sekt/ v.t. дели́ть, раз- попола́м

bisexual /baɪ'sekʃʊəl/ adj. бисексуа́льный

bishop /'bɪʃəp/ n. (eccl.) епи́скоп; (chess) слон

bison /'baɪs(ə)n/ n. (pl. ~) бизо́н

bistro /'bi:strəʊ/ n. (pl. ~s) бистро́ (nt. indecl.)

↙ **bit**[1] /bɪt/ n. **1** кусо́к, кусо́чек; **a ~ of paper** листо́к бума́ги **2** (abstract uses): **a ~ of news** но́вость; **a ~ of advice** сове́т; **I am a ~ late** я немно́го опозда́л; **~ by ~** ма́ло-пома́лу; **a ~ of a coward** трусова́тый

bit[2] /bɪt/ n. (comput.) бит

bit[3] /bɪt/ n. (of bridle) уд|ила́ (-и́л)

bit[4] /bɪt/ past of ▸ **bite**

bitch /bɪtʃ/ n. **1** (female dog) су́ка **2** (infml, spiteful woman) су́ка (vulg.), сте́рва (sl.)

bitchy /'bɪtʃɪ/ adj. (**bitchier, bitchiest**) (infml) стерво́зный

bite /baɪt/ n. **1** (act of biting) куса́ние **2** (mouthful): **I haven't had a ~ to eat** у меня́ куска́ не́ было во рту **3** (wound caused by biting) уку́с
● v.t. (past **bit**, p.p. **bitten**) **1** куса́ть, укуси́ть **2** (fig.): **~ sb's head off** откуси́ть (pf.) кому́-н. го́лову
● v.i. (past **bit**, p.p. **bitten**): **does your dog ~?** ва́ша соба́ка куса́ется?; **the fish won't ~** ры́ба не клюёт

biting /'baɪtɪŋ/ adj. (of wind) ре́зкий; (of satire) е́дкий, язви́тельный

bitten /'bɪt(ə)n/ p.p. of ▸ **bite**

bitter /'bɪtə(r)/ adj. (lit., fig.) го́рький; **a ~ wind** ре́зкий ве́тер; **~ enemy** зле́йший/закля́тый враг; **to the ~ end** до са́мого конца́

bivouac /'bɪvʊæk/ n. откры́тый ла́герь (без пала́ток и тенто́в), бива́к
● v.i. (**bivouacked, bivouacking**) распол|ага́ться, -ожи́ться откры́тым ла́герем, бива́ком

bizarre /bɪ'zɑ:(r)/ adj. чудно́й; (behaviour) чудакова́тый

↙ **black** /blæk/ n. **1** (colour) чернота́, чёрное; **be in the ~** не име́ть долго́в **2** (person) черноко́жий
● adj. **1** (colour) чёрный; **a ~ eye** подби́тый глаз **2** (person) черноко́жий **3**: **~ and white** чёрно-бе́лый; **in ~ and white** (in writing) чёрным по бе́лому
● v.i.: **~ out** (lose consciousness) теря́ть, по- созна́ние
■ **~berry** n. (plant; berries) ежеви́ка (collect.); (single berry) я́года ежеви́ки; **~bird** n. чёрный дрозд; **~board** n. кла́ссная доска́; **~currant**

n. чёрная сморо́дина; **~head** n. у́горь (m.); **~ ice** n. гололе́дица; **~mail** n. шанта́ж, вымога́тельство ● v.t. шантажи́ровать (impf.); **~mailer** n. шантажи́ст, вымога́тель (m.); **~ market** n. чёрный ры́нок; **~out** n. (in wartime) затемне́ние; (electricity failure) авари́йное отключе́ние электроэне́ргии; (loss of consciousness) поте́ря созна́ния; **B~ Sea** n. Чёрное мо́ре; **~smith** n. кузне́ц; **~ tie** n. (bow tie) чёрный га́лстук-ба́бочка; (evening dress) стро́гий вече́рний костю́м

blacken /'blækən/ v.t. (reputation) черни́ть, о-

bladder /'blædə(r)/ n. пузы́рь (m.)

blade /bleɪd/ n. **1** (of knife etc.) ле́звие **2** (of oar etc.) ло́пасть, лопа́тка **3** (of grass etc.) были́нка, стебелёк

↙ **blame** /bleɪm/ n. (censure) порица́ние; осужде́ние; (fault) вина́
● v.t. порица́ть (impf.); вини́ть (impf.); осу|жда́ть, -ди́ть (кого́ за что); **he was ~d for the mistake** вину́ за оши́бку возложи́ли на него́; **he is entirely to ~** э́то по́лностью его́ вина́; **~ sth on sb** взва́л|ивать, -и́ть вину́ за что-н. на кого́-н.

blameless /'bleɪmlɪs/ adj. безупре́чный; неви́нный

bland /blænd/ adj. (mild) мя́гкий; (insipid) пре́сный

blank /blæŋk/ n. про́пуск; **my mind is a ~ on this subject** у меня́ э́то вы́летело из головы́
● adj. **1** (empty): **a ~ sheet of paper** чи́стый лист бума́ги; **a ~ cheque** незапо́лненный чек; (fig.) карт-бла́нш **2** (fig.): **look ~** (of person) вы́глядеть (impf.) озада́ченным

blanket /'blæŋkɪt/ n. одея́ло; (horse ~) попо́на; **the hills lay under a ~ of snow** холмы́ бы́ли покры́ты сло́ем сне́га

blankly /'blæŋklɪ/ adv. бессмы́сленно, ту́по

blare /bleə(r)/ v.t. (**~ out**) труби́ть, про-
● v.i. труби́ть, про-; реве́ть (impf.)

blaspheme /blæs'fi:m/ v.t. (revile) поноси́ть (impf.), хули́ть (impf.)
● v.i. богоху́льствовать (impf.), богоху́льничать (impf.)

blasphemous /'blæsfiməs/ adj. богоху́льный

blasphemy /'blæsfimɪ/ n. богоху́льство

blast /blɑ:st/ n. **1**: **~ of wind** поры́в ве́тра **2** (from explosion) взрыв **3**: **at full ~** (fig.) в по́лном разга́ре; по́лным хо́дом
● v.t. взрыва́ть, -орва́ть
● v.i.: **~ off** (rocketry) взлет|а́ть, -е́ть; старт|ова́ть (impf., pf.)
■ **~-off** n. взлёт; моме́нт ста́рта

blatant /'bleɪt(ə)nt/ adj. (flagrant) я́вный, вопию́щий

blaze[1] /bleɪz/ n. **1** (of fire) пла́мя (nt.) **2** (fig.): **~e of publicity** шу́мная рекла́ма
● v.i.: **a fire was ~ing in the hearth** в ками́не пыла́л ого́нь; **the building was ~ing** зда́ние полыха́ло
□ **~e up** v.i. взл|ётывать, -ыхнуть (lit., fig.)

blaze[2] /bleɪz/ v.t.: **~ a trail** про|кла́дывать, -ложи́ть путь

b

blazer /'bleɪzə(r)/ *n.* ≈ ку́ртка, (клу́бный/ шко́льный) пиджа́к, бле́йзер

bleach /bliːtʃ/ *n.* отбе́ливатель (*m.*)
• *v.t.* бели́ть (*impf.*); отбе́л|ивать, -и́ть; (hair) обесцве́|чивать, -тить
• *v.i.* беле́ть (*impf.*)

bleak /bliːk/ *adj.* уны́лый, безра́достный; (gloomy) мра́чный

bleary-eyed /blɪə(r)/ *adj.* с затума́ненными/ му́тными глаза́ми

bleat /bliːt/ *v.t. & i.* мыча́ть (*impf.*), бле́ять (*impf.*)

bleed /bliːd/ *v.t.* (*past and p.p.* **bled** /bled/): ~ sb (for money) об|ира́ть, -обра́ть кого́-н.
• *v.i.* (*past and p.p.* **bled** /bled/) (of person) ист|ека́ть, -е́чь кро́вью; (of wound) кровоточи́ть (*impf.*); his nose is ~ing у него́ но́сом идёт кровь

bleep /bliːp/ *n.* сигна́л
• *v.i.* сигна́лить, про-
• *v.t.* (summon) вызыва́ть, вы́звать сигна́лом

bleeper /'bliːpə(r)/ *n.* (BrE) пе́йджер

blemish /'blemɪʃ/ *n.* недоста́ток, изъя́н

blend /blend/ *n.* смесь
• *v.t.* сме́ш|ивать, -а́ть; (colours, ideas) сочета́ть (*impf.*)
• *v.i.* сме́ш|иваться, -а́ться; (of colours, ideas) сочета́ться (*impf.*); гармони́ровать (*impf.*)

blender /'blendə(r)/ *n.* (cul.) смеси́тель (*m.*), ми́ксер, бле́ндер

bless /bles/ *v.t.* (*past and p.p.* **blessed**)
1 (relig.) благослов|ля́ть, -и́ть; ~ you! дай вам Бог здоро́вья!; (after sneeze) бу́дьте здоро́вы! **2** (prosper, favour): he was ~ed with good health Бог награди́л его́ здоро́вьем

blessing /'blesɪŋ/ *n.* **1** благослове́ние **2**: it is a ~ in disguise! ≈ не́ было бы сча́стья, да несча́стье помогло́!

blew /bluː/ *past of* ▶ blow[1]

blight /blaɪt/ *n.* головня́
• *v.t.*: ~ sb's hopes разру́ш|ать, -у́шить чьи-н. наде́жды

blind /blaɪnd/ *n.* што́ра, ста́вень (*m.*); **Venetian** ~ жалюзи́ (*nt. indecl.*)
• *adj.* **1** слепо́й; the ~ (*as n.*) слепы́е, слепцы́ (*m. pl.*); go ~ сле́пнуть, о-; a ~ spot слепо́е пятно́; (fig.) пробе́л; turn a ~ eye to sth закр|ыва́ть, -ы́ть глаза́ на что-н. **2** (concealed): a ~ corner непросма́тривающийся, закры́тый поворо́т; a ~ spot (on the road) мёртвая зо́на; a ~ date (infml) свида́ние с незнако́мым/ незнако́мой **3** (closed up): a ~ alley (lit., fig.) тупи́к
• *v.t.* ослеп|ля́ть, -и́ть; (also fig., temporarily) слепи́ть (*impf.*)
■ ~**fold** *adv.* с завя́занными глаза́ми • *v.t.* завя́з|ывать, -а́ть глаза́ + *d.*

blindly /'blaɪndlɪ/ *adv.* (gropingly) на о́щупь; (recklessly) сле́по

blindness /'blaɪndnɪs/ *n.* слепота́; (fig.) слепота́, ослепле́ние

bling /blɪŋ/ *n.* (infml) (clothing) гламу́рная оде́жда; (jewellery) ца́цки (*f. pl.*) (sl.), побряку́шки (*f. pl.*) (infml); ((containing) diamonds) брю́лики (*m. pl.*) (infml)

blink /blɪŋk/ *n.* морга́ние, мига́ние
• *v.t. & i.* (of person) мига́ть, -ну́ть; морг|а́ть, -ну́ть; (of light) мерца́ть (*impf.*)

blinkers /'blɪŋkəz/ *n. pl.* (BrE) шо́р|ы (*pl., g.* —) (also fig.)

blip /blɪp/ *n.* (on screen) отражённый и́мпульс

bliss /blɪs/ *n.* блаже́нство

blissful /'blɪsfʊl/ *adj.* блаже́нный

blister /'blɪstə(r)/ *n.* волдьı́рь (*m.*)
• *v.i.* покр|ыва́ться, -ы́ться волдыря́ми/ пузыря́ми

blithe /'blaɪð/, **blithesome** /'blaɪðsəm/ *adjs.* жизнера́достный, беспе́чный

blitz /blɪts/ *n.* бомбёжка
• *v.t.* разбомби́ть (*pf.*)

blizzard /'blɪzəd/ *n.* бура́н, вью́га

bloated /'bləʊtɪd/ *adj.* разду́тый, разду́вшийся

blob /blɒb/ *n.* (small mass) ка́пля; ша́рик; (spot of colour) кля́кса

ⓢ **block** /blɒk/ *n.* **1** (of wood) чурба́н, коло́да; (of stone, marble) глы́ба **2** (for execution) пла́ха **3** (of houses) кварта́л; ~ of flats (BrE) многокварти́рный дом **4** (typ.): ~ capitals печа́тные бу́квы
• *v.t.* (obstruct physically): roads ~ed by snow доро́ги, занесённые сне́гом; the sink is ~ed ра́ковина засори́лась
■ ~**buster** *n.* (infml) блокба́стер, ка́ссовый фильм

blockade /blɒˈkeɪd/ *n.* блока́да
• *v.t.* блоки́ровать (*impf., pf.*)

ⓢ **blog** /blɒg/ *n.* (comput.) блог

blogger /'blɒɡə(r)/ *n.* (comput.) бло́ггер, бло́гер

blogosphere /'blɒɡəsfɪə(r)/ *n.* (comput.) блогосфе́ра

bloke /bləʊk/ *n.* (BrE, infml) тип; па́рень (*m.*)

blonde, blond /blɒnd/ *n.* блонди́нка
• *adj.* белоку́рый, све́тлый

ⓢ **blood** /blʌd/ *n.* **1** кровь **2** (*attr.*): ~ **bank** до́норский пункт; ~ **donor** до́нор; ~ **group** гру́ппа кро́ви; ~ **test** ана́лиз кро́ви; (for paternity) иссле́дование кро́ви **3** (var. fig. uses): **in cold** ~ хладнокро́вно; **we need new** ~ нам нужны́ но́вые си́лы
■ ~ **pressure** *n.* кровяно́е давле́ние; ~**shed** *n.* кровопроли́тие; ~**shot** *adj.* нали́тый кро́вью; ~**stained** *adj.* запа́чканный кро́вью; ~**stream** *n.* ток кро́ви; ~**thirsty** *adj.* кровожа́дный

bloody /'blʌdɪ/ *adj.* (**bloodier, bloodiest**)
1 крова́вый **2** (BrE, sl.): a ~ **liar** отча́янный лгун
• *adv.* (sl.): ~ **awful** черто́вский; скве́рный, дрянно́й

bloom /bluːm/ *n.* (single flower) цвето́к; **in** ~ в цвету́
• *v.i.* цвести́ (*impf.*); (come into ~) расцве|та́ть, -сти́

blossom /'blɒsəm/ *n.* цвет, цвете́ние
• *v.i.* цвести́ (*impf.*)

b

blot /blɒt/ *n.* (on paper) кля́кса; (blemish) пятно́
- *v.t.* (**blotted, blotting**) (sully) ~ one's copybook (BrE, fig.) пятна́ть, за- свою́ репута́цию
□ ~ **out** *v.t.* (from one's memory) изгла́|живать, -дить (*or* стира́ть, -ере́ть) из па́мяти

blouse /blaʊz/ *n.* ко́фточка, блу́зка

◆ **blow¹** /bləʊ/ *v.t.* (*past* **blew**, *p.p.* **blown**)
1 дуть, ду́нуть; ~ a whistle свисте́ть, за- в свисто́к; дава́ть, дать свисто́к; ~ one's nose сморка́ться, вы- **2** (of wind): the wind blew the papers out of my hand ве́тер вы́рвал бума́ги у меня́ из рук **3** (elec.): ~ a fuse переж|ига́ть, -е́чь про́бку
- *v.i.* (*past* **blew**, *p.p.* **blown**) **1** (of wind or person) дуть, по-, ду́нуть **2** (of thing): the door blew open дверь распахну́лась; the fuse blew про́бка перегоре́ла
□ ~ **away** *v.t. & i.* ун|оси́ть(ся), -ести́(сь)
□ ~ **down** *v.t.* вали́ть, по-
- *v.i.*: the tree blew down бу́ря повали́ла де́рево
□ ~ **out** *v.t.*: he blew the candle out он заду́л свечу́
□ ~ **over** *v.i.*: the storm blew over бу́ря ути́хла
□ ~ **up** *v.t.*: ~ up a bridge взрыва́ть, взорва́ть мост; ~ up a tyre нака́ч|ивать, -а́ть ши́ну/ колесо́; ~ up a photograph увели́чи|вать, -ть фотогра́фию
- *v.i.*: the mine blew up ми́на взорвала́сь
■ ~**out** *n.* (of tyre) разры́в; (infml, feast) оби́льное засто́лье, кутёж; ~**torch** *n.* пая́льная ла́мпа

blow² /bləʊ/ *n.* уда́р

blown /bləʊn/ *p.p. of* ▸ **blow¹**

blub /blʌb/ *v.i.* (**blubbed, blubbing**) (infml) реве́ть (*impf.*)

blubber¹ /ˈblʌbə(r)/ *n.* (whale fat) во́рвань

blubber² /ˈblʌbə(r)/ *v.i.* = blub

bludgeon /ˈblʌdʒ(ə)n/ *v.t.* бить (*impf.*) дуби́нкой; (fig.) принужда́ть, -уди́ть

◆ **blue** /bluː/ *n.* **1** (colour) синева́, голубизна́ **2** (sky): out of the ~ (fig.) ни с того́ ни с сего́; he arrived out of the ~ он нагря́нул неожи́данно **3**: the ~s (infml) тоска́, уны́ние, хандра́ **4**: ~s (mus.) блюз
- *adj.* (**bluer, bluest**) **1** (colour) (dark) си́ний; (light) голубо́й **2** (infml, sad): feel ~ хандри́ть (*impf.*) **3** (infml, obscene) неприли́чный, непристо́йный
■ ~**bell** *n.* ди́кий/лесно́й гиаци́нт; ~**collar worker** *n.* произво́дственный рабо́чий; ~**print** *n.* (phot.) светоко́пия, си́нька; (fig.) план

bluff /blʌf/ *n.*: call sb's ~ заст|авля́ть, -а́вить кого́-н. раскры́ть ка́рты
- *v.i.* блефова́ть (*impf.*)
- *v.t.* втира́ть (*impf.*) очки́ + *d.*; ~ one's way out of sth вы́крутиться (*pf.*) из чего́-л.

bluish /ˈbluːɪʃ/ *adj.* (dark) синева́тый; (light) голубова́тый

blunder /ˈblʌndə(r)/ *n.* оши́бка, опло́шность
- *v.i.* блужда́ть (*impf.*); (grope) пробира́ться/

◆ ключева́я ле́ксика

дви́гаться (*impf.*) о́щупью; ~ into a table нат|ыка́ться, -кну́ться на стол

blunt /blʌnt/ *adj.* (not sharp) тупо́й; (plain-spoken) прямо́й
- *v.t.* тупи́ть (*impf.*)

blur /blɜː(r)/ *n.* ды́мка
- *v.t.* (**blurred, blurring**) сма́з|ывать, -ать

blurb /blɜːb/ *n.* (infml) (изда́тельская) аннота́ция

blurt /blɜːt/ *v.t.*: ~ out выпа́ливать, вы́палить

blush /blʌʃ/ *v.i.* красне́ть, по-

blusher /ˈblʌʃə(r)/ *n.* (cosmetic) румя́на

bluster /ˈblʌstə(r)/ *n.* (of storm) рёв; (of person) гро́мкие слова́ (*nt. pl.*), угро́зы (*f. pl.*)
- *v.i.* (of storm) реве́ть (*impf.*); (of person) расшуме́ться (*pf.*), разбушева́ться (*pf.*)

BO *abbr.* (*of* **body odour**) за́пах по́та

boar /bɔː(r)/ *n.* каба́н

◆ **board** /bɔːd/ *n.* **1** (piece of wood) доска́ (*also for chess etc.*) **2** (food) стол; ~ and lodging, bed and ~ пита́ние и прожива́ние; ночле́г и пита́ние **3**: above ~ в откры́тую, че́стно **4** (council) правле́ние; ~ of directors правле́ние директоро́в **5** (naut. etc.): on ~ на борту́
- *v.t.* **1** (cover with ~s) (*also* ~ up) общ|ива́ть, -и́ть (*or* покр|ыва́ть, -ы́ть) доска́ми **2**: ~ a ship (go on ~) сади́ться, сесть на кора́бль
■ ~ **game** *n.* насто́льная игра́; ~**room** *n.* зал заседа́ний сове́та директоро́в

boarder /ˈbɔːdə(r)/ *n.* (lodger) жиле́ц, постоя́лец; (at school) учени́|к (-ца), живу́щий (-ая) в шко́ле-интерна́те

boarding /ˈbɔːdɪŋ/ *n.* (naut.) аборда́ж; (aeron.) поса́дка
■ ~ **card**, ~ **pass** *nn.* поса́дочный биле́т/ тало́н; ~ **school** *n.* шко́ла-интерна́т

boast /bəʊst/ *n.* хвастовство́
- *v.t. & i.* (~ of) хва́стать(ся), по- + *i.*; хвали́ться, по- + *i.*

boastful /ˈbəʊstfʊl/ *adj.* хвастли́вый

◆ **boat** /bəʊt/ *n.* (small, rowing ~) ло́дка, шлю́пка; (vessel) су́дно; (large ~) кора́бль (*m.*), парохо́д; in the same ~ (fig.) в одина́ковом положе́нии
- *v.i.* (go ~ing) ката́ться (*indet.*) на ло́дке
■ ~**house** *n.* сара́й для ло́док

boater /ˈbəʊtə(r)/ *n.* соло́менная шля́па

bob¹ /bɒb/ *n.* (hairstyle) коро́ткая стри́жка

bob² /bɒb/ *v.i.* (**bobbed, bobbing**) (move up and down) подпры́г|ивать, -нуть; подск|а́кивать, -очи́ть

bobsled /ˈbɒbsled/ *n.* (AmE) = bobsleigh

bobsleigh /ˈbɒbsleɪ/ *n.* (BrE) бобсле́й

bode /bəʊd/ *v.t. & i.*: ~ ill/well предвеща́ть/ сули́ть (*impf.*) недо́брое/хоро́шее

bodice /ˈbɒdɪs/ *n.* корса́ж, лиф

bodily /ˈbɒdɪlɪ/ *adj.* теле́сный, физи́ческий

◆ **body** /ˈbɒdɪ/ *n.* **1** (of person or animal) те́ло **2** (dead person) мёртвое те́ло; уби́т|ый (-ая) **3** (of ship) ко́рпус; (of car) ку́зов; (of aircraft) фюзеля́ж **4** (quantity) ма́сса, гру́ппа; ~ of

b

evidence совокупность доказа́тельств
5 (group): public ∼ обще́ственная
организа́ция **6** (strength, consistency)
консисте́нция, вя́зкость
■ ∼**builder** n. (person) культури́ст; (apparatus)
эспа́ндер; ∼**building** n. культури́зм,
бодибилдинг; ∼**guard** n. (group) ли́чная
охра́на; (individual) телохрани́тель (m.); ∼
piercing n. пи́рсинг; ∼**work** n. (of vehicle)
ку́зов
bog /bɒg/ n. боло́то, тряси́на
 ● v.t. (**bogged, bogging**): get ∼ged down
(fig.) вя́знуть, за-, у-
boggle /ˈbɒg(ə)l/ v.i.: the mind ∼s уму́
непостижи́мо
boggy /ˈbɒgɪ/ adj. (**boggier, boggiest**)
болоти́стый
bogus /ˈbəʊgəs/ adj. фикти́вный, притво́рный
bohemian /bəʊˈhiːmɪən/ n. представи́тель
(-ница) боге́мы
boil[1] /bɔɪl/ n. (swelling) гно́йный нары́в,
фуру́нкул
boil[2] /bɔɪl/ n. (state of ∼ing) кипе́ние; bring to
the ∼ довести́ (pf.) до кипе́ния; вскипяти́ть
(pf.)
 ● v.t.: ∼ water кипяти́ть, вс- во́ду; ∼ fish/an
egg вари́ть, с- ры́бу/яйцо́
 ● v.i.: the water is ∼ing вода́ кипи́т; the egg
has ∼ed яйцо́ свари́лось
 □ ∼ down v.i.: it ∼s down to this, that … э́то
сво́дится к тому́, что…
 □ ∼ over v.i. (lit.) уходи́ть, уйти́ (or убе|га́ть,
-жа́ть) че́рез край
boiler /ˈbɔɪlə(r)/ n. отопи́тельный котёл;
бо́йлер
 ■ ∼ suit n. (BrE) комбинезо́н
boiling /ˈbɔɪlɪŋ/ adj. кипя́щий; ∼ hot
горя́чий, как кипято́к
 ■ ∼ point n. то́чка кипе́ния
boisterous /ˈbɔɪstərəs/ adj. бу́йный,
шумли́вый, шу́мный
bold /bəʊld/ n. (typ.) жи́рный шрифт
 ● adj. **1** сме́лый, отва́жный; (impudent)
наха́льный **2**: ∼ strokes (in painting) широ́кие
мазки́
Bolivia /bəˈlɪvɪə/ n. Боли́вия
Bolivian /bəˈlɪvɪən/ n. боливи́|ец (-йка)
 ● adj. боливи́йский
bollard /ˈbɒlɑːd/ n. (BrE) ту́мба
Bolshevik /ˈbɒlʃəvɪk/ n. большеви́|к (-чка)
 ● adj. большевистский
Bolshevism /ˈbɒlʃəvɪz(ə)m/ n. большеви́зм
bolster /ˈbəʊlstə(r)/ n. ва́лик
 ● v.t. подп|ира́ть, -ере́ть
bolt[1] /bəʊlt/ n. **1** (on door etc.) засо́в **2** (screw)
болт
 ● adv.: ∼ upright пря́мо; вы́тянувшись
 ● v.t.: ∼ the door зап|ира́ть, -ере́ть дверь на
засо́в
bolt[2] /bəʊlt/ v.t. (gulp down) глота́ть, проглоти́ть
 ● v.i. (of horse) понести́ (pf.); (of person)
ри́нуться (pf.), помча́ться (pf.), удра́ть (pf.)
⚡ **bomb** /bɒm/ n. бо́мба
 ● v.t. & i. бомби́ть, раз-

■ ∼ **disposal** n. обезвре́живание
неразорва́вшихся бомб; ∼**shell** n.
артиллери́йский снаря́д; the news came
as a ∼shell to them весть их как гро́мом
порази́ла; ∼**site** n. райо́н разру́шенный
бомбардиро́вк|ой/-ами
bombard /bɒmˈbɑːd/ v.t. **1** бомби́ть, раз-;
бомбардирова́ть (impf.); обстре́л|ивать, -я́ть
2 (fig.): ∼ sb with questions бомбардирова́ть
(impf.) кого́-н. вопро́сами
bombardment /bɒmˈbɑːdmənt/ n.
бомбардиро́вка, бомбёжка; (with shells)
артиллери́йский обстре́л
bombastic /bɒmˈbæstɪk/ adj. высокопа́рный,
напы́щенный
bomber /ˈbɒmə(r)/ n. (aircraft)
бомбардиро́вщик; (person) террори́ст
bombing /ˈbɒmɪŋ/ n. бомбомета́ние,
бомбардиро́вка
bona fide /ˈbəʊnə ˈfaɪdɪ/ adj.
добросо́вестный, че́стный
bond /bɒnd/ n. **1** (link) связь **2** (fin.)
облига́ция; (in pl.) бо́ны (f. pl.)
 ● v.i. (form a relationship) устан|а́вливать, -ови́ть
кре́пкие отноше́ния (c + i.)
⚡ **bone** /bəʊn/ n. **1** кость; I have a ∼ to pick with
you у меня́ к вам прете́нзия **2** (substance) кость
 ● v.t.: ∼ fish/meat отдел|я́ть, -и́ть ры́бу/мя́со
от косте́й
 ■ ∼ **china** n. твёрдый англи́йский фарфо́р;
∼ **dry** adj. соверше́нно сухо́й; ∼ **idle** adj.
ужа́сно лени́вый
bonfire /ˈbɒnfaɪə(r)/ n. костёр
bonk /bɒnk/ v.i. (BrE, vulg.) тра́х|аться, -нуться
bonnet /ˈbɒnɪt/ n. **1** (woman's hat) ка́пор;
чепе́ц, че́пчик **2** (BrE, of car) капо́т
bonny /ˈbɒnɪ/ adj. (**bonnier, bonniest**) (Sc.,
attractive, beautiful) хоро́шенький; (healthy): a ∼
baby кре́пкий ребёнок
bonus /ˈbəʊnəs/ n. пре́мия, премиа́льные
(pl.); (fig.) дополни́тельное преиму́щество,
бо́нус
bony /ˈbəʊnɪ/ adj. (**bonier, boniest**)
костяно́й, кости́стый
boo /buː/ n. гул/свист неодобре́ния
 ● v.t. (**boos, booed**) освист|ывать, -а́ть;
∼ an actor off the stage гу́лом/сви́стом
неодобре́ния прогна́ть (pf.) актёра со сце́ны
 ● v.i. (**boos, booed**) улюлю́кать (impf.)
 ● int. фу!
boob[1] /buːb/ n. **1** (BrE, infml, mistake) прома́шка
2 (AmE, infml, simpleton) простофи́ля (c.g.),
дуралей
 ● v.i. (BrE, infml) оплоша́ть (pf.); дать (pf.)
прома́шку
boob[2] /buːb/ n. (usu. in pl.) (sl., breasts) буфера́
(m. pl.) (sl.)
booby trap /ˈbuːbɪ/ n. (mil.) ми́на-лову́шка
 ● v.t. (**booby-trap**) устан|а́вливать, -ови́ть
ми́ны-лову́шки в/на + p.
⚡ **book** /bʊk/ n. **1** кни́га; (small) кни́жка **2** (set):
∼ of matches/stamps кни́жечка спи́чек/
ма́рок **3** (account): keep the ∼s вести́ (det.)
бухга́лтерские/счётные кни́ги; in sb's good/

b

bad ~s на хоро́шем/плохо́м счету́ у кого́-н.
● *v.t.* (ticket, table, taxi) зака́з|ывать, -а́ть; (hotel room, seat) брони́ровать, за-; ~ **sb in at a hotel** брони́ровать, за- для кого́-н. но́мер в гости́нице
■ ~**case** *n.* кни́жный шкаф; (open-fronted) кни́жные по́лки (*f. pl.*); ~ **club** *n.* клуб книголю́бов; ~**keeping** *n.* бухгалте́рия, счетово́дство; ~**maker** *n.* букме́кер; ~**mark** *n.* (also comput.) закла́дка; ~**seller** *n.* книготорго́вец; ~**shelf** *n.* кни́жная по́лка; ~**shop**, (AmE) ~**store** *nn.* кни́жный магази́н

bookie /'bʊkɪ/ *n.* (infml) букме́кер

booking /'bʊkɪŋ/ *n.* зака́з
■ ~ **office** *n.* (BrE) биле́тная ка́сса

booklet /'bʊklɪt/ *n.* брошю́ра, букле́т

boom[1] /buːm/ *n.* (of gun, thunder) гул, ро́кот; (of voice) гул
● *v.t. & i.* (of gun) бу́хать (*impf.*), грохота́ть (*impf.*); (of thunder) глу́хо грохота́ть (*impf.*)

boom[2] /buːm/ *n.* (comm.) бум, оживле́ние
● *v.i.* **business is** ~**ing** де́ло процвета́ет

boomerang /'buːməræŋ/ *n.* бумера́нг

boorish /'bʊərɪʃ/ *adj.* ха́мский, мужи́цкий

boost /buːst/ *n.* (increase) увеличе́ние; (stimulus) толчо́к, сти́мул; **give a** ~ **to the economy** стимули́ровать (*impf., pf.*) эконо́мику
● *v.t.* (increase) увели́чи|вать, -ть

booster /'buːstə(r)/ *n.:* ~ **injection** (med.) повто́рная приви́вка

boot /buːt/ *n.* **1** (footwear) боти́нок, башма́к; (knee-length) сапо́г; **football** ~**s** бу́тсы (*f. pl.*) **2** (BrE, of a car) бага́жник
● *v.t.* (comput.) загру|жа́ть, -зи́ть
■ ~**leg** *adj.* (fig.): ~**leg whisky** контраба́ндное ви́ски; ~**legger** *n.* самого́нщик

booth /buːð/ *n.* (for telephoning) бу́дка; (polling ~) каби́на для голосова́ния

booty /'buːtɪ/ *n.* добы́ча

booze /buːz/ *n.* вы́пивка; попо́йка
● *v.i.* пья́нствовать (*impf.*), выпива́ть (*impf.*)

bop /bɒp/ (BrE, infml) *n.* та́нец под популя́рную му́зыку; (party) та́нцы под популя́рную му́зыку (*m. pl.*)
● *v.i.* танцева́ть, с- под популя́рную му́зыку

✧ **border** /'bɔːdə(r)/ *n.* **1** (side, edging): ~ **of a lake** бе́рег о́зера; **herbaceous** ~ бордю́р из многоле́тних цвето́в **2** (frontier) грани́ца; (fig.) грань
● *v.t.* **our garden** ~**s his field** наш сад грани́чит с его́ по́лем
● *v.i.* **these countries** ~ **on one another** э́ти стра́ны грани́чат друг с дру́гом; **this** ~**s on fanaticism** э́то грани́чит с фанати́змом
■ ~**line** *n.* (fig.) грань; **a** ~**line case** промежу́точный слу́чай

bore[1] /bɔː(r)/ *n.* кали́бр, кана́л ствола́
● *v.t.* сверли́ть, про-; бури́ть, про-

bore[2] /bɔː(r)/ *n.* (person) скучный челове́к; зану́да (*c.g.*); (thing): **it's such a bore cooking every day** така́я тоска́ ка́ждый день гото́вить

● *v.t.* надо|еда́ть, -е́сть + *d.*; ~ **sb to death, tears** надо|еда́ть, -е́сть кому́-н. до́ сме́рти

bore[3] /bɔː(r)/ *past of* ▸ **bear**[2]

bored /bɔːd/ *adj.* скуча́ющий; **I am** ~ мне ску́чно; **in a** ~ **voice** ску́чным/скуча́ющим го́лосом; **I am** ~ **with him** он мне надое́л

boredom /'bɔːdəm/ *n.* ску́ка, тоска́

boring /'bɔːrɪŋ/ *adj.* ску́чный, надое́дливый

✧ **born** /bɔːn/ *adj. and p.p. of* ▸ **bear**[2] **1**: **a** ~ **poet** прирождённый поэ́т **2**: **be** ~ роди́ться (*pf.*)

borne /bɔːn/ *p.p. of* ▸ **bear**[2]

Borneo /'bɔːnɪəʊ/ *n.* Борне́о (*nt. indecl.*)

borough /'bʌrə/ *n.* райо́н

borrow /'bɒrəʊ/ *v.t. & i.* (take for a time) брать, взять на вре́мя; заи́мствовать, по-; зан|има́ть, -я́ть; (money) брать, взять взаймы́

borscht /bɔːʃt/, **borsch** /bɔːʃ/ *n.* борщ

Bosnia /'bɒznɪə/ *n.* Бо́сния

Bosnia-Herzegovina /'bɒznɪə həːtsə'ɡɒvɪnə/ *n.* (*also* **Bosnia and Herzegovina**) Бо́сния и Герцегови́на

bosom /'bʊz(ə)m/ *n.* **1** (breast) грудь **2** (fig.) се́рдце, душа́
■ ~ **friend** *n.* закады́чный друг

Bosporus /'bɒspərəs/ *n.* Босфо́р

✧ **boss** /bɒs/ *n.* (master) босс, хозя́ин, нача́льник
● *v.t.:* ~ **sb about** кома́ндовать (*impf.*) кем-н.

bossy /'bɒsɪ/ *adj.* (**bossier, bossiest**) (voice, tone) команди́рский; **your husband is really** ~ твой муж привы́к ве́чно кома́ндовать

botanical /bə'tænɪk(ə)l/ *adj.* ботани́ческий

botanist /'bɒtənɪst/ *n.* бота́ник

botany /'bɒtənɪ/ *n.* бота́ника

botch /bɒtʃ/ *v.t.* зава́л|ивать, -и́ть

✧ **both** /bəʊθ/ *pron. & adj.* о́ба (*m., nt.*), о́бе (*f.*); и тот и друго́й; ~ **sledges** о́бе па́ры сане́й; ~ **of us** мы о́ба
● *adv.:* ~ ... **and** ... и... и...; **my sister and I** ~ **helped him** мы о́ба помогли́ ему́, и я, и сестра́

bother /'bɒðə(r)/ *n.* беспоко́йство; хло́п|оты (-о́т); возня́; **I had no** ~ **finding the book** я нашёл кни́гу без труда́
● *v.t.* (disturb) беспоко́ить, по-; трево́жить, по-; (pester): **he is always** ~**ing me to lend him money** он ве́чно пристаёт ко мне с про́сьбой одолжи́ть ему́ де́нег; ~ **(it)!** (BrE) чёрт возьми́!; **I can't be** ~**ed** мне лень, мне недосу́г
● *v.i.* беспоко́иться, по-; **don't** ~ **to make tea** не вози́тесь с ча́ем

Botox® /'bəʊtɒks/ *n.* (med.) бо́токс (*медици́нский/космети́ческий препара́т*)

✧ **bottle** /'bɒt(ə)l/ *n.* буты́лка; (BrE, for infants) буты́лочка, рожо́к
● *v.t.* (preserve in ~s) храни́ть в буты́лках; ~ **up** (put in ~s) разл|ива́ть, -и́ть по буты́лкам; (conceal) скры|ва́ть, -ть
■ ~**fed** *adj.* иску́сственно вско́рмленный; ~**neck** *n.* (fig.) зато́р; про́бка; у́зкое ме́сто; ~**opener** *n.* открыва́лка (infml); ~**top** *n.* колпачо́к на буты́лку

bottled /'bɒt(ə)ld/ *adj.:* ~ **beer** буты́лочное пи́во

ℰ **bottom** /'bɒtəm/ *n.* **1** (lowest part) дно; (of mountain) подно́жие, подо́шва; (of page) низ, коне́ц; (of stairs) низ, основа́ние; ~ **shelf** ни́жняя по́лка; at the ~ of the class отстаю́щий в кла́ссе **2** (further end): ~ of the garden/street коне́ц са́да/у́лицы **3** (BrE, buttocks) зад; за́дняя часть **4** (fig.): get to the ~ of sth добира́ться, -ра́ться до су́ти чего́-н.; he came ~ in algebra он был са́мым неуспева́ющим по а́лгебре
■ ~ **line** *n.* (crux of the matter) суть де́ла

boudoir /'buːdwɑː(r)/ *n.* будуа́р
bougainvillea, bougainvillaea /buːgən'vɪlɪə/ *n.* (bot.) бугенвилле́я (*scientific name*), бугенви́ллия

bough /baʊ/ *n.* сук
bought /bɔːt/ *past and p.p. of* ▸ buy
boulder /'bəʊldə(r)/ *n.* валу́н
boulevard /'buːləvɑːd/ *n.* бульва́р
bounce /baʊns/ *n.* подпры́гивание, отско́к
● *v.t.*: ~ a ball бить (*impf.*) мячо́м об пол (о зем́лю, об сте́нку и т. п.)
● *v.i.* (of ball etc.) отск|а́кивать, -очи́ть; подпры́г|ивать, -нуть; (infml, of cheque) верну́ться (*pf.*); ~ **back** (fig.) бы́стро опра́виться

bouncer /'baʊnsə(r)/ *n.* вышиба́ла (*m.*)
bound¹ /baʊnd/ *n.* (*usu. in pl.*) (limit) грани́ца, преде́л; the town is out of ~s to troops вход в го́род солда́там воспрещён

bound² /baʊnd/ *v.i.* пры́г|ать, -нуть; скак|а́ть, -нуть; he ~ed off to fetch the book он подпры́гнул, что́бы доста́ть кни́гу

bound³ /baʊnd/ *adj.* **1** (certain): he is ~ to win он непреме́нно вы́играет **2** (obliged): you are not ~ to go вам не обяза́тельно идти́ **3** (en route): the ship is ~ for New York парохо́д направля́ется в Нью-Йо́рк

bound⁴ /baʊnd/ *past and p.p. of* ▸ bind
boundary /'baʊndrɪ/ *n.* **1** (of a field etc.) грани́ца, рубе́ж; (fig.) преде́л; (*attr.*) пограни́чный
boundless /'baʊndlɪs/ *adj.* безграни́чный, беспреде́льный
bountiful /'baʊntɪfʊl/ *adj.* ще́дрый; оби́льный
bouquet /buː'keɪ/ *n.* (of flowers, wine) буке́т
bourbon /'bɔːbən/ *n.* (whisky) бурбо́н
bourgeois /'bʊəʒwɑː/ *adj.* буржуа́зный
bourgeoisie /ˌbʊəʒwɑː'ziː/ *n.* буржуази́я
bout /baʊt/ *n.* **1** (at games) бой, встре́ча, схва́тка **2** (of illness) при́ступ
boutique /buː'tiːk/ *n.* (небольшо́й) мо́дный магази́н; бути́к
bow¹ /baʊ/ *n.* **1** (weapon) лук **2** (of violin etc.) смычо́к **3** (knot) бант
■ ~-**legged** *adj.* кривоно́гий; ~ **tie** *n.* (га́лстук-)ба́бочка

bow² /baʊ/ *n.* (salutation) покло́н
● *v.t.* (bend): ~ one's head склоня́ть, -и́ть го́лову; the wind ~ed the trees ве́тер гнул/клони́л дере́вья
● *v.i.* **1** (salute) кла́няться, поклони́ться **2** (defer) склон|я́ться, -и́ться (to, before: пе́ред + *i.*)

bow³ /baʊ/ *n.* (naut.) нос
bowel /'baʊəl/ *n.* **1** кишка́ **2**: ~s of the earth не́дра (*pl., g.* —) земли́
bowl¹ /bəʊl/ *n.* ча́ша, ва́за, ми́ска
bowl² /bəʊl/ *n.*: play ~s игра́ть (*impf.*) в бо́улинг/ке́гли/шары́
● *v.t.*: ~ over (lit.) сшиб|а́ть, -и́ть; (fig.): he was ~ed over by her она́ срази́ла его́
● *v.i.* **1** (cricket) под|ава́ть, -а́ть мяч **2** (play bowls) игра́ть (*impf.*) в бо́улинг/ке́гли/шары́
■ ~**ing alley** *n.* зал для игры́ в бо́улинг; кегельба́н; ~**ing green** *n.* лужа́йка для игры́ в бо́улинг/шары́

bowler¹ /'bəʊlə(r)/ *n.* (at games) подаю́щий/ броса́ющий мяч
bowler² /'bəʊlə(r)/ *n.* (*in full* ~ hat) котело́к
ℰ **box¹** /bɒks/ *n.* **1** (receptacle) коро́бка, я́щик **2** (theatr.) ло́жа **3** (typ.) ра́мка
● *v.t.* класть, положи́ть в коро́бку/я́щик
■ ~ **number** *n.* но́мер абоне́нтского я́щика; ~ **office** *n.* (театра́льная) ка́сса

box² /bɒks/ *v.t.*: ~ sb's ears да|ва́ть, -ть кому́-н. оплеу́ху (*or* по́ уху)
● *v.i.* (sport) бокси́ровать (*impf.*)
boxer /'bɒksə(r)/ *n.* (sportsman; dog) боксёр
■ ~ **shorts** *n. pl.* боксёрские трусы́
boxing /'bɒksɪŋ/ *n.* (sport) бокс
Boxing Day /'bɒksɪŋ/ *n.* (BrE) второ́й день Рождества́

ℰ **boy** /bɔɪ/ *n.* **1** (child) ма́льчик **2** (son) сын
■ ~**friend** *n.* ≈ па́рень (*m.*), ≈ молодо́й челове́к, бойфре́нд; B~ **Scout** *n.* бойска́ут
boycott /'bɔɪkɒt/ *n.* бойко́т
● *v.t.* бойкоти́ровать (*impf., pf.*)
boyish /'bɔɪʃ/ *adj.* мальчи́ческий
bra /brɑː/ *n.* (*pl.* **bras**) (infml) ли́фчик, бюстга́льтер
brace /breɪs/ *n.* **1** (support) подпо́рка, распо́рка **2**: ~s (BrE, for trousers) подтя́ж|ки (-ек) **3** (dentistry etc.) ши́на
● *v.t.* **1** (support) подп|ира́ть, -ере́ть; he ~d himself against the wall он опёрся о сте́ну **2** (of nerves): he ~d himself to do it он собра́лся с ду́хом что́бы сде́лать э́то

bracelet /'breɪslɪt/ *n.* брасле́т
bracing /'breɪsɪŋ/ *adj.* бодря́щий, укрепля́ющий
bracken /'brækən/ *n.* па́поротник-орля́к
bracket /'brækɪt/ *n.* **1** (support) кронште́йн **2** (typ.) ско́бка **3** (fig.): the higher income ~s гру́ппа населе́ния с бо́лее высо́кими дохо́дами
● *v.t.* (**bracketed, bracketing**) **1** (enclose in ~s) заключ|а́ть, -и́ть в ско́бки **2** (fig.): do not ~ me with him не равня́йте меня́ с ним
brag /bræg/ *v.i.* (**bragged, bragging**) хва́стать(ся), по- (*чем*)
braid /breɪd/ *n.* (of hair) коса́; (decorative) галу́н
Braille /breɪl/ *n.* шрифт Бра́йля; а́збука Бра́йля

ℰ **brain** /breɪn/ *n.* (anat.) мозг; (*in pl.*) (cul.) мозги́
■ ~**child** *n.* плод ра́зума/воображе́ния; ~ **drain** *n.* «уте́чка мозго́в»; ~**storming session** *n.* коллекти́вное обсужде́ние

b

проблем; ~**wash** *v.t.* пром|ыва́ть, -ы́ть мозги́ (+ *d.*); ~**washing** *n.* промыва́ние мозго́в; ~**wave** *n.*: he had a ~wave ему́ пришла́ счастли́вая мысль; его́ осени́ла иде́я

brainy /'breɪnɪ/ *adj.* (**brainier, brainiest**) (infml) башкови́тый, мозгови́тый

braise /breɪz/ *v.t.* туши́ть (*impf.*)

brake /breɪk/ *n.* (on vehicle) то́рмоз
● *v.t. & i.* тормози́ть, за-

bramble /'bræmb(ə)l/ *n.* ежеви́ка

bran /bræn/ *n.* о́труб|и (-е́й)

✎ **branch** /brɑːntʃ/ *n.* (of tree) ветвь; ве́тка; (of family, genus) ли́ния, ветвь; (of railway line) ве́тка; (comm.) филиа́л, отделе́ние; (of knowledge, subject, industry) о́трасль
● *v.i.* (of organization): ~ out разветв|ля́ться, -и́ться; (of road or railway) (*also* ~ **off**) разветв|ля́ться, -и́ться; ответв|ля́ться, -и́ться

✎ **brand** /brænd/ *n.* сорт, ма́рка, бренд
● *v.t.* **1** (cattle etc.) клейми́ть, за- **2** (stigmatize) клейми́ть, за- **3** (comm.): ~ed goods фи́рменные това́ры
■ ~ **name** *n.* фи́рменное назва́ние; ~ **new** *adj.* соверше́нно но́вый, с иго́лочки

branding /'brændɪŋ/ *n.* (comm.) бре́ндинг (*создание и продвижение на рынке торговых марок*)

brandish /'brændɪʃ/ *v.t.* разма́хивать (*impf.*) + *i.*

brandy /'brændɪ/ *n.* коньяк; бре́нди (*nt. indecl.*)

brash /bræʃ/ *adj.* наха́льный, наглова́тый, де́рзкий

brass /brɑːs/ *n.* **1** (metal) лату́нь, жёлтая медь **2** (mus.): the ~ духовы́е инструме́нты (*m. pl.*); медь
■ ~ **band** *n.* духово́й орке́стр

brat /bræt/ *n.* (pej.) невоспи́танный ребёнок

bravado /brə'vɑːdəʊ/ *n.* брава́да

brave /breɪv/ *adj.* хра́брый, сме́лый
● *v.t.* бр|оса́ть, -о́сить вы́зов + *d.*; ~ publicity не боя́ться (*impf.*) гла́сности

bravery /'breɪvərɪ/ *n.* хра́брость, сме́лость

bravo /brɑː'vəʊ/ *int.* бра́во!

brawl /brɔːl/ *n.* сканда́л
● *v.i.* сканда́лить (*impf.*)

brawny /'brɔːnɪ/ *adj.* (**brawnier, brawniest**) мускули́стый

brazen /'breɪz(ə)n/ *adj.* на́глый, бессты́дный
● *v.t.*: ~ sth out на́гло выкру́чиваться, выкрути́ться из чего́-н.

brazier /'breɪzɪə(r)/ *n.* (portable heater) жаро́вня

Brazil /brə'zɪl/ *n.* Брази́лия

Brazilian /brə'zɪljən/ *n.* брази́л|ец (-ья́нка)
● *adj.* брази́льский

breach /briːtʃ/ *n.* **1** (violation, interruption) наруше́ние; ~ of trust злоупотребле́ние дове́рием **2** (gap) проло́м, брешь
● *v.t.* проры|ва́ть, -ва́ть

bread /bred/ *n.* хлеб; ~ and butter (fig.) хлеб с ма́слом
■ ~-**and-butter** *adj.* насу́щный; ~ **bin** *n.* (BrE) хле́бница; ~**board** *n.* хле́бная доска́;

~**crumb** *n.* кро́шка; (*in pl.*) (cul.) толчёные сухари́ (*m. pl.*); ~**line** *n.*: on the ~line (BrE) в тяжёлом материа́льном положе́нии; ~**winner** *n.* корми́лец

breadth /bredθ/ *n.* **1** (width) ширина́ **2** (fig.): ~ of mind широта́ ума́

✎ **break** /breɪk/ *n.* **1** (broken place, gap) тре́щина, разры́в **2** (interval) переры́в, па́уза; (rest) переды́шка **3** (change) переме́на **4** (infml, opportunity) возмо́жность; lucky ~ счастли́вый слу́чай
● *v.t.* (*past* **broke**, *p.p.* **broken**) **1** (fracture, destroy) лома́ть, с-; (glass, china) бить (*or* разбива́ть), раз-; he broke his leg он слома́л но́гу **2** (fig.): ~ a record поби́ть (*pf.*) реко́рд **3** (convey): ~ the news сообщ|а́ть, -и́ть (неприя́тные) но́вости **4** (weaken): ~ a fall осл|абля́ть, -а́бить си́лу паде́ния **5** (violate) нар|уша́ть, -у́шить; ~ a secret разгл|аша́ть, -аси́ть та́йну **6** (interrupt, put an end to): ~ one's journey прер|ыва́ть, -ва́ть путеше́ствие
● *v.i.* (*past* **broke**, *p.p.* **broken**) **1** (fracture, disperse) лома́ться, с-; обл|а́мываться, -ома́ться; (of glass, china) би́ться (*or* разбива́ться), раз-; ~ in two лома́ться, с- попола́м **2** (fig.): ~ing point преде́л **3** (burst, dawn): the storm broke разрази́лась гроза́; the news broke at 5 o'clock об э́том ста́ло изве́стно в 5 часо́в **4** (change): his voice broke (at puberty) у него́ слома́лся го́лос; the weather broke пого́да испо́ртилась **5** (var.): ~ even ост|ава́ться, -а́ться при свои́х; we broke for lunch мы сде́лали переры́в на обе́д
● (*with preps.*): burglars broke into the house граби́тели ворвали́сь в дом; the house was broken into в до́ме произошла́ кра́жа со взло́мом

□ ~ **away** *v.i.*: ~ away from one's jailers выры|ва́ться, вы́рваться из рук тюре́мщиков; ~ away from a group отк|а́лываться, -оло́ться от гру́ппы

□ ~ **down** *v.t.*: ~ down a door выла́мывать, вы́ломать дверь; ~ down resistance сломи́ть (*pf.*) сопротивле́ние; ~ down expenditure разб|ива́ть, -и́ть расхо́ды по статья́м
● *v.i.*: the car broke down маши́на слома́лась; he broke down он не вы́держал

□ ~ **in** *v.t.*: ~ in a door вл|а́мываться, -оми́ться в дверь; ~ in a horse выезжа́ть, вы́ездить ло́шадь; ~ in a new pair of shoes разна́шивать, -оси́ть но́вые ту́фли
● *v.i.*: ~ in on a conversation вме́ш|иваться, -а́ться в разгово́р

□ ~ **off** *v.t.*: ~ off a twig отл|а́мывать, -оми́ть ве́точку; ~ off relations пор|ыва́ть, -ва́ть отноше́ния (с + *i.*); ~ off an engagement раст|орга́ть, -о́ргнуть помо́лвку
● *v.i.* (be severed) отл|а́мываться, -оми́ться ве́точку; he broke off (speaking) он замолча́л

□ ~ **out** *v.i.*: the prisoner broke out заключённый сбежа́л; war broke out разрази́лась/вспы́хнула война́; his face broke out in pimples на его́ лице́ вы́сыпали прыщи́

□ ~ **up** *v.t.*: ~ up the ground взры|ва́ть, -ть зе́млю; ~ up a meeting прекра|ща́ть, -ти́ть собра́ние; ~ up a family (separate) разб|ива́ть,

-и́ть семью́

● *v.i.*: school ∼s up tomorrow (BrE) уча́щихся за́втра распуска́ют на кани́кулы; she broke up with her boyfriend она́ разошла́сь с дру́гом

■ ∼**away** *n.*: a ∼away faction отколо́вшаяся фра́кция; (sport) отры́в; ∼**down** *n.* (mechanical) поло́мка; (of health) расстро́йство; (of negotiations) срыв; (analysis) подразделе́ние, разби́вка; ∼**-in** *n.* взлом; ∼**neck** *adj.*: ∼neck speed головокружи́тельная ско́рость; ∼**through** *n.* (mil.) проры́в; (fig.) скачо́к, перело́м, проры́в; ∼**-up** *n.* разва́л, распа́д; (of friendship) разры́в; ∼**water** *n.* волноре́з

✦ **breakfast** /'brekfəst/ *n.* за́втрак

● *v.i.* за́втракать, по-

breast /brest/ *n.* **1** грудь **2** (cul.): ∼ of lamb бара́нья груди́нка

■ ∼**fed** *adj.* вско́рмленный гру́дью; ∼**feeding** *n.* кормле́ние гру́дью; ∼**stroke** *n.* брасс

breath /breθ/ *n.* дыха́ние; (single ∼) вздох; out of ∼ задыха́ясь; bad ∼ дурно́й за́пах изо рта; catch, hold one's ∼ зата́|ивать, -и́ть дыха́ние; take sb's ∼ away захва́т|ывать, -и́ть дух у кого́-н.

■ ∼**taking** *adj.* захва́тывающий

breathalyse /'breθəlaɪz/ (AmE **breathalyze**) *v.t.* пров|еря́ть, -е́рить на алкого́ль

breathalyser /'breθəlaɪzə(r)/ (AmE **Breathalyzer**®) *n.* алкоме́тр, алкого́льно-респира́торная тру́бка

breathe /briːð/ *v.t.* **1**: ∼ fresh air дыша́ть (*impf.*) све́жим во́здухом **2** (utter softly): ∼ a sigh изд|ава́ть, -а́ть вздох; don't ∼ a word! ни сло́ва бо́льше!

● *v.i.* дыша́ть (*impf.*)

breather /'briːðə(r)/ *n.* переды́шка

breathing /'briːðɪŋ/ *n.* дыха́ние

■ ∼ space *n.* переды́шка

breathless /'breθlɪs/ *adj.* задыха́ющийся, запыха́вшийся

bred /bred/ *past and p.p. of* ▶ breed

breed /briːd/ *n.* поро́да

● *v.t.* (*past and p.p.* **bred**) **1** (cause) поро|жда́ть, -ди́ть **2** (animals) раз|води́ть, -вести́

● *v.i.* (*past and p.p.* **bred**) размн|ожа́ться, -о́житься; плоди́ться, рас-

breeder /'briːdə(r)/ *n.* животново́д, скотово́д

breeding /'briːdɪŋ/ *n.* **1** (by stockbreeders) разведе́ние **2** (manners etc.) воспи́танность

■ ∼ ground *n.* (fig.) расса́дник, оча́г

breeze /briːz/ *n.* ветеро́к; бриз

● *v.i.*: ∼ in/out (infml) влете́ть/вы́лететь (*pf.*)

breezy /'briːzɪ/ *adj.* (**breezier**, **breeziest**) (of weather) све́жий; (fig., of person) живо́й, беззабо́тный

brevity /'brevɪtɪ/ *n.* кра́ткость

brew /bruː/ *v.t.* (beer) вари́ть, с-; (tea) зава́р|ивать, -и́ть

● *v.i.* **1** (of tea etc.) зава́р|иваться, -и́ться **2**: a storm is ∼ing (lit. and fig.) гроза́ надвига́ется; there's trouble ∼ing быть беде́

brewer /'bruːə(r)/ *n.* пивова́р

brewery /'bruːərɪ/ *n.* пивова́ренный заво́д

bribe /braɪb/ *n.* взя́тка, по́дкуп

● *v.t.* да|ва́ть, -ть взя́тку + *d.*; ∼ sb to do sth по́дкупом доб|ива́ться, -и́ться чего́-н. от кого́-н.

bribery /'braɪbərɪ/ *n.* взя́точничество

brick /brɪk/ *n.* кирпи́ч; ∼s (collect.) кирпи́ч; (attr.) кирпи́чный

● *v.t.*: ∼ up за|кла́дывать, -ложи́ть кирпичо́м

■ ∼**layer** *n.* ка́менщик

bridal /'braɪd(ə)l/ *adj.* сва́дебный

bride /braɪd/ *n.* неве́ста

■ ∼**groom** *n.* жени́х; ∼**smaid** *n.* подру́жка неве́сты

✦ **bridge¹** /brɪdʒ/ *n.* **1** (also dentistry) мост **2** (naut.) капита́нский мо́стик **3** (of nose) перено́сица **4** (of violin) подста́вка

● *v.t.*: ∼ a river наво́|дить, -ести́ мост че́рез ре́ку; (join by bridging) соедин|я́ть, -и́ть мосто́м; (fig.): ∼ a gap восп|олня́ть, -о́лнить пробе́л

bridge² /brɪdʒ/ *n.* (game) бридж

bridle /'braɪd(ə)l/ *n.* узда́, узде́чка

● *v.t.* (a horse) взну́зд|ывать, -а́ть; (fig.) обу́зд|ывать, -а́ть

● *v.i.* (fig.) зад|ира́ть, -ра́ть нос

■ ∼ path *n.* (BrE) верхова́я тропа́

brief /briːf/ *n.* **1** (lawyer's) изложе́ние де́ла **2** (BrE, instructions) инстру́кция **3** (in pl.) (infml, underpants) трус|ы́ (-о́в)

● *adj.* коро́ткий, недо́лгий; in ∼ вкра́тце

● *v.t.* **1**: ∼ a lawyer (BrE) поруч|а́ть, -и́ть адвока́ту веде́ние де́ла **2** (mil. etc.) инструкти́ровать (*impf., pf.*)

■ ∼**case** *n.* портфе́ль (*m.*)

briefing /'briːfɪŋ/ *n.* инструкта́ж; (press) бри́финг

briefly /'briːflɪ/ *adv.* кра́тко, сжа́то

brigade /brɪ'geɪd/ *n.* брига́да

brigadier /brɪgə'dɪə(r)/ *n.* (also ∼ **general**) брига́дный генера́л

brigand /'brɪgənd/ *n.* разбо́йник

✦ **bright** /braɪt/ *adj.* **1** (clear, shining) я́ркий, све́тлый; a ∼ day я́сный день; ∼ red я́рко-кра́сный; a ∼ room све́тлая ко́мната **2** (cheerful): look on the ∼ side смотре́ть (*impf.*) на ве́щи оптимисти́чески **3** (clever): a ∼ girl толко́вая де́вочка; a ∼ idea блестя́щая мысль

brighten /'braɪt(ə)n/ *v.t.* (also ∼ up) ожив|ля́ть, -и́ть

● *v.i.* (also ∼ up): the weather ∼ed (up) пого́да проясни́лась

brightness /'braɪtnɪs/ *n.* (lustre) я́ркость; (cleverness) блеск, смышлёность

brilliance /'brɪlɪəns/ *n.* (brightness) я́ркость; (intelligence) блеск (ума́)

brilliant /'brɪlɪənt/ *adj.* (lit., fig.) сверка́ющий, блестя́щий; (BrE, infml, excellent) замеча́тельный

brim /brɪm/ *n.* край; (of hat) поля́ (*nt. pl.*)

brine /braɪn/ *n.* рассо́л

✦ **bring** /brɪŋ/ *v.t.* (*past and p.p.* **brought**)

b

(cause to come, deliver) (a thing) принос|и́ть, -ести́; (a person) привод|и́ть, -ести́; **it brought tears to my eyes** э́то вы́звало у меня́ слёзы

□ ~ **about** v.t. (cause) вызыва́ть, вы́звать; производ|и́ть, -ести́

□ ~ **back** v.t. принос|и́ть, -ести́ (or привод|и́ть, -ести́) наза́д

□ ~ **down** v.t. (an aircraft) сби|ва́ть, -ть; ~ **prices down** сни|жа́ть, -и́зить це́ны

□ ~ **forward** v.t. (advance date of) перенос|и́ть, -ести́ на бо́лее ра́нний срок

□ ~ **in** v.t. внос|и́ть, -ести́; ввод|и́ть, -ести́; ~ **in a verdict** выноси́ть, вы́нести верди́кт

□ ~ **off** v.t.: ~ **off a manoeuvre** успе́шно заверш|а́ть, -и́ть опера́цию

□ ~ **on** v.t.: **this brought on a bad cold** э́то вы́звало си́льный на́сморк

□ ~ **out** v.t. выноси́ть, вы́нести; выводи́ть, вы́вести; (make evident) выявля́ть, вы́явить; (publish) выпуска́ть, вы́пустить; **the curtains ~ out the green in the carpet** занаве́ски оттеня́ют зе́лень ковра́

□ ~ **round** v.t. (restore to consciousness) привод|и́ть, -ести́ в себя́; (persuade) убе|жда́ть, -ди́ть

□ ~ **up** v.t. (educate) воспи́т|ывать, -а́ть; (vomit): **he brought up his dinner** его́ вы́рвало по́сле обе́да; ~ **up a subject** подн|има́ть, -я́ть вопро́с; завод|и́ть, -ести́ разгово́р о чём-н.

brink /brɪŋk/ n. край (also fig.)

brisk /brɪsk/ adj. (of movement) ско́рый; (of air, wind) све́жий

bristle /ˈbrɪs(ə)l/ n. щети́на
● v.i. (of hair) стоя́ть (impf.) ды́бом; встать (pf.) ды́бом; (of animal, also fig., of person) ощети́ни|ваться, -ться

Britain /ˈbrɪt(ə)n/ n. Брита́ния

ꙮ **British** /ˈbrɪtɪʃ/ n.: **the** ~ брита́нцы (m. pl.)
● adj. брита́нский
■ ~ **Isles** n. pl. Брита́нские острова́

Briton /ˈbrɪt(ə)n/ n. брита́н|ец (-ка)

brittle /ˈbrɪt(ə)l/ adj. ло́мкий, хру́пкий

broach /brəʊtʃ/ v.t.: ~ **a subject** подн|има́ть, -я́ть вопро́с

ꙮ **broad** /brɔːd/ adj. **1** (wide) широ́кий **2**: in ~ **daylight** средь бе́ла дня **3** (decided): **a** ~ **hint** то́лстый намёк; **a** ~ **accent** си́льный акце́нт **4** (approximate): **in** ~ **outline** в о́бщих черта́х
■ ~ **band** n. (comput.) широкополо́сная переда́ча да́нных; ~ **bean** n. фасо́ль; ~ **cast** n. трансля́ция ● v.t. (on radio/TV) трансли́ровать (impf., pf.); перед|ава́ть, -а́ть по ра́дио, телеви́дению; (spread news etc.) распростран|я́ть, -и́ть ● v.i. (on radio/TV) вести́ (det.) радиопереда́чу, телепереда́чу; ~ **caster** n. (radio) радиожурнали́ст; (TV) тележурнали́ст; ~ **casting** n. (radio) радиовеща́ние; (TV) телевеща́ние; трансля́ция; ~ **minded** adj. широ́ких взгля́дов; ~ **sheet** n. газе́та большо́го форма́та

broaden /ˈbrɔːd(ə)n/ v.t. & i. расш|иря́ть(ся), -и́рить(ся)

broadly /ˈbrɔːdlɪ/ adv. (in the main) в основно́м; ~ **speaking** вообще́ говоря́

broccoli /ˈbrɒkəlɪ/ n. бро́кколи (nt. indecl.)

brochure /ˈbrəʊʃə(r)/ n. брошю́ра

broil /brɔɪl/ v.t. (AmE, cul.) жа́рить, за- на откры́том огне́

broke /brəʊk/ adj. (infml) разори́вшийся, безде́нежный

broken /ˈbrəʊkən/ adj. **1**: **a** ~ **leg** сло́манная нога́; ~ **English** ло́маный англи́йский язы́к **2** (~-down): **a** ~ **marriage** расстро́енный брак; **a** ~ **home** разби́тая семья́ **3** (crushed): **a** ~ **man** сло́мленный челове́к
■ ~ **down** adj. (of machine) сло́манный; ~ **hearted** adj. с разби́тым се́рдцем

broker /ˈbrəʊkə(r)/ n. ма́клер, бро́кер

brolly /ˈbrɒlɪ/ n. (BrE, infml) = umbrella

bronchitis /brɒŋˈkaɪtɪs/ n. бронхи́т

bronze /brɒnz/ n. бро́нза; (attr.) бро́нзовый

brooch /brəʊtʃ/ n. брошь

brood /bruːd/ n. пото́мство
● v.i. **1** (of bird) сиде́ть (impf.) на я́йцах **2**: ~ **over an insult** копи́ть (impf.) в себе́ оби́ду

broody /ˈbruːdɪ/ adj. (**broodier, broodiest**) **1** (thoughtful) заду́мчивый; (morose) угрю́мый **2**: **a** ~ **hen** (хоро́шая) насе́дка **3** (of a woman): **she's feeling** ~ в ней просну́лся матери́нский инсти́нкт

brook /brʊk/ n. (stream) руче́й

broom /bruːm/ n. метла́
■ ~ **stick** n. (witch's) помело́

brothel /ˈbrɒθ(ə)l/ n. борде́ль (m.), публи́чный дом

ꙮ **brother** /ˈbrʌðə(r)/ n. брат
■ ~ **in-law** n. (sister's husband, husband's sister's husband) зять (m.); (wife's) ~ шу́рин; (husband's ~) де́верь (m.); (wife's sister's husband) своя́к

brotherly /ˈbrʌðəlɪ/ adj. бра́тский

brought /brɔːt/ past and p.p. of ▶ bring

brow /braʊ/ n. (forehead) лоб, чело́; (of hill) гре́бень (m.)

brown /braʊn/ n. кори́чневый цвет
● adj. **1** кори́чневый; (grey-~) бу́рый **2** (tanned) загоре́лый
● v.t. поджа́ри|вать, -ть
■ ~ **bread** n. се́рый хлеб; ~ **paper** n. обёрточная бума́га

brownish /ˈbraʊnɪʃ/ adj. коричнева́тый

browse /braʊz/ v.i. щипа́ть (impf.) траву́

browser /ˈbraʊzə(r)/ n. (comput.) бра́узер

bruise /bruːz/ n. синя́к, кровоподтёк; (on fruit) вмя́тина
● v.t. ста́вить, по- синя́к + d.; (fruit) помя́ть, поби́ть (both pf.); **I ~ d my shoulder** я уши́б плечо́

brunette /bruːˈnet/ n. брюне́тка

brunt /brʌnt/ n. гла́вный уда́р; **bear the** ~ **of the work** выноси́ть, вы́нести всю тя́жесть рабо́ты

brush /brʌʃ/ n. (for sweeping) щётка; (painter's) кисть

ꙮ ключева́я ле́ксика

b

● *v.t.* (clean) чи́стить, по-; (touch slightly):
the branches ~ed my cheek ве́тви слегка́
косну́лись мое́й щеки́
● *v.i.*: **~ against sth** слегка́ каса́ться,
косну́ться чего́-н.; **~ past sb** прон|оси́ться,
-ести́сь ми́мо кого́-н.
□ **~ aside** *v.t.*: **~ aside difficulties** отме|та́ть,
-сти́ тру́дности
□ **~ up** *v.t.*: **~ up one's French** освеж|а́ть, -и́ть в
па́мяти францу́зский
● *v.i.*: **~ up on a subject** освеж|а́ть, -и́ть
зна́ния по како́му-н. предме́ту
■ **~wood** *n.* хво́рост, вале́жник
brusque /bruːsk/ *adj.* ре́зкий
Brussels /ˈbrʌs(ə)lz/ *n.* Брюссе́ль (*m.*)
■ **~ sprouts** *n. pl.* брюссе́льская капу́ста
brutal /ˈbruːt(ə)l/ *adj.* жесто́кий
brutality /bruːˈtælɪtɪ/ *n.* жесто́кость
brutalize /ˈbruːtəlaɪz/ *v.t.* ожесточ|а́ть, -и́ть;
огруб|ля́ть, -и́ть
brute /bruːt/ *n.* (animal) живо́тное, зверь (*m.*);
(person) скоти́на (*c.g.*)
● *adj.*: **~ force** гру́бая, физи́ческая си́ла
B.Sc. *abbr.* (*of* **Bachelor of Science**)
бакала́вр (есте́ственных) нау́к
BSE *abbr.* (*of* **bovine spongiform
encephalopathy**) бы́чья губкови́дная
энцефалопати́я
bubble /ˈbʌb(ə)l/ *n.* пузы́рь (*m.*); (of air, gas)
пузырёк
● *v.i.* (of water) пузыри́ться (*impf.*), кипе́ть
(*impf.*)
■ **~ bath** *n.* пе́на для ва́нны
Bucharest /buːkəˈrest/ *n.* Бухаре́ст
buck¹ /bʌk/ *n.* **1** (male animal) саме́ц **2** (AmE,
infml, dollar) до́ллар **3**: **pass the ~** (infml)
снима́ть, снять с себя́ отве́тственность
buck² /bʌk/ *v.i.* (of horse) брыка́ться (*impf.*)
bucket /ˈbʌkɪt/ *n.* ведро́
● *v.i.* (**bucketed, bucketing**) (BrE, rain): **it's
~ing down** льёт как из ведра́
■ **~ list** *n.* спи́сок всех дел, кото́рые челове́к
хоте́л бы сде́лать пе́ред сме́ртью
buckle /ˈbʌk(ə)l/ *n.* пря́жка
● *v.t.* **1** (coat, shoe) застёг|ивать, -ну́ть **2** (wheel)
гнуть, по-; деформи́ровать (*impf., pf.*)
● *v.i.* **1** (of coat, shoe) застёг|иваться, -ну́ться
2 (of wheel) гну́ться, по-; деформи́роваться
(*impf., pf.*) **3** (of knees) под|гиба́ться, -огну́ться
buckwheat /ˈbʌkwiːt/ *n.* гречи́ха; (*attr.*)
гре́чневый
bud /bʌd/ *n.* по́чка; (flower not fully opened)
буто́н
● *v.i.* (**budded, budding**) (of plant)
покр|ыва́ться, -ы́ться по́чками; (fig.)
распус|ка́ться, -ти́ться; **he's a ~ding musician**
он многообеща́ющий музыка́нт
Budapest /buːdəˈpest/ *n.* Будапе́шт
Buddhism /ˈbʊdɪz(ə)m/ *n.* будди́зм
Buddhist /ˈbʊdɪst/ *n.* будди́ст
● *adj.* будди́йский, будди́стский
buddleia /ˈbʌdlɪə/ *n.* (bot.) буд(д)ле́я
buddy /ˈbʌdɪ/ *n.* (AmE, infml) дружи́ще (*m.*),
прия́тель (*m.*)

budge /bʌdʒ/ *v.t.*: **I cannot ~ this rock** я не
могу́ сдви́нуть э́тот ка́мень
● *v.i.*: **the bookcase won't ~ an inch** кни́жный
шкаф невозмо́жно сдви́нуть с ме́ста
budgerigar /ˈbʌdʒərɪɡɑː(r)/ *n.* волни́стый
попуга́йчик
✒ **budget** /ˈbʌdʒɪt/ *n.* бюдже́т
● *v.t. & i.* (**budgeted, budgeting**): **~
(funds) for a project** ассигнова́ть (*impf., pf.*)
определённую су́мму на прое́кт
budgie /ˈbʌdʒɪ/ *n.* (infml) = **budgerigar**
Buenos Aires /bweɪnɒs ˈaɪrɪz/ *n.* Буэ́нос-А́йрес
buff /bʌf/ *n.* (colour) тёмно-жёлтый цвет
buffalo /ˈbʌfələʊ/ *n.* (*pl.* **~ or ~es**) (wild ox)
бу́йвол
buffer /ˈbʌfə(r)/ *n.* (rail., comput., also fig.) бу́фер
buffet¹ /ˈbʌfɪt/ *v.t.* (**buffeted, buffeting**)
уд|аря́ть, -а́рить в + *a.*
buffet² /ˈbʊfeɪ/ *n.* (refreshment bar) буфе́т; (meal)
а-ля фурше́т
bug /bʌɡ/ *n.* (small insect) бука́шка, жучо́к;
(infml, germ) зара́за; (microphone) жучо́к;
(comput., error) оши́бка, баг (sl.)
● *v.t.* (**bugged, bugging**): **the room was
~ged** (infml) в ко́мнате бы́ли устано́влены
подслу́шивающие устро́йства; (infml, annoy)
раздраж|а́ть, -и́ть
bugger /ˈbʌɡə(r)/ (BrE, vulg.) *n.* (as term of abuse)
сво́лочь; **poor ~** несча́стный
● *v.t.*: **~ (it)!** чёрт возьми́!; **~ them!** да хрен с
ни́ми!; **~ all** ни хрена́
● *v.i.*: **~ off!** прова́ливай!; убира́йся!
buggy /ˈbʌɡɪ/ *n.* (in full **baby ~**) лёгкая
де́тская коля́ска
bugle /ˈbjuːɡ(ə)l/ *n.* горн
✒ **build** /bɪld/ *n.* телосложе́ние
● *v.t.* (past and p.p. **built**) **1** стро́ить, по-;
выстра́ивать, вы́строить; **~ a nest** вить,
с- гнездо́ **2**: **a well-built man** хорошо́
сло́женный челове́к **3** (fig.): **~ a new world**
созд|ава́ть, -а́ть но́вый мир
□ **~ up** *v.t.*: **~ sb up** (in health) укреп|ля́ть, -и́ть
кому́-н. здоро́вье; (in prestige) популяризи́ровать
(*impf., pf.*) кого́-н.; созд|ава́ть, -а́ть и́мя кому́-н.;
~ up a business созд|ава́ть, -а́ть де́ло
● *v.i.*: **work has built up over the past year** за
после́дний год накопи́лось мно́го рабо́ты
■ **~-up** *n.* (accumulation) скопле́ние; рост,
разви́тие, развёртывание; (infml, boosting)
популяриза́ция, созда́ние и́мени
builder /ˈbɪldə(r)/ *n.* строи́тель (*m.*)
✒ **building** /ˈbɪldɪŋ/ *n.* **1** (structure) зда́ние,
постро́йка, строе́ние; (premises) помеще́ние
2 (activity) (по)стро́йка; (esp. large-scale)
строи́тельство
■ **~ site** *n.* стро́йка; **~ society** *n.* (BrE)
(жили́щно-)строи́тельное о́бщество; ≈
ипоте́чный банк
built past and p.p. of ▶ **build**
■ **~-in** *adj.*: **a ~ cupboard** встро́енный/стенно́й
шкаф; **~-up** *adj.*: **~ area** застро́енный райо́н
bulb /bʌlb/ *n.* (bot., anat.) лу́ковица; (of lamp)
ла́мпочка

Bulgaria /bʌlˈgeəriə/ *n.* Болга́рия

Bulgarian /bʌlˈgeəriən/ *n.* (person) болга́р|ин (-ка); (language) болга́рский язы́к
• *adj.* болга́рский

bulge /bʌldʒ/ *n.* вы́пуклость
• *v.i.* (swell) выпя́чиваться, вы́пятиться; (of bag etc.) над|ува́ться, -у́ться

bulimia /buˈlɪmɪə/ *n.* булими́я

bulimic /buˈlɪmɪk/ *adj.* страда́ющий булими́ей

bulk /bʌlk/ *n.* **1** (size) величина́, ма́сса, объём **2** (greater part) основна́я ма́сса/часть
■ ~ **buying** *n.* опто́вые заку́пки

bulky /ˈbʌlkɪ/ *adj.* (**bulkier, bulkiest**) громо́здкий

bull /bʊl/ *n.* (ox) бык; (elephant, whale, etc.) саме́ц
■ ~**dog** *n.* бульдо́г; ~**dozer** *n.* бульдо́зер; ~**fight** *n.* бой быко́в; ~**fighter** *n.* тореадо́р; ~**ring** *n.* аре́на для бо́я быко́в; ~**seye** *n.* (of target) я́блочко

bullet /ˈbʊlɪt/ *n.* пу́ля
■ ~**proof** *adj.* пуленепробива́емый; ~**proof vest** бронежиле́т

bulletin /ˈbʊlɪtɪn/ *n.* (official statement) бюллете́нь (*m.*); (news report) сво́дка (новосте́й), вы́пуск, сообще́ние

bullock /ˈbʊlək/ *n.* вол

bully /ˈbʊlɪ/ *n.* громи́ла (*m.*), задира (*c.g.*)
• *v.t.* запу́г|ивать, -а́ть

bum /bʌm/ *n.* (infml) **1** (BrE, buttocks) зад, за́дница **2** (AmE, vagrant) бродя́га (*m.*)

bumblebee /ˈbʌmb(ə)lbiː/ *n.* шмель (*m.*)

bump /bʌmp/ *n.* **1** (thump) глухо́й уда́р; (collision) толчо́к **2** (swelling, protuberance) ши́шка
• *v.t.* уд|аря́ть, -а́рить; ушиб|а́ть, -и́ть; I ~ed **my knee as I fell** я уши́б коле́но при паде́нии
• *v.i.*: his car ~ed into ours его́ маши́на вре́залась в на́шу; I ~ed into him in London я наткну́лся на него́ в Ло́ндоне

bumper /ˈbʌmpə(r)/ *n.* **1** (of car) ба́мпер **2**: ~ **crop** небыва́лый/невида́нный урожа́й

bumpkin /ˈbʌmpkɪn/ *n.* мужла́н

bumptious /ˈbʌmpʃəs/ *adj.* самоуве́ренный, зазна́вшийся

bumpy /ˈbʌmpɪ/ *adj.* (**bumpier, bumpiest**) (of road) уха́бистый, тря́ский; a ~ **flight** ≈ болта́нка

bun /bʌn/ *n.* **1** (cul.) бу́лочка, плю́шка **2** (of hair) пучо́к

bunch /bʌntʃ/ *n.* **1** (of flowers) буке́т; (of grapes) кисть, гроздь; (of bananas) гроздь; ~ **of keys** свя́зка ключе́й **2** (infml, group) компа́ния, гру́ппа

bundle /ˈbʌnd(ə)l/ *n.* **1** (of clothes etc.) у́зел; (of sticks) вяза́нка; (of hay) оха́пка **2**: she is a ~ of **nerves** она́ о́чень не́рвная
• *v.t.* **1**: ~ **up** свя́з|ывать, -а́ть в у́зел/вяза́нку **2** (shove) запи́х|ивать, -а́ть

bung /bʌŋ/ *n.* заты́чка, вту́лка
• *v.t.* **1** (cask etc.) зат|ыка́ть, -кну́ть; закупо́ри|вать, -ть; the sink is ~ed up

ра́ковина засори́лась; my nose is ~ed up у меня́ зало́жен нос **2** (BrE, sl., throw) швыр|я́ть, -ну́ть

bungalow /ˈbʌŋgələʊ/ *n.* бу́нгало (*nt. indecl.*)

bungle /ˈbʌŋg(ə)l/ *v.t.* по́ртить, на-; пу́тать, с-

bunk¹ /bʌŋk/ *n.* (sleeping berth) ко́йка
■ ~ **bed** *n.* двухъя́русная крова́ть

bunk² /bʌŋk/ *v.i.* (BrE, infml, slip away) см|ыва́ться, -ы́ться; **to ~ off lessons/school** прог|у́ливать, -уля́ть уро́ки, сачкова́ть (*impf.*)

bunker /ˈbʌŋkə(r)/ *n.* (underground shelter) бу́нкер, блинда́ж; (golf) я́ма

buoy /bɔɪ/ *n.* буй, ба́кен; (life~) спаса́тельный буй/круг
• *v.t.*: ~ **up** (fig., support) подде́рж|ивать, -а́ть; (cheer up) подб|а́дривать, -одри́ть

buoyant /ˈbɔɪənt/ *adj.* плаву́чий; (of person) жизнера́достный; (of hopes, market) оживлённый; (of prices) име́ющий тенде́нцию к повыше́нию

burden /ˈbɜːd(ə)n/ *n.* (load) но́ша, груз; (fig.) бре́мя (*nt.*); обу́за
• *v.t.* (load) нагру|жа́ть, -зи́ть; (fig.) обремен|я́ть, -и́ть

bureau /ˈbjʊərəʊ/ *n.* (*pl.* ~**x** *or* ~**s**) (BrE, desk) бюро́ (*indecl.*), конто́рка; (AmE, chest) комо́д; (office) бюро́; ~ **de change** обме́нный пункт

bureaucracy /bjʊəˈrɒkrəsɪ/ *n.* бюрокра́тия

bureaucrat /ˈbjʊərəkræt/ *n.* бюрокра́т, чино́вник

bureaucratic /bjʊərəˈkrætɪk/ *adj.* бюрократи́ческий

bureaux /ˈbjʊərəʊz/ *pl. of* ▶ **bureau**

burgeon /ˈbɜːdʒ(ə)n/ *v.i.* да|ва́ть, -ть по́чки; распус|ка́ться, -ти́ться

burger /ˈbɜːgə(r)/ *n.* га́мбургер, котле́та
■ ~ **bar** *n.* га́мбургерная, котле́тная

burglar /ˈbɜːglə(r)/ *n.* кварти́рный вор, взло́мщик

burglarize /ˈbɜːgləraɪz/ *v.t.* (AmE) = burgle

burglary /ˈbɜːglərɪ/ *n.* ограбле́ние (до́ма/ о́фиса), кра́жа с взло́мом

burgle /ˈbɜːg(ə)l/ *v.t.* гра́бить, о-

burial /ˈberɪəl/ *n.* погребе́ние, захороне́ние

burly /ˈbɜːlɪ/ *adj.* (**burlier, burliest**) здорове́нный, дю́жий

Burma /ˈbɜːmə/ *n.* Би́рма

✒ **burn** /bɜːn/ *n.* ожо́г
• *v.t.* (*past and p.p.* **burnt** *or* **burned**) (destroy by fire) сж|ига́ть, -ечь; ~ **oneself** обж|ига́ться, -е́чься; the meat is ~t мя́со сгоре́ло/подгоре́ло
• *v.i.* (*past and p.p.* **burnt** *or* **burned**) горе́ть (*impf.*)
□ ~ **down** *v.t.* сж|ига́ть, -ечь
• *v.i.*: the house ~t down дом сгоре́л дотла́
□ ~ **out** *v.t.*: the fire ~t itself out пожа́р вы́жег всё до́ что и стих/костёр догоре́л (до угле́й) и поту́х; ~ **oneself out** (fig.) сгоре́ть (*pf.*)

burner /ˈbɜːnə(r)/ *n.* **1** (of stove etc.) горе́лка, конфо́рка; **to put on the back burner**

b

отодв|ига́ть, -и́нуть на за́дний план **2** (for CDs/DVDs) (CD/DVD)-реза́к (sl.) (*устройство для записи информации на компакт-диск*)

burning /'bə:nɪŋ/ *n.* горе́ние
• *adj.* (of fever) сжига́ющий; (of shame) жгу́чий; (of zeal) неи́стовый

burnt /bə:nt/ *past and p.p. of* ▸ burn

burp /bə:p/ (infml) *n.* отры́жка, рыга́ние
• *v.i.* рыг|а́ть, -ну́ть

burrow /'bʌrəʊ/ *n.* нора́
• *v.i.* рыть, вы́- нору́; рыть, про- ходы́

bursary /'bə:sərɪ/ *n.* (BrE, grant) стипе́ндия

burst /bə:st/ *n.* взрыв; a ~ of energy вспы́шка/взрыв эне́ргии; ~ of applause взрыв аплодисме́нтов; ~ of machine-gun fire пулемётная о́чередь
• *v.t.* (*past and p.p.* **burst**) раз|рыва́ть, -орва́ть; **the river ~ its banks** река́ вы́шла из берего́в
• *v.i.* (*past and p.p.* **burst**): **the balloon ~** возду́шный шар ло́пнул; **he is ~ing with health** он пы́шет здоро́вьем; **he was ~ing with pride** его́ распира́ло от го́рдости; **the door ~ open** дверь распахну́лась
• *with preps.*: ~ **into tears** разрыда́ться (*pf.*); ~ **into a room** врыва́ться, ворва́ться в ко́мнату; ~ **into flame(s)** вспы́х|ивать, -нуть
□ ~ **out** *v.i.* (exclaim) вы́палить (*pf.*); ~ **out laughing** расхохота́ться (*pf.*)

bury /'berɪ/ *v.t.* **1** (inter) хорони́ть, по- **2** (hide in earth) зар|ыва́ть, -ы́ть

ᵇ **bus** /bʌs/ *n.* (*pl.* **buses** or AmE **busses**) авто́бус
■ ~ **conductor** *n.* конду́ктор авто́буса; ~ **driver** *n.* води́тель (*m.*) авто́буса; ~ **station** *n.* авто́бусная ста́нция; ~ **stop** *n.* авто́бусная остано́вка

bush /bʊʃ/ *n.* (shrub) куст; (wild land) некульти́вированная земля́

bushy /'bʊʃɪ/ *adj.* (**bushier, bushiest**) (of beard etc.) густо́й; (of plant) кусти́стый; (of tail) пуши́стый

ᵇ **business** /'bɪznɪs/ *n.* **1** (affair) де́ло; **it is none of your ~** э́то не ва́ше де́ло; э́то вас не каса́ется; **mind your own ~** не вме́шивайтесь/су́йтесь не в своё де́ло **2** (work): **get down to ~** бра́ться, взя́ться за де́ло **3** (comm. etc.): ~ **hours, hours of ~** (of an office) часы́ приёма/рабо́ты; **he is in the wool ~** он занима́ется торго́влей ше́рстью; **go into ~** заня́ться (*pf.*) комме́рцией; **on ~** по де́лу **4** (establishment) фи́рма, предприя́тие
■ ~ **card** *n.* визи́тка, визи́тная ка́рточка; ~**like** *adj.* делово́й, практи́чный; ~**man** *n.* коммерса́нт, бизнесме́н, делбе́ц; ~**woman** *n.* бизнес-ле́ди, бизнесву́мен (*both f. indecl.*), делова́я же́нщина

busker /'bʌskə(r)/ *n.* у́личный музыка́нт

busses /'bʌsɪz/ (AmE) *pl. of* ▸ bus

bust¹ /bʌst/ *n.* (sculpture; bosom) бюст

bust² /bʌst/ (infml) *v.t.* (*past and p.p.* **busted** or **bust**) (fracture, destroy) лома́ть, с-
• *v.i.* (*past and p.p.* **busted** or **bust**) лома́ться, с-; (*also* **go ~**) **the business went**

~ де́ло ло́пнуло

bustle /'bʌs(ə)l/ *n.* суматоха, суета́
• *v.i.* (*also* ~ **about**) суети́ться, тормоши́ться (*both impf.*)

bustling /'bʌslɪŋ/ *adj.* сует|ли́вый; a ~ **city** оживлённый го́род

ᵇ **busy** /'bɪzɪ/ *adj.* (**busier, busiest**)
1 (occupied) за́нятый; **I had a ~ day** я весь день был(а́) в дела́х; **he was ~ packing** он был за́нят упако́вкой; **the line is ~** (AmE) но́мер за́нят **2**: a ~ **street** шу́мная/оживлённая у́лица
• *v.t.*: ~ **oneself** зан|има́ться, -я́ться

ᵇ **but** /bʌt/ *adv.*: **we can ~ try** попы́тка — не пы́тка
• *prep. & conj.* (except): **no one ~ me** никто́, кроме меня́; **she is anything ~ beautiful** она́ далеко́ не краса́вица; **the last ~ one** предпосле́дний; **next door ~ one** че́рез одну́ дверь; ~ **for me he would have stayed** е́сли бы не я, он бы оста́лся; **I cannot help ~ think ...** я не могу́ не ду́мать, что...
• *conj.* но

butcher /'bʊtʃə(r)/ *n.* мясни́к; ~**'s (shop)** мясна́я ла́вка, мясно́й павильо́н
• *v.t.* (cattle) забива́ть (*impf.*); (people) истреб|ля́ть, -и́ть

butchery /'bʊtʃərɪ/ *n.* (trade) торго́вля мя́сом; (massacre) резня́

butler /'bʌtlə(r)/ *n.* дворе́цкий

butt¹ /bʌt/ *n.* (fig., target): a ~ **for ridicule** мише́нь для насме́шек

butt² /bʌt/ *n.* (of rifle) прикла́д; (of cigarette) оку́рок; (AmE, infml, buttocks) зад, за́дница

butt³ /bʌt/ *v.i.*: ~ **in** (interrupt) встр|ева́ть, -ять

butter /'bʌtə(r)/ *n.* ма́сло
• *v.t.* нама́з|ывать, -ать ма́слом; ~ **up** (fig.) льсти́ть, по- + *d.*
■ ~**cup** *n.* лю́тик; ~**fingers** *n.* растя́па (*c.g.*)

butterfly /'bʌtəflaɪ/ *n.* **1** ба́бочка; **I have butterflies in my stomach** у меня́ се́рдце ёкает **2** (swimming): ~ **stroke** баттерфля́й

buttock /'bʌtək/ *n.* я́годица

button /'bʌt(ə)n/ *n.* **1** пу́говица **2** (knob) кно́пка; **press a ~** наж|има́ть, -а́ть кно́пку **3** (AmE, badge) значо́к
• *v.t.* (*also* ~ **up**) застёг|ивать, -ну́ть
■ ~**hole** *n.* пе́тля́, петли́ца; (BrE, flower) цвето́к в петли́це • *v.t.* (fig.) заде́рж|ивать, -а́ть разгово́ром

buttress /'bʌtrɪs/ *n.* (archit.) подпо́р(к)а; (fig.) опо́ра

ᵇ **buy** /baɪ/ *n.*: a good ~ вы́годная поку́пка
• *v.t.* (**buys, buying,** *past and p.p.* **bought**) покупа́ть, купи́ть; ~ **sb a drink** ста́вить, по- кому́-н. вы́пивку
□ ~ **off** *v.t.* откуп|а́ться, -и́ться (*от кого*)
□ ~ **out** *v.t.*: ~ **sb out** выкупа́ть, вы́купить чью-н. до́лю
□ ~ **up** *v.t.* скуп|а́ть, -и́ть
■ ~**out** *n.* (comm.) вы́куп

buyer /'baɪə(r)/ *n.* покупа́тель (*m.*)

buzz /bʌz/ *n.* жужжа́ние; (of talk) гул, жужжа́ние

b

c

● *v.t.* (summon with buzzer) звони́ть, по-; вызыва́ть, вы́звать сигна́лом

● *v.i.* (of insect, projectile) жужжа́ть (*impf.*)

buzzard /ˈbʌzəd/ *n.* сары́ч, каню́к; (AmE, turkey vulture) гриф-инде́йка

buzzer /ˈbʌzə(r)/ *n.* (elec.) зу́ммер

✎ **by** /baɪ/ *adv.* (near) побли́зости; (alongside) ря́дом; (past) ми́мо; **the days went ~** дни шли оди́н за други́м

● *prep.* **1** (near): **sit ~ the fire** сиде́ть (*impf.*) у ками́на; **I was going ~ the house** я шёл ми́мо до́ма; **~ oneself** (alone) (соверше́нно) оди́н/одна́; (unaided) сам/сама́, самостоя́тельно; **a path ~ the river** доро́жка у/вдоль реки́; **~ the way** кста́ти **2** (along, via): **~ land and sea** по су́ше и по мо́рю; **~ the nearest road** ближа́йшей доро́гой **3** (of time limit): **~ Thursday** к четвергу́; **~ now** тепе́рь; **he should know ~ now** пора́ бы уж ему́ зна́ть; **~ then** к тому́ вре́мени **4** (means) (*often expr. by i. case*) (**~** means of) при по́мощи + *g.*; **a book ~ Tolstoy** кни́га Толсто́го; **~ my watch** по мои́м часа́м; **~ rail** по желе́зной доро́ге; **~ taxi** на/в такси́; **~ law** по зако́ну; **a letter written ~ hand** письмо́, напи́санное от руки́ **5** (of rate or measurement): **little ~ little** ма́ло-пома́лу; **bread came down in price ~1**

rouble хлеб подешеве́л на оди́н рубль; **sell sth ~ the yard** прод|ава́ть, -а́ть что-н. на я́рды; **one ~ one** оди́н за други́м; по одному́, поодино́чке; **day ~ day** день за днём; **you must divide thirty ~ five** вам на́до раздели́ть 30 на 5; **a room 13 feet ~ 12** ко́мната трина́дцать фу́тов на двена́дцать

bye-bye /ˈbaɪbaɪ, bəˈbaɪ/ *int.* пока́!; всего́ хоро́шего!

by-election /ˈbaɪlekʃ(ə)n/ *n.* (BrE) дополни́тельные вы́боры (*m. pl.*)

bygone /ˈbaɪɡɒn/ *n.* (*usu. in pl.*): **let ~s be ~s** что бы́ло, то прошло́

● *adj.* проше́дший, мину́вший

bypass /ˈbaɪpɑːs/ *n.* объе́зд, обхо́д; (med.) шунт; **heart ~** корона́рное шунти́рование

● *v.t.* об|ходи́ть, -ойти́ (also fig.)

by-product /ˈbaɪprɒdʌkt/ *n.* побо́чный проду́кт

bystander /ˈbaɪstændə(r)/ *n.* зри́тель (*m.*)

byte /baɪt/ *n.* (comput.) байт

Byzantine /baɪˈzæntaɪn/ *adj.* (lit., fig.) византи́йский

■ **~ Empire** *n.* Византи́я, Византи́йская импе́рия

Byzantium /bɪˈzæntɪəm/ *n.* (city) Виза́нтий

Cc

C¹ /siː/ *n.* **1** (mus.) до (*nt. indecl.*) **2** (academic mark) «удовлетвори́тельно», тро́йка

C² /siː/ *n.* (*abbr. of* **Celsius** *or* **centigrade**) C (= *градусов по Цельсию*)

c. *abbr. of* **1** (**century**) в. (век); столе́тие **2** (**circa**) ок. (о́коло) **3** (**cent(s)**) це́нт(ы)

cab /kæb/ *n.* **1** (taxi) такси́ (*nt. indecl.*); кеб **2** (of lorry etc.) каби́на води́теля

■ **~ driver** *n.* шофёр такси́

cabaret /ˈkæbəreɪ/ *n.* кабаре́ (*nt. indecl.*), эстра́дное представле́ние

cabbage /ˈkæbɪdʒ/ *n.* капу́ста

cabby /ˈkæbɪ/ *n.* (infml) такси́ст

cabin /ˈkæbɪn/ *n.* каби́на; (in ship etc.) каю́та

cabinet /ˈkæbɪnɪt/ *n.* **1** (piece of furniture) го́рка, (застеклённый) шка́ф(чик) **2** (pol.) кабине́т (мини́стров)

cable /ˈkeɪb(ə)l/ *n.* (elec.) ка́бель (*m.*)

■ **~ TV** *n.* ка́бельное телеви́дение

cackle /ˈkæk(ə)l/ *v.t. & i.* гогота́ть

cactus /ˈkæktəs/ *n.* (*pl.* **cacti** /-taɪ/ *or* **cactuses**) ка́ктус

CAD *abbr.* (*of* **computer-aided design**) автоматизи́рованное проекти́рование

caddy /ˈkædɪ/ *n.* ча́йница

cadet /kəˈdet/ *n.* (mil.) каде́т, курса́нт

cadge /kædʒ/ *v.t. & i.* выкля́нчивать, вы́клянчить; (infml) стрел|я́ть, -ьну́ть (*что у кого*)

Caesarean /sɪˈzeərɪən/ (AmE *also* **Cesarean**) *adj.*: **~ birth, operation, section** ке́сарево сече́ние

✎ **cafe** /ˈkæfeɪ/ *n.* кафе́ (*nt. indecl.*)

cafeteria /kæfɪˈtɪərɪə/ *n.* кафете́рий

caffeine /ˈkæfiːn/ *n.* кофеи́н

cage /keɪdʒ/ *n.* кле́тка

Cairo /ˈkaɪrəʊ/ *n.* Каи́р

cajole /kəˈdʒəʊl/ *v.t.* обха́живать (*impf.*)

✎ **cake** /keɪk/ *n.* **1** (sponge ~) кекс; (with cream) торт **2** (fig.): **a piece of ~** (infml) пустяко́вое де́ло

calamity /kəˈlæmɪtɪ/ *n.* бе́дствие

calcium /ˈkælsɪəm/ *n.* ка́льций

calculat|e /ˈkælkjʊleɪt/ *v.t.* **1** (compute) вычисля́ть, вы́числить **2** (estimate) рассчи́т|ывать, -а́ть **3** (plan): **a ~ed risk** обду́манный риск

C

calculating /'kælkjʊleɪtɪŋ/ *adj.* расчётливый, себе на уме

calculation /kælkjʊ'leɪʃ(ə)n/ *n.* вычисление

calculator /'kælkjʊleɪtə(r)/ *n.* калькулятор

Calcutta /kæl'kʌtə/ *n.* Калькутта

calendar /'kælɪndə(r)/ *n.* календарь

calf¹ /kɑːf/ *n.* (*pl.* **calves**) (of cattle) телёнок
■ ~**skin** *n.* опоек

calf² /kɑːf/ *n.* (*pl.* **calves**) (of leg) икра

calibrate /'kælɪbreɪt/ *v.t.* калибровать (*impf., pf.*), градуировать (*impf., pf.*)

calibre /'kælɪbə(r)/ (AmE **caliber**) *n.* калибр

California /kælɪ'fɔːnɪə/ *n.* Калифорния

♂ **call** /kɔːl/ *n.* **1** (cry) зов, оклик **2** (of bird) крик **3** (teleph.): **telephone** ~ звонок по телефону **4** (visit): **pay a** ~ нан|осить, -ести визит **5** (summons, demand) зов, клич, призыв; **the doctor is on** ~ врач на вызове **6** (need): **there is no** ~ **for him to worry** ему нечего волноваться
• *v.t.* **1** (name) наз|ывать, -вать; **he is** ~**ed John** его зовут Джон(ом); ~ **a strike** приз|ывать, -вать к забастовке **2** (summon): ~ **a doctor/taxi!** вызовите врача/такси! **3** (announce): ~ **a meeting** соз|ывать, -вать собрание
• *v.i.* **1** (cry) звать, по-; окл|икать, -икнуть **2** (visit) за|ходить, -йти; **I** ~**ed on him** я зашёл к нему; **the train** ~**s at every station** поезд останавливается на каждой станции **3** ~ **for** (pick up): **I** ~**ed for him at 6** я зашёл за ним в 6 часов; (demand): **the situation** ~**s for courage** обстоятельства требуют мужества **4** ~ **on: the president** ~**ed on the world community for help** президент призвал на помощь мировое сообщество
□ ~ **back** *v.t. & i.* (on telephone) позвонить (*pf.*) снова + *d.*
□ ~ **in** *v.t.* (a specialist) вызывать, вызвать
□ ~ **off** *v.t.* (cancel) отмен|ять, -ить
□ ~ **out** *v.t.* (summon away) от|зывать, -звать; (doctor) вызывать, вызвать
• *v.i.* выклик|ать, выкликнуть
□ ~ **up** *v.t.* (telephone) звонить, по- (*кому*) по телефону; (evoke) вызывать, вызвать; (for mil. service) приз|ывать, -вать
■ ~ **box** *n.* (BrE) телефонная будка; ~ **centre** *n.* колл-центр, информационно-справочная служба

caller /'kɔːlə(r)/ *n.* (visitor) посетитель (-ница); (telephone) позвонивший (по телефону)

calligraphy /kə'lɪɡrəfɪ/ *n.* каллиграфия

callous /'kæləs/ *adj.* чёрствый

calm /kɑːm/ *n.* спокойствие, тишина
• *adj.* спокойный
• *v.t. & i.* (*also* ~ **down**) успок|аивать(ся), -оить(ся)

calorie /'kælərɪ/ *n.* калория

calves /kɑːvz/ *pl. of* ▸ **calf¹**, ▸ **calf²**

camaraderie /kæmə'rɑːdərɪ/ *n.* товарищеские отношения

Cambodia /kæm'bəʊdɪə/ *n.* Камбоджа

Cambodian /kæm'bəʊdɪən/ *n.* (person) камбоджи|ец (-йка)
• *adj.* камбоджийский

camcorder /'kæmkɔːdə(r)/ *n.* портативная видеокамера

came /keɪm/ *past of* ▸ **come**

camel /'kæm(ə)l/ *n.* верблюд

camellia /kə'miːlɪə/ *n.* камелия

♂ **camera** /'kæmrə/ *n.* фотоаппарат
■ ~**man** *n.* оператор; ~ **phone** *n.* камерофон, мобильный телефон с фото-/видео|камерой

camomile /'kæməmaɪl/ *n.* ромашка

camouflage /'kæməflɑːʒ/ *n.* маскировка
• *v.t.* маскировать, за-

♂ **camp¹** /kæmp/ *n.* лагерь
• *v.i.* (pitch camp) разб|ивать, -ить лагерь
■ ~ **bed** *n.* (BrE) раскладушка; ~**fire** *n.* походный костёр; ~**site** *n.* кемпинг, турбаза

camp² /kæmp/ *adj.* женоподобный

♂ **campaign** /kæm'peɪn/ *n.* кампания
• *v.i.* участвовать (*impf.*) в походе; (fig.) вести (*det.*) кампанию

campaigner /kæm'peɪnə(r)/ *n.* участник кампании

camper /'kæmpə(r)/ *n.* (person) ночующий на открытом воздухе; (vehicle) (BrE *also* ~ **van**) автодом (*автомобиль, не прицеп*); (AmE) жилой/туристский автоприцеп

camping /'kæmpɪŋ/ *n.* кемпинг; **go** ~ жить (*impf.*) в палатках

campus /'kæmpəs/ *n.* (*pl.* ~**es**) университетский городок

can¹ /kæn/ *n.* **1** (for liquids) бидон **2** (for food) (консервная) банка
• *v.t.* (**canned, canning**) консервировать (*impf., pf.*)
■ ~ **opener** *n.* консервный нож

♂ **can²** /kæn/ *v.i.* (*3rd pers. sg. pres.* **can,** *past* **could,** *neg.* **cannot, can't**) (expr. ability or permission) мочь (*impf.*); (expr. capability) уметь (*impf.*); **he can't clean his teeth yet** он ещё не умеет чистить зубы; **I** ~ **see him** я вижу его; **I** ~ **understand that** я понимаю (*or* могу понять) это; **as soon as you** ~ как только сможете; как можно скорее

Canada /'kænədə/ *n.* Канада

♂ **Canadian** /kə'neɪdɪən/ *n.* (person) канад|ец (-ка)
• *adj.* канадский

canal /kə'næl/ *n.* канал

canary /kə'neərɪ/ *n.* канарейка
■ **C**~ **Islands** *n. pl.* Канарские острова

Canberra /'kænbərə/ *n.* Канберра

cancel /'kæns(ə)l/ *v.t.* (**cancelled, cancelling,** AmE *also* **canceled, canceling**) отмен|ять, -ить. (*impf.*)

cancellation /kænsə'leɪʃ(ə)n/ *n.* отмена, аннулирование

♂ **cancer** /'kænsə(r)/ *n.* **1** (med.) рак **2** (**C**~) (astron., astrol.) Рак

candid /'kændɪd/ *adj.* искренний

♂ **candidate** /'kændɪdət/ *n.* кандидат

candle /'kænd(ə)l/ *n.* свеча
■ ~**light** *n.* свет свечи/свечей; ~**stick** *n.* подсвечник

candour /ˈkændə(r)/ (AmE **candor**)
n. откровéнность, и́скренность;
беспристрáстность

candy /ˈkændɪ/ *n.* (AmE) конфéты, слáсти (*f. pl.*)

cane /keɪn/ *n.* **1** (bot.) камы́ш, тростни́к **2** (for
punishment) рóзга

canine /ˈkeɪnaɪn/ *adj.* собáчий
■ **~ tooth** *n.* клык

cannabis /ˈkænəbɪs/ *n.* (resin) гаши́ш; (dried
leaves) анашá, марихуáна

cannibal /ˈkænɪb(ə)l/ *n.* каннибáл

cannibalism /ˈkænɪbəlɪz(ə)m/ *n.*
каннибали́зм, людоéдство

cannon /ˈkænən/ *n.* пýшка, орýдие
■ **~ball** *n.* пýшечное ядрó

◌̎ **cannot** /ˈkænɒt, kəˈnɒt/ *neg. of* ▶ **can²**

canoe /kəˈnuː/ *n.* канóэ (*nt. indecl.*)
● *v.i.* (**canoes, canoed, canoeing**) плыть
(*det.*) в челнокé (*or* на канóэ)

canopy /ˈkænəpɪ/ *n.* **1** (covering over bed etc.)
балдахи́н, пóлог **2** (of parachute) кýпол
3 (fig.) пóлог, покрóв

◌̎ **can't** /ˈkɑːnt/ *neg. of* ▶ **can²**

cantankerous /kænˈtæŋkərəs/ *adj.*
сварли́вый

canteen /kænˈtiːn/ *n.* **1** (eating place) столóвая
2 (water container) фля́га

canter /ˈkæntə(r)/ *v.i.* éхать (*impf.*) лёгким
галóпом

canvas /ˈkænvəs/ *n.* холст

canvass /ˈkænvəs/ *v.t. & i.:* **~ a constituency**
вести́ (*det.*) предвы́борную агитáцию
в избирáтельном óкруге; **~ opinions**
соб|ирáть, -рáть мнéния

canvasser /ˈkænvəsə(r)/ *n.* агитáтор

canyon /ˈkænjən/ *n.* каньóн

cap /kæp/ *n.* **1** (of uniform) фурáжка; (baseball **~**)
кéпка **2** (of bottle) кры́шка; (of pen) колпачóк
● *v.t.* (**capped, capping**) (excel)
прев|осходи́ть, -зойти́; **to ~ it all** в
довершéние ко всемý

capability /keɪpəˈbɪlɪtɪ/ *n.* спосóбность

◌̎ **capable** /ˈkeɪpəb(ə)l/ *adj.* **1** (gifted) спосóбный
2: **~ of** спосóбный на + *a.*

capacious /kəˈpeɪʃəs/ *adj.* простóрный

◌̎ **capacity** /kəˈpæsɪtɪ/ *n.* **1** (ability to hold)
вмести́мость; **the hall's seating ~ is 500**
вмести́мость зáла — пятьсóт мест; **the room
was filled to ~** кóмната былá запóлнена до
откáза **2** (of engine) (наибóльшая) мóщность
3 (position): **in my ~ as critic** как кри́тик

cape¹ /keɪp/ *n.* (garment) наки́дка, плащ

cape² /keɪp/ *n.* (geog.) мыс

capers /ˈkeɪpəz/ *n. pl.* (cul.) кáперсы (*m. pl.*)

capillary /kəˈpɪlərɪ/ *adj.* капилля́рный
■ **~ action** *n.* капилля́рное притяжéние,
капилля́рность

◌̎ **capital** /ˈkæpɪt(ə)l/ *n.* **1** (principal city) столи́ца
2 (upper-case letter) прописнáя/заглáвная

бýква **3** (wealth) капитáл
● *adj.* **1** (involving death penalty): **~ punishment**
смéртная казнь **2** (econ.): **~ expenditure**
капитáльные затрáты **3** (upper-case)
прописнóй

capitalism /ˈkæpɪtəlɪz(ə)m/ *n.* капитали́зм

capitalist /ˈkæpɪtəlɪst/ *n.* капитали́ст
● *adj.* капиталисти́ческий

capitalize /ˈkæpɪtəlaɪz/ *v.t. & i.:* **~ on sb's
misfortune** нажـ|ивáться, -и́ться на чьём-н.
несчáстье

capitulate /kəˈpɪtjʊleɪt/ *v.t.* капитули́ровать
(*impf., pf.*)

cappuccino /ˌkæpʊˈtʃiːnəʊ/ *n.* (*pl.* **~s**)
капуч(ч)и́но (*m. & nt. indecl.*)

capricious /kəˈprɪʃəs/ *adj.* прихотли́вый,
капри́зный

Capricorn /ˈkæprɪkɔːn/ *n.* Козерóг

capsize /kæpˈsaɪz/ *v.t. & i.* опроки́|дывать(ся),
-нуть(ся)

capsule /ˈkæpsjuːl/ *n.* (med.) кáпсула

captain /ˈkæptɪn/ *n.* **1** (head of team) капитáн
комáнды **2** (army rank) капитáн **3** (naval rank)
капитáн пéрвого рáнга

caption /ˈkæpʃ(ə)n/ *n.* (title) пóдпись к
карти́нке

captivating /ˈkæptɪveɪtɪŋ/ *adj.* плени́тельный

captive /ˈkæptɪv/ *n.* плéнник, плéнный

captivity /kæpˈtɪvɪtɪ/ *n.* плен, пленéние

◌̎ **capture** /ˈkæptʃə(r)/ *n.* пои́мка, захвáт
● *v.t.* брать, взять в плен; **~ sb's attention**
прикóв|ывать, -áть чьё-н. внимáние

◌̎ **car** /kɑː(r)/ *n.* (легковóй) автомоби́ль, маши́на
■ **~ boot sale** *n.* (BrE) продáжа (прямо) из
багáжника; **~ ferry** *n.* автопарóм; **~ hire** *n.*
прокáт автомоби́лей; **~ park** *n.* (BrE) пáркинг,
автостоя́нка; **~sick** *adj.*: **do you get ~sick?**
вас укáчивает в маши́не?

carafe /kəˈræf/ *n.* графи́н

caramel /ˈkærəmel/ *n.* карамéль

carat /ˈkærət/ *n.* (AmE *also* **karat**) карáт

caravan /ˈkærəvæn/ *n.* (horse-drawn) фургóн,
кры́тая телéга; (BrE, trailer) жилóй/тури́стский
автоприцéп, трéйлер
● *v.i.* (**caravanned, caravanning**) (BrE):
go ~ning путешéствовать (*impf.*) в трéйлере

caraway /ˈkærəweɪ/ *n.* тмин
■ **~ seed** *n.* тми́нное сéмя

carbohydrate /ˌkɑːbəˈhaɪdreɪt/ *n.* углевóд

carbon /ˈkɑːbən/ *n.* **1** (element) углерóд **2**: **~
copy** (fig.) (тóчная) кóпия
■ **~ dioxide** *n.* углеки́слый газ; **~
monoxide** *n.* угáрный газ; **~-neutral** *adj.*
углерóдно-нейтрáльный; **~ offsetting**
n. компенсацио́нное снижéние вы́бросов
двуóкиси углерóда

carburettor /ˌkɑːbəˈretə(r)/ (AmE
carburetor) *n.* карбюрáтор

carcass /ˈkɑːkəs/ *n.* **1** (of animal) тýша; **~
meat** (BrE) парнóе мя́со **2** (of building, ship, etc.)
каркáс, óстов, кóрпус

carcinogenic /ˌkɑːsɪnəˈdʒenɪk/ *adj.*
канцерогéнный

carcinoma /ˌkɑːsɪˈnəʊmə/ n. (pl. ~s or ~ta) карцинóма, рáковое новообразовáние

ⓕ **card** /kɑːd/ n. **1** (material) картóн; (piece) кáрточка; (postcard) открытка **2** (playing ~) игрáльная кáрта; play ~s игрáть, сыгрáть в кáрты

cardboard /ˈkɑːdbɔːd/ n. картóн
■ ~ box n. картóнная корóбка

cardiac /ˈkɑːdɪæk/ adj. сердéчный
■ ~ arrest n. останóвка сéрдца

cardigan /ˈkɑːdɪɡən/ n. шерстянáя кóфта, кардигáн; (man's) вязаная кýртка

cardinal /ˈkɑːdɪn(ə)l/ n. (eccl.) кардинáл
● adj. (principal) кардинáльный; a matter of ~ importance дéло чрезвычáйной вáжности
■ ~ number n. колúчественное числúтельное

cardiologist /ˌkɑːdɪˈɒlədʒɪst/ n. кардиóлог

cardiology /ˌkɑːdɪˈɒlədʒɪ/ n. кардиолóгия

ⓕ **care** /keə(r)/ n. **1** (serious attention) осторóжность; handle this with ~ обращáйтесь с этим осторóжно; take ~ you don't fall смотрúте, не упадúте **2** (charge) забóта, попечéние; take a child into ~ (BrE) взять (pf.) ребёнка под опéку госудáрства **3** (anxiety): free from ~ свобóдный от забóт
● v.i. **1** (feel anxiety): I don't ~ what they say мне всё равнó, что онú скáжут; who ~s? не всё ли равнó?; I couldn't ~ less (infml) мне-то что?; мне наплевáть **2** (feel inclination): would you ~ for a walk? не хотúте ли пойтú погулять? **3** (look after): he is well ~d for за ним хорóший ухóд
■ ~free adj. беззабóтный; ~taker n. сторож, смотрúтель (m.) здáния

ⓕ **career** /kəˈrɪə(r)/ n. карьéра, профéссия
● v.i. мчáться (impf.)

careful /ˈkeəfʊl/ adj. **1** (attentive) осторóжный; be ~ not to fall бýдьте осторóжны, не упадúте; he is ~ with his money он не трáтит дéнег зря **2** (of work) тщáтельный

careless /ˈkeəlɪs/ adj. (thoughtless) неосторóжный; a ~ mistake ошúбка по невнимáтельности; (negligent) небрéжный

carer /ˈkeərə(r)/ n. (BrE) человéк, ухáживающий за ребёнком, больным, инвалúдом и т. д.

caress /kəˈres/ v.t. ласкáть (impf.)

cargo /ˈkɑːɡəʊ/ n. (pl. ~es or ~s) груз
■ ~ ship n. торгóвое сýдно

Caribbean /ˌkærɪˈbiːən, kəˈrɪbɪən/ adj. карúбский; (as n.) the ~ (Sea) Карúбское мóре

caricature /ˈkærɪkətjʊə(r)/ n. карикатýра

caring /ˈkeərɪŋ/ adj. забóтливый

carnage /ˈkɑːnɪdʒ/ n. бóйня

carnation /kɑːˈneɪʃ(ə)n/ n. гвоздúка (декоративное растение)

carnival /ˈkɑːnɪv(ə)l/ n. (annual merrymaking) ежегóдный карнавáл; (Shrovetide) Мáсленица

carnivore /ˈkɑːnɪvɔː(r)/ n. плотоядное/ хúщное живóтное

carnivorous /kɑːˈnɪvərəs/ adj. плотоядный

carol /ˈkær(ə)l/ n. ≈ колядка; рождéственская пéсня

■ ~-singing n. рождéственские песнопéния; ≈ колядки

carousel /ˌkærəˈsel/ n. карусéль

carpenter /ˈkɑːpɪntə(r)/ n. плóтник

carpentry /ˈkɑːpɪntrɪ/ n. (occupation) плóтничество, плóтницкое дéло

carpet /ˈkɑːpɪt/ n. ковёр
● v.t. (carpeted, carpeting) уст|илáть, -лáть коврáми

carriage /ˈkærɪdʒ/ n. **1** (road vehicle) экипáж **2** (BrE, of train) пассажúрский вагóн **3** (BrE, transport of goods) перевóзка, достáвка
■ ~way n. (BrE) проéзжая часть (дорóги)

carrier /ˈkærɪə(r)/ n. **1** (transport agent) транспортёр **2** (of disease) перенóсчик (болéзни)
■ ~ bag n. (BrE) сýмка для покýпок

carrot /ˈkærət/ n. морквóвь

ⓕ **carry** /ˈkærɪ/ v.t. **1** (transport) носúть (indet.), нестú (det.); (of or by vehicle) возúть (indet.), везтú (det.); pipes ~ water водá идёт по трýбам; wires ~ sound звук передаётся по проводáм; what weight will the bridge ~? на какóй вес рассчúтан этот мост? **2** (have): I always ~ an umbrella (money) with me у меня всегдá с собóй зóнтик (всегдá при себé есть дéньги); this crime carries a heavy penalty это преступлéние влечёт за собóй тяжёлое наказáние
● v.i.: the shot carried 200 yards снаряд пролетéл 200 ярдов
□ ~ away v.t. (fig.): he was carried away by his feelings он оказáлся во влáсти чувств; он увлёкся
□ ~ forward, over vv.t. (transfer) перен|осúть, -ести
□ ~ off v.t. (remove) ун|осúть, -ести; he carried the situation off well он удáчно вышел из положéния
□ ~ on v.t. (conduct, perform): ~ on a conversation/ business вестú (det.) разговóр/дéло
● v.i. (continue) прод|олжáть, -óлжить; ~ on with your work продолжáйте рабóту; (talk, behave excitedly) волновáться (impf.)
□ ~ out v.t. (execute) выполнять, выполнить
■ ~cot n. (BrE) переноснáя дéтская кровáтка

cart /kɑːt/ n. телéжка
■ ~wheel n. колесó телéги; turn ~wheels кувыркáться, -нýться колесóм

carte blanche /ˌkɑːt ˈblɑːʃ/ n. карт-блáнш (m. indecl.)

cartel /kɑːˈtel/ n. (comm.) картéль (m.)

cartilage /ˈkɑːtɪlɪdʒ/ n. хрящ

cartographer /kɑːˈtɒɡrəfə(r)/ n. картóграф

cartography /kɑːˈtɒɡrəfɪ/ n. картогрáфия

carton /ˈkɑːt(ə)n/ n. (large box) картóнка; (for milk etc.) пакéт

cartoon /kɑːˈtuːn/ n. (in newspaper) карикатýра; (film) мультфúльм

cartoonist /kɑːˈtuːnɪst/ n. карикатурúст

cartridge /ˈkɑːtrɪdʒ/ n. (mil.) патрóн; (for printer) кáртридж; (for camera) кассéта

ⓕ **carve** /kɑːv/ v.t. (cut) рéзать (impf.); (shape by cutting): ~ a statue out of wood вырезáть,

вы́резать ста́тую из де́рева; **he ~d out a career for himself** он сде́лал карье́ру; **~ meat** ре́зать, на- мя́со
□ **~ up** *v.t.* (fig.) раздел|я́ть, -и́ть

carving /ˈkɑːvɪŋ/ *n.* (object) резна́я рабо́та, резьба́

cascade /kæsˈkeɪd/ *n.* каска́д; водопа́д
● *v.i.* па́дать/ниспада́ть (*both impf.*) каска́дом

✧ **case¹** /keɪs/ *n.* **1** (instance) слу́чай, обстоя́тельство, де́ло; **in that ~** в тако́м/э́том слу́чае; **in any ~** во вся́ком слу́чае; **in ~ of fire** в слу́чае пожа́ра **2** (med.) слу́чай, заболева́ние **3** (hypothesis): **take an umbrella in ~ it rains** (*or* **in ~ of rain**) возьми́те зо́нтик на слу́чай дождя́; **just in ~** на вся́кий слу́чай **4** (law) суде́бное де́ло **5** (gram.) паде́ж
■ **~ history** *n.* (med.) исто́рия боле́зни

✧ **case²** /keɪs/ *n.* (container) я́щик, ларе́ц, коро́бка; (for spectacles, violin, etc.) футля́р; (BrE, suitcase) чемода́н; **glass ~** витри́на

✧ **cash** /kæʃ/ *n.* нали́чные (де́н|ьги (*pl., g.* -ег)); **~ on delivery** нало́женным платежо́м
● *v.t.*: **~ a cheque** получ|а́ть, -и́ть де́ньги по че́ку; **~ in** получ|а́ть, -и́ть де́ньги по + *d.*
● *v.i.*: **~ in on** (fig.) воспо́льзоваться (*pf.*) (+ *i.*)
■ **~ desk** *n.* (BrE) ка́сса; **~ machine** *n.* банкома́т, де́нежный автома́т; **~ register** *n.* ка́ссовый аппара́т, ка́сса

cashback /ˈkæʃbæk/ *n.* кешбэ́к (*получение наличных денег с дебетовой карточки в предприятии розничной торговли при оплате покупки; компенсационная скидка с цены покупки*)

cashcard /ˈkæʃkɑːd/ *n.* (BrE) ка́рточка для банкома́та

cashew /ˈkæʃuː/ *n.* (оре́х) ке́шью (*m. indecl.*)

cashier /kæˈʃɪə(r)/ *n.* касси́р

cashmere /ˈkæʃmɪə(r)/ *n.* кашеми́р

cashpoint /ˈkæʃpɔɪnt/ *n.* (BrE) банкома́т

casino /kəˈsiːnəʊ/ *n.* (*pl.* **~s**) казино́ (*nt. indecl.*)

casket /ˈkɑːskɪt/ *n.* шкату́лка; (AmE, coffin) гроб

Caspian /ˈkæspɪən/ *n.* (*in full* **the ~ (Sea)**) Каспи́йское мо́ре

casserole /ˈkæsərəʊl/ *n.* (container) кастрю́ля для туше́ния; (food) рагу́ (*nt. indecl.*)

cassette /kəˈset/ *n.* кассе́та
■ **~ player** *n.* пле́ер; **~ recorder** *n.* кассе́тный магнитофо́н

cassock /ˈkæsək/ *n.* ря́са

✧ **cast** /kɑːst/ *n.* **1** (mould) фо́рма для отли́вки; (object) plaster **~** ги́псовый сле́пок **2** (theatr., cin.) соста́в актёров
● *v.t.* (*past and p.p.* **~**) **1** (throw) бр|оса́ть, -о́сить **2** (fig.): **~ a vote** проголосова́ть (*pf.*); отда́ть (*pf.*) го́лос; **~ doubt on** подв|ерга́ть, -е́ргнуть сомне́нию; **~ a spell (up)on** окол|до́вывать, -ова́ть **3** (pour) отл|ива́ть, -и́ть **4** (theatr.): **~ a play** распредел|я́ть, -и́ть ро́ли в пье́се
■ **~away** *n. & adj.* потерпе́вший кораблекруше́ние; **~ iron** *n.* чугу́н; **~-iron**

adj. чугу́нный; (fig.) стально́й, желе́зный; **~-off** *n. & adj.*: **~-off clothing** обно́ск|и (-ов), старьё

castanets /kæstəˈnets/ *n. pl.* кастанье́ты (*f. pl.*) (*ударный музыкальный инструмент в виде скреплённых пластин, надеваемых на пальцы рук*)

caste /kɑːst/ *n.* ка́ста

caster /ˈkɑːstə(r)/ *n.*: **~ sugar** (BrE) са́харный песо́к

castigate /ˈkæstɪgeɪt/ *v.t.* бичева́ть (*impf.*)

casting /ˈkɑːstɪŋ/ *n.* (theatr., cin.) распределе́ние роле́й

castle /ˈkɑːs(ə)l/ *n.* за́мок; (at chess) ладья́

castrate /kæˈstreɪt/ *v.t.* кастри́ровать (*impf., pf.*)

casual /ˈkæʒʊəl/ *adj.* **1** (chance) случа́йный **2** (careless) небре́жный, беспе́чный; (familiar) развя́зный; **clothes for ~ wear** проста́я/повседне́вная оде́жда

casualty /ˈkæʒʊəltɪ/ *n.* (person) пострада́вший от несча́стного слу́чая; (mil.) уби́тый
■ **~ department** *n.* (BrE) травматологи́ческое отделе́ние

✧ **cat** /kæt/ *n.* **1** ко́шка **2** (idioms): **let the ~ out of the bag** проб|а́лтываться, -олта́ться; выба́лтывать, вы́болтать секре́т; **it's raining ~s and dogs** дождь льёт как из ведра́
■ **~nap** *v.i.* вздремну́ть (*pf.*); **~walk** *n.* рабо́чие мостк|и́ (-о́в); (in fashion house) по́диум

catalogue /ˈkætəlɒg/ (AmE **catalog**) *n.* катало́г
● *v.t.* (**catalogues, catalogued, cataloguing**, AmE **catalogs, cataloged, cataloging**) каталогизи́ровать (*impf., pf.*)

catalyst /ˈkætəlɪst/ *n.* катализа́тор

catalytic /kætəˈlɪtɪk/ *adj.*: **~ converter** каталити́ческий нейтрализа́тор (выхлопны́х га́зов)

catapult /ˈkætəpʌlt/ *n.* (BrE, toy) рога́тка

cataract /ˈkætərækt/ *n.* (med.) катара́кта

catarrh /kəˈtɑː(r)/ *n.* ката́р

catastrophe /kəˈtæstrəfɪ/ *n.* катастро́фа

catastrophic /kætəˈstrɒfɪk/ *adj.* катастрофи́ческий

✧ **catch** /kætʃ/ *n.* **1** (act of catching) по́имка, захва́т **2** (amount caught) уло́в, добы́ча **3** (trap) уло́вка, лову́шка; **there must be a ~ in it** здесь есть како́й-то подво́х **4** (fastener) щеко́лда, защёлка, шпинга́лет
● *v.t. & i.* (*past and p.p.* **caught**) **1** (seize) лови́ть, пойма́ть; **he caught the ball** он пойма́л мяч; **~ a fish** пойма́ть (*pf.*) ры́бу; **~ a fugitive** пойма́ть (*pf.*) беглеца́ **2** (of entanglement, fastening, etc.): **her dress caught on a nail** она́ зацепи́лась пла́тьем за гвоздь; **he caught his foot** у него́ застря́ла нога́ **3** (intercept, detect): **I caught him stealing** я заста́л его́, за воровство́м; **we were caught in the storm** нас засти́гла бу́ря **4** (be in time for): **~ a train** успе́ть (*pf.*) на по́езд **5** (fig.): **I didn't ~ what you said** я прослу́шал, что вы сказа́ли; **~ sb's eye** привле́чь (*pf.*) чьё-н. внима́ние; **~ fire** загоре́ться (*pf.*); **a glimpse of** уви́деть (*pf.*) ме́льком; **~ hold of** схвати́ть, улови́ть (*both pf.*) **6** (be infected

✧ ключева́я ле́ксика

by) схвати́ть, получи́ть (*both pf.*); ~ **cold** простуди́ться (*pf.*)

□ ~ **on** *v.i.*: the fashion did not ~ on э́та мо́да не привила́сь

□ ~ **out** *v.t.* (BrE): he was caught out in a mistake его́ пойма́ли/подлови́ли на оши́бке

□ ~ **up** *v.t. & i.*: he caught the others up; he caught up with the others он догна́л остальны́х; I must ~ up on my work я запусти́л рабо́ту — тепе́рь на́до нагоня́ть

■ ~**phrase** *n.* мо́дное выраже́ние, слове́чко; ~-**22 situation** *n.* безвы́ходное положе́ние; парадокса́льная ситуа́ция

catching /'kætʃɪŋ/ *adj.* зара́зный

catchy /'kætʃɪ/ *adj.* (**catchier, catchiest**) легко́ запомина́ющийся, прили́пчивый

categorical /kætɪ'ɡɒrɪk(ə)l/ *adj.* категори́ческий

categorize /'kætɪɡəraɪz/ *v.t.* распредел|я́ть, -и́ть по катего́риям

✧ **category** /'kætɪɡərɪ/ *n.* катего́рия

cater /'keɪtə(r)/ *v.i.*: ~ **for** (BrE) пост|авля́ть, -а́вить прови́зию для + *g.*; (fig.) обслу́ж|ивать, -и́ть

caterer /'keɪtərə(r)/ *n.* (*often in pl.*) (company) фи́рма, обслу́живающая банке́ты, сва́дьбы *и т. п.*

caterpillar /'kætəpɪlə(r)/ *n.* гу́сеница

catharsis /kə'θɑːsɪs/ *n.* (*pl.* **catharses** /-siːz/) ка́тарсис

cathartic /kə'θɑːtɪk/ *adj.* очища́ющий

cathedral /kə'θiːdr(ə)l/ *n.* (кафедра́льный) собо́р

✧ **Catholic** /'kæθəlɪk/ *n.* като́л|ик (-и́чка)
● *adj.* (relig.) католи́ческий; **Roman** ~ ри́мско-католи́ческий

Catholicism /kə'θɒlɪsɪz(ə)m/ *n.* католици́зм, католи́чество

cattle /'kæt(ə)l/ *n.* скот, скоти́на

catty /'kætɪ/ *adj.* (**cattier, cattiest**) ехи́дный

Caucasus /'kɔːkəsəs/ *n.* Кавка́з

caught /kɔːt/ *past and p.p. of* ▶ **catch**

cauldron /'kɔːldrən/ *n.* коте́л

cauliflower /'kɒlɪflaʊə(r)/ *n.* цветна́я капу́ста

✧ **cause** /kɔːz/ *n.* **1** (reason) причи́на, по́вод **2** (need) причи́на, основа́ние; there is no ~ **for** alarm нет основа́ний/причи́н для беспоко́йства **3** (purpose): the ~ of peace де́ло ми́ра; a good ~ пра́вое де́ло
● *v.t.* вызыва́ть, вы́звать; ~ sb trouble (*or* a loss) причин|я́ть, -и́ть кому́-н. беспоко́йство/убы́тки; what ~d the accident? что послужи́ло причи́ной несча́стного слу́чая?

caution /'kɔːʃ(ə)n/ *n.* **1** (prudence) осторо́жность **2** (BrE, warning) предостереже́ние, предостороро́жность
● *v.t.* предостер|ега́ть, -е́чь

cautious /'kɔːʃəs/ *adj.* осторо́жный, осмотри́тельный

cavalier /kævə'lɪə(r)/ *n.* (gallant; royalist) кавале́р
● *adj.* бесцеремо́нный, надме́нный

cavalry /'kævəlrɪ/ *n.* кавале́рия, ко́нница

cave[1] /keɪv/ *n.* пеще́ра

■ ~**man** *n.* пеще́рный челове́к, троглоди́т

cave[2] /keɪv/ *v.i.*: ~ **in** (lit.) прова́л|иваться, -и́ться; (fig.) сд|ава́ться, -а́ться

cavernous /'kæv(ə)nəs/ *adj.* пеще́ристый

caviar /'kævɪɑː(r)/ *n.* икра́

cavity /'kævɪtɪ/ *n.* по́лость; (in tooth) дупло́

cavort /kə'vɔːt/ *v.i.* скака́ть (*impf.*)

caw /kɔː/ *v.t. & i.* ка́рк|ать, -нуть

cayenne /keɪ'en/ *n.*: ~ **pepper** кайе́нский пе́рец

CCTV *abbr.* (*of* **closed-circuit TV**) систе́ма видеонаблюде́ния, видеонаблюде́ние

CD *abbr.* (*of* **compact disc**) компа́кт-ди́ск

■ ~ **player** *n.* прои́грыватель (*m.*) компа́кт-ди́сков, CD-пле́ер

CD-ROM *abbr.* (*of* **compact disc — read-only memory**) компа́кт-ди́ск (*штампо́ванный*)

■ ~ **drive** *n.* приво́д компа́кт-ди́сков

cease /siːs/ *v.t.* прекра|ща́ть, -ти́ть
● *v.i.* прекра|ща́ться, -ти́ться

■ ~**fire** *n.* прекраще́ние огня́

ceaseless /'siːslɪs/ *adj.* непреста́нный, непреры́вный

cedar /'siːdə(r)/ *n.* кедр

cede /siːd/ *v.t.* сда|ва́ть, -ть

ceilidh /'keɪlɪ/ *n.* вечери́нка с шотла́ндской и́ли ирла́ндской наро́дной му́зыкой и та́нцами

ceiling /'siːlɪŋ/ *n.* потоло́к

✧ **celebrate** /'selɪbreɪt/ *v.t. & i.* **1** (mark an occasion) пра́здновать, от- **2** : ~ **a marriage** соверша́ть, -и́ть обря́д бракосочета́ния

celebrated /'selɪbreɪtɪd/ *adj.* знамени́тый

celebration /selɪ'breɪʃ(ə)n/ *n.* пра́зднование, торжества́ (*nt. pl.*), просла́вле́ние; ~ **of marriage** соверше́ние обря́да бракосочета́ния

celebrity /sɪ'lebrɪtɪ/ *n.* (fame) знамени́тость; (person) знамени́тость

■ ~ **culture** *n.* культ знамени́тостей; культу́ра, сформиро́ванная ку́льтом знамени́тостей

celery /'selərɪ/ *n.* (листово́й) сельдере́й

celestial /sɪ'lestɪəl/ *adj.* (astron., fig.) небе́сный

■ ~ **globe** *n.* гло́бус звёздного не́ба

celibate /'selɪbət/ *adj.* безбра́чный, да́вший обе́т безбра́чия

✧ **cell** /sel/ *n.* **1** (in prison) ка́мера **2** (biol.) кле́тка

■ ~**phone** *n.* со́товый телефо́н

cellar /'selə(r)/ *n.* по́греб, подва́л

cellist /'tʃelɪst/ *n.* виолончели́ст (-ка)

cello /'tʃeləʊ/ *n.* (*pl.* ~**s**) виолонче́ль

cellophane® /'seləfeɪn/ *n.* целлофа́н; (*attr.*) целлофа́новый

Celt /kelt/ *n.* кельт

Celtic /'keltɪk/ *adj.* кельтский

cement /sɪ'ment/ *n.* цеме́нт

■ ~ **mixer** *n.* бетономеша́лка

cemetery /'semɪtərɪ/ *n.* кла́дбище

censor /'sensə(r)/ *n.* це́нзор
● *v.t.* подв|ерга́ть, -е́ргнуть цензу́ре

censorious /sen'sɔːrɪəs/ *adj.*
сверхкрити́чный, приди́рчивый

censorship /'sensəʃɪp/ *n.* цензу́ра

censure /'sensjə(r)/ *n.* кри́тика
● *v.t.* критикова́ть (*impf.*)

census /'sensəs/ *n.* (*pl.* ∼**es**) пе́репись (населе́ния)

cent /sent/ *n.* цент

centenary /sen'tiːnərɪ/ *n.* (BrE) столе́тие

centennial /sen'tenɪəl/ *n.* (AmE) = centenary

center /'sentə(r)/ *n.*, *v.t.* & *v.i.* (AmE) = centre

centigrade /'sentɪɡreɪd/ *adj.*: 20° ∼ 20 гра́дусов Це́льсия (*or* по Це́льсию)

centilitre /'sentɪliːtə(r)/ (AmE **centiliter**) *n.* сантили́тр

centimetre /'sentɪmiːtə(r)/ (AmE **centimeter**) *n.* сантиме́тр

centipede /'sentɪpiːd/ *n.* многоно́жка

⚬ **central** /'sentr(ə)l/ *adj.* **1** (pert. to a centre) центра́льный; **the house is very** ∼ дом нахо́дится в са́мом це́нтре го́рода **2** (principal) центра́льный, гла́вный
■ **C**∼ **America** *n.* Центра́льная Аме́рика; **C**∼ **Asia** *n.* Сре́дняя А́зия

centralize /'sentrəlaɪz/ *v.t.* централизова́ть (*impf., pf.*)

⚬ **centre** /'sentə(r)/ (AmE **center**) *n.* **1** (middle) центр; ∼ **of gravity** центр тя́жести **2** (fig.): **shopping** ∼ торго́вый центр **3** (pol.) центр
● *v.t.* поме|ща́ть, -сти́ть в це́нтре
● *v.i.* сосредото́ч|иваться, -и́ться; **the discussion** ∼**d round this point** диску́ссия сосредото́чилась вокру́г э́того вопро́са
■ ∼ **forward** *n.* (sport) центра́льный напада́ющий; ∼**piece** *n.* орнамента́льная ва́за в середи́не стола́; (fig.) гла́вное украше́ние

⚬ **century** /'sentʃərɪ/ *n.* столе́тие, век

CEO *abbr.* (*of* **chief executive officer**) гла́вный исполни́тельный дире́ктор

ceramic /sɪ'ræmɪk/ *adj.* керами́ческий

ceramics /sɪ'ræmɪks/ *n.* кера́мика

cereal /'sɪərɪəl/ *n.* хле́бный злак; (*in full* **breakfast** ∼) хло́пья (к за́втраку) (*корнфлекс и т. п.*)

cerebral /'serɪbr(ə)l/ *adj.* мозгово́й, церебра́льный
■ ∼ **palsy** *n.* (med.) де́тский церебра́льный парали́ч, ДЦП

ceremonial /serɪ'məʊnɪəl/ *adj.* церемониа́льный, обря́довый

ceremonious /serɪ'məʊnɪəs/ *adj.* церемо́нный

ceremony /'serɪmənɪ/ *n.* (rite) обря́д, церемо́ния; (formal behaviour) церемо́нность; **stand (up)on** ∼ церемо́ниться (*impf.*)

⚬ **certain** /'sɜːt(ə)n/ *adj.* **1** (undoubted) несомне́нный; **I cannot say for** ∼ я не могу́ сказа́ть наверняка́; **make** ∼ **of** (ascertain) удостов|еря́ться, -е́риться в чём-н.; **he is** ∼ **to succeed** наверняка́ он добьётся

успе́ха **2** (confident) уве́ренный; **I am** ∼ **he will come** я уве́рен, что он придёт **3** (unspecified) изве́стный, не́который; **a** ∼ **person** не́кто, не́кое лицо́; **under** ∼ **conditions** при изве́стных усло́виях; **a** ∼ (*sc. some*) **pleasure** не́которое удово́льствие

⚬ **certainly** /'sɜːtənlɪ/ *adv.* (without doubt) несомне́нно, наверняка́, наве́рно(е); (expr. obedience or consent) коне́чно, безусло́вно

certainty /'sɜːtəntɪ/ *n.* **1** (being certainly true) несомне́нность **2** (certain fact) несомне́нный факт

certificate /sə'tɪfɪkət/ *n.* удостовере́ние, свиде́тельство, сертифика́т

certify /'sɜːtɪfaɪ/ *v.t.* удостов|еря́ть, -е́рить

cervical /sə'vaɪk(ə)l/ *adj.* ше́йный
■ ∼ **smear** *n.* (BrE) мазо́к с ше́йки ма́тки

cervix /'sɜːvɪks/ *n.* (*pl.* **cervices** /-siːz/) ше́я; (of womb) ше́йка (ма́тки)

Cesarean /sɪ'zeərɪən/ *adj.* (AmE) = Caesarean

cessation /se'seɪʃ(ə)n/ *n.* прекраще́ние, остано́вка; ∼ **of hostilities** прекраще́ние вое́нных де́йствий

cf. *abbr.* (*of Latin* **confer**) (= **compare with**) ср., сравни́

CFCs *abbr.* (*of* **chlorofluorocarbons**) фрео́ны (*m. pl.*)

chafe /tʃeɪf/ *v.i.* нат|ира́ться, -ере́ться

chaffinch /'tʃæfɪntʃ/ *n.* зя́блик

⚬ **chain** /tʃeɪn/ *n.* цепь; (*in pl.*) (fetters) це́пи (*f. pl.*), око́в|ы (*pl., g.* —); (fig.): ∼ **of events, consequences** цепь собы́тий/после́дствий
● *v.t.* прико́в|ывать, -а́ть це́пью
■ ∼ **reaction** *n.* цепна́я реа́кция; ∼**smoke** *v.t.* кури́ть (*impf.*) одну́ сигаре́ту за друго́й; ∼**smoker** *n.* зая́длый кури́льщик; ∼ **store** *n.* оди́н из сети фи́рменных магази́нов

⚬ **chair** /tʃeə(r)/ *n.* **1** стул **2** (∼**man**) председа́тель (*m.*)
● *v.t.* (preside over) председа́тельствовать (*impf.*) на + *p.*
■ ∼**lift** *n.* подвесно́й подъёмник; ∼**man**, ∼**person** *nn.* = chair *n.* 2

chaise longue /ʃeɪz 'lɒŋ(ɡ)/ *n.* (*pl.* **chaise longues** *or* **chaises longues** *pronunc. same*) шезло́нг

chalet /'ʃæleɪ/ *n.* шале́ (*nt. indecl.*)

chalk /tʃɔːk/ *n.* мел

⚬ **challenge** /'tʃælɪndʒ/ *n.* вы́зов
● *v.t.* вызыва́ть, вы́звать; (dispute) оспа́ривать (*impf.*); ∼ **sb to a race** вызыва́ть, вы́звать кого́-н. на состяза́ние

challenger /'tʃælɪndʒə(r)/ *n.* претенде́нт (-ка)

challenging /'tʃælɪndʒɪŋ/ *adj.* тру́дный, но интере́сный

chamber /'tʃeɪmbə(r)/ *n.* **1** (room) ко́мната; (*in pl.*) (apartment) кварти́ра **2** (hall, e.g. of parliament) зал, за́ла **3** (official body) пала́та; **C**∼ **of Commerce** торго́вая пала́та
■ ∼**maid** *n.* го́рничная; ∼ **music** *n.* ка́мерная му́зыка

chameleon /kə'miːlɪən/ *n.* хамелео́н

champagne /ʃæm'peɪn/ *n.* шампа́нское

⚬ ключева́я ле́ксика

♂ **champion** /'tʃæmpɪən/ n. **1** (defender)
побо́рни|к, защи́тни|к (-ца) **2** (prizewinner)
чемпио́н (-ка) (infml)

championship /'tʃæmpɪənʃɪp/ n. (advocacy)
защи́та; (sport) (contest) чемпиона́т,
пе́рвенство; (title) чемпио́нство

♂ **chance** /tʃɑːns/ n. **1** (casual occurrence) слу́чай,
случа́йность; **by ~** случа́йно; **game of ~**
аза́ртная игра́ **2** (possibility, opportunity) шанс,
возмо́жность; **the ~s are that he will come**
все ша́нсы за то, что он придёт; **I had no ~**
of winning у меня́ не́ было никаки́х ша́нсов
на успе́х

chancellor /'tʃɑːnsələ(r)/ n. ка́нцлер; (BrE,
of university) ре́ктор; **C~ of the Exchequer**
ка́нцлер казначе́йства, мини́стр фина́нсов

chancy /'tʃɑːnsɪ/ adj. (**chancier, chanciest**)
(infml) риско́ванный

chandelier /ʃændə'lɪə(r)/ n. лю́стра

♂ **change** /tʃeɪndʒ/ n. **1** (alteration) измене́ние;
(substitution) переме́на; **~ of air, scene**
переме́на обстано́вки; **for a ~** для
разнообра́зия **2** (spare set) сме́на; **he took a**
~ of underwear with him он взял с собо́й
сме́ну белья́ **3** (money) ме́лкие де́н|ьги
(-ег); (returned as balance) сда́ча; **have you ~**
for a pound? вы не разме́няете оди́н фунт
(ме́лочью)? **4** (of trains etc.) переса́дка
● v.t. **1** (alter, replace) меня́ть, по-; **~** (**one's**)
clothes переод|ева́ться, -е́ться; **~ one's mind**
разду́м|ывать, -ать; переду́м|ывать, -ать; **~**
the subject смен|я́ть, переме́нить (both pf.)
те́му разгово́ра; **~ trains** перес|а́живаться,
-е́сть на друго́й по́езд **2** (reclothe etc.): **~**
a baby перепел|ена́ть, -ена́ть; **~ a bed**
меня́ть, по- посте́льное бельё **3** (money):
~ a five pound note разменя́ть (pf.)
пятифу́нтовую бума́жку; **~ euros into**
pounds обменя́ть (pf.) е́вро на фу́нты
(сте́рлингов) **4** (exchange): **~ places with sb**
(lit.) поменя́ться (pf.) места́ми с кем-н.
● v.i. **1**: **he has ~d a lot** он си́льно
измени́лся/перемени́лся; **caterpillars ~**
into butterflies гу́сеницы превраща́ются в
ба́бочек **2** (rail.) перес|а́живаться, -е́сть
■ **~over** n. (of leader etc.) сме́на

changeable /'tʃeɪndʒəb(ə)l/ adj. (of person,
weather) изме́нчивый

changing room /'tʃeɪndʒɪŋ/ n. (sport)
раздева́лка; (BrE, in shop) приме́рочная

♂ **channel** /'tʃæn(ə)l/ n. **1** (strait) проли́в, кана́л;
the English C~ Ла-Ма́нш; **the C~ Islands**
Норма́ндские острова́ **2** (fig.): **through the**
usual ~s обы́чным путём **3** (television) кана́л
● v.t. (**channelled, channelling**, AmE
channeled, channeling) (fig.): **his**
energies are ~led into sport вся его́ эне́ргия
ухо́дит на спорт
■ **C~ Tunnel** n. тонне́ль под Ла-Ма́ншем

channel-hop /'tʃæn(ə)lhɒp/ v.i. (infml)
1 (television) (ча́сто) переключа́ть (impf.)
телевизио́нные кана́лы **2** (across the English
Channel) пересека́ть (impf.) Ла-Ма́нш

chant /tʃɑːnt/ n. песнь; (eccl.) пе́ние
● v.t. восп|ева́ть, -е́ть

● v.i. петь (impf.)

chaos /'keɪɒs/ n. ха́ос

chaotic /keɪ'ɒtɪk/ adj. хаоти́ческий, хаоти́чный

chap¹ /tʃæp/ v.t. (**chapped, chapping**):
~ped hands потре́скавшиеся ру́ки

chap² /tʃæp/ n. (BrE, infml) па́рень (m.), ма́лый

chapel /'tʃæp(ə)l/ n. часо́вня, моле́льня

chaperone, chaperon /'ʃæpərəʊn/ n.
компаньо́нка
● v.t. сопрово|жда́ть, -ди́ть

chaplain /'tʃæplɪn/ n. капелла́н, свяще́нник

♂ **chapter** /'tʃæptə(r)/ n. глава́

char /tʃɑː(r)/ v.t. (**charred, charring**)
обу́гли|вать, -ть

♂ **character** /'kærɪktə(r)/ n. **1** (nature) сво́йство,
ка́чество **2** (personal qualities) хара́ктер
3 (distinctive person): **she is quite a ~** она́
оригина́льная ли́чность **4** (fictional) персона́ж
5 (letter, symbol) бу́ква, ли́тера, знак; **Chinese**
~s кита́йские иеро́глифы (m. pl.)

characteristic /kærɪktə'rɪstɪk/ n. характе́рная
черта́
● adj. хара́ктерный, типи́чный

characterization /kærɪktəraɪ'zeɪʃ(ə)n/ n.
1 (description) характери́стика **2** (by author or
actor) созда́ние о́браза; тракто́вка

characterize /'kærɪktəraɪz/ v.t. **1** (describe)
характеризова́ть (impf., pf.) **2** (distinguish)
отлич|а́ть, -и́ть

characterless /'kærɪktəlɪs/ adj. (undistinguished)
бесхара́ктерный, заура́дный

charade /ʃə'rɑːd/ n. шара́да

charcoal /'tʃɑːkəʊl/ n. древе́сный у́голь
■ **~-grey** n. & adj. тёмно-се́рый, пе́пельный
(цвет)

♂ **charge** /tʃɑːdʒ/ n. **1** (for gun) заря́д **2** (elec.)
заря́д **3** (expense) цена́, расхо́ды (m. pl.);
what is the ~? ско́лько э́то сто́ит?; **a ~**
account счёт в магази́не; **free of ~** беспла́тно
4 (duty, care): **she's in ~ of the hospital** она́
возглавля́ет больни́цу; **take ~ of a business**
взять (pf.) на себя́ руково́дство де́лом
5 (person entrusted): **the nurse took her ~s**
for a walk ня́ня повела́ свои́х пито́мцев на
прогу́лку **6** (accusation) обвине́ние; **bring a ~**
against sb выдвига́ть, вы́двинуть обвине́ние
про́тив кого́-н. **7** (attack) нападе́ние, ата́ка
● v.t. **1** (accuse) обвин|я́ть, -и́ть; **he is ~d with**
murder его́ обвиня́ют в уби́йстве **2** (debit):
~ the amount/goods to me запиши́те су́мму/
това́ры на мой счёт **3** (ask price): **he ~d £5**
for the book он запроси́л 5 фу́нтов за э́ту
кни́гу **4** (also v.i.) (attack): **the troops ~d the**
enemy войска́ атакова́ли неприя́теля
■ **~ card** n. креди́тная ка́рточка

chariot /'tʃærɪət/ n. колесни́ца

charisma /kə'rɪzmə/ n. хари́зма, обая́ние

charismatic /kærɪz'mætɪk/ adj.
харизмати́ческий

charitable /'tʃærɪtəb(ə)l/ adj. ми́лостивый,
снисходи́тельный

♂ **charity** /'tʃærɪtɪ/ n. **1** (kindness) любо́вь к
бли́жнему **2** (institution) благотвори́тельная
организа́ция

c

■ ~ **concert** *n.* благотвори́тельный конце́рт; ~ **shop** *n.* благотвори́тельный магази́н поде́ржанных веще́й

charlatan /'ʃɑːlət(ə)n/ *n.* шарлата́н

charm /tʃɑːm/ *n.* **1** (attraction) обая́ние, очарова́ние **2** (talisman) амуле́т
● *v.t.* очаро́в|ывать, -а́ть

charming /'tʃɑːmɪŋ/ *adj.* очарова́тельный

chart /tʃɑːt/ *n.* **1** (record) табли́ца, гра́фик **2** (*in pl.*) (hit parade) хит-пара́д
● *v.t.* черти́ть, на- ка́рту + *g.*; ~ sb's progress де́лать, с- диагра́мму чьего́-н. продвиже́ния

charter /'tʃɑːtə(r)/ *n.* **1** (grant of rights) ха́ртия, гра́мота **2** (hire) фрахто́вка, наём
● *v.t.* **1** (grant diploma to): ~ed accountant (BrE) бухга́лтер-экспе́рт, ауди́тор **2** (hire) фрахтова́ть, за-
■ ~ **flight** *n.* ча́ртерный рейс

chase /tʃeɪs/ *n.* пого́ня
● *v.t.* гоня́ться (*indet.*), гна́ться (*det.*), погна́ться (*pf.*) за (+ *i.*); ~ away отгоня́ть, отогна́ть; he owes us a reply — please ~ him up! (infml) мы ждём его́ отве́та — поторопи́те-ка его́!
● *v.i.*: ~ after гна́ться, по- за (+ *i.*); охо́титься (*impf.*) за + *i.*

chasm /'kæz(ə)m/ *n.* бе́здна, про́пасть (also fig.)

chassis /'ʃæsɪ/ *n.* (*pl.* ~ /-sɪz/) шасси́ (*nt. indecl.*)

chaste /tʃeɪst/ *adj.* целому́дренный

chasten /'tʃeɪs(ə)n/ *v.t.* (punish, subdue) смир|я́ть, -и́ть; the rebuke had a ~ing effect упрёк поде́йствовал отрезвля́юще

chastise /tʃæs'taɪz/ *v.t.* нака́з|ывать, -а́ть; кара́ть, по-

chastity /'tʃæstɪtɪ/ *n.* целому́дрие

chat /tʃæt/ *n.* болтовня́, бесе́да
● *v.t.* (**chatted, chatting**): ~ sb up (BrE, infml) заи́грывать (*impf.*) с кем-н.
● *v.i.* (**chatted, chatting**) болта́ть, по-
■ ~**line** *n.* кана́л многосторо́нней свя́зи (*для обще́ния по телефо́ну и́ли в Интерне́те*); ~ **room** *n.* (comput.) разде́л ча́та; ~ **show** *n.* (BrE) бесе́да/интервью́ (*nt. indecl.*) со знамени́тостями

château /'ʃætəʊ/ *n.* (*pl.* ~x *pronunc. same or* /-təʊz/) за́мок

chatter /'tʃætə(r)/ *n.* болтовня́, трескотня́
● *v.i.* **1** болта́ть, тарато́рить (*both impf.*) **2**: his teeth are ~ing у него́ зу́бы стуча́т (от хо́лода/испу́га)

chatty /'tʃætɪ/ *adj.* (**chattier, chattiest**) болтли́вый, говорли́вый; (style) разгово́рный

chauffeur /'ʃəʊfə(r)/ *n.* (персона́льный) шофёр

chauvinism /'ʃəʊvɪnɪz(ə)m/ *n.* шовини́зм

chauvinist /'ʃəʊvɪnɪst/ *n.* шовини́ст (-ка); male ~ сторо́нник дискримина́ции же́нщин; мужско́й шовини́ст

chauvinistic /ʃəʊvɪ'nɪstɪk/ *adj.* шовинисти́ческий

chav /tʃæv/ *n.* (BrE, sl.) го́пни|к (-ца) (*особенно по вне́шним атрибу́там*) (sl.), (collect.

also) гопота́ (sl.); па́рень (*m.*) /де́вушка из рабо́чего райо́на (*по интере́сам*)

✔ **cheap** /tʃiːp/ *adj.* дешёвый

cheapen /'tʃiːpən/ *v.t.* (degrade) ун|ижа́ть, -и́зить; ~ oneself (fig.) роня́ть (*impf.*) себя́

cheat /tʃiːt/ *n.* (person) обма́нщик, плут, жу́лик
● *v.t. & i.* обма́н|ывать, -у́ть

Chechen /'tʃetʃen/ *n.* чече́н|ец (-ка)
● *adj.* чече́нский

Chechnya /'tʃetʃnjə/ *n.* Чечня́

✔ **check¹** /tʃek/ *n.* **1** (restraint) заде́ржка **2** (verification) контро́ль (*m.*) **3** (at chess) шах (*also as int.*) **4** (AmE, used for paying) чек **5** (AmE, bill in restaurant) счёт (-а́) **6** (AmE, for hat, luggage, etc.) номеро́к; квита́нция **7** (AmE, tick) га́лочка
● *v.t.* **1** (restrain) сде́рж|ивать, -а́ть **2** (verify) контроли́ровать, про-; пров|еря́ть, -е́рить **3** (AmE, tick) отм|еча́ть, -е́тить га́лочкой
□ ~ in *v.i.* (at hotel) регистри́роваться, за-
● *v.t.* (baggage) сд|ава́ть, -ать
□ ~ out *v.i.* (from hotel) выпи́сываться, вы́писаться
□ ~ up *v.i.*: ~ up on sth пров|еря́ть, -е́рить что-н.
■ ~**list** *n.* контро́льный спи́сок, пе́речень (*m.*); ~**out** *n.* ка́сса; ~**point** *n.* контро́льный пункт; ~**-up** *n.* прове́рка

check² /tʃek/ *n.* (pattern) кле́тка
● *attr. adj.* (*also* ~**ed**) кле́тчатый

checker /'tʃekə(r)/ *v.t.* (AmE) = chequer

checkers /'tʃekəz/ *n.* (AmE) ша́ш|ки (-ек)

checkmate /'tʃekmeɪt/ *n.* шах и мат

cheek /tʃiːk/ *n.* **1** (part of face) щека́ **2** (impudence) на́глость
■ ~**bone** *n.* скула́

cheeky /'tʃiːkɪ/ *adj.* (**cheekier, cheekiest**) наха́льный

cheer /tʃɪə(r)/ *n.* **1** (shout): three ~s for our visitors! троекра́тное ура́ на́шим гостя́м!; ~s! (as toast) (за) ва́ше здоро́вье! **2** (*in pl., as int.*) (BrE, infml) спаси́бо
● *v.t.* приве́тствовать (*impf.*)
● *v.i.* (utter ~s) изд|ава́ть, -а́ть восто́рженные кри́ки
□ ~ up *v.t. & i.* ободр|я́ть(ся), -и́ть(ся)
● *v.i.* повеселе́ть (*pf.*); ~ up! не уныва́йте!
■ ~**leader** *n.* де́вушка из гру́ппы подде́ржки (спорти́вной кома́нды), чирли́дер

cheerful /'tʃɪəfʊl/ *adj.* весёлый, ра́достный

cheese /tʃiːz/ *n.* сыр
■ ~**burger** *n.* чи́збургер; ~**cake** *n.* чизке́йк

cheetah /'tʃiːtə/ *n.* гепа́рд

chef /ʃef/ *n.* шеф-по́вар

✔ **chemical** /'kemɪk(ə)l/ *n.* хими́ческий проду́кт; (*in pl.*) химика́ты (*m. pl.*)
● *adj.* хими́ческий

chemist /'kemɪst/ *n.* **1** (scientist) хи́мик **2** (BrE, pharmacist) апте́карь (*m.*)
■ ~'s shop *n.* (BrE) апте́ка

chemistry /'kemɪstrɪ/ *n.* хи́мия

chemo /'kiːməʊ/ *n.* (infml) химиотерапи́я

chemotherapy /kiːmə'θerəpɪ/ *n.* химиотерапи́я

✔ ключева́я ле́ксика

cheque /tʃek/ (AmE **check**) *n.* чек; he made the ~ out to me он выписал чек на моё имя
■ ~**book** *n.* чéковая книжка; ~**book journalism** *n.* заказнáя журналистика

chequer /'tʃekə(r)/ (AmE **checker**) *v.t.* (fig.): ~ed career бурная жизнь
■ ~**ed flag** *n.* клéтчатый, шáхматный флажóк

cherish /'tʃerɪʃ/ *v.t.* **1** (love) нéжно любить (*impf.*) **2** (of hopes etc.) лелéять (*impf.*)

cherry /'tʃeri/ *n.* **1** (sour) (fruit) вишня; (tree) вишня, вишнёвое дéрево **2** (sweet) (fruit) черéшня; (tree) черéшня, черéшневое дéрево
■ ~**pick** *v.t. & i.* (things) отбирáть, -обрáть лучшее; (people, animals) отбирáть, -обрáть лучших

cherub /'tʃerəb/ *n.* херувим

chess /tʃes/ *n.* шáхматы (*pl., g.* —)
■ ~**board** *n.* шáхматная доскá; ~ **player** *n.* шахматист (-ка)

chest /tʃest/ *n.* **1** (furniture) сундýк; ~ of drawers шкаф с выдвижными ящиками **2** (anat.) груднáя клéтка; **get sth off one's ~** облегчить (*pf.*) дýшу

chestnut /'tʃesnʌt/ *n.* (tree, fruit) каштáн

chew /tʃuː/ *v.t. & i.* жевáть (*impf.*); ~ **upon**, ~ **over** (fig.) пережёвывать (*impf.*); ~**ing gum** жевáтельная резинка, жвáчка (infml)

chewy /'tʃuːɪ/ *adj.* (**chewier**, **chewiest**) (infml) тягýчий

chic /ʃiːk/ *adj.* (**chicer**, **chicest**) элегáнтный, шикáрный

chick /tʃɪk/ *n.* птенéц
■ ~**peas** *n. pl.* (bot.) нут (обыкновéнный/ культýрный), турéцкий/бáраний горóх

chicken /'tʃɪkɪn/ *n.* цыплёнок; (as food) курятина, цыплёнок, кýрица
■ ~**pox** *n.* ветряная óспа, ветрянка (infml)

chicory /'tʃɪkəri/ *n.* (bot.) цикóрий (корневóй)

☞ **chief** /tʃiːf/ *n.* **1** (leader) вождь (*m.*), главá (*m.*) **2** (senior official) шеф, начáльник; ~ of staff начáльник штáба
● *adj.* **1** (most important) глáвный, основнóй, важнéйший **2** (senior) глáвный, стáрший

chiefly /'tʃiːfli/ *adv.* глáвным óбразом

chiffon /'ʃɪfɒn/ *n.* шифóн

chilblain /'tʃɪlbleɪn/ *n.* обморóженное мéсто

☞ **child** /tʃaɪld/ *n.* (*pl.* **children**) дитя (*nt.*), ребёнок
■ ~ **benefit** *n.* пособие на ребёнка; ~**birth** *n.* рóды (-ов); ~**care** *n.* ухóд за детьми (*особенно в детских садах и яслях*)

childhood /'tʃaɪldhʊd/ *n.* дéтство

childish /'tʃaɪldɪʃ/ *adj.* дéтский, ребяческий

childless /'tʃaɪldlɪs/ *adj.* бездéтный

childlike /'tʃaɪldlaɪk/ *adj.* дéтский

children /'tʃɪldr(ə)n/ *pl. of* ▶ **child**

Chile /'tʃɪli/ *n.* Чили (*f. indecl.*)

Chilean /'tʃɪliən/ *n.* чилиéц (-йка)
● *adj.* чилийский

chill /tʃɪl/ *n.* **1** (physical) (also fig.) хóлод **2** (med.) простýда; **catch a ~** простужáться, -диться
● *adj.* холóдный

● *v.t.* (lit.) охлаждáть, -дить; (fig.) остужáть, -дить

● *v.i.*: ~ **out** (infml) расслабляться, -áбиться

chilled /tʃɪld/ *adj.* (of wine etc.) охлаждённый; (infml, relaxed) расслáбленный

chilli /'tʃɪli/ (AmE **chili**) *n.* (*pl.* **-es**) крáсный стручкóвый пéрец

chilly /'tʃɪli/ *adj.* (**chillier**, **chilliest**) холóдный

chime /tʃaɪm/ *n.* перезвóн
● *v.t.*: the clock ~d midnight часы́ пробили пóлночь

chimney /'tʃɪmni/ *n.* трубá, дымохóд

chimpanzee /tʃɪmpæn'ziː/ *n.* шимпанзé (*m. indecl.*)

chin /tʃɪn/ *n.* подборóдок

China /'tʃaɪnə/ *n.* Китáй

china /'tʃaɪnə/ *n.* фарфóр

☞ **Chinese** /tʃaɪ'niːz/ *n.* (*pl.* ~) китáец (-янка); (language) китáйский язы́к
● *adj.* китáйский

chink[1] /tʃɪŋk/ *n.* (crevice) щель; a ~ of light ýзкая полóска свéта

chink[2] /tʃɪŋk/ *n.* (sound) звяканье

chintz /tʃɪnts/ *n.* ситец; (*attr.*) ситцевый

chip /tʃɪp/ *n.* **1** (of wood) щéпка; стрýжка; (of china) оскóлок **2** (fig.): he has a ~ on his shoulder он дéржится вызывáюще **3** (piece missing): the cup has a ~ у чáшки откóлот кусóк **4** (*in pl.*) (food) (BrE) картóфель (*m.*) соломкой/фри; (AmE) чипсы (*m. pl.*) **5** (at games) фишка, мáрка **6** (in microelectronics) чип, микросхéма
● *v.t.* (**chipped**, **chipping**) стругáть, выстругать; откáлывать, -олóть; отбивáть, -ить; оббивáть, -ить
● *v.i.* (**chipped**, **chipping**): ~ **in** (infml) вмéшиваться, -áться; влезáть, -ть (в разговóр)
■ ~**board** *n.* фибролит; (*attr.*) фибролитовый

chipmunk /'tʃɪpmʌŋk/ *n.* бурундýк

chiropodist /kɪ'rɒpədɪst/ *n.* специалист (-ка) по лечéнию заболевáний стопы

chiropody /kɪ'rɒpədi/ *n.* лечéние заболевáний стопы

chiropractor /'kaɪərəʊpræktə(r)/ *n.* хиропрáктик

chirp /tʃəːp/ *v.t. & i.* чирикать (*impf.*); щебетáть (*impf.*)

chirpy /'tʃəːpi/ *adj.* (**chirpier**, **chirpiest**) (infml) бóдрый

chisel /'tʃɪz(ə)l/ *n.* долотó, стамéска
● *v.t.* (**chiselled**, **chiselling**, AmE **chiseled**, **chiseling**) ваять, из-

chit-chat /'tʃɪttʃæt/ *n.* болтовня, пересýды (-ов)

chivalrous /'ʃɪvəlrəs/ *adj.* ры́царский

chivalry /'ʃɪvəlri/ *n.* ры́царство

chive /tʃaɪv/ *n.* лук-рéзанец

chivvy /'tʃɪvi/ *v.t.* (BrE, infml) гонять (*impf.*)

chloride /'klɔːraɪd/ *n.* хлорид

chlorine /'klɔːriːn/ *n.* хлор

chock /tʃɒk/ *n.* клин; подпóрка
■ ~**a-block** *adj.* загромождённый; ~**full** *adj.* битком набитый

C

chocolate /'tʃɒkələt/ *n.* (also drink) шокола́д; (~-coated sweet) шокола́дная конфе́та; ~ **biscuit** шокола́дное пече́нье
■ ~ **bar** *n.* пли́тка шокола́да

✎ **choice** /tʃɔɪs/ *n.* **1** (choosing) вы́бор, отбо́р **2** (thing chosen) вы́бор **3** (variety) вы́бор

choir /'kwaɪə(r)/ *n.* хор
■ ~**boy** *n.* пе́вчий; ~**master** *n.* хормейстер

choke /tʃəʊk/ *n.* (in car) возду́шная засло́нка; дро́ссель (*m.*)
● *v.t.* **1** (throttle) души́ть, за- **2** (block) заку́пор|ивать, -ить; **the garden is** ~**d with weeds** сорняки́ заглуши́ли сад
● *v.i.* зад|ыха́ться, -охну́ться

choker /'tʃəʊkə(r)/ *n.* коро́ткое ожере́лье, колье́ (*nt. indecl.*)

cholera /'kɒlərə/ *n.* холе́ра

cholesterol /kə'lestərɒl/ *n.* холестери́н

✎ **choose** /tʃuːz/ *v.t.* (*past* **chose**, *p.p.* **chosen**) выбира́ть, вы́брать; **there are five to** ~ **from** мо́жно выбира́ть из пяти́; **I chose to remain** я предпочёл оста́ться

choosy /'tʃuːzɪ/ *adj.* (**choosier, choosiest**) разбо́рчивый

chop /tʃɒp/ *n.* **1** (cut) ру́бящий уда́р **2** (of meat) отбивна́я котле́та
● *v.t.* (**chopped, chopping**) (*also* ~ **up**) (wood) руби́ть (*impf.*); (food) нар|еза́ть, -е́зать; крош|и́ть (*impf.*); ~ **a tree down** руби́ть, с- де́рево

choppy /'tʃɒpɪ/ *adj.* (**choppier, choppiest**) (of sea) неспоко́йный

chopstick /'tʃɒpstɪk/ *n.* па́лочка для еды́

choral /'kɔːr(ə)l/ *adj.* хорово́й

chord /kɔːd/ *n.* (mus.) аккорд

chore /tʃɔː(r)/ *n.* (*usu. in pl.*) (routine task) рути́нная рабо́та; **household** ~**s** дома́шняя рабо́та; (tedious task) бре́мя (*nt.*)

choreographer /kɒrɪ'ɒɡrəfə(r)/ *n.* балетмейстер, хорео́граф

choreography /kɒrɪ'ɒɡrəfɪ/ *n.* хореогра́фия

chorister /'kɒrɪstə(r)/ *n.* хори́ст (-ка)

chortle /'tʃɔːt(ə)l/ *v.i.* фы́ркать (*impf.*); дави́ться (*impf.*) от сме́ха

chorus /'kɔːrəs/ *n.* (*pl.* ~**es**) **1** (singers) хор **2** (refrain) припе́в, рефре́н

chose /tʃəʊz/ *past of* ▸ **choose**

chosen /'tʃəʊz(ə)n/ *p.p. of* ▸ **choose**

Christ /kraɪst/ *n.* Христо́с

christen /'krɪs(ə)n/ *v.t.* крести́ть (*impf., pf.*); **he was** ~**ed John** при креще́нии ему́ да́ли и́мя Джон

christening /'krɪs(ə)nɪŋ/ *n.* креще́ние

✎ **Christian** /'krɪstɪən/ *n.* христи|ани́н (-а́нка)
● *adj.* христиа́нский
■ ~ **name** *n.* и́мя (*nt.*) (*в противоположность фамилии*)

Christianity /krɪstɪ'ænɪtɪ/ *n.* христиа́нство

✎ **Christmas** /'krɪsməs/ *n.* (*pl.* ~**es**) Рождество́
■ ~ **cake** *n.* (BrE) рожде́ственский пиро́г; ~ **card** *n.* рожде́ственская откры́тка; ~ **Day**

n. пе́рвый день Рождества́; ~ **Eve** *n.* кану́н Рождества́; ~ **tree** *n.* рожде́ственская, нового́дняя ёлка

chrome /krəʊm/ *n.* хром

chromosome /'krəʊməsəʊm/ *n.* хромосо́ма

chronic /'krɒnɪk/ *adj.* **1** (med.) хрони́ческий **2** (fig., incessant) хрони́ческий, постоя́нный

chronicle /'krɒnɪk(ə)l/ *n.* хро́ника, ле́топись
● *v.t.* вести́ (*det.*) хро́нику + g.

chronological /krɒnə'lɒdʒɪk(ə)l/ *adj.* хронологи́ческий

chronology /krə'nɒlədʒɪ/ *n.* хроноло́гия

chrysanthemum /krɪ'sænθəməm/ *n.* хризанте́ма

chubby /'tʃʌbɪ/ *adj.* (**chubbier, chubbiest**) то́лстенький, пу́хленький

chuck /tʃʌk/ *v.t.* (infml, throw) швыр|я́ть, -ну́ть
□ ~ **away** *v.t.* (lit.) выбра́сывать, вы́бросить
□ ~ **out** *v.t.* (thing or person) вы́кинуть (*pf.*); вы́швырнуть (*pf.*)

chuckle /'tʃʌk(ə)l/ *n.* сда́вленный смешо́к, смех
● *v.i.* фы́ркать (*impf.*) от сме́ха, посме́иваться (*impf.*)

chuffed /tʃʌft/ *adj.* (BrE, infml) дово́льный

chum /tʃʌm/ *n.* прия́тель (*m.*), дружо́к

chunk /tʃʌŋk/ *n.* то́лстый кусо́к/ло́моть (*m.*)

chunky /'tʃʌŋkɪ/ *adj.* (**chunkier, chunkiest**) (person) корена́стый; (jumper) то́лстый

✎ **church** /tʃɜːtʃ/ *n.* це́рковь; (building) це́рковь; (esp. Orthodox) храм
■ ~**goer** *n.*: **he is a regular** ~**goer** он регуля́рно хо́дит в це́рковь; ~**yard** *n.* пого́ст, кла́дбище при це́ркви

churlish /'tʃɜːlɪʃ/ *adj.* ха́мский, гру́бый

churn /tʃɜːn/ *n.* (tub) масло́бойка; (BrE, can) бидо́н
● *v.t.*: ~ **butter** сби|ва́ть, -ть ма́сло; (fig.): **he** ~**s out novels** он печёт рома́ны (как блины́); **the propeller** ~**ed up the waves** винт взвихри́л во́лны

chute /ʃuːt/ *n.* (slide, slope) жёлоб, спуск; (for amusement) гора́, го́рка; (for rubbish) мусоропрово́д

chutney /'tʃʌtnɪ/ *n.* ча́тни (*nt. indecl.*) (*инди́йская припра́ва из фру́ктов или овоще́й с доба́влением у́ксуса, о́стрых спе́ций и са́хара*)

CIA *abbr.* (*of* **Central Intelligence Agency**) ЦРУ (Центра́льное разве́дывательное управле́ние)

cicada /sɪ'kɑːdə/ *n.* (zool.) цика́да

cider /'saɪdə(r)/ *n.* (BrE, alcoholic drink) сидр; (AmE, non-alcoholic drink) я́блочный напи́ток

cigar /sɪ'ɡɑː(r)/ *n.* сига́ра

cigarette /sɪɡə'ret/ *n.* сигаре́та; (of Russian type) папиро́са
■ ~**lighter** *n.* зажига́лка

cinder /'sɪndə(r)/ *n.* (*in pl.*) шлак, зола́, пе́пел

cine camera /'sɪnɪkæmrə/ *n.* (BrE) кинока́мера, киноаппара́т

cinema /'sɪnɪmə/ *n.* кино́ (*nt. indecl.*)

cinematography /sɪnɪmə'tɒɡrəfɪ/ *n.*
кинематогра́фия

cinnamon /'sɪnəmən/ *n.* кори́ца

circa /'sɜːkə/ *prep.* приблизи́тельно; о́коло + *g.*

circle /'sɜːk(ə)l/ *n.* **1** (math.) (*also* fig.)
круг, окру́жность; a ~ of trees кольцо́
дере́вьев; go round in a ~ (fig., e.g. argument)
возвраща́ться (*impf.*) к исхо́дной то́чке
2 (theatr.): dress ~ бельэта́ж; upper ~ балко́н
• *v.t.*: the earth ~s the sun земля́ враща́ется
вокру́г со́лнца
• *v.i.*: the hawk ~d я́стреб кружи́л в не́бе (*or*
опи́сывал круги́)

circuit /'sɜːkɪt/ *n.* **1** (distance, journey round): he
made a ~ of the camp он обошёл ла́герь
2 (elec.) цепь
■ ~-**breaker** *n.* автомати́ческий выключа́тель

circuitous /sɜː'kjuːɪtəs/ *adj.* кру́жный,
око́льный

circular /'sɜːkjʊlə(r)/ *n.* циркуля́р
• *adj.* кругово́й

circulate /'sɜːkjʊleɪt/ *v.i.* циркули́ровать
(*impf., pf.*); she ~d among the guests она́
обходи́ла госте́й

circulation /sɜːkjʊ'leɪʃ(ə)n/ *n.* (of blood)
кровообраще́ние; (of air) циркуля́ция

circumcise /'sɜːkəmsaɪz/ *v.t.* соверша́ть, -и́ть
обре́зание + *d.*

circumcision /sɜːkəm'sɪʒ(ə)n/ *n.* обре́зание

circumference /sə'kʌmfərəns/ *n.*
окру́жность

circumnavigate /sɜːkəm'nævɪɡeɪt/ *v.t.*
пла́вать (*indet.*) вокру́г + *g.*; Drake ~d
the globe Дрейк соверши́л кругосве́тное
пла́вание

circumspect /'sɜːkəmspekt/ *adj.*
осмотри́тельный

circumstance /'sɜːkəmstəns/ *n.* **1** (fact,
detail) обстоя́тельство, усло́вие; in, under the
~s в да́нных усло́виях/обстоя́тельствах;
under no ~s ни при каки́х усло́виях/
обстоя́тельствах **2** (condition of life)
материа́льное положе́ние

circumstantial /sɜːkəm'stænʃ(ə)l/ *adj.*: ~
evidence ко́свенные ули́ки (*f. pl.*)

circumvent /sɜːkəm'vent/ *v.t.* обходи́ть,
-ойти́; (outwit, cheat) перехитри́ть (*pf.*)

circus /'sɜːkəs/ *n.* (*pl.* ~**es**) цирк; (fig.) балага́н

cirrhosis /sɪ'rəʊsɪs/ *n.* цирро́з

CIS *abbr.* (*of* **Commonwealth of
Independent States**) СНГ (Содру́жество
Незави́симых Госуда́рств); (*attr.*) эсэнгэ́шный
(*infml*)

cistern /'sɪst(ə)n/ *n.* цисте́рна, бак

citadel /'sɪtədel/ *n.* (lit., fig.) цитаде́ль

cite /saɪt/ *v.t.* (quote) цити́ровать, про-

citizen /'sɪtɪz(ə)n/ *n.* граждани́н (-а́нка); (of
city) жи́тель (-ница)

citizenship /'sɪtɪzənʃɪp/ *n.* гражда́нство,
по́дданство

citrus /'sɪtrəs/ *n.*: ~ **fruit** цитрусовые (*nt. pl.*)

city /'sɪtɪ/ *n.* го́род; (of London) Си́ти (*m. indecl.*)
■ ~ **centre**, (AmE) ~ **center** *n.* центр го́рода

civic /'sɪvɪk/ *adj.* гражда́нский

civil /'sɪv(ə)l/ *adj.* **1** (relating to citizens)
гражда́нский; ~ **rights** гражда́нские права́;
~ **war** гражда́нская война́; ~ **partner**
гражда́нский супру́г/гражда́нская супру́га,
партнёр однопо́лого бра́ка; ~ **partnership**
гражда́нский брак, однопо́лый брак
2 (relating to the state) госуда́рственный;
~ **servant** госуда́рственный слу́жащий,
чино́вник; ~ **service** госуда́рственная
слу́жба **3** (polite) ве́жливый

civilian /sɪ'vɪlɪən/ *n. & adj.* шта́тский

civilization /sɪvɪlaɪ'zeɪʃ(ə)n/ *n.* цивилиза́ция

civilize /'sɪvɪlaɪz/ *v.t.* цивилизова́ть (*impf., pf.*)

claim /kleɪm/ *n.* **1** (assertion of right) притяза́ние
2 (assertion) утвержде́ние, заявле́ние
3 (demand) тре́бование
• *v.t.* **1** (demand) тре́бовать, по- + *g.* **2** (assert
as fact) утвержда́ть, -ди́ть; he ~s to own the
land он заявля́ет, что э́та земля́ принадлежи́т
ему́

claimant /'kleɪmənt/ *n.* претенде́нт (-ка)
(*на что*)

clairvoyant /kleə'vɔɪənt/ *n. & adj.*
яснови́дящий (-ая)

clam /klæm/ *n.* двуство́рчатый морско́й
моллю́ск
• *v.i.* (**clammed, clamming**): ~ **up** (infml)
уходи́ть, уйти́ в себя́

clamber /'klæmbə(r)/ *v.i.* кара́бкаться, вс- (*на
что*)

clammy /'klæmɪ/ *adj.* (**clammier,
clammiest**) холо́дный и ли́пкий

clamour /'klæmə(r)/ (AmE **clamor**) *n.* шум
(*m. pl.*)
• *v.i.* шуме́ть (*impf.*)

clamp /klæmp/ *n.* (implement) зажи́м
• *v.t.* заж|има́ть, -а́ть
• *v.i.*: ~ **down on** (fig.) заж|има́ть, -а́ть
■ ~**down** *n.* стро́гий запре́т, стро́гие ме́ры
(*против чего*)

clan /klæn/ *n.* клан

clandestine /klæn'destɪn/ *adj.* та́йный

clang /klæŋ/ *n.* лязг
• *v.t. & i.* ля́зг|ать, -нуть; звене́ть (*impf.*)

clap /klæp/ *n.* (of thunder) уда́р; (of applause)
хлопо́к, хло́панье; let's give him a ~!
похло́паем ему́!
• *v.t.* (**clapped, clapping**) (strike, slap): ~
one's hands хло́п|ать, -нуть в ладо́ши
• *v.i.* (**clapped, clapping**) хло́пать (*impf.*)

clarification /klærɪfɪ'keɪʃ(ə)n/ *n.* проясне́ние

clarify /'klærɪfaɪ/ *v.t.* вн|оси́ть, -ести́ я́сность
в + *a.*

clarinet /klærɪ'net/ *n.* кларне́т

clarinettist /klærɪ'netɪst/ *n.* кларнети́ст (-ка)

clarity /'klærɪtɪ/ *n.* я́сность

clash /klæʃ/ *n.* **1** (sound) гул **2** (conflict): ~ of
views расхожде́ние во взгля́дах
• *v.t.*: he ~ed the cymbals он уда́рил в
цимба́лы
• *v.i.* **1** (sound): the cymbals ~ed зазвене́ли
цимба́лы **2** (conflict): the armies ~ed а́рмии
столкну́лись; (coincide inconveniently): the

c

two concerts ~ óба концéрта совпадáют по врéмени; **the colours** ~ э́ти цветá не гармонúруют друг с дрýгом

clasp /klɑːsp/ *n.* пря́жка
● *v.t.:* ~ **sb by the hand** сж|имáть, -áть комý-н. рýку

✓ **class** /klɑːs/ *n.* **1** (group) класс, разря́д; (railway etc.): **he went first** ~ он éхал пéрвым клáссом **2** (social) класс **3** (scholastic) класс; (period of instruction): **a maths** ~ урóк математики; **he attended** ~**es in French** он посещáл заня́тия по французскому (языкý); (AmE, graduates): **the** ~ **of 1955** вы́пуск 1955 гóда **4** (distinction) класс, шик
● *v.t.* классифицúровать (*impf., pf.*)
■ ~**-conscious** *adj.* клáссово-сознáтельный; ~**mate** *n.* одноклáссни|к (-ца); ~**room** *n.* клáссная кóмната, класс

✓ **classic** /ˈklæsɪk/ *n.* **1** клáссик **2** (*in pl.*) (studies): **he studied** ~**s** он изучáл классúческую филолóгию
● *adj.* классúческий

classical /ˈklæsɪk(ə)l/ *adj.* классúческий
classifiable /ˈklæsɪfaɪəb(ə)l/ *adj.* поддаю́щийся классификáции
classification /ˌklæsɪfɪˈkeɪʃ(ə)n/ *n.* классификáция
classif|y /ˈklæsɪfaɪ/ *v.t.* классифицúровать (*impf., pf.*); ~**ied** (secret) засекрéченный
■ ~**ied ad** *n.* темати́ческое объявлéние
classy /ˈklɑːsɪ/ *adj.* (**classier, classiest**) стúльный (infml)
clatter /ˈklætə(r)/ *n.* (of metal) грóхот; (of hoofs, plates, cutlery, etc.) стук, звон, звя́канье
● *v.i.* гремéть; грохотáть (*both impf.*)
clause /klɔːz/ *n.* **1** (gram.) предложéние **2** (law) статья́
claustrophobia /ˌklɔːstrəˈfəʊbɪə/ *n.* клаустрофóбия
claustrophobic /ˌklɔːstrəˈfəʊbɪk/ *adj.*: **I'm** ~ я страдáю клаустрофóбией
claw /klɔː/ *n.* (of animal, bird) кóготь (*m.*); (of crustacean) клешня́; (of machinery) кулáк, лáпа, клéщ|и (-éй)
clay /kleɪ/ *n.* глúна

✓ **clean** /kliːn/ *adj.* **1** (not dirty) чúстый; **keep a room** ~ содержáть (*impf.*) кóмнату в чистотé **2** (fresh): **a** ~ **sheet of paper** чúстый лист бумáги **3** (pure, unblemished) чúстый, незапя́тнанный **4** (neat, smooth): ~ **lines** чéткие очертáния; чúстые лúнии
● *v.t.* чúстить (*impf.*); ~ **one's teeth** чúстить, по- зýбы; ~ **a car** мыть, вы- машúну; ~ **a window** прот|ирáть, -ерéть окнó; **he had his suit** ~**ed** он óтдал костю́м в чúстку
□ ~ **out** *v.t.:* ~ **out a room** убрáть (*pf.*) кóмнату
□ ~ **up** *v.t.:* ~ **oneself up** прив|одúть, -ести́ себя́ в поря́док; ~ **up a city** (fig.) очúстить (*pf.*) гóрод
■ ~**-cut** *adj.* рéзко очéрченный; ~**-shaven** *adj.* чúсто вы́бритый

✓ ключевáя лéксика

cleaner /ˈkliːnə(r)/ *n.* (person) убóрщи|к (-ца); **he sent the suit to the** ~**'s** он óтдал костю́м в чúстку; (substance) мóющее срéдство; очисти́тель (*m.*)
cleanliness /ˈklenlɪnɪs/ *n.* чистотá
cleanse /klenz/ *v.t.* оч|ищáть, -úстить
cleanser /ˈklenzə(r)/ *n.* срéдство для очищéния кóжи

✓ **clear** /klɪə(r)/ *adj.* **1** (easy to see) я́сный, отчётливый; (evident) я́вный, очевúдный **2** (bright) я́ркий, я́сный; **on a** ~ **day** в погóжий день **3** (transparent) прозрáчный **4** (of sound) чúстый **5** (intelligible, certain): **make sth** ~ **to sb** объясн|я́ть, -úть что-н. комý-н.; **make oneself** ~ объясн|я́ться, -úться; **I am not** ~ **what he wants** мне нея́сно, чегó он хóчет **6** (safe, free) свобóдный; ~ **of debt** свобóдный от долгóв; ~ **of suspicion** вне подозрéний; **my conscience is** ~ моя́ сóвесть чистá; **keep a** ~ **head** сохраня́ть (*impf.*) я́сный ум
● *adv.:* **stand** ~ **of the gates** стоя́ть (*impf.*) в сторонé от ворóт; **keep** ~ **of** держáться (*impf.*) в сторонé от + *g.*
● *v.t.* **1** (make ~) оч|ищáть, -úстить; **the streets were** ~**ed of snow** ýлицы очúстили от снéга; ~ **land** расчищáть, -úстить зéмлю; **she** ~**ed the table** онá убралá со столá; **he was** ~**ed for security** егó засекрéтили; **he** ~**ed his throat** он откáшлялся; **he** ~**ed the things out of the drawer** он освободúл я́щик **2** (jump over; get past): **the horse** ~**ed the hedge** лóшадь взялá барьéр **3** (make profit of): **we** ~**ed £50** мы получúли 50 фýнтов прúбыли **4**: ~ **a debt** погасúть (*pf.*) долг
● *v.i. see* ▶ **clear up**
□ ~ **away** *v.t.* уб|ирáть, -рáть
● *v.i.* (disperse) рассé|иваться, -яться
□ ~ **off** *v.i.* (infml, go away) уб|ирáться, -рáться
□ ~ **out** *v.t.:* **she** ~**ed out the cupboard** онá очúстила шкаф
● *v.i.* (infml, go away) убрáться (*pf.*)
□ ~ **up** *v.t.* (tidy, remove) уб|ирáть, -рáть; ~ **up a mystery** разгадáть (*pf.*) тáйну
● *v.i.:* **the weather** ~**ed up** погóда проясни́лась
■ ~**-cut** *adj.* (fig.) чёткий; ~**-headed** *adj.* толкóвый
clearance /ˈklɪərəns/ *n.* **1** (removal of obstruction etc.) очúстка, расчúстка **2**: **security** ~ дóпуск к секрéтной рабóте
■ ~ **sale** *n.* распродáжа
clearing /ˈklɪərɪŋ/ *n.* прóсека, поля́на

✓ **clearly** /ˈklɪəlɪ/ *adv.* (distinctly) я́сно; (evidently) очевúдно, конéчно
cleavage /ˈkliːvɪdʒ/ *n.* «ручеёк», ложбúнка бю́ста
cleaver /ˈkliːvə(r)/ *n.* нож мясникá
clef /klef/ *n.* (mus.) ключ; **treble** ~ скрипúчный ключ
cleft /kleft/ *adj.* расщеплённый
■ ~ **palate** *n.* расщеплённое нёбо
clematis /ˈklemətɪs/ *n.* климáтис, ломонóс
clench /klentʃ/ *v.t.:* ~ **one's teeth** стúснуть (*pf.*) зýбы; ~ **one's fists** сж|имáть, -áть кулакú

clergy /ˈklɜːdʒɪ/ *n.* духове́нство, клир
■ ~**man** *n.* духо́вное лицо́; (Protestant) па́стор
cleric /ˈklerɪk/ *n.* церко́вник, духо́вное лицо́
clerical /ˈklerɪk(ə)l/ *adj.* **1** (of clergy)
клерика́льный **2** (of clerks) канцеля́рский,
ко́нторский
■ ~ **error** *n.* канцеля́рская оши́бка
clerk /klɑːk/ *n.* **1** (in office) секрета́рь
(*m.*), делопроизводи́тель (*m.*); bank ~
ба́нковский слу́жащий **2** (official) слу́жащий;
(of court) регистра́тор **3** (AmE, shop assistant)
продаве́ц; (AmE, hotel receptionist) (дежу́рный)
администра́тор
clever /ˈklevə(r)/ *adj.* (**cleverer, cleverest**)
у́мный; (skilful) ло́вкий; **he is** ~ **with his
fingers** у него́ уме́лые ру́ки
cliché /ˈkliːʃeɪ/ *n.* клише́ (*nt. indecl.*)
⚿ **click** /klɪk/ *n.* щёлканье, щелчо́к
  ● *v.t.* щёлк|ать, -нуть + *i.*
  ● *v.i.* щёлк|ать, -нуть; (comput.): ~ **on an icon**
щёлк|ать, -нуть (мы́шкой) на ико́нке
⚿ **client** /ˈklaɪənt/ *n.* клие́нт (-ка)
clientele /kliːɒnˈtel/ *n.* клиенту́ра
cliff /klɪf/ *n.* утёс, скала́
climactic /klaɪˈmæktɪk/ *adj.*
кульминацио́нный
⚿ **climate** /ˈklaɪmət/ *n.* кли́мат; (fig.) атмосфе́ра
■ ~ **change** *n.* измене́ние кли́мата
climatic /klaɪˈmætɪk/ *adj.* климати́ческий
climatologist /klaɪməˈtɒlədʒɪst/ *n.*
климато́лог
climax /ˈklaɪmæks/ *n.* кульмина́ция
  ● *v.i.* (culminate) дост|ига́ть, -и́чь
кульмина́ции, апоге́я
⚿ **climb** /klaɪm/ *n.* подъём, восхожде́ние
  ● *v.t.* вл|еза́ть, -езть на + *a.*
  ● *v.i.* ла́зить (indet.), лезть (det.); ~ **up a
tree** влез|а́ть, -ть на де́рево; ~ **over a wall**
перел|еза́ть, -езть че́рез сте́ну; ~ **down a
ladder** слез|а́ть, -ть с ле́стницы; ~ **on to a
table** зал|еза́ть, -езть на стол
■ ~**down** *n.* (BrE) отступле́ние, усту́пка
climber /ˈklaɪmə(r)/ *n.* альпини́ст (-ка); (plant)
вью́щееся расте́ние
climbing /ˈklaɪmɪŋ/ *n.* альпини́зм
clime /klaɪm/ *n.* (poet., region) край, сторона́
clinch /klɪntʃ/ *v.t.*: ~ **a bargain** заключи́ть
(*pf.*) сде́лку (*окончательно согласовав все
условия*)
cling /klɪŋ/ *v.i.* (past and p.p. **clung**) (adhere)
цепля́ться (impf.) (**to**: за + *a.*); (fig.): **they
clung together** они́ держа́лись вме́сте; **a**
~**ing dress** облега́ющее пла́тье
clinic /ˈklɪnɪk/ *n.* кли́ника
⚿ **clinical** /ˈklɪnɪk(ə)l/ *adj.* **1** клини́ческий
2 (fig.) бесстра́стный
clink /klɪŋk/ *v.t.* звене́ть (impf.) + *i.*
  ● *v.i.* звене́ть (impf.); чо́к|аться, -нуться
clip¹ /klɪp/ *n.* (for hair) зако́лка
  ● *v.t.* (**clipped, clipping**) (secure) заж|има́ть,
-а́ть
■ ~**board** *n.* доска́ с зажи́мом для бума́ги;
~**-on** *adj.* пристёгивающийся

clip² /klɪp/ *n.* (cin.) отры́вок (из фи́льма)
  ● *v.t.* (**clipped, clipping**) (cut): ~ **a hedge**
подстр|ига́ть, -и́чь живу́ю и́згородь; ~
sb's wings (fig.) подре́зать (*pf.*) кому́-н.
кры́лышки
clipper /ˈklɪpə(r)/ *n.* (in pl.) (for nails) куса́ч|ки
(-ек)
clipping /ˈklɪpɪŋ/ *n.* (from newspaper) газе́тная
вы́резка
cloak /kləʊk/ *n.* плащ, ма́нтия
  ● *v.t.* (fig.) прикр|ыва́ть, -ы́ть
■ ~**room** *n.* (for clothes) гардеро́б, раздева́лка;
(BrE, lavatory) убо́рная
clock /klɒk/ *n.* час|ы́ (-о́в); **he works round
the** ~ он рабо́тает кру́глые су́тки; **put the** ~
forward ста́вить, по- часы́ вперёд; **put the**
~ **back** (lit.) перев|оди́ть, -ести́ часы́ наза́д;
(fig.) поверну́ть (*pf.*) вре́мя вспять
  ● *v.i.*: ~ **in, on** (BrE) отм|еча́ться, -е́титься
по прихо́де на рабо́ту; ~ **out, off** (BrE)
отм|еча́ться, -е́титься при ухо́де с рабо́ты
■ ~**work** *n.* часово́й механи́зм; **the ceremony
went like** ~**work** церемо́ния прошла́ без
сучка́, без задо́ринки
clockwise /ˈklɒkwaɪz/ *adj. & adv.*
(дви́жущийся) по часово́й стре́лке
clog¹ /klɒg/ *n.* (shoe) башма́к на деревя́нной
подо́шве; сабо́ (*nt. indecl.*)
clog² /klɒg/ *v.t.* (**clogged, clogging**)
засор|я́ть, -и́ть; **the sink is** ~**ged** ра́ковина
засори́лась
cloister /ˈklɔɪstə(r)/ *n.* арка́да
clone /kləʊn/ *n.* клон
  ● *v.t.* разм|ножа́ть, -ожи́ть вегетати́вным
путём; клони́ровать (impf., pf.)
cloning /ˈkləʊnɪŋ/ *n.* клони́рование
⚿ **close**¹ /kləʊs/ *adj.* **1** (near) бли́зкий; **he had a**
~ **shave, call** он был на волосо́к от ги́бели;
~ **resemblance** большо́е схо́дство **2** (intimate)
бли́зкий; **a** ~ **friend** бли́зкий друг **3** (compact):
~ **texture** пло́тная ткань **4** (attentive): **keep
a** ~ **watch on sb** тща́тельно следи́ть (impf.)
за кем-н.; ~ **examination** тща́тельное
обсле́дование; ~ **attention** при́стальное
внима́ние **5** (of games etc.): **a** ~ **contest**
упо́рная борьба́ **6** (stuffy) ду́шный
  ● *adv.*: **he lives** ~ **to, by the church** он живёт
побли́зости от це́ркви; **follow** ~ **behind
sb** сле́довать (impf.) непосре́дственно за
кем-н.
■ ~**-fitting** *adj.* облега́ющий; ~**-up** *n.* (cin.)
кру́пный план
⚿ **close**² /kləʊz/ *n.* (end) коне́ц; **bring to a** ~
заверш|а́ть, -и́ть, зак|а́нчивать, -о́нчить; **the
meeting drew to a** ~ собра́ние подошло́ к
концу́
  ● *v.t.* **1** (shut) закр|ыва́ть, -ы́ть; **the museum is**
~**d** музе́й не рабо́тает **2** (end, complete): ~ **a
meeting** закр|ыва́ть, -ы́ть собра́ние; ~ **a deal**
заключ|а́ть, -и́ть сде́лку; **the closing scene
of the play** заключи́тельная сце́на пье́сы;
the closing date is December 1 после́дний
срок — пе́рвое декабря́
  ● *v.i.* **1** (shut) закр|ыва́ться, -ы́ться; **the
door** ~**d** дверь закры́лась **2** (cease): **he**

c

~d with this remark он зако́нчил э́тим замеча́нием **3** (come closer) сбли|жа́ться, -зи́ться; **the soldiers ~d up** солда́ты сомкну́ли ряды́

□ **~ down** v.t. закр|ыва́ть, -ы́ть

• v.i. (e.g. of a factory) закр|ыва́ться, -ы́ться

□ **~ off** v.t. блоки́ровать (impf., pf.)

□ **~ up** v.t. & i. закр|ыва́ть(ся), -ы́ть(ся)

⚭ **closely** /ˈkləʊslɪ/ adv.: **it ~ resembles pork** э́то о́чень напомина́ет свини́ну; (attentively) внима́тельно; **watch ~** при́стально следи́ть (impf.) за + i.; **~ connected** те́сно/про́чно свя́занный

closet /ˈklɒzɪt/ n. (AmE) (стенно́й) шкаф

closure /ˈkləʊʒə(r)/ n. закры́тие

clot /klɒt/ n. сгу́сток, комо́к; (BrE, sl., stupid person) болва́н, тупи́ца (c.g.)

• v.i. (**clotted**, **clotting**) свёртываться, сверну́ться

cloth /klɒθ/ n. **1** (material) ткань, мате́рия **2** (piece of ~) тря́пка

⚭ **clothes** /kləʊðz/ n. pl. пла́тье, оде́жда

■ **~ brush** n. платяна́я щётка; **~ line** n. верёвка для белья́; **~peg** (BrE), **~pin** (AmE) nn. прище́пка

clothing /ˈkləʊðɪŋ/ n. оде́жда

cloud /klaʊd/ n. **1** (in the sky) о́блако; ту́ча **2** (of unhappiness etc.): **this cast a ~ over our meeting** э́то омрачи́ло на́шу встре́чу

• v.t. покр|ыва́ть, -ы́ть облака́ми; (fig.) омрач|а́ть, -и́ть; **eyes ~ed with tears** глаза́, помутне́вшие от слёз

• v.i.: **the sky ~ed over, up** (AmE) не́бо затяну́ло облака́ми/ту́чами

cloudy /ˈklaʊdɪ/ adj. (**cloudier**, **cloudiest**) о́блачный; (of liquid) му́тный

clout /klaʊt/ n. (infml) (blow) затре́щина; (influence) влия́ние

• v.t. (hit) тре́снуть (pf.)

clove /kləʊv/ n.: **a ~ of garlic** зу́бчик чеснока́

clover /ˈkləʊvə(r)/ n. кле́вер

cloves /kləʊvz/ n. pl. (aromatic) гвозди́ка (пряность)

clown /klaʊn/ n. кло́ун

• v.i. стро́ить (impf.) из себя́ шута́

club¹ /klʌb/ n. (weapon) дуби́нка; (at golf) клю́шка; (in pl.) (at cards) тре́фы (f. pl.)

⚭ **club²** /klʌb/ n. (society) клуб

• v.i. (**clubbed**, **clubbing**): **they ~bed together to pay the fine** они́ сложи́лись и уплати́ли штраф; **they're always going out ~bing** (infml) они́ — постоя́нные посети́тели ночны́х клу́бов

cluck /klʌk/ v.i. куда́хтать, клохта́ть (both impf.)

clue /kluː/ n. ключ, нить; (for crossword) определе́ние; **the police found a ~** поли́ция нашла́ ули́ку; **I haven't a ~** (infml) поня́тия не име́ю

clueless /ˈkluːlɪs/ adj. (infml) бестолко́вый; не в ку́рсе

clump /klʌmp/ n. (cluster) гру́ппа

• v.t. (plant in groups) сажа́ть, посади́ть

гру́ппами; (gather into a group) соб|ира́ть, -ра́ть в ку́чу

clumsy /ˈklʌmzɪ/ adj. (**clumsier**, **clumsiest**) неуклю́жий, нело́вкий

clung /klʌŋ/ past and p.p. of ▸ **cling**

cluster /ˈklʌstə(r)/ n. скопле́ние

• v.i. соб|ира́ться, -ра́ться гру́ппами; **the children ~ed round the teacher** де́ти столпи́лись вокру́г учи́теля

clutch /klʌtʃ/ n. **1** (in pl.) (grasp) ла́пы (f. pl.), ко́гти (m. pl.) **2** (of car) сцепле́ние

• v.t. & i. хвата́ться, схвати́ться (**at**: за + a.); **he ~ed (at) the rope** он ухвати́лся за верёвку

■ **~ pedal** n. педа́ль сцепле́ния

clutter /ˈklʌtə(r)/ n. сумато́ха, суета́

• v.t. (also ~ **up**) загромо|жда́ть, -зди́ть

cm /ˈsentɪmiːtə(r)(z)/ n. (abbr. of **centimetre(s)**) см (сантиме́тр(ы))

Co. /kəʊ/ n. (abbr. of **company**) К° (компа́ния)

c/o abbr. (of **care of**) че́рез; **John Smith c/o David Green** Дэ́виду Гри́ну для переда́чи Джо́ну Сми́ту

coach¹ /kəʊtʃ/ n. **1** (horse-drawn) каре́та, экипа́ж **2** (railway) пассажи́рский ваго́н **3** (BrE, bus) (туристи́ческий, междугоро́дный) авто́бус

■ **~ tour** n. авто́бусная экску́рсия

⚭ **coach²** /kəʊtʃ/ n. (trainer) тре́нер

• v.t. репети́ровать (impf.); (train) тренирова́ть, на-

coagulate /kəʊˈæɡjʊleɪt/ v.t. сгу|ща́ть, -сти́ть; (phys., chem.) коагули́ровать (impf., pf.); (med., blood) свёртывать, сверну́ть

• v.i. сгу|ща́ться, -сти́ться; (phys., chem.) коагули́роваться (impf., pf.); (med., of blood) свёртываться, сверну́ться

coal /kəʊl/ n. (mineral) ка́менный у́голь; (BrE, piece of ~) у́голь (m.); (fig.): **haul sb over the ~s** да|ва́ть, -ть нагоня́й кому́-н.

■ **~field** n. ка́менноу́гольный бассе́йн; **~ mine** n. у́гольная ша́хта; **~ miner** n. шахтёр

coalition /kəʊəˈlɪʃ(ə)n/ n. (pol.) коали́ция

coarse /kɔːs/ adj. (of material) гру́бый; (of sand, sugar) кру́пный; **~ manners** гру́бые/вульга́рные мане́ры

coast /kəʊst/ n. морско́й бе́рег

• v.i. **1** (bicycle downhill) кати́ться (impf.) на велосипе́де с горы́ **2** (do sth with little effort) де́лать (impf.) что-л. без осо́бых уси́лий

■ **~guard** n. (officer) сотру́дник (тамо́женной) берегово́й охра́ны; (collect.) берегова́я охра́на; **~line** n. берегова́я ли́ния

coastal /ˈkəʊst(ə)l/ adj. берегово́й, прибре́жный

coaster /ˈkəʊstə(r)/ n. подно́с, подста́вка

coat /kəʊt/ n. **1** (overcoat) пальто́ (nt. indecl.); **~ of arms** герб **2** (of animal) шерсть, мех **3** (of paint etc.) слой

• v.t. покр|ыва́ть, -ы́ть; **the pill was ~ed with sugar** пилю́ля в са́харной оболо́чке

■ **~ hanger** n. ве́шалка

coating /ˈkəʊtɪŋ/ n. (layer) слой

co-author /kəʊˈɔːθə(r)/ n. соа́втор

coax /kəʊks/ v.t. угов|а́ривать, -ори́ть

⚭ ключева́я ле́ксика

cobble¹ /'kɒb(ə)l/ *n.* (*also* **cobblestone**) булы́жник

cobble² /'kɒb(ə)l/ *v.t.* (*usu.* ~ **together**) де́лать (*impf.*) ко́е-ка́к

cobbled /'kɒb(ə)ld/ *adj.*: ~ street булы́жная мостова́я

cobra /'kəʊbrə/ *n.* ко́бра; очко́вая змея́

cobweb /'kɒbweb/ *n.* паути́на

cocaine /kə'keɪn/ *n.* кокаи́н

cock¹ /kɒk/ *n.* **1** (male domestic fowl) пету́х **2** (male bird) пету́х, саме́ц ■ ~ **and bull** *adj.*: ~ and bull story вздор, небыли́ца; ~**pit** *n.* (aeron.) каби́на; ~**roach** *n.* тарака́н; ~**tail** *n.* (drink) кокте́йль (*m.*)

cock² /kɒk/ *v.t.* **1** (stick up etc.): the horse ~ed (up) its ears ло́шадь навостри́ла у́ши **2** (of gun) взв|оди́ть, -ести́ куро́к + *g.*

cockerel /'kɒkər(ə)l/ *n.* петушо́к

cockle /'kɒk(ə)l/ *n.* сердцеви́дка, съедо́бный моллю́ск

cockney /'kɒknɪ/ *n. & adj.* (person) ко́кни (*c.g. indecl.*); (language) ко́кни (*m. indecl.*); ~ **accent** акце́нт ко́кни

cocky /'kɒkɪ/ *adj.* (**cockier, cockiest**) наха́льный

cocoa /'kəʊkəʊ/ *n.* кака́о (*nt. indecl.*)

coconut /'kəʊkənʌt/ *n.* коко́с, коко́совый оре́х

cocoon /kə'ku:n/ *n.* ко́кон

COD *abbr.* (*of* **cash on delivery**) упла́та при доста́вке

cod /kɒd/ *n.* (*pl.* ~) треска́

coda /'kəʊdə/ *n.* (mus.) ко́да

⚲ **code** /kəʊd/ *n.* (of laws, conduct) ко́декс; (set of symbols) код ● *v.t.* (encode) коди́ровать (*impf., pf.*)

codeine /'kəʊdi:n/ *n.* кодеи́н

co-educational /kəʊedju:'keɪʃən(ə)l/ *adj.* совме́стного обуче́ния

coerce /kəʊ'ə:s/ *v.t.* прин|ужда́ть, -у́дить

coercion /kəʊ'ə:ʃ(ə)n/ *n.* принужде́ние; he paid under ~ он заплати́л под давле́нием; его́ принуди́ли заплати́ть

coercive /kəʊ'ə:sɪv/ *adj.* принуди́тельный

coexist /kəʊɪɡ'zɪst/ *v.i.* сосуществова́ть (*impf.*)

coexistence /kəʊɪɡ'zɪst(ə)ns/ *n.* сосуществова́ние

C. of E. *abbr.* (*of* **Church of England**) Англика́нская це́рковь

⚲ **coffee** /'kɒfɪ/ *n.* ко́фе (*m. indecl.*); two ~s два ко́фе; black ~ чёрный ко́фе; white ~ ко́фе с молоко́м ■ ~ **bar** *n.* буфе́т; ~ **bean** *n.* (on tree) кофе́йный боб; (as product) кофе́йное зерно́; (in pl.) ко́фе в зёрнах; ~ **break** *n.* переры́в на ко́фе; ~ **pot** *n.* кофе́йник; ~ **table** *n.* кофе́йный/ журна́льный сто́лик

coffer /'kɒfə(r)/ *n.* (chest) сунду́к; (in pl.) (fig., funds) казна́

coffin /'kɒfɪn/ *n.* гроб

cog /kɒɡ/ *n.* зуб (-ья); зубе́ц

cogent /'kəʊdʒ(ə)nt/ *adj.* убеди́тельный

cogitate /'kɒdʒɪteɪt/ *v.i.* размышля́ть (*impf.*) (on/over: о чём *or* над чем)

cognac /'kɒnjæk/ *n.* конья́к

cognizant /'kɒɡnɪz(ə)nt/ *adj.* зна́ющий, осведомлённый

cohabit /kəʊ'hæbɪt/ *v.i.* (**cohabited, cohabiting**) сожи́тельствовать (*impf.*)

coherent /kəʊ'hɪərənt/ *adj.* свя́зный, после́довательный

cohesion /kəʊ'hi:ʒ(ə)n/ *n.* сцепле́ние; сплочённость

cohort /'kəʊhɔ:t/ *n.* кого́рта

coil /kɔɪl/ *n.* вито́к; кольцо́ ● *v.t. & i.* (*also* ~ **up**) свёртывать(ся), сверну́ть(ся) кольцо́м (*or* в кольцо́)

coin /kɔɪn/ *n.* моне́та ● *v.t.*: ~ a phrase созд|ава́ть, -а́ть выраже́ние ■ ~ **box** *n.* (BrE, telephone) телефо́н-автома́т; ~**operated** *adj.* моне́тный

coincide /kəʊɪn'saɪd/ *v.i.* совп|ада́ть, -а́сть

coincidence /kəʊ'ɪnsɪd(ə)ns/ *n.* совпаде́ние

coincidental /kəʊɪnsɪ'dent(ə)l/ *adj.* случа́йный

coke¹ /kəʊk/ *n.* (fuel) кокс

coke² /kəʊk/ *n.* (sl., cocaine) кокаи́н

colander /'kʌləndə(r)/ *n.* дуршла́г

⚲ **cold** /kəʊld/ *n.* **1** хо́лод **2** (illness) просту́да; catch (a) ~ просту́|жа́ться, -ди́ться ● *adj.* **1** (at low temperature) холо́дный; I am, feel ~ мне хо́лодно **2** (fig.): in ~ blood хладнокро́вно; get ~ feet (infml) тру́сить, с- **3** (unfeeling): a ~ person холо́дный челове́к ■ ~**-blooded** *adj.* (of reptile, fish) холоднокро́вный; (fig.) бесчу́вственный, безжа́лостный; ~**-shoulder** *v.t.* ока́з|ывать, -а́ть кому́-н. холо́дный приём

coleslaw /'kəʊlslɔ:/ *n.* капу́стный сала́т (*свежие капуста, морковь, лук под майонезом*)

colic /'kɒlɪk/ *n.* ко́лик|и (*pl., g.* —)

collaborate /kə'læbəreɪt/ *v.i.* сотру́дничать (*impf.*)

collaboration /kəlæbə'reɪʃ(ə)n/ *n.* сотру́дничество

⚲ **collapse** /kə'læps/ *n.* (of a building; of prices, market, etc.) обва́л; (of negotiations etc.) прова́л; (of hopes etc.) круше́ние; (of resistance etc.) разва́л; (med.) колла́пс ● *v.i.* (of a building etc.) обва́л|иваться, -и́ться; (of person) вали́ться, с-

collapsible /kə'læpsɪb(ə)l/ *adj.* складно́й

collar /'kɒlə(r)/ *n.* **1** (of garment) воротни́к; hot under the ~ (fig., excited, vexed) рассе́рженный **2** (of dog) оше́йник ● *v.t.* (seize) схва́т|ывать, -и́ть ■ ~**bone** *n.* (anat.) ключи́ца

collate /kə'leɪt/ *v.t.* слич|а́ть, -и́ть

collateral /kə'lætər(ə)l/ *adj.* побо́чный, дополни́тельный; ~ **security** (fin.) дополни́тельное обеспече́ние (*кредита*)

⚲ **colleague** /'kɒli:ɡ/ *n.* колле́га (*c.g.*)

⚲ **collect** /kə'lekt/ *v.t.* **1** (gather together) соб|ира́ть, -ра́ть; ~**ed works** (по́лное) собра́ние

c

c

сочине́ний **2** (debts, taxes) соб|ира́ть, -ра́ть **3** (stamps etc.) коллекциони́ровать (*impf.*) **4** (fetch) заб|ира́ть, -ра́ть
• *v.i.* соб|ира́ться, -ра́ться

collected /kə'lektɪd/ *adj.* (calm) со́бранный

ᵔ **collection** /kə'lekʃ(ə)n/ *n.* (of valuables etc.) колле́кция; (accumulation) скопле́ние; (for charity) сбор; (of mail) вы́емка

collective /kə'lektɪv/ *n.* (cooperative unit) коллекти́в
• *adj.* коллекти́вный
■ ~ **farm** *n.* колхо́з

collector /kə'lektə(r)/ *n.* (of stamps etc.) коллекционе́р; a ~'s **piece** ре́дкий/ уника́льный экземпля́р; (of taxes, debts) сбо́рщик

ᵔ **college** /'kɒlɪdʒ/ *n.* **1** (school) ко́лледж **2** (university) университе́т; институ́т **3** (within university) университе́тский ко́лледж

collide /kə'laɪd/ *v.i.* ст|а́лкиваться, -олкну́ться

colliery /'kɒlɪərɪ/ *n.* каменноу́гольная ша́хта

collision /kə'lɪʒ(ə)n/ *n.* столкнове́ние

colloquial /kə'ləʊkwɪəl/ *adj.* разгово́рный

colloquialism /kə'ləʊkwɪəlɪz(ə)m/ *n.* разгово́рное выраже́ние/сло́во

collusion /kə'lu:ʒ(ə)n/ *n.* сго́вор; **act in** ~ де́йствовать (*impf.*) по сго́вору

Colombia /kə'lɒmbɪə/ *n.* Колу́мбия

Colombian /kə'lɒmbɪən/ *n.* колумби́|ец (-йка)
• *adj.* колумби́йский

colon¹ /'kəʊlɒn/ *n.* (anat.) то́лстая/ободо́чная кишка́

colon² /'kəʊlɒn/ *n.* (gram.) двоето́чие

colonel /'kɜ:n(ə)l/ *n.* полко́вник

colonial /kə'ləʊnɪəl/ *adj.* колониа́льный

colonialism /kə'ləʊnɪəlɪz(ə)m/ *n.* колониали́зм

colonist /'kɒlənɪst/ *n.* колони́ст (-ка)

colonization /'kɒlənaɪ'zeɪʃ(ə)n/ *n.* колониза́ция

colonize /'kɒlənaɪz/ *v.t.* колонизова́ть, колонизи́ровать (*both impf., pf.*)

colonizer /'kɒlənaɪzə(r)/ *n.* колониза́тор

colony /'kɒlənɪ/ *n.* коло́ния

colossal /kə'lɒs(ə)l/ *adj.* колосса́льный, грома́дный

ᵔ **colour** /'kʌlə(r)/ (AmE **color**) *n.* **1** (lit.) цвет; **change** ~ (lit.) меня́ть, по- цвет; (fig.) (go pale) бледне́ть, по-; (blush) красне́ть, по-; **the film is in** ~ э́то цветно́й фильм **2** (of face) цвет лица́ **3** (*in pl.*) (paints) кра́ски **4** (of race): **a person of** ~ представи́тель (-ница) небе́лой ра́сы
• *v.t.* **1** (paint) кра́сить, по- **2** (imbue): **his action was** ~**ed by envy** его́ посту́пок был отча́сти продикто́ван за́вистью
• *v.i.* (blush) красне́ть, по-
■ ~-**blind** *adj.* страда́ющий дальтони́змом; ~ **film** *n.* цветна́я плёнка; ~ **scheme** *n.* цветова́я га́мма; ~ **television** *n.* цветно́е телеви́дение

ᵔ ключева́я ле́ксика

coloured /'kʌləd/ (AmE **colored**) *adj.* (not black or white) цветно́й

colourful /'kʌləfʊl/ (AmE **colorful**) *adj.* кра́сочный, я́ркий; a ~ **personality** я́ркая/ колори́тная ли́чность

colouring /'kʌlərɪŋ/ (AmE **coloring**) *n.* окра́ска; (complexion) цвет лица́

colourless /'kʌlələs/ (AmE **colorless**) *adj.* (lit., fig.) бесцве́тный

colt /kəʊlt/ *n.* (young horse) жеребёнок

ᵔ **column** /'kɒləm/ *n.* **1** (pillar) коло́нна **2** (in book etc.) столбе́ц **3** (regular feature in newspaper): **weekly** ~ еженеде́льная коло́нка/ру́брика **4** (mil. etc.) коло́нна

columnist /'kɒləmnɪst/ *n.* обозрева́тель (*m.*)

coma /'kəʊmə/ *n.* (*pl.* ~**s**) ко́ма

comb /kəʊm/ *n.* расчёска
• *v.t.* расчёс|ывать, -а́ть; причёс|ывать, -а́ть

combat /'kɒmbæt/ *n.* бой
• *v.t.* (**combated, combating**) боро́ться (*impf.*) с + *i.* (*or* про́тив + *g.*)

combatant /'kɒmbət(ə)nt/ *n.* бое́ц; вою́ющая сторона́

ᵔ **combination** /kɒmbɪ'neɪʃ(ə)n/ *n.* сочета́ние

combine¹ /'kɒmbaɪn/ *n.* **1** (group of people or companies) объедине́ние **2** (in full ~ **harvester**) комба́йн

ᵔ **combine²** /kəm'baɪn/ *v.t.* сочета́ть (*impf.*); ~ **forces** объедин|я́ть, -и́ть (*or* соедин|я́ть, -и́ть) си́лы

combustion /kəm'bʌstʃ(ə)n/ *n.* воспламене́ние; сгора́ние; **spontaneous** ~ самовоспламене́ние; **internal** ~ **engine** дви́гатель (*m.*) вну́треннего сгора́ния

ᵔ **come** /kʌm/ *v.i.* (*past* **came**, *p.p.* **come**) **1** (move near, arrive) при|ходи́ть, -йти́; **he has** ~ **a hundred miles** он прие́хал за сто миль; ~ **along!** пойдёмте!; ~ **into the house!** заходи́те/зайди́те в дом! **2** (of inanimate things, lit., fig.): **the dress** ~**s to her knees** пла́тье дохо́дит ей до коле́н; **the feeling** ~**s and goes** э́то чу́вство то появля́ется, то исчеза́ет; **it came as a shock to me** э́то бы́ло для меня́ уда́ром **3** (fig. uses with 'into'): **he has** ~ **into a fortune** он получи́л большо́е насле́дство; **the party came into power** па́ртия пришла́ к вла́сти **4** (happen) случа́ться, быва́ть (*both impf.*); **Christmas** ~**s once a year** Рождество́ быва́ет раз в году́; **how** ~ **he was late?** как получи́лось, что он опозда́л?; **in years to** ~ в после́дующие го́ды; в бу́дущем; ~ **what may** будь, что бу́дет; **how** ~? (infml) э́то почему́ же?; как так? **5** (amount): **the bill** ~**s to £5** счёт равня́ется пяти́ фу́нтам; **his plans came to nothing** из его́ пла́нов ничего́ не вы́шло **6** (become, prove to be): **her dreams came true** её мечты́ осуществи́лись/ сбыли́сь; **his shoelace came undone** у него́ шнуро́к развяза́лся **7** (fig., find oneself in a position): **I have** ~ **to see that he is right** я убеди́лся, что он прав **8** (of person, originate) прои|схо́дить, -зойти́; **he** ~**s from Scotland** он уроже́нец Шотла́ндии; (of thing, originate) **wine** ~**s from grapes** вино́ получа́ется из виногра́да

• *with preps.*: ~ **across** (encounter) нат|а́лкиваться, -олкну́ться на + *a.*; ~ **into** (inherit): **she came into a large estate** ей доста́лось большо́е име́ние; ~ **off** (become detached (from)): **a button came off my coat** от моего́ пальто́ оторвала́сь пу́говица; ~ **over** (fig.): **what came over you?** что на вас нашло́?; ~ **under** (be categorized): **what heading does this ~ under?** к како́й ру́брике э́то отно́сится?

□ ~ **across (as)** показа́ться (*pf.*) + *i.*

□ ~ **apart** *v.i.* (become unfastened) ра|сходи́ться, -зойти́сь

□ ~ **away** *v.i.* (become detached) отл|а́мываться, -ома́ться *or* -оми́ться (**from:** от + *g.*)

□ ~ **back** *v.i.* (return) возвра|ща́ться, -ти́ться; верну́ться (*pf.*)

□ ~ **down** *v.i.*: **her hair ~s down to her waist** её во́лосы дохо́дят до по́яса; (of prices) па́дать, упа́сть; (fig.): **he came down with influenza** он слёг с гри́ппом

□ ~ **forward** *v.i.* (offer one's services) предл|ага́ть, -ожи́ть свои́ услу́ги

□ ~ **in** *v.i.* (lit.) входи́ть, войти́; **the tide came in** наступи́л прили́в; **it came in handy** э́то пригоди́лось

□ ~ **off** *v.i.* (become detached) отва́л|иваться, -и́ться; (happen, succeed): **the experiment came off** о́пыт уда́лся; (finish work): **he ~s off at 10 on** ухо́дит со слу́жбы в 10

□ ~ **on** *v.i.* (follow) сле́довать (*impf.*); (progress) де́лать (*impf.*) успе́хи; (start, set in): **I have a cold coming on** у меня́ начина́ется просту́да; (*in imper.*) ~ **on!** (expr. encouragement) ну́-ка!; (expr. impatience) ну!; ну́ же!; (of actor, appear) появл|я́ться, -и́ться

□ ~ **out** *v.i.* (lit.) выходи́ть, вы́йти; **the sun came out** появи́лось/вы́глянуло со́лнце; (become known, appear): **the book came out** кни́га вы́шла; (disappear): **the stains came out** пя́тна сошли́; (declare oneself): **he came out against the plan** он вы́ступил про́тив пла́на; (publicly acknowledge one's homosexuality) откры́то призн|ава́ть, -а́ть свою́ гомосексуа́льность; (BrE, go on strike) забастова́ть (*pf.*); **she came out in a rash** (BrE) она́ покры́лась сы́пью

□ ~ **over** *v.i.*: **they came over to England** они́ прие́хали в А́нглию

□ ~ **round** *v.i.* (change mind): **he came round to my view** он пришёл-таки к мое́й то́чке зре́ния; (yield): **she'll ~ round** (BrE) она́ усту́пит/согласи́тся; (recover consciousness) при|ходи́ть, -йти́ в себя́; очну́ться (*pf.*)

□ ~ **through** *v.i.* (survive experience) пережи́ть (*pf.*)

□ ~ **to** *v.i.* (recover one's senses) при|ходи́ть, -йти́ в себя́

□ ~ **up** *v.i.*: **the sun came up** со́лнце взошло́; **the seeds came up** семена́ взошли́; **the water came up to my waist** вода́ доходи́ла мне до по́яса; **the question came up** встал вопро́с; **the case ~s tomorrow** э́то де́ло разбира́ется за́втра; **he came up against a difficulty** он столкну́лся с тру́дностями; **he came up with a suggestion** он внёс предложе́ние

■ ~**back** *n.* (return) возвраще́ние; ~**uppance** /kʌm'ʌpəns/ *n.* (infml): **he got his ~uppance** он

получи́л по заслу́гам

comedian /kə'miːdɪən/ *n.* ко́мик

comedy /'kɒmədɪ/ *n.* коме́дия

comet /'kɒmɪt/ *n.* коме́та

comfort /'kʌmfət/ *n.* **1** (physical ease) комфо́рт **2** (relief of suffering) утеше́ние, отра́да **3** (thing that brings ~) утеше́ние, успокое́ние
• *v.t.* ут|еша́ть, -е́шить

✓ **comfortabl|e** /'kʌmftəb(ə)l/ *adj.* удо́бный, ую́тный, комфорта́бельный, комфо́ртный; **the car holds six people ~y** э́та маши́на свобо́дно вмеща́ет шесть челове́к; **he is ~y off** он живёт в доста́тке

comforter /'kʌmfətə(r)/ *n.* (AmE, quilt for bed) стёганое одея́ло

comforting /'kʌmfətɪŋ/ *adj.* утеши́тельный, успокои́тельный

comfy /'kʌmfɪ/ *adj.* (infml) удо́бный, ую́тный

comic /'kɒmɪk/ *n.* **1** (infml, comedian) ко́мик, юмори́ст **2** (magazine) ко́микс
• *adj.* коми́ческий, юмористи́ческий
■ ~ **strip** *n.* ко́микс

comical /'kɒmɪk(ə)l/ *adj.* коми́чный, смешно́й

coming /'kʌmɪŋ/ *n.* прие́зд, прихо́д; ~ **and going** движе́ние взад-вперёд
• *adj.* бу́дущий, наступа́ющий

comma /'kɒmə/ *n.* запята́я

✓ **command** /kə'mɑːnd/ *n.* **1** (order, also comput.) кома́нда **2** (authority) кома́ндование; **he is in ~ of the army** он кома́ндует а́рмией **3** (control) контро́ль (*m.*) **4** (knowledge): **she has a good ~ of French** она́ непло́хо владе́ет францу́зским (языко́м) **5** (mil.) кома́ндование
• *v.t.* **1** (give orders to) прика́з|ывать, -а́ть + *d.* **2** (have authority over) кома́ндовать (*impf.*) + *i.* **3** (be able to use or enjoy) располага́ть (*impf.*) + *i.*; **he ~s respect** он заслу́живает уваже́ния
■ ~ **post** *n.* кома́ндный пункт, КП

commandant /kɒmən'dænt/ *n.* коменда́нт

commandeer /kɒmən'dɪə(r)/ *v.t.* реквизи́ровать (*impf.*, *pf.*)

commander /kə'mɑːndə(r)/ *n.* команди́р, кома́ндующий

commanding /kə'mɑːndɪŋ/ *adj.*: ~ **officer** команди́р; **a ~ presence** внуши́тельная оса́нка

commando /kə'mɑːndəʊ/ *n.* (*pl.* ~**s**) деса́нтник-диверса́нт, диверса́нт-разве́дчик; (*in pl.*) кома́ндос (*indecl.*, *pl.*)

commemorate /kə'meməreɪt/ *v.t.* (celebrate memory of) отм|еча́ть, -е́тить (*годовщину*, *событие*)

commemorative /kə'memərətɪv/ *adj.* па́мятный, мемориа́льный

commence /kə'mens/ *v.t. & i.* нач|ина́ть(ся), -а́ть(ся)

commend /kə'mend/ *v.t.* **1** (entrust) вв|еря́ть, -е́рить; поруч|а́ть, -и́ть; **he ~ed his soul to God** он посвяти́л себя́ Бо́гу **2** (praise) хвали́ть, по-

commendable /kə'mendəb(ə)l/ *adj.* похва́льный

commensurate /kə'menʃərət/ *adj.* разме́рный

✓ **comment** /'kɒment/ *n.* замеча́ние,

коммента́рий; **no ∼!** без коммента́риев!
 • *v.t. & i.* комменти́ровать (*impf., pf.*);
 толкова́ть (*impf.*)
commentary /'kɒməntərɪ/ *n.* коммента́рий
commentator /'kɒmənteɪtə(r)/ *n.*
 коммента́тор
commerce /'kɒmə:s/ *n.* комме́рция
⚘ **commercial** /kə'mə:ʃ(ə)l/ *n.* рекла́ма,
 рекла́мная переда́ча
 • *adj.* комме́рческий, торго́вый
commercialize /kə'mə:ʃəlaɪz/ *v.t.* ста́вить, по-
 на комме́рческую осно́ву; вн|оси́ть, -ести́
 комме́рческий дух в + *a.*
commiserate /kə'mɪzəreɪt/ *v.i.* выража́ть,
 вы́разить соболе́знование (**with:** + *d.*)
commissar /'kɒmɪsɑ:(r)/ *n.* комисса́р
⚘ **commission** /kə'mɪʃ(ə)n/ *n.* **1** (authorization)
 полномо́чие **2** (comm.) комиссио́нн|ые (-ых)
 3 (committee) коми́ссия
 • *v.t.* поруч|а́ть, -и́ть (*что кому*); **he ∼ed
 me to buy this** он поручи́л мне купи́ть э́то;
 he ∼ed a portrait from the artist он заказа́л
 худо́жнику портре́т; **a ∼ed officer** офице́р
commissioner /kə'mɪʃənə(r)/ *n.* член
 коми́ссии
⚘ **commit** /kə'mɪt/ *v.t.* (**committed,
 committing**) **1** (perform) соверш|а́ть, -и́ть
 2 (pledge): **he ∼ted himself to helping her** он
 взя́лся помо́чь ей **3**: **a ∼ted writer** иде́йный
 писа́тель
⚘ **commitment** /kə'mɪtmənt/ *n.* обяза́тельство
⚘ **committee** /kə'mɪtɪ/ *n.* комите́т, коми́ссия
commodity /kə'mɒdɪtɪ/ *n.* това́р, предме́т
 потребле́ния
commodore /'kɒmədɔ:(r)/ *n.* (in navy or
 merchant marine) коммодо́р, капита́н пе́рвого
 ра́нга; (of yacht club) командо́р
⚘ **common** /'kɒmən/ *n.* **1** (land) пусты́рь (*m.*),
 вы́гон **2** (sth usual or shared): **you have a lot in
 ∼ with her** у вас с ней мно́го о́бщего
 • *adj.* (**commoner, commonest**)
 1 (belonging to more than one, general) о́бщий;
 it is ∼ knowledge that … общеизве́стно,
 что… **2** (belonging to the public): **∼ land**
 обще́ственная земля́ **3** (ordinary, usual)
 обы́чный, обы́денный, обыкнове́нный;
 the ∼ people (просто́й) наро́д **4** (vulgar)
 вульга́рный, по́шлый
 ▪ **∼-law** *adj.*: **∼-law marriage**
 незарегистри́рованный брак; **∼-law wife**
 сожи́тельница; **∼place** *n.* бана́льность
 • *adj.* бана́льный; **∼ room** *n.* (BrE) (senior)
 учи́тельская, преподава́тельская; (junior)
 студе́нческая ко́мната о́тдыха; **∼ sense** *n.*
 здра́вый смысл
commonly /'kɒmənlɪ/ *adv.* (usually) обы́чно,
 обыкнове́нно
Commonwealth /'kɒmənwelθ/ *n.*: **the ∼ (of
 Nations)** Брита́нское Содру́жество (на́ций);
 the ∼ of Independent States Содру́жество
 Незави́симых Госуда́рств
commotion /kə'məʊʃ(ə)n/ *n.* волне́ние, возня́

communal /'kɒmjʊn(ə)l/ *adj.*
 обще́ственный, коммуна́льный
commune /'kɒmju:n/ *n.* (administrative unit)
 общи́на, комму́на; (Russian hist., peasant ∼) мир
communicate /kə'mju:nɪkeɪt/ *v.t.* сообщ|а́ть,
 -и́ть
 • *v.i.* свя́з|ываться, -а́ться; сообщ|а́ть, -и́ть
 (*кому о чём*); **∼ with sb** обща́ться (*impf.*)
 с кем-н.
⚘ **communication** /kəmju:nɪ'keɪʃ(ə)n/ *n.*
 обще́ние; связь, сообще́ние, коммуника́ция
communicative /kə'mju:nɪkətɪv/ *adj.*
 общи́тельный, разгово́рчивый
communion /kə'mju:nɪən/ *n.* прича́стие
communism /'kɒmjʊnɪz(ə)m/ *n.* коммуни́зм
communist /'kɒmjʊnɪst/ *n.* коммуни́ст (-ка)
 • *adj.* коммунисти́ческий
⚘ **community** /kə'mju:nɪtɪ/ *n.* (political, social, etc.
 group) общи́на, гру́ппа населе́ния; (society)
 о́бщество
commute /kə'mju:t/ *v.i.* (to work) е́здить
 (*indet.*) ка́ждый день на значи́тельное
 расстоя́ние на рабо́ту
 • *v.t.* замен|я́ть, -и́ть; (law) смягч|а́ть, -и́ть
 (*пригово́р*)
commuter /kə'mju:tə(r)/ *n.* (traveller) жи́тель
 (-ница) при́города, (регуля́рно) е́здящ|ий
 (-ая) на рабо́ту в го́род (на авто́бусе, по́езде
 и т. п.)
compact /kəm'pækt/ *adj.* (concise) сжа́тый,
 компа́ктный
 ▪ **∼ disc** /'kɒmpækt/ *n.* компа́кт-ди́ск; **∼ disc
 player** прои́грыватель (*m.*) компа́кт-ди́сков
companion /kəm'pænjən/ *n.* спу́тни|к (-ца)
companionship /kəm'pænjənʃɪp/ *n.*
 дру́жеское обще́ние; дру́жеские отноше́ния
⚘ **company** /'kʌmpənɪ/ *n.* **1** (companionship):
 I was glad of his ∼ я был рад его́ о́бществу;
 keep sb ∼ сост|авля́ть, -а́вить кому́-н.
 компа́нию **2** (associates, guests): **we have ∼
 this evening** у нас сего́дня бу́дут го́сти
 3 (commercial firm) това́рищество, компа́ния;
 ∼ car служе́бная маши́на **4** (theatr.) тру́ппа
 5 (mil.) ро́та
comparable /'kɒmpərəb(ə)l/ *adj.* сравни́мый
comparative /kəm'pærətɪv/ *adj.*
 1 сравни́тельный **2** (relative) относи́тельный
⚘ **compare** /kəm'peə(r)/ *v.t.* сра́вн|ивать, -и́ть
 • *v.i.* сра́вн|иваться, -и́ться
⚘ **comparison** /kəm'pærɪs(ə)n/ *n.* сравне́ние;
 in, by ∼ with по сравне́нию с + *i.*
compartment /kəm'pɑ:tmənt/ *n.* (section)
 отделе́ние, отсе́к; (on train) купе́ (*nt. indecl.*)
compass /'kʌmpəs/ *n.* **1** (mariner's) ко́мпас;
 points of the ∼ стра́ны све́та **2** (*in full pair
 of ∼es*) (geom.) ци́ркуль (*m.*)
compassion /kəm'pæʃ(ə)n/ *n.* сострада́ние
compassionate /kəm'pæʃənət/ *adj.*
 сострада́тельный
compatible /kəm'pætɪb(ə)l/ *adj.* совмести́мый
compatriot /kəm'pætrɪət/ *n.* сооте́чественник
compel /kəm'pel/ *v.t.* (**compelled,
 compelling**) заст|авля́ть, -а́вить

⚘ ключева́я ле́ксика

compelling /kəmˈpelɪŋ/ *adj.* непреодоли́мый, неотрази́мый

compensate /ˈkɒmpenseɪt/ *v.t.*: ~ sb for sth компенси́ровать (*impf., pf.*) (*кому что*); **they expressed a willingness to** ~ **fans for their expenditure** они́ вы́разили гото́вность компенси́ровать боле́льщикам затра́ты; **he was** ~d **for his injuries** он получи́л компенса́цию за свои́ уве́чья ● *v.i.*: ~ **for** возме|ща́ть, -сти́ть; компенси́ровать (*impf., pf.*); **his personality** ~s **for his appearance** его́ ли́чные ка́чества компенси́руют его́ вне́шность

compensation /kɒmpenˈseɪʃ(ə)n/ *n.* компенса́ция; **pay** ~ выпла́чивать, вы́платить компенса́цию

compete /kəmˈpiːt/ *v.i.* (vie) конкури́ровать (*impf.*); ~ **with, against sb for sth** конкури́ровать (*impf.*) с кем-н. из-за чего́-н.; (in sport) состяза́ться (*impf.*)

competence /ˈkɒmpɪt(ə)ns/, **competency** /ˈkɒmpɪtənsɪ/ *nn.* уме́ние, компете́нтность

competent /ˈkɒmpɪt(ə)nt/ *adj.* компете́нтный

competition /kɒmpəˈtɪʃ(ə)n/ *n.* **1** (rivalry) сопе́рничество **2** (contest) состяза́ние

competitive /kəmˈpetɪtɪv/ *adj.* (person) честолюби́вый; ~ **prices** конкурентоспосо́бные це́ны

competitor /kəmˈpetɪtə(r)/ *n.* конкуре́нт (-ка)

compilation /kɒmpɪˈleɪʃ(ə)n/ *n.* (act) собира́ние; (result) сбо́рник

compile /kəmˈpaɪl/ *v.t.* соб|ира́ть, -ра́ть

complacent /kəmˈpleɪs(ə)nt/ *adj.* самодово́льный

complain /kəmˈpleɪn/ *v.i.* жа́ловаться, по- (**about, of**: на + *a.*); **he** ~s **of frequent headaches** он жа́луется на ча́стые головны́е бо́ли

complaint /kəmˈpleɪnt/ *n.* жа́лоба

complement /ˈkɒmplɪmənt/ *v.t.* доп|олня́ть, -о́лнить

complementary /kɒmplɪˈmentərɪ/ *adj.* дополни́тельный; ~ **medicine** (BrE) альтернати́вная, нетрадицио́нная медици́на

complete /kəmˈpliːt/ *adj.* **1** (whole) по́лный **2** (finished) зако́нченный, завершённый; **when will the work be** ~? когда́ бу́дет завершён э́тот труд? **3** (thorough) соверше́нный ● *v.t.* зака́нчивать, -о́нчить; (fill in) зап|олня́ть, -о́лнить

completely /kəmˈpliːtlɪ/ *adv.* соверше́нно, по́лностью

completion /kəmˈpliːʃ(ə)n/ *n.* заверше́ние

complex /ˈkɒmpleks/ *n.* ко́мплекс ● *adj.* сло́жный, ко́мплексный

complexion /kəmˈplekʃ(ə)n/ *n.* цвет лица́

complexity /kəmˈpleksɪtɪ/ *n.* сло́жность

compliance /kəmˈplaɪəns/ *n.* усту́пчивость

compliant /kəmˈplaɪənt/ *adj.* усту́пчивый

complicate /ˈkɒmplɪkeɪt/ *v.t.* осложн|я́ть, -и́ть

complicated /ˈkɒmplɪkeɪtɪd/ *adj.* сло́жный

complication /kɒmplɪˈkeɪʃ(ə)n/ *n.* (complicating circumstance) осложне́ние; (med.):

~s **set in** после́довали осложне́ния

complicity /kəmˈplɪsɪtɪ/ *n.* соуча́стие

compliment *n.* /ˈkɒmplɪmənt/ комплиме́нт; похвала́ ● *v.t.* /ˈkɒmplɪment/ говори́ть (*impf.*) комплиме́нты (+ *d.*) (*по поводу чего*)

complimentary /kɒmplɪˈmentərɪ/ *adj.* **1** (laudatory) похва́льный, ле́стный **2**: ~ **ticket** контрама́рка, пригласи́тельный биле́т

comply /kəmˈplaɪ/ *v.i.*: ~ **with** уступ|а́ть, -и́ть + *d.*

component /kəmˈpəʊnənt/ *n.* компоне́нт ● *adj.* составно́й

compose /kəmˈpəʊz/ *v.t. & i.* **1** (make up) сост|авля́ть, -а́вить; **the party was** ~d **of teachers** гру́ппа состоя́ла из учителе́й **2** (liter., mus.) сочин|я́ть, -и́ть **3** (calm): ~ **oneself** успок|а́иваться, -о́иться; **a** ~d **manner** сде́ржанная мане́ра

composer /kəmˈpəʊzə(r)/ *n.* (mus.) компози́тор

composite /ˈkɒmpəzɪt/ *adj.* составно́й

composition /kɒmpəˈzɪʃ(ə)n/ *n.* **1** (act of composing) сочине́ние, составле́ние **2** (litererary or musical work) произведе́ние, сочине́ние **3** (school exercise) сочине́ние **4** (make-up) соста́в; ~ **of the soil** соста́в по́чвы

compost /ˈkɒmpɒst/ *n.* компо́ст

composure /kəmˈpəʊʒə(r)/ *n.* споко́йствие

compound¹ /ˈkɒmpaʊnd/ *n.* (enclosure) огоро́женное ме́сто

compound² *n.* /ˈkɒmpaʊnd/ (mixture) смесь; (gram.) сло́жное сло́во; (chem.) соедине́ние ● *adj.* /ˈkɒmpaʊnd/ составно́й, сло́жный ● *v.t.* /kəmˈpaʊnd/ (worsen) обостр|я́ть, -и́ть; **her interference** ~ed **the problem** её вмеша́тельство то́лько обостри́ло пробле́му ■ ~ **fracture** *n.* осложнённый перело́м

comprehend /kɒmprɪˈhend/ *v.t.* пон|има́ть, -я́ть

comprehensible /kɒmprɪˈhensɪb(ə)l/ *adj.* поня́тный, постижи́мый

comprehension /kɒmprɪˈhenʃ(ə)n/ *n.* понима́ние, постиже́ние

comprehensive /kɒmprɪˈhensɪv/ *adj.* (of wide scope) всеобъе́млющий, исче́рпывающий ■ ~ **school** *n.* (BrE) общеобразова́тельная шко́ла со ста́ршими кла́ссами

compress¹ /ˈkɒmpres/ *n.* (to relieve inflammation) компре́сс

compress² /kəmˈpres/ *v.t.* (physically) сж|има́ть, -а́ть

comprise /kəmˈpraɪz/ *v.t.* включ|а́ть, -и́ть в себя́

compromise /ˈkɒmprəmaɪz/ *n.* компроми́сс ● *v.t.* компромети́ровать, с- ● *v.i.* при|ходи́ть, -йти́ к компроми́ссу

compulsion /kəmˈpʌlʃ(ə)n/ *n.* принужде́ние; **on, under** ~ по принужде́нию

compulsive /kəmˈpʌlsɪv/ *adj.* (irresistible) непреодоли́мый; (inveterate) зая́длый

compulsory /kəmˈpʌlsərɪ/ *adj.* обяза́тельный

computer /kəmˈpjuːtə(r)/ *n.* компью́тер ■ ~-**aided design** *n.* автоматизи́рованное

проекти́рование; ~**-aided learning** n.
маши́нное обуче́ние; ~ **dating** n. подбо́р
супру́гов с по́мощью компью́тера; ~ **game**
n. компью́терная игра́; ~ **graphics** n. pl.
компью́терная гра́фика; ~**-literate** adj.
со зна́нием компью́тера; ~ **programmer**
n. программи́ст (-ка); ~ **programming**
n. программи́рование; ~ **science** n.
вычисли́тельная те́хника

computerize /kəm'pju:təraɪz/ v.t.
компьютеризи́ровать (impf., pf.)

comrade /'kɒmreɪd/ n. това́рищ

comradeship /'kɒmreɪdʃɪp/ n. това́рищество

con /kɒn/ (infml) v.t. (**conned, conning**)
над|ува́ть, -у́ть
● n. жу́льничество, моше́нничество

conceal /kən'si:l/ v.t. утаи́вать, -и́ть

concede /kən'si:d/ v.t. уступ|а́ть, -и́ть

conceit /kən'si:t/ n. самомне́ние,
самонаде́янность

conceited /kən'si:tɪd/ adj. самонаде́янный

conceivabl|e /kən'si:vəb(ə)l/ adj. мы́слимый,
постижи́мый; **he may** ~**y be right** не
исключено́, что он пра́в

conceive /kən'si:v/ v.t. (imagine) заду́м|ывать,
-ать
● v.i. зач|ина́ть, -а́ть, забере́менеть (pf.)

⚜ **concentrate** /'kɒnsəntreɪt/ v.t.
сосредото́чи|вать, -ть
● v.i. сосредото́чи|ваться, -ться; **she** ~**d on
her work** она́ сосредото́чилась на свое́й
рабо́те

⚜ **concentration** /kɒnsən'treɪʃ(ə)n/ n. **1** (of
attention) сосредото́ченность **2** (of people or
things) сосредото́чение, концентра́ция
■ ~ **camp** n. концентрацио́нный ла́герь,
концла́герь (m.)

⚜ **concept** /'kɒnsept/ n. поня́тие

conception /kən'sepʃ(ə)n/ n. **1** (notion)
конце́пция **2** (physiol.) зача́тие

conceptual /kən'septʃʊəl/ adj. концептуа́льный
■ ~ **art** n. концептуа́льное иску́сство

⚜ **concern** /kən'sə:n/ n. **1** (anxiety, worry)
беспоко́йство **2** (matter) де́ло; (matter of interest)
заинтересо́ванное отноше́ние **3** (business)
конце́рн; **a going** ~ де́йствующее
предприя́тие
● v.t. **1** (have to do with) каса́ться (impf.) + g.;
~**ed** (involved) заинтересо́ванный; **the parties**
~**ed** заинтересо́ванные сто́роны; **as far
as that is** ~**ed** что каса́ется э́того **2** (cause
anxiety to) беспоко́ить (impf.); ~**ed** (anxious)
озабо́ченный; **I am** ~**ed about the future**
меня́ беспоко́ит бу́дущее

concerning /kən'sə:nɪŋ/ prep. относи́тельно
+ g.

concert /'kɒnsət/ n. конце́рт
■ ~ **hall** n. конце́ртный зал

concerted /kən'sə:tɪd/ adj.: **a** ~ **effort to
eradicate poverty** совме́стные уси́лия,
напра́вленные на искорене́ние бе́дности

concertina /kɒnsə'ti:nə/ n. концерти́но (nt.
indecl.), гармо́ника

⚜ ключева́я ле́ксика

concerto /kən'tʃeətəʊ/ n. (pl. ~**s**) конце́рт

concession /kən'seʃ(ə)n/ n. **1** (yielding; thing
yielded) усту́пка; **as a special** ~ в ви́де навстре́чу
2 (preferential rate) льго́та; (reduction) ски́дка

conciliation /kənsɪlɪ'eɪʃ(ə)n/ n. примире́ние

conciliatory /kən'sɪlɪətərɪ/ adj.
примири́тельный

concise /kən'saɪs/ adj. кра́ткий, сжа́тый

conclave /'kɒŋkleɪv/ n. конкла́в; (fig.) та́йное
совеща́ние

⚜ **conclud|e** /kən'klu:d/ v.t. **1** (terminate)
зак|а́нчивать, -о́нчить; ~**ing** заключи́тельный,
заверша́ющий; (session etc.) закр|ыва́ть, -ы́ть
2 (infer) де́лать, с- вы́вод, что…
● v.i. (end) зак|а́нчиваться, -о́нчиться

⚜ **conclusion** /kən'klu:ʒ(ə)n/ n. заключе́ние; **in**
~ в заключе́ние

conclusive /kən'klu:sɪv/ adj. реша́ющий

concoct /kən'kɒkt/ v.t. (a drink etc.) стря́пать,
со-; (a story etc.) стря́пать, со-

concoction /kən'kɒkʃ(ə)n/ n. (drink etc.)
смесь; (story invented) вы́думка

concrete /'kɒŋkri:t/ n. бето́н
● adj. **1** (made of ~) бето́нный **2** (specific,
definite) конкре́тный

concur /kən'kə:(r)/ v.i. (**concurred,
concurring**) **1** (of circumstance etc.) совп|ада́ть,
-а́сть; сходи́ться, сойти́сь **2** (agree, consent)
согла|ша́ться, -си́ться (**with:** c + i.)

concurrent /kən'kʌrənt/ adj. (simultaneous)
одновреме́нный; ~**ly** одновреме́нно

concuss /kən'kʌs/ v.t. (med.) вызыва́ть,
вы́звать сотрясе́ние мо́зга у + g.

concussion /kən'kʌʃ(ə)n/ n. (med.)
сотрясе́ние мо́зга

condemn /kən'dem/ v.t. осу|жда́ть, -ди́ть;
(blame) порица́ть (impf.); (declare unfit for use)
призн|ава́ть, -а́ть него́дным
■ ~**ed cell** n. (BrE) ка́мера сме́ртника

condemnation /kɒndem'neɪʃ(ə)n/ n.
осужде́ние; порица́ние; (of building) призна́ние
него́дным

condensation /kɒnden'seɪʃ(ə)n/ n. (water
droplets): **the inside of the tent was covered in**
~ пала́тка изнутри́ запоте́ла

condense /kən'dens/ v.t. **1** (phys.)
конденси́ровать (impf., pf.) **2** (fig.): **a** ~**d
account of events** сжа́тый отчёт о собы́тиях
● v.i. (phys.) конденси́роваться (impf., pf.)
■ ~**d milk** n. сгущённое молоко́

condescend /kɒndɪ'send/ v.i. сни|сходи́ть,
-зойти́

condescending /kɒndɪ'sendɪŋ/ adj.
снисходи́тельный

condescension /kɒndɪ'senʃ(ə)n/ n.
снисхожде́ние, снисходи́тельность

⚜ **condition** /kən'dɪʃ(ə)n/ n. **1** (state) состоя́ние,
положе́ние **2** (fitness): **the athlete is out of** ~
спортсме́н не в фо́рме **3** (in pl.) (circumstances)
усло́вия (nt. pl.) **4** (requisite, stipulation) усло́вие;
on ~ **that** … при усло́вии, что…

conditional /kən'dɪʃən(ə)l/ adj.: **the** ~
(**mood**) (gram.) усло́вное наклоне́ние

conditioner /kən'dɪʃənə(r)/ *n.* бальза́м для воло́с

condolence /kən'dəʊləns/ *n.* (*also in pl.*) соболе́знование

condom /'kɒndɒm/ *n.* презервати́в

condominium /kɒndə'mɪnɪəm/ *n.* (AmE) кондоми́ниум

condone /kən'dəʊn/ *v.t.* проща́ть, -сти́ть

conducive /kən'dju:sɪv/ *adj.* спосо́бствующий

conduct¹ /'kɒndʌkt/ *n.* поведе́ние

⚡ **conduct²** /kən'dʌkt/ *v.t.* **1** (lead, guide) води́ть (*indet.*), вести́ (*det.*); ~ **an experiment** ста́вить, по- о́пыт **3** (mus.) (*also v.i.*) дирижи́ровать (*impf.*) + *i.* **4** (phys.) проводи́ть (*impf.*)

conductive /kən'dʌktɪv/ *adj.* (tech.) проводя́щий

conductor /kən'dʌktə(r)/ *n.* **1** (mus.) дирижёр **2** (of bus, tram) конду́ктор; (AmE, of train) проводни́к **3** (phys.) проводни́к

cone /kəʊn/ *n.* **1** (geom.) ко́нус **2** (for ice cream) ва́фельная трубо́чка

confectioner /kən'fekʃənə(r)/ *n.* конди́тер

confectionery /kən'fekʃən(ə)rɪ/ *n.* (wares) конди́терские изде́лия

confederation /kənfedə'reɪʃ(ə)n/ *n.* сою́з; федера́ция; конфедера́ция

confer¹ /kən'fɜː(r)/ *v.t.* (**conferred, conferring**) (grant) присв|а́ивать, -о́ить (**on** + *d.*)

confer² /kən'fɜː(r)/ *v.i.* (**conferred, conferring**) (consult) совеща́ться (*impf.*) (**with:** c + *i.*)

⚡ **conference** /'kɒnfərəns/ *n.* конфере́нция, совеща́ние

■ ~ **call** *n.* телеконфере́нция, селе́кторное совеща́ние

confess /kən'fes/ *v.t. & i.* **1** призн|ава́ть, -а́ть; **he** ~**ed to the crime** он созна́лся в преступле́нии **2** (relig., ~ **one's sins**) испове́д|оваться, -аться

confession /kən'feʃ(ə)n/ *n.* **1** (avowal) призна́ние, созна́ние **2** (relig.) и́споведь

confetti /kən'fetɪ/ *n.* конфетти́ (*nt. indecl.*)

confidant, *fem.* **confidante** /'kɒndænt/ *n.* дове́ренное лицо́

confide /kən'faɪd/ *v.i.:* ~ **in sb** (impart secrets to) дели́ться, по- (*своими планами и т. п.*) c + *i.*

⚡ **confidence** /'kɒnfɪd(ə)ns/ *n.* **1** (confiding of secrets) дове́рие; **I tell you this in** ~ я говорю́ вам э́то конфиденциа́льно (*or* по секре́ту) **2** (secret) та́йна; конфиденциа́льное сообще́ние **3** (trust): ~ **in him** я уве́рен в нём; я ве́рю в него́ **4** (certainty, assurance) уве́ренность **5**: ~ **trick** моше́нничество

confident /'kɒnfɪd(ə)nt/ *adj.* уве́ренный; (self-confident) самоуве́ренный

confidential /kɒnfɪ'denʃ(ə)l/ *adj.* конфиденциа́льный

confidentiality /kɒnfɪdenʃɪ'ælɪtɪ/ *n.* конфиденциа́льность

configuration /kənfɪgə'reɪʃ(ə)n/ *n.* конфигура́ция

confine¹ /'kɒnfaɪn/ *n.* (*usu. in pl.*) грани́цы (*f. pl.*)

confine² /kən'faɪn/ *v.t.* ограни́чи|вать, -ть

confinement /kən'faɪnmənt/ *n.* (imprisonment) заключе́ние; **solitary** ~ одино́чное заключе́ние

⚡ **confirm** /kən'fɜːm/ *v.t.* **1** (establish as certain) утвер|жда́ть, -ди́ть; подтвер|жда́ть, -ди́ть; **his appointment was** ~**ed** его́ назначе́ние бы́ло утверждено́ **2** (of person): **a** ~**ed drunkard** го́рький пья́ница; **a** ~**ed bachelor** убеждённый холостя́к **3** (relig.): **be** ~**ed** про|ходи́ть, -йти́ обря́д конфирма́ции

confirmation /kɒnfə'meɪʃ(ə)n/ *n.* **1** (of report etc.) подтвержде́ние **2** (relig.) конфирма́ция

confiscate /'kɒnfɪskeɪt/ *v.t.* конфискова́ть (*impf., pf.*)

⚡ **conflict¹** /'kɒnflɪkt/ *n.* конфли́кт

conflict² /kən'flɪkt/ *v.i.* быть в конфли́кте (**with:** c + *i.*); ~**ing reports** противоречи́вые сообще́ния

conform /kən'fɔːm/ *v.i.* подчин|я́ться, -и́ться + *d.*

conformist /kən'fɔːmɪst/ *n.* конформи́ст

conformity /kən'fɔːmɪtɪ/ *n.* (correspondence, accordance) соотве́тствие; (compliance) подчине́ние; (conformism) конформи́зм

confound /kən'faʊnd/ *v.t.* **1** (amaze) пора|жа́ть, -зи́ть; потряс|а́ть, -ти́ **2** (confuse) сме́ш|ивать, -а́ть; спу́т|ывать, -ать **3** (as expletive): ~ **it!** чёрт возьми́!; **he is a** ~**ed nuisance** он ужа́сно доку́члив

confront /kən'frʌnt/ *v.t.* смотре́ть (*impf.*) в лицо́ + *d.*; встр|еча́ть, -е́тить

confrontation /kɒnfrʌn'teɪʃ(ə)n/ *n.* конфронта́ция

confuse /kən'fju:z/ *v.t.* **1** (throw into confusion) сму|ща́ть, -ти́ть; **his question** ~**d me** его́ вопро́с смути́л меня́ **2** (mistake) спу́т|ывать, -ать; **he** ~**d Austria with Australia** он спу́тал А́встрию с Австра́лией

confusion /kən'fju:ʒ(ə)n/ *n.* смуще́ние; (mix-up) пу́таница

congeal /kən'dʒiːl/ *v.i.* свёр|тываться, -ну́ться

congenial /kən'dʒiːnɪəl/ *adj.* бли́зкий по ду́ху

congenital /kən'dʒenɪt(ə)l/ *adj.:* ~ **defect** врождённый дефе́кт

congested /kən'dʒestɪd/ *adj.* (roads) перегру́женный

congestion /kən'dʒestʃ(ə)n/ *n.* перегру́женность

■ **congestion charge** *n.* пла́та за въезд в центр го́рода

conglomerate /kən'glɒmərət/ *n.* конгломера́т

conglomeration /kənglɒmə'reɪʃ(ə)n/ *n.* конгломера́т

Congo /'kɒngəʊ/ *n.* (country) Ко́нго (*nt. indecl.*); **Democratic Republic of the Congo** (formerly Zaire) Демократи́ческая Респу́блика Ко́нго

Congolese /kɒngə'liːz/ *n.* (native of Congo or Democratic Republic of the Congo) конголе́з|ец (-ка)

c

● *adj.* конголе́зский

congratulate /kənˈgrætjʊleɪt/ *v.t.*
поздр|авля́ть, -а́вить (*кого с чем*)

congratulation /kəngrætjʊˈleɪʃ(ə)n/ *n.*
поздравле́ние; ~s! поздравля́ю!

congratulatory /kənˈgrætjʊlətərɪ/ *adj.*
поздрави́тельный

congregate /ˈkɒŋgrɪgeɪt/ *v.i.* соб|ира́ться,
-ра́ться; сходи́ться, сойти́сь

congregation /kɒŋgrɪˈgeɪʃ(ə)n/ *n.*
прихожа́не (*m. pl.*)

congress /ˈkɒŋgres/ *n.* **1** (organized meeting)
конгре́сс, съезд **2** (pol., hist.) конгре́сс; C~
(AmE) конгре́сс США

■ C~**man** *n.* член конгре́сса, конгрессме́н;
C~**woman** *n.* же́нщина-член конгре́сса

conifer /ˈkɒnɪfə(r)/ *n.* хво́йное де́рево

coniferous /kəˈnɪfərəs/ *adj.* хво́йный

conjecture /kənˈdʒektʃə(r)/ *n.*
предположе́ние, дога́дка
● *v.t. & i.* предпол|ага́ть, -ожи́ть; гада́ть (*impf.*)

conjugal /ˈkɒndʒʊg(ə)l/ *adj.* супру́жеский,
бра́чный

conjugate /ˈkɒndʒʊgeɪt/ *v.t.* (gram.) спряга́ть,
про-

conjugation /kɒndʒʊˈgeɪʃ(ə)n/ *n.* (gram.)
спряже́ние

conjunction /kənˈdʒʌŋkʃ(ə)n/ *n.* (gram.) сою́з

conjunctivitis /kəndʒʌŋktɪˈvaɪtɪs/ *n.* (med.)
конъюнктиви́т

conjure /ˈkʌndʒə(r)/ *v.t. & i.* **1** (fig.): ~ up
вызыва́ть, вы́звать в воображе́нии **2** (perform
tricks) пока́з|ывать, -а́ть фо́кусы

conjurer, **conjuror** /ˈkʌndʒərə(r)/ *n.*
фо́кусник

✔ **connect** /kəˈnekt/ *v.t.* (join) соедин|я́ть, -и́ть;
the towns are ~ed by railway э́ти города́
соединены́ желе́зной доро́гой; (associate)
свя́з|ывать, -а́ть
● *v.i.* соедин|я́ться, -и́ться; the train ~s with
the one from London э́тот по́езд согласо́ван
по расписа́нию с ло́ндонским (по́ездом)

✔ **connection** /kəˈnekʃ(ə)n/ *n.* **1** (joining up)
соедине́ние, связь **2** (fig., link) связь **3** (of
transport) согласо́ванность расписа́ния; I
missed my ~ я не успе́л сде́лать переса́дку
4 (association) связь **5** (teleph.): the ~ was bad
телефо́н пло́хо рабо́тал

connive /kəˈnaɪv/ *v.i.*: ~ at потво́рствовать
(*impf.*) + *d.*; ~ with сгов|а́риваться, -ори́ться
c + *i.*

connoisseur /kɒnəˈsə:(r)/ *n.* знато́к,
цени́тель (*m.*)

connotation /kɒnəˈteɪʃ(ə)n/ *n.* побо́чное
значе́ние

conquer /ˈkɒŋkə(r)/ *v.t.* (overcome; obtain by
conquest) завоёв|ывать, -а́ть

conqueror /ˈkɒŋkərə(r)/ *n.* завоева́тель (*m.*)

conquest /ˈkɒŋkwest/ *n.* завоева́ние

conscience /ˈkɒnʃ(ə)ns/ *n.* со́весть; clear ~
чи́стая со́весть; guilty ~ нечи́стая со́весть

conscientious /kɒnʃɪˈenʃəs/ *adj.* созна́тельный

■ ~ **objector** *n.* отка́зывающийся от вое́нной
слу́жбы по убежде́нию

conscious /ˈkɒnʃəs/ *adj.* **1** (physically aware)
сознаю́щий, ощуща́ющий **2** (mentally aware)
сознаю́щий, понима́ющий; I was ~ of having
offended him я сознава́л, что оскорби́л его́
3 (realized) сознаю́щий, созна́тельный; a ~
effort созна́тельное уси́лие

consciousness /ˈkɒnʃəsnɪs/ *n.* **1** (physical)
созна́ние; he lost ~ он потеря́л созна́ние;
she regained ~ она́ пришла́ в себя́/
созна́ние **2** (mental) созна́тельность

conscript /ˈkɒnskrɪpt/ *n.* новобра́нец,
призывни́к

conscription /kənˈskrɪpʃ(ə)n/ *n.* во́инская
пови́нность

consecrate /ˈkɒnsɪkreɪt/ *v.t.* осв|яща́ть, -яти́ть

consecutive /kənˈsekjʊtɪv/ *adj.*
после́довательный

consensus /kənˈsensəs/ *n.* согла́сие,
единоду́шие; (pol.) консе́нсус

consent /kənˈsent/ *n.* согла́сие
● *v.i.* согла|ша́ться, -си́ться

✔ **consequence** /ˈkɒnsɪkwəns/ *n.* **1** (result)
сле́дствие, после́дствие **2** (importance)
ва́жность, значе́ние

consequential /kɒnsɪˈkwenʃ(ə)l/ *adj.*
1 (consequent) сле́дующий/вытека́ющий (*из
чего*) **2** (important) ва́жный, значи́тельный

consequently /ˈkɒnsɪkwentlɪ/ *adv.*
сле́довательно, зна́чит, (infml) ста́ло быть

conservation /kɒnsəˈveɪʃ(ə)n/ *n.*
сохране́ние, охра́на

■ ~ **area** *n.* запове́дник

conservationist /kɒnsəˈveɪʃənɪst/ *n.* боре́ц
за охра́ну приро́ды

✔ **conservative** /kənˈsə:vətɪv/ *n.* консерва́тор
● *adj.* консервати́вный

conservatory /kənˈsə:vətərɪ/ *n.* **1** (BrE,
room) застеклённая вера́нда **2** (mus.)
консервато́рия

conserve /kənˈsə:v, *n. only also* ˈkɒnsə:v/ *n.*
(preserved fruit) варе́нье
● *v.t.* (fruit) консерви́ровать, за-; (protect)
сохран|я́ть, -и́ть; ~ one's strength бере́чь
(*impf.*) свои́ си́лы

✔ **consider** /kənˈsɪdə(r)/ *v.t. & i.* рассм|а́тривать,
-отре́ть; we are ~ing going to Canada
мы поду́мываем о пое́здке в Кана́ду; ~
yourself under arrest счита́йте, что вы
аресто́ваны; he is ~ed clever его́ счита́ют
у́мным; он счита́ется у́мным; (make allowance
for) счита́ться (*impf.*) c + *i.*; we must ~
his feelings мы должны́ счита́ться с его́
чу́вствами

✔ **considerable** /kənˈsɪdərəb(ə)l/ *adj.*
значи́тельный

considerate /kənˈsɪdərət/ *adj.*
внима́тельный, забо́тливый

✔ **consideration** /kənsɪdəˈreɪʃ(ə)n/ *n.*
1 (reflection) рассмотре́ние; take into ~
прин|има́ть, -я́ть во внима́ние **2** (making
allowance): he showed ~ for my feelings он

✔ ключевая лексика

считался с мои́ми чу́вствами; он щади́л мои́ чу́вства **3** (reason, factor) соображе́ние

considering /kənˈsɪdərɪŋ/ *prep. & adv.* учи́тывая, принима́я во внима́ние; **that is not so bad,** ~ (infml) в о́бщем, э́то не так уж пло́хо

consign /kənˈsaɪn/ *v.t.* (send) посыла́ть, -ла́ть; (to hand over (to), commit (to)): ~ **to oblivion** преда|ва́ть, -ть забве́нию

consignment /kənˈsaɪnmənt/ *n.* (consigning) отпра́вка; (goods) груз, па́ртия това́ра

✔ **consist** /kənˈsɪst/ *v.i.*: ~ **of** состоя́ть (*impf.*) из + *g.*; ~ **in** состоя́ть (*impf.*) в + *i.*; **his task ~s in defining work norms** его́ рабо́та состои́т в определе́нии норм вы́работки

consistency /kənˈsɪst(ə)nsɪ/ *n.* **1** (of mixture etc.) консисте́нция **2** (adherence to logic) после́довательность

✔ **consistent** /kənˈsɪst(ə)nt/ *adj.* (of argument etc.) после́довательный; (of person) после́довательный

consolation /kɒnsəˈleɪʃ(ə)n/ *n.* утеше́ние, отра́да

console[1] /ˈkɒnsəʊl/ *n.* (panel) пульт управле́ния

console[2] /kənˈsəʊl/ *v.t.* ут|еша́ть, -е́шить

consolidate /kənˈsɒlɪdeɪt/ *v.t.* укреп|ля́ть, -и́ть

consonant /ˈkɒnsənənt/ *n.* (ling.) согла́сный (звук)

consorti|um /kənˈsɔːtɪəm/ *n.* (*pl.* ~**a** *or* ~**ums**) консо́рциум

conspicuous /kənˈspɪkjʊəs/ *adj.* заме́тный

conspiracy /kənˈspɪrəsɪ/ *n.* за́говор; конспира́ция

conspirator /kənˈspɪrətə(r)/ *n.* загово́рщик

conspiratorial /kənspɪrəˈtɔːrɪəl/ *adj.* загово́рщический, конспира́торский

conspire /kənˈspaɪə(r)/ *v.t. & i.* устр|а́ивать, -о́ить за́говор

constable /ˈkʌnstəb(ə)l/ *n.* (BrE) полице́йский

✔ **constant** /ˈkɒnst(ə)nt/ *adj.* постоя́нный

constantly /ˈkɒnst(ə)ntlɪ/ *adj.* постоя́нно

constellation /kɒnstəˈleɪʃ(ə)n/ *n.* созве́здие

consternation /kɒnstəˈneɪʃ(ə)n/ *n.* смяте́ние, у́жас

constipate /ˈkɒnstɪpeɪt/ *v.t.*: **I am ~d** у меня́ запо́р

constipation /kɒnstɪˈpeɪʃ(ə)n/ *n.* запо́р

constituency /kənˈstɪtjʊənsɪ/ *n.* избира́тельный о́круг

constituent /kənˈstɪtjʊənt/ *n.* (elector) избира́тель (-ница); (element) составна́я часть

constitute /ˈkɒnstɪtjuːt/ *v.t.* сост|авля́ть, -а́вить

constitution /kɒnstɪˈtjuːʃ(ə)n/ *n.* **1** (make-up) строе́ние, структу́ра **2** (pol.) конститу́ция

constitutional /kɒnstɪˈtjuːʃən(ə)l/ *adj.* (pol.) конституцио́нный

constrain /kənˈstreɪn/ *v.t.* (force) прин|ужда́ть, -у́дить; заст|авля́ть, -а́вить; вынужда́ть, вы́нудить; (restrict) ограни́чи|вать, -ть; ~**ed**

(embarrassed) стеснённый

constraint /kənˈstreɪnt/ *n.* ограниче́ние

constrict /kənˈstrɪkt/ *v.t.* сж|има́ть, -а́ть

constriction /kənˈstrɪkʃ(ə)n/ *n.* сжа́тие, суже́ние

✔ **construct** /kənˈstrʌkt/ *v.t.* стро́ить, по-

✔ **construction** /kənˈstrʌkʃ(ə)n/ *n.* построе́ние, строи́тельство, стро́йка; (thing constructed) постро́йка, сооруже́ние; **the road is under** ~ доро́га стро́ится

constructive /kənˈstrʌktɪv/ *adj.* (pert. to construction; helpful) конструкти́вный

construe /kənˈstruː/ *v.t.* (**construes, construed, construing**) (interpret) истолко́в|ывать, -а́ть

consul /ˈkɒns(ə)l/ *n.* ко́нсул

consulate /ˈkɒnsjʊlət/ *n.* ко́нсульство

consult /kənˈsʌlt/ *v.t.*: ~ **a book** спр|авля́ться, -а́виться в кни́ге; ~ **a lawyer** сове́товаться, по- с юри́стом
● *v.i.* сове́товаться, по-, консульти́роваться (*impf., pf.*) (**with:** c + *i.*)
■ ~**ing room** *n.* кабине́т (врача́)

consultancy /kənˈsʌlt(ə)nsɪ/ *n.* (company) консульти́рующая фи́рма; (job) до́лжность консульта́нта

consultant /kənˈsʌlt(ə)nt/ *n.* консульта́нт

consultation /kɒnsəlˈteɪʃ(ə)n/ *n.* консульта́ция

consultative /kənˈsʌltətɪv/ *adj.* консультати́вный, совеща́тельный

consume /kənˈsjuːm/ *v.t.* **1** (eat or drink) съ|еда́ть, -е́сть **2** (use up) потреб|ля́ть, -и́ть **3** (destroy) истреб|ля́ть, -и́ть; **the fire ~d the huts** пожа́р уничто́жил лачу́ги **4**: **he was ~d with envy/curiosity** его́ снеда́ла за́висть; его́ снеда́ло любопы́тство

✔ **consumer** /kənˈsjuːmə(r)/ *n.* потреби́тель (*m.*)
■ ~ **goods** *n. pl.* потреби́тельские това́ры; ~ **society** *n.* о́бщество потребле́ния

consummate *v.t.* /ˈkɒnsjʊmeɪt/ (marriage) осуществ|ля́ть, -и́ть (*бра́чные отноше́ния*)
● *adj.* /ˈkɒns(j)əmət/ зако́нченный

consumption /kənˈsʌmpʃ(ə)n/ *n.* потребле́ние, поглоще́ние

✔ **contact** /ˈkɒntækt/ *n.* **1** (lit., fig.) конта́кт, соприкоснове́ние; **bring, come into** ~ **with** устан|овля́ть (*pf.*) конта́кт с + *i.* **2** (of person): **he made useful ~s** он завяза́л поле́зные знако́мства
● *v.t.* связа́ться (*pf.*) c + *i.*
■ ~ **lenses** *n. pl.* конта́ктные ли́нзы

contagion /kənˈteɪdʒ(ə)n/ *n.* зара́за

contagious /kənˈteɪdʒəs/ *adj.* зара́зный

✔ **contain** /kənˈteɪn/ *v.t.* **1** (hold within itself) содержа́ть (*impf.*) в себе́ **2** (be capable of holding) вмеща́ть (*impf.*); **how much does this bottle ~?** ско́лько вмеща́ет э́та буты́лка? **3** (control) сде́рж|ивать, -а́ть; **he could not ~ his enthusiasm** он не мог сдержа́ть своего́ восто́рга

container /kənˈteɪnə(r)/ *n.* **1** (receptacle) сосу́д **2** (for transport) конте́йнер
■ ~ **ship,** ~ **truck** *nn.* контейнерово́з

c

contaminate /kən'tæmɪneɪt/ v.t. зара|жа́ть, -зи́ть

contamination /kəntæmɪ'neɪʃ(ə)n/ v.t. зараже́ние

contemplate /'kɒntəmpleɪt/ v.t. **1** (gaze at) созерца́ть (impf.) **2** (envisage, plan) обду́м|ывать, -ать

contemplation /kɒntəm'pleɪʃ(ə)n/ n. (gazing) созерца́ние; (thought) размышле́ние, обду́мывание

contemplative /kən'templətɪv/ adj. созерца́тельный

✒ **contemporary** /kən'tempərərɪ/ n. совреме́нни|к, све́рстни|к (-ца)
● adj. совреме́нный

contempt /kən'tempt/ n. презре́ние; ~ of court оскорбле́ние суда́, неуваже́ние к суду́

contemptible /kən'temptɪb(ə)l/ adj. презре́нный

contemptuous /kən'temptʃʊəs/ adj. презри́тельный

contend /kən'tend/ v.t. (maintain) утвержда́ть (impf.)
● v.i. (compete) состяза́ться (impf.); сопе́рничать (impf.)

✒ **content¹** /'kɒntent/ n. (lit., fig.) содержа́ние; (in pl.) содержи́мое; (in full **table of** ~s) оглавле́ние, содержа́ние

content² /kən'tent/ adj. дово́льный
● v.t. удовлетвор|я́ть, -и́ть; a ~ed look дово́льный вид

contention /kən'tenʃ(ə)n/ n. (strife) спор

contentious /kən'tenʃəs/ adj. вздо́рный, задири́стый

contentment /kən'tentmənt/ n. удовлетворённость

contest n. /'kɒntest/ ко́нкурс, состяза́ние
● v.t. & i. /kən'test/ **1** (dispute) осп|а́ривать, -о́рить **2** (contend for) отст|а́ивать, -оя́ть; боро́ться (impf.) за + a.

contestant /kən'test(ə)nt/ n. конкуре́нт (-ка)

✒ **context** /'kɒntekst/ n. конте́кст; in the ~ of today's America в усло́виях совреме́нной Аме́рики

continent /'kɒntɪnənt/ n. контине́нт

continental /kɒntɪ'nent(ə)l/ adj. континента́льный
■ ~ **breakfast** n. лёгкий у́тренний за́втрак; ~ **quilt** n. (BrE) стёганое одея́ло

contingency /kən'tɪndʒənsɪ/ n. возмо́жное обстоя́тельство
■ ~ **plan** n. вариа́нт пла́на; альтернати́вный план

contingent /kən'tɪndʒ(ə)nt/ n. (mil.) континге́нт

continual /kən'tɪnjʊəl/ adj. постоя́нный

continuation /kəntɪnjʊ'eɪʃ(ə)n/ n. продолже́ние

✒ **continue** /kən'tɪnju:/ v.t. (**continues, continued, continuing**) прод|олжа́ть,

-о́лжить; **'to be** ~**d'** (of story etc.) продолже́ние сле́дует
● v.i. (**continues, continued, continuing**) прод|олжа́ться, -о́лжиться; the wet weather ~s сыра́я пого́да де́ржится

continuity /kɒntɪ'nju:ɪtɪ/ n. непреры́вность

continuous /kən'tɪnjʊəs/ adj. непреры́вный; (gram.) дли́тельный

continu|um /kən'tɪnjʊəm/ n. (pl. ~a) конти́нуум

contort /kən'tɔ:t/ v.t. иска|жа́ть, -зи́ть

contortion /kən'tɔ:ʃ(ə)n/ n. искаже́ние; искривле́ние

contour /'kɒntʊə(r)/ n. ко́нтур
■ ~ **line** n. горизонта́ль

contraband /'kɒntrəbænd/ n. контраба́нда

contraception /kɒntrə'sepʃ(ə)n/ n. предупрежде́ние бере́менности

contraceptive /kɒntrə'septɪv/ n. противозача́точное сре́дство
● adj. противозача́точный

✒ **contract¹** /'kɒntrækt/ n. (agreement) контра́кт, догово́р
■ ~ **killer** n. ки́ллер, наёмный уби́йца; ~ **killing** n. заказно́е уби́йство

contract² /kən'trækt/ v.t. (an illness) подхв|а́тывать, -ати́ть
● v.i. (agree) прин|има́ть, -я́ть на себя́ обяза́тельство; he ~ed to build a bridge он подряди́лся постро́ить мост

contract³ /kən'trækt/ v.t. (shorten) сокра|ща́ть, -ти́ть; (tighten) сж|има́ть, -а́ть
● v.i. (shorten) сокра|ща́ться, -ти́ться; metal ~s мета́лл сжима́ется; (tighten) сж|има́ться, -а́ться

contraction /kən'trækʃ(ə)n/ n. (of metal) сжа́тие; (med.) родова́я схва́тка

contractor /kən'træktə(r)/ n. (person) подря́дчик

contradict /kɒntrə'dɪkt/ v.t. противоре́чить (impf.) + d.

contradiction /kɒntrə'dɪkʃ(ə)n/ n. противоре́чие

contradictory /kɒntrə'dɪktərɪ/ adj. противоречи́вый

contralto /kən'træltəʊ/ n. (pl. ~s) (singer) контра́льто (f. indecl.); (voice) контра́льто (nt. indecl.)

contraption /kən'træpʃ(ə)n/ n. (infml) приспособле́ние

contrary /'kɒntrərɪ/ n. противополо́жность; on the ~ (как раз) наоборо́т; there is no evidence to the ~ нет доказа́тельств проти́вного/обра́тного
● adj. **1** противополо́жный, проти́вный, обра́тный **2** /kən'treərɪ/ своево́льный, своенра́вный
● adv.: ~ to my expectations вопреки́ мои́м ожида́ниям

✒ **contrast** n. /'kɒntrɑ:st/ контра́ст; in ~ to в противополо́жность + d.; by ~ with по сравне́нию с + i.
● v.t. /kən'trɑ:st/ противопост|авля́ть, -а́вить
● v.i. /kən'trɑ:st/ контрасти́ровать (impf., pf.)

contravene /kɒntrə'viːn/ *v.t.* противоре́чить (*impf.*) + *d.*; he ~d the law он нару́шил зако́н

contravention /kɒntrə'venʃ(ə)n/ *n.* наруше́ние; in ~ of в наруше́ние + *g.*

⚹ **contribute** /kən'trɪbjuːt/ *v.t.* (money etc.) же́ртвовать, по-; he ~d £5 он внёс 5 фу́нтов • *v.i.* соде́йствовать (*impf.*) (to: + *d.*); she ~s to our magazine она́ пи́шет для на́шего журна́ла

⚹ **contribution** /kɒntrɪ'bjuːʃ(ə)n/ *n.*: a ~ of £5 поже́ртвование/взнос в пять фу́нтов; his ~ to our success его́ вклад в наш успе́х

contributor /kən'trɪbjʊtə(r)/ *n.* (writer) (постоя́нный) сотру́дник; (of funds) же́ртвователь (*m.*)

contributory /kən'trɪbjʊtərɪ/ *adj.* соде́йствующий, спосо́бствующий; ~ factor спосо́бствующий фа́ктор; a ~ pension scheme (BrE) пенсио́нная систе́ма, осно́ванная на отчисле́ниях из за́работка рабо́тающих

■ ~ negligence *n.* (law) встре́чная вина́, вина́ потерпе́вшего

contrite /kən'traɪt/ *adj.* ка́ющийся

contrition /kən'trɪʃ(ə)n/ *n.* раска́яние

contrive /kən'traɪv/ *v.t.* (devise) заду́м|ывать, -ать; (succeed): he ~d to offend everybody он умудри́лся оби́деть всех; ~d (artificial) иску́сственный

⚹ **control** /kən'trəʊl/ *n.* 1 (power to direct etc.) управле́ние, регули́рование; he lost ~ of the car он потеря́л управле́ние автомоби́лем; he is in ~ of the situation он хозя́ин положе́ния; the situation is under ~ ситуа́ция нормализова́лась/находи́тся под контро́лем; the children are out of ~ де́ти не слу́шаются 2 (means of regulating) контро́ль (*m.*) 3 (in pl.) (of a machine etc.) рычаги́ (*m. pl.*) управле́ния 4: ~ panel прибо́рная доска́; пульт управле́ния; ~ room пункт управле́ния; ~ tower (aeron.) контро́льно-диспе́тчерский пункт
• *v.t.* (**controlled, controlling**) контроли́ровать, про-; регули́ровать (*impf., pf.*); ~ one's temper владе́ть (*impf.*) собо́й; ~ prices регули́ровать це́ны

controversial /kɒntrə'vɜːʃ(ə)l/ *adj.* спо́рный

controversy /'kɒntrəvɜːsɪ/ *n.* поле́мика, спор

convalesce /kɒnvə'les/ *v.i.* выздора́вливать, поправля́ться (*both impf.*)

convalescence /kɒnvə'les(ə)ns/ *n.* выздоровле́ние

convalescent /kɒnvə'les(ə)nt/ *adj.* выздора́вливающий, поправля́ющийся

convene /kən'viːn/ *v.t.* (people) соб|ира́ть, -ра́ть; (meeting) соз|ыва́ть, -ва́ть
• *v.i.* соб|ира́ться, -ра́ться

convenience /kən'viːnɪəns/ *n.* удо́бство; at your ~ когда́ вам бу́дет удо́бно; marriage of ~ фикти́вный брак

■ ~ foods *n. pl.* пищевы́е полуфабрика́ты; ~ store *n.* магази́н ша́говой досту́пности, (круглосу́точный) магази́н това́ров

повседне́вного спро́са

convenient /kən'viːnɪənt/ *adj.* удо́бный; if it is ~ for you е́сли вам удо́бно

convent /'kɒnv(ə)nt/ *n.* (же́нский) монасты́рь

convention /kən'venʃ(ə)n/ *n.* 1 (congress) съезд 2 (treaty) конве́нция 3 (custom) обы́чай

conventional /kən'venʃ(ə)n(ə)l/ *adj.* обы́чный; a ~ person челове́к, кото́рый приде́рживается усло́вностей

converge /kən'vɜːdʒ/ *v.i.* сходи́ться, сойти́сь

conversant /kən'vɜːs(ə)nt/ *adj.* знако́мый (with: с + *i.*); осведомлённый (with: в + *p.*)

⚹ **conversation** /kɒnvə'seɪʃ(ə)n/ *n.* разгово́р, бесе́да, речь

converse /kən'vɜːs/ *v.i.* бесе́довать (*impf.*)

conversion /kən'vɜːʃ(ə)n/ *n.* 1 (transformation) превраще́ние, перехо́д 2 (relig. etc.) обраще́ние (to: в + *a.*) 3 (comm.): ~ of pounds into dollars перево́д фу́нтов в до́ллары

convert[1] /'kɒnvɜːt/ *n.* (ново)обращённый

convert[2] /kən'vɜːt/ *v.t.* 1 (change) превра|ща́ть, -ти́ть; the house was ~ed into flats дом был разби́т на кварти́ры 2 (relig. etc.) обра|ща́ть, -ти́ть 3 (comm.): ~ pounds into euros перевести́ (*pf.*) фу́нты (сте́рлингов) в е́вро
• *v.i.*: he ~ed to Buddhism он обрати́лся в будди́зм

convertible /kən'vɜːtɪb(ə)l/ *n.* (car) автомоби́ль (*m.*) с откидны́м/открыва́ющимся ве́рхом

convex /'kɒnveks/ *adj.* вы́пуклый

convey /kən'veɪ/ *v.t.* 1 (carry, transmit) перев|ози́ть, -езти́ 2 (impart) перед|ава́ть, -а́ть

conveyancing /kən'veɪənsɪŋ/ *n.* (law) составле́ние нотариа́льных а́ктов о переда́че иму́щества

conveyor /kən'veɪə(r)/ *n.*: ~ belt конве́йерная ле́нта

convict[1] /'kɒnvɪkt/ *n.* осуждённый

convict[2] /kən'vɪkt/ *v.t.* (law) осу|жда́ть, -ди́ть (of: за + *a.*)

conviction /kən'vɪkʃ(ə)n/ *n.* 1 (law) осужде́ние 2 (settled opinion) убежде́ние, убеждённость 3 (persuasive force) убежде́ние

convince /kən'vɪns/ *v.t.* убе|жда́ть, -ди́ть

convincing /kən'vɪnsɪŋ/ *adj.* убеди́тельный

convivial /kən'vɪvɪəl/ *adj.* весёлый

convoy /'kɒnvɔɪ/ *n.* тра́нспортная коло́нна с конво́ем

convulsion /kən'vʌlʃ(ə)n/ *n.* (in pl.) (med.) конву́льсия, су́дорога

coo /kuː/ *v.t. & i.* (**coos, cooed**) воркова́ть (*impf.*)

cook /kʊk/ *n.* (male) по́вар; (female) куха́рка
• *v.t.* гото́вить, при-
• *v.i.* (food) гото́виться, при-; (person) гото́вить (*impf.*)

■ ~book *n.* (AmE) пова́ренная кни́га

cooker /'kʊkə(r)/ *n.* (BrE, stove) плита́

cookery /'kʊkərɪ/ *n.* кулинари́я, стряпня́

■ ~ book *n.* (BrE) пова́ренная кни́га

cookie /'kʊkɪ/ *n.* (AmE, sweet biscuit) пече́нье

cooking /'kʊkɪŋ/ *n.* (cuisine) ку́хня
● *adj.*: ~ **apple** я́блоко для запека́ния

⚡ **cool** /ku:l/ *n.* **1** прохла́да **2**: lose one's ~ (infml) вы́йти (*pf.*) из себя́, потеря́ть (*pf.*) самооблада́ние
● *adj.* **1** (lit.) прохла́дный, све́жий **2** (unexcited) хладнокро́вный **3** (unenthusiastic) прохла́дный **4** (infml, splendid) клёвый, кла́ссный; ~! класс!, кру́то!
● *v.t.* охла|жда́ть, -ди́ть
● *v.i.* охла|жда́ться, -ди́ться; ~ **down, off** ост|ыва́ть, -ы́ть; ~ing-off period пери́од обду́мывания

coop /ku:p/ *n.* куря́тник
● *v.t.*: ~ **up** (fig.) держа́ть (*impf.*) взаперти́

cooperate /kəʊ'ɒpəreɪt/ *v.i.* сотру́дничать (*impf.*)

cooperation /kəʊɒpə'reɪʃ(ə)n/ *n.* сотру́дничество

cooperative /kəʊ'ɒpərətɪv/ *n.* кооперати́в
● *adj.* кооперати́вный

co-opt /kəʊ'ɒpt/ *v.t.* коопти́ровать (*impf., pf.*)

coordinate *n.* /kəʊ'ɔ:dɪnət/ (math., geog.) координа́та; (*in pl.*) о́си (*f. pl.*) координа́т
● *v.t.* /kəʊ'ɔ:dɪneɪt/ координи́ровать (*impf., pf.*)

coordination /kəʊɔ:dɪ'neɪʃ(ə)n/ *n.* координа́ция

cop /kɒp/ *n.* (sl., policeman) полице́йский, коп

cope /kəʊp/ *v.i.* спр|авля́ться, -а́виться (with: c + *i.*)

Copenhagen /kəʊpən'heɪɡən/ *n.* Копенга́ген

copious /'kəʊpɪəs/ *adj.* оби́льный

copper /'kɒpə(r)/ *n.* медь

copulate /'kɒpjʊleɪt/ *v.i.* совокуп|ля́ться, -и́ться

⚡ **copy** /'kɒpɪ/ *n.* **1** (version) ко́пия, ру́копись **2** (of book etc.) экземпля́р
● *v.t. & i.* перепи́с|ывать, -а́ть; (imitate) подража́ть (*impf.*) + *d.*; ~ **out a letter** переписа́ть (*pf.*) письмо́; **he copied in the examination** он спи́сывал на экза́мене
■ ~**right** *n.* а́вторское пра́во

cord /kɔ:d/ *n.* (rope, string) верёвка; (flex) шнур

cordial /'kɔ:dɪəl/ *n.* (BrE) подслащённый напи́ток
● *adj.* серде́чный, раду́шный

cordless /'kɔ:dlɪs/ *adj.* беспроводно́й
■ ~ **(tele)phone** *n.* радиотелефо́н

cordon /'kɔ:d(ə)n/ *n.* (of police etc.) оцепле́ние, кордо́н
● *v.t.* (*also* ~ **off**) оцеп|ля́ть, -и́ть

corduroy /'kɔ:dərɔɪ/ *n.* вельве́т
● *adj.* вельве́товый

⚡ **core** /kɔ:(r)/ *n.* (of fruit) сердцеви́на; (fig.) центр, ядро́, суть; ~ **of a problem** суть пробле́мы

Corfu /kɔ:'fu:/ *n.* Ко́рфу (*m. indecl.*)

coriander /kɒrɪ'ændə(r)/ *n.* кориа́ндр; (of fresh leaves, usu.) кинза́

cork /kɔ:k/ *n.* про́бка; (*attr.*) про́бковый

⚡ ключева́я ле́ксика

■ ~**screw** *n.* што́пор

corn[1] /kɔ:n/ *n.* **1** (BrE, grain, seed) зерно́ **2** (BrE, wheat) пшени́ца **3** (AmE, maize) кукуру́за
■ ~**flakes** *n. pl.* кукуру́зные хло́пья; ~**flour** *n.* (BrE) кукуру́зная/ри́совая мука́; ~ **on the cob** *n.* кукуру́за в поча́тках

corn[2] /kɔ:n/ *n.* (on foot) мозо́ль

cornea /'kɔ:nɪə/ *n.* рогови́ца; рогова́я оболо́чка

⚡ **corner** /'kɔ:nə(r)/ *n.* **1** (place where lines etc. meet) у́гол; at, on the ~ на углу́; round the ~ (lit.) за угло́м; (fig., near) ря́дом; in a tight ~ в затрудне́нии; he looked out of the ~ of his eye он следи́л кра́ешком гла́за **2** (football) углово́й уда́р, ко́рнер
● *v.t.* заг|оня́ть, -на́ть в у́гол; the fugitive was ~ed беглеца́ загна́ли в у́гол; he ~ed the market он завладе́л ры́нком, скупи́в весь това́р
■ ~**stone** *n.* (fig.) краеуго́льный ка́мень

cornet /'kɔ:nɪt/ *n.* **1** (mus. instrument) корне́т, корне́т-а-писто́н **2** (BrE, for ice cream) ва́фельный рожо́к

cornice /'kɔ:nɪs/ *n.* карни́з

corny /'kɔ:nɪ/ *adj.* (**cornier, corniest**) (infml) пло́ский, изби́тый

coronary /'kɒrənərɪ/ *adj.* (med.): ~ **artery** вене́чная арте́рия
● *n.* (*in full* ~ **thrombosis**) коронаротромбо́з

coronation /kɒrə'neɪʃ(ə)n/ *n.* корона́ция

coroner /'kɒrənə(r)/ *n.* сле́дователь (*m.*) (*по делам о насильственной или скоропостижной смерти*)

corporal[1] /'kɔ:pr(ə)l/ *n.* (officer) капра́л

corporal[2] /'kɔ:pr(ə)l/ *adj.*: ~ **punishment** теле́сное наказа́ние

⚡ **corporate** /'kɔ:pərət/ *adj.* **1** (collective) о́бщий **2** (of, forming a corporation) корпорати́вный

corporation /kɔ:pə'reɪʃ(ə)n/ *n.* (company) акционе́рное о́бщество
■ ~ **tax** *n.* нало́г с дохо́дов компа́ний

corps /kɔ:(r)/ *n.* (*pl.* ~ /kɔ:z/) (mil., diplomacy) ко́рпус

corpse /kɔ:ps/ *n.* труп

corpuscle /'kɔ:pʌs(ə)l/ *n.* корпу́скула, те́льце, части́ца

⚡ **correct** /kə'rekt/ *adj.* **1** (right, true) пра́вильный, ве́рный, то́чный **2** (of behaviour) корре́ктный
● *v.t.* испр|авля́ть, -а́вить

correction /kə'rekʃ(ə)n/ *n.* исправле́ние
■ ~ **fluid** *n.* корректи́рующая жи́дкость

correspond /kɒrɪ'spɒnd/ *v.i.* **1** (match, harmonize) соотве́тствовать (*impf.*) (to: + *d.*) **2** (exchange letters) перепи́сываться (*impf.*) (with: c + *i.*)

correspondence /kɒrɪ'spɒnd(ə)ns/ *n.* корреспонде́нция, перепи́ска
■ ~ **course** *n.* курс зао́чного обуче́ния

correspondent /kɒrɪ'spɒnd(ə)nt/ *n.* корреспонде́нт (-ка)

corresponding /kɒrɪ'spɒndɪŋ/ *adj.* соотве́тственный, соотве́тствующий

corridor /'kɒrɪdɔ:(r)/ *n.* коридо́р

corroborate /kə'rɒbəreɪt/ *v.t.* подтвер|жда́ть, -ди́ть

corrode /kə'rəʊd/ *v.t.* разъ|еда́ть, -е́сть
● *v.i.* ржаве́ть, за-

corrosion /kə'rəʊʒ(ə)n/ *n.* корро́зия, ржа́вчина

corrosive /kə'rəʊsɪv/ *adj.* коррози́йный, разъеда́ющий, е́дкий; (fig.) разъеда́ющий

corrugate /'kɒrʊgeɪt/ *v.t.*: ~d iron волни́стое/ рифлёное желе́зо

corrupt /kə'rʌpt/ *adj.* **1** (depraved) развращённый **2** (dishonest) прода́жный **3** (comput.) повреждённый
● *v.t.* **1** (deprave) развра|ща́ть, -ти́ть **2** (comput.) иска|жа́ть, -зи́ть

corruption /kə'rʌpʃ(ə)n/ *n.* разложе́ние; развраще́ние

corset /'kɔ:sɪt/ *n.* корсе́т

Corsica /'kɔ:sɪkə/ *n.* Ко́рсика

cortisone /'kɔ:tɪzəʊn/ *n.* (med.) кортизо́н

cosh /kɒʃ/ *n.* (BrE) дуби́нка

cosmetic /kɒz'metɪk/ *n.* косме́тика
● *adj.* космети́ческий

cosmic /'kɒzmɪk/ *adj.* косми́ческий

cosmology /kɒz'mɒlədʒɪ/ *n.* космоло́гия

cosmonaut /'kɒzmənɔ:t/ *n.* космона́вт

cosmopolitan /kɒzmə'pɒlɪt(ə)n/ *adj.* космополити́ческий

cosmos /'kɒzmɒs/ *n.* ко́смос

Cossack /'kɒsæk/ *n.* каза́|к (-чка); (*attr.*) каза́цкий, каза́чий

cosset /'kɒsɪt/ *v.t.* (**cosseted, cosseting**) балова́ть (*impf.*); не́жить (*impf.*)

ᶜ **cost** /kɒst/ *n.* **1** (monetary) цена́, сто́имость; ~ **price** себесто́имость; ~ **of living** прожи́точный ми́нимум **2** (expense, loss) цена́; **at all** ~**s** любо́й цено́й
● *v.t. & i.* **1** (*past and p.p.* ~) (involve expense) сто́ить (*impf.*); **this** ~ **me £5** э́то сто́ило мне 5 фу́нтов; э́то обошло́сь мне в 5 фу́нтов **2** (*past and p.p.* ~**ed**) (assess ~ of) оце́н|ивать, -и́ть изде́ржки (*предприятия и т. п.*)
■ ~**-effective** *adj.* рента́бельный

co-star /'kəʊstɑ:(r)/ *n.* партнёр (-ша) (в друго́й гла́вной ро́ли)
● *v.t.*: **a picture** ~**ring X and Y** фильм с уча́стием двух звёзд — X и Y
● *v.i.*: **they** ~**red in that picture** они́ снима́лись в э́том фи́льме в гла́вных роля́х

costly /'kɒstlɪ/ *adj.* (**costlier, costliest**) дорого́й

costume /'kɒstju:m/ *n.* костю́м
■ ~ **jewellery** *n.* бижуте́рия

cosy /'kəʊzɪ/ (AmE **cozy**) *adj.* (**cosier, cosiest**) ую́тный

cot /kɒt/ *n.* (BrE, child's bed) де́тская крова́тка; (AmE, camp bed) раскладу́шка
■ ~ **death** *n.* (BrE) внеза́пная смерть (ребёнка грудно́го во́зраста)

cottage /'kɒtɪdʒ/ *n.* котте́дж; да́ча; ~ **cheese** (прессо́ванный) творо́г

cotton /'kɒt(ə)n/ *n.* **1** (plant) хло́пок, хлопча́тник **2** (fabric) хло́пок **3** (thread) ни́тки (*f. pl.*) **4** (*attr.*) хлопчатобума́жный
■ ~ **wool** *n.* (BrE) ва́та

couch /kaʊtʃ/ *n.* (sofa) куше́тка, дива́н; (bed) крова́ть

couchette /ku:'ʃet/ *n.* спа́льное ме́сто

cough /kɒf/ *n.* ка́шель (*m.*)
● *v.i.* ка́шлять (*impf.*)
■ ~ **medicine, ~ mixture** (BrE) *nn.* миксту́ра от ка́шля

ᶜ **could** /kʊd/ *v. aux., see* ▶ **can²**

couldn't /'kʊd(ə)nt/ *neg. of* ▶ **could**

ᶜ **council** /'kaʊns(ə)l/ *n.* сове́т; **town** ~ городско́й сове́т; муниципалите́т
■ ~ **house** *n.* (BrE, dwelling) муниципа́льный дом; жило́й дом, принадлежа́щий муниципа́льному сове́ту

councillor /'kaʊnsələ(r)/ (AmE *also* **councilor**) *n.* член сове́та

counsel /'kaʊns(ə)l/ *n.* (barrister(s)) адвока́т
● *v.t.* (**counselled, counselling,** AmE **counseled, counseling**) сове́товать, по- + *d.*

counsellor /'kaʊnsələ(r)/ (AmE **counselor**) *n.* сове́тник

count¹ /kaʊnt/ *n.* (nobleman) граф (*не брита́нский*)

ᶜ **count²** /kaʊnt/ *n.* **1** (reckoning) счёт, подсчёт; **keep** ~ вести́ (*det.*) счёт **2** (total) ито́г; **the** ~ **was 200** ито́г равня́лся 200 (двумста́м) **3** (law) пункт обвини́тельного заключе́ния
● *v.t.* **1** (number, reckon) счита́ть, со- + *d.*; ~ **your change!** прове́рьте сда́чу!; **50 people, not** ~**ing the children** 50 челове́к, не счита́я дете́й
● *v.i.* **1** (reckon, number) счита́ть (*impf.*); ~ **up to 10!** счита́йте до десяти́! **2** (be reckoned) счита́ться (*impf.*); **that doesn't** ~ э́то не в счёт (*or* не счита́ется) **3** (rely) рассчи́тывать (*impf.*) (**on:** на + *a.*); **I** ~ (**up)on you to help** я рассчи́тываю на ва́шу по́мощь
■ ~**down** *n.* (обра́тный) отсчёт вре́мени

countenance /'kaʊntɪnəns/ *n.* (face) лицо́, о́блик; выраже́ние лица́
● *v.t.* подде́рж|ивать, -а́ть

counter¹ /'kaʊntə(r)/ *n.* **1** (at games) фи́шка, ма́рка **2** (in shop) прила́вок; **under the** ~ (fig.) из-под полы́/прила́вка

counter² /'kaʊntə(r)/ *v.t. & i.* (oppose, parry) противоде́йствовать (*impf.*) + *d.*

counteract /kaʊntə'rækt/ *v.t.* противоде́йствовать (*impf.*) + *d.*

counter-attack /'kaʊntərətæk/ *n.* контрата́ка

counterclockwise /kaʊntə'klɒkwaɪz/ *adj. & adv.* (AmE) (дви́жущийся) про́тив часово́й стре́лки

counter-espionage /kaʊntər'espɪənɑːʒ/ *n.* контрразве́дка

counterfeit /'kaʊntəfɪt/ *adj.* подде́льный, подло́жный
● *v.t.* подде́л|ывать, -ать; (fig., simulate) подража́ть (*impf.*) + *d.*

counterfoil /'kaʊntəfɔɪl/ *n.* (BrE) корешо́к (че́ка, квита́нции и т. п.)

counterpart /'kaʊntəpɑːt/ n. па́ра (к чему), дополне́ние; (person) колле́га (c.g.)

counterproductive /kaʊntəprə'dʌktɪv/ adj. нецелесообра́зный

countersign /'kaʊntəsaɪn/ v.t. ста́вить, вто́рую по́дпись на + p.

countess /'kaʊntɪs/ n. графи́ня

countless /'kaʊntlɪs/ adj. бесчи́сленный

⚜ **country** /'kʌntrɪ/ n. **1** (geog., pol.) страна́ **2** (opp. town) дере́вня; **in the ~** за́ го́родом, на да́че; **(~side)** приро́да **3** (terrain) ме́стность; **difficult ~** труднопроходи́мая ме́стность
■ **~ club** n. за́городный клуб; **~ house** (also **~ seat**) n. поме́стье; **~side** n. се́льская ме́стность; ландша́фт

⚜ **county** /'kaʊntɪ/ n. гра́фство

coup /kuː/ n. (pl. **coups** /kuːz/) уда́чный ход
■ **~ d'état** n. госуда́рственный переворо́т

coupé /'kuːpeɪ/ n. закры́тый двухдве́рный автомоби́ль

⚜ **couple** /'kʌp(ə)l/ n. (objects or people) па́ра

coupon /'kuːpɒn/ n. купо́н, тало́н

courage /'kʌrɪdʒ/ n. хра́брость, сме́лость, му́жество; **take, pluck up ~** мужа́ться (impf.); соб|ира́ться, -ра́ться с ду́хом

courageous /kə'reɪdʒəs/ adj. хра́брый

courgette /kʊə'ʒet/ n. (BrE) кабачо́к

courier /'kʊrɪə(r)/ n. (messenger) курье́р; (travel guide) экскурсово́д

⚜ **course** /kɔːs/ n. **1** (movement, process) ход, тече́ние; **~ of events** ход собы́тий; **in due ~** в до́лжное/своё вре́мя; **of ~** коне́чно **2** (direction) курс, направле́ние; **we are on ~** мы идём по ку́рсу **3** (race~) скорово́й круг **4** (series) курс; **a ~ of lectures** курс ле́кций; **a ~ of treatment** курс лече́ния **5** (cul.) блю́до; **main ~** второ́е блю́до

⚜ **court** /kɔːt/ n. **1** (yard) двор **2** (space for playing games) площа́дка для игр; (tennis) корт **3** (sovereign's etc.) двор **4** (law) суд; **~ of law, justice** суд
● v.t. (a woman) уха́живать (impf.) за + i.
■ **~house** n. зда́ние суда́; **~ martial** n. вое́нный суд; **~-martial** v.t. (**-martialled, -martialling,** AmE **-martialed, -martialing**) суди́ть (impf.) вое́нным судо́м; **~room** n. зал суда́; **~yard** n. двор

courteous /'kɜːtɪəs/ adj. ве́жливый, учти́вый

courtesan /kɔːtɪ'zæn/ n. куртиза́нка

courtesy /'kɜːtɪsɪ/ n. ве́жливость, учти́вость
■ **~ bus** n. беспла́тный авто́бус

courtier /'kɔːtɪə(r)/ n. придво́рный

courtship /'kɔːtʃɪp/ n. уха́живание

cousin /'kʌz(ə)n/ n. (male) двою́родный брат; (female) двою́родная сестра́; **second ~** трою́родный брат (трою́родная сестра́)

cove /kəʊv/ n. бу́хточка

covenant /'kʌvənənt/ n. соглаше́ние, догово́р; **C~ of the League of Nations** уста́в Ли́ги На́ций; (relig.) заве́т
● v.t. & i. заключ|а́ть, -и́ть соглаше́ние;

догов|а́риваться, -ори́ться (с кем о чём)

⚜ **cover** /'kʌvə(r)/ n. **1** (lid) кры́шка **2** (loose ~ing of chair etc.) чехо́л; (in pl.) (bedclothes) посте́ль **3** (of book etc.) переплёт, обло́жка **4** (shelter, protection) укры́тие, прикры́тие; **take ~** укр|ыва́ться, -ы́ться **5** (at table): **~ charge** пла́та за дополни́тельное обслу́живание (му́зыку в рестора́не и т. п.) **6** (BrE, insurance) страхова́ние
● v.t. **1** (overspread etc.) (also **~ up, ~ over**) покр|ыва́ть, -ы́ть; **~ a chair** об|ива́ть, -и́ть стул; **she ~ed her face in, with her hands** она́ закры́ла лицо́ рука́ми; **the roads are ~ed with snow** доро́ги занесены́ сне́гом **2** (fig.) покр|ыва́ть, -ы́ть **3** (protect) закр|ыва́ть, -ы́ть; **are you ~ed against theft?** вы застрахо́ваны от кра́жи? **4** (aim weapon at) це́литься (impf.) в + a. **5** (meet, satisfy) покр|ыва́ть, -ы́ть **6** (deal with): **the lectures ~ a wide field** ле́кции охва́тывают широ́кий круг вопро́сов **7** (of correspondence): **~ing letter** сопроводи́тельное письмо́
■ **~-up** n. сокры́тие; **~ version** n. (mus.) ка́вер-ве́рсия (пе́сни)

⚜ **coverage** /'kʌvərɪdʒ/ n. охва́т

covert /'kəʊvət/ adj. скры́тый

covet /'kʌvɪt/ v.t. (**coveted, coveting**) жа́ждать (impf.) + g.; (infml) за́риться (impf.) на + a.

cow /kaʊ/ n. коро́ва
■ **~boy** n. ковбо́й

coward /'kaʊəd/ n. трус (-и́ха)

cowardice /'kaʊədɪs/ n. тру́сость

cowardly /'kaʊədlɪ/ adj. трусли́вый

cower /'kaʊə(r)/ v.i. съёжи|ваться, -ться

cowslip /'kaʊslɪp/ n. первоцве́т

coy /kɔɪ/ adj. (**coyer, coyest**) стыдли́вый

cozy /'kəʊzɪ/ adj. (AmE) = cosy

crab /kræb/ n. краб; (astron., astrol.): **the C~** Рак

crack /kræk/ n. **1** (in a cup, ice, etc.) тре́щина; (in wall, floor, etc.) щель **2** (sudden noise) треск, щёлканье **3** (infml, attempt) попы́тка; **have a ~ at sth** попыта́ть (pf.) свои́ си́лы в чём-н. **4**: **at the ~ of dawn** с (пе́рвой) зарёй **5**: **a ~ shot** первокла́ссный стрело́к **6** (drug) крэк
● v.t. **1** (a plate, a bone) раск|а́лывать, -оло́ть; **~ a nut** расколо́ть (pf.) оре́х; **~ a code** разгада́ть (pf.) шифр **2**: **~ a whip** щёлк|ать, -нуть кнуто́м; **~ a joke** отпусти́ть (pf.) шу́тку
● v.i. **1** (get broken or fissured) да|ва́ть, -ть тре́щину; **the glass ~ed** стекло́ тре́снуло; (fig., give way): **he did not ~ under torture** пы́тки не сломи́ли его́ **2** (of sound) щёлк|ать, -нуть
□ **~ down** v.i.: **~ down on** прин|има́ть, -я́ть круты́е ме́ры про́тив + g.
□ **~ up** v.i. (of person: suffer collapse) надломи́ться (pf.); развал|иваться, -и́ться

cracker /'krækə(r)/ n. **1** (biscuit) кре́кер **2** (Christmas **~**) хлопу́шка

crackle /'kræk(ə)l/ n. (sound) треск, потре́скивание
● v.i. (of sound) потре́скивать (impf.)

cradle /'kreɪd(ə)l/ n. (lit., fig.) колыбе́ль

⚜ ключева́я ле́ксика

• *v.t.*: ~ a child in one's arms держа́ть (*impf.*) ребёнка на рука́х

craft /krɑːft/ *n.* **1** (skill) ло́вкость, уме́ние **2** (occupation) ремесло́; **arts and ~s** иску́сства и ремёсла (*nt. pl.*) **3** (*pl.* ~) (boat) су́дно
■ ~**sman** *n.* реме́сленник, ма́стер

crafty /ˈkrɑːftɪ/ *adj.* (**craftier, craftiest**) хи́трый

crag /kræɡ/ *n.* скала́, утёс

cram /kræm/ *v.t.* (**crammed, cramming**) **1** (insert forcefully) запи́х|ивать, -а́ть/-ну́ть; (fill): **the shelves are ~med with books** по́лки ло́мятся от книг **2** *v.t. & i.* (study intensively) уси́ленно занима́ться (пе́ред экза́меном) (*impf.*)

cramp /kræmp/ *n.* су́дорога
• *v.t.* стесн|я́ть, -и́ть

cranberry /ˈkrænbərɪ/ *n.* клю́ква (*collect.*)

crane /kreɪn/ *n.* (bird) жура́вль (*m.*); (machine) (грузо)подъёмный кран

crank[1] /kræŋk/ *n.* (handle) кривоши́п

crank[2] /kræŋk/ *n.* (person) чуда́к (-чка)

cranny /ˈkrænɪ/ *n.* тре́щина

crap /kræp/ *n.* (vulg.) (sth of poor quality) говно́ (vulg.); (nonsense) вздор, чепуха́

⚔ **crash** /kræʃ/ *n.* **1** (noise) гро́хот **2** (smash) ава́рия, круше́ние; **he was killed in a car/ plane** ~ он поги́б в автомоби́льной/ авиацио́нной катастро́фе; (comput.) фата́льный сбой **3**: **a** ~ (*sc.* intensive) **course** уско́ренный курс
• *v.t.* разб|ива́ть, -и́ть; гро́хнуть (*pf.*); **he ~ed the aircraft** он разби́л самолёт
• *v.i.* **1**: **the plane ~ed** самолёт потерпе́л ава́рию (*or* разби́лся) **2** (comput.) зав|иса́ть, -и́снуть
■ ~ **helmet** *n.* шлем автого́нщика/ мотоцикли́ста; мотошле́м; ~**land** *v.i.* соверш|а́ть, -и́ть авари́йную поса́дку; ~**landing** *n.* авари́йная поса́дка

crass /kræs/ *adj.* глу́пый; ~ **stupidity** непроходи́мая ту́пость, полне́йшая глу́пость

crate /kreɪt/ *n.* я́щик

crater /ˈkreɪtə(r)/ *n.* кра́тер; (bomb ~) воро́нка

cravat /krəˈvæt/ *n.* широ́кий га́лстук; ше́йный плато́к

crave /kreɪv/ *v.t. & i.* (desire) жа́ждать (*impf.*) + g.

craving /ˈkreɪvɪŋ/ *n.* стра́стное жела́ние

crawfish *see* ▸ **crayfish**

crawl /krɔːl/ *n.* **1** (~ing motion) по́лзание; **traffic was reduced to a** ~ тра́нспорт тащи́лся е́ле-е́ле **2** (swimming stroke) кроль (*m.*)
• *v.i.* **1** по́лзать (*indet.*), ползти́ (*det.*); **he ~ed on his hands and knees** он полз на четвере́ньках **2** (kowtow) пресмыка́ться (*impf.*) (**to**: пе́ред + *i.*) **3**: **the ground is ~ing with ants** земля́ кишма́ киши́т муравья́ми

crayfish /ˈkreɪfɪʃ/, **crawfish** /ˈkrɔːfɪʃ/ *nn.* (freshwater) речно́й рак; (marine) лангу́ст

crayon /ˈkreɪən/ *n.* цветно́й каранда́ш; цветно́й мело́к; пасте́ль

craze /kreɪz/ *n.* ма́ния, помеша́тельство

crazy /ˈkreɪzɪ/ *adj.* (**crazier, craziest**) безу́мный, сумасше́дший; ~ **about sth** помеша́нный на чём-н.; **he is** ~ **about her** он без ума́ от неё

creak /kriːk/ *v.i.* скрипе́ть (*impf.*)

cream /kriːm/ *n.* **1** (top part of milk) сли́в|ки (-ок) **2** (dish or sweet) крем **3** (polish, cosmetic, etc.) крем, мазь; **face** ~ крем для лица́ **4** (*attr.*) (~-coloured) кре́мового цве́та
• *v.t.* (apply ~ to) на|кла́дывать, -ложи́ть крем на (+ *a*); ~ **off** от|бира́ть, -обра́ть
■ ~ **cake** *n.* торт с кре́мом; кре́мовое пиро́жное

creamy /ˈkriːmɪ/ *adj.* (**creamier, creamiest**) жи́рный

crease /kriːs/ *n.* скла́дка
• *v.t.* (newspaper, trousers) мять, с-/из-
• *v.i.* (form ~s) мя́ться, с-/из-

⚔ **create** /kriːˈeɪt/ *v.t.* созд|ава́ть, -а́ть

⚔ **creation** /kriːˈeɪʃ(ə)n/ *n.* **1** (act, process) созда́ние, созида́ние **2** (product of imagination) творе́ние

⚔ **creative** /kriːˈeɪtɪv/ *adj.* тво́рческий

creativity /kriːeɪˈtɪvɪtɪ/ *n.* тво́рческий дар

creator /kriːˈeɪtə(r)/ *n.* созда́тель (*m.*)

creature /ˈkriːtʃə(r)/ *n.* созда́ние, тварь, существо́

crèche /kreʃ/ *n.* (BrE) (де́тские) я́сл|и (-ей)

credential /krɪˈdenʃ(ə)l/ *n.* (*usu. in pl.*) квалифика́ция

credibility /kredɪˈbɪlɪtɪ/ *n.* убеди́тельность

credible /ˈkredɪb(ə)l/ *adj.* (of person) заслу́живающий дове́рия

⚔ **credit** /ˈkredɪt/ *n.* **1** (belief, trust, confidence) ве́ра, дове́рие **2** (honour): **the work does you** ~ э́та рабо́та де́лает вам честь **3** (fin.) креди́т; **buy on** ~ покупа́ть (*pf.*) в креди́т
• *v.t.* (**credited, crediting**) **1** (believe sth) ве́рить, по- + *d.* **2**: **I ~ed him with more sense** я счита́л его́ бо́лее благоразу́мным
■ ~ **card** *n.* креди́тная ка́рточка; ~ **crisis** *n.* (fin.) креди́тный кри́зис, фина́нсовый кри́зис; ~ **crunch** *n.* (fin.) нехва́тка ба́нковских креди́тов; ~**worthiness** *n.* кредитоспосо́бность; ~**worthy** *adj.* кредитоспосо́бный

creditable /ˈkredɪtəb(ə)l/ *adj.* (praiseworthy) похва́льный; (believable) правдоподо́бный, вероя́тный

creditor /ˈkredɪtə(r)/ *n.* кредито́р

credulous /ˈkredjʊləs/ *adj.* легкове́рный, дове́рчивый

creed /kriːd/ *n.* вероуче́ние; (fig.) убежде́ния (*nt. pl.*)

creek /kriːk/ *n.* (inlet) зали́в, бу́хта; (small river) ре́чка

creep /kriːp/ *n.* (infml) несно́сный/ отврати́тельный тип
• *v.i.* (*past and p.p.* **crept**) по́лзать (*indet.*), ползти́ (*det.*); **old age ~s up on one unnoticed** ста́рость подкра́дывается незаме́тно

creeper /ˈkriːpə(r)/ *n.* (plant) ползу́чее/ вью́щееся расте́ние

creepy /'kri:pɪ/ adj. (**creepier, creepiest**)
1 жу́ткий **2** (of flesh) в мура́шках
■ ~**crawly** n. бука́шка
cremate /krɪ'meɪt/ v.t. креми́ровать (*impf., pf.*)
cremation /krɪ'meɪʃ(ə)n/ n. крема́ция
crematori|um /kremə'tɔːrɪəm/ n. (pl. ~**a or** ~**ums**) кремато́рий
crept /krept/ *past and p.p. of* ► creep
crescent /'krez(ə)nt/ n. **1** (moon) лу́нный серп **2** (symbol of Islam) полуме́сяц
cress /kres/ n. кресс-сала́т
crest /krest/ n. **1** (tuft of feathers; top of a wave, hill) гре́бень (*m.*) **2** (heraldic device) герб
crevasse /krə'væs/ n. рассе́лина в леднике́
crevice /'krevɪs/ n. щель, расще́лина
✔ **crew** /kru:/ n. **1** (of vessel) кома́нда, экипа́ж; (of aircraft) экипа́ж **2** (team) брига́да, арте́ль **3**: ~ **cut** стри́жка ёжиком
crib /krɪb/ n. де́тская крова́тка с се́ткой
cricket¹ /'krɪkɪt/ n. (insect) сверчо́к
cricket² /'krɪkɪt/ n. (game) кри́кет
✔ **crime** /kraɪm/ n. (offence) преступле́ние; (*collect.*) престу́пность
Crimea /kraɪ'mɪə/ n. Крым
Crimean /kraɪ'mɪən/ adj. кры́мский
✔ **criminal** /'krɪmɪn(ə)l/ n. престу́пни|к (-ца)
● adj. **1** (guilty) престу́пный; **he has a** ~ **history** у него́ престу́пное про́шлое **2** (pert. to crime) уголо́вный, кримина́льный
criminologist /krɪmɪ'nɒlədʒɪst/ n. криминóлог
criminology /krɪmɪ'nɒlədʒɪ/ n. криминоло́гия
crimson /'krɪmz(ə)n/ n. мали́новый цвет
● adj. мали́новый
cringe /krɪndʒ/ v.i. (**cringing**) раболе́пствовать (*impf.*)
crippl|e /'krɪp(ə)l/ n. (archaic or offens.) кале́ка (*c.g.*)
● v.t. кале́чить, ис-; (fig.): **strikes are** ~**ing industry** забасто́вки расша́тывают промы́шленность
✔ **crisis** /'kraɪsɪs/ n. (pl. **crises** /-si:z/) кри́зис
crisp /krɪsp/ n. (BrE) (in pl.) хрустя́щий карто́фель, чи́пс|ы (-ов)
● adj. (of substance) хрустя́щий; **a** ~ **biscuit** рассы́пчатое пече́нье; **a** ~ **lettuce** све́жий сала́т; (of style, orders, etc.) чека́нный
■ ~**bread** n. сухари́ (*m. pl.*); хрустя́щие хле́бцы (*m. pl.*)
criss-cross /'krɪskrɒs/ adj. перекре́щивающийся
● v.t. расчер|чивать, -ти́ть крест-на́крест
criteri|on /kraɪ'tɪərɪən/ n. (pl. ~**a**) крите́рий
✔ **critic** /'krɪtɪk/ n. кри́тик
✔ **critical** /'krɪtɪk(ə)l/ adj. **1** (decisive) крити́ческий; **the patient's condition is** ~ больно́й в крити́ческом состоя́нии **2** (fault-finding) крити́ческий, крити́чный
✔ **criticism** /'krɪtɪsɪz(ə)m/ n. кри́тика; **I have only one** ~ **to make** у меня́ то́лько одно́

замеча́ние
✔ **criticize** /'krɪtɪsaɪz/ v.t. (adversely) критикова́ть (*impf.*)
critique /krɪ'tiːk/ n. кри́тика; (review) реце́нзия, крити́ческая статья́
croak /krəʊk/ v.t. & i. ква́кать (*impf.*)
Croat /'krəʊæt/ n. хорва́т (-ка)
Croatia /krəʊ'eɪʃə/ n. Хорва́тия
Croatian /krəʊ'eɪʃ(ə)n/ adj. хорва́тский
crochet /'krəʊʃeɪ/ n. вя́зка крючко́м
● v.t. & i. (**crocheted** /-ʃeɪd/, **crocheting** /-ʃeɪɪŋ/) вяза́ть (*impf.*) крючко́м
crockery /'krɒkərɪ/ n. гли́няная/фая́нсовая посу́да
crocodile /'krɒkədaɪl/ n. крокоди́л
crocus /'krəʊkəs/ n. (pl. **crocuses** or **croci** /-kaɪ/) кро́кус, шафра́н
croissant /'krwʌsɑ̃/ n. круасса́н, францу́зский рога́лик
crony /'krəʊnɪ/ n. дружо́к, закады́чный друг
crook /krʊk/ n. моше́нник, жу́лик
crooked /'krʊkɪd/ adj. (**crookeder, crookedest**) **1** (bent) со́гнутый, изо́гнутый **2** (infml, dishonest) бесче́стный
crop /krɒp/ n. урожа́й, жа́тва
● v.i. (**cropped, cropping**) (fig.): **difficulties** ~**ped up** появи́лись/возни́кли тру́дности
croquet /'krəʊkeɪ/ n. кроке́т
✔ **cross** /krɒs/ n. **1** крест **2** (mixing of breeds) по́месь, гибри́д
● adj. **1** (transverse) попере́чный, перекрёстный **2** (angry) серди́тый; злой (**with:** на + *a.*)
● v.t. **1** (go across, traverse) (*also* ~ **over**) ~ **a road/bridge** пере|ходи́ть, -йти́ че́рез доро́гу/ мост; ~ **the Channel** перепл|ыва́ть, -ы́ть Ла-Ма́нш; **the idea never** ~**ed my mind** э́та мысль никогда́ не приходи́ла мне в го́лову **2** (draw lines across): ~ **a cheque** (BrE) перечёрк|ивать, -ну́ть чек **3** (place across) скре́щ|ивать, -сти́ть; ~ **one's legs** скрести́ть (*pf.*) но́ги **4**: ~ **oneself** крести́ться, пере-
● v.i.: **he** ~**ed to where I was sitting** он перешёл к тому́ ме́сту, где я сиде́л; **he** ~**ed from Dover to Calais** он перепра́вился из Ду́вра в Кале́
□ ~ **off, out** vv.t. вычёркивать, вы́черкнуть
■ ~**check** n. све́рка ● v.t. сверя́ть, -е́рить; ~**country** adj.: **a** ~**country race** бег по пересечённой ме́стности, кросс; ~**country runner** кроссме́н; ~**examine** v.t. подв|ерга́ть, -е́ргнуть перекрёстному допро́су; (fig.) допр|а́шивать, -оси́ть; ~**eyed** adj. косогла́зый, косо́й; ~**fire** n. (mil.) перекрёстный ого́нь; ~**legged** adj. (сидя́щий) положи́в но́гу на́ ногу; ~ **purposes** n. pl. недоразуме́ние; ~**question** v.t. допр|а́шивать, -оси́ть; ~**reference** n. перекрёстная ссы́лка; ~**road** n. перекрёсток, пересека́ющая доро́га; **at the** ~ **roads** (fig.) на распу́тье; ~ **section** n. попере́чное сече́ние; ~**word** n. кроссво́рд
crossing /'krɒsɪŋ/ n. перехо́д

crotch /krɒtʃ/ *n.* промежность
crotchet /'krɒtʃɪt/ *n.* (BrE, mus.) четвертная нота
crouch /krautʃ/ *v.i.* сгибаться, согнуться
croupier /'kru:pɪeɪ/ *n.* (at gambling) крупьé (*m. indecl.*)
crouton /'kru:tɒn/ *n.* (cul.) грéнка
crow[1] /krəʊ/ *n.* ворóна
■ ~**'s-nest** *n.* (naut.) наблюдáтельный пост на мáчте, «воронье гнездо»
crow[2] /krəʊ/ *n.* (of cock) кукарéканье
● *v.i.* кукарéкать (*impf.*)
crowbar /'krəʊbɑ:(r)/ *n.* лом
⚘ **crowd** /kraʊd/ *n.* толпá
● *v.t.* зап|олнять, -óлнить; ~ed street многолюдная улица; the room was ~ed with furniture кóмната былá загромождéна мéбелью
● *v.i.* (assemble in a ~) толпиться, с-; they ~ed into the room они набились в кóмнату
■ ~**sourcing** *n.* краудсóрсинг (*осуществление каких-л. работ с помощью большого числа людей, привлечённых через Интернет*)
crown /kraʊn/ *n.* **1** корóна, венéц **2** (dental work) корóнка **3** (*attr.*) C~ jewels королéвские/цáрские регáлии (*f. pl.*)
● *v.t.* **1**: he was ~ed king его короновáли (на цáрство) **2**: ~ a tooth стáвить, по- корóнку на зуб
⚘ **crucial** /'kru:ʃ(ə)l/ *adj.* (decisive) решáющий
crucible /'kru:sɪb(ə)l/ *n.* тúгель (*m.*); (fig.) горнúло (rhet.)
crucifix /'kru:sɪfɪks/ *n.* распятие, крест
crucifixion /kru:sɪ'fɪkʃ(ə)n/ *n.* распятие (на крестé)
crucify /'kru:sɪfaɪ/ *v.t.* расп|инáть, -ять
crude /kru:d/ *adj.* **1** (of materials): ~ oil сырáя нефть **2** (graceless) грубый, неотёсанный **3** (ill-made): ~ paintings аляповáтые картины
cruel /'kru:əl/ *adj.* (**crueller, cruellest** *or* **crueler, cruelest**) жестóкий
cruelty /'kru:əltɪ/ *n.* жестóкость
cruise /kru:z/ *n.* (pleasure voyage) морскóе путешéствие, круúз
● *v.i.* (sail or drive about) курсúровать (*impf.*); (go on cruise(s)) совершáть (*impf.*) круúз(ы)
■ ~ **missile** *n.* крылáтая ракéта
cruiser /'kru:zə(r)/ *n.* (warship) крéйсер; **cabin** ~ прогýлочный кáтер с каютой
crumb /krʌm/ *n.* крóшка
crumble /'krʌmb(ə)l/ *v.t.* (bread etc.) крошúть, рас-
● *v.i.* крошúться (*impf.*); (of a wall) обвáл|иваться, -úться; (fig., of hopes etc.) рýшиться (*impf., pf.*)
crumpet /'krʌmpɪt/ *n.* ≈ сдóбная лепёшка
crumple /'krʌmp(ə)l/ *v.t.* мять, с-/из-; ~ up a sheet of paper скóмкать (*pf.*) лист бумáги
crunch /krʌntʃ/ *v.t. & i.* грызть (*impf.*) с хрýстом
crusade /kru:'seɪd/ *n.* (lit., fig.) крестóвый похóд
crusader /kru:'seɪdə(r)/ *n.* крестонóсец; (fig.) борéц

crush /krʌʃ/ *n.* **1** (crowd) дáвка **2** (infatuation): she has a ~ on him онá без умá от негó
● *v.t.* **1** (squash) раздáв|ливать, -úть **2** (crumple) мять, из-/с- **3** (defeat) сокруш|áть, -úть; our hopes were ~ed нáши надéжды рýхнули; a ~ing defeat пóлное поражéние, разгрóм
crust /krʌst/ *n.* (of bread) кóрка; (of pastry) кóрочка; the earth's ~ земнáя корá
crustacean /krʌ'steɪʃ(ə)n/ *n.* ракообрáзное
crutch /krʌtʃ/ *n.* костыль (*m.*)
crux /krʌks/ *n.* (*pl.* ~**es** *or* **cruces** /'kru:si:z/) суть
⚘ **cry** /kraɪ/ *n.* крик
● *v.i.* **1** (weep) плáкать (*impf.*) **2** (shout) кричáть (*impf.*)
□ ~ **off** *v.t. & i.* (an engagement) отмен|ять, -úть (свидáние)
□ ~ **out** (in pain or distress) вскрúк|ивать, -нуть
crypt /krɪpt/ *n.* склеп
cryptic /'krɪptɪk/ *adj.* таúнственный, загáдочный
crystal /'krɪst(ə)l/ *n.* **1** (substance) гóрный хрустáль **2** (glassware) хрустáль (*m.*)
■ ~ **ball** *n.* магúческий кристáлл; ~ **clear** *adj.* (fig.) ясный как бóжий день
crystallize /'krɪstəlaɪz/ *v.t.* **1** (form into crystals) кристаллизовáть (*impf., pf.*), за- (*pf.*) **2** (clarify) вопло|щáть, -тúть в определённую фóрму **3**: ~d fruit засáхаренные фрýкты
● *v.i.* **1** (form into crystals) кристаллизовáться (*impf., pf.*); вы- (*pf.*) **2**: our plans ~d нáши плáны определúлись
CT *abbr.* (*of* **computerized tomography**) (med.) компьютерная томогрáфия; ~ **scan** исслéдование с пóмощью компьютерной томогрáфии
cub /kʌb/ *n.* детёныш
Cuba /'kju:bə/ *n.* Кýба; **in** ~ на Кýбе
Cuban /'kju:bən/ *n.* кубúн|ец (-ка)
● *adj.* кубúнский
cube /kju:b/ *n.* **1** (math.) куб **2** (solid) кýбик
● *v.t.* (cut into ~s) нар|езáть, -éзать кýбиками
cubic /'kju:bɪk/ *adj.* кубúческий
cubicle /'kju:bɪk(ə)l/ *n.* (at a swimming pool; in a toilet) кабúнка; (in a shop) примéрочная
cubism /'kju:bɪz(ə)m/ *n.* кубúзм
cubist /'kju:bɪst/ *n.* кубúст (-ка)
cuckoo /'kʊku:/ *n.* кукýшка
cucumber /'kju:kʌmbə(r)/ *n.* огурéц
cuddle /'kʌd(ə)l/ *v.t.* обнимáть
● *v.i.* обнимáться
cue[1] /kju:/ *n.* (theatr.) рéплика
cue[2] /kju:/ *n.* (sport) кий
cuff /kʌf/ *n.* **1** (part of sleeve) манжéта; **off the** ~ (fig.) экспрóмтом **2** (AmE, trouser turn-up) отворóт
■ ~**links** *n. pl.* зáпонки (*f. pl.*)
cuisine /kwɪ'zi:n/ *n.* (национáльная) кýхня
cul-de-sac /'kʌldəsæk/ *n.* (also fig.) тупúк
culinary /'kʌlɪnərɪ/ *adj.* кулинáрный
cull /kʌl/ *n.* (of wild animals) отстрéл
● *v.t.* **1** (slaughter) бить (*impf.*) **2** (select) от|бирáть, -обрáть; под|бирáть, -обрáть

culminate /'kʌlmɪneɪt/ v.i.: ~ in завершш|а́ться, -и́ться + i.

culpable /'kʌlpəb(ə)l/ adj. вино́вный

culprit /'kʌlprɪt/ n. престу́пник

cult /kʌlt/ n. культ

cultivate /'kʌltɪveɪt/ v.t. (land) возде́л|ывать, -ать; (crops) культиви́ровать (impf.)

cultivator /'kʌltɪveɪtə(r)/ n. (person) земледе́лец; (implement) культива́тор

✧ **cultural** /'kʌltʃər(ə)l/ adj. культу́рный

✧ **culture** /'kʌltʃə(r)/ n. (civilization) культу́ра, быт

cultured /'kʌltʃəd/ adj. (of person) интеллиге́нтный, культу́рный

cumbersome /'kʌmbəsəm/ adj. громо́здкий, обремени́тельный

cumin /'kjuːmɪn/ n. тмин

cumulative /'kjuːmjʊlətɪv/ adj. кумуляти́вный

cunning /'kʌnɪŋ/ n. хи́трость
● adj. (**cunninger, cunningest**) хи́трый

cunt /kʌnt/ n. (vulg., genitals) пизда́ (vulg.); (as term of abuse) су́ка

cup /kʌp/ n. **1** ча́шка, (liter.) ча́ша **2** (as prize) ку́бок
● v.t. (**cupped, cupping**): ~ one's hand держа́ть (impf.) ру́ку го́рстью

cupboard /'kʌbəd/ n. шкаф, буфе́т

cupola /'kjuːpələ/ n. ку́пол

curable /'kjʊərəb(ə)l/ adj. излечи́мый

curate /'kjʊərət/ n. вика́рий

curator /kjʊə'reɪtə(r)/ n. (of museum etc.) храни́тель (m.)

curb /kə:b/ n. **1** узда́ **2** = **kerb**
● v.t. (fig.) обу́зд|ывать, -а́ть

curd /kə:d/ n. творо́г
■ ~ **cheese** n. (BrE) творо́г

curdle /'kə:d(ə)l/ v.i. свёр|тываться, -ну́ться

cure /'kjʊə(r)/ n. (medicine, remedy) лека́рство, сре́дство; (treatment) лече́ние
● v.t. **1** (a person) выле́чивать, вы́лечить; he was ~d of asthma он вы́лечился от а́стмы **2** (a disease) выле́чивать, вы́лечить **3** (meat) соли́ть, по-; вя́лить, про-

curfew /'kə:fjuː/ n. коменда́нтский час

curiosity /kjʊəri'ɒsɪtɪ/ n. любопы́тство, любозна́тельность

curious /'kjʊəriəs/ adj. **1** (inquisitive) любопы́тный, любозна́тельный **2** (odd) стра́нный; ~ly enough как ни стра́нно

curl /kə:l/ n. (of hair) ло́кон, завито́к
● v.t.: ~ one's hair зав|ива́ть, -и́ть во́лосы
● v.i.: her hair ~s naturally у неё во́лосы вьются от приро́ды; the dog ~ed up by the fire соба́ка сверну́лась клубко́м у ками́на

curlers /'kə:ləz/ n. pl. бигуди́ (nt. pl., indecl.)

curly /'kə:lɪ/ adj. (**curlier, curliest**) кудря́вый

currant /'kʌrənt/ n. изю́м, кори́нка

currency /'kʌrənsɪ/ n. валю́та; де́ньги (-ег)

✧ **current** /'kʌrənt/ n. **1** (of air, water) струя́, пото́к

2 (elec.) ток
● adj. теку́щий; the ~ issue of a magazine теку́щий/очередно́й но́мер журна́ла
■ ~ **account** n. (BrE, comm.) теку́щий счёт; теку́щие собы́тия; ~ **affairs** (also ~ **events**) n. pl. теку́щие собы́тия

✧ **currently** /'kʌrəntlɪ/ adv. тепе́рь, в настоя́щее вре́мя

curriculum /kə'rɪkjʊləm/ n. (pl. ~a) курс обуче́ния
■ ~um vitae n. (кра́ткая) биогра́фия

curry¹ /'kʌrɪ/ n. (cul.) ка́рри (nt. indecl.)

curry² /'kʌrɪ/ v.t.: ~ favour with sb подли́з|ываться, -а́ться к кому́-н.

curse /kə:s/ n. **1** (execration) прокля́тие **2** (bane) прокля́тие, бич **3** (oath) богоху́льство
● v.t. **1** (pronounce ~ on) прокл|ина́ть, -я́сть **2** (abuse, scold) руга́ть (impf.) **3**: he is ~d with a violent temper Госпо́дь награди́л его́ необу́зданным нра́вом
● v.i. (swear, utter ~s) руга́ться (impf.)

cursor /'kə:sə(r)/ n. (comput.) курсо́р

cursory /'kə:sərɪ/ adj. бе́глый, пове́рхностный

curt /kə:t/ adj. отры́вистый, ре́зкий

curtail /kə:'teɪl/ v.t. сокра|ща́ть, -ти́ть

curtain /'kə:t(ə)n/ n. занаве́ска, што́ра

curtsy, curtsey /'kə:tsɪ/ n. реве́ранс, приседа́ние
● v.i. прис|еда́ть, -е́сть

curve /kə:v/ n. (line) крива́я; (bend in road) изги́б
● v.t. сгиба́ть, согну́ть
● v.i. из|гиба́ться, -огну́ться; the road ~s доро́га извива́ется

cushion /'kʊʃ(ə)n/ n. (дива́нная) поду́шка
● v.t.: ~ a blow смягч|а́ть, -и́ть уда́р

cushy /'kʊʃɪ/ adj. (**cushier, cushiest**) (infml): ~ job непы́льная рабо́та

cusp /kʌsp/ n. **1** (of moon) рог; (of leaf) о́стрый коне́ц; (of tooth) ко́нчик **2** (beginning) поро́г

custard /'kʌstəd/ n. сла́дкий крем/со́ус из яи́ц и молока́

custodian /kʌ'stəʊdɪən/ n. (of property etc.) администра́тор; (of museum etc.) храни́тель (m.)

custody /'kʌstədɪ/ n. **1** (guardianship) опе́ка, попече́ние **2** (arrest): take, give into ~ брать, взять под стра́жу

custom /'kʌstəm/ n. **1** (habit) обы́чай **2** (BrE, clientele) клиенту́ра **3** (in pl.) (establishment) тамо́жня; (in pl.) (duties) тамо́женные по́шлины (f. pl.)
■ ~-made adj. сде́ланный/изгото́вленный на зака́з; ~s officer n. тамо́женник

customary /'kʌstəmərɪ/ adj. обы́чный, привы́чный

✧ **customer** /'kʌstəmə(r)/ n. (purchaser) покупа́тель (m.)

customize /'kʌstəmaɪz/ v.t. под|гоня́ть, -огна́ть в соотве́тствии с тре́бованиями зака́зчика; изгот|а́вливать, -о́вить по индивидуа́льному зака́зу

✧ **cut** /kʌt/ n. **1** (act of ~ting) ре́зка; (in finger) поре́з; (slit) разре́з **2** (reduction) сниже́ние

✧ ключева́я ле́ксика

cute | Czech

3 (omission) купю́ра
● *v.t.* (**cutting**, *past and p.p.* **cut**) **1** (divide, separate, wound, extract by ~ting) ре́зать (*impf.*); разр|еза́ть, -еза́ть; отр|еза́ть, -еза́ть; he ~ himself on the tin он поре́зался/пора́нился о консе́рвную ба́нку; ~ sth in two разр|еза́ть, -еза́ть что-н. попола́м **2** (make by ~ting): ~ me a piece of cake отре́жьте мне кусо́к то́рта; ~ a key выта́чивать, вы́точить ключ; ~ a jewel грани́ть, о-, драгоце́нный ка́мень **3** (trim) подстр|ига́ть, -и́чь; ~ one's nails подстр|ига́ть, -и́чь но́гти; have one's hair ~ стри́чься, по- **4** (reduce) сн|ижа́ть, -и́зить **5**: the baby ~ a tooth у ребёнка проре́зался зуб
● *v.i.* (**cutting**, *past and p.p.* **cut**) **1** (make incision) ре́зать (*impf.*); this knife doesn't ~ э́тот нож не ре́жет **2** (in pass. sense) ре́заться (*impf.*); sandstone ~s easily песча́ник легко́ ре́жется **3** (run, take short ~): we ~ across the fields мы прошли́ кратча́йшим путём, напряму́ю че́рез поля́
▫ ~ **back** *v.t.* (prune) подр|еза́ть, -еза́ть; (fig., reduce, limit) сокра|ща́ть, -ти́ть
▫ ~ **down** *v.t.* (e.g. a tree) руби́ть, с-; ~ down expenses сокра|ща́ть, -ти́ть расхо́ды
▫ ~ **off** *v.t.*: she ~ the chicken's head off она́ отруби́ла цыплёнку го́лову; I was ~ off while talking меня́ разъедини́ли/прерва́ли во вре́мя разгово́ра; they ~ off our electricity у нас отключи́ли/вы́ключили электри́чество; we were ~ off by the tide прили́в отре́зал нас от су́ши; he ~ himself off from the world он отгороди́лся от ми́ра
▫ ~ **out** *v.t.*: she ~ out a picture from the paper она́ вы́резала карти́нку из газе́ты; ~ out smoking бро́сить (*pf.*) кури́ть
▫ ~ **up** *v.t.*: he ~ up his meat он наре́зал мя́со
■ ~ **and paste** *v.t.* (comput.) вы́резать и вста́вить; ~**back** *n.* (reduction) сокраще́ние; ~ **glass** *n.* гранёное стекло́; хруста́ль (*m.*); ~**-price** *adj.* продава́емый по сни́женной цене́; ~**-rate** (AmE) = cut-price; ~**-throat** *n.* головоре́з; (*attr.*) ~**-throat competition** ожесточённая/беспоща́дная конкуре́нция
cute /kjuːt/ *adj.* симпати́чный, ми́лый
cutlery /ˈkʌtləri/ *n.* столо́вые прибо́ры
cutlet /ˈkʌtlɪt/ *n.* отбивна́я котле́та
cutting /ˈkʌtɪŋ/ *n.* **1** (BrE, press ~) вы́резка **2** (of plant) отро́сток
● *adj.*: a ~ retort язви́тельный/ре́зкий отве́т; the ~ edge of technology са́мая совреме́нная

те́хника
C.V. *abbr.* (*of* **curriculum vitae**) (кра́ткая) автобиогра́фия
cyanide /ˈsaɪənaɪd/ *n.* циани́д
cyberattack /ˈsaɪbərətæk/ *n.* кибератáка
cyberbullying /ˈsaɪbəbʊlɪŋ/ *n.* киберзапу́гивание (*использование информационных технологий, чтобы запугивать или унижать других*)
cybercafe /ˈsaɪbəkæfeɪ/ *n.* интерне́т-кафе́
cybercrime /ˈsaɪbəkraɪm/ *n.* **1** (offence) киберпреступле́ние **2** (collect.) киберпресту́пность
cybernetics /saɪbəˈnetɪks/ *n.* киберне́тика
cyberspace /ˈsaɪbəspeɪs/ *n.* киберпростра́нство
cyclamen /ˈsɪkləmən/ *n.* (*pl.* ~ *or* ~s) цикламе́н
✍ **cycle** /ˈsaɪk(ə)l/ *n.* **1** (series, rotation) цикл, круг **2** (bicycle) велосипе́д
● *v.i.* е́здить (*indet.*) на велосипе́де
■ ~ **lane** *n.* (BrE) велосипе́дная доро́жка
cyclic /ˈsɪklɪk/, **cyclical** /ˈsɪklɪk(ə)l/ *adjs.* цикли́ческий
cycling /ˈsaɪklɪŋ/ *n.* езда́ на велосипе́де
cyclist /ˈsaɪklɪst/ *n.* велосипеди́ст
cyclone /ˈsaɪkləʊn/ *n.* цикло́н
cygnet /ˈsɪɡnɪt/ *n.* молодо́й ле́бедь
cylinder /ˈsɪlɪndə(r)/ *n.* цили́ндр
cylindrical /sɪˈlɪndrɪk(ə)l/ *adj.* цилиндри́ческий
cymbal /ˈsɪmb(ə)l/ *n.* таре́лка (*музыкальный инструмент*)
cynic /ˈsɪnɪk/ *n.* ци́ник
cynical /ˈsɪnɪk(ə)l/ *adj.* цини́чный
cynicism /ˈsɪnɪsɪz(ə)m/ *n.* цини́зм
cypress /ˈsaɪprəs/ *n.* кипари́с
Cypriot /ˈsɪprɪət/ *n.* киприо́т (-ка)
● *adj.* ки́прский
Cyprus /ˈsaɪprəs/ *n.* Кипр
Cyrillic /sɪˈrɪlɪk/ *adj.* кири́ллический
■ ~ **alphabet** *n.* кири́ллица
cyst /sɪst/ *n.* киста́
cystitis /sɪˈstaɪtɪs/ *n.* цисти́т
cytology /saɪˈtɒlədʒɪ/ *n.* цитоло́гия
czar /zɑː(r)/ *n.* = **tsar**
Czech /tʃek/ *n.* чех (че́шка); (language) че́шский язы́к
● *adj.* че́шский; ~ **Republic** Че́хия

Dd

d

D /diː/ *n.* **1** (mus.) ре (*nt. indecl.*) **2** (academic mark) «неудовлетвори́тельно», дво́йка
■ ~-**Day** *n.* день (*m.*) нача́ла вое́нной опера́ции, день «Д»

dab /dæb/ *n.* (small quantity) мазо́к
• *v.t. & i.* (**dabbed**, **dabbing**) прикла́дывать, -ложи́ть; she ~bed (at) her eyes with a handkerchief она́ прикла́дывала к глаза́м плато́к

dabble /'dæb(ə)l/ *v.i.*: he ~s in politics он игра́ет в поли́тику

dacha /'dætʃə/ *n.* да́ча

dachshund /'dækshʊnd/ *n.* та́кса (*порода собак*)

dad /dæd/, **daddy** /'dædɪ/ *nn.* (infml) па́па (*m.*), па́почка (*m.*)

daddy /'dædɪ/ *n.* = dad

daffodil /'dæfədɪl/ *n.* нарци́сс жёлтый

daft /dɑːft/ *adj.* (BrE, person) тро́нутый (infml); (action) бестолко́вый, глу́пый

Dagestan /dægɪ'stɑːn/ *n.* Дагеста́н

Dagestani /dægɪ'stɑːnɪ/ *n.* (*pl.* ~**s**) дагеста́н|ец (-ка)
• *adj.* дагеста́нский

dagger /'dægə(r)/ *n.* кинжа́л; she looked ~s at him она́ пронзи́ла его́ взгля́дом

dahlia /'deɪlɪə/ *n.* георги́н

✍ **daily** /'deɪlɪ/ *n.* (newspaper) ежедне́вная газе́та
• *adj.* ежедне́вный
• *adv.* ежедне́вно, ка́ждый день

dainty /'deɪntɪ/ *n.* ла́комство, деликате́с
• *adj.* (**daintier**, **daintiest**) изя́щный, изы́сканный

dairy /'deərɪ/ *n.* **1** (room or building) маслоде́льня **2** (shop) моло́чный магази́н; (*attr.*) моло́чный

daisy /'deɪzɪ/ *n.* маргари́тка

dally /'dælɪ/ *v.i.* **1** (play, toy) балова́ться (*impf.*) (with: + *i.*) **2** (flirt) флиртова́ть (*impf.*) **3** (waste time) тра́тить (*impf.*) вре́мя по́пусту

Dalmatian /dæl'meɪʃ(ə)n/ *n.* (dog) далма́тский дог, далмати́н

dam /dæm/ *n.* да́мба, плоти́на, запру́да

✍ **damage** /'dæmɪdʒ/ *n.* **1** (harm, injury) вред, поврежде́ние **2** (*in pl.*) (law) убы́тк|и (-ов)
• *v.t.* (physically) повре|жда́ть, -ди́ть + *d.*; (morally) вреди́ть, на-, причин|я́ть, -и́ть вред + *d.*

dame /deɪm/ *n.* **1** (female equivalent of knight) дейм, кавале́рственная да́ма **2** (AmE, infml, woman) ба́бёнка (infml)

damn /dæm/ *n.* (negligible amount): I don't care a ~ мне наплева́ть
• *v.t.* **1** (doom to hell) прокл|ина́ть, -я́сть

✍ ключева́я ле́ксика

2 (as expletive): ~ (it all)! чёрт возьми́!

damned /dæmd/ *n.*, *adj.*, & *adv.*: a ~ fool по́лный дура́к; it's a ~ nuisance (э́то) черто́вски доса́дно

damp /dæmp/ *n.* вла́жность, сы́рость
• *adj.* вла́жный, сыро́й
• *v.t.* (*also* **dampen**) **1** (lit.) сма́|чивать, -очи́ть; увлажн|я́ть, -и́ть **2** (fig.): ~ sb's ardour осту|жа́ть, -ди́ть чей-н. пыл

✍ **dance** /dɑːns/ *n.* **1** та́нец **2** (party) танцева́льный ве́чер; та́нцы (*m. pl.*)
• *v.t.* танцева́ть, с-
• *v.i.* танцева́ть, с-; пляса́ть, с-

dancer /'dɑːnsə(r)/ *n.* (professional) танцо́р, танцо́вщи|к (-ца); (non-professional): she's a good ~ она́ хорошо́ танцу́ет

dancing /'dɑːnsɪŋ/ *n.* та́нцы (*m. pl.*)

dandelion /'dændɪlaɪən/ *n.* одува́нчик

dandruff /'dændrʌf/ *n.* пе́рхоть

dandy /'dændɪ/ *n.* щёголь (*m.*), франт
• *adj.* (**dandier**, **dandiest**) (AmE, infml) превосхо́дный; пе́рвый класс (*pred.*)

Dane /deɪn/ *n.* датча́н|ин (-ка)

✍ **danger** /'deɪndʒə(r)/ *n.* опа́сность; in ~ в опа́сности; he is in ~ of falling он риску́ет упа́сть

✍ **dangerous** /'deɪndʒərəs/ *adj.* опа́сный, риско́ванный

dangle /'dæŋɡ(ə)l/ *v.t.* болта́ть (*impf.*) + *i.*
• *v.i.* болта́ться (*impf.*)

Danish /'deɪnɪʃ/ *n.* (language) да́тский язы́к
• *adj.* да́тский

dank /dæŋk/ *adj.* вла́жный, сыро́й

dapper /'dæpə(r)/ *adj.* щеголева́тый

dare /deə(r)/ *n.* вы́зов
• *v.t.* бр|оса́ть, -о́сить вы́зов + *d.*; I ~ you to jump over the wall! а ну, перепры́гни че́рез э́ту сте́ну!
• *v.i.* **1** (have courage) осме́ли|ваться, -ться **2** (have impudence) сметь, по- **3**: I ~ say (that) … на́до ду́мать (*or* полага́ю), что…
■ ~**devil** *adj.* отча́янный, бесшаба́шный

daring /'deərɪŋ/ *adj.* отва́жный, де́рзкий

✍ **dark** /dɑːk/ *n.* темнота́, тьма; before/after ~ до/по́сле наступле́ния темноты́; (ignorance): I am in the ~ as to his plans я в неве́дении относи́тельно его́ пла́нов
• *adj.* **1** (lacking light) тёмный **2** (in colour) тёмный; тёмного цве́та; (with names of colours) тёмно- **3** (of complexion) сму́глый **4** (fig.) тёмный, покры́тый мра́ком
■ ~ **blue** *n.* тёмно-си́ний; ~ **glasses** *n. pl.* (spectacles) тёмные/со́лнечные очки́; ~ **green** *n.* тёмно-зелёный; ~-**haired** *adj.* темноволо́сый; ~-**skinned** *adj.* темноко́жий

darken /'dɑ:kən/ *v.t.* затемн|я́ть, -и́ть
● *v.i.* темне́ть, по-

darkness /'dɑ:knɪs/ *n.* темнота́

darling /'dɑ:lɪŋ/ *n.* дорого́й, родно́й, люби́мый; **she's a ~** она́ пре́лесть

darn /dɑ:n/ *v.t. & i.* (mend) што́пать, за-

dart /dɑ:t/ *n.* стрела́, дро́тик
■ **~board** *n.* мише́нь для стрел

dash /dæʃ/ *n.* **1** (sudden rush, race) рыво́к, бросо́к; **let's make a ~ for it** дава́й(те) побежи́м туда́ **2** (admixture): **a ~ of pepper** щепо́тка пе́рца **3** (written stroke) тире́ (*nt. indecl.*)
● *v.t.* **1** (hurl) швыр|я́ть, -ну́ть; **the ship was ~ed against the rocks** су́дно вы́бросило на ска́лы **2** (perform rapidly): **he ~ed off a sketch** он сде́лал набро́сок **3** (fig., disappoint) разр|уша́ть, -у́шить; **his hopes were ~ed** его́ наде́жды ру́хнули
● *v.i.* (rush) мча́ться (*impf.*); **she ~ed into the shop** она́ ворвала́сь в магази́н; **he ~ed off to town** он умча́лся в го́род

dashboard /'dæʃbɔ:d/ *n.* прибо́рная пане́ль/ доска́

dashing /'dæʃɪŋ/ *adj.* сти́льный

✧ **data** /'deɪtə/ *n.* (*with sg. or pl. v.*) да́нные (*nt. pl.*); **~ capture** сбор да́нных; **~ processing** обрабо́тка информа́ции

database /'deɪtəbeɪs/ *n.* ба́за да́нных

date¹ /deɪt/ *n.* (fruit) фи́ник

✧ **date²** /deɪt/ *n.* **1** (indication of time) да́та, число́; **what's the ~ today?** како́е сего́дня число́? **2** (period) пери́од; **at an early ~** (soon) в ближа́йшем бу́дущем; **out of ~** устаре́лый; **up to ~** нове́йший, совреме́нный **3** (appointment) свида́ние
● *v.t.* **1** (indicate ~ on) дати́ровать (*impf., pf.*) **2** (AmE, go out with) встреча́ться (*impf.*) с + *i.*; **dating agency** аге́нтство знако́мств
● *v.i.*: **this church ~s from the 14th century** э́та це́рковь отно́сится к XIV ве́ку

dated /'deɪtɪd/ *adj.* (out of date) устаре́вший, устаре́лый

dative /'deɪtɪv/ *adj. & n.* да́тельный (паде́ж)

✧ **daughter** /'dɔ:tə(r)/ *n.* дочь
■ **~-in-law** *n.* неве́стка, сноха́

daunt /dɔ:nt/ *v.t.* устраш|а́ть, -и́ть; обескура́жи|вать, -ть

dawdle /'dɔ:d(ə)l/ *v.i.* ме́шкать (*impf.*)

dawn /dɔ:n/ *n.* рассве́т, заря́; **at ~** на рассве́те; **на заре́**
● *v.i.* **1** (of daybreak) света́ть (*impf.*) **2** (fig.): **it ~ed on me that...** меня́ осени́ло, что...

✧ **day** /deɪ/ *n.* **1** (time of daylight) день (*m.*); (*attr.*) дневно́й; **twice a ~** два ра́за в день **2** (24 hours) день (*m.*), су́т|ки (-ок); **a ~ and a half** полтора́ дня **3** (as point of time): **what ~ (of the week) is it?** како́й сего́дня день (неде́ли)?; **one ~** (past) одна́жды; (future) когда́-нибудь; **every other ~** че́рез день; **some ~** когда́-нибудь; **~ in, ~ out; ~ after ~** изо дня в день; **(on) the ~ I met you** в день на́шей встре́чи; **(on) the ~ before** накану́не (*чего*); **I took a ~ off** я взял выходно́й; **we**

had a ~ out (BrE) мы провели́ день вне до́ма **4** (as work period): **he works a 5-hour ~** у него́ пятичасово́й рабо́чий день **5** (period) пора́, вре́мя (*nt.*); **these ~s** (nowadays) тепе́рь, в на́ши дни; **in those ~s** в те дни; в то вре́мя **6** (denoting contest): **his arrival saved the ~** его́ прие́зд спас положе́ние
■ **~break** *n.* рассве́т; **~care** *adj.*: **~-care facilities** (for children) детса́д; (for babies, toddlers) я́сл|и (-ей); **~dream** *n.* грёза, мечта́ ● *v.i.* мечта́ть (*impf.*); **~light** *n.* (period): **in broad ~light** средь бе́ла дня; **~ nursery** *n.* (crèche) де́тские я́сл|и (-ей); **~time** *n.* день (*m.*); **in the ~time** днём; (*attr.*) дневно́й; **~-to-~** *adj.* повседне́вный

daze /deɪz/ *n.*: **he was in a ~** он был поражён/ как в тума́не
● *v.t.* пора|жа́ть, -зи́ть

dazzle /'dæz(ə)l/ *v.t.* **1** (lit.) ослеп|ля́ть, -и́ть **2** (fig.) пора|жа́ть, -зи́ть

dB *abbr.* (*of* decibel(s)) дБ (дециве́л)

DC *abbr.* (*of* direct current) постоя́нный ток

deacon /'di:kən/ *n.* дья́кон

✧ **dead** /ded/ *n.*: **at ~ of night** глубо́кой но́чью
● *adj.* **1** (no longer living) мёртвый, уме́рший; (in accident etc.) поги́бший, уби́тый; (of animal) до́хлый; **~ body** труп, мёртвое те́ло; **~ flowers/leaves** увя́дшие цветы́/ли́стья; **he is ~** он у́мер; (killed) он уби́т; (*as n.*) **the ~** уме́ршие, поко́йные **2** (inert): **~ end** (lit., fig.) тупи́к; **a ~-end job** бесперспекти́вная рабо́та **3** (spent, uncharged): **the telephone went ~** телефо́н отключи́лся **4** (abrupt, exact, complete) внеза́пный; **a ~ certainty** по́лная уве́ренность
● *adv.*: **he stopped ~** он останови́лся как вко́панный; **~ on time** мину́та в мину́ту; **~ tired** сме́ртельно уста́лый; **he is ~ set on going to London** он реши́л пое́хать в Ло́ндон во что бы то ни ста́ло
■ **~line** *n.* преде́льный/кра́йний срок; **~lock** *n.* мёртвая то́чка; тупи́к; **~ loss** *n.* (fig., failure) по́лный прова́л; **he's a ~ loss** он неуда́чник, от него́ то́лку не бу́дет; **~pan** *adj.* (infml) невырази́тельный

deaden /'ded(ə)n/ *v.t.* осл|абля́ть, -а́бить; **the drug ~s pain** лека́рство притупля́ет боль

deadly /'dedlɪ/ *adj.* (**deadlier**, **deadliest**) смерте́льный; **~ enemy** смерте́льный враг

deaf /def/ *adj.* **1** глухо́й; (*as n.*) **the ~** глухи́е **2** (fig.): **turn a ~ ear to** не слу́шать (*impf.*); не обраща́ть (*impf.*) внима́ния на + *a.*
■ **~ aid** *n.* (BrE) слухово́й аппара́т; **~ mute** *n.* (often offens.) глухонемо́й

deafening /'defənɪŋ/ *adj.* оглуши́тельный

✧ **deal** /di:l/ *n.* **1** (amount) коли́чество; **a great, good ~ (of)** мно́го + *g.* **2** (business agreement) сде́лка; **it's a ~!** договори́лись!; по рука́м!
● *v.t.* (*past and p.p.* **dealt**) (cards) сда|ва́ть, -ть
● *v.i.* (*past and p.p.* **dealt**) **1** (do business) торгова́ть (*impf.*); **he ~s in furs** он торгу́ет меха́ми **2**: **~ with** (treat) обраща́ться (*impf.*) с + *i.*; (cope with) справля́ться, спра́виться с + *i.*; **he ~t with the problem skilfully** он

умело подошёл к этому вопросу **3**: ~ **with** (discuss a subject etc.) (of person) занима́ться, -я́ться (*impf.*) + *i.*; (of book) рассма́тривать, -отре́ть

dealer /'di:lə(r)/ *n.* торго́вец, ди́лер

dealing /'di:lɪŋ/ *n.* **1** (trade): ~ **in real estate** торго́вля недви́жимостью **2** (*in pl.*) (association) торго́вые дела́; сде́лки (*f. pl.*)

dealt /delt/ *past and p.p of* ▶ **deal**

dean /di:n/ *n.* (eccl.) дека́н, настоя́тель (*m.*); (academic) дека́н

dear /dɪə(r)/ *n.* ми́лый, дорого́й
● *adj.* **1** (beloved) люби́мый, дорого́й **2** (lovable) сла́вный, ми́лый **3** (in informal letters) дорого́й; (in formal letters) уважа́емый **4** (costly) дорого́й
● *int.*: **oh ~!/~ me!** о, Го́споди!; Бо́же ты мой!

dearly /'dɪəlɪ/ *adv.* (very much) о́чень; (at a high price) до́рого

dearth /dɜ:θ/ *n.* нехва́тка, недоста́ток

death /deθ/ *n.* **1** (act or fact of dying) смерть; **drink oneself to ~** умира́ть, -ере́ть от пья́нства; **work oneself to ~** рабо́тать (*impf.*) на изно́с; **at ~'s door** на поро́ге сме́рти **2** (instance of dying) ги́бель **3** (utmost limit): **he was bored to ~** ему́ бы́ло до́ смерти ску́чно; **I'm sick to ~ of it** мне э́то надое́ло до сме́рти
■ **~bed** *n.* сме́ртное ло́же; ~ **penalty** *n.* сме́ртная казнь; ~ **toll** *n.* число́ поги́бших; ~ **trap** *n.*: **this theatre is a ~ trap in case of fire** в слу́чае пожа́ра э́тот теа́тр су́щая западня́

deathly /'deθlɪ/ *adj. & adv.* (**deathlier**, **deathliest**) смерте́льный; ~ **pale** сме́ртельно бле́дный; ~ **silence** мёртвая тишина́

debar /dɪ'bɑ:(r)/ *v.t.* (**debarred**, **debarring**) препя́тствовать, вос- + *d.*

debarkation /di:bɑ:'keɪʃ(ə)n/ *n.* = disembarkation

debatable /dɪ'beɪtəb(ə)l/ *adj.* спо́рный

debate /dɪ'beɪt/ *n.* диску́ссия; (in parliament) деба́т|ы (-ов)

debauched /dɪ'bɔ:tʃt/ *adj.* (dissolute) распу́тный

debauchery /dɪ'bɔ:tʃərɪ/ *n.* разврат, распу́щенность

debit /'debɪt/ *n.* дебет
● *v.t.* (**debited**, **debiting**) дебетова́ть (*impf., pf.*)
■ ~ **card** *n.* дебето́вая ка́рточка

debonair /debə'neə(r)/ *adj.* обходи́тельный, учти́вый

debrief /di:'bri:f/ *v.t.* расспра́|шивать, -оси́ть; ~ **sb** заслу́ш|ивать, -ать чей-н. отчёт

debris /'debri:/ *n.* оско́лки (*m. pl.*); обло́мки (*m. pl.*)

debt /det/ *n.* долг; **get into ~** входи́ть, войти́ в долги́

debtor /'detə(r)/ *n.* должни́к

debugger /di:'bʌɡə(r)/ *n.* (comput.) програ́мма отла́дки, отла́дчик

debunk /di:'bʌŋk/ *v.t.* (infml) развенч|ивать, -а́ть

debut /'debju:/ *n.* дебю́т

debutante /'debjutɑ:nt/ *n.* (making first appearance in fashionable society) де́вушка, впервы́е выезжа́ющая в свет; (theatr., sport) дебюта́нтка

decade /'dekeɪd/ *n.* десятиле́тие

decadence /'dekəd(ə)ns/ *n.* упа́док, декаде́нтство

decadent /'dekəd(ə)nt/ *adj.* упа́дочный, декаде́нтский

decaffeinated /di:'kæfɪneɪtɪd/ *adj.* без кофеи́на

decant /dɪ'kænt/ *v.t.* (pour wine) сце́|живать, -ди́ть; перел|ива́ть, -и́ть (*из буты́лки в графи́н*)

decanter /dɪ'kæntə(r)/ *n.* графи́н

decapitate /dɪ'kæpɪteɪt/ *v.t.* обезгла́в|ливать, -ить

decay /dɪ'keɪ/ *n.* разложе́ние; **tooth ~** разруше́ние зубо́в
● *v.i.* разл|ага́ться, -ожи́ться

deceased /dɪ'si:st/ *adj.* поко́йный; (*as n.*) **the ~** поко́йник

deceit /dɪ'si:t/ *n.* обма́н, ложь

deceitful /dɪ'si:tfʊl/ *adj.* обма́нчивый, лжи́вый

deceive /dɪ'si:v/ *v.t.* обма́н|ывать, -у́ть; ~ **oneself** обма́н|ываться, -у́ться

December /dɪ'sembə(r)/ *n.* дека́брь (*m.*)

decency /'di:s(ə)nsɪ/ *n.* прили́чие

decent /'di:s(ə)nt/ *adj.* **1** (not obscene) прили́чный, присто́йный **2** (proper, adequate) прили́чный, подходя́щий **3** (honest, moral) поря́дочный **4** (good, satisfactory) хоро́ший, неплохо́й **5** (BrE, infml, kind, generous) до́брый, любе́зный

decentralize /di:'sentrəlaɪz/ *v.t.* децентрализова́ть (*impf., pf.*)

deception /dɪ'sepʃ(ə)n/ *n.* обма́н

deceptive /dɪ'septɪv/ *adj.* обма́нчивый

decibel /'desɪbel/ *n.* дециба́л

decide /dɪ'saɪd/ *v.t.* реш|а́ть, -и́ть; ~ **a question** реш|а́ть, -и́ть вопро́с
● *v.i.* реш|а́ться, -и́ться; ~ **between alternatives** де́лать, с- вы́бор; ~ **on going** реши́ть (*pf.*) пое́хать; ~ **against going** реши́ть (*pf.*) не е́хать

deciduous /dɪ'sɪdjʊəs/ *adj.* ли́ственный, листопа́дный

decimal /'desɪm(ə)l/ *adj.* десяти́чный
■ ~ **point** *n.* запята́я, отделя́ющая це́лое от дро́би (*в стра́нах англи́йского языка́ в чи́слах с десяти́чными дробя́ми вме́сто запято́й испо́льзуется то́чка: 7,1 пи́шется как 7.1*)

decipher /dɪ'saɪfə(r)/ *v.t.* (fig., make out) раз|бира́ть, -обра́ть

decision /dɪ'sɪʒ(ə)n/ *n.* реше́ние; **make, take, come to a ~** прин|има́ть, -я́ть реше́ние

decisive /dɪ'saɪsɪv/ *adj.* реши́тельный

decisiveness /dɪ'saɪsɪvnɪs/ *n.* реши́тельность

deck /dek/ *n.* **1** (of ship) па́луба **2** (AmE, of cards) коло́да
■ ~**chair** *n.* шезло́нг

---

declaim /dɪ'kleɪm/ *v.t. & i.* декламировать (*impf.*)

declaration /deklə'reɪʃ(ə)n/ *n.* декларация

✓ **declare** /dɪ'kleə(r)/ *v.t. & i.* **1** (say solemnly) заявля|ть, -ить; **he ~d that he was innocent** он заявил о своей невиновности **2** (pronounce) объявля|ть, -ить; **l ~ the meeting open** объявляю собрание открытым **3** (at customs) декларировать (*impf., pf.*)

declassify /diː'klæsɪfaɪ/ *v.t.* рассекре́|чивать, -тить (*документы*)

declension /dɪ'klenʃ(ə)n/ *n.* (gram.) склонение

✓ **decline** /dɪ'klaɪn/ *n.* **1** (fall) падение **2** (decay) упадок, закат
● *v.t.* **1** отклон|ять, -ить; **he ~d the invitation** он отклонил приглашение **2** (gram.) склонять, про-
● *v.i.* **1** (sink) падать, упасть; при|ходить, -йти в упадок **2** (refuse) отказ|ываться, -аться

declutter /diː'klʌtə(r)/ *v.t.* (tidy up) убира́ть, убра́ть, приводить, привести в порядок (*комнату, рабочее пространство, и т. п.*)

decode /diː'kəʊd/ *v.t.* расшифро́в|ывать, -ать

decompose /diːkəm'pəʊz/ *v.i.* (decay) разл|ага́ться, -ожи́ться

decontaminate /diːkən'tæmɪneɪt/ *v.t.* обеззара́|живать, -зить; (remove radioactivity from) дезактиви́ровать (*impf., pf.*)

decor /'deɪkɔː(r)/ *n.* (of room) убра́нство; (of stage) декора́ции (*f. pl.*)

decorate /'dekəreɪt/ *v.t.* **1** (adorn) укр|аша́ть, -а́сить (*impf.*) **2** (paint, furnish, etc.) отде́л|ывать, -ать

decoration /dekə'reɪʃ(ə)n/ *n.* украше́ние, убра́нство

decorative /'dekərətɪv/ *adj.* декорати́вный

decorator /'dekəreɪtə(r)/ *n.* (painter) маля́р; (paperer) окле́йщик обо́ев

decorum /dɪ'kɔː rəm/ *n.* вне́шнее прили́чие; этике́т, деко́рум

decoy /'diː kɔɪ/ *n.* прима́нка
● *v.t.* прима́н|ивать, -и́ть

decrease *n.* /'diː kriː s/ уменьше́ние, убыва́ние
● *v.i.* /dɪ'kriː s/ ум|еньша́ться, -е́ньшиться; убыва́ть, -ы́ть

decree /dɪ'kriː/ *n.* **1** (pol.) указ **2** (law) суде́бное реше́ние

decrepit /dɪ'krepɪt/ *adj.* дря́хлый, ве́тхий

dedicate /'dedɪkeɪt/ *v.t.* **1** (devote) посвя|ща́ть, -ти́ть (*что-н. кому-н.*); (assign) предназн|ача́ть, -а́чить (*что-н. кому-н.*)

dedicated /'dedɪkeɪtɪd/ *adj.* пре́данный, беззаве́тный

dedication /dedɪ'keɪʃ(ə)n/ *n.* (devotion) пре́данность, самоотве́рженность; (inscription) посвяще́ние

deduce /dɪ'djuː s/ *v.t.* выводи́ть, вы́вести; заключ|а́ть, -и́ть

deduct /dɪ'dʌkt/ *v.t.* вычита́ть, вы́честь

deduction /dɪ'dʌkʃ(ə)n/ *n.* (subtraction) вы́чет; (inference) вы́вод, заключе́ние

deed /diː d/ *n.* **1** (sth done) де́йствие, посту́пок **2** (law) акт, докуме́нт

deem /diː m/ *v.t.* полага́ть (*impf.*), счита́ть, счесть

✓ **deep** /diː p/ *adj.* **1** глубо́кий **2** (with measurement): **a hole 6 feet ~** я́ма глубино́й в 6 фу́тов **3** (submerged, lit., fig.): **~ in thought** заду́мавшийся; погружённый в разду́мья **4** (extreme) глубо́кий **5** (of colour) тёмный, насы́щенный **6** (low-pitched) ни́зкий
● *adv.* глубо́ко
■ **~-freeze** *n.* морози́льник; **~-frozen** *adj.* заморо́женный; **~-fry** *v.t.* зажа́ри|вать, -ть; **~-rooted** *adj.*: **~-rooted belief** глубоко́ укорени́вшееся мне́ние; **~-sea** *adj.*: **~-sea fishing** глубоково́дный лов; **~-vein thrombosis** *n.* (med.) тромбо́з глубо́ких вен

deepen /'diː pən/ *v.t. & i.* **1** (make, become deeper) углуб|ля́ть(ся), -и́ть(ся) **2** (intensify) усили|вать(ся), -ть(ся) **3** (make, become lower in pitch) пон|ижа́ть(ся), -и́зить(ся)

✓ **deeply** /'diː plɪ/ *adv.* глубо́ко; **he is ~ in debt** он влез в долги́ по́ уши

deer /dɪə(r)/ *n.* (*pl.* ~) оле́нь (*m.*)

deface /dɪ'feɪs/ *v.t.* иска|жа́ть, -зи́ть

defamatory /dɪ'fæmətərɪ/ *adj.* клеветни́ческий

default *n.* /dɪ'fɔː lt, 'diː fɔː lt/ **1** (neglect): **he won the match by ~** он вы́играл матч из-за нея́вки проти́вника **2** (comput.) значе́ние по умолча́нию; **~ font** шрифт по умолча́нию **3** (fin.) дефо́лт
● *v.i.* /dɪ'fɔː lt/ не выполня́ть, вы́полнить обяза́тельства

✓ **defeat** /dɪ'fiː t/ *n.* пораже́ние
● *v.t.* нан|оси́ть, -ести́ пораже́ние + *d.*; **they were ~ed** они́ потерпе́ли пораже́ние

defeatism /dɪ'fiː tɪz(ə)m/ *n.* пораже́нчество

defeatist /dɪ'fiː tɪst/ *n.* пессими́ст
● *adj.* пораже́нческий, пессимисти́ческий

defecate /'defɪkeɪt/ *v.i.* испражн|я́ться, -и́ться

defect¹ /'diː fekt/ *n.* дефе́кт; поро́к

defect² /dɪ'fekt/ *v.i.* перебе|га́ть, -жа́ть (**from:** от + *g.*) (**to:** к + *d.*, на + *a.*)

defection /dɪ'fekʃ(ə)n/ *n.* дезерти́рство; **there were several ~s from the party** не́сколько челове́к вы́шло/вы́шли из па́ртии

defective /dɪ'fektɪv/ *adj.* несоверше́нный

defector /dɪ'fektə(r)/ *n.* перебе́жчи|к (-ца)

✓ **defence** /dɪ'fens/ (AmE **defense**) *n.* оборо́на, защи́та; **in ~ of** в защи́ту + *g.*

defenceless /dɪ'fenslɪs/ (AmE **defenseless**) *adj.* беззащи́тный

✓ **defend** /dɪ'fend/ *v.t.* обороня́ть (*impf.*)

defendant /dɪ'fend(ə)nt/ *n.* отве́тчик

defender /dɪ'fendə(r)/ *n.* защи́тник

defense /dɪ'fens/ *n.* (AmE) = **defence**

defenseless /dɪ'fenslɪs/ *adj.* (AmE) = **defenceless**

defensive /dɪ'fensɪv/ *adj.* оборони́тельный; **he has a ~ manner** он как бу́дто опра́вдывается

defer¹ /dɪ'fɜː(r)/ *v.t.* (**deferred**, **deferring**) (postpone) отсро́чи|вать, -ть

defer² /dɪ'fɜː(r)/ *v.i.* (**deferred**, **deferring**): **~ to** счита́ться (*impf.*) с + *i.*

deference /'defərəns/ n. уваже́ние, почти́тельность

deferential /defə'renʃ(ə)l/ adj. почти́тельный

defiance /dɪ'faɪəns/ n. вы́зов; **in ~ of** вопреки́ + d.

defiant /dɪ'faɪənt/ adj. вызыва́ющий

deficiency /dɪ'fɪʃənsɪ/ n. **1** (lack) нехва́тка, отсу́тствие **2** (in pl.) (shortcomings) недоста́тки (m. pl.)

deficient /dɪ'fɪʃ(ə)nt/ adj. недоста́точный, непо́лный

deficit /'defɪsɪt/ n. дефици́т, недочёт

defile /dɪ'faɪl/ v.t. оскверн|я́ть, -и́ть

꙰ **define** /dɪ'faɪn/ v.t. определ|я́ть, -и́ть

definite /'defɪnɪt/ adj. **1** (specific) определённый **2** (clear, exact) то́чный, чёткий ∎ **~ article** n. (gram.) определённый арти́кль

꙰ **definitely** /'defɪnɪtlɪ/ adv. определённо, то́чно; **he is ~ coming** он непреме́нно/то́чно придёт

꙰ **definition** /defɪ'nɪʃ(ə)n/ n. (clearness of outline) я́сность, чёткость; (statement of meaning) определе́ние

definitive /dɪ'fɪnɪtɪv/ adj. оконча́тельный

deflect /dɪ'flekt/ v.t. & i. отклон|я́ть(ся), -и́ть(ся)

deflection /dɪ'flekʃ(ə)n/ n. отклоне́ние

deforestation /di:fɒrɪ'steɪʃ(ə)n/ n. обезле́сение

deform /dɪ'fɔ:m/ v.t. уро́довать, из-

deformity /dɪ'fɔ:mɪtɪ/ n. уро́дливость, уро́дство

defraud /dɪ'frɔ:d/ v.t. обма́н|ывать, -у́ть

defrost /di:'frɒst/ v.t. (food, refrigerator) размор|а́живать, -о́зить

deft /deft/ adj. ло́вкий, иску́сный

defunct /dɪ'fʌŋkt/ adj. несуществу́ющий, исче́знувший

defuse /di:'fju:z/ v.t. сн|има́ть, -я́ть взрыва́тель (m.) + g.; (fig.) разря|жа́ть, -ди́ть

defy /dɪ'faɪ/ v.t. **1** (challenge) вызыва́ть, вы́звать **2** (fig.): **the problem defies solution** пробле́ма неразреши́ма

degenerate adj. /dɪ'dʒenərət/ вы́родившийся, дегенерати́вный
● v.i. /dɪ'dʒenəreɪt/ вырожда́ться, вы́родиться (impf.)

degradation /degrə'deɪʃ(ə)n/ n. (moral) упа́док, деграда́ция

degrade /dɪ'greɪd/ v.t. прин|ижа́ть, -и́зить

degrading /dɪ'greɪdɪŋ/ adj. унизи́тельный

꙰ **degree** /dɪ'gri:/ n. **1** (unit of measurement) гра́дус **2** (step, stage) сте́пень; у́ровень (m.); **by ~s** постепе́нно; **to a ~** до изве́стной сте́пени **3** (academic) (учёная) сте́пень

dehumanize /di:'hju:mənaɪz/ v.t. дегуманизи́ровать (impf., pf.)

dehydrate /di:haɪ'dreɪt/ v.t. обезво́|живать, -дить

de-icer /di:'aɪsə(r)/ n. антиобледени́тель (m.)

deify /'deɪɪfaɪ/ v.t. обожествл|я́ть, -и́ть; боготвори́ть, о-

deign /deɪn/ v.t.: **he did not ~ to answer us** он не соизво́лил отве́тить нам

deity /'deɪtɪ/ n. божество́

dejected /dɪ'dʒektɪd/ adj. удручённый, пода́вленный

꙰ **delay** /dɪ'leɪ/ n. заде́ржка, отсро́чка, промедле́ние; **without ~** неме́дленно
● v.t. от|кла́дывать, -ложи́ть

delegate n. /'delɪgət/ делега́т, представи́тель (m.)
● v.t. /'delɪgeɪt/ **~ sb** делеги́ровать (impf., pf.) кого́-н.; **~ a task** поруч|а́ть, -и́ть рабо́ту (кому)

delegation /delɪ'geɪʃ(ə)n/ n. делега́ция

delete /dɪ'li:t/ v.t. вычёркивать, вы́черкнуть; (comput.) удал|я́ть, -и́ть

Delhi /'delɪ/ n. Де́ли (m. indecl.)

deliberate /dɪ'lɪbərət/ adj. (intentional) наме́ренный; (slow) осмотри́тельный

deliberately /dɪ'lɪbərətlɪ/ adv. наме́ренно

deliberation /dɪlɪbə'reɪʃ(ə)n/ n. (pondering) обду́мывание; (in pl.) диску́ссия; (slowness) медли́тельность, неторопли́вость

delicacy /'delɪkəsɪ/ n. (exquisiteness) утончённость, то́нкость; (proneness to injury) хру́пкость; (critical nature) щекотли́вость, делика́тность

delicate /'delɪkət/ adj. **1** (fine, exquisite) то́нкий **2** (easily injured) хру́пкий **3** (ticklish) щекотли́вый

delicatessen /delɪkə'tes(ə)n/ n. гастроно́м

delicious /dɪ'lɪʃəs/ adj. о́чень вку́сный

delight /dɪ'laɪt/ n. удово́льствие, наслажде́ние; **take ~ in sth** на|ходи́ть, -йти́ удово́льствие в чём-н.
● v.t. дост|авля́ть, -а́вить наслажде́ние + d.; **I am ~ed to accept the invitation** я с ра́достью принима́ю приглаше́ние

delightful /dɪ'laɪtfʊl/ adj. восхити́тельный, очарова́тельный

delineate /dɪ'lɪnɪeɪt/ v.t. (e.g. a frontier) оче́р|чивать, -ти́ть; (e.g. character) изобра|жа́ть, -зи́ть

delinquency /dɪ'lɪŋkwənsɪ/ n. престу́пность

delinquent /dɪ'lɪŋkwənt/ n. правонаруши́тель (-ница)

delirious /dɪ'lɪrɪəs/ adj. в бреду́ (pred.)

delirium /dɪ'lɪrɪəm/ n. бред
∎ **~ tremens** n. /'tri:menz/ бе́лая горя́чка

꙰ **deliver** /dɪ'lɪvə(r)/ v.t. **1** (of birth): **she delivered a child** (assisted at birth) она́ приняла́ ребёнка **2** (give, present): **~ judgement** выноси́ть, вы́нести реше́ние; **~ a speech** произн|оси́ть, -ести́ речь **3** (send out, convey) дост|авля́ть, -а́вить

꙰ **delivery** /dɪ'lɪvərɪ/ n. **1** (childbirth) ро́ды (-ов) **2** (distribution) доста́вка; **charges payable on ~** опла́та при доста́вке

delphinium /del'fɪnɪəm/ n. (pl. ~s) (bot.) дельфи́ниум

delta /'deltə/ n. де́льта

delude /dɪ'lu:d/ v.t. вв|оди́ть, -ести́ в заблужде́ние; **he ~d himself into believing that …** он уве́рил себя́ в том, что…

deluge /'delju:dʒ/ n. **1** (lit.) пото́п **2** (fig.) пото́к

delusion /dɪˈluːʒ(ə)n/ *n.* заблужде́ние

de luxe /də ˈlʌks/ *adj.* роско́шный; a ~ **cabin** каю́та люкс

delve /delv/ *v.i.*: ~ **in(to) one's pockets** ры́ться (*impf.*) в карма́нах

ơ **demand** /dɪˈmɑːnd/ *n.* **1** (claim) тре́бование; **there are many** ~**s on my time** у меня́ мно́го дел **2** (desire to obtain) потре́бность, спро́с; **there is no** ~ **for this article** на э́тот това́р нет спро́са
● *v.t.* тре́бовать, по- + *g. or a.*

demanding /dɪˈmɑːndɪŋ/ *adj.* тре́бовательный

demean /dɪˈmiːn/ *v.t.*: ~ **oneself** роня́ть, урони́ть своё досто́инство

demented /dɪˈmentɪd/ *adj.* сумасше́дший

dementia /dɪˈmenʃə/ *n.* слабоу́мие

demilitarize /diːˈmɪlɪtəraɪz/ *v.t.* демилитаризова́ть (*impf., pf.*)

demise /dɪˈmaɪz/ *n.* кончи́на

demo /ˈdeməʊ/ *n.* (*pl.* ~**s**) (infml) = demonstration

demobilize /diːˈməʊbɪlaɪz/ *v.t.* демобилизова́ть (*impf., pf.*)

ơ **democracy** /dɪˈmɒkrəsɪ/ *n.* демокра́тия

democrat /ˈdeməkræt/ *n.* демокра́т

ơ **democratic** /deməˈkrætɪk/ *adj.* демократи́ческий

demographic /deməˈɡræfɪk/ *adj.* демографи́ческий

demography /dɪˈmɒɡrəfɪ/ *n.* демогра́фия

demolish /dɪˈmɒlɪʃ/ *v.t.* сн|оси́ть, -ести́

demolition /deməˈlɪʃ(ə)n/ *n.* разруше́ние, снос

demon /ˈdiːmən/ *n.* де́мон

demonic /dɪˈmɒnɪk/ *adj.* дья́вольский

demonize /ˈdiːmənaɪz/ *v.t.* демонизи́ровать (*impf., pf.*)

demonstrable /ˈdemənstrəb(ə)l/ *adj.* доказу́емый

ơ **demonstrate** /ˈdemənstreɪt/ *v.t.* **1** (prove) дока́з|ывать, -а́ть **2** (show in operation) демонстри́ровать, про-
● *v.i.* уча́ствовать (*impf.*) в демонстра́ции

demonstration /demənˈstreɪʃ(ə)n/ *n.* (proof) доказа́тельство; (public manifestation) демонстра́ция

demonstrative /dɪˈmɒnstrətɪv/ *adj.* экспанси́вный

demonstrator /ˈdemənstreɪtə(r)/ *n.* демонстра́нт

demoralize /dɪˈmɒrəlaɪz/ *v.t.* деморализова́ть (*impf., pf.*)

demote /dɪˈməʊt/ *v.t.* пон|ижа́ть, -и́зить (в до́лжности)

demure /dɪˈmjʊə(r)/ *adj.* (**demurer**, **demurest**) скро́мный

den /den/ *n.* **1** (animal's lair) берло́га **2** (of thieves) прито́н **3** (study) кабине́т

denationalization /diːnæʃənəlaɪˈzeɪʃ(ə)n/ *n.* денационализа́ция

denationalize /diːˈnæʃənəlaɪz/ *v.t.* денационализи́ровать (*impf., pf.*)

denial /dɪˈnaɪəl/ *n.* отрица́ние; ~ **of justice** отка́з в правосу́дии

denim /ˈdenɪm/ *n.* джинсо́вая ткань
● *adj.* джинсо́вый

Denmark /ˈdenmɑːk/ *n.* Да́ния

denomination /dɪnɒmɪˈneɪʃ(ə)n/ *n.* **1** (name, nomenclature) наименова́ние **2** (relig.) вероиспове́дание **3**: **money of small** ~**s** де́нежные зна́ки (*m. pl.*) ма́лого досто́инства

denote /dɪˈnəʊt/ *v.t.* обозн|ача́ть, -а́чить

denounce /dɪˈnaʊns/ *v.t.* **1** (speak against) осу|жда́ть, -ди́ть **2** (inform against) дон|оси́ть, -ести́ на + *a.*

dense /dens/ *adj.* густо́й

density /ˈdensɪtɪ/ *n.* густота́

dent /dent/ *n.* (mark) вмя́тина; (hollow) вы́боина
● *v.t.* ост|авля́ть, -а́вить вмя́тину в/на + *p.*

dental /ˈdent(ə)l/ *adj.* (of teeth) зубно́й
■ ~ **floss** *n.* зубна́я нить; ~ **surgeon** *n.* = dentist

dentist /ˈdentɪst/ *n.* зубно́й врач, данти́ст, стомато́лог

dentistry /ˈdentɪstrɪ/ *n.* стоматоло́гия

dentures /ˈdentʃəz/ *n. pl.* зубно́й проте́з

ơ **deny** /dɪˈnaɪ/ *v.t.* **1** (contest truth of) отрица́ть (*impf.*) **2** (repudiate) отр|ека́ться, -е́чься от + *g.* **3** (refuse) отка́з|ывать, -а́ть (*кому в чём*)

deodorant /diːˈəʊdərənt/ *n.* дезодора́нт

depart /dɪˈpɑːt/ *v.i.* **1** (go away) отпр|авля́ться, -а́виться **2**: ~ **from** (custom, plan, etc.) отступ|а́ть, -и́ть от + *g.*

ơ **department** /dɪˈpɑːtmənt/ *n.* **1** отде́л **2** (of government) департа́мент, ве́домство **3** (of university) ка́федра
■ ~ **store** *n.* универма́г

departmental /diːpɑːtˈment(ə)l/ *adj.* ве́домственный

departure /dɪˈpɑːtʃə(r)/ *n.* (going away) отъе́зд; (of train) отправле́ние

ơ **depend** /dɪˈpend/ *v.i.* **1** (be conditional) зави́сеть (*impf.*) (**on**: от + *g.*); **that** ~**s; it all** ~**s** как сказа́ть **2** (rely) пол|ага́ться, -ожи́ться (**on**: на + *a.*)

dependable /dɪˈpendəb(ə)l/ *adj.* надёжный

dependant /dɪˈpend(ə)nt/ (AmE **dependent**) *n.* иждиве́н|ец (-ка)

dependence /dɪˈpend(ə)ns/ *n.* зави́симость (**on**: от + *g.*); (reliance) дове́рие (**on**: к + *d.*)

dependency /dɪˈpendənsɪ/ *n.* (pol.) коло́ния

dependent /dɪˈpend(ə)nt/ *adj.* зави́симый

depict /dɪˈpɪkt/ *v.t.* изобра|жа́ть, -зи́ть

depiction /dɪˈpɪkʃ(ə)n/ *n.* описа́ние, изображе́ние

deplete /dɪˈpliːt/ *v.t.* истощ|а́ть, -и́ть

deplorable /dɪˈplɔːrəb(ə)l/ *adj.* плаче́вный

deplore /dɪˈplɔː(r)/ *v.t.* сожале́ть (*impf.*) о + *p.*

deploy /dɪˈplɔɪ/ *v.t.* развёр|тывать, -ну́ть

deployment /dɪˈplɔɪmənt/ *n.* развёртывание; размеще́ние

depopulate /diːˈpɒpjʊleɪt/ *v.t.* истреб|ля́ть, -и́ть/уничт|ожа́ть, -о́жить/ум|еньша́ть,

-éньшить населéние + g.

depopulation /di:pɒpjʊ'leɪʃ(ə)n/ n. сокращéние населéния

deport /dɪ'pɔːt/ v.t. депортировать (impf., pf.)

deportation /di:pɔː'teɪʃ(ə)n/ n. депортáция, вы́сылка

depose /dɪ'pəʊz/ v.t. све|ргáть, -éргнуть (с престóла)

deposit /dɪ'pɒzɪt/ n. **1** (sum in bank) вклад **2** (advance payment) задáток **3** (layer) отложéние; (of ore etc.) зáлежь; (of precious metals and stones) рóссыпь

• v.t. (**deposited, depositing**) класть, положи́ть; (place in bank) депони́ровать (impf., pf.)

■ ~ **account** n. (BrE) депози́тный счёт

depot /'depəʊ/ n. (place of storage) склад; (AmE, train or bus station) стáнция

deprave /dɪ'preɪv/ v.t. развра|щáть, -ти́ть

depravity /dɪ'prævɪtɪ/ n. разврáт, развращённость

depreciate /dɪ'priːʃɪeɪt/ v.i. обесцéни|ваться, -ться

depreciation /dɪpriːʃɪ'eɪʃ(ə)n/ n. обесцéнивание, обесцéнение

depress /dɪ'pres/ v.t. **1** (push down) наж|имáть, -áть на + a. **2** (fig.): ~ed area райóн, пострадáвший от экономи́ческой депрéссии **3** (make sad) удруч|áть, -и́ть

depressing /dɪ'presɪŋ/ adj. удручáющий

depression /dɪ'preʃ(ə)n/ n. депрéссия, тоскá

deprivation /deprɪ'veɪʃ(ə)n/ n. лишéние

deprive /dɪ'praɪv/ v.t. лиш|áть, -и́ть (кого чего); ~d (underprivileged) обездóленный

depth /depθ/ n. **1** (deepness) глубинá; **6 feet in** ~ глубинóй в шесть фу́тов; **be out of one's** ~ не доставáть (impf.) ногáми до дна; (fig.): **I am out of my** ~ **in this job** э́та рабóта мне не по плечу́ **2** (extremity): ~ **of despair** глубóкое отчáяние; ~ **of winter** глубóкая зимá

deputize /'depjʊtaɪz/ v.i.: ~ **for sb** замещáть (impf.) когó-н.

deputy /'depjʊtɪ/ n. **1** (substitute) замести́тель (m.) **2** (member of parliament) депутáт

■ ~ **chairman** n. замести́тель (m.) председáтеля

derail /di:'reɪl/ v.t.: **be derailed** (of train) сходи́ть, сойти́ с рéльсов

derailment /dɪ'reɪlmənt/ n. сход с рéльсов

derange /dɪ'reɪndʒ/ v.t. сво|ди́ть, -ести́ с умá

deregulate /di:'regjʊleɪt/ v.t. отмен|я́ть, -и́ть (госудáрственное) регули́рование

deregulation /di:regjʊ'leɪʃ(ə)n/ n. отмéна (госудáрственного) регули́рования

derelict /'derəlɪkt/ adj. забрóшенный

dereliction /derɪ'lɪkʃ(ə)n/ n. забрóшенность, запу́щенность; ~ **of duty** нарушéние (служéбного) дóлга

deride /dɪ'raɪd/ v.t. высмéивать, вы́смеять; осмé|ивать, -я́ть

derision /dɪ'rɪʒ(ə)n/ n. осмея́ние, высмéивание

derisive /dɪ'raɪsɪv/ adj. (scornful) насмéшливый

derisory /dɪ'raɪsərɪ/ adj. (ludicrous) смешнóй, ничтóжный

derive /dɪ'raɪv/ v.t. извл|екáть, -éчь; ~ **pleasure from** получ|áть, -и́ть удовóльствие от + g.

dermatitis /də:mə'taɪtɪs/ n. дермати́т

dermatologist /də:mə'tɒlədʒɪst/ n. дерматóлог

derogatory /dɪ'rɒgətərɪ/ adj. пренебрежи́тельный

descend /dɪ'send/ v.t. сходи́ть, сойти́ с + g.

• v.i. **1** (go down) спус|кáться, -ти́ться **2** (originate) происходи́ть (impf.); **he is** ~ed **from a ducal family** он происхóдит из гéрцогского рóда **3** (attack) набр|áсываться, -óситься

descendant /dɪ'send(ə)nt/ n. потóмок

descent /dɪ'sent/ n. **1** (act of descending) спуск **2** (ancestry) происхождéние

✍ **describe** /dɪ'skraɪb/ v.t. опи́с|ывать, -áть; ~ **sb as** наз|ывáть, -вáть когó-н. (кем-н./каки́м-н.)

✍ **description** /dɪ'skrɪpʃ(ə)n/ n. описáние

descriptive /dɪ'skrɪptɪv/ adj. описáтельный

desecrate /'desɪkreɪt/ v.t. оскверн|я́ть, -и́ть

desegregate /di:'segrɪgeɪt/ v.t. десегреги́ровать (impf., pf.) (отменять сегрегацию)

desert¹ /'dezət/ n. (waste land) пусты́ня

• adj. пусты́нный

■ ~ **island** n. необитáемый óстров

desert² /dɪ'zə:t/ v.t. **1** (go away from) ост|авля́ть, -áвить; **the streets were** ~ed **на у́лицах не́ было ни души́ 2** (abandon) пок|идáть, -и́нуть

• v.i. дезерти́ровать (impf., pf.)

deserter /dɪ'zə:[tə(r)/ n. дезерти́р

desertion /dɪ'zə:ʃ(ə)n/ n. дезерти́рство

deserts /dɪ'zə:ts/ n. pl.: **get one's** ~ получ|áть, -и́ть по заслу́гам

✍ **deserve** /dɪ'zə:v/ v.t. & i. заслу́ж|ивать, -и́ть

deserving /dɪ'zə:vɪŋ/ adj. похвáльный

desiccate /'desɪkeɪt/ v.t. высу́шивать, вы́сушить

■ ~d **coconut** n. сушёный кокóс

✍ **design** /dɪ'zaɪn/ n. **1** (drawing, plan) план, проéкт **2** (art of drawing) рисовáние **3** (tech., layout, system) констру́кция, проéкт; ~ **of a car** констру́кция автомоби́ля; ~ **of a building** проéкт здáния **4** (pattern) узóр, рисýнок **5** (version of product) модéль

• v.t. сост|авля́ть, -áвить план + g.

designate /'dezɪgneɪt/ v.t. (specify a time) etc.) обозн|ачáть, -áчить; (appoint to a post) назн|ачáть, -áчить

designer /dɪ'zaɪnə(r)/ n. (of dresses, decorations) модельéр; (tech.) констру́ктор; (industrial) дизáйнер

■ ~ **baby** n. ребёнок, рождённый из эмбриóна, вы́бранного из нéскольких эмбриóнов, котóрые бы́ли полу́чены мéтодом экстракорпорáльного оплодотворéния

desirable /dɪ'zaɪərəb(ə)l/ *adj.* жела́тельный; (attractive) привлека́тельный

◇ **desire** /dɪ'zaɪə(r)/ *n.* жела́ние, стремле́ние
● *v.t.* жела́ть, по-; **it leaves much to be ∼d** э́то оставля́ет жела́ть лу́чшего *or* мно́гого

desk /desk/ *n.* пи́сьменный стол; (with sloping top) конто́рка; (information point) спра́вочный стол

desktop /'desktɒp/ *adj.* насто́льный
● *n.* (also comput.) рабо́чий стол
■ ∼ **publishing** *n.* насто́льная полиграфи́я; ∼ **publishing system** насто́льная изда́тельская систе́ма

desolate /'desələt/ *adj.* забро́шенный

despair /dɪ'speə(r)/ *n.* отча́яние
● *v.i.* отча́|иваться, -́яться; **I ∼ of him** я утра́тил ве́ру в него́

despatch /dɪ'spætʃ/ *v.t.* (BrE) = dispatch

desperate /'despərət/ *adj.* **1** (wretched) отча́янный **2** (in extreme need): **he is ∼ for money** он испы́тывает кра́йнюю нужду́ в деньга́х

desperation /despə'reɪʃ(ə)n/ *n.* отча́яние

despicable /dɪ'spɪkəb(ə)l/ *adj.* презре́нный

despise /dɪ'spaɪz/ *v.t.* презира́ть (*impf.*)

◇ **despite** /dɪ'spaɪt/ *prep.* несмотря́ на + *a.*

despondency /dɪ'spɒndənsɪ/ *n.* уны́ние

despondent /dɪ'spɒnd(ə)nt/ *adj.* уны́лый

despot /'despɒt/ *n.* де́спот

despotic /de'spɒtɪk/ *adj.* (system, rule) деспоти́ческий; (person, style) деспоти́чный

despotism /'despətɪz(ə)m/ *n.* деспоти́зм

dessert /dɪ'zɜːt/ *n.* десе́рт
■ ∼**spoon** *n.* десе́ртная ло́жка

destabilize /diː'steɪbɪlaɪz/ *v.t.* дестабилизи́ровать (*impf., pf.*)

destination /destɪ'neɪʃ(ə)n/ *n.* ме́сто назначе́ния

destine /'destɪn/ *v.t.* предназн|ача́ть, -а́чить; **the plan was ∼d to fail** э́тот план был обречён на прова́л

destiny /'destɪnɪ/ *n.* судьба́

destitute /'destɪtjuːt/ *adj.* нужда́ющийся

◇ **destroy** /dɪ'strɔɪ/ *v.t.* (building) разр|уша́ть, -у́шить; (friendship, hope) разб|ива́ть, -и́ть; (kill) истреб|ля́ть, -и́ть

destroyer /dɪ'strɔɪə(r)/ *n.* **1** (one who destroys) разруши́тель (*m.*) **2** (naut.) эсми́нец; эска́дренный миноно́сец

◇ **destruction** /dɪ'strʌkʃ(ə)n/ *n.* уничтоже́ние, разруше́ние

destructive /dɪ'strʌktɪv/ *adj.* разруши́тельный

desultory /'dezəltərɪ/ *adj.* отры́вочный; ∼ **reading** бессисте́мное чте́ние

detach /dɪ'tætʃ/ *v.t.* отдел|я́ть, -и́ть

detachable /dɪ'tætʃəb(ə)l/ *adj.* съёмный, отделя́емый

detached /dɪ'tætʃt/ *adj.* (unemotional) равноду́шный, отчуждённый; **a ∼ house** отде́льный дом

detachment /dɪ'tætʃmənt/ *n.* (indifference) отчуждённость, равноду́шие; (mil., body of troops etc.) отря́д

◇ **detail** /'diːteɪl/ *n.* дета́ль; **go into ∼(s)** входи́ть, вдава́ться (*both impf.*) в подро́бности; **in ∼** подро́бно, дета́льно
● *v.t.* входи́ть (*impf.*) в подро́бности + *g.*

detain /dɪ'teɪn/ *v.t.* заде́рж|ивать, -а́ть; **he was ∼ed by the police** он был заде́ржан поли́цией

detainee /diː'teɪ'niː/ *n.* заде́ржанный

detect /dɪ'tekt/ *v.t.* (discover) обнару́жи|вать, -ть; (discern) ул|а́вливать, -ови́ть

detection /dɪ'tekʃ(ə)n/ *n.* (of crime) рассле́дование, раскры́тие

detective /dɪ'tektɪv/ *n.* сы́щик, детекти́в
■ ∼ **novel** *n.* детекти́в, детекти́вный рома́н

detector /dɪ'tektə(r)/ *n.* (radio) дете́ктор

detention /dɪ'tenʃ(ə)n/ *n.* (at school) оставле́ние по́сле уро́ков; (confinement) заключе́ние (под стра́жу)
■ ∼ **centre** *n.* (for asylum seekers) приёмник-распредели́тель (*m.*) (*для (нелега́льных) мигра́нтов*)

deter /dɪ'tɜː(r)/ *v.t.* (**deterred**, **deterring**) уде́рж|ивать, -а́ть

detergent /dɪ'tɜːdʒ(ə)nt/ *n.* мо́ющее сре́дство; (washing powder) стира́льный порошо́к

deteriorate /dɪ'tɪərɪəreɪt/ *v.i.* ух|удша́ть(ся), -у́дшить(ся)

determination /dɪtɜːmɪ'neɪʃ(ə)n/ *n.* **1** (deciding upon) реше́ние **2** (resoluteness) реши́мость

◇ **determine** /dɪ'tɜːmɪn/ *v.t.* реш|а́ть, -и́ть; **he is ∼d to go** (*or* **on going**) он твёрдо реши́л е́хать

determined /dɪ'tɜːmɪnd/ *adj.* реши́тельный

deterrent /dɪ'terənt/ *n.* сре́дство устраше́ния/сде́рживания

detest /dɪ'test/ *v.t.* ненави́деть (*impf.*)

detestable /dɪ'testəb(ə)l/ *adj.* отврати́тельный

detonate /'detəneɪt/ *v.t.* детони́ровать (*impf., pf.*)

detour /'diːtʊə(r)/ *n.* (on foot) обхо́д; (by transport) объе́зд

detract /dɪ'trækt/ *v.i.*: ∼ **from** умал|я́ть, -и́ть

detriment /'detrɪmənt/ *n.*: **he works long hours to the ∼ of his health** он рабо́тает сверх но́рмы в уще́рб своему́ здоро́вью

detrimental /detrɪ'ment(ə)l/ *adj.* вре́дный

deuce /djuːs/ *n.* (tennis) ра́вный счёт

devaluation /diː'væljuː'eɪʃ(ə)n/ *n.* обесце́нение; (fin.) девальва́ция

devalue /diː'væljuː/ *v.t.* (**devalues**, **devalued**, **devaluing**) обесце́ни|вать, -ть; (fin.) девальви́ровать (*impf., pf.*)
● *v.i.* (**devalues**, **devalued**, **devaluing**) пров|оди́ть, -ести́ девальва́цию

devastat|e /'devəsteɪt/ *v.t.* (fig.) убива́ть, уби́ть; **a ∼ing remark** уничтожа́ющее/убий́ственное замеча́ние

devastation /devə'steɪʃ(ə)n/ *n.* опустоше́ние, разоре́ние

◇ **develop** /dɪ'veləp/ *v.t.* (**developed**,

developing) **1** (cause to unfold) разв|ива́ть, -и́ть; (work up, polish) обраб|а́тывать, -о́тать **2** (phot.) проявля́ть, -и́ть **3** (contract): he ~ed a cough у него́ появи́лся ка́шель **4** (open up for residence etc.) разв|ива́ть, -и́ть
● *v.i.* (**developed, developing**) разв|ива́ться, -и́ться; ~ into превра|ща́ться, -ти́ться в + *a.*

developer /dɪ'veləpə(r)/ *n.* (builder) застро́йщик

✎ **development** /dɪ'veləpmənt/ *n.* **1** (unfolding) разви́тие, рост **2** (event) собы́тие, обстоя́тельство **3** (of land etc.) разви́тие (райо́на); (building) застро́йка

deviate /'di:vɪeɪt/ *v.i.* отклон|я́ться, -и́ться (from: от + g.)

deviation /di:vɪ'eɪʃ(ə)n/ *n.* отклоне́ние, отхо́д

✎ **device** /dɪ'vaɪs/ *n.* **1** (method) приём; he was left to his own ~s он был предоста́влен самому́ себе́ **2** (instrument) приспособле́ние, прибо́р

devil /'dev(ə)l/ *n.* чёрт, дья́вол

devious /'di:vɪəs/ *adj.* (road) изви́листый, око́льный; (fig.) лука́вый, неи́скренний

devise /dɪ'vaɪz/ *v.t.* (think out) приду́м|ывать, -ать

devoid /dɪ'vɔɪd/ *adj.* лишённый; ~ of fear бесстра́шный

devolution /di:və'lu:ʃ(ə)n/ *n.* переда́ча/ делеги́рование вла́сти

devolve /dɪ'vɒlv/ *v.t.* (delegate) перед|ава́ть, -а́ть
● *v.i.* пере|ходи́ть, -йти́; the work ~d on/ to me рабо́ту пе́редали мне; the estate ~d on/to a distant cousin име́ние перешло́ к да́льнему ро́дственнику

devote /dɪ'vəʊt/ *v.t.* посвя|ща́ть, -ти́ть; he ~s his time to study он посвяща́ет всё своё вре́мя учёбе; she is ~d to her children она́ пре́дана свои́м де́тям; a ~d friend пре́данный друг

devotee /devə'ti:/ *n.* приве́рженец

devotion /dɪ'vəʊʃ(ə)n/ *n.* **1** (being devoted) пре́данность **2** (love) пре́данность

devour /dɪ'vaʊə(r)/ *v.t.* пож|ира́ть, -ра́ть

devout /dɪ'vaʊt/ *adj.* благочести́вый

dew /dju:/ *n.* роса́

dexterity /dek'sterɪtɪ/ *n.* ло́вкость, прово́рство

dexterous, dextrous /'dekstrəs/ *adj.* ло́вкий, прово́рный

diabetes /daɪə'bi:ti:z/ *n.* диабе́т

diabetic /daɪə'betɪk/ *n.* диабе́тик
● *adj.* диабети́ческий

diabolical /daɪə'bɒlɪk(ə)l/, **diabolic** /daɪə'bɒlɪk/ *adjs.* дья́вольский

diagnose /'daɪəgnəʊz/ *v.t.* диагности́ровать (*impf., pf.*)

diagnosis /daɪəg'nəʊsɪs/ *n.* (*pl.* **diagnoses** /-si:z/) диа́гноз

diagnostic /daɪəg'nɒstɪk/ *adj.* диагности́ческий

diagonal /daɪ'ægən(ə)l/ *n.* диагона́ль
● *adj.* диагона́льный; ~ly по диагона́ли

diagram /'daɪəgræm/ *n.* диагра́мма

✎ ключева́я ле́ксика

dial /'daɪ(ə)l/ *n.* **1** (of clock) цифербла́т **2** (of radio etc.) шкала́
● *v.t. & i.* (**dialled, dialling**, AmE **dialed, dialing**): ~ a number наб|ира́ть, -ра́ть но́мер; ~ the police station звони́ть, по- в поли́цию
■ ~ling tone *n.* дли́нный гудо́к; сигна́л «ли́ния свобо́дна»

dialect /'daɪəlekt/ *n.* диале́кт, го́вор

dialogue /'daɪəlɒg/ (AmE *also* **dialog**) *n.* диало́г

dialysis /daɪ'ælɪsɪs/ *n.* диа́лиз

diameter /daɪ'æmɪtə(r)/ *n.* диа́метр

diametric /daɪə'metrɪk/, **diametrical** /daɪə'metrɪk(ə)l/ *adjs.* диаметра́льный

diamond /'daɪəmənd/ *n.* **1** (precious stone) алма́з **2** (geom.) ромб **3** (at cards) бу́б|ны (-ен)

diaper /'daɪəpə(r)/ *n.* (AmE) подгу́зник

diaphragm /'daɪəfræm/ *n.* диафра́гма

diarrhoea /daɪə'rɪə/ (AmE **diarrhea**) *n.* поно́с

diary /'daɪərɪ/ *n.* (journal) дневни́к; (engagement book) календа́рь (*m.*)

diaspora /daɪ'æspərə/ *n.* диа́спора

dice /daɪs/ *n.* (cube) игра́льные ко́сти (*f. pl.*); (game of ~) игра́ в ко́сти
● *v.t.* нар|еза́ть, -е́зать куби́ками

dichotomy /daɪ'kɒtəmɪ/ *n.* дихотоми́я; (contrast) противопоставле́ние

Dictaphone® /'dɪktəfəʊn/ *n.* диктофо́н

dictate /dɪk'teɪt/ *v.t. & i.* (as dictation; command) диктова́ть, про-; I won't be ~d to я не позво́лю ста́вить мне усло́вия

dictation /dɪk'teɪʃ(ə)n/ *n.* (to class) дикта́нт; (to secretary) дикто́вка

dictator /dɪk'teɪtə(r)/ *n.* дикта́тор

dictatorial /dɪktə'tɔ:rɪəl/ *adj.* дикта́торский

dictatorship /dɪk'teɪtəʃɪp/ *n.* диктату́ра

dictionary /'dɪkʃənrɪ/ *n.* словарь (*m.*)

did /dɪd/ *past of* ▶ **do**

didactic /daɪ'dæktɪk/ *adj.* поучи́тельный, дидакти́ческий

didn't /'dɪdn(ə)nt/ *neg. of* ▶ **did**

✎ **die** /daɪ/ *v.i.* (**dies, died, dying**) **1** (of person) ум|ира́ть, -ере́ть (*pf.*); (in accident, in war) ги́бнуть, по-; (of animals) под|ыха́ть, -о́хнуть; (of plants) ув|яда́ть, -я́нуть; пог|иба́ть, -и́бнуть **2** (fig.): I'm dying to see him я до́ сме́рти хочу́ его́ ви́деть
□ ~ **down** *v.i.* (of fire) уг|аса́ть, -а́снуть; (of noise) ут|иха́ть, -и́хнуть; the wind ~d down ве́тер ути́х; (of feeling) ум|ира́ть, -ере́ть
□ ~ **out** *v.i.* вымира́ть, вы́мереть

diesel /'di:z(ə)l/ *n.* (*also* ~ **engine**) ди́зель (*m.*); (*also* ~ **oil**) ди́зельное то́пливо

diet /'daɪət/ *n.* **1** (customary food) пи́ща, пита́ние **2** (medical régime) дие́та; go on a ~ сади́ться, сесть на дие́ту; he is on a ~ он (сиди́т) на дие́те

dietitian /daɪə'tɪʃ(ə)n/ *n.* (врач-)дието́лог

differ /'dɪfə(r)/ *v.i.* **1** (be different) отлича́ться (*impf.*); they ~ in size они́ различа́ются разме́ром, по разме́ру **2** (disagree) ра|сходи́ться, -зойти́сь во мне́ниях; we

d

agreed to ~ мы реши́ли прекрати́ть
бесполе́зный спор

⌀ **difference** /'dɪfrəns/ *n.* **1** (state of being unlike)
отли́чие, разли́чие, ра́зница; it makes no
~ whether you go or not соверше́нно
безразли́чно, идёте вы и́ли нет **2** (dispute)
разногла́сие, спор

⌀ **different** /'dɪfrənt/ *adj.* друго́й, ра́зный,
разли́чный; they live in ~ houses они́ живу́т
в ра́зных дома́х; she wears a ~ hat each day
на ней ка́ждый день друга́я шля́па; of ~
kinds ра́зного ро́да; he became a ~ person он
стал други́м челове́ком; ~ from непохо́жий
на + *a.*; отли́чный от + *g.*

differentiate /dɪfə'renʃɪeɪt/ *v.t.* различ|а́ть,
-и́ть

differently /'dɪfrəntlɪ/ *adv.* по-ино́му; по-
друго́му

⌀ **difficult** /'dɪfɪkəlt/ *adj.* (of thing or person)
тру́дный

⌀ **difficulty** /'dɪfɪkəltɪ/ *n.* тру́дность,
затрудне́ние; I have ~ in understanding him я
с трудо́м его́ понима́ю

diffident /'dɪfɪd(ə)nt/ *adj.* неуве́ренный в
себе́; засте́нчивый, стесни́тельный

diffuse[1] /dɪ'fju:s/ *adj.* (of light etc.) рассе́янный;
(of style) расплы́вчатый

diffuse[2] /dɪ'fju:z/ *v.t.* (light, heat, etc.)
рассе́|ивать, -ять; (learning, etc.)
распростран|я́ть, -и́ть

dig /dɪg/ *n.* **1** (poke) толчо́к **2** (fig.) насме́шка
3 (archaeological expedition) раско́пки (*f. pl.*)
● *v.t. & i.* (**digging**, *past and p.p.* **dug**)
копа́ть, вы́-; he dug a hole он вы́рыл я́му;
they are ~ging for gold они́ и́щут зо́лото
□ ~ **out** *v.t.* выка́лывать, вы́копать
□ ~ **up** *v.t.* отк|а́пывать, -опа́ть

digest /daɪ'dʒest/ *v.t.* (food) перева́р|ивать,
-и́ть; (information etc.) усв|а́ивать, -о́ить
● *v.i.* перева́р|иваться, -и́ться

digestion /daɪ'dʒestʃ(ə)n/ *n.* перева́ривание

digger /'dɪgə(r)/ *n.* (machine) экскава́тор

digit /'dɪdʒɪt/ *n.* (finger or toe) па́лец; (numeral)
ци́фра

⌀ **digital** /'dɪdʒɪt(ə)l/ *adj.* цифрово́й
■ ~ **camera** *n.* цифрова́я (фо́то)ка́мера; ~
clock *n.* цифровы́е/электро́нные час|ы́ (-о́в)

digitize /'dɪdʒɪtaɪz/ *v.t.* оцифр|о́вывать,
-ова́ть; преобраз|о́вывать, -ова́ть в
цифрову́ю фо́рму

dignified /'dɪgnɪfaɪd/ *adj.* по́лный
досто́инства

dignitary /'dɪgnɪtərɪ/ *n.* сано́вник;
высокопоста́вленное лицо́

dignity /'dɪgnɪtɪ/ *n.* досто́инство

digress /daɪ'gres/ *v.i.* отклон|я́ться, -и́ться
(от те́мы)

digression /daɪ'greʃ(ə)n/ *n.* отклоне́ние

dilapidated /dɪ'læpɪdeɪtɪd/ *adj.* ве́тхий

dilate /daɪ'leɪt/ *v.t.* расш|иря́ть, -и́рить
● *v.i.* расш|иря́ться, -и́риться

dilemma /daɪ'lemə/ *n.* диле́мма

diligent /'dɪlɪdʒ(ə)nt/ *adj.* приле́жный

dill /dɪl/ *n.* укро́п
■ ~ **pickle** *n.* марино́ванный огуре́ц

dilute /daɪ'lju:t/ *v.t.* разв|оди́ть, -ести́

dim /dɪm/ *adj.* (**dimmer, dimmest**) (of light
etc.) ту́склый; (of memory etc.) сму́тный
● *v.t.* (**dimmed, dimming**) затума́ни|вать,
-ть; ~ one's headlights пере|ходи́ть, -йти́ на
бли́жний свет

dime /daɪm/ *n.* десятице́нтовик

dimension /daɪ'menʃ(ə)n/ *n.* **1** (extent)
разме́р **2** (direction of measurement) измере́ние

diminish /dɪ'mɪnɪʃ/ *v.t.* ум|еньша́ть, -е́ньшить

diminutive /dɪ'mɪnjʊtɪv/ *n.* (gram.)
уменьши́тельное сло́во
● *adj.* (small) миниатю́рный

dimple /'dɪmp(ə)l/ *n.* я́мочка; (ripple) рябь

din /dɪn/ *n.* гам

din|e /daɪn/ *v.i.* у́жинать, по-
■ ~**ing car** *n.* ваго́н-рестора́н; ~**ing room** *n.*
столо́вая (ко́мната)

diner /'daɪnə(r)/ *n.* **1** (person) у́жинающий
2 (AmE, restaurant) дешёвый рестора́н
(*оформленный по типу вагона-ресторана*)

dinghy /'dɪŋgɪ/ *n.* ма́ленькая шлю́пка, я́лик;
(inflatable) надувна́я ло́дка

dingy /'dɪndʒɪ/ *adj.* (**dingier, dingiest**)
тёмный, мра́чный

⌀ **dinner** /'dɪnə(r)/ *n.* у́жин; have ~ обе́дать,
по-/у́жинать, по-
■ ~ **hour** *n.* час обе́да/у́жина; ~ **jacket** *n.*
смо́кинг; ~ **party** *n.* зва́ный обе́д; ~ **time** *n.*
вре́мя у́жина

dinosaur /'daɪnəsɔ:(r)/ *n.* диноза́вр

dip /dɪp/ *n.* **1** (immersion) погруже́ние **2** (bathe)
ныря́ние **3** (slope) спуск, укло́н **4** (cul.) со́ус
● *v.t.* (**dipped, dipping**) **1** (immerse)
окуна́ть, -у́ть; мак|а́ть, -ну́ть; погру|жа́ть,
-зи́ть **2** (lower briefly) приспус|ка́ть, -ти́ть; ~
headlights (BrE) переключ|а́ть, -и́ть фа́ры на
(*or* включ|а́ть, -и́ть) бли́жний свет
● *v.i.* (**dipped, dipping**) **1** (go below surface)
окуна́ться, -у́ться **2** (fig.): ~ into one's purse
раскоше́ли|ваться, -ться **3** (slope away): the
(plot of) land ~s to the south уча́сток име́ет
накло́н к ю́гу **4** (fall slightly) пони|жа́ться,
-зи́ться
■ ~**stick** *n.* уровнеме́р, щуп

diphtheria /dɪf'θɪərɪə/ *n.* дифтери́я, дифтери́т

diphthong /'dɪfθɒŋ/ *n.* дифто́нг

diploma /dɪ'pləʊmə/ *n.* дипло́м

diplomacy /dɪ'pləʊməsɪ/ *n.* диплома́тия;
(tact) дипломати́чность

diplomat /'dɪpləmæt/ *n.* (lit., fig.) диплома́т

diplomatic /dɪplə'mætɪk/ *adj.* (lit., fig.)
дипломати́ческий

dire /'daɪə(r)/ *adj.* ужа́сный; he is in ~ need of
help он кра́йне нужда́ется в по́мощи

⌀ **direct** /daɪ'rekt/ *adj.* **1** (straight) прямо́й;
(straightforward) прямо́й; he has a ~ way of
speaking он говори́т всё пря́мо в лицо́
● *adv.* пря́мо
● *v.t.* **1** (indicate the way): can you ~ me to
the station? вы не ска́жете, как пройти́ на

вокзáл? **2** (address) адресовáть (*impf., pf.*); напр|авлять, -áвить; **my remarks were ~ed to him** мои замечáния были адресóваны ему **3** (manage, control) руководить (*impf.*) + *i.*; **he ~ed the play** он постáвил пьéсу

■ **~ flight** *n.* прямóй/беспересáдочный полёт/ рейс

✍ **direction** /daɪˈrekʃ(ə)n/ *n.* **1** (course) направлéние; **they dispersed in all ~s** они разошлись в рáзные стóроны **2** (*in pl.*) (instructions) указáния (*nt. pl.*)

directive /daɪˈrektɪv/ *n.* директива, указáние

✍ **directly** /daɪˈrektlɪ/ *adv.* **1** (in var. senses of direct) прямо **2** (at once) немéдленно, тóтчас

✍ **director** /daɪˈrektə(r)/ *n.* **1** (of company etc.) дирéктор **2** (theatr.) режиссёр

directory /daɪˈrektərɪ/ *n.* (reference work) спрáвочник, указáтель (*m.*)

■ **~ assistance** (AmE), **~ enquiries** (BrE) *nn.* спрáвочная

dirge /dɜːdʒ/ *n.* погребáльное пéние

dirt /dɜːt/ *n.* **1** (unclean matter) грязь **2** (earth) грунт, земля

■ **~ track** *n.* мотоциклéтный трек

dirty /ˈdɜːtɪ/ *adj.* (**dirtier, dirtiest**) **1** (not clean) грязный **2** (obscene) похáбный **3** (nasty) грязный, гáдкий; **he played a ~ trick on me** он подложил мне свинью; **he gave me a ~ look** (infml) он посмотрéл на меня сердито

● *v.t.* грязнить, за-; пáчкать, за-

disability /dɪsəˈbɪlɪtɪ/ *n.* (a limiting mental or physical condition) дефéкт; (being disabled) инвалидность

disable /dɪsˈeɪb(ə)l/ *v.t.* (physically) калéчить, ис-; **~d person** инвалид

disadvantage /dɪsədˈvɑːntɪdʒ/ *n.* невыгодное положéние; **be at a ~** окáз|ываться, -áться в невыгодном положéнии

● *v.t.* дéйствовать (*impf.*) в ущéрб + *d.*; **~d** (underprivileged) обездóленный

disaffected /dɪsəˈfektɪd/ *adj.* недовóльный

disagree /dɪsəˈɡriː/ *v.i.* (**disagrees, disagreed, disagreeing**) **1** (differ) не соотвéтствовать (*impf.*) (with: + *d.*) **2** (in opinion) не согла|шáться, -ситься; **I ~ with you** я с вáми не соглáсен **3** (have adverse effect): **oysters ~ with me** от устриц мне плóхо

disagreeable /dɪsəˈɡriːəb(ə)/ *adj.* (unpleasant) неприятный; (of person) непривéтливый

disagreement /dɪsəˈɡriːmənt/ *n.* разноглáсие

disallow /dɪsəˈlaʊ/ *v.t.* (reject) отклон|ять, -ить; (goal) не засчит|ывать, -итáть

✍ **disappear** /dɪsəˈpɪə(r)/ *v.i.* исч|езáть, -éзнуть

disappearance /dɪsəˈpɪərəns/ *n.* исчезновéние

disappoint /dɪsəˈpɔɪnt/ *v.t.* разочарóв|ывать, -áть

disappointing /dɪsəˈpɔɪntɪŋ/ *adj.* разочарóвывающий

disappointment /dɪsəˈpɔɪntmənt/ *n.* разочарование; **to my ~** к моему огорчéнию

disapproval /dɪsəˈpruːv(ə)l/ *n.* неодобрéние

disapprove /dɪsəˈpruːv/ *v.i.* (**~ of**) не одобрять (*impf.*)

disapproving /dɪsəˈpruːvɪŋ/ *adj.* неодобрительный

disarm /dɪsˈɑːm/ *v.t.* разоруж|áть, -ить

disarmament /dɪsˈɑːməmənt/ *n.* разоружéние

disarray /dɪsəˈreɪ/ *n.* смятéние, расстрóйство

disassociate /dɪsəˈsəʊsɪeɪt/ *v.t.* = **dissociate**

✍ **disaster** /dɪˈzɑːstə(r)/ *n.* бéдствие

disastrous /dɪˈzɑːstrəs/ *adj.* гибельный

disband /dɪsˈbænd/ *v.t.* распус|кáть, -тить; расформирóв|ывать, -áть

● *v.i.* расп|адáться, -áсться; **the (theatre) company ~ed** трýппа распáлась

disbelief /dɪsbɪˈliːf/ *n.* невéрие

disbelieve /dɪsbɪˈliːv/ *v.t.* (person) не вéрить (*impf.*) + *d.*; (account, evidence) не вéрить (*impf.*) + *d.* (*or* в + *a.*)

✍ **disc** /dɪsk/ *n.* **1** (AmE **disk**) диск **2** (**disk**) (comput.): **floppy disk** гибкий диск

■ **disk drive** *n.* дисковóд; **~ jockey** *n.* диск-жокéй, диджéй

discard /dɪˈskɑːd/ *v.t.* выбрáсывать, выбросить

discernible /dɪˈsɜːnɪb(ə)l/ *adj.* различимый

discerning /dɪˈsɜːnɪŋ/ *adj.* проницáтельный

discernment /dɪˈsɜːnmənt/ *n.* проницáтельность

discharge *n.* /ˈdɪstʃɑːdʒ/ **1** (of fluid) слив; (of gas) выброс **2** (med.) выделéния (*pl.*) **3** (performance, e.g. of duty) исполнéние; (of a debt) уплáта **4** (release, dismissal) увольнéние, освобождéние

● *v.t.* /dɪsˈtʃɑːdʒ/ **1** (emit liquid) слив|áть, слить **2** (med.) выдел|ять, выделить **3** (from hospital) выписывать, выписать

disciple /dɪˈsaɪp(ə)l/ *n.* (relig.) апóстол

disciplinarian /dɪsɪplɪˈneərɪən/ *n.* сторóнник дисциплины; **she is a good ~** онá умéет поддéрживать дисциплину

disciplinary /dɪsɪˈplɪnərɪ/ *adj.* дисциплинáрный; **take ~ action** прин|имáть, -ять дисциплинáрные мéры

discipline /ˈdɪsɪplɪn/ *n.* дисциплина

disclaim /dɪsˈkleɪm/ *v.t.* отр|екáться, -éчься от + *g.*

disclose /dɪsˈkləʊz/ *v.t.* разоблач|áть, -ить

disco /ˈdɪskəʊ/ *n.* (*pl.* **~s**) (infml) = **discotheque**

discolor *v.i. & v.t.* (AmE) = **discolour**

discolour /dɪsˈkʌlə(r)/ (AmE **discolor**) *v.i.* (lose colour) обесцвé|чиваться, -титься

● *v.t.* **1** (make change colour) мен|ять, по- цвет + *g.*; **rain ~ed the water** дождь поменял цвет воды; **smoking had ~ed his teeth** его зýбы пожелтéли от курéния; (make lose colour) обесцвé|чивать, -тить

discomfort /dɪsˈkʌmfət/ *n.* неудóбство

disconcert /dɪskənˈsɜːt/ *v.t.* волновáть, вз-

disconnect /dɪskə'nekt/ v.t. (gas etc.)
отключ|а́ть, -и́ть; **we were ~ed** (telephone)
нас разъедини́ли/прерва́ли

disconnection /dɪskə'nekʃ(ə)n/ n.
разъедине́ние, отключе́ние

discontent /dɪskən'tent/ n. недово́льство

discontented /dɪskən'tentɪd/ adj.
недово́льный

discontinue /dɪskən'tɪnju:/ v.t.
(**discontinues**, **discontinued**,
discontinuing) прекра|ща́ть, -ти́ть

discord /'dɪskɔ:d/ n. (disagreement) разногла́сие;
(disharmony) разла́д, раздо́р; (mus.) диссона́нс

discotheque /'dɪskətek/ n. дискоте́ка

discount n. /'dɪskaʊnt/ ски́дка
• v.t. /dɪs'kaʊnt/ снижа́ть, сни́зить це́ну на + a.;
(not consider) не прин|има́ть, -я́ть в расчёт

discourage /dɪs'kʌrɪdʒ/ v.t. обескура́жи|вать,
-ть

discourteous /dɪs'kə:tɪəs/ adj. неве́жливый

꜀ **discover** /dɪ'skʌvə(r)/ v.t. (place, fact)
откр|ыва́ть, -ы́ть; (find out) узн|ава́ть, -а́ть

discovery /dɪ'skʌvərɪ/ n. откры́тие;
обнаруже́ние

discredit /dɪs'kredɪt/ n. (loss of repute)
дискредита́ция; **bring sb into ~** (or **bring
~ upon sb**) компромети́ровать, с- кого́-н.;
дискредити́ровать (impf., pf.) (кого́-н.)
• v.t. (**discredited**, **discrediting**)
дискредити́ровать (impf., pf.)

discreditable /dɪs'kredɪtəb(ə)l/ adj. (shameful)
позо́рный

discreet /dɪ'skri:t/ adj. (**discreeter**,
discreetest) такти́чный

discrepancy /dɪs'krepənsɪ/ n. расхожде́ние

discrete /dɪ'skri:t/ adj. обосо́бленный

discretion /dɪ'skreʃ(ə)n/ n. **1** (prudence, good
judgement) осмотри́тельность **2** (freedom to
judge) усмотре́ние; **I leave this to your ~** я
оставля́ю э́то на ва́ше усмотре́ние

discretionary /dɪ'skreʃənərɪ/ adj.
дискрецио́нный (позволяющий
распоряжаться по своему усмотрению)

discriminate /dɪ'skrɪmɪneɪt/ v.i.: **~ against**
дискримини́ровать (impf., pf.)

discriminating /dɪ'skrɪmɪneɪtɪŋ/ adj.
разбо́рчивый

discrimination /dɪskrɪmɪ'neɪʃ(ə)n/ n.
дискримина́ция

discriminatory /dɪ'skrɪmɪnətərɪ/ adj.
пристра́стный

discus /'dɪskəs/ n. (pl. ~es) (sport) диск

꜀ **discuss** /dɪ'skʌs/ v.t. дискути́ровать (impf.)

꜀ **discussion** /dɪ'skʌʃ(ə)n/ n. обсужде́ние,
диску́ссия

disdain /dɪs'deɪn/ n. презре́ние
• v.t. презира́ть, -ре́ть; пренебр|ега́ть,
-е́чь + i.; **he ~ed to reply** он не соизво́лил
отве́тить

disdainful /dɪs'deɪnfʊl/ adj. презри́тельный

꜀ **disease** /dɪ'zi:z/ n. боле́знь

diseased /dɪ'zi:zd/ adj. (lit., fig.) больно́й

disembark /dɪsɪm'bɑ:k/ v.t. & i.
выса́живать(ся), вы́садить(ся)

disembarkation /dɪsɪmbɑ:'keɪʃ(ə)n/ n.
вы́садка, вы́грузка

disembod|y /dɪsɪm'bɒdɪ/ v.t. (set free from
the body) освобо|жда́ть, -ди́ть от теле́сной
оболо́чки; a **~ied spirit** освобождённая душа́

disenchant /dɪsɪn'tʃɑ:nt/ v.t.
разочаро́в|ывать, -а́ть

disentangle /dɪsɪn'tæŋg(ə)l/ v.t.
распу́т|ывать, -ать; выпу́тывать, вы́путать

disfigure /dɪs'fɪgə(r)/ v.t. уро́довать, из-;
обезобра́|живать, -зить

disfigurement /dɪs'fɪgəmənt/ n. (act)
обезобра́живание; (result) уро́дство

disgrace /dɪs'greɪs/ n. **1** (loss of respect)
бесче́стье, позо́р **2** (disfavour) неми́лость,
опа́ла; **he is in ~** он в неми́лости **3** (cause of
shame) позо́р
• v.t. позо́рить, о-; (bring shame upon): **he ~d
the family name** он покры́л позо́ром свою́
семью́

disgraceful /dɪs'greɪsfʊl/ adj. позо́рный,
недосто́йный

disgruntled /dɪs'grʌnt(ə)ld/ adj.
недово́льный; раздражённый

disguise /dɪs'gaɪz/ n. маскиро́вка
• v.t. (weapons, objects, intentions) маскирова́ть,
за-; (with clothing) переод|ева́ть, -е́ть; (emotions)
скры|ва́ть, -ть

disgust /dɪs'gʌst/ n. отвраще́ние
• v.t. внуш|а́ть, -и́ть отвраще́ние + d.

disgusting /dɪs'gʌstɪŋ/ adj. отврати́тельный

dish /dɪʃ/ n. **1** (vessel, contents) блю́до; **wash, do
the ~es** мыть, вы- посу́ду **2** (infml, TV satellite
~) таре́лка
• v.t.: **~ out** (food) ра|скла́дывать, -зложи́ть
по таре́лкам (еду)
■ **~cloth** n. ку́хонная/посу́дная тря́пка;
~ towel n. (AmE) ку́хонное/посу́дное
полоте́нце; **~washer** n. посудомо́ечная
маши́на

dishearten /dɪs'hɑ:t(ə)n/ v.t. прив|оди́ть,
-ести́ в уны́ние; **I was ~ed** я упа́л ду́хом

dishevelled /dɪ'ʃev(ə)ld/ (AmE **disheveled**)
adj. взъеро́шенный

dishonest /dɪs'ɒnɪst/ adj. нече́стный,
бесче́стный

dishonesty /dɪs'ɒnɪstɪ/ n. нече́стность,
бесче́стность

dishonour /dɪs'ɒnə(r)/ (AmE **dishonor**) n.
бесче́стье, позо́р

dishonourable /dɪs'ɒnərəb(ə)l/ (AmE
dishonorable) adj. бесче́стный

dishy /'dɪʃɪ/ adj. (**dishier**, **dishiest**) (BrE,
infml) аппети́тный, привлека́тельный

disillusion /dɪsɪ'lu:ʒ(ə)n/ v.t.
разочаро́в|ывать, -а́ть

disillusionment /dɪsɪ'lu:ʒənmənt/ n.
разочарова́ние

disincentive /dɪsɪn'sentɪv/ n. сде́рживающее
обстоя́тельство

disinfect /dɪsɪn'fekt/ *v.t.* дезинфици́ровать (*impf., pf.*)

disinfectant /dɪsɪn'fekt(ə)nt/ *n.* дезинфици́рующее сре́дство

disingenuous /dɪsɪn'dʒenjʊəs/ *adj.* нейскренний

disinherit /dɪsɪn'herɪt/ *v.t.* (**disinherited, disinheriting**) лиш|а́ть, -и́ть насле́дства

disintegrate /dɪs'ɪntɪɡreɪt/ *v.i.* расп|ада́ться, -а́сться

disinterested /dɪs'ɪntrɪstɪd/ *adj.* (impartial) бескоры́стный

disjointed /dɪs'dʒɔɪntɪd/ *adj.* бессвя́зный

disk /dɪsk/ *n.* (AmE and comput.) = disc

diskette /dɪs'ket/ *n.* (comput.) дискéта

dislike /dɪs'laɪk/ *n.* (feeling) неприя́знь; (*often in pl.*) (disliked thing) антипа́тия; **I took a ~ to him** я невзлюби́л его́
● *v.t.* не люби́ть (*impf.*) + *g.*

dislocate /'dɪsləkeɪt/ *v.t.* вы́вихнуть (*pf.*)

dislodge /dɪs'lɒdʒ/ *v.t.* сме|ща́ть, -сти́ть

disloyal /dɪs'lɔɪəl/ *adj.* нелоя́льный

disloyalty /dɪs'lɔɪəltɪ/ *n.* нелоя́льность, неве́рность

dismal /'dɪzm(ə)l/ *adj.* мра́чный, уны́лый, гнету́щий

dismantle /dɪs'mænt(ə)l/ *v.t.* раз|бира́ть, -обра́ть

dismay /dɪs'meɪ/ *n.* смяте́ние

✒ **dismiss** /dɪs'mɪs/ *v.t.* **1** (send away) распус|ка́ть, -ти́ть **2** (discharge from service) уво́ль|нять, -о́лить **3** (reject): **I ~ed the idea** я оста́вил э́ту мысль **4** (law, a case) прекра|ща́ть, -ти́ть

dismissal /dɪs'mɪs(ə)l/ *n.* увольне́ние

dismissive /dɪs'mɪsɪv/ *adj.* презри́тельный

dismount /dɪs'maʊnt/ *v.i.* (from horse) спе́ши|ваться, -ться; (from bicycle) слез|а́ть, -ть

disobedient /dɪsə'biːdɪənt/ *adj.* непослу́шный

disobey /dɪsə'beɪ/ *v.t.* не слу́шаться, по- + *g.*; не повинова́ться (*impf., pf.*) + *d.*

disorder /dɪs'ɔːdə(r)/ *n.* (untidiness) беспоря́док; (riot) беспоря́дки (*m. pl.*); (med.) расстро́йство

disorderly /dɪs'ɔːdəlɪ/ *adj.* (untidy) беспоря́дочный; (unruly) буйный
■ **~ conduct** *n.* хулига́нство

disorganized /dɪs'ɔːɡənaɪzd/ *adj.* неорганизо́ванный

disorient /dɪs'ɔːrɪənt/ *v.t.* дезориенти́ровать (*impf., pf.*)

disorientate /dɪs'ɔːrɪənteɪt/ *v.t.* (BrE) = disorient

disown /dɪs'əʊn/ *v.t.* отка́з|ываться, -а́ться от + *g.*

disparage /dɪ'spærɪdʒ/ *v.t.* (belittle) преум|еньша́ть, -е́ньшить; говори́ть (*impf.*) с пренебреже́нием о + *p.*

✒ ключева́я ле́ксика

disparate /'dɪspərət/ *adj.* несхо́жий

disparity /dɪ'spærɪtɪ/ *n.* расхожде́ние; (incongruity) несоотве́тствие

dispassionate /dɪ'spæʃənət/ *adj.* бесстра́стный

dispatch /dɪ'spætʃ/ *n.* сообще́ние
● *v.t.* **1** (send off) отпр|авля́ть, -а́вить **2** (deal with) спр|авля́ться, -а́виться с + *i.*

dispel /dɪ'spel/ *v.t.* (**dispelled, dispelling**) рассе́|ивать, -ять

dispensable /dɪ'spensəb(ə)l/ *adj.* необяза́тельный

dispensary /dɪ'spensərɪ/ *n.* апте́ка; (in hospital) пункт разда́чи лека́рств

dispensation /dɪspen'seɪʃ(ə)n/ *n.* **1** (dealing out) разда́ча **2** (order) зако́н; **under the Mosaic ~** по Моисе́еву зако́ну **3** (exemption) освобожде́ние, исключе́ние; (permission) разреше́ние

dispense /dɪ'spens/ *v.t.* **1** (deal out) разд|ава́ть, -а́ть **2** (medicines) пригот|овля́ть, -о́вить
● *v.i.*: **~ with** (do without) об|ходи́ться, -ойти́сь без + *g.*

dispenser /dɪ'spensə(r)/ *n.* **1** (of medicines) фармаце́вт **2** (machine) торго́вый автома́т

disperse /dɪ'spɜːs/ *v.t.* рассе́|ивать, -ять; **the policeman ~d the crowd** полице́йский разогна́л толпу́
● *v.i.* рассе́|иваться, -яться

displace /dɪs'pleɪs/ *v.t.* сме|ща́ть, -сти́ть
■ **~d persons** *n. pl.* перемещённые ли́ца

✒ **display** /dɪ'spleɪ/ *n.* **1** (manifestation) пока́з, проявле́ние **2** (of goods etc.) вы́ставка **3** (of computer) дисплей
● *v.t.* (quality, emotion) проявля́ть, -и́ть; обнару́жи|вать, -ть; (on screen, in a picture) демонстри́ровать, про-; (goods etc.) выставля́ть, вы́ставить

displeased /dɪs'pliːzd/ *adj.* недово́льный; **I am ~ with you** я недово́лен ва́ми

displeasure /dɪs'pleʒə(r)/ *n.* недово́льство, неудово́льствие; **incur sb's ~** навл|ека́ть, -е́чь на себя́ (*or* вызыва́ть, вы́звать) чьё-н. недово́льство

disposable /dɪ'spəʊzəb(ə)l/ *adj.* ра́зовый, однора́зовый

disposal /dɪ'spəʊz(ə)l/ *n.* **1** (getting rid of) удале́ние, устране́ние **2** (control): **the money is at your ~** де́ньги в ва́шем распоряже́нии

dispose /dɪ'spəʊz/ *v.t.*: **he is well ~d towards me** он хорошо́ ко мне отно́сится
● *v.i.* (*with prep.* **of**) изб|авля́ться, -а́виться от + *g.*

disposition /dɪspə'zɪʃ(ə)n/ *n.* **1** (arrangement) расположе́ние **2** (character) нрав, хара́ктер; **he has a cheerful ~** у него́ весёлый нрав

dispossess /dɪspə'zes/ *v.t.* лиш|а́ть, -и́ть (*кого чего*); от|бира́ть, -обра́ть (*что у кого*)

disproportionate /dɪsprə'pɔːʃənət/ *adj.* непропорциона́льный

disprove /dɪs'pruːv/ *v.t.* опров|ерга́ть, -е́ргнуть

disputable /dɪ'spjuːtəb(ə)l/ *adj.* спо́рный

dispute /dɪ'spjuːt/ *n.* **1** (argument) диспут; (disagreement) спор **2** (quarrel) ссора, разногласие
● *v.t.* (call in question, oppose) оспа|ривать, -орить

disqualify /dɪs'kwɒlɪfaɪ/ *v.t.* дисквалифицировать (*impf., pf.*)

disquiet /dɪs'kwaɪət/ *n.* беспокойство, тревога
● *v.t.* беспокоить, о-, тревожить, вс-

disregard /dɪsrɪ'ɡɑːd/ *n.* пренебрежение + *i.*; **he showed ~ for his teachers** он проявлял неуважение к учителям
● *v.t.* игнорировать (*impf., pf.*)

disrepair /dɪsrɪ'peə(r)/ *n.* неисправность; **fall into ~** при|ходить, -йти в упадок/ запустение

disreputable /dɪs'repjʊtəb(ə)l/ *adj.* (behaviour) позорный; (company, person) пользующийся дурной славой

disrepute /dɪsrɪ'pjuːt/ *n.* дурная слава; **fall into ~** приобре|тать, -сти дурную славу

disrespect /dɪsrɪ'spekt/ *n.* неуважение (**for, towards:** к + *d.*)

disrespectful /dɪsrɪ'spektfʊl/ *adj.* непочтительный

disrupt /dɪs'rʌpt/ *v.t.* (event) срывать, сорвать; (process, system) прер|ывать, -вать

disruption /dɪs'rʌpʃ(ə)n/ *n.* срыв

disruptive /dɪs'rʌptɪv/ *adj.* разрушительный, подрывной

dissatisfaction /dɪsætɪs'fækʃ(ə)n/ *n.* неудовлетворённость

dissatisfied /dɪ'sætɪsfaɪd/ *adj.* недовольный; **she is ~ with her job** она недовольна своей работой

dissect /dɪ'sekt/ *v.t.* вскр|ывать, -ыть

disseminate /dɪ'semɪneɪt/ *v.t.* распростран|ять, -ить

dissent /dɪ'sent/ *n.* несогласие

dissertation /dɪsə'teɪʃ(ə)n/ *n.* диссертация

disservice /dɪs'sɜːvɪs/ *n.* плохая услуга; ущерб; **he did me a ~** он нанёс мне ущерб; он навредил мне; **her words did great ~ to the cause** её слова нанесли большой ущерб делу

dissident /'dɪsɪd(ə)nt/ *n.* (pol.) диссидент
● *adj.* несогласный

dissimilar /dɪ'sɪmɪlə(r)/ *adj.* несходный

dissipated /'dɪsɪpeɪtɪd/ *adj.* беспутный; (life style) разгульный

dissociate /dɪ'səʊʃɪeɪt/ *v.t.*: **~ oneself** отмеж|ёвываться, -еваться (**from:** от + *g.*); **I ~ myself from what has been said** я отмежёвываюсь от того, что было сказано

dissolute /'dɪsəluːt/ *adj.* распущенный, беспутный, распутный

dissolve /dɪ'zɒlv/ *v.t.* **1** (phys.) раствор|ять, -ить **2**: **the queen ~d parliament** королева распустила парламент
● *v.i.* (phys.) раствор|яться, -иться

dissuade /dɪ'sweɪd/ *v.t.* отгов|аривать, -орить (*кого от чего*)

distance /'dɪst(ə)ns/ *n.* **1** (measure of space) дистанция, расстояние; **she lives within walking ~ of the office** от её дома до работы можно дойти пешком; **in the ~** вдалеке; **from a ~** издали, издалека **2** (fig.): **keep one's ~** держаться (*impf.*) в стороне (**from:** от + *g.*)

distant /'dɪst(ə)nt/ *adj.* **1** (in space) далёкий, дальний **2** (fig., remote): **a ~ cousin** дальний родственник **3** (reserved) сдержанный, холодный

distaste /dɪs'teɪst/ *n.* отвращение (**for:** к + *d.*)

distasteful /dɪs'teɪstfʊl/ *adj.* отвратительный, неприятный

distillery /dɪ'stɪlərɪ/ *n.* ликёроводочный завод

distinct /dɪ'stɪŋkt/ *adj.* **1** (sound) внятный; (picture) отчётливый; (advantage, possibility) очевидный **2** (different) отличный (**from:** от + *g.*)

distinction /dɪ'stɪŋkʃ(ə)n/ *n.* **1** (difference) отличие **2** (discrimination) различие **3** (special quality) отличительная особенность; **a writer of ~** выдающийся писатель **4** (mark of honour) отличие

distinctive /dɪ'stɪŋktɪv/ *adj.* отличительный

distinguish /dɪ'stɪŋɡwɪʃ/ *v.t.* различ|ать, -ить

distinguished /dɪ'stɪŋɡwɪʃt/ *adj.* выдающийся, видный

distort /dɪ'stɔːt/ *v.t.* искрив|лять, -ить; **~ facts** извра|щать, -тить факты

distract /dɪ'strækt/ *v.t.* отвл|екать, -ечь; **it ~s me from my work** это отвлекает меня от работы

distraction /dɪ'strækʃ(ə)n/ *n.* помеха

distraught /dɪ'strɔːt/ *adj.* обезумевший

distress /dɪ'stres/ *n.* **1** (physical suffering) изнурение, изнеможение **2** (mental suffering) тревога, депрессия **3** (danger) бедствие; **a ship in ~** судно, терпящее бедствие
● *v.t.* огорч|ать, -ить

distressing /dɪ'stresɪŋ/ *adj.* огорчительный

distribute /dɪ'strɪbjuːt/ *v.t.* **1** (deal out) распредел|ять, -ить; (goods) распростран|ять, -ить **2** (spread) распредел|ять, -ить

distribution /dɪstrɪ'bjuːʃ(ə)n/ *n.* распределение; (of goods) распространение

distributor /dɪ'strɪbjʊtə(r)/ *n.* (comm.) дистрибьютор

district /'dɪstrɪkt/ *n.* район, округ; (*attr.*) районный, окружной
■ **~ attorney** *n.* (AmE) окружной прокурор

distrust /dɪs'trʌst/ *v.t.* не доверять (*impf.*) + *d.*

distrustful /dɪs'trʌstfʊl/ *adj.* недоверчивый

disturb /dɪ'stɜːb/ *v.t.* беспокоить, о-; (peace) нар|ушать, -ушить; **he was ~ed by the news** он был обеспокоен новостью

disturbance /dɪ'stɜːb(ə)ns/ *n.* (act of troubling) нарушение; (riot) волнения (*nt. pl.*)

disturbing /dɪ'stɜːbɪŋ/ *adj.* тревожный

disuse /dɪs'juːs/ *n.*: **fall into ~** выходить, выйти из употребления

disused /dɪs'juːzd/ *adj.*: **a ~ well** заброшенный колодец

ditch /dɪtʃ/ *n.* кана́ва; ров
- *v.t.* (infml): ~ one's plans забр|а́сывать,
-о́сить свои́ пла́ны; ~ sb бр|оса́ть, -о́сить
кого́-н.

dither /'dɪðə(r)/ *v.i.* (infml) колеба́ться, по-

ditto /'dɪtəʊ/ *n.* (*pl.* ~s) то же

diva /'diːvə/ *n.* (*pl.* ~s) примадо́нна, ди́ва

divan /dɪ'væn/ *n.* тахта́, дива́н
- ■ ~ **bed** *n.* дива́н-крова́ть

dive /daɪv/ *n.* ныро́к, ныря́ние; (of aircraft)
пики́рование
- *v.i.* (*past and p.p.* **dived** or AmE also **dove**)
(plunge into water) ныр|я́ть, -ну́ть; (in diving suit)
погру|жа́ться, -зи́ться

diver /'daɪvə(r)/ *n.* ныра́льщик; водола́з

diverge /daɪ'vɜːdʒ/ *v.i.* ра|сходи́ться, -зойти́сь

diverse /daɪ'vɜːs/ *adj.* разнообра́зный

diversify /daɪ'vɜːsɪfaɪ/ *v.t.* разнообра́зить
(*impf.*); диверсифици́ровать (*impf., pf.*)

diversion /daɪ'vɜːʃ(ə)n/ *n.* **1** (turning aside)
отклоне́ние; traffic ~ (BrE) объе́зд
2 (amusement) развлече́ние, заба́ва **3**: create
a ~ отвл|ека́ть, -е́чь внима́ние

diversity /daɪ'vɜːsɪtɪ/ *n.* разнообра́зие

divert /daɪ'vɜːt/ *v.t.* (deflect) отклон|я́ть, -и́ть;
(entertain) развл|ека́ть, -е́чь

divest /daɪ'vest/ *v.t.*: ~ sb of sth лиш|а́ть, -и́ть
(*кого чего-л.*); ~ oneself of responsibilities
слож|и́ть (*pf.*) с себя́ обя́занности

✓ **divide** /dɪ'vaɪd/ *n.* расхожде́ние
- *v.t.* **1** (share) дели́ть, по-, раз-; they ~d
the money equally они́ раздели́ли де́ньги
по́ровну **2** (math.) дели́ть, раз-; ~ 27 by 3
27 дели́ть, раз- на́ 3 **3** (separate) разде́л|я́ть,
-и́ть; dividing line разграничи́тельная ли́ния
4 (cause disagreement) разъедин|я́ть, -и́ть
- *v.i.* дели́ться, раз-; the road ~s доро́га
разветвля́ется

dividend /'dɪvɪdend/ *n.* (fin.) дивиде́нд

divine /dɪ'vaɪn/ *adj.* (**diviner**, **divinest**)
боже́ственный

diving /'daɪvɪŋ/ *n.* ныря́ние
- ■ ~ **board** *n.* трампли́н, вы́шка (для прыжко́в
в во́ду); ~ **suit** *n.* скафа́ндр

divisible /dɪ'vɪzɪb(ə)l/ *adj.* (раз)дели́мый

✓ **division** /dɪ'vɪʒ(ə)n/ *n.* **1** (math.) деле́ние
2 (dividing) разделе́ние, разде́л **3** (mil.)
диви́зия **4** (department) отде́л

divisive /dɪ'vaɪsɪv/ *adj.* вызыва́ющий
разногла́сия

divorce /dɪ'vɔːs/ *n.* (law) разво́д
- *v.t.* (law) разв|оди́ть, -ести́; he ~d his
wife он развёлся с жено́й; she is ~d она́
разведена́
- *v.i.* разв|оди́ться, -ести́сь

divorcee /dɪvɔː'siː/ *n.* (AmE **divorcé**, *f.*
divorcée) разведённый (муж), разведённая
(жена́)

divulge /daɪ'vʌldʒ/ *v.t.* разгла|ша́ть, -си́ть

DIY (BrE) *abbr.* (*of* **do it yourself**): ~ store
магази́н «Уме́лые ру́ки»

✓ ключева́я ле́ксика

dizzy /'dɪzɪ/ *adj.* (**dizzier, dizziest**)
испы́тывающий головокруже́ние; I feel ~ у
меня́ кру́жится голова́

DJ *abbr.* (*of* **disc jockey**) диджѐй

DNA *abbr.* (*of* **deoxyribonucleic acid**)
ДНК (дезоксирибонуклеи́новая кислота́)

✓ **do** /duː/ *v.t. & aux.* (3rd pers. sing. pres. **does**,
past **did**, *p.p.* **done**) **1** (as aux. or substitute
for v. already used; not translated unless emph.): I ~
not smoke я не курю́; did you not see me?
ра́зве вы меня́ не ви́дели?; I ~ want to go
я о́чень хочу́ пойти́; ~ tell me пожа́луйста,
расскажи́те мне; they promised to help, and
they did они́ обеща́ли помо́чь и помогли́;
so ~ I я то́же **2** (perform, carry out): what can
I ~ for you? чем могу́ служи́ть?; what ~es
he ~ (for a living)? чем он занима́ется?;
the team did well кома́нда вы́ступила
успе́шно; easier said than ~ne легко́
сказа́ть; well ~ne! молоде́ц! **3** (render):
it ~es him credit э́то де́лает ему́ честь;
it won't ~ any good э́то бесполе́зно, э́то
ничего́ не даст **4** (solve): ~ a sum реш|а́ть,
-и́ть арифмети́ческую зада́чу **5** (attend
to): he ~es book reviews он рецензи́рует
кни́ги; we did geography today сего́дня мы
занима́лись геогра́фией **6** (arrange, clean, tidy):
~ one's hair прич|ёсываться, -еса́ться; ~ the
dishes мыть, по- посу́ду **7** (cook): well ~ne
хорошо́ прожа́ренный; the potatoes are ~ne
карто́шка свари́лась/гото́ва **8** (infml, swindle)
над|ува́ть, -у́ть **9**: ~ne! (agreed) по рука́м!
- *v.i.* (3rd pers. sing. pres. **does**: past **did**,
p.p. **done**) **1** (act, behave): ~ as I tell you
де́лай, что тебе́ говоря́т **2** (be satisfactory,
fitting or advisable): the scraps will ~ for the dog
объе́дки пойду́т собáке; this will never ~ э́то
никуда́ не годи́тся; так не пойдёт; that will
~! (is enough) хва́тит!; дово́льно!; tomorrow
will ~ мо́жно и за́втра **3** (fare, succeed): how
~ you ~? здра́вствуйте!; как пожива́ете?;
how did he ~ in his exams? как он сдал
экза́мены?; my roses are ~ing well мои́ ро́зы
хорошо́ расту́т; the patient is ~ing well
больно́й поправля́ется
- *with preps.*: what shall we ~ about lunch?
как насчёт обе́да?; ~ sb out of sth (cheat,
deprive of) выма́нивать, вы́манить что-н. у
кого́-н.; what have you ~ne with the keys?
куда́ вы де́ли ключи́?; I could ~ with a drink
я охо́тно (or с удово́льствием) вы́пил бы;
that coat could ~ with a clean не помеша́ло
бы вы́чистить э́то пальто́; he ~esn't know
what to ~ with himself он не зна́ет, чем
заня́ться; it is nothing to ~ with you э́то
вас не каса́ется; these books are ~ne with
э́ти кни́ги бо́льше не нужны́; we must ~
without luxuries мы должны́ обойти́сь без
ро́скоши; I can ~ without his silly jokes мне
надое́ли его́ дура́цкие шу́тки
- □ ~ **away** *v.i.*: ~ away with конча́ть, ко́нчить
с + *i.*
- □ ~ **in** *v.t.* (sl., kill) уб|ира́ть, -ра́ть; (infml, exhaust):
I am ~ne in я изм ота́н
- □ ~ **out** *v.t.* (BrE, clean, e.g. a room) уб|ира́ть, -ра́ть;
(BrE, clear, e.g. a cupboard) вычища́ть, вы́чистить

□ ~ **up** *v.t.* (repair, refurnish): ~ up a room отдéл|ывать, -áть кóмнату; (fasten): ~ up a parcel завя́з|ывать, -áть пакéт; ~ up a dress застёг|ивать, -нýть плáтье

■ ~**-it-yourself** *adj.* самодéльный

Dobermann /ˈdəʊbəmən/, **Dobermann pinscher** /ˈdəʊbəmən ˈpɪnʃə(r)/ (AmE **Doberman**) *n.* доберма́н(-пи́нчер)

docile /ˈdəʊsaɪl/ *adj.* послýшный, покóрный

dock[1] /dɒk/ *n.* (in court) скамья́ подсудúмых

dock[2] /dɒk/ *n.* **1** (naut.) док **2** (*in pl.*) (port facilities) верфь **3** (wharf) прúстань
● *v.i.* (go into ~) входúть, войтú в док; (of space vehicles) стыкова́ться, со-

■ ~**yard** *n.* верфь

dock[3] /dɒk/ *v.t.* (reduce) урéз|ывать, -áть

docker /ˈdɒkə(r)/ *n.* дóкер; портóвый рабóчий

◇ **doctor** /ˈdɒktə(r)/ *n.* **1** (of medicine) врач, дóктор **2** (academic) дóктор
● *v.t.* (falsify) поддéл|ывать, -ать

doctoral /ˈdɒktər(ə)l/ *adj.* дóкторский

doctorate /ˈdɒktərət/ *n.* стéпень дóктора

doctrine /ˈdɒktrɪn/ *n.* доктрúна

◇ **document** *n.* /ˈdɒkjʊmənt/ докумéнт
● *v.t.* /ˈdɒkjʊment/ документи́ровать (*impf.*, *pf.*)

documentary /dɒkjʊˈmentərɪ/ *n.* документáльный фильм

documentation /dɒkjʊmenˈteɪʃ(ə)n/ *n.* документáция

doddery /ˈdɒdərɪ/ *adj.* трясýщийся от стáрости; дрýхлый

dodge /dɒdʒ/ *n.* увёртка
● *v.t.* увúл|ивать, -ьнýть от + *g.*; ~ a blow увора́чиваться, увернýться от удáра
● *v.i.* уклон|я́ться, -úться (от + *g.*)

dodgy /ˈdɒdʒɪ/ *adj.* (**dodgier**, **dodgiest**) (BrE, infml) (suspicious) подозрúтельный; (risky) рискóванный

does /dʌz/ *3rd pers. sing. pres. of* ▸ **do**

doesn't /ˈdʌz(ə)nt/ *neg. of* ▸ **does**

doff /dɒf/ *v.t.* сн|имáть, -ять (*шля́пу*)

◇ **dog** /dɒg/ *n.* **1** собáка, пёс (also fig., pej.) **2** (male) кобéль (*m.*) **3** (fig.): **go to the** ~**s** разорúться (*pf.*), пойтú (*pf.*) прáхом

■ ~ **collar** *n.* ошéйник; (infml, clergyman's) крýглый стоя́чий воротнúк; ~**-eared** *adj.* потрёпанный; ~**house** *n.* (AmE) конурá; **in the** ~**house** (infml) в немúлости; ~**-paddle** *v.i.* плáвать (*indet.*) по-собáчьи; ~**sbody** *n.* (BrE) ишáк, работя́га (*c.g.*)

dogged /ˈdɒgɪd/ *adj.* упóрный

dogma /ˈdɒgmə/ *n.* дóгма; (specific) дóгмат

dogmatic /dɒgˈmætɪk/ *adj.* (views) догматúческий; (person) догматúчный

dogmatism /ˈdɒgmətɪz(ə)m/ *n.* догматúзм

doing /ˈduːɪŋ/ *n.*: **this was her** ~ э́то её рук дéло; **it will take some** ~ придётся постарáться; э́то не тáк прóсто

doldrums /ˈdɒldrəmz/ *n. pl.* (fig.) уны́ние, хандрá; **be in the** ~ быть в уны́нии, хандрúть (*impf.*)

dole /dəʊl/ *n.* (BrE, infml, benefit) пособúе по безрабóтице; **he is on the** ~ он получáет пособúе по безрабóтице
● *v.t.*: ~ **out** раздавáть, -áть

doleful /ˈdəʊlfʊl/ *adj.* скóрбный

doll /dɒl/ *n.* кýкла

◇ **dollar** /ˈdɒlə(r)/ *n.* дóллар

dollop /ˈdɒləp/ *n.* (infml) солúдная пóрция

dolphin /ˈdɒlfɪn/ *n.* дельфúн

domain /dəˈmeɪn/ *n.* (fig.) óбласть; (comput.) домéн

dome /dəʊm/ *n.* кýпол

domed /dəʊmd/ *adj.* куполообрáзный

◇ **domestic** /dəˈmestɪk/ *adj.* **1** (of the home; of animals) домáшний **2** (not foreign) отéчественный, внýтренний

domesticate /dəˈmestɪkeɪt/ *v.t.* (tame) приручáть, -úть

domesticity /dɒmeˈstɪsɪtɪ/ *n.* семéйная/ домáшняя жизнь

domicile /ˈdɒmɪsaɪl/ *n.* (dwelling) мéсто жúтельства
● *v.t.*: ~**d in England** имéющий постоя́нное местожúтельство в А́нглии

dominance /ˈdɒmɪnəns/ *n.* преобладáние, госпóдство

dominant /ˈdɒmɪnənt/ *adj.* доминúрующий

◇ **dominate** /ˈdɒmɪneɪt/ *v.t. & i.* **1** (prevail) доминúровать (*impf.*) (над + *i.*) **2** (influence) подавля́ть (*impf.*); **she** ~**s her daughter** онá подавля́ет дочь

domination /dɒmɪˈneɪʃ(ə)n/ *n.* госпóдство

domineering /dɒmɪˈnɪərɪŋ/ *adj.* влáстный

Dominican /dəˈmɪnɪkən/ *adj.*: **the** ~ **Republic** Доминикáнская Респýблика

domino /ˈdɒmɪnəʊ/ *n.* (*pl.* ~**es**) кость доминó; (*in pl.*) (game) доминó (*nt. indecl.*)

don /dɒn/ *n.* **1** (Spanish title) дон **2** (university teacher) преподавáтель (*m.*)

■ **D**~ **Juan** *n.* (fig.) донжуáн

donate /dəʊˈneɪt/ *v.t.* дарúть, по-

donation /dəʊˈneɪʃ(ə)n/ *n.* дар

done /dʌn/ *p.p. of* ▸ **do**

donkey /ˈdɒŋkɪ/ *n.* осёл (also fig.)

donor /ˈdəʊnə(r)/ *n.* дарúтель (-ница); (of blood, transplant) дóнор

◇ **don't** /dəʊnt/ *neg. of* ▸ **do**

doodle /ˈduːd(ə)l/ *v.i.* чúркать (*impf.*)

doom /duːm/ *n.* (ruin) гúбель
● *v.t.* обрекáть, -éчь на + *a.*

◇ **door** /dɔː(r)/ *n.* **1** (of room etc.) дверь; (of cupboard etc.) двéрца; **behind closed** ~**s** (in secret) за закры́тыми дверя́ми **2** (fig.): **a** ~ **to success** путь к успéху

■ ~**bell** *n.* двернóй звонóк; ~ **handle** *n.* дверна́я рýчка; ~ **keeper** *n.* привра́тник; швейца́р; ~**knob** *n.* крýглая дверна́я рýчка; ~**man** *n.* = doorkeeper; ~**mat** *n.* половúк; ~**step** *n.* порóг; ~**-to-**~ *adj.*: ~**-to-**~ **salesman** коммивояжёр; ~**way** *n.* двернóй проём

d

dope /dəʊp/ n. infml **1** (drug) дурма́н, нарко́тик **2** (fool) ду́рень (m.)
● v.t. **1** (make unconscious) дурма́нить, о- **2** (put narcotic in) нака́ч|ивать, -а́ть нарко́тиками

dopey /'dəʊpɪ/ adj. (**dopier, dopiest**) (bemused by drug or sleep) одурма́ненный; (infml, foolish) чо́кнутый

dormant /'dɔ:mənt/ adj. (of animals) в спя́чке; ~ volcano спя́щий вулка́н

dormitory /'dɔ:mɪtərɪ/ n. о́бщая спа́льня

dormouse /'dɔ:maʊs/ n. (pl. **dormice**) со́ня

DOS /dɒs/ abbr. (of **disk operating system**) ДОС (ди́сковая операцио́нная систе́ма)

dose /dəʊs/ n. до́за

doss /dɒs/ v.i. (BrE, infml) **1** (also ~ **down**) ночева́ть, пере- **2** (also ~ **around**) безде́льничать (impf.)
■ ~**house** n. ночле́жка

dossier /'dɒsɪə(r)/ n. досье́ (nt. indecl.), де́ло

dot /dɒt/ n. то́чка; **on the** ~ то́чно
● v.t. (**dotted, dotting**) (place ~ on): ~ one's i's (lit., fig.) ста́вить, по- то́чки над «i»
■ ~**ted line** n. пункти́р; пункти́рная ли́ния

dotage /'dəʊtɪdʒ/ n. ста́рческое слабоу́мие, мара́зм; **he is in his** ~ он впал в де́тство/ мара́зм

dot-com company /dɒt'kɒm/ n. интерне́т-компа́ния

dote /dəʊt/ v.i.: ~ **on** (child, friend) обожа́ть (impf.)

✓ **double** /'dʌb(ə)l/ n. **1** (two shots of spirits) двойна́я ме́ра **2** (person resembling another) двойни́к **3** (running pace): **at the** ~ (BrE), **on the** ~ (AmE) бе́глым ша́гом **4** (tennis) па́рная игра́; **mixed** ~s сме́шанные па́ры (f. pl.)
● adj. (in two parts; twice as much) двойно́й; **'Anna' is spelt with a** ~ **'n'** «А́нна» пи́шется с двумя́ «н»
● adv. вдво́е; **bend** ~ сгиба́ть(ся), согну́ть(ся) вдво́е; **pay** ~ плати́ть, за- вдвойне́; **she sees** ~ у неё дво́ится в глаза́х
● v.t. удв|а́ивать, -о́ить
● v.i. **1** (become twice as great) удв|а́иваться, -о́иться **2** (turn sharply): **he** ~**d back on his tracks** он пошёл обра́тно по своему́ сле́ду **3** (bend) корчиться, с-; **she** ~**d up with the pain** она́ скорчилась от бо́ли **4** (combine roles): **I** ~**d for him** я дубли́ровал его́; **the porter** ~**s as waiter** носи́льщик рабо́тает официа́нтом по совмести́тельству
■ ~**-barrelled name** n. (BrE) двойна́я фами́лия; ~ **bass** n. контраба́с; ~ **bed** n. дву(х)спа́льная крова́ть; ~**-breasted** adj. двубо́ртный; ~**-check** v.t. перепров|еря́ть, -е́рить; ~**-click** v.i. (comput.) два́жды щёлк|ать, -нуть; ~**-cross** v.t. обма́н|ывать, -у́ть; ~**-decker** n. (bus) двухэта́жный авто́бус; ~**-dip recession** n. (econ.) двойно́е паде́ние; ~ **Dutch** n. (BrE) тарабáрщина, кита́йская гра́мота; ~**-park** v.t. & i. ста́вить, по- (маши́ну) во второ́й ряд; ~ **room** n. (in hotel) двухме́стный но́мер; ~ **take** n. (fig.) заме́дленная реа́кция

✓ ключева́я ле́ксика

✓ **doubt** /daʊt/ n. сомне́ние; **there is no** ~ **that ...** нет сомне́ния в том, что...; **the question is in** ~ э́тот вопро́с ещё не я́сен; **without** ~ вне сомне́ния; несомне́нно; **no** ~ несомне́нно, безусло́вно
● v.t. & i. сомнева́ться (impf.) (в + p.); **I** ~ **that, whether she will come** (я) сомнева́юсь, что она́ придёт

doubtful /'daʊtfʊl/ adj. **1** (feeling doubt) сомнева́ющийся **2** (causing doubt) сомни́тельный

dough /dəʊ/ n. те́сто
■ ~**nut** n. по́нчик

dour /dʊə(r)/ adj. суро́вый

douse /daʊs/ v.t. (drench) зал|ива́ть, -и́ть; (extinguish) гаси́ть, по-

dove /dʌv/ n. го́лубь (m.)

dowdy /'daʊdɪ/ adj. (**dowdier, dowdiest**) неэлега́нтный

down¹ /daʊn/ n. (hair, fluff) пух, пушо́к

✓ **down²** /daʊn/ n. невзго́да; **ups and** ~s взлёты (m. pl.) и паде́ния (nt. pl.)
● adj. напра́вленный вниз/кни́зу
● adv. **1** (expr. motion/place) вниз/внизу́; **the blinds are** ~ што́ры спу́щены; **prices are** ~ це́ны упа́ли; (fig.): **he is £15** ~ он в убы́тке на 15 фу́нтов **2** (expr. movement to lower level): **climb** ~ слез|а́ть, -ть; **come** ~ спус|ка́ться, -ти́ться **3** (expr. change of position): **sit** ~ сади́ться, сесть; **lie** ~ ложи́ться, лечь; **fall** ~ па́дать, упа́сть; **knock sb** ~ сби|ва́ть, -ть; **be bent** ~ он нагну́лся **4** (reduction): **the wind died** ~ ве́тер ути́х; **the house burnt** ~ дом сгоре́л дотла́ **5**: ~ **with the government!** доло́й прави́тельство!
● prep. **1** (expr. downward direction): **we walked** ~ **the hill** мы шли с горы́ (or под го́ру); **tears ran** ~ **her face** слёзы текли́/кати́лись у неё по лицу́ **2** (at, to a lower or further part of): **further** ~ **the river** да́льше вниз по реке́; **we sailed** ~ **the Volga** мы плы́ли вниз по Во́лге; **she lives** ~ **the street** она́ живёт да́льше по э́той у́лице **3** (along): **he walked** ~ **the street** он шёл по у́лице

down-and-out /daʊnə'naʊt/ n. бродя́га (m.); бездо́мный

downcast /'daʊnkɑ:st/ adj. (dejected) удручённый; пода́вленный

downfall /'daʊnfɔ:l/ n. паде́ние

downgrade /'daʊngreɪd/ v.t. пон|ижа́ть, -и́зить в чи́не

downhearted /daʊn'hɑ:tɪd/ adj. пода́вленный

downhill /'daʊnhɪl/ adv. под го́ру; вниз; **go** ~ (fig.) кати́ться (det.) по накло́нной пло́скости

download /daʊn'ləʊd/ v.t. (comput.) загру|жа́ть, -зи́ть; ска́ч|ивать, скача́ть

downmarket /daʊn'mɑ:kɪt/ adj. (BrE) дешёвый

downpour /'daʊnpɔ:(r)/ n. ли́вень (m.)

downright /'daʊnraɪt/ adj. (straightforward, blunt) прямо́й; (absolute) соверше́нный; я́вный

downshift /'daʊnʃɪft/ v.i. **1** (AmE, motoring) переключ|а́ть, -и́ть на ни́жнюю ско́рость

2 (at work) пере|ходи́ть, -йти́ на ме́нее напряжённую, хотя́ и нижеопла́чиваемую рабо́ту

downsize /'daʊnsaɪz/ *v.t. & i.* (comm.) ум|еньша́ть, -е́ньшить разме́ры (компа́нии) за счёт увольне́ния рабо́тников

Down's syndrome /daʊnz/ *n.* боле́знь/ синдро́м Да́уна

downstairs *adj.* /'daʊnsteəz/: ~ **rooms** ко́мнаты пе́рвого этажа́
● *adv.* /daʊn'steəz/ (expr. place) внизу́; (expr. motion) вниз

downstream /daʊn'stri:m/ *adv.* вниз по тече́нию

down-to-earth /'daʊntəə:θ/ *adj.* практи́чный

downtown /'daʊntaʊn/ *adj.* (AmE) располо́женный в делово́й ча́сти го́рода

downtrodden /'daʊntrɒd(ə)n/ *adj.* угнетённый

downturn /'daʊntə:n/ *n.* (fall, reduction) паде́ние, спад

downward /'daʊnwəd/ *adj.* спуска́ющийся

downwards /'daʊnwədz/ *adv.* вниз

doze /dəʊz/ *v.i.* дрема́ть (*impf.*); ~ **off** задрема́ть (*pf.*)

♂ **dozen** /'dʌz(ə)n/ *n.* **1** (*pl.* ~) дю́жина **2**: ~s **of** мно́жество, ма́сса + *g.*

dozy /'dəʊzɪ/ *adj.* (**dozier**, **doziest**) сонли́вый; (BrE, not alert) рассе́янный

drab /dræb/ *adj.* (**drabber**, **drabbest**) се́рый

draft /drɑ:ft/ *n.* (see also ▸ **draught**) **1** (outline, rough copy) набро́сок, чернови́к **2** (order for payment) чек, тра́тта **3** (AmE, conscription) призы́в
● *v.t.* **1** (detach for duty) наря|жа́ть, -ди́ть **2** (conscript) приз|ыва́ть, -ва́ть **3** (prepare ~ of) набр|а́сывать, -оса́ть чернови́к + *g.*
■ ~ **dodger** *n.* лицо́, уклоня́ющееся от вое́нной слу́жбы

draftsman /'drɑ:ftsmən/ *n.* (of contracts etc.) состави́тель (*m.*) (*законопрое́кта и т. п.*); (AmE, one who draws) чертёжник

drafty /'drɑ:ftɪ/ *adj.* (AmE) = **draughty**

drag /dræg/ *n.* (infml, person) зану́да; (thing) тоска́ зелёная
● *v.t.* (**dragged**, **dragging**) (pull) тяну́ть, волочи́ть, тащи́ть (*all impf.*); **I had to** ~ **him to the party** мне пришло́сь тащи́ть его́ на вечери́нку; ~ **one's feet** (fig.) тяну́ть, ме́длить (*both impf.*)
● *v.i.* (**dragged**, **dragging**) **1** (trail) волочи́ться (*impf.*) **2** (be slow or tedious) тяну́ться (*impf.*)
▫ ~ **on** *v.i.*: **the performance** ~**ged on till 11** представле́ние затяну́лось до оди́ннадцати часо́в

dragon /'drægən/ *n.* (fabulous beast) драко́н
■ ~**fly** *n.* стрекоза́

dragoon /drə'gu:n/ *v.t.* прин|ужда́ть, -у́дить; **she was** ~**ed into obeying** её заста́вили подчини́ться

drain /dreɪn/ *n.* (channel carrying off sewage etc.) водосто́к; (*in pl.*) (system of ~s) канализа́ция
● *v.t.* **1** (water etc.) отв|оди́ть, -ести́ **2** (land etc.) осуш|а́ть, -и́ть (*impf.*) **3** (exhaust) истощ|а́ть, -и́ть
● *v.i.* **1** (flow away) ут|ека́ть, -е́чь **2** (lose moisture) высыха́ть, вы́сохнуть
■ ~**ing board** (BrE), ~**board** (AmE) *nn.* суши́лка; ~**pipe** *n.* дрена́жная труба́

drainage /'dreɪnɪdʒ/ *n.* **1** (draining or being drained) дрена́ж, осуше́ние **2** (system of drains) канализа́ция

drake /dreɪk/ *n.* се́лезень (*m.*)

drama /'drɑ:mə/ *n.* дра́ма

dramatic /drə'mætɪk/ *adj.* (pert. to drama) драмати́ческий; (exciting) драмати́чный

dramatics /drə'mætɪks/ *n.* (staging of plays) драмати́ческое иску́сство; теа́тр; **amateur** ~ люби́тельский/самоде́ятельный теа́тр

dramatist /'dræmətɪst/ *n.* драмату́рг

dramatize /'dræmətaɪz/ *v.t.* (turn into a play) инсцени́ровать (*impf., pf.*); (exaggerate) драматизи́ровать (*impf., pf.*)

drank /dræŋk/ *past of* ▸ **drink**

drape /dreɪp/ *n.* (usu. *in pl.*) за́навес, портье́ра
● *v.t.* драпирова́ть, за-

drastic /'dræstɪk/ *adj.* реши́тельный, круто́й

draught /drɑ:ft/ (AmE **draft**) *n.* **1** (current of air) тя́га; **there is a** ~ **in here** здесь сквози́т **2** (of liquor): ~ **beer, beer on** ~ пи́во из бо́чки **3** (in pl., BrE, game) ша́шки (*f. pl.*)

draughtsman /'drɑ:ftsmən/ *n.* чертёжник

draughty /'drɑ:ftɪ/ (AmE **drafty**) *adj.* (**draughtier**, **draughtiest**): **this is a** ~ **room** в э́той ко́мнате постоя́нный сквозня́к

♂ **draw** /drɔ:/ *n.* (in lottery) ро́зыгрыш; (~n **game**) ничья́
● *v.t.* (*past* **drew**, *p.p.* **drawn**) **1** (pull, move) тяну́ть (*impf.*); таска́ть (*indet.*), тащи́ть (*det.*); ~ **the curtains** (close) задв|ига́ть, -и́нуть занаве́ски; (open) раздв|ига́ть, -и́нуть занаве́ски **2** (extract) выта́скивать, вы́тащить; ~ **a knife** выхва́тывать, вы́хватить нож; ~ **blood** ра́нить (*impf., pf.*) кого́-н. до кро́ви; ~ **lots** тяну́ть, вы́жребий **3** (obtain from a source): ~ **money out of the bank** снима́ть, снять де́ньги в ба́нке; ~ **on one's savings** тра́тить, по-свои́ сбереже́ния **4** (attract) привл|ека́ть, -е́чь; **I drew him into the conversation** я втяну́л/вовлёк его́ в разгово́р **5** (trace, depict) рисова́ть, на-; черти́ть, на- **6** (of mental operations): ~ **a distinction/comparison** пров|оди́ть, -ести́ разли́чие/сравне́ние; ~ **conclusions** при|ходи́ть, -йти́ к вы́водам **7** (of contest): **the match was** ~**n** матч зако́нчился вничью́
● *v.i.* (*past* **drew**, *p.p.* **drawn**) (move, come) прид|вига́ться, -ви́нуться; **the day drew to a close** день бли́зился к концу́
▫ ~ **in** *v.i.*: **the train drew in** по́езд подошёл к перро́ну; (shorten): **the days are** ~**ing in** дни стано́вятся коро́че
▫ ~ **out** *v.t.* (extract) выта́скивать, вы́тащить;

выти́гивать, вы́тянуть; (prolong) затя́|гивать,
-ну́ть; (encourage to speak): ~ **sb out** вызыва́ть,
вы́звать кого́-н. на разгово́р
• *v.i.*: **the train drew out** по́езд отошёл
□ ~ **up** *v.t.* (plan, contract, etc.) сост|авля́ть, -а́вить
■ ~**back** *n.* (disadvantage) недоста́ток

drawer /drɔ:(r)/ *n.* (in table etc.) (выдвижно́й)
я́щик

d **drawing** /'drɔ:ɪŋ/ *n.* **1** (technique) рисова́ние
2 (piece of ~) рису́нок
■ ~ **board** *n.* чертёжная доска́; ~ **pin** *n.* (BrE)
кно́пка; ~ **room** *n.* гости́ная

drawl /drɔ:l/ *n.* протя́жное произноше́ние

drawn /drɔ:n/ *p.p. of* ▸ draw

dread /dred/ *v.t.* боя́ться (*impf.*) + *g.*; **I ~
to think what may happen** мне стра́шно
поду́мать, что мо́жет случи́ться

dreadful /'dredfʊl/ *adj.* ужа́сный

✦ **dream** /dri:m/ *n.* **1** (appearance in sleep) сон,
сновиде́ние **2** (fantasy) мечта́, мечта́ние
• *v.t. & i.* (*past and p.p.* **dreamed** /dremt,
dri:md/ *or* **dreamt** /dremt/) **1** (in sleep)
ви́деть (*impf.*) сон; **I ~t of you** вы мне
сни́лись; я ви́дел вас во сне **2** (imagine)
пом|ышля́ть, -ы́слить о + *p.*; **I never ~t of
doing so** у меня́ и в мы́слях не́ было де́лать
э́того; **he ~t up a plan** (infml) он сочини́л
план

dreamer /'dri:mə(r)/ *n.* (dreamy person)
мечта́тель (*m.*); (visionary) фантазёр

dreamt /dremt/ *past and p.p. of* ▸ dream

dreamy /'dri:mɪ/ *adj.* (**dreamier**,
dreamiest) мечта́тельный; (infml, lovely)
восхити́тельный

dreary /'drɪərɪ/ *adj.* (**drearier**, **dreariest**)
(gloomy) тоскли́вый; (dull) се́рый

dregs /dregz/ *n. pl.* отсто́й, оса́док

drench /drentʃ/ *v.t.* пром|а́чивать, -очи́ть

✦ **dress** /dres/ *n.* **1** (clothing, costume) оде́жда,
наря́д, туале́т **2** (woman's garment) пла́тье
• *v.t.* **1** (clothe) од|ева́ть, -е́ть (*кого во что*)
2 (prepare) припр|авля́ть, -а́вить; ~ **a salad**
запр|авля́ть, -а́вить сала́т **3** (a wound)
перевя́з|ывать, -а́ть
• *v.i.* **1** (put on one's clothes) од|ева́ться, -е́ться;
~ **up** (~ elaborately) наря|жа́ться, -ди́ться;
they ~ed up as pirates они́ наряди́лись
пира́тами **2** (choose clothes) од|ева́ться,
-е́ться; **he ~es well** он хорошо́ одева́ется
■ ~ **circle** *n.* бельэта́ж; ~ **code** *n.* дресс-
код (*правила-ограничения в отношении
допустимой одежды*); ~**maker** *n.* портни́ха;
~ **rehearsal** *n.* генера́льная репети́ция

dresser[1] /'dresə(r)/ *n.*: **she is a stylish ~** она́
шика́рно одева́ется

dresser[2] /'dresə(r)/ *n.* (sideboard) буфе́т;
(AmE, chest of drawers) шкаф с выдвижны́ми
я́щиками

dressing /'dresɪŋ/ *n.* **1** (med.) повя́зка **2** (AmE,
stuffing) начи́нка **3** (of salad etc.) запра́вка

✦ ключева́я ле́ксика

■ ~ **gown** *n.* хала́т; ~ **room** *n.* (theatr.)
артисти́ческая убо́рная; ~ **table** *n.*
туале́тный сто́лик

dressy /'dresɪ/ *adj.* (**dressier**, **dressiest**)
шика́рный, наря́дный

drew /dru:/ *past of* ▸ draw

dribble /'drɪb(ə)l/ *n.* (trickle) стру́йка
• *v.t.*: ~ **a ball** вести́ (*det.*) мяч
• *v.i.* (of baby) пус|ка́ть, -ти́ть слю́ни

drier /'draɪə(r)/ *n.* = dryer

drift /drɪft/ *n.* **1** (of tide etc.) тече́ние **2** (heap
of snow, leaves, etc.) нано́с, ку́ча **3** (meaning)
смысл; **I get his ~** я понима́ю, куда́ он
кло́нит
• *v.i.* дрейфова́ть (*impf.*); **the boat ~ed out to
sea** ло́дку отнесло́ в мо́ре; **they were friends
but ~ed apart** они́ бы́ли друзья́ми, но их
пути́ постепе́нно разошли́сь

drill[1] /drɪl/ *n.* (instrument) (small) дрель; (large)
бур, бура́в; (dentist's) бормаши́на
• *v.t.* сверли́ть, про-; бури́ть, про-; ~ **a hole**
сверли́ть, про- отве́рстие
• *v.i.* бури́ть (*impf.*); ~ **for oil** бури́ть (*impf.*)
нефтяну́ю сква́жину

drill[2] /drɪl/ *n.* (mil.) строева́я подгото́вка
• *v.t.* (troops) обуч|а́ть, -и́ть строево́й
подгото́вке

✦ **drink** /drɪŋk/ *n.* **1** (liquid) напи́ток, питьё
2 (quantity) глото́к **3** (alcoholic) вы́пивка,
спиртно́й напи́ток
• *v.t. & i.* (*past* **drank**, *p.p.* **drunk**) пить, вы́-
■ ~**driving** *n.* (BrE) вожде́ние в нетре́звом
состоя́нии; ~**ing water** *n.* питьева́я вода́

drinkable /'drɪŋkəb(ə)l/ *adj.* (safe to drink)
питьево́й, го́дный для питья́; (tasty) вку́сный

drip /drɪp/ *n.* **1** (action) ка́панье; (drop) ка́пля;
(weak person) тря́пка; (med.) ка́пельница; **be on
a ~** быть под ка́пельницей
• *v.i.* (**dripped**, **dripping**) ка́пать (*impf.*)

dripping /'drɪpɪŋ/ *n.* **1** (in pl.) (AmE, liquid)
ка́пли (*f. pl.*) **2** (BrE, cul.) топлёный жир

✦ **drive** /draɪv/ *n.* **1** (ride in vehicle) езда́; **go for
a ~** прокати́ться, поката́ться (*both pf.*) (на
маши́не); **the station is an hour's ~ away** до
ста́нции час езды́ **2** (private road) подъездна́я
доро́га **3** (hit, stroke, at tennis etc.) драйв,
си́льный уда́р **4** (energy) напо́ристость,
напо́р **5** (organized effort) кампа́ния; **a ~ for
new members** кампа́ния по привлече́нию
но́вых чле́нов **6** (driving gear) переда́ча,
при́вод **7** (comput.) при́вод; **disk ~** дисково́д;
hard ~ жёсткий диск
• *v.t.* (*past* **drove**, *p.p.* **driven**) **1** (force to
move) гоня́ть (*indet.*), гнать (*det.*); выбива́ть,
вы́бить **2** (operate) управля́ть (*impf.*) + *i.*;
~ **a car** води́ть (*indet.*) маши́ну **3** (impel,
of objects): **he drove a nail into the plank** он
вбил гвоздь в до́ску **4** (impel, fig.): ~ **sb mad**
сво|ди́ть, -ести́ кого́-н. с ума́
• *v.i.* (*past* **drove**, *p.p.* **driven**) **1** (operate
vehicle) води́ть (*indet.*), вести́ (*det.*) маши́ну
2 (be impelled): **driving rain** проливно́й дождь

driven /'drɪv(ə)n/ *p.p. of* ▸ drive

driver /ˈdraɪvə(r)/ n. **1** (of vehicle) води́тель (m.), шофёр **2** (comput.) дра́йвер
■ ~'s **license** n. (AmE) води́тельские права́

driving /ˈdraɪvɪŋ/ n. езда́
■ ~ **instructor** n. преподава́тель (m.) автошко́лы; ~ **licence** n. (BrE) води́тельские права́; ~ **school** n. автошко́ла; ~ **test** n. экза́мен на вожде́ние

drizzle /ˈdrɪz(ə)l/ n. и́зморось
• v.i. мороси́ть (impf.)

dromedary /ˈdrɒmɪdərɪ/ n. дромаде́р, одного́рбый верблю́д

drone /drəʊn/ n. **1** (of bee) тру́тень (m.) **2** (of engine) гуде́ние; (of voice) жужжа́ние
• v.i. (hum) жужжа́ть (impf.); ~ гуде́ть (impf.); (speak monotonously) бубни́ть (impf.) (infml)

drool /druːl/ v.i. пус|ка́ть, -ти́ть слю́ни

droop /druːp/ v.i. (of flowers, head) ни́кнуть, по-

drop /drɒp/ n. **1** (small quantity of liquid) ка́пля; (fig.): a ~ in the bucket (AmE), ocean ка́пля в мо́ре **2** (fall) паде́ние; ~ in prices/ temperature паде́ние цен; пониже́ние температу́ры; there is a ~ of 30 feet behind this wall за э́той стено́й 30-фу́товый обры́в
• v.t. (dropped, dropping) **1** (allow, cause to fall) роня́ть, урони́ть; ~ a parcel at sb's house оставля́ть, -а́вить паке́т у чьего́-н. до́ма **2** (bomb etc.) сбр|а́сывать, -о́сить **3** (lower): ~ one's voice пон|ижа́ть, -и́зить го́лос **4** (send, utter casually): ~ sb a line черкну́ть (pf.) кому́-н. па́ру строк; ~ a hint оброни́ть (pf.) намёк **5** (allow to descend, disembark) выса́живать, вы́садить; please ~ me at the station пожа́луйста, вы́садите меня́ у ста́нции
• v.i. (dropped, dropping) **1** (fall, descend) па́дать, упа́сть **2** (become weaker or lower) па́дать, упа́сть; the wind ~ped ве́тер стих/ути́х **3** (sink, collapse) па́дать, упа́сть; he ~ped (on) to his knees он упа́л/опусти́лся на коле́ни
□ ~ **in** v.i. (infml): he ~ped in on me он загляну́л ко мне
□ ~ **off** v.i. (become fewer or less) ум|еньша́ться, -е́ньшиться; (infml, doze off) засну́ть (pf.)
□ ~ **out** v.i.: five runners ~ped out пять бегуно́в вы́были из соревнова́ния; he ~ped out of school он бро́сил шко́лу
■ ~**out** n. челове́к, поста́вивший себя́ вне о́бщества

droppings /ˈdrɒpɪŋz/ n. pl. (of animals and birds) помёт

dross /drɒs/ n. шлак, ока́лина; (fig.) отбро́сы (m. pl.)

drought /draʊt/ n. за́суха

drove /drəʊv/ past of ▶ drive

drown /draʊn/ v.t. **1** (kill by immersion) топи́ть, у- **2** (of sound) приглуш|а́ть, -и́ть
• v.i. тону́ть, у-

drowsy /ˈdraʊzɪ/ adj. (**drowsier, drowsiest**) (feeling sleepy) со́нный

drudgery /ˈdrʌdʒərɪ/ n. изнури́тельная рабо́та

drug /drʌg/ n. **1** (medicinal substance) медикаме́нт,

лека́рство **2** (narcotic or stimulant) нарко́тик
• v.t. (**drugged, drugging**) (food etc.) подме́ш|ивать, -а́ть нарко́тики в + a.; (person) да|ва́ть, -ть нарко́тики + d.
■ ~ **abuse** adj. употребле́ние нарко́тиков; ~ **addict** n. наркома́н; ~ **addiction** n. наркома́ния; ~**store** n. (AmE) ≈ апте́ка; ~ **trafficker** (also ~ **pusher**) n. наркоде́лец

drum /drʌm/ n. **1** (instrument) бараба́н **2** (container for oil etc.) металли́ческая бо́чка
• v.t. (**drummed, drumming**) бараба́нить (impf.); ~ **up support** соз|ыва́ть, -ва́ть подмо́гу; ~ **sth into sb's head** вд|а́лбливать, -олби́ть что-л. кому́-н. в го́лову
• v.i. (**drummed, drumming**) бараба́нить (impf.)
■ ~**stick** n. бараба́нная па́лочка; (of fowl) но́жка

drummer /ˈdrʌmə(r)/ n. бараба́нщ|ик (-ица)

drunk[1] /drʌŋk/ n. пья́ный
• adj. пья́ный

drunk[2] /drʌŋk/ p.p. of ▶ drink

drunkard /ˈdrʌŋkəd/ n. пья́ница (c.g.), алкого́лик

drunken /ˈdrʌŋkən/ adj. пья́ный

dry /draɪ/ adj. (**drier** /ˈdraɪə(r)/, **driest** /ˈdraɪɪst/) **1** (free from moisture) сухо́й **2**: ~ **run** (trial) про́бный забе́г **3** (of humour) сухо́й; (of remark etc.) ирони́ческий
• v.t. суши́ть (or высу́шивать), вы́-; ~ **oneself** вытира́ться, вы́тереться; ~ **the dishes** вытира́ть, вы́тереть посу́ду; ~ **one's hands** вытира́ть, вы́тереть ру́ки; **dried fruit(s)** сушёные фру́кты
• v.i. со́хнуть, вы́-; суши́ться (or высу́шиваться), вы́-
■ ~**-clean** v.t. подв|ерга́ть, -е́ргнуть хими́ческой чи́стке

dryer /ˈdraɪə(r)/ n. суши́лка, суши́льный автома́т

DSL abbr. (of **digital subscriber line**) (teleph., comput.) (цифрова́я) вы́деленная ли́ния

DTD n. (abbr. of **Document Type Definition**) (comput.) описа́ние шабло́на докуме́нта

dual /ˈdjuːəl/ adj. дво́йственный, двойно́й
■ ~ **carriageway** n. (BrE) доро́га с двусторо́нним движе́нием и раздели́тельным барье́ром; ~ **nationality** n. двойно́е гражда́нство

dub /dʌb/ v.t. (**dubbed, dubbing**) (film) дубли́ровать (impf.)

dubious /ˈdjuːbɪəs/ adj. (feeling doubt) сомнева́ющийся; (inspiring mistrust) сомни́тельный

Dublin /ˈdʌblɪn/ n. Ду́блин

duchess /ˈdʌtʃɪs/ n. герцоги́ня

duchy /ˈdʌtʃɪ/ n. ге́рцогство, кня́жество

duck[1] /dʌk/ n. (pl. ~ or ~s) (bird) у́тка; (as food) ути́ное мя́со

duck[2] /dʌk/ v.t. погру|жа́ть, -зи́ть; ~ **one's head** бы́стро наг|иба́ть, -ну́ть го́лову; (evade): ~ **a question** уклон|я́ться, -и́ться от отве́та
• v.i. окун|а́ться, -у́ться

duckling /ˈdʌklɪŋ/ n. утёнок

duct /'dʌkt/ *n.* (anat.) кана́л, прото́к

dud /dʌd/ *adj.* (useless) непригóдный; (counterfeit) подде́льный

dude /duːd/ *n.* пижóн (infml)

✍ **due** /djuː/ *n.* дóлжное
● *adj.* **1** (payable) причита́ющийся; **when is the rent ~?** когда́ на́до плати́ть за кварти́ру? **2** (proper) дóлжный, надлежа́щий; **in ~ time** в своё вре́мя; **in ~ course** в свою́ óчередь, свои́м чередóм; **I am ~ for a haircut** мне пора́ постри́чься **3** (expected): **he is ~ to speak twice** он дóлжен вы́ступить два́жды **4**: **~ to** (infml, owing to) благодаря́ + *d.*; (because of) из-за + *g.*
● *adv.* тóчно, пря́мо; **the village lies ~ south** дере́вня лежи́т пря́мо на юг отсю́да

duel /'djuːəl/ *n.* дуэ́ль

duet /djuː'et/ *n.* дуэ́т

duffel, duffle /'dʌf(ə)l/ *n.* **1** (text.): **~ coat** пальтó из шерстянóй ба́йки с капюшóном **2**: **~ bag** ≈ веще́вой мешóк

dug /dʌɡ/ *past and p.p. of* ▶ **dig**

duke /djuːk/ *n.* ге́рцог

dull /dʌl/ *adj.* **1** (not clear or bright) ту́склый; **~ weather** па́смурная погóда **2** (uninteresting) ску́чный
● *v.t.* притуп|ля́ть, -и́ть

duly /'djuːlɪ/ *adv.* (in the proper manner) дóлжным óбразом; (at the right time) в дóлжное вре́мя, своевре́менно

dumb /dʌm/ *adj.* **1** (unable to speak) немóй **2** (AmE, infml, stupid) глу́пый
● *v.t.*: **~ down** (infml) популяризи́ровать (*impf., pf.*)
■ **~bell** *n.* ганте́ль

dumbfound, dumfound /dʌm'faʊnd/ *v.t.* ошара́ш|ивать, -ить

dummy /'dʌmɪ/ *n.* ку́кла; **tailor's ~** манеке́н; **baby's ~** (BrE) сóска
● *adj.* (imitation) подставнóй
■ **~ run** *n.* прóбный забе́г

dump /dʌmp/ *n.* **1** (rubbish tip) (му́сорная) сва́лка **2** (ammunition store) вре́менный полевóй склад **3** (seedy place) дыра́ (infml)
● *v.t.* **1** (throw away) выбра́сывать, вы́бросить **2** (deposit carelessly) сва́л|ивать, -и́ть **3** (infml, abandon) броса́ть, брóсить

dumpy /'dʌmpɪ/ *adj.* (**dumpier, dumpiest**) призе́мистый

dune /djuːn/ *n.* дю́на

dung /dʌŋ/ *n.* (manure) навóз

dungarees /dʌŋɡə'riːz/ *n. pl.* комбинезóн

dungeon /'dʌndʒ(ə)n/ *n.* темни́ца

duo /'djuːəʊ/ *n.* (*pl.* **~s**) дуэ́т

dupe /djuːp/ *n. v.t.* ост|авля́ть, -а́вить в дурака́х; над|ува́ть, -у́ть

duplicate[1] /'djuːplɪkət/ *n.* дублика́т; кóпия
● *adj.* запаснóй

duplicate[2] /'djuːplɪkeɪt/ *v.t.* удв|а́ивать, -óить

duplicity /djuː'plɪsɪtɪ/ *n.* двули́чность

durable /'djʊərəb(ə)l/ *adj.* прóчный; долгове́чный

duration /djʊə'reɪʃ(ə)n/ *n.* продолжи́тельность

duress /djʊə'res/ *n.*: **under ~** под нажи́мом/ давле́нием

✍ **during** /'djʊərɪŋ/ *prep.* (throughout) в тече́ние + *g.*; (at some point in) во вре́мя + *g.*

dusk /dʌsk/ *n.* су́мер|ки (-ек)

dust /dʌst/ *n.* пыль
● *v.t.* **1** (remove ~ from) ст|ира́ть, -ере́ть пыль с + *g.* **2** (sprinkle) пос|ыпа́ть, -ы́пать
■ **~bin** *n.* (BrE) му́сорный я́щик; **~ cover** *n.* (for chair etc.) чехóл; (of book) супероблóжка; **~cart** *n.* (BrE) мусоровóз; **~man** *n.* (BrE) му́сорщик; **~pan** *n.* совóк для му́сора

duster /'dʌstə(r)/ *n.* (BrE) тря́пка для пы́ли

dusty /'dʌstɪ/ *adj.* (**dustier, dustiest**) пы́льный

Dutch /dʌtʃ/ *n.* **1** (language) голла́ндский/ нидерла́ндский язы́к **2** (*as pl.*) (people) голла́ндцы (*m. pl.*)
■ **~man** *n.* голла́ндец; **~woman** *n.* голла́ндка

dutiful /'djuːtɪfʊl/ *adj.* пре́данный; (obedient) послу́шный

✍ **duty** /'djuːtɪ/ *n.* **1** (moral obligation) долг, обя́занность **2** (official employment) служе́бные обя́занности; дежу́рство; **on ~** на дежу́рстве; **off ~** свобóдный; вне слу́жбы; в свобóдное/неслуже́бное вре́мя **3** (fin.) пóшлина, сбор; **customs ~** тамóженная пóшлина
■ **~-free** *adj.* беспóшлинный

duvet /'duːveɪ/ *n.* (BrE) стёганое одея́ло

DVD *abbr.* (*of* **digital versatile disk**) DVD, Ди-ви-ди́ (*m. indecl.*)
■ **~ player** *n.* DVD-пле́ер

dwarf /dwɔːf/ *n.* (*pl.* **dwarfs** *or* **dwarves**) (person, offens.) ка́рлик; (in folklore) гном

dwell /dwel/ *v.i.* (*past and p.p.* **dwelt** *or* **dwelled**): **~ (up)on** (expatiate on) распространя́ться (*impf.*) о + *p.*

dwelling /'dwelɪŋ/ *n.* жильё, жили́ще
■ **~ house** *n.* жилóй дом; **~ place** *n.* местожи́тельство

dwelt /dwelt/ *past and p.p. of* ▶ **dwell**

dwindle /'dwɪnd(ə)l/ *v.i.* сокра|ща́ться, -ти́ться

dye /daɪ/ *n.* кра́ска
● *v.t.* (**dyeing**) кра́сить, по-

dying /'daɪɪŋ/ *adj.* умира́ющий, предсме́ртный

dynamic /daɪ'næmɪk/ *n.* (force) дви́жущая си́ла; (*in pl.*) (science) дина́мика
● *adj.* (pertaining to force) динами́ческий; (energetic) динами́чный

dynamism /'daɪnəmɪz(ə)m/ *n.* динами́зм

dynamite /'daɪnəmaɪt/ *n.* динами́т (also fig.)

dynamo /'daɪnəməʊ/ *n.* (*pl.* **~s**) дина́мо (*nt. indecl.*); дина́мо-маши́на

dynasty /'dɪnəstɪ/ *n.* дина́стия

dysentery /'dɪsəntrɪ/ *n.* дизентери́я

dyslexia /dɪs'leksɪə/ *n.* (med.) дисле́ксия (*неспосóбность к чте́нию*)

dyslexic /dɪs'leksɪk/ *adj.*: **he is ~** он дисле́ктик

Ee

E /iː/ *n.* **1** (mus.) ми (*nt. indecl.*) **2** (academic mark) «кол», единица

e|- *prefix* (comput.) электро́нный

■ ~**-banking** *n.* ба́нковские услу́ги че́рез Интерне́т, Интерне́т-ба́нкинг; ~**-book** *n.* электро́нная кни́га; ~**-commerce** *n.* электро́нная комме́рция; ~**-learning** *n.* электро́нное обуче́ние; ~**-ticket** *n.* электро́нный биле́т (*на самолёт и т. п.*)

✧ **each** /iːtʃ/ *pron. & adj.* ка́ждый; he gave ~ (one) of us a book он ка́ждому из нас дал по кни́ге; he sat with a child on ~ side of him он сиде́л ме́жду двумя́ детьми́; the apples cost 20 pence ~ я́блоки стоя́т два́дцать пе́нсов шту́ка (*or* за шту́ку); ~ other друг дру́га; 2 ~ по два/дво́е; 500 ~ по пятьсо́т

eager /ˈiːɡə(r)/ *adj.* стремя́щийся (**for:** к + *d.*); he is ~ to go он рвётся идти́

eagerness /ˈiːɡənɪs/ *n.* рве́ние, стремле́ние

eagle /ˈiːɡ(ə)l/ *n.* орёл

✧ **ear¹** /ɪə(r)/ *n.* **1** (anat.) у́хо **2**: ~ for music музыка́льный слух; she plays by ~ она́ игра́ет на слух; play it by ~ (fig.) пол|ага́ться, -ожи́ться на чутьё

■ ~**ache** *n.* боль в у́хе; ~**drum** *n.* бараба́нная перепо́нка; ~**mark** *v.t.* (designate) предназн|ача́ть, -а́чить; ассигнова́ть (*impf.*, *pf.*); ~**phone**, ~**piece** *nn.* нау́шник; ~**phone** ра́ковина телефо́нной тру́бки; ~**plug** *n.* затычка для уше́й; ~**ring** *n.* серьга́

ear² /ɪə(r)/ *n.* (bot.) ко́лос

earl /əːl/ *n.* (брита́нский) граф

✧ **earl|y** /ˈəːlɪ/ *adj.* (**earlier, earliest**) ра́нний; in one's ~y days, life в ю́ности/мо́лодости; in the ~y part of this century в нача́ле э́того столе́тия; we are ~y мы пришли́ ра́но; on Tuesday at (the) ~iest не ра́ньше вто́рника
• *adv.* ра́но; come as ~y as possible приходи́те как мо́жно ра́ньше; two hours ~ier на два часа́ ра́ньше

✧ **earn** /əːn/ *v.t. & i.* зараб|а́тывать, -о́тать; (deserve) заслу́ж|ивать, -и́ть; ~ one's living зараба́тывать (*impf.*) на жизнь

earnest /ˈəːnɪst/ *n.*: in ~ серьёзно, всерьёз
• *adj.* серьёзный

earnings /ˈəːnɪŋz/ *n. pl.* за́работок

✧ **earth** /əːθ/ *n.* **1** (planet, world) земля́; why on ~? с како́й ста́ти?; заче́м то́лько?; who on ~? кто то́лько?; кто же?; like nothing on ~ ни на что не похо́жий **2** (dry land) земля́ **3** (soil) земля́, по́чва **4** (BrE, elec.) земля́, заземле́ние

earthenware /ˈəːθ(ə)nweə(r)/ *n.* гонча́рные изде́лия; гли́няная посу́да

earthly /ˈəːθlɪ/ *adj.* земно́й; there is no ~ reason to … нет ни мале́йшей причи́ны

(+ *inf.*); he hasn't an ~ (BrE, infml) у него́ нет ни мале́йшего ша́нса

earthquake /ˈəːθkweɪk/ *n.* землетрясе́ние

earthy /ˈəːθɪ/ *adj.* (**earthier, earthiest**) (smell etc.) земляно́й; (fig.) приземлённый, грубова́тый

ease /iːz/ *n.* **1** (facility) лёгкость **2** (comfort) поко́й, о́тдых, досу́г; be, feel at ~ чу́вствовать (*impf.*) себя́ непринуждённо; put sb at his/her ~ приободри́ть (*pf.*) кого́-н.
• *v.t.*: ~ tension осл|абля́ть, -а́бить напряжённость; ~ congestion разгру|жа́ть, -зи́ть движе́ние; ~ sb's anxiety успок|а́ивать, -о́ить кого́-н.
• *v.i.*: ~ off on drinking (infml) пить (*impf.*) ме́ньше; the pressure of work ~d (up) напряжённость рабо́ты спа́ла

easel /ˈiːz(ə)l/ *n.* мольбе́рт

✧ **easily** /ˈiːzɪlɪ/ *adv.* легко́, без труда́; he is ~ the best он безусло́вно са́мый лу́чший; he may ~ be late он вполне́ мо́жет опозда́ть

✧ **east** /iːst/ *n.* восто́к; to the ~ of London к восто́ку от Ло́ндона
• *adv.* на восто́к; к восто́ку; travel ~ дви́гаться (*impf.*) на восто́к; ~ of Moscow к восто́ку от Москвы́
• *adj.* восто́чный; ~ wind восто́чный ве́тер

Easter /ˈiːstə(r)/ *n.* Па́сха; at ~ на Па́сху
■ ~ **Day/Sunday** *n.* Све́тлое/Христо́во воскресе́нье, Па́сха; ~ **Monday** *n.* Све́тлый понеде́льник; ~ **egg** *n.* пасха́льное яйцо́

easterly /ˈiːstəlɪ/ *n.* (wind) восто́чный ве́тер
• *adj.* восто́чный

✧ **eastern** /ˈiːst(ə)n/ *adj.* восто́чный

eastward /ˈiːstwəd/ *adj.* восто́чный
• *adv.* (*also* ~**s**) на восто́к; к восто́ку, в восто́чном направле́нии

✧ **easy** /ˈiːzɪ/ *adj.* (**easier, easiest**) **1** (not difficult) лёгкий; the book is ~ to read кни́га легко́ чита́ется; he is ~ to get on with у него́ лёгкий хара́ктер **2** (comfortable) споко́йный, лёгкий; he leads an ~ life у него́ лёгкая жизнь; I am ~ (infml, have no preference) мне всё равно́
• *adv.*: take it ~! (don't exert yourself) расслабьтесь!; (don't worry) не волну́йтесь!; (don't hurry) не спеши́те!
■ ~**-going** *adj.* благоду́шный

✧ **eat** /iːt/ *v.t. & i.* (*past* **ate**, *p.p.* **eaten**) есть, съ-; (politely, of others) ку́шать, по-/с-; ~ one's dinner пообе́дать/поу́жинать (*pf.*)
□ ~ **out** *v.i.* есть (*impf.*) вне до́ма
□ ~ **up** *v.t.* дое|да́ть, -́сть; (fig.): he is ~en up with curiosity его́ съеда́ет любопы́тство

eaten /ˈiːt(ə)n/ *p.p. of* ▶ **eat**

eavesdrop /ˈiːvzdrɒp/ *v.i.* подслу́ш|ивать, -ать

e

ebb /eb/ *n.* отли́в
• *v.i.* (of tide) уб|ыва́ть, -ы́ть; (fig.) ослаб|ева́ть, -е́ть

ebony /'ebənɪ/ *n.* эбе́новое/чёрное де́рево; (fig., black) чёрный как смоль

ebullient /ɪ'bʌlɪənt/ *adj.* кипу́чий, по́лный энтузиа́зма

eccentric /ɪk'sentrɪk/ *n.* чуда́к; оригина́л
• *adj.* эксцентри́чный

eccentricity /eksen'trɪsɪtɪ/ *n.* (quality) чуда́чество, эксцентри́чность; (eccentric habit) стра́нность

ecclesiastical /ɪkliːzɪ'æstɪk(ə)l/ *adj.* духо́вный, церко́вный

ECG *abbr.* (*of* **electrocardiogram**) ЭКГ (электрокардиогра́мма)

echelon /'eʃəlɒn/ *n.* **1** (level, rank) чин, ранг **2** (mil. formation) эшело́н

echo /'ekəʊ/ *n.* (*pl.* **echoes**) э́хо
• *v.t.* (**echoes, echoed**) вто́рить (*impf.*) + *d.*; ~ sb's words вто́рить чьим-н. слова́м
• *v.i.* (**echoes, echoed**) отд|ава́ться, -а́ться э́хом

eclair /ɪ'kleə(r)/ *n.* экле́р

eclectic /ɪ'klektɪk/ *adj.* эклекти́ческий, эклекти́чный

eclipse /ɪ'klɪps/ *n.* (astron.) затме́ние
• *v.t.* (lit., fig.) затм|ева́ть, -и́ть

eco-friendly /'iːkəʊfrendlɪ/ *adj.* экологи́чески безвре́дный

eco-label /'iːkəʊleɪb(ə)l/ *n* экологи́ческий я́рлык

ecological /iːkə'lɒdʒɪk(ə)l/ *adj.* экологи́ческий

ecologist /ɪ'kɒlədʒɪst/ *n.* эко́лог

ecology /ɪ'kɒlədʒɪ/ *n.* эколо́гия

✐ **economic** /iːkə'nɒmɪk, ek-/ *adj.*
1 экономи́ческий, хозя́йственный **2** (profitable) рента́бельный
■ ~ **migrant** *n.* экономи́ческий мигра́нт

economical /iːkə'nɒmɪk(ə)l, ek-/ *adj.* эконо́мный, бережли́вый

economics /iːkə'nɒmɪks, ek-/ *n. pl.* (*often treated as sg.*) эконо́мика

economist /ɪ'kɒnəmɪst/ *n.* экономи́ст

economize /ɪ'kɒnəmaɪz/ *v.i.* эконо́мить, с-; ~ **on fuel** эконо́мить, с- то́пливо

✐ **economy** /ɪ'kɒnəmɪ/ *n.* **1** (thrift) эконо́мия, хозя́йственность, бережли́вость **2** (economic system) эконо́мика, хозя́йство
■ ~ **class** *n.* эконо́м-класс

ecosystem /'iːkəʊsɪstəm/ *n.* экосисте́ма

ecotourism /iːkəʊ'tʊərɪz(ə)m/ *n.* экотури́зм

ecotourist /'iːkəʊtʊərɪst/ *n.* экотури́ст

ecstasy /'ekstəsɪ/ *n.* **1** (strong emotion) экста́з **2** (the drug) э́кстези (*m. indecl.*)

ecstatic /ɪk'stætɪk/ *adj.* экстати́ческий, в экста́зе

Ecuador /'ekwədɔː(r)/ *n.* Эквадо́р

Ecuadorean /ekwə'dɔːrɪən/ *n.* эквадо́р|ец (-ка)
• *adj.* эквадо́рский

✐ ключева́я ле́ксика

eczema /'eksɪmə/ *n.* экзе́ма

✐ **edge** /edʒ/ *n.* **1** (sharpened side) острие́, ле́звие **2** (fig.): **be on** ~ быть в не́рвном состоя́нии **3** (border) грань; край
• *v.t. & i.* **1** (border) окайм|ля́ть, -и́ть; ~ **a path with plants** обса́|живать, -ди́ть доро́жку цвета́ми **2** (move obliquely): ~ **one's way through a crowd** проб|ира́ться, -ра́ться че́рез толпу́; **he** ~**d closer to me** он пододви́нулся ко мне

edgeways /'edʒweɪz/, **edgewise** /'edʒwaɪz/ *advs.* бо́ком; **I could not get a word in** ~ я не мог сло́ва вста́вить

edible /'edɪb(ə)l/ *adj.* съедо́бный

edifice /'edɪfɪs/ *n.* зда́ние; (fig.) структу́ра, систе́ма

edifying /'edɪfaɪɪŋ/ *adj.* назида́тельный, поучи́тельный

Edinburgh /'edɪnbərə/ *n.* Эдинбу́рг

edit /'edɪt/ *v.t.* (**edited, editing**) (a text, newspaper) редакти́ровать, от-; (film etc.) монти́ровать, с-

✐ **edition** /ɪ'dɪʃ(ə)n/ *n.* изда́ние; (e.g. of newspaper) вы́пуск

✐ **editor** /'edɪtə(r)/ *n.* реда́ктор

editorial /edɪ'tɔːrɪəl/ *n.* передови́ца, передова́я статья́
• *adj.* редакцио́нный; реда́кторский
■ ~ **office** *n.* реда́кция

educate /'edjʊkeɪt/ *v.t.* да|ва́ть, -ть образова́ние + *d.*; ~**d speech** культу́рная речь

✐ **education** /edjʊ'keɪʃ(ə)n/ *n.* образова́ние, культу́ра; (upbringing) воспита́ние

educational /edjʊ'keɪʃən(ə)l/ *adj.* (pert. to education) образова́тельный; (instructive) воспита́тельный, уче́бный

EEC *abbr.* (*of* **European Economic Community**) ЕЭС (Европе́йское экономи́ческое соо́бщество)

eel /iːl/ *n.* у́горь (*m.*)

eerie /'ɪərɪ/ (AmE **eery**) *adj.* (**eerier, eeriest**) жу́ткий

✐ **effect** /ɪ'fekt/ *n.* **1** (result) результа́т; **punishment had no** ~ **on him** наказа́ние на него́ не поде́йствовало; **to no** ~ безрезульта́тно; **take** ~ (e.g. medicine) де́йствовать, по- **2** (validity) де́йствие; **come into** ~ вступ|а́ть, -и́ть в си́лу **3** (sensual etc. impression) впечатле́ние, эффе́кт
• *v.t.* осуществ|ля́ть, -и́ть; выполня́ть, вы́полнить

✐ **effective** /ɪ'fektɪv/ *adj.* **1** (efficacious) эффекти́вный **2** (operative) име́ющий си́лу; де́йствующий

effeminate /ɪ'femɪnət/ *adj.* женоподо́бный

effervesce /efə'ves/ *v.i.* пузыри́ться (*impf.*); (fig.) искри́ться (*impf.*)

effervescence /efə'ves(ə)ns/ *n.* шипе́ние; (fig.) весёлое оживле́ние, кипе́ние

effervescent /efə'ves(ə)nt/ *adj.* пузыря́щийся, шипя́щий; (fig.) искря́щийся, кипу́чий

effete /ɪ'fiːt/ *adj.* сла́бый, упа́дочный; (degenerate) вы́родившийся

efficacious /ˌefɪˈkeɪʃəs/ *adj.* эффекти́вный, де́йственный

efficacy /ˈefɪkəsɪ/ *n.* эффекти́вность, де́йственность

efficiency /ɪˈfɪʃənsɪ/ *n.* делови́тость; эффекти́вность, производи́тельность

efficient /ɪˈfɪʃ(ə)nt/ *adj.* делови́тый, исполни́тельный; эффекти́вный, производи́тельный

effigy /ˈefɪdʒɪ/ *n.* изображе́ние; **burn sb in** ~ сжечь (*pf.*) чьё-н. изображе́ние/чу́чело

ˢ **effort** /ˈefət/ *n.* уси́лие, попы́тка; (*in pl.*) рабо́та; **make an** ~ приложи́ть (*pf.*) уси́лие

effortless /ˈefətlɪs/ *adj.* непринуждённый; не тре́бующий уси́лий; **with** ~ **skill** с непринуждённой ло́вкостью

effrontery /ɪˈfrʌntərɪ/ *n.* на́глость, наха́льство

effusive /ɪˈfjuːsɪv/ *adj.* экспанси́вный; **he was** ~ **in his gratitude** он рассыпа́лся в благода́рностях

e.g. *abbr.* (*of* **exempli gratia**) напр. (наприме́р)

egalitarian /ɪˌɡælɪˈteərɪən/ *adj.* эгалита́рный

egalitarianism /ɪˌɡælɪˈteərɪənɪz(ə)m/ *n.* эгалитари́зм

ˢ **egg¹** /eɡ/ *n.* яйцо́
■ ~ **cup** *n.* рю́мка для яйца́; ~**plant** *n.* (AmE) баклажа́н

egg² /eɡ/ *v.t.:* ~ **on** подстрека́ть, -ну́ть

ego /ˈiːɡəʊ/ *n.* (*pl.* **egos**) (self-esteem) самолю́бие

egocentric /ˌiːɡəʊˈsentrɪk/ *adj.* эгоцентри́ческий, эгоцентри́чный

egoism /ˈiːɡəʊɪz(ə)m/ *n.* эгои́зм

egoist /ˈiːɡəʊɪst/ *n.* эгои́ст (-ка)

egotist /ˈiːɡətɪst/ *n.* эгоцентри́ст (-ка)

egotistic /ˌiːɡəˈtɪstɪk/, **egotistical** /ˌiːɡəˈtɪstɪk(ə)l/ *adjs.* эгоцентри́ческий

Egypt /ˈiːdʒɪpt/ *n.* Еги́пет

Egyptian /ɪˈdʒɪpʃ(ə)n/ *n.* египтя́н|ин (-ка)
● *adj.* еги́петский

eiderdown /ˈaɪdədaʊn/ *n.* (BrE, quilt) пухо́вое одея́ло

ˢ **eight** /eɪt/ *n.* (число́/но́мер) во́семь; (figure; thing numbered 8; group of ~) восьмёрка
● *adj.* во́семь + *g. pl.*

eighteen /eɪˈtiːn/ *n.* восемна́дцать
● *adj.* восемна́дцать + *g. pl.*

eighteenth /eɪˈtiːnθ/ *n.* (date) восемна́дцатое число́; (fraction) одна́ восемна́дцатая
● *adj.* восемна́дцатый

eighth /eɪtθ/ *n.* (date) восьмо́е (число́); (fraction) одна́ восьма́я
● *adj.* восьмо́й

eightieth /ˈeɪtɪɪθ/ *n.* одна́ восьмидеся́тая
● *adj.* восьмидеся́тый

eight|y /ˈeɪtɪ/ *n.* во́семьдесят; **he is in his** ~**ies** ему́ за во́семьдесят

ˢ **either** /ˈaɪðə(r)/ *pron. & adj.* (one or other) любо́й, ка́ждый; тот и́ли друго́й; **do** ~ **of these roads lead to town?** кака́я-нибу́дь из э́тих доро́г ведёт к го́роду?; ~ **book will do** люба́я из э́тих книг годи́тся; **I do not like** ~

(one) мне не нра́вится ни тот, ни друго́й; **on** ~ **side of the window** по обе́им сторона́м окна́
● *adv. & conj.:* **I do not like Smith, or Jones** ~ я не люблю́ ни Сми́та, ни Джо́нса; (intensive) **it was not long ago** ~ э́то бы́ло не так уж давно́; ~ ... **or** и́ли... и́ли; ли́бо... ли́бо; то ли... то ли; не то... не то

ejaculate /ɪˈdʒækjʊleɪt/ *v.t.* (utter suddenly) воскл|ица́ть, -и́кнуть
● *v.i.* (physiol.) эякули́ровать (*impf., pf.*), изв|ерга́ть, -е́ргнуть се́мя

ejaculation /ɪˌdʒækjʊˈleɪʃ(ə)n/ *n.* (physiol.) эякуля́ция

eject /ɪˈdʒekt/ *v.t.* (lit., fig.) выбра́сывать, вы́бросить
● *v.i.* (aeron.): **the pilot** ~**ed** лётчик катапульти́ровался

eke /iːk/ *v.t.:* ~ **out** (supplement) восп|олня́ть, -о́лнить; ~ **out a livelihood** ко́е-как перебива́ться (*impf.*)

elaborate¹ /ɪˈlæbərət/ *adj.* иску́сно сде́ланный

elaborate² /ɪˈlæbəreɪt/ *v.t.* разраб|а́тывать, -о́тать; ~ **on** (develop) разв|ива́ть, -и́ть; (make more precise) уточн|я́ть, -и́ть

elapse /ɪˈlæps/ *v.i.* про|ходи́ть, -йти́

elastic /ɪˈlæstɪk/ *n.* рези́нка
● *adj.* (lit.) эласти́чный; упру́гий; (fig.) ги́бкий
■ ~ **band** *n.* (BrE) рези́нка

elate /ɪˈleɪt/ *v.t.:* **she was** ~**d at the news** но́вость окрыли́ла её

elation /ɪˈleɪʃ(ə)n/ *n.* ликова́ние, восто́рг

elbow /ˈelbəʊ/ *n.* ло́коть (*m.*)
■ ~ **grease** *n.* (joc.) уси́ленная полиро́вка

elder¹ /ˈeldə(r)/ *adj.* ста́рший

elder² /ˈeldə(r)/ *n.* (bot.) бузина́ (*красная, чёрное*)
■ ~**berry** *n.* я́года бузины́

elderly /ˈeldəlɪ/ *adj.* пожило́й

eldest /ˈeldɪst/ *adj.* са́мый ста́рший

ˢ **elect** /ɪˈlekt/ *adj.* и́збранный; **president-**~ и́збранный президе́нт
● *v.t.* изб|ира́ть, -ра́ть; выбира́ть, вы́брать; **they** ~**ed him king** они́ избра́ли его́ королём; **he** ~**ed to go** он предпочёл пойти́

ˢ **election** /ɪˈlekʃ(ə)n/ *n.* вы́боры (*m. pl.*)
■ ~ **campaign** *n.* предвы́борная/ избира́тельная кампа́ния

electoral /ɪˈlektər(ə)l/ *adj.* избира́тельный

electorate /ɪˈlektərət/ *n.* (body of voters) избира́тели (*m. pl.*)

ˢ **electric** /ɪˈlektrɪk/ *adj.* электри́ческий
■ ~ **blanket** *n.* одея́ло-гре́лка; ~ **shock** *n.* уда́р электри́ческим то́ком

electrical /ɪˈlektrɪk(ə)l/ *adj.* электри́ческий
■ ~ **engineering** *n.* электроте́хника

electrician /ɪˌlekˈtrɪʃ(ə)n/ *n.* эле́ктрик (infml), (электро)монтёр

ˢ **electricity** /ɪˌlekˈtrɪsɪtɪ/ *n.* электри́чество

electrify /ɪˈlektrɪfaɪ/ *v.t.* (also fig.) электризова́ть, -

electrocardiogram /ɪˌlektrəʊˈkɑːdɪəɡræm/ *n.* электрокардиогра́мма

e

e

electrocute /ɪˈlektrəkjuːt/ v.t. (execute) казни́ть (impf., pf.) на электри́ческом сту́ле; **he was ~d** (by accident) его́ уби́ло то́ком

electrode /ɪˈlektrəʊd/ n. электро́д

electromagnetic /ɪlektrəʊmæɡˈnetɪk/ adj. электромагни́тный

electron /ɪˈlektrɒn/ n. электро́н
■ **~ microscope** n. электро́нный микроско́п

✒ **electronic** /ɪlekˈtrɒnɪk/ adj. электро́нный
■ **~ tagging** n. электро́нная слёжка

electronics /ɪlekˈtrɒnɪks/ n. электро́ника

elegance /ˈelɪɡ(ə)ns/ n. элега́нтность, изя́щество

elegant /ˈelɪɡ(ə)nt/ adj. элега́нтный, изя́щный

✒ **element** /ˈelɪmənt/ n. **1** (earth, air, etc.) стихи́я; (fig.): **in one's ~** в свое́й стихи́и **2** (chem.) элеме́нт **3** (feature, constituent) элеме́нт; составна́я часть **4** (elec.) элеме́нт

elementary /elɪˈmentərɪ/ adj. элемента́рный
■ **~ school** n. нача́льная шко́ла

elephant /ˈelɪfənt/ n. (pl. ~ or ~s) слон

elevate /ˈelɪveɪt/ v.t. (lit.) подн|има́ть, -я́ть; **~d railway** надзе́мная желе́зная доро́га

elevated /ˈelɪveɪtɪd/ adj. (lofty) высо́кий, возвы́шенный

elevator /ˈelɪveɪtə(r)/ n. **1** (machine) грузоподъёмник, элева́тор **2** (AmE, lift) лифт

eleven /ɪˈlev(ə)n/ n. оди́ннадцать
● adj. оди́ннадцать + g. pl.

elevenses /ɪˈlevənzɪz/ n. pl. (BrE, infml) лёгкий за́втрак о́коло оди́ннадцати часо́в утра́

eleventh /ɪˈlevənθ/ n. (date) оди́ннадцатое (число́); (fraction) одна́ оди́ннадцатая
● adj. оди́ннадцатый

elf /elf/ n. (pl. **elves**) эльф

elicit /ɪˈlɪsɪt/ v.t. (**elicited, eliciting**) извл|ека́ть, -е́чь; допы́т|ываться, -а́ться; **~ a fact** выявля́ть, вы́явить факт; **~ a reply** доби́ться (pf.) отве́та

eligibility /elɪdʒɪˈbɪlɪtɪ/ n. пра́во на избра́ние

eligible /ˈelɪdʒɪb(ə)l/ adj. могу́щий быть и́збранным; **to be ~ for** име́ть пра́во на + a.

eliminate /ɪˈlɪmɪneɪt/ v.t. **1** (rule out) исключ|а́ть, -и́ть **2** (sport): **he was ~d in the first round** он вы́был в пе́рвом ту́ре

elimination /ɪlɪmɪˈneɪʃ(ə)n/ n. устране́ние

elite /eɪˈliːt/ n. эли́та; **an ~ regiment** отбо́рный полк

elitist /ɪˈliːtɪst/ adj. элита́рный

elixir /ɪˈlɪksɪə(r)/ n. эликси́р

Elizabethan /ɪlɪzəˈbiːθ(ə)n/ n. совреме́нник эпо́хи короле́вы Елизаве́ты
● adj. елизаве́тинский, относя́щийся к эпо́хе короле́вы Елизаве́ты

elk /elk/ n. (pl. ~ or ~s) лось (m.)

ellipse /ɪˈlɪps/ n. э́ллипс, ова́л

elliptical /ɪˈlɪptɪkəl/ adj. (math., gram.) эллипти́ческий

elm /elm/ n. (tree; wood) вяз

elongate /ˈiːlɒŋɡeɪt/ v.t. удлин|я́ть, -и́ть

elongation /iːlɒŋˈɡeɪʃ(ə)n/ n. удлине́ние

elope /ɪˈləʊp/ v.i. (тáйно) бежа́ть (det.) (с возлю́бленным)

eloquent /ˈeləkwənt/ adj. красноречи́вый

El Salvador /el ˈsælvədɔː(r)/ n. Сальвадо́р

✒ **else** /els/ adj. & adv. друго́й; **no one ~** никто́ друго́й; бо́льше никто́; **everyone ~** все остальны́е; **nowhere ~** ни в како́м друго́м ме́сте; **everywhere ~** везде́, то́лько не здесь/там; **what ~ could I say?** что ещё я мог сказа́ть?; **do you want anything ~?** вы хоти́те ещё что-нибудь?; **or ~** и́ли же

elsewhere /elsˈweə(r)/ adv. (in another place) где-нибудь ещё, в друго́м ме́сте; (to another place) куда́-нибудь ещё, в друго́е ме́сто

elude /ɪˈluːd/ v.t. изб|ега́ть, -ежа́ть, -е́гнуть + g.; ускольз|а́ть, -ну́ть от + g.

elusive /ɪˈluːsɪv/ adj. неулови́мый

elves /elvz/ pl. of ▶ **elf**

emaciated /ɪˈmeɪsɪeɪtɪd/ adj. истощённый

✒ **email, e-mail** /ˈiːmeɪl/ n. (system, letters) электро́нная по́чта; (letter) электро́нное письмо́
● v.t. (a person) пос|ыла́ть, -ла́ть электро́нное письмо́ (кому-н.); (information, a document) пос|ыла́ть, -ла́ть электро́нной по́чтой
■ **~ address** n. электро́нный а́дрес

emanate /ˈeməneɪt/ v.i. излуча́ться (impf.); истека́ть (impf.)

emancipate /ɪˈmænsɪpeɪt/ v.t. эмансипи́ровать (impf., pf.)

emancipation /ɪmænsɪˈpeɪʃ(ə)n/ n. эмансипа́ция

embalm /ɪmˈbɑːm/ v.t. бальзами́ровать (impf., pf.) (pf. also за-, на-)

embankment /ɪmˈbæŋkmənt/ n. (wall etc.) на́сыпь, гать; (roadway) на́бережная

embargo /emˈbɑːɡəʊ/ n. (pl. ~es) эмба́рго (nt. indecl.); **lift, raise an ~** сн|има́ть, -ять эмба́рго (**from:** c + g.)

embark /ɪmˈbɑːk/ v.i. (go on board) грузи́ться, по-; сади́ться, сесть на кора́бль; (fig.) пус|ка́ться, -ти́ться (**on:** в + a.); **~ on an undertaking** предприн|има́ть, -я́ть де́ло

embarkation /embɑːˈkeɪʃ(ə)n/ n. (of goods) погру́зка; (of people) поса́дка

embarrass /ɪmˈbærəs/ v.t. смущ|а́ть, -ти́ть

embarrassing /ɪmˈbærəsɪŋ/ adj. щекотли́вый, вызыва́ющий смуще́ние

embarrassment /ɪmˈbærəsmənt/ n. смуще́ние, замеша́тельство

embassy /ˈembəsɪ/ n. посо́льство

embattled /ɪmˈbæt(ə)ld/ adj. (ready for war) приведённый в боеву́ю гото́вность; (in difficulties) в тру́дном положе́нии

embed /ɪmˈbed/ v.t. (**embedded, embedding**): **stones ~ded in rock** ка́мни, вмуро́ванные в скалу́; **facts ~ded in one's memory** фа́кты, вре́завшиеся в па́мять

embellish /ɪmˈbelɪʃ/ v.t. укр|аша́ть, -а́сить; (a tale etc.) приукра́|шивать, -сить

embellishment /ɪmˈbelɪʃmənt/ n. приукра́шивание

―――――――――

✒ ключева́я ле́ксика

embers /'embəz/ *n. pl.* (coals etc.) тлеющие угольки (*m. pl.*)

embezzle /ɪm'bez(ə)l/ *v.t.* растрá|чивать, -тить

embezzlement /ɪm'bezəlmənt/ *n.* растрáта

emblem /'embləm/ *n.* эмблéма; (national) герб

embodiment /ɪm'bɒdɪmənt/ *n.* воплощéние, олицетворéние

embody /ɪm'bɒdɪ/ *v.t.* вопло|щáть, -тить

embrace /ɪm'breɪs/ *n.* объятие
● *v.t.* **1** (clasp in one's arms) обн|имáть, -ять
2 (include) включ|áть, -ить
● *v.i.* обн|имáться, -яться

embroider /ɪm'brɔɪdə(r)/ *v.t.* вышивáть, вышить; (a story etc.) приукрá|шивать, -сить

embroidery /ɪm'brɔɪdərɪ/ *n.* вышивáние, вышивка

embroil /ɪm'brɔɪl/ *v.t.* впут|ывать, -ать; вовл|екáть, -éчь

embryo /'embrɪəʊ/ *n.* (*pl.* **~s**) эмбрион

embryology /embrɪ'ɒlədʒɪ/ *n.* эмбриология

embryonic /embrɪ'ɒnɪk/ *adj.* эмбрионáльный; (fig.) недорáзвитый; в зáродыше

emerald /'emər(ə)ld/ *n.* изумрýд
■ **~ green** *n.* изумрýдно-зелёный

✍ **emerge** /ɪ'mɜ:dʒ/ *v.i.* всплы|вáть, -ть; появ|ляться, -иться; (fig.) возн|икáть, -икнуть

emergence /ɪ'mɜ:dʒ(ə)ns/ *n.* появлéние, возникновéние

✍ **emergency** /ɪ'mɜ:dʒənsɪ/ *n.* авáрия; крáйняя необходимость; (for use in ~) запаснóй, запáсный, врéменный
■ **~ exit** *n.* запáсный выход; **~ landing** *n.* вынужденная посáдка

emigrant /'emɪgrənt/ *n.* эмигрáнт (-ка)

emigrate /'emɪgreɪt/ *v.i.* эмигрировать (*impf.*, *pf.*)

emigration /emɪ'greɪʃ(ə)n/ *n.* эмигрáция

émigré /'emɪgreɪ/ *n.* эмигрáнт (-ка) (*особенно политический*)

eminence /'emɪnəns/ *n.* **1** (high ground) высотá; возвышéние **2** (celebrity) знаменитость; reach, win, attain ~ добиться (*pf.*) слáвы/извéстности **3** (title): His E~ Егó Высокопреосвящéнство

eminent /'emɪnənt/ *adj.* (of person) выдающийся, знаменитый

emission /ɪ'mɪʃ(ə)n/ *n.* (of gas, heat) выделéние; (of light) излучéние; (in pl.) выбросы

emit /ɪ'mɪt/ *v.t.* (**emitted, emitting**) (smoke, smell) испус|кáть, -тить; (light) излучáть, -ить; (gas, heat) выделять, выделить; (sound) изд|авáть, -áть

emoticon /ɪ'məʊtɪkɒn/ *n.* эмóтикон, смáйл(ик)

✍ **emotion** /ɪ'məʊʃ(ə)n/ *n.* (feeling) эмóция; (agitation) волнéние

✍ **emotional** /ɪ'məʊʃən(ə)l/ *adj.* эмоционáльный

emotive /ɪ'məʊtɪv/ *adj.* эмоционáльно волнýющий

empathy /'empəθɪ/ *n.* сопережитвáние

emperor /'empərə(r)/ *n.* империáтор

emphasis /'emfəsɪs/ *n.* (*pl.* **emphases** /-si:z/) ударéние, выразительность; **lay ~ on** подчёрк|ивать, -нýть

✍ **emphasize** /'emfəsaɪz/ *v.t.* подчёрк|ивать, -нýть

emphatic /ɪm'fætɪk/ *adj.* эмфатический, выразительный

emphysema /emfɪ'si:mə/ *n.* (med.) эмфизéма

empire /'empaɪə(r)/ *n.* импéрия

empirical /ɪm'pɪrɪk(ə)l/ *adj.* эмпирический

empiricism /ɪm'pɪrɪsɪz(ə)m/ *n.* эмпиризм

✍ **employ** /ɪm'plɔɪ/ *v.t.* **1** (engage to work) нан|имáть, -ять; дав|áть, дать рабóту + *d.*; **be ~ed** рабóтать (*impf.*), служить (*impf.*) **2** (use) примен|ять, -ить

✍ **employee** /em'plɔɪ/ *n.* служащий

✍ **employer** /ɪm'plɔɪə(r)/ *n.* работодáтель (*m.*)

✍ **employment** /ɪm'plɔɪmənt/ *n.* **1** (service for pay) рабóта, служба **2** (occupation) занятие **3** (use) применéние, использование
■ **~ agency** *n.* кáдровое агéнтство; бюрó по трудоустрóйству

empower /ɪm'paʊə(r)/ *v.t.* уполномóчи|вать, -ть

empress /'emprɪs/ *n.* императрица

emptiness /'emptɪnɪs/ *n.* (lit., fig.) пустотá

empt|y /'emptɪ/ *adj.* (**emptier, emptiest**) пустóй; порóжний; (fig.): **~y words** пустые словá
● *v.t.* опорожн|ять, -ить; **~y water out of a jug** вылить (*pf.*) вóду из кувшина
● *v.i.* опорожн|яться, -иться; **the streets ~ied** улицы опустéли
■ **~y-handed** *adj.* с пустыми рукáми

EMS *abbr. of* **1** (**European Monetary System**) ЕВС (Еврoпéйская валютная система) **2** (**Enhanced Message/ Messaging Service**): **~ message** EMS-сообщéние

emu /'i:mju:/ *n.* эму (*m. indecl.*)

emulate /'emjʊleɪt/ *v.t.* подражáть (*impf.*) + *d.*

emulsion /ɪ'mʌlʃ(ə)n/ *n.* эмýльсия

✍ **enable** /ɪ'neɪb(ə)l/ *v.t.* (make able) да|вáть, -ть возмóжность + *d.*; (make possible) дéлать, с- возмóжным

enact /ɪ'nækt/ *v.t.* (make law) вв|одить, -ести в дéйствие; утвер|ждáть, -дить; (act) игрáть, сыгрáть (*роль*); разы|грывать, -áть; (carry out) соверш|áть, -ить

enactment /ɪ'næktmənt/ *n.* введéние закóна в силу; утверждéние (закóна *и т. п.*); (of sb's fantasies) игрá

enamel /ɪ'næm(ə)l/ *n.* эмáль

encampment /ɪn'kæmpmənt/ *n.* расположéние лáгерем; (camp) лáгерь (*m.*)

encapsulate /ɪn'kæpsjʊleɪt/ *v.t.* (fig.) заключ|áть, -ить в себé

enchant /ɪn'tʃɑ:nt/ *v.t.* обвор|áживать, -ожить; очарóв|ывать, -áть

enchanting /ɪn'tʃɑ:ntɪŋ/ *adj.* чарýющий, обворожительный

encircle /ɪnˈsɜːk(ə)l/ v.t. окруж|а́ть, -и́ть
enclave /ˈenkleɪv/ n. анкла́в
enclos|e /ɪnˈkləʊz/ v.t. **1** (surround, fence) окруж|а́ть, -и́ть; ~e a garden with a wall обн|оси́ть, -ести́ сад стено́й **2** (in letter etc.) при|кла́дывать, -ложи́ть; a letter ~ing an invoice письмо́ с приложе́нием счёта
enclosure /ɪnˈkləʊʒə(r)/ n. (fence) огражде́ние, огра́да; (in letter) приложе́ние
encode /ɪnˈkəʊd/ v.t. коди́ровать (impf., pf.) (pf. also за-); шифрова́ть, за-
encompass /ɪnˈkʌmpəs/ v.t. (surround) окруж|а́ть, -и́ть; (contain, comprise) заключ|а́ть, -и́ть; (envelop) оку́т|ывать, -ать
encore /ˈɒŋkɔː(r)/ n. & int. бис
encounter /ɪnˈkaʊntə(r)/ n. встре́ча
• v.t. встр|еча́ться, -е́титься с + i.
ᴄ **encourage** /ɪnˈkʌrɪdʒ/ v.t. обод|ря́ть, -ри́ть; I ~d him to go я угова́ривал его́ идти́
encouragement /ɪnˈkʌrɪdʒmənt/ n. ободре́ние, поощре́ние, подде́ржка
encouraging /ɪnˈkʌrɪdʒɪŋ/ adj. ободря́ющий
encroach /ɪnˈkrəʊtʃ/ v.i. поку|ша́ться, -си́ться (on: на + a.); ~ on sb's rights посяг|а́ть, -ну́ть на чьи-н. права́
encrypt /enˈkrɪpt/ v.t. шифрова́ть, за-
encumber /ɪnˈkʌmbə(r)/ v.t. (burden) обремен|я́ть, -и́ть; ~ oneself with luggage взва́л|ивать, -и́ть на себя́ бага́ж
encumbrance /ɪnˈkʌmbrəns/ n. обу́за, препя́тствие
encyclopedia /ensaɪkləˈpiːdɪə, ɪn-/ n. энциклопе́дия
encyclopedic /ɪnsaɪkləˈpiːdɪk/ adj. энциклопеди́ческий
ᴄ **end** /end/ n. **1** (extremity, lit., fig.) коне́ц; two hours on ~ (in succession) два часа́ кря́д; third from the ~ тре́тий с кра́ю; at the ~ of August в конце́ (or в после́дних чи́слах) а́вгуста **2** (of elongated object) коне́ц, край; he stood the box on (its) ~ он поста́вил я́щик стоймя́ (infml) **3** (remnant, small part): candle ~ ога́рок; cigarette ~ оку́рок **4** (conclusion) оконча́ние; in the ~ в конце́ концо́в, в коне́чном счёте; come to an ~ ок|а́нчиваться, -о́нчиться; конча́ться, ко́нчиться; put an ~ to класть, положи́ть коне́ц + d.; he stayed till the bitter ~ он остава́лся на ме́сте до са́мого конца́ **5** (purpose) цель; to this ~ с э́той це́лью; any means to an ~ все сре́дства хороши́
• v.t. конча́ть, ко́нчить; ~ a quarrel прекра|ща́ть, -ти́ть ссо́ру; ~ one's days рассчита́ться с жи́знью
• v.i. конча́ться, ко́нчиться; the road ~s here доро́га конча́ется здесь; the story ~s happily э́то расска́з со счастли́вым концо́м
▢ ~ up v.i.: he ~ed up in jail он ко́нчил тюрьмо́й; he ~ed up at the opera в конце́ концо́в он попа́л-таки в о́перу
■ ~ product n. коне́чный проду́кт

endanger /ɪnˈdeɪndʒə(r)/ v.t. подв|ерга́ть, -е́ргнуть опа́сности; ста́вить (impf.) под угро́зу
■ ~ed species n. вымира́ющий вид
endear /ɪnˈdɪə(r)/ v.t.: this speech ~ed her to me э́та речь расположи́ла меня́ к ней; an ~ing smile покоря́ющая/подкупа́ющая улы́бка
endearment /ɪnˈdɪəmənt/ n. ла́ска; term of ~ ла́сковое обраще́ние
endeavour /ɪnˈdevə(r)/ (AmE **endeavor**) n. стара́ние, стремле́ние
• v.i. стара́ться, по-
ending /ˈendɪŋ/ n. (action) оконча́ние (also gram.); (of book, play) коне́ц
endive /ˈendaɪv/ n. сала́т энди́вий; (AmE, chicory crown) цико́рий (верхняя наземная часть)
endless /ˈendlɪs/ adj. бесконе́чный
endorse /ɪnˈdɔːs/ v.t. **1** (sign) индосси́ровать (impf., pf.); ~ a cheque распи́с|ываться, -а́ться на че́ке **2** (support) подвер|жда́ть, -ди́ть
endorsement /ɪnˈdɔːsmənt/ n. **1** переда́точная на́дпись; индосса́мент; резолю́ция (начальника на документе) **2** (support) подтвержде́ние
endow /ɪnˈdaʊ/ v.t. одар|я́ть, -и́ть
endowment /ɪnˈdaʊmənt/ n. **1** (act of endowing) поже́ртвование **2** (funds) вклад, поже́ртвование **3** (talent) одарённость
endurable /ɪnˈdjʊərəb(ə)l/ adj. прие́млемый, сно́сный
endurance /ɪnˈdjʊərəns/ n. (physical) про́чность; (mental) выно́сливость
endure /ɪnˈdjʊə(r)/ v.t. выноси́ть, вы́нести
• v.i. (last) прод|олжа́ться, -о́лжиться
enema /ˈenɪmə/ n. (med.) кли́зма
ᴄ **enemy** /ˈenəmɪ/ n. враг, не́друг
ᴄ **energetic** /enəˈdʒetɪk/ adj. энерги́чный
ᴄ **energy** /ˈenədʒɪ/ n. (physical or mental) эне́ргия
■ ~ drink n. энергети́ческий напи́ток, энерге́тик (infml)
enforce /ɪnˈfɔːs/ v.t.: ~ a judg(e)ment (law) прив|оди́ть, -ести́ в исполне́ние суде́бное реше́ние; ~ a law следи́ть (impf.) за соблюде́нием зако́на
enforceable /ɪnˈfɔːsəb(ə)l/ adj. осуществи́мый, обеспе́ченный правово́й са́нкцией
enforcement /ɪnˈfɔːsmənt/ n. осуществле́ние; law ~ наблюде́ние за соблюде́нием зако́нов
ᴄ **engage** /ɪnˈɡeɪdʒ/ v.t. **1** (occupy) зан|има́ть, -я́ть; he is ~d in reading он за́нят чте́нием; he ~d me in conversation он вовлёк меня́ в разгово́р; the line is ~d (teleph.) но́мер за́нят; ~d signal, tone (BrE) коро́ткие гудки́; сигна́л «за́нято»; the lavatory is ~d убо́рная занята́ **2** (pledge to marry): Tom and Mary are ~d Том и Мэ́ри помо́лвлены; they got ~d они́ обручи́лись **3** (tech.) зацеп|ля́ть, -и́ть; включ|а́ть, -и́ть
• v.i. **1** (undertake) бра́ться, взя́ться **2** (embark, busy oneself) зан|има́ться, -я́ться чем-н.; he ~d in this venture он взя́лся за э́то предприя́тие

ᴄ ключева́я ле́ксика

engagement /ɪn'geɪdʒmənt/ *n.* **1** (to marry) помо́лвка **2** (appointment to meet etc.) свида́ние, встре́ча
■ ~ **ring** *n.* обруча́льное кольцо́
engender /ɪn'dʒendə(r)/ *v.t.* (fig.) поро|жда́ть, -ди́ть
♂ **engine** /'endʒɪn/ *n.* дви́гатель (*m.*); мото́р
■ ~ **driver** *n.* (BrE) машини́ст
♂ **engineer** /endʒɪ'nɪə(r)/ *n.* инжене́р, меха́ник
● *v.t.* (tech.) проекти́ровать, с-; (fig.) зат|ева́ть, -е́ять
engineering /endʒɪ'nɪərɪŋ/ *n.* инжене́рное де́ло; машинострое́ние; **civil** ~ гражда́нское строи́тельство
England /'ɪŋglənd/ *n.* А́нглия
♂ **English** /'ɪŋglɪʃ/ *n.* **1** (language) англи́йский язы́к **2**: **the** ~ (people) англича́не
● *adj.* англи́йский
■ ~**man** *n.* англича́нин; ~**woman** *n.* англича́нка
engrave /ɪn'greɪv/ *v.t.* гравирова́ть, вы-
engraving /ɪn'greɪvɪŋ/ *n.* гравю́ра
engross /ɪn'grəʊs/ *v.t.*: **he was** ~**ed in his work** он был поглощён рабо́той
engulf /ɪn'gʌlf/ *v.t.* погло|ща́ть, -ти́ть
♂ **enhance** /ɪn'hɑ:ns/ *v.t.* усили|вать, -ть
enhancement /ɪn'hɑ:nsmənt/ *n.* усиле́ние, повыше́ние
enigma /ɪ'nɪgmə/ *n.* зага́дка
enigmatic /enɪg'mætɪk/ *adj.* зага́дочный
♂ **enjoy** /ɪn'dʒɔɪ/ *v.t.* **1** (get pleasure from) насла|жда́ться, -ди́ться + *i.*; **I** ~**ed talking to him** мне доставля́ло удово́льствие говори́ть с ним; **we** ~**ed our holiday** мы хорошо́ провели́ о́тпуск; ~ **oneself** весели́ться (*impf.*); наслажда́ться (*impf.*); хорошо́ пров|оди́ть, -ести́ вре́мя **2** (possess) располага́ть (*impf.*) + *i.*; ~ **good/bad health** облада́ть хоро́шим/плохи́м здоро́вьем
enjoyable /ɪn'dʒɔɪəb(ə)l/ *adj.* прия́тный
enjoyment /ɪn'dʒɔɪmənt/ *n.* наслажде́ние, удово́льствие
enlarge /ɪn'lɑ:dʒ/ *v.t.* увели́чи|вать, -ть
● *v.i.* расши|ря́ться, -́риться; **he** ~**d on the point** он подро́бнее останови́лся на э́том
enlargement /ɪn'lɑ:dʒmənt/ *n.* увеличе́ние; расшире́ние
enlighten /ɪn'laɪt(ə)n/ *v.t.* просве|ща́ть, -ти́ть
enlightening /ɪn'laɪt(ə)nɪŋ/ *adj.* поучи́тельный
enlightenment /ɪn'laɪtənmənt/ *n.* просвещённость; **the E**~ (hist.) Просвеще́ние
enlist /ɪn'lɪst/ *v.t.* вербова́ть, за-; ~ **sb's support** заручи́ться, -́ться чьей-н. подде́ржкой
● *v.i.* поступ|а́ть, -и́ть на вое́нную слу́жбу
enlistment /ɪn'lɪstmənt/ *n.* **1** (of workers) вербо́вка **2** (mil.) поступле́ние на вое́нную слу́жбу
enliven /ɪn'laɪv(ə)n/ *v.t.* ожив|ля́ть, -и́ть
en masse /ɑ̃ 'mæs/ *adv.* в ма́ссе
enmity /'enmɪtɪ/ *n.* вражда́
enormity /ɪ'nɔ:mɪtɪ/ *n.* чудо́вищность

enormous /ɪ'nɔ:məs/ *adj.* грома́дный, огро́мный; ~**ly** чрезвыча́йно
♂ **enough** /ɪ'nʌf/ *n.* доста́точное коли́чество; дово́льно, доста́точно; **£5 is** ~ пяти́ фу́нтов доста́точно; **(that's)** ~**!** доста́точно!; дово́льно!; **there is** ~ **to go round** хва́тит на всех; **I have had** ~ **of your lies** надое́ла мне ва́ша ложь
● *adj.* доста́точный; **I have just** ~ **money** де́нег у меня́ в обре́з **(for:** на + *a.*)
● *adv.* доста́точно; **are you warm** ~? вы не замёрзли?; вам тепло́?; **curiously** ~ как ни стра́нно
enquire /ɪn'kwaɪə(r)/ *v.t.* спр|а́шивать, -оси́ть
● *v.i.* осве|домля́ться, -́домиться; ~ **into a matter** рассле́довать (*pf.*) де́ло; ~ **after sb** спр|а́шивать, -оси́ть о ком-н.
enquiring /ɪn'kwaɪərɪŋ/ *adj.*: **an** ~ **look** вопроси́тельный взгляд; **an** ~ **mind** пытли́вый ум
enquir|y /ɪn'kwaɪərɪ/ *n.* расспро́сы (*m. pl.*); **make** ~**ies** нав|оди́ть, -ести́ спра́вки
enrage /ɪn'reɪdʒ/ *v.t.* беси́ть, вз-
enrich /ɪn'rɪtʃ/ *v.t.* обога|ща́ть, -ти́ть
enrol /ɪn'rəʊl/ *v t. & i.* **(enrolled, enrolling)** зач|исля́ть(ся), -и́слить(ся)
enrolment /ɪn'rəʊlmənt/ *n.* зачисле́ние, приём
ensconce /ɪn'skɒns/ *v.t.*: ~ **oneself** устр|а́иваться, -о́иться, укр|ыва́ться, -ы́ться
ensemble /ɒn'sɒmb(ə)l/ *n.* анса́мбль (*m.*)
enshrine /ɪn'ʃraɪn/ *v.t.* поме|ща́ть, -сти́ть в ра́ку; (fig.) храни́ть (*impf.*)
ensign /'ensaɪn/ *n.* **1** (flag) (кормово́й) флаг **2** (hist., standard-bearer) пра́порщик **3** (AmE, naut.) мла́дший лейтена́нт
enslave /ɪn'sleɪv/ *v.t.* порабо|ща́ть, -ти́ть
ensue /ɪn'sju:/ *v.i.* **(ensues, ensued, ensuing)** сле́довать (*impf.*) (*из чего*); **in** ~**ing years** в после́дующие го́ды
♂ **ensure** /ɪn'ʃʊə(r)/ *v.t.* (make certain; secure) обеспе́чи|вать, -ть
entail /ɪn'teɪl/ *v.t.* влечь (*impf.*) за собо́й
entangle /ɪn'tæŋg(ə)l/ *v.t.* (lit.) запу́т|ывать, -ать; (fig.) впу́т|ывать, -ать; **he** ~**d himself with women** он запу́тался в отноше́ниях с же́нщинами
♂ **enter** /'entə(r)/ *v.t. & i.* **1** (go into) входи́ть, войти́ в + *a.*; ~ **the army** вступ|а́ть, -и́ть в а́рмию; **the idea never** ~**ed my head** э́та мысль никогда́ не приходи́ла мне в го́лову **2** (include in record) запи́с|ывать, -а́ть; (comput.) вводи́ть, ввести́; ~ **a horse for a race** заявл|я́ть, -и́ть ло́шадь для ска́чек; ~ **(oneself) for an examination** под|ава́ть, -а́ть докуме́нты на уча́стие в экза́мене
● *with prep.*: ~ **into conversation** вступ|а́ть, -и́ть в разгово́р; **he** ~**ed into the spirit of the game** он прони́кся ду́хом игры́
enterprise /'entəpraɪz/ *n.* **1** (undertaking) предприя́тие **2** (initiative) предприи́мчивость **3** (econ.): **free** ~ свобо́дное предпринима́тельство
enterprising /'entəpraɪzɪŋ/ *adj.* предприи́мчивый

e

entertain /entə'teɪn/ v.t. развл|екáть, -éчь; прин|имáть, -ять; ~ **friends** уго|щáть, -стúть друзéй; (amuse) развл|екáть, -éчь

entertainer /entə'teɪnə(r)/ n. артúст эстрáды

entertaining /entə'teɪnɪŋ/ adj. интерéсный, занимáтельный

entertainment /entə'teɪnmənt/ n. **1** (social) приём гостéй **2** (amusement) развлечéние **3** (spectacle) представлéние

enthral /ɪn'θrɔ:l/ (AmE **enthrall**) v.t. (**enthralled, enthralling**) (fascinate) увл|екáть, -éчь; an ~**ling play** захвáтывающая пьéса

enthuse /ɪn'θju:z/ v.i. (infml) восторгáться (impf.) (чем)

enthusiasm /ɪn'θju:zɪæz(ə)m/ n. востóрг, энтузиáзм

enthusiast /ɪn'θju:zɪæst/ n. энтузиáст (-ка)

enthusiastic /ɪnθju:zɪ'æstɪk/ adj. востóрженный; пóлный энтузиáзма

entice /ɪn'taɪs/ v.t. соблазн|ять, -úть

enticement /ɪn'taɪsmənt/ n. (action) замáнивание; (enticing) примáнка, соблáзн

 ✧ **entire** /ɪn'taɪə(r)/ adj. цéлый, пóлный, цéльный; ~**ly** целикóм, совершéнно

entirety /ɪn'taɪərəti/ n. полнотá, цéльность

 ✧ **entitle** /ɪn'taɪt(ə)l/ v.t. **1** (authorize) да|вáть, -ть прáво на + a.; **you are** ~**d to two books a month** вам полагáется две кнúги в мéсяц **2**: **a book** ~**d 'Progress'** кнúга под заглáвием «Прогрéсс»

entitlement /ɪn'taɪt(ə)lmənt/ n. (right) прáво

entity /'entɪti/ n. существó

entomologist /entə'mɒlədʒɪst/ n. энтомóлог

entomology /entə'mɒlədʒɪ/ n. энтомолóгия

entourage /'ɒntʊərɑːʒ/ n. антурáж, окружéние

entrance¹ /'entrəns/ n. вход
 ■ ~ **examination** n. вступúтельный экзáмен; ~ **fee** n. вступúтельный взнос; ~ **hall** n. прихóжая, вестибюль (m.)

entrance² /ɪn'trɑːns/ v.t. восторгáть (impf.)

entrant /'entrənt/ n. (person entering school, profession, etc.) поступáющий; (competitor) учáстник

entreat /ɪn'tri:t/ v.t. умол|ять, -úть

entreaty /ɪn'tri:tɪ/ n. мольбá

entrench /ɪn'trentʃ/ v.t. окруж|áть, -úть окóпами; **the enemy were** ~**ed nearby** враг окопáлся вблизú; ~ **oneself** окáпываться, -опáться; (fig.): **customs** ~**ed by tradition** обычаи, закреплённые традúцией

entrepreneur /ɒntrəprə'nɜ:(r)/ n. предпринимáтель (m.)

entrepreneurial /ɒntrəprə'nɜ:rɪəl/ adj. предпринимáтельский

entrust /ɪn'trʌst/ v.t. вв|ерять, -éрить; **I** ~**ed the task to him** (or ~**ed him with the task**) я дал емý, поручéние

 ✧ **entry** /'entrɪ/ n. **1** (going in) вход **2** (access) дóступ; **he gained** ~ **to the house** он

пробрáлся в дом **3** (item) зáпись; **dictionary** ~ словáрная статья; ~ **in a diary** зáпись в дневникé **4** (inscription; competitor): **there was a large** ~ **for the race** на скáчки записáлось мнóго учáстников
 ■ ~ **form** n. вступúтельная анкéта

entryphone® /'entrɪfəʊn/ n. (BrE) домофóн

enunciate /ɪ'nʌnsɪeɪt/ v.t. (express) формулúровать, с-; (pronounce) произн|осúть, -ести

envelop /ɪn'veləp/ v.t. (**enveloped, enveloping**) об|орáчивать, -ернýть; окýт|ывать, -ать; **hills** ~**ed in mist** холмы́, окýтанные тумáном; **a baby** ~**ed in a shawl** младéнец, завёрнутый в шаль; ~**ed in mystery** покры́тый тáйной

envelope /'ɒnvələʊp/ n. конвéрт

enviable /'envɪəb(ə)l/ adj. завúдный

envious /'envɪəs/ adj. завúстливый

 ✧ **environment** /ɪn'vaɪərənmənt/ n. окружéние, средá; **the** ~ окружáющая средá
 ■ ~**-friendly** adj. экологúчески безврéдный

 ✧ **environmental** /ɪnvaɪərən'ment(ə)l/ adj. окружáющий
 ■ ~ **studies** n. pl. изучéние окружáющей среды́

environmentalism /ɪnvaɪərən'mentəlɪz(ə)m/ n. защúта окружáющей среды́

environmentalist /ɪnvaɪərən'mentəlɪst/ n. сторóнник защúты окружáющей среды́

environs /ɪn'vaɪərənz/ n. pl. окрéстности (f. pl.)

envisage /ɪn'vɪzɪdʒ/ v.t. (consider) рассм|áтривать, -отрéть; (visualize) предвúдеть (impf.)

envoy /'envɔɪ/ n. дипломáт

envy /'envɪ/ n. зáвисть
 ● v.t. завúдовать, по- + d.; **I** ~ **him** я емý завúдую; **I** ~ **his patience** я завúдую егó терпéнию

enzyme /'enzaɪm/ n. энзúм

epaulette /'epəlet/ n. эполéт

ephemeral /ɪ'femər(ə)l/ adj. эфемéрный

epic /'epɪk/ n. эпúческая поэ́ма, эпопéя
 ● adj. эпúческий; (on a grand scale) грандиóзный

epicentre /'epɪsentə(r)/ (AmE **epicenter**) n. эпицéнтр

epidemic /epɪ'demɪk/ n. эпидéмия

epidural /epɪ'djʊər(ə)l/ n. эпидурáльная инъéкция

epilepsy /'epɪlepsɪ/ n. эпилéпсия

epileptic /epɪ'leptɪk/ n. эпилéптик
 ● adj. эпилептúческий

 ✧ **episode** /'epɪsəʊd/ n. (occurrence) эпизóд; (instalment) часть

episodic /epɪ'sɒdɪk/ adj. (composed of episodes) состоящий из отдéльных эпизóдов; (incidental, occasional) эпизодúческий

epitaph /'epɪtɑːf/ n. эпитáфия, надгрóбная нáдпись

epitome /ɪ'pɪtəmɪ/ n. воплощéние

epitomize /ɪ'pɪtəmaɪz/ v.t. вопло|щáть, -тúть

epoch /ˈiːpɒk/ *n.* эпо́ха

eponymous /ɪˈpɒnɪməs/ *adj.* и́менем кото́рого на́зван (-а, -о) (+ *nom.*); (hero) загла́вный (*роль, герой*)

🗸 **equal** /ˈiːkw(ə)l/ *n.* ро́вня; our boss treats us all as ~s наш нача́льник обраща́ется со все́ми на́ми на ра́вных
• *adj.* **1** (same, equivalent) ра́вный, одина́ковый **2** (adequate) спосо́бный; she is ~ to the task она́ вполне́ мо́жет спра́виться с э́той зада́чей
• *v.t. & i.* (**equalled, equalling**, AmE **equaled, equaling**) **1** (math.) равня́ться (*impf.*) (*чему*) **2**: he ~s me in strength мы с ним равны́ по си́ле

equality /ɪˈkwɒlɪtɪ/ *n.* ра́венство, равнопра́вие

equalize /ˈiːkwəlaɪz/ *v.t. & i.* ура́вн|ивать, -я́ть

equalizer /ˈiːkwəlaɪzə(r)/ *n.* (sport) гол, сра́внивающий счёт

🗸 **equally** /ˈiːkwəlɪ/ *adv.* **1** (to an equal extent) одина́ково **2** (also, likewise) ра́вным о́бразом; наравне́ **3** (evenly): he divided the money ~ он раздели́л де́ньги по́ровну

equanimity /ekwəˈnɪmɪtɪ/ *n.* душе́вное равнове́сие; споко́йствие; with ~ споко́йно

equate /ɪˈkweɪt/ *v.t.* отождествл|я́ть, -и́ть; she ~s wealth with happiness она́ отождествля́ет бога́тство со сча́стьем

equation /ɪˈkweɪʒ(ə)n/ *n.* уравне́ние

equator /ɪˈkweɪtə(r)/ *n.* эква́тор

equidistant /iːkwɪˈdɪst(ə)nt/ *adj.* равноотстоя́щий; these towns are ~ from London э́ти города́ располо́жены на одина́ковом расстоя́нии от Ло́ндона

equilibrium /iːkwɪˈlɪbrɪəm/ *n.* (lit., fig.) равнове́сие

equinox /ˈekwɪnɒks/ *n.* равноде́нствие

equip /ɪˈkwɪp/ *v.t.* (**equipped, equipping**) снаря|жа́ть, -ди́ть

🗸 **equipment** /ɪˈkwɪpmənt/ *n.* снаряже́ние, экипиро́вка

equitable /ˈekwɪtəb(ə)l/ *adj.* справедли́вый

equity /ˈekwɪtɪ/ *n.* **1** (fairness) справедли́вость **2** (in pl.) (fin.) обыкнове́нные а́кции (*f. pl.*)

equivalent /ɪˈkwɪvələnt/ *n.* эквивале́нт
• *adj.* эквивале́нтный

equivocal /ɪˈkwɪvək(ə)l/ *adj.* двусмы́сленный, сомни́тельный

🗸 **era** /ˈɪərə/ *n.* э́ра

eradicate /ɪˈrædɪkeɪt/ *v.t.* искорен|я́ть, -и́ть

erase /ɪˈreɪz/ *v.t.* ст|ира́ть, -ере́ть

eraser /ɪˈreɪzə(r)/ *n.* рези́нка

erect /ɪˈrekt/ *adj.* прямо́й
• *v.t.* (build, set up) воздв|ига́ть, -и́гнуть; соору|жа́ть, -ди́ть

erection /ɪˈrekʃ(ə)n/ *n.* (setting up) сооруже́ние; (building) зда́ние; (physiol.) эре́кция

ergonomic /ˌɜːgəˈnɒmɪk/ *adj.* эргономи́чный

Eritrea /erɪˈtreɪə/ *n.* Эритре́я

ERM *abbr.* (of **Exchange Rate Mechanism**) МВК (механи́зм валю́тных ку́рсов)

ermine /ˈɜːmɪn/ *n.* (pl. ~ or ~s) (animal, fur) горноста́й

erode /ɪˈrəʊd/ *v.t.* разъ|еда́ть, -е́сть; (fig.) подт|а́чивать, -очи́ть

erosion /ɪˈrəʊʒ(ə)n/ *n.* разъеда́ние, эро́зия; (fig.): the ~ of his hopes постепе́нное разруше́ние его́ наде́жд

erotic /ɪˈrɒtɪk/ *adj.* эроти́ческий

eroticism /ɪˈrɒtɪsɪz(ə)m/ *n.* эроти́зм

err /ɜː(r)/ *v.i.* ошиб|а́ться, -и́ться; заблужда́ться (*impf.*)

errand /ˈerənd/ *n.* поруче́ние

errant /ˈerənt/ *adj.* **1** (misbehaving) заблу́дший **2** (stray, wandering) стра́нствующий; knight ~ стра́нствующий ры́царь

erratic /ɪˈrætɪk/ *adj.* неусто́йчивый; (of person) беспоря́дочный; ~ally нерегуля́рно

erroneous /ɪˈrəʊnɪəs/ *adj.* оши́бочный

🗸 **error** /ˈerə(r)/ *n.* оши́бка, заблужде́ние; the letter was sent in ~ письмо́ бы́ло отпра́влено по оши́бке

erstwhile /ˈɜːstwaɪl/ *adj.* да́вний, давни́шний; an ~ friend да́вний/стари́нный друг

erudite /ˈeruːdaɪt/ *adj.* эруди́рованный, учёный

erudition /eruˈdɪʃ(ə)n/ *n.* эруди́ция

erupt /ɪˈrʌpt/ *v.i.* (of volcano) изверга́ться (*impf.*)

eruption /ɪˈrʌpʃ(ə)n/ *n.* **1** (of volcano etc.) изверже́ние **2** (fig.) взрыв

escalate /ˈeskəleɪt/ *v.i.* разраста́ться (*impf.*)

escalation /eskəˈleɪʃ(ə)n/ *n.* эскала́ция

escalator /ˈeskəleɪtə(r)/ *n.* эскала́тор

escapade /ˈeskəpeɪd/ *n.* (эктравага́нтная) вы́ходка

🗸 **escape** /ɪˈskeɪp/ *n.* **1** (becoming free) побе́г; бе́гство **2** (avoidance) спасе́ние, избавле́ние; he had a narrow ~ from shipwreck он едва́ спа́сся при кораблекруше́нии
• *v.t.* избе|га́ть, -жа́ть + *g.*; she ~d death она́ оста́лась в живы́х; nothing ~s you! всё-(то) вы замеча́ете!
• *v.i.* бежа́ть (*det.*); уход|и́ть, уйти́; соверш|и́ть (*pf.*) побе́г; an ~d prisoner бе́глый ареста́нт

escapism /ɪˈskeɪpɪz(ə)m/ *n.* бе́гство от действи́тельности; эскапи́зм

escort[1] /ˈeskɔːt/ *n.* (mil.) конво́й, эско́рт; police ~ (of criminal) конво́й; her ~ to the ball её кавале́р на балу́

escort[2] /ɪˈskɔːt/ *v.t.* сопрово|жда́ть, -ди́ть; (mil.) эскорти́ровать (*impf., pf.*); I ~ed him to his seat я провёл его́ на ме́сто

Eskimo /ˈeskɪməʊ/ *n.* (pl. ~ or ~s) эскимо́с (-ка)
• *adj.* эскимо́сский

esophagus /iːˈsɒfəgəs/ *n.* (AmE) = **oesophagus**

esoteric /iːsəˈterɪk/ *adj.* эзотери́ческий

🗸 **especially** /ɪˈspeʃ(ə)lɪ/ *adj.* осо́бенно

espionage /ˈespɪənɑːʒ/ *n.* шпиона́ж

espouse /ɪˈspaʊz/ *v.t.*: ~ a cause (целико́м) отд|ава́ться, -а́ться де́лу

espresso /eˈspresəʊ/ *n.* (pl. ~s) (coffee) ко́фе «эспре́ссо»

essay /'eseɪ/ *n.* (literary composition) óчерк, эссé (*nt. indecl.*); (in school) сочинéние

essence /'es(ə)ns/ *n.* **1** (intrinsic nature) сýщность, существó **2** (extract) эссéнция

✓ **essential** /ɪ'senʃ(ə)l/ *n.* сýщность
● *adj.* **1** (necessary) необходи́мый; **it is** ~ **that I should know** óчень вáжно, чтóбы я знал **2** (fundamental) существéнный; ~**ly** существéнно; по существý; в сýщности **3**: ~ **oils** эфи́рные маслá

✓ **establish** /ɪ'stæblɪʃ/ *v.t.* **1** (found, set up) учре|ждáть, -ди́ть; устан|áвливать, -ови́ть **2** (prove, gain acceptance for) утвер|ждáть, -ди́ть; ~ **one's reputation** созд|авáть, -áть себé репутáцию
■ **E**~**ed Church** *n.* госудáрственная цéрковь

establishment /ɪ'stæblɪʃmənt/ *n.* **1** (setting up) учреждéние, установлéние **2** (of a fact etc.) установлéние **3** (institution) учреждéние, заведéние; **educational** ~ учéбное заведéние **4** (business concern) заведéние, дéло **5** (set of institutions or key persons): **the E**~ «истéблишмент»

✓ **estate** /ɪ'steɪt/ *n.* **1** (landed property) помéстье, имéние; **housing** ~ (BrE) жилóй масси́в **2** (property) имýщество; **real** ~ недви́жимость
■ ~ **agent** (BrE) агéнт по продáже недви́жимости; ~ **car** *n.* (BrE) автомоби́ль (*m.*) с кýзовом «универсáл»; универсáл (infml)

esteem /ɪ'sti:m/ *n.* уважéние

estimate[1] /'estɪmət/ *n.* **1** (assessment) оцéнка **2** (comm.) смéта

✓ **estimate**[2] /'estɪmeɪt/ *v.t.* оцéн|ивать, -и́ть

estimation /estɪ'meɪʃ(ə)n/ *n.* (judgement) оцéнка, суждéние

Estonia /ɪ'stəʊnɪə/ *n.* Эстóния

Estonian /ɪ'stəʊnɪən/ *n.* эстóн|ец (-ка)
● *adj.* эстóнский

estrange /ɪ'streɪndʒ/ *v.t.* отдал|я́ть, -и́ть; **his** ~**d wife** женá, с котóрой он живёт раздéльно

estrogen /'i:strədʒ(ə)n/ *n.* (AmE) = **oestrogen**

estuary /'estjʊərɪ/ *n.* эстуáрий, ýстье

✓ **etc.** /et 'setərə/ *adv.* (*abbr. of* **et cetera**) и т. д., и т. п. (и так дáлее; и тому подóбное)

etch /etʃ/ *v.t.* трави́ть, вы́-; гравировáть, вы́-; (fig.): **it is** ~**ed on my memory** э́то запечатлéлось у меня́ в пáмяти

etching /'etʃɪŋ/ *n.* офóрт, гравю́ра

eternal /ɪ'tɜ:n(ə)l/ *adj.* вéчный (also fig.)

eternity /ɪ'tɜ:nɪtɪ/ *n.* вéчность

ether /'i:θə(r)/ *n.* (phys., chem.) эфи́р

ethereal /ɪ'θɪərɪəl/ *adj.* эфи́рный, неземнóй; ~ **beauty** неземнáя красотá

ethical /'eθɪk(ə)l/ *adj.* эти́чный

ethics /'eθɪk/ *n. pl.* э́тика; морáль

Ethiopia /i:θɪ'əʊpɪə/ *n.* Эфиóпия

Ethiopian /i:θɪ'əʊpɪən/ *n.* эфиóп (-ка)
● *adj.* эфиóпский

ethnic /'eθnɪk/ *adj.* этни́ческий
■ ~ **cleansing** *n.* этни́ческая чи́стка

ethos /'i:θɒs/ *n.* дух, харáктер

etiquette /'etɪket/ *n.* этикéт

etymological /etɪmə'lɒdʒɪk(ə)l/ *adj.* этимологи́ческий

etymology /etɪ'mɒlədʒɪ/ *n.* этимолóгия

EU *abbr.* (*of* **European Union**) ЕС (Европéйский сою́з)

eucalyp|tus /ju:kə'lɪptəs/ *n.* (*pl.* ~**tuses** or ~**ti** /-taɪ/) эвкали́пт

Eucharist /'ju:kərɪst/ *n.* евхари́стия, святóе причáстие

eulogy /'ju:lədʒɪ/ *n.* хвалéбная речь, панеги́рик; (at funeral) надгрóбная речь

euphemism /'ju:fɪmɪz(ə)m/ *n.* эвфеми́зм

euphemistic /ju:fɪ'mɪstɪk/ *adj.* эвфемисти́ческий

euphoria /ju:'fɔ:rɪə/ *adj.* эйфори́я

euphoric /ju:'fɒrɪk/ *adj.* в припóднятом настроéнии

eureka /jʊə'ri:kə/ *int.* э́врика

euro /'jʊərəʊ/ *n.* (*pl.* ~**s**) éвро (*m. indecl.*)

Euro|- /'jʊərəʊ/ *comb. form* евро...
■ ~**-MP** *n.* депутáт Европарлáмента; ~**sceptic** *n.* европескéптик; **e**~**zone** *n.* Еврозóна

Europe /'jʊərəp/ *n.* Еврóпа

✓ **European** /jʊərə'pɪən/ *n.* европé|ец (-йка)
● *adj.* европéйский

euthanasia /ju:θə'neɪzɪə/ *n.* эвтанáзия, умерщвлéние из милосéрдия

evacuate /ɪ'vækjʊeɪt/ *v.t.* эвакуи́ровать (*impf., pf.*)

evacuation /ɪvækjʊ'eɪʃ(ə)n/ *n.* (removal) эвакуáция; (physiol.) очищéние кишéчника, испражнéние

evacuee /ɪvækju:'i:/ *n.* эвакуи́рованный

evade /ɪ'veɪd/ *v.t.* избе|гáть, -жáть + *g.*; ~ **a blow/question** уклон|я́ться, -и́ться от удáра/ отвéта

evaluate /ɪ'væljʊeɪt/ *v.t.* оцéн|ивать, -и́ть

evaluation /ɪvæljʊ'eɪʃ(ə)n/ *n.* оцéнка

evangelical /i:væn'dʒelɪk(ə)l/ *adj.* евангели́ческий

evangelism /ɪ'vændʒəlɪz(ə)m/ *n.* прóповедь Евáнгелия; (fig.) проповéдничество

evangelist /ɪ'vændʒəlɪst/ *n.* (author of gospel) евангели́ст; (preacher) проповéдник Евáнгелия

evaporate /ɪ'væpəreɪt/ *v.t. & i.* испар|я́ть(ся), -и́ть(ся) (also fig.)

evaporation /ɪvæpə'reɪʃ(ə)n/ *n.* испарéние

evasion /ɪ'veɪʒ(ə)n/ *n.* (avoidance) уклонéние; (prevarication) увёртка

evasive /ɪ'veɪsɪv/ *adj.* (of answer) уклóнчивый; (of person) увёртливый

eve /i:v/ *n.* (day or evening before) канýн (also fig.); **on the** ~ **of** наканýне + *g.*

✓ **even** /'i:v(ə)n/ *adj.* (**evener**, **evenest**) **1** (level, smooth) рóвный **2** (equal) рáвный; **the score is** ~ счёт рáвный; **get** ~ **with sb** расквитáться (*pf.*) с кем-н. **3** (divisible by 2) чётный
● *adv.* дáже; и; хотя́ бы; **she won't** ~ **notice**

она́ и не заме́тит; **not ~** да́же не; **this applies ~ more to French** э́то ещё в бо́льшей сте́пени отно́сится к францу́зскому языку́
　● *v.t.* (make even or equal) выра́внивать, вы́ровнять

✧ **evening** /ˈiːvnɪŋ/ *n.* ве́чер; **in the ~** ве́чером; **one ~** одна́жды ве́чером; **this ~** сего́дня ве́чером; **tomorrow ~** за́втра ве́чером; **~ dress, clothes** (of either sex) вече́рний туале́т; **~ dress, gown** (woman's) вече́рнее пла́тье

evenness /ˈiːvənnɪs/ *n.* (physical smoothness) гла́дкость; (uniformity) равноме́рность; (of temper, tone, etc.) ро́вность, уравнове́шенность; (of odds, contest, etc.) ра́венство

✧ **event** /ɪˈvent/ *n.* **1** (occurrence) собы́тие **2** (hypothesis) слу́чай; **in the ~ of his coming** в слу́чае его́ прихо́да; **in any ~** в любо́м слу́чае **3** (sports race) забе́г, зае́зд; (type of sport) вид спо́рта

eventful /ɪˈventfʊl/ *adj.* насы́щенный собы́тиями

eventual /ɪˈventʃʊəl/ *adj.* коне́чный

eventuality /ɪventjuˈælɪtɪ/ *n.* возмо́жность, слу́чай

✧ **eventually** /ɪˈventjʊəlɪ/ *adv.* со вре́менем; в конце́ концо́в

✧ **ever** /ˈevə(r)/ *adv.* **1** (always) всегда́; **for ~** навсегда́, наве́чно; **~ after, since** с тех (са́мых) пор; **~ since** (as conj.) с тех пор, как… **2** (at any time): **do you ~ see him?** вы его́ хоть иногда́ ви́дите?; **scarcely, hardly ~** почти́ никогда́; о́чень ре́дко; **as good as ~** не ху́же, чем ра́ньше; **better than ~** лу́чше, чем когда́-либо **3** (intensive): **why ~ did you do it?** заче́м же вы э́то сде́лали?; **~ so rich** (BrE) невероя́тно бога́тый; (infml): **thank you ~ so much** (BrE) я вам чрезвыча́йно благода́рен
　■ **~green** (bot.) *n.* вечнозелёное расте́ние
　● *adj.* вечнозелёный; **~lasting** *adj.* ве́чный

✧ **every** /ˈevrɪ/ *adj.* ка́ждый, вся́кий; **I have ~ confidence in him** я в нём соверше́нно уве́рен; **~ ten minutes** ка́ждые де́сять мину́т; **~ other car** ка́ждый второ́й автомоби́ль; **~ other day** че́рез день; **~ now and again; ~ so often; ~ once in a while** вре́мя от вре́мени; по времена́м; иногда́
　■ **~day** *adj.* повседне́вный; обыкнове́нный; бытово́й

everybody /ˈevərɪbɒdɪ/ *pron.* ка́ждый; вся́кий; все (*pl.*); **~body else** все остальны́е

everyone /ˈevrɪwʌn/ *pron.* = **everybody**

everything /ˈevrɪθɪŋ/ *pron.* всё

everywhere /ˈevrɪweə(r)/ *adv.* везде́, повсю́ду

evict /ɪˈvɪkt/ *v.t.* выселя́ть, вы́селить

eviction /ɪˈvɪkʃ(ə)n/ *n.* выселе́ние

✧ **evidence** /ˈevɪd(ə)ns/ *n.* **1** (indication) доказа́тельство, свиде́тельство **2** (law) свиде́тельские показа́ния (*nt. pl.*); ули́ка; да́нные (*nt. pl.*); **give ~** да|ва́ть, -ть свиде́тельские показа́ния
　● *v.t.* служи́ть, по- доказа́тельством, ули́кой (*чего*)

evident /ˈevɪd(ə)nt/ *adj.* очеви́дный, я́сный; **it was ~ from his behaviour that …** бы́ло ви́дно по его́ поведе́нию, что…

✧ **evil** /ˈiːvɪl/ *n.* зло
　● *adj.* злой, дурно́й

evocation /evəˈkeɪʃ(ə)n/ *n.* вызыва́ние; воскреше́ние в па́мяти

evocative /ɪˈvɒkətɪv/ *adj.* навева́ющий воспомина́ния

evoke /ɪˈvəʊk/ *v.t.* вызыва́ть, вы́звать; пробу|жда́ть, -ди́ть; нап|омина́ть, -о́мнить

evolution /iːvəˈluːʃ(ə)n/ *n.* эволю́ция

evolutionary /iːvəˈluːʃənərɪ/ *adj.* эволюцио́нный

evolve /ɪˈvɒlv/ *v.i.* разв|ива́ться, -и́ться

ewe /juː/ *n.* овца́

ex /eks/ *n.* (infml) бы́вший муж, бы́вшая жена́

ex- /eks/ *pref.* (former) экс-…, бы́вший

exacerbate /ɪɡˈzæsəbeɪt/ *v.t.* (pain etc.) обостр|я́ть, -и́ть

exact /ɪɡˈzækt/ *adj.* то́чный

✧ **exactly** /ɪɡˈzæktlɪ/ *adv.* то́чно; (of numbers, quantities) ро́вно

exaggerate /ɪɡˈzædʒəreɪt/ *v.t.* преувели́чи|вать, -ть

exaggeration /ɪɡzædʒəˈreɪʃ(ə)n/ *n.* преувеличе́ние

exalt /ɪɡˈzɔːlt/ *v.t.* (make higher in rank etc.) повы́ша́ть, -ы́сить; (praise) превозн|оси́ть, -ести́

exaltation /eɡzɔːlˈteɪʃ(ə)n/ *n.* **1** (raising in rank etc.) повыше́ние **2** (worship) возвели́чение, возвели́чивание **3** (mental or emotional transport) экзальта́ция

exam /ɪɡˈzæm/ *n.* = **examination**

examination /ɪɡzæmɪˈneɪʃ(ə)n/ *n.* экза́мен; **take an ~** сдава́ть (*impf.*) экза́мен; **pass an ~** сдать (*pf.*) экза́мен
　■ **~ paper** *n.* (written by examinee) экзаменацио́нная рабо́та; (questions set) вопро́сы (*m. pl.*) (для экзаменацио́нной рабо́ты)

✧ **examine** /ɪɡˈzæmɪn/ *v.t.* **1** (inspect) осм|а́тривать, -отре́ть; **~ passports** пров|еря́ть, -е́рить паспорта́; **~ a patient** осм|а́тривать, -отре́ть больно́го **2** (academic) экзаменова́ть, про-

examiner /ɪɡˈzæmɪnə(r)/ *n.* экзамена́тор

✧ **example** /ɪɡˈzɑːmp(ə)l/ *n.* **1** (illustration, model) приме́р; **for ~** наприме́р **2** (warning) уро́к; **let this be an ~ to you** пусть э́то послу́жит вам уро́ком

exasperate /ɪɡˈzɑːspəreɪt/ *v.t.* изв|оди́ть, -ести́

exasperation /ɪɡzɑːspəˈreɪʃ(ə)n/ *n.* раздраже́ние

excavate /ˈekskəveɪt/ *v.t.* копа́ть (*impf.*); выка́пывать, вы́копать; раск|а́пывать, -опа́ть

excavation /ekskəˈveɪʃ(ə)n/ *n.* (site) раско́пки (*f. pl.*); (action) выка́пывание

excavator /ˈekskəveɪtə(r)/ *n.* (person) землеко́п; (machine) экскава́тор

exceed /ɪkˈsiːd/ *v.t.* превы́|ша́ть, -ы́сить

e

exceedingly /ɪk'siːdɪŋlɪ/ adv. весьма́, чрезвыча́йно

excel /ɪk'sel/ v.i. (**excelled, excelling**) выделя́ться (impf.); he ~s in sport он превосхо́дный спортсме́н

Excellency /'eksələnsɪ/ n.: His ~ его́ превосходи́тельство

✧ **excellent** /'eksələnt/ adj. отли́чный

✧ **except** /ɪk'sept/ prep. (also **excepting**) исключа́я + a.; кро́ме + g.; за исключе́нием + g.; ра́зве лишь/то́лько; the essay is good ~ for the spelling mistakes сочине́ние хоро́шее, е́сли не счита́ть орфографи́ческих оши́бок

✧ **exception** /ɪk'sepʃ(ə)n/ n. **1** исключе́ние; with the ~ of за исключе́нием + g. **2**: take ~ to обижа́ться, -и́деться на + a.

exceptional /ɪk'sepʃən(ə)l/ adj. исключи́тельный

excerpt /'eksɜːpt/ n. вы́держка, цита́та

excess /ɪk'ses/ n. изли́шек, избы́ток; in ~ of £20 свы́ше двадцати́ фу́нтов

■ ~ **baggage** /'ekses/ n. изли́шек багажа́

excessive /ɪk'sesɪv/ adj. изли́шний; (extreme) чрезме́рный

✧ **exchange** /ɪks'tʃeɪndʒ/ n. **1** (act of exchanging) обме́н (of: + g./i.); in ~ for в обме́н на + a. **2** (fin.) размо́н, обме́н; ~ rate/control валю́тный курс/контро́ль **3** (teleph.) (центра́льная) телефо́нная ста́нция ● v.t. меня́ть, об-/по- (что на что); (reciprocally) меня́ться, об-/по- (+ i.); we ~d places мы поменя́лись места́ми

exchequer /ɪks'tʃekə(r)/ n. казначе́йство, казна́

excise¹ /'eksaɪz/ n. акци́з

■ ~ **officer** n. акци́зный чино́вник

excise² /ɪk'saɪz/ v.t. выреза́ть, вы́резать; отре́зать, -е́зать

excision /ɪk'sɪʒ(ə)n/ n. выреза́ние, отреза́ние; (med.) иссече́ние, удале́ние

excitable /ɪk'saɪtəb(ə)l/ adj. легко́ возбуди́мый

excite /ɪk'saɪt/ v.t. волнова́ть, вз-; don't ~ yourself (or get ~d)! не волну́йтесь!

excitement /ɪk'saɪtmənt/ n. возбужде́ние, волне́ние

✧ **exciting** /ɪk'saɪtɪŋ/ adj. захва́тывающий

exclaim /ɪk'skleɪm/ v.t. & i. воскли́цать, -и́кнуть

exclamation /eksklə'meɪʃ(ə)n/ n. восклица́ние

■ ~ **mark** n. восклица́тельный знак

exclude /ɪk'skluːd/ v.t. исключ|а́ть, -и́ть

exclusion /ɪk'skluːʒ(ə)n/ n. исключе́ние

exclusive /ɪk'skluːsɪv/ adj. **1** (sole) исключи́тельный, еди́нственный **2**: ~ of (not counting) без + g., не счита́я + g. **3** (high-class) эксклюзи́вный; an ~ club клуб для и́збранных

exclusivity /ekskluː'sɪvɪtɪ/ n. эксклюзи́вность

excommunicate /ekskə'mjuːnɪkeɪt/ v.t. отлуч|а́ть, -и́ть от це́ркви

excrement /'ekskrɪmənt/ n. экскреме́нты (m. pl.)

excrete /ɪk'skriːt/ v.t. выделя́ть, вы́делить

excruciating /ɪk'skruːʃɪeɪtɪŋ/ adj. мучи́тельный

excursion /ɪk'skɜː(ʃ(ə)n/ n. (trip) экску́рсия

excuse¹ /ɪk'skjuːs/ n. извине́ние, оправда́ние, отгово́рка; a poor ~ сла́бая отгово́рка; please make my ~s to the hostess пожа́луйста, переда́йте мои́ извине́ния хозя́йке

excuse² /ɪk'skjuːz/ v.t. **1** (forgive) извин|я́ть, -и́ть; про|ща́ть, -сти́ть; please ~ my coming late (or me for coming late) извини́те, что я пришёл по́здно; ~ me, what time is it? прости́те, кото́рый час? **2** (release): I ~d him from attending я позво́лил ему́ не прису́тствовать

ex-directory /ɪk'skjuːz/ adj. (BrE) не внесённый в телефо́нную кни́гу; he's ~ его́ но́мера нет в телефо́нной кни́ге

execute /'eksɪkjuːt/ v.t. **1** (carry out) выполня́ть, вы́полнить; осуществля́ть, -ли́ть **2** (put to death) казни́ть (impf., pf.)

execution /eksɪ'kjuːʃ(ə)n/ n. **1** (carrying out) исполне́ние, выполне́ние **2** (capital punishment) казнь

executioner /eksɪ'kjuːʃənə(r)/ n. пала́ч

✧ **executive** /ɪg'zekjʊtɪv/ n. (руководя́щий) рабо́тник ● adj. **1** (executing laws etc.) исполни́тельный **2** (managing) руководя́щий

executor /ɪg'zekjʊtə(r)/ n. (of a will) исполни́тель (m.) завеща́ния, душеприка́зчик

exemplary /ɪg'zemplərɪ/ adj. приме́рный, образцо́вый

exemplify /ɪg'zemplɪfaɪ/ v.t. служи́ть, по- приме́ром + g.

exempt /ɪg'zempt/ adj. освобождённый, свобо́дный (от чего) ● v.t. освобо|жда́ть, -ди́ть

exemption /ɪg'zempʃ(ə)n/ n. освобожде́ние (от чего)

✧ **exercise** /'eksəsaɪz/ n. **1** (physical activity) заря́дка, упражне́ние; you should take more ~ вам ну́жно бо́льше вре́мени уделя́ть физи́ческим упражне́ниям **2** (trial of skill): military ~s вое́нные уче́ния; (in lesson) упражне́ние; (fig.): the object of the ~ цель э́того предприя́тия ● v.t. **1** (exert, use) выка́зывать, вы́казать; проявл|я́ть, -и́ть; ~ authority примен|я́ть, -и́ть власть **2** (physically) упражня́ть (impf.) ● v.i. упражня́ться (impf.)

■ ~ **book** n. (BrE) (учени́ческая) тетра́дь

exert /ɪg'zɜːt/ v.t. осуществл|я́ть, -и́ть; ~ oneself постара́ться (pf.)

exertion /ɪg'zɜː(ʃ(ə)n/ n. напряже́ние, уси́лие

exhale /eks'heɪl/ v.i. выдыха́ть, вы́дохнуть

exhaust /ɪg'zɔːst/ n. (apparatus) вы́хлоп, вы́пуск; (expelled gas) отрабо́танный газ ● v.t. истощ|а́ть, -и́ть; изнур|я́ть, -и́ть; I feel ~ed я соверше́нно без сил

✧ ключева́я ле́ксика

exhausting /ɪgˈzɔːstɪŋ/ adj. изнури́тельный, утоми́тельный

exhaustion /ɪgˈzɔːstʃ(ə)n/ n. переутомле́ние, изнеможе́ние

exhaustive /ɪgˈzɔːstɪv/ adj. исче́рпывающий, всесторо́нний

exhibit /ɪgˈzɪbɪt/ n. (in museum etc.) экспона́т
• v.t. (**exhibited, exhibiting**) **1** (e.g. painting) экспони́ровать (impf., pf.) **2** (fig., display) проявля́ть, -и́ть

⚙ **exhibition** /eksɪˈbɪʃ(ə)n/ n. (public show) вы́ставка; **he made an ~ of himself** он сде́лал себя́ посме́шищем

exhibitionist /eksɪˈbɪʃənɪst/ n. хвасту́н (infml)

exhilarat|e /ɪgˈzɪləreɪt/ v.t. весели́ть, раз-; **~ing news** ра́достное изве́стие

exhilaration /ɪgzɪləˈreɪʃ(ə)n/ n. весе́лье; прия́тное возбужде́ние

exhort /ɪgˈzɔːt/ v.t. призы́вать, -ва́ть (кого к чему); увещева́ть (impf.)

exhortation /egzɔːˈteɪʃ(ə)n/ n. призы́в, увещева́ние

exhume /eksˈhjuːm/ v.t. эксгуми́ровать (impf., pf.); выка́пывать, вы́копать

exile /ˈeksaɪl/ n. **1** (banishment) изгна́ние **2** (person) изгна́нник
• v.t. изг|оня́ть, -на́ть; ссыла́ть, сосла́ть

⚙ **exist** /ɪgˈzɪst/ v.i. существова́ть (impf.)

⚙ **existence** /ɪgˈzɪst(ə)ns/ n. существова́ние

existential /egzɪˈstenʃ(ə)l/ adj. экзистенциа́льный

existentialism /egzɪˈstenʃəlɪz(ə)m/ n. экзистенциали́зм

exit /ˈeksɪt/ n. (also comput.) вы́ход
• v.i. (**exited, exiting**) уходи́ть, уйти́; (comput.) выходи́ть, вы́йти

exonerate /ɪgˈzɒnəreɪt/ v.t. опра́вд|ывать, -а́ть; сн|има́ть, -я́ть обвине́ние с (+ g.) (в чём)

exorbitant /ɪgˈzɔːbɪt(ə)nt/ adj. непоме́рный, чрезме́рный

exorcism /ˈeksɔːsɪz(ə)m/ n. экзорци́зм, изгна́ние злых ду́хов

exorcize /ˈeksɔːsaɪz/ v.t. изг|оня́ть, -на́ть злых ду́хов из + g.

exotic /ɪgˈzɒtɪk/ adj. экзоти́ческий

⚙ **expand** /ɪkˈspænd/ v.t. (lit., fig.) расш|иря́ть, -и́рить; **heat ~s metals** при нагрева́нии мета́ллы расширя́ются
• v.i. расш|иря́ться, -и́риться; увели́чи|ваться, -ться в объёме

expanse /ɪkˈspæns/ n. протяже́ние

expansion /ɪkˈspænʃ(ə)n/ n. расшире́ние; (pol.) экспа́нсия; (increase) подъём

expatriate /eksˈpætrɪət/ n. & adj. экспатриа́нт (-ка)

⚙ **expect** /ɪkˈspekt/ v.t. **1** (of future or probable event) ждать (impf.), ожида́ть (impf.) + g.; **I ~ to see him** я рассчи́тываю встре́титься с ним **2** (require) ожида́ть (impf.) + g.; **I ~ you to be punctual** я наде́юсь/рассчи́тываю, что

вы бу́дете пунктуа́льны **3** (suppose) полага́ть (impf.); **I ~ you are hungry** я полага́ю, вы голодны́ **4**: **she is ~ing** (infml, pregnant) она́ ожида́ет ребёнка

expectancy /ɪkˈspekt(ə)nsɪ/ n. ожида́ние; предвкуше́ние

expectant /ɪkˈspekt(ə)nt/ adj. выжида́ющий; **an ~ mother** бу́дущая мать

⚙ **expectation** /ekspekˈteɪʃ(ə)n/ n. ожида́ние; **contrary to ~** вопреки́ ожида́ниям; **come up to ~s** опра́вдать (pf.) ожида́ния

expectorant /ekˈspektərənt/ n. (med.) отха́ркивающее сре́дство

expediency /ɪkˈspiːdɪənsɪ/ n. вы́года

expedient /ɪkˈspiːdɪənt/ n. приём, спо́соб
• adj. целесообра́зный; (advantageous) вы́годный

expedition /ekspɪˈdɪʃ(ə)n/ n. экспеди́ция

expeditionary /ekspɪˈdɪʃənərɪ/ adj. экспедицио́нный
■ **~ force** n. экспедицио́нные войска́

expel /ɪkˈspel/ v.t. (**expelled, expelling**) (compel to leave) исключ|а́ть, -и́ть; выгоня́ть, вы́гнать

expend /ɪkˈspend/ v.t. (money) расхо́довать, из-; тра́тить, ис-; (ammunition) расхо́довать, из-; (time, efforts) тра́тить, ис-/по-

expenditure /ɪkˈspendɪtʃə(r)/ n. расхо́д, тра́та

⚙ **expense** /ɪkˈspens/ n. **1** (monetary cost) расхо́д; **at my ~** (lit.) за мой счёт; **go to ~** нести́ (det.) расхо́ды; **spare no ~** не жале́ть (impf.) средств **2** (detriment): **a joke at my ~** шу́тка на мой счёт
■ **~ account** n. ава́нсовый отчёт

⚙ **expensive** /ɪkˈspensɪv/ adj. дорого́й, дорогосто́ящий

⚙ **experience** /ɪkˈspɪərɪəns/ n. **1** (process of gaining knowledge etc.) о́пыт **2** (event) слу́чай; **an unpleasant ~** неприя́тный слу́чай
• v.t. испы́т|ывать, -а́ть

experienced /ɪkˈspɪərɪənst/ adj. о́пытный

⚙ **experiment** /ɪkˈsperɪmənt/ n. экспериме́нт, о́пыт
• v.i. эксперименти́ровать (impf.)

experimental /ɪksperɪˈment(ə)l/ adj. эксперимента́льный, про́бный

experimentation /ɪksperɪmenˈteɪʃ(ə)n/ n. эксперименти́рование

⚙ **expert** /ˈekspəːt/ n. экспе́рт, знато́к, специали́ст (по чему)
• adj. квалифици́рованный; уме́лый; **an ~ driver** о́пытный шофёр; **~ advice** сове́т специали́ста; **she is ~ at persuading people** она́ ма́стер угова́ривать

expertise /ekspəːˈtiːz/ n. (skill, knowledge) компете́нтность

expire /ɪkˈspaɪə(r)/ v.i. (of period, licence, etc.) ист|ека́ть, -е́чь

expiry /ɪkˈspaɪərɪ/ n. истече́ние (сро́ка)

⚙ **explain** /ɪkˈspleɪn/ v.t. объясн|я́ть, -и́ть; изъясн|я́ть, -и́ть

✔ **explanation** /ɛksplə'neɪʃ(ə)n/ *n.* объяснéние

explanatory /ɪk'splænətərɪ/ *adj.* объяснительный

expletive /ɪk'spliːtɪv/ *n.* (oath) брáнное выражéние; (gram.) вставнóе слóво

explicable /ɪk'splɪkəb(ə)l/ *adj.* объясни́мый

explicit /ɪk'splɪsɪt/ *adj.* я́сный, чёткий, тóчный

explode /ɪk'spləʊd/ *v.t.* вз|рывáть, -орвáть
• *v.i.* взрывáться, -орвáться

exploit[1] /'eksplɔɪt/ *n.* пóдвиг

exploit[2] /ɪk'splɔɪt/ *v.t.* **1** (use or develop economically; misuse) эксплуати́ровать (*impf.*) **2** (an advantage etc.) испóльзовать (*impf., pf.*)

exploitation /eksplɔɪ'teɪʃ(ə)n/ *n.* (of person or resources) эксплуатáция

exploitative /ɪk'splɔɪtətɪv/ *adj.* эксплуатáторский, эксплуатациóнный

exploration /eksplə'reɪʃ(ə)n/ *n.* (geog.) исслéдование; (of possibilities etc.) изучéние

exploratory /ɪk'splɒrətərɪ/ *adj.* исслéдовательский; ~ **talks** предвари́тельные переговóры

✔ **explore** /ɪk'splɔː(r)/ *v.t.* **1** (geog.) исслéдовать (*impf., pf.*) **2** (possibilities etc.) изуч|áть, -и́ть

explorer /ɪk'splɔːrə(r)/ *n.* исслéдователь (*m.*) (-ница)

explosion /ɪk'spləʊʒ(ə)n/ *n.* (of bomb etc.) взрыв; (of rage etc.) вспы́шка; **population** ~ демографи́ческий взрыв

explosive /ɪk'spləʊsɪv/ *n.* взры́вчатое вещество
• *adj.* взры́вчатый, взрывнóй; (situation) взрывоопáсный

exponent /ɪk'spəʊnənt/ *n.* (advocate) сторóнник; представи́тель (*m.*)

exponential /ekspə'nenʃ(ə)l/ *adj.* (math.) экспоненциáльный, показáтельный

export[1] /'ekspɔːt/ *n.* э́кспорт, вы́воз

export[2] /ek'spɔːt/ *v.t.* экспорти́ровать (*impf., pf.*); вывози́ть, вы́везти

exportation /ekspɔː'teɪʃ(ə)n/ *n.* экспорти́рование

exporter /ek'spɔːtə(r)/ *n.* экспортёр

✔ **expose** /ɪk'spəʊz/ *v.t.* **1** (physically) выставля́ть, вы́ставить; ~ **oneself** (indecently) обнаж|áться, -и́ться **2** (unmask) разоблач|áть, -и́ть

exposition /ekspə'zɪʃ(ə)n/ *n.* (setting forth facts etc.) изложéние; (exhibition) экспози́ция, вы́ставка

exposure /ɪk'spəʊʒə(r)/ *n.* **1** (physical): ~ **to light** выставлéние на свет; **he died of** ~ он поги́б от хóлода **2** (unmasking) разоблачéние **3** (phot.) экспози́ция

expound /ɪk'spaʊnd/ *v.t.* (a theory) изл|агáть, -ожи́ть; (a text) толковáть (*impf.*)

express[1] /ɪk'spres/ *n.* (~ **train**) экспрéсс; курьéрский пóезд
• *adj.* (urgent, high-speed) срóчный
• *adv.* срóчно, спéшно; **the goods were sent** ~ (urgently) товáр был отпрáвлен экспрéссом

✔ ключевáя лéксика

■ ~ **letter** *n.* срóчное письмó; ~ **mail** *n.* э́кстренная пóчта

✔ **express**[2] /ɪk'spres/ *v.t.* (show in words etc.) выражáть, вы́разить; выскáзывать, вы́сказать; ~ **oneself** выражáться, вы́разиться

✔ **expression** /ɪk'spreʃ(ə)n/ *n.* **1** (act of expressing) выражéние **2** (word, term) выражéние (also math.)

expressionism /ɪk'spreʃənɪz(ə)m/ *n.* экспрессиони́зм

expressionist /ɪkspreʃə'nɪst/ *n.* экспрессиони́ст

expressive /ɪk'spresɪv/ *adj.* вырази́тельный

expulsion /ɪk'spʌlʃ(ə)n/ *n.* изгнáние; исключéние

expurgate /'ekspəgeɪt/ *v.t.*: ~ **a book** исключ|áть, -и́ть (*or* изымáть, изъя́ть) нежелáтельные местá из кни́ги

exquisite /ek'skwɪzɪt/ *adj.* (perfected) утончённый

extemporize /ɪk'stempəraɪz/ *v.t. & i.* и|мпровизи́ровать, сы-; **he** ~**d a speech** он произнёс импровизи́рованную речь

✔ **extend** /ɪk'stend/ *v.t.* **1** (stretch out) протя́|гивать, -нýть **2** (make longer, wider or larger) удлин|я́ть, -и́ть; расш|иря́ть, -и́рить; ~ **a railway** продли́ть (*pf.*) железнодорóжную ли́нию; ~ **one's premises** расш|иря́ть, -и́рить помещéние **3** (prolong) продл|евáть, -и́ть; ~ **one's leave/passport** продл|евáть, -и́ть óтпуск/пáспорт; **an** ~**ed** (*sc. lengthy*) **visit** дли́тельный визи́т
• *v.i.* простирáться (*impf.*); **the garden** ~**s to the river** сад простирáется до рекú

extension /ɪk'stenʃ(ə)n/ *n.* **1** (stretching out) вытя́гивание, удлинéние **2** (enlarging in space or time) расширéние, увеличéние; ~ **of leave** продлéние óтпуска **3** (additional part of building etc.) пристрóйка (**to:** к + *d.*) **4** (teleph., telephone) параллéльный телефóн; (number) добáвочный (нóмер); **my number is 5652,** ~ **10** мой нóмер 5652, добáвочный 10
■ ~ **lead** *n.* (elec.) удлини́тель (*m.*)

extensive /ɪk'stensɪv/ *adj.* (wide, far-reaching) прострáнный

✔ **extent** /ɪk'stent/ *n.* **1** (physical size, length, etc.) протяжéние **2** (fig., range) размéр; круг; диапазóн **3** (degree) стéпень; **to some** (*or* **certain**) ~ до нéкоторой/извéстной стéпени

extenuat|e /ɪk'stenjʊeɪt/ *v.t.* преум|еньшáть, -éньшить; ~**ing circumstances** смягчáющие обстоя́тельства

exterior /ɪk'stɪərɪə(r)/ *n.* (of object) внéшняя сторонá; (archit.) экстерьéр
• *adj.* внéшний

exterminate /ɪk'stɜːmɪneɪt/ *v.t.* истреб|ля́ть, -и́ть

extermination /ɪkstɜːmɪ'neɪʃ(ə)n/ *n.* истреблéние

external /ɪk'stɜːn(ə)l/ *n.* внéшность
• *adj.* внéшний; **for** ~ **use only** тóлько для наружного употреблéния

extinct /ɪk'stɪŋkt/ *adj.* (of volcano) потýхший; (of species, custom) вы́мерший

extinction /ɪk'stɪŋkʃ(ə)n/ *n.* угасáние; (of species etc.) вымирáние

extinguish /ɪk'stɪŋgwɪʃ/ *v.t.* (light, fire) гасить, по-; (hopes etc.) убивáть, -ить

extinguisher /ɪk'stɪŋgwɪʃə(r)/ *n.* огнетуши́тель (*m.*)

extol /ɪk'stəʊl/ *v.t.* (**extolled, extolling**) превозн|оси́ть, -ести́

extort /ɪk'stɔːt/ *v.t.* вымогáть (*impf.*)

extortion /ɪk'stɔːʃ(ə)n/ *n.* вымогáтельство

extortionate /ɪk'stɔːʃənət/ *adj.* вымогáтельский

extortionist /ɪk'stɔːʃənə(r)/ *n.* вымогáтель (*m.*)

♂ **extra** /'ekstrə/ *n.* **1** (additional item) что-н. дополни́тельное **2** (minor performer) стати́ст (-ка), актёр (актри́са) массóвки
● *adj.* (additional) добáвочный, дополни́тельный; **it costs £1, postage ~** э́то сто́ит 1 фунт без пересы́лки
● *adv.* сверх-, осóбо; **~ strong** (e.g. drink) осóбой крéпости
■ **~ time** *n.* (sport) дополни́тельное врéмя

extract¹ /'ekstrækt/ *n.* вы́держка

extract² /ɪk'strækt/ *v.t.* (cork) вытáскивать, вы́тащить; (tooth) удал|я́ть, -и́ть

extra-curricular /ekstrəkə'rɪkjʊlə(r)/ *adj.* проводи́мый сверх учéбного плáна

extradite /'ekstrədaɪt/ *v.t.* (hand over) выдавáть, вы́дать (*обвиня́емого преступника*); экстради́ровать (*impf., pf.*)

extradition /ekstrə'dɪʃ(ə)n/ *n.* вы́дача (престýпника); экстради́ция

extramarital /ekstrə'mærɪt(ə)l/ *adj.*: **~ affair** внебрáчная связь

extramural /ekstrə'mjʊər(ə)l/ *adj.* (BrE, of education) заóчный; **~ student** заóчни|к (-ца)

extraneous /ɪk'streɪnɪəs/ *adj.* посторóнний, чужóй

extraordinary /ɪk'strɔːdɪnərɪ/ *adj.* (unusual) необы́чный; (impressive) необычáйный; (specially convened) чрезвычáйный

extrapolate /ɪk'stræpəlet/ *v.t. & i.* (math.) (*also* fig.) экстраполи́ровать (*impf., pf.*)

extraterrestrial /ekstrətɪ'restrɪəl/ *adj.* внеземнóй
● *n.* инопланетя́н|ин (-ка)

extravagance /ɪk'strævəɡ(ə)ns/ *n.* (lack of thrift) расточи́тельство; (luxury) изли́шество; (unusualness) экстравагáнтность

extravagant /ɪk'strævəɡ(ə)nt/ *adj.* расточи́тельный; **she was ~ with water** онá расхóдовала сли́шком мнóго воды́

extravaganza /ɪkstrævə'ɡænzə/ *n.* фееéрия

extreme /ɪk'striːm/ *n.* **1** (high degree) крáйность **2** (of conduct etc.) крáйность; **he**

went to **~s to satisfy them** он пошёл на крáйние мéры, чтóбы угоди́ть им
● *adj.* крáйний, предéльный; **the ~ edge of the city** сáмая окрáина гóрода

♂ **extremely** /ɪk'striːmlɪ/ *adv.* крáйне

extremism /ɪk'striːmɪz(ə)m/ *n.* экстреми́зм

extremist /ɪk'striːmɪst/ *n.* экстреми́ст
● *adj.* экстреми́стский

extremity /ɪk'stremɪtɪ/ *n.* **1** (end, extreme point) край **2** (*in pl.*) (hands and feet) конéчности (*f. pl.*) **3** (extreme quality) крáйность; **the ~ of his grief** безмéрность егó гóря **4** (hardship) крáйность; **reduced to ~** доведённый до крáйности **5** (*in pl.*) (extreme measures) крáйние мéры (*f. pl.*)

extricate /'ekstrɪkeɪt/ *v.t.* высвобождáть, вы́свободить; **~ oneself from a difficulty** вы́путаться (*pf.*) из затруднéния

extrovert /'ekstrəvɔːt/ *n.* экстравéрт

exuberance /ɪɡ'zjuːbərəns/ *n.* (profusion) изоби́лие; (of character) экспанси́вность

exuberant /ɪɡ'zjuːbərənt/ *adj.* (of imagination etc.) богáтый, бýйный; (of spirits etc.) экспанси́вный

exude /ɪɡ'zjuːd/ *v.i.* проступ|áть, -и́ть; выдел|я́ть, -ить; **she ~d cheerfulness** онá излучáла весéлье

exult /ɪɡ'zʌlt/ *v.i.* торжествовáть, ликовáть (*both impf.*)

exultant /ɪɡ'zʌlt(ə)nt/ *adj.* торжествýющий, ликýющий

exultation /ɪɡzʌl'teɪʃ(ə)n/ *n.* торжествó, ликовáние

♂ **eye** /aɪ/ *n.* **1** (organ of vision) глаз **2** (var. idioms): **make ~s at sb** (infml) стрóить (*impf.*) глáзки комý-н.; **keep an ~ on** (e.g. a saucepan, children, the time) следи́ть (*impf.*) за + *i.*; **an ~ for an ~** óко за óко; **before sb's very ~s** на глазáх у когó-н.; **he has an ~ for colour** он чýвствует цвет; **I caught her ~** я поймáл её взгляд; **see ~ to ~ with** сходи́ться (*impf.*) во взгля́дах с + *i.* **3** (special sense): **~ of a needle** игóльное ушкó
● *v.t.* (**eyes, eyed, eyeing** *or* **eying**) разгля́д|ывать, -éть; наблюдáть (*impf.*)
■ **~ball** *n.* глазнóе я́блоко; **~brow** *n.* бровь; **~brow pencil** карандáш для бровéй; **~-catching** *adj.* эффéктный; **~ drops** *n. pl.* глазны́е кáпли; **~ hospital** *n.* глазнáя больни́ца; **~lash** *n.* ресни́ца; **~lid** *n.* вéко; **without batting an ~lid** (infml) глáзом не моргнýв; **~liner** *n.* карандáш для подведéния глаз; **~shadow** *n.* тéни (*f. pl.*) для век; **~sight** *n.* зрéние; **she has good ~sight** у неё хорóшее зрéние; **~sore** *n.* урóдство; **~witness** *n.* очеви́дец

-eyed /aɪd/ *comb. form*: **blue~** голубоглáзый

Ff

F¹ /ef/ *n.* (mus.) фа (*nt. indecl.*)

F² /ef/ *n.* (*abbr. of* **Fahrenheit**) F (= *градусов по Фаренгейту*)

fable /'feɪb(ə)l/ *n.* ба́сня

fabric /'fæbrɪk/ *n.* (text.) ткань, мате́рия; (of a building etc., fig.) структу́ра

fabricate /'fæbrɪkeɪt/ *v.t.* **1** (invent) выду́мывать, вы́думать **2** (construct) стро́ить, по-

fabrication /fæbrɪ'keɪʃ(ə)n/ *n.* **1** (invented story, lie) вы́думка; **complete ~** сплошна́я вы́думка **2** (manufacturing) изготовле́ние

fabulous /'fæbjʊləs/ *adj.* роско́шный, баснословный

facade /fə'sɑːd/ *n.* (archit.) фаса́д

✎ **face** /feɪs/ *n.* **1** (front part of head) лицо́; **look sb in the ~** посмотре́ть (*pf.*) кому́-н. в глаза́; **I came ~ to ~ with him** я столкну́лся с ним лицо́м к лицу́; **I told him so to his ~** я сказа́л ему́ э́то в лицо́; **she laughed in my ~** она́ рассмея́лась мне в лицо́; **he shut the door in my ~** он захло́пнул дверь пе́ред мои́м но́сом; **in the ~ of danger** пе́ред лицо́м опа́сности **2** (facial expression) лицо́; выраже́ние лица́; **he made/pulled a ~** он ско́рчил/состро́ил ро́жу; **his ~ fell** он измени́лся в лице́; у него́ вы́тянулось лицо́ **3** (respect): **he saved ~** он спас свою́ репута́цию **4** (physical surface) лицо́; (of clock) циферблат; **he laid the card ~ down** он положи́л ка́рту лицо́м вниз (*or* руба́шкой вверх)

• *v.t.* **1** (physically) стоя́ть (*impf.*) лицо́м к + *d.*; **the man facing us** челове́к, сидя́щий *и т. n.* про́тив нас **2** (confront) смотре́ть (*impf.*) в лицо́ *чему*; **we must ~ facts** на́до смотре́ть фа́ктам в лицо́; **let's ~ it!** (infml) на́до гляде́ть пра́вде в глаза́!

• *v.i.*: **the house ~s south** дом обращён фаса́дом на юг; **their house ~s ours** их дом напро́тив на́шего; **he ~d up to the difficulties** он не испуга́лся тру́дностей

■ **F~book®** *n.* социа́льная сеть «Фейсбу́к»; **~lift** *n.* подтя́жка ко́жи на лице́; (fig.) вне́шнее обновле́ние, космети́ческий ремо́нт; **~ value** *n.* (of currency) номина́льная сто́имость; **I took his words at ~ value** я при́нял его́ слова́ за чи́стую моне́ту

faceless /'feɪsləs/ *adj.* (anonymous) безли́чный, безли́кий

facet /'fæsɪt/ *n.* грань; (fig.) аспе́кт

facetious /fə'siːʃəs/ *adj.* шутли́вый, шу́точный

facetiousness /fə'siːʃəsnɪs/ *n.* (неуме́стная) шутли́вость

facial /'feɪʃ(ə)l/ *n.* масса́ж лица́
• *adj.* лицево́й

facile /'fæsaɪl/ *adj.* (easy, fluent) лёгкий, свобо́дный; (superficial) пове́рхностный

✎ **facilitate** /fə'sɪlɪteɪt/ *v.t.* спосо́бствовать (*impf.*) + *d.*

✎ **facilit|y** /fə'sɪlɪtɪ/ *n.* (ease) лёгкость; (appliance, installation) сооруже́ние; **~ies for study** усло́вия (*nt. pl.*) для учёбы; **sports ~ies** спорти́вное обору́дование; помеще́ния (*nt. pl.*) для заня́тия спо́ртом

facsimile /fæk'sɪmɪlɪ/ *n.* (exact copy) факси́миле (*nt. indecl.*); (fax) факс

✎ **fact** /fækt/ *n.* факт; **as a matter of ~** факти́чески; на са́мом де́ле; **the ~ is that …** де́ло в том, что…; **in ~** (actually) факти́чески; в/на са́мом де́ле; (intensifying): **I think so, in ~ I'm quite sure** я так ду́маю, бо́лее того́, я уве́рен в э́том

■ **~-finding** *adj.* занима́ющийся установле́нием фа́ктов, рассле́дованием обстоя́тельств

faction /'fækʃ(ə)n/ *n.* фра́кция, группиро́вка

factional /'fækʃən(ə)l/ *adj.* фракцио́нный

✎ **factor** /'fæktə(r)/ *n.* фа́ктор

factory /'fæktərɪ/ *n.* фа́брика, заво́д

factual /'fæktʃʊəl/ *adj.* факти́ческий

faculty /'fækəltɪ/ *n.* **1** (power, aptitude) спосо́бность **2** (BrE, part of university) факульте́т **3** (AmE, body of teachers) профе́ссорско-преподава́тельский соста́в

fad /fæd/ *n.* (craze) увлече́ние; (whim) при́хоть

fade /feɪd/ *v.t.* **1** (cause to lose colour) обесцве́|чивать, -тить **2** (cin., radio): **~ out** постепе́нно уме́ньшать, -е́ньшить си́лу зву́ка; **~ in** постепе́нно увели́чи|вать, -ть си́лу зву́ка

• *v.i.* **1** (lose colour) обесцве́|чиваться, -титься **2** (fig.): **his hopes ~d** его́ наде́жды растая́ли

faeces /'fiːsiːz/ (AmE **feces**) *n. pl.* фека́лии (*f. pl.*); испражне́ния (*nt. pl.*)

fag¹ /fæg/ *n.* (BrE, infml, tedious task) изнури́тельная рабо́та

fag² /fæg/ *n.* (BrE, infml, cigarette) сигаре́та, папиро́са

■ **~ end** *n.* (butt) оку́рок; (fig.) коне́ц (*чего*); оста́ток (*чего*)

fagged /'fægd/ *adj.* (BrE, infml) измо́танный; **I am ~ out** я вконе́ц вы́мотался

Fahrenheit /'færənhaɪt/ *n.* (*abbr* **F**) Фаренге́йт

✎ **fail** /feɪl/ *n.*: **without ~** обяза́тельно, непреме́нно
• *v.t.* **1** (exam) не сдава́ть, -ть; (drugs test; of sportsman/addict) не про|ходи́ть, -йти́ (тест

на до́пинг/нарко́тики) **2** (disappoint, desert) подв|оди́ть, -ести́; **words ~ me** я не нахожу́ слов
● *v.i.* **1** (decline) ух|удша́ться, -у́дшиться; (fall short) недостава́ть (*impf.*); **the crops ~ed** хлеб не уроди́лся; **his eyesight is ~ing** его́ зре́ние слабе́ет; **he is in ~ing health** его́ здоро́вье ухудша́ется **2** (not succeed): **he ~ed in the exam** он провали́лся на экза́мене; **he ~ed to convince her** ему́ не удало́сь (*or* он не суме́л) убеди́ть её **3** (omit) упус|ка́ть, -ти́ть; **he never ~s to write** он никогда́ не забыва́ет писа́ть

failing /'feɪlɪŋ/ *n.* (defect) недоста́ток
● *prep.* за неиме́нием + *g.*

failure /'feɪljə(r)/ *n.* **1** (unsuccess) неуда́ча, неуспе́х, прова́л **2** (person) неуда́чник **3** (non-functioning) ава́рия; **heart ~** остано́вка се́рдца **4** (omission): **his ~ to answer is a nuisance** о́чень доса́дно, что он не отвеча́ет

faint /feɪnt/ *n.* (med.) о́бморок; **in a dead ~** в глубо́ком о́бмороке
● *adj.* **1** (weak, indistinct) сла́бый, неотчётливый; **I haven't the ~est idea** я не име́ю ни мале́йшего поня́тия **2** (giddy): **I feel ~** мне ду́рно
● *v.i.* (lose consciousness) па́дать, упа́сть в о́бморок; (grow weak) слабе́ть (*impf.*)
■ **~-hearted** *adj.* трусли́вый, малоду́шный

fair¹ /feə(r)/ *n.* (trade fair) (вы́ставка-)я́рмарка; (fun fair) я́рмарка; аттракцио́ны *m.pl.*
■ **~ground** *n.* я́рмарочная пло́щадь

fair² /feə(r)/ *adj.* **1** (beautiful) прекра́сный, краси́вый; **the ~ sex** прекра́сный пол **2** (of weather) я́сный **3** (abundant): **a ~ amount** (a lot) значи́тельное/изря́дное коли́чество **4** (average) сно́сный; **she has a ~ chance of success** у неё неплохи́е ша́нсы на успе́х; **her performance was only ~** её выступле́ние бы́ло та́к себе́ **5** (equitable): **~ share** зако́нная до́ля; **it is ~ to say that ...** со всей справедли́востью мо́жно сказа́ть, что... **6** (of hair) све́тлый; (blond) белоку́рый; **a ~ complexion** све́тлый цвет лица́
■ **~-haired** *adj.* белоку́рый; **~-minded** *adj.* справедли́вый; **~ play** *n.* че́стная игра́; справедли́вость

fairly /'feəlɪ/ *adv.* **1** (moderately) дово́льно, сно́сно, терпи́мо **2** (justly) че́стно, справедли́во

fairness /'feənɪs/ *n.* (equity) справедли́вость, че́стность; **in all ~** со всей справедли́востью

fairy /'feərɪ/ *n.* фе́я
■ **~ story**, **~ tale** *nn.* ска́зка; (fig.) ска́зка, небыли́ца

fait accompli /feɪt ə'kɒmplɪ/ *n.* (*pl.* **faits accomplis** *pronunc. same*) сверши́вшийся факт

faith /feɪθ/ *n.* **1** (trust) ве́ра, дове́рие; **I have no ~ in doctors** я не ве́рю доктора́м **2** (relig.) ве́ра **3** (sincerity): **in good ~** че́стно, добросо́вестно

faithful /'feɪθfʊl/ *adj.* то́чный, достове́рный; (*as n. pl.*) **the ~** (believers) правове́рные

faithfully /'feɪθfʊlɪ/ *adv.* то́чно, ве́рно; **yours ~** (BrE, formal letter ending) с уваже́нием;

искренне Ваш

faithless /'feɪθlɪs/ *adj.* вероло́мный

fake /feɪk/ *n.* (sham) подде́лка; (*attr.*) подде́льный
● *v.t.* подде́л|ывать, -ать

falcon /'fɔ:lkən/ *n.* со́кол

fall /fɔ:l/ *n.* **1** (physical drop) паде́ние **2** (moral) паде́ние; **~ from grace** нра́вственное паде́ние **3** (diminution) пониже́ние; **~ in prices** паде́ние цен **4** (*in pl.*) (waterfall) водопа́д **5** (AmE, autumn) о́сень
● *v.i.* (*past* **fell**, *p.p.* **fallen**) **1** па́дать, упа́сть; **he fell over a chair** он упа́л, споткну́вшись о стул; **he fell off his horse** он упа́л с ло́шади **2** (drop, sink) па́дать, упа́сть; **prices fell** це́ны сни́зились/упа́ли; **the temperature fell** температу́ра упа́ла; **my spirits fell ~** я упа́л/пал ду́хом **3** (of defeat etc.) па́|дать, -сть; **the government fell** прави́тельство па́ло **4** (pass into a state): **he fell ill** он заболе́л; **he fell in love with her** он влюби́лся в неё **5** (come): **darkness fell** наступи́ла темнота́
□ **~ apart** распа́|даться, -сться
□ **~ back** (mil.) отступ|а́ть, -и́ть; **~ back on sth** прибе́га|ть, -́гнуть к чему́-н.
□ **~ behind** (e.g. in walking) отст|ава́ть, -а́ть; (with rent) зап|а́здывать, -озда́ть с упла́той за кварти́ру
□ **~ down** па́дать, упа́сть
□ **~ for** (**~** in love with) увл|ека́ться, -е́чься + *i.*; (be taken in by): **he fell for her story** он пове́рил её слова́м
□ **~ in** впасть (*во что*); **the roof fell in** кры́ша ру́хнула/обвали́лась; **the soldiers fell in** солда́ты постро́ились
□ **~ off** па́дать, упа́сть (*с чего*); **attendance is ~ing off** посеща́емость па́дает
□ **~ out** выпа|да́ть, вы́пасть; **his hair fell out** у него́ вы́пали во́лосы; (quarrel) поссо́риться (*pf.*)
□ **~ over** па́дать, упа́сть
□ **~ through** прова́л|иваться, -и́ться
■ **~out** *n.* (nuclear) радиоакти́вные оса́дки (*m. pl.*)

fallacious /fə'leɪʃəs/ *adj.* оши́бочный, ло́жный

fallacy /'fæləsɪ/ *n.* (false belief) заблужде́ние

fallen /'fɔ:l(ə)n/ *p.p. of* ▸ **fall**

fallible /'fælɪb(ə)l/ *adj.* подве́рженный оши́бкам

Fallopian tube /fə'ləʊpɪən/ *n.* фалло́пиева труба́

fallow /'fæləʊ/ *adj.* (agric.) вспа́ханный под пар; (земля́): **lie ~** ост|ава́ться, -а́ться под па́ром
■ **~ land** *n.* пар

false /fɔ:ls/ *adj.* **1** (wrong) ло́жный, оши́бочный, фальши́вый **2** (deceitful) лжи́вый, вероло́мный **3** (sham) фальши́вый
■ **~ alarm** *n.* ло́жная трево́га; **~ bottom** *n.* двойно́е дно; **~ pretences** *n. pl.* обма́н; притво́рство; **~ start** *n.* (racing, also fig.) фальста́рт; срыв в са́мом нача́ле; **~ teeth** *n. pl.* иску́сственные зу́бы

falsehood /ˈfɔːlshʊd/ *n.* ложь, непра́вда; **he told a ~** он сказа́л непра́вду

falsify /ˈfɔːlsɪfaɪ/ *v.t.* подде́л|ывать, -ать

falsity /ˈfɔːlsɪtɪ/ *n.* (falsehood, inaccuracy) ло́жность, оши́бочность

falter /ˈfɔːltə(r)/ *v.i.* (move or act hesitatingly) спот|ыка́ться, -кну́ться; (in speaking) зап|ина́ться, -ну́ться

fame /feɪm/ *n.* сла́ва; репута́ция

◆ **familiar** /fəˈmɪlɪə(r)/ *adj.* **1** (common, usual) обы́чный, привы́чный **2** (of acquaintance) знако́мый; **I am ~ with the subject** я знако́м с э́тим предме́том

familiarity /fəˌmɪlɪˈærɪtɪ/ *n.* **1** (close acquaintance) бли́зкое знако́мство (**with:** c + *i.*) **2** (of manner) фамилья́рность

familiarize /fəˈmɪlɪəraɪz/ *v.t.* ознак|омля́ть, -о́мить (*кого с чем*); **~ oneself with sth** ознако́миться (*pf.*) с чем-н.

◆ **family** /ˈfæmɪlɪ/ *n.* **1** (parents and children) семья́ **2** (*attr.*) семе́йный
■ **~ name** *n.* (surname) фами́лия; **~ planning** *n.* контро́ль (*m.*) над рожда́емостью; **~ tree** *n.* родосло́вное де́рево

famine /ˈfæmɪn/ *n.* го́лод

famished /ˈfæmɪʃt/ *adj.* (infml): **I'm ~** я си́льно проголода́лся; я умира́ю с го́лоду

◆ **famous** /ˈfeɪməs/ *adj.* знамени́тый, просла́вленный

fan[1] /fæn/ *n.* ве́ер; (ventilator) вентиля́тор
● *v.t.* (**fanned, fanning**): **~ oneself** обма́хиваться (*impf.*) ве́ером
● *v.i.* (**fanned, fanning**): **~ out** (e.g. roads) расходи́ться (*impf.*) ве́ером; (e.g. soldiers) разв|ора́чиваться, -ерну́ться ве́ером

◆ **fan**[2] /fæn/ *n.* (infml, devotee) боле́льщи|к (-ца), фана́т (-ка), люби́тель (*m.*) (-ница)
■ **~ mail** *n.* пи́сьма (*nt. pl.*) от покло́нников

fanatic /fəˈnætɪk/ *n.* фана́тик

fanatical /fəˈnætɪk(ə)l/ *adj.* фанати́чный

fanaticism /fəˈnætɪsɪz(ə)m/ *n.* фанати́зм

fanciful /ˈfænsɪfʊl/ *adj.* капри́зный; причу́дливый

fancy /ˈfænsɪ/ *n.* **1** (imagination) фанта́зия **2** (thing imagined) фанта́зия **3** (liking) скло́нность; **he took a ~ to her** он увлёкся е́ю
● *adj.* (**fancier, fanciest**) (elaborate) прихотли́вый; **this dress is too ~ to wear to work** для рабо́ты ну́жно пла́тье поскромне́е; (fashionable) мо́дный
● *v.t.* **1** (imagine): **~ (that)!** вообрази́(те)! **2** (BrE, like) хоте́ть (*impf.*) + *g.*; жела́ть (*impf.*); **she fancies him** (infml) он ей нра́вится; **what do you ~ for dinner?** чего́ бы вам хоте́лось на у́жин?
■ **~ dress** *n.* маскара́дный костю́м; **~-dress ball** костюми́рованный бал

fanfare /ˈfænfeə(r)/ *n.* фанфа́ра

fang /fæŋ/ *n.* (of wolf etc.) клык; (of snake) ядови́тый зуб

fantasize /ˈfæntəsaɪz/ *v.i.* фантази́ровать (*impf.*)

fantastic /fænˈtæstɪk/ *adj.* (wild, strange) фантасти́ческий, фантасти́чный; (infml, marvellous) потряса́ющий, изуми́тельный

fantasy /ˈfæntəsɪ/ *n.* фанта́зия; (genre) фанта́стика

FAQ *abbr.* (*of* **frequently asked questions**) (comput.) ча́сто задава́емые вопро́сы

◆ **far** /fɑː(r)/ *adj.* (**further, furthest** *or* **farther, farthest**) да́льний, далёкий, отдалённый; **the F~ East** Да́льний Восто́к; **at the ~ end of the street** на друго́м конце́ у́лицы
● *adv.* (**further, furthest** *or* **farther, farthest**) далеко́; **~ away, off** о́чень далеко́; **they came from ~ and wide** они́ съе́хались отовсю́ду (*or* со всех концо́в); **better** (на)мно́го/гора́здо лу́чше; **it is ~ from true** э́то совсе́м не так; **so ~** (until now) до сих пор; пока́ (что); **as, so ~ as** (of distance) до (*чего*); (of extent) наско́лько; поско́льку; **as ~ as I know** наско́лько мне изве́стно; **as ~ as I am concerned** что каса́ется меня́; **he went so ~ as to say …** он да́же сказа́л…; **how ~** (of distance) как далеко́; (of extent) наско́лько; **he will go ~** (succeed) он далеко́ пойдёт; **he has gone too ~ this time** на э́тот раз он зашёл сли́шком далеко́
■ **~away** *adj.* (distant) далёкий, отдалённый; **~-fetched** *adj.* с натя́жкой; притя́нутый за́ волосы/уши; **~-off** *adj.* отдалённый; **~-reaching** *adj.* далеко́ иду́щий; **~-sighted** *adj.* (prudent etc.) дальнови́дный, предусмотри́тельный; (long-sighted) дальнозо́ркий

farce /fɑːs/ *n.* (theatr., fig.) фарс

farcical /ˈfɑːsɪk(ə)l/ *adj.* смехотво́рный

fare /feə(r)/ *n.* (cost) пла́та за прое́зд

farewell /feəˈwel/ *n.* проща́ние

◆ **farm** /fɑːm/ *n.* фе́рма
● *v.t. & i.* **1** (agric.) занима́ться (*impf.*) се́льским хозя́йством **2**: **~ out work** отд|ава́ть, -а́ть рабо́ту
■ **~house** *n.* фе́рмерский дом; **~yard** *n.* двор фе́рмы

◆ **farmer** /ˈfɑːmə(r)/ *n.* фе́рмер
■ **~'s market** *n.* ры́нок сельскохозя́йственной проду́кции

farming /ˈfɑːmɪŋ/ *n.* се́льское хозя́йство, фе́рмерство

farther /ˈfɑːðə(r)/ (see also ▸ **further**) *adj.* бо́лее отдалённый; дальне́йший
● *adv.* да́льше, да́лее

farthest /ˈfɑːðɪst/ (see also ▸ **furthest**) *adj.* са́мый да́льний
● *adv.* да́льше всего́

fascinate /ˈfæsɪneɪt/ *v.t.* очаро́в|ывать, -а́ть

fascinating /ˈfæsɪneɪtɪŋ/ *adj.* очарова́тельный

fascination /ˌfæsɪˈneɪʃ(ə)n/ *n.* очарова́ние, обая́ние, пре́лесть

Fascism /ˈfæʃɪz(ə)m/ *n.* фаши́зм

Fascist /ˈfæʃɪst/ *n.* фаши́ст (-ка)
● *adj.* фаши́стский

◆ **fashion** /ˈfæʃ(ə)n/ *n.* **1** (way) о́браз, мане́ра; **after a ~** (indifferently) до не́которой сте́пени

2 (prevailing style) мо́да; **in ~** в мо́де; **out of ~** вы́шедший из мо́ды
● *v.t.* (e.g. an object) прид|ава́ть, -а́ть фо́рму + *d.*
■ **~ designer** *n.* модельéр; **~ house** *n.* дом моде́лей; **~ show** *n.* пока́з мод

fashionable /ˈfæʃənəb(ə)l/ *adj.* мо́дный

fast¹ /fɑːst/ *n.* (relig.) пост
● *v.i.* пости́ться (*impf.*)

fast² /fɑːst/ *adv.* (firmly) про́чно, кре́пко; **she was ~ asleep** она́ кре́пко спала́; **the car stuck ~** маши́на застря́ла/завя́зла

🗸 **fast³** /fɑːst/ *adj.* (rapid) ско́рый, бы́стрый; **my watch is ~** мои́ часы́ спеша́т
● *adv.* бы́стро
■ **~-food restaurant** *n.* рестора́н бы́строго обслу́живания; **~ lane** *n.* (on road) скоростно́й ряд

fasten /ˈfɑːs(ə)n/ *v.t.* (coat) застёг|ивать, -ну́ть; (laces) завя́з|ывать, -а́ть; (seat belt) пристёг|ивать, -ну́ть
● *v.i.* зап|ира́ться, -ере́ться; **the dress ~s down the back** пла́тье застёгивается на спине́

fastener /ˈfɑːsənə(r)/, **fastening** /ˈfɑːsnɪŋ/ *nn.* запо́р, задви́жка

fastidious /fæˈstɪdɪəs/ *adj.* привере́дливый, щепети́льный; разбо́рчивый

🗸 **fat** /fæt/ *n.* жир
● *adj.* (**fatter**, **fattest**) **1** (of person etc.) то́лстый, жи́рный, ту́чный; **get ~** толсте́ть, по- **2** (rich): **a ~ profit** больша́я при́быль

fatal /ˈfeɪt(ə)l/ *adj.* **1** (causing death) смерте́льный; **a ~ accident** несча́стный слу́чай со смерте́льным исхо́дом **2** (disastrous) роково́й, фата́льный

fatalism /ˈfeɪtəlɪz(ə)m/ *n.* фатали́зм

fatalistic /feɪtəˈlɪstɪk/ *adj.* фаталисти́ческий

fatality /fəˈtælətɪ/ *n.* (death) смерть (*от несча́стного слу́чая и т. п.*); (fate) неотврати́мая судьба́

fate /feɪt/ *n.* судьба́, у́часть, уде́л, до́ля

fateful /ˈfeɪtfʊl/ *adj.* роково́й

🗸 **father** /ˈfɑːðə(r)/ *n.* **1** (male parent, also fig.) оте́ц, роди́тель (*m.*) **2** (in personifications): **F~ Christmas** Дед Моро́з **3** (priest) оте́ц, ба́тюшка
● *v.t.* поро|жда́ть, -ди́ть
■ **~-in-law** *n.* (husband's ~) свёкор; (wife's ~) тесть (*m.*); **~land** *n.* оте́чество

fatherhood /ˈfɑːðəhʊd/ *n.* отцо́вство

fatherly /ˈfɑːðəlɪ/ *adj.* оте́ческий

fathom /ˈfæð(ə)m/ *n.* морска́я саже́нь
● *v.t.* (fig.) пост|ига́ть, -и́гнуть

fatigue /fəˈtiːɡ/ *n.* (also, tech., metal ~) уста́лость; (mil.) (*in pl.*) (menial tasks) хозя́йственная рабо́та

fatten /ˈfæt(ə)n/ *v.t.* (animal) отк|а́рмливать, -орми́ть на убо́й

fattening /ˈfæt(ə)nɪŋ/ *adj.* калори́йный

fatty /ˈfætɪ/ *adj.* (**fattier**, **fattiest**) жи́рный, жирово́й

fatuous /ˈfætʃʊəs/ *adj.* самодово́льно-глу́пый; бессмы́сленный

faucet /ˈfɔːsɪt/ *n.* (AmE, tap) кран

fault /fɔːlt/ *n.* **1** (imperfection) недоста́ток,

дефе́кт; **find ~ with sb** на|ходи́ть, -йти́ недоста́тки у кого́-н. **2** (in mechanism) дефе́кт **3** (error) оши́бка **4** (blame) вина́; **it's (all) your ~** э́то ва́ша вина́; э́то всё из-за вас **5** (at tennis etc.) непра́вильная пода́ча; **double ~** двойна́я оши́бка **6** (geol.) разло́м, сдвиг
● *v.t.* на|ходи́ть, -йти́ недоста́тки в + *p.*; **I could not ~ his argument** я не мог придра́ться к его́ аргумента́ции

faultless /ˈfɔːltlɪs/ *adj.*: **~ precision** безупре́чная то́чность

faulty /ˈfɔːltɪ/ *adv.* (**faultier**, **faultiest**) повреждённый

fauna /ˈfɔːnə/ *n.* (*pl.* **~s**) фа́уна

faux pas /fəʊ ˈpɑː/ *n.* (*pl.* **~**) беста́ктность

🗸 **favour** /ˈfeɪvə(r)/ (AmE **favor**) *n.* **1** (goodwill) благоскло́нность; **find ~ in sb's eyes** сниска́ть (*pf.*) чьё-н. расположе́ние; **I am in ~ of the plan** я — за э́тот план **2** (kindly act) одолже́ние, любе́зность, услу́га; **he did me a ~** он оказа́л мне любе́зность **3** (advantage) по́льза; **this is in his ~** э́то говори́т в его́ по́льзу; **the exchange rate is in our ~** курс обме́на валю́ты вы́годен для нас
● *v.t.* **1** (support) благоприя́тствовать (*impf.*) + *d.* **2** (treat with partiality) ока́з|ывать, -а́ть предпочте́ние + *d.*

favourable /ˈfeɪvərəb(ə)l/ (AmE **favorable**) *adj.* благоприя́тный, благоскло́нный; **a ~ report** положи́тельный отчёт

🗸 **favourite** /ˈfeɪvərɪt/ (AmE **favorite**) *n.* (person) люби́мец, фавори́т; (horse) фавори́т
● *adj.* люби́мый, излю́бленный

favouritism /ˈfeɪvərɪtɪz(ə)m/ (AmE **favoritism**) *n.*: **a teacher shouldn't show ~** у учи́теля не должно́ быть люби́мчиков

fawn¹ /fɔːn/ *n.* (deer) оленёнок

fawn² /fɔːn/ *v.i.* (of person): **~ on sb** подли́з|ываться, -а́ться к кому́-н.

fax /fæks/ *n.* факс
● *v.t.* пос|ыла́ть, -ла́ть фа́ксом
■ **~ machine** *n.* факс, факси́мильный аппара́т

faze /feɪz/ *v.t.* сму|ща́ть, -ти́ть

FBI *abbr.* (*of* **Federal Bureau of Investigation**) ФБР (Федера́льное бюро́ рассле́дований)

FC *abbr.* (*of* **football club**) футбо́льный клуб, ФК

🗸 **fear** /fɪə(r)/ *n.* **1** (terror) страх, боя́знь, опасе́ние; **your ~s are groundless** ва́ши опасе́ния напра́сны **2** (likelihood): **I was silent for ~ of offending him** я молча́л, боя́сь оби́деть его́; **there is no ~ of my losing the money** не бо́йтесь, де́ньги я не потеря́ю
● *v.t. & i.* боя́ться (*impf.*) + *g.*; опаса́ться (*impf.*) + *g.*; **she ~s death** она́ бои́тся сме́рти; **I ~ the worst** я опаса́юсь ху́дшего; **I ~ for his life** я опаса́юсь за его́ жизнь

fearful /ˈfɪəfʊl/ *adj.* (terrible) ужа́сный; (timid) боязли́вый; **I was ~ of waking her** я боя́лся разбуди́ть её

fearless /ˈfɪəlɪs/ *adj.* бесстра́шный

fearsome /ˈfɪəsəm/ *adj.* устраша́ющий, гро́зный

feasible /'fiːzɪb(ə)l/ *adj.* осуществимый
feast /fiːst/ *n.* **1** (relig.) (церковный) праздник **2** (meal) пир
●*v.t. & i.* пировать (*impf.*); праздновать (*impf.*); he ~ed his eyes on the scene он любовался этим зрелищем
feat /fiːt/ *n.* подвиг; ~ of engineering выдающееся достижение инженерного искусства
feather /'feðə(r)/ *n.* перо
⚹ **feature** /'fiːtʃə(r)/ *n.* **1** (part of face) черта **2** (aspect) черта, особенность **3** (main item): this journal makes a ~ of sport этот журнал широко освещает спортивные события; ~ (film) художественный фильм
●*v.t.* (give prominence to) поме|щать, -стить на видном месте
●*v.i.* (figure prominently) быть/являться (*impf.*) характерной чертой
⚹ **February** /'februərɪ/ *n.* февраль (*m.*)
feckless /'feklɪs/ *adj.* безалаберный
fed /fed/ *past and p.p. of* ▸ feed
⚹ **federal** /'fedər(ə)l/ *adj.* федеральный
federalism /'fedərəlɪz(ə)m/ *n.* федерализм
federation /fedə'reɪʃ(ə)n/ *n.* федерация
⚹ **fee** /fiː/ *n.* (professional charge) гонорар; school ~s плата за обучение
feeble /'fiːb(ə)l/ *adj.* (feebler, feeblest) хилый, слабый
⚹ **feed** /fiːd/ *n.* (animal's) корм; (baby's) кормление
●*v.t.* (*past and p.p.* fed) **1** (give food to) корм|ить, на-; (fig.): I am fed up (infml) я сыт по горло; мне надоело **2** (fig.): he fed information into the computer он ввёл данные в компьютер
■ ~back *n.* (elec.) обратная связь; (fig.) отклик, отзыв(ы); реакция
⚹ **feel** /fiːl/ *n.* (sensation) ощущение; (contact) осязание; he has a ~ for language у него есть чувство языка
●*v.t.* (*past and p.p.* felt) **1** (explore by touch) щупать, по-; ~ the edge of a knife трогать, по- лезвие ножа; ~ the weight of this box! чувствуете, сколько весит этот ящик! **2** (grope) пробираться (*impf.*) ощупью; he felt his way in the dark он пробирался ощупью в темноте **3** (be aware of) чувствовать, по-; did you ~ the earthquake? вы почувствовали землетрясение? **4** (be affected by) чувствовать, по-; he ~s (or is ~ing) the heat жара плохо действует на него; он плохо переносит жару **5** (be of opinion) считать (*impf.*); I ~ you should go по-моему, вам следует пойти/сходить
●*v.i.* (*past and p.p.* felt) **1** (experience sensation): I ~ cold мне холодно; I ~ hungry я голоден; I ~ sure я уверен; I ~ bad about not inviting him мне совестно, что я не пригласил его; I ~ like (going for) a walk мне хочется прогуляться; I don't ~ up to going я не в состоянии идти/идти; it ~s like rain похоже, будет дождь; I ~ for you я вам

⚹ ключевая лексика

сочувствую **2** (produce sensation) да|вать, -ть ощущение (*чего*); your hands ~ cold у вас холодные руки; how does it ~ to be home? каково оказаться дома? **3** (grope): he felt in his pocket for a coin он пошарил в кармане, ища монету; he felt along the wall for the door он пытался нащупать дверь в стене
feeler /'fiːlə(r)/ *n.* (zool.) щупальце, усик; (fig.): he put out ~s он прозондировал почву; он закинул удочку
⚹ **feeling** /'fiːlɪŋ/ *n.* **1** (power of sensation) ощущение, чувство **2** (sense) сознание, чувство **3** (opinion): I have a ~ he won't come у меня предчувствие, что он не придёт **4** (emotion) чувство, страсть; he spoke with ~ он говорил с чувством **5** (sensitivity) чувствительность; you hurt his ~s вы его обидели
feet /fiːt/ *pl. of* ▸ foot
feign /feɪn/ *v.t.* симулировать (*impf., pf.*); ~ madness симулировать безумие
feisty /'faɪstɪ/ *adj.* (feistier, feistiest) (person) храбрый, смелый; (dog) смелый, бесстрашный; (action) смелый, решительный; (spirit) решительный
feline /'fiːlaɪn/ *n.* животное из семейства кошачьих
●*adj.* кошачий
fell[1] /fel/ *v.t.* (person) сби|вать, -ть с ног; (tree) рубить, с-; валить, с-/по-
fell[2] /fel/ *past of* ▸ fall
⚹ **fellow** /'feləʊ/ *n.* **1** (chap) парень (*m.*) **2** (academic or professional) коллега; сотрудник; (BrE, of a college) член совета колледжа
■ ~ countryman *n.* соотечественник; ~ countrywoman *n.* соотечественница
fellowship /'feləʊʃɪp/ *n.* (companionship) товарищество; братство; (association) корпорация; коллегия (*адвокатов и т. п.*)
felony /'felənɪ/ *n.* (тяжкое) уголовное преступление
felt[1] /felt/ *n.* (material) войлок, фетр; ~ hat фетровая шляпа
■ ~-tip pen *n.* фломастер
felt[2] /felt/ *past and p.p. of* ▸ feel
⚹ **female** /'fiːmeɪl/ *n.* (woman or girl) женщина; (animal) самка, матка
●*adj.* женский
feminine /'femɪnɪn/ *adj.* женский
femininity /femɪ'nɪnɪtɪ/ *n.* женственность
feminism /'femɪnɪz(ə)m/ *n.* феминизм
feminist /'femɪnɪst/ *n.* феминист (-ка)
femme fatale /fæm fə'tɑːl/ *n.* (*pl.* femmes fatales* pronunc. same*) роковая женщина
femur /'fiːmə(r)/ *n.* бедро
fen /fen/ *n.* топь, болото
fence /fens/ *n.* забор, изгородь, ограда; sit on the ~ занимать (*impf.*) нейтральную/выжидательную позицию
●*v.t.* (*also* ~ in, off, round) огор|аживать, -одить
fencer /'fensə(r)/ *n.* фехтовальщик
fencing /'fensɪŋ/ *n.* фехтование

fend /fend/ *v.i.:* ~ **for oneself** полага́ться (*impf.*) на себя́

fender /'fendə(r)/ *n.* **1** (in front of fire) ≈ ками́нная решётка **2** (AmE, of car) крыло́

feng shui /feŋ 'ʃuːi/ *n.* фэн-шу́й (*m. & nt. indecl.*)

fennel /'fen(ə)l/ *n.* фе́нхель (*m.*), сла́дкий укро́п

fern /fəːn/ *n.* (*pl.* ~ *or* ~**s**) па́поротник

ferocious /fə'rəʊʃəs/ *adj.* свире́пый, лю́тый

ferocity /fə'rɒsɪti/ *n.* свире́пость, лю́тость

ferret /'ferɪt/ *n.* (zool.) хорёк
• *v.t.* (**ferreted, ferreting**): ~ **out** (fig.) выи́скивать, вы́искать
• *v.i.* (**ferreted, ferreting**): ~ **about** (fig.) ры́скать (*impf.*)

Ferris wheel /'ferɪs/ *n.* чёртово колесо́; колесо́ обозре́ния

ferry /'ferɪ/ *n.* (boat) паро́м
• *v.t.* (convey to and fro) перев|ози́ть, -ти́ (*or* перепр|авля́ть, -а́вить) на паро́ме; отв|ози́ть, -ези́

fertile /'fəːtaɪl/ *adj.* **1** (of soil) плодоро́дный; (of humans, animals) плодови́тый **2** (fig.): a ~ **imagination** бога́тое воображе́ние

fertility /fə'tɪlɪti/ *n.* плодоро́дие; плодови́тость
■ ~ **drug** *n.* препара́т от беспло́дия

fertilize /'fəːtɪlaɪz/ *v.t.* (biol.) оплодотвор|я́ть, -и́ть; (hort.) уд|обря́ть, -о́брить

fertilizer /'fəːtɪlaɪzə(r)/ *n.* (hort.) удобре́ние

fervent /'fəːv(ə)nt/ *adj.* (fig.) горя́чий, пы́лкий

fervid /'fəːvɪd/ *adj.* пы́лкий, пла́менный

fervour /'fəːvə(r)/ (AmE **fervor**) *n.* жар, пыл, страсть

fester /'festə(r)/ *v.i.* гно́иться, за-/на-; нагн|а́иваться, -ои́ться

ˢ **festival** /'festɪv(ə)l/ *n.* фестива́ль (*m.*)

festive /'festɪv/ *adj.* пра́здничный

festivity /fe'stɪvɪti/ *n.* пра́зднество, торжество́

festoon /fe'stuːn/ *n.* гирля́нда
• *v.t.* укр|аша́ть, -а́сить гирля́ндами

fetal /'fiːt(ə)l/ *adj.* заро́дышевый, эмбриона́льный
■ ~ **position** *n.* положе́ние эмбрио́на (в ма́тке)

fetch /fetʃ/ *v.t.* **1** (go and get) прин|оси́ть, -ести́; (children from school, dry-cleaning) заб|ира́ть, -ра́ть; **they** ~**ed the doctor** они́ вы́звали врача́ **2** (of price): **his house** ~**ed £150,000** он вы́ручил 150 000 фу́нтов за свой дом

fetching /'fetʃɪŋ/ *adj.* привлека́тельный

fete /feɪt/ *n.* пра́зднество, пра́здник

fetid /'fetɪd/ *adj.* воню́чий, злово́нный

fetish /'fetɪʃ/ *n.* фети́ш

fetter /'fetə(r)/ *n.* (*in pl.*) ножны́е кандал|ы́ (-о́в); (fig.) око́в|ы (*pl., g.* —)
• *v.t.* зако́в|ывать, -а́ть в кандалы́; (fig.) ско́в|ывать, -а́ть

fettle /'fet(ə)l/ *n.*: **in fine** ~ (condition) в хоро́шем состоя́нии; (mood) в хоро́шем настрое́нии

fetus /'fiːtəs/ (*pl.* ~**es**) *n.* плод, заро́дыш

feud /fjuːd/ *n.* вражда́
• *v.i.* враждова́ть (*с кем*) (*impf.*)

feudal /'fjuːd(ə)l/ *adj.* феода́льный

fever /'fiːvə(r)/ *n.* жар; **he has a high** ~ у него́ жар

feverish /'fiːvərɪʃ/ *adj.* лихора́дочный

ˢ **few** /fjuː/ *n. & adj.* немно́гие (*pl.*); немно́го + *g.*; ма́ло + *g.*; ~ (**people**) **know the truth** немно́гие зна́ют пра́вду; a ~ (**people**) немно́гие (лю́ди); не́сколько челове́к; a **good** ~ (BrE), **quite a** ~ дово́льно мно́го (+ *g.*); ~ **and far between** ре́дкие; **every** ~ **minutes** ка́ждые не́сколько мину́т

fewer /'fjuːə(r)/ *n. & adj.* ме́нее, ме́ньше; **he wrote no** ~ **than 60 books** он написа́л ни мно́го ни ма́ло 60 книг

fiancé /fɪ'ɒnseɪ/ *n.* жени́х

fiancée /fɪ'ɒnseɪ/ *n.* неве́ста

fiasco /fɪ'æskəʊ/ *n.* (*pl.* ~**s**) фиа́ско (*nt. indecl.*), прова́л

fib /fɪb/ *n.* вы́думка, непра́вда
• *v.i.* (**fibbed, fibbing**) прив|ира́ть, -ра́ть (infml)

fibre /'faɪbə(r)/ (AmE **fiber**) *n.* **1** (filament) волокно́ **2** (in diet) клетча́тка
■ ~**glass** *n.* стекловолокно́; стеклопла́стик; ~-**optic** *adj.* волоко́нно-опти́ческий

fickle /'fɪk(ə)l/ *adj.* переме́нчивый, непостоя́нный

fiction /'fɪkʃ(ə)n/ *n.* **1** (invention, pretence) вы́мысел, вы́думка, фи́кция **2** (novels etc.) беллетри́стика; **work of** ~ худо́жественное произведе́ние

fictional /'fɪkʃən(ə)l/ *adj.* вы́мышленный; беллетристи́ческий

fictitious /fɪk'tɪʃəs/ *adj.* подло́жный, фикти́вный; a ~ **name** вы́мышленное и́мя

fiddle /'fɪd(ə)l/ *v.t.* (BrE, falsify) подде́л|ывать, -ать
• *v.i.* (fidget, tamper) верте́ться (*impf.*); крути́ться (*impf.*); вози́ться (*impf.*); **he** ~**d with his tie** он тереби́л свой га́лстук; **don't** ~ **with my papers!** не тро́гайте мои́ бума́ги!

fidelity /fɪ'delɪti/ *n.* (loyalty) ве́рность

fidget /'fɪdʒɪt/ *v.i.* (**fidgeted, fidgeting**) ёрзать (*impf.*)

fidgety /'fɪdʒɪti/ *adj.* суетли́вый, непосе́дливый

ˢ **field** /fiːld/ *n.* **1** (piece of ground) по́ле **2** (physical range, area) по́ле **3** (area of activity or study) о́бласть; по́ле/сфе́ра де́ятельности
■ ~ **day** *n.* (fig., day of successful exploits) знамена́тельный/па́мятный день; ~ **events** *n. pl.* лёгкая атле́тика; ~**work** *n.* (research) иссле́дования (*nt. pl.*) в есте́ственных усло́виях

fiend /fiːnd/ *n.* (devil) дья́вол; (evil person) злоде́й, и́зверг; (fig.): **dope** ~ наркома́н; **fresh air** ~ (зая́длый) люби́тель све́жего во́здуха

fiendish /'fiːndɪʃ/ *adj.* дья́вольский, злоде́йский

fierce /fɪəs/ *adj.* (**fiercer, fiercest**) свире́пый, лю́тый; ~ **competition** жесто́кая конкуре́нция

f

fiery /'faɪərɪ/ adj. (**fierier, fieriest**) огненный, пламенный; a ~ temper вспыльчивый/горячий характер; a ~ horse горячая лошадь

fifteen /fɪf'tiːn/ n. пятнадцать; she is ~ ей пятнадцать лет
• adj. пятнадцать + g. pl.

fifteenth /fɪf'tiːnθ/ n. (date) пятнадцатое (число); (fraction) одна пятнадцатая
• adj. пятнадцатый

fifth /fɪfθ/ n. (date) пятое (число); (fraction) одна пятая
• adj. пятый

fiftieth /'fɪftɪɪθ/ n. (fraction) одна пятидесятая
• adj. пятидесятый

fift|y /'fɪftɪ/ n. пятьдесят, полсотни; the ~ies (decade) пятидесятые годы; he is in his ~ies ему за пятьдесят (лет); ему пошёл шестой десяток; we shared expenses ~y-~y мы разделили расходы пополам
• adj. пятьдесят + g. pl.

fig /fɪɡ/ n. (fruit) инжир
■ ~ leaf n. фиговый листок; ~ tree n. инжир, фиговое дерево

⚓ **fight** /faɪt/ n. бой, схватка, драка
• v.t. & i. (past and p.p. **fought**) драться, по-; сражаться, -зиться; (wage war) воевать (impf.); the boys/dogs are ~ing мальчики/ собаки дерутся; ~ a battle вести (det.) бой; ~ an election вести (det.) предвыборную борьбу; ~ a lawsuit судиться (impf.); he fought his way forward он пробивался/ проталкивался вперёд; he fought off a cold он (быстро) справился с простудой; they fought off the enemy они отбили врага; ~ back v.i. отбиваться, -иться

fighter /'faɪtə(r)/ n. 1 (one who fights) боец; (fig.) борец 2 (~ aircraft) истребитель (m.)

fighting /'faɪtɪŋ/ n. бой, сражение
• adj. боевой; we have a ~ chance стоит попытаться

figment /'fɪɡmənt/ n. вымысел; a ~ of the imagination плод воображения

figurative /'fɪɡərətɪv/ adj. переносный

⚓ **figure** /'fɪɡə(r)/ n. 1 (numerical sign) цифра; double ~s двузначные числа; a six-~ number шестизначное число 2 (diagram, illustration) рисунок 3 (human form) фигура; I saw a ~ approaching я увидел приближавшуюся ко мне фигуру; she has a good ~ у неё хорошая фигура 4 (person of importance) фигура, выдающаяся личность
• v.t.: ~ out (calculate) вычислять, вычислить; (understand) понимать, -ять; I can't ~ him out я не могу его понять
• v.i. 1 (appear) фигурировать (impf.); this did not ~ in my plans это не входило в мои планы 2 (AmE, infml): it ~s (makes sense, is plausible) это похоже на правду; I ~ they'll be late я думаю, что они опоздают
■ ~head n. носовое украшение, фигура на носу корабля; (fig.) номинальный руководитель; ~ skating n. фигурное катание

figurine /fɪɡjʊ'riːn/ n. фигурка, статуэтка

Fiji /'fiːdʒiː/ n. Фиджи (indecl.)

filament /'fɪləmənt/ n. (thread) волокно, нить; (elec.) нить накала

file¹ /faɪl/ n. (tool) напильник
• v.t. подпил|ивать, -ить; ~ one's nails подпил|ивать, -ить ногти

⚓ **file²** /faɪl/ n. 1 (for papers) папка, скоросшиватель (m.) 2 (set of papers etc.) дело, досье (nt. indecl.) 3 (comput.) файл
• v.t. 1 (documents) подшив|ать, -ить 2 (submit): ~ a complaint под|авать, -ать жалобу; ~ suit against sb возбу|ждать, -дить судебное дело против кого-н.
• v.i.: ~ for divorce под|авать, -ать на развод

file³ /faɪl/ n. (row) ряд, шеренга; колонна; in single ~ гуськом; по одному
• v.i. идти (det.) гуськом/колонной; the prisoners ~d out заключённые выходили гуськом друг за другом

filing /'faɪlɪŋ/ n. (of papers) регистрация бумаг
■ ~ cabinet n. шкаф, сейф

Filipino /fɪlɪ'piːnəʊ/ n. (pl. ~s) филиппин|ец (-ка)
• adj. филиппинский

⚓ **fill** /fɪl/ v.t. 1 (make full) нап|олнять, -олнить; зап|олнять, -олнить; he ~ed the hole with sand он заполнил яму песком; I was ~ed with admiration я был полон восхищения 2: ~ a tooth пломбировать, за- 3 (fig., of office etc.) зан|имать, -ять; ~ a vacancy зап|олнять, -олнять вакантную должность 4: ~ a need удовлетвор|ять, -ить потребность
• v.i. (become full) нап|олняться, -олниться
□ ~ in v.t. (BrE, complete) зап|олнять, -олнить; he ~ed in the form (BrE) он заполнил бланк/ анкету; (infml, inform): I ~ed him in я ввёл его в курс дела
□ ~ out v.t. (AmE, a form) зап|олнять, -олнять
• v.i. расши|ряться, -ириться
□ ~ up v.t. (make full) нап|олнять, -олнить
• v.i. (become full) нап|олняться, -олниться

fillet /'fɪlɪt/ n. филе (nt. indecl.)
• v.t. (**filleted, filleting**) (of fish, take off bone) отдел|ять, -ить мясо от костей

filling /'fɪlɪŋ/ n. (in tooth) пломба; (in pie) начинка
• adj. (of food) сытный
■ ~ station n. автозаправочная or бензозаправочная станция; (бензо)заправка

⚓ **film** /fɪlm/ n. 1 (thin coating) плёнка 2 (phot.) фотоплёнка; (cin.) киноплёнка 3 (motion picture) фильм
• v.t. & i. сн|имать, -ять
■ ~ crew n. съёмочная группа; ~ star n. кинозвезда; ~ studies n. pl. киноведение; ~ studio n. киностудия

filter /'fɪltə(r)/ n. (for liquid) фильтр; (for light) светофильтр
• v.t. (purify) фильтровать, от-/про-

filth /fɪlθ/ n. грязь

filthy /'fɪlθɪ/ adj. (**filthier, filthiest**) грязный

⚓ ключевая лексика

fin /fɪn/ n. плавни́к

final /'faɪn(ə)l/ n. **1** (in pl.) (BrE, exam at end of degree course) выпускно́й экза́мен; (AmE, exam at end of term, year, class) ито́говый экза́мен **2** (match) фина́л
 • adj. **1** (last in order) после́дний **2** (decisive) оконча́тельный, реша́ющий

finale /fɪ'nɑ:lɪ/ n. (mus., fig.) фина́л

finalist /'faɪnəlɪst/ n. финали́ст (-ка)

finalize /'faɪnəlaɪz/ v.t. (give final form to) заверш|а́ть, -и́ть; (settle, e.g. arrangements) (оконча́тельно) ула́|живать, -дить

finally adv. (after a long time) в конце́ концо́в; (once and for all) оконча́тельно; (lastly) наконе́ц

finance /'faɪnæns/ n. фина́нсы (m. pl.); дохо́ды (m. pl.)
 • v.t. финанси́ровать (impf., pf.)

financial /faɪ'næns(ə)l/ adj. фина́нсовый

financier /faɪ'nænsɪə(r)/ n. финанси́ст

finch /fɪntʃ/ n. зя́блик

find /faɪnd/ n. (discovery, esp. valuable) нахо́дка
 • v.t. (past and p.p. **found**) **1** (discover, encounter) на|ходи́ть, -йти́; (by search) раз|ыска́ть, от- (both pf.); pine trees are found in many countries сосна́ растёт/встреча́ется во мно́гих стра́нах; I ~ it hard to understand him мне тру́дно поня́ть его́ **2** (judge): the jury found him guilty прися́жные призна́ли его́ вино́вным **3** (obtain) получ|а́ть, -и́ть; he found time to read он находи́л вре́мя для чте́ния **4**: ~ out (detect) узн|ава́ть, -а́ть; (ascertain) выясня́ть, вы́яснить; have you found out (about) the trains? вы узна́ли расписа́ние поездо́в?

finding /'faɪndɪŋ/ n. (also in pl.) (conclusion) вы́вод(ы)

fine¹ /faɪn/ n. (punishment) штраф, пе́ня
 • v.t. штрафова́ть, о-; he was ~d £5 его́ оштрафова́ли на 5 фу́нтов

fine² /faɪn/ adj. **1** (of weather) я́сный, хоро́ший **2** (handsome, excellent) прекра́сный, замеча́тельный; a ~ view прекра́сный вид **3** (exquisite) то́нкий; ~ workmanship то́нкая рабо́та **4** (of small particles) ме́лкий; ~ dust ме́лкая пыль **5** (thin) то́нкий, о́стрый; a pencil with a ~ point о́стро отто́ченный каранда́ш **6** (subtle) утончённый, то́нкий; a ~ distinction то́нкое разли́чие; the ~ arts изобрази́тельные/изя́щные иску́сства
 • adv.: he cut it ~ (of time) он оста́вил себе́ вре́мени в обре́з; that suits me ~ (infml) э́то меня́ вполне́ устра́ивает

fineness /'faɪnnɪs/ n. (delicacy) то́нкость, утончённость, изя́щество

finery /'faɪnərɪ/ n. пы́шный наря́д

finesse /fɪ'nes/ n. (delicacy) делика́тность, то́нкость

finger /'fɪŋɡə(r)/ n. (of hand or glove) па́лец
 • v.t. тро́гать, по-
 ■ ~nail n. но́готь (m.); ~print n. отпеча́ток па́льца • v.t. (take sb's ~prints) сн|има́ть, -я́ть отпеча́тки па́льцев у + g.; ~tip n. ко́нчик па́льца

finicky /'fɪnɪkɪ/ adjs. (чересчу́р) разбо́рчивый, привере́дливый

finish /'fɪnɪʃ/ n. **1** (conclusion) оконча́ние, коне́ц **2** (polish) отде́лка
 • v.t. **1** (end) зак|а́нчивать, -о́нчить; конча́ть, ко́нчить; I ~ed the book я (за)ко́нчил кни́гу; he ~ed (off, up) the pie он дое́л весь пиро́г; we will ~ the job мы зако́нчим рабо́ту **2** (perfect) соверше́нствовать (impf.) **3** (infml, exhaust, kill) изнур|я́ть, -и́ть; the fever ~ed him off лихора́дка докона́ла/приконча́ла его́
 • v.i. конча́ться, ко́нчиться; зак|а́нчиваться, -о́нчиться; have you ~ed with that book? вам бо́льше не нужна́ э́та кни́га?
 ■ ~ing post n. фи́ниш; ~ing touch n. после́дний штрих

finite /'faɪnaɪt/ adj. коне́чный; име́ющий преде́л

Finland /'fɪnlənd/ n. Финля́ндия

Finn /fɪn/ n. финн (-ка)

Finnish /'fɪnɪʃ/ n. (language) фи́нский язы́к
 • adj. фи́нский

fiord /fjɔ:d/ n. = fjord

fir /fə:(r)/ n. (in full ~ **tree**) ель

fire /'faɪə(r)/ n. **1** (phenomenon of combustion) ого́нь (m.); the house is on ~ дом загоре́лся/гори́т; set ~ to подж|ига́ть, -е́чь; catch ~ загор|а́ться, -е́ться **2** (burning fuel) ого́нь (m.); light a ~ разж|ига́ть, -е́чь ками́н; топи́ть, за- печь **3** (conflagration) пожа́р; ~! пожа́р! **4** (of ~arms) ого́нь (m.), стрельба́; open ~ откр|ыва́ть, -ы́ть ого́нь
 • v.t. **1** (set fire to) подж|ига́ть, -е́чь **2** (of ~arms) стреля́ть (impf.) из + g.; a ~ rifle стреля́ть (impf.) из ружья́; a ~ shot вы́стрелить (pf.)
 • v.i. (of ~arms) стреля́ть (impf.); the troops ~d at the enemy войска́ стреля́ли по врагу́
 ■ ~ alarm n. (alert) пожа́рная трево́га; (device) автомати́ческий пожа́рный сигна́л; ~arm n. огнестре́льное ору́жие; ~ bomb n. зажига́тельная бо́мба; ~ brigade n. (BrE) пожа́рная кома́нда; ~ engine n. пожа́рная маши́на; ~ escape n. пожа́рная ле́стница; ~ extinguisher n. огнетуши́тель (m.); ~fighter n. пожа́рный; пожа́рник (infml); ~guard n. ками́нная решётка; ~lighter n. (BrE) расто́пка; ~man n. пожа́рный; пожа́рник (infml); ~place n. ками́н, оча́г; ~proof adj. огнеупо́рный • v.t. прид|ава́ть, -а́ть огнесто́йкость + d.; ~side n. ме́сто о́коло ками́на; (fig.) дома́шний оча́г; ~ station n. пожа́рное депо́ (nt. indecl.); ~wood n. дрова́ (pl., g. —); ~work(s) n. (pl.) фейерве́рк

firing /'faɪərɪŋ/ n. (shooting) стрельба́
 ■ ~ line n. ли́ния огня́

firm¹ /fə:m/ n. фи́рма

firm² /fə:m/ adj. **1** (physically) кре́пкий, твёрдый **2** (fig.) усто́йчивый, сто́йкий, непоколеби́мый; you must be ~ with him вы должны́ быть с ним постро́же; a ~ offer твёрдое предложе́ние
 • adv. твёрдо, усто́йчиво; stand ~ стоя́ть (impf.) твёрдо

firmament /'fɜ:məmənt/ *n.* небе́сный свод

firmware /'fɜ:mweə(r)/ *n.* (comput.) микропрогра́мма, встро́енная програ́мма; проши́вка (sl.)

⚹ **first** /fɜ:st/ *n.* **1** (beginning): **at ~** снача́ла, сперва́ **2** (date) пе́рвое (число́); **on the ~ of May** пе́рвого ма́я **3** (BrE, academic) вы́сшая оце́нка/отме́тка
● *adj.* **1** (in time or place) пе́рвый; **on the ~ floor** (BrE) на второ́м этаже́; (AmE) на пе́рвом этаже́; **at ~ glance** на пе́рвый взгляд; **hear sth at ~ hand** узн|ава́ть, -а́ть что-н. из пе́рвых рук; **in the ~ place** во-пе́рвых, в пе́рвую о́чередь; **I will go there ~ tomorrow** за́втра я пе́рвым де́лом зайду́ туда́; **the ~ time I saw him** когда́ я в пе́рвый раз уви́дел его́ **2** (in rank or importance) пе́рвый
● *adv.* **1** (before all) (*also* **~ and foremost** *or* **~ of all**) пре́жде всего́; в пе́рвую о́чередь **2** (initially) сперва́, снача́ла; (in the ~ place) во-пе́рвых; (for the ~ time) впервы́е; **I ~ met him last year** я познако́мился с ним в про́шлом году́
■ **~ aid** *n.* пе́рвая по́мощь; **~-aid kit** санита́рная су́мка; апте́чка; **~-class** *adj.* (excellent) первокла́ссный ● *adv.* (of travel) пе́рвым кла́ссом; **~ cousin** *n.* двою́родный брат, двою́родная сестра́; **~ name** *n.* и́мя; **~ night** *n.* (theatr.) премье́ра; **~-night nerves** волне́ние пе́ред премье́рой; **~-rate** *adj.* первокла́ссный

firstly /'fɜ:stlɪ/ *adv.* во-пе́рвых

fiscal /'fɪsk(ə)l/ *adj.* фиска́льный, фина́нсовый

⚹ **fish** /fɪʃ/ *n.* (*pl.* **~** *or* **~es**) ры́ба
● *v.i.* лови́ть/уди́ть (*impf.*) ры́бу; (fig.): **~ for compliments** напра́шиваться (*impf.*) на комплиме́нты; **~ for information** выу́живать, вы́удить сведе́ния
■ **~-monger** *n.* торго́вец ры́бой; **~net** *n.*: **~net stockings** ажу́рные чулки́

fisherman /'fɪʃəmən/ *n.* рыба́к; (angler for pleasure) рыболо́в

fishery /'fɪʃərɪ/ *n.* (fish farm) рыбово́дческое хозя́йство

fishing /'fɪʃɪŋ/ *n.* ры́бная ло́вля; **the boys have gone ~** ма́льчики ушли́ на рыба́лку
■ **~ line** *n.* ле́ска; **~ net** *n.* рыболо́вная сеть; **~ rod** *n.* уди́лище

fishy /'fɪʃɪ/ *adj.* (**fishier, fishiest**) ры́бий, ры́бный; (infml, suspect) нечи́стый, подозри́тельный

fissure /'fɪʃə(r)/ *n.* тре́щина, расще́лина
● *v.i.* тре́скаться, по-; тре́снуть (*pf.*)

fist /fɪst/ *n.* кула́к

fit¹ /fɪt/ *n.* **1** (attack of illness) при́ступ, припа́док **2** (outburst): **~ of coughing** при́ступ ка́шля; **his jokes had us in ~s** от его́ шу́ток мы пока́тывались со́ смеху **3**: **in ~s and starts** уры́вками

⚹ **fit²** /fɪt/ *n.* (of a garment etc.): **this jacket is a tight ~** э́тот пиджа́к узкова́т
● *adj.* (**fitter, fittest**) **1** (suitable) го́дный, приго́дный, подходя́щий; **see, think ~**

счита́ть, счесть ну́жным; **a meal ~ for a king** ца́рская тра́пеза; **you are not ~ to be seen** вам нельзя́ пока́зываться в тако́м ви́де **2** (in good health) здоро́вый; **keep (oneself) ~** подде́рживать (*impf.*) хоро́шую (спорти́вную) фо́рму
● *v.t.* (**fitted, fitting**) **1** (equip) (*also* **~ out, ~ up**) снаря|жа́ть, -ди́ть; снаб|жа́ть, -ди́ть; экипирова́ть (*impf., pf.*); обору́довать (*impf., pf.*) **2** (install): **he ~ted a new lock on the door** он вста́вил но́вый замо́к в дверь; (fig., accommodate): **I can ~ you in next week** я могу́ назна́чить вам встре́чу на сле́дующей неде́ле **3** (make suitable, adapt) приспос|а́бливать, -о́бить; (correspond to in dimensions) под|ходи́ть, -ойти́ + *d.*; **the dress ~s you** э́то пла́тье хорошо́ на вас сиди́т **4** (insert): **he ~ted the cigarette into the holder** он вста́вил сигаре́ту в мундшту́к
● *v.i.* (**fitted, fitting**) **1** (be of the correct dimensions) под|ходи́ть, -ойти́; **this dress ~s well** э́то пла́тье сиди́т хорошо́; **that ~s (in) with my plans** э́то вполне́ совпада́ет с мои́ми пла́нами **2** (be inserted): **tubes that ~ into one another** тру́бки, вставля́ющиеся одна́ в другу́ю
■ **~ted carpet** *n.* (BrE) ковёр во всю ко́мнату; **~ted kitchen** *n.* (BrE) встро́енная ку́хня

fitful /'fɪtfʊl/ *adj.* неро́вный, преры́вистый

fitness /'fɪtnɪs/ *n.* хоро́шее здоро́вье

fitter /'fɪtə(r)/ *n.* (of machinery) монтёр, сбо́рщик

fitting /'fɪtɪŋ/ *n.* **1** (of clothes) приме́рка **2** (fixture in building) обору́дование
● *adj.* подходя́щий, го́дный
■ **~ room** *n.* приме́рочная

⚹ **five** /faɪv/ *n.* (число́/но́мер) пять; (**~ people**) пя́теро; пять челове́к; **in ~s, ~ at a time** по пяти́, пятёрками; (figure, number 5, group of **~**) пятёрка; **~ (o'clock)** пять (часо́в); **he is ~** ему́ пять лет; **~ to 4 (o'clock)** без пяти́ четы́ре; **~ past 6** пять мину́т седьмо́го
● *adj.* пять + *g. pl.*; **~ sixes are thirty** пя́тью шесть — три́дцать

fiver /'faɪvə(r)/ *n.* (BrE, infml, five pounds, five-pound note) пятёрка (infml)

⚹ **fix** /fɪks/ *n.* (dilemma) затрудни́тельное положе́ние; (infml, injection of drug) уко́л
● *v.t.* **1** (make firm) укреп|ля́ть, -и́ть; (fig.): **~ the blame on sb** взва́л|ивать, -и́ть вину́ на кого́-н. **2** (direct steadily) напр|авля́ть, -а́вить; **~ed gaze** при́стальный/неподви́жный взгляд **3** (determine, settle) (*also v.i.*) **let us ~ (on) a date** дава́йте договори́мся о да́те **4** (provide) (*also* **~ up**) **can you ~ (up) a room for me?** (*or* **~ me up with a room?**) мо́жете ли вы найти́/подыска́ть для меня́ ко́мнату? **5** (infml, repair): **he ~ed the radio in no time** он в два счёта почини́л радиоприёмник; (AmE, prepare): **I will ~ the drinks** я пригото́влю напи́тки

fixation /fɪk'seɪʃ(ə)n/ *n.* (psych.) фикса́ция

fixed /'fɪkst/ *adj.* неподви́жный, закреплённый, постоя́нный; **~ idea** навя́зчивая иде́я, иде́я фикс

■ ~ **rate** *n.* фикси́рованная ста́вка

fixer /'fɪksə(r)/ *n.* (phot.) фикса́ж; (sl., organizer) посре́дник

fixture /'fɪkstʃə(r)/ *n.* **1** (fitting in building) приспособле́ние **2** (BrE, sporting event) предстоя́щее спорти́вное состяза́ние/ мероприя́тие

fizzle /'fɪz(ə)l/ *v.i.* (~ **out**) око́нчиться (*pf.*) ниче́м

fizzy /'fɪzɪ/ *adj.* (**fizzier, fizziest**) шипу́чий

fjord, fiord /fjɔːd/ *n.* фьорд, фио́рд

flabby /'flæbɪ/ *adj.* (**flabbier, flabbiest**) вя́лый, дря́блый

flag[1] /flæg/ *n.* (emblem) флаг, зна́мя (*nt.*)
• *v.t.* (**flagged, flagging**) **1** (mark for attention) ме́тить, по- **2** (signal to stop): ~ (**down**) *a passing car* остан|а́вливать, -ови́ть проезжа́ющую маши́ну
■ ~**pole** *n.* флагшто́к

flag[2] /flæg/ *v.i.* (**flagged, flagging**) (grow weary) ослаб|ева́ть, -е́ть; (fig.): *the conversation was* ~ging разгово́р не кле́ился

flagon /'flægən/ *n.* графи́н/кувши́н для вина́

flagrant /'fleɪgrənt/ *adj.* вопию́щий, возмути́тельный

flail /fleɪl/ *v.i.* (fig.) маха́ть (*impf.*) + *i.*; *he charged with his hands* ~*ing* он наступа́л, разма́хивая рука́ми

flair /'fleə(r)/ *n.* нюх, чутьё; *a* ~ *for languages* спосо́бность (*f. pl.*) к языка́м

flake /fleɪk/ *n.* (*in pl.*) хло́пь|я (-ев); ~**s of snow** снежи́нки (*f. pl.*)
• *v.i.* (peel) шелуши́ться (*impf.*); слои́ться (*impf.*); *the rust* ~**d off** ржа́вчина отслои́лась

flamboyance /flæm'bɔɪəns/ *n.* цвети́стость; я́ркость

flamboyant /flæm'bɔɪənt/ *adj.* (person, behaviour) колори́тный; (clothing) бро́ский, я́ркий; (style) цвети́стый

flame /fleɪm/ *n.* ого́нь (*m.*), пла́мя (*nt.*); *burst into* ~(**s**) вспы́х|ивать, -нуть; *the house was in* ~**s** дом был охва́чен пла́менем

flaming /'fleɪmɪŋ/ *adj.* **1** (ablaze) пыла́ющий, горя́щий **2** (fig., violent): *they had a* ~ *row* у них произошёл стра́шный сканда́л

flamingo /flə'mɪŋgəʊ/ *n.* (*pl.* ~**s or** ~**es**) флами́нго (*m. indecl.*)

flammable /'flæməb(ə)l/ *adj.* горю́чий; легко́ воспламеня́ющийся

flan /flæn/ *n.* откры́тый пиро́г

flank /flæŋk/ *n.* (mil.) фланг
• *v.t.*: *he was* ~**ed by guards** по о́бе сто́роны от него́ шла/стоя́ла стра́жа

flannel /'flæn(ə)l/ *n.* **1** (a kind of cloth) флане́ль **2**: *face* ~ (BrE) махро́вая салфе́тка для лица́

flap /flæp/ *n.* **1** (hinged piece etc.): *the table has two* ~**s** у стола́ две откидны́е доски́; (of pocket, envelope) кла́пан **2** (waving motion) взмах
• *v.t. & i.* (**flapped, flapping**) взма́х|ивать, -ну́ть + *i.*; *the bird* ~**ped its wings** пти́ца взмахну́ла кры́льями

flare[1] /'fleə(r)/ *n.* (effect of flame) сверка́ние; (illuminating device) сигна́льная раке́та; освети́тельный патро́н
• *v.i.* сверк|а́ть, -ну́ть; горе́ть (*impf.*) неро́вным пла́менем; (fig.): *she* ~**s up at the least thing** она́ взрыва́ется из-за ка́ждого пустяка́

flare[2] /'fleə(r)/ *n.*: ~**s** (trousers) брю́ки клёш
• *v.i.* расш|иря́ться, -и́риться; ~**d skirt** ю́бка клёш

flash /flæʃ/ *n.* **1** (burst of light) вспы́шка, про́блеск; *a* ~ **of lightning** вспы́шка мо́лнии; *he had a* ~ **of inspiration** на него́ нашло́ вдохнове́ние **2** (instant) мгнове́ние, миг; *he answered in a* ~ он мгнове́нно отве́тил
• *v.t.*: *he* ~**ed the light in my face** он напра́вил свет мне в лицо́; (fig.): *he* ~**ed a glance at her** он метну́л на неё взгля́д
• *v.i.* сверк|а́ть, -ну́ть; вспы́х|ивать, -нуть; мельк|а́ть, -ну́ть; *the light* ~**ed on and off** свет то вспы́хивал, то гас; *cars* ~**ed by** маши́ны мча́лись ми́мо
■ ~**back** *n.* (cin. etc.) ретроспекти́ва; ~**bulb** *n.* (phot.) ла́мпа-вспы́шка; ~ **flood** *n.* ли́вневый па́водок; ~**light** *n.* (AmE) карма́нный/ электри́ческий фона́рь; ~ **memory** *n.* (comput.) флеш-па́мять

flashy /'flæʃɪ/ *adj.* (**flashier, flashiest**) крича́щий, показно́й, эффе́ктный

flask /flɑːsk/ *n.* фля́га, фля́жка

⚥ **flat** /flæt/ *n.* **1** (BrE, apartment) кварти́ра **2** (mus.) бемо́ль (*m.*) **3** (level object or area) пло́скость; *the* ~ **of the hand** ладо́нь
• *adj.* (**flatter, flattest**) **1** (level) пло́ский, ро́вный; ~ **screen** пло́ский экра́н; (no longer inflated or charged): ~ **tyre** (BrE), **tire** (AmE) спу́щенная ши́на; *the battery is* ~ (BrE) батаре́я се́ла **2** (uniform) однообра́зный **3** (unqualified) прямо́й, категори́ческий **4** (dull, insipid) ску́чный, вя́лый, бесцве́тный
• *adv.* (**flatter, flattest**) **1** (in or into a horizontal position): *he fell* ~ **on his back** он упа́л на́взничь **2** (infml, with expressions of time): *in ten seconds* ~ ро́вно за де́сять секу́нд **3** (mus., below true pitch): *she sings* ~ **on the high notes** она́ фальши́вит на высо́ких но́тах
■ ~**bed** *adj.* (comput.) планше́тный; ~**bed scanner** планше́тный ска́нер; ~**mate** *n.* (BrE) сосе́д (-ка) по кварти́ре; ~ **out** *adv.*: *drive out* (infml, at top speed) гнать (*impf.*) на по́лной ско́рости; ~ **rate** *n.* еди́ная ста́вка

flatly /'flætlɪ/ *adv.* (refuse) категори́чески

flatten /'flæt(ə)n/ *v.t.* **1** (make smooth) выра́внивать, вы́ровнять **2** (reduce thickness of) распло́щ|ивать, -ть; *he* ~**ed himself against the wall** он прижа́лся к стене́ **3** (lay low): *the gale* ~**ed the corn** бу́рей примя́ло хлеба́

flatter /'flætə(r)/ *v.t.* льсти́ть, по- + *d.*

flattering /'flætərɪŋ/ *adj.* ле́стный, льсти́вый; (of person) льсти́вый

flattery /'flætərɪ/ *n.* лесть

flatulence /'flætjʊləns/ *n.* скопле́ние га́зов; (fig.) напы́щенность, высокопа́рность

flaunt /flɔːnt/ *v.t.* афиши́ровать (*impf.*); щего́л|я́ть, -ьну́ть + *i.*

flautist /'flɔ:tɪst/ *n.* флейти́ст (-ка)

flavour /'fleɪvə(r)/ (AmE **flavor**) *n.* арома́т, вкус
• *v.t.* припр|авля́ть, -а́вить

flavouring /'fleɪvərɪŋ/ (AmE **flavoring**) *n.* припра́ва; спе́ции (*f. pl.*)

flaw /flɔ:/ *n.* (defect) изъя́н, недоста́ток

flawed /flɔ:d/ *adj.* име́ющий недоста́тки

flawless /'flɔ:lɪs/ *adj.* безупре́чный

flax /flæks/ *n.* (plant) лён; (fibre) куде́ль (*волокно льна*)

flea /fli:/ *n.* блоха́

fleck /flek/ *n.* кра́пинка, пятно́; (of dust) пыли́нка
• *v.t.* покр|ыва́ть, -ы́ть пя́тнами/кра́пинками

fled /fled/ *past and p.p. of* ▸ **flee**

fledgling, fledgeling /'fledʒlɪŋ/ *n.* то́лько что опери́вшийся птене́ц

flee /fli:/ *v.t.* (*past and p.p.* **fled**) избе|га́ть, -жа́ть
• *v.i.* (*past and p.p.* **fled**) бежа́ть, с-

fleece /fli:s/ *n.* руно́, ове́чья шерсть

fleecy /'fli:sɪ/ *adj.* (**fleecier, fleeciest**) шерсти́стый

fleet /fli:t/ *n.* **1** (collection of vessels) флоти́лия, флот **2** (of vehicles) парк

fleeting /'fli:tɪŋ/ *adj.* бе́глый, мимолётный; a ~ glimpse бе́глый взгляд

Flemish /'flemɪʃ/ *n.* (language) флама́ндский язы́к; the ~ (people) флама́ндцы (*m. pl.*)
• *adj.* флама́ндский

flesh /fleʃ/ *n.* **1** (bodily tissue) плоть, те́ло **2** (fig.): my own ~ and blood (children) моя́ плоть и кровь; (relatives) моя́ родня́ **3** (of fruit) мя́коть

fleshy /'fleʃɪ/ *adj.* (**fleshier, fleshiest**) (of persons) то́лстый, ту́чный

flew /flu:/ *past of* ▸ **fly³**

flex¹ /fleks/ *n.* (BrE) (ги́бкий) шнур

flex² /fleks/ *v.t.* сгиба́ть, согну́ть; ~ one's muscles напр|яга́ть, -я́чь му́скулы

flexibility /ˌfleksɪ'bɪlɪtɪ/ *n.* эласти́чность; (fig.) ги́бкость

flexible /'fleksɪb(ə)l/ *adj.* эласти́чный, ги́бкий; (fig.) ги́бкий

flexitime /'fleksɪtaɪm/ *n.* ненорми́рованный рабо́чий день

flick /flɪk/ *n.* (jerk) толчо́к; (light touch): a ~ of the whip лёгкий уда́р хлысто́м
• *v.t.* (shake with a jerk) встр|я́хивать, -яхну́ть; (propel with finger end) щёлк|ать, -нуть; (touch, e.g. with whip) стегну́ть (*pf.*)
• *v.i.*: ~ through просм|а́тривать, -отре́ть

flicker /'flɪkə(r)/ *n.* (of light) мерца́ние; (fig.): a ~ of hope про́блеск наде́жды
• *v.i.* (flutter) трепета́ть (*impf.*); (burn or shine fitfully) мерца́ть (*impf.*)

⚡ **flight¹** /flaɪt/ *n.* **1** полёт; (journey by air): a non-stop ~ беспоса́дочный полёт; (a particular ~) рейс; the next ~ from London to Paris сле́дующий рейс по маршру́ту

Ло́ндон — Пари́ж **2** (fig.): ~ of fancy полёт фанта́зии **3**: ~ of stairs ле́стничный марш
■ ~ **attendant** *n.* стю́ард (-е́сса); ~ **engineer** *n.* бортмеха́ник; ~ **path** *n.* курс полёта; ~ **recorder** *n.* бортово́й самопи́сец

flight² /flaɪt/ *n.* бе́гство, побе́г; take ~ обра|ща́ться, -ти́ться в бе́гство

flighty /'flaɪtɪ/ *adj.* (**flightier, flightiest**) ве́треный, капри́зный

flimsy /'flɪmzɪ/ *adj.* (**flimsier, flimsiest**) то́нкий, непро́чный; a ~ structure непро́чная постро́йка; a ~ excuse сла́бое оправда́ние

flinch /flɪntʃ/ *v.i.* вздр|а́гивать, -о́гнуть

fling /flɪŋ/ *n.* **1** (sexual) коро́ткий рома́н, интри́жка **2**: he had his ~ он повесели́лся/ нагуля́лся вво́лю
• *v.t.* (*past and p.p.* **flung**): ~ oneself into a chair бр|оса́ться, -о́ситься в кре́сло; she flung her arms around me она́ обняла́ меня́
• *with adv.*: ~ open the window распа́х|ивать, -ну́ть окно́

flint /flɪnt/ *n.* креме́нь (*m.*)

flip /flɪp/ *n.* щелчо́к
• *adj.* (flippant) де́рзкий
• *v.t.* (**flipped, flipping**) (a coin) подбр|а́сывать, -о́сить
• *v.i.* (infml, go crazy) сходи́ть, сойти́ с ума́

flip-flop /'flɪpflɒp/ *n.* (*usu. in pl.*) (footwear) вьетна́мка, сла́нец

flippancy /'flɪpənsɪ/ *n.* легкомы́слие, ве́треность

flippant /'flɪpənt/ *adj.* легкомы́сленный, ве́треный

flipper /'flɪpə(r)/ *n.* плавни́к, ласт; (diver's appendage) ласт

flirt /flɜ:t/ *n.* коке́тка; люби́тель (*m.*) поуха́живать
• *v.i.* коке́тничать (*impf.*) (with: с + *i.*); (fig.): ~ with (an idea etc.) поду́мывать о + *p.*

flirtation /flɜ:'teɪʃ(ə)n/ *n.* флирт; коке́тство; (fig.) игра́

flirtatious /flɜ:'teɪʃəs/ *adj.* коке́тливый

flit /flɪt/ *v.i.* (**flitted, flitting**) порх|а́ть, -ну́ть

float /fləʊt/ *n.* **1** (for line or net) поплаво́к, буй; (for learning to swim) пла́вательная доска́ **2** (BrE, cart) платфо́рма на колёсах
• *v.t.* спус|ка́ть, -ти́ть на́ воду; (comm.): ~ a company учре|жда́ть, -ди́ть акционе́рное о́бщество
• *v.i.* **1** пла́вать (*indet.*), плыть (*det.*); the boat ~ed downriver ло́дку несло́ тече́нием вниз по реке́ **2** (in air) плыть (*det.*)

floating /'fləʊtɪŋ/ *adj.* пла́вающий, плаву́чий
■ ~ **voter** *n.* коле́блющийся избира́тель

flock /flɒk/ *n.* (of birds) ста́я; (of sheep or goats) ста́до
• *v.i.* стека́ться (*impf.*)

flog /flɒɡ/ *v.t.* (**flogged, flogging**) стега́ть, от-

flood /flʌd/ *n.* **1** (inundation) наводне́ние, полово́дье, разли́в **2** (fig.): she burst into ~s of tears она́ разрыда́лась

- *v.t.* затоп|ля́ть, -и́ть; **the basement was** ~ed подва́л затопи́ло
- *v.i.* разл|ива́ться, -и́ться

■ ~**gate** *n.* шлюз; **open the** ~**gates (to)** (fig.) да|ва́ть, -ть во́лю (чему); ~**light** *n.* проже́ктор
- *v.t.* осве|ща́ть, -ти́ть проже́кторами

❡ **floor** /flɔː(r)/ *n.* **1** пол **2**: **take the** ~ (in public assembly) брать, взять сло́во; (in dance hall) пойти́ (*pf.*) танцева́ть **3** (storey) эта́ж
- *v.t.* (infml, knock down) сби|ва́ть, -ть с ног; (fig., nonplus) сра|жа́ть, -зи́ть; **the question** ~ed **him** вопро́с срази́л его́

■ ~**board** *n.* полови́ца; ~**cloth** *n.* (BrE) полова́я тря́пка; ~ **lamp** *n.* (AmE) торше́р; ~ **show** *n.* представле́ние в кабаре́

flooring /ˈflɔːrɪŋ/ *n.* насти́л, пол

flop /flɒp/ *n.* (failure) прова́л
- *v.i.* (**flopped, flopping**) **1** (move limply): ~ **down in a chair** плюх|аться, -нуться в кре́сло **2** (infml, fail) прова́л|иваться, -и́ться

floppy /ˈflɒpɪ/ *adj.* (**floppier, floppiest**) болта́ющийся, свиса́ющий

■ ~ **disk** *n.* (comput.) диске́та, ги́бкий диск

flora /ˈflɔːrə/ *n.* (*pl.* **floras** *or* **florae** /-riː/) фло́ра

floral /ˈflɔːr(ə)l/ *adj.* цвето́чный

florid /ˈflɒrɪd/ *adj.* (ornate) цвети́стый, витиева́тый; (ruddy) кра́сный, багро́вый

florist /ˈflɒrɪst/ *n.* продаве́ц цвето́в (цвето́чница)

floss /flɒs/ *n.*: **dental** ~ зубна́я нить

flotation /fləʊˈteɪʃ(ə)n/ *n.* распрода́жа а́кций компа́нии

flotilla /fləˈtɪlə/ *n.* флоти́лия (ме́лких судо́в)

flotsam /ˈflɒtsəm/ *n.* (вы́брошенный и) пла́вающий на пове́рхности груз, му́сор

flounce[1] /flaʊns/ *v.i.* бр|оса́ться, -о́ситься; ~ **out (of a room)** вылета́ть, вы́лететь из ко́мнаты

flounce[2] /flaʊns/ *n.* (trimming) обо́рка

flounder /ˈflaʊndə(r)/ *v.i.* бара́хтаться (*impf.*); (fig.) пу́таться в слова́х

flour /ˈflaʊə(r)/ *n.* мука́

flourish /ˈflʌrɪʃ/ *n.* **1** (wave of hand etc.) широ́кий жест **2** (literary embellishment) цвети́стость
- *v.t.* разма́хивать (*impf.*) + *i.*
- *v.i.* процвета́ть (*impf.*)

flourishing /ˈflʌrɪʃɪŋ/ *adj.* процвета́ющий, преуспева́ющий

flout /flaʊt/ *v.t.* поп|ира́ть, -ра́ть

❡ **flow** /fləʊ/ *n.* тече́ние, пото́к; **in full** ~ в разга́ре
- *v.i.* **1** течь, ли́ться (*both impf.*); **the Oka** ~s **into the Volga** Ока́ впада́ет в Во́лгу **2** (fig., move freely) ли́ться, течь (*both impf.*)

■ ~ **chart/diagram** *n.* блок-схе́ма

❡ **flower** /ˈflaʊə(r)/ *n.* цвето́к; цветко́вое расте́ние; **in** ~ в цвету́
- *v.i.* (blossom; flourish) цвести́ (*impf.*)

■ ~ **arrangement** *n.* цвето́чная компози́ция; ~ **bed** *n.* клу́мба; ~**pot** *n.* цвето́чный горшо́к

flowery /ˈflaʊərɪ/ *adj.* покры́тый цвета́ми; (fig.) цвети́стый

flown /fləʊn/ *p.p. of* ▸ **fly**[3]

flu /fluː/ *n.* (infml) грипп

fluctuate /ˈflʌktʃʊeɪt/ *v.i.* колеба́ться (*impf.*)

fluctuation /flʌktʃʊˈeɪʃ(ə)n/ *n.* колеба́ние

flue /fluː/ *n.* дымохо́д

■ ~ **pipe** *n.* (tech.) жарова́я труба́

fluency /ˈfluːənsɪ/ *n.* пла́вность, бе́глость

fluent /ˈfluːənt/ *adj.* пла́вный, бе́глый; **he speaks Russian** ~**ly** он свобо́дно говори́т по-ру́сски

fluff /flʌf/ *n.* пух, пушо́к
- *v.t.* **1** (make fluffy) взби|ва́ть, -ть **2** (infml, bungle) пу́тать, с-; ~ **one's lines** заб|ыва́ть, -ы́ть свои́ слова́

fluffy /ˈflʌfɪ/ *adj.* (**fluffier, fluffiest**) пуши́стый

fluid /ˈfluːɪd/ *n.* жи́дкость
- *adj.* жи́дкий, теку́чий; (fig.) неопределённый, переме́нчивый

■ ~ **ounce** *n.* жи́дкая у́нция

fluidity /fluːˈɪdɪtɪ/ *n.* теку́честь; (fig.) переме́нчивость, неопределённость

fluke /fluːk/ *n.* (lucky stroke) (неожи́данная) уда́ча, случа́йность

flung /flʌŋ/ *past and p.p. of* ▸ **fling**

fluorescent /flʊəˈres(ə)nt/ *adj.* флюоресци́рующий

fluoride /ˈflʊəraɪd/ *n.* фтори́д

flurry /ˈflʌrɪ/ *n.* (gust) шквал; (agitation) волне́ние, сумато́ха

flush /flʌʃ/ *n.* (flow of water) внеза́пный прили́в; (blush) прили́в кро́ви
- *v.t.* **1** (swill clean) пром|ыва́ть, -ы́ть; ~ **the lavatory** спус|ка́ть, -ти́ть во́ду в туале́т **2** (make red) зал|ива́ть, -и́ть кра́ской
- *v.i.* красне́ть, по-

fluster /ˈflʌstə(r)/ *v.t.* волнова́ть, вз-; будора́жить, вз-

flute /fluːt/ *n.* (instrument) фле́йта

flutter /ˈflʌtə(r)/ *n.* трепета́ние, дрожь
- *v.t.* мах|а́ть, -ну́ть + *i.*
- *v.i.* трепета́ть (*impf.*); (of birds) переп|а́рхивать, -орхну́ть

flux /flʌks/ *n.* постоя́нная сме́на; **everything was in a state of** ~ всё находи́лось в состоя́нии непреры́вного измене́ния

fly[1] /flaɪ/ *n.* му́ха

■ ~ **spray** *n.* (fluid) жи́дкость от мух; (instrument) аэрозо́ль (*m.*) от мух

fly[2] /flaɪ/ *n.* (on trousers) ширинка

❡ **fly**[3] /flaɪ/ *v.t.* (*past* **flew**, *p.p.* **flown**): ~ **an aircraft** управля́ть (*impf.*) самолётом; ~ **home the wounded** дост|авля́ть, -а́вить ра́неных в тыл самолётом
- *v.i.* (*past* **flew**, *p.p.* **flown**) **1** (move through the air) лета́ть (*indet.*), лете́ть (*det.*), по-; **he has never flown** он никогда́ не лета́л **2** (move swiftly): **I must** ~! ну, я побежа́л!; **he flew downstairs** он ку́барем скати́лся с ле́стницы; ~ **into a passion** вспыли́ть (*pf.*); ~ **off the handle** (infml) сорва́ться (*pf.*); **send** ~**ing** швыр|я́ть, -ну́ть; (of person) сби|ва́ть, -ть с ног; **time flies** вре́мя лети́т

● *with advs.*: leaves were ⁓ing about повсю́ду кружи́лись ли́стья; ⁓ away улет|а́ть, -е́ть; **the plane flew in to refuel and flew off again** самолёт прилете́л на запра́вку и вновь/сно́ва улете́л

■ ⁓**-by-night** *n.* ненадёжный челове́к; ⁓**over** *n.* (BrE, bridge, overpass) эстака́да; путепрово́д

flyer /'flaɪə(r)/ *n.* (handbill) рекла́мный листо́к

flying /'flaɪɪŋ/ *n.* полёт; **he likes** ⁓ он лю́бит лета́ть

● *adj.*: **pass with** ⁓ **colours** пройти́, сдать (*both pf.*) с блéском; **get off to a** ⁓ **start** сра́зу пойти́ (*pf.*) хорошо́ (*or* в го́ру)

■ ⁓ **saucer** *n.* лета́ющая таре́лка; ⁓ **visit** *n.* блицвизи́т; кра́ткое посеще́ние

foal /fəʊl/ *n.* жеребёнок

foam /fəʊm/ *n.* пе́на; ⁓ **rubber** по́ристая рези́на

● *v.i.* пе́ниться (*impf.*); **he was** ⁓**ing at the mouth** (fig., infml) он весь кипе́л от зло́сти

fob /fɒb/ *v.t.* (**fobbed, fobbing**): ⁓ **sb off with promises** корми́ть (*impf.*) кого́-н. обеща́ниями

focal /'fəʊk(ə)l/ *adj.*: ⁓ **point** фока́льная то́чка; (fig.): **the** ⁓ **point in his argument** гла́вный пункт его́ доказа́тельств

foci /'fəʊsaɪ/ *pl. of* ▶ **focus**

ꝛ **focus** /'fəʊkəs/ *n.* (*pl.* **focuses** *or* **foci** /-saɪ/) (math., phys., phot.) фо́кус; **out of** ⁓ не в фо́кусе; (fig.) центр, средото́чие; **he became the** ⁓ **of interest** он оказа́лся в це́нтре внима́ния

● *v.t.* (**focused, focusing** *or* **focussed, focussing**) (binoculars, camera) настр|а́ивать, -о́ить; (rays) фокуси́ровать, с-; (attention) сосредо|то́чивать, -то́чить

● *v.i.* (**focused, focusing** *or* **focussed, focussing**) (concentrate) сосредо|то́чиваться, -то́читься (**on**: на + *p.*)

■ ⁓ **group** *n.* фо́кус-гру́ппа

fodder /'fɒdə(r)/ *n.* корм для скота́

foe /fəʊ/ *n.* враг, не́друг

foetal /'fiːt(ə)l/ *adj.* (BrE) = fetal

foetus /'fiːtəs/ *n.* (BrE) = fetus

fog /fɒg/ *n.* тума́н

● *v.t.* (**fogged, fogging**) (fig.): **the windows are** ⁓**ged up** о́кна запоте́ли

■ ⁓**horn** *n.* тума́нный горн, тума́нная сире́на; ⁓ **lamp/light** *n.* противотума́нная фа́ра

fogey, fogy /'fəʊgɪ/ *n.* (*pl.* **fogeys** *or* **fogies**) старомо́дный/отста́лый челове́к

fogg|y /'fɒgɪ/ *adj.* (**foggier, foggiest**) тума́нный

foible /'fɔɪb(ə)l/ *n.* сла́бость; сла́бая стру́нка

foil¹ /fɔɪl/ *n.* (thin metal) фольга́, станио́ль (*m.*)

foil² /fɔɪl/ *v.t.* сби|ва́ть, -ть со сле́да

foist /fɔɪst/ *v.t.* навя́з|ывать, -а́ть (*что кому*)

fold¹ /fəʊld/ *n.* скла́дка; **the** ⁓**s of a dress** скла́дки пла́тья

● *v.t.* скла́дывать, сложи́ть; свё|ртывать (*or* -ора́чивать), -ерну́ть; ⁓ **one's arms** скре́|щивать, -сти́ть ру́ки на груди́

● *v.i.* скла́дываться, сложи́ться; (fig.): **the play** ⁓**ed after a week** пье́са сошла́ со сце́ны че́рез

неде́лю; **their business** ⁓**ed** они́ сверну́ли де́ло

fold² /fəʊld/ *n.* (for sheep) заго́н; **return to the** ⁓ (fig.) верну́ться (*pf.*) в ло́но (*церкви и т. п.*)

-fold /fəʊld/ *comb. form.* -кра́тный; **threefold** трёхкра́тный

folder /'fəʊldə(r)/ *n.* (container for papers) скоросшива́тель (*m.*); (also comput.) па́пка

folding /'fəʊldɪŋ/ *adj.* складно́й

foliage /'fəʊlɪɪdʒ/ *n.* листва́

ꝛ **folk** /fəʊk/ *n.* (*pl.* **folk** *or* **folks**) наро́д, лю́д|и (-е́й)

folklore /'fəʊklɔː(r)/ *n.* фолькло́р

ꝛ **follow** /'fɒləʊ/ *v.t. & i.* **1** (proceed or happen after) сле́довать, по- за + *i.*; **he** ⁓**ed (in) his father's footsteps** он пошёл по стопа́м отца́; **as** ⁓**s** сле́дующим о́бразом; **как сле́дует ни́же**; **his plan was as** ⁓**s** его́ план был тако́в **2** (as inference) сле́довать (*impf.*) из + *g.*; **it does not** ⁓ **that ...** э́то во́все не зна́чит, что... **3** (pursue) следи́ть (*impf.*) за + *i.*; **don't look now, we're being** ⁓**ed** не огля́дывайтесь, за на́ми следя́т **4** (keep to) приде́рживаться (*impf.*) + *g.*; (fig., be guided by): ⁓ **sb's advice/example** сле́довать, по- чьему́-н. сове́ту/приме́ру **5** (fig., keep track of): **I don't** ⁓ **you** я вас не понима́ю; ⁓ **the news in the papers** следи́ть (*impf.*) за новостя́ми в газе́тах

□ ⁓ **through** *v.t. & i.* сле́довать (*impf.*) (за + *i.*) до конца́

□ ⁓ **up** *v.t.* (look into) раз|бира́ть, -обра́ть; ⁓ **up a suggestion** уч|и́тывать, -е́сть чьё-н. предложе́ние

■ ⁓**-up** *n.* продолже́ние; (med.) контро́ль (*m.*)

follower /'fɒləʊə(r)/ *n.* после́дователь (*m.*) (-ница); сторо́нни|к (-ца)

following /'fɒləʊɪŋ/ *n.* после́дователи (*m. pl.*); приве́рженцы (*m. pl.*)

● *adj.* (ensuing) сле́дующий; **(on) the** ⁓ **day** на сле́дующий день; (about to be specified): **we shall need the** ⁓ нам потре́буется сле́дующее

folly /'fɒlɪ/ *n.* глу́пость

foment /fə'ment/ *v.t.* (hatred etc.) подстрек|а́ть, -ну́ть

ꝛ **fond** /fɒnd/ *adj.* **1** ⁓ **of: he became** ⁓ **of her** он привяза́лся к ней; **are you** ⁓ **of music?** вы лю́бите му́зыку? **2** (loving) не́жный, лю́бящий; ⁓ **memories** прия́тные/до́брые воспомина́ния

fondle /'fɒnd(ə)l/ *v.t.* ласка́ть (*impf.*)

font /fɒnt/ *n.* (eccl.) купе́ль

ꝛ **food** /fuːd/ *n.* пи́ща, пита́ние; еда́; (fig.): ⁓ **for thought** пи́ща для размышле́ний

■ ⁓ **poisoning** *n.* пищево́е отравле́ние; ⁓ **processor** *n.* ку́хонный комба́йн; ⁓**stuff** *n.* пищево́й проду́кт

fool /fuːl/ *n.* (simpleton) дура́к, глупе́ц; (jester) шут; **play the** ⁓ дура́читься (*impf.*); валя́ть (*impf.*) дурака́; **make a** ⁓ **(out) of sb** дура́чить, о- кого́-н.

● *v.t.* (deceive) одура́чи|вать, -ть

● *v.i.*: ⁓ **about, around** валя́ть (*impf.*) дурака́

■ ⁓**-proof** *adj.* (reliable) безотка́зный, ве́рный

foolhardy /'fuːlhɑːdɪ/ *adj.* (**foolhardier, foolhardiest**) безрассу́дно хра́брый

ꝛ ключева́я ле́ксика

foolish /'fuːlɪʃ/ *adj.* глу́пый; дура́цкий

foolishness /'fuːlɪʃnɪs/ *n.* глу́пость

✐ **foot** /fʊt/ *n.* (*pl.* **feet**) **1** (extremity of leg) ступня́, нога́; стопа́ ноги́; (lowest part, bottom): at the ~ of the hill у подно́жия холма́; at the ~ of the page в конце́ страни́цы; at the ~ of the stairs внизу́ ле́стницы; at the ~ of the bed в нога́х крова́ти **2** (unit of length) фут; six ~ (*or* feet) tall шести́ фу́тов ро́стом ● *phrr.*: we came here on ~ мы пришли́ сюда́ пешко́м; put one's ~ down (fig.) зан|има́ть, -я́ть твёрдую/реши́тельную пози́цию; put one's ~ in it (fig.) дать (*pf.*) ма́ху; stand on one's own (two) feet стоя́ть (*impf.*) на нога́х; быть самостоя́тельным ● *v.t.*: ~ the bill опла́|чивать, -ти́ть счёт

■ ~-and-mouth disease *n.* я́щур; ~bridge *n.* пешехо́дный мо́стик; ~hold *n.* то́чка опо́ры; ~lights *n. pl.* ра́мпа (*sg.*); ~note *n.* сно́ска; ~path *n.* тропа́, тропи́нка; ~print *n.* след ноги́; ~step *n.* шаг, по́ступь; ~stool *n.* скаме́ечка для ног; ~wear *n.* о́бувь

footage /'fʊtɪdʒ/ *n.* киноматериа́л

football /'fʊtbɔːl/ *n.* (BrE) футбо́л; (AmE) америка́нский футбо́л; ~ match (BrE) футбо́льный матч; ~ player футболи́ст

footballer /'fʊtbɔːlə(r)/ *n.* (BrE) футболи́ст

footer /'fʊtə(r)/ *n.* (line of text) ни́жний колонти́тул

footing /'fʊtɪŋ/ *n.* (foothold) опо́ра для ног(и́); lose one's ~ оступи́ться (*pf.*); (fig.) потеря́ть (*pf.*) по́чву под нога́ми; on an equal ~ на ра́вной ноге́

✐ **for** /fɔː(r)/ *prep.* **1** (with the object or purpose of) для + *g.*; ра́ди + *g.*; ~ example наприме́р; they have gone ~ a walk они́ пошли́ гуля́ть; (destination) на + *a.*; к + *d.*; the train ~ Moscow по́езд на Москву́; (aspiration): prospecting ~ oil разве́дка нефтяны́х месторожде́ний **2** (denoting reason; on account of) ра́ди + *g.*, для + *g.*; he is known ~ his generosity он изве́стен свое́й ще́дростью; (accorded to) the penalty ~ treason is death наказа́ние за госуда́рственную изме́ну — сме́ртная казнь; (on the occasion of): I gave him a book ~ his birthday я подари́л ему́ кни́гу на день рожде́ния; he went abroad ~ his holidays в о́тпуск он пое́хал за грани́цу **3** (representative of): A ~ Anna «А» как в сло́ве «А́нна»; (in support; in favour of): a vote ~ freedom го́лос за свобо́ду; (denoting purpose): they need premises ~ a school им ну́жно помеще́ние под шко́лу; ready ~ departure гото́в(ый) к отъе́зду; (on behalf of) за + *a.*, от + *g.*; speak ~ yourself! говори́те за себя́! **4** (denoting intended recipient): there is a letter ~ you вам письмо́ **5** (denoting duration or extent): ~ a long time на до́лгое вре́мя; в тече́ние до́лгого вре́мени; I haven't seen him ~ (some) days я не ви́дел его́ не́сколько дней; there is no house ~ miles на мно́го киломе́тров вокру́г нет ни еди́ного до́ма; (intended duration): ~ ever and ever навсегда́, на ве́ки ве́чные; they are going away ~ a few days они́ уезжа́ют на не́сколько

дней **6** (denoting relationship; in respect of): as ~ me, myself что каса́ется меня́; luckily ~ her на её сча́стье, к сча́стью для неё; (in relation to what is normal or suitable): warm ~ the time of year тепло́ для э́того вре́мени го́да; it's cold enough ~ snow хо́лодно — того́ и гляди́ пойдёт снег; not bad ~ a beginner непло́хо для новичка́ **7** (in return ~, instead of): get something ~ nothing получ|а́ть, -и́ть что-н. да́ром; once (and) ~ all раз и навсегда́ **8** (despite): ~ all that, I still love him но несмотря́ на всё, я его́ люблю́ **9** (with certain expressions of time): ~ the first time в пе́рвый раз; the wedding is arranged ~ June the 1st сва́дьба назна́чена на пе́рвое ию́ня

forage /'fɒrɪdʒ/ *n.* фура́ж, корм ● *v.i.* (search) разы́скивать (*impf.*) ■ ~ cap *n.* фура́жка

foray /'fɒreɪ/ *n.* набе́г

forbade /fəˈbæd, fəˈbeɪd/, **forbad** /fəˈbæd/ *past of* ▸ forbid

forbearance /fɔːˈbeərəns/ *n.* возде́ржанность, терпели́вость, терпе́ние

forbid /fəˈbɪd/ *v.t.* (**forbidding**, *past* **forbade** *or* **forbad**, *p.p.* **forbidden**) запре|ща́ть, -ти́ть (*кому что*)

forbidden /fəˈbɪd(ə)n/ *adj.* запрещённый, запре́тный

forbidding /fəˈbɪdɪŋ/ *adj.* (unfriendly) неприя́зненный; (threatening) гро́зный

✐ **force** /fɔːs/ *n.* **1** (strength, lit., fig.) си́ла; use ~ приб|ега́ть, -е́гнуть к си́ле; in full ~ в по́лном соста́ве; by ~ си́лой, наси́льно **2** (body of men, usu. armed) вооружённый отря́д; (Police) F~ поли́ция; (*in pl.*) the (armed) F~s а́рмия, вооружённые си́лы **3** (binding power, validity) де́йственность; in ~ (of law etc.) в си́ле **4** (phys.) си́ла ● *v.t.* **1** (compel, constrain) заст|авля́ть, -а́вить; he was ~d to sell the house он был вы́нужден прода́ть дом; ~d (laugh etc.) принуждённый **2** (apply ~ to): ~ (open) the door выла́мывать, вы́ломать дверь ■ ~-feed *v.t.* корми́ть (*impf.*) наси́льно

forceful /'fɔːsfʊl/ *adj.* си́льный, убеди́тельный

forceps /'fɔːseps/ *n. pl.* хирурги́ческие щипц|ы́ (-о́в)

forcible /'fɔːsɪb(ə)l/ *adj.* наси́льственный; (forceful) убеди́тельный; ~ entry наси́льственное вторже́ние

ford /fɔːd/ *n.* брод ● *v.t.* пере|ходи́ть, -йти́ вброд

fore /fɔː(r)/ *n.*: come to the ~ выдвига́ться, вы́двинуться ● *adj.* (*as pref.*) пред…

forearm /'fɔːrɑːm/ *n.* предпле́чье

foreboding /fɔːˈbəʊdɪŋ/ *n.* дурно́е предчу́вствие

forecast /'fɔːkɑːst/ *n.* предсказа́ние; (*also* **weather** ~) прогно́з пого́ды ● *v.t.* (*past and p.p.* ~ *or* ~ed) предска́з|ывать, -а́ть

forecaster /'fɔːkɑːstə(r)/ *n.*: weather ~ сино́птик

forecourt /'fɔːkɔːt/ *n.* пере́дний двор

forefather /'fɔːfɑːðə(r)/ *n.* пре́док, пра́отец

forefinger /'fɔːfɪŋɡə(r)/ *n.* указа́тельный па́лец

forefront /'fɔːfrʌnt/ *n.* аванга́рд; **in the ~ of the battle** на передово́й (ли́нии)

forego /fɔː'ɡəʊ/ *v.i.*: **a ~ne conclusion** предрешённый исхо́д

foreground /'fɔːɡraʊnd/ *n.* пере́дний план

forehand /'fɔːhænd/ *adj.* (tennis): **~ stroke** уда́р спра́ва

forehead /'fɒrɪd, 'fɔːhed/ *n.* лоб

ꝙ **foreign** /'fɒrən/ *adj.* **1** (of or pertaining to another country or countries) иностра́нный, заграни́чный **2** (alien) чужо́й, чу́ждый
■ **~ affairs** *n. pl.* междунаро́дные отноше́ния; **F~ Secretary** *n.* (BrE) мини́стр иностра́нных дел; **~ trade** *n.* вне́шняя торго́вля

foreigner /'fɒrənə(r)/ *n.* иностра́н|ец (-ка)

foreleg /'fɔːleɡ/ *n.* пере́дняя ла́па/нога́

foreman /'fɔːmən/ *n.* ма́стер, деся́тник; **~ of the jury** старшина́ (*m.*) прися́жных

foremost /'fɔːməʊst/ *adj.* са́мый пере́дний
• *adv.*: **first and ~** пре́жде всего́; в пе́рвую о́чередь

forename /'fɔːneɪm/ *n.* и́мя (*nt.*) (*в отли́чие от фами́лии*)

forensic /fə'rensɪk/ *adj.* суде́бный; **~ expert, scientist** суде́бно-медици́нский экспе́рт

foreplay /'fɔːpleɪ/ *n.* предвари́тельные ла́ски, прелю́дия (*перед половы́м а́ктом*)

forerunner /'fɔːrʌnə(r)/ *n.* предше́ственни|к (-ца)

fore|see /fɔː'siː/ *v.t.* (*past* **~saw**, *p.p.* **~seen**) предви́деть (*impf.*)

foreseeable /fɔː'siːəb(ə)l/ *adj.*: **in the ~ future** в обозри́мом бу́дущем

foreshadow /fɔː'ʃædəʊ/ *v.t.* предвеща́ть (*impf.*)

foreshore /'fɔːʃɔː(r)/ *n.* берегова́я полоса́, затопля́емая прили́вом

foresight /'fɔːsaɪt/ *n.* предусмотри́тельность

foreskin /'fɔːskɪn/ *n.* кра́йняя плоть

ꝙ **forest** /'fɒrɪst/ *n.* лес

forestall /fɔː'stɔːl/ *v.t.* предвосх|ища́ть, -и́тить; опере|жа́ть, -ди́ть; предупре|жда́ть, -ди́ть

forester /'fɒrɪstə(r)/ *n.* лесни́к

forestry /'fɒrɪstrɪ/ *n.* лесово́дство

foretaste /'fɔːteɪst/ *n.* предвкуше́ние

fore|tell /fɔː'tel/ *v.t.* (*past and p.p.* **~told**) предска́з|ывать, -а́ть

forethought /'fɔːθɔːt/ *n.* предусмотри́тельность

forever /fə'revə(r)/ *adv.* навсегда́, наве́чно; (continually) постоя́нно, ве́чно

forewarn /fɔː'wɔːn/ *v.t.* предупре|жда́ть, -ди́ть

foreword /'fɔːwɜːd/ *n.* предисло́вие

forfeit /'fɔːfɪt/ *n.* (penalty) штраф, конфиска́ция

• *v.t.* (**forfeited, forfeiting**) теря́ть, по-(пра́во на) + *a.*

forgave /fə'ɡeɪv/ *past of* ▸ **forgive**

forge /fɔːdʒ/ *n.* (workshop) ку́зница
• *v.t. & i.* **1** (shape metal) кова́ть (*impf.*) **2** (fabricate) изобре|та́ть, -сти́; (counterfeit) подде́л|ывать, -ать **3**: **~ ahead** вырыва́ться, вы́рваться вперёд

forger /'fɔːdʒə(r)/ *n.* подде́лыватель (*m.*); фальсифика́тор; (of money) фальшивомоне́тчик

forgery /'fɔːdʒərɪ/ *n.* подде́лка

ꝙ **forget** /fə'ɡet/ *v.t. & i.* (**forgetting**, *past* **forgot**, *p.p.* **forgotten** *or* esp. AmE **forgot**) забы|ва́ть, -ть; **I forgot all about the lecture** я соверше́нно забы́л о ле́кции
■ **~-me-not** *n.* (bot.) незабу́дка

forgetful /fə'ɡetfʊl/ *adj.* забы́вчивый

forgivable /fə'ɡɪvəb(ə)l/ *adj.* прости́тельный

forgive /fə'ɡɪv/ *v.t.* (*past* **forgave**, *p.p.* **forgiven**) про|ща́ть, -сти́ть; **I ~ you (for) everything** я вам всё проща́ю

forgiveness /fə'ɡɪvnɪs/ *n.* проще́ние

forgo /fɔː'ɡəʊ/ *v.t.* (**forgoes** /-'ɡəʊz/; *past* **forwent**, *p.p.* **forgone** /-'ɡɒn/) отка́з|ываться, -а́ться от + *g.*

forgot /fə'ɡɒt/ *past and* (esp. AmE) *p.p. of* ▸ **forget**

forgotten /fə'ɡɒt(ə)n/ *p.p. of* ▸ **forget**

fork /fɔːk/ *n.* **1** (cul.) ви́лка **2** (hort.) ви́лы (*f. pl.*) **3** (bifurcation) разви́лка
• *v.i.* (bifurcate) разд|валя́ться, -вои́ться; **~ out** (sl., provide money) отва́л|ивать, -и́ть; раскоше́ли|ваться, -ться (**for**: на + *a.*)
■ **~-lift n.** (*in full* **~-lift truck**) автопогру́зчик

forked /fɔːkt/ *adj.*: **~ lightning** зигзагообра́зная мо́лния

forlorn /fə'lɔːn/ *adj.* забро́шенный

ꝙ **form** /fɔːm/ *n.* **1** (shape) фо́рма, вид; (figure) фигу́ра **2** (kind, variant) вид, фо́рма **3** (of health) состоя́ние; **in good ~** в хоро́шей фо́рме; (of spirits): **he appeared in great ~** он был в отли́чной фо́рме **4** (document) бланк, анке́та **5** (BrE, class in school) класс
• *v.t.* **1** (fashion) формирова́ть, с-; **he ~ed the clay into a vase** гли́на под его́ рука́ми преврати́лась в ва́зу; (by discipline, training, etc.) тренирова́ть, на-; **his character was ~ed at school** его́ хара́ктер сформирова́лся в шко́ле **2** (organize, create) организо́в|ывать, -а́ть; **they ~ed an alliance** они́ созда́ли/образова́ли сою́з; **he was unable to ~ a government** он не смог сформирова́ть прави́тельство **3** (conceive): **they ~ed a plan** они́ вы́работали план **4** (mil. etc.) стро́|ить, по-; **~ a queue** (BrE) **line** (AmE) образо́в|ывать, -ова́ть о́чередь **5** (constitute) сост|авля́ть, -а́вить; **this ~s the basis of our discussion** э́то составля́ет осно́ву на́шей диску́ссии
• *v.i.* (take shape, appear): **ice ~ed on the window** на окне́ образова́лся/возни́к моро́зный узо́р; **an idea ~ed in his mind** в его́ мозгу́ возни́кла иде́я

formal /'fɔːm(ə)l/ *adj.* официа́льный

ꝙ ключева́я ле́ксика

formality /fɔːˈmælɪtɪ/ n. форма́льность

formalize /ˈfɔːməlaɪz/ v.t. оф|ормля́ть, -о́рмить

format /ˈfɔːmæt/ n. (also comput.) форма́т
* v.t. (comput.) формати́ровать, от-

formation /fɔːˈmeɪʃ(ə)n/ n. образова́ние, формирова́ние

formative /ˈfɔːmətɪv/ adj. формиру́ющий, образу́ющий; he spent his ~ years in France го́ды, когда́ скла́дывался/формирова́лся его́ хара́ктер, он провёл во Фра́нции

⚹ **former** /ˈfɔːmə(r)/ adj. 🔟 (earlier) предше́ствующий; my ~ husband мой бы́вший муж 🔼 (first mentioned of two) пе́рвый

formerly /ˈfɔːməlɪ/ adv. пре́жде, ра́ньше

formidable /ˈfɔːmɪdəb(ə)l/ adj. (frightening) устраша́ющий, гро́зный; (huge) огро́мный

formless /ˈfɔːmlɪs/ adj. бесфо́рменный

formula /ˈfɔːmjʊlə/ n. (pl. **formulas** or **formulae** /-liː/) (math., chem.) фо́рмула

formulate /ˈfɔːmjʊleɪt/ v.t. формули́ровать, с-

forsake /fɔːˈseɪk/ v.t. (past **forsook** /-ˈsʊk/; p.p. **forsaken** /-ˈseɪk(ə)n/) пок|ида́ть, -и́нуть; ост|авля́ть, -а́вить; бр|оса́ть, -о́сить

fort /fɔːt/ n. форт

forte /ˈfɔːteɪ/ n. (strong point) си́льная сторона́

forth /fɔːθ/ adv. вперёд, да́льше; and so ~ и так да́лее; from this day ~ с э́того дня; впредь

forthcoming /fɔːθˈkʌmɪŋ/ adj. предстоя́щий; the clerk was not very ~ with information чино́вник был не о́чень охо́тно дава́л све́дения

forthright /ˈfɔːθraɪt/ adj. прямо́й, прямолине́йный

fortieth /ˈfɔːtɪɪθ/ n. (fraction) одна́ сороков́ая
* adj. сороков́ой

fortification /fɔːtɪfɪˈkeɪʃ(ə)n/ n. укрепле́ние

fortif|y /ˈfɔːtɪfaɪ/ v.t. укреп|ля́ть, -и́ть; ~ied wines креплёные ви́на

fortitude /ˈfɔːtɪtjuːd/ n. сто́йкость; си́ла ду́ха

fortnight /ˈfɔːtnaɪt/ (BrE) n. две неде́ли

fortnightly /ˈfɔːtnaɪtlɪ/ adj. двухнеде́льный
* adv. раз в две неде́ли

fortress /ˈfɔːtrɪs/ n. кре́пость

fortuitous /fɔːˈtjuːɪtəs/ adj. случа́йный

fortunate /ˈfɔːtʃənət/ adj. счастли́вый, уда́чный; ~ly к сча́стью

fortune /ˈfɔːtʃuːn/ n. 🔟 (chance) уда́ча, сча́стье, форту́на; by good ~ по сча́стью 🔼 (fate) судьба́; the Gypsy (woman) told my ~ цыга́нка (по/на)гада́ла мне 🔺 (large sum) состоя́ние, бога́тство; make a ~ разбогате́ть (pf.)
■ ~ teller n. гада́лка, вороже́я

fort|y /ˈfɔːtɪ/ n. со́рок; the ~ies (decade) сороковы́е го́ды (m. pl.); they are both in their ~ies им обо́им за со́рок
* adj. со́рок (+ g. pl.)

⚹ **forward** /ˈfɔːwəd/ n. (sport) напада́ющий
* adj. (situated to the fore) пере́дний; (progressive) прогресси́вный; (pert) нагло́ва́тый, развя́зный
* adv. (onward; towards one) вперёд; please come ~ пожа́луйста, вы́йдите вперёд; the meeting has been brought ~ a day собра́ние перенесли́ на́ день ра́ньше; (towards the future):

I look ~ to meeting her я с нетерпе́нием жду встре́чи с ней
* v.t. (send) пос|ыла́ть, -ла́ть; отпр|авля́ть, -а́вить; (send on) перес|ыла́ть, -ла́ть
■ ~ slash n. коса́я черта́, слеш

forwards /ˈfɔːwədz/ adv. вперёд

forwent /fɔːˈwent/ past of ▸ **forgo**

fossil /ˈfɒs(ə)l/ n. окамене́лость

foster /ˈfɒstə(r)/ v.t. 🔟 (bring up) воспи́т|ывать, -а́ть (чужо́го ребёнка); (also ~ out) (BrE) assign to someone else to bring up) отд|ава́ть, -а́ть на воспита́ние 🔼 (fig., hope) пита́ть (impf.); (hatred) се́ять, по-
■ ~-child n. приёмный ребёнок, воспи́танник; ~-father n. приёмный оте́ц; ~-mother n. приёмная мать

fought /fɔːt/ past and p.p. of ▸ **fight**

foul /faʊl/ n. (sport) наруше́ние (пра́вил игры́)
* adj. гря́зный, отврати́тельный; a ~ smell злово́ние; ~ language сквернослов́ие, ру́гань; ~ weather отврати́тельная пого́да; непого́да
* v.t. (defile) загрязн|я́ть, -и́ть; па́чкать, за-; засор|я́ть, -и́ть; (obstruct) образо́в|ывать, -а́ть зато́р в + p.
■ ~-mouthed adj. сквернослов́ящий; ~ play n. (sport) гру́бая игра́; (violence) нечи́стое де́ло

found[1] /faʊnd/ v.t. осно́в|ывать, -а́ть; за|кла́дывать, -ложи́ть; (base) осно́в|ывать, -а́ть

found[2] /faʊnd/ past and p.p. of ▸ **find**

⚹ **foundation** /faʊnˈdeɪʃ(ə)n/ n. 🔟 (establishing) основа́ние, учрежде́ние 🔼 (base of building etc.) фунда́мент; (fig.) осно́ва 🔺: ~ cream крем под пу́дру

founder /ˈfaʊndə(r)/ n. основа́тель (m.) (-ница)

foundry /ˈfaʊndrɪ/ n. лите́йная

fountain /ˈfaʊntɪn/ n. фонта́н
■ ~ pen n. авторучка

⚹ **four** /fɔː(r)/ n. (число́/но́мер) четы́ре; (~ people) че́тверо; (figure; thing numbered 4; group of ~) четвёрка; he got down on all ~s он опусти́лся на четвере́ньки
* adj. четы́ре + g. sg.
■ ~-letter adj.: ~-letter word (fig.) руга́тельство; непристо́йное сло́во; ~-wheel adj.: ~-wheel drive (attr.) с при́водом на четы́ре колеса́; (n.) внедоро́жник, вездехо́д

fourteen /fɔːˈtiːn/ n. четы́рнадцать
* adj. четы́рнадцать + g. pl.

fourteenth /fɔːˈtiːnθ/ n. (date) четы́рнадцатое (число́); (fraction) одна́ четы́рнадцатая
* adj. четы́рнадцатый

⚹ **fourth** /fɔːθ/ n. 🔟 (date) четвёртое (число́) 🔼 (fraction) одна́ четвёртая
* adj. четвёртый

fowl /faʊl/ n. (pl. ~ or ~s) (domestic) дома́шняя пти́ца

fox /fɒks/ n. лиса́, лиси́ца
■ ~-hound n. го́нчая; ~-hunting n. (верхова́я) охо́та на лис

foyer /ˈfɔɪeɪ/ n. фойе́ (nt. indecl.)

fracking /'frækɪŋ/ n. (tech.) гидравли́ческий перело́м

fraction /'frækʃ(ə)n/ n. дробь

fractious /'frækʃəs/ adj. капри́зный

fracture /'fræktʃə(r)/ n. (of a bone) перело́м ● v.t. & i. лома́ть(ся), с-

fragile /'frædʒaɪl/ adj. хру́пкий

fragility /frə'dʒɪlɪtɪ/ n. ло́мкость, хру́пкость

fragment /'frægmənt/ n. обло́мок, оско́лок; (of writing) фрагме́нт

fragmentary /'frægməntərɪ/ adj. отры́вочный, фрагмента́рный

fragrance /'freɪgrəns/ n. арома́т

fragrant /'freɪgrənt/ adj. арома́тный

frail /freɪl/ adj. хру́пкий

✔ **frame** /freɪm/ n. **1** (structural skeleton) скеле́т, костя́к **2** (wood or metal surround) ра́ма, ра́мка **3**: ~ **of mind** настрое́ние; расположе́ние ду́ха **4** (cin.) кадр ● v.t. **1** (a picture) вставля́ть, -а́вить в ра́м(к)у **2** (a proposal, a reply) составля́ть, -а́вить; созд|ава́ть, -а́ть **3** (an innocent person, infml) подста́вля́ть, -а́вить

■ ~**work** n. карка́с, о́стов; (fig.): **within the** ~**work of the constitution** в ра́мках конститу́ции

France /frɑːns/ n. Фра́нция

franchise /'fræntʃaɪz/ n. (right to vote) пра́во го́лоса; (comm.) привиле́гия, франши́за

frank /fræŋk/ adj. открове́нный, и́скренний

frankfurter /'fræŋkfɜːtə(r)/ n. соси́ска (копчёная)

frantic /'fræntɪk/ adj. неи́стовый, безу́мный; **she became** ~ **with grief** она́ обезу́мела от го́ря

fraternal /frə'tɜːn(ə)l/ adj. бра́тский

fraternity /frə'tɜːnɪtɪ/ n. бра́тство

fraternize /'frætənaɪz/ v.i. брата́ться (impf.)

fraud /frɔːd/ n. (fraudulent act) обма́н, моше́нничество; (impostor) обма́нщик, моше́нник

fraudulent /'frɔːdjʊlənt/ adj. обма́нный, фальши́вый, моше́ннический

fraught /frɔːt/ adj. по́лный; **the expedition is** ~ **with danger** экспеди́ция чрева́та опа́сностями; (tense) напряжённый

fray /freɪ/ v.t. проти́ра́ться, -ере́ться

frazzle /'fræz(ə)l/ n.: **worn to a** ~ доведённый до изнеможе́ния

freak /friːk/ n. (unusual occurrence): ~ **weather conditions** необы́чные пого́дные усло́вия; (abnormal person or thing) уро́д, вы́родок; ~ **of nature** оши́бка приро́ды; (enthusiast) фана́т; **health** ~ поме́шанный на здоро́вье ● v.i.: ~ (**out**) (infml) при|ходи́ть, -йти́ в возбужде́ние

freakish /'friːkɪʃ/ adj. причу́дливый, чудно́й

freckle /'frek(ə)l/ n. весну́шка

✔ **free** /friː/ adj. (**freer** /'friːə(r)/, **freest** /'friːɪst/) **1** свобо́дный, во́льный; **you are** ~ **to leave** вы мо́жете уйти́; **they gave us a** ~ **hand**

они́ предоста́вили нам по́лную свобо́ду де́йствий; **set** ~ освобо|жда́ть, -ди́ть **2** (without constraint) непринуждённый, раско́ванный **3** (without payment) беспла́тный; ~ **of charge** беспла́тный **4** (unoccupied) свобо́дный, незаня́тый **5** (liberal) ще́дрый; ~ **with one's money** ще́дрый, расточи́тельный ● v.t. (release, e.g. a rope) высвобожда́ть; (liberate) освобо|жда́ть, -ди́ть

■ ~ **fall** n. свобо́дное паде́ние; ~-**for-all** n. (competition) откры́тый (для всех) ко́нкурс; ~ **gift** n. полу́ченное да́ром; ~**lance(r)** n. лицо́ свобо́дной профе́ссии; внешта́тный сотру́дник; **F~mason** n. масо́н; **F~masonry** n. масо́нство; **F~phone** n. (BrE) беспла́тный телефо́н; ~-**range** adj.: ~-**range eggs** я́йца от кур на свобо́дном вы́гуле; ~ **speech** n. свобо́да сло́ва; ~**way** n. (AmE) скоростна́я автостра́да; ~ **will** n. свобо́да во́ли; **he left of his own** ~ **will** он ушёл добро́вольно/сам (or по свое́й во́ле)

✔ **freedom** /'friːdəm/ n. свобо́да; ~ **of speech** свобо́да сло́ва

freesia /'friːʒə/ n. (bot.) фре́зия

freez|e /friːz/ n. (period of frost) замора́живание; **wage** ~**e** замора́живание за́работной пла́ты ● v.t. (past **froze**, p.p. **frozen**) замор|а́живать, -о́зить; **frozen food** моро́женые проду́кты; ~**e assets/prices** замор|а́живать, -о́зить фо́нды/це́ны ● v.i. (past **froze**, p.p. **frozen**) **1** (impers.) моро́зить (impf.); **it's** ~**ing outside** на дворе́ стра́шный моро́з **2** (congeal with cold): **the roads are frozen** доро́ги покры́лись льдом; **the pipes are frozen (up)** тру́бы промёрзли; ~**ing point** то́чка замерза́ния **3** (fig., become rigid) заст|ыва́ть, -ы́ть; (as command): ~**e!** стоя́ть!, ни с ме́ста! **4** (become chilled) зам|ерза́ть, -ёрзнуть; **I'm** ~**ing** я замёрз

freezer /'friːzə(r)/ n. (domestic appliance) морози́льник

■ ~ **compartment** n. морози́лка

freight /freɪt/ n. фрахт

freighter /'freɪtə(r)/ n. (vessel) грузово́е су́дно; (aircraft) грузово́й самолёт

✔ **French** /frentʃ/ n. (language) францу́зский язы́к; **the** ~ (people) францу́зы (m. pl.) ● adj. францу́зский

■ ~ **Canadian** n. франкокана́д|ец (-ка); ~ **fries** n. pl. карто́фель (m.) соло́мкой/фри; ~**man** n. францу́з; ~ **Riviera** n. Лазу́рный Бе́рег; ~ **window** n. двуство́рчатое окно́ до по́ла; (in pl.) две́ри в сад; ~**woman** n. францу́женка

frenetic /frə'netɪk/ adj. неи́стовый

frenzied /'frenzɪd/ adj. неи́стовый, взбешённый

frenzy /'frenzɪ/ n. неи́стовство, бе́шенство

frequency /'friːkwənsɪ/ n. частота́

frequent /'friːkwənt/ adj. ча́стый

✔ **frequently** /'friːkwəntlɪ/ adv. ча́сто

fresco /'freskəʊ/ n. (pl. ~**s** or ~**es**) фре́ска

✔ **fresh** /freʃ/ adj. **1** (new) све́жий, но́вый **2** (recent in origin): ~ **bread** све́жий хлеб; **it is still** ~ **in my memory** э́то ещё свежо́ в мое́й

✔ ключева́я ле́ксика

па́мяти **3** (as opposed to salt) пре́сный **4** (cool, refreshing) све́жий, прохла́дный **5** (unspoilt, unsullied) све́жий, незапя́тнанный; ~ **air** све́жий во́здух **6** (lively) бо́дрый, живо́й **7** (impudent) развя́зный, де́рзкий
■ ~**water** adj. пресново́дный

freshen /'freʃ(ə)n/ v.i.: she's gone to ~ up она́ пошла́ привести́ себя́ в поря́док

freshly /'freʃlɪ/ adv. (recently) неда́вно; то́лько что

fret /fret/ v.i. (**fretted, fretting**) волнова́ться; му́читься (both impf.)

fretful /'fretful/ adj. раздражи́тельный, капри́зный

Freudian /'frɔɪdɪən/ adj.: ~ slip огово́рка по Фре́йду

friction /'frɪkʃ(ə)n/ n. тре́ние; (fig.) тре́ния (nt. pl.)

ℱ **Friday** /'fraɪdeɪ/ n. пя́тница

fridge /frɪdʒ/ n. холоди́льник
■ ~-**freezer** n. (BrE) двухка́мерный холоди́льник

ℱ **friend** /frend/ n. (male) друг, прия́тель; (female) подру́га, прия́тельница; **be** ~**s** дружи́ть (impf.) (с кем); **make** ~**s** подружи́ться (pf.) (с кем)

friendly /'frendlɪ/ adj. (**friendlier, friendliest**) дру́жеский, това́рищеский

friendship /'frendʃɪp/ n. дру́жба

frieze /friːz/ n. (decorative band) бордю́р, фриз

frigate /'frɪgət/ n. (hist.) фрега́т; (small destroyer) эска́дренный миноно́сец; сторожево́й кора́бль

fright /fraɪt/ n. страх, испу́г; **give sb a** ~ испуга́ть (pf.) кого́-н.; напуга́ть (pf.) кого́-н.; I got the ~ of my life я жу́тко испуга́лся

frighten /'fraɪt(ə)n/ v.t. пуга́ть, на-/ис-; **she is** ~**ed of the dark** она́ бои́тся темноты́

frightening /'fraɪtnɪŋ/ adj. стра́шный

frightful /'fraɪtful/ adj. (terrible) ужа́сный, стра́шный; (infml, hideous) безобра́зный

frigid /'frɪdʒɪd/ adj. **1** (cold) холо́дный **2** (unfeeling) холо́дный, безразли́чный; (sexually) холо́дный, фриги́дный
■ ~ **zone** n. аркти́ческий по́яс

frill /frɪl/ n. обо́рочка

frilly /'frɪlɪ/ adj. (**frillier, frilliest**) с обо́рками

fringe /frɪndʒ/ n. **1** (ornamental border) бахрома́ **2** (BrE, of hair) чёлка **3** (fig., edge, margin) край, кайма́
■ ~ **benefits** n. pl. дополни́тельные льго́ты (f. pl.)

frisk /frɪsk/ v.t. (search) обы́ск|ивать, -а́ть

frisky /'frɪskɪ/ adj. (**friskier, friskiest**) ре́звый, игри́вый

frisson /'friːsɔ̃/ n. дрожь (от предвкушаемого удовольствия)

fritter /'frɪtə(r)/ v.t.: ~ away транжи́рить, рас-

frivolity /frɪ'vɒlɪtɪ/ n. легкомы́слие

frivolous /'frɪvələs/ adj. легкомы́сленный, пусто́й

frizzy /'frɪzɪ/ adj. (**frizzier, frizziest**) вью́щийся, курча́вый

frock /frɒk/ n. пла́тье; **party** ~ вече́рнее пла́тье
■ ~ **coat** n. сюрту́к

frog /frɒg/ n. лягу́шка; I've got a ~ in my throat (fig.) я охри́п
■ ~**man** n. ныря́льщик с аквала́нгом

frolic /'frɒlɪk/ v.i. (**frolicked, frolicking**) шали́ть (impf.); резви́ться (impf.)

ℱ **from** /frɒm/ prep. **1** (denoting origin of movement, measurement or distance): the train ~ London to Paris по́езд из Ло́ндона в Пари́ж; **guests** ~ Ukraine го́сти с Украи́ны; 10 miles ~ here в десяти́ ми́лях отсю́да; ~ the beginning of the book с нача́ла кни́ги; ~ end to end от одного́ конца́ до друго́го; far ~ it! отню́дь!; во́все нет! **2** (expr. separation): I took the key ~ him я взял у него́ ключ; released ~ prison вы́пущенный из тюрьмы́ **3** (denoting personal origin): a letter ~ my son письмо́ от моего́ сы́на **4** (expr. material origin): wine is made ~ grapes вино́ де́лается из виногра́да **5** (expr. origin in time): ~ the very beginning с са́мого нача́ла; ~ beginning to end с нача́ла до конца́; ~ now on с э́того моме́нта; ~ February to October с февраля́ по октя́брь; ~ time to time вре́мя от вре́мени **6** (expr. source or model): he quoted ~ memory он цити́ровал по па́мяти; he spoke ~ the heart он говори́л от души́ **7** (expr. cause) от/с + g.; suffer ~ arthritis страда́ть (impf.) артри́том **8** (expr. difference): I can't tell him ~ his brother я не могу́ отличи́ть его́ от его́ бра́та **9** (expr. change): things went ~ bad to worse дела́ шли всё ху́же и ху́же **10** (with numbers): ~ 1 to 10 от одного́ до десяти́; it will last ~ 10 to 15 days э́то продли́тся 10-15 дней; they cost ~ £5 (upwards) они́ сто́ят от 5 фу́нтов и вы́ше **11** (with advs.): ~ above све́рху; ~ below сни́зу; ~ inside изнутри́; ~ outside снару́жи; ~ afar издалека́; ~ under the table из-под стола́

frond /frɒnd/ n. ветвь с ли́стьями; лист (па́поротника)

ℱ **front** /frʌnt/ n. **1** (foremost side or part) перёд; пере́дняя сторона́; he walked in ~ of the procession он шёл впереди́ проце́ссии; in ~ of the house пе́ред до́мом; in ~ of the children при де́тях; back to ~ за́дом наперёд **2** (archit.) фаса́д **3** (fighting line) фронт; he was sent to the ~ его́ посла́ли на фронт; in the ~ line на передово́й ли́нии **4** (BrE, road bordering sea) на́бережная **5** (meteor.) фронт
■ ~ **benches** n. pl. (pol.) скамьи́ для мини́стров и ли́деров оппози́ции в парла́менте; ~ **door** n. пара́дная дверь; ~ **page** n. пе́рвая страни́ца/полоса́; ~ **page news** основны́е но́вости в газе́те

frontier /'frʌntɪə(r)/ n. грани́ца

frost /frɒst/ n. моро́з
● v.t.: the windows were ~ed over о́кна замёрзли
■ ~**bite** n. обмороже́ние, отмороже́ние; ~**ed glass** n. ма́товое стекло́

frosting /'frɒstɪŋ/ n. (AmE, cul.) глазу́рь

frosty /'frɒstɪ/ adj. (**frostier, frostiest**) моро́зный; (fig., unfriendly) холо́дный, ледяно́й

f

froth /frɒθ/ n. пе́на

frothy /'frɒθɪ/ adj. (**frothier, frothiest**)
пе́нистый; (fig.) пустой

frown /fraʊn/ v.i. хму́риться, на-; the
authorities ~ on gambling вла́сти
неодобри́тельно отно́сятся к аза́ртным и́грам

froze /frəʊz/ past of ▶ **freeze**

frozen /'frəʊz(ə)n/ adj. замёрзший,
засты́вший; (ice-bound) ско́ванный льдом

frugal /'fruːɡ(ə)l/ adj. бережли́вый

✧ **fruit** /fruːt/ n. фрукт
 ■ ~ **cake** n. фрукто́вый кекс; ~ **juice** n.
фрукто́вый сок; ~ **machine** n. (BrE) игрово́й
автома́т; ~ **salad** n. фрукто́вый сала́т

fruitful /'fruːtfʊl/ adj. плодотво́рный

fruition /fruː'ɪʃ(ə)n/ n.: come to ~
осуществ|ля́ться, -и́ться

fruitless /'fruːtlɪs/ adj. беспло́дный

fruity /'fruːtɪ/ adj. (**fruitier, fruitiest**)
фрукто́вый

frustrate /frʌ'streɪt/ v.t. разочаро́в|ывать,
-а́ть; I feel ~d я обескура́жен

frustration /frʌ'streɪʃ(ə)n/ n. **1** (thwarting)
круше́ние (планов/надежд) **2** (disappointment)
разочарова́ние

fr|y /fraɪ/ v.t. жа́рить, за-/из-/по-; ~**ied egg(s)**
яи́чница; ~**ied potato** жа́реная карто́шка
 ● v.i. жа́риться (impf.)
 ■ ~**ying pan** n. сковорода́

ft abbr. (of **foot, feet**) фут(ы)

fuchsia /'fjuːʃə/ n. фу́ксия

fuck /fʌk/ (vulg.) n.: he doesn't give a ~ ему́
по́ хую (or по́ хуй); (euph.) ему́ по́ фигу (or
по́ фиг)
 ● v.t. еба́ть, вы-; (euph.) тра́х|ать, -нуть; ~ it!
чёрт возьми́/побери́! (euph.) блядь!, (euph.)
блин!; ~ all (BrE) ни хуя́, (euph.) ни хрена́; to
do ~ all ни хуя́ не де́лать
 ● v.i. еба́ться, по-; (euph.) тра́х|аться, -нуться
 ● with advs.: ~ about/around занима́ться,
страда́ть (both impf.) хуйнёй; (euph.)
занима́ться, страда́ть (both impf.) хернёй; ~
off! отъеби́сь (от меня́)!; пошёл/иди́ на́ хуй!,
(euph.) пошёл/иди́ на́ фиг!; ~ up v.t. (sth)
зап|а́рывать, -оро́ть (no vulg. equivalent); (a game,
contest, etc.) прос|ира́ть, -ра́ть; про|ёбывать,
-еба́ть; (sb) док|а́нывать, -она́ть (no vulg.
equivalent); (v.i.) лажа́ть (impf.), облажа́ться
(pf.) (no vulg. equivalents); порта́чить, на- (no
vulg. equivalent)

fucking /'fʌkɪŋ/ adj. (vulg.) ёбаный, (euph.)
долба́ный

fudge /fʌdʒ/ n. (sweetmeat) сли́вочная пома́дка
 ● v.t. & i. (an issue, question) уклон|я́ться, -и́ться
от + g.; (facts, figures) подтасо́в|ывать, -а́ть; ~
accounts подде́л|ывать, -ать счета́

✧ **fuel** /'fjuːəl/ n. то́пливо, горю́чее
 ● v.t. (**fuelled, fuelling,** AmE **fueled,
fueling**) снаб|жа́ть, -ди́ть (or запр|авля́ть,
-а́вить) то́пливом

fugitive /'fjuːdʒɪtɪv/ n. бегл|е́ц (-я́нка)

fugue /fjuːɡ/ n. (mus.) фу́га

✧ ключева́я ле́ксика

fulcr|um /'fʊlkrəm/ n. (pl. ~**a** or ~**ums**)
то́чка опо́ры; то́чка приложе́ния си́лы

fulfil /fʊl'fɪl/ (AmE **fulfill**) v.t. (**fulfilled,
fulfilling**) выполня́ть, вы́полнить

fulfilment /fʊl'fɪl mənt/ (AmE **fulfillment**)
n. (accomplishment) выполне́ние, исполне́ние;
(satisfaction) удовлетворе́ние

✧ **full** /fʊl/ adj. **1** (filled to capacity) по́лный; the
hotel is ~ (up) все ко́мнаты в гости́нице
за́няты; (having plenty): ~ of ideas по́лон иде́й/
за́мыслов; ~ of life жизнера́достный; по́лон
жи́зни **2** (complete): we waited a ~ hour мы
жда́ли це́лый час
 ● adv. **1** (very): you know ~ well вы са́ми
прекра́сно зна́ете **2** (completely): she turned
the radio on ~ она́ включи́ла ра́дио на
по́лную мо́щность/гро́мкость
 ■ ~**back** n. защи́тник; ~**-grown** adj.
взро́слый; ~**-length** adj. во всю длину́;
~**-length dress** пла́тье до пят; ~ **moon**
n. полнолу́ние; ~**-scale** adj. в по́лном
объёме; ~ **stop** n. то́чка; ~**-time** adj. (of job)
занима́ющий всё (рабо́чее) вре́мя

✧ **fully** /'fʊlɪ/ adv. вполне́, по́лностью,
соверше́нно, до конца́

fulsome /'fʊlsəm/ adj. чрезме́рный,
тошнотво́рный

fumble /'fʌmb(ə)l/ v.t. тереби́ть (impf.) в
рука́х; ~ a ball упусти́ть (pf.) мяч
 ● v.i. ры́ться (impf.); he ~d in his pockets for
a key он ры́лся в карма́нах, ища́ ключ

fume /fjuːm/ n. дым, ко́поть
 ● v.i. (fig.): fuming with rage кипя́щий от гне́ва

fumigate /'fjuːmɪɡeɪt/ v.t. оку́р|ивать, -и́ть

✧ **fun** /fʌn/ n. весе́лье, заба́ва; make ~ of, poke
~ at насмеха́ться (impf.) над + i.; he is ~ to
be with с ним не соску́чишься; we had ~ at
the party в гостя́х бы́ло ве́село
 ■ ~**fair** n. (BrE) увесели́тельный парк

✧ **function** /'fʌŋkʃ(ə)n/ n. **1** (purpose) фу́нкция,
назначе́ние **2** (social gathering) ве́чер **3**: ~ **key**
(comput.) функциона́льная кла́виша
 ● v.i. функциони́ровать, де́йствовать (both
impf.)

functional /'fʌŋkʃən(ə)l/ adj. функциона́льный

functionary /'fʌŋkʃənərɪ/ n. функционе́р,
должностно́е лицо́

✧ **fund** /fʌnd/ n. фонд, запа́с, резе́рв; (in pl.)
(resources) фо́нды (m. pl.); he is in ~s (BrE) он
при деньга́х
 ● v.t. финанси́ровать (impf., pf.); (fin.)
консолиди́ровать (impf., pf.)
 ■ ~**-raising** n. сбор средств; a ~**-raising dinner**
(for charity) благотвори́тельный банке́т

fundamental /fʌndə'ment(ə)l/ adj.
основно́й, суще́ственный

fundamentalism /fʌndə'mentəlɪz(ə)m/ n.
фундаментали́зм

fundamentalist /fʌndə'mentəlɪst/ n.
фундаментали́ст

funeral /'fjuːnər(ə)l/ n. по́хор|оны (-о́н)
 ■ ~ **parlour** (BrE), ~ **home** (AmE) nn.
похоро́нное бюро́

funereal /fjuː'nɪərɪəl/ adj. мра́чный; тра́урный

fungi /'fʌŋgaɪ, 'fʌndʒaɪ/ *pl. of* ▶ fungus

fungicide /'fʌndʒɪsaɪd/ *n.* фунгици́д; (med.) противогрибко́вое сре́дство, противогрибко́вый препара́т

fungus /'fʌŋgəs/ *n.* (*pl.* **fungi** *or* **funguses**) грибо́к; (ни́зший) гриб

funnel /'fʌn(ə)l/ *n.* воро́нка; (of ship) дымова́я труба́

ℱ **funny** /'fʌnɪ/ *adj.* (**funnier, funniest**)
1 (amusing) смешно́й, заба́вный **2** (strange) стра́нный; I have a ~ feeling you're right! я подозрева́ю, что вы пра́вы!

fur /fə:(r)/ *n.* **1** (animal hair) шерсть **2** (as worn) мех

furious /'fjʊərɪəs/ *adj.* **1** (violent) бу́йный, неи́стовый **2** (enraged) взбешённый; she was ~ with him она́ разозли́лась на него́ не на шу́тку

furnace /'fə:nɪs/ *n.* горн, оча́г, печь, то́пка

furnish /'fə:nɪʃ/ *v.t.* обст|авля́ть, -а́вить

furnishings /'fə:nɪʃɪŋz/ *n. pl.* обстано́вка

furniture /'fə:nɪtʃə(r)/ *n.* ме́бель

furore /fjʊə'rɔ:rɪ/ *n.* фуро́р

furrier /'fʌrɪə(r)/ *n.* меховщи́к, скорня́к

furrow /'fʌrəʊ/ *n.* **1** (in the earth etc.) борозда́, жёлоб; plough a lonely ~ (fig.) де́йствовать (*impf.*) в одино́чку **2** (wrinkle) глубо́кая морщи́на
● *v.t.* (fig.): ~ed brow намо́рщенный лоб

furry /'fə:rɪ/ *adj.* (**furrier, furriest**) покры́тый ме́хом; пушно́й

ℱ **further** /'fə:ðə(r)/ (*see also* ▶ farther) *adj.*
1 дальне́йший; (additional) доба́вочный, дополни́тельный; until ~ notice впредь до дальне́йшего уведомле́ния **2** (more distant) да́льний
● *adv.* да́лее, да́льше; I can go no ~ я не могу́ да́льше идти́
● *v.t.* продв|ига́ть, -и́нуть; соде́йствовать (*impf.*) + *d.*; спосо́бствовать (*impf.*) + *d.*
■ ~ education *n.* (BrE) дальне́йшее образова́ние (*после шко́лы, не вы́сшее*)

furtherance /'fə:ðərəns/ *n.* продвиже́ние; in ~ of this plan для осуществле́ния э́того пла́на

furthermore /'fə:ðə'mɔ:(r)/ *adv.* к тому́ же; кро́ме того́

furthest /'fə:ðɪst/ *adj.* са́мый да́льний
● *adv.* да́льше всего́

furtive /'fə:tɪv/ *adj.* скры́тный

fury /'fjʊərɪ/ *n.* я́рость

fuse¹ /fju:z/ *n.* (elec.) предохрани́тель (*m.*), про́бка
● *v.t. & i.* (BrE, elec.): he ~d the lights он пережёг про́бки; the lights ~d про́бки перегоре́ли
■ ~ box *n.* распредели́тельный щит(о́к) (с предохрани́телями/про́бками); ~ wire *n.* про́волока для предохрани́теля

fuse², fuze /fju:z/ *n.* (igniting device) запа́л, фити́ль (*m.*)

fuselage /'fju:zəlɑ:ʒ/ *n.* фюзеля́ж

fusion /'fju:ʒ(ə)n/ *n.* (blending, coalition) сплав, слия́ние

fuss /fʌs/ *n.* суета́, шум (из-за пустяко́в); make a ~ about, over sth суети́ться (*impf.*) вокру́г чего́-н.; make a ~ of sb (BrE) суетли́во опека́ть (*impf.*) кого́-н.
● *v.i.* суети́ться (*impf.*); she ~es over her children она́ ве́чно во́зится со свои́ми детьми́

fussy /'fʌsɪ/ *adj.* (**fussier, fussiest**) разбо́рчивый; I'm not ~ (about) what I eat я не привере́длив в еде́

futile /'fju:taɪl/ *adj.* напра́сный, тще́тный

futility /fju:'tɪlɪtɪ/ *n.* тще́тность, бесполе́зность

futon /'fu:tɒn/ *n.* япо́нский матра́с (*в скла́дной деревя́нной ра́ме; рассти́лается на полу́ в ка́честве крова́ти и́ли кре́сла*)

ℱ **future** /'fju:tʃə(r)/ *n.* **1** бу́дущее; in (the) ~ в бу́дущем **2** (gram.) бу́дущее вре́мя
● *adj.* бу́дущий; belief in a ~ life ве́ра в загро́бную жизнь

futuristic /fju:tʃə'rɪstɪk/ *adj.* футуристи́ческий

fuze /fju:z/ *n.* = fuse²

fuzzy /'fʌzɪ/ *adj.* (**fuzzier, fuzziest**) (fluffy) пуши́стый; (blurred) расплы́вчатый

Gg

G /dʒiː/ n. (mus.) соль (nt. indecl.)

gab /gæb/ n. (infml): **he has the gift of the ~** у него хорошо подвешен язык

gabble /ˈgæb(ə)l/ n. бормотание; (sl.) трёп, болтовня
• v.t. & i. бормотать, про-

gaberdine /gæbəˈdiːn/ n. (material) габардин; (attr.) габардиновый

gadget /ˈgædʒɪt/ n. (infml) штуковина, хитроумное приспособление; (for a computer, mobile phone, etc.) гаджет

gaffe /gæf/ n. ложный шаг, оплошность

gag /gæg/ n. **1** (to prevent speech etc.) кляп **2** (joke) шутка, хохма
• v.t. (**gagged, gagging**) вст|авлять, -авить кляп + d.; (fig.) зат|ыкать, -кнуть рот + d.
• v.i. (**gagged, gagging**) (retch) давиться (impf.)

gaga /ˈgɑːgɑː/ adj. (sl.) чокнутый, слабоумный; **go ~** впа|дать, -сть в маразм; выжива́ть, выжить из ума

gage /geɪdʒ/ n. & v.t. (AmE) = **gauge**

gaiety /ˈgeɪətɪ/ (AmE **gayety**) n. весёлость, веселье

ৎ gain /geɪn/ n. **1** (profit) прибыль **2** (increase) увеличение
• v.t. овлад|евать, -еть; доб|иваться, -иться + g.; доб|ывать, -ыть; приобре|тать, -сти; **he ~ed 5 pounds in weight** он поправился на 5 фунтов; **the patient is ~ing strength** пациент набирается сил
• v.i. **1** (reap profit, benefit, advantage) изв|лекать, -ечь пользу/выгоду; **how do I stand to ~ from it?** какая мне от этого польза/выгода? **2** (move ahead): **my watch ~s (three minutes a day)** мои часы спешат (на три минуты в день); **he ~ed on his rival** он нагонял соперника

gainful /ˈgeɪnfʊl/ adj. прибыльный; доходный; **~ employment** хорошо оплачиваемая работа

galaxy /ˈgæləksɪ/ n. галактика; (**the G~**) Галактика

gale /geɪl/ n. буря

gallant /ˈgælənt/ adj. **1** (attentive to ladies) галантный **2** (brave) доблестный

gallery /ˈgælərɪ/ n. **1** (walk, passage) галерея **2** (picture **~**) картинная галерея **3** (theatr.) балкон

galley /ˈgælɪ/ n. (pl. **~s**) **1** (ship) галера **2** (ship's kitchen) камбуз; (in aircraft) кухня на борту самолёта

■ **~ slave** n. раб на галерах

Gallic /ˈgælɪk/ adj. (Gaulish) галльский; (French) французский

galling /ˈgɔːlɪŋ/ adj. (fig.) раздражающий

gallivant /ˈgælɪvænt/ v.i. (infml) шляться (impf.); слоняться (impf.)

gallon /ˈgælən/ n. галлон

gallop /ˈgæləp/ n. галоп
• v.i. скакать (impf.) (галопом); (fig.): **we ~ed through our work** мы в спешке закончили (нашу/свою) работу

gallows /ˈgæləʊz/ n. pl. виселица; **send sb to the ~** отправить (pf.) кого-н. на виселицу
■ **~ humour**, (AmE) **humor** n. юмор висельника

galore /gəˈlɔː(r)/ adv. (infml) в изобилии, сколько угодно

galvanize /ˈgælvənaɪz/ v.t. оцинков|ывать, -ать; (fig.) побу|ждать, -дить

Gambia /ˈgæmbɪə/ n. Гамбия

gamble /ˈgæmb(ə)l/ n. азартная игра; (risky undertaking) рискованное предприятие
• v.t. & i. играть (impf.) в азартные игры; **~ away a fortune** проиграть (pf.) состояние

gambler /ˈgæmblə(r)/ n. игрок; картёжник

gambling /ˈgæmblɪŋ/ n. азартные игры (f. pl.)

ৎ game /geɪm/ n. **1** игра; **we had a ~ of golf** мы сыграли партию в гольф **2** (plan, trick) игра; **he gave the ~ away** он раскрыл свои карты **3** (hunted animal) дичь; зверь (m.)
■ **~keeper** n. охраняющий дичь егерь; **~ plan** n. стратегия; **~ reserve** n. охотничий заказник/заповедник; **~s console** n. игровая консоль, игровая приставка; **~ show** n. телеигра, игровое шоу (indecl.)

gammon /ˈgæmən/ n. (BrE) окорок

gamut /ˈgæmət/ n. (mus.) гамма; (fig.) диапазон, гамма; **she ran the ~ of the emotions** она передала всю гамму чувств

gang /gæŋ/ n. (of workmen) бригада; (of prisoners) партия (заключённых); (of criminals) шайка, банда
• v.i.: **they ~ed up on me** они ополчились против/на меня
■ **~land** n. преступный мир; **~master** n. (BrE) бригадир; **~way** n. (from ship to shore or aircraft to ground) трап

gangrene /ˈgæŋgriːn/ n. гангрена

gangster /ˈgæŋstə(r)/ n. бандит

gannet /ˈgænɪt/ n. (bird) олуша; (BrE, fig., glutton) обжора

gantry /ˈgæntrɪ/ n. помост
■ **~ crane** n. эстакадный кран

ৎ ключевая лексика

gap /gæp/ n. (in a wall etc.) брешь, пролóм; (in conversation) пáуза; (of 5 years etc.) перерьíв; (between rich and poor, theory and practice) разрьíв; (in application form, sb's knowledge) пробéл

■ ~ **year** n. (BrE) год пéред поступлéнием в университéт (*котóрый выпускникá шкóлы проводит рабóтая или путешéствуя*)

gap|e /geɪp/ v.i. (stare) зевáть (*impf.*) (по сторонáм); a ~ing wound зияющая рáна; the chasm ~ed before him пéред ним зияла прóпасть

garage /'gæra:dʒ/ n. (for keeping a car) гарáж; (where petrol is sold) бензозапрáвочная стáнция; (for repairing cars) автосéрвис

garbage /'ga:bɪdʒ/ n. (AmE, rubbish) мýсор (also fig.); хлам; (nonsense) чепухá, вздор

■ ~ **can** n. (AmE, outside) мýсорный бак; (in kitchen) мýсорное ведрó; ~ **dump** n. свáлка; ~ **truck** n. (AmE) мусоровóз

garble /'ga:b(ə)l/ v.t. (distort) искажáть, -зить

garden /'ga:d(ə)n/ n. **1** (plot of ground) сад; vegetable **2** (attr.) садóвый • v.i. занимáться (*impf.*) садовóдством

■ ~ **centre**, (AmE) **center** n. садóвый центр; ~ **party** n. свéтский приём на открьíтом вóздухе

gardener /'ga:dnə(r)/ n. садóвник

gargle /'ga:g(ə)l/ v.i. полоскáть, про- гóрло

garish /'geərɪʃ/ adj. пёстрый

garland /'ga:lənd/ n. гирлянда

garlic /'ga:lɪk/ n. чеснóк

garment /'ga:mənt/ n. предмéт одéжды

garnish /'ga:nɪʃ/ n. (cul.) гарнир • v.t. (cul.) подавáть, áть (*что с чем*)

garret /'gærɪt/ n. мансáрда; чердáк

garrison /'gærɪs(ə)n/ n. гарнизóн

garter /'ga:tə(r)/ n. подвязка

■ ~ **belt** n. (AmE) пóяс с подвязками

gas /gæs/ n. (pl. ~es) **1** газ **2** (attr.) гáзовый **3** (AmE, petrol) бензин, горючее • v.t. (**gases, gassed, gassing**) умер|щвлять, -твить, -твить гáзом

■ ~ **cooker** n. (BrE) гáзовая плитá; ~ **fire** n. (BrE) гáзовый камин; ~ **mask** n. противогáз; ~ **oven** n. (domestic) гáзовая духóвка; ~ **station** n. (AmE) бензозапрáвочная стáнция

gash /gæʃ/ n. разрéз • v.t. разрéз|áть, -ать

gasoline, gasolene /'gæsəli:n/ n. газолин; (AmE, petrol) бензин

gasp /ga:sp/ n. глотóк вóздуха; at one's last ~ при послéднем издыхáнии • v.i. зад|ыхáться, -охнýться; he was ~ing for breath он задыхáлся; he ~ed with astonishment он открьíл рот от удивлéния

gastric /'gæstrɪk/ adj. желýдочный

■ ~ **band** n. желýдочный бандáж; ~ **juice** n. желýдочный сок; ~ **ulcer** n. язва желýдка

gastroenteritis /ˌgæstrəʊentə'raɪtɪs/ n. гастроэнтерит

gastronomic /ˌgæstrə'nɒmɪk/ adj. гастрономический

gastronomy /gæ'strɒnəmɪ/ n. гастронóмия

gate /geɪt/ n. ворóта (-óт); (city ~) городскиé ворóта; (at airport) вьíход

■ ~**crash** v.t. & i. при|ходить, -йти (на вечеринку и т. п.) без приглашéния; ~**crasher** n. незвáный гость

gateau /'gætəʊ/ n. (pl. ~s or ~x /-əʊz/) (BrE) торт

gather /'gæðə(r)/ n. (in cloth) сбóрки (f. pl.) • v.t. **1** (pick, e.g. flowers, harvest) (also ~ in) соб|ирáть, -рáть **2** (collect) (also ~ up) соб|ирáть, -рáть **3** (understand) заключ|áть, -ить; I ~ he's abroad он как бýдто за границей **4** (pull together): ~ one's thoughts, wits соб|ирáться, -рáться с мьíслями **5** (sewing) соб|ирáть, -рáть в склáдки • v.i. соб|ирáться, -рáться; a crowd ~ed собралáсь толпá

gathering /'gæðərɪŋ/ n. собрáние

gaudy /'gɔ:dɪ/ adj. (**gaudier, gaudiest**) кричáщий

gauge /geɪdʒ/ (AmE **gage**) n. **1** (thickness, diameter, etc.) размéр; (rail.): standard ~ стандáртная колея **2** (instrument) шаблóн • v.t. **1** (measure) изм|ерять, -éрить **2** (fig., estimate) оцéн|ивать, -ить

gaunt /gɔ:nt/ adj. (person) исхудáлый

gauntlet /'gɔ:ntlɪt/ n. рукавица; (armoured glove) лáтная рукавица; throw down the ~ (fig.) брóсить (*pf.*) перчáтку/вьíзов; pick up the ~ принять (*pf.*) вьíзов

gauze /gɔ:z/ n. мáрля, газ

gave /geɪv/ past of ► **give**

gawk /gɔ:k/ v.i. = **gawp**

gawp /gɔ:p/ v.i. (BrE) глазéть (*impf.*); пялить (*impf.*) глазá (at: на + a.)

gay /geɪ/ adj. (**gayer, gayest**) весёлый; (infml, homosexual) гомосексуáльный, голубóй • n. (infml, homosexual) гей, гомосексуалист

■ ~ **marriage** n. (infml) однопóлый граждáнский брак

gayety /'geɪətɪ/ n. (AmE) = **gaiety**

gaze /geɪz/ n. пристальный взгляд • v.i. пристально глядéть

gazebo /gə'zi:bəʊ/ n. (pl. ~s or ~es) бельведéр

gazelle /gə'zel/ n. газéль

GB abbr. (of **Great Britain**) Великобритáния

GBH (BrE, law) abbr. (of **grievous bodily harm**) тяжёлые телéсные поврежéния

GCSE (BrE) abbr. (of **General Certificate of Secondary Education**) ≈ аттестáт о непóлном срéднем образовáнии

GDP abbr. (of **gross domestic product**) ВВП (валовóй внýтренний продýкт)

gear /gɪə(r)/ n. **1** (equipment, clothing) принадлéжности (f. pl.); аксессуáры (m. pl.); одéжда; hunting ~ охóтничье снаряжéние **2** (of car etc.) зубчáтая передáча; change ~ переключáть, -ить передáчу; the car is in ~ машина на передáче • v.t.: ~ up готóвить (*impf.*); пригот|áвливать, -óвить

■ ~**box** n. корóбка передáч; ~ **lever** n. (BrE)

рыча́г переключе́ния переда́ч/скоросте́й; ~ **shift** *n.* (AmE) = gear lever

geek /giːk/ *n.* (infml) (computer etc. enthusiast) челове́к, увлечённый компью́терными техноло́гиями и т. п.; (socially inept person) социа́льно нело́вкий челове́к

geese /giːs/ *pl. of* ► **goose**

gel /dʒel/ *n.* гель (*m.*)

gelateria /dʒelæˈtɪərɪə/ *n.* кафе́-моро́женое

gelatine /ˈdʒelətiːn/ *n.* желати́н

gem /dʒem/ *n.* драгоце́нный ка́мень

Gemini /ˈdʒemɪnaɪ/ *n.* Близнецы́ (*m. pl.*)

gender /ˈdʒendə(r)/ *n.* (sex) пол; (gram.) род
■ ~ **reassignment** *n.* опера́ция по измене́нию по́ла

✍ **gene** /dʒiːn/ *n.* ген
■ ~ **therapy** *n.* ге́нная терапи́я

genealogical /dʒiːnɪəˈlɒdʒɪk(ə)l/ *adj.* родосло́вный; генеалоги́ческий

genealogist /dʒiːnɪˈælədʒɪst/ *n.* специали́ст по генеало́гии

genealogy /dʒiːnɪˈælədʒɪ/ *n.* генеало́гия

genera /ˈdʒenərə/ *pl. of* ► **genus**

✍ **general** /ˈdʒenər(ə)l/ *n.* генера́л
• *adj.* **1** (universal or nearly so) о́бщий; генера́льный **2** (usual) обы́чный; ~ **opinion** о́бщее мне́ние; **in** ~ вообще́
■ ~ **election** *n.* всео́бщие вы́боры; ~ **knowledge** *n.* о́бщие зна́ния; ~ **practitioner** *n.* участко́вый врач; терапе́вт; ~ **strike** *n.* всео́бщая забасто́вка

generalization /dʒenərəlaɪˈzeɪʃ(ə)n/ *n.* обобще́ние

generalize /ˈdʒenərəlaɪz/ *v.i.* обобщённо говори́ть (*impf.*)

✍ **generally** /ˈdʒenərəlɪ/ *adv.* **1** (usually) обы́чно **2** (widely) широко́ **3** (approximately) вообще́; ~ **speaking** вообще́ говоря́

✍ **generate** /ˈdʒenəreɪt/ *v.t.* порожда́ть, -ди́ть; ~ **heat** выделя́ть (*impf.*) тепло́; ~ **hatred** вызыва́ть (*impf.*) не́нависть

✍ **generation** /dʒenəˈreɪʃ(ə)n/ *n.* **1** (of heat etc.) генера́ция **2** (of people) поколе́ние; **the** ~ **gap** пробле́ма отцо́в и дете́й

generator /ˈdʒenəreɪtə(r)/ *n.* генера́тор

generic /dʒɪˈnerɪk/ *adj.* (of a class) родово́й; (general) о́бщий; (of drug) непатенто́ванный, о́бщего ти́па

generosity /dʒenəˈrɒsɪtɪ/ *n.* великоду́шие

generous /ˈdʒenərəs/ *adj.* **1** (liberal) ще́дрый **2** (plentiful) оби́льный

genesis /ˈdʒenɪsɪs/ *n.* ге́незис; возникнове́ние; **(Book of) G**~ кни́га Бытия́

genetic /dʒɪˈnetɪk/ *adj.* генети́ческий
■ ~**ally modified** *adj.* генети́чески модифици́рованный; ~ **engineering** *n.* ге́нная инжене́рия; ~ **fingerprinting** *n.* ге́нная дактилоскопи́я; ~ **modification** *n.* генети́ческая модифика́ция; ~ **profiling** *n.* генети́ческое профили́рование; ~ **screening** *n.* генети́ческий скри́нинг

geneticist /dʒɪˈnetɪsɪst/ *n.* гене́тик

genetics /dʒɪˈnetɪks/ *n.* гене́тика

genial /ˈdʒiːnɪəl/ *adj.* серде́чный

geniality /dʒiːnɪˈælɪtɪ/ *n.* раду́шие; доброду́шие

genie /ˈdʒiːnɪ/ *n.* джинн, дух

genital /ˈdʒenɪt(ə)l/ *adj.* полово́й; (*in pl.*) половы́е о́рганы (*m. pl.*), генита́лии (*f. pl.*)

genitive /ˈdʒenɪtɪv/ *n. & adj.* роди́тельный (паде́ж)

genius /ˈdʒiːnɪəs/ *n.* ге́ний

genocide /ˈdʒenəsaɪd/ *n.* геноци́д

genome /ˈdʒiːnəʊm/ *n.* гено́м

genre /ˈʒɑːrə/ *n.* жанр

genteel /dʒenˈtiːl/ *adj.* благовоспи́танный; «благоро́дный»; с аристократи́ческими зама́шками

Gentile /ˈdʒentaɪl/ *n.* невре́й
• *adj.* невре́йский

gentle /ˈdʒent(ə)l/ *adj.* (**gentler**, **gentlest**) мя́гкий, ти́хий, делика́тный; a ~ **slope** поло́гий склон; a ~ **breeze** лёгкий ветеро́к; a ~ **hint** то́нкий намёк

gentleman /ˈdʒent(ə)lmən/ *n.* джентльме́н

gently /ˈdʒentlɪ/ *adv.* мя́гко; делика́тно

gentry /ˈdʒentrɪ/ *n.* нетитуло́ванное дворя́нство

Gents /dʒent/ *n.* (**the** ~) (*sg.*) (BrE, lavatory) мужско́й туале́т

genuine /ˈdʒenjʊɪn/ *adj.* настоя́щий; по́длинный; ~ **sorrow** и́скренняя печа́ль; a ~ **person** прямо́й/и́скренний челове́к

genus /ˈdʒiːnəs/ *n.* (*pl.* **genera**) род

geographer /dʒɪˈɒɡrəfə(r)/ *n.* гео́граф

geographical /dʒiːəˈɡræfɪk(ə)l/, **geographic** /dʒiːəˈɡræfɪk/ *adjs.* географи́ческий

geography /dʒɪˈɒɡrəfɪ/ *n.* геогра́фия

geological /dʒiːəˈlɒdʒɪk(ə)l/ *adj.* геологи́ческий

geologist /dʒɪˈɒlədʒɪst/ *n.* гео́лог

geology /dʒɪˈɒlədʒɪ/ *n.* геоло́гия

geometric /dʒiːəˈmetrɪk/, **geometrical** /dʒiːəˈmetrɪkəl/ *adjs.* геометри́ческий

geometry /dʒɪˈɒmɪtrɪ/ *n.* геоме́трия

geopolitical /dʒiːəʊpəˈlɪtɪk(ə)l/ *adj.* геополити́ческий

Georgia /ˈdʒɔːdʒɪə/ *n.* (in Caucasus) Гру́зия

Georgian /ˈdʒɔːdʒ(ə)n/ *n.* грузи́н (-ка)
• *adj.* грузи́нский

geranium /dʒəˈreɪnɪəm/ *n.* гера́нь

geriatric /dʒerɪˈætrɪk/ *adj.* гериатри́ческий

geriatrics /dʒerɪˈætrɪks/ *n.* гериатри́я

germ /dʒɜːm/ *n.* микро́б, бакте́рия; (fig.) зача́ток
■ ~ **warfare** *n.* бактериологи́ческая война́

✍ **German** /ˈdʒɜːmən/ *n.* **1** (person) не́м|ец (-ка) **2** (language) неме́цкий язы́к
• *adj.* неме́цкий; (esp. pol.) герма́нский
■ ~ **measles** *n. pl.* красну́ха; ~ **shepherd (dog)** *n.* неме́цкая овча́рка

germane /dʒɜːˈmeɪn/ *adj.* уме́стный; подходя́щий

Germanic /dʒɜ:'mænɪk/ *adj.* германский
Germany /'dʒɜ:mənɪ/ *n.* Германия
germinate /'dʒɜ:mɪneɪt/ *v.i.* прораст|а́ть, -и́
germination /dʒɜ:mɪ'neɪʃ(ə)n/ *n.*
прораста́ние; (fig.) зарожде́ние; разви́тие
gerontology /dʒerən'tɒlədʒɪ/ *n.*
геронтоло́гия
gerund /'dʒerənd/ *n.* геру́ндий
gestation /dʒe'steɪʃ(ə)n/ *n.* бере́менность;
(fig.) созрева́ние
gesticulate /dʒe'stɪkjʊleɪt/ *v.i.*
жестикули́ровать (*impf.*)
gesture /'dʒestʃə(r)/ *n.* жест
  ● *v.i.* жестикули́ровать (*impf.*)

✍ **get** /get/ *v.t.* (**getting**, *past* **got**, *p.p.* **got** or
AmE **gotten**) **1** (obtain, receive) получ|а́ть,
-и́ть; **I've got it!** (answer to problem, etc.) эврика!;
I ~ you (infml, understand) по́нял!; **this room ~s
a lot of sun** э́та ко́мната о́чень со́лнечная;
I got (sc. *bought*) **a new suit** я приобрёл/
купи́л но́вый костю́м **2** (of suffering, etc.):
he got 2 years (sentence) он получи́л 2 го́да
(тюрьмы́); **he got the measles** он заболе́л
ко́рью; **he got a blow on the head** он
получи́л уда́р по голове́; **she got her feet
wet** она́ промочи́ла но́ги **3** (fetch, lay hands on)
дост|ава́ть, -а́ть; доб|ыва́ть, -ы́ть; **I got him a
chair** я принёс ему́ стул; **~ me the manager!**
позови́те мне заве́дующего! **4** (bring into
a position or state): **we got him home** мы
доста́вили его́ домо́й; **we got the piano
through the door** мы пронесли́ пиани́но
че́рез дверь **5** (p.p., expr. possession): **he has
got a book** у него́ есть кни́га **6** (p.p., expr.
obligation): **I have got to go** я до́лжен идти́
7 (persuade) заст|авля́ть, -а́вить; **I got him to
tell me everything** я заста́вил его́ рассказа́ть
мне всё; **I got the fire to burn** мне удало́сь
разже́чь ого́нь **8** (cause sth to be done):
I got my hair cut я постри́гся **9** (denoting
progress or achievement): **I got to know him** я
познако́мился с ним бли́же; **I got to like
travelling** я полюби́л путеше́ствия; **he got to
be manager** он стал дире́ктором
  ● *v.i.* (**getting**, *past* **got**, *p.p.* **got** or AmE
gotten) **1** (become, be) ста|нови́ться, -ть;
he got red in the face он покрасне́л; **he
got angry** он разозли́лся; **he got drunk** он
напи́лся; **he got married** он жени́лся; **he
got ready** он пригото́вился; **he got killed**
его́ уби́ли; он поги́б; **we got talking** мы
разговори́лись **2** (arrive) приб|ыва́ть,
-ы́ть; **when did you ~ here?** когда́ вы сюда́
при́были? **where has my book got to?** куда́
де́лась/дева́лась моя́ кни́га?
  ● *with preps.*: **the officer got his troops across
the river** офице́р перепра́вил свои́ войска́
че́рез ре́ку; **I cannot ~ at the books** я не
могу́ добра́ться до э́тих книг; **we must
~ at the truth** мы должны́ добра́ться до
и́стины; **what is he ~ting at?** (trying to say) что
он хо́чет сказа́ть?; куда́ он кло́нит?; **she is
always ~ting at me** (BrE, criticizing) она́ всегда́
ко мне придира́ется; **he got in(to) the taxi** он
сел в такси́; **I cannot ~ into these shoes** я не

могу́ влезть в э́ти ту́фли; **he got into the club**
его́ при́няли в клуб; **he got off his horse** он
соскочи́л с коня́; **he got on his bicycle** он сел
на велосипе́д; **the lion got out of its cage** лев
вы́скочил из кле́тки; **I got out of going to the
party** я отверте́лся/уклони́лся от вечери́нки;
I got £6 out of him я вы́жал из него́ 6
фу́нтов; **we got over the wall** мы переле́зли
че́рез сте́ну; **I cannot ~ over his rudeness**
я не могу́ прийти́ в себя́ от его́ гру́бости;
we got round the difficulty мы спра́вились
с э́той пробле́мой; **she got round him** ей
удало́сь его́ уговори́ть/провести́; **I got
through the work** я проде́лал всю рабо́ту;
he got through his exam он сдал экза́мен;
we got to Paris by noon мы добра́лись до
Пари́жа к полу́дню; **the children got up to
mischief** (BrE) де́ти расшали́лись; **we got up
to chapter 5** мы дошли́ до 5-й (пя́той) главы́
  □ **~ about** *v.i.*: **he ~s about a great deal** он
постоя́нно в разъе́здах; **a car makes it easier to
~ about** с маши́ной ле́гче поспева́ть всю́ду
  □ **~ across** *v.t.*: **the speaker got his point across**
выступа́ющий чётко изложи́л свою́ то́чку
зре́ния
  □ **~ along** *v.i.*: **they ~ along** (sc. *be agreeable to
each other*) **very well** они́ отли́чно ла́дят
  □ **~ around** *v.i.* = get about, get round
  □ **~ away** *v.i.*: **the prisoner got away**
заключённый бежа́л; **he got away with
cheating** ему́ удало́сь сжу́льничать
  □ **~ back** *v.t.*: **he got his books back** он получи́л
обра́тно/наза́д свои́ кни́ги
    ● *v.i.*: **he got back from the country** он
верну́лся из дере́вни
  □ **~ by** *v.i.*: **please let me ~ by** (pass) разреши́те
мне пройти́, пожа́луйста
  □ **~ down** *v.t.*: **he got a book down from the
shelf** он снял кни́гу с по́лки
    ● *v.i.*: **he got down from his horse** он
соскочи́л/слез с коня́; **he got down to his
work** он засе́л за рабо́ту
  □ **~ in** *v.i.*: **the burglar got in through the
window** вор прони́к в дом че́рез окно́; **the
train got in early** по́езд пришёл ра́но; **we
didn't ~ in to the concert** мы не попа́ли на
конце́рт; **he got in** (sc. *was elected*) **for Chester**
он прошёл на вы́борах в Че́стере
  □ **~ off** *v.t.* (remove) сн|има́ть, -я́ть; **his lawyer
got him off** (acquitted) адвока́т доби́лся его́
оправда́ния
    ● *v.i.*: **he got off at the next station** он сошёл
(с по́езда) на сле́дующей ста́нции; **I got off
(to sleep) early** я ра́но засну́л; **we got off
(sc. *started*) at 9 a.m.** мы вы́шли/вы́ехали/
отпра́вились в 9 часо́в; **he got off with a fine**
он отде́лался штра́фом
  □ **~ on** *v.t.*: **~ your clothes on!** оде́ньтесь!
    ● *v.i.*: **how are you ~ting on?** как дела́?; **she
is ~ting on** (BrE) (making progress) она́ де́лает
успе́хи; (growing old) она́ старе́ет; **~ting on
for** (nearly) почти́; **~ting on with your work!**
займи́тесь свое́й рабо́той!; **they ~ on** (well)
together (BrE) они́ ла́дят ме́жду собо́й
  □ **~ out** *v.t.*: **he got out his spectacles** он вы́нул
очки́; **they got the book out** (published) они́
изда́ли/вы́пустили кни́гу

g

● *v.i.*: ~ out! убира́йтесь!; the secret got out секре́т стал изве́стен

□ ~ **round** *v.i.*: I haven't got round to writing to him я ника́к не соберу́сь написа́ть ему́

□ ~ **through** *v.t.* (an exam) выде́рживать, вы́держать экза́мен

□ ~ **together** *v.t.*: he got an army together он собра́л а́рмию

● *v.i.*: we must ~ together and have a talk мы должны́ встре́титься и поговори́ть

□ ~ **up** *v.t.*: they got me up at 7 они́ по́дняли меня́ в 7 часо́в

● *v.i.* (from bed, chair, etc.) встава́ть, -ть; the wind/sea is ~ting up поднима́ется ве́тер; мо́ре начина́ет волнова́ться

■ ~**together** *n.* (meeting, gathering) встре́ча, сбо́рище

Ghana /'gɑːnə/ *n.* Га́на

Ghanaian /gɑːˈneɪən/ *n.* га́н|ец (-ка)

● *adj.* га́нский

ghastly /'gɑːstlɪ/ *adj.* (**ghastlier, ghastliest**) ужа́сный

gherkin /'gɜːkɪn/ *n.* корнишо́н

ghetto /'getəʊ/ *n.* (*pl.* ~**s** *or* ~**es**) ге́тто (*nt. indecl.*)

■ ~ **blaster** *n.* (infml) переносно́й магнитофо́н, магнито́ла

ghost /gəʊst/ *n.* привиде́ние; дух

ghostly /'gəʊstlɪ/ *adj.* (**ghostlier, ghostliest**) похо́жий на привиде́ние

GI *abbr.* (*of* **government issue**) (American soldier) (америка́нский) солда́т

giant /'dʒaɪənt/ *n.* гига́нт

gibber /'dʒɪbə(r)/ *v.i.* тарато́рить (*impf.*); говори́ть (*impf.*) невня́тно; лопота́ть (*impf.*) (infml)

gibberish /'dʒɪbərɪʃ/ *n.* тараба́рщина

gibbon /'gɪbən/ *n.* гиббо́н

giblets /'dʒɪblɪts/ *n. pl.* потрох|а́ (-о́в)

Gibraltar /dʒɪˈbrɔːltə/ *n.* Гибралта́р

giddy /'gɪdɪ/ *adj.* (**giddier, giddiest**) головокружи́тельный; I feel ~ у меня́ кру́жится голова́

♂ **gift** /gɪft/ *n.* **1** (thing given) пода́рок **2** (talent) дарова́ние; дар; he has a ~ for languages у него́ спосо́бности *(f. pl.)* /тала́нт к языка́м

■ ~ **shop** *n.* магази́н пода́рков; ~ **voucher** (BrE), ~ **token** (BrE), ~ **certificate** (AmE) *n.* пода́рочный тало́н/ купо́н

gifted /'gɪftɪd/ *adj.* одарённый

gig[1] /gɪg/ *n.* (infml, performance) выступле́ние, конце́рт

gig[2] /gɪg/ *n.* (*abbr. of* **gigabyte**) (comput., infml) гиг

giga- /'gɪgə/ *comb. form* гига...

■ ~**byte** *n.* гигаба́йт; ~**watt** *n.* гигава́тт

gigantic /dʒaɪˈgæntɪk/ *adj.* гига́нтский

giggle /'gɪg(ə)l/ *n.* хихи́канье

● *v.i.* хихи́к|ать, -нуть

gilt /gɪlt/ *n.* позоло́та

♂ ключева́я ле́ксика

gimmick /'gɪmɪk/ *n.* трюк

gin /dʒɪn/ *n.* джин; ~ and tonic джин-то́ник

ginger /'dʒɪndʒə(r)/ *n.* (bot., cul.) имби́рь (*m.*); *(attr.)* имби́рный

gingerly /'dʒɪndʒəlɪ/ *adj.* (кра́йне) осторо́жный

● *adv.* осторо́жно

Gipsy, Gypsy /'dʒɪpsɪ/ *n.* цыга́н (-ка)

● *adj.* цыга́нский

giraffe /dʒɪˈrɑːf/ *n.* (*pl.* ~ *or* ~**s**) жира́ф

girder /'gɜːdə(r)/ *n.* (beam) ба́лка

girdle /'gɜːd(ə)l/ *n.* **1** (belt etc.) по́яс; куша́к **2** (corset) корсе́т

♂ **girl** /gɜːl/ *n.* (child) де́вочка; (young woman) де́вушка; (pej.) девчо́нка

■ ~**friend** *n.* (female friend) подру́га; (female sexual partner) де́вушка; **G~ Guide** (also **G~ Scout**) *n.* де́вочка-ска́ут, гёрлска́ут

girlish /'gɜːlɪʃ/ *adj.* деви́ческий; (of a boy) изне́женный, (infml) как девчо́нка

girth /gɜːθ/ *n.* (of horse) подпру́га; (of tree, person, etc.) обхва́т; разме́р

gist /dʒɪst/ *n.* суть

♂ **give** /gɪv/ *n.* **1** (elasticity) пода́тливость, эласти́чность **2**: ~ and take взаи́мные усту́пки *(f. pl.)*

● *v.t.* (*past* **gave**, *p.p.* **given** /'gɪv(ə)n/)
1 да|ва́ть, -ть; I gave the porter my luggage я о́тдал свой бага́ж носи́льщику; two years, ~ or take a month or so о́коло двух лет — ме́сяцем бо́льше и́ли ме́ньше **2** (as a present) дари́ть, по-; he was ~ n a book ему́ подари́ли кни́гу **3** (~ in exchange): I gave a good price for it я за э́то хорошо́ заплати́л; he gave as good as he got он отплати́л той же моне́той **4** (provide, inflict): he ~s me a lot of trouble он доставля́ет мне мно́го хлопо́т; he has ~ n me his cold я зарази́лся от него́ на́сморком; he gave (*sc. cited*) an example (cited) он привёл приме́р; ~ him my regards переда́йте ему́ приве́т от меня́; ~ pleasure дост|авля́ть, -а́вить удово́льствие **5** (devote) уделя́ть, -и́ть; посвя|ща́ть, -ти́ть; he gave a lot of time to the work он удели́л э́той рабо́те мно́го вре́мени; he gave his life for her он о́тдал за неё жизнь **6** (allow): I ~ you an hour to get ready я даю́ вам час на сбо́ры/ приготовле́ния **7** (organize) устр|а́ивать, -о́ить; they gave a dance они́ устро́или танцева́льный ве́чер **8** (special uses of given): at a ~n (*sc. specified, agreed, particular*) time в определённое вре́мя; he is ~ n to boasting он скло́нен к хвастовству́; ~n that ... при том, что...

● *v.i.* (*past* **gave**, *p.p.* **given** /'gɪv(ə)n/) (yield) подд|ава́ться, -а́ться; под|ава́ться, -а́ться

□ ~ **away** *v.t.* дари́ть, по-; he gave away the secret он вы́дал секре́т; he gave the game away (revealed a secret) он проболта́лся; он вы́дал секре́т

□ ~ **back** *v.t.* (restore) возвра|ща́ть, -ти́ть

□ ~ **in** *v.t.* (submit): he gave in his exam paper (BrE) он сдал свою́ экзаменацио́нную рабо́ту

● *v.i.* (yield) подд|ава́ться, -а́ться; уступ|а́ть, -и́ть; he gave in to my persuasion он подда́лся мои́м угово́рам

□ **~ off** *v.t.* (emit) испус|ка́ть, -ти́ть; изд|ава́ть, -а́ть

□ **~ out** *v.t.* (distribute) распредел|я́ть, -и́ть
● *v.i.* конча́ться, ко́нчиться; **his strength gave out** его́ си́лы исся́кли

□ **~ up** *v.t.* ост|авля́ть, -а́вить; (resign, surrender) отка́з|ываться, -а́ться + *g.*; **he gave up his seat to her** он уступи́л ей ме́сто; **the murderer gave himself up** уби́йца сда́лся; (desist from) бр|оса́ть, -о́сить; **he gave up smoking** он бро́сил кури́ть; (abandon hope of): **they gave him up for lost** они́ реши́ли, что он пропа́л; **we gave it up as a bad job** мы махну́ли руко́й на э́то де́ло
● *v.i.*: **I ~ up!** сдаю́сь!

■ **~away** *n.* (infml, betrayal of secret etc.): **her tears were a ~away** слёзы выдава́ли её; **~n name** *n.* (forename) и́мя (*nt.*)

glacier /'glæsɪə(r)/ *n.* ледни́к

glad /glæd/ *adj.* (**gladder, gladdest**) дово́льный; **I am ~ to meet you** рад с ва́ми познако́миться

gladden /'glæd(ə)n/ *v.t.* ра́довать, об-; **flowers ~ the scene** цветы́ оживля́ют вид; **wine ~s the heart** вино́ весели́т ду́шу

gladiator /'glædɪeɪtə(r)/ *n.* гладиа́тор

gladio|lus /glædɪ'əʊləs/ *n.* (*pl.* **~li** /-laɪ/ *or* **~luses**) гладио́лус

gladly /'glædlɪ/ *adv.* охо́тно

glamor /'glæmə(r)/ *n.* (AmE) = **glamour**

glamorize, glamourize /'glæməraɪz/ *v.t.* приукра́|шивать, -сить

glamorous /'glæmərəs/ *adj.* обольсти́тельный; (of job etc.) зама́нчивый

glamour /'glæmə(r)/ (AmE **glamor**) *n.* волшебство́

glanc|e /glɑːns/ *n.* взгляд
● *v.t. & i.* **1** (look) взгляну́ть (*pf.*); **he ~ed at the clock** он взгляну́л на часы́; **he ~ed round the room** он огляде́л ко́мнату **2** (bounce) отск|а́кивать, -очи́ть; **a ~ing blow** скользя́щий уда́р

gland /glænd/ *n.* железа́

glandular /'glændjʊlə(r)/ *adj.*: **~ fever** воспале́ние гланд

glare /gleə(r)/ *n.* (fierce light) ослепи́тельный свет/блеск; (angry look) свире́пый взгляд
● *v.i.*: **~ at sb** испепел|я́ть, -и́ть кого́-н. взгля́дом

glaring /'gleərɪŋ/ *adj.* (e.g. headlights) слепя́щий; (of mistake etc.) гру́бый

✑ **glass** /glɑːs/ *n.* **1** (substance) стекло́ **2** (for drinking) (tumbler) стака́н; (wine ~) рю́мка, бока́л **3** (~ware) стекля́нная посу́да **4** (BrE, mirror) зе́ркало **5** (*in pl.*) (spectacles) очк|и́ (-о́в)

glaucoma /glɔː'kəʊmə/ *n.* глауко́ма

glaze /gleɪz/ *n.* глазу́рь
● *v.t.* (pottery) покр|ыва́ть, -ы́ть глазу́рью

gleam /gliːm/ *n.* про́блеск
● *v.i.* поблёскивать (*impf.*)

glean /gliːn/ *v.t.* (information) соб|ира́ть, -ра́ть

glee /gliː/ *n.* (delight) весе́лье; ликова́ние

gleeful /'gliːfʊl/ *adj.* лику́ющий

glen /glen/ *n.* лощи́на

glib /glɪb/ *adj.* (**glibber, glibbest**) бо́йкий на язы́к; **a ~ excuse** благови́дный предло́г

glide /glaɪd/ *v.i.* скольз|и́ть, -ну́ть; (in aircraft) плани́ровать, с-

glider /'glaɪdə(r)/ *n.* пла́нер

gliding /'glaɪdɪŋ/ *n.* (sport) планери́зм

glimmer /'glɪmə(r)/ *n.*: **a ~ of hope** про́блеск/луч наде́жды

glimpse /glɪmps/ *n.* про́блеск; **I caught a ~ of him** он промелькну́л у меня́ пе́ред глаза́ми
● *v.t.* уви́деть (*pf.*) ме́льком

glint /glɪnt/ *n.* блеск; (reflection) о́тблеск
● *v.i.* блесте́ть (*impf.*); (flash) вспы́х|ивать, -нуть

glisten /'glɪs(ə)n/ *v.i.* сверк|а́ть, -ну́ть

glitch /glɪtʃ/ *n.* небольшо́е затрудне́ние

glitter /'glɪtə(r)/ *n.* блеск, сверка́ние
● *v.i.* блесте́ть (*impf.*); сверка́ть (*impf.*)

glitz /glɪts/ *n.* (показно́й) блеск, лоск, шик

glitzy /'glɪtsɪ/ *adj.* (**glitzier, glitziest**) гламу́рный

gloat /gləʊt/ *v.i.* злора́дствовать (*impf.*)

✑ **global** /'gləʊb(ə)l/ *adj.* (total) всео́бщий; (worldwide) глоба́льный
■ **~ warming** *n.* глоба́льное потепле́ние

globalization /gləʊbəlaɪ'zeɪʃ(ə)n/ *n.* глобализа́ция

globe /gləʊb/ *n.* шар
■ **~trotter** *n.* зая́длый тури́ст

globule /'glɒbjuːl/ *n.* ша́рик; ка́пелька

gloom /gluːm/ *n.* (dark) тьма; (despondency) мра́чность

gloomy /'gluːmɪ/ *adj.* (**gloomier, gloomiest**) (dark) мра́чный; (depressing) гнету́щий; (depressed) хму́рый; уны́лый

glorify /'glɔːrɪfaɪ/ *v.t.* просл|авля́ть, -а́вить

glorious /'glɔːrɪəs/ *adj.* сла́вный, великоле́пный; **a ~ day** (weather) изуми́тельный день

glory /'glɔːrɪ/ *n.* **1** (renown, honour) сла́ва **2** (splendour) великоле́пие
● *v.i.* упива́ться (*impf.*) + *i.*; **~ in one's strength** упива́ться свое́й си́лой

gloss /glɒs/ *n.* (lit., fig.) лоск
● *v.t.*: **~ over faults** обойти́ (*pf.*) оши́бки молча́нием
■ **~ paint** *n.* блестя́щий лак

glossary /'glɒsərɪ/ *n.* глосса́рий

glossy /'glɒsɪ/ *adj.* (**glossier, glossiest**) гля́нцевый; лощёный; **a ~ photograph** гля́нцевая фотогра́фия; **~ magazines** гля́нцевые журна́лы

glove /glʌv/ *n.* перча́тка
■ **~ compartment** *n.* (in car) бардачо́к (infml)

glow /gləʊ/ *n.* (of fire, sunset, etc.) за́рево; (of feelings) пыл
● *v.i.* (incandesce) накал|я́ться, -и́ться; (shine) свети́ться (*impf.*); **he ~ed with pride** его́ распира́ла го́рдость; **he described the trip in ~ing colours** он опи́сывал путеше́ствие в ра́дужных тона́х

glower /'glaʊə(r)/ *v.i.* серди́то смотре́ть (*impf.*) (**at**: на + *a.*)

glucose /'ɡluːkəʊs/ *n.* глюко́за

glue /ɡluː/ *n.* клей
● *v.t.* (**glues, glued, gluing** *or* **glueing**) прикле́и|вать, -ть
■ ∼-**sniffer** *n.* токсикома́н; ∼-**sniffing** *n.* токсикома́ния

glum /ɡlʌm/ *adj.* (**glummer, glummest**) угрю́мый

glut /ɡlʌt/ *n.* избы́ток

gluten /'ɡluːt(ə)n/ *n.* клейкови́на

glutton /'ɡlʌt(ə)n/ *n.* обжо́ра (*c.g.*); a ∼ **for work** жа́дный к рабо́те

gluttonous /'ɡlʌtənəs/ *adj.* прожо́рливый

gluttony /'ɡlʌtəni/ *n.* обжо́рство

glycerine /'ɡlɪsəriːn/ (AmE **glycerin**) *n.* глицери́н

GM *abbr.* (*of* **genetically modified**): ∼ **foods** генети́чески модифици́рованные проду́кты

GMT *n.* = Greenwich Mean time

gnarled /nɑːld/, **gnarly** /'nɑːlɪ/ *adjs.* шишкова́тый; сучкова́тый

gnash /næʃ/ *v.t.*: ∼ **one's teeth** скрежета́ть (*impf.*) зуба́ми

gnat /næt/ *n.* кома́р, мо́шка

gnaw /nɔː/ *v.t. & i.* грызть (*impf.*)

gnome /nəʊm/ *n.* гном

GNP *abbr.* (*of* **gross national product**) ВНП (валово́й национа́льный проду́кт)

GNVQ *n.* (*abbr. of* **General National Vocational Qualification**) (BrE) Общенациона́льное свиде́тельство о профессиона́льной квалифика́ции

✍ **go** /ɡəʊ/ *n.* (*pl.* ∼**es**) **1** (movement, animation): she's **on the** ∼ **from morning to night** она́ с утра́ до ве́чера на нога́х **2** (turn, attempt): **now it's my** ∼ тепе́рь моя́ о́чередь
● *v.i.* (*3rd pers. sing. pres.* **goes**, *past* **went**, *p.p.* **gone**) (*see also* ▸ **gone**) **1** (on foot) ходи́ть (*indet.*), идти́ (*det.*), пойти́ (*pf.*); (by transport) е́здить (*indet.*), е́хать (*det.*) пое́хать (*pf.*); (by plane) лета́ть (*indet.*), лете́ть (*det.*), полете́ть (*pf.*) (самолётом); **this train** ∼**es to London** э́тот по́езд идёт в Ло́ндон **2** (fig., with general idea of motion or direction): **this road** ∼**es to York** э́та доро́га ведёт в Йорк; **he** ∼**es to school** (is a schoolboy) он хо́дит в шко́лу; **let me** ∼! отпусти́те меня́!; **there is still an hour to** ∼ ещё час в запа́се; **his plans went wrong** его́ пла́ны сорвали́сь **3** (with cognate etc. object): **he went a long way** он пошёл/ушёл далеко́; **they went halves** они́ раздели́ли всё попола́м; **the balloon went 'pop'** шар ло́пнул **4** (idea of progress or outcome): **how's it** ∼**ing?** (health, affairs) как дела́?; как пожива́ете?; **everything is** ∼**ing well** всё (идёт) хорошо́; **the party/ play went well** вечери́нка/пье́са прошла́ хорошо́ **5** (expr. tenor or tendency): **the story** ∼**es that …** расска́зывают, что… **6** (set out, depart): **the post** ∼**es at 5 p.m.** по́чта ухо́дит в 5 часо́в

дня **7** (pass, disappear): **our holiday went in a flash** на́ши кани́кулы пролете́ли мгнове́нно; **it's** ∼**ne 4** (o'clock) уже́ бо́льше четырёх; пошёл пя́тый час; **I wish this pain would** ∼! хоть бы прошла́ э́та боль!; **all my money is** ∼**ne** все мои́ де́ньги уплы́ли **8** (become): **the milk went sour** молоко́ проки́сло; **she went red in the face** она́ покрасне́ла **9** (function): **I can't get my watch to** ∼ у меня́ не заво́дятся часы́ **10** (sound): **come in when the bell** ∼**es** входи́те, когда́ зазвони́т звоно́к **11** (be known, accepted, usual): **what he says** ∼**es** его́ сло́во — зако́н; **anything** ∼**es** всё сойдёт; **it** ∼**es without saying** э́то само́ собо́й разуме́ется **12** (expr. impending or predicted action): **I'm** ∼**ing to sneeze** я сейча́с чихну́; **it's** ∼**ing to rain** собира́ется дождь **13** (expr. intention): **I am** ∼**ing to ask him** я реши́л спроси́ть его́ **14** (be sold): **the picture went for a song** карти́ну про́дали за бесце́нок; **these cakes are** ∼**ing cheap** э́ти пиро́жные сто́ят дёшево (*or* иду́т по дешёвке)
● *with preps.*: **how shall I** ∼ **about this?** как мне за э́то взя́ться?; **he went about his business** он заня́лся свои́ми дела́ми; **the dog went after the hare** соба́ка погнала́сь за за́йцем; **the decision went against them** реше́ние бы́ло не в их по́льзу; **he went** (sc. passed) **by the window** он прошёл ми́мо окна́; **I went for a drink** я отпра́вился вы́пить; **the dog went for his legs** соба́ка хвата́ла его́ за но́ги; **he will always** ∼ **for the best** он всегда́ бу́дет стреми́ться к лу́чшему; **he went into the house** он вошёл в дом; **he had to** ∼ **into hospital** ему́ пришло́сь лечь в больни́цу; **it won't** ∼ **into the box** (is too big) э́то не войдёт в коро́бку; **I've** ∼**ne off prawns** (BrE, infml) я разлюби́л креве́тки; **I am** ∼**ing on a course** я поступа́ю на ку́рсы; **all my money went on food** все его́ де́ньги пошли́/уходи́ли на еду́; **we have no evidence to** ∼ **on** для э́того у нас нет никаки́х основа́ний; **I went over his work with him** вме́сте с ним я прошёлся по его́ рабо́те; **we have** ∼**ne over** (sc. discussed) **that** мы э́то обсужда́ли; **we went round the gallery** мы обошли́ галере́ю; ∼ **through the main gate!** проходи́те че́рез гла́вные воро́та!; **she went through his pockets** она́ обша́рила у него́ все карма́ны; **he has** ∼**ne through a lot** ему́ довело́сь мно́гое испыта́ть; **I'll** ∼ **through the main points again** я хочу́ повтори́ть гла́вные пу́нкты; **he went through the money in a week** он растра́тил де́ньги за неде́лю; **the estate went to her nephew** иму́щество перешло́ её племя́ннику; **the prize went to him** он вы́играл приз; **the money will** ∼ **towards a new car** де́ньги пойду́т на поку́пку но́вой маши́ны; **he went up the stairs** он стал поднима́ться (*or* пошёл вверх) по ле́стнице; **this tie** ∼**es with your suit** э́тот га́лстук подхо́дит к ва́шему костю́му; **he has been** ∼**ing** (out) **with her for several months** он встреча́ется с ней уже́ не́сколько ме́сяцев; **we went without a holiday** мы обошли́сь без о́тпуска
□ ∼ **ahead!** вперёд!

□ ~ **along** *v.i.*: I cannot ~ along with that я не могу́ с э́тим согласи́ться

□ ~ **around** *v.i.* **1**: he is ~ing around with my sister он встреча́ется с мое́й сестро́й **2** (AmE) = go round *v.i.*

□ ~ **away** *v.i.* уходи́ть, уйти́; ~ away! уходи́те!

□ ~ **back** *v.i.* идти́ (*det.*) наза́д; возвра|ща́ться, -ти́ться; he went back on his word он не сдержа́л своего́ сло́ва; this custom ~es back to the 15th century э́тот обы́чай восхо́дит к пятна́дцатому ве́ку

□ ~ **by** *v.i.*: as the years ~ by с года́ми

□ ~ **down** *v.i.* спус|ка́ться, -ти́ться; he went down on his knees он опусти́лся на коле́ни; the sun went down со́лнце се́ло; she went down with flu (BrE) она́ слегла́ с гри́ппом; prices are ~ing down це́ны па́дают; his story went down well его́ расска́з был хорошо́ при́нят

□ ~ **in** *v.i.* (enter) входи́ть, войти́; the sun went in со́лнце зашло́; he went in for the competition он при́нял уча́стие в ко́нкурсе

□ ~ **off** *v.i.*: he went off without a word он ушёл без еди́ного сло́ва; the alarm clock went off буди́льник зазвене́л; the light has ~ne off свет пога́с; the fruit has ~ne off (BrE) фру́кты погни́ли; his work has ~ne off lately в после́днее вре́мя он стал рабо́тать ху́же; the party went off well вечери́нка прошла́ хорошо́

□ ~ **on** *v.i.*: the lights went on загоре́лся свет; I can't ~ on any longer я так бо́льше не могу́; shall we ~ on to the next item? дава́йте перейдём к сле́дующему пу́нкту?; ~ on playing! продолжа́йте игра́ть!; what is ~ing on here? что тут происхо́дит?; ~ on at (nag) пили́ть (*impf.*); набра́сываться (*impf.*) на + *a.*; he went on (*sc. stage*) after the interval он вы́шел на сце́ну по́сле антра́кта; as time ~es on со вре́менем

□ ~ **out** *v.i.* (exit) выходи́ть, вы́йти; the light went out свет пога́с; the tide was ~ing out шёл отли́в

□ ~ **over** *v.i.*: he went over to France он перепра́вился во Фра́нцию; the country went over to decimal coinage страна́ перешла́ на десяти́чную моне́тную систе́му

□ ~ **round** *v.i.* **1** (revolve) враща́ться (*impf.*), кружи́ться, за- **2** (BrE): I went round to see him я пошёл его́ навести́ть; we had to ~ round by the park нам пришло́сь идти́ в обхо́д че́рез парк; he ~es round collecting money он обхо́дит всех и собира́ет де́ньги; is there enough food to ~ round? хва́тит ли еды́ на всех?

□ ~ **through** *v.i.*: I cannot ~ through with the plan я не могу́ осуществи́ть э́тот план; the deal went through сде́лка состоя́лась; has their divorce ~ne through? они́ уже́ развели́сь?

□ ~ **together** *v.i.*: they were ~ing (keeping company) together for years они́ встреча́лись мно́гие го́ды; these colours ~ together э́ти цвета́ гармони́руют

□ ~ **under** *v.i.*: his business went under его́ де́ло ло́пнуло

□ ~ **up** *v.i.* подн|има́ться, -я́ться; he went up to bed он пошёл спать; prices have ~ne up це́ны повы́сились

■ ~-**ahead** *n.* разреше́ние, «добро́», «зелёная у́лица»; ~-**between** *n.* посре́дник; ~-**cart** (*also* ~-**kart**) *n.* карт; ~-**slow** *n.* (BrE) части́чная забасто́вка

goad /ɡəʊd/ *n. v.t.* погоня́ть (*impf.*); (prod) пришпо́ри|вать, -ть; (tease, torment) раздража́ть (*impf.*)

⚘ **goal** /ɡəʊl/ *n.* **1** (objective) цель **2** (sport) воро́т|а (*pl., g.* —)

■ ~**keeper** *n.* врата́рь (*m.*); ~**post** *n.* шта́нга

goalie /ˈɡəʊlɪ/ *n.* (infml) врата́рь (*m.*)

goat /ɡəʊt/ *n.* коза́; (male) козёл

gobble[1] /ˈɡɒb(ə)l/ *v.t.* жрать, по-/со-

gobble[2] /ˈɡɒb(ə)l/ *v.i.* (of a turkey) кулды́кать (*impf.*)

gobbledygook /ˈɡɒb(ə)ldɪɡuːk/ *n.* (sl.) болтоло́гия, (пусто́й) набо́р слов; (in speech of politicians, also) витиева́тая демаго́гия; (in documents) бюрократи́ческий жарго́н, канцеляри́т

goblin /ˈɡɒblɪn/ *n.* домово́й, го́блин

⚘ **god** /ɡɒd/ *n.* (a deity) бог; (G~: supreme being) Бог; боже́ство; my G~! Бо́же мой!; Го́споди!

■ ~**child** *n.* крёстни|к (-ца); ~-**daughter** *n.* крёстница; ~**father** *n.* крёстный (оте́ц); ~**forsaken place** *n.* медве́жий у́гол; ~**mother** *n.* крёстная (мать); ~**parent** *n.* крёстный (оте́ц); крёстная (мать); ~**send** *n.* нахо́дка; ≈ сам Бог посла́л; ~**son** *n.* крёстник

goddess /ˈɡɒdɪs/ *n.* боги́ня

goes /ɡəʊz/ *3rd pers. sing. pres. of* ▶ go

goggles /ˈɡɒɡ(ə)lz/ *n. pl.* тёмные/защи́тные очк|и́ (-о́в)

going /ˈɡəʊɪŋ/ *n.* **1** (departure) отъе́зд, ухо́д **2** (progress, speed) ско́рость; fifty miles an hour is good ~ 50 миль в час — хоро́шая ско́рость; this book is heavy ~ э́та кни́га тру́дно чита́ется; the conversation was heavy ~ разгово́р не кле́ился

● *adj.* **1** (working): a ~ concern де́йствующее предприя́тие **2** (BrE, to be had): one of the best newspapers ~ одна́ из лу́чших ны́нешних газе́т

■ ~-**s-on** *n. pl.* (infml) поведе́ние; посту́пки (*m. pl.*); дела́ (*nt. pl.*); «дели́шки» (*nt. pl.*)

⚘ **gold** /ɡəʊld/ *n.* (metal) зо́лото; he's as good as ~ (of child) он зо́лото, а не ребёнок

● *adj.* (made of gold, gold-coloured) золото́й; ~ medal золота́я меда́ль

■ ~ **dust** *n.* золото́й песо́к; ~**fish** *n.* золота́я ры́бка; ~ **mine** *n.* золото́й рудни́к; (fig.): the shop is a ~ mine э́тот магази́н — золото́е дно; ~ **medal** *n.* золота́я меда́ль; ~ **rush** *n.* золота́я лихора́дка

golden /ˈɡəʊld(ə)n/ *adj.* (lit., fig.) золото́й; (of colour) золоти́стый; the ~ age золото́й век; receive a ~ handshake on retirement получи́ть (*pf.*) вознагражде́ние при ухо́де на пе́нсию; miss a ~ opportunity упусти́ть (*pf.*) редча́йшую возмо́жность

golf /ɡɒlf/ *n.* гольф

■ ~ **club** *n.* (association) клуб люби́телей игры́

в гольф; (implement) клю́шка; ~ **course** n. площа́дка/по́ле для игры́ в гольф

golfer /'gɒlfə(r)/ n. игро́к в гольф

gondola /'gɒndələ/ n. (boat; airship car) гондо́ла

gone /gɒn/ adj. (see also ▶ **go**) **1** (departed, past) уе́хавший **2** (dead) уме́рший, усо́пший

gong /gɒŋ/ n. (instrument) гонг

gonorrhoea /ɡɒnə'rɪə/ (AmE **gonorrhea**) n. гонорея́

✎ **good** /ɡʊd/ n. **1** (~ness, ~ action) добро́, бла́го; **he is up to no ~** он заду́мал что́-то недо́брое **2** (benefit) по́льза; **drink it! it will do you ~** вы́пейте э́то — вам поле́зно; **it's no ~ complaining** что то́лку жа́ловаться? **3**: **for ~** (permanently) навсегда́ **4** (in pl.) (property) добро́ **5** (in pl.) (merchandise) това́р(ы)
● adj. (**better, best**) **1** (in most senses) хоро́ший; до́брый; (of food) вку́сный; ~ **idea!** прекра́сная мысль!; a ~ **player** си́льный игро́к; ~ **heavens!** Бо́же мой! **2** (of health, condition, etc.) хоро́ший; здоро́вый; **I don't feel so ~ today** (infml) я себя́ нева́жно чу́вствую сего́дня; **apples are ~ for you** я́блоки поле́зны для здоро́вья **3** (favourable, fortunate): ~ **luck!** жела́ю успе́ха!; **it's a ~ thing we stayed at home** хорошо́, что мы оста́лись до́ма **4** (kind) любе́зный, до́брый; **that's very ~ of you** э́то о́чень ми́ло с ва́шей стороны́ **5** (of skill): ~ **at maths** спосо́бный к + d.; си́льный в + p.; **she's ~ at maths** она́ спосо́бна к матема́тике; **he is no ~ at his job** он взя́лся не за своё де́ло **6** (suitable) подходя́щий **7** (well behaved) воспи́танный; послу́шный; **be ~!** веди́ себя́ прили́чно! **8** (var.): ~ **morning!** до́брое у́тро!; **it's ~ to see you** прия́тно вас ви́деть; **a ~ while ago** давны́м-давно́; **he was as ~ as his word** он сдержа́л своё сло́во; **he as ~ as refused to go** он факти́чески отказа́лся идти́
■ ~-**for-nothing** n. безде́льник, никчёмный челове́к; **G~ Friday** n. Страстна́я пя́тница; ~-**humoured**, (AmE) -**humored** adj. добро́душный; ~-**looking** adj. краси́вый; хоро́ш/хороша́ собо́й; ~-**natured** adj. добро́душный; ~**night** int. споко́йной но́чи!; ~**s train** n. това́рный по́езд; ~**will** n. (friendship) доброжела́тельность; (of business) репута́ция

goodbye /ɡʊd'baɪ/ n. проща́ние
● int. до свида́ния!; проща́йте!

goodness /'ɡʊdnɪs/ n. **1** (virtue) доброта́ **2** (kindness) любе́зность **3** (nourishment): **these apples are full of ~** э́ти я́блоки о́чень поле́зны/пита́тельны **4** (euph., God): ~ **me!** вот те на́!; **thank ~!** сла́ва Бо́гу!

gooey /'ɡuːɪ/ adj. (**gooier, gooiest**) (infml) кле́йкий; ли́пкий

google /'ɡuːɡ(ə)l/ v.t. & i. иска́ть (impf.) в Интерне́те (особенно в поисковой системе Google (propr.))

goose /ɡuːs/ n. (pl. **geese**) **1** гусь (m.) (fem. also гусы́ня) **2** (simpleton) простофи́ля (c.g.)
■ ~**berry** n. крыжо́вник (collect.); я́года

крыжо́вника; **play ~berry** (BrE, infml) ока́зываться, -а́ться тре́тьим ли́шним; ~**flesh** n. гуся́тина; **it gives me ~flesh** у меня́ от э́того мура́шки по те́лу бе́гают; ~-**step** n. (mil.) гуси́ный шаг

gorge /ɡɔːdʒ/ n. уще́лье
● v.t. & i. объ|еда́ться, -е́сться; **the lion ~d (itself) on its prey** лев жа́дно поглоща́л свою́ добы́чу

gorgeous /'ɡɔːdʒəs/ adj. (magnificent) великоле́пный; (richly coloured) кра́сочный

gorilla /ɡə'rɪlə/ n. гори́лла

gormless /'ɡɔːmlɪs/ adj. (BrE, infml) безду́мный; дура́шливый

gorse /ɡɔːs/ n. (bot.) утёсник обыкнове́нный

gory /'ɡɔːrɪ/ adj. (**gorier, goriest**) кровопроли́тный; ~ **details** крова́вые подро́бности

gosh /ɡɒʃ/ int. (infml) Бо́же мой!

gosling /'ɡɒzlɪŋ/ n. гусёнок

gospel /'ɡɒsp(ə)l/ n. **1** Ева́нгелие **2** (in full **g. music**) го́спел

gossip /'ɡɒsɪp/ n. **1** (talk) спле́тня **2** (person) спле́тни|к (-ца) **3** (attr.): ~ **column** коло́нка све́тской хро́ники
● v.i. (**gossiped, gossiping**) спле́тничать, на-

got /ɡɒt/ past and p.p. of ▶ **get**

Gothic /'ɡɒθɪk/ n. го́тика, готи́ческий стиль
● adj. готи́ческий

gotten /'ɡɒt(ə)n/ (AmE) p.p. of ▶ **get**

gouache /ɡʊ'ɑːʃ/ n. гуа́шь

goulash /'ɡuːlæʃ/ n. гуля́ш

gourmet /'ɡʊəmeɪ/ n. гурма́н

gout /ɡaʊt/ n. пода́гра

govern /'ɡʌv(ə)n/ v.t. **1** (rule; also v.i.) пра́вить (impf.) + i.; (control, influence) руководи́ть (impf.) + i.; ~**ing body** (of hospital, school, etc.) дире́кция, правле́ние **2** (apply to): **the same principle ~s both cases** оди́н и тот же при́нцип примени́м в обо́их слу́чаях

governess /'ɡʌvənɪs/ n. гуверна́нтка

✎ **government** /'ɡʌvənmənt/ n. (rule) правле́ние; (system) фо́рма правле́ния

governmental /ɡʌvən'ment(ə)l/ adj. прави́тельственный

✎ **governor** /'ɡʌvənə(r)/ n. **1** (ruling official) губерна́тор **2** (member of governing body) член правле́ния

gown /ɡaʊn/ n. (woman's) пла́тье; (academic or official) ма́нтия

GP abbr. (of **general practitioner**) врач о́бщей пра́ктики; уча́стковый врач

GPS n. (abbr. of **Global Positioning System**) глоба́льная спу́тниковая навигацио́нная систе́ма

✎ **grab** /ɡræb/ v.t. & i. (**grabbed, grabbing**) схва́т|ывать, -и́ть; **he ~bed me by the lapels** он схвати́л меня́ за ла́цканы

grace /ɡreɪs/ n. **1** (elegance) гра́ция, изя́щество; **airs and ~s** (iron.) жема́нство **2** (dispensation) отсро́чка; **the law allows 3 days' ~** по зако́ну полага́ется 3 дня отсро́чки (*or* льго́тных дня); (prayer before meal) моли́тва; **say** ~ моли́ться (*impf.*) пе́ред едо́й

graceful /'greɪsfʊl/ *adj.* грацио́зный; изя́щный

gracious /'greɪʃəs/ *adj.* ми́лостивый; любе́зный; ~ **living** краси́вая жизнь
• *int.*: **good(ness)** ~ **(me)!** Бо́же мой!

grade /greɪd/ *n.* **1** (assessed category) сте́пень; (of quality) сорт; (of rank) сте́пень; класс; (AmE, class in school) класс **2** (school rating) отме́тка; оце́нка **3** (AmE): ~ **crossing** (железнодоро́жный) перее́зд
• *v.t.* сортирова́ть, рас-
■ ~ **school** *n.* (AmE) нача́льная шко́ла

gradient /'greɪdɪənt/ *n.* градие́нт

gradual /'grædʒʊəl/ *adj.* постепе́нный

gradually /'grædʒʊəlɪ/ *adv.* постепе́нно

ᔕ **graduate¹** /'grædʒʊət/ *n.* (of university, school, etc.) выпускни́к (-ца)

ᔕ **graduate²** /'grædʒʊeɪt/ *v.i.* (from university, college) ока́нчивать, -о́нчить университе́т/вуз; (AmE, from school) шко́лу

graduation /grædʒʊ'eɪʃ(ə)n/ *n.* (receiving degree) получе́ние дипло́ма/сте́пени; (AmE) оконча́ние шко́лы

graffiti /grə'fiːtɪ/ *n.* (*sing.* **graffito** /-təʊ/) граффи́ти (*indecl., pl.*), на́дписи (*f. pl.*) (на сте́нах/забо́рах)

graft /grɑːft/ *n.* (tissue) переса́женная ткань
• *v.t.* (med.) переса́|живать, -ди́ть; (hort., also fig.) прив|ива́ть, -и́ть

grain /greɪn/ *n.* **1** (collect.) (seed of cereal plants) зерно́; (single seed) зерно́ **2** (small particle) зёрнышко; ~ **of sand** песчи́нка; **there is not a** ~ **of truth in it** в э́том нет ни крупи́цы/гра́на/ка́пли пра́вды **3** (of wood) волокно́ **4**: **it goes against the** ~ **with me** (fig.) э́то мне не по душе́/нутру́

gram /græm/ *n.* грамм

grammar /'græmə(r)/ *n.* грамма́тика
■ ~ **school** *n.* (BrE) сре́дняя шко́ла с гуманита́рным укло́ном

grammatical /grə'mætɪk(ə)l/ *adj.* граммати́ческий

gramme /græm/ *n.* (BrE) = gram

gramophone /'græməfəʊn/ *n.* граммофо́н
■ ~ **record** *n.* грампласти́нка

gran /græn/ *n.* (BrE) = granny

granary /'grænərɪ/ *n.* амба́р

grand /grænd/ *adj.* **1** (great, important) вели́кий; грандио́зный **2** (elevated, imposing) вели́чественный **3** (all-embracing): ~ **total** о́бщая су́мма
■ ~**child** *n.* внук (вну́чка); ~**(d)ad** *n.* (infml) де́душка (*m.*); ~**daughter** *n.* вну́чка; ~**father** *n.* де́душка (*m.*); ~**father clock** высо́кие напо́льные часы́; ~**ma** *n.* (infml) ба́бушка; ~**mother** *n.* ба́бушка; ~**pa** *n.* (infml) де́душка (*m.*); ~**parent** *n.* де́душка (ба́бушка); ~ **piano** *n.* роя́ль (*m.*); ~**son** *n.* внук; ~**stand** *n.* трибу́на

grandeur /'grændʒə(r)/ *n.* вели́чие; великоле́пие

grandiose /'grændɪəʊs/ *adj.* грандио́зный

granite /'grænɪt/ *n.* грани́т

granny /'grænɪ/ *n.* (infml) ба́бушка

ᔕ **grant** /grɑːnt/ *n.* (sum etc. conferred) дота́ция; (to student) стипе́ндия
• *v.t.* **1** (bestow) дарова́ть (*impf., pf.*); жа́ловать, по- **2** (concede) призн|ава́ть, -а́ть; ~**ed, he has done all that he could** согла́сен: он сде́лал всё, что мог **3**: **he takes my help for** ~**ed** он принима́ет мою́ по́мощь как до́лжное

granulate /'grænjʊleɪt/ *v.t. & i.*: ~**d sugar** са́харный песо́к

granule /'grænjuːl/ *n.* зерно́, гра́нула

grape /greɪp/ *n.* (a single fruit) виногра́дина; **bunch of** ~**s** гроздь виногра́да
■ ~**fruit** *n.* грейпфру́т; ~**vine** *n.* виногра́дная лоза́; (fig.): **I heard on the** ~**vine that …** до меня́ дошли́ слу́хи (о том), что…

graph /grɑːf/ *n.* гра́фик
■ ~ **paper** *n.* бума́га в кле́тку, миллиметро́вка (infml)

graphic /'græfɪk/ *adj.* **1** (pertaining to drawing etc.) изобрази́тельный **2** (vivid) кра́сочный

graphics /'græfɪks/ *n.* гра́фика
■ ~ **card** *n.* (comput.) видеока́рта, графи́ческая пла́та

grapple /'græp(ə)l/ *v.i.*: ~ **with a problem** бра́ться, взя́ться за пробле́му

grasp /grɑːsp/ *n.* **1** (grip) хва́тка **2** (comprehension) понима́ние
• *v.t.* (seize) схва́т|ывать, -и́ть; (comprehend) схва́т|ывать, -и́ть смысл + g.
• *v.i.*: ~ **at, for** (lit., fig.) ухвати́ться (*pf.*) за + a.

grass /grɑːs/ *n.* **1** трава́ **2** (lawn) газо́н **3** (sl., marijuana) марихуа́на, «тра́вка»
■ ~**hopper** *n.* кузне́чик; ~**roots** *adj.* (infml) низово́й, из низо́в; ~**roots opinion is against the plan** рядовы́е гра́ждане настро́ены про́тив э́того пла́на; ~ **snake** *n.* уж

grassy /'grɑːsɪ/ *adj.* (**grassier**, **grassiest**) травяно́й; травяни́стый

grate¹ /greɪt/ *n.* (fireplace) ками́нная решётка; ками́н

grate² /greɪt/ *v.t.* тере́ть (*impf.*); ~**d cheese** тёртый сыр
• *v.i.* **1**: ~ **on** (fig.) раздража́ть (*impf.*) **2** (make harsh sound) скр|ипе́ть, -и́пнуть

grateful /'greɪtfʊl/ *adj.* благода́рный; призна́тельный

grater /'greɪtə(r)/ *n.* тёрка

gratify /'grætɪfaɪ/ *v.t.* дост|авля́ть, -а́вить удово́льствие + d.

grating /'greɪtɪŋ/ *n.* решётка

gratis /'grɑːtɪs/ *adj.* беспла́тный
• *adv.* беспла́тно

gratitude /'grætɪtjuːd/ *n.* благода́рность

gratuitous /grə'tjuːɪtəs/ *adj.* **1** (unwarranted) беспричи́нный; **a** ~ **insult** незаслу́женное оскорбле́ние **2** (free) даровой; безвозме́здный; ~ **advice** беспла́тный сове́т

gratuity /grə'tjuːɪtɪ/ *n.* (tip) чаевы́|е (-х)

grave¹ /greɪv/ *n.* моги́ла

■ ~**stone** *n.* надгро́бная плита́; ~**yard** *n.* кла́дбище

grave² /ɡreɪv/ *adj.* серьёзный

gravel /'ɡræv(ə)l/ *n.* гра́вий

gravitate /'ɡrævɪteɪt/ *v.i.* (fig.) тяготе́ть (*impf.*) (**to(wards)**: к + *d.*)

gravity /'ɡrævɪtɪ/ *n.* **1** (force) си́ла притяже́ния **2** (weight) тя́жесть; **centre of** ~ центр тя́жести; **law of** ~ зако́н всеми́рного тяготе́ния **3** (seriousness) серьёзность; тя́жесть

gravy /'ɡreɪvɪ/ *n.* подли́вка

gray /ɡreɪ/ *n. & adj.* (AmE) = **grey**

grayish /'ɡreɪɪʃ/ *adj.* (AmE) = **greyish**

graze¹ /ɡreɪz/ *n.* (abrasion) цара́пина; сса́дина
● *v.t.* зад|ева́ть, -е́ть; **he fell and** ~**d his knee** он упа́л и оцара́пал коле́но

graze² /ɡreɪz/ *v.i.*: **he has 40 sheep out to** ~ у него́ (в ста́де/ота́ре) пасётся 40 ове́ц

grease /ɡriːs/ *n.* (fat) жир; (lubricant) сма́зка
● *v.t.* сма́з|ывать, -ать

■ ~**paint** *n.* грим

greasy /'ɡriːsɪ/ *adj.* (**greasier, greasiest**) жи́рный

ℯ **great** /ɡreɪt/ *adj.* **1** большо́й, вели́кий; (famous) знамени́тый; **they are** ~ **friends** они́ больши́е друзья́; **a** ~ **many people** ма́сса наро́ду; **a** ~ **deal of courage** неза уря́дная хра́брость **2** (infml, splendid) замеча́тельный; **we had a** ~ **time** мы замеча́тельно провели́ вре́мя **3** (eminent, distinguished) вели́кий; **a** ~ **occasion** торже́ственное собы́тие **4**: **G**~ **Britain** Великобрита́ния

■ ~**aunt** *n.* двою́родная ба́бушка; ~**granddaughter** *n.* пра́внучка; ~**grandfather** *n.* пра́дед; ~**grandmother** *n.* прабабушка; ~**grandson** *n.* пра́внук; ~**nephew** *n.* внуча́тый племя́нник; ~**niece** *n.* внуча́тая племя́нница; ~**uncle** *n.* двою́родный дед

greatly /'ɡreɪtlɪ/ *adv.* о́чень, си́льно, значи́тельно; **I was** ~ **amused** э́то меня́ си́льно позаба́вило

Greece /ɡriːs/ *n.* Гре́ция

greed /ɡriːd/ *n.* жа́дность; (for food) прожо́рливость

greedy /'ɡriːdɪ/ *adj.* (**greedier, greediest**) (for money etc.) жа́дный; (for food) прожо́рливый

Greek /ɡriːk/ *n.* **1** (person) гре|к (-ча́нка) **2** (language) гре́ческий язы́к; **Ancient** ~ древнегре́ческий язы́к; **it's (all)** ~ **to me** э́то для меня́ кита́йская гра́мота
● *adj.* гре́ческий

ℯ **green** /ɡriːn/ *n.* **1** (colour) зелёный цвет; зелёное; **dressed in** ~ оде́тый в зелёное **2** (*in pl.*) (vegetables) зе́лень **3** (grassy area) лужа́йка; (on golf course) площа́дка вокру́г лу́нки
● *adj.* зелёный; (unripe) незре́лый; (fig., inexperienced) «зелёный»

■ ~**grocer** *n.* (BrE) продав|е́ц (-щи́ца) зе́лени; ~**house** *n.* тепли́ца; ~**house effect**

парнико́вый *or* тепли́чный эффе́кт

greenery /'ɡriːnərɪ/ *n.* зе́лень

greenish /'ɡriːnɪʃ/ *adj.* зеленова́тый

Greenland /'ɡriːnlənd/ *n.* Гренла́ндия
● *adj.* гренла́ндский

Greenwich Mean time, Greenwich time /'ɡrenɪtʃ, 'ɡrɪnɪdʒ/ *n.* вре́мя по Гри́нвичу

greet /ɡriːt/ *v.t.* (socially) здоро́ваться, по- с + *i.*; (welcome) приве́тствовать (*impf.*)

greeting /'ɡriːtɪŋ/ *n.* (on meeting) приве́тствие; ~**s!** приве́т!; (on a special occasion) **birthday** ~**s** поздравле́ние с днём рожде́ния

■ ~**s card** *n.* поздрави́тельная откры́тка

gregarious /ɡrɪ'ɡeərɪəs/ *adj.* ста́дный; (fig. also) общи́тельный

grenade /ɡrɪ'neɪd/ *n.* грана́та

grew /ɡruː/ *past of* ▶ **grow**

grey /ɡreɪ/ (AmE **gray**) *n.* се́рый цвет; се́рое
● *adj.* се́рый; **he has gone very** ~ он си́льно поседе́л; **his face turned** ~ он побледне́л

■ ~ **area** *n.* (fig.) о́бласть неопределённости; ~**haired, ~headed** *adjs.* седо́й, седовла́сый; ~**hound** *n.* англи́йская борза́я

greyish /'ɡreɪɪʃ/ (AmE **grayish**) *adj.* серова́тый

grid /ɡrɪd/ *n.* **1** (grating) решётка **2** (map reference squares) координа́тная се́тка **3** (power supply system) энергосисте́ма

griddle /'ɡrɪd(ə)l/ *n.* ≈ сковоро́дка

gridlock /'ɡrɪdlɒk/ *n.* зато́р

grief /ɡriːf/ *n.* (sorrow) го́ре, печа́ль; (disaster): **he will come to** ~ он пло́хо ко́нчит

grievance /'ɡriːv(ə)ns/ *n.* прете́нзия; недово́льство

grieve /ɡriːv/ *v.t.* огорч|а́ть, -и́ть
● *v.i.* горева́ть (*impf.*); **she** ~**d for her husband** она́ горева́ла о му́же

grievous /'ɡriːvəs/ *adj.* го́рестный; ~ **bodily harm** (law) тяжёлые теле́сные поврежде́ния (*nt. pl.*)

grill /ɡrɪl/ *n.* (BrE, on cooker) гриль (*m.*)
● *v.t.* (BrE, cook) жа́рить, за- на гри́ле; (infml, interrogate) учин|я́ть, -и́ть допро́с + *d.*

grille /ɡrɪl/ *n.* решётка

grim /ɡrɪm/ *adj.* (**grimmer, grimmest**) суро́вый, мра́чный, гро́зный

grimace /'ɡrɪməs/ *n.* грима́са
● *v.i.* грима́сничать (*impf.*)

grime /ɡraɪm/ *n.* са́жа; грязь

grimy /'ɡraɪmɪ/ *adj.* (**grimier, grimiest**) чума́зый; гря́зный

grin /ɡrɪn/ *n.* усме́шка; ухмы́лка
● *v.i.* (**grinned, grinning**) усмех|а́ться, -ну́ться; ухмыл|я́ться, -ьну́ться

grind /ɡraɪnd/ *n.* (infml) изнури́тельный труд
● *v.t.* (*past and p.p.* **ground**) **1** (crush) моло́ть, с-; **ground almonds** мо́лотый минда́ль **2** (wear down) изн|а́шивать, -оси́ть **3**: ~ **one's teeth** скрежета́ть/скрипе́ть (*both impf.*) зуба́ми
● *v.i.* (*past and p.p.* **ground**) **1** (rub, grate) тере́ть (*impf.*) **2**: ~ **to a halt** остан|а́вливаться, -ови́ться (с ля́згом)

■ ~**stone** *n.* точи́ло; **he kept his nose to the** ~**stone** он труди́лся без о́тдыха

grip /grɪp/ *n.* схва́тывание; (fig.) понима́ние; **come to** ~**s with a problem** вплотну́ю заня́ться (*pf.*) пробле́мой; **take a** ~ **of yourself!** возьми́те себя́ в ру́ки!; **he is losing his** ~ хва́тка у него́ уже́ не та
● *v.t.* (**gripped, gripping**) (hold tightly) схва́т|ывать, -и́ть; (hold the attention of) захва́т|ывать, -и́ть; **a** ~**ping story** захва́тывающий расска́з

gripe /graɪp/ *n.* **1** (*in pl.*) (colic pains) ко́лик|и (*pl., g.* —) **2** (grumble, complaint) ворча́ние
● *v.i.* (complain) ворча́ть (*impf.*)

grisly /ˈɡrɪzlɪ/ *adj.* (**grislier, grisliest**) ужаса́ющий

grist /grɪst/ *n.* (fig.): **it will bring** ~ **to the mill** э́то принесёт дохо́д; **all is** ~ **to his mill** он из всего́ извлека́ет вы́году

gristle /ˈɡrɪs(ə)l/ *n.* хрящ

grit /grɪt/ *n.* гра́вий
● *v.t.* (**gritted, gritting**) **1** (spread ~ on): **the streets were** ~**ted at the first sign of frost** при пе́рвых при́знаках моро́за у́лицы посы́пали песко́м **2**: ~ **one's teeth** (fig.) сти́снуть (*pf.*) зу́бы

gritty /ˈɡrɪtɪ/ *adj.* (**grittier, grittiest**) песча́ный; (fig., of style) шерохова́тый

grizzle /ˈɡrɪz(ə)l/ *v.i.* (BrE, infml, fret) капри́зничать (*impf.*); хны́кать (*impf.*)

groan /ɡrəʊn/ *n.* стон
● *v.i.* стона́ть, за-

grocer /ˈɡrəʊsə(r)/ *n.* бакале́йщик
■ ~'**s shop** *n.* бакале́я

grocery /ˈɡrəʊsərɪ/ *n.* (*in pl.*) (goods) бакале́я

groggy /ˈɡrɒɡɪ/ *adj.* (**groggier, groggiest**) нетвёрдо стоя́щий на нога́х

groin /ɡrɔɪn/ *n.* (anat.) пах

groom /ɡruːm/ *n.* (for horses) ко́нюх; (bride~) жени́х
● *v.t.* **1**: ~ **a horse** чи́стить, по- ло́шадь **2** (prepare, coach) гото́вить; **he is being** ~**ed for President** его́ про́чат в президе́нты

groove /ɡruːv/ *n.* желобо́к

grope /ɡrəʊp/ *v.t. & i.* идти́ (*det.*) о́щупью; о́щуп|ывать, -ать; **he** ~**d his way towards the door** он о́щупью добра́лся до две́ри

gross /ɡrəʊs/ *n.* (*pl.* ~) (number) гросс (*12 дю́жин*)
● *adj.* **1** (coarse) гру́бый **2** (obese) ту́чный **3** (opp. net) валово́й; ~ **domestic product** валово́й вну́тренний проду́кт; ~ **national product** валово́й национа́льный проду́кт; ~ **weight** вес бру́тто
● *v.t.*: **we** ~**ed £1,000** мы получи́ли о́бщую при́быль в 1000 фу́нтов

grotesque /ɡrəʊˈtesk/ *adj.* гроте́скный

grotto /ˈɡrɒtəʊ/ *n.* (*pl.* ~**es** *or* ~**s**) грот

grouchy /ˈɡraʊtʃɪ/ *adj.* (**grouchier, grouchiest**) (infml) ворчли́вый; брюзгли́вый

⚘ **ground**[1] /ɡraʊnd/ *n.* **1** (surface of earth) земля́; грунт; **it suits me down to the** ~ э́то меня́

вполне́ устра́ивает **2** (soil, also fig.) по́чва **3** (position) положе́ние; **this opinion is gaining** ~ э́та то́чка зре́ния получа́ет всё бо́льше распростране́ние; **they held their** ~ **well** они́ сто́йко держа́лись **4** (area, distance) расстоя́ние; **we covered a lot of** ~ (distance) мы покры́ли большо́е расстоя́ние; (fig., work) мы заме́тно продви́нулись вперёд **5** (defined area of activity) площа́дка; **football** ~ футбо́льная площа́дка; **sports** ~ спорти́вная площа́дка **6** (*in pl.*) (estate) сад, парк, зе́мли (*f. pl.*) **7** (*in pl.*) (dregs) гу́ща **8** (reason) основа́ние; **I have no** ~**s for complaint** у меня́ нет основа́ний жа́ловаться
● *v.t.* **1** (run aground) сажа́ть, посади́ть на мель **2** (prevent from flying) запре|ща́ть, -ти́ть полёты + *g.*
■ ~ **floor** *n.* (BrE) пе́рвый эта́ж; ~ **forces** *n. pl.* сухопу́тные войска́; ~**nut** *n.* земляно́й оре́х; ~**work** *n.* фунда́мент, осно́вы (*f. pl.*)

ground[2] /ɡraʊnd/ *past and p.p. of* ▶ **grind**

grounding /ˈɡraʊndɪŋ/ *n.* (basic instruction) подгото́вка

groundless /ˈɡraʊndlɪs/ *adj.* беспричи́нный, беспо́чвенный, необосно́ванный

⚘ **group** /ɡruːp/ *n.* **1** (assemblage) гру́ппа; коллекти́в; (political etc. unit) группиро́вка; фра́кция **2** (*attr.*) группово́й
● *v.t. & i.* группирова́ть(ся), с-
■ ~ **therapy** *n.* группова́я психотерапи́я

grouse /ɡraʊs/ *n.* (*pl.* ~) (bird) шотла́ндская куропа́тка

grout /ɡraʊt/ *n.* (mortar) цеме́нтный раство́р
● *v.t.* зал|ива́ть, -и́ть цеме́нтом

grove /ɡrəʊv/ *n.* ро́ща

grovel /ˈɡrɒv(ə)l/ *v.i.* (**grovelled, grovelling**, AmE **groveled, groveling**) лежа́ть (*impf.*) ниц/распростёршись; (fig.) пресмыка́ться (*impf.*) (**to**: пе́ред + *i.*)

⚘ **grow** /ɡrəʊ/ *v.t.* (*past* **grew**, *p.p.* **grown**) расти́ть, вы́-; выра́щивать (*impf.*); разводи́ть (*impf.*); **he is** ~**ing a beard** он отра́щивает бо́роду
● *v.i.* (*past* **grew**, *p.p.* **grown**) **1** (of habitat) расти́, вы́расти; **ivy** ~**s on walls** плющ растёт на стена́х **2** (of development): **he grew (by) 5 inches** он вы́рос на 5 дю́ймов; **she has** ~**n into a young lady** она́ преврати́лась в молоду́ю же́нщину; **she is letting her hair** ~ она́ отра́щивает во́лосы; **he looks quite** ~**n up** он вы́глядит совсе́м взро́слым; ~**n-ups** взро́слые (*pl.*); **I grew to like him** со вре́менем он стал мне нра́виться; **it's a habit I've never** ~**n out of** э́то привы́чка, от кото́рой я никогда́ не мог изба́виться; **he grew out of his clothes** он вы́рос из оде́жды; **the tune** ~**s on one** э́тот моти́в начина́ет нра́виться со вре́менем; (increase) увели́чи|ваться, -ться; уси́ли|ваться, -ться; **he listened with** ~**ing impatience** он слу́шал с расту́щим нетерпе́нием **3** (become) ста|нови́ться, -ть; **as he grew older, he …** с во́зрастом он …; **she grew pale** она́ побледне́ла

grower /ˈɡrəʊə(r)/ *n.* (cultivator) садово́д

g

growl /graʊl/ *n.* рыча́ние
• *v.i.* рыча́ть (*impf.*)

grown /grəʊn/ *p.p.* of ▶ **grow**

✐ **growth** /grəʊθ/ *n.* (development) рост; (increase) приро́ст; (path.) наро́ст

grubby /'grʌbɪ/ *adj.* (**grubbier, grubbiest**) гря́зный, запа́чканный

grudge /grʌdʒ/ *n.* прете́нзия, недоброжела́тельность; **I bear him no ~e** я на него́ не в оби́де
• *v.t.* зави́довать, по- (*чему*); **I do not ~e him his success** я не зави́дую его́ успе́ху; **I ~e paying so much** мне жаль сто́лько плати́ть; **he obeyed ~ingly** он неохо́тно вы́полнил приказа́ние

gruel /'gru:əl/ *n.* жи́дкая (овся́ная) ка́ша, каши́ца

gruelling /'gru:əlɪŋ/ (AmE **grueling**) *adj.* изма́тывающий

gruesome /'gru:səm/ *adj.* жу́ткий

gruff /grʌf/ *adj.* (of voice) хри́плый

grumble /'grʌmb(ə)l/ *v.i.* (complain) ворча́ть (*impf.*); (rumble) грохота́ть (*impf.*)

grumpy /'grʌmpɪ/ *adj.* (**grumpier, grumpiest**) сварли́вый

grunt /grʌnt/ *n.* (animal) хрю́канье; (human) ворча́ние
• *v.i.* (of animals) хрю́к|ать, -нуть; (of humans) ворча́ть, про-

guarantee /ɡærən'tiː/ *n.* гара́нтия
• *v.t.* (**guarantees, guaranteed**) страхова́ть, за-; **it is ~d to last 10 years** срок го́дности/гара́нтии — 10 лет; **~d against rust** гаранти́рованный от корро́зии

✐ **guard** /ɡɑːd/ *n.* ◆ (state of alertness) настороже́нность; **he was caught off his ~** его́ заста́ли враспло́х; (mil.): **on ~ duty** на часа́х; **в карау́ле** ◆ (man appointed to keep ~) охра́нник, карау́льный; (*collect.*) охра́на, стра́жа ◆ (BrE, of a train) проводни́к ◆ (protective device) защи́тное устро́йство
• *v.t.* охраня́ть (*impf.*); бере́чь (*impf.*)
• *v.i.* бере́чься (*impf.*), остерега́ться (*impf.*) (against: + *g.*); **everything was done to ~ against infection** бы́ли при́няты все ме́ры про́тив инфе́кции
■ **~ dog** *n.* сторожева́я соба́ка; **~sman** *n.* гварде́ец

guarded /'ɡɑːdɪd/ *adj.* сде́ржанный; осторо́жный

guardian /'ɡɑːdɪən/ *n.* ◆ (protector) опеку́н ◆ (law) опеку́н
■ **~ angel** *n.* а́нгел-храни́тель (*m.*)

Guatemala /ɡwɑːtə'mɑːlə/ *n.* Гватема́ла

Guatemalan /ɡwɑːtə'mɑːlən/ *n.* гватема́л|ец (-ка)
• *adj.* гватема́льский

guerrilla /ɡə'rɪlə/ *n.* партиза́н
■ **~ warfare** *n.* партиза́нская война́

✐ **guess** /ɡes/ *n.* дога́дка; **at a rough ~** гру́бо/ориентиро́вочно
• *v.t.* ◆ (estimate) прики́|дывать, -нуть;

I would ~ his age at 40 я бы дал ему́ лет 40 ◆ (conjecture) дога́д|ываться, -аться (*о чём*) ◆ (infml, expect, suppose) полага́ть (*impf.*); **I ~ you are right** вероя́тно, вы пра́вы
• *v.i.* гада́ть (*impf.*); **she likes to keep him ~ing** ей нра́вится держа́ть его́ в неве́дении
■ **~work** *n.* дога́дки (*f. pl.*)

✐ **guest** /ɡest/ *n.* ◆ (one privately entertained) гость (*m.*) ◆ (at a hotel etc.) постоя́лец
■ **~ house** *n.* пансио́н; **~ room** *n.* ко́мната для госте́й

guffaw /ɡʌ'fɔː/ *n.* го́гот (*смех*)
• *v.i.* гогота́ть (*impf.*) (*смея́ться*)

guidance /'ɡaɪd(ə)ns/ *n.* руково́дство

✐ **guide** /ɡaɪd/ *n.* ◆ (leader) руководи́тель (*m.*); (for travellers, tourists, etc.) гид, экскурсово́д ◆ (directing principle) руково́дство ◆ (manual) уче́бник; **~ to fishing** руково́дство по ры́бной ло́вле ◆ **(Girl) G~** де́вочка-ска́ут
• *v.t.* води́ть (*indet.*), вести́ (*det.*), по-; **руководи́ть** (*impf.*) + *i.*; **be ~d by principles** руково́дствоваться (*impf.*) при́нципами
■ **~book** *n.* путеводи́тель (*m.*); **~ dog** *n.* соба́ка-поводы́рь; **~line** *n.* директи́ва

guild /ɡɪld/ *n.* ◆ (hist.) ги́льдия ◆ ассоциа́ция, сою́з

guillotine /'ɡɪləti:n/ *n.* ◆ гильоти́на ◆ (for paper, metal, etc.) ре́зальная маши́на

guilt /ɡɪlt/ *n.* вина́

✐ **guilty** /'ɡɪltɪ/ *adj.* (**guiltier, guiltiest**) вино́вный; **he pleaded ~ to the crime** он призна́л себя́ вино́вным в преступле́нии; **~ conscience** нечи́стая со́весть; **a verdict of ~/not ~** обвини́тельный/оправда́тельный пригово́р

guinea pig /'ɡɪnɪ pɪɡ/ *n.* морска́я сви́нка; (fig.) «подо́пытный кро́лик»

guise /ɡaɪz/ *n.* (dress) наря́д; (pretence) предло́г; **under the ~ of friendship** под ви́дом дру́жбы

guitar /ɡɪ'tɑː(r)/ *n.* гита́ра

guitarist /ɡɪ'tɑːrɪst/ *n.* гитари́ст (-ка)

gulf /ɡʌlf/ *n.* ◆ (deep bay) зали́в; бу́хта; **the G~ Stream** Гольфстри́м ◆ (abyss) бе́здна ◆ (fig.) про́пасть

gull /ɡʌl/ *n.* (bird) ча́йка

gullet /'ɡʌlɪt/ *n.* пищево́д; **it sticks in my ~** (fig.) э́то стои́т у меня́ поперёк го́рла

gullible /'ɡʌlɪb(ə)l/ *adj.* легкове́рный

gully /'ɡʌlɪ/ *n.* лощи́на

gulp /ɡʌlp/ *n.* большо́й глото́к; **he took a ~ of tea** он глотну́л ча́ю
• *v.t.* глот|а́ть, -ну́ть

gum¹ /ɡʌm/ *n.* (anat.) десна́

gum² /ɡʌm/ *n.* (adhesive) клей; (resin) каме́дь; (chewing ~) жева́тельная рези́нка

gumption /'ɡʌmpʃ(ə)n/ *n.* (infml) смышлёность; нахо́дчивость

✐ **gun** /ɡʌn/ *n.* (cannon) пу́шка, ору́дие; (pistol) пистоле́т; (rifle) ружьё; **he stuck to his ~s** (fig.) он не сдал пози́ций; **jump the ~** (fig.) сова́ться, су́нуться ра́ньше вре́мени
• *v.t.* (**gunned, gunning**) стреля́ть (*impf.*); **the refugees were ~ned down** бе́женцев расстре́ляли

✐ ключева́я ле́ксика

■ ∼**fire** *n.* оруди́йный ого́нь; ∼**man** *n.* банди́т; террори́ст; ∼**point** *n.*: at ∼**point** угрожа́я ору́жием; под ду́лом пистоле́та; ∼**powder** *n.* по́рох; ∼**shot** *n.* руже́йный вы́стрел

gunner /'gʌnə(r)/ *n.* канони́р; артиллери́ст

gurgle /'gɜːg(ə)l/ *n.* бу́льканье
• *v.i.* бу́лькать (*impf.*)

guru /'guru:/ *n.* гуру́ (*m. indecl.*)

gush /gʌʃ/ *v.i.* хлы́нуть (*pf.*)

gust /gʌst/ *n.* поры́в ве́тра

gusto /'gʌstəʊ/ *n.* (relish) смак; (zeal) жар

gusty /'gʌstɪ/ *adj.* (gustier, gustiest) бу́рный; поры́вистый; a ∼ day ве́треный день

gut /gʌt/ *n.* **1** (intestine) кишка́ **2** (*in pl.*) (intestines, stomach) кишки́ (*f. pl.*); (fig., courage and determination) вы́держка; he hadn't the ∼s to tackle the burglar у него́ не хвати́ло му́жества задержа́ть граби́теля; ∼ reaction инстинкти́вная реа́кция
• *v.t.* (**gutted, gutting**) **1** (eviscerate) потроши́ть, вы- **2** (destroy contents of) опустош|а́ть, -и́ть

gutsy /'gʌtsɪ/ *adj.* (gutsier, gutsiest) упо́рный, де́рзкий

gutter /'gʌtə(r)/ *n.* (under eaves) водосто́чный жёлоб; (at roadside) сто́чная кана́ва

guttural /'gʌtər(ə)l/ *adj.* горта́нный; горлово́й; (ling.) веля́рный, задненёбный

⚡ **guy** /gaɪ/ *n.* ма́лый; wise ∼ у́мник

guzzle /'gʌz(ə)l/ *v.t.* (eat) есть, съ- с жа́дностью; (drink) пить, вы- с жа́дностью; (fig., consume) про|еда́ть, -е́сть

gym /dʒɪm/ *n.* (gymnasium) гимнасти́ческий зал; (gymnastics) гимна́стика
■ ∼ shoe *n.* спорти́вная та́почка

gymkhana /dʒɪm'kɑːnə/ *n.* конноспорти́вные состяза́ния (*nt. pl.*)

gymnasi|um /dʒɪm'neɪzɪəm/ *n.* (*pl.* ∼ums *or* ∼a) гимнасти́ческий зал

gymnast /'dʒɪmnæst/ *n.* гимна́ст (-ка)

gymnastic /dʒɪm'næstɪk/ *adj.* гимнасти́ческий

gymnastics /dʒɪm'næstɪks/ *n.* гимна́стика

gynaecological /gaɪnəkə'lɒdʒɪk(ə)l/ (AmE **gynecological**) *adj.* гинекологи́ческий

gynaecologist /gaɪnə'kɒlədʒɪst/ (AmE **gynecologist**) *n.* гинеко́лог

gynaecology /gaɪnə'kɒlədʒɪ/ (AmE **gynecology**) *n.* гинеколо́гия

Gypsy /'dʒɪpsɪ/ *n. & adj.* = Gipsy

gyrate /dʒaɪə'reɪt/ *v.i.* враща́ться (*impf.*)

g

h

Hh

haberdashery /'hæbədæʃərɪ/ *n.* (BrE) (shop) галантере́йный магази́н; (wares) галантере́я

habit /'hæbɪt/ *n.* **1** (settled practice) привы́чка; get into the ∼ of ...ing прив|ыка́ть, -ы́кнуть + *inf.*; get out of the ∼ of ...ing отв|ыка́ть, -ы́кнуть + *inf. or* от + *g.* **2** (nun's/monk's dress) ря́са

habitable /'hæbɪtəb(ə)l/ *adj.* приго́дный для жилья́

habitat /'hæbɪtæt/ *n.* есте́ственная среда́ (*растения, животного*)

habitual /hə'bɪtʃʊəl/ *adj.* привы́чный; обы́чный; a ∼ liar неисправи́мый лгун

hack /hæk/ *v.t.* разруб|а́ть, -и́ть; руби́ть (*impf.*)
• *v.i.*: ∼ into (comput.) прон|ика́ть, -и́кнуть в + *a.*; взл|а́мывать, -ома́ть

hacker /'hækə(r)/ *n.* (comput.) ха́кер

hackneyed /'hæknɪd/ *adj.* изби́тый

had /hæd/ *past and p.p. of* ▶ have

haddock /'hædək/ *n.* (*pl.* ∼) пи́кша

hadn't /'hæd(ə)nt/ *neg. of* ▶ had

haematologist /hi:mə'tɒlədʒɪst/ (AmE **hematologist**) *n.* гемато́лог

haematology /hi:mə'tɒlədʒɪ/ (AmE **hematology**) *n.* гематоло́гия

haemoglobin /hi:mə'gləʊbɪn/ (AmE **hemoglobin**) *n.* гемоглоби́н

haemophilia /hi:mə'fɪlɪə/ (AmE **hemophilia**) *n.* гемофили́я

haemophiliac /hi:mə'fɪlɪæk/ (AmE **hemophiliac**) *n.* гемофи́лик

haemorrhage /'hemərɪdʒ/ (AmE **hemorrhage**) *n.* кровоизлия́ние; (fig.) отто́к

haemorrhoids /'hemərɔɪdz/ (AmE **hemorrhoids**) *n. pl.* геморро́й

hag /hæg/ *n.* карга́, ве́дьма (usu. fig.)

haggard /'hægəd/ *adj.* изможждённый

haggle /'hæg(ə)l/ *v.i.* торгова́ться (*impf.*)

hail¹ /heɪl/ *n.* (frozen rain) град
• *v.i.*: it is ∼ing идёт град
■ ∼stone *n.* гра́дина; ∼storm *n.* гроза́ с гра́дом

hail² /heɪl/ *v.t.* **1** (acclaim) провозгла|ша́ть, -си́ть; (praise) превозноси́ть (*impf.*) **2** (summon) под|зыва́ть, -озва́ть; he ∼ed a taxi он подозва́л такси́

⚡ **hair** /heə(r)/ *n.* **1** (single strand) во́лос, волосо́к **2** (head of ∼) во́лосы (*m. pl.*) **3** (of animals) шерсть, щети́на
■ ∼brush *n.* щётка для воло́с; ∼cut *n.*

стри́жка; **have a** ~**cut** стри́чься, по-; ~**do** n.
(infml) причёска; ~**dresser** n. парикма́хер;
~**dresser's** n. (shop, salon) парикма́херская;
~**dryer** n. фен; ~**grip** n. (BrE) зако́лка;
~**pin** n. шпи́лька; ~**pin bend** (BrE), **turn** (AmE)
круто́й поворо́т; ~**raising** adj. жу́ткий;
~**spray** n. лак для воло́с; ~**style** n. причёска

hairy /ˈheərɪ/ adj. (**hairier, hairiest**)
волоса́тый

Haiti /ˈheɪtɪ/ n. Гаи́ти (m. indecl.)

hake /heɪk/ n. хек

halcyon /ˈhælsɪən/ attr. adj. ти́хий,
безмяте́жный

hale /heɪl/ adj. кре́пкий; ~ **and hearty**
кре́пкий и бодрый

♂ **half** /hɑːf/ n. (pl. **halves**) **1** (one of two equal
parts) полови́на; **one and a** ~ полтора́; **he
cut the loaf in** ~ он разре́зал хлеб попола́м;
~ **an hour** полчаса́; ~ **past two** полови́на
тре́тьего; **they agreed to go halves** они́
согласи́лись подели́ть попола́м **2** (of a game)
пери́од, тайм
● adv.: ~ **asleep** со́нный; ~ **dead** полуживо́й;
~ **as much** вдво́е ме́ньше; ~ **as much again** в
полтора́ ра́за бо́льше; **I** ~ **expected it** я почти́
ждал э́того

■ ~**back** n. полузащи́тник; ~**brother**
n. (having same father) единокро́вный брат;
(having same mother) единоутро́бный брат;
~**hearted** adj. нереши́тельный; без
энтузиа́зма; ~**hour** n. (also ~ **an hour**)
полчаса́; **every** ~**hour** ка́ждые полчаса́; ~
mast n.: **at** ~ **mast** приспу́щенный (флаг);
~**moon** n. полуме́сяц; ~**pound** n. also ~
a pound полфу́нта; ~**price** adj. полцены́;
at ~**price** за полцены́; ~**sister** n. (having
same father) единокро́вная сестра́; (having same
mother) единоутро́бная сестра́; ~**term** n.:
~**term (holiday)** (BrE) кани́кулы (pl., g. —) в
середи́не триме́стра; ~**time** n. коне́ц тайма;
the teams changed ends at ~**time** кома́нды
поменя́лись места́ми после пе́рвого тайма;
~**way** adj. лежа́щий на полпути́; ~**way
house** (fig.) компроми́сс; полуме́ра ● adv. на
полпути́; **we met** ~**way from the station** мы
встре́тились на полпути́ от вокза́ла

halibut /ˈhælɪbət/ n. (pl. ~) па́лтус

halitosis /ˌhælɪˈtəʊsɪs/ n. дурно́й за́пах изо рта́

♂ **hall** /hɔːl/ n. **1** (place of assembly) зал **2** (lobby)
(also **hallway**) пере́дняя, холл; ~ **of
residence** (BrE) общежи́тие

■ ~**mark** n. проби́рное клеймо́; (fig.)
отличи́тельный при́знак ● v.t. ста́вить, по-
про́бу на + p.

hallelujah /ˌhælɪˈluːjə/ n. & int. аллилу́йя

hallo see ▶ hello

Halloween /ˌhæləʊˈiːn/ n. кану́н Дня Всех
Святы́х (31 октября́)

hallucination /həˌluːsɪˈneɪʃ(ə)n/ n.
галлюцина́ция

halo /ˈheɪləʊ/ n. (pl. ~**es** or ~**s**) (round saint's
head) нимб; (fig.) орео́л

♂ ключева́я ле́ксика

halt /hɒlt/ n. остано́вка; **come to a** ~
остан|а́вливаться, -ови́ться; **call a** ~ де́лать,
с- прива́л; (fig.) да|ва́ть, -ть отбо́й
● v.t. остан|а́вливать, -ови́ть
● v.i. (stop) остан|а́вливаться, -ови́ться; ~!
who goes there? стой! кто идёт?

halter /ˈhɒltə(r)/ n. (for a horse) по́вод

halve /hɑːv/ v.t. (divide in two) дели́ть,
раз- попола́м; (reduce by half) ум|еньша́ть,
-е́ньшить (or сокра|ща́ть, -ти́ть) наполови́ну

halves /hɑːvz/ pl. of ▶ half

ham /hæm/ n. ветчина́

hamburger /ˈhæmbɜːgə(r)/ n. **1** га́мбургер
2 (AmE, minced beef) говя́жий фарш

hamlet /ˈhæmlɪt/ n. дереву́шка

hammer /ˈhæmə(r)/ n. молото́к
● v.t. (beat) уд|аря́ть, -а́рить; (defeat) бить, по-;
~ **in** вби|ва́ть, -ть; **we** ~**ed out a plan** мы
разрабо́тали план
● v.i. стуча́ть (impf.); колоти́ть (impf.);
someone was ~**ing on the door** кто́-то
колоти́л в дверь

hammock /ˈhæmək/ n. гама́к

hamper[1] /ˈhæmpə(r)/ n. корзи́на с кры́шкой

hamper[2] /ˈhæmpə(r)/ v.t. меша́ть, по- + d.;
стесня́ть (impf.)

hamster /ˈhæmstə(r)/ n. хомя́к

♂ **hand** /hænd/ n. **1** (lit., fig.) рука́, кисть;
~ **luggage** (BrE), **baggage** (AmE) ручна́я
кладь; **I shall have my** ~**s full next week** на
сле́дующей неде́ле я бу́ду о́чень за́нят;
~ **in** ~ (lit., fig.) рука́ о́б руку; (lit. only):
walk ~ **in** ~ ходи́ть (impf.) (держа́сь) за́
руку **2** (vbl. phrr.): **let me give, lend you a**
~! дава́йте я вам помогу́!; **she had a** ~ **in
his downfall** в его́ паде́нии она́ сыгра́ла не
после́днюю роль; **they were holding** ~s
они́ держа́лись за́ руки; **try one's** ~ **at sth**
про́бовать, по- себя́ в чём-н. **3** (prepositional
phrr.): **you should take that child in** ~ вы
должны́ взять э́того ребёнка на́ руки; **on** ~
в нали́чии; в распоряже́нии; **he has a sick
father on his** ~s у него́ на рука́х больно́й
оте́ц; **things are getting out of** ~ собы́тия
выхо́дят из-под контро́ля **4** (member of crew
or team): **all** ~s **on deck!** все наве́рх!; **farm** ~
рабо́тник на фе́рме **5** (side): **on the one** ~ ...,
on the other ~ (fig.) с одно́й стороны́..., с
друго́й стороны́ **6** (of a clock) стре́лка **7** (set
of cards) ка́рты (f. pl.); **show one's** ~ (fig.)
раскр|ыва́ть, -ы́ть ка́рты
● v.t. перед|ава́ть, -а́ть; ~ **me the paper,
please** переда́йте мне газе́ту, пожа́луйста
● with advs.: **he** ~**ed back the money** он
верну́л де́ньги; **the custom was** ~**ed down**
э́тот обы́чай передава́лся из поколе́ния в
поколе́ние; **will you** ~ **in your resignation?**
вы пода́дите заявле́ние об ухо́де?; **the
teacher** ~**ed out books** учи́тель разда́л
кни́ги; **the king** ~**ed over his authority
to parliament** коро́ль пе́редал власть
парла́менту

■ ~**bag** n. (BrE) су́мочка, да́мская су́мка;
~**ball** n. (game) ручно́й мяч, гандбо́л;
~**book** n. посо́бие; руково́дство; ~**brake**

n. ручно́й то́рмоз; ~**cuff** *n.* нару́чник ● *v.t.* над|ева́ть, -е́ть нару́чники + *d. or* на + *a.*;
~ **grenade** *n.* ручна́я грана́та; ~**made** *adj.* сде́ланный вручну́ю; ручно́й рабо́ты; ~**out** *n.* (gift) подая́ние; ми́лостыня; (for publicity) рекла́мный листо́к; ~**picked** *adj.* тща́тельно ото́бранный; ~**set** *n.* (telephone) тру́бка; ~**s-free** *adj.* (device etc.) оставля́ющий ру́ки свобо́дными (*прибор и m. n.*); ~**shake** *n.* рукопожа́тие; ~**s-on** *adj.* практи́ческий, свя́занный с жи́знью; ~**s-on experience** практи́ческий о́пыт; ~**stand** *n.* сто́йка на рука́х; ~**writing** *n.* по́черк; ~**written** *adj.* напи́санный от руки́

handful /'hændfʊl/ *n.* горсть; (infml): **this child is a** ~ с э́тим ребёнком хлопо́т не оберёшься

handicap /'hændɪkæp/ *n.* поме́ха, препя́тствие
● *v.t.* (**handicapped**, **handicapping**) чини́ть (*impf.*) препя́тствия (*кому*); ~**ped person** (sometimes offens.) (physically) инвали́д; челове́к с ограни́ченными возмо́жностями; (mentally) у́мственно отста́лый челове́к

handicraft /'hændɪkrɑ:ft/ *n.* ремесло́, ручна́я рабо́та

handiwork /'hændɪwɜ:k/ *n.* ручна́я рабо́та

handkerchie|f /'hæŋkətʃi:f/ *n.* (*pl.* ~**fs** *or* ~**ves**) носово́й плато́к

⚘ **handle** /'hænd(ə)l/ *n.* (of door, cup) ру́чка; (of sword, tool) рукоя́ть, рукоя́тка
● *v.t.* **1** (take or hold in the hands) тро́гать (*impf.*) **2** (manage, deal with, treat) обраща́ться (*impf.*) с + *i.*; обходи́ться (*impf.*) с + *i.*; спр|авля́ться, -а́виться с + *i.*; **he** ~**d the affair very well** он прекра́сно спра́вился с э́тим де́лом; **the officer** ~**d his men well** офице́р уме́ло кома́ндовал свои́ми солда́тами
■ ~**bars** *n. pl.* (of a bicycle) руль (*m.*)

handsome /'hænsəm/ *adj.* (**handsomer**, **handsomest**) краси́вый

handy /'hændɪ/ *adj.* (**handier**, **handiest**) **1** (to hand, available) (име́ющийся) под руко́й **2** (convenient) удо́бный, (infml) сподру́чный; **it may come in** ~ э́то мо́жет пригоди́ться
■ ~**man** *n.* разнорабо́чий

⚘ **hang** /hæŋ/ *n.*: **I can't get the** ~ **of this machine** (*or* of his argument) я не могу́ разобра́ться в э́той маши́не (*or* в его́ до́водах)
● *v.t.* (*past and p.p.* **hung**, *except in sense 3: past and p.p.* **hanged**) **1** (suspend) ве́шать, пове́сить **2** (decorate) разве́|шивать, -сить **3** (execute by ~ing) ве́шать, пове́сить; **Judas** ~**ed himself** Иу́да пове́сился
● *v.i.* (*past and p.p.* **hung**, *except in sense 3: past and p.p.* **hanged**) **1** (be suspended) висе́ть (*impf.*); (fig.): **the threat of dismissal hung over him** над ним нави́сла угро́за увольне́ния **2** (lean) све́|шиваться, -ситься; **don't** ~ **out of the window** не высо́вывайтесь из окна́ **3** (be executed): **he will** ~ **for it** он попадёт за э́то на ви́селицу **4** (loiter, stay close): **he hung round the door** он задержа́лся у две́ри

□ ~ **about** *v.i.* (BrE) = hang around

□ ~ **around** *v.i.* болта́ться (*impf.*); шата́ться (*impf.*)

□ ~ **back** *v.i.* отст|ава́ть, -а́ть

□ ~ **on** *v.i.* (cling) держа́ться (*impf.*) (**to**: за + *a.*); (persist) упо́рствовать (*impf.*); ~ **on!** (infml) погоди́те!

□ ~ **out** *v.t.* выве́шивать, вы́весить; **she hung out the washing** она́ вы́весила бельё
● *v.i.* (protrude): **his shirt was** ~**ing out** руба́шка вы́лезла у него́ из брюк; (infml, relax) тусова́ться (*impf.*)

□ ~ **together** *v.i.* (make sense): **the story doesn't** ~ **together** ≈ концы́ с конца́ми не схо́дятся

□ ~ **up** *v.t.* (fasten on peg, nail, etc.) ве́шать, пове́сить
● *v.i.* (end telephone conversation) ве́шать, пове́сить тру́бку

■ ~**glider** *n.* (craft) дельтапла́н; ~**gliding** *n.* дельтапланери́зм; ~**over** *n.* (from drink) похме́лье, перепо́й; ~**up** *n.* (infml) ко́мплекс

hangar /'hæŋə(r)/ *n.* анга́р

hanger /'hæŋə(r)/ *n.* (for clothes) ве́шалка
■ ~**on** *n.* приспе́шник

hanging /'hæŋɪŋ/ *n.* **1** висе́ние; (execution) пове́шение **2** (*in pl.*) (tapestry etc.) портье́ры (*f. pl.*)

hanker /'hæŋkə(r)/ *v.i.*: ~ **after/for** жа́ждать + *g.*

hanky /'hæŋkɪ/ *n.* (infml) = handkerchief

Hanoi /hæ'nɔɪ/ *n.* Хано́й

haphazard /hæp'hæzəd/ *adj.* случа́йный

hapless /'hæplɪs/ *adj.* несча́стный; злополу́чный

⚘ **happen** /'hæp(ə)n/ *v.i.* **1** (occur) случ|а́ться, -и́ться; прои|сходи́ть, -зойти́; получ|а́ться, -и́ться; **I hope nothing has** ~**ed to him** наде́юсь, с ним ничего́ не случи́лось **2** (chance): **as it** ~**s I can help you** в да́нном слу́чае я могу́ вам помо́чь; **we** ~**ed to meet** мы неожи́данно/случа́йно встре́тились

happily /'hæpɪlɪ/ *adv.* **1** (contentedly) сча́стливо **2** (fortunately) к сча́стью **3** (gladly) с удово́льствием

happiness /'hæpɪnɪs/ *n.* сча́стье

⚘ **happy** /'hæpɪ/ *adj.* (**happier**, **happiest**) **1** (contented) сча́стливый **2** (fortunate) счастли́вый, уда́чливый; ~ **birthday!** с днём рожде́ния!; ~ **Christmas!** с Рождество́м (Христо́вым)! **3** (pleased) дово́льный (*чем*); **we shall be** ~ **to come** мы с удово́льствием придём
■ ~**-go-lucky** *adj.* беззабо́тный; беспе́чный; ~ **medium** *n.* золота́я середи́на

harangue /hə'ræŋ/ *v.t.* увещева́ть (*impf.*)

harass /'hærəs/ *v.t.* изв|оди́ть, -ести́

harassment /'hærəsmənt/ *n.* тра́вля; изма́тывание; **sexual** ~ сексуа́льное домога́тельство

harbinger /'hɑ:bɪndʒə(r)/ *n.* предве́стник

harbour /'hɑ:bə(r)/ (AmE **harbor**) *n.* га́вань, порт
● *v.t.* да|ва́ть, -ть убе́жище + *d.*; ~**ing a criminal** укрыва́тельство престу́пника; (fig.):

I ~ **no grudge against him** я не держу́ на него́ зла

◇ **hard** /hɑːd/ *adj.* **1** (firm, solid) твёрдый; про́чный; ~ **core** (fig., nucleus of resistance etc.) ядро́; ~ **and fast rules** жёсткие пра́вила **2** (difficult) тру́дный; **bargains are** ~ **to come by** достава́ть ве́щи по невысо́ким це́нам непро́сто **3** (unsentimental, relentless): **don't be too** ~ **on her!** не бу́дьте к ней сли́шком стро́ги! **4** (vigorous, harsh): ~ **times** тяжёлые времена́; **it's a** ~ **life** жизнь трудна́; тру́дно живётся; ~ **liquor** кре́пкие напи́тки; ~ **drugs** сильноде́йствующие нарко́тики; ~ **water** жёсткая вода́ **5** (intensive): ~ **work** тяжёлая/тру́дная рабо́та **6** (infml, unfortunate): ~ **luck!** (BrE) не везёт!; **his parents are** ~ **up** его́ роди́тели — лю́ди небога́тые **7** **8**; ~ **of hearing** глухова́тый; тугой на́ ухо **8** (of money): ~ **cash** нали́чность; нали́чные (де́ньги); ~ **currency** твёрдая валю́та ● *adv.* **1** (solid): **the ground froze** ~ земля́ промёрзла **2** (with force): **it is raining** ~ идёт си́льный дождь **3** (persistently): **work** ~ (study) усе́рдно занима́ться (*impf.*); **I tried** ~ **to make him understand** я изо всех сил стара́лся разъясни́ть ему́ (*что*) ◼ ~**back** *n.* (book) кни́га в жёстком переплёте *or* в твёрдой обло́жке; ~**board** *n.* древе́сно-волокни́стая плита́, ДВП; ~**boiled** *adj.*: a ~**boiled egg** яйцо́ вкруту́ю; ~**copy** *n.* (comput.) распеча́тка; ~**core** *adj.* (criminal) закоренелый; (pornography) открове́нный; жёсткий; ~ **disk** *n.* (comput.) жёсткий диск; ~**earned** *adj.* зарабо́танный тяжёлым трудо́м; ~ **hat** *n.* защи́тный шлем; ~**headed** *adj.* трёзвый; практи́чный; ~**hearted** *adj.* бессерде́чный; неумоли́мый; ~**hitting** *adj.* (e.g. speech) жёсткий; бескомпроми́ссный; ~ **labour** *n.* исправи́тельно-трудовы́е рабо́ты; (fig.) ка́торга; ~**liner** *n.* сторо́нник жёсткой ли́нии; ~**nosed** *adj.* упря́мый, непримири́мый; ~**pressed** *adj.* находя́щийся в тру́дном положе́нии; ~**ware** *n.* скобяны́е изде́лия/ това́ры; (mil., infml) те́хника; (comput.) аппарату́ра; ~**wearing** *adj.* но́ский; ~**working** *adj.* рабо́тящий; (at studies) усидчивый

harden /ˈhɑːd(ə)n/ *v.t.* (make hard) де́лать, с- твёрдым; (fig.) ожесточа́ть, -и́ть; **he** ~**ed his heart** его́ се́рдце ожесточи́лось; **a** ~**ed criminal** закоренелый престу́пник; рецидиви́ст ● *v.i.* тверде́ть, за-; (fig.): **opinion** ~**ed** мне́ние укорени́лось

◇ **hardly** /ˈhɑːdlɪ/ *adv.* **1** (with difficulty) с трудо́м **2** (only just) едва́; **I had** ~ **sat down when the phone rang** я сел, как зазвони́л телефо́н **3** (not reasonably) вряд ли; **you can** ~ **expect her to agree** вы едва́ (*or* вряд) ли мо́жете рассчи́тывать на её согла́сие **4** (almost not): ~ **ever** почти́ никогда́; **I** ~ **know him** я его́ почти́ не зна́ю; **there's** ~ **any money left** де́нег почти́ не

оста́лось

hardship /ˈhɑːdʃɪp/ *n.* невзго́ды (*f. pl.*)

hardy /ˈhɑːdɪ/ *adj.* (**hardier, hardiest**) закалённый; (of plants) морозосто́йкий

hare /heə(r)/ *n.* за́яц

harem /ˈhɑːriːm/ *n.* гаре́м

haricot /ˈhærɪkəʊ/ *n.* (in full ~ **bean**) фасо́ль (обыкнове́нная) (collect.)

harm /hɑːm/ *n.* вред, уще́рб; **there's no** ~ (in) **trying** попы́тка не пы́тка ● *v.t.* вреди́ть, по- + *d.*; причин|я́ть, -и́ть (*or* нан|оси́ть, -ести́) вред + *d.*

harmful /ˈhɑːmfʊl/ *adj.* вре́дный

harmless /ˈhɑːmlɪs/ *adj.* (not injurious) безвре́дный; (innocent) безоби́дный

harmonic /hɑːˈmɒnɪk/ *adj.* гармони́ческий

harmonica /hɑːˈmɒnɪkə/ *n.* губна́я гармо́ника

harmonious /hɑːˈməʊnɪəs/ *adj.* (lit., fig.) гармони́чный

harmonize /ˈhɑːmənaɪz/ *v.t.* (mus.) гармонизи́ровать (*impf., pf.*)

harmony /ˈhɑːmənɪ/ *n.* гармо́ния

harness /ˈhɑːnɪs/ *n.* у́пряжь ● *v.t.* запр|яга́ть, -я́чь; (fig., natural forces) обу́зд|ывать, -а́ть; (energy etc.) мобилизова́ть (*impf., pf.*)

harp /hɑːp/ *n.* а́рфа ● *v.i.* (fig.): ~ **on sth** тверди́ть (*impf.*) о чём-н.

harpist /ˈhɑːpɪst/ *n.* арфи́ст (-ка)

harpoon /hɑːˈpuːn/ *n.* гарпу́н

harpsichord /ˈhɑːpsɪkɔːd/ *n.* клавеси́н

harrowing /ˈhærəʊɪŋ/ *adj.*: a ~ **tale** душераздира́ющая исто́рия

harsh /hɑːʃ/ *adj.* **1** (rough) гру́бый, ре́зкий **2** (severe) суро́вый

hart /hɑːt/ *n.* саме́ц оле́ня

harvest /ˈhɑːvɪst/ *n.* (yield) урожа́й; (process) жа́тва, сбор урожа́я ● *v.t.* соб|ира́ть, -ра́ть; жать, с- ◼ ~ **festival** *n.* пра́здник урожа́я

has /hæz/ *3rd pers. sg. pres. of* ▸ **have**

hash[1] /hæʃ/ *n.*: (fig.): **he made a** ~ **of it** он загуби́л всё де́ло

hash[2] /hæʃ/ *n.* (also ~ **sign**) си́мвол но́мера (#), решётка, знак решётки ◼ ~**tag** *n.* хеште́г

hashish /ˈhæʃiːʃ/ *n.* гаши́ш

hasn't /ˈhæz(ə)nt/ *neg. of* ▸ **has**

hassle /ˈhæs(ə)l/ *n.* (infml) каните́ль

hassock /ˈhæsək/ *n.* **1** (BrE) поду́шечка для коленопреклоне́ния **2** (AmE) пуф

haste /heɪst/ *n.* спе́шка

hasten /ˈheɪs(ə)n/ *v.t.* (hurry) торопи́ть, по- ● *v.i.* торопи́ться, по-, спеши́ть (*impf.*); **I** ~ **to add that ...** спешу́ доба́вить, что...

hasty /ˈheɪstɪ/ *adj.* (**hastier, hastiest**) (hurried) поспе́шный; (rash, ill-considered) поспе́шный

hat /hæt/ *n.* шля́па; (fur, knitted) ша́пка ◼ ~**trick** *n.*: **he scored a** ~**trick** (fig., of footballer etc.) он сде́лал хет-три́к

◇ ключева́я ле́ксика

hatch¹ /hætʃ/ *n.* (opening) люк; (cover) крышка
■ **~back** *n.* хетчбэк (*автомобиль с открывающейся вверх задней двервю*)

hatch² /hætʃ/ *v.t.* (egg) высиживать, высидеть; (fig., plot) вынашивать, выносить; зам|ышлять, -ыслить
● *v.i.* (*also* ~ **out**) (of bird) вылупляться, вылупиться

hatchet /'hætʃɪt/ *n.* топор, топорик

⚹ **hate** /heɪt/ *n.* ненависть
● *v.t.* ненавидеть (*impf.*); (dislike strongly) ненавидеть (*impf.*); I ~ **getting up early** я ненавижу рано вставать

hateful /'heɪtfʊl/ *adj.* ненавистный

hatred /'heɪtrɪd/ *n.* ненависть (for: к + *d.*)

haughty /'hɔːtɪ/ *adj.* (**haughtier, haughtiest**) высокомерный

haul /hɔːl/ *n.* **1**: **a long** ~ (fig.) долгое дело **2**: **a** ~ **of fish** улов; (fig., booty) добыча, улов
● *v.t. & i.* тянуть (*impf.*); тащить (*impf.*)

haulage /'hɔːlɪdʒ/ *n.* транспортировка

haulier /'hɔːlɪə(r)/ *n.* (BrE) перевозчик

haunch /hɔːntʃ/ *n.* бедро

haunt /hɔːnt/ *n.* излюбленное место
● *v.t.* неотступно преследовать (*impf.*); a ~ed **house** дом с привидениями; a ~ing **melody** навязчивая мелодия

⚹ **have** /hæv/ *n.*: **the** ~s **and the** ~-**nots** имущие и неимущие
● *v.t.* (*3rd pers. sg. pres.* **has**, *past and p.p.* **had**) **1** иметь; (possess) обладать + *i.*; (often expr. by) y + *g.*; **she has blue eyes** y неё голубые глаза; I ~ **no doubt** у меня нет сомнений; **he had the courage to refuse** у него хватило мужества отказаться; I ~ **no idea** понятия не имею **2** (contain): **June has 30 days** в июне 30 дней **3** (experience): ~ **a good time!** желаю вам хорошо провести время!; (suffer from): **he has a cold** у него насморк **4** (bear) родить (*impf., pf.*); **she is having a baby in May** в мае у неё родится ребёнок **5** (receive, obtain): **we had news of him yesterday** вчера мы получили известие о нём; (tolerate): I **won't** ~ **it!** этого я не потерплю! **6** (show, exercise): ~ **pity on me** сжальтесь надо мной!; **he had no mercy on** был безжалостен **7** (undertake, perform): ~ **a game of tennis** сыграть (*pf.*) в теннис; ~ **a go** (infml) пытаться, по- **8** (partake of, enjoy): ~ **dinner** ужинать (*impf.*) **9** (infml, swindle): **you've been had** вас провели/ надули **10** (with inf., be obliged to, need to): I ~ **to finish by tomorrow** я должен закончить к завтрашнему дню; I ~ **to sit down** мне надо сесть; (be obliged) быть обязанным; **you don't** ~ **to go** вы не обязаны идти; (having no choice) быть вынужденным; I **had to accept the invitation** я был вынужден принять приглашение **11** (phrr. with it): **let him** ~ **it!** (sl., attack him) дай ему хорошенько!; покажи ему!; **he has it in for me** (infml) у него зуб на меня; ~ **it out with sb** объясн|яться, -иться с кем-н.
● *with advs.*: **can** I ~ **my watch back?** могу я получить свои часы обратно?; **he had his**

coat off он был без пальто; **she had a red dress on** на ней было красное платье; ~ **sb on** (BrE) разыгр|ывать, -ать кого-н.; **he was had up for speeding** (BrE, infml) его задержали за превышение скорости
● *miscellaneous phrr.*: **you had better/best give the book back** вам не мешало бы вернуть книгу; **it has nothing to do with you** к вам это (никоим образом) не относится; I'll ~ **nothing to do with it** я не желаю иметь никакого отношения к этому

haven /'heɪv(ə)n/ *n.* гавань; (fig.) приют

haven't /'hæv(ə)nt/ *neg. of* ▶ **have**

haversack /'hævəsæk/ *n.* рюкзак

havoc /'hævək/ *n.* (destruction) разгром; (fig.): **play** ~ **with** вн|осить, -ести беспорядок/ хаос в + *a.*

Hawaii /hə'waɪɪ/ *n.* Гавайи (*m. pl.*)

hawk /hɔːk/ *n.* ястреб (also fig., pol.)

hawthorn /'hɔːθɔːn/ *n.* боярышник

hay /heɪ/ *n.* сено
■ ~ **fever** *n.* поллиноз, аллергия на пыльцу растений; ~**stack** *n.* стог сена; ~**wire** *n.* (sl.): **everything went** ~**wire** всё пошло наперекосяк

hazard /'hæzəd/ *n.* опасность
● *v.t.* отва́ж|иваться, -иться + *inf. or* на + *a.*; **he** ~**ed a remark** он отважился высказать замечание
■ ~ **lights** *n. pl.* аварийные фары (*f. pl.*)

hazardous /'hæzədəs/ *adj.* рискованный
■ ~ **waste** *n.* вредные отходы *m. pl.*

haze /heɪz/ *n.* дымка

hazel /'heɪz(ə)l/ *n.* (tree) лесной орех; (colour) ореховый цвет; ~ **eyes** карие глаза
■ ~**nut** *n.* лесной орех

hazy /'heɪzɪ/ *adj.* (**hazier, haziest**) подёрнутый дымкой; (fig.) смутный, туманный

HDTV *abbr.* (*of* **high-definition television**) ТВЧ (телевидение высокой чёткости)

⚹ **he** /hiː/ *pers. pron.* (*obj.* **him**) он; (obj. **him**) он, тот

⚹ **head** /hed/ *n.* **1** голова; **from** ~ **to foot, toe** с головы до ног; I **cannot make** ~ **or tail of it** я не могу в этом разобраться; **this is all completely over my** ~ всё это выше моего понимания; **shake one's** ~ качать, по- головой; **a** ~ **cold** насморк **2** (mind, brain): **he has a good** ~ **for figures** он хорошо считает; **he's off his** ~ он спятил (infml); (faculties): **the wine went to his** ~ вино ударило ему в голову; **success went to his** ~ успех вскружил ему голову; (balance, composure): **he lost/kept his** ~ он потерял голову / он не терял головы **3** (on a coin): ~s **or tails?** орёл или решка? **4** (unit): **£5 a** ~ пять фунтов с каждого **5** (upper or principal end): **at the** ~ **of the table** во главе стола **6** (principal member) глава (*c.g.*), старший; ~ **of state** глава государства; ~ **of the family** глава семьи; (*attr.*) (principal): ~ **office** главная контора, центр **7** (culmination): **to come to a** ~ назр|евать, -еть
● *v.t.* **1** (direct): **he is** ~**ed for home** он

направля́ется домо́й **2** (strike with head): **he ~ed the ball into the net** он заби́л мяч в се́тку голово́й **3** (be in charge of) возгла|вля́ть, -а́вить; **he ~ed the team** он возглавля́л кома́нду
● *v.i.* (move, steer) напр|авля́ться, -а́виться; (fig.): **he is ~ing for disaster** он пло́хо ко́нчит
■ **~ache** *n.* головна́я боль; **I have a ~ache** у меня́ боли́т голова́; **~band** *n.* головна́я повя́зка; **~dress** *n.* (замыслова́тый/ экзоти́ческий) головно́й убо́р; **~ first** *n. pl.* голово́й вперёд; **~hunter** *n.* (fig.) челове́к, перема́нивающий специали́стов из други́х организа́ций; **~lamp, ~light** *nn.* фа́ра; **~line** *n.* заголо́вок; (*in pl.*) (гла́вные) но́вости дня; **he hit the ~lines** его́ и́мя не сходи́ло с пе́рвых поло́с газе́т; **~long** *adv.* голово́й вперёд; (in a rush) стремгла́в; **~master, ~mistress** *nn.* (BrE) дире́ктор шко́лы; **~-on** *adj.* лобово́й, встре́чный; **a ~-on collision** лобово́е столкнове́ние; **~phone** *n.* нау́шник; **~quarters** *n.* штаб-кварти́ра; (mil.) штаб, ста́вка; **~rest** *n.* подголо́вник; **~scarf** *n.* косы́нка; **~set** *n.* (pair of ~phones) нау́шники (*m. pl.*); **~stone** *n.* (tombstone) надгро́бный ка́мень; **~strong** *adj.* своево́льный, упря́мый; **~ teacher** *n.* дире́ктор шко́лы; **~way** *n.* продвиже́ние вперёд; (fig.): **we are not making much ~way** мы продвига́емся сли́шком ме́дленно

headed /'hedɪd/ *adj.*: **~ notepaper** (of organization) ге́рбовая бума́га; (of person) именна́я бума́га

header /'hedə(r)/ *n.* **1** (in soccer) уда́р голово́й **2** (line of text) колонти́тул

heading /'hedɪŋ/ *n.* (title) заголо́вок, загла́вие; (section) ру́брика

heady /'hedɪ/ *adj.* (**headier, headiest**) хмельно́й; (also fig.) пьяня́щий

heal /hiːl/ *v.t.* (person) исцел|я́ть, -и́ть; (wound) залеч́|ивать, -и́ть
● *v.i.* заж|ива́ть, -и́ть

healer /'hiːlə(r)/ *n.* ле́карь (*m.*)

healing /'hiːlɪŋ/ *n.* лече́ние

✒ **health** /helθ/ *n.* здоро́вье; **in good ~** здоро́вый
■ **~ centre** *n.* поликли́ника; **~ food** *n.* натура́льная пи́ща; **~ insurance** *n.* медици́нская страхо́вка; **~ service** *n.* слу́жба здравоохране́ния, здравоохране́ние

✒ **healthy** /'helθɪ/ *adj.* (**healthier, healthiest**) здоро́вый

heap /hiːp/ *n.* **1** (pile) ку́ча, гру́да **2** (*in pl.*) (infml, large quantity) ма́сса, ку́ча, у́йма; **he has ~s of money** у него́ у́йма/ку́ча де́нег
● *v.t.*: **a ~ed** (BrE), **heaping** (AmE) **spoonful** ло́жка с ве́рхом; **they ~ed honours on him** его́ осы́пали по́честями

✒ **hear** /hɪə(r)/ *v.t. & i.* (*past and p.p.* **heard** /hɜːd/) **1** (perceive with ear) слы́шать, у-; **I can't ~ a word** я не слы́шу ни сло́ва; **I ~d him shout** я услы́шал, как он закрича́л; **I ~ someone coming** я слы́шу, что кто-то идёт

or (чьи́-то) шаги́ **2** (listen to): **~ evidence** слу́шать, за- показа́ния свиде́телей; **his prayer was ~d** его́ моли́твы бы́ли услы́шаны; **I won't ~ of it!** я и слы́шать об э́том не хочу́! **3** (learn) слы́шать, у-; **have you ~d the news?** вы слы́шали но́вости?; **have you ~d from your brother?** что слы́шно от ва́шего бра́та?; **I've never ~d of him** я о нём никогда́ не слы́шал **4**: **~!, ~!** пра́вильно!; ве́рно ска́зано!
■ **~say** *n.* слу́хи (*m. pl.*)

✒ **hearing** /'hɪərɪŋ/ *n.* **1** (perception) слух **2** (law) слу́шание
■ **~ aid** *n.* слухово́й аппара́т

hearse /hɜːs/ *n.* катафа́лк

✒ **heart** /hɑːt/ *n.* **1** (organ) се́рдце **2** (soul; seat of emotions) се́рдце, душа́; **he had set his ~ on winning** он стра́стно жела́л вы́играть; **don't take it to ~** не принима́йте э́то бли́зко к се́рдцу; (enthusiasm): **his ~ is not in his work** у него́ душа́ не лежи́т к рабо́те; (courage): **he lost ~** он пал ду́хом; **take ~!** не па́дайте ду́хом!; (memory): **I learnt it by ~** я вы́учил э́то наизу́сть **3** (centre) середи́на, сердцеви́на; **this book gets to the ~ of the matter** э́та кни́га затра́гивает са́мую суть де́ла **4** (*in pl.*) (cards) че́рв|и (-е́й)
■ **~ache** *n.* серде́чная боль; **~ attack** *n.* серде́чный при́ступ; инфа́ркт; **~beat** *n.* серде́чное бие́ние; **~breaking** *adj.* душераздира́ющий; **~broken** *adj.* с разби́тым се́рдцем; **~burn** *n.* изжо́га; **~ disease** *n.* боле́знь се́рдца; **~ failure** *n.* разры́в се́рдца; **~felt** *adj.* душе́вный, глубоко́ прочу́вствованный; **~throb** *n.* (infml) люби́мец; **~-to-~** *adj.*: **a ~-to-~ talk** разгово́р по душа́м; **~ transplant** *n.* переса́дка се́рдца

hearten /'hɑːt(ə)n/ *v.t.* ободр|я́ть, -и́ть

hearth /hɑːθ/ *n.* оча́г

heartless /'hɑːtlɪs/ *adj.* бессерде́чный

hearty /'hɑːtɪ/ *adj.* (**heartier, heartiest**) **1** (cordial) серде́чный **2** (healthy): **a ~ appetite** прекра́сный аппети́т **3** (cheerful) весёлый

✒ **heat** /hiːt/ *n.* **1** (hotness) жара́; (warmth) тепло́ **2** (warmth of feeling) теплота́; (passion) горя́чность; **in the ~ of the moment** сгоряча́ **3** (in running) забе́г; (in horse racing) зае́зд; (in swimming) заплы́в **4** (of animals) те́чка; **our dog is on ~** у на́шей соба́ки те́чка
● *v.t.* **1** (raise temperature of) нагр|ева́ть, -е́ть; **the potatoes were ~ed up** карто́шку разогре́ли; **~ed swimming pool** бассе́йн с подогре́вом **2**: **a ~ed argument** жа́ркий спор
■ **~stroke** *n.* теплово́й уда́р; **~wave** *n.* полоса́/пери́од си́льной жары́

heater /'hiːtə(r)/ *n.* обогрева́тель (*m.*)

heath /hiːθ/ *n.* **1** (BrE, waste land) пу́стошь **2** (shrub) ве́реск

heathen /'hiːð(ə)n/ *n.* язы́чник
● *adj.* язы́ческий

heather /'heðə(r)/ *n.* ве́реск

heating /'hiːtɪŋ/ *n.* обогрева́ние, отопле́ние

h

heave /hiːv/ *v.t.* (*past and p.p.* **heaved**)
(lift) подн|имáть, -я́ть; (throw) бр|осáть,
-óсить; ~ **a sigh** (тяжелó) взд|ыхáть,
-охнýть
● *v.i.* (*past and p.p.* **heaved** *or esp.* naut.,
hove) **1** (pull): they ~**d on the rope** они́
вы́брали канáт **2** (retch) тýжиться (*impf.*)
(при рвóте) **3** (rise and fall) вздымáться
(*impf.*)

heaven /ˈhev(ə)n/ *n.* **1** (sky, firmament) нéбо,
небéсный свод **2** (paradise) рай, цáрство
небéсное **3** (God): thank ~ **for that** слáва
Бóгу; for ~'s sake рáди Бóга; **(good)** ~**s!**
Гóсподи!; Бóже мой!

heavenly /ˈhevənlɪ/ *adj.* **1** (in or of heaven)
небéсный **2** (infml, wonderful) изуми́тельный;
ди́вный

heavily /ˈhevɪlɪ/ *adv.* значи́тельно, си́льно;
he fell ~ он тяжелó рýхнул; they were ~
defeated они́ потерпéли тяжёлое поражéние

♂ **heavy** /ˈhevɪ/ *adj.* (**heavier**, **heaviest**)
тяжёлый; a ~ **blow** (lit., fig.) тяжёлый удáр;
a ~ **cold** си́льный нáсморк; **he is a ~ drinker**
он си́льно пьёт; **with a ~ heart** с тяжёлым
сéрдцем; ~ **rain** си́льный/проливнóй дождь;
he is a ~ sleeper у негó крéпкий сон; a ~
sky хмýрое нéбо; ~ **traffic** интенси́вное
движéние
■ ~**-handed** *adj.* неуклю́жий; ~ **metal** *n.*
(infml, mus.) хéви-метáл; ~**weight** *n.* (sport, fig.)
тяжеловéс

Hebrew /ˈhiːbruː/ *n.* (language)
древнееврéйский язы́к; (modern) иври́т
● *adj.* древнееврéйский; (modern) иври́тский

heckle /ˈhek(ə)l/ *v.t.* переби|вáть, -и́ть
● *v.i.* переби|вáть, -и́ть орáтора

heckler /ˈheklə(r)/ *n.* человéк, котóрый
пытáется переби́ть орáтора; крикýн

hectare /ˈhekteə(r)/ *n.* (10,000 square metres)
гектáр

hectic /ˈhektɪk/ *adj.* (busy) лихорáдочный,
бýрный

hector /ˈhektə(r)/ *v.t.* запýг|ивать, -áть

hedge /hedʒ/ *n.* живáя и́згородь
● *v.t.*: ~ **one's bets** (fig.) перестрах|óвываться,
-овáться
● *v.i.* (prevaricate) уви́л|ивать, -ьнýть
■ ~**hog** *n.* ёж; ~**row** *n.* живáя и́згородь,
шпалéра

hedonism /ˈhedənɪz(ə)m/ *n.* гедони́зм

hedonist /ˈhedənɪst/ *n.* гедони́ст

hedonistic /hedəˈnɪstɪk/ *adj.*
гедонисти́ческий

heed /hiːd/ *n.* внимáние
● *v.t.* учи́т|ывать, -éсть; вн|имáть, -ять + *d.*

heedless /ˈhiːdlɪs/ *adj.* беззабóтный,
беспéчный; she continued, ~ **of danger** онá
продолжáла, невзирáя на опáсность

heel /hiːl/ *n.* пя́тка; he fell head over ~s он
полетéл вверх тормáшками; he took to his
~s он брóсился наутёк

hefty /ˈheftɪ/ *adj.* (**heftier**, **heftiest**) (person)
здоровéнный; (blow) здорóвый

heifer /ˈhefə(r)/ *n.* тёлка, нéтель

---

height /haɪt/ *n.* **1** высотá; (of person) рост
2 (high ground) верши́на, верхýшка **3** (utmost
degree) вы́сшая стéпень; the ~ **of fashion**
послéдний крик мóды; the gale was at its ~
шторм был в разгáре

heighten /ˈhaɪt(ə)n/ *v.t.* (intensify) уси́ли|вать, -ть
● *v.i.* уси́ли|ваться, -ться

heinous /ˈheɪnəs/ *adj.* гнýсный, омерзи́тельный

heir /eə(r)/ *n.* наслéдник

heiress /ˈeərɪs/ *n.* наслéдница

heirloom /ˈeəluːm/ *n.* фами́льная рели́квия

held /held/ *past and p.p. of* ▸ hold

helicopter /ˈhelɪkɒptə(r)/ *n.* вертолёт

heliport /ˈhelɪpɔːt/ *n.* вертолётный аэродрóм;
(small, or at the top of building) вертолётная
площáдка

helium /ˈhiːlɪəm/ *n.* гéлий

hell /hel/ *n.* **1** (place or state) ад; he went
through ~ он перенёс мýки áда **2** (infml or sl.,
expr. vexation or emphasis): oh ~! чёрт возьми́!;
go to ~! иди́ к чёрту!; what the ~ **do you
want?** что вам нýжно, чёрт возьми́/побери́?;
they made the ~ **of a noise** они́ ужáсно
шумéли; we had a ~ **of a time** мы чертóвски
хорошó повесели́лись; just for the ~ **of it** за
здорóво живёшь, прóсто так

hellish /ˈhelɪʃ/ *adj.* áдский

hello, **hallo** /həˈləʊ/ *int.* (greeting)
здрáвствуй(те)!; (infml) привéт!; (on telephone)
аллó!

helm /helm/ *n.* (tiller) руль, рýмпель (*both
m.*); take the ~ (lit., fig.) встаǀвáть, -ть у
штурвáла/руля́

helmet /ˈhelmɪt/ *n.* шлем; (modern soldier's or
fireman's) кáска

♂ **help** /help/ *n.* пóмощь; he walks with the ~ of
a stick он хóдит с пáлкой; your advice was a
great ~ to us ваш совéт нам óчень помóг
● *v.t.* **1** (assist) помǀогáть, -óчь + *d.*; please
~ me up помоги́те мне, пожáлуйста,
подня́ться **2** (serve with food etc.) угоǀщáть,
-сти́ть; may I ~ you to (some more) salad?
могý я положи́ть вам (ещё) немнóго
салáта?; ~ yourself! угощáйтесь!; бери́те,
пожáлуйста! **3** (prevent; also v.i.): I can't ~ it я
не могý ничегó подéлать; I can't ~ laughing
я не могý удержáться от смéха; я не могý
не смея́ться; it can't be ~ed ничегó не
подéлаешь
● *v.i.* (avail, be of use) быть полéзным; crying
won't ~ слезáми гóрю не помóжешь
■ ~**line** *n.* слýжба/телефóн довéрия

helper /ˈhelpə(r)/ *n.* помóщник; (of a craftsman)
подрýчный

helpful /ˈhelpfʊl/ *adj.* полéзный; (obliging)
услýжливый

helping /ˈhelpɪŋ/ *n.* пóрция

helpless /ˈhelplɪs/ *adj.* беспóмощный

Helsinki /ˈhelsɪŋkɪ, helˈsɪŋkɪ/ *n.* Хéльсинки
(*m. indecl.*)

hem /hem/ *n.* край, подóл
● *v.t.* (**hemmed**, **hemming**) **1** (sew the edge
of) подшиǀвáть, -и́ть **2**: ~ **in** окружǀáть, -и́ть

h

hematologist etc. (AmE) see **haematologist** etc.

hemisphere /'hemɪsfɪə(r)/ n. полуша́рие

hemoglobin etc. (AmE) see **haemoglobin** etc.

hemp /hemp/ n. (plant) конопля́; (fibre) пенька́; **Indian** ~ (plant) конопля́ инди́йская; (drug, dried leaves and flowers) марихуа́на, анаша́; (resin) гаши́ш

hen /hen/ n. (domestic fowl) ку́рица; (female of bird species) са́мка пти́цы

■ ~ **party** n. (infml) деви́чник; ~**pecked** adj.: **he is** ~**pecked** жена́ де́ржит его́ под каблуко́м

hence /hens/ adv. (from here) отсю́да; (from now): **3 years** ~ че́рез три го́да; (consequently) отсю́да, сле́довательно

henchman /'hentʃmən/ n. приспе́шник

hepatitis /hepə'taɪtɪs/ n. гепати́т

heptathlon /hep'tæθlən/ n. семибо́рье

◢ **her** /hɜː(r)/ pron. (obj. of ▶ **she**); **he loves** ~ он лю́бит её; **he looks at** ~ он смо́трит на неё
● poss. adj. её; ~ **husband** её муж; (referring to subj. of sentence) свой; **she loves** ~ **husband** она́ лю́бит своего́ му́жа

herald /'her(ə)ld/ v.t. возвеща́ть, -сти́ть

heraldic /he'rældɪk/ adj. герáльди́ческий

heraldry /'herəldrɪ/ n. гера́льдика

herb /hɜːb/ n. трава́

■ ~ **tea** n. (camomile etc.) травяно́й чай; (blackcurrant etc.) фрукто́вый чай

herbaceous /hɜː'beɪʃəs/ adj. травяно́й

■ ~ **border** n. цвето́чный бордю́р

herbal /'hɜːb(ə)l/ n. травни́к
● adj. травяно́й

■ ~ **medicine** n. траволече́ние; ~ **tea** n. (camomile etc.) травяно́й чай; (blackcurrant etc.) фрукто́вый чай

herbalist /'hɜːbəlɪst/ n. специали́ст по лека́рственным расте́ниям

herbivore /'hɜːbɪvɔː(r)/ n. травоя́дное живо́тное

Herculean /hɜːkju'liːən/ adj. геркуле́сов; (fig.): ~ **efforts** титани́ческие уси́лия

herd /hɜːd/ n. ста́до
● v.t. сгоня́ть, согна́ть (вме́сте)

◢ **here** /hɪə(r)/ adv. **1** (in or at this place) здесь, тут; **my house is near** ~ мой дом ря́дом; **from** ~ **to there** отсю́да — туда́ **2** (to this place, in this direction) сюда́; **come** ~ **!** иди́те сюда́! **3** (demonstrative) вот; ~ **I am!** вот и я!; я тут!; ~ **he comes!** вот и он!; ~ **we are at last!** наконе́ц-то (мы) пришли́/ прие́хали/при́были!; ~'**s to our victory!** за на́шу побе́ду! **4** (with offers): ~ **you are!** пожа́луйста! **5** (phr.): **he looked** ~ **and there** он поиска́л там и сям (infml)

hereabouts /hɪərə'baʊts/ adv. поблизо́сти

hereafter /hɪər'ɑːftə(r)/ n.: **the** ~ загро́бная жизнь

hereby /hɪə'baɪ/ adv. сим (archaic); э́тим; настоя́щим

hereditary /hɪ'redɪtərɪ/ adj. насле́дственный

heredity /hɪ'redɪtɪ/ n. насле́дственность

◢ ключева́я ле́ксика

heresy /'herəsɪ/ n. е́ресь

heretic /'herətɪk/ n. ерети́|к (-чка)

heretical /hɪ'retɪk(ə)l/ adj. ерети́ческий

heritage /'herɪtɪdʒ/ n. насле́дство; (fig.) насле́дие

hermaphrodite /hɜː'mæfrədaɪt/ n. гермафроди́т

hermetic /hɜː'metɪk/ adj. гермети́ческий; ~**ally sealed** гермети́чески закры́тый

hermit /'hɜːmɪt/ n. отше́льник

hernia /'hɜːnɪə/ n. гры́жа

◢ **hero** /'hɪərəʊ/ n. (pl. ~**es**) геро́й

■ ~ **worship** n. преклоне́ние пе́ред геро́ями

heroic /hɪ'rəʊɪk/ adj. (person, attempt) геро́йческий

heroin /'herəʊɪn/ n. герои́н

heroine /'herəʊɪn/ n. герои́ня

heroism /'herəʊɪz(ə)m/ n. герои́зм

heron /'herən/ n. ца́пля

herpes /'hɜːpiːz/ n. лиша́й

herring /'herɪŋ/ n. сельдь; (as food) селёдка

hers /hɜːz/ pron. её; **is this handkerchief** ~**?** э́то её плато́к?; **friends of** ~ её друзья́

◢ **herself** /hɜː'self/ pron. **1** (refl.) себя́ (d., p. себе́, i. собо́й); -сь (suff.); **she looked at** ~ **in the mirror** она́ посмотре́ла на себя́ в зе́ркало; **she fell down and hurt** ~ она́ упа́ла и уши́блась **2** (emph.) сама́; **she said so** ~ она́ сама́ э́то сказа́ла **3** (after preps.) одна́; сама́; **she did it by** ~ она́ сде́лала э́то сама́; **she lives by** ~ она́ живёт одна́ **4** (her normal state): **she is not** ~ **today** сего́дня она́ сама́ не своя́

hertz /hɜːts/ n. (pl. ~) герц

hesitant /'hezɪt(ə)nt/ adj. коле́блющийся

hesitate /'hezɪteɪt/ v.i. колеба́ться (impf.); **don't** ~ **to ask** непреме́нно спроси́те

hesitation /hezɪ'teɪʃ(ə)n/ n. колеба́ние

hessian /'hesɪən/ n. (cloth) мешкови́на

heterogeneous /hetərəʊ'dʒiːnɪəs/ adj. неоднородный, разнохарáктерный

heterosexual /hetərəʊ'sekʃʊəl/ n. гетеросексуа́л(ьный челове́к)
● adj. гетеросексуа́льный

hexagon /'heksəgən/ n. шестиуго́льник

hexagonal /hek'sægən(ə)l/ adj. шестиуго́льный

hey /heɪ/ int. (used to attract attention) эй!; (as an informal greeting) приве́т!

heyday /'heɪdeɪ/ n. расцве́т, зени́т

HGV (BrE) abbr. (of **heavy goods vehicle**) большегрузный автомоби́ль

hi /haɪ/ int. приве́т!

hiatus /haɪ'eɪtəs/ n. (pl. ~**es**) **1** (gap) про́пуск, пробе́л **2** (between vowels) зия́ние

hibernate /'haɪbəneɪt/ v.i. впада́ть (impf.) в зи́мнюю спя́чку

hibiscus /hɪ'bɪskəs/ n. (pl. ~**es**) (bot.) гиби́скус

hiccup, hiccough /'hɪkʌp/ n. ико́та; (slight delay) зами́нка
● v.i. (**hiccuped, hiccuping**) ик|а́ть, -ну́ть

hid /hɪd/ *past of* ▸ **hide²**
hidden /'hɪd(ə)n/ *p.p. of* ▸ **hide²**
hide¹ /haɪd/ *n.* (skin) шкýра; (leather) кóжа
✧ **hide²** /haɪd/ *v.t.* (*past* **hid**, *p.p.* **hidden**)
прятать, с-; скры|вáть, -ть
● *v.i.* (*past* **hid**, *p.p.* **hidden**) прятаться, с-;
скр|ывáться, -ыться
■ **~-and-seek** *n.* прят|ки (-ок); **~away**, **~out**
nn. укрытие
hideous /'hɪdɪəs/ *adj.* урóдливый,
безобрáзный; (unpleasant) мéрзкий
hiding¹ /'haɪdɪŋ/ *n.* (infml, thrashing): **she gave
him a good ~** онá егó выпорола как слéдует
hiding² /'haɪdɪŋ/ *n.* (concealment) укрытие; **he
went into ~** он скрылся
■ **~ place** *n.* укрытие
hierarchical /haɪə'rɑ:kɪk(ə)l/ *adj.*
иерархический
hierarchy /'haɪərɑ:kɪ/ *n.* иерáрхия
hieroglyph /'haɪərəglɪf/ *n.* иерóглиф
hieroglyphic /haɪərə'glɪfɪk/ *adj.*
иероглифический
hieroglyphics /haɪərə'glɪfɪks/ *n. pl.*
иерóглифы, иероглифическое письмó
hi-fi /haɪfaɪ/ *n.* (*abbr. of* **high fidelity**)
(*pl.* **~s**) (infml) (высококáчественная)
стереосистéма
higgledy-piggledy /hɪgəldɪ'pɪgəldɪ/ *adj.*
беспорядочный; сумбýрный
● *adv.* вперемéшку; беспорядочно
✧ **high** /haɪ/ *n.*: **prices reached a new ~** цéны
достигли небывáло высóкого ýровня
● *adj.* ▮ (tall, elevated) высóкий (also mus.); **ten
feet ~** высотóй в 10 фýтов ▮ (chief, important):
~ command вы́сшее комáндование; **in ~
places** (fig.) в верхáх, в вы́сших сфéрах
▮ (greater than average; extreme): **~ blood
pressure** высóкое (кровянóе) давлéние; **in ~
spirits** в отли́чном/припóднятом настроéнии
▮ (at its peak): **~ noon** пóлдень; **~ summer**
середи́на/разгáр лéта; **it is ~ time** давнó
порá; **it is ~ time I was gone** мне ужé давнó
порá идти ▮ (drugs) под кáйфом; **to be ~
on cocaine** быть под кокаи́ном
● *adv.*: **~ up** высóко; (of direction) ввысь
■ **~brow** *n.* интеллектуáл ● *adj.*
интеллектуáльный, серьёзный; **~-class**
adj. первоклáссный, высóкого клáсса;
~-flyer *n.* (person likely to succeed) подаю́щий
больши́е надéжды (*or* многобещáющий)
человéк; **~-handed** *adj.* влáстный,
своевóльный; **~-heeled** *adj.* на высóком
каблукé; **~ heels** *n. pl.* тýфли на высóком
каблукé; **~ jump** *n.* прыжóк в высотý;
the H~lands *n. pl.* сéвер и сéверо-зáпад
Шотлáндии; **~lighter** *n.* флома́стер;
~-pitched *adj.* высóкий; **~-ranking**
adj. высокопостáвленный; **~-rise**
adj.: **~-rise apartment blocks** высóтные
многоквартирные домá; **~ road** *n.* шоссé
(*nt. indecl.*); **~-speed** *adj.* скоростнóй; **~
street** *n.* (BrE) глáвная ýлица; **~-tech** *adj.*
высокотехнологичный; **~ tide** *n.* больша́я
водá, прили́в; **~way** *n.* шоссé (*nt. indecl.*);
H~way Code прáвила дорóжного движéния

higher /'haɪə(r)/ *adj.* (senior, advanced) вы́сший;
~ education вы́сшее образовáние
● *adv.*: **~ up the hill** вы́ше на холмé
highlight /'haɪlaɪt/ *n.* (*in pl.*) (in hair) цветны́е
пряди (*f. pl.*); (fig.) кульминацио́нный
момéнт
● *v.t.* (fig., emphasize) выделя́ть, вы́делить (also
comput.); заостр|я́ть, -и́ть внимáние на + *p.*
✧ **highly** /'haɪlɪ/ *adv.* весьмá, óчень; **~ paid**
высокооплáчиваемый; **he speaks ~ of you**
он о вас óчень хорошó отзывáется; **she is ~
thought of** её óчень цéнят
■ **~ strung** *n.* (BrE) взви́нченный, нервóзный
Highness /'haɪnɪs/ *n.*: **His Royal ~** Егó
Королéвское Высóчество
hijack /'haɪdʒæk/ *v.t.* уг|оня́ть, -нáть;
пох|ищáть, -и́тить
hijacker /'haɪdʒækə(r)/ *n.* угóнщик,
похити́тель (*m.*)
hike¹ /haɪk/ *n.* (walk) турпохóд
● *v.i.* гуля́ть (*impf.*); ходи́ть (*indet.*), идти́
(*det.*) пешкóм
hike² /haɪk/ (infml) *n.* (rise) подъём
● *v.t.* (raise) подн|имáть, -я́ть
hiker /'haɪkə(r)/ *n.* пéший тури́ст
hiking /'haɪkɪŋ/ *n.* пéший тури́зм
hilarious /hɪ'leərɪəs/ *adj.* весёлый
hilarity /hɪ'lærɪtɪ/ *n.* весéлье, потéха
hill /hɪl/ *n.* холм
■ **~side** *n.* склон холмá; **~top** *n.* верши́на
холмá
hillock /'hɪlək/ *n.* хóлмик, бугóр
hilly /'hɪlɪ/ *adj.* (**hillier**, **hilliest**) холми́стый
✧ **him** /hɪm/ *obj. of* ▸ **he**
Himalayas /hɪmə'leɪəz/ *n. pl.* Гималáи (-ев)
✧ **himself** /hɪm'self/ *pron.* ▮ (refl.) себя́ (*d.,
p.* себé, *i.* собóй); -ся (*suff.*); **I hope he
behaves ~** надéюсь, что он бýдет вести́
себя́ прили́чно; **he fell and hurt ~** он упáл
и уши́бся ▮ (emph.) сам; **he did the job ~**
он сам сдéлал э́ту рабóту ▮ (after preps.)
оди́н; сам; **he did it by ~** он сдéлал э́то сам;
he lives by ~ он живёт оди́н ▮ (in his normal
state): **he is not ~ today** он сегóдня сам не
свой
hind /haɪnd/ *adj.*: **the dog stood on its ~ legs**
собáка встáла на зáдние лáпы
■ **~sight** *n.*: **he spoke with ~sight** он говори́л,
зная, чем кóнчилось дéло
hinder /'hɪndə(r)/ *v.t.* мешáть, по- + *d.*
Hindi /'hɪndɪ/ *n.* (language) хи́нди (*m. indecl.*)
hindrance /'hɪndrəns/ *n.* помéха,
препя́тствие
Hindu /'hɪndu:/ *n.* (*pl.* **~s**) индýс (-ка)
● *adj.* индýсский
Hinduism /'hɪndu:ɪz(ə)m/ *n.* индуи́зм
Hindustani /hɪndʊ'stɑ:nɪ/ *n.* (language)
хиндустáни (*m. indecl.*)
hinge /hɪndʒ/ *n.* шарни́р; (on door) петля́
● *v.i.* (**hingeing** *or* **hinging**): **it all ~d
on this event** всё бы́ло свя́зано с э́тим
событием

h

hint /hɪnt/ n. (suggestion) намёк; **he is always dropping ~s** он всегда говорит намёками; **there was a ~ of frost** начинало подмораживать; (written advice) совет
• v.t. & i. намек|ать, -нуть на + a.; **I ~ed that I needed a holiday** я намекнул, что мне нужен отпуск; **what are you ~ing (at)?** на что вы намекаете?

hip¹ /hɪp/ n. (anat.) бедро

hip² /hɪp/ int.: **~, ~, hooray!** гип-гип, ура!

hip³ /hɪp/ adj. (**hipper, hippest**) (infml) модный, крутой (sl.)

hippie, hippy /ˈhɪpɪ/ n. хиппи (c.g., indecl.)

hippo /ˈhɪpəʊ/ n. (pl. **~s**) (infml) гиппопотам, бегемот

hippopotamus /hɪpəˈpɒtəməs/ n. бегемот

✧ **hire** /ˈhaɪə(r)/ n. (engagement of person) наём; (of thing) наём, прокат; **cars for ~** машины напрокат
• v.t. (BrE, a place) сн|имать, -ять; (BrE, equipment, a car) брать, взять напрокат; (a worker) н|анимать, -анять
■ **~ purchase** n. (BrE) покупка в рассрочку

✧ **his** /hɪz/ pron. его; **is this book ~?** это его книга?; **friends of ~** его друзья
• poss. adj. его; **this is a ~ book** это его книга; (referring to subj. of sentence) свой; **he loves ~ children** он любит своих детей

Hispanic /hɪˈspænɪk/ adj. испанский; латиноамериканский
• n. латиноамерикан|ец (-ка)

hiss /hɪs/ n. шипение
• v.i. (of snake) шипеть, за-; (of audience) свистеть (impf.)

historian /hɪˈstɔːrɪən/ n. историк

historic /hɪˈstɒrɪk/ adj. исторический

✧ **historical** /hɪˈstɒrɪk(ə)l/ adj. исторический

✧ **history** /ˈhɪstərɪ/ n. история

histrionic /hɪstrɪˈɒnɪk/ adj. (theatrical) театральный, мелодраматический

✧ **hit** /hɪt/ n. (blow) удар, толчок; (infml, success) успех; (popular song) хит; шлягер
• v.t. (**hitting**, past and p.p. **hit**) **1** (strike) уд|арять, -арить; **he fell and ~ his head on a stone** он упал и ударился головой о камень; **the bullet ~ him in the shoulder** пуля попала ему в плечо; **the car ~ a tree** машина врезалась в дерево; **to ~ the target/mark** поп|адать, -асть в цель **2** (fig. uses): **the idea suddenly ~ me** меня вдруг осенило **3** (encounter): **he ~ a bad patch** (infml) у него началась полоса неудач
□ **~ back** v.t.: **if he ~s you, ~ him back** если он вас ударит, ударьте его тоже; (fig., at critics etc.) да|вать, -ть отпор + d.
□ **~ off** v.t.: **~ it off** ладить (impf.)
■ **~ man** n. наёмный/профессиональный убийца, киллер

hitch /hɪtʃ/ n. задержка
• v.t. **1** (fasten) привяз|ывать, -ать; прицеп|лять, -ить **2** (infml): **~ a lift** подъ|езжать, -ехать на попутной машине

✧ ключевая лексика

• v.i. (infml) (also **~-hike**) ездить автостопом
■ **~-hiker** n. путешествующий автостопом; **~-hiking** n. «голосование», езда автостопом (or на попутных машинах)

hither /ˈhɪðə(r)/ adv. сюда
■ **~to** adv. до сих пор

HIV abbr. of (**human immunodeficiency virus**) (med.) ВИЧ (вирус иммунодефицита человека)
■ **~-positive** adj. ВИЧ-инфицированный

hive /haɪv/ n. улей; (fig.): **the office is a ~ of industry** работа в офисе кипит

HND (BrE) abbr. (of **Higher National Diploma**) диплом о высшем техническом образовании

hoar /hɔː(r)/ adj. седой
■ **~ frost** n. иней, изморозь

hoard /hɔːd/ n. (тайный) запас, склад
• v.t. припрят|ывать, -ать

hoarding /ˈhɔːdɪŋ/ n. **1** (BrE, for poster display) рекламный щит **2** (BrE, fence round building site) забор/ограда вокруг стройплощадки

hoarse /hɔːs/ adj. хриплый

hoax /həʊks/ n. надувательство

hob /hɒb/ n. (BrE) поверхность кухонной плиты

hobble /ˈhɒb(ə)l/ v.i. ковылять (impf.)

hobby /ˈhɒbɪ/ n. хобби (nt. indecl.)

hobnob /ˈhɒbnɒb/ v.i. (**hobnobbed, hobnobbing**) водиться (impf.) (с кем), знаться (impf.) (с кем)

hockey /ˈhɒkɪ/ n. (on field) хоккей на траве; **ice ~** хоккей (с шайбой/на льду)
■ **~ stick** n. клюшка

hoe /həʊ/ n. мотыга, тяпка
• v.t. & i. (**hoes, hoed, hoeing**) разрыхлять (impf.) мотыгой

hog /hɒɡ/ n. боров; (AmE, also fig.) свинья; **go the whole ~** дов|одить, -ести дело до конца; идти, пойти на всё
• v.t. (**hogged, hogging**) (monopolize): **he ~ged the conversation** он не давал никому слова вставить

Hogmanay /ˈhɒɡməneɪ/ n. (Sc.) канун Нового года

hoist /hɔɪst/ v.t. подн|имать, -ять

✧ **hold** /həʊld/ n. **1** (grasp, grip) удерживание, захват; **he caught ~ of the rope** он ухватился за канат; **he kept ~ of the reins** он не выпускал поводья из рук; **he seized, took ~ of my arm** он схватил/взял меня за руку; **I got ~ of a plumber** я нашёл/отыскал водопроводчика; **where did you get ~ of those tickets?** где вы достали эти билеты; **it's difficult to get ~ of her** её трудно застать **2** (means of pressure): **she has a ~ on, over him** она имеет над ним власть **3** (ship's) трюм
• v.t. (past and p.p. **held**) **1** (clasp, grip) держать (impf.); **they sat ~ing hands** они сидели держась за руки **2** (maintain, keep in a certain position): **~ it!** (infml) (don't move) не двигайтесь!; не шевелитесь!; (fig., keep): **they were held to a draw** их принудили

к ничьей!; ~ the line! (teleph.) не кладите трубку! **3** (detain) зад|ёрживать, -ержа́ть; he was held prisoner его держа́ли в плену **4** (contain) вме|ща́ть, -сти́ть; the hall ~s a thousand зал вмеща́ет ты́сячу челове́к **5** (consider) полага́ть (impf.), счита́ть (impf.); the court held that ... суд призна́л, что...; he was held responsible ему́ пришло́сь держа́ть отве́т; I don't ~ it against him я не ста́влю ему́ э́то в вину́ **6** (restrain): she held her breath она́ затаи́ла дыха́ние **7** (have, own) владе́ть (impf.) + i.; we ~ the same views мы приде́рживаемся одина́ковых взгля́дов **8** (occupy, remain in possession of): he held his ground он не уступа́л; он не сдава́лся; I can ~ my own against anyone я могу́ потяга́ться с кем уго́дно **9** (carry on, conduct) пров|оди́ть, -ести́; the meeting was held at noon собра́ние состоя́лось (or провели́) в по́лдень
• v.i. (past and p.p. **held**) **1** (grasp): ~ tight! держи́тесь кре́пче/кре́пко! **2** (remain): ~ still! не дви́гайтесь! **3** (remain unbroken, unchanged, intact): will the rope ~? вы́держит ли верёвка?; how long will the weather ~? до́лго ли проде́ржится/просто́ит така́я пого́да?

□ ~ **back** v.t. (restrain) удёрж|ивать, -а́ть; I couldn't ~ him back я не мог его́ удержа́ть; (withhold) удёрж|ивать, -а́ть
• v.i. (refrain) воздёрж|иваться, -а́ться (от чего)

□ ~ **down** v.t.: (fig.): do you think you can ~ the job down? суме́ете ли вы удержа́ться на э́той до́лжности?; we will try to ~ prices down мы постара́емся сдержа́ть рост цен

□ ~ **forth** v.i. (infml, orate) разглаго́льствовать (impf.); веща́ть (impf.)

□ ~ **off** v.t. (keep away, repel): they held off the attack они́ отби́ли ата́ку; (postpone): he held off going to the doctor он откла́дывал визи́т к врачу́
• v.i. (stay away): the rain held off all morning дождя́ так и не́ было всё у́тро

□ ~ **on** v.t. (keep in position) прикреп|ля́ть, -и́ть
• v.i. (cling) держа́ться (to: за + a.); she held on to the banisters она́ держа́лась за пери́ла; (fig.): you should ~ on to those shares вам на́до держа́ться за э́ти а́кции; (infml, wait): ~ on a minute till I'm ready подожди́те: я бу́ду гото́в че́рез мину́ту; (on the telephone): ~ on, please! не ве́шайте тру́бку!

□ ~ **out** v.t. (extend) проти́гивать, -яну́ть; he greeted me and held out his hand он поздоро́вался и протяну́л мне ру́ку; (fig., offer): I can't ~ out any hope я не могу́ вас ниче́м обнадёжить
• v.i. (endure, refuse to yield) держа́ться, про-; the men are ~ing out for more money рабо́чие наста́ивают на повыше́нии зарпла́ты; (last): supplies cannot ~ out much longer запа́сов хва́тит не надо́лго

□ ~ **over** v.t. (defer) откла́дывать, -ложи́ть

□ ~ **up** v.t. (lift, hold erect) подн|има́ть, -я́ть; the boy held up his hand ма́льчик по́днял ру́ку; (delay) задёрж|ивать, -а́ть; we were held up on the way по доро́ге нас задержа́ли; traffic was

held up by fog движе́ние останови́лось из-за тума́на; (waylay): the robbers held them up at pistol point банди́ты огра́били их, угрожа́я пистоле́том
• v.i.: do you think the table will ~ up under the weight? вы ду́маете, стол вы́держит тако́й вес?

■ ~**all** n. (BrE) вещево́й мешо́к; ~**-up** n. (delay) заде́ржка; (robbery) вооружённый грабёж

holder /ˈhəʊldə(r)/ n. **1** (possessor) владе́лец; облада́тель (m.) **2** (container, also fin.) держа́тель (m.)

⚐ **hole** /həʊl/ n. **1** (cavity) дыра́ **2** (opening) отве́рстие **3** (burrow) нора́ **4** (phr.): the purchase made a ~ in his savings поку́пка оста́вила брешь в его́ сбереже́ниях; ~ in the wall (BrE, infml) банкома́т

■ ~ **punch(er)** n. дыроко́л

⚐ **holiday** /ˈhɒlɪdeɪ/ n. (BrE) **1** (day off) выходно́й (день); bank ~ официа́льный нерабо́чий день **2** (annual leave) о́тпуск, о́тдых; (school, university vacation) кани́кул|ы (pl., g. —); (leisure time) о́тдых; he is on ~ он в о́тпуске/отпуску́; у него́ кани́кулы

■ ~ **camp** n. (ле́тний) ла́герь; ~**maker** n. отдыха́ющий; тури́ст (-ка)

holistic /hɒˈlɪstɪk/ adj. це́лостный

Holland /ˈhɒlənd/ n. (country or province) Голла́ндия

hollow /ˈhɒləʊ/ n. вы́емка
• adj. **1** (not solid) пусто́й, по́лый **2** (of sounds) глухо́й **3** (fig., false, insincere) фальши́вый, лжи́вый; ~ laughter неесте́ственный смех **4** (sunken) вва́лившийся, впа́лый; ~ cheeks вва́лившиеся щёки

holly /ˈhɒlɪ/ n. остроли́ст

hollyhock /ˈhɒlɪhɒk/ n. алте́й ро́зовый

holocaust /ˈhɒləkɔːst/ n. ма́ссовое уничтоже́ние; the H~ холоко́ст

holster /ˈhəʊlstə(r)/ n. кобура́

holy /ˈhəʊlɪ/ adj. (**holier, holiest**) свяще́нный, свято́й; the H~ Ghost, Spirit Свято́й Дух; the H~ Land Свята́я земля́ (об Израиле и Палестине)

homage /ˈhɒmɪdʒ/ n. почте́ние, преклоне́ние; we pay ~ to his genius мы преклоня́емся пе́ред его́ ге́нием

⚐ **home** /həʊm/ n. **1** (place where one resides or belongs) дом; (attr.) дома́шний; she left ~ она́ поки́нула (роди́тельский) дом; at home (in one's house) до́ма; (on one's ~ ground) у себя́; (e.g. football) на своём по́ле; make yourself at ~ бу́дьте как до́ма; I feel at ~ here я чу́вствую себя́ здесь как до́ма **2** (institution) a ~ for the disabled дом инвали́дов; he put his parents into a ~ он помести́л свои́х роди́телей в дом престаре́лых **3** (attr.) (opp. foreign; native, local): ~ affairs вну́тренние дела́; ~ team кома́нда хозя́ев по́ля; ~ town родно́й го́род
• adv. **1** (at or to one's own house): he was on his way ~ он шёл/е́хал домо́й; is he ~ yet? он (уже́) до́ма? **2** (in or to one's own country):

h

he came ~ **from abroad** он верну́лся из-за грани́цы **3** (to the point aimed at): **bring sth ~ to sb** дов|оди́ть, -ести́ что-н. до чьего́-н. созна́ния; **his remarks struck ~** его́ замеча́ния попа́ли в цель

■ ~ **economics** n. pl. домово́дство; ~ **entertainment system** n. дома́шний развлека́тельный центр; ~**-grown** adj. (vegetables) дома́шний, с огоро́да; (not foreign) оте́чественный; ~ **help** n. (BrE) приходя́щая домрабо́тница; ~**land** n. ро́дина, родна́я страна́; ~**-made** adj. дома́шний; H~ **Office** n. (BrE) Министе́рство вну́тренних дел; ~ **page** n. (comput.) ста́ртовая страни́ца в Интерне́те; H~ **Secretary** n. (BrE) мини́стр вну́тренних дел; ~**sick** adj. скуча́ющий/ тоску́ющий по до́му/ро́дине; ~**work** n. дома́шнее зада́ние

homeless /ˈhəʊmlɪs/ adj. бездо́мный

homely /ˈhəʊmlɪ/ adj. (**homelier**, **homeliest**) **1** (BrE, cosy) дома́шний, ую́тный **2** (BrE, unpretentious): a ~ meal неприхотли́вая еда́ **3** (AmE, unattractive) некраси́вый

homeopath /ˈhəʊmɪəpæθ, ˈhɒm-/ n. гомеопа́т

homeopathic /həʊmɪəˈpæθɪk, hɒm-/ adj. гомеопати́ческий

homeopathy /həʊmɪˈɒpəθɪ, hɒmɪ-/ n. гомеопа́тия

homeward /ˈhəʊmwəd/ adv. (also **homewards**) домо́й

homicidal /hɒmɪˈsaɪd(ə)l/ adj. замышля́ющий уби́йство

homicide /ˈhɒmɪsaɪd/ n. (crime) уби́йство

homogeneous /hɒməˈdʒiːnɪəs/ adj. одноро́дный

homophobia /həʊməˈfəʊbɪə/ n. не́нависть к гомосексуали́стам, гомофо́бия

homosexual /hɒməˈsekʃʊəl/ n. гомосексуали́ст
● adj. гомосексуа́льный

homosexuality /hɒməsekʃʊˈælɪtɪ/ n. гомосексуали́зм

Honduran /hɒnˈdjʊərən/ n. гондура́с|ец (-ка)
● adj. гондура́сский

Honduras /hɒnˈdjʊərəs/ n. Гондура́с

hone /həʊn/ v.t. (sharpen) точи́ть, за-; (fig.) отт|а́чивать, -очи́ть

honest /ˈɒnɪst/ adj. (fair) че́стный; (candid): **to be ~ (with you)** че́стно говоря́

honestly /ˈɒnɪstlɪ/ adv. **1** (straightforwardly) че́стно **2** (candidly) пря́мо, чистосерде́чно; ~! че́стное сло́во!

honesty /ˈɒnɪstɪ/ n. **1** (integrity) че́стность **2** (candour) прямота́, и́скренность

honey /ˈhʌnɪ/ n. мёд; (AmE, infml, darling) дорого́й, ми́лый
■ ~**moon** n. медо́вый ме́сяц ● v.i. пров|оди́ть, -ести́ медо́вый ме́сяц

Hong Kong /hɒŋ ˈkɒŋ/ n. Гонко́нг

honk /hɒŋk/ v.i. гуде́ть (impf.)

---

honor /ˈɒnə(r)/ n. & v.t. (AmE) = honour

honorable /ˈɒnərəb(ə)l/ adj. (AmE)
= honourable

honorari|um /ɒnəˈreərɪəm/ n. (pl. ~ums or ~a) гонора́р

honorary /ˈɒnərərɪ/ adj. почётный

⚹ **honour** /ˈɒnə(r)/ (AmE **honor**) n. **1** (good character, reputation) честь **2** (dignity, credit) честь; **the reception was held in his ~** приём был устро́ен в его́ честь **3** (as title): **Your H~** ва́ша честь **4** (in pl.) (academic distinction): ~**s degree** ≈ сте́пень балака́вра
● v.t. **1** (respect, do ~ to) ока́з|ывать, -а́ть честь + d. **2** (fulfil obligation) выполня́ть, вы́полнить; **he failed to ~ the agreement** он не вы́полнил соглаше́ния; **will the cheque be ~ed?** бу́дет ли упла́чено по э́тому че́ку?

honourable /ˈɒnərəb(ə)l/ (AmE **honorable**) adj. че́стный, досто́йный

hood /hʊd/ n. **1** (headgear) капюшо́н **2** (BrE, of car) складно́й верх **3** (AmE, of car engine) капо́т

hoodie /ˈhʊdɪ/ n. (infml) толсто́вка с капюшо́ном; молодо́й челове́к, нося́щий толсто́вку с капюшо́ном

hoodwink /ˈhʊdwɪŋk/ v.t. одура́чи|вать, -ть; пров|оди́ть, -ести́ (infml)

hoof /huːf/ n. (pl. **hoofs** or **hooves**) копы́то

hook /hʊk/ n. **1** (curved device, also for fishing and as fastening) крючо́к, крюк; **the receiver was off the ~** тру́бка была́ снята́; **get off the ~** (infml) вызволя́ть, вы́зволить; **let off the ~** (infml) выруча́ть, вы́ручить **2** (boxing blow) хук, боково́й уда́р
● v.t. (usu. with advs., fasten): **she ~ed up her dress** она́ застегну́ла пла́тье (на крючки́)

hooligan /ˈhuːlɪɡən/ n. хулига́н

hooliganism /ˈhuːlɪɡənɪz(ə)m/ n. хулига́нство

hoop /huːp/ n. **1** (plaything) о́бруч **2** (BrE, croquet) воро́т|а (pl., g. —)

hooray! /hʊˈreɪ/ int. ура́

hoot /huːt/ n. (owl's cry) у́ханье; (warning note) гудо́к, сигна́л
● v.i. (of a car etc.) гуде́ть, про-; (of an owl) у́х|ать, -нуть; (of a person): **we ~ed with laughter** мы пока́тывались со́ смеху

hooter /ˈhuːtə(r)/ n. **1** (of car, factory) гудо́к **2** (sl., nose) руби́льник (нос)

Hoover® /ˈhuːvə(r)/ (BrE) n. пылесо́с
● v.t. (**h~**) пылесо́сить, про-

hooves /huːvz/ pl. of ▸ hoof

hop¹ /hɒp/ n. подско́к, скачо́к (на одно́й ноге́)
● v.i. (**hopped**, **hopping**) пры́гать, скака́ть (both impf.)

hop² /hɒp/ n. (bot.) хмель (m.)

⚹ **hope** /həʊp/ n. наде́жда; **don't raise my ~s in vain** не обнадёживайте меня́ понапра́сну
● v.t. & i. наде́яться (impf.); **I ~ to see you soon** наде́юсь, ско́ро вас уви́жу; **let's ~ so!** бу́дем наде́яться!; **I ~ not** наде́юсь, что нет

hopeful /ˈhəʊpfʊl/ adj. **1** (having hope): **I am ~ of success** я наде́юсь/рассчи́тываю на успе́х **2** (inspiring hope) обнадёживающий; **a ~ sign** обнадёживающий знак

hopefully /'hɒpfʊli/ *adv.*: ~ he will arrive soon надо надеяться, он скоро приедет

hopeless /'həʊplɪs/ *adj.* **1** (affording no hope) безнадёжный; a ~ situation безнадёжное положение **2** (infml, incapable): he's quite ~ at science точные науки ему совершенно не даются

horde /hɔ:d/ *n.* полчище

horizon /həˈraɪz(ə)n/ *n.* (lit., fig.) горизонт

horizontal /hɒrɪˈzɒnt(ə)l/ *adj.* горизонтальный

hormonal /hɔ:ˈməʊn(ə)l/ *adj.* гормональный

hormone /'hɔ:məʊn/ *n.* гормон; ~ replacement therapy гормональная терапия

horn /hɔ:n/ *n.* **1** (of cattle) рог **2** (mus., French horn) валторна; (hunting horn) рог **3** (of car) гудок

hornet /'hɔ:nɪt/ *n.* шершень (*m.*); his words stirred up a ~'s nest (fig.) его слова потревожили осиное гнездо

hornist /'hɔ:nɪst/ *n.* валторнист (-ка)

horoscope /'hɒrəskəʊp/ *n.* гороскоп

horrendous /həˈrendəs/ *adj.* ужасный

horrible /'hɒrɪb(ə)l/, **horrid** /'hɒrɪd/ *adjs.* ужасный

horrific /həˈrɪfɪk/ *adj.* ужасающий

horrify /'hɒrɪfaɪ/ *v.t.* потрясать, -ти

horror /'hɒrə(r)/ *n.* ужас; (extreme dislike): I have a ~ of cats я терпеть не могу кошек
■ ~ film *n.* фильм ужасов

hors d'oeuvre /ɔːˈdəːvz/ *n.* (*pl.* ~ or ~s pronunc. same or /-ˈdəːvz/) закуска

horse /hɔ:s/ *n.* лошадь, конь (*m.*); I had it straight from the ~'s mouth я узнал это из первых рук
■ ~back *n.*: on ~back верхом; ~back riding (AmE) = horse riding; ~ chestnut *n.* каштан конский; ~power *n.* лошадиная сила; 20 ~power 20 лошадиных сил; ~ race, ~ racing *nn.* скачки (*f. pl.*), бега (*m. pl.*); ~radish *n.* хрен; ~ riding *n.* верховая езда; ~shoe *n.* подкова

horticultural /hɔ:tɪˈkʌltʃər(ə)l/ *adj.* садоводческий

horticulture /'hɔ:tɪkʌltʃə(r)/ *n.* садоводство

horticulturist /hɔ:tɪˈkʌltʃərɪst/, **horticulturalist** /hɔ:tɪˈkʌltʃərəlɪst/ *nn.* садовод

hose /həʊz/ *n.* (*also* **hosepipe**) шланг

hosiery /'həʊzɪərɪ/ *n.* чулочно-носочные изделия (*nt. pl.*)

hospice /'hɒspɪs/ *n.* хоспис

hospitable /hɒˈspɪtəb(ə)l/ *adj.* гостеприимный

hospital /'hɒspɪt(ə)l/ *n.* больница; he is in ~ он (лежит) в больнице
■ ~ trust *n.* (BrE) больничный трест (*больница Национальной службы здравоохранения, управляемая на правах доверительной собственности*)

hospitality /hɒspɪˈtælɪtɪ/ *n.* гостеприимство

hospitalize /'hɒspɪtəlaɪz/ *v.t.* госпитализировать (*impf., pf.*)

host¹ /həʊst/ *n.* хозяин
● *v.t.* организовать (*impf., pf.*)

host² /həʊst/ *n.* (multitude) множество, масса

hostage /'hɒstɪdʒ/ *n.* заложник

hostel /'hɒst(ə)l/ *n.* общежитие

hostelry /'hɒstəlrɪ/ *n.* (archaic or joc.) постоялый двор

hostess /'həʊstɪs/ *n.* хозяйка

hostile /'hɒstaɪl/ *adj.* враждебный

hostility /hɒˈstɪlɪtɪ/ *n.* враждебность

hot /hɒt/ *adj.* (**hotter, hottest**) **1** (water, object) горячий; (weather) жаркий; I am ~ мне жарко; a ~ flush прилив крови; in the ~ seat (infml) на ответственной должности **2** (spicy) острый **3**: ~ on the scent, trail по горячему следу
● *v.i.* (**hotted, hotting**) (BrE, infml, become livelier): the game ~ted up игра оживилась
■ ~bed *n.* парник; (fig.) рассадник, очаг; ~-blooded *adj.* пылкий, страстный; ~ dog *n.* хот-дог; ~-headed *adj.* вспыльчивый, горячий; ~line *n.* (for enquiries) горячая линия; (between governments) прямая телефонная связь; ~plate *n.* плитка; ~-tempered *adj.* вспыльчивый; ~-water bottle *n.* грелка

hotel /həʊˈtel/ *n.* гостиница, отель (*m.*)

hotelier /həʊˈteliə(r)/ *n.* хозяин гостиницы

hound /haʊnd/ *n.* охотничья собака
● *v.t.* **1** (harrass) не давать кому-н. проходу **2** (~ out) (force to leave) выживать, выжить

hour /aʊə(r)/ *n.* **1** (period) час; boats for hire by the ~ прокат лодок с почасовой оплатой **2** (of clock time): every ~ on the ~ в начале каждого часа **3**: in office ~s в рабочее время; out of ~s в нерабочее время

hourly /'aʊəlɪ/ *adj.* **1** (occurring once an hour) ежечасный **2**: an ~ wage почасовая оплата
● *adv.* ежечасно; (at any time) с часу на час

house¹ /haʊs/ *n.* **1** (habitation) дом, здание; (pol.): H~ of Commons палата общин; H~ of Lords палата лордов; H~ of Representatives палата представителей **2** (audience) зал, аудитория; they played to a full ~ на их выступлении зал был полон; (BrE, performance) представление
■ ~boat *n.* плавучий дом; ~bound *adj.*: he is ~bound он не выходит из дома; ~holder *n.* домовладелец; ~ husband *n.* муж, ведущий домашнее хозяйство; ~keeper *n.* экономка; ~keeping *n.* домашнее хозяйство; ~-proud *adj.* любящий заниматься благоустройством и украшением дома; ~-to-~, a ~-to-~ search обыск всех домов подряд; повальный обыск; ~-trained *adj.* (BrE) приученный жить (*or* не пачкать) в доме (*о собаке, кошке*); ~-warming *n.* новоселье; ~wife *n.* домохозяйка; ~work *n.* домашние дела

house² /haʊz/ *v.t.* **1** (provide house(s) for) селить, по- **2** (accommodate) вмещать, -стить; this building ~s the city council в этом здании размещается муниципалитет **3** (store) хранить (*impf.*)

household /'haʊshəʊld/ *n.* дом; домашний круг; (*attr.*) ~ appliances бытовые приборы;

she is a ~ name её все зна́ют

☞ **housing** /ˈhaʊzɪŋ/ *n.* жильё
■ ~ **association** *n.* жили́щно-строи́тельная ассоциа́ция; ~ **benefit** *n.* (BrE) посо́бие на вы́плату квартпла́ты; ~ **development,** ~ **estate** (BrE), ~ **project** (AmE) *nn.* жило́й микрорайо́н

hovel /ˈhɒv(ə)l/ *n.* лачу́га

hover /ˈhɒvə(r)/ *v.i.* пари́ть (*impf.*); (fig.): to ~ around sb ви́ться (*impf.*) вокру́г + *g.*
■ ~**craft** *n.* хове́ркра́фт; су́дно на возду́шной поду́шке

☞ **how** /haʊ/ *adv.* **1** (in direct and indirect questions) как; каки́м о́бразом?; ~ **come?** (infml) как э́то?; ~ **come you are late?** почему́ э́то вы опа́здываете?; ~ **are you?** как пожива́ете?; ~ **do you know that?** отку́да вы э́то зна́ете?; ~ **about a drink?** не хоти́те ли вы́пить?; **2** (with adjs. and advs.): ~ **far is it?** как далеко́ э́то нахо́дится?; ~ **many, much?** ско́лько?; ~ **old is she?** ско́лько ей лет? **3** (in indirect statements or questions): **I told him** ~ **I'd been abroad** я рассказа́л ему́, как я съе́здил за грани́цу **4** (in exclamations): ~ **I wish I were there!** как бы мне хоте́лось сейча́с быть там!

☞ **however** /haʊˈevə(r)/ *adv.* (with adj.) како́й бы ни; как ни; ~ **strong he is** како́й бы он ни был си́льный; (with adv.) как бы ни; ~ **hard he tried** как ни он стара́лся; (in questions) как же; ~ **did you find out that?** как же вы узна́ли э́то?; (nevertheless) одна́ко, и всё же; ~, **he forgot** одна́ко он забы́л

howl /haʊl/ *n.* вой
● *v.t. & i.* выть (*impf.*); **listen to the wolves** ~**ing!** послу́шайте, как во́ют во́лки!

howler /ˈhaʊlə(r)/ *n.* (infml, error) грубе́йшая оши́бка, ля́псус

HQ *abbr.* (*of* **headquarters**) штаб-кварти́ра; (mil.) штаб, ста́вка

HR *abbr.* (*of* **human resources**) отде́л ка́дров

HRH (BrE) *abbr.* (*of* **Her/His Royal Highness**) Её/Его́ Короле́вское Высо́чество

HRT *abbr.* (*of* **hormone replacement therapy**) гормона́льная терапи́я

hub /hʌb/ *n.* сту́пица; (fig.) центр; (comput.) хаб
■ ~**cap** *n.* колпа́к

hubbub /ˈhʌbʌb/ *n.* шум, го́вор, го́мон, гвалт

huddle /ˈhʌd(ə)l/ *v.i.* толпи́ться, с-; **they** ~**d together for warmth** они́ прижа́лись друг к дру́гу, что́бы согре́ться

hue[1] /hju:/ *n.* (colour) отте́нок, тон (-á)

hue[2] /hju:/ *n.*: ~ **and cry** крик; (outcry) возмуще́ние

huff /hʌf/ *n.*: **he walked off in a** ~ он ушёл вконе́ц разоби́женный

hug /hʌg/ *n.* объя́тие
● *v.t. & i.* (**hugged, hugging**) обн|има́ть(ся), -я́ть(ся)

☞ **huge** /hju:dʒ/ *adj.* огро́мный, грома́дный; (event) грандио́зный

hull /hʌl/ *n.* (of ship) ко́рпус; (of aircraft) фюзеля́ж

hum /hʌm/ *n.* (of insects) жужжа́ние; (of machines) гуде́ние, гул
● *v.t. & i.* (**hummed, humming**) **1** (make murmuring sound) (of insects) жужжа́ть (*impf.*); (of cars) гуде́ть (*impf.*) **2** (sing with closed lips) напева́ть (*impf.*)

☞ **human** /ˈhju:mən/ *n.* челове́к
● *adj.* челове́ческий; ~ **being** челове́к; ~ **nature** челове́ческая приро́да; ~ **resources** (department) отде́л ка́дров; ~ **rights** права́ челове́ка; **human shield** живо́й щит

humane /hju:ˈmeɪn/ *adj.* гума́нный, челове́чный

humanism /ˈhju:məniz(ə)m/ *n.* гумани́зм

humanist /ˈhju:mənɪst/ *n.* гумани́ст

humanitarian /hju:mænɪˈteəriən/ *adj.* гуманита́рный; гума́нный

humanit|y /hju:ˈmænɪti/ *n.* **1** (the human race) челове́чество **2** (humaneness) гума́нность **3**: the ~**ies** гуманита́рные нау́ки (*f. pl.*)

humble /ˈhʌmb(ə)l/ *adj.* (**humbler, humblest**) скро́мный, поко́рный, смире́нный

humbug /ˈhʌmbʌg/ *n.* (deceit, hypocrisy) надува́тельство; (fraud) обма́нщик; (nonsense) чушь, вздор; (BrE, sweet) ледене́ц

humdrum /ˈhʌmdrʌm/ *adj.* однообра́зный, ну́дный

humid /ˈhju:mɪd/ *adj.* вла́жный

humidifier /hju:ˈmɪdɪfaɪ(ə)r/ *n.* увлажни́тель (*m.*) во́здуха

humidity /hju:ˈmɪdɪti/ *n.* вла́жность

humiliate /hju:ˈmɪlieɪt/ *v.t.* ун|ижа́ть, -и́зить

humiliation /hju:mɪliˈeɪʃ(ə)n/ *n.* униже́ние

humility /hju:ˈmɪlɪti/ *n.* смире́ние; скро́мность

hummock /ˈhʌmək/ *n.* буго́р, приго́рок

humor /ˈhju:mə(r)/ *n. & v.t.* (AmE) = **humour**

humorist /ˈhju:mərɪst/ *n.* (facetious person) остря́к, весельча́к; (humorous writer etc.) юмори́ст

humorless /ˈhju:məlɪs/ *adj.* (AmE) = **humourless**

humorous /ˈhju:mərəs/ *adj.* юмористи́ческий

humour /ˈhju:mə(r)/ (AmE **humor**) *n.* **1** (disposition) нрав, душе́вный склад **2** (amusement) ю́мор; **he has little sense of** ~ у него́ сла́бое чу́вство ю́мора
● *v.t.* пота́кать (*impf.*) + *d.*

humourless /ˈhju:məlɪs/ (AmE **humorless**) *adj.* лишённый чу́вства ю́мора; ску́чный

hump /hʌmp/ *n.* горб

hunch /hʌntʃ/ *n.* чутьё, интуи́ция
● *v.t.*: **he** ~**ed (up) his shoulders** он ссуту́лился/сгорбился

hundred /ˈhʌndrəd/ *n.* (*pl.* ~**s** or (*with numeral or qualifying word*) ~) (число́, но́мер) сто; (*collect.*) со́тня; **a** ~ **and fifty** сто пятьдеся́т, полтора́ста; ~**s of people** со́тни люде́й; **I'm one** ~ **per cent behind you** я стопроце́нтно на ва́шей стороне́; **in the nineteen** ~**s** в девятисо́тые го́ды
● *adj.* сто + *g. pl.*; **a** ~ **miles away** (fig.) за ты́сячу вёрст

☞ ключева́я ле́ксика

■ ~**weight** *n.* (BrE, approximately 50.8 kilograms) английский це́нтнер; (AmE, approximately 45.4 kilograms) америка́нский це́нтнер

hundredth /'hʌndrədθ/ *n.* (fraction) одна́ со́тая
• *adj.* со́тый

hung /hʌŋ/ *past and p.p. of* ▶ hang

Hungarian /hʌŋ'geəriən/ *n.* (person) венгр (венге́рка); (language) венге́рский язы́к
• *adj.* венге́рский

Hungary /'hʌŋɡəri/ *n.* Ве́нгрия

hunger /'hʌŋɡə(r)/ *n.* го́лод
■ ~ **strike** *n.* голодо́вка

hungry /'hʌŋɡri/ *adj.* (**hungrier**, **hungriest**) голо́дный

hunk /hʌŋk/ *n.* большо́й кусо́к; (of bread) ломо́ть (*m.*) хле́ба

hunt /hʌnt/ *n.* **1** (~ing expedition) охо́та **2** (search) охо́та (**for:** на + *a.*); по́иск|и (-ов) (**for:** + *g.*)
• *v.t. & i.* (pursue for food or sport) охо́титься (*impf.*) (на + *a.*); (search for) охо́титься (*impf.*) (за + *i.*); вести́ (*det.*) по́иски (+ *g.*); иска́ть (*impf.*)

hunter /'hʌntə(r)/ *n.* охо́тник

hunting /'hʌntɪŋ/ *n.* охо́та

hurdle /'hɜ:d(ə)l/ *n.* (in athletics & fig.) барье́р, препя́тствие

hurl /hɜ:l/ *v.t.* бр|оса́ть, -о́сить; he ~ed abuse at me он осы́пал меня́ оскорбле́ниями

hurrah /hʊ'rɑ:/, **hurray** /hʊ'reɪ/ *int.* ура́!

hurricane /'hʌrɪkən/ *n.* урага́н

hurr|y /'hʌri/ *n.* спе́шка, поспе́шность; he was in no ~y to go он не спеши́л уходи́ть; in his ~y, he forgot his briefcase в спе́шке он забы́л взять портфе́ль
• *v.t.* **1** (cause to move hastily) торопи́ть, по- **2** (perform hastily): don't ~y the job рабо́тайте не спеша́
• *v.i.* (move hastily) спеши́ть, по-; торопи́ться, по-; he ~ied home он спеши́л домо́й; they ~ied to finish the work они́ спеши́ли зако́нчить рабо́ту
• *with advs.:* ~y along there, please! потора́пливайтесь, пожа́луйста!; ~y up! потора́пливайтесь!

✍ **hurt** /hɜ:t/ *n.* (offence) оби́да
• *v.t.* (*past and p.p.* ~) (inflict pain on) ушиб|а́ть, -и́ть; причин|я́ть, -и́ть боль + *d.*; I won't ~ you я не причиню́ вам бо́ли (*or* не сде́лаю вам бо́льно); these shoes ~ (me) э́ти ту́фли мне жмут; (injure) ушиб|а́ть, -и́ть; he fell and ~ his back он упа́л и ушиб спи́ну; ~ oneself ушиб|а́ться, -и́ться, удара́ться, уда́риться; (damage) вреди́ть, по-; (offend, pain) об|ижа́ть, -и́деть; заде|ва́ть, -́ть; now you've ~ his feelings вот ну, вы его́ и оби́дели
• *v.i.* (*past and p.p.* ~) (be sore) боле́ть (*impf.*); my arm ~s у меня́ боли́т/но́ет рука́; (do damage): it won't ~ to wait не меша́ло бы подожда́ть

hurtful /'hɜ:tfʊl/ *adj.* оби́дный

hurtle /'hɜ:t(ə)l/ *v.i.* нести́сь (*impf.*), мча́ться (*impf.*)

✍ **husband** /'hʌzbənd/ *n.* муж (-ья́)

hush /hʌʃ/ *v.t.*: she ~ed the baby to sleep она́ убаю́кала ребёнка; the scandal was ~ed up сканда́л замя́ли
• *v.i.* (as int.): ~! ти́ше!; молчи́те!
■ ~~ *adj.* (infml) та́йный, засекре́ченный

husk /hʌsk/ *n.* шелуха́; (of nuts) скорлупа́
• *v.t.* очища́ть, очи́стить; лущи́ть, об-

husky[1] /'hʌski/ *n.* (dog) эскимо́сская ла́йка, ха́ски (*f. indecl.*)

husky[2] /'hʌski/ *adj.* (**huskier**, **huskiest**) (hoarse) сухо́й, хри́плый

hustle /'hʌs(ə)l/ *n.* су́толока, да́вка
• *v.t.*: the police ~d him away его́ уволокли́ полице́йские

hut /hʌt/ *n.* (small building) хи́жина; (barrack) бара́к

hutch /hʌtʃ/ *n.* (for pets) кле́тка

hyacinth /'haɪəsɪnθ/ *n.* гиаци́нт

hybrid /'haɪbrɪd/ *n.* гибри́д

hybridize /'haɪbrɪdaɪz/ *v.t.* скре́|щивать, -сти́ть; гибридизи́ровать (*impf.*)

hydrangea /haɪ'dreɪndʒə/ *n.* горте́нзия

hydraulic /haɪ'drɒlɪk/ *adj.* гидравли́ческий

hydrochloric /haɪdrə'klɒrɪk/ *adj.*: ~ **acid** соля́ная кислота́

hydroelectric /haɪdrəʊɪ'lektrɪk/ *adj.* гидроэлектри́ческий

hydrofoil /'haɪdrəfɔɪl/ *n.* су́дно на подво́дных кры́льях; раке́та

hydrogen /'haɪdrədʒ(ə)n/ *n.* водоро́д

hyena /haɪ'i:nə/ *n.* гие́на

hygiene /'haɪdʒi:n/ *n.* гигие́на

hygienic /haɪ'dʒi:nɪk/ *adj.* гигиени́ческий

hygienist /'haɪdʒi:nɪst/ *n.* ассисте́нт зубно́го врача́ (*специалист по гигиене полости рта*)

hymn /hɪm/ *n.* (церко́вный) гимн

hype /haɪp/ *n.* (infml) крикли́вая рекла́ма
• *adj.*: ~d-up ду́тый, ли́повый

hyperactive /haɪpə'ræktɪv/ *adj.* чрезме́рно акти́вный

hyperbole /haɪ'pɜ:bəli/ *n.* гипе́рбола, преувеличе́ние

hyperlink /'haɪpəlɪŋk/ *n.* (comput.) гиперссы́лка, гиперте́кстовая ссы́лка

hypermarket /'haɪpəmɑ:kɪt/ *n.* (BrE) гиперма́ркет

hypertension /haɪpə'tenʃ(ə)n/ *n.* (med.) высо́кое кровяно́е давле́ние

hypertext /'haɪpətekst/ *n.* (comput.) гиперте́кст

hyphen /'haɪf(ə)n/ *n.* дефи́с, чёрточка (infml)

hypnosis /hɪp'nəʊsɪs/ *n.* гипно́з

hypnotic /hɪp'nɒtɪk/ *adj.* гипноти́ческий

hypnotism /'hɪpnətɪz(ə)m/ *n.* гипноти́зм

hypnotist /'hɪpnətɪst/ *n.* гипнотизёр

hypnotize /'hɪpnətaɪz/ *v.t.* гипнотизи́ровать, за-

hypochondriac /haɪpə'kɒndriæk/ *n.* ипохо́ндрик

hypocrisy /hɪ'pɒkrɪsi/ *n.* лицеме́рие

hypocrite /'hɪpəkrɪt/ *n.* лицеме́р

hypocritical /hɪpə'krɪtɪk(ə)l/ *adj.* лицеме́рный, неи́скренний

hypodermic /haɪpə'dɜ:mɪk/ *adj.*: ~ **syringe/ needle** шприц/игла́ для подко́жных

инъе́кций

hypothermia /haɪpəʊ'θɜːmɪə/ *n.* гипотерми́я
hypothesis /haɪ'pɒθɪsɪs/ *n.* (*pl.* **hypotheses** /-siːz/) гипо́теза
hypothetical /haɪpə'θetɪk(ə)l/ *adj.* гипотети́ческий

hysterectomy /hɪstə'rektəmɪ/ *n.* удале́ние ма́тки
hysteria /hɪ'stɪərɪə/ *n.* истери́я
hysterical /hɪ'sterɪk(ə)l/ *adj.* истери́чный
hysterics /hɪ'sterɪks/ *n.* исте́рика
Hz *abbr.* (*of* **hertz**) Гц (герц)

h

i

✔ **I** /aɪ/ *pers. pron.* (*obj.* **me**) я; he and ~ were there мы с ним бы́ли там; he is older than ~ он ста́рше меня́
Iberian /aɪ'bɪərɪən/ *adj.* ибери́йский
✔ **ice** /aɪs/ *n.* лёд
 ● *v.t.* **1** (cover with ~): the pond was soon ~d over пруд вско́ре затяну́ло/сковáло льдо́м **2** (cul.) глазировáть (*impf., pf.*)
 ■ ~-**cold** *adj.* ледяно́й; ~ **cream** *n.* моро́женое; ~ **cube** *n.* ку́бик льда; ~ **hockey** *n.* хокке́й (на льду); ~(**d**) **lolly** *n.* (BrE) моро́женое на пáлочке; ~ **rink** *n.* като́к; ~ **skate** *n.* конёк; ~-**skate** *v.i.* катáться (*impf.*) на конькáх
iceberg /'aɪsbɜːg/ *n.* áйсберг
Iceland /'aɪslənd/ *n.* Исла́ндия
Icelandic /aɪs'lændɪk/ *n.* исла́ндский язы́к
 ● *adj.* исла́ндский
icicle /'aɪsɪk(ə)l/ *n.* сосу́лька
icing /'aɪsɪŋ/ *n.* (on cake) сáхарная глазу́рь
icon /'aɪkɒn/ *n.* икóна; (comput.) икóн(к)а, пиктогрáмма
iconoclastic /aɪkɒnə'klæstɪk/ *adj.* иконоборческий
icy /'aɪsɪ/ *adj.* (**icier**, **iciest**) (cold, lit., fig.) ледяно́й; (covered with ice) покры́тый льдо́м
ID *abbr.* (*of* **identification**) удостовере́ние ли́чности
✔ **idea** /aɪ'dɪə/ *n.* **1** (mental concept; suggestion, plan) иде́я; a good ~ хоро́шая иде́я **2** (thought) мысль; I can't bear the ~ of it (одна́) мысль об э́том мне проти́вна **3** (notion; impression) поня́тие, представле́ние; I've no ~ (я) поня́тия не име́ю **4** (aim, intention) иде́я, за́мысел, наме́рение **5** (opinion, belief) мне́ние, взгляд
✔ **ideal** /aɪ'diːəl/ *n.* идеа́л
 ● *adj.* идеа́льный
idealism /aɪ'dɪəlɪz(ə)m/ *n.* идеали́зм
idealist /aɪ'dɪəlɪst/ *n.* идеали́ст
idealistic /aɪdɪə'lɪstɪk/ *adj.* идеалисти́ческий
ideally /aɪ'dɪəlɪ/ *adv.* идеа́льно; (as sentence adverb) в идеа́ле

identical /aɪ'dentɪk(ə)l/ *adj.* тожде́ственный, иденти́чный
 ■ ~ **twins** *n. pl.* одноя́йцевые близнецы́
identification /aɪdentɪfɪ'keɪʃ(ə)n/ *n.*: ~ of a body опознáние тру́па; (*attr.*) опознавáтельный
✔ **identif|y** /aɪ'dentɪfaɪ/ *v.t.* **1** (establish identity of) опозн|авáть, -áть; идентифици́ровать (*impf., pf.*) **2** (associate) (*also v.i.*) (infml): he ~ied (himself) with the movement он стал убеждённым сторо́нником э́того движе́ния
identikit® /aɪ'dentɪkɪt/ *n.*: an ~ (picture) фоторобо́т
✔ **identity** /aɪ'dentɪtɪ/ *n.* ли́чность
 ■ ~ **card** *n.* удостовере́ние ли́чности; ~ **theft** *n.* крáжа ли́чной информáции (*с целью получить доступ к банковскому счёту и т. п.*)
ideological /aɪdɪə'lɒdʒɪk(ə)l/ *adj.* идеологи́ческий, иде́йный
ideology /aɪdɪ'ɒlədʒɪ/ *n.* идеоло́гия
idiocy /'ɪdɪəsɪ/ *n.* (stupidity; stupid behaviour) идио́тство
idiom /'ɪdɪəm/ *n.* (expression) идио́ма; (language; way of speaking) наре́чие, го́вор, язы́к
idiomatic /ɪdɪə'mætɪk/ *adj.* идиомати́ческий; he speaks ~ Russian он свобо́дно владе́ет ру́сским языко́м; он говори́т по-ру́сски как ру́сский
idiosyncrasy /ɪdɪəʊ'sɪŋkrəsɪ/ *n.* своеобрáзие
idiosyncratic /ɪdɪəʊsɪŋ'krætɪk/ *adj.* своеобрáзный
idiot /'ɪdɪət/ *n.* идио́т (-ка)
idiotic /ɪdɪ'ɒtɪk/ *adj.* идио́тский
idle /'aɪd(ə)l/ *adj.* (**idler**, **idlest**) **1** (not working) нерабо́тающий; (unemployed) безрабо́тный; (of factories etc.) безде́йствующий; (of machinery) простáивающий **2** (lazy) прáздный, лени́вый **3** (purposeless) пусто́й; out of ~ curiosity из прáздного/пусто́го любопы́тства; ~ talk пустáя болтовня́
 ● *v.t.*: he ~d away his life он растрáтил свою́ жизнь впусту́ю
 ● *v.i.* **1** (be ~) безде́льничать (*impf.*) **2** (of an engine): the motor ~s well мото́р хорошо́ рабо́тает на холосто́м ходу́

idol /'aɪd(ə)l/ *n.* и́дол, куми́р
idolatry /aɪ'dɒlətrɪ/ *n.* идолопокло́нство; (fig.) обожа́ние
idolize /'aɪdəlaɪz/ *v.t.* (fig.) боготвори́ть (*impf.*)
idyll /'ɪdɪl/ *n.* иди́ллия
idyllic /ɪ'dɪlɪk/ *adj.* идилли́ческий
i.e. *abbr.* (*of* **id est**) т. е. (то есть)
IED *n.* (*abbr. of* **improvized explosive device**) (mil.) самоде́льное взрывно́е устро́йство
♂ **if** /ɪf/ *conj.* **1** (condition or supposition) е́сли, е́сли бы; ~ **he comes** е́сли он придёт; ~ **I were you** на ва́шем ме́сте; **he talks as** ~ **he were the boss** он говори́т, как бу́дто он нача́льник **2** (though) хотя́, пусть; **a pleasant,** ~ **chilly, day** прия́тный, хотя́ и прохла́дный день **3** (whether): **do you know** ~ **he is at home?** вы не зна́ете, он до́ма?; **see** ~ **the door is locked** посмотри́те, заперта́ ли дверь
igloo /'ɪɡlu:/ *n.* и́глу (*nt. indecl.*)
ignite /ɪɡ'naɪt/ *v.t.* заж|ига́ть, -е́чь
   ● *v.i.* заж|ига́ться, -е́чься
ignition /ɪɡ'nɪʃ(ə)n/ *n.* (~ system in engine) зажига́ние
  ■ ~ **key** *n.* ключ зажига́ния
ignoble /ɪɡ'nəʊb(ə)l/ *adj.* (**ignobler, ignoblest**) (base) по́длый, ни́зкий, посты́дный; (of lowly birth) ни́зкого происхожде́ния
ignominious /ɪɡnə'mɪnɪəs/ *adj.* позо́рный, посты́дный; **an** ~ **death** бессла́вная смерть
ignominy /'ɪɡnəmɪnɪ/ *n.* (dishonour) позо́р, бесче́стье
ignoramus /ɪɡnə'reɪməs/ *n.* (*pl.* ~**es**) неве́жда
ignorance /'ɪɡnərəns/ *n.* (in general) неве́жество; (of certain facts) незна́ние, неве́дение
ignorant /'ɪɡnərənt/ *adj.* неве́жественный; **I was** ~ **of his intentions** я не знал о его́ наме́рениях
♂ **ignore** /ɪɡ'nɔ:(r)/ *v.t.* игнори́ровать (*impf., pf.*) (*pf. also* про-)
iguana /ɪɡ'wɑ:nə/ *n.* игуа́на
ilk /ɪlk/ *n.*: **and others of his** ~ (infml) и други́е того́ же ро́да; и ему́ подо́бные
ill /ɪl/ *n.* зло; **I meant him no** ~ я не жела́л ему́ зла
   ● *adj.* **1** (unwell) больно́й, нездоро́вый; **he looks** ~ он вы́глядит больны́м; **he was taken** (*or* **fell**) ~ **with a fever** он заболе́л лихора́дкой; **I feel** ~ мне нехорошо́; я пло́хо себя́ чу́вствую **2** (bad) дурно́й; ~ **effects** па́губные после́дствия; ~ **health** нездоро́вье, нездоро́вие; ~ **humour** (BrE); **humor** (AmE), ~ **temper** (mood) дурно́е настрое́ние; ~-**treatment** дурно́е обраще́ние; ~ **will** зла́я во́ля, зло́ба; **I bear you no** ~ **will** я не жела́ю вам зла
   ● *adv.* пло́хо, ду́рно; ~ **at ease** не по себе́; **to feel** ~ **at ease** чу́вствовать, по- себя́ нело́вко; **I can** ~ **afford it** я с трудо́м могу́ себе́ э́то позво́лить; **I have never spoken** ~ **of him** я никогда́ не отзыва́лся о нём пло́хо
  ■ ~-**informed** *adj.* пло́хо осведомлённый; ~-**mannered** *adj.* невоспи́танный, пло́хо

воспи́танный; ~-**treat**, ~-**use** *vv.t.* пло́хо об|ходи́ться, -ойти́сь с + *i.*
♂ **illegal** /ɪ'li:ɡ(ə)l/ *adj.* незако́нный, нелега́льный
illegible /ɪ'ledʒɪb(ə)l/ *adj.* неразбо́рчивый
illegitimate /ɪlɪ'dʒɪtɪmət/ *adj.* незаконнорождённый
illicit /ɪ'lɪsɪt/ *adj.* незако́нный, недозво́ленный
illiterate /ɪ'lɪtərət/ *adj.* негра́мотный
♂ **illness** /'ɪlnɪs/ *n.* боле́знь
illogical /ɪ'lɒdʒɪk(ə)l/ *adj.* нелоги́чный
illuminate /ɪ'lu:mɪneɪt/ *v.t.* осве|ща́ть, -ти́ть; **an** ~**d sign** светя́щаяся рекла́ма
illumination /ɪlu:mɪ'neɪʃ(ə)n/ *n.* освеще́ние
illusion /ɪ'lu:ʒ(ə)n/ *n.* иллю́зия, обма́н; **I was under an** ~ я был во вла́сти иллю́зии; **I have no** ~**s about him** относи́тельно него́ у меня́ нет никаки́х иллю́зий
illusionist /ɪ'lu:ʒənɪst/ *n.* иллюзиони́ст, фо́кусник
illusive /ɪ'lu:sɪv/, **illusory** /ɪ'lu:sərɪ/ *adjs.* иллюзо́рный, при́зрачный
illustrate /'ɪləstreɪt/ *v.t.* иллюстри́ровать (*impf., pf.*)
illustration /ɪlə'streɪʃ(ə)n/ *n.* иллюстра́ция
illustrative /'ɪləstrətɪv/ *adj.* иллюстрати́вный, поясни́тельный; **a work** ~ **of his genius** произведе́ние, пока́зывающее его́ гениа́льность/тала́нт
illustrator /'ɪləstreɪtə(r)/ *n.* иллюстра́тор
illustrious /ɪ'lʌstrɪəs/ *adj.* просла́вленный, знамени́тый
♂ **image** /'ɪmɪdʒ/ *n.* **1** (representation) изображе́ние **2** (likeness) ко́пия, портре́т; **he was the** ~ **of his father** он был то́чной ко́пией (*or* живы́м портре́том) своего́ отца́ **3** (impression made on others) и́мидж, репута́ция
  ■ ~ **consultant** *n.* консульта́нт по и́миджу
imagery /'ɪmɪdʒərɪ/ *n.* (in writing) о́бразность
imaginable /ɪ'mædʒɪnəb(ə)l/ *adj.* вообрази́мый; **we had the greatest trouble** ~ у нас бы́ли невообрази́мые хло́поты
imaginary /ɪ'mædʒɪnərɪ/ *adj.* вообража́емый
imagination /ɪmædʒɪ'neɪʃ(ə)n/ *n.* воображе́ние
imaginative /ɪ'mædʒɪnətɪv/ *adj.* (person) одарённый/облада́ющий (больши́м/ бога́тым) воображе́нием; (literature) худо́жественный
♂ **imagine** /ɪ'mædʒɪn/ *v.t.* **1** (form mental picture of) вообра|жа́ть, -зи́ть **2** (conceive) предст|авля́ть, -а́вить себе́; **I cannot** ~ **how it happened** я не могу́ предста́вить себе́, как э́то случи́лось **3** (suppose) предпол|ага́ть, -ожи́ть **4** (guess) дога́д|ываться, -а́ться; пон|има́ть, -я́ть
imam /ɪ'mɑ:m/ *n.* има́м
imbalance /ɪm'bæləns/ *n.* отсу́тствие равнове́сия, неусто́йчивость; несоотве́тствие
imbecile /'ɪmbɪsi:l/ *n.* глупе́ц, дура́к (ду́ра) (infml)
   ● *adj.* глу́пый
imbibe /ɪm'baɪb/ *v.t.* (drink) погло|ща́ть, -ти́ть; пить, вы́-; (fig., assimilate) усв|а́ивать, -о́ить;

впи́т|ывать, -а́ть; he ~d new ideas он впита́л но́вые иде́и

imbue /ɪmˈbjuː/ *v.t.* (**imbues, imbued, imbuing**) **1** (lit., saturate) пропи́т|ывать, -а́ть; (dye) окра́шивать, -сить **2** (fig., inspire) вселя́ть, -и́ть (*что в кого*); (fill): ~d with hatred прони́кнутый не́навистью

IMF *abbr.* (*of* **International Monetary Fund**) МВФ (Междунаро́дный валю́тный фонд)

imitate /ˈɪmɪteɪt/ *v.t.* копи́ровать (*impf.*); и|мити́ровать, сы-

imitation /ɪmɪˈteɪʃ(ə)n/ *n.* имита́ция, подде́лка; ~ **leather** иску́сственная ко́жа

immaculate /ɪˈmækjʊlət/ *adj.* безупре́чный

immaterial /ɪməˈtɪərɪəl/ *adj.* (unimportant) несуще́ственный

immature /ɪməˈtjʊə(r)/ *adj.* незре́лый

immeasurable /ɪˈmeʒərəb(ə)l/ *adj.* неизмери́мый

i ◆ **immediate** /ɪˈmiːdɪət/ *adj.* **1** (direct, closest possible) непосре́дственный; (next in order) очередно́й; **in the ~ neighbourhood** в непосре́дственной бли́зости; **my ~ neighbours** мои́ ближа́йшие сосе́ди; **on his ~ left** сра́зу нале́во от него́; **in the ~ future** в ближа́йшем бу́дущем **2** (without delay) неме́дленный, мгнове́нный **3** (urgent) безотлага́тельный

◆ **immediately** /ɪˈmiːdɪətlɪ/ *adv.* неме́дленно, то́тчас (же), сра́зу, мгнове́нно

immemorial /ɪmɪˈmɔːrɪəl/ *adj.* незапа́мятный; **from time ~** с незапа́мятных времён

immense /ɪˈmens/ *adj.* огро́мный, грома́дный

immensity /ɪˈmensɪtɪ/ *n.* безме́рность, необъя́тность

immerse /ɪˈmɜːs/ *v.t.* погр|ужа́ть, -узи́ть

immersion /ɪˈmɜːʃ(ə)n/ *n.* (lit., fig.) погруже́ние; ∎ **~ heater** *n.* водонагрева́тель (*m.*) (погружа́емого ти́па)

immigrant /ˈɪmɪɡrənt/ *n.* иммигра́нт (-ка)

immigration /ɪmɪˈɡreɪʃ(ə)n/ *n.* иммигра́ция

imminent /ˈɪmɪnənt/ *adj.* надвига́ющийся

immobile /ɪˈməʊbaɪl/ *adj.* неподви́жный

immobilize /ɪˈməʊbɪlaɪz/ *v.t.* лиш|а́ть, -и́ть подви́жности; **I was ~d by a broken leg** я не мог дви́гаться из-за сло́манной ноги́

immoderate /ɪˈmɒdərət/ *adj.* неуме́ренный

immoral /ɪˈmɒr(ə)l/ *adj.* безнра́вственный

immorality /ɪməˈrælɪtɪ/ *n.* безнра́вственность

immortal /ɪˈmɔːt(ə)l/ *n. & adj.* бессме́ртный

immortality /ɪmɔːˈtælɪtɪ/ *n.* бессме́ртие

immortalize /ɪˈmɔːtəlaɪz/ *v.t.* увекове́чи|вать, -ть

immovable *adj.* недви́жимый

immune /ɪˈmjuːn/ *adj.*: **~ to disease** невосприи́мчивый к боле́зни; **~ to criticism** неподвла́стный кри́тике
∎ **~ system** *n.* имму́нная систе́ма

immunity /ɪˈmjuːnɪtɪ/ *n.* (to disease etc.) иммуните́т, невосприи́мчивость (**to/**

against: к + *d.*, про́тив + *g.*); (in law) неприкоснове́нность, иммуните́т (**from:** от/ про́тив + *g.*); **diplomatic ~** дипломати́ческий иммуните́т

immunization /ɪmjuːnaɪˈzeɪʃ(ə)n/ *n.* иммуниза́ция

immunize /ˈɪmjuːnaɪz/ *v.t.* вакцини́ровать (*impf., pf.*) (**against:** от + *g.*); де́лать, с- невосприи́мчивым (**against:** к + *d.*)

immutable /ɪˈmjuːtəb(ə)l/ *adj.* неизме́нный, непрело́жный

imp /ɪmp/ *n.* (also fig., mischievous child) дьяволёнок, чертёнок, бесёнок; (fig. only) постре́л

◆ **impact** /ˈɪmpækt/ *n.* (collision) столкнове́ние; (striking force) уда́р, толчо́к; (fig., effect, influence) возде́йствие, влия́ние

impair /ɪmˈpeə(r)/ *v.t.* (damage) повре|жда́ть, -ди́ть; (ruin; mar) по́ртить, ис-

impairment /ɪmˈpeəmənt/ *n.* (damage) поврежде́ние; (deterioration) ухудше́ние; (disability) дефе́кт

impale /ɪmˈpeɪl/ *v.t.* прок|а́лывать, -оло́ть; пронз|а́ть, -и́ть; прот|ыка́ть, -кну́ть; **he ~d himself on his sword** он пронзи́л себя́ мечо́м; **he fell and was ~d on the railings** он свали́лся на огра́ду и проткну́л себе́ живо́т

impart /ɪmˈpɑːt/ *v.t.* перед|ава́ть, -а́ть

impartial /ɪmˈpɑːʃ(ə)l/ *adj.* беспристра́стный

impartiality /ɪmpɑːʃɪˈælɪtɪ/ *n.* беспристра́стность

impassable /ɪmˈpɑːsəb(ə)l/ *adj.* (on foot) непроходи́мый; (for vehicles) непрое́зжий

impasse /ˈæmpɑːs/ *n.* тупи́к; **things reached an ~** дела́ зашли́ в тупи́к

impassioned /ɪmˈpæʃ(ə)nd/ *adj.* стра́стный, пы́лкий

impassive /ɪmˈpæsɪv/ *adj.* безмяте́жный

impatience /ɪmˈpeɪʃ(ə)ns/ *n.* нетерпе́ние; (irritation) раздраже́ние

impatient /ɪmˈpeɪʃ(ə)nt/ *adj.* нетерпели́вый; (irritable) раздражи́тельный, раздражённый; **he was getting ~** он теря́л терпе́ние, он раздража́лся; **he is ~ to begin** ему́ не те́рпится нача́ть

impeach /ɪmˈpiːtʃ/ *v.t.* (pol.) обвин|я́ть, -и́ть (*кого в чём*)

impeachment /ɪmˈpiːtʃmənt/ *n.* (pol.) импи́чмент

impeccable /ɪmˈpekəb(ə)l/ *adj.* безупре́чный

impecunious /ɪmpɪˈkjuːnɪəs/ *adj.* безде́нежный, малообеспе́ченный

impedance /ɪmˈpiːd(ə)ns/ *n.* (elec.) по́лное сопротивле́ние, импеда́нс

impede /ɪmˈpiːd/ *v.t.* (obstruct) препя́тствовать (*impf.*) (+ *d.*); (hinder) меша́ть, по- (+ *d.*)

impediment /ɪmˈpedɪmənt/ *n.* **1** (obstruction) препя́тствие; **an ~ to progress** препя́тствие на пути́ прогре́сса **2** (speech defect) дефе́кт ре́чи

impel /ɪmˈpel/ *v.t.* (**impelled, impelling**) (drive; force) прин|ужда́ть, -уди́ть; заст|авля́ть, -а́вить; побу|жда́ть, -ди́ть; **conscience ~led**

◆ ключева́я ле́ксика

him to speak the truth со́весть принуди́ла его говори́ть пра́вду; **I feel ~led to say** я вы́нужден сказа́ть

impending /ɪmˈpendɪŋ/ *adj.* предстоя́щий

impenetrable /ɪmˈpenɪtrəb(ə)l/ *adj.* непроница́емый

imperative /ɪmˈperətɪv/ *n.* (gram.) повели́тельное наклоне́ние, императи́в
● *adj.* (essential): **it is ~ that you come at once** вам необходи́мо то́тчас яви́ться

imperceptible /ɪmpəˈseptɪb(ə)l/ *adj.* незаме́тный; незначи́тельный

imperfect /ɪmˈpɜːfɪkt/ *n.* (gram.) проше́дшее несовершѐнное вре́мя, имперфе́кт
● *adj.* несовершѐнный, дефе́ктный

imperfection /ɪmpəˈfekʃ(ə)n/ *n.* (incompleteness, faultiness) несовершѐнство, неполнота́; (fault) дефе́кт, изъя́н; недоста́ток

imperfective /ɪmpəˈfektɪv/ *n. & adj.* (gram.) несовершѐнный (вид)

imperial /ɪmˈpɪərɪəl/ *adj.* импе́рский

imperialism /ɪmˈpɪərɪəlɪz(ə)m/ *n.* империали́зм

imperialist /ɪmˈpɪərɪəlɪst/ *n.* империали́ст
● *adj.* империалисти́ческий

impermeable /ɪmˈpɜːmɪəb(ə)l/ *adj.* непроница́емый

impersonal /ɪmˈpɜːsən(ə)l/ *adj.* безли́чный

impersonate /ɪmˈpɜːsəneɪt/ *v.t.* (act the part of) игра́ть (*impf.*) роль + *g.*; (pretend to be) выдава́ть (*impf.*) себя́ за + *a.*

impersonator /ɪmˈpɜːsəneɪtə(r)/ *n.* пароди́ст, имита́тор

impertinence /ɪmˈpɜːtɪnəns/ *n.* де́рзость, на́глость, наха́льство

impertinent /ɪmˈpɜːtɪnənt/ *adj.* де́рзкий, на́глый, наха́льный

imperturbable /ɪmpəˈtɜːbəb(ə)l/ *adj.* невозмути́мый

impervious /ɪmˈpɜːvɪəs/ *adj.* непроница́емый; (fig.): **~ to criticism** глухо́й к кри́тике

impetuous /ɪmˈpetʃʊəs/ *adj.* (impulsive) импульси́вный; (unpremeditated) необду́манный

impetus /ˈɪmpɪtəs/ *n.* толчо́к; и́мпульс; (fig.) толчо́к, сти́мул

impinge /ɪmˈpɪndʒ/ *v.i.* (**impinging**): **~ on** посяга́ть, -ну́ть на + *a.*

implacable /ɪmˈplækəb(ə)l/ *adj.* неумоли́мый

implant *v.t.* /ɪmˈplɑːnt/ (med.) вживля́ть, -и́ть; (fig., instil) внедря́ть, -и́ть
● *n.* /ˈɪmplɑːnt/ (med.) импланта́т

implausible /ɪmˈplɔːzɪb(ə)l/ *adj.* неправдоподо́бный

implement[1] /ˈɪmplɪmənt/ *n.* ору́дие, инструме́нт; **farm ~s** сельскохозя́йственные ору́дия

⚥ **implement[2]** /ˈɪmplɪment/ *v.t.* выполня́ть, вы́полнить

implementation /ɪmplɪmenˈteɪʃ(ə)n/ *n.* выполне́ние, осуществле́ние

implicate /ˈɪmplɪkeɪt/ *v.t.* вовле|ка́ть, -е́чь; **the evidence ~d him** ули́ки пока́зывали на его́ прича́стность

implication /ɪmplɪˈkeɪʃ(ə)n/ *n.* (thing implied) скры́тый смысл; (significance) значе́ние

implicit /ɪmˈplɪsɪt/ *adj.* **1** (implied) подразумева́емый, недоска́занный **2** (unquestioning) безогово́рочный

implore /ɪmˈplɔː(r)/ *v.t.* умоля́ть, -и́ть; **he ~d my forgiveness** он моли́л меня́ о проще́нии

impl|y /ɪmˈplaɪ/ *v.t.* **1** (hint) намека́ть (*impf.*) на + *a.*; **he ~ied that I was wrong** он намека́л на то (*or* дал поня́ть), что я не прав **2** (mean) подразумева́ть (*impf.*); **what do his words ~y?** что означа́ют его́ слова́?

impolite /ɪmpəˈlaɪt/ *adj.* неве́жливый

imponderable /ɪmˈpɒndərəb(ə)l/ *adj.* неулови́мый

import[1] /ˈɪmpɔːt/ *n.* (bringing from abroad) и́мпорт, ввоз; (in pl.) (goods introduced) и́мпортные/ввози́мые това́ры (*m. pl.*)

import[2] /ɪmˈpɔːt/ *v.t.* импорти́ровать (*impf., pf.*); ввозить, -и́ть

⚥ **importance** /ɪmˈpɔːt(ə)ns/ *n.* значе́ние, ва́жность; **it is of no ~** э́то не име́ет значе́ния

⚥ **important** /ɪmˈpɔːt(ə)nt/ *adj.* ва́жный; **it is ~ for you to realize it** ва́жно, чтобы вы по́няли э́то

importer /ɪmˈpɔːtə(r)/ *n.* импортёр

⚥ **impose** /ɪmˈpəʊz/ *v.t.* (tax, penalty, etc.) нал|ага́ть, -ожи́ть (*что на кого*); **the government ~d a tax on wealth** госуда́рство обложи́ло бога́тых нало́гом; **he ~s his views on everyone** он всем навя́зывает свои́ взгля́ды
● *v.i.*: (**~ on**) (take advantage of): **he ~s on his friends** он испо́льзует свои́х друзе́й

imposing /ɪmˈpəʊzɪŋ/ *adj.* внуши́тельный

imposition /ɪmpəˈzɪʃ(ə)n/ *n.* **1** (imposing of obligation, burden, etc.) возложе́ние, наложе́ние **2** (of tax, etc.) обложе́ние **3** (unreasonable demand) чрезме́рное тре́бование

impossibility /ɪmpɒsɪˈbɪlɪtɪ/ *n.* невозмо́жность

⚥ **impossible** /ɪmˈpɒsɪb(ə)l/ *adj.* невозмо́жный; **don't ask me to do the ~** не тре́буйте от меня́ невозмо́жного

impostor /ɪmˈpɒstə(r)/ *n.* обма́нщи|к (-ца)

impotence /ˈɪmpət(ə)ns/ *n.* бесси́лие; (sexual) импоте́нция

impotent /ˈɪmpət(ə)nt/ *adj.* бесси́льный

impound /ɪmˈpaʊnd/ *v.t.* конфискова́ть (*impf., pf.*)

impoverished /ɪmˈpɒvərɪʃt/ *adj.* бе́дный, обедне́вший

impracticable /ɪmˈpræktɪkəb(ə)l/ *adj.* нереа́льный, неосуществи́мый

impractical /ɪmˈpræktɪk(ə)l/ *adj.* непракти́чный

imprecise /ɪmprɪˈsaɪs/ *adj.* нето́чный

impregnable /ɪmˈpregnəb(ə)l/ *adj.* непристу́пный

impregnate /ˈɪmpregneɪt/ *v.t.* (fertilize) оплодотвор|я́ть, -и́ть; (saturate) пропи́т|ывать, -а́ть

i

impresario /ˌɪmprɪˈsɑːrɪəʊ/ n. (pl. ~s) импреса́рио (m. indecl.), антрепенёр

impress /ɪmˈpres/ v.t. **1** (on the mind) запечатл|ева́ть, -е́ть; **we ~ed on them the need for caution** мы внуши́ли им необходи́мость соблюда́ть осторо́жность **2** (have a strong effect on) произв|оди́ть, -ести́ впечатле́ние на + a.; **he did not ~ me at all** он не произвёл на меня́ никако́го впечатле́ния
• v.i. произв|оди́ть, -ести́ впечатле́ние

impression /ɪmˈpreʃ(ə)n/ n. **1** (imprint) отпеча́ток, о́ттиск **2** (effect) эффе́кт, результа́т; впечатле́ние; **make, create an ~** произв|оди́ть, -ести́ впечатле́ние **3** (notion) впечатле́ние, представле́ние; **I was under the ~ that ...** я полага́л, что...; **I have a strong ~ that ...** я почти́ уве́рен, что...

impressionable /ɪmˈpreʃənəb(ə)l/ adj. впечатли́тельный

impressionism /ɪmˈpreʃənɪz(ə)m/ n. импрессиони́зм

impressionist /ɪmˈpreʃənɪst/ n. **1** (art) импрессиони́ст **2** (mimic) пароди́ст, имита́тор

⚬ **impressive** /ɪmˈpresɪv/ adj. внуши́тельный, впечатля́ющий, си́льный

imprint[1] /ˈɪmprɪnt/ n. (lit., fig.) отпеча́ток; (fig.) печа́ть

imprint[2] /ɪmˈprɪnt/ v.t. отпеча́т|ывать, -ать; (fig.) запечатл|ева́ть, -е́ть

imprison /ɪmˈprɪz(ə)n/ v.t. заключ|а́ть, -и́ть в тюрьму́; зато́ч|а́ть, -и́ть

imprisonment /ɪmˈprɪzənmənt/ n. тюре́мное заключе́ние

improbability /ɪmˌprɒbəˈbɪlɪtɪ/ n. неправдоподо́бие, невероя́тность

improbable /ɪmˈprɒbəb(ə)l/ adj. неправдоподо́бный, невероя́тный

impromptu /ɪmˈprɒmptjuː/ adj. импровизи́рованный

improper /ɪmˈprɒpə(r)/ adj. **1** (unsuitable) неподходя́щий, несоотве́тствующий; неуме́стный **2** (incorrect) непра́вильный **3** (unseemly) неприли́чный, непристо́йный

impropriety /ˌɪmprəˈpraɪətɪ/ n. (inappropriateness) неуме́стность; (indecency) непристо́йность, неприли́чие; (irregularity) непра́вильность

⚬ **improv|e** /ɪmˈpruːv/ v.t. (make better) ул|учша́ть, -у́чшить; **he has ~ed his French** он де́лает успе́хи во францу́зском (языке́)
• v.i. **1** (become better) ул|учша́ться, -у́чшиться; **wine ~es with age** с года́ми вино́ стано́вится лу́чше; **his health is ~ing** он (or его́ здоро́вье) поправля́ется **2** **~e on** (produce sth better than): **I can ~e on that** я могу́ предложи́ть не́что лу́чшее

⚬ **improvement** /ɪmˈpruːvmənt/ n. улучше́ние; **there has been an ~ in the weather** пого́да улу́чшилась; (rebuilding etc.)

перестро́йка; перестано́вка

improvidence /ɪmˈprɒvɪd(ə)ns/ n. непредусмотри́тельность; расточи́тельность, небережли́вость

improvident /ɪmˈprɒvɪd(ə)nt/ adj. (heedless of the future) непредусмотри́тельный; (wasteful) расточи́тельный, небережли́вый

improvisation /ˌɪmprəvaɪˈzeɪʃ(ə)n/ n. импровиза́ция

improvise /ˈɪmprəvaɪz/ v.t. & i. (music, speech, etc.) импровизи́ровать (impf.); (arrange as makeshift) мастери́ть, с-; **an ~d dinner** импровизи́рованный у́жин

imprudent /ɪmˈpruːd(ə)nt/ adj. опроме́тчивый, неблагоразу́мный, неосторо́жный

impudence /ˈɪmpjʊd(ə)ns/ n. де́рзость; бессты́дство; наха́льство; на́глость

impudent /ˈɪmpjʊd(ə)nt/ adj. наха́льный, на́глый

impulse /ˈɪmpʌls/ n. толчо́к

impulsive /ɪmˈpʌlsɪv/ adj. импульси́вный

impunity /ɪmˈpjuːnɪtɪ/ n.: **with ~** безнака́занно

impure /ɪmˈpjʊə(r)/ adj. нечи́стый, гря́зный

impurity /ɪmˈpjʊərɪtɪ/ n. нечистота́, грязь; (in pl.) (foreign substances) при́меси (f. pl.)

⚬ **in** /ɪn/ adj. (infml, fashionable) популя́рный, мо́дный; **he knows all the '~' people** он зна́ет всех ну́жных люде́й
• adv. **1** (at home) до́ма; **tell them I'm not ~** скажи́те, что меня́ нет до́ма; (~ one's office etc.): **the boss is not ~ yet** нача́льника ещё нет (у себя́ в кабине́те) **2** (arrived at station, port, etc.). **the train has been ~ (for) 10 minutes** по́езд пришёл 10 мину́т тому́ наза́д **3** (~ fashion): **short skirts are ~ again** коро́ткие ю́бки опя́ть в мо́де **4** (~ power): **which party was ~ then?** кака́я па́ртия была́ тогда́ у вла́сти?
• prep. **1** (position) в/на + p.; (inhabited places): **~ Moscow** в Москве́; (countries and territories): **~ France** во Фра́нции; **the Crimea** в Крыму́; (open spaces and flat areas): **~ the street** на у́лице; **in the country(side)** в дере́вне; **~ the garden** в саду́; (buildings): **~ the school** в шко́ле; (activities): **~ the lesson** на уро́ке; **~ the war** на войне́; во вре́мя войны́; (groups): **~ the crowd** в толпе́; (points of compass): **~ the (Far) East** на (Да́льнем) Восто́ке; (vehicles): **let's go ~ the car** пое́дем на маши́не; (natural phenomena): **~ the fresh air** на све́жем во́здухе; **~ darkness** в темноте́; **~ the rain** под дождём; (books): **~ the Bible** в Би́блии **2** (motion) в (rarely на) + a.; **they arrived ~ the city** они́ прибыли в го́род; **look ~ the mirror** посмотри́те в зе́ркало **3** (time, specific centuries, years and decades): **~ the 20th century** в двадца́том ве́ке; **~ 1975** в ты́сяча девятьсо́т се́мьдесят пя́том году́; **~ May** в ма́е; **~ (the) future** в бу́дущем; (ages of history, events, periods): **~ the Middle Ages** в Сре́дние века́; **3 times ~ one day** три ра́за в/за оди́н день; (seasons): **~ spring** весно́й; (times of day): **~ the morning** у́тром; **~ the**

mornings по утра́м; (at the end of): **I shall finish this book** ∼ **3 days' time** я зако́нчу/дочита́ю э́ту кни́гу че́рез три дня; (in the course of): **he completed it** ∼ **6 weeks** он зако́нчил э́то за шесть неде́ль **4** (condition, situation): ∼ **his absence** в его́ отсу́тствие; ∼ **these circumstances** при/в э́тих усло́виях; ∼ **power** у вла́сти **5** (manner): ∼ **a whisper** шёпотом; ∼ **detail** подро́бно; ∼ **secret** под секре́том, по секре́ту; ∼ **turn** по о́череди **6** (language): ∼ **Russian** по-ру́сски **7** (material): **a statue** ∼ **marble** ста́туя из мра́мора **8** (ratio: out of): **only 1** ∼ **every 10 survived** из ка́ждых десяти́ вы́жил то́лько оди́н

inability /ɪnəˈbɪlɪtɪ/ n. неспосо́бность

in absentia /ɪn æbˈsentɪə/ adv. зао́чно

inaccessible /ɪnəkˈsesɪb(ə)l/ adj. недосту́пный, непристу́пный

inaccuracy /ɪnˈækjʊrəsɪ/ n. нето́чность

inaccurate /ɪnˈækjʊrət/ adj. нето́чный

inaction /ɪnˈækʃ(ə)n/ n. безде́йствие

inactive /ɪnˈæktɪv/ adj. безде́йственный, безде́йствующий

inactivity /ɪnækˈtɪvɪtɪ/ n. безде́йствие

inadequacy /ɪnˈædɪkwəsɪ/ n. недоста́точность; (personal) неспосо́бность, неполноце́нность

inadequate /ɪnˈædɪkwət/ adj. недоста́точный; (personally) неполноце́нный

inadvertent /ɪnədˈvɜː(ɹ)t(ə)nt/ adj. неумы́шленный, неча́янный, нево́льный

inadvisable /ɪnədˈvaɪzəb(ə)l/ adj. нецелесообра́зный, нежела́тельный

inane /ɪˈneɪn/ adj. глу́пый, пусто́й, неле́пый

inanimate /ɪnˈænɪmət/ adj. неодушевлённый

inanity /ɪnˈænɪtɪ/ n. глу́пость; неле́пость

inapplicable /ɪnˈæplɪkəb(ə)l, ɪnəˈplɪk-/ adj. неприменимый

inappropriate /ɪnəˈprəʊprɪət/ adj. неуме́стный, неподходя́щий

inarticulate /ɪnɑːˈtɪkjʊlət/ adj. косноязы́чный

inasmuch as /ɪnəzˈmʌtʃ/ conj. так как; ввиду́ того́, что

inattentive /ɪnəˈtentɪv/ adj. невнима́тельный

inaudible /ɪnˈɔːdɪb(ə)l/ adj. неслы́шный

inaugural /ɪˈnɔːɡjʊr(ə)l/ n. торже́ственная речь при вступле́нии в до́лжность ● adj. вступи́тельный, инаугурацио́нный

inaugurate /ɪˈnɔːɡjʊreɪt/ v.t. **1** (install with ceremony) (торже́ственно) вво|ди́ть, -ести́ в до́лжность; **the President was** ∼**d** президе́нт вступи́л в до́лжность **2** (launch; officiate at opening of) откр|ыва́ть, -ы́ть; (fig.): **they** ∼**d many reforms** они́ провели́ мно́го рефо́рм; **he** ∼**d a new policy** он положи́л нача́ло но́вой поли́тике; **a new era was** ∼**d** начала́сь но́вая э́ра

inauguration /ɪnɔːɡjʊˈreɪʃ(ə)n/ n. (of official) вступле́ние в до́лжность

inauspicious /ɪnɔːˈspɪʃəs/ adj. злове́щий

inbox /ˈɪnbɒks/ n. (comput.) входя́щие (сообще́ния)

inbuilt /ɪnˈbɪlt/ adj. врождённый

incalculable /ɪnˈkælkjʊləb(ə)l/ adj. неисчисли́мый

incandescent /ɪnkænˈdes(ə)nt/ adj. (of electric light) накалённый, раскалённый; (emitting light) светя́щийся от нагре́ва; (furious) взбешённый; (passionate) пы́лкий

incantation /ɪnkænˈteɪʃ(ə)n/ n. заклина́ние, закля́тие

incapable /ɪnˈkeɪpəb(ə)l/ adj. неспосо́бный; **he is** ∼ **of understanding** он неспосо́бен поня́ть (что); ∼ **of lying** неспосо́бный на ложь

incapacitate /ɪnkəˈpæsɪteɪt/ v.t.: **he was** ∼**d for 3 weeks** он вы́был из стро́я на три неде́ли

incapacity /ɪnkəˈpæsɪtɪ/ n. неспосо́бность

incarcerate /ɪnˈkɑːsəreɪt/ v.t. заточ|а́ть, -и́ть (в тюрьму́)

incarceration /ɪnkɑːsəˈreɪʃ(ə)n/ n. заточе́ние (в тюрьму́)

incarnation /ɪnkɑːˈneɪʃ(ə)n/ n. воплоще́ние, олицетворе́ние

incendiary /ɪnˈsendɪərɪ/ n. (in full ∼ **bomb**) зажига́тельная бо́мба

incense[1] /ˈɪnsens/ n. ла́дан, фимиа́м

incense[2] /ɪnˈsens/ v.t. разгне́вать (pf.); **she was** ∼**d at, by his behaviour** его́ поведе́ние привело́ её в я́рость

incentive /ɪnˈsentɪv/ n. побужде́ние, сти́мул; ∼ **bonus** поощри́тельная пре́мия

inception /ɪnˈsepʃ(ə)n/ n. нача́ло, начина́ние

incessant /ɪnˈses(ə)nt/ adj. непреста́нный, непреры́вный

incest /ˈɪnsest/ n. кровосмеше́ние

incestuous /ɪnˈsestjʊəs/ adj. кровосмеси́тельный

◆ **inch** /ɪntʃ/ n. дюйм

incidence /ˈɪnsɪd(ə)ns/ n. **1** (range or scope of effect) охва́т, сфе́ра де́йствия; **the** ∼ **of a disease** число́ заболе́вших (or слу́чаев заболева́ния) **2** (phys., falling; contact) паде́ние, накло́н; **angle of** ∼ у́гол паде́ния

◆ **incident** /ˈɪnsɪd(ə)nt/ n. слу́чай, собы́тие; происше́ствие, инциде́нт

incidental /ɪnsɪˈdent(ə)l/ adj. (casual) случа́йный; (secondary) побо́чный ■ ∼ **music** n. музыка́льное сопровожде́ние

incidentally /ɪnsɪˈdentəlɪ/ adv. (in passing) попу́тно

incinerate /ɪnˈsɪnəreɪt/ v.t. испепел|я́ть, -и́ть

incinerator /ɪnˈsɪnəreɪtə(r)/ n. мусоросжига́тельная печь

incision /ɪnˈsɪʒ(ə)n/ n. надре́з

incisive /ɪnˈsaɪsɪv/ adj. ре́жущий; (fig.): **an** ∼ **tone** ре́зкий тон; **an** ∼ **mind** о́стрый/ проница́тельный ум

incite /ɪnˈsaɪt/ v.t. (stir up) возбу|жда́ть, -ди́ть; (urge) побу|жда́ть, -ди́ть; **he** ∼**d them to revolt** он подстрека́л их к мятежу́

i

incitement /ɪnˈsaɪtmənt/ *n.* (inciting) подстрека́тельство; (spur, stimulus) побужде́ние, сти́мул

inclination /ɪnklɪˈneɪʃ(ə)n/ *n.* **1** (tendency) накло́нность **2** (desire) охо́та, жела́ние; **he has lost all ~ to work** он потеря́л вся́кое жела́ние рабо́тать

incline /ɪnˈklaɪn/ *v.t.* **1** (bend forward or down) склоня́ть, -и́ть **2** (fig., dispose) склоня́ть, -и́ть; **I am ~d to agree with you** я скло́нен согласи́ться с ва́ми; **if you feel ~d (to do so)** е́сли вы располо́жены э́то сде́лать ● *v.i.* **1** (lean, slope) наклоня́ться, -и́ться **2** (tend) склоня́ться, -и́ться; **he ~s to(wards) leniency** он скло́нен проявля́ть снисходи́тельность

✍ **includ|e** /ɪnˈkluːd/ *v.t.* включа́ть, -и́ть; **5 members, ~ing the President** пять чле́нов, включа́я президе́нта; **service ~ed** включа́я услу́ги

inclusion /ɪnˈkluːʒ(ə)n/ *n.* включе́ние

inclusive /ɪnˈkluːsɪv/ *adj. & adv.* **1**: **~ of** (including) включа́я; включа́ющий в себя́; содержа́щий в себе́ **2**: **from February 2nd to 20th ~** со второ́го февраля́ по двадца́тое включи́тельно

incognito /ɪnkɒɡˈniːtəʊ/ *adv.* инко́гнито

incoherent /ɪnkəʊˈhɪərənt/ *adj.* бессвя́зный

✍ **income** /ˈɪŋkʌm/ *n.* дохо́д
■ **~ tax** *n.* подохо́дный нало́г

incoming /ˈɪnkʌmɪŋ/ *adj.* входя́щий, поступа́ющий, прибыва́ющий; **the ~ tide** прили́в; **~ calls** поступа́ющие/входя́щие звонки́; **~ mail** входя́щая по́чта

incommunicado /ɪnkəmjuːnɪˈkɑːdəʊ/ *adj. & adv.* лишённый пра́ва перепи́ски и сообще́ния; в изоля́ции

incomparable /ɪnˈkɒmpərəb(ə)l/ *adj.* несравне́нный, бесподо́бный

incompatible /ɪnkəmˈpætɪb(ə)l/ *adj.* несовмести́мый

incompetence /ɪnˈkɒmpɪt(ə)ns/ *n.* неспосо́бность, некомпете́нтность; неуме́ние

incompetent /ɪnˈkɒmpɪt(ə)nt/ *adj.* (person) неспосо́бный, некомпете́нтный; (work) неуме́лый

incomplete /ɪnkəmˈpliːt/ *adj.* (not full) непо́лный; (unfinished) незавершённый, незако́нченный

incomprehensible /ɪnkɒmprɪˈhensɪb(ə)l/ *adj.* непоня́тный, непостижи́мый

inconceivable /ɪnkənˈsiːvəb(ə)l/ *adj.* невообрази́мый

inconclusive /ɪnkənˈkluːsɪv/ *adj.* (of argument etc.) неубеди́тельный; **the vote was ~** голосова́ние не́ дало определённых результа́тов

incongruity /ɪnkɒnˈɡruːɪtɪ/ *n.* несоотве́тствие; неуме́стность

incongruous /ɪnˈkɒnɡruəs/ *adj.* (out of keeping) несоотве́тствующий, неподходя́щий; (out of place) неуме́стный

inconsequential /ɪnkɒnsɪˈkwenʃ(ə)l/ *adj.* (insignificant) незначи́тельный; (irrelevant, immaterial) несуще́ственный

inconsiderate /ɪnkənˈsɪdərət/ *adj.* невнима́тельный (к други́м), нечу́ткий

inconsistency /ɪnkənˈsɪst(ə)nsɪ/ *n.* непосле́довательность; противоречи́вость

inconsistent /ɪnkənˈsɪst(ə)nt/ *adj.* (of a person) непосле́довательный; (of an account) противоречи́вый

inconsolable /ɪnkənˈsəʊləb(ə)l/ *adj.* неуте́шный, безуте́шный

inconspicuous /ɪnkənˈspɪkjʊəs/ *adj.* незаме́тный

incontestable /ɪnkənˈtestəb(ə)l/ *adj.* неоспори́мый

incontinent /ɪnˈkɒntɪnənt/ *adj.* (unrestrained) несде́ржанный; (med.): **he was ~** он страда́л недержа́нием (мочи́/ка́ла)

incontrovertible /ɪnkɒntrəˈvɜːtɪb(ə)l/ *adj.* неоспори́мый

inconvenience /ɪnkənˈviːnɪəns/ *n.* неудо́бство, беспоко́йство
● *v.t.* причиня́ть, -и́ть неудо́бство + *d.*

inconvenient /ɪnkənˈviːnɪənt/ *adj.* неудо́бный

incorporate /ɪnˈkɔːpəreɪt/ *v.t.* **1** (combine) объединя́ть, -и́ть **2** (include) включа́ть, -и́ть

incorrect /ɪnkəˈrekt/ *adj.* (inaccurate) непра́вильный; (untrue) неве́рный

incorrigible /ɪnˈkɒrɪdʒɪb(ə)l/ *adj.* неисправи́мый

✍ **increase¹** /ˈɪnkriːs/ *n.* рост, возраста́ние; увеличе́ние; **unemployment is on the ~** безрабо́тица растёт/увели́чивается; (amount of ~) приро́ст; **my shares show an ~ of 5%** мои́ а́кции подняли́сь на пять проце́нтов

✍ **increase²** /ɪnˈkriːs/ *v.t.* увели́чи|вать, -ть; (extend): **~ one's influence** расш|иря́ть, -и́рить своё влия́ние; (raise): **~ prices** пов|ыша́ть, -ы́сить це́ны; (intensify): **this merely ~d his determination** э́то то́лько укрепи́ло его́ реши́мость
● *v.i.* увели́чи|ваться, -ться; (grow) расти́ (*impf.*); (intensify) уси́ли|ваться, -ться; (expand) расш|иря́ться, -и́риться; (rise): **sugar ~d in price** са́хар повы́сился в цене́ (*or* подорожа́л)

✍ **increasingly** /ɪnˈkriːsɪŋlɪ/ *adv.* всё бо́лее; **it becomes ~ difficult** стано́вится всё трудне́е

incredibl|e /ɪnˈkredɪb(ə)l/ *adj.* невероя́тный; **he was ~y stupid** он был невероя́тно глуп

incredulous /ɪnˈkredjʊləs/ *adj.* недове́рчивый

increment /ˈɪnkrɪmənt/ *n.* (regular salary increase) приба́вка

incriminating /ɪnˈkrɪmɪneɪtɪŋ/ *adj.* изоблича́ющий

incubate /ˈɪŋkjʊbeɪt/ *v.t.* (of a bird) сиде́ть (*impf.*) на (я́йцах); (hatch by artificial heat) инкуби́ровать (*impf., pf.*)
● *v.i.* (of a disease) находи́ться (*impf.*) в инкубацио́нном пери́оде

✍ ключева́я ле́ксика

incubator /'ɪŋkjʊbeɪtə(r)/ *n.* инкуба́тор
inculcate /'ɪnkʌlkeɪt/ *v.t.* внедря́ть, -и́ть; внуш|а́ть, -и́ть
incumbent /ɪn'kʌmbənt/ *n.* **1** (eccl.) прихо́дский свяще́нник **2** (holder of a post) занима́ющий (*какую-н.*) до́лжность
  ● *adj.* (holding office) занима́ющий пост, до́лжность; the ~ **president** ны́нешний президе́нт; (necessary as a duty): ~ **upon** возлежа́щий на + *p.*; возло́женный на + *a.*; it is ~ **upon you to warn them** вы обя́заны предупреди́ть их
incur /ɪn'kə:(r)/ *v.t.* (**incurred, incurring**) навл|ека́ть, -е́чь на себя́; he ~red heavy expenses он понёс больши́е расхо́ды
incurable /ɪn'kjʊərəb(ə)l/ *adj.* (of sick person) безнадёжный; (fig.): an ~ **optimist** неисправи́мый оптими́ст; (of disease) неизлечи́мый
incursion /ɪn'kə:ʃ(ə)n/ *n.* вторже́ние, налёт, набе́г
indebted /ɪn'detɪd/ *adj.* (owing money) в долгу́, до́лжный; (owing gratitude) обя́занный
indecency /ɪn'di:s(ə)nsɪ/ *n.* неприли́чие, непристо́йность; an **act of gross** ~ непристо́йное де́йствие
indecent /ɪn'di:s(ə)nt/ *adj.* неприли́чный, непристо́йный
  ■ ~ **exposure** *n.* непристо́йное обнаже́ние те́ла
indecipherable /ɪndɪ'saɪfərəb(ə)l/ *adj.* не поддаю́щийся расшифро́вке; (of handwriting etc.) неразбо́рчивый
indecision /ɪndɪ'sɪʒ(ə)n/ *n.* нереши́тельность
indecisive /ɪndɪ'saɪsɪv/ *adj.* (irresolute) нереши́тельный; (not producing a result) не реша́ющий
indeclinable /ɪndɪ'klaɪnəb(ə)l/ *adj.* (gram.) несклоня́емый
✧ **indeed** /ɪn'di:d/ *adv.* **1** (really, actually) действи́тельно; в са́мом де́ле; вот и́менно **2** (expr. emphasis): thanks very much ~ премно́го вам благода́рен; "Will you come?" — "I will ~" «Вы придёте?» — «Непреме́нно/обяза́тельно» **3** (expr. intensification) к тому́ же; ма́ло/бо́лее того́; да́же
indefatigable /ɪndɪ'fætɪgəb(ə)l/ *adj.* неутоми́мый
indefensible /ɪndɪ'fensɪb(ə)l/ *adj.* (mil.) неприго́дный для оборо́ны; (unjustified) не име́ющий оправда́ния, непрости́тельный; an ~ **statement** неприе́млемое утвержде́ние
indefinable /ɪndɪ'faɪnəb(ə)l/ *adj.* неопредели́мый
indefinite /ɪn'defɪnɪt/ *adj.* **1** (not clearly defined) неопределённый **2** (unlimited) неограни́ченный **3** (gram.): ~ **article** неопределённый арти́кль
indefinitely /ɪn'defɪnɪtlɪ/ *adv.* на неопределённое вре́мя
indelible /ɪn'delɪb(ə)l/ *adj.* (lit., fig.) несмыва́емый
indentation /ɪnden'teɪʃ(ə)n/ *n.* (notch, cut) зубе́ц, вы́рез, зазу́брина; (in coastline etc.)

изви́лина
independence /ɪndɪ'pend(ə)ns/ *n.* незави́симость (from: от + *g.*)
✧ **independent** /ɪndɪ'pend(ə)nt/ *adj.* незави́симый, самостоя́тельный; не зави́сящий (of: от + *g.*); (in adv. sense) ~ of незави́симо от + *g.*; поми́мо + *g.*
in-depth /ɪn'depθ/ *adj.* обстоя́тельный
indescribable /ɪndɪ'skraɪbəb(ə)l/ *adj.* неопису́емый
indestructible /ɪndɪ'strʌktɪb(ə)l/ *adj.* неразруши́мый
indeterminate /ɪndɪ'tə:mɪnət/ *adj.* (not fixed; indefinite) неопределённый; an ~ **sentence** неопределённый пригово́р; (not settled; undecided) нерешённый; неоконча́тельный; an ~ **result** неоконча́тельный результа́т; (vague; indefinable) нея́сный, сму́тный
index /'ɪndeks/ *n.* **1** (indicative figure) и́ндекс; **retail price** ~ и́ндекс ро́зничных цен **2** (alphabetical) указа́тель (*m.*); card ~ картоте́ка **3**: ~ **finger** указа́тельный па́лец
  ● *v.t.* (econ.) (also ~**-link**, BrE) индекси́ровать (impf., pf.)
  ■ ~ **card** *n.* (картоте́чная) ка́рточка
India /'ɪndɪə/ *n.* Инди́я
✧ **Indian** /'ɪndɪən/ *n.* **1** (native of India) инди́|ец (-а́нка) **2** (in full **American** ~) инд|е́ец (-иа́нка)
  ● *adj.* **1** (of India) инди́йский **2** (North American) инде́йский
  ■ ~ **Ocean** *n.* Инди́йский океа́н; ~ **summer** *n.* ба́бье ле́то
✧ **indicate** /'ɪndɪkeɪt/ *v.t.* (point to) ука́зывать, -а́ть; (be a sign of) свиде́тельствовать (impf.) o + *p.*
indication /ɪndɪ'keɪʃ(ə)n/ *n.* (sign) знак, указа́тель (*m.*); (hint) при́знак, намёк; he gave no ~ of his feelings он ниче́м не вы́дал свои́х чувств
indicative /ɪn'dɪkətɪv/ *n.* (gram.) изъяви́тельное наклоне́ние
  ● *adj.*: ~ of (suggesting, showing) ука́зывающий на (+ *a.*)
indicator /'ɪndɪkeɪtə(r)/ *n.* **1** (pointer of instrument) стре́лка; указа́тель (*m.*) **2** (BrE, on vehicle) указа́тель (*m.*) поворо́та
indict /ɪn'daɪt/ *v.t.* предъяв|ля́ть, -и́ть обвине́ние + *d.*
indictment /ɪn'daɪtmənt/ *n.* (charge) обвини́тельный акт; (fig.): these figures are an ~ of government policy э́ти ци́фры слу́жат обвини́тельным докуме́нтом про́тив поли́тики прави́тельства
indifference /ɪn'dɪfrəns/ *n.* безразли́чие; равноду́шие
indifferent /ɪn'dɪfrənt/ *adj.* (without interest) безразли́чный; (mediocre) посре́дственный
indigenous /ɪn'dɪdʒɪnəs/ *adj.* тузе́мный
indigestible /ɪndɪ'dʒestɪb(ə)l/ *adj.* трудноперева́риваемый
indigestion /ɪndɪ'dʒestʃ(ə)n/ *n.* несваре́ние желу́дка
indignant /ɪn'dɪgnənt/ *adj.* возмущённый; I was ~ at his remark его́ замеча́ние

возмути́ло меня́

indignation /ˌɪndɪɡˈneɪʃ(ə)n/ *n.* возмуще́ние

indignit|y /ɪnˈdɪɡnɪti/ *n.* униже́ние, оскорбле́ние; **we were subjected to various ~ies** мы подве́рглись вся́ческим униже́ниям

indirect /ˌɪndaɪˈrekt/ *adj.* непрямо́й, ко́свенный

indiscreet /ˌɪndɪˈskriːt/ *adj.* беста́ктный

indiscretion /ˌɪndɪˈskreʃ(ə)n/ *n.* нескро́мность; (indiscreet act) неосторо́жный посту́пок

indiscriminate /ˌɪndɪˈskrɪmɪnət/ *adj.*
1 (undiscriminating) неразбо́рчивый **2** (random) де́йствующий без разбо́ра

indispensable /ˌɪndɪˈspensəb(ə)l/ *adj.* необходи́мый

indisposed /ˌɪndɪˈspəʊzd/ *adj.* (unwell) (немно́го) нездоро́вый; **the Queen is ~** короле́ва нездоро́вится

indisposition /ˌɪndɪspəˈzɪʃ(ə)n/ *n.* (feeling unwell) недомога́ние

indisputable /ˌɪndɪˈspjuːtəb(ə)l/ *adj.* неоспори́мый

indistinct /ˌɪndɪˈstɪŋkt/ *adj.* (of things seen or heard) нея́сный; невня́тный; (vague) сму́тный, расплы́вчатый

indistinguishable /ˌɪndɪˈstɪŋɡwɪʃəb(ə)l/ *adj.* (not recognizably different) неразличи́мый, неотличи́мый; **he is ~ from his brother** его́ невозмо́жно отличи́ть от бра́та; **the two are ~** э́ти дво́е неразличи́мы

✎ individual /ˌɪndɪˈvɪdʒʊəl/ *n.* **1** (single being) ли́чность, индиви́дуум, едини́ца, о́собь **2** (type of person) челове́к, тип
● *adj.* **1** (single, particular) отде́льный **2** (of or for one person) ли́чный, ча́стный; **the teacher gave each pupil ~ attention** учи́тель уделя́л внима́ние ка́ждому ученику́ **3** (distinctive) характе́рный, осо́бенный

individualism /ˌɪndɪˈvɪdʒʊəlɪz(ə)m/ *n.* индивидуали́зм

individuality /ˌɪndɪvɪdʒʊˈælɪti/ *n.* индивидуа́льность

indoctrinate /ɪnˈdɒktrɪneɪt/ *v.t.* внуш|а́ть, -и́ть при́нципы + *d.*

indolent /ˈɪndələnt/ *adj.* лени́вый, вя́лый

indomitable /ɪnˈdɒmɪtəb(ə)l/ *adj.* неукроти́мый

Indonesia /ˌɪndəˈniːzə/ *n.* Индоне́зия

Indonesian /ˌɪndəˈniːz(ə)n/ *n.* (person) индонези́|ец (-йка); (language) индонези́йский язы́к
● *adj.* индонези́йский

indoor /ˈɪndɔː(r)/ *adj.* ко́мнатный; **~ games** ко́мнатные и́гры; **~ swimming pool** закры́тый бассе́йн

indoors /ɪnˈdɔːz/ *adv.* (expr. position) в до́ме; взаперти́; (expr. motion) в дом, внутрь

induce /ɪnˈdjuːs/ *v.t.* **1** (persuade, prevail on) убе|жда́ть, -ди́ть; **nothing will ~ him to change his mind** ничто́ не заста́вит его́

✎ ключева́я ле́ксика

измени́ть реше́ние **2** (bring about) вызыва́ть, вы́звать; **illness ~d by fatigue** боле́знь, вы́званная переутомле́нием

inducement /ɪnˈdjuːsmənt/ *n.* (motive, incentive) сти́мул; **there is no ~ for me to stay here** ничто́ не уде́рживает меня́ здесь; (bribe) подкуп

induction /ɪnˈdʌkʃ(ə)n/ *n.* введе́ние, вступле́ние

indulge /ɪnˈdʌldʒ/ *v.t.* (gratify, give way to) потво́рствовать (*impf.*) + *d.*; (spoil) по́ртить, ис-; балова́ть, из-
● *v.i.* (allow oneself pleasure) увлека́ться (*impf.*) (*чем*); **he ~s in a cigar** он позволя́ет себе́ вы́курить сига́ру

indulgence /ɪnˈdʌldʒ(ə)ns/ *n.* **1** (gratification) потво́рство **2** (pleasure indulged in) удово́льствие; **smoking is his only ~** куре́ние — его́ еди́нственная сла́бость

indulgent /ɪnˈdʌldʒ(ə)nt/ *adj.* потво́рствующий; **~ parents** не сли́шком стро́гие роди́тели

✎ industrial /ɪnˈdʌstrɪəl/ *adj.* промы́шленный, индустриа́льный; **~ accident** несча́стный слу́чай на произво́дстве
■ **~ action** *n.* (BrE) забасто́вочные де́йствия; **~ estate** *n.* (BrE) промы́шленная зо́на; **~ relations** *n. pl.* произво́дственные отноше́ния (ме́жду работода́телями и (их) рабо́тниками)

industrialist /ɪnˈdʌstrɪəlɪst/ *n.* промы́шленник; фабрика́нт

industrialization /ɪndʌstrɪəlaɪˈzeɪʃ(ə)n/ *n.* индустриализа́ция

industrialize /ɪnˈdʌstrɪəlaɪz/ *v.t.* индустриализи́ровать (*impf., pf.*)

industrious /ɪnˈdʌstrɪəs/ *adj.* трудолюби́вый

✎ industry /ˈɪndəstri/ *n.* **1** (branch of manufacture) о́трасль **2** (the world of manufacture) индустри́я; промы́шленность; **he intends to go into ~** он хо́чет заня́ться произво́дством **3** (diligence) трудолю́бие

inebriated /ɪˈniːbrɪeɪtɪd/ *adj.* пья́ный

inedible /ɪnˈedɪb(ə)l/ *adj.* несъедо́бный

ineffective /ˌɪnɪˈfektɪv/ *adj.* неэффекти́вный

ineffectual /ˌɪnɪˈfektʃʊəl/ *adj.* безрезульта́тный

inefficiency /ˌɪnɪˈfɪʃ(ə)nsi/ *n.* (of persons) неуме́ние, неспосо́бность; (of organizations, etc.) неэффекти́вность

inefficient /ˌɪnɪˈfɪʃ(ə)nt/ *adj.* (of persons) неуме́лый, неспосо́бный; (of organizations, etc.) неэффекти́вный; (of machines) непроизводи́тельный

ineligible /ɪnˈelɪdʒɪb(ə)l/ *adj.* (for office) неподходя́щий; (for a benefit) не име́ющий пра́ва (**for:** на + *a.*)

inept /ɪˈnept/ *adj.* неуме́лый

ineptitude /ɪˈneptɪtjuːd/ *n.* неуме́ние; (act) глу́пая вы́ходка

inequality /ˌɪnɪˈkwɒlɪti/ *n.* нера́венство

inequity /ɪnˈekwɪti/ *n.* несправедли́вость

inert /ɪˈnɜːt/ *adj.* (fig.) вя́лый, безде́ятельный

inertia /ɪˈnɜːʃə/ *n.* инéртность; (phys.) инéрция

inescapable /ɪnɪˈskeɪpəb(ə)l/ *adj.* неизбéжный

inevitability /ɪnevɪtəˈbɪlɪti/ *n.* неизбéжность

inevitable /ɪnˈevɪtəb(ə)l/ *adj.* неизбéжный, неминýемый

inexcusable /ɪnɪkˈskjuːzəb(ə)l/ *adj.* непрости́тельный

inexhaustible /ɪnɪɡˈzɔːstɪb(ə)l/ *adj.* (unfailing) неистощи́мый, неисчерпáемый

inexpensive /ɪnɪkˈspensɪv/ *adj.* недорогóй

inexperienced /ɪnɪkˈspɪərɪənst/ *adj.* неóпытный

inexplicable /ɪnɪkˈsplɪkəb(ə)l/ *adj.* необъясни́мый

in extremis /ɪn ekˈstriːmɪs/ *adv.* в крáйнем слýчае

infallible /ɪnˈfælɪb(ə)l/ *adj.* надёжный

infamous /ˈɪnfəməs/ *adj.* (person) бесслáвный; (behaviour) позóрный

infancy /ˈɪnf(ə)nsɪ/ *n.* младéнчество

infant /ˈɪnf(ə)nt/ *n.* младéнец
■ ~ **school** *n.* (BrE) шкóла для малышéй, млáдшие клáссы начáльной шкóлы

infantile /ˈɪnfəntaɪl/ *adj.* **1** дéтский, младéнческий; ~ **paralysis** дéтский парали́ч **2** (childish) инфанти́льный

infantry /ˈɪnfəntrɪ/ *n.* пехóта
■ ~**man** *n.* пехоти́нец

infatuate /ɪnˈfætʃʊeɪt/ *v.t.*: he is ~d with her онá покори́ла/плени́ла егó

infatuation /ɪnfætʃʊˈeɪʃ(ə)n/ *n.* влюблённость, увлечéние

infect /ɪnˈfekt/ *v.t.* (lit., fig.) зарa|жáть, -зи́ть; the wound became ~ed рáна загнои́лась

infection /ɪnˈfekʃ(ə)n/ *n.* инфéкция; he caught the ~ from his brother он зарази́лся от брáта

infectious /ɪnˈfekʃəs/ *adj.* (disease) зарáзный, инфекцио́нный; (person) зарáзный; (fig.) зарази́тельный

infer /ɪnˈfɜː(r)/ *v.t.* (**inferred**, **inferring**) заключ|áть, -и́ть; предпол|агáть, -ожи́ть

inferior /ɪnˈfɪərɪə(r)/ *n.* подчинённый
● *adj.* **1** (lower in position, rank, etc.) ни́зший **2** (poorer in quality) хýдший **3** (of less importance) неполноцéнный; he makes me feel ~ в егó прису́тствии у меня́ появля́ется кóмплекс неполноцéнности

inferiority /ɪnfɪərɪˈɒrɪti/ *n.* (of position) бóлее ни́зкое положéние; (of quality) низкосóртность
■ ~ **complex** *n.* кóмплекс неполноцéнности

infernal /ɪnˈfɜːn(ə)l/ *adj.* **1** (of hell) áдский **2** (devilish, abominable) áдский, дья́вольский; an ~ **machine** áдская маши́на **3** (infml, confounded) чертóвский; an ~ **nuisance** прокля́тие

inferno /ɪnˈfɜːnəʊ/ *n.* (*pl.* ~**s**) (lit., fig.) ад

infertile /ɪnˈfɜːtaɪl/ *adj.* (soil) неплодорóдный; (woman, man) бесплóдный

infertility /ɪnfəˈtɪlɪti/ *n.* неплодорóдность; бесплóдность

infest /ɪnˈfest/ *v.t.* наводн|я́ть, -и́ть; the house is ~ed with rats дом наводнён кры́сами

infidel /ˈɪnfɪd(ə)l/ *n. & adj.* (relig.) невéрный

infidelity /ɪnfɪˈdelɪti/ *n.* невéрность, измéна (супрýжеская)

in-fighting /ˈɪnfaɪtɪŋ/ *n.* междоусóбица, внýтренняя борьбá

infiltrate /ˈɪnfɪltreɪt/ *v.t.* прон|икáть, -и́кнуть

infinite /ˈɪnfɪnɪt/ *adj.* бесконéчный, беспредéльный

infinitesimal /ɪnfɪnɪˈtesɪm(ə)l/ *adj.* бесконéчно мáлый

infinitive /ɪnˈfɪnɪtɪv/ *n.* инфинити́в, неопределённая фóрма глагóла

infinity /ɪnˈfɪnɪti/ *n.* бесконéчность

infirm /ɪnˈfɜːm/ *adj.* (physically) нéмощный, дря́хлый

infirmary /ɪnˈfɜːmərɪ/ *n.* больни́ца

inflame /ɪnˈfleɪm/ *v.t.*: the wound became ~d рáна воспали́лась

inflammable /ɪnˈflæməb(ə)l/ *adj.* легкó воспламеня́ющийся, горю́чий

inflammation /ɪnfləˈmeɪʃ(ə)n/ *n.* воспалéние

inflammatory /ɪnˈflæmətərɪ/ *adj.* **1** (seditious) зажигáтельный; подстрекáтельский **2** (med.) воспали́тельный

inflatable /ɪnˈfleɪtəb(ə)l/ *adj.* надувнóй

inflate /ɪnˈfleɪt/ *v.t.* над|увáть, -ýть

inflation /ɪnˈfleɪʃ(ə)n/ *n.* (econ.) инфля́ция

inflection /ɪnˈflekʃ(ə)n/ *n.* (gram.) флéксия

inflexible /ɪnˈfleksɪb(ə)l/ *adj.* неги́бкий, жёсткий; (fig.) непреклóнный, непоколеби́мый

inflict /ɪnˈflɪkt/ *v.t.* (a blow) нан|оси́ть, -ести́; (pain) причин|я́ть, -и́ть

influence /ˈɪnflʊəns/ *n.* (power to affect or change) влия́ние, воздéйствие; she is a good ~ on him онá на негó хорошó влия́ет; under the ~ (of drink) под воздéйствием (алкогóля)
● *v.t.* влия́ть, по- на + *a.*; окáз|ывать, -áть влия́ние на + *a.*; he was ~d by what he saw уви́денное повлия́ло на негó

influential /ɪnflʊˈenʃ(ə)l/ *adj.* влия́тельный

influenza /ɪnflʊˈenzə/ *n.* грипп

influx /ˈɪnflʌks/ *n.* (fig.) наплы́в

inform /ɪnˈfɔːm/ *v.t.* сообщ|áть, -и́ть + *d.*; информи́ровать (*impf., pf.*); осв|едомля́ть, -éдомить; стáвить, по- в извéстность; I was not ~ed of the facts мне не сообщи́ли о фáктах; keep me ~ed держи́те меня́ в кýрсе дел
● *v.i.* дон|оси́ть, -ести́; he ~ed against, on his comrades он доноси́л на свои́х товáрищей

informal /ɪnˈfɔːm(ə)l/ *adj.* неофициáльный; непринуждённый; it will be an ~ **party** вéчер бýдет дрýжеский; ~ **dress** повседнéвная одéжда

information /ɪnfəˈmeɪʃ(ə)n/ *n.* информáция; свéдения (*nt. pl.*); спрáвка; дáнные (*nt. pl.*); a useful piece of ~ полéзная информáция
■ ~ **desk** *n.* спрáвочный стол; ~ **technology** *n.* информáтика

informative /ɪnˈfɔːmətɪv/ *adj.*
информати́вный

informer /ɪnˈfɔːmə(r)/ *n.* (police ~)
осведоми́тель (-ница); (against sb) доно́счик
(-ца)

infra-red /ˌɪnfrəˈred/ *adj.* инфракра́сный

infrastructure /ˈɪnfrəstrʌktʃə(r)/ *n.*
инфраструкту́ра

infrequent /ɪnˈfriːkwənt/ *adj.* ре́дкий

infringe /ɪnˈfrɪndʒ/ *v.t. & i.* нар|уша́ть,
-у́шить; this does not ~ on your rights э́то не
ущемля́ет ва́ших прав

infringement /ɪnˈfrɪndʒmənt/ *n.* наруше́ние

infuriat|e /ɪnˈfjʊərɪeɪt/ *v.t.* прив|оди́ть, -ести́ в
я́рость/бе́шенство; разъяр|я́ть, -и́ть; an ~ing
delay возмути́тельная заде́ржка

ingenious /ɪnˈdʒiːnɪəs/ *adj.*
изобрета́тельный; остроу́мный

ingenuity /ˌɪndʒɪˈnjuːɪtɪ/ *n.*
изобрета́тельность; оригина́льность

ingenuous /ɪnˈdʒenjʊəs/ *adj.* простоду́шный,
наи́вный

ingot /ˈɪŋgət/ *n.* сли́ток

ingrained /ɪnˈgreɪnd/ *adj.* **1** ~ dirt въе́вшаяся
грязь **2** (fig.) закорене́лый, врождённый

ingratitude /ɪnˈgrætɪtjuːd/ *n.*
неблагода́рность

ingredient /ɪnˈgriːdɪənt/ *n.* (of mixture)
компоне́нт; (cul.) ингредие́нт; hard work is
an important ~ of success упо́рный труд —
ва́жная составля́ющая успе́ха

inhabit /ɪnˈhæbɪt/ *v.t.* (inhabited,
inhabiting) жить (*impf.*) в + *p.*; обита́ть
(*impf.*) в + *p.*; is the island ~ed? э́тот о́стров
обита́ем?

inhabitant /ɪnˈhæbɪt(ə)nt/ *n.* жи́тель
(-ница); жиле́ц

inhale /ɪnˈheɪl/ *v.t.* вд|ыха́ть, -охну́ть
● *v.i.* затя́гиваться (*сигаре́той и т. п.*)

inhaler /ɪnˈheɪlə(r)/ *n.* (device) ингаля́тор

inherent /ɪnˈherənt/ *adj.* сво́йственный,
прису́щий

inherit /ɪnˈherɪt/ *v.t.* (inherited, inheriting)
насле́довать (*impf., pf.*) (*pf. also* у-)
● *v.i.* (inherited, inheriting) получ|а́ть,
-и́ть насле́дство

inheritance /ɪnˈherɪt(ə)ns/ *n.* (inheriting)
насле́дование; (sth inherited) насле́дство

inhibit /ɪnˈhɪbɪt/ *v.t.* (inhibited, inhibiting)
(restrain) угнета́ть (*impf.*); ско́в|ывать, -а́ть;
an ~ed person ско́ванный челове́к

inhibition /ˌɪnhɪˈbɪʃ(ə)n/ *n.* торможе́ние

inhospitable /ˌɪnhɒˈspɪtəb(ə)l/ *adj.*
негостеприи́мный

inhuman /ɪnˈhjuːmən/ *adj.* бесчелове́чный

inhumane /ˌɪnhjuːˈmeɪn/ *adj.* негума́нный

inhumanity /ˌɪnhjuːˈmænɪtɪ/ *n.*
бесчелове́чность, жесто́кость

✍ **initial** /ɪˈnɪʃ(ə)l/ *n.* нача́льная бу́ква; (in pl.)
(as signature) инициа́лы (*m. pl.*)
● *adj.* нача́льный

● *v.t.* (initialled, initialling, AmE
initialed, initialing): ~ a document
ста́вить, по- инициа́лы под докуме́нтом

✍ **initially** /ɪˈnɪʃəlɪ/ *adv.* внача́ле, снача́ла

initiate¹ /ɪˈnɪʃɪət/ *n.* посвящённый

initiate² /ɪˈnɪʃɪeɪt/ *v.t.* **1** (set in motion)
начина́ть, -а́ть **2** (introduce) приобщ|а́ть, -и́ть
(into: к + *d.*); he was ~d into the mysteries of
science его́ посвяти́ли в та́йны нау́ки

✍ **initiative** /ɪˈnɪʃətɪv/ *n.* инициати́ва; he took
the ~ он взял инициати́ву на себя́

inject /ɪnˈdʒekt/ *v.t.* вв|оди́ть, -ести́;
впры́с|кивать, -нуть; the drug was ~ed into
the bloodstream лека́рство ввели́ в ве́ну; he
learned to ~ himself with insulin он научи́лся
де́лать себе́ уко́лы/инъе́кции инсули́на

injection /ɪnˈdʒekʃ(ə)n/ *n.* впры́скивание;
инъе́кция

injunction /ɪnˈdʒʌŋkʃ(ə)n/ *n.* (law) суде́бный
запре́т

✍ **injure** /ˈɪndʒə(r)/ *v.t.* (physically) ушиб|а́ть,
-и́ть; повре|жда́ть, -ди́ть; ра́нить (*impf., pf.*);
(fig.): he will ~ his own reputation он сам
испо́ртит себе́ репута́цию

injured /ˈɪndʒəd/ *adj.* (suffering injury) ра́неный;
(as n. pl.) the dead and ~ уби́тые и ра́неные;
(offended) оби́женный

✍ **injury** /ˈɪndʒərɪ/ *n.* ра́на, ране́ние, уши́б, тра́вма

injustice /ɪnˈdʒʌstɪs/ *n.* несправедли́вость

ink /ɪŋk/ *n.* черни́л|а (*pl., g.* —)
■ ~jet *adj.*: ~jet printer (comput.) стру́йный
при́нтер

inkling /ˈɪŋklɪŋ/ *n.* (hint) намёк; (suspicion)
подозре́ние

inland /ˈɪnlənd/ *adj.* располо́женный внутри́
страны́
● *adv.* (motion) внутрь/вглубь страны́; (place)
внутри́ страны́
■ I~ Revenue *n.* (BrE) Госуда́рственная
нало́говая слу́жба

in-law /ˈɪnlɔː/ *n.*: ~s ро́дственники (*m. pl.*) со
стороны́ му́жа/жены́, своя́ки (infml) (*m. pl.*)

inla|y /ɪnˈleɪ/ *n.* инкруста́ция
● *v.t.* инкрусти́ровать (*impf., pf.*); an ~id
floor парке́тный пол с инкруста́цией

in loco parentis /ɪn ˌləʊkəʊ pəˈrentɪs/ *adv.* в
ка́честве роди́телей

inmate /ˈɪnmeɪt/ *n.* (of hospital, home, etc.)
больно́й, пацие́нт; (of prison) заключённый

inn /ɪn/ *n.* тракти́р

innate /ɪˈneɪt/ *adj.* врождённый

inner /ˈɪnə(r)/ *adj.* вну́тренний

innocence /ˈɪnəs(ə)ns/ *n.* невино́вность

innocent /ˈɪnəs(ə)nt/ *adj.* **1** (law) невино́вный
2 (harmless) неви́нный **3** (without sin)
неви́нный, безгре́шный

innocuous /ɪˈnɒkjʊəs/ *adj.* безвре́дный,
безоби́дный

innovation /ˌɪnəˈveɪʃ(ə)n/ *n.* нововведе́ние

innovative /ˈɪnəvətɪv/ *adj.* нова́торский

innovator /ˈɪnəveɪtə(r)/ *n.* нова́тор

innuendo /ˌɪnjuˈendəʊ/ *n.* (pl. ~es or ~s)
инсинуа́ция; (hint) намёк

inoculate /ɪ'nɒkjʊleɪt/ v.t. де́лать, с-
приви́вку; прив|ива́ть, -и́ть; **he was ~d
against smallpox** ему́ сде́лали приви́вку от
о́спы/ему́ приви́ли о́спу
inoculation /ɪnɒkjʊ'leɪʃ(ə)n/ n. приви́вка
inoffensive /ɪnə'fensɪv/ adj. необи́дный
inoperable /ɪn'ɒpərəb(ə)l/ adj. (untreatable
by surgery) неопера́бельный; (unworkable)
непримени́мый; **the plan proved to be ~**
план оказа́лся неприменими́мым
inordinate /ɪn'ɔ:dɪnət/ adj. непоме́рный,
чрезме́рный, неуме́ренный
inorganic /ɪnɔ:'gænɪk/ adj. неоргани́ческий
inpatient /'ɪnpeɪʃ(ə)nt/ n. стациона́рный/
ко́ечный больно́й
input /'ɪnpʊt/ n. (investment, resources) вложе́ние;
(contribution) вклад; (comput., of data) ввод
• v.t. (comput.) вв|оди́ть, -ести́ (into: в + a.)
inquest /'ɪŋkwest/ n. (in criminal case)
сле́дствие; (investigation) рассле́дование
inquire /ɪn'kwaɪə(r)/ (see also ▸ enquire) v.i.
спр|авля́ться, -а́виться; нав|оди́ть, -ести́
спра́вки
ℐ **inquiry** /ɪn'kwaɪərɪ/ (see also ▸ enquiry) n.
(investigation) рассле́дование; (in criminal case)
сле́дствие; **court of ~** сле́дственная коми́ссия
inquisition /ɪnkwɪ'zɪʃ(ə)n/ n. (questioning)
допро́с; **he was subjected to an ~** он был под
сле́дствием; (hist.) инквизи́ция
inquisitive /ɪn'kwɪzɪtɪv/ adj. любопы́тный
inroad /'ɪnrəʊd/ n. (usu. in pl.) (encroachment)
посяга́тельство; **the holiday will make large
~s into/on my savings** кани́кулы поглотя́т
бо́льшую часть мои́х сбереже́ний
insane /ɪn'seɪn/ adj. безу́мный,
сумасше́дший; (law) невменя́емый
insanitary /ɪn'sænɪtərɪ/ adj. антисанита́рный,
негигиени́чный
insanity /ɪn'sænɪtɪ/ n. (madness) сумасше́ствие;
безу́мие; (law) невменя́емость
insatiable /ɪn'seɪʃəb(ə)l/ adj. ненасы́тный
inscribe /ɪn'skraɪb/ v.t. ~ (engrave) высека́ть,
вы́сечь; выреза́ть, вы́резать; начерта́ть (pf.);
the stone was ~d with their names их имена́
бы́ли вы́сечены на ка́мне; **a verse is ~d on
his tomb** на его́ надгро́бном ка́мне вы́сечена
стихотво́рная эпита́фия 2 (autograph)
надпи́с|ывать, -а́ть; **please ~ your name in
the book** пожа́луйста, распиши́тесь в кни́ге
inscription /ɪn'skrɪpʃ(ə)n/ n. на́дпись
inscrutable /ɪn'skru:təb(ə)l/ adj. (smile)
зага́дочный; (face) непроница́емый
insect /'ɪnsekt/ n. насеко́мое; **~ bite** уку́с
насеко́мого
insecticide /ɪn'sektɪsaɪd/ n. инсектици́д
insecure /ɪnsɪ'kjʊə(r)/ adj. 1 (unsafe; unreliable)
ненадёжный, небезопа́сный; **his position in
the firm is ~** его́ положе́ние в фи́рме ша́ткое
2 (lacking confidence) неуве́ренный (в себе́)
insecurity /ɪnsɪ'kjʊrɪtɪ/ n. ненадёжность,
небезопа́сность; неуве́ренность
insemination /ɪnsemɪ'neɪʃ(ə)n/ n.
оплодотворе́ние; **artificial ~** иску́сственное

оплодотворе́ние
insensible /ɪn'sensɪb(ə)l/ adj. (numb)
нечувстви́тельный; **his hands were ~
with cold** от хо́лода его́ ру́ки потеря́ли
чувстви́тельность; (unconscious)
бесчу́вственный; (unaware) не созна|ю́щий;
he was ~ of the danger он не сознава́л
опа́сности
insensitive /ɪn'sensɪtɪv/ adj.
нечувстви́тельный; невосприи́мчивый,
равноду́шный
inseparable /ɪn'sepərəb(ə)l/ adj.
неразде́льный, неразры́вный
insert /ɪn'sɜ:t/ v.t. вст|авля́ть, -а́вить;
поме|ща́ть, -сти́ть; **he ~ed the key in(to) the
lock** он вста́вил ключ в замо́к
insertion /ɪn'sɜ:ʃ(ə)n/ n. (inserting) вкла́дывание,
помеще́ние, введе́ние; (sth inserted) вста́вка
ℐ **inside** /ɪn'saɪd/ n. 1 (interior) вну́треннее
простра́нство; вну́тренняя часть 2 (of road):
it is forbidden to pass on the ~ (when driving on
the right/left) обго́н спра́ва/сле́ва запрещён
• adj. вну́тренний; **~ pocket** вну́тренний
карма́н; **he received ~ information** он
получи́л информа́цию из вну́тренних
исто́чников
• adv. 1 (in the interior) внутри́; **I opened the
box and there was nothing ~** я откры́л
коро́бку — внутри́ бы́ло пу́сто 2 (indoors)
внутри́, в помеще́нии, до́ма
• prep. 1 (of motion into a place) в + a., внутрь
+ g.; **dogs are not allowed ~ the shop** с
соба́ками вход в магази́н запрещён; (of
position) в + p., внутри́ + g.; **have you seen ~
the house?** вы ви́дели дом изнутри́? 2 (of
time) в преде́лах + g., в тече́ние + g.; **I shall
be back ~ (of) a week** я верну́сь не поздне́е,
чем че́рез неде́лю
■ **~ out** adv. наизна́нку; **the thieves turned
everything ~ out** во́ры переверну́ли всё вверх
дном; **he knows the subject ~ out** он зна́ет
предме́т вдоль и поперёк
insider /ɪn'saɪdə(r)/ n. (comm.) свой/
непосторо́нний челове́к; **~ trading**
инса́йдерская торго́вля (незаконное участие
в би́ржевых сде́лках с использованием
информации из вну́тренних источников)
insight /'ɪnsaɪt/ n. проница́тельность;
понима́ние; **gain an ~ into sth** пости́|гнуть,
-чь (both pf.) что-н.
insignificant /ɪnsɪg'nɪfɪk(ə)nt/ adj.
малова́жный, ничто́жный
insincere /ɪnsɪn'sɪə(r)/ adj. неи́скренний
insinuate /ɪn'sɪnjʊeɪt/ v.t. (hint) намек|а́ть,
-ну́ть на + a.
insinuation /ɪnsɪnjʊ'eɪʃ(ə)n/ n. (hint) намёк,
инсинуа́ция
insipid /ɪn'sɪpɪd/ adj. ску́чный, вя́лый
ℐ **insist** /ɪn'sɪst/ v.t. & i. наст|а́ивать, -оя́ть на +
p.; тре́бовать; **he ~ed on his rights**
он наста́ивал на свои́х права́х; **he ~ed on
my accompanying him** он настоя́л на том,
чтобы я его́ сопровожда́л
insistence /ɪn'sɪst(ə)ns/ n. (quality)
насто́йчивость; (act) настоя́ние,

настойчивое требование

insistent /ɪnˈsɪst(ə)nt/ *adj.* настойчивый; **he was ~ that I should go** он настаивал на том, чтобы я пошёл

insofar as /ɪnsəʊˈfɑː(r)/ *conj.* (постольку) поскольку

insole /ˈɪnsəʊl/ *n.* стелька

insolence /ˈɪnsələns/ *n.* нахальство

insolent /ˈɪnsələnt/ *adj.* нахальный

insolvent /ɪnˈsɒlv(ə)nt/ *adj.* неплатёжеспособный; несостоятельный

insomnia /ɪnˈsɒmnɪə/ *n.* бессонница

insomniac /ɪnˈsɒmnɪæk/ *n.* страдающий бессонницей

insouciance /ɪnˈsuːsɪəns/ *n.* небрежность

insouciant /ɪnˈsuːsɪənt/ *adj.* небрежный

inspect /ɪnˈspekt/ *v.t.* осм|атривать, -отреть

inspection /ɪnˈspekʃ(ə)n/ *n.* осмотр, инспекция

inspector /ɪnˈspektə(r)/ *n.* (inspecting official) инспектор; (police officer) инспектор (полиции)

inspiration /ɪnspɪˈreɪʃ(ə)n/ *n.* вдохновение

 ✎ **inspire** /ɪnˈspaɪə(r)/ *v.t.* **1** (influence creatively) вдохновл|ять, -ить; **he is an ~d musician** он вдохновенный музыкант **2** (instil) всел|ять, -ить; **his work does not ~ me with confidence** его работа не вызывает у меня доверия

instability /ɪnstəˈbɪlɪti/ *n.* нестабильность, неустойчивость; (of character) неуравновешенность

 ✎ **install** /ɪnˈstɔːl/ *v.t.* (**installed, installing**) **1** (a person in office) вв|одить, -ести в должность **2** (machine, also comput.) устан|авливать, -овить

installation /ɪnstəˈleɪʃ(ə)n/ *n.* (of thing) установка; (art) инсталляция; (comput.) инсталляция, установка

instalment /ɪnˈstɔːlmənt/ *n.* (AmE also **installment**) *n.* **1** (partial payment) взнос; **we are paying for our carpet in ~s** мы платим за ковёр в рассрочку **2** (of published work) отрывок, выпуск

 ✎ **instance** /ˈɪnst(ə)ns/ *n.* **1** (example) пример; **for ~** например **2** (particular case) случай; **in this ~** в этом/данном случае

instant /ˈɪnst(ə)nt/ *n.* мгновение; **come here this ~!** иди сюда сию же минуту!
 • *adj.* **1** (immediate) мгновенный; немедленный **2** (cul.): **~ coffee** растворимый кофе

instantaneous /ɪnstənˈteɪnɪəs/ *adj.* мгновенный

 ✎ **instead** /ɪnˈsted/ *adv.* взамен + *g.*; **~ of** вместо + *g.*; **let me go ~ (of you)** давайте я пойду вместо вас; **if the steak is off I'll have chicken ~** если бифштексов нет, я возьму курицу

instep /ˈɪnstep/ *n.* подъём (ноги)

instigate /ˈɪnstɪɡeɪt/ *v.t.* подстрекать (*impf.*), провоцировать, с-

instil /ɪnˈstɪl/ *v.t.* (**instilled, instilling**) внуш|ать, -ить; прив|ивать, -ить

instinct /ˈɪnstɪŋkt/ *n.* инстинкт

instinctive /ɪnˈstɪŋktɪv/ *adj.* инстинктивный, безотчётный

institute /ˈɪnstɪtjuːt/ *n.* институт
 • *v.t.* устан|авливать, -овить; учре|ждать, -дить

 ✎ **institution** /ɪnstɪˈtjuːʃ(ə)n/ *n.* учреждение, организация, заведение, институт; **charitable ~** благотворительное учреждение

institutional /ɪnstɪˈtjuːʃən(ə)l/ *adj.* институциональный; **she is in need of ~ care** её следует госпитализировать; **~ reform** реформа учреждений

instruct /ɪnˈstrʌkt/ *v.t.* **1** (teach) учить, на- (*кого чему*) **2** (order) инструктировать (*impf., pf.*) (*pf. also* про-); **I was ~ed to call on you** мне было приказано зайти к вам

instruction /ɪnˈstrʌkʃ(ə)n/ *n.* (direction) указание; руководство; **follow the ~s on the packet** следуйте указаниям на пакете; (order) распоряжение, приказ
 ■ **~ book** *n.* руководство

instructive /ɪnˈstrʌktɪv/ *adj.* поучительный

instructor /ɪnˈstrʌktə(r)/ *n.* (sport) инструктор; (teacher) учитель (-ница)

 ✎ **instrument** /ˈɪnstrəmənt/ *n.* **1** (implement) инструмент **2** (mus.) (музыкальный) инструмент
 ■ **~ panel** *n.* пульт управления

instrumental /ɪnstrəˈment(ə)l/ *n.* (gram.) творительный падеж
 • *adj.* **1** (serving as means): **~ to our purpose** полезный для нашей цели **2** (mus.) инструментальный **3** (gram.) творительный

instrumentalist /ɪnstrəˈmentəlɪst/ *n.* инструменталист

insubordinate /ɪnsəˈbɔːdɪnət/ *adj.* непокорный

insubordination /ɪnsəbɔːdɪˈneɪʃ(ə)n/ *n.* неподчинение; непокорность

insubstantial /ɪnsəbˈstænʃ(ə)l/ *adj.* (not real, imaginary) нереальный, иллюзорный; (building, structure) непрочный; (evidence) слабый, неубедительный; (meal) несытный

insufferable /ɪnˈsʌf(ə)rəb(ə)l/ *adj.* невыносимый

insufficient /ɪnsəˈfɪʃ(ə)nt/ *adj.* недостаточный

insular /ˈɪnsjʊlə(r)/ *adj.* островной; (fig.) ограниченный, узкий

insulate /ˈɪnsjʊleɪt/ *v.t.* (protect from escape of electricity) изолировать (*impf., pf.*); (protect from escape of heat) утепл|ять, -ить, теплоизолировать (*impf., pf.*)

insulation /ɪnsjʊˈleɪʃ(ə)n/ *n.* (against escape of electricity) изоляция; (against escape of heat) теплоизоляция

insulin /ˈɪnsjʊlɪn/ *n.* инсулин

insult[1] /ˈɪnsʌlt/ *n.* оскорбление; обида

insult[2] /ɪnˈsʌlt/ *v.t.* оскорб|лять, -ить; **~ing language** оскорбительные выражения

insuperable /ɪnˈsuːpərəb(ə)l/ *adj.* непреодолимый

insupportable /ɪnsə'pɔːtəb(ə)l/ *adj.*
нестерпи́мый, невыноси́мый, несно́сный

⚘ **insurance** /ɪn'ʃʊərəns/ *n.* страхова́ние,
страхо́вка; **National I~** (BrE) госуда́рственное
страхова́ние; **take out ~** страхова́ться, за-
■ **~ company** *n.* страхова́я компа́ния; **~
policy** *n.* страхово́й по́лис

insure /ɪn'ʃʊə(r)/ *v.t.* страхова́ть, за-

insurgent /ɪn'sɜːdʒ(ə)nt/ *n.* повста́нец

insurmountable /ɪnsə'maʊntəb(ə)l/ *adj.*
непреодоли́мый

insurrection /ɪnsə'rekʃ(ə)n/ *n.* восста́ние

intact /ɪn'tækt/ *adj.* нетро́нутый, це́лый

intake /'ɪnteɪk/ *n.* (BrE, of recruits, students, etc.)
набо́р; (amount taken into body) потребле́ние; ~
of breath вздох

intangible /ɪn'tændʒɪb(ə)l/ *adj.* **1** (non-
material) неосяза́емый, неулови́мый **2** (vague,
obscure): ~ **ideas** сму́тные/нея́сные
представле́ния

integral /'ɪntɪgr(ə)l/ *adj.* неотъе́млемый,
суще́ственный

integrate /'ɪntɪgreɪt/ *v.t.* интегри́ровать
(*impf., pf.*)
● *v.i.* объедин|я́ться, -и́ться

integration /ɪntɪ'greɪʃ(ə)n/ *n.* интегра́ция

integrity /ɪn'tegrɪtɪ/ *n.* че́стность, це́льность

intellect /'ɪntəlekt/ *n.* интелле́кт, ум, рассу́док;
the great ~s of the age вели́кие умы́ эпо́хи

intellectual /ɪntɪ'lektʃʊəl/ *n.* интеллиге́нт
(-ка), интеллектуа́л (-ка)
● *adj.* интеллектуа́льный, у́мственный

⚘ **intelligence** /ɪn'telɪdʒ(ə)ns/ *n.* **1** (mental
power) ум, интелле́кт; **I had the ~ to refuse
his offer** у меня́ хвати́ло ума́ не приня́ть его́
предложе́ния **2** (mil.) разве́дка

intelligent /ɪn'telɪdʒ(ə)nt/ *adj.* у́мный,
смышлёный, сообрази́тельный

intelligentsia /ɪntelɪ'dʒentsɪə/ *n.*
интеллиге́нция

intelligible /ɪn'telɪdʒɪb(ə)l/ *adj.* поня́тный,
вня́тный

⚘ **intend** /ɪn'tend/ *v.t.* **1** (have in mind)
намерева́ться, хоте́ть, собира́ться (*all impf.*)
2 (mean) предназн|ача́ть, -а́чить; **a book ~ed
for advanced students** кни́га, рассчи́танная
на продви́нутый эта́п обуче́ния

intense /ɪn'tens/ *adj.* (**intenser, intensest**)
1 (extreme) си́льный, интенси́вный **2** (ardent)
напряжённый

intensify /ɪn'tensɪfaɪ/ *v.t.* уси́ли|вать, -ть;
увели́чи|вать, -ть

intensity /ɪn'tensɪtɪ/ *n.* си́ла, интенси́вность

intensive /ɪn'tensɪv/ *adj.* интенси́вный; ~
care unit отделе́ние реанима́ции

intent¹ /ɪn'tent/ *n.*: **to all ~s and purposes**
факти́чески, на са́мом де́ле

intent² /ɪn'tent/ *adj.* **1** (earnest, eager)
увлечённый, ре́вностный; (expression)
сосредото́ченный **2** (resolved): **he was ~
on getting a first** он был по́лон реши́мости
получи́ть дипло́м с отли́чием

⚘ **intention** /ɪn'tenʃ(ə)n/ *n.* наме́рение; у́мысел;

I have no ~ of going to the party у меня́ нет
наме́рения идти́ на вечери́нку

intentional /ɪn'tenʃən(ə)l/ *adj.*
умы́шленный, наме́ренный; **he ignored me
~ly** он наме́ренно не заме́тил меня́

interact /ɪntər'ækt/ *v.i.* взаимоде́йствовать
(*impf.*)

⚘ **interaction** /ɪntər'ækʃ(ə)n/ *n.* взаимоде́йствие

interactive /ɪntər'æktɪv/ *adj.* (comput.)
интеракти́вный, диало́говый

intercept /ɪntə'sept/ *v.t.* перехва́т|ывать, -и́ть

interchange /'ɪntətʃeɪndʒ/ *n.* **1** обме́н; ~
of views обме́н мне́ниями **2** (road junction)
перекрёсток с эстака́дой; ~ **of views** обме́н
мне́ниями

interchangeable /ɪntə'tʃeɪndʒəb(ə)l/ *adj.*
взаимозаменя́емый

intercity /ɪntə'sɪtɪ/ *adj.* междугоро́дный

intercom /'ɪntəkɒm/ *n.* (in an office, plane)
селе́ктор; (to get into a house) домофо́н

interconnect /ɪntəkə'nekt/ *v.i.* соедин|я́ться,
-и́ться

intercontinental /ɪntəkɒntɪ'nent(ə)l/ *adj.*
межконтинента́льный; ~ **ballistic missile**
межконтинента́льная баллисти́ческая
раке́та

intercourse /'ɪntəkɔːs/ *n.* (sexual) (полово́е)
сноше́ние

interdependent /ɪntədɪ'pend(ə)nt/ *adj.*
взаимозави́симый

⚘ **interest** /'ɪntrest/ *n.* **1** (attention, curiosity)
интере́с; **show a great ~ in sth** проявля́ть,
-и́ть большо́й интере́с к чему́-н. **2** (quality
arousing ~) занима́тельность; **his books
lack ~ for me** меня́ его́ кни́ги не
занима́ют **3** (pursuit) интере́с; **a man of
wide ~s** челове́к с широ́ким кру́гом
интере́сов **4** (often in pl.) (advantage)
интере́сы (*m. pl.*), по́льза, вы́года; **it is
in your ~ to listen to his advice** в ва́ших
же интере́сах прислу́шаться к его́
сове́там **5** (charge on loan) (paid) ссу́дный
проце́нт; проце́нты (*m. pl.*); (received)
проце́нтный дохо́д; **rate of ~, ~ rate**
проце́нтная ста́вка; (fig.): **my kindness was
repaid with ~** меня́ щедро вознаградили за
мою́ доброту́
● *v.t.* интересова́ть (*impf.*); (cause a person to
take interest) заинтересова́ть (*pf.*)
■ **~-free** *adj.* беспроце́нтный

interested /'ɪntrestɪd/ *adj.* **1** (having interest)
интересу́ющийся; **are you ~ in football?**
вы интересу́етесь футбо́лом? **2** (not
impartial) заинтересо́ванный; **an ~ party**
заинтересо́ванная сторона́

⚘ **interesting** /'ɪntrestɪŋ/ *adj.* интере́сный

interface /'ɪntəfeɪs/ *n.* (comput.) интерфе́йс;
(fig.) взаимосвя́зь, взаимоде́йствие

interfer|e /ɪntə'fɪə(r)/ *v.i.* вме́ш|иваться,
-а́ться; **don't ~e in my affairs** не
вме́шивайтесь в мои́ дела́; **she is an ~ing old
lady** она́ назо́йливая стару́ха

interference /ɪntə'fɪərəns/ *n.* вмеша́тельство,
поме́ха; (radio, TV) поме́хи (*f. pl.*)

intergovernmental /ɪntəgʌvən'ment(ə)l/ *adj.* межправительственный

interim /'ɪntərɪm/ *n.* промежуток времени; **in the ~** тем временем
● *adj.* (temporary) временный; (provisional) промежуточный

interior /ɪn'tɪərɪə(r)/ *n.* ▮ (inside) внутренняя часть, пространство внутри ▮ (of building) интерьер ▮ (home affairs): **Minister of the I~** министр внутренних дел
● *adj.* внутренний
■ **~ decorator** *n.* художник по интерьеру

interject /ɪntə'dʒekt/ *v.t.* вст|авлять, -авить; **'It's not true,' he ~ed** «Это неправда», — вставил он

interjection /ɪntə'dʒekʃ(ə)n/ *n.* восклицание; (gram.) междометие

interlock /ɪntə'lɒk/ *v.t. & i.* соедин|ять(ся), -ить(ся), сцеп|лять(ся), -ить(ся)

interloper /'ɪntələupə(r)/ *n.* незваный гость

interlude /'ɪntəlu:d/ *n.* перерыв; (theatr.) антракт

intermarry /ɪntə'mærɪ/ *v.i.* смеш|иваться, -аться; родниться, по- путём брака

intermediary /ɪntə'mi:dɪərɪ/ *n.* посредни|к (-ца)
● *adj.* посреднический

intermediate /ɪntə'mi:dɪət/ *adj.* промежуточный

interminable /ɪn'tə:mɪnəb(ə)l/ *adj.* бесконечный, нескончаемый, вечный

intermission /ɪntə'mɪʃ(ə)n/ *n.* антракт

intermittent /ɪntə'mɪt(ə)nt/ *adj.* прерывистый

intern[1] /'ɪntə:n/ *n.* (trainee) стажёр, практикант; (AmE, medical student) молодой врач, интерн

intern[2] /ɪn'tə:n/ *v.t.* интернировать (*impf., pf.*)

☞ **internal** /ɪn'tə:n(ə)l/ *adj.* внутренний; **I~ Revenue Service** (AmE) *see* ▸ **IRS**

☞ **international** /ɪntə'næʃən(ə)l/ *n.* (BrE, sporting event) международные соревнования (*nt. pl.*)
● *adj.* международный, интернациональный; **I~ Monetary Fund** Международный валютный фонд

internee /ɪntə:'ni:/ *n.* интернированный

☞ **Internet** *n.* (**the ~**) Интернет; **on the ~** в Интернете; **~ service provider** (интернет-)провайдер

internment /ɪn'tə:nmənt/ *n.* интернирование
■ **~ camp** *n.* лагерь (*m.*) для интернированных (лиц)

interplay /'ɪntəpleɪ/ *n.* взаимодействие, взаимосвязь

interpolate /ɪn'tə:pəleɪt/ *v.t.* интерполировать (*impf., pf.*); вст|авлять, -авить

interpret /ɪn'tə:prɪt/ *v.t.* (**interpreted**, **interpreting**) ▮ (explain) толковать (*impf.*); истолк|овывать, -овать; **how do you ~ this dream?** как вы объясняете этот сон? ▮ (understand) истолк|овывать, -ать

● *v.i.* перев|одить, -ести (устно)

interpretation /ɪntə:prɪ'teɪʃ(ə)n/ *n.* интерпретация, толкование

interpreter /ɪn'tə:prɪtə(r)/ *n.* (устный) переводчи|к (-ца)

interracial /ɪntə'reɪʃ(ə)l/ *adj.* межрасовый

interregn|um /ɪntə'regnəm/ *n.* (*pl.* **~ums** *or* **~a**) междуцарствие; междувластие

interrogate /ɪn'terəgeɪt/ *v.t.* допр|ашивать, -осить

interrogation /ɪnterə'geɪʃ(ə)n/ *n.* допрос

interrogative /ɪntə'rɒgətɪv/ *adj.* вопросительный

interrupt /ɪntə'rʌpt/ *v.t. & i.* прер|ывать, -вать; переб|ивать, -ить; **don't ~ when I am speaking** не перебивайте, когда я говорю; **he ~ed me as I was reading** он прервал моё чтение

interruption /ɪntə'rʌpʃ(ə)n/ *n.* помеха; нарушение; вторжение

intersect /ɪntə'sekt/ *v.t. & i.* перес|екать(ся), -ечь(ся)

intersection /ɪntə'sekʃ(ə)n/ *n.* (crossroads) перекрёсток; (intersecting) пересечение

intersperse /ɪntə'spə:s/ *v.t.* разбр|асывать, -осать; рассыпать, -ыпать; **red flowers ~d with yellow ones** красные цветы вперемежку с жёлтыми; **his talk was ~d with anecdotes** он пересыпал/разбавлял (infml) своё выступление анекдотами

interstate /ɪntə'steɪt/ *adj.* (between regions of country) межштатный; (between countries) межгосударственный

interval /'ɪntəv(ə)l/ *n.* ▮ (of time) промежуток, отрезок времени; интервал; **we see each other at ~s** мы видимся время от времени; **at ~s of an hour** с интервалами в час ▮ (of place) расстояние; **the posts were set at ~s of 10 feet** столбы были расставлены на расстоянии десяти футов (друг от друга) ▮ (BrE, theatr.) антракт

intervene /ɪntə'vi:n/ *v.i.* вмеш|иваться, -аться; **the government ~d in the dispute** в конфликт вмешалось правительство

☞ **intervention** /ɪntə'venʃ(ə)n/ *n.* вмешательство

☞ **interview** /'ɪntəvju:/ *n.* деловая встреча; собеседование; (with the media) интервью (*nt. indecl.*); **an ~ for a job** собеседование при приёме на работу; **he gave an ~ to the press** он дал интервью журналистам
● *v.t.* (with the media) интервьюировать (*impf., pf.*); **only certain candidates were ~ed** собеседование провели только с несколькими кандидатами

interviewee /ɪntəvju:'i:/ *n.* интервьюируемый, дающий интервью

interviewer /'ɪntəvju:ə(r)/ *n.* (for media) интервьюер; (for job) проводящий собеседование

interwar /ɪntə'wɔ:(r)/ *adj.*: **~ period** период между двумя мировыми войнами

intestate /ɪn'testeɪt/ *adj.*: **to die ~** умир|ать, -еть, не оставив завещания

intestine /ɪn'testɪn/ *n.* кишечник

☞ ключевая лексика

intimacy /'ɪntɪməsɪ/ *n.* инти́мность, бли́зость

intimate /'ɪntɪmət/ *adj.* **1** (close) бли́зкий **2** (private, personal) инти́мный, ли́чный; the ~ **details of his life** подро́бности его́ ли́чной жи́зни **3** (detailed) основа́тельный; **he has an ~ knowledge of the subject** он доскона́льно зна́ет предме́т

intimidate /ɪn'tɪmɪdeɪt/ *v.t.* запу́г|ивать, -а́ть; угрожа́ть (*impf.*) + *d.*

⚘ **into** /'ɪntʊ/ *prep.* **1** (expr. motion to a point within) в + *a.* **2** (expr. extent) до; **far ~ the night** до по́здней но́чи **3** (expr. change or process) в + *a. or* на + *a.*; **the rain turned ~ snow** дождь перешёл в снег; **translate ~ French** перев|оди́ть, -ести́ на францу́зский **4** (infml, of a devotee): **he's ~ jazz** он увлека́ется джа́зом

intolerable /ɪn'tɒlərəb(ə)l/ *adj.* невыноси́мый

intolerance /ɪn'tɒlərəns/ *n.* нетерпи́мость

intolerant /ɪn'tɒlərənt/ *n.* нетерпи́мый; ~ **of** (unable to bear) не вынося́щий + *g.*

intone /ɪn'təʊn/ *v.t.* (utter in particular tone) интони́ровать (*impf.*); (recite with prolonged sounds) чита́ть нараспе́в (*impf.*)

intoxicate /ɪn'tɒksɪkeɪt/ *v.t.* (lit., fig.) опьян|я́ть, -и́ть

intoxication /ɪntɒksɪ'keɪʃ(ə)n/ *n.* опьяне́ние

intractable /ɪn'træktəb(ə)l/ *adj.* (of person) упря́мый, непоко́рный, несгово́рчивый; (of problems, metal) неподда́тливый; ~ **illness** трудноизлечи́мое заболева́ние; ~ **pain** неустрани́мая боль

intransigent /ɪn'trænsɪdʒ(ə)nt/ *adj.* непреклю́нный

intransitive /ɪn'trænsɪtɪv/ *adj.* (gram.) непереходный

intravenous /ɪntrə'viːnəs/ *adj.* внутриве́нный

in tray /'ɪntreɪ/ *n.* (BrE) насто́льная корзи́на для входя́щей корреспонде́нции

intrepid /ɪn'trepɪd/ *adj.* неустраши́мый, бесстра́шный

intricate /'ɪntrɪkət/ *adj.* запу́танный, сло́жный

intrigu|e *n.* /'ɪntriːg/ интри́га; про́иски (*m. pl.*) ● *v.t.* /ɪn'triːg/ (**intrigues**, **intrigued**, **intriguing**) интригова́ть, за-; интересова́ть, за-; **I was ~ed to learn** мне бы́ло интере́сно узна́ть; **an ~ing prospect** зама́нчивая перспекти́ва

intrinsic /ɪn'trɪnzɪk/ *adj.* прису́щий, по́длинный; ~ **value** по́длинная це́нность

⚘ **introduce** /ɪntrə'djuːs/ *v.t.* **1** (bring in) вв|оди́ть, -ести́; (при)вн|оси́ть, -ести́; **many improvements have been ~d** введи́ мно́го усоверше́нствований **2** (present) предст|авля́ть, -а́вить; знако́мить, по- (*кого с кем*); **may I ~ my fiancée?** разреши́те предста́вить (вам) мою́ неве́сту

⚘ **introduction** /ɪntrə'dʌkʃ(ə)n/ *n.* **1** (bringing in) введе́ние, установле́ние **2** (sth brought in) но́вшество, нововведе́ние **3** (presentation) представле́ние; **letter of ~** рекоменда́тельное письмо́ **4** (preliminary matter in book, speech, etc.) введе́ние, вступле́ние

introductory /ɪntrə'dʌktərɪ/ *adj.* вступи́тельный, вво́дный

introspection /ɪntrə'spekʃ(ə)n/ *n.* интроспе́кция, самоана́лиз

introvert /'ɪntrəvɜːt/ *n.* за́мкнутый челове́к, интрове́рт

intrud|e /ɪn'truːd/ *v.t.* нав|я́зывать, -яза́ть ● *v.i.* вт|орга́ться, -о́ргнуться; **you are ~ing on my time** вы посяга́ете на моё вре́мя

intruder /ɪn'truːdə(r)/ *n.* граби́тель (*m.*)

intrusion /ɪn'truːʒ(ə)n/ *n.* вторже́ние

intrusive /ɪn'truːsɪv/ *adj.* назо́йливый

intuition /ɪntjuː'ɪʃ(ə)n/ *n.* интуи́ция; чутьё

intuitive /ɪn'tjuːɪtɪv/ *adj.* интуити́вный

inundate /'ɪnʌndeɪt/ *v.t.* наводн|я́ть, -и́ть; **I was ~d with letters** меня́ засы́пали пи́сьмами

invade /ɪn'veɪd/ *v.t.* вторга́ться, вто́ргнуться в + *a.*

invader /ɪn'veɪdə(r)/ *n.* захва́тчик

invalid[1] /'ɪnvəlɪd/ *n.* больно́й

invalid[2] /ɪn'vælɪd/ *adj.* недействи́тельный, не име́ющий (зако́нной) си́лы

invalidate /ɪn'vælɪdeɪt/ *v.t.* аннули́ровать (*impf.*, *pf.*)

invaluable /ɪn'væljʊəb(ə)l/ *adj.* неоцени́мый, бесце́нный

invariable /ɪn'veərɪəb(ə)l/ *adj.* неизме́нный, постоя́нный

invariably /ɪn'veərɪəblɪ/ *adv.* неизме́нно

invasion /ɪn'veɪʒ(ə)n/ *n.* вторже́ние, наше́ствие; ~ **of privacy** вторже́ние в ли́чную жизнь

inveigle /ɪn'veɪg(ə)l/ *v.t.* соблазн|я́ть, -и́ть; обол|ьща́ть, -сти́ть; **they ~d him into the conspiracy** они́ вовлекли́ его́ в за́говор; **he was ~d into signing a cheque** его́ обма́ном заста́вили подписа́ть чек

invent /ɪn'vent/ *v.t.* изобре|та́ть, -сти́; (think up) приду́м|ывать, -ать

invention /ɪn'venʃ(ə)n/ *n.* изобрете́ние

inventive /ɪn'ventɪv/ *adj.* изобрета́тельный, нахо́дчивый

inventor /ɪn'ventə(r)/ *n.* изобрета́тель (*m.*)

inventory /'ɪnvəntərɪ/ *n.* инвента́рь (*m.*)

invert /ɪn'vɜːt/ *v.t.* (turn upside down) перев|ора́чивать, -ерну́ть; ~**ed commas** (BrE, gram.) кавы́чки (*f. pl.*)

invertebrate /ɪn'vɜːtɪbrət/ *n.* беспозвоно́чное (живо́тное)

⚘ **invest** /ɪn'vest/ *v.t.* вкла́д|ывать, вложи́ть; инвести́ровать (*impf.*, *pf.*) ● *v.i.* вкла́д|ывать, вложи́ть де́ньги/капита́л; (infml, spend money usefully): **I must ~ in a new hat** мне придётся потра́титься на но́вую шля́пу

⚘ **investigate** /ɪn'vestɪgeɪt/ *v.t.* (crime, facts) рассле́довать (*impf.*, *pf.*); (study) иссле́довать (*impf.*, *pf.*)

⚘ **investigation** /ɪnvestɪ'geɪʃ(ə)n/ *n.* (criminal) рассле́дование, сле́дствие; (study) иссле́дование

investigative /ɪn'vestɪgətɪv/ *adj.*: ~ **journalism** журнали́стика рассле́дований

investigator /ɪn'vestɪɡeɪtə(r)/ *n.* (in police)
следователь (*m.*); (researcher) исследователь
(*m.*)

⚡ **investment** /ɪn'vestmənt/ *n.* (investing)
инвестирование; (sum invested) инвестиция
■ ~ **bank** *n.* инвестиционный банк

⚡ **investor** /ɪn'vestə(r)/ *n.* вкладчик, инвестор
inveterate /ɪn'vetərət/ *adj.* закоренелый,
заядлый

invidious /ɪn'vɪdiəs/ *adj.* оскорбительный;
обидный; an ~ **comparison** обидное/
оскорбительное сравнение

invigilate /ɪn'vɪdʒɪleɪt/ *v.i.* (BrE) наблюдать
(*impf.*) за экзаменующимися

invigilator /ɪn'vɪdʒɪleɪtə(r)/ *n.* официальный
наблюдатель (*на экзамене*)

invigorating /ɪn'vɪɡəreɪtɪŋ/ *adj.* бодрящий

invincible /ɪn'vɪnsɪb(ə)l/ *adj.* непобедимый

invisible /ɪn'vɪzɪb(ə)l/ *adj.* невидимый,
незримый

invitation /ɪnvɪ'teɪʃ(ə)n/ *n.* приглашение

⚡ **invite** /ɪn'vaɪt/ *v.t.* **1** (request to come)
приглаша|ть, -сить; **she** ~**d him into her flat**
она пригласила его к себе на квартиру; **I
am seldom** ~**d out** меня редко куда-либо
приглашают **2** (request) предл|агать,
-ожить; **we were** ~**d to choose** нам был
предоставлен выбор

invoice /'ɪnvɔɪs/ *n.* счёт, счёт-фактура
● *v.t.* выпи́сывать, выписать счёт кому-н.
(на товары)

invoke /ɪn'vəʊk/ *v.t.* взывать, воззвать;
приз|ывать, -вать; ~ **the law** взывать,
воззвать к закону

involuntary /ɪn'vɒləntəri/ *adj.* (accidental)
нечаянный; (uncontrollable) непроизвольный

⚡ **involve** /ɪn'vɒlv/ *v.t.* **1** (implicate)
вовл|екать, -ечь; **it will not** ~ **you in any
expense** это не потребует от вас никаких
расходов **2** (entail) влечь, по- за собой;
вызыва́ть, вызвать; **it would** ~ **my living in
London** в таком случае мне бы пришлось
жить в Лондоне

involved /ɪn'vɒlvd/ *adj.* сложный,
запутанный

involvement /ɪn'vɒlvmənt/ *n.* (participation)
причастность; (personal) связь, вовлечённость

invulnerable /ɪn'vʌlnərəb(ə)l/ *adj.*
неуязвимый

inward /'ɪnwəd/ *adj.* (lit., fig.) внутренний
● *adv.* = inwards

inwards /'ɪnwədz/ *adv.* (expr. motion) внутрь

in-your-face /ɪnjɔ:'feɪs/ *adj.* (infml) жёсткий,
провокационный

iodine /'aɪədi:n/ *n.* йод

iota /aɪ'əʊtə/ *n.* йота; **we will not yield one** ~
мы не отступим ни на йоту; **I don't care one**
~ мне решительно всё равно

IOU /aɪəʊ'ju:/ *n.* долговая расписка

IQ *abbr.* (*of* **intelligence quotient**)
коэффициент интеллекта/умственного

развития

IRA *abbr. of* **1** (**Irish Republican Army**)
ИРА (Ирландская республиканская армия)
2 (**individual retirement account**)
(AmE) индивидуальные пенсионные вклады
(*m. pl.*)

Iran /ɪ'rɑ:n/ *n.* Иран

Iranian /ɪ'reɪniən/ *n.* иран|ец (-ка)
● *adj.* иранский

Iraq /ɪ'rɑ:k/ *n.* Ирак

Iraqi /ɪ'rɑ:ki/ *n.* (*pl.* ~**s**) иракец, житель
(-ница) Ирака
● *adj.* иракский

irascible /ɪ'ræsɪb(ə)l/ *adj.* раздражительный,
вспыльчивый

irate /aɪ'reɪt/ *adj.* сердитый, гневный

Ireland /'aɪələnd/ *n.* Ирландия

iridescent /ɪrɪ'des(ə)nt/ *adj.* радужный,
переливчатый

iris /'aɪərɪs/ *n.* **1** (plant) ирис **2** (of eye)
радужная оболочка

⚡ **Irish** /'aɪərɪʃ/ *n.* **1** (language) ирландский
язык **2**: the ~ ирландцы (*m. pl.*)
● *adj.* ирландский
■ ~**man** *n.* ирландец; ~**woman** *n.* ирландка

iron /'aɪən/ *n.* **1** (metal) железо **2** (for ironing)
утюг
● *adj.* (lit., fig.) железный
● *v.t.* (clothes) гладить, по-/вы-; ~ **out** (fig.)
сгла́|живать, -дить
● *v.i.* гладить (*impf.*); **she spent the whole
evening** ~**ing** она гладила весь вечер
■ ~**monger** *n.* (BrE) торговец скобяными
изделиями; ~**monger's (shop)** *n.* (BrE)
магазин скобяных изделий/товаров

ironic /aɪ'rɒnɪk/, **ironical** /aɪ'rɒnɪk(ə)l/ *adjs.*
иронический

ironing /'aɪənɪŋ/ *n.* **1** (action) глаженье
2 (linen) бельё для глаженья
■ ~ **board** *n.* гладильная доска

irony /'aɪrəni/ *n.* ирония

irrational /ɪ'ræʃ(ə)l/ *adj.* (not endowed
with reason) неразумный; (illogical; absurd)
иррациональный

irreconcilable /ɪ'rekənsaɪləb(ə)l/ *adj.*
непримиримый

irrefutable /ɪrɪ'fju:təb(ə)l/ *adj.*
неопровержимый

irregular /ɪ'reɡjʊlə(r)/ *adj.* **1** (contrary to
rule) неправильный; (contrary to custom,
norm) непринятый **2** (variable in occurrence)
нерегулярный; **he keeps** ~ **hours** у него
неупорядоченный режим **3** (uneven)
неровный; ~ **teeth** неровные зубы
4 (unequal) неодинаковый; **at** ~ **intervals**
с неодинаковыми интервалами **5** (gram.)
неправильный

irregularity /ɪreɡjʊ'lærɪti/ *n.*
неправильность, нерегулярность

irrelevant /ɪ'reliv(ə)nt/ *adj.* неуместный,
неподходящий

irreparable /ɪ'repərəb(ə)l/ *adj.*: **an** ~
mistake непоправимая ошибка; **an** ~ **loss**
безвозвратная потеря/утрата; **my watch**

suffered ~ **damage** мои часы́ оконча́тельно
слома́лись

irreplaceable /ɪrɪˈpleɪsəb(ə)l/ *adj.*
незамени́мый

irrepressible /ɪrɪˈpresɪb(ə)l/ *adj.*
неукроти́мый, неугомо́нный, неудержи́мый

irreproachable /ɪrɪˈprəʊtʃəb(ə)l/ *adj.*
безупре́чный

irresistible /ɪrɪˈzɪstɪb(ə)l/ *adj.* неотрази́мый

irresolute /ɪˈrezəluːt/ *adj.* нереши́тельный

irrespective /ɪrɪˈspektɪv/ *adj.*: ~ **of** невзира́я/
несмотря́ на + *a.*

irresponsible /ɪrɪˈspɒnsɪb(ə)l/ *adj.*
безотве́тственный

irreverence /ɪˈrevərəns/ *n.*
непочти́тельность, неуваже́ние

irreverent /ɪˈrevərənt/ *adj.* непочти́тельный

irreversible /ɪrɪˈvɜːsɪb(ə)l/ *adj.* (process)
необрати́мый; (decision) неотменя́емый

irrevocable /ɪˈrevəkəb(ə)l/ *adj.*
бесповоро́тный

irrigate /ˈɪrɪɡeɪt/ *v.t.* оро|ша́ть, -си́ть

irrigation /ɪrɪˈɡeɪʃ(ə)n/ *n.* ороше́ние,
иррига́ция

irritability /ɪrɪtəˈbɪlɪtɪ/ *n.* раздражи́тельность;
(of skin etc.) чувстви́тельность

irritable /ˈɪrɪtəb(ə)l/ *adj.* **1** (easily
annoyed) раздражи́тельный **2** (of skin etc.)
чувстви́тельный

irritant /ˈɪrɪt(ə)nt/ *n.* раздражи́тель (*m.*)

irritate /ˈɪrɪteɪt/ *v.t.* раздража́ть (*impf.*)

irritation /ɪrɪˈteɪʃ(ə)n/ *n.* раздраже́ние

IRS (AmE) *abbr.* (of **Internal Revenue
Service**) Госуда́рственная нало́говая
слу́жба

is /ɪz/ *3rd pers. sing. pres. of* ▶ **be**

Islam /ˈɪzlɑːm/ *n.* исла́м, мусульма́нство

Islamic /ɪzˈlæmɪk/ *adj.* мусульма́нский,
исла́мский

⚡ **island** /ˈaɪlənd/ *n.* о́стров; **traffic** ~ острово́к
безопа́сности

islander /ˈaɪləndə(r)/ *n.* островитя́н|ин (-ка)

isle /aɪl/ *n.* о́стров

isn't /ˈɪz(ə)nt/ *neg. of* ▶ **is**

isolate /ˈaɪsəleɪt/ *v.t.* изоли́ровать (*impf., pf.*)
(also med.); разобща́ть, -и́ть; **an** ~**d village**
отдалённая дере́вня

isolation /aɪsəˈleɪʃ(ə)n/ *n.* изоля́ция,
разобще́ние; **a case considered in** ~ отде́льно
взя́тый слу́чай

isolationism /aɪsəˈleɪʃəˌnɪz(ə)m/ *n.*
изоляциони́зм

ISP *abbr.* (of **Internet service provider**)
(интерне́т-)прова́йдер

Israel /ˈɪzreɪl/ *n.* (bibl., pol.) Изра́иль (*m.*)

Israeli /ɪzˈreɪlɪ/ *n.* (*pl.* ~**s**) израильтя́н|ин (-ка)
● *adj.* изра́ильский

⚡ **issue** /ˈɪʃuː/ *n.* **1** (publication, production) вы́пуск,

изда́ние; (sth published or produced) вы́пуск,
изда́ние; (of a magazine) после́дние
номера́ журна́ла **2** (topic) вопро́с; предме́т
обсужде́ния; **I don't want to make an** ~ **of it**
я не хочу́ де́лать из э́того пробле́му
● *v.t.* (**issues, issued, issuing**) **1** (publish)
выпуска́ть, вы́пустить; изд|ава́ть, -а́ть;
a book ~**d last year** кни́га, и́зданная в
про́шлом году́ **2** (supply) выдава́ть, вы́дать;
снаб|жа́ть, -ди́ть

Istanbul /ɪstænˈbʊl/ *n.* Стамбу́л

isthmus /ˈɪsθməs/ *n.* (*pl.* ~**es**) переше́ек,
перемы́чка

IT *abbr.* (of **information technology**)
информа́тика

⚡ **it** /ɪt/ *pers. pron.* **1** он (она́, оно́); (impersonal,
often untranslated) э́то; **who is** ~? кто э́то?; ~**'s
the postman** э́то почтальо́н; **I don't speak
Russian but I understand** ~ я не говорю́ по-
ру́сски, но понима́ю **2** (impersonal or indefinite):
~ **is cold** хо́лодно; ~ **is 6 o'clock** (сейча́с)
шесть часо́в; ~ **is raining** идёт дождь;
~ **is 5 miles to Oxford** до О́ксфорда пять
миль **3** (emph. another word): ~ **was John who
laughed** э́то Джон смея́лся

Italian /ɪˈtæljən/ *n.* (person) италья́н|ец (-ка);
(language) италья́нский язы́к
● *adj.* италья́нский

italics /ɪˈtælɪks/ *n.* курси́в; **in** ~ курси́вом

Italy /ˈɪtəlɪ/ *n.* Ита́лия

itch /ɪtʃ/ *n.* зуд
● *v.i.* чеса́ться (*impf.*)

itchy /ˈɪtʃɪ/ *adj.* (**itchier, itchiest**) (skin)
зудя́щий; (causing itchiness) вызыва́ющий зуд

⚡ **item** /ˈaɪtəm/ *n.* пункт, но́мер; **news** ~
(коро́ткое) сообще́ние

itemize /ˈaɪtəmaɪz/ *v.t.* переч|исля́ть, -и́слить;
сост|авля́ть, -а́вить пе́речень + *g.*; **an** ~**d
account** подро́бный счёт

itinerary /aɪˈtɪnərərɪ/ *n.* маршру́т, план пути́
(*m.*)

⚡ **its** /ɪts/ *poss. adj.* его́, её; (pert. to subject of
sentence) свой; **the horse broke** ~ **leg** ло́шадь
слома́ла но́гу

⚡ **itself** /ɪtˈself/ *n.* **1** (refl.) себя́ (*d., p.* себе́, *i.*
собо́й); -ся/-сь (*suff.*); **the cat was washing**
~ кот умыва́лся; **the monkey saw** ~
in the mirror обезья́на уви́дела себя́ в
зе́ркале **2** (emph.) сам; **she is kindness** ~ она́
сама́ доброта́; **by** ~ (alone) оди́н, одино́ко, в
отдале́нии; (automatically) самостоя́тельно

ITV (BrE) *abbr.* (of **Independent
Television**) Незави́симое (комме́рческое)
телеви́дение (*телеканал в Великобритании*)

IVF *n.* (abbr. of **in vitro fertilization**)
экстракорпора́льное оплодотворе́ние

ivory /ˈaɪvərɪ/ *n.* **1** (substance) слоно́вая кость;
the I~ **Coast** Кот-д'Ивуа́р **2** (colour) цвет
слоно́вой ко́сти

ivy /ˈaɪvɪ/ *n.* плющ

i

Jj

jab /dʒæb/ n. **1** (sharp blow) тычо́к **2** (BrE, infml, injection) уко́л
● v.t. (**jabbed, jabbing**) **1** (poke) ты́кать, ткнуть **2** (thrust) втыка́ть, воткну́ть

jabber /'dʒæbə(r)/ n. трескотня́
● v.t. тарато́рить, про-
● v.i. треща́ть (impf.), тарато́рить (impf.)

jack /dʒæk/ n. **1** (name): ~ of all trades ма́стер на все ру́ки **2** (card) вале́т **3** (lifting device) домкра́т
● v.t.: ~ in (BrE, infml, give up) бро́са|ть, -о́сить
■ ~daw n. га́лка; ~knife v.i.: the lorry ~knifed грузови́к занесло́; ~pot n. джекпо́т; he hit the ~pot (fig.) ему́ кру́пно повезло́

jackal /'dʒæk(ə)l/ n. шака́л

jacket /'dʒækɪt/ n. (informal style) ку́ртка; (part of suit) пиджа́к

jade /dʒeɪd/ n. (min.) нефри́т

jaded /'dʒeɪdɪd/ adj.: you look ~ у вас утомлённый вид

jagged /'dʒægɪd/ adj. зубча́тый

jaguar /'dʒægjʊə(r)/ n. ягуа́р

jail /dʒeɪl/ n. тюрьма́
● v.t. заключ|а́ть, -и́ть в тюрьму́

jailer /'dʒeɪlə(r)/ n. тюре́мщик

jam¹ /dʒæm/ n. (BrE, preserve) джем

jam² /dʒæm/ n. (crush) да́вка; traffic ~ про́бка
● v.t. (**jammed, jamming**) **1** (cram) зап|и́хивать, -ихну́ть; she ~med everything into the cupboard она́ всё запихну́ла в шка́ф; (force): he ~med the brakes on он ре́зко затормози́л **2** (cause to stick or stop): the machine got ~med ста́нок засто́порило/ закли́нило **3** (obstruct) заб|ива́ть, -и́ть; the crowds ~med every exit толпа́ заби́ла все вы́ходы; (radio) глуши́ть, за-
● v.i. (**jammed, jamming**) (get stuck) застр|ева́ть, -я́ть
■ ~-packed adj. наби́тый до отка́за

Jamaica /dʒə'meɪkə/ n. Яма́йка

Jamaican /dʒə'meɪkən/ n. яма́|ец (-йка)
● adj. яма́йский

jangle /'dʒæŋg(ə)l/ n. ре́зкий звук
● v.i. бренча́ть (impf.)
● v.t. звя́к|ать, -нуть в + a.

janitor /'dʒænɪtə(r)/ n. вахтёр

♂ **January** /'dʒænjʊərɪ/ n. янва́рь (m.)

Japan /dʒə'pæn/ n. Япо́ния

♂ **Japanese** /dʒæpə'niːz/ n. (pl. ~) (person) япо́н|ец (-ка); (language) япо́нский язы́к
● adj. япо́нский

japonica /dʒə'pɒnɪkə/ n. айва́ япо́нская

jar¹ /dʒɑː(r)/ n. (vessel) ба́нка

jar² /dʒɑː(r)/ v.t. (**jarred, jarring**) сотряс|а́ть, -ти́
● v.i. (**jarred, jarring**) **1** (sound discordantly) дисгармони́ровать (impf.) **2**: ~ on (irritate) раздраж|а́ть, -и́ть

jargon /'dʒɑːgən/ n. жарго́н

jasmine /'dʒæzmɪn/ n. жасми́н

jaundice /'dʒɔːndɪs/ n. желту́ха
● v.t. (usu. p.p.): he took a ~d view of the affair он мра́чно смотре́л на э́то де́ло

jaunt /dʒɔːnt/ n. увесели́тельная пое́здка/ прогу́лка

jaunty /'dʒɔːntɪ/ adj. (**jauntier, jauntiest**) бо́йкий

javelin /'dʒævəlɪn/ n. (мета́тельное) копьё

jaw /dʒɔː/ n. че́люсть

jay /dʒeɪ/ n. со́йка
■ ~walk v.i. пере|ходи́ть, -йти́ у́лицу неосторо́жно; ~walker n. неосторо́жный пешехо́д

jazz /dʒæz/ n. джаз
● v.t.: ~ up (fig., enliven) ожив|ля́ть, -и́ть
■ ~ band n. джаз-орке́стр, джаз-ба́нд

jazzy /'dʒæzɪ/ adj. (**jazzier, jazziest**) бро́ский, я́ркий

JCB® /dʒeɪsiː'biː/ n. (BrE) экскава́тор

JCR (BrE) abbr. (of **Junior Common Room**) студе́нческая ко́мната о́тдыха

jealous /'dʒeləs/ adj. **1** (of affection etc.) ревни́вый; she was ~ of her husband's secretary она́ ревнова́ла му́жа к секрета́рше **2** (envious) зави́стливый; I am ~ of his success я зави́дую его́ успе́ху

jealousy /'dʒeləsɪ/ n. ре́вность; (envy) за́висть

jeans /dʒiːnz/ n. pl. джи́нс|ы (-ов)

jeep® /dʒiːp/ n. джип

jeer /dʒɪə(r)/ v.t. & i. (taunt) глуми́ться (impf.) (at: над + i.); (deride) насмеха́ться (impf.) (at: над + i.)

jelly /'dʒelɪ/ n. **1** (BrE) желе́ (nt. indecl.) **2** (AmE, jam) джем
■ ~fish n. меду́за

jeopardize /'dʒepədaɪz/ v.t. (endanger) подв|ерга́ть, -е́ргнуть опа́сности; (put at risk) рискова́ть (impf.) + i.

jeopardy /'dʒepədɪ/ n. опа́сность; his life was in ~ его́ жизнь была́ в опа́сности

jerk /dʒɜːk/ n. **1** (pull) рыво́к; (jolt) уда́р **2** (twitch) су́дорожное вздра́гивание **3** (infml, idiot) ду́рень (m.), тупи́ца (c.g.)
● v.t. дёр|гать, -нуть
● v.i.: the train ~ed to a halt по́езд ре́зко

останови́лся

jerky /'dʒɜːkɪ/ *adj.* (**jerkier**, **jerkiest**)
судоро́жный

jersey /'dʒɜːzɪ/ *n.* (*pl.* ~**s**) сви́тер

jest /dʒest/ *n.* шу́тка; **in** ~ в шу́тку
● *v.i.* шути́ть, по-

jester /'dʒestə(r)/ *n.* (hist.) шут

Jesus /'dʒiːzəs/ *n.* Иису́с; (as expletive): ~
(Christ)! Бо́же!

jet¹ /dʒet/ *n.* (min.) гага́т
● *adj.* (~**-black**) чёрный как смоль

jet² /dʒet/ *n.* **1** (stream of water etc.) струя́ **2** (*in
full* ~ **engine**) реакти́вный дви́гатель; (*in
full* ~ **aircraft**) реакти́вный самолёт
● *v.i.* (**jetted**, **jetting**) лета́ть (*indet.*) на
реакти́вном самолёте
■ ~ **lag** *n.* наруше́ние су́точного ри́тма; ~ **set**
n. междунаро́дная эли́та

jettison /'dʒetɪs(ə)n/ *v.t.* (lit., fig.)
выбра́сывать, вы́бросить (за́ борт)

jetty /'dʒetɪ/ *n.* при́стань, мол

Jew /dʒuː/ *n.* евре́й (-ка)

jewel /'dʒuːəl/ *n.* (precious stone) драгоце́нный
ка́мень; (fig.) сокро́вище

jeweller /'dʒuːələ(r)/ (AmE **jeweler**) *n.*
ювели́р

jewellery /'dʒuːəlrɪ/ (AmE *also* **jewelry**) *n.*
ювели́рные изде́лия; драгоце́нности (*f. pl.*)

✧ **Jewish** /'dʒuːɪʃ/ *adj.* евре́йский

jib /dʒɪb/ *n.* **1** (naut.) кли́вер **2** (of crane) стрела́

jibe /dʒaɪb/ *n.* (taunt) насме́шка

jiffy /'dʒɪfɪ/ *n.* (infml) миг; **in a** ~ ми́гом

jig /dʒɪg/ *n.* (dance) джи́га

jiggle /'dʒɪg(ə)l/ *v.t.* пока́чивать (*impf.*)

jigsaw /'dʒɪgsɔː/ *n.* (puzzle) (составна́я)
карти́нка-зага́дка, пазл

jihad *n.* (relig.) джиха́д

jilt /dʒɪlt/ *v.t.* бр|оса́ть, -о́сить

jingle /'dʒɪŋg(ə)l/ *n.* (ringing sound) звя́канье;
(advertising tune) рекла́мная пе́сенка
● *v.t. & i.* звя́к|ать, -нуть + *i.*

jingoistic /dʒɪŋgəʊ'ɪstɪk/ *adj.*
шовинисти́ческий

jinx /dʒɪŋks/ *n.* (infml) злы́е ча́ры (*f. pl.*); **put a**
~ **on** сгла́зить (*pf.*)

jitter /'dʒɪtə(r)/ *n.* (infml): **have the** ~**s**
не́рвничать (*impf.*)

jittery /'dʒɪtərɪ/ *adj.* (infml) не́рвный

jive /dʒaɪv/ *n.* джайв (*танец*)
● *v.i.* исп|олня́ть, -о́лнить (*impf.*) джайв

✧ **job** /dʒɒb/ *n.* **1** (piece of work) рабо́та;
зада́ние; **my** ~ **is to wash the dishes** моя́
обя́занность — мыть посу́ду; (difficult task):
we had a ~ **finding them** мы с трудо́м
их отыска́ли **2** (product of work): **you've
made a good** ~ **of that** вы сде́лали э́то
хорошо́ **3** (employment; position) рабо́та; ме́сто;
what is your ~? кака́я у вас рабо́та?; **get
a** ~ на|ходи́ть, -йти́ рабо́ту **4** (circumstance,
fact): **it's a good** ~ **you stayed at home** (BrE)
хорошо́, что вы оста́лись до́ма
■ ~**-seeker** *n.* лицо́, и́щущее рабо́ту; ~**-share**
v.i. дели́ть (*impf.*) рабо́чее ме́сто и за́рплату

jobcentre /'dʒɒbsentə(r)/ *n.* (BrE) центр по
трудоустро́йству, би́ржа труда́

jobless /'dʒɒblɪs/ *adj.* безрабо́тный

jockey /'dʒɒkɪ/ *n.* (*pl.* ~**s**) жоке́й

jockstrap /'dʒɒkstræp/ *n.* суспензо́рий

jocular /'dʒɒkjʊlə(r)/ *adj.* весёлый

jodhpurs /'dʒɒdpəz/ *n. pl.* брю́к|и (*pl., g.* —)
для верхово́й езды́

jog /dʒɒg/ *n.* **1** (nudge) толчо́к **2** (trot) бег
трусцо́й
● *v.t.* (**jogged**, **jogging**): ~ **sb's elbow**
толк|а́ть, -ну́ть кого́-н. под ло́коть; ~ **sb's
memory** освеж|а́ть, -и́ть чью-н. па́мять
● *v.i.* (**jogged**, **jogging**) бе́гать (*indet.*)
трусцо́й

jogger /'dʒɒgə(r)/ *n.* люби́тель (*m.*)
оздорови́тельного бе́га

jogging /'dʒɒgɪŋ/ *n.* оздорови́тельный бе́г;
бег трусцо́й

✧ **join** /dʒɔɪn/ *n.* связь, соедине́ние
● *v.t.* **1** (connect) соедин|я́ть, -и́ть; **the towns
are** ~**ed by a railway** э́ти города́ соединя́ет
желе́зная доро́га **2** (enter) вступ|а́ть, -и́ть
в + *a.*; ~ **a club** вступ|а́ть, -и́ть в клуб; ~
the army идти́, пойти́ в а́рмию **3** (enter sb's
company) присоедин|я́ться, -и́ться к + *d.*;
(meet) встр|еча́ться, -е́титься с + *i.*; **may
I** ~ **you?** разреши́те присоедини́ться к
вам? **4** (flow or lead into) соедин|я́ться, -и́ться
с + *i.*; сл|ива́ться, -и́ться с + *i.*
● *v.i.* **1** (be connected) соедин|я́ться, -и́ться; (be
united) объедин|я́ться, -и́ться; (come together)
сходи́ться, сойти́сь; (flow together) сл|ива́ться,
-и́ться **2** (become a member) стать (*impf.*)
чле́ном (*чего*)
□ ~ **in** *v.i.* (take part) прин|има́ть, -я́ть уча́стие;
(in conversation, discussion, etc.) вступ|а́ть, -и́ть в
+ *a.*
□ ~ **up** *v.t. & i.* (unite) соедин|я́ть(ся), -и́ть(ся)
● *v.i.* (infml, enlist) идти́, пойти́ в а́рмию

joiner /'dʒɔɪnə(r)/ *n.* столя́р

joinery /'dʒɔɪnərɪ/ *n.* столя́рная рабо́та; **do,
practise** ~ столя́рничать (*impf.*)

✧ **joint** /dʒɔɪnt/ *n.* **1** (place of juncture; means of
joining) соедине́ние; стык **2** (anat.) суста́в,
сочлене́ние **3**: **a** ~ **of meat** (BrE) кусо́к
мя́са (*к обеду*) **4** (infml, place) прито́н **5** (sl.,
marijuana cigarette) кося́к
● *adj.* **1** (combined; shared) совме́стный;
(common) о́бщий; ~ **efforts** о́бщие/
совме́стные уси́лия **2** (sharing): ~ **owner**
совладе́лец
■ ~ **account** *n.* о́бщий/совме́стный счёт; ~
action *n.* совме́стные де́йствия (*nt. pl.*); ~
venture *n.* совме́стное предприя́тие

joist /dʒɔɪst/ *n.* ба́лка

jok|e /dʒəʊk/ *n.* **1** шу́тка; (story) анекдо́т;
(witticism) остро́та; (laughing stock) посме́шище;
it's no ~**e!** э́то не шу́тка!; **crack, make a** ~**e**
шути́ть, по-; **play a** ~**e on sb** сыгра́ть (*pf.*)
шу́тку с кем-н.
● *v.i.* шути́ть, по-; **I was only** ~**ing** я всего́
лишь пошути́л

joker /'dʒəʊkə(r)/ *n.* (one who jokes) шутни́к;
(cards) джо́кер

j

jollity /'dʒɒlɪtɪ/ n. весе́лье, увеселе́ние

jolly /'dʒɒlɪ/ adj. (**jollier, jolliest**) (cheerful) весёлый; (entertaining) ра́достный
• adv. (BrE, infml, very) о́чень

jolt /dʒɒlt/ n. толчо́к; (fig.) уда́р, потрясе́ние
• v.t. & i. трясти́(сь) (impf.)

Jordan /'dʒɔːd(ə)n/ n. (country) Иорда́ния; (river) Иорда́н

Jordanian /dʒɔː'deɪnɪən/ n. иорда́н|ец (-ка)
• adj. иорда́нский

jostle /'dʒɒs(ə)l/ v.t. толк|а́ть, -ну́ть

jot /dʒɒt/ v.t. (**jotted, jotting**): ~ down набр|а́сывать, -оса́ть

journal /'dʒɜːn(ə)l/ n. журна́л

journalism /'dʒɜːnəlɪz(ə)m/ n. журнали́стика

ɗ **journalist** /'dʒɜːnəlɪst/ n. журнали́ст (-ка)

ɗ **journey** /'dʒɜːnɪ/ n. (pl. ~s) (expedition; trip) (long) путеше́ствие; (shorter) пое́здка; **be, go on a ~** путеше́ствовать (impf.); (travel; travelling time) путь
• v.i. (**journeys, journeyed**) путеше́ствовать (impf.)

joust /dʒaʊst/ n. (ры́царский) турни́р
• v.i. состяза́ться (impf.) на турни́ре

jovial /'dʒəʊvɪəl/ adj. весёлый

joy /dʒɔɪ/ n. (gladness) ра́дость
■ ~**rider** n. лиха́ч, управля́ющий у́гнанным автомоби́лем; ~**riding** n. риско́ванная езда́ на у́гнанном автомоби́ле

joyful /'dʒɔɪfʊl/ adj. ра́достный

joyless /'dʒɔɪlɪs/ adj. безра́достный

joyous /'dʒɔɪəs/ adj. ра́достный; (happy) весёлый

jubilant /'dʒuːbɪlənt/ adj. лику́ющий

jubilee /'dʒuːbɪliː/ n. юбиле́й

Judaism /'dʒuːdeɪɪz(ə)m/ n. иудаи́зм

ɗ **judge** /dʒʌdʒ/ n. **1** (legal functionary) судья́ (m.) **2** (arbiter) арби́тр, судья́ **3** (expert) знато́к, цени́тель (m.)
• v.t. **1** (pass judgement on) суди́ть (impf.) o + i.; (assess) оце́н|ивать, -и́ть **2** (consider) счита́ть (impf.); **he was ~d to be innocent** его́ сочли́ невино́вным
• v.i. суди́ть (impf.); **to ~ from what you say** су́дя по тому́, что вы сказа́ли

ɗ **judgement, judgment** /'dʒʌdʒmənt/ n. **1** (sentence) суде́бное реше́ние, пригово́р **2** (opinion; estimation) мне́ние; сужде́ние

judicial /dʒuː'dɪʃ(ə)l/ adj. суде́бный

judiciary /dʒuː'dɪʃərɪ/ n. су́дьи (m. pl.); суде́бная власть

judicious /dʒuː'dɪʃəs/ adj. рассуди́тельный

judo /'dʒuːdəʊ/ n. дзюдо́ (nt. indecl.)

jug /dʒʌg/ n. кувши́н

juggernaut /'dʒʌgənɔːt/ n. (BrE, lorry) многото́нный грузови́к

juggle /'dʒʌg(ə)l/ v.i. (lit., fig.) жонгли́ровать (impf.)

juggler /'dʒʌglə(r)/ n. жонглёр

ɗ ключевая лексика

jugular /'dʒʌgjʊlə(r)/ n. (in full ~ **vein**) яре́мная ве́на

juice /dʒuːs/ n. сок

juicer /'dʒuːsə(r)/ n. соковыжима́лка

juicy /'dʒuːsɪ/ adj. (**juicier, juiciest**) со́чный; (infml, scandalous) сма́чный

jukebox /'dʒuːkbɒks/ n. музыка́льный автома́т (для проигрывания дисков)

ɗ **July** /dʒuː'laɪ/ n. июль (m.)

jumble /'dʒʌmb(ə)l/ n. (untidy heap) ку́ча; (muddle) беспоря́док, пу́таница; (infml, unwanted articles) хлам
• v.t. (also ~ **up**) переме́ш|ивать, -а́ть
■ ~ **sale** n. (BrE) дешёвая распрода́жа (в благотворительных целях)

jumbo /'dʒʌmbəʊ/ n. (pl. ~s) (also ~ **jet**) реакти́вный ла́йнер; (attr.) гига́нтский

ɗ **jump** /dʒʌmp/ n. прыжо́к, скачо́к; (obstacle) препя́тствие; (fig., abrupt rise) скачо́к; (fig., start, shock) вздра́гивание
• v.t. **1** (~ over, across) перепры́г|ивать, -нуть че́рез + a. **2** (var. fig. uses): ~ **the queue** про|ходи́ть, -йти́ без о́череди; **you've ~ed a few lines** вы пропусти́ли (or перескочи́ли че́рез) не́сколько строк
• v.i. **1** пры́г|ать, -нуть; (on horseback) вск|а́кивать, -очи́ть **2** (fig.) переска́кивать (impf.); **he ~ed from one topic to another** он переска́кивал с одно́й те́мы на другу́ю **3** (start) подск|а́кивать, -очи́ть; **the noise made me ~** звук заста́вил меня́ подскочи́ть **4** (make sudden movement) подск|а́кивать, -очи́ть; **shares ~ed to a new level** а́кции подскочи́ли в цене́ **5** (fig. uses): **I would ~ at the chance** я бы ухвати́лся за э́ту возмо́жность; ~ **on sb** (attack) набр|а́сываться, -о́ситься на кого́-н.; (rebuke) ре́зко оса|жда́ть, -ди́ть кого́-н.
• with advs.: **he ~ed back in surprise** он отпря́нул в удивле́нии; **she ~ed down from the fence** она́ спры́гнула с забо́ра; **if you want a lift, ~ in!** е́сли хоти́те, что́бы я вас подбро́сил, залеза́йте (в маши́ну)!; ~ **up from one's chair** вск|а́кивать, -очи́ть со сту́ла; ~ **up and down** пры́гать/подпры́гивать (impf.) вверх и вниз
■ ~ **lead** n. (BrE) электри́ческий ка́бель (для за́пуска дви́гателя автомоби́ля от посторо́ннего исто́чника эне́ргии)

jumper /'dʒʌmpə(r)/ n. (BrE, sweater) дже́мпер; (AmE, pinafore dress) сарафа́н

jumpy /'dʒʌmpɪ/ adj. (**jumpier, jumpiest**) не́рвный, дёрганый

junction /'dʒʌŋkʃ(ə)n/ n. (meeting point: of railways) у́зел; (of roads) пересече́ние (доро́г); (of rivers) слия́ние

juncture /'dʒʌŋktʃə(r)/ n. (joining) соедине́ние; **at a critical ~** в крити́ческий моме́нт; **at this ~** в да́нный моме́нт

ɗ **June** /dʒuːn/ n. ию́нь (m.)

jungle /'dʒʌŋg(ə)l/ n. джу́нгли (-ей)

junior /'dʒuːnɪə(r)/ n.: **he is my ~ by 5 years** он на пять лет мла́дше меня́
• adj. мла́дший; ~ **partner** мла́дший партнёр
■ ~ **high school** n. (AmE) непо́лная сре́дняя

шко́ла (*7, 8, 9 классы*); ∼ **school** *n.* (BrE) нача́льная шко́ла (*для детей 7—11 лет*)

juniper /'dʒu:nɪpə(r)/ *n.* можжеве́льник; (*attr.*) можжеве́ловый

junk /dʒʌŋk/ *n.* (rubbish) хлам
■ ∼ **food** *n.* неполноце́нная пи́ща; ∼ **mail** *n.* рекла́мные рассы́лки; ∼ **shop** *n.* ла́вка старьёвщика

junkie, junky /'dʒʌŋkɪ/ *n.* (sl., drug addict) наркома́н

Jupiter /'dʒu:pɪtə(r)/ *n.* (myth., astron.) Юпи́тер

jurisdiction /dʒʊərɪs'dɪkʃ(ə)n/ *n.* (legal authority) юрисди́кция; **have** ∼ **over** име́ть (*impf.*) юрисди́кцию над + *i.*

jurisprudence /dʒʊərɪs'pru:d(ə)ns/ *n.* юриспруде́нция

juror /'dʒʊərə(r)/ *n.* прися́жный (заседа́тель)

jury /'dʒʊərɪ/ *n.* прися́жные (заседа́тели) (*m. pl.*)
■ ∼ **box** *n.* скамья́ прися́жных

✍ **just** /dʒʌst/ *adj.* (equitable) справедли́вый; (deserved) справедли́вый, заслу́женный
● *adv.* **1** то́чно, как раз, и́менно; **it was** ∼ **3 o'clock** бы́ло ро́вно три часа́ **2**: ∼ **like, as** (expr. comparison) то́чно так же, как (и); то́чно, как; **that's** ∼ **like him** (typical) э́то так похо́же на него́; **he is** ∼ **as lazy as ever** он всё тако́й же лени́вый; **it's** ∼ **as well I warned you** хорошо́, что я вас предупреди́л **3** ∼ **about** (approximately): ∼ **about right** почти́ так/ пра́вильно; (almost): **I've** ∼ **about finished** я почти́ (за)ко́нчил **4** (expr. time) то́лько что; (very recently): **I saw him** ∼ **now** я то́лько что ви́дел его́; ∼ **as** (expr. time) (как) то́лько; ∼ **as he entered the room** то́лько он вошёл в ко́мнату; (at this moment): **I'm** ∼ **off** я ухожу́ пря́мо сейча́с/как раз сейча́с **5** (barely) едва́; **I** ∼ **caught the train** я едва́ успе́л на по́езд; **he had** ∼ **come in when the phone rang** то́лько

он вошёл, как зазвони́л телефо́н; **(wait)** ∼ **a minute!** (одну́) мину́т(к)у! **6** (merely) то́лько; ∼ **listen to this!** вы то́лько послу́шайте!; **I went** ∼ **to hear him** я пошёл то́лько, что́бы послу́шать его́; ∼ **fancy!** поду́майте то́лько!; ∼ **you wait!** ну, погоди́!; ∼ **in case** на вся́кий слу́чай **7** (positively, absolutely) так и; про́сто(-на́просто); **it's** ∼ **splendid!** э́то про́сто великоле́пно!; **not** ∼ **yet** ещё не/нет

✍ **justice** /'dʒʌstɪs/ *n.* **1** (fairness; equity) справедли́вость; **to do him** ∼ отдава́я ему́ до́лжное **2** (system of institutions) правосу́дие, юсти́ция; **bring sb to** ∼ отдава́ть, -а́ть кого́-н. под суд **3**: **J**∼ **of the Peace** (BrE) мирово́й судья́

justifiable /'dʒʌstɪfaɪəb(ə)l/ *adj.* опра́вданный

justification /dʒʌstɪfɪ'keɪʃ(ə)n/ *n.* оправда́ние; **he objected, and with** ∼ он возрази́л и не без основа́ний

✍ **justif|y** /'dʒʌstɪfaɪ/ *v.t.* опра́в|дывать, -а́ть; **I was** ∼**ied in suspecting ...** я име́л все основа́ния подозрева́ть...; ∼**y oneself** опра́вд|ываться, -а́ться

jut /dʒʌt/ *v.i.* (**jutted, jutting**) (*usu.* ∼ **out**) выступа́ть (*impf.*); выдава́ться (*impf.*)

juvenile /'dʒu:vənaɪl/ *n.* подро́сток
● *adj.* ю́ный, ю́ношеский
■ ∼ **delinquency** *n.* престу́пность среди́ несовершенноле́тних, подростко́вая престу́пность; ∼ **delinquent** *n.* несовершенноле́тний престу́пник/ правонаруши́тель

juxtapose /dʒʌkstə'pəʊz/ *v.t.* поме|ща́ть, -сти́ть бок о́ бок; сопост|авля́ть, -а́вить (*кого с кем or что с чем*)

juxtaposition /dʒʌkstəpə'zɪʃ(ə)n/ *n.* сосе́дство, бли́зость; (for comparison) сопоставле́ние

j

k

Kk

Kabul /'kɑ:bʊl/ *n.* Кабу́л

kale /keɪl/ *n.* листова́я капу́ста

kaleidoscope /kə'laɪdəskəʊp/ *n.* калейдоско́п

kangaroo /kæŋgə'ru:/ *n.* кенгуру́ (*m. indecl.*)

karaoke /kærɪ'əʊkɪ/ *n.* карао́ке (*nt. indecl.*)

karate /kə'rɑ:tɪ/ *n.* карате́ (*nt. indecl.*)

Kashmir /kæʃ'mɪə(r)/ *n.* Кашми́р

kayak /'kaɪæk/ *n.* кая́к (*эскимосская лодка; лёгкая спортивная одноместная лодка*)

Kazakh /kə'zæk/ *n.* (*pl.* ∼**s**) (person) каза́|х (-шка); (language) каза́хский язы́к

Kazakhstan /kæzək'stɑ:n/ *n.* Казахста́н

kebab /kɪ'bæb/ *n.* шашлы́к

keel /ki:l/ *n.* киль (*m.*)
● *v.i.*: ∼ **over** опроки́|дываться, -нуться

keen /ki:n/ *adj.* (lit., fig., sharp, acute) о́стрый; ∼ **eyesight** о́строе зре́ние; (piercing) пронзи́тельный; (strong, intense) си́льный; ∼ **interest** живо́й интере́с; (eager; energetic) ре́вностный; **a** ∼ **pupil** усе́рдный учени́к; ∼ **competition** трудно́е соревнова́ние; (enthusiastic) стра́стный; **a** ∼ **sportsman** стра́стный спортсме́н; **be** ∼ **on** си́льно/ стра́стно увл|ека́ться, -е́чься + *i.*; **I am not** ∼ **on chess** я не осо́бенно увлека́юсь ша́хматами; **he is** ∼ **on your coming** ему́ о́чень хо́чется, что́бы вы пришли́

⚔ **keep** /kiːp/ *n.* **1** (sustenance) пропита́ние; **earn one's** ~ зараба́тывать, -о́тать себе́ на пропита́ние **2**: **for** ~s насовсе́м (infml) • *v.t.* (*past and p.p.* **kept**) **1** (retain possession of) держа́ть (*impf.*), не отдава́ть (*impf.*); оста́вля́ть, -а́вить (себе́ *or* при себе́); (preserve) храни́ть (*impf.*); сохран|я́ть, -и́ть; (save, put by): **I shall** ~ **this paper to show my mother** я сохраню́ э́ту газе́ту, что́бы показа́ть ма́тери **2** (cause to remain): **the traffic kept me awake** у́личное движе́ние не дава́ло мне спать; **the garden** ~s **me busy** сад не даёт мне сиде́ть сложа́ ру́ки; ~ **the house clean** содержа́ть (*impf.*) дом в чистоте́/поря́дке; ~ **it to yourself** пома́лкивайте об э́том; (infml): ~ **an eye on sth** пригля́дывать (*impf.*) за чем-н.; **where do you** ~ **the salt?** где вы храни́те соль? **3** (cause to continue): **I don't like to be kept waiting** я не люблю́, когда́ меня́ заставля́ют ждать; **that will** ~ **you going till lunchtime** тепе́рь вы продержитесь до обе́да **4** (remain in, on): ~ **one's seat** (remain sitting) не встава́ть (*impf.*); (retain, preserve): ~ **one's balance** сохраня́ть/уде́рживать (*both impf.*) равнове́сие **5** (have charge of; manage; maintain) име́ть, держа́ть, содержа́ть (*all impf.*); **the shop was kept by an Italian** владе́льцем ла́вки был италья́нец; **he wants to** ~ **pigs** он хо́чет держа́ть свине́й **6** (accounts, records, diary) вести́ (*det.*) **7** (detain) заде́рж|ивать, -а́ть; **I won't** ~ **you** я вас не задержу́ **8** (fulfil, be faithful to) соде́рж|ивать, -а́ть; соблюда́ть, -сти́; ~ **the law** соблюда́ть зако́н; ~ **one's word** держа́ть, с- сло́во; **I can't** ~ **the appointment** я не могу́ прийти́ на встре́чу • *v.i.* (*past and p.p.* **kept**) **1** (remain) держа́ться (*impf.*); остава́ться (*impf.*); **the weather kept fine** стоя́ла хоро́шая пого́да; **I can't** ~ **warm here** я не могу́ здесь согре́ться; **how are you** ~ing? (BrE) как пожива́ете?; как жизнь? (infml) **I exercise to** ~ **fit** я занима́юсь гимна́стикой/спо́ртом, что́бы быть в фо́рме; **we still** ~ **in touch** мы всё ещё подде́рживаем отноше́ния/связь **2** (continue) продолжа́ть (*impf.*) (+ *inf.*); **she** ~s **giggling** она́ всё хихи́кает **3** (remain fresh): **the food will** ~ **in the refrigerator** еда́ в холоди́льнике не испо́ртится • *with preps.*: **you must** ~ **at it till it's finished** не отвлека́йтесь, пока́ не (за)ко́нчите; **what are you trying to** ~ **from me?** что вы скрыва́ете от меня́?; '~ **off the grass!** «по газо́нам не ходи́ть»; ~ **out of sb's way** (avoid him) избега́ть (*impf.*) кого́-н.; **he cannot** ~ **out of trouble for long** он ве́чно попада́ет в исто́рии; **he** ~s **himself to himself** он замыка́ется в себе́; ~ **to the path** держа́ться (*impf.*) тропи́нки; ~ **to the point** не отклоня́ться (*impf.*) от те́мы

□ ~ **away** *v.t.*: **the rain kept people away** дождь отпугну́л наро́д; **she kept her daughter away from school** она́ не пуска́ла дочь в шко́лу

• *v.i.*: **he tried to** ~ **away from them** он стара́лся их избега́ть

□ ~ **back** *v.t.* (restrain) сде́рж|ивать, -а́ть; (retain): **they** ~ **back £100 from my wages** из мое́й зарпла́ты уде́рживают сто фу́нтов; (repress): **she could hardly** ~ **back her tears** она́ едва́ сде́рживала слёзы

□ ~ **down** *v.t.*: ~ **your voice down!** не повыша́йте го́лос!; (limit, control): **they tried to** ~ **down expenses** они́ стара́лись расхо́довать как мо́жно ме́ньше; (oppress) держа́ть (*impf.*) в подчине́нии; (digest): **he can't** ~ **anything down** его́ желу́док ничего́ не принима́ет

□ ~ **off** *v.t.* (ward off, repel): **my hat will** ~ **the rain off** моя́ шля́па защити́т меня́ от дождя́ • *v.i.* (stay at a distance): **I hope the rain** ~s **off** я наде́юсь, что дождь не начнётся

□ ~ **on** *v.t.* (continue to wear): **women** ~ **their hats on in church** в це́ркви же́нщины не снима́ют шляп; (continue to employ): **they won't** ~ **you on after 60** они́ уво́лят вас, когда́ вам испо́лнится 60 лет; (leave in place): ~ **the lid on** не снима́йте кры́шку • *v.i.* (*with pres. part.*) (continue): **he kept on reading** он продолжа́л чита́ть; **she kept on glancing out of the window** она́ то и де́ло выгля́дывала из окна́; **she kept on** (working) **till the job was finished** она́ рабо́тала, пока́ всё не зако́нчила

□ ~ **out** *v.t.* (exclude): **we put up a fence to** ~ **out trespassers** мы постро́или/поста́вили забо́р, что́бы посторо́нние не заходи́ли на террито́рию • *v.i.*: '**Private** — ~ **out!**' (notice) «посторо́нним вход воспрещён!»

□ ~ **up** *v.t.* (prevent from falling or sinking): **he could not** ~ **his trousers up** у него́ всё вре́мя сва́ливались брю́ки; (fig., sustain, maintain): ~ **one's strength up** подкрепля́ть (*impf*) си́лы; **the house is expensive to** ~ **up** э́тот дом до́рого содержа́ть; (continue): ~ **up the good work!** продолжа́йте в том же ду́хе!; **he could not** ~ **up the payments** он был не в состоя́нии регуля́рно плати́ть; (prevent from going to bed): **the baby kept us up half the night** ребёнок не дава́л нам спать полно́чи • *v.i.* (stay level): **we kept up with them the whole way** всю доро́гу мы не отстава́ли от них; ~ **up with the times** не отстава́ть (*impf*) от собы́тий; шага́ть (*impf*) в но́гу со вре́менем; (remain in touch): **I** ~ **up with several old friends** я подде́рживаю отноше́ния ко́е с кем из ста́рых друзе́й

keeper /ˈkiːpə(r)/ *n.* (in zoo) служи́тель (*m.*) (зоопа́рка); (BrE, museum ~) смотри́тель (*m.*)

keeping /ˈkiːpɪŋ/ *n.* **1**: **in safe** ~ в надёжных рука́х **2**: **be in** ~ **with** соотве́тствовать (*impf.*) + *d.*

keg /keg/ *n.* бочо́нок

kennel /ˈken(ə)l/ *n.* конура́

Kenya /ˈkenjə/ *n.* Ке́ния

Kenyan /ˈkenjən/ *n.* кени́|ец (-йка) • *adj.* кени́йский

kept /kept/ *past and p.p. of* ▶ **keep**

kerb /kɜːb/ (AmE **curb**) *n.* обо́чина

kerfuffle /kə'fʌf(ə)l/ *n.* (BrE, infml) шум, завару́ха

kernel /'kɜ:n(ə)l/ *n.* (of nut or fruit stone) ядро́

kerosene, kerosine /'kerəsi:n/ *n.* кероси́н; (*attr.*) кероси́новый

kestrel /'kestr(ə)l/ *n.* (zool.) пустельга́

ketchup /'ketʃʌp/ *n.* ке́тчуп

kettle /'ket(ə)l/ *n.* ча́йник

key /ki:/ *n.* (*pl.* **keys**) **1** ключ **2** (fig.) ключ; the ~ to understanding the political situation ключ к понима́нию полити́ческой ситуа́ции **3** (*attr.*) (important, essential) ключево́й, важне́йший **4** (of piano or computer) кла́виша; (*in pl.*) клавиату́ра **5** (mus.) тона́льность
• *v.t.* (**keys, keyed**) (comput.) вв|оди́ть, -ести́ (into: в + *a.*); ~ up взви́н|чивать, -ти́ть
▪ ~**board** *n.* (mus., comput.) клавиату́ра; ~**boarder** *n.* опера́тор компью́тера; ~**board(s)** *n.* (mus. instrument) кла́вишные (*pl.*); ~**hole** *n.* замо́чная сква́жина; ~**hole surgery** *n.* (BrE) полостна́я опера́ция с минима́льным вскры́тием; ~ **ring** *n.* кольцо́ для ключе́й

kg /'kɪləgræm(z)/ *n.* (*abbr. of* **kilogram(s)**) кг (килогра́мм)

KGB *abbr.* (hist.) КГБ (Комите́т госуда́рственной безопа́сности)

khaki /'kɑ:kɪ/ *n.* (*pl.* ~**s**) ха́ки (*nt. indecl.*)
• *adj.*: a ~ shirt руба́шка цве́та ха́ки

kick /kɪk/ *n.* **1** уда́р, пино́к **2** (recoil) отда́ча **3** (infml, stimulus): **get a ~ out of sth** получ|а́ть, -и́ть удово́льствие от чего́-н.
• *v.t.* уд|аря́ть, -а́рить ного́й; **he ~ed me on the shin** он уда́рил меня́ по го́лени; **he ~ed the ball** он уда́рил по мячу́; **I could have ~ed myself** я рвал на себе́ во́лосы; ~ **the habit** (infml, give up addiction) бро́сить (*pf.*) употребля́ть нарко́тики/кури́ть/пить и т. д.
• *v.i.* (of animals) ляга́ться (*impf.*); брыка́ться (*impf.*)
□ ~ **about, around** *vv.t.*: **they were ~ing a ball about** они́ гоня́ли мяч
□ ~ **off** *v.i.* (football) нач|ина́ть, -а́ть игру́; (infml, begin) нач|ина́ть, -а́ть
□ ~ **out** *v.t.* (infml, eject, expel) выгоня́ть, вы́гнать
□ ~ **up** *v.t.* (infml, create): ~ **up a row** устр|а́ивать, -о́ить сканда́л
▪ ~**-boxing** *n.* кикбо́ксинг; ~**off** *n.* нача́ло (игры́); ~**-start** *v.t.* (lit. and fig.): **to ~-start the economy** дать толчо́к эконо́мике

kid¹ /kɪd/ *n.* **1** (young goat) козлёнок **2** (leather) ла́йка **3** (infml, child) малы́ш; **my ~ brother** мой мла́дший брат
▪ ~ **gloves** *n. pl.* ла́йковые перча́тки

kid² /kɪd/ *v.t.* (**kidded, kidding**) **1** (infml, deceive) над|ува́ть, -у́ть; **who are you ~ding?** кого́ вы хоти́те обману́ть? **2** (tease) дразни́ть (*impf.*)
• *v.i.* (**kidded, kidding**) (tease with untruths): **you're ~ding!** врёшь!

kidnap /'kɪdnæp/ *v.t.* (**kidnapped, kidnapping**, AmE **kidnaped, kidnaping**) пох|ища́ть, -и́тить

kidnapper /'kɪdnæpə(r)/ *n.* похити́тель (*m.*)

kidney /'kɪdnɪ/ *n.* (*pl.* ~**s**) по́чка
▪ ~ **bean** *n.* фасо́ль (*collect.*)

Kiev /'ki:ef/ *n.* Ки́ев

kill /kɪl/ *v.t.* **1** уб|ива́ть, -и́ть; (rats etc.) трави́ть (*impf.*); ~ **oneself** ко́нчить самоуби́йством; (fig., infml): **my feet are ~ing me** я без за́дних ног; ~ **time** уб|ива́ть, -и́ть вре́мя **2** (animals for food) ре́зать, за- **3** (destroy) уничт|ожа́ть, -о́жить; **this drug ~s the pain** э́то лека́рство снима́ет боль
▪ ~**joy** *n.* брюзга́ (*c.g.*)

killer /'kɪlə(r)/ *n.* (murderer) уби́йца (*c.g.*); (infml, sth hilarious) что-н. умори́тельное
▪ ~ **whale** *n.* коса́тка

killing /'kɪlɪŋ/ *n.* (murder) уби́йство; (slaughter of animals) убо́й, забо́й

kiln /kɪln/ *n.* печь

kilo /'ki:ləʊ/ *n.* (*pl.* ~**s**) кило́ (*nt. indecl.*)

kilobyte /'kɪləbaɪt/ *n.* килоба́йт

kilogram /'kɪləgræm/ *n.* килогра́мм

kilohertz /'kɪləhɜ:ts/ *n.* килоге́рц

kilometre /'kɪləmi:tə(r)/ (AmE **kilometer**) *n.* киломе́тр

kilowatt /'kɪləwɒt/ *n.* килова́тт

kilt /kɪlt/ *n.* (шотла́ндская) ю́бка, килт

kimono /kɪ'məʊnəʊ/ *n.* (*pl.* ~**s**) кимоно́ (*nt. indecl.*)

kin /kɪn/ *n.* (family) семья́; (relations) родня́ (*collect.*); ро́дственники (*m. pl.*); **kith and ~** родны́е и бли́зкие; **next of ~** ближа́йш|ий ро́дственни|к (-а́я -ца)

kind /kaɪnd/ *n.* **1** (sort, variety) род, сорт, разнови́дность; **all ~s of goods** вся́кие/ра́зные това́ры; a ~ of сво́его ро́да; **what ~ of?** что за?; како́й?; **what ~ of a painter is he?** что он за худо́жник? **2** ~ **of** (infml, to some extent): **I ~ of expected it** я как бы ожида́л э́того **3**: **in ~** натýрой; **pay in ~** плати́ть, за- нату́рой
• *adj.* до́брый, любе́зный
▪ ~**-hearted** *adj.* добросерде́чный

kindergarten /'kɪndəgɑ:t(ə)n/ *n.* де́тский сад

kindle /'kɪnd(ə)l/ *v.t.* разж|ига́ть, -е́чь; (fig., arouse) возбу|жда́ть, -ди́ть

kindliness /'kaɪndlɪnɪs/ *n.* доброта́

kindling /'kɪndlɪŋ/ *n.* (firewood) расто́пка; ще́пки (*f. pl.*)

kindly /'kaɪndlɪ/ *adj.* (**kindlier, kindliest**) до́брый, доброду́шный
• *adv.* **1** (in a kind manner) любе́зно, ми́ло **2** (please): ~ **ring me tomorrow** бу́дьте добры́, позвони́те мне за́втра **3**: **he does not take ~ to criticism** он не лю́бит кри́тики

kindness /'kaɪndnɪs/ *n.* **1** (benevolence) доброта́ **2** (kind act) любе́зность

kindred /'kɪndrɪd/ *adj.* (lit., fig.) ро́дственный; ~ **ideas** ро́дственные иде́и; a ~ **spirit** родна́я душа́

kinetic /kɪ'netɪk/ *adj.* кинети́ческий

king /kɪŋ/ *n.* **1** коро́ль (*m.*) **2** (chess) коро́ль; (draughts, checkers) да́мка; (cards): ~ **of diamonds** бубно́вый коро́ль
▪ ~**fisher** *n.* (голубо́й) зимородо́к

kingdom /'kɪŋdəm/ n. короле́вство; **the animal ~** живо́тное ца́рство

kink /kɪŋk/ n. (in rope etc.) переги́б; (in metal) изги́б

kinky /'kɪŋkɪ/ adj. (**kinkier, kinkiest**) (twisted) кручёный; (infml, perverted) извращённый; со стра́нностями

kinsfolk /'kɪnzfəʊk/ n. родня́ (collect.)

kinsman /'kɪnzmən/ n. ро́дственник

kinswoman /'kɪnzwʊmən/ n. ро́дственница

kiosk /'kiːɒsk/ n. кио́ск; **telephone ~** (BrE) телефо́нная бу́дка, автома́т

kip /kɪp/ (BrE) n. (infml, sleep) сон
• v.i. (**kipped, kipping**) **1**: **~ down for the night** устро́иться (pf.) на ночь **2** (sleep) кема́рить, по- (infml)

kipper /'kɪpə(r)/ n. копчёная селёдка

Kirghiz /'kɜːgɪz/ n. = Kyrgyz

Kirghizia /kɜː'gɪzɪə/ n. = Kyrgyzstan

kiss /kɪs/ n. поцелу́й; **give sb a ~ on the cheek** поцелова́ть (pf.) кого́-н. в щёку; **~ of life** иску́сственное дыха́ние
• v.t. целова́ть, по-; **they ~ed each other goodbye** они́ поцелова́лись на проща́ние
• v.i. целова́ться, по-

kit /kɪt/ n. (BrE, personal equipment, esp. clothing) снаряже́ние; (for particular activity) набо́р/ компле́кт (спорти́вных) принадле́жностей; (set of parts for assembly) констру́ктор
• v.t. (**kitted, kitting**) (BrE) (usu. **~ out**) снаря|жа́ть, -ди́ть
■ **~bag** n. вещмешо́к

⚹ **kitchen** /'kɪtʃɪn/ n. ку́хня

kite /kaɪt/ n. (возду́шный/бума́жный) змей; **fly a ~** (lit.) запус|ка́ть, -ти́ть зме́я

kitsch /kɪtʃ/ n. китч

kitten /'kɪt(ə)n/ n. котёнок

kitty /'kɪtɪ/ n. (at cards etc.) банк

kiwi /'kiːwiː/ n. (pl. **kiwis**) ки́ви (m. indecl.)
■ **~ fruit** n. ки́ви (m. & nt. indecl.)

kleptomania /kleptəʊ'meɪnɪə/ n. клептома́ния

kleptomaniac /kleptəʊ'meɪnɪæk/ n. клептома́н (-ка)

km /'kɪləmiːtə(r)(z)/ n. (abbr. of **kilometre(s)**) км (киломе́тр)

knack /næk/ n. (skill, faculty) сноро́вка, уме́ние; **have the ~** име́ть (impf.) сноро́вку (**of/for:** в + p.)

knacker /'nækə(r)/ n. (BrE) ску́пщик ста́рых живо́тных
■ **~'s yard** n. живодёрня

knackered /'nækəd/ adj. (BrE, infml) измо́танный

knapsack /'næpsæk/ n. ра́нец

knead /niːd/ v.t. меси́ть, за-

knee /niː/ n. коле́н|о (pl. -и); **he was on his ~s** он стоя́л на коле́нях
• v.t. (**knees, kneed, kneeing**) уд|аря́ть, -а́рить коле́ном
■ **~cap** n. коле́нная ча́шечка; **~-deep** pred.

⚹ ключева́я ле́ксика

adj. & adv.: **he stood ~-deep in water** он стоя́л по коле́но в воде́; **~-length** adj. до коле́н

kneel /niːl/ v.i. (past and p.p. **knelt** or esp. AmE **kneeled**) **1** (also **~ down**) (go down on one's knees) ста|нови́ться, -ть на коле́ни **2** (be in ~ing position) стоя́ть (impf.) на коле́нях

knelt /nelt/ past and p.p. of ▶ kneel

knew /njuː/ past of ▶ know

knickers /'nɪkəz/ n. pl. (BrE, undergarment) тру́сик|и (-ов)

knick-knack /'nɪknæk/ n. безделу́шка

knife /naɪf/ n. (pl. **knives**) нож
• v.t. (kill) зак|а́лывать, -оло́ть ножо́м; (injure) ра́нить (impf.)
■ **~-edge** n.: **on a ~-edge** (fig.) вися́щий на волоске́; **~point** n.: **at ~point** угрожа́я ножо́м

knight /naɪt/ n. **1** (hist.) ры́царь (m.) **2** (member of order) кавале́р **3** (chess) конь (m.)
• v.t. ≈ присв|а́ивать, -о́ить (кому) ры́царское (ненасле́дственное дворя́нское) зва́ние

knighthood /'naɪthʊd/ n. ры́царство; ры́царское зва́ние

knit /nɪt/ v.t. (**knitting**, past and p.p. **knitted** or **knit**) вяза́ть, с-
• v.i. (**knitting**, past and p.p. **knitted** or **knit**) **1** (do ~ting) вяза́ть (impf.) **2** (of bones) сраст|а́ться, -и́сь
■ **~wear** n. трикота́жные изде́лия

knitting /'nɪtɪŋ/ n. (action) вяза́ние; (thing being knitted) вяза́нье
■ **~ needle** n. вяза́льная спи́ца

knives /naɪvz/ pl. of ▶ knife

knob /nɒb/ n. (handle) ру́чка; (button) кно́пка

knobbly /'nɒblɪ/ adj. шишкова́тый, бугорча́тый

knock /nɒk/ n. **1** (rap) стук **2** (blow) уда́р **3** (fig.): **the pound has taken some ~s lately** в после́днее вре́мя положе́ние фу́нта (сте́рлингов) си́льно пошатну́лось
• v.t. **1** (hit) удар|я́ть, -а́рить; **the blow ~ed him flat** уда́р сбил его́ с ног; **he ~ed the glass off the table** он смахну́л стака́н со стола́; **I ~ed the gun out of his hand** я вы́бил из его́ руки́ пистоле́т **2** (fig. uses): **~ into shape** прив|оди́ть, -ести́ в поря́док; **I'll ~ a pound off the price** я сбро́шу/ски́ну/сба́влю фунт с цены́ **3** (criticize) ха́ять (impf.) (infml)
• v.i. **1** (rap) стуча́ть; **~ at the door** стуча́ть(ся), по- в дверь **2**: **~ against** (collide with) нат|ыка́ться, -кну́ться на + a. **3** (of engine) стуча́ть (impf.)
□ **~ back** v.t. (BrE, disconcert): **the news ~ed me back** изве́стие привело́ меня́ в замеша́тельство; (infml, consume): **he can ~ back 5 pints in as many minutes** он за пять мину́т мо́жет опроки́нуть/вы́лакать пять кру́жек (пи́ва); (BrE, infml, cost): **that will ~ me back a bit** э́то вста́нет/вле́тит мне в копе́ечку
□ **~ down** v.t. (strike to ground) сби|ва́ть, -ть с ног; вали́ть, с-; **he was ~ed down by a car** его́ сби́ла маши́на; (demolish) сн|оси́ть, -ести́
□ **~ off** v.t. (lit.) сби|ва́ть, -ть; (infml uses) (deduct from price) сб|а́влять, -а́вить; (BrE, steal)

тащи́ть, c-/y-
• *v.i.* (infml, stop work) свора́чиваться, сверну́ться (sl.)

▫ ∼ **out** *v.t.* (make unconscious) оглуш|а́ть, -и́ть; **the blow on his head** ∼ed **him out** он был оглушён уда́ром по голове́; (eliminate from contest): **he was** ∼ed **out in the first round** он вы́был в пе́рвом ту́ре

▫ ∼ **over** *v.t.* опроки́д|ывать, -нуть

■ ∼-**down** *adj.*: **at a** ∼-**down price** по дешёвке (infml); ∼**out** *n.* (boxing) нока́ут; (BrE, competition) соревнова́ния (*nt. pl.*) по олимпи́йской систе́ме; (*attr.*) ∼out **blow** сокруши́тельный уда́р

knocker /'nɒkə(r)/ *n.* (on door) (дверно́й) молото́к

knocking /'nɒkɪŋ/ *n.* (noise) стук

knot /nɒt/ *n.* (in rope etc.; in wood; measure of speed) у́зел; **tie a** ∼ **in a rope** завя́з|ывать, -а́ть у́зел на верёвке; **tie sth in a** ∼ завя́з|ывать, -а́ть что-н. узло́м
• *v.t.* (**knotted, knotting**) завя́з|ывать, -а́ть

⚘ **know** /nəʊ/ *n.*: **be in the** ∼ быть в ку́рсе де́ла
• *v.t.* (*past* **knew,** *p.p.* **known**) ◨ (be aware, have knowledge of) знать (*impf.*); **I** ∼ **nothing about it** я об э́том ничего́ не зна́ю; **for all I** ∼ кто его́ зна́ет; **who** ∼**s?** как знать?; **I knew it!** (я) так и знал! ◨ (recognize, distinguish) знать (*impf.*); узн|ава́ть, -а́ть; отлич|а́ть, -и́ть; **I** ∼ **him by sight** я зна́ю его́ в лицо́; **he knew her at once** он сра́зу её узна́л ◨ (be acquainted, familiar with) знать (*impf.*); быть знако́мым с + *i.*; **get to** ∼ **sb** знако́миться, по- с кем-н.; **I have** ∼**n him since childhood** я знако́м с ним с де́тства ◨ (be versed in; understand; have experience in) зна́ть (*impf.*), понима́ть (*impf.*), разбира́ться (*impf.*) в + *p.*; **he** ∼**s Russian** он зна́ет ру́сский язы́к; он владе́ет ру́сским языко́м; ∼ **how to** уме́ть, c-
• *v.i.* (*past* **knew,** *p.p.* **known**): **let sb** ∼ сообщ|а́ть, -и́ть (*or* да|ва́ть, -ть знать) кому́-н.; **will you let me** ∼? вы сообщи́те мне?; **do you** ∼ **of a good restaurant?** вы зна́ете (*or* вы мо́жете порекомендова́ть) хоро́ший рестора́н?; **I don't** ∼ **him, but I** ∼ **of** **him** ли́чно я с ним не знако́м, но наслы́шан о нём; **did you** ∼ **about the accident?** вы зна́ли об э́том несча́стном слу́чае?

■ ∼-**all** (BrE), ∼-**it-all** (AmE) *nn.* всезна́йка (*c.g.*);

∼-**how** *n.* уме́ние; но́у-ха́у (*nt. indecl.*); о́пыт

knowing /'nəʊɪŋ/ *adj.* (significant): **a** ∼ **look** понима́ющий/многозначи́тельный взгляд

⚘ **knowledge** /'nɒlɪdʒ/ *n.* зна́ние; (understanding): **our** ∼ **of the subject is as yet limited** на́ши позна́ния в э́той о́бласти пока́ ограни́чены; (range of information or experience): **to the best of my** ∼ наско́лько мне изве́стно

knowledgeable /'nɒlɪdʒəb(ə)l/ *adj.* хорошо́ осведомлённый

known /nəʊn/ *adj.* изве́стный; *see also* ▸ know

knuckle /'nʌk(ə)l/ *n.* (anat.) костя́шка (па́льца)
• *v.i.*: ∼ **down to one's work** прин|има́ться, -я́ться за де́ло

koala /kəʊ'ɑːlə/ *n.* (*in full* ∼ **bear**) коа́ла (*m.*), су́мчатый медве́дь

Kolkata /kɒl'kɑːtə/ *n.* Калькутта

kopek /'kəʊpek/ *n.* копе́йка

Koran /kə'rɑːn/ *n.* Кора́н

Korea /kə'rɪːə/ *n.* Коре́я

Korean /kə'rɪːən/ *n.* (person) коре́|ец (-я́нка); (language) коре́йский язы́к
• *adj.* коре́йский

kosher /'kəʊʃə(r)/ *adj.* (relig.) коше́рный

Kosovo /'kɒsəvə/ *n.* Ко́сово

kowtow, kotow /kaʊ'taʊ/ *n.* ни́зкий покло́н
• *v.i.* де́лать, c- ни́зкий покло́н; (fig.) раболе́пствовать (*impf.*), пресмыка́ться (*impf.*) (**to:** пе́ред + *i.*)

kudos /'kjuːdɒs/ *n.* сла́ва

kumquat /'kʌmkwɒt/ *n.* кумква́т (*дерево семейства цитрусовых с очень маленькими плодами оранжевого цвета; плоды этого дерева*)

kung fu /kʊŋ 'fuː/ *n.* кун-фу́ (*nt. indecl.*)

Kurd /kɜːd/ *n.* курд (-я́нка)

Kurdish /'kɜːdɪʃ/ *n.* ку́рдский язы́к
• *adj.* ку́рдский

Kurdistan /kɜːdɪ'stɑːn/ *n.* Курдиста́н

Kuwait /kʊ'weɪt/ *n.* Куве́йт

Kuwaiti /kʊ'weɪtɪ/ *n.* (*pl.* ∼**s**) куве́йт|ец (-ка)
• *adj.* куве́йтский

kvass /kvɑːs/ *n.* квас

Kyrgyz /'kɜːgɪz/ *n.* (*pl.* ∼) (person) кирги́з (-ка); (language) кирги́зский язы́к
• *adj.* кирги́зский

Kyrgyzstan /kɜːgɪ'stɑːn/ *n.* Кыргызста́н

k

Ll

L (BrE) *abbr.* (*of* **learner**): ∼-**plate** ≈ «У» (*на учебной машине*)

l /'li:tə(r)(z)/ *n.* (*abbr. of* **litre(s)**) л (литр)

lab /læb/ *n.* (infml) = laboratory

∘ **label** /'leɪb(ə)l/ *n.* ярлы́к, этике́тка
 ● *v.t.* (**labelled, labelling**, AmE **labeled, labeling**) (stick ∼ on) накле́и|вать, -ть ярлы́к на + *a.*; (fig.): he was ∼led a fascist ему́ прикле́или ярлы́к фаши́ста

labor /'leɪbə(r)/ *etc.* see ▸ **labour** *etc.* ∼ **union** (AmE) профсою́з

laboratory /lə'bɒrətərɪ/ *n.* лаборато́рия
 ■ ∼ **assistant** *n.* лабора́нт (-ка)

laborious /lə'bɔːrɪəs/ *adj.* (difficult) тру́дный, тяжёлый; (toilsome) трудоёмкий

∘ **labour** /'leɪbə(r)/ (AmE **labor**) *n.* **1** (toil, work) труд, рабо́та **2** (workforce) рабо́чие (*pl.*) **3** (*in full* **L∼ Party**) лейбори́стская па́ртия, лейбори́сты (*m. pl.*); the **L∼ government** лейбори́стское прави́тельство **4** (childbirth) ро́д|ы (-ов); be in ∼ рожа́ть (*impf.*)
 ● *v.t.*: ∼ a point вдава́ться (*impf.*) в изли́шние подро́бности
 ● *v.i.* **1** (toil) труди́ться (*impf.*) **2** (strive): he is ∼ing to finish his book он прилага́ет все уси́лия, что́бы за|ко́нчить кни́гу
 ■ ∼-**intensive** *adj.* трудоёмкий; ∼-**saving** *adj.* рационализа́торский

labourer /'leɪbərə(r)/ (AmE **laborer**) *n.* рабо́чий

Labrador /'læbrədɔː(r)/ *n.* Лабрадо́р; (dog) лабрадо́р

laburnum /lə'bɜːnəm/ *n.* (bot.) бобо́вник, золото́й дождь

labyrinth /'læbərɪnθ/ *n.* (lit., fig.) лабири́нт

labyrinthine /læbə'rɪnθaɪn/ *adj.* (lit.) лабири́нтный; (fig.) запу́танный

lace /leɪs/ *n.* **1** (openwork fabric) кру́жево, кружева́ (*nt. pl.*) **2** (of shoe etc.) шнуро́к
 ● *v.t.* (fasten or tighten with ∼) шнурова́ть, за-; he ∼d up his shoes он зашнурова́л боти́нки
 ■ ∼-**ups** *n. pl.* (BrE) о́бувь на шнуро́вке/шнурка́х

lacerate /'læsəreɪt/ *v.t.* (lit., fig.) терза́ть, рас-/ис-; растер́з|ывать, -а́ть; (wound) ра́нить (*impf., pf.*)

∘ **lack** /læk/ *n.* недоста́ток
 ● *v.t. & i.*: he ∼s sth ему́ чего́-то недостаёт; he ∼s, is ∼ing in courage у него́ не хвата́ет хра́брости
 ■ ∼**lustre,** (AmE) ∼**luster** *adj.* ту́склый, без бле́ска

lackadaisical /lækə'deɪzɪk(ə)l/ *adj.* вя́лый, апати́чный

lackey /'lækɪ/ *n.* (*pl.* ∼s) (lit., fig.) лаке́й; (fig.) подхали́м

laconic /lə'kɒnɪk/ *adj.* лакони́чный

lacquer /'lækə(r)/ *n.* политу́ра (*no pl.*); лак

lad /læd/ *n.* (boy) ма́льчик; (fellow, youth) па́рень (*m.*)

ladder /'lædə(r)/ *n.* **1** ле́стница **2** (BrE, in stocking) спусти́вшаяся петля́
 ● *v.t. & i.* (BrE): I have ∼ed my stocking; my stocking has ∼ed у меня́ спусти́лась петля́ на чулке́

laden /'leɪd(ə)n/ *adj.*: he returned ∼ with books он верну́лся нагру́женный кни́гами; the table was ∼ with food стол ломи́лся от еды́; she was ∼ with cares она́ была́ обременена́ забо́тами

ladies /'leɪdɪz/ *n.* see ▸ **lady 2**

ladle /'leɪd(ə)l/ *n.* поло́вник

∘ **lady** /'leɪdɪ/ *n.* **1** (woman) да́ма; (as title) ле́ди (*f. indecl.*); **Ladies and Gentlemen** да́мы и господа́ **2**: the **Ladies** (*sg.*), (AmE) **ladies' room** (lavatory) же́нский туале́т
 ■ ∼**bird** (BrE), ∼**bug** (AmE) *nn.* бо́жья коро́вка

lag[1] /læg/ *n.* (delay) запа́здывание
 ● *v.i.* (**lagged, lagging**) отст|ава́ть, -а́ть; the children were ∼ging (behind) де́ти плели́сь позади́

lag[2] /læg/ *v.t.* (**lagged, lagging**) (wrap in felt etc.) изоли́ровать/покрыва́ть (*impf.*) (во́йлоком)

lager /'lɑːgə(r)/ *n.* све́тлое пи́во

lagoon /lə'guːn/ *n.* лагу́на

laid /leɪd/ *past and p.p. of* ▸ **lay**[2]

laid-back /leɪd'bæk/ *adj.* непринуждённый, споко́йный

lain /leɪn/ *p.p. of* ▸ **lie**[2]

lair /leə(r)/ *n.* ло́гово

laissez-faire /leseɪ'feə(r)/ *n.* невмеша́тельство (*политика невмешательства правительства в экономику*)

lake /leɪk/ *n.* о́зеро

lama /'lɑːmə/ *n.* (relig.) ла́ма (*m.*)

lamb /læm/ *n.* ягнёнок, бара́шек; (meat) бара́шек
 ■ ∼ **chop** *n.* бара́нья котле́та

lambaste /læm'beɪst/ *v.t.* дуба́сить, от- (infml)

lame /leɪm/ *adj.* **1** (archaic when used of people) хромо́й **2** (fig., of excuse etc.) сла́бый

lament /lə'ment/ *n.* плач
 ● *v.t.* опла́к|ивать, -ать

lamentable /'læməntəb(ə)l/ *adj.* плаче́вный

lamentation /læmən'teɪʃ(ə)n/ *n.* (lamenting) се́тование; (lament) плач

laminate /'læmɪneɪt/ *v.t.* (overlay with protective layer) ламини́ровать (*impf., pf.*)

lamp /læmp/ *n.* ла́мпа
■ ~ **post** *n.* фона́рный столб; ~**shade** *n.* абажу́р

lampoon /læm'pu:n/ *n.* па́сквиль (*m.*)
● *v.t.* писа́ть, на- па́сквиль на + *a.*

LAN *abbr.* (*of* **local area network**) (comput.) лока́льная сеть

lance /lɑ:ns/ *n.* пи́ка
● *v.t.* (med.) вскры|ва́ть, -ть ланце́том

ᕱ **land** /lænd/ *n.* **1** земля́; (dry ~) су́ша; **travel by** ~ е́хать (*det.*) су́шей (*or* по су́ше); **reach** ~ дост|ига́ть, -и́гнуть бе́рега **2** (ground, soil) грунт, по́чва; **work the** ~ обраба́тывать (*impf.*) зе́млю; **a house with some** ~ дом с земе́льным уча́стком **3** (country) земля́, страна́; (state) госуда́рство **4** (property) земля́, име́ние; **his** ~**s extend for several miles** его́ владе́ния простира́ются на не́сколько миль
● *v.t.* **1**: ~ **an aircraft** сажа́ть, посади́ть (*or* приземл|я́ть, -и́ть) самолёт **2**: ~ **a fish** выта́скивать, вы́тащить ры́бу на бе́рег **3** (win) выи́грывать, вы́играть; (secure): **he** ~**ed himself a good job** он пристро́ился на хоро́шую рабо́ту **4** (get, involve): **he** ~**ed himself with a lot of work** он загрузи́л себя́ рабо́той
● *v.i.* **1** (of passengers) выса́живаться, вы́садиться **2** (of aircraft) приземл|я́ться, -и́ться; (spacecraft on moon) прилун|я́ться, -и́ться **3** (of athlete, after jump) приземл|я́ться, -и́ться **4** (fall, lit. or fig.): **she** ~**ed in trouble** она́ попа́ла в беду́; **the ball** ~**ed on his head** мяч попа́л ему́ в го́лову **5**: ~ **up** (infml, arrive) прибыва́ть, -ы́ть; **I** ~**ed up in the wrong street** я очути́лся не на той у́лице
■ ~**lady** *n.* (BrE, of pub) хозя́йка; (of building) домовладе́лица, хозя́йка; ~**line** *n.* назе́мная ли́ния свя́зи; ~**lord** *n.* (BrE, of pub) хозя́ин; (owner of ~) землевладе́лец; (of building) домовладе́лец, хозя́ин; ~**mark** *n.* (prominent feature) заме́тный объе́кт на ме́стности, ориенти́р; (fig.) ве́ха; ~**mine** *n.* фуга́с; ~**owner** *n.* землевладе́л|ец (-ица); ~**slide** *n.* о́ползень (*m.*); (pol.) **they won by a** ~**slide** они́ победи́ли с огро́мным переве́сом (голосо́в)

landed /'lændɪd/ *adj.* **1** (possessing land) землевладе́льческий **2** (consisting of land): ~ **property** земе́льные владе́ния
■ ~ **gentry** *n. pl.* поме́щики (*m. pl.*)

landing /'lændɪŋ/ *n.* **1** (bringing or coming to earth) поса́дка, приземле́ние; (on the moon) прилуне́ние **2** (putting ashore; depositing by air) вы́садка **3** (mil.) деса́нт **4** (on stairs) (ле́стничная) площа́дка
■ ~ **gear** *n.* шасси́ (*nt. indecl.*); ~ **strip** *n.* поса́дочная полоса́

landscape /'lændskeɪp/ *n.* (picture) пейза́ж; (scenery) ландша́фт
■ ~ **gardening** *n.* ландша́фтный диза́йн

lane /leɪn/ *n.* **1** (narrow street) переу́лок; (country road) доро́жка **2** (of traffic) ряд **3** (air route) тра́сса **4** (for shipping) морско́й путь **5** (on racetrack, swimming pool) доро́жка

ᕱ **language** /'læŋgwɪdʒ/ *n.* язы́к; (esp. spoken) речь; **bad** ~ скверносло́вие
■ ~ **laboratory** *n.* лингафо́нный кабине́т

languid /'læŋgwɪd/ *adj.* то́мный, вя́лый

languish /'læŋgwɪʃ/ *v.i.* томи́ться (*impf.*)

languor /'læŋgə(r)/ *n.* то́мность, вя́лость; (pleasant) исто́ма

languorous /'læŋgərəs/ *adj.* то́мный; по́лный исто́мы

lank /læŋk/ *adj.*: ~ **hair** гла́дкие/прямы́е во́лосы

lanky /'læŋkɪ/ *adj.* (**lankier**, **lankiest**) долговя́зый

lantern /'læntə)n/ *n.* фона́рь (*m.*)

lap¹ /læp/ *n.*: **the boy sat on his mother's** ~ ма́льчик сиде́л у ма́тери на коле́нях; **he lives in the** ~ **of luxury** ≈ он живёт в (обстано́вке) ро́скоши
■ ~ **dance** *n.* эроти́ческий та́нец, исполня́емый в непосре́дственной близости к клие́нту, заказа́вшему его́; ~**top** (**computer**) *n.* портати́вный компью́тер; лэпто́п

lap² /læp/ *n.* (circuit of racetrack) круг

lap³ /læp/ *v.t.* (**lapped**, **lapping**) **1** (drink with tongue) лака́ть, вы́-; **the cat** ~**ped up the milk** ко́шка выла́кала молоко́ **2** (fig., accept eagerly) жа́дно глота́ть (*impf.*); **he** ~**ped up their compliments** он жа́дно лови́л их комплиме́нты

lapel /lə'pel/ *n.* ла́цкан, отворо́т

Lapp /læp/ *n.* **1** (person) саа́ми (*m. & f. indecl.*); лопа́р|ь (-ка) **2** (language) (*also* ~**ish**) саа́мский/лопа́рский язы́к; язы́к саа́ми
● *adj.* **1** (*also* ~**ish**) лопа́рский, саа́мский **2** (of Lapland) лапла́ндский

lapse /læps/ *n.* **1** (slight mistake) упуще́ние; (of memory) прова́л (в) па́мяти **2** (interval) промежу́ток
● *v.i.* **1** (decline morally) пасть (*pf.*); **he** ~**d into his old ways** он принялся́ за ста́рое; ~ **into silence** зам|олка́ть, -о́лкнуть **2** (law, become void) теря́ть, по- си́лу

larch /lɑ:tʃ/ *n.* (tree) ли́ственница

lard /lɑ:d/ *n.* са́ло

larder /'lɑ:də(r)/ *n.* кладова́я

ᕱ **large** /lɑ:dʒ/ *n.*: **at** ~ (free) на во́ле, на свобо́де; (in general) целико́м; во всём объёме; **the public at** ~ широ́кая пу́блика
● *adj.* большо́й, кру́пный
● *adv.*: **by and** ~ вообще́ говоря́
■ ~**scale** *adj.* крупномасшта́бный

ᕱ **largely** /'lɑ:dʒlɪ/ *adv.* (to a great extent) по бо́льшей ча́сти; в значи́тельной сте́пени

lark¹ /lɑ:k/ *n.* (bird) жа́воронок

lark² /lɑ:k/ *n.* (infml, amusement) заба́ва; **for a** ~ шу́тки ра́ди

larva /'lɑ:və/ *n.* (*pl.* **larvae** /-vi:/) личи́нка

laryngitis /lærɪn'dʒaɪtɪs/ *n.* ларинги́т

larynx /'lærɪŋks/ *n.* (*pl.* **larynges**) горта́нь

lascivious /lə'sɪvɪəs/ *adj.* похотли́вый

laser /'leɪzə(r)/ *n.* ла́зер; (*attr.*) ла́зерный

lash¹ /læʃ/ *n.* (*in full* **eye** ~) ресни́ца

l

lash² /læʃ/ *n.* (stroke) уда́р (пле́тью)
- *v.t.* (with whip, wind, rain) хлест|а́ть, -ну́ть
- *v.i.:* **the rain ~ed against the window** дождь хлеста́л в окно́
□ **~ out** *v.i.* (with fists) наки́|дываться, -ну́ться (*на кого*); (verbally) набр|а́сываться, -о́ситься (с кри́тикой) (*на кого*)
lasso /læ'su:/ *n.* (*pl.* **~s** *or* **~es**) арка́н, лассо́ (*nt. indecl.*)
- *v.t.* (**lassoes, lassoed**) арка́нить, за-
⚹ **last** /lɑːst/ *n.* (final or most recent person or thing): **he was the ~ of his line** он был после́дним в роду́; **our house is the ~ in the road** наш дом после́дний/кра́йний на у́лице; **at ~** наконе́ц; (as excl.) наконе́ц-то!
- *adj.* **1** (latest; final; ~ of series) после́дний; **in the ~ 7 years** в после́дние 7 лет; **at the very ~ moment** в са́мый после́дний моме́нт; **~ but one** предпосле́дний **2** (preceding, of time) про́шлый; **~ week** на про́шлой неде́ле; **~ night we got home late** вчера́ ве́чером мы по́здно верну́лись (домо́й) **3** (least likely or suitable): **she is the ~ person to help** от неё ме́ньше всего́ мо́жно ожида́ть по́мощи; **that's the ~ thing I would have expected** э́того я никаќ не ожида́л
- *adv.* **1** (in order) по́сле всех; **he finished ~** он ко́нчил после́дним **2** (on the ~ occasion) в после́дний раз **3** (~ly, in the ~ place) на после́днем ме́сте
- *v.i.* **1** (go on, continue) дли́ться, про-; прод|олжа́ться, -о́лжиться; **the rain won't ~ long** дождь ско́ро пройдёт **2** (endure, be sustained) выде́рживать, вы́держать; **as long as my health ~s (out)** пока́ у меня́ хва́тит здоро́вья; (be preserved, survive) сохран|я́ться, -и́ться; **the tradition has ~ed until today** э́та тради́ция сохрани́лась до настоя́щего вре́мени **3** (remain usable): **this suit has ~ed well** э́тот костю́м хорошо́ но́сится; **this car is built to ~ 4** (of the dying): **he won't ~ long** он до́лго не протя́нет (infml)
- *v.i.* & *t.* (be sufficient) хват|а́ть, -и́ть (**for sb:** + *d.*; **for a certain amount of time:** на + *a.*); **£100 ~s (me) a week** ста фу́нтов (мне) хвата́ет на неде́лю; **the bread won't ~ us today** хле́ба нам на сего́дня не хва́тит
■ **~-ditch** *adj.* отча́янный; **~-minute** *adj.* (сде́ланный) в после́днюю мину́ту; **~ name** *n.* фами́лия; **~ rites** *n. pl.* причаще́ние пе́ред сме́ртью
lasting /lɑːstɪŋ/ *adj.* (enduring) про́чный, продолжи́тельный
lastly /lɑːstlɪ/ *adv.* в заключе́ние; наконе́ц
latch /lætʃ/ *n.* (bar) щеко́лда; (lock) защёлка
- *v.i.:* **~ on to** смекну́ть (*pf.*) (infml)
⚹ **late** /leɪt/ *adj.* **1** (far on in time) по́здний; **it is ~** по́здно; **in ~ May** к концу́/в конце́ ма́я; **the ~ 19th century** коне́ц 19 ве́ка; **he is in his ~ 40s** ему́ почти́/под пятьдеся́т **2** (behind time): **be ~ for the train** опа́з|дывать, -да́ть на по́езд; **he was an hour ~** он опозда́л на час; **I was ~ in replying** я опозда́л отве́тить (*or* с отве́том) **3** (recent) неда́вний; после́дний; **his**

~**st book** его́ после́дняя кни́га **4** (deceased) поко́йный
- *adv.* по́здно; **stay up ~** по́здно ложи́ться (*impf.*); **a year ~r** спустя́ год
latecomer /leɪtkʌmə(r)/ *n.* опозда́вший
lately /leɪtlɪ/ *adv.* в после́днее вре́мя
latent /leɪt(ə)nt/ *adj.* скры́тый
lateral /lætər(ə)l/ *adj.* боково́й, горизонта́льный; **~ section** попере́чный разре́з
latest /leɪtɪst/ *adj.* после́дний; са́мый но́вый
lathe /leɪð/ *n.* тока́рный стано́к
lather /lɑːðə(r)/ *n.* (мы́льная) пе́на
Latin /lætɪn/ *n.* латы́нь; лати́нский язы́к
- *adj.* лати́нский
■ **~ America** *n.* Лати́нская Аме́рика; **~ American** *adj.* латиноамерика́нский ● *n.* латиноамерика́н|ец (-ка)
Latino /lə'ti:nəʊ/ *n.* (*pl.* **~s**) вы́ходец из Лати́нской Аме́рики
latitude /lætɪtju:d/ *n.* (geog., also fig.) широта́
⚹ **latter** /lætə(r)/ *pron.* & *adj.* после́дний, второ́й; **of cream and yogurt, the ~ is healthier** что каса́ется сли́вок и йо́гурта, то после́дний поле́знее
latterly /lætəlɪ/ *adv.* (of late) (в/за) после́днее вре́мя; (towards the end) к концу́, под коне́ц
lattice /lætɪs/ *n.* решётка; (*attr.; also* **~d**) решётчатый
Latvia /lætvɪə/ *n.* Ла́твия
Latvian /lætvɪən/ *n.* (person) латви́|ец (-йка) латы́ш (-ка); (language) латы́шский язы́к
- *adj.* латви́йский, латы́шский
⚹ **laudable** /lɔːdəb(ə)l/ *adj.* похва́льный
⚹ **laugh** /lɑːf/ *n.* смех; **we had a good ~ over it** мы от души́ посмея́лись над э́тим
- *v.t.:* **he was ~ing his head off** он хохота́л как безу́мный
- *v.i.* смея́ться (*impf.*) (**at:** над + *i.*); **burst out ~ing** рассмея́ться (*pf.*); расхохота́ться (*pf.*); **he ~s at my jokes** он смеётся, когда́ я шучу́; **it's nothing to ~ at** в э́том нет ничего́ смешно́го; **I couldn't stop ~ing** я смея́лся так, что не мог останови́ться
□ **~ off** *v.t.:* **~ sth off** отде́л|ываться, -аться от чего́-н. шу́ткой
laughable /lɑːfəb(ə)l/ *adj.* смешно́й, смехотво́рный
laughing /lɑːfɪŋ/ *n.* смех
■ **~ stock** *n.* посме́шище
laughter /lɑːftə(r)/ *n.* смех
launch¹ /lɔːntʃ/ *n.* (motor boat) ка́тер
⚹ **launch²** /lɔːntʃ/ *n.* (of ship) спуск (на́ воду); (of rocket or spacecraft) за́пуск; (of product) вы́пуск
- *v.t.* (set afloat): **~ a ship** спус|ка́ть, -ти́ть кора́бль на́ воду; (send into air): **~ a rocket** запус|ка́ть, -ти́ть раке́ту; (initiate): **~ a campaign** нач|ина́ть, -а́ть (*or* откр|ыва́ть, -ы́ть) кампа́нию; **~ an enterprise/product** пус|ка́ть, -ти́ть предприя́тие/проду́кт в прода́жу
■ **~(ing) pad** *n.* ста́ртовая площа́дка
launder /lɔːndə(r)/ *v.t.* **1** стира́ть, вы́- **2** (fig.): **~ money** отм|ыва́ть, -ы́ть де́ньги

launderette, laundrette /lɔːnˈdret/ *n.* (BrE) пра́чечная самообслу́живания

laundry /ˈlɔːndrɪ/ *n.* **1** (establishment) пра́чечная **2** (clothes) бельё (для сти́рки *or* из сти́рки)

laurel /ˈlɒr(ə)l/ *n.* лавр

lava /ˈlɑːvə/ *n.* ла́ва

lavatory /ˈlævətərɪ/ *n.* убо́рная, туале́т

lavender /ˈlævɪndə(r)/ *n.* лава́нда

lavish /ˈlævɪʃ/ *adj.* ще́дрый
- *v.t.:* ~ money on sth пром|а́тывать, -ота́ть де́ньги на что-н.; ~ praise on sb расточа́ть (*impf.*) похвалы́ кому́-н.

◆ **law** /lɔː/ *n.* **1** (rule or body of rules for society) зако́н; by ~ по зако́ну; break the ~ нар|уша́ть, -у́шить зако́н **2** (as subject of study, profession, system) пра́во, юсти́ция; ~ and order правопоря́док; read, study ~ изуч|а́ть, -и́ть пра́во **3** (phys., math.): ~ of gravity зако́н всеми́рного тяготе́ния; ~ of probability тео́рия вероя́тностей
■ ~-abiding *adj.* законопослу́шный; ~ court *n.* суд; ~-enforcement *n.* (*attr.*): ~-enforcement agencies правоохрани́тельные о́рганы; ~giver, ~maker *nn.* законода́тель (*m.*); ~ school *n.* юриди́ческий вуз; ~suit *n.* суде́бный проце́сс

lawful /ˈlɔːfʊl/ *adj.* зако́нный

lawless /ˈlɔːlɪs/ *adj.* (of country etc.) ди́кий; (of person) непоко́рный

lawn /lɔːn/ *n.* газо́н
■ ~mower *n.* газонокоси́лка

◆ **lawyer** /ˈlɔːjə(r)/ *n.* юри́ст; (advocate, barrister) адвока́т

lax /læks/ *adj.* нестро́гий

laxative /ˈlæksətɪv/ *n.* слаби́тельное (сре́дство)

lay¹ /leɪ/ *past of* ▸ lie²

◆ **lay²** /leɪ/ *v.t.* (*past and p.p.* laid) **1** (put down, deposit) класть, положи́ть; ~ an egg нести́, с- яйцо́; (set in position): ~ bricks класть (*impf.*) кирпичи́; ~ a foundation (lit., fig.) за|кла́дывать, -ложи́ть фунда́мент; ~ a trap ста́вить, по- лову́шку **2** (prepare): ~ a fire пригото́вить (*pf.*) всё, что́бы развести́ ого́нь; ~ the table for dinner накр|ыва́ть, -ы́ть стол к обе́ду
- *v.i.* (*past and p.p.* laid) (sc. eggs) нести́сь (*impf.*)

□ ~ down *v.t.:* ~ down one's arms (surrender) скла́дывать, сложи́ть ору́жие; (formulate, prescribe): ~ down conditions/rules устан|а́вливать, -ови́ть (*or* формули́ровать, с-) усло́вия/пра́вила; (sacrifice): ~ down one's life for one's friends же́ртвовать, по- жи́знью (*or* отд|ава́ть, -а́ть жизнь) за друзе́й

□ ~ off *v.t.* (suspend from work) ув|ольня́ть, -о́лить (со слу́жбы)

□ ~ on *v.t.* (BrE, provide supply of) пров|оди́ть, -ести́; (infml): he promised to ~ on some drinks он обеща́л поста́вить вы́пивку; (arrange) устр|а́ивать, -о́ить

□ ~ out *v.t.* (arrange for display etc.) выставля́ть, вы́ставить; (garden etc.) разб|ива́ть, -и́ть
■ ~about *n.* (infml) лентя́й (-ка); ~-by *n.* (BrE) придоро́жная площа́дка для стоя́нки автомоби́лей; ~-off *n.* (of workers) сокраще́ние

шта́тов; ~out *n.* (arrangement) расположе́ние; (of town etc.) плани́ровка; (of garden etc.) разби́вка; (plan) чертёж, план

lay³ /leɪ/ *adj.* **1** (opp. clerical) мирско́й **2** (opp. professional): ~ opinion непрофессиона́льное мне́ние
■ ~man *n.* (non-specialist) непрофессиона́л, неспециали́ст

◆ **layer** /ˈleɪə(r)/ *n.* слой, пласт

laze /leɪz/ *v.i.:* ~ about слоня́ться (*impf.*) без де́ла

laziness /ˈleɪzɪnɪs/ *n.* лень, ле́ность

lazy /ˈleɪzɪ/ *adj.* (lazier, laziest) лени́вый; be ~ лени́ться (*impf.*); I was too ~ to write to him мне бы́ло лень ему́ (на)писа́ть

lb /paʊnd(z)/ *n.* (*abbr. of* libra) фунт

LCD *abbr.* (*of* liquid crystal display) ЖК-диспле́й (жидкокристалли́ческий диспле́й)

leach /liːtʃ/ *v.t. & i.* выщела́чивать(ся), вы́щелочить(ся) (*о почве, горной породе*)

lead¹ /led/ *n.* **1** (metal) свине́ц **2** (in pencil) графи́т, гри́фель (*m.*)
■ ~-free *adj.* неэтили́рованный

◆ **lead²** /liːd/ *n.* **1** (direction, guidance; initiative) руково́дство; take the ~ брать, взять на (себя́) руково́дство/инициати́ву **2** (first place): be in the ~ стоя́ть (*impf.*) во главе́; (sport) быть впереди́; вести́ (*det.*); (fig.) стоя́ть (*impf.*) во главе́, пе́рвенствовать (*impf.*); take the ~ (sport) выходи́ть, вы́йти вперёд **3** (clue): the police are looking for a ~ поли́ция пыта́ется напа́сть на след **4** (BrE, cord, strap) поводо́к, привя́зь **5** (elec.) про́вод (-á)
- *v.t.* (*past and p.p.* led) **1** (conduct) води́ть (*indet.*), вести́ (*det.*), повести́(*pf.*); he led his troops into battle он повёл солда́т в бой **2** (fig., bring, incline, induce): ~ sb to believe созда́ть (*pf.*) впечатле́ние у кого́-н., что… **3** (be in charge of): ~ an expedition/orchestra руково́дить (*impf.*) экспеди́цией/орке́стром; (command) кома́ндовать (*impf.*) (+ *i.*); (act as chief or head of) возгл|авля́ть, -а́вить **4** (pass, spend): ~ an idle life вести́ (*det.*) пра́здную жизнь
- *v.i.* (*past and p.p.* led) **1** (of a road etc.) вести́ (*det.*) **2** (be first or ahead) быть впереди́

□ ~ away *v.t.* отв|оди́ть, -ести́; ув|оди́ть, -ести́

□ ~ in *v.t.* вв|оди́ть, -ести́

□ ~ up *v.i.:* ~ up to (lit.) подв|оди́ть, -ести́ к + *d.*; (precede, form preparation for) подгот|овля́ть, -о́вить; the events that led up to the war собы́тия, приве́дшие к войне́

leaded /ˈledɪd/ *adj.* (petrol) этили́рованный

leaden /ˈled(ə)n/ *adj.* (lit., fig.) свинцо́вый

◆ **leader** /ˈliːdə(r)/ *n.* **1** руководи́тель (*m.*), ли́дер; (comm.) ли́дер **2** (mil.) команди́р **3** (BrE, in newspaper) передова́я (статья́)

◆ **leadership** /ˈliːdəʃɪp/ *n.* (role of leader; group of leaders) руково́дство; (qualities of a leader) ли́дерство

leading /ˈliːdɪŋ/ *adj.* (foremost) веду́щий; (outstanding) выдаю́щийся; ~ question наводя́щий вопро́с
■ ~ lady *n.* исполни́тельница гла́вной ро́ли

leaf /liːf/ *n.* (*pl.* **leaves**) **1** (of tree or plant) лист (-ья) **2** (of book) лист (-ы́); (fig.): **turn over a new** ~ нач|ина́ть, -а́ть но́вую жизнь, испра́виться (*pf.*)
● *v.t.*: ~ **through** перели́ст|ывать, -а́ть
leaflet /ˈliːflɪt/ *n.* листо́вка
leafy /ˈliːfɪ/ *adj.* (**leafier**, **leafiest**) густоли́ственный
✍ **league** /liːg/ *n.* (alliance) ли́га; **in** ~ **with** в сою́зе с + *i.*; (pej.) в сго́воре с + *i.*; **be not in the same** ~ **as sb** быть не того́ кла́сса; **football** ~ футбо́льная ли́га
■ ~ **table** *n.* (BrE) (sport) табли́ца результа́тов; (fig.) сравни́тельный гра́фик
leak /liːk/ *n.* (hole) течь; (escape of fluid) уте́чка; (fig., of information) уте́чка информа́ции
● *v.t.* (fig.) выдава́ть, вы́дать
● *v.i.* (roof, boat) течь (*impf.*); **leak out** (liquid, gas) прос|а́чиваться, -очи́ться; (fig.): **the affair** ~**ed out** де́ло вы́плыло нару́жу
■ ~-**proof** *adj.* непроница́емый
leakage /ˈliːkɪdʒ/ *n.* (lit., fig.) уте́чка
leaky /ˈliːkɪ/ *adj.* (**leakier**, **leakiest**) дыря́вый, име́ющий течь; **a** ~ **pipe/roof** протека́ющая труба́/кры́ша
lean[1] /liːn/ *adj.* **1** (thin) то́щий; (fig.): ~ **years** ску́дные го́ды **2** (of meat) нежи́рный
lean[2] /liːn/ *v.t.* (*past and p.p.* **leaned** /liːnd, lent/ or esp. BrE **leant**) прислон|я́ть, -и́ть (*что к чему*); оп|ира́ть, -ере́ть (*что обо что*)
● *v.i.* (*past and p.p.* **leaned** /liːnd, lent/ or esp. BrE **leant**) **1** (incline from vertical) наклон|я́ться, -и́ться; ~ **out of the window** высо́вываться, вы́сунуться из окна́ **2** (support oneself) прислон|я́ться, -и́ться; оп|ира́ться, -ере́ться; **he was** ~**ing against a tree** он стоя́л, прислони́вшись к де́реву; (fig.): **he** ~**s** (*sc.* depends) **on his wife for support** он опира́ется на подде́ржку жены́; (infml, put pressure): **I had to** ~ **on him to get results** мне пришло́сь нажа́ть на него́, что́бы доби́ться результа́тов
leaning /ˈliːnɪŋ/ *n.* (inclination) скло́нность; (tendency) пристра́стие
leant /lent/ (esp. BrE) *past and p.p. of* ▶ **lean**[2]
leap /liːp/ *n.* прыжо́к, скачо́к
● *v.t.* (*past and p.p.* **leaped** /liːpt, lept/ or **leapt** /lept/) (~ over) переск|а́кивать, -очи́ть (*or* перепры́г|ивать, -нуть) че́рез + *a.*
● *v.i.* (*past and p.p.* **leaped** /liːpt, lept/ or **leapt** /lept/) пры́г|ать, -нуть; **my heart** ~**t for joy** у меня́ се́рдце подскочи́ло от ра́дости; ~ **to one's feet** вск|а́кивать, -очи́ть; (fig.): **he** ~**t at my offer** он ухвати́лся за моё предложе́ние
■ ~**frog** *n.* чехарда́; ~ **year** *n.* високо́сный год
✍ **learn** /lɜːn/ *v.t.* (*past and p.p.* **learned** /lɜːnt, lɜːnd/ or esp. BrE **learnt** /lɜːnt/) учи́ться, на- (+ *d. or inf.*); изуч|а́ть, -и́ть; (study) занима́ться (*impf.*) (+ *i.*); **he** ~**ed** (**how**) **to ride** он научи́лся е́здить верхо́м; **he is** ~**ing to be an interpreter** он у́чится на

перево́дчика; **where did you** ~ **Russian?** где вы изуча́ли ру́сский язы́к?
● *v.i.* (*past and p.p.* **learned** /lɜːnt, lɜːnd/ or esp. BrE **learnt** /lɜːnt/): **you can** ~ **from his mistakes** учи́тесь на его́ оши́бках
learned /ˈlɜːnɪd/ *adj.* учёный
learner /ˈlɜːnə(r)/ *n.* начина́ющий; (~ **driver**) начина́ющий води́тель, (не име́ющий води́тельских прав)
✍ **learning** /ˈlɜːnɪŋ/ *n.* (process) уче́ние; изуче́ние; (body of knowledge) нау́ка
■ ~ **curve** *n.* ско́рость приобрете́ния на́выка; ~ **difficulty/disability** *n.* у́мственный недоста́ток; **person with** ~ **difficulties/ disabilities** у́мственно отста́лый челове́к
learnt /lɜːnt/ (esp. BrE) *past and p.p. of* ▶ **learn**
lease /liːs/ *n.* аре́нда
● *v.t.* (of lessee) арендова́ть (*impf., pf.*); брать, взять в аре́нду/внаём; (of lessor) сд|ава́ть, -ать в аре́нду
■ ~**hold** *n.* аре́нда; ~**holder** *n.* аренда́тор
leash /liːʃ/ *n.* поводо́к
✍ **least** /liːst/ *n.*: **to say the** ~ мя́гко говоря́; **the** ~ **he could do is to pay for the damage** он мог бы по кра́йней ме́ре возмести́ть уще́рб; **at** ~ по кра́йней ме́ре; не ме́ньше + *g.*; **at** ~ **once a year** не ре́же, чем раз в год; **he is at** ~ **as tall as you** он ва́шего ро́ста, а мо́жет быть и вы́ше; **you should at** ~ **have warned me** вы бы хоть предупреди́ли меня́; **not in the** ~ ничу́ть, ниско́лько; **he is not in the** ~ **interested** он совсе́м не заинтересо́ван (*pred.*)
● *adj.* (smallest) наиме́ньший; **that's the** ~ **of my worries** э́то меня́ ме́ньше всего́ волну́ет; (slightest) мале́йший; **he hasn't a** ~ **idea about it** он не име́ет ни мале́йшего поня́тия об э́том
● *adv.* ме́ньше всего́; **it is the** ~ **successful of his books** э́то наиме́нее уда́чная из его́ книг; **with the** ~ **possible trouble** с наиме́ньшими хло́потами; с наиме́ньшей затра́той сил
leather /ˈleðə(r)/ *n.* ко́жа
● *adj.* ко́жаный
✍ **leave** /liːv/ *n.* о́тпуск; **he is on** ~ он в о́тпуске
● *v.t.* (*past and p.p.* **left**) **1** (allow or cause to remain) ост|авля́ть, -а́вить; **the wound left a scar** от ра́ны оста́лся шрам; **has anyone left a message?** никто́ ничего́ не передава́л?; (with indication of state or circumstances): ~ **me alone!** оста́вьте меня́ (в поко́е)!; ~ **the door open!** оста́вьте дверь откры́той!; (*p.p.*) (remaining): **I have no money left** у меня́ не оста́лось де́нег **2** (~ **behind by accident**) заб|ыва́ть, -ы́ть; **I left my umbrella at home** я забы́л зо́нтик до́ма **3** (bequeath) завеща́ть (*impf., pf.*); **she was left a large inheritance by her uncle** дя́дя оста́вил ей большо́е насле́дство **4** (abandon) бр|оса́ть, -о́сить; пок|ида́ть, -и́нуть; **he left his wife for another woman** он бро́сил свою́ жену́ ра́ди друго́й же́нщины **5** (entrust) предост|авля́ть, -а́вить; ~ **it to him** пусть он э́то сде́лает; ~ **it to me** я э́тим займу́сь **6** (go away from) выходи́ть, вы́йти из + *g.*; (by vehicle) выезжа́ть, вы́ехать из + *g.*; (by air) вылета́ть,

вы́лететь из + g.; I ~ **the house at eight** я выхожу́ и́з дому в во́семь часо́в; (~ **for good,** quit) броса́ть, -о́сить; пок|ида́ть, -и́нуть; **he left his job** он бро́сил свою́ рабо́ту; **he ~s school this year** он конча́ет шко́лу в э́том году́

● *v.i.* (*past and p.p.* **left**) **1** (of person on foot) уходи́ть, уйти́; (by transport) уезжа́ть, уе́хать; (by air) улет|а́ть, -е́ть **2** (of train) от|ходи́ть, -ойти́; (of boat) от|ходи́ть, -ойти́; отпл|ыва́ть, -ы́ть; (of aircraft) вылета́ть, вы́лететь

□ ~ **behind** *v.t.* ост|авля́ть, -а́вить по́сле себя́; (forget to take): **he left his hat behind** он забы́л свою́ шля́пу; (abandon): **he was left behind on the island** он оказа́лся бро́шенным на о́строве; (outstrip): **we left him far behind** мы оста́вили его́ далеко́ позади́

□ ~ **on** *v.t.*: **I left the light on** я оста́вил свет включённым

□ ~ **out** *v.t.*: **she left the washing out in the rain** она́ оста́вила бельё под дождём; (omit) пропус|ка́ть, -ти́ть; **I felt left out** я почу́вствовал себя́ ли́шним

□ ~ **over** *v.t.* (*pass.*) (remain) ост|ава́ться, -а́ться; **a lot was left over after dinner** по́сле обе́да оста́лось ещё мно́го еды́

leaves /liːvz/ *pl. of* ▸ **leaf**

Lebanese /lebəˈniːz/ *n.* (*pl.* ~) лива́н|ец (-ка)
● *adj.* лива́нский

Lebanon /ˈlebənən/ *n.* Лива́н

lecher /ˈletʃə(r)/ *n.* развра́тник, распу́тник

lecherous /ˈletʃərəs/ *adj.* развра́тный, распу́тный

lechery /ˈletʃərɪ/ *n.* развра́т

lectern /ˈlektəːn/ *n.* анало́й (*в церкви*); (in lecture room) пюпи́тр

lecture /ˈlektʃə(r)/ *n.* ле́кция
● *v.t.* чита́ть, про- ле́кцию/нота́цию + *d.*
● *v.i.*: **he ~s in Russian** он чита́ет ле́кции по ру́сскому языку́
■ ~ **hall,** ~ **room,** ~ **theatre** *nn.* аудито́рия

lecturer /ˈlektʃərə(r)/ *n.* ле́ктор; (BrE, in university) преподава́тель (*m.*)

led /led/ *past and p.p. of* ▸ **lead²**

ledge /ledʒ/ *n.* (shelf) пла́нка, по́лочка; (projection) вы́ступ

ledger /ˈledʒə(r)/ *n.* (book) гроссбу́х; (гла́вная) учётная кни́га

leech /liːtʃ/ *n.* пия́вка

leek /liːk/ *n.* лук-поре́й

leer /lɪə(r)/ *n.* ухмы́лка
● *v.i.* ухмыл|я́ться, -ьну́ться; ~ **at** хи́тро/злобно смотре́ть, по- на + *a.*

leeway /ˈliːweɪ/ *n.* свобо́да де́йствий

✧ **left¹** /left/ *n.* **1** (side, direction): **from the** ~ сле́ва; **to the** ~ нале́во; **on, to my** ~ нале́во от меня́; **on, from my** ~ сле́ва от меня́ **2** (pol.): **the L**~ ле́вые (*pl.*)
● *adj.* ле́вый; ~ **wing** (pol.) ле́вое крыло́
● *adv.* нале́во; **turn** ~ сво́|ра́чивать, -ерну́ть нале́во
■ ~-**hand** *adj.* ле́вый; **on the** ~-**hand side of the street** на ле́вой стороне́ у́лицы; **car with** ~-**hand drive** маши́на с левосторо́нним

управле́нием (*or* с рулём сле́ва); ~-**handed** *adj.* де́лающий всё ле́вой руко́й, леворуки́й; ~-**handed person** левша́ (*c.g.*); ~-**wing** *adj.* ле́вый

left² /left/ *past and p.p. of* ▸ **leave**

leftovers /ˈleftəʊvəz/ *n. pl.* оста́тк|и (-ов); (food) обе́дки (-ов)

✧ **leg** /leg/ *n.* **1** нога́; (dim.) но́жка; **pull sb's** ~ разы́гр|ывать, -а́ть кого́-н. **2** (meat): ~ **of lamb** бара́нья нога́ **3** (of furniture etc.) но́жка **4** (of garment): **trouser** ~ штани́на **5** (stage of journey etc.) эта́п

legacy /ˈlegəsɪ/ *n.* насле́дство, насле́дие

✧ **legal** /ˈliːg(ə)l/ *adj.* **1** (pert. to or based on law) юриди́ческий, правово́й; take ~ **advice** консульти́роваться, про- с юри́стом **2** (permitted or ordained by law) зако́нный, лега́льный; **within one's** ~ **rights (to)** впра́ве (*по закону*) (+ *inf.*) **3** (involving court proceedings) суде́бный
■ ~ **action** *n.* суде́бный иск; **take** ~ **action against** возбу|жда́ть, -ди́ть де́ло про́тив + *g.*; предъявля́ть, -и́ть иск (к) + *d.*; ~ **aid** *n.* (BrE) беспла́тная юриди́ческая по́мощь неиму́щим; ~ **holiday** *n.* (AmE) официа́льный нерабо́чий день; ~ **tender** *n.* зако́нное платёжное сре́дство

legality /lɪˈgælɪtɪ/ *n.* зако́нность, лега́льность

legalization /liːgəlaɪˈzeɪʃ(ə)n/ *n.* узако́нивание, легализа́ция

legalize /ˈliːgəlaɪz/ *v.t.* узако́ни|вать, -ть; легализова́ть (*impf., pf.*)

legato /lɪˈgɑːtəʊ/ *n. & adv.* (*pl.* ~**s**) (mus.) лега́то (*nt. indecl.*)

legend /ˈledʒ(ə)nd/ *n.* леге́нда

legendary /ˈledʒəndərɪ/ *adj.* легенда́рный

leggings /ˈlegɪŋz/ *n. pl.* (stretch trousers) ле́гинс|ы (-ов)

legible /ˈledʒɪb(ə)l/ *adj.* разбо́рчивый

legislate /ˈledʒɪsleɪt/ *v.i.* изд|ава́ть, -а́ть зако́ны

✧ **legislation** /ledʒɪsˈleɪʃ(ə)n/ *n.* законода́тельство

legislative /ˈledʒɪslətɪv/ *adj.* законода́тельный

legislature /ˈledʒɪslətʃə(r)/ *n.* (assembly) законода́тельный о́рган; (institutions) законода́тельные учрежде́ния

legitimacy /lɪˈdʒɪtɪməsɪ/ *n.* зако́нность

legitimate /lɪˈdʒɪtɪmət/ *adj.* (lawful) зако́нный; (justifiable): ~ **demands** справедли́вые тре́бования

legitimize /lɪˈdʒɪtɪmaɪz/ *v.t.* узако́ни|вать, -ть

leisure /ˈleʒə(r)/ *n.* свобо́дное вре́мя; **at one's** ~ (in free time) в свобо́дное вре́мя; (unhurriedly) не спеша́
■ ~ **centre** *n.* спорти́вно-развлека́тельный ко́мплекс; ~ **time** *n.* вре́мя досу́га

leisured /ˈleʒəd/ *adj.* досу́жий, пра́здный; **the** ~ **classes** нерабо́тающие кла́ссы/слои́ о́бщества

leisurely /ˈleʒəlɪ/ *adj.* неспе́шный, нетороли́вый

leitmotif, leitmotiv /ˈlaɪtməʊtiːf/ *n.* лейтмоти́в

lemon /ˈlemən/ *n.* лимо́н; (*attr.*) лимо́нный

lemonade /leməˈneɪd/ n. **1** (BrE, carbonated drink) лимона́д **2** (drink of lemon juice and water) напи́ток из со́ка лимо́на с водо́й

lemur /ˈliːmə(r)/ n. лему́р

lend /lend/ v.t. (past and p.p. **lent**) **1** да|ва́ть, -ть взаймы́; од|а́лживать, -олжи́ть; ссу|жа́ть, -ди́ть (кого чем or что кому); одолжи́те мне (or да́йте мне взаймы́) пять фу́нтов; ~ me the book for a while да́йте мне кни́гу на вре́мя **2** (impart) прид|ава́ть, -а́ть **3** (proffer): ~ a hand (help) ока́з|ывать, -а́ть по́мощь (кому); (help out in difficulty) выруча́ть, вы́ручить

lender /ˈlendə(r)/ n. заимода́вец, кредито́р

length /leŋkθ/ n. **1** (dimension, measurement) длина́; two metres in ~ два ме́тра длино́й **2** (racing etc.): the horse won by a ~ ло́шадь опереди́ла други́х на ко́рпус **3** (of time) продолжи́тельность, дли́тельность, срок; the chief fault of this film is its ~ гла́вный недоста́ток э́того фи́льма — его́ растя́нутость; at ~ (finally) наконе́ц; (in detail) во всех подро́бностях **4** (extent, degree): he went to great ~s not to offend them он сде́лал всё возмо́жное, что́бы не оби́деть их **5** (piece of material) кусо́к; отре́з

lengthen /ˈleŋkθ(ə)n/ v.t. & i. удлин|я́ть(ся), -и́ть(ся)

lengthy /ˈleŋkθɪ/ adj. (**lengthier**, **lengthiest**) дли́нный, затя́нутый; (in time) дли́тельный

leniency /ˈliːnɪənsɪ/ n. снисхожде́ние; мя́гкость

lenient /ˈliːnɪənt/ adj. (of person) снисходи́тельный; (of punishment etc.) мя́гкий

Leningrad /ˈleningræd/ n. (hist.) Ленингра́д; (attr.) ленингра́дский

lens /lenz/ n. (anat., optics) ли́нза; (phot.) объекти́в

Lent /lent/ n. Вели́кий пост

lent /lent/ past and p.p. of ▶ **lend**

lentil /ˈlentɪl/ n. чечеви́ца

Leo /ˈliːəʊ/ n. (pl. ~s) (astron., astrol.) Лев

leopard /ˈlepəd/ n. леопа́рд

leotard /ˈliːətɑːd/ n. трико́ (nt. indecl.)

leper /ˈlepə(r)/ n. прокажённый

leprosy /ˈleprəsɪ/ n. прока́за

lesbian /ˈlezbɪən/ n. лесбия́нка
• adj. лесби́йский

lesion /ˈliːʒ(ə)n/ n. поврежде́ние, пораже́ние

✎ **less** /les/ n. ме́ньшее коли́чество; you should eat ~ вам сле́дует ме́ньше есть; ~ than £50 ме́нее 50 фу́нтов; in ~ than an hour ме́нее чем за час
• adj. **1** (smaller) ме́ньший **2** (not so much) ме́ньше; eat ~ meat! е́шьте ме́ньше мя́са!
• adv. ме́ньше, ме́нее; не так, не сто́лько; he is ~ intelligent than his sister он не так умён, как его́ сестра́; the ~ you think about it the better чем ме́ньше об э́том ду́мать, тем лу́чше; ~ and ~ всё ме́ньше и ме́ньше
• prep. ми́нус; за вы́четом + g.; I paid him

his wages, ~ what he owed me я вы́дал ему́ зарпла́ту за вы́четом су́ммы, кото́рую он мне задолжа́л

lessen /ˈles(ə)n/ v.t. & i. ум|еньша́ть(ся), -е́ньшить(ся)

lesser /ˈlesə(r)/ adj. ме́ньший

✎ **lesson** /ˈles(ə)n/ n. уро́к, заня́тие; English ~s уро́ки англи́йского языка́; teach sb a ~ (rebuke, punish) дать (pf.) уро́к кому́-н.

let[1] /let/ n. (BrE, of property) аре́нда; take a house on a long ~ снять (pf.) дом на дли́тельный срок
• v.t. (**letting**, past and p.p. **let**) (also ~ out) сда|ва́ть, -ть внаём

✎ **let**[2] /let/ v.t. (**letting**, past and p.p. **let**)
1 (allow) позв|оля́ть, -о́лить + d.; разреш|а́ть, -и́ть + d.; he will help you позво́льте вам помо́чь; he won't ~ me work он не даёт мне рабо́тать; ~ go (relax grip on) выпуска́ть, вы́пустить из рук; отпус|ка́ть, -ти́ть; ~ oneself go увл|ека́ться, -е́чься; (set free) выпуска́ть, вы́пустить; ~ one's hair grow отпус|ка́ть, -ти́ть во́лосы **2** (cause to): ~ sb know да|ва́ть, -ть кому́-н. знать; сообщ|а́ть, -и́ть кому́-н. **3** (in imper. or hortatory sense): ~ me see (reflect) погоди́те; да́йте поду́мать; just ~ him try it! пусть то́лько попро́бует! **4** (~ come or go): shall I ~ you into a secret? хоти́те я раскро́ю вам та́йну?; he was ~ out of prison его́ вы́пустили из тюрьмы́

□ ~ **alone** v.t.: ~ alone (not to mention) не то́лько что, не говоря́ уже́ о + p.; they haven't got a radio, ~ alone television у них и ра́дио нет, не говоря́ уже́ о телеви́зоре

□ ~ **down** v.t. (disappoint) разочаро́в|ывать, -а́ть; (fail to support) подв|оди́ть, -ести́ (infml); (BrE, deflate) ~ down tyres спус|ка́ть, -ти́ть ши́ны; (lengthen) ~ down a dress отпуска́ть, отпусти́ть пла́тье

□ ~ **in** v.t. (admit) впус|ка́ть, -ти́ть; the window doesn't ~ in much light че́рез э́то окно́ проника́ет ма́ло све́та; my shoes ~ in water мои́ ту́фли протека́ют/промока́ют; he ~ himself in он сам откры́л дверь и вошёл; what have I ~ myself in for? во что я ввяза́лся?

□ ~ **off** v.t. (discharge) разря|жа́ть, -ди́ть; ~ off fireworks запуска́ть (impf.) фейерве́рк; (not punish) не нака́зывать (impf.); he was ~ off lightly он легко́ отде́лался; (excuse) про|ща́ть, -сти́ть + d.; they ~ him off his debt ему́ прости́ли долг

□ ~ **on** v.i. (infml, divulge) прогов|а́риваться, -ори́ться

□ ~ **out** v.t.: ~ out a scream завизжа́ть (pf.); взви́згнуть (pf.); ~ out a secret прогов|а́риваться, -ори́ться; проболта́ться (pf.)

□ ~ **up** v.i. (weaken, diminish) осла́б|евать, -е́ть; (stop for a while) приостан|а́вливаться, -ови́ться; (relax) переду́х|ать, -ну́ть

■ ~-**down** n. (disappointment, anticlimax) разочарова́ние

lethal /ˈliːθ(ə)l/ adj. (fatal) смерте́льный; (designed to kill) смертоно́сный

lethargic /lɪˈθɑːdʒɪk/ adj. вя́лый

lethargy /ˈleθədʒɪ/ n. вя́лость

ℐ **letter** /'letə(r)/ n. **1** (of alphabet) бу́ква **2** (written communication) письмо́
■ ~ **bomb** n. бо́мба в конве́рте; ~ **box** n. (BrE) почто́вый я́щик

lettuce /'letɪs/ n. сала́т (*растение*)

leukaemia /luː'kiːmɪə/ (AmE **leukemia**) n. белокро́вие, лейкеми́я

ℐ **level** /'lev(ə)l/ n. у́ровень; on a ~ with на одно́м у́ровне с + *i.*; talks at Cabinet ~ перегово́ры на прави́тельственном у́ровне
● *adj.* (even) ро́вный; (flat) пло́ский; (horizontal) горизонта́льный; the water was ~ with the banks вода́ была́ вро́вень с берега́ми; draw ~ with наг|оня́ть, -на́ть
● *v.t.* (**levelled**, **levelling**, AmE **leveled**, **leveling**) **1** (make ~) ур|а́внивать, -овня́ть; выра́внивать, вы́ровнять **2** (raze to ground) ср|а́внивать, -овня́ть с землёй **3** (aim) нав|оди́ть, -ести́; нацели|вать, -ть; she ~led a gun at his head она́ прице́лилась ему́ в го́лову; (criticism, accusation) напр|авля́ть, -а́вить (**at:** про́тив + *g.*)
□ ~ **off**, ~ **out** *vv.t.* (smooth out) сгла́|живать, -дить; (make ~, even, identical) ур|а́внивать, -овня́ть
■ ~ **crossing** n. (BrE) (железнодоро́жный) перее́зд; ~**-headed** adj. тре́звый, рассуди́тельный

lever /'liːvə(r)/ n. рыча́г

leverage /'liːvərɪdʒ/ n. (action) де́йствие/ уси́лие рычага́; use ~ **on sb** (fig.) повлия́ть (*pf.*) на кого́-н.

levitation /levɪ'teɪʃ(ə)n/ n. левита́ция

levity /'levɪtɪ/ n. легкомы́слие

levy /'levɪ/ n. взима́ть (*impf.*) (**on:** c + *g.*)
● *v.t.* обложе́ние

lewd /ljuːd/ adj. (of person) развра́тный; (of joke, suggestion) непристо́йный, гря́зный

lexical /'leksɪk(ə)l/ adj. лекси́ческий

lexicon /'leksɪkən/ n. (dictionary) слова́рь, лексико́н; (vocabulary of writer etc.) ле́ксика

liability /laɪə'bɪlɪtɪ/ n. **1** (responsibility) отве́тственность **2** (*in pl.*) (debts) долги́ (*m. pl.*) **3** (handicap): he's nothing but a ~ он про́сто обу́за

liable /'laɪəb(ə)l/ adj. **1** (answerable) отве́тственный (**for:** за + *a.*) **2** (subject): he is ~ to a heavy fine его́ мо́гут подве́ргнуть большо́му штра́фу **3** (apt, likely): she is ~ to forget it она́ скло́нна забыва́ть об э́том

liaise /lɪ'eɪz/ *v.i.* устана́вливать/подде́рживать связь (**with:** c + *i.*) (*impf.*)

liaison /lɪ'eɪzɒn/ n. связь

liar /'laɪə(r)/ n. лгун (-ья)

libel /'laɪb(ə)l/ n. клевета́
● *v.t.* (**libelled**, **libelling**, AmE **libeled**, **libeling**) клевета́ть (*на кого*), о- (*кого*), на- (*на кого*); they ~led me они́ оклевета́ли меня́, они́ наклевета́ли на меня́

libellous /'laɪbələs/ (AmE **libelous**) adj. клеветни́ческий

liberal /'lɪbər(ə)l/ n. либера́л
● *adj.* **1** (generous) ще́дрый; (abundant) оби́льный **2** (broadminded): a man of ~

views челове́к широ́ких взгля́дов **3** (pol.) либера́льный
■ **L~ Democrat** n. (pol.) либера́л-демокра́т

liberalization /lɪbərəlaɪ'zeɪʃ(ə)n/ n. демократиза́ция, либерализа́ция

liberalize /'lɪbərəlaɪz/ *v.t.* либерализова́ть (*impf., pf.*)

liberate /'lɪbəreɪt/ *v.t.* освобо|жда́ть, -ди́ть

liberation /lɪbə'reɪʃ(ə)n/ n. освобожде́ние

liberator /'lɪbəreɪtə(r)/ n. освободи́тель (-ница)

Liberia /laɪ'bɪərɪə/ n. Либе́рия

Liberian /laɪ'bɪərɪən/ n. либери́|ец (-йка)
● *adj.* либери́йский

libertarian /lɪbə'teərɪən/ n. (advocate of freedom) боре́ц за демократи́ческие свобо́ды

liberty /'lɪbətɪ/ n. свобо́да; at ~ находя́щийся на свобо́де; you are at ~ to go вы вольны́ уйти́

libido /lɪ'biːdəʊ/ n. (*pl.* ~s) либи́до (*nt. indecl.*)

Libra /'liːbrə/ n. (astron., astrol.) Весы́ (-о́в)

librarian /laɪ'breərɪən/ n. библиоте́карь (*m.*)

ℐ **library** /'laɪbrərɪ/ n. библиоте́ка

Libya /'lɪbɪə/ n. Ли́вия

Libyan /'lɪbɪən/ n. ливи́|ец (-йка)
● *adj.* ливи́йский

licence /'laɪs(ə)ns/ (AmE also **license**) n. **1** (permission) разреше́ние; (for trade) лице́нзия **2** (permit) свиде́тельство; driving ~ води́тельские права́ **3** (freedom) во́льность
■ ~ **plate** n. (AmE) номерно́й знак

ℐ **license** /'laɪs(ə)ns/ (AmE also **licence**) *v.t.* **1** (authorize) разреш|а́ть, -и́ть *что*; да|ва́ть, -ть разреше́ние на *что* **2** (grant permit, permission to) разреш|а́ть, -и́ть + *d.*; ~d premises заведе́ние, облада́ющее лице́нзией на прода́жу спиртны́х напи́тков

licensee /laɪsən'siː/ n. облада́тель (-ница) разреше́ния/лице́нзии; (of public house) хозя́|ин (-йка) ба́ра

licensing /'laɪsənsɪŋ/ n. лицензи́рование

licentious /laɪ'senʃəs/ adj. распу́щенный

lichen /'laɪkən/ n. лиша́йник

lick /lɪk/ *v.t.* **1** лиз|а́ть, -ну́ть; ~ one's lips/ (infml) chops обли́з|ываться, -а́ться; гу́бы; обли́з|ываться, -а́ться; (fig.): ~ one's wounds зали́з|ывать, -а́ть ра́ны **2** (infml, defeat) поб|ива́ть, -и́ть

licorice /'lɪkərɪs, -rɪʃ/ n. (AmE) = liquorice

lid /lɪd/ n. кры́шка

lido /'liːdəʊ, 'laɪ-/ n. (*pl.* ~s) (обще́ственный) пляж

lie¹ /laɪ/ n. (falsehood) ложь; tell a ~ лгать, со-
● *v.i.* (**lies**, **lied**, **lying**) лгать, со-; врать, со-/на-; he ~d to me он мне солга́л

ℐ **lie²** /laɪ/ *v.i.* (**lying**, *past* **lay**, *p.p.* **lain**) **1** (repose) лежа́ть, по-; ~ **low** притаи́ться (*pf.*) **2** (be; be situated) находи́ться (*impf.*); быть располо́женным **3** (fig., reside, rest): the choice ~s with you вы́бор зави́сит от вас; вам выбира́ть; she knows where her interests ~ она́ своего́ не упу́стит **4** (~ down) ложи́ться, лечь; приле́чь (*pf.*); **he went and lay on the bed** он лёг на крова́ть

□ ~ **about**, ~ **around** *vv.i.* валя́ться (*impf.*)

□ ~ **ahead** *v.i.* предстоя́ть (*impf.*)

□ ~ **down** *v.i.* ложи́ться, лечь; **I shall ~ down for an hour** я приля́гу на час/часо́к

■ ~-**down** *n.* (BrE): **she had a ~-down** она́ полежа́ла; ~-**in** *n.* (BrE): **we had a ~-in** мы вста́ли по́здно

lieu /lu:/ *n.*: **in ~ of** вме́сто + *g.*

lieutenant /lefˈtenənt/ *n.* лейтена́нт

◆ **life** /laɪf/ *n.* (*pl.* **lives**) **1** (being alive) жизнь; **save sb's ~** спасти́ (*pf.*) жизнь кому́-н.; (existence): **that's ~!** такова́ жизнь!; (way or style of ~) быт; **family ~** дома́шний быт; **country, village ~** дереве́нская жизнь **2** (period, span of ~): **have the time of one's ~** прекра́сно проводи́ть (*impf.*) вре́мя; **he has had a good/ quiet ~** он про́жил хоро́шую/споко́йную жизнь **3** (animation) жизнь; **the ~ and soul of the party** душа́ о́бщества; **the child is full of ~** ребёнок о́чень живо́й; **the play came to ~ in the third act** пье́са оживи́лась к тре́тьему де́йствию; **is there ~ on Mars?** есть ли жизнь на Ма́рсе?; **animal ~** живо́тный мир

■ ~-**belt** *n.* (BrE) спаса́тельный круг; ~**boat** *n.* спаса́тельная ло́дка; ~ **coach** *n.* персона́льный наста́вник; ~ **expectancy** *n.* вероя́тная продолжи́тельность жи́зни; ~**guard**, ~**saver** *nn.* спаса́тель (-ница) (на пля́же); ~ **insurance** *n.* страхова́ние жи́зни; ~ **jacket** *n.* спаса́тельный жиле́т; ~**like** *adj.* реалисти́чный; ~**line** *n.* (fig.) еди́нственная наде́жда; спаси́тельное сре́дство; (of communication line) связу́ющий мост (to: **c** + *i.*); ~**long** *adj.* пожи́зненный; **they were ~long friends** они́ бы́ли друзья́ми всю жизнь; ~-**saving** *n.* спасе́ние; ~ **sentence** *n.* пожи́зненное заключе́ние (*как приговор*); (of inanimate things, durability) долгове́чность; срок слу́жбы; ~-**size(d)** *adjs.* в натура́льную величину́; ~**span** *n.* (of person, animal) продолжи́тельность жи́зни; (of machine, tool) срок эксплуата́ции; ~-**style** *n.* о́браз жи́зни; ~-**support** *adj.*: ~-**support system** систе́ма жизнеобеспече́ния; ~**time** *n.* жизнь; **in sb's ~time** при жи́зни кого́-н.; **the chance of a ~time** ре́дкий/исключи́тельный слу́чай; **it's a ~time since I saw her** я не ви́дел её це́лую ве́чность

lifeless /ˈlaɪflɪs/ *adj.* (dead) мёртвый; (inanimate) неживо́й; (inert) безжи́зненный

◆ **lift** /lɪft/ *n.* **1** (in car etc.): **give sb a ~** подв|ози́ть, -езти́ кого́-н. **2** (fig., of spirits): **the news gave her a ~** от э́той но́вости она́ воспря́нула ду́хом **3** (BrE, apparatus) лифт

● *v.t.* **1** (raise) подн|има́ть, -я́ть **2** (remove): ~ **a ban** сн|има́ть, -ять запре́т

● *v.i.* (disperse) рассе́|иваться, -яться; (cease) прекра|ща́ться, -ти́ться

□ ~ **off** *v.t.* сн|има́ть, -я́ть

● *v.i.* (of rocket) отр|ыва́ться, -орва́ться от земли́

□ ~ **up** *v.t.* подн|има́ть, -я́ть

◆ ключева́я ле́ксика

■ ~-**off** *n.* отры́в от земли́

ligament /ˈlɪɡəmənt/ *n.* свя́зка

◆ **light**[1] /laɪt/ *n.* **1** свет; **stand against the ~** стоя́ть (*impf.*) про́тив све́та; **bring to ~** выводи́ть, вы́вести на чи́стую во́ду; **come to ~** обнару́жи|ваться, -ться; выплыва́ть, вы́плыть; **shed, throw ~ on sth** прол|ива́ть, -и́ть свет на что-н.; (in a picture): **effects of ~ and shade** эффе́кты све́та и те́ни; (lighting) освеще́ние; (fig.): **this book shows him in a bad ~** э́та кни́га пока́зывает его́ в невы́годном све́те; (point of ~): **the ~s of the town** огни́ го́рода **2** (lamp) ла́мпа; (of car) фа́ра; **traffic ~s** светофо́р **3** (flame) ого́нь (*m.*); **have you a ~?** у вас огонька́ не бу́дет?

● *adj.* **1** (opp. dark) све́тлый; **get ~** рассве|та́ть, -сти́ **2** (in colour) све́тлый; све́тлого цве́та; ~-**haired** светловоло́сый; ~-**skinned** светлоко́жий; (with names of colours) све́тло-; ~ **green** све́тло-зелёный; ~ **blue** све́тло-голубо́й

● *v.t.* (*past* **lit**, *p.p.* **lit** *or* (*attr.*) **lighted**) (*also* ~ **up**) **1** (kindle) заж|ига́ть, -е́чь; ~ **a fire** разв|оди́ть, -ести́ ого́нь; ~ (**up**) **a cigarette** заку́р|ивать, -и́ть папиро́су **2** (illuminate) осве|ща́ть, -ти́ть; ~ **the way for sb** свети́ть, по- кому́-н.; (fig.): **a smile lit up his face** улы́бка озари́ла его́ лицо́

■ ~ **bulb** *n.* ла́мпочка; ~**house** *n.* мая́к; ~**weight** *n.* (sport, also fig.) легкове́с; ~ **year** *n.* светово́й год

◆ **light**[2] /laɪt/ *adj.* (opp. heavy) лёгкий; **our casualties were ~** на́ши поте́ри бы́ли незначи́тельны; **a ~ sentence** мя́гкий пригово́р; **I am a ~ sleeper** я чу́тко сплю

■ ~-**headed** *adj.*: **she felt ~-headed** у неё закружи́лась голова́; ~-**hearted** *adj.* (carefree) беспе́чный; (of action) необду́манный; ~ **music** *n.* лёгкая му́зыка; ~ **reading** *n.* лёгкое чте́ние; ~**weight** *adj.* (suit) лёгкий; (fig.) несерьёзный, легкове́сный

lighten[1] /ˈlaɪt(ə)n/ *v.t.* (make less heavy or easier) облегч|а́ть, -и́ть

lighten[2] /ˈlaɪt(ə)n/ *v.i.* (grow brighter) светле́ть, по-

lighter /ˈlaɪtə(r)/ *n.* (for cigarettes etc.) зажига́лка

lighting /ˈlaɪtɪŋ/ *n.* освеще́ние

lightly /ˈlaɪtlɪ/ *adv.* легко́; **you have got off ~** вы легко́ отде́лались

lightning /ˈlaɪtnɪŋ/ *n.* мо́лния; **he was struck by ~** в него́ уда́рила мо́лния

● *attr. adj.*: **with ~ speed** молниено́сно

◆ **like**[1] /laɪk/ *n.* (sth equal or similar) подо́бное; **music, dancing and the ~** му́зыка, та́нцы и тому́ подо́бное; (person) подо́бный; **the ~s of me, us** наш брат

● *adj.* (**more like**, **most like**) подо́бный, похо́жий

● *prep.* **1** (similar to, characteristic of) похо́жий на + *a.*; **she is ~ her mother** она́ похо́жа на мать; **what's she ~?** что она́ за челове́к?; **a house ~ yours** дом вро́де ва́шего; **it sounds ~ thunder** как бу́дто гром греми́т; **it sounds ~ a good idea** э́то, пожа́луй, хоро́шая иде́я; **a person ~ that** тако́й челове́к **2** (inclined towards): **I don't feel ~ it** мне (что́-то) не

хо́чется; **I felt ~ crying** мне хоте́лось
пла́кать; **I feel ~ an ice cream** я бы не прочь
съесть моро́женое
■ **~-minded** *adj.* приде́рживающийся тех же
взгля́дов

✓ **like²** /laɪk/ *v.t.* (take pleasure in) люби́ть (*impf.*),
цени́ть (*impf.*); **he ~s living in Paris** ему́
нра́вится жить в Пари́же; **she ~d dancing**
она́ люби́ла танцева́ть; **I ~ him** он мне
нра́вится; **we ~d the play** пье́са нам
понра́вилась; **would you ~ a drink?** хоти́те
вы́пить (чего́-нибудь)?; **if you ~** е́сли
хоти́те; **I should ~ to meet him** мне хоте́лось
бы познако́миться с ним; **he would ~ to
come** он хоте́л бы прийти́; **as you ~** как
уго́дно

likeable /'laɪkəb(ə)l/ *adj.* симпати́чный

likelihood /'laɪklɪhʊd/ *n.* вероя́тность; **in all
~** по всей вероя́тности

✓ **likely** /'laɪklɪ/ *adj.* (**likelier, likeliest**)
1 (probable) вероя́тный; (plausible)
правдоподо́бный **2** (to be expected): **he is ~ to
come** он, вероя́тно, придёт

liken /'laɪkən/ *v.t.* упод|обля́ть, -о́бить (*кого/
что кому/чему*)

likeness /'laɪknɪs/ *n.* схо́дство, подо́бие; **a
family ~** фами́льное схо́дство

likewise /'laɪkwaɪz/ *adv.* подо́бно

liking /'laɪkɪŋ/ *n.* симпа́тия (*к кому*); **I took a
~ to him** я почу́вствовал к нему́ симпа́тию;
is the meat done to your ~? э́то мя́со
пригото́влено, как вы лю́бите?

lilac /'laɪlək/ *n.* сире́нь

lilt /lɪlt/ *n.* (tune) напе́в; (rhythm) ритм
● *v.i.*: **a ~ing melody** мелоди́чный напе́в

lily /'lɪlɪ/ *n.* ли́лия
■ **~ of the valley** *n.* ла́ндыш

limb /lɪm/ *n.* **1** (of body, also fig.) член;
коне́чность **2** (branch of tree) сук, ветвь

limber /'lɪmbə(r)/ *v.i.*: **~ up** разм|ина́ться,
-я́ться

limbo /'lɪmbəʊ/ *n.* (*pl.* **~s**) **1** (relig.) лимб
2 (fig.): **our plans are in ~** на́ши пла́ны вися́т
в во́здухе

lime¹ /laɪm/ *n.* (fruit) лайм
■ **~ juice** *n.* сок ла́йма

lime² /laɪm/ *n.* (tree) ли́па

lime³ /laɪm/ *n.* (calcium oxide) и́звесть
■ **~light** *n.* (lit.) свет ра́мпы; (fig.): **be in the
~light** быть знамени́тостью; **~stone** *n.*
известня́к

✓ **limit** /'lɪmɪt/ *n.* **1** (terminal point) преде́л;
set, fix a ~ to sth устан|а́вливать, -ови́ть
преде́л чему́-н.; **I am willing to help you,
within ~s** я гото́в помо́чь вам в преде́лах
возмо́жного **2** (boundary) грани́ца **3** (time
~) (преде́льный) срок; **age ~** преде́льный
во́зраст
● *v.t.* (**limited, limiting**) ограни́чи|вать,
-ть (*кого/что чем*)
■ **~ed (liability) company** *n.* (BrE) компа́ния
с ограни́ченной отве́тственностью

limitation /lɪmɪ'teɪʃ(ə)n/ *n.* (condition)
огово́рка; (drawback) недоста́ток; **he has his**

~s он не лишён недоста́тков; (limiting, being
limited) ограниче́ние

limitless /'lɪmɪtlɪs/ *adj.* безграни́чный,
беспреде́льный; (of time) бесконе́чный

limousine /'lɪmʊ'ziːn/ *n.* лимузи́н

limp¹ /lɪmp/ *n.* хромота́; **he has a ~** он
хрома́ет/прихра́мывает
● *v.i.* хрома́ть (*impf.*)

limp² /lɪmp/ *adj.* **1** (flexible) мя́гкий **2** (flabby)
вя́лый

linchpin, lynchpin /'lɪntʃpɪn/ *n.* чека́;
(fig., of person or thing) тот/то, на ком/чём всё
де́ржится

✓ **line¹** /laɪn/ *n.* **1** (cord) верёвка; **hang washing
on the ~** разве́сить (*pf.*) бельё на верёвке;
(fishing ~) ле́ска **2** (wire, cable for communication)
ли́ния (свя́зи); ка́бель (*m.*); про́вод; **he is
on the ~** он говори́т по телефо́ну; он у
телефо́на **3** (rail.) ли́ния; (track) полотно́;
ре́льсы (*m. pl.*) **4** (transport system) ли́ния;
air ~s возду́шные ли́нии **5** (long narrow
mark) ли́ния, черта́; (imagined straight ~):
~ of fire направле́ние стрельбы́ **6** (on
face, etc.) скла́дка **7** (drawn, painted, etc.)
штрих **8** (boundary) грани́ца, преде́л;
черта́ **9** (row) ряд, ли́ния; **stand in a ~**
стоя́ть (*impf.*) в ряд; **stand in ~** (AmE, queue)
стоя́ть (*impf.*) в о́череди; **in ~ with** в одну́
ли́нию (*or* в ряд) с + *i.*; (fig.) в согла́сии/
соотве́тствии с + *i.*; **bring into ~** (fig.)
привле́чь (*pf.*) (*кого*) на свою́ сто́рону;
come, fall into ~ (fig.) согласова́ться (*impf.,
pf.*) **10** (mil., entrenched position): **front ~**
ли́ния фро́нта **11** (of print or writing) строка́;
on ~ 10 there's a mistake в деся́той строке́
оши́бка; (*in pl.*) (actor's part) роль **12** (lineage)
ли́ния **13** (course, direction, track) направле́ние,
ли́ния; **take a firm, hard, strong ~** занима́ть,
-я́ть твёрдую пози́цию; стро́го обіходи́ться,
-ойти́сь (*с кем*) **14** (province): **his ~ of
business** род его́ заня́тий **15** (class of goods)
сорт, род, моде́ль (това́ра)
● *v.t.* **1** (mark with ~s): **~d paper** лино́ванная
бума́га; **his face was deeply ~d** его́ лицо́
бы́ло изборождено́ морщи́нами **2** (form a
~ along) стоя́ть (*impf.*) вдоль + *g*; **police ~d
the street** полице́йские стоя́ли по обе́им
сторона́м у́лицы
□ **~ up** *v.t.* (align) выстра́ивать, вы́строить в
ряд/ли́нию
● *v.i.* (queue up) ста|нови́ться, -ть в о́чередь
■ **~sman** *n.* (sport) боково́й судья́; **~-up**
n. (sport) соста́в кома́нды; (mus.) соста́в
анса́мбля/(поп-)гру́ппы; (TV) расписа́ние
переда́ч

line² /laɪn/ *v.t.* **1** (put lining into) ста́вить, по- на
подкла́дку; **her coat is ~d with silk** у неё
пальто́ на шёлковой подкла́дке **2** (fig.)
заст|авля́ть, -а́вить; **the wall was ~d with
books** стена́ была́ заста́влена кни́гами

lineage /'lɪnɪɪdʒ/ *n.* (ancestry) происхожде́ние;
(genealogy) родосло́вная

linear /'lɪnɪə(r)/ *adj.* лине́йный

linen /'lɪnɪn/ *n.* **1** (smooth) лён; (coarse) холст
2 (~ articles) бельё; (bed ~) посте́льное бельё

● *adj.* полотня́ный

liner /'laɪnə(r)/ *n.* ла́йнер

linger /'lɪŋɡə(r)/ *v.i.* (take one's time) ме́длить (*impf.*); (stay on) заде́рж|иваться, -а́ться; **I have** ⁓**ing doubts** мои́ сомне́ния не рассе́ялись

□ ⁓ **on** *v.i.* (remain) ост|ава́ться, -а́ться

lingerie /'læʒərɪ/ *n.* да́мское бельё

linguist /'lɪŋɡwɪst/ *n.* лингви́ст, языкове́д

linguistic /lɪŋ'ɡwɪstɪk/ *adj.* лингвисти́ческий

linguistics /lɪŋ'ɡwɪstɪks/ *n.* лингви́стика

lining /'laɪnɪŋ/ *n.* подкла́дка

✎ **link** /lɪŋk/ *n.* **1** (of chain, also fig.) звено́ **2** (connection) связь; (comput.) ссы́лка
● *v.t.* (unite) соедин|я́ть, -и́ть; (join) свя́з|ывать, -а́ть; ⁓ **arms with sb** идти́ (*det.*) под руку с кем-н.

□ ⁓ **up** *v.t. & i.* соедин|я́ть(ся), -и́ть(ся)

■ ⁓-**up** *n.* связь, соедине́ние

lino /'laɪnəʊ/ *n.* (*pl.* ⁓**s**) (BrE) = **linoleum**

linoleum /lɪ'nəʊlɪəm/ *n.* линоле́ум

linseed /'lɪnsiːd/ *n.* льняно́е се́мя

■ ⁓ **oil** *n.* льняно́е ма́сло

lintel /'lɪnt(ə)l/ *n.* при́толока (*ве́рхний брус дверно́й/око́нной ра́мы*)

lion /'laɪən/ *n.* лев

■ ⁓ **cub** *n.* львёнок

lioness /'laɪənes/ *n.* льви́ца

lip /lɪp/ *n.* **1** губа́; (dim.) гу́бка **2** (edge of cup, wound, etc.) край

■ ⁓-**read** *v.t. & i.* чита́ть (*impf.*) с губ; ⁓**salve** *n.* (BrE) гигиени́ческая губна́я пома́да; ⁓ **service** *n.*: **pay** ⁓ **service to sth** призн|ава́ть, -а́ть что-н. то́лько на слова́х; ⁓**stick** *n.* (substance) губна́я пома́да; (applicator) тю́бик губно́й пома́ды

liqueur /lɪ'kjʊə(r)/ *n.* ликёр

liquid /'lɪkwɪd/ *n.* жи́дкость
● *adj.* жи́дкий

■ ⁓ **assets** *n. pl.* (fin.) ликви́дные акти́вы

liquidate /'lɪkwɪdeɪt/ *v.t.* ликвиди́ровать (*impf., pf.*)

liquidation /lɪkwɪ'deɪʃ(ə)n/ *n.* ликвида́ция

liquidize /'lɪkwɪdaɪz/ *v.t.* (BrE, cul.) превра|ща́ть, -ти́ть в жи́дкость; пропус|ка́ть, -ти́ть че́рез смеси́тель/ми́ксер

liquidizer /'lɪkwɪdaɪzə(r)/ *n.* (BrE, cul.) смеси́тель (*m.*), ми́ксер

liquor /'lɪkə(r)/ *n.* (спиртно́й) напи́ток

■ ⁓ **store** *n.* (AmE) ви́нный магази́н

liquorice /'lɪkərɪs, -rɪʃ/ (AmE **licorice**) *n.* (plant) соло́дка, лакри́чник; (substance) лакри́ца

lisp /lɪsp/ *n.* шепеля́вость; **he has a** ⁓ он шепеля́вит

✎ **list¹** /lɪst/ *n.* (inventory, enumeration) спи́сок, пе́речень (*m.*); ⁓ **price** цена́ по прейскура́нту
● *v.t.* (make a ⁓ of) сост|авля́ть, -а́вить спи́сок + *g.*; (enter on a ⁓) вн|оси́ть, -ести́ в спи́сок

■ ⁓**ed building** *n.* зда́ние, находя́щееся под охра́ной госуда́рства

list² /lɪst/ *v.i.* (of ship) накреня́ться (*impf.*)

✎ ключева́я ле́ксика

✎ **listen** /'lɪs(ə)n/ *v.i.* слу́шать, по-; ⁓ **to** слу́шать, по- + *a.*; **do you** ⁓ **to the radio?** вы слу́шаете ра́дио?; (pay attention) прислу́ш|иваться, -аться к + *d.*; **don't** ⁓ **to him!** не обраща́йте на него́ внима́ния!; **I was** ⁓**ing for the bell** я (напряжённо) ждал звонка́; **he** ⁓**ed in on their conversation** он подслу́шал их разгово́р

listener /'lɪsənə(r)/ *n.* слу́шатель (*m.*)

listing /'lɪstɪŋ/ *n.* (list) спи́сок; (mentioning) упомина́ние

listless /'lɪstlɪs/ *adj.* вя́лый

lit /lɪt/ *past and p.p. of* ▶ **light¹**

litany /'lɪtəni/ *n.* (Orthodox) ектенья́; (Catholic) лита́ния; (fig., tedious enumeration) ску́чное перечисле́ние

literacy /'lɪtərəsi/ *n.* гра́мотность

literal /'lɪtər(ə)l/ *adj.* буква́льный

literary /'lɪtərəri/ *adj.* литерату́рный

literate /'lɪtərət/ *adj.* гра́мотный

✎ **literature** /'lɪtrətʃə(r)/ *n.* литерату́ра

lithe /laɪð/ *adj.* ги́бкий

lithograph /'lɪθəɡrɑːf/ *n.* литогра́фия

lithography /lɪ'θɒɡrəfi/ *n.* литогра́фия

Lithuania /lɪθʊ'eɪnɪə/ *n.* Литва́

Lithuanian /lɪθʊ'eɪnɪən/ *n.* (person) лито́в|ец (-ка); (language) лито́вский язы́к
● *adj.* лито́вский

litigate /'lɪtɪɡeɪt/ *v.i.* суди́ться (*impf.*)

litigation /lɪtɪ'ɡeɪʃ(ə)n/ *n.* тя́жба; суде́бный проце́сс

litigious /lɪ'tɪdʒəs/ *adj.* **1** (fond of going to law) сутя́жнический; **a** ⁓ **person** сутя́жни|к (-ца) **2** (pert. to litigation): ⁓ **procedure** процеду́ра суде́бного разбира́тельства

litmus /'lɪtməs/ *n.* ла́кмус

■ ⁓ **paper** *n.* ла́кмусовая бума́га

litre /'liːtə(r)/ (AmE **liter**) *n.* литр

litter /'lɪtə(r)/ *n.* **1** (refuse) сор, отбро́с|ы (-ов) **2**: **cat** ⁓ коша́чья подсти́лка **3** (newly-born animals) помёт
● *v.t.* сори́ть, на-; **the table is** ⁓**ed with books** стол зава́лен кни́гами

■ ⁓ **bin** *n.* (BrE) му́сорный я́щик

✎ **little** /'lɪt(ə)l/ *n.* **1** (not much) ма́ло, немно́го, немно́жко + *g.*; **I see** ⁓ **of him now** я тепе́рь ре́дко ви́жу его́; ⁓ **or nothing** почти́ ничего́; ма́ло что; (small amount): **he knows a** ⁓ **Japanese** он немно́го зна́ет япо́нски; ⁓ **by** ⁓ ма́ло-пома́лу; постепе́нно
● *adj.* (**littler**, **littlest**) **1** (small) ма́ленький, небольшо́й **2** (young): ⁓ **boy** (ма́ленький) ма́льчик; ⁓ **girl** (ма́ленькая) де́вочка **3** (trivial) ме́лкий; незначи́тельный **4** (not tall or long) невысо́кий; недли́нный; **wait here for a** ⁓ **while** подожди́те здесь немно́жко **5** (**less**, **least**) (small, of quantity) ма́ло, немно́го, немно́жко + *g.*; **there is** ⁓ **butter left** ма́сла оста́лось ма́ло
● *adv.* (**less**, **least**) **1** (not much) ма́ло; **I see him very** ⁓ я ма́ло/ре́дко с ним ви́жусь; ⁓ **more** ненамно́го/немно́гим бо́льше; **he is** ⁓ **better than a thief** он про́сто-на́просто вор; (not at all): ⁓ **did he know I was following him**

liturgy /'lɪtədʒɪ/ *n.* (eccl.) литургия

✧ **live¹** /laɪv/ *adj.* **1** (living) живой **2** (not spent or exploded): ~ ammunition боевые патроны; a ~ wire (lit.) провод под током/напряжением; (fig.) человек с изюминкой **3** (not recorded): ~ broadcast прямая передача; прямой эфир; ~ music живая музыка; the game was broadcast ~ матч транслировался непосредственно со стадиона (*or* шёл в прямой трансляции) ● *adv.* (as or at actual event) живьём (infml); he sang ~ он пел живьём
　■ ~stock *n.* домашний скот

✧ **live²** /lɪv/ *v.i.* **1** (be alive) жить (*impf.*) **2** (subsist): they ~ on vegetables они питаются овощами **3** (depend for one's living) жить (*impf.*); he ~s off his friends он живёт за счёт друзей; he ~s on his reputation он живёт за счёт былых заслуг **4** (conduct oneself) жить (*impf.*); he ~d up to my expectations он не обманул моих ожиданий; (arrange one's diet, habits, etc.): he ~s well он живёт хорошо (*or* на широкую ногу) **5** (continue alive): the doctors think he won't ~ врачи думают, что он не выживет; he ~d to regret it впоследствии он об этом жалел; (fig., survive): his fame will ~ for ever слава его не умрёт **6** (reside) жить, проживать (*both impf.*); обитать (*impf.*); where do you ~? где вы живёте; ~ with (fig., tolerate) мириться, при- с + *i.*
　□ ~ in *v.i.* (of student) жить (*impf.*) в общежитии
　□ ~ on *v.i.*: his memory ~s on память о нём жива
　□ ~ up *v.t.*: ~ it up (infml) жить (*impf.*) широко, вести (*impf.*) бурную жизнь
　■ ~-in *adj.*: ~-in nanny няня, живущая в семье; ~-in lover сожитель (-ница)

livelihood /'laɪvlɪhʊd/ *n.* средства (*nt. pl.*) к существованию

lively /'laɪvlɪ/ *adj.* (**livelier, liveliest**) живой

liven /'laɪv(ə)n/ *v.t. & i.* (*also* ~ up) оживлять(ся), -ить(ся)

liver /'lɪvə(r)/ *n.* (anat.) печень; (food) печёнка

livery /'lɪvərɪ/ *n.* (of servants) ливрея; (of a guild etc.) форма; (for horses) прокорм
　■ ~ stable *n.* платная конюшня

lives¹ /laɪvz/ *pl. of* ▸ life

lives² /lɪvz/ *2nd pers. sg. pres. of* ▸ live²

livid /'lɪvɪd/ *adj.* (furious) в ярости; (crimson) багровый

✧ **living** /'lɪvɪŋ/ *n.* **1** (process, manner of ~): ~ conditions условия жизни; cost of ~ стоимость жизни; standard of ~ жизненный уровень **2** (livelihood) средства (*nt. pl.*) к жизни; earn one's ~ зарабатывать, -отать себе на жизнь ● *adj.* живой; within ~ memory на памяти живущих
　■ ~ room *n.* гостиная

lizard /'lɪzəd/ *n.* ящерица

llama /'lɑːmə/ *n.* лама (*животное*)

✧ **load** /ləʊd/ *n.* **1** (burden) ноша; груз, нагрузка; тяжесть; (fig.) бремя **2** (amount carried) груз; a ~ of bricks груз кирпичей **3** (*in pl.*) (infml, large amount) уйма, масса ● *v.t.* **1** (cargo, etc.) грузить, по- **2** (ship, vehicle, etc.) грузить, на- **3** (fig., with cares, etc.) обременять, -ить (*кого чем*) **4** (with gifts, praises, etc.) осыпать, -ыпать (*кого чем*) **5** (firearm, camera, etc.) заряжать, -дить **6** (fig.): a ~ed question провокационный вопрос **7** (sl.): he's ~ed (rich) он (полностью/хорошо) упакован **8** (comput.) загружать, -зить
　□ ~ down *v.t.* обременять, -ить
　□ ~ up *v.t.* нагружать, -зить
　● *v.i.* грузиться, на-

loaf¹ /ləʊf/ *n.* (*pl.* **loaves**) буханка

loaf² /ləʊf/ *v.i.* (infml) (*also* ~ about) лодырничать (*impf.*)

loafer /'ləʊfə(r)/ *n.* (person) лодырь (*m.*); (shoe) кожаная туфля типа мокасин

loam /ləʊm/ *n.* суглинок

✧ **loan** /ləʊn/ *n.* **1** (sum lent) заём, ссуда **2** (lending or being lent): take on ~; have the ~ of (of money) брать, взять взаймы; (of objects) брать, взять на время ● *v.t.* (lend, borrow) одалживать, -олжить (*что-н. кому-н., что-н. у кого-н.*)
　■ ~ shark *n.* (infml) ростовщик

loath /ləʊθ/ *pred. adj.*: he was ~ to do anything он ничего не хотел делать

loathe /ləʊð/ *v.t.* ненавидеть (*impf.*)

loathing /'ləʊðɪŋ/ *n.* отвращение; feel ~ for испытывать (*impf.*) отвращение к + *d.*

loathsome /'ləʊðsəm/ *adj.* отвратительный, омерзительный

loaves /ləʊvz/ *pl. of* ▸ loaf¹

lob /lɒb/ *n.* (high-pitched ball) свеча ● *v.t.* (**lobbed, lobbing**): ~ a ball подавать, -ать свечу

lobby /'lɒbɪ/ *n.* вестибюль (*m.*); (theatr.) фойе (*nt. indecl.*); (group) лобби (*nt. indecl.*) ● *v.i.* агитировать (*impf.*) ● *v.t.* агитировать, с- (infml)

lobbying /'lɒbɪɪŋ/ *n.* агитация

lobe /ləʊb/ *n.* (of ear) мочка

lobelia /lə'biːlɪə/ *n.* (bot.) лобелия

lobster /'lɒbstə(r)/ *n.* омар

✧ **local** /'ləʊk(ə)l/ *n.* (inhabitant) местный житель; (BrE, public house) местный паб, местная пивная ● *adj.* местный; (of this place) здешний; 2 o'clock ~ time два часа по местному времени
　■ ~ anaesthetic *n.* местный наркоз; ~ authority *n.* (BrE) местные власти; ~ call *n.* местный телефонный разговор; ~ government *n.* местное самоуправление

locale /ləʊ'kɑːl/ *n.* место (действия); местность

locality /ləʊ'kælɪtɪ/ *n.* местность; (neighbourhood): there is no cinema in the ~ нигде поблизости нет кино

localize /'ləʊkəlaɪz/ *v.t.* локализовать (*impf., pf.*)

locally /'ləʊkəlɪ/ *adv.*: he is well known ~ он известен в этих краях; he works ~ он работает поблизости

♂ **locate** /ləʊˈkeɪt/ *v.t.* **1**: be ~d (situated) находи́ться (*impf.*) **2** (determine position of) определя́ть, -и́ть ме́сто/местоположе́ние + *g.*; has the fault been ~d? нашли́ поврежд́ение?; определи́ли ли ме́сто поврежд́ение?

♂ **location** /ləʊˈkeɪʃ(ə)n/ *n.* **1** (determining of place) определе́ние (ме́ста) **2** (position) местонахожде́ние **3**: on ~ (cin.) на нату́ре; shooting on ~ нату́рная съёмка

locative /ˈlɒkətɪv/ *n.* & *adj.* (gram.) ме́стный (паде́ж)

loch /lɒk/ *n.* о́зеро (*в Шотландии*); L~ Ness о́зеро Лох-Не́сс

lock¹ /lɒk/ *n.* (of hair) ло́кон

lock² /lɒk/ *n.* **1** (on door or firearm) замо́к; under ~ and key под замко́м; (on door or gate) запо́р **2** (on canal) шлюз
• *v.t.* **1** (secure; restrict movement of) запира́ть, -ере́ть (на замо́к); I was ~ed out дверь была́ заперта́, и я не мог войти́ **2** (cause to stop moving or revolving) тормози́ть, за-; he ~ed the steering он заблоки́ровал руль **3** (interlace) сплета́ть, -сти́; his fingers were ~ed together он сцепи́л ру́ки
• *v.i.*: does this chest ~? э́тот сунду́к запира́ется?
□ ~ in *v.t.* запира́ть, -ере́ть (*кого*) в ко́мнате/до́ме *и т. п.*; he ~ed himself in он за́перся на ключ
□ ~ out *v.t.* запира́ть, -ере́ть дверь и не впуска́ть
□ ~ up *v.t.* запира́ть, -ере́ть на замо́к; (imprison) сажа́ть, посади́ть (*в тюрьму*)
■ ~smith *n.* сле́сарь (*m.*)

locker /ˈlɒkə(r)/ *n.* (cupboard) шка́фчик
■ ~ room *n.* раздева́лка

locket /ˈlɒkɪt/ *n.* медальо́н

locomotion /ləʊkəˈməʊʃ(ə)n/ *n.* передвиже́ние

locomotive /ləʊkəˈməʊtɪv/ *n.* локомоти́в

locum /ˈləʊkəm/ *n.* (*pl.* ~s) (infml) = locum tenens

locum tenens /ˈləʊkəm ˈtiːnenz/ *n.* (*pl.* locum tenentes* /ˈləʊkəm tɪˈnentiːz/) (doctor or clergyman) вре́менный замести́тель (*m.*)

locust /ˈləʊkəst/ *n.* саранча́ (*also collect.*)

lodge /lɒdʒ/ *n.* **1** (cottage) дом привра́тника **2** (porter's apartment) сторо́жка
• *v.t.*: ~ a complaint/appeal обра|ща́ться, -ти́ться с жа́лобой/апелля́цией
• *v.i.* **1** (live) жить (*impf.*); прожива́ть (*impf.*); he ~s with us он у нас живёт **2** (become stuck) застре́ва|ть, -ять; a bone ~d in his throat кость застря́ла у него́ в го́рле

lodger /ˈlɒdʒə(r)/ *n.* жиле́ц

lodging /ˈlɒdʒɪŋ/ *n.* прожива́ние (see ▶ board *n.* 2); (*in pl.*) меблиро́ванные ко́мнаты (*f. pl.*)

loft /lɒft/ *n.* черда́к

lofty /ˈlɒftɪ/ *adj.* (loftier, loftiest) (high) высо́кий; (exalted) возвы́шенный; (haughty) надме́нный

log¹ /lɒg/ *n.* **1** (of wood) бревно́, чурба́н **2** (for fire) поле́но; he slept like a ~ он спал как уби́тый
■ ~ cabin *n.* (бреве́нчатая) хи́жина

log² /lɒg/ *n.* (*in full* ~book) ва́хтенный журна́л; (of aircraft) бортово́й журна́л; (of car) формуля́р
• *v.t.* (logged, logging) (record) зано́с|и́ть, -ести́ в ва́хтенный журна́л; ~ in/on (comput.) входи́ть, войти́ в систе́му; ~ out/off (comput.) выходи́ть, вы́йти из систе́мы
■ ~book *n.* = log² *n.*

loganberry /ˈləʊgənbərɪ/ *n.* лога́нова я́года (*гибрид малины с ежевикой*)

logarithm /ˈlɒgərɪð(ə)m/ *n.* логари́фм

loggerheads /ˈlɒgəhedz/ *n. pl.*: they are at ~ они́ в ссо́ре (*or* не в лада́х) друг с дру́гом

logic /ˈlɒdʒɪk/ *n.* ло́гика

logical /ˈlɒdʒɪk(ə)l/ *adj.* (based on logic, e.g. conclusion, explanation) логи́ческий; (reasonable, e.g. action) логи́чный

logistic /ləˈdʒɪstɪk/ *adj.* организацио́нный

logistical /ləˈdʒɪstɪk(ə)l/ *adj.* = logistic

logistics /ləˈdʒɪstɪks/ *n. pl.* организа́ция; (mil.) материа́льно-техни́ческое обеспе́чение

logo /ˈləʊgəʊ/ *n.* (*pl.* ~s) эмбле́ма

loin /lɔɪn/ *n.* (meat) филе́ (*nt. indecl.*) (*мясное*)

loiter /ˈlɔɪtə(r)/ *v.i.* ме́шкать (*impf.*)

loll /lɒl/ *v.i.* **1** (sit or stand in lazy attitude) сиде́ть/стоя́ть (*impf.*) развали́сь, **2** (of tongue etc.: hang loose) выва́ливаться (*impf.*)

lollipop /ˈlɒlɪpɒp/ *n.* ледене́ц на па́лочке

London /ˈlʌnd(ə)n/ *n.* Ло́ндон

lone /ləʊn/ *adj.* одино́кий, уединённый

lonely /ˈləʊnlɪ/ *adj.* (lonelier, loneliest) **1** (solitary, alone) одино́кий; lead a ~ existence вести́ (*det.*) одино́кий о́браз жи́зни **2** (isolated) уединённый

loner /ˈləʊnə(r)/ *n.* (infml) одино́чка (*c.g.*)

lonesome /ˈləʊnsəm/ *adj.* одино́кий

♂ **long¹** /lɒŋ/ *n.*: I shan't be away for ~ я уезжа́ю ненадо́лго; я ско́ро верну́сь; it won't take ~ э́то не займёт мно́го вре́мени
• *adj.* **1** (of space, measurement) дли́нный; the table is 2 metres ~ длина́ э́того стола́ — два ме́тра; how ~ is this river? какова́ длина́ э́той реки́? **2** (of distance) да́льний; a ~ journey да́льний/до́лгий путь **3** (of time) до́лгий; my holiday is 2 weeks ~ мой о́тпуск дли́тся две неде́ли; for a ~ time до́лго, давно́; надо́лго; a ~ time ago мно́го вре́мени тому́ наза́д; давны́м-давно́ **4** (prolonged) дли́тельный; a ~ illness затяжна́я боле́знь
• *adv.* **1** (a ~ time): I shan't be ~ я ско́ро верну́сь; я не задержу́сь; ~ after *prep.* до́лгое вре́мя по́сле + *g.*; ~ before *prep.* задо́лго до + *g.*; ~ ago (давны́м-)давно́; before ~ вско́ре, ско́ро; (for a ~ time): have you been here ~? вы здесь давно́?; ~ live the Queen! да здра́вствует короле́ва! **3** (throughout): all day ~ це́лый день; all night ~ всю ночь напролёт **4**: as ~ as I live пока́ я жив; stay as ~ as you like

оставайтесь, сколько хотите; **as ~ as you don't mind** если вам всё равно; если вы не возражаете **5**; **so ~!** (infml) пока! **6**; **no ~er** больше не; **she no ~er lives here** она больше здесь не живёт; **I can't wait much ~er** намного дольше ждать я не могу

■ **~-awaited** adj. долгожданный; **~-distance** adj.: **~-distance call** междугородный/международный вызов; **~-distance runner** бегун на длинные дистанции; **~-haired** adj. длинноволосый; **~ johns** n. pl. кальсон|ы (pl., g. —); **~ jump** n. прыжок в длину; **~-range** adj. (of gun) дальнобойный; (of forecast, policy, etc.) долгосрочный; **~-sighted** adj. дальнозоркий; **~-standing** adj. старинный, долголетний; **~-term** adj. долгосрочный; (of plans, etc.) перспективный; **~-winded** adj. многословный

long² /lɒŋ/ v.i.: **~ for sth** жаждать (impf.) чего-н.; **~ to do sth** мечтать (impf.) делать что-то

longevity /lɒnˈdʒevɪtɪ/ n. (of person) долголетие; (of thing) долговечность

longing /ˈlɒŋɪŋ/ n. (eager desire) жажда (**for:** + g.); (melancholy desire) тоска (**for:** по + d.)

longitude /ˈlɒŋɡɪtju:d/ n. долгота

loo /lu:/ n. (BrE, infml, lavatory) сортир (infml)

✎ **look** /lʊk/ n. **1** (glance) взгляд n. **2**: **have, take a ~ at** (examine) осм|атривать, -отреть; рассм|атривать, -отреть **3**: **have a ~ for** (search) иск|ать, по- **4** (expression) выражение; **there was a ~ of** horror on his face его лицо выражало ужас **5** (appearance) вид; **he has given the shop a new ~** он (полностью) преобразил магазин; (in pl.) (personal appearance) наружность, внешность
• v.t. **1** (inspect, scrutinize): **~ sb in the face, eye** смотреть, по- в глаза кому-н. **2** (have the appearance of) выглядеть (impf.) + i.; **he made me ~ a fool** он поставил меня в дурацкое положение; **he ~s his age** ему вполне дашь его годы; **she is thirty, but she does not ~ it** ей тридцать, но ей столько не дашь
• v.i. **1** (use one's eyes; pay attention) смотреть, по-; **he ~ed out of the window to see if she was coming** он посмотрел в окно, не идёт ли она; (search) искать, по- **2** (face) выходить (impf.); **the windows ~ on to the garden/street** окна выходят в сад/на улицу **3** (appear) выглядеть (impf.) + i.; **she is ~ing well** она хорошо выглядит; **everybody ~ed tired** у всех был усталый вид; **that ~s tasty** у этого блюда аппетитный вид; **things ~ black** плохо дело; **this ~s suspicious** это подозрительно; **~ like** (resemble) выглядеть (impf.) + i.; походить (impf.) на + a.; **he ~s like his father** он похож на отца; (give expectation of): **it ~s like rain** собирается (or похоже, что) будет дождь

□ **~ after** v.t. (care for, tend to) ухаживать (impf.) за + i.; (keep safe) хранить (impf.); (be responsible for) заниматься (impf.) + i.

□ **~ at** v.i. (direct gaze on) смотреть, по- на + a; **he was ~ing at a book** он смотрел на книгу; (inspect, examine) смотреть, по- на + a.; осм|атривать, -отреть; **the customs men ~ed**

at our luggage таможенники осмотрели наш багаж

□ **~ back** v.i.: **once started, there was no ~ing back** раз уж мы начали, отступать было поздно; **~ back on** вспоминать (impf.)

□ **~ down** v.i. (lower one's gaze) опус|кать, -тить глаза; **~ down on** смотреть (impf.) свысока на + a.; презирать (impf.)

□ **~ for** v.i. (seek) искать, по-; **he is ~ing for a job** он ищет место/работу

□ **~ forward** v.i.: **~ forward to** предвкушать (impf.); ждать (impf.) + g. с нетерпением; **I ~ forward to meeting you** жду с нетерпением, когда увижусь с вами

□ **~ in on** v.i. (visit) загля|дывать, -нуть к кому-н., забе|гать, -жать к кому-н.

□ **~ into** v.i. (investigate, examine) исследовать (impf.); рассм|атривать, -отреть

□ **~ on** v.i. (watch without getting involved) наблюдать, смотреть (both impf.); (regard) считать (impf.); **I ~ on him as my son** я считаю его своим сыном; **~ on to** (face) see ▸ **look** v.i. 2

□ **~ out** v.i. (be careful) быть начеку/настороже; **~ out!** осторожно!; (keep one's eyes open): **she stood at the door ~ing out for the postman** она стояла в дверях, высматривая почтальона; **we are ~ing out for a house** мы присматриваем дом

□ **~ round** v.i. (turn one's head) огля|дываться, -нуться; (make an inspection) осм|атриваться, -отреться; озираться (impf.); (inspect) осм|атривать, -отреть

□ **~ through** v.i.: **they ~ed through** (sc. examined) **our papers** они просмотрели наши бумаги; **he quickly ~ed through the newspaper** он быстро пробежал глазами газету

□ **~ to** v.i. (turn to) обра|щаться, -титься к + d.; **we ~ed to him for help** мы рассчитывали на его помощь

□ **~ up** v.t. (visit) наве|щать, -стить; (seek information on) отыск|ивать, -ать
• v.i. (raise one's eyes) подн|имать, -ять глаза (**at sb:** на кого-н.); (improve) ул|учшаться, -учшиться; **things are ~ing up** дела идут на поправку; **~ up to** (respect) уважать (impf.)

■ **~alike** n. двойник; **~-in** n. (BrE, infml) шанс, возможность; **~out** n. (post) наблюдательный пункт; (watch): **be on the ~out for** (e.g. a house) присматривать (impf.) себе

loom¹ /lu:m/ n. ткацкий станок

loom² /lu:m/ v.i. **1** (appear indistinctly) (also ~ **up**) неясно вырисовываться (impf.) **2** (impend) нав|исать, -иснуть

loop /lu:p/ n. (also comput.) петля

loophole /ˈlu:phəʊl/ n. (fig.) лазейка

loose /lu:s/ n.: **on the ~** в загуле; на свободе; на воле
• adj. **1** (free, unconfined) свободный; **break ~** вырваться (pf.) на свободу; **let ~** (e.g. a dog) спус|кать, -тить с цепи **2** (not fastened or held together): **~ papers** отдельные листы **3** (not secure or firm): **at a ~ end** (fig.) без дела; **I have a ~ tooth** у меня зуб шатается; **the nut is ~** гайка разболталась; **the button is ~** пуговица болтается **4** (slack) слабо натянутый; **~ clothes**

широ́кая/просто́рная оде́жда **5** (not compact or dense): ~ **weave** неплотная ткань **6** (imprecise): a ~ **translation** приблизи́тельный/во́льный перево́д **7** (morally lax) распу́щенный

loosen /'luːs(ə)n/ *v.t.* (tongue) развя́з|ывать, -а́ть; (screw) отви́н|чивать, -ти́ть; (by shaking or pulling) расша́т|ывать, -а́ть; (tie, rope, belt, etc.) осл|абля́ть, -а́бить

loot /luːt/ *n.* добы́ча
• *v.t.* гра́бить, раз-

looter /'luːtə(r)/ *n.* мароде́р, граби́тель (*m.*)

lopsided /lɒp'saɪdɪd/ *adj.* (grin) криво́й; (fig.) неравноме́рный, односторо́нний

loquacious /lə'kweɪʃəs/ *adj.* словоохо́тливый, болтли́вый

lord /lɔːd/ *n.* **1** (BrE, nobleman) лорд **2** (ruler, also fig.) власти́тель (*m.*); ~ **of the manor** владе́лец поме́стья **3** (God) Госпо́дь; **Our L**~ (Christ) Госпо́дь
• *v.t.:* ~ **it over sb** кома́ндовать (*impf.*) кем-н.

Lordship /'lɔːdʃɪp/ *n.:* **Your** ~ ва́ша све́тлость/ ми́лость

lorry /'lɒrɪ/ *n.* (BrE) грузови́к

✎ **los|e** /luːz/ *v.t.* (*past and p.p.* **lost**) **1** теря́ть, по-; ~**e patience** выходи́ть, вы́йти из терпе́ния; ~**e one's temper** серди́ться, рас-**2**: **be, get** ~**t** (~**e one's way**) заблуди́ться (*pf.*); **get** ~**t!** исче́зни!, кати́сь! (infml); (fig.): ~**t in thought** заду́мавшись **3** (in contest, sport, gambling) про́иг|рывать, -а́ть; **he** ~**t the argument** его́ победи́ли в спо́ре; **they** ~**t the match** они́ проигра́ли **4** (of a clock) отст|ава́ть, -а́ть на + *a.*
• *v.i.* **1** прои́гр|ывать, -а́ть; теря́ть, по-; ~**e out** (infml) потерпе́ть (*pf.*) неуда́чу **2** (of a clock): **my watch is** ~**ing** мои́ часы́ отстаю́т
■ ~**t property office** (BrE), ~**t and found department** (AmE) *nn.* бюро́ нахо́док

loser /'luːzə(r)/ *n.* (at a game) проигра́вший; (person who habitually fails) неуда́чник; **he is a good (bad)** ~ он (не) уме́ет досто́йно прои́грывать

✎ **loss** /lɒs/ *n.* **1** поте́ря **2** (monetary) убы́ток **3: I am at a** ~ **to answer** я затрудня́юсь отве́тить

lost /lɒst/ *past and p.p. of* ▶ **lose**

✎ **lot** /lɒt/ *n.* **1: draw** ~**s** тяну́ть (*impf.*) жре́бий; (fig., destiny) судьба́, уча́сть, до́ля **2** (plot of land) уча́сток **3** (in auction) лот **4: the** ~ (BrE, infml, everything) всё; **that's the** ~! вот и всё! **5** (**a** ~, ~**s**) (a large number, amount) мно́го; **a** ~ **of people** мно́го наро́ду; мно́гие; **I don't see a** ~ **of him nowadays** тепе́рь мы с ним ма́ло/ре́дко ви́димся; **there were** ~**s of apples left** оста́лась у́йма/ку́ча я́блок; **he plays a** ~ **of football** он мно́го игра́ет в футбо́л
• *adv.* (**a** ~) **1** (often) ча́сто; **we went to the theatre a** ~ мы ча́сто ходи́ли в теа́тр **2** (with comps.) (much) гора́здо, намно́го; **a** ~ **worse** гора́здо ху́же

lotion /'ləʊʃ(ə)n/ *n.* лосьо́н

lottery /'lɒtərɪ/ *n.* лотере́я

---

loud /laʊd/ *adj.* шу́мный; (fig.): ~ **colours** крича́щие кра́ски
• *adv.* гро́мко; out ~ вслух
■ ~**speaker** *n.* громкоговори́тель (*m.*), дина́мик

lounge /laʊndʒ/ *n.* (BrE, sitting room) гости́ная; (at airport) зал ожида́ния; (bar) бар пе́рвого кла́сса
• *v.i.:* ~ **about** (idly) безде́льничать (*impf.*)

lousy /'laʊzɪ/ *adj.* (**lousier, lousiest**) (infml) парши́вый, отврати́тельный

lout /laʊt/ *n.* хам

loutish /'laʊtɪʃ/ *adj.* ха́мский; неотёсанный

lovable /'lʌvəb(ə)l/ *adj.* ми́лый

✎ **love** /lʌv/ *n.* **1** любо́вь; **he sent you his** ~ он проси́л переда́ть вам серде́чный приве́т; **be in** ~ (**with sb**) быть влюблённым в кого́-н.; **fall in** ~ **with sb** влюб|ля́ться, -и́ться в кого́-н.; **make** ~ (have sexual intercourse) зан|има́ться, -я́ться любо́вью; (my) ~! (мой) ми́лый!; (моя́) ми́лая! **2** (zero score) ноль (*m.*)
• *v.t.* люби́ть (*impf.*); **I** ~ **the way he smiles** мне ужа́сно нра́вится, как он улыба́ется; **I** ~ **walking in the rain** я обожа́ю гуля́ть под дождём
■ ~ **affair** *n.* рома́н; (pej.) любо́вная связь

loveless /'lʌvlɪs/ *adj.* нелю́бящий, без любви́; ~ **marriage** брак без любви́

lovely /'lʌvlɪ/ *adj.* (**lovelier, loveliest**) (beautiful) краси́вый; (charming) преле́стный

lover /'lʌvə(r)/ *n.* **1** любо́вник (*in pl.*) влюблённые **2** (devotee) люби́тель *m.* (-ница)

loving /'lʌvɪŋ/ *adj.* лю́бящий; (tender) не́жный

✎ **low** /ləʊ/ *n.* **1** (meteor.) цикло́н **2** (~ point or level): **the pound fell to an all-time** ~ фунт дости́г небыва́ло ни́зкого у́ровня
• *adj.* **1** ни́зкий, невысо́кий; (of pitch of sound) ни́зкий; (of volume of sound) негро́мкий, ти́хий; **he spoke in a** ~ **voice** он говори́л, пони́зив го́лос (*or* ти́хим го́лосом); **keep a** ~ **profile** вести́ себя́ сде́ржанно **2** (base) ни́зкий, по́длый; **a** ~ **trick** по́длая уло́вка **3** (nearly empty; scanty): **a** ~ **attendance** ни́зкая/плоха́я посеща́емость; **we are getting** ~ **on sugar** у нас остаётся малова́то са́хара **4** (depressed): **I was feeling** ~ мне бы́ло невесело
• *adv.* ни́зко
■ ~**-alcohol** *adj.* слабоалкого́льный; ~**brow** *adj.* неразвито́й; ~**-calorie** *adj.* малокалори́йный; ~**-carb** *adj.* низкоуглево́дный; ~**-carbon** *adj.* низкоуглеро́дистый; ~**-cut** *adj.* с ни́зким/ глубо́ким вы́резом; ~**-down** *n.* (information) подного́тная (infml) • *adj.* по́длый, скве́рный; ~**-fat** *adj.* маложи́рный; ~**-key** *adj.* (fig.) сде́ржанный; ~**-land** *n.* (*usu. in pl.*) ни́зменность; ~**-lying** *adj.* ни́зменный; ~**-paid** *adj.* малооплачиваемый; ~**-tide** (also ~ **water**) *n.* ма́лая вода́, отли́в

lower /'ləʊə(r)/ *adj.* ни́жний
• *v.t.* **1** (e.g. boat, flag) спус|ка́ть, -ти́ть; (eyes) опус|ка́ть, -ти́ть; (price) сни|жа́ть, -и́зить; (voice) пони|жа́ть, -и́зить **2** (decrease) ум|еньша́ть,

-е́ньшить **3** (debase) ун|ижа́ть, -и́зить

lowly /'ləʊlɪ/ adj. (**lowlier, lowliest**) (humble) скро́мный; (primitive) ни́зший

loyal /'lɔɪəl/ adj. (faithful) ве́рный; (devoted) пре́данный; (pol.) лоя́льный

loyalist /'lɔɪəlɪst/ n. лояли́ст (-ка)

loyalty /'lɔɪəltɪ/ n. ве́рность, пре́данность, лоя́льность

lozenge /'lɒzɪndʒ/ n. табле́тка(-ледене́ц)

LP abbr. (of **long-playing record**) долгоигра́ющая пласти́нка

LSD abbr. of (chem.) (**lysergic acid diethylamide**) ЛСД (диэтилами́д лизерги́новой кислоты́)

Ltd /'lɪmɪtɪd/ abbr. (of **limited liability company**) (BrE, comm.) ООО (о́бщество с ограни́ченной отве́тственностью)

lubricate /'lu:brɪkeɪt/ v.t. сма́з|ывать, -ать

lubrication /lu:brɪ'keɪʃ(ə)n/ n. сма́зывание

lucid /'lu:sɪd/ adj. я́сный

lucidity /lu:'sɪdɪtɪ/ n. я́сность

luck /lʌk/ n.: good/bad ~ сча́стье/несча́стье; good ~!; the best of ~! жела́ю сча́стья/ уда́чи/успе́ха!; bad, hard ~! не повезло́!

luckily /'lʌkɪlɪ/ adv. к сча́стью

lucky /'lʌkɪ/ adj. (**luckier, luckiest**) **1** (of person) счастли́вый, уда́чливый; (of things, actions, events) уда́чный; you're ~ to be alive скажи́ спаси́бо, что оста́лся в живы́х **2** (bringing luck): a ~ charm счастли́вый талисма́н

lucrative /'lu:krətɪv/ adj. при́быльный

lucre /'lu:kə(r)/ n. при́быль, нажи́ва; filthy ~ презре́нный мета́лл

ludicrous /'lu:dɪkrəs/ adj. смехотво́рный

lug /lʌg/ v.t. (**lugged, lugging**) (infml) тащи́ть (impf.)

luggage /'lʌgɪdʒ/ n. бага́ж
■ ~ **rack** n. (on train, bus) се́тка/по́лка для багажа́

lugubrious /lʊ'gu:brɪəs/ adj. (mournful) скро́бный; (dismal) мра́чный

lukewarm /lu:k'wɔ:m/ adj. теплова́тый

lull /lʌl/ n. (in storm, fighting, etc.) зати́шье; (in conversation) па́уза, переры́в
• v.t. (~ to sleep) убаю́к|ивать, -ать; ~ sb into a false sense of security усып|ля́ть, -и́ть чью-н. бди́тельность

lullaby /'lʌləbaɪ/ n. колыбе́льная (пе́сня)

lumbar /'lʌmbə(r)/ adj. поясни́чный

lumber¹ /'lʌmbə(r)/ n. (AmE, timber) пиломатериа́лы (m. pl.)
• v.t. (BrE, encumber) обременя́ть (impf.); I'm ~ed with my mother-in-law тёща сиди́т у меня́ на ше́е
■ ~jack n. лесору́б

lumber² /'lʌmbə(r)/ v.i. (also ~ along) дви́гаться (impf.) тяжело́

luminary /'lu:mɪnərɪ/ n. свети́ло

luminous /'lu:mɪnəs/ adj. светя́щийся

lump /lʌmp/ n. **1** (of earth, dough, etc.) ком; ~ of sugar кусо́к са́хара; ~ in the throat комо́к в го́рле **2** (swelling) ши́шка, о́пухоль
• v.t.: ~ together (treat alike) ста́вить (impf.)

■ ~ **sum** n. единовре́менно выпла́чиваемая су́мма

lumpectomy /lʌm'pektəmɪ/ n. (med.) удале́ние о́пухоли моло́чной железы́

lumpy /'lʌmpɪ/ adj. (**lumpier, lumpiest**) комкова́тый

lunacy /'lu:nəsɪ/ n. безу́мие

lunar /'lu:nə(r)/ adj. лу́нный

lunatic /'lu:nətɪk/ n. сумасше́дший

lunch /lʌntʃ/ n. обе́д
• v.i. обе́дать, по-
■ ~ **break**, ~ **hour**, ~**time** nn. обе́денный переры́в

lung /lʌŋ/ n. лёгкое

lunge /lʌndʒ/ v.i. (**lungeing** or **lunging**) бро́ситься (pf.) (forward: вперёд; at: на + a.)

lupin /'lu:pɪn/ n. люпи́н

lurch¹ /lɜ:tʃ/ n.: leave sb in the ~ пок|ида́ть, -и́нуть кого́-н. в беде́

lurch² /lɜ:tʃ/ v.i. шата́ться (impf.); the drunken man ~ed across the street пья́ный, пошатываясь, перешёл у́лицу

lure /ljʊə(r)/ n. (decoy) прима́нка; (fig., enticement) собла́зн; the ~ of foreign travel зама́нчивость заграни́чных путеше́ствий
• v.t. (persons) зама́н|ивать, -и́ть; a rival firm ~d him away конкури́рующая фи́рма перемани́ла его́ (к себе́)

lurid /'ljʊərɪd/ adj. (gaudy) крича́щий; (sensational) сенсацио́нный; ~ details жу́ткие подро́бности

lurk /lɜ:k/ v.i. прита́|иваться, -и́ться

luscious /'lʌʃəs/ adj. (succulent) со́чный

lush /lʌʃ/ adj. пы́шный, роско́шный

lust /lʌst/ n. **1** (sexual passion) по́хоть **2** (craving): ~ for power жа́жда вла́сти
• v.i.: ~ for, after sb испы́т|ывать, -а́ть вожделе́ние к кому́-н.

luster /'lʌstə(r)/ n. (AmE) = lustre

lustful /'lʌstfʊl/ adj. похотли́вый

lustre /'lʌstə(r)/ (AmE **luster**) n. блеск

lustrous /'lʌstrəs/ adj. (brilliant) блестя́щий; (glossy) глянцеви́тый

lusty /'lʌstɪ/ adj. (**lustier, lustiest**) (healthy) здоро́вый; (vigorous) бо́дрый

lute /lu:t/ n. (mus.) лю́тня

Luxembourg /'lʌksəmbɜ:g/ n. Люксембу́рг
• adj. люксембу́ргский

Luxembourger /'lʌksəmbɜ:gə(r)/ n. люксембу́рж|ец (-енка)

luxuriance /lʌg'zjʊərɪəns/ n. изоби́лие; пы́шность

luxuriant /lʌg'zjʊərɪənt/ adj. (of growth) бу́йный

luxuriate /lʌg'zjʊərɪeɪt/ v.i. (enjoy oneself): ~ in sth наслажда́ться (impf.) чем-н.

luxurious /lʌg'zjʊərɪəs/ adj. роско́шный

luxury /'lʌkʃərɪ/ n. **1** (luxuriousness) ро́скошь **2** (object of ~) предме́т ро́скоши; ~ apartment роско́шная кварти́ра

lying /'laɪŋ/ n. (telling lies) ложь
• adj. лжи́вый

lymph /lɪmf/ *n.* (physiol.) ли́мфа
■ ~ **gland/node** *nn.* лимфати́ческий у́зел
lynch /lɪntʃ/ *v.t.* линчева́ть (*impf., pf.*)
lynchpin /'lɪntʃpɪn/ *n.* = linchpin
lyre /'laɪə(r)/ *n.* ли́ра
■ ~**bird** *n.* пти́ца-ли́ра, лирохво́ст

lyric /'lɪrɪk/ *n.* (*usu. in pl.*) (words of song) слова́ (*nt. pl.*), текст
lyrical /'lɪrɪk(ə)l/ *adj.* лири́ческий; **he waxed** ~ **about, over ...** он расчу́вствовался, говоря́ о...
lyricist /'lɪrɪsɪst/ *n.* а́втор слов/те́кста (*песни/ мюзикла*)

Mm

m /'miːtə(r)(z)/ *n.* (*abbr. of* **metre(s)**) м (метр)
m|- *pref.* моби́льный; ~**-commerce** моби́льная комме́рция
MA *abbr.* (*of* **Master of Arts**) маги́стр гуманита́рных нау́к
mac /mæk/ *n.* (BrE, infml) = mackintosh
macabre /mə'kɑːbr(ə)/ *adj.* мра́чный
macaroni /mækə'rəʊnɪ/ *n.* макаро́н|ы (*pl., g.* —)
Macedonia /mæsə'dəʊnɪə/ *n.* Македо́ния
Macedonian /mæsɪ'dəʊnɪən/ *n.* македо́н|ец (-ка)
● *adj.* македо́нский
machination /mækɪ'neɪʃ(ə)n/ *n.* (*usu. in pl.*) махина́ция; ко́зни (*f. pl.*); интри́га
♂ **machine** /mə'ʃiːn/ *n.* маши́на, механи́зм
■ ~ **gun** *n.* пулемёт; ~**-readable** *adj.* (comput.) машиночита́емый
machinery /mə'ʃiːnərɪ/ *n.* (*collect.*) (machines) маши́ны (*f. pl.*); (fig.): **the** ~ **of government** прави́тельственные структу́ры (*f. pl.*)
machinist /mə'ʃiːnɪst/ *n.* машини́ст; (BrE, sewing machine operator) швё́йник (швея́)
macho /'mætʃəʊ/ *adj.* мужско́й, мужи́цкий; му́жественный
macintosh *see* ▶ mackintosh
mackerel /'mækr(ə)l/ *n.* (*pl.* ~ *or* ~**s**) ску́мбрия
mackintosh, macintosh /'mækɪntɒʃ/ *n.* (BrE) дождеви́к (*плащ*)
macro /'mækrəʊ/ *n.* (*pl.* ~**s**) (comput.) макрокома́нда
macrocosm /'mækrəʊkɒz(ə)m/ *n.* макрокосм(ос)
mad /mæd/ *adj.* (**madder, maddest**)
1 (insane) сумасше́дший; **go** ~ сходи́ть, сойти́ с ума́; **drive sb** ~ сво|ди́ть, -ести́ кого́-н. с ума́ **2** (of animals) бе́шеный **3** (wildly foolish) шально́й; ~**ly in love** безу́мно влюблённый **4** (infml, angry) серди́тый; **be, get** ~ вы́йти (*pf.*) из себя́; **she was** ~ **with me for breaking the vase** она́ разозли́лась на меня́ за то, что я разби́л ва́зу **5**: ~ **about**

(infatuated with, enthusiastic for) в восто́рге (*or* без па́мяти) от + *g.*
■ ~ **cow disease** *n.* коро́вье бе́шенство; ~**man** *n.* сумасше́дший
Madagascar /mædə'gæskə(r)/ *n.* Мадагаска́р
madam /'mædəm/ *n.* (form of address) мада́м, госпожа́
maddening /'mædənɪŋ/ *adj.* несно́сный
made /meɪd/ *past and p.p. of* ▶ make
■ ~**-to-measure** *adj.* сде́ланный (как) на зака́з
Madeira /mə'dɪərə/ *n.* Маде́йра; (wine) маде́ра
madness /'mædnɪs/ *n.* (insanity) сумасше́ствие; (folly) безу́мие
Madrid /mə'drɪd/ *n.* Мадри́д
madrigal /'mædrɪg(ə)l/ *n.* мадрига́л
maestr|o /'maɪstrəʊ/ *n.* ~**i** *or* ~**os** маэ́стро (*m. indecl.*)
Mafia /'mæfɪə/ *n.* ма́фия
magazine[1] /mægə'ziːn/ *n.* (cartridge chamber) магази́н (*автома́та*)
♂ **magazine**[2] /mægə'ziːn/ *n.* (periodical) журна́л
magenta /mə'dʒentə/ *n. & adj.* красновато-лило́вый/пурпу́рный цвет
maggot /'mægət/ *n.* личи́нка
magic /'mædʒɪk/ *n.* (lit., fig.) ма́гия, волшебство́
● *adj.* волше́бный, маги́ческий
magical /'mædʒɪk(ə)l/ *adj.* волше́бный
magician /mə'dʒɪʃ(ə)n/ *n.* (sorcerer) волше́бник; (conjurer) фо́кусник
magisterial /mædʒɪ'stɪərɪəl/ *adj.* (of a magistrate) суде́йский; (authoritative) авторите́тный
magistrate /'mædʒɪstrət/ *n.* мирово́й судья́ (*m.*)
magnanimous /mæg'nænɪməs/ *adj.* великоду́шный
magnate /'mægneɪt/ *n.* магна́т
magnesium /mæg'niːzɪəm/ *n.* ма́гний
magnet /'mægnɪt/ *n.* (lit., fig.) магни́т
magnetic /mæg'netɪk/ *adj.* магни́тный
magnetism /'mægnɪtɪz(ə)m/ *n.* магнети́зм
magnetize /'mægnɪtaɪz/ *v.t.* намагни́|чивать, -тить; (fig.) гипнотизи́ровать, за-

magnification /ˌmægnɪfɪˈkeɪʃ(ə)n/ *n.*
увеличе́ние; (of a radio signal) усиле́ние;
(exaggeration) преувеличе́ние

magnificence /mægˈnɪfɪs(ə)ns/ *n.*
великоле́пие

magnificent /mægˈnɪfɪs(ə)nt/ *adj.*
великоле́пный

magnify /ˈmægnɪfaɪ/ *v.t.* увели́чи|вать, -ть
■ ~**ing glass** *n.* увеличи́тельное стекло́, лу́па

magnitude /ˈmægnɪtjuːd/ *n.* (size) величина́;
(importance) ва́жность

magnolia /mægˈnəʊlɪə/ *n.* **1** (tree) магно́лия
2 (colour) кре́мовый цвет

magpie /ˈmægpaɪ/ *n.* соро́ка

mahogany /məˈhɒɡənɪ/ *n.* (wood, tree)
кра́сное де́рево

maid /meɪd/ *n.* (domestic servant) прислу́га; (in
hotel) го́рничная
■ ~**servant** *n.* прислу́га, служа́нка

maiden /ˈmeɪd(ə)n/ *n.* де́ва
● *adj.* **1** (of a girl) де́вичий **2** (first): ~
speech пе́рвая речь (новоизбранного чле́на
парла́мента); ~ **voyage** пе́рвый рейс
■ ~ **name** *n.* де́вичья фами́лия

mail /meɪl/ *n.* **1** (postal system) по́чта **2** (letters)
по́чта, пи́сьма (*nt. pl.*)
● *v.t.* отпр|авля́ть, -а́вить (по по́чте); **the firm
has me on its** ~**ing list** я состою́ в спи́ске
подпи́счиков фи́рмы
■ ~**box** *n.* (AmE, also comput.) почто́вый я́щик;
~**man** *n.* (AmE) почтальо́н; ~ **order** *n.*
почто́вый зака́з; ~**-order** *adj.* торгу́ющий по
почто́вым зака́зам; ~**shot** *n.* (BrE) рекла́мная
рассы́лка

maim /meɪm/ *v.t.* кале́чить, ис-

main /meɪn/ *n.* (in sg. and (BrE) in pl.)
(principal supply line) магистра́ль; (sewerage)
канализа́ция; (water) водопрово́д,
водопрово́дная магистра́ль; (gas)
газопрово́д; (electricity) ка́бель (*m.*)
● *adj.* гла́вный, основно́й; ~ **street** гла́вная
у́лица
■ ~ **course** *n.* (of meal) основно́е блю́до;
~**land** *n.* (continent) матери́к; (opp. island): **they
live on the** ~**land** они́ живу́т на большо́й
земле́; ~ **line** *n.* (rail.) железнодоро́жная
магистра́ль; ~ **road** *n.* магистра́ль, гла́вная
доро́га; ~**stream** *n.* (fig.) госпо́дствующая
тенде́нция

mainframe /ˈmeɪnfreɪm/ *adj.*: ~ **computer**
больша́я ЭВМ

mainly /ˈmeɪnlɪ/ *adv.* гла́вным о́бразом

maintain /meɪnˈteɪn/ *v.t.* **1** (keep up)
подде́рживать (*impf.*); (preserve) сохран|я́ть,
-и́ть **2** (support) содержа́ть (*impf.*); **he has
a wife and child to** ~ ему́ прихо́дится
содержа́ть жену́ и ребёнка **3** (keep in
repair) обслу́живать (*impf.*) **4** (assert as true)
утвержда́ть (*impf.*); **he** ~**ed his innocence** он
наста́ивал на свое́й невино́вности

maintenance /ˈmeɪntənəns/ *n.* **1** (maintaining)
подде́ржка **2** (of dependants) содержа́ние
3 (of machinery etc.) (техни́ческое)
обслу́живание

maisonette /ˌmeɪzəˈnet/ *n.* двухэта́жная
кварти́ра

maize /meɪz/ *n.* кукуру́за, ма́ис

majestic /məˈdʒestɪk/ *adj.* вели́чественный

majesty /ˈmædʒɪstɪ/ *n.* (stateliness)
вели́чественность; (title): **His/Her M**~ Его́/Её
Вели́чество

major /ˈmeɪdʒə(r)/ *n.* **1** (rank) майо́р **2** (mus.)
мажо́р; **C** ~ до мажо́р **3** (AmE, main subject of
study) основно́й предме́т (*в колле́дже*)
● *adj.* **1** (greater) бо́льший; (principal, more
important) гла́вный; ~ **road** гла́вная доро́га
2 (significant) кру́пный; **a** ~ **operation**
кру́пная опера́ция **3** (mus.) мажо́рный; ~
key мажо́рная тона́льность
● *v.i.*: **he** ~**ed in physics** (AmE) он
специализи́ровался по фи́зике

Majorca /məˈjɔːkə/ *n.* Майо́рка

majority /məˈdʒɒrɪtɪ/ *n.* большинство́;
бо́льшая часть; (in elections etc.): **the
government have a** ~ **of 60** у прави́тельства —
большинство́ в 60 голосо́в

make /meɪk/ *n.* (brand): **a good** ~ **of car**
автомоби́ль хоро́шей ма́рки
● *v.t.* (*past and p.p.* **made**) **1** (create, construct)
де́лать, с-; (build) стро́ить, по-; **what is this
made of?** из чего́ э́то сде́лано? **2** (sew) шить,
с-; **a suit made to order** костю́м, сши́тый на
зака́з **3** (manufacture) изгот|а́вливать, -о́вить;
произв|оди́ть, -ести́; **the factory** ~**s shoes**
фа́брика произво́дит о́бувь **4** (prepare)
гото́вить, при-; вари́ть, с-; **she made breakfast**
она́ пригото́вила за́втрак; ~ **a bed** (prepare it for
sleeping) стели́ть, по- посте́ль; (tidy it after use)
уб|ира́ть, -ра́ть посте́ль **5** (equal) равня́ться
(*impf.*) + *d.*; **four plus two** ~**s six** четы́ре
плюс два равня́ется шести́; (constitute): **it** ~**s
sense** э́то разу́мно **6** (understand) пон|има́ть,
-я́ть; **what do you** ~ **of this sentence?** как
вы понима́ете э́то предложе́ние?; (estimate):
what do you ~ **the time?** кото́рый час на
ва́ших часа́х? **7** (reach) дост|ига́ть, -и́чь + *g.*;
he made it (*sc. succeeded*) **after three years**
он дости́г успе́ха че́рез три го́да; (earn)
зараб|а́тывать, -о́тать; **he** ~**s a good living** он
хорошо́ зараба́тывает **8** (cause to be) де́лать,
с- + *a. and i.*; **the rain** ~**s the road slippery**
от дождя́ доро́га стано́вится ско́льзкой;
~ **sb angry** серди́ть, рас- кого́-н.; (appoint,
elect): **they made him chairman** его́ вы́брали
председа́телем **9** (compel, cause to) заст|авля́ть,
-а́вить; **I'll** ~ **you pay for this!** вы у меня́ за э́то
заплати́те!; **don't** ~ **me laugh!** не смеши́те
меня́!; ~ **do with/without sth** об|ходи́ться,
-ойти́сь чем-н./без чего́-н.
● *v.i.* (*past and p.p.* **made**) (with ceratin
preps.: move, proceed): ~ **after** пус|ка́ться,
-ти́ться вслед за + *i.*; ~ **for** (head towards)
напр|авля́ться, -а́виться на + *a. or* к + *d.*
□ ~ **off** *v.i.* (hurry away) сбе|га́ть, -жа́ть
□ ~ **out** *v.t.* (write out): ~ **out a bill/cheque**
выпи́сывать, вы́писать счёт/чек; (assert)
утвержда́ть (*impf.*); **they** ~ **out he was drunk**
они́ утвержда́ют, что он был пьян; (understand)
раз|бира́ться, -обра́ться в + *p.*; **I can't** ~ **him
out** я не могу́ его́ поня́ть; (discern, distinguish)

m

различ|а́ть, -и́ть

□ ~ **up** v.t. (pay; pay the residue of) допла́|чивать, -ти́ть; **I shall** ~ **up the difference out of my own pocket** я доплачу́ ра́зницу из своего́ карма́на; (repay) возме|ща́ть, -сти́ть; **we must** ~ **it up to him somehow** мы должны́ ка́к-то возмести́ть ему́ э́то; (prepare) гото́вить, при-/из-; ~ **up a bed** заст|ила́ть, -ели́ть посте́ль; (fig.): ~ **up one's mind** реш|а́ть, -и́ть; (form, compose) сост|авля́ть, -а́вить; **life is made up of disappointments** жизнь полна́ разочарова́ний; (invent) выду́мывать, вы́думать; сочин|я́ть, -и́ть; **the whole story was made up** вся э́та исто́рия была́ вы́думана; (assemble) соб|ира́ть, -ра́ть; ~ **(it) up** (be reconciled) мири́ться, по-; (with cosmetics) кра́сить, по-; **she was heavily made up** она́ была́ си́льно накра́шена

□ ~ **up for** (compensate for) возме|ща́ть, -сти́ть; **this will** ~ **up for everything** э́тим всё бу́дет компенси́ровано

■ ~-**believe** n.: **he lives in a world of** ~-**believe** он живёт в ми́ре грёз; ~**shift** adj.: **a** ~**shift shelter** на́скоро сколо́ченное укры́тие; ~-**up** n. (composition): **there is some cowardice in his** ~-**up** он не́сколько трусова́т; (cosmetics) макия́ж, косме́тика; (theatr., etc.) грим; ~-**up artist** n. визажи́ст; ~-**up room** n. гримёрная

maker /'meɪkə(r)/ n. производи́тель (m.)

making /'meɪkɪŋ/ n. **1** (in pl.) (potential qualities): **he has all the** ~**s of a general** у него́ есть все зада́тки, что́бы стать генера́лом **2** (creation) созда́ние; **the difficulties were not of my** ~ э́ти тру́дности возни́кли не из-за меня́; (manufacture, production) изготовле́ние, произво́дство; (preparation) приготовле́ние

malachite /'mæləkaɪt/ n. малахи́т; (attr.) малахи́товый

maladjusted /ˌmælə'dʒʌstɪd/ adj. (fig., of person) пло́хо приспосо́бленный

malady /'mælədɪ/ n. (lit., fig.) неду́г, боле́знь

malaise /mə'leɪz/ n. (bodily discomfort) недомога́ние; (disquiet) беспоко́йство

malaria /mə'leərɪə/ n. маляри́я

Malay /mə'leɪ/ n. & adj. = Malayan

Malaya /mə'leɪə/ n. Мала́йя

Malayan /mə'leɪən/ n. (person) мала́|ец (-йка); (language) мала́йский язы́к
● adj. мала́йский

Malaysia /mə'leɪʒə/ n. Мала́йзия

Malaysian /mə'leɪʒ(ə)n/ adj. малайзи́йский
● n. малайзи́|ец (-йка)

malcontent /'mælkəntent/ n. & adj. недово́льный

♂ **male** /meɪl/ n. (person) мужчи́на (m.); (animal etc.) саме́ц
● adj. мужско́й; ~ **pigeon** го́лубь-саме́ц

malevolence /mə'levələns/ n. недоброжела́тельство, злора́дство

malevolent /mə'levələnt/ adj. недоброжела́тельный, злора́дный

malformation /ˌmælfɔː'meɪʃ(ə)n/ n. непра́вильное образова́ние, поро́к разви́тия;

уро́дство

malformed /mæl'fɔːmd/ adj. непра́вильно/ пло́хо сформиро́ванный

malfunction /mæl'fʌŋkʃ(ə)n/ n. неиспра́вная рабо́та, отка́з
● v.i. неиспра́вно де́йствовать (impf.)

malice /'mælɪs/ n. зло́ба; **I bear you no** ~ я не пита́ю к вам зло́бы

malicious /mə'lɪʃəs/ adj. (of person) злой; (of thought, act, etc.) зло́бный

malign /mə'laɪn/ v.t. клевета́ть, о- (кого), на- (на кого); **he** ~**ed me** он оклевета́л меня́, он наклевета́л на меня́

malignant /mə'lɪgnənt/ adj. злой, зло́бный; (med.) злока́чественный

malinger /mə'lɪŋgə(r)/ v.i. симули́ровать (impf., pf.) боле́знь

malingerer /mə'lɪŋgərə(r)/ n. симуля́нт (-ка)

mall /mæl/ n. торго́вый центр

mallard /'mælɑːd/ n. (pl. ~ or ~s) кря́ква

malleable /'mælɪəb(ə)l/ adj. пода́тливый

mallet /'mælɪt/ n. деревя́нный молото́к

malnutrition /ˌmælnjuː'trɪʃ(ə)n/ n. недоеда́ние

malpractice /mæl'præktɪs/ n. (of doctor) престу́пная небре́жность (врача́); (law, abuse of trust) злоупотребле́ние дове́рием

Malta /'mɔːltə/ n. Ма́льта

Maltese /mɔːl'tiːz/ n. (pl. ~) (person) мальти́|ец (-йка); (language) мальти́йский язы́к
● adj. мальти́йский

maltreat /mæl'triːt/ v.t. ду́рно обраща́ться (impf.) с + i.

maltreatment /mæl'triːtmənt/ n. дурно́е обраще́ние (с кем)

mammal /'mæm(ə)l/ n. млекопита́ющее (живо́тное)

mammogram /'mæməgræm/ n. маммогра́мма

mammoth /'mæməθ/ n. ма́монт
● adj. (huge) гига́нтский, грома́дный

♂ **man** /mæn/ n. (pl. **men**) **1** (adult male) мужчи́на (m.); **they talked** ~ **to** ~ они́ говори́ли как мужчи́на с мужчи́ной; **old** ~ стари́к **2** (mankind) челове́к, челове́чество **3** (person) челове́к (лю́ди) **4** (husband) муж **5** (piece in chess) ша́хматная фигу́ра; (in draughts) ша́шка
● v.t. (**manned**, **manning**) **1** (a post) зан|има́ть, -я́ть **2** (guns, machines) обслу́живать (impf.)

■ ~**hole** n. люк; ~-**made** adj. иску́сственный; (text.) синтети́ческий; ~**power** n. рабо́чая си́ла

♂ **manage** /'mænɪdʒ/ v.t. **1** (control, conduct) управля́ть, руководи́ть, заве́довать (all impf. + i.); **they** ~**ed the business between them** они́ вдвоём управля́ли предприя́тием **2** (handle) владе́ть (impf.) + i.; **I can't** ~ **it** э́то мне не по си́лам **3** (be ~er of): **he has** ~**ed the team for 10 years** он руководи́л кома́ндой в тече́ние десяти́

♂ ключева́я ле́ксика

лет; **the singer was looking for someone to ~e him** певец подыскивал себе импрессарио **4** (cope with) спр|авля́ться, -а́виться с + i.; **I can't ~e this work** я не спра́влюсь с э́той рабо́той **5** (contrive) суме́ть (pf.); **I ~ed to convince him** мне удало́сь убеди́ть его́
• v.i. (cope) спр|авля́ться, -а́виться; (get by, make do) об|ходи́ться, -ойти́сь
■ **~ing director** n. дире́ктор-распоряди́тель (m.)

manageable /'mænɪdʒəb(ə)l/ adj. выполни́мый

ℱ **management** /'mænɪdʒmənt/ n. **1** (control, controlling) управле́ние (чем), ме́неджмент **2** (handling person or thing) обраще́ние; **staff ~** обраще́ние с ли́чным соста́вом **3** (managers) администра́ция, дире́кция

ℱ **manager** /'mænɪdʒə(r)/ n. (controller of business etc.) заве́дующий (чем); (sport) ста́рший тре́нер; (of sb's career) ме́неджер

manageress /mænɪdʒə'res/ n. заве́дующая (чем)

managerial /mænɪ'dʒɪərɪəl/ adj. администрати́вный; управле́нческий

mandarin /'mændərɪn/ n. (orange) мандари́н

mandate /'mændeɪt/ n. (official order) манда́т; (given by voters) нака́з

mandatory /'mændətərɪ/ adj. обяза́тельный

mandolin /mændə'lɪn/ n. мандоли́на

mane /meɪn/ n. гри́ва

maneuver /mə'nu:və(r)/ n., v.t., & v.i. (AmE) = manoeuvre

manful /'mænfʊl/ adj. му́жественный

manger /'meɪndʒə(r)/ n. я́сли pl (-ей)

mangle /'mæŋg(ə)l/ v.t. (mutilate) уро́довать, из-

mango /'mæŋgəʊ/ n. (pl. ~es or ~s) ма́нго (nt. indecl.)

mangy /'meɪndʒɪ/ adj. (**mangier**, **mangiest**) парши́вый, шелуди́вый (infml)

manhandle /'mænhænd(ə)l/ v.t. (move by manual effort) та|ска́ть (indet.), -щи́ть (det.) (вручну́ю); (treat roughly) изб|ива́ть, -и́ть

mania /'meɪnɪə/ n. ма́ния

maniac /'meɪnɪæk/ n. манья́к

manic /'mænɪk/ n. безу́мный

manicure /'mænɪkjʊə(r)/ n. маникю́р
• v.t. де́лать, с- маникю́р + d.

manicurist /'mænɪkjʊərɪst/ n. (female) маникю́рша

manifest /'mænɪfest/ adj. я́вный, очеви́дный
• v.t. (show clearly) я́сно пока́з|ывать, -а́ть; (exhibit) проявля́ть, -и́ть

manifestation /mænɪfe'steɪʃ(ə)n/ n. проявле́ние

manifesto /mænɪ'festəʊ/ n. (pl. ~s) манифе́ст

manifold /'mænɪfəʊld/ adj. (numerous) многочи́сленный; (various) разнообра́зный

manikin /'mænɪkɪn/ n. (very small person) челове́чек; (artist's dummy) манеке́н

Manila /mə'nɪlə/ n. Мани́ла
• adj. мани́льский
■ **~ paper** n. мани́льская бума́га

manipulate /mə'nɪpjʊleɪt/ v.t. (lit., fig., also pej.) манипули́ровать (impf.) (+ i.)

manipulation /mənɪpjʊ'leɪʃ(ə)n/ n. манипуля́ция

manipulative /mə'nɪpjʊlətɪv/ adj. (person) жуликова́тый (infml); (behaviour, practice) жу́льнический (infml)

mankind /mæn'kaɪnd/ n. челове́чество

manliness /'mænlɪnɪs/ n. му́жественность

manly /'mænlɪ/ adj. (**manlier**, **manliest**) подоба́ющий мужчи́не

mannequin /'mænɪkɪn/ n. (person) манеке́нщица; (dummy) манеке́н

ℱ **manner** /'mænə(r)/ n. **1** (way, fashion, mode) о́браз; **in a ~ of speaking** в не́котором смы́сле **2** (in pl.) (ways of life; customs) обы́чаи (m. pl.) **3** (style of behaviour) мане́ра; **he has an awkward ~** он де́ржится нело́вко **4** (in pl.) (behaviour) мане́ры (f. pl.); **good, bad ~s** хоро́шие/плохи́е мане́ры; (polite behaviour): **have you no ~s?** как ты себя́ веде́шь?

mannered /'mænəd/ adj. (affected) мане́рный

mannerism /'mænərɪz(ə)m/ n. (affected habitual gesture etc.) мане́ра; (excessive use of these) мане́рность

manoeuvrable /mə'nu:vrəb(ə)l/ (AmE **maneuverable**) adj. манёвренный, подвижно́й

manoeuvre /mə'nu:və(r)/ (AmE **maneuver**) n. манёвр
• v.t. маневри́ровать (impf.) + i.; **I ~d him to his chair** мне удало́сь подвести́ его́ к сту́лу
• v.i. (lit., fig.) маневри́ровать (impf.)

manor /'mænə(r)/ n. (estate) поме́стье; (~ house) особня́к

mansion /'mænʃ(ə)n/ n. особня́к

manslaughter /'mænslɔ:tə(r)/ n. непредумы́шленное уби́йство

mantel /'mænt(ə)l/, **mantelpiece** /'mænt(ə)lpi:s/ nn. ками́нная по́лка

mantra /'mæntrə/ n. ма́нтра

manual /'mænjʊəl/ n. (handbook) посо́бие
• adj. (operated by hand) ручно́й
■ **~ labour** n. физи́ческий труд

manufacture /mænjʊ'fæktʃə(r)/ n. изготовле́ние; (on large scale) произво́дство
• v.t. изгот|а́вливать, -о́вить; произв|оди́ть, -ести́; **~ed goods** промтова́ры (m. pl.)

ℱ **manufacturer** /mænjʊ'fæktʃərə(r)/ n. изготови́тель (m.), производи́тель (m.)

manure /mə'njʊə(r)/ n. наво́з

manuscript /'mænjʊskrɪpt/ n. ру́копись

ℱ **many** /'menɪ/ adj. (**more**, **most**) мно́гие; **~ times** мно́го раз; **half as ~** вдво́е ме́ньше; **twice as ~** вдво́е бо́льше; **as, so ~** (as) сто́лько(, ско́лько); **not as ~ as** не так мно́го, как; **not ~** немно́го, не так уж мно́го

ℱ **map** /mæp/ n. ка́рта; (of railway system) схе́ма; **town ~** план го́рода
• v.t. (**mapped**, **mapping**): **~ out** (make ~ of): **he ~ped out his route before leaving** он соста́вил маршру́т пе́ред отъе́здом; (fig., plan) плани́ровать, рас-; **he ~ped out his**

plans он прики́нул, что ему́ ну́жно де́лать

maple /'meɪp(ə)l/ *n.* клён; (*attr.*) кленóвый

marathon /'mærəθ(ə)n/ *n.* марафо́н
■ **~ runner** *n.* марафо́нец

maraud /mə'rɔːd/ *v.i.* мародёрствовать (*impf., pf.*)

marble /'mɑːb(ə)l/ *n.* **1** (substance) мра́мор **2** (in child's game) стекля́нный ша́рик; **play ~s** игра́ть (*impf.*) в ша́рики
● *adj.* мра́морный

❖ **March** /mɑːtʃ/ *n.* март

march /mɑːtʃ/ *n.* (mil.) марш; (pol.) марш, демонстра́ция
● *v.i.* **1** (mil.) маршировáть, про-; **we watched them ~ past** мы смотре́ли, как они́ прошли́ стро́ем; **quick ~!** шáгом марш! **2** (walk determinedly) **he ~ed into the room** он сме́ло вошёл в кóмнату
□ **~ along** *v.i.*: **they were ~ing along singing** они́ маршировáли с пе́снями

mare /meə(r)/ *n.* кобы́ла

margarine /mɑːdʒə'riːn/ *n.* маргари́н

margin /'mɑːdʒɪn/ *n.* **1** (edge) край; (of page) по́ле (*usu. in pl.*); **in the ~** на поля́х **2** (extra amount) запа́с; **he won by a narrow ~** он победи́л с небольши́м преиму́ществом

marginal /'mɑːdʒɪn(ə)l/ *adj.* (insignificant) незначи́тельный; минима́льный

marguerite /mɑːgə'riːt/ *n.* ниáвник (*крупная полевая ромашка*)

marigold /'mærɪgəʊld/ *n.* (*also called* **common/pot ~**) (genus Calendula) ноготки́ (*m. pl.*); (*also called* **French/African ~**) (genus Tagetes) бáрхатцы (*m. pl.*)

marijuana /mærɪ'(h)wɑːnə/ *n.* марихуáна

marina /mə'riːnə/ *n.* мари́на, при́стань для яхт

marinade /'mærɪneɪd/ *n.* марина́д
● *v.t.* (*also* **marinate**) маринова́ть, за-

marine /mə'riːn/ *n.* **1** (fleet): **mercantile, merchant ~** торго́вый флот **2** (naval infantryman) солда́т морско́й пехо́ты, морско́й пехоти́нец
● *adj.* морско́й

marital /'mærɪt(ə)l/ *adj.*: **~ relations** супру́жеские отноше́ния; **~ status** семе́йное положе́ние

maritime /'mærɪtaɪm/ *adj.* (of the sea): **~ law** морско́е прáво; (situated by the sea) примо́рский

marjoram /'mɑːdʒərəm/ *n.* майорáн садо́вый

❖ **mark** /mɑːk/ *n.* **1** (imperfection; stain, spot, etc.) пятнó **2** (trace) след; **you have left dirty ~s on the floor** вы наследи́ли на полу́ **3** (sign, symbol) знак; **as a ~ of goodwill** в знак расположе́ния **4** (reference point) ме́тка; (fig., standard): **his work was not up to the ~** его́ рабо́та была́ не на высоте́ **5** (starting line) старт; **on your ~s, get set, go!** на старт, внима́ние, марш! **6** (assessment of performance) отме́тка; **he always gets good ~s** он всегда́ получáет хорóшие отме́тки; (preceded by number) балл
● *v.t.* **1** (stain, scar, scratch, etc.): **a tablecloth ~ed with coffee stains** скáтерть, забры́зганная ко́фе; **the table was badly ~ed** стол был си́льно запáчкан **2** (indicate) отм|ечáть, -е́тить; **is our village ~ed on this map?** нáша дере́вня нанесенá на э́ту кáрту?; **the prices are clearly ~ed** це́ны чётко простáвлены **3** (observe and remember): **a ~ed man** челове́к, взя́тый на заме́тку; (BrE, football, etc.: follow closely) закр|ывáть, -ы́ть; (notice) зам|ечáть, -е́тить; **~ my words!** помяни́те моё слóво! **4** (assign ~s to): **~ an exercise** пров|еря́ть, -е́рить упражне́ние
□ **~ down** *v.t.* (reduce price of): **all the goods were ~ed down for the sale** для распродáжи це́ны на все товáры бы́ли сни́жены
□ **~ off** *v.t.* отм|ечáть, -е́тить
□ **~ out** *v.t.*: **a tennis court had been ~ed out** те́ннисный корт был расчéрчен/размéчен; (preselect; destine): **he was ~ed out for promotion** его́ реши́ли повы́сить в дóлжности
□ **~ up** *v.t.* (raise price of): **goods were ~ed up after the budget** це́ны бы́ли повы́шены после объявле́ния финáнсовой сме́ты

marked /mɑːkt/ *adj.* (noticeable) заме́тный

markedly /'mɑːkɪdlɪ/ *adv.*: **they were ~ different** они́ заме́тно отличáлись друг от дру́га

marker /'mɑːkə(r)/ *n.* (indicator) индикáтор; (flag) сигнáльный флажóк; (pen) фломáстер

❖ **market** /'mɑːkɪt/ *n.* **1** (gathering; event; place of business) ры́нок, базáр; (*attr.*) ры́ночный, базáрный **2** (trade) торгóвля; **there is no ~ for these goods** на э́ти товáры нет спрóса **3** (share prices) це́ны (*f. pl.*); **the ~ is falling** це́ны пáдают **4** **on the ~** (available for purchase): **he put his house on the ~** он вы́ставил свой дом на продáжу
● *v.t.* (**marketed, marketing**) (advertise) реклами́ровать (*impf.*); (sell) продавáть (*impf.*)
■ **~ day** *n.* (BrE) базáрный день; **~ economy** *n.* ры́ночная эконóмика; **~ forces** *n. pl.* ры́ночные си́лы (*f. pl.*); **~ gardener** *n.* (BrE) владе́лец огорóдного хозя́йства; **~ leader** *n.* ли́дер ры́нка; **~ place** *n.* базáрная плóщадь; (fig.) ры́нок; **~ research** *n.* исслéдование ры́нка; **~ share** *n.* дóля ры́нка; **~ town** *n.* (небольшóй) гóрод с ры́нком; **~ value** *n.* ры́ночная стóимость

marketable /'mɑːkɪtəb(ə)l/ *adj.* (produced for sale) товáрный; (selling quickly) хóдкий

❖ **marketing** /'mɑːkɪtɪŋ/ *n.* мáркетинг
■ **~ manager** *n.* мéнеджер по мáркетингу

marking /'mɑːkɪŋ/ *n.* **1** (on animals etc.) окрáска **2** (for identification) знак

marksman /'mɑːksmən/ *n.* стрелóк

marmalade /'mɑːməleɪd/ *n.*: **orange ~** апельси́новый джем

maroon[1] /mə'ruːn/ *n. & adj.* (colour) тёмно-бордóвый (цвет)

maroon[2] /mə'ruːn/ *v.t.* высáживать, вы́садить на необитáемый óстров *и т. п.*; (fig.) (*in pass.*) застре|вáть, -я́ть; **we were ~ed in Paris**

мы застря́ли в Пари́же

marquee /mɑːˈkiː/ *n.* (BrE) (больша́я) пала́тка

♂ **marriage** /ˈmærɪdʒ/ *n.* **1** (married state) брак; ~ **of convenience** фикти́вный брак **2** (ceremony) сва́дьба; бракосочета́ние **3** (*attr.*) бра́чный; ~ **certificate** свиде́тельство о бра́ке; ~ **guidance** (BrE) семе́йная консульта́ция

married /ˈmærɪd/ *adj.* **1** (of man) жена́тый (**to:** на + *p.*); (of woman) заму́жняя, (*pred.*) за́мужем (**to:** за + *i.*); **they are** ~ (to each other) они́ жена́ты **2** (pert. to marriage) супру́жеский; **a** ~ **couple** супру́жеская па́ра

marrow /ˈmærəʊ/ *n.* **1** (anat.) (ко́стный) мозг **2** (*in full* **vegetable** ~) (BrE) кабачо́к

♂ **marry** /ˈmærɪ/ *v.t.* **1** (of man) жени́ться (*impf., pf.*) на + *p.* **2** (of woman) выходи́ть, вы́йти за́муж за + *a.* **3** (of priest) венча́ть, об-
 ● *v.i.* (of man) жени́ться (*impf., pf.*); (of woman) выходи́ть, вы́йти за́муж; (of couple) пожени́ться (*pf.*); (relig.) венча́ться, об-

Mars /mɑːz/ *n.* (myth., astron.) Марс

marsh /mɑːʃ/ *n.* боло́то
 ■ ~**land** *n.* боло́тистая ме́стность

marshal /ˈmɑːʃ(ə)l/ *n.* **1** (mil.) ма́ршал **2** (organizer) распоряди́тель (*m.*) **3** (AmE, head of police) нача́льник полице́йского уча́стка
 ● *v.t.* (**marshalled, marshalling**, AmE **marshaled, marshaling**) **1** (draw up in order): ~ **troops** выстра́ивать, вы́строить войска́; (fig.): ~ **one's forces** соб|ира́ть, -ра́ть си́лы **2** (direct): ~ **a crowd** напр|авля́ть, -а́вить толпу́

marshy /ˈmɑːʃɪ/ *adj.* (**marshier, marshiest**) боло́тистый

marsupial /mɑːˈsuːpɪəl/ *n.* су́мчатое живо́тное
 ● *adj.* су́мчатый

martial /ˈmɑːʃ(ə)l/ *adj.* (military) вое́нный
 ■ ~ **arts** *n. pl.* спорти́вная борьба́; ~ **law** *n.* вое́нное положе́ние

martyr /ˈmɑːtə(r)/ *n.* му́чени|к (-ца)
 ● *v.t.* му́чить, за-

martyrdom /ˈmɑːtədəm/ *n.* му́ченичество

marvel /ˈmɑːv(ə)l/ *n.* чу́до
 ● *v.i.* (**marvelled, marvelling**, AmE **marveled, marveling**) (wonder) диви́ться (*impf.*) + *d.*; удив|ля́ться, -и́ться + *d.*

marvellous /ˈmɑːvələs/ (AmE **marvelous**) *adj.* (astonishing) изуми́тельный; (splendid) чуде́сный

Marxism /ˈmɑːksɪz(ə)m/ *n.* маркси́зм

Marxist /ˈmɑːksɪst/ *n.* маркси́ст (-ка)
 ● *adj.* маркси́стский

marzipan /ˈmɑːzɪpæn/ *n.* марципа́н (*кондитерское изделие; начинка, глазурь*)

mascara /mæˈskɑːrə/ *n.* тушь для ресни́ц

mascot /ˈmæskɒt/ *n.* талисма́н

masculine /ˈmæskjʊlɪn/ *adj.* мужско́й

masculinity /mæskjʊˈlɪnɪtɪ/ *n.* му́жественность

mash /mæʃ/ *n.* (BrE, potato) пюре́ (*nt. indecl.*)
 ● *v.t.* (cul.): ~**ed potatoes** карто́фельное пюре́
 ■ ~**-up** *n.* (mixture, fusion) (infml) смесь

несхо́дных элеме́нтов

mask /mɑːsk/ *n.* ма́ска
 ● *v.t.* над|ева́ть, -е́ть ма́ску на + *a.*; (fig.): **she** ~**ed her feelings** она́ скрыва́ла свои́ чу́вства

masochism /ˈmæsəkɪz(ə)m/ *n.* мазохи́зм

masochist /ˈmæsəkɪst/ *n.* мазохи́ст (-ка)

masochistic /mæsəˈkɪstɪk/ *adj.* мазохи́стский

mason /ˈmeɪs(ə)n/ *n.* ка́менщик; (**M**~, **Free**~) масо́н

masonry /ˈmeɪsənrɪ/ *n.* ка́менная кла́дка

masquerade /mæskəˈreɪd/ *n.* (lit., fig.) маскара́д
 ● *v.i.*: **he** ~**d as a general** он выдава́л себя́ за генера́ла

Mass /mæs/ *n.* (relig.) ме́сса, литурги́я; (in Orthodox church) обе́дня

♂ **mass** /mæs/ *n.* **1** (phys. etc.) ма́сса **2** (large number) мно́жество; ~**es of people** ма́сса наро́ду; **the** ~**es** (наро́дные/широ́кие) ма́ссы; (*in pl.*) (infml, a large amount): **there's** ~**es of food** полно́ еды́ **3** (*attr.*) ма́ссовый; **the** ~ **media** сре́дства ма́ссовой информа́ции (*abbr.* СМИ); масс-ме́диа (*pl. indecl.*)
 ● *v.t.* соб|ира́ть, -ра́ть; ~ **troops** сосредото́чи|вать, -ть, войска́
 ● *v.i.* соб|ира́ться, -ра́ться; **the clouds are** ~**ing** собира́ются облака́
 ■ ~ **destruction** *n.* ма́ссовое уничтоже́ние; ~**-produce** *v.t.*: **these toys are** ~**-produced** э́ти игру́шки ма́ссового произво́дства; ~ **production** *n.* ма́ссовое произво́дство

massacre /ˈmæsəkə(r)/ *n.* бо́йня
 ● *v.t.* переб|ива́ть, -и́ть

massage /ˈmæsɑːʒ/ *n.* масса́ж
 ● *v.t.* масси́ровать (*impf., pf.*)

masseur /mæˈsɜː(r)/ *n.* массажи́ст

masseuse /mæˈsɜːz/ *n.* массажи́стка

♂ **massive** /ˈmæsɪv/ *adj.* (large and heavy) масси́вный; (substantial) огро́мный

mast /mɑːst/ *n.* ма́чта

mastectomy /mæˈstektəmɪ/ *n.* мастэктоми́я (*ампутация молочной железы*)

♂ **master** /ˈmɑːstə(r)/ *n.* **1** (one in control, boss) хозя́ин; (owner) владе́лец **2** (BrE, teacher) учи́тель (*m.*); (in university): **M**~ **of Arts** маги́стр гуманита́рных нау́к **3** (skilled craftsman, expert) ма́стер **4** (original) по́длинник
 ● *v.t.* **1** (gain control of) спр|авля́ться, -а́виться с + *i.* **2** (acquire knowledge of, skill in) овлад|ева́ть, -е́ть + *i.*; **it is a language which can be** ~**ed in 6 months** э́тим языко́м мо́жно овладе́ть за шесть ме́сяцев **3** (overcome) овлад|ева́ть, -е́ть + *i.*; ~ **one's feelings** владе́ть, о- свои́ми чу́вствами
 ■ ~ **bedroom** *n.* гла́вная спа́льня; ~ **builder** *n.* строи́тель-подря́дчик; ~ **key** *n.* отмы́чка; ~**mind** *n.* руководи́тель (*m*) ● *v.t.*: **he** ~**minded the plan** он разрабо́тал весь план; ~ **of ceremonies** *n.* распоряди́тель (*m.*), конферансье́ (*nt. indecl.*); ~**piece** *n.* шеде́вр; ~ **plan** *n.* генера́льный план

masterful /ˈmɑːstəfʊl/ *adj.* вла́стный

m

masterly /ˈmɑːstəlɪ/ adj. ма́стерский
mastery /ˈmɑːstərɪ/ n. **1** (authority) власть
2 (skill) мастерство́ **3** (knowledge) владе́ние
masturbate /ˈmæstəbeɪt/ v.i. мастурби́ровать
(impf.)
masturbation /mæstəˈbeɪʃ(ə)n/ n.
мастурба́ция
mat¹ /mæt/ n. **1** (floor covering) ко́врик **2** (to
protect table) подста́вка
mat² /mæt/ v.t. (**matted, matting**): his hair
was ~ted with blood его́ во́лосы сли́плись
от кро́ви
matador /ˈmætədɔː(r)/ n. матадо́р
match¹ /mætʃ/ n. (for producing flame) спи́чка
■ ~box n. спи́чечная коро́бка
◦ **match²** /mætʃ/ n. **1** (equal) па́ра, ро́вня; he's
no ~ for her он ей не па́ра **2** (thing resembling
or suiting another): these curtains are a good
~ for the carpet э́ти занаве́ски подхо́дят к
ковру́ **3** (game) соревнова́ние, состяза́ние;
матч, игра́; football ~ футбо́льный матч
● v.t. (suit; correspond to) под|ходи́ть, -ойти́ к
+ d.; гармони́ровать (impf.) c + i.; her hat
doesn't ~ her dress её шля́па не подхо́дит
к пла́тью; (find a ~ for): we try to ~ the jobs
to the applicants мы стара́емся подбира́ть
подходя́щую рабо́ту для кандида́тов
● v.i. (correspond: be identical): the handbag
and gloves don't ~ су́мочка и перча́тки не
гармони́руют друг с дру́гом
■ ~ point n. очко́, реша́ющее исхо́д ма́тча;
матч-по́йнт
mate /meɪt/ n. **1** (BrE, infml, companion, also as
form of address) брат, друг **2** (one of a pair of
animals or birds) саме́ц (са́мка) **3** (assistant)
помо́щник **4** (ship's) помо́щник капита́на
● v.t. & i. спа́ри|вать(ся), -ть(ся)
◦ **material** /məˈtɪərɪəl/ n. **1** (substance) материа́л;
raw ~(s) сырьё; (fig., of person): he is good
officer ~ из него́ вы́йдет хоро́ший офице́р;
(subject matter): there is good ~ there for
a novel там есть хоро́ший материа́л для
рома́на **2** (fabric) мате́рия **3** (in pl.): writing
~s пи́сьменные принадле́жности
● adj. материа́льный
materialism /məˈtɪərɪəlɪz(ə)m/ n.
материали́зм
materialist /məˈtɪərɪəlɪst/ n. материали́ст
materialistic /mətɪərɪəˈlɪstɪk/ adj.
материалисти́ческий
materialize /məˈtɪərɪəlaɪz/ v.i.
материализова́ться (impf., pf.)
maternal /məˈtɜːn(ə)l/ adj. (motherly)
матери́нский
maternity /məˈtɜːnɪtɪ/ n. матери́нство
■ ~ leave n. декре́тный о́тпуск
math /mæθ/ n. (AmE, infml) (abbr.)
= mathematics
mathematical /mæθəˈmætɪk(ə)l/ adj.
математи́ческий
mathematician /mæθəməˈtɪʃ(ə)n/ n.
матема́тик

mathematics /mæθəˈmætɪks/ n. матема́тика
maths /mæθs/ n. (BrE, infml) (abbr.)
= mathematics
matinee /ˈmætɪneɪ/ n. дневно́е представле́ние
mating /ˈmeɪtɪŋ/ n. спа́ривание
■ ~ season n. сезо́н спа́ривания
matriarchal /meɪtrɪˈɑːk(ə)l/ матриарха́льный
matriculate /məˈtrɪkjʊleɪt/ v.i. быть
при́нятым в вы́сшее уче́бное заведе́ние
matriculation /mətrɪkjʊˈleɪʃ(ə)n/ n.
зачисле́ние в вы́сшее уче́бное заведе́ние
matrimonial /mætrɪˈməʊnɪəl/ adj.
супру́жеский; бра́чный
matrimony /ˈmætrɪmənɪ/ n. брак
matri|x /ˈmeɪtrɪks/ n. (pl. ~ces /-siːz/ or
~xes) ма́трица
matron /ˈmeɪtrən/ n. **1** (BrE, in hospital)
ста́ршая сестра́ **2** (in school) эконо́мка
matt /mæt/ adj. ма́товый; ~ paint ма́товая
кра́ска
◦ **matter** /ˈmætə(r)/ n. **1** (phys., phil.) мате́рия;
(substance) вещество́ **2** (physiol.): grey ~
се́рое вещество́; (pus) гной **3** (material
for reading) материа́л (m. pl.); printed ~
печа́тный материа́л **4** (question; issue) вопро́с;
де́ло; that's quite another ~ э́то совсе́м
друго́е де́ло; it is a ~ of course само́ собо́й
разуме́ется; as a ~ of fact (to tell the truth) по
пра́вде сказа́ть; (in reality) на са́мом де́ле;
(incidentally) со́бственно (говоря́); it is a ~ for
the police э́то де́ло поли́ции; a ~ of life and
death вопро́с жи́зни и сме́рти; that's a ~ of
opinion э́то спо́рный вопро́с; (in pl.) (affairs)
дела́; to make ~s worse в доверше́ние ко
всем бе́дам **5** (the ~) (sth wrong, amiss): what's
the ~? в чём де́ло?; is (there) anything the
~? что-нибудь не ла́дно?; what's the ~ with
him? что с ним?; there's nothing the ~ (with
me) (у меня́) всё в поря́дке **6** (importance): no
~ what I do, the result will be the same что
бы я ни сде́лал, результа́т бу́дет тот же
● v.i. име́ть (impf.) значе́ние; it doesn't ~ to
me э́то не име́ет для меня́ значе́ния
■ ~-of-fact adj. приземлённый, лишённый
фанта́зии; сухо́й, делово́й
mattress /ˈmætrɪs/ n. матра́с, матра́ц
mature /məˈtjʊə(r)/ adj. (**maturer,
maturest**) зре́лый
● v.i. **1** (lit., fig., ripen, develop) созр|ева́ть,
-е́ть; children ~ earlier nowadays в на́ши
дни де́ти развива́ются быстре́е **2** (become
due for payment): the policy ~s next year в
бу́дущем году́ наступа́ет срок вы́платы по
страхово́му по́лису
■ ~ student n. (BrE) студе́нт (-ка) зре́лого
во́зраста
maturity /məˈtjʊərɪtɪ/ n. зре́лость
maudlin /ˈmɔːdlɪn/ adj. слюня́во
сентимента́льный; плакси́вый во хмелю́
maul /mɔːl/ v.t. терза́ть, рас~; he was ~ed to
death by a tiger его́ растерза́л тигр
Mauritania /mɒrɪˈteɪnɪə/ n. Маврита́ния
mausoleum /mɔːsəˈliːəm/ n. мавзоле́й

◦ ключева́я ле́ксика

m

mauve /məʊv/ n. & adj. розова́то-лило́вый (цвет)

maverick /'mævərɪk/ n. (fig., dissenter) диссиде́нт; (attr.) неприка́янный

mawkish /'mɔːkɪʃ/ adj. при́торный

maxim /'mæksɪm/ n. (aphorism) афори́зм

maximize /'mæksɪmaɪz/ v.t. максима́льно увели́чи|вать, -ть

maximum /'mæksɪməm/ n. ма́ксимум
● adj. максима́льный

❧ **May** /meɪ/ n. май; ~ **Day** Пе́рвое ма́я; пра́здник Пе́рвого ма́я
■ ~**day** n. (distress signal) сигна́л бе́дствия

❧ **may** /meɪ/ v. aux. (3rd pers. sing. pres. **may**, past **might**) **1** (expr. possibility) мо́жет быть; пожа́луй; it ~ be true возмо́жно, э́то пра́вда; it ~ not be true возмо́жно, э́то не так; he might have lost his way without my help без мое́й по́мощи он мог бы заблуди́ться; you ~ well be right вполне́ возмо́жно, вы и пра́вы **2** (expr. permission): ~ I come and see you? мо́жно мне (or могу́ я) к вам зайти́?; you ~ go if you wish е́сли хоти́те, мо́жете идти́ **3** (expr. reproach): you might have asked my permission мо́жно бы́ло бы спроси́ть моего́ согла́сия **4** (in main clause, expr. wish or hope): ~ the best man win! да победи́т сильне́йший!
■ ~**be** adv. мо́жет быть

maybe /'meɪbɪ/ adv. мо́жет быть

mayhem /'meɪhem/ n. разгро́м

mayonnaise /meɪə'neɪz/ n. майоне́з

mayor /meə(r)/ n. мэр

mayoress /'meərɪs/ n. (mayor's wife) жена́ мэ́ра; (female mayor) же́нщина-мэр

maze /meɪz/ n. лабири́нт; (fig.) пу́таница

MBA abbr. (of **Master of Business Administration**) маги́стр ме́неджмента

MBE n. (abbr. of **Member of the Order of the British Empire**) кавале́р о́рдена Брита́нской импе́рии 5-й (низшей) сте́пени

MC abbr. (of **Master of Ceremonies**) конферансье́ (nt. indecl.), распоряди́тель (m.)

MD (BrE) abbr. (of **Managing Director**) дире́ктор-распоряди́тель (m.)

ME abbr. (of **myalgic encephalitis**) миалги́ческий энцефали́т, синдро́м хрони́ческой уста́лости

❧ **me** /miː/ obj. of ▶ **I**

meadow /'medəʊ/ n. луг

meagre /'miːɡə(r)/ (AmE **meager**) adj. ску́дный

❧ **meal** /miːl/ n. еда́, тра́пеза; we have 3 ~s a day мы еди́м три ра́за в день

❧ **mean¹** /miːn/ n. (average) середи́на
■ ~**time** n.: in the ~**time** ме́жду тем

mean² /miːn/ adj. **1** (niggardly) скупо́й **2** (spiteful) зло́бный; don't be ~ to him не обижа́йте его́ **3** (inferior): he is a man of no ~ abilities он челове́к незауря́дных спосо́бностей

❧ **mean³** /miːn/ v.t. (past and p.p. **meant**) **1** (intend) име́ть (impf.) в виду́; намерева́ться (impf.); I ~ to solve this problem я наме́рен

реши́ть э́тот вопро́с; I ~t no harm я не жела́л зла; I ~t it as a joke я хоте́л пошути́ть; I didn't ~ to hurt you я не хоте́л вас оби́деть **2** (design, destine) предназн|а́чать, -а́чить; they were ~t for each other они́ бы́ли со́зданы друг для дру́га **3** (of person, intend to convey) хоте́ть (impf.) сказа́ть; what do you ~? что вы э́тим хоти́те сказа́ть? **4** (of words etc., signify) зна́чить (impf.), означа́ть (impf.); this sentence ~s nothing to me э́то предложе́ние ничего́ мне не говори́т; does my friendship ~ nothing to you? неуже́ли моя́ дру́жба ничего́ для вас не зна́чит?; (entail, involve): organizing a fete ~s a lot of hard work подгото́вка к пра́зднику тре́бует мно́го уси́лий

meander /mɪ'ændə(r)/ v.i. (of streams, roads, etc.) извива́ться, ви́ться (both impf.)

❧ **meaning** /'miːnɪŋ/ n. значе́ние

meaningful /'miːnɪŋfʊl/ adj. значи́тельный

meaningless /'miːnɪŋlɪs/ adj. бессмы́сленный

meanness /'miːnnɪs/ n. по́длость, ни́зость; ску́пость

means /miːnz/ n. **1** (instrument, method) спо́соб; a ~ to an end сре́дство для достиже́ния це́ли; by ~ of посре́дством + g.; с по́мощью + g.; by all ~ (AmE, without fail) непреме́нно; (expr. permission) коне́чно; пожа́луйста; it was by no ~ easy э́то бы́ло отню́дь не про́сто **2** (facilities): ~ of communication (transport) сре́дства сообще́ния; (telecommunication) сре́дства свя́зи **3** (resources) сре́дства; a man of ~ челове́к со сре́дствами; live beyond one's ~ жить (impf.) не по сре́дствам
■ ~ **test** n. прове́рка нужда́емости

meant /ment/ past and p.p. of ▶ **mean³**

meanwhile /'miːnwaɪl/ adv. ме́жду тем, тем вре́менем

measles /'miːz(ə)lz/ n. корь

measly /'miːzlɪ/ adj. (**measlier**, **measliest**) жа́лкий

measurable /'meʒərəb(ə)l/ adj. измери́мый

❧ **measure** /'meʒə(r)/ n. **1** (standard unit for expressing size, quantity, degree) ме́ра; (portion, of whisky etc.) по́рция **2** (graduated rod or tape for measuring) измери́тельная лине́йка; руле́тка **3** (step) ме́ра, мероприя́тие **4** (degree, extent) сте́пень; in some ~ до не́которой сте́пени; she was irritated beyond ~ она́ пришла́ в невероя́тное раздраже́ние
● v.t. **1** (find size etc. of) ме́рить, с-; изм|еря́ть, -е́рить; he was ~d for a suit с него́ сня́ли ме́рку для костю́ма **2** (amount to when measured): the room ~s 12 ft across ко́мната ширино́й в двена́дцать фу́тов
□ ~ **off**, ~ **out** v.t. отм|еря́ть, -е́рить
□ ~ **up** v.i.: the team has not ~d up to our expectations кома́нда не оправда́ла на́ших ожида́ний

measured /'meʒəd/ adj. **1** (steps) разме́ренный; ~ tread ме́рная по́ступь **2** (tone) уме́ренный; (considered; careful) обду́манный, осторо́жный

m

measurement /ˈmeʒəmənt/ *n.* (measuring) измере́ние; (dimension) разме́р; **take sb's ~s** снять (*pf.*) ме́рку с кого́-н.; **waist ~** объём та́лии

meat /miːt/ *n.* мя́со

meaty /ˈmiːtɪ/ *adj.* (**meatier, meatiest**) мяси́стый

Mecca /ˈmekə/ *n.* Ме́кка

mechanic /mɪˈkænɪk/ *n.* меха́ник

mechanical /mɪˈkænɪk(ə)l/ *adj.* механи́ческий
■ **~ engineering** *n.* машинострое́ние

mechanics /mɪˈkænɪks/ *n.* меха́ника

⚹ **mechanism** /ˈmekənɪz(ə)m/ *n.* механи́зм

mechanization /mekənaɪˈzeɪʃ(ə)n/ *n.* механиза́ция

mechanize /ˈmekənaɪz/ *v.t. & i.* механизи́ровать(ся) (*impf., pf.*)

Med /med/ *n.* (BrE, infml) (*abbr.*): **the ~** Средизе́мное мо́ре

medal /ˈmed(ə)l/ *n.* меда́ль; (mil. award) о́рден (-á)

medallion /məˈdæljən/ *n.* медальо́н

medallist /ˈmedəlɪst/ (AmE **medalist**) *n.* (recipient) медали́ст (-ка)

meddle /ˈmed(ə)l/ *v.i.*: **~ in** (interfere in) вме́ш|иваться, -а́ться в + *a.*; **~ with** (touch, tamper with) тро́|гать, -нуть

meddlesome /ˈmedəlsəm/ *adj.* надо́йливый; **he is a ~ person** он всё вре́мя вме́шивается не в свои́ дела́

⚹ **media** /ˈmiːdɪə/ *see* ▶ **medium** *n.* 4

mediate /ˈmiːdɪeɪt/ *v.i.* выступа́ть, вы́ступить посре́дником

mediation /miːdɪˈeɪʃ(ə)n/ *n.* посре́дничество

mediator /ˈmiːdɪeɪtə(r)/ *n.* посре́дник

medic /ˈmedɪk/ *n.* (infml) (студе́нт-)ме́дик

⚹ **medical** /ˈmedɪk(ə)l/ *n.* (infml, **~ examination**): **have a ~** про|ходи́ть, -йти́ медици́нский осмо́тр (*abbr.* медосмо́тр)
● *adj.* медици́нский; целе́бный
■ **~ certificate** *n.* спра́вка от врача́

medicament /mɪˈdɪkəmənt/ *n.* лека́рство, медикаме́нт

medication /medɪˈkeɪʃ(ə)n/ *n.* (medicine) лека́рство; (treatment) лече́ние

medicinal /məˈdɪsɪn(ə)l/ *adj.* (of medicine) лека́рственный; (curative) целе́бный

⚹ **medicine** /ˈmedɪsɪn/ *n.* ◗ (science, practice) медици́на ◖ (substance) лека́рство; медикаме́нт, миксту́ра
■ **~ cabinet** *n.* апте́чка; **~ man** *n.* зна́харь (*m.*)

medieval /medrˈiːv(ə)l/ *adj.* средневеко́вый

mediocre /miːdɪˈəʊkə(r)/ *adj.* посре́дственный

mediocrity /miːdɪˈɒkrɪtɪ/ *n.* посре́дственность

meditate /ˈmedɪteɪt/ *v.i.* размышля́ть (*impf*) (on: о + *p.*); (relig.) медити́ровать (*impf.*)

meditation /medɪˈteɪʃ(ə)n/ *n.* размышле́ние; (relig.) медита́ция

meditative /ˈmedɪtətɪv/ *adj.* заду́мчивый

Mediterranean /medɪtəˈreɪnɪən/ *n.* (*in full* **~ Sea**) Средизе́мное мо́ре
● *adj.* средиземномо́рский

medium /ˈmiːdɪəm/ *n.* (*pl.* **media** *or* **mediums**) ◗ (middle quality) середи́на; **he strikes a happy ~** он приде́рживается золото́й середи́ны ◖ (means, agency) сре́дство ◗ (spiritualist) ме́диум ◔ **the media** (mass media) сре́дства ма́ссовой информа́ции
● *adj.* (intermediate) промежу́точный; (average) сре́дний
■ **~ dry** *adj.* полусухо́й; **~-sized** *adj.* сре́днего разме́ра

medley /ˈmedlɪ/ *n.* (*pl.* **medleys**) смесь; (mus.) попурри́ (*nt. indecl.*)

meek /miːk/ *adj.* кро́ткий

⚹ **meet** /miːt/ *n.* (of sportsmen, etc.) сбор
● *v.t.* (*past and p.p.* **met**) ◗ (encounter) встре|ча́ть, -е́тить; (make acquaintance of) знако́миться, по- с + *i.*; **I met your sister in Moscow** я познако́мился с ва́шей сестро́й в Москве́ ◖ (face): **I am ready to ~ your challenge** я гото́в приня́ть ваш вы́зов ◗ (experience, suffer): **~ one's death** поги́бнуть (*pf.*) ◔ (pay, settle): **this will barely ~ my expenses** э́то с трудо́м покро́ет мои́ расхо́ды
● *v.i.* (*past and p.p.* **met**) ◗ (of persons, come together) встре|ча́ться, -е́титься; **our eyes met** на́ши глаза́ встре́тились; (become acquainted) знако́миться, по-; **we met at a dance** мы познако́мились на та́нцах ◖ (assemble) соб|ира́ться, -ра́ться; **the council met to discuss the situation** сове́т собра́лся, что́бы обсуди́ть положе́ние ◗ (of things, qualities, etc.: come into contact) сходи́ться (*impf.*); **the rivers Oka and Volga ~ at Nizhni Novgorod** Ни́жний Но́вгород — ме́сто слия́ния рек Оки́ и Во́лги; **make (both) ends ~** (fig.) св|оди́ть, -ести́ концы́ с конца́ми ◔ **~ with**: **~ with difficulties** испы́т|ывать, -а́ть затрудне́ния; **he met with an accident** с ним произошёл несча́стный слу́чай
□ **~ up** *v.i.* (infml): **we met up** (*or* **I met up with him/her/them**) **in London** мы встре́тились в Ло́ндоне

⚹ **meeting** /ˈmiːtɪŋ/ *n.* ◗ (encounter) встре́ча; (by arrangement) свида́ние ◖ (gathering) собра́ние ◗ (sports **~**) (спорти́вное) состяза́ние; (race **~**) ска́чки (*f. pl.*)
■ **~ place**, **~ point** *nn.* ме́сто встре́чи

meg /meg/ *n.* (comput., infml) (*abbr.*) мег (infml)

megabyte /ˈmegəbaɪt/ *n.* (comput.) мегаба́йт

megalomania /megələˈmeɪnɪə/ *n.* ма́ния вели́чия, мегалома́ния

megalomaniac /megələˈmeɪnɪæk/ *n.* страда́ющий ма́нией вели́чия

megaphone /ˈmegəfəʊn/ *n.* мегафо́н

megapixel /ˈmegəpɪks(ə)l/ *n.* (comput.) мегапи́ксель (*m.*)

melancholy /ˈmelənkəlɪ/ *n.* уны́ние
● *adj.* (of person) уны́лый; (of things) гру́стный

mellow /ˈmeləʊ/ *adj.* ◗ (of voice, sound, colour, light) со́чный ◖ (of wine) вы́держанный ◗ (of character) подобре́вший

● *v.t.*: age has ~ed him го́ды смягчи́ли его́ хара́ктер

● *v.i.* (of person) смягча́ться, -и́ться

melodic /mɪ'lɒdɪk/ *adj.* мелоди́чный

melodious /mɪ'ləʊdɪəs/ *adj.* мелоди́чный; ~ voice певу́чий го́лос

melodrama /'melədrɑːmə/ *n.* мелодра́ма

melodramatic /melədrə'mætɪk/ *adj.* мелодрамати́ческий

melody /'melədɪ/ *n.* мело́дия

melon /'melən/ *n.* ды́ня

melt /melt/ *v.t.* **1** (reduce to liquid) раст|а́пливать, -опи́ть **2** (fig., soften) размягч|а́ть, -и́ть

● *v.i.* **1** (become liquid) та́ять, рас- **2** (fig., soften) смягч|а́ться, -и́ться; her heart ~ed at the sight её се́рдце смягчи́лось при ви́де э́того

□ ~ **down** *v.t.* распл|авля́ть, -а́вить

melting point /'meltɪŋ pɔɪnt/ *n.* температу́ра плавле́ния

◆ **member** /'membə(r)/ *n.* член, уча́стни|к (-ца) (*о́бщества и т. п.*)

membership /'membəʃɪp/ *n.* (being a member) чле́нство; (*collect.*) (members) чле́ны (*m. pl.*)

membrane /'membreɪn/ *n.* перепо́нка, мембра́на

memento /mə'mentəʊ/ *n.* (*pl.* ~es *or* ~s) сувени́р

memo /'meməʊ/ *n.* (*pl.* ~s) = memorandum

memoir /'memwɑː(r)/ *n.* (*in pl.*) (autobiography) воспомина́ния (*nt. pl.*), мемуа́р|ы (-ов)

memorable /'memərəb(ə)l/ *adj.* па́мятный; незабыва́емый

memorandum /memə'rændəm/ *n.* запи́ска

memorial /mə'mɔːrɪəl/ *n.* па́мятник

memorize /'meməraɪz/ *v.t.* зау́ч|ивать, -и́ть (наизу́сть)

◆ **memory** /'memərɪ/ *n.* **1** (faculty; its use) па́мять; I have a bad ~ for faces у меня́ плоха́я па́мять на ли́ца; in ~ of в па́мять + *g.* **2** (recollection) воспомина́ние **3** (comput.) па́мять

■ **Memory Stick**® *n.* (comput.) флеш-па́мять; флёшка (infml)

men /men/ *pl. of* ▶ **man**

■ ~'s **room** *n.* (AmE) мужско́й туале́т

menace /'menɪs/ *n.* угро́за

● *v.t.* угрожа́ть (*impf.*) + *d.*

ménage /meɪ'nɑːʒ/ *n.* хозя́йство

■ ~ **à trois** *n.* брак втроём

menagerie /mɪ'nædʒərɪ/ *n.* звери́нец

mend /mend/ *n.*: be on the ~ идти́ (*det.*) на попра́вку

● *v.t.* **1** (repair) чини́ть, по-; заш|ива́ть, -и́ть **2** (improve, reform) испр|авля́ть, -а́вить; ~ one's ways испр|авля́ться, -а́виться

● *v.i.* (regain health) выздора́вливать, вы́здороветь; his leg is ~ing nicely его́ нога́ зажива́ет хорошо́

mendacious /men'deɪʃəs/ *adj.* лжи́вый

menial /'miːnɪəl/ *adj.* лаке́йский

■ ~ **work** *n.* чёрная рабо́та

meningitis /menɪn'dʒaɪtɪs/ *n.* менинги́т

menopause /'menəpɔːz/ *n.* кли́макс

menstrual /'menstrʊəl/ *adj.* менструа́льный

menstruate /'menstrʊeɪt/ *v.i.* менструи́ровать (*impf.*)

menstruation /menstrʊ'eɪʃ(ə)n/ *n.* менструа́ция

menswear /'menzweə(r)/ *n.* мужска́я оде́жда

◆ **mental** /'ment(ə)l/ *adj.* **1** (of the mind) у́мственный; ~ly handicapped (sometimes offens.) у́мственно отста́лый **2** (pert. to ~ health) психи́ческий; ~ illness психи́ческая боле́знь **3** (carried out in the mind) мы́сленный

■ ~ **hospital** *n.* (often offens.) психиатри́ческая больни́ца

mentality /men'tælɪtɪ/ *n.* менталите́т

◆ **mention** /'menʃ(ə)n/ *n.* упомина́ние; there was a ~ of him in the paper в газе́те упомина́лось его́ и́мя

● *v.t.* упом|ина́ть, -яну́ть (*кого́/что or о ком/чём*); I shall ~ it to him я скажу́ ему́ об э́том; ~ sb's name наз|ыва́ть, -ва́ть чьё-н. и́мя; don't ~ it! не за что!; ничего́; не сто́ит!; not to ~ (*or* without ~ing) не говоря́ уже́ о + *p.*

mentor /'mentɔː(r)/ *n.* наста́вник, ме́нтор

menu /'menjuː/ *n.* (also comput.) меню́ (*nt. indecl.*)

MEP *abbr.* (*of* **Member of the European Parliament**) депута́т Европарла́мента

mercantile /'mɜːkəntaɪl/ *adj.* торго́вый

■ ~ **marine** *n.* торго́вый флот

mercenary /'mɜːsɪnərɪ/ *n.* наёмник

● *adj.* коры́стный

merchandise /'mɜːtʃəndaɪz/ *n.* **1** това́ры (*m. pl.*) **2** (of a football club etc.) атрибу́тика

merchant /'mɜːtʃ(ə)nt/ *n.* **1** (hist.) купе́ц; (with qualifying word: dealer) торго́вец; wine ~ торго́вец ви́нами

■ ~ **bank** *n.* (BrE) комме́рческий банк; ~ **marine** (AmE), ~ **navy** (BrE) *nn.* торго́вый флот

merciful /'mɜːsɪfʊl/ *adj.* милосе́рдный, сострада́тельный; his death was a ~ release смерть была́ для него́ бла́гом

merciless /'mɜːsɪlɪs/ *adj.* беспоща́дный, безжа́лостный

mercurial /mɜː'kjʊərɪəl/ *adj.* **1** (of mercury) рту́тный; ~ poisoning отравле́ние рту́тью **2** (of person, lively) живо́й; (volatile) непостоя́нный, изме́нчивый

mercury /'mɜːkjʊrɪ/ *n.* ртуть

mercy /'mɜːsɪ/ *n.* **1** (compassion, clemency) милосе́рдие; поща́да; beg for ~ проси́ть (*impf.*) поща́ды; show ~ to (*or* have ~ on) щади́ть, по- **2** (power): at the ~ of во вла́сти + *g.*

mere /mɪə(r)/ *adj.* (**merest**) **1** (simple; pure) просто́й; чи́стый; (nothing but) не бо́лее чем; всего́ лишь; то́лько; he is a ~ child он всего́ лишь ребёнок **2** (alone) оди́н (то́лько); the ~ sight of him disgusts me оди́н его́ вид вызыва́ет у меня́ отвраще́ние

◆ **merely** /'mɪəlɪ/ *adv.* (simply) про́сто; (only) то́лько

merge /mɜːdʒ/ *v.t. & i.* сл|ива́ть(ся), -и́ть(ся)

m

merger /'mɜːdʒə(r)/ *n.* объединение

meringue /mə'ræŋ/ *n.* безе (*nt. indecl.*)

merit /'merɪt/ *n.* (deserving quality, worth) достоинство
 ● *v.t.* (**merited, meriting**) заслуж|ивать, -и́ть

meritocracy /merɪ'tɒkrəsɪ/ *n.* общество, управля́емое людьми́ с наибо́льшими способностями

mermaid /'mɜːmeɪd/ *n.* руса́лка

merriment /'merɪmənt/ *n.* весе́лье

merry /'merɪ/ *adj.* (**merrier, merriest**) (happy, full of gaiety) весёлый; M~ Christmas! с Рождество́м (Христо́вым)!
 ■ ~-go-round *n.* карусе́ль

mesh /meʃ/ *n.* **1** (space in net etc.) яче́йка **2** (*in pl.*) (network) сеть
 ● *v.i.* (interlock) зацеп|ля́ться, -и́ться

mesmerize /'mezməraɪz/ *v.t.* (lit., fig.) гипнотизи́ровать, за-

mess¹ /mes/ *n.* **1** (disorder) беспоря́док; **the room was in a complete ~** ко́мната была́ в соверше́нном беспоря́дке; **make a ~ of** (spoil; bungle) провал|ивать, -и́ть **2** (confusion) пу́таница **3** (trouble) неприя́тность, беда́, го́ре; **get oneself into a ~** вли́пнуть (*pf.*) (*infml*)
 ● *v.i.*: ~ **with** (interfere with) вме́шиваться (*impf.*) в + *a.*
 □ ~ **about** *v.t.* (BrE, inconvenience) причиня́ть (*impf.*) неудо́бство + *d.*
 ● *v.i.* (work half-heartedly or without plan) ковыря́ться (*impf.*); (potter, idle about) каните́литься (*impf.*)
 □ ~ **about with** (fiddle with) вози́ться (*impf.*) c + *i.*
 □ ~ **around** *v.t. & i.* = mess about
 □ ~ **up** *v.t.* (make dirty) па́чкать, пере-; (bungle) провал|ивать, -и́ть; (put into confusion) перепу́т|ывать, -ать

mess² /mes/ *n.* (eating place) столо́вая

 ✐ **message** /'mesɪdʒ/ *n.* (formal) сообще́ние; (informal) запи́ска, за́пись

messenger /'mesɪndʒə(r)/ *n.* курье́р, посы́льный

Messiah /mɪ'saɪə/ *n.* Месси́я (*m.*)

Messrs /'mesəz/ *pl. of* ▶ Mr

messy /'mesɪ/ *adj.* (**messier, messiest**) (untidy) неубра́нный; (slovenly) неря́шливый; (unpleasant) неприя́тный

Met /met/ *abbr. of* **1** (**the Met (Office)**) Метеорологи́ческое бюро́ (*во Великобрита́нии*) **2** (**the Met**) поли́ция Ло́ндона **3** (**the Met**) Метрополи́тен-о́пера (*в Нью-Йо́рке*)

met /met/ *past and p.p. of* ▶ meet

metabolic /metə'bɒlɪk/ *adj.*: ~ **rate** ско́рость обме́на веще́ств

metabolism /mɪ'tæbəlɪz(ə)m/ *n.* обме́н веще́ств

 ✐ **metal** /'met(ə)l/ *n.* мета́лл
 ● *adj.* металли́ческий

─────────────────────
 ✐ ключева́я ле́ксика

metallic /mə'tælɪk/ *adj.* металли́ческий

metallurgist /me'tælədʒɪst/ *n.* металлу́рг

metallurgy /mɪ'tælədʒɪ/ *n.* металлурги́я

metamorphosis /metə'mɔːfəsɪs/ *n.* (*pl.* **metamorphoses** /-siːz/) метаморфо́за

metaphor /'metəfɔː(r)/ *n.* мета́фора

metaphorical /metə'fɒrɪk(ə)l/ *adj.* метафори́ческий; ~**ly speaking** о́бразно говоря́

metaphysical /metə'fɪzɪk(ə)l/ *adj.* метафизи́ческий

metaphysics /metə'fɪzɪks/ *n.* метафи́зика

mete /miːt/ *v.t.* (~ **out**) распредел|я́ть, -и́ть

meteor /'miːtɪə(r)/ *n.* метео́р

meteoric /miːtɪ'ɒrɪk/ *adj.* (fig.) головокружи́тельный

meteorite /'miːtɪəraɪt/ *n.* метеори́т

meteorological /miːtɪərə'lɒdʒɪk(ə)l/ *adj.* метеорологи́ческий
 ■ ~ **office** (BrE), ~ **center** (AmE) *nn.* слу́жба пого́ды

meteorologist /miːtɪə'rɒlədʒɪst/ *n.* метеоро́лог

meteorology /miːtɪə'rɒlədʒɪ/ *n.* метеороло́гия

meter¹ /'miːtə(r)/ *n.* (apparatus) счётчик; **gas ~** га́зовый счётчик
 ● *v.t.* изм|еря́ть, -е́рить; зам|еря́ть, -е́рить

meter² /'miːtə(r)/ *n.* (AmE) = metre

methane /'miːθeɪn/ *n.* мета́н

 ✐ **method** /'meθəd/ *n.* (way) ме́тод, спо́соб; (system) систе́ма, мето́дика

methodical /mɪ'θɒdɪk(ə)l/ *adj.* системати́ческий

Methodist /'meθədɪst/ *n.* (relig.) методи́ст (-ка); (*attr.*) методи́стский

methodology /meθə'dɒlədʒɪ/ *n.* методоло́гия

meths /meθs/ *n.* (BrE, infml) денатура́т

methylated /'meθɪleɪtɪd/ *adj.*: ~ **spirit** денатура́т

meticulous /mə'tɪkjʊləs/ *adj.* тща́тельный

meticulousness /mə'tɪkjʊləsnɪs/ *n.* тща́тельность, аккура́тность

 ✐ **metre** /'miːtə(r)/ (AmE **meter**) *n.* метр

metric /'metrɪk/ *adj.* метри́ческий

metronome /'metrənəʊm/ *n.* метроно́м

metropolis /mɪ'trɒpəlɪs/ *n.* столи́ца

metropolitan /metrə'pɒlɪt(ə)n/ *adj.* столи́чный

mettle /'met(ə)l/ *n.* си́ла хара́ктера

mews /mjuːz/ *n. pl.* (BrE) коню́шни (*f. pl.*) (переде́ланные в жило́е помеще́ние)

Mexican /'meksɪkən/ *n.* мексика́н|ец (-ка)
 ● *adj.* мексика́нский

Mexico /'meksɪkəʊ/ *n.* Ме́ксика; ~ **City** Ме́хико (*m. indecl.*)

mezzanine /'metsəniːn/ *n.* мезони́н, полуэта́ж

mezzo /'metsəʊ/ *adv.* полу-
 ■ ~ **forte** *adv.* дово́льно гро́мко; ~**-soprano** *n.* (*pl.* ~**s**) (singer) ме́ццо-сопра́но (*f. indecl.*); (voice) ме́ццо-сопра́но (*nt. indecl.*)

miaow /mɪ'aʊ/ *v.i.* мяу́кать (*impf.*)

mice /maɪs/ *pl. of* ▶ **mouse**

microbe /'maɪkrəʊb/ *n.* микро́б

microbiologist /maɪkrəʊbaɪ'ɒlədʒɪst/ *n.* микробио́лог

microbiology /maɪkrəʊbaɪ'ɒlədʒɪ/ *n.* микробиоло́гия

microblog /'maɪkrəʊblɒg/ *n.* (comput.) микробло́г

microchip /'maɪkrəʊtʃɪp/ *n.* микросхе́ма, чип

microclimate /'maɪkrəʊklaɪmət/ *n.* микрокли́мат

microcosm /'maɪkrəkɒz(ə)m/ *n.* микроко́см

microfiche /'maɪkrəʊfiːʃ/ *n.* микрофи́ша (*несколько фотографий на микроплёнке*)

microfilm /'maɪkrəʊfɪlm/ *n.* микрофи́льм, микроплёнка

microlight /'maɪkrəʊlaɪt/ *n.* (BrE) сверхлёгкий персона́льный самолёт

microorganism /maɪkrəʊ'ɔːgənɪz(ə)m/ *n.* микрооргани́зм

microphone /'maɪkrəfəʊn/ *n.* микрофо́н

microprocessor /maɪkrəʊ'prəʊsesə(r)/ *n.* микропроце́ссор

microscope /'maɪkrəskəʊp/ *n.* микроско́п

microscopic /maɪkrə'skɒpɪk/ *adj.* микроскопи́ческий

microwave /'maɪkrəʊweɪv/ *n.*: ~ **oven** микроволно́вая печь

mid /mɪd/ *adj. & pref.*: in ~ **air** (высоко́) в во́здухе; from ~ June to ~ July с середи́ны ию́ня до середи́ны ию́ля

■ ~**day** *n.* по́лдень (*m.*); ~**night** *n.* по́лночь; ~**summer** *n.* середи́на ле́та; (*attr.*) M~**summer Day** Ива́нов день (*24 ию́ня*); ~**way** *adv.* на полпути́; **the M~west** *n.* Сре́дний За́пад США; ~**winter** *n.* середи́на зимы́

◌ **middle** /'mɪd(ə)l/ *n.* **1** середи́на; in the ~ of среди́ + *g.*; (of time): in the ~ of the night посреди́ но́чи; I was in the ~ of getting ready в тот моме́нт я как раз собира́лся **2** (waist) та́лия

● *adj.* сре́дний; the M~ Ages Сре́дние века́; the ~ classes сре́дние слои́ о́бщества; сре́дний класс

■ ~**aged** *adj.* сре́дних лет; ~**class** *adj.* относя́щийся к сре́днему кла́ссу; M~ East *n.* Бли́жний Восто́к; ~**man** *n.* посре́дник; ~ **school** *n.* (BrE) сре́дняя шко́ла; ~**weight** *n. & adj.* (бокс.) сре́днего ве́са

middling /'mɪdlɪŋ/ *adj.* сре́дний, второсо́ртный; fair to ~ так себе́

midge /mɪdʒ/ *n.* кома́р, мо́шка

midget /'mɪdʒɪt/ *n.* (offens.) ка́рлик

midriff /'mɪdrɪf/ *n.* ве́рхняя часть живота́

midst /mɪdst/ *n.* середи́на; in the ~ of среди́, в разга́р + *g.*, ме́жду + *i.*; a stranger in our ~ чужо́й среди́ нас

midwife /'mɪdwaɪf/ *n.* акуше́рка

miff /mɪf/ *v.t.* (infml): he was ~ed by my remark моё замеча́ние оби́дело его́

might[1] /maɪt/ *n.* **1** (power) мощь **2** (strength) си́ла; with (all his) ~ and main изо всех сил,

что бы́ло мо́чи

◌ **might**[2] /maɪt/ *v. aux. see* ▶ **may**

mighty /'maɪtɪ/ *adj.* (**mightier**, **mightiest**) мо́щный

migraine /'miːɡreɪn/ *n.* мигре́нь

migrant /'maɪgrənt/ *n.* переселе́нец
● *adj.* кочу́ющий

migrate /maɪ'greɪt/ *v.i.* пересел|я́ться, -и́ться; (of birds) соверш|а́ть, -и́ть перелёт

migration /maɪ'greɪʃ(ə)n/ *n.* мигра́ция; перелёт

migratory /maɪ'greɪtərɪ/ *adj.* перелётный

mike /maɪk/ *n.* (infml) = microphone

mild /maɪld/ *adj.* мя́гкий; a ~ day тёплый день

mildew /'mɪldjuː/ *n.* пле́сень

◌ **mile** /maɪl/ *n.* ми́ля; (fig.): I was ~s away я замечта́лся; it sticks out a ~ э́то броса́ется в глаза́

■ ~**stone** *n.* ка́мень с указа́нием расстоя́ния; (fig.) ве́ха

mileage /'maɪlɪdʒ/ *n.* **1** (distance in miles) расстоя́ние в ми́лях; (of car) пробе́г автомоби́ля в ми́лях **2** (travel expenses) проездны́е (*pl.*)

milieu /mɪ'ljɜː/ *n.* (*pl.* ~**x** *or* ~**s**) окруже́ние, среда́

militancy /'mɪlɪt(ə)nsɪ/ *n.* вои́нственность

militant /'mɪlɪt(ə)nt/ *n.* бое́ц, боре́ц
● *adj.* вои́нствующий

militarism /'mɪlɪtərɪz(ə)m/ *n.* милитари́зм

militaristic /mɪlɪtə'rɪstɪk/ *adj.* милитари́стский, милитаристи́ческий

◌ **military** /'mɪlɪtərɪ/ *n.*: the ~ военнослу́жащие (*m. pl.*), войска́ (*nt. pl.*)
● *adj.* вое́нный

■ ~ **service** *n.* вое́нная слу́жба; (as liability) во́инская пови́нность

militate /'mɪlɪteɪt/ *v.i.*: ~ against препя́тствовать (*impf.*) + *d.*; говори́ть (*impf.*) про́тив + *g.*; his age ~s against him ему́ меша́ет во́зраст

militia /mɪ'lɪʃə/ *n.* мили́ция

milk /mɪlk/ *n.* молоко́
● *v.t.* дои́ть, по-; (fig.): they ~ed him of all his cash они́ вы́качали из него́ все де́ньги

■ ~**man** *n.* продаве́ц молока́, моло́чник; ~**shake** *n.* моло́чный кокте́йль

milky /'mɪlkɪ/ *adj.* (**milkier**, **milkiest**) моло́чный; the M~ Way Мле́чный Путь

mill /mɪl/ *n.* **1** (for grinding corn) ме́льница; (factory) фа́брика
● *v.t.* моло́ть, пере-
● *v.i.* (infml): a crowd was ~ing around the entrance лю́ди толпи́лись у вхо́да

millenni|um /mɪ'lenɪəm/ *n.* (*pl.* ~**ums** *or* ~**a**) тысячеле́тие

miller /'mɪlə(r)/ *n.* ме́льник

milligram, milligramme /'mɪlɪgræm/ *n.* миллигра́мм

millimetre /'mɪlɪmiːtə(r)/ (AmE **-meter**) *n.* миллиме́тр

milliner /'mɪlɪnə(r)/ *n.* ма́стер/мастери́ца по изготовле́нию же́нских шляп

m

million /'mɪljən/ *n. & adj.* (*pl.* ~**s** *or* (*with numeral or qualifying word*) ~) миллио́н + *g.*

millionaire /mɪljə'neə(r)/ *n.* миллионе́р

millionth /'mɪljənθ/ *n.* миллио́нная часть
● *adj.* миллио́нный

milometer /maɪ'lɒmɪtə(r)/ *n.* (BrE) счётчик пробе́га

mime /maɪm/ *n.* (performance; technique) пантоми́ма; (artist) арти́ст пантоми́мы
● *v.t.* (act by miming) изобра|жа́ть, -зи́ть пантоми́мой
● *v.i.* (pretend to sing) петь, с-/про- под фоногра́мму

mimic /'mɪmɪk/ *n.* имита́тор
● *v.t.* (**mimicked, mimicking**) передра́зн|ивать, -и́ть

mimicry /'mɪmɪkrɪ/ *n.* (imitation) имити́рование; подража́ние + *d.*

minaret /mɪnə'ret/ *n.* минаре́т

minc|e /mɪns/ *n.* (BrE) фарш
● *v.t.* руби́ть (*impf.*)
■ ~**ed beef** *n.* говя́жий фарш; ~**ing machine** *n.* мясору́бка

✎ **mind** /maɪnd/ *n.* **1** (intellect) ум; **you must be out of your ~** вы с ума́ сошли́ **2** (remembrance): **bear in ~** по́мнить (*impf.*); **the tune went clean out of my ~** я на́чисто забы́л э́ту мело́дию **3** (opinion) мне́ние; **he spoke his ~ on the subject** он открове́нно вы́сказался на э́ту те́му; **he doesn't know his own ~** он сам не зна́ет, чего́ он хо́чет; **try to keep an open ~!** постара́йтесь быть объекти́вн|ым (-ой)! **4** (intention) наме́рение; **he changed his ~** он переду́мал; **I have made up my ~ to stay** я реши́л оста́ться **5** (thought) мы́сли (*f. pl.*); **I had something on my ~** меня́ что́-то трево́жило; **I set his ~ at rest** я его́ успоко́ил; **it took her ~ off her troubles** э́то отвлекло́ её от (её) забо́т/невзго́д; **I cannot read his ~** я не могу́ угада́ть/проче́сть его́ мы́сли; **I can see him in my ~'s eye** он стои́т у меня́ пе́ред глаза́ми **6** (way of thinking) настрое́ние; **to my ~** на мой взгляд; мне ка́жется (*or* я счита́ю), что **7** (attention): **keep your ~ on what you are doing** не отвлека́йтесь
● *v.t.* **1** (take care, charge of) присм|а́тривать, -отре́ть за + *i.*; **~ your own business!** не вме́шивайтесь не в своё де́ло! **2** (worry about) забо́титься (*impf.*) о + *p.*; беспоко́иться о + *p.*; **never ~ the expense** не ду́майте о расхо́дах; **~ your head!** осторо́жнее, не ушиби́те го́лову! **3** (object to) возра|жа́ть, -зи́ть на + *a.*; име́ть (*impf.*) что-н. про́тив + *g.*; **I don't ~ the cold** я не бою́сь хо́лода; **would you ~ opening the door?** откро́йте, пожа́луйста, дверь; **I wouldn't ~ going for a walk** я не прочь прогуля́ться
● *v.i.* **1** (worry) беспоко́иться (*impf.*); трево́житься (*impf.*); **we're rather late, but never ~!** мы немно́го опа́здываем, ну, ничего́! **2** (object) возра|жа́ть, -зи́ть; **do you ~ if I smoke?** вы не про́тив, е́сли я закурю́?

✎ ключева́я ле́ксика

■ ~**-boggling** *adj.* порази́тельный

minder /'maɪndə(r)/ *n.* (BrE) (child minder) ня́ня; (infml, bodyguard) телохрани́тель (*m.*)

mindful /'maɪndfʊl/ *adj.* забо́тливый; **we must be ~ of the children** мы должны́ ду́мать о де́тях; **I was ~ of his advice** я по́мнил его́ сове́т; **he was ~ of his duty** он сознава́л свой долг

mindless /'maɪndlɪs/ *adj.* **1** (thoughtless) безду́мный; (stupid) глу́пый **2** (not requiring intelligence): ~ **drudgery** механи́ческий труд

mine[1] /maɪn/ *n.* **1** (excavation) ша́хта; рудни́к **2** (explosive device) ми́на
● *v.t.* **1** (excavate): ~ **coal/ore** добыва́ть (*impf.*) у́голь/руду́ **2** (mil.) мини́ровать, за-
● *v.i.* разраб|а́тывать, -о́тать рудни́к
■ ~**field** *n.* ми́нное по́ле

✎ **mine**[2] /maɪn/ *pron.*: **that book is ~** э́то моя́ кни́га; **a friend of ~** (оди́н) мой друг/знако́мый

miner /'maɪnə(r)/ *n.* (coal ~) шахтёр

mineral /'mɪnər(ə)l/ *n.* минера́л, руда́
● *adj.* минера́льный
■ ~ **water** *n.* минера́льная вода́

mineralogical /mɪnərə'lɒdʒɪk(ə)l/ *adj.* минералоги́ческий

mineralogist /mɪnə'rælədʒɪst/ *n.* минерало́г

mineralogy /mɪnə'rælədʒɪ/ *n.* минерало́гия

minestrone /mɪnɪ'strəʊnɪ/ *n.* италья́нский овощно́й суп с ме́лкими макаро́нными изде́лиями

mingle /'mɪŋg(ə)l/ *v.i.* сме́шиваться (*impf.*); ~ **with** (frequent) обща́ться (*impf.*) с + *i.*

mini /'mɪnɪ/ *n.* (*pl.* ~**s**) (garment) ми́ни (*юбка и т. д.*)

miniature /'mɪnɪtʃə(r)/ *n.* миниатю́ра
● *adj.* миниатю́рный

minibus /'mɪnɪbʌs/ *n.* микроавто́бус

minicab /'mɪnɪkæb/ *n.* (BrE) такси́ (*nt. indecl.*)

minidisc /'mɪnɪdɪsk/ *n.* ми́ни-ди́ск

minim /'mɪnɪm/ *n.* (BrE, mus.) полови́нная но́та

minimal /'mɪnɪm(ə)l/ *adj.* минима́льный

minimalism /'mɪnɪməlɪz(ə)m/ *n.* минимали́зм

minimalist /'mɪnɪməlɪst/ *n.* минимали́ст
● *adj.* минимали́стский

minimize /'mɪnɪmaɪz/ *v.t.* (reduce to minimum) дов|оди́ть, -ести́ до ми́нимума; (make light of) преум|еньша́ть, -е́ньшить

✎ **minimum** /'mɪnɪməm/ *n.* ми́нимум; (*attr.*) минима́льный

mining /'maɪnɪŋ/ *n.* го́рное де́ло, го́рная промы́шленность

minion /'mɪnjən/ *n.* приспе́шник

miniskirt /'mɪnɪskɜːt/ *n.* ми́ни-ю́бка

✎ **minister** /'mɪnɪstə(r)/ *n.* **1** (head of government dept.) мини́стр **2** (clergyman) свяще́нник, па́стор
● *v.i.*: ~ **to** служи́ть (*impf.*) + *d.*; прислу́живать (*impf.*) + *d.*

ministerial /mɪnɪ'stɪərɪəl/ *adj.* министе́рский

ministry /'mɪnɪstrɪ/ *n.* министе́рство

mink /mɪŋk/ *n.* но́рка

minnow /'mɪnəʊ/ *n.* песка́рь (*m.*)

♂ **minor** /'maɪnə(r)/ *n.* **1** (person under age) несовершенноле́тний **2** (mus.) мино́р; A ~ ля мино́р
● *adj.* **1** (of lesser importance) второстепе́нный; малозначи́тельный, ме́лкий, небольшо́й **2** (mus.) мино́рный; ~ **key** мино́рная тона́льность

♂ **minority** /maɪ'nɒrɪtɪ/ *n.* меньшинство́, ме́ньшая часть; (*attr.*) ~ **group** меньшинство́

Minsk *n.* Минск

minstrel /'mɪnstr(ə)l/ *n.* менестре́ль (*m.*)

mint¹ /mɪnt/ *n.* (bot.) мя́та; (a sweet) мя́тная конфе́та

mint² /mɪnt/ *n.* (fin.) моне́тный двор
● *v.t.* чека́нить (*impf.*)

minuet /mɪnju'et/ *n.* менуэ́т

minus /'maɪnəs/ *n.* ми́нус
● *adj.* отрица́тельный
● *prep.* ми́нус; без + *g.*; ~ **1** ми́нус оди́н; **he came back** ~ **an arm** он верну́лся без руки́
■ ~ **sign** *n.* (знак) ми́нус

minuscule /'mɪnəskjuːl/ *adj.* кро́хотный, о́чень ма́ленький

♂ **minute¹** /'mɪnɪt/ *n.* **1** (fraction of hour or degree) мину́та; **he left everything till the last** ~ он отложи́л всё до после́дней мину́ты **2** (moment) мгнове́ние, моме́нт, миг; **just a** ~! (одну́) мину́тку!; **I'll tell him the** ~ **he arrives** как то́лько он придёт, я ему́ скажу́ **3** (*usu. in pl.*) (record) протоко́л

minute² /maɪ'njuːt/ *adj.* (**minutest**, *no comp.*) (tiny) ме́лкий, кро́хотный

minutiae /maɪ'njuːʃɪaɪ/ *n.* ме́лочи (*f. pl.*); дета́ли (*f. pl.*)

minx /mɪŋks/ *n.* (joc.) озорни́ца; (coquette) коке́тка

miracle /'mɪrək(ə)l/ *n.* чу́до

miraculous /mɪ'rækjʊləs/ *adj.* чуде́сный

mirage /'mɪrɑːʒ/ *n.* мира́ж

mire /'maɪə(r)/ *n.* тряси́на; боло́то; **his name was dragged through the** ~ его́ смеша́ли с гря́зью

mirror /'mɪrə(r)/ *n.* зе́ркало
● *v.t.* отра|жа́ть, -зи́ть

mirth /mɜːθ/ *n.* (gladness) весе́лье; (laughter) смех

misadventure /mɪsəd'ventʃə(r)/ *n.* несча́стье, несча́стный слу́чай; **death by** ~ смерть от несча́стного слу́чая

misapprehension /mɪsæprɪ'henʃ(ə)n/ *n.* превра́тное понима́ние; **I was under a** ~ я заблужда́лся

misappropriate /mɪsə'prəʊprɪeɪt/ *v.t.* (незако́нно) присв|а́ивать, -о́ить

misappropriation /mɪsəprəʊprɪ'eɪʃ(ə)n/ *n.* незако́нное присвое́ние

misbehave /mɪsbɪ'heɪv/ *v.i.* ду́рно себя́ вести́ (*det.*)

miscalculate /mɪs'kælkjʊleɪt/ *v.t.* пло́хо рассчи́т|ывать, -а́ть
● *v.i.* просчи́т|ываться, -а́ться

miscalculation /mɪskælkjʊ'leɪʃ(ə)n/ *n.* просчёт

miscarriage /'mɪskærɪdʒ/ *n.* **1** (biol.) вы́кидыш; **she had a** ~ у неё произошёл вы́кидыш **2**: ~ **of justice** оши́бка правосу́дия

miscarr|y /mɪs'kærɪ/ *v.i.* **1** (of a woman) име́ть (*impf.*) вы́кидыш **2** (fail) терпе́ть (*impf.*) неуда́чу; **his plans** ~**ied** его́ пла́ны провали́лись

miscellaneous /mɪsə'leɪnɪəs/ *adj.* сме́шанный; разнообра́зный

mischief /'mɪstʃɪf/ *n.* озорство́; прока́зы (*f. pl.*); **he is always getting into** ~ он всегда́ прока́зничает/шали́т

mischievous /'mɪstʃɪvəs/ *adj.* озорно́й, шаловли́вый

misconception /mɪskən'sepʃ(ə)n/ *n.* непра́вильное представле́ние/понима́ние

misconduct /mɪs'kɒndʌkt/ *n.* дурно́е поведе́ние; **professional** ~ наруше́ние профессиона́льной э́тики; должностно́е преступле́ние

misconstrue /mɪskən'struː/ *v.t.* непра́вильно истолко́в|ывать, -а́ть

misdeed /mɪs'diːd/ *n.* преступле́ние

misdemeanour /mɪsdɪ'miːnə(r)/ (AmE **misdemeanor**) *n.* просту́пок

misdiagnose /mɪsdaɪəg'nəʊz/ *v.t.* (med.) ста́вить, по- неве́рный диа́гноз; **her depression was** ~**d as stress** у неё была́ депре́ссия, а ей оши́бочно поста́вили диа́гноз «стре́сс»

miser /'maɪzə(r)/ *n.* скря́га (*c.g.*), скуп|о́й (-а́я)

miserable /'mɪzərəb(ə)l/ *adj.* **1** (unhappy) жа́лкий, несча́стный **2** (causing wretchedness) плохо́й, скве́рный; **what** ~ **weather!** кака́я скве́рная пого́да! **3** (mean): a ~ **sum (of money)** ничто́жная/ми́зерная су́мма

miserly /'maɪzəlɪ/ *adj.* скупо́й

misery /'mɪzərɪ/ *n.* **1** (suffering) страда́ние; муче́ние **2** (extreme poverty) нищета́, бе́дность **3** (BrE, infml, person who complains) зану́да (*c.g.*), ны́тик

misfire /mɪs'faɪə(r)/ *v.i.* да|ва́ть, -ть осе́чку; (tech., of ignition) не срабо́тать, -выпада́ть, вы́пасть; (fig.) не состоя́ться (*impf.*); **his plans** ~**d** его́ план сорва́лся

misfit /'mɪsfɪt/ *n.* неприспосо́бленный челове́к

misfortune /mɪs'fɔːtʃuːn/ *n.* (bad luck) беда́, несча́стье; **I had the** ~ **to lose my purse** я име́л несча́стье потеря́ть кошелёк; (stroke of bad luck) несча́стье, неуда́ча

misgiving /mɪs'gɪvɪŋ/ *n.* опасе́ние; дурно́е предчу́вствие

misguided /mɪs'gaɪdɪd/ *adj.*: **I was** ~ **enough to trust him** я име́л неосторо́жность дове́риться ему́; ~ **enthusiasm** энтузиа́зм, досто́йный лу́чшего примене́ния

mishandle /mɪs'hænd(ə)l/ *v.t.* (ill-treat) пло́хо/ду́рно обраща́ться (*impf.*) с + *i.*; (manage inefficiently) пло́хо вести́ (*det.*) (де́ло)

mishap /'mɪshæp/ *n.* неуда́ча

mishear /mɪs'hɪə(r)/ *v.t.* нето́чно расслы́шать (*pf.*)

m

misinform /ˌmɪsɪnˈfɔːm/ v.t. непрáвильно информи́ровать (impf., pf.)

misinformation /ˌmɪsɪnfəˈmeɪʃ(ə)n/ n. невéрная информáция; дезинформáция

misinterpret /ˌmɪsɪnˈtɜːprɪt/ v.t. непрáвильно пон|имáть, -я́ть

misinterpretation /ˌmɪsɪntɜːprɪˈteɪʃ(ə)n/ n. непрáвильное понимáние/толковáние

misjudge /mɪsˈdʒʌdʒ/ v.t. невéрно оцéн|ивать, -и́ть

mislay /mɪsˈleɪ/ v.t. затеря́ть (pf.)

mislead /mɪsˈliːd/ v.t. вв|оди́ть, -ести́ в заблуждéние

mismanage /mɪsˈmænɪdʒ/ v.t. плóхо управля́ть (impf.) + i.

mismanagement /mɪsˈmænɪdʒmənt/ n. плохóе управлéние/руковóдство; (inefficiency) нераспоряди́тельность

misnomer /mɪsˈnəʊmə(r)/ n. непрáвильное назвáние/и́мя

misogynist /mɪˈsɒdʒɪnɪst/ n. женоненави́стник

misogyny /mɪˈsɒdʒɪnɪ/ n. женоненави́стничество

misplaced /mɪsˈpleɪst/ adj. (inappropriate) неумéстный; (unfounded) безоснóвáтельный

misprint /ˈmɪsprɪnt/ n. опечáтка

mispronounce /ˌmɪsprəˈnaʊns/ v.t. непрáвильно произн|оси́ть, -ести́

misquote /mɪsˈkwəʊt/ v.t. нетóчно цити́ровать, про-; **I have been ~d** мои́ словá искази́ли

misread /mɪsˈriːd/ v.t. (read incorrectly) читáть, про- непрáвильно; (misinterpret) непрáвильно истолкóв|ывать, -áть

misrepresent /ˌmɪsreprɪˈzent/ v.t. иска|жáть, -зи́ть

misrepresentation /ˌmɪsreprɪzenˈteɪʃ(ə)n/ n. искажéние (фáктов)

misrule /mɪsˈruːl/ n. (bad government) плохóе правлéние; (lawlessness) беспоря́док, анáрхия

◆ **miss¹** /mɪs/ n. (failure to hit etc.) прóмах; **I gave the meeting a ~** (BrE) я не пошёл на собрáние
● v.t. **1** (fail to hit or catch): **he ~ed the ball** он пропусти́л мяч; **he ~ed the bus** он опоздáл на автóбус **2** (fig., fail to grasp) не пон|имáть, -я́ть; не улови́ть (pf.); **you have ~ed the point** вы не пóняли сути́ **3** (fail to hear or see) не услы́шать (pf.); пропус|кáть, -ти́ть; **you must not ~ this film** не пропусти́те этот фильм **4** (fail to meet): **you've just ~ed him!** вы с ним чуть-чýть разминýлись! **5** (escape by chance) избе|гáть, -жáть; **we just ~ed having an accident** мы чуть не попáли в катастрóфу **6** (regret absence of) скучáть (impf.), соскýчиться (pf.) по (+ d.); **she ~es her husband** онá скучáет по мýжу; **he ~ed Moscow** он соскучи́лся по Москвé
● v.i. (fail to hit target) промáх|иваться, -нýться; не поп|адáть, -áсть в цель
□ **~ out** v.t. упус|кáть, -ти́ть; пропус|кáть,

-ти́ть; **you have ~ed out the most important thing** вы пропусти́|ли/упусти́ли сáмое вáжное
● v.i. (infml): **he ~ed out on all the fun** он пропусти́л сáмое весéлье; **I felt I was ~ing out** я чýвствовал, что мнóгое упускáю

miss² /mɪs/ n. мисс

mis-sell /mɪsˈsel/ v.t. прод|авáть, -áть обмáнным/нечéстным путём

misshapen /mɪsˈʃeɪpən/ adj. урóдливый

missile /ˈmɪsaɪl/ n. **1** (object thrown) метáтельный предмéт **2** (weapon thrown or fired) снаря́д **3** (rocket weapon) ракéта

missing /ˈmɪsɪŋ/ adj. недостаю́щий; потеря́вшийся; **there is a page ~** не хватáет страни́цы; **he went ~** он пропáл (бéз вести)

◆ **mission** /ˈmɪʃ(ə)n/ n. **1** (mil.) задáние **2** (pol., relig.) ми́ссия

missionary /ˈmɪʃənərɪ/ n. миссионéр (-ка)

missive /ˈmɪsɪv/ n. послáние

misspell /mɪsˈspel/ v.t. & i. непрáвильно написáть (pf.); сдéлать (pf.) орфографи́ческую оши́бку

mist /mɪst/ n. (lit., fig.) тумáн, ды́мка, мгла
● v.t. & i. затумáни|вать(ся), -ть(ся); **my glasses have ~ed over** у меня́ запотéли очки́

◆ **mistake** /mɪˈsteɪk/ n. оши́бка; заблуждéние; **by ~** по оши́бке; **make no ~ (about it)** бýдьте увéрены
● v.t. (misunderstand) ошиб|áться, -и́ться в + p.; (misrecognize): **he mistook me for my brother** он приня́л меня́ за моегó брáта

mistaken /mɪˈsteɪkən/ adj. **1** (in error): **if I am not ~** éсли я не ошибáюсь **2** (ill-judged; erroneous) неосмотри́тельный

mistletoe /ˈmɪs(ə)ltəʊ/ n. омéла

mistress /ˈmɪstrɪs/ n. **1** (woman in charge) хозя́йка **2** (lover) любóвница

mistrial /mɪsˈtraɪəl/ n. непрáвильное судéбное разбирáтельство

mistrust /mɪsˈtrʌst/ n. недовéрие
● v.t. не доверя́ть (impf.) + d.

misty /ˈmɪstɪ/ adj. (mistier, mistiest) тумáнный

misunder|stand /ˌmɪsʌndəˈstænd/ v.t. непрáвильно пон|имáть, -я́ть; **she felt ~stood** онá чýвствовала, что её не понимáют

misunderstanding /ˌmɪsʌndəˈstændɪŋ/ n. недоразумéние

misuse¹ /mɪsˈjuːs/ n. непрáвильное употреблéние; злоупотреблéние (чем)

misuse² /mɪsˈjuːz/ v.t. (use improperly) непрáвильно употреб|ля́ть, -и́ть; (treat badly) дýрно обращáться (impf.) с + i.

miter /ˈmaɪtə(r)/ n. (AmE) = mitre

mitigat|e /ˈmɪtɪɡeɪt/ v.t. смягч|áть, -и́ть; **~ing circumstances** смягчáющие обстоя́тельства

mitigation /ˌmɪtɪˈɡeɪʃ(ə)n/ n. смягчéние, ослаблéние; **a plea in ~** ходáтайство о смягчéнии пригово́ра

mitre /ˈmaɪtə(r)/ (AmE **miter**) n. (bishop's headgear) ми́тра

mitten /ˈmɪt(ə)n/ n. рукави́ца

m

ᔯ **mix** /mɪks/ *n.* смесь
- *v.t.* **1** (mingle) смеш|ивать, -áть; (combine) сочетáть (*impf.*); **I like to ~ business with pleasure** я люблю сочетáть приятное с полéзным **2** (prepare by ~ing) смеш|ивать, -áть; перемéш|ивать, -áть
- *v.i.* (of persons) общáться (*impf., pf.*); **she won't ~ with her neighbours** онá не хóчет общáться с сосéдями
- □ **~ up** *v.t.* (~ thoroughly) (хорошó) перемéш|ивать, -áть; (confuse) перепýт|ывать, -ать; **I ~ed him up with his father** я перепýтал его с его отцóм; **a ~ed-up child** (infml) трýдный ребёнок; (involve) впýт|ывать, -ать
- ▪ **~-up** *n.* недоразумéние

mixed /mɪkst/ *adj.* смéшанный, перемéшанный; **(place for) ~ bathing** óбщий пляж; **I have ~ feelings about it** у меня на этот счёт противоречивые чýвства
- ▪ **~-race** *adj.* имéющий родителей рáзных рас, состоящий из людéй рáзных рас

mixer /ˈmɪksə(r)/ *n.* (for cement) мешáлка; (for food) миксер

mixture /ˈmɪkstʃə(r)/ *n.* смесь

ml *abbr. of* **1** (**millilitre(s)**) /ˈmɪlɪliːtə(r)(z)/ мл (миллилитр) **2** (**mile(s)**) /maɪl(z)/ миля

mm /ˈmɪlɪmiːtə(r)(z)/ *n.* (*abbr. of* **millimetre(s)**) мм (миллимéтр)

MMR (med.) (*of* **measles, mumps, and rubella**) *abbr.*, MMR, прививка «корь-свинка-краснýха»

MMS *abbr.* (*of* **Multimedia Message/ Messaging Service**): **~ message** MMS-сообщéние

moan /məʊn/ *n.* стон; (infml, complaint) стон, нытьё
- *v.i.* стонáть (*impf.*); (infml, complain) ныть (*impf.*)

moat /məʊt/ *n.* ров с водóй

mob /mɒb/ *n.* толпá
- *v.t.* (**mobbed, mobbing**) нап|адáть, -áсть на + *a.*

ᔯ **mobile** /ˈməʊbaɪl/ *n.* (BrE) мобильный/сóтовый телефóн
- *adj.* **1** (easily moved) передвижнóй, переноснóй; (troops) подвижный **2** (person) мобильный
- ▪ **~ phone** *n.* (BrE) мобильный/сóтовый телефóн

mobility /məˈbɪlɪtɪ/ *n.* подвижность, мобильность

mobilization /ˌməʊbɪlaɪˈzeɪʃ(ə)n/ *n.* мобилизáция

mobilize /ˈməʊbɪlaɪz/ *v.t.* мобилизовáть (*impf., pf.*)
- *v.i.* мобилизовáться (*impf., pf.*)

moccasin /ˈmɒkəsɪn/ *n.* мокасин

mock /mɒk/ *adj.* поддéльный, фальшивый
- *v.t.* насмехáться (*impf.*) над + *i.*
- ▪ **~ examination** *n.* (BrE) предэкзаменационная провéрка

mockery /ˈmɒkərɪ/ *n.* (ridicule) издевáтельство; (parody) парóдия

MOD *abbr.* (*of* **Ministry of Defence**) Министéрство оборóны

mod /mɒd/ *adj.* (*attr.*): **~ cons** (BrE) совремéнные удóбства; **with all ~ cons** (BrE, in advertisement) со всéми удóбствами

mode /məʊd/ *n.* мéтод

ᔯ **model** /ˈmɒd(ə)l/ *n.* **1** (representation) модéль, схéма **2** (pattern) образéц, стандáрт; **he is a ~ of gallantry** он образéц галáнтности; **a ~ husband** идеáльный муж **3** (person posing for artist) натýрщик(-ца) **4** (woman displaying clothes etc.) манекéнщица, модéль **5** (design) модéль, тип
- *v.t.* (**modelled, modelling**, AmE **modeled, modeling**) дéлать, с- модéль + *g.*; **she ~led the dress** (wore it as a ~) онá демонстрировала плáтье; (fig.): **he ~s himself upon his father** он слéдует примéру своегó отцá

modem /ˈməʊdem/ *n.* модéм

moderate[1] /ˈmɒdərət/ *adj.* умéренный; срéдний; **~ drinker** умéренно пьющий человéк

moderate[2] /ˈmɒdəreɪt/ *v.t.* ум|ерять, -éрить; смягч|áть, -ить
- *v.i.* смягч|áться, -иться

moderation /ˌmɒdəˈreɪʃ(ə)n/ *n.* умéренность; **in ~** умéренно

ᔯ **modern** /ˈmɒd(ə)n/ *adj.* совремéнный
- ▪ **~ languages** *n. pl.* нóвые языки

modernism /ˈmɒdənɪz(ə)m/ *n.* модернизм

modernization /ˌmɒdənaɪˈzeɪʃ(ə)n/ *n.* модернизáция

modernize /ˈmɒdənaɪz/ *v.t.* модернизировать (*impf., pf.*)

modest /ˈmɒdɪst/ *adj.* скрóмный

modesty /ˈmɒdɪstɪ/ *n.* скрóмность

modicum /ˈmɒdɪkəm/ *n.* чýточка, толика

modification /ˌmɒdɪfɪˈkeɪʃ(ə)n/ *n.* модификáция

modify /ˈmɒdɪfaɪ/ *v.t.* модифицировать (*impf.*)

modish /ˈməʊdɪʃ/ *adj.* мóдный

modulate /ˈmɒdjʊleɪt/ *v.t.* (vary pitch of, also radio) модулировать (*impf.*)

module /ˈmɒdjuːl/ *n.* (independent unit) блок, сéкция; (unit of study) курс

mogul /ˈməʊg(ə)l/ *n.* (fig., tycoon) магнáт

mohair /ˈməʊheə(r)/ *n.* мохéр; (*attr.*) мохéровый

moist /mɔɪst/ *adj.* влáжный, сырóй

moisten /ˈmɔɪs(ə)n/ *v.t.* увлажн|ять, -ить; смá|чивать, -очить

moisture /ˈmɔɪstʃə(r)/ *n.* влáжность, влáга

moisturize /ˈmɔɪstʃəraɪz/ *v.t.* увлажн|ять, -ить

moisturizer /ˈmɔɪstʃəraɪzə(r)/ *n.* увлажняющий крем

mold /məʊld/ *n.* (AmE) = **mould**[1], **mould**[2]

Moldova /mɒlˈdəʊvə/ *n.* Молдóва

Moldovan /mɒlˈdəʊv(ə)n/ *n.* молдавáн|ин (-ка)
- *adj.* молдáвский

m

moldy /ˈməʊldɪ/ adj. (AmE) = mouldy

mole¹ /məʊl/ n. (on skin) ро́динка

mole² /məʊl/ n. (zool.) крот; (secret agent) аге́нт, внедри́вшийся в иностра́нную разве́дку

molecular /məˈlekjʊlə(r)/ adj. молекуля́рный

molecule /ˈmɒlɪkjuːl/ n. моле́кула

molest /məˈlest/ v.t. прист|ава́ть, -а́ть к + d.

mollify /ˈmɒlɪfaɪ/ v.t. смягч|а́ть, -и́ть; успок|а́ивать, -о́ить

mollusc /ˈmɒləsk/ n. моллю́ск

mollycoddle /ˈmɒlɪkɒd(ə)l/ v.t. не́жить (impf.)

Molotov cocktail /ˈmɒlətɒf ˈkɒkteɪl/ n. буты́лка с зажига́тельной сме́сью

molt /məʊlt/ v.i. (AmE) = moult

molten /ˈməʊlt(ə)n/ adj. распла́вленный

✓ **moment** /ˈməʊmənt/ n. моме́нт, миг; **he will be here (at) any ~ now** он здесь бу́дет с мину́ты на мину́ту; **I am busy at the ~** я сейча́с за́нят

momentarily /ˈməʊməntərɪlɪ/ adv. на мгнове́ние; (AmE, very soon) че́рез не́сколько мину́т

momentary /ˈməʊməntərɪ/ adj. мгнове́нный

momentous /məˈmentəs/ adj. ва́жный

momentum /məˈmentəm/ n. (pl. **momenta**) (phys.) ине́рция; (fig., impetus) дви́жущая си́ла; и́мпульс

monarch /ˈmɒnək/ n. мона́рх

monarchist /ˈmɒnəkɪst/ n. монархи́ст (-ка) ● adj. монархи́стский

monarchy /ˈmɒnəkɪ/ n. мона́рхия

monastery /ˈmɒnəstrɪ/ n. монасты́рь (m.)

monastic /məˈnæstɪk/ adj. (of monasteries) монасты́рский; **~ life** мона́шеская жизнь; **~ order** мона́шеский о́рден

✓ **Monday** /ˈmʌndeɪ/ n. понеде́льник

monetarism /ˈmʌnɪtərɪz(ə)m/ n. монетари́зм

monetarist /ˈmʌnɪtərɪst/ n. монетари́ст ● adj. монетари́стский

monetary /ˈmʌnɪtərɪ/ adj. де́нежный

✓ **money** /ˈmʌnɪ/ n. (pl. **moneys** or **monies**) де́нь|ги (-ег); **I got my ~'s worth** я получи́л сполна́ за свои́ де́ньги; **make ~** (earn money) зараб|а́тывать, -о́тать; (become rich) разбогате́ть (pf.)
■ **~ box** n. (BrE) копи́лка; **~ laundering** n. отмыва́ние де́нег; **~lender** n. ростовщи́к; **~ order** n. почто́вый перево́д

Mongolia /mɒŋˈɡəʊlɪə/ n. Монго́лия

Mongolian /mɒŋˈɡəʊlɪən/ n. (person) монго́л (-ка); (language) монго́льский язы́к ● adj. монго́льский

mongrel /ˈmʌŋɡr(ə)l/ n. дворня́га

monitor /ˈmɒnɪtə(r)/ n. (TV, comput.) монито́р ● v.t. следи́ть (impf.) за + i.

monk /mʌŋk/ n. мона́х

monkey /ˈmʌŋkɪ/ n. (pl. **~s**) обезья́на

mono /ˈmɒnəʊ/ n. мо́но; **recorded in ~** запи́санный монофони́чески

monochrome /ˈmɒnəkrəʊm/ n. однокра́сочное изображе́ние ● adj. одноцве́тный, монохро́мный

monogamous /məˈnɒɡəməs/ adj. монога́мный, единобра́чный

monogamy /məˈnɒɡəmɪ/ n. монога́мия, единобра́чие

monogram /ˈmɒnəɡræm/ n. моногра́мма

monograph /ˈmɒnəɡrɑːf/ n. моногра́фия

monolith /ˈmɒnəlɪθ/ n. моноли́т

monolithic /mɒnəˈlɪθɪk/ adj. (lit., fig.) моноли́тный

monologue /ˈmɒnəlɒɡ/ n. моноло́г

monopolize /məˈnɒpəlaɪz/ v.t.: **he ~s the conversation** он не даёт никому́ вста́вить сло́ва

monopoly /məˈnɒpəlɪ/ n. монопо́лия

monosodium glutamate /mɒnəˈsəʊdɪəm ˈɡluːtəmeɪt/ n. глутама́т на́трия (пищевая добавка)

monosyllabic /mɒnəsɪˈlæbɪk/ adj. односло́жный

monotone /ˈmɒnətəʊn/ n.: **in a ~** без вся́кого выраже́ния, моното́нно

monotonous /məˈnɒtənəs/ adj. моното́нный

monotony /məˈnɒtənɪ/ n. моното́нность, однообра́зие

monsoon /mɒnˈsuːn/ n. сезо́н дожде́й

monster /ˈmɒnstə(r)/ n. (misshapen creature) уро́д; (imaginary animal) чудо́вище; (person of exceptional cruelty etc.) чудо́вище, и́зверг

monstrosity /mɒnˈstrɒsɪtɪ/ n. (unsightly thing) чудо́вище

monstrous /ˈmɒnstrəs/ adj. (monsterlike) ужа́сный; (huge) грома́дный, исполи́нский

Montenegro /mɒntɪˈniːɡrəʊ/ n. Черного́рия

✓ **month** /mʌnθ/ n. ме́сяц

monthly /ˈmʌnθlɪ/ n. (periodical) ежеме́сячник ● adj. ме́сячный ● adv. ежеме́сячно

monument /ˈmɒnjʊmənt/ n. па́мятник, монуме́нт

monumental /mɒnjʊˈment(ə)l/ adj. монумента́льный; (fig.) колосса́льный

moo /muː/ v.i. (**moos, mooed**) мыча́ть, про-

mooch /muːtʃ/ v.i. **1** (usu. **~ about/ around**) (BrE, infml, loiter) слоня́ться (impf.) (без де́ла) **2** (AmE, infml, cadge) попроша́йничать (impf.)

mood /muːd/ n. (state of mind) настрое́ние; **I am not in the ~ for conversation** я не расположе́н к разгово́ру

moody /ˈmuːdɪ/ adj. (**moodier, moodiest**) (gloomy) угрю́мый; (subject to changes of mood) капри́зный; переме́нчивого настрое́ния

moon /muːn/ n. луна́; (astron.) Луна́; **new ~** молодо́й ме́сяц, новолу́ние
■ **~light** n. лу́нный свет; **by ~light** при луне́ ● v.i. (infml) подхалту́ри|вать, -ть; **~lighting** n. (infml) халту́ра; **~lit** adj. за́литый лу́нным све́том

moor¹ /mʊə(r)/ n. ме́стность, поро́сшая ве́реском

■ ~**land** *n.* вересковая пустошь

moor² /mʊə(r)/ *v.t.* ставить, по- на причал; швартовать, при-
● *v.i.*: **they** ~**ed in the harbour** они пришвартовались в гавани

mooring /ˈmʊərɪŋ/ *n.* причал

Moorish /ˈmʊərɪʃ/ *adj.* мавританский

moose /muːs/ *n.* (*pl.* ~) американский лось

moot /muːt/ *adj.*: **a** ~ **point** спорный пункт
● *v.t.*: **the question was** ~**ed** вопрос поставили на обсуждение

mop /mɒp/ *n.* швабра; ~ **of hair** копна волос
● *v.t.* (**mopped, mopping**) прот|ирать, -ереть; вытирать, вытереть; **she** ~**ped the floor** она протёрла пол; **he** ~**ped his brow** он вытер лоб
□ ~ **up** *v.t.* (spilt liquid) вытирать, вытереть

mope /məʊp/ *v.i.* хандрить (*impf.*)

moped /ˈməʊped/ *n.* мопед

◊ **moral** /ˈmɒr(ə)l/ *n.* **1** мораль **2** (*in pl.*) нрав|ы (-ов)
● *adj.* **1** (ethical) моральный; нравственный **2** (virtuous) нравственный

morale /məˈrɑːl/ *n.* моральное состояние

moralist /ˈmɒrəlɪst/ *n.* моралист (-ка)

morality /məˈrælɪtɪ/ *n.* нравственность, этика

moralize /ˈmɒrəlaɪz/ *v.i.* морализировать (*impf.*)

morass /məˈræs/ *n.* болото; трясина

moratorium /ˌmɒrəˈtɔːrɪəm/ *n.* (*pl.* **moratoriums** *or* **moratoria**) мораторий; **impose a** ~ объявл|ять, -ить мораторий

morbid /ˈmɔːbɪd/ *adj.* болезненный, нездоровый

◊ **more** /mɔː(r)/ *n. & adj.* (greater amount or number) больше, более; **a little** ~ побольше; **he received** ~ **than I did** он получил больше меня; (additional amount or number) ещё; больше; ~ **tea** ещё чаю; **have you any** ~ **matches?** у вас ещё остались спички?; **there is no** ~ **soup** супа больше нет
● *adv.* больше, более; (rather) скорее; ~ **or less** более или менее; **I like beef** ~ **than lamb** я предпочитаю говядину баранине; **she is** ~ **beautiful than her sister** она красивее своей сестры; ~ **and** ~ всё более и более; **the** ~ **the better** чем больше, тем лучше; ~ **than once** не раз; **once** ~ снова, опять, ещё раз

moreover /mɔːˈrəʊvə(r)/ *adv.* кроме того; сверх того

morgue /mɔːg/ *n.* морг

moribund /ˈmɒrɪbʌnd/ *adj.* умирающий, отмирающий

◊ **morning** /ˈmɔːnɪŋ/ *n.* **1** утро; **in the** ~ утром; **it began to rain in the** ~ дождь пошёл с утра; **on Monday** ~ в понедельник утром; **this** ~ сегодня утром; **good** ~! доброе утро! **2** (*attr.*) утренний

Moroccan /məˈrɒkən/ *n.* марокка́н|ец (-ка)
● *adj.* марокканский

Morocco /məˈrɒkəʊ/ *n.* Марокко (*nt. indecl.*)

moron /ˈmɔːrɒn/ *n.* (infml) идиот (-ка)

morose /məˈrəʊs/ *adj.* (gloomy) мрачный; (unsociable) необщительный

morphine /ˈmɔːfiːn/ *n.* морфий

morris dance /ˈmɒrɪs/ *n.* моррис (*народный английский танец*)

Morse /mɔːs/ *n.* (*in full* ~ **code**) азбука Морзе

morsel /ˈmɔːs(ə)l/ *n.* кусочек

mortal /ˈmɔːt(ə)l/ *n.* смертный
● *adj.* смертельный, смертоносный; **a** ~ **wound** смертельная рана

mortality /mɔːˈtælɪtɪ/ *n.* смертность

mortar /ˈmɔːtə(r)/ *n.* (building material) известковый раствор

mortgage /ˈmɔːgɪdʒ/ *n.* ссуда на покупку дома
● *v.t.* за|кладывать, -ложить

mortician /mɔːˈtɪʃ(ə)n/ *n.* (AmE) похоронных дел мастер

mortify /ˈmɔːtɪfaɪ/ *v.t.* (shame, humiliate) об|ижать, -идеть; ун|ижать, -изить; **a** ~**ing defeat** унизительное поражение

mortuary /ˈmɔːtjʊərɪ/ *n.* морг, покойницкая

mosaic /məʊˈzeɪk/ *n.* мозаика
● *adj.* мозаичный

Moscow /ˈmɒskəʊ/ *n.* Москва; (*attr.*) московский

mosque /mɒsk/ *n.* мечеть

mosquito /mɒˈskiːtəʊ/ *n.* (*pl.* ~**es**) комар

moss /mɒs/ *n.* мох

◊ **most** /məʊst/ *n.* (greatest part) большая часть; **I was in bed** ~ **of the time** большую часть времени я провёл в постели; (greatest amount) наибольшее количество; **£5 at the** ~ максимум 5 фунтов; **you must make the** ~ **of your chances** вам нужно наилучшим образом использовать свои возможности
● *adj.*: ~ **people** большинство людей; ~ **of us** большинство из нас; **who has the** ~ **money?** у кого больше всех денег?
● *adv.* **1** (expr. comparison): **what I** ~ **desire** чего я больше всего хочу; **the** ~ **beautiful** самый красивый **2** (very) очень, весьма

◊ **mostly** /ˈməʊstlɪ/ *adv.* главным образом

MOT (BrE) *abbr.* (*of* **Ministry of Transport**) Министерство транспорта; ~ (**test**) ≈ техосмотр

motel /məʊˈtel/ *n.* мотель (*m.*)

moth /mɒθ/ *n.* мотылёк, ночная бабочка

◊ **mother** /ˈmʌðə(r)/ *n.* **1** мать **2** (*attr.*) материнский
● *v.t.* относиться (*impf.*) по-матерински к + *d.*
■ ~**board** *n.* (comput.) материнская плата; ~ **country** *n.* родина; ~**in-law** *n.* (wife's mother) тёща; (husband's mother) свекровь; ~**of-pearl** *n.* перламутр ● *adj.* перламутровый; ~ **tongue** *n.* родной язык

motherhood /ˈmʌðəhʊd/ *n.* материнство

motherly /ˈmʌðəlɪ/ *adj.* нежный, заботливый

motif /məʊˈtiːf/ *n.* мотив

◊ **motion** /ˈməʊʃ(ə)n/ *n.* **1** (movement) движение; **the car was in** ~ машина двигалась; **he set the plan in** ~ он приступил

m

к осуществле́нию пла́на **2** (proposal)
предложе́ние
● *v.t. & i.*: **he** ~**ed to them to leave** он показа́л
жéстом, чтóбы они́ ушли́

motionless /'məʊʃənlıs/ *adj.* неподви́жный

motivate /'məʊtıveıt/ *v.t.* (induce) побужда́ть,
-ди́ть; **he is highly ~d** у негó есть мóщный
сти́мул

motivation /məʊtı'veıʃ(ə)n/ *n.* побужде́ние,
сти́мул

motive /'məʊtıv/ *n.* пóвод, моти́в,
побужде́ние

motley /'mɒtlı/ *adj.*: **a ~ crew** пёстрая толпа́

motor /'məʊtə(r)/ *n.* **1** (engine) дви́гатель
(*m.*), мотóр **2** (*in full* BrE ~ **car**) (легковóй)
автомоби́ль (*m.*); **the ~ trade** торгóвля
автомоби́лями
■ ~**bike** *n.* мотоци́кл; ~ **boat** *n.* мотóрная
лóдка; ~**cycle** *n.* мотоци́кл; ~**cyclist**
n. мотоцикли́ст; ~ **racing** *n.* (BrE)
автомоби́льные гóнки (*abbr.* автогóнки) (*f.
pl.*); ~ **scooter** *n.* моторóллер; ~ **show**
n. автосалóн; ~**way** *n.* (BrE) автостра́да,
автомагистра́ль

motorcade /'məʊtəkeıd/ *n.* автоколóнна

motorist /'məʊtərıst/ *n.* автомоби́лист (-ка)

motorize /'məʊtəraız/ *v.t.* моторизова́ть
(*impf., pf.*)

mottled /'mɒt(ə)ld/ *adj.* пятни́стый,
кра́пчатый

motto /'mɒtəʊ/ *n.* (*pl.* ~**es** *or* ~**s**) деви́з;
лóзунг

mould¹ /məʊld/ (AmE **mold**) *n.* (container)
фóрма
● *v.t.* лепи́ть, с-; (fig.) формирова́ть, с-

mould² /məʊld/ (AmE **mold**) *n.* (fungus)
плéсень

mouldy /'məʊldı/ (AmE **moldy**)
adj. (**mo(u)ldier, mo(u)ldiest**)
заплéсневелый

moult /məʊlt/ (AmE **molt**) *v.i.* линя́ть (*impf.*)

mound /maʊnd/ *n.* (for burial or fortification)
на́сыпь; (heap) ку́ча

mount /maʊnt/ *n.*: **M~ Everest** гора́ Эвере́ст
● *v.t.* **1** (ascend, get on to) взбира́ться,
-обра́ться на + *a.*; подн|има́ться, -я́ться на +
a.; **he ~ed his horse** он сел на лóшадь **2** (put,
fix on a ~) вст|авля́ть, -а́вить в опра́ву;
опр|авля́ть, -а́вить **3** (set up): **the enemy ~ed
an offensive** враг предприня́л наступле́ние
● *v.i.* (increase) расти́ (*impf.*); (*also* ~ **up**)
нак|а́пливаться, -опи́ться

✍ **mountain** /'maʊntın/ *n.* **1** гора́ **2** (*attr.*)
гóрный

mountaineer /maʊntı'nıə(r)/ *n.* альпини́ст
(-ка)

mountaineering /maʊntı'nıərıŋ/ *n.*
альпини́зм

mountainous /'maʊntınəs/ *adj.* гори́стый

mourn /mɔːn/ *v.t.* опла́кивать (*impf.*)
● *v.i.* скорбе́ть (*impf.*); печа́литься (*impf.*);
she ~ed for her child она́ опла́кивала смерть

✍ ключева́я ле́ксика

своегó ребёнка

mourner /'mɔːnə(r)/ *n.* прису́тствующий на
похорона́х

mournful /'mɔːnfʊl/ *adj.* скóрбный,
тра́урный

mourning /'mɔːnıŋ/ *n.* скорбь; тра́ур

mouse /maʊs/ *n.* (*pl.* **mice**) мышь; (comput.
pl. also ~**s**) мышь, мы́шка
■ ~ **mat** (BrE), ~ **pad** (AmE) *nn.* (comput.)
кóврик для мы́ши; ~**over** *n.* (comput.)
маусóвер (sl.)

mousse /muːs/ *n.* мусс

moustache /məˈstɑːʃ/ (AmE **mustache**) *n.*
усы́ (-óв)

✍ **mouth¹** /maʊθ/ *n.* рот; (fig.): ~ **of a cave** вход
в пеще́ру; ~ **of a river** у́стье реки́
■ ~ **organ** *n.* губна́я гармóника; ~**wash**
n. полоска́ние для рта; ~**watering** *adj.*
вку́сный, аппети́тный

mouth² /maʊð/ *v.t.*: **the actor ~ed his words**
актёр напы́щенно деклами́ровал

mouthful /'maʊθfʊl/ *n.* кусóк, глотóк

✍ **move** /muːv/ *n.* **1** (in games) ход; **it's
your ~!** ваш ход!; (fig., action) посту́пок;
ход, шаг **2** (initiation of action) движе́ние;
it's time we made a ~ (BrE) нам пора́
дви́гаться; **get a ~ on!** дви́гайтесь!,
потора́пливайтесь! **3** (change of residence)
переéзд
● *v.t.* **1** (change position of; put in motion) дви́гать
(*impf.*); передв|ига́ть, -и́нуть; **he ~d his
chair nearer the fire** он пододви́нул стул к
ками́ну **2** (affect, provoke) трóгать, трóнуть;
волнова́ть, вз-; **the sight ~d him to tears**
зре́лище трóнуло егó до слёз
● *v.i.* **1** (change position; be in motion) дви́|гаться,
-нуться; **the lever won't ~** рыча́г не
сдвига́ется; **don't ~!** не дви́гайтесь!; **a
moving staircase** эскала́тор **2** (change one's
residence) пере|езжа́ть, -éхать **3** (make progress)
развива́ться (*impf.*) **4** (stir) шевели́ться
(*impf.*); **nobody ~d to help him** никтó не
пошевели́лся, чтóбы ему́ помóчь
□ ~ **about, ~ around** *v.i.* пере|езжа́ть, -éхать;
разъезжа́ть (*impf.*); **he ~s about a lot** он
мнóго разъезжа́ет
□ ~ **along** *v.i.*: ~ **along there, please!**
проходи́те, пожа́луйста!
□ ~ **away** *v.t. & i.* удал|я́ть(ся), -и́ть(ся); **they
~d away from here** они́ переéхали отсю́да
□ ~ **in** *v.i.* (take up abode): **they ~d in next door**
они́ посели́лись в сосе́днем дóме
□ ~ **on** *v.i.* продв|ига́ться, -и́нуться; идти́ (*det.*)
да́льше; **she stopped and then ~d on** она́
останови́лась, а зате́м опя́ть продóлжила
путь; ~ **on to a better job** он перешёл на
бóлее подходя́щую рабóту
□ ~ **out** *v.i.*: **we have to ~ out tomorrow** мы
должны́ съéхать за́втра
□ ~ **over** *v.i.* (to make room) подв|ига́ться,
-и́нуться
□ ~ **up** *v.i.* подв|ига́ться, -и́нуться; ~ **up and let
me sit down!** подви́ньтесь и да́йте мне сесть!

✍ **movement** /'muːvmənt/ *n.* **1** (state of moving,
motion) движе́ние, перемеще́ние **2** (of the body)

or part of it) жест, телодвиже́ние **3** (group united by common purpose) движе́ние

ℐ **movie** /'mu:vɪ/ n. (infml) фильм, кинокарти́на; **he's gone to the ~s** он пошёл в кино́

moving /'mu:vɪŋ/ adj. волну́ющий, тро́гательный

mow /məʊ/ v.t. & i. (p.p. **mowed** or **mown**) коси́ть, с-; **he ~ed the lawn** он подстри́г траву́/газо́н

mower /'məʊə(r)/ n. коси́лка

Mozambican /məʊzæm'bi:kən/ n. мозамби́кец; жи́тель (-ница) Мозамби́ка
● adj. мозамби́кский

Mozambique /məʊzæm'bi:k/ n. Мозамби́к

MP abbr. (of **Member of Parliament**) член парла́мента

MP3 n. (comput.) MP3, МП3 (формат сжатия аудиоданных); **MP3 player** MP3-пле́ер

mpg abbr. (of **miles per gallon**) миль на галло́н (бензи́на)

mph abbr. (of **miles per hour**) миль в час

ℐ **Mr** /'mɪstə(r)/ n. (abbr. of **mister**) (pl. **Messrs** /'mesəz/) г-н (господ|и́н (pl. -á))

MRI abbr. (of **magnetic resonance imaging**) МРТ (магни́тно-резона́нсная томогра́фия)(); **~ scan** иссле́дование с по́мощью МРТ

ℐ **Mrs** /'mɪsɪz/ n. (abbr. of **mistress**) (pl. ~) г-жа (госпожа́)

MS abbr. (of **multiple sclerosis**) рассе́янный склеро́з

ℐ **Ms** /mɪz, məz/ n. г-жа (госпожа́)

M.Sc. abbr. (of **Master of Science**) маги́стр (есте́ственных) нау́к

Mt /maʊnt/ n. (abbr. of **Mount**) г. (гора́)

ℐ **much** /mʌtʃ/ n. & adj. (**more, most**) мно́гое; мно́го + g.; **his work is not up to ~** его́ рабо́та не отлича́ется высо́ким ка́чеством; **too ~** сли́шком (мно́го); мно́го; **I don't see ~ of him** я его́ ре́дко ви́жу; **he doesn't read ~** он ма́ло чита́ет; **he is not ~ of an actor** он актёр нева́жный; **how ~** ско́лько + g.; **very ~** о́чень (мно́го); о́чень си́льно; **as ~ again** ещё сто́лько же; **I thought as ~** я так и ду́мал; **so ~** сто́лько + g.
● adv. (**more, most**) **1** (by far) гора́здо; **~ better** гора́здо лу́чше; **~ the best** гора́здо лу́чше други́х/остальны́х **2** (greatly) о́чень; нема́ло; **I am ~ obliged to you** премно́го вам обя́зан; **it doesn't ~ matter** э́то не име́ет большо́го значе́ния; **so ~ the better** тем лу́чше; **how ~ do you love me?** как си́льно ты меня́ лю́бишь?; **~ to my surprise** к моему́ вели́кому удивле́нию; **~ as I should like to go** как бы я ни хоте́л пойти́; **not ~!** (infml, very ~) о́чень да́же!; а как же! **3** (about) приме́рно, почти́; **his condition is ~ the same** его́ состоя́ние приме́рно тако́е же

muck /mʌk/ n. (infml) грязь; (anything disgusting) дрянь

□ **~ about** (BrE) v.t. (inconvenience) причин|я́ть, -и́ть неудо́бство + d.
● v.i.: **he was ~ing about with the radio** он вози́лся с ра́дио

mud /mʌd/ n. грязь; сля́коть

muddle /'mʌd(ə)l/ n. **1** (mess; disorder) беспоря́док; неразбери́ха; **things have got into a ~** всё перепу́талось/ смеша́лось **2** (confusion of mind) пу́таница
● v.t. **1** (bring into disorder) перепу́т|ывать, -ать; вн|оси́ть, -ести́ беспоря́док в + a.; **you have ~d (up) my papers** вы смеша́ли мои́ бума́ги **2** (confuse) пу́тать, на-; сби|ва́ть, -ть с то́лку; **don't ~ me (up)** не сбива́йте меня́ с то́лку

muddy /'mʌdɪ/ adj. (**muddier, muddiest**) гря́зный

muesli /'m(j)u:zlɪ/ n. мю́сли (смесь злаков, орехов и сухих фруктов) (nt. indecl.)

muffin /'mʌfɪn/ n. ма́ффин, ма́ленький куполови́дный кекс; (AmE **English ~**) ≈ горя́чая бу́лочка, ≈ ола́дья

muffle /'mʌf(ə)l/ v.t. **1** (wrap up) ку́тать, за-; **he was ~d up in an overcoat** он был заку́тан в пальто́ **2** (of sound) глуши́ть, за-

mug¹ /mʌɡ/ n. (vessel) кру́жка

mug² /mʌɡ/ n. (BrE, infml, simpleton) балбе́с

mug³ /mʌɡ/ v.t. (**mugged, mugging**) (BrE, infml) (attack) нап|ада́ть, -а́сть на (+ a.); (rob) гра́бить, о-

mugger /'mʌɡə(r)/ n. у́личный граби́тель

mugging /'mʌɡɪŋ/ n. у́личный грабёж

muggy /'mʌɡɪ/ adj. (**muggier, muggiest**) (damp and warm) вла́жный и тёплый; (close) ду́шный

mulberry /'mʌlbərɪ/ n. (tree) ту́товое де́рево, шелкови́ца; (fruit) ту́товая я́года; (attr.) (colour) багро́вый

mulch /mʌltʃ/ n. му́льча (защитная подстилка из сухой травы, листьев, навоза и т. п.)
● v.t. мульчи́ровать (impf., pf.)

mule¹ /mju:l/ n. мул; (fig., of person) упря́мый осёл

mule² /mju:l/ n. (slipper) шлёпанец

mull¹ /mʌl/ v.t.: **~ wine** вари́ть, с- глинтве́йн

mull² /mʌl/ v.t.: **~ over** (ponder) размышля́ть (impf.) над + i.

mullah /'mʌlə/ n. мулла́ (m.)

mullet /'mʌlɪt/ n. кефа́ль

multicoloured /'mʌltɪkʌləd/ (AmE **multicolored**) adj. многоцве́тный, кра́сочный

multicultural /mʌltɪ'kʌltʃər(ə)l/ adj. многокульту́рный, многонациона́льный

multiculturalism /mʌltɪ'kʌltʃərəlɪz(ə)m/ n. мультикультурали́зм

multifarious /mʌltɪ'feərɪəs/ adj. разнообра́зный

multilateral /mʌltɪ'lætər(ə)l/ adj. многосторо́нний

multimedia /mʌltɪ'mi:dɪə/ n. мультиме́диа (pl. indecl.); (attr.) мультимеди́йный

multinational /mʌltɪ'næʃən(ə)l/ adj. многонациона́льный

ℐ **multiple** /'mʌltɪp(ə)l/ n. кра́тное число́
● adj. многочи́сленный

m

■ ~ **sclerosis** *n.* рассе́янный склеро́з

multiplication /mʌltɪplɪˈkeɪʃ(ə)n/ *n.* умноже́ние

multiplicity /mʌltɪˈplɪsɪtɪ/ *n.* многочи́сленность, разнообра́зие

multiply /ˈmʌltɪplaɪ/ *v.t.* умн|ожа́ть, -о́жить
● *v.i.* размн|ожа́ться, -о́житься

multipurpose /mʌltɪˈpɜːpəs/ *adj.* многоцелево́й

multiracial /mʌltɪˈreɪʃ(ə)l/ *adj.* многонациона́льный, многора́совый

multistorey /mʌltɪˈstɔːrɪ/ *adj.* многоэта́жный

multitask /ˈmʌltɪtɑːsk/ *v.i.* **1** (comput.) рабо́тать (*impf.*) в многозада́чном режи́ме **2** (fig.) де́лать, с- мно́го дел одновре́менно

multitude /ˈmʌltɪtjuːd/ *n.* мно́жество, ма́сса

mum /mʌm/ *n.* (BrE, infml, mother) ма́ма

mumble /ˈmʌmb(ə)l/ *v.t. & i.* (mutter) бормота́ть, про-

mumbo-jumbo /mʌmbəʊˈdʒʌmbəʊ/ *n.* тараба́рщина

mummy¹ /ˈmʌmɪ/ *n.* (embalmed corpse) му́мия

mummy² /ˈmʌmɪ/ *n.* (BrE, infml, mother) ма́ма, ма́мочка

mumps /mʌmps/ *n.* сви́нка (*заболева́ние*)

munch /mʌntʃ/ *v.t. & i.* жева́ть (*impf.*)

mundane /mʌnˈdeɪn/ *adj.* земно́й, мирско́й

municipal /mjuːˈnɪsɪp(ə)l/ *adj.* муниципа́льный, городско́й

municipality /mjuːnɪsɪˈpælɪtɪ/ *n.* муниципалите́т

munitions /mjuːˈnɪʃ(ə)ns/ *n. pl.* снаряже́ние, вооруже́ние
■ ~ **factory** *n.* вое́нный заво́д

mural /ˈmjʊər(ə)l/ *n.* фре́ска

⚜ **murder** /ˈmɜːdə(r)/ *n.* уби́йство
● *v.t.* уб|ива́ть, -и́ть

murderer /ˈmɜːdərə(r)/ *n.* уби́йца (*c.g.*)

murderous /ˈmɜːdərəs/ *adj.* смертоно́сный

murky /ˈmɜːkɪ/ *adj.* (**murkier**, **murkiest**) мра́чный, тёмный

murmur /ˈmɜːmə(r)/ *n.* ро́пот
● *v.t. & i.* говори́ть (*impf.*) ти́хо; бормота́ть, про-; шепта́ть, про-

⚜ **muscle** /ˈmʌs(ə)l/ *n.* мы́шца, му́скул
● *v.i.* (infml): he ~d in on the conversation он ввяза́лся в разгово́р

Muscovite /ˈmʌskəvaɪt/ *n.* москви́ч (-ка)
● *adj.* моско́вский

muscular /ˈmʌskjʊlə(r)/ *adj.* (pert. to muscle) мы́шечный; (with strong muscles) мускули́стый; си́льный

muse¹ /mjuːz/ *n.* (myth.) му́за

muse² /mjuːz/ *v.i.* размышля́ть (*impf.*); заду́мываться (*impf.*)

⚜ **museum** /mjuːˈzɪəm/ *n.* музе́й

mushroom /ˈmʌʃruːm/ *n.* гриб

mushy /ˈmʌʃɪ/ *adj.* (**mushier**, **mushiest**) мя́гкий; (fig.) слаща́вый

⚜ **music** /ˈmjuːzɪk/ *n.* му́зыка

⚜ **musical** /ˈmjuːzɪk(ə)l/ *n.* мю́зикл
● *adj.* музыка́льный

musician /mjuːˈzɪʃ(ə)n/ *n.* музыка́нт

musicologist /mjuːzɪˈkɒlədʒɪst/ *n.* музыкове́д

musicology /mjuːzɪˈkɒlədʒɪ/ *n.* музыкове́дение

musket /ˈmʌskɪt/ *n.* мушке́т

⚜ **Muslim** /ˈmʊzlɪm, ˈmʌ-/ *n.* мусульма́н|ин (-ка)
● *adj.* мусульма́нский

mussel /ˈmʌs(ə)l/ *n.* ми́дия

⚜ **must** /mʌst/ *n.* (infml, necessary item): **the Tower of London is a ~ for visitors** тури́сты должны́ непреме́нно посмотре́ть Ло́ндонский Та́уэр
● *v. aux.* (3rd pers. sing. pres. **must**, *past* **had to** *or in indirect speech* **must**) **1** (expr. necessity): **one ~ eat to live** что́бы жить, ну́жно есть; **~ you go so soon?** неуже́ли вам уже́ на́до уходи́ть?; **~ you behave like that?** неуже́ли вы ина́че не мо́жете?; (expr. obligation): **we ~ not be late** нам нельзя́ опа́здывать; **I ~ admit** я до́лжен призна́ть **2** (with neg., expr. prohibition): **cars ~ not be parked here** стоя́нка маши́н запрещена́ **3** (expr. certainty or strong probability): **you ~ be tired** вы, наве́рно, уста́ли; **you ~ have known that** вы мо́жет быть, чтобы вы э́того не зна́ли

mustache /məˈstɑːʃ/ *n.* (AmE) = **moustache**

mustard /ˈmʌstəd/ *n.* (plant; relish) горчи́ца

muster /ˈmʌstə(r)/ *n.*: **will his work pass ~?** (fig.) его́ рабо́та годи́тся?
● *v.t.* (summon together) соб|ира́ть, -ра́ть; (fig.): **he ~ed (up) all his courage** он собра́лся с ду́хом
● *v.i.* (assemble) соб|ира́ться, -ра́ться

mustn't /ˈmʌs(ə)nt/ *neg. of* ▶ **must**

musty /ˈmʌstɪ/ *adj.* (**mustier**, **mustiest**) за́тхлый

mutant /ˈmjuːt(ə)nt/ *n.* (biol.) мута́нт

mutate /mjuːˈteɪt/ *v.i.* (biol.) мути́ровать (*impf., pf.*); (change) видоизмен|я́ться, -и́ться

mutation /mjuːˈteɪʃ(ə)n/ *n.* (biol.) мута́ция; (change) измене́ние

mute /mjuːt/ *adj.* **1** (silent) безмо́лвный **2** (unable to speak) (often offens.) немо́й
● *v.t.* приглуш|а́ть, -и́ть

mutilate /ˈmjuːtɪleɪt/ *v.t.* уве́чить, из-

mutilation /mjuːtɪˈleɪʃ(ə)n/ *n.* уве́чье

mutineer /mjuːtɪˈnɪə(r)/ *n.* мяте́жник

mutinous /ˈmjuːtɪnəs/ *adj.* мяте́жный

mutiny /ˈmjuːtɪnɪ/ *n.* мяте́ж
● *v.i.* бунтова́ть, взбунтова́ться

mutter /ˈmʌtə(r)/ *v.t. & i.* бормота́ть (*impf.*); говори́ть (*impf.*) невня́тно

mutton /ˈmʌt(ə)n/ *n.* бара́нина

mutual /ˈmjuːtʃʊəl/ *adj.* взаи́мный
■ ~ **aid** *n.* взаимопо́мощь

muzzle /ˈmʌz(ə)l/ *n.* **1** (animal's) мо́рда **2** (guard for this) намо́рдник **3** (of firearm) ду́ло
● *v.t.* над|ева́ть, -е́ть намо́рдник на + *a.*; (fig.) заст|авля́ть, -а́вить молча́ть

⚜ **my** /maɪ/ *poss. adj.* мой; (belonging to speaker) свой; **I lost ~ pen** я потеря́л свою́ ру́чку

Myanmar /maɪənˈmɑː(r)/ *n.* Мья́нма

myopia /maɪˈəʊpɪə/ *n.* миопи́я, близору́кость

myopic /maɪˈɒpɪk/ *adj.* близору́кий

⚜ ключева́я ле́ксика

myriad /'mɪrɪəd/ n. несмётное число; мириа́д|ы (pl., g. —)
• adj. несчётный
myrrh /mɜː(r)/ n. (fragrant resin) ми́рра
♂ **myself** /maɪˈself/ pron. **1** (refl.) себя́ (d., p. себе́, i. собо́й), -ся/-сь (suff.); I said to ~ я сказа́л себе́; I felt pleased with ~ я был дово́лен собо́й; I hurt ~ я уши́бся/уши́блась **2** (emph.) сам; I did it ~ я сам э́то сде́лал; I did it by ~ (without help) я э́то сде́лал сам; I am not ~ today я сего́дня немно́го не в фо́рме (or сам не свой) **3** (after preps.): dancing takes me out of ~ та́нцы развлека́ют меня́
mysterious /mɪˈstɪərɪəs/ adj. таи́нственный, зага́дочный

mystery /'mɪstərɪ/ n. та́йна, секре́т, зага́дка
mystic /'mɪstɪk/ n. ми́стик
• adj. (also ~**al** /'mɪstɪk(ə)l/) мисти́ческий
mysticism /'mɪstɪsɪz(ə)m/ n. ми́стика
mystify /'mɪstɪfaɪ/ v.t. озада́чи|вать, -ть
mystique /mɪˈstiːk/ n. таи́нственность, зага́дочность
myth /mɪθ/ n. (lit., fig.) миф
mythical /'mɪθɪk(ə)l/ adj. мифи́ческий
mythological /mɪθəˈlɒdʒɪk(ə)l/ adj. мифологи́ческий
mythology /mɪˈθɒlədʒɪ/ n. мифоло́гия
myxomatosis /mɪksəmə'təʊsɪs/ n. миксомато́з (заболевание кроликов)

Nn

nab /næb/ v.t. (**nabbed, nabbing**) захва́т|ывать, -и́ть; заст|ава́ть, -а́ть
naff /næf/ adj. (BrE) безвку́сный
nag /næg/ v.t. (**nagged, nagging**) пили́ть (impf.)
nagging /'nægɪŋ/ adj. приди́рчивый; a ~ pain ною́щая боль
nail /neɪl/ n. **1** (on finger or toe) но́готь (m.) **2** (metal spike) гвоздь (m.)
• v.t. **1** приби|ва́ть, -и́ть (что к чему); пригво|жда́ть, -зди́ть **2** (pin down): he tried to evade the issue but I ~ed him down он пыта́лся уйти́ от пробле́мы, но я прижа́л его́ к сте́нке
■ ~ **brush** n. щёт(оч)ка для ногте́й; ~ **file** n. пи́л(оч)ка (для ногте́й); ~ **polish** n. лак для ногте́й; ~ **varnish** n. (BrE) лак для ногте́й
naive /naɪˈiːv/ adj. наи́вный, простоду́шный
naivety, naïvety /naɪˈiːvɪtɪ/ n. наи́вность, простоду́шие
naked /'neɪkɪd/ adj. го́лый
nakedness /'neɪkɪdnɪs/ n. нагота́, обнажённость
♂ **name** /neɪm/ n. **1** (esp. **fore**~) и́мя (nt.); (surname) и́мя, фами́лия; (of pet) кли́чка; **what is his** ~? как его́ зову́т/фами́лия? **2** (of a thing) назва́ние **3** (reputation) и́мя, репута́ция; he made a ~ for himself он со́здал/сде́лал себе́ и́мя **4**: call sb ~s руга́ть (impf.) кого́-н. (нехоро́шими слова́ми)
• v.t. **1** (give ~ to) наз|ыва́ть, -ва́ть; да|ва́ть, -ть и́мя + d.; they haven't yet ~d the baby они́ ещё не́ да́ли ребёнку и́мя; he was ~d Andrew after his grandfather его́ назва́ли Андре́ем в честь де́да **2** (recite) наз|ыва́ть, -ва́ть; the pupil ~d the chief cities of Europe учени́к назва́л/перечи́слил гла́вные города́

Евро́пы; (state) наз|ыва́ть, -ва́ть; ~ your price! назна́чьте це́ну!; (identify): how many stars can you ~? ско́лько звёзд вы мо́жете определи́ть?
■ ~-**dropping** n. (infml) ≈ хвастовство́ свои́ми знако́мствами/свя́зями; ~**sake** n. (with same first ~) тёзка (c.g.)
namely /'neɪmlɪ/ adv. (a) и́менно; то есть
Namibia /nəˈmɪbɪə/ n. Нами́бия
Namibian /nəˈmɪbɪən/ n. намиби́|ец (-йка)
• adj. намиби́йский
nanny /'nænɪ/ n. (for child) ня́ня, ня́нечка
■ ~ **goat** n. коза́
nanotechnology /nænəʊtekˈnɒlədʒɪ/ n. нанотехноло́гия
nap /næp/ n. (short sleep) коро́ткий сон; have, take a ~ вздремну́ть (pf.)
napalm /'neɪpɑːm/ n. напа́лм; (attr.) напа́лмовый
nape /neɪp/ n. загри́вок
napkin /'næpkɪn/ n. (in full **table** ~) салфе́тка
nappy /'næpɪ/ n. (BrE, infml) подгу́зник
narcissistic /nɑːsɪˈsɪstɪk/ adj. самовлюблённый
narcis|sus /nɑːˈsɪsəs/ n. (pl. ~**si** /-saɪ/) нарци́сс
narcotic /nɑːˈkɒtɪk/ n. нарко́тик
• adj. наркоти́ческий
narrate /nəˈreɪt/ v.t. **1** (story) расска́з|ывать, -а́ть **2**: ~ a film/broadcast чита́ть (impf.) текст от а́втора
narrative /'nærətɪv/ n. (story) расска́з
• adj. повествова́тельный
narrator /nəˈreɪtə(r)/ n. расска́зч|ик (-ица); (theatr., cin.) а́вторский го́лос, ди́ктор
narrow /'nærəʊ/ adj. (**narrower, narrowest**) (lit., fig.) **1** у́зкий **2** (with little margin): a ~

majority незначи́тельное большинство́; **he had a ~ escape from death** он чу́дом избежа́л сме́рти
• *v.t.*: **the choice was ~ed down to two candidates** вы́бор свёлся к двум кандидату́рам
• *v.i.* (of river, road) су́|живаться, -зи́ться
■ **~-gauge** *adj.* узкоколе́йный; **~-minded** *adj.* узколо́бый, ограни́ченный

nasal /'neɪz(ə)l/ *adj.* (of, for the nose) носово́й; (of the voice) гнуса́вый

nasturtium /nə'stɜːʃəm/ *n.* насту́рция

nasty /'nɑːstɪ/ *adj.* (**nastier, nastiest**)
1 (offensive, e.g. smell or taste) неприя́тный, проти́вный **2** (morally offensive) ме́рзкий, га́дкий, гну́сный **3** (unkind, unpleasant) злой; **a ~ remark** зло́е замеча́ние; **a ~ temper** тяжёлый хара́ктер; **he played a ~ trick on me** он сыгра́л со мной злу́ю шу́тку; (of the elements): **~ weather** скве́рная пого́да **4** (threatening) опа́сный; **there was a ~ look in his eye** его́ вид не предвеща́л ничего́ до́брого **5** (difficult): **that's a ~ rock to climb** на э́ту ска́лу нелегко́ взобра́ться

⚘ **nation** /'neɪʃ(ə)n/ *n.* (population) на́ция; (people) наро́д; (country) страна́
■ **~wide** *adj.* общенациона́льный, всенаро́дный; **a ~wide search** ро́зыск/по́иски (*m. pl.*) по всей стране́

⚘ **national** /'næʃən(ə)l/ *n.* гражд|ани́н (-а́нка)
• *adj.* (of the state) госуда́рственный; (of the country or population as a whole) наро́дный, всенаро́дный; (central; opp. provincial) центра́льный; (pert. to a particular nation or ethnic group) национа́льный; **~ newspapers** центра́льные газе́ты
■ **~ anthem** *n.* госуда́рственный гимн; **N~ Health Service** *n.* Национа́льная слу́жба здравоохране́ния; **N~ Insurance** *n.* Госуда́рственное страхова́ние; **~ service** *n.* во́инская пови́нность

nationalism /'næʃənəlɪz(ə)m/ *n.* национали́зм

nationalist /'næʃənəlɪst/ *n.* национали́ст (-ка)

nationalistic /ˌnæʃənə'lɪstɪk/ *adj.* националисти́ческий

nationality /ˌnæʃə'nælɪtɪ/ *n.* по́дданство; гражда́нство; (ethnic group, e.g. within Russia) национа́льность

nationalization /ˌnæʃənəlaɪ'zeɪʃ(ə)n/ *n.* национализа́ция

nationalize /'næʃənəlaɪz/ *v.t.* национализи́ровать (*impf., pf.*)

native /'neɪtɪv/ *n.* **1** (indigenous inhabitant) тузе́м|ец (-ка) *n.* уроже́н|ец (-ка) + *g.* **3** (of animal, plant): **the kangaroo/eucalyptus is a ~ of Australia** ро́дина кенгуру́/эвкали́пта — Австра́лия
• *adj.* **1** (of one's birth) родно́й; **~ language** родно́й язы́к **2** (indigenous) тузе́мный; **~ population** тузе́мное/коренно́е/ме́стное населе́ние
■ **N~ American** *n.* америка́нск|ий инде́ец (-ая индиа́нка)

nativity /nə'tɪvɪtɪ/ *n.* Рождество́ Христо́во

NATO /'neɪtəʊ/ *n.* (*abbr. of* **North Atlantic Treaty Organization**) НА́ТО (Организа́ция Североатланти́ческого догово́ра)

natter /'nætə(r)/ (BrE, infml) *n.*: **I came in for a ~** я зашёл поболта́ть
• *v.i.* болта́ть (*impf.*)

⚘ **natural** /'nætʃr(ə)l/ *adj.* **1** (found in, pertaining to nature) есте́ственный, приро́дный; стихи́йный; **~ phenomena** явле́ния приро́ды **2** (normal, not surprising) есте́ственный, норма́льный; **it is ~ for parents to love their children** для роди́телей есте́ственно люби́ть свои́х дете́й **3** (simple, unaffected) просто́й; простоду́шный
■ **~-born** *adj.* прирождённый; **~ resources** *n. pl.* приро́дные ресу́рсы/бога́тства

naturalism /'nætʃərəlɪz(ə)m/ *n.* натурали́зм

naturalist /'nætʃərəlɪst/ *n.* натурали́ст

naturalistic /ˌnætʃərə'lɪstɪk/ *adj.* натуралисти́ческий

naturalization /ˌnætʃərəlaɪ'zeɪʃ(ə)n/ *n.* натурализа́ция; акклиматиза́ция

naturalize /'nætʃərəlaɪz/ *v.t.* (admit to citizenship) натурализова́ть (*impf., pf.*); (of animals, plants: introduce to another country) акклиматизи́ровать (*impf., pf.*)

naturally /'nætʃərəlɪ/ *adv.* есте́ственно

⚘ **nature** /'neɪtʃə(r)/ *n.* **1** (force, natural phenomena) приро́да **2** (temperament) нату́ра, хара́ктер; **human ~** челове́ческая приро́да; **it was his ~ to be proud** он был го́рдым по нату́ре **3** (essential quality) приро́да, хара́ктер; **by, in the (very) ~ of things** по приро́де веще́й
■ **~ reserve** *n.* запове́дник

naturism /'neɪtʃərɪz(ə)m/ *n.* (nudism) нуди́зм

naturist /'neɪtʃərɪst/ *n.* (nudist) нуди́ст (-ка)

naughtiness /'nɔːtɪnɪs/ *n.* озорство́

naughty /'nɔːtɪ/ *adj.* (**naughtier, naughtiest**) **1** (e.g. child's behaviour) непослу́шный, шаловли́вый, озорно́й; **be ~** озорнича́ть (*impf.*); **you were ~ today** ты сего́дня пло́хо себя́ вёл **2** (risqué) риско́ванный

nausea /'nɔːzɪə/ *n.* тошнота́

nauseat|e /'nɔːzɪeɪt/ *v.t.* вызыва́ть, вы́звать тошноту́ у + *g.*; **~ing** тошнотво́рный

nauseous /'nɔːzɪəs/ *adj.* тошнотво́рный; **I feel ~** меня́ тошни́т

nautical /'nɔːtɪk(ə)l/ *adj.* морско́й

naval /'neɪv(ə)l/ *adj.* морско́й; (of the navy) вое́нно-морско́й
■ **~ base** *n.* вое́нно-морска́я ба́за; **~ officer** *n.* морско́й офице́р

nave /neɪv/ *n.* (of church) неф

navel /'neɪv(ə)l/ *n.* пупо́к (infml)

navigable /'nævɪgəb(ə)l/ *adj.* (of river, sea) судохо́дный

navigate /'nævɪgeɪt/ *v.t.* (of person): **~ a ship/aircraft** управля́ть (*impf.*) корабле́м/самолётом; **~ a river/sea** пла́вать (*indet.*), плыть (*det.*) по реке́/мо́рю
• *v.i.* (in ship) пла́вать (*indet.*), плыть (*det.*);

(in aircraft) лет|а́ть (*indet.*), -е́ть (*det.*)

navigation /næviˈgeiʃ(ə)n/ *n.* навига́ция

navigator /ˈnævigeitə(r)/ *n.* (naut., aeron.) штурма́н, навига́тор

navy /ˈneivi/ *n.* **1** (naval forces) вое́нно-морски́е си́лы (*f. pl.*); (ships of war) вое́нно-морско́й флот **2** (*in full* ~ **blue**) тёмно-си́ний цвет
● *adj.* = navy-blue
■ ~-blue *adj.* тёмно-си́ний

Nazi /ˈnɑːtsi/ *n.* (*pl.* ~s) наци́ст (-ка)
● *adj.* наци́стский

Nazism /ˈnɑːtsiz(ə)m/ *n.* наци́зм

⚹ **near** /niə(r)/ *adj.* **1** (close at hand, in space or time) бли́зкий; **the station is quite** ~ **(to) our house** ста́нция (нахо́дится) совсе́м бли́зко от на́шего до́ма; **in the** ~ **future** в ближа́йшем бу́дущем **2**: **the** ~ **side** (of road or vehicle in Britain) ле́вая сторона́ **3** (narrowly achieved): ~ **miss** непрямо́е попада́ние; **we won, but it was a** ~ **thing** мы победи́ли, но с трудо́м
● *adv.* **1** (of place or time) бли́зко; **come a little** ~er подойди́те побли́же **2** (fig.): **the bus was nowhere** ~ **full** авто́бус был далеко́ не по́лный; **she is nowhere** ~ **as old as her husband** она́ гора́здо не так стара́, как её муж
● *v.t.* приближа́ться, -и́зиться к + *d.*; **he is** ~ing **his end** он при́ смерти
● *prep.* о́коло, во́зле, близ, бли́зко от, у (*all* + *g.*); ~ **here** недалеко́ отсю́да; **come** ~er **the fire!** подвига́йтесь к ками́ну!; **we are no** ~er **a solution** мы ничу́ть не приблизи́лись/бли́же к реше́нию
■ ~by *adj.*, *adv.* располо́женный побли́зости; близлежа́щий, сосе́дний; **he was standing** ~by он стоя́л бли́зко/ря́дом; ~sighted *adj.* близору́кий

⚹ **nearly** /ˈniəli/ *adv.* (almost) почти́; **he** ~ **fell** он чуть не упа́л; **we are** ~ **there** мы почти́ прие́хали/пришли́; **there is not** ~ **enough to eat** еды́ далеко́ не доста́точно

nearness /ˈniənis/ *n.* бли́зость

neat /niːt/ *adj.* **1** (of appearance) опря́тный, аккура́тный **2** (clear, precise) чёткий, изя́щный **3** (of liquor etc., undiluted) неразба́вленный **4** (AmE, infml, excellent) отли́чный, кла́ссный

nebulous /ˈnebjʊləs/ *adj.* (fig.) тума́нный

⚹ **necessarily** /nesəˈserili/ *adv.* обяза́тельно; **it is not** ~ **true** э́то не обяза́тельно так

⚹ **necessary** /ˈnesəsəri/ *adj.* (indispensable) необходи́мый; (compulsory) необходи́мый, обяза́тельный; (inevitable) неизбе́жный; **it is** ~ **to eat in order to live** что́бы жить, необходи́мо есть/пита́ться; **it is not** ~ **to dress for dinner** переодева́ться к обе́ду необяза́тельно; мо́жно не одева́ться к обе́ду

necessitate /niˈsesiteit/ *v.t.* вызыва́ть, вы́звать; обусло́вливать, -ить

necessity /niˈsesiti/ *n.* **1** (inevitability) неизбе́жность **2** (need) нужда́, необходи́мость; **of** ~ по необходи́мости **3** (necessary thing): **the telephone is a** ~ телефо́н не ро́скошь, а предме́т пе́рвой необходи́мости

neck /nek/ *n.* **1** ше́я; **stick one's** ~ **out** (infml) ста́вить, по- себя́ под уда́р; ~ **and** ~ но́здря в но́здрю; **голова́ в го́лову 2** (of var. objects): ~ **of a bottle** го́рлышко буты́лки; ~ **of a shirt** во́рот руба́шки
■ ~lace *n.* ожере́лье; ~line *n.* вы́рез (пла́тья); ~tie *n.* га́лстук

nectar /ˈnektə(r)/ *n.* некта́р

nectarine /ˈnektərin/ *n.* нектари́н, гла́дкий пе́рсик

née /nei/ *adj.* урождённая

⚹ **need** /niːd/ *n.* (want, requirement) нужда́; **the house is in** ~ **of repair** дом нужда́ется в ремо́нте; **my** ~**s are few** у меня́ скро́мные потре́бности; (necessity) необходи́мость; **if** ~ **be** в слу́чае необходи́мости; **there's no** ~ **to get upset** не́зачем расстра́иваться; **there is no** ~ **for him to read the whole book** ему́ необяза́тельно/не́зачем чита́ть всю кни́гу
● *v.t.* **1** (require) нужда́ться (*impf.*) в + *p.*; **the grass** ~**s cutting** газо́н сле́дует подстри́чь; **he** ~**s a haircut** ему́ пора́ (по)стри́чься **2** (*with inf.*) (be obliged, under necessity): ~ **I come today?** мне ну́жно приходи́ть сего́дня?; **you** ~**n't do it all tomorrow** вам не обяза́тельно ко́нчить всю рабо́ту за́втра; **you** ~ **not have bothered** напра́сно вы беспоко́ились; **I** ~ **not** (have no reason to) мне не́зачем; **he** ~ **not come** он мо́жет не приходи́ть

needle /ˈniːd(ə)l/ *n.* игла́, иго́лка
● *v.t.* (irritate, tease) подде́в|а́ть, -е́ть
■ ~work *n.* рукоде́лие

needless /ˈniːdlis/ *adj.* (unnecessary) нену́жный; (inappropriate) неуме́стный; ~ **to say** (само́ собо́й) разуме́ется

needy /ˈniːdi/ *adj.* (**needier, neediest**) нужда́ющийся

nefarious /niˈfeəriəs/ *adj.* злоде́йский

negate /niˈgeit/ *v.t.* сво|ди́ть, -ести́ на нет

negation /niˈgeiʃ(ə)n/ *n.* опроверже́ние

⚹ **negative** /ˈnegətiv/ *n.* **1** (statement, reply, word) отрица́ние **2** (phot.) негати́в
● *adj.* отрица́тельный

neglect /niˈglekt/ *n.* **1** (failure to attend to) пренебреже́ние + *i.*; ~ **of one's duties** пренебреже́ние свои́ми обя́занностями **2** (lack of care) запу́щенность; ~ **of one's children** отсу́тствие забо́ты о свои́х де́тях **3** (failure to notice) невнима́ние (**of**: к + *d.*) **4** (uncared-for state) запу́щенность, забро́шенность; **the house was in a state of** ~ дом был запу́щен/забро́шен
● *v.t.* **1** (work) запус|ка́ть, -ти́ть; забр|а́сывать, -о́сить; (duty) пренебр|ега́ть, -е́чь + *i.* **2** (leave uncared for) забр|а́сывать, -о́сить, оставля́ть, -а́вить без внима́ния; **he** ~ed **his family** он забро́сил свою́ семью́; ~ed **children** безнадзо́рные/забро́шенные де́ти; **a** ~ed **garden** запу́щенный/забро́шенный сад **3** (*with inf.*) (fail) заб|ыва́ть, -ы́ть; **he** ~ed **to wind up the clock** он забы́л завести́ часы́

neglectful /niˈglektful/ *adj.* небре́жный, невнима́тельный; **he is** ~ **of his interests** он не забо́тится о со́бственных интере́сах

n

negligence /'neglɪdʒ(ə)ns/ *n.* небрéжность
negligent /'neglɪdʒ(ə)nt/ *adj.* (careless) небрéжный; (inattentive) невнимáтельный
negligible /'neglɪdʒɪb(ə)l/ *adj.* незначи́тельный
negotiable /nɪ'ɡəʊʃəb(ə)l/ *adj.*
1: ~ **conditions, terms** усло́вия, котóрые мóгут служи́ть предмéтом переговóров **2** (navigable) проходи́мый; (of roads) проéзжий
negotiate /nɪ'ɡəʊʃɪeɪt/ *v.t.* **1** (conduct negotiations over) вести́ (*impf.*) переговóры о + *p.*; (conclude agreement on) при|ходи́ть, -йти́ к соглашéнию о + *p.* **2** (get over or through) проб|ира́ть, -ра́ться чéрез + *a.*; ~ **a corner** брать, взять поворóт
• *v.i.* догов|áриваться, -ори́ться
negotiation /nɪɡəʊʃɪ'eɪʃ(ə)n/ *n.* (process) обсуждéние; (*in pl.*) (talks) переговóры (*m. pl.*)
negotiator /nɪ'ɡəʊʃɪeɪtə(r)/ *n.* учáстник переговóров
Negro /'niːɡrəʊ/ *n.* (*pl.* ~**es**) (often offens.) негр
• *adj.* негритя́нский
neigh /neɪ/ *v.i.* ржáть (*impf.*)
♂ **neighbour** /'neɪbə(r)/ (AmE **neighbor**) *n.* сосéд (-ка)
♂ **neighbourhood** /'neɪbəhʊd/ (AmE **neighborhood**) *n.* **1** (locality) мéстность, окрéстность; (district) райóн **2** (neighbours) сосéди (*m. pl.*)
neighbouring /'neɪbərɪŋ/ (AmE **neighboring**) *adj.* сосéдний
neighbourly /'neɪbəlɪ/ (AmE **neighborly**) *adj.* добрососéдский; **in a** ~ **fashion** по-сосéдски; **that's not a** ~ **thing to do** э́то не по-сосéдски
♂ **neither** /'naɪðə(r)/ *pron. & adj.* ни тот, ни другóй; ~ **of them knows** ни оди́н (*or* никтó) из них не знáет
• *adv.* **1**: ~ … **nor** ни… ни; ~ **he nor I went** ни он, ни я не пошли́ **2** (*after neg. clause*): **he didn't go and** ~ **did I** он не пошёл, и я тóже
neoclassical /niːəʊ'klæsɪk(ə)l/ *adj.* неокласси́ческий
neon /'niːɒn/ *adj.* неóновый
■ ~ **light** *n.* неóновый свет; ~ **sign** *n.* неóновая реклáма
neo-Nazi /niːəʊ'nɑːtsɪ/ *n.* (*pl.* ~**s**) неонаци́ст (-ка)
Nepal /nɪ'pɔːl/ *n.* Непáл
Nepal|ese /nepə'liːz/, **Nepali** /nɪ'pɔːlɪ/ *nn.* (*pl.* ~**ese**, ~**i**, ~**is**) непáл|ец (-ка)
• *adjs.* непáльский
nephew /'nefjuː/ *n.* племя́нник
nepotism /'nepətɪz(ə)m/ *n.* семéйственность, кумовствó
Neptune /'neptjuːn/ *n.* Нептýн
nerd /nɜːd/ *n.* занýда (*c.g.*)
nerve /nɜːv/ *n.* **1** нерв; **he doesn't know what** ~**s are** он не знáет, что такóе нéрвы; **he gets on my** ~**s** он дéйствует мне на нéрвы

2 (courage, assurance) смéлость; **lose one's** ~ робéть, о-; (infml, impudence) нáглость; **he's got a** ~! ну и наглéц!
■ ~**-racking** *adj.* (situation) нервóзный; (time) напряжённый
nervous /'nɜːvəs/ *adj.* **1** (pert. to nerves) нéрвный; **he had a** ~ **breakdown** у негó бы́ло нéрвное расстрóйство; **he's a** ~ **wreck** э́то человéк с подóрванной нéрвной систéмой **2** (highly strung) нéрвный **3** (agitated) нéрвный, взволнóванный; **I'm** ~ я нéрвничаю **4** (apprehensive) нéрвный, нéрвничающий
nervousness /'nɜːvəsnɪs/ *n.* нéрвность, нервóзность
nest /nest/ *n.* гнездó; ~ **of tables** комплéкт стóликов (*вставляющихся один в другой*)
• *v.i.* (of birds) гнезди́ться (*impf.*)
■ ~ **egg** *n.* (fig., savings) сбережéния (*nt. pl.*)
nestle /'nes(ə)l/ *v.t. & i.*: ~ (one's head/ face) **against sb/sth** приж|имáться, -áться (головóй/лицóм) к комý/чемý-н.; **a village (lay)** ~**d at the foot of the hill** у поднóжия горы́ приюти́лась дерéвня
♂ **net¹** /net/ *n.* **1** (for protecting fruit, against mosquitoes etc.) сéтка; (snare for birds, fishing ~, also fig.) сеть, сéти (*f. pl.*) **2** (fabric) тюль (*m.*) **3**: **the Net** (comput.) Сеть, Интернéт
• *v.t.* (**netted, netting**) (fish etc.) лови́ть, пойма́ть в сеть/сéти; **he** ~**ted the ball** он заки́нул мяч в сéтку; (at football) он заби́л гол
■ ~**ball** *n.* нетбóл (*род баскетбола*); ~ **curtains** *n. pl.* тю́левые занавéски; ~**work** *n.* сеть в + *a.* (BrE, TV, radio) передавáть, -áть по (телевизиóнной/радиотрансляциóнной) сéти; (comput.) свя́з|ывать, -áть в óбщую сеть • *v.i.* (fig.) нала́ж|ивать, -дить контáкты/свя́зи
net², **nett** /net/ *adj.* чи́стый
• *v.t.* (**netted, netting**) (obtain as profit) получáть, -и́ть чи́стыми; дéлать, с-
■ ~ **income** *n.* чи́стый дохóд
nether /'neðə(r)/ *adj.* ни́жний
■ ~**most** *adj.* сáмый ни́жний; ~ **regions** *n. pl.* преиспóдняя
Netherlands /'neðələndz/ *n. pl.* Нидерлáнд|ы (-ов)
nett /net/ *adj. & v.t.* (BrE) = **net²**
netting /'netɪŋ/ *n.* сéтка
nettle /'net(ə)l/ *n.* крапи́ва
neuralgia /njʊə'rældʒə/ *n.* невралги́я
neurological /njʊərə'lɒdʒɪk(ə)l/ *adj.* неврологи́ческий
neurologist /njʊə'rɒlədʒɪst/ *n.* невропатóлог, неврóлог
neurology /njʊə'rɒlədʒɪ/ *n.* неврологи́я
neurosis /njʊə'rəʊsɪs/ *n.* (*pl.* **neuroses** /-siːz/) неврóз
neurotic /njʊə'rɒtɪk/ *adj.* невроти́ческий
neuter /'njuːtə(r)/ *n.* срéдний род
• *adj.* (gram.) срéдний; срéднего рóда
• *v.t.* кастри́ровать (*impf., pf.*)
neutral /'njuːtr(ə)l/ *n.* (of gears): **in** ~ в нейтрáльном положéнии; на нейтрáльной

переда́че; **put the car in(to)** ~ поста́вить (*pf.*) маши́ну на нейтра́льную переда́чу
● *adj.* нейтра́льный

neutrality /njuːˈtrælɪtɪ/ *n.* нейтралите́т

neutralize /ˈnjuːtrəlaɪz/ *v.t.* нейтрализова́ть (*impf., pf.*)

neutron /ˈnjuːtrɒn/ *n.* нейтро́н

Neva /ˈniːvə/ *n.* Нева́

✍ **never** /ˈnevə(r)/ *adv.* никогда́ (… не); (not once) ни ра́зу (… не); **you** ~ **know** как знать?; ~ **before** никогда́ ра́ньше; **I believed him once, but** ~ **again** одна́жды я ему́ пове́рил, но бо́льше никогда́ не пове́рю; (emphatic for not) так и не; **he** ~ **even tried** он да́же не попро́бовал; (BrE, expr. incredulity): ~! не мо́жет быть!
■ ~**-ending** *adj.* бесконе́чный; **it's a** ~**-ending job** э́той рабо́те конца́ нет; ~**theless** *adv.* одна́ко; (*conj.*) тем не ме́нее

✍ **new** /njuː/ *adj.* **1** но́вый; **as good as** ~ совсе́м как но́вый **2** (modern, advanced) нове́йший, после́дний; **the** ~**est fashions** нове́йшие/после́дние мо́ды **3** (fresh) молодо́й **4** (unaccustomed): **I am** ~ **to this work** я в э́том де́ле новичо́к; (unfamiliar): **this work is** ~ **to me** э́та рабо́та для меня́ непривы́чна
■ **N**~ **Age** *n.* филосо́фская систе́ма, бази́рующаяся на ве́ре в альтернати́вный о́браз жи́зни; ~**born** *adj.* новорождённый; ~**comer** *n.* новичо́к; ~**found** *adj.*: **a** ~**-found interest** но́вое увлече́ние + *i.*; ~ **moon** *n.* молодо́й ме́сяц, новолу́ние; ~ **potatoes** *n. pl.*. молодо́й карто́фель; **N**~ **Year** *n.* Но́вый год; **Happy N**~ **Year!** с Но́вым го́дом!; **N**~ **Year's Day** день Но́вого го́да; **N**~ **Year's Eve** кану́н Но́вого го́да

newel /ˈnjuːəl/ *n.* **1** коло́нна винтово́й ле́стницы **2** (*also* ~ **post**) баля́сина пери́л

newly /ˈnjuːlɪ/ *adv.* **1** (recently) неда́вно, но́во-; ~ **arrived** неда́вно прибы́вший, новоприбы́вший **2** (anew) вновь; **a** ~ **painted gate** свежевы́крашенная кали́тка
■ ~**-wed** *n.*: **the** ~**-weds** молодожён|ы (-ов)

newness /ˈnjuːnɪs/ *n.* новизна́

✍ **news** /njuːz/ *n.* **1** но́вости (*f. pl.*); (piece of ~) но́вость, весть; **have you heard the** ~? вы слы́шали но́вость? **2** (in press or radio) но́вости (*f. pl.*), после́дние изве́стия
■ ~ **agency** *n.* информацио́нное аге́нтство; ~**agent** *n.* (shop) газе́тный кио́ск; (person) = newsvendor; ~ **bulletin** *n.* (BrE) вы́пуск новосте́й; ~**caster** *n.* ди́ктор; ~ **conference** *n.* пресс-конфере́нция; ~ **flash** *n.* э́кстренное сообще́ние; ~**letter** *n.* информацио́нный бюллете́нь; ~**reader** *n.* (BrE) ди́ктор (*после́дних изве́стий*); ~**vendor** *n.* (BrE) продав|е́ц (-щи́ца) газе́т

newspaper /ˈnjuːspeɪpə(r)/ *n.* газе́та; (*attr.*) газе́тный

newt /njuːt/ *n.* трито́н

New York /njuː ˈjɔːk/ *n.* Нью-Йо́рк

New Zealand /njuː ˈziːlənd/ *n.* Но́вая Зела́ндия

New Zealander /njuː ˈziːləndə(r)/ *n.* новозела́нд|ец (-ка)

✍ **next** /nekst/ *n.* (in order): **the week after** ~ че́рез неде́лю; ~, **please!** сле́дующий!; ~ **of kin** ближа́йший ро́дственник
● *adj.* **1** (of place: nearest) ближа́йший; (adjacent) сосе́дний, сме́жный; **he lives** ~ **door** он живёт ря́дом **2** : ~ **to** (fig., almost) почти́; **I got it for** ~ **to nothing** я купи́л э́то за бесце́нок **3** (in a series) очередно́й; (future) бу́дущий, сле́дующий; ~ **day** на друго́й/ сле́дующий день; ~ **Friday** в сле́дующую пя́тницу; ~ **October** в сле́дующем октябре́; ~ **week** на бу́дущей/сле́дующей неде́ле; ~ **year** в бу́дущем году́; ~ **time we'll go to London** в сле́дующий раз мы пое́дем в Ло́ндон
● *adv.*: **what** ~? э́того ещё не хвата́ло!; **what will he do** ~? а тепе́рь что он наду́мает?; ~ **to** ря́дом с (+ *i.*); **he stood** ~ **to the fire** он стоя́л во́зле ками́на
■ ~**-door** *adj.* сосе́дний; ~**-door neighbour** ближа́йший сосе́д

NHS *abbr.* (*of* **National Health Service**) Национа́льная слу́жба здравоохране́ния

nib /nɪb/ *n.* перо́

nibble /ˈnɪb(ə)l/ *v.t.* поку́сывать (*impf.*)
● *v.i.*: ~ **at sth** грызть (*impf.*) что-н.

Nicaragua /nɪkəˈrægjʊə/ *n.* Никара́гуа (*nt. & f. indecl.*)

Nicaraguan /nɪkəˈrægjʊən/ *n.* никарагуа́н|ец (-ка)
● *adj.* никарагуа́нский

✍ **nice** /naɪs/ *adj.* (agreeable) прия́тный, ми́лый; (good) хоро́ший; (of person) прия́тный, ми́лый, симпати́чный, любе́зный; **that's very** ~ **of you** э́то о́чень ми́ло с ва́шей стороны́; **this soup tastes** ~ э́тот суп вку́сный; **the children were** ~ **and clean** де́ти бы́ли чи́стенькие
■ ~**-looking** *adj.* ми́лый, симпати́чный

nicely /ˈnaɪslɪ/ *adv.* (well, satisfactorily) хорошо́; (agreeably) прия́тно; (kindly) ми́ло

nicety /ˈnaɪsɪtɪ/ *n.* **1** (*usu. in pl.*) (subtle detail or distinction) то́нкость, ме́лкая подро́бность **2** (exactness) то́чность; (accuracy) аккура́тность; **to a** ~ то́чно

niche /niːʃ/ *n.* ни́ша

nick /nɪk/ *n.* **1** (notch) зару́бка **2**: **in the** ~ **of time** в (са́мый) после́дний моме́нт; как раз во́время
● *v.t.* **1** (cut) де́лать, с- зару́бку на + *p.*; **he** ~**ed his chin shaving** он поре́зал себе́ подборо́док во вре́мя бритья́ **2** (BrE, sl., arrest) брать, взять **3** (BrE, sl., steal) спере́ть (*pf.*) (sl.)

nickel /ˈnɪk(ə)l/ *n.* **1** (metal) ни́кель (*m.*); (AmE coin) пятице́нтовик

nickname /ˈnɪkneɪm/ *n.* про́звище, кли́чка
● *v.t.* прозва́ть (*pf.*) (*sb sth + a. and i.*)

nicotine /ˈnɪkətiːn/ *n.* никоти́н

niece /niːs/ *n.* племя́нница

Nigeria /naɪˈdʒɪərɪə/ *n.* Ниге́рия

Nigerian /naɪˈdʒɪərɪən/ *n.* нигери́|ец (-йка)
● *adj.* нигери́йский

niggardly /ˈnɪɡədlɪ/ *adj.* скупо́й

niggle /ˈnɪɡ(ə)l/ *v.t.* дёргать, придира́ться (*both impf.*) к + *d.*

niggling /'nɪglɪŋ/ *adj.* придирчивый

nigh /naɪ/ *adj., adv., & prep.* (archaic) = **near**

↶ **night** /naɪt/ *n.* ночь; (waking hours of darkness) вечер; **all ~ (long)** всю ночь (напролёт); **last ~** вчера вечером/ночью; **at, by ~** ночью; **on Saturday ~** в субботу вечером; **good ~!** (infml): **~-~!** спокойной ночи!
■ **~club** *n.* ночной клуб; **~dress** *n.* ночная рубашка; **~ life** *n.* ночная жизнь (города); **~mare** *n.* (also fig.) кошмар; **have a ~mare** видеть (*impf.*) кошмарный сон; **~marish** *adj.* кошмарный; **~ school** *n.* вечерняя школа; **~ shift** *n.* ночная смена; **~-time** *n.* ночное время; **in the ~-time** ночью; **~watchman** *n.* ночной сторож

nightie /'naɪtɪ/ *n.* ночная рубашка/сорочка

nightingale /'naɪtɪŋgeɪl/ *n.* соловей

nightly /'naɪtlɪ/ *adj.* (happening every night) еженощный; ежевечерний; **~ performances** ежедневные вечерние представления
● *adv.* еженощно; каждую ночь; каждый вечер

nil /nɪl/ *n.* нуль (*m.*)

Nile /naɪl/ *n.* Нил

nimble /'nɪmb(ə)l/ *adj.* (**nimbler, nimblest**) (agile) проворный, шустрый (infml); (dextrous) ловкий

↶ **nine** /naɪn/ *n.* (число/номер) девять; (figure; thing numbered 9; group of ~) девятка; **~ (o'clock)** пять (часов); **he is ~** ему девять лет
● *adj.* девять + *g. pl.*

nineteen /naɪn'tiːn/ *n.* девятнадцать; **talk ~ to the dozen** тараторить (*impf.*)
● *adj.* девятнадцать + *g. pl.*

nineteenth /naɪn'tiːnθ/ *n.* (date) девятнадцатое число; (fraction) одна девятнадцатая
● *adj.* девятнадцатый

ninetieth /'naɪntɪɪθ/ *n.* одна девяностая
● *adj.* девяностый

ninet|y /'naɪntɪ/ *n.* девяносто; **he is in his ~ies** ему за девяносто; **in the ~ies** (decade) в девяностых годах
● *adj.* девяносто + *g. pl.*

ninth /naɪnθ/ *n.* (date) девятое число; (fraction) одна девятая
● *adj.* девятый

nip /nɪp/ *n.* **1** (pinch) щипок **2** (small bite) укус **3** (of frost): **there's a ~ in the air today** сегодня мороз пощипывает
● *v.t.* (**nipped, nipping**) **1** (pinch) щип|ать, -нуть **2** (bite) укусить, куснуть (*both pf.*)
● *v.i.* (**nipped, nipping**) **1** (pinch) щипаться (*impf.*) **2** (BrE, usu. with advs., move smartly): **I must ~ along to the shop** мне нужно сбегать в магазин; **he ~ped out to have a smoke** он выскочил покурить

nipple /'nɪp(ə)l/ *n.* сосок

nippy /'nɪpɪ/ *adj.* (**nippier, nippiest**) **1** (nimble) проворный **2** (chilly): **the weather is ~** морозит

nirvana /nə:'vɑːnə/ *n.* нирвана

nit /nɪt/ *n.* гнида
■ **~pick** *v.i.* (sl.) придираться (*impf.*) к мелочам

nitrate /'naɪtreɪt/ *n.* нитрат

nitrogen /'naɪtrədʒ(ə)n/ *n.* азот

nitty-gritty /ˌnɪtɪ'grɪtɪ/ *n.* (sl.) суть дела; **the ~ of politics** политическая кухня

nitwit /'nɪtwɪt/ *n.* олух (infml)

↶ **no** /nəʊ/ *adj.* **1** (not any) никакой; **there's ~ food in the house** в доме нет (никакой) еды; **it's ~ use complaining** нет (никакого) смысла жаловаться; **~ doubt** несомненно; **~ one** никто; **I spoke to ~ one** я ни с кем не говорил; *see also* ▶ **nobody 2** (not a; quite other than) не; **he's ~ fool** он (вовсе) не дурак; **in ~ time** (very quickly) в короткий срок, в два счёта (infml) **3** (expr. refusal or prohibition): **~ smoking** курить воспрещается; **~ entry** вход воспрещён; нет входа
● *adv.* (with comps., not at all, in no way) не; **~ better than before** ничуть не лучше, чем раньше; **he ~ longer lives there** он там больше не живёт; **there is ~ more bread** хлеба больше нет; **~ sooner said than done!** сказано — сделано!; **~ sooner had he said it than ...** не успел он сказать, как...
● *particle* нет; **~ thank you** нет, спасибо; (after negative statement or question, sometimes) да; **"You don't like him, do you?" — "No, I don't"** «Ведь он вам не нравится?» — «Да, не нравится»
■ **~-fly** *adj.*: **~-fly zone** запретная воздушная зона; **~-go** *adj.*: **~-go area** (BrE) запретная область

nobble /'nɒb(ə)l/ *v.t.* (BrE, infml) **1** (horse) портить, ис- **2** (bribe) подмаз|ывать, -ать; подкуп|ать, -ить

nobility /nəʊ'bɪlɪtɪ/ *n.* (quality) благородство; (titled class) дворянство

noble /'nəʊb(ə)l/ *n.* (*in full* **~man, ~woman**) двор|янин (-янка)
● *adj.* (**nobler, noblest**) **1** (of character) благородный **2** (belonging to the nobility) дворянский

↶ **nobody** /'nəʊbədɪ/ *n.* ничтожный человек, ничтожество
● *pron.* (*also* **no one**) никто (... не); **~ knows** никто не знает; **there was ~ present** никого не было; **I spoke to ~** я ни с кем не говорил

nocturnal /nɒk'tə:n(ə)l/ *adj.* ночной

nod /nɒd/ *n.* кивок; **give sb a ~ of the head** кив|ать, -нуть головой кому-н.
● *v.t.* (**nodded, nodding**): **~ one's head** кив|ать, -нуть
● *v.i.* (**nodded, nodding**) кив|ать, -нуть

node /nəʊd/ *n.* (bot., phys.) узел; (astron., math.) точка пересечения

nodule /'nɒdjuːl/ *n.* (bot., med.) узелок

↶ **noise** /nɔɪz/ *n.* **1** (din) шум; **make a ~** шуметь, за- **2** (sound) звук

noisy /'nɔɪzɪ/ *adj.* (**noisier, noisiest**) (of thing) шумный; (of person) шумливый

nomad /'nəʊmæd/ *n.* кочевник

nomenclature /nəʊ'menklətʃə(r)/ *n.* номенклатура

nominal /'nɒmɪn(ə)l/ *adj.* номина́льный

nominate /'nɒmɪneɪt/ *v.t.* (appoint, e.g. person) назн|ача́ть, -а́чить; (propose, e.g. candidate) выставля́ть, вы́ставить кандидату́ру + *g.*; (for a prize) номини́ровать (*impf., pf.*)

nomination /nɒmɪ'neɪʃ(ə)n/ *n.* назначе́ние; (for a prize) номина́ция

nominative /'nɒmɪnətɪv/ *adj. & n.* имени́тельный (паде́ж)

nominee /nɒmɪ'niː/ *n.* кандида́т; (for a prize) номина́нт

non- /nɒn/ *pref.* не…

non-alcoholic /nɒnælkə'hɒlɪk/ *adj.* безалкого́льный

non-aligned /nɒnə'laɪnd/ *adj.* (pol.) неприсоедини́вшийся (к полити́ческим бло́кам)

non-believer /nɒnbɪ'liːvə(r)/ *n.* неве́рующий

nonchalance /'nɒnʃələns/ *n.* беззабо́тность; безразли́чие

nonchalant /'nɒnʃələnt/ *adj.* беззабо́тный

non-committal /nɒnkə'mɪt(ə)l/ *adj.* (evasive) укло́нчивый

non-compliance /nɒnkəm'plaɪəns/ *n.*: ~ with regulations несоблюде́ние пра́вил

nonconformist /nɒnkən'fɔːmɪst/ *adj.* нонконформи́стский

non-cooperation /nɒnkəʊɒpə'reɪʃ(ə)n/ *n.* отка́з от сотру́дничества

nondescript /'nɒndɪskrɪpt/ *adj.* невзра́чный, безли́чный

♂ none /nʌn/ *pron.* (person) никто́; ~ of us is perfect никто́ из нас не явля́ется соверше́нством; ~ of the people died ни оди́н челове́к не у́мер; (thing) ничто́; there is ~ of it left из э́того ничего́ не оста́лось; it's ~ of your business э́то не ва́ше де́ло
• *adv.*: he is ~ the worse for his accident он ничу́ть не пострада́л по́сле ава́рии

nonentity /nɒ'nentɪtɪ/ *n.* (person) ничто́жество

non-essential /nɒnɪ'senʃ(ə)l/ *adj.* несуще́ственный

non-event /nɒnɪ'vent/ *n.* собы́тие сомни́тельной ва́жности

non-existence /nɒnɪg'zɪst(ə)ns/ *n.* небытие́

non-existent /nɒnɪg'zɪst(ə)nt/ *adj.* несуществу́ющий

non-fiction /nɒn'fɪkʃ(ə)n/ *n.* документа́льная про́за/литерату́ра

non-interference /nɒnɪntə'fɪərəns/ *n.* невмеша́тельство

non-intervention /nɒnɪntə'venʃ(ə)n/ *n.* невмеша́тельство

non-member /nɒn'membə(r)/ *n.* не член

no-nonsense /nəʊ'nɒns(ə)ns/ *adj.* (businesslike) делово́й; (strict) стро́гий

nonplus /nɒn'plʌs/ *v.t.* (**nonplussed**, **nonplussing**) прив|оди́ть, -ести́ в замеша́тельство

non-profit /nɒn'prɒfɪt/ *adj.* некомме́рческий

non-profit-making /nɒn'prɒfɪt,meɪkɪŋ/ *adj.* (BrE) = non-profit

nonsense /'nɒns(ə)ns/ *n.* **1** (sth without meaning) бессмы́слица; (rubbish) вздор; ерунда́ (infml); **talk ~** говори́ть (*impf.*) вздор/ерунду́ **2** (foolish conduct) глу́пость; **let's have no more ~!** хва́тит валя́ть дурака́!

nonsensical /nɒn'sensɪk(ə)l/ *adj.* бессмы́сленный

non-smoker /nɒn'sməʊkə(r)/ *n.* некуря́щий

non-smoking /nɒn'sməʊkɪŋ/ *adj.*: ~ compartment купе́ (*nt. indecl.*) для некуря́щих

non-starter /nɒn'stɑːtə(r)/ *n.* (infml, of plan, idea) дохлый но́мер, до́хлое де́ло

non-stick /nɒn'stɪk/ *adj.*: a ~ saucepan кастрю́ля с непригора́ющим покры́тием

non-stop /nɒn'stɒp/ *adj.* **1** (of train or coach) иду́щий/е́дущий без остано́вок; (of aircraft or flight) беспоса́дочный **2** (continuous) непреры́вный
• *adv.* **1** беспоса́дочно **2**: he talks ~ он говори́т без у́молку

noodles /'nuːd(ə)lz/ *n. pl.* (cul.) лапша́

nook /nʊk/ *n.* уголо́к; I searched every ~ and cranny я обша́рил ка́ждый уголо́к

noon /nuːn/ *n.* по́лдень (*m.*); 12 ~ двена́дцать часо́в дня

no one /'nəʊwʌn/ *pron. see* ▶ nobody

noose /nuːs/ *n.* (loop) петля́; (lasso) арка́н

♂ nor /nɔː(r)/ *conj.*: they had neither arms ~ provisions у них нé бы́ло ни ору́жия, ни провиа́нта; you are not well, ~ am I вам нездоро́вится, и мне то́же

norm /nɔːm/ *n.* но́рма, пра́вило

♂ normal /'nɔːm(ə)l/ *adj.* (regular, standard) норма́льный; (usual) обы́чный; I ~ly use the bus обы́чно я е́ду авто́бусом; (sane, well balanced) норма́льный

normality /nɔː'mælɪtɪ/ *n.* норма́льность

♂ north /nɔːθ/ *n.* се́вер; (naut.) норд; the ~ of England се́вер А́нглии/се́верная часть А́нглии; in the ~ на се́вере; from the ~ с се́вера; to the ~ на се́вер
• *adj.* се́верный
• *adv.*: we went ~ мы пое́хали на се́вер
■ N~ America *n.* Се́верная Аме́рика; N~ American *n.* североамерика́н|ец (-ка)
• *adj.* североамерика́нский; ~bound *adj.* направля́ющийся на се́вер; ~-east *n.* се́веро-восто́к • *adj.* се́веро-восто́чный; ~-east wind норд-о́ст • *adv.* к се́веро-восто́ку; на се́веро-восто́к; ~-easterly *adj.* се́веро-восто́чный; ~-eastern *adj.* се́веро-восто́чный; N~ Pole *n.* Се́верный по́люс; N~ Sea *n.* Се́верное мо́ре; ~-west *n.* се́веро-за́пад • *adj.* се́веро-за́падный; ~-west wind норд-ве́ст • *adv.* к се́веро-за́паду; на се́веро-за́пад; ~-westerly *adj.* се́веро-за́падный; ~-western *adj.* се́веро-за́падный

northerly /'nɔːðəlɪ/ *n.* (wind) се́верный ве́тер
• *adj.* се́верный

n

◦ **northern** /'nɔːð(ə)n/ *adj.* северный
  ∎ **N~ Ireland** *n.* Северная Ирландия; **N~ Irish** *adj.* североирландский
northerner /'nɔːðənə(r)/ *n.* северян|ин (-ка)
northward /'nɔːθwəd/ *adj.* северный
  ● *adv.* (*also* **~s**) на север; к северу, в северном направлении
Norway /'nɔːweɪ/ *n.* Норвегия
Norwegian /nɔː'wiːdʒ(ə)n/ *n.* (person) норвеж|ец (-ка); (language) норвежский язык
  ● *adj.* норвежский
nose /nəʊz/ *n.* **1** нос; (dim.) носик; **blow one's ~** сморкаться, вы-; **look down one's ~ at sb** смотреть, по- свысока на кого-н.; **rub sb's ~ in sth** тыкать, ткнуть кого-н. носом во что-н.; **turn up one's ~ at sth** воротить (*impf.*) нос от чего-н. **2** (sense of smell) нюх, чутьё
  ● *v.t.*: **~ into** (pry, meddle) соваться, сунуться (*or* совать, сунуть нос) в + *a.*
  ∎ **~bleed** *n.*: **he has frequent ~bleeds** у него часто идёт носом (*or* из носа) кровь; **~dive** *n.* пикирование; **prices took a ~dive** цены резко упали ● *v.i.* пикировать (*impf., pf.*)
nosey /'nəʊzɪ/ *adj.* = **nosy**
nostalgia /nɒ'stældʒə/ *n.* ностальгия
nostalgic /nɒ'stældʒɪk/ *adj.* (person): **be ~ for** тосковать по + *d.*; (thing) ностальгический
nostril /'nɒstrɪl/ *n.* ноздря
nosy, nosey /'nəʊzɪ/ *adj.* (**nosier, nosiest**) (infml) любопытный

◦ **not** /nɒt/ *adv.* **1** не; (*as pred.*) нет; **she is ~ here** её здесь нет **2** (elliptical phrr.): **guilty or ~, he is my son** виновен он или нет, а он мой сын; **whether or ~** так или иначе; **I hope ~** надеюсь, что нет **3** (~ even): **~ one of them moved** ни один из них не подвинулся **4** (~ at all): 'Do you mind if I smoke?' — '**N~** at all!' «Вы не возражаете, если я закурю?» — «Нисколько/ничуть»; **'Many thanks!'** — '**N~** at all!' «Большое спасибо!» — «Не стоит! (*or* Пожалуйста!)» **5** (var. phrr.): **~ on your life** ни в коем случае; **~ in the least** ничуть; нисколько
notable /'nəʊtəb(ə)l/ *n.* знаменитость
  ● *adj.* (perceptible) заметный; (remarkable) замечательный; (well known) известный
notably /'nəʊtəblɪ/ *adv.* заметно
notary /'nəʊtərɪ/ *n.* (*also* **~ public**) нотариус
notch /nɒtʃ/ *n.* зарубка
  ● *v.t.* **1** (mark with ~) делать, с- зарубку на + *p.* **2**: **~ up a point** (in game) выигрывать, выиграть очко

◦ **note** /nəʊt/ *n.* **1** (communication) записка; **he left a ~ for you** он оставил вам записку **2** (written record) запись; **make a ~ of sth** записы|вать, -ать что-н. **3** (attention, notice) внимание; **take ~ of** (observe) прин|имать, -ять во внимание; (heed) прин|имать, -ять к сведению **4** (mus.) нота; (key of instrument) клавиша **5** (BrE, currency) банкнота
  ● *v.t.* **1** (observe, notice) зам|ечать, -етить;

(heed) обра|щать, -тить внимание на + *a.*
  2: **~ down** (in writing) запис|ывать, -ать
  ∎ **~book** *n.* записная книжка; **~book computer** *n.* ноутбук; **~pad** *n.* блокнот; **~paper** *n.* писчая бумага; **~worthy** *adj.* достойный внимания
noted /'nəʊtɪd/ *adj.* известный, знаменитый; **~ for his courage** известный своим мужеством
◦ **nothing** /'nʌθɪŋ/ *pron.* ничто, ничего (infml); **she is ~ to me** она для меня ничто; **there's ~ to be ashamed of** в этом нет ничего постыдного; **there's ~ worse than getting wet through** нет ничего хуже, чем промокнуть насквозь; **there's ~ like a hot bath** нет ничего лучше горячей ванны; **~ much** мало; **there's ~ wrong with that** ничего в этом плохого нет; **he did ~ to help** он ничем не помог; **I have ~ to do** мне нечего делать; **it has ~ to do with me** это меня не касается; **they had ~ to eat** им нечего было есть, у них не было никакой еды; **I have ~ but praise for him** я не могу им нахвалиться; **he had ~ on** (was naked) он был совершенно голый; **~ of the kind** ничего подобного; **he will stop at ~** он ни перед чем не остановится; **for ~** (without cause) ни за что, ни про что; (to no purpose) зря, напрасно, даром; (free of charge) бесплатно
  ● *adv.*: **she is ~ like her sister** она совсем не похожа на сестру; **this exam is ~ like as hard as the last** этот экзамен гораздо/куда легче предыдущего
◦ **notice** /'nəʊtɪs/ *n.* **1** (intimation) предупреждение **2** (time limit): **I have to give my employer a month's ~** (of resignation) я должен предупредить хозяина за месяц (об уходе с работы); **at short ~** в последнюю минуту; в срочном порядке; **till further ~** впредь до дальнейшего уведомления **3** (written announcement) объявление **4** (attention) внимание; **he took no ~ of me** он не обращал на меня внимания
  ● *v.t.* (observe) зам|ечать, -етить
  ∎ **~ board** *n.* (BrE) доска объявлений
noticeable /'nəʊtɪsəb(ə)l/ *adj.* заметный
notifiable /'nəʊtɪfaɪəb(ə)l/ *adj.* (of disease etc.) подлежащий регистрации
notification /ˌnəʊtɪfɪ'keɪʃ(ə)n/ *n.* извещение
notif|y /'nəʊtɪfaɪ/ *v.t.* **1** (inform) изве|щать, -стить; сообщ|ать, -ить + *d.*; **I was ~ied of your arrival** меня известили/мне сообщили о вашем (предстоящем) приезде; **he ~ied me of his address** он сообщил мне свой адрес **2** (register) регистрировать (*impf., pf.*); **all births must be ~ied** все рождения подлежат регистрации
◦ **notion** /'nəʊʃ(ə)n/ *n.* понятие, представление
notional /'nəʊʃən(ə)l/ *adj.* (ostensible, imaginary) воображаемый, мнимый
notoriety /ˌnəʊtə'raɪətɪ/ *n.* дурная слава, печальная известность; **his arrest won him a brief ~** его арест создал/принёс ему на время печальную известность

n

notorious /nəʊ'tɔ:rɪəs/ *adj.* (well known) (обще)изве́стный; (pej.) пресловꙋ́тый; печа́льно изве́стный

notwithstanding /nɒtwɪð'stændɪŋ/ *adv.* всё-таки
• *prep.* несмотря́ на + *a.*

nought /nɔ:t/ *n.* **1** (zero) нуль (*m.*) **2** (figure 0) ноль (*m.*)

noun /naʊn/ *n.* (и́мя) существи́тельное

nourish /'nʌrɪʃ/ *v.t.* пита́ть (*impf.*)

nourishment /'nʌrɪʃmənt/ *n.* пита́ние

nouveau riche /nu:vəʊ 'ri:ʃ/ *n.* (*pl.* **nouveaux riches** *pronunc. same*) нувори́ш

ᕷ **novel** /'nɒv(ə)l/ *n.* рома́н
• *adj.* необы́чный

novelist /'nɒvəlɪst/ *n.* писа́тель (-ница) романи́ст (-ка)

novelty /'nɒvəltɪ/ *n.* (newness) новизна́; (new thing) нови́нка; но́вшество

ᕷ **November** /nəʊ'vembə(r)/ *n.* ноя́брь (*m.*)

novice /'nɒvɪs/ *n.* **1** (relig.) послꙋ́шни|к (-ца) **2** (beginner) новичо́к

ᕷ **now** /naʊ/ *adv.* **1** (at the present time) тепе́рь, сейча́с, ны́не; в настоя́щее вре́мя; (opp. previously): **I'm married** ~ я тепе́рь жена́т; **(every)** ~ **and then** вре́мя от вре́мени; порой; (with preps.): **before** ~ (hitherto) до сих пор; (in the past) в про́шлом; **by** ~ к э́тому вре́мени; **he should be here by** ~ он до́лжен ужé быть здесь; **from** ~ **on** впредь; отны́не **2** (this time): ~ **you've broken the glass** ну, вот вы и разби́ли стака́н **3** (at once; at this moment) сейча́с; **I must go** ~ мне пора́ (уходи́ть); **he was here just** ~ он то́лько что был здесь; **only** ~ то́лько тепе́рь **4** (emphatic) ну, так, ита́к; ~ **you just listen to me** нет, вы послꙋ́шайте, что я вам скажꙋ́; ~ **why didn't I think of that?** как же я об э́том не поду́мал?
• *conj.* (*also* ~ **that**) по́сле того́ как

nowadays /'naʊədeɪz/ *adv.* в на́ши дни; в на́ше вре́мя; ны́не

nowhere /'nəʊweə(r)/ *adv.* нигде́; (motion) никуда́; **the house was** ~ **near the park** дом стоя́л о́чень далеко́ от па́рка; **he was** ~ **near** 60 ему́ ещё бы́ло далеко́ до шести́десяти (лет); **this conversation is getting us** ~ э́тот разгово́р нас ни к чему́ не приведёт; **there's** ~ **to sit** не́где сесть

noxious /'nɒkʃəs/ *adj.* вре́дный, па́губный

nozzle /'nɒz(ə)l/ *n.* сопло́

nuance /'nju:ɑ̃s/ *n.* отте́нок, нюа́нс

nub /nʌb/ *n.* (fig., point, gist) суть

nubile /'nju:baɪl/ *adj.* (mature) зре́лый, созре́вший; (alluring) прельсти́тельный

ᕷ **nuclear** /'nju:klɪə(r)/ *adj.* **1** (phys.) я́дерный **2**: ~ **family** ма́лая/нукле́арная семья́
■ ~ **bomb** *n.* я́дерная бо́мба; ~ **energy** *n.* я́дерная эне́ргия; ~ **power station** *n.* а́томная электроста́нция; ~ **reactor** *n.* а́томный/я́дерный реа́ктор

nucleus /'nju:klɪəs/ *n.* (*pl.* **nuclei**) (phys., fig.) ядро́; (biol.) заро́дыш

nude /nju:d/ *n.* **1** (art) обнажённая (фигꙋ́ра) **2**: **in the** ~ в го́лом ви́де, нагишо́м (infml)

• *adj.* го́лый, обнажённый, наго́й

nudge /nʌdʒ/ *v.t.* подт|а́лкивать, -олкнꙋ́ть

nudist /'nju:dɪst/ *n.* нуди́ст (-ка)

nudity /'nju:dɪtɪ/ *n.* нагота́

nugget /'nʌgɪt/ *n.* саморо́док (*зо́лота*)

nuisance /'nju:s(ə)ns/ *n.* (annoyance) доса́да; (inconvenience) неудо́бство; **what a** ~! кака́я доса́да!

null /nʌl/ *adj.*: **become** ~ **and void** утра́чивать, -тить (зако́нную) си́лу

nullify /'nʌlɪfaɪ/ *v.t.* аннули́ровать (*impf., pf.*)

numb /nʌm/ *adj.* **1** (of body) онеме́лый, онеме́вший; (of extremities, ~ **with cold**) окочене́лый **2** (of mind, senses) онеме́вший, оцепене́вший; **go** ~ неме́ть, о-; цепене́ть, о-
• *v.t.*: **the cold had** ~**ed my hands** мои́ рꙋ́ки окочене́ли от хо́лода; **morphine** ~**ed the pain** мо́рфий притупи́л боль

ᕷ **number** /'nʌmbə(r)/ *n.* **1** (numeral) число́, ци́фра **2** (quantity, amount) число́, коли́чество; **the average** ~ **in a class is** 30 сре́дняя чи́сленность кла́сса — три́дцать челове́к/ученико́в; **there were a large** ~ **of people** там бы́ло мно́го наро́ду/большо́е коли́чество людéй; **a** ~ **of professors attended the lecture** ле́кцию слꙋ́шали не́сколько профессоро́в **3** (identifying) но́мер; **he was** ~ 3 **on the list** он шёл тре́тьим но́мером в спи́ске; **look after** ~ **one** (fig.) забо́титься (*impf.*) о со́бственной персо́не; **telephone** ~ но́мер телефо́на; **you have the wrong** ~ вы не туда́ звони́те/попа́ли; (song or item in stage performance) но́мер
• *v.t.* **1** (count) переч|исля́ть, -и́слить; **his days are** ~**ed** егó дни сочтены́ **2** (give ~ **to**) нумерова́ть, про- **3** (amount to) насчи́тываться (*impf.*)
■ ~ **plate** *n.* (BrE) номерно́й знак

numeracy /'nju:mərəsɪ/ *n.* зна́ние арифме́тики

numeral /'nju:mər(ə)l/ *n.* ци́фра

numerical /nju:'merɪk(ə)l/ *adj.* чи́сленный, числово́й

ᕷ **numerous** /'nju:mərəs/ *adj.* многочи́сленный

nun /nʌn/ *n.* мона́хиня, мона́шенка

nunnery /'nʌnərɪ/ *n.* же́нский монасты́рь

nuptial /'nʌpʃ(ə)l/ *adj.* сва́дебный

nuptials /'nʌpʃ(ə)lz/ *n. pl.* сва́дьба

ᕷ **nurse** /nɜ:s/ *n.* **1** (~ **maid**) ня́ня, ня́нька (infml) **2** (of the sick) сиде́лка; (orderly) санита́рка; (senior ~) медсестра́; **male** ~ (orderly) санита́р; (senior) медбра́т
• *v.t.* **1** (suckle) корми́ть (*impf.*) (грꙋ́дью) **2** (attend to) уха́живать (*impf.*) за + *i.* **3** (fig.): ~ **hopes** леле́ять (*impf.*) наде́жду

nursery /'nɜ:sərɪ/ *n.* **1** (room) де́тская **2** (institution etc. for care of young): **day** ~ (дневны́е) я́сл|и (-ей) **3**: ~ **nurse** (BrE) воспита́тельница я́слей/де́тского са́да; ~ **school** де́тский сад, детса́д; ~ **rhyme** де́тские сти́шки (*m. pl.*); де́тская пе́сенка **4** (hort.) пито́мник

nursing /'nɜ:sɪŋ/ *n.* (career) профе́ссия медсестры́

■ ~ **home** *n.* (частная) лечéбница, (частный) санатóрий; (old people's home) дом (для) престарéлых

nurture /'nɜ:tʃə(r)/ *v.t.* (nourish) питáть (*impf.*); (rear) воспи́т|ывать, -áть

nut /nʌt/ *n.* **1** орéх **2** (for securing bolt) гáйка
■ ~**crackers** *n. pl.* щипц|ы́ (-óв) для орéхов; ~**shell** *n.* орéховая скорлупá; **in a** ~**shell** (fig.) крáтко; в двух словáх

nutmeg /'nʌtmeg/ *n.* мускáтный орéх

nutrient /'nju:trɪənt/ *n.* питáтельное вещество́

nutrition /nju:'trɪʃ(ə)n/ *n.* питáние

nutritional /nju:'trɪʃən(ə)l/ *adj.* (deficiency, value) питáтельный; (advice) диети́ческий

nutritious /nju:'trɪʃəs/ *adj.* питáтельный

nutty /'nʌtɪ/ *adj.* (**nuttier, nuttiest**) **1** (of taste) с при́вкусом орéха **2** (crazy) чóкнутый (infml)

nuzzle /'nʌz(ə)l/ *v.t. & i.:* ~ (**against, up to**) sb/ sth ты́каться (*impf.*) нóсом в когó-н./что-н.

nylon /'naɪlɒn/ *n.* нейлóн
● *adj.* нейлóновый

nymph /nɪmf/ *n.* ни́мфа

nymphomaniac /nɪmfə'meɪnɪæk/ *n.* нимфомáнка

Oo

O /əʊ/ *n.* (nought) нуль (*m.*), ноль (*m.*)

oak /əʊk/ *n.* (tree; wood) дуб; (*attr.*) дубóвый

OAP (BrE) *abbr.* (*of* **old-age pensioner**) пенсионéр (-ка) (по стáрости)

oar /ɔ:(r)/ *n.* веслó

oasis /əʊ'eɪsɪs/ *n.* (*pl.* **oases** /-si:z/) оáзис

oast house /'əʊsthaʊs/ *n.* хмелесуши́льня

oat /əʊt/ *n.* (in *pl.*) овёс; **sow one's wild** ~**s** (fig.) прож|игáть, -éчь мóлодость; перебеси́ться (*pf.*)
■ ~**meal** *n.* толокнó; овся́ная крупá

oath /əʊθ/ *n.* **1** прися́га; **on** (BrE), **under** ~ под прися́гой **2** (profanity) прокля́тие

obdurate /'ɒbdjʊrət/ *adj.* (stubborn) упря́мый; (hard-headed) ожесточённый

OBE *abbr.* (*of* **Officer of the Order of the British Empire**) кавалéр óрдена Британской импéрии 4-й стéпени

obedience /ə'bi:dɪəns/ *n.* повиновéние

obedient /ə'bi:dɪənt/ *adj.* послу́шный, покóрный

obelisk /'ɒbəlɪsk/ *n.* обели́ск

obese /əʊ'bi:s/ *adj.* тýчный

obesity /əʊ'bi:sɪtɪ/ *n.* тýчность

obey /ə'beɪ/ *v.t.* (comply with): ~ **the laws** подчин|я́ться, -и́ться закóнам; (be obedient to): ~ **one's parents** слýшаться, по- роди́телей
● *v.i.* повиновáться (*impf., pf.*)

obfuscate /'ɒbfʌskeɪt/ *v.t.* (darken, obscure) затемн|я́ть, -и́ть; (confuse) сму|щáть, -ти́ть

obfuscation /ɒbfʌs'keɪʃ(ə)n/ *n.* затемнéние; смущéние

obituary /ə'bɪtjʊərɪ/ *n.* некролóг

♂ **object**[1] /'ɒbdʒɪkt/ *n.* **1** (material thing) предмéт, вещь **2** (focus) предмéт, объéкт **3** (purpose, aim) цель; **I had no particular** ~ **in view** никакóй определённой цéли я не преслéдовал **4** (gram.) дополнéние

object[2] /əb'dʒekt/ *v.i.* возра|жáть, -зи́ть (**to:** прóтив + *g.*); протестовáть (*impf.*) (**to:** прóтив + *g.*); выдвигáть, выдвинуть возражéния (**to:** прóтив + *g.*); **I** ~ **to being treated like this** я протестýю прóтив такóго обращéния; **do you** ~ **to my smoking?** вам не мешáет, что я курю́?; **I'll open a window if you don't** ~ я открóю окнó, éсли вы не возражáете

objection /əb'dʒekʃ(ə)n/ *n.* возражéние, протéст; **I have no** ~ **to your going abroad** я не возражáю (*or* я ничегó не имéю) прóтив вáшей поéздки за грани́цу

objectionable /əb'dʒekʃənəb(ə)l/ *adj.* нежелáтельный; неприéмлемый

objective /əb'dʒektɪv/ *n.* цель
● *adj.* объекти́вный

objectivity /ɒbdʒek'tɪvɪtɪ/ *n.* объекти́вность

objector /əb'dʒektə(r)/ *n.* возражáющий; **conscientious** ~ человéк, откáзывающийся от воéнной слýжбы из принципиáльных соображéний

obligate /'ɒblɪgeɪt/ *v.t.* обя́з|ывать, -áть

obligation /ɒblɪ'geɪʃ(ə)n/ *n.* (promise, commitment) обязáтельство; (duty, responsibility) обя́занность; **be under an** ~ **to sb** быть обя́занным комý-н.

obligatory /ə'blɪgətərɪ/ *adj.* обязáтельный

oblige /ə'blaɪdʒ/ *v.t.* **1** (compel) вынуждáть, вы́нудить; **we are** ~**d to remind you** мы вы́нуждены напóмнить вам **2** (do favour to) обя́з|ывать, -áть; **I am much** ~**d to you** я вам óчень обя́зан/благодáрен

obliging /ə'blaɪdʒɪŋ/ *adj.* услýжливый

oblique /ə'bli:k/ *adj.* **1** (slanting) косóй **2** (gram. and fig.) кóсвенный

obliterate /əˈblɪtəreɪt/ *v.t.* (lit., fig.) ст|ира́ть, -ере́ть (с лица́ земли́)

obliteration /əblɪtəˈreɪʃ(ə)n/ *n.* стира́ние

oblivion /əˈblɪvɪən/ *n.* забве́ние

oblivious /əˈblɪvɪəs/ *adj.*: to be ~ of не име́ть никако́го поня́тия о + *p.*; he was ~ to her objections он был глух к её возраже́ниям

oblong /ˈɒblɒŋ/ *n.* продолгова́тая фигу́ра
● *adj.* продолгова́тый

obnoxious /əbˈnɒkʃəs/ *adj.* проти́вный

oboe /ˈəʊbəʊ/ *n.* гобо́й

oboist /ˈəʊbəʊɪst/ *n.* гобои́ст (-ка)

obscene /əbˈsiːn/ *adj.* непристо́йный

obscenity /əbˈsenɪtɪ/ *n.* непристо́йность

obscure /əbˈskjʊə(r)/ *adj.* **1** (not easily understood) нея́сный **2** (little known) малоизве́стный
● *v.t.* (darken, also fig.) затемн|я́ть, -и́ть; (conceal from sight) заслон|я́ть, -и́ть

obscurity /əbˈskjʊərɪtɪ/ *n.* (lack of clarity) нея́сность; (being unknown) безве́стность

obsequious /əbˈsiːkwɪəs/ *adj.* подобостра́стный, раболе́пный

observable /əbˈzɜːvəb(ə)l/ *adj.* заме́тный, различи́мый

observance /əbˈzɜːv(ə)ns/ *n.* **1** (of rule, law, custom, etc.) соблюде́ние **2** (rite, ceremony) обря́д; (ritual) ритуа́л

observant /əbˈzɜːv(ə)nt/ *adj.* наблюда́тельный; внима́тельный

⚡ **observation** /ɒbzəˈveɪʃ(ə)n/ *n.* наблюде́ние; keep sb under ~ держа́ть (*impf.*) кого́-н. под наблюде́нием

observatory /əbˈzɜːvətərɪ/ *n.* обсервато́рия

⚡ **observe** /əbˈzɜːv/ *v.t.* **1** (notice) зам|еча́ть, -е́тить; (see) ви́деть, у- **2** (watch) наблюда́ть (*impf.*) за + *i.* **3** (remark) зам|еча́ть, -е́тить

observer /əbˈzɜːvə(r)/ *n.* наблюда́тель (*m.*)

obsess /əbˈses/ *v.t.* завлад|ева́ть, -е́ть (чьим-н.) умо́м

obsession /əbˈseʃ(ə)n/ *n.* (being obsessed) одержи́мость; (fixed idea) навя́зчивая иде́я

obsessive /əbˈsesɪv/ *adj.* навя́зчивый

obsolescence /ɒbsəˈles(ə)ns/ *n.* устарева́ние; planned, built-in ~ заплани́рованная устаре́лость (*товара*)

obsolescent /ɒbsəˈles(ə)nt/ *adj.* устарева́ющий

obsolete /ˈɒbsəliːt/ *adj.* устаре́лый; become ~ выходи́ть, вы́йти из употребле́ния; отж|ива́ть, -и́ть

obstacle /ˈɒbstək(ə)l/ *n.* препя́тствие
■ ~ course *n.* (sport) полоса́ препя́тствий; ~ race *n.* бег/ска́чки с препя́тствиями

obstetric /əbˈstetrɪk/, **obstetrical** /əbˈstetrɪk(ə)l/ *adjs.* акуше́рский, родовспомога́тельный

obstetrician /ɒbstəˈtrɪʃ(ə)n/ *n.* акуше́р (-ка)

obstetrics /əbˈstetrɪks/ *n.* акуше́рство

obstinate /ˈɒbstɪnət/ *adj.* (stubborn) упря́мый; (persistent) насто́йчивый

obstruct /əbˈstrʌkt/ *v.t.* меша́ть (*impf.*) + *d.*, препя́тствовать (*impf.*) + *d.*; ~ the road

загра|жда́ть, -ди́ть доро́гу; ~ the view заслон|я́ть, -и́ть вид

obstruction /əbˈstrʌkʃ(ə)n/ *n.* загражде́ние; (hindrance) препя́тствие

obstructive /əbˈstrʌktɪv/ *adj.* (policy) препя́тствующий; (object) загора́живающий; (pol.) обструкцио́нный

⚡ **obtain** /əbˈteɪn/ *v.t.* (procure) доб|ыва́ть, -ы́ть; (acquire) приобре|та́ть, -сти́
● *v.i.* (formal, be current, prevalent) существова́ть (*impf.*)

obtainable /əbˈteɪnəb(ə)l/ *adj.* достижи́мый, досту́пный; is this model still ~? э́ту моде́ль мо́жно ещё приобрести́?

obtrusive /əbˈtruːsɪv/ *adj.* навя́зчивый, назо́йливый

obtuse /əbˈtjuːs/ *adj.* (lit., fig.) тупо́й

obviate /ˈɒbvɪeɪt/ *v.t.* (evade, circumvent) избе|га́ть, -жа́ть + *g.*; (remove) устран|я́ть, -и́ть

⚡ **obvious** /ˈɒbvɪəs/ *adj.* очеви́дный, я́сный; ~ly очеви́дно

⚡ **occasion** /əˈkeɪʒ(ə)n/ *n.* слу́чай; on many ~s во мно́гих слу́чаях; ча́сто; on the ~ of his marriage по слу́чаю его́ бра́ка; today is a special ~ сего́дня осо́бый день; rise to the ~ оказ|ываться, -а́ться на высоте́ положе́ния

occasional /əˈkeɪʒən(ə)l/ *adj.* случа́йный; (infrequent) ре́дкий

occasionally /əˈkeɪʒən(ə)lɪ/ *adv.* вре́мя от вре́мени, поро́й, иногда́, и́зредка

occult /ɒˈkʌlt/ *n.*: the ~ окульти́зм

occupancy /ˈɒkjʊpənsɪ/ *n.* заня́тие; (taking, holding possession) завладе́ние; (holding on lease) аре́нда, владе́ние

occupant /ˈɒkjʊpənt/ *n.* **1** (tenant) жиле́ц, аренда́тор, нанима́тель (*m.*) **2**: the ~s of the car е́хавшие в маши́не

occupation /ɒkjʊˈpeɪʃ(ə)n/ *n.* **1** (taking possession) завладе́ние **2** (mil.) оккупа́ция; army of ~ оккупацио́нная а́рмия **3** (pastime) заня́тие, время(пре)провожде́ние **4** (employment) заня́тие; профе́ссия

occupational /ɒkjʊˈpeɪʃən(ə)l/ *adj.* профессиона́льный
■ ~ hazard *n.* риск, свя́занный с хара́ктером рабо́ты; профессиона́льный/ произво́дственный риск

occupier /ˈɒkjʊpaɪə(r)/ *n.* (BrE) прожива́ющий

⚡ **occupy** /ˈɒkjʊpaɪ/ *v.t.* **1** (take over, take possession of) зан|има́ть, -я́ть; завлад|ева́ть, -е́ть + *i.* **2** (employ): he ~ies his time with crossword puzzles он посвяща́ет всё своё вре́мя разга́дыванию/реше́нию кроссво́рдов

⚡ **occur** /əˈkɜː(r)/ *v.i.* (occurred, occurring) **1** (take place) случа́ться, -и́ться **2** (of thought) при|ходи́ть, -йти́ в го́лову, на ум; it ~red to me that … мне пришло́ в го́лову, что…

occurrence /əˈkʌrəns/ *n.* происше́ствие, слу́чай

OCD *abbr.* (of **obsessive-compulsive disorder**) (med.) ОКР (обсесси́вно-компульси́вное расстро́йство)

ocean /ˈəʊʃ(ə)n/ *n.* океа́н

oceanic /ˌəʊʃɪˈænɪk/ adj. океани́ческий, океа́нский

oceanographer /ˌəʊʃəˈnɒɡrəfə(r)/ n. океано́граф

oceanography /ˌəʊʃəˈnɒɡrəfi/ n. океаногра́фия

ochre /ˈəʊkə(r)/ (AmE **ocher**) n. о́хра

o'clock /əˈklɒk/ adv.: two ~ два часа́; at 10 ~ at night в де́сять часо́в ве́чера

octagon /ˈɒktəɡən/ n. восьмиуго́льник

octagonal /ɒkˈtæɡən(ə)l/ adj. восьмиуго́льный

octave /ˈɒktɪv/ n. (mus.) окта́ва

✧ **October** /ɒkˈtəʊbə(r)/ n. октя́брь (m.)

octopus /ˈɒktəpəs/ n. (pl. **octopuses**) осьмино́г, спрут

✧ **odd** /ɒd/ adj. **1** (not even): ~ **numbers** нечётные чи́сла **2** (not matching) непа́рный; I was wearing ~ **socks** я был в ра́зных носка́х **3** (not in a set) разро́зненный **4** (with some remainder) с ли́шним; 40 ~ со́рок с ли́шним (or с чем-то) **5** (occasional) случа́йный; ~ **jobs** случа́йная рабо́та; he made the ~ **mistake** (infml) ему́ случа́лось ошиба́ться **6** (strange) стра́нный, эксцентри́чный, чудно́й

oddity /ˈɒdɪti/ n. (person) чуда́|к (-чка); (thing) причу́дливая вещь

oddly /ˈɒdli/ adv.: ~ **enough** как (э́то) ни стра́нно; представля́ть себе́

odds /ɒdz/ n. pl. **1** (balance of advantage): the ~ are in our favour переве́с на на́шей стороне́; the ~ were against his winning у него́ бы́ло ма́ло ша́нсов на вы́игрыш **2** (betting): long ~ нера́вные ша́нсы (m. pl.); short ~ почти́ ра́вные ша́нсы **3** (variance): be at ~ with sb не ла́дить (impf.) с кем-н. **4**: ~ and ends (leftovers) оста́тки (m. pl.); (sundries) вся́кая вся́чина

ode /əʊd/ n. о́да

odious /ˈəʊdɪəs/ adj. (hateful) ненави́стный, одио́зный; (foul, vile) гну́сный; (repulsive) отврати́тельный

odour /ˈəʊdə(r)/ (AmE **odor**) n. (smell) за́пах

odyssey /ˈɒdɪsi/ n. (pl. ~**s**) одиссе́я, приключе́ния (nt. pl.)

oedema /ɪˈdiːmə/ (AmE **edema**) n. отёк

oesopha|gus /iːˈsɒfəɡəs/ (AmE **esophagus**) n. (pl. ~**gi** /-dʒaɪ/ or ~**guses**) пищево́д

oestrogen /ˈiːstrədʒ(ə)n/ (AmE **estrogen**) n. эстроге́н

✧ **of** /ɒv/ prep. (expr. by g. and/or var. preps.) **1** (origin): **Lawrence** ~ **Arabia** Ло́уренс Арави́йский **2** (cause): he died ~ **fright** он у́мер от испу́га **3** (material) из + g.; **what is it made** ~? из чего́ э́то сде́лано? **4** (composition): a bunch ~ **keys** свя́зка ключе́й; a family ~ 8 семья́ из восьми́ челове́к **5** (contents): a bottle ~ **milk** (full) буты́лка молока́ **6** (qualities): a man ~ **ability** спосо́бный челове́к **7** (possession): the property ~ the state госуда́рственная

со́бственность **8** (partitive): some ~ us не́которые/ко́е-кто из нас; a quarter ~ an hour че́тверть часа́; most ~ all осо́бенно; бо́льше всего́/всех; a friend ~ ours оди́н из на́ших знако́мых **9** (separation, distance): within 10 miles ~ **London** в десяти́ ми́лях от Ло́ндона

✧ **off** /ɒf/ adj. **1** (nearer to centre of road): on the ~ **side** (in Britain) на пра́вой стороне́ **2** (improbable): I went on the ~ **chance** of finding him in я пошёл туда́ науда́чу — вдруг заста́ну (его́) **3** (substandard): it was one of my ~ **days** в тот день я был не в са́мой лу́чшей фо́рме **4** (inactive): the ~ **season** мёртвый сезо́н, межсезо́нье

• adv. **1** (away): two miles ~ в двух ми́лях отту́да/отсю́да; the elections are still two years ~ до вы́боров ещё два го́да; it's time I was ~; I must be ~ мне пора́ (уходи́ть) **2** (disconnected): the electricity was ~ электри́чество бы́ло отключено́ **3** (ended, cancelled): their engagement is ~ их помо́лвка расто́ргнута; the match is ~ матч отмене́н **4** (not working): day ~ выходно́й (день); he was ~ sick он отсу́тствовал/не́ был на рабо́те по боле́зни **5** (not fresh): the fish is ~ ры́ба испо́ртилась (or с душко́м (infml))

• prep. (from; away from; up or down from): the car went ~ the road маши́на съе́хала с доро́ги; ~ work на рабо́те; he fell ~ the ladder он упа́л с ле́стницы; he took 50p ~ the price он сни́зил це́ну на пятьдеся́т пе́нсов; он сба́вил с цены́ пятьдеся́т пе́нсов; (disinclined for): he is ~ his food он потеря́л аппети́т

offal /ˈɒf(ə)l/ n. (of meat) потроха́ (m. pl.); (entrails) требуха́

✧ **offence** /əˈfens/ (AmE **offense**) n. **1** (crime) правонаруше́ние, преступле́ние **2** (affront) оби́да; cause, give ~ to оскорб|ля́ть, -и́ть **3** (mil.) наступле́ние

offend /əˈfend/ v.t. об|ижа́ть, -и́деть
• v.i. греши́ть (impf.)

offender /əˈfendə(r)/ n. (against law) правонаруши́тель (m.) (-ница)

offense /əˈfens/ n. (AmE) = offence

offensive /əˈfensɪv/ n. нападе́ние; (mil.) наступле́ние; go on the ~ пере|ходи́ть, -йти́ в наступле́ние; (fig.) зан|има́ть, -я́ть наступа́тельную пози́цию
• adj. (causing offence) оскорби́тельный; (of person) отврати́тельный, проти́вный

✧ **offer** /ˈɒfə(r)/ n. **1** предложе́ние **2**: be on ~ (BrE, for sale at reduced price) прод|ава́ться, -а́ться со ски́дкой
• v.t. предл|ага́ть, -ожи́ть; he ~ed me a drink он предложи́л мне вы́пить; ~ an opinion выража́ть, вы́разить своё мне́ние; he did not ~ to help он не предложи́л помо́чь

offering /ˈɒfərɪŋ/ n. **1** (sacrifice) подноше́ние, же́ртва **2** (contribution) поже́ртвование

offhand /ˌɒfˈhænd, ˈɒfhænd/ adj. развя́зный, бесцеремо́нный
• adv. (right now, without thought) сра́зу

✧ **office** /ˈɒfɪs/ n. **1** (position of responsibility) до́лжность, слу́жба; the party in ~ па́ртия,

находя́щаяся у вла́сти; **he held ~ for 10 years** он занима́л до́лжность/пост де́сять лет **2** (premises) о́фис, конто́ра, канцеля́рия **3** (for services) бюро́ (*nt. indecl.*); **booking ~** биле́тная ка́сса
■ **~ block** *n.* администрати́вное зда́ние; **~ hours** *n. pl.* часы́ рабо́ты; рабо́чее/служе́бное вре́мя

◦' **officer** /'ɒfɪsə(r)/ *n.* **1** (in armed forces) офице́р **2** (official) должностно́е лицо́, чино́вник; **customs ~** тамо́женник

◦' **official** /ə'fɪʃ(ə)l/ *n.* должностно́е лицо́, чино́вник
  ● *adj.* (authoritative) официа́льный; (relating to office) служе́бный, должностно́й

officiate /ə'fɪʃɪeɪt/ *v.i.* (be in charge) распоряжа́ться (*impf.*); (at church service) соверш|а́ть, -и́ть богослуже́ние; **~ at a wedding** соверш|а́ть, -и́ть обря́д бракосочета́ния; **~ as chairman** председа́тельствовать (*impf.*)

officious /ə'fɪʃəs/ *adj.* навя́зчивый, назо́йливый

offing /'ɒfɪŋ/ *n.*: **in the ~** (fig.) в перспекти́ве

off-key /ɒf'kiː/ *adj.* (mus., also fig.) фальши́вый

off-licence /'ɒflaɪs(ə)ns/ *n.* (BrE) ви́нный магази́н

offline /ɒf'laɪn/ *adj.* (comput.) автоно́мный, офла́йновый; (disconnected) отключённый

offload /ɒf'ləʊd/ *v.t.* разгру|жа́ть, -зи́ть

off-peak /ɒfpiːk/ *adj.* непи́ковый

off-piste /ɒf'piːst/ *adj., adv.* вне горнолы́жной тра́ссы; (fig.) вдали́ от проторённых маршру́тов

off-putting /'ɒfpʊtɪŋ/ *adj.* (infml) отта́лкивающий

offset /'ɒfset/ *v.t.* **1** (take into consideration) засчи́т|ывать, -а́ть; **donations to charity can be ~ against tax** поже́ртвования на благотвори́тельные це́ли мо́гут засчи́тываться при упла́те нало́гов **2** (compensate for) возме|ща́ть, -сти́ть

offshoot /'ɒfʃuːt/ *n.* побе́г; (fig.) о́трасль

offshore /'ɒfʃɔː(r)/ *adj.* **1** (close to the shore) прибре́жный; (at a distance from the shore) морско́й; (foreign) заграни́чный; (fin.) офшо́рный
  ● *adv.* (in the open sea) в откры́том мо́ре; (abroad) за грани́цей
■ **~ wind** *n.* берегово́й ве́тер

offside /ɒf'saɪd/ (football) *n.* положе́ние вне игры́, офса́йд
  ● *adv.* вне игры́, офса́йд

offspring /'ɒfsprɪŋ/ *n.* (*pl.* **~**) пото́мок, о́тпрыск; (*in pl.*) пото́мство

offstage /ɒf'steɪdʒ/ *adj.* закули́сный
  ● *adv.* за кули́сами

off-the-cuff /ɒfðə'kʌf/ *adj.* импровизи́рованный

off-the-record /ɒfðə'rekɔːd/ *adj.* неофициа́льный

off-white /'ɒfwaɪt/ *adj. & n.* гря́зно-бе́лый (цвет)

◦' **often** /'ɒf(ə)n/ *adv.* (**oftener, oftenest**)

ча́сто; **every so ~** вре́мя от вре́мени

ogle /'əʊɡ(ə)l/ *v.t.* пожира́ть (*impf.*) глаза́ми

ogre /'əʊɡə(r)/ *n.* велика́н-людое́д; (fig.) стра́шный челове́к

◦' **oh** /əʊ/ *int.* о!, ах!; (expr. surprise, fright, pain) ой!

ohm /əʊm/ *n.* ом

◦' **oil** /ɔɪl/ *n.* **1** ма́сло; **engine ~** маши́нное ма́сло **2** (petroleum) нефть
  ● *v.t.* (lubricate) сма́з|ывать, -ать
■ **~field** *n.* месторожде́ние не́фти; **~ painting** *n.* ма́сло, холст, карти́на; **~ rig** *n.* нефтяна́я вы́шка; **~skin** *n.* непромока́емый костю́м; **~ slick** *n.* плёнка не́фти на воде́; **~ tanker** *n.* (ship) та́нкер; (vehicle) нефтево́з; **~ well** *n.* нефтяна́я сква́жина

oily /'ɔɪli/ *adj.* (**oilier, oiliest**) ма́сляный

ointment /'ɔɪntmənt/ *n.* мазь

OK, okay /əʊ'keɪ/ *n.* (*pl.* **~s**) (infml) одобре́ние, «добро́»
  ● *adj.* (safe, well): **she is ~** она́ в поря́дке; (acceptable): **are you sure it's ~?** э́то ничего́?; **I'll be back soon, ~?** я ско́ро верну́сь, ла́дно?
  ● *adv.*: **the meeting went off ~** собра́ние прошло́ норма́льно; **he is doing ~** у него́ всё хорошо́/норма́льно
  ● *v.t.* (**OK's, OK'd, OK'ing**) од|обря́ть, -о́брить
  ● *int.* ла́дно!, хорошо́!

◦' **old** /əʊld/ *n.*: **the ~** (people) старики́ (*m. pl.*), пожилы́е/престаре́лые (лю́ди)
  ● *adj.* (**older, oldest**) **1** ста́рый; (object, house) стари́нный; **grow ~** ста́риться, со- **2** (expr. age): **how ~ is he?** ско́лько ему́ лет?; **my son is 4 years ~** моему́ сы́ну четы́ре го́да **3** (longstanding) стари́нный, давни́шний; **they are ~ friends** они́ стари́нные/да́вние друзья́ **4** (former) бы́вший, пре́жний
■ **~ age** *n.* ста́рость; **~-age pension** (BrE) пе́нсия по ста́рости; **~-fashioned** *adj.* старомо́дный; **~ man** *n.* (also infml, husband or father) стари́к; **~ people's/folk's home** *n.* дом престаре́лых; **~ woman** *n.* (also infml, wife) стару́ха

oligarch /'ɒlɪɡɑːk/ *n.* олига́рх

oligarchy /'ɒlɪɡɑːki/ *n.* олига́рхия

olive /'ɒlɪv/ *n.* масли́на
  ● *adj.* оли́вковый
■ **~ oil** *n.* оли́вковое ма́сло

Olympic /ə'lɪmpɪk/ *adj.*: **~ Games, ~s** Олимпи́йские и́гры

ombudsman /'ɒmbʊdzmən/ *n.* о́мбудсмен; уполномо́ченный по права́м челове́ка

omelette /'ɒmlɪt/ (AmE *also* **omelet**) *n.* омле́т

omen /'əʊmən/ *n.* знак

ominous /'ɒmɪnəs/ *adj.* злове́щий

omission /ə'mɪʃ(ə)n/ *n.* про́пуск

omit /ə'mɪt/ *v.t.* (**omitted, omitting**) пропус|ка́ть, -ти́ть

omnibus /'ɒmnɪbəs/ *n.* **1** (obs.) о́мнибус, авто́бус **2** (~ volume) сбо́рник, антоло́гия

omnipotence /ɒm'nɪpət(ə)ns/ *n.* всемогу́щество

omnipotent /ɒm'nɪpət(ə)nt/ *adj.* всемогу́щий

o

omnipresent /ˌɒmnɪˈprez(ə)nt/ *adj.*
вездесу́щий

omniscience /ɒmˈnɪsɪəns/ *n.* всеве́дение

omniscient /ɒmˈnɪsɪənt/ *adj.* всеве́дущий

omnivorous /ɒmˈnɪvərəs/ *adj.* всея́дный

⚹ **on** /ɒn/ *adv.* **1** (expr. continuation): **straight ~** пря́мо; **and so ~** и так да́лее; **from now ~** (начина́я) с э́того дня; **he went ~ (and ~)** about his dog он без конца́ говори́л о свое́й соба́ке; (expr. extension): **further ~** да́льше; **later ~** по́зже **2** (placed, spread, etc. **~** sth): **he had his glasses ~** он был в очка́х; он наде́л очки́ **3** (arranged, available): **what's ~ tonight?** (TV) что сего́дня по програ́мме?; что сего́дня пока́зывают?; **is the match still ~?** матч не отмени́ли/отменён? **4** (turned, switched **~**): **the kettle is ~** ча́йник поста́влен/включён; **the light is ~** свет включён; **the radio was ~ full blast** ра́дио бы́ло включено́ на всю мощь **5**: **it's not ~** (infml) (not feasible) так не пойдёт; (not acceptable) недопусти́мо
● *prep.* **1** (expr. position): на **+** *p.*; **~ the table** на столе́; (supported by): **stand ~ one leg** стоя́ть (*impf.*) на одно́й ноге́; **the look ~ his face** выраже́ние его́ лица́; (as means of transport) на **+** *p.*; **~ horseback** верхо́м; **~ foot** пешко́м; **I came ~ the bus** я прие́хал на авто́бусе; (**~** one's person): **I have no money ~ me** у меня́ нет при себе́ де́нег; (expr. relative position): **~ my left** сле́ва от меня́ **2** (expr. final position) на **+** *a.*; **he sat down ~ the sofa** он сел на дива́н **3** (expr. point of contact): **he hit me ~ the head** он уда́рил меня́ по голове́; **he knocked ~ the door** он постуча́л в дверь; **she dried her hands ~ a towel** она́ вы́терла ру́ки полоте́нцем **4** (of a medium of communication) по **+** *d.*; **~ the radio/telephone/television** по ра́дио/телефо́ну/телеви́зору **5** (expr. time): **~ Tuesday** во вто́рник; **~ time** во́время; своевре́менно; **~ the 8th of May** восьмо́го ма́я; **~ Tuesdays** по вто́рникам **6** (immediately after): **~ his arrival** по его́ прие́зде; **~ seeing him she ran off** уви́дев его́, она́ убежа́ла; (during): **~ my way home** по доро́ге домо́й **7** (concerning): **an article ~ Pushkin** статья́ о Пу́шкине **8** (at the expense of): **drinks are ~ me** я угоща́ю; **the joke was ~ me** шу́тка оберну́лась про́тив меня́ **9** (taking drugs etc.): **he's ~ drugs** он (регуля́рно) принима́ет нарко́тики

on-board /ˈɒnbɔːd/ *adj.* бортово́й

⚹ **once** /wʌns/ *adv.* **1** (оди́н) раз; **~ again, more** ещё раз **2** (as soon as): **you hesitate you are lost** сто́ит (то́лько) заколеба́ться, и ты пропа́л **3** (at one time, formerly) не́когда; одно́ вре́мя; одна́жды; когда́-то; **~ upon a time there was** (давны́м-давно́) жил-был **4**: **at ~** (immediately) сейча́с же; (simultaneously) в то же вре́мя
■ **~-over** *n.* (infml): **give sb/sth the ~-over** бе́гло осма́тривать, -отре́ть кого́/что-н.

oncologist /ɒŋˈkɒlədʒɪst/ *n.* онко́лог

oncology /ɒŋˈkɒlədʒɪ/ *n.* онколо́гия

oncoming /ˈɒnkʌmɪŋ/ *adj.* приближа́ющийся, наступа́ющий

⚹ **one** /wʌn/ *n.* **1** (number) оди́н; (in counting): **~, two, three** раз/оди́н, два, три **2** (hour) час; **~ o'clock** (a.m.) час но́чи; (p.m.) час дня **3** (age): **he's only ~** ему́ всего́/то́лько год(ик) **4** (person): **little ~s** де́ти; **our loved ~s** на́ши бли́зкие; **he is not ~ to refuse** он не из тех, кто отка́зывается **5** (member of a group) оди́н; **~ of my friends** оди́н из мои́х друзе́й; **the ~ with the beard** тот(, кото́рый) с бородо́й; **I for ~ don't believe him** что каса́ется меня́, то я не ве́рю ему́; **~ of these days** ка́к-нибудь на днях; **~ another** друг дру́га; **~ after the other; ~ by ~** оди́н за други́м; **~ at a time** по одному́; по о́череди **6** (referring to category understood): **which book do you want, the red or the green ~?** каку́ю кни́гу вы хоти́те, кра́сную и́ли зелёную?
● *pron.*: **~ never knows** никогда́ не зна́ешь; **~ gets used to anything** челове́к ко всему́ привыка́ет
● *adj.* **1** оди́н; **price ~ rouble** цена́ (оди́н) рубль; (with pluralia tantum) одни́; **~ watch** одни́ часы́ **2** (only) еди́нственный; **the ~ way to do it** еди́нственный спо́соб сде́лать э́то **3** (the same) тот же са́мый **4** (particular but unspecified): **~ evening** ка́к-то/одна́жды ве́чером; **~ day** (in past) одна́жды; (in future) когда́-нибудь
■ **~-off** *adj.* (BrE, infml) уника́льный, еди́нственный; **~-parent family** *n.* семья́ с одни́м роди́телем; **~-sided** *adj.* (prejudiced) односторо́нний; **~-time** *adj.* бы́вший; было́й; **~-to-one** *adj.* непосре́дственный; **~-way** *adj.*: **~-way traffic** односторо́ннее движе́ние; **~-way street** у́лица с односторо́нним движе́нием; **~-way ticket** биле́т в одну́ сто́рону (*or* в одно́м направле́нии)

onerous /ˈəʊnərəs/ *adj.* обремени́тельный, тя́гостный

oneself /wʌnˈself/ *pron.* **1** (refl.) себя́, -ся *suff.*; **talk to ~** говори́ть (*impf.*) с сами́м собо́й **2** (emph.) сам; **it's best to do it ~** лу́чше сде́лать э́то самому́

ongoing /ˈɒngəʊɪŋ/ *adj.* (continuing): **~ process** поступа́тельный проце́сс; (in progress) теку́щий

onion /ˈʌnjən/ *n.* лу́ковица; (*pl., collect.*) (ре́пчатый) лук

⚹ **online** /ɒnˈlaɪn/ (comput.) *adj.* (information, program) онла́йновый, диало́говый, интеракти́вный; (connected) подключённый; **~ dating** знако́мство в Интерне́те; **~ dating site** сайт знако́мств
● *adv.* (в режи́ме) онла́йн, в Интерне́те; **we watched the film ~** мы смотре́ли фильм в Интерне́те

onlooker /ˈɒnlʊkə(r)/ *n.* зри́тель (*m.*)

⚹ **only** /ˈəʊnlɪ/ *adj.* еди́нственный; **she was an ~ child** она́ была́ еди́нственным ребёнком; **I was the ~ one there** кро́ме меня́ там никого́ не́ было
● *adv.* то́лько; всего́; **~ just** (recently) то́лько что; (barely) едва́; **I have ~ just arrived** я то́лько что при́был; **he was ~ just in time**

он едва успел; **if** ~ **you knew** если бы вы только знали; **the soup was** ~ **warm** суп был еле тёплый
• *conj.* но; **I would go myself,** ~ **I'm tired** я пошёл бы сам, но я устал

onomatopoeia /ˌɒnəmætəˈpiːə/ *n.* звукоподражание

on-screen /ˌɒnˈskriːn/ *adj.* (comput.) экранный; **follow the** ~ **instructions** следуйте инструкциям на экране

onset /ˈɒnset/ *n.* начало, наступление

on-site /ˈɒnsaɪt/ *adj.* на местах/месте

onslaught /ˈɒnslɔːt/ *n.* атака, нападение

✎ **onto** /ˈɒntuː/ *prep.* (= **on** *prep.* 2) на + *a.*; **she climbed** ~ **the roof** она влезла на крышу

onus /ˈəʊnəs/ *n.* бремя, ответственность

onward /ˈɒnwəd/ *adj.* продвигающийся
• *adv.* (*also* **onwards**) вперёд, далее; **from now** ~ впредь, отныне; **from then** ~ с тех пор; (in future) с того времени

oops! /ʊps/ *int.* (infml) ой!

ooze /uːz/ *v.t.* (emit): **the wound** ~**d blood** из раны сочилась кровь; (fig.): **he** ~**d self-confidence** он источал самоуверенность
• *v.i.* медленно течь (*impf.*)

opal /ˈəʊp(ə)l/ *n.* опал

opaque /əʊˈpeɪk/ *adj.* (**opaquer, opaquest**) непрозрачный

✎ **open** /ˈəʊpən/ *n.* ◼ (~ **space;** ~ **air**) открытое пространство; **in the** ~ под открытым небом ◻ (fig.): **bring sth into the** ~ выявлять, выявить
• *adj.* ◼ открытый; **in the** ~ **air** на открытом воздухе; ~ **contempt** явное/нескрываемое презрение; **in** ~ **country** на открытой местности; **have an** ~ **mind on sth** не иметь предвзятого мнения о + *p.*; **on the** ~ **road** на пустой/свободной дороге; **the door flew** ~ дверь распахнулась ◻ (accessible, available) доступный; **the road is** ~ **to traffic** дорога открыта для движения ◻ (frank) открытый, откровенный
• *v.t.* ◼ открывать, -ыть; (book, newspaper) открывать, -ыть; раскрывать, -ыть ◻ (fig.): **he** ~**ed an account** он открыл счёт; **a new business has been** ~**ed** открыли новый бизнес
• *v.i.* ◼ открываться, -ыться ◻ (fig., begin) начинаться, -аться; **the play** ~**s with a long speech** пьеса начинается длинным монологом; **the new play** ~**s on Saturday** новая пьеса идёт с субботы ◻ (of door etc.): **the windows** ~ **on to a courtyard** окна выходят во двор
◻ ~ **up** *v.t.*: ~ **up!** (command to open) откройте дверь!; **he** ~**ed up the boot (of the car)** он открыл багажник
• *v.i.*: **he** ~**ed up about his visit** он откровенно рассказал о своей поездке
◼ ~-**air** *adj.*: ~-**air life** жизнь на открытом воздухе; ~ **competition** *n.* открытое соревнование; ~ **day** *n.* (BrE, at school) день открытых дверей; ~-**heart** *adj.*: ~-**heart surgery** операция, проводимая на отключённом сердце; ~ **market** *n.* открытый рынок; ~-**minded** *adj.*

непредвзятый, непредубеждённый; ~-**plan** *adj.* с открытой планировкой; ~ **ticket** *n.* билет с открытой датой

opener /ˈəʊpənə(r)/ *n.* (in full **can** ~) консервный нож

opening /ˈəʊpənɪŋ/ *n.* ◼ (aperture) отверстие ◻ (beginning) начало; (of play, speech) вступление ◻ (job) место, вакансия
• *adj.* (initial) начальный, первый; ~ **remarks** вступительные замечания; (working): ~ **hours** рабочие часы; часы работы

openly /ˈəʊpənlɪ/ *adv.* открыто; (frankly) откровенно; (publicly) публично, открыто

openness /ˈəʊpənnɪs/ *n.* (frankness) открытость, откровенность; (pol.) гласность

opera /ˈɒpərə/ *n.* опера
◼ ~ **glass** *n.* театральный бинокль; ~ **house** *n.* оперный театр

operable /ˈɒpərəb(ə)l/ *adj.* ◼ (med.) операбельный ◻ (workable) действующий, функционирующий

✎ **operate** /ˈɒpəreɪt/ *v.t.* ◼ (control work of) управлять (*impf.*) + *i.*; **the machine is** ~**d by electricity** эта машина работает на электричестве ◻ (put into effect): **we** ~ **a simple system** мы применяем простую систему
• *v.i.* ◼ (work, act) работать (*impf.*); **the brakes failed to** ~ тормоза отказали ◻ ~ **on** (med.) оперировать (*impf., pf.*) (**for:** по поводу + *g.*)

operatic /ˌɒpəˈrætɪk/ *adj.* оперный

operating /ˈɒpəreɪtɪŋ/ *adj.* ◼ (med.): ~ **room** (AmE), **theatre** (BrE) операционная ◻ (comput.): ~ **system** операционная система

✎ **operation** /ˌɒpəˈreɪʃ(ə)n/ *n.* ◼ (action, effect) действие; работа; **bring into** ~ приводить, -ести в действие ◻ (process) процесс, операция ◻ (control) эксплуатация, управление ◻ (med.) операция ◻ (mil.) операция, действия (*nt. pl.*)

operational /ˌɒpəˈreɪʃən(ə)l/ *adj.* действующий; **the factory is fully** ~ завод полностью готов к эксплуатации

operative /ˈɒpərətɪv/ *n.* ◼ (machine operator) станочник; квалифицированный рабочий; оператор (*какого-н. устройства*)
• *adj.* действенный

operator /ˈɒpəreɪtə(r)/ *n.* ◼ (one who works a machine) оператор ◻ (telephonist) телефонист (-ка)

operetta /ˌɒpəˈretə/ *n.* оперетта

ophthalmic /ɒfˈθælmɪk/ *adj.* глазной
◼ ~ **optician** *n.* (BrE) окулист

ophthalmologist /ˌɒfθælˈmɒlədʒɪst/ *n.* офтальмолог

ophthalmology /ˌɒfθælˈmɒlədʒɪ/ *n.* офтальмология

opiate /ˈəʊpɪət/ *n.* опиат; (fig.) опиум

✎ **opinion** /əˈpɪnjən/ *n.* (judgement) мнение; (view) взгляд; **in my** ~ по моему мнению, по-моему, на мой взгляд; (estimate): **have a high/low** ~ **of** быть высокого/невысокого мнения о + *p.*
◼ ~ **poll** *n.* опрос общественного мнения

opinionated /əˈpɪnjəneɪtɪd/ *adj.* догматичный

opium /ˈəʊpɪəm/ *n.* óпиум

✍ **opponent** /əˈpəʊnənt/ *n.* оппонéнт, противник; (sport) противник, сопéрник

opportune /ˈɒpətjuːn/ *adj.* своеврéменный, умéстный

opportunism /ɒpəˈtjuːnɪz(ə)m/ *n.* оппортунизм

opportunist /ɒpəˈtjuːnɪst/ *n.* оппортунист ● *adj.* оппортунистический

opportunistic /ɒpətjuːˈnɪstɪk/ *adj.* оппортунистический

✍ **opportunity** /ɒpəˈtjuːnɪtɪ/ *n.* (favourable circumstance) удóбный слýчай; (good chance) возмóжность; **he took the ~ to …** он воспóльзовался слýчаем, чтóбы…

✍ **oppos|e** /əˈpəʊz/ *v.t.* **1** (set against): **as ~ed to** в отличие от + *g.*; **I am firmly ~ed to the idea** я решительно прóтив этой идéи **2** (set oneself against): **the ~ing side** противная сторонá; (sport) комáнда противника; (show opposition to) противиться (*impf.*) + *d.*

opposite /ˈɒpəzɪt/ *n.* противополóжность; **just the ~** как раз наоборóт ● *adj.* противополóжный; **his house is ~ ours** егó дом (стоит) напрóтив нáшего; **in the ~ direction** в обрáтном направлéнии; **~ number** лицó, занимáющее такýю же дóлжность в другóй организáции ● *adv.* напрóтив ● *prep.* (на)прóтив (+ *g.*)

✍ **opposition** /ɒpəˈzɪʃ(ə)n/ *n.* **1** (resistance) сопротивлéние, противодéйствие; **he offered no ~** он не оказáл никакóго сопротивлéния **2** (BrE, pol.) оппозиция

oppress /əˈpres/ *v.t.* угнетáть (*impf.*)

oppression /əˈpreʃ(ə)n/ *n.* (oppressing) угнетéние, гнёт, притеснéние, тирания; (being oppressed) угнетённость

oppressive /əˈpresɪv/ *adj.* угнетáющий, давящий; **~ weather** угнетáющая/дýшная погóда

oppressor /əˈpresə(r)/ *n.* угнетáтель (*m.*)

opt /ɒpt/ *v.i.*: **~ for** выбирáть, выбрать; **~ out of** откáзываться, -áться от учáстия в + *p.* ■ **~-out** *n.* откáз от учáстия в чём-н.

optic /ˈɒptɪk/ *adj.*: **~ nerve** зрительный нерв

optical /ˈɒptɪk(ə)l/ *adj.* оптический ■ **~ illusion** *n.* оптический обмáн

optician /ɒpˈtɪʃ(ə)n/ *n.* окулист

optics /ˈɒptɪks/ *n.* óптика

optimism /ˈɒptɪmɪz(ə)m/ *n.* оптимизм

optimist /ˈɒptɪmɪst/ *n.* оптимист (-ка)

optimistic /ɒptɪˈmɪstɪk/ *adj.* оптимистический, оптимистичный

optimize /ˈɒptɪmaɪz/ *v.t.* оптимизировать (*impf., pf.*)

optimum /ˈɒptɪməm/ *adj.* оптимáльный

✍ **option** /ˈɒpʃ(ə)n/ *n.* выбор; **I have no ~ but to …** у меня нет другóго выбора, (крóме) как…

optional /ˈɒpʃən(ə)l/ *adj.* необязáтельный

optometrist /ɒpˈtɒmɪtrɪst/ *n.* (AmE) окулист

opulence /ˈɒpjʊləns/ *n.* богáтство, обилие, изобилие

opulent /ˈɒpjʊlənt/ *adj.* (wealthy) богáтый; (abundant) обильный

✍ **or** /ɔː(r)/ *conj.* **1** или; **two ~ three** два-три **2** (~ else) или, инáче; или же; а (не) то; **we must hurry ~ we'll be late** нýжно поторáпливаться, а то опоздáем **3**: **there were 20 ~ so people present** там было человéк 20 (*or* óколо двадцати человéк)

oral /ˈɔːr(ə)l/ *n.* ýстный экзáмен ● *adj.* (by word of mouth) ýстный; (pert. to mouth) стоматологический; (pert. to contraceptive, sex) орáльный ■ **~ hygiene** *n.* гигиéна пóлости рта

orange /ˈɒrɪndʒ/ *n.* **1** (fruit) апельсин **2** (tree) апельсиновое дéрево **3** (colour) орáнжевый цвет ● *adj.* (colour) орáнжевый ■ **~ juice** *n.* апельсиновый сок

orang-utan /ɔːræŋəˈtæn/ *n.* орангутáн(г)

oration /ɔːˈreɪʃ(ə)n/ *n.* речь

orator /ˈɒrətə(r)/ *n.* орáтор

orbit /ˈɔːbɪt/ *n.* орбита ● *v.t.* (**orbited**, **orbiting**) (move in ~ round) вращáться (*impf*) вокрýг (+ *g.*) ● *v.i.* (**orbited**, **orbiting**) (move in ~) вращáться (*impf*) по орбите

orchard /ˈɔːtʃəd/ *n.* (фруктóвый) сад

orchestra /ˈɔːkɪstrə/ *n.* оркéстр

orchestral /ɔːˈkestr(ə)l/ *adj.* оркестрóвый

orchestrate /ˈɔːkɪstreɪt/ *v.t.* оркестровáть (*impf., pf.*); (fig.) организóв|ывать, -áть

orchestration /ɔːkɪˈstreɪʃ(ə)n/ *n.* оркестрóвка

orchid /ˈɔːkɪd/ *n.* орхидéя

ordain /ɔːˈdeɪn/ *v.t.* **1** (eccl.) посвя|щáть, -тить в духóвный сан **2** (destine) предпис|ывать, -áть

ordeal /ɔːˈdiːl/ *n.* мýка

✍ **order** /ˈɔːdə(r)/ *n.* **1** (arrangement) порядок; (sequence, succession) послéдовательность; **in alphabetical ~** в алфавитном порядке; **in ~ of importance** по стéпени вáжности **2** (result of arrangement or control) порядок; **everything is in ~** всё в порядке; (settled state): **restore ~** восстан|áвливать, -овить порядок; **out of ~** неисправный, в плохóм состоянии **3** (instruction) прикáз, распоряжéние, поручéние; **give an, the ~** отд|авáть, -áть прикáз; **under sb's ~s** под комáндой когó-н. **4** (direction to supply) закáз (**for:** на + *a.*); **on ~** по закáзу **5** (*in pl.*) (eccl.): **holy ~s** духóвный сан; **take ~s** прин|имáть, -ять духóвный сан **6**: **in ~ to** (для тогó,) чтóбы (+ *inf.*); **in ~ that** (для тогó,) чтóбы (+ *past tense*) ● *v.t.* **1** (arrange) прив|одить, -ести в порядок **2** (command) прикáз|ывать, -áть; распоря|жáться, -диться; **he ~ed the soldiers to leave** он прикáзал солдáтам разойтись **3** (reserve; request) закáз|ывать, -áть **4**: **~ sb about** комáндовать (*impf.*) + *i.*

■ ~ **form** *n.* бланк заказа

orderliness /'ɔ:dəlɪnɪs/ *n.* (order) поря́док; (methodical nature) аккура́тность

orderly /'ɔ:dəlɪ/ *n.* санита́р
● *adj.* **1** (organized) организо́ванный **2** (quiet, well behaved) ти́хий, послу́шный

ordinal /'ɔ:dɪn(ə)l/ *n.* (*in full* ~ **number**) поря́дковое числи́тельное

⚡ **ordinary** /'ɔ:dɪnərɪ/ *n.*: out of the ~ необы́чный, незауря́дный
● *adj.* (usual) обы́чный; (average) обыкнове́нный; (normal) норма́льный

ordination /ɔ:dɪ'neɪʃ(ə)n/ *n.* (eccl.) рукоположе́ние

ore /ɔ:(r)/ *n.* руда́

oregano /ɒrɪ'gɑ:nəʊ/ *n.* души́ца обыкнове́нная, ди́кий майора́н

organ /'ɔ:gən/ *n.* **1** (mus.) орга́н **2** (biol., pol., etc.) о́рган
■ ~ **donor** *n.* до́нор; ~ **transplant** *n.* переса́дка о́ргана

organic /ɔ:'gænɪk/ *adj.* органи́ческий; ~ **food** натура́льные пищевы́е проду́кты

organism /'ɔ:gənɪz(ə)m/ *n.* органи́зм

organist /'ɔ:gənɪst/ *n.* органи́ст (-ка)

⚡ **organization** /ɔ:gənaɪ'zeɪʃ(ə)n/ *n.* организа́ция

organizational /ɔ:gənaɪ'zeɪʃən(ə)l/ *adj.* организацио́нный

⚡ **organize** /'ɔ:gənaɪz/ *v.t.* организо́в|ывать, -а́ть; устр|а́ивать, -о́ить; ~d **crime** организо́ванная престу́пность

organizer /'ɔ:gənaɪzə(r)/ *n.* организа́тор

orgasm /'ɔ:gæz(ə)m/ *n.* орга́зм

orgy /'ɔ:dʒɪ/ *n.* о́ргия; (fig.) разгу́л

Orient /'ɔ:rɪənt/ *n.* Восто́к

orient /'ɒrɪənt, 'ɔ:r-/, **orientate** /'ɒrɪənteɪt, 'ɔ:r-/ *v.t.* (determine position of) ориенти́ровать (*impf., pf.*) (*pf. also* c-); ~ **oneself** ориенти́роваться (*impf., pf.*) (*pf. also* c-)

oriental /ɔ:rɪ'ent(ə)l/ *adj.* восто́чный

orientation /ɔ:rɪen'teɪʃ(ə)n/ *n.* (lit., fig.) ориентиро́вка, ориента́ция

orienteering /ɔ:rɪen'tɪərɪŋ/ *n.* спорти́вное ориенти́рование, ориенти́рование на ме́стности

orifice /'ɒrɪfɪs/ *n.* (aperture) отве́рстие; (mouth) у́стье

⚡ **origin** /'ɒrɪdʒɪn/ *n.* нача́ло, исто́чник

⚡ **original** /ə'rɪdʒɪn(ə)l/ *n.* по́длинник, оригина́л
● *adj.* **1** (first, earliest) первонача́льный; the ~ **inhabitants** исконные жи́тели **2** (inventive) оригина́льный, самобы́тный

originality /ərɪdʒɪ'nælɪtɪ/ *n.* оригина́льность, самобы́тность

⚡ **originally** /ə'rɪdʒɪnəlɪ/ *adv.* (in the first place) первонача́льно, исхо́дно; (in origin) по происхожде́нию

originate /ə'rɪdʒɪneɪt/ *v.i.* брать, взять нача́ло; (arise) возн|ика́ть, -и́кнуть

ornament /'ɔ:nəmənt/ *n.* **1** (adornment) украше́ние **2** (decorative article) орна́мент

ornamental /ɔ:nə'ment(ə)l/ *adj.* декорати́вный

ornamentation /ɔ:nəmen'teɪʃ(ə)n/ *n.* украше́ние

ornate /ɔ:'neɪt/ *adj.* бога́то укра́шенный

ornithological /ɔ:nɪθə'lɒdʒɪk(ə)l/ *adj.* орнитологи́ческий

ornithologist /ɔ:nɪ'θɒlədʒɪst/ *n.* орнито́лог

ornithology /ɔ:nɪ'θɒlədʒɪ/ *n.* орнитоло́гия

orphan /'ɔ:f(ə)n/ *n.* сирота́ (*c.g.*)

orphanage /'ɔ:fənɪdʒ/ *n.* прию́т для сиро́т

orthodox /'ɔ:θədɒks/ *adj.* ортодокса́льный, правове́рный; the O~ **Church** правосла́вная це́рковь

orthodoxy /'ɔ:θədɒksɪ/ *n.* (relig.) ортодокса́льность, правове́рность; (fig.) ортодокса́льность

orthographic /ɔ:θə'græfɪk/, **orthographical** /ɔ:θə'græfɪk(ə)l/ *adjs.* орфографи́ческий

orthography /ɔ:'θɒgrəfɪ/ *n.* правописа́ние, орфогра́фия

orthopaedic /ɔ:θə'pi:dɪk/ (AmE **orthopedic**) *adj.* ортопеди́ческий

orthopaedics /ɔ:θə'pi:dɪks/ (AmE **orthopedics**) *n.* ортопе́дия

orthopaedist /ɔ:θə'pi:dɪst/ (AmE **orthopedist**) *n.* ортопе́д

oscillate /'ɒsɪleɪt/ *v.t.* кача́ть (*impf.*)
● *v.i.* (swing) кача́ться (*impf.*) (elec., radio, also fig.), колеба́ться (*impf.*); (elec., radio, also fig.) колеба́ться (*impf.*)

oscillation /ɒsɪ'leɪʃ(ə)n/ *n.* колеба́ние; (elec.) осцилля́ция

Oslo /'ɒzləʊ/ *n.* О́сло (*m. indecl.*)

osmosis /ɒz'məʊsɪs/ *n.* (biol., chem.) о́смос

ostensibl|e /ɒ'stensɪb(ə)l/ *adj.* (for show) показно́й; (professed) мни́мый; he called ~y to thank me он пришёл я́кобы для того́, чтобы поблагодари́ть меня́

ostentation /ɒsten'teɪʃ(ə)n/ *n.* (display) показна́я ро́скошь

ostentatious /ɒsten'teɪʃəs/ *adj.* показно́й, хвастли́вый

osteopath /'ɒstɪəpæθ/ *n.* остеопа́т

osteopathy /ɒstɪ'ɒpəθɪ/ *n.* остеопа́тия

ostracize /'ɒstrəsaɪz/ *v.t.* подв|ерга́ть, -е́ргнуть остраки́зму

ostrich /'ɒstrɪtʃ/ *n.* стра́ус (*африка́нский*); (*attr.*) страуси́ный

⚡ **other** /'ʌðə(r)/ *pron.* друго́й, ино́й; ~s may disagree with you други́е/ины́е мо́гут с ва́ми не согласи́ться; one after the ~ оди́н за други́м; someone or ~ кто́-нибудь; (expr. reciprocity): they were in love with each ~ они́ бы́ли влюблены́ друг в дру́га; (in pl.) (additional ones; more) ещё + g.; (remaining ones) остальны́е
● *adj.* **1** друго́й; on the ~ side of the road на друго́й/той стороне́ доро́ги; some ~ time в друго́й раз **2** (additional) ещё + g. **3** (remaining) остально́й; we shall visit the ~ museums tomorrow мы посети́м

o

остальны́е музе́и за́втра **4**: the ~ day на дня́х; every ~ day че́рез день

otherwise /ˈʌðəwaɪz/ *adv.* **1** (in a different way) ина́че, по-друго́му, други́м спо́собом **2** (in other respects) в други́х отноше́ниях; **the house is cold but** ~ **comfortable** дом холо́дный, но в остально́м удо́бный; **3** (if not; or else) ина́че, а то; **I went,** ~ **I would have missed them** я пошёл, ина́че я бы их не заста́л

Ottawa /ˈɒtəwə/ *n.* Отта́ва

otter /ˈɒtə(r)/ *n.* вы́дра

Ottoman /ˈɒtəmən/ *n.* (*pl.* ~**s**) **1** (hist.) оттома́н **2** (**o**~) (sofa) оттома́нка, тахта́ ● *adj.* оттома́нский

ouch /aʊtʃ/ *int.* ой!, ай!

ought /ɔːt/ *v. aux.* **1** (expr. duty) до́лжен; **you** ~ **to go there** вы должны́ (*or* вам сле́дует) туда́ пойти́; **you** ~ **to have gone yesterday** вам сле́довало пойти́ туда́ вчера́ **2** (expr. desirability) до́лжен; на́до + *d.*; **you** ~ **to have seen his face** на́до бы́ло ви́деть его́ лицо́ **3** (expr. probability) должно́ быть, вероя́тно; **he** ~ **to be there by now** сейча́с он, вероя́тно (*or* должно́ быть), уже́ там

ounce /aʊns/ *n.* (weight) у́нция (= *28,35 г*)

our /ˈaʊə(r)/ *poss. adj.* наш

ours /ˈaʊəz/ *pron. & pred. adj.* наш; ~ **is a blue car** на́ша маши́на си́няя; **this tree is** ~ э́то де́рево на́ше

ourselves /aʊəˈselvz/ *pron.* **1** (refl.) себя́ (*d., p.* себе́, *i.* собо́й); -сь (*suff.*); **we washed** ~ мы умы́лись; (after preps): **we can only depend on** ~ мы мо́жем полага́ться то́лько на себя́ (сами́х); **we were not satisfied with** ~ мы бы́ли недово́льны собо́й **2** (emph.) са́ми; **we** ~ **were not present** са́ми мы не прису́тствовали **3**: **by** ~ (alone) са́ми (по себе́); (without aid) са́ми, одни́

oust /aʊst/ *v.t.* (force out, also fig.) вытесня́ть, вы́теснить; (expel) выгоня́ть, вы́гнать

out /aʊt/ *pred. adj. & adv.* **1** (away from home, room, usual place, etc.): **he is** ~ его́ нет до́ма; (sport) вне игры́ **2** (~ of doors) на дворе́; на у́лице; **it is quite warm** ~ **today** сего́дня на дворе́ тепло́; **he was** ~ **and about all day** он был на нога́х весь день; **we were** ~ **in the garden** мы бы́ли в саду́; (fig., intent): **they are** ~ **to get him** они́ (во что бы то ни ста́ло) наме́рены его́ пойма́ть **3** (visible): **the stars are** ~ вы́сыпали звёзды; **the sun will be** ~ **this afternoon** по́сле полу́дня пока́жется/поя́вится со́лнце; (revealed): **the secret is, was** ~ секре́т раскры́лся (*or* стал всем изве́стен); (published): **my book is** ~ **at last** моя́ кни́га наконе́ц вы́шла (из печа́ти) **4** (at departure): **he stumbled on the way** ~ выходя́, он споткну́лся; (at a distance): **the tide is** ~ сейча́с отли́в **5** (astray, wrong): **I wasn't far** ~ я не намно́го оши́бся **6** (infml, ~ of favour, fashion): **short hair is** ~ коро́ткая стри́жка сейча́с не в мо́де **7** (over): **before the week is** ~ до оконча́ния неде́ли; (extinguished): **the fire is** ~ ого́нь поту́х **8**: ~ **of** (movement) из

+ *g.*; **he fell** ~ **of the window** он вы́пал из окна́; (material): **made** ~ **of silk** (сши́тый) из шёлка, шёлковый; (from among): **two students** ~ **of forty** два студе́нта из сорока́; (motive): ~ **of pity/love/respect** из жа́лости/любви́/уваже́ния (**for:** к + *d.*); ~ **of grief/joy** с го́ря/ра́дости; ~ **of boredom** от/со ску́ки; (outside): ~ **of danger** вне опа́сности; ~ **of doors** на у́лице, на дворе́, на во́здухе; **feel** ~ **of it** чу́вствовать (*impf.*) себя́ чужи́м (*or* ни при чём); ~ **of control** вне контро́ля; ~ **of fashion** не в мо́де; (without): ~ **of breath** запыха́вшийся; ~ **of work** безрабо́тный ● *v.t.* (infml, expose as being homosexual) изоблича́ть, -и́ть в гомосексуали́зме

out-and-out /aʊtəndˈaʊt/ *adj.* соверше́нный, по́лный, отъя́вленный

outback /ˈaʊtbæk/ *n.* глушь

outboard /ˈaʊtbɔːd/ *adj.*: ~ **motor** подвесно́й мото́р

outbox /ˈaʊtbɒks/ *n.* (comput.) исходя́щие (сообще́ния)

outbreak /ˈaʊtbreɪk/ *n.* вспы́шка

outbuilding /ˈaʊtbɪldɪŋ/ *n.* надво́рное строе́ние, надво́рная постро́йка

outburst /ˈaʊtbɜːst/ *n.* вспы́шка, взры́в

outcast /ˈaʊtkɑːst/ *n.* изгна́нник, отве́рженный

outcome /ˈaʊtkʌm/ *n.* исхо́д, результа́т

outcry /ˈaʊtkraɪ/ *n.* проте́ст, (обще́ственное) негодова́ние

outdo /aʊtˈduː/ *v.t.* превосходи́ть, -зойти́

outdoor /ˈaʊtdɔː(r)/ *adj.*: ~ **games** и́гры на откры́том во́здухе, подви́жные и́гры; ~ **clothes** ве́рхнее пла́тье

outdoors /aʊtˈdɔːz/ *adv.* на откры́том во́здухе, на дворе́; (expr. motion) на во́здух

outer /ˈaʊtə(r)/ *adj.* (external) вне́шний ■ ~ **space** *n.* ко́смос

outfit /ˈaʊtfɪt/ *n.* комплéкт (оде́жды)

outgoing /ˈaʊtɡəʊɪŋ/ *adj.* **1** (departing): **the** ~ **president** президе́нт, уходя́щий с поста́; ~ **mail** исходя́щая по́чта **2** (sociable): **an** ~ **person** общи́тельный/ужи́вчивый челове́к

outgoings /ˈaʊtɡəʊɪŋz/ *n. pl.* (BrE) расхо́ды (*m. pl.*)

outgrow /aʊtˈɡrəʊ/ *v.t.* **1** (grow too large for) выраста́ть, вы́расти из + *g.* **2** (discard with time) выраста́ть, вы́расти из + *g.*

outhouse /ˈaʊthaʊs/ *n.* надво́рное строе́ние; (AmE, lavatory) убо́рная во дворе́, отхо́жее ме́сто

outing /ˈaʊtɪŋ/ *n.* прогу́лка, экску́рсия

outlandish /aʊtˈlændɪʃ/ *adj.* дико́винный, чудно́й

outlast /aʊtˈlɑːst/ *v.t.* (outlive) переж|ива́ть, -и́ть

outlaw /ˈaʊtlɔː/ *n.* лицо́, объя́вленное вне зако́на ● *v.t.* объявл|я́ть, -и́ть вне зако́на

outlay /ˈaʊtleɪ/ *n.* изде́ржки (*f. pl.*)

outlet /ˈaʊtlet/ *n.* **1** (lit.) выходно́е/выпускно́е отве́рстие **2** (shop) фи́рменный магази́н **3** (for energies etc.) отду́шина, вы́ход

outline /'aʊtlaɪn/ n. **1** (contour) ко́нтур, очерта́ние (*often in pl.*) **2** (of speech, article) конспе́кт
● *v.t.* нам|еча́ть, -е́тить в о́бщих черта́х

outlive /aʊt'lɪv/ v.t. пережи|ва́ть, -и́ть

outlook /'aʊtlʊk/ n. **1** (lit., fig., prospect) вид, перспекти́ва; (weather etc.) прогно́з **2** (point of view) то́чка зре́ния

outlying /'aʊtlaɪɪŋ/ adj. отдалённый, удалённый

outmoded /aʊt'məʊdɪd/ adj. старомо́дный, немо́дный, устаре́лый

outnumber /aʊt'nʌmbə(r)/ v.t. прев|осходи́ть, -зойти́ *кого/что* чи́сленно

out-of-court settlement /aʊtəv'kɔːt/ n. (law) мирова́я сде́лка, урегули́рованная вне суда́

out-of-date /aʊtəv'deɪt/ adj. устаре́лый, старомо́дный

outpatient /'aʊtpeɪʃ(ə)nt/ n. амбулато́рный больно́й
■ ~ **department** n. поликли́ника, амбулато́рная отделе́ние

outpost /'aʊtpəʊst/ n. отдалённое поселе́ние

output /'aʊtpʊt/ n. **1** (production) вы́пуск, проду́кция, произво́дство **2** (productivity) производи́тельность
● *v.t.* (comput.) выводи́ть, вы́вести

outrage /'aʊtreɪdʒ/ n. (outrageous situation) безобра́зие; (outrageous act) безобра́зный посту́пок; (anger) негодова́ние

outrageous /aʊt'reɪdʒəs/ adj. безобра́зный, возмути́тельный

outrider /'aʊtraɪdə(r)/ n. (*usu. in pl.*) эско́рт

outright adj. /'aʊtraɪt/ (direct) прямо́й, откры́тый; (total) соверше́нный
● adv. /aʊt'raɪt/ (directly, openly) пря́мо, откры́то; (totally) соверше́нно; (fully) по́лностью; (instantly) сра́зу

outset /'aʊtset/ n. нача́ло; **at the** ~ внача́ле; **from the** ~ с са́мого нача́ла

⚤ **outside** n. /aʊt'saɪd/ нару́жная сторона́; **from, on the** ~ снару́жи; **at the (very)** ~ са́мое бо́льшее
● adj. /'aʊtsaɪd/ **1** (external, exterior) нару́жный, вне́шний **2** (extreme) кра́йний; **he has an** ~ **chance of winning** у него́ есть при́зрачные ша́нсы на вы́игрыш
● adv. /aʊt'saɪd/ снару́жи; извне́; (to the ~) нару́жу
● prep. /aʊt'saɪd/ вне + g., из + g.; (beyond bounds of) за преде́лами + g.; ~ **the door/ window** за две́рью/окно́м

outsider /aʊt'saɪdə(r)/ n. посторо́нний; (in contest, lit., fig.) аутса́йдер

outsize /'aʊtsaɪz/ adj. нестанда́ртный

outskirts /'aʊtskɜːts/ n. pl. (of town) окра́ина

outsource /aʊt'sɔːs/ v.t. (econ.) отд|ава́ть, -а́ть на́ сторону/на субподря́д

outspoken /aʊt'spəʊkən/ adj. прямо́й, открове́нный

outstanding /aʊt'stændɪŋ/ adj. (prominent, eminent) выдаю́щийся; (still to be done) невы́полненный; (unpaid) неопла́ченный

outstay /aʊt'steɪ/ v.t.: ~ **one's welcome** загости́ться (*pf.*)

outstretched /aʊt'stretʃt, aʊt'stretʃt/ adj. (hand) протя́нутый

outstrip /aʊt'strɪp/ v.t. (lit., fig.) опере|жа́ть, -ди́ть

outward /'aʊtwəd/ adj. (external) нару́жный, вне́шний

outwardly /'aʊtwədlɪ/ adv. вне́шне, на вид

outwards /'aʊtwədz/ adv. нару́жу

outweigh /aʊt'weɪ/ v.t. переве́|шивать, -сить

outwit /aʊt'wɪt/ v.t. (**outwitted, outwitting**) перехитри́ть (*pf.*)

oval /'əʊv(ə)l/ n. ова́л
● adj. ова́льный

ovarian /ə'veərɪən/ adj. яи́чниковый
■ ~ **cancer** n. рак яи́чников

ovary /'əʊvərɪ/ n. яи́чник

ovation /əʊ'veɪʃ(ə)n/ n. ова́ция

oven /'ʌv(ə)n/ n. духо́вка

⚤ **over** /'əʊvə(r)/ adv. **1** (across; to, on the other side): ~ **there** (вон) там; **I asked him** ~ я пригласи́л его́ к себе́ **2** (covering surface): **all** ~ (everywhere) повсю́ду; **I felt hot and cold all** ~ меня́ (всего́) броса́ло то в жар, то в хо́лод **3** (at an end): **the meeting is** ~ собра́ние ко́нчилось **4** (*also* ~ **again**) (once more) опя́ть, сно́ва, ещё раз; ~ **and** ~ **again** ты́сячу раз, сно́ва и сно́ва **5** (in excess): **sums of £5 and** ~ су́ммы в/от 5 фу́нтов и вы́ше; **I had £3 (left)** ~ у меня́ ещё оста́валось три фу́нта
● prep. **1** (above) над + i.; **a roof** ~ **one's head** кры́ша над голово́й; (expr. division): **five** ~ **two** (math.) пять дробь два **2** (to the far side of) че́рез + a.; **a bridge** ~ **the river** мост че́рез ре́ку; **I threw the ball** ~ **the wall** я переки́нул мяч че́рез сте́ну; **he jumped** ~ **the puddles** он перепры́гнул (че́рез) лу́жи; (down from): **he fell** ~ **the cliff** он упа́л со скалы́; (against): **he tripped** ~ **a stone** он споткну́лся о ка́мень **3** (on the far side of): **he lives** ~ **the way** он живёт че́рез у́лицу **4** (resting on): **he pulled his cap** ~ **his eyes** он надви́нул ша́пку на глаза́; **crossing one leg** ~ **the other** заки́нув но́гу на́ ногу; (across, ~ the surface of) по + d.; **all** ~ **the world** во всём ми́ре; по всему́ све́ту **5** (more than) бо́льше/ свы́ше + g.; ~ **a year ago** бо́льше/свы́ше го́да (тому́) наза́д; **children** ~ **5** де́ти ста́рше пяти́ лет; ~ **600** свы́ше шестисо́т **6** (during): **much has happened** ~ **the past two years** за после́дние два го́да мно́гое случи́лось/ произошло́ **7** (on the subject of): **he gets angry** ~ **nothing** он зли́тся из-за пустяко́в; **a quarrel** ~ **money** ссо́ра из-за де́нег

⚤ **overall** n. /'əʊvərɔːl/ (BrE) рабо́чий хала́т; (*in pl.*) комбинезо́н
● adj. /'əʊvərɔːl/ (total) по́лный; (general) (все)о́бщий
● adv. /əʊvər'ɔːl/ (taken as a whole) в це́лом

overawe /əʊvər'ɔː/ v.t. внуш|а́ть, -и́ть благогове́йный страх + d.

overbalance /əʊvə'bæləns/ (BrE) v.i. теря́ть, по- равнове́сие

o

overbearing /ˌəʊvəˈbeərɪŋ/ *adj.* властный
overboard /ˈəʊvəbɔːd/ *adv.*: **man ~!** человек за бортом!
overbook /ˌəʊvəˈbʊk/ *v.t.*: **the plane was ~ed** билетов на самолёт было продано больше, чем имелось мест
overcast /ˈəʊvəkɑːst/ *adj.* покрытый облаками
overcharge /ˌəʊvəˈtʃɑːdʒ/ *v.t.* назн|ачать, -ачить завышенную цену (*кому*) (**for:** за + *a.*)
overcoat /ˈəʊvəkəʊt/ *n.* пальто (*nt. indecl.*)
overcome /ˌəʊvəˈkʌm/ *v.t.* (prevail over) преодол|евать, -еть; (of emotion) охват|ывать, -ить
overconfident /ˌəʊvəˈkɒnfɪd(ə)nt/ *adj.* самонадеянный
overcook /ˌəʊvəˈkʊk/ *v.t.* (by roasting, frying) пережар|ивать, -ить; (by boiling) перевар|ивать, -ить
overcrowd /ˌəʊvəˈkraʊd/ *v.t.* перепол|нять, -олнить
overdo /ˌəʊvəˈduː/ *v.t.* (by roasting, frying) пережар|ивать, -ть; (by boiling) перевар|ивать, -ить; **~ it** перестараться (*pf.*); переб|арщивать, -орщить (infml); переусердствовать (*pf.*) (*в чём*)
overdose /ˈəʊvədəʊs/ *n.* передозировка, чрезмерная доза
overdraft /ˈəʊvədrɑːft/ *n.* (deficit in bank account) овердрафт, перерасход; (agreement) разрешение на превышение кредита
overdraw /ˌəʊvəˈdrɔː/ *v.t.*: **I am £100 ~n** я превысил кредит в банке на 100 фунтов
overdue /ˌəʊvəˈdjuː/ *adj.* запоздалый; **the baby is 2 weeks ~** ребёнок должен был родиться две недели тому назад; (of payment) просроченный
overeat /ˌəʊvərˈiːt/ *v.i.* пере|едать, -есть; объ|едаться, -есться
overestimate /ˌəʊvərˈestɪmeɪt/ *v.t.* переоцен|ивать, -ить
overexcited /ˌəʊvərɪkˈsaɪtɪd/ *adj.* крайне возбуждённый
overflow /ˈəʊvəfləʊ/ *v.t. & i.* перел|иваться, -иться (*через что*); **the river ~s its banks** река заливает берега (*or* выходит из берегов); **~ing with** (fig.) преисполненный + *g.*
overground /ˈəʊvəɡraʊnd/ *adj.* надземный
overgrow /ˌəʊvəˈɡrəʊ/ *v.t.*: **be ~n (with)** зараст|ать, -и + *i.*
overhaul /ˈəʊvəhɔːl/ *n.* (of machine) осмотр; (of system) пересмотр
  ● *v.t.* осм|атривать, -отреть; ремонти|ровать, от-; пересм|атривать, -отреть
overhead *n.* /ˈəʊvəhed/ (*usu. in pl.*) накладные расходы (*m. pl.*)
  ● *adj.*: /ˈəʊvəhed/ **~ projector** диапроектор; **~ railway** надземная железная дорога
  ● *adv.* /ˌəʊvəˈhed/ наверху, вверху; (in the sky) на небе

overhear /ˌəʊvəˈhɪə(r)/ *v.t.* нечаянно услышать (*pf.*)
overheat /ˌəʊvəˈhiːt/ *v.t. & i.* перегр|евать(ся), -еть(ся)
overindulge /ˌəʊvərɪnˈdʌldʒ/ *v.i.*: **~ in sth** злоупотреб|лять, -ить чем-н.
overjoyed /ˌəʊvəˈdʒɔɪd/ *adj.* вне себя от радости
overkill /ˈəʊvəkɪl/ *n.* (fig.) выход за пределы необходимости
overland /ˈəʊvəlænd/ *adj.* сухопутный
  ● *adv.* по суше
overlap /ˈəʊvəlæp/ *v.i.* за|ходить, -йти один на другой; (coincide) (частично) совп|адать, -асть
overleaf /ˈəʊvəliːf/ *adv.* на обороте (страницы)
overload /ˈəʊvələʊd/ *v.t.* перегру|жать, -зить
overlook /ˌəʊvəˈlʊk/ *v.t.* **1** (open on to) выходить (*impf.*) на + *a.*; **our house is not ~ed** наш дом защищён от посторонних взглядов; **a view ~ing the lake** вид на озеро **2** (fail to notice) просмотреть (*pf.*), проглядеть (*pf.*), пропус|кать, -тить; (disregard) упус|кать, -тить
overly /ˈəʊvəlɪ/ *adv.* слишком, чересчур
overnight /ˌəʊvəˈnaɪt/ *adj.*: **an ~ stay** ночёвка, ночлег
  ● *adv.* (through the night) всю ночь; (during the night) за ночь; **stay ~** ночевать, за-
  ■ **~ bag** *n.* дорожная сумка, небольшой чемодан
overpass /ˈəʊvəpɑːs/ *n.* эстакада
overpayment /ˌəʊvəˈpeɪmənt/ *n.* переплата
overpopulated /ˌəʊvəˈpɒpjʊleɪtɪd/ *adj.* перенаселённый
overpower /ˌəʊvəˈpaʊə(r)/ *v.t.* одол|евать, -еть; (overwhelm) сокруш|ать, -ить; **~ing smell** очень сильный запах
overrate /ˌəʊvəˈreɪt/ *v.t.* переоцен|ивать, -ить
overreach /ˌəʊvəˈriːtʃ/ *v.t.* (outwit) перехитрить (*pf.*); **~ oneself** (defeat one's object) перестараться (*pf.*)
overreact /ˌəʊvərɪˈækt/ *v.i.* реаги́ровать, от-/про- чрезмерно резко
overrid|e /ˌəʊvəˈraɪd/ *v.t.* (reject) отв|ергать, -ергнуть; **~ing** (aim) основной, первостепенный; (consideration) главный, решающий
overrule /ˌəʊvəˈruːl/ *v.t.* (annul) аннули́ровать (*impf., pf.*); **I was ~d** моё возражение отвергли
overrun /ˌəʊvəˈrʌn/ *v.t.* **1** (of enemy) соверш|ать, -ить набег на + *a.* **2** (infest): **the garden is ~ with weeds** сад зарос сорняками; **the house is ~ with rats** дом кишит крысами
  ● *v.i.*: **the broadcast is ~ning by 20 minutes** передача идёт на 20 минут дольше положенного времени
overseas *adj.* /ˈəʊvəsiːz/ (trip) заграничный; (visitor) иностранный
  ● *adv.* /ˌəʊvəˈsiːz/ за границей
oversee /ˌəʊvəˈsiː/ *v.t.* надзирать (*impf.*) за + *i.*
overseer /ˈəʊvəsiːə(r)/ *n.* надсмотрщик, надзиратель (*m.*)

overshadow /əʊvə'ʃædəʊ/ v.t. (lit., fig.) заслон|ять, -и́ть

overshoot /əʊvə'ʃuːt/ v.t. (junction, traffic lights) про|езжа́ть, -е́хать; проск|а́кивать, -очи́ть; ~ the mark (lit.) брать, взять вы́ше це́ли; (fig.) за|ходи́ть, -йти́ сли́шком далеко́
• v.i.: the plane overshot on landing (при поса́дке) самолёт перелете́л то́чку приземле́ния

oversight /'əʊvəsaɪt/ n. недосмо́тр, упуще́ние

oversimplify /əʊvə'sɪmplɪfaɪ/ v.t. сли́шком упро|ща́ть, -сти́ть

oversleep /əʊvə'sliːp/ v.i. прос|ыпа́ть, -па́ть

overspend /əʊvə'spend/ v.i. тра́тить, по-сли́шком мно́го

overstep /əʊvə'step/ v.t. переступ|а́ть, -и́ть

oversubscribed /əʊvəsəb'skraɪbd/ adj.: the course is ~ курс перепо́лнен

overt /əʊ'vɜːt/ adj. я́вный, очеви́дный

overtake /əʊvə'teɪk/ v.t. об|гоня́ть, -огна́ть

over the top /əʊvə ðə 'tɒp/ adj. чрезме́рный

overthrow /əʊvə'θrəʊ/ v.t. ниспров|ерга́ть, -е́ргнуть

overtime /'əʊvətaɪm/ n. сверхуро́чная рабо́та
• adv. сверхуро́чно

overtone /'əʊvətəʊn/ n. отте́нок

overture /'əʊvətjʊə(r)/ n. уверть́ра

overturn /əʊvə'tɜːn/ v.t. & i. опроки́|дывать(ся), -нуть(ся)

overview /'əʊvəvjuː/ n. обзо́р

overweight /'əʊvəweɪt/ adj. ве́сящий бо́льше но́рмы

overwhelm /əʊvə'welm/ v.t. (in battle) сокруш|а́ть, -и́ть; (fig.): his kindness ~ed me я был ошеломлён/потрясён его́ добро́той; ~ing majority подавля́ющее большинство́

overwork /əʊvə'wɜːk/ v.t. & i. переутом|ля́ть(ся), -и́ть(ся)

overwrought /əʊvə'rɔːt/ adj. сли́шком возбуждённый, не́рвный; she is ~ у неё не́рвное истоще́ние

ovulate /'ɒvjʊleɪt/ v.i. овули́ровать (impf., pf.)

ovulation /ɒvjʊ'leɪʃ(ə)n/ n. овуля́ция

owe /əʊ/ v.t. & i. быть до́лжным + d.; you ~ us £50 вы должны́ нам 50 фу́нтов; I ~ you for the ticket я до́лжен вам за биле́т

owing /'əʊɪŋ/ adj. 1 (yet to be paid) причита́ющийся 2: ~ to (attributable to) по причи́не + g.; (on account of, because of) из-за + g.

owl /aʊl/ n. сова́

own /əʊn/ pron.: get one's ~ back on sb поквита́ться (pf.) с кем-н.; on one's ~ (alone) в одино́честве; (independently) самостоя́тельно, сам (по себе́)
• adj. со́бственный, свой; my ~ house мой со́бственный дом; this house is not my ~ э́тот дом мне не принадлежи́т; can I have a room of my ~? мо́жно получи́ть отде́льную ко́мнату?; of one's ~ accord по со́бственному побужде́нию; по со́бственной во́ле; my ~ father мой родно́й оте́ц
• v.t. владе́ть (impf.) + i.; who ~s this bag? чья э́то су́мка?; the land was ~ed by my father (э́та) земля́ принадлежа́ла моему́ отцу́ (or э́той землёй владе́л мой оте́ц)
• v.i. 1: ~ to (liter., acknowledge, admit) призн|ава́ть, -а́ть (что); she ~ed to feelings of jealousy она́ призна́лась в том, что ревнова́ла 2: ~ up (to sth) призн|ава́ться, -а́ться (в чём-н.); I ~ed up to having told a lie я призна́лся, что солга́л

owner /'əʊnə(r)/ n. владе́л|ец (-ица)

ownership /'əʊnəʃɪp/ n. владе́ние (of: + i.); со́бственность (of: на + a.)

ox /ɒks/ n. (pl. **oxen**) бык

oxide /'ɒksaɪd/ n. о́кись, окси́д

oxidize /'ɒksɪdaɪz/ v.t. окисл|я́ть, -и́ть

oxygen /'ɒksɪdʒ(ə)n/ n. кислоро́д

oyster /'ɔɪstə(r)/ n. у́стрица

ozone /'əʊzəʊn/ n. озо́н
■ ~ layer n. озо́нный/озо́новый слой

Pp

p abbr. 1 (of **penny, pence**) (BrE) пе́нни (nt. indecl.), пенс 2 (of **page**) с(тр). (страни́ца)

PA abbr. of 1 (BrE) (**personal assistant**) ли́чный секрета́рь 2 (**public address (system**)) звукоусили́тельная аппарату́ра

pace /peɪs/ n. 1 (step) шаг 2 (speed): keep ~ with посп|ева́ть, -е́ть за + i.
• v.i.: he ~d up and down он ходи́л взад и вперёд
■ ~maker n. (leader) ли́дер, задаю́щий темп; (med.) (электро)кардиостимуля́тор, электри́ческий стимуля́тор се́рдца

Pacific /pə'sɪfɪk/ n. (in full the ~ (Ocean)) Ти́хий океа́н

pacifier /'pæsɪfaɪə(r)/ n. (AmE, child's dummy) со́ска

pacifism /'pæsɪfɪz(ə)m/ n. пацифи́зм

pacifist /'pæsɪfɪst/ n. пацифи́ст (-ка)

pacify /'pæsɪfaɪ/ v.t. успок|а́ивать, -о́ить

o

p

⚹ **pack** /pæk/ *n.* **1** (rucksack) рюкза́к **2** (packet) па́чка, паке́т **3** (collection) набо́р; **it's all a ~ of lies** э́то сплошна́я ложь **4** (animals): **~ of wolves** ста́я волко́в **5** (BrE, cards) коло́да
● *v.t.* **1** (put into container) упако́в|ывать, -а́ть; укла́дывать, уложи́ть **2** (put into small space): **they were ~ed in there like sardines** они́ наби́лись туда́ как се́льди в бо́чке **3** (cover for protection) упако́в|ывать, -а́ть; **the glass is ~ed in cotton wool** стекло́ упако́вано в ва́ту **4** (fill) зап|олня́ть, -о́лнить; **he ~ed his bags and left** он уложи́л чемода́ны и уе́хал; **the hall was ~ed** зал был битко́м наби́т
● *v.i.* **1** (for travelling) укла́дываться, уложи́ться **2** (crowd together): **they ~ed into the car** они́ вти́снулись в автомоби́ль
□ **~ in** *v.t.* (infml, stop, give up) прекра|ща́ть, -ти́ть
□ **~ up** *v.t.*: **have the presents been ~ed up yet?** пода́рки уже́ упако́ваны?; (infml, stop): **I ~ed up smoking last year** я бро́сил кури́ть в про́шлом году́
● *v.i.*: **we spent the day ~ing up** мы це́лый день укла́дывались; (infml, stop working): **the workmen ~ed up at 5** рабо́чие зако́нчили в 5 часо́в; **the engine ~ed up** (BrE) мото́р отказа́л
■ **~ed lunch** *n.* бутербро́ды с собо́й

⚹ **package** /'pækɪdʒ/ *n.* (parcel) посы́лка; (comput.) паке́т; (*in full* **~ deal**) ко́мплексная сде́лка
● *v.t.* упако́в|ывать, -а́ть
■ **~ holiday, ~ tour** *nn.* (BrE) организо́ванная тури́стическая пое́здка

packet /'pækɪt/ *n.* (of cigarettes, biscuits) па́чка; (of crisps) паке́т

packing /'pækɪŋ/ *n.* упако́вка

pact /pækt/ *n.* соглаше́ние, догово́р

pad /pæd/ *n.* **1** (small cushion) поду́шечка; (for protection) прокла́дка **2** (block of paper) блокно́т **3** (launching platform) ста́ртовая площа́дка
● *v.t.* (**padded**, **padding**) **1** (cushion) наб|ива́ть, -и́ть; (coat) подб|ива́ть, -и́ть **2** (*also* **~ out**) (fig.) (lengthen unnecessarily) разб|авля́ть, -а́вить
● *v.i.* (**padded**, **padding**) (infml, move softly) бесшу́мно дви́гаться (*impf.*)

padding /'pædɪŋ/ *n.* наби́вка

paddle[1] /'pæd(ə)l/ *n.* гребо́к (*весло́*)
● *v.t. & i.* грести́ (*impf.*)

paddle[2] /'pæd(ə)l/ *n.*: **the children have gone for a ~e** де́ти пошли́ поплеска́ться в воде́
● *v.i.* (walk in shallow water) шлёпать (*impf.*) по воде́
■ **~ing pool** *n.* (BrE) де́тский бассе́йн, лягуша́тник (infml)

paddock /'pædək/ *n.* (small field, esp. for horses) вы́гул; (at racecourse, track) падцо́к (*техническая зона на ипподроме между конюшнями и беговой дорожкой, где лошадей готовят к забегу; аналогичное место для гоночных машин непосредственно возле трассы*)

padlock /'pædlɒk/ *n.* вися́чий замо́к
● *v.t.* ве́шать, пове́сить замо́к на + *a.*

⚹ ключева́я ле́ксика

paediatric /ˌpiːdɪˈætrɪk/ (AmE **pediatric**) *adj.* педиатри́ческий

paediatrician /ˌpiːdɪəˈtrɪʃ(ə)n/ (AmE **pediatrician**) *n.* педиа́тр

paediatrics /ˌpiːdɪˈætrɪks/ (AmE **pediatrics**) *n.* педиатри́я

paedophile /'piːdəfaɪl/ (AmE **pedophile**) *n.* педофи́л

paedophilia /ˌpiːdəˈfɪlɪə/ (AmE **pedophilia**) *n.* педофили́я

pagan /'peɪɡən/ *n.* язы́чни|к (-ца)
● *adj.* язы́ческий

paganism /'peɪɡənɪz(ə)m/ *n.* язы́чество

⚹ **page**[1] /peɪdʒ/ *n.* (of a book etc.) страни́ца

page[2] /peɪdʒ/ *n.* ма́льчик-слуга́
● *v.t.*: **please ~ Mr Smith!** пожа́луйста, вы́зовите господи́на Сми́та по пе́йджеру!

pageant /'pædʒ(ə)nt/ *n.* представле́ние, де́йство

pageantry /'pædʒəntrɪ/ *n.* пы́шность, пара́дность

pager /'peɪdʒə(r)/ *n.* пе́йджер

paid /peɪd/ *past and p.p. of* ▶ **pay**; **put ~ to** (infml) класть, положи́ть коне́ц + *d.*

pail /peɪl/ *n.* ведро́

⚹ **pain** /peɪn/ *n.* **1** (suffering) боль; **he is in great ~** его́ му́чают бо́ли; (localized): **he had severe stomach ~s** у него́ бы́ли о́стрые бо́ли в желу́дке; **he is a ~ in the neck** (infml) он стои́т всем поперёк го́рла **2** (*in pl.*) (trouble, effort) стара́ния (*nt. pl.*), хлоп|о́ты (-о́т); **he takes great ~s over every picture** он подо́лгу рабо́тает над ка́ждой карти́ной
■ **~killer** *n.* болеутоля́ющее (сре́дство)

painful /'peɪnfʊl/ *adj.* (of part of body) больно́й; (causing pain) боле́зненный, мучи́тельный

painless /'peɪnlɪs/ *adj.* безболе́зненный

painstaking /'peɪnzteɪkɪŋ/ *adj.* стара́тельный, усе́рдный

⚹ **paint** /peɪnt/ *n.* кра́ска
● *v.t.* **1** (portray in colours) рисова́ть, на- **2** (cover with ~) кра́сить, по-/вы́- ● *v.i.* рисова́ть (*impf.*); писа́ть (*impf.*) кра́сками
■ **~box** *n.* набо́р кра́сок; **~brush** *n.* кисть

painter /'peɪntə(r)/ *n.* (artist) худо́жник; (decorator) маля́р

⚹ **painting** /'peɪntɪŋ/ *n.* **1** (profession) жи́вопись **2** (work of art) карти́на

⚹ **pair** /peə(r)/ *n.* па́ра; **they walked along in ~s** они́ шли па́рами; **~ of scissors** но́жницы (*pl., g.* —); **two ~s of trousers** дво́е (*or* две па́ры) брюк
□ **~ off** *v.t. & i.* разб|ива́ть(ся), -и́ть(ся) на па́ры; (infml, marry) жени́ться (*impf., pf.*), пожени́ться (*pf.*)

pajamas /pɪˈdʒɑːməz/ *n. pl.* (AmE) = pyjamas

Pakistan /ˌpɑːkɪˈstɑːn/ *n.* Пакиста́н

Pakistani /ˌpɑːkɪˈstɑːnɪ/ *n.* (*pl.* **~s**) пакиста́н|ец (-ка)
● *adj.* пакиста́нский

pal /pæl/ *n.* (infml) дружо́к

palace /'pælɪs/ *n.* дворе́ц

palaeography /ˌpælɪˈɒɡrəfɪ/ (AmE **paleography**) n. палеогра́фия

palatable /ˈpælətəb(ə)l/ adj. вку́сный

palate /ˈpælət/ n. нёбо

palatial /pəˈleɪʃ(ə)l/ adj. роско́шный, великоле́пный

palaver /pəˈlɑːvə(r)/ n. (infml) суета́

pale /peɪl/ adj. (of complexion) бле́дный; she turned ~ она́ побледне́ла; (of colours) све́тлый; ~ blue све́тло-голубо́й
• v.i. бледне́ть, по-; (fig.): **the event ~d into insignificance** э́то собы́тие отошло́ на за́дний план

Palestine /ˈpælɪstaɪn/ n. Палести́на

Palestinian /ˌpælɪˈstɪnɪən/ n. палести́н|ец (-ка)
• adj. палести́нский

palette /ˈpælɪt/ n. (lit., fig.) пали́тра

pall[1] /pɔːl/ n. покро́в; **a ~ of smoke hung over the city** пелена́ ды́ма висе́ла над го́родом
■ ~-**bearer** n. несу́щий гроб

pall[2] /pɔːl/ v.i. при|еда́ться, -е́сться, надо|еда́ть, -е́сть (on: + d.)

pallet /ˈpælɪt/ n. (for loads) поддо́н

palliative /ˈpælɪətɪv/ n. паллиати́в, полуме́ра
• adj. паллиати́вный; смягча́ющий

pallid /ˈpælɪd/ adj. -бле́дный

pallor /ˈpælə(r)/ n. бле́дность

pally /ˈpælɪ/ adj. (**pallier, palliest**) (infml, friendly) дружелю́бный; **be ~ with sb** быть с кем-н. на коро́ткой ноге́

palm[1] /pɑːm/ n. (tree) па́льма
■ **P~ Sunday** n. Ве́рбное воскресе́нье

palm[2] /pɑːm/ n. (of hand) ладо́нь
• v.t.: ~ **sth off on sb** (or **sb off with sth**) подс|о́вывать, -у́нуть что-н. кому́-н.

palmistry /ˈpɑːmɪstrɪ/ n. хирома́нтия

palpable /ˈpælpəb(ə)l/ adj. ощути́мый

palpitate /ˈpælpɪteɪt/ v.i. пульси́ровать (impf.)

palpitation /ˌpælpɪˈteɪʃ(ə)n/ n. сердцебие́ние; **just to watch him gave me ~s** оди́н его́ вид приводи́л меня́ в тре́пет

paltry /ˈpɔːltrɪ/ adj. (**paltrier, paltriest**) (worthless) ничто́жный; (petty, mean) ме́лкий

pamper /ˈpæmpə(r)/ v.t. балова́ть, из-

pamphlet /ˈpæmflɪt/ n. (printed leaflet) брошю́ра

pan[1] /pæn/ n. кастрю́ля; (in full **frying ~**) сковорода́
• v.t. (**panned, panning**) (infml, criticize severely) разн|оси́ть, -ести́
• v.i. (**panned, panning**) (fig.): **everything ~ned out well** (всё) вы́шло как нельзя́ лу́чше

pan[2] /pæn/ v.i. (**panned, panning**) (of camera) повора́чиваться (impf.)

panacea /ˌpænəˈsiːə/ n. панаце́я

panache /pəˈnæʃ/ n. (flamboyance) рисо́вка, щегольство́

Panama /ˌpænəˈmɑː/ n. Пана́ма
■ ~ **Canal** n. Пана́мский кана́л

pancake /ˈpænkeɪk/ n. блин; ола́дья
■ **P~ Day** n. вто́рник на Ма́сленой неде́ле, в кото́рый пеку́т блины́

pancreas /ˈpæŋkrɪəs/ n. поджелу́дочная железа́

pancreatic /ˌpæŋkrɪˈætɪk/ adj. панкреати́ческий

panda /ˈpændə/ n. па́нда

pandemonium /ˌpændɪˈməʊnɪəm/ n. стра́шный шум; (скандал) смяте́ние, столпотворе́ние

pander /ˈpændə(r)/ v.i. (minister) потво́рствовать (impf.) (**to**: + d.)

pane /peɪn/ n. око́нное стекло́

☞ **panel** /ˈpæn(ə)l/ n. **1** (of door etc.) пане́ль **2**: ~ **of judges** жюри́ (nt. indecl.), суде́йская гру́ппа **3** (for instruments) пульт; **control ~** пульт управле́ния
■ ~ **game** n. (BrE) виктори́на

panellist /ˈpænəlɪst/ (AmE **panelist**) n. (in discussion) уча́стник диску́ссии/кру́глого стола́; (judge) член жюри́

pang /pæŋ/ n. **1** (sharp pain) ко́лики (f. pl.); ~**s of hunger** голо́дные бо́ли **2** (mental) му́ки (f. pl.); **a ~ of conscience** угрызе́ния (nt. pl.) со́вести

panic /ˈpænɪk/ n. па́ника
• v.t. (**panicked, panicking**) (infml): **they were ~ked into surrender** они́ впа́ли в па́нику и сдали́сь
• v.i. (**panicked, panicking**) паникова́ть (impf.)
■ ~-**stricken** adj. охва́ченный па́никой

panicky /ˈpænɪkɪ/ adj. (infml, action) пани́ческий; (person): **he was ~** он паникова́л

pannier /ˈpænɪə(r)/ n. корзи́на

panorama /ˌpænəˈrɑːmə/ n. панора́ма

panoramic /ˌpænəˈræmɪk/ adj. панора́мный

pansy /ˈpænzɪ/ n. анюти́н|ы гла́з|ки (-ых -ок)

pant /pænt/ v.i. тяжело́ дыша́ть (impf.)

panther /ˈpænθə(r)/ n. панте́ра; (AmE) пу́ма

panties /ˈpæntɪz/ n. pl. (infml) тру́сик|и (-ов)

pantomime /ˈpæntəmaɪm/ n. (BrE, entertainment) рожде́ственское представле́ние

pantry /ˈpæntrɪ/ n. кладова́я

pants /pænts/ n. pl. (BrE, underwear) трус|ы́ (pl., g. -о́в); (AmE, trousers) брю́к|и (pl., g. —)

pantyhose /ˈpæntɪhəʊz/ n. (AmE) колго́т|ки pl. g. -ок

papacy /ˈpeɪpəsɪ/ n. па́пство

papara|zzo /ˌpæpəˈrætsəʊ/ n. (pl. ~**zzi** /-tsɪ/) папара́цци (c.g. indecl.); фотокорреспонде́нт, рабо́тающий на бульва́рную пре́ссу

☞ **paper** /ˈpeɪpə(r)/ n. **1** бума́га **2** (newspaper) газе́та **3** (in pl.) (documents) докуме́нты (m. pl.), бума́ги (f. pl.) **4** (in full **examination ~**) (BrE) экзаменацио́нная рабо́та **5** (essay, lecture) докла́д **6** (wallpaper) обо́|и (-ев)
• v.t. (apply wallpaper to) окле́и|вать, -ть обо́ями
■ ~-**back** n. кни́га в бума́жном/мя́гком переплёте; ~ **bag** n. бума́жный паке́т; ~ **clip** n. канцеля́рская скре́пка; ~ **handkerchief** n. бума́жная салфе́тка; ~ **round** n. доста́вка газе́т (на́ дом); ~ **shop** n. газе́тный кио́ск; ~**work** n. канцеля́рская рабо́та

paprika /ˈpæprɪkə/ n. (spice) па́прика

Papua New Guinea /ˌpæpjʊə njuː ˈgɪnɪ/ n. Па́пуа — Но́вая Гвине́я

par /pɑː(r)/ n. **1** (equality) ра́венство; **this is on a ~ with his other work** (э́та) рабо́та на

p

у́ровне его други́х **2** (face value) цена́; **above** ∼ вы́ше номина́льной цены́; **below** ∼ ни́же номина́льной цены́ **3** (standard): **I feel below** ∼ **today** я сего́дня нева́жно себя́ чу́вствую

parable /'pærəb(ə)l/ n. при́тча

parabola /pə'ræbələ/ n. (pl. **parabolas** or **parabolae** /-li:/) пара́бола

parabolic /pærə'bɒlɪk/ adj. (geom.) параболи́ческий

paracetamol /pærə'si:təmɒl/ n. (BrE) парацетамо́л

parachute /'pærəʃu:t/ n. парашю́т
• v.t. сбра́сывать, сбро́сить с парашю́том
• v.i.: **the pilot** ∼**d out of the aircraft** пило́т вы́бросился из самолёта с парашю́том
■ ∼ **jump** n. прыжо́к с парашю́том

parachutist /'pærəʃu:tɪst/ n. парашюти́ст (-ка)

parade /pə'reɪd/ n. **1** (public procession) ше́ствие, пара́д **2** (of troops) пара́д
• v.t. выставля́ть, вы́ставить напока́з
• v.i. ше́ствовать (impf.)
■ ∼ **ground** n. плац

paradise /'pærədaɪs/ n. рай

paradox /'pærədɒks/ n. парадо́кс

paradoxical /pærə'dɒksɪk(ə)l/ adj. парадокса́льный

paraffin /'pærəfɪn/ n. **1** (BrE, ∼ oil) кероси́н **2** (∼ wax) парафи́н

paragon /'pærəgən/ n. образе́ц

paragraph /'pærəɡrɑ:f/ n. абза́ц, пара́граф

Paraguay /'pærəgwaɪ/ n. Парагва́й

parallel /'pærəlel/ n. **1** (line) паралле́льная ли́ния; (of latitude) паралле́ль **2** (fig.) паралле́ль
• adj. паралле́льный; (similar) аналоги́чный

parallelogram /pærə'leləɡræm/ n. параллелогра́мм

Paralympics /pærə'lɪmpɪks/ n. pl. Параолимпи́йские и́гры f. pl.

paralyse /'pærəlaɪz/ (AmE **paralyze**) v.t. парализова́ть (impf., pf.)

paralysis /pə'rælɪsɪs/ n. (pl. **paralyses** /-si:z/) парали́ч

paralytic /pærə'lɪtɪk/ adj. (med.) паралити́ческий, парализо́ванный; (BrE, incapably drunk) мертве́цки пья́ный

paramedic /pærə'medɪk/ n. медрабо́тник (без высшего образования)

parameter /pə'ræmɪtə(r)/ n. (math., comput., also fig.) пара́метр

paramilitary /pærə'mɪlɪtəri/ adj. военизи́рованный

paramount /'pærəmaʊnt/ adj. первостепе́нный

paranoia /pærə'nɔɪə/ n. парано́йя

paranoid /'pærənɔɪd/ n. парано́ик
• adj. парано́идный

paranormal /pærə'nɔ:m(ə)l/ adj. паранорма́льный

parapet /'pærəpɪt/ n. (low wall) парапе́т; (trench defence) бру́ствер

paraphernalia /pærəfə'neɪlɪə/ n. причинда́л|ы (-ов) (infml, joc.)

paraphrase /'pærəfreɪz/ v.t. переска́з|ывать, -а́ть

paraplegic /pærə'pli:dʒɪk/ adj. парализо́ванный

parasailing n. (sport) парасе́йлинг (полёты на парашюте за катером)

parasite /'pærəsaɪt/ n. парази́т

parasitic /pærə'sɪtɪk/ adj. (lit., fig.) паразити́ческий

parasol /'pærəsɒl/ n. зо́нтик (от со́лнца)

paratrooper /'pærətru:pə(r)/ n. (авиа)деса́нтник

parcel /'pɑ:s(ə)l/ n. паке́т, бандеро́ль, посы́лка
• v.t. (**parcelled, parcelling**, AmE **parceled, parceling**) **1** (also ∼ **up**) (pack up) пакова́ть, у- **2** (also ∼ **out**) (divide) дроби́ть, раз-

parch /pɑ:tʃ/ v.t. иссуш|а́ть, -и́ть; **the ground was** ∼**ed** земля́ вы́сохла; **my lips are** ∼**ed** у меня́ запекли́сь гу́бы

parchment /'pɑ:tʃmənt/ n. перга́мент

pardon /'pɑ:d(ə)n/ n. **1** извине́ние, проще́ние **2** (law) поми́лование; **they were granted a free** ∼ их поми́ловали
• v.t. (forgive) про|ща́ть, -сти́ть; (excuse) извин|я́ть, -и́ть; (law) ми́ловать, по-

✍ **parent** /'peərənt/ n. (father or mother) роди́тель (-ница)
■ ∼ **company** n. компа́ния-учреди́тель

parentage /'peərəntɪdʒ/ n. происхожде́ние; **he is of mixed** ∼ он происхо́дит от сме́шанного бра́ка

parental /pə'rent(ə)l/ adj. роди́тельский

parenthes|is /pə'renθəsɪs/ n. (pl. **parentheses** /-si:z/) (word) вво́дное сло́во; (sentence) вво́дное предложе́ние; (in pl.) (text mark) кру́глые ско́бки (f. pl.); **in** ∼**es** в ско́бках

parenthood /'peərənthʊd/ n. (fatherhood) отцо́вство; (motherhood) матери́нство

parenting /'peərəntɪŋ/ n. воспита́ние

Paris /'pærɪs/ n. Пари́ж

parish /'pærɪʃ/ n. (eccl.) прихо́д; (BrE, civil) о́круг

parishioner /pə'rɪʃənə(r)/ n. прихожа́н|ин (-ка)

parity /'pærɪti/ n. (equality) ра́венство, парите́т

✍ **park** /pɑ:k/ n. **1** (public garden) парк **2** (protected area of countryside) парк **3** (grounds of country mansion) уго́д|ья (-ий)
• v.t. паркова́ть, при-
• v.i. паркова́ться, при-
■ **park-and-ride** n. «парку́йся и поезжа́й (да́льше)» (система периферийных автостоянок, где автовладельцы оставляют свои автомобили и пересаживаются на общественный транспорт)

parking /'pɑ:kɪŋ/ n. (авто)стоя́нка; **'no** ∼**!'** «стоя́нка запрещена́!»
■ ∼ **lot** n. (AmE) стоя́нка; ме́сто стоя́нки; ∼ **meter** n. счётчик на стоя́нке; ∼ **place** n.

ме́сто для парко́вки; ~ **ticket** n. штраф за
наруше́ние пра́вил стоя́нки/парко́вки

Parkinson's disease /'pɑːkɪns(ə)nz/ n.
боле́знь Паркинсо́на

parlance /'pɑːləns/ n. язы́к; мане́ра
выраже́ния; **in common ~** в простаре́чии

parliament /'pɑːləmənt/ n. парла́мент

parliamentarian /pɑːləmen'teərɪən/ n.
(member of parliament) парламента́рий

parliamentary /pɑːlə'mentərɪ/ adj.
парла́ментский, парламента́рный

parlour /'pɑːlə(r)/ (AmE **parlor**) n. (in house)
гости́ная; **beauty ~** космети́ческий кабине́т/
сало́н; **funeral ~** похоро́нное бюро́ (nt.
indecl.); **ice cream ~** кафе́-моро́женое

parochial /pə'rəʊkɪəl/ adj. прихо́дский; (fig.)
ограни́ченный, у́зкий

parochialism /pə'rəʊkɪəlɪz(ə)m/ n.
ограни́ченность, у́зость

parody /'pærədɪ/ n. паро́дия
• v.t. пароди́ровать (impf., pf.)

parole /pə'rəʊl/ n. че́стное сло́во; **he was
released on ~** его́ освободи́ли под че́стное
сло́во

paroxysm /'pærəksɪz(ə)m/ n. (med., also fig.)
при́ступ

parquet /'pɑːkɪ, -keɪ/ n. парке́т
■ **~ floor** n. парке́тный пол

parrot /'pærət/ n. попуга́й

parry /'pærɪ/ v.t. (blow) отра|жа́ть, -зи́ть;
(question) пари́ровать (impf., pf.)

parsimonious /pɑːsɪ'məʊnɪəs/ adj. скупо́й

parsley /'pɑːslɪ/ n. петру́шка

parsnip /'pɑːsnɪp/ n. пастерна́к

parson /'pɑːs(ə)n/ n. па́стор
■ **~'s nose** n. (of fowl) «архиере́йский нос»,
кури́ная гу́зка

✎ **part** /pɑːt/ n. ◼ часть; (portion) до́ля; **for the
most ~** бо́льшей ча́стью; **in ~** части́чно,
отча́сти; (component) **spare ~s** запасны́е
ча́сти; (gram.): **~s of speech** ча́сти ре́чи
◼ (share) уча́стие; **take ~ in** прин|има́ть, -я́ть
уча́стие в + p. ◼ (actor's role or lines) роль
◼ (side in dispute etc.) сторона́; **for my ~** с мое́й
стороны́, что каса́ется меня́ ◼ (AmE, in one's
hair) пробо́р
• adv. части́чно, ча́стью, отча́сти; **the wall is
~ brick and ~ stone** стена́ сло́жена части́чно
из кирпича́, части́чно из ка́мня
• v.t. разделя́|ть, -и́ть; **the policeman ~ed the
crowd** полице́йский раздви́нул толпу́; **his
hair was ~ed in the middle** его́ во́лосы бы́ли
расче́саны на прямо́й пробо́р
• v.i. (of people) расст|ава́ться, -а́ться; **the
crowd ~ed** толпа́ расступи́лась; **she has ~ed
from her husband** она́ разошла́сь с му́жем;
he hates to ~ with his money он о́чень не
лю́бит расстава́ться с деньга́ми
■ **~ exchange** n. (BrE) сде́лка, при кото́рой
ста́рая вещь обме́нивается на но́вую с
допла́той; **~-time** adj., adv. на полста́вки;
I want a ~-time job я хочу́ рабо́тать на
полста́вки; **he works ~-time** он рабо́тает на
полста́вки

partial /'pɑːʃ(ə)l/ adj. ◼ (opp. total) части́чный
◼ (biased) пристра́стный ◼: **~ to** (fond of)
неравноду́шный к + d.

✎ **participant** /pɑː'tɪsɪpənt/ n. уча́стник

✎ **participate** /pɑː'tɪsɪpeɪt/ v.i. уча́ствовать
(impf.)

participation /pɑːtɪsɪ'peɪʃ(ə)n/ n. уча́стие

participle /'pɑːtɪsɪp(ə)l/ n. прича́стие

particle /'pɑːtɪk(ə)l/ n. (also gram.) части́ца
■ **~ accelerator** n. ускори́тель части́ц

✎ **particular** /pə'tɪkjʊlə(r)/ n. ча́стность; **in ~**
(specifically) в ча́стности; (especially) осо́бенно;
(in pl.) да́нные (pl.); **let me take down your
~s** разреши́те мне записа́ть ва́ши да́нные
• adj. ◼ (specific) осо́бенный, осо́бый; **for no
~ reason** без осо́бой причи́ны ◼ (fastidious)
привере́дливый; **she is not ~ about what she
wears** ей всё равно́, что наде́ть

✎ **particularly** /pə'tɪkjʊləlɪ/ adv. осо́бенно

parting /'pɑːtɪŋ/ n. ◼ (leave-taking) проща́ние
◼ (BrE, of the hair) пробо́р

partisan /pɑːtɪ'zæn/ n. партиза́н (-ка)
• adj. пристра́стный

partition /pɑː'tɪʃ(ə)n/ n. (division) разде́л;
(dividing structure) перегоро́дка
• v.t. дели́ть, раз-/по-; **~ off** оттор|а́живать,
-оди́ть

partly /'pɑːtlɪ/ adv. части́чно, отча́сти

✎ **partner** /'pɑːtnə(r)/ n. (business, sexual, cards,
dancing, etc.) партнёр (-ша (infml)); (in marriage)
супру́г (-а)

partnership /'pɑːtnəʃɪp/ n. това́рищество;
партнёрство; **to go into ~** входи́ть, войти́ в
партнёрство (with: с + i.)

partridge /'pɑːtrɪdʒ/ n. (pl. ~ or ~s)
куропа́тка

✎ **party** /'pɑːtɪ/ n. ◼ (political group) па́ртия
◼ (group) компа́ния, гру́ппа ◼ (social gathering)
вечери́нка ◼ (participant in contract etc.) сторона́
■ **~ line** n. (pol.) поли́тика (or полити́ческий
курс) па́ртии; (teleph.) о́бщая телефо́нная
ли́ния; **~ political** парти́йный; **~ political
broadcast** (BrE) пропаганди́стское выступле́ние
па́ртии по ра́дио и́ли телеви́дению

✎ **pass** /pɑːs/ n. ◼ (qualifying standard in exam) сда́ча
экза́мена ◼ (document) про́пуск ◼ (transfer of
ball in game) пас, переда́ча ◼ (lunge) вы́пад;
(infml, amorous approach): **he made a ~ at her**
он к ней пристава́л (infml) ◼ (mountain defile)
уще́лье, перева́л
• v.t. ◼ (go by) про|ходи́ть, -йти́ (ми́мо + g.);
I ~ed him in the street я прошёл ми́мо него́
на у́лице ◼ (go, get through) про|ходи́ть, -йти́;
will your car ~ the test пройдёт ли ва́ша
маши́на прове́рку?; **~ an exam** сдать (pf.)
экза́мен ◼ (spend) пров|оди́ть, -ести́ ◼ (accept)
пропус|ка́ть, -ти́ть; (approve) одобр|я́ть,
-о́брить ◼ (hand over) переда|ва́ть, -а́ть; **~
(me) the salt, please!** переда́йте мне соль,
пожа́луйста! ◼ (utter) произн|оси́ть, -ести́; **the
judge ~ed sentence** судья́ вы́нес пригово́р
• v.i. ◼ (proceed, move) про|ходи́ть, -йти́;
перепр|авля́ться, -а́виться; (get through):
let me ~! да́йте мне пройти́!, разреши́те

p

пройти! **2** (go by, elapse) про|ходи́ть, -йти́; **time** ~es **slowly** вре́мя прохо́дит ме́дленно **3** (qualify in exam etc.) про|ходи́ть, -йти́

□ ~ **away** *v.i.* (die) сконча́ться (*pf.*)

□ ~ **by** *v.t. & i.* про|ходи́ть, -йти́ (ми́мо + *g.*)

□ ~ **down** *v.t.* перед|ава́ть, -а́ть

□ ~ **off** *v.t.* (dismiss): **he** ~ed **off the whole affair as a joke** он обрати́л всё де́ло в шу́тку; (falsely represent): **he tried to** ~ **off the picture as genuine** он выдава́л карти́ну за по́длинник • *v.i.* (go away) прекра|ща́ться, -ти́ться; **the pain was slow to** ~ **off** боль проходи́ла ме́дленно; (be carried through) про|ходи́ть, -йти́; **the wedding** ~ed **off without a hitch** сва́дьба прошла́ без пробле́м

□ ~ **on** *v.t.* перед|ава́ть, -а́ть • *v.i.* про|ходи́ть, -йти́; (euph., die) сконча́ться (*pf.*)

□ ~ **out** *v.i.* (infml, lose consciousness) отключ|а́ться, -и́ться

■ ~ **key** *n.* отмы́чка; **P~over** *n.* евре́йская Па́сха; ~**word** *n.* (also comput.) паро́ль (*m.*)

passable /'pɑːsəb(ə)l/ *adj.* (affording passage) проходи́мый; (tolerable) сно́сный

passage /'pæsɪdʒ/ *n.* **1** (going by) прохо́д; (going across, over) перее́зд; перелёт; **a bird of** ~ перелётная пти́ца; (transition, change) перехо́д; (going through, way through) прохо́д **2** (crossing by ship etc.) рейс **3** (corridor) коридо́р **4** (literary excerpt) отры́вок, текст

■ ~**way** *n.* коридо́р

passé /'pæseɪ/ *adj.* устаре́лый, немо́дный

⚥ **passenger** /'pæsɪndʒə(r)/ *n.* пассажи́р

■ ~ **train** *n.* пассажи́рский по́езд

passer-by /pɑːsə'baɪ/ *n.* прохо́жий

passing /'pɑːsɪŋ/ *n.*: **I will mention in** ~ я заме́чу ме́жду про́чим • *adj.* (transient): **a** ~ **fancy** мимолётное увлече́ние

passion /'pæʃ(ə)n/ *n.* страсть

passionate /'pæʃənət/ *adj.* стра́стный, пы́лкий

passive /'pæsɪv/ *n.* (gram.) страда́тельный зало́г • *adj.* пасси́вный

■ ~ **smoking** *n.* пасси́вное куре́ние; (gram.) пасси́вный, страда́тельный

passivity /pæ'sɪvɪtɪ/ *n.* пасси́вность

passport /'pɑːspɔːt/ *n.* па́спорт

⚥ **past** /pɑːst/ **1** про́шлое **2** (gram.) проше́дшее вре́мя • *adj.* **1** (bygone) мину́вший, про́шлый; (*pred.*) (gone by) ми́мо; **the time for that is** ~ вре́мя (для) э́того давно́ минова́ло **2** (preceding) про́шлый, после́дний; **for the** ~ **few days** за после́дние не́сколько дней; **during the** ~ **week** за после́днюю/э́ту неде́лю **3** (gram.) проше́дший • *adv.* ми́мо; **the soldiers marched** ~ солда́ты прошли́ ми́мо • *prep.* **1** (after) по́сле + *g.*; **it is** ~ **eight (o'clock)** сейча́с девя́тый час; **ten** ~ **one** де́сять мину́т второ́го **2** (by) ми́мо + *g.*; **he drove** ~ **the house** он прое́хал ми́мо

до́ма **3** (to the far side of) за + *a.*; (on the far side of) за + *i.*; **you've gone** ~ **the turning** вы прое́хали поворо́т **4** (beyond) свы́ше + *g.*, сверх + *g.*; **he was a fine actor, but he's** ~ **it now** (infml) когда́-то он был хоро́шим актёром, но э́то в про́шлом; **I wouldn't put it** ~ **him to steal the money** я ду́маю, что он спосо́бен укра́сть де́ньги

■ ~ **participle** *n.* прича́стие проше́дшего вре́мени; ~ **tense** *n.* проше́дшее вре́мя

pasta /'pæstə/ *n.* макаро́н|ы (*pl., g.* —)

paste /peɪst/ *n.* (adhesive) клей • *v.t.* **1** (stick) накле́|ивать, -ить; прикле́|ивать, -ить **2** (comput.) вст|авля́ть, -а́вить

pastel /'pæst(ə)l/ *n.* (crayon) пасте́ль; ~ **shades** пасте́льные кра́ски

pasteurize /'pɑːstʃəraɪz/ *v.t.* пастеризова́ть (*impf., pf.*)

pastiche /pæ'stiːʃ/ *n.* (literary imitation) стилиза́ция (**of:** под + *a.*); подде́лка

pastime /'pɑːstaɪm/ *n.* вре́мя(пре)провожде́ние

pastor /'pɑːstə(r)/ *n.* па́стор

pastoral /'pɑːstər(ə)l/ *adj.* пастора́льный

pastry /'peɪstrɪ/ *n.* (dough) те́сто; (tart) пиро́жное

pasturage /'pɑːstʃərɪdʒ/ *n.* (grazing land) па́стбище; (grazing) вы́пас

pasture /'pɑːstʃə(r)/ *n.* па́стбище

pat¹ /pæt/ *n.* **1** (light touch) хлопо́к; шлепо́к **2** (of butter) кусо́чек • *v.t.* (**patted, patting**) похло́п|ывать, -ать; (a dog) гла́дить, по-

pat² /pæt/ *adj.* гото́вый; **he had his lesson off** ((AmE) **down**) ~ он вы́учил уро́к назубо́к

patch /pætʃ/ *n.* **1** (covering over hole) запла́та; (over eye) повя́зка; (comput.) патч, «запла́т(к)а» **2** (distinctive area) клочо́к; ~es **of blue sky** клочки́ голубо́го не́ба; **there were** ~es **of ice on the road** на доро́ге места́ми была́ гололе́дица **3** (piece of ground) уча́сток **4** (scrap) лоску́т • *v.t.* (mend) лата́ть, за-

□ ~ **up** *v.t.* (repair) чини́ть, по-; (fig.) ула́|живать, -дить

patchy /'pætʃɪ/ *adj.* (fig., of knowledge) отры́вочный; (fig., of uneven quality) неро́вный

patent /'peɪt(ə)nt/ *n.* пате́нт • *adj.* **1**: ~ **leather** лакиро́ванная ко́жа **2** (obvious) очеви́дный • *v.t.* патентова́ть, за-

paternal /pə'tɜːn(ə)l/ *adj.* отцо́вский

paternalistic /pətɜːnə'lɪstɪk/ *adj.* (pol.) патернали́стский; (manner, tone) покрови́тельственный

paternity /pə'tɜːnɪtɪ/ *n.* отцо́вство

■ ~ **leave** *n.* о́тпуск по ухо́ду за ребёнком (для отца́)

⚥ **path** /pɑːθ/ *n.* (track for walking) тропа́, тропи́нка; доро́жка; (fig.) путь (*m.*); (course, trajectory) траекто́рия; **the** ~ **of a bullet** траекто́рия полёта пу́ли

pathetic /pə'θetɪk/ *adj.* жа́лкий

pathological /pæθə'lɒdʒɪk(ə)l/ *adj.* патологи́ческий

⚥ ключева́я ле́ксика

pathologist /pə'θɒlədʒɪst/ *n.* пато́лог
pathology /pə'θɒlədʒɪ/ *n.* патоло́гия
pathos /'peɪθɒs/ *n.* го́речь, печа́ль
patience /'peɪʃ(ə)ns/ *n.* **1** терпе́ние; she lost ~ with him она́ потеря́ла с ним вся́кое терпе́ние **2** (BrE, card game) пасья́нс
ⷯ **patient** /'peɪʃ(ə)nt/ *n.* пацие́нт, больно́й
   ● *adj.* терпели́вый
patio /'pætɪəʊ/ *n.* (*pl.* ~s) дво́рик
patriarchal /peɪtrɪ'ɑːk(ə)l/ *adj.* патриарха́льный
patriot /'peɪtrɪət/ *n.* патрио́т (-ка)
patriotic /ˌpeɪtrɪ'ɒtɪk/ *adj.* патриоти́ческий
patriotism /'pætrɪətɪz(ə)m/ *n.* патриоти́зм
patrol /pə'trəʊl/ *n.* **1** (action) патрули́рование, дозо́р **2** (~ling body) патру́ль (*m.*)
   ● *v.t. & i.* (**patrolled, patrolling**) патрули́ровать (*impf.*)
   ■ ~ **car** *n.* (полице́йская) патру́льная маши́на; ~ **vessel** *n.* сторожево́й кора́бль
patron /'peɪtrən/ *n.* **1** (supporter) покрови́тель (*m.*), патро́н; a ~ of the arts покрови́тель иску́сств, мецена́т **2** (customer) (постоя́нный) клие́нт
   ■ ~ **saint** *n.* свят|о́й засту́пни|к (-а́я -ца)
patronage /'pætrənɪdʒ/ *n.* покрови́тельство, ше́фство
patroniz|e /'pætrənaɪz/ *v.t.* (visit as customer) постоя́нно посеща́ть (*impf.*); (treat condescendingly) отн|оси́ться, -ести́сь свысока́ к + *d.*; ~ing manner снисходи́тельная мане́ра
patronymic /ˌpætrə'nɪmɪk/ *n.* о́тчество
patter[1] /'pætə(r)/ *n.* (of salesman) скорогово́рка
patter[2] /'pætə(r)/ *n.* (tapping sound) стук, посту́кивание
   ● *v.i.* (of rain) бараба́нить (*impf.*); (of feet) топота́ть (*impf.*)
ⷯ **pattern** /'pæt(ə)n/ *n.* **1** (decorative design) узо́р **2** (example) образе́ц **3** (model for production) вы́кройка; dress ~ вы́кройка пла́тья **4** (system) о́браз, мане́ра; new ~s of behaviour но́вые но́рмы (*f. pl.*) поведе́ния
   ● *v.t.*: a ~ed dress пла́тье с узо́рами
paucity /'pɔːsɪtɪ/ *n.* нехва́тка, ску́дость
paunch /pɔːntʃ/ *n.* брюшко́, живо́т
pauper /'pɔːpə(r)/ *n.* бедня́к
pause /pɔːz/ *n.* (intermission) переры́в; (in speaking) па́уза
   ● *v.i.* остан|а́вливаться, -ови́ться
pave /peɪv/ *v.t.* мости́ть, вы́-; (fig.): his proposal ~d the way to a lasting peace его́ предложе́ние проложи́ло путь к про́чному ми́ру
pavement /'peɪvmənt/ *n.* **1** (BrE, footway) тротуа́р **2** (AmE, paved surface) мостова́я
pavilion /pə'vɪljən/ *n.* (BrE, sport) павильо́н
paving stone /'peɪvɪŋ stəʊn/ *n.* брусча́тка
paw /pɔː/ *n.* ла́па
pawn[1] /pɔːn/ *n.* (chessman, also fig.) пе́шка
pawn[2] /pɔːn/ *v.t.* за|кла́дывать, -ложи́ть
   ■ ~**broker** *n.* челове́к, даю́щий де́ньги под зало́г (веще́й); ~**shop** *n.* ломба́рд

ⷯ **pay** /peɪ/ *n.* (wages) зарпла́та; жа́лованье
   ● *v.t.* (*past and p.p.* **paid**) **1** (give in return for sth) плати́ть, за-, у-; she always ~s cash она́ всегда́ пла́тит нали́чными; (contribute): everyone must ~ their share ка́ждый до́лжен внести́ свою́ до́лю **2** (remunerate) плати́ть, за-, опла́|чивать, -ти́ть (sb: + *d.*); we are paid on Fridays нам пла́тят по пя́тницам; мы получа́ем зарпла́ту по пя́тницам **3** (bestow): ~ attention to me! послу́шайте меня́!; ~ sb a compliment де́лать, с- кому́-н. комплиме́нт; ~ sb a visit наве|ща́ть, -сти́ть кого́-н. **4** (benefit, profit): it will ~ you to wait вам сто́ит подожда́ть
   ● *v.i.* (*past and p.p.* **paid**) **1** (give money) распла́|чиваться, -ти́ться (for: за + *a.*) **2** (suffer) плати́ть, за-; плати́ться, по- (for: за + *a.*); he paid for his carelessness он поплати́лся за своё легкомы́слие **3** (yield a return) окуп|а́ться, -и́ться; дава́ть, дать при́быль
   □ ~ **back** *v.t.* (reimburse): he paid me back in person он ли́чно верну́л мне де́ньги; (have revenge on) отплати́ть (*pf.*) + *d.*
   □ ~ **in** *v.t.* вн|оси́ть, -ести́
   □ ~ **off** *v.t.* рассчи́т|ываться, -а́ться с + *i.*; (~ wages and discharge) рассчи́т|ывать, -а́ть
   ● *v.i.* (bring profit) окуп|а́ться, -и́ться
   □ ~ **out** *v.t.* (expend) выпла́чивать, вы́платить
   □ ~ **up** *v.i.* (~ amount due) рассчи́т|ываться, -а́ться сполна́
   ■ ~ **day** *n.* платёжный день; ~ **packet** *n.* (BrE) *n.* за́работок, (infml) получка; ~**phone** *n.* телефо́н-автома́т; ~**slip** *n.* (BrE) квита́нция о вы́даче зарпла́ты; ~ **TV** *n.* пла́тное телеви́дение; ~**wall** *n.* (comput.) систе́ма пла́тного до́ступа, пла́тная подпи́ска
payable /'peɪəb(ə)l/ *adj.* опла́чиваемый; подлежа́щий упла́те
PAYE (BrE) *abbr.* (*of* **pay-as-you-earn**) автомати́ческое отчисле́ние подохо́дного нало́га из зарпла́ты
ⷯ **payment** /'peɪmənt/ *n.* (paying) опла́та, платёж; (sum paid) пла́та; (of debt etc.) упла́та
PC *abbr. of* **1** (**personal computer**) ПК (персона́льный компью́тер) **2** (**politically correct**) полити́чески корре́ктный, политкорре́ктный
PDA *n.* (*abbr. of* **Personal Digital Assistant**) «электро́нный помо́щник»
PE *abbr.* (*of* **physical education**) физкульту́ра
pea /piː/ *n.* горо́шина
   ■ ~**nut** *n.* ара́хис, земляно́й оре́х; ~**nut butter** па́ста из тёртого ара́хиса
ⷯ **peace** /piːs/ *n.* **1** (freedom from war) мир **2** (freedom from civil disorder) споко́йствие, поря́док **3** (quiet) споко́йствие, поко́й; can we have some ~ and quiet? нельзя́ ли поти́ше?; ~ of mind споко́йствие ду́ха
   ■ ~**keeping** *adj.*: ~keeping force миротво́рческие войска́ (*nt. pl.*) /си́лы (*f. pl.*); ~**maker** *n.* миротво́рец; ~ **talks** *n. pl.* ми́рные перегово́ры; ~**time** *n.* ми́рное вре́мя
peaceful /'piːsfʊl/ *adj.* ми́рный

peach /piːtʃ/ n. **1** (fruit) пе́рсик **2** (tree) пе́рсиковое де́рево

peacock /ˈpiːkɒk/ n. павли́н

peak /piːk/ n. **1** (mountain top) пик, верши́на **2** (of cap) козырёк **3** (fig., highest point) пик, верши́на; ~ **viewing hours** прайм-та́йм
• v.i.: **demand** ~**ed** спрос дости́г вы́сшей то́чки

peaked /piːkt/ adj. **1** остроконе́чный; ~ **cap** (фо́рменная) фура́жка **2** (haggard) (also **peaky**) осу́нувшийся

peaky /ˈpiːkɪ/ adj. (**peakier, peakiest**) = **peaked** 2

peal /piːl/ n. (of bells) трезво́н; (of laughter) взрыв

pear /peə(r)/ n. **1** (fruit) гру́ша **2** (tree) гру́шевое де́рево, гру́ша

pearl /pɜːl/ n. жемчу́жина

peasant /ˈpez(ə)nt/ n. крестья́н|ин (-ка)

peat /piːt/ n. торф

pebble /ˈpeb(ə)l/ n. га́лька

pebbly /ˈpeblɪ/ adj. покры́тый га́лькой

pecan /ˈpiːkən/ n. оре́х пека́н

peck /pek/ n. (made by beak) клево́к; (fig., hasty kiss): **he gave her a** ~ **on the cheek** он чмо́кнул её в щё(ч)ку
• v.t. клева́ть, клю́нуть; поклева́ть (pf.)
• v.i. (fig.): **she** ~**ed at her food** она́ едва́ дотро́нулась до еды́
■ ~**ing order** n. ≈ неофициа́льная иера́рхия

peckish /ˈpekɪʃ/ adj. (BrE, infml) голо́дный

pectoral /ˈpektər(ə)l/ adj. (anat.) грудно́й

peculiar /pɪˈkjuːlɪə(r)/ adj. **1** (exclusive) осо́бенный, своеобра́зный **2** (strange) стра́нный

peculiarity /pɪkjuːlɪˈærɪtɪ/ n. (characteristic) сво́йство; (oddity) стра́нность

pecuniary /pɪˈkjuːnɪərɪ/ adj. де́нежный

pedagogical /pedəˈɡɒɡɪk(ə)l/, **pedagogic** /pedəˈɡɒɡɪk/ adjs. педагоги́ческий

pedal /ˈped(ə)l/ n. педа́ль
• v.i. (**pedalled, pedalling**, AmE **pedaled, pedaling**) е́хать (det.) на велосипе́де

pedant /ˈped(ə)nt/ n. педа́нт (fem. also -ка)

pedantic /pɪˈdæntɪk/ adj. педанти́чный

pedantry /ˈped(ə)ntrɪ/ n. педанти́чность

peddle /ˈped(ə)l/ v.t. торгова́ть (impf.) вразно́с

peddler /ˈpedlə(r)/ n. (of drugs) торго́вец нарко́тиками

pedestal /ˈpedɪst(ə)l/ n. пьедеста́л

pedestrian /pɪˈdestrɪən/ n. пешехо́д
• adj. пешехо́дный
■ ~ **crossing** n. (BrE) перехо́д; ~ **precinct** n. пешехо́дная зо́на

pediatric /piːdɪˈætrɪk/ adj. (AmE) = paediatric

pediatrician /piːdɪəˈtrɪʃ(ə)n/ n. (AmE) = paediatrician

pediatrics /piːdɪˈætrɪks/ n. (AmE) = paediatrics

pedicure /ˈpedɪkjʊə(r)/ n. (treatment) педикю́р; (person) педикю́рша

pedigree /ˈpedɪɡriː/ n. происхожде́ние; (attr.) ~ **cattle** племенно́й скот

pedophile /ˈpiːdəfaɪl/ n. (AmE) = paedophile

pedophilia /piːdəˈfɪlɪə/ n. (AmE) = paedophilia

pee /piː/ (infml) n. (urination) пи-пи́ (nt. indecl.); (urine) моча́
• v.i. (**pees, peed**) мочи́ться, по-

peek /piːk/ n. (infml) взгляд укра́дкой

peel /piːl/ n. (thin skin of fruit) кожура́; (of vegetables) шелуха́; (rind of orange etc.) ко́рка
• v.t. **1** (remove skin from) очища́ть, -и́стить **2** (remove from surface) сн|има́ть, -ять
• v.i. **1** (lose skin) шелуши́ться (impf.) **2** (come away from surface) (also ~ **away**, ~ **off**) слез|а́ть, -ть; обл|еза́ть, -е́зть; **the paint has begun to** ~ (off) кра́ска начала́ облеза́ть

peeling /ˈpiːlɪŋ/ n. (of fruit) кожура́; (of vegetables) шелуха́

peep¹ /piːp/ n. (furtive or hasty look) взгляд укра́дкой; **take, have a** ~ **at** взгляну́ть (pf.) на + a.
• v.i. погля́д|ывать, -е́ть; **he** ~**ed in at the window** он загляну́л в окно́
■ ~**hole** n. глазо́к

peep² /piːp/ n. (chirp) писк; (fig.): **not a** ~! ни сло́ва!
• v.i. (chirp) пища́ть, пи́скнуть

peer¹ /pɪə(r)/ n. **1** (equal) ра́вн|ый (-ая); (person of the same age) рове́сни|к (-ца), све́рстни|к (-ца) **2** (noble) пэр
■ ~ **group** n. рове́сники, све́рстники (m. pl.); ~ **(group) pressure** давле́ние гру́ппы (све́рстников)

peer² /pɪə(r)/ v.i. (look closely) всм|а́триваться, -отре́ться (**at/into**: в + a.)

peerage /ˈpɪərɪdʒ/ n. пэ́рство, ти́тул пэ́ра

peeved /piːvd/ adj. (infml): **he looks** ~ у него́ недово́льный вид

peg /peɡ/ n. (for holding sth down) ко́лышек; (in full **clothes** ~) (BrE) прище́пка; (for hat, coat) ве́шалка, крючо́к

pejorative /pɪˈdʒɒrətɪv/ adj. уничижи́тельный

pelican /ˈpelɪkən/ n. пелика́н

pellet /ˈpelɪt/ n. ша́рик

pelt /pelt/ v.t. (assail) заб|ра́сывать, -оса́ть; **they** ~**ed him with stones/insults** они́ заброса́ли его́ камня́ми/оскорбле́ниями
• v.i. стуча́ть, бараба́нить (both impf.); **the rain was** ~**ing down** дождь бараба́нил вовсю́

pelvic /ˈpelvɪk/ adj. та́зовый
■ ~ **girdle** n. та́зовый по́яс

pelvis /ˈpelvɪs/ n. (pl. **pelvises**) (anat.) таз

pen¹ /pen/ n. (writing instrument) ру́чка
■ ~**friend** n. (BrE) друг (подру́га по перепи́ске); ~**knife** n. перочи́нный нож(ик); ~ **pal** n. (AmE) = penfriend

pen² /pen/ n. (enclosure) заго́н

penal /ˈpiːn(ə)l/ adj.: ~ **code** уголо́вный ко́декс; ~ **colony** исправи́тельная коло́ния

penalize /ˈpiːnəlaɪz/ v.t. нака́з|ывать, -а́ть

✔ **penalty** /ˈpen(ə)ltɪ/ n. (punishment) наказа́ние; (fine) штраф; (football) (in full ~ **kick**) пена́льти (*m. indecl.*)

penance /'penəns/ *n.* епитимья́; покая́ние; **he must do ~ for his sins** он до́лжен замоли́ть/искупи́ть свои́ грехи́

pence /pens/ *n. see* ▶ **penny**

penchant /'pɑ̃ʃɑ̃/ *n.* скло́нность (**for:** к + *d.*)

pencil /'pensɪl/ *n.* каранда́ш
• *v.t.* (**pencilled, pencilling,** AmE **penciled, penciling**): **~ in** (arrange provisionally) де́лать, с- предвари́тельную заме́тку насчёт + *g.*
■ **~ case** *n.* пена́л; **~ sharpener** *n.* точи́лка

pendant /'pend(ə)nt/ *n.* куло́н

pending /'pendɪŋ/ *adj.* рассма́триваемый
• *prep.* до + *g.*; в ожида́нии + *g.*

pendulous /'pendjʊləs/ *adj.* подвесно́й

pendulum /'pendjʊləm/ *n.* ма́ятник

penetrate /'penɪtreɪt/ *v.t.* прон|ика́ть, -и́кнуть в + *a.*

penetrating /'penɪtreɪtɪŋ/ *adj.* си́льный; о́стрый; **a ~ voice** пронзи́тельный го́лос

penguin /'peŋgwɪn/ *n.* пингви́н

penicillin /penɪ'sɪlɪn/ *n.* пеницилли́н

peninsula /pə'nɪnsjʊlə/ *n.* полуо́стров

penis /'piːnɪs/ *n.* (*pl.* **penises**) пе́нис, половой член

penitence /'penɪt(ə)ns/ *n.* раска́яние

penitent /'penɪt(ə)nt/ *adj.* раска́ивающийся

penitentiary /penɪ'tenʃərɪ/ *n.* тюрьма́

pennant /'penənt/ *n.* флажо́к, вы́мпел

penniless /'penɪlɪs/ *adj.* безде́нежный, без гроша́ (*pred.*)

penny /'penɪ/ *n.* (*pl. for separate coins* **pennies**, *for a sum of money* **pence**) пе́нни (*nt. indecl.*), пенс; (AmE cent) цент; **at last the ~ has dropped!** (BrE, infml) наконе́ц-то дошло́!

pension /'penʃ(ə)n/ *n.* пе́нсия; **old-age ~** пе́нсия по ста́рости

pensionable /'penʃənəb(ə)l/ *adj.*: **~ age** пенсио́нный во́зраст; **his job is ~** его́ рабо́та даёт ему́ пра́во на пе́нсию

pensioner /'penʃənə(r)/ *n.* пенсионе́р (-ка)

pensive /'pensɪv/ *adj.* заду́мчивый

pent /pent/ *adj.*: **~-up feelings** сде́рживаемые чу́вства

pentagon /'pentəgən/ *n.* пятиуго́льник; **the P~** (AmE War Department) Пентаго́н

pentathlon /pen'tæθlən/ *n.* пятибо́рье

Pentecost /'pentɪkɒst/ *n.* Пятидеся́тница (*христиа́нский пра́здник*)

penthouse /'penthaʊs/ *n.* (apartment) роско́шная кварти́ра на после́днем этаже́; пентха́ус

penultimate /pɪ'nʌltɪmət/ *adj.* предпосле́дний

penury /'penjʊrɪ/ *n.* бе́дность, нужда́

peony /'piːənɪ/ *n.* пио́н

✓ **people** /'piːp(ə)l/ *n.* ❶ (persons) лю́д|и (-е́й); **few ~** ма́ло люде́й; **most ~ will object** большинство́ (люде́й) бу́дет про́тив ❷ (nation; proletariat) наро́д ❸ (inhabitants) жи́тели (*m. pl.*); (citizens) гра́ждане (*m. pl.*) ❹ (persons grouped by type): **young ~** молодёжь,

молоды́е лю́ди; **old ~** старики́ (*m. pl.*)

pep /pep/ *n.*: **~ talk** нака́чка
• *v.t.* (**pepped, pepping**) (*usu.* **~ up**) ожив|ля́ть, -и́ть

pepper /'pepə(r)/ *n.* (condiment) пе́рец; (vegetable, sweet ~) (сла́дкий) пе́рец
■ **~corn** *n.* перчи́нка; **~ mill** *n.* ме́льница для пе́рца; **~mint** *n.* (sweet) мя́тный ледене́ц

peptic /'peptɪk/ *adj.* пепти́ческий, пищевари́тельный
■ **~ ulcer** *n.* я́зва желу́дка

✓ **per** /pɜː(r)/ *prep.* в + *a.*; на + *a.*; с + *g.*; **60 miles ~ hour** 60 миль в час; **they collected 20 pence ~ man** они́ собра́ли по 20 пе́нсов с челове́ка

per capita /pə 'kæpɪtə/ *adv.* на ду́шу (населе́ния)

perceive /pə'siːv/ *v.t.* (with mind) пост|ига́ть, -и́гнуть, -и́чь; (through senses) восприн|има́ть, -я́ть

✓ **per cent** /pə 'sent/ (AmE **percent**) *n., adv.* проце́нт

percentage /pə'sentɪdʒ/ *n.* (of people/things) проце́нт; (of substance) проце́нтное содержа́ние
■ **~ point** *n.* проце́нтный пункт

perceptible /pə'septɪb(ə)l/ *adj.* ощути́мый

perception /pə'sepʃ(ə)n/ *n.* (process) восприя́тие, ощуще́ние; (discernment) осозна́ние, понима́ние

perceptive /pə'septɪv/ *adj.* восприи́мчивый; (observant) проница́тельный

perch /pɜːtʃ/ *n.* (of bird) насе́ст
• *v.t. & i.* сади́ться, сесть; **he ~ed on a stool** он присе́л на табуре́т

percipient /pə'sɪpɪənt/ *adj.* воспринима́ющий

percolate /'pɜːkəleɪt/ *v.t.* про|ходи́ть, -йти́ че́рез + *a.*
• *v.i.* прос|а́чиваться, -очи́ться; **water ~s through sand** вода́ проса́чивается/прохо́дит сквозь песо́к; **I'm waiting for the coffee to ~ through** (fig., news, idea, fashion) (постепе́нно) распростран|я́ться, -и́ться, получ|а́ть, -и́ть распростране́ние (*среди́ люде́й, в о́бществе*); (of news, also) (постепе́нно) ста|нови́ться, -ть изве́стным (**to:** + *d.*)

percolator /'pɜːkəleɪtə(r)/ *n.* (cul.) перколя́тор, кофева́рка

percussion /pə'kʌʃ(ə)n/ *n.* (*in full* **~ instruments**) уда́рные инструме́нты (*m. pl.*)

peremptory /pə'remptərɪ/ *adj.* (imperious) повели́тельный; непререка́емый

perennial /pə'renɪəl/ *adj.* (plant) многоле́тний; (enduring) ве́чный

perestroika /perɪ'strɔɪkə/ *n.* перестро́йка

✓ **perfect¹** /'pɜːfɪkt/ *adj.* ❶ (complete; absolute) соверше́нный; по́лный; **I am ~ly sure of it** я соверше́нно/по́лностью уве́рен в э́том ❷ (faultless) соверше́нный, безупре́чный; **he speaks ~ English** он в соверше́нстве владе́ет англи́йским (языко́м) ❸ (exact, precise) абсолю́тный; **~ pitch** (mus.) абсолю́тный

p

слух; (corresponding to requirements): **the dress is a ~ fit** плáтье сидúт безупрéчно **4** (gram.) перфéктный, совершéнный

■ **~ tense** n. перфéкт

perfect² /pə'fekt/ v.t. совершéнствовать, у-

perfection /pə'fekʃ(ə)n/ n. совершéнство; **she dances to ~** онá безупрéчно танцýет

perfectionist /pə'fekʃənɪst/ n. взыскáтельный человéк

perfidious /pə:'fɪdɪəs/ adj. веролóмный, ковáрный

perforate /'pə:fəreɪt/ v.t. перфорúровать (impf.); **a ~d appendix** прободнóй/ перфорáтивный аппендицúт

⚡ **perform** /pə'fɔ:m/ v.t. **1** (task) выполнять, вы́полнить **2** (piece of music) исп|олнять, -óлнить; (play) игрáть, сыгрáть
  • v.i. **1** (in public) игрáть, сыгрáть; выступáть, вы́ступить **2** (function) рабóтать (impf.); **my car ~s well on hills** моя́ машúна хорошó идёт в гóру

⚡ **performance** /pə'fɔ:məns/ n. **1** (of task) выполнéние **2** (of a machine, vehicle, etc.) ход, характерúстика **3** (public appearance) выступлéние **4** (of play, etc.) представлéние

performer /pə'fɔ:mə(r)/ n. исполнúтель (m.) (-ница)

perfume /'pə:fju:m/ n. дух|ú (-óв), парфю́м
  • v.t. (impart odour to) дéлать, с- благоухáнным

perfumery /pə'fju:mərɪ/ n. (business) парфюмéрия; (shop) парфюмéрный магазúн

■ **~ department** n. парфюмéрия

perfunctory /pə'fʌŋktərɪ/ adj. (glance, inspection) повéрхностный; (kiss, smile) небрéжный

pergola /'pə:gələ/ n. садóвая áрка, áрка из вью́щихся растéний

⚡ **perhaps** /pə'hæps/ adv. мóжет быть; возмóжно; пожáлуй

peril /'perɪl/ n. опáсность; риск

perilous /'perɪləs/ adj. опáсный; рискóванный

perimeter /pə'rɪmɪtə(r)/ n. перúметр

⚡ **period** /'pɪərɪəd/ n. **1** перúод; **she has ~s of depression** у неё бывáют перúоды депрéссии; **for a long ~** дóлгое врéмя **2** (previous age) эпóха; **~ furniture** старúнная мéбель **3** (lesson) урóк **4** (menstruation) мéсячные (pl.) **5** (AmE, full stop) тóчка

■ **~ pains** n. pl. (BrE) мéсячные бóли (f. pl.)

periodic /pɪərɪ'ɒdɪk/ adj. периодúческий

periodical /pɪərɪ'ɒdɪk(ə)l/ n. периодúческое издáние

peripatetic /perɪpə'tetɪk/ adj. (teacher) приходя́щий; (itinerant) бродя́чий

peripheral /pə'rɪfər(ə)l/ n. (comput.) периферúйное устрóйство
  • adj. (lit.) периферúйный; (fig.) несущéственный, побóчный

periphery /pə'rɪfərɪ/ n. (boundary) гранúца, чертá; (also fig.) периферúя

periscope /'perɪskəʊp/ n. перискóп

perish /'perɪʃ/ v.i. **1** пог|ибáть, -úбнуть **2**: **the rubber has ~ed** резúна пришлá в негóдность

perishable /'perɪʃəb(ə)l/ adj. скоропóртящийся; (in pl., as n.) скоропóртящийся товáр

perjure /'pə:dʒə(r)/ v.t.: **~ oneself** да|вáть, -ть лóжное показáние под прися́гой, лжесвидéтельствовать (impf.)

perjury /'pə:dʒərɪ/ n. лжесвидéтельство

perk /pə:k/ v.i. & t.: **~ up** (liven up) ожив|ля́ть(ся), -úть(ся)

perky /'pə:kɪ/ adj. (**perkier, perkiest**) (infml) весёлый, оживлённый

perm /pə:m/ n. перманéнтная завúвка, перманéнт
  • v.t.: **she had her hair ~ed** онá сдéлала себé перманéнтную завúвку/перманéнт

permafrost /'pə:məfrɒst/ n. вéчная мерзлотá

permanence /'pə:mənəns/ n. неизмéнность

permanent /'pə:mənənt/ adj. постоя́нный

permeable /'pə:mɪəb(ə)l/ adj. пр/ица́емый

permeate /'pə:mɪeɪt/ v.t. пропúт|ывать, -áть; прон|икáть, -úкнуть в + a.

permissible /pə'mɪsɪb(ə)l/ adj. допустúмый, позволúтельный

permission /pə'mɪʃ(ə)n/ n. позволéние, разрешéние

permissive /pə'mɪsɪv/ adj.: **~ society** óбщество вседозвóленности

permit¹ /'pə:mɪt/ n. разрешéние, прóпуск (-á); **work ~** разрешéние на рабóту

permit² /pə'mɪt/ v.t. (**permitted, permitting**) разреш|áть, -úть, позв|оля́ть, -óлить; **smoking ~ted** курúть разрешáется
  • v.i. (**permitted, permitting**): **if circumstances ~** éсли обстоя́тельства позвóлят

permutation /pə:mju'teɪʃ(ə)n/ n. (math.) перестанóвка; (fig.) вариáнт, модификáция

pernicious /pə'nɪʃəs/ adj. пáгубный, врéдный; **~ anaemia** злокáчественное малокрóвие

pernickety /pə'nɪkɪtɪ/ adj. (infml) привередлúвый

peroxide /pə'rɒksaɪd/ n. пéрекись; **a ~ blonde** крáшеная блондúнка

perpendicular /pə:pən'dɪkjʊlə(r)/ adj. перпендикуля́рный

perpetrate /'pə:pɪtreɪt/ v.t. соверш|áть, -úть

perpetrator /'pə:pɪtreɪtə(r)/ n. винóвник (+ g.), винóвный (в + p.)

perpetual /pə'petʃʊəl/ adj. вéчный

perpetuate /pə'petʃʊeɪt/ v.t. увековéчи|вать, -ть

perpetuity /pə:pɪ'tju:ɪtɪ/ n. вéчность; **in ~** навсегдá, (на)вéчно

perplex /pə'pleks/ v.t. озадáчи|вать, -ть

persecute /'pə:sɪkju:t/ v.t. преслéдовать (impf.)

persecution /pə:sɪ'kju:ʃ(ə)n/ n. преслéдование

persecutor /'pə:sɪkju:tə(r)/ n. преслéдователь (m.) (-ница)

perseverance /pə:sɪ'vɪərəns/ n. упóрство, настóйчивость

p

persevere /ˌpɜːsɪˈvɪə(r)/ v.i. прояв|лять, -ить упорство/настойчивость (в + p.); you must ~ in (at, with) your work вы должны проявить упорство/настойчивость в своей работе

Persian /ˈpɜːʃ(ə)n/ adj.: ~ Gulf Персидский залив

persist /pəˈsɪst/ v.i. (continue stubbornly) упорно/настойчиво продолжать (impf.); (continue) сохран|яться, -иться; fog will ~ all day туман продержится весь день

persistence /pəˈsɪst(ə)ns/ n. упорство, настойчивость

persistent /pəˈsɪst(ə)nt/ adj. (stubborn) упорный, настойчивый; (continuous) постоянный

ɗ **person** /ˈpɜːs(ə)n/ n. **1** (individual) человек **2** (of particular category, also gram.) лицо; first ~ singular первое лицо единственного числа

personable /ˈpɜːsənəb(ə)l/ adj. привлекательный

ɗ **personal** /ˈpɜːsən(ə)l/ adj. личный; don't make ~ remarks! не переходите на личности!

■ ~ **column** n. (of newspaper) колонка частных объявлений; ~ **computer** n. персональный компьютер; ~ **organizer** n. органайзер; ~ **stereo** n. плеер

personality /ˌpɜːsəˈnælɪtɪ/ n. **1** (character) личность **2** (famous person) знаменитость

personally /ˈpɜːsənəlɪ/ adv. лично

personification /pəˌsɒnɪfɪˈkeɪʃ(ə)n/ n. олицетворение, воплощение; he is the ~ of selfishness он является воплощением эгоизма

personif|y /pəˈsɒnɪfaɪ/ v.t. воплo|щать, -тить; she was kindness ~ied она была воплощением доброты

personnel /ˌpɜːsəˈnel/ n. персонал; штат; кадры (m. pl.)

■ ~ **department** n. = HR

ɗ **perspective** /pəˈspektɪv/ n. **1** перспектива **2** (fig.): you must see, get things in ~ надо видеть вещи в их истинном свете

perspex® /ˈpɜːspeks/ n. (BrE) плексиглас, органическое стекло, оргстекло

perspicacious /ˌpɜːspɪˈkeɪʃəs/ adj. проницательный

perspicacity /ˌpɜːspɪˈkæsɪtɪ/ n. проницательность

perspicuous /pəˈspɪkjʊəs/ adj. ясный, понятный

perspiration /ˌpɜːspɪˈreɪʃ(ə)n/ n. пот

perspire /pəˈspaɪə(r)/ v.i. потеть, вс-

persuade /pəˈsweɪd/ v.t. **1** (convince) убе|ждать, -дить; I ~d him of my innocence я убедил его в моей невиновности **2** (induce) угов|аривать, -орить; he was ~d to sing его уговорили спеть

persuasion /pəˈsweɪʒ(ə)n/ n. (persuading) убеждение; (conviction) убеждение; (denomination) вероисповедание

persuasive /pəˈsweɪsɪv/ adj. убедительный; (of person) обладающий даром убеждения

pert /pɜːt/ adj. дерзкий, нахальный

pertain /pəˈteɪn/ v.i. (relate) относиться (impf.) (to: к + d.)

pertinent /ˈpɜːtɪnənt/ adj. уместный

perturb /pəˈtɜːb/ v.t. тревожить, вс-

Peru /pəˈruː/ n. Перу (nt. & f. indecl.)

peruse /pəˈruːz/ v.t. рассм|атривать, -отреть

Peruvian /pəˈruːvɪən/ n. перуан|ец (-ка)
● adj. перуанский

pervade /pəˈveɪd/ v.t. прониз|ывать, -ать

pervasive /pəˈveɪsɪv/ adj. пронизывающий

perverse /pəˈvɜːs/ adj. превратный

perversion /pəˈvɜːʃ(ə)n/ n. (distortion; sexual deviation) извращение

perversity /pəˈvɜːsɪtɪ/ n. превратность

pervert[1] /ˈpɜːvɜːt/ n. (sexual deviant) извращенец

pervert[2] /pəˈvɜːt/ v.t. извра|щать, -тить; ~ the course of justice иска|жать, -зить ход правосудия

pessimism /ˈpesɪmɪz(ə)m/ n. пессимизм

pessimist /ˈpesɪmɪst/ n. пессимист (-ка)

pessimistic /ˌpesɪˈmɪstɪk/ adj. пессимистический; (person) пессимистичный

pest /pest/ n. (harmful creature) вредитель (m.); (of person) зануда (c.g.)

pester /ˈpestə(r)/ v.t. докучать (impf.); he keeps ~ing me for money он всё время пристаёт ко мне насчёт денег

pesticide /ˈpestɪsaɪd/ n. пестицид

pestilence /ˈpestɪləns/ n. чума

pet /pet/ n. **1** (animal, bird, etc.) питомец, домашнее животное **2** (favourite) любим|ец (-ица), баловень (m.); his ~ subject его излюбленная тема
● v.t. (**petted, petting**) (fondle) ласкать, при-
● v.i. (**petted, petting**) (infml, fondle each other) обнима́ться (impf.)

■ ~ **food** n. корм для домашних животных; ~ **name** n. ласкательное/уменьшительное имя

petal /ˈpet(ə)l/ n. лепесток

peter /ˈpiːtə(r)/ v.i. (usu. ~ **out**) (run dry, low) исс|якать, -якнуть; (of a path) постепенно исч|езать, -езнуть

petite /pəˈtiːt/ adj. миниатюрный

petition /pɪˈtɪʃ(ə)n/ n. (signed by many people) петиция; (application to court) исковое заявление
● v.t. (a person/an organization) под|авать, -ать прошение кому or во что
● v.i.: ~ for divorce под|авать, -ать заявление о разводе

petrif|y /ˈpetrɪfaɪ/ v.t. (fig.) прив|одить, -ести в оцепенение; I was ~ied я оцепенел

petrochemicals /ˌpetrəʊˈkemɪk(ə)ls/ n. pl. нефтепродукты (m. pl.), нефтехимические продукты (m. pl.)

petrol /ˈpetr(ə)l/ n. (BrE) бензин; fill up with ~ запр|авляться, -авиться бензином

■ ~ **pump** n. (at garage) бензоколонка; ~ **station** n. бензозаправочная станция, бензоколонка; ~ **tank** n. бензобак

petroleum /pəˈtrəʊlɪəm/ n. нефть

petticoat /ˈpetɪkəʊt/ n. нижняя юбка

p

petty /ˈpetɪ/ *adj.* (**pettier, pettiest**) **1** (trivial) ме́лкий, малова́жный **2** (small-minded) ме́лочный **3** (of small amounts): ~ **cash** де́ньги на ме́лкие расхо́ды; ~ **theft** ме́лкая кра́жа

petulance /ˈpetjʊləns/ *n.* раздражи́тельность

petulant /ˈpetjʊlənt/ *adj.* раздражи́тельный

petunia /pɪˈtjuːnɪə/ *n.* пету́ния

pew /pjuː/ *n.* (церко́вная) скамья́

pewter /ˈpjuːtə(r)/ *n.* (alloy) сплав о́лова с ме́дью/со свинцо́м; (vessels made of ~) оловя́нная посу́да
• *adj.* оловя́нный

phallic /ˈfælɪk/ *adj.* фалли́ческий
■ ~ **symbol** *n.* фалли́ческий си́мвол

phallus /ˈfæləs/ *n.* (*pl.* **phalli** /-laɪ, -lɪ/ *or* **phalluses**) фа́ллос

phantom /ˈfæntəm/ *n.* фанто́м

Pharaoh /ˈfeərəʊ/ *n.* фарао́н

pharmaceutical /ˌfɑːməˈsjuːtɪk(ə)l/ *adj.* фармацевти́ческий

pharmacist /ˈfɑːməsɪst/ *n.* фармаце́вт

pharmacology /ˌfɑːməˈkɒlədʒɪ/ *n.* фармаколо́гия

pharmacy /ˈfɑːməsɪ/ *n.* (dispensary) апте́ка; (science, practice) апте́чное де́ло

pharynx /ˈfærɪŋks/ *n.* (*pl.* **pharynges** /fəˈrɪndʒiːz/) зев; гло́тка

ꝑ **phase** /feɪz/ *n.* фа́за; (stage) ста́дия
• *v.t.*: **a** ~**d withdrawal** поэта́пный вы́вод; ~ **out** (weapons) поэта́пно сн|има́ть, -я́ть с вооруже́ния

Ph.D. *abbr.* (*of* **Doctor of Philosophy**) ≈ сте́пень кандида́та нау́к

pheasant /ˈfez(ə)nt/ *n.* фаза́н

phenomena /fɪˈnɒmɪnə/ *pl. of* ▶ **phenomenon**

phenomenal /fɪˈnɒmɪn(ə)l/ *adj.* феномена́льный

phenomenon /fɪˈnɒmɪnən/ *n.* (*pl.* **phenomena**) феноме́н

philanderer /fɪˈlændərə(r)/ *n.* волоки́та (*m.*)

philanthropic /ˌfɪlənˈθrɒpɪk/ *adj.* филантропи́ческий

philanthropist /fɪˈlænθrəpɪst/ *n.* филантро́п (-ка)

philanthropy /fɪˈlænθrəpɪ/ *n.* филантро́пия

philatelist /fɪˈlætəlɪst/ *n.* филатели́ст (-ка)

philately /fɪˈlætəlɪ/ *n.* филатели́я

Philippines /ˈfɪlɪpiːnz/ *n. pl.* (*in full* **the** ~) Филиппи́н|ы (*pl., g.* —)

philistine /ˈfɪlɪstaɪn/ *n.* (fig.) обыва́тель (*m.*)

philological /ˌfɪləˈlɒdʒɪk(ə)l/ *adj.* языкове́дческий; филологи́ческий

philologist /fɪˈlɒlədʒɪst/ *n.* языкове́д; фило́лог

philology /fɪˈlɒlədʒɪ/ *n.* (language) языкове́дение; (language and literature) филоло́гия

philosopher /fɪˈlɒsəfə(r)/ *n.* фило́соф

philosophical /ˌfɪləˈsɒfɪk(ə)l/, **philosophic** /ˌfɪləˈsɒfɪk/ *adjs.* филосо́фский

ꝑ ключева́я ле́ксика

philosophize /fɪˈlɒsəfaɪz/ *v.i.* филосо́фствовать (*impf.*)

philosophy /fɪˈlɒsəfɪ/ *n.* филосо́фия

phishing /ˈfɪʃɪŋ/ *n.* (comput.) фи́шинг (*рассы́лка электро́нных сообще́ний по́льзователям се́ти Интерне́т от и́мени соли́дных компа́ний с це́лью получе́ния их ли́чных да́нных*)

phlegm /flem/ *n.* (secretion) мокро́та; (fig.) флегмати́чность

phlegmatic /flegˈmætɪk/ *adj.* флегмати́чный

phobia /ˈfəʊbɪə/ *n.* фо́бия, страх

phoenix /ˈfiːnɪks/ *n.* (myth.) фе́никс

ꝑ **phone** /fəʊn/ (*see also* ▶ **telephone**) *n.* телефо́н
• *v.t. & i.* звони́ть, по- (*кому*)
□ ~ **back** *v.t. & i.* перезвони́ть (*pf.*)
□ ~ **up** *v.t. & i.* звони́ть, по- (*кому*)
■ ~**card** *n.* телефо́нная ка́рточка; ~ **hacker** *n.* взло́мщик моби́льных телефо́нов; ~ **hacking** *n.* взлом моби́льных телефо́нов; ~**-in** *n.* горя́чая ли́ния в прямо́м эфи́ре

phonetic /fəˈnetɪk/ *adj.* фонети́ческий

phoney, phony /ˈfəʊnɪ/ (sl.) *n.* (*pl.* **phoneys** *or* **phonies**) (person) шарлата́н; (thing) подде́лка
• *adj.* (**phonier, phoniest**) подде́льный

phony /ˈfəʊnɪ/ *n. & adj.* = **phoney**

phosphate /ˈfɒsfeɪt/ *n.* фосфа́т

phosphorus /ˈfɒsfərəs/ *n.* фо́сфор

ꝑ **photo** /ˈfəʊtəʊ/ *n.* (*pl.* **photos**) фо́то (*nt. indecl.*), сни́мок
■ ~**call** *n.* (BrE) = photo opportunity; ~**copier** *n.* фотокопирова́льный аппара́т; ~**copy** *n.* фотоко́пия, ксероко́пия • *v.t.* сн|има́ть, -я́ть фотоко́пию (c) + *g.*; ~ **opportunity** *n.* сеа́нс фотосъёмки, фотосе́ссия (*для пре́ссы*)

photogenic /ˌfəʊtəʊˈdʒenɪk/ *adj.* фотогени́чный

ꝑ **photograph** /ˈfəʊtəgrɑːf/ *n.* фотогра́фия
• *v.t.* фотографи́ровать, с-

photographer /fəˈtɒgrəfə(r)/ *n.* фото́граф

photographic /ˌfəʊtəˈgræfɪk/ *adj.* фотографи́ческий

photography /fəˈtɒgrəfɪ/ *n.* фотогра́фия, фотосъёмка

photosynthesis /ˌfəʊtəʊˈsɪnθɪsɪs/ *n.* фотоси́нтез

phrase /freɪz/ *n.* фра́за
• *v.t.* формули́ровать, с-
■ ~ **book** *n.* разгово́рник

phraseology /ˌfreɪzɪˈɒlədʒɪ/ *n.* фразеоло́гия

ꝑ **physical** /ˈfɪzɪk(ə)l/ *adj.* физи́ческий; (relating to the body): ~ **education/training** физи́ческое воспита́ние/трениро́вка; физкульту́ра; ~**ly handicapped** (sometimes offens.) физи́чески неполноце́нный; **have you had your** ~ **(examination)?** вы прошли́ медици́нский осмо́тр?

physician /fɪˈzɪʃ(ə)n/ *n.* врач

physicist /ˈfɪzɪsɪst/ *n.* фи́зик

physics /ˈfɪzɪks/ *n.* фи́зика

physiognomy /ˌfɪzɪˈɒnəmɪ/ *n.* (facial features) физионо́мия

physiological /ˌfɪzɪəˈlɒdʒɪk(ə)l/ *adj.* физиологи́ческий

physiology /ˌfɪzɪˈɒlədʒɪ/ *n.* физиоло́гия

physiotherapist /ˌfɪzɪəʊˈθerəpɪst/ *n.* физиотерапе́вт

physiotherapy /ˌfɪzɪəʊˈθerəpɪ/ *n.* физиотерапи́я

physique /fɪˈziːk/ *n.* телосложе́ние

pianist /ˈpɪənɪst/ *n.* пиани́ст (-ка)

piano /pɪˈænəʊ/ *n.* (*pl.* ~s) фортепиа́но, фортепья́но (*nt. indecl.*); (upright) пиани́но (*nt. indecl.*)

piccolo /ˈpɪkələʊ/ *n.* (*pl.* ~s) пи́кколо (*nt. indecl.*)

✓ **pick** /pɪk/ *n.* **1** (~axe) кирка́ **2** (selection): take your ~! выбира́йте!; the ~ of the bunch са́мый лу́чший
• *v.t.* **1** (pluck) рвать, со-; (gather) соб|ира́ть, -ра́ть **2** (probe) ковыря́ть (*impf.*); stop ~ing your nose! не ковыря́й в носу́! **3** (make by ~ing): he ~ed a hole in the cloth он продыря́вил ткань **4** (select) выбира́ть, вы́брать; she ~ed her way through the mud она́ осторо́жно ступа́ла по гря́зи; the captains ~ed sides капита́ны определи́ли соста́в(ы) кома́нд; he's trying to ~ a quarrel он и́щет по́вод(а) для ссо́ры
• *v.i.* (select) выбира́ть, вы́брать; ~ and choose быть разбо́рчивым
• *with preps.*: ~ at ковыря́ть, по-; the child ~ed at (*sc.* trifled with) his food ребёнок поковыря́л еду́ ви́лкой; ~ on (find fault with) прид|ира́ться, -ра́ться к + *d.*
□ ~ out *v.t.* (select): he ~ed out the best for himself са́мое лу́чшее он отобра́л для себя́; (distinguish): I ~ed him out in the crowd я узна́л его́ в толпе́
□ ~ up *v.t.* (lift) подн|има́ть, -я́ть; (acquire, gain) приобре|та́ть, -сти́; he has ~ed up an American accent он приобрёл америка́нский акце́нт; the car began to ~ up speed маши́на начала́ набира́ть ско́рость; (provide transport for) заб|ира́ть, -ра́ть, под|бира́ть, -обра́ть; I never ~ up hitch-hikers я никогда́ не беру́ «голосу́ющих» на доро́ге; (apprehend) заде́рж|ивать, -а́ть; the culprit was ~ed up by the police престу́пник был заде́ржан поли́цией; (resume) возобнов|ля́ть, -и́ть; he ~ed up the thread where he had left off он возобнови́л бесе́ду с того́ ме́ста, где останови́лся
• *v.i.* (recover health) опр|авля́ться, -а́виться, попр|авля́ться, -а́виться; (improve) ул|учша́ться, -у́чшиться; trade is ~ing up торго́вля оживля́ется
■ ~axe, (AmE) also ~ax *n.* кирка́; ~-me-up *n.* тонизи́рующее сре́дство; ~pocket *n.* карма́нник, карма́нный вор; ~up *n.* (van) пика́п

picket /ˈpɪkɪt/ *n.* (of strikers) пике́т
• *v.t.* (**picketed, picketing**) пикети́ровать (*impf.*); the workers are ~ing the factory рабо́чие пикети́руют фа́брику

picking /ˈpɪkɪŋ/ *n.* **1** (gathering) сбор **2** (*in pl.*) (remains) оста́тки (*m. pl.*); объе́дки (*m. pl.*)

pickle /ˈpɪk(ə)l/ *n.* **1** (*usu. in pl.*) (preserved vegetables) соле́нья (*pl.*) **2** (*infml*, predicament) напа́сть
• *v.t.* маринова́ть, за-

picky /ˈpɪkɪ/ *adj.* (**pickier, pickiest**) (*infml*) разбо́рчивый

picnic /ˈpɪknɪk/ *n.* пикни́к

pictorial /pɪkˈtɔːrɪəl/ *n.* иллюстри́рованное изда́ние
• *adj.* изобрази́тельный; (illustrated) иллюстри́рованный

✓ **picture** /ˈpɪktʃə(r)/ *n.* **1** (depiction) карти́на; (drawing) рису́нок; (image on TV screen) карти́нка, изображе́ние **2** (embodiment) олицетворе́ние; he looks the ~ of health он пы́шет здоро́вьем **3** (*infml*, of information): he will soon put you in the ~ он вско́ре введёт вас в курс (де́ла) **4** (film) (кино)фи́льм, (кино)карти́на; (*in pl.*) (cinema show, cinema) кино́ (*nt. indecl.*)
• *v.t.*: ~ to yourself вообрази́те/предста́вьте себе́
■ ~ book *n.* кни́жка с карти́нками

picturesque /ˌpɪktʃəˈresk/ *adj.* живопи́сный

pie /paɪ/ *n.* пиро́г; (small one) пирожо́к

✓ **piece** /piːs/ *n.* **1** (portion, bit) кусо́к; a ~ of bread кусо́к хле́ба; a ~ of paper листо́к бума́ги, бума́жка; to pull, tear to ~s раз|рыва́ть, -орва́ть на ча́сти/куски́; to go to ~s (of person) поддава́ться, подда́ться эмо́циям **2** (example): a ~ of news но́вость; a ~ of advice сове́т; I gave him a ~ of my mind я его́ отчита́л **3** (object of art etc.) произведе́ние (иску́сства); a ~ of furniture предме́т ме́бели **4** (chess) фигу́ра **5** (coin) моне́та
□ ~ together *v.t.* соедин|я́ть, -и́ть; (*fig.*) свя́з|ывать, -а́ть
■ ~meal *adj.* части́чный • *adv.* по частя́м

pier /pɪə(r)/ *n.* (structure projecting into sea) пирс; (landing stage) прича́л; (breakwater) мол

pierc|e /pɪəs/ *v.t.* прок|а́лывать, -оло́ть; she had her ears ~ed она́ проколо́ла у́ши; a ~ing cry пронзи́тельный крик

piercing /ˈpɪəsɪŋ/ *n.* (of body) пи́рсинг

piety /ˈpaɪɪtɪ/ *n.* набо́жность

pig /pɪg/ *n.* (animal) свинья́; (greedy person): he made a ~ of himself он нае́лся, как свинья́
■ ~-headed *adj.* упря́мый (как осёл); ~sty *n.* (*lit., fig.*) свина́рник

pigeon /ˈpɪdʒɪn/ *n.* го́лубь (*m.*)
■ ~hole *n.* (compartment) отделе́ние для бума́г
• *v.t.* (categorize) классифици́ровать (*impf., pf.*)

piggy /ˈpɪgɪ/ *n.* (piglet) поросёнок
■ ~back *n.*: give sb a ~back носи́ть (*indet.*), нести́ (*det.*) кого́-н на спине́; ~ bank *n.* копи́лка

piglet /ˈpɪglɪt/ *n.* поросёнок

pigment /ˈpɪgmənt/ *n.* пигме́нт

pigmentation /ˌpɪgmənˈteɪʃ(ə)n/ *n.* пигмента́ция

pike /paɪk/ *n.* (*pl.* ~) (fish) щу́ка

pile /paɪl/ *n.* (heap) ку́ча, гру́да; (*infml*, large quantity) (*often in pl.*) ку́ча, ма́сса

● *v.t.* **1** (heap up) свáл|ивать, -и́ть в кýчу **2** (load) нав|áливать, -али́ть; заст|авля́ть, -áвить

□ ~ **in** *v.i.* (infml, crowd into) наб|ивáться, -и́ться

□ ~ **up** *v.i.* (accumulate) (of objects) нагромо|ждáться, -зди́ться; (of work, debts) нак|áпливаться, -опи́ться

■ ~-**up** *n.* (crash) столкновéние нéскольких маши́н

piles /paɪlz/ *n. pl.* (med.) геморрóй (*see also* ▶ **pile** *n.*)

pilfer /'pɪlfə(r)/ *v.t. & i.* ворова́ть (*impf.*)

pilgrim /'pɪlgrɪm/ *n.* палóмник

pilgrimage /'pɪlgrɪmɪdʒ/ *n.* паломничество

pill /pɪl/ *n.* пилю́ля, табле́тка; **she is on the** ~ онá принимáет противозача́точные табле́тки

pillage /'pɪlɪdʒ/ *n.* мародёрство, грабёж
● *v.t.* грáбить, раз-
● *v.i.* мародёрствовать (*impf.*); грáбить (*impf.*)

pillar /'pɪlə(r)/ *n.* столб, колóнна

pillion /'pɪljən/ *n.*: **she rode** ~ онá éхала на зáднем сидéнье мотоци́кла

pillow /'pɪləʊ/ *n.* подýшка
■ ~**case**, ~**slip** *nn.* нáволочка

⚡ **pilot** /'paɪlət/ *n.* **1** (of aircraft) лётчи|к (-ца), пилóт **2** (*attr.*) (fig.) прóбный, óпытный
● *v.t.* (**piloted**, **piloting**) (lit.) пилоти́ровать (*impf.*)
■ ~ **scheme** *n.* эксперимéнт

pimp /pɪmp/ *n.* сутенёр

pimple /'pɪmp(ə)l/ *n.* прыщ, пры́щик

pimply /'pɪmplɪ/ *adj.* прыщáвый

PIN /pɪn/ *n.* (*abbr. of* **personal identification number**) персонáльный код

pin /pɪn/ *n.* **1** булáвка **2** (securing peg) прище́пка
● *v.t.* (**pinned**, **pinning**) **1** (fasten) прик|áлывать, -олóть; (fig.): ~ **blame on sb** свáл|ивать, -и́ть вину́ на когó-н. **2** (immobilize) приж|имáть, -áть; **the bandits** ~**ned him against the wall** банди́ты прижáли егó к стенé

□ ~ **down** *v.t.* (lit.) прик|áлывать, -олóть; (fig., commit to an action or opinion) прип|ирáть, -ерéть к сте́нке

□ ~ **up** *v.t.* прик|áлывать, -олóть; вéшать, повéсить

■ ~**ball** *n.* (game, machine) пинбóл; ~**point** *n.* (lit.) острие́ булáвки ● *v.t.* (fig.) тóчно определ|я́ть, -и́ть; ~**stripe** (suit) *n.* костю́м в тóнкую свéтлую полóску; ~-**up** *n.* фотогрáфия красóтки (в журнáле)

pinafore /'pɪnəfɔ:(r)/ *n.* (BrE, apron) фáртук
■ ~ **dress** *n.* плáтье-сарафáн

pincers /'pɪnsəz/ *n. pl.* **1** (of crab) клешн|и́ (-éй) **2** (tech.) клéщ|и (-éй)

pinch /pɪntʃ/ *n.* **1** (nip) щипóк **2** (small amount) щепóтка
● *v.t.* **1** (squeeze) (objects) прищем|ля́ть, -и́ть; (person) щипáть, ущипнýть **2** (BrE, infml, steal) стащи́ть (*pf.*)

pine¹ /paɪn/ *n.* соснá

■ ~**apple** *n.* ананáс; ~ **cone** *n.* соснóвая ши́шка

pin|e² /paɪn/ *v.i.* **1** (languish) чáхнуть, за-; томи́ться (*impf.*); **she is** ~**ing away** онá чáхнет **2** (long): ~**e for** жáждать (*impf.*) + *g.*

ping-pong /'pɪŋpɒŋ/ *n.* пинг-пóнг

pink /pɪŋk/ *n.* (flower) гвозди́ка; (colour) рóзовый цвет
● *adj.* (of colour) рóзовый

pinnacle /'pɪnək(ə)l/ *n.* (fig.) верши́на

pint /paɪnt/ *n.* пи́нта

pioneer /paɪə'nɪə(r)/ *n.* пионéр, новáтор
● *v.t. & i.* быть пионéром (*в чём*)

pious /'paɪəs/ *adj.* нáбожный

pip /pɪp/ *n.* (BrE) сéмечко; зёрнышко

pipe /paɪp/ *n.* **1** (conduit) трубá **2** (mus. instrument) ду́дка; (*in pl.*) (bagpipes) волы́нка **3** (for smoking) трýбка
● *v.t.* **1** (convey by ~s) пус|кáть, -ти́ть по трубáм **2**: ~**d music** музыкáльная трансля́ция (в общéственном мéсте)

■ ~ **dream** *n.* несбы́точная мечтá; ~**line** *n.* (for oil) нефтепровóд; (fig.): **in the** ~**line** на подхóде (infml)

piper /'paɪpə(r)/ *n.* (bagpipe player) волы́нщи|к (-ца); **he who pays the** ~ **calls the tune** кто плáтит, тот и распоряжáется

piping /'paɪpɪŋ/ *adv.*: ~ **hot** с пы́лу, с жáру

piquancy /'pi:kənsɪ/ *n.* пикáнтность

piquant /'pi:kɑ:nt/ *adj.* пикáнтный

pique /pi:k/ *n.* досáда; **in a fit of** ~ в порыве раздражéния

piracy /'paɪrəsɪ/ *n.* пирáтство

pirate /'paɪərət/ *n.* пирáт; (infringer of copyright) нарýши|тель (*m.*) áвторского прáва, пирáт
● *v.t.* (video, software) выпуск|áть, выпустить пирáтскую кóпию + *g.*

pirouette /pɪrʊ'et/ *n.* пируэ́т

Pisces /'paɪsi:z/ *n.* (*pl.* ~) (astron., astrol.) Ры́бы (*f. pl.*)

piss /pɪs/ *v.i.* (vulg.) ссать, по- (vulg.); ~ **off!** (BrE) отвали́!; провáливай!

pissed /pɪst/ *adj.* (BrE, vulg., drunk) в жóпу пья́ный (vulg.); ~ **off** (AmE *also* ~) обозлённый

pistachio /pɪ'stɑ:ʃɪəʊ/ *n.* (*pl.* ~**s**) фистáшка

piste /pi:st/ *n.* (skiing) горнолы́жная трáсса

pistol /'pɪst(ə)l/ *n.* пистолéт

piston /'pɪst(ə)n/ *n.* пóршень (*m.*)

pit¹ /pɪt/ *n.* **1** (a large hole) котловáн; (for gravel) карьéр **2**: **the** ~**s** (sl.) хýже нéкуда
● *v.t.* (**pitted**, **pitting**): **he** ~**ted his wits against the law** он пытáлся обойти́ закóн
■ ~**fall** *n.* западня́, капкáн

pit² /pɪt/ *n.* (AmE, fruit stone) кóсточка

pitch¹ /pɪtʃ/ *n.* **1** (of voice or instrument) высотá **2** (BrE, area for games) пóле, площáдка
● *v.t.* **1** (set up, erect): **they** ~**ed camp for the night** они́ разби́ли на ночь лáгерь **2** (throw) бр|осáть, -óсить **3** (mus.): **the song is** ~**ed too high for me** э́та пéсня сли́шком высокá для моегó гóлоса
● *v.i.* (of ship): **the ship was** ~**ing** корáбль испы́тывал килевýю кáчку; (of person, fall

forwards) па́дать, упа́сть на́взничь

□ ~ **in** v.i. (join in with vigour) горячо́/энерги́чно бра́ться, взя́ться (*за что*)

■ ~**fork** n. (сенны́е) ви́л|ы (pl., g. —)

pitch² /pɪtʃ/ n. (substance) смола́

■ ~**-black** adj. чёрный как смоль; ~**-dark** adj.: it is ~**-dark** here здесь тьма кроме́шная; здесь темны́м-темно́ (infml)

pitcher /ˈpɪtʃə(r)/ n. (jug) кувши́н; (at baseball) подаю́щий

piteous /ˈpɪtɪəs/ adj. жа́лкий; (voice, song, words) жа́лобный

pith /pɪθ/ n. (plant tissue) сердцеви́на, мя́коть; (essential part) суть; (vigour, force) эне́ргия, си́ла

pithy /ˈpɪθɪ/ adj. (**pithier**, **pithiest**) (fig.) сжа́тый; содержа́тельный

pitiful /ˈpɪtɪfʊl/ adj. жа́лкий

pitiless /ˈpɪtɪlɪs/ adj. безжа́лостный

pittance /ˈpɪt(ə)ns/ n. жа́лкие гроши́ (m. pl.)

pitted /ˈpɪtɪd/ adj. (with its stone removed) без ко́сточки

pituitary /pɪˈtjuːɪtərɪ/ n. (in full ~ **gland**) гипо́физ

pity /ˈpɪtɪ/ n. **1** (compassion) жа́лость; **have, take** ~ **on** сжа́литься (pf.) над + i. **2** (cause for regret) жаль; **what a** ~! как жаль/жа́лко!
● v.t. жале́ть, по-

pivot /ˈpɪvət/ v.i. (**pivoted**, **pivoting**) враща́ться (impf.)

pixel /ˈpɪks(ə)l/ n. (comput.) пи́ксель (m.), элеме́нт изображе́ния

pixy, pixie /ˈpɪksɪ/ n. эльф

pizza /ˈpiːtsə/ n. пи́цца

placard /ˈplækɑːd/ n. плака́т

placate /pləˈkeɪt/ v.t. умиротвор|я́ть, -и́ть

✐ **place** /pleɪs/ n. **1** ме́сто; **all over the** ~ (everywhere) повсю́ду; (in confusion) повсю́ду, в беспоря́дке; **everything is in** ~ всё на ме́сте; **your laughter is out of** ~ ваш смех неуме́стен; **that put him in his** ~ э́то поста́вило его́ на ме́сто; **he took his** ~ **in the queue** (BrE), **in (the) line** (AmE) он за́нял ме́сто в о́череди; (seat): **he gave up his** ~ **to a lady** он уступи́л своё ме́сто да́ме; (fig., position): **put yourself in my** ~ поста́вьте себя́ на моё ме́сто; (fig.): **take** ~ состоя́ться (pf.); име́ть (impf.) ме́сто; **in** ~ **of** вме́сто + g. **2** (locality) ме́сто; **in** ~**s** (here and there) места́ми **3** (building) дом; жили́ще; ~ **of work** ме́сто рабо́ты; **come round to my** ~! заходи́те ко мне! **4** (position) ме́сто; **our team took first** ~ на́ша кома́нда заняла́ пе́рвое ме́сто; **in the first** ~ во-пе́рвых
● v.t. **1** (stand) ста́вить, по-; (lay) класть, положи́ть (comm.): **I** ~**d an order with them** я сде́лал у них зака́з **3** (identify) определ|я́ть, -и́ть; **I know those lines, but I cannot** ~ **them** мне знако́мы э́ти стро́чки, но я не могу́ вспо́мнить, отку́да они́

■ ~ **mat** n. подста́вка/салфе́тка под столо́вый прибо́р; ~ **name** n. географи́ческое назва́ние

placebo /pləˈsiːbəʊ/ n. (pl. ~**s**) (med.) плаце́бо (nt. indecl.); имита́ция лека́рственного сре́дства

placen|ta /pləˈsentə/ n. (pl. ~**tae** /-tiː/ or ~**tas**) плаце́нта

placid /ˈplæsɪd/ adj. споко́йный

plagiarism /ˈpleɪdʒərɪz(ə)m/ n. плагиа́т

plagiarize /ˈpleɪdʒəraɪz/ v.i. занима́ться (impf.) плагиа́том
● v.t.: **he** ~**d my book** его́ рабо́та целико́м спи́сана с мое́й кни́ги

plague /pleɪɡ/ n. **1** (pestilence) чума́ **2** (infestation): **a** ~ **of rats** наше́ствие крыс
● v.t. (**plagues, plagued, plaguing**) (pester) докуча́ть (impf.) + d.

plaice /pleɪs/ n. (pl. ~) ка́мбала

plaid /plæd/ n. (fabric) шотла́ндка (ткань)

plain /pleɪn/ n. равни́на
● adj. **1** (clear) я́сный, я́вный; **her distress was** ~ **to see** она́ я́вно страда́ла **2** (easy to understand) я́сный, поня́тный **3** (not patterned): ~ **blue shirt** одното́нная (or гла́дкая) голуба́я руба́шка; ~ **paper** нелино́ванная бума́га; (simple, ordinary) просто́й; ~ **food** проста́я пи́ща **4** (unattractive) некраси́вый
■ ~ **chocolate** n. чёрный шокола́д; ~**-clothes** adj. оде́тый в штатское; ~ **flour** n. (BrE) мука́ без доба́вок

plaintiff /ˈpleɪntɪf/ n. исте́ц (-и́ца)

plaintive /ˈpleɪntɪv/ adj. печа́льный

plait /plæt/ n. (BrE) коса́
● v.t. запле|та́ть, -сти́

✐ **plan** /plæn/ n. (map; drawing) чертёж; (schedule): **all went according to** ~ всё прошло́ по пла́ну; (project) план, прое́кт
● v.t. (**planned, planning**) плани́ровать, за-; (design) проекти́ровать, с-
● v.i. (**planned, planning**) намерева́ться, плани́ровать (both impf.); **we must** ~ **ahead** на́до ду́мать о бу́дущем

plane¹ /pleɪn/ n. (tool) руба́нок, струг
● v.t. строга́ть, вы́-

✐ **plane²** /pleɪn/ n. **1** (flat surface) пло́скость **2** (aeroplane) самолёт **3** (fig., level of existence, thought) у́ровень (m.)

✐ **planet** /ˈplænɪt/ n. плане́та

plank /plæŋk/ n. доска́

plankton /ˈplæŋkt(ə)n/ n. планкто́н

✐ **planning** /ˈplænɪŋ/ n. плани́рование
■ ~ **permission** n. (BrE) разреше́ние на строи́тельство

✐ **plant** /plɑːnt/ n. **1** (vegetable organism) расте́ние **2** (industrial machinery) обору́дование **3** (factory) заво́д
● v.t. **1** (put in ground) сажа́ть, посади́ть; (seeds) се́ять, по- **2** (fig.): ~ **evidence** подбр|а́сывать, -о́сить ули́ки; подде́л|ывать, -ать доказа́тельства

plantation /plɑːnˈteɪʃ(ə)n/ n. планта́ция

planter /ˈplɑːntə(r)/ n. (person who plants seeds, bulbs, trees) сажа́льщик, се́ятель (m.); (of seeds only, plantation owner) планта́тор; (agricultural machine) се́ялка; (container for plants) декорати́вный горшо́к (для расте́ний)

plaque /plæk/ n. (tablet) доще́чка; (on teeth) зубно́й ка́мень

plasma /ˈplæzmə/ n. пла́зма

p

■ ~ **screen** n. (TV, comput.) пла́зменный экра́н
plaster /ˈplɑːstə(r)/ n. **1** (for coating walls etc.)
штукату́рка **2** (BrE, med.) пла́стырь (m.)
● v.t. **1** (wall) штукату́рить, о- **2** (cover)
обле́п|ля́ть, -и́ть; his boots were ~ed with
mud его́ боти́нки бы́ли обле́плены гря́зью
■ ~ **cast** n. ги́псовый сле́пок
plasterer /ˈplɑːstərə(r)/ n. штукату́р
♂ **plastic** /ˈplæstɪk/ n. пла́стик, пластма́сса;
(infml, credit card) креди́тная ка́рточка
● adj. **1** (made of ~) пластма́ссовый;
пла́стиковый **2** (art) пласти́ческий
■ ~ **bag** n. полиэтиле́новый мешо́к/паке́т; ~
surgery n. (practice) пласти́ческая хирурги́я;
(operation) пласти́ческая опера́ция
plasticine® /ˈplæstɪsiːn/ n. пластили́н
♂ **plate** /pleɪt/ n. **1** (shallow dish) (ме́лкая)
таре́лка **2** (sheet of metal, glass, etc.) лист,
пласти́н(к)а **3** (illustration) вкладна́я
иллюстра́ция, вкле́йка **4** (in full dental ~)
вставна́я че́люсть
● v.t.: silver-~d spoons посеребрённые ло́жки
■ ~**glass** adj. из зерка́льного стекла́
plateau /ˈplætəʊ/ n. (pl. ~x /-z/ or ~s) плато́
(nt. indecl.)
♂ **platform** /ˈplætfɔːm/ n. **1** (at station) платфо́рма,
перро́н **2** (for speakers) трибу́на; (fig., pol.)
(полити́ческая) платфо́рма **3** (comput.)
платфо́рма
platinum /ˈplætɪnəm/ n. пла́тина
platitude /ˈplætɪtjuːd/ n. изби́тая фра́за,
бана́льность
platonic /pləˈtɒnɪk/ adj. платони́ческий
platoon /pləˈtuːn/ n. взвод
platter /ˈplætə(r)/ n. блю́до
plaudit /ˈplɔːdɪt/ n. (usu. in pl.) (applause)
аплодисме́нт|ы (-ов); (praise) похвала́ (sg.)
plausibility /ˌplɔːzɪˈbɪlɪtɪ/ n. вероя́тность,
правдоподо́бие
plausible /ˈplɔːzɪb(ə)l/ adj. (statement)
правдоподо́бный, вероя́тный; (person)
убеди́тельный
♂ **play** /pleɪ/ n. **1** (dramatic work) пье́са; (in theatre)
спекта́кль (m.) **2** (recreation) игра́; ~ **on**
words игра́ слов **3** (sport): the ball was out of
~ мяч был вне игры́ **4** (fig., action) де́йствие,
де́ятельность; all his strength was brought
into ~ он мобилизова́л все свои́ си́лы
● v.t. **1** (perform, take part in) игра́ть, сыгра́ть в
+ a.; ~ **football** игра́ть (impf.) в футбо́л
2 (perform on) игра́ть, сыгра́ть на + p.; can
you ~ **the piano?** вы игра́ете на роя́ле?
3 (perform piece of music) исп|олня́ть, -о́лнить;
(CD) про|и́грывать, -игра́ть **4** (perpetrate): he
is always ~ing tricks on me он всегда́ на́до
мной подшу́чивает **5** (enact role of) игра́ть,
сыгра́ть **6** (cards): he ~ed the ace он пошёл
с туза́
● v.i. игра́ть, сыгра́ть; (have fun) игра́ть,
забавля́ться (both impf.); (take part in game)
игра́ть (impf.); they ~ed to win они́ игра́ли
с аза́ртом

□ ~ **down** v.t. (represent as not important)
преум|еньша́ть, -е́ньшить
□ ~ **up** v.i. (BrE, misbehave) распус|ка́ться, -ти́ться
■ ~**boy** n. плейбо́й; ~**ground** n. площа́дка
для игр; ~**group** n. (BrE) дошко́льная гру́ппа;
~**house** n. теа́тр; ~**mate** n. прия́тель
(-ница); ~**off** n. реша́ющая встре́ча;
повто́рная встре́ча по́сле ниче́й; ~**school**
n. ≈ де́тский сад; ~**thing** n. игру́шка;
~**time** n. (шко́льная) переме́на; ~**wright**
n. драмату́рг
♂ **player** /ˈpleɪə(r)/ n. **1** (of game) игро́к;
спортсме́н **2** (actor) актёр **3** (musician)
исполни́тель (-ница)
playful /ˈpleɪfʊl/ adj. игри́вый, шаловли́вый
playfulness /ˈpleɪfʊlnɪs/ n. игри́вость
playing /ˈpleɪɪŋ/ n. игра́
■ ~ **card** n. игра́льная ка́рта; ~ **field** n.
спорти́вное по́ле
plaza /ˈplɑːzə/ n. пло́щадь
PLC, plc (BrE) abbr. (of **public limited**
company) откры́тая/публи́чная компа́ния
с ограни́ченной отве́тственностью
plea /pliː/ n. **1** (law) заявле́ние (отве́тчика);
he entered a ~ of guilty он призна́л себя́
вино́вным **2** (appeal) про́сьба
plead /pliːd/ v.t. **1** (case) вести́ (impf.) **2** (offer
as excuse) ссыла́ться, сосла́ться на + a.;
the defendant ~ed insanity подсуди́мый
сосла́лся на невменя́емость **3** (declare
oneself): my client ~s (not) guilty мой клие́нт
(не) признаёт себя́ вино́вным
● v.i. приз|ыва́ть, -ва́ть; умоля́ть (impf.); he
~ed with me to stay он умоля́л меня́ оста́ться
pleasant /ˈplez(ə)nt/ adj. (**pleasanter**,
pleasantest) прия́тный
pleasantry /ˈplezəntrɪ/ n. (amiable remark)
любе́зность
♂ **please** /pliːz/ v.t. нра́виться, по- + d.;
ра́довать, по-; дост|авля́ть, -а́вить
удово́льствие + d.; I was not very ~d at,
by, with the results я был не о́чень дово́лен
результа́тами; I shall be ~d to attend я бу́ду
рад приня́ть уча́стие
● v.i. **1** (give pleasure) уго|жда́ть, -ди́ть **2** (think
fit) изво́лить (impf.); as you ~ де́лайте,
как хоти́те **3** (polite request): ~ **shut the door**
пожа́луйста, закро́йте дверь
pleasing /ˈpliːzɪŋ/ adj. прия́тный
pleasurable /ˈpleʒərəb(ə)l/ adj. прия́тный
pleasure /ˈpleʒə(r)/ n. удово́льствие; it's a ~!
(I'm delighted to oblige) не сто́ит!
pleat /pliːt/ n. скла́дка
● v.t.: ~ed skirt плисси́рованная ю́бка
plectr|um /ˈplektrəm/ n. (pl. ~ums or ~a)
(mus., for guitar etc.) медиа́тор, плектр
pledge /pledʒ/ n. обе́т, обеща́ние
● v.t. отд|ава́ть, -а́ть в зало́г
plenteous /ˈplentɪəs/ adj. оби́льный
plentiful /ˈplentɪfʊl/ adj. оби́льный
♂ **plenty** /ˈplentɪ/ n. (a lot) мно́го; мно́жество;
we have ~ у нас мно́го; we have ~ of time
to spare у нас мно́го вре́мени в запа́се;
he has ~ of money у него́ мно́го, де́нег;

♂ ключева́я ле́ксика

(sufficient): **that will be ~** э́того бу́дет доста́точно

plethora /'pleθərə/ *n.* (med.) полнокро́вие; (fig., overabundance) избы́ток

pleurisy /'plʊərɪsɪ/ *n.* (med.) плеври́т

pliable /'plaɪəb(ə)l/ *adj.* ги́бкий

pliers /'plaɪəz/ *n. pl.* кле́щ|и (-е́й)

plight /plaɪt/ *n.* (незави́дная) у́часть

plimsoll /'plɪms(ə)l/ *n.* (BrE, light shoe): ~s паруси́новые ту́фли *f. pl.*

plinth /plɪnθ/ *n.* цо́коль; постаме́нт

plod /plɒd/ *v.t. & i.* (**plodded, plodding**) тащи́ться (*impf.*)

plonk /plɒŋk/ *n.* (BrE, sl., cheap wine) дешёвое вино́, бормоту́ха (infml)
  ● *v.t.* (infml, put down heavily) гро́х|ать, -нуть; ба́х|ать, -нуть

♂ **plot** /plɒt/ *n.* **1** (piece of ground) уча́сток (земли́) **2** (outline of play etc.) фа́була, сюже́т **3** (conspiracy) за́говор
  ● *v.t.* (**plotted, plotting**) **1** (conspire to achieve): **they ~ted his ruin** они́ гото́вили ему́ ги́бель **2** (mark on a graph) нан|оси́ть, -ести́ (*данные*) на ка́рту/гра́фик
  ● *v.i.* (**plotted, plotting**) (conspire) организо́вывать, организова́ть (*both impf.*) за́говор

plough /plaʊ/ (AmE **plow**) *n.* плуг
  ● *v.t.* паха́ть, вс-
  ● *v.i.* (fig.) продв|ига́ться, -и́нуться; **I ~ed through the book** я с трудо́м оси́лил кни́гу
  □ **~ back** *v.t.*: **profits are ~ed back** при́быль вкла́дывается в де́ло/реинвести́руется
  □ **~ up** *v.t.* распа́х|ивать, -а́ть

ploy /plɔɪ/ *n.* уло́вка

pluck /plʌk/ *v.t.* **1** (flowers) срыва́ть, сорва́ть **2** (bird) ощи́п|ывать, -а́ть **3** (eyebrows) выщи́пывать, вы́щипать **4** (mus.) перебира́ть (*impf.*) стру́ны + *g.* **5** (twitch, pull at; also v.i.) дёр|гать, -нуть
  □ **~ up** *v.t.*: **~ up courage** соб|ира́ться, -ра́ться с ду́хом

plucky /'plʌkɪ/ *adj.* (**pluckier, pluckiest**) (infml) сме́лый, отва́жный

plug /plʌg/ *n.* **1** (stopper, e.g. of bath) про́бка, заты́чка **2** (elec.) (connector with pins) ви́лка; (socket) розе́тка **3** (spark **~**) свеча́ зажига́ния **4** (infml, advertisement) рекла́ма
  ● *v.t.* (**plugged, plugging**) (stop up) зат|ыка́ть, -кну́ть; (infml, advertise) реклами́ровать (*impf., pf.*)
  □ **~ in** *v.t.* включ|а́ть, -и́ть
  ■ **~hole** *n.* (BrE) сто́чное отве́рстие; **~-in** *adj.* вставно́й

plum /plʌm/ *n.* **1** (fruit, tree) сли́ва **2** (fig.): **a ~ job** тёплое месте́чко

plumage /'pluːmɪdʒ/ *n.* опере́ние

plumb /plʌm/ *adj.* (vertical) вертика́льный
  ● *adv.* (infml, exactly) то́чно; (AmE, utterly) соверше́нно, совсе́м
  ● *v.t.* (sound) изм|еря́ть, -е́рить ло́том; (fig.): **he ~ed the depths of absurdity** он дошёл до по́лного абсу́рда

plumber /'plʌmə(r)/ *n.* водопрово́дчик

plumbing /'plʌmɪŋ/ *n.* канализа́ция, водопрово́дно-канализацио́нная сеть

plume /pluːm/ *n.* **1** (feather) перо́; **a ~ of smoke** шлейф ды́ма **2** (in headdress) султа́н, плюма́ж

plummet /'plʌmɪt/ *v.i.* (**plummeted, plummeting**) обр|ыва́ться, -орва́ться

plump /plʌmp/ *adj.* пу́хлый

plunder /'plʌndə(r)/ *n.* (looting) грабёж; (loot) добы́ча
  ● *v.t.* гра́бить, раз-

plunge /plʌndʒ/ *n.* (fig.): **he took the ~** он реши́л: была́ не была́
  ● *v.t.* погру|жа́ть, -зи́ть; **the room was ~d into darkness** ко́мната погрузи́лась во мрак
  ● *v.i.* оку|на́ться, -ться

pluperfect /pluː'pɜːfɪkt/ *n.* (gram.) плюсквамперфе́кт, давнопроше́дшее вре́мя
  ● *adj.* плюсквамперфе́ктный, давнопроше́дший

plural /'plʊər(ə)l/ *n.* мно́жественное число́
  ● *adj.*: **~ noun** существи́тельное во мно́жественном числе́

pluralism /'plʊərəlɪz(ə)m/ *n.* плюрали́зм

♂ **plus** /plʌs/ *n.* плюс
  ● *adj.* доба́вочный
  ● *prep.* плюс; **3 ~ 4 is 7** три плюс четы́ре — семь
  ■ **~ sign** *n.* (знак) плюс

plush /plʌʃ/ *n.* плюш
  ● *adj.* **1** (made of ~) плю́шевый **2** (sl., sumptuous) (*also* **plushy**) шика́рный

plutonium /pluː'təʊnɪəm/ *n.* плуто́ний

ply[1] /plaɪ/ *n.* (layer) слой; (strand) нить; **three-~** (plywood) трёхсло́йная фане́ра; **three-~ yarn** трёхни́точная пря́жа
  ■ **~wood** *n.* фане́ра ● *adj.* фане́рный

ply[2] /plaɪ/ *v.t.* **1** (work at): **he plies an honest trade** он зараба́тывает на хлеб че́стным трудо́м **2** (keep supplied) корми́ть, на-; **I was plied with food** меня́ хорошо́ накорми́ли
  ● *v.i.* (travel regularly) курси́ровать (*impf.*)

PM *abbr.* (*of* **Prime Minister**) премье́р-мини́стр

p.m. *abbr.* (*of* **post meridiem**) по́сле полу́дня; **at 3 p.m.** в три часа́ дня

PMT (BrE) *abbr.* (*of* **premenstrual tension**) предменструа́льное напряже́ние

pneumatic /njuː'mætɪk/ *adj.* пневмати́ческий
  ■ **~ drill** *n.* пневмати́ческий отбо́йный молото́к

pneumonia /njuː'məʊnɪə/ *n.* воспале́ние лёгких, пневмони́я

PO *abbr.* (*of* **Post Office**) по́чта
  ■ **~ box** *n.* абоне́нтский я́щик

poach[1] /pəʊtʃ/ *v.t.* (cul.) _вари́ть, с- на ме́дленном огне́; **~ed egg** яйцо́-пашо́т

poach[2] /pəʊtʃ/ *v.t. & i.*: **~ game** занима́ться (*impf.*) браконье́рством; браконье́рствовать (*impf.*)

poacher /'pəʊtʃə(r)/ *n.* браконье́р

pocket /'pɒkɪt/ *n.* **1** (in clothing) карма́н **2** (at billiards) лу́за **3** (*attr.*) (miniature) карма́нный

p

• *v.t.* (**pocketed, pocketing**) класть, положи́ть в карма́н

■ **-book** *n.* (AmE, handbag) су́мочка; (AmE, wallet) бума́жник; **~knife** *n.* карма́нный но́ж(ик); **~ money** *n.* (BrE) карма́нные де́ньги (-ег)

pod /pɒd/ *n.* стручо́к

podgy /'pɒdʒɪ/ *adj.* (**podgier, podgiest**) (BrE) то́лстенький, призе́мистый

podium /'pəʊdɪəm/ *n.* возвыше́ние/по́диум

⚘ **poem** /'pəʊɪm/ *n.* стихотворе́ние; (long narrative) поэ́ма

poet /'pəʊɪt/ *n.* поэ́т

poetic /pəʊ'etɪk/ *adj.* поэти́ческий

poetry /'pəʊɪtrɪ/ *n.* (also fig.) поэ́зия

pogrom /'pɒɡrəm/ *n.* погро́м

poignant /'pɔɪnjənt/ *adj.* о́стрый, го́рький

⚘ **point** /pɔɪnt/ *n.* **1** (sharp end) остриё **2** (tip) ко́нчик **3** (promontory) мыс **4** (dot) то́чка; **decimal ~** (in Russian usage) запята́я (*отделяющая десятичную дробь от целого числа*); **two ~ five (2.5)** две це́лых (и) пять деся́тых **5** (mark, position) ме́сто, пункт; **~ of view** то́чка зре́ния **6** (moment) моме́нт; **at this ~** he turned round в э́тот моме́нт/тут он поверну́лся; **I was on the ~ of leaving** я уже́ собра́лся уходи́ть **7** (unit, e.g. on shares index) едини́ца; **up to a ~** до изве́стной сте́пени **8** (unit of evaluation) пункт, очко́; **they won on ~s** они́ вы́играли по очка́м **9** (chief idea, meaning, purpose) суть, вопро́с, смысл; **that is beside the ~** не в э́том суть/де́ло; **come to the ~** до|ходи́ть, -йти́ до гла́вного/су́ти (де́ла); **I don't see the ~ of the joke** э́та шу́тка мне непоня́тна; **I made a ~ of seeing him** я счёл необходи́мым повида́ться с ним; **you missed the ~** вы не по́няли су́ти (де́ла); **there was no ~ in staying** не имело смы́сла остава́ться; **what's the ~ of it?** како́й в э́том смысл? **10** (item) пункт; **we agree on certain ~s** по не́которым пу́нктам мы схо́димся **11** (quality) черта́; **singing is not my strong ~** я не силён в пе́нии

• *v.t.* ука́з|ывать, -а́ть; пока́з|ывать, -а́ть; **he ~ed a gun at her** он навёл на неё пистоле́т

• *v.i.* ука́з|ывать, -а́ть (**at, to**: на + *a.*); **everything ~s to his guilt** всё ука́зывает на его́ вину́

□ **~ out** *v.t.* ука́з|ывать, -а́ть на + *a.*

■ **~-blank** *adj.* (lit.) прямо́й; (fig.) категори́ческий • *adv.* пря́мо, в упо́р

pointed /'pɔɪntɪd/ *adj.* **1** (e.g. a stick) острконе́чный **2** (significant) о́стрый, ко́лкий; подчёркнутый

pointer /'pɔɪntə(r)/ *n.* **1** (of balance etc.) стре́лка, указа́тель (*m.*) **2** (indication) намёк

pointing /'pɔɪntɪŋ/ *n.* (of wall etc.) расши́вка швов

pointless /'pɔɪntlɪs/ *adj.* бессмы́сленный

poise /pɔɪz/ *n.* уравнове́шенность, самооблада́ние

• *v.t.*: **he is ~d to attack** он гото́в к нападе́нию

poison /'pɔɪz(ə)n/ *n.* яд, отра́ва

• *v.t.* (lit., fig.) отрав|ля́ть, -и́ть; **food ~ing** пищево́е отравле́ние; **he has food ~ing** он отрави́лся

poisonous /'pɔɪz(ə)nəs/ *adj.* ядови́тый; (fig.) вре́дный

poke /pəʊk/ *n.* толчо́к

• *v.t.* **1** (prod) ты́кать, ткнуть; **to ~ the fire** меша́ть, по- у́гли в ками́не **2** (thrust) пиха́ть, пихну́ть/сова́ть, су́нуть; **he ~d his tongue out** он вы́сунул язы́к; **he ~s his nose into other people's business** он суёт нос не в своё де́ло

• *v.i.*: **he ~d about among the rubbish** он ры́лся в му́соре

poker /'pəʊkə(r)/ *n.* **1** (for a fire) кочерга́ **2** (game) по́кер

■ **~-faced** *adj.* с ка́менным лицо́м

poky /'pəʊkɪ/ *adj.* (**pokier, pokiest**) (infml) те́сный

Poland /'pəʊlənd/ *n.* По́льша

polar /'pəʊlə(r)/ *adj.* поля́рный

■ **~ bear** *n.* бе́лый медве́дь

Pole /pəʊl/ *n.* (person) поля́к (по́лька)

pole¹ /pəʊl/ *n.* (of earth, elec., and fig.) по́люс

■ **P~ Star** *n.* Поля́рная звезда́

pole² /pəʊl/ *n.* (post) столб, шест

■ **~ vault** *n.* прыжо́к с шесто́м; **~-vaulter** *n.* прыгу́н (-нья) с шесто́м, шестови́к

polemic /pə'lemɪk/ *n.* поле́мика, спор

• *adj.* (**also polemical**) полеми́ческий, спо́рный

⚘ **police** /pə'liːs/ *n.* поли́ция; (in Russia) мили́ция

• *v.t.* охраня́ть, подде́рживать (*both impf.*) поря́док в (+ *p.*)

■ **~ constable** *n.* (BrE) полице́йский; **~ force** *n.* поли́ция; **~man** *n.* полице́йский; (in Russia) милиционе́р; **~ officer** *n.* полице́йский; **~ station** *n.* (полице́йский) уча́сток; (in Russia) отделе́ние мили́ции; **~woman** *n.* же́нщина-полице́йский/милиционе́р

⚘ **policy** /'pɒlɪsɪ/ *n.* (planned action) поли́тика; (insurance) (страхово́й) по́лис

■ **~holder** *n.* держа́тель (*m.*) страхово́го по́лиса

polio /'pəʊlɪəʊ/ *n.* полиомиели́т

Polish /'pəʊlɪʃ/ *n.* (language) по́льский язы́к

• *adj.* по́льский

polish /'pɒlɪʃ/ *n.* **1** (brightness) полиро́вка **2** (substance used for ~ing) полирова́льная па́ста **3** (fig., refinement) лоск, блеск

• *v.t.* полирова́ть, от-; (metal, also fig.) шлифова́ть, от-

□ **~ off** *v.t.* (infml, finish) разде́л|ывать, -аться с + *i.*; поко́нчить (*pf.*) с + *i.*

polite /pə'laɪt/ *adj.* (**politer, politest**) ве́жливый

politic /'pɒlɪtɪk/ *adj.* **1** (prudent) благоразу́мный **2**: **the body ~** госуда́рство

⚘ **political** /pə'lɪtɪk(ə)l/ *adj.* полити́ческий; **~ly correct** полит(и́чески)корре́ктный

■ **~ correctness** *n.* полит(и́ческая) корре́ктность; **~ prisoner** *n.* полит(и́ческий) заключённый

⚘ **politician** /pɒlɪ'tɪʃ(ə)n/ *n.* поли́тик

politicize /pə'lɪtɪsaɪz/ *v.t.* политизи́ровать (*impf., pf.*)

⚘ ключева́я ле́ксика

ᵍ **politics** /'pɒlɪtɪks/ *n.* поли́тика; (political views) полити́ческие взгля́ды (*m. pl.*) /убежде́ния (*nt. pl.*)

ᵍ **poll** /pəʊl/ *n.* (voting process) голосова́ние; (opinion canvass) опро́с
• *v.t.* **1** (receive) получа́ть, -и́ть/наб|ира́ть, -ра́ть **2** (take votes of): **they ~ed the meeting** они́ поста́вили вопро́с на голосова́ние

pollen /'pɒlən/ *n.* цвето́чная пыльца́

pollinate /'pɒlɪneɪt/ *v.t.* опыл|я́ть, -и́ть

polling /'pəʊlɪŋ/ *n.* голосова́ние
■ **~ booth** *n.* (BrE) каби́на для голосова́ния; **~ day** *n.* день вы́боров; **~ station** *n.* избира́тельный уча́сток

pollutant /pə'luːtənt/ *n.* загрязни́тель (*m.*)

pollute /pə'luːt/ *v.t.* загрязн|я́ть, -и́ть

pollution /pə'luːʃ(ə)n/ *n.* загрязне́ние

polo /'pəʊləʊ/ *n.* по́ло (*nt. indecl.*)
■ **~ neck** *n.* (BrE) сви́тер с кру́глым высо́ким воротнико́м

polyester /pɒlɪ'estə(r)/ *n.* (fabric) полиэ́стер

polygamy /pə'lɪɡəmɪ/ *n.* полига́мия

polygon /'pɒlɪɡɒn/ *n.* многоуго́льник

Polynesia /pɒlɪ'niːʒə/ *n.* Полине́зия

Polynesian /pɒlɪ'niːʒ(ə)n/ *n.* полинези́|ец (~йка)
• *adj.* полинези́йский

polyp /'pɒlɪp/ *n.* (zool., med.) поли́п

polystyrene /pɒlɪ'staɪriːn/ *n.* полистиро́л

polytechnic /pɒlɪ'teknɪk/ *n.* политехни́ческий институ́т

polythene /'pɒlɪθiːn/ *n.* (BrE) полиэтиле́н; (*attr.*) полиэтиле́новый

polyurethane /pɒlɪ'jʊərəθeɪn/ *n.* полиурета́н

pomegranate /'pɒmɪɡrænɪt/ *n.* (tree, fruit) грана́т

pomp /pɒmp/ *n.* пы́шность, по́мпа

pompom /'pɒmpɒm/, **pompon** /'pɒmpɒn/ *nn.* (tuft) помпо́н

pomposity /pɒm'pɒsɪtɪ/ *n.* помпе́зность; (of person) напы́щенность

pompous /'pɒmpəs/ *adj.* помпе́зный; (of person) напы́щенный

poncho /'pɒntʃəʊ/ *n.* (*pl.* ~s) по́нчо (*nt. indecl.*)

pond /pɒnd/ *n.* пруд

ponder /'pɒndə(r)/ *v.t.* обду́м|ывать, -ать
• *v.i.* размышля́ть (*impf.*)

pong /pɒŋ/ *n.* (BrE, infml) вонь, злово́ние

pontiff /'pɒntɪf/ *n.*: **supreme ~** (the Pope) Па́па Ри́мский

pontificate /pɒn'tɪfɪkeɪt/ *v.i.* (fig., speak pompously) веща́ть (*impf.*) (*говорить важно, напыщенно*)

pony /'pəʊnɪ/ *n.* (horse) по́ни (*m. indecl.*)
■ **~tail** *n.* хво́стик (*причёска*)

poodle /'puːd(ə)l/ *n.* пу́дель (*m.*)

ᵍ **pool¹** /puːl/ *n.* (small body of water) пруд; (puddle) лу́жа; (*in full* **swimming ~**) (пла́вательный) бассе́йн

pool² /puːl/ *n.* **1** (total of staked money) совоку́пность ста́вок; (in cards) банк; **football**

~s футбо́льный тотализа́тор **2** (common reserve) о́бщий фонд **3** (billiards game) пул
• *v.t.* объедин|я́ть, -и́ть (в о́бщий фонд)

ᵍ **poor** /pɔː(r)/ *n.* (collect.): **the ~** беднота́, бедняки́ (*m. pl.*), бе́дные (*pl.*)
• *adj.* **1** (indigent) бе́дный **2** (unfortunate) бе́дный, несча́стный **3** (small) ску́дный; плохо́й; **a ~ harvest** ни́зкий урожа́й **4** (of low quality) плохо́й; **~ health** плохо́е здоро́вье

poorly /'pɔːlɪ/ *adj.* нездоро́вый
• *adv.* пло́хо; **this book is ~ written** э́та кни́га пло́хо напи́сана

pop¹ /pɒp/ *n.* (explosive sound) щелчо́к, хлопо́к; (infml, gaseous drink) газиро́вка
• *adv.*: **the balloon went ~** ша́рик ло́пнул
• *v.t.* (**popped, popping**) **1** (cause to explode): **~ a balloon** прок|а́лывать, -оло́ть ша́рик **2** (put suddenly) сова́ть, су́нуть
• *v.i.* (**popped, popping**) (make explosive sound) хло́п|ать, -нуть, щёлк|ать, -нуть
• *with advs.* (infml): **they ~ped in for a drink** они́ заскочи́ли/забежа́ли вы́пить; **she kept ~ping out all day** она́ весь день куда́-то выска́кивала; **he ~ped up unexpectedly** он появи́лся неожи́данно
■ **~corn** *n.* попко́рн, возду́шная кукуру́за; **~-up** *n.* (comput.) всплыва́ющее окно́

ᵍ **pop²** /pɒp/ *n.* (infml, music) поп-му́зыка
• *adj.*: **~ group** поп-гру́ппа; **~ star** поп-звезда́

pope /pəʊp/ *n.* (*also* **the Pope**) Па́па Ри́мский (*m.*)

poplar /'pɒplə(r)/ *n.* то́поль (*m.*)

poppy /'pɒpɪ/ *n.* мак
■ **~ seed** *n.* мак

populace /'pɒpjʊləs/ *n.* (the masses) ма́ссы (*f. pl.*)

ᵍ **popular** /'pɒpjʊlə(r)/ *adj.* **1** (of the people) наро́дный **2** (of or for the masses): **the ~ press** ма́ссовая пре́сса/печа́ть **3** (generally liked) по́льзующийся о́бщей симпа́тией; **he is ~ with the ladies** он име́ет успе́х у же́нщин

popularity /pɒpjʊ'lærɪtɪ/ *n.* популя́рность; успе́х

popularize /'pɒpjʊləraɪz/ *v.t.* популяризи́ровать (*impf., pf.*)

populate /'pɒpjʊleɪt/ *v.t.* насел|я́ть, -и́ть

ᵍ **population** /pɒpjʊ'leɪʃ(ə)n/ *n.* населе́ние; жи́тели (*m. pl.*)

populous /'pɒpjʊləs/ *adj.* многолю́дный, густонаселённый

porcelain /'pɔːsəlɪn/ *n.* фарфо́р; (*attr.*) фарфо́ровый

porch /pɔːtʃ/ *n.* (covered entrance) крыльцо́; (AmE, veranda) вера́нда

porcupine /'pɔːkjʊpaɪn/ *n.* дикобра́з

pore¹ /pɔː(r)/ *n.* по́ра

pore² /pɔː(r)/ *v.i.*: **he likes to ~ over old books** он лю́бит сиде́ть над ста́рыми кни́гами

pork /pɔːk/ *n.* свини́на

porn /pɔːn/, **porno** /'pɔːnəʊ/ *nn.* (infml) порногра́фия, по́рно (*nt. indecl.*) (infml), порну́ха (infml)

pornographic /pɔːnə'ɡræfɪk/ *adj.* порнографи́ческий

p

pornography /pɔːˈnɒɡrəfɪ/ *n.* порногра́фия

porridge /ˈpɒrɪdʒ/ *n.* овся́ная ка́ша

port¹ /pɔːt/ *n.* (harbour) порт, га́вань; ~ of call порт захо́да

port² /pɔːt/ *n.* (wine) портве́йн

port³ /pɔːt/ *n.* (comput.) порт

port⁴ /pɔːt/ *n.* (left side) ле́вый борт
● *adj.* ле́вый; ~ **side** ле́вый борт; ~ **wind** ве́тер с ле́вого бо́рта

portable /ˈpɔːtəb(ə)l/ *adj.* портати́вный

portal /ˈpɔːt(ə)l/ *n.* (comput.) порта́л

portcullis /pɔːtˈkʌlɪs/ *n.* опускна́я решётка

portend /pɔːˈtend/ *v.t.* предвеща́ть (*impf.*)

portent /ˈpɔːt(ə)nt/ *n.* (omen) предзнаменова́ние; (marvel) чу́до

porter /ˈpɔːtə(r)/ *n.* **1** (carrier of luggage) носи́льщик **2** (AmE, sleeping car attendant) проводни́к **3** (BrE, doorkeeper) швейца́р

portfolio /pɔːtˈfəʊlɪəʊ/ *n.* (*pl.* ~**s**) **1** (case) портфе́ль (*m.*); (artist's) па́пка (*с образца́ми работ*); (fashion model's) портфо́лио (*nt. indecl.*) **2** (pol., fin.) портфе́ль (*m.*)

porthole /ˈpɔːthəʊl/ *n.* иллюмина́тор

portion /ˈpɔːʃ(ə)n/ *n.* (part, share) часть; до́ля; (of food) по́рция

portly /ˈpɔːtlɪ/ *adj.* (**portlier**, **portliest**) доро́дный, по́лный, ту́чный

portrait /ˈpɔːtrɪt/ *n.* портре́т

portray /pɔːˈtreɪ/ *v.t.* (depict, describe) рисова́ть, на- портре́т + *g.*; (act part of) игра́ть, сыгра́ть

portrayal /pɔːˈtreɪəl/ *n.* изображе́ние

Portugal /ˈpɔːtjʊɡ(ə)l/ *n.* Португа́лия

Portuguese /pɔːtjʊˈɡiːz/ *n.* (*pl.* ~) **1** (person) португа́л|ец (-ка) **2** (language) португа́льский язы́к
● *adj.* португа́льский

pose /pəʊz/ *n.* по́за
● *v.t.* (put forward) предлаг|а́ть, -ожи́ть; изл|ага́ть, -ожи́ть
● *v.i.* **1** (take up a position) пози́ровать (*impf.*); he ~**s as an expert** он выдаёт себя́ за знатока́/специали́ста **2** (behave in an affected way) рисова́ться (*impf.*)

poser /ˈpəʊzə(r)/ *n.* (problem) головоло́мка; (person) позёр

posh /pɒʃ/ *adj.* (infml) шика́рный; (people) све́тский

⚹ **position** /pəˈzɪʃ(ə)n/ *n.* **1** (place occupied by sb or sth) ме́сто, положе́ние **2** (situation) положе́ние; **that puts me in an awkward ~** э́то ста́вит меня́ в нело́вкое положе́ние; **I am not in a ~ to say** я не в состоя́нии сказа́ть **3** (attitude, opinion) пози́ция **4** (post) до́лжность, ме́сто
● *v.t.* поме|ща́ть, -сти́ть

⚹ **positive** /ˈpɒzɪtɪv/ *adj.* **1** (definite) несомне́нный, определённый **2** (certain) уве́ренный, убеждённый; **are you ~ you saw him?** вы уве́рены, что ви́дели его́? **3** (assertive) самоуве́ренный **4** (practical, helpful) позити́вный, конструкти́вный

5 (gram., math., elec., med.) положи́тельный
■ ~ **discrimination** *n.* дискримина́ция в по́льзу определённой гру́ппы

positively /ˈpɒzɪtɪvlɪ/ *adv.* (with conviction) с уве́ренностью; (definitely) несомне́нно; (for emphasis): **she was ~ rude to me** она́ была́ со мной про́сто груба́

possess /pəˈzes/ *v.t.* **1** (own, have) владе́ть (*impf.*) + *i.*; (good qualities) облада́ть (*impf.*) + *i.* **2** (influence) овлад|ева́ть, -е́ть; **whatever ~ed him to do that?** что его́ заста́вило поступи́ть таки́м о́бразом?

possession /pəˈzeʃ(ə)n/ *n.* **1** (ownership, occupation) владе́ние; **they took ~ of the house** они́ ста́ли владе́льцами до́ма **2** (property) иму́щество, со́бственность

possessive /pəˈzesɪv/ *n.* (gram.) притяжа́тельный паде́ж
● *adj.* **1** (gram.) притяжа́тельный **2** (of person) со́бственнический; (jealous) ревни́вый

⚹ **possibility** /pɒsɪˈbɪlɪtɪ/ *n.* возмо́жность; вероя́тность

⚹ **possible** /ˈpɒsɪb(ə)l/ *adj.* возмо́жный; **as soon as ~** как мо́жно скоре́е; **I have done everything ~ to help** я сде́лал всё возмо́жное, что́бы помо́чь

⚹ **possibly** /ˈpɒsɪblɪ/ *adv.* возмо́жно; **how can I ~ do that?** как же я могу́ э́то сде́лать?; **I can't ~ ~** я ника́к не смогу́

⚹ **post¹** /pəʊst/ *n.* (of wood, metal, etc.) столб
● *v.t.* (display publicly) выве́шивать, вы́весить; **the results will be ~ed (up) on the board** результа́ты бу́дут вы́вешены на доске́

⚹ **post²** /pəʊst/ *n.* (BrE, mail) по́чта; **by return of ~** с обра́тной по́чтой; **I must take these letters to the ~** я до́лжен отнести́ э́ти пи́сьма на по́чту; **if you hurry you will catch the ~** е́сли вы поспеши́те, то успе́ете до отпра́вки по́чты; **has the ~ come yet?** по́чта уже́ была́/пришла́?
● *v.t.* **1** (BrE, dispatch by mail) отпр|авля́ть, -а́вить по по́чте **2** (fig.) изве|ща́ть, -сти́ть; **keep me ~ed (of events)** держи́те меня́ в ку́рсе (дел)
■ ~**box** *n.* почто́вый я́щик; ~**card** *n.* откры́тка; ~**code** *n.* (BrE) почто́вый и́ндекс; ~**man** *n.* (BrE) почтальо́н; ~**mark** *n.* почто́вый ште́мпель; ~**office** *n.* по́чта; ~**woman** *n.* (BrE) почтальо́н, почтальо́нка (infml)

⚹ **post³** /pəʊst/ *n.* **1** (place of duty) пост; **at one's ~** на посту́ **2** (job) до́лжность, пост
● *v.t.* **1** (assign to place of duty) назн|ача́ть, -а́чить на до́лжность **2** (mil., guard, sentry) выставля́ть, вы́ставить

postage /ˈpəʊstɪdʒ/ *n.* почто́вые расхо́ды (*m. pl.*); почто́вый сбор

postal /ˈpəʊst(ə)l/ *adj.* почто́вый
■ ~ **order** *n.* (BrE) (де́нежный) почто́вый перево́д

post-date /pəʊstˈdeɪt/ *v.t.* **1** (give a date later than the actual one) дати́ровать (*impf.*) бо́лее по́здним число́м **2** (occur later than) сле́довать, по- за + *i.*

poste-haste /pəʊstˈheɪst/ *adv.* о́чень бы́стро, неме́дленно

⚹ ключева́я ле́ксика

poster /'pəʊstə(r)/ *n.* (placard) афи́ша, плака́т;
(advertising) по́стер

posterior /pɒ'stɪərɪə(r)/ *n.* зад
● *adj.* (subsequent) после́дующий; (behind)
за́дний

posterity /pɒ'sterɪtɪ/ *n.* пото́мк|и (-ов)

postgraduate /pəʊst'grædjʊət/ *n.*: ~ student
аспира́нт (-ка)
● *adj.* аспира́нтский

posthumous /'pɒstjʊməs/ *adj.* посме́ртный

post-impressionism /pəʊstɪm'preʃənɪz(ə)m/
n. постимпрессиони́зм

postmodern /pəʊst'mɒd(ə)n/ *adj.*
постмодерни́стский

postmodernism /pəʊst'mɒdənɪz(ə)m/ *n.*
постмодерни́зм

post-mortem /pəʊst'mɔːtəm/ *n.* вскры́тие
(тру́па), аутопси́я

postnatal /pəʊst'neɪt(ə)l/ *adj.* послеродово́й

post-operative /pəʊst'ɒpərətɪv/ *adj.*
послеопераци́онный

postpone /pəʊs'pəʊn/ *v.t.* отсро́чи|вать, -ть;
от|кла́дывать, -ложи́ть

postscript /'pəʊskrɪpt/ *n.* постскри́птум

postulate /'pɒstjʊleɪt/ *v.t.* постули́ровать
(*impf., pf.*)

posture /'pɒstʃə(r)/ *n.* оса́нка
● *v.i.* пози́ровать (*impf.*)

post-war /pəʊst'wɔː(r)/ *adj.* послевое́нный

posy /'pəʊzɪ/ *n.* буке́т цвето́в

pot[1] /pɒt/ *n.* горшо́к; ~s and pans ку́хонная
посу́да/у́тварь; a ~ of tea ча́йник с
зава́ренным ча́ем; his work is going to ~
(*infml*) его́ рабо́та идёт насма́рку
● *v.t.* (**potted, potting**) **1** (preserves)
консерви́ровать, за- **2** (plants) сажа́ть,
посади́ть в горшо́к **3** (fig., abridge): ~ted
history кра́ткая исто́рия **4** (billiards)
заг|оня́ть, -на́ть в лу́зу
■ ~ **belly** *n.* (большо́й) живо́т, пу́зо; ~**hole**
n. (in road) вы́боина; ~**holing** *n.* (BrE)
спелеоло́гия; ~ **plant** *n.* (BrE) горше́чное
расте́ние

pot[2] /pɒt/ *n.* (infml, marijuana) анаша́

potash /'pɒtæʃ/ *n.* пота́ш, углеки́слый ка́лий

potassium /pə'tæsɪəm/ *n.* ка́лий; (*attr.*)
ка́лиевый, кали́йный

potato /pə'teɪtəʊ/ *n.* (*pl.* ~**es**) (*collect., and in*
pl.) карто́фель (*m.*); (single ~) карто́фелина
■ ~ **chips** (AmE), ~ **crisps** (BrE) *nn. pl.*
хрустя́щий карто́фель, чи́пс|ы (*pl., g.* -ов)

potent /'pəʊt(ə)nt/ *adj.* (powerful) си́льный,
могу́щественный; (of alcoholic drink) кре́пкий

potential /pə'tenʃ(ə)l/ *n.* потенциа́л
● *adj.* потенциа́льный

potion /'pəʊʃ(ə)n/ *n.* насто́йка, сна́добье; love
~ любо́вный напи́ток

potter[1] /'pɒtə(r)/ *n.* гонча́р

potter[2] /'pɒtə(r)/ *v.i.* (e.g. in garden) копа́ться,
ковыря́ться (*both impf.*)

pottery /'pɒtərɪ/ *n.* кера́мика

potty[1] /'pɒtɪ/ *n.* (infml, chamber pot) горшо́к

potty[2] /'pɒtɪ/ *adj.* (**pottier, pottiest**) (BrE,
crazy) чо́кнутый (infml)

pouch /paʊtʃ/ *n.* су́мочка, мешо́чек;
(kangaroo's) су́мка

pouffe, pouf /puːf/ *n.* (seat) пуф

poultry /'pəʊltrɪ/ *n.* дома́шняя пти́ца
(*collect.*)

pounce /paʊns/ *v.i.* набр|а́сываться, -о́ситься;
the cat ~d on the mouse ко́шка бро́силась
на мы́шь

pound[1] /paʊnd/ *n.* **1** (weight) фунт **2** (money)
фунт (сте́рлингов)

pound[2] /paʊnd/ *n.* (enclosure) заго́н

pound[3] /paʊnd/ *v.t.* **1** (crush) разб|ива́ть,
-и́ть **2** (thump) колоти́ть (*impf.*)
● *v.i.* **1** (thump): he ~ed at the door он
колоти́л в дверь; her heart was ~ing
with excitement её се́рдце колоти́лось от
волне́ния **2** (run heavily) мча́ться/нести́сь
(*both impf.*) с гро́хотом

pour /pɔː(r)/ *v.t.* лить (*impf.*); нал|ива́ть,
-и́ть; will you ~ me (out) a cup of tea?
нале́йте мне, пожа́луйста, ча́шку ча́я; (fig.):
he ~ed scorn on the idea он вы́смеял э́ту
иде́ю
● *v.i.* ли́ться (*impf.*); (fig.): the crowd ~ed
out of the theatre толпа́ повали́ла из теа́тра
(infml); (of rain) лить (*impf.*) как из ведра́; it
was ~ing with rain шёл проливно́й дождь,
дождь лил как из ведра́
● with advs. (fig.): letters ~ed in посы́пались
пи́сьма; she ~ed out a tale of woe она́
излила́ своё го́ре

pout /paʊt/ *v.i.* над|ува́ть, -у́ть гу́бы; ду́ться, на-

poverty /'pɒvətɪ/ *n.* бе́дность, нищета́; on the
~ line на гра́ни нищеты́
■ ~-**stricken** *adj.* ни́щий

POW *abbr.* (*of* **prisoner of war**)
военнопле́нный

powder /'paʊdə(r)/ *n.* (chem., med., etc.)
порошо́к; (cosmetic) пу́дра
● *v.t.* **1** (reduce to ~) превра|ща́ть, -ти́ть в
порошо́к **2** (apply ~ to) пу́дрить, на-
■ ~ed milk *n.* порошко́вое/сухо́е молоко́

powdery /'paʊdərɪ/ *adj.* порошкообра́зный;
рассы́пчатый

power /'paʊə(r)/ *n.* **1** (ability, capacity) си́ла,
мощь; purchasing ~ покупа́тельная
спосо́бность **2** (*in pl.*) (faculties): he was
at the height of his ~s он был в расцве́те
сил **3** (vigour) эне́ргия **4** (electrical energy)
эне́ргия; there was a ~ cut электроэне́ргию
вре́менно отключи́ли; (mechanical energy)
мо́щность **5** (control) власть; I have him in my
~ он в мое́й вла́сти; in ~ у вла́сти **6** (right)
полномо́чия (*nt. pl.*), пра́во **7** (influential
person or organization) си́ла **8** (state) держа́ва
9 (supernatural force) си́ла **10** (infml, large
amount) ма́сса, мно́жество; this medicine
has done me a ~ of good э́то лека́рство
принесло́ мне огро́мную по́льзу **11** (math.):
two to the ~ of ten два в деся́той сте́пени
● *v.t.* (supply with electrical energy) снаб|жа́ть,
-ди́ть эне́ргией; (supply with mechanical energy)
прив|оди́ть, -ести́ в де́йствие

p

■ ~**boat** *n.* мото́рный ка́тер; ~ **drill** *n.* электри́ческая дрель; ~ **line** *n.* ли́ния электропереда́чи; ~-**point** *n.* штéпсельная розéтка; ~ **plant,** ~ **station** *nn.* электроста́нция

✓ **powerful** /'paʊəfəl/ *adj.* си́льный, мо́щный; a ~ **speech** я́ркая речь

powerless /'paʊəlɪs/ *adj.* бесси́льный

pp *abbr.* (*of* per procurationem): John Brown pp A. Smith по довéренности Джо́на Бра́уна подписа́л А. Смит

pp. *abbr.* (*of* **pages**) стр./сс. (страни́цы)

PR *abbr. of* **1** (**public relations**) пиа́р **2** (**proportional representation**) пропорциона́льное представи́тельство

practicable /'præktɪkəb(ə)l/ *adj.* (feasible) осуществи́мый, реа́льный

✓ **practical** /'præktɪk(ə)l/ *adj.* **1** (concerned with practice) практи́ческий; a ~ **joke** ро́зыгрыш, шу́тка; he is a ~ **man** он практи́чный человéк **2** (workable, feasible) осуществи́мый, реа́льный

practicality /præktɪ'kælɪtɪ/ *n.* практи́чность

practically /'præktɪkəlɪ/ *adv.* **1** (in a practical manner) практи́чески; на дéле **2** (almost) практи́чески, факти́чески

✓ **practice** /'præktɪs/ *n.* **1** (performance) пра́ктика; the idea will not work in ~ э́та идéя на пра́ктике неосуществи́ма **2** (habitual performance) обы́чай, обыкновéние **3** (repeated exercise) упражнéние, трениро́вка, пра́ктика; I am badly out of ~ я давно́ не упражня́лся/ практикова́лся **4** (work of doctor, lawyer, etc.) пра́ктика
● *v.t. & i.* (AmE) = **practise**

✓ **practis|e** /'præktɪs/ (AmE **practice**) *v.t.* **1** (perform habitually) дéлать, с- по привы́чке; (for exercise) упражня́ть (*impf.*) отраб|а́тывать, -о́тать; (sport, game, etc.) упражня́ться (*impf.*) в + *p.*; (instrument): she was ~ing the piano она́ упражня́лась на роя́ле/фортепиа́но **2** (a profession etc.) практикова́ть (*impf.*); a ~ing physician практику́ющий врач
● *v.i.* упражня́ться (*impf.*); трениров́аться (*impf.*)

practitioner /præk'tɪʃənə(r)/ *n.* практику́ющий специали́ст

pragmatic /præg'mætɪk/ *adj.* прагмати́ческий

pragmatism /'prægmətɪz(ə)m/ *n.* прагмати́зм

pragmatist /'prægmətɪst/ *n.* прагма́тик

Prague /prɑːɡ/ *n.* Пра́га

prairie /'preərɪ/ *n.* прéрия

✓ **praise** /preɪz/ *n.* похвала́
● *v.t.* (voice admiration of) хвали́ть, по-; (give glory to) восхвал|я́ть, -и́ть
■ ~**worthy** *adj.* досто́йный похвалы́, похва́льный

pram /præm/ *n.* (BrE) (дéтская) коля́ска

prance /prɑːns/ *v.i.* (of horse) гарцева́ть (*impf.*); (of person) ва́жничать (*impf.*)

prank /præŋk/ *n.* вы́ходка, продéлка

prankster /'præŋkstə(r)/ *n.* шутни́к, прока́зник

prat /præt/ *n.* (BrE, infml, idiot) идио́т (-ка)

prattle /'præt(ə)l/ *n.* болтовня́; (childish) лéпет
● *v.i.* болта́ть (*impf.*); (of child) лепета́ть, про-

prawn /prɔːn/ *n.* кревéтка

pray /preɪ/ *v.i.* моли́ться, по-; the farmers ~ed for rain фéрмеры моли́ли Бо́га, что́бы пошёл дождь; we will ~ for the Queen мы бу́дем моли́ться за короле́ву

prayer /'preə(r)/ *n.* моли́тва; say one's ~s моли́ться, по-

preach /priːtʃ/ *v.t.* проповéдовать (*impf.*)
● *v.i.* чита́ть про́поведь

preacher /'priːtʃə(r)/ *n.* проповéдник

preamble /priː'æmb(ə)l/ *n.* преа́мбула

prearrange /priːə'reɪndʒ/ *v.t.* организо́в|ывать, -а́ть зара́нее

precarious /prɪ'keərɪəs/ *adj.* **1** (uncertain) ненадёжный; a ~ **foothold** ненадёжная опо́ра **2** (dangerous, risky) опа́сный, риско́ванный

precaution /prɪ'kɔːʃ(ə)n/ *n.* предосторо́жность

precautionary /prɪ'kɔːʃənərɪ/ *adj.* предупреди́тельный

precede /prɪ'siːd/ *v.t.* предшéствовать (*impf.*) + *d.*

precedence /'presɪd(ə)ns/ *n.* первоочерёдность; this question takes ~ э́тот вопро́с до́лжен рассма́триваться в пéрвую о́чередь

precedent /'presɪd(ə)nt/ *n.* прецедéнт; set a ~ созд|ава́ть, -а́ть прецедéнт

precept /'priːsept/ *n.* (moral instruction) наставлéние; (rule) пра́вило

precinct /'priːsɪŋkt/ *n.* **1** (BrE, area of restricted access): pedestrian ~ пешехо́дная зо́на; shopping ~ торго́вый центр **2** (AmE, police or electoral district) уча́сток

precious /'preʃəs/ *adj.* (valued) цéнный; (stone) драгоцéнный

precipice /'presɪpɪs/ *n.* про́пасть, обры́в

precipitate[1] /prɪ'sɪpɪtət/ *adj.* (rash) опромéтчивый

precipitate[2] /prɪ'sɪpɪteɪt/ *v.t.* **1** вв|ерга́ть, -éргнуть; the country was ~d into war страну́ ввéргли в войну́ **2** (bring on rapidly) уск|оря́ть, -о́рить

precipitation /prɪsɪpɪ'teɪʃ(ə)n/ *n.* (rain etc.) оса́д|ки (-ов)

precipitous /prɪ'sɪpɪtəs/ *adj.* (steep) обры́вистый, круто́й; (hasty) поспéшный

precise /prɪ'saɪs/ *adj.* то́чный, аккура́тный

precisely /prɪ'saɪslɪ/ *adv.* то́чно; (with numbers or quantities) ро́вно; (as reply: 'quite so') совершéнно вéрно; вот и́менно

precision /prɪ'sɪʒ(ə)n/ *n.* то́чность; аккура́тность

preclude /prɪ'kluːd/ *v.t.* (prevent) предотвра|ща́ть, -ти́ть; (make impossible) исключ|а́ть, -и́ть

✓ ключева́я лéксика

precocious /prɪˈkəʊʃəs/ *adj.* ра́но
развившийся; ра́нний

preconceived /priːkənˈsiːvd/ *adj.* предвзя́тый

preconception /priːkənˈsepʃ(ə)n/ *n.*
предвзя́тое мне́ние

precondition /priːkənˈdɪʃ(ə)n/ *n.*
предвари́тельное усло́вие

precursor /priːˈkɜːsə(r)/ *n.* предше́ственни|к
(-ца); (of event) предве́стник

pre-date /priːˈdeɪt/ *v.t.* предше́ствовать
(*impf.*) + *d.*

predator /ˈpredətə(r)/ *n.* хи́щник

predatory /ˈpredətərɪ/ *adj.* хи́щный

predecease /priːdɪˈsiːs/ *v.t.:* he ~d her он
у́мер ра́ньше её

predecessor /ˈpriːdɪsesə(r)/ *n.*
предше́ственни|к (-ца)

predetermine /priːdɪˈtɜːmɪn/ *v.t.*
предреш|а́ть, -и́ть

predicament /prɪˈdɪkəmənt/ *n.* тру́дное
положе́ние

predicate /ˈpredɪkət/ *n.* (gram.) сказу́емое

predicative /prɪˈdɪkətɪv/ *adj.* (gram.)
предикати́вный

♂ **predict** /prɪˈdɪkt/ *v.t.* предска́з|ывать, -а́ть

predictable /prɪˈdɪktəb(ə)l/ *adj.*
предска́зуемый

prediction /prɪˈdɪkʃ(ə)n/ *n.* предсказа́ние

predilection /priːdɪˈlekʃ(ə)n/ *n.* пристра́стие,
скло́нность (for: к + *d.*)

predispose /priːdɪˈspəʊz/ *v.t.*
предраспол|ага́ть, -ожи́ть

predominance /prɪˈdɒmɪnəns/ *n.* (control;
superiority) госпо́дство; (preponderance)
преоблада́ние

predominant /prɪˈdɒmɪnənt/ *adj.*
преоблада́ющий

predominantly /prɪˈdɒmɪnəntlɪ/ *adv.*
преиму́щественно

predominate /prɪˈdɒmɪneɪt/ *v.i.* преоблада́ть
(*impf.*)

pre-eminence /priːˈemɪnəns/ *n.*
превосхо́дство, преиму́щество

pre-eminent /priːˈemɪnənt/ *adj.* выдаю́щийся

pre-empt /priːˈempt/ *v.t.* предупре|жда́ть, -ди́ть

pre-emptive /priːˈemptɪv/ *adj.:* ~ strike
упрежда́ющий уда́р

preen /priːn/ *v.t.* (of bird): ~ one's feathers
чи́стить, по- пе́рья; (of person): ~ oneself
прихор|а́шиваться, -оши́ться (infml)

prefabricate /priːˈfæbrɪkeɪt/ *v.t.:* ~d house
(*or* infml **prefab**) сбо́рный дом

preface /ˈprefəs/ *n.* предисло́вие

prefect /ˈpriːfekt/ *n.* (BrE, at school) ста́роста (*c.g.*)

♂ **prefer** /prɪˈfɜː(r)/ *v.t.* (**preferred, preferring**)
1 (like better) предпоч|ита́ть, -е́сть; I ~ juice
to water я предпочита́ю сок воде́ **2** (submit):
~ charges предъяв|ля́ть, -и́ть обвине́ния

preferable /ˈprefərəb(ə)l/ *adj.*
предпочти́тельный

preference /ˈprefərəns/ *n.* предпочте́ние

preferential /prefəˈrenʃ(ə)l/ *adj.*
предпочти́тельный; льго́тный

prefix /ˈpriːfɪks/ *n.* приста́вка, пре́фикс

pregnancy /ˈpregnənsɪ/ *n.* бере́менность

pregnant /ˈpregnənt/ *adj.* бере́менная;
become ~ забере́менеть (*pf.*)

preheat /priːˈhiːt/ *v.t.* предвари́тельно
подогр|ева́ть, -е́ть

prehistoric /priːhɪˈstɒrɪk/ *adj.*
доистори́ческий

prejudge /priːˈdʒʌdʒ/ *v.t.* предреш|а́ть, -и́ть

prejudice /ˈpredʒʊdɪs/ *n.* предрассу́док,
предубежде́ние
• *v.t.* **1** (cause to have a ~): you are ~d
against him вы отно́ситесь к нему́ с
предубежде́нием **2** (harm) нан|оси́ть, -ести́
ущерб + *d.*

prejudiced /ˈpredʒʊdɪst/ *adj.* предубеждённый

preliminary /prɪˈlɪmɪnərɪ/ *adj.*
предвари́тельный

prelude /ˈpreljuːd/ *n.* (mus., fig.) прелю́дия

premarital /priːˈmærɪt(ə)l/ *adj.* доба́рачный

premature /preməˈtjʊə(r)/ *adj.*
преждевре́менный
■ ~ baby *n.* недоно́шенный ребёнок

premeditate /priːˈmedɪteɪt/ *v.t.:* ~d murder
преднаме́ренное уби́йство

premenstrual /priːˈmenstrʊəl/ *adj.*
предменструа́льный

premier /ˈpremɪə(r)/ *n.* премье́р(-мини́стр)
• *adj.* пе́рвый; гла́вный

premiere /ˈpremɪeə(r)/ *n.* премье́ра

premiership /ˈpremɪəʃɪp/ *n.* премье́рство

premise /ˈpremɪs/ *n.* (phil.) посы́лка;
предположе́ние

premises /ˈpremɪsɪz/ *n. pl.* помеще́ние

premium /ˈpriːmɪəm/ *n.* (*pl.* ~s) **1** (payment
for insurance) (страхова́я) пре́мия **2** (additional
payment) приплата **3**: at a ~ вы́ше номина́ла

premonition /preməˈnɪʃ(ə)n/ *n.* предчу́вствие

prenatal /priːˈneɪt(ə)l/ *adj.* предродово́й

preoccupation /priːɒkjʊˈpeɪʃ(ə)n/ *n.*
озабо́ченность

preoccupy /priːˈɒkjʊpaɪ/ *v.t.* забо́тить, о-

preparation /prepəˈreɪʃ(ə)n/ *n.* подгото́вка,
приготовле́ние; she was packing in ~ for
the journey она́ укла́дывала ве́щи, гото́вясь
к пое́здке; (in pl.) (preparatory measures)
приготовле́ния (nt. pl.)

preparatory /prɪˈpærətərɪ/ *adj.*
подготови́тельный

♂ **prepare** /prɪˈpeə(r)/ *v.t.* гото́вить (*impf.*);
пригот|а́вливать, -о́вить; подгот|а́вливать,
-о́вить; the tutor ~d him for his exams
учи́тель подгото́вил его́ к экза́менам
• *v.i.* подгот|а́вливаться, -о́виться;
пригот|а́вливаться, -о́виться

preponderance /prɪˈpɒndərəns/ *n.* переве́с,
преиму́щество

preposition /prepəˈzɪʃ(ə)n/ *n.* (gram.) предло́г

prepositional /prepəˈzɪʃənəl/ *n. & adj.* (gram.)
предло́жный (паде́ж)

prepossessing /priːpəˈzesɪŋ/ *adj.*
располага́ющий, привлека́тельный

p

preposterous /prɪ'pɒstərəs/ *adj.*
возмути́тельный

prerequisite /pri:'rekwɪzɪt/ *n.* предпосы́лка

prerogative /prɪ'rɒgətɪv/ *n.* (of ruler, etc.)
прерогати́ва; (privilege) привиле́гия

Presbyterian /ˌprezbɪ'tɪəriən/ *n.*
пресвитериа́н|ин (-ка)
● *adj.* пресвитериа́нский

preschool /ˈpriːskuːl/ *adj.* дошко́льный

prescribe /prɪ'skraɪb/ *v.t.* **1** (impose)
предпи́с|ывать, -а́ть **2** (med.) пропи́с|ывать,
-а́ть

prescription /prɪ'skrɪpʃ(ə)n/ *n.* (from doctor)
реце́пт; (medicine) лека́рство

prescriptive /prɪ'skrɪptɪv/ *adj.* (imposing a rule
or method) предпи́сывающий

♂ **presence** /ˈprez(ə)ns/ *n.* прису́тствие; ~ of
mind прису́тствие ду́ха

♂ **present¹** /ˈprez(ə)nt/ *n.* **1** (time now at hand)
настоя́щее (вре́мя); at ~ в настоя́щее вре́мя;
сейча́с **2** (gram., ~ tense) настоя́щее вре́мя
● *adj.* **1** (at hand) прису́тствующий; no one
else was ~ никого́ бо́льше не́ было
2 (in question) да́нный; in the ~ case в
да́нном слу́чае **3** (existent) настоя́щий;
at the ~ time в настоя́щее вре́мя;
сейча́с; under ~ circumstances в да́нных
обстоя́тельствах **4** (gram.) настоя́щего
вре́мени
■ ~**-day** *adj.* совреме́нный, ны́нешний; ~
participle *n.* прича́стие настоя́щего вре́мени

present² /ˈprez(ə)nt/ *n.* (gift) пода́рок

♂ **present³** /prɪ'zent/ *v.t.* **1** (offer, put forward)
дари́ть, по-; вруч|а́ть, -и́ть; преподн|оси́ть,
-ести́; as soon as an opportunity ~s itself как
то́лько предста́вится слу́чай; he ~ed his case
well он хорошо́ изложи́л свои́ до́воды; (give)
предост|авля́ть, -а́вить; I was ~ed with a
choice мне предоста́вили вы́бор **2** (introduce)
предст|авля́ть, -а́вить

presentable /prɪ'zentəb(ə)l/ *adj.* прили́чный

♂ **presentation** /ˌprezən'teɪʃ(ə)n/ *n.* **1** (making a
present) подноше́ние, вруче́ние **2** (production)
предъявле́ние **3** (exposition) изложе́ние,
пода́ча

presenter /prɪ'zentə(r)/ *n.* (TV, radio) веду́щ|ий
(-ая)

presentiment /prɪ'zentɪmənt/ *n.*
предчу́вствие; he had a ~ of danger он
предчу́вствовал опа́сность

presently /ˈprezntlɪ/ *adv.* (soon) вско́ре;
(AmE, at present) сейча́с, в настоя́щее вре́мя, в
да́нный моме́нт

preservation /ˌprezə'veɪʃ(ə)n/ *n.* (act of
preserving) сохране́ние; консерви́рование;
(of materials) консерва́ция; (of monuments, etc.)
охра́на

preservative /prɪ'zɜ:vətɪv/ *n.* (in food)
консерва́нт

preserve /prɪ'zɜ:v/ *n.* **1** (jam) варе́нье **2** (area for
protection of game, etc.) запове́дник
● *v.t.* **1** (save; protect) сохран|я́ть, -и́ть **2** (keep

from decomposition, etc.) консерви́ровать, за-
3 (maintain) подде́рж|ивать, -а́ть; храни́ть, со-

preside /prɪ'zaɪd/ *v.i.* председа́тельствовать
(*impf.*)

presidency /ˈprezɪdənsɪ/ *n.* президе́нтство

♂ **president** /ˈprezɪd(ə)nt/ *n.* (of state, bank, etc.)
президе́нт

presidential /ˌprezɪ'denʃ(ə)l/ *adj.*
президе́нтский

♂ **press** /pres/ *n.* **1** (act of ~ing): she gave his
trousers a ~ она́ погла́дила ему́ брю́ки
2 (machine for ~ing or printing) пресс
3 (newspaper world) печа́ть, пре́сса; (newspaper
reaction) о́тклик, реце́нзия; a good ~ helps
to sell a book хоро́шие о́тклики в печа́ти
спосо́бствуют сбы́ту кни́ги
● *v.t.* **1** (exert physical pressure on) наж|има́ть,
-а́ть; ~ the button наж|има́ть, -а́ть (на)
кно́пку **2** (push) приж|има́ть, -а́ть; he ~ed
his nose against the window он прижа́л
нос к окну́ **3** (iron) гла́дить, по- **4** (clasp)
сжима́ть, сжать; he ~ed her hand он сжал
ей ру́ку **5** (fig., sustain vigorously): ~ charges
выдвига́ть, вы́двинуть обвине́ние **6** (urge):
they ~ed me to stay они́ угова́ривали меня́
оста́ться
● *v.i.*: if you ~ too hard, the pencil will
break е́сли сли́шком нажима́ть, каранда́ш
слома́ется (*impf.*); ~ for (reform, enqiury, etc.)
добива́ться (*impf.*) + g.
□ ~ forward *v.i.* прот|а́лкиваться, -олкну́ться
(вперёд)
□ ~ on *v.i.* продолжа́ть (*impf.*)
■ ~ agency *n.* аге́нтство печа́ти; ~
conference *n.* пресс-конфере́нция; ~ stud
n. (BrE) кно́пка (на оде́жде); ~-up *n.* (BrE)
отжима́ние; do ~-ups отж|има́ться, -а́ться
(от по́ла)

pressing /ˈpresɪŋ/ *adj.* настоя́тельный,
неотло́жный

♂ **pressure** /ˈpreʃə(r)/ *n.* **1** давле́ние
2 (compulsive influence) давле́ние, возде́йствие;
put ~ on ока́з|ывать, -а́ть давле́ние/нажи́м
на + a.; наж|има́ть, -а́ть на + a. (infml)
■ ~ cooker *n.* скорова́рка; ~ group *n.* ≈
инициати́вная гру́ппа; движе́ние

pressurize /ˈpreʃəraɪz/ *v.t.* **1** гермети́зировать
(*impf.*) **2** (fig.) ока́з|ывать, -а́ть давле́ние на
+ a.; he was ~d into writing a confession его́
заста́вили написа́ть призна́ние

prestige /pre'sti:ʒ/ *n.* прести́ж

prestigious /pre'stɪdʒəs/ *adj.* прести́жный

presumably /prɪ'zju:məblɪ/ *adv.* вероя́тно

presume /prɪ'zju:m/ *v.t.* **1** (assume) полага́ть
(*impf.*) **2** (with inf.: venture) брать, взять на
себя́ сме́лость; I would not ~ to argue with
you я не возьму́ на себя́ сме́лость с ва́ми
спо́рить

presumptuous /prɪ'zʌmptʃʊəs/ *adj.*
самонаде́янный

presuppose /ˌpri:sə'pəʊz/ *v.t.* (заране́е)
предпол|ага́ть, -ожи́ть; допус|ка́ть, -ти́ть

pre-tax /ˈpri:tæks/ *adj.* до вы́чета нало́гов

♂ ключева́я ле́ксика

pretence /prɪˈtens/ (AmE **pretense**) *n.*
1 (pretending) притво́рство; he made a ~
of reading the newspaper он притвори́лся,
что чита́ет газе́ту; **by/under/on false** ~s
обма́нным путём **2** (pretext, excuse) предло́г;
he called under the ~ of asking advice он
зашёл под предло́гом спроси́ть сове́та

pretend /prɪˈtend/ *v.t. & i.* притворя́ться
(*impf.*); де́лать (*impf.*) вид; she is ~ing to be
asleep она́ притворя́ется, что спит; ~ to be
pirates игра́ть в пира́тов (*о детях*)

pretense /prɪˈtens/ *n.* (AmE) = pretence

pretension /prɪˈtenʃ(ə)n/ *n.* претенцио́зность

pretentious /prɪˈtenʃəs/ *adj.* претенцио́зный;
показно́й

pretext /ˈpriːtekst/ *n.* предло́г; on/under the
~ of под предло́гом + *g.*

ꝺ **pretty** /ˈprɪtɪ/ *adj.* (**prettier, prettiest**)
краси́вый, хоро́шенький
● *adv.* доста́точно, дово́льно; ~ **much** (nearly)
почти́

prevail /prɪˈveɪl/ *v.i.* **1** (win) торжествова́ть,
вос-; (of idea) возобладáть (*impf.*) **2** (be
widespread) преоблада́ть (*impf.*); ~ing
winds преоблада́ющие ве́тры **3**: ~ (up)on
(persuade) убе|жда́ть, -ди́ть

prevalence /ˈprevələns/ *n.* распростране́ние

prevalent /ˈprevələnt/ *adj.*
распространённый

ꝺ **prevaricate** /prɪˈværɪkeɪt/ *v.i.* виля́ть (*impf.*)

prevarication /prɪˌværɪˈkeɪʃ(ə)n/ *n.* ува́ливание

ꝺ **prevent** /prɪˈvent/ *v.t.* (stop happening)
предотвра|ща́ть, -ти́ть; (make unable to do)
меша́ть, по- + *d.*; illness ~ed him from
coming боле́знь помеша́ла ему́ прийти́

preventable /prɪˈventəb(ə)l/ *adj.*
предотврати́мый

preventative /prɪˈventətɪv/ *adj.* = preventive

prevention /prɪˈvenʃ(ə)n/ *n.*
предотвраще́ние, предупрежде́ние

preventive /prɪˈventɪv/ *adj.*
предупреди́тельный
■ ~ **medicine** *n.* профила́ктика

preview /ˈpriːvjuː/ *n.* (of film)
(предвари́тельный) просмо́тр; (of exhibition)
верниса́ж

ꝺ **previous** /ˈpriːvɪəs/ *adj.* (earlier, former)
предыду́щий

ꝺ **previously** /ˈpriːvɪəslɪ/ *adv.* ра́ньше

pre-war /priːˈwɔː(r)/ *adj.* довое́нный,
предвое́нный

prey /preɪ/ *n.* добы́ча
● *v.i.* охо́титься (*impf.*); owls ~ on mice со́вы
охо́тятся на мыше́й; (fig.): the crime ~ed
upon his mind (соверше́нное) преступле́ние
мучи́ло его́, не дава́ло ему́ поко́я

ꝺ **price** /praɪs/ *n.* **1** цена́; they wanted peace
at any ~ им ну́жен был мир любо́й цено́й
2 (value) це́нность
● *v.t.* (fix ~ of) оце́н|ивать, -и́ть
■ ~ **list** *n.* прейскура́нт; ~ **tag** *n.* це́нник,
ярлы́к (*с указанием цены*)

priceless /ˈpraɪslɪs/ *adj.* (invaluable) бесце́нный;
(infml, amusing) беспод́обный

pricey /ˈpraɪsɪ/ *adj.* (**pricier, priciest**) (infml)
дорого́й

prick /prɪk/ *n.* шип; колю́чка
● *v.t.* прок|а́лывать, -оло́ть
□ ~ **up** *v.t.*: ~ **up one's ears** навостри́ть (*pf.*) у́ши

prickle /ˈprɪk(ə)l/ *n.* (thorn) колю́чка, шип; (of
hedgehog etc.) игла́
● *v.t. & i.* коло́ть(ся), у-

prickly /ˈprɪklɪ/ *adj.* (**pricklier, prickliest**)
(having spines or thorns) колю́чий; (causing a
prickling sensation) ко́лкий, ко́лющий(ся); (fig.,
easily offended) оби́дчивый

pride /praɪd/ *n.* го́рдость; he takes ~ in his
work он горди́тся свое́й рабо́той
● *v.t.*: ~ **oneself on** горди́ться (*impf.*) + *i.*

priest /priːst/ *n.* свяще́нник

priesthood /ˈpriːsthʊd/ *n.* свяще́нство

prig /prɪg/ *n.* педа́нт; (hypocrite) ханжа́ (*c.g.*)

priggish /ˈprɪgɪʃ/ *adj.* педанти́чный;
(hypocritical) ха́нжеский

prim /prɪm/ *adj.* (**primmer, primmest**)
(*also* ~ **and proper**) чо́порный

prima /ˈpriːmə/ *adj.*: ~ **ballerina** при́ма-
балери́на; ~ **donna** (lit.) примадо́нна, ди́ва;
(fig.) примадо́нна

primarily /ˈpraɪmərɪlɪ/ *adv.* (principally) в
основно́м

ꝺ **primary** /ˈpraɪmərɪ/ *n.* (AmE, election)
предвари́тельные вы́бор|ы (-ов)
● *adj.* **1** (original) первонача́льный **2** (basic,
principal) основно́й; of ~ **importance**
первостепе́нной ва́жности
■ ~ **colours,** (AmE) ~ **colors** *n. pl.* основны́е
цвета́; ~ **school** *n.* (BrE) нача́льная шко́ла

primate /ˈpraɪmeɪt/ *n.* (archbishop) прима́с;
(mammal) прима́т

prime /praɪm/ *n.*: in the ~ of life в расцве́те
сил; he is past his ~ его́ лу́чшие дни/го́ды
(оста́лись) позади́
● *adj.* **1** (principal) гла́вный **2** (best) лу́чший;
~ **beef** говя́дина вы́сшего со́рта
● *v.t.* **1** (firearm) заря|жа́ть, -ди́ть; (engine,
pump) запр|авля́ть, -а́вить **2** (supply with facts
etc.) инструкти́ровать (*impf., pf.*)
■ ~ **minister** *n.* премье́р-мини́стр; ~
number *n.* (math.) просто́е число́; ~ **time** *n.*
(TV, radio) прайм-та́йм

primeval /praɪˈmiːv(ə)l/ *adj.* первобы́тный

primitive /ˈprɪmɪtɪv/ *adj.* примити́вный; (of
earliest man, tribes) первобы́тный

primordial /praɪˈmɔːdɪəl/ *adj.* перви́чный,
первобы́тный; (fundamental) основно́й

primrose /ˈprɪmrəʊz/ *n.* первоцве́т (*лесное
растение*)

primula /ˈprɪmjʊlə/ *n.* при́мула

prince /prɪns/ *n.* князь (*m.*); (son of royalty) принц

princely /ˈprɪnslɪ/ *adj.* (**princelier,
princeliest**) кня́жеский; (splendid)
великоле́пный; (generous): ~ **sum** ца́рская
су́мма

princess /prɪnˈses/ *n.* принце́сса

p

principal /ˈprɪnsɪp(ə)l/ *n.* дире́ктор, ре́ктор ● *adj.* гла́вный, основно́й

principality /ˌprɪnsɪˈpælɪtɪ/ *n.* кня́жество

principally /ˈprɪnsɪpəlɪ/ *adv.* гла́вным о́бразом, преиму́щественно

⚘ **principle** /ˈprɪnsɪp(ə)l/ *n.* при́нцип, нача́ло; in ∼ в при́нципе; on ∼ из при́нципа

⚘ **print** /prɪnt/ *n.* **1** (mark made on surface by pressure) след; отпеча́ток **2** (letters, etc.) шрифт; печа́ть; the book is in ∼ кни́га ещё продаётся; the book is out of ∼ кни́га бо́льше не продаётся **3** (picture) гравю́ра, эста́мп; (by photography) репроду́кция ● *v.t.* **1** (impress) впеча́тать, на-/от-; (fig.) запечатл|ева́ть, -е́ть **2** (produce by ∼ing process) печа́тать, на-/от- **3** (write in imitation of ∼) писа́ть, на- печа́тными бу́квами □ ∼ **out** *v.t.* (comput.) распеча́т|ывать, -ать ■ ∼**out** *n.* (comput.) распеча́тка

printer /ˈprɪntə(r)/ *n.* (person) печа́тник, типо́граф; (printing house) типогра́фия; (comput.) при́нтер

⚘ **prior** /ˈpraɪə(r)/ *adj.* (earlier) пре́жний; (more important) первоочередно́й ● *adv.*: ∼ to до + g.

prioritize /praɪˈɒrɪtaɪz/ *v.t.* (determine the order for dealing with) определ|я́ть, -и́ть свои́ приорите́ты в + p.; (designate or treat as most important) удел|я́ть, -и́ть первостепе́нное внима́ние + d.

⚘ **priority** /praɪˈɒrɪtɪ/ *n.* приорите́т

priory /ˈpraɪərɪ/ *n.* монасты́рь (*m.*)

prise /praɪz/ (*AmE* **prize**) *v.t.* взл|а́мывать, -ома́ть; the box was ∼d open я́щик взлома́ли; (fig.) разн|има́ть, -я́ть; they ∼d the combatants apart они́ разня́ли деру́щихся

prism /ˈprɪz(ə)m/ *n.* при́зма

⚘ **prison** /ˈprɪz(ə)n/ *n.* **1** тюрьма́ **2** (*attr.*) тюре́мный ■ ∼ **camp** *n.* исправи́тельно-трудово́й ла́герь; ∼ **sentence** *n.* тюре́мный срок

⚘ **prisoner** /ˈprɪznə(r)/ *n.* **1** (detained by civil authorities) заключённый **2** (∼ of war) пле́нный, военноплённый

prissy /ˈprɪsɪ/ *adj.* (**prissier**, **prissiest**) чо́порный, жема́нный; (of style) вы́чурный

pristine /ˈprɪstiːn/ *adj.* чи́стый; нетро́нутый

privacy /ˈprɪvəsɪ/ *n.* уедине́ние

⚘ **private** /ˈpraɪvət/ *n.* **1** (soldier) рядово́й **2**: in ∼ (meet, talk) с гла́зу на глаз ● *adj.* **1** (personal) ча́стный, ли́чный; in ∼ life в ли́чной жи́зни; for ∼ reasons по ли́чным причи́нам **2** (not open to the general public) закры́тый **3** (secret) та́йный, секре́тный **4** (without official status) ча́стный, неофициа́льный ■ ∼ **eye** *n.* (infml) ча́стный сы́щик, детекти́в; ∼ **property** *n.* ча́стная со́бственность

privation /praɪˈveɪʃ(ə)n/ *n.* (hardship) лише́ние (*nt. pl.*); нужда́; (loss) утра́та; лише́ние

privatization /ˌpraɪvətaɪˈzeɪʃ(ə)n/ *n.* приватиза́ция

privatize /ˈpraɪvətaɪz/ *v.t.* приватизи́ровать (*impf., pf.*)

privet /ˈprɪvɪt/ *n.* (bot.) бирючи́на

privilege /ˈprɪvɪlɪdʒ/ *n.* привиле́гия

privileged /ˈprɪvɪlɪdʒd/ *adj.* привилегиро́ванный

⚘ **prize**[1] /praɪz/ *n.* **1** (reward for merit in sport etc.) приз; (esp. monetary) пре́мия **2** (*attr.*) (awarded as prize) призово́й; (∼-winning) премиро́ванный; (possession) бесце́нный ■ ∼**-giving** *n.* (BrE) церемо́ния вруче́ния награ́д; ∼ **money** *n.* призовы́е де́н|ьги (-ег); ∼**winner** *n.* призёр

prize[2] /praɪz/ *v.t.* (AmE) = prise

pro[1] /prəʊ/ *n.* (*pl.* ∼s) (point in favour): ∼s and cons за и про́тив ● *prep.* (infml, in favour of) за + *a.*

pro[2] /prəʊ/ *n.* (*pl.* ∼s) (infml, professional) профессиона́л (-ка); про́фи (*c.g. indecl.*) (infml)

proactive /prəʊˈæktɪv/ *adj.* де́йственный

probability /ˌprɒbəˈbɪlɪtɪ/ *n.* вероя́тность; in all ∼ по всей вероя́тности

probable /ˈprɒbəb(ə)l/ *adj.* вероя́тный

⚘ **probably** /ˈprɒbəblɪ/ *adv.* вероя́тно

probate /ˈprəʊbeɪt/ *n.* утвержде́ние завеща́ния

probation /prəˈbeɪʃ(ə)n/ *n.*: be on ∼ (at work) про|ходи́ть, -йти́ испыта́тельный срок; (law) быть усло́вно осуждённым ■ ∼ **officer** *n.* должностно́е лицо́, осуществля́ющее надзо́р за усло́вно осуждёнными

probationary /prəˈbeɪʃənərɪ/ *adj.* испыта́тельный

probationer /prəˈbeɪʃənə(r)/ *n.* (trainee) стажёр; практика́нт; (offender on probation) усло́вно осуждённый

probe /prəʊb/ *n.* (instrument) зонд; (fig., investigation) рассле́дование ● *v.t. & i.* иссле́довать (*impf., pf.*)

⚘ **problem** /ˈprɒbləm/ *n.* пробле́ма, вопро́с; (math. etc.) зада́ча ■ ∼ **child** *n.* тру́дный ребёнок

problematic /ˌprɒbləˈmætɪk/, **problematical** /ˌprɒbləˈmætɪkəl/ *adjs.* проблемати́чный

⚘ **procedure** /prəˈsiːdjə(r)/ *n.* процеду́ра

⚘ **proceed** /prəˈsiːd/ *v.i.* **1** (go on) прод|олжа́ть, -о́лжить **2** (start) прин|има́ться, -я́ться (with: за + *a.*); she ∼ed to lay the table она́ приняла́сь накрыва́ть на стол

proceedings /prəˈsiːdɪŋz/ *n. pl.* **1** (activity) де́ятельность **2** (legal action) суде́бное де́ло, иск

proceeds /ˈprəʊsiːdz/ *n. pl.* вы́ручка, дохо́д

⚘ **process** /ˈprəʊses/ *n.* **1** проце́сс **2** (course) тече́ние, ход; we're in the ∼ of buying a house сейча́с мы покупа́ем дом ● *v.t.* **1** (treat in special way, also comput.) обраб|а́тывать, -о́тать **2** (subject to routine handling) оф|ормля́ть, -о́рмить

procession /prəˈseʃ(ə)n/ *n.* проце́ссия, ше́ствие

p

processor /'prəʊsesə(r)/ n. (comput.) процéссор
proclaim /prə'kleɪm/ v.t. провозгла|шáть, -сúть
proclamation /prɒklə'meɪʃ(ə)n/ n.
  провозглашéние
proclivity /prə'klɪvɪtɪ/ n. склóнность,
  наклóнность
procrastinate /prəʊ'kræstɪneɪt/ v.i. мéдлить
  (impf.)
procreate /'prəʊkrɪeɪt/ v.t. & i. произв|одúть,
  -естú (потóмство)
procreation /prəʊkrɪ'eɪʃ(ə)n/ n.
  воспроизведéние
procure /prə'kjʊə(r)/ v.t. дост|авáть, -áть
procurement /prə'kjʊəmənt/ n.
  приобретéние, получéние; (of equipment etc.)
  постáвка
prod /prɒd/ n. тычóк
  ● v.t. (**prodded, prodding**) тыкать, ткнуть
pro-democracy /prəʊdɪ'mɒkrəsɪ/ adj.
  продемократúческий, защищáющий
  демокрáтию
prodigal /'prɒdɪg(ə)l/ adj. (wasteful)
  расточúтельный; the P∼ Son (bibl.) блýдный
  сын; (lavish) щéдрый
prodigious /prə'dɪdʒəs/ adj. (amazing)
  потрясáющий; (enormous) огрóмный
prodigy /'prɒdɪdʒɪ/ n. вундеркúнд
produce¹ /'prɒdjuːs/ n. продýкты (m. pl.)
  (пищевые)
ᵖ **produce²** /prə'djuːs/ v.t. 1 (make, manufacture)
  произв|одúть, -естú; выпускáть, выпустить
  2 (bring about) вызывáть, вызвать; прин|осúть,
  -естú 3 (present) предст|авлять, -áвить; can
  you ∼ proof of your words? мóжете ли вы
  предстáвить чтó-либо в доказáтельство/
  подтверждéние вáших слов? 4 (show)
  предъявлять, -úть; you must ∼ a ticket
  вы должны предъявúть билéт 5 (yield)
  произв|одúть, -естú; this soil ∼s good crops
  эта пóчва даёт хорóший урожáй 6 (theatr.)
  стáвить, по-; (cin.) выпускáть, выпустить
ᵖ **producer** /prə'djuːsə(r)/ n. 1 (of goods)
  производúтель (m.) 2 (stage, TV) режиссёр-
  постанóвщик 3 (film) продюсер
ᵖ **product** /'prɒdʌkt/ n. продýкт, издéлие; (in
  pl.) продýкция; (collect.) товáры (m. pl.)
ᵖ **production** /prə'dʌkʃ(ə)n/ n. 1 (manufacture)
  произвóдство 2 (yield) производúтельность
  3 (stage, film) постанóвка, режиссýра
  ■ ∼ line n. произвóдственная лúния
productive /prə'dʌktɪv/ adj. (tending to produce)
  производúтельный; (yielding well) плодорóдный
productivity /prɒdʌk'tɪvɪtɪ/ n.
  производúтельность, продуктúвность
profane /prə'feɪn/ adj. (secular) мирскóй;
  (heathen) языческий; (irreverent) богохýльный
  ● v.t. профанúровать (impf., pf.);
  осквернять, -úть
profanit|y /prə'fænɪtɪ/ n. (irreverence)
  богохýльство; (swearing) сквернослóвие; to
  utter ∼ies сквернослóвить (impf.)
profess /prə'fes/ v.t. 1 (claim to have or feel)
  заяв|лять, -úть; he ∼es an interest in

architecture он заявляет, что интересýется
  архитектýрой 2 (claim, pretend) претендовáть
  (impf.); I don't ∼ to know much about music
  я не претендýю на большúе познáния в
  мýзыке; he ∼es to be an expert at chess он
  выдаёт себя за первоклáссного шахматúста
profession /prə'feʃ(ə)n/ n. профéссия
ᵖ **professional** /prə'feʃən(ə)l/ n. профессионáл
  ● adj. профессионáльный
professionalism /prə'feʃənəlɪz(ə)m/ n.
  профессионалúзм
ᵖ **professor** /prə'fesə(r)/ n. (holder of university
  chair) профéссор; (AmE, university teacher)
  преподавáтель (-ница)
proffer /'prɒfə(r)/ n. предложéние
  ● v.t. предл|агáть, -ожúть; he ∼ed his hand
  он протянýл рýку
proficiency /prə'fɪʃ(ə)nsɪ/ n. мастерствó,
  умéние
proficient /prə'fɪʃ(ə)nt/ adj. умéлый
profile /'prəʊfaɪl/ n. прóфиль (m.); he kept a
  low ∼ он старáлся не выделяться
ᵖ **profit** /'prɒfɪt/ n. прúбыль
  ● v.t. (**profited, profiting**) прин|осúть,
  -естú пóльзу + d.
  ● v.i. (**profited, profiting**) пóльзоваться,
  вос- (from: + g.); извл|екáть, -éчь пóльзу
  (from: из + g.); he has not ∼ed from his
  experience он не воспóльзовался свойм
  óпытом
profitability /prɒfɪtə'bɪlɪtɪ/ n. дохóдность,
  прúбыльность, рентáбельность
profitable /'prɒfɪtəb(ə)l/ adj. (advantageous)
  полéзный, выгодный; (lucrative) дохóдный
profiteer /prɒfɪ'tɪə(r)/ n. спекулянт (-ка)
  ● v.i. спекулúровать (impf.)
profligate /'prɒflɪgət/ adj. (extravagant)
  расточúтельный; (dissolute) распýтный
  ● n. (dissolute person) разврáтник
profound /prə'faʊnd/ adj. (**profounder,
  profoundest**) глубóкий
profundity /prə'fʌndɪtɪ/ n. глубинá
profuse /prə'fjuːs/ adj. (plentiful) обúльный;
  (lavish) щéдрый; he apologized ∼ly он
  рассыпáлся в извинéниях
profusion /prə'fjuːʒ(ə)n/ n. изобúлие
progesterone /prəʊ'dʒestərəʊn/ n.
  прогестерóн
prognosis /prɒg'nəʊsɪs/ n. (pl. **prognoses**
  /-siːz/) прогнóз
ᵖ **program** /'prəʊgræm/ n. (comput.) прогрáмма;
  (AmE) = programme
  ● v.t. (**programmed, programming**)
  (comput., also fig.) программúровать, за-; (AmE)
  = programme
ᵖ **programme** /'prəʊgræm/ n. прогрáмма;
  (radio, TV) передáча; (plan) прогрáмма, план
  ● v.t. (**programmed, programming**)
  (schedule): the meeting is ∼d for today
  собрáние назнáчено на сегóдня
programmer /'prəʊgræmə(r)/ n. (comput.)
  программúст (-ка)
ᵖ **progress¹** /'prəʊgres/ n. 1 (forward movement)

p

движе́ние вперёд **2** (advance, development)
прогре́сс; **a meeting is in** ~ идёт заседа́ние
■ ~ **report** *n*. докла́д о хо́де рабо́ты

progress² /prə'gres/ *v.i.* прогресси́ровать
(*impf.*); продв|ига́ться, -и́нуться (вперёд)

progression /prə'greʃ(ə)n/ *n.* продвиже́ние

progressive /prə'gresɪv/ *adj.* **1** (favouring
progress) прогресси́вный, передово́й
2 (gradual) поступа́тельный, постепе́нный

prohibit /prə'hɪbɪt/ *v.t.* (**prohibited**,
prohibiting) запре|ща́ть, -ти́ть

prohibition /prəʊhr'bɪʃ(ə)n, prəʊɪ'b-/ *n.*
запреще́ние

prohibitive /prə'hɪbɪtɪv/ *adj.*
запрети́тельный, запреща́ющий

✤ **project¹** /'prɒdʒekt/ *n.* (scheme) прое́кт, план;
(at school) рабо́та

project² /prə'dʒekt/ *v.t.* (throw) выбра́сывать,
вы́бросить; (fig.): **she** ~**ed a positive image**
она́ производи́ла позити́вное впечатле́ние
● *v.i.* (protrude) выдава́ться (*impf.*); выступа́ть
(*impf.*)

projectile /prə'dʒektaɪl/ *n.* снаря́д

projection /prə'dʒekʃ(ə)n/ *n.* **1** (planning)
проекти́рование **2** (throwing, propulsion)
отбра́сывание **3** (cin.) прое́кция
(изображе́ния) **4** (psych., geom.) прое́кция
5 (protrusion) вы́ступ
■ ~ **room** *n.* (кино)проекцио́нная каби́на

projector /prə'dʒektə(r)/ *n.* (apparatus)
прое́ктор

proletarian /prəʊlɪ'teərɪən/ *n.* пролета́рий
● *adj.* пролета́рский

proletariat /prəʊlɪ'teərɪət/ *n.* пролетариа́т

pro-life /prəʊ'laɪf/ *adj.* возража́ющий про́тив
або́ртов

proliferate /prə'lɪfəreɪt/ *v.i.* (бы́стро)
распростран|я́ться, -и́ться

proliferation /prəlɪfə'reɪʃ(ə)n/ *n.* (бы́строе)
размноже́ние, пролифера́ция; (fig.)
распростране́ние

prolific /prə'lɪfɪk/ *adj.* (lit.) плодоро́дный; (fig.)
плодови́тый

prologue /'prəʊlɒg/ (AmE **prolog**) *n.* проло́г

prolong /prə'lɒŋ/ *v.t.* продл|ева́ть, -и́ть

prom /prɒm/ *n.* (infml) **1** = promenade **2** (AmE,
students' ball) бал, выпускно́й

promenade /prɒmə'nɑːd/ *n.* (BrE, esp. at
seaside) ме́сто для гуля́ния

prominence /'prɒmɪnəns/ *n.* (importance)
ви́дное положе́ние

prominent /'prɒmɪnənt/ *adj.* **1** (projecting)
выступа́ющий **2** (important) выдаю́щийся

promiscuity /prɒmɪ'skju:ɪtɪ/ *n.*
распу́щенность

promiscuous /prə'mɪskjʊəs/ *adj.*
распу́щенный

✤ **promise** /'prɒmɪs/ *n.* **1** (assurance) обеща́ние;
he kept his ~ он сдержа́л своё обеща́ние
2 (ground for expectation) наде́жда; **he shows** ~

он подаёт наде́жды
● *v.t. & i.* обеща́ть, по-; **he** ~**d to be here by 7**
он обеща́л быть здесь к 7 часа́м; **I** ~**d myself
a quiet evening** я реши́л споко́йно провести́
ве́чер

promising /'prɒmɪsɪŋ/ *adj.* перспекти́вный;
многообеща́ющий, подаю́щий наде́жды

promontory /'prɒməntərɪ/ *n.* мыс

✤ **promote** /prə'məʊt/ *v.t.* **1** (raise to higher rank)
продв|ига́ть, -и́нуть; пов|ыша́ть, -ы́сить (в
чи́не/зва́нии) **2** (encourage, support) поощр|я́ть,
-и́ть; подде́рж|ивать, -а́ть **3** (publicize)
реклами́ровать (*impf.*)

promoter /prə'məʊtə(r)/ *n.* (of event) аге́нт,
промо́утер; (of cause) пропаганди́ст (-ка)

promotion /prə'məʊʃ(ə)n/ *n.* продвиже́ние,
повыше́ние; (encouragement, support) поощре́ние,
подде́ржка; (publicizing) рекла́ма, промоу́шен

prompt¹ /prɒmpt/ *v.t.* **1** (assist memory
of) подска́з|ывать, -а́ть + *d.*; (theatr.)
суфли́ровать (*impf.*) + *d.* **2** (impel)
побу|жда́ть, -ди́ть

prompt² /prɒmpt/ *adj.* бы́стрый,
неме́дленный; **he arrived** ~**ly at 9** он
прие́хал то́чно в де́вять

prompter /'prɒmptə(r)/ *n.* (theatr.) суфлёр

prone /prəʊn/ *adj.* **1** (face downwards)
лежа́щий ничко́м, лежа́щий вниз лицо́м
2: ~ **to** (liable to) скло́нный к + *d.*

prong /prɒŋ/ *n.* зубе́ц

pronoun /'prəʊnaʊn/ *n.* местоиме́ние

pronounce /prə'naʊns/ *v.t.* произн|оси́ть, -ести́

pronounced /prə'naʊnst/ *adj.* (decided)
я́вный; **he walks with a** ~ **limp** он си́льно/
заме́тно хрома́ет

pronouncement /prə'naʊnsmənt/ *n.*
заявле́ние; выска́зывание

pronunciation /prənʌnsɪ'eɪʃ(ə)n/ *n.*
произноше́ние

proof /pru:f/ *n.* доказа́тельство; (typ.)
корректу́ра
■ ~**reader** *n.* корре́ктор

prop¹ /prɒp/ *n.* (support) сто́йка; подпо́рка;
(fig.) опо́ра, подде́ржка
● *v.t.* (**propped**, **propping**) (*also* **prop
up**) **1** подп|ира́ть, -ере́ть; ~ **the ladder
against the wall!** приста́вьте ле́стницу к
стене́! **2** (fig.) подде́рж|ивать, -а́ть

prop² /prɒp/ *n.* (*usu. in pl.*) (theatr.) бутафо́рия,
реквизи́т

propaganda /prɒpə'gændə/ *n.* пропага́нда

propagate /'prɒpəgeɪt/ *v.t.* (plants) разв|оди́ть,
-ести́; (ideas) распростран|я́ть, -и́ть

propagation /prɒpə'geɪʃ(ə)n/ *n.*
размноже́ние; (fig.) распростране́ние

propagator /'prɒpəgeɪtə(r)/ *n.* (person)
распространи́тель (-ница); (for plants)
микропарни́к

propel /prə'pel/ *v.t.* (**propelled**,
propelling) прив|оди́ть, -ести́ в движе́ние

propeller /prə'pelə(r)/ *n.* пропе́ллер

propensity /prə'pensɪtɪ/ *n.*
предрасположе́ние, скло́нность

ꝏ **proper** /ˈprɒpə(r)/ *adj.* **1** (suitable)
подходя́щий, ну́жный **2** (decent)
(благо)присто́йный, прили́чный **3** (correct)
пра́вильный; in the ~ sense of the word в
прямо́м смы́сле сло́ва

ꝏ **properly** /ˈprɒpəlɪ/ *adv.* (correctly) подоба́юще,
как сле́дует; you must be ~ dressed вы
должны́ оде́ться подоба́юще

ꝏ **property** /ˈprɒpətɪ/ *n.* **1** (possession(s))
со́бственность; иму́щество **2** (house)
дом; (estate) име́ние; (real estate)
недви́жимость **3** (attribute) сво́йство

prophecy /ˈprɒfɪsɪ/ *n.* проро́чество

prophesy /ˈprɒfɪsaɪ/ *v.t.* проро́чить, на-

prophet /ˈprɒfɪt/ *n.* проро́к

prophetic /prəˈfetɪk/ *adj.* проро́ческий

prophylactic /ˌprɒfɪˈlæktɪk/ *n.*
профилакти́ческое сре́дство
● *adj.* профилакти́ческий

proponent /prəˈpəʊnənt/ *n.* пропаганди́ст,
побо́рник (*чего*)

proportion /prəˈpɔːʃ(ə)n/ *n.* **1** (part) часть,
до́ля **2** (ratio) пропо́рция, соотноше́ние; in
~ пропорциона́льно, соразме́рно **3** (due
relation) соразме́рность; his ambitions are out
of all ~ его́ честолю́бие выхо́дит за вся́кие
ра́мки **4** (*in pl.*) (dimensions) разме́р, разме́ры
(*m. pl.*)

proportional /prəˈpɔːʃən(ə)l/ *adj.*
пропорциона́льный
■ ~ representation *n.* (pol.)
пропорциона́льное представи́тельство

proportionate /prəˈpɔːʃənət/ *adj.*
соразме́рный; payment will be ~ to effort
опла́та бу́дет соотве́тствовать затра́ченным
уси́лиям

ꝏ **proposal** /prəˈpəʊz(ə)l/ *n.* предложе́ние

ꝏ **propose** /prəˈpəʊz/ *v.t.* **1** (suggest)
предл|ага́ть, -ожи́ть; he ~d (marriage) to her
он сде́лал ей предложе́ние (*стать жено́й*)
2 (put forward) выдвига́ть, вы́двинуть
3 (intend) предпол|ага́ть, -ожи́ть;
намерева́ться (*impf.*); I ~ to leave tomorrow
я намерева́юсь е́хать за́втра

proposition /ˌprɒpəˈzɪʃ(ə)n/ *n.* **1** (statement)
заявле́ние **2** (proposed scheme) предложе́ние

propound /prəˈpaʊnd/ *v.t.* предл|ага́ть,
-ожи́ть на обсужде́ние; изл|ага́ть, -ожи́ть

proprietor /prəˈpraɪətə(r)/ *n.* владе́лец, хозя́ин

proprietorial /prəpraɪəˈtɔːrɪəl/ *adj.*
со́бственнический

propriety /prəˈpraɪətɪ/ *n.* (fitness) уме́стность;
(correctness of behaviour) пра́вила поведе́ния;
пра́вила прили́чия, (благо)присто́йность

pro rata /prəʊ ˈrɑːtə/ *adv.* пропорциона́льно;
соотве́тственно

prosaic /prəˈzeɪk/ *adj.* прозаи́ческий

proscribe /prəˈskraɪb/ *v.t.* запре|ща́ть, -ти́ть

prose /prəʊz/ *n.* про́за

prosecute /ˈprɒsɪkjuːt/ *v.t.* (law) возбу|жда́ть,
-ди́ть де́ло про́тив + *g.*

prosecution /ˌprɒsɪˈkjuːʃ(ə)n/ *n.* **1** (carrying
on legal proceedings) обвине́ние; предъявле́ние

и́ска **2** (prosecuting party) обвине́ние; counsel
for the ~ обвини́тель (*m.*) (в уголо́вном
проце́ссе)

prosecutor /ˈprɒsɪkjuːtə(r)/ *n.* обвини́тель
(*m.*)

ꝏ **prospect** /ˈprɒspekt/ *n.* перспекти́ва; there is
no ~ of success нет наде́жды на успе́х; a job
without ~s рабо́та без перспекти́в

prospective /prəˈspektɪv/ *adj.* бу́дущий

prospector /prəˈspektə(r)/ *n.* разве́дчик,
стара́тель (*m.*)

prospectus /prəˈspektəs/ *n.* (*pl.* ~es)
проспе́кт (*рекламное издание*)

prosper /ˈprɒspə(r)/ *v.i.* преусп|ева́ть, -е́ть

prosperity /prɒˈsperɪtɪ/ *n.* процвета́ние

prosperous /ˈprɒspərəs/ *adj.* процвета́ющий

prostate /ˈprɒsteɪt/ *n.* (*in full* ~ gland)
проста́та, предста́тельная железа́

prosthe|sis /ˈprɒsθɪsɪs/ *n.* (*pl.* ~ses /-siːz/)
проте́з

prosthetic /prɒsˈθetɪk/ *adj.* проте́зный

prostitute /ˈprɒstɪtjuːt/ *n.* проститу́тка; male
~ мужчи́на-проститу́тка
● *v.t.*: ~ oneself зан|има́ться, -я́ться
проститу́цией; (fig.) торгова́ть (*impf.*) собо́й

prostitution /ˌprɒstɪˈtjuːʃ(ə)n/ *n.* (lit., fig.)
проститу́ция

prostrate /ˈprɒstreɪt/ *adj.* **1** (lying face down)
распросте́ртый **2** (overcome): she was ~ with
grief она́ была́ сло́млена го́рем

protagonist /prəˈtæɡənɪst/ *n.* гла́вный геро́й

ꝏ **protect** /prəˈtekt/ *v.t.* защи|ща́ть, -ти́ть

ꝏ **protection** /prəˈtekʃ(ə)n/ *n.* **1** (defence)
защи́та **2** (care) попече́ние
■ ~ racket *n.* рэ́кет

protectionism /prəˈtekʃ(ə)nɪz(ə)m/ *n.*
протекциони́зм

protectionist /prəˈtekʃ(ə)nɪst/ *n.*
протекциони́ст
● *adj.* протекциони́стский

protective /prəˈtektɪv/ *adj.* защи́тный

protégé /ˈprɒtɪʒeɪ/ *n.* (*f.* **protégée**) протеже́
(*c.g., indecl.*)

ꝏ **protein** /ˈprəʊtiːn/ *n.* протеи́н, бело́к

pro tem /prəʊ ˈtem/ *adv.* на вре́мя, вре́менно

ꝏ **protest**[1] /ˈprəʊtest/ *n.* проте́ст; возраже́ние
■ ~ march *n.* марш проте́ста

protest[2] /prəˈtest/ *v.t.* **1** (affirm) утвержда́ть
(*impf.*); he continued to ~ his innocence
он продолжа́л наста́ивать на свое́й
невино́вности **2** (AmE, object to) возража́ть/
протестова́ть (*impf.*) про́тив + *g.*
● *v.i.:* ~ against протестова́ть (*impf.*)
про́тив + *g.*; ~ about выража́ть, вы́разить
недово́льство + *i.*

Protestant /ˈprɒtɪst(ə)nt/ *n.* протеста́нт (-ка)
● *adj.* протеста́нтский

protestation /ˌprɒtɪˈsteɪʃ(ə)n/ *n.* (affirmation)
(торже́ственное) заявле́ние; ~s of innocence
торже́ственные заявле́ния о невино́вности

protester /prəˈtestə(r)/ *n.* протесту́ющий (-ая)

protocol /ˈprəʊtəkɒl/ *n.* протоко́л

proton /ˈprəʊtɒn/ *n.* прото́н

p

prototype /'prəʊtətaɪp/ *n.* прототи́п

protract /prə'trækt/ *v.t.* затя́|гивать, -ну́ть; a ~ed visit затяну́вшийся визи́т; a ~ed war затяжна́я война́

protractor /prə'træktə(r)/ *n.* (geom.) транспорти́р

protrud|e /prə'truːd/ *v.i.* выдава́ться (*impf.*); ~ing teeth выпира́ющие зу́бы

◌ **proud** /praʊd/ *adj.* го́рдый; to be ~ (of) горди́ться + *i.*; this is a ~ day for the school э́то торже́ственный/ра́достный день для шко́лы; (arrogant) надме́нный

◌ **prove** /pruːv/ *v.t.* (*p.p.* **proved** *or* **proven** /'pruːv(ə)n, 'prəʊ-/) доказа́|ывать, -а́ть; he ~d his worth он показа́л себя́ досто́йным челове́ком; he needs to ~ himself to others ему́ на́до утверди́ть себя́ в глаза́х други́х ● *v.i.* (*p.p.* **proved** *or* **proven** /'pruːv(ə)n, 'prəʊ-/) (turn out) ока́з|ываться, -а́ться; the alarm ~d (to be) a hoax трево́га оказа́лась ло́жной

provenance /'prɒvɪnəns/ *n.* происхожде́ние

proverb /'prɒvɜːb/ *n.* посло́вица

proverbial /prə'vɜːbɪəl/ *adj.* **1** (pert. to provs.) воше́дший в погово́рку/посло́вицу, как; как *кто-н./что-н.* из той погово́рки/посло́вицы; ~ wisdom наро́дная му́дрость **2** (notorious) общеизве́стный

◌ **provide** /prə'vaɪd/ *v.t.* **1**: ~ sb with sth обеспе́чи|вать, -ть кого́-н. чем-н.; снаб|жа́ть, -ди́ть кого́-н. чем-н. **2** (prescribe) предус|ма́тривать, -отре́ть ● *v.i.* (prepare oneself) пригот|а́вливаться, -о́виться; she had three children to ~ for у неё на содержа́нии бы́ло тро́е дете́й

provided /prə'vaɪdɪd/, **providing** /prə'vaɪdɪŋ/ *conjs.* при усло́вии, что; е́сли

providence /'prɒvɪd(ə)ns/ *n.* **1** (foresight) предусмотри́тельность; (thrift) расчётливость **2** (divine care): he escaped by a special ~ его́ спасло́ (то́лько) провиде́ние; (P~: God or nature) Провиде́ние, про́мысл Бо́жий

provider /prə'vaɪdə(r)/ *n.* снабже́нец, поставщи́|к (-ца); (breadwinner): her husband is a good ~ её муж хорошо́ обеспе́чивает семью́; (comput., Internet service ~) прова́йдер

province /'prɒvɪns/ *n.* о́бласть; in the ~s в провинции, на перифери́и

provincial /prə'vɪnʃ(ə)l/ *adj.* провинциа́льный

◌ **provision** /prə'vɪʒ(ə)n/ *n.* **1** (supplying) снабже́ние **2** (*in pl.*) (supplies, esp. food) прови́зия **3** (preparation) обеспе́чение; their father had made ~ for them оте́ц обеспе́чил их на бу́дущее

provisional /prə'vɪʒən(ə)l/ *adj.* вре́менный

proviso /prə'vaɪzəʊ/ *n.* (*pl.* ~s) усло́вие, огово́рка; with the ~ that ... с усло́вием (*or* с огово́ркой), что...

provocation /prɒvə'keɪʃ(ə)n/ *n.* провока́ция; I did it under ~ меня́ спровоци́ровали на э́то

provocative /prə'vɒkətɪv/ *adj.* (challenging) вызыва́ющий; (alluring) соблазни́тельный

provoke /prə'vəʊk/ *v.t.* **1** (cause) вызыва́ть, вы́звать; провоци́ровать, с- **2** (anger) серди́ть, рас-

prow /praʊ/ *n.* нос (*судна*)

prowess /'praʊɪs/ *n.* (skill) мастерство́; (valour) до́блесть

prowl /praʊl/ *v.t.* (a place) ры́скать (*impf.*) по + *d.* ● *v.i.* ры́скать (*impf.*)

proximity /prɒk'sɪmɪtɪ/ *n.* бли́зость; сосе́дство

proxy /'prɒksɪ/ *n.* (authorization) полномо́чие, дове́ренность; they voted by ~ они́ голосова́ли по дове́ренности

prude /pruːd/ *n.* ханжа́ (*c.g.*)

prudence /'pruːd(ə)ns/ *n.* благоразу́мие

prudent /'pruːd(ə)nt/ *adj.* благоразу́мный

prudish /'pruːdɪʃ/ *adj.* стыдли́вый; (pej.) ха́нжеский

prune¹ /pruːn/ *n.* черносли́в

prune² /pruːn/ *v.t.* (trim) обр|еза́ть, -е́зать; подр|еза́ть, -е́зать

prurient /'prʊərɪənt/ *adj.* похотли́вый

pry /praɪ/ *v.i.* вме́ш|иваться, -а́ться (в чужи́е дела́)

PS *abbr.* (*of* **postscript**) постскри́птум, припи́ска

psalm /sɑːm/ *n.* псало́м

pseudonym /'sjuːdənɪm/ *n.* псевдони́м

psych /saɪk/ *v.t.*: ~ oneself up настр|а́ивать, -о́ить себя́

psyche /'saɪkɪ/ *n.* душа́; дух

psychedelic /saɪkə'delɪk/ *adj.* (experience) психодели́ческий; (clothes, colours) чудно́й; (drug) галлюциноге́нный

psychiatric /saɪkɪ'ætrɪk/ *adj.* психиатри́ческий

psychiatrist /saɪ'kaɪətrɪst/ *n.* психиа́тр

psychiatry /saɪ'kaɪətrɪ/ *n.* психиатри́я

psychic /'saɪkɪk/ *n.* экстрасе́нс ● *adj.* ◌ яснови́дящий (-ая)

psychoanalyse /saɪkəʊ'ænəlaɪz/ (AmE **-analyze**) *v.t.* подв|ерга́ть, -е́ргнуть психоана́лизу

psychoanalysis /saɪkəʊə'nælɪsɪs/ *n.* психоана́лиз

psychoanalyst /saɪkəʊ'ænəlɪst/ *n.* психоанали́тик

psychological /saɪkə'lɒdʒɪk(ə)l/ *adj.* психологи́ческий

psychologist /saɪ'kɒlədʒɪst/ *n.* психо́лог

psychology /saɪ'kɒlədʒɪ/ *n.* психоло́гия

psychopath /'saɪkəpæθ/ *n.* психопа́т (-ка)

psychopathic /saɪkə'pæθɪk/ *adj.* психопати́ческий; he is ~ он психопа́т

psychosis /saɪ'kəʊsɪs/ *n.* (*pl.* **psychoses** /-sɪːz/) психо́з

psychosomatic /saɪkəʊsə'mætɪk/ *adj.* психосомати́ческий

psychotherapist /saɪkəʊ'θerəpɪst/ *n.* психотерапе́вт

psychotherapy /saɪkəʊ'θerəpɪ/ *n.* психотерапи́я

p

◌ ключева́я ле́ксика

psychotic /saɪˈkɒtɪk/ *adj.* психоти́ческий, душевнобольно́й

PTA *abbr.* (*of* **parent-teacher association**) ассоциа́ция учителе́й и роди́телей, учи́тельско-роди́тельский комите́т

PTO *abbr.* (*of* **please turn over**) см. на об. (смотри́ на оборо́те)

pub /pʌb/ *n.* (BrE, infml) пивна́я; паб; каба́к

puberty /ˈpjuːbəti/ *n.* полово́е созрева́ние

pubescent /pjuːˈbes(ə)nt/ *adj.* дости́гший полово́й зре́лости, половозре́лый

pubic /ˈpjuːbɪk/ *adj.* лобко́вый, ло́нный
■ ∼ **hair** *n.* лобко́вые во́лосы

⚡ **public** /ˈpʌblɪk/ *n.* **1** (community) обще́ственность; наро́д; **the library is open to the** ∼ вход в библиоте́ку свобо́дный **2** (audience) пу́блика; **I have never spoken in** ∼ я никогда́ не выступа́л пе́ред пу́бликой
● *adj.* **1** (pert. to people in general) обще́ственный; **in the** ∼ **interest** в интере́сах о́бщества/госуда́рства **2** (pert. to politics or the state) обще́ственный, госуда́рственный; **a** ∼ **figure** обще́ственный де́ятель **3** (shared by the community) публи́чный, обще́ственный **4** (done openly, in view of others) публи́чный, гла́сный, откры́тый
■ ∼ **address system** *n.* набо́р звукоусили́тельной аппарату́ры для выступле́ний; ∼ **convenience** *n.* (BrE) обще́ственный туале́т; ∼ **holiday** *n.* устано́вленный зако́ном пра́здник; ∼ **house** *n.* (BrE) пивна́я, паб; ∼ **inquiry** *n.* публи́чное/откры́тое рассле́дование; ∼ **opinion** *n.* обще́ственное мне́ние; ∼ **prosecutor** *n.* прокуро́р; ∼ **relations** *n. pl.* свя́зи с обще́ственностью; ∼ **sector** *n.* госуда́рственный се́ктор; ∼ **school** *n.* (BrE) ча́стная шко́ла; (AmE) госуда́рственная шко́ла; ∼ **transport** *n.* обще́ственный тра́нспорт

publican /ˈpʌblɪkən/ *n.* (BrE) содержа́тель (*m.*) ба́ра/па́ба

⚡ **publication** /pʌblɪˈkeɪʃ(ə)n/ *n.* публика́ция, опубликова́ние, изда́ние

publicity /pʌbˈlɪsɪti/ *n.* **1** (public notice, dissemination) гла́сность, огла́ска **2** (advertisement) реклами́рование, рекла́ма, па́блисити (*nt. indecl.*)
■ ∼ **campaign** *n.* рекла́мная кампа́ния

publicize /ˈpʌblɪsaɪz/ *v.t.* реклами́ровать (*impf.*); огла|ша́ть, -си́ть

⚡ **publish** /ˈpʌblɪʃ/ *v.t.* **1** (books, newspapers) изд|ава́ть, -а́ть; выпуска́ть, вы́пустить **2** (letter, article, information, author) публикова́ть, о-

publisher /ˈpʌblɪʃə(r)/ *n.* изда́тель (*m.*)

publishing /ˈpʌblɪʃɪŋ/ *n.* изда́тельское де́ло; ∼ **house** *n.* изда́тельство

pudding /ˈpʊdɪŋ/ *n.* пу́динг, запека́нка; (BrE, sweet course) сла́дкое; **black** ∼ кровяна́я колбаса́

puddle /ˈpʌd(ə)l/ *n.* (pool) лу́жа

puerile /ˈpjʊəraɪl/ *adj.* де́тский, инфанти́льный

Puerto Rican /pwɜːˈtəʊ ˈriːkən/ *n.* пуэрторика́н|ец (-ка)
● *adj.* пуэрторика́нский

Puerto Rico /pwɜːˈtəʊ ˈriːkəʊ/ *n.* Пуэ́рто-Ри́ко (*nt. indecl.*)

puff /pʌf/ *n.* **1** (of breath) вы́дох **2** (of smoke) дымо́к, клуб **3** (of air or wind) дунове́ние
● *v.t.* **1** (breathe out) выдыха́ть, вы́дохнуть; ∼**ed smoke in my face** он вы́дохнул дым мне в лицо́ **2** (make out of breath): **I was** ∼**ed after the climb** по́сле подъёма у меня́ появи́лась оды́шка **3** ∼ **out** (smoke) выпуска́ть, вы́пустить; (chest): **he** ∼**ed out his chest with pride** он го́рдо вы́пятил грудь **4**: ∼**ed-up** (haughty) наду́тый
● *v.i.* **1** (breathe quickly): **he was** ∼**ing and panting** он пыхте́л **2** (emit smoke) дыми́ться (*impf.*) **3** ∼ **up** (swell) расп|уха́ть, -у́хнуть
■ ∼ **pastry** *n.* слоёное те́сто

puffin /ˈpʌfɪn/ *n.* ту́пик, топо́рик (*птица*)

puffy /ˈpʌfi/ *adj.* (**puffier**, **puffiest**) (eyes) опу́хший; (face) отёчный

pugnacious /pʌɡˈneɪʃəs/ *adj.* драчли́вый, вои́нственный

puke /pjuːk/ *n.* (infml) рво́та, блевоти́на
● *v.i.* блева́ть (*impf.*) (infml); **he** ∼**d** его́ вы́рвало

⚡ **pull** /pʊl/ *n.* (traction) тя́га; (act) дёрганье; **he gave a** ∼ **on the rope** он дёрнул за (за) верёвку
● *v.t.* **1** (draw towards one, tug, jerk) тяну́ть, по-; тащи́ть, по-; **he** ∼**ed me by the sleeve** он потяну́л меня́ за рука́в **2** (fig.): **she** ∼**ed a face at him** она́ скорчи́ла ему́ грима́су **3** (extract): **he** ∼**ed a gun on me** он вы́хватил пистоле́т и навёл его́ на меня́ **4** (strain) растя́г|ивать, -ну́ть
● *v.i.* тяну́ть, по-; **they** ∼**ed on the rope** они́ потяну́ли за верёвку
□ ∼ **apart** *v.t.* (*also* ∼ **to pieces**) раз|рыва́ть, -орва́ть (на куски́); (fig., criticize severely) разн|оси́ть, -ести́ в пух и прах
□ ∼ **away** *v.i.* (move off) от|ходи́ть, -ойти́
□ ∼ **back** *v.t.* отта́|скивать, -щи́ть; оття́г|ивать, -ну́ть; **he** ∼**ed her back from the window** он оттащи́л её от окна́
● *v.i.* отступ|а́ть, -и́ть
□ ∼ **down** *v.t.* (lower by ∼ing) спус|ка́ть, -ти́ть; (demolish) сн|оси́ть, -ести́
□ ∼ **in** *v.i.* (drive or move to a standstill) остан|а́вливаться, -ови́ться; **the train** ∼**ed in** по́езд подошёл к перро́ну; **he** ∼**ed in to the kerb** (BrE), **up to the curb** (AmE) он подъе́хал к тротуа́ру; (drive or move towards near side of road): **he** ∼**ed in to avoid a collision** он прижа́лся к обо́чине, что́бы избежа́ть столкнове́ния
□ ∼ **off** *v.t.* (remove, detach) стя́г|ивать, -ну́ть; сн|има́ть, -ять; (infml, achieve) успе́шно заверш|а́ть, -и́ть
□ ∼ **on** *v.t.* натя́г|ивать, -ну́ть
□ ∼ **out** *v.t.* (extract) выта́скивать, вы́тащить; (withdraw) выводи́ть, вы́вести; **the troops should be** ∼**ed out** войска́ сле́дует вы́вести
● *v.i.* (drive or move away) от|ходи́ть, -ойти́; (of driving manoeuvres) отъ|езжа́ть, -е́хать; **he** ∼**ed out to overtake** он пошёл на обго́н; (withdraw, of troops) от|ходи́ть, -ойти́; (from an enterprise): **he** ∼**ed out** он отказа́лся от

p

участия в этом деле
□ ~ **through** *v.i.* (recover from illness) поправляться, -авиться
□ ~ **together** *v.t.*: ~ **yourself together!** возьмите себя в руки!
● *v.i.* (fig.) срабатываться, -отаться; **if we all ~ together, we shall win** объединившись, мы победим
□ ~ **up** *v.t.* (uproot) вырывать, вырвать; (raise) вытягивать, вытянуть; (draw nearer) придвигать, -инуть; ~ **up a chair!** придвиньте стул!; (bring to a halt) останавливать, -овить; (reprimand) отчитывать, -ать
● *v.i.* (come to a halt) останавливаться, -овиться
■ ~**-up** *n.* (gymnastic exercise) подтягивание

pulley /'pʊlɪ/ *n.* (*pl.* **pulleys**) шкив

pullover /'pʊləʊvə(r)/ *n.* пуловер, свитер

pulp /pʌlp/ *n.* **1** (of fruit) мякоть **2** (fig.) месиво; бесформенная масса

pulpit /'pʊlpɪt/ *n.* кафедра (*в церкви*)

pulsate /pʌl'seɪt/ *v.i.* пульсировать (*impf.*)

pulse /pʌls/ *n.* пульс

pulverize /'pʌlvəraɪz/ *v.t.* (reduce to powder) размельчать, -ить; (fig., smash, demolish) уничтожать, -ожить

puma /'pju:mə/ *n.* пума

pummel /'pʌm(ə)l/ *v.t.* (**pummelled**, **pummelling**, AmE **pummeled**, **pummeling**) колотить, по-, бить, из- (*кулаками*)

pump /pʌmp/ *n.* насос, помпа
● *v.t.* **1** (transfer by ~ing) качать, на- **2** (fig.): **I ~ed him for information** я выспрашивал его; я выведывал у него сведения **3** (*also* ~ **up**) (inflate) накачивать, -ать

pumpkin /'pʌmpkɪn/ *n.* тыква

pun /pʌn/ *n.* игра слов, каламбур

punch /pʌntʃ/ *n.* **1** (blow with fist) удар кулаком **2** (fig., energy) энергия, огонь (*m.*) **3** (tool for perforating, e.g. paper) дырокол
● *v.t.* **1** (hit with fist) ударять, -арить кулаком **2** (perforate) компостировать (*impf.*)
■ ~**line** *n.* концовка, развязка (*анекдота и т. n.*); ~**-up** *n.* (BrE, infml) драка

punctilious /pʌŋk'tɪlɪəs/ *adj.* скрупулёзный

punctual /'pʌŋktjʊəl/ *adj.* пунктуальный, точный

punctuate /'pʌŋktjʊeɪt/ *v.t.* (insert punctuation marks in) ставить, по- знаки препинания в + *a.*; (fig., interrupt, intersperse) прерывать, -вать

punctuation /pʌŋktjʊ'eɪʃ(ə)n/ *n.* пунктуация
■ ~ **mark** *n.* знак препинания

puncture /'pʌŋktʃə(r)/ *n.* прокол
● *v.t.* прокалывать, -олоть

pundit /'pʌndɪt/ *n.* знаток, специалист

pungent /'pʌndʒ(ə)nt/ *adj.* острый

punish /'pʌnɪʃ/ *v.t.* наказывать, -ать; карать, по-

punishment /'pʌnɪʃmənt/ *n.* наказание

punitive /'pju:nɪtɪv/ *adj.* карательный; ~ **taxation** высокое налогообложение

---

punk /pʌŋk/ *n.* **1** (admirer of ~ rock) панк; (~ rock) панк-рок **2** (AmE, infml, worthless person) дрянь
● *adj.* панковский

punnet /'pʌnɪt/ *n.* (BrE) корзин(оч)ка

punt /pʌnt/ *n.* (boat) плоскодонка

punter /'pʌntə(r)/ *n.* **1** (at cards) понтёр; (at races) игрок; (client) клиент (-ка) **2** (in American football and rugby) игрок, бьющий по подброшенному мячу

puny /'pju:nɪ/ *adj.* (**punier**, **puniest**) (undersized, feeble) тщедушный, хилый

pup /pʌp/ *n.* (young dog) щенок

⚔ **pupil** /'pju:p(ə)l/ *n.* **1** (one being taught) ученик (-ца) **2** (of eye) зрачок

puppet /'pʌpɪt/ *n.*: **glove ~** кукла; **string ~** марионетка; (fig.) марионетка

puppy /'pʌpɪ/ *n.* щенок
■ ~ **fat** *n.* детская пухлость; ~ **love** *n.* детская любовь

⚔ **purchase** /'pɜ:tʃɪs/ *n.* (buying; thing bought) покупка, приобретение
● *v.t.* (buy) покупать, купить

purchaser /'pɜ:tʃɪsə(r)/ *n.* покупатель (-ница)

pure /pjʊə(r)/ *adj.* чистый

purée /'pjʊəreɪ/ *n.* пюре (*nt. indecl.*)

purely /'pjʊəlɪ/ *adv.* исключительно, совершенно, чисто

purgatory /'pɜ:gətərɪ/ *n.* чистилище; (fig.) ад

purge /pɜ:dʒ/ *n.* очищение
● *v.t.* (lit., fig.) очищать, -истить

purify /'pjʊərɪfaɪ/ *v.t.* очищать, -истить

purist /'pjʊərɪst/ *n.* пурист

puritan /'pjʊərɪt(ə)n/ *n.* (**P~**) (hist.) пуританин (-ка); (fig.) пуританин (-ка)
● *adj.* пуританский

puritanical /pjʊərɪ'tænɪk(ə)l/ *adj.* пуританский

purity /'pjʊərɪtɪ/ *n.* чистота

purple /'pɜ:p(ə)l/ *n.* лиловый/фиолетовый цвет
● *adj.* лиловый, фиолетовый

purport¹ /'pɜ:pɔ:t/ *n.* смысл, суть

purport² /pə'pɔ:t/ *v.t.* (state) подразумевать (*impf.*); (claim): **this book is not all it ~s to be** эта книга не совсем такая, какой она претендует быть

⚔ **purpose** /'pɜ:pəs/ *n.* (aim) цель; (intention) намерение; **on ~** нарочно, специально; **she went out with the ~ of buying clothes** она вышла с целью купить одежду
■ ~**-built** *adj.* (BrE) выстроенный специально

purposeful /'pɜ:pəsfʊl/ *adj.* целеустремлённый

purposely /'pɜ:pəslɪ/ *adv.* нарочно, (пред)намеренно, специально

purr /pɜ:(r)/ *v.i.* мурлыкать (*impf.*)

purse /pɜ:s/ *n.* (for money) кошелёк; (AmE, handbag) сумочка
● *v.t.* морщить, с-; **he ~d (up) his lips** он поджал губы
■ ~ **strings** *n. pl.*: **her husband holds the ~ strings** (fig.) её муж распоряжается деньгами

⚔ **pursue** /pə'sju:/ *v.t.* (**pursues**, **pursued**, **pursuing**) **1** (chase) преследовать (*impf.*)

2 (strive after) добива́ться (*impf.*) + *g.* **3** (course) сле́довать (*impf.*) + *d.*; (interest) занима́ться (*impf.*) + *i.*; (activity) предприн|има́ть, -я́ть; (policy) проводи́ть (*impf.*)

pursuer /pə'sju:ə(r)/ *n.* пресле́дователь (*m.*)

pursuit /pə'sju:t/ *n.* **1** (chase) пресле́дование; пого́ня; **he escaped, with the police in hot ~** он бежа́л, пресле́дуемый поли́цией по пята́м **2** (seeking) по́иск|и (-ов); **he will stop at nothing in ~ of his ends** он не остано́вится ни пе́ред чем для достиже́ния свои́х це́лей **3** (recreation) заня́тие

pus /pʌs/ *n.* гной

☞ **push** /pʊʃ/ *n.* толчо́к
 ● *v.t.* **1** (exert pressure to move) толк|а́ть, -ну́ть; пих|а́ть, -ну́ть **2** (fig., urge) подт|а́лкивать, -олкну́ть; вынужда́ть, вы́нудить **3** (press) наж|има́ть, -а́ть **4** (promote) реклами́ровать (*impf.*); прот|а́лкивать, -олкну́ть
 ● *v.i.* **1** (exert force) толка́ться (*impf.*); **don't ~!** не толка́йтесь! **2** (force one's way) прот|а́лкиваться, -олкну́ться; **he ~ed past me** он проле́з вперёд, оттолкну́в меня́
 □ **~ around** *v.t.* (fig.): **I won't be ~ed around** я не позво́лю кома́ндовать над(о) мной
 □ **~ aside/away** *v.t.* отт|а́лкивать, -олкну́ть
 □ **~ in** *v.t.* вт|а́лкивать, -олкну́ть
 ● *v.i.* втира́ться, втере́ться; **don't ~ in!** (intrude) не ле́зьте!
 □ **~ on** *v.i.* продв|ига́ться, -и́нуться (вперёд)
 □ **~ over** *v.t.* опроки́д|ывать, -нуть
 □ **~ past** *v.i.* прот|а́лкиваться, -олкну́ться
 □ **~ through** *v.t.* (lit., fig.) прот|а́лкивать, -олкну́ть
 ■ **~chair** *n.* (BrE) (де́тская) прогу́лочная коля́ска; **~-up** *n.* (AmE) отжима́ние; **do ~-ups** отж|има́ться, -а́ться (от по́ла)

pusher /'pʊʃə(r)/ *n.* (infml, drug ~) наркоторго́вец

pushy /'pʊʃi/ *adj.* (**pushier**, **pushiest**) напо́ристый

puss /pʊs/ *n.* (cat) ко́шечка, ки́ска

☞ **put** /pʊt/ *v.t.* (**putting**, *past and p.p.* **put**)
 1 (move into a certain position) класть, положи́ть; (stand) ста́вить, по-; (set) сажа́ть, посади́ть; **~ the money in your pocket!** положи́те де́ньги в карма́н!; **~ yourself in my place!** поста́вьте себя́ на моё ме́сто!; **I ~ the matter into the hands of my lawyer** я поручи́л э́то де́ло своему́ адвока́ту; **she ~ a cloth on the table** она́ накры́ла стол ска́тертью; **she ~ the children to bed** она́ уложи́ла дете́й; **where did I ~ that book?** куда́ я дел э́ту кни́гу? **2** (thrust) вонз|а́ть, -и́ть; **he ~ his fist through the window** он проби́л окно́ кулако́м **3** (bring into a certain state or relationship): **that ~s me at a disadvantage** э́то ста́вит меня́ в невы́годное положе́ние; **his cold ~ him off his food** из-за просту́ды он потеря́л аппети́т; (impose, bring in): **the tax ~s a heavy burden on the rich** нало́г ложи́тся тяжёлым бре́менем на бога́тых; (set, arrange): **~ in order** прив|оди́ть, -ести́ в поря́док; (appoint to a job) ста́вить, по-; **~ sb in charge of** ста́вить, по- кого́-н. во главе́ + *g.*; (offer): **they ~ their house**

on the market они́ объяви́ли о прода́же до́ма; (invest) вкла́дывать, вложи́ть; поме|ща́ть, -сти́ть **4** (estimate, consider): **I would ~ her (age) at about 65** я дал бы ей лет 65; **I wouldn't ~ it past him to be lying** с него́ ста́нется: совра́т и де́нег не возьмёт; **he ~s a high value on courtesy** он высоко́ це́нит ве́жливость **5** (submit) выдвига́ть, вы́двинуть; зад|ава́ть, -а́ть; **may I ~ a suggestion?** мо́жно мне внести́ предложе́ние? **6** (express) изл|ага́ть, -ожи́ть; **how can I ~ it?** как бы э́то сказа́ть?; **will you ~ that in writing?** вы мо́жете изложи́ть э́то на бума́ге?
 □ **~ across** *v.t.* (make clear, communicate) объясн|я́ть, -и́ть
 □ **~ away** *v.t.* (tidy) уб|ира́ть, -ра́ть; (save) от|кла́дывать, -ложи́ть
 □ **~ back** *v.t.* (replace, restore) класть, положи́ть на ме́сто; (of clock) перев|оди́ть, -ести́ наза́д; (postpone) от|кла́дывать, -ложи́ть
 □ **~ by** *v.t.* (save) от|кла́дывать, -ложи́ть
 □ **~ down** *v.t.* (place on ground, etc.) класть, положи́ть на зе́млю; **~ your gun down!** бро́сьте ору́жие!; опусти́те ружьё!; (allow to alight): **the bus stopped to ~ down passengers** авто́бус останови́лся, что́бы вы́садить пассажи́ров; (make deposit of) вн|оси́ть, -ести́ (зада́ток); (lower) сн|ижа́ть, -и́зить; (repress) подав|ля́ть, -и́ть; **the rebellion was quickly ~ down** восста́ние бы́ло бы́стро пода́влено; (write down) запи́с|ывать, -а́ть; (kill sick animal) усып|ля́ть, -и́ть; умерщв|ля́ть, -и́ть
 □ **~ forward** *v.t.* (advance): **the clocks are ~ forward in spring** весно́й часы́ перево́дят вперёд; (propose) выдвиг|а́ть, вы́двинуть; **his name was ~ forward** была́ вы́двинута его́ кандидату́ра; (bring nearer) передв|ига́ть, -и́нуть вперёд
 □ **~ in** *v.t.* (cause to enter; insert) вст|авля́ть, -а́вить; (install) вст|авля́ть, -а́вить; (contribute): **I ~ in a word for him** я вста́вил за него́ слове́чко; (submit, present) под|ава́ть, -а́ть; **I ~ in an application** я по́дал заявле́ние; **~ in an appearance** появ|ля́ться, -и́ться; (work): **I ~ in 6 hours today** я сего́дня отрабо́тал 6 часо́в
 ● *v.i.* (of boat or crew) за|ходи́ть, -йти́ в порт; **the ship ~ in at Gibraltar** кора́бль зашёл в Гибралта́р; (apply): **she ~ in for a job as secretary** она́ подала́ заявле́ние на до́лжность/ме́сто секретаря́
 □ **~ off** *v.t.* (postpone) от|кла́дывать, -ложи́ть; отсро́ч|ивать, -ть; (fob off): **he ~ me off with promises** он отде́лался от меня́ обеща́ниями; (deter) отпу́г|ивать, -ну́ть; **we were ~ off by the weather** мы переду́мали из-за пого́ды; (repel) отт|а́лкивать, -олкну́ть; **I was ~ off by his tactlessness** меня́ оттолкну́ла его́ беста́ктность; (distract): **I can't recite if you keep ~ting me off** я не могу́ деклами́ровать, когда́ вы меня́ отвлека́ете
 □ **~ on** *v.t.* (clothes, etc.) над|ева́ть, -е́ть; (place in position): **when the pot is full, ~ the lid on** когда́ кастрю́ля напо́лнится, накро́йте её кры́шкой; (assume): **he ~ on an air of innocence** он напусти́л на себя́ неви́нный вид; (increase) увели́чи|вать, -ть; **you're ~ting on weight**

вы полнéете/поправля́етесь; (light, radio, etc.)
включ|а́ть, -и́ть; (play, concert, etc.) ста́вить, по-

□ ~ **out** v.t. (place outside door) выставля́ть,
вы́ставить за дверь; (extend, protrude): ~
your tongue out! покажи́те язы́к!; **he ~
out his hand in welcome** он протяну́л ру́ку
для приве́тствия; (arrange so as to be seen)
выставля́ть, вы́ставить; выкла́дывать,
вы́ложить; (hang up outside) выве́шивать,
вы́весить; **she ~ the washing out to dry**
она́ вы́весила бельё суши́ться; (extinguish)
туши́ть, по-; гаси́ть, по-; ~ **the lights out!**
потуши́те свет!; ~ **your cigarette out!**
погаси́те сигаре́ту!; (dislocate) выви́хивать,
вы́вихнуть; (inconvenience) нар|уша́ть, -у́шить
пла́ны + g.; **would it ~ you out to come at
3?** вас не затрудни́т прийти́ в 3 часа́?; (vex)
раздраж|а́ть, -и́ть

□ ~ **through** v.t. (accomplish) осуществ|ля́ть,
-и́ть; (connect by telephone) соедин|я́ть, -и́ть

□ ~ **together** v.t. (bring close or into contact)
соедин|я́ть, -и́ть; (assemble) сост|авля́ть,
-а́вить; (construct from components) соб|ира́ть,
-ра́ть

□ ~ **up** v.t. (raise, hold up) подн|има́ть, -я́ть;
~ **up your hand if you know the answer!**
кто зна́ет отве́т, подними́те ру́ку!; (display)
выставля́ть, вы́ставить; (erect) возд|вига́ть,
-и́гнуть; стро́ить, по-; **shall we ~ the
curtains up?** бу́дем ве́шать занаве́ски?;
(increase) пов|ыша́ть, -ы́сить; ~ **up prices** (BrE)
подн|има́ть, -я́ть це́ны; (offer) выдвига́ть,
вы́двинуть; **he ~ up no resistance** он не
оказа́л никако́го сопротивле́ния; **they ~
up three candidates** они́ вы́двинули трёх
кандида́тов; (supply) вн|оси́ть, -ести́; **I will
~ up £1,000 to support him** я вношу́ ты́сячу
фу́нтов в его́ по́льзу; (accommodate) **he ~ me**

up for the night я переночева́л у него́; (infml,
introduce): **I ~ him up to that trick** я его́ научи́л
э́тому приёму/трю́ку

● v.i. (tolerate) мири́ться, при- (*с кем/чем*); **I
won't ~ up with any nonsense** я не потерплю́
никаки́х глу́постей

■ ~-**down** n. (snub) ре́зкость

putrefy /ˈpjuːtrɪfaɪ/ v.i. (go bad) гнить, с-;
(fester) разл|ага́ться, -ожи́ться

putrid /ˈpjuːtrɪd/ adj. (decomposed) гнило́й;
(infml, unpleasant) отврати́тельный

putt /pʌt/ n. уда́р, загоня́ющий мяч в лу́нку
(*в гольфе*)

● v.i. (**putted**, **putting**) заг|оня́ть, -на́ть
мяч в лу́нку

■ ~**ing green** n. лужа́йка с лу́нками
(*в гольфе*)

putty /ˈpʌtɪ/ n. зама́зка, шпаклёвка

puzzle /ˈpʌz(ə)l/ n. зага́дка; (for entertainment)
головоло́мка, пазл

● v.t. озада́ч|ивать, -ть; прив|оди́ть, -ести́ в
недоуме́ние

PVC abbr. (*of* **polyvinyl chloride**) ПВХ
(поливинилхлори́д)

pygmy /ˈpɪɡmɪ/ n. пигме́й

pyjamas /pəˈdʒɑːməz/ (AmE **pajamas**) n. pl.
пижа́ма; **pyjama trousers** пижа́мные штаны́

pylon /ˈpaɪlən/ n. (for electricity) опо́ра (*линии
электропереда́ч*)

pyramid /ˈpɪrəmɪd/ n. пирами́да

pyre /ˈpaɪə(r)/ n. погреба́льный костёр

Pyrenees /ˌpɪrəˈniːz/ n. pl. Пирене́|и (-ев)

pyrotechnics /ˌpaɪərəʊˈteknɪks/ n. pl.
(treated as sg. or pl.) (art of making fireworks)
пироте́хника; (firework display, also fig.)
фейерве́рк

python /ˈpaɪθ(ə)n/ n. пито́н

p

q

Qq

Qatar /kæˈtɑː(r)/ n. Ка́тар

QE abbr. (*of* **quantitative easing**) (econ.)
коли́чественное смягче́ние

quack /kwæk/ n. (sound) кря́канье
● v.i. кря́кать (*impf.*)

quadruple /ˈkwɒdrʊp(ə)l/ adj. учетверённый
● v.t. & i. увели́чи|вать(ся), -ть(ся) в четы́ре
ра́за

quagmire /ˈkwɒɡmaɪə(r)/ n. (also fig.) боло́то

quail /kweɪl/ v.i. тру́сить, с-

quaint /kweɪnt/ adj. причу́дливый, чудно́й

quake /kweɪk/ v.i. дрожа́ть (*impf.*);
содрог|а́ться, -ну́ться

qualification /ˌkwɒlɪfɪˈkeɪʃ(ə)n/ n. **1** (skill)
квалифика́ция **2** (modification) ограниче́ние

qualifier /ˈkwɒlɪfaɪə(r)/ n. (match) отбо́рочное
соревнова́ние, отбо́рочный матч; (person,
team) челове́к, проше́дший (*or* кома́нда,
проше́дшая) отбо́рочные соревнова́ния

◗ **qualif|y** /ˈkwɒlɪfaɪ/ v.t. **1** (for job) гото́вить
(*impf.*); **I am not ~ied to advise you** я
недоста́точно компете́нтен, что́бы дава́ть
вам сове́ты; (make entitled) дава́ть, дать пра́во
(+ d.) (to + inf.; for: на + a.); **he is a ~ied**

doctor он дипломи́рованный врач **2** (modify) огов|а́ривать, -ори́ть; уточн|я́ть, -и́ть; **I must ~y my statement** я до́лжен сде́лать огово́рку ● *v.i.* (be eligible) име́ть (*impf.*) пра́во (**for:** на + *a.*); **will you ~y for a pension?** бу́дете ли вы име́ть пра́во на пе́нсию?; (sport): **our team failed to ~y** на́ша кома́нда не прошла́ отбо́рочные соревнова́ния

qualitative /ˈkwɒlɪtətɪv/ *adj.* ка́чественный

◇ **quality** /ˈkwɒlɪtɪ/ *n.* **1** (degree of merit) ка́чество; (excellence) высо́кое ка́чество, доброка́чественность **2** (characteristic) ка́чество, сво́йство
● *adj.* (высоко)ка́чественный

qualm /kwɑːm/ *n.* сомне́ние, колеба́ние

quandary /ˈkwɒndərɪ/ *n.* затрудни́тельное положе́ние

quango /ˈkwæŋɡəʊ/ *n.* (*pl.* ~s) (BrE, infml) полуавтоно́мная организа́ция

quantifiable /ˈkwɒntɪfaɪəb(ə)l/ *adj.* измери́мый

quantitative /ˈkwɒntɪtətɪv/ *adj.* коли́чественный
■ **~ easing** *n.* (econ.) коли́чественная смягче́ние

quantity /ˈkwɒntɪtɪ/ *n.* коли́чество
■ **~ surveyor** *n.* (BrE) инжене́р-планови́к

quantum /ˈkwɒntəm/ *n.* (*pl.* **quanta**) (phys.) квант; **~ leap** скачо́к; **~ mechanics** ква́нтовая меха́ника; **~ theory** ква́нтовая тео́рия

quarantine /ˈkwɒrəntiːn/ *n.* каранти́н
● *v.t.* содержа́ть (*impf.*) в каранти́не

quarrel /ˈkwɒr(ə)l/ *n.* **1** (altercation) ссо́ра **2** (cause for complaint) по́вод для ссо́ры, прете́нзия; **I have no ~ with him on that score** у меня́ нет к нему́ прете́нзий по э́тому по́воду
● *v.i.* (**quarrelled, quarrelling**, AmE **quarreled, quarreling**) (have an argument) ссо́риться, по-; (take issue): **I cannot ~ with his logic** я не могу́ не согласи́ться с его́ ло́гикой

quarrelsome /ˈkwɒrəlsəm/ *adj.* сварли́вый

quarry¹ /ˈkwɒrɪ/ *n.* (prey) добы́ча

quarry² /ˈkwɒrɪ/ *n.* (for stone etc.) карье́р
● *v.t.* (extract) доб|ыва́ть, -ы́ть

◇ **quarter** /ˈkwɔːtə(r)/ *n.* **1** (fourth part) че́тверть; (of hour): **a ~ to six** без че́тверти шесть; **a ~ past six** че́тверть седьмо́го; (of year) кварта́л **2** (AmE coin) два́дцать пять це́нтов **3** (district) кварта́л **4** (in *pl.*) (lodgings) каза́рмы (*f. pl.*); кварти́ры (*f. pl.*) **5**: **at close ~s** в те́сном сосе́дстве, вблизи́
● *v.t.* (divide into four) дели́ть, раз- на четы́ре ча́сти
■ **~-final** *n.* четвертьфина́л

quarterly /ˈkwɔːtəlɪ/ *adj.* кварта́льный
● *adv.* ежеква́ртально; раз в три ме́сяца

quartet /kwɔːˈtet/ *n.* (mus.) кварте́т

quartz /kwɔːts/ *n.* кварц

quash /kwɒʃ/ *v.t.* подав|ля́ть, -и́ть

quaver /ˈkweɪvə(r)/ *n.* **1** (trembling tone) дрожа́ние **2** (BrE, mus.) восьма́я но́та
● *v.i.* дрожа́ть (*impf.*)

quay /kiː/ *n.* прича́л

■ **~side** *n.* при́стань

queasy /ˈkwiːzɪ/ *adj.* (**queasier, queasiest**): **I feel a little ~** меня́ немно́го тошни́т

queen /kwiːn/ *n.* **1** короле́ва **2** (fig.) короле́ва, цари́ца **3** (*also* **~ bee**) ма́тка **4** (at chess) ферзь (*m.*) **5** (at cards) да́ма
■ **Q~'s Counsel** *n.* адвока́т вы́сшего ра́нга

queer /kwɪə(r)/ *adj.* стра́нный

quell /kwel/ *v.t.* подавля́ть, -и́ть

quench /kwentʃ/ *v.t.*: **~ one's thirst** утол|я́ть, -и́ть жа́жду

querulous /ˈkwerʊləs/ *adj.* ворчли́вый

query /ˈkwɪərɪ/ *n.* вопро́с
● *v.t.* выража́ть, вы́разить сомне́ние в + *p.*; усомни́ться (*pf.*) в + *p.*

quest /kwest/ *n.* по́иски (*m. pl.*); **the ~ for happiness** по́иски сча́стья

◇ **question** /ˈkwestʃ(ə)n/ *n.* **1** (interrogation; problem) вопро́с; **it is only a ~ of finding the money** де́ло то́лько в том, что́бы найти́ де́ньги; **a holiday is out of the ~** об о́тпуске не мо́жет быть и ре́чи; **the man in ~** челове́к, о кото́ром идёт речь **2** (doubt, objection) сомне́ние; **his statements were called into ~** его́ заявле́ния бы́ли поста́влены под сомне́ние
● *v.t.* **1** (interrogate) допр|а́шивать, -оси́ть **2** (cast doubt on) ста́вить, по- под сомне́ние
■ **~ mark** *n.* вопроси́тельный знак

questionable /ˈkwestʃənəb(ə)l/ *adj.* сомни́тельный

questioner /ˈkwestʃənə(r)/ *n.* задаю́щий/зада́вший вопро́с(ы)

questionnaire /kwestʃəˈneə(r)/ *n.* анке́та

queue /kjuː/ (BrE) *n.* о́чередь; **he was trying to jump the ~** он пыта́лся пройти́ без о́череди
● *v.i.* (**queues, queued, queuing** *or* **queueing**) (*also* **~ up**) станови́ться, стать в о́чередь

quibble /ˈkwɪb(ə)l/ *v.i.* (argue) пререка́ться (*impf.*)

quiche /kiːʃ/ *n.* откры́тый пиро́г с сы́ром, беко́ном, о́вощами *и т. п.*

◇ **quick** /kwɪk/ *n.*: **he bit his nails to the ~** он иску́сал все но́гти; **his words cut me to the ~** его́ слова́ заде́ли меня́ за живо́е
● *adj.* **1** (rapid) бы́стрый, ско́рый; **he is a ~ worker** он бы́стро рабо́тает **2** (lively) живо́й; (quick-minded) сообрази́тельный; **he has a ~ temper** он о́чень вспы́льчив
● *adv.* бы́стро; **~, get a doctor!** скоре́е позови́те врача́!
■ **~sand(s)** *n.* зыбу́чий песо́к; зыбу́чие пески́; **~-tempered** *adj.* вспы́льчивый; **~-witted** *adj.* смышлёный, нахо́дчивый

quicken /ˈkwɪkən/ *v.t.* (make quicker) уск|оря́ть, -о́рить; (stimulate) возбу|жда́ть, -ди́ть
● *v.i.* (become quicker) уск|оря́ться, -о́риться

quid /kwɪd/ *n.* (*pl.* ~) (BrE, infml, £1) фунт (сте́рлингов)

◇ **quiet** /ˈkwaɪət/ *n.* (silence) тишина́; (repose) поко́й
● *adj.* (**quieter, quietest**) **1** (making little or no sound) ти́хий; бесшу́мный; **can't you keep**

q

~**?** ты не мо́жешь помолча́ть? **2** (undisturbed) споко́йный, ми́рный; **we had a ~ night** ночь прошла́ споко́йно **3** (of gentle disposition) споко́йный, ти́хий **4** (private; concealed) та́йный; скры́тый; **on the ~** (infml, secretly) тайко́м; втихомо́лку; (in confidence) под (больши́м) секре́том
● *int.* ти́ше!

quieten /'kwaɪət(ə)n/ *v.t. & i.* (BrE *also* ~ **down**) успок|а́ивать(ся), -о́ить(ся)

quietness /'kwaɪətnɪs/ *n.* (stillness) тишина́; (repose) поко́й; (of manner) невозмути́мость, споко́йствие

quiff /kwɪf/ *n.* (BrE) чёлка; (tuft) зачёс

quill /kwɪl/ *n.* перо́; (of porcupine) игла́ (*дикобра́за*)

quilt /kwɪlt/ *n.* стёганое одея́ло
● *v.t.:* ~**ed bathrobe, bedcover** стёганый хала́т, стёганое покрыва́ло

quip /kwɪp/ *n.* остро́та
● *v.i.* (**quipped, quipping**) остри́ть, с-

quirk /kwə:k/ *n.* причу́да

quirky /'kwə:kɪ/ *adj.* (**quirkier, quirkiest**) причу́дливый

quit /kwɪt/ *v.t.* (**quitting,** *past and p.p.* **quitted** *or* **quit**) **1** (leave) ост|авля́ть, -а́вить **2** (infml, stop) прекра|ща́ть, -ти́ть
● *v.i.* (**quitting,** *past and p.p.* **quitted** *or* **quit**) **1** (leave job etc.): **the maid was given notice to ~** го́рничную предупреди́ли об увольне́нии **2** (leave off) перест|ава́ть, -а́ть

✓ **quite** /kwaɪt/ *adv.* **1** (entirely) совсе́м,

совершённо, вполне́; **I ~ agree** я вполне́/ совершённо согла́сен; ~ **right!** совершённо ве́рно!; **have you ~ finished?** ну, вы ко́нчили?; **that is ~ another matter** э́то совсе́м друго́е де́ло **2** (to a certain extent) дово́льно; **it is ~ cold here** здесь дово́льно хо́лодно; **I ~ like cycling** я не прочь поката́ться на велосипе́де; ~ **a long time** дово́льно мно́го вре́мени; ~ **a few** дово́льно мно́го; нема́ло

quits /kwɪts/ *pred. adj.:* **now we are ~** тепе́рь мы кви́ты

quiver /'kwɪvə(r)/ *v.i.* дрожа́ть, за-

quiz /kwɪz/ *n.* (*pl.* **quizzes**) (test of knowledge) виктори́на; (AmE, school test) контро́льная (рабо́та)
● *v.t.* (**quizzed, quizzing**) выспра́шивать, вы́спросить

quizzical /'kwɪzɪk(ə)l/ *adj.* насме́шливый, ирони́ческий

quorum /'kwɔ:rəm/ *n.* кво́рум

quota /'kwəʊtə/ *n.* (*pl.* ~**s**) кво́та, но́рма

quotation /kwəʊ'teɪʃ(ə)n/ *n.* **1** (passage quoted) цита́та **2** (estimate of cost) цена́, сто́имость
■ ~ **marks** *n. pl.* кавы́ч|ки (-ек)

✓ **quote** /kwəʊt/ *n.* **1** (infml, quotation) цита́та **2** (in *pl.*) (infml, quotation marks) кавы́ч|ки (-ек)
● *v.t.* **1** (repeat words of) цити́ровать, про- **2** (refer to) ссыла́ться, сосла́ться на + *a.* **3**: ~ **a price** назн|ача́ть, -а́чить це́ну

Rr

rabbi /'ræbaɪ/ *n.* (*pl.* ~**s**) равви́н

rabbit /'ræbɪt/ *n.* кро́лик

rabble /'ræb(ə)l/ *n.* сброд, чернь
■ ~-**rouser** *n.* демаго́г; ~-**rousing** *adj.* демагоги́ческий

rabid /'ræbɪd/ *adj.* (with rabies, also fig.) бе́шеный

rabies /'reɪbi:z/ *n.* бе́шенство

raccoon, racoon /rə'ku:n/ *n.* ено́т

✓ **race¹** /reɪs/ *n.* **1** бег на ско́рость, го́нка; забе́г; (horse) ~**s** ска́чки (*f. pl.*)
● *v.t.:* **I'll ~ you to the corner** посмо́трим, кто быстре́е добежи́т до угла́
● *v.i.* **1** (compete in speed) состяза́ться (*impf.*) в ско́рости **2** (move at speed) нести́сь (*impf.*); мча́ться, по-
■ ~**horse** *n.* скакова́я ло́шадь; ~**track** *n.* трек

race² /reɪs/ *n.* (ethnic) páca

racer /'reɪsə(r)/ *n.* (person) го́нщик; (car, yacht, etc.) го́ночная маши́на/я́хта *и т. п.*

racial /'reɪʃ(ə)l/ *adj.* pácовый

racing /'reɪsɪŋ/ *n.* (in full **horse** ~) ска́чки (*f. pl.*); (in full **motor** ~) автого́нки (*f. pl.*)
■ ~ **car** *n.* го́ночный автомоби́ль; ~ **driver** *n.* го́нщик

racism /'reɪsɪz(ə)m/ *n.* раси́зм

racist /'reɪsɪst/ *n.* раси́ст (-ка)
● *adj.* раси́стский

rack¹ /ræk/ *n.* сто́йка с по́лками; стелла́ж; (plate ~) подста́вка для посу́ды; (luggage ~) бага́жная по́лка/се́тка

rack² /ræk/ *v.t.* му́чить, из-; **he was ~ed with pain** он ко́рчился от бо́ли; (fig.): **I ~ed my brains for an answer** я лома́л го́лову над отве́том

racket¹, racquet /'rækɪt/ *n.* раке́тка

racket² /'rækɪt/ *n.* **1** (din) шум, гам **2** (infml, dishonest scheme) жу́льническое предприя́тие

q
r

racketeer /ˌrækɪˈtɪə(r)/ n. рэкетир

raconteur /ˌrækɒnˈtɜː(r)/ n. хороший рассказчик

racoon /rəˈkuːn/ n. = raccoon

racy /ˈreɪsɪ/ adj. (**racier, raciest**) (piquant, lively) острый, пряный; a ~ **style** бойкий/яркий стиль

radar /ˈreɪdɑː(r)/ n. радиолокация; (apparatus) радар; ~ **screen** экран радара

radiance /ˈreɪdɪəns/ n. сияние, блеск; the sun's ~ солнечное сияние

radiant /ˈreɪdɪənt/ adj. сияющий; she was ~ with happiness она сияла от счастья

radiate /ˈreɪdɪeɪt/ v.t. & i. излуч|ать(ся), -ить(ся); (fig.): his face ~d happiness его лицо светилось радостью

radiation /ˌreɪdɪˈeɪʃ(ə)n/ n. радиация, излучение

radiator /ˈreɪdɪeɪtə(r)/ n. (heating device) батарея, радиатор; (of car) радиатор

radical /ˈrædɪk(ə)l/ n. (pol., chem., math.) радикал
● adj. (fundamental) коренной; (pol.) радикальный

radicalization /ˌrædɪkəlaɪˈzeɪʃ(ə)n/ n. радикализация

radicalize /ˈrædɪkəlaɪz/ v.t. радикализировать (impf., pf.)

ᵇ **radio** /ˈreɪdɪəʊ/ n. (pl. ~s) (means of communication) радио (nt. indecl.); (receiving apparatus) радиоприёмник
● v.t. (**radioes, radioed**) 1 (send by ~) перед|авать, -ать (по радио) 2 (contact by ~) ради́ровать (pf.) + d.
■ ~-controlled adj. радиоуправляемый; ~ station n. радиостанция

radioactive /ˌreɪdɪəʊˈæktɪv/ adj. радиоактивный

radioactivity /ˌreɪdɪəʊækˈtɪvɪtɪ/ n. радиоактивность

radiographer /ˌreɪdɪˈɒɡrəfə(r)/ n. рентгенолог, радиографист

radiography /ˌreɪdɪˈɒɡrəfɪ/ n. рентгенография, радиография

radiologist /ˌreɪdɪˈɒlədʒɪst/ n. радиолог, рентгенолог

radiology /ˌreɪdɪˈɒlədʒɪ/ n. рентгенология, радиология

radiotherapy /ˌreɪdɪəʊˈθerəpɪ/ n. радиотерапия

radish /ˈrædɪʃ/ n. редиска; (in pl., collect.) редис

radius /ˈreɪdɪəs/ n. радиус

raffle /ˈræf(ə)l/ n. лотерея

raft /rɑːft/ n. (сплавной) плот

rafter /ˈrɑːftə(r)/ n. стропило

rag /ræɡ/ n. (cloth) тряпка, лоскут; (in pl.) (torn or tattered clothing) лохмоть|я (-ев)

rag|e /reɪdʒ/ n. 1 (violent anger) ярость, гнев 2 (dominant fashion) последний крик моды
● v.i.: he ~ed at his wife он накинулся на свою жену; the wind ~ed all day ветер бушевал весь день; a ~ing thirst

мучительная жажда

ragged /ˈræɡɪd/ adj. 1 (torn) рваный, потрёпанный; (wearing torn clothes) оборванный 2 (rough): a ~ **beard** косматая борода; ~ **clouds** рваные облака

raid /reɪd/ n. (by police) облава, рейд; (by criminals) налёт; (mil.) рейд, налёт
● v.t.: our bombers ~ed Hamburg наши бомбардировщики совершили налёт на Гамбург; the flat was ~ed in his absence в его отсутствие квартиру ограбили

rail /reɪl/ n. 1 (bar for support etc.) перекладина, рейка; (of staircase) перил|а (pl., g. —); (for hanging things on) вешалка 2 (of railway track) рельс; (railway transport): by ~ поездом
■ ~road n. (AmE) железная дорога ● v.t. (infml): they were ~roaded into agreement их с ходу втянули в соглашение; ~way n. железная дорога; (attr.) железнодорожный

railing /ˈreɪlɪŋ/, **railings** /ˈreɪlɪŋz/ nn. ограда, решётка

ᵇ **rain** /reɪn/ n. дождь (m.)
● v.i.: it is ~ing идёт дождь; it was ~ing hard шёл сильный дождь
■ ~bow n. радуга; ~ check n. (AmE) обещание принять приглашение в другой раз; ~coat n. плащ; ~drop n. капля дождя; ~fall n. осадк|и (-ов); ~forest n. тропический лес

rainy /ˈreɪnɪ/ adj. (**rainier, rainiest**) дождливый; save, keep for a ~ **day** откладывать, отложить на чёрный день

ᵇ **raise** /reɪz/ n. (AmE, rise in salary) прибавка
● v.t. 1 (lift) подн|имать, -ять; (make higher) пов|ышать, -ысить; the government ~d the duty on tobacco правительство повысило пошлину на табак; the news ~d my hopes известие укрепило мои надежды; (make louder): don't ~ your voice! не повышайте голоса! 2 (bring up): may I ~ one question? можно мне задать вопрос?; (evoke): you ~d a doubt in my mind вы заронили мне в душу сомнение 3 (give voice to): she ~d the alarm она подняла тревогу 4 (collect): she ~d money for charity она собрала деньги на благотворительные цели 5 (rear): they ~d a family они вырастили детей

raisin /ˈreɪz(ə)n/ n. изюминка

rake /reɪk/ n. (tool) граб|ли (pl., g. -лей/-ель)
● v.t.: he ~d the soil level он разрыхлил грунт
□ ~ **in** v.t.: he ~d in the money (fig., infml) он загребал деньги лопатой
□ ~ **up** v.t. сгре|бать, -сти; (fig.): why ~ up an old quarrel? зачем ворошить старую ссору?

rakish /ˈreɪkɪʃ/ adj. (of man) распутный, бесшабашный; (of hat) залихватски/лихо/небрежно надетый

rall|y /ˈrælɪ/ n. 1 (mass gathering) митинг 2 (at tennis etc.) (затяжной) обмен ударами, серия 3 (motor race) авторалли (nt. indecl.)
● v.t. (reassemble) соб|ирать, -рать (в строй)
● v.i. 1 (reassemble) соб|ираться, -раться 2 (revive): he ~ied from his illness он оправился от болезни; the market ~ied рынок ожил/оживился

r

RAM /ræm/ *n.* (*abbr. of* **random-access memory**) (comput.) операти́вная па́мять, ОЗУ (операти́вное запомина́ющее устро́йство)

ram /ræm/ *n.* бара́н
• *v.t.* (**rammed, ramming**) **1** (drive by force): **stakes were ~med into the ground** ко́лья бы́ли вби́ты в зе́млю **2** (strike with force): **the ship ~med the bridge** кора́бль наскочи́л на мост
■ **~ raid** *n.* ограбле́ние с испо́льзованием тяжёлой (строи́тельной) те́хники

Ramadan /ˈræmədæn/ *n.* (relig.) Рамаза́н, Рамада́н

rambl|e /ˈræmb(ə)l/ *n.* прогу́лка
• *v.i.* **1** (walk) прогу́л|иваться, -я́ться **2** (fig., of speech) болта́ть (*impf.*); языко́м; a **~ing speaker** многосло́вный ора́тор; a **~ing speech** бессвя́зная речь

rambler /ˈræmblə(r)/ *n.* (hiker) люби́тель (-ница) пешехо́дного тури́зма

ramification /ræmɪfɪˈkeɪʃ(ə)n/ *n.* разветвле́ние; (consequence) после́дствие

ramp /ræmp/ *n.* (slope) скат, укло́н

rampage *n.*: /ˈræmpeɪdʒ/ **go on the ~** нейстовствовать (*impf.*)
• *v.i.* /ræmˈpeɪdʒ/ бу́йствовать, буя́нить (*both impf.*)

rampant /ˈræmpənt/ *adj.* свире́пствующий, безу́держный

rampart /ˈræmpɑːt/ *n.* крепостно́й вал

ramshackle /ˈræmʃæk(ə)l/ *adj.* обветша́лый

ran /ræn/ *past of* ▸ **run**

ranch /rɑːntʃ/ *n.* ра́нчо (*nt. indecl.*), фе́рма

rancher /ˈrɑːntʃə(r)/ *n.* владе́лец ра́нчо; ското́вод

rancid /ˈrænsɪd/ *adj.* прого́рклый, ту́хлый

rancour /ˈræŋkə(r)/ (AmE **rancor**) *n.* зло́ба

R & B *abbr.* (*of* **rhythm and blues**) ритм-энд-блюз; (modern style) ар-эн-би́ (*m. indecl.*) (*usu. written in Roman*)

R & D *abbr.* (*of* **research and development**) нау́чно-иссле́довательская рабо́та

random /ˈrændəm/ *n.*: **at ~** наобу́м, науга́д, науда́чу
• *adj.* случа́йный

randy /ˈrændɪ/ *adj.* (**randier, randiest**) (BrE, infml) сексуа́льно возбуждённый, похотли́вый

rang /ræŋ/ *past of* ▸ **ring²**

✍ **range** /reɪndʒ/ *n.* **1** (row, series) цепь, ряд **2** (grazing area) неогоро́женное па́стбище; (hunting ground) охо́тничье уго́дье **3** (area for firing, bombing, etc.) полиго́н; **rifle ~** стре́льбище **4** (operating distance) да́льность, ра́диус; **they fired at close ~** они́ стреля́ли с бли́зкого расстоя́ния **5** (extent) диапазо́н **6** (selection) набо́р; (assortment) ассортиме́нт **7** (stove) ку́хонная плита́
• *v.i.* **1** (wander): **tigers ~d through the jungle** ти́гры броди́ли по джу́нглям **2** (extend)

простира́ться (*impf.*); **my research ~s over a wide field** мои́ иссле́дования охва́тывают широ́кую о́бласть **3** (vary between limits) колеба́ться (*impf.*)

ranger /ˈreɪndʒə(r)/ *n.* лесни́к, объе́здчик

✍ **rank¹** /ræŋk/ *n.* **1** (row) ряд; (*in full* **taxi ~**) (BrE) стоя́нка такси́ **2** (line of soldiers) шере́нга; **the men broke ~(s)** солда́ты нару́шили строй; **among the ~s of the unemployed** в ряда́х безрабо́тных **3** (common soldiers) рядовы́е **4** (position in armed forces etc.) зва́ние, чин **5** (social position): **people of all ~s of society** представи́тели всех слоёв о́бщества
• *v.t.* (class) классифици́ровать (*impf., pf.*); **he was ~ed among the great poets** его́ причисля́ли к вели́ким поэ́там
• *v.i.* (have a place): **a high-~ing officer** ста́рший офице́р
■ **~ and file** *n. pl.* (ordinary members of organization) рядовы́е

rank² /ræŋk/ *adj.* **1** (foul; offensive): **the skunk gives off a ~ odour** от ску́нса исхо́дит злово́ние **2** (gross) чрезме́рный; **~ outsider** соверше́нно посторо́нний челове́к

rankle /ˈræŋk(ə)l/ *v.i.* терза́ть, му́чить (*both impf.*)

ransack /ˈrænsæk/ *v.t.* **1** (search) обша́ри|вать, -ть **2** (plunder) гра́бить, раз-

ransom /ˈrænsəm/ *n.* вы́куп; **he was held to ~** (lit.) за него́ тре́бовали вы́куп; (fig.) его́ шантажи́ровали

rant /rænt/ *v.i.* разглаго́льствовать (*impf.*)

rap /ræp/ *n.* **1** (light blow) лёгкий уда́р, стук **2** (*also* **~ music**) рэп
• *v.t.* (**rapped, rapping**) слегка́ уд|аря́ть, -а́рить по + *d.*
• *v.i.* (**rapped, rapping**) сту|ча́ть, -́кнуть; **he ~ped on the door** он постуча́л в дверь

rapacious /rəˈpeɪʃəs/ *adj.* жа́дный, ненасы́тный

rape¹ /reɪp/ *n.* изнаси́лование
• *v.t.* наси́ловать, из-

rape² /reɪp/ *n.* (bot.) рапс

rapid /ˈræpɪd/ *adj.* (**rapider, rapidest**) бы́стрый, ско́рый

rapidity /rəˈpɪdɪtɪ/ *n.* быстрота́, ско́рость

rapist /ˈreɪpɪst/ *n.* наси́льник

rapper /ˈræpə(r)/ *n.* исполни́тель (*m.*) рэ́па, рэ́ппер

rapport /ræˈpɔː(r)/ *n.* взаимопонима́ние, конта́кт

rapture /ˈræptʃə(r)/ *n.* восто́рг

rapturous /ˈræptʃərəs/ *adj.* восто́рженный

✍ **rare¹** /reə(r)/ *adj.* (**rarer, rarest**) (uncommon) ре́дкий

rare² /reə(r)/ *adj.* (**rarer, rarest**) (bloody): **a ~ steak** бифште́кс с кро́вью

rarefied /ˈreərɪfaɪd/ *adj.* (phys.) разрежённый; (fig.) утончённый, изы́сканный

rarely /ˈreəlɪ/ *adv.* ре́дко, неча́сто, и́зредка

raring /ˈreərɪŋ/ *adj.* (infml): **he was ~ to go** ему́ не терпе́лось приступи́ть к де́лу

✍ ключева́я ле́ксика

rarity /'reərɪtɪ/ *n.* (uncommonness) ре́дкость; (thing valued for this) (больша́я) ре́дкость

rascal /'rɑ:sk(ə)l/ *n.* моше́нник, плут

rash¹ /ræʃ/ *n.* сыпь

rash² /ræʃ/ *adj.* опроме́тчивый

rasher /'ræʃə(r)/ *n.* ло́мтик (беко́на)

rasp /rɑ:sp/ *n.* (file) ра́шпиль (*m.*), напи́льник; (grating sound) скре́жет
● *v.t.* (scrape) скрести́, скобли́ть, тере́ть (*all impf.*)
● *v.i.* скрежета́ть (*impf.*); a ~ing voice скрипу́чий го́лос
▫ ~ **away**, ~ **off** *vv.t.* соск|а́бливать, -обли́ть
▫ ~ **out** *v.t.* (e.g. an order) га́ркнуть (*pf.*)

raspberry /'rɑ:zbərɪ/ *n.* мали́на (*collect.*)

Rastafarian /ræstə'feərɪən/ *n.* (relig.) растафа́ри (*c.g. indecl.*)
● *adj.* растафариа́нский

rat /ræt/ *n.* кры́са
■ ~ **race** *n.* бе́шеная пого́ня за успе́хом/бога́тством

⚡ **rate** /reɪt/ *n.* **1** (proportion) но́рма, разме́р; ~ **of exchange** курс обме́на; **birth** ~ рожда́емость **2** (speed) ско́рость; **we shall never get there at this** ~ при таки́х те́мпах мы туда́ никогда́ не добере́мся **3** (price) расце́нка, тари́ф **4** (BrE, tax on property etc.) ме́стный нало́г **5**: **at any** ~ (in any case) во вся́ком слу́чае
● *v.t.* оце́н|ивать, -и́ть
■ ~**payer** *n.* (BrE) плате́льщик ме́стных нало́гов

⚡ **rather** /'rɑ:ðə(r)/ *adv.* **1** (by preference): **I would** ~ **die than consent** я скоре́е умру́, чем соглашу́сь; **I'd** ~ **have coffee** я предпочёл бы ко́фе; **I'd** ~ **not say** я лу́чше промолчу́ **2** (somewhat) дово́льно, не́сколько; **the result was** ~ **surprising** результа́т был дово́льно неожи́данным; **it is** ~ **a pity** а жаль всё же; **the effect was** ~ **spoiled** эффе́кт был сма́зан/подпо́рчен

ratification /rætɪfɪ'keɪʃ(ə)n/ *n.* ратифика́ция

ratify /'rætɪfaɪ/ *v.t.* ратифици́ровать (*impf., pf.*)

rating /'reɪtɪŋ/ *n.* ре́йтинг

ratio /'reɪʃɪəʊ/ *n.* (*pl.* ~**s**) отноше́ние, соотноше́ние

ration /'ræʃ(ə)n/ *n.* рацио́н, паёк
● *v.t.* (fetch): **they were** ~**ed to one loaf a week** их паёк своди́лся к одно́й буха́нке в неде́лю; **meat was severely** ~**ed** мя́со бы́ло стро́го норми́ровано

rational /'ræʃən(ə)l/ *adj.* разу́мный, рациона́льный

rationale /ræʃə'nɑ:l/ *n.* основна́я причи́на

rationalism /'ræʃənəlɪz(ə)m/ *n.* рационали́зм

rationality /ræʃə'nælɪtɪ/ *n.* разу́мность, рациона́льность

rationalize /'ræʃənəlaɪz/ *v.t.* (give reasons for) разу́мно объясн|я́ть, -и́ть; (make more efficient) рационализи́ровать (*impf., pf.*)

rattle /'ræt(ə)l/ *n.* **1** (sound) треск, гро́хот **2** (child's toy) погрему́шка
● *v.t.*: **he** ~**d the money box** он встряхну́л копи́лку

● *v.i.*: **the hail** ~**d on the roof** град бараба́нил по кры́ше
■ ~**snake** *n.* грему́чая змея́

ratty /'rætɪ/ *adj.* (**rattier**, **rattiest**) (BrE, infml, irritable) злой, раздражи́тельный

raucous /'rɔ:kəs/ *adj.* ре́зкий, хри́плый

raunchy /'rɔ:ntʃɪ/ *adj.* (**raunchier**, **raunchiest**) распу́тный

ravage /'rævɪdʒ/ *v.t.* опустош|а́ть, -и́ть

rave /reɪv/ *n.* (party) весёлая вечери́нка
● *adj.*: ~ **review** восто́рженный о́тзыв
● *v.i.* (in delirium) бре́дить (*impf.*); (in delight): **they** ~**d about the play** они́ бы́ли в восто́рге от пье́сы

raven /'reɪv(ə)n/ *n.* во́рон
■ ~-**haired** *adj.* с волоса́ми цве́та во́ронова крыла́ (*or* чёрными как смоль)

ravenous /'rævənəs/ *adj.*: **I am** ~ я го́лоден как волк

ravine /rə'vi:n/ *n.* овра́г, лощи́на

raving /'reɪvɪŋ/ *adj. & adv.* (insane): a ~ **lunatic** бу́йно поме́шанный; **you must be** ~ **mad** ты совсе́м спяти́л

ravioli /rævɪ'əʊlɪ/ *n.* равио́л|и (-ей)

ravishing /'rævɪʃɪŋ/ *adj.* восхити́тельный

raw /rɔ:/ *adj.* **1** (uncooked) сыро́й **2** (unprocessed) необрабо́танный; ~ **data** необрабо́танные да́нные; ~ **materials** сырьё **3** (inexperienced) нео́пытный, зелёный **4** (of weather) сыро́й **5** (harsh): **he got a** ~ **deal** (infml) с ним суро́во обошли́сь

Rawlplug® /'rɔ:lplʌg/ *n.* (BrE) пла́стиковый дю́бель (*для вкру́чивания шуру́пов в сте́ну и т. п.*)

ray /reɪ/ *n.* луч

raze /reɪz/ *v.t.* разр|уша́ть, -у́шить до основа́ния

razor /'reɪzə(r)/ *n.* бри́тва; **electric** ~ электробри́тва
■ ~ **blade** *n.* ле́звие

re /ri:/ *prep.* каса́тельно + *g.*

⚡ **reach** /ri:tʃ/ *n.* **1** (extent of stretch) разма́х рук, длина́ руки́; (fig.): **we are within easy** ~ **of London** от нас легко́ добра́ться до Ло́ндона; от нас до Ло́ндона руко́й пода́ть **2** (*usu. in pl.*) (stretch of river): **the upper** ~**es of the Thames** верхо́вья (*nt. pl.*) Те́мзы
● *v.t.* (fetch) дотя́|гиваться, -ну́ться до + *g.*; **I can just** ~ **the shelf** я е́ле-е́ле достаю́ (*or* могу́ дотяну́ться) до по́лки **2** (arrive at) дост|ига́ть, -и́гнуть + *g.*; **your letter** ~**ed me only yesterday** ва́ше письмо́ дошло́ до меня́ то́лько вчера́; ~ **agreement** прийти́ (*pf.*) к соглаше́нию
● *v.i.* **1** (stretch out hand) тяну́ться, по- руко́й; **he** ~**ed for his rifle** он потяну́лся к винто́вке **2** (extend) простира́ться, тяну́ться (*both impf.*)
▫ ~ **down** *v.i.*: **he** ~**ed down and picked up the coin** он нагну́лся и по́днял моне́ту
▫ ~ **up** *v.i.* протяну́ть (*pf.*) ру́ку вверх

react /rɪ'ækt/ *v.i.* реаги́ровать, от-/про-/с-

⚡ **reaction** /rɪ'ækʃ(ə)n/ *n.* реа́кция

reactionary /rɪ'ækʃənərɪ/ *n.* реакционе́р

● *adj.* реакцио́нный

reactor /rɪˈæktə(r)/ *n.* (tech.) реа́ктор

✍ **read** /riːd/ *v.t.* (*past and p.p.* **read** /red/)
1 (peruse) чита́ть, про- *or* проче́сть; **have you read this book?** вы чита́ли э́ту кни́гу?; **can you ~ music?** вы уме́ете игра́ть по но́там?
2 (discern) **he read my thoughts** он (про)чита́л мои́ мы́сли **3** (BrE, study) изуча́ть (*impf.*); **he is ~ing law** он у́чится на юриди́ческом факульте́те **4** (examine): **~ a meter** сн|има́ть, -я́ть показа́ния счётчика
● *v.i.* (*past and p.p.* **read** /red/): **he can neither ~ nor write** он не уме́ет ни чита́ть, ни писа́ть
□ **~ out** *v.t.* прочи́т|ывать, -а́ть; огла|ша́ть, -си́ть
□ **~ through** *v.t.* прочи́т|ывать, -а́ть
□ **~ up on** *v.i.* мно́го чита́ть (*impf.*); **he read up on the subject** он подчита́л ко́е-что по э́тому предме́ту

readable /ˈriːdəb(ə)l/ *adj.* **1** (legible) разбо́рчивый **2** (enjoyable, infml) интере́сный

✍ **reader** /ˈriːdə(r)/ *n.* чита́тель (-ница)

readily /ˈredɪlɪ/ *adv.* (willingly) охо́тно; (without difficulty) легко́, без труда́

✍ **reading** /ˈriːdɪŋ/ *n.* **1** (pursuit) чте́ние **2** (interpretation) толкова́ние **3** (of instrument) показа́ние
■ **~ room** *n.* чита́льный зал

readjust /riːəˈdʒʌst/ *v.t.* попр|авля́ть, -а́вить
● *v.i.*: **after the war he found it hard to ~** по́сле войны́ ему́ бы́ло тру́дно приспосо́биться к ми́рной жи́зни

✍ **ready** /ˈredɪ/ *adj.* (**readier**, **readiest**) (prepared) гото́вый (*к чему*); пригото́вленный, подгото́вленный; **I'm just getting ~** я почти́ гото́в; **she got the children ~ for school** она́ собрала́ дете́й в шко́лу; (willing) гото́вый; **I am ~ to admit I was wrong** гото́в призна́ть, что я был непра́в
● *adv.*: **they sell meat ~ cooked** там продаётся мясна́я кулинари́я
■ **~-made** *adj.* гото́вый

✍ **real** /rɪəl/ *adj.* (actual) настоя́щий; реа́льный; **in ~ life** в жи́зни; **~ silver** настоя́щее серебро́
■ **~ estate** *n.* недви́жимость; **~ time** *adj.* (comput.) (рабо́тающий/происходя́щий) в режи́ме реа́льного вре́мени

realign /riːəˈlaɪn/ *v.t.* перестр|а́ивать, -о́ить

realism /ˈriːəlɪz(ə)m/ *n.* реали́зм

realist /ˈrɪəlɪst/ *n.* реали́ст (-ка)

realistic /rɪəˈlɪstɪk/ *adj.* реалисти́чный, практи́чный

✍ **reality** /rɪˈælɪtɪ/ *n.* реа́льность, действи́тельность
■ **~ TV** *n.* реа́лити-ТВ (*nt. indecl.*)

realization /rɪəlaɪˈzeɪʃ(ə)n/ *n.* осозна́ние

✍ **realize** /ˈrɪəlaɪz/ *v.t.* **1** (be aware of) осозн|ава́ть, -а́ть; (grasp mentally) сообра|жа́ть, -зи́ть; **he ~d his mistake at once** он сра́зу же созна́л свою́ оши́бку; **do you ~ what you have done?** вы понима́ете, что вы сде́лали?; **I didn't ~ you wanted it** до меня́ не дошло́, что э́то вам

нужно **2** (convert into fact) осуществ|ля́ть, -и́ть; **I will help you to ~ your ambition** я помогу́ вам осуществи́ть ва́ши стремле́ния

✍ **really** /ˈrɪəlɪ/ *adv.* действи́тельно; в/на са́мом де́ле; **do you ~ mean it?** вы серьёзно?; **I am ~ sorry for you** мне вас и́скренне жаль; **~?** (expr. surprise) серьёзно?; (acknowledging information) да?, пра́вда?; **~!** (expr. indignation) ну, зна́ете!; **not ~** не о́чень, не осо́бенно

realm /relm/ *n.* короле́вство; (fig.) сфе́ра, о́бласть, мир

reap /riːp/ *v.t. & i.* жать, с-

reappear /riːəˈpɪə(r)/ *v.i.* сно́ва появ|ля́ться, -и́ться

reappraise /riːəˈpreɪz/ *v.t.* пересм|а́тривать, -отре́ть

rear¹ /rɪə(r)/ *n.* за́дняя часть, сторона́
● *adj.*: **~ entrance** чёрный ход; **~ wheel** за́днее колесо́
■ **~-view mirror** *n.* зе́ркало за́днего ви́да

rear² /rɪə(r)/ *v.t.* (bring up) расти́ть, вы́-; (breed) разв|оди́ть, -ести́
● *v.i.* (*also* **~ up**) ста|нови́ться, -ть на дыбы́; **the horse ~ed in terror** ло́шадь (в)ста́ла на дыбы́ от испу́га

rearm /riːˈɑːm/ *v.t. & i.* перевооруж|а́ть(ся), -и́ть(ся)

rearmament /riːˈɑːməmənt/ *n.* перевооруже́ние

rearrange /riːəˈreɪndʒ/ *v.t.* (objects) перест|авля́ть, -а́вить; (a meeting) передв|ига́ть, -и́нуть вре́мя + *g.*

rearrangement /riːəˈreɪndʒmənt/ *n.* перестано́вка

✍ **reason** /ˈriːz(ə)n/ *n.* **1** (cause, ground) причи́на; **with ~** обосно́ванно **2** (good sense) благоразу́мие; **he will not listen to ~** он не прислу́шивается к го́лосу ра́зума
● *v.i.*: **it is useless to ~ with him** его́ бесполе́зно убежда́ть; ло́гика на него́ не де́йствует

✍ **reasonable** /ˈriːzənəb(ə)l/ *adj.* **1** (sensible) (благо)разу́мный **2** (fairly good) дово́льно хоро́ший, неплохо́й

reasoning /ˈriːzənɪŋ/ *n.* рассужде́ние

reassert /riːəˈsɜːt/ *v.t.* сно́ва подтвер|жда́ть, -ди́ть

reassess /riːəˈses/ *v.t.* переоце́н|ивать, -и́ть

reassessment /riːəˈsesmənt/ *n.* переоце́нка

reassurance /riːəˈʃʊərəns/ *n.* (повто́рное) завере́ние, подтвержде́ние

reassur|e /riːəˈʃɔː(r)/ *v.t.* успок|а́ивать, -о́ить; подбодр|я́ть, -и́ть; **his words were most ~ing** его́ слова́ звуча́ли са́мым ободря́ющим о́бразом

rebate /ˈriːbeɪt/ *n.* возвра́т перепла́ченной су́ммы

rebel¹ /ˈreb(ə)l/ *n.* повста́нец

rebel² /rɪˈbel/ *v.i.* (**rebelled**, **rebelling**) восст|ава́ть, -а́ть

rebellion /rɪˈbeljən/ *n.* восста́ние, мяте́ж, бунт

rebellious /rɪˈbeljəs/ *adj.* (in revolt) восста́вший, мяте́жный; (disobedient) непоко́рный

r

reboot /ri:'bu:t/ *v.t.* (comput.) перезагру|жа́ть, -зи́ть

rebound¹ /rɪ'baʊnd/ *n.* отско́к; **on the ～** на отско́ке; (fig.): **he married her on the ～** он жени́лся на ней по́сле разочарова́ния в любви́ к друго́й

rebound² /rɪ'baʊnd/ *v.i.* отск|а́кивать, -очи́ть

rebranding /ri:'brændɪŋ/ *n.* (comm.) ребре́ндинг (*пересоздание и продвижение на рынке торговых марок*)

rebuff /rɪ'bʌf/ *n.* отпо́р, ре́зкий отка́з ● *v.t.* дава́ть, дать отпо́р + *d.*; ре́зко отклон|я́ть, -и́ть; (mil.): **the enemy's attack was ～ed** ата́ка неприя́теля была́ отражена́

rebuild /ri:'bɪld/ *v.t.* сно́ва стро́ить, по-

rebuke /rɪ'bju:k/ *n.* упрёк, уко́р ● *v.t.* упрек|а́ть, -ну́ть; укоря́ть (*impf.*)

rebut /rɪ'bʌt/ *v.t.* (**rebutted, rebutting**) опров|ерга́ть, -е́ргнуть

rebuttal /rɪ'bʌt(ə)l/ *n.* опроверже́ние

recalcitrant /rɪ'kælsɪtrənt/ *adj.* непоко́рный

recall¹ /'ri:kɔ:l/ *n.* воспомина́ние

⚹ **recall²** /rɪ'kɔ:l/ *v.t.* **1** (summon back) от|зыва́ть, -озва́ть **2** (to mind) нап|омина́ть, -о́мнить

recant /rɪ'kænt/ *v.t. & i.* публи́чно ка́яться, по- (*в чём*); отр|ека́ться, -е́чься (*от чего*)

recap /'ri:kæp/ *n.* повторе́ние ● *v.t. & i.* (**recapped, recapping**) повтор|я́ть, -и́ть; резюми́ровать (*impf., pf.*)

recapture /ri:'kæptʃə(r)/ *v.t.* взять (*pf.*) обра́тно; (fig.) восстан|а́вливать, -ови́ть в па́мяти

recce /'reki/ *n.* (BrE, infml) = **reconnaissance**

recede /rɪ'si:d/ *v.i.* **1** (move back) отступ|а́ть, -и́ть; (move away) удал|я́ться, -и́ться; **the tide was ～ing** вода́ спада́ла; **～ing hair** реде́ющие во́лосы **2** (diminish) ум|еньша́ться, -е́ньшиться

receipt /rɪ'si:t/ *n.* **1** (receiving) получе́ние **2** (in *pl.*) (money received) де́нежные поступле́ния, прихо́д **3** (written acknowledgement) распи́ска, квита́нция

⚹ **receive** /rɪ'si:v/ *v.t.* **1** (get, be given) получ|а́ть, -и́ть; **he ～s stolen goods** (BrE) он укрыва́ет кра́деное **2** (admit) прин|има́ть, -я́ть; (greet) прин|има́ть, -я́ть; **how was your speech ～d?** как бы́ло встре́чено ва́ше выступле́ние?

receiver /rɪ'si:və(r)/ *n.* **1** (*also* **telephone ～**) (телефо́нная) тру́бка **2** (*also* **radio ～**) (ра́дио)приёмник

⚹ **recent** /'ri:s(ə)nt/ *adj.* **1** (occurring lately) неда́вний **2** (modern) совреме́нный

⚹ **recently** /'ri:səntli/ *adv.* неда́вно, на днях, за после́днее вре́мя; **until quite ～** ещё совсе́м неда́вно

receptacle /rɪ'septək(ə)l/ *n.* вмести́лище

reception /rɪ'sepʃ(ə)n/ *n.* **1** (of guests etc.) приём **2** (greeting) встре́ча, приём; **he was given a great ～** ему́ устро́или великоле́пный приём **3** (of radio signals) приём
■ **～ desk** *n.* (in hotel) регистра́ция; (in hospital) регистрату́ра

receptionist /rɪ'sepʃənɪst/ *n.* (in hotel, hospital) регистра́тор, дежу́рный; (in a business firm) секрета́рь (*m.*) по приёму посети́телей

receptive /rɪ'septɪv/ *adj.* восприи́мчивый

recess /rɪ'ses, 'ri:ses/ *n.* **1** (vacation) переры́в; (AmE, between classes) переме́на **2** (niche) ни́ша, алько́в

recession /rɪ'seʃ(ə)n/ *n.* спад

recharge /ri:'tʃɑ:dʒ/ *v.t.* перезаря|жа́ть, -ди́ть

recipe /'resɪpɪ/ *n.* реце́пт

recipient /rɪ'sɪpɪənt/ *n.* получа́тель (-ница)

reciprocal /rɪ'sɪprək(ə)l/ *adj.* взаи́мный

reciprocate /rɪ'sɪprəkeɪt/ *v.t.* отв|еча́ть, -е́тить взаи́мностью ● *v.i.* отпла́|чивать, -ти́ть

reciprocity /resɪ'prɒsɪtɪ/ *n.* взаи́мность; взаимоде́йствие; обме́н

recital /rɪ'saɪt(ə)l/ *n.* изложе́ние

recite /rɪ'saɪt/ *v.t.* деклами́ровать, про-

reckless /'reklɪs/ *adj.* безрассу́дный; **he drove ～ly** он неосторо́жно вёл маши́ну

reckon /'rekən/ *v.t.* **1** (calculate) счита́ть, по- **2** (think, consider) счита́ть (*impf.*) ● *v.i.* **1** (count) счита́ть (*impf.*); **he is a man to be ～ed with** с таки́м челове́ком, как он, ну́жно счита́ться **2** (rely) рассчи́тывать (*impf.*) (*на кого/что*); **he ～ed on making a clear profit** он рассчи́тывал на чи́стую при́быль

reckoning /'rekənɪŋ/ *n.* счёт, вычисле́ние

reclaim /rɪ'kleɪm/ *v.t.* **1** (bring under cultivation) осв|а́ивать, -о́ить **2** (demand return of) тре́бовать, по- обра́тно **3** (recycle) утилизи́ровать (*impf., pf.*)

reclamation /reklə'meɪʃ(ə)n/ *n.* (of land) освое́ние; (of waste) утилиза́ция

recline /rɪ'klaɪn/ *v.i.* (полу)лежа́ть (*impf.*); **～ing nude** лежа́щая обнажённая

recluse /rɪ'klu:s/ *n.* затво́рни|к (-ца), отше́льни|к (-ца)

recognition /rekəg'nɪʃ(ə)n/ *n.* **1** (knowing again) опознава́ние, узнава́ние; (comput.) распознава́ние **2** (acknowledgement) призна́ние

recognizable /'rekəgnaɪzəb(ə)l/ *adj.* опознава́емый

⚹ **recognize** /'rekəgnaɪz/ *v.t.* **1** (know again) узн|ава́ть, -а́ть **2** (acknowledge) призн|ава́ть, -а́ть; **he was ～d as the lawful heir** он был при́знан зако́нным насле́дником

recoil /'ri:kɔɪl/ *v.i.* отпря́нуть (*pf.*)

recollect /rekə'lekt/ *v.t.* всп|омина́ть, -о́мнить

recollection /rekə'lekʃ(ə)n/ *n.* па́мять

⚹ **recommend** /rekə'mend/ *v.t.* **1** (suggest as suitable) рекомендова́ть (*impf., pf.*), от-/по- (*pf.*) **2** (advise sb) рекомендова́ть, по- + *d.*

recommendation /rekəmen'deɪʃ(ə)n/ *n.* рекоменда́ция

recompense /'rekəmpens/ *n.* компенса́ция

reconcile /'rekənsaɪl/ *v.t.* **1** (make friendly) мири́ть, по- **2** (make compatible) совме|ща́ть, -сти́ть **3** (resign): **～ oneself** смир|я́ться,

-и́ться (**to**: с + *i.*)

reconciliation /rekənsılı'eıʃ(ə)n/ *n.*
примире́ние

reconnaissance /rı'kɒnıs(ə)ns/ *n.* разве́дка,
рекогносциро́вка

reconnoitre /rekə'nɔıtə(r)/ (AmE
reconnoiter) *v.t. & i.* разве́дывать (*impf.*);
производи́ть (*impf*) разве́дку

reconsider /ri:kən'sıdə(r)/ *v.t.*
пересм|а́тривать, -отре́ть
● *v.i.* переду́мать (*pf.*)

reconstitute /ri:'kɒnstıtju:t/ *v.t.*
воспроизв|оди́ть, -ести́

reconstruct /ri:kən'strʌkt/ *v.t.*
восстан|а́вливать, -ови́ть; воссозд|ава́ть,
-а́ть; (fig.): **the police ~ed the crime** поли́ция
воспроизвела́ карти́ну преступле́ния

reconstruction /ri:kən'strʌkʃ(ə)n/ *n.*
восстановле́ние, воссозда́ние; (of acts etc.)
воспроизведе́ние, воссозда́ние

⚜ **record¹** /'rekɔ:d/ *n.* **1** (written note, document)
за́пись, учёт; **the teacher keeps a ~
of attendance** учи́тель ведёт учёт
посеща́емости; **weather ~s** да́нные
наблюде́ний за пого́дными явле́ниями
2 (state of being recorded, esp. as evidence)
за́пись; **this is off the ~** э́то не должно́
быть пре́дано огла́ске **3** (past conduct,
achievement) про́шлое; **this firm has a
bad ~ for strikes** э́та фи́рма изве́стна
многочи́сленными забасто́вками; **the
defendant had a (criminal) ~** у обвиня́емого
ра́нее име́лись суди́мости **4** (sound recording)
(грам)пласти́нка **5** (best performance) реко́рд;
world ~ мирово́й реко́рд; (*attr.*) реко́рдный,
небыва́лый; **cars have had ~ sales** про́дано
реко́рдное коли́чество маши́н
■ **~-breaking** *adj.* реко́рдный; **~ holder**
n. рекордсме́н (-ка); **~ player** *n.*
про́игрыватель (*m.*)

⚜ **record²** /rı'kɔ:d/ *v.t.* **1** (set down in writing, also
fig.) запи́с|ывать, -а́ть **2** (on tape, film, etc.)
запи́с|ывать, -а́ть (на плёнку) **3** (of instrument:
register) регистри́ровать, за-

recorder /rı'kɔ:də(r)/ *n.* (mus.) (англи́йская)
фле́йта

recording /rı'kɔ:dıŋ/ *n.* за́пись

recount¹ /ri:'kaʊnt/ *n.* (second count) пересчёт
● *v.t.* пересчи́т|ывать, -а́ть

recount² /rı'kaʊnt/ *v.t.* (narrate) расска́з|ывать,
-а́ть

recoup /rı'ku:p/ *v.t.*: **~ one's losses** возвраща́ть,
верну́ть поте́рянное

recourse /rı'kɔ:s/ *n.*: **have ~ to** приб|ега́ть,
-е́гнуть к + *d.*

⚜ **recover** /rı'kʌvə(r)/ *v.t.* (regain) получ|а́ть,
-и́ть обра́тно; верну́ть (*pf.*); **he tried to ~
his losses** он пыта́лся верну́ть поте́рянное;
(win back) отвоёв|ывать, -а́ть
● *v.i.* попр|авля́ться, -а́виться; **we must help
the country to ~** мы должны́ помо́чь стране́
сно́ва встать на́ ноги

⚜ ключева́я ле́ксика

recovery /rı'kʌvərı/ *n.* **1** (regaining possession)
возвра́т; возмеще́ние; **the ~ of your money
will take time** пройдёт вре́мя, пре́жде чем
вы полу́чите свои́ де́ньги обра́тно **2** (revival)
выздоровле́ние; **he made a rapid ~** он
бы́стро попра́вился **3** (rehabilitation)
восстановле́ние
■ **~ vehicle** *n.* авари́йный автомоби́ль

recreate /ri:krı'eıt/ *v.t.* вновь созд|ава́ть, -а́ть

recreation /rekrı'eıʃ(ə)n/ *n.* о́тдых;
развлече́ние

recrimination /rıkrımı'neıʃ(ə)n/ *n.*
встре́чное обвине́ние

recruit /rı'kru:t/ *n.* (mil.) новобра́нец
● *v.t.* (enlist) вербова́ть, за-; наб|ира́ть, -ра́ть

recruitment /rı'kru:tmənt/ *n.* вербо́вка

rectangle /'rektæŋɡ(ə)l/ *n.* прямоуго́льник

rectangular /rek'tæŋɡʊlə(r)/ *adj.*
прямоуго́льный

rectify /'rektıfaı/ *v.t.* испр|авля́ть, -а́вить

rector /'rektə(r)/ *n.* (BrE, clergyman) ≈
прихо́дский свяще́нник

rectory /'rektərı/ *n.* (BrE) дом прихо́дского
свяще́нника

rectum /'rektəm/ *n.* (*pl.* **rectums** or **recta**)
пряма́я кишка́

recuperate /rı'ku:pəreıt/ *v.i.* попр|авля́ться,
-а́виться

recuperation /rıku:pə'reıʃ(ə)n/ *n.*
выздоровле́ние

recur /rı'kə:(r)/ *v.i.* (**recurred, recurring**)
повтор|я́ться, -и́ться; **a ~ring headache**
хрони́ческие головны́е бо́ли (*f. pl.*)

recurrence /rı'kʌrəns/ *n.* повторе́ние

recurrent /rı'kʌrənt/ *adj.* повторя́ющийся

recycle /ri:'saık(ə)l/ *v.t.* перераб|а́тывать, -о́тать

recycling /ri:'saıklıŋ/ *n.* повто́рное
испо́льзование, перерабо́тка

⚜ **red** /red/ *n.* **1** кра́сный цвет; **~ doesn't suit
her** кра́сное ей не идёт; **she was dressed in
~** она́ была́ оде́та в кра́сное **2** (debit side
of account) долг, задо́лженность; **in the ~** в
долга́х
● *adj.* (**redder, reddest**) кра́сный; а́лый;
she went ~ in the face она́ покрасне́ла
■ **R~ Crescent** *n.* Кра́сный Полуме́сяц;
R~ Cross *n.* Кра́сный Крест; **~currant**
n. кра́сная сморо́дина; **~-handed** *adj.*: **he
was caught ~-handed** его́ пойма́ли на ме́сте
преступле́ния (*or* с поли́чным); **~head** *n.*
ры́жий (*челове́к*); **~-headed** *adj.* ры́жий;
~-hot *adj.* раскалённый докрасна́; **~-light
district** *n.* кварта́л публи́чных домо́в; **~
tape** *n.* (fig.) (канцеля́рская) волоки́та

redden /'red(ə)n/ *v.t.* окра́ш|ивать, -сить в
кра́сный цвет
● *v.i.* красне́ть, по-

reddish /'redıʃ/ *adj.* красновá́тый

redecorate /ri:'dekəreıt/ *v.t.* отде́л|ывать,
-ать; ремонти́ровать, от-

redeem /rı'di:m/ *v.t.* **1** (get back, recover)
выкупа́ть, вы́купить **2** (relig.): **Christ came
to ~ sinners** Христо́с пришёл искупи́ть

грехи людей **3** (compensate): he has one ~ing feature у него есть одно положительное качество

redemption /rɪ'dempʃ(ə)n/ *n.* (relig.) искупление; past ~ без надежды на спасение

redeploy /ri:dɪ'plɔɪ/ *v.t. & i.* (mil.) передислоци́ровать(ся) (*impf., pf.*)

redeployment /ri:dɪ'plɔɪmənt/ *n.* передислокация; перераспределение

redevelop /ri:dɪ'veləp/ *v.t.* перестр|а́ивать, -о́ить

redial /ri:'daɪ(ə)l/ *v.t. & i.* повторно наб|ира́ть, -ра́ть (но́мер)

rediscover /ri:dɪ'skʌvə(r)/ *v.t.* откр|ыва́ть, -ы́ть за́ново

redo /ri:'du:/ *v.t.* переде́л|ывать, -ать

redouble /ri:'dʌb(ə)l/ *v.t. & i.* удв|а́ивать(ся), -о́ить(ся); he ~d his efforts он удво́ил свои усилия

redoubtable /rɪ'daʊtəb(ə)l/ *adj.* гро́зный; устраша́ющий

redress /rɪ'dres/ *n.* возмеще́ние; I shall seek ~ я бу́ду добива́ться компенса́ции
● *v.t.* возме|ща́ть, -сти́ть; their victory ~ed the balance of forces их побе́да восстанови́ла равнове́сие сил

⚡ **reduce** /rɪ'dju:s/ *v.t.* **1** (make less or smaller) ум|еньша́ть, -е́ньшить; сокра|ща́ть, -ти́ть; (lower) сн|ижа́ть, -и́зить; сб|авля́ть, -а́вить; all prices are ~d все це́ны сни́жены **2** (bring, compel) дов|оди́ть, -ести́ (*до чего*); вынужда́ть, вы́нудить; the film ~d her to tears фильм растро́гал её до слёз; the family was ~d to begging семья́ была́ обречена́ на нищету́

⚡ **reduction** /rɪ'dʌkʃ(ə)n/ *n.* сокраще́ние; сниже́ние; a ~ in numbers коли́чественное сокраще́ние; price ~s сниже́ние цен

redundancy /rɪ'dʌnd(ə)nsɪ/ *n.* (BrE, dismissal) увольне́ние

redundant /rɪ'dʌnd(ə)nt/ *adj.* (superfluous) изли́шний; (BrE, at work): many workers were made ~ мно́гих рабо́чих уво́лили

reed /ri:d/ *n.* **1** (bot.) тростни́к, камы́ш **2** (mus.) язычо́к

reef /ri:f/ *n.* риф

reek /ri:k/ *v.i.* воня́ть, про-; his clothes ~ed of tobacco от его́ оде́жды несло́ табако́м

reel¹ /ri:l/ *n.* (winding device) кату́шка; руло́н
● *with advs.*: the fisherman ~ed in the line рыба́к смота́л у́дочку; the guide ~ed off a lot of dates гид вы́палил це́лый ряд истори́ческих дат

reel² /ri:l/ *v.i.* кружи́ться (*impf.*); he ~ed under the blow он зашата́лся от уда́ра

re-elect /ri:ɪ'lekt/ *v.t.* переизб|ира́ть, -ра́ть

re-emerge /ri:ɪ'mɜ:dʒ/ *v.i.* вновь появ|ля́ться, -и́ться

re-examine /ri:ɪg'zæmɪn/ *v.t.* вновь рассм|а́тривать, -отре́ть

ref /ref/ *n.* (infml) = referee *n.* 2

refectory /rɪ'fektərɪ/ *n.* (in monastery) тра́пезная; (in school, college) столо́вая

⚡ **refer** /rɪ'fɜ:(r)/ *v.t.* (referred, referring) (pass on, direct) от|сыла́ть, -осла́ть; the clerk ~red me to the manager слу́жащий отосла́л меня́ к нача́льнику
● *v.i.* (referred, referring) **1** (have recourse) спр|авля́ться, -а́виться; he ~red to the dictionary он спра́вился в словаре́; the speaker ~red to his notes ора́тор загляну́л в конспе́кт **2** (allude): ~ to (mention) упом|ина́ть, -яну́ть; (cite) ссыла́ться, сосла́ться на + *a.*

referee /refə'ri:/ *n.* **1** (arbitrator) арби́тр **2** (at games) судья́ (*m.*); ре́фери (*m. indecl.*) **3** (person supplying testimonial) поручи́тель (*m.*)
● *v.t. & i.* (referees, refereed): he agreed to ~ the match он согласи́лся суди́ть матч

⚡ **reference** /'refərəns/ *n.* **1** (referring for decision etc.) отсы́лка; he acted without ~ to his superiors он де́йствовал без согласова́ния с нача́льством **2** (relation) отноше́ние; with ~ to your letter в связи́ с ва́шим письмо́м **3** (allusion) упомина́ние, ссы́лка; the book contains many ~s to the Queen в кни́ге ча́сто упомина́ется короле́ва **4** (in text) ссы́лка, сно́ска **5** (referring for information) спра́вка **6** (testimonial) о́тзыв, рекоменда́ция; характери́стика; (person supplying ~) поручи́тель (*m.*)
■ ~ book *n.* спра́вочник

referend|um /refə'rendəm/ *n.* (*pl.* ~ums or ~a) рефере́ндум

referral /rɪ'fɜ:r(ə)l/ *n.* направле́ние

refill¹ /'ri:fɪl/ *n.* (for pen etc.) запасно́й сте́ржень

refill² /ri:'fɪl/ *v.t.* нап|олня́ть, -о́лнить вновь

refine /rɪ'faɪn/ *v.t.* **1** (purify) оч|ища́ть, -и́стить **2** (make more cultured) соверше́нствовать, у-; ~d manners утончённые/изы́сканные мане́ры

refinement /rɪ'faɪnmənt/ *n.* **1** (good manners) благовоспи́танность **2** (improving change, addition) улучше́ние, усоверше́нствование

refinery /rɪ'faɪnərɪ/ *n.* (oil) нефтеочисти́тельный заво́д

refit¹ /'ri:fɪt/ *n.* ремо́нт, переоборудование

refit² /ri:'fɪt/ *v.t.* чини́ть, по-; переоборудовать (*impf., pf.*); ремонти́ровать, от-

⚡ **reflect** /rɪ'flekt/ *v.t.* отра|жа́ть, -зи́ть
● *v.i.* **1** (produce a reflection) отра|жа́ться, -зи́ться; (fig., bring discredit): your behaviour ~s on us all ва́ше поведе́ние ложи́тся пятно́м на нас всех **2** (consider) заду́маться (*pf.*) (on: над + *i.*); I ~ed (on/upon) how fortunate I had been я поду́мал о том, как мне повезло́

reflection /rɪ'flekʃ(ə)n/ *n.* **1** (of light, heat, etc.) отраже́ние **2** (consideration) размышле́ние; on ~, I may have been wrong поразмы́слив, я реши́л, что, возмо́жно, (я) был непра́в

reflex /'ri:fleks/ *n.* (also ~ **action**) рефле́кс

reflexive /rɪ'fleksɪv/ *adj.* возвра́тный

reflexologist /ri:flek'sɒlədʒɪst/ *n.* рефлексотерапе́вт

reflexology /ri:flek'sɒlədʒɪ/ *n.* (med.) рефлексоло́гия

r

⚡ **reform** /rɪ'fɔːm/ *n.* рефо́рма
- *v.t.* (a system) улу́чшать, -у́чшить;
реформи́ровать (*impf., pf.*); (a person)
перевоспи́т|ывать, -а́ть; испр|авля́ть,
-а́вить
- *v.i.* испр|авля́ться, -а́виться

reformat /riː'fɔːmæt/ *v.t.* (comput.)
формати́ровать, от- за́ново

Reformation /refə'meɪʃ(ə)n/ *n.* Реформа́ция

reformer /rɪ'fɔːmə(r)/ *n.* реформа́тор

reformist /rɪ'fɔːmɪst/ *n.* реформи́ст

refraction /rɪ'frækʃ(ə)n/ *n.* преломле́ние;
рефра́кция

refrain¹ /rɪ'freɪn/ *n.* припе́в

refrain² /rɪ'freɪn/ *v.i.* сде́рж|иваться, -а́ться;
I could hardly ~ from laughing я е́ле
сде́рживался от сме́ха

refresh /rɪ'freʃ/ *v.t.* освеж|а́ть, -и́ть; let me ~
your memory позво́льте напо́мнить вам

refresher /rɪ'freʃə(r)/ *n.* (also ~ **course**)
курс переподгото́вки

refreshing /rɪ'freʃɪŋ/ *adj.* освежа́ющий

refreshment /rɪ'freʃmənt/ *n.* еда́; питьё;
~s are served on the train в по́езде мо́жно
перекуси́ть

refrigerate /rɪ'frɪdʒəreɪt/ *v.t.* замор|а́живать,
-о́зить

refrigeration /rɪfrɪdʒə'reɪʃ(ə)n/ *n.*
замора́живание

refrigerator /rɪ'frɪdʒəreɪtə(r)/ *n.*
холоди́льник

refuel /riː'fjuːəl/ *v.i.* запр|авля́ться, -а́виться

refuge /'refjuːdʒ/ *n.* убе́жище; приста́нище;
the cat took ~ beneath the table кот
спря́тался под столо́м

refugee /refjʊ'dʒiː/ *n.* бе́жен|ец (-ка)
■ ~ **camp** *n.* ла́герь (*m.*) бе́женцев

refund¹ /'riːfʌnd/ *n.* возмеще́ние убы́тков

refund² /rɪ'fʌnd/ *v.t.* возме|ща́ть, -сти́ть (*что
кому*)

refurbish /riː'fɜːbɪʃ/ *v.t.* отде́л|ывать, -ать

refurbishment /riː'fɜːbɪʃmənt/ *n.*
(капита́льный) ремо́нт

refusal /rɪ'fjuːz(ə)l/ *n.* отка́з

refuse¹ /'refjuːs/ *n.* му́сор
■ ~ **collection** *n.* убо́рка му́сора

⚡ **refuse²** /rɪ'fjuːz/ *v.t. & i.* (decline to give)
отка́з|ывать, -а́ть (*кому в чём*); (reject)
отв|ерга́ть, -е́ргнуть; (decline sth offered)
отка́з|ываться, -а́ться от + *g.*

refute /rɪ'fjuːt/ *v.t.* опров|ерга́ть, -е́ргнуть

regain /rɪ'geɪn/ *v.t.* получ|а́ть, -и́ть обра́тно;
he never ~ed consciousness он так и не
пришёл в созна́ние

regal /'riːg(ə)l/ *adj.* короле́вский

regale /rɪ'geɪl/ *v.t.* уго|ща́ть, -сти́ть; по́тчевать
(*impf.*)

⚡ **regard** /rɪ'gɑːd/ *n.* 1 (respect) отноше́ние; in
this ~ в э́том отноше́нии; in, with ~ to your
request что каса́ется ва́шей про́сьбы
2 (consideration) внима́ние, забо́та; he paid

no ~ to her feelings он не счита́лся с её
чу́вствами 3 (esteem) уваже́ние (for: к
+ *d.*); he holds your opinion in high ~ он
о́чень высоко́ це́нит ва́ше мне́ние 4 (in pl.)
(greetings) приве́т; give him my warmest ~s
переда́йте ему́ от меня́ серде́чный приве́т
- *v.t.* 1 (consider) расце́н|ивать, -и́ть;
сч|ита́ть, -есть; he was ~ed as a hero его́
счита́ли геро́ем 2 (concern): as ~s, ~ing
относи́тельно + *g.*; что каса́ется + *g.*; насчёт
+ *g.* 3 (look at) разгля́д|ывать, -е́ть

regardless /rɪ'gɑːdlɪs/ *adj.* невнима́тельный
(of: к + *d.*); ~ of expense не счита́ясь с
расхо́дами

regatta /rɪ'gætə/ *n.* рега́та

regenerate /rɪ'dʒenəreɪt/ *v.t. & i.*
возро|жда́ть(ся), -ди́ть(ся)

regent /'riːdʒ(ə)nt/ *n.* ре́гент

reggae /'regeɪ/ *n.* ре́гги (*m. indecl.*)

⚡ **regime** /reɪ'ʒiːm/ *n.* режи́м, строй; under the
old ~ при ста́ром режи́ме

regiment /'redʒɪmənt/ *n.* полк

regimental /redʒɪ'ment(ə)l/ *adj.* полково́й

⚡ **region** /'riːdʒ(ə)n/ *n.* райо́н, о́бласть; регио́н;
in the ~ of £5,000 приблизи́тельно 5000
фу́нтов

⚡ **regional** /'riːdʒən(ə)l/ *adj.* райо́нный,
областно́й; региона́льный

⚡ **register** /'redʒɪstə(r)/ *n.* (record, list) рее́стр;
за́пись; (in school) журна́л
- *v.t.* 1 (enter on official record) регистри́ровать,
за-; оф|ормля́ть, -о́рмить; ~ed letter
заказно́е письмо́ 2 (of an instrument: record)
пока́з|ывать, -а́ть; отм|еча́ть, -е́тить
3 (express) выраж|а́ть, вы́разить
- *v.i.* (record one's name) регистри́роваться, за-

registrar /redʒɪs'trɑː(r)/ *n.* (keeper of
records) регистра́тор; (BrE, in hospital) врач,
проходя́щий пра́ктику по специа́льности

registration /redʒɪ'streɪʃ(ə)n/ *n.*
регистра́ция; ~ number of a car (BrE)
(регистрацио́нный) но́мер маши́ны

registry /'redʒɪstrɪ/ *n.* регистрату́ра; ~
office (BrE): they were married at a ~
office они́ расписа́лись в за́гсе; они́
зарегистри́ровались

regress /rɪ'gres/ *v.i.* дви́гаться (*impf.*) в
обра́тном направле́нии, регресси́ровать
(*impf.*)

regret /rɪ'gret/ *n.* сожале́ние; I found to my
~ that I was late я обнару́жил, к своему́
сожале́нию, что опозда́л; I have no ~s я ни о
чём не жале́ю
- *v.t.* (**regretted, regretting**) сожале́ть
(*impf.*); I ~ losing my temper я сожале́ю, что
вы́шел из себя́; I ~ to say ... к сожале́нию, я
до́лжен сказа́ть...; you will live to ~ this вы
ещё пожале́ете об э́том

regretful /rɪ'gretfʊl/ *adj.* опеча́ленный;
по́лный сожале́ния

regrettable /rɪ'gretəb(ə)l/ *adj.* приско́рбный

⚡ **regular** /'regjʊlə(r)/ *n.* 1 (in full ~ **soldier**)
солда́т регуля́рной а́рмии 2 (in full ~
customer) завсегда́тай; постоя́нный

посети́тель
● *adj.* **1** (orderly in appearance, symmetrical)
пра́вильный, регуля́рный **2** (steady, unvarying)
регуля́рный, норма́льный; a ~ **pulse**
ритми́чный пульс; **he keeps** ~ **hours** у
него́ стро́гий/чёткий режи́м (дня) **3** (AmE,
ordinary) регуля́рный, обы́чный

regularity /ˌregjʊˈlærɪti/ *n.* регуля́рность

regularly /ˈregjʊləli/ *adv.* регуля́рно

regulate /ˈregjʊleɪt/ *v.t.* регули́ровать (*impf.*)

⚬ **regulation** /ˌregjʊˈleɪʃ(ə)n/ *n.* **1** (control)
регули́рование **2** (rule) пра́вило

regulator /ˈregjʊleɪtə(r)/ *n.* (person)
отве́тственное лицо́; (body) отве́тственная
организа́ция; (device) регуля́тор, стабилиза́тор

regulatory /ˌregjʊˈleɪtəri/ *adj.* регули́рующий
■ ~ **body** *n.* о́рган управле́ния

regurgitate /rɪˈɡɜːdʒɪteɪt/ *v.t.* отры́г|ивать,
-ну́ть

rehabilitate /ˌriːhəˈbɪlɪteɪt/ *v.t.*
перевоспи́т|ывать, -а́ть

rehabilitation /ˌriːhəbɪlɪˈteɪʃ(ə)n/ *n.*
перевоспита́ние; реабилита́ция

rehearsal /rɪˈhɜːs(ə)l/ *n.* репети́ция

rehearse /rɪˈhɜːs/ *v.t.* репети́ровать, от-

rehouse /riːˈhaʊz/ *v.t.* пересел|я́ть, -и́ть

reign /reɪn/ *n.* ца́рствование, власть
● *v.i.* ца́рствовать (*impf.*); (fig.) цари́ть (*impf.*)

reimburse /ˌriːɪmˈbɜːs/ *v.t.* возме|ща́ть, -сти́ть
(*что кому*)

reimbursement /ˌriːɪmˈbɜːsmənt/ *n.*
возмеще́ние, возвраще́ние

reincarnation /ˌriːɪnkɑːˈneɪʃ(ə)n/ *n.*
перевоплоще́ние

reindeer /ˈreɪndɪə(r)/ *n.* (*pl.* ~ *or* ~s)
се́верный оле́нь

reinforce /ˌriːɪnˈfɔːs/ *v.t.* усил|и́|вать, -ть

reinforcement /ˌriːɪnˈfɔːsmənt/ *n.* усиле́ние;
(*in pl.*) (troops) подкрепле́ние

reins /reɪnz/ *n. pl.* во́ж|жи (-же́й)

reinstate /ˌriːɪnˈsteɪt/ *v.t.* восстан|а́вливать,
-ови́ть в права́х/до́лжности/положе́нии

reinstatement /ˌriːɪnˈsteɪtmənt/ *n.*
восстановле́ние в права́х/до́лжности/
положе́нии

reissue /riːˈɪʃuː/ *v.t.* переизд|ава́ть, -а́ть

reiterate /riːˈɪtəreɪt/ *v.t.* повтор|я́ть, -и́ть

reject[1] /ˈriːdʒekt/ *n.* (discarded article)
неподходя́щая вещь; (comm.) брако́ванное
изде́лие; (*pl., collect.*) брак

⚬ **reject**[2] /rɪˈdʒekt/ *v.t.* откло́н|я́ть, -и́ть;
отв|ерга́ть, -е́ргнуть; **my offer was** ~**ed
out of hand** моё предложе́ние сра́зу же
отклони́ли

rejection /rɪˈdʒekʃ(ə)n/ *n.* отка́з, отклоне́ние

rejoice /rɪˈdʒɔɪs/ *v.i.* ра́доваться, об- (*чему*)

rejuvenate /rɪˈdʒuːvəneɪt/ *v.t.* омол|а́живать,
-оди́ть

rekindle /riːˈkɪnd(ə)l/ *v.t.* разж|ига́ть, -е́чь
вновь

relapse *n.* /ˈriːlæps/ рециди́в
● *v.i.* /rɪˈlæps/ сно́ва преда́ться (*pf.*) (*чему*); he

~**d into bad ways** он сно́ва сби́лся с пути́;
she ~**d into silence** она́ (сно́ва) замолча́ла

⚬ **relate** /rɪˈleɪt/ *v.t.* **1** (narrate) расска́з|ывать,
-а́ть о + *p.* **2** (establish relation between)
свя́з|ывать, -а́ть (*что с чем*)
● *v.i.* относи́ться (*impf.*) (**to:** к + *d.*)

⚬ **related** /rɪˈleɪtɪd/ *adj.* **1** (logically connected)
свя́занный (с + *i.*); взаимосвя́занный (друг с
дру́гом) **2** (by blood or marriage): **he and I are** ~
мы с ним ро́дственники

⚬ **relation** /rɪˈleɪʃ(ə)n/ *n.* **1** (connection)
отноше́ние; **in, with** ~ **to** относи́тельно + *g.*
2 (*in pl.*) (dealings) отноше́ния (*nt. pl.*);
international ~**s** междунаро́дные отноше́ния
3 (family member) ро́дственни|к (-ца)

⚬ **relationship** /rɪˈleɪʃənʃɪp/ *n.* (relevance)
связь, отноше́ние; (between people or groups)
взаимоотноше́ния (*nt. pl.*), связь; (kinship)
родство́

⚬ **relative** /ˈrelətɪv/ *n.* (family member)
ро́дственни|к (-ца)
● *adj.* **1** (comparative) относи́тельный,
сравни́тельный; **he is a** ~ **newcomer** он
здесь относи́тельно неда́вно **2** (gram.): ~
pronoun относи́тельное местоиме́ние

⚬ **relatively** /ˈrelətɪvli/ *adv.* относи́тельно; ~
speaking вообще́ говоря́

relativity /ˌreləˈtɪvɪti/ *n.* относи́тельность;
theory of ~ тео́рия относи́тельности

relax /rɪˈlæks/ *v.i.* (rest) рассл|абля́ться,
-а́биться; отдыха́ть (*impf.*); **I like to** ~ **in the
sun** я люблю́ посиде́ть на со́лнце; **a** ~**ed
atmosphere** споко́йная атмосфе́ра; (slacken)
осл|абева́ть, -абе́ть
● *v.t.* (control, attention) осл|абля́ть, -а́бить;
he ~**ed his grip** он разжа́л ру́ку; (person)
рассл|абля́ть, -а́бить

relaxation /ˌriːlækˈseɪʃ(ə)n/ *n.* **1** (rest,
recreation) о́тдых, развлече́ние **2** (of control)
ослабле́ние **3** (of tension) разря́дка

relay /ˈriːleɪ/ *n.* **1** (fresh team) сме́на **2** (*in full*
~ **race**) эстафе́тный бег
● *v.t.* (transmit) трансли́ровать (*impf., pf.*)

⚬ **release** /rɪˈliːs/ *n.* **1** (liberation) освобожде́ние
2 (unfastening) освобожде́ние **3** (device for doing
this) спуск **4** (of book, recording, film) вы́пуск
● *v.t.* **1** (liberate) освобо|жда́ть, -ди́ть
2 (unfasten) отпус|ка́ть, -ти́ть; выпуска́ть,
вы́пустить; **do not** ~ **the brake** не
отпуска́йте то́рмоз **3** (book, CD, film)
выпуска́ть, вы́пустить

relegate /ˈreləɡeɪt/ *v.t.* от|сыла́ть, -осла́ть;
the team was ~**d to the second division** (BrE)
кома́нду перевели́ во второ́й дивизио́н

relegation /ˌreləˈɡeɪʃ(ə)n/ *n.* пониже́ние,
перево́д (в бо́лее ни́зкий класс *и т. п.*)

relent /rɪˈlent/ *v.i.* смягч|а́ться, -и́ться;
подобре́ть (*pf.*)

relentless /rɪˈlentlɪs/ *adj.* безжа́лостный

relevance /ˈreləv(ə)ns/ *n.* отноше́ние к де́лу;
уме́стность

⚬ **relevant** /ˈreləv(ə)nt/ *adj.* относя́щийся к

r

де́лу; уме́стный; ~ **to** относя́щийся к + *d*.

reliability /rɪlaɪəˈbɪlɪtɪ/ *n*. надёжность; достове́рность

reliable /rɪˈlaɪəb(ə)l/ *adj*. надёжный; (of a statement) достове́рный

reliance /rɪˈlaɪəns/ *n*. (trust) дове́рие; **I place great ~ upon him** я ему́ о́чень доверя́ю; (dependence) зави́симость; ~ **on drugs** зави́симость от нарко́тиков

reliant /rɪˈlaɪənt/ *adj*. (dependent) зави́симый, зави́сящий; **they are completely ~ on their pension** они́ по́лностью зави́сят от свое́й пе́нсии

relic /ˈrelɪk/ *n*. рели́квия

✓ **relief** /rɪˈliːf/ *n*. **1** (alleviation) облегче́ние **2** (assistance) посо́бие; **a ~ fund for flood victims** фонд по́мощи же́ртвам наводне́ния **3** (sculpture etc.) релье́ф
   ■ ~ **agency** *n*. организа́ция по оказа́нию по́мощи; ~ **map** *n*. релье́фная ка́рта

relieve /rɪˈliːv/ *v.t*. **1** (alleviate) облегч|а́ть, -и́ть; **I was ~d to get your letter** я был рад получи́ть ва́ше письмо́ **2** (bring assistance to) при|ходи́ть, -йти́ на по́мощь + *d*. **3** (unburden) освобо|жда́ть, -ди́ть (*кого от чего*); **this ~s me of the necessity to speak** э́то освобожда́ет меня́ от необходи́мости говори́ть **4** (replace on duty) смен|я́ть, -и́ть

✓ **religion** /rɪˈlɪdʒ(ə)n/ *n*. рели́гия, ве́ра; вероиспове́дание

✓ **religious** /rɪˈlɪdʒəs/ *adj*. религио́зный

relinquish /rɪˈlɪŋkwɪʃ/ *v.t*. (abandon) ост|авля́ть, -а́вить; (surrender) сд|ава́ть, -ать; **he ~ed his claims** он отказа́лся от свои́х тре́бований

relish /ˈrelɪʃ/ *n*. **1** (zest) (большо́е/ нескрыва́емое) удово́льствие; **he ate with ~** он ел с аппети́том **2** (sauce) припра́ва
   ● *v.t*. получ|а́ть, -и́ть удово́льствие от + *g*.; (infml): **I don't ~ the prospect** меня́ не прельща́ет перспекти́ва

relocate /riːləʊˈkeɪt/ *v.t. & i*. переме|ща́ть(ся), -сти́ть(ся)

relocation /riːləʊˈkeɪʃən/ *n*. перемеще́ние

reluctance /rɪˈlʌkt(ə)ns/ *n*. нежела́ние; неохо́та

reluctant /rɪˈlʌkt(ə)nt/ *adj*. неохо́тный; **she was ~ to leave home** ей не хоте́лось покида́ть дом

✓ **rely** /rɪˈlaɪ/ *v.i*. полага́ться (*impf*.); наде́яться (*impf*.) (*both* на + *a*.); **you can ~ on me** вы мо́жете на меня́ положи́ться

✓ **remain** /rɪˈmeɪn/ *v.i*. ост|ава́ться, -а́ться; (stay) пребыва́ть (*impf*.); **he ~ed silent** он храни́л молча́ние

remainder /rɪˈmeɪndə(r)/ *n*. (rest) оста́т|ок, -ки (*m. pl*.); (of people) остальны́е (*pl*.)

remains /rɪˈmeɪnz/ *n*. оста́тки (*m. pl*.), оста́нк|и (-ов)

remand /rɪˈmɑːnd/ *n*.: **on ~** под стра́жей
   ● *v.t*.: **he was ~ed in custody** он содержа́лся под стра́жей

■ ~ **home** *n*. (BrE) исправи́тельный дом для несовершенноле́тних

remark /rɪˈmɑːk/ *n*. замеча́ние
   ● *v.t*. зам|еча́ть, -е́тить

remarkable /rɪˈmɑːkəb(ə)l/ *adj*. удиви́тельный; замеча́тельный

remarry /riːˈmærɪ/ *v.i*. вступ|а́ть, -и́ть в но́вый брак

remedial /rɪˈmiːdɪəl/ *adj*. (of education) корректи́вный

remedy /ˈremɪdɪ/ *n*. (cure) сре́дство, лека́рство (**for:** от + *g*.)
   ● *v.t*. испр|авля́ть, -а́вить

✓ **remember** /rɪˈmembə(r)/ *v.t*. **1** (have in one's memory) по́мнить (*impf*.); **I ~ you saying it** я по́мню, что вы э́то сказа́ли; **I ~ her as a girl** я по́мню её де́вочкой **2** (recall) всп|омина́ть, -о́мнить; **he couldn't ~ how many meetings he had had in the past days** он не смог вспо́мнить число́ встреч, на кото́рых он побыва́л за после́дние дни **3** (not forget) не заб|ыва́ть, -ы́ть, име́ть (*impf*.) в виду́; ~ **to turn out the light** не забу́дьте погаси́ть свет

remembrance /rɪˈmembrəns/ *n*. па́мять; **in ~ of** в па́мять о + *p*.

✓ **remind** /rɪˈmaɪnd/ *v.t*. нап|омина́ть, -о́мнить (*кому что, о чём, or* + *inf*.); **he ~s me of my father** он напомина́ет мне отца́; **he ~ed me to buy bread** он напо́мнил мне купи́ть хле́ба

reminder /rɪˈmaɪndə(r)/ *n*. напомина́ние

reminisce /remɪˈnɪs/ *v.i*. пред|ава́ться, -а́ться воспомина́ниям

reminiscence /remɪˈnɪs(ə)ns/ *n*. воспомина́ние

reminiscent /remɪˈnɪs(ə)nt/ *adj*. **1** (of person, recalling the past): **he became ~** он преда́лся воспомина́ниям **2**: ~ **of** (tending to remind one of sth or suggest sth) напомина́ющий; вызыва́ющий воспомина́ния о + *p*.; **his music is ~ of Brahms** его́ му́зыка напомина́ет Бра́мса

remiss /rɪˈmɪs/ *adj*. хала́тный; неради́вый; **that was very ~ of me** с мое́й стороны́ э́то бы́ло недобросо́вестно

remission /rɪˈmɪʃ(ə)n/ *n*. (med.) реми́ссия

remit /ˈriːmɪt/ *n*. зада́чи (*f. pl*.), компете́нция

remnant /ˈremnənt/ *n*. (remains) оста́ток; (of cloth) оста́ток

remodel /riːˈmɒd(ə)l/ *v.t*. переде́л|ывать, -ать

remonstrate /ˈremənstreɪt/ *v.i*. протестова́ть (*impf*.); возра|жа́ть, -зи́ть; (exhort): **he ~d with me** он увещева́л меня́

remorse /rɪˈmɔːs/ *n*. угрызе́ния (*nt. pl*.) со́вести

remorseful /rɪˈmɔːsfʊl/ *adj*. по́лный рака́яния

remorseless /rɪˈmɔːslɪs/ *adj*. безжа́лостный

remortgage /riːˈmɔːɡɪdʒ/ *v.t*. (fin.) переза|кла́дывать, -ложи́ть

remote /rɪˈməʊt/ *adj*. (remoter, remotest) отдалённый, глухо́й; **a ~ ancestor** далёкий

пре́док; **there is a ~ possibility of its happening** не исключено́, что э́то случи́тся; **I haven't the ~st idea** не име́ю ни мале́йшего поня́тия; **he was not even ~ly interested** он не прояви́л ни мале́йшего интере́са (к + d.)
- **~ control** n. (control) дистанцио́нное управле́ние; (device) пульт ДУ, пульт дистанцио́нного управле́ния; **~-controlled** adj. с дистанцио́нным управле́нием

remoteness /rɪˈməʊtnɪs/ n. отдалённость

removal /rɪˈmuːv(ə)l/ n. (taking away) удале́ние; (BrE, of furniture) перево́зка

◆ **remove** /rɪˈmuːv/ v.t. **1** (take away, off) уб|ира́ть, -ра́ть; ун|оси́ть, -ести́; **how can I ~ these stains?** как мо́жно вы́вести э́ти пя́тна? **2** (dismiss): **he was ~d from office** его́ сня́ли с рабо́ты

remover /rɪˈmuːvə(r)/ n.: **furniture ~** (BrE) перево́зчик ме́бели; **stain ~** пятновыводи́тель (m.)

remunerate /rɪˈmjuːnəreɪt/ v.t. (person) вознагра|жда́ть, -ди́ть; (work) опла́|чивать, -ти́ть

remuneration /rɪmjuːnəˈreɪʃ(ə)n/ n. вознагражде́ние

Renaissance /rɪˈneɪs(ə)ns/ n. (hist.) Ренесса́нс, Возрожде́ние; (**r~**) (revival) возрожде́ние

rename /riːˈneɪm/ v.t. переимено́в|ывать, -а́ть

render /ˈrendə(r)/ v.t. (cause to be): **he was ~ed speechless** он онеме́л

rendezvous /ˈrɒndeɪvuː/ n. (pl. ~ /-vuːz/) рандеву́ (nt. indecl.), свида́ние
- v.i. (**rendezvouses** /-vuːz/, **rendezvoused** /-vuːd/, **rendezvousing** /-vuːɪŋ/) встр|еча́ться, -е́титься

rendition /renˈdɪʃ(ə)n/ n. (performance) исполне́ние; (translation) перево́д

renegade /ˈrenɪɡeɪd/ n. ренега́т, отсту́пник
- adj. ренега́тский, отсту́пнический

renege, renegue /rɪˈneɪɡ/ v.i.: **he ~d on his promise** он нару́шил своё обеща́ние

renew /rɪˈnjuː/ v.t. возобнов|ля́ть, -и́ть

renewable /rɪˈnjuːəb(ə)l/ adj.: **~ resources** возобновля́емые ресу́рсы

renewal /rɪˈnjuːəl/ n. возобновле́ние

renounce /rɪˈnaʊns/ v.t. отка́з|ываться, -а́ться от + g.

renouncement /rɪˈnaʊnsmənt/ n. отрече́ние, отка́з

renovate /ˈrenəveɪt/ v.t. ремонти́ровать, от-; реставри́ровать (impf., pf.) (pf. also от-)

renovation /renəˈveɪʃ(ə)n/ n. реставра́ция; ремо́нт

renown /rɪˈnaʊn/ n. сла́ва; изве́стность; **a preacher of ~** пропове́дник, по́льзующийся большо́й изве́стностью; **he won ~ on the battlefield** он завоева́л сла́ву на по́ле бо́я

renowned /rɪˈnaʊnd/ adj. изве́стный

rent¹ /rent/ n. (tear, split) дыра́

◆ **rent²** /rent/ n. (for premises) аре́ндная пла́та; (for a flat) квартпла́та
- v.t. **1** (car, equipment) брать, взять напрока́т;

(a place) сн|има́ть, -я́ть **2**: **~ (out)** (car) дава́ть, дать напрока́т; (building) сд|ава́ть, -а́ть
- **~ boy** n. (BrE, infml) мужчи́на-прости́тутка

rental /ˈrent(ə)l/ n. разме́р аре́ндной пла́ты

renunciation /rɪnʌnsɪˈeɪʃ(ə)n/ n. отрече́ние, отка́з

reorganization /riːɔːɡənaɪˈzeɪʃ(ə)n/ n. реорганиза́ция

reorganize /riːˈɔːɡənaɪz/ v.t. реорганизо́в|ывать, -а́ть

rep¹ /rep/ n. (infml) = representative 1

rep² /rep/ n. (infml) = repertory 2

repair /rɪˈpeə(r)/ n. **1** (restoring) ремо́нт **2** (condition): **the house is in good ~** дом в хоро́шем состоя́нии
- v.t. (mend) ремонти́ровать, от-; чини́ть, по-; (restore) восстан|а́вливать, -ови́ть
- **~man** n. ма́стер

reparation /repəˈreɪʃ(ə)n/ n. компенса́ция; возмеще́ние уще́рба; (in pl.) (compensation for war damage) (вое́нные) репара́ции (f. pl.)

repartee /repɑːˈtiː/ n. остроу́мный разгово́р

repatriate /riːˈpætrɪeɪt/ v.t. репатрии́ровать (impf., pf.)

repatriation /riːpætrɪˈeɪʃ(ə)n/ n. репатриа́ция

repay /riːˈpeɪ/ v.t. (debt) выпла́чивать, вы́платить (кому́)

repayable /riːˈpeɪəb(ə)l/ adj. подлежа́щий упла́те

repayment /riːˈpeɪmənt/ n. вы́плата, возмеще́ние

repeal /rɪˈpiːl/ n. отме́на, аннули́рование
- v.t. аннули́ровать (impf., pf.)

◆ **repeat** /rɪˈpiːt/ n. повторе́ние
- v.t. повтор|я́ть, -и́ть; **after ~ed attempts** по́сле неоднокра́тных попы́ток

repeatedly /rɪˈpiːtɪdlɪ/ adv. неоднокра́тно

repel /rɪˈpel/ v.t. (**repelled, repelling**) **1** (enemy, attack) отб|ива́ть, -и́ть **2** (be repulsive to) отта́лкивать (impf.)

repellent /rɪˈpelənt/ n.: **insect ~** сре́дство от насеко́мых
- adj. (repulsive) отта́лкивающий

repent /rɪˈpent/ v.t. & i. ка́яться (impf.); раска́|иваться, -яться (в чём)

repentance /rɪˈpent(ə)ns/ n. раска́яние

repentant /riːˈpent(ə)nt/ adj. раска́ивающийся

repercussion /riːpəˈkʌʃ(ə)n/ n. (usu. in pl.) после́дствия (nt. pl.)

repertoire /ˈrepətwɑː(r)/ n. репертуа́р

repertory /ˈrepətərɪ/ n. **1** (repertoire) репертуа́р **2** (also **rep**: infml): **~ company** постоя́нная тру́ппа с определённым репертуа́ром; **~ theatre** (BrE), **theater** (AmE) репертуа́рный теа́тр **3** (fig., store) запа́с

repetition /repɪˈtɪʃ(ə)n/ n. повторе́ние

repetitious /repɪˈtɪʃəs/ adj. = repetitive

repetitive /rɪˈpetɪtɪv/ adj. повторя́ющийся; ску́чный
- **~ strain injury** n. тра́вма, вы́званная повторя́ющимся движе́нием

r

⚡ **replace** /rɪˈpleɪs/ v.t. **1** (put back) класть, положить (or ставить, по-) на место; возвра|щать, -тить **2** (provide substitute for) замен|ять, -ить; **the vase cannot be ~d** это уникальная ваза **3** (take the place of) заме|щать, -стить; **he ~d me as secretary** он замещал/сменил меня в должности секретаря

replacement /rɪˈpleɪsmənt/ n. (provision of substitute) замещение, замена; (substitute) замена

replay[1] /ˈriːpleɪ/ n. (of a game) переигровка

replay[2] /riːˈpleɪ/ v.t. (sport) переигрыв|ать, -ать

replenish /rɪˈplenɪʃ/ v.t. (one's wardrobe) поп|олнять, -олнить; **he ~ed his glass** он снова наполнил стакан

replete /rɪˈpliːt/ adj. наполненный; сытый, богатый (чем); **~ with food** наевшийся вдоволь

replica /ˈreplɪkə/ n. копия

replicate /ˈreplɪkeɪt/ v.t. копировать, с-

⚡ **reply** /rɪˈplaɪ/ n. ответ
  ● v.i. отв|ечать, -етить

⚡ **report** /rɪˈpɔːt/ n. доклад, отчёт; **newspaper ~** сообщение, известие, репортаж; **school ~** (BrE), **~ card** (AmE) отчёт об успеваемости
  ● v.t. **1** (give news or account of) сообщ|ать, -ить; сост|авлять, -авить отчёт о + p.; **it has been ~ed that ...** сообщалось, что... **2** (inform against) жаловаться, по- на + a.; **I shall ~ you for insolence** я пожалуюсь на вас за вашу дерзость
  ● v.i. **1** (give information) до|кладывать, -ложить; делать, с- доклад; предст|авлять, -авить отчёт **2** (present oneself) яв|ляться, -иться (куда-н.)

⚡ **reporter** /rɪˈpɔːtə(r)/ n. репортёр

repository /rɪˈpɒzɪtəri/ n. (receptacle) храни|лище, вместилище; (store) склад; (fig.): **he is a ~ of information** он неиссякаемый источник информации

repossess /riːpəˈzes/ v.t. из|ымать, -ъять за неплатёж

reprehensible /reprɪˈhensɪb(ə)l/ adj. предосудительный

⚡ **represent** /reprɪˈzent/ v.t. **1** (speak or act for) представлять (impf.) **2** (constitute, amount to) представлять (impf.) собой **3** (portray) изобра|жать, -зить; **what does this picture ~?** что изображено на этой картине?; (make out): **he ~ed himself as an expert** он выдавал себя за знатока **4** (symbolize, correspond to) символизировать (impf., pf.), изображать (impf.), обозначать (impf.)

representation /reprɪzenˈteɪʃ(ə)n/ n. **1** (portrayal) изображение **2** (in pl.) (statements): **diplomatic ~s** дипломатические представления (заявления) **3** (being represented) представительство

⚡ **representative** /reprɪˈzentətɪv/ n. представитель (m.) (-ница)
  ● adj. показательный, типичный

_____
⚡ ключевая лексика

⚡ **repress** /rɪˈpres/ v.t. **1** (put down) подав|лять, -ить **2** (restrain) сдерж|ивать, -ать

repression /rɪˈpreʃ(ə)n/ n. (of feelings) подавление; (of people) репрессия

repressive /rɪˈpresɪv/ adj. репрессивный

reprieve /rɪˈpriːv/ n. (law) отсрочка исполнения (смертного) приговора

reprimand /ˈreprɪmɑːnd/ n. выговор, замечание
  ● v.t. делать, с- выговор/замечание + d.

reprint[1] /ˈriːprɪnt/ n. перепечатка

reprint[2] /riːˈprɪnt/ v.t. перепечат|ывать, -ать

reprisal /rɪˈpraɪz(ə)l/ n. ответное действие

reproach /rɪˈprəʊtʃ/ n. упрёк, укор
  ● v.t. упрек|ать, -нуть; укорять (impf.)

reproachful /rɪˈprəʊtʃfʊl/ adj. укоризненный

reprobate /ˈreprəbeɪt/ n. негодяй, нечестивец
  ● adj. нечестивый; безнравственный

reproduce /riːprəˈdjuːs/ v.t. (copy) воспроизв|одить, -ести
  ● v.i. (biol.) размн|ожаться, -ожиться

reproduction /riːprəˈdʌkʃ(ə)n/ n. (biol.) размножение; (art) репродукция

reproductive /riːprəˈdʌktɪv/ adj. (biol.) половой

reproof /rɪˈpruːf/ n. порицание

reprove /rɪˈpruːv/ v.t. делать, с- выговор + d.

reptile /ˈreptaɪl/ n. пресмыкающееся, рептилия

republic /rɪˈpʌblɪk/ n. республика

republican /rɪˈpʌblɪkən/ n. республикан|ец (-ка)
  ● adj. республиканский

repudiate /rɪˈpjuːdɪeɪt/ v.t. отв|ергать, -ергнуть

repugnance /rɪˈpʌgnəns/ n. отвращение

repugnant /rɪˈpʌgnənt/ adj. отвратительный

repulse /rɪˈpʌls/ v.t. (drive back) отб|ивать, -ить; (refuse) отт|алкивать, -олкнуть

repulsion /rɪˈpʌlʃ(ə)n/ n. отвращение

repulsive /rɪˈpʌlsɪv/ adj. отвратительный

reputable /ˈrepjʊtəb(ə)l/ adj. почтенный

⚡ **reputation** /repjʊˈteɪʃ(ə)n/ n. репутация

repute /rɪˈpjuːt/ n.: **an artist of ~** художник с именем
  ● v.t.: **he is ~d to be rich** он считается богатым; говорят, что он богат; **the ~d father** предполагаемый отец

reputedly /rɪˈpjuːtɪdli/ adv. по общему мнению

⚡ **request** /rɪˈkwest/ n. просьба; **a programme of ~s** концерт по заявкам
  ● v.t. просить, по-

requiem /ˈrekwɪəm/ n. (mus.) реквием; (relig.) панихида

⚡ **require** /rɪˈkwaɪə(r)/ v.t. **1** (need) нуждаться (impf.) в + p.; **the matter ~s some thought** над этим надо подумать **2** (demand) требовать, по- + g.; **my attendance is ~d by law** по закону я обязан присутствовать; **I have done all that is ~d** я сделал всё, что требуется

⚡ **requirement** /rɪˈkwaɪəmənt/ n. **1** (need)

потре́бность **2** (demand) тре́бование

requisite /'rekwɪzɪt/ adj. необходи́мый

requisition /rekwɪ'zɪʃ(ə)n/ v.t. реквизи́ровать (impf., pf.)

reschedule /ri:'ʃedju:l/ v.t. перен|оси́ть, -ести́

⚘ **rescue** /'reskju:/ n. спасе́ние, вы́ручка; **he came to my ~** он пришёл мне на по́мощь/ вы́ручку
• v.t. (**rescues, rescued, rescuing**) спас|а́ть, -ти́

rescuer /'reskju:ə(r)/ n. спаси́тель (-ница)

⚘ **research** /rɪ'sə:tʃ/ n. изуче́ние, иссле́дование, изыска́ние; **~ and development** нау́чно-иссле́довательская рабо́та
• v.t. & i. иссле́довать (impf., pf.)

⚘ **researcher** /rɪ'sə:tʃə(r)/ n. иссле́дователь (-ница)

resemblance /rɪ'zembləns/ n. схо́дство

resemble /rɪ'zemb(ə)l/ v.t. походи́ть (impf.) на + a.

resend /ri:'send/ v.t. отпр|авля́ть, -а́вить повто́рно; пос|ыла́ть, -ла́ть повто́рно

resent /rɪ'zent/ v.t. возму|ща́ться, -ти́ться + i.; **I ~ your interfering in my affairs** мне о́чень не нра́вится, что вы вме́шиваетесь в мои́ дела́

resentful /rɪ'zentfʊl/ adj. возмущённый

resentment /rɪ'zentmənt/ n. возмуще́ние

reservation /rezə'veɪʃ(ə)n/ n. **1** (booking) (предвари́тельный) зака́з **2** (limitation) огово́рка **3** (for indigenous people) резерва́ция

⚘ **reserve** /rɪ'zə:v/ n. **1** (store) запа́с, резе́рв **2** (mil.) резе́рв **3** (~ player) запасно́й (игро́к) **4** (area) запове́дник; **game ~** охо́тничий запове́дник **5** (reticence) сде́ржанность
• v.t. **1** (save) бере́чь, с-; прибер|ега́ть, -е́чь **2** (set aside) резерви́ровать, за-; (ticket, table) зака́з|ывать, -а́ть; (hotel room) брони́ровать, за-

reserved /rɪ'zə:vd/ adj. **1** (booked) зака́занный (зара́нее) **2** (reticent) сде́ржанный

reservist /rɪ'zə:vɪst/ n. резерви́ст

reservoir /'rezəvwɑ:(r)/ n. водохрани́лище, водоём

reset /ri:'set/ v.t. (clock) перест|авля́ть, -а́вить; (trap) сно́ва ста́вить, по-

resettle /ri:'set(ə)l/ v.t. пересел|я́ть, -и́ть
• v.i. пересел|я́ться, -и́ться

resettlement /ri:'setəlmənt/ n. переселе́ние

reshuffle /ri:'ʃʌf(ə)l/ n.: **Cabinet ~** перестано́вки в Кабине́те мини́стров

reside /rɪ'zaɪd/ v.i. прожива́ть (impf.); жить (impf.)

residence /'rezɪd(ə)ns/ n. **1** (residing) прожива́ние **2** (home, mansion) дом, резиде́нция

⚘ **resident** /'rezɪd(ə)nt/ n. (inhabitant) (постоя́нный) жи́тель; (BrE, in hotel) постоя́лец
• adj. постоя́нно прожива́ющий

residential /rezɪ'denʃ(ə)l/ adj.: **a ~ area** жило́й райо́н

residual /rɪ'zɪdʒʊəl/ adj. оста́точный, оста́вшийся

residue /'rezɪdju:/ n. оста́ток

resign /rɪ'zaɪn/ v.t. **1** (give up) отка́з|ываться, -а́ться от + g.; **he ~ed his post as Chancellor** он по́дал в отста́вку с поста́ ка́нцлера **2** (reconcile): **he ~ed himself to defeat** он смири́лся с пораже́нием
• v.i. под|ава́ть, -а́ть (or уходи́ть, уйти́) в отста́вку; уходи́ть, уйти́ с рабо́ты

resignation /rezɪg'neɪʃ(ə)n/ n. **1** (resigning of office) отста́вка; **he handed in his ~** он по́дал заявле́ние об отста́вке/ухо́де **2** (acceptance of fate) поко́рность

resigned /rɪ'zaɪnd/ adj. поко́рный, смири́вшийся (to: с + i.)

resilience /rɪ'zɪliəns/ n. эласти́чность; (fig.) вы́носливость

resilient /rɪ'zɪliənt/ adj. эласти́чный; (fig.) вы́носливый

resin /'rezɪn/ n. смола́

resist /rɪ'zɪst/ v.t. **1** (oppose) сопротивля́ться (impf.) + d. **2** (refrain from) возде́рж|иваться, -а́ться от + g.; **I could not ~ the temptation to smile** я не мог удержа́ться от улы́бки; **she cannot ~ chocolates** она́ не мо́жет устоя́ть пе́ред шокола́дом

⚘ **resistance** /rɪ'zɪst(ə)ns/ n. сопротивле́ние; (political movement) движе́ние сопротивле́ния

resistant /rɪ'zɪst(ə)nt/ adj. сопротивля́ющийся

resit /ri:'sɪt/ v.t. (BrE): **~ an examination** пересдава́ть (impf.) экза́мен

resolute /'rezəlu:t/ adj. реши́тельный

⚘ **resolution** /rezə'lu:ʃ(ə)n/ n. **1** (firmness of purpose) реши́мость **2** (vow): **New Year ~** нового́дний заро́к **3** (expression of intent) резолю́ция **4** (comput., TV, phot., etc., of screen, camera, etc.) разреше́ние

⚘ **resolve** /rɪ'zɒlv/ n. (determination) реши́тельность, реши́мость
• v.t. & i. **1** (decide) реш|а́ть, -и́ть; прин|има́ть, -я́ть реше́ние **2** (settle) (раз)реш|а́ть, -и́ть; **their quarrel was ~d** их спор разреши́лся

resonance /'rezənəns/ n. резона́нс, гул

resonant /'rezənənt/ adj. звуча́щий

resonate /'rezəneɪt/ v.i. резони́ровать, звуча́ть (both impf.)

resort /rɪ'zɔ:t/ n. **1** (recourse): **in the last ~** в кра́йнем слу́чае **2** (place): **holiday ~** куро́рт; **seaside ~** морско́й куро́рт
• v.i. (have recourse) приб|ега́ть, -е́гнуть (**to:** к + d.)

resound /rɪ'zaʊnd/ v.i. звуча́ть (impf.); **the hall ~ed with voices** в за́ле раздава́лись голоса́; (fig.): **a ~ing success** оглуши́тельный успе́х

⚘ **resource** /rɪ'zɔ:s/ n. (source) исто́чник; (in pl.) запа́сы (m. pl.); ресу́рсы (m. pl.)
• v.t. снаб|жа́ть, -ди́ть кого́-н. (де́ньгами, обору́дованием и т. п.)

resourceful /rɪ'zɔ:sfʊl/ adj. изобрета́тельный

resourcefulness /rɪ'zɔ:sfʊlnɪs/ n. изобрета́тельность, нахо́дчивость

⚘ **respect** /rɪ'spekt/ n. **1** (esteem) уваже́ние

r

2 (reference): with ~ to что каса́ется + g.

3 (in pl.) (polite greetings) почте́ние;
he came to pay his ~s он пришёл
засвиде́тельствовать своё почте́ние
● v.t. уважа́ть (impf.); почита́ть (impf.)

respectability /rɪspektə'bɪlɪtɪ/ n.
респекта́бельность

respectable /rɪ'spektəb(ə)l/ adj. прили́чный

respectful /rɪ'spektfʊl/ adj. почти́тельный

respective /rɪ'spektɪv/ adj. соотве́тственный;
we went off to our ~ rooms мы разошли́сь
по свои́м ко́мнатам; the boys and girls
were taught woodwork and sewing ~ly
ма́льчиков и де́вочек учи́ли соотве́тственно
столя́рному де́лу и шитью́

respiration /respɪ'reɪʃ(ə)n/ n. дыха́ние

respirator /'respɪreɪtə(r)/ n. респира́тор

respiratory /rɪ'spɪrətərɪ/ adj. дыха́тельный

respite /'respaɪt/ n. (rest) переды́шка

resplendent /rɪ'splend(ə)nt/ adj.
блиста́тельный

✓ **respond** /rɪ'spɒnd/ v.i. **1** (reply) отв|еча́ть,
-е́тить (to: на + a.) **2** (react) реаги́ровать, от-
(to: на + a.); his illness is ~ing to treatment
его́ боле́знь поддаётся лече́нию

✓ **response** /rɪ'spɒns/ n. **1** (reply) отве́т; in ~
to your enquiry в отве́т на ваш запро́с
2 (reaction) реа́кция, о́тклик

✓ **responsibility** /rɪspɒnsɪ'bɪlɪtɪ/ n.
отве́тственность; I take full ~ for my actions
я беру́ на себя́ по́лную отве́тственность за
свои́ де́йствия

✓ **responsible** /rɪ'spɒnsɪb(ə)l/ adj. **1** (accountable)
отве́тственный; she is ~ for cleaning my
room убо́рка мое́й ко́мнаты вхо́дит в её
обя́занности **2** (to blame): who's ~? кто
винова́т?; who was ~ for breaking the
window? кто разби́л окно́? **3** (trustworthy)
надёжный **4** (involving responsibility) ва́жный

responsive /rɪ'spɒnsɪv/ adj. отзы́вчивый

✓ **rest¹** /rest/ n. **1** (relaxation) о́тдых; I'm going
(up) to have a ~ (я) пойду́ приля́гу
2 (undisturbed state) поко́й; I set his mind at ~
я его́ успоко́ил **3** (intermission) переды́шка;
they took a short ~ они́ сде́лали небольшу́ю
переды́шку **4** (prop) опо́ра
● v.t. **1** (give ~ to) дава́ть, -ть о́тдых + d.
2 (place for support) класть, положи́ть (on: на
+ a.); прислоня́ть, -и́ть (что к чему)
● v.i. **1** (relax) лежа́ть (impf.); отд|ыха́ть,
-охну́ть **2** (fig., remain) ост|ава́ться, -а́ться;
the decision ~s with you реше́ние зави́сит
от вас **3** (be supported) опира́ться (impf.)
(на что)
■ ~room n. (AmE, toilet) туале́т

✓ **rest²** /rest/ n. (remainder) оста́ток; (remaining
things, people) остальны́е (pl.)

restart /ri:'stɑ:t/ v.t. (begin again) вновь
нач|ина́ть, -а́ть; (car) сно́ва зав|оди́ть, -ести́

✓ **restaurant** /'restərɒnt/ n. рестора́н
■ ~ car n. ваго́н-рестора́н

restful /'restfʊl/ adj. успока́ивающий

restive /'restɪv/ adj. (of horse) норови́стый; (of
person) стропти́вый; (restless) беспоко́йный

restless /'restlɪs/ adj. беспоко́йный

restock /ri:'stɒk/ v.t. поп|олня́ть, -о́лнить
запа́сы

restoration /restə'reɪʃ(ə)n/ n. реставра́ция

✓ **restore** /rɪ'stɔ:(r)/ v.t. **1** (goods to owner)
возвра|ща́ть, -ти́ть (or верну́ть); (former
state or situation) восстан|а́вливать,
-ови́ть; order was ~d поря́док был
восстано́влен **2** (monument, work of art)
реставри́ровать (impf., pf.) (pf. also от-)

restorer /rɪ'stɔ:rə(r)/ n. реставра́тор

restrain /rɪ'streɪn/ v.t. сде́рж|ивать, -а́ть; his
manner was ~ed он был сде́ржан

restraint /rɪ'streɪnt/ n. **1** (self-control)
сде́ржанность **2** (constraint) ограниче́ние

restrict /rɪ'strɪkt/ v.t. ограни́чи|вать, -ть

restriction /rɪ'strɪkʃ(ə)n/ n. ограниче́ние

restrictive /rɪ'strɪktɪv/ adj. ограничи́тельный

✓ **result** /rɪ'zʌlt/ n. результа́т, сле́дствие; he died
as a ~ of his injuries он у́мер от ран
● v.i. **1** (arise) сле́довать (impf.) (из чего)
2 (end) конча́ться, ко́нчиться (in: + i.); the
quarrel ~ed in bloodshed ссо́ра ко́нчилась
кровопроли́тием

resume /rɪ'zju:m/ v.t. (continue) прод|олжа́ть,
-о́лжить; (take again): he ~d command он
сно́ва при́нял кома́ндование (чем)
● v.i.: let us ~ after lunch продо́лжим по́сле
обе́да

résumé /'rezjʊmeɪ/ n. (summary; CV) резюме́
(nt. indecl.)

resumption /rɪ'zʌmpʃ(ə)n/ n. продолже́ние

resurface /ri:'sɜ:fɪs/ v.t. меня́ть, смени́ть
покры́тие + g.
● v.i. всплы|ва́ть, -ть

resurgence /rɪ'sɜ:dʒ(ə)ns/ n. возрожде́ние

resurrect /rezə'rekt/ v.t. воскре|ша́ть, -си́ть

resurrection /rezə'rekʃ(ə)n/ n. (of Christ)
воскресе́ние; (fig.) воскреше́ние

resuscitate /rɪ'sʌsɪteɪt/ v.t. прив|оди́ть, -ести́
в созна́ние; реаними́ровать (impf., pf.)

resuscitation /rɪsʌsɪ'teɪʃ(ə)n/ n. реанима́ция
(иску́сственное дыха́ние)

retail /'ri:teɪl/ n. ро́зничная прода́жа
● v.i. продава́ться (impf.) в ро́зницу

retailer /'ri:teɪlə(r)/ n. ро́зничный торго́вец

✓ **retain** /rɪ'teɪn/ v.t. уде́рживать (impf.);
сохран|я́ть, -и́ть

retainer /rɪ'teɪnə(r)/ n. **1** (hist.) васса́л;
(servant) слуга́ (m.) **2** (fee) предвари́тельный
гонора́р

retaliate /rɪ'tælɪeɪt/ v.i. отпла́|чивать, -ти́ть
той же моне́той

retaliation /rɪtælɪ'eɪʃ(ə)n/ n. отпла́та,
возме́здие

retarded /rɪ'tɑ:dɪd/ adj.: (offens.) a ~ child
у́мственно отста́лый ребёнок

retentive /rɪ'tentɪv/ adj.: a ~ memory
це́пкая па́мять; a soil ~ of moisture по́чва,
сохраня́ющая вла́гу

rethink /ri:'θɪŋk/ v.t. пересма́|тривать, -отре́ть

✓ ключева́я ле́ксика

reticent /ˈretɪs(ə)nt/ *adj.* молчали́вый

retina /ˈretɪnə/ *n.* (*pl.* **retinas** or **retinae** /-niː/) сетча́тка

retinue /ˈretɪnjuː/ *n.* сви́та

retir|e /rɪˈtaɪə(r)/ *v.i.* **1** (from employment) уходи́ть, уйти́ в отста́вку **2** (withdraw) удал|я́ться, -и́ться; **he has a ~ing disposition** он засте́нчивый челове́к

retired /rɪˈtaɪəd/ *adj.* (находя́щийся) на пе́нсии

retirement /rɪˈtaɪəmənt/ *n.* отста́вка, вы́ход на пе́нсию (*or* в отста́вку)
■ **~ age** *n.* пенсио́нный во́зраст

retort /rɪˈtɔːt/ *n.* возраже́ние
● *v.i.* отв|еча́ть, -е́тить ре́зко (*or* тем же)

retrace /rɪˈtreɪs/ *v.t.*: **~ one's steps** возвраща́ться, верну́ться тем же путём

retract /rɪˈtrækt/ *v.t.* отка́з|ываться, -а́ться от + *g.*
● *v.i.* втя́|гиваться, -ну́ться

retrain /riːˈtreɪn/ *v.t. & i.* переквалифици́ровать(ся) (*impf., pf.*)

retreat /rɪˈtriːt/ *n.* отступле́ние, отхо́д
● *v.i.* (withdraw) удал|я́ться, -и́ться

retrench /rɪˈtrentʃ/ *v.i.* (economize) эконо́мить, с-

retrial /ˈriːtraɪəl/ *n.* повто́рное слу́шание де́ла

retribution /retrɪˈbjuːʃ(ə)n/ *n.* возме́здие, ка́ра

retrieval /rɪˈtriːv(ə)l/ *n.* (recovery, getting back) возвраще́ние

retrieve /rɪˈtriːv/ *v.t.* брать, взять обра́тно

retriever /rɪˈtriːvə(r)/ *n.* охо́тничья поиско́вая соба́ка; ретри́вер

retrograde /ˈretrəɡreɪd/ *adj.* реакцио́нный

retrogressive /retrəˈɡresɪv/ *adj.* регресси́рующий

retrospect /ˈretrəspekt/ *n.*: **in ~** ретроспекти́вно

retrospective /retrəˈspektɪv/ *adj.* ретроспекти́вный; **a ~ law** зако́н, име́ющий обра́тную си́лу
● *n.* (exhibition) ито́говая вы́ставка рабо́т худо́жника

⚬ **return** /rɪˈtɜːn/ *n.* **1** (coming or going back) возвраще́ние; **many happy ~s (of the day)!** с днём рожде́ния!; **~ fare** сто́имость обра́тного прое́зда; (*in full* **~ ticket**) (BrE) обра́тный биле́т, биле́т в о́ба конца́ **3** (profit) дохо́д **4** (giving, sending, putting) отда́ча, возвра́т **5** (reciprocation): **in ~ (for)** взаме́н (+ *g.*); (in response to) в отве́т (на + *a.*) **6** (report) отчёт, ра́порт; **income tax ~** нало́говая деклара́ция **7** (comput.) возвра́т
● *v.t.* **1** (give, send, put, back) возвра|ща́ть, -ти́ть (*or* верну́ть); **he ~ed the ball accurately** он хорошо́ отби́л мяч **2** (declare) до|кла́дывать, -ложи́ть; **the jury ~ed a verdict of guilty** прися́жные призна́ли обвиня́емого вино́вным
● *v.i.* возвра|ща́ться, -ти́ться (*or* верну́ться)

reunion /riːˈjuːnjən/ *n.* (reuniting) воссоедине́ние; (meeting of old friends etc.) встре́ча (ста́рых друзе́й)

reunite /riːjuːˈnaɪt/ *v.t. & i.* воссоедин|я́ть(ся), -и́ть(ся)

reusable /riːˈjuːzəb(ə)l/ *adj.* многокра́тного по́льзования

reuse /riːˈjuːz/ *v.t.* сно́ва испо́льзовать (*impf., pf.*)

rev /rev/ *v.t. & i.* (**revved, revving**) (*also* **~ up**) увели́чи|вать, -ть оборо́ты (мото́ра)

revamp /riːˈvæmp/ *v.t.* обнов|ля́ть, -и́ть

⚬ **reveal** /rɪˈviːl/ *v.t.* обнару́жи|вать, -ть; **this account is very ~ing** э́тот отчёт о́чень показа́телен; **she wore a ~ing dress** она́ была́ в откры́том пла́тье

revel /ˈrev(ə)l/ *v.i.* (**revelled, revelling**, AmE **reveled, reveling**) наслажда́ться (*impf.*) + *i.*; **she ~s in gossip** она́ обожа́ет спле́тни

revelation /revəˈleɪʃ(ə)n/ *n.* откры́тие, открове́ние

reveller /ˈrevələ(r)/ (AmE **reveler**) *n.* кути́ла (*m.*), гуля́ка (*c.g.*)

revelry /ˈrevəlrɪ/ *n.* попо́йка, разгу́л

revenge /rɪˈvendʒ/ *n.* месть; **he took his ~ on me** он мне отомсти́л
● *v.t.*: **he ~d himself on his enemies** он отомсти́л свои́м врага́м

⚬ **revenue** /ˈrevənjuː/ *n.* дохо́д

reverberate /rɪˈvɜːbəreɪt/ *v.i.* отра|жа́ться, -зи́ться

revere /rɪˈvɪə(r)/ *v.t.* почита́ть (*impf.*)

reverence /ˈrevərəns/ *n.* почита́ние, почте́ние

Reverend /ˈrevərənd/ *adj.*: **the ~ John Smith** его́ преподо́бие Джон Смит

reverent /ˈrevərənt/, **reverential** /revəˈrenʃ(ə)l/ *adjs.* почти́тельный

reverie /ˈrevərɪ/ *n.* мечта́ние

reversal /rɪˈvɜːs(ə)l/ *n.* по́лная переме́на

reverse /rɪˈvɜːs/ *n.* **1** (opposite) противополо́жность; **the ~ is true** де́ло обстои́т как раз наоборо́т **2** (~ gear): **he put the car into ~** он включи́л за́дний ход
● *adj.* обра́тный, противополо́жный; **in ~ order** в обра́тном поря́дке; **in ~ gear** за́дним хо́дом
● *v.t.* **1** (turn round, invert) пов|ора́чивать, -ерну́ть обра́тно **2** (drive backwards): **he ~d (the car) into a wall** он дал за́дний ход и вре́зался в сте́ну
● *v.i.* (of driver) да|ва́ть, -ть за́дний ход

reversible /rɪˈvɜːsɪb(ə)l/ *adj.* (process etc.) обрати́мый; (garment) двусторо́нний

revert /rɪˈvɜːt/ *v.i.* возвра|ща́ться, -ти́ться; **the fields have ~ed to scrub** поля́ вновь поросли́ куста́рником; **he ~ed to his old ways** он взя́лся за ста́рое; (of property, rights, etc.) пере|ходи́ть, -йти́ (*к пре́жнему владе́льцу*)

⚬ **review** /rɪˈvjuː/ *n.* **1** (re-examination, retrospect) пересмо́тр **2** (of mil. forces etc.) пара́д **3** (of book etc.) реце́нзия **4** (periodical) обозре́ние
● *v.t.* **1** (re-examine) пересм|а́тривать, -отре́ть **2** (inspect) просм|а́тривать, -отре́ть **3** (write critical account of) рецензи́ровать, от-

reviewer /rɪˈvjuːə(r)/ *n.* рецензе́нт

r

revise /rɪ'vaɪz/ *v.t.* (one's views)
пересм|а́тривать, -отре́ть; (correct a text, an opinion) испр|авля́ть, -а́вить
● *v.i.* (BrE): **I must ~ for the exams** я до́лжен повтори́ть материа́л к экза́менам

revision /rɪ'vɪʒ(ə)n/ *n.* (of text) прове́рка, перерабо́тка; (for exams) повторе́ние

revitalize /riː'vaɪtəlaɪz/ *v.t.* вновь ожив|ля́ть, -и́ть

revival /rɪ'vaɪv(ə)l/ *n.* (return to consciousness, health, etc.) возвраще́ние созна́ния; a ~ **of interest** оживле́ние интере́са; (return to use, popularity) возрожде́ние

revive /rɪ'vaɪv/ *v.t.* (bring back to life, enliven) ожив|ля́ть, -и́ть; (custom, hope) возро|жда́ть, -ди́ть
● *v.i.* (of flowers, person) ож|ива́ть, -и́ть; (regain consciousness) при|ходи́ть, -йти́ в себя́

revoke /rɪ'vəʊk/ *v.t.* отмен|я́ть, -и́ть

revolt /rɪ'vəʊlt/ *n.* восста́ние
● *v.t.* вызыва́ть, вы́звать отвраще́ние у + *g.*; a ~ing sight отврати́тельное зре́лище
● *v.i.* восст|ава́ть, -а́ть; бунтова́ть (*impf.*); взбунтова́ться (*pf.*)

revolution /revə'luːʃ(ə)n/ *n.* 1 (one complete rotation) оборо́т 2 (pol., also fig.) револю́ция

revolutionary /revə'luːʃənərɪ/ *n.* революционе́р (-ка)
● *adj.* революцио́нный

revolutionize /revə'luːʃənaɪz/ *v.t.* революционизи́ровать (*impf., pf.*)

revolv|e /rɪ'vɒlv/ *v.i.* враща́ться (*impf.*); (fig.): **he thinks everything ~es around him** он мнит себя́ це́нтром вселе́нной
■ ~ing doors *n. pl.* враща́ющиеся две́ри

revolver /rɪ'vɒlvə(r)/ *n.* револьве́р

revue /rɪ'vjuː/ *n.* (theatr.) обозре́ние, ревю́ (*nt. indecl.*)

revulsion /rɪ'vʌlʃ(ə)n/ *n.* отвраще́ние

reward /rɪ'wɔːd/ *n.* 1 (for achievement) награ́да (**for:** за + *a.*) 2 (sum offered) пре́мия
● *v.t.* (воз)награ|жда́ть, -ди́ть; **it was a ~ing task** де́ло сто́ило того́

rewind /riː'waɪnd/ *v.t.* перем|а́тывать, -ота́ть

rewire /riː'waɪə(r)/ *v.t.*: ~ **a house** замен|я́ть, -и́ть прово́дку в до́ме

reword /riː'wɜːd/ *v.t.* переформули́ровать (*impf., pf.*)

rework /riː'wɜːk/ *v.t.* перераб|а́тывать, -о́тать

rewrite /riː'raɪt/ *v.t.* (copy out) перепи́с|ывать, -а́ть; (rework) перераб|а́тывать, -о́тать

rhapsod|y /'ræpsədɪ/ *n.* (mus.) рапсо́дия; (fig.): **he went into ~ies over her dress** он пел дифира́мбы её туале́ту/наря́ду

rhetoric /'retərɪk/ *n.* рито́рика

rhetorical /rɪ'tɒrɪk(ə)l/ *adj.* ритори́ческий

rheumatic /ruː'mætɪk/ *n.* (sufferer from rheumatism) ревма́тик; (in pl.) (infml, rheumatism) ревмати́зм
● *adj.* ревмати́ческий
■ ~ fever *n.* ревмати́зм

rheumatism /'ruːmətɪz(ə)m/ *n.* ревмати́зм

rheumatoid /'ruːmətɔɪd/ *adj.* ревмато́идный, ревмати́ческий
■ ~ arthritis *n.* ревмато́идный артри́т

rhino /'raɪnəʊ/ *n.* (*pl.* ~s or ~) = rhinoceros

rhinoceros /raɪ'nɒsərəs/ *n.* (*pl.* ~ or ~es) носоро́г

Rhodes /rəʊdz/ *n.* Ро́дос

rhododendron /rəʊdə'dendrən/ *n.* рододе́ндрон

rhubarb /'ruːbɑːb/ *n.* реве́нь (*m.*)

rhyme /raɪm/ *n.* ри́фма; (poem) стих
● *v.t. & i.* рифмова́ть(ся) (*impf.*)

rhythm /'rɪð(ə)m/ *n.* ритм

rhythmic /'rɪðmɪk/ *adj.* ритми́чный, ритми́ческий

rib /rɪb/ *n.* (anat.) ребро́; **spare ~s** (of meat) рёбрышки (*nt. pl.*)

ribald /'rɪb(ə)ld/ *adj.* непристо́йный, скабрёзный

ribbon /'rɪbən/ *n.* ле́нта, тесьма́

rice /raɪs/ *n.* рис

✇ **rich** /rɪtʃ/ *n.* (collect.): **the ~** бога́тые (*pl.*)
● *adj.* 1 (wealthy) бога́тый 2 (fertile) плодоро́дный 3 (of food) жи́рный

riches /'rɪtʃɪz/ *n. pl.* бога́тство

richness /'rɪtʃnɪs/ *n.* бога́тство; (of food) жи́рность

Richter scale /'rɪktə/ *n.* шкала́ Ри́хтера

rickety /'rɪkɪtɪ/ *adj.* ша́ткий, неусто́йчивый

ricochet /'rɪkəʃeɪ/ *n.* рикоше́т; ~ **fire** стрельба́ на рикоше́тах
● *v.i.* (**ricocheted** /-ʃeɪd/, **ricocheting** /-ʃeɪɪŋ/ or **ricochetted** /-ʃetɪd/, **ricochetting** /-ʃetɪŋ/) рикошети́ровать (*impf., pf.*); бить (*impf.*) рикоше́том

rid /rɪd/ *v.t.* (**ridding**, *past and p.p.* **rid**) освобо|жда́ть, -ди́ть; изб|авля́ть, -а́вить; **get ~ of** изб|авля́ться, -а́виться от + *g.*; **we were glad to be, get ~ of him** мы бы́ли ра́ды от него́ изба́виться

riddance /'rɪd(ə)ns/ *n.*: **good ~ to him!** ≈ скатертью доро́га!

ridden /'rɪd(ə)n/ *p.p. of* ▶ ride

riddle¹ /'rɪd(ə)l/ *n.* зага́дка

riddle² /'rɪd(ə)l/ *v.t.* (pierce all over) решети́ть, из-; **he was ~d with bullets** пу́ли изрешети́ли его́ те́ло

✇ **ride** /raɪd/ *n.* 1 (on horseback) прогу́лка верхо́м; (by vehicle) пое́здка, езда́ 2 (excursion) прогу́лка 3 (fairground feature) аттракцио́н
● *v.t. & i.* (*past* **rode**, *p.p.* **ridden**) 1 (on horseback) е́здить (*indet.*), е́хать (*det.*), по- (верхо́м) (на + *p.*); ката́ться (*impf.*) (верхо́м) (на + *p.*) 2 (on a vehicle) е́здить (*indet.*), е́хать (*det.*), по- (на + *p.*); **I ~ a bicycle to work** я е́зжу на рабо́ту на велосипе́де
□ ~ **out** *v.t.*: **we shall ~ out our present troubles** мы переживём ны́нешние тру́дности
□ ~ **up** *v.i.* (approach on horseback) подъ|езжа́ть, -е́хать верхо́м; (of clothing) зад|ира́ться, -ра́ться

rider /'raɪdə(r)/ *n.* (horseman) вса́дни|к (-ца); (cyclist) велосипеди́ст (-ка)

✇ ключева́я ле́ксика

ridge /rɪdʒ/ *n.* **1** край; спи́нка **2** (of high land) го́рный хребе́т

ridicule /'rɪdɪkjuːl/ *n.* насме́шка
● *v.t.* подн|има́ть, -я́ть на́ смех

ridiculous /rɪ'dɪkjʊləs/ *adj.* (funny) смехотво́рный; (stupid) (*attr.*) смешно́й; (stupid) (*pred.*) глу́пый; **don't be ~!** не бу́дь(те) посме́шищем!; **~ly low prices** до смешно́го ни́зкие це́ны

riding /'raɪdɪŋ/ *n.* верхова́я езда́
■ **~ school** *n.* шко́ла верхово́й езды́

rife /raɪf/ *adj.* распространённый

riff /rɪf/ *n.* (mus.) рифф

riff-raff /'rɪfræf/ *n.* подо́нки (*m. pl.*) о́бщества; сброд

rifle /'raɪf(ə)l/ *n.* винто́вка

rift /rɪft/ *n.* **1** тре́щина, щель **2** (fig.) разла́д

rig /rɪg/ *n.* бурова́я вы́шка
● *v.t.* (**rigged, rigging**) (conduct fraudulently): **the elections were ~ged** результа́ты вы́боров бы́ли подтасо́ваны
□ **~ up** *v.t.* (на́скоро) сору|жа́ть, -ди́ть

Riga /'riːɡə/ *n.* Ри́га

rigging /'rɪɡɪŋ/ *n.* такела́ж

right /raɪt/ *n.* **1** (what is morally good) правота́; справедли́вость; **the child must learn the difference between ~ and wrong** ребёнка сле́дует научи́ть отлича́ть добро́ от зла́ **2** (entitlement) пра́во; **by ~s** по справедли́вости; че́стно говоря́; **~ of way** пра́во прохо́да/прое́зда **3** (~-hand side etc.) пра́вая сторона́; **on, to the ~** напра́во; **on, from the ~** спра́ва **4** (pol.): **the R~** пра́вые (*pl.*)
● *adj.* **1** (just, morally good) пра́вый, справедли́вый; **I try to do what is ~** я стара́юсь поступа́ть че́стно; **you were ~ to refuse** вы пра́вильно сде́лали, что отказа́лись **2** (correct, true) пра́вильный, ве́рный; **what is the ~ time?** вы мо́жете сказа́ть то́чное вре́мя?; **~ side up** в пра́вильном положе́нии; **that's ~!** пра́вильно!; ве́рно!; **I set him ~ on a few points** я ему́ ко́е-что разъясни́л **3** (in order, good health): **I don't feel ~** я пло́хо себя́ чу́вствую; **this medicine will soon put you ~** от э́того лека́рства вы ско́ро попра́витесь; **are you all ~?** с ва́ми всё в поря́дке?; (expr. doubt) вам нехорошо́?; вам пло́хо?; **all ~, I'll come with you** ла́дно, я пойду́ с ва́ми; **~!** (expr. agreement or consent) ве́рно!; хорошо́! **4** (opp. left) пра́вый
● *adv.* **1** (straight) пря́мо; **carry ~ on!** всё вре́мя пря́мо! **2** (exactly) то́чно; **~ here/there** пря́мо здесь/там; **~ now** сейча́с; в да́нный моме́нт **3** (immediately) сра́зу (же); **~ away** сра́зу (же), пря́мо сейча́с, неме́дленно, сию́ мину́ту **4** (all the way) по́лностью; **he turned ~ round** он поверну́лся круго́м; **I went ~ back to the beginning** я верну́лся к са́мому нача́лу; **he came ~ up to me** он подошёл ко мне вплотну́ю **5** (correctly, properly) справедли́во; пра́вильно; **he can do nothing ~** у него́ ничего́ не ла́дится; **have I guessed ~?** я угада́л? **6** (of direction) напра́во

● *v.t.* (correct) испр|авля́ть, -а́вить
■ **~ angle** *n.* прямо́й у́гол; **~-hand** *adj.* пра́вый; **~-hand drive** правосторо́ннее управле́ние; **~-hand man** (fig.) ве́рный помо́щник, пра́вая рука́; **~-handed** *adj.* де́лающий всё пра́вой руко́й, праворукий; **~-wing** *adj.* (pol.) пра́вых взгля́дов; пра́вый

righteous /'raɪtʃəs/ *adj.* пра́ведный

rightful /'raɪtfʊl/ *adj.* зако́нный

rightly /'raɪtlɪ/ *adv.* **1** (correctly) пра́вильно; **~ or wrongly, I believe he is lying** так э́то и́ли нет, но я ду́маю, он лжёт **2** (justly) справедли́во

rigid /'rɪdʒɪd/ *adj.* жёсткий; (fig.) неги́бкий; **~ discipline** стро́гая дисципли́на

rigidity /rɪ'dʒɪdɪtɪ/ *n.* жёсткость; (fig.) неги́бкость

rigmarole /'rɪɡmərəʊl/ *n.* каните́ль

rigorous /'rɪɡərəs/ *adj.* стро́гий

rigour /'rɪɡə(r)/ (AmE **rigor**) *n.* стро́гость

rile /raɪl/ *v.t.* (infml) серди́ть, рас-; раздраж|а́ть, -и́ть; **it ~d him to lose the game** его́ зли́ло, что он проигра́л

rim /rɪm/ *n.* о́бод; край

rind /raɪnd/ *n.* (of orange, cheese) ко́рка; (of bacon) кожура́, шку́рка

ring¹ /rɪŋ/ *n.* **1** (ornament) кольцо́; (with stone; signet ~) пе́рстень (*m.*); **engagement ~** кольцо́, пода́ренное при помо́лвке; **wedding ~** обруча́льное кольцо́ **2** (circle) кольцо́, круг; **he had ~s under his eyes** у него́ бы́ли тёмные круги́ под глаза́ми **3** (conspiracy) ша́йка, ба́нда; **spy ~** шпио́нская организа́ция **4** (of circus, boxing, etc.) аре́на, ринг **5** (of cooker) конфо́рка
■ **~ binder** *n.* скоросшива́тель (*m.*); **~leader** *n.* глава́рь (*m.*); **~ road** *n.* (BrE) кольцева́я доро́га

ring² /rɪŋ/ *n.* **1** (sound of bell) звоно́к; **there was a ~ at the door** в дверь позвони́ли **2** (BrE, telephone call) звоно́к; **give me a ~ tomorrow** позвони́те мне за́втра
● *v.t.* (*past* **rang**, *p.p.* **rung**) **1** звони́ть, по- в + *a.* **2** (BrE, telephone) (*also* **~ up**) звони́ть, по- + *d.*
● *v.i.* (*past* **rang**, *p.p.* **rung**) **1** звони́ть, по-; **the bells are ~ing** звоня́т колокола́; **the telephone rang** зазвони́л телефо́н; (fig.): **his words ~ true** его́ слова́ звуча́т правдоподо́бно **2** (BrE, telephone) звони́ть, по-; **we must ~ for the doctor** мы должны́ вы́звать врача́ (по телефо́ну) **3** (resound) огла|ша́ться, -си́ться (*чем*)
● *with advs.*: **~ off** (BrE) пове́сить (*pf.*) тру́бку; **a shot rang out** разда́лся вы́стрел
■ **~tone** *n.* мело́дия звонка́, рингто́н (*в моби́льном телефо́не*)

ringing /'rɪŋɪŋ/ *adj.* зво́нкий

ringlet /'rɪŋlɪt/ *n.* (curl) ло́кон

rink /rɪŋk/ *n.* като́к

rinse /rɪns/ *n.* полоска́ние
● *v.t.* полоска́ть, про-

Rio /'riːəʊ/, **Rio de Janeiro** /'riːəʊ də dʒə'nɪərəʊ/ *n.* Ри́о-де-Жане́йро (*m. indecl.*)

r

riot /'raɪət/ *n.* **1** (revolt) мятёж, бунт **2** (fig.): she allowed her imagination to run ~ она дала полную волю воображёнию; the weeds are running ~ сорняки буйно разрастаются; the garden was a ~ of colour сад пестрёл всёми красками
• *v.i.* (rebel) бесчинствовать (*impf.*)

rioter /'raɪətə(r)/ *n.* бунтарь (*m.*), мятёжник

riotous /'raɪətəs/ *adj.* (rebellious) мятёжный; (wildly enthusiastic) безудержный, шумный

rip /rɪp/ *v.t.* (**ripped, ripping**) рвать, разо-; he ~ped his trousers on a nail он порвал брюки о гвоздь; he ~ped open the envelope он разорвал конвёрт; ~ off (infml, steal) об|дирать, -одрать; she ~ped up the letter она разорвала письмо
• *v.i.* (**ripped, ripping**) рваться, разо-
■ ~-**off** *n.* (infml): it's a ~-off это обдираловка

ripe /raɪp/ *adj.* спёлый, зрёлый; the corn is ~ хлеба поспёли/созрёли; ~ cheese выдержанный сыр

ripen /'raɪpən/ *v.i.* зреть (*or* созревать), со-
• *v.t.*: the sun ~ed the tomatoes помидоры созрёли на солнце

ripple /'rɪp(ə)l/ *n.* рябь
• *v.t. & i.* покр|ывать(ся), -ыть(ся) рябью

rise /raɪz/ *n.* **1** (slope, also fig., ascent) подъём **2** (increase) повышёние, увеличёние; a ~ in temperature повышёние температуры; they asked for a ~ (BrE) они попросили об увеличёнии зарплаты **3** (origin): give ~ to вызывать, вызвать
• *v.i.* (*past* **rose**, *p.p.* **risen** /'rɪz(ə)n/) **1** (get up from bed) вста|вать, -ть (на ноги); (from seated or kneeling position) вста|вать, -ть; подн|иматься, -яться; (into the air) подн|иматься, -яться; (from the dead) воскр|есать, -ёснуть; (above the horizon) восходить, взойти; when the sun ~s когда восходит солнце; he will always ~ to the occasion он не растеряется в любой ситуации **2** (slope upwards) подн|иматься, -яться; (tower): the cliffs rose sheer above them над ними круто возвышались скалы **3** (increase in amount) возрастать (*impf.*); увели́чи|ваться, -ться; rising costs увеличивающиеся расходы; (in level): the waters are rising вода поднимается/ прибывает; the bread has ~n хлеб поднялся (*на дрожжах*); the temperature is rising температура повышается; (in price) пов|ышаться, -ыситься в ценё; дорожать, по-; (in pitch): his voice rose in anger в гнёве он повысил голос

risible /'rɪzɪb(ə)l/ *adj.* смешной, смехотворный

risk /rɪsk/ *n.* риск; he takes many ~s он любит рисковать; he ran the ~ of defeat он рисковал потерпёть поражёние
• *v.t.* рисковать (*impf.*) + i.

risky /'rɪskɪ/ *adj.* (**riskier, riskiest**) рискованный, опасный

risotto /rɪ'zɒtəʊ/ *n.* (*pl.* ~**s**) ризотто (*nt. indecl.*)

risqué /'rɪskeɪ/ *adj.* рискованный

rite /raɪt/ *n.* обряд

ritual /'rɪtʃʊəl/ *n.* ритуал; (*collect.*) обрядность
• *adj.* ритуальный

rival /'raɪv(ə)l/ *n.* сопёрник; (in business) конкурёнт
• *adj.* сопёрничающий; the ~ team команда противника
• *v.t.* (**rivalled, rivalling,** AmE **rivaled, rivaling**) сопёрничать (*impf.*) с + i.

rivalry /'raɪvəlrɪ/ *n.* сопёрничество; (in business) конкурёнция

◌ **river** /'rɪvə(r)/ *n.* река; (*attr.*) речной; up/down ~ вверх/вниз по рекё
■ ~**side** *n.* прибрёжная полоса • *adj.* прибрёжный, стоящий на берегу реки

rivet /'rɪvɪt/ *n.* заклёпка
• *v.t.* (**riveted, riveting**) клепать (*impf.*); склёп|ывать, -ать

riveting /'rɪvɪtɪŋ/ *adj.* (infml) захватывающий

Riyadh /'riːæd/ *n.* Эр-Рияд

◌ **road** /rəʊd/ *n.* **1** (thoroughfare) дорога; (*attr.*) дорожный **2** (fig.) путь (*m.*), дорога; he is on the ~ to recovery он на пути к выздоровлёнию
■ ~**block** *n.* блокпост; ~ **map** *n.* карта (автомобильных) дорог; (fig.) путеводная нить; ~ **rage** *n.* (BrE) приступ гнёва/ярости водителя автомобиля; ~**show** *n.* (radio, TV) репортаж с мёста событий; (pol.) выездное заседание, встрёча с избирателями; ~**side** *n.* обочина дороги; ~**works** *n. pl.* (BrE) дорожно-ремонтные работы; ~**worthy** *adj.* пригодный для езды по дорогам

roam /rəʊm/ *v.t. & i.* бродить, странствовать, скитаться (*all impf.*); he ~ed the streets он бродил по улицам

roar /rɔː(r)/ *n.* (of animal, people) рёв; ~s of laughter взрывы хохота
• *v.t. & i.* ревёть (*impf.*); he ~ed with laughter он хохотал во всё горло

roast /rəʊst/ *n.* жаркое
• *v.t.* жарить, за-, из-; ~ beef жареная/ запечённая говядина
• *v.i.* грёться (*impf.*)

rob /rɒb/ *v.t.* (**robbed, robbing**) (person) обкра́|дывать, обокрасть; грабить, о-; (building) грабить, о-; I have been ~bed меня обокрали/ограбили; the bank was ~bed банк ограбили; they ~bed him of his watch они украли у него часы; (fig., deprive) лиш|ать, -ить (*кого-н. чего-н.*)

robber /'rɒbə(r)/ *n.* грабитель (*m.*), вор

robbery /'rɒbərɪ/ *n.* (of person, building) ограблёние, грабёж; (when life-threatening) разбой

robe /rəʊb/ *n.* **1** мантия **2** (AmE, dressing gown) (*also* **bath**~) (купальный) халат

robin /'rɒbɪn/ *n.* малиновка

robot /'rəʊbɒt/ *n.* робот

robust /rəʊ'bʌst/ *adj.* (**robuster, robustest**) крёпкий, сильный

◌ **rock¹** /rɒk/ *n.* (solid part of earth's crust) горная

поро́да; (boulder) валу́н; **the firm is on the ～s** (infml) фи́рма прогоре́ла; (AmE, stone, pebble) ка́мень (*m.*); **whisky on the ～s** (infml) ви́ски со льдом

■ ～ **bottom** *n.* (fig.): **at ～-bottom prices** по са́мым ни́зким це́нам; ～ **climber** *n.* скалола́з; ～ **climbing** *n.* скалола́зание; ～ **face** *n.* скала́; ～**fall** *n.* камнепа́д; ～ **garden** *n.* = **rockery**

⚘ **rock²** /rɒk/ *n.* (music) рок
  ● *v.t.* (sway gently) кач|а́ть, -ну́ть; ука́ч|ивать, -а́ть; **she ～ed the baby to sleep** она́ укача́ла/ убаю́кала ребёнка; (shake) трясти́, по-; **the earthquake ～ed the house** дом шата́лся от землетрясе́ния
  ● *v.i.* (sway gently) кача́ться (*impf.*)

■ ～**ing chair** *n.* кача́лка; ～ **'n' roll** *n.* рок-н-ро́лл; ～ **star** *n.* рок-звезда́

rockery /'rɒkərɪ/ *n.* альпина́рий, альпи́йская го́рка

rocket /'rɒkɪt/ *n.* раке́та
  ● *v.i.* (**rocketed, rocketing**) (fig.): **prices ～ed** це́ны ре́зко подскочи́ли

rocky /'rɒkɪ/ *adj.* (**rockier, rockiest**) **1** (of rock; full of rocks) скали́стый, камени́стый; **the R～ Mountains, the Rockies** (infml) Скали́стые го́ры (*f. pl.*) **2** (unsteady) неусто́йчивый, ша́ткий

rococo /rə'kəʊkəʊ/ *n.* рококо́ (*nt. indecl.*)
  ● *adj.* в сти́ле рококо́

rod /rɒd/ *n.* **1** (slender stick) прут; (fishing ～) у́дочка; (instrument of chastisement) ро́зга **2** (metal bar) сте́ржень (*m.*)

rode /rəʊd/ *past of* ▸ **ride**

rodent /'rəʊd(ə)nt/ *n.* грызу́н

rogue /rəʊg/ *n.* жу́лик, моше́нник
  ■ ～ **state** *n.* (pol.) госуда́рство-изго́й; ～ **trader** *n.* (fin.) афери́ст

roguish /'rəʊgɪʃ/ *adj.* (villainous) жуликова́тый; (playful) прока́зливый, озорно́й

⚘ **role** /rəʊl/ *n.* роль; **title ～** загла́вная роль
  ■ ～ **model** *n.* образе́ц для подража́ния; ～**-play** *v.i.* разы́гр|ывать, -а́ть ро́ли

⚘ **roll** /rəʊl/ *n.* **1** (of cloth, paper, film, etc.) руло́н **2** (list) рее́стр, спи́сок **3** (of bread) бу́лочка **4** (rumbling sound) раска́т; бой бараба́на
  ● *v.t.* **1** (move by revolving) ката́ть (*indet.*), кати́ть (*det.*), по- **2** (flatten by use of cylinder) ката́ть, рас-; раска́тывать (*impf.*); **she was ～ing pastry** она́ раска́тывала те́сто **3** (shape into cylinder or sphere) свёр|тывать, -ну́ть; свора́чивать (*impf.*)
  ● *v.i.* **1** (move by revolving) кати́ться (*impf.*); ска́тываться (*impf.*); **the car began to ～ downhill** маши́на покати́лась вниз **2** (sway) кача́ться (*impf.*); колыха́ться (*impf.*) **3** (make deep sound) греме́ть (*impf.*); грохота́ть (*impf.*)
  □ ～ **along** *v.i.*: **we were ～ing along at 30 mph** маши́на кати́лась со ско́ростью 30 миль в час
  □ ～ **over** *v.i.*: **he ～ed over and went to sleep again** он переверну́лся на друго́й бок и сно́ва засну́л
  □ ～ **up** *v.t.* свёр|тывать, -ну́ть; (sleeves) засу́ч|ивать, -и́ть

■ ～**ing pin** *n.* ска́лка; ～**-up** *n.* (BrE, cigarette) самокру́тка

roller /'rəʊlə(r)/ *n.* ро́лик; като́к; (for paint) ва́лик; (*in pl.*) (for hair) бигуди́ (*nt. pl., indecl.*)
  ■ ～ **blades®** *n. pl.* одноря́дные ро́ликовые коньки́ (*m. pl.*); ～ **coaster** *n.* америка́нские го́рки (*f. pl.*); ～ **skate** *v.i.* ката́ться (*indet.*) на ро́ликах; ～ **skates** *n. pl.* ро́ликовые коньки́ (*m. pl.*)

ROM /rɒm/ *n.* (*abbr. of* **read-only memory**) (comput.) ПЗУ (постоя́нное запомина́ющее устро́йство)

Roman /'rəʊmən/ *n.* (also hist.) ри́млян|ин (-ка)
  ● *adj.* (of Rome) ри́мский; **the ～ alphabet** лати́нский алфави́т
  ■ ～ **Catholic** *n.* като́л|ик (-и́чка) ● *adj.* католи́ческий

romance /rəʊ'mæns/ *n.* **1** (novel, love affair) рома́н **2** (romantic atmosphere) рома́нтика **3**: **R～ languages** рома́нские языки́

Romanesque /rəʊmə'nesk/ *n. & adj.* рома́нский (стиль)

Romania /rəʊ'meɪnɪə/ *n.* Румы́ния

Romanian /rəʊ'meɪnɪən/ *n.* (person) румы́н (-ка); (language) румы́нский язы́к
  ● *adj.* румы́нский

romantic /rəʊ'mæntɪk/ *n.* рома́нтик
  ● *adj.* романти́ческий, романти́чный

romanticism /rəʊ'mæntɪsɪz(ə)m/ *n.* романти́зм

romanticize /rəʊ'mæntɪsaɪz/ *v.t.* романтизи́ровать (*impf., pf.*)

Romany /'rɒmənɪ/ *n.* (Gypsy) цыга́н (-ка); (language) цыга́нский язы́к
  ● *adj.* цыга́нский

Rome /rəʊm/ *n.* Рим

romp /rɒmp/ *n.* возня́
  ● *v.i.* резви́ться (*impf.*)

roof /ru:f/ *n.* кры́ша; ～ **of the mouth** нёбо
  ■ ～ **rack** *n.* бага́жник (на кры́ше автомоби́ля)

rook /rʊk/ *n.* (bird) грач; (chess) ладья́

⚘ **room** /ru:m/ *n.* **1** ко́мната **2** (space) ме́сто, простра́нство; **there's plenty of ～** полно́ ме́ста **3** (scope) возмо́жность
  ■ ～**-mate** *n.* сосе́д (-ка) по ко́мнате; ～ **service** *n.* обслу́живание в но́мере

roomy /'ru:mɪ/ *adj.* (**roomier, roomiest**) просто́рный, вмести́тельный

rooster /'ru:stə(r)/ *n.* (AmE) пету́х

⚘ **root** /ru:t/ *n.* **1** (of plant) ко́рень (*m.*); **take ～** пус|ка́ть, -ти́ть ко́рни; **the idea took ～ in his mind** э́та мысль засе́ла у него́ в голове́ **2** (fig., source) причи́на; ～ **cause** основна́я причи́на; **money is the ～ of all evil** де́ньги — ко́рень зла
  ● *v.t.* **1** (fig.): **he is a man of deeply ～ed prejudices** он челове́к с укорени́вшимися предрассу́дками **2** (transfix): **he stood ～ed to the ground** он стоя́л как вко́панный
  □ ～ **about** *v.i.* ры́ться (*impf.*)
  □ ～ **out** *v.t.* вырыва́ть, вы́рвать с ко́рнем

rope /rəʊp/ *n.* (cord) верёвка, кана́т; (fig.): **he knows the ～s** он зна́ет все ходы́ и вы́ходы; он зна́ет, что к чему́

r

● *v.t.* привя́з|ывать, -а́ть (*что к чему*)

□ **~ in** *v.t.* (infml, enlist) втя́г|ивать, -ну́ть; **I was ~d in to help me**ня запрягли в э́то де́ло

rosary /ˈrəʊzəri/ *n.* чёт|ки (-ок)

rose¹ **~** /rəʊz/ *n.* ро́за

■ **~bud** *n.* буто́н ро́зы; **~ bush** *n.* ро́зовый куст; **~-coloured,** (AmE) **-colored** *adj.* ро́зовый; **he sees the world through ~-coloured spectacles** (BrE), **glasses** (AmE) он смо́трит на мир че́рез ро́зовые очки́

rose² /rəʊz/ *past of* ▶ **rise**

rosemary /ˈrəʊzməri/ *n.* розмари́н

rosette /rəʊˈzet/ *n.* розе́тка (*украшение*)

roster /ˈrɒstə(r)/ *n.* гра́фик дежу́рств

rostrum /ˈrɒstrəm/ *n.* трибу́на

rosy /ˈrəʊzi/ *adj.* (**rosier, rosiest**) ро́зовый; **~ cheeks** румя́ные щёки

rot /rɒt/ *n.* гние́ние; гниль
● *v.t.* (**rotted, rotting**) по́ртить, ис-
● *v.i.* (**rotted, rotting**) гнить, с-; по́ртиться, ис-

rota /ˈrəʊtə/ *n.* (BrE) гра́фик дежу́рств

rotary /ˈrəʊtəri/ *adj.* враща́ющийся

rotate /rəʊˈteɪt/ *v.t. & i.* враща́ть(ся) (*impf.*)

rotation /rəʊˈteɪʃ(ə)n/ *n.* враще́ние; оборо́т

rote /rəʊt/ *n.*: **he learnt the poem by ~** он вы́учил стихотворе́ние наизу́сть

■ **~ learning** *n.* механи́ческое запомина́ние

rotten /ˈrɒt(ə)n/ *adj.* (**rottener, rottenest**) (decayed) гнило́й; (corrupt) разложи́вшийся; испо́рченный; (very unfortunate) отврати́тельный; **I'm feeling ~** я себя́ пога́но чу́вствую

Rottweiler /ˈrɒtvaɪlə(r)/ *n.* ротве́йлер

rotund /rəʊˈtʌnd/ *adj.* (spherical) округлённый; (corpulent, plump) по́лный

rouble /ˈruːb(ə)l/ *n.* рубль (*m.*)

rouge /ruːʒ/ *n.* (cosmetic) румя́н|а (*pl., g. —*)
● *v.t. & i.* румя́нить(ся), на-

rough /rʌf/ *adj.* **1** (opp. smooth, even, level) шерохова́тый, неро́вный **2** (opp. calm, gentle) бу́рный; **a ~ crowd** хамова́тая пу́блика; **the students were ~ly handled by the police** поли́ция гру́бо обраща́лась со студе́нтами **3** (arduous) тру́дный; **he had a ~ time** ему́ пришло́сь ту́го **4** (crude) гру́бый; **a ~-and-ready meal** еда́, пригото́вленная на ско́рую ру́ку **5** (rudimentary) черново́й; **a ~ sketch** черново́й набро́сок **6** (approximate) приблизи́тельный; **at a ~ guess** по приблизи́тельной оце́нке; **~ly speaking** гру́бо говоря́
● *v.t.*: **~ it** (infml) жить (*impf.*) без удо́бств

■ **~shod** *adv.* (fig.): **he rode ~shod over their feelings** он соверше́нно не щади́л их чувств

roughage /ˈrʌfɪdʒ/ *n.* гру́бая пи́ща

roughen /ˈrʌf(ə)n/ *v.t. & i.* де́лать(ся), с- гру́бым/шерохова́тым

roulette /ruːˈlet/ *n.* руле́тка

⚘ **round** /raʊnd/ *n.* **1** (circular or ~ed object) круг, окру́жность; (BrE, slice) ло́мтик **2** (regular cycle)

cycle; обхо́д; круговоро́т; **the doctor is on his ~s** до́ктор де́лает обхо́д **3** (stage in contest) тур, эта́п, ра́унд **4** (set, series): **he bought a ~ of drinks** он поста́вил по стака́нчику всем прису́тствующим; **a ~ of applause** аплодисме́нты (*m. pl.*) **5** (of ammunition) патро́н
● *adj.* **1** (circular, spherical) кру́глый; **~ shoulders** суту́лые пле́чи **2** (involving circular motion) кругово́й **3** (of numbers) кру́глый; **a ~ dozen** це́лая дю́жина
● *adv.* (BrE): **all the year ~** кру́глый год; **the tree is six feet ~** э́то де́рево шесть фу́тов в окру́жности; **he went a long way ~** он сде́лал изря́дный крюк; **he was ~ at our house** он зашёл к нам
● *prep.* (BrE) **1** (encircling) вокру́г, круго́м, о́коло (*all + g.*); **they sat ~ the table** они́ сиде́ли вокру́г стола́ **2** (to or at all points of): **he looked ~ the room** он осмотре́л (всю) ко́мнату; **they went ~ the galleries** они́ обошли́ карти́нные галере́и **3**: **~ the corner** (of position) за угло́м; (of motion) за́ угол
● *v.t.* **1** (go ~) огиба́ть, обогну́ть; об|ходи́ть, -ойти́ круго́м; **we ~ed the corner** мы заверну́ли/сверну́ли за́ угол **2** (~ a number up or down) округл|я́ть, -и́ть
● *v.i.* (turn aggressively): **he ~ed on me with abuse** он обру́шился на меня́ с бра́нью; **he ~ed on his pursuers** он набро́сился на свои́х пресле́дователей

□ **~ off** *v.t.* (smooth) выра́внивать, вы́ровнять; (bring to a conclusion) заверш|а́ть, -и́ть

□ **~ up** *v.t.* сгоня́ть, согна́ть; **the courier ~ed up the party** гид собра́л свою́ гру́ппу

■ **~about** *n.* (merry-go-round) карусе́ль; (BrE, traffic island) кольцева́я тра́нспортная развя́зка ● *adj.* око́льный; **~ about** *adv.* приблизи́тельно; **~-the-clock** *adj.* круглосу́точный; **~-the-world** *adj.* кругосве́тный; **~ trip** *n.* пое́здка в о́ба конца́; **~-up** *n.* (of news) сво́дка новосте́й; (of cattle) заго́н скота́; (raid) обла́ва

rounders /ˈraʊndəz/ *n.* англи́йская лапта́ (*командная игра, напоминающая бейсбол*)

rouse /raʊz/ *v.t.* **1** (wake) буди́ть, раз- **2** (stimulate to action, interest, etc.) подстрека́ть (*impf.*); побу|жда́ть, -ди́ть

rout /raʊt/ *n.* разгро́м
● *v.t.* разб|ива́ть, -и́ть на́голову

⚘ **route** /ruːt/ *n.* (of bus etc.) маршру́т; (way) путь, доро́га

routine /ruːˈtiːn/ *n.* **1** (regular course of action) заведённый поря́док; (*attr.*) регуля́рный; повседне́вный **2** (theatr.) но́мер, выступле́ние

rov|e /rəʊv/ *v.i.* скита́ться (*impf.*); **he has a ~ing disposition** он лю́бит стра́нствовать; **a ~ing correspondent** разъездно́й корреспонде́нт

⚘ **row¹** /rəʊ/ *n.* (line) ряд

row² /rəʊ/ *v.t.*: **he ~ed the boat in to shore** он привёл ло́дку к бе́регу
● *v.i.* грести́ (*impf.*)

■ **~boat** (AmE), **~ing boat** (BrE) *nn.* гребна́я шлю́пка

⚘ ключева́я ле́ксика

row³ /raʊ/ *n.* (BrE) **1** (noise) шум **2** (argument) ссо́ра; спор; (dispute) ди́спут, диску́ссия; **I had a ~ with the neighbours** я поруга́лся с сосе́дями
● *v.i.* (quarrel) ссо́риться, по-

rowan /'rəʊən/ *n.* ряби́на

rowdy /'raʊdɪ/ *adj.* (**rowdier, rowdiest**) гру́бый, шу́мный

rowing /'rəʊɪŋ/ *n.* (sport) гре́бля

rowlock /'rɒlək/ *n.* уключи́на

royal /'rɔɪəl/ *adj.* короле́вский, ца́рский; **His R~ Highness** Его́ Короле́вское Высо́чество
■ **~ blue** *n.* я́рко-си́ний цвет

royalist /'rɔɪəlɪst/ *n.* рояли́ст (-ка)
● *adj.* рояли́стский

royalty /'rɔɪəltɪ/ *n.* **1** (royal person(s)) член|(ы) короле́вской семьи́ **2** (payment) а́вторский гонора́р

RSI *abbr.* (*of* repetitive strain injury) тра́вма, вы́званная повторя́ющимся движе́нием

RSVP *abbr.* (*of* répondez, s'il vous plaît) бу́дьте любе́зны отве́тить

rub /rʌb/ *v.t.* (**rubbed, rubbing**) (part of the body) тере́ть (*impf.*); пот|ира́ть, -ере́ть; (chafe) нат|ира́ть, -ере́ть; (sth with a substance) нат|ира́ть, -ере́ть + *i.*
● *v.i.* (**rubbed, rubbing**) тере́ться (*impf.*)
□ **~ in** *v.t.* вт|ира́ть, -ере́ть; **it was my fault; don't ~ it in!** я винова́т, но ско́лько мо́жно упрека́ть?!
□ **~ off** *v.t.* ст|ира́ть, -ере́ть
□ **~ out** *v.t.* отт|ира́ть, -ере́ть; ст|ира́ть, -ере́ть
□ **~ up** *v.t.* нач|ища́ть, -и́стить; полирова́ть, от-; **you ~bed him (up) the wrong way** вы к нему́ не так подошли́

rubber /'rʌbə(r)/ *n.* **1** (substance) рези́на; (*attr.*) рези́новый **2** (BrE, eraser) ла́стик, рези́нка
■ **~ band** *n.* рези́нка; **~ gloves** *n. pl.* рези́новые перча́тки; **~-stamp** *v.t.* (infml) подпи́с|ывать, -а́ть не гля́дя

rubbish /'rʌbɪʃ/ *n.* (BrE) (refuse) му́сор; хлам (also fig.); (nonsense) чепуха́, вздор
■ **~ bin** *n.* му́сорное ведро́; **~ dump, ~ tip** *nn.* сва́лка

rubble /'rʌb(ə)l/ *n.* булы́жник, ще́бень (*m.*)

rubella /ru:'belə/ *n.* (med.) красну́ха

ruble /'ru:b(ə)l/ *n.* = rouble

ruby /'ru:bɪ/ *n.* руби́н

rucksack /'rʌksæk/ *n.* рюкза́к

rudder /'rʌdə(r)/ *n.* руль (*m.*)

ruddy /'rʌdɪ/ *adj.* (**ruddier, ruddiest**) румя́ный

rude /ru:d/ *adj.* **1** (impolite) гру́бый; невоспи́танный; **don't be ~!** не груби́те!; **he was ~ to the teacher** он нагруби́л учи́телю **2** (indecent) гру́бый, непристо́йный

rudiment /'ru:dɪmənt/ *n.* (*in pl.*) элемента́рные зна́ния

rudimentary /ru:dɪ'mentərɪ/ *adj.* элемента́рный

rueful /'ru:fʊl/ *adj.* печа́льный, удручённый

ruffian /'rʌfɪən/ *n.* головоре́з, банди́т

ruffle /'rʌf(ə)l/ *n.* (frill) обо́рка
● *v.t.:* **a breeze ~d the surface of the lake** от ве́тра о́зеро покры́лось ря́бью; **she ~d his hair** она́ взъеро́шила ему́ во́лосы; **the bird ~d up its feathers** пти́ца взъеро́шила пе́рья; **he never gets ~d** он всегда́ невозмути́м

rug /rʌg/ *n.* ковёр

rugby /'rʌgbɪ/ *n.* (*also* rugby football) ре́гби (*nt. indecl.*)
■ **~ player** *n.* регби́ст; **~ shirt** *n.* руба́шка-ре́гби

rugged /'rʌgɪd/ *adj.* **1** (rough, uneven) неро́вный; **a ~ coast** скали́стый бе́рег **2** (irregular) гру́бый; **~ features** ре́зкие черты́

rugger /'rʌgə(r)/ *n.* (BrE, infml) = rugby

ruin /'ru:ɪn/ *n.* **1** (downfall) ги́бель, круше́ние **2** (collapsed or destroyed state; building in this state) разва́лины, руи́ны (*both f. pl.*); **the town lay in ~s** го́род лежа́л в руи́нах; **the house fell into ~** дом соверше́нно развали́лся; (fig.): **their plans lay in ~s** их пла́ны ру́хнули
● *v.t.* разр|уша́ть, -у́шить; уничт|ожа́ть, -о́жить; губи́ть, по-; **he was ~ed** (in business) он разори́лся; **the rain ~ed my suit** дождь испо́ртил мой костю́м; **a ~ed building** разру́шенное зда́ние

✎ **rule** /ru:l/ *n.* **1** (regulation; principle) пра́вило; **smoking is against the ~s** кури́ть не разреша́ется **2** (normal practice) привы́чка, обы́чай; **as a ~** как пра́вило **3** (government) правле́ние, госпо́дство **4** (measuring stick) лине́йка
● *v.t.* **1** (govern) управля́ть (*impf.*) + *i.*; руководи́ть (*impf.*) + *i.* **2** (decree) постан|а́вливать, -ови́ть; **the umpire ~d that the ball was not out** судья́ объяви́л, что мяч не́ был в а́уте **3**: **~d paper** лино́ванная бума́га
● *v.i.* (hold sway) пра́вить (*impf.*); управля́ть (*impf.*); **ruling classes** пра́вящие кла́ссы
□ **~ out** *v.t.* (exclude) исключ|а́ть, -и́ть

ruler /'ru:lə(r)/ *n.* **1** (reigning person) прави́тель (*m.*); (measuring stick) лине́йка

ruling /'ru:lɪŋ/ *n.* (decree) постановле́ние; реше́ние

rum /rʌm/ *n.* ром

rumba /'rʌmbə/ *n.* ру́мба
● *v.i.* (**rumbas, rumbaed** /-bəd/ *or* **rumba'd, rumbaing** /-bə(r)ɪŋ/) танцева́ть, с- ру́мбу

rumble /'rʌmb(ə)l/ *n.* громыха́ние, гул
● *v.i.* громыха́ть (*impf.*); греме́ть, за-/про-; **thunder was ~ing in the distance** вдалеке́ греме́л гром

ruminant /'ru:mɪnənt/ *n.* жва́чное живо́тное
● *adj.* жва́чный

ruminate /'ru:mɪneɪt/ *v.i.* (ponder) разду́мывать (*impf.*)

rumination /ru:mɪ'neɪʃ(ə)n/ *n.* (fig.) размышле́ние

rummage /'rʌmɪdʒ/ *v.i.* ры́ться (*impf.*)

rumour /'ru:mə(r)/ (AmE rumor) *n.* слух; то́лк|и (-ов)

r

● *v.t.*: the ~ed visit визи́т, о кото́ром прошёл слух

rumple /'rʌmp(ə)l/ *v.t.* (clothes) мять, по-; (hair) еро́шить, взъ-

rumpus /'rʌmpəs/ *n.* (*pl.* **rumpuses**) шум; сканда́л; **kick up a** ~ подн|има́ть, -я́ть шум

■ ~ **room** *n.* (AmE) ко́мната для игр и развлече́ний

♂ **run** /rʌn/ *n.* **1** (action of ~ning) бег; пробе́г; **he went for a** ~ **before breakfast** он сде́лал пробе́жку пе́ред за́втраком; **the prisoner made a** ~ **for it** заключённый бежа́л/удра́л; **the prisoner is on the** ~ заключённый нахо́дится в бега́х **2** (trip, journey, route) пое́здка, рейс, маршру́т **3** (continuous stretch) пери́од; отре́зок вре́мени; **he had a** ~ **of good luck** у него́ была́ полоса́ везе́ния; **the play had a long** ~ пье́са шла до́лго; **in the long** ~ в коне́чном счёте **4** (score at cricket etc.) очко́ **5** (for fowls etc.) заго́н **6** (AmE, ladder in stocking) спусти́вшаяся петля́

● *v.t.* (**running**, *past* **ran**, *p.p.* **run**) **1** (execute): **he ran a good race** он хорошо́ пробежа́л (диста́нцию) **2** (cover) бежа́ть (*det.*), про-; **he can** ~ **the mile in under a minute** он мо́жет пробежа́ть ми́лю ме́ньше чем за мину́ту **3** (convey in car) подв|ози́ть, -езти́ (на маши́не); **shall I** ~ **you home?** хоти́те, я подвезу́ вас домо́й? **4** (cause to go): **he ran his fingers over the keys** он пробежа́л па́льцами по кла́вишам; **he ran his eye over the page** он пробежа́л глаза́ми страни́цу; **I shall** ~ (water into) **the bath** я напущу́ воды́ в ва́нну **5** (operate) управля́ть (*impf.*) (+ *i.*); **who is** ~ning **the shop?** кто ве́дает ла́вкой?; **he** ~s **a small business** у него́ своё небольшо́е де́ло; **she** ~s **the house single-handed** она́ сама́ ведёт хозя́йство; **she ran the engine for a few minutes** он завёл мото́р на не́сколько мину́т

● *v.i.* (**running**, *past* **ran**, *p.p.* **run**) **1** (move quickly) бе́гать (*indet.*), бежа́ть (*det.*), побежа́ть (*pf.*); **I had to** ~ **for the train** мне пришло́сь бежа́ть, что́бы поспе́ть на по́езд; **he ran for his life** он удира́л изо всех сил; ~ **for it!** беги́! **2** (come by chance) столкну́ться (*pf.*) (с + *i.*); натолкну́ться (*pf.*) (на + *a.*); **I ran into, across an old friend** я случа́йно встре́тил ста́рого това́рища **3** (compete) соревнова́ться (*impf.*); (fig.): **he ran for president** он баллоти́ровался в президе́нты **4** (of public transport) ходи́ть (*indet.*); **there are no trains** ~ning **поезда́** не хо́дят **5** (of machines etc.: function) де́йствовать (*impf.*); **most cars** ~ **on petrol** (BrE), **gasoline** (AmE) большинство́ маши́н рабо́тает на бензи́не; **leave the engine** ~ning! не выключа́йте мото́р! **6** (flow) течь, протека́ть, стру́иться (*all impf.*); **tears/sweat ran down his face** слёзы кати́лись (*or* пот стру́йся) по его́ щека́м; **his nose was** ~ning у него́ текло́ из но́су **7** (of colour, ink) линя́ть, по- **8** (extend) тяну́ться (*impf.*); простира́ться (*impf.*); **the gardens** ~ **down**

to the river сады́ тя́нутся до реки́; **his income** ~s **into five figures** его́ дохо́д измеря́ется пятизна́чной ци́фрой **9** (continue) быть де́йствительным; **the lease has seven years to** ~ догово́р о на́йме действи́телен ещё семь лет; **the play has been** ~ning **for five years** пье́са идёт пять лет; **it** ~s **in their family** э́то у них насле́дственное

● *further phr. with preps.*: ~ (collide with) **into** налете́ть (*impf.*) на + *a.*; (encounter): **he ran into debt** он зале́з/влез в долги́; ~ **over, through** (review) повтор|я́ть, -и́ть

☐ ~ **about** *v.i.* бе́гать (*indet.*)

☐ ~ **away** *v.i.* убе|га́ть, -жа́ть; уд|ира́ть, -ра́ть

☐ ~ **back** *v.i.*: **he ran back to apologize** он прибежа́л наза́д, что́бы извини́ться

☐ ~ **down** *v.t.*: **don't** ~ **your battery down** не тра́тьте батаре́ю; **she is always** ~ning **down her neighbours** она́ ве́чно поно́сит сосе́дей; **you look very** ~ **down** у вас о́чень утомлённый вид

☐ ~ **off** *v.i.* убе|га́ть, -жа́ть; уд|ира́ть, -ра́ть; **he ran off with the jewels** он сбежа́л с драгоце́нностями

☐ ~ **out** *v.i.* (come to an end) конча́ться, ко́нчиться; **he will soon** ~ **out of money** у него́ ско́ро ко́нчатся де́ньги

☐ ~ **over** *v.t.* задави́ть (*pf.*); **he was** ~ **over by a car** его́ задави́ла маши́на

☐ ~ **up** *v.t.*: **he ran up a bill at the tailor's** он задолжа́л портно́му

● *v.i.*: **she ran up to tell me the news** она́ прибежа́ла, что́бы сообщи́ть мне но́вость

■ ~away *n.* (fugitive) бегле́ц (-я́нка); (*attr.*) a ~away **horse** ло́шадь, кото́рая понесла́; ~-**in** *n.* (fight, squabble) схва́тка; ~-**of-the-mill** *adj.* обы́чный, сре́дний; ~-**up** *n.* (run preparatory to action) разбе́г; (fig.): **the** ~-**up to the election** (BrE) предвы́борная пора́/кампа́ния; ~**way** *n.* (aeron.) взлётно-поса́дочная полоса́

rung[1] /rʌŋ/ *n.* (of ladder) ступе́нька

rung[2] /rʌŋ/ *p.p. of* ▸ **ring**[2]

runner /'rʌnə(r)/ *n.* **1** (athlete) бегу́н **2** (horse in race) рыса́к, (бегова́я) ло́шадь **3** (narrow cloth, rug) доро́жка **4** (bot., shoot) побе́г

■ ~ **bean** *n.* (BrE) зелёная (стручко́вая) фасо́ль; ~-**up** *n.* уча́стник/кандида́т, заня́вший второ́е ме́сто

running /'rʌnɪŋ/ *n.* **1** (sport) бег; **I shall take up** ~ я займу́сь бе́гом **2** (contest) состяза́ние; **they are out of the** ~ **for the Cup** они́ вы́были из соревнова́ний на ку́бок **3** (operation) управле́ние (*чем*)

● *adj.* **1** (performed while events proceed) теку́щий **2** (continuous) непреры́вный **3** (in succession) подря́д, кря́ду; **he won three times** ~ он вы́играл три ра́за подря́д

■ ~ **commentary** *n.* репорта́ж (с ме́ста собы́тия); ~ **costs** *n. pl.* (of business) теку́щие расхо́ды (*m. pl.*); (of car) расхо́ды (*m. pl.*) на содержа́ние маши́ны; ~ **shoes** *n. pl.* кроссо́в|ки (-ок); ~ **water** *n.* водопрово́д

runny /'rʌnɪ/ *adj.* (**runnier, runniest**) теку́чий, жи́дкий; a ~ **nose** на́сморк

r

rupture /'rʌptʃə(r)/ n. проры́в; перело́м
- v.t. (burst, break) прор|ыва́ть, -ва́ть
- v.i. раз|рыва́ться, -орва́ться

ꝰ **rural** /'rʊər(ə)l/ adj. се́льский

ruse /ru:z/ n. уло́вка, ухищре́ние

rush¹ /rʌʃ/ n. (bot.) тростни́к

rush² /rʌʃ/ n. стреми́тельное движе́ние; he made a ~ for the goal он бро́сился к воро́там; (bustle) спе́шка; (increase in activity): the Christmas ~ предрожде́ственская суета́; in the ~ hour в часы́ пик
- v.t. **1** (speed) торопи́ть, по-; troops were ~ed to the front войска́ бы́ли сро́чно перебро́шены на фронт; the order was ~ed through зака́з бы́стро проверну́ли; I refuse to be ~ed into a decision я отка́зываюсь принима́ть реше́ние в спе́шке **2** (charge) брать, взять штурмом
- v.i. мча́ться, по-; бр|оса́ться, -о́ситься; кида́ться, ки́нуться; she ~ed off without saying goodbye она́ убежа́ла, не попроща́вшись; they ~ed to congratulate her они́ бро́сились её поздравля́ть

rusk /rʌsk/ n. суха́рь (m.)

Russia /'rʌʃə/ n. Росси́я

ꝰ **Russian** /'rʌʃ(ə)n/ n. **1** (person of Russian nationality) ру́сск|ий (-ая); (person of Russian citizenship) россия́н|ин (-ка) **2** (language) ру́сский язы́к; do you speak ~? вы говори́те по-ру́сски?
- adj. ру́сский
■ ~ doll n. матрёшка; ~-speaking adj. русскоязы́чный

rust /rʌst/ n. ржа́вчина
- v.i. ржаве́ть, за-

rustic /'rʌstɪk/ adj. дереве́нский, се́льский

rustle /'rʌs(ə)l/ n. ше́лест, шо́рох
- v.t. шелесте́ть (impf.) + i.; шурша́ть (impf.) + i.
- v.i. шелесте́ть (impf.); шурша́ть (impf.)

rusty /'rʌstɪ/ adj. (rustier, rustiest) ржа́вый; (fig., out of practice): his Russian is ~ он подзабы́л ру́сский

rut /rʌt/ n. (wheel track) колея́, вы́боина; (fig.) рути́на; it is easy to get into a ~ легко́ погря́знуть в рути́не

ruthless /'ru:θlɪs/ adj. безжа́лостный, жесто́кий

Rwanda /rʊ'ændə/ n. Руа́нда

rye /raɪ/ n. рожь; ~ bread ржано́й хлеб; (~ whisky) ржано́е ви́ски (nt. indecl.)

Ss

sabbath /'sæbəθ/ n. (Jewish) суббо́та; (Christian) воскресе́нье

sabbatical /sə'bætɪk(ə)l/ n. (also ~ leave) тво́рческий о́тпуск

sabotage /'sæbətɑ:ʒ/ n. диве́рсия, сабота́ж
- v.t. саботи́ровать (impf., pf.)

saboteur /sæbə'tɜ:(r)/ n. сабота́жни|к (-ца), диверса́нт

sabre /'seɪbə(r)/ n. са́бля

saccharine /'sækəri:n/ adj. са́харный, сахари́стый; (fig.) слаща́вый, при́торный

sachet /'sæʃeɪ/ n. (BrE) паке́тик (шампуня и m. n.)

sack¹ /sæk/ n. **1** (bag) мешо́к **2** (infml, dismissal) увольне́ние; I got the ~ меня́ вы́гнали/уво́лили
- v.t. (infml, dismiss) выгоня́ть, вы́гнать; увол|ьня́ть, -ить

sack² /sæk/ v.t. (plunder) гра́бить, раз-

sacrament /'sækrəmənt/ n. та́инство

sacred /'seɪkrɪd/ adj. свяще́нный, свято́й

sacrifice /'sækrɪfaɪs/ n. же́ртва
- v.t. (lit., at altar) прин|оси́ть, -ести́ (кого/что) в же́ртву; (give up) же́ртвовать, по- + i.

sacrificial /sækrɪ'fɪʃ(ə)l/ adj. же́ртвенный

sacrilege /'sækrɪlɪdʒ/ n. святота́тство

sacrilegious /sækrɪ'lɪdʒəs/ adj. святота́тственный, кощу́нственный

sacrosanct /'sækrəʊsæŋkt/ adj. свяще́нный

ꝰ **sad** /sæd/ adj. (sadder, saddest) гру́стный, печа́льный; I feel ~ мне гру́стно; a ~ event печа́льное собы́тие; (regrettable) приско́рбный; it is ~ that you failed the exams о́чень жаль, что вы провали́лись на экза́менах

sadden /'sæd(ə)n/ v.t. печа́лить, о-

saddle /'sæd(ə)l/ n. седло́
- v.t. **1** седла́ть, о- **2** (fig.) (burden): ~ sb with sth взва́л|ивать, -и́ть что-н. на кого́-н.

sadism /'seɪdɪz(ə)m/ n. сади́зм

sadist /'seɪdɪst/ n. сади́ст (-ка)

sadistic /sə'dɪstɪk/ adj. сади́стский

sadness /'sædnɪs/ n. грусть, печа́ль, тоска́

sae (BrE) abbr. (of stamped addressed envelope) конве́рт с ма́ркой и обра́тным а́дресом

safari /sə'fɑ:rɪ/ n. (pl. ~s) сафа́ри (nt. indecl.)
■ ~ park n. сафа́ри-парк

safe¹ /seɪf/ n. сейф

ꝰ **safe²** /seɪf/ adj. **1** (affording security, not dangerous) безопа́сный; (reliable) надёжный; **in sb's ~ keeping** у кого́-н. на сохране́нии; **to be on the ~ side** на вся́кий слу́чай, для (бо́льшей) ве́рности **2** (free from danger): **we are ~ from attack** мы мо́жем не опаса́ться нападе́ния; (unhurt, undamaged): **we saw them home ~ and sound** мы доста́вили их домо́й це́лыми и невреди́мыми (*or* в це́лости и сохра́нности) **3** (cautious, moderate) осторо́жный; **better ~ than sorry** бережёного Бог бережёт; **I decided to play ~** я реши́л не рискова́ть **4** (certain): **it's a ~ bet** мо́жно быть уве́ренным

■ **~ conduct** *n.* (document) охра́нная гра́мота; **~ deposit** *n.* храни́лище с се́йфами; **~guard** *n.* охра́на, страхо́вка, гара́нтия (**against:** от + *g.*); защи́тная ме́ра, ме́ры безопа́сности ● *v.t.* гаранти́ровать (*impf., pf.*); охран|я́ть, -и́ть; **~ house** *n.* конспирати́вная кварти́ра; укры́тие; **~ sex** *n.* безопа́сный секс

safely /ˈseɪflɪ/ *adv.* **1** (unharmed) благополу́чно, в сохра́нности; **we returned ~** мы благополу́чно верну́лись; **the parcel arrived ~** посы́лка пришла́ в це́лости и сохра́нности **2** (with confidence) уве́ренно, с уве́ренностью; **I can ~ say that …** я могу́ с уве́ренностью сказа́ть, что… **3** (securely) надёжно

♂ **safety** /ˈseɪftɪ/ *n.* безопа́сность; **road ~** безопа́сность на доро́гах

■ **~ belt** *n.* реме́нь (*m.*) безопа́сности; **~ net** *n.* (fig.) страхо́вка; **~ pin** *n.* англи́йская була́вка

saffron /ˈsæfrən/ *n.* (substance) шафра́н; (colour) шафра́нный/шафра́новый цвет (*оранжево-жёлтый*)
● *adj.* шафра́нный

sag /sæg/ *v.i.* (**sagged, sagging**) (of rope, curtain) пров|иса́ть, -и́снуть; (of ceiling) прог|иба́ться, -ну́ться; (of cheeks, breasts) обв|иса́ть, -и́снуть

saga /ˈsɑːɡə/ *n.* са́га; (fig.): **he told me the ~ of his escape** он пове́дал мне (фантасти́ческую) исто́рию своего́ побе́га

sagacious /səˈɡeɪʃ(ə)s/ *adj.* **1** (of person) му́дрый; (of animal) у́мный **2** (perspicacious) проница́тельный, му́дрый; (of action: far-sighted) дальнови́дный, прозорли́вый

sage[1] /seɪdʒ/ *n.* (bot.) шалфе́й

sage[2] /seɪdʒ/ *n.* (wise man) мудре́ц

Sagittarius /sædʒɪˈteərɪəs/ *n.* Стреле́ц

Sahara /səˈhɑːrə/ *n.* Caха́ра

▶ **said** /sed/ *past and p.p. of* ▶ **say**

sail /seɪl/ *n.* **1** па́рус; **in full ~** на всех паруса́х; **make, set ~ for** отпл|ыва́ть, -ы́ть в/ на + *a.*; отпр|авля́ться, -а́виться в/на + *a.* **2** (voyage on water) пла́вание
● *v.t.* **1** (of person or ship) пла́вать (*indet.*), плыть (*det.*) в (+ *p.*); (cover a distance) проппл|ыва́ть, -ы́ть; **we ~ed 150 miles** мы проплы́ли/прошли́ 150 миль **2** (control navigation of) управля́ть (*impf.*) (+ *i.*)
● *v.i.* **1** пл|а́вать (*indet.*), -ы́ть (*det.*),

поплы́ть (*pf.*); **the ship ~ed into harbour** кора́бль вошёл в га́вань; **we ~ed out to sea** мы вы́шли в мо́ре; **they ~ed up the coast** они́ плы́ли вдоль бе́рега **2** (fig., move gracefully) плыть (*det.*); пла́вно дви́гаться (*impf.*); **пропл|ыва́ть, -ы́ть; she ~ed through** the exams он с лёгкостью (*or* без труда́) сдал экза́мены

■ **~boat** *n.* (AmE) па́русная ло́дка

sailboard /ˈseɪlbɔːd/ *n.* виндсёрф(ер)

sailboarder /ˈseɪlbɔːdə(r)/ *n.* виндсёрфинги́ст (-ка)

sailboarding /ˈseɪlbɔːdɪŋ/ *n.* виндсёрфинг

sailing /ˈseɪlɪŋ/ *n.* (as sport) па́русный спорт

■ **~ boat** *n.* (BrE) па́русная ло́дка; **~ ship** *n.* па́русное су́дно, па́русник

sailor /ˈseɪlə(r)/ *n.* моря́к, матро́с

saint /seɪnt/ *n.* свято́й; **S~ Valentine's Day** день свято́го Валенти́на

sainthood /ˈseɪnthʊd/ *n.* свя́тость

saintly /ˈseɪntlɪ/ *adj.* (**saintlier, saintliest**) свято́й

sake /seɪk/ *n.*: **for the ~ of** ра́ди + *g.*; **for God's, heaven's, goodness ~** ра́ди Бо́га (*or* всего́ свято́го); **for old times' ~** по ста́рой па́мяти

salable /ˈseɪləb(ə)l/ *adj.* (AmE) = saleable

salacious /səˈleɪʃəs/ *adj.* (indecent) непристо́йный, скабрёзный

salad /ˈsæləd/ *n.* сала́т

■ **~ dressing** *n.* запра́вка для сала́та

salami /səˈlɑːmɪ/ *n.* (*pl.* **~s**) копчёная колбаса́, саля́ми (*f. indecl.*)

salary /ˈsælərɪ/ *n.* зарпла́та

♂ **sale** /seɪl/ *n.* **1** прода́жа, сбыт; **be on, for ~** име́ться (*impf.*) в прода́же; **~** (*sc. selling*) **price** прода́жная цена́ **2** (event, clearance **~**) распрода́жа; **~** (*sc. reduced*) **price** сни́женная цена́, цена́ со ски́дкой

■ **~s assistant, ~s clerk** (AmE) *nn.* продаве́ц (-щи́ца); **~sman** *n.* (in shop) продаве́ц; (travelling door-to-door) коммивояжёр; **~swoman** *n.* (in shop) продавщи́ца

saleable /ˈseɪləb(ə)l/ (AmE *also* **salable**) *adj.* ходово́й, хо́дкий (both infml)

salient /ˈseɪlɪənt/ *adj.* (noticeable, important) выдаю́щийся, я́ркий

saline /ˈseɪlaɪn/ *n.* (salt in water) соляно́й раство́р; (med.) физиологи́ческий раство́р
● *adj.* солёный, соляно́й

■ **~ solution** *n.* соляно́й раство́р

saliva /səˈlaɪvə/ *n.* слюна́

salivate /ˈsælɪveɪt/ *v.i.* выделя́ть, вы́делить слюну́

salmon /ˈsæmən/ *n.* лосо́сь (*m.*); сёмга

salmonella /sælməˈnelə/ *n.* сальмоне́лла

salon /ˈsælɒn/ *n.* сало́н

saloon /səˈluːn/ *n.* (on ship) сало́н; (*in full ~ **bar***) (BrE) бар; (*in full ~ **car***) (BrE) седа́н

salt /sɔːlt/ *n.* соль
● *adj.*: **~ water** морска́я вода́
● *v.t.* **1** (cure in brine) соли́ть, за- **2** (sprinkle with **~**) соли́ть, по-

S

■ ~ **cellar** *n.* соло́нка

salty /'sɔːltɪ/ *adj.* (**saltier, saltiest**) солёный

salubrious /sə'luːbrɪəs/ *adj.* (healthy) здоро́вый; (curative) целе́бный, цели́тельный

salutary /'sæljʊtərɪ/ *adj.* благотво́рный

salute /sə'luːt/ *n.* отда́ние че́сти; во́инское приве́тствие
   ● *v.t. & i.* отдава́ть, -а́ть честь (*кому*)

Salvadorean /sælvə'dɔːrɪən/ *n.* сальвадо́р|ец (-ка)
   ● *adj.* сальвадо́рский

salvage /'sælvɪdʒ/ *n.* (action of saving) спасе́ние (иму́щества); (what is saved) спасённое иму́щество; спасённый груз *и т. п.*
   ● *v.t.* (save) спас|а́ть, -ти́; (preserve) сохран|я́ть, -и́ть

salvation /sæl'veɪʃ(ə)n/ *n.* спасе́ние (души́), избавле́ние
■ **S~ Army** *n.* А́рмия спасе́ния

salve /sælv/ *n.* (lit., fig.) бальза́м
   ● *v.t.* (fig., soothe) успок|а́ивать, -о́ить

Samaritan /sə'mærɪt(ə)n/ *n.*: **good ~** (bibl.) до́брый самаритя́нин

samba /'sæmbə/ *n.* са́мба

⚜ **same** /seɪm/ *adj.* тот же (са́мый); тако́й же; оди́н (и тот же); (unvarying) одина́ковый, неизме́нный, ро́вный; **is that the ~ man we saw yesterday?** э́то тот же челове́к, кото́рого мы ви́дели вчера́?; **we are the ~ age** мы одни́х лет (*or* одного́ во́зраста); **in the ~ way** таки́м же о́бразом; **at the ~ time** в то же вре́мя, одновре́менно; (however) в то же вре́мя, ме́жду тем; **the village looks just the ~ as ever** дере́вня вы́глядит тако́й же, как всегда́; **it's the ~ everywhere** везде́ одина́ково
   ● *pron.* тот же (са́мый); **it's all the ~ to me** мне всё равно́; **~ again, please!** то же са́мое, пожа́луйста!; **... and the ~ to you!** ... и вам та́кже (*or* того́ же)!
   ● *adv.*: **I don't feel the ~ towards him** я измени́л своё отноше́ние к нему́; **all the ~** (nevertheless) всё-таки; всё равно́; всё же; **just the ~** (despite that) тем не ме́нее; **~ here!** я то́же!

samovar /'sæməvɑː(r)/ *n.* самова́р

⚜ **sample** /'sɑːmp(ə)l/ *n.* (comm., fig.) образе́ц, обра́зчик, приме́р; (med.) про́ба
   ● *v.t.* про́бовать, по-

sanatorium /sænə'tɔːrɪəm/ (AmE **sanitarium**) *n.* санато́рий

sanctify /'sæŋktɪfaɪ/ *v.t.* освя|ща́ть (*or* святи́ть) -ти́ть; (justify) опра́вд|ывать, -а́ть

sanctimonious /sæŋktɪ'məʊnɪəs/ *adj.* ха́нжеский

sanction /'sæŋkʃ(ə)n/ *n.* са́нкция
   ● *v.t.* (authorize) санкциони́ровать (*impf., pf.*); (approve) од|обря́ть, -о́брить

sanctity /'sæŋktɪtɪ/ *n.* свя́тость

sanctuary /'sæŋktjʊərɪ/ *n.* **1** (holy place) святи́лище **2** (asylum) убе́жище **3** (for wild life) запове́дник

sanctum /'sæŋktəm/ *n.* (*pl.* **~s**) святи́лище; (fig., 'den') прибе́жище

sand /sænd/ *n.* песо́к
   ● *v.t.* (polish) (*also* **~ down**) шлифова́ть, от-
■ **~ paper** *n.* (шлифова́льная) шку́рка ● *v.t.* чи́стить, за- (*or* шлифова́ть, от-) шку́ркой; **~stone** *n.* песча́ник

sandal /'sænd(ə)l/ *n.* санда́лия

sandwich /'sænwɪdʒ/ *n.* бутербро́д; **ham ~** бутербро́д с ветчино́й
   ● *v.t.*: **his car was ~ed between two lorries** его́ маши́на была́ зажа́та ме́жду двумя́ грузовика́ми
■ **~ bar** *n.* бутербро́дная; **~ course** *n.* (BrE) курс обуче́ния, череду́ющий тео́рию с пра́ктикой

sandy /'sændɪ/ *adj.* (**sandier, sandiest**) **1** (consisting of sand) песча́ный; (resembling sand) песо́чный **2** (hair) рыжева́тый

sane /seɪn/ *adj.* (opp. mad) норма́льный, психи́чески здоро́вый; (idea, plan) здра́вый

San Francisco /sæn fræn'sɪskəʊ/ *n.* Сан-Франци́ско (*m. indecl.*)

sang /sæŋ/ *past of* ▸ **sing**

sanguine /'sæŋgwɪn/ *adj.* (optimistic) оптимисти́чный

sanitarium /sænɪ'teərɪəm/ *n.* (AmE) = **sanatorium**

sanitary /'sænɪtərɪ/ *adj.* санита́рный, гигиени́ческий
■ **~ towel** (BrE), **~ napkin** (AmE) *nn.* гигиени́ческая прокла́дка

sanitation /sænɪ'teɪʃ(ə)n/ *n.* санита́рия; канализацио́нная систе́ма

sanitize /'sænɪtaɪz/ *v.t.* де́лать, с- бо́лее прие́млемым

sanity /'sænɪtɪ/ *n.* (state of being sane) здра́вый ум

sank /sæŋk/ *past of* ▸ **sink**

Santa Claus /'sæntə klɔːz/ *n.* (in Russia) ≈ Дед Моро́з; (in Britain, US, etc.) Са́нта-Кла́ус

sap /sæp/ *n.* (of plants) сок
   ● *v.t.* (**sapped, sapping**) (fig.): **~ sb's strength** истощ|а́ть, -и́ть чьи-н. си́лы

sapling /'sæplɪŋ/ *n.* (tree) молодо́е де́ревце

sapphire /'sæfaɪə(r)/ *n.* (stone) сапфи́р; (colour) лазу́рь

sarcasm /'sɑːkæz(ə)m/ *n.* сарка́зм

sarcastic /sɑː'kæstɪk/ *adj.* саркасти́ческий

sarcopha|gus /sɑː'kɒfəgəs/ *n.* (*pl.* **~gi** /-gaɪ/) саркофа́г

sardine /sɑː'diːn/ *n.* сарди́н(к)а

sardonic /sɑː'dɒnɪk/ *adj.* зло́бно-насме́шливый, язви́тельный

sari /'sɑːrɪ/ *n.* (*pl.* **~s**) са́ри (*nt. indecl.*) (*индийская национальная женская одежда*)

sarong /sə'rɒŋ/ *n.* саро́нг (*малай(зий)ская/индонезийская национальная одежда*)

SARS /sɑːz/ *n.* (*abbr. of* **severe acute respiratory syndrome**) атипи́чная пневмони́я, САРС (*тяжёлый о́стрый респирато́рный синдро́м*)

s

sash /sæʃ/ n. (round waist) по́яс; (over shoulder) (о́рденская) ле́нта

sat /sæt/ past and p.p. of ▶ sit

Satan /'seɪt(ə)n/ n. сатана́ (m.)

satanic /sə'tænɪk/ adj. сатани́нский, а́дский

satanism /'seɪtənɪz(ə)m/ n. сатани́зм

satchel /'sætʃ(ə)l/ n. ра́нец

satellite /'sætəlaɪt/ n. (иску́сственный) спу́тник; ~ television broadcasting спу́тниковое телеви́дение
■ ~ **dish** n. спу́тниковая анте́нна

satiate /'seɪʃɪeɪt/ v.t. нас|ыща́ть, -ы́тить

satin /'sætɪn/ n. а́тлас
● adj. атла́сный

satire /'sætaɪə(r)/ n. сати́ра

satirical /sə'tɪrɪk(ə)l/ adj. сатири́ческий

satirist /'sætɪrɪst/ n. сати́рик

satirize /'sætɪraɪz/ v.t. высме́ивать, вы́смеять

satisfaction /sætɪs'fækʃ(ə)n/ n. удовлетворе́ние, удовлетворённость

satisfactory /sætɪs'fæktərɪ/ adj. удовлетвори́тельный, хоро́ший

✎ **satisf|y** /'sætɪsfaɪ/ v.t. **1** удовлетвор|я́ть, -и́ть; ~y one's hunger утол|я́ть, -и́ть го́лод; a ~ied customer дово́льный клие́нт **2** (convince) убе|жда́ть, -ди́ть; I ~ied him of my innocence я убеди́л его́ в мое́й невино́вности **3** (fulfil): ~y an obligation выполня́ть, вы́полнить обяза́тельство **4** (of food): a ~ying lunch сы́тный обе́д

satphone /'sætfəʊn/ n. спу́тниковый телефо́н

satsuma /sæt'suːmə/ n. мандари́н

saturate /'sætʃəreɪt/ v.t. нас|ыща́ть, -ы́тить; the carpet became ~d with water ковёр пропита́лся водо́й; I was ~d я весь промо́к

saturation /sætʃə'reɪʃ(ə)n/ n. насыще́ние, насы́щенность

✎ **Saturday** /'sætədeɪ/ n. суббо́та

Saturn /'sæt(ə)n/ n. (astron., myth.) Сату́рн

sauce /sɔːs/ n. (cul.) со́ус, подли́вка
■ ~**pan** n. кастрю́ля

saucer /'sɔːsə(r)/ n. блю́дце

saucy /'sɔːsɪ/ adj. (**saucier**, **sauciest**) (cheeky) де́рзкий; (BrE, coquettish) коке́тливый

Saudi /'saʊdɪ/ n. (pl. ~s) сау́дов|ец (-ка)
● adj. сау́довский
■ ~ **Arabia** n. Сау́довская Ара́вия

sauerkraut /'saʊəkraʊt/ n. ки́слая/ква́шеная капу́ста

sauna /'sɔːnə/ n. са́уна, фи́нская (парна́я) ба́ня

saunter /'sɔːntə(r)/ v.i. идти́ (det.) не торопя́сь

sausage /'sɒsɪdʒ/ n. соси́ска
■ ~ **roll** n. (BrE) соси́ска в те́сте

savage /'sævɪdʒ/ n. дика́р|ь (-ка)
● adj. **1** (of animals: fierce) свире́пый **2** (of attack, blow, etc.) жесто́кий, я́ростный
● v.t. (жесто́ко) иск|уса́ть, -уса́ть; (fig.)

раст|ёрзывать, -ерза́ть

✎ **sav|e** /seɪv/ n. (football etc.): the goalkeeper made a brilliant ~e врата́рь блестя́ще отби́л уда́р
● v.t. **1** (rescue) спас|а́ть, -ти́; изб|авля́ть, -а́вить; he ~ed my life он спас мне жизнь; she was ~ed from drowning ей не да́ли утону́ть; (protect) храни́ть (impf.) **2** (put by) бере́чь, с-; от|кла́дывать, -ложи́ть; копи́ть, на-; I ~ed (up) £100 towards a holiday я скопи́л 100 фу́нтов на о́тпуск; ~e me something to eat! оста́вьте мне что́-нибудь пое́сть!; (collect) соб|ира́ть, -ра́ть; (avoid using or spending) эконо́мить, с-; he took the bus to ~e time он пое́хал авто́бусом, что́бы сэконо́мить вре́мя; (obviate need for, expense of, etc.) эконо́мить, с-; that will ~e me £100 я сэконо́млю на э́том сто фу́нтов; I ~ed him the trouble of replying я изба́вил его́ от необходи́мости отвеча́ть; (comput.) сохран|я́ть, -и́ть
● v.i. эконо́мить, с-; копи́ть (impf.); he is ~ing up for a bicycle он откла́дывает/ко́пит де́ньги (or он ко́пит) на велосипе́д

saver /'seɪvə(r)/ n. (investor) вкла́дчик

saving /'seɪvɪŋ/ n. **1** (salvation) спасе́ние **2** (economy) эконо́мия **3** (in pl.) (money laid by) сбереже́ния (nt. pl.)
● adj.: ~ grace положи́тельное/спаси́тельное сво́йство/ка́чество
■ ~**s account** n. сберега́тельный счёт; ~**s bank** n. сберега́тельная ка́сса, сберега́тельный банк

saviour /'seɪvjə(r)/ (AmE **savior**) n. спаси́тель (m.)

savour /'seɪvə(r)/ (AmE **savor**) n. вкус
● v.t. смакова́ть (impf.)

savoury /'seɪvərɪ/ (AmE **savory**) adj. несла́дкий

saw¹ /sɔː/ n. (tool) пила́
● v.t. (p.p. **sawn** /sɔːn/ or **sawed**) пили́ть (impf.); распил|ива́ть, -и́ть
● v.i. (p.p. **sawn** /sɔːn/ or **sawed**) пили́ть (impf.)
□ ~ **off** v.t. отпил|ива́ть, -и́ть; ~n-off (or AmE ~ed-off) shotgun обре́з
■ ~**dust** n. опи́л|ки (-ок)

saw² /sɔː/ past of ▶ see

sax /sæks/ n. (infml) = saxophone

saxophone /'sæksəfəʊn/ n. саксофо́н

saxophonist /sæk'sɒfənɪst/ n. саксофони́ст (-ка)

✎ **say** /seɪ/ n. (expression of opinion): let sb have his ~ да|ва́ть, -ть кому́-н. вы́сказаться; we had no ~ in the matter с на́шим мне́нием в э́том де́ле не счита́лись
● v.t. & i. (3rd pers. sing. pres. **says** /sez/; past and p.p. **said**) **1** говори́ть, сказа́ть; he ~s I am lazy он говори́т, что я лени́в; I must ~ призна́ться; she is said to be rich говоря́т, она́ бога́та; when all is said and done в конце́ концо́в, в коне́чном счёте; ~ good morning to sb здоро́ваться, по- с кем-н.; that is to ~ (in other words; viz.) то есть; други́ми слова́ми; it goes without ~ing (само́ собо́й)

✎ ключева́я ле́ксика

разуме́ется; слов нет **2** (of inanimate objects: indicate): **the signpost** ∼**s London** на указа́теле напи́сано «Ло́ндон»; **the clock** ∼**s 5 o'clock** часы́ пока́зывают пять **3** (formulate, express): ∼ **a prayer** произн|оси́ть, -ести́ моли́тву

saying /'seɪŋ/ n. погово́рка

scab /skæb/ n. струп, ко́рка

scaffold /'skæfəʊld/ n. **1** эшафо́т, пла́ха; **die on the** ∼ умира́ть, умере́ть на эшафо́те **2** = scaffolding

scaffolding /'skæfəʊldɪŋ/ n. лес|а́ (-о́в) (*строительные*)

scald /skɔːld/ v.t. ошпа́ри|вать, -ть; ∼**ing water** круто́й кипято́к

scale[1] /skeɪl/ n. **1** (of fish, reptile, etc.) чешу́йка; (*pl.*, *collect.*) чешуя́ **2** (on teeth) (зубно́й) ка́мень (*m.*)

scale[2] /skeɪl/ n. (*usu.* ∼ **pan**) ча́ш(к)а (весо́в)

♂ **scale**[3] /skeɪl/ n. **1** (graded system of charges) шкала́ расце́нок **2** (of map, also fig.) масшта́б **3** (size) разме́р **4** (mus.) га́мма
● v.t. (climb): ∼ **a wall** влез|а́ть, -ть (*or* зал|еза́ть, -е́зть) на сте́ну; ∼ **a mountain** вз|бира́ться, -обра́ться на́ гору
□ ∼ **down** v.t. ум|еньша́ть, -е́ньшить; сокра|ща́ть, -ти́ть
■ ∼ **drawing** n. масшта́бный чертёж

scales /skeɪlz/ n. pl. (weighing machine) вес|ы́ (-о́в)

scalp /skælp/ n. скальп

scalpel /'skælp(ə)l/ n. ска́льпель (*m.*)

scam /skæm/ n. (sl.) обма́н, надува́тельство

scamper /'skæmpə(r)/ v.i. мча́ться (*impf.*), бе́гать (*indet.*); **the dog** ∼**ed off** соба́ка умча́лась

scampi /'skæmpɪ/ n. креве́тки (*f. pl.*) (*крупные, приготовленные*)

scan /skæn/ v.t. (**scanned**, **scanning**) **1** (survey) обв|оди́ть, -ести́ взгля́дом; (glance through) пробе|га́ть, -жа́ть (глаза́ми) **2** (comput., med.) скани́ровать (*impf.*)
● n. **1** (act of surveying or looking) внима́тельное просма́тривание **2** (med.) *see* ▶ **CT**, ▶ **MRI**, ▶ **ultrasound** **3** (image obtained by scanning) изображе́ние, фотогра́фия

scandal /'skænd(ə)l/ n. сканда́л; **it is a** ∼ э́то безобра́зие

scandalize /'skændəlaɪz/ v.t. шоки́ровать (*impf.*, *pf.*)

scandalous /'skændələs/ adj. (shocking) сканда́льный; (disgraceful) позо́рный, безобра́зный, возмути́тельный

Scandinavia /skændɪ'neɪvɪə/ n. Скандина́вия

Scandinavian /skændɪ'neɪvɪən/ n. скандина́в (-ка)
● adj. скандина́вский

scanner /'skænə(r)/ n. (comput., med.) ска́нер

scant /skænt/ adj. (inadequate) недоста́точный

scanty /'skæntɪ/ adj. (**scantier**, **scantiest**) ску́дный

scapegoat /'skeɪpɡəʊt/ n. козёл отпуще́ния

scar /skɑː(r)/ n. шрам, рубе́ц; (fig.) след, ра́на
● v.t. (**scarred**, **scarring**) (mark with ∼)

ост|авля́ть, -а́вить шра́мы на + *p.*; (fig.) ра́нить (*impf.*, *pf.*)

scarce /skeəs/ adj. ре́дкий

scarcely /'skeəslɪ/ adv. едва́; почти́ не

scarcity /'skeəsɪtɪ/ n. **1** (insufficiency) недоста́ток, нехва́тка, дефици́т; **it was a time of great** ∼ э́то бы́ло вре́мя больши́х лише́ний **2** (rarity) ре́дкость
■ ∼ **value** n. сто́имость, определя́емая дефици́том

scare /skeə(r)/ n. (fright) испу́г; **give sb a** ∼ пуга́ть, ис- кого́-н.; (alarm, panic) па́ника
● v.t. пуга́ть, ис-; **I felt** ∼**d** я боя́лся; **they were** ∼**d stiff** они́ до́ сме́рти перепуга́лись
□ ∼ **away,** ∼ **off** vv.t. отпу́г|ивать, -ну́ть; спу́г|ивать, -ну́ть
■ ∼**crow** n. пу́гало, (огоро́дное) чу́чело; ∼**monger** n. паникёр (-ша)

scarf /skɑːf/ n. (*pl.* **scarves** *or* ∼**s**) шарф

scarlet /'skɑːlɪt/ n. а́лый цвет
● adj. а́лый
■ ∼ **fever** n. скарлати́на

scarves /skɑːvz/ pl. of ▶ scarf

scary /'skeərɪ/ adj. (**scarier**, **scariest**) (infml) стра́шный, жу́ткий

scathing /'skeɪðɪŋ/ adj. е́дкий

scatter /'skætə(r)/ v.t. **1** (throw here and there) разбр|а́сывать, -оса́ть; (sprinkle) рас|сыпа́ть, -ы́пать; пос|ыпа́ть, -ы́пать **2** (pass.): ∼**ed villages** разбро́санные (там и тут) сёла **3** (disperse) раз|гоня́ть, -огна́ть
● v.i. (disperse) рассе́|иваться, -яться

scavenge /'skævɪndʒ/ v.i. ры́ться/копа́ться (*impf.*) в отбро́сах

scavenger /'skævɪndʒə(r)/ n. (animal) живо́тное, пита́ющееся па́далью; (person) помо́ечник; челове́к, собира́ющий ве́щи и/ и́ли еду́ на помо́йках

scenario /sɪ'nɑːrɪəʊ/ n. (*pl.* ∼**s**) сцена́рий

♂ **scene** /siːn/ n. **1** (stage, of play) сце́на **2** (place) ме́сто; **change of** ∼ переме́на обстано́вки **3** (set, decor) декора́ция; (fig.): **behind the** ∼**s** за кули́сами **4** (view) карти́на

scenery /'siːnərɪ/ n. (theatr.) декора́ции (*f. pl.*); (landscape) пейза́ж, вид

scenic /'siːnɪk/ adj. **1** (picturesque) живопи́сный; ∼ **beauty** живопи́сность (ландша́фта) **2** (theatr.) сцени́ческий; ∼ **effects** сцени́ческие эффе́кты (*m. pl.*)

scent /sent/ n. **1** (odour) за́пах, арома́т, благоуха́ние **2** (perfume) дух|и́ (-о́в) **3** (trail, also fig.) след
● v.t.: ∼**ed candle** аромати́ческая свеча́

sceptic /'skeptɪk/ (AmE **skeptic**) n. ске́птик

sceptical /'skeptɪk(ə)l/ (AmE **skeptical**) adj. скепти́ческий

scepticism /'skeptɪsɪz(ə)m/ (AmE **skepticism**) n. скептици́зм

sceptre /'septə(r)/ (AmE **scepter**) n. ски́петр

♂ **schedule** /'ʃedjuːl/ n. **1** (list) спи́сок, пе́речень (*m.*) **2** (timetable) план, расписа́ние; **a full** ∼ больша́я програ́мма; **be behind** ∼ опа́здывать, -озда́ть; **be ahead of** ∼ опере|жа́ть, -ди́ть

S

гра́фик; **on** ~ во́время/то́чно
- *v.t.* **1** (tabulate) сост|авля́ть, -а́вить спи́сок + *g.*; **a** ~**d flight** регуля́рный рейс **2** (time; plan) рассчи́т|ывать, -а́ть; нам|еча́ть, -е́тить; **we are** ~**d to finish by May** по пла́ну мы должны́ ко́нчить к ма́ю

schematic /skɪˈmætɪk/ *adj.* схемати́ческий; (simplistic, formulaic) схемати́чный

♂ **scheme** /skiːm/ *n.* **1** (plan) прое́кт, план **2** (plot) про́иск|и (-ов)
- *v.i.* интригова́ть (*impf.*)

schism /ˈsɪz(ə)m/ *n.* раско́л; (relig. also) схи́зма

schizophrenia /ˌskɪtsəˈfriːnɪə/ *n.* шизофрени́я

schizophrenic /ˌskɪtsəˈfrenɪk/ *n.* шизофре́н|ик (-и́чка)
- *adj.* шизофрени́ческий

scholar /ˈskɒlə(r)/ *n.* учёный

scholarly /ˈskɒləlɪ/ *adj.* учёный, академи́ческий

scholarship /ˈskɒləʃɪp/ *n.* (erudition) учёность; (grant) стипе́ндия

♂ **school** /skuːl/ *n.* **1** (for educating children) шко́ла; **at** ~ в шко́ле; **go to** ~ ходи́ть (*indet.*) в шко́лу; учи́ться (*impf.*) в шко́ле; **we were at** ~ **together** мы учи́лись в одно́й шко́ле; **boys'/girls'** ~ мужска́я/же́нская шко́ла **2** (AmE, university) университе́т; (department of university): ~ **of law** юриди́ческий факульте́т **3** (for specialist education) учи́лище; **military** ~ вое́нное учи́лище; ~ **of art** худо́жественное учи́лище
- ■ ~**bag** *n.* шко́льная су́мка; ~ **book** *n.* уче́бник; ~**boy** *n.* шко́льник; ~**children** *n. pl.* шко́льники (*m. pl.*); ~ **fees** *n. pl.* пла́та за обуче́ние; ~**girl** *n.* шко́льница; ~-**leaver** *n.* (BrE) выпускни́|к (-ца); ~-**leaving** *adj.*: ~-**leaving age** (BrE) во́зраст, до кото́рого обуче́ние в шко́ле обяза́тельно; ~ **report** *n.* шко́льный та́бель; ~ **run** *n.* путь, кото́рый ежедне́вно проде́лывают роди́тели, отвозя́щие дете́й в шко́лу на автомоби́ле; ~ **teacher** *n.* учи́тель (-ница)

schooling /ˈskuːlɪŋ/ *n.* (об)уче́ние

schooner /ˈskuːnə(r)/ *n.* (naut.) шху́на; (BrE, for sherry) фуже́р; (AmE, for beer) большо́й пивно́й бока́л

♂ **science** /ˈsaɪəns/ *n.* **1** (systematic knowledge) нау́ка **2** (natural ~s) есте́ственные нау́ки
- ■ ~ **fiction** *n.* нау́чная фанта́стика

♂ **scientific** /ˌsaɪənˈtɪfɪk/ *adj.* нау́чный

♂ **scientist** /ˈsaɪəntɪst/ *n.* учёный (*в о́бласти есте́ственных нау́к*)

sci-fi /ˈsaɪfaɪ/ *n.* (infml) нау́чная фанта́стика

scintillating /ˈsɪntɪleɪtɪŋ/ *adj.* блестя́щий

scissors /ˈsɪzəz/ *n. pl.* но́жниц|ы (*pl., g.* —)

scoff[1] /skɒf/ *v.i.* (mock) смея́ться (*impf.*); ~ **at** издева́ться/глуми́ться/насмеха́ться (*all impf.*) над + *i.*

scoff[2] /skɒf/ (BrE, infml) *v.t. & i.* жрать, со-

scold /skəʊld/ *v.t.* руга́ть, об-

scone /skɒn/ *n.* ≈ небольшо́й кекс

scoop /skuːp/ *n.* **1** (for food) ло́жка **2** (journalism) ≈ сенса́ция
- *v.t.* **1** (lift with ~) заче́рп|ывать, -ну́ть; (*also* ~ **out**) вычё́рп|ывать, вы́черпать **2** (win) выи́грывать, вы́играть

scooter /ˈskuːtə(r)/ *n.* (child's) самока́т; (motor ~) мотороллер

scope /skəʊp/ *n.* **1** (range) разма́х, охва́т; **this is beyond the** ~ **of our enquiry** э́то выхо́дит за преде́лы/ра́мки на́шего рассле́дования **2** (outlet): **the game offers** ~ **for the children's imagination** э́та игра́ даёт просто́р де́тскому воображе́нию

scorch /skɔːtʃ/ *v.t.* (burn, dry up) жечь, с-; выжига́ть, вы́жечь; (clothes etc.) подпа́л|ивать, -и́ть

♂ **score** /skɔː(r)/ *n.* **1** (in games) счёт; **what's the** ~? како́й счёт?; **keep the** ~ вести́ (*det.*) счёт **2** (mus.) партиту́ра **3** (twenty) два́дцать; (about twenty) о́коло двадцати́ **4**: **on that/this** ~ на э́тот счёт
- *v.t.* **1** (scratch) цара́пать, ис-; ~ **out, through** вычё́ркивать, вы́черкнуть **2** (win) выи́грывать, вы́играть; ~ **a goal** (football) заб|ива́ть, -и́ть гол
- *v.i.* выи́грывать, вы́играть очко́; (football) заб|ива́ть, -и́ть гол

scorn /skɔːn/ *n.* презре́ние
- *v.t.* презира́ть (*impf.*); пренебр|ега́ть, -е́чь + *i.*

scornful /ˈskɔːnfʊl/ *adj.* (person): **he was** ~ **of the idea** он отнёсся к э́той иде́е с презре́нием; (glance etc.) презри́тельный

Scorpio /ˈskɔːpɪəʊ/ *n.* (*pl.* ~**s**) Скорпио́н

Scot /skɒt/ *n.* шотла́нд|ец (-ка)

Scotch /skɒtʃ/ *n.* (whisky) шотла́ндское ви́ски (*nt. indecl.*), скотч
- *adj.* шотла́ндский
- ■ ~ **tape**® *n.* кле́йкая ле́нта, скотч

scot-free /skɒtˈfriː/ *adv.*: **go/get off** ~ (unpunished) ост|ава́ться, -а́ться безнака́занным

Scotland /ˈskɒtlənd/ *n.* Шотла́ндия

Scots /skɒts/ *n.* (ling.) шотла́ндский го́вор
- *adj.* шотла́ндский
- ■ ~**man** *n.* шотла́ндец; ~**woman** *n.* шотла́ндка

♂ **Scottish** /ˈskɒtɪʃ/ *adj.* шотла́ндский

scoundrel /ˈskaʊndr(ə)l/ *n.* подле́ц

scour[1] /ˈskaʊə(r)/ *v.t.* (cleanse) чи́стить, вы́-

scour[2] /ˈskaʊə(r)/ *v.t.* (range in search or pursuit) обры́скать (*pf.*); **he** ~**ed the town for his daughter** он обе́гал весь го́род в по́исках до́чери

scourer /ˈskaʊərə(r)/ *n.* (for saucepans etc.) металли́ческая моча́лка; ёж

scourge /skɜːdʒ/ *n.* бич

scout /skaʊt/ *n.* **1** (mil.) разве́дчик **2** (Boy S~) ска́ут, бойска́ут; (Girl S~) де́вочка-ска́ут
- *v.i.*: **I have been** ~**ing about for a present** я обхо́дил все магази́ны в по́исках пода́рка

scowl /skaʊl/ *n.* серди́тый/хму́рый взгляд

♂ ключева́я ле́ксика

● *v.i.*: he ∼ed at me он хму́ро/серди́то посмотре́л на меня́

Scrabble® /'skræb(ə)l/ *n.* скрэбл, ≈ игра́ «Эруди́т»

scrabble /'skræb(ə)l/ *v.i.*: ∼ **about** ша́рить (*impf.*); ∼ **about for sth** разы́скивать (*impf.*) что-н.

scramble /'skræmb(ə)l/ *n.* **1** (climb with hands and feet) кара́бканье **2** (struggle to get sth) сва́лка; (fig.) борьба́, схва́тка
● *v.t.*: ∼d **eggs** яи́чница-болту́нья
● *v.i.* кара́бкаться, вс-; вз|бира́ться, -обра́ться; **the boys** ∼d **over the wall** ма́льчики переле́зли че́рез забо́р

scrap /skræp/ *n.* **1** (small piece) кусо́чек; (of metal) обло́мок; (of cloth) обре́зок; лоску́т; (fragment) обры́вок; ∼s **of paper** клочки́ (*m. pl.*) бума́ги **2** (*in pl.*) (waste food) объе́дк|и (-ов) **3** (waste material) ути́ль (*m.*); (∼ metal) металлоло́м; (∼ paper) макулату́ра
● *v.t.* (**scrapped**, **scrapping**) **1** (make into ∼) превра|ща́ть, -ти́ть в лом **2** (infml, discard, plan) отмен|я́ть, -и́ть
■ ∼**book** *n.* альбо́м для накле́ивания вы́резок; ∼ **heap** *n.* сва́лка; ∼ **iron** *n.* металли́ческий лом; ∼**yard** *n.* (BrE) сва́лка

scrape /skreɪp/ *n.*: **get into a** ∼ вли́пнуть (*pf.*) в исто́рию (infml)
● *v.t.* **1** (abrade) скобли́ть, вы-; (graze) сса́|живать, -ди́ть; (scratch): **he** ∼d **his car against a tree** он поцара́пал маши́ну о де́рево **2** (clean) выска́бливать (*or* скобли́ть) вы́скоблить
● *v.i.* **1** (rub): **my hand** ∼d **against the wall** я ссади́л себе́ ру́ку о сте́ну **2** (get through): **she just** ∼d **into the final** она́ с трудо́м вы́шла в фина́л
□ ∼ **along**, ∼ **by** *vv.i.* (get by) переб|ива́ться, -и́ться; **we can just** ∼ **by** мы ко́е-как перебива́емся
□ ∼ **through** *v.i.* проти́с|киваться, -ну́ться; **she** ∼d **through (her exam)** она́ с трудо́м сдала́ экза́мен
□ ∼ **together** *v.t.* (money etc.) наскре|ба́ть, -сти́

scratch /skrætʃ/ *n.* **1** (mark) цара́пина **2** (noise) цара́панье **3** (wound) цара́пина, сса́дина **4** (fig.): **come up to** ∼ де́лать (*impf.*) то, что поло́жено; **start from** ∼ нач|ина́ть, -а́ть с нача́ла/нуля́
● *v.t.* **1** цара́пать, о-; **he** ∼ed **letters on the wall** он наца́рапал бу́квы на стене́ **2** (to relieve itching) чеса́ть, по-; ∼ **one's head** чеса́ть (*impf.*) го́лову
● *v.i.* **1** (of person, ∼ oneself) чеса́ться, по- **2** (of animal): **does your cat** ∼? ва́ша ко́шка цара́пается?
□ ∼ **about**, ∼ **around** *vv.i.*: **the chickens** ∼ed **around for food** ку́ры клева́ли зе́млю в по́исках пи́щи
□ ∼ **out** *v.t.*: ∼ **sb's eyes out** выцара́пывать, вы́царапать глаза́ кому́-н.

scrawl /skrɔːl/ *n.* кара́кули (*f. pl.*)
● *v.t.* черк|а́ть, -ну́ть; цара́пать, на-
● *v.i.* писа́ть (*impf.*) кара́кулями

scrawny /'skrɔːnɪ/ *adj.* (**scrawnier**, **scrawniest**) костля́вый, то́щий

scream /skriːm/ *n.* **1** пронзи́тельный крик; (shriek) вопль (*m.*); (high-pitched ∼) визг **2** (infml, funny affair): **it was a** ∼! (э́то была́) умо́ра!
● *v.t.* выкри́кивать, вы́крикнуть
● *v.i.* вопи́ть (*impf.*); (high-pitched) визжа́ть (*impf.*); **he was** ∼**ing for help** он взыва́л о по́мощи

screech /skriːtʃ/ *n.* пронзи́тельный крик, визг; (of object) скрип, скре́жет
● *v.i.* пронзи́тельно крича́ть, за-; (of gears, tyres, etc.) скрежета́ть (*impf.*)

♂ **screen** /skriːn/ *n.* **1** (partition) перегоро́дка **2** (furniture) ши́рма **3** (shelter) прикры́тие; **behind a** ∼ **of trees** под прикры́тием дере́вьев **4** (cin., TV, comput.) экра́н
● *v.t.* **1** (protect) защи|ща́ть, -ти́ть **2** (hide) укр|ыва́ть, -ы́ть **3** (separate) отгор|а́живать, -оди́ть; **we** ∼ed **off the kitchen from the dining room** мы отгороди́ли ку́хню от столо́вой **4** (cin., also med.) investigate; **be** ∼ed **(for)** про|ходи́ть, -йти́ прове́рку на + *a.* **5** (show on ∼) пока́з|ывать, -а́ть
■ ∼ **grab** *n.* (comput.) скриншо́т; ∼**play** *n.* сцена́рий; ∼**saver** *n.* (comput.) скринсе́йвер; ∼**shot** *n.* (comput.) скриншо́т; ∼**writer** *n.* сценари́ст

screw /skruː/ *n.* винт, шуру́п
● *v.t.* **1** зави́н|чивать, -ти́ть; **the cupboard was** ∼ed **to the wall** шкаф был приви́нчен к стене́
□ ∼ **up** *v.t.* зави́н|чивать, -ти́ть; (crumple) ко́мкать, с-; ∼ **up one's eyes** щу́рить, со- глаза́; **a face** ∼ed **up with pain** лицо́, искажённое от бо́ли; ∼ **up one's courage** соб|ира́ться, -ра́ться с ду́хом; (sl., spoil) напорта́чить (*pf.*); зава́л|ивать, -и́ть
■ ∼ **cap**, ∼ **top** *nn.* нави́нчивающаяся кры́шка; ∼**driver** *n.* отвёртка

scribble /'skrɪb(ə)l/ *v.i.* (make marks) исчёркивать, исчерка́ть; **the children** ∼d **all over the wall** де́ти исчерка́ли всю сте́ну
● *v.t.* (write hastily) начерка́ть (*pf.*); ∼ **down** бы́стро написа́ть (*pf.*); (write untidily) цара́пать, на-

scribe /skraɪb/ *n.* (hist.) писе́ц

scrimp /skrɪmp/ *v.i.* = **skimp**

script /skrɪpt/ *n.* (writing system) письмо́; (text) текст; (theatr. etc.) сцена́рий; (comput.) скрипт, сцена́рий
■ ∼**writer** *n.* сценари́ст

scripture /'skrɪptʃə(r)/ *n.* Писа́ние

scroll /skrəʊl/ *n.* (of parchment) сви́ток; (archit.) завито́к
● *v.i.* (comput.) (∼ down/up) прокр|у́чивать, -ути́ть (вниз/вверх)
■ ∼ **bar** *n.* (comput.) полоса́ прокру́тки

scrot|um /'skrəʊtəm/ *n.* (*pl.* ∼**a** *or* ∼**ums**) мошо́нка

scrounge /skraʊndʒ/ *v.t.* (infml, cadge) стрел|я́ть, -ьну́ть (infml)
● *v.i.* (cadge) попроша́йничать (*impf.*)

scrounger /'skraʊndʒə(r)/ *n.* (infml) попроша́йка (*c.g.*)

s

scrub[1] /skrʌb/ *n.* (brushwood) куста́рник; (area) за́росли (*f. pl.*)

scrub[2] /skrʌb/ *n.*: **give sth a** ～ вычища́ть, вы́чистить что-н.

• *v.t.* (**scrubbed, scrubbing**) (scour) скрести́ (*impf.*); (wipe) тере́ть (*impf.*); (clean) чи́стить, по-; дра́ить, на-; ～ **the floor** мыть, вы- пол

■ ～**bing brush** *n.* жёсткая щётка

scruff /skrʌf/ *n.*: **take sb by the** ～ **of the neck** хвата́ть, схвати́ть кого-н. за ши́ворот/ загри́вок

scruffy /'skrʌfɪ/ *adj.* (**scruffier, scruffiest**) (infml) неопря́тный

scrumptious /'skrʌmpʃəs/ *adj.* (infml) о́чень вку́сный, сма́чный

scruple /'skruːp(ə)l/ *n.* сомне́ния (*nt. pl.*); **have** ～**s about doing sth** со́вести́ться, по- сде́лать что-н.; **have no** ～**s about doing sth** не стесня́ться, по- сде́лать что-н.

scrupulous /'skruːpjʊləs/ *adj.* тща́тельный, скрупулёзный, педанти́чный

scrutinize /'skruːtɪnaɪz/ *v.t.* (examine) рассм|а́тривать, -отре́ть; (stare at) при́стально смотре́ть (*impf.*) на + *a.*

scrutiny /'skruːtɪnɪ/ *n.* ◼1 (searching gaze) внима́тельный/испыту́ющий взгляд ◼2 (close investigation) тща́тельное рассле́дование/ рассмотре́ние/иссле́дование

scuba /'skuːbə/ *n.* скуба, аквала́нг

■ ～**-diver** *n.* аквалангист; ～**-diving** *n.* подво́дное пла́вание со скубой

scud /skʌd/ *v.i.* (**scudded, scudding**) нести́сь, про-; (naut.) идти́ (*det.*) под ве́тром

scuff /skʌf/ *v.t.*: ～ (sc. wear away) **one's** shoes сн|а́шивать, -оси́ть о́бувь

scuffle /'skʌf(ə)l/ *n.* потасо́вка, схва́тка

scullery /'skʌlərɪ/ *n.* судомо́йня

sculpt /skʌlpt/ *v.t.* вая́ть, из-; (model in clay etc.) лепи́ть, вы́-; (in stone) высека́ть, вы́сечь; (in wood) ре́зать, вы́-

• *v.i.* быть/рабо́тать (*impf.*) ску́льптором

sculptor /'skʌlptə(r)/ *n.* ску́льптор

sculpture /'skʌlptʃə(r)/ *n.* скульпту́ра

scum /skʌm/ *n.* пе́на; (fig.) подо́нки (*m. pl.*)

scurry /'skʌrɪ/ *n.* суета́, спе́шка; **there was a** ～ **towards the exit** все бро́сились к вы́ходу; **the** ～ **of mice under the floor** возня́ мыше́й под по́лом

• *v.i.* (also ～ **about**) суетли́во бе́гать (*impf.*); снова́ть (*impf.*); ～ **through one's work** на́спех проде́л|ывать, -ать рабо́ту

□ ～ **away**, ～ **off** *vv.i.* убе|га́ть, -жа́ть; (disperse) разбе|га́ться, -жа́ться

scuttle /'skʌt(ə)l/ *v.i.* юркну́ть (*pf.*); снова́ть (*impf.*)

scythe /saɪð/ *n.* коса́

⚷ **sea** /siː/ *n.* мо́ре; **at** ～ в мо́ре; **be all at** ～ не знать что де́лать; **by** ～ мо́рем; **by the** ～ у мо́ря, на мо́ре; (*attr.*) ～ **air** морско́й во́здух; ～ **voyage** морско́е путеше́ствие

■ ～**food** *n.* морепроду́кты (*m. pl.*); ～**front** *n.*

примо́рский бульва́р, на́бережная; ～**gull** *n.* ча́йка; ～ **horse** *n.* морско́й конёк; ～ **level** *n.* у́ровень (*m.*) мо́ря; ～ **lion** *n.* морско́й лев; ～**man** *n.* моря́к, матро́с; ～**plane** *n.* гидросамолёт; ～**shell** *n.* морска́я ра́ковина; ～**shore** *n.* морско́й бе́рег, взмо́рье; ～**sick** *adj.*: **I was** ～**sick** меня́ укача́ло (на корабле́); ～**side** *n.* морско́е побере́жье • *adj.* примо́рский; ～**side resort** морско́й куро́рт; ～ **urchin** *n.* морско́й ёж; ～**water** *n.* морска́я вода́; ～**weed** *n.* морска́я во́доросль; ～**worthy** *adj.* морехо́дный, го́дный к пла́ванию

seal[1] /siːl/ *n.* (zool.) тюле́нь (*m.*); (in full **fur** ～) ко́тик

seal[2] /siːl/ *n.* (on document etc.) печа́ть

• *v.t.* ◼1 (affix ～ to) при|кла́дывать, -ложи́ть печа́ть к + *d.* ◼2 (confirm): ～ **a bargain** скреп|ля́ть, -и́ть сде́лку ◼3 (close securely) запеча́т|ывать, -ать; плотно/ на́глухо закр|ыва́ть, -ы́ть; **a** ～**ed envelope** запеча́танный конве́рт; **the police** ～**ed off all exits from the square** поли́ция перекры́ла все вы́ходы с пло́щади ◼4 (decide): **his fate is** ～**ed** его́ у́часть решена́

seam /siːm/ *n.* шов, рубе́ц

seamless /'siːmlɪs/ *adj.* без шва; из одного́ куска́

seamstress /'semstrɪs/ *n.* швея́

seance /'seɪɒns/ *n.* спирити́ческий сеа́нс

⚷ **search** /səːtʃ/ *n.* ◼1 (quest, also comput.) по́иск (*usu. in pl.*); **make a** ～ **for sb/sth** иска́ть (*impf.*) кого́-н./что-н.; **a man in** ～ **of a wife** мужчи́на, и́щущий себе́ жену́ ◼2 (examination) о́быск

• *v.t.* ◼1 (examine) обы́ск|ивать, -а́ть; пров|оди́ть, -ести́ осмо́тр + *g.*; (rummage through) обша́ри|вать, -ть ◼2 (peer at) обв|оди́ть, -ести́ взгля́дом ◼3 (penetrate): ～**ing questions** подро́бные вопро́сы

• *v.i.* иска́ть (*impf.*); (of police, customs) пров|оди́ть, -ести́ о́быск; ～ **for** иска́ть (*impf.*), разы́скивать (*impf.*); ～ **through** просм|а́тривать, -отре́ть; **he** ～**ed through all his papers for the contract** он перебра́л/ перебра́л все свои́ бума́ги в по́исках догово́ра

■ ～ **engine** *n.* (comput.) поиско́вая систе́ма/ маши́на; ～**light** *n.* прожектор; ～ **party** *n.* поиско́вая гру́ппа; ～ **warrant** *n.* о́рдер на о́быск

⚷ **season** /'siːz(ə)n/ *n.* ◼1 сезо́н; (of year) вре́мя го́да; **strawberries are in** ～ сейча́с сезо́н клубни́ки; **holiday** ～ сезо́н отпуско́в ◼2 (BrE) (*in full* ～ **ticket**) сезо́нный/проездно́й биле́т; (for concerts, etc.) абонеме́нт

• *v.t.* ◼1 (mature: of timber, wine, etc.) выде́рживать, вы́держать ◼2 (acclimatize): **a** ～**ed traveller** о́пытный путеше́ственник ◼3 (spice) припр|авля́ть, -а́вить; **a highly** ～**ed dish** о́строе блю́до

seasonable /'siːzənəb(ə)l/ *adj.* (suited to the season) соотве́тствующий сезо́ну; (opportune) своевре́менный

seasonal /'siːzən(ə)l/ *adj.* сезо́нный

⚷ ключева́я ле́ксика

seasoning /'si:zənɪŋ/ n. (cul.) припра́ва

◆ **seat** /si:t/ n. **1** (place to sit) сиде́нье; (chair) стул; (bench) скамья́, скаме́йка **2** (place in vehicle, theatre, etc.) ме́сто; **take one's ~** зан|има́ть, -я́ть ме́сто; **he booked a ~** он заказа́л биле́т **3** (of chair) сиде́нье **4** (of trousers) зад (у) брюк
● v.t. **1** (make sit) сажа́ть, посади́ть **2** (provide with ~s) вме|ща́ть, -сти́ть; **this table ~s twelve** за э́тот стол мо́жно посади́ть двена́дцать челове́к
■ **~ belt** n. реме́нь (m.) безопа́сности

seating /'si:tɪŋ/ n. (allocation of places) расса́живание; (placing at table) размеще́ние госте́й за столо́м

secateurs /seka'tə:z/ n. pl. (BrE) садо́вые но́жниц|ы (pl., g. —)

secede /sɪ'si:d/ v.i. отдел|я́ться, -и́ться (from: от + g.); выходи́ть, вы́йти (from: из + g.)

secession /sɪ'seʃ(ə)n/ n. отделе́ние (from: от + g.); вы́ход (from: из + g.)

secluded /sɪ'klu:dɪd/ adj.: a ~d spot уединённый/укро́мный уголо́к

seclusion /sɪ'klu:ʒ(ə)n/ n. уедине́ние, изоля́ция

◆ **second** /'sekənd/ n. **1** второ́й; **on the ~ of May** второ́го ма́я **2** (in pl.) (imperfect goods) второсо́ртный/брако́ванный това́р **3** (measure of time) секу́нда; **wait a ~!** одну́ секу́нду!; **~(s) hand** (of clock) секу́ндная стре́лка
● adj. второ́й; (other) друго́й; **Charles the S~** Карл Второ́й; **on the ~ floor**, (AmE) **third floor** на тре́тьем этаже́; **the ~ largest city** второ́й по величине́ го́род; (additional) доба́вочный; **~ helping** доба́вка; **have ~ thoughts** переду́мать, разду́мать (both pf.)
● v.t. (support) поддерж|ива́ть, -а́ть
■ **~ best** adj. не са́мый лу́чший; (inferior) второсо́ртный; **~-class** adj.: **~-class cabin** каю́та второ́го кла́сса; **~-class citizens** гра́ждане второ́го со́рта ● adv.: **we travel ~-class** мы е́здим вторы́м кла́ссом; **~ cousin** n. трою́родный брат (трою́родная сестра́); **~ hand** n. see ▶ **second** n. **3**; **~-hand** adj. (previously used) поде́ржанный; **~-hand bookshop** букинисти́ческий магази́н; (indirect): **~-hand information** информа́ция из вторы́х рук ● adv.: **I bought the car ~-hand** я купи́л поде́ржанную маши́ну; **~ name** n. (BrE) фами́лия; **~-rate** adj. (of goods) второсо́ртный; (mediocre) посре́дственный

secondary /'sekəndərɪ/ adj. (less important) втори́чный; (school) сре́дний

secondly /'sekəndlɪ/ adv. во-вторы́х

secondment /sɪ'kɒndmənt/ n. (BrE) командиро́вка

secrecy /'si:krɪsɪ/ n. секре́тность

◆ **secret** /'si:krɪt/ n. секре́т; та́йна; **keep a ~** храни́ть, со- секре́т; **in ~** секре́тно, та́йно
● adj. секре́тный, та́йный; (hidden) потайно́й, секре́тный; (undisclosed): **I was ~ly glad to see him** в глубине́ души́ я был рад его́ ви́деть

secretarial /sekrɪ'teərɪəl/ adj. секрета́рский

◆ **secretary** /'sekrɪtərɪ/ n. секрета́р|ь; (female typist, receptionist, etc.) секрета́рша (infml)
■ **S~ of State** n. (in UK) мини́стр; (in US) госуда́рственный секрета́рь, мини́стр иностра́нных дел

secrete /sɪ'kri:t/ v.t. **1** (physiol. etc.) выдел|я́ть, вы́делить **2** (conceal) укр|ыва́ть, -ы́ть; пря́тать, с-; **~ oneself** укр|ыва́ться, -ы́ться; пря́таться, с-

secretive /'si:krɪtɪv/ adj. скры́тный, за́мкнутый

sect /sekt/ n. се́кта

sectarian /sek'teərɪən/ adj. секта́нтский

◆ **section** /'sekʃ(ə)n/ n. **1** (separate or distinct part) се́кция; (severed portion) кусо́к; **~ of the population** часть населе́ния; **~ of a book** разде́л кни́ги; (department) отде́л, отделе́ние **2** (geom. etc.) разре́з; **~ drawing** чертёж в разре́зе; сече́ние

◆ **sector** /'sektə(r)/ n. се́ктор

secular /'sekjʊlə(r)/ adj. (worldly) мирско́й; (lay, non-religious) све́тский

◆ **secure** /sɪ'kjʊə(r)/ adj. **1** (free from care) споко́йный; **feel ~ about sth** не беспоко́иться (impf.) о чём-н. **2** (safe) про́чный, надёжный; (reliable) надёжный; (assured): **a ~ income** гаранти́рованный/ве́рный дохо́д
● v.t. **1** (make safe) закреп|ля́ть, -и́ть; застрахо́в|ывать, -а́ть **2** (insure) страхова́ть, за- **3** (obtain) дост|ава́ть, -а́ть

◆ **security** /sɪ'kjʊərɪtɪ/ n. **1** (safety) безопа́сность; **he is a ~ risk** он неблагонадёжен **2** (guarantee) гара́нтия **3** (pledge) зало́г; гара́нтия; **~ for a loan** гара́нтия за́йма; закла́д **4** (in pl.) (bonds) це́нные бума́ги (f. pl.)
■ **~ guard** n. охра́нник, секью́рити (m. indecl.)

sedate¹ /sɪ'deɪt/ adj. степе́нный, уравнове́шенный

sedate² /sɪ'deɪt/ v.t. да|ва́ть, -ть успокои́тельное + d.

sedation /sɪ'deɪʃ(ə)n/ n. успокое́ние; **under ~** под де́йствием успокои́тельного

sedative /'sedətɪv/ n. успокои́тельное (сре́дство)

sedentary /'sedəntərɪ/ adj. (of posture etc.) сидя́чий; **a ~ way of life** сидя́чий/малоподви́жный о́браз жи́зни; (of person) неподви́жный, малоподви́жный

sediment /'sedɪmənt/ n. оса́док, отсто́й

sedimentary /sedɪ'mentərɪ/ adj. оса́дочный

sedition /sɪ'dɪʃ(ə)n/ n. подстрека́тельство к мятежу́

seduce /sɪ'dju:s/ v.t. соблазн|я́ть, -и́ть

seducer /sɪ'dju:sə(r)/ n. соблазни́тель (m.); обольсти́тель (m.)

seduction /sɪ'dʌkʃ(ə)n/ n. (act of seducing sb) обольще́ние; (temptation) собла́зн

seductive /sɪ'dʌktɪv/ adj. соблазни́тельный

◆ **see** /si:/ v.t. (past **saw**, p.p. **seen**) **1** ви́деть; **I saw her arrive** я ви́дел, как она́ прие́хала;

S

did you ~ anyone leaving? вы ви́дели, чтобы кто́-нибудь выходи́л? **2** (look at, watch) смотре́ть, по- на + *a.*; ~ p 4 см. стр./с. 4; let me ~ that да́йте мне на э́то посмотре́ть; the film is worth ~ing э́тот фильм сто́ит посмотре́ть; the sights осм|а́тривать, -отре́ть достопримеча́тельности **3** (imagine) предст|авля́ть, -а́вить себе́ (*что*) **4** (find out) посмотре́ть (*pf.*) узн|ава́ть, -а́ть; I'll ~ if I can get tickets я посмотрю́, смогу́ ли я доста́ть биле́ты **5** (comprehend) ви́деть, у-; пон|има́ть, -я́ть; I don't ~ what good that is я не ви́жу, кака́я от э́того по́льза; as far as I can ~ насколько я понима́ю **6** (consider) ду́мать, по-; I'll ~ я поду́маю; посмо́трим **7** (meet) ви́деть, у-; встр|еча́ть, -е́тить; (associate) ви́деться (*impf.*), встреча́ться (*impf.*) (*с кем*); they stopped ~ing each other они́ разошли́сь (*or* переста́ли встреча́ться); (visit) посе|ща́ть, -ти́ть; наве|ща́ть, -сти́ть; we went to ~ our friends мы навести́ли на́ших друзе́й; come and ~ me, us sometime заходи́те ка́к-нибудь; ~ you on Tuesday! до вто́рника! **8** (consult): I went to ~ him about a job я пошёл к нему́ поговори́ть о рабо́те; can I ~ you for a moment? мо́жно вас на мину́тку? **9** (escort) прово|жа́ть, -ди́ть; he saw her to the door он проводи́л её до две́ри **10** (ensure) следи́ть, про-; ~ (to it) that the door is locked проследи́те, чтобы за́перли дверь
● *v.i.* (*past* **saw**, *p.p.* **seen**) **1** ви́деть (*impf.*); can you ~ from where you are? вам отту́да ви́дно?; he cannot ~ (is blind) он не ви́дит; он слеп; we saw through him мы раскуси́ли его́ **2** (make provision; take care; give attention; organize) забо́титься, по- (*о чём*); (arrange, organize) забо́титься, по-; she ~s to the laundry она́ ве́дает сти́ркой; I have to ~ to the children мне прихо́дится забо́титься о де́тях; he saw to it that I got the money он позабо́тился о том, чтобы я получи́л де́ньги
□ ~ **off** *v.t.* (accompany) прово|жа́ть, -ди́ть; we saw them off at the station мы проводи́ли их на по́езд
□ ~ **out** *v.t.* прово|жа́ть, -ди́ть до вы́хода; I can ~ myself out ≈ я сам найду́ доро́гу
□ ~ **through** *v.t.*: who will ~ the job through? кто доведёт де́ло до конца́?
■ ~-**through** *adj.* прозра́чный

⚲ **seed** /siːd/ *n.* **1** (lit., fig.) се́мя (*nt.*); (of apple, melon, sunflower) се́мечко; go, run to ~ (lit.) идти́, пойти́ на семена́; (fig., of person) сд|ава́ть, -ать **2** (sport: ~ed player) посе́янный игро́к

seedling /ˈsiːdlɪŋ/ *n.* сея́нец

seedy /ˈsiːdɪ/ *adj.* (**seedier**, **seediest**) (shabby) потрёпанный; (sleazy) захуда́лый

⚲ **seek** /siːk/ *v.t.* (*past and p.p.* **sought**) (look for) иска́ть (*impf.*) (+ *a./g. of concrete/abstract object*); (try to get) иска́ть (*impf.*) (+ *g.*); (ask for): ~ advice проси́ть, по- сове́та; ~ out разыска́ть (*pf.*); отыска́ть (*pf.*)

⚲ **seem** /siːm/ *v.i.* каза́ться, по-; предст|авля́ться,

-а́виться; it ~s to me мне ка́жется; по-мо́ему; it ~s like only yesterday как бу́дто э́то бы́ло вчера́; she ~s young она́ мо́лодо вы́глядит; I ~ed to hear a voice мне показа́лось, что я слы́шал чей-то го́лос

seen /siːn/ *p.p. of* ▸ see

seep /siːp/ *v.i.* (*usu.* ~ **out, through**) прос|а́чиваться, -очи́ться

see-saw /ˈsiːsɔː/ *n.* (доска́-)каче́л|и (-ей)
● *v.i.* (fig.) колеба́ться (*impf.*)

seethe /siːð/ *v.i.* (of liquids, also fig.) бурли́ть (*impf.*); the streets were ~ing with people у́лицы кише́ли наро́дом/людьми́

segment /ˈsegmənt/ *n.* сегме́нт; (of fruit) до́лька

segregate /ˈsegrɪgeɪt/ *v.t.* отдел|я́ть, -и́ть; раздел|я́ть, -и́ть

segregation /segrɪˈgeɪʃ(ə)n/ *n.* (separation) отделе́ние, изоля́ция; (racial) (ра́совая) сегрега́ция

seismologist /saɪzˈmɒlədʒɪst/ *n.* сейсмологи́ческий

seismology /saɪzˈmɒlədʒɪ/ *n.* сейсмоло́гия

seize /siːz/ *v.t.* **1** (grasp; lay hold of) хвата́ть, схвати́ть; he ~d (hold of) the rope он схвати́л (*or* ухвати́лся за) верёвку; ~ an opportunity ухва|та́ться, -ти́ться за возмо́жность; по́льзоваться, вос- слу́чаем **2** (power, land) захва́т|ывать, -и́ть; брать, взять
● *v.i.* (jam) (*also* ~ **up**) за|еда́ть, -е́сть; застр|ева́ть, -я́ть

seizure /ˈsiːʒə(r)/ *n.* (capture) захва́т; (confiscation) конфиска́ция; (attack of illness) при́ступ, припа́док; (stroke) уда́р

seldom /ˈseldəm/ *adv.* ре́дко

⚲ **select** /sɪˈlekt/ *adj.* и́збранный, элита́рный
● *v.t.* выбира́ть, вы́брать; от|бира́ть, -обра́ть; под|бира́ть, -обра́ть

⚲ **selection** /sɪˈlekʃ(ə)n/ *n.* **1** (choice) вы́бор **2** (assortment) подбо́р, ассортиме́нт

selective /sɪˈlektɪv/ *adj.* (choosing carefully) разбо́рчивый; (partial) вы́борочный

⚲ **self** /self/ *n.* (*pl.* **selves**) (individuality) су́щность; (personality) ли́чность; I am not my former ~ я уже́ не тот, что пре́жде

self-absorbed /selfəbˈzɔːbd/ *adj.* поглощённый собо́й

self-addressed /selfəˈdrest/ *adj.*: ~ envelope конве́рт с обра́тным а́дресом отправи́теля

self-adhesive /selfədˈhiːsɪv/ *adj.* самокле́ящийся

self-assurance /selfəˈʃʊərəns/ *n.* уве́ренность (в себе́)

self-assured /selfəˈʃʊəd/ *adj.* (само)уве́ренный

self-awareness /selfəˈweənɪs/ *n.* самосозна́ние

self-catering /selfˈkeɪtərɪŋ/ *n.* (BrE): ~ apartment жильё с самообслу́живанием; ~ holiday путёвка, включа́ющая жильё с самообслу́живанием

self-centred /self'sentəd/ (AmE **-centered**) *adj.* эгоцентри́чный

self-confessed /selfkən'fest/ *adj.* открове́нный

self-confidence /self'kɒnfɪd(ə)ns/ *n.* уве́ренность (в себе́)

self-confident /self'kɒnfɪd(ə)nt/ *adj.* уве́ренный (в себе́)

self-conscious /self'kɒnʃəs/ *adj.* (awkward) нело́вкий; (shy) засте́нчивый; (embarrassed) смущённый

self-contained /selfkən'teɪnd/ *adj.* (person) самостоя́тельный, незави́симый; (BrE, of accommodation) отде́льный

self-control /selfkən'trəʊl/ *n.* самооблада́ние

self-controlled /selfkən'trəʊld/ *adj.* вы́держанный

self-criticism /self'krɪtɪsɪz(ə)m/ *n.* самокри́тика

self-defence /selfdɪ'fens/ (AmE **-defense**) *n.* самооборо́на, самозащи́та

self-denial /selfdɪ'naɪəl/ *n.* самоотрече́ние; **practise** ~ отка́зывать (*impf.*) себе́ во всём; ограни́чивать (*impf.*) себя́

self-destruct /selfdɪ'strʌkt/ *v.i.* (tech.) самоликвиди́роваться (*impf., pf.*)

self-destructive /selfdɪ'strʌktɪv/ *adj.* самоуби́йственный

self-determination /selfdɪtə:mɪ'neɪʃ(ə)n/ *n.* самоопределе́ние

self-discipline /self'dɪsɪplɪn/ *n.* вну́тренняя дисципли́на

self-effacing /selfɪ'feɪsɪŋ/ *adj.* скро́мный

self-employed /selfɪm'plɔɪd/ *adj.* рабо́тающий не по на́йму

self-esteem /selfɪ'sti:m/ *n.* самоуваже́ние, самолю́бие

self-evident /self'evɪd(ə)nt/ *adj.* очеви́дный

self-explanatory /selfɪk'splænətərɪ/ *adj.* не тре́бующий разъясне́ний

self-expression /selfɪk'spreʃ(ə)n/ *n.* самовыраже́ние

self-fulfilling /selffʊl'fɪlɪŋ/ *adj.*: ~ **prophecy** предсказа́ние, влия́ющее на результа́т

self-governing /self'gʌvənɪŋ/ *adj.* самоуправля́ющийся, автоно́мный

self-government /self'gʌvənmənt/ *n.* самоуправле́ние

self-help /self'help/ *n.* самопо́мощь

self-image /self'ɪmɪdʒ/ *n.* самооце́нка, со́бственное представле́ние о себе́

self-important /selfɪm'pɔ:t(ə)nt/ *adj.* ва́жный, самонадея́нный

self-indulgent /selfɪn'dʌldʒ(ə)nt/ *adj.* избало́ванный

self-inflicted /selfɪn'flɪktɪd/ *adj.* нанесённый самому́ себе́

self-interest /self'ɪntrest/ *n.* со́бственный интере́с; коры́сть

selfish /'selfɪʃ/ *adj.* эгоисти́чный, эгоисти́ческий, коры́стный

selfishness /'selfɪʃnɪs/ *n.* эгоисти́чность, эго́изм

selfless /'selflɪs/ *adj.* самоотве́рженный, беззаве́тный

self-made /'selfmeɪd/ *adj.*: **he is a** ~ **man** он сам себя́ сде́лал; он челове́к, вы́бившийся из низо́в

self-pity /self'pɪtɪ/ *n.* жа́лость к себе́

self-portrait /self'pɔ:trɪt/ *n.* автопортре́т

self-possessed /selfpə'zest/ *adj.* хладнокро́вный, невозмути́мый

self-possession /selfpə'zeʃ(ə)n/ *n.* хладнокро́вие, невозмути́мость

self-preservation /selfprezə'veɪʃ(ə)n/ *n.* самосохране́ние

self-proclaimed /selfprə'kleɪmd/ *adj.* самозва́ный

self-raising /self'reɪzɪŋ/ (AmE **self-rising**) *adj.*: ~ **flour** мука́ с разрыхли́телем

self-reliant /selfrɪ'laɪənt/ *adj.* самостоя́тельный

self-respect /selfrɪ'spekt/ *n.* самоуваже́ние

self-righteous /selfraɪtʃəs/ *adj.* ха́нжеский

self-rule /self'ru:l/ *n.* самоуправле́ние

self-sacrifice /self'sækrɪfaɪs/ *n.* самопоже́ртвование

self-satisfied /self'sætɪsfaɪd/ *adj.* самодово́льный

self-sealing /self'si:lɪŋ/ *adj.* самозакле́ивающийся

self-service /self'sə:vɪs/ *n.* самообслу́живание

self-sufficient /selfsə'fɪʃ(ə)nt/ *adj.* самостоя́тельный; (econ.): **Russia is 70%** ~ **in oil/food production** Росси́я обеспе́чивает свои́ потре́бности в не́фти/продово́льствии на 70% за счёт вну́тренних ресу́рсов

self-taught /self'tɔ:t/ *adj.*: **a** ~ **man, woman** самоу́чка (*c.g.*)

self-willed /self'wɪld/ *adj.* своево́льный

✒ **sell** /sel/ *v.t.* (*past and p.p.* **sold**) **1** прода|ва́ть, -а́ть; торгова́ть (*impf.*) + *i.*; **I'll** ~ **you this carpet for £20** я прода́м вам э́тот ковёр за 20 фу́нтов; ~**ing price** прода́жная цена́; **this shop** ~**s stamps** в э́том магази́не продаю́тся почто́вые ма́рки **2** (infml, put across): **he was unable to** ~ **his idea to the management** ему́ не удало́сь убеди́ть правле́ние приня́ть его́ предложе́ние

• *v.i.* (*past and p.p.* **sold**) **1** (of person): **you were wise to** ~ **when you did** вы во́время про́дали свой това́р **2** (of goods): **the house sold for £90,000** за дом вы́ручили 90 000 фу́нтов

□ ~ **off** *v.t.* распрода|ва́ть, -а́ть; **they sold off the goods at a reduced price** они́ распро́дали това́р по сни́женной цене́

□ ~ **out** *v.i.*: **the book sold out** э́та кни́га разошла́сь; **the shop sold out of cigarettes** магази́н распро́дал все сигаре́ты; **they have sold out of tickets** все биле́ты про́даны; **they were accused of** ~**ing out to the enemy** их обвини́ли в том, что они́ продали́сь врагу́

■ ~**-by date** *n.* (BrE) срок го́дности; ~**-out** *n.* спекта́кль/конце́рт/спорти́вный матч с

seller /'selə(r)/ n. продав|е́ц (-щи́ца); торго́в|ец (-ка)

Sellotape® /'seləteɪp/ n. (BrE) скотч, кле́йкая ле́нта

selves /selvz/ pl. of ▶ self

semantic /sɪ'mæntɪk/ adj. семанти́ческий, смысловой

semaphore /'seməfɔ:(r)/ n. семафо́р
 ● v.t. & i. сигнализи́ровать (impf., pf.) флажка́ми

semen /'si:mən/ n. се́мя (nt.), спе́рма

semester /sɪ'mestə(r)/ n. семе́стр

semi /'semɪ/ n. (pl. ~s) (BrE, infml, house) оди́н из двух особняко́в, име́ющих о́бщую сте́ну
 ● pref. полу…
 ■ ~-**automatic** adj. полуавтомати́ческий; ~**breve** n. (BrE, mus.) це́лая но́та; ~**circle** n. полукру́г; ~**circular** adj. полукру́глый; ~**colon** n. то́чка с запято́й; ~**conductor** n. полупроводни́к; ~-**conscious** adj. в полубессозна́тельном состоя́нии; ~-**detached** adj.: ~-**detached house** оди́н из двух особняко́в, име́ющих о́бщую сте́ну; ~-**final** n. полуфина́л; ~-**finalist** n. полуфинали́ст (-ка); ~-**skimmed** adj. (BrE) обезжи́ренный; ~**tone** n. (mus.) полуто́н

seminal /'semɪn(ə)l/ adj. **1** семенно́й **2** (fig., work) эпоха́льный; (idea) плодотво́рный
 ■ ~ **fluid** n. семенна́я жи́дкость

seminar /'semɪnɑ:(r)/ n. семина́р

seminary /'semɪnəri/ n. семина́рия

Semitic /sɪ'mɪtɪk/ adj. семити́ческий, семи́тский; (language) семи́тский

semolina /semə'li:nə/ n. ма́нная крупа́, ма́нка (infml)

senate /'senɪt/ n. сена́т; (of university) сове́т

senator /'senətə(r)/ n. сена́тор

send /send/ v.t. (past and p.p. **sent**) (dispatch) пос|ыла́ть, -ла́ть; отпр|авля́ть, -а́вить; **he sent me a book** он присла́л мне кни́гу; **I shall ~ you to bed** я отпра́влю тебя́ спать; **the teacher sent him out of the room** учи́тель вы́ставил/вы́гнал его́ из кла́сса
 ● v.i. (past and p.p. **sent**): **he sent for a doctor** он вы́звал врача́; он посла́л за врачо́м
 □ ~ **away** v.i.: ~ **away for sth** выпи́сывать, вы́писать что-н., зак|а́зывать, -аза́ть что-н.
 □ ~ **back** v.t. (person) пос|ыла́ть, -ла́ть наза́д; (thing) от|сыла́ть, -осла́ть
 □ ~ **in** v.t.: **he sent in his bill** он посла́л счёт; ~ **in a report** представля́ть, -а́вить отчёт
 □ ~ **off** v.t. (dispatch) отпр|авля́ть, -а́вить; **he was sent off by the referee** судья́ удали́л его́ с по́ля
 □ ~ **on** v.t. (forward) перес|ыла́ть, -ла́ть
 □ ~ **out** v.t. высыла́ть, вы́слать; (distribute) ра|ссыла́ть, -зосла́ть; (emit): ~ **out heat** выделя́ть, вы́делить тепло́
 □ ~ **up** v.t. (infml, ridicule) высме́ивать, вы́смеять
 ■ ~-**off** n. про́воды pl. (-ов); **he got a marvellous ~-off from his friends** друзья́ устро́или ему́ замеча́тельные про́воды; ~-**up** n. (infml, parody,

satire) паро́дия, сати́ра

sender /'sendə(r)/ n. отправи́тель (m.)

Senegal /senɪ'gɔ:l/ n. Сенега́л

senile /'si:naɪl/ adj. ста́рческий
 ■ ~ **dementia** n. ста́рческое слабоу́мие; (of person) дря́хлый

senility /sɪ'nɪlɪti/ n. (physical) дря́хлость; (mental) ста́рческое слабоу́мие

senior /'si:nɪə(r)/ n.: **he is my ~ by 5 years** он на пять лет ста́рше меня́
 ● adj. (in age) ста́рший (во́зрастом, года́ми); (in position) ста́рший (по чи́ну/зва́нию)
 ■ ~ **citizen** n. пожило́й челове́к, челове́к пенсио́нного во́зраста

seniority /si:nɪ'ɒrɪti/ n. старшинство́

sensation /sen'seɪʃ(ə)n/ n. **1** (feeling) ощуще́ние **2** (exciting event) сенса́ция

sensational /sen'seɪʃən(ə)l/ adj. сенсацио́нный

sensationalism /sen'seɪʃənəlɪz(ə)m/ n. сенсацио́нность

sense /sens/ n. **1** (faculty) чу́вство; **the five ~s** пять чувств; **a keen ~ of hearing** о́стрый слух **2** (feeling; perception; appreciation) чу́вство, ощуще́ние; **have you no ~ of shame?** у вас стыда́ нет!; ~ **of humour** чу́вство ю́мора **3** (in pl.) (sanity) ум; **take leave of one's ~s** сходи́ть, сойти́ с ума́; **come to one's ~s** бра́ться, взя́ться за ум **4** (common ~) здра́вый смысл; **he had the ~ to call the police** у него́ хвати́ло ума́ вы́звать поли́цию **5** (meaning) смысл, значе́ние; **in a ~** в изве́стном/не́котором смы́сле; **make ~ of** пон|има́ть, -я́ть; раз|бира́ться, -обра́ться в + p.; **it makes ~** это разу́мно
 ● v.t. чу́вствовать, по-; ощу|ща́ть, -ти́ть

senseless /'senslɪs/ adj. **1** (foolish) бессмы́сленный **2** (unconscious) бесчу́вственный; **knock sb ~** оглуш|а́ть, -и́ть кого́-н.

sensible /'sensɪb(ə)l/ adj. (благо)разу́мный; ~ **shoes** практи́чная о́бувь

sensitive /'sensɪtɪv/ adj. чувстви́тельный, восприи́мчивый; (tender) ~ **skin** не́жная ко́жа; (painful): ~ **tooth** больно́й зуб; (potentially embarrassing): **a ~ topic** щекотли́вая/делика́тная те́ма

sensitivity /sensɪ'tɪvɪti/ n. чувстви́тельность

sensor /'sensə(r)/ n. (tech.) да́тчик

sensual /'sensjʊəl/ adj. чу́вственный

sensuous /'sensjʊəs/ adj. чу́вственный

sent /sent/ past and p.p. of ▶ send

sentence /'sent(ə)ns/ n. **1** (gram.) предложе́ние **2** (law) пригово́р
 ● v.t. пригов|а́ривать, -ори́ть

sentiment /'sentɪmənt/ n. **1** (feeling) чу́вство **2** (opinion) мне́ние, то́чка зре́ния; **those are my ~s** таково́ моё мне́ние

sentimental /sentɪ'ment(ə)l/ adj. сентимента́льный

sentimentality /sentɪmen'tælɪti/ n. сентимента́льность

sentry /'sentri/ n. часово́й

Seoul /səʊl/ *n.* Сеу́л

ⵢ **separate¹** /'sepərət/ *adj.* отде́льный; (distinct) осо́бый; (not together) разде́льный; **two ~ questions** два самостоя́тельных/ра́зных вопро́са; **they are living ~ly** они́ живу́т/ прожива́ют отде́льно/разде́льно

separate² /'sepəreit/ *v.t.* (set apart) отдел|я́ть, -и́ть; (part) разлуч|а́ть, -и́ть; **he is ~d from his family** он не живёт с семьёй
● *v.i.* **1** (become detached) отдел|я́ться, -и́ться **2** (of man and wife) ра|сходи́ться, -зойти́сь

separation /sepə'reiʃ(ə)n/ *n.* отделе́ние, разделе́ние; (of spouses) разде́льное прожива́ние

separatism /'sepərətiz(ə)m/ *n.* сепарати́зм

separatist /'sepərətist/ *n.* сепарати́ст (-ка)

ⵢ **September** /sep'tembə(r)/ *n.* сентя́брь (*m.*)

septic /'septik/ *adj.* септи́ческий; **the wound has gone ~** ра́на загнои́лась

sepulchral /sɪ'pʌlkr(ə)l/ *adj.* (of a tomb): **~ stone** надгро́бный/моги́льный ка́мень; (gloomy): **~ voice** замоги́льный го́лос

sepulchre /'sepəlkə(r)/ (AmE **sepulcher**) *n.* гробни́ца; (in cave) склеп

sequel /'si:kw(ə)l/ *n.* продолже́ние (**to:** + *g.*); си́квел (**to:** + *g. or* к + *d.*)

sequence /'si:kwəns/ *n.* **1** (succession) после́довательность; поря́док; **~ of events** ход/после́довательность собы́тий **2** (part of film) эпизо́д

sequential /sɪ'kwenʃ(ə)l/ *adj.* после́довательный

sequester /sɪ'kwestə(r)/ *v.t.* **1** (isolate, detach) изоли́ровать (*impf., pf.*); **~ oneself from the world** удал|я́ться, -и́ться от ми́ра; **a ~ed village** уединённая дере́вня **2** (law etc., confiscate) (*also* **sequestrate**) (take temporary possession) секвестрова́ть (*impf., pf.*); (confiscate) конфискова́ть (*impf., pf.*)

sequestrate /'si:kwistreit/ *v.t.* = sequester 2

sequestration /si:kwi'streiʃ(ə)n/ *n.* секве́стр, аре́ст иму́щества

sequin /'si:kwin/ *n.* (spangle) блёстка

Serb /sə:b/ *n.* серб (-ка)

Serbia /'sə:biə/ *n.* Се́рбия

Serbian /'sə:biən/ *n.* (person) серб (-ка); (language) се́рбский язы́к
● *adj.* се́рбский

Serbo-Croat /sə:bəʊ'krəʊæt/, **Serbo-Croatian** /sə:bəʊkrəʊ'eiʃ(ə)n/ *nn.* серб(ск)охорва́тский язы́к
● *adjs.* серб(ск)охорва́тский

serenade /serə'neid/ *n.* серена́да
● *v.t. & i.* петь, с- серена́ду (*кому*)

serene /sɪ'ri:n/ *adj.* (**serener, serenest**) безмяте́жный, споко́йный

serf /sə:f/ *n.* крепостно́й; **emancipation of the ~s** раскрепоще́ние крестья́н

sergeant /'sa:dʒ(ə)nt/ *n.* сержа́нт

serial /'siəriəl/ *n.* (story etc.) рома́н, выходя́щий отде́льными вы́пусками; (TV) многосери́йный телефи́льм; сериа́л
● *adj.*: **~ killer** сери́йный уби́йца; **~ number** сери́йный но́мер

serialize /'siəriəlaiz/ *v.t.* (publish in successive parts) изд|ава́ть, -а́ть вы́пусками; (screen in successive parts) выпуска́ть, вы́пустить се́риями

series /'siəri:z/ *n.* (*pl.* **~**) **1** (succession) се́рия **2** (TV) цикл програ́мм

ⵢ **serious** /'siəriəs/ *adj.* **1** (thoughtful) серьёзный; **I am ~ about this** я говорю́ э́то всерьёз; **you can't be ~** вы шу́тите; **take sth ~ly** отн|оси́ться, -ести́сь серьёзно к + *d.*; (words) (вос)прин|има́ть, -я́ть что-н. всерьёз **2** (important; not slight) серьёзный, суще́ственный, ва́жный; **~ crime** тя́жкое/ серьёзное преступле́ние; **he is ~ly ill** он серьёзно/тяжело́ бо́лен

seriousness /'siəriəsnis/ *n.* серьёзность; ва́жность; **in all ~** без шу́ток; со всей серьёзностью

sermon /'sə:mən/ *n.* про́поведь

serpent /'sə:pənt/ *n.* змея́; (bibl.) змий

serrated /sə'reitid/ *adj.* зубча́тый, зазу́бренный

serum /'siərəm/ *n.* сы́воротка

servant /'sə:v(ə)nt/ *n.* (male, also fig.) слуга́ (*m.*); (female) служа́нка, прислу́га

ⵢ **serve** /sə:v/ *n.* (at tennis) пода́ча
● *v.t.* **1** (be servant to; give service to) служи́ть (*impf.*) + *d.*; **if my memory ~s me correctly/ well** е́сли па́мять мне не изменя́ет **2** (meet needs of, satisfy): **~ a purpose** служи́ть (*impf.*) це́ли; **this box has ~d its purpose** э́та коро́бка сослужи́ла свою́ слу́жбу; (provide service to) обслу́ж|ивать, -и́ть; **the railway ~s all these villages** желе́зная доро́га обслу́живает все э́ти сёла **3** (supply with food, goods, etc.) под|ава́ть, -а́ть + *d.*; **the waiter ~d us with vegetables** официа́нт по́дал (нам) о́вощи; **are you being ~d?** вас кто́-нибудь обслу́живает? **4** (proffer) под|ава́ть, -а́ть; **dinner is ~d** обе́д по́дан; **~ a ball** под|ава́ть, -а́ть мяч **5** (fulfil, go through): **~ one's sentence** отб|ыва́ть, -ы́ть срок **6** (treat): **it ~s him right** так ему́ и на́до; поде́лом ему́
● *v.i.* служи́ть (*impf.*); **he ~d in the army** он служи́л в а́рмии; **~ on a jury** быть прися́жным; **the plank ~d as a bench** доска́ служи́ла ла́вкой/скамьёй

server /'sə:və(r)/ *n.* (at tennis) подаю́щий; (comput.) се́рвер

ⵢ **service** /'sə:vis/ *n.* **1** (employment) слу́жба; **length of ~** стаж **2** (branch of public work) слу́жба; **public, civil ~** госуда́рственная слу́жба; **do one's military ~** отб|ыва́ть, -ы́ть во́инскую пови́нность; **the ~s** вооружённые си́лы (*f. pl.*) **3** (work done for sb or sth) услу́га; (by hotel staff etc.) обслу́живание, се́рвис **4** (system to meet public need): **postal ~** почто́вая слу́жба; **a frequent train ~ to London** регуля́рное железнодоро́жное сообще́ние с Ло́ндоном **5** (technical maintenance) техобслу́живание **6** (eccl.) слу́жба; обря́д; **marriage/burial ~** венча́ние/ отпева́ние **7** (in tennis) пода́ча
● *v.t.*: **~ a vehicle** пров|оди́ть, -ести́ осмо́тр и теку́щий ремо́нт маши́ны

S

■ ~ **charge** *n.* плáта за обслýживание; ~**man** *n.* военнослýжащий; ~ **station** *n.* (for petrol) бензозапрáвочная стáнция, бензоколóнка; (for repairs) стáнция техни́ческого обслýживания; ~**woman** *n.* военнослýжащая

serviceable /'sɜːvɪsəb(ə)l/ *adj.* полéзный, гóдный

serviette /sɜːvɪ'et/ *n.* (BrE) салфéтка

servile /'sɜːvaɪl/ *adj.* раболéпный, подобострáстный

servility /sɜː'vɪlɪtɪ/ *n.* подобострáстие

serving /'sɜːvɪŋ/ *n.* (of food) пóрция

servitude /'sɜːvɪtjuːd/ *n.* рáбство; **penal** ~ кáторжные рабóты (*f. pl.*)

⚥ **session** /'seʃ(ə)n/ *n.* (meeting) заседáние; (period) сéссия

⚥ **set** /set/ *n.* **1** (collection) набóр; (complete set) комплéкт; (pictures, coins, etc. collected) коллéкция; **chess** ~ шáхматы (*pl., g.* —); **dinner** ~ столóвый серви́з; ~ **of teeth** (dentures) зубнóй протéз **2** (receiving apparatus): **television** ~ телеви́зор **3** (tennis) сет, пáртия **4** (theatr.) декорáция **5** (cin.): **on** ~ на съёмочной площáдке

● *adj.* **1** (fixed): a ~ **smile** засты́вшая улы́бка; **he has** ~ **opinions** у негó установи́вшиеся взгля́ды; **he is** ~ **in his ways** он не изменя́ет свои́м привы́чкам; ~ **phrase** клишé (*indecl.*); шаблóнное выражéние; (prearranged): **at the** ~ **time** в устанóвленное врéмя; ~ **menu** кóмплексное меню́; (prescribed): ~ **books** обязáтельная литератýра **2** (ready): **all** ~**?** готóвы?; **we were all** ~ **to go** мы совсéм ужé собрали́сь идти́ **3** (resolved): **he is** ~ **on going to the cinema** он настрóился идти́ в кинó; **he was dead** ~ **against the idea** он был реши́тельно/категори́чески прóтив э́того предложéния

● *v.t.* (**setting**, *past and p.p.* ~) **1** (lay) класть, положи́ть; (place) размещáть, -сти́ть; распол|агáть, -ожи́ть; (arrange; ~ out) расст|авля́ть, -áвить **2** (adjust, prepare) стáвить, по-; **I always** ~ **my watch by the station clock** я всегдá стáвлю часы́ по станциóнным часáм; **they** ~ **a trap for him** они́ устрóили емý ловýшку; ~ **the table** накр|ывáть, -ы́ть (на) стол **3** (make straight or firm): ~ **a bone** впр|авля́ть, -áвить кость; ~ **sb's hair** укл|áдывать, уложи́ть комý-н. вóлосы **4** (fig., apply): ~ **one's heart on** стрáстно желáть (*impf.*) + *g.* **5** (make or put into specified state) прив|оди́ть, -ести́; **he** ~ **the boat in motion** он привёл лóдку в движéние; ~ **sb's mind at ease, rest** успок|áивать, -óить когó-н.; ~ **on fire** подж|игáть, -éчь; (incite): **he** ~ **his dog on me** он натрави́л на меня́ свою́ собáку **6** (start) заст|авля́ть, -áвить (+ *inf.*); **the smoke** ~ **her coughing** онá закáшлялась от ды́ма **7** (present) зад|авáть, -áть **8** (establish): **he is** ~**ting his children a bad example** он подаёт свои́м дéтям дурнóй примéр **9** (an exam) сост|авля́ть, -áвить **10** ~ **sth to music** класть, положи́ть что-н. на мýзыку

11 (situate): **he** ~ **the scene in Paris** мéстом дéйствия он избрáл Пари́ж

● *v.i.* (**setting**, *past and p.p.* ~) **1** (of sun) сади́ться, сесть **2** (become firm or solid) затверд|евáть, -éть; твердéть (*impf.*); (of jelly) заст|ывáть, -ы́ть; (of cement) схвáт|ываться, -и́ться

● *with preps.*: ~ **about (doing) sth** прин|имáться, -я́ться за что-н.; ~ **(up)on sb** нап|адáть, -áсть на когó-н.

□ ~ **aside** *v.t.* (allocate) выдел|я́ть, вы́делить; (reserve) от|клáдывать, -ложи́ть

□ ~ **back** *v.t.* (delay, damage) зам|едля́ть, -éдлить; отбр|áсывать, -óсить назáд; нан|оси́ть, -ести́ урóн + *d.*; (infml, cost): **the trip** ~ **him back a few pounds** поéздка влетéла емý в копéечку

□ ~ **down** *v.t.* (make statement or record): **he** ~ **down his complaint in writing** он изложи́л свою́ жáлобу в пи́сьменном ви́де; **she** ~ **down her impressions in a diary** онá заноси́ла/запи́сывала свои́ впечатлéния в дневни́к

□ ~ **forth** *v.t.* (declare) изл|агáть, -ожи́ть
● *v.i.* (leave) отпр|авля́ться, -áвиться

□ ~ **in** *v.i.* (take hold): **winter is** ~**ting in** наступáет зимá; **the rain** ~ **in early** дождь начался́ рáно

□ ~ **off** *v.t.* (cause to explode): **they were** ~**ting off fireworks** они́ устрóили фейервéрк; (cause): **his arrest** ~ **off a wave of protest** егó арéст вы́звал волнý протéстов; (enhance): **the ribbon will** ~ **off your complexion** лéнта оттени́т/подчеркнёт цвет вáшего лицá; (compensate) возме|щáть, -сти́ть; ~ **off gains against losses** баланси́ровать, с- при́быль и убы́тки; (cause to start): **the story** ~ **them off laughing** э́тот расскáз рассмеши́л их
● *v.i.* (leave, on foot) пойти́ (*pf.*); (by transport) поéхать (*pf.*); отпр|авля́ться, -áвиться

□ ~ **out** *v.t.* (arrange, display) распол|агáть, -ожи́ть; (expound) изл|агáть, -ожи́ть
● *v.i.* (leave) пойти́, поéхать (*both pf.*); отпр|авля́ться, -áвиться; (attempt): **he** ~ **out to conquer Europe** он задýмал покори́ть Еврóпу

□ ~ **to** *v.i.* (make a start) прин|имáться, -я́ться; (begin to fight or argue) сцеп|ля́ться, -и́ться (infml); схв|áтываться, -ати́ться

□ ~ **up** *v.t.* (erect) устан|áвливать, -ови́ть; (form): **we** ~ **up a committee** мы организовáли комитéт; (establish): ~ **up a school** осн|óвывать, -áть шкóлу; (claim, put forward): **he** ~**s himself up to be a scholar** он изображáет из себя́ учёного; (restore to health): **a holiday will** ~ **you up** óтдых вас постáвит нá ноги
● *v.i.*: **she** ~ **up in business** онá организовáла своё дéло

■ ~**back** *n.* (delay) задéржка; (failure) неудáча; (difficulty) затруднéние; ~**-to** *n.* (infml, fight) схвáтка; ~**-up** *n.* (infml, arrangement) поря́дки (*m. pl.*); обстанóвка; (comput.) устанóвка

settee /se'tiː/ *n.* (небольшóй) дивáн

⚥ **setting** /'setɪŋ/ *n.* **1** (of sun etc.) захóд, закáт **2** (of gems) опрáва **3** (background) обстанóвка, окружéние

⚥ **settle** /'set(ə)l/ *v.t.* **1** (place securely): ~ **oneself in an armchair** ус|áживаться, -éсться

⚥ ключевáя лéксика

в кре́сло **2** (install) поме|ща́ть, -сти́ть; устр|а́ивать, -о́ить **3** (calm) успок|а́ивать, -о́ить **4** (reconcile) упла́|живать, -дить; **their differences were soon ~d** их разногла́сия бы́ли ско́ро ула́жены **5** (decide) реш|а́ть, -и́ть; **that ~s it** тогда́ всё (я́сно) **6** (pay): **~ a bill** плати́ть, за- по счёту; **~ a debt** гаси́ть, по-/упл|а́чивать, -ати́ть долг
• *v.i.* **1** (sink down; come to rest) ос|еда́ть, -е́сть; **the dust will soon ~** (fig.) шуми́ха ско́ро уля́жется; (alight) ус|а́живаться, -е́сться **2** (become fixed) устан|а́вливаться, -ови́ться **3** (become comfortable, accustomed) (*also* **~ down**) **the dog ~d in its basket** соба́ка улегла́сь в свое́й корзи́не **4** (make one's home) посел|я́ться, -и́ться
□ **~ down** *v.i.* (in home) устр|а́иваться, -о́иться; (in job) осв|а́иваться, -о́иться; (adopt sober ways) остепен|я́ться, -и́ться; (become quiet) успок|а́иваться, -о́иться; **he ~d down to write letters** он приня́лся/усе́лся писа́ть пи́сьма
□ **~ in** *v.i.* осв|а́иваться, -о́иться
□ **~ up** *v.i.* распла́|чиваться, -ти́ться (*с кем*)

⚔ **settlement** /'setəlmənt/ *n.* **1** (colony) поселе́ние; (settled place) посёлок **2** (agreement) соглаше́ние; **reach a ~** дост|ига́ть, -и́чь соглаше́ния **3** (payment) упла́та, расчёт; **~ of an account** упла́та по счёту

⚔ **settler** /'setlə(r)/ *n.* поселе́н|ец (-ка)

⚔ **seven** /'sev(ə)n/ *n.* (число́/но́мер) семь; (**~** people) се́меро, семь челове́к; (figure; thing numbered 7; group of **~**) семёрка
• *adj.* семь + *g. pl.*

seventeen /sevən'ti:n/ *n.* семна́дцать
• *adj.* семна́дцать + *g. pl.*

seventeenth /sevən'ti:nθ/ *n.* (date) семна́дцатое (число́); (fraction) одна́ семна́дцатая
• *adj.* семна́дцатый

seventh /'sev(ə)nθ/ *n.* (date) седьмо́е (число́); (fraction) одна́ седьма́я
• *adj.* седьмо́й

seventieth /'sevəntɪɪθ/ *n.* одна́ семидеся́тая
• *adj.* семидеся́тый

seventy /'sevəntɪ/ *n.* се́мьдесят; **he is in his ~ies** ему́ за се́мьдесят; ему́ (пошёл) восьмо́й деся́ток; **in the ~ies** (decade) в семидеся́тых года́х; в семидеся́тые го́ды
• *adj.* се́мьдесят + *g. pl.*

sever /'sevə(r)/ *v.t.* отдел|я́ть, -и́ть; **~ a rope** перер|еза́ть, -е́зать верёвку; **~ one's connection with** пор|ыва́ть, -ва́ть связь с + *i.*

⚔ **several** /'sevr(ə)l/ *pron.*: **~ of my friends** не́которые из мои́х друзе́й
• *adj.* не́сколько + *g. pl.*; **myself and ~ others** я и не́сколько други́х люде́й

severance /'sevərəns/ *n.* отделе́ние, разры́в
■ **~ pay** *n.* выходно́е посо́бие; компенса́ция при увольне́нии

⚔ **severe** /sɪ'vɪə(r)/ *adj.* **1** (stern, strict) стро́гий, суро́вый **2** (violent) жесто́кий, си́льный; **~ pain** си́льная/стра́шная боль

severity /sɪ'verɪtɪ/ *n.* (strictness) стро́гость, суро́вость; (seriousness) серьёзность

sew /səʊ/ *v.t. & i.* (*p.p.* **sewn** or **sewed**) шить, с-; **~ a button on to a dress** приш|ива́ть, -и́ть пу́говицу к пла́тью

sewage /'su:ɪdʒ/ *n.* сто́чные во́ды (*f. pl.*)

sewer /'su:ə(r)/ *n.* (conduit) сто́чная труба́, канализацио́нная труба́

sewing /'səʊɪŋ/ *n.* шитьё; (*attr.*) швейный
■ **~ machine** *n.* швейная маши́н(к)а

sewn /səʊn/ *p.p. of* ▶ **sew**

⚔ **sex** /seks/ *n.* **1** пол; (*attr.*) половой **2** (sexual activity) секс; (sexual intercourse) полово́е сноше́ние; **have ~ with sb** (infml) спать, пере- с кем-н.
□ **~ up** *v.t.* (infml) оживл|я́ть, -и́ть (*делать более ярким, выразительным*)
■ **~ change** *n.* опера́ция по измене́нию по́ла; **~ education** *n.* полово́е воспита́ние

sexiness /'seksɪnɪs/ *n.* сексуа́льность

sexism /'seksɪz(ə)m/ *n.* секси́зм

sexist /'seksɪst/ *adj.* секси́стский

⚔ **sexual** /'seksʊəl/ *adj.* (organ, disease, reproduction) половой; (relations) сексуа́льный; **~ harassment** сексуа́льное домога́тельство; **~ relations** сексуа́льные отноше́ния (*nt. pl.*)

sexuality /seksjʊ'ælɪtɪ/ *n.* сексуа́льность

sexy /'seksɪ/ *adj.* (**sexier**, **sexiest**) (infml) сексуа́льный; (film, novel) эроти́ческий

shabbiness /'ʃæbɪnɪs/ *n.* (of clothes) изно́шенность; (of building, room, area) убо́гость; (of behaviour) по́длость

shabby /'ʃæbɪ/ *adj.* (**shabbier**, **shabbiest**) (clothes, personal appearance) потрёпанный; (building, room, area) убо́гий; (behaviour) по́длый

shack /ʃæk/ *n.* лачу́га

shackle /'ʃæk(ə)l/ *n.* (*in pl.*) (fetters) (also fig.) око́в|ы (*pl., g.* —)
• *v.t.* **1** (lit., fetter) зако́в|ывать, -а́ть в око́вы; (impede) ско́в|ывать, -а́ть; стесня́ть (*impf.*)

shade /ʃeɪd/ *n.* **1** (unilluminated area) тень; **put in(to) the ~** (fig.) затм|ева́ть, -и́ть **2** (tint, nuance) отте́нок, тон **3** (of lamp) абажу́р **4** (AmE, blind) што́ра
• *v.t.* **1** (screen from light) затен|я́ть, -и́ть; (shield from light etc.) заслон|я́ть, -и́ть **2** (restrict light of) приглуш|а́ть, -и́ть

shadow /'ʃædəʊ/ *n.* тень; **he has ~s under his eyes** у него́ (чёрные/тёмные) круги́ под глаза́ми
• *v.t.* (follow secretly) (та́йно) следи́ть/сле́довать (*impf.*) за (+ *i.*)
■ **~ cabinet** *n.* (BrE) теневой кабине́т

shadowy /'ʃædəʊɪ/ *adj.* (shady) тени́стый; (dim) нея́сный; (vague) сму́тный

shady /'ʃeɪdɪ/ *adj.* (**shadier**, **shadiest**) **1** (in shadow) теневой **2** (infml, suspect) сомни́тельный, тёмный

shaft /ʃɑ:ft/ *n.* **1** (of spear) дре́вко; (handle) ру́чко, рукоя́тка **2** (of light) луч **3** (tech., rod) вал **4** (of mine) ша́хта, ствол ша́хты

shag /ʃæg/ *n.* (BrE, vulg.) *v.t.* тра́х|ать, -нуть
• *v.i.* тра́х|аться, -нуться

shaggy /'ʃægɪ/ *adj.* (**shaggier**, **shaggiest**) лохма́тый

S

⚡ **shake** /ʃeɪk/ *n.* встря́ска; **give sb/sth a ~** встря́х|ивать, -ну́ть кого́-н./что́-н.
● *v.t.* (*past* **shook**, *p.p.* **shaken** /ʃeɪk(ə)n/)
1 тря|сти́, -хну́ть; сотряс|а́ть, -ти́ (*что, чем*); **they shook hands** они́ пожа́ли друг дру́гу ру́ки; **he shook his head** он покача́л голово́й **2** (shock) потряс|а́ть, -ти́; (morally) колеба́ть, по-
● *v.i.* (*past* **shook**, *p.p.* **shaken** /ʃeɪk(ə)n/)
1 (vibrate) трясти́сь (*impf.*); сотряса́ться (*impf.*) **2** (tremble) дрожа́ть, за-; **his hands shook** у него́ дрожа́ли ру́ки; **he was shaking with fever** его́ трясла́ лихора́дка
□ **~ off** *v.t.* (fig., of pursuers, illness, habit, etc.) отдел|я́ться, -я́ться от + *g.*; изб|авля́ться, -а́виться от + *g.*
□ **~ up** *v.t.* встря́х|ивать, -ну́ть; (mix by shaking): **~ up a medicine** взб|а́лтывать, -олта́ть лека́рство
■ **~-up** *n.* (in cabinet, etc.) ка́дровая перестано́вка; (in a system, in a service) коренны́е переме́ны (*f. pl.*)

shaky /ʃeɪkɪ/ *adj.* (**shakier, shakiest**) ша́ткий, нетвёрдый; **his position in the party is ~** его́ положе́ние в па́ртии ша́ткое/непро́чное; **a ~ voice** дрожа́щий го́лос

⚡ **shall** /ʃæl/ *v. aux.* **1** (in 1st person, usu. translated by future tense): **I ~ go** я пойду́ **2** (interrog.): **~ I wait?** мне подожда́ть?; **~ we have dinner now?** не пообе́дать ли нам сейча́с?; **давайте пообе́даем**

shallot /ʃəˈlɒt/ *n.* (лук-)шало́т

shallow /ˈʃæləʊ/ *adj.* ме́лкий; (fig.): **~ mind** пове́рхностный/неглубо́кий ум

sham /ʃæm/ *n.* **1** (pretence) притво́рство; **his illness is only a ~** его́ боле́знь то́лько/одно́ притво́рство; (hypocrisy) лицеме́рие **2** (counterfeit) подде́лка
● *adj.* **1** (feigned) притво́рный **2** (counterfeit) подде́льный; **~ marriage** фикти́вный брак
● *v.i.* (**shammed, shamming**): **he is ~ming** он притворя́ется

shaman /ˈʃeɪmən/ *n.* шама́н

shambles /ˈʃæmb(ə)lz/ *n.* (infml, mess) беспоря́док, ха́ос, барда́к

shame /ʃeɪm/ *n.* **1** (sense of guilt) стыд; **~ on you!** как тебе́ (*or* вам) не сты́дно! **2** (disgrace) позо́р, срам; **bring ~ on** позо́рить, о- **3** (sth regrettable) жа́лость, доса́да; **what a ~!** как жаль!
● *v.t.* **1** (cause to feel ashamed) сму|ща́ть, -ти́ть; стыди́ть, при- **2** (disgrace) позо́рить, о-

shameful /ˈʃeɪmfʊl/ *adj.* позо́рный, посты́дный

shameless /ˈʃeɪmlɪs/ *adj.* бессты́дный; (unscrupulous) бессо́вестный

shampoo /ʃæmˈpuː/ *n.* шампу́нь (*m.*)
● *v.t.* (**shampoos, shampooed**) мыть, вы- шампу́нем

shandy /ˈʃændɪ/ *n.* смесь пи́ва с лимона́дом

shan't /ʃɑːnt/ *neg. of* ▶ **shall**

shanty /ˈʃæntɪ/ *n.*: **~ town** трущо́бный посёлок

⚡ **shape** /ʃeɪp/ *n.* **1** (outward form) фо́рма; (outline) очерта́ние; **take ~** (become clear) проясн|я́ться, -и́ться **2** (vague figure) о́браз **3** (order) поря́док; **put** *or* (infml) **knock sth into ~** прив|оди́ть, -ести́ что-н. в поря́док; (condition) фо́рма, состоя́ние; **he is exercising to get into ~** он трениру́ется, чтобы обрести́ (спорти́вную) фо́рму
● *v.t.* прид|ава́ть, -а́ть фо́рму + *d.*; (from wood) выреза́ть, вы́резать; (from clay) лепи́ть, вы́-/с-; (fig.): **~ sb's character** формирова́ть, с- чей-н. хара́ктер
□ **~ up** *v.i.* (take ~) скла́дываться, сложи́ться

shapeless /ˈʃeɪplɪs/ *adj.* бесфо́рменный

shapely /ˈʃeɪplɪ/ *adj.* (**shapelier, shapeliest**) хорошо́ сложённый; стро́йный; **~ legs** стро́йные но́ги

shard /ʃɑːd/ *n.* (broken piece) черепо́к

⚡ **share** /ʃeə(r)/ *n.* **1** (part) часть; (portion) до́ля; **fair ~** справедли́вая часть **2** (of capital) а́кция
● *v.t.* дели́ть, раз- (*что с кем*); **he ~s all his secrets with me** (*or* **I ~ all his secrets**) он де́лится со мной все́ми свои́ми секре́тами; **~ an office with sb** рабо́тать (*impf.*) с кем-н. в одно́й ко́мнате; **we must all ~ the blame** мы все несём отве́тственность за э́то; **I ~ your views** я разделя́ю ва́ши взгля́ды; **I ~ your grief** я разделя́ю ва́ше го́ре
● *v.i.*: **I ~ in your grief** я разделя́ю ва́ше го́ре
□ **~ out** *v.t.* (divide) дели́ть, раз-; (allocate) распредел|я́ть, -и́ть
■ **~holder** *n.* акционе́р

shark /ʃɑːk/ *n.* аку́ла

⚡ **sharp** /ʃɑːp/ *n.* (mus.) дие́з
● *adj.* **1** (edged, pointed) (also fig., of senses etc.) о́стрый; ре́зкий; **~ knife** о́стрый нож; **~ pencil** о́стрый каранда́ш; **~ features** ре́зкие черты́ лица́; (keen): **~ eyes** о́строе зре́ние; **~ ears** то́нкий слух; **~ wits** о́стрый ум; (of sounds): **~ voice** ре́зкий го́лос; (severe): **a ~ remark** ко́лкое замеча́ние; **~ tongue** злой/о́стрый язы́к; **~ frost** си́льный моро́з; **~ wind** ре́зкий ве́тер; **~ pain** о́страя/ре́зкая боль; (sour) ки́слый **2** (abrupt) круто́й, ре́зкий; **~ turn** круто́й поворо́т; **a ~ drop in the temperature** ре́зкое паде́ние температу́ры; **a ~ rise in prices** ре́зкое повыше́ние цен **3** (artful) хи́трый
● *adv.* **1** (at a ~ angle): **turn ~ right** кру́то пов|ора́чивать, -ерну́ть напра́во **2** (punctually): **at four o'clock ~** то́чно/ро́вно в четы́ре (часа́) **3** (mus.): **he sings ~** он поёт сли́шком высоко́

sharpen /ˈʃɑːpən/ *v.t.* (knife etc.) точи́ть, на-; зат|а́чивать, -очи́ть; (pencil) заостр|я́ть, -и́ть; точи́ть, под-

sharpener /ˈʃɑːpənə(r)/ *n.* (pencil ~) точи́лка

sharpness /ˈʃɑːpnɪs/ *n.* (of knife, etc.) острота́; (of voice, etc.) ре́зкость; (of outline, photograph, etc.) чёткость; (astringency) те́рпкость, е́дкость

shatter /ˈʃætə(r)/ *v.t.* (breakables, hopes) разб|ива́ть, -и́ть; (of health or nerves) расстра́|ивать, -о́ить; **I was ~ed** (BrE, infml, exhausted) я вы́мотался до преде́ла; **I was ~ed by the news** я был потрясён/уби́т э́той

S

новостью
- *v.i.* разб|ива́ться, -и́ться

shave /ʃeɪv/ *n.* **1** бритьё; **have a ~** побри́ться (*pf.*) **2** (infml, escape): **we had a close ~** мы бы́ли на волосо́к от ги́бели
- *v.t.* (*p.p.* **shaved** *or* (*as adj.*) **shaven**): **~ one's chin/beard** выбрива́ть, вы́брить подборо́док; брить, по- бо́роду
- *v.i.* (*p.p.* **shaved**) бри́ться, по-; **he does not ~ every day** он бре́ется не ка́ждый день
- □ **~ off** *v.t.* сбри|ва́ть, -ть

shaver /ˈʃeɪvə(r)/ *n.* (razor) бри́тва; **electric ~** электробри́тва

shaving /ˈʃeɪvɪŋ/ *n.* **1** (action) бритьё **2** (**~s**) (of wood or metal) стру́жка
- **~ brush** *n.* помазо́к; **~ cream, ~ foam** *nn.* крем, пе́на для бритья́

shawl /ʃɔːl/ *n.* шаль

ᵔ **she** /ʃiː/ *pers. pron.* (*obj.* **her**) она́; **~ and I** я и она́; **мы с ней**

sheaf /ʃiːf/ *n.* (*pl.* **sheaves**) (of corn) сноп; **~ of papers** па́чка/свя́зка бума́г

shear /ʃɪə(r)/ *n.* (*in pl.*) (pair of **~s**) (садо́вые) но́жниц|ы (*pl., g.* —)
- *v.t.* (*past* **sheared**, *p.p.* **shorn** *or* **sheared**) (sheep) стричь, о-

sheath /ʃiːθ/ *n.* (of weapon) но́ж|ны (-ен); (BrE, condom) презервати́в

sheaves /ʃiːvz/ *pl. of* ▶ **sheaf**

shed[1] /ʃed/ *n.* сара́й; (for aircraft) анга́р

shed[2] /ʃed/ *v.t.* (**shedding**, *past and p.p.* **~**) **1** (load, skin) сбр|а́сывать, -о́сить; **trees ~ their leaves** дере́вья роня́ют ли́стья/ листву́ **2** (blood, tears) прол|ива́ть, -и́ть **3** (diffuse): **~ light on** (lit., fig.) пролива́ть, проли́ть (*or* бр|оса́ть, -о́сить) свет на + *a.* **4**: **~ jobs** сокра|ща́ть, -ти́ть рабо́чие места́

sheen /ʃiːn/ *n.* (gloss) лоск; (brightness) блеск, сия́ние

sheep /ʃiːp/ *n.* (*pl.* **~**) овца́; (male) бара́н
- **~skin** *n.* овчи́на; ове́чья шку́ра; бара́нья ко́жа

sheepish /ˈʃiːpɪʃ/ *adj.* сконфу́женный

sheer /ʃɪə(r)/ *adj.* **1** (absolute) соверше́нный, су́щий, я́вный **2** (precipitous) отве́сный, перпендикуля́рный; **a ~ drop** круто́й обры́в **3** (text., diaphanous) прозра́чный

sheet /ʃiːt/ *n.* **1** (bed linen) простыня́ **2** (flat piece) лист (-ы́); **~ of water/ice** слой воды́/льда
- **~ music** *n.* но́ты (*f. pl.*)

sheikh, sheik /ʃeɪk/ *n.* шейх

shelf /ʃelf/ *n.* (*pl.* **shelves**) **1** по́лка; **set of shelves** стелла́ж **2** (ledge of rock etc.) вы́ступ
- **~ life** *n.* срок хране́ния

shell /ʃel/ *n.* **1** (of mollusc etc.) ра́ковина, раку́шка; (of tortoise) па́нцирь (*m.*); (of egg, nut) скорлупа́ **2** (of building) нару́жные сте́ны **3** (of bomb) оболо́чка; (missile) снаря́д
- *v.t.* **1**: **~ peas** лущи́ть, об- горо́х; **~ eggs** чи́стить, о- я́йца **2** (bombard) обстре́л|ивать, -я́ть (артиллери́йскими снаря́дами)
- □ **~ out** (infml) *v.i.* раскоше́ли|ваться, -ться (infml)
- *v.i.* отва́л|ивать, -и́ть (infml)

~fish *n.* (mollusc) моллю́ск; (crustacean) ракообра́зное

shelter /ˈʃeltə(r)/ *n.* **1** (protection) укры́тие, защи́та; **take ~ from** укр|ыва́ться, -ы́ться от + *g.* **2** (building etc. providing **~**) прию́т, убе́жище; (for homeless people) ночле́жка
- *v.t.* **1** (provide refuge for) приюти́ть (*pf.*) **2** (protect) оберега́ть (*impf.*); защи|ща́ть, -ти́ть
- *v.i.* укр|ыва́ться, -ы́ться; пря́таться, с- (**from:** от + *g.*)
- **~ed housing** *n.* (BrE) дома́, обору́дованные необходи́мыми удо́бствами для престаре́лых/ инвали́дов

shelves /ʃelvz/ *pl. of* ▶ **shelf**

shelving /ˈʃelvɪŋ/ *n.* стелла́ж

shepherd /ˈʃepəd/ *n.* пасту́х

sheriff /ˈʃerɪf/ *n.* шери́ф

sherry /ˈʃerɪ/ *n.* хе́рес

Shetland /ˈʃetlənd/ *n.* (*in full* **the ~s** *or* **the ~ Islands**) Шетле́ндские острова́ (*m. pl.*)

shield /ʃiːld/ *n.* щит
- *v.t.* заслон|я́ть, -и́ть; защи|ща́ть, -ти́ть; (fig.) огра|жда́ть, -ди́ть

ᵔ **shift** /ʃɪft/ *n.* **1** (change of position etc.) сдвиг, измене́ние, перемеще́ние **2** (of workers) сме́на; **work (in) ~s** рабо́тать (*impf.*) посме́нно; **he is on the night ~** он рабо́тает в ночну́ю сме́ну
- *v.t.* (move) сме|ща́ть, -сти́ть; дви́|гать, -нуть; (transfer) переме|ща́ть, -сти́ть; (remove) уб|ира́ть, -ра́ть
- *v.i.* переме|ща́ться, -сти́ться
- **~ work** *n.* (по)сме́нная рабо́та

shifty /ˈʃɪftɪ/ *adj.* (**shiftier, shiftiest**): **a ~ fellow** ско́льзкий тип; **~ eyes** бе́гающие гла́зки (*m. pl.*)

Shiite /ˈʃiːaɪt/ *n.* шии́т

shilly-shally /ˈʃɪlɪʃælɪ/ *v.i.* колеба́ться (*impf.*)

shimmer /ˈʃɪmə(r)/ *v.i.* мерца́ть (*impf.*)

shin /ʃɪn/ *n.* го́лень

shin|e /ʃaɪn/ *n.* **1** (brightness) блеск; (gloss) гля́нец, лоск **2** (infml): **take a ~e to sb** увлека́ться, -е́чься кем-н.
- *v.t.* (*past and p.p.* **shined**) **1** (polish) чи́стить, вы́-/по-; **~e shoes** чи́стить, вы́-/по- ту́фли **2**: **~e a light in sb's face** осве|ща́ть, -ти́ть фонарём чье́-н. лицо́
- *v.i.* (*past and p.p.* **shone** *or* **shined**) **1** (emit light) свети́ть(ся) (*impf.*); (brightly) сия́ть (*impf.*); **the sun ~es** со́лнце сия́ет; (fig.): **his face shone with happiness** его́ лицо́ сия́ло от сча́стья; **~ing eyes** сия́ющие глаза́ **2** (glitter) блиста́ть (*impf.*); блес|те́ть, -ну́ть **3** (fig., excel) блиста́ть (*impf.*); блесте́ть (*impf.*); **he is a ~ing example of industry** он явля́ет собо́й замеча́тельный приме́р трудолю́бия

shingle /ˈʃɪŋg(ə)l/ *n.* (pebbles) га́лька

shingles /ˈʃɪŋg(ə)lz/ *n.* (med.) опоя́сывающий лиша́й

shiny /ˈʃaɪnɪ/ *adj.* (**shinier, shiniest**) блестя́щий

S

ship /ʃɪp/ n. корабль (m.); су́дно
 • v.t. (**shipped, shipping**) отпр|авля́ть, -а́вить
■ ~**building** n. судострое́ние, кораблестрое́ние; ~**owner** n. судовладе́лец; ~**wreck** n. кораблекруше́ние • v.t. (in pass.) be ~**wrecked** терпе́ть, по-кораблекруше́ние; ~**yard** n. верфь; судострои́тельный заво́д
shipment /ˈʃɪpmənt/ n. **1** (dispatch) отпра́вка, отгру́зка **2** (goods shipped) па́ртия това́ра
shipping /ˈʃɪpɪŋ/ n. **1** (transport) перево́зка, транспортиро́вка **2** (ships) флот
shirk /ʃɜːk/ v.t. уклон|я́ться, -и́ться от + g.
 • v.i. ло́дырничать (impf.)
shirt /ʃɜːt/ n. руба́шка; соро́чка
■ ~**sleeve** n.: in ~**sleeves** без пиджака́
shirty /ˈʃɜːtɪ/ adj. (**shirtier, shirtiest**) (BrE, infml): get ~ раздраж|а́ться, -и́ться
shit /ʃɪt/ n. (vulg.) говно́; (as expletive) чёрт!
shitty /ˈʃɪtɪ/ adj. (**shittier, shittiest**) (vulg.) говённый, говня́ный; (euph.) дерьмо́вый
shiver /ˈʃɪvə(r)/ n. дрожь; it gives me the ~s to think of it от одно́й мы́сли об э́том меня́ броса́ет в дрожь
 • v.i. дрожа́ть (impf.)
shoal /ʃəʊl/ n. (of fish) кося́к (рыб)
shock¹ /ʃɒk/ n. **1** (violent jar or blow) толчо́к, уда́р; I got an electric ~ меня́ уда́рило то́ком **2** (disturbing impression) потрясе́ние, шок; the news gave him a ~ но́вость потрясла́ его́; (distressing surprise) уда́р **3** (med.) шок
 • v.t. **1** (distress): I was ~ed to hear of the disaster я был потрясён сообще́нием о катастро́фе **2** (offend sense of decency) шоки́ровать (impf., pf.)
■ ~ **absorber** n. амортиза́тор; ~ **wave** n. взрывна́я волна́
shock² /ʃɒk/ n. (of hair) копна́ воло́с
shocking /ˈʃɒkɪŋ/ adj. (disturbing) ужаса́ющий; (scandalous) шоки́рующий, сканда́льный
shod /ʃɒd/ past and p.p. of ▸ shoe
shoddy /ˈʃɒdɪ/ adj. (**shoddier, shoddiest**) дрянно́й, некаче́ственный
shoe /ʃuː/ n. **1** ту́фля **2** (in full horse~) подко́ва
 • v.t. (**shoes, shoeing,** past and p.p. **shod**) (horse) подко́в|ывать, -а́ть
■ ~**lace** n. шнуро́к; ~ **shop** n. обувно́й магази́н
shone /ʃɒn/ past and p.p. of ▸ shine
shoo /ʃuː/ v.t. (**shoos, shooed**) (often ~ away, ~ off) отпу́г|ивать, -ну́ть
shook /ʃʊk/ past of ▸ shake
shoot /ʃuːt/ n. **1** (bot.) росто́к, побе́г **2** (~ing expedition) охо́та
 • v.t. (past and p.p. **shot**) **1** (discharge, fire): to ~ an arrow пус|ка́ть, -ти́ть стрелу́; these guns ~ rubber bullets э́ти ру́жья стреля́ют рези́новыми пу́лями **2** (kill) застрели́ть (pf.); (wound) ра́нить (impf., pf.); he was shot in the head пу́ля попа́ла

ему́ в го́лову **3** (propel): ~ a bolt (on door) задв|ига́ть, -и́нуть засо́в **4** (cin., film, scene) сн|има́ть, -я́ть, засня́ть (pf.) (фильм, эпизо́д)
 • v.i. (past and p.p. **shot**) **1** (fire, of person or weapon) стреля́ть (impf.) (at: в + a.); he was shot at twice в него́ два́жды стреля́ли **2** (dart) прон|оси́ться, -ести́сь; he shot out of the doorway он вы́скочил из подъе́зда; a ~ing pain стреля́ющая боль; a ~ing star па́дающая звезда́ **3** (football etc.) бить (impf.) по мячу́
□ ~ **down** v.t.: we shot down five enemy aircraft мы сби́ли пять самолётов проти́вника
□ ~ **up** v.i. (of prices etc.) подск|а́кивать, -очи́ть; (sl., inject drugs) ширя́ться, на-
■ ~**-out** n. (infml) перестре́лка
shooting /ˈʃuːtɪŋ/ n. (marksmanship; attack) стрельба́; (hunting) охо́та
■ ~ **range** n. тир; (outdoor) стре́льбище, полиго́н
shop /ʃɒp/ n. **1** магази́н; (small ~) ла́вка; talk ~ разгова́ривать/говори́ть (both impf.) о (свои́х профессиона́льных) дела́х **2** (work~) мастерска́я, цех; on the ~ floor (BrE) в цеху́/це́хе
 • v.i. (**shopped, shopping**) де́лать, с-поку́пки; she ~ped around она́ ходи́ла по магази́нам и прице́нивалась
■ ~ **assistant** n. (BrE) продаве́ц (-щи́ца); ~**keeper** n. владе́л|ец (-ица) магази́на; ~**lifter** n. магази́нный вор; ~**lifting** n. воровство́ в магази́нах; магази́нная кра́жа; ~**-soiled** (BrE), ~**worn** (AmE) adjs. залежа́вшийся; ~ **window** n. витри́на
shopper /ˈʃɒpə(r)/ n. покупа́тель (-ница)
shopping /ˈʃɒpɪŋ/ n. поку́пки (f. pl.); do one's ~ де́лать, с- поку́пки
■ ~ **bag** n. хозя́йственная су́мка; ~ **centre** n. торго́вый центр
shore¹ /ʃɔː(r)/ n. бе́рег; on the ~ на берегу́
shore² /ʃɔː(r)/ v.t.: ~ up подп|ира́ть, -ере́ть; креп|и́ть (impf.)
shorn /ʃɔːn/ p.p. of ▸ shear
short /ʃɔːt/ n. **1** (~ film) короткометра́жный фильм **2** (BrE, ~ drink) кре́пкий напи́ток
 • adj. **1** коро́ткий; (of ~ duration) кра́ткий, недо́лгий; (of stature) невысо́кого ро́ста; (small) небольшо́й; this dress is too ~ э́то пла́тье сли́шком ко́ротко; the days are getting ~er дни стано́вятся коро́че; a ~ time ago неда́вно; at ~ range с бли́зкого расстоя́ния; make ~ work of sth бы́стро распр|авля́ться, -а́виться с чем-н.; I want my hair cut ~ я хочу́ коро́тко постри́чься **2** (brief): in ~ коро́че говоря́; (одни́м) сло́вом; for ~ сокращённо; для кра́ткости **3** (curt, sharp) ре́зкий **4** (insufficient): in ~ supply дефици́тный; I am 2 pounds ~ мне не хвата́ет двух фу́нтов **5**: be ~ of sth (lacking) испы́тывать (impf.) недоста́ток в чём-н.; be ~ of breath запыха́ться (impf.) **6**: ~ of (except) кро́ме + g. **7** (of pastry) рассы́пчатый, песо́чный
 • adv. **1** (abruptly): he stopped ~ он вдруг останови́лся; (while speaking) он вдруг замолча́л **2** ~ of (without reaching): fall ~ of a

target не дост|ига́ть, -и́чь це́ли; **we ran ~ of potatoes** у нас ко́нчилась карто́шка
■ **~bread, ~cake** *nn.* песо́чное пече́нье; **~-change** *v.t.* (infml) обсчи́т|ывать, -а́ть; **~ circuit** *n.* коро́ткое замыка́ние; **~circuit** *v.t.* зам|ыка́ть, -кну́ть короотко́); **~coming** *n.* недоста́ток, **~ cut** *n.* (route) кратча́йший путь; **~fall** *n.* недоста́ток, дефици́т; **~hand** *n.* стеногра́фия; **~hand typist** (BrE) стенографи́ст(ка); **~list** *n.* шорт-ли́ст, коро́ткий спи́сок кандида́тов, соиска́телей *и т. п.* ● *v.t.* зан|оси́ть, -ести́ в шорт-ли́ст (*or* коро́ткий спи́сок); **~lived** *adj.* недолгове́чный, мимолётный; **~-range** *adj.* (of gun) с небольшо́й да́льностью стрельбы́; (of missile) бли́жнего де́йствия; (of forecast) краткосро́чный; **~sighted** *adj.* (lit., fig.) близору́кий; **~-sleeved** *adj.* (shirt) с коро́ткими рука́вами; **~-staffed** *adj.* страда́ющий недоста́тком рабо́тников; **~ story** *n.* расска́з; **~-term** *adj.* краткосро́чный; **~-wave** *adj.* коротковолно́вый

shortage /ˈʃɔːtɪdʒ/ *n.* недоста́ток, нехва́тка, дефици́т

shorten /ˈʃɔːt(ə)n/ *v.t. & i.* укор|а́чивать(ся), -оти́ть(ся)

shortly /ˈʃɔːtlɪ/ *adv.* **1** (soon) ско́ро; **~ before** незадо́лго до + *g.*; **~ after** вско́ре по́сле + *g.* **2** (sharply) ре́зко

shorts /ʃɔːts/ *n. pl.* (short trousers) шо́рт|ы (*pl.*, *g.* —/ -ов); (AmE, underpants) трус|ы́ (*pl.*, *g.* -о́в)

shot[1] /ʃɒt/ *n.* **1** (discharge of firearm) вы́стрел; **take a ~ at** вы́стрелить (*pf.*) в + *a. or* по + *d.* **2** (stroke, at games etc.) уда́р **3** (of person) стрело́к; **he's a good ~** он хоро́ший стрело́к **4** (phot.) сни́мок; (cin.) кадр **5** (small dose): **~ of liquor** глото́к спиртно́го; (injection) уко́л
■ **~gun** *n.* дробови́к; **~put(ting)** *n.* (sport) толка́ние ядра́

shot[2] /ʃɒt/ *past and p.p. of* ▸ **shoot**

should /ʃʊd/ *v. aux.* **1** (conditional): **I ~ say** я бы сказа́л; **I ~ have thought so** на́до полага́ть, что так бы; **~ he die** (в слу́чае) е́сли он умрёт; **I ~n't think so** не ду́маю **2** (expr. duty): **you ~ tell him** вы должны́ ему́ сказа́ть **3** (expr. probability or expectation): **we ~ be there by noon** мы должны́ поспе́ть туда́ к полу́дню; **how ~ I know?** отку́да мне знать? **4** (expr. purpose): **he suggested that I ~ go** он предложи́л мне уйти́

shoulder /ˈʃəʊldə(r)/ *n.* плечо́
● *v.t.*: (lit.): **~ a heavy load** взва́л|ивать, -и́ть на себя́ тяжёлый груз; (fig.): **~ responsibility** брать, взять на себя́ отве́тственность
■ **~ blade** *n.* лопа́тка

shouldn't /ˈʃʊd(ə)nt/ *neg. of* ▸ **should**

shout /ʃaʊt/ *n.* крик
● *v.t.* выкри́кивать, вы́крикнуть
● *v.i.* кр|ича́ть, -и́кнуть; **don't ~ at me** не кричи́те на меня́; **~ for help** звать, по- на по́мощь
□ **~ down** *v.t.*: **he was ~ed down** его́ слова́

бы́ли заглушены́ кри́ком/кри́ками
□ **~ out** *v.t.* выкри́кивать, вы́крикнуть
● *v.i.* закрича́ть (*pf.*)

shove /ʃʌv/ *n.* толчо́к; **give sb a ~** пихну́ть/ толкну́ть (*pf.*) кого́-н.
● *v.t.* толк|а́ть, -ну́ть; **~ sth into one's pocket** совать, су́нуть что-н. себе́ в карма́н; **he ~d his way forward** он протисну́лся вперёд
□ **~ aside, ~ away** *vv.t.* отт|а́лкивать, -олкну́ть

shovel /ˈʃʌv(ə)l/ *n.* лопа́та; (mechanical) экскава́тор
● *v.t.* (**shovelled, shovelling**, AmE **shoveled, shoveling**): **~ snow off a path** сгре|ба́ть, -сти́ снег с доро́жки; расч|ища́ть, -и́стить доро́жку от сне́га

show /ʃəʊ/ *n.* **1** (manifestation): **make a ~ of force** демонстри́ровать, про- си́лу; (semblance) ви́димость **2** (exhibition) пока́з, вы́ставка; шо́у; **for ~** для ви́ду; напока́з; (ostentation) пы́шность, пара́дность **3** (entertainment) представле́ние; шо́у
● *v.t.* (*p.p.* **shown** *or* **showed**) **1** (disclose, reveal, offer for inspection) пока́з|ывать, -а́ть; **this dress will not ~ the dirt** на э́том пла́тье грязь не бу́дет заме́тна; **he has nothing to ~ for his efforts** он зря стара́лся; **~ oneself** (appear) появ|ля́ться, -и́ться; пока́з|ываться, -а́ться **2** (exhibit publicly) выставля́ть, вы́ставить; (a film) пок|а́зывать, -аза́ть **3** (display) проявля́ть, -и́ть; демонстри́ровать, про- **4** (point out) ука́з|ывать, -а́ть на + *a.*; (demonstrate) пок|а́зывать, -аза́ть; **he ~ed me how to play** он показа́л мне, как игра́ть; (explain) объясн|я́ть, -и́ть **5** (conduct) прово|жа́ть, -ди́ть; **he ~ed me to the door** он проводи́л меня́ до две́ри
● *v.i.* (*p.p.* **shown** *or* **showed**) **1** (be visible) видне́ться (*impf.*); **the stain will not ~** пятно́ не бу́дет заме́тно **2** (be exhibited): **what films are ~ing?** каки́е фи́льмы пока́зывают/иду́т?
□ **~ in** *v.t.* вв|оди́ть, -ести́/пров|оди́ть, -ести́ в ко́мнату/дом
□ **~ off** *v.t.* (display to advantage) вы́годно подчёркивать (*impf.*); **the frame ~s off the picture** в э́той ра́мке карти́на подчёркнуто хорошо́ смо́трится; (boastfully) выставля́ть (*impf.*) напока́з, щеголя́ть (*impf.*) + *i.*
● *v.i.* рисова́ться (*impf.*)
□ **~ out** *v.t.* пров|оди́ть, -ести́ к вы́ходу
□ **~ up** *v.t.* (make conspicuous) выделя́ть, вы́делить
● *v.i.* (infml, appear) появ|ля́ться, -и́ться; (be conspicuous): **the flowers ~ed up against the white background** цветы́ выделя́лись на бе́лом фо́не
■ **~ business** *n.* шо́у-би́знес; **~case** *n.* витри́на; **~down** *n.* про́ба сил; оконча́тельная прове́рка; **~jumping** *n.* ко́нкур; **~-off** *n.* позёр (-ка); хвасту́н (-ья) (infml); **~room** *n.* демонстрацио́нный зал

shower /ˈʃaʊə(r)/ *n.* **1** (of rain/snow) кратковре́менный дождь/снег **2** (for washing oneself) душ; **take a ~** прин|има́ть, -я́ть душ

S

● *v.t.* **1** (with water etc.) зал|ива́ть, -и́ть **2** (with bullets etc.) ос|ыпа́ть, -ы́пать гра́дом (*пуль и m. n.*)

● *v.i.* прин|има́ть, -я́ть душ

showery /'ʃaʊərɪ/ *adj.* дождли́вый

shown /ʃəʊn/ *p.p. of* ▶ show

showy /'ʃəʊɪ/ *adj.* (**showier**, **showiest**) я́ркий, бро́ский

shrank /ʃræŋk/ *past of* ▶ shrink

shrapnel /'ʃræpn(ə)l/ *n.* шрапне́ль

shred /ʃred/ *n.* **1** (of cloth) клочо́к; **tear to ~s** раз|рыва́ть, -орва́ть в клочья́ **2** (fig., bit): **not a ~ of evidence** ни мале́йших доказа́тельств; **not a ~ of truth** ни ка́пли пра́вды

● *v.t.* (**shredded**, **shredding**) (tear) раз|рыва́ть, -орва́ть; (cut) разре|за́ть, -́зать

shredder /'ʃredə(r)/ *n.* (for documents) маши́на для уничтоже́ния бума́ги

shrew /ʃru:/ *n.* (zool.) землеро́йка; (woman) сварли́вая же́нщина

shrewd /ʃru:d/ *adj.* проница́тельный

shriek /ʃri:k/ *n.* визг; **~s of laughter** визгли́вый смех

● *v.i.* визжа́ть (*impf.*); взви́зг|ивать, -нуть

shrill /ʃrɪl/ *adj.* пронзи́тельный

shrimp /ʃrɪmp/ *n.* креве́тка

shrine /ʃraɪn/ *n.* (tomb) гробни́ца; (chapel) часо́вня; (lit., fig., hallowed place) святы́ня, храм

shrink /ʃrɪŋk/ *v.t.* (*past* **shrank**, *p.p.* **shrunk** *or esp. as adj.* **shrunken**): **hot water will ~ this fabric** от горя́чей воды́ э́тот материа́л ся́дет

● *v.i.* (*past* **shrank**, *p.p.* **shrunk**) **1** (of clothes) сади́ться, сесть; (of wood) сс|ыха́ться, -о́хнуться **2** (grow smaller) сокра|ща́ться, -ти́ться **3** (recoil) отпря́нуть (*pf.*); **he shrank (back) from the fire** он отпря́нул от огня́

shrivel /'ʃrɪv(ə)l/ *v.t.* (**shrivelled**, **shrivelling**, AmE **shriveled**, **shriveling**) (dry up) высу́шивать, вы́сушить; (wrinkle) мо́рщить, с-

● *v.i.* (**shrivelled**, **shrivelling**, AmE **shriveled**, **shriveling**) (dry up) высыха́ть, вы́сохнуть; (wrinkle up) смо́рщи|ваться, -ться

shroud /ʃraʊd/ *n.* са́ван

● *v.t.* оку́т|ывать, -ать

Shrove Tuesday /ʃrəʊv/ *n.* вто́рник на Ма́сленой неде́ле

shrub /ʃrʌb/ *n.* (bot.) куст

shrubbery /'ʃrʌbərɪ/ *n.* куста́рник; уча́сток са́да, заса́женный куста́рником

shrug /ʃrʌg/ *n.*: **with a ~** (of the shoulders) пожа́в плеча́ми

● *v.t. & i.* (**shrugged**, **shrugging**): **~ (one's shoulders)** пож|има́ть, -а́ть плеча́ми; **~ sth off** отм|а́хиваться, -ахну́ться от чего́-н.

shrunk /ʃrʌŋk/ *p.p. of* ▶ shrink

shrunken /'ʃrʌŋk(ə)n/ *adj.* (*p.p. of* ▶ shrink) (old person; body, face) иссо́хший, вы́сохший (infml)

shudder /'ʃʌdə(r)/ *n.* дрожь

● *v.i.* дрожа́ть, за-; содрог|а́ться, -ну́ться

shuffle /'ʃʌf(ə)l/ *v.t.* **1**: **~ one's feet** ша́ркать (*impf.*) нога́ми **2**: **~ cards** тасова́ть, пере-; ка́рты

● *v.i.*: **~ along, about** волочи́ть (*impf.*) но́ги

shun /ʃʌn/ *v.t.* (**shunned**, **shunning**) избега́ть (*impf.*) + g.

shunt /ʃʌnt/ *v.t.* (rail.) перев|оди́ть, -ести́ (*поезд, вагон*)

● *v.i.* маневри́ровать (*impf.*)

✍ **shut** /ʃʌt/ *v.t.* (**shutting**, *past and p.p.* **~**) закр|ыва́ть, -ы́ть

● *v.i.* (**shutting**, *past and p.p.* **~**) закр|ыва́ться, -ы́ться

□ **~ off** *v.t.* (stop supply of) отключ|а́ть, -и́ть

□ **~ down** *v.t.* закр|ыва́ть, -ы́ть; (comput.) выключа́ть, вы́ключить; заверш|а́ть, -и́ть рабо́ту

● *v.i.* закр|ыва́ться, -ы́ться

□ **~ out** *v.t.* (exclude) исключ|а́ть, -и́ть; **~ out light/noise** не пропус|ка́ть, -ти́ть све́та/шу́ма

□ **~ up** *v.t.* (close) зап|ира́ть, -ере́ть; **their house is ~ up for the winter** дом у них заколо́чен на́ зиму; (confine): **the boy was ~ up in his room** ма́льчик был за́перт в ко́мнате; (silence): **they soon ~ him up** они́ ско́ро заста́вили его́ замолча́ть

● *v.i.* (be, become silent): **~ up!** замолчи́!, закни́сь! (infml)

■ **~down** *n.* закры́тие; (comput.) выключе́ние, заверше́ние рабо́ты

shutter /'ʃʌtə(r)/ *n.* **1** (on window) ста́вень (*m.*) **2** (phot.) затво́р

shuttle /'ʃʌt(ə)l/ *n.*: **~ service** регуля́рное движе́ние/сообще́ние

● *v.i.* снова́ть (*impf.*)

■ **~cock** *n.* вола́н

shy /ʃaɪ/ *adj.* (**shyer**, **shyest**) (bashful) засте́нчивый; (timid) ро́бкий

● *v.i.* (of person): **~ away from sth** шара́х|аться, -нуться от чего́-н.

Siamese /saɪə'mi:z/ *n.* (*pl.* **~**) (*also* **~ cat**) сиа́мская ко́шка

● *adj.* сиа́мский

■ **~ twins** *n. pl.* сиа́мские близнецы́ (*m. pl.*)

Siberia /saɪ'bɪərɪə/ *n.* Сиби́рь

Siberian /saɪ'bɪərɪən/ *n.* сибиря́|к (-чка)

● *adj.* сиби́рский

sibling /'sɪblɪŋ/ *n.* (brother) родно́й брат; (sister) родна́я сестра́

✍ **sick** /sɪk/ *adj.* **1** (unwell) больно́й **2** (nauseated): **I feel ~** меня́ тошни́т/мути́т; **he was ~** его́ вы́рвало **3 ~ of: I am ~ to death of her** она́ мне надое́ла до́ смерти **4** (morbid) ме́рзкий, жу́ткий; **~ joke** ме́рзкий анекдо́т

■ **~bay** *n.* лазаре́т; **~ leave** *n.* о́тпуск по боле́зни; **he is on ~ leave** он на больни́чном (infml); **~ pay** *n.* опла́та по больни́чному листу́

sicken /'sɪkən/ *v.t.* (fig., disgust) вызыва́ть, вы́звать отвраще́ние у (*кого*); **~ing** отврати́тельный, проти́вный

● *v.i.* (become ill) забол|ева́ть, -е́ть; **he is ~ing for influenza** (BrE) он заболева́ет гри́ппом

sickle /'sɪk(ə)l/ *n.* серп

sickly /'sɪklɪ/ *adj.* (**sicklier, sickliest**)
(unhealthy) боле́зненный; (inducing nausea)
тошнотво́рный

sickness /'sɪknɪs/ *n.* (ill health) нездоро́вье;
(nausea) тошнота́

side /saɪd/ *n.* **1** сторона́; **on the right/left**
~ с пра́вой/с ле́вой стороны́; спра́ва/
сле́ва; **on the** ~ (infml, additionally, illicitly) на
стороне́ **2** (edge) край; **by the** ~ **of the lake**
на берегу́ о́зера; **on the** ~ **of the mountain**
на скло́не горы́ **3** (of room, table) коне́ц **4** (of
the body) бок; **at my** ~ ря́дом со мной; **they
were standing** ~ **by** ~ они́ стоя́ли бок о́
бок/ря́дом **5** (of a building) бокова́я стена́; ~
entrance боково́й вход **6** (aspect) сторона́;
I can see the funny ~ **of the affair** мне
очеви́дна смешна́я сторона́ (де́ла) **7** (party)
сторона́; **take** ~**s with sb** принима́ть,
-я́ть (*or* станови́ться, -ть на) чью-н.
сто́рону **8** (BrE, team) кома́нда **9** (*attr.*)
боково́й
● *v.i.:* ~ **with sb** станови́ться, -ть на чью-н.
сто́рону

■ ~**board** *n.* буфе́т, серва́нт; ~**boards** (Br)
(*also* ~**burns**) *n. pl.* (infml) бакенба́рды
(*pl., g.* —); ~ **effect** *n.* побо́чное де́йствие;
~**line** *n.* (work) побо́чная рабо́та; (goods)
неоснов но́й това́р ● *v.t.* оттесн я́ть -и́ть на
за́дний план; ~**long** *adj.* косо́й; ~ **plate**
n. ма́ленькая таре́лка; ~**show** *n.* (at fair)
аттракцио́н; ~**step** *v.t.* (fig.) уклон я́ться,
-и́ться от + *g.*; ~ **street** *n.* переу́лок;
~**track** *v.t.* (distract): **I meant to finish the job,
but I was** ~**tracked** я собира́лся зако́нчить
(э́ту) рабо́ту, но меня́ отвлекли́; ~**walk** *n.*
(AmE) тротуа́р; ~**ways** *adj.* боково́й ● *adv.*
(to one ~) вбок; (of motion) бо́ком

siding /'saɪdɪŋ/ *n.* (rail.) запа́сный путь

sidle /'saɪd(ə)l/ *v.i.:* ~ **up to sb** под ходи́ть,
-ойти́ к кому́-н. бочко́м

siege /siːdʒ/ *n.* оса́да, блока́да; **lay** ~ **to**
оса жда́ть, -ди́ть

siesta /sɪ'estə/ *n.* сие́ста

sieve /sɪv/ *n.* си́то
● *v.t.* просе́ ивать, -ять

sift /sɪft/ *v.t.* просе́ ивать, -ять; (fig.): ~ **the facts**
тща́тельно рассма́тривать, -отре́ть фа́кты

sigh /saɪ/ *n.* вздох
● *v.i.* взд ыха́ть, -охну́ть

sight /saɪt/ *n.* **1** (faculty) зре́ние **2** (seeing,
being seen) вид; **I can't bear the** ~ **of him** я
его́ ви́деть не могу́; **catch** ~ **of** зам еча́ть,
-е́тить; **lose** ~ **of** теря́ть, по- из ви́ду; **at first**
~ с пе́рвого взгля́да; на пе́рвый взгляд;
(range of vision): **come into** ~ пока́з ываться,
-а́ться; появл я́ться, -и́ться; **in** ~ на виду́;
keep out of ~ не пока́з ывать(ся), -а́ть(ся)
(на глаза́); **he would not let her out of his**
~ он с неё глаз не спуска́л **3** (spectacle)
вид, зре́лище; **a** ~ **for sore eyes** (infml)
прия́тное зре́лище; **see the** ~**s** осм а́тривать,
-отре́ть достопримеча́тельности **4** (aiming
device) прице́л; **he set his** ~**s on becoming a
professor** он ме́тил в профессора́ (infml)
● *v.t.* (spot) зам еча́ть, -е́тить; ви́деть, у-

■ ~**seeing** *n.* осмо́тр
достопримеча́тельностей; ~**seer** *n.* тури́ст
(-ка); экскурса́нт (-ка)

sign /saɪn/ *n.* **1** (mark; gesture) знак; (symbol)
си́мвол; **plus/minus/equals** ~ знак плюс/
ми́нус/ра́венства **2** (indication) при́знак;
there's still no ~ **of him** его́ всё нет и нет
3 (board with information) вы́веска; **road/traffic**
~ доро́жный знак
● *v.t. & i.* подпи́с ывать(ся), -а́ть(ся);
распи́с ываться, -а́ться

□ ~ **on** *v.i.* (BrE, as unemployed) регистри́роваться,
за- в спи́сках безрабо́тных; (*also* ~ **up**)
(register) регистри́роваться, за-
● *v.t. & i.* (for job) нан има́ть(ся), -я́ть(ся)

■ ~ **language** *n.* язы́к жéстов; ~**post** *n.*
указа́тель (*m.*)

signal /'sɪɡn(ə)l/ *n.* (also as needed for mobile phone
to work) сигна́л
● *v.i.* (**signalled, signalling,** AmE
signaled, signaling) сигнализи́ровать
(*impf., pf.*)

signatory /'sɪɡnətərɪ/ *n.* подписа́вшийся
● *adj.:* ~ **powers** держа́вы, подписа́вшие
догово́р

signature /'sɪɡnətʃə(r)/ *n.* **1** по́дпись
2 (mus.): ~ **tune** (BrE) (музыка́льная)
заста́вка

signet /'sɪɡnɪt/ *n.* печа́тка

■ ~ **ring** *n.* кольцо́ с печа́ткой

significance /sɪɡ'nɪfɪkəns/ *n.* значе́ние

significant /sɪɡ'nɪfɪk(ə)nt/ *adj.* значи́тельный;
(important) ва́жный

signify /'sɪɡnɪfaɪ/ *v.t.* означа́ть (*impf.*)

Sikh /siːk/ *n.* сикх
● *adj.* си́кхский

Sikhism /'siːkɪz(ə)m/ *n.* сикхи́зм

silage /'saɪlɪdʒ/ *n.* си́лос

silence /'saɪləns/ *n.* молча́ние; тишина́; **in** ~ в
молча́нии/тишине́; мо́лча
● *v.t.* заст авля́ть, -а́вить замолча́ть

silencer /'saɪlənsə(r)/ *n.* глуши́тель (*m.*)

silent /'saɪlənt/ *adj.* (saying nothing)
безмо́лвный; **keep** ~ молча́ть (*impf.*);
(taciturn) молчали́вый; **fall, become** ~
замолча́ть (*pf.*); умолка́ть, умо́лкнуть;
(mute): ~ **film** немо́й фильм

silhouette /ˌsɪluː'et/ *n.* силуэ́т

silicon /'sɪlɪkən/ *n.*: ~ **chip** кре́мниевый чип

silicone /'sɪlɪkəʊn/ *n.* силико́н; (*attr.*)
силико́новый

silk /sɪlk/ *n.* шёлк; (*attr.*) шёлковый

silky /'sɪlkɪ/ *adj.* (**silkier, silkiest**)
шелкови́стый

sill /sɪl/ *n.* подоко́нник

silly /'sɪlɪ/ *adj.* (**sillier, silliest**) глу́пый

silo /'saɪləʊ/ *n.* (*pl.* ~**s**) (tower; pit on farm)
си́лосная ба́шня/я́ма; (for missile) ста́ртовая
ша́хта (*ракеты*)

silt /sɪlt/ *n.* ил
● *v.t. & i.* (*usu.* ~ **up**) зай ли вать(ся), -ть(ся)

S

silver /'sɪlvə(r)/ *n.* **1** (metal; silverware) серебро́
2 (colour) сере́бряный цвет
• *adj.* (made of ~) сере́бряный; (resembling ~)
серебри́стый
■ ~ **birch** *n.* бе́лая берёза; ~ **paper** *n.* (BrE)
фольга́

silvery /'sɪlvərɪ/ *adj.* серебри́стый

SIM /sɪm/ (*in full* **SIM card**) *n.* сим-ка́рта,
SIM-ка́рта

ᕀ **similar** /'sɪmɪlə(r)/ *adj.* **1** (alike) схо́дный,
похо́жий **2**: ~ **to** похо́жий на + *a.*;
подо́бный + *d.*

similarity /sɪmɪ'lærɪtɪ/ *n.* схо́дство

similarly /'sɪmɪləlɪ/ *adv.* так же

simile /'sɪmɪlɪ/ *n.* сравне́ние

simmer /'sɪmə(r)/ *v.i.* кипе́ть (*impf.*) на
ме́дленном огне́; (fig.): ~ **with indignation**
кипе́ть (*impf.*) негодова́нием; ~ **down** (fig.)
успок|а́иваться, -о́иться

simper /'sɪmpə(r)/ *n.* жема́нная улы́бка
• *v.i.* жема́нно улыб|а́ться, -ну́ться

ᕀ **simple** /'sɪmp(ə)l/ *adj.* (**simpler, simplest**)
1 просто́й **2** (easy) лёгкий

simpleton /'sɪmp(ə)lt(ə)n/ *n.* проста́к

simplicity /sɪm'plɪsɪtɪ/ *n.* простота́

simplification /sɪmplɪfɪ'keɪʃ(ə)n/ *n.*
упроще́ние

simplify /'sɪmplɪfaɪ/ *v.t.* упро|ща́ть, -сти́ть

simplistic /sɪm'plɪstɪk/ *adj.* (чрезме́рно)
упрощённый

ᕀ **simply** /'sɪmplɪ/ *adv.* про́сто; **the weather was**
~ **dreadful** пого́да была́ про́сто ужа́сная

simulate /'sɪmjʊleɪt/ *v.t.* (feeling etc.)
изобра|жа́ть, -зи́ть, симули́ровать (*impf.,*
pf.); (leather, stone) и|мити́ровать, сы-;
(conditions) модели́ровать, с-

simulation /sɪmjʊ'leɪʃ(ə)n/ *n.* симуля́ция; (of
conditions) модели́рование

simulator /'sɪmjʊleɪtə(r)/ *n.* (person)
симуля́нт, притво́рщик; (device)
модели́рующее/имити́рующее устро́йство;
flight ~ пилота́жный тренажёр

simultaneous /sɪməl'teɪnɪəs/ *adj.*
одновреме́нный

sin /sɪn/ *n.* грех
• *v.i.* (**sinned, sinning**) греши́ть, со-

ᕀ **since** /sɪns/ *adv.* с тех пор; **the house has**
~ **been rebuilt** с тех пор (*or* поздне́е) дом
перестро́или
• *prep.* с + *g.*; **nothing has happened**
~ **Christmas** с Рождества́ ничего́ не
произошло́; ~ **yesterday** со вчера́шнего дня
• *conj.* **1** (from, during the time when): **how**
long is it ~ **we last met?** ско́лько вре́мени
прошло́ с на́шей после́дней встре́чи?;
I have moved house ~ **I saw you** с тех пор
как мы с ва́ми (после́дний раз) ви́делись,
я перее́хал **2** (seeing that) так как, поско́льку;
~ **you ask** е́сли хоти́те знать

sincere /sɪn'sɪə(r)/ *adj.* (**sincerer, sincerest**)
и́скренний; **yours** ~**ly** и́скренне Ваш

sincerity /sɪn'serɪtɪ/ *n.* и́скренность

sinew /'sɪnjuː/ *n.* сухожи́лие

sinful /'sɪnfʊl/ *adj.* гре́шный

ᕀ **sing** /sɪŋ/ *v.t.* (*past* **sang**, *p.p.* **sung**) петь,
с-; (fig.): ~ **sb's praises** восхваля́ть (*impf.*)
кого́-н.
• *v.i.* (*past* **sang**, *p.p.* **sung**) петь, с-

Singapore /sɪŋə'pɔː(r)/ *n.* Сингапу́р

Singaporean /sɪŋə'pɔːrɪən/ *n.* сингапу́р|ец
(-ка)
• *adj.* сингапу́рский

singe /sɪndʒ/ *v.t.* (**singeing**) пали́ть, о-;
(slightly) подпа́л|ивать, -и́ть

singer /'sɪŋə(r)/ *n.* пев|е́ц (-и́ца)

singing /'sɪŋɪŋ/ *n.* пе́ние

ᕀ **single** /'sɪŋɡ(ə)l/ *n.* (BrE, ticket) биле́т в оди́н
коне́ц; (CD, vinyl) сингл; (*in pl.*) (of tennis etc.)
одино́чная игра́; одино́чный разря́д
• *adj.* **1** (one) оди́н; (only one) еди́нственный,
еди́ный; **in** ~ **file** гусько́м **2** (unmarried)
одино́кий; (man) холосто́й; (woman)
незаму́жняя
• *v.t.* ~ **out**: **he was** ~**d out** его́ вы́делили
■ ~ **bed** *n.* односпа́льная крова́ть; ~**-handed**
adj. & adv. без посторо́нней по́мощи; ~
-minded *adj.* целеустремлённый; ~
mother *n.* мать-одино́чка; ~ **parent** *n.*
роди́тель-одино́чка; ~ **room** *n.* (in hotel)
одноме́стный но́мер; ~**-sex** *adj.*: ~**-sex school**
шко́ла разде́льного обуче́ния

singlet /'sɪŋɡlɪt/ *n.* (BrE) ма́йка

singular /'sɪŋɡjʊlə(r)/ *n.* (gram.) еди́нственное
число́
• *adj.*: ~ **noun** существи́тельное в
еди́нственном числе́

sinister /'sɪnɪstə(r)/ *adj.* злове́щий

sink /sɪŋk/ *n.* (in kitchen etc.) ра́ковина
• *v.t.* (*past* **sank** *or* **sunk**, *p.p.* **sunk**)
1: ~ **a ship** топи́ть, по-/за- су́дно **2** (plunge)
вби|ва́ть, -ть; (fig.): **the dog sank its teeth**
into his leg соба́ка вонзи́ла зу́бы ему́ в
но́гу **3** (excavate): ~ **a well** рыть, вы- коло́дец
• *v.i.* (*past* **sank** *or* **sunk**, *p.p.* **sunk** *or as*
adj. **sunken**) **1** (in water etc.) тону́ть, у-;
(of objects) тону́ть, за-; **the ship sank** су́дно
затону́ло **2** (below the horizon) за|ходи́ть, -йти́;
the sun ~**s in the west** со́лнце захо́дит на
за́паде **3** (subside, of water) спа|да́ть, -сть; (of
building or soil) осе|да́ть, -́сть **4** (get lower)
па́дать, упа́сть; **his voice sank** он пони́зил
го́лос **5** (fall): **I sank into a deep sleep** я
погрузи́лся в глубо́кий сон; (fig.): **my heart**
sank (with a sudden shock) у меня́ се́рдце
оборвало́сь; **his heart sank when he saw**
how much he had to do ему́ ста́ло ду́рно,
когда́ он уви́дел, ско́лько ему́ предстоя́ло
сде́лать **6** (penetrate) впи́т|ываться, -а́ться;
(fig.): **his words sank in** его́ слова́ дошли́ до
меня́ *и т. п.*

sinner /'sɪnə(r)/ *n.* гре́шни|к (-ца)

sinus /'saɪnəs/ *n.* па́зуха

sinusitis /saɪnə'saɪtɪs/ *n.* (med.) синуси́т

sip /sɪp/ *n.* глото́к
• *v.t.* (**sipped, sipping**) потя́гивать (*impf.*)

siphon, syphon /'saɪf(ə)n/ *n.* сифо́н
(*трубка для переливания жидкостей*)
● *v.t.:* ~ **off, out** выка́чивать, вы́качать
сифо́ном

sir /sə:(r)/ *n.* (form of address; title) сэр, господи́н;
Dear S~ (in letters) Уважа́емый господи́н

siren /'saɪərən/ *n.* сире́на

sirloin /'sə:lɔɪn/ *n.* филе́ (*nt. indecl.*)
(*говядины*)

ơ **sister** /'sɪstə(r)/ *n.* сестра́; (BrE, nursing ~)
ста́ршая медици́нская сестра́
■ **~-in-law** *n.* (brother's wife) неве́стка; (husband's
sister) золо́вка; (wife's sister) своя́ченица

sisterly /'sɪstəlɪ/ *adj.* сёстринский

ơ **sit** /sɪt/ *v.t.* (**sitting,** *past and p.p.* **sat**) (BrE): ~
an examination сдава́ть (*impf.*) экза́мен
● *v.i.* (**sitting,** *past and p.p.* **sat**) **1** (take a
seat) сади́ться, сесть **2** (be seated) сиде́ть
(*impf.*); **he can't ~ still** ему́ не сиди́тся (на
ме́сте); **~ on a committee** бы́ть чле́ном
комите́та **3** (pose): **~ for an artist** пози́ровать
(*impf.*) худо́жнику; **~ for one's photograph**
фотографи́роваться, с- **4** (be in session)
заседа́ть (*impf.*); **the committee ~s at 10**
заседа́ние комите́та начина́ется в 10 (часо́в)
□ **~ down** *v.i.* сади́ться, сесть
□ **~ in** *v.i.:* **~ in on a meeting** прису́тствовать
(*impf.*) на собра́нии
□ **~ up** *v.i.* (from lying position): **he sat up in bed**
он приподня́лся и сел в посте́ли/крова́ти;
(straighten one's back) сиде́ть (*impf.*) пря́мо
■ **~ting duck** (also **~ting target**) *n.* (fig.)
лёгкая добы́ча/мише́нь

sitcom /'sɪtkɒm/ *n.* (infml) коме́дия положе́ний
(*комедийный сериал с участием одних и
тех же героев в разных ситуациях*)

ơ **site** /saɪt/ *n.* (place) ме́сто; (position) положе́ние;
(location) местоположе́ние

sitter /'sɪtə(r)/ *n.* **1** (person sitting for portrait)
моде́ль; **she was his ~ many times** она́ мно́го
раз ему́ пози́ровала; (paid one) нату́рщи|к
(-ца) **2** (baby**~**) ≈ приходя́щая ня́ня

sitting /'sɪtɪŋ/ *n.* (of assembly) заседа́ние; (for
serving meals) сме́на
■ **~ room** *n.* (BrE) гости́ная

situate /'sɪtʃʊeɪt/ *v.t.* распол|ага́ть, -ожи́ть

ơ **situation** /sɪtʃʊ'eɪʃ(ə)n/ *n.* **1** (place) ме́сто;
(position) местоположе́ние **2** (circumstances)
положе́ние, ситуа́ция; **what is the ~?** каково́
положе́ние дел? **3** (job): **~s vacant** (BrE, as
column heading) вака́нтные до́лжности

ơ **six** /sɪks/ *n.* (число́/но́мер) шесть; (~ people)
ше́стеро, шесть челове́к; (figure; thing numbered
6; group of ~) шестёрка
● *adj.* шесть + *g. pl.*

sixteen /sɪks'ti:n/ *n.* шестна́дцать
● *adj.* шестна́дцать + *g. pl.*

sixteenth /sɪks'ti:nθ/ *n.* (date) шестна́дцатое
(число́); (fraction) одна́ шестна́дцатая
● *adj.* шестна́дцатый

sixth /sɪksθ/ *n.* (date) шесто́е (число́); (fraction)
одна́ шеста́я
● *adj.* шесто́й; **in the ~ form** (BrE) в ста́ршем
кла́ссе

■ **~-form college** *n.* (BrE) шко́ла со ста́ршими
кла́ссами; **~ sense** *n.* шесто́е чу́вство

sixtieth /'sɪkstɪɪθ/ *n.* одна́ шестидеся́тая
● *adj.* шестидеся́тый

sixt|y /'sɪkstɪ/ *n.* шестьдеся́т; **he is in his ~ies**
ему́ за шестьдеся́т(лет); **in the ~ies** (decade)
в шестидеся́тых года́х; **в шестидеся́тые
го́ды**
● *adj.* шестьдеся́т + *g. pl.*

sizable /'saɪzəb(ə)l/ *adj.* = sizeable

ơ **size** /saɪz/ *n.* **1** (dimension) разме́р; величина́;
these books are all the same ~ все э́ти кни́ги
одного́ форма́та; **cut sb down to ~** (infml)
ста́вить, по- кого́-н. на ме́сто **2** (of clothes
etc.): **I take ~ 12** я ношу́/у меня́ двена́дцатый
разме́р; **I take ~ 10 in shoes** я ношу́ о́бувь
деся́того разме́ра
● *v.t.:* **~ sb up** соста|вля́ть, -а́вить о ком-н.
мне́ние; **~ up the situation** оц|е́нивать,
-ени́ть обстано́вку

sizeable, sizable /'saɪzəb(ə)l/ *adj.*
значи́тельного разме́ра

sizzle /'sɪz(ə)l/ *v.i.* шипе́ть (*impf.*)

skate[1] /skeɪt/ *n.* (ice ~) конёк; (*in full* **roller
~**) ро́лик; (*in sg. usu.*) боти́нок
● *v.i.* (on ice) ката́ться/бе́гать (*both indet.*) на
конька́х; (on roller-~s) ката́ться (*indet.*) на
ро́ликах
■ **~board** *n.* скейтбо́рд; **~boarder** *n.*
скейтборди́ст (-ка); **~boarding** *n.*
скейтбо́рдинг

skate[2] /skeɪt/ *n.* (fish) скат

skater /'skeɪtə(r)/ *n.* (figure ~) фигури́ст (-ка)

skating /'skeɪtɪŋ/ *n.* (figure ~) ката́ние на
конька́х
■ **~ rink** *n.* като́к

skeleton /'skelɪt(ə)n/ *n.* **1** скеле́т **2** (*attr.*): **~
key** отмы́чка

skeptic /'skeptɪk/ *n.* (AmE) = sceptic

skeptical /'skeptɪk(ə)l/ *n.* (AmE) = sceptical

skepticism /'skeptɪsɪz(ə)m/ *n.* (AmE)
= scepticism

sketch /sketʃ/ *n.* **1** (artistic) эски́з, набро́сок,
зарисо́вка **2** (brief outline) кра́ткое описа́ние;
(of plan) о́бщее представле́ние **3** (play) скетч
● *v.t.* (draw) набр|а́сывать, -оса́ть; (fig. also)
опи́с|ывать, -а́ть в о́бщих черта́х
● *v.i.* де́лать, с- эски́з/зарисо́вку
■ **~book** *n.* альбо́м для эски́зов/рисова́ния

sketchy /'sketʃɪ/ *adj.* (**sketchier,
sketchiest**) пове́рхностный

skewer /'skju:ə(r)/ *n.* ве́ртел
● *v.t.* наса́|живать, -ди́ть на ве́ртел

ski /ski:/ *n.* (*pl.* **~s**) лы́жа
● *v.i.* (**skis, skied** /ski:d/, **skiing**) (cross-
country) ходи́ть (*indet.*) на лы́жах; (downhill)
ката́ться (*impf.*) на лы́жах
■ **~ boots** *n. pl.* лы́жные боти́нки (*m. pl.*);
~ jumping *n.* прыжки́ (*m. pl.*) на лы́жах
с трампли́на; **~ lift** *n.* (горнолы́жный)
подъёмник

skid /skɪd/ *n.* (of car) скольже́ние; юз, зано́с;
the car went into a ~ маши́ну занесло́

S

● *v.i.* (**skidded, skidding**) (of car, wheels) пойти́ (*pf.*) ю́зом

skier /'ski:ə(r)/ *n.* лы́жник

skiing /'ski:ɪŋ/ *n.* ката́ние на лы́жах

skilful /'skɪlfʊl/ (AmE **skillful**) *adj.* иску́сный, уме́лый

ᵒ⚲ **skill** /skɪl/ *n.* мастерство́, иску́сство; (specific ability) на́вык

skilled /skɪld/ *adj.* (skilful) иску́сный; (trained) квалифици́рованный

skillet /'skɪlɪt/ *n.* (AmE) сковорода́

skillful /'skɪlfʊl/ *adj.* (AmE) = skilful

skim /skɪm/ *v.t.* (**skimmed, skimming**) **1**: ~ a liquid сн|има́ть, -я́ть на́кипь/пе́нку с жи́дкости **2** (move lightly over) лете́ть (*det.*) над са́мой пове́рхностью + g. **3** (scan through) бегло́ просм|а́тривать, -отре́ть
■ ~**med milk** *n.* обезжи́ренное молоко́

skimp /skɪmp/ *v.i.* скупи́ться, эконо́мить (*both impf.*)

skimpy /'skɪmpɪ/ *adj.* (**skimpier, skimpiest**) (meagre, of knowledge) ску́дный; (of clothes) те́сный, у́зкий

ᵒ⚲ **skin** /skɪn/ *n.* **1** ко́жа; I got soaked to the ~ я промо́к до ни́тки; escape by the ~ of one's teeth чу́дом спаса́ться, -ти́сь **2** (of animal) шку́ра **3** (of fruit) кожура́
● *v.t.* (**skinned, skinning**) (remove ~ from) сн|има́ть, -я́ть шку́ру с + g.; свежева́ть, о-
■ ~**deep** *adj.* пове́рхностный; ~ **diving** *n.* подво́дное пла́вание (с аквала́нгом); ~**flint** *n.* скря́га (*c.g.*); ~**head** *n.* (BrE) «бритоголо́вый», скинхе́д; ~**tight** *adj.*: ~**tight trousers** брю́ки в обтя́жку

skinny /'skɪnɪ/ *adj.* (**skinnier, skinniest**) то́щий

skint /skɪnt/ *adj.* (BrE, infml): I'm ~ я без копе́йки, я на мели́

skip¹ /skɪp/ *n.* скачо́к, прыжо́к
● *v.t.* (**skipped, skipping**) (lesson etc.) пропус|ка́ть, -ти́ть
● *v.i.* (**skipped, skipping**) (use ~ping rope) скака́ть/пры́гать (*impf.*) (че́рез скака́лку); (jump): she ~ped for joy она́ подпры́гнула от ра́дости
■ ~**ping rope** *n.* (BrE) скака́лка

skip² /skɪp/ *n.* (BrE, for rubbish) конте́йнер для (перево́зки) му́сора

skipper /'skɪpə(r)/ *n.* (captain) шки́пер, капита́н

skirmish /'skɜ:mɪʃ/ *n.* схва́тка

skirt /skɜ:t/ *n.* ю́бка
● *v.t.* (go round) об|ходи́ть, -ойти́; we ~ed the town мы обошли́ го́род; (form border of): the road ~s the forest доро́га обрамля́ет лес
■ ~**ing board** *n.* (BrE) пли́нтус

skittish /'skɪtɪʃ/ *adj.* (of horse etc.) норови́стый; (of person) капри́зный

skittle /'skɪt(ə)l/ *n.* ке́гля; (in pl.) (game) ке́гли (*f. pl.*)

skive /skaɪv/ *v.i.* (BrE, infml) сачкова́ть (*impf.*) (sl.)

skiver /'skaɪvə(r)/ *n.* (BrE, infml) сачо́к (sl.)

skulduggery /skʌl'dʌgərɪ/ *n.* надува́тельство

skulk /skʌlk/ *v.i.* зата́иваться (*impf.*)

skull /skʌl/ *n.* че́реп

skunk /skʌŋk/ *n.* скунс

ᵒ⚲ **sky** /skaɪ/ *n.* не́бо
■ ~**diving** *n.* затяжны́е прыжки́ с парашю́том; ~**high** *adv.* до небе́с; ~**light** *n.* фона́рь (*m.*); ~**line** *n.* (horizon) горизо́нт; (silhouette against the sky) силуэ́т (на фо́не не́ба); ~ **marshal** *n.* сотру́дник слу́жбы безопа́сности, сопровожда́ющий возду́шные ре́йсы; ~**scraper** *n.* небоскрёб

slab /slæb/ *n.* (of stone etc.) плита́; (of cake etc.) кусо́к

slack /slæk/ *adj.* **1** (slow) ме́дленный **2** (negligent) небре́жный **3** (loose): ~ rope прови́сшая верёвка **4** (quiet): ~ season, period мёртвый сезо́н
● *v.i.* (BrE) ло́дырничать (*impf.*); we ~ed towards five к пяти́ часа́м мы сба́вили темп (рабо́ты)

slacken /'slækən/ *v.t.* **1** (rope, rein) отпус|ка́ть, -ти́ть; (screw, nut) ослабля́ть, осла́бить **2** (diminish): ~ speed сб|авля́ть, -а́вить ско́рость
● *v.i.* **1** (of rope) пров|иса́ть, -и́снуть; (of screw, nut) слабе́ть, о- **2** (die down): demand is ~ing спрос уменьша́ется

slag /slæg/ *n.* (slagged, slagging): ~ off (BrE, infml, criticize) разн|оси́ть, -ести́
■ ~ heap *n.* гру́да шла́ка

slain /sleɪn/ *p.p. of* ▸ slay

slalom /'slɑːləm/ *n.* сла́лом

slam /slæm/ *v.t.* (**slammed, slamming**) **1** (shut with a bang): ~ a door хло́п|ать, -нуть две́рью **2** (other violent action): he ~med the brakes on он ре́зко нажа́л на тормоза́
● *v.i.* (**slammed, slamming**) (of door etc.) захло́п|ываться, -нуться

slander /'slɑːndə(r)/ *n.* клевета́
● *v.t.* клевета́ть (*на кого*), о- (*кого*), на- (*на кого*); he ~ed me он оклевета́л меня́, он наклевета́л на меня́

slanderous /'slɑːndərəs/ *adj.* клеветни́ческий

slang /slæŋ/ *n.* жарго́н; сленг

slant /slɑːnt/ *n.* (oblique position) накло́н; укло́н
● *v.t.* (incline) накло́н|я́ть, -и́ть
● *v.i.*: his handwriting ~s to the right он пи́шет с накло́ном впра́во

slap /slæp/ *n.* шлепо́к; ~ in the face (lit., fig.) пощёчина
● *adv.* (exactly) пря́мо
● *v.t.* (**slapped, slapping**) шлёпать, от-; ~ sb's face да|ва́ть, -ть кому́-н. пощёчину
■ ~**dash** *adj.* небре́жный

slash /slæʃ/ *n.* (slit) разре́з; (oblique mark; also, forward ~) коса́я черта́
● *v.t.* **1** (wound with knife etc.) ра́нить, по- **2** (cut slits in) разр|еза́ть, -е́зать **3** (reduce): ~ prices ре́зко сн|ижа́ть, -и́зить це́ны

slat /slæt/ *n.* пла́нка; (of blind) пласти́нка (жалюзи́)

slate /sleɪt/ *n.* **1** (material) сла́нец **2** (piece of ~ for roofing) ши́ферная пли́тка **3** (fig.): **wipe the ~ clean** поко́нчить (*pf.*) с про́шлым
● *v.t.* **1** (cover with ~s) крыть, по- ши́фером **2** (BrE, criticize) разн|оси́ть, -ести́

slaughter /'slɔːtə(r)/ *n.* избие́ние, резня́; (of animals) убо́й
● *v.t.* **1** (kill animals, people) ре́зать, за- **2** (infml, defeat heavily) разб|ива́ть, -и́ть в пух и прах
■ **~house** *n.* (ското)бо́йня

Slav /slɑːv/ *n.* слав|яни́н (-я́нка)
● *adj.* славя́нский

slave /sleɪv/ *n.* раб (-ы́ня)
● *v.i.* (also ~ **away**) рабо́тать (*impf.*) как раб

slavery /'sleɪvərɪ/ *n.* ра́бство

Slavic /'slɑːvɪk/ *adj.* славя́нский

slavish /'sleɪvɪʃ/ *adj.* ра́бский

Slavonic /slə'vɒnɪk/ *adj.* славя́нский

slay /sleɪ/ *v.t.* (*past* **slew**, *p.p.* **slain**) (liter.) умер|щвля́ть, -тви́ть

sleazy /'sliːzɪ/ *adj.* (**sleazier**, **sleaziest**) (infml, squalid) захука́лый, убо́гий

sled /sled/ (AmE) *n.* = sledge *n.*
● *v.i.* (**sledded**, **sledding**) = sledge *v.i.*

sledge /sledʒ/ *n.* са́н|и (-е́й)
● *v.i.* ката́ться (*indet.*) на саня́х

sledgehammer /'sledʒhæmə(r)/ *n.* кува́лда

sleek /sliːk/ *adj.* (of animal) гла́дкий, лосня́щийся; (of person's hair) прили́занный

ꝛ **sleep** /sliːp/ *n.* сон; **have a ~** поспа́ть (*pf.*); **go to ~** зас|ыпа́ть, -ну́ть, усну́ть (*pf.*); **send to ~** усып|ля́ть, -и́ть; **we had our dog put to ~** нам пришло́сь усыпи́ть соба́ку
● *v.i.* **1** (*past and p.p.* **slept**) спать (*impf.*); ~ **like a log** спать (*impf.*) как уби́тый; **I can't ~** я не могу́ засну́ть; ~ **on a decision** откла́дывать, отложи́ть реше́ние до утра́ **2** (have sex) спать, пере- (with: c + *i.*)
□ ~ **around** *v.i.* спать (*impf.*) с кем попа́ло
□ ~ **in** *v.i.* (intentionally) поспа́ть (*pf.*) всласть; (oversleep) прос|ыпа́ть, -па́ть
■ **~walk** *v.i.* ходи́ть (*impf.*) во сне; **~walker** *n.* луна́тик

sleeper /'sliːpə(r)/ *n.* (person): **he is a light/ heavy ~** он чу́тко/кре́пко спит; (BrE, rail support) шпа́ла; (sleeping car) спа́льный ваго́н

sleeping /'sliːpɪŋ/**:**
■ ~ **bag** *n.* спа́льный мешо́к; ~ **pill** *n.* снотво́рная табле́тка, снотво́рное

sleepless /'sliːplɪs/ *adj.* бессо́нный

sleepy /'sliːpɪ/ *adj.* (**sleepier**, **sleepiest**) (lit., fig.) со́нный; сонли́вый; **I feel ~** мне хо́чется (or я хочу́) спать

sleet /sliːt/ *n.* мо́крый снег
● *v.i.*: **it is ~ing** идёт мо́крый снег

sleeve /sliːv/ *n.* **1** рука́в; **have sth up one's ~** (fig.) име́ть (*impf.*) что-н. про запа́с **2** (record cover) конве́рт (пласти́нки)

sleeveless /'sliːvlɪs/ *adj.* без рукаво́в

sleigh /sleɪ/ *n.* са́н|и (-е́й)

sleight of hand /slaɪt/ *n.* ло́вкость рук

slender /'slendə(r)/ *adj.* (**slenderer**, **slenderest**) **1** (thin) то́нкий; (of person, slim)

стро́йный **2** (scanty) ску́дный; ~ **means** ску́дные сре́дства

slept /slept/ *past and p.p. of* ▸ sleep

sleuth /sluːθ/ *n.* сы́щик

slew /sluː/ *past of* ▸ slay

slice /slaɪs/ *n.* **1** (of bread, meat) ло́моть (*m.*); (of cake, apple) кусо́к **2** (share) часть, до́ля
● *v.t.* нар|еза́ть, -е́зать ломтя́ми/ло́мтиками
■ **~d bread** *n.* (предвари́тельно) наре́занный хлеб

slick /slɪk/ *adj.* (skilful) ло́вкий, бо́йкий; (smooth, also fig.) гла́дкий; (slippery) ско́льзкий

slid|e /slaɪd/ *n.* **1** (chute) спуск, жёлоб **2** (of microscope) предме́тное стекло́ **3** (for projection on screen) слайд, диапозити́в **4** (BrE, hair~e) зако́лка
● *v.t.* (*past and p.p.* **slid** /slɪd/): ~**e a drawer into place** задв|ига́ть, -и́нуть я́щик на ме́сто
● *v.i.* (*past and p.p.* **slid** /slɪd/) **1** скользи́ть (*impf.*); ~**ing door** раздвижна́я дверь; **the papers ~ off my lap** бума́ги соскользну́ли у меня́ с коле́н **2**: ~**ing scale** (econ.) скользя́щая шкала́
■ ~**e projector** *n.* прое́ктор; ~**e rule** *n.* логарифми́ческая лине́йка

slight¹ /slaɪt/ *n.* (offence) оби́да
● *v.t.* об|ижа́ть, -и́деть

slight² /slaɪt/ *adj.* **1** (slender) то́нкий **2** (not serious) лёгкий; **she has a ~ cold** у неё лёгкая просту́да **3** (small): **there is a ~ risk of infection** есть не́которая опа́сность зараже́ния **4**: ~**est** мале́йший; **this is not the ~est use** от э́того ни мале́йшей по́льзы

ꝛ **slightly** /'slaɪtlɪ/ *adv.* слегка́; **I know them ~** я с ни́ми немно́го знако́м; ~ **younger** немно́го/чуть моло́же

slim /slɪm/ *adj.* (**slimmer**, **slimmest**) то́нкий, худо́й
● *v.i.* (**slimmed**, **slimming**) худе́ть, по-

slime /slaɪm/ *n.* (mud) ил; (viscous substance) слизь

slimy /'slaɪmɪ/ *adj.* (**slimier**, **slimiest**) **1** сли́зистый, ско́льзкий **2** (fig., infml, of person) нейскренний

sling /slɪŋ/ *n.* переви́зь
● *v.t.* (*past and p.p.* **slung**) швыр|я́ть, -ну́ть

slink /slɪŋk/ *v.i.* (*past and p.p.* **slunk**): ~ **off, away** (stealthily) выска́льзывать, вы́скользнуть; (in a guilty way) уходи́ть, уйти́ поджа́в хвост

slinky /'slɪŋkɪ/ *adj.* (**slinkier**, **slinkiest**): a ~ **dress** облега́ющее пла́тье

slip /slɪp/ *n.* **1** (error) оши́бка (по небре́жности); ~ **of the tongue/pen** огово́рка/опи́ска **2** (petticoat) комбина́ция (же́нское белье́) **3** (of paper) поло́ска
● *v.t.* (**slipped**, **slipping**) **1** (slide; pass covertly): **he ~ped the ring on to her finger** он наде́л ей на па́лец кольцо́; **I ~ped the waiter a coin** я су́нул официа́нту моне́ту **2** (escape from) выска́льзывать, вы́скользнуть из + *g.*; **his name ~ped my memory/mind** его́ и́мя вы́скочило у меня́ из па́мяти/головы́
● *v.i.* (**slipped**, **slipping**) **1** (slide) скользи́ть

(*impf.*); (fall over) поскользну́ться (*pf.*); she ∼ped on the ice она́ поскользну́лась на льду **2** (move quickly) выска́льзывать, вы́скользнуть; she ∼ped out of the room она́ вы́скользнула из ко́мнаты; I'll ∼ into another dress я (бы́стренько) переоде́нусь; ∼ through проск|а́льзывать, -ользну́ть (че́рез + *a.*)

□ ∼ up *v.i.*: he ∼ped up and hurt his back он поскользну́лся и повреди́л себе́ спи́ну; I ∼ped up in my calculations я оши́бся в подсчётах; (fig.) я просчита́лся

■ ∼ped disc *n.* смещённый межпозвоно́чный диск; ∼ road *n.* (BrE) подъездна́я доро́га; ∼shod *adj.* небре́жный; ∼-up *n.* (infml) оши́бка

slipper /'slɪpə(r)/ *n.* та́почка

slippery /'slɪpərɪ/ *adj.* (also fig.) ско́льзкий

slit /slɪt/ *n.* (cut) разре́з; (slot) щель, щёлка
• *v.t.* (**slitting**, *past and p.p.* ∼): ∼ open an envelope вскр|ыва́ть, -ы́ть/раз|рыва́ть, -орва́ть конве́рт; ∼ sb's throat перер|еза́ть, -е́зать кому́-н. го́рло

slither /'slɪðə(r)/ *v.i.*: ∼ about in the mud скользи́ть (*impf.*) по гря́зи

sliver /'slɪvə(r)/ *n.* (of glass) оско́лок; (of cake, cheese) кусо́чек

slob /slɒb/ *n.* (sl.) недотёпа (*c.g.*)

slobber /'slɒbə(r)/ *v.i.* (lit., fig.) распус|ка́ть, -ти́ть слю́ни

slog /slɒg/ *n.* (infml, arduous work) тяжёлая рабо́та
• *v.i.* (**slogged**, **slogging**) (work hard) вка́лывать (*impf.*) (infml); he was ∼ging along the road он упо́рно шага́л по доро́ге; he is ∼ging away at Latin он корпи́т над латы́нью (infml)

slogan /'sləʊgən/ *n.* (advertising) сло́ган; (political) ло́зунг

slop /slɒp/ *n.* (in pl.) (waste liquid) помо́|и (-ев)
• *v.t.* (**slopped**, **slopping**): ∼ beer over the table расплёск|ивать, -а́ть пи́во по столу́

slope /sləʊp/ *n.* (area of land) склон; (of 90 degrees etc.) укло́н, накло́н
• *v.i.*: ∼ back(wards)/forwards коси́ться, по-наза́д/вперёд; ∼ down спуска́ться (*impf.*); ∼ up(wards) поднима́ться (*impf.*)

sloping /'sləʊpɪŋ/ *adj.* (roof, shoulders) пока́тый; (surface, handwriting) накло́нный; (ground) понижа́ющийся

sloppy /'slɒpɪ/ *adj.* (**sloppier**, **sloppiest**) **1** (careless) неря́шливый **2** (sentimental) сентимента́льный

slot /slɒt/ *n.* **1** (slit) паз; (aperture) отве́рстие **2** (in timetable) специа́льно отведённое вре́мя; вре́менной интерва́л
• *v.t.* (**slotted**, **slotting**) **1**: ∼ together соедин|я́ть, -и́ть на шипа́х **2**: ∼ in вст|авля́ть, -а́вить
■ ∼ machine *n.* (BrE, vending machine) торго́вый автома́т; (fruit machine) игрово́й автома́т

sloth /sləʊθ/ *n.* **1** (zool.) лени́вец **2** (idleness) ле́ность

slothful /'sləʊθfʊl/ *adj.* лени́вый

slouch /slaʊtʃ/ *v.i.* суту́литься (*impf.*); he sat ∼ed in a chair он сиде́л развали́вшись в кре́сле

Slovak /'sləʊvæk/ *n.* (person) слова́|к (-чка); (language) слова́цкий язы́к
• *adj.* слова́цкий

Slovakia /slə'vækɪə/ *n.* Слова́кия

Slovene /'sləʊviːn/, **Slovenian** /slə'viːnɪən/ *nn.* (person) слове́н|ец (-ка); (language) слове́нский язы́к
• *adjs.* слове́нский

Slovenia /slə'viːnɪə/ *n.* Слове́ния

slovenly /'slʌvənlɪ/ *adj.* неря́шливый

⚷ **slow** /sləʊ/ *adj.* **1** ме́дленный; in ∼ motion в заме́дленном де́йствии **2** (of clock): my watch is 10 minutes ∼ мои́ часы́ отстаю́т на де́сять мину́т **3** (dull-witted) тупо́й **4** (not lively): business is ∼ дела́ иду́т вя́ло
• *adv.* ме́дленно
• *v.t.* (*also* ∼ down, ∼ up) зам|едля́ть, -е́длить
• *v.i.* (*also* ∼ down, ∼ up) зам|едля́ться, -е́длиться
■ ∼-moving *adj.* ме́дленный

sludge /slʌdʒ/ *n.* грязь

slug /slʌg/ *n.* (zool.) слизня́к

sluggish /'slʌgɪʃ/ *adj.* **1**: ∼ market вя́лый ры́нок; (slow-moving) ме́дленный **2** (lazy) лени́вый

sluice /sluːs/ *n.* (in full ∼ gate) шлюз

slum /slʌm/ *n.* трущо́ба

slumber /'slʌmbə(r)/ *n.* дремо́та; disturb sb's ∼s нар|уша́ть, -у́шить чей-н. сон
• *v.i.* дрема́ть, за-

slump /slʌmp/ *n.* (fall in prices etc.) паде́ние; (trade recession) упа́док
• *v.i.* **1** (of person) сва́л|иваться, -и́ться **2** (of price, trade) ре́зко па́дать, упа́сть

slung /slʌŋ/ *past and p.p. of* ▸ sling

slunk /slʌŋk/ *past and p.p. of* ▸ slink

slur /slɜː(r)/ *n.* пятно́
• *v.t.* (**slurred**, **slurring**) (pronounce indistinctly) говори́ть, сказа́ть невня́тно

slush /slʌʃ/ *n.* **1** сля́коть **2**: ∼ fund де́ньги для по́дкупа госуда́рственных чино́вников

slushy /'slʌʃɪ/ *adj.* (**slushier**, **slushiest**) сля́котный, мо́крый; (sentimental) сентимента́льный

slut /slʌt/ *n.* (pej.) (loose woman) шлю́ха, потаску́ха (both vulg.); (sloven) неря́ха (infml)

sly /slaɪ/ *adj.* (**slyer**, **slyest**) хи́трый; on the ∼ укра́дкой, потихо́ньку

smack¹ /smæk/ *n.* **1** (sound) хлопо́к **2** (slap) шлепо́к; ∼ in the face пощёчина
• *v.t.* хло́п|ать, -нуть; шлёпать, от-

smack² /smæk/ *v.i.*: ∼ of (lit., fig.) отдава́ть (*impf.*) + *i.*

⚷ **small** /smɔːl/ *n.*: ∼ of the back поясни́ца
• *adj.* **1** ма́ленький, небольшо́й, ма́лый; (of eggs, berries, stones, etc.) ме́лкий; (not big enough): this coat is too ∼ for me э́то пальто́ мне мало́; make sb look ∼ (fig.) ун|ижа́ть, -и́зить

кого-н.; **I felt very ~** я (по)чу́вствовал себя́ соверше́нно уничто́женным **2** (unimportant, of ~ value) ме́лкий, незначи́тельный

● *adv.*: **chop sth up ~** ме́лко наруб|а́ть, -и́ть что-н.

■ **~ ad** *n.* коро́ткое объявле́ние; **~ change** *n.* ме́лкие де́ньги, ме́лочь; **~ print** *n.* ме́лкий шрифт; **~-scale** *adj.* (map, drawing) маломасшта́бный; **~ talk** *n.* све́тский разгово́р

smarmy /'smɑːmɪ/ *adj.* (**smarmier, smarmiest**) (infml) льсти́вый

smart¹ /smɑːt/ *v.i.* **1** (of wound) жечь (*impf.*); **my eyes are ~ing** у меня́ глаза́ щи́плет **2** (of person) страда́ть (*impf.*)

ơ **smart²** /smɑːt/ *adj.* **1** (sharp) ре́зкий, суро́вый, о́стрый **2** (brisk): **he walked off at a ~ pace** он удали́лся бы́стрым ша́гом **3** (clever) сообрази́тельный **4** (elegant): **a ~ hat** элега́нтная шля́па; **you look ~** вы вы́глядите про́сто превосхо́дно

■ **~ card** *n.* пла́стиковая ка́рточка со встро́енным микропроце́ссором; смарт-ка́рта

smarten /'smɑːt(ə)n/ *v.t.* (*also* **~ up**): **~ oneself up** прихора́шиваться (*impf.*) (infml); (a room, house, ship, etc.) прив|оди́ть, -ести́ в поря́док

● *v.i.* (**~ up**) (in appearance): **he has ~ed up** он привёл себя́ в поря́док

smartphone /'smɑːtfəʊn/ *n.* (comput.) смартфо́н

smash /smæʃ/ *n.* **1** (sound) гро́хот; (collision) столкнове́ние **2** (at tennis etc.) смэш **3**: **~ hit** (infml) суперхи́т; **be a ~ hit** име́ть (*impf.*) оглуши́тельный успе́х

● *v.t.* **1** (shatter) разб|ива́ть, -и́ть **2** (drive with force): **he ~ed the ball over the net** си́льным уда́ром он посла́л мяч че́рез се́тку

● *v.i.* **1** (be broken) разб|ива́ться, -и́ться **2** (crash) вр|еза́ться, -е́заться; **the car ~ed into a wall** маши́на вре́залась в сте́ну

smashing /'smæʃɪŋ/ *adj.* (BrE, infml): **a ~ film** замеча́тельный/потряса́ющий фильм

smattering /'smætərɪŋ/ *n.*: **he has a ~ of German** он чуть-чу́ть зна́ет неме́цкий

smear /smɪə(r)/ *n.* **1** (blotch) пятно́ **2** (infml, slander) клевета́

● *v.t.* ма́зать, на-; разма́з|ывать, -ать; **he ~ed grease paint on his face** он наложи́л грим (себе́) на лицо́

■ **~ campaign** *n.* клеветни́ческая кампа́ния; **~ test** *n.* мазо́к с ше́йки ма́тки

smell /smel/ *n.* **1** (faculty) обоня́ние **2** (odour) за́пах

● *v.t.* (*past and p.p.* **smelt** *or* **smelled**) **1** (perceive ~ of) чу́вствовать, по-; (наличие чего-л.) **1 ~ something burning** я чу́вствую за́пах га́ри; (of animals, also fig.) чу́ять (*impf.*) **2** (sniff) ню́хать, по-

● *v.i.* (*past and p.p.* **smelt** *or* **smelled**) (emit ~) па́хнуть (*impf.*); (pleasantly) издава́ть (*impf.*) арома́т; **the soup ~s good** суп хорошо́/вку́сно па́хнет; **the room smelt of cigarettes** в ко́мнате па́хло табако́м; (unpleasantly) ду́рно/пло́хо па́хнуть (*impf.*)

■ **~ing salts** *n. pl.* нюха́тельная соль

smelly /'smelɪ/ *adj.* (**smellier, smelliest**) ду́рно па́хнущий, воню́чий

smelt /smelt/ *past and p.p. of* ▸ **smell**

smidgen /'smɪdʒ(ə)n/ *n.* (infml) чуто́к, немно́го

ơ **smile** /smaɪl/ *n.* улы́бка

● *v.i.* улыб|а́ться, -ну́ться; **~ on** (fig.): **fortune ~d on him** сча́стье ему́ улыба́лось

ơ **smil|ey** /'smaɪlɪ/ *n.* (*pl.* **~eys, ~ies**) (symbol) сма́йл(ик)

smirk /smɜːk/ *n.* самодово́льная улы́бка, ухмы́лка

● *v.i.* ухмыл|я́ться, -ьну́ться

smith /smɪθ/ *n.* (*in full* black**~**) кузне́ц

smithereens /smɪðə'riːnz/ *n. pl.* (infml): **to ~** вдре́безги

smithy /'smɪðɪ/ *n.* ку́зница

smock /smɒk/ *n.* пла́тье/блу́за со сбо́рками

smog /smɒɡ/ *n.* смог

ơ **smoke** /sməʊk/ *n.* дым

● *v.t.* **1** (preserve with ~) копти́ть, за-; **~d fish** копчёная ры́ба **2** (tobacco etc.) кури́ть, вы-

● *v.i.* **1** (of person) кури́ть (*impf.*) **2** (of chimney etc.) дыми́ться (*impf.*)

■ **~screen** *n.* (lit., fig.) дымова́я заве́са

smokeless /'sməʊklɪs/ *adj.* безды́мный; **~ zone** (BrE) безды́мная городска́я зо́на

smoker /'sməʊkə(r)/ *n.* куря́щий; кури́льщи|к (-ца)

smoking /'sməʊkɪŋ/ *n.* куре́ние; **'No S~!'** «кури́ть воспреща́ется!»; «не кури́ть!»

smoky /'sməʊkɪ/ *adj.* (**smokier, smokiest**) ды́мный

smolder /'sməʊldə(r)/ *v.i.* (AmE) = smoulder

smooch /smuːtʃ/ *v.i.* (infml) **1** (kiss and cuddle) обнима́ться, целова́ться, прижима́ться (infml), ти́скаться (infml) (*all impf.*) **2** (BrE, dance in close embrace) обнима́ться, прижима́ться (infml) (*both impf.*) в та́нце (*or* танцу́я)

smooth /smuːð/ *adj.* **1** (even, level) гла́дкий, ро́вный; **a ~ paste** те́сто без комко́в **2** (not harsh): **~ wine** нете́рпкое вино́ **3** (suave) гала́нтный

● *v.t.* **1** (make level) выра́внивать, вы́ровнять **2** (flatten) пригла́|живать, -дить **3** (make easy) смягч|а́ть, -и́ть

□ **~ away** *v.t.*: **he ~ed away our difficulties** он устрани́л на́ши тру́дности

□ **~ over** *v.t.* смягч|а́ть, -и́ть; **~ things over** ула́|живать, -дить де́ло

smother /'smʌðə(r)/ *v.t.* **1** (suffocate) души́ть, за-; **~ a fire** туши́ть, по- ого́нь **2** (cover) покр|ыва́ть, -ы́ть **3** (suppress, conceal) подав|ля́ть, -и́ть

smoulder /'sməʊldə(r)/ (AmE *also* **smolder**) *v.i.* (lit., fig.) тлеть (*impf.*); **~ing hatred** затаённая не́нависть

SMS *n.* (*abbr. of* **Short Message/ Messaging Service**): **~ message** SMS/ CMC-сообще́ние, (infml) SMS (*pronounced* эс-эм-э́с)

smudge /smʌdʒ/ *n.* пятно́

● *v.t.* сма́з|ывать, -ать

S

smug /smʌg/ *adj.* (**smugger, smuggest**) самодово́льный

smuggle /'smʌg(ə)l/ *v.t.* пров|ози́ть, -ез-ти́ контраба́ндой; (fig.): he was ~d into the house его́ тайко́м провели́ в дом

smuggler /'smʌglə(r)/ *n.* контрабанди́ст (-ка)

smuggling /'smʌglɪŋ/ *n.* контраба́нда

smutty /'smʌtɪ/ *adj.* (**smuttier, smuttiest**): ~ face гря́зное/запа́чканное лицо́; ~ joke гря́зный/поха́бный (infml) анекдо́т

snack /snæk/ *n.* заку́ска; have a ~ переку́с|ывать, -и́ть
■ ~ **bar** *n.* заку́сочная, буфе́т

snag /snæg/ **1** (obstacle) препя́тствие; (difficulty) затрудне́ние **2** (tear) разры́в

snail /sneɪl/ *n.* ули́тка

snake /sneɪk/ *n.* змея́

snap /snæp/ *n.* **1** (noise) щелчо́к, щёлканье; (of sth breaking) треск **2** (infml, photograph) сни́мок
● *adj.*: ~ decision внеза́пное реше́ние
● *v.t.* (**snapped, snapping**) **1** (make ~ping noise with) щёлк|ать, -нуть (+ *i.*) **2** (break) разл|а́мывать, -ома́ть; he ~ped the stick in two он разлома́л па́лку на́двое **3** (infml, photograph) сни|ма́ть, -я́ть
● *v.i.* (**snapped, snapping**) **1** (make biting motion): ~ at огрыз|а́ться, -ну́ться на (+ *a.*); (speak sharply) груби́ть, на- (at: + *d.*); don't ~ at me! не груби́те (мне)! **2** (break) тре́снуть, слома́ться (*both pf.*)
□ ~ **off** *v.t.*: ~ sb's head off (infml) набр|а́сываться, -о́ситься на кого́-н.
□ ~ **up** *v.t.* (buy eagerly) расхва́т|ывать, -а́ть
■ ~shot *n.* (люби́тельский) сни́мок

snappy /'snæpɪ/ *adj.* (**snappier, snappiest**): make it ~! жи́во!

snare /sneə(r)/ *n.* западня́, лову́шка

snarl /snɑːl/ *v.i.* рыча́ть, за-

snatch /snætʃ/ *n.* обры́вок, отры́вок
● *v.t.* хвата́ть, схвати́ть; ~ sth from sb вырыва́ть, вы́рвать что-н. у кого́-н.
● *v.i.* хвата́ть (*impf.*); ~ at sth хвата́ться, схвати́ться за что-н.

sneak /sniːk/ *v.i.* (*past and p.p.* **sneaked** or AmE, infml **snuck**) кра́сться (*impf.*); ~ into a room прокра́д|ываться, -сться в ко́мнату; ~ out of a room выска́льзывать, вы́скользнуть из ко́мнаты

sneakers /'sniːkəz/ *n. pl.* (AmE) кроссо́вки (*f. pl.*)

sneaking /'sniːkɪŋ/ *adj.*: ~ feeling сму́тное подозре́ние

sneaky /'sniːkɪ/ *adj.* (**sneakier, sneakiest**) **1** (person) хи́трый **2** = sneaking

sneer /snɪə(r)/ *n.* презри́тельная усме́шка
● *v.i.* усмех|а́ться, -ну́ться; ~ at глуми́ться/насмеха́ться (*both impf.*) над + *i.*

sneeze /sniːz/ *n.* чиха́нье
● *v.i.* чих|а́ть, -ну́ть

snide /snaɪd/ *adj.* (infml) еха́дный

sniff /snɪf/ *n.* вдох
● *v.t.* (inhale) вд|ыха́ть, -охну́ть; (smell at) ню́хать, по-
● *v.i.* шмы́г|ать, -ну́ть (но́сом) (infml)

sniffle /'snɪf(ə)l/ *n.* сопе́ние; (*in pl.*) на́сморк
● *v.i.* шмы́г|ать, -ну́ть (но́сом)

snigger /'snɪgə(r)/ *v.i.* хихи́к|ать, -нуть

snip /snɪp/ *v.t.* (**snipped, snipping**) подр|еза́ть, -е́зать

sniper /'snaɪpə(r)/ *n.* сна́йпер

snippet /'snɪpɪt/ *n.* (*in pl.*) (of news etc.) обры́вки (*m. pl.*)

snivel /'snɪv(ə)l/ *v.i.* (**snivelled, snivelling**, AmE **sniveled, sniveling**) хны́кать (*impf.*)

snob /snɒb/ *n.* сноб

snobbery /'snɒbərɪ/ *n.* сноби́зм

snobbish /'snɒbɪʃ/ *adj.* сноби́стский

snog /snɒg/ *v.i.* (**snogged, snogging**) (BrE, infml) лиза́ться (*impf.*) (infml)

snooker /'snuːkə(r)/ *n.* сну́кер (*игра на бильярде*)

snoop /snuːp/ *v.i.* (infml) подгл|я́дывать, -яде́ть чужи́е та́йны

snooty /'snuːtɪ/ *adj.* (**snootier, snootiest**) (infml) наду́тый, зазна́вшийся

snooze /snuːz/ (infml) *n.*: have, take a ~ вздремну́ть (*pf.*)
● *v.i.* дрема́ть (*impf.*)

snore /snɔː(r)/ *n.* храп
● *v.i.* храпе́ть, за-

snorkel /'snɔːk(ə)l/ *n.* (дыха́тельная) тру́бка (*для подводного плавания*)

snort /snɔːt/ *v.i.* фы́рк|ать, -нуть

snout /snaʊt/ *n.* (of animal) мо́рда; (of pig) ры́ло

snow /snəʊ/ *n.* снег
● *v.i.*: it is ~ing идёт снег
□ ~ **in** *v.t.*: we were ~ed in наш дом занесло́ сне́гом
□ ~ **under** *v.t.* (fig.): we are ~ed under with work мы зава́лены рабо́той
■ ~ball *n.* снежо́к ● *v.i.* (fig., increase) расти́ (*impf.*) как сне́жный ком; ~board *n.* сноубо́рд; ~boarding *n.* сноубо́рдинг; ~drift *n.* сугро́б; ~drop *n.* подсне́жник; ~fall *n.* снегопа́д; ~flake *n.* снежи́нка; (*in pl.*) (large) (сне́жные) хло́пья; ~man *n.* сне́жная ба́ба; ~plough *n.* снегоубо́рочная маши́на

snowy /'snəʊɪ/ *adj.* (**snowier, snowiest**): ~ weather сне́жная пого́да; ~ roofs заснё́женные кры́ши

snub /snʌb/ *n.* (rebuff) оби́да
● *v.t.* (**snubbed, snubbing**) ун|ижа́ть, -и́зить

snuck /snʌk/ (AmE, infml) *past and p.p. of*
▶ sneak

snuff /snʌf/ *n.* ню́хательный таба́к; pinch of ~ поню́шка; take ~ ню́хать, по- таба́к
■ ~box *n.* табаке́рка

snug /snʌg/ *adj.* (**snugger, snuggest**) ую́тный

snuggle /'snʌg(ə)l/ *v.i.*: ~ down in bed свёр|тываться, -ну́ться в посте́ли; ~ up to sb

---

приж|има́ться, -а́ться к кому́-н.

❖ **so** /səʊ/ *adv.* **1** так; **is that ~?** э́то так?; (э́то) пра́вда?; **that being ~** раз так; **I'm ~ glad to see you** я так рад вас ви́деть; **would you be ~ kind as to visit her?** бу́дьте так добры́, навести́те её; **he is not ~ silly as to ask her** он не насто́лько глуп, что́бы проси́ть её; **he was ~ overworked that …** он был так/ до тако́й сте́пени загру́жен рабо́той, что…; **~ far** (up to now) до сих пор, пока́; **~ far as I know** наско́лько я зна́ю; **and ~ forth, on** и так да́лее; **~ long as** (provided that) е́сли то́лько; **~ many** сто́лько + *g.*, так мно́го + *g.*; **thank you ~ much!** большо́е (вам) спаси́бо!; **~ much the worse/better** тем ху́же/лу́чше; **~ to say, speak** так сказа́ть; **~ what** ну и что? **2** (also) то́же; **(and) ~ do I** и я то́же **3** (consequently, accordingly) поэ́тому, так что; ита́к, зна́чит; **he is ill, (and) ~ he can't come** он нездоро́в, поэ́тому не мо́жет прийти́; **~ you did see him after all** зна́чит/ ита́к, вы всё-таки его́ ви́дели **4** (that the foregoing is true or will happen): **I suppose/hope ~** я ду́маю/наде́юсь, что да; **do you think ~?** вы так ду́маете? **5**: **~ as to** (in order to) для того́, что́бы; (in such a way as to) так, что́бы **6** (thereabouts): **there were 100 or ~ people there** там бы́ло приме́рно сто челове́к (*or* о́коло ста челове́к)

■ **~-called** *adj.* так называ́емый; **~-so** *adj. & adv.* ничего́; так себе́

soak /səʊk/ *v.t.* **1** (wet) зам|а́чивать, -очи́ть; выма́чивать, вы́мочить; **she ~s the laundry overnight** она́ зама́чивает бельё на́ ночь **2** (wet through): **the shower ~ed me to the skin** дождь промочи́л меня́ до ни́тки/наскво́зь
● *v.i.* **1** (remain immersed) мо́кнуть (*impf.*) **2** (drain) впи́т|ываться, -а́ться; **the rain ~ed into the ground** дождь пропита́л по́чву; **the water ~ed through my shoes** вода́ просочи́лась мне в ту́фли
□ **~ up** *v.t.* (lit., fig.) впи́т|ывать, -а́ть

soaking /ˈsəʊkɪŋ/ *adj. & adv.*: **you are ~ (wet)** вы промо́кли наскво́зь

soap /səʊp/ *n.* мы́ло
■ **~ opera** *n.* мы́льная о́пера, телесериа́л; **~ powder** *n.* стира́льный порошо́к

soapy /ˈsəʊpɪ/ *adj.* (**soapier, soapiest**) **1** (covered with soap) мы́льный, намы́ленный **2** (resembling, containing, consisting of soap) мы́льный

soar /sɔ:(r)/ *v.i.* **1** (of birds) высоко́ взлет|а́ть, -е́ть **2** (fig.): **her spirits ~ed** она́ испыта́ла душе́вный подъём **3** (of prices) (ре́зко) пов|ыша́ться, -ы́ситься **4** (of mountains, buildings) возвыша́ться (*impf.*)

sob /sɒb/ *n.* всхлип, всхли́пывание
● *v.i.* (**sobbed, sobbing**) всхли́п|ывать, -нуть

sober /ˈsəʊbə(r)/ *adj.* (**soberer, soberest**) **1** (not drunk, not fanciful) тре́звый **2** (of colour) споко́йный
● *v.t.* (*usu.* **~ up**) отрезв|ля́ть, -и́ть
● *v.i.*: **~ up** протрезв|ля́ться, -и́ться

sobriety /səˈbraɪɪtɪ/ *n.* тре́звость

soccer /ˈsɒkə(r)/ *n.* футбо́л
■ **~ match** *n.* футбо́льный матч; **~ player** *n.* футболи́ст

sociable /ˈsəʊʃəb(ə)l/ *adj.* общи́тельный

❖ **social** /ˈsəʊʃ(ə)l/ *adj.* **1** (pert. to the community) обще́ственный, социа́льный **2** (convivial): **~ gathering** дру́жеская встре́ча
■ **S~ Democrat** *n.* социа́л-демокра́т; **~ media** *n. pl.* социа́льные се́ти; **~ network** *n.* социа́льная сеть; **~ networking** *n.* по́льзование социа́льной се́тью; **~ sciences** *n. pl.* обще́ственные нау́ки; **~ security** *n.* (system) социа́льное обеспе́чение; (money received) посо́бие; **~ services** *n. pl.* систе́ма социа́льного обеспе́чения; **~ worker** *n.* социа́льный рабо́тник

socialism /ˈsəʊʃəlɪz(ə)m/ *n.* социали́зм

socialist /ˈsəʊʃəlɪst/ *n.* социали́ст (-ка)
● *adj.* социалисти́ческий

socialite /ˈsəʊʃəlaɪt/ *n.* све́тская знамени́тость

socialize /ˈsəʊʃəlaɪz/ *v.i.* обща́ться (*impf.*)

❖ **society** /səˈsaɪətɪ/ *n.* о́бщество; (association) о́бщество, объедине́ние, организа́ция

sociological /ˌsəʊsɪəˈlɒdʒɪk(ə)l/ *adj.* социологи́ческий

sociologist /ˌsəʊsɪˈɒlədʒɪst/ *n.* социо́лог

sociology /ˌsəʊsɪˈɒlədʒɪ/ *n.* социоло́гия

sock /sɒk/ *n.* носо́к

socket /ˈsɒkɪt/ *n.* **1** (anat.) впа́дина; **eye ~** глазна́я впа́дина, глазни́ца **2** (for plug) розе́тка; (slot for connecting electrical device) разъём; (for bulb) патро́н

sod /sɒd/ (BrE, sl.) *n.* сво́лочь (*f.*)
● *v.i.* (**sodded, sodding**) **~ off:** I told him to **~ off** я его́ посла́л; **~ off!** иди́ на́ фиг!
● *v.t.* (**sodded, sodding**): **~ it!** чёрт возьми́!

soda /ˈsəʊdə/ *n.* **1** со́да; **washing ~** стира́льная/кристалли́ческая со́да **2** (*also* **~ water**) со́довая (вода́)

sodden /ˈsɒd(ə)n/ *adj.* промо́кший

sodium /ˈsəʊdɪəm/ *n.* на́трий

sofa /ˈsəʊfə/ *n.* дива́н
■ **~ bed** *n.* дива́н-крова́ть

Sofia /ˈsəʊfɪə/ *n.* Со́фия

❖ **soft** /sɒft/ *adj.* **1** мя́гкий **2** (compassionate) мя́гкий; отзы́вчивый; **have a ~ spot for sb** пита́ть (*impf.*) сла́бость к кому́-н.; (indulgent) мя́гкий, нестро́гий; **she is too ~ with her children** она́ недоста́точно строга́ с детьми́
■ **~ drink** *n.* безалкого́льный напи́ток; **~ drugs** *n. pl.* лёгкие нарко́тики; **~ sign** *n.* (gram.) мя́гкий знак; **~ toy** *n.* мя́гкая игру́шка

soften /ˈsɒf(ə)n/ *v.t.* смягч|а́ть, -и́ть
● *v.i.* смягч|а́ться, -и́ться
□ **~ up** *v.t.*: **~ sb up** (fig.) осл|абля́ть, -а́бить чьё-н. сопротивле́ние

software /ˈsɒftweə(r)/ *n.* (comput.) програ́ммное обеспе́чение

soggy /ˈsɒgɪ/ *adj.* (**soggier, soggiest**) сыро́й, вла́жный

S

soil¹ /sɔɪl/ *n.* по́чва

soil² /sɔɪl/ *v.t.* па́чкать, за-/ис-/вы́-; ~ed linen гря́зное бельё

soirée /ˈswɑːreɪ/ *n.* зва́ный ве́чер

sojourn /ˈsɒdʒ(ə)n/ (liter.) *n.* (вре́менное) пребыва́ние
● *v.i.* пребыва́ть, (вре́менно) жить, прожива́ть (*all impf.*)

solace /ˈsɒləs/ *n.* утеше́ние, отра́да

solar /ˈsəʊlə(r)/ *adj.* со́лнечный
■ ~ **system** *n.* Со́лнечная систе́ма

sold /səʊld/ *past and p.p. of* ▶ sell

solder /ˈsəʊldə(r)/ *v.t.* пая́ть (*impf.*); ~ sth to sth припа́|ивать, -я́ть что-н. к чему́-н.; ~ together спая́ть (*pf.*)

♂ **soldier** /ˈsəʊldʒə(r)/ *n.* солда́т
● *v.i.*: ~ on (fig., persevere doggedly) не сдава́ться (*impf.*)

sole¹ /səʊl/ *n.* (*pl.* ~) (fish) морско́й язы́к (*род камбалы*)

sole² /səʊl/ *n.* (of foot) ступня́, подо́шва (infml); (of shoe) подо́шва, подмётка

sole³ /səʊl/ *adj.* (only) еди́нственный; (exclusive) исключи́тельный

solecism /ˈsɒlɪsɪz(ə)m/ *n.* (of language) солеци́зм; гру́бая (языкова́я) оши́бка; (of behaviour) гру́бая вы́ходка, гру́бость

solely /ˈsəʊllɪ/ *adv.* то́лько, еди́нственно, исключи́тельно

solemn /ˈsɒləm/ *adj.* торже́ственный; (serious) серьёзный, ва́жный

solemnity /səˈlemnɪtɪ/ *n.* торже́ственность; (gravity) ва́жность; (of appearance) серьёзность

solicit /səˈlɪsɪt/ *v.t.* (**solicited, soliciting**) (petition): ~ sb's help проси́ть, по- кого́-н. о по́мощи
● *v.i.* (**solicited, soliciting**) (of prostitute) пристава́ть (*impf.*) к мужчи́нам

solicitor /səˈlɪsɪtə(r)/ *n.* (BrE) адвока́т

solicitous /səˈlɪsɪtəs/ *adj.* забо́тливый, внима́тельный; she is ~ for, about your safety она́ забо́тится о ва́шей безопа́сности

solicitude /səˈlɪsɪtjuːd/ *n.* забо́тливость

♂ **solid** /ˈsɒlɪd/ *n.* (phys.) твёрдое те́ло
● *adj.* (**solider, solidest**) **1** (not liquid) твёрдый; become ~ тверде́ть, за- **2** (not hollow) це́льный **3** (homogeneous): ~ silver чи́стое серебро́ **4** (unbroken): a ~ line сплошна́я черта́; it rained for 3 ~ days дождь лил три дня подря́д **5** (firmly built) про́чный **6** (sound, reliable) соли́дный; надёжный

solidarity /sɒlɪˈdærɪtɪ/ *n.* солида́рность

solidify /səˈlɪdɪfaɪ/ *v.i.* тверде́ть, за-

solidity /səˈlɪdɪtɪ/ *n.* твёрдость; (sturdiness) про́чность; (reliability) надёжность; (soundness) основа́тельность

soliloquy /səˈlɪləkwɪ/ *n.* моноло́г

solitary /ˈsɒlɪtərɪ/ *adj.* (secluded) уединённый; (lonely) одино́кий; (single) едини́чный, еди́нственный

■ ~ **confinement** *n.* одино́чное заключе́ние

solitude /ˈsɒlɪtjuːd/ *n.* уедине́ние, одино́чество

solo /ˈsəʊləʊ/ *n.* (mus.) со́ло (*nt. indecl.*)
● *adj.* со́льный; (aeron.) самостоя́тельный

soloist /ˈsəʊləʊɪst/ *n.* соли́ст (-ка)

solstice /ˈsɒlstɪs/ *n.* солнцестоя́ние

soluble /ˈsɒljʊb(ə)l/ *adj.* раствори́мый

♂ **solution** /səˈluːʃ(ə)n/ *n.* **1** (result of dissolving) раство́р **2** (solving, answer) реше́ние

♂ **solve** /sɒlv/ *v.t.*: ~ an equation/problem реш|а́ть, -и́ть уравне́ние/зада́чу; ~ a mystery раскр|ыва́ть, -ы́ть та́йну

solvent /ˈsɒlv(ə)nt/ *n.* раствори́тель (*m.*)
● *adj.* (fin.) платёжеспосо́бный
■ ~ **abuse** *n.* токсикома́ния

Somali /səˈmɑːlɪ/ *n.* (*pl.* ~ *or* ~s) (person) сомали́|ец (-йка); (language) сомали́ (*m. indecl.*)
● *adj.* сомали́йский

Somalia /səˈmɑːlɪə/ *n.* Сомали́ (*nt. indecl.*)

sombre /ˈsɒmbə(r)/ (AmE *also* **somber**) *adj.* угрю́мый

♂ **some** /sʌm/ *pron.* **1** (of persons) не́которые, одни́; ~ left and others stayed одни́ ушли́, други́е оста́лись; ~ of these girls не́которые/ кое́-кто из э́тих де́вушек **2** (of things, an indefinite number) не́сколько; can I have ~? мо́жно (мне) взять не́сколько?; (an indefinite amount): have ~ more! возьми́те ещё! **3** (a part) часть; I agree with ~ of what you said части́чно я согла́сен с ва́шими слова́ми
● *adj.* **1** (definite though unspecified) како́й-то; ~ fool has locked the door како́й-то дура́к за́пер дверь; ~ day/time когда́-нибудь **2** (no matter what) како́й-нибудь, како́й-либо **3** (one or two) кое-каки́е (*pl.*); (a certain amount, may be expr. by g.): I bought ~ milk я купи́л молока́; (a certain number) не́сколько; (or untranslated): I bought ~ envelopes я купи́л конве́рты; for ~ time now с не́которого вре́мени **4** (approximately) приме́рно, о́коло

♂ **somebody** /ˈsʌmbədɪ/ *pron.* (*also* **someone**) (in particular) кто́-то; there is ~ in the cellar в по́гребе кто́-то есть; (only in nom.) не́кто; (no matter who) кто́-нибудь, кто́-либо; ~ else can do it кто́-нибудь друго́й мо́жет э́то сде́лать

♂ **somehow** /ˈsʌmhaʊ/ *adv.* (no matter how) ка́к-нибудь; так и́ли ина́че; we shall manage ~ мы ка́к-нибудь спра́вимся; (in some unspecified way) ка́к-то, каки́м-то о́бразом; he found out my name ~ он каки́м-то о́бразом узна́л, как меня́ зову́т; (for some reason): ~ I never liked him он мне почему́-то никогда́ не нра́вился

♂ **someone** /ˈsʌmwʌn/ *pron.* = somebody

someplace /ˈsʌmpleɪs/ *adv.* (AmE)
= somewhere 1

somersault /ˈsʌməsɒlt/ *n.* (in the air) са́льто (*nt. indecl.*); (on the ground) кувыро́к
● *v.i.* кувырк|а́ться, -ну́ться; де́лать, с- са́льто

♂ **something** /ˈsʌmθɪŋ/ *pron.* (definite) что́-то; (only in nom.) не́что; (indefinite) что́-нибудь, что́-либо; I must get ~ to eat я до́лжен что-нибудь поесть; **she lectures in** ∼ **or other** она читает лекции по какому-то (там) предмету; **there is** ∼ **about him** в нём что-то такое есть; **she has a cold or** ∼ у неё простуда или что-то в этом роде; (expr. approximation): **he left** ∼ **like a million** он оставил что-то порядка миллиона

sometime /ˈsʌmtaɪm/ *adv.* когда-нибудь, когда-либо; ∼ **soon** как-нибудь, скоро

✧ **sometimes** /ˈsʌmtaɪmz/ *adv.* иногда

✧ **somewhat** /ˈsʌmwɒt/ *adv.* как-то, несколько, довольно

✧ **somewhere** /ˈsʌmweə(r)/ *adv.* **1** (AmE also **someplace**) (place, specific) где-то; (place, anywhere) где-нибудь, где-либо; (motion, specific) куда-то; (motion, anywhere) куда-нибудь, куда-либо **2** (approximately) около + g.

✧ **son** /sʌn/ *n.* сын
■ ∼**-in-law** *n.* зять (*m.*) (*муж дочери*)

sonata /səˈnɑːtə/ *n.* соната

✧ **song** /sɒŋ/ *n.* песня

sonic /ˈsɒnɪk/ *adj.* звуковой

sonnet /ˈsɒnɪt/ *n.* сонет

sonorous /ˈsɒnərəs/ *adj.* звучный

✧ **soon** /suːn/ *adv.* **1** (in a short while) скоро, вскоре; **write** ∼! напишите (по)скорее!; **as** ∼ **as possible** как можно скорее **2** (early) рано; ∼**er or later** рано или поздно **3**: **as** ∼ **as** как только; **as** ∼ **as I saw him, I recognized him** я узнал его, как только увидел **4** (willingly): **I would** ∼**er die than permit it** я скорее умру, чем допущу это; **what would you** ∼**er do: go now or wait?** что вы предпочитаете: уйти или подождать?

soot /sʊt/ *n.* сажа, копоть

soothe /suːð/ *v.t.* (calm) успок|а́ивать, -о́ить; (relieve) облегч|а́ть, -и́ть

soothing /ˈsuːðɪŋ/ *adj.* (tone) утешительный; (cream) успокойтельный

sooty /ˈsʊti/ *adj.* (**sootier, sootiest**) (blackened with soot) закопчённый, закопте́лый; (black as soot) чёрный как сажа; (containing soot): ∼ **deposit** слой сажи

sophisticated /səˈfɪstɪkeɪtɪd/ *adj.* **1** (complicated) ∼ **techniques** сложная техника **2** (refined) ∼ **taste** утончённый вкус

sophistication /səfɪstɪˈkeɪʃ(ə)n/ *n.* (refinement) утончённость, искушённость

soporific /sɒpəˈrɪfɪk/ *adj.* снотворный, усыпляющий

soppy /ˈsɒpi/ *adj.* (**soppier, soppiest**) (BrE, infml, sentimental) сентиментальный

soprano /səˈprɑːnəʊ/ *n.* (*pl.* ∼**s**) (singer) сопрано (*f. indecl.*); (voice) сопрано (*nt. indecl.*)

sorbet /ˈsɔːbeɪ/ *n.* щербет

sorcerer /ˈsɔːsərə(r)/ *n.* колдун, волшебник

sorceress /ˈsɔːsərɪs/ *n.* колдунья, волшебница

sorcery /ˈsɔːsəri/ *n.* колдовство, волшебство

sordid /ˈsɔːdɪd/ *adj.* (squalid) убогий; (morally bad) гнусный

sore /sɔː(r)/ *n.* болячка, язва

● *adj.*: **a** ∼ **tooth** больной зуб; **I have a** ∼ (*sc.* grazed) **knee** я ссадил себе колено; **he has a** ∼ **throat** у него болит горло; **it is a** ∼ **point with him** это у него больное место

sorrow /ˈsɒrəʊ/ *n.* (sadness) печаль, горе; (*in pl.*) горести (*pl., f.*)

sorrowful /ˈsɒrəʊfʊl/ *adj.* печальный, горестный

✧ **sorry** /ˈsɒri/ *adj.* (**sorrier, sorriest**) **1** (regretful): **be** ∼ **for sth** сожалеть (*impf.*) о чём-н., жалеть, по- о чём-н.; **we were** ∼ **to hear of your father's death** мы с грустью узнали о смерти вашего отца; ∼! виноват!; простите!; извините!; **say you're** ∼! (по)проси прощения!; ∼, **I'm busy** извините, но я занят; **I'm** ∼ **I came** я жалею, что пришёл **2** (expr. pity, sympathy): **I feel** ∼ **for you** мне жалко/жаль тебя; **it's the children I feel** ∼ **for** кого мне жалко/жаль — так это детей; **feel** ∼ **for oneself** жалеть (*impf.*) себя **3** (wretched) жалкий; **in a** ∼ **state** в жалком состоянии

✧ **sort** /sɔːt/ *n.* **1** (kind, species) род, сорт, разряд, вид; **he is not the** ∼ (of person) **to complain** он не из тех, кто жалуется; **what** ∼ **of man is he?** что он за человек?; **what** ∼ **of music do you like?** какую музыку вы любите?; **people of all** ∼**s** самые разные люди **2**: ∼ **of** (infml) вроде, как бы; в общем-то; **he** ∼ **of suggested I took him with me** он как бы дал мне понять, что хочет пойти со мной **3**: **out of** ∼**s** (BrE) не в духе
● *v.t.* раз|бирать, -обрать; **they** ∼**ed themselves into groups of six** они разбились на группы по шесть человек; (letters etc., also comput.) сортировать, рас-
□ ∼ **out** *v.t.* (select) от|бирать, -обрать; (separate) отдел|ять, -ить; (arrange) раз|бирать, -обрать; (fig., put in order): **I have to go home to** ∼ **things out** мне нужно пойти домой и во всём разобраться

sortie /ˈsɔːtiː/ *n.* (sally) вылазка (also fig.); (flight) вылет

SOS *n.* (*pl.* ∼**s**) (радио)сигнал бедствия

sought /sɔːt/ *past and p.p. of* ▶ **seek**

✧ **soul** /səʊl/ *n.* **1** душа **2** (music) соул

soulful /ˈsəʊlfʊl/ *adj.* проникновенный, задушевный

soulless /ˈsəʊllɪs/ *adj.* бездушный

✧ **sound**¹ /saʊnd/ *n.* **1** звук; (of rain, sea, wind, etc.) шум **2**: **I don't like the** ∼ **of it** мне это (что-то) не нравится
● *v.t.*: **they** ∼**ed the bell** они позвонили в колокол; ∼ **the alarm** бить, за- тревогу
● *v.i.* **1** (emit sound) звучать, про- **2** (give impression) казаться, по-; **it** ∼**s like thunder** похоже на гром; **the statement** ∼**s improbable** это заявление кажется маловероятным
■ ∼ **barrier** *n.* звуковой барьер; ∼ **card** *n.* (comput.) звуковая карта; ∼ **effects** *n. pl.* звуковое сопровождение, шумовые эффекты; ∼**proof** *adj.* звуконепроницаемый; ∼**track** *n.* саундтрек

sound² /saʊnd/ *n.* (strait) пролив

S

ˢ **sound³** /saʊnd/ *v.t.* (fig.): ~ **(out)** sb (*or* sb's **intentions, opinions**) зонди́ровать, прокого́-н.

sound⁴ /saʊnd/ *adj.* **1** (healthy) здоро́вый; **of** ~ **mind** в здра́вом уме́; (in good condition) испра́вный **2** (thorough) хоро́ший; **he slept** ~**ly** он кре́пко спал; **he was** ~**ly thrashed** его́ си́льно изби́ли

soup /suːp/ *n.* суп
▪ ~ **kitchen** *n.* беспла́тная столо́вая для нужда́ющихся

sour /ˈsaʊə(r)/ *adj.* **1** (of fruit etc.) ки́слый **2** (of milk) проки́сший, ски́сший; **go, turn** ~ ск|иса́ть, -и́снуть **3** (of person) мра́чный, озло́бленный

ˢ **source** /sɔːs/ *n.* **1** (of stream etc.) исто́к **2** (fig.) исто́чник

ˢ **south** /saʊθ/ *n.* юг; (naut.) зюйд; **in the** ~ на ю́ге; **from the** ~ с ю́га; **to the** ~ **of** к ю́гу от + *g.*
● *adj.* ю́жный
● *adv.*: **the ship sailed due** ~ су́дно шло пря́мо на юг; **our village is** ~ **of London** на́ша дере́вня нахо́дится к ю́гу от Ло́ндона
▪ ~**-east** *n.* ю́го-восто́к ● *adj.* ю́го-восто́чный; ~**-east wind** зюйд-о́ст ● *adv.* к ю́го-восто́ку; на ю́го-восто́к; ~**-easterly** *adj.* ю́го-восто́чный; ~**-eastern** *adj.* ю́го-восто́чный; **S**~ **Pole** *n.* Ю́жный по́люс; ~**-west** *n.* ю́го-за́пад ● *adj.* ю́го-за́падный; ~**-west wind** зюйд-ве́ст ● *adv.* к ю́го-за́паду; на ю́го-за́пад; ~**-westerly** *adj.* ю́го-за́падный; ~**-western** *adj.* ю́го-за́падный; ~ **wind** *n.* ю́жный ве́тер

South Africa /saʊθ ˈæfrɪkə/ *n.* Ю́жная А́фрика

South African /saʊθ ˈæfrɪkən/ *n.* южноафрика́н|ец (-ка)
● *adj.* южноафрика́нский

South America /saʊθ əˈmerɪkə/ *n.* Ю́жная Аме́рика

South American /saʊθ əˈmerɪkən/ *n.* южноамерика́н|ец (-ка)
● *adj.* южноамерика́нский

southerly /ˈsʌðəlɪ/ *n.* (wind) ю́жный ве́тер
● *adj.* ю́жный

ˢ **southern** /ˈsʌð(ə)n/ *adj.* ю́жный

southerner /ˈsʌðənə(r)/ *n.* южа́н|ин (-ка)

southward /ˈsaʊθwəd/ *adj.* ю́жный
● *adv.* (*also* **southwards**) на юг; к ю́гу, в ю́жном направле́нии

souvenir /suːvəˈnɪə(r)/ *n.* сувени́р

sovereign /ˈsɒvrɪn/ *n.* (monarch) госуда́р|ь (-ыня); (coin) совере́н
● *adj.* сувере́нный

sovereignty /ˈsɒvrɪntɪ/ *n.* суверените́т

ˢ **Soviet** /ˈsəʊvɪət/ (hist.) *n.* сове́т
● *adj.* сове́тский; **the** ~ **Union** Сове́тский Сою́з

sow¹ /saʊ/ *n.* (pig) свинья́ (*самка*)

sow² /səʊ/ *v.t.* (*past* **sowed** /səʊd/; *p.p.* **sown** *or* **sowed**) **1** (seed) се́ять, по- **2** (ground) зас|е́ивать, -е́ять

ˢ ключева́я ле́ксика

soy /sɔɪ/, **soya** /ˈsɔɪə/ *nn.* со́я
● *adj.* со́евый; ~ **sauce** со́евый со́ус

sozzled /ˈsɒz(ə)ld/ *adj.* (sl.) пья́ный вдре́безги

spa /spɑː/ *n.* во́ды (*f. pl.*); куро́рт с минера́льными исто́чниками

ˢ **space** /speɪs/ *n.* **1** (expanse) простра́нство, просто́р **2** (outer ~) ко́смос; (*attr.*) косми́ческий **3** (distance, interval) расстоя́ние **4** (of time, distance) промежу́ток/пери́од вре́мени; **in the** ~ **of an hour** за час; **в тече́ние часа́ 5** (area) ме́сто; **blank** ~ пусто́е ме́сто
● *v.t.* (*also* ~ **out**): **the posts were** ~**d six feet apart** столбы́ бы́ли располо́жены на расстоя́нии шести́ фу́тов друг от дру́га
▪ ~**craft** (also ~**ship**) *n.* косми́ческий кора́бль; ~**suit** *n.* скафа́ндр (*космона́вта*)

spacious /ˈspeɪʃəs/ *adj.* просто́рный

spade /speɪd/ *n.* **1** (tool) лопа́та **2** (cards) пи́ка; **queen of** ~**s** пи́ковая да́ма, да́ма пик

spaghetti /spəˈɡetɪ/ *n.* спаге́тти (*nt. and pl. indecl.*)

Spain /speɪn/ *n.* Испа́ния

span¹ /spæn/ *n.* **1** (distance between supports) пролёт **2** (of time) промежу́ток/пери́од вре́мени **3**: **wing** ~ разма́х кры́льев
● *v.t.* (**spanned**, **spanning**) перекр|ыва́ть, -ы́ть; (fig.): **the movement** ~**s almost two centuries** э́то движе́ние охва́тывает почти́ два столе́тия

span² /spæn/ *past of* ▶ **spin**

span³ /spæn/ *see* ▶ **spick**

Spaniard /ˈspænjəd/ *n.* испа́н|ец (-ка)

spaniel /ˈspænj(ə)l/ *n.* спание́ль (*m.*)

Spanish /ˈspænɪʃ/ *n.* **1** (language) испа́нский (язы́к) **2**: **the** ~ (collect.) испа́нцы (*m. pl.*)
● *adj.* испа́нский

spank /spæŋk/ *v.t.* шлёпать, от-

spanner /ˈspænə(r)/ *n.* (BrE) га́ечный ключ

spar /spɑː(r)/ *v.i.* (**sparred**, **sparring**) бокси́ровать (*impf.*)

spare /speə(r)/ *n.* **1** (in full ~ **part**) запасна́я часть, запча́сть **2** (in full ~ **wheel**) запасно́е колесо́
● *adj.* (extra) ли́шний; (additional, reserve) запасно́й, резе́рвный
● *v.t.* **1** (withhold use of) жале́ть, по- **2** (dispense with, do without) об|ходи́ться, -ойти́сь без + *g.*; **we cannot** ~ **him** мы не мо́жем обойти́сь без него́ **3** (afford): **can you** ~ **a cigarette?** у вас не найдётся сигаре́ты?; **I can** ~ **you only a few minutes** я могу́ удели́ть вам то́лько не́сколько мину́т **4 to** ~ (available, left over): **I have no time to** ~ у меня́ нет ли́шнего вре́мени; **we got there with an hour to** ~ когда́ мы прие́хали туда́, у нас остава́лся це́лый час в запа́се **5** (show leniency to) щади́ть, по-; **I tried to** ~ **his feelings** я стара́лся щади́ть его́ чу́вства **6** (save from) изб|авля́ть, -а́вить (*кого от чего*); **I will** ~ **you the trouble of replying** я изба́влю вас от необходи́мости отвеча́ть
▪ ~ **room** *n.* ко́мната для госте́й; ~ **time** *n.* свобо́дное вре́мя

spark /spɑːk/ *n.* искра
- *v.t.* (*also* ~ **off**) (cause) вызыва́ть, вы́звать; (friendship) дава́ть, -ть нача́ло + *d.*
- ~ **plug** *n.* свеча́ зажига́ния, запа́льная свеча́

sparkl|e /'spɑːk(ə)l/ *n.* сверка́ние, блеск, блиста́ние; блёстка, и́скорка
- *v.i.* сверка́ть, за-; (flash) блесте́ть, за-; ~ing **wine** шипу́чее/игри́стое вино́

sparkler /'spɑːklə(r)/ *n.* (firework) бенга́льский ого́нь

sparrow /'spærəʊ/ *n.* воробе́й

sparse /spɑːs/ *adj.* ре́дкий; (scattered) разбро́санный; ~ly **populated** малонаселённый

Spartan /'spɑːt(ə)n/ *n.* спарта́н|ец (-ка)
- *adj.* спарта́нский

spasm /'spæz(ə)m/ *n.* (of muscles) спа́зм; (mental or physical reaction) при́ступ, припа́док

spasmodic /spæz'mɒdɪk/ *adj.* спазмати́ческий

spastic /'spæstɪk/ *n.* (often offens.) (спасти́ческий) парали́тик

spat /spæt/ *past and p.p. of* ▶ spit²

spate /speɪt/ *n.* (BrE, sudden flood) разли́в; (fig.) пото́к

spatial /'speɪʃ(ə)l/ *adj.* простра́нственный

spatter /'spætə(r)/, **splatter** /'splætə(r)/ *vv.t. & i.* бры́з|гать, -нуть; забры́згать (*pf.*); ~ed **with mud** забры́зганный гря́зью

spatula /'spætjʊlə/ *n.* (med.) шпа́тель (*m.*); (cul.) лопа́точка

♂ **speak** /spiːk/ *v.t.* (*past* **spoke**, *p.p.* **spoken**)
1 (say) говори́ть, сказа́ть; произн|оси́ть, -ести́; (express): ~ **one's mind** выска́зывать, вы́сказать своё мне́ние **2** (converse in) говори́ть (*impf.*); he ~s **Russian well** он хорошо́ говори́т по-ру́сски
- *v.i.* (*past* **spoke**, *p.p.* **spoken**) говори́ть (*impf.*); (converse) говори́ть, по-; разгова́ривать (*impf.*); вести́ (*indet.*) разгово́р; (make a speech) выступа́ть, вы́ступить; произн|оси́ть, -ести́ речь; 'Smith ~ing' «(с ва́ми) говори́т Смит»; **roughly**, **broadly** ~ing гру́бо говоря́; в о́бщих черта́х; **strictly** ~ing стро́го говоря́; ~ **of** (mention, refer to) упом|ина́ть, -яну́ть о + *p.*
□ ~ **out** *v.i.* (express oneself plainly) выска́зываться, вы́сказаться (открове́нно)
□ ~ **up** *v.i.* (~ louder) говори́ть (*impf.*) гро́мче; (express support): ~ **up for sb** подде́рж|ивать, -а́ть кого́-н.

♂ **speaker** /'spiːkə(r)/ *n.* **1**: the ~ **was a man of about 40** говоря́щему бы́ло лет со́рок **2**: a **Russian** ~ челове́к, владе́ющий ру́сским языко́м **3** (public ~) ора́тор, докла́дчик, выступа́ющий **4** (*in full* **loud** ~) громкоговори́тель (*m.*). **5** (pol.) спи́кер

spear /spɪə(r)/ *n.* копьё, дро́тик
- ~**head** *v.t.*: ~**head a movement** возгл|авля́ть, -а́вить движе́ние

spec¹ /spek/ *n.* (infml): he **went there on** ~ он пошёл туда́ науда́чу

spec² /spek/ *n.* (infml, specification) специфика́ция

♂ **special** /'speʃ(ə)l/ *adj.* **1** (exceptional) осо́бый, осо́бенный; (for a particular purpose) специа́льный **2** (extraordinary) специа́льный, э́кстренный
- ~ **delivery** *n.* сро́чная доста́вка; ~ **effect** *n.* спецэффе́кт

specialist /'speʃəlɪst/ *n.* специали́ст (-ка) (in: по + *d.*)

speciality /speʃɪ'ælɪtɪ/ (AmE **specialty**) *n.* **1** (pursuit) специа́льность, специализа́ция **2** (product, recipe, etc.): ~ **of the house** фи́рменное блю́до

specialize /'speʃəlaɪz/ *v.i.* специализи́роваться (*impf.*, *pf.*) (in: по + *d.*; в/на + *p.*)

specially /'speʃəlɪ/ *adv.* **1** (for specific purpose) специа́льно **2** (exceptionally) осо́бенно, исключи́тельно; **be** ~ **careful** быть осо́бенно осторо́жным

specialty /'speʃəltɪ/ *n.* (AmE) = speciality

♂ **species** /'spiːʃɪz/ *n.* (*pl.* ~) (биологи́ческий) вид

♂ **specific** /spə'sɪfɪk/ *adj.* определённый

♂ **specifically** /spə'sɪfɪkəlɪ/ *adv.* (exactly) определённо; (specially) специа́льно

specification /spesɪfɪ'keɪʃ(ə)n/ *n.* (tech.) специфика́ция; (*in pl.*) техни́ческие характери́стики (*f. pl.*)

specify /'spesɪfaɪ/ *v.t.* определ|я́ть, -и́ть

specimen /'spesɪmən/ *n.* (of rock, handwriting) образе́ц; (of plant, animal) экземпля́р; (of urine) моча́ для ана́лиза

speck /spek/ *n.* (of dirt) пя́тнышко; ~ **of dust** пыли́нка

specs /speks/ *n. pl.* (infml) = spectacle 2

spectacle /'spektək(ə)l/ *n.* **1** (public show; sight) зре́лище **2** (BrE) (*in pl.*) (glasses) очк|и́ (-о́в)

spectacular /spek'tækjʊlə(r)/ *adj.* эффе́ктный, впечатля́ющий

spectator /spek'teɪtə(r)/ *n.* зри́тель (-ница)

spectre /'spektə(r)/ (AmE **specter**) *n.* привиде́ние, при́зрак

spectrum /'spektrəm/ *n.* спектр

speculate /'spekjʊleɪt/ *v.i.* **1** (meditate) размышля́ть (*impf.*) (*о чем*); (conjecture) гада́ть (*impf.*) **2** (risk, invest money) спекули́ровать (*impf.*), игра́ть (*impf.*) на би́рже; he ~s **in oil shares** он спекули́рует а́кциями нефтяны́х компа́ний

speculation /spekjʊ'leɪʃ(ə)n/ *n.* (meditation) размышле́ние; (conjecture) дога́дка; (investment) спекуля́ция

speculative /'spekjʊlətɪv/ *adj.* (investment) спекуляти́вный

speculator /'spekjʊleɪtə(r)/ *n.* спекуля́нт (-ка)

sped /sped/ *past and p.p. of* ▶ speed *v.i.* 1

♂ **speech** /spiːtʃ/ *n.* речь; **make a** ~ произн|оси́ть, -ести́ речь
- ~ **therapist** *n.* логопе́д

speechless /'spiːtʃlɪs/ *adj.*: I **was** ~ **with surprise** я онеме́л от удивле́ния

♂ **speed** /spiːd/ *n.* (rapidity) быстрота́, ско́рость; (rate) ско́рость; **at full**, **top** ~ на по́лной

S

скóрости

• *v.t.* (*past and p.p.* **speeded**) (*also* ~ **up**) ускор|я́ть, -óрить

• *v.i.* **1** (*past and p.p.* **sped**) (move quickly) мча́ться (*impf.*), нести́сь (*impf.*) **2** (*past and p.p.* **speeded**) (go too fast:) he was fined for ~ing его́ оштрафова́ли за превыше́ние скóрости **3** ~ **up** (*past and p.p.* **speeded**) ускор|я́ться, -óриться

■ ~**boat** *n.* быстрохóдный ка́тер; ~ **camera** *n.* ка́мера-рада́р, спид-ка́мера (*фиксирует скорость автомобиля для последующего доказательства превышения скорости*); ~ **dating** *n.* экспрéсс-знакóмства (*nt. pl.*)

speedometer /spiː'dɒmɪtə(r)/ *n.* спидóметр

speedy /'spiːdɪ/ *adj.* (**speedier**, **speediest**) (rapid) скóрый, бы́стрый; (hasty) поспéшный; (prompt, undelayed) скóрый, немéдленный

spell¹ /spel/ *n.* (magical formula) ча́р|ы (*pl., g.* —); колдовствó; **cast a** ~ **over** заколдóв|ывать, -а́ть

■ ~**bound** *adj.* очарóванный, зачарóванный

spell² /spel/ *n.* (interval) перѝод; промежу́ток врéмени; **we're in for a** ~ **of fine weather** ожида́ется полоса́ хорóшей погóды

spell³ /spel/ *v.t.* (*past and p.p.* **spelled** *or esp.* BrE **spelt**) **1** (write or name letters in sequence) произно́с|ить, -ести́ (*or* писа́ть, на-) по бу́квам; **how do you** ~ **your name?** как пи́шется ва́ша фамѝлия?; **he cannot** ~ **his own name** он не мóжет пра́вильно написа́ть свою́ фамѝлию **2** (fig., signify) означа́ть (*impf.*); **these changes** ~ **disaster** э́ти перемéны суля́т несча́стье

• *v.i.* (*past and p.p.* **spelled** *or esp.* BrE **spelt**) писа́ть (*impf.*) пра́вильно/гра́мотно

■ ~**checker** *n.* (comput.) програ́мма провéрки орфогра́фии

spelling /'spelɪŋ/ *n.* правописа́ние, орфогра́фия

spelt /spelt/ *past and p.p. of* ▸ **spell³**

⚡ **spend** /spend/ *v.t.* (*past and p.p.* **spent**) **1** (pay out) тра́тить, ис-; расхóдовать, из- **2** (pass) пров|оди́ть, -ести́; **how do you** ~ **your leisure time?** как вы провóдите свой досу́г?

• *v.i.* (*past and p.p.* **spent**) (~ money) тра́титься, по-; **they went on a** ~ing **spree** онѝ пошлѝ транжи́рить дéньги

spent /spent/ *past and p.p. of* ▸ **spend**

sperm /spɜːm/ *n.* (*pl.* ~ *or* ~**s**) спéрма; (*in full* ~ **whale**) кашалóт

spew /spjuː/ (infml) *v.t.* (vomit) выблёвывать, вы́блевать (sl.); (lit., fig.) изрыга́ть (*impf.*); **a machine gun** ~ing **out bullets** пулемёт, полива́ющий (неприя́теля) огнём

• *v.i.* (vomit) блева́ть (*impf.*) (sl.)

sphere /sfɪə(r)/ *n.* сфéра; ~ **of influence** сфéра влия́ния

spherical /'sferɪk(ə)l/ *adj.* сфери́ческий

sphinx /sfɪŋks/ *n.* сфинкс

spice /spaɪs/ *n.* **1** спéция, пря́ность, припра́ва **2** (fig., piquancy) острота́

⚡ ключевая лексика

spick /spɪk/ *adj.:* ~ **and span** (clean, tidy) сверка́ющий чистотóй

spicy /'spaɪsɪ/ *adj.* (**spicier**, **spiciest**) пря́ный; (fig.) пика́нтный

spider /'spaɪdə(r)/ *n.* пау́к; ~'s **web** паути́на

spike /spaɪk/ *n.* острие́

spiky /'spaɪkɪ/ *adj.* (**spikier**, **spikiest**) остроконéчный; ~ **hairstyle** ёжик

spill /spɪl/ *v.t.* (*past and p.p.* **spilt** *or* **spilled**) (liquid) прол|ива́ть, -и́ть; (powder etc.) расс|ыпа́ть, -ы́пать

• *v.i.* (*past and p.p.* **spilt** *or* **spilled**) (of liquids) разл|ива́ться, -и́ться; (of salt etc.) расс|ыпа́ться, -ы́паться

□ ~ **over** *v.i.* перел|ива́ться, -и́ться (чéрез край)

spin /spɪn/ *n.* **1** (whirl) круже́ние, враще́ние **2** (of ball) враще́ние; **put** ~ **on a ball** закру́|чивать, -ти́ть мяч **3** (outing): **go for a** ~ **in the car** прокати́ться/поката́ться (*both pf.*) на маши́не **4** (bias) пристра́стие

• *v.t.* (**spinning**, *past* **spun** *or* **span**, *p.p.* **spun**) **1** (yarn, wool, etc.) прясть, с-; ~ning **wheel** пря́лка; **the spider** ~s **its web** пау́к плетёт паути́ну **2** (cause to revolve) вертéть, за-; крути́ть, за-; кружи́ть, за-; ~ **a coin** подбр|а́сывать, -óсить монéту

• *v.i.* (**spinning**, *past* **spun** *or* **span**, *p.p.* **spun**) вертéться, за-; крути́ться, за-; кружи́ться, за-; (of wheel) бы́стро враща́ться/ крути́ться (*impf.*); (of one's head): **my head is** ~ning **у** меня́ голова́ идёт кру́гом

□ ~ **out** *v.t.:* ~ **out a story** растя́г|ивать, -ну́ть расска́з

□ ~ **round** *v.t. & i.* бы́стро пов|ора́чивать(ся), -ерну́ть(ся) (круго́м)

■ ~ **doctor** *n.* (pol.) политтехнóлог; ~ **dryer** *n.* (BrE) суши́лка, суши́льный автома́т; ~**-off** *n.* (infml) побóчный результа́т

spina bifida /spaɪnə 'bɪfɪdə/ *n.* расщеплéние позвонóчника

spinach /'spɪnɪdʒ/ *n.* шпина́т

spinal /'spaɪn(ə)l/ *adj.* спиннóй, позвонóчный

■ ~ **column** *n.* позвонóчный столб; ~ **cord** *n.* спиннóй мозг

spindle /'spɪnd(ə)l/ *n.* (axis, rod) ось, шпѝндель (*m.*)

spine /spaɪn/ *n.* **1** (backbone) позвонóчник, спиннóй хребéт **2** (of hedgehog, plant) игла́ **3** (of book) корешóк

spineless /'spaɪnlɪs/ *adj.* (fig.) бесхребéтный, бесхара́ктерный

spinster /'spɪnstə(r)/ *n.* (old maid) ста́рая дéва; (law, unmarried woman) незаму́жняя жéнщина

spiral /'spaɪər(ə)l/ *n.* спира́ль

• *adj.* спира́льный

• *v.i.* (**spiralled**, **spiralling**, AmE **spiraled**, **spiraling**): **the crime rate is** ~ling (upwards) престу́пность (*or* у́ровень престу́пности) растёт бы́стрыми тéмпами

■ ~ **staircase** *n.* винтова́я лéстница

spire /'spaɪə(r)/ *n.* (of church etc.) шпиль (*m.*)

⚡ **spirit** /'spɪrɪt/ *n.* **1** (soul) душа́; духóвное нача́ло **2** (courage) хра́брость; **show some** ~

прояв|ля́ть, -и́ть му́жество/хара́ктер **3** (*in pl.*) (humour) настрое́ние; **he was in high ~s** он был в припо́днятом настрое́нии; **keep one's ~s up** мужа́ться (*impf.*); **не** па́дать (*impf.*) ду́хом **4** (*in pl.*) (BrE, alcoholic drink) спиртно́й напи́ток

■ **~ level** *n.* ватерпа́с

spirited /'spɪrɪtɪd/ *adj.* живо́й; **a ~ reply** бо́йкий отве́т; **a ~ horse** горя́чий конь

spiritual /'spɪrɪtʃʊəl/ *adj.* духо́вный

spiritualism /'spɪrɪtʃʊəlɪz(ə)m/ *n.* спирити́зм

spiritualist /'spɪrɪtʃʊəlɪst/ *n.* спири́т (-ка)

spirituality /ˌspɪrɪtʃʊˈælɪtɪ/ *n.* одухотворённость

spit¹ /spɪt/ *n.* (for roasting) ве́ртел

spit² /spɪt/ *n.* (spittle) слюна́
  • *v.t.* (**spitting**, *past and p.p.* **spat** *or* ~) (*also* ~ **out**) выплёвывать, вы́плюнуть
  • *v.i.* (**spitting**, *past and p.p.* **spat** *or* ~) **1** плева́ть, -ю́нуть; (of cat etc.) фы́рк|ать, -нуть **2** (of fire) сы́пать (*impf.*) и́скрами **3** (BrE, infml, rain) накра́пывать (*impf.*)

■ **~ting image** *n.*: **the ~ting image of his father** то́чная ко́пия своего́ отца́

spite /spaɪt/ *n.* **1** (ill will) зло́ба, злость **2**: **in ~ of** несмотря́ на + *a.*
  • *v.t.*: **he does it to ~ me** он де́лает э́то мне назло́

spiteful /'spaɪtfʊl/ *adj.* зло́бный, злора́дный

spitefulness /'spaɪtfʊlnɪs/ *n.* зло́бность, злора́дство

spittle /'spɪt(ə)l/ *n.* плево́к; слюна́

splash /splæʃ/ *n.* **1** (sound) всплеск, плеск **2** (liquid) бры́зги (*m. pl.*); **I felt a ~ of rain** на меня́ упа́ли ка́пли дождя́ **3** (of blood, mud, etc.) пятно́; **a ~ of colour** кра́сочное пятно́
  • *v.t.* бры́з|гать, -нуть (*чем на что*); забры́згать (*pf.*) (*что чем*); **he ~ed paint on her dress** он забры́згал ей пла́тье кра́ской
  • *v.i.* **1** (of liquid etc.) разбры́зг|иваться, -аться; (of waves) плеска́ться (*impf.*) **2** (move or fall with ~): **the ducks ~ed about in the pond** у́тки плеска́лись в пруду́; (BrE, infml, fig.): **they ~ed out on a new carpet** они́ разори́лись на но́вый ковёр

splatter /'splætə(r)/ *v.t. & i.* = spatter

splay /spleɪ/ *v.t.*: **~ one's legs** раски́|дывать, -нуть но́ги

spleen /spli:n/ *n.* (anat.) селезёнка

splendid /'splendɪd/ *adj.* (excellent) прекра́сный, великоле́пный; **what a ~ idea!** замеча́тельная/прекра́сная мысль!

splendour /'splendə(r)/ (AmE **splendor**) *n.* великоле́пие, пышность

splice /splaɪs/ *v.t.* **1** (rope) сра́|щивать, -сти́ть **2** (tape) скле́и|вать, -ть

splint /splɪnt/ *n.* (for broken bone) ши́на, лубо́к

splinter /'splɪntə(r)/ *n.* **1** (of wood) лучи́на, ще́пка; (in finger) зано́за **2** (fig.): **~ group** отколо́вшаяся фра́кция
  • *v.t. & i.* расщеп|ля́ть(ся), -и́ть(ся)

split /splɪt/ *n.* **1** (crack, fissure) тре́щина, щель, расще́лина **2** (fig., schism) раско́л **3**: **do the ~s** (BrE) де́лать, с- шпага́т

• *v.t.* (**splitting**, *past and p.p.* ~) **1** коло́ть, рас-; расщеп|ля́ть, -и́ть; (crack open) раск|а́лывать, -оло́ть **2** (divide) раздел|я́ть, -и́ть; (share) дели́ть, по- **3** (cause dissension in) раск|а́лывать, -оло́ть
  • *v.i.* (**splitting**, *past and p.p.* ~) **1** (of hard substance) раск|а́лываться, -оло́ться; тре́снуть (*pf.*); (divide) раздел|я́ться, -и́ться **2** (become disunited) разъедин|я́ться, -и́ться; раск|а́лываться, -оло́ться
  □ **~ up** *v.t. & i.* (separate) ра|сходи́ться, -зойти́сь; раз|бива́ть(ся), -би́ть(ся); **we ~ up into two groups** мы разби́лись на две гру́ппы; **he and his wife ~ up** они́ с жено́й разошли́сь

■ **~ second** *n.* до́ля секу́нды

splutter /'splʌtə(r)/ *v.t. & i.* (of person) говори́ть (*impf.*) захлёбываясь; (of fire) шипе́ть (*impf.*)

spoil /spɔɪl/ *v.t.* (*past and p.p.* **spoiled** *or* esp. BrE **spoilt**) **1** (impair, ruin) по́ртить, ис-; **the rain ~t our holiday** дождь испо́ртил нам о́тпуск **2** (overindulge) балова́ть, из-; **a ~t child** избало́ванный ребёнок
  • *v.i.* (*past and p.p.* **spoilt**, esp. BrE *or* **spoiled**) (go bad etc.) по́ртиться, ис-

■ **~sport** *n.* тот, кто по́ртит удово́льствие други́м

spoilt /spɔɪlt/ *past and p.p. of* ▶ spoil

spoke¹ /spəʊk/ *n.* (of wheel) спи́ца

spoke² /spəʊk/ *past of* ▶ speak

spoken /'spəʊkən/ *p.p. of* ▶ speak

spokesman /'spəʊksmən/ *n.* представи́тель (*m.*)

spokesperson /'spəʊkspɜ:s(ə)n/ *n.* представи́тель (*m.*) (-ница)

spokeswoman /'spəʊkswʊmən/ *n.* представи́тельница

sponge /spʌndʒ/ *n.* **1** (zool, toilet article) гу́бка **2** (cake) бискви́т
  • *v.t.* (**sponging** *or* **spongeing**) обт|ира́ть, -ере́ть гу́бкой
  • *v.i.* (**sponging** *or* **spongeing**) (fig.): **he ~s off his brother** он сиди́т на ше́е у бра́та

■ **~ bag** *n.* (BrE) су́мка для туале́тных принадле́жностей; **~ cake** *n.* бискви́т

sponsor /'spɒnsə(r)/ *n.* **1** (guarantor) поручи́тель (-ница); (of new member etc.) рекоменда́тель (-ница) **2** (providing finance) спо́нсор
  • *v.t.* руча́ться, поручи́ться за + *a.*; рекомендова́ть (*impf., pf.*); (on TV etc.) финанси́ровать (*impf., pf.*)

sponsorship /'spɒnsəʃɪp/ *n.* поручи́тельство, пору́ка; спо́нсорство

spontaneity /ˌspɒntəˈneɪɪtɪ/ *n.* спонта́нность, стихи́йность, непосре́дственность

spontaneous /spɒnˈteɪnɪəs/ *adj.* спонта́нный, стихи́йный, непосре́дственный

spoof /spu:f/ *n.* (infml) паро́дия

spook /spu:k/ *n.* (joc.) привиде́ние, при́зрак

spooky /'spu:kɪ/ *adj.* (**spookier**, **spookiest**) (infml) злове́щий; **~ house** дом с привиде́ниями

S

spool /spuːl/ *n.* шпу́лька, кату́шка

spoon /spuːn/ *n.* ло́жка

spoonful /'spuːnfʊl/ *n.* (по́лная) ло́жка (*чего*)

sporadic /spə'rædɪk/ *adj.* споради́ческий, едини́чный, отде́льный

⚔ **sport** /spɔːt/ *n.* **1** (outdoor pastime(s)) спорт; (*in pl.*) спорт, ви́ды (*m. pl.*) спо́рта **2** (*in pl.*) (BrE, athletic events) спорти́вные и́гры (*f. pl.*) **3** (infml, person) молодчи́на (*m.*)

■ ~**s car** *n.* спорти́вный автомоби́ль

sporting /'spɔːtɪŋ/ *adj.* **1** (connected with, fond of sport) спорти́вный **2** (sportsmanlike) че́стный, поря́дочный

sportsman /'spɔːtsmən/ *n.* спортсме́н

sportswoman /'spɔːtswʊmən/ *n.* спортсме́нка

sporty /'spɔːtɪ/ *adj.* (**sportier**, **sportiest**) (person, clothing) спорти́вный

⚔ **spot** /spɒt/ *n.* **1** (patch) пятно́; (speck) пя́тнышко, кра́пинка; **come out in** ~**s** (rash) покры́ва|ться, -́ться сы́пью **2** (stain) пятно́ **3** (pimple) прыщ(ик) **4** (place) ме́сто; **the police were on the** ~ **within minutes** поли́ция прибыла́ на ме́сто (уже́) че́рез не́сколько мину́т; **we were in a (tight)** ~ нам пришло́сь ту́го **5** (BrE, infml, small amount): **I have a** ~ **of work to do** мне ну́жно немно́го порабо́тать; ~ **of bother** небольша́я неприя́тность **6**: ~ **on** (BrE, infml, exactly right) в са́мую то́чку

• *v.t.* (**spotted**, **spotting**) **1** (stain) па́чкать, за-; (with liquid) зака́пать (*pf.*) **2** (*p.p.*) (covered, decorated with ~s): **a** ~**ted tie** га́лстук в кра́пинку **3** (infml, notice) зам|еча́ть, -е́тить; (catch sight of) уви́деть (*pf.*)

■ ~ **check** *n.* вы́борочная прове́рка; ~**light** *n.* освети́тельный проже́ктор; (fig.): **turn the** ~**light on sth** привл|ека́ть, -е́чь внима́ние к чему́-н.; **be in the** ~**light** быть в це́нтре внима́ния

spotless /'spɒtlɪs/ *adj.* сверка́ющий чистото́й; без еди́ного пя́тнышка

spotty /'spɒtɪ/ *adj.* (**spottier**, **spottiest**) (of colour) пятни́стый; (BrE, pimply) прыщева́тый

spouse /spaʊs/ *n.* супру́г (-а)

spout /spaʊt/ *n.* но́сик

• *v.t.* **1**: **a whale** ~**s water** кит выбра́сывает струю́ воды́ **2** (infml, declaim) говори́ть (*impf.*) о + *p.*; ~ **poetry** деклами́ровать, про- стихи́

• *v.i.* **1** бить (*impf.*); ли́ться (*impf.*) пото́ком **2** (fig., infml, make speeches) разглаго́льствовать (*impf.*)

sprain /spreɪn/ *n.* растяже́ние

• *v.t.*: ~ **one's wrist/ankle** раст|я́гивать, -яну́ть запя́стье/лоды́жку

sprang /spræŋ/ *past of* ▸ **spring²**

sprat /spræt/ *n.* шпрот(а), ки́лька

sprawl /sprɔːl/ *n.*: **urban** ~ беспоря́дочный рост го́рода

• *v.i.* **1** (person) раст|я́гиваться, -яну́ться **2** (buildings) раски́|дываться, -нуться

⚔ ключева́я ле́ксика

spray /spreɪ/ *n.* **1** (water droplets) бры́зг|и (*pl., g.* —) **2** (liquid preparation, e.g. fly spray) жи́дкость (для пульвериза́ции) **3** (device for ~ing) спрей

■ ~ **can** *n.* аэрозо́ль (*m.*), спрей

⚔ **spread** /spred/ *n.* **1** (dissemination, expansion) распростране́ние **2** (span) разма́х **3** (cul.) па́ста (*на хлеб*)

• *v.t.* (*past and p.p.* ~) **1** (extend) распростран|я́ть, -и́ть; (unfold) ра|скла́дывать, -зложи́ть; (cover) расст|ила́ть, -ели́ть (*or* разостла́ть); ~ **butter on bread** (*or* **bread with butter**) нама́з|ывать, -ать ма́сло на хлеб (*or* хлеб ма́слом); **the bird** ~ **its wings** пти́ца распра́вила кры́лья; ~ **(out) a map** ра|скла́дывать, -зложи́ть ка́рту **2** (diffuse) распростран|я́ть, -и́ть

• *v.i.* (*past and p.p.* ~) распростран|я́ться, -и́ться; расстила́ться (*impf.*); **the news soon** ~ но́вость/весть бы́стро распространи́лась; **the fire is** ~**ing** пожа́р разраста́ется

■ ~**eagle** *v.t.*: **lie** ~**eagled** лежа́ть (*impf.*) распласта́вшись; ~**sheet** *n.* (comput.) (электро́нная) табли́ца

spree /spriː/ *n.* (infml) весе́лье

sprig /sprɪg/ *n.* ве́точка

sprightly /'spraɪtlɪ/ *adj.* (**sprightlier**, **sprightliest**) живо́й, бо́йкий

⚔ **spring¹** /sprɪŋ/ *n.* (season) весна́; **in** ~ весно́й; (attr.) весе́нний

■ ~**clean** *v.t. & i.* произв|оди́ть, -ести́ генера́льную убо́рку (+ *g.*); ~ **onion** *n.* (BrE) зелёный лук; ~**time** *n.* весна́

spring² /sprɪŋ/ *n.* **1** (leap) прыжо́к, скачо́к **2** (elasticity) упру́гость, эласти́чность **3** (elastic device) пружи́на **4** (of water) исто́чник, ключ, родни́к

• *v.t.* (*past* **sprang** *or* AmE **sprung**, *p.p.* **sprung**) (produce suddenly): ~ **a surprise on sb** заст|ига́ть, -и́чь кого́-н. враспло́х; ~ **a leak** дава́ть, -ть течь

• *v.i.* (*past* **sprang** *or* AmE **sprung**, *p.p.* **sprung**) **1** (leap) пры́г|ать, -нуть; скак|а́ть, -ну́ть; ~ **out of bed** вск|а́кивать, -очи́ть с посте́ли **2** (come into being) появ|ля́ться, -и́ться; возн|ика́ть, -и́кнуть; **a breeze sprang up** подня́лся лёгкий ветеро́к

■ ~**board** *n.* (lit., fig.) трампли́н

sprinkle /'sprɪŋk(ə)l/ *v.t.*: ~ **sth with water**, ~ **water on sth** кропи́ть, о-/обры́зг|ивать, -ать что-н. водо́й; ~ **sth with salt/sand**, ~ **salt/ sand on sth** пос|ыпа́ть, -ы́пать что-н. со́лью/ песко́м

sprinkler /'sprɪŋklə(r)/ *n.* разбры́згиватель (*m.*), пульвериза́тор; (in fire safety) спри́нклер

sprint /sprɪnt/ *n.* спринт

• *v.i.* бежа́ть (*det.*) с максима́льной ско́ростью

sprinter /'sprɪntə(r)/ *n.* спри́нтер

sprocket /'sprɒkɪt/ *n.* **1** звёздочка (це́пи) **2** (*also* ~ **wheel**) цепно́е/зубча́тое колесо́; (in film, tape) зубча́тый бараба́н

sprout /spraʊt/ *n.* (in pl., *also* **Brussels** ~**s**) брюссе́льская капу́ста

• *v.i.* (of plant) пус|ка́ть, -ти́ть ростки́; (of seed)

прораст|а́ть, -и́

spruce[1] /spruːs/ *n.* (tree) ель

spruce[2] /spruːs/ *adj.* опря́тный, наря́дный
• *v.t.*: ~ **up** наво|ди́ть, -ести́ красоту́/блеск на + *a.*; ~ **oneself up** прихора́шиваться (*impf.*)

sprung /sprʌŋ/ *p.p. and* AmE *past of* ▶ **spring**[2]

spun /spʌn/ *past and p.p. of* ▶ **spin**

spur /spɜː(r)/ *n.* **1** (on rider's heel) шпо́ра **2** (fig.) побужде́ние, сти́мул; **on the ~ of the moment** в сиюмину́тном поры́ве
• *v.t.* (**spurred**, **spurring**) (fig.) побу|жда́ть, -ди́ть; под|гоня́ть, -огна́ть; ~**red on by ambition** подгоня́емый честолю́бием

spurious /ˈspjʊəriəs/ *adj.* подде́льный

spurn /spɜːn/ *v.t.* отв|ерга́ть, -е́ргнуть

spurt[1] /spɜːt/ *n.* (sudden effort) поры́в; (in race) рыво́к; **put on a ~** рвану́ться (*pf.*)

spurt[2] /spɜːt/ *n.* (jet) струя́
• *v.i.* бить (*impf.*) струёй; хлы́нуть (*pf.*)

sputnik /ˈspʊtnɪk/ *n.* (иску́сственный) спу́тник

spy /spaɪ/ *n.* шпио́н
• *v.t.* (discern) разгля́д|ывать, -е́ть
• *v.i.* (engage in espionage) шпио́нить (*impf.*); ~ **on sb** подгля́дывать (*impf.*) за кем-н.

spying /ˈspaɪɪŋ/ *n.* шпиона́ж

squabble /ˈskwɒb(ə)l/ *v.i.* пререка́ться (*impf.*) (*с кем*); вздо́рить, по-

squad /skwɒd/ *n.* **1** (mil.) гру́ппа, кома́нда, отделе́ние **2** (gang, group) отря́д; рабо́чая брига́да
■ ~ **car** *n.* полице́йская патру́льная (авто)маши́на

squadron /ˈskwɒdrən/ *n.* (aeron.) эскадри́лья; (mil.) эскадро́н; (naut.) эска́дра

squalid /ˈskwɒlɪd/ *adj.* ни́зкий, ни́зменный, гну́сный

squall /skwɔːl/ *n.* шквал; поры́вистый ве́тер

squalor /ˈskwɒlə(r)/ *n.* убо́жество; (sordidness) ни́зость, гну́сность

squander /ˈskwɒndə(r)/ *v.t.* пром|а́тывать, -ота́ть; растра́|чивать, -тить

square /skweə(r)/ *n.* **1** (shape) квадра́т **2** (on chessboard etc.) кле́тка; **we are back to ~ one** (fig.) мы верну́лись в исхо́дное положе́ние **3** (open space in town) пло́щадь
• *adj.* **1** (geom., math., shape) квадра́тный; ~ **metre** квадра́тный метр; ~ **root (of)** квадра́тный ко́рень (из + *g.*); (right-angled) прямоуго́льный **2** (even) то́чный; в поря́дке; **we are all ~** мы кви́ты
• *adv.* **1** (at right angles) перпендикуля́рно **2** (straight) пря́мо **3**: **ten feet ~** де́сять фу́тов в ширину́ и де́сять в длину́
• *v.t.* **1** (straighten) выпрямля́ть, вы́прямить; ~ **one's shoulders** распр|авля́ть, -а́вить пле́чи **2** (settle) ула́д|живать, -дить **3** (math.) возв|оди́ть, -ести́ в квадра́т; **3 ~d is 9** три в квадра́те равно́ девяти́
• *v.i.* **1** (agree) согласо́в|ываться, -а́ться; ~ **with** сходи́ться (*impf.*) с + *i.*; **this statement does not ~ with the facts** э́то заявле́ние

расхо́дится с фа́ктами **2**: ~ **up** (*sc.* settle accounts) **with sb** поквита́ться (*pf.*) с кем-н.

squash[1] /skwɒʃ/ *n.* (crush) да́вка; (BrE, drink) фрукто́вый напи́ток; (game) сквош
• *v.t.* (crush) дави́ть, раз-; (compress) сж|има́ть, -а́ть; **I ~ed the fly against the wall** я раздави́л му́ху на стене́; **the tomatoes were ~ed** помидо́ры помя́лись
• *v.i.* (crowd) потесни́ться (*pf.*); **they ~ed up to make room for me** они́ потесни́лись, что́бы дать мне ме́сто

squash[2] /skwɒʃ/ *n.* (*pl.* ~ *or* ~**es**) (bot.) (winter ~) ты́ква; (summer ~) кабачо́к

squat /skwɒt/ *adj.* (**squatter**, **squattest**) призе́мистый
• *v.i.* (**squatted**, **squatting**) **1** (be crouching) сиде́ть (*impf.*) на ко́рточках **2** (occupy building illegally) незако́нно всел|я́ться, -и́ться в чужо́й дом

squatter /ˈskwɒtə(r)/ *n.* (illegal occupant) челове́к, незако́нно всели́вшийся в (чужо́й) дом

squawk /skwɔːk/ *v.i.* пронзи́тельно крича́ть, за-

squeak /skwiːk/ *n.* **1** (of mouse etc.) писк **2** (of hinge etc.) скрип, визг
• *v.i.* **1** (of person or animal) пища́ть, пи́скнуть **2** (of object) скрипе́ть, скри́пнуть

squeaky /ˈskwiːkɪ/ *adj.* (**squeakier**, **squeakiest**) пискли́вый, визгли́вый; скрипу́чий

squeal /skwiːl/ *v.i.* визжа́ть, за-

squeamish /ˈskwiːmɪʃ/ *adj.* брезгли́вый; **feel ~** чу́вствовать, по- тошноту́

squeeze /skwiːz/ *n.* **1** (pressure) сжа́тие, пожа́тие **2** (crush) теснота́, да́вка; **we got in, but it was a tight ~** нам удало́сь вти́снуться, но бы́ло о́чень те́сно **3** (fin.) ограниче́ние креди́та
• *v.t.* **1** (compress) сж|има́ть, -а́ть; сда́в|ливать, -и́ть; (to extract moisture etc.) выжима́ть, вы́жать; (extort): ~ **a confession from sb** вынужда́ть, вы́нудить призна́ние у кого́-н. **2** (force, cram) вти́с|кивать, -нуть
• *v.i.* проти́с|киваться, -нуться

squid /skwɪd/ *n.* кальма́р

squiggle /ˈskwɪɡ(ə)l/ *n.* загогу́лина, кара́кул|я (*g. pl.* -ей)

squint /skwɪnt/ *n.* косогла́зие; **she has a ~ in her right eye** она́ коси́т на пра́вый глаз
• *v.i.* **1** коси́ть (*impf.*) **2** (half-shut one's eyes) щу́риться (*impf.*); прищу́ри|ваться, -ться **3**: ~ **at sth** смотре́ть, по- и́скоса на что-н.

squirm /skwɜːm/ *n.* извива́ться (*impf.*); ко́рчиться (*impf.*); **he made me ~ with embarrassment** он меня́ так смути́л, что я не знал, куда́ де́ться

squirrel /ˈskwɪr(ə)l/ *n.* бе́лка

squirt[1] /skwɜːt/ *v.t.* прыс|кать, -нуть; ~ **water in the air** пус|ка́ть, -ти́ть струю́ воды́ в во́здух; ~ **scent from an atomizer** бры́згать, по- духа́ми из пульвериза́тора
• *v.i.* бить (*impf.*) струёй; разбры́зг|иваться, -аться

Sri Lanka /ʃriː ˈlæŋkə/ *n.* Шри-Ланка́

St *abbr. of* (**Saint**) св., Св. (свят|о́й, -а́я)

St. *abbr. of* (**street**) ул. (у́лица)

stab /stæb/ *n.* **1** уда́р (о́стрым ору́жием); ~ **in the back** (fig.) нож/уда́р в спи́ну **2** (fig., sharp pain) внеза́пная о́страя боль; уко́л
• *v.t.* (**stabbed, stabbing**): ~ **sb in the chest with a knife** нан|оси́ть, -ести́ кому́-н. уда́р в грудь ножо́м

stability /stə'bɪlɪtɪ/ *n.* стаби́льность, усто́йчивость

stabilize /'steɪbɪlaɪz/ *v.t. & i.* стабилизи́ровать(ся) (*impf., pf.*)

stable¹ /'steɪb(ə)l/ *n.* коню́шня

stable² /'steɪb(ə)l/ *adj.* (**stabler, stablest**) усто́йчивый, стаби́льный

staccato /stə'kɑːtəʊ/ *n.* (*pl.* ~s) & *adv.* стакка́то (*nt. indecl.*)
• *adj.* отры́вистый

stack /stæk/ *n.* **1** (of hay etc.) стог; скирда́ **2** (pile): ~ **of wood** поле́нница, шта́бель (*m.*) дров; ~ **of papers** ки́па/сто́пка бума́г; ~ **of plates** стопа́/сто́пка таре́лок **3** (infml) (*usu. in pl.*) (large amount) ма́сса, ку́ча, гру́да
• *v.t.*: ~ **books on the floor** скла́дывать, сложи́ть кни́ги сто́пками на полу́

stadium /'steɪdɪəm/ *n.* стадио́н

⚜ **staff** /stɑːf/ *n.* (employees) штат; **teaching** ~ преподава́тельский соста́в
• *v.t.* укомплектов|ывать, -а́ть (*что or штат чего*)
■ ~ **meeting** *n.* (of teachers) педагоги́ческий сове́т; ~ **room** *n.* (BrE, at school) учи́тельская

stag /stæg/ *n.* (deer) оле́нь-саме́ц (*m.*)
■ ~ **party** *n.* (infml) мальчи́шник

⚜ **stage** /steɪdʒ/ *n.* **1** (theatr.) сце́на, подмо́стки; (as profession) теа́тр, сце́на; **go on the** ~ идти́, пойти́ на сце́ну **2** (phase) ста́дия, фа́за, эта́п; **the war reached a critical** ~ война́ вступи́ла в крити́ческую фа́зу; **I shall do it in** ~s я сде́лаю э́то постепе́нно
• *v.t.*: ~ **a play** ста́вить, по- пье́су; (organize) устр|а́ивать, -о́ить; организова́ть (*impf., pf.*)
■ ~ **manager** *n.* постано́вщик

stagger /'stægə(r)/ *v.t.* **1** (disconcert) потряс|а́ть, -ти́; пора|жа́ть, -зи́ть; ошелом|ля́ть, -и́ть; ~ing **success** потряса́ющий успе́х **2**: ~ **working hours, holidays,** *etc.* распредел|я́ть, -и́ть часы́ рабо́ты, отпуска́ *и т. п.*
• *v.i.* шата́ться (*impf.*); пошатыва́ться (*impf.*)

stagnant /'stægnənt/ *adj.* (water) стоя́чий; (pond) засто́явшийся

stagnate /stæg'neɪt/ *v.i.* заст|а́иваться, -оя́ться

stagnation /stæg'neɪʃ(ə)n/ *n.* засто́й

staid /steɪd/ *adj.* степе́нный

stain /steɪn/ *n.* **1** пятно́ **2** (for colouring) краси́тель (*m.*)
• *v.t.* **1** (soil) па́чкать, за-/ис- **2** (colour) окра́|шивать, -сить; ~ **wood** мори́ть, за- де́рево
■ ~ed **glass** *n.* цветно́е стекло́; ~ed-glass **window** витра́ж

⚜ ключева́я ле́ксика

stainless /'steɪnlɪs/ *adj.*: ~ **steel** нержаве́ющая сталь

stair /steə(r)/ *n.* **1** (step) ступе́нька **2** (*in pl.*) ле́стница; **he ran up the** ~s он взбежа́л по ле́стнице
■ ~**case,** ~**way** *nn.* ле́стница; ле́стничная кле́тка

stake /steɪk/ *n.* **1** (post) столб, кол (ко́лья) **2** (wager) ста́вка, закла́д **3** (share in a business) до́ля; (an interest) заинтересо́ванность **4**: **his reputation was at** ~ его́ репута́ция была́ поста́влена на ка́рту
• *v.t.* **1** (support with ~) укреп|ля́ть, -и́ть колó́м **2** (wager) ста́вить, по-; (risk, gamble) рискова́ть (*impf.*) + *i.*
□ ~ **out** *v.t.*: ~ **out a boundary** отм|еча́ть, -е́тить ве́хами грани́цу; ~ **out a place** (infml, keep under surveillance) вести́ (*det.*) наблюде́ние за (+ *i.*)
■ ~**holder** *n.* посре́дник; ~**-out** *n.* (infml) полице́йский надзо́р

stalactite /'stæləktaɪt/ *n.* сталакти́т

stalagmite /'stæləgmaɪt/ *n.* сталагми́т

stale /steɪl/ *adj.* (**staler, stalest**) несве́жий; ~ **bread** чёрствый хлеб; (of air) спёртый, за́тхлый

stalemate /'steɪlmeɪt/ *n.* (chess) пат; (fig., impasse) тупи́к, безвы́ходное положе́ние

stalk¹ /stɔːk/ *n.* (stem) сте́бель (*m.*); черешо́к

stalk² /stɔːk/ **1** (pursue stealthily) высле́живать, вы́следить **2** (persecute obsessively) пресле́довать (*impf.*)

stalker /'stɔːkə(r)/ *n.* челове́к, патологи́чески пресле́дующий предме́т своего́ внима́ния; навя́зчивый пресле́дователь

stall¹ /stɔːl/ *n.* **1** (for animal) сто́йло **2** (in market etc.) прила́вок, стóйка; **book** ~ кио́ск **3** (*in pl.*) (BrE, theatr.) парте́р, кре́сла (*nt. pl.*)
• *v.i.* (of engine) гло́хнуть, за-
■ ~**holder** *n.* (BrE) владе́лец (-ица) пала́тки (на ры́нке)

stall² /stɔːl/ *v.i.* (play for time) тяну́ть, затя́гивать (*both impf.*) вре́мя

stallion /'stæljən/ *n.* жеребе́ц

stalwart /'stɔːlwət/ *adj.*: ~ **supporter** я́р|ый сторо́нни|к (-ая -ца), сто́йкий приве́рженец

stamina /'stæmɪnə/ *n.* выно́сливость

stammer /'stæmə(r)/ *n.* заика́ние
• *v.i.* заика́ться (*impf.*)

stamp /stæmp/ *n.* **1** (instrument) штамп, печа́ть, клеймо́ **2** (mark) печа́ть, клеймо́; (postage etc.) ма́рка
• *v.t.* **1** (imprint) штампова́ть, про-; ста́вить, по- штамп/печа́ть на + *a.* **2** (beat on ground): ~ **one's feet** то́пать, -нуть нога́ми
• *v.i.* (feet) то́п|ать, -нуть
□ ~ **out** *v.t.* (lit.): ~ **out a fire** зат|а́птывать, -опта́ть ого́нь; (fig., exterminate, destroy) уничт|ожа́ть, -о́жить; (fig., suppress) подав|ля́ть, -и́ть (*восста́ние*)
■ ~ **collecting** *n.* коллекциони́рование ма́рок; ~ **duty** *n.* ге́рбовый сбор

stampede /stæm'piːd/ *n.* бе́гство
• *v.i.* разбе|га́ться, -жа́ться врассыпну́ю

stance /stɑːns/ *n.* пози́ция

⚲ **stand** /stænd/ *n.* **1** (support) подста́вка **2** (stall) сто́йка; (BrE, for display) стенд **3** (for spectators) трибу́на **4** (for taxis etc.) стоя́нка **5** (position) ме́сто; (fig.): take a firm ~ зан|има́ть, -я́ть твёрдую пози́цию; make a ~ against sb/sth ока́з|ывать, -а́ть сопротивле́ние кому́-н./ чему́-н.

● *v.t.* (*past and p.p.* **stood**) **1** (place, set) ста́вить; **he stood the ladder against the wall** он приста́вил ле́стницу к стене́ **2** (bear) терпе́ть, вы́-; выноси́ть, вы́нести; перен|оси́ть, -ести́; **she can't ~ him** она́ его́ не выно́сит (*or* терпе́ть не мо́жет)

● *v.i.* (*past and p.p.* **stood**) **1** (be or stay in upright position) стоя́ть (*impf.*) **2** (remain): **our house will ~ for another fifty years** наш дом простои́т ещё пятьдеся́т лет **3** (hold good) ост|ава́ться, -а́ться в си́ле **4** (be situated) стоя́ть (*impf.*); находи́ться (*impf.*) **5** (find oneself, be): **I shall leave the text as it ~s** я оставля́ю текст, как он есть; **as matters ~** при да́нном положе́нии веще́й; **how do we ~ for money?** как у нас (обстои́т) с деньга́ми? **6** (rise to one's feet) вста|ва́ть, -ть **7** (assume or move to specified position): **I'll ~ here** я (в)ста́ну сюда́; **we had to ~ in a queue** (BrE), **in line** (AmE) нам пришло́сь постоя́ть в о́череди; **~ back!** (отступи́те) наза́д!

● *with preps.*: **we will ~ by** (*sc.* support) **you** мы вас подде́ржим; **I ~ by what I said** я не отступа́юсь от свои́х слов; **~ for office** (BrE) выставля́ть, вы́ставить свою́ кандидату́ру; **~ for Parliament** (BrE) баллоти́роваться (*impf.*) в парла́мент; **we ~ for freedom** мы стои́м за свобо́ду; **'Mg' ~s for magnesium** Mg обознача́ет ма́гний; **I will not ~ for such impudence** я не потерплю́ тако́й на́глости; **he ~s to win/lose £1,000** его́ ждёт вы́игрыш/ про́игрыш в ты́сячу фу́нтов

□ **~ about**, **~ around** *vv.i.* стоя́ть (*impf.*) без де́ла

□ **~ aside** *v.i.* стоя́ть (*impf.*) в стороне́

□ **~ back** *v.i.* (also fig.) от|ходи́ть, -ойти́ в сто́рону

□ **~ by** *v.i.* (be ready) быть/стоя́ть (*impf.*) нагото́ве

□ **~ down** *v.i.*: **he stood down in favour of his brother** он снял свою́ кандидату́ру в по́льзу бра́та; (of minister etc.) под|ава́ть, -а́ть в отста́вку

□ **~ in** *v.i.* (substitute): **~ in for sb else** замен|я́ть, -и́ть кого́-н. друго́го

□ **~ out** *v.i.* (be prominent) выделя́ться (*impf.*); выдава́ться (*impf.*)

□ **~ up** *v.t.*: **he stood his bicycle up against the wall** он прислони́л свой велосипе́д к стене́; (infml): **his girlfriend stood him up** его́ подру́га не пришла́ на свида́ние

● *v.i.*: **he stood up as I entered** он встал, когда́ я вошёл; **he ~s up for his rights** он отста́ивает свои́ права́; **he stood up bravely to his opponent** он оказа́л му́жественное сопротивле́ние проти́внику

■ **~-alone** *adj.* (comput.) автоно́мный; **~by**

n. (state of readiness) гото́вность; **keep on ~by** держа́ть (*impf.*) нагото́ве; (dependable thing or person) надёжная опо́ра; испы́танное сре́дство; **~-in** *n.* замести́тель (-ница); **~-offish** *adj.* (aloof) сде́ржанный; (haughty) высокоме́рный; **~point** *n.* то́чка зре́ния; **~still** *n.*: **come to a ~still** остан|а́вливаться, -ови́ться; засто́пориться (*pf.*) (infml); **at a ~still** на мёртвой то́чке; **many factories are at a ~still** мно́го фа́брик безде́йствует/ проста́ивает

⚲ **standard** /'stændəd/ *n.* **1** (flag) зна́мя, штанда́рт **2** (norm) станда́рт; (level) у́ровень (*m.*); **come up to ~** соотве́тствовать (*impf.*) тре́буемому у́ровню; **~ of living** жи́зненный у́ровень, у́ровень жи́зни

● *adj.* **1** станда́ртный **2** (model, basic) норма́тивный, образцо́вый; (general) типово́й **3**: **~ lamp** (BrE) напо́льная ла́мпа, торше́р

standardize /'stændədaɪz/ *v.t.* стандартизи́ровать (*impf., pf.*)

standing /'stændɪŋ/ *n.* **1** (rank) положе́ние; (reputation) репута́ция **2** (duration) продолжи́тельность; **a custom of long ~** стари́нный обы́чай

● *adj.*: **~ army** регуля́рная/постоя́нная а́рмия; **~ invitation** приглаше́ние приходи́ть в любо́е вре́мя; **~ order** (BrE, to banker) прика́з о регуля́рных платежа́х

stank /stæŋk/ *past of* ▶ **stink**

stanza /'stænzə/ *n.* строфа́

staple[1] /'steɪp(ə)l/ *n.* (for papers) ско́бка (*для сте́плера*)

● *v.t.*: **~ papers together** скреп|ля́ть, -и́ть бума́ги сте́плером

staple[2] /'steɪp(ə)l/ *n.* **1** (principal commodity) основно́й това́р/проду́кт **2** (chief material) осно́ва

● *adj.* основно́й, гла́вный

stapler /'steɪplə(r)/ *n.* (for paper) сте́плер

⚲ **star** /stɑː(r)/ *n.* **1** звезда́; **five-~ hotel** пятизвёздочная гости́ница **2** (famous actor etc.) звезда́; **film ~** кинозвезда́ **3** (asterisk) звёздочка

● *v.i.* (**starred**, **starring**): **~ in a film** игра́ть (*impf.*) гла́вную роль в фи́льме

■ **~-fish** *n.* морска́я звезда́; **~ sign** *n.* знак зодиа́ка; **~-studded** *adj.* (fig.) с уча́стием мно́жества звёзд

starboard /'stɑːbəd/ (naut.) *n.* пра́вый борт

● *adj.* пра́вый; **~ side** пра́вый борт; **~ wind** ве́тер с пра́вого бо́рта

starch /stɑːtʃ/ *n.* крахма́л

stardom /'stɑːdəm/ *n.*: **rise to ~** ста|нови́ться, -ть звездо́й

stare /steə(r)/ *n.* при́стальный взгляд

● *v.i.* глазе́ть (*impf.*); **~ at sb** при́стально смотре́ть/гляде́ть на кого́-н.

stark /stɑːk/ *adj.* **1** (desolate) го́лый **2** (sharply evident) я́вный; **be in ~ contrast to** ре́зко контрасти́ровать (*impf.*) с + *i.*

● *adv.*: **~ naked** соверше́нно го́лый; в чём мать родила́ (infml)

starling /'stɑːlɪŋ/ *n.* скворе́ц

S

✔ **start** /stɑːt/ *n.* **1** (sudden movement)
вздра́гивание, содрога́ние; **he woke with a**
∼ он вздро́гнул и просну́лся **2** (beginning)
нача́ло; (of journey) отправле́ние; (of race) старт
● *v.t.* **1** (begin) нач|ина́ть, -а́ть; **it is ∼ing to**
rain начина́ется дождь; **we ∼ed our journey**
мы отпра́вились в путь; **she ∼ed crying**
она́ начала́ пла́кать/распла́калась (*with*
many verbs, the pf. formed with за- means
'to start …ing') **2** (set in motion): **∼ (up) an**
engine зав|оди́ть, -ести́ (*or* запус|ка́ть,
-ти́ть) мото́р/дви́гатель **3** (initiate): **∼ (up)**
a business осно́в|ывать, -а́ть (*or* нач|ина́ть,
-а́ть) би́знес/де́ло; **∼ a family** зав|оди́ть,
-ести́ семью́
● *v.i.* **1** (make sudden movement) вздр|а́гивать,
-о́гнуть; содрог|а́ться, -ну́ться **2** (begin)
нач|ина́ться, -а́ться; (arise) появ|ля́ться,
-и́ться; возн|ика́ть, -и́кнуть; **it ∼ed raining**
пошёл/начался́ дождь; **we had to ∼ again**
from scratch пришло́сь нача́ть всё с нача́ла;
there were 12 of us to ∼ with снача́ла/
сперва́ нас бы́ло 12 (челове́к); **to ∼ with,**
you should write to him пре́жде всего́ (*or*
для нача́ла) вы должны́ написа́ть ему́ **3** (set
out) отпр|авля́ться, -а́виться **4** (of engine etc.):
the car ∼ed without any trouble маши́на
завела́сь без пробле́м
□ **∼ off** *v.i.* (leave) пойти́, пое́хать (*both pf.*);
she ∼ed off by apologizing for being late она́
начала́ с извине́ний за своё опозда́ние
□ **∼ out** *v.i.* (leave) отпр|авля́ться, -а́виться;
пойти́, пое́хать (*both pf.*)
□ **∼ over** *v.i.* (AmE) нач|ина́ть, -а́ть сно́ва
□ **∼ up** *v.t. see* ▶ **start** v.t. 2, ▶ **start** v.t. 3
■ **∼ing price** *n.* нача́льная/ста́ртовая цена́
starter /ˈstɑːtə(r)/ *n.* (BrE, first course) заку́ска;
for ∼s (infml) для нача́ла
✔ **startle** /ˈstɑːt(ə)l/ *v.t.* (scare) пуга́ть, ис-;
вспу́г|ивать, -ну́ть
startling /ˈstɑːtlɪŋ/ *adj.* порази́тельный,
потряса́ющий
starvation /stɑːˈveɪʃ(ə)n/ *n.* го́лод,
голода́ние; **die of ∼** ум|ира́ть, -ере́ть от
го́лода (*or* с го́лоду)
starv|e /stɑːv/ *v.t.* мори́ть, у-/за- (го́лодом);
(fig.): **the child was ∼ed of affection** ребёнок
страда́л от отсу́тствия любви́
● *v.i.* (go hungry) голода́ть (*impf.*); **I'm ∼ing!** я
ужа́сно проголода́лся!; я го́лоден как волк!
stash /stæʃ/ *n.* скры́тый запа́с
● *v.t.* (infml): **he has £1,000 ∼ed away** у него́
припря́тана ты́сяча фу́нтов
✔ **state**[1] /steɪt/ *n.* **1** (condition) состоя́ние,
положе́ние **2** (country, government) госуда́рство;
(*attr.*) госуда́рственный; **United S∼s**
Соединённые Шта́ты (Аме́рики) (*abbr.*
США) **3** (pomp.): **∼ apartments** пара́дные
поко́и (*m. pl.*); **∼ visit** госуда́рственный
визи́т
■ **∼-aided** *adj.* получа́ющий дота́цию/
субси́дию от госуда́рства; **S∼ Department**
adj. (AmE) госуда́рственный департа́мент,
министе́рство иностра́нных дел; **∼-of-the-**

art *adj.* ультрасовреме́нный, нове́йший
✔ **state**[2] /steɪt/ *v.t.* (declare; say clearly) заяв|ля́ть,
-и́ть о + *p.*; сказа́ть (*pf.*) что; утвержда́ть
(*impf.*) что; сообщ|а́ть, -и́ть о + *p.*; (indicate)
ука́з|ывать, -а́ть
stateless /ˈsteɪtlɪs/ *adj.* не име́ющий
гражда́нства
stately /ˈsteɪtlɪ/ *adj.* (**statelier, stateliest**)
вели́чественный, велича́вый
■ **∼ home** *n.* (BrE) дом-дворе́ц
✔ **statement** /ˈsteɪtmənt/ *n.* (declaration)
заявле́ние; (fin.) отчёт
statesman /ˈsteɪtsmən/ *n.* госуда́рственный
де́ятель
static /ˈstætɪk/ *n.* **1** (**∼ electricity**) стати́ческое
электри́чество **2** (as radio interference)
(атмосфе́рные) поме́хи (*f. pl.*)
● *adj.* **1** (stationary) неподви́жный,
стациона́рный **2** (opp. dynamic) стати́ческий,
стати́чный
✔ **station** /ˈsteɪʃ(ə)n/ *n.* **1** (base, headquarters)
ста́нция; **police ∼** полице́йский уча́сток; (in
Russia) отделе́ние мили́ции **2** (rail.) ста́нция;
(large, mainline **∼**) вокза́л
● *v.t.* распол|ага́ть, -ожи́ть; **∼ a guard at the**
gate выставля́ть, вы́ставить карау́л у воро́т;
(mil.) разме|ща́ть, -сти́ть; дислоци́ровать
(*impf., pf.*)
■ **∼ wagon** *n.* (AmE) универса́л (infml) (*тип*
ку́зова)
stationary /ˈsteɪʃənərɪ/ *adj.* неподви́жный
stationery /ˈsteɪʃənərɪ/ *n.* канцеля́рские
принадле́жности (*f. pl.*) /това́ры (*m. pl.*)
statistical /stəˈtɪstɪk(ə)l/ *adj.* статисти́ческий
statistician /ˌstætɪˈstɪʃ(ə)n/ *n.* стати́стик
statistics /stəˈtɪstɪks/ *n.* статисти́ческие
да́нные
statue /ˈstætjuː/ *n.* ста́туя
statuesque /ˌstætjʊˈesk/ *adj.* велича́вый,
вели́чественный
statuette /ˌstætjʊˈet/ *n.* статуэ́тка
stature /ˈstætʃə(r)/ *n.* **1** (height) рост **2** (fig.)
масшта́б, кали́бр
✔ **status** /ˈsteɪtəs/ *n.* ста́тус
■ **∼ quo** *n.* ста́тус-кво́ (*m. & nt. indecl.*)
statute /ˈstætjuːt/ *n.* стату́т; (law) зако́н
statutory /ˈstatjʊtərɪ/ *adj.* предусмо́тренный
зако́ном
staunch /stɔːntʃ/ *adj.* (loyal) лоя́льный;
(devoted): **a ∼ socialist** непрекло́нный/
убеждённый социали́ст
stave /steɪv/ *v.t.*: **∼ off** предотвра|ща́ть, -ти́ть
✔ **stay** /steɪ/ *n.* **1** (sojourn) пребыва́ние **2**: **∼ of**
execution отсро́чка исполне́ния
● *v.i.* **1** (stop, put up) (at a place)
остан|а́вливаться, -ови́ться; (with sb) гости́ть
(*impf.*); остан|а́вливаться, -ови́ться; **we are**
∼ing with friends мы останови́лись/гости́м
у друзе́й **2** (remain) ост|ава́ться, -а́ться; **he**
уходи́ть (*impf.*); **∼ at home** сиде́ть (*impf.*)
до́ма; **I ∼ed away from work** я не пошёл/
вы́шел на рабо́ту; **can you ∼, for tea?** вы
мо́жете оста́ться на чай?; **I am ∼ing in today**
сего́дня я не выхожу́ (*or* я сижу́ до́ма); **he**

~ed on at the university он остáлся при университéте; **she is allowed to** ~ **out till midnight** ей разрешáют не приходи́ть домóй до 12 часóв нóчи; ~ **up late** не ложи́ться (*impf.*) (спать) допозднá **3** (*endure in race etc.*): **he has no** ~**ing power** у негó нет никакóй выно́сливости

STD *abbr.* (*of* **sexually transmitted disease**) заболевáние, передавáемое половы́м путём

stead /sted/ *n.*: **stand sb in good** ~ сослужи́ть (*pf.*) комý-н. хорóшую слýжбу

steadfast /ˈstedfɑːst/ *adj.* (reliable) надёжный; (unwavering) непоколеби́мый

steady /ˈstedɪ/ *adj.* (**steadier, steadiest**) **1** (firmly fixed) прóчный, усто́йчивый, твёрдый; **keep the camera** ~! не дви́гайте фотоаппарáт!; (unfaltering): **a** ~ **gaze** твёрдый взгляд **2** (even) рóвный; (constant) постоя́нный; **he works steadily** он упóрно рабóтает; ~ **demand** постоя́нный спрос
● *v.t.* (strengthen): **the doctor gave him sth to** ~ **his nerves** дóктор дал емý лекáрство для укреплéния нéрвов

steak /steɪk/ *n.* (of beef) бифштéкс (натурáльный)

⚷ **steal** /stiːl/ *v.t.* (*past* **stole**, *p.p.* **stolen**) **1** воровáть (*impf.*); красть, у-; **I had my handbag stolen** у меня укрáли сýмку **2** (fig.): ~ **a glance at sb** взглянýть (*pf.*) укрáдкой на когó-н.
● *v.i.* (*past* **stole**, *p.p.* **stolen**) **1** (thieve) воровáть (*impf.*) **2** (move secretly or silently) крáсться (*impf.*); **he stole round to the back door** он прокрáлся к зáдней двéри

stealth /stelθ/ *n.*: **by** ~ тайкóм, укрáдкой, втихомóлку (infml)

stealthy /ˈstelθɪ/ *adj.* (**stealthier, stealthiest**): ~ **glance** взгляд укрáдкой; ~ **tread** крадýщаяся похóдка

steam /stiːm/ *n.* пар; **let off** ~ (lit.) выпускáть, вы́пустить пары́; (fig.) давáть, -ть вы́ход чýвствам; **run out of** ~ (fig.) выдыхáться, вы́дохнуться
● *v.t.* **1** (cook with ~) пáрить (*impf.*); ~ed **fish** ры́ба, пригото́вленная на парý **2** (cover with ~): **the carriage windows were** ~ed **up** вагóнные óкна запотéли
● *v.i.* выделя́ть (*impf.*) пар/испарéния; пус|кáть, -ти́ть пар
■ ~ **engine** *n.* паровóз; ~**roller** *n.* паровóй катóк

steamer /ˈstiːmə(r)/ *n.* (ship) парохóд

steamy /ˈstiːmɪ/ *adj.* (**steamier, steamiest**) (full of steam) пóлный пáра; (infml, sexy) любóвный

steed /stiːd/ *n.* (poet.) конь (*m.*)

steel /stiːl/ *n.* сталь; (*attr.*) стальнóй
● *v.t.*: ~ **oneself** (pluck up courage) соб|ирáться, -рáться с дýхом
■ ~**mill**, ~**works** *nn.* сталелитéйный завóд

steely /ˈstiːlɪ/ *adj.* (**steelier, steeliest**) (fig., unyielding) желéзный, непреклóнный; (stern) сурóвый

steep¹ /stiːp/ *adj.* **1** крутóй; (fig.): **there has been a** ~ **decline in trade** в торгóвле произошёл рéзкий спад **2** (infml, excessive) чрезмéрный, непомéрный; **we had to pay a** ~ **price** нам э́то влетéло в копéечку

steep² /stiːp/ *v.t.* (soak) замáчивать, -очи́ть

steeple /ˈstiːp(ə)l/ *n.* (bell tower) колокóльня; (spire) шпиль (*m.*)
■ ~**chase** *n.* стипль-чéз; скáчки (*f. pl.*) /бег с препя́тствиями

steer¹ /stɪə(r)/ *n.* (animal) вол

steer² /stɪə(r)/ *v.t.* **1** (ship, vehicle, etc.) управля́ть (*impf.*) + *i.* **2** (person, activity, etc.) вести́ (*det.*); напр|авля́ть, -áвить
● *v.i.* **1** (of steersman) управля́ть/прáвить (*both impf.*) рулём **2** (of person): ~ **clear of** избегáть (*impf.*) + *g.*

steering wheel /ˈstɪərɪŋ wiːl/ *n.* (of car) руль (*m.*)

stem¹ /stem/ *n.* **1** (bot.) стéбель (*m.*) **2** (of wine glass) нóжка **3** (gram.) оснóва
■ ~ **cell** *n.* (biol.) стволовáя клéтка

stem² /stem/ *v.t.* (**stemmed, stemming**) (check, stop) остан|áвливать, -ови́ть

stench /stentʃ/ *n.* вонь

stencil /ˈstensɪl/ *n.* трафарéт
● *v.t.* (**stencilled, stencilling**, AmE **stenciled, stenciling**) расписывать, -áть при пóмощи трафарéта

⚷ **step** /step/ *n.* **1** (movement, distance, sound, manner of ~ping) шаг **2** (fig., action) шаг, мéра; **take** ~s **towards** предприн|имáть, -я́ть шаги́ к + *d.* **3** (raised surface) ступéнь; (of staircase etc.) ступéнька **4** (*in pl.*) (BrE) (*also* ~**ladder**) стремя́нка
● *v.i.* (**stepped, stepping**) шаг|áть, -нýть; ступ|áть, -и́ть; **someone** ~ped **on my foot** ктó-то наступи́л мне нá ногу
□ ~ **aside** *v.i.* сторони́ться, по-; (fig.) уступ|áть, -и́ть (дорóгу) другóму
□ ~ **back** *v.i.* отступ|áть, -и́ть
□ ~ **down** *v.i.*: **he** ~ped **down off the ladder** он спусти́лся/сошёл с лéстницы; **he** ~ped **down in favour of a more experienced man** он уступи́л мéсто бóлее óпытному человéку
□ ~ **in** *v.i.* (intervene) вмéш|иваться, -áться; (replace sb): **thanks for** ~ping **in** спаси́бо, что вы́ручили
□ ~ **up** *v.t.* (increase) пов|ышáть, -ы́сить; уси́ли|вать, -ть
■ ~**-by-**~ *adj.* постепéнный ● *adv.* постепéнно; ~**ping stone** *n.* кáмень для перехóда (*через ручéй и т. п.*); (fig.) трампли́н; **a** ~**ping stone to success** ступéнь к успéху; ~**ladder** *n.* = **step** *n.* 4

step|- /step/ *comb. form*: ~**brother** *n.* свóдный брат; ~**child** *n.* (boy) пáсынок; (girl) пáдчерица; ~**daughter** *n.* пáдчерица; ~**father** *n.* óтчим; ~**mother** *n.* мáчеха; ~**sister** *n.* свóдная сестрá; ~**son** *n.* пáсынок

steppe /step/ *n.* степь

stereo /ˈsterɪəʊ/ *n.* (*pl.* ~s) (~**phonic system**) стереосистéма; **personal** ~ плéер

stereotype /ˈsterɪəʊtaɪp/ *n.* стереоти́п; (*attr.*) стереоти́пный

S

stereotypical /ˌsterɪəʊˈtɪpɪk(ə)l/ *adj.* стереотипный

sterile /ˈsteraɪl/ *adj.* **1** (of land) неплодородный; (of person or animal) бесплодный **2** (germ-free) стерильный

sterility /stəˈrɪlɪtɪ/ *n.* бесплодие

sterilize /ˈsterɪlaɪz/ *v.t.* стерилизовать (*impf., pf.*)

sterling /ˈstɜːlɪŋ/ *n.* стерлинг; фунт стерлингов

stern[1] /stɜːn/ *n.* (of ship) корма

stern[2] /stɜːn/ *adj.* (severe) суровый

stern|um /ˈstɜːnəm/ *n.* (*pl.* ∼ums *or* ∼a) грудина

steroid /ˈsterɔɪd/ *n.* стероид

stethoscope /ˈsteθəskəʊp/ *n.* стетоскоп

stew /stjuː/ *n.* рагу (*nt. indecl.*)
 ● *v.t.* (meat, fish, vegetables) тушить, по-; (fruit) варить (*impf.*); ∼ed fruit компот

steward /ˈstjuːəd/ *n.* (of estate, club, etc.) управляющий, эконом, стюард; (of race meeting) распорядитель (*m.*); (on ship) стюард; (on train) проводник; (on plane) бортпроводник, стюард

stewardess /ˌstjuːəˈdes/ *n.* (on plane) стюардесса, бортпроводница

stick[1] /stɪk/ *n.* **1** (for support, punishment) палка; (*in full* **walking** ∼) трость; (*in full* **hockey** ∼) клюшка **2** (∼ shaped object): ∼ of chalk мелок; ∼ of celery/rhubarb стебель (*m.*) сельдерея/ревеня; ∼ of dynamite динамитная шашка

⚡ **stick**[2] /stɪk/ *v.t.* (*past and p.p.* **stuck**) **1** (insert point of) втыкать, воткнуть; **I stuck a pin in the map** я воткнул булавку в карту **2** (cause to adhere) приклеивать, -ть (*что к чему*); наклеивать, -ть (*что на что*); (affix): ∼ a notice on the door вешать, повесить объявление на дверь **3** (infml, put): ∼ that book on the shelf суньте эту книгу на полку; **he stuck his head round the door** он просунул голову в дверь **4** (BrE, infml, endure) терпеть, вы- **5** (infml uses of pass. with preps.): **get stuck into sth** (BrE, make serious start on) прин|иматься, -яться за что-н. всерьёз; **be stuck with sth** (unable to get rid of) быть не в состоянии отделаться от чего-н.
 ● *v.i.* (*past and p.p.* **stuck**) **1** (be implanted): **a dagger** ∼ing **in his back** кинжал, торчащий у него в спине **2** (remain attached, adhere) прил|ипать, -ипнуть (*к чему*); приклеи|ваться, -ться; **these pages have stuck (together)** эти страницы склеились; ∼ing plaster (BrE) лейкопластырь (*m.*), липкий пластырь **3** (cling, cleave): ∼ to the point не отступать (*impf.*) от темы; ∼ to one's principles ост|аваться, -аться верным своим принципам; **the accused stuck to his story** обвиняемый упорно стоял на своём **4** (*also* **be stuck, get stuck**) (become embedded, fixed) застр|евать, -ять; **the drawer** ∼s ящик застрял; **can you help with this problem? I'm stuck** помогите мне,

⚡ ключевая лексика

пожалуйста, с этой задачей — я совсем запутался; **one thing** ∼s **in my mind** одно у меня засело в памяти

□ ∼ **around** *v.i.* (infml) не уходить (*impf.*)

□ ∼ **down** *v.t.* (seal): **have you stuck the envelope down?** вы заклеили конверт?

□ ∼ **on** *v.t.* (affix) приклеи|вать, -ть

□ ∼ **out** *v.t.*: ∼ **one's tongue out** высовывать, высунуть язык; ∼ **one's head out** высовываться, высунуться
 ● *v.i.* (project) торчать (*impf.*); **his ears** ∼ **out** у него торчат уши

□ ∼ **together** *v.t.* (with glue) склеи|вать, -ть
 ● *v.i.*: **good friends** ∼ **together** настоящие друзья стоят друг за друга (горой)

□ ∼ **up** *v.i.* (protrude upwards) торчать (*impf.*); ∼ **up for** (defend) заступ|аться, -иться за (*кого/ что*)

sticker /ˈstɪkə(r)/ *n.* наклейка

sticky /ˈstɪkɪ/ *adj.* (**stickier, stickiest**) клейкий, липкий

stiff /stɪf/ *adj.* **1** (not flexible or soft) жёсткий **2** (not working smoothly) тугой; ∼ **hinges** тугие петли **3** (of tension or parts of body) онемелый, окостенелый; **I have a** ∼ **neck** у меня шея онемела; **he has a** ∼ **leg** у него нога плохо сгибается; **I feel** ∼ я не могу ни согнуться, ни разогнуться **4** (forceful) сильный; **a** ∼ **drink** хороший глоток спиртного **5** (difficult) трудный, тяжёлый; **a** ∼ **examination** трудный экзамен; (severe) суровый; **he got a** ∼ **sentence** ему вынесли суровый приговор **6** (constrained) натянутый, чопорный **7** (*pred.*) (infml): **he was scared** ∼ он перепугался до смерти; **I was bored** ∼ я чуть не умер со скуки

stiffen /ˈstɪf(ə)n/ *v.t.* прид|авать, -ать жёсткость + *d.*
 ● *v.i.* (become rigid) делаться, с- жёстким; (of body) коченеть, о-, костенеть, о-

stifl|e /ˈstaɪf(ə)l/ *v.t.* **1** (smother, suffocate) душить, за-; **it is** ∼ing **in here** здесь душно **2** (e.g. rebellion, feelings) подав|лять, -ить

stigma /ˈstɪgmə/ *n.* позор, пятно

stigmatize /ˈstɪgmətaɪz/ *v.t.* клеймить, за-

stile /staɪl/ *n.* (steps) перелаз (*ступеньки у забора, стены*)

stiletto /stɪˈletəʊ/ *n.* (*pl.* ∼s) (*usu. in pl.*) (thin high heel) шпилька; (shoe) туфля на шпильке

⚡ **still** /stɪl/ *adj.* **1** (quiet, calm) тихий **2** (motionless) неподвижный; **sit/stand** ∼ сидеть/стоять (*impf.*) спокойно **3** (BrE, not fizzy) негазированный
 ● *adv.* **1** (even now, then; as formerly) (всё) ещё; до сих пор; по-прежнему **2** (nevertheless) тем не менее, всё-таки, всё равно **3** (*with comp.*) (even, yet) ещё
 ■ ∼ **life** *n.* (art) натюрморт

stilt /stɪlt/ *n.* **1** ходуля; **walk on** ∼s ходить (*indet.*) на ходулях **2** (supporting a building) свая

stilted /ˈstɪltɪd/ *adj.* (of style etc.) высокопарный

stimulant /ˈstɪmjʊlənt/ *n.* (med.) стимулирующее средство

stimulate /'stɪmjʊleɪt/ *v.t.* **1** (rouse, incite) (*sb to do sth*) побу|ждáть, -дить (*кого + inf. or к чему*); стимулировать (*impf., pf.*) **2** (excite, arouse) возбу|ждáть, -дить; **the story ∼d my curiosity** рассказ возбудил моё любопытство

stimu|lus /'stɪmjʊləs/ *n.* (*pl.* ∼**li** /-laɪ/) (incentive) стимул, побуждéние

sting /stɪŋ/ *n.* **1** (of insect, etc.) жáло **2** (by insect) укýс
• *v.t.* (*past and p.p.* **stung**) **1** (of insect, etc.) жáлить, у-; кусáть, укусить; (of plant) обж|игáть, -éчь; жечь (*impf.*) **2** (of pain, smoke, etc.) обж|игáть, -éчь
• *v.i.* (*past and p.p.* **stung**) **1** (of insect, etc.) жáлиться (*impf.*); кусáться (*impf.*) **2** (feel pain) жечь (*impf.*); **the smoke made my eyes ∼** дым ел мне глазá
■ ∼**ing nettle** *n.* (жгýчая) крапива

stingy /'stɪndʒɪ/ *adj.* (**stingier, stingiest**) скупóй

stink /stɪŋk/ *n.* вонь
• *v.i.* (*past* **stank** *or* **stunk**, *p.p.* **stunk**) вонять (*impf.*); **the room ∼s of onions** в комнате воняет лýком

stint /stɪnt/ *n.* урóк
• *v.t.*: **he did not ∼ on his praise** он не скупился на похвалы

stipend /'staɪpend/ *n.* (of clergyman) жáлованье; (of student) стипéндия

stipulate /'stɪpjʊleɪt/ *v.t.* (demand) обуслóв|ливать, -ить

stir /stɜː(r)/ *n.*: **the news caused a ∼** это извéстие надéлало мнóго шýма
• *v.t.* (**stirred, stirring**): **the wind ∼s the trees** вéтер колышет дерéвья; ∼ **one's tea** размéш|ивать, -áть чай; ∼ **the soup** мешáть, по- суп
• *v.i.* (**stirred, stirring**) шевелиться, за-
□ ∼ **up** *v.t.* (arouse): ∼ **up rebellion** сéять (*impf.*) смýту

stirrup /'stɪrəp/ *n.* стрéмя (*nt.*)

stitch /stɪtʃ/ *n.* **1** (sewing) стежóк; (knitting) петля **2** (med.) шов **3** (pain in side) кóлик|и (*pl., g.* —) в бокý
• *v.t.* (sew together) сши|вáть, -ть; (esp. med.) заш|ивáть, -йть

stoat /stəʊt/ *n.* горностáй (в лéтнем мехý)

✑ **stock** /stɒk/ *n.* **1** (store, supply) запáс, инвентáрь (*m.*); **in ∼** в ассортимéнте; **take ∼ of** (fig., appraise) критически оцéн|ивать, -ить **2** (lineage) семья́, происхождéние **3** (of farm) (*in full* **live∼**) скот, поголóвье скотá **4** (cul.) (крéпкий) бульóн **5** (comm.) áкции (*f. pl.*); фóнды (*m. pl.*)
• *adj.* (regularly used) обычный, шаблóнный
• *v.t.* **1** (equip with ∼) снаб|жáть, -дить (*что чем*); оборýдовать (*impf., pf.*) **2** (keep in ∼) держáть (*impf.*); имéть (*impf.*) в наличии
• *v.i.* (∼ **up**): **we ∼ed up with fuel for the winter** мы запаслись тóпливом на зиму
■ ∼**broker** *n.* биржевóй мáклер; ∼ **cube** *n.* бульóнный кýбик; **S∼ Exchange** *n.* фóндовая биржа; ∼ **market** *n.* фóндовая биржа; ∼**pile** *v.t.* запас|áть, -ти + *a. or g.*; ∼**still** *adv.* неподвижно; ∼**taking** *n.*

инвентаризáция

Stockholm /'stɒkhəʊm/ *n.* Стокгóльм

stocking /'stɒkɪŋ/ *n.* чулóк

stockist /'stɒkɪst/ *n.* (BrE) рóзничный продавéц (*определённых товаров*)

stocky /'stɒkɪ/ *adj.* (**stockier, stockiest**) коренáстый, приземистый

stodgy /'stɒdʒɪ/ *adj.* (**stodgier, stodgiest**) (BrE, of food) тяжёлый

stoic /'stəʊɪk/ *n.* (of either sex) стóик
• *adj.* стоический

stoical /'stəʊɪk(ə)l/ *adj.* стоический

stoicism /'stəʊɪsɪz(ə)m/ *n.* стоицизм

stoke /stəʊk/ *v.t.* (*also* ∼ **up**) (put more fuel on) загру|жáть, -зить (*топку*)

stole /stəʊl/ *past of* ▸ **steal**

stolen /'stəʊlən/ *p.p. of* ▸ **steal**

stomach /'stʌmək/ *n.* **1** (internal organ) желýдок **2** (external part of body; belly) живóт, брюхо
• *v.t.* (fig., tolerate): **I can't ∼ him** я егó не переношý; я егó терпéть не могý
■ ∼ **ache** *n.* кóлик|и (*pl., g.* —) в животé

stomp /stɒmp/ *v.i.* (infml, tread heavily) тóпать, про-

✑ **stone** /stəʊn/ *n.* (*sense 4: pl.* ∼) **1** кáмень (*m.*) **2** (rock, material): **built of local ∼** пострóенный из мéстного кáмня **3** (of plum etc.) кóсточка **4** (BrE, weight) стóун (*6,35 кг*)
• *v.t.* **1** (pelt with ∼s) поб|ивáть, -ить камня́ми **2**: ∼ **cherries** оч|ищáть, -истить вишни от кóсточек **3**: ∼**d** (infml) (drunk) пьяный вдрéбезги (infml); (with drugs) обдóлбанный (sl.)
■ **S∼ Age** *n.* кáменный век; ∼ **circle** *n.* крóмлех; ∼ **cold** *adj.* холóдный как лёд; ∼**-deaf** *adj.* совершéнно глухóй; ∼**mason** *n.* кáменщик

stony /'stəʊnɪ/ *adj.* (**stonier, stoniest**) камени́стый; (fig., unfeeling) кáменный

stood /stʊd/ *past and p.p. of* ▸ **stand**

stooge /stuːdʒ/ *n.* (sl.) (comedian's foil) партнёр кóмика; (deputy of low standing) подставнóе лицó

stool /stuːl/ *n.* табурéт(ка)

stoop /stuːp/ *n.* сутýлость; **he walks with a ∼** он сутýлится при ходьбé
• *v.i.* **1** (of posture) сутýлиться, с-; (bend down) наг|ибáться, -нýться; гибáться, согнýться **2** (lower oneself): **he never ∼ed to lying** он никогдá не унижáлся до лжи

✑ **stop** /stɒp/ *n.* **1** (halt, halting place) останóвка; **come to a ∼** остан|áвливаться, -овиться; **put a ∼ to** положить (*pf.*) конéц (+ *d.*) **2** (in telegram) (full ∼) тóчка (*abbr.* тчк)
• *v.t.* (**stopped, stopping**) **1** (*also* ∼ **up**) (close, plug) закр|ывáть, -ыть; зат|ыкáть, -кнýть; задéл|ывать, -ать **2** (arrest motion of) остан|áвливать, -овить; **he ∼ped the car** он останови́л маши́ну **3** (arrest progress of; bring to an end) остан|áвливать, -овить; задéрж|ивать, -áть; прекра|щáть, -тить; **rain ∼ped play** дождь сорвáл игрý; **I ∼ped the cheque** (BrE), **check** (AmE) я приостанови́л платёж по этому чéку; (cut off, disallow, ∼ provision of): **my**

father ~ped my allowance отéц перестáл
выделя́ть мне де́ньги **4** (prevent): ~ sb
from удéрж|ивать, -áть кого́-н. от + g.; не
да|ва́ть, -ть (кому́) (+ inf.); **I tried to** ~ **him
(from) telling me** я пыта́лся помеша́ть ему́
сказа́ть ей **5** (with gerund: discontinue, leave off)
перест|ава́ть, -а́ть (+ inf.); прекра|ща́ть,
-ти́ть (+ n. obj.); ~ **teasing the cat!**
переста́ньте дразни́ть ко́шку!; **they** ~ped
talking when I came in когда́ я вошёл, они́
умо́лкли
- *v.i.* (**stopped**, **stopping**) **1** (come to
a halt) остан|а́вливаться, -ови́ться **2** (in
speaking) зам|олка́ть, -о́лкнуть; замолча́ть
(*pf.*) **3** (cease activity) перест|ава́ть, -а́ть;
конча́ть, ко́нчить **4** (come to an end)
прекра|ща́ться, -ти́ться; конча́ться,
ко́нчиться; перест|ава́ть, -а́ть; **the rain** ~ped
дождь конча́лся/переста́л; **the road** ~ped
suddenly неожи́данно доро́га ко́нчилась
□ ~ **by** *v.i.* за|ходи́ть, -йти́; (in a vehicle)
за|езжа́ть, -éхать
□ ~ **off**, ~ **over** *vv.i.* остан|а́вливаться, -ови́ться
- ~**gap** *n.* (person) вре́менная заме́на; (thing)
заты́чка; вре́менная ме́ра; ~**-off**, ~**over** *nn.*
остано́вка (в пути́); ~**watch** *n.* секундоме́р
stoppage /'stɒpɪdʒ/ *n.* (strike) забасто́вка;
(stopping, discontinuing) прекраще́ние
stopper /'stɒpə(r)/ *n.* (of bottle etc.) про́бка
storage /'stɔːrɪdʒ/ *n.* (storing) хране́ние; (in
warehouse) складирова́ние
- ~ **heater** *n.* (BrE) электрообогрева́тель (*m.*),
аккумули́рующий тепло́
ꝏ **store** /stɔː(r)/ *n.* **1** (stock, reserve) запа́с, резе́рв,
припа́сы (*m. pl.*); **he has a surprise in** ~ **for
you** у него́ для вас припасён сюрпри́з **2** (in
pl.) (supplies) припа́сы (*m. pl.*), резе́рвы (*m.
pl.*) **3** (AmE, shop) магази́н, ла́вка; **department**
~ универма́г
- *v.t.* **1** (keep) храни́ть (*impf.*) **2**: ~ **up**
запас|а́ть, -ти́ **3** (deposit in ~) сда|ва́ть, -ть на
хране́ние
- ~**keeper** *n.* ла́вочни|к (-ца); ~**room** *n.*
кладова́я
storey /'stɔːrɪ/ (AmE **story**) *n.* эта́ж
stork /stɔːk/ *n.* а́ист
storm /stɔːm/ *n.* бу́ря; (thunder ~) гроза́
- *v.t.* (mil.) штурмова́ть (*impf.*); брать, взять
шту́рмом/при́ступом
- *v.i.*: **he** ~ed **out of the room** он в гне́ве
вы́бежал из ко́мнаты
- ~ **cloud** *n.* грозова́я ту́ча
stormy /'stɔːmɪ/ *adj.* (**stormier**, **stormiest**)
бу́рный (also fig.)
ꝏ **story**[1] /'stɔːrɪ/ *n.* **1** (tale, account) расска́з,
исто́рия; (fairy tale) ска́зка; **short** ~ расска́з,
нове́лла **2** (newspaper report) отчёт, статья́
- ~**book** *n.* сбо́рник расска́зов; ~**teller** *n.*
расска́зчи|к (-ца)
story[2] /'stɔːrɪ/ *n.* (AmE) = **storey**
stout /staʊt/ *n.* (beer) тёмное пи́во
- *adj.* **1** (strong) кре́пкий, про́чный
2 (corpulent) по́лный, доро́дный

ꝏ ключева́я ле́ксика

stove /stəʊv/ *n.* печь, пе́чка; (for cooking) плита́
stow /stəʊ/ *v.t.* укла́дывать, уложи́ть
- ~**away** *n.* безбиле́тный пассажи́р, «за́яц»
St Petersburg /s(ə)nt 'piːtəzbɜːg/ *n.* Санкт-
Петербу́рг
straddle /'stræd(ə)l/ *v.t.* (extend across)
охва́т|ывать, -и́ть; (sit with legs on either side of):
~ **a fence** сиде́ть, сесть верхо́м на забо́ре
straggl|e /'stræg(ə)l/ *v.i.*: **the children** ~ed
home from school де́ти брели́/тащи́лись
из шко́лы домо́й; **a** ~**ing line of houses**
беспоря́дочный ряд домо́в
straggler /'stræglə(r)/ *n.* отста́вший
straggly /'stræglɪ/ *adj.* (**stragglier**,
straggliest) (hair) всклоко́ченный,
растрёпанный; (plants) увя́дший
ꝏ **straight** /streɪt/ *n.* (of racecourse): **home** ~
фи́нишная пряма́я
- *adj.* **1** прямо́й; **in a** ~ **line** пря́мо в ряд;
she had ~ **hair** у неё бы́ли прямы́е во́лосы;
I couldn't keep a ~ **face** я не мог удержа́ться
от улы́бки **2** (level) ро́вный; (neat, in order)
у́бранный, приведённый в поря́док;
put the record ~ (fig.) вн|оси́ть, -ести́
я́сность; **let's get this** ~ дава́йте внесём
определённость в э́тот вопро́с **3** (frank,
honest) прямо́й, че́стный **4** (orthodox): ~
play (theatr.) (чи́стая) дра́ма; (heterosexual)
гетеросексуа́льный **5** (undiluted)
неразба́вленный
- *adv.* **1** пря́мо; **sit (up)** ~! сиди́(те) пря́мо!;
keep ~ **on!** иди́(те) пря́мо!; (directly): **I am
going** ~ **to Paris** я е́ду пря́мо в Пари́ж; **I told
him** ~ **(out)** я сказа́л ему́ пря́мо **2**: ~ **away**,
off сра́зу, то́тчас
- ~**forward** *adj.* (frank) прямо́й; (uncomplicated)
просто́й
straighten /'streɪt(ə)n/ *v.t.* **1** выпрямля́ть,
вы́прямить; распрям|ля́ть, -и́ть; **he** ~ed
his back он вы́прямился; он распрями́л
спи́ну **2** (put in order) прив|оди́ть, -ести́ в
поря́док; ула́|живать, -дить; **I will try to** ~
things out я постара́юсь всё ула́дить
strain /streɪn/ *n.* **1** (tension) натяже́ние;
(wearing effect): **the** ~**s of modern life**
напряжённость/стресс совреме́нной жи́зни;
(muscular ~) растяже́ние (мы́шц) **2** (of animals,
plants) поро́да
- *v.t.* **1** (exert) напр|яга́ть, -я́чь; **I** ~ed **my
ears to catch his words** я напря́г слух, что́бы
улови́ть его́ слова́ **2** (overexert): ~ **one's
eyes** переутом|ля́ть, -и́ть глаза́; по́ртить,
ис- зре́ние; ~ **oneself** над|рыва́ться,
-орва́ться **3** (overtax): ~ **sb's patience**
испы́тывать (*impf.*) чьё-н. терпе́ние **4** (filter)
(*also* ~ **off**) проце́|живать, -ди́ть;
отце́|живать, -ди́ть; сце́|живать, -ди́ть
- *v.i.* (exert oneself) напр|яга́ться, -я́чься
strainer /'streɪnə(r)/ *n.* си́то; (tea ~) си́течко
strait /streɪt/ *n.* **1** (of water) проли́в **2**: **in dire**
~s в отча́янном положе́нии
- ~**jacket** *n.* смири́тельная руба́шка; ~**-laced**
adj. пурита́нский
straitened /'streɪtənd/ *adj.*: ~ **circumstances**
стеснённые обстоя́тельства

strand¹ /strænd/ v.t. (usu. in pass.) сажа́ть, посади́ть на мель; **I was ~ed in Paris** я застря́л в Пари́же

strand² /strænd/ n. (fibre, thread) прядь, нить

strange /streɪndʒ/ adj. **1** (unfamiliar) незнако́мый, неизве́стный **2** (remarkable) стра́нный, необыкнове́нный, необы́чный; **~ to say (or ~ly enough) he loves her** как (э́то) ни стра́нно, он лю́бит её

strangeness /ˈstreɪndʒnɪs/ n. (remarkableness) стра́нность; (unfamiliarity) непривы́чность

stranger /ˈstreɪndʒə(r)/ n. **1** (unknown person) незнако́м|ец (-ка); посторо́нний (челове́к) **2** (foreigner): **I am a ~ here** я здесь чужо́й

strangle /ˈstræŋɡ(ə)l/ v.t. души́ть, за-; удави́ть (pf.)
- **~hold** n. (lit., fig.) заси́лье

strap /stræp/ n. реме́нь (m.); (of dress) брете́лька
- v.t. (**strapped**, **strapping**) стя́|гивать, -ну́ть ремнём

strapless /ˈstræplɪs/ adj. без брете́лек

strapping /ˈstræpɪŋ/ adj. ро́слый, здоро́вый (infml)

Strasbourg /ˈstræzbɜːɡ/ n. Стра́сбург

strata /ˈstrɑːtə/ pl. of ▶ **stratum**

stratagem /ˈstrætədʒəm/ n. уло́вка

strategic /strəˈtiːdʒɪk/ adj. стратеги́ческий

strategist /ˈstrætɪdʒɪst/ n. страте́г

strategy /ˈstrætədʒɪ/ n. страте́гия

stratif|y /ˈstrætɪfaɪ/ v.t. (arrange in strata) насл|а́ивать, -ои́ть; **~ied rock** сло́истый ка́мень

stratosphere /ˈstrætəsfɪə(r)/ n. стратосфе́ра

strat|um /ˈstrɑːtəm/ n. (pl. **~a**) слой

straw /strɔː/ n. **1** (collect.) соло́ма; (attr.) соло́менный **2** (single ~) соло́минка; **clutch at ~s** (fig.) хвата́ться, схвати́ться за соло́минку; **that was the last ~** э́то бы́ло после́дней ка́плей
- **~ poll, ~ vote** (AmE) nn. (неофициа́льный) опро́с; голосова́ние

strawberry /ˈstrɔːbərɪ/ n. (in pl., collect.) клубни́ка; (wild) земляни́ка

stray /streɪ/ adj. **1** (wandering, lost) заблуди́вшийся, бездо́мный; **~ dog** бездо́мная соба́ка **2** (off-target): **a ~ bullet** шальна́я пу́ля
- v.i. **1** (wander) заблуди́ться (pf.); сбива́ться, сби́ться с пути́; **we must not ~ too far from the path** мы не должны́ отклоня́ться сли́шком далеко́ от тропи́нки **2** (of thoughts, affections) блужда́ть (impf.)

streak /striːk/ n. **1** поло́ска, прожи́лка; **~ of lightning** вспы́шка мо́лнии **2** (fig., trace, tendency) черта́, накло́нность
- v.t.: **~ed with** кра́сными поло́сками
- v.i. (infml, move rapidly) прон|оси́ться, -ести́сь

stream /striːm/ n. **1** (brook) ручёй; (rivulet) ре́чка **2** (flow) пото́к, тече́ние; **~ of abuse** пото́к руга́тельств (nt. pl.) /бра́ни
- v.i. течь, струи́ться, ли́ться (all impf.); **tears ~ed down her cheeks** слёзы струи́лись/

лили́сь/текли́ у неё по щека́м; **light ~ed in at the window** свет струи́лся в окно́; **her eyes were ~ing** у неё из глаз лили́сь слёзы
- **~line** v.t. прид|ава́ть, -а́ть обтека́емую фо́рму + d.; (fig.) упро|ща́ть, -сти́ть, рационализи́ровать (impf., pf.); **~lined** adj. стро́йный; упрощённый

streamer /ˈstriːmə(r)/ n. руло́н бума́жной ле́нты; (flag) вы́мпел

streaming /ˈstriːmɪŋ/ adj. **1** (of a cold): **he had a ~ cold** у него́ был стра́шный на́сморк **2**: (comput.): **~ video** пото́ковое ви́део

street /striːt/ n. у́лица; **he lives in the next ~ (to us)** он живёт на сосе́дней у́лице
- **~car** n. (AmE) трамва́й; **~ credibility** (infml) (also **~ cred**) n. и́мидж; **~ lamp** n. у́личный фона́рь; **~wise** adj. (infml) о́пытный, у́шлый

strength /streŋθ/ n. **1** си́ла; (of structure, material, beam) про́чность; (of wine, solution) кре́пость **2** (basis): **on the ~ of** на основа́нии + g.

strengthen /ˈstreŋkθ(ə)n/ v.t. укреп|ля́ть, -и́ть; уси́ли|вать, -ть

strenuous /ˈstrenjʊəs/ adj. (requiring effort) напряжённый; (energetic) уси́ленный, интенси́вный

stress /stres/ n. **1** (tension) напряже́ние; (pressure) давле́ние, нажи́м; (psych.) стресс **2** (emphasis) ударе́ние; **lay ~ on** де́лать, с- ударе́ние на + p.
- v.t. **1** (subject to ~) напр|яга́ть, -я́чь; **I'm ~ed out** я живу́ в постоя́нном стре́ссе/ напряже́нии **2** (emphasize) подчёрк|ивать, -ну́ть; де́лать, с- упо́р на + a.

stressful /ˈstresfʊl/ adj. стре́ссовый

stretch /stretʃ/ n. **1** (elasticity) растяжи́мость, эласти́чность **2** (expanse) простра́нство **3** (of time) отре́зок; **he works 8 hours at a ~** он рабо́тает во́семь часо́в подря́д
- v.t. **1** (lengthen) вытя́|гивать, вы́тянуть; (broaden) раст|я́гивать, -ну́ть **2** (pull to fullest extent): **~ a rope between two posts** натя́|гивать, -ну́ть верёвку ме́жду двумя́ столба́ми; **~ oneself** потя́|гиваться, -ну́ться; **~ one's legs** разм|ина́ть, -я́ть но́ги **3** (strain, exert): **~ the truth** преувели́чи|вать, -ть
- v.i. **1** (be elastic) растя́гиваться (impf.) **2** (extend) прост|ира́ться, -ере́ться; (of time) дли́ться, про- **3** (~ oneself) потя́|гиваться, -ну́ться
- **~ fabric** n. эласти́чная мате́рия

stretcher /ˈstretʃə(r)/ n. носи́л|ки (-ок)

strew /struː/ v.t. (p.p. **strewn** or **strewed**) разбр|а́сывать, -оса́ть

stricken /ˈstrɪkən/ adj. (lit.) ра́неный; (fig.) поражённый

strict /strɪkt/ adj. **1** (precise) стро́гий, то́чный **2** (stringent): **in ~ confidence** в строжа́йшей та́йне **3** (stern) стро́гий, взыска́тельный

stride /straɪd/ n. (широ́кий) шаг; **he took the exam in his ~** он с лёгкостью сдал экза́мен; **science has made great ~s** нау́ка доби́лась больши́х успе́хов

S

• *v.i.* (*past* **strode**, *p.p.* **stridden** /'strɪd(ə)n/) шага́ть (*impf.*)

strident /'straɪd(ə)nt/ *adj.* ре́зкий, пронзи́тельный

strife /straɪf/ *n.* борьба́, вражда́

◆ **strike** /straɪk/ *n.* **1** (of workers) забасто́вка; **be on ~** бастова́ть (*impf.*); **go on ~** забастова́ть (*pf.*) **2** (attack; blow) нападе́ние; уда́р; налёт
• *v.t.* (*past* **struck**, *p.p.* **struck** *or archaic* **stricken**) **1** (hit) удар|я́ть, -а́рить (*чем по чему; что обо что; кого чем*); **the ship struck a rock** кора́бль наскочи́л на скалу́ **2** (fig., impress) пора|жа́ть, -зи́ть; каза́ться, по- + *d.*; **he was struck by her beauty** он был поражён её красото́й; **the idea ~s me as a good one** э́та мысль ка́жется мне уда́чной **3** (fig., discover) нап|ада́ть, -а́сть на + *a.*; на|ходи́ть, -йти́; откр|ыва́ть, -ы́ть; **they struck oil** они́ откры́ли нефтяно́е месторожде́ние **4**: **~ a match** чи́рк|ать, -нуть спи́чкой **5** (of bell, clock, etc.) бить (*impf.*), проб|ива́ть, -и́ть; **the clock struck midnight** часы́ проби́ли по́лночь **6** (arrive at): **~ a bargain** заключ|а́ть, -и́ть сде́лку; **~ a balance** подв|оди́ть, -ести́ бала́нс/ито́ги; (fig.) на|ходи́ть, -йти́ компроми́сс
• *v.i.* (*past* **struck**, *p.p.* **struck** *or archaic* **stricken**) **1** (hit) удар|я́ть, -а́рить **2** (of clock, etc.) бить, про- **3** (go on ~) бастова́ть (*impf.*) (**for:** чтобы доби́ться + *g.*)

□ **~ down** *v.t.* (fell) сби|ва́ть, -ть с ног; сра|жа́ть, -зи́ть; (of illness, etc.) сва́л|ивать, -и́ть; сра|жа́ть, -зи́ть

□ **~ off** *v.t.* (delete): **~ sb** (*or* sb's name) **off** вычёркивать, вы́черкнуть кого́-н. (*or* чьё-н. и́мя) (из спи́ска *и т. п.*)

□ **~ out** *v.t.* (delete) вычёркивать, вы́черкнуть

□ **~ up** *v.t.*: **~ up an acquaintance** завя́з|ывать, -а́ть знако́мство
• *v.i.* (begin playing/singing) заигра́ть, запе́ть (*both pf.*)

striker /'straɪkə(r)/ *n.* **1** (person on strike) забасто́вщи|к (-ца) **2** (sport) напада́ющий

striking /'straɪkɪŋ/ *adj.* порази́тельный, замеча́тельный

string /strɪŋ/ *n.* **1** верёвка, бечёвка; **pull ~s** наж|има́ть, -а́ть на все кно́пки **2** (of mus. instrument, racket) струна́; **the ~s** (of orchestra) стру́нные инструме́нты (*m. pl.*) **3** (set of objects): **~ of pearls** ни́тка же́мчуга; **~ of onions/sausages** свя́зка лу́ка/соси́сок; **~ of boats/houses** ряд ло́док/домо́в
• *v.t.* (*past and p.p.* **strung**) **1** (furnish with ~): **~ a bow** натя́|гивать, -ну́ть тетиву́; **~ a racket** натя́|гивать, -ну́ть стру́ны **2** (thread on ~) нани́з|ывать, -а́ть **3** (remove ~y fibre from): **~ beans** чи́стить, по- фасо́ль

□ **~ along** *v.i.*: **~ along with sb** (infml, accompany) тащи́ться, по- за кем-н.
• *v.t.* (infml, deceive) води́ть (*impf.*) за́ нос

□ **~ out** *v.t.* (extend) растя́|гивать, -ну́ть; **the houses were strung out along the beach** дома́ тяну́лись вдоль побере́жья

■ **~ quartet** *n.* стру́нный кварте́т

stringent /'strɪndʒ(ə)nt/ *adj.* стро́гий, то́чный

strip[1] /strɪp/ *n.* полоса́; (of cloth) поло́ска, ле́нта; **~ of land** поло́ска земли́

■ **~ cartoon** *n.* расска́з в карти́нках; **~ lighting** *n.* (BrE) нео́новое освеще́ние

strip[2] /strɪp/ *v.t.* (**stripped**, **stripping**) **1** (tear off) сдира́ть, содра́ть **2** (denude) разд|ева́ть, -е́ть; **the room was ~ped bare** из ко́мнаты вы́несли всю ме́бель; **~ (down)** a machine/weapon раз|бира́ть, -обра́ть (*or* демонти́ровать (*impf., pf.*)) маши́ну/ору́жие
• *v.i.* (**stripped**, **stripping**): **~ (naked)**, **~ off** разд|ева́ться, -е́ться (донага́)

stripe /straɪp/ *n.* полоса́, поло́ска

striped /straɪpt/ *adj.* полоса́тый

stripling /'strɪplɪŋ/ *n.* юне́ц

stripper /'strɪpə(r)/ *n.* стриптизёр (-ка/-ша)

strive /straɪv/ *v.i.* (*past* **strove** *or* **strived**, *p.p.* **striven** /'strɪv(ə)n/ *or* **strived**) стреми́ться (*impf.*) (**after, for:** к + *d.*)

strode /strəʊd/ *past of* ▶ **stride**

stroke[1] /strəʊk/ *n.* **1** уда́р; **at a ~** (fig.) одни́м уда́ром/ма́хом **2** (paralytic attack) уда́р, инсу́льт **3** (in swimming) стиль (*m.*) **4** (single instance): **~ of genius** гениа́льная мысль; **~ of luck** (неожи́данная) уда́ча; везе́ние **5** (with pen etc.) штрих; (with brush) мазо́к

stroke[2] /strəʊk/ *v.t.* гла́дить, по-

stroll /strəʊl/ *n.* прогу́лка
• *v.i.* гуля́ть (*impf.*); прогу́л|иваться, -я́ться

stroller /'strəʊlə(r)/ *n.* (AmE, for child) прогу́лочная коля́ска

◆ **strong** /strɒŋ/ *adj.* (**stronger** /'strɒŋɡə(r)/, **strongest** /'strɒŋɡɪst/) **1** (powerful) си́льный, кре́пкий; **~ measures** круты́е ме́ры; **~ argument** ве́ский аргуме́нт; **~ evidence** убеди́тельное доказа́тельство **2** (tough; durable) кре́пкий; про́чный; **~ cloth** кре́пкая мате́рия; **~ walls** про́чные сте́ны **3** (robust) кре́пкий, здоро́вый **4** (of faculties): **oratory is his ~ point** его́ си́ла в красноре́чии **5** (of smell, taste, etc.): **~ flavour** о́стрый/ре́зкий при́вкус **6** (concentrated): **~ drink** кре́пкий напи́ток; **a ~ cup of tea** ча́шка кре́пкого ча́я **7** (sharply defined): **~ light** ре́зкий свет; **~ accent** си́льный акце́нт; **~ colour** я́ркий/ насы́щенный цвет
• *adv.*: **going ~** в прекра́сной фо́рме

■ **~-hold** *n.* кре́пость, тверды́ня; **~-willed** *adj.* реши́тельный, волево́й

◆ **strongly** /'strɒŋlɪ/ *adv.* си́льно, кре́пко; (fig.) твёрдо; **I ~ believe that** я твёрдо убеждён, что; **I feel ~ about** я про́сто уве́рен в чём (*or* в том, что); **I am ~ opposed to** я (настро́ен) реши́тельно про́тив + *g.*

stroppy /'strɒpɪ/ *adj.* (**stroppier**, **stroppiest**) (BrE, infml) несгово́рчивый, сварли́вый, стропти́вый

strove /strəʊv/ *past of* ▶ **strive**

struck /strʌk/ *past and p.p. of* ▶ **strike**

structural /'strʌktʃər(ə)l/ *adj.*: **~ defects** дефе́кты (в) констру́кции

■ **~ engineer** *n.* инжене́р-строи́тель (*m.*)

◆ ключева́я ле́ксика

S

⚡ **structure** /'strʌktʃə(r)/ n. **1** (abstract) структу́ра **2** (concrete) строе́ние, сооруже́ние; (building) зда́ние
● v.t. стро́ить, по-; организо́в|ывать, -а́ть

⚡ **struggle** /'strʌg(ə)l/ n. (lit., fig.) борьба́; (tussle) схва́тка, потасо́вка
● v.i. **1** (fight) боро́ться (impf.); би́ться (impf.) **2** (try hard) боро́ться (impf.); he ~d to make himself heard он изо всех сил пыта́лся перекрича́ть други́х; he ~d for breath он хвата́л ртом во́здух; he ~d to his feet он с трудо́м подня́лся на́ ноги

strum /strʌm/ v.t. & i. (**strummed**, **strumming**) бренча́ть (impf.) (на + p.)

strung /strʌŋ/ past and p.p. of ▸ **string**

strut¹ /strʌt/ v.i. (**strutted**, **strutting**) ходи́ть (indet.) с ва́жным ви́дом

strut² /strʌt/ n. (support) сто́йка, распо́рка, подпо́рка

stub /stʌb/ n. (of pencil) огры́зок; (of cigarette) оку́рок; (of cheque etc.) корешо́к
● v.t. (**stubbed**, **stubbing**) **1**: ~ (out) a cigarette гаси́ть, по- папиро́су **2**: ~ one's toe on sth спот|ыка́ться, -кну́ться о(бо) что-н.

stubble /'stʌb(ə)l/ n. (in field) жнивьё, стерня́ (сжатое поле с остатками соломы на корню); (of beard) щети́на

stubborn /'stʌbən/ adj. упря́мый

stuck /stʌk/ past and p.p. of ▸ **stick**²

stuck-up /'stʌkʌp/ adj. (infml, conceited) высокоме́рный

stud¹ /stʌd/ n. (of horses) ко́нный заво́д

stud² /stʌd/ n. (metal decoration) кно́пка; (on boots) шип; (collar ~) за́понка

⚡ **student** /'stju:d(ə)nt/ n. студе́нт (-ка); (attr.) студе́нческий; (pupil) учени|к (-ца), уча́щ|ийся (-аяся)
■ ~ **teacher** n. учи́тель-практика́нт (учи́тельница-практика́нтка)

⚡ **studio** /'stju:dɪəʊ/ n. (pl. ~s) **1** (of artist etc.) мастерска́я, сту́дия, ателье́ (nt. indecl.) **2** (broadcasting ~) (radio) радиосту́дия; (TV) телесту́дия **3** (cin.) киносту́дия

studious /'stju:dɪəs/ adj. усе́рдный

⚡ **stud|y** /'stʌdɪ/ n. **1** (learning) изуче́ние, учёба, нау́ка; ~ies заня́тия (nt. pl.) **2** (room) кабине́т
● v.t. изуч|а́ть, -и́ть; иссле́довать (impf., pf.)
● v.i. учи́ться (impf.)

⚡ **stuff** /stʌf/ n. **1** (substance) материа́л, вещество́, вещь **2** (infml, things) ве́щи (f. pl.)
● v.t. **1** (fill) наб|ива́ть, -и́ть (что чем); (cul.) фаршировáть, за-, начин|я́ть, -и́ть **2** (cram) запи́х|ивать, -а́ть/-ну́ть (что во что)

stuffing /'stʌfɪŋ/ n. **1** (of cushion etc.) наби́вка **2** (cul.) начи́нка, фарш

stuffy /'stʌfɪ/ adj. (**stuffier**, **stuffiest**) (of room) ду́шный; (of person) чо́порный

stultify /'stʌltɪfaɪ/ v.t. (deaden) притуп|ля́ть, -и́ть

stumbl|e /'stʌmb(ə)l/ v.i. **1** (miss one's footing) оступ|а́ться, -и́ться; спот|ыка́ться, -кну́ться **2** (speak haltingly) зап|ина́ться, -ну́ться; спот|ыка́ться, -кну́ться **3**: ~e across, upon

(find by chance) нат|а́лкиваться, -олкну́ться на + a.
■ ~**ing block** n. ка́мень (m.) преткнове́ния

stump /stʌmp/ n. (of tree) пень (m.); (of limb) культя́, обру́бок; (of pencil) огры́зок
● v.t.: I was ~ed by the question э́тот вопро́с поста́вил меня́ в тупи́к

stun /stʌn/ v.t. (**stunned**, **stunning**) **1** (knock unconscious) оглуш|а́ть, -и́ть **2** (amaze) пора|жа́ть, -зи́ть; a ~ning dress потряса́ющее пла́тье

stung /stʌŋ/ past and p.p. of ▸ **sting**

stunk /stʌŋk/ past and p.p. of ▸ **stink**

stunt /stʌnt/ n. трюк, но́мер
● v.t.: ~ growth заде́рж|ивать, -а́ть рост; ~ed trees низкоро́слые дере́вья
■ ~ **man** n. (cin.) каскадёр

stupefy /'stju:pɪfaɪ/ v.t. ошело́м|ля́ть, -и́ть

stupendous /stju:'pendəs/ adj. изуми́тельный; (in size) огро́мный, колосса́льный

stupid /'stju:pɪd/ adj. (**stupider**, **stupidest**) глу́пый

stupidity /stju:'pɪdɪtɪ/ n. глу́пость

stupor /'stju:pə(r)/ n. остолбене́ние, сту́пор

sturdy /'stɜːdɪ/ adj. (**sturdier**, **sturdiest**) (person) кре́пкий; (thing) про́чный

sturgeon /'stɜːdʒ(ə)n/ n. осётр; (as food) осётр, осетри́на

stutter /'stʌtə(r)/ n. заика́ние
● v.i. заика́ться (impf.)

sty, **stye** /staɪ/ n. (on eye) ячме́нь (m.)

⚡ **style** /staɪl/ n. **1** (manner) стиль (m.), мане́ра **2** (elegance): she has ~ у неё есть вкус; live in ~ жить (impf.) широко́ **3** (fashion) мо́да, фасо́н
● v.t.: she had her hair ~d она́ сде́лала себе́ причёску

stylish /'staɪlɪʃ/ adj. (fashionable) мо́дный; (smart) элега́нтный, сти́льный

stylishness /'staɪlɪʃnɪs/ n. элега́нтность

stylist /'staɪlɪst/ n. стили́ст; hair ~ парикма́хер-моделье́р

stylistic /staɪ'lɪstɪk/ adj. стилисти́ческий

stylize /'staɪlaɪz/ v.t. стилизова́ть (impf., pf.)

stymie /'staɪmɪ/ v.t. (**stymies**, **stymied**, **stymieing**) (fig.) меша́ть (impf.) + d.; препя́тствовать (impf.) + d.

suave /swɑːv/ adj. обходи́тельный, учти́вый

subconscious /sʌb'kɒnʃəs/ n. (the ~) подсозна́ние
● adj. подсозна́тельный

subcontinent /sʌb'kɒntɪnənt/ n. субконтине́нт

subcontract /sʌbkən'trækt/ v.t.: the work was ~ed out рабо́ту о́тдали субподря́дчику

subcontractor /sʌbkən'træktə(r)/ n. субподря́дчик

subculture /'sʌbkʌltʃə(r)/ n. субкульту́ра

subdivide /sʌbdɪ'vaɪd/ v.t. & i. подразде́л|я́ть(ся), -и́ть(ся)

subdivision /'sʌbdɪvɪʒ(ə)n/ n. подразделе́ние

subdue /səb'dju:/ v.t. (**subdues**, **subdued**, **subduing**) **1** (subjugate) подавл|я́ть,

S

-и́ть **2** (soften) смягч|а́ть, -и́ть; ~d light мя́гкий свет **3** (restrain): he seems ~d today он сего́дня что-то прити́х

subedit /'sʌbedɪt/ v.t. (**subedited, subediting**) (BrE) редакти́ровать, от- пе́ред набо́ром; гото́вить, под- к набо́ру

subeditor /'sʌbedɪtə(r)/ n. (BrE) помо́щник реда́ктора; техни́ческий реда́ктор (abbr. техре́д) (infml)

subhuman /sʌb'hjuːmən/ n. недочелове́к
  ● adj. нечелове́ческий

♂ **subject¹** /'sʌbdʒɪkt/ n. **1** (pol.) по́дданный **2** (gram.) подлежа́щее **3** (theme) те́ма, предме́т; change the ~ переводи́ть, -ести́ разгово́р на другу́ю те́му **4** (branch of study) предме́т
  ● adj. **1** (subordinate) подчинённый; all citizens are ~ to the law зако́н распространя́ется на всех гра́ждан **2** (liable): he is ~ to changes of mood он подве́ржен (бы́стрым) сме́нам настрое́ния; trains are ~ to delay возмо́жны опозда́ния поездо́в **3**: ~ to (conditional upon) подлежа́щий + d.; the treaty is ~ to ratification догово́р подлежи́т ратифика́ции
  ■ ~ **matter** n. содержа́ние, предме́т (чего)

subject² /səb'dʒekt/ v.t. (expose) подв|ерга́ть, -е́ргнуть (кого/что чему); he was ~ed to insult его́ подве́ргли оскорбле́нию

subjective /səb'dʒektɪv/ adj. субъекти́вный

subjectivity /sʌbdʒek'tɪvɪtɪ/ n. субъекти́вность

sub judice /sʌb 'dʒuːdɪsɪ/ adj. находя́щийся на рассмотре́нии (суда́)

subjugate /'sʌbdʒʊgeɪt/ v.t. покор|я́ть, -и́ть

subjunctive /səb'dʒʌŋktɪv/ n. сослага́тельное наклоне́ние

sub|let /'sʌblet/ (~**letting**, past and p.p. ~**let**) v.t. перед|ава́ть, -а́ть в субаре́нду

sublime /sə'blaɪm/ adj. (**sublimer, sublimest**) возвы́шенный

subliminal /sʌb'lɪmɪn(ə)l/ adj. подсозна́тельный

submachine gun /sʌbmə'ʃiːn gʌn/ n. автома́т (оружие)

submarine /sʌbmə'riːn/ n. подво́дная ло́дка

submerge /səb'mɜːdʒ/ v.t. & i. погру|жа́ть(ся), -зи́ть(ся)

submission /səb'mɪʃ(ə)n/ n. **1** (subjection) подчине́ние **2** (presentation) представле́ние, предъявле́ние

submissive /səb'mɪsɪv/ adj. поко́рный, смире́нный

♂ **submit** /səb'mɪt/ v.t. (**submitted, submitting**) (present) предст|авля́ть, -а́вить
  ● v.i. (**submitted, submitting**) подчин|я́ться, -и́ться

subordinate /sə'bɔːdɪnət/ n. подчинённый
  ● adj. подчинённый

subpoena /sə'piːnə/ v.t. (past and p.p. **subpoenaed** or **subpoena'd**) вызыва́ть, вы́звать в суд

♂ ключева́я ле́ксика

sub-prime /sʌb'praɪm/ adj субстанда́ртный; ~ mortgage ипоте́чный заём, вы́данный заёмщику с плохо́й креди́тной исто́рией

subscribe /səb'skraɪb/ v.i.: ~ to a journal подпи́с|ываться, -а́ться на журна́л; I cannot ~ to that view я не могу́ согласи́ться с э́тим мне́нием

subscriber /səb'skraɪbə(r)/ n. подпи́счик

subscription /səb'skrɪpʃ(ə)n/ n. (fee) взнос; ~ to a newspaper подпи́ска на газе́ту

subsequent /'sʌbsɪkwənt/ adj. после́дующий, сле́дующий; ~ly впосле́дствии

subservience /səb'sɜːvɪəns/ n. раболе́пие, послуша́ние

subservient /səb'sɜːvɪənt/ adj. раболе́пный

subset /'sʌbset/ n. гру́ппа (в составе чего-л.)

subside /səb'saɪd/ v.i. **1** (of ground or building) ос|еда́ть, -е́сть **2** (of water) спа|да́ть, -сть **3** (of fever) па́дать, упа́сть; (of wind, storm, etc.) ут|иха́ть, -и́хнуть

subsidence /səb'saɪd(ə)ns/ n. (of ground) оседа́ние, оса́дка

subsidiary /səb'sɪdɪərɪ/ n. (comm.) филиа́л
  ● adj. вспомога́тельный, второстепе́нный; (of company) дочерний

subsidize /'sʌbsɪdaɪz/ v.t. субсиди́ровать (impf., pf.)

subsidy /'sʌbsɪdɪ/ n. субси́дия

subsist /səb'sɪst/ v.i. существова́ть (impf.)

subsistence /səb'sɪst(ə)ns/ n. существова́ние

substance /'sʌbst(ə)ns/ n. **1** (essential elements) суть **2** (type of matter) вещество́ **3** (solidity): a piece of writing that lacks ~ сочине́ние, лишённое содержа́ния; there is no ~ in the rumour э́тот слух ниче́м не подкреплён

substandard /sʌb'stændəd/ adj. нестанда́ртный, низкока́чественный

♂ **substantial** /səb'stænʃ(ə)l/ adj. **1** (solid) кре́пкий; a ~ building соли́дное зда́ние; a ~ dinner сы́тный обе́д **2** (considerable): a ~ sum поря́дочная су́мма; a ~ improvement значи́тельное/заме́тное улучше́ние

substantiate /səb'stænʃɪeɪt/ v.t. обоснов|ывать, -а́ть

substitute /'sʌbstɪtjuːt/ n. (person) заме́на, замести́тель (m.); (in sport) запасно́й (игрок)
  ● v.t. (use instead) испо́льзовать (impf., pf.) (for: вме́сто + g.)
  ● v.i.: ~ for заме|ща́ть, -сти́ть; подмен|я́ть, -и́ть; (sport) замен|я́ть, -и́ть (игрока)

substitution /sʌbstɪ'tjuːʃ(ə)n/ n. заме́на, замеще́ние, подме́на

subsume /səb'sjuːm/ v.t. включ|а́ть, -и́ть в каку́ю-н. катего́рию; отн|оси́ть, -ести́ к како́й-н. катего́рии, гру́ппе и т. п.

subterfuge /'sʌbtəfjuːdʒ/ n. уло́вка

subterranean /sʌbtə'reɪnɪən/ adj. подзе́мный

subtitles /'sʌbtaɪt(ə)lz/ n. pl. (cin.) субти́тры (m. pl.)

subtle /'sʌt(ə)l/ adj. (**subtler, subtlest**) (fine, perceptive) то́нкий; (refined) утончённый

subtlety /'sʌtəltɪ/ n. тóнкость; утончённость

subtotal /'sʌbtəʊt(ə)l/ n. промежýточный итóг

subtract /səb'trækt/ v.t. вычитáть, вы́честь

subtraction /səb'trækʃ(ə)n/ n. вычитáние

subtropical /sʌb'trɒpɪk(ə)l/ adj. субтропи́ческий

suburb /'sʌbɜːb/ n. при́город

suburban /sə'bɜːbən/ adj. при́городный

suburbia /sə'bɜːbɪə/ n. (collect.) при́городы m. pl.

subversion /səb'vɜːʃ(ə)n/ n. подрывнáя дéятельность

subversive /səb'vɜːsɪv/ adj. подрывнóй

subway /'sʌbweɪ/ n. (BrE, passage under road) подзéмный перехóд; (AmE, railway) метрó (nt. indecl.), подзéмка (infml)

sub-zero /sʌb'zɪərəʊ/ adj.: ∼ temperatures минусовы́е температýры

ℐ **succeed** /sək'siːd/ v.t. (as heir) наслéдовать (impf., pf.) + d.; (as replacement) сменя́ть, -и́ть • v.i. (be, become successful) преуспевáть, -éть; добивáться, -и́ться успéха/своегó; he ∼ed in tricking us all емý удалóсь всех нас обманýть

ℐ **success** /sək'ses/ n. успéх, удáча; my holidays were not a ∼ this year мои́ кани́кулы в э́том годý бы́ли неудáчными

ℐ **successful** /sək'sesfʊl/ adj. успéшный, удáчный; I tried to persuade him, but was not ∼ я пытáлся убеди́ть егó, но мне э́то не удалóсь

succession /sək'seʃ(ə)n/ n. **1** (sequence) послéдовательность; in ∼ подря́д **2** (series) ряд, цепь **3** (succeeding to office etc.) наслéдство, наслéдование (о порядке передачи)

successive /sək'sesɪv/ adj. послéдовательный; on three ∼ occasions три рáза подря́д

successor /sək'sesə(r)/ n. преéмни|к (-ца), наслéдни|к (-ца)

succinct /sək'sɪŋkt/ adj. сжáтый

succulent /'sʌkjʊlənt/ adj. сóчный

succumb /sə'kʌm/ v.i. уступ|áть, -и́ть; подд|авáться, -áться; they ∼ed to the enemy's superior force они́ уступи́ли превосходя́щей си́ле проти́вника; she did not ∼ to temptation онá не поддалáсь искушéнию

ℐ **such** /sʌtʃ/ adj. **1** (of the kind mentioned; of this, that kind) такóй; ∼ places такúе местá; I have never seen ∼ a sight я никогдá не ви́дел подóбного зрéлища; I said no ∼ thing я ничегó подóбного не говори́л; some ∼ thing чтó-то в э́том рóде; how could you do ∼ a thing? как вы моглú так поступи́ть? **2** ∼ as (of a kind …): ∼ grapes as you never saw такóй виногрáд, какóго вы в жи́зни не ви́дели; I am not ∼ a fool as to believe him я не такóй дурáк, чтóбы повéрить емý; (like): a picture ∼ as that is valuable такóго рóда карти́ны высóко цéнятся

■ ∼-and-∼ adj. такóй-то; ∼like pron. что-н. подóбное; theatres, cinemas, and ∼like

театры, кино и томý подóбное

suck /sʌk/ v.t. **1** сосáть (impf.); (∼ in, imbibe) вс|áсывать, -осáть; тянýть (impf.) (через соломинку и т. n.) **2** (squeeze or dissolve in mouth) сосáть (impf.)
□ ∼ out v.t. (with pump etc.) выс|áсывать, вы́сосать
□ ∼ up v.t. (dust etc.) вс|áсывать, -осáть
□ ∼ up to v.t. (infml, behave obsequiously to) подли́з|ываться, -áться к комý-н.

sucker /'sʌkə(r)/ n. **1** (organ, device) присóска, присóсок **2** (bot.) отрóсток, боковóй побéг **3** (sl., gullible person) простá|к (-чкá), лох (sl.)

suction /'sʌkʃ(ə)n/ n. всáсывание

Sudan /suː'dɑːn/ n. Судáн

Sudanese /suːdə'niːz/ n. (pl. ∼) судáн|ец (-ка)
• adj. судáнский

sudden /'sʌd(ə)n/ n.: (all) of a ∼ внезáпно, вдруг
• adj. (unexpected) внезáпный, неожи́данный

ℐ **suddenly** /'sʌd(ə)nlɪ/ adv. внезáпно, вдруг

suddenness /'sʌd(ə)nnɪs/ n. внезáпность, неожи́данность

suds /sʌdz/ n. pl. мы́льная пéна

sue /sjuː/ v.t. (**sues**, **sued**, **suing**) возбу|ждáть, -ди́ть иск/дéло прóтив + g.; ∼ (sb) for libel/for damages возбу|ждáть, -ди́ть иск/дéло прóтив + g. за клеветý/о возмещéнии убы́тков
• v.i. под|авáть, -áть в суд (на + a.)

suede /sweɪd/ n. зáмша; (attr.) зáмшевый

suet /'suːɪt/ n. нутряное сáло; пóчечный жир

ℐ **suffer** /'sʌfə(r)/ v.t. испы́т|ывать, -áть; претерп|евáть, -éть; (defeat) терпéть, по-
• v.i. страдáть (impf.) (from: от + g.); he ∼s from shyness он (óчень) застéнчив; he is ∼ing from measles он болéет кóрью; у негó корь

sufferance /'sʌfərəns/ n.: on ∼ из ми́лости; с молчали́вого соглáсия

sufferer /'sʌfrə(r)/ n. страдáлец

suffering /'sʌfrɪŋ/ n. страдáние

suffice /sə'faɪs/ v.i. быть достáточным; хватá|ть, -и́ть

sufficient /sə'fɪʃ(ə)nt/ adj. достáточный

suffix /'sʌfɪks/ n. сýффикс

suffocat|**e** /'sʌfəkeɪt/ v.t. души́ть, за-; he was ∼ed by poisonous fumes он задохнýлся от ядови́того ды́ма; ∼ing heat удýшливая жарá
• v.i. задыхáться, -охнýться

suffocation /sʌfə'keɪʃ(ə)n/ n. удушéние, удýшье

suffrage /'sʌfrɪdʒ/ n. избирáтельное прáво

sugar /'ʃʊɡə(r)/ n. сáхар
■ ∼ **beet** n. сáхарная свёкла; ∼ **cane** n. сáхарный тростни́к; ∼ **lump** n. кусó(че)к сáхара

sugary /'ʃʊɡərɪ/ adj. **1** сáхарный, сáхари́стый **2** (fig., of tone, smile, etc.) слáдкий, слащáвый

ℐ **suggest** /sə'dʒest/ v.t. предл|агáть, -ожи́ть; совéтовать, по-; I ∼ you try again я совéтую вам попрóбовать ещё раз(óк)

ℐ **suggestion** /sə'dʒestʃ(ə)n/ n. **1** (proposal) предложéние, совéт **2** (implication) намёк, доля; (tinge) оттенок

suggestive /sə'dʒɛstɪv/ *adj.*: ~ of напоминающий; (improper) непристойный

suicidal /su:ɪ'saɪd(ə)l/ *adj.* (person) склонный к самоубийству; (action) самоубийственный

ⸯ **suicide** /'su:ɪsaɪd/ *n.* **1** (also fig.) самоубийство; **commit** ~ кончать, (по)кончить с собой **2** (person) самоубийца (*c.g.*)

ⸯ **suit** /sju:t/ *n.* **1** (of clothes) костюм **2** (law) иск, дело **3** (of cards) масть
● *v.t.* **1** (be convenient for) под|ходить, -ойти + *d.*; устр|аивать, -оить; **would Sunday** ~ **you?** воскресенье вам подойдёт (*or* вас устроит)? **2** (be appropriate or good for) под|ходить, -ойти + *d.*; **the role does not** ~ **him** эта роль ему не подходит; **they are** ~ed **to one another** они подходят друг другу **3** (please): **he tries to** ~ **everybody** он старается всем угодить **4** (enhance): **that hat** ~s **her** эта шляпа ей идёт
■ ~**case** *n.* чемодан

suitable /'sju:təb(ə)l/ *adj.* подходящий, годный

suitably /'sju:təblɪ/ *adv.* соответственно, правильно

suite /swi:t/ *n.* (set): ~ **of furniture** мебельный гарнитур; (in hotel) (номер) люкс

suitor /'sju:tə(r)/ *n.* (wooer) жених, поклонник

sulfur /'sʌlfə(r)/ *n.* (AmE) = sulphur

sulfuric /sʌl'fjʊərɪk/ *adj.* (AmE) = sulphuric

sulk /sʌlk/ *v.i.* быть в дурном настроении; дуться (*impf.*) (infml)

sulky /'sʌlkɪ/ *adj.* (**sulkier, sulkiest**) надутый, мрачный

sullen /'sʌlən/ *adj.* (sulky) надутый; (sombre) мрачный

sulphur /'sʌlfə(r)/ (AmE **sulfur**) *n.* сера

sulphuric /sʌl'fjʊərɪk/ (AmE **sulfuric**) *adj.*: ~ **acid** серная кислота

sultana /sʌl'tɑ:nə/ *n.* изюминка; (*collect.*) кишмиш (*об изюме*)

sultry /'sʌltrɪ/ *adj.* (**sultrier, sultriest**) знойный

sum /sʌm/ *n.* **1** (total) итог **2** (amount) сумма **3** (calculation) (арифметическая), задача
● *v.t.* (**summed, summing**) (*usu.* ~ **up**) суммировать (*impf., pf.*); подв|одить, -ести итоги + *g.*
● *v.i.* (**summed, summing**): ~ **up** суммировать (*impf., pf.*)

summarize /'sʌməraɪz/ *v.t.* суммировать (*impf., pf.*); резюмировать (*impf., pf.*)

summary /'sʌmərɪ/ *n.* резюме (*nt. indecl.*), сводка

ⸯ **summer** /'sʌmə(r)/ *n.* лето; **in** ~ летом; (*attr.*) летний
■ ~ **house** *n.* беседка; ~ **school** *n.* летняя школа; ~**time** *n.* лето

summery /'sʌmərɪ/ *adj.*: ~ **weather** летняя/тёплая погода; ~ **clothes** лёгкая/летняя одежда

summit /'sʌmɪt/ *n.* (lit., fig.) вершина, верх; ~ (**meeting**) саммит, встреча в верхах

summon /'sʌmən/ *v.t.* **1** (send for) призывать, -вать; (also law) вызывать, вызвать **2**: ~ **up one's energy/courage** соб|ираться, -раться с силами/духом

summons /'sʌmənz/ *n.* (*pl.* ~**es**) вызов; (law) судебная повестка, вызов в суд
● *v.t.* вызывать, вызвать в суд

sumptuous /'sʌmptʃʊəs/ *adj.* роскошный

ⸯ **sun** /sʌn/ *n.* солнце; (astron.) Солнце; **lie in the** ~ лежать (*impf.*) на солнце
■ ~**bathe** *v.i.* загорать (*impf.*); ~**bed** *n.* (BrE, lounger) шезлонг; (for acquiring tan) солярий; ~**burn** *n.* (inflammation) солнечный ожог; ~**burnt** *adj.* (tanned) загорелый; (inflamed) обожжённый солнцем; ~**dial** *n.* солнечные часы (*m. pl.*); ~**flower** *n.* подсолнечник; ~**glasses** *n. pl.* солнцезащитные очки; ~**hat** *n.* шляпа от солнца; ~**lamp** *n.* кварцевая лампа; ~**light** *n.* солнечный свет; ~**rise** *n.* восход (солнца); **at** ~**rise** на заре; ~**roof** *n.* (of car) раздвижная крыша; ~**set** *n.* заход солнца, закат; **at** ~**set** на закате; ~**shade** *n.* (солнечный) зонтик; ~**shine** *n.* солнечный свет; ~**stroke** *n.* солнечный удар; ~**tan** *n.* загар; ~**tan lotion** крем для загара

ⸯ **Sunday** /'sʌndeɪ/ *n.* воскресенье

sundries /'sʌndrɪz/ *n. pl.* разное

sundry /'sʌndrɪ/ *adj.* разный, различный; **all and** ~ всё и вся; все без исключения

sung /sʌŋ/ *p.p. of* ▶ sing

sunk /sʌŋk/ *past and p.p. of* ▶ sink

sunken /'sʌŋkən/ *adj.* (of cheeks etc.) впалый; (submerged) подводный

Sunni /'sʊnɪ/ *n.* суннит

sunny /'sʌnɪ/ *adj.* (**sunnier, sunniest**) солнечный; **a** ~ **disposition** жизнерадостный характер

super /'su:pə(r)/ *adj.* замечательный, превосходный

superb /su:'pɜ:b/ *adj.* превосходный, великолепный

supercilious /su:pə'sɪlɪəs/ *adj.* высокомерный

superficial /su:pə'fɪʃ(ə)l/ *adj.* поверхностный

superficiality /su:pəfɪʃɪ'ælɪtɪ/ *n.* поверхностность

superfluous /su:'pɜ:fluəs/ *adj.* излишний

superhuman /su:pə'hju:mən/ *adj.* сверхчеловеческий

superimpose /su:pərɪm'pəʊz/ *v.t.* на|кладывать, -ложить (*что на что*)

superinjunction /su:pərɪn'dʒʌnkʃ(ə)n/ *n.* суперзапрет (*судебное решение, запрещающее разглашать некую информацию, а также упоминать сам факт существования запрета*)

superintendent /su:pərɪn'tend(ə)nt/ *n.* (manager) заведующий; (of police) начальник; (AmE, of a building) комендант

ⸯ **superior** /su:'pɪərɪə(r)/ *n.* старший, начальник
● *adj.* **1** (of higher rank) старший, высший **2** (better) превосходный, превосходящий **3** (supercilious): **a** ~ **smile** презрительная улыбка; **don't look so** ~! бросьте эту вашу

S

высокоме́рную мане́ру!

superiority /suːˌpɪərɪˈɒrɪtɪ/ n. старшинство́

superlative /suːˈpɜːlətɪv/ n. (gram.) превосхо́дная сте́пень
● adj. величайший, высо́чайший

superman /ˈsuːpəmæn/ n. (pl. **supermen**) сверхчелове́к, супермен

supermarket /ˈsuːpəmɑːkɪt/ n. суперма́ркет

supermodel /ˈsuːpəmɒd(ə)l/ n. супермоде́ль

supernatural /suːpəˈnætʃər(ə)l/ n.: a belief in the ~ ве́ра в сверхъесте́ственное
● adj. сверхъесте́ственный

superpower /ˈsuːpəpaʊə(r)/ n. сверхдержа́ва

supersede /suːpəˈsiːd/ v.t. сменя́ть, -и́ть

supersonic /suːpəˈsɒnɪk/ adj. сверхзвуково́й

superstar /ˈsuːpəstɑː(r)/ n. суперзвезда́

superstition /suːpəˈstɪʃ(ə)n/ n. суеве́рие

superstitious /suːpəˈstɪʃəs/ adj. суеве́рный

superstore /ˈsuːpəstɔː(r)/ n. гиперма́ркет

superstructure /ˈsuːpəstrʌktʃə(r)/ n. надстро́йка

supervise /ˈsuːpəvaɪz/ v.t. надзира́ть (impf.) за + i.

supervision /suːpəˈvɪʒ(ə)n/ n. надсмо́тр/ надзо́р (of: за + i.)

supervisor /ˈsuːpəvaɪzə(r)/ n. надсмо́трщи|к (-ца); (academic) (нау́чный) руководи́тель

supervisory /suːpəˈvaɪzərɪ/ adj. контро́льный, надзира́ющий; ~ body контро́льный о́рган; ~ duties обя́занности по надзо́ру

supine /ˈsuːpaɪn/ adj. (face up) лежа́щий на́взничь; (fig.) безде́ятельный, ине́ртный, вя́лый

supper /ˈsʌpə(r)/ n. у́жин; have ~ у́жинать, по-

supplant /səˈplɑːnt/ v.t. (replace) вытесня́ть, вы́теснить; (oust) выжива́ть, вы́жить

supple /ˈsʌp(ə)l/ adj. (**suppler, supplest**) ги́бкий

supplement[1] /ˈsʌplɪmənt/ n. 1 (dietary) доба́вка 2 (of book etc.) дополне́ние 3 (surcharge) допла́та

supplement[2] /ˈsʌplɪment/ v.t. доп|олня́ть, -о́лнить

supplementary /sʌplɪˈmentərɪ/ adj. дополни́тельный, доба́вочный

supplier /səˈplaɪə(r)/ n. поставщи́|к (-ца)

♂ **suppl|y** /səˈplaɪ/ n. 1 (providing) снабже́ние (чем) 2 (thing supplied, stock) запа́с; take, lay in a ~y of sth запаса́ться, -ти́сь чем-н.; bread is in short ~y хлеб в дефици́те; ~ies (mil.) (бое)припа́сы (m. pl.) 3 (econ.) предложе́ние; ~y and demand спро́с и предложе́ние
● v.t. 1 (furnish, equip) снаб|жа́ть, -ди́ть; обеспе́чи|вать, -ть (both кого/чем чем); пита́ть (impf.) 2 (give, yield) да|ва́ть, -ть; дост|авля́ть, -а́вить (что кому/чему); cows ~y milk коро́вы даю́т молоко́
■ ~y teacher n. (BrE) внешта́тный учи́тель, рабо́тающ|ий (-ая -ница, -ая) по замеще́нию

♂ **support** /səˈpɔːt/ n. подде́ржка; give, lend ~

оказ|ывать, -а́ть подде́ржку + d.; in ~ of в подде́ржку + g.
● v.t. 1 (hold up) подде́рж|ивать, -а́ть; подп|ира́ть, -ере́ть; (fig., assist): which party do you ~? каку́ю па́ртию вы подде́рживаете? 2 (provide subsistence for) содержа́ть (impf.); he cannot ~ a family он не в состоя́нии содержа́ть семью́ 3 (confirm) подкреп|ля́ть, -и́ть 4 (a particular sports team) боле́ть (impf.) за + a.
■ ~ing actor n. актёр (-ри́са) второ́го пла́на

♂ **supporter** /səˈpɔːtə(r)/ n. (of cause, motion, etc.) сторо́нни|к (-ца), приве́рженец; (BrE, of sports team) боле́льщи|к (-ца)

supportive /səˈpɔːtɪv/ adj. подде́рживающий, лоя́льный

♂ **suppose** /səˈpəʊz/ v.t. 1 (assume) предпол|ага́ть, -ожи́ть; допус|ка́ть, -ти́ть; supposing he came, what would you say? е́сли бы он пришёл, что бы вы сказа́ли?; ~ they find out? а вдруг они́ узна́ют? 2 (imagine, believe): he is ~d to be rich счита́ется/говоря́т, что он бога́т 3 (pass.) (be expected): this is ~d to help you sleep э́то должно́ помо́чь вам засну́ть; he is ~d to wash the dishes ему́ поло́жено мыть посу́ду

supposedly /səˈpəʊzɪdlɪ/ adv. предположи́тельно

supposition /sʌpəˈzɪʃ(ə)n/ n. предположе́ние, гипо́теза, дога́дка

suppository /səˈpɒzɪtərɪ/ n. (med.) суппозито́рий, свеча́

suppress /səˈpres/ v.t. 1 (prevent; restrain) подав|ля́ть, -и́ть; сде́рж|ивать, -а́ть 2 (conceal) скры|ва́ть, -ть; they succeeded in ~ing the truth им удало́сь скрыть пра́вду

suppression /səˈpreʃ(ə)n/ n. (restraining) подавле́ние, сде́рживание; (banning) запреще́ние; (silencing) зама́лчивание

supremacy /suːˈpreməsɪ/ n. госпо́дство, превосхо́дство

supreme /suːˈpriːm/ adj. 1 (of authority) верхо́вный 2 (greatest): he made the ~ sacrifice он поже́ртвовал (свое́й) жи́знью

surcharge /ˈsɜːtʃɑːdʒ/ n. допла́та, припла́та

♂ **sure** /ʃɔː(r)/ adj. 1 (certain, confident) уве́ренный, убеждённый; he is very ~ of himself он о́чень уве́рен в себе́; I'm ~ you are right я уве́рен (or не сомнева́юсь), что вы пра́вы; I'm not ~ whether to go or not я не зна́ю, пойти́ и́ли нет 2 (safe) ве́рный, надёжный; there can be no ~ proof абсолю́тных доказа́тельств не мо́жет быть 3 (with inf., certain, to be relied on): he is ~ to come он непреме́нно придёт; it is ~ to be wet нависня́ка бу́дет дождли́во
4: for ~ несомне́нно, непреме́нно; то́чно, наверняка́ 5: make ~ (convince, satisfy oneself) убежда́ться, -ди́ться; удостов|еря́ться, -е́риться (all в чём) 6: I made ~ (sc. ensured) that he would come я позабо́тился о том, что́бы он (обяза́тельно) пришёл
● adv.: ~ enough действи́тельно, конечно
■ ~-fire adj. (infml) ве́рный, надёжный

♂ **surely** /ˈʃɔːlɪ/ adv. 1 (without doubt)

несомне́нно, ве́рно, наверняка́ **2** (expr. strong hope or belief): ∼ **I have met you before** я уве́рен, что мы с ва́ми встреча́лись

surf /səːf/ *n.* прибо́й
- *v.i.* занима́ться (*impf.*) сёрфингом
- *v.t.:* ∼ **the Internet** путеше́ствовать (*impf.*) по Интерне́ту
- ∼**board** *n.* доска́ для сёрфинга

surface /'səːfɪs/ *n.* пове́рхность; **his politeness is only on the** ∼ его́ ве́жливость чи́сто вне́шняя/показна́я
- *v.t.:* ∼ **a road** покр|ыва́ть, -ы́ть доро́гу асфа́льтом *и т. п.*
- *v.i.* вспл|ыва́ть, -ы́ть на пове́рхность

surfeit /'səːfɪt/ *n.* (excess of eating etc.) изли́шество, избы́ток; (repletion, satiety, also fig.) пресыще́ние
- *v.t.* (**surfeited, surfeiting**) (satiate) прес|ыща́ть, -ы́тить

surfer /'səːfə(r)/ *n.* сёрфинги́ст (-ка); челове́к, занима́ющийся сёрфингом

surfing /'səːfɪŋ/ *n.* сёрфинг

surge /səːdʒ/ *n.* (of waves, water) во́лны (*f. pl.*); вал; (of crowd, emotion, etc.) волна́, прили́в; (of elec. current) и́мпульс
- *v.i.* **1** (of waves, water) вздыма́ться (*impf.*) **2** (of crowd): **the crowd** ∼**d forward** толпа́ подала́сь вперёд **3** (of emotions) нахлы́нуть (*pf.*)

surgeon /'səːdʒ(ə)n/ *n.* хиру́рг

surgery /'səːdʒərɪ/ *n.* **1** (operation) опера́ция **2** (BrE, office) приёмная/кабине́т (врача́); **the doctor holds a** ∼ **every morning** врач принима́ет ка́ждое у́тро

surgical /'səːdʒɪk(ə)l/ *adj.* хирурги́ческий
- ∼ **spirit** *n.* медици́нский спирт

surly /'səːlɪ/ *adj.* (**surlier, surliest**) неприве́тливый

surmise /sə'maɪz/ *n.* (conjecture) дога́дка; (supposition) предположе́ние
- *v.i.* предпол|ага́ть, -ожи́ть

surmount /sə'maʊnt/ *v.t.* (overcome) преодол|ева́ть, -е́ть

surmountable /sə'maʊntəb(ə)l/ *adj.* преодоли́мый

surname /'səːneɪm/ *n.* фами́лия

surpass /sə'pɑːs/ *v.t.* прев|осходи́ть, -зойти́

surplice /'səːplɪs/ *n.* стиха́рь (*m.*) (*дли́нное одея́ние с широ́кими рукава́ми, надева́емое свяще́нниками на вре́мя слу́жбы*)

surplus /'səːpləs/ *n.* изли́шек
- *adj.* изли́шний, избы́точный

surprise /sə'praɪz/ *n.* **1** (astonishment) удивле́ние **2** (unexpected news, gift, etc.) неожи́данность, сюрпри́з **3** (unexpected action): **catch, take sb by** ∼ заст|ига́ть, -и́чь кого́-н. враспло́х
- *v.t.* **1** (astonish) удив|ля́ть, -и́ть; **I was** ∼**d to hear you had been ill** я с удивле́нием узна́л, что вы бы́ли больны́ **2** (capture by ∼) захва́т|ывать, -и́ть враспло́х; **we** ∼**d him in the act of stealing** мы пойма́ли

его́ с поли́чным на воровстве́ (*or* при соверше́нии кра́жи)

surprising /sə'praɪzɪŋ/ *adj.* удиви́тельный, порази́тельный; **he eats** ∼**ly little** он удиви́тельно/на удивле́ние ма́ло ест

surreal /sə'rɪəl/ *adj.* сюрреалисти́ческий

surrealism /sə'rɪəlɪz(ə)m/ *n.* сюрреали́зм

surrealist /sə'rɪəlɪst/ *n.* сюрреали́ст
- *adj.* сюрреалисти́ческий

surrender /sə'rendə(r)/ *n.* (handing over) сда́ча; (giving up) отка́з (**of:** от + *g.*); (capitulation) капитуля́ция
- *v.t.* **1** (yield) сда|ва́ть, -ть **2** (give up) отка́з|ываться, -а́ться от + *g.*
- *v.i.* сд|ава́ться, -а́ться; капитули́ровать (*impf., pf.*)

surreptitious /sʌrəp'tɪʃəs/ *adj.* та́йный

surrogate /'sʌrəgət/ *n.* суррога́т
- ∼ **mother** *n.* суррога́тная мать

surround /sə'raʊnd/ *v.t.* окруж|а́ть, -и́ть; **the** ∼**ing countryside** окре́стности (*f. pl.*)

surroundings /sə'raʊndɪŋz/ *n. pl.* ме́стность, окре́стности (*f. pl.*); обстано́вка

surveillance /sə'veɪləns/ *n.* надзо́р
- ∼ **camera** *n.* ка́мера скры́того наблюде́ния

survey¹ /'səːveɪ/ *n.* **1** (inspection, investigation) иссле́дование, обсле́дование; (BrE, of building) оце́нка состоя́ния до́ма/зда́ния; (by asking questions) опро́с **2** (of land) съёмка, проме́р

survey² /sə'veɪ/ *v.t.* **1** (view) обозр|ева́ть, -е́ть **2** (inspect) осм|а́тривать, -отре́ть **3** (land etc.) межева́ть (*impf.*); произв|оди́ть, -ести́ съёмку + *g.*

surveyor /sə'veɪə(r)/ *n.* **1** (BrE, of houses) строи́тельный инспе́ктор **2** (of land etc.) землеме́р

survival /sə'vaɪv(ə)l/ *n.* выжива́ние

survive /sə'vaɪv/ *v.t.* **1** (outlive) переж|ива́ть, -и́ть (*во вре́мени*) **2** (come alive through): ∼ **an illness** перен|оси́ть, -ести́ боле́знь
- *v.i.* выжива́ть, вы́жить; (be preserved) сохран|я́ться, уцеле́ть (*both pf.*); **the custom still** ∼**s** э́тот обы́чай ещё сохрани́лся

survivor /sə'vaɪvə(r)/ *n.* оста́вшийся в живы́х, уцеле́вший

susceptible /sə'septɪb(ə)l/ *adj.*: ∼ **to** восприи́мчивый к + *d.*; **he is** ∼ **to colds** он подве́ржен просту́де

suspect¹ /'sʌspekt/ *n.* подозрева́емый
- *adj.* подозри́тельный; не внуша́ющий дове́рия

suspect² /sə'spekt/ *v.t.* **1** подозрева́ть (*impf.*); **I** ∼**ed him to be lying** я подозрева́л, что он лжёт **2** (doubt) сомнева́ться, усомни́ться в + *p.*

suspend /sə'spend/ *v.t.* **1** (hang up) подве́|шивать, -сить **2** (stop for a time) приостан|а́вливать, -ови́ть; ∼**ed sentence** усло́вное осужде́ние/наказа́ние **3** (from office etc.) вре́менно отстран|я́ть, -и́ть

suspender /sə'spendə(r)/ *n.* (AmE) (*in pl.*) (braces) подтя́ж|ки (-ек)
- ∼ **belt** *n.* (BrE) (же́нский) по́яс с подвя́зками

---

suspense /sə'spens/ *n.* напряже́ние, напряжённость; **keep sb in ~** держа́ть (*impf.*) кого́-н. в неизве́стности

suspension /sə'spenʃ(ə)n/ *n.* **1** (stoppage) приостановле́ние **2** (from office etc.) отстране́ние

suspicion /sə'spɪʃ(ə)n/ *n.* подозре́ние; **arouse ~** возбужда́ть, -ди́ть подозре́ния

suspicious /sə'spɪʃəs/ *adj.* **1** (mistrustful) подозри́тельный, недове́рчивый (**towards, of:** к + *d.*) **2** (arousing suspicion) подозри́тельный

suss /sʌs/ *v.t.* (BrE, infml): **she's got him ~ed** она́ его́ раскуси́ла; **he ~ed out the best route** он разузна́л лу́чший маршру́т

sustain /sə'steɪn/ *v.t.* **1** (lit., fig., support) подде́рж|ивать, -а́ть **2** (suffer) нести́, по-; **the enemy ~ed heavy losses** проти́вник понёс тяжёлые поте́ри; **~ an injury** перен|оси́ть, -ести́ тра́вму; получ|а́ть, -и́ть уве́чье **3** (maintain): **~ one's efforts** не ослабля́ть (*impf.*) уси́лий

sustainability /səsteɪnə'bɪlɪtɪ/ *n.* усто́йчивость

sustenance /'sʌstɪnəns/ *n.* пита́ние, пи́ща

suture /'su:tʃə(r)/ *n.* (med.) шов

swab /swɒb/ *n.* (med.) тампо́н

swagger /'swægə(r)/ *v.i.* расха́живать (*impf.*) с ва́жным ви́дом

Swahili /swə'hi:lɪ/ *n.* (pl. **~**) (language, people) суахи́ли (*m. indecl.*)

swallow¹ /'swɒləʊ/ *n.* (bird) ла́сточка

swallow² /'swɒləʊ/ *n.* (gulp) глото́к
 • *v.t.* прогл|а́тывать, -оти́ть; загл|а́тывать, -оти́ть; **he had to ~ his pride** ему́ пришло́сь поступи́ться свои́м самолю́бием
 • *v.i.* глота́ть (*impf.*)

swam /swæm/ *past of* ▶ **swim**

swamp /swɒmp/ *n.* боло́то
 • *v.t.* **1** (with water) зал|ива́ть, -и́ть **2** (fig., overwhelm): **we were ~ed with applications** мы бы́ли зава́лены заявле́ниями

swampy /'swɒmpɪ/ *adj.* (**swampier, swampiest**) боло́тистый

swan /swɒn/ *n.* ле́бедь (*m.*)

swank /swæŋk/ *n.* (infml) показу́ха
 • *v.i.*: **~ about sth** хва́стать (*impf.*) чем-н.

swanky /'swæŋkɪ/ *adj.* (**swankier, swankiest**) (infml) шика́рный

swap, swop /swɒp/ *n.* обме́н
 • *v.t.* (**swapped, swapping** *or* **swopped, swopping**) (sth for sth else) меня́ть, по- (**for:** на + *a.*); **he ~ped his car for a motorbike** он поменя́л маши́ну на мотоци́кл; (exchange with sb else) меня́ться, по- + *i.* (with sb: с + *i.*); **will you ~ places with me?** вы не поменя́етесь со мной места́ми?

swarm /swɔ:m/ *n.*: **~ of ants/bees** мураьи́ный/пчели́ный рой
 • *v.i.* **1** (of bees, ants, etc.) рои́ться (*impf.*) **2** (of people): **children ~ed around him** де́ти столпи́лись вокру́г него́ **3** (teem) кише́ть (*impf.*) + *i.*; **the town is ~ing with tourists** го́род наводнён тури́стами

swarthy /'swɔ:ðɪ/ *adj.* (**swarthier, swarthiest**) сму́глый

swastika /'swɒstɪkə/ *n.* сва́стика

swat /swɒt/ *v.t.* (**swatted, swatting**) (an insect) прихло́пнуть (*pf.*)

swathe /sweɪð/ *v.t.* (wrap) **~d in bandages** обмо́танный бинта́ми; **~d in blankets** заку́танный одея́лами

sway /sweɪ/ *n.*: **have, hold ~ over sb** держа́ть (*impf.*) кого́-н. в подчине́нии
 • *v.t.* **1** (rock) кача́ть, -ну́ть **2** (influence) влия́ть, по-; колеба́ть, по-
 • *v.i.* кача́ться, качну́ться

swear /sweə(r)/ *v.t. & i.* (*past* **swore**, *p.p.* **sworn**) **1** (promise) кля́сться, по-; **they swore eternal friendship** они́ покляли́сь в ве́чной дру́жбе **2** (bind by an oath) прив|оди́ть, -ести́ к прися́ге; **the jury was sworn in** прися́жных привели́ к прися́ге; **he was sworn to secrecy** с него́ взя́ли кля́тву о неразглаше́нии та́йны; **sworn enemies** закля́тые враги́
 • *v.i.* (*past* **swore**, *p.p.* **sworn**) **1** (take an oath) кля́сться, по-; (fig.): **he ~s by aspirin** он (безгранично) ве́рит в по́льзу аспири́на **2** (curse) брани́ться (*impf.*); руга́ться (*impf.*)
 ■ **~ word** *n.* руга́тельство

swearing /'sweərɪŋ/ *n.* брань, руга́нь

sweat /swet/ *n.* **1** пот, испа́рина **2** (state of ~ing) потѐ́ние, пот; **a cold ~** холо́дный пот
 • *v.i.* (*past and p.p.* **sweated** *or* AmE **~**) потѐ́ть, вс-
 ■ **~shirt** *n.* хлопчатобума́жный (спорти́вный) сви́тер, толсто́вка

sweater /'swetə(r)/ *n.* сви́тер

sweaty /'swetɪ/ *adj.* (**sweatier, sweatiest**): **~ hands** по́тные ру́ки

Swede /swi:d/ *n.* (person) швед (-ка); (**s~**) (BrE, vegetable) брю́ква

Sweden /'swi:d(ə)n/ *n.* Шве́ция

Swedish /'swi:dɪʃ/ *n.* (language) шве́дский язы́к
 • *adj.* шве́дский

sweep /swi:p/ *n.* **1** (with broom etc.): **give a room a good ~** хороше́нько подме|та́ть, -сти́ ко́мнату **2** (~ing movement) взмах, разма́х **3** (long flowing curve) изги́б **4** (*in full* **chimney ~**) трубочи́ст
 • *v.t.* (*past and p.p.* **swept**) **1** (rush over): **the waves swept the shore** во́лны набега́ли на бе́рег **2** (carry forcefully): **a wave swept him overboard** его́ смы́ло волно́й (за́ борт); **he swept her off her feet** (fig.) он вскружи́л ей го́лову **3** (clean, brush) подме|та́ть, -сти́; чи́стить, вы́-; **he swept the litter into a corner** он замёл му́сор в у́гол; **~ a chimney** проч|ища́ть, -и́стить трубу́; (fig.): **~ sth under the carpet** заме|та́ть, -сти́ что-н. под ковёр
 • *v.i.* (*past and p.p.* **swept**) **1** (rush, dash) прон|оси́ться, -ести́сь; **rain swept across the country** дождь прошёл по всей стране́; **fear swept over him** страх охвати́л его́ **2** (walk majestically): **she swept into the room** она́

S

го́рдо вошла́ в ко́мнату **3** (brush) мести́, под-; подме|та́ть, -сти́

□ ~ **aside** v.t.: he swept aside my protestations он не стал слу́шать мои́х возраже́ний

□ ~ **away** v.t. сме|та́ть, -сти́; the storm swept everything away бу́ря всё смела́

□ ~ **up** v.t.: be sure and ~ up all the dirt смотри́те, вы́метите весь му́сор как сле́дует

• v.i.: I had to ~ up after them мне пришло́сь по́сле них убира́ть

sweeping /'swi:pɪŋ/ adj. (comprehensive) всеобъе́млющий; ~ **changes** радика́льные измене́ния; (too general): a ~ **statement** огу́льное утвержде́ние

⚘ **sweet** /swi:t/ n. **1** (BrE, piece of confectionery) конфе́та **2** (BrE, dessert) сла́дкое, тре́тье

• adj. **1** (to taste) сла́дкий; my brother has a ~ **tooth** мой брат — сладкое́жка (c.g.) **2** (fragrant) сла́дкий, души́стый; how ~ the roses smell! как сла́дко па́хнут ро́зы! **3** (infml, charming, nice) ми́лый; a ~ **little dog** симпати́чная соба́чка

■ ~**-and-sour** adj. ки́сло-сла́дкий; ~**corn** n. (столо́вая) кукуру́за; ~**heart** n. возлю́бленн|ый (-ая); (as form of address) дорого́й, ми́лый, люби́мый; ~ **talk** n. (infml) лесть; ~**-talk** v.t. (infml) загов|а́ривать, -ори́ть кому́-н. зу́бы

sweeten /'swi:t(ə)n/ v.t. подсла́|щивать, -сти́ть

sweetener /'swi:tənə(r)/ n. (sugar substitute) замени́тель (m.) са́хара; (BrE, bribe) взя́тка

swell /swel/ n. (of sea) зыбь

• v.t. (p.p. **swollen** or **swelled**) **1** (increase size of) разд|ува́ть, -у́ть; my finger is swollen у меня́ па́лец опу́х/распу́х **2** (increase number of) увели́чи|вать, -ть

• v.i. (p.p. **swollen** or **swelled**) **1** (expand, dilate) (also ~ **up**) над|ува́ться, -у́ться; (of part of body) оп|уха́ть, -у́хнуть **2** (increase in size or volume) выраста́ть, вы́расти; the crowd ~ed to over six thousand толпа́ увели́чилась до шести́ с ли́шним ты́сяч (челове́к)

swelling /'swelɪŋ/ n. о́пухоль

sweltering /'sweltərɪŋ/ adj. нестерпи́мо жа́ркий

s **swept** /swept/ past and p.p. of ▶ sweep

swerve /swə:v/ v.i. (кру́то) пов|ора́чиваться, -ерну́ться

swift /swɪft/ n. (bird) стриж

• adj. (rapid) бы́стрый; (prompt) ско́рый

swig /swɪɡ/ (infml) n. глото́к

• v.t. (**swigged, swigging**) хлеба́ть (impf.)

swill /swɪl/ n. по́йло; (pig food) помо́|и (-ев)

• v.t. **1** (BrE, wash, rinse) мыть, вы́-; полоска́ть, вы́- **2** (drink heavily) лака́ть, вы́-, хлеба́ть, вы́-, хлеста́ть, вы́- (all infml)

swim /swɪm/ n.: have, go for a ~ купа́ться, ис-

• v.i. (**swimming**, past **swam**, p.p. **swum**) **1** (cross by ~ming) перепл|ыва́ть, -ы́ть **2** (cover by ~ming): ~ a mile пропл|ыва́ть, -ы́ть ми́лю

• v.i. (**swimming**, past **swam**, p.p. **swum**) **1** пла́вать (indet.), плыть (det.), по- **2** (fig., swirl): everything was ~ming before my eyes всё поплы́ло у меня́ пе́ред глаза́ми

■ ~**suit** n. купа́льник

swimmer /'swɪmə(r)/ n. плов|е́ц (-чи́ха)

swimming /'swɪmɪŋ/ n. пла́вание

■ ~ **bath** (BrE), ~ **pool** nn. (пла́вательный) бассе́йн

swindle /'swɪnd(ə)l/ n. моше́нничество

• v.t. обма́н|ывать, -у́ть; ~ **money out of sb** выма́нивать, вы́манить у кого́-н. де́ньги

swindler /'swɪndlə(r)/ n. моше́нник

swine /swaɪn/ n. (pl. ~, also (fig.) ~**s**) (lit., fig.) свинья́

swing /swɪŋ/ n. **1** (movement) кача́ние, колеба́ние; in full ~ (fig.) в (по́лном) разга́ре **2** (shift): the polls showed a ~ to the left вы́боры показа́ли ре́зкое увеличе́ние популя́рности «ле́вых» **3** (rhythm) ритм; I can't get into the ~ of things я ника́к не мог включи́ться в де́ло **4** (seat on rope) каче́л|и (-ей)

• v.t. (past and p.p. **swung**) **1** (apply circular motion to): ~ **one's arms** разма́хивать (impf.) рука́ми **2** (cause to turn) пов|ора́чивать, -ерну́ть; разв|ора́чивать, -ерну́ть

• v.i. (past and p.p. **swung**) **1** (sway) кача́ться (impf.), колеба́ться (impf.); (dangle) висе́ть, свиса́ть, болта́ться (all impf.) **2** (turn) пов|ора́чиваться, -ерну́ться; враща́ться (impf.); the door swung open in the wind дверь распахну́лась от ве́тра

■ ~ **doors**, ~**ing doors** (AmE) nn. pl. свобо́дно распа́хивающаяся (двуство́рчатая) дверь

swingeing /'swɪndʒɪŋ/ adj. (BrE): a ~ **blow** ошеломля́ющий уда́р; a ~ **majority** подавля́ющее большинство́; a ~ **fine** грома́дный/огро́мный/ штраф

swipe /swaɪp/ v.t. (infml) (hit) с си́лой уд|аря́ть, -а́рить по + d.; (steal) стащи́ть (pf.)

■ ~ **card** n. магни́тная ка́рточка

swirl /swə:l/ v.i. (of water) крути́ться (impf.) в водоворо́те; (of snow) ви́хриться (impf.); (of leaves etc.) кружи́ться, за-

Swiss /swɪs/ n. (pl. ~) швейца́р|ец (-ка)

• adj. швейца́рский

⚘ **switch** /swɪtʃ/ n. **1** (elec.) выключа́тель (m.), переключа́тель (m.) **2** (change) поворо́т, переме́на

• v.t. (transfer) перев|оди́ть, -ести́; переключ|а́ть, -и́ть

• v.i.: he ~ed from one extreme to the other он перешёл/бро́сился из одно́й кра́йности в другу́ю

□ ~ **off** v.t. выключа́ть, вы́ключить; ~ off a lamp гаси́ть, по- ла́мпу

□ ~ **on** v.t. включ|а́ть, -и́ть; (light) заж|ига́ть, -е́чь

■ ~**board** n. коммута́тор; ~**board operator** телефони́ст (-ка)

Switzerland /'swɪtsələnd/ n. Швейца́рия

swivel /'swɪv(ə)l/ v.t. & i. (**swivelled, swivelling**, AmE **swiveled, swiveling**) пов|ора́чивать(ся), -ерну́ть(ся) (на

⚘ ключева́я ле́ксика

шарни́рах)

swollen /'swəʊlən/ *p.p. of* ▶ swell

swoop /swuːp/ *v.i.* (aeron.) пики́ровать,
с-; **the eagle ~ed (down) on its prey** орёл
стреми́тельно упа́л на свою́ же́ртву;
the enemy ~ed on the town неприя́тель
соверши́л внеза́пный налёт на го́род

swop /swɒp/ *n. & v.t.* = swap

sword /sɔːd/ *n.* (cutting weapon) меч; (light thrust
weapon) шпа́га

swore /swɔː(r)/ *past of* ▶ swear

sworn /swɔːn/ *p.p. of* ▶ swear

swot /swɒt/ (BrE) *n.* зубри́ла (*c.g.*)
• *v.i.* (**swotted, swotting**) зубри́ть (*impf.*)

swum /swʌm/ *p.p. of* ▶ swim

swung /swʌŋ/ *past and p.p. of* ▶ swing

sycamore /'sɪkəmɔː(r)/ *n.* я́вор

sycophantic /ˌsɪkə'fæntɪk/ *adj.* подхали́мский,
льсти́вый

Sydney /'sɪdnɪ/ *n.* Си́дней

syllable /'sɪləb(ə)l/ *n.* слог

syllabus /'sɪləbəs/ *n.* програ́мма (*учебная*)

symbiosis /ˌsɪmbaɪ'əʊsɪs/ *n.* симбио́з

symbol /'sɪmb(ə)l/ *n.* си́мвол; (sign, e.g. math.) знак

symbolic /sɪm'bɒlɪk/ *adj.* символи́ческий,
символи́чный

symbolism /'sɪmbəlɪz(ə)m/ *n.* символи́зм

symbolize /'sɪmbəlaɪz/ *v.t.* символизи́ровать
(*impf., pf.*)

symmetrical /sɪ'metrɪk(ə)l/ *adj.*
симметри́чный

symmetry /'sɪmɪtrɪ/ *n.* симме́трия

sympathetic /ˌsɪmpə'θetɪk/ *adj.*
1 (compassionate) сочу́вственный
2 (supportive): **I am ~ towards his ideas** его́
иде́и мне близки́

sympathize /'sɪmpəθaɪz/ *v.i.* сочу́вствовать
(*impf.*) (**with:** + *d.*)

sympathizer /'sɪmpəθaɪzə(r)/ *n.* сторо́нни|к
(-ца)

sympathy /'sɪmpəθɪ/ *n.* (compassion)
сочу́вствие, сострада́ние; (agreement)
согла́сие; **the power workers came out in ~**
рабо́тники электроста́нции забастова́ли в
знак солида́рности

symphony /'sɪmfənɪ/ *n.* симфо́ния

■ **~ concert** *n.* симфони́ческий конце́рт; **~
orchestra** *n.* симфони́ческий орке́стр

symposi|um /sɪm'pəʊzɪəm/ *n.* (*pl.* **~a** *or*
~ums) симпо́зиум

◆ **symptom** /'sɪmptəm/ *n.* симпто́м

symptomatic /ˌsɪmptə'mætɪk/ *adj.*
симптомати́чный, симптомати́ческий

synagogue /'sɪnəgɒg/ *n.* синаго́га

sync /sɪŋk/ *n.* (infml): **out of ~** несинхро́нный

synchronize /'sɪŋkrənaɪz/ *v.t.*
синхронизи́ровать (*impf., pf.*)

■ **~d swimming** *n.* синхро́нное пла́вание

syncopation /ˌsɪŋkə'peɪʃ(ə)n/ *n.* синко́па

syndicate /'sɪndɪkət/ *n.* синдика́т

syndrome /'sɪndrəʊm/ *n.* синдро́м

synonym /'sɪnənɪm/ *n.* сино́ним

synonymous /sɪ'nɒnɪməs/ *adj.* (fig.)
равнозна́чный (**with:** + *d.*)

synopsis /sɪ'nɒpsɪs/ *n.* (*pl.* **synopses** /-siːz/)
резюме́ (*nt. indecl.*)

syntax /'sɪntæks/ *n.* си́нтаксис

synthesis /'sɪnθɪsɪs/ *n.* (*pl.* **syntheses** /-siːz/)
си́нтез

synthesize /'sɪnθɪsaɪz/ *v.t.* синтези́ровать
(*impf., pf.*)

synthesizer /'sɪnθɪsaɪzə(r)/ *n.* синтеза́тор

synthetic /sɪn'θetɪk/ *adj.* синтети́ческий
• *n.* (*usu. in pl.*) синте́тика (*collect.*)

syphilis /'sɪfɪlɪs/ *n.* си́филис

Syria /'sɪrɪə/ *n.* Си́рия

Syrian /'sɪrɪən/ *n.* сири́|ец (-йка)
• *adj.* сири́йский

syringe /sɪ'rɪndʒ/ *n.* шприц

syrup /'sɪrəp/ *n.* (juice) сиро́п; (treacle) па́тока;
golden ~ све́тлая па́тока

◆ **system** /'sɪstəm/ *n.* **1** (complex; method)
систе́ма **2** (network) сеть **3** (body as a whole)
органи́зм; **get sth out of one's ~** (fig.)
изб|авля́ться, -а́виться от чего́-н.

■ **~s analysis** *n.* систе́мный ана́лиз; **~s
analyst** *n.* систе́мный анали́тик

systematic /ˌsɪstə'mætɪk/ *adj.*
системати́ческий

systemic /sɪ'stemɪk/ *adj.* относя́щийся ко
всему́ органи́зму, сомати́ческий; **~ poison**
общеядови́тое отравля́ющее вещество́

S

Tt

tab /tæb/ *n.* **1** (projecting flap) ушко́ **2** (infml, check): **the police are keeping ~s on him** поли́ция присма́тривает за ним

⚬ **table** /'teɪb(ə)l/ *n.* **1** стол **2** (arrangement of data) табли́ца
● *v.t.* **1** (BrE, present for discussion) ста́вить, по- на обсужде́ние **2** (AmE, postpone) от|кла́дывать, -ложи́ть
■ **~cloth** *n.* ска́терть; **~ mat** *n.* (BrE) подста́вка (*под тарелку и т. п.*); **~spoon** *n.* столо́вая ло́жка; **~ tennis** *n.* насто́льный те́ннис, пинг-по́нг

tablet /'tæblɪt/ *n.* **1** табле́тка **2** (comput.) пла́ншетный компью́тер, планше́т

tabloid /'tæblɔɪd/ *n.* табло́ид; **the ~s** бульва́рная пре́сса

taboo /tə'buː/ *n.* табу́ (*nt. indecl.*)

tacit /'tæsɪt/ *adj.* молчали́вый (*согласие, одобрение*)

taciturn /'tæsɪtə:n/ *adj.* неразгово́рчивый, молчали́вый

taciturnity /ˌtæsɪ'tə:nɪtɪ/ *n.* неразгово́рчивость, молчали́вость

tack /tæk/ *n.* **1** (small nail) гво́здик **2** (fig.): **he is on the wrong ~** он на ло́жном пути́
● *v.t.* **1** (fasten) прикреп|ля́ть, -и́ть гво́здиками **2** (stitch) намёт|ывать, -а́ть **3**: **~ on** (fig., add) доб|авля́ть, -а́вить

tackle /'tæk(ə)l/ *n.* **1** (football) блокиро́вка **2**: **fishing ~** рыбол́овные сна́сти (*f. pl.*)
● *v.t.* (grapple with) бра́ться, взя́ться за + *a.*; **I ~d him on the subject** я по́днял э́тот вопро́с в разгово́ре с ним; (football) блоки́ровать (*impf., pf.*)

tacky[1] /'tækɪ/ *adj.* (**tackier, tackiest**) (sticky) ли́пкий, кле́йкий

tacky[2] /'tækɪ/ *adj.* (**tackier, tackiest**) (infml, tasteless) безвку́сный (*вульга́рный*)

tact /tækt/ *n.* такт

tactful /'tæktfʊl/ *adj.* такти́чный

tactic /'tæktɪk/ *n.* та́ктика; (*in pl.*) (mil.) та́ктика

tactical /'tæktɪk(ə)l/ *adj.* такти́ческий

tactician /tæk'tɪʃ(ə)n/ *n.* та́ктик

tactile /'tæktaɪl/ *adj.* осяза́тельный, такти́льный

tactless /'tæktlɪs/ *adj.* беста́ктный

tadpole /'tædpəʊl/ *n.* голова́стик

tag /tæg/ *n.* ярлы́к
● *v.i.* (**tagged, tagging**) (follow): **the children ~ged along behind** де́ти тащи́лись сза́ди; **to ~ along with sb** увя́з|ываться, -а́ться за кем-н.

Tahiti /tə'hi:tɪ/ *n.* Таи́ти (*m. indecl.*)

t'ai chi ch'uan /taɪ tʃi: 'tʃwɑːn/, **t'ai chi** /taɪ 'tʃi:/ *n.* тайцзицюа́нь (*f. indecl.*)

tail /teɪl/ *n.* **1** (of animal) хвост **2** (of a coin) ре́шка **3**: **~s** (coat) фрак
● *v.t.* (shadow) висе́ть (*impf.*) на хвосте́ у + *g.*
● *v.i.* уб|ыва́ть, -ы́ть; **the attendance figures ~ed off** посеща́емость упа́ла; **his voice ~ed away into silence** его́ го́лос (постепе́нно) зати́х
■ **~back** *n.* (BrE) дли́нная верени́ца автомоби́лей в про́бке; многокиломе́тровая про́бка

tailor /'teɪlə(r)/ *n.* портно́й
● *v.t.* (fig.) приспос|а́бливать, -о́бить; **his speech was ~ed to the situation** его́ речь была́ соста́влена с учётом ситуа́ции
■ **~-made** *adj.* (clothes) сде́ланный на зака́з; (fig.) подходя́щий

taint /teɪnt/ *v.t.* по́ртить, ис-; **~ed money** гря́зные де́ньги; **~ed reputation** подмо́ченная репута́ция

Taiwan /'taɪwɑːn/ *n.* Тайва́нь (*m.*)

Tajik /tɑː'dʒiːk/ *n.* **1** (person) таджи́к (-чка) **2** (language) таджи́кский язы́к
● *adj.* таджи́кский

Tajikistan /təˌdʒiːkɪ'stɑːn/ *n.* Таджикиста́н

⚬ **take** /teɪk/ *n.* (cin.) дубль (*m.*), монта́жный кадр
● *v.t.* (*past* **took**, *p.p.* **taken** /'teɪk(ə)n/) **1** (pick up, grasp) брать, взять; **he took her by the hand** он взял её за́ руку; **she took a coin out of her purse** она́ вы́нула моне́ту из кошелька́; **the last mile took it out of me** на после́дней ми́ле я вы́дохся **2** (capture) брать, взять; **he was ~n captive** его́ взя́ли в плен; (assume) прин|има́ть, -я́ть на себя́; **you must ~ the initiative** вы должны́ взять на себя́ инициати́ву; **he took control** он взял управле́ние в свои́ ру́ки; (win) выи́грывать, вы́играть; **she took first prize** она́ получи́ла пе́рвый приз **3** (acquire): **these seats are ~n** э́ти места́ за́няты; (in payment): **they took £50 in one evening** они́ вы́ручили 50 фу́нтов за оди́н ве́чер; (by enquiry or examination) определ|я́ть, -и́ть; **the doctor took my temperature** врач изме́рил мне температу́ру; (unlawfully): **the thieves took all her jewellery** во́ры забра́ли все её драгоце́нности **4** (avail oneself of): **please ~ a seat** пожа́луйста, сади́тесь; (travel by): **let's ~ a taxi** дава́йте возьмём такси́ **5** (accept) прин|има́ть, -я́ть; **will you ~ a cheque?** вы при́мете чек?; **will you ~ £50 for it?** вы отдади́те э́то за 50 фу́нтов?; **~ my advice!** послу́шайте меня́!; **I ~ responsibility** я беру́

на себя́ отве́тственность; **can't you ~ a joke?** вы что, шу́ток не понима́ете?; (receive) брать (*impf.*); **she ~s lessons in Spanish** она́ берёт уро́ки испа́нского языка́; (submit to): **when do you ~ your exams?** когда́ вы сдаёте экза́мены? **6** (use regularly) прин|има́ть, -я́ть; **he has begun to ~ drugs** он на́чал принима́ть нарко́тики; **do you ~ sugar in your tea?** вы пьёте чай с са́харом?; (of size in clothes): **I ~ a ten in shoes** у меня́ деся́тый разме́р о́буви **7** (make or obtain from original source): **may I ~ your photograph?** позво́льте мне вас сфотографи́ровать? **8** (convey) (on foot) отн|оси́ть, -ести́; (by transport) отв|ози́ть, -езти́; брать, взять; перед|ава́ть, -а́ть; **he was ~n to hospital** его́ отвезли́ в больни́цу **9** (require): **the job will ~ a long time** рабо́та займёт мно́го вре́мени; **how long does it ~ to get there?** ско́лько (вре́мени) туда́ добира́ться?; **it took us 3 hours to get there** нам потре́бовалось три часа́, что́бы добра́ться туда́; **he's got what it ~s** (infml) у него́ есть для э́того все зада́тки

● *v.i.* (*past* **took**, *p.p.* **taken** /'teɪk(ə)n/) **1** (~ effect; succeed): **the vaccination has not ~n** вакци́на не привила́сь **2** ~ **after** (resemble): **he ~s after his father** он похо́ж на (своего́) отца́ **3** ~ **to** (resort to) приб|ега́ть, -е́гнуть к + *d.*; **she took to her bed** она́ слегла́; **he took to drink** он за́пил; **he has ~n to getting up early** он стал ра́но встава́ть; (feel well disposed towards): **I took to him from the start** он мне сра́зу понра́вился

□ ~ **apart** *v.t.* (dismantle) раз|бира́ть, -обра́ть

□ ~ **away** *v.t.* (remove) уб|ира́ть, -ра́ть; заб|ира́ть, -ра́ть; **the police took his gun away** поли́ция отобрала́ у него́ пистоле́т; **he was ~n away to prison** его́ отвезли́ в тюрьму́; (subtract) вычита́ть, вы́честь

□ ~ **back** *v.t.* (return) верну́ть (*pf.*); (retract): **I ~ back everything I said** я беру́ наза́д всё, что сказа́л

□ ~ **down** *v.t.* (remove) сн|има́ть, -я́ть; (lengthen): **she took her dress down an inch** она́ отпусти́ла пла́тье на дюйм; (dismantle) он|оси́ть, -ести́; **the shed was ~n down** сара́й снесли́; (write down) запи́с|ывать, -а́ть

□ ~ **in** *v.t.* (lit.) вн|оси́ть, -ести́; (give shelter to): **they took him in when he was starving** они́ приюти́ли его́, когда́ он голода́л; (let accommodation to): **she ~s in lodgers** она́ берёт постоя́льцев; (make smaller): **she took in her dress** она́ уши́ла пла́тье; (comprehend) усв|а́ивать, -о́ить; (deceive) обма́н|ывать, -у́ть

□ ~ **off** *v.t.* (remove) сн|има́ть, -я́ть; (deduct from price): **I will ~ 10% off for cash** е́сли вы пла́тите нали́чными, я сбро́шу 10 проце́нтов; (BrE, infml, mimic) имити́ровать (*impf.*), копи́ровать (*impf.*)

● *v.i.* (become airborne) взлет|а́ть, -е́ть

□ ~ **on** *v.t.* (hire) брать, взять; (undertake) брать, взять на себя́; **he took on too much** он взял на себя́ сли́шком мно́го; (assume) приобре|та́ть, -сти́

□ ~ **out** *v.t.* (extract) вынима́ть, вы́нуть; **he took out his wallet** он вы́нул бума́жник; **he had**

all his teeth ~n out ему́ удали́ли все зу́бы; **he took his girlfriend out to dinner** он повёл свою́ подру́гу в рестора́н; (vent one's feelings) срыва́ть, сорва́ть; **he took it out on his wife** он сорва́л всё на свое́й жене́

□ ~ **over** *v.t. & i.* (assume control (of)) прин|има́ть, -я́ть руково́дство (+ *i.*)

● *v.i.* (replace sb): **let me ~ over!** я вас сменю́!

□ ~ **up** *v.t.* (lift) подн|има́ть, -я́ть; (accept) прин|има́ть, -я́ть; **will he ~ up the challenge?** он при́мет вы́зов?; (shorten): **she had to ~ up her dress** ей пришло́сь укороти́ть пла́тье; (occupy) зан|има́ть, -я́ть; (pursue): **I shall ~ the matter up with the Minister** я обращу́сь с э́тим де́лом к мини́стру; (accept challenge or offer): **I'll ~ you up on that!** (я) ловлю́ вас на сло́ве!; (interest oneself in) бра́ться, взя́ться за + *a.*

● *v.i.* (consort) свя́з|ываться, -а́ться (**with:** с + *i.*)

■ ~**away** *n.* (BrE) (shop) рестора́н, продаю́щий еду́ на вы́нос; (meal) еда́ на вы́нос; ~**-home** *attr. adj.*: ~**-home pay** чи́стый за́работок; ~**-off** *n.* (impersonation) подража́ние, паро́дия; (of aircraft, also fig.) взлёт; ~**out** *n.* (AmE) = takeaway; ~**over** *n.* (comm.) поглоще́ние (*како́й-н. компа́нии друго́й компа́нией*)

taking /'teɪkɪŋ/ *n.* взя́тие; овладе́ние; **the money was there for the ~** де́ньги текли́ пря́мо в ру́ки

● *adj.* привлека́тельный

takings /'teɪkɪŋz/ *n. pl.* (money taken) вы́ручка; **the ~ were lower than expected** сбор оказа́лся ме́ньше, чем рассчи́тывали

talcum /'tælkəm/ *n.*: ~ **powder** тальк

tale /teɪl/ *n.* **1** расска́з, по́весть **2** (malicious or idle report): **tell ~s** я́бедничать, на- (**about:** на + *a.*)

✍ **talent** /'tælənt/ *n.* тала́нт, дар

✍ **talented** /'tæləntɪd/ *adj.* тала́нтливый

talisman /'tælɪzmən/ *n.* (*pl.* ~**s**) талисма́н

✍ **talk** /tɔːk/ *n.* **1** (speech, conversation) разгово́р, бесе́да **2** (lecture) ле́кция; докла́д; **give a ~** чита́ть, про- ле́кцию **3** (discussion) (*usu. in pl.*) перегово́ры (*m. pl.*)

● *v.t.* **1** (express) говори́ть (*impf.*); **you are ~ing nonsense** вы говори́те чепуху́ **2** (discuss) обсу|жда́ть, -ди́ть; **they were ~ing politics** они́ говори́ли о поли́тике **3** (bring or make by ~ing): **he ~ed me into it** он угово́рил меня́ сде́лать э́то; **I tried to ~ her out of it** я пыта́лся отговори́ть её от э́того

● *v.i.* говори́ть (*impf.*) (**about:** о + *p.*); **a ~ing parrot** говоря́щий попуга́й

□ ~ **over** *v.t.* (discuss) обсу|жда́ть, -ди́ть

■ ~ **show** *n.* ток-шо́у (*nt. indecl.*)

talkative /'tɔːkətɪv/ *adj.* разгово́рчивый, болтли́вый

talking-to /'tɔːkɪŋ/ *n.* (infml) вы́говор

tall /tɔːl/ *adj.* высо́кий, высо́кого ро́ста; **how ~ are you?** како́го вы ро́ста?; **six feet ~** ро́стом в шесть фу́тов

Tallinn /'tælɪn/ *n.* Та́ллин

tally /'tælɪ/ *n.* счёт

● *v.i.* соотве́тствовать (*impf.*)

talon /'tælən/ *n.* ко́готь (*m.*)

tambourine /tæmbə'riːn/ *n.* бу́бен

t

tame /teɪm/ adj. (domesticated) ручно́й, дома́шний; (submissive) послу́шный; (dull) пре́сный
• v.t. прируч|а́ть, -и́ть; (of savage animals) укро|ща́ть, -ти́ть

Tamil /ˈtæmɪl/ n. (person) тами́л (-ка); (language) тами́льский язы́к
• adj. тами́льский

tamper /ˈtæmpə(r)/ v.i.: ~ with (meddle in) вме́ш|иваться, -а́ться в + a.

tampon /ˈtæmpɒn/ n. тампо́н

tan /tæn/ n. (colour) (желтова́то-/рыжева́то-)кори́чневый цвет; (tint of skin) зага́р; he went to Spain to get a ~ он пое́хал загора́ть в Испа́нию
• adj. (желтова́то-/рыжева́то-)кори́чневый
• v.t. (tanned, tanning) (make brown): a ~ned face загоре́лое лицо́
• v.i. (tanned, tanning): she ~s easily она́ бы́стро загора́ет

tangent /ˈtændʒ(ə)nt/ n. (geom.) каса́тельная; (fig.): he went off at a ~ он отклони́лся от те́мы

tangerine /ˌtændʒəˈriːn/ n. мандари́н, танжери́н

tangible /ˈtændʒɪb(ə)l/ adj. осяза́емый

tangle /ˈtæŋɡ(ə)l/ n. сплете́ние
• v.t. спу́т|ывать, -ать; the wool had got ~d up ни́тки спу́тались
• v.i. (infml) свя́з|ываться, -а́ться

tango /ˈtæŋɡəʊ/ n. (pl. ~s) та́нго (nt. indecl.)
• v.i. (tangoes, tangoed) танцева́ть, с- та́нго

tangy /ˈtæŋɪ/ adj. (tangier, tangiest) о́стрый, те́рпкий

tank /tæŋk/ n. **1** (container) бак, цисте́рна; petrol ~ бензоба́к; water ~ бак для воды́ **2** (armoured vehicle) танк

tankard /ˈtæŋkəd/ n. высо́кая пивна́я кру́жка

tanker /ˈtæŋkə(r)/ n. (ship) та́нкер; (vehicle) автоцисте́рна

tantalize /ˈtæntəlaɪz/ v.t. (tease) дразни́ть (impf.)

tantamount /ˈtæntəmaʊnt/ adj.: ~ to равноси́льный + d.

tantrum /ˈtæntrəm/ n. вспы́шка раздраже́ния; the child is in a ~ ребёнок капри́зничает

Tanzania /ˌtænzəˈniːə/ n. Танза́ния

Tanzanian /ˌtænzəˈniːən/ n. танзани́|ец (-йка)
• adj. танзани́йский

tap¹ /tæp/ n. кран
• v.t. (tapped, tapping) (fig.): the line is being ~ped разгово́р подслу́шивают

tap² /tæp/ n. (light blow) стук
• v.t. (tapped, tapping) легко́ уд|аря́ть, -а́рить; стуча́ть, по-
• v.i. (tapped, tapping) стуча́ться, по-; he ~ped on the door он постуча́лся в дверь
■ ~dance, ~-dancing nn. чечётка

tape /teɪp/ n. (strip of fabric etc.) тесьма́, ле́нта; adhesive ~ ли́пкая ле́нта; (magnetic ~)

(магнитофо́нная) ле́нта/плёнка
• v.t. **1** (bind with ~) свя́з|ывать, -а́ть тесьмо́й **2** (record) запи́с|ывать, -а́ть (на плёнку)
■ ~ **measure** n. руле́тка, (санти)ме́тр; ~ **recorder** n. магнитофо́н; ~**worm** n. ле́нточный червь

taper /ˈteɪpə(r)/ v.t. & i. сужа́ть(ся), су́зить(ся)

tapestry /ˈtæpɪstrɪ/ n. гобеле́н

tar /tɑː(r)/ n. дёготь (m.)

tarantula /təˈræntjʊlə/ n. тара́нтул

tardy /ˈtɑːdɪ/ adj. (tardier, tardiest) (slow-moving) медли́тельный; (late in coming, belated) запозда́вший, запозда́лый

🗝 **target** /ˈtɑːɡɪt/ n. (for shooting etc.) мише́нь (also fig.), цель; (objective) цель
• v.t. (targeted, targeting) **1** (select as object) де́лать, с- мише́нью **2** (aim) напр|авля́ть, -а́вить

tariff /ˈtærɪf/ n. (duty) тари́ф

tarmac® /ˈtɑːmæk/ n. гудро́н, асфа́льт; (aeron.) бетони́рованная площа́дка

tarnish /ˈtɑːnɪʃ/ v.t.: ~ed by damp потускне́вший от вла́ги; he has a ~ed reputation он запятна́л свою́ репута́цию
• v.i. тускне́ть, по-

tarpaulin /tɑːˈpɔːlɪn/ n. брезе́нт

tarragon /ˈtærəɡən/ n. эстраго́н, тарху́н

tart¹ /tɑːt/ n. (flat pie) откры́тый пиро́г с фру́ктами/я́годами
• v.t.: ~ up (BrE, infml, embellish) приукра́|шивать, -сить; she was all ~ed up она́ была́ разоде́та с головы́ до ног

tart² /tɑːt/ adj. (of taste) ки́слый

tartan /ˈtɑːt(ə)n/ n. (fabric) шотла́ндка (кле́тчатая ткань)

Tartar /ˈtɑːtə(r)/ (hist.) n. тата́ро(-)монго́л
• adj. тата́ро(-)монго́льский

Tashkent /tæʃˈkent/ n. Ташке́нт

🗝 **task** /tɑːsk/ n. зада́ча, зада́ние
■ ~ **force** n. (mil.) операти́вная гру́ппа; ~**master** n.: he is a hard ~master он из тебя́ все со́ки выжима́ет

Tasmania /tæzˈmeɪnɪə/ n. Тасма́ния

tassel /ˈtæs(ə)l/ n. ки́сточка (украше́ние)

🗝 **taste** /teɪst/ n. (sense; flavour) вкус; (act of tasting; small portion for tasting): have a ~ of this! попро́буйте/отве́дайте э́того!; (fig., liking): she has expensive ~s in clothes она́ лю́бит носи́ть дороги́е ве́щи; (fig., discernment) вкус; he is a man of ~ он челове́к со вку́сом; bad ~ дурно́й вкус
• v.t. **1** (perceive flavour of) чу́вствовать, по-; can you ~ the garlic? вы чу́вствуете чесно́к? **2** (eat small amount of) есть, по- **3** (experience) вку|ша́ть, -си́ть; изве́д|ывать, -ать
• v.i.: the meat ~s horrible у мя́са отврати́тельный вкус; ~ of име́ть (impf.) при́вкус + g.

tasteful /ˈteɪstfʊl/ adj. изя́щный; со вку́сом

tasteless /ˈteɪstlɪs/ adj. (insipid; showing no taste) безвку́сный; (behaviour) беста́ктный

tasty /ˈteɪstɪ/ adj. (tastier, tastiest) вку́сный, ла́комый

🗝 ключева́я ле́ксика

t

Tatar /'tɑ:tə(r)/ (inhabitant of Tatarstan etc.) татáр|ин (-ка)
● adj. татáрский

tattered /'tætəd/ adj. пóрванный, разóрванный

tatters /'tætəz/ n. pl. клóчь|я (-ев), лохмóть|я (-ев)

tattoo /tæ'tu:/ n. (pl. ~s) (on skin) татуирóвка
● v.t. (**tattoos, tattooed**) татуúровать (impf., pf.)

tatty /'tæti/ adj. (**tattier, tattiest**) (infml) потрёпанный

taught /tɔ:t/ past and p.p. of ▸ teach

taunt /tɔ:nt/ v.t. дразнúть (impf.)

Taurus /'tɔ:rəs/ n. (astron.) Телéц

taut /tɔ:t/ adj. (tight) тугóй, тýго натя́нутый

tautological /ˌtɔ:tə'lɒdʒɪk(ə)l/ adj. тавтологúческий

tautology /tɔ:'tɒlədʒɪ/ n. тавтолóгия

tavern /'tæv(ə)n/ n. (archaic) тавéрна

tawdry /'tɔ:drɪ/ adj. (**tawdrier, tawdriest**) кричáщий, безвкýсный

✿ **tax** /tæks/ n. налóг
● v.t. обл|агáть, -ожúть налóгом; (fig.): he ~es my patience он испы́тывает моё терпéние
■ ~ **collector** n. сбóрщик налóгов; ~ **disc** n. (BrE) наклéйка об уплáте дорóжного налóга; ~**free** adjs. не облагáемый налóгом; ~ **haven** n. странá с нúзкими налóгами; ~**payer** n. налогоплатéльщик

taxable /'tæksəb(ə)l/ adj. подлежáщий обложéнию налóгом

taxation /tæk'seɪʃ(ə)n/ n. налогообложéние

taxi /'tæksɪ/ n. (pl. ~s) таксú (nt. indecl.)
● v.i. (**taxies, taxied, taxiing**) (of aircraft) рулúть (impf.)
■ ~ **rank**, ~ **stand** (AmE) nn. стоя́нка таксú

taxidermist /'tæksɪdə:mɪst/ n. таксидермúст, набúвщик чýчел

taxidermy /'tæksɪdə:mɪ/ n. таксидермúя, набúвка чýчел

taxonomic /ˌtæksə'nɒmɪk/ adj. таксономúческий

taxonomy /tæk'sɒnəmɪ/ n. системáтика, таксонóмия

TB abbr. (of **tuberculosis**) туберкулёз

TBA abbr. (of **to be announced, to be arranged**) бýдет объя́влено дополнúтельно

Tbilisi /təbɪ'li:sɪ/ n. Тбилúси (m. indecl.)

tea /ti:/ n. (plant, beverage) чай; (BrE, meal) пóлдник; **make (the)** ~ завáр|ивать, -úть чай; **have** ~ пить, вы́- чай/чáя/чáю
■ ~ **bag** n. пакéтик чáя, чáйный пакéтик; ~ **break** n. (BrE) перерЫ́в на чай; ~**cup** n. чáйная чáшка; ~**pot** n. чáйник (для завáрки); ~ **shop** n. кафé (nt. indecl.); ~**spoon** n. чáйная лóжечка; ~**spoonful** n. однá/цéлая чáйная лóжка; ~**strainer** n. чáйное сúтечко; ~**time** n. (BrE) рáнний вéчер, врéмя (вечéрнего) чаепúтия; ~**towel** n. (BrE) кýхонное/посýдное полотéнце

✿ **teach** /ti:tʃ/ v.t. (past and p.p. **taught**)
❶ (instruct) учúть, на-; обуч|áть, -úть; **she taught me Russian** онá учúла меня́ рýсскому языкý ❷ v.t. & i. (give instruction) (school etc.) учúть (impf.); (university etc.) преподавáть (impf.); ~**ing staff** преподавáтельский состáв ❸ (elliptical): **that will** ~ **you!** э́то бýдет вам урóком!; **I'll** ~ **you (a lesson)!** я вас проучý!

✿ **teacher** /'ti:tʃə(r)/ n. учúтель (m.) (-ница); педагóг
■ ~ **training college** n. педагогúческий институ́т

✿ **teaching** /'ti:tʃɪŋ/ n. преподавáние

teak /ti:k/ n. (wood) тик; (tree) тик, тúковое дéрево

✿ **team** /ti:m/ n. (sport) комáнда; (of workers etc.) бригáда
■ ~ **game** n. (sport) комáндная игрá; ~ **spirit** n. коллективúзм; (sport) комáндный дух; ~**work** n. коллектúвная рабóта

✿ **tear¹** /tɪə(r)/ n. слезá; **burst into** ~s расплáкаться (pf.)
■ ~**drop** n. слезúнка; ~ **gas** n. слезоточúвый газ

tear² /teə(r)/ n. (rent) разрЫ́в, дырá
● v.t. (past **tore**, p.p. **torn**) ❶ (rip) раз|рывáть, -орвáть; рвать, по-; **I tore my shirt on a nail** я порвáл рубáшку о гвоздь; **he tore open the envelope** он разорвáл/вскрыл конвéрт ❷ (remove by force) от|рывáть, -орвáть; срывáть, сорвáть
● v.i. (past **tore**, p.p. **torn**) ❶ (become torn) рвáться, по- ❷ (rush) мчáться, по-; нестúсь, по-
● with advs.: **I could not** ~ **myself away** я не мог оторвáться; **several pages had been torn out** нéсколько странúц бЫ́ло вЫ́рвано; **the letter was torn up** письмó разорвáли

tearful /'tɪəfʊl/ adj. заплáканный

tease /ti:z/ v.t. дразнúть (impf.)

teat /ti:t/ n. сосóк

✿ **technical** /'teknɪk(ə)l/ adj. технúческий; ~ **term** специáльный тéрмин

technicality /ˌteknɪ'kælɪtɪ/ n. технúческая детáль

technician /tek'nɪʃ(ə)n/ n. тéхник

✿ **technique** /tek'ni:k/ n. (skill) тéхника; (method) приём

technocrat /'teknəkræt/ n. технокрáт

technological /ˌteknə'lɒdʒɪk(ə)l/ adj. технúческий

technologist /tek'nɒlədʒɪst/ n. тéхник; (in particular area) технóлог

✿ **technology** /tek'nɒlədʒɪ/ n. тéхника; (in particular area) технолóгия

teddy /'tedɪ/ n. (also ~ **bear**) (плю́шевый) мúшка

tedious /'ti:dɪəs/ adj. нýдный

teem /ti:m/ v.i.: **the house is** ~**ing with ants** дом кишúт муравья́ми

teen /ti:n/ n.: **he is in his** ~s емý ещё нет двадцатú (лет); он подрóсток
■ ~**age** adj. (characteristic of teenagers) подросткóвый, ю́ношеский; (girl, boy)

несовершеннолéтний; **~ager** *n.* подрóсток, юноша (*m.*) /дéвушка до двадцатú лет; тинéйджер

teeter /'ti:tə(r)/ *v.i.* качáться (*impf.*)

teeth /ti:θ/ *pl. of ▸* **tooth**

teeth|e /ti:ð/ *v.i.*: baby is **~ing** у ребёнка рéжутся зýбы
■ **~ing troubles** *n. pl.* (fig.) «дéтские болéзни» (*f. pl.*)

teetotal /ti:'təʊt(ə)l/ *adj.* непьющий

TEFL /'tef(ə)l/ *abbr.* (*of* **teaching of English as a foreign language**) преподавáние англúйского языкá как инострáнного

Tehran, **Teheran** /teə'rɑ:n/ *n.* Тегерáн

Tel Aviv /'tel ə'vi:v/ *n.* Тель-Авúв

telecommunications /ˌtelɪkəmjuːnɪ'keɪʃ(ə)nz/ *n. pl.* телекоммуникáции (*f. pl.*)

teleconference /'telɪkɒnfərəns/ *n.* телеконферéнция

telegram /'telɪɡræm/ *n.* телегрáмма

telegraph /'telɪɡrɑ:f/ *n.* телегрáф
● *v.t. & i.* телеграфúровать (*impf., pf.*)
■ **~ pole** *n.* телегрáфный столб

telepathic /ˌtelɪ'pæθɪk/ *adj.* телепатúческий

telepathy /tɪ'lepəθɪ/ *n.* телепáтия

⚬ **telephone** /'telɪfəʊn/ *n.* телефóн; **he is (talking) on the ~** (BrE) он разговáривает по телефóну; **someone wants you on the ~** вас прóсят к телефóну; **he picked up the ~** он пóднял трýбку; **public ~** телефóн-автомáт
● *v.t. & i.* звонúть, по- (*кому*) по телефóну
■ **~ booth, ~ box** (BrE) *nn.* телефóнная бýдка; **~ call** *n.* телефóнный звонóк; **~ directory** *n.* телефóнный спрáвочник; **~ number** *n.* телефóнный нóмер, (infml) телефóн; **~ operator** *n.* телефонúст (-ка)

telephonist /tɪ'lefənɪst/ *n.* (BrE) телефонúст (-ка)

telesales /'telɪseɪlz/ *n. pl.* продáжа по телефóну

telescope /'telɪskəʊp/ *n.* телескóп

telescopic /ˌtelɪ'skɒpɪk/ *adj.* ❶ (of or constituting a telescope) телескопúческий ❷ (visible by telescope) вúдимый посрéдством телескóпа ❸ (consisting of retracting and extending sections) складнóй, выдвижнóй
■ **~ aerial** *n.* выдвижнáя антéнна; **~ lens** *n.* телескопúческий объектúв

teletext /'telɪtekst/ *n.* телетéкст

televise /'telɪvaɪz/ *v.t.* покáз|ывать, -áть по телевúдению

⚬ **television** /'telɪvɪʒ(ə)n, -'vɪʒ(ə)n/ *n.* (system, process) телевúдение; **what's on ~?** что покáзывают по телевúдению?; (apparatus) (*also* **~ set**) телевúзор
■ **~ camera** *n.* телекáмера; **~ programme** *n.* телевизиóнная передáча, телепередáча, телепрогрáмма; **~ studio** *n.* телестýдия

⚬ **tell** /tel/ *v.t.* (*past and p.p.* **told**) ❶ (relate; inform of; make known) рассказ|ывать, -áть; сообщ|áть, -úть; укáз|ывать, -áть; **~ me all about it!** расскажúте мне всё как есть/бы́ло! ❷ (speak,

say) говорúть, сказáть; **are you ~ing the truth?** вы говорúте прáвду? ❸ (decide, know) определ|я́ть, -úть; узн|авáть, -áть; **can she ~ the time yet?** онá ужé умéет определя́ть врéмя?; **you never can ~** никогдá не знáешь ❹ (distinguish) отлич|áть, -úть; различ|áть, -úть; **I can't ~ them apart** я не могý их различúть ❺ (instruct) прикáз|ывать, -áть; говорúть, сказáть; **he was told to wait outside** емý сказáли/велéли подождáть за двéрью; **~ him not to wait** скажúте емý, чтóбы он не ждал ❻ (predict) предскáз|ывать, -áть; **I told you so!** я вам говорúл!
● *v.i.* (*past and p.p.* **told**) ❶ (give information) рассказ|ывать, -áть; **he told of his adventures** он рассказáл о своúх приключéниях; **don't ~ on me!** (infml) не выдавáй меня́!; **he promised not to ~** (divulge secret) он обещáл молчáть ❷ (have an effect) скáз|ываться, -áться
□ **~ off** *v.t.* (infml, reprove) отчúт|ывать, -áть
■ **~tale** *n.* сплéтник, я́беда (*c.g.*); (attr.) предáтельский

telling /'telɪŋ/ *adj.* сúльный; **a ~ argument** убедúтельный дóвод; **a ~ example** нагля́дный примéр; **a ~ blow** ощутúмый удáр

telly /'telɪ/ *n.* (BrE, infml) тéлик (infml)

temerity /tɪ'merɪtɪ/ *n.* смéлость

temp /temp/ *n.* (infml) рабóтающ|ий (-ая) врéменно
● *v.i.* рабóтать (*impf.*) врéменно

temper /'tempə(r)/ *n.* ❶ (disposition) нрав; (mood) настроéние; **he lost his ~** он вы́шел из себя́ ❷ (anger) вспы́льчивость; несдéржанность; **he has a quick ~** он вспы́льчив(ый); **he flew into a ~** он вспылúл; **he left in a ~** он разозлúлся и ушёл
● *v.t.* ❶ (harden) закáл|ивать, -úть ❷ (mitigate) ум|еря́ть, -éрить

temperament /'temprəmənt/ *n.* темперáмент

temperamental /ˌtemprə'ment(ə)l/ *adj.* капрúзный

temperate /'tempərət/ *adj.* умéренный

⚬ **temperature** /'temprɪtʃə(r)/ *n.* температýра; (fever) жар; **he has (or is running) a ~** у негó температýра/жар

tempest /'tempɪst/ *n.* бýря

tempestuous /tem'pestjʊəs/ *adj.* бýрный

tempi /'tempi:/ *pl. of ▸* **tempo**

template /'templeɪt/ *n.* модéль; (comput.) шаблóн

temple[1] /'temp(ə)l/ *n.* (relig.) храм, святúлище

temple[2] /'temp(ə)l/ *n.* (anat.) висóк

temp|o /'tempəʊ/ *n.* (*pl.* **~os** *or* **~i**) темп

temporal /'tempər(ə)l/ *adj.* (of time) временнóй; (of this life; secular) мирскóй, свéтский; (anat.) височнáй

temporarily /'tempərərɪlɪ/ *adv.* врéменно

temporary /'tempərərɪ/ *adj.* врéменный

tempt /tempt/ *v.t.* соблазн|я́ть, -и́ть; иску|ша́ть, -си́ть; **I was ~ed to agree with him** я был скло́нен с ним согласи́ться; **~ing** соблазни́тельный

temptation /temp'teɪʃ(ə)n/ *n.* собла́зн, искуше́ние

temptress /'temptrɪs/ *n.* искуси́тельница, соблазни́тельница

✧ **ten** /ten/ *n.* де́сять; (figure; thing numbered 10; group of ~) деся́тка
  ● *adj.* де́сять + *g. pl.*
  ■ **~pin bowling** *n.* ке́гл|и (-ей); **~pins** *n. pl.* (AmE) = tenpin bowling

tenable /'tenəb(ə)l/ *adj.* **1** (defensible) разу́мный, здра́вый; **a ~ argument** разу́мный до́вод **2** (to be held): **the office is ~ for three years** срок полномо́чий — три го́да

tenacious /tɪ'neɪʃəs/ *adj.* насто́йчивый

tenacity /tɪ'næsɪtɪ/ *n.* це́пкость; насто́йчивость

tenancy /'tenənsɪ/ *n.* наём помеще́ния

tenant /'tenənt/ *n.* (one renting from landlord) (private individual) жиле́ц, квартира́нт; (company) аренда́тор

tend¹ /tend/ *v.t.* (look after) присм|а́тривать, -отре́ть за + *i.*

✧ **tend²** /tend/ *v.i.* (be inclined) склоня́ться (*impf.*) (*к чему*); **he ~s to get excited** он легко́ возбужда́ется

tendency /'tendənsɪ/ *n.* скло́нность; **he has a ~ to forget** он забы́вчив(ый)

tender¹ /'tendə(r)/ *n.* (comm.) предложе́ние
  ● *v.t.* предл|ага́ть, -ожи́ть; **he ~ed his resignation** он по́дал заявле́ние об отста́вке

tender² /'tendə(r)/ *adj.* (**tenderer**, **tenderest**) **1** (sensitive, loving) не́жный; **my finger is still ~** мой па́лец всё ещё боли́т **2** (not tough): **a ~ steak** мя́гкий бифште́кс

tenderness /'tendənɪs/ *n.* не́жность; (of meat etc.) мя́гкость

tendon /'tend(ə)n/ *n.* сухожи́лие

tendril /'tendrɪl/ *n.* у́сик (*растения*)

tenement /'tenɪmənt/ *n.* (block of flats) многокварти́рный дом; (flat) кварти́ра

tenet /'tenɪt/ *n.* до́гмат, при́нцип

tenner /'tenə(r)/ *n.* (BrE, infml, ten pounds, ten-pound note) деся́тка

tennis /'tenɪs/ *n.* те́ннис
  ■ **~ court** *n.* те́ннисный корт; **~ player** *n.* тенниси́ст (-ка)

tenor /'tenə(r)/ *n.* (mus.) те́нор

tense¹ /tens/ *n.* (gram.) вре́мя (*nt.*)

tense² /tens/ *adj.* натя́нутый, напряжённый
  ● *v.t.* натя́|гивать, -ну́ть; напр|яга́ть, -я́чь

tension /'tenʃ(ə)n/ *n.* (stretching; mental strain) напряже́ние; (stretched state) натяже́ние

tent /tent/ *n.* пала́тка

tentacle /'tentək(ə)l/ *n.* щу́пальце

tentative /'tentətɪv/ *adj.* осторо́жный

tenterhooks /'tentəhʊks/ *n. pl.*: **I was on ~** я сиде́л как на иго́лках

tenth /tenθ/ *n.* **1** (date) деся́тое число́ **2** (fraction) деся́тая часть; **one ~** одна́ деся́тая
  ● *adj.* деся́тый

tenuous /'tenjʊəs/ *adj.* сла́бый

tenure /'tenjə(r)/ *n.* (holding of office) пребыва́ние в до́лжности; (period of office) срок полномо́чий; (in school etc.) (of property) усло́вия (*nt. pl.*) владе́ния иму́ществом; (security of ~) постоя́нная шта́тная до́лжность

tepid /'tepɪd/ *adj.* теплова́тый

tera- /'terə/ *comb. form* тера...
  ■ **~byte** *n.* терабайт; **~watt** *n.* терава́тт

✧ **term** /tɜːm/ *n.* **1** (fixed or limited period) пери́од; **~ of office** срок полномо́чий; (in school etc.) триме́стр, уче́бная че́тверть **2** (expression) те́рмин; **in ~s of** с то́чки зре́ния + *g.*; в смы́сле + *g.* **3** (*in pl.*) (conditions) усло́вия (*nt. pl.*); **they came to ~s** они́ пришли́ к соглаше́нию **4** (*in pl.*) (relations) отноше́ния (*nt. pl.*); **I kept on good ~s with him** я подде́рживал с ним хоро́шие отноше́ния
  ● *v.t.* наз|ыва́ть, -ва́ть

terminal /'tɜːmɪn(ə)l/ *n.* **1** (of transport) коне́чный пункт; (rail) вокза́л; **air ~** (in city) (городско́й) аэровокза́л **2** (at airport) термина́л **3** (elec.) кле́мма, зажи́м **4** (comput., also, where oil/gas are stored) термина́л
  ● *adj.* (coming to or forming the end point) коне́чный
  ■ **~ illness** *n.* смерте́льная боле́знь

terminate /'tɜːmɪneɪt/ *v.t.* заверш|а́ть, -и́ть
  ● *v.i.* зак|а́нчиваться, -о́нчиться

termination /tɜːmɪ'neɪʃ(ə)n/ *n.* завершо́ние; коне́ц; **~ of pregnancy** прекраще́ние бере́менности, або́рт

terminology /tɜːmɪ'nɒlədʒɪ/ *n.* терминоло́гия, номенклату́ра

terminus /'tɜːmɪnəs/ *n.* (BrE) коне́чный пункт

terrace /'terəs/ *n.* (raised area) терра́са; (BrE, row of houses) ряд одноти́пных домо́в, примыка́ющих друг к дру́гу

terraced /'terəst/ *adj.* (of land, a garden) терра́сный; (of house) стоя́щий в ряду́ одноти́пных домо́в

terracotta /terə'kɒtə/ *n.* террако́та (*жёлтая/красная обожжённая гончарная глина*); (*attr.*) террако́товый (*из такой глины*; *цвет*)

terrain /te'reɪn/ *n.* ме́стность

terrapin /'terəpɪn/ *n.* пресново́дная черепа́ха

terrestrial /tə'restrɪəl/ *adj.* земно́й

terrible /'terɪb(ə)l/ *adj.* стра́шный

terribly /'terɪblɪ/ *adv.* ужа́сно, стра́шно

terrier /'terɪə(r)/ *n.* терье́р

terrific /tə'rɪfɪk/ *adj.* (infml, huge) колосса́льный; (infml, marvellous) потряса́ющий

terrify /'terɪfaɪ/ *v.t.* ужас|а́ть, -ну́ть

territorial /terɪ'tɔːrɪəl/ *adj.* территориа́льный

✧ **territory** /'terɪtərɪ/ *n.* террито́рия

terror /'terə(r)/ *n.* у́жас, страх

✧ **terrorism** /'terərɪz(ə)m/ *n.* террори́зм

✧ **terrorist** /'terərɪst/ *n.* террори́ст (-ка)

terrorize /'terəraɪz/ *v.t.* терроризи́ровать (*impf., pf.*)

terse /tɜːs/ *adj.* (**terser**, **tersest**) кра́ткий, сжа́тый

terseness /'tɜːsnɪs/ *n.* кра́ткость, сжа́тость

tertiary /'tɜːʃərɪ/ *adj.* (geol., med., etc.) трети́чный; ~ **education** вы́сшее образова́ние

✍ **test** /test/ *n.* испыта́ние, прове́рка; **his promises were put to the** ~ его́ обеща́ния подве́рглись прове́рке на де́ле; (examination in school) контро́льная рабо́та; (at college) зачёт; (oral) опро́с, зачёт; **blood** ~ ана́лиз кро́ви ● *v.t.* **1** (make trial of) подв|ерга́ть, -е́ргнуть испыта́нию; пров|еря́ть, -е́рить **2** (subject to ~s) пров|еря́ть, -е́рить
■ ~ **case** *n.* показа́тельный слу́чай; (law) де́ло-прецеде́нт; **T~ match** *n.* (cricket, rugby) междунаро́дный матч; ~ **pilot** *n.* лётчик-испыта́тель (*m.*); ~ **tube** *n.* проби́рка; ~-**tube baby** ребёнок «из проби́рки» (*зачатый вне материнского чрева*)

testament /'testəmənt/ *n.* (clear sign) свиде́тельство; (bibl.): **the Old/New T~** Ве́тхий/Но́вый Заве́т

testicle /'testɪk(ə)l/ *n.* (anat.) яи́чко

testify /'testɪfaɪ/ *v.i.* **1** (affirm) свиде́тельствовать (*impf.*) **2**: ~ **to** (be evidence of) свиде́тельствовать (*impf.*) о + *p.*

testimonial /testɪ'məʊnɪəl/ *n.* рекоменда́ция

testimony /'testɪmənɪ/ *n.* (statement) показа́ния (*nt. pl.*); (evidence) доказа́тельство

testosterone /te'stɒstərəʊn/ *n.* тестостеро́н

tetanus /'tetənəs/ *n.* (med.) столбня́к

tetchy /'tetʃɪ/ *adj.* (**tetchier**, **tetchiest**) раздражи́тельный; оби́дчивый

tête-à-tête /teɪtɑː'teɪt/ *n.* тет-а-те́т ● *adv.* (to talk) тет-а-те́т; с гла́зу на гла́з; (to dine) вдвоём

tether /'teðə(r)/ *n.* при́вязь; (fig.): **he was at the end of his** ~ он дошёл до ру́чки (infml) ● *v.t.* привя́з|ывать, -а́ть

Teutonic /tjuː'tɒnɪk/ *adj.* тевто́нский, герма́нский

✍ **text** /tekst/ *n.* текст ● *v.t.* пос|ыла́ть, -ла́ть SMS/CMC (*pron.* эс-эм-э́с) (*кому*)
■ ~**book** *n.* уче́бник; ~ **message** *n.* SMS/CMC-сообще́ние

textile /'tekstaɪl/ *n.* ткань

textual /'tekstʃʊəl/ *adj.* текстово́й; ~ **criticism** текстоло́гия

texture /'tekstʃə(r)/ *n.* (of fabric): **this cloth has a smooth** ~ э́та ткань мя́гкая на о́щупь

Thai /taɪ/ *n.* (*pl.* ~ **or** ~**s**) таила́нд|ец (-ка) ● *adj.* таила́ндский

Thailand /'taɪlænd/ *n.* Таила́нд

Thames /temz/ *n.* Те́мза

✍ **than** /ðæn/ *conj.* чем; **he's got more money** ~ **me** у него́ бо́льше де́нег, чем у меня́; **he is taller** ~ **me** он вы́ше меня́; **the visitor was none other** ~ **his father** посети́телем был не кто ино́й, как его́ оте́ц

✍ **thank** /θæŋk/ *v.t.* благодари́ть, по-; (by returning favour) отблагодари́ть (*pf.*); ~ **you (very much)** (большо́е) спаси́бо; ~ **God you are**

safe сла́ва бо́гу, вы в безопа́сности
■ ~ **you** *n.*: **he left without as much as a** ~ **you** он ушёл, да́же не сказа́в спаси́бо; (*attr.*) ~-**you letter** благода́рственное письмо́

thankful /'θæŋkfʊl/ *adj.* благода́рный

thankless /'θæŋklɪs/ *adj.* неблагода́рный

✍ **thanks** /θæŋks/ *n. pl.* благода́рность; ~ **for everything** спаси́бо за всё; ~ **to** благодаря́ + *d.*
■ ~**giving** *n.* **1** благодаре́ние **2**: **T~giving (Day)** День благодаре́ния

✍ **that** /ðæt/ *pron.* (*pl.* **those**) **1** (demonstrative) э́то; **those were the days!** вот э́то бы́ли времена́!; **what is** ~? что э́то (тако́е)?; **who is** ~? кто э́то?; ~'**s a nice hat!** кака́я краси́вая шля́пка!; ~'**s it!** (sc. the point) вот и́менно!; (sc. right) пра́вильно!; так!; ~ **is how the war began** вот как начала́сь война́; ~'**s right!** пра́вильно!; ве́рно!; ~'**s all** э́то всё; вот и всё!; **I'm going, and** ~'**s** я ухожу́: всё; ~ **is (to say)** то́ есть **2** (*rel.*) кото́рый; **the book** ~ **I am talking about** кни́га, о кото́рой я говорю́; **he was the best man** ~ **I ever knew** он был са́мым лу́чшим челове́ком, како́го я когда́-л. знал
● *adj.* (*pl.* **those**) э́тот, тот; **I'll take** ~ **one** я возьму́ (вот) э́тот; **at** ~ **time** в то вре́мя
● *adv.*: **I can't walk** ~ **far** я не могу́ так мно́го ходи́ть; **it is not all** ~ **cold** не так уж (и) хо́лодно
● *conj.* что; **I think** ~ **you're wrong** я ду́маю, что вы непра́вы; (expr. wish) что́бы; **I wish** ~ **he would go away** я хочу́, что́бы он ушёл

thatch /θætʃ/ *n.* (straw) соло́ма; (reeds) тростни́к
● *v.t.* крыть, по- соло́мой/тростнико́м; **a** ~**ed roof** соло́менная/тростнико́вая кры́ша

thatched /θætʃt/ *adj.* соло́менный

thaw /θɔː/ *n.* (also fig.) о́ттепель
● *v.t.* (ground, river) отта́|ивать, -ять; (food) размор|а́живать, -о́зить
● *v.i.* (ground, river) отта́|ивать, -ять; (of food) размор|а́живаться, -о́зиться; (fig.) смягч|а́ться, -и́ться

✍ **the** /ðə, ðiː/ *definite article* (*usu. untranslated*) (if more emphatic) э́тот, тот (са́мый); ~ **one with** ~ **blue handle** тот, что с голубо́й ру́чкой; **he is** ~ **man for** ~ **job** он са́мый подходя́щий челове́к для э́той рабо́ты
● *adv.*: ~ **more** ~ **better** чем бо́льше, тем лу́чше; **he was none** ~ **worse (for it)** он (при э́том) ниско́лько не пострада́л

✍ **theatre** /'θɪətə(r)/ (AmE **theater**) *n.* теа́тр
■ ~**goer** *n.* театра́л

theatrical /θɪ'ætrɪk(ə)l/ *adj.* театра́льный

theft /θeft/ *n.* кра́жа

✍ **their** /ðeə(r)/ *adj.* их; (referring to grammatical subject) свой; **they want a house of** ~ **own** они́ хотя́т име́ть (свой) со́бственный дом

theirs /ðeəz/ *pron.* их, свой; **the money was** ~ **by right** де́ньги принадлежа́ли им по пра́ву; **it is a habit of** ~ у них така́я привы́чка

✍ **them** /ðem/ *obj. of* ▸ **they**

thematic /θɪ'mætɪk/ *adj.* темати́ческий

theme /θi:m/ *n.* тéма

■ ~ **park** *n.* тематический парк; ~ **song** (also ~ **tune**) *n.* лейтмотив

themselves /ðəm'selvz/ *pron.* **1** (refl.) себя (*d., p.* себé, *i.* собóй); -сь (*suff.*); **they blamed** ~ они винили себя; **they were proud of** ~ они гордились собóй; **did they hurt** ~? они ушиблись?; **they live by** ~ они живут одни; **they did it by** ~ они сдéлали это сáми; **they have only** ~ **to blame** они сáми виновáты **2** (emph.): **they did the work** ~ они сдéлали эту рабóту сáми

then /ðen/ *n.*: **before** ~ до этого/тогó врéмени; **by** ~ к этому/томý врéмени; **since** ~ с тех пор
  ● *adv.* **1** (at that time) тогдá **2** (next) дáльше, дáлее **3** (furthermore) крóме тогó; опять-таки (infml) **4** (in that case) тогдá; ~ **what do you want?** чегó же вы тогдá (*or* в такóм слýчае) хотите?

thence /ðens/ *adv.* оттýда

theologian /θɪə'ləʊdʒ(ə)n/ *n.* богослóв, теóлог

theological /θɪə'lɒdʒɪk(ə)l/ *adj.* богослóвский, теологический

theology /θɪ'ɒlədʒɪ/ *n.* богослóвие, теолóгия

theorem /'θɪərəm/ *n.* теорéма

theoretical /θɪə'retɪk(ə)l/ *adj.* теоретический

theorist /'θɪərɪst/ *n.* теорéтик

theorize /'θɪəraɪz/ *v.i.* теоретизировать (*impf.*)

theory /'θɪərɪ/ *n.* теóрия; **in** ~ в теóрии; теоретически

therapeutic /θerə'pju:tɪk/ *adj.* терапевтический, лечéбный

therapist /'θerəpɪst/ *n.* терапéвт

therapy /'θerəpɪ/ *n.* терапия, лечéние

there /ðeə(r)/ *adv.* **1** (in or at that place) там; вон (infml); вон тáм; **that man** ~ **is my uncle** (вот) тот человéк — мой дядя **2** (to that place) тудá **3** (at that point) тут, здесь **4** (demonstrative): ~ **you go again!** опять вы за своё!; ~ **you are, take it!** вот вам, держите!; **oh,** ~ **you are!: I was looking for you** вот и вы! А я вас искáл **5** (with v. 'to be', expr. presence, availability, etc.): ~**'s a fly in my soup** у меня в сýпе мýха; **is** ~ **a doctor here?** тут есть врач?; ~ **seems to have been a mistake** тут, кáжется, произошлá ошибка; ~ **was plenty to eat** еды былó полнó
  ● *int.*: ~! **what did I tell you?** ну вот! что я вам говорил?

thereabouts /ðeərə'baʊts/ *adv.* (nearby) поблизости; (approximately) óколо этого; приблизительно

thereby /ðeə'baɪ/ *adv.* этим

therefore /'ðeəfɔ:(r)/ *adv.* поэтому, слéдовательно

thereupon /ðeərə'pɒn/ *adv.* за этим

thermal /'θə:m(ə)l/ *n.* (aeron.) восходящий потóк тёплого вóздуха
  ● *adj.*: ~ **capacity** теплоёмкость; ~ **reactor** (ядерный) реáктор на теплових нейтрóнах, теплової ядерный реáктор; ~ **springs** горячие истóчники; ~ **underwear**

термобельё

thermodynamics /θə:məʊdaɪ'næmɪks/ *n.* термодинáмика

thermometer /θə'mɒmɪtə(r)/ *n.* термóметр

Thermos® /'θə:məs/ *n.* (*in full* ~ **flask**) тéрмос

thermostat /'θə:məstæt/ *n.* термостáт

thesaurus /θɪ'sɔ:rəs/ *n.* тезáурус

these /ði:z/ *pl.* of ▶ this

thesis /'θi:sɪs/ *n.* (*pl.* **theses** /-si:z/) (dissertation) диссертáция; (contention) тéзис

thespian /'θespɪən/ *n.* (joc.) актёр (-риса)

they /ðeɪ/ *pers. pron.* (*obj.* **them**, *poss.* **their**, **theirs**) они; ~ **who ...** те, котóрые/кто...; **both of them** они óба

thick /θɪk/ *n.*: **in the** ~ **of the crowd** в гýще толпы; **in the** ~ **of the fighting** в сáмом пéкле бóя
  ● *adj.* **1** (of solid substance) тóлстый; (of liquid) густóй **2** (dense) густóй **3** (infml, stupid) тупóй
  ● *adv.* гýсто, чáсто; **the blows came** ~ **and fast** удáры сыпались один за другим

■ ~**set** *adj.* коренáстый; ~**-skinned** *adj.* (lit., fig.) толстокóжий

thicken /'θɪkən/ *v.t.* сгущáть, -стить; дéлать, с- бóлее густым
  ● *v.i.* (liquid) дéлаться, с- бóлее густым; (fog) сгущáться, -ститься

thicket /'θɪkɪt/ *n.* зáросл|и (-ей)

thickness /'θɪknɪs/ *n.* толщинá, густотá; (layer) слой

thief /θi:f/ *n.* (*pl.* **thieves**) вор

thieve /θi:v/ *v.i.* крáсть, у-; воровáть, (infml pf.) с-

thieves /θi:vz/ *pl.* of ▶ thief

thigh /θaɪ/ *n.* бедрó

thimble /'θɪmb(ə)l/ *n.* напёрсток

thin /θɪn/ *adj.* (**thinner**, **thinnest**) **1** (not fat; of person) худóй; (of body, parts of body) тóнкий; **she has got** ~ онá похудéла **2** (not thick; of paper, blanket) тóнкий **3** (not dense; of hair) рéдкий **4** (of liquids) жидкий
  ● *adv.* тóнко
  ● *v.t.* (**thinned**, **thinning**) (liquid) разбавлять, -áвить
  ● *v.i.* (**thinned**, **thinning**): **the crowd** ~**ned (out)** толпá поредéла; **his hair is** ~**ning** у негó рéдеют вóлосы

thing /θɪŋ/ *n.* **1** (object) вещь, предмéт **2** (*in pl.*) (belongings) имýщество; вéщи (*f. pl.*) **3** (*in pl.*) (equipment) принадлéжности (*f. pl.*) **4** (matter) дéло; вещь; **for one** ~, **he's too old** начнём с тогó, что он слишком стар; **how are** ~**s?** как делá?; **all** ~**s considered** принимáя во внимáние всё **5** (act) дéйствие; постýпок; **that was a silly** ~ **to do** это был глýпый постýпок **6** (event): **what a terrible** ~ **to happen!** какóе ужáсное несчáстье! **7** (remark): **what a** ~ **to say!** как мóжно сказáть такóе! **8** (issue): **the** ~ **is, can you afford it?** хвáтит ли у вас на это дéнег? — **вот в чём дéло 9** (**a** ~): (something): **it's a** ~ **I have never done before** я этого никогдá рáньше не дéлал; (*with neg.*) nothing; **I can't**

t

see a ~ я ничего не ви́жу **10** (of persons or animals) созда́ние; **poor ~** бедня́га (c.g.)

⚔ **think** /θɪŋk/ v.t. & i. (past and p.p. **thought**) (opine) ду́мать, по-; полага́ть (impf.); счита́ть (impf.); **I ~** (я) ду́маю; мне ка́жется; **I don't ~ so** не ду́маю; **yes, I ~ so** да, пожа́луй; **I ~ I'll go** я, пожа́луй, пойду́; (judge) ду́мать, счита́ть, полага́ть (all impf.); **do you ~ she's pretty?** вы ду́маете она́ хоро́шенькая?/вы счита́ете её хоро́шенькой?; (reflect) ду́мать, по-; мы́слить (impf.); (expect) ду́мать (impf.); предполага́ть (impf.); (imagine): **I can't ~ how he does it** я не могу́ себе́ предста́вить, как э́то он э́то де́лает; (with preps. about/of) **I have other things to ~ about** у меня́ мно́го други́х забо́т; **have you thought about going to the police?** вы не ду́мали пойти́ в поли́цию?; **I couldn't ~ of his name** я не мог вспо́мнить, как его́ зову́т; **who first thought of the idea?** кому́ пе́рвому пришла́ в го́лову э́та иде́я?

● with advs.: ~ **it over!** обду́майте э́то!; **he never ~s his answers through** он никогда́ не проду́мывает свои́ отве́ты (до конца́); ~ **up** (devise) приду́м|ывать, -ать; (invent) выду́мывать, вы́думать

■ ~ **tank** n. (infml) мозгово́й центр

thinker /'θɪŋkə(r)/ n. мысли́тель (m.); **he is a quick ~** он бы́стро сообража́ет

thinking /'θɪŋkɪŋ/ n. **1** (process of thought) размышле́ние **2** (opinion) мне́ние; **to my way of ~** на мой взгляд

⚔ **third** /θɜːd/ n. **1** (date) тре́тье (число́); **my birthday is on the ~** мой день рожде́ния тре́тьего (числа́) **2** (fraction) треть; **two ~s** две тре́ти

● adj. тре́тий; **the T~ World** тре́тий мир

■ ~-**class** adj. тре́тьего кла́сса; ~-**generation** adj. тре́тьего поколе́ния; ~ **party** n. (law etc.) тре́тья сторона́

thirdly /'θɜːdlɪ/ adv. в-тре́тьих

thirst /θɜːst/ n. жа́жда; ~ **for knowledge** жа́жда зна́ний

thirsty /'θɜːstɪ/ adj. (**thirstier, thirstiest**) испы́тывающий жа́жду; **I am/feel ~** мне хо́чется (or я хочу́) пить

thirteen /θɜːˈtiːn/ n. трина́дцать

● adj. трина́дцать + g. pl.

thirteenth /θɜːˈtiːnθ/ n. (date) трина́дцатое число́; (fraction) одна́ трина́дцатая

● adj. трина́дцатый

thirtieth /'θɜːtɪəθ/ n. (date) тридца́тое число́; (fraction) одна́ тридца́тая

● adj. тридца́тый

thirt|y /'θɜːtɪ/ n. три́дцать; **in the ~ies** в тридца́тых года́х; **he is in his ~ies** ему́ за три́дцать

● adj. три́дцать + g. pl.

⚔ **this** /ðɪs/ pron. (pl. **these**) э́то; ~ **is what I think** вот, что я ду́маю; **are these your shoes?** э́то ва́ши ту́фли?; **we talked of ~ and that** мы (по)говори́ли о том, о сём

● adj. (pl. **these**) э́тот; да́нный; ~ **book here** вот э́та кни́га; **come here ~ minute!** иди́

⚔ ключева́я ле́ксика

сюда́ сию́ же мину́ту!; **these days** (nowadays) в настоя́щее вре́мя, в на́ши дни

● adv.: **about ~ high** приме́рно тако́й высоты́

thistle /'θɪs(ə)l/ n. чертополо́х

thong /θɒŋ/ n. **1** реме́нь (m.) **2** (garment) тру́сик|и (pl., g. -ов) «та́нга», та́нга (pl. indecl.); стри́нг|и (pl., g. -ов)

thorn /θɔːn/ n. колю́чка, шип

thorny /'θɔːnɪ/ adj. (**thornier, thorniest**) колю́чий; (fig.): **a ~ problem** сло́жная пробле́ма

thorough /'θʌrə/ adj. (search, investigation) тща́тельный, всесторо́нний; (person) скрупулёзный

■ ~**bred** n. чистопоро́дное живо́тное ● adj. чистокро́вный, чистопоро́дный; ~**fare** n. тра́нспортная магистра́ль; '**No ~fare!**' «прохо́да/прое́зда нет!»

thoroughly /'θʌrəlɪ/ adv. (satisfied, ashamed) соверше́нно; (study) тща́тельно

thoroughness /'θʌrənɪs/ n. тща́тельность; основа́тельность; скрупулёзность

those /ðəʊz/ pl. of ▸ that

⚔ **though** /ðəʊ/ adv. & conj. хотя́, хоть; несмотря́ на то, что…; **even ~ it's late** пусть уже́ по́здно, но…; **he said he would come; he didn't, ~** он сказа́л, что придёт; одна́ко же не пришёл; **as ~** как бу́дто бы; **it looks as ~ he will lose** похо́же на то, что он проигра́ет

⚔ **thought¹** /θɔːt/ n. **1** (thinking) мысль; **modern scientific ~** совреме́нная нау́чная мысль **2** (reflection) размышле́ние; **deep in ~** погружённый в размышле́ния; **on second ~s** поду́мав **3** (idea, opinion) мысль, иде́я, соображе́ние

■ ~-**provoking** adj. заставля́ющий (серьёзно) заду́маться

thought² /θɔːt/ past and p.p. of ▸ think

thoughtful /'θɔːtfʊl/ adj. **1** (well considered): **a ~ essay** вду́мчивое/содержа́тельное эссе́ **2** (considerate) внима́тельный, чу́ткий

thoughtless /'θɔːtlɪs/ adj. (careless) неосмотри́тельный; (inconsiderate) невнима́тельный

⚔ **thousand** /'θaʊz(ə)nd/ n. & adj. (pl. ~**s** or (with numeral or qualifying word) ~) ты́сяча + g. pl.

thousandth /'θaʊzəndθ/ n. ты́сячная часть

● adj. ты́сячный

thrash /θræʃ/ v.t. (beat) изб|ива́ть, -и́ть; (fig., defeat) побе|жда́ть, -ди́ть

● v.i.: **the swimmer ~ed about in the water** плове́ц изо всех сил колоти́л рука́ми и нога́ми по воде́; **he ~ed about in bed** он мета́лся в посте́ли

□ ~ **out** v.t. (fig.) обстоя́тельно обсу|жда́ть, -ди́ть; **let us ~ out this problem** дава́йте разберём э́тот вопро́с по пу́нктам

thread /θred/ n. **1** (spun fibre) нить, ни́тка; **he lost the ~ of his argument** он потеря́л нить рассужде́ний **2** (of a screw etc.) резьба́

● v.t. прод|ева́ть, -е́ть ни́тку в + a.; нани́з|ывать, -а́ть

■ ~**bare** adj. потёртый

✔ **threat** /θret/ *n.* угро́за

✔ **threaten** /'θret(ə)n/ *v.t. & i.* грози́ть, при- + *d.*; **he ~ed to leave** он угрожа́л, что уйдёт; он грози́лся уйти́

✔ **three** /θri:/ *n.* (число́/но́мер) три; (**~ people**) тро́е; (figure, thing numbered 3; group of **~**) тро́йка
● *adj.* три + *sg.*
■ **~-cornered** *adj.* треуго́льный;
~-dimensional *adj.* (lit.) трёхме́рный;
~-fold *adv.* втро́е; **~-piece** *adj.*: **~-piece suit** (костю́м-)тро́йка; **~-piece suite** дива́н с двумя́ кре́слами; **~-year-old** *adj.* трёхле́тний

threshold /'θreʃhəʊld/ *n.* поро́г

threw /θru:/ *past of* ▶ **throw**

thrift /θrɪft/ *n.* бережли́вость, эконо́мность

thrifty /'θrɪftɪ/ *adj.* (**thriftier, thriftiest**) бережли́вый, эконо́мный

thrill /θrɪl/ *n.* (physical sensation) дрожь, тре́пет; (excitement) восто́рг, восхище́ние
● *v.t.* восхи|ща́ть, -ти́ть; **a ~ing finish** захва́тывающий коне́ц

thriller /'θrɪlə(r)/ *n.* три́ллер

thrive /θraɪv/ *v.i.* (prosper) процвета́ть (*impf.*); (grow vigorously) разраст|а́ться, -и́сь

throat /θrəʊt/ *n.* го́рло; **I have a sore ~** у меня́ боли́т го́рло

throb /θrɒb/ *v.i.* (**throbbed, throbbing**) стуча́ть (*impf.*)

thrombosis /θrɒm'bəʊsɪs/ *n.* (*pl.* **thromboses** /-si:z/) (med.) тромбо́з

throne /θrəʊn/ *n.* трон, престо́л

throng /θrɒŋ/ *n.* толпа́
● *v.i.* ст|ека́ться, -е́чься

throttle /'θrɒt(ə)l/ *v.t.* души́ть, за-

✔ **through** /θru:/ *adj.* **1** прямо́й; сквозно́й; **'No ~ road!'** (as notice) «прое́зда нет!»; **a ~ train** прямо́й по́езд **2** (various pred. uses): **you must wait till I'm ~** (finished) вам придётся подожда́ть, пока́ я дочита́ю газе́ту; **she told him she was ~ with him** она́ ему́ сказа́ла, что ме́жду ни́ми всё ко́нчено
● *adv.* (from beginning to end; completely) до конца́; **have you read it ~?** вы всё прочита́ли?; **you will get wet ~** вы промо́кнете наскво́зь; **the whole night ~** всю ночь напролёт; (all the way): **the train goes ~ to Paris** по́езд идёт пря́мо до Пари́жа
● *prep.* **1** че́рез + *a.*; **he came ~ the window** он влез че́рез окно́; (esp. suggesting difficulty) сквозь + *a.*; (into, in) в + *a.*; **look ~ the window!** посмотри́(те) в окно́!; (via): **we drove ~ Germany** мы е́хали че́рез Герма́нию **2** (during) в тече́ние + *g.* **3** (from, because of) из-за + *g.*; по + *d.*; **~ laziness** из-за ле́ни; **~ stupidity** по глу́пости; (of desirable result) благодаря́ + *d.* **4** (AmE, up to and including): **from Monday ~ Saturday** с понеде́льника по суббо́ту (включи́тельно) **5** (over the area of): **the news quickly spread ~ the town** весть бы́стро распространи́лась по го́роду
■ **~way** *n.* (AmE) автостра́да

✔ **throughout** /θru:'aʊt/ *adv.* (in every part) везде́; повсю́ду; (in all respects) во всём
● *prep.* (from end to end of) че́рез + *a.*; **~ the country** по всей стране́; (for the duration of): **~ the 20th century** на протяже́нии всего́ XX/ двадца́того ве́ка; **it rained ~ the night** всю ночь шёл дождь

✔ **throw** /θrəʊ/ *n.* **1** (act of **~ing**) броса́ние, мета́ние **2** (in wrestling) бросо́к
● *v.t.* (*past* **threw**, *p.p.* **thrown**) **1** бр|оса́ть, -о́сить; кида́ть, ки́нуть; **his horse threw him** ло́шадь сбро́сила его́; **the news threw me** (infml) изве́стие потрясло́ меня́ **2** (organize) устр|а́ивать, -о́ить; **let's ~ a party** дава́йте устро́им вечери́нку
□ **~ away** *v.t.* (discard) выбра́сывать, вы́бросить; (forgo) упус|ка́ть, -ти́ть
□ **~ back** *v.t.* отбр|а́сывать, -о́сить наза́д
□ **~ in** *v.t.* вбр|а́сывать, -о́сить; (fig., include) доб|авля́ть, -а́вить; (contribute): **may I ~ in a suggestion?** разреши́те мне внести́ предложе́ние?
□ **~ off** *v.t.* сбр|а́сывать, -о́сить; **he threw off his clothes** он сбро́сил с себя́ оде́жду
□ **~ on** *v.t.*: **he threw on a coat** он набро́сил пальто́
□ **~ out** *v.t.* выбра́сывать, вы́бросить; (reject) отклон|я́ть, -и́ть; (expel) исключ|а́ть, -и́ть; выбра́сывать, вы́бросить
□ **~ together** *v.t.* (compile) сост|авля́ть, -а́вить; (bring into contact) соб|ира́ть, -ра́ть вме́сте
□ **~ up** *v.t.* подбр|а́сывать, -о́сить
● *v.i.* (vomit): **he threw up** его́ вы́рвало
■ **~away** *adj.* ра́зового по́льзования; **~-in** *n.* вбра́сывание (мяча́) (*в футбо́ле и ре́гби*)

thrown /θrəʊn/ *p.p. of* ▶ **throw**

thrush¹ /θrʌʃ/ *n.* (bird) дрозд

thrush² /θrʌʃ/ *n.* (disease) моло́чница

thrust /θrʌst/ *n.* толчо́к
● *v.t.* (*past and p.p.* **thrust**) толк|а́ть, -ну́ть; **he ~ a note into my hand** он су́нул мне в ру́ку запи́ску

thud /θʌd/ *n.* глухо́й звук; стук
● *v.i.* (**thudded, thudding**) глу́хо уд|аря́ться, -а́риться

thug /θʌɡ/ *n.* банди́т, головоре́з

thuggery /'θʌɡərɪ/ *n.* бандити́зм, хулига́нство

thuggish /'θʌɡɪʃ/ *adj.* хулига́нский

thumb /θʌm/ *n.* большо́й па́лец (руки́); **~s down** знак неодобре́ния; **~s up** знак одобре́ния; **he is completely under her ~** он по́лностью у неё под каблуко́м
● *v.t.* **1**: **~ through** перели́ст|ывать, -а́ть **2**: **~ a lift** (infml) голосова́ть (*impf.*)
■ **~tack** *n.* (AmE) кно́пка

thump /θʌmp/ *n.* (blow) тяжёлый уда́р; (noise) глухо́й стук/шум
● *v.t.* бить (*impf.*); колоти́ть (*impf.*)
● *v.i.* би́ться (*impf.*); колоти́ться (*impf.*)

thunder /'θʌndə(r)/ *n.* гром
● *v.i.*: **it is ~ing** гром греми́т
■ **~bolt** *n.* уда́р мо́лнии; **~clap** *n.* уда́р гро́ма; **~storm** *n.* гроза́; **~struck** *adj.* (fig.) ошеломлённый

✔ **Thursday** /'θɜ:zdeɪ/ *n.* четве́рг

✔ **thus** /ðʌs/ *adv.* (in this way) таки́м о́бразом;

t

(accordingly) сле́довательно, таки́м о́бразом

thwart /θwɔːt/ *v.t.* меша́ть, по- + *d.*; **~ sb's plans** расстр|а́ивать, -о́ить чьи-н. пла́ны

thyme /taɪm/ *n.* тимья́н

thyroid /'θaɪrɔɪd/ *n.* (*in full* **~ gland**) щитови́дная железа́

tiara /tɪ'ɑːrə/ *n.* тиа́ра, диаде́ма

Tibet /tɪ'bet/ *n.* Тибе́т

Tibetan /tɪ'bet(ə)n/ *n.* тибе́т|ец (-ка)
● *adj.* тибе́тский

tick¹ /tɪk/ *n.* **1** (of clock etc.) ти́канье; **~-tock** тик-та́к **2** (checking mark) га́лочка, пти́чка
● *v.i.* ти́кать (*impf.*)
● *v.t.* отм|еча́ть, -е́тить га́лочкой
□ **~ off** *v.t.* (infml, reprove) отчи́т|ывать, -а́ть; (mark with **~**): **she ~ed off the items** она́ отмеча́ла предме́ты га́лочками

tick² /tɪk/ *n.* (parasite) клещ

🗝 **ticket** /'tɪkɪt/ *n.* (for travel, seating, etc.) биле́т; (tag) ярлы́к; (AmE, list of election candidates) спи́сок кандида́тов на вы́борах; (printed notice of offence): **he got a ~ for speeding** он получи́л штраф за превыше́ние ско́рости
■ **~ office** *n.* биле́тная ка́сса

tickle /'tɪk(ə)l/ *v.t.* щекота́ть, по-

ticklish /'tɪklɪʃ/ *adj.*: **she is ~** она́ бои́тся щеко́тки; (tricky) щекотли́вый

tidal /'taɪd(ə)l/ *adj.* прили́вный
■ **~ wave** *n.* прили́вная волна́

tidbit /'tɪdbɪt/ *n.* (AmE) = titbit

tide /taɪd/ *n.* (rise) морско́й прили́в; (fall) морско́й отли́в; (fig.) волна́, тече́ние; **the rising ~ of excitement** уси́ливающееся возбужде́ние

tidiness /'taɪdɪnɪs/ *n.* аккура́тность, опря́тность

tidings /'taɪdɪŋz/ *n. pl.* (liter. and joc.) ве́сти (*f. pl.*), но́вости (*f. pl.*)

tidy /'taɪdɪ/ *adj.* (**tidier**, **tidiest**) (neat) опря́тный, аккура́тный; (considerable): **a ~ sum** прили́чная су́мма
● *v.t.* (*also* **~ up**) прив|оди́ть, -ести́ в поря́док; приб|ира́ть, -ра́ть
● *v.i.* (*usu.* **~ up**) нав|оди́ть, -ести́ поря́док

🗝 **tie** /taɪ/ *n.* **1** (*also* **neck ~**) га́лстук **2** (part that fastens or connects) завя́зка, связь; шнуро́к **3** (fig., bond) у́з|ы (*pl., g.* —) **4** (fig., restriction) обу́за **5** (equal score) ничья́; **the match ended in a ~** матч зако́нчился ничье́й/вничью́
● *v.t.* (**tying**) **1** (fasten) свя́з|ывать, -а́ть; привя́з|ывать, -а́ть **2** (arrange in bow or knot) перевя́з|ывать, -а́ть; завя́з|ывать, -а́ть; шнурова́ть, за-
● *v.i.* (**tying**) **1** (fasten) завя́з|ываться, -а́ться **2** (make equal score) равня́ть, с- счёт; игра́ть, сыгра́ть вничью́
□ **~ back** *v.t.*: **she wore her hair ~d back** она́ завя́зывала во́лосы сза́ди
□ **~ down** *v.t.* (lit.) привя́з|ывать, -а́ть; (fig., restrict) свя́з|ывать, -а́ть
□ **~ in (with)** *v.i.* соотве́тствовать (*impf.*)

(+ *d.*); согласо́в|ываться, -а́ться (с + *i.*)
□ **~ up** *v.t.* (lit.) привя́з|ывать, -а́ть; свя́з|ывать, -а́ть; (fig.): **I'm ~d up this week** на э́той неде́ле у меня́ дел под завя́зку; **his capital is ~d up** его́ капита́л инвести́рован
■ **~breaker** *n.* реша́ющая игра́ (*после ничьей*)

tier /tɪə(r)/ *n.* ряд; я́рус

tiff /tɪf/ *n.* (infml) размо́лвка

tiger /'taɪɡə(r)/ *n.* тигр

tight /taɪt/ *adj.* **1** (with no slack) туго́й; (close-fitting) те́сный; (of clothes) облега́ющий; **my shoes are too ~** мои́ ту́фли жмут **2** (strict) стро́гий **3** (under pressure): **I have a ~ schedule** у меня́ жёсткое расписа́ние
● *adv.* (fitting) те́сно, пло́тно; (screwed) кре́пко; (stretched) ту́го; **hold ~!** держи́тесь кре́пко!; **shut your eyes ~!** кре́пко зажму́рьте глаза́!
■ **~-fisted** *adj.* скупо́й, прижи́мистый; **~(ly)-fitting** *adj.* пло́тно облега́ющий; **~rope** *n.* натя́нутый кана́т

tighten /'taɪt(ə)n/ *v.t.* (grip) сж|има́ть, -а́ть; (bonds) закреп|ля́ть, -и́ть; (screw, belt) зат|я́гивать, -яну́ть

tights /taɪts/ *n. pl.* (BrE) колго́т|ки (-ок)

tigress /'taɪɡrɪs/ *n.* тигри́ца

tile /taɪl/ *n.* (for roof) черепи́ца; (for floor etc.) пли́тка
● *v.t.* (roof) крыть, по- черепи́цей; (walls) крыть, по- пли́ткой

till¹ /tɪl/ *n.* ка́сса

till² /tɪl/ *n.* (*see also* ▶ **until**) *prep.* до + *g.*; **he will not come ~ after dinner** он придёт то́лько по́сле у́жина
● *conj.* пока́… (не); до тех пор пока́ (не); **don't go ~ I come back** не уходи́те, пока́ я не верну́сь

tilt /tɪlt/ *v.t.* наклон|я́ть, -и́ть
● *v.i.* (slope) наклон|я́ться, -и́ться

timber /'tɪmbə(r)/ *n.* (wood) древеси́на; (trees) лес; (beam) ба́лка

timbre /'tæmbə(r)/ *n.* тембр

🗝 **time** /taɪm/ *n.* **1** вре́мя (*nt.*); **in ~, with ~** с тече́нием вре́мени; **~ will tell** вре́мя пока́жет **2** (duration, period, opportunity): **after a ~** че́рез не́которое вре́мя; **all the ~** всё вре́мя, всегда́; **all in good ~** всему́ своё вре́мя; **in no ~ (at all)** момента́льно; **I haven't seen him for a long ~** я его́ давно́ не ви́дел; **take your ~!** не торопи́тесь! **3** (experience): **have a good ~!** жела́ю вам прия́тно провести́ вре́мя; **we had the ~ of our lives** мы отли́чно провели́ вре́мя **4** (~ of day or night) час, вре́мя; **what's the ~?** кото́рый час?, ско́лько вре́мени?; **what ~ do you make it?** ско́лько на ва́ших (часа́х)?; **the ~ is 8 o'clock** сейча́с 8 часо́в; **at that ~** (hour) в э́тот час; **what ~ do you go to bed?** в кото́ром часу́ вы ложи́тесь спать? **5** (moment) вре́мя; **I was away at the ~** меня́ тогда́ (or в то вре́мя) не́ было; **at ~s** иногда́, времена́ми; **at all ~s** всегда́; во всех слу́чаях; **by the ~ I got back he had gone** (к тому́ вре́мени,) когда́ я верну́лся, его́ уже́ не́ было; **from ~ to ~** иногда́, вре́мя от вре́мени; **it's ~ for bed** пора́ спать; **the train was on ~** по́езд пришёл

во́время **6** (occasion) раз; **nine ~s out of ten** в девяти́ слу́чаях из десяти́; **another ~** когда́-нибудь; в друго́й раз; **one at a ~**! по одному́; не все сра́зу!; **the first ~ I saw him** когда́ я впервы́е (or в пе́рвый раз) уви́дел его́ **7** (in multiplication): **6 ~s 2 is 12** 6 (умно́жить) на 2 — 12; ше́стью два — двена́дцать **8** (period) вре́мя, времена́ (nt. pl.), эпо́ха **9** (mus.) такт, ритм; **in ~ with the music** в такт му́зыке
• v.t. **1** (do at a chosen ~) выбира́ть, вы́брать вре́мя для + g. **2** (measure ~ of or for) зас|ека́ть, -е́чь вре́мя + g. **3** (schedule): **the train was ~d to leave at 6** по́езд до́лжен был отойти́ в 6 часо́в
■ **~ bomb** n. бо́мба заме́дленного де́йствия; **~-consuming** adj. тре́бующий мно́го вре́мени; **~ limit** n. преде́льный срок; **~ off** n. о́тпуск; **~share** n. та́ймшер, совме́стное владе́ние куро́ртным помеще́нием; **~table** n. расписа́ние; гра́фик; **~ zone** n. часово́й по́яс

timeless /'taɪmlɪs/ adj. ве́чный

timely /'taɪmlɪ/ adj. (**timelier, timeliest**) своевре́менный

timer /'taɪmə(r)/ n. та́ймер, часово́й механи́зм

timid /'tɪmɪd/ adj. (**timider, timidest**) засте́нчивый

timing /'taɪmɪŋ/ n. (choosing of appropriate ~) вы́бор (наибо́лее подходя́щего) вре́мени

timpani, tympani /'tɪmpənɪ/ n. лита́вры (f. pl.)

timpanist, tympanist /'tɪmpənɪst/ n. литаври́ст

tin /tɪn/ n. **1** (metal) о́лово **2** (container) (жестяна́я) ба́нка; (also **tin can**) (BrE, for preserving food) консе́рвная ба́нка; (for biscuits) (металли́ческая) коро́бка **3** (for baking cakes) фо́рма; (for roasting) противень (m.)
• v.t. (**tinned, tinning**) консерви́ровать, за-; **~ned goods** консерви́рованные проду́кты
■ **~foil** n. фольга́; **~ opener** n. (BrE) консе́рвный нож

tinge /tɪndʒ/ n. отте́нок
• v.t. (**tinging** or **tingeing**) слегка́ окра́|шивать, -сить; (fig.): **her voice was ~d with regret** в её го́лосе звуча́ло лёгкое сожале́ние

tingl|e /'tɪŋg(ə)l/, **tingling** /'tɪŋglɪŋ/ nn. пощи́пывание; (of pleasure etc.) тре́пет
• v.i.: **a ~ing sensation** ощуще́ние пощи́пывания; **they were ~ing with excitement** они́ дрожа́ли от возбужде́ния

tinker /'tɪŋkə(r)/ v.i. (meddle etc.) вози́ться (impf.) (с чем)

tinkle /'tɪŋk(ə)l/ n. (sound) звон; звя́канье
• v.i.: **the bell ~d** колоко́льчик звене́л

tinsel /'tɪns(ə)l/ n. мишура́

tint /tɪnt/ n. отте́нок; тон
• v.t.: **~ed glasses** тёмные очки́

⚇ **tiny** /'taɪnɪ/ adj. (**tinier, tiniest**) кро́шечный

tip¹ /tɪp/ n. **1** (pointed end) ко́нчик; верху́шка; (part attached, e.g. of arrow) наконе́чник; **the ~s**

of my fingers are freezing у меня́ мёрзнут ко́нчики па́льцев
■ **~toe** n.: **on ~toe(s)** на цы́почках • v.i. ходи́ть (indet.) на цы́почках

tip² /tɪp/ n. (BrE, for rubbish) сва́лка
• v.t. (**tipped, tipping**) **1** (tilt) накло́н|я́ть, -и́ть **2** (overturn) выва́ливать, вы́валить; опорожн|я́ть, -и́ть
□ **~ over** v.t. & i. опроки́|дывать(ся), -нуть(ся); **the boat ~ped over** ло́дка переверну́лась

tip³ /tɪp/ n. **1** (piece of advice) сове́т; намёк **2** (gratuity) чаев|ы́е (-ы́х)
• v.t. (**tipped, tipping**) **1** (BrE, predict): **the horse was ~ped to win** предска́зывали, что победи́т э́та ло́шадь **2** (remunerate) да|ва́ть, -ть на чай + d.
□ **~ off** v.t. (infml) предупре|жда́ть, -ди́ть
■ **~-off** n. (infml): **the police had a ~-off** поли́цию предупреди́ли

Tipp-Ex®, Tippex /'tɪpeks/ n. (BrE) корректи́рующая жи́дкость

tipple /'tɪp(ə)l/ n. (infml) напи́ток, питьё
• v.i. выпива́ть (impf.)

tipster /'tɪpstə(r)/ n. (at races) «жучо́к» (на ска́чках)

tipsy /'tɪpsɪ/ adj. (**tipsier, tipsiest**) подвы́пивший; (pred.) навеселе́

tirade /taɪˈreɪd/ n. тира́да

tire¹ /'taɪə(r)/ n. (AmE) = **tyre**

tire² /'taɪə(r)/ v.t. утом|ля́ть, -и́ть
• v.i. утом|ля́ться, -и́ться; уст|ава́ть, -а́ть

tired /'taɪəd/ adj. уста́лый; **she's ~** она́ уста́ла; **I'm ~ out** я соверше́нно вы́мотался (infml); **you will soon get ~ of him** вы ско́ро от него́ уста́нете

tireless /'taɪəlɪs/ adj. неутоми́мый

tiresome /'taɪəsəm/ adj. надое́дливый, ну́дный

tissue /'tɪʃuː/ n. (handkerchief) салфе́тка; (text., biol.) ткань
■ **~ paper** n. то́нкая обёрточная бума́га

tit¹ /tɪt/ n. (bird) сини́ца

tit² /tɪt/ n. (vulg., breast) си́ська (infml)

titbit /'tɪtbɪt/ (AmE **tidbit** /'tɪdbɪt/) n. ла́комый кусо́чек; (fig.): **a ~ of news** пика́нтная но́вость

titillate /'tɪtɪleɪt/ v.t. (tickle) щекота́ть (impf.); (excite) прия́тно возбу|жда́ть, -ди́ть

titivate /'tɪtɪveɪt/ v.i. прихора́шиваться (impf.)

⚇ **title** /'taɪt(ə)l/ n. **1** (of book etc.) назва́ние **2** (of rank etc.) ти́тул
■ **~-holder** n. чемпио́н; **~ role** n. загла́вная роль

titter /'tɪtə(r)/ n. хихи́канье
• v.i. хихи́кать (impf.)

tiz /tɪz/, **tizzy** /'tɪzɪ/ nn. (infml) возбужде́ние, ажиота́ж; **she got into a ~** она́ пришла́ в стра́шное возбужде́ние

⚇ **to** /tuː/ adv. **1**: **pull the door ~!** закро́й дверь! **2**: **~ and fro** взад и вперёд; **he went ~ and fro in his search for a compromise** он колеба́лся в своём вы́боре, ища́

компроми́ссное реше́ние
- *prep.* **1** (expr. indirect obj., recipient) (usu. expr. by d. case): **a letter ~ my wife** письмо́ мое́й жене́; **~ me that is absurd** по-мо́ему, э́то глу́по; (expr. support): **here's ~ our victory** за на́шу побе́ду (*тост*) **2** (expr. destination, with place names, countries, etc.) в + *a.*; **~ Moscow** в Москву́; **~ Russia** в Росси́ю; **~ the theatre** в теа́тр (BrE), theater (AmE); (expr. direction): **the road ~ London** доро́га в Ло́ндон; (with islands, planets, left and right, etc.) на + *a.*; **~ Cyprus** на Кипр; **back ~ Earth** обра́тно на Зе́млю; **turn ~ the right!** поверни́те напра́во!; **~ a concert** на конце́рт; **~ war** на войну́; **~ the factory** на заво́д/фа́брику; **~ the station** на ста́нцию; (with persons) к + *d.*; **he went ~ his parents'** он поéхал к роди́телям; (towards) к + *d.* **3** (up to, as far as) до + *g.*; на + *a.*; по + *a.*; **is it far ~ town?** до го́рода далеко́?; **~ the bottom** на са́мое дно; **from 10 ~ 4** с десяти́ до четырёх; **from morning ~ night** с утра́ до́ ночи; **ten (minutes) ~ six** (BrE) без десяти́ (мину́т) шесть; **from April to June** с апре́ля по ию́нь **4** (expr. end state): **smash ~ pieces** разб|ива́ть, -и́ть на куски́; **from bad ~ worse** всё ху́же и ху́же **5** (expr. response) на + *a.*; к + *d.*; **an answer ~ my letter** отве́т на моё письмо́ **6** (expr. result or reaction) к + *d.*; **~ my surprise** к моему́ удивле́нию **7** (expr. attachment, suitability) к + *d.*; от + *g.*; в + *a.*; **the key ~ the door** ключ от две́ри **8** (expr. reference or relationship): **he is good ~ his employees** он хорошо́ отно́сится к свои́м сотру́дникам; **attention ~ detail** внима́ние к дета́лям **9** (expr. ratio or proportion): **ten ~ one he won't succeed** де́сять про́тив одного́, что ему́ э́то не уда́стся **10** (expr. score) на + *a.*; **we won by six goals ~ four** мы вы́играли со счётом 6:4 **11** (expr. position): **~ my right** спра́ва от меня́; **~ the south of Minsk** к ю́гу от Ми́нска
- *particle with v. forming inf.* **1** (as subj. or obj. of v.): **~ err is human** челове́ку сво́йственно ошиба́ться; **he learnt ~ swim** он научи́лся пла́вать **2** (as extension of adj.): **this book is easy ~ read** э́та кни́га легко́ чита́ется; **too hot ~ touch** тако́й горя́чий, что не дотро́нуться **3** (expr. purpose) (с тем *or* для того́), что́бы…; (with inf. only): **I came ~ help** я пришёл(, что́бы) помо́чь; (expr. request): **I asked him ~ help** я попроси́л его́ помо́чь; (expr. result, sequel): **I arrived only ~ find him gone** когда́ я прие́хал, оказа́лось, что его́ уже́ нет **4** (as substitute for complete inf.): **I was going ~ write but I forgot ~** я собира́лся написа́ть, но забы́л

toad /təʊd/ *n.* жа́ба
- **~stool** *n.* пога́нка

toady /ˈtəʊdɪ/ *n.* лизоблю́д, подхали́м
- *v.i.* подли́зываться (*impf.*) (к кому)

toast¹ /təʊst/ *n.* (toasted bread) тост, гре́нка
- *v.t.* поджа́ри|вать, -ть

toast² /təʊst/ *n.*: **drink a ~ to sth** пить, вы́- за что-н.

- *v.t.* пить, вы́- за (чьё-н.) здоро́вье

toaster /ˈtəʊstə(r)/ *n.* то́стер

tobacco /təˈbækəʊ/ *n.* (*pl.* **~s**) таба́к

tobacconist /təˈbækənɪst/ *n.* (BrE) торго́вец таба́чными изде́лиями

toboggan /təˈbɒɡən/ *n.* са́н|и (-éй); тобо́гган, тобога́н

⚹ **today** /təˈdeɪ/ *adv. & n.* сего́дня; сего́дняшний день; **what's ~?** како́й сего́дня день?; **~'s newspaper** сего́дняшняя газе́та; (fig., the present time) настоя́щее вре́мя, сего́дня; **young people of ~** совреме́нная молодёжь

toddler /ˈtɒdlə(r)/ *n.* ребёнок, начина́ющий ходи́ть

toe /təʊ/ *n.* **1** (of foot) па́лец (ноги́); **big ~** большо́й па́лец (ноги́); **little ~** мизи́нец (ноги́) **2** (of shoe or sock) носо́к
- *v.t.* (**toes, toed, toeing**): **~ the line** (fig., conform) ходи́ть (*indet.*) по стру́нке (infml)

toffee /ˈtɒfɪ/ *n.* ири́ска

⚹ **together** /təˈɡeðə(r)/ *adv.* **1** (in company) вме́сте; **~ with** (in addition to) вме́сте с + *i.* **2** (simultaneously) одновре́менно

toggle /ˈtɒɡ(ə)l/ *n.* (comput.) тýмблер

toil /tɔɪl/ *v.i.* (work hard) труди́ться (*impf.*)

toilet /ˈtɔɪlɪt/ *n.* туале́т
- **~ paper** *n.* туале́тная бума́га

toiletries /ˈtɔɪlɪtrɪz/ *n. pl.* туале́тные принадле́жности

token /ˈtəʊkən/ *n.* **1** (sign) знак **2** (substitute for coin) жето́н **3** (attr.) символи́ческий

Tokyo /ˈtəʊkjəʊ/ *n.* То́кио (*m. indecl.*)

told /təʊld/ *past and p.p. of* ▶ **tell**

tolerable /ˈtɒlərəb(ə)l/ *adj.* терпи́мый

tolerance /ˈtɒlərəns/ *n.* (forbearance) терпи́мость; (resistance to hard conditions etc.) выно́сливость

tolerant /ˈtɒlərənt/ *adj.* терпи́мый

tolerate /ˈtɒləreɪt/ *v.t.* (endure) терпе́ть (*impf.*); (permit) допус|ка́ть, -ти́ть

toll¹ /təʊl/ *n.* (tax) по́шлина, сбор
- **~ call** *n.* (AmE) междугоро́дный разгово́р

toll² /təʊl/ *n.* (of bell) колоко́льный звон
- *v.i.* звони́ть (*impf.*)

tom /tɒm/:
- **~boy** *n.* девчо́нка-сорване́ц; **~cat** *n.* кот

tomato /təˈmɑːtəʊ/ *n.* (*pl.* **~es**) помидо́р
- **~ paste** (also **~ purée**) *n.* тома́тная па́ста; **~ juice** *n.* тома́тный сок; **~ sauce** *n.* тома́тный со́ус

tomb /tuːm/ *n.* моги́ла
- **~stone** *n.* (standing) надгро́бный па́мятник; (laid over) надгро́бная плита́

tome /təʊm/ *n.* (liter.) том

⚹ **tomorrow** /təˈmɒrəʊ/ *adv. & n.* за́втра; **~ morning** за́втра у́тром; **the day after ~** послеза́втра; **~ week** (BrE) че́рез 8 дней

ton /tʌn/ *n.* то́нна; (fig.): **he has ~s of money** у него́ ку́ча де́нег

⚹ **tone** /təʊn/ *n.* **1** (quality of sound, colour) тон; (teleph.) гудо́к **2** (character) хара́ктер
- **~ down** *v.t.* смягч|а́ть, -и́ть
- **~ in** *v.i.* гармони́ровать (*impf.*)

□ ~ **up** *v.t.* укреп|ля́ть, -и́ть

■ ~**-deaf** *adj.* лишённый музыка́льного слу́ха

toner /'təʊnə(r)/ *n.* (for printer) то́нер

tongs /tɒŋz/ *n. pl.* щипц|ы́ (-о́в)

tongue /tʌŋ/ *n.* **1** (lit., and as food) язы́к; **put, stick one's ~ out** высо́вывать, вы́сунуть язы́к **2** (fig., article so shaped) язы́к, язычо́к **3** (language) язы́к; **mother/native ~** родно́й язы́к

■ ~**-tied** *adj.* лиши́вшийся да́ра ре́чи; ~**-twister** *n.* скорогово́рка

tonic /'tɒnɪk/ *n.* **1** (medicine) тонизи́рующее сре́дство; (fig.) подде́ржка **2** (~ water) то́ник

✓ **tonight** /tə'naɪt/ *adv. & n.* (this evening) сего́дня ве́чером; (this night) сего́дня но́чью

tonne /tʌn/ *n.* (метри́ческая) то́нна

tonsil /'tɒns(ə)l/ *n.* минда́лина

tonsillitis /tɒnsɪ'laɪtɪs/ *n.* тонзилли́т, анги́на

✓ **too** /tu:/ *adv.* **1** (also) та́кже, то́же **2** (excessively) сли́шком; **it's ~ cold for swimming** сли́шком хо́лодно, что́бы купа́ться; **that is ~ much!** э́то уж сли́шком!

took /tʊk/ *past of* ▸ **take**

✓ **tool** /tu:l/ *n.* инструме́нт, ору́дие

■ ~**bar** *n.* (comput.) пане́ль инструме́нтов

tooth /tu:θ/ *n.* (*pl.* **teeth**) зуб

■ ~**ache** *n.* зубна́я боль; ~**brush** *n.* зубна́я щётка; ~**paste** *n.* зубна́я па́ста; ~**pick** *n.* зубочи́стка

toothless /'tu:θlɪs/ *adj.* беззу́бый

✓ **top**[1] /tɒp/ *n.* **1** (summit; highest part) верх (-и́); верху́шка, верши́на; (of hill, tree, head) маку́шка (infml); **at the ~ of the hill** на верши́не холма́; **at the ~ of the page** в нача́ле страни́цы; **she cleaned the house from ~ to bottom** она́ тща́тельно убрала́ дом **2** (fig., highest rank, foremost place) веду́щее положе́ние; пе́рвое ме́сто; **he came ~ of the class** он стал пе́рвым в кла́ссе **3** (fig., utmost degree) верх; **at the ~ of his voice** во весь го́лос **4** (upper surface) пове́рхность; верх; **on ~** (lit.) наверху́; (fig.): **I feel on ~ of the world** я чу́вствую себя́ на седьмо́м не́бе; **on ~ of everything I caught a cold** вдоба́вок ко всему́ я ещё (и) простуди́лся **5** (lid) верх; кры́шка **6** (*attr.*): **~ secret** соверше́нно секре́тный; **at ~ speed** на максима́льной ско́рости

● *v.t.* (**topped, topping**) **1** (serve as ~ to) венча́ть, у- **2** (be higher than; exceed) превыша́ть, -ы́сить

□ ~ **up** *v.t.* дол|ива́ть, -и́ть; **may I ~ you up?** вам доли́ть?

■ ~ **hat** *n.* цили́ндр; ~**-heavy** *adj.* неусто́йчивый; ~**-up** *n.* (BrE): **can I give you a ~-up?** вам доли́ть?

top[2] /tɒp/ *n.* (toy) волчо́к

topaz /'təʊpæz/ *n.* топа́з; (*attr.*) топа́зовый

topiary /'təʊpɪərɪ/ *adj.*: **the ~ art** фигу́рная стри́жка кусто́в

✓ **topic** /'tɒpɪk/ *n.* те́ма

topical /'tɒpɪk(ə)l/ *adj.* актуа́льный

topicality /tɒpɪ'kælɪtɪ/ *n.* актуа́льность

topless /'tɒplɪs/ *adj.* с обнажённой гру́дью

● *adv.* то́плес(с)

topmost /'tɒpməʊst/ *adj.* (highest) са́мый ве́рхний; (most important) са́мый ва́жный

topographical /tɒpə'græfɪk(ə)l/ *adj.* топографи́ческий

topography /tə'pɒɡrəfɪ/ *n.* топогра́фия; (features) релье́ф

topping /'tɒpɪŋ/ *n.* (cul.) ве́рхний слой; (sauce) подли́вка

topple /'tɒp(ə)l/ *v.t.* вали́ть, с-

● *v.i.* вали́ться, с-

topsy-turvy /tɒpsɪ'tɜ:vɪ/ *adj.* перевёрнутый вверх дном (infml)

● *adv.* вверх дном

Torah /'tɔ:rɑ:/ *n.* (relig.) То́ра

torch /tɔ:tʃ/ *n.* (flaming) фа́кел; (BrE): **electric ~** (электри́ческий) фона́рь

tore /tɔ:(r)/ *past of* ▸ **tear**[2]

torment[1] /'tɔ:ment/ *n.* муче́ние

torment[2] /tɔ:'ment/ *v.t.* му́чить (*impf.*)

tormentor /tɔ:'mentə(r)/ *n.* мучи́тель (-ница)

torn /tɔ:n/ *p.p. of* ▸ **tear**[2]

tornado /tɔ:'neɪdəʊ/ *n.* (*pl.* **~es** *or* **~s**) смерч

torpedo /tɔ:'pi:dəʊ/ *n.* (*pl.* **~es**) торпе́да

torpid /'tɔ:pɪd/ *adj.* вя́лый, апати́чный; (in hibernation) находя́щийся в состоя́нии спя́чки

torpidity /tɔ:'pɪdɪtɪ/, **torpor** /'tɔ:pə(r)/ *nn.* вя́лость, апа́тия

torrent /'tɒrənt/ *n.* (lit., fig.) пото́к

torrential /tə'renʃ(ə)l/ *adj.*: **~ rain** проливно́й дождь

torrid /'tɒrɪd/ *adj.* жа́ркий; (passionate) стра́стный

torso /'tɔ:səʊ/ *n.* (*pl.* **~s**) ту́ловище, торс

tortoise /'tɔ:təs/ *n.* черепа́ха

tortuous /'tɔ:tʃʊəs/ *adj.* изви́листый

torture /'tɔ:tʃə(r)/ *n.* (physical) пы́тка; (mental) му́ки (*f. pl.*)

● *v.t.* пыта́ть (*impf.*); му́чить (*impf.*)

torturer /'tɔ:tʃərə(r)/ *n.* мучи́тель (*m.*), пала́ч

Tory /'tɔ:rɪ/ *n.* (infml) то́ри (*m. indecl.*)

toss /tɒs/ *n.* бросо́к

● *v.t.* **1** (throw) бр|оса́ть, -о́сить; **they ~ed a coin to decide** они́ подки́нули моне́ту, что́бы реши́ть исхо́д де́ла **2** (agitate) швыр|я́ть, -ну́ть

● *v.i.* мета́ться (*impf.*); **the child ~ed in its sleep** ребёнок мета́лся во сне

□ ~ **off** *v.t.* (do quickly) де́лать, с- на́спех

□ ~ **up** *v.i.*: **shall we ~ up to see who goes?** дава́йте бро́сим жре́бий, кому́ идти́

tot[1] /tɒt/ *n.* (BrE, of liquor) глото́к

tot[2] /tɒt/ *v.t.* (BrE) (**totted, totting**): **~ up** сост|авля́ть, -а́вить (*су́мму*); сумми́ровать (*impf., pf.*); **he ~ted up the figures** он подвёл ито́г

✓ **total** /'təʊt(ə)l/ *n.* су́мма, ито́г

● *adj.* (whole) о́бщий; **the ~ figure** о́бщая ци́фра; (complete): **~ failure** по́лный прова́л

● *v.t.* (**totalled, totalling**, AmE **totaled, totaling**) (*also* **~ up**) подсчи́т|ывать, -а́ть

totalitarian /təʊtælɪ'teərɪən/ *adj.* тоталита́рный

t

totalitarianism /təʊtælɪ'teərɪənɪz(ə)m/ *n.* тоталитари́зм

totality /təʊ'tælɪtɪ/ *n.* (sum total) вся су́мма, о́бщее коли́чество; (the whole of sth) (по́лная) совоку́пность; ~ **of** sth что́-л. в по́лном объёме; **in** sth's ~ в це́лом, в совоку́пности, во всей полноте́; (astron.) вре́мя по́лного затме́ния

ᴃ **totally** /'təʊtəlɪ/ *adv.* соверше́нно, абсолю́тно

totter /'tɒtə(r)/ *v.i.* ковыля́ть (*impf.*)

ᴃ **touch** /tʌtʃ/ *n.* **1** (light pressure) прикоснове́ние **2** (sense) осяза́ние **3** (of pen or brush) штрих **4** (tinge) чу́точка, отте́нок, налёт; **a** ~ **of frost in the air** лёгкий моро́зец **5** (style) стиль (*m.*); **you must have lost your** ~ вы я́вно утра́тили (бы́лую) хва́тку **6** (communication) конта́кт, обще́ние; **we must keep in** ~ мы должны́ подде́рживать конта́кт друг с дру́гом; **how can I get in** ~ **with you?** как мо́жно с ва́ми связа́ться?; **we lost** ~ **with him** мы потеря́ли с ним конта́кт/связь **7** (football) пло́щадь за боковы́ми ли́ниями по́ля; **to kick a ball into** ~ выбива́ть, вы́бить мяч за боковую́ (ли́нию)
● *v.t.* **1** (contact physically) тро́гать, -нуть; каса́ться, косну́ться + *g.*; **he** ~**ed her (on the) arm** он косну́лся её руки́; **it was** ~ **and go** исхо́д был неизве́стен до са́мого конца́ **2** (reach) достава́ть, -а́ть до + *g.*; дост|ига́ть, -и́гнуть + *g.* **3** (approach in excellence) равня́ться (*impf.*) с + *i.*; сравни́ться (*pf.*) с + *i.*; идти́ (*det.*) в сравне́ние с + *i.* **4** (affect) тро́|гать, -нуть; волнова́ть, вз- **5** (taste) прик|аса́ться, -осну́ться к + *d.*; **I never** ~ **a drop** (of alcohol) я не прикаса́юсь к спиртно́му **6** (concern) каса́ться (*impf.*) + *g.* **7** (treat lightly) (*also v.i. with prep.* **on**) затр|а́гивать, -о́нуть; каса́ться, косну́ться + *g.*
● *v.i.* соприк|аса́ться, -осну́ться

■ ~**down** *n.* (aeron.) поса́дка; (rugby) попы́тка; (American football) тачда́ун; ~**line** *n.* боковая́ ли́ния (*поля*); ~**type** *v.i.* печа́тать (*impf.*) вслепу́ю/слепы́м ме́тодом

touched /tʌtʃt/ *adj.* тро́нутый

touching /'tʌtʃɪŋ/ *adj.* тро́гательный

touchy /'tʌtʃɪ/ *adj.* (**touchier, touchiest**) оби́дчивый

ᴃ **tough** /tʌf/ *adj.* **1** (of meat) жёсткий **2** (strong, hardy) кре́пкий; (person) выно́сливый **3** (difficult) тру́дный; (stubborn) упря́мый **4** (severe) круто́й; жёсткий

toughen /'tʌf(ə)n/ *v.t.* де́лать, с- жёстким; (body, character) де́лать, с- выно́сливым

toughness /'tʌfnɪs/ *n.* (of food, regime, etc.) жёсткость; (strength; hardiness) про́чность; (uncompromising nature) несговорчивость; упря́мство

toupee /'tu:peɪ/ *n.* небольшо́й пари́к, накла́дка

ᴃ **tour** /tʊə(r)/ *n.* **1** (extended visit) путеше́ствие; (short) пое́здка; (of museum, garden) экску́рсия **2** (of performer, sports team, politician) турне́ (*nt. indecl.*), тур; (of performer) гастро́ли (*f. pl.*); **to be on** ~ быть в турне́/на гастро́лях;

гастроли́ровать (*impf.*)
● *v.t. & i.* соверш|а́ть, -и́ть экску́рсию (по + *d.*)

■ ~ **operator** *n.* (company) турфи́рма, туропера́тор

tourism /'tʊərɪz(ə)m/ *n.* тури́зм

ᴃ **tourist** /'tʊərɪst/ *n.* тури́ст (-ка)

tournament /'tʊənəmənt/ *n.* турни́р

tousled /'taʊz(ə)ld/ *adj.:* ~ **hair** взъеро́шенные во́лосы

tow /təʊ/ *n.:* **can I give you a** ~? взять вас на букси́р?
● *v.t.* букси́ровать (*impf.*); **they** ~**ed the car away** маши́ну отбукси́ровали

ᴃ **towards** /təˈwɔːdz/, **toward** /təˈwɔːd/ *prep.* **1** (in the direction of) к + *d.*; на + *a.*; по направле́нию к + *d.* **2** (in relation to) к + *d.*; по отноше́нию к + *d.*; относи́тельно + *g.*; **they seemed friendly** ~ **us** каза́лось, что они́ бы́ли располо́жены к нам дру́жески **3** (for the purpose of) для + *g.* **4** (near) к + *d.*; о́коло + *g.*; ~ **evening** к ве́черу, под ве́чер

towel /'taʊəl/ *n.* полоте́нце

tower /'taʊə(r)/ *n.* ба́шня; (fig.): **a** ~ **of strength** опло́т; надёжная опо́ра
● *v.i.* вы́ситься, возвыша́ться (*both impf.*)

■ ~ **block** *n.* (BrE) многоэта́жный/высо́тный дом, высо́тка

ᴃ **town** /taʊn/ *n.* **1** го́род; **go to** ~ (infml) разверну́ться (*pf.*) вовсю́ **2** (attr.) городско́й

■ ~ **council** *n.* мэ́рия; ~ **hall** *n.* мэ́рия; ра́туша; ~ **planning** *n.* градострои́тельство

township /'taʊnʃɪp/ *n.* **1** (hist., in South Africa) негритя́нский кварта́л **2** (AmE) райо́н

toxic /'tɒksɪk/ *adj.* ядови́тый

toxicologist /tɒksɪ'kɒlədʒɪst/ *n.* токсико́лог

toxicology /tɒksɪ'kɒlədʒɪ/ *n.* токсиколо́гия

toxin /'tɒksɪn/ *n.* токси́н

toy /tɔɪ/ *n.* игру́шка
● *v.i.:* **he** ~**ed with his pencil** он верте́л в рука́х каранда́ш; **he** ~**ed with her affections** он игра́л её чу́вствами

■ ~ **boy** *n.* (infml) молодо́й любо́вник; ~**shop** *n.* магази́н игру́шек

trac|e /treɪs/ *n.* след
● *v.t.* **1** (delineate) черти́ть, на-; (with transparent paper) перев|оди́ть, -ести́; ~**ing paper** ка́лька **2** (follow the tracks of) высле́живать, вы́следить; **the thief was** ~**ed to London** следы́ во́ра вели́ в Ло́ндон **3** (discover by search) устан|а́вливать, -ови́ть

traceable /'treɪsəb(ə)l/ *adj.* просле́живаемый

trachea /trəˈkiːə/ *n.* (*pl.* **tracheae** /-'kiːiː/ *or* **tracheas**) (anat.) трахе́я

tracheotomy /træki'ɒtəmɪ/ *n.* трахеотоми́я

ᴃ **track** /træk/ *n.* **1** (mark) след; **we lost** ~ **of him** мы потеря́ли его́ след **2** (path) путь (*m.*), тра́сса **3** (for racing etc.) (бегова́я) доро́жка; (for bicycle and motor racing) трек **4** (of railway) путь **5** (of tank etc.) гу́сеница **6** (recording of one song etc.) за́пись, трек
● *v.t.* следи́ть за + *i.*; высле́живать, вы́следить

□ ~ **down** *v.t.* (person) высле́живать,

вы́следить; (object) оты́ск|ивать, -а́ть
■ ~**suit** *n.* трениро́вочный костю́м
tracker /'trækə(r)/ *n.* (hunter) охо́тник
■ ~ **dog** *n.* соба́ка-ище́йка
tract /trækt/ *n.* (region) уча́сток, райо́н
traction /'trækʃ(ə)n/ *n.* тя́га
■ ~ **engine** *n.* тя́говый дви́гатель (*m.*); тяга́ч
tractor /'træktə(r)/ *n.* тра́ктор
◆ **trade** /treɪd/ *n.* **1** (business) ремесло́;
профе́ссия; **he is a builder by** ~ он по
профе́ссии строи́тель **2** (commerce) торго́вля
● *v.t.* (exchange) меня́ть (*impf.*); **they** ~**d furs
for food** они́ меня́ли меха́ на проду́кты
● *v.i.* торгова́ть (*impf.*); **he** ~**s in sables** он
торгу́ет соболя́ми
□ ~ **in** *v.t.*: **I** ~**d in my old car for a new one** я
отда́л ста́рую маши́ну в счёт поку́пки но́вой
■ ~**mark** *n.* това́рный знак; ~ **name** *n.*
назва́ние фи́рмы; ~**off** *n.* компроми́сс;
~ **secret** *n.* профессиона́льный секре́т;
~**sman** *n.* торго́вец; ~**smen's entrance**
чёрный ход; ~**(s) union** *n.* профсою́з
trader /'treɪdə(r)/ *n.* торго́вец
◆ **tradition** /trə'dɪʃ(ə)n/ *n.* тради́ция
◆ **traditional** /trə'dɪʃən(ə)l/ *adj.* традицио́нный
traditionalist /trə'dɪʃənəlɪst/ *n.*
традиционали́ст
◆ **traffic** /'træfɪk/ *n.* **1** (movement of vehicles etc.)
(доро́жное) движе́ние, тра́нспорт; **heavy** ~
большо́е движе́ние **2** (trade) торго́вля
● *v.i.* (**trafficked, trafficking**) торгова́ть
(*чем*)
■ ~ **jam** *n.* про́бка; ~ **lights** *n. pl.*
светофо́р; ~ **warden** *n.* (BrE) инспе́ктор,
контроли́рующий соблюде́ние пра́вил
парко́вки и стоя́нки (*в че́рте го́рода*)
trafficker /'træfɪkə(r)/ *n.* (pej.) деле́ц,
торго́вец; **drug** ~ наркоделе́ц
tragedy /'trædʒɪdɪ/ *n.* траге́дия
tragic /'trædʒɪk/ *adj.* траги́ческий
trail /treɪl/ *n.* (path) доро́жка, тропи́нка; (mark
left) след; **the storm left a** ~ **of destruction**
бу́ря оста́вила по́сле себя́ полосу́
разруше́ния
● *v.t.* **1** (draw or drag behind) тащи́ть (*impf.*);
волочи́ть (*impf.*) **2** (pursue) идти́ (*det.*) по
сле́ду + *g.*
● *v.i.* **1** (be drawn or dragged) тащи́ться (*impf.*);
волочи́ться (*impf.*) **2** (straggle) плести́сь
(*impf.*) **3** (grow or hang loosely) све́шиваться
(*impf.*)
trailer /'treɪlə(r)/ *n.* **1** (vehicle) прице́п; (AmE,
caravan) жило́й автоприце́п, тре́йлер **2** (cin.,
TV) ано́нс
◆ **train** /treɪn/ *n.* **1** (also **railway** ~) по́езд; **I
came by** ~ я прие́хал по́ездом **2** (procession)
проце́ссия; карава́н; (mil.) обо́з **3** (fig.) ряд,
цепь; **I don't follow your** ~ **of thought** мне
тру́дно улови́ть ход ва́ших мы́слей **4** (of
dress etc.) шлейф
● *v.t.* **1** (give instruction to) учи́ть, об-/обуч|а́ть,
-и́ть (**in**: + *d.*); **2** (prepare for a career) гото́вить
(*impf.*); (sportsman) тренирова́ть (*impf.*);
(animals) дрессирова́ть (*impf.*) **2** (direct)

● *v.i.* (learn skill) учи́ться, об-/обуч|а́ться,
-и́ться; (undertake preparation) готови́ться
(*impf.*); (of sportsman) тренирова́ться (*impf.*);
she is ~**ing to be a teacher** она́ гото́вится
стать учи́телем
■ ~ **driver** *n.* машини́ст
trainee /treɪ'niː/ *n.* стажёр; учени́|к (-ца)
trainer /'treɪnə(r)/ *n.* **1** тре́нер; (of horses
etc.) дрессиро́вщи|к (-ца) **2** (BrE, sports shoe)
кроссо́вка
◆ **training** /'treɪnɪŋ/ *n.* **1** (instruction) подгото́вка,
обуче́ние **2** (physical preparation) трениро́вка
traipse /treɪps/ *v.i.* (infml) таска́ться (*impf.*)
(*по у́лицам и т. п.*)
trait /treɪt/ *n.* осо́бенность, сво́йство
traitor /'treɪtə(r)/ *n.* преда́тель (*m.*) (-ница),
изме́нни|к (-ца)
trajectory /trə'dʒektərɪ/ *n.* траекто́рия
tram /træm/ *n.* (BrE) трамва́й
tramp /træmp/ *n.* бродя́га
trample /'træmp(ə)l/ *v.t.* топта́ть, по-,
раст|а́птывать, -опта́ть
● *v.i.* тяжело́ ступа́ть (*impf.*); (fig.): **he** ~**d
on everyone's feelings** он не счита́лся ни с
чьи́ми чу́вствами
trampoline /'træmpəliːn/ *n.* бату́т
trampolining /'træmpəliːnɪŋ/ *n.* прыжки́ (*m.
pl.*) на бату́те
trance /trɑːns/ *n.* транс
tranquil /'træŋkwɪl/ *adj.* споко́йный, ми́рный
tranquillity /træŋ'kwɪlɪtɪ/ *n.* споко́йствие
tranquillizer /'træŋkwɪlaɪzə(r)/ (AmE
tranquilizer) *n.* успокои́тельное сре́дство,
транквилиза́тор
transaction /træn'zækʃ(ə)n/ *n.* сде́лка
transatlantic /trænzət'læntɪk/ *adj.*
трансатланти́ческий
transcend /træn'send/ *v.t.* превы|ша́ть,
-́ысить
transcendental /trænsen'dent(ə)l/ *adj.*
(phil.) трансцендента́льный
transcontinental /trænzkɒntɪ'nent(ə)l/ *adj.*
трансконтинента́льный
transcribe /træn'skraɪb/ *v.t.* перепи́с|ывать,
-а́ть
transcript /'trænskrɪpt/ *n.* ко́пия
transcription /træn'skrɪpʃ(ə)n/ *n.*
перепи́сывание; ко́пия, транскри́пция;
phonetic ~ фонети́ческая транскри́пция
◆ **transfer¹** /'trænsfɜː(r)/ *n.* (of object)
перенесе́ние, перено́с; (of worker, money)
перево́д; (of footballer) перехо́д; (conveyance,
handing over) переда́ча
◆ **transfer²** /træns'fɜː(r)/ *v.t.* (**transferred,
transferring**) **1** (object) перен|оси́ть, -ести́
2 (hand over) перед|ава́ть, -а́ть **3** (footballer,
worker, money) перев|оди́ть, -ести́
● *v.i.* (**transferred, transferring**) (of
footballer, worker) пере|ходи́ть, -йти́; (to another
vehicle) пере|са́живаться, -се́сть
transferable /træns'fɜːrəb(ə)l/ *adj.* (ticket,
vote) тот, кото́рый мо́жет быть пе́редан

t

другому лицу; (skills) универса́льный, приго́дный в любо́й ситуа́ции

transference /'trænsfərəns/ *n.* перенесе́ние; перево́д; **thought** ∼ переда́ча мы́сли на расстоя́ние

transfix /træns'fɪks/ *v.t.* прико́в|ывать, -а́ть к ме́сту; **he was** ∼**ed with horror** он оцепене́л от у́жаса

ꝺ **transform** /træns'fɔ:m/ *v.t.* преобразо́в|ывать, -а́ть

transformation /trænsfə'meɪʃ(ə)n/ *n.* преобразова́ние

transformer /træns'fɔ:mə(r)/ *n.* (elec.) трансформа́тор

transfusion /træns'fju:ʒ(ə)n/ *n.* перелива́ние (кро́ви)

transgress /trænz'gres/ *v.t. & i.* (infringe) пере|ходи́ть, -йти́ грани́цы + *g.*; нар|уша́ть, -у́шить (*закон и т. n.*)

transgression /trænz'greʃ(ə)n/ *n.* (infringement) просту́пок; (offence) наруше́ние; (sin) грех

transience /'trænzɪəns/ *n.* быстроте́чность; мимолётность

transient /'trænzɪənt/ *adj.* (impermanent) вре́менный; (brief) мимолётный

transistor /træn'zɪstə(r)/ *n.* транзи́стор

transit /'trænzɪt/ *n.* транзи́т, перево́зка; **lost in** ∼ поте́рянный при перево́зке; **in** ∼ транзи́том

■ ∼ **camp** *n.* транзи́тный ла́герь

transition /træn'zɪʃ(ə)n/ *n.* перехо́д

transitional /træn'zɪʃən(ə)l/ *adj.* перехо́дный; промежу́точный

transitive /'trænsɪtɪv/ *adj.* (gram.) перехо́дный

transitory /'trænsɪtərɪ/ *adj.* преходя́щий, мимолётный

translate /trænz'leɪt/ *v.t. & i.* перев|оди́ть, -ести́; **these poems do not** ∼ **well** э́ти стихи́ не поддаю́тся перево́ду

translation /trænz'leɪʃ(ə)n/ *n.* перево́д

translator /trænz'leɪtə(r)/ *n.* перево́дчи|к (-ца)

transliterate /trænz'lɪtəreɪt/ *v.t.* транслитери́ровать (*impf., pf.*)

translucence /trænz'lu:s(ə)ns/ *n.* просве́чиваемость, полупрозра́чность

translucent /trænz'lu:s(ə)nt/ *adj.* просве́чивающий, полупрозра́чный

transmission /trænz'mɪʃ(ə)n/ *n.* переда́ча, трансми́ссия

transmit /trænz'mɪt/ *v.t. & i.* перед|ава́ть, -а́ть

transmitter /trænz'mɪtə(r)/ *n.* переда́тчик

transparency /træn'spærənsɪ/ *n.*
1 прозра́чность **2** (picture) транспара́нт

transparent /træn'spærənt/ *adj.* прозра́чный

transpire /træn'spaɪə(r)/ *v.i.* (come to be known) обнару́жи|ваться, -ться; (infml, happen) случ|а́ться, -и́ться

transplant¹ /'trænsplɑ:nt/ *n.* переса́дка

transplant² /træns'plɑ:nt/ *v.t.* (hort., med.) переса|́живать, -ади́ть

transplantation /trænsplɑ:n'teɪʃ(ə)n/ *n.* переса́дка, транспланта́ция; (fig.) переселе́ние

ꝺ **transport¹** /'trænspɔ:t/ *n.* тра́нспорт; **public** ∼ обще́ственный тра́нспорт

transport² /træn'spɔ:t/ *v.t.* перев|ози́ть, -езти́; транспорти́ровать (*impf., pf.*)

transportation /trænspɔ:'teɪʃ(ə)n/ *n.* (of goods etc.) перево́зка, транспортиро́вка

transpose /træns'pəʊz/ *v.t.* перест|авля́ть, -а́вить

transsexual /trænz'sekʃʊəl/ *n.* транссексуа́л

Trans-Siberian /trænzsaɪ'bɪərɪən/ *adj.:* ∼ **Railway** (BrE), **Railroad** (AmE) Транссиби́рская магистра́ль

transvestite /trænz'vestaɪt/ *n.* трансвести́т

trap /træp/ *n.* **1** (for animals etc.) западня́ **2** (light vehicle) рессо́рная двуко́лка
• *v.t.* (**trapped, trapping**) лови́ть, пойма́ть в лову́шку/капка́н; (fig., catch): **his fingers were** ∼**ped in the door** он защеми́л па́льцы две́рью
■ ∼**door** *n.* люк

trapeze /trə'pi:z/ *n.* трапе́ция (*циркова́я*)

trapezi|um /trə'pi:zɪəm/ *n.* (*pl.* ∼**a** *or* ∼**ums**) (geom.) трапе́ция

trapper /'træpə(r)/ *n.* охо́тник(, ста́вящий капка́ны) на пушно́го зве́ря

trappings /'træpɪŋz/ *n. pl.* (harness) сбру́я; (fig.): **the** ∼ **of office** вне́шние атрибу́ты (*m. pl.*) вла́сти

trash /træʃ/ *n.* му́сор
■ ∼ **can** *n.* (AmE) му́сорное ведро́; (outside) му́сорный бак

trauma /'trɔ:mə/ *n.* (*pl.* ∼**s**) тра́вма

traumatic /trɔ:'mætɪk/ *adj.* (distressing) тя́жкий; (of physical injury) травмати́ческий

traumatize /'trɔ:mətaɪz/ *v.t.* травми́ровать (*impf., pf.*)

ꝺ **travel** /'træv(ə)l/ *n.* путеше́ствие, пое́здка
• *v.t.* (**travelled, travelling**, AmE usu. **traveled, traveling**) путеше́ствовать (*impf.*) по + *d.*; е́здить (indet.) по + *d.*
• *v.i.* (**travelled, travelling**, AmE usu. **traveled, traveling**) путеше́ствовать (*impf.*); е́здить, съ-; (move) дви́гаться (*impf.*); перемеща́ться (*impf.*)
■ ∼ **agency** *n.* туристи́ческое аге́нтство, тураге́нтство; ∼ **agent** *n.* туристи́ческий аге́нт; ∼**sickness** *n.* тошнота́ при езде́

traveller /'trævələ(r)/ (AmE **traveler**) *n.* путеше́ственник
■ ∼**'s cheque** (BrE), **traveler's check** (AmE) *nn.* доро́жный чек

travelling /'trævəlɪŋ/ *n.* путеше́ствие
• *adj.* путеше́ствующий
■ ∼ **salesman** *n.* коммивояжёр

traverse /'trævəs, trə'və:s/ *v.t.* перес|ека́ть, -е́чь

travesty /'trævɪstɪ/ *n.* паро́дия (**of:** на + *a.*)

trawl /trɔ:l/ *n.* (in full ∼ **net**) трал, тра́ловая сеть; до́нный не́вод

ꝺ ключева́я ле́ксика

•*v.t. & i.* тра́лить (*impf.*); лови́ть (*impf.*) ры́бу тра́лом; **the fishermen ~ed their nets for herring** они́ тра́лили сельдь; (fig., search thoroughly) проч|ёсывать, -еса́ть

trawler /'trɔ:lə(r)/ *n.* тра́улер

tray /treɪ/ *n.* подно́с

treacherous /'tretʃərəs/ *adj.* преда́тельский

treachery /'tretʃərɪ/ *n.* преда́тельство

treacle /'tri:k(ə)l/ *n.* (BrE) па́тока

tread /tred/ *n.* **1** (manner or sound of walking) похо́дка **2** (of tyre) проте́ктор
•*v.t.* (*past* **trod**, *p.p.* **trodden** *or* **trod**) ступа́ть (*impf.*) по + *d.*; шага́ть (*impf.*) по + *d.*
•*v.i.* (*past* **trod**, *p.p.* **trodden** *or* **trod**): ~ **on that cockroach!** растопчи́те/раздави́те э́того тарака́на!; **don't ~ on the grass!** по газо́нам не ходи́ть!
■ ~**mill** *n.* бегова́я доро́жка; (fig.) однообра́зная рабо́та

treason /'tri:z(ə)n/ *n.* (госуда́рственная) изме́на

treasonable /'tri:zənəb(ə)l/ *adj.* изме́ннический

treasure /'treʒə(r)/ *n.* сокро́вище
•*v.t.* (store up) храни́ть, со-; (value highly) высоко́ цени́ть (*impf.*); **~d memories** дороги́е воспомина́ния

treasurer /'treʒərə(r)/ *n.* казначе́й

treasury /'treʒərɪ/ *n.* (public department) казна́

✍ **treat** /tri:t/ *n.* удово́льствие; **it's my ~!** я угоща́ю!
•*v.t.* **1** (behave towards) обраща́ться (*impf.*) с + *i.*; **he ~s me like a child** он обраща́ется со мной, как с ребёнком **2** (regard) рассма́тривать (*impf.*); отн|оси́ться, -ести́сь к + *d.* **3** (deal with; discuss) осве|ща́ть, -ти́ть; рассм|а́тривать, -отре́ть; **he ~ed the subject in detail** он подро́бно освети́л те́му **4** (give medical care to) лечи́ть (*impf.*) **5** (apply chemical process to) обраб|а́тывать, -о́тать **6** (give sb sth at one's own expense) уго|ща́ть, -сти́ть; **he ~ed me to a whisky** он угости́л меня́ ви́ски; **I shall ~ myself to a holiday** я устро́ю себе́ о́тпуск

treatise /'tri:tɪs/ *n.* тракта́т; нау́чный труд

✍ **treatment** /'tri:tmənt/ *n.* **1** (handling) обраще́ние; рассмотре́ние **2** (chem. etc.) обрабо́тка **3** (med.) лече́ние; (session of therapy) процеду́ра

treaty /'tri:tɪ/ *n.* догово́р

treble /'treb(ə)l/ *n.* **1** (voice) ди́скант; ~ **clef** скрипи́чный ключ
•*adj.* тройно́й
•*v.t. & i.* утр|а́ивать(ся), -о́ить(ся)

✍ **tree** /tri:/ *n.* де́рево

trek /trek/ *n.* перехо́д
•*v.i.* (**trekked**, **trekking**) соверш|а́ть, -и́ть дли́тельный похо́д

trellis /'trelɪs/ *n.* шпале́ра

tremble /'tremb(ə)l/ *v.i.* дрожа́ть (*impf.*); трясти́сь (*impf.*)

tremendous /trɪ'mendəs/ *adj.* (huge) огро́мный; (infml, splendid) замеча́тельный

tremor /'tremə(r)/ *n.* (quivering) содрога́ние, дрожь; (thrill) тре́пет; **there was a ~ in his voice** его́ го́лос дрожа́л; **earth ~** подзе́мный толчо́к

tremulous /'tremjʊləs/ *adj.* (trembling) дрожа́щий

trench /trentʃ/ *n.* ров, кана́ва; (mil.) транше́я

✍ **trend** /trend/ *n.* направле́ние, тенде́нция; **set a ~** вв|оди́ть, -ести́ мо́ду (**for:** на + *a.*)

trendy /'trendɪ/ *adj.* (**trendier**, **trendiest**) (infml) мо́дный

trepidation /trepɪ'deɪʃ(ə)n/ *n.* тре́пет, дрожь; **in ~** трепеща́

trespass /'trespəs/ *v.i.* вт|орга́ться, -о́ргнуться в чужи́е владе́ния

trespasser /'trespəsə(r)/ *n.* лицо́, вторга́ющееся в чужи́е владе́ния; ~**s will be prosecuted** наруши́тели бу́дут пресле́доваться

✍ **trial** /'traɪəl/ *n.* **1** (test) испыта́ние, про́ба; **I discovered the truth by ~ and error** я пришёл к и́стине путём проб и оши́бок; **he took the car on a week's ~** он взял автомаши́ну на неде́льное испыта́ние **2** (*attr.*) про́бный **3** (judicial examination) суде́бный проце́сс; **he went on ~ for murder** его́ суди́ли за уби́йство
■ ~ **run** *n.* испыта́тельный пробе́г

triangle /'traɪæŋɡ(ə)l/ *n.* треуго́льник

triangular /traɪ'æŋɡjʊlə(r)/ *adj.* треуго́льный; **a ~ argument** спор ме́жду тремя́ ли́цами

triathlon /traɪ'æθlən/ *n.* троебо́рье

tribal /'traɪb(ə)l/ *adj.* племенно́й

tribe /traɪb/ *n.* пле́мя (*nt.*)

tribulation /trɪbjʊ'leɪʃ(ə)n/ *n.* страда́ние, беда́

tribunal /traɪ'bju:n(ə)l/ *n.* трибуна́л

tributary /'trɪbjʊtərɪ/ *n.* прито́к

tribute /'trɪbju:t/ *n.* дань; **he paid a ~ to his wife's help** он вы́разил благода́рность свое́й жене́ за по́мощь

trice /traɪs/ *n.*: **in a ~** вмиг, ми́гом

trick /trɪk/ *n.* **1** (dodge) приём, хи́трость; **he knows all the ~s of the trade** он зна́ет все хо́ды и вы́ходы **2** (deception) обма́н, трюк; (prank) шу́тка; **he is always playing ~s on me** он всегда́ надо мной подшу́чивает **3** (feat) шту́ка; **that will do the ~** э́то срабо́тает наверняка́ **4** (knack) хва́тка **5** (at cards) взя́тка
•*v.t.* обма́н|ывать, -у́ть; над|ува́ть, -у́ть; **they ~ed him out of a fortune** они́ вы́манили у него́ ма́ссу де́нег

trickery /'trɪkərɪ/ *n.* обма́н, надува́тельство

trickle /'trɪk(ə)l/ *n.* стру́йка
•*v.t.* ка́пать (*impf.*)
•*v.i.* сочи́ться (*impf.*); ка́пать (*impf.*); (fig.): **the crowd began to ~ away** толпа́ ста́ла постепе́нно расходи́ться

tricky /'trɪkɪ/ *adj.* (**trickier**, **trickiest**) (awkward) сло́жный, мудрёный; (crafty) хи́трый, кова́рный

tricycle /'traɪsɪk(ə)l/ *n.* трёхколёсный
велосипéд

trifle /'traɪf(ə)l/ *n.* **1** (thing of small value)
пустя́к, мéлочь **2** (BrE, sweet dish) бисквит со
взби́тыми сли́вками
● *v.i.* относи́ться (*impf.*) несерьёзно к +
d.; **he ~d with her affections** он игра́л её
чу́вствами

trifling /'traɪflɪŋ/ *adj.* пустяко́вый;
незначи́тельный

trigger /'trɪgə(r)/ *n.* куро́к
● *v.t.* (*usu.* **~ off**) вызыва́ть, вы́звать

trigonometry /trɪgə'nɒmɪtrɪ/ *n.*
тригономéтрия

trilby /'trɪlbɪ/ *n.* (BrE) мя́гкая фéтровая шля́па

trill /trɪl/ *n.* трель
● *v.i.*: **the birds were ~ing** пти́цы залива́лись
трéлями

trillion /'trɪljən/ *n.* (*pl.* **~s** or (*with numeral
or qualifying word*) **~**) (10^{12}, million million)
триллио́н

trilogy /'trɪlədʒɪ/ *n.* трило́гия

trim /trɪm/ *n.* **1** (order, fitness) поря́док;
состоя́ние гото́вности; **we must get into ~
before the race** нам ну́жно набра́ть фо́рму
пéред соревнова́нием **2** (light cut) подрéзка,
стри́жка
● *adj.* (**trimmer**, **trimmest**) аккура́тный,
опря́тный
● *v.t.* (**trimmed**, **trimming**) **1** (cut to desired
shape) подр|еза́ть, -éзать; подр|а́внивать,
-овня́ть **2** (decorate) отдé|лывать, -лать; **a hat
~med with fur** ша́пка, отде́ланная мéхом

trimming /'trɪmɪŋ/ *n.* (on dress etc.) отдéлка;
(infml, accessory) гарни́р

Trinity /'trɪnɪtɪ/ *n.* Тро́ица
■ **~ Sunday** *n.* день Свято́й Тро́ицы

trinket /'trɪŋkɪt/ *n.* безделу́шка

trio /'triːəʊ/ *n.* (*pl.* **~ s**) (group of three) тро́йка;
(mus.) три́о (*nt. indecl.*)

♂ **trip** /trɪp/ *n.* (excursion) поéздка; (longer one)
путешéствие
● *v.t.* (**tripped**, **tripping**) (cause to stumble)
(*also* **~ up**) ста́вить, по- подно́жку + *d.*;
(fig.) запу́т|ывать, -ать, сби|ва́ть, -ть с то́лку
● *v.i.* (**tripped**, **tripping**) **1** (run lightly):
she came ~ping down the stairs она́ легко́
сбежа́ла вниз по лéстнице **2** (stumble) (*also*
~ up) спот|ыка́ться, -кну́ться

tripartite /traɪ'pɑːtaɪt/ *adj.* трёхсторо́нний

tripe /traɪp/ *n.* (offal) требуха́; (infml, rubbish)
чепуха́, вздор

triple /'trɪp(ə)l/ *adj.* тройно́й, утро́енный
■ **~ jump** *n.* тройно́й прыжо́к

triplet /'trɪplɪt/ *n.*: **~s** (children) тройня́ (*sg.*)

triplicate /'trɪplɪkət/ *n.*: **in ~** в трёх
экземпля́рах

tripod /'traɪpɒd/ *n.* тренога

trite /traɪt/ *adj.* бана́льный, изби́тый

triumph /'traɪʌmf/ *n.* (joy at success) торжество́;
(success) триу́мф
● *v.i.* побе|жда́ть, -ди́ть; восторжествова́ть

(*pf.*); **he ~ed over adversity** он преодолéл
все невзго́ды

triumphant /traɪ'ʌmf(ə)nt/ *adj.* (victorious)
победоно́сный; (exultant) торжеству́ющий

trivia /'trɪvɪə/ *n.* мéлочи (*f. pl.*)

trivial /'trɪvɪəl/ *adj.* (trifling) мéлкий,
незначи́тельный; (everyday) обы́денный

triviality /trɪvɪ'ælɪtɪ/ *n.* незначи́тельность,
тривиа́льность

trivialize /'trɪvɪəlaɪz/ *v.t.* оп|ошля́ть, -о́шлить

trod /trɒd/ *past and p.p. of* ▸ **tread**

trodden /'trɒd(ə)n/ *p.p. of* ▸ **tread**

trolley /'trɒlɪ/ *n.* (*pl.* **~s**) (BrE, for luggage,
purchases) телéжка; (AmE, streetcar) трамва́й
■ **~bus** *n.* троллéйбус; **~ car** *n.* (AmE) трамва́й

trombone /trɒm'bəʊn/ *n.* тромбо́н

trombonist /trɒm'bəʊnɪst/ *n.* тромбони́ст

♂ **troop** /truːp/ *n.* **1** (mil. unit) батарéя **2** (in pl.)
(soldiers) войск|а́ (*pl., g.* —)

trooper /'truːpə(r)/ *n.* **1** (soldier) (in armoured
unit) танки́ст; (in cavalry) кавалери́ст **2** (AmE,
policeman) полицéйский

trophy /'trəʊfɪ/ *n.* трофéй

tropic /'trɒpɪk/ *n.* тро́пик; **in the ~s** в
тро́пиках

tropical /'trɒpɪk(ə)l/ *adj.* тропи́ческий

trot /trɒt/ *n.* рысь; **on the ~** (BrE) подря́д
● *v.i.* (**trotted**, **trotting**) (of a horse) идти́
(*det.*) ры́сью; (of person) семени́ть (*impf.*)
□ **~ out** *v.t.* (infml): **he ~ted out the usual
excuses** он, как обы́чно, привёл свои́ ста́рые
отгово́рки

♂ **trouble** /'trʌb(ə)l/ *n.* **1** (anxiety) волнéние,
трево́га; беспоко́йство; (misfortune) го́ре,
беда́, несча́стье **2** (difficulties) хло́п|оты (-о́т),
тру́дности (*f. pl.*); (difficulty) затруднéние;
money ~s дéнежные затруднéния; **I am
having ~ with the car** у меня́ непола́дки
(*f. pl.*) с маши́ной; **what's the ~?** в чём
дéло? **3** (predicament) неприя́тность;
he's always getting into ~ он вéчно
попада́ет в исто́рии **4** (inconvenience): **he
saved me the ~** он изба́вил меня́ от э́той
необходи́мости **5** (care, effort) забо́та, труд,
хло́п|оты (-о́т); **she took a lot of ~ over
the cake** она́ приложи́ла нема́ло стара́ний,
что́бы пригото́вить э́тот торт **6** (unrest)
волнéния (*nt. pl.*)
● *v.t.* **1** (worry) трево́жить (*impf.*); волнова́ть
(*impf.*); **don't let it ~ you** не принима́йте
э́то бли́зко к сéрдцу **2** (afflict) беспоко́ить
(*impf.*); му́чить (*impf.*); **he is ~d with a cough**
его́ му́чит ка́шель **3** (put to inconvenience)
беспоко́ить, по-, затрудн|я́ть, -и́ть; **don't ~
yourself** не беспоко́йтесь; **sorry to ~ you!**
прости́те за беспоко́йство!
■ **~-free** *adj.* (reliable) надёжный, безотка́зный;
~maker *n.* смутья́н (-ка); **~shooter** *n.*
специали́ст по разрешéнию конфли́ктных/
кри́зисных ситуа́ций (*в компа́нии и т. п.*); **~
spot** *n.* горя́чая то́чка

troublesome /'trʌb(ə)ls(ə)m/ *adj.* тру́дный;
хло́потный

♂ ключевáя лéксика

trough /trɒf/ *n.* **1** (food ~) кормушка; (drinking ~) поилка **2** (dip) впадина

troupe /tru:p/ *n.* труппа

trousers /'traʊzəz/ *n. pl.* штан|ы́ (-о́в), брюк|и (*pl., g.* —); **a pair of ~** па́ра брюк

trout /traʊt/ *n.* форе́ль

trowel /'traʊəl/ *n.* (for bricklaying etc.) мастеро́к; (for gardening) (садо́вый) сово́к, лопа́тка

truancy /'tru:ənsɪ/ *n.* прогу́л

truant /'tru:ənt/ *n.* прогу́льщик; **did you ever play ~?** вы когда́-нибудь прогу́ливали уро́ки?

truce /tru:s/ *n.* переми́рие

truck /trʌk/ *n.* (BrE, railway wagon) откры́тая грузова́я платфо́рма; (lorry) грузови́к; (barrow) теле́жка

trucker /'trʌkə(r)/ *n.* води́тель (*m.*) грузовика́

truculent /'trʌkjʊlənt/ *adj.* агресси́вный, драчли́вый

trudge /trʌdʒ/ *v.i.* тащи́ться (*impf.*)

✍ **true** /tru:/ *adj.* (**truer**, **truest**) **1** (in accordance with fact) ве́рный, правди́вый; **is it ~ that ...?** (э́то) пра́вда, что...?; **a ~ story** правди́вый расска́з; **all my dreams came ~** все мои́ мечты́ сбыли́сь/осуществи́лись **2** (in accordance with reason; genuine) правди́вый; настоя́щий; и́стинный **3** (conforming accurately) ве́рный, пра́вильный; **~ to life** правди́вый **4** (loyal; dependable) пре́данный, ве́рный; надёжный

truffle /'trʌf(ə)l/ *n.* (fungus, candy) трю́фель (*m.*)

truism /'tru:ɪz(ə)m/ *n.* изби́тая и́стина, трюи́зм; **it is a ~ that** общеизве́стно, что...

✍ **truly** /'tru:lɪ/ *adv.* **1** (truthfully) и́скренне; (accurately) правди́во **2** (sincerely) и́скренне; **yours ~** (at end of letter) пре́данный Вам

trump /trʌmp/ *n.* (*in full* ~ **card**) ко́зырь (*m.*); **the weather turned up ~s** (BrE) нам (неожи́данно) повезло́ с пого́дой

trumpet /'trʌmpɪt/ *n.* труба́; **blow one's own ~** (fig.) хвали́ться (*impf.*)

trumpeter /'trʌmpɪtə(r)/ *n.* труба́ч

truncate /trʌŋ'keɪt/ *v.t.* усека́ть, -е́чь; **a ~d cone** усечённый ко́нус; **his speech was ~d** его́ речь уре́зали

truncheon /'trʌntʃ(ə)n/ *n.* (BrE) (полице́йская) дуби́нка

trundle /'trʌnd(ə)l/ *v.t. & i.* кати́ть(ся) (*impf.*)

trunk /trʌŋk/ *n.* **1** (of tree) ствол **2** (of body) ту́ловище **3** (box) сунду́к **4** (of elephant) хо́бот **5** (*in pl.*) (garment) пла́в|ки (-ок) **6** (AmE, boot of car) бага́жник
■ **~ road** *n.* (BrE) магистра́ль

✍ **trust** /trʌst/ *n.* **1** (confidence) дове́рие; ве́ра **2** (law) довери́тельная со́бственность
● *v.t.* **1** (have confidence in, rely on) дов|еря́ть, -е́рить + *d.* **2** (entrust) вв|еря́ть, -е́рить
● *v.i.* **1** (have faith, confidence) дов|еря́ться, -е́риться (**in:** + *d.*); **she ~ed in God** она́ отдала́сь на во́лю Бо́жью **2** (commit oneself with confidence) дов|еря́ться, -е́риться (**to:** + *d.*); **he ~ed to luck** он дове́рился уда́че
■ **~ fund** *n.* целево́й фонд

trustee /trʌs'ti:/ *n.* довери́тельный со́бственник; опеку́н

trusting /'trʌstɪŋ/ *adj.* дове́рчивый

trustworthiness /'trʌstwə:ðɪnɪs/ *n.* надёжность

trustworthy /'trʌstwə:ðɪ/ *adj.* надёжный

trusty /'trʌstɪ/ *adj.* (**trustier**, **trustiest**) ве́рный, надёжный

✍ **truth** /tru:θ/ *n.* пра́вда; (verity) и́стина

truthful /'tru:θfʊl/ *adj.* (of person) правди́вый; (of statement etc.) правди́вый, ве́рный, то́чный

truthfulness /'tru:θfʊlnɪs/ *n.* правди́вость; ве́рность, то́чность

✍ **try** /traɪ/ *n.* **1** (attempt) попы́тка **2** (test): **why not give it a ~?** почему́ бы не попро́бовать? **3** (rugby) прохо́д с мячо́м в зачётное по́ле сопе́рника, попы́тка
● *v.t.* **1** (attempt) пыта́ться, по-; стара́ться, по-; **he tried his best** он стара́лся изо всех сил; **he tried hard** он о́чень стара́лся **2** (sample) про́бовать, по-; (taste) отве́д|ывать, -ать; (experiment with): **have you tried aspirin?** вы про́бовали аспири́н? **3** (law, a person) суди́ть (*impf.*) **4** (subject to strain): **he tries my patience** он испы́тывает моё терпе́ние; **a ~ing situation** тру́дное положе́ние **5** (test) испы́т|ывать, -а́ть; пров|еря́ть, -е́рить
● *v.i.:* **~ harder next time!** в сле́дующий раз приложи́те бо́льше уси́лий!; **I tried for a prize** я добива́лся при́за; я претендова́л на приз
□ **~ on** *v.t.* прим|еря́ть, -е́рить
□ **~ out** *v.t.* испы́т|ывать, -а́ть; опро́бовать (*pf.*)

tsar, tzar /za:(r)/ *n.* царь (*m.*)

T-shirt /'ti:ʃə:t/ *n.* футбо́лка

tsunami /tsu:'nɑ:mɪ/ *n.* (*pl.* ~**s**) цуна́ми (*nt. indecl.*)

tub /tʌb/ *n.* **1** ка́дка; бо́чка **2** (bath) ва́нна **3** (of margarine) упако́вка; (of ice cream, yogurt) стака́нчик

tuba /'tju:bə/ *n.* ту́ба

tubby /'tʌbɪ/ *adj.* (**tubbier**, **tubbiest**) (of person) коротконо́гий и то́лстый

tube /tju:b/ *n.* **1** (of metal, glass, etc.) труба́, тру́бка **2** (of toothpaste, etc.) тю́бик **3** (of tyre) ка́мера (ши́ны) **4** (in the body) труба́ **5** (BrE, infml, underground railway) метро́ (*nt. indecl.*)

tuberculosis /tjʊbɜ:kjʊ'ləʊsɪs/ *n.* туберкулёз

tuck¹ /tʌk/ *v.t.* (stow) пря́тать, с-; под|бира́ть, -обра́ть
□ **~ away** *v.t.* запря́т|ывать, -ать
□ **~ in** *v.t.* запр|авля́ть, -а́вить; **~ your shirt in!** запра́вьте руба́шку!
□ **~ up** *v.t.:* **he ~ed up his sleeves** он засучи́л рукава́; **he ~ed the children up** (in bed) дете́й уложи́ли в крова́ть и укры́ли одея́лом

tuck² /tʌk/ *v.i.:* **they ~ed into their supper** они́ уплета́ли у́жин за о́бе щёки; **~ in!** налета́й(те)! (*на еду*)

✍ **Tuesday** /'tju:zdeɪ/ *n.* вто́рник

tuft /tʌft/ *n.* (of grass, hair, etc.) пучо́к

tug /tʌɡ/ *n.* **1** (pull) рыво́к, дёрганье **2** (boat) букси́р
● *v.t.* (**tugged**, **tugging**) тащи́ть (*impf.*)

t

• *v.i.* (**tugged, tugging**) дёр|гать, -нуть; he ~ged at my sleeve он дёрнул меня́ за рука́в

■ ~ **of war** *n.* перетя́гивание кана́та

tuition /tjuː'ɪʃ(ə)n/ *n.* обуче́ние

tulip /'tjuːlɪp/ *n.* тюльпа́н

tumble /'tʌmb(ə)l/ *n.* **1** (fall) паде́ние; **take a ~** упа́сть (*pf.*) **2** (acrobatic feat) кувыро́к
• *v.i.* сва́л|иваться, -и́ться
• *with adv.*: **the house seemed about to ~ down** дом, каза́лось, вот-во́т разва́лится

■ ~ **dryer** *n.* (BrE) электри́ческая суши́лка для белья́

tumbler /'tʌmblə(r)/ *n.* (glass) стака́н

tummy /'tʌmɪ/ *n.* (infml) живо́т(ик)

tumour /'tjuːmə(r)/ (AmE **tumor**) *n.* о́пухоль

tumult /'tjuːmʌlt/ *n.* сумато́ха

tumultuous /tjʊ'mʌltʃʊəs/ *adj.* шу́мный, беспоко́йный; **he received a ~ welcome** ему́ устро́или бу́рную встре́чу

tuna /'tjuːnə/ *n.* туне́ц

tundra /'tʌndrə/ *n.* ту́ндра

tune /tjuːn/ *n.* **1** (melody) мело́дия; моти́в **2** (correct pitch): **you are not singing in ~** вы фальши́вите; **he plays out of ~** он игра́ет фальши́во; **the piano is out of ~** фортепиа́но расстро́ено
• *v.t.* **1** (mus., bring to right pitch) настр|а́ивать, -о́ить; **tuning fork** камерто́н **2** (adjust running of) настр|а́ивать, -о́ить; регули́ровать, от-
□ ~ **in** *v.t. & i.* настр|а́ивать(ся), -о́ить(ся); **he ~d in to the BBC** он настро́ил приёмник на Би-би-си́

tuneful /'tjuːnfʊl/ *adj.* музыка́льный, мелоди́чный

tuneless /'tjuːnlɪs/ *adj.* немузыка́льный, немелоди́чный

tuner /'tjuːnə(r)/ *n.* (of pianos etc.) настро́йщик; (radio component) тю́нер; (receiver) (ра́дио)приёмник

tunic /'tjuːnɪk/ *n.* (ancient garment) туни́ка; (part of uniform) ки́тель (*m.*)

Tunisia /tjuː'nɪzɪə/ *n.* Туни́с

Tunisian /tjuː'nɪzɪən/ *n.* туни́с|ец (-ка)
• *adj.* туни́сский

tunnel /'tʌn(ə)l/ *n.* тонне́ль (*m.*), тунне́ль (*m.*)
• *v.t.* (**tunnelled, tunnelling**, AmE **tunneled, tunneling**): **they ~led their way out (of prison)** они́ сде́лали подко́п и сбежа́ли (из тюрьмы́)
• *v.i.* (**tunnelled, tunnelling**, AmE **tunneled, tunneling**) про|кла́дывать, -ложи́ть тонне́ль

turban /'tɜːbən/ *n.* тюрба́н

turbine /'tɜːbaɪn/ *n.* турби́на

turbulence /'tɜːbjʊləns/ *n.* бу́рность; (aeron.) турбуле́нтность; (fig.) суета́, сумато́ха

turbulent /'tɜːbjʊlənt/ *adj.* бу́рный; (fig.) беспоко́йный

turf /tɜːf/ *n.* (*pl.* **turfs** *or* **turves**) (grassy topsoil) дёрн; (peat) торф
• *v.t.* **1** (cover with ~) (*also* ~ **over**) покр|ыва́ть, -ы́ть дёрном **2**: ~ **out** (BrE, infml, eject) выбра́сывать, вы́бросить

turgid /'tɜːdʒɪd/ *adj.* (fig.) напы́щенный

Turk /tɜːk/ *n.* ту́р|ок (-ча́нка)

Turkey /'tɜːkɪ/ *n.* **1** (country) Ту́рция **2** (**t~**, *pl.* **t~s**) (bird) инд|ю́к (-е́йка); (as food) инде́йка, индю́шка

Turkish /'tɜːkɪʃ/ *n.* туре́цкий язы́к
• *adj.* туре́цкий

■ ~ **delight** *n.* раха́т-луку́м

Turkmen /'tɜːkmən/ *n.* (*pl.* ~ *or* ~**s**) (person) туркме́н (-ка); (language) туркме́нский язы́к
• *adj.* туркме́нский

Turkmenistan /tɜːkmenɪ'stɑːn/ *n.* Туркмениста́н

turmeric /'tɜːmərɪk/ *n.* курку́ма (*азиатская пряность*)

turmoil /'tɜːmɔɪl/ *n.* беспоря́док; смяте́ние

◆ **turn** /tɜːn/ *n.* **1** (rotation) поворо́т, оборо́т **2** (change of direction) поворо́т; **I took a right ~** я поверну́л напра́во **3** (change in condition) переме́на; поворо́т; **his condition took a ~ for the worse** его́ состоя́ние уху́дшилось **4** (chance of doing sth in proper order) о́чередь; **it's your ~ next** вы сле́дующий; **they all spoke in ~** (*or* **took ~s to speak**) они́ говори́ли по о́череди **5** (service) услу́га; **he did me a good ~** он оказа́л мне до́брую услу́гу **6** (performance) но́мер **7** (infml, shock) потрясе́ние; **you gave me quite a ~** вы меня́ поря́дком испуга́ли
• *v.t.* **1** (cause to move round) пов|ора́чивать, -ерну́ть; **he ~ed his head** он поверну́л го́лову; **she ~ed the pages** она́ перелиста́ла страни́цы **2** (direct) напр|авля́ть, -а́вить; **he can ~ his hand to anything** он всё уме́ет; (incline): ~ **sb against sb/sth** настр|а́ивать, -о́ить кого́-н. про́тив + *g.* **3** (pass round or beyond) пов|ора́чивать, -ерну́ть за + *a.*; slow down as you ~ **the corner** повора́чивая за у́гол, сба́вьте ско́рость; **it has ~ed two o'clock** уже́ два часа́; **he has ~ed fifty** ему́ испо́лнилось 50 лет **4** (transform) превра|ща́ть, -ти́ть; **he ~ed the water into wine** он обрати́л во́ду в вино́ **5** (cause to become): **the shock ~ed his hair white** он поседе́л от потрясе́ния **6** (send forcibly) прог|оня́ть, -на́ть; **he was ~ed out of the house** его́ вы́гнали из до́ма/из до́му
• *v.i.* **1** (move round) пов|ора́чиваться, -ерну́ться; враща́ться (*impf.*); **the key won't ~** ключ не повора́чивается; (fig.): **everything ~s on his answer** всё зави́сит от его́ отве́та; (revolve): **the discussion ~ed upon the meaning of democracy** спор враща́лся вокру́г по́длинного значе́ния демокра́тии **2** (change direction) свора́чиваться, сверну́ться; направля́ться (*impf.*); **right ~!** напра́во!; **who can I ~ to?** к кому́ я могу́ обрати́ться?; **he ~ed on his attackers** он бро́сился на свои́х оби́дчиков **3** (change) превра|ща́ться,

-ти́ться; **the tadpoles** ⁓ed **into frogs** голова́стики преврати́лись в лягу́шек; **he** ⁓ed **into a miser** он стал скря́гой **4** (become) ста|нови́ться, -ть; де́латься, с-; **she** ⁓ed **pale** она́ побледне́ла; **it has** ⁓ed **warm** потепле́ло

□ ⁓ **away** v.t. (refuse admittance to) прог|оня́ть, -на́ть; не пус|ка́ть, -ти́ть
 ● v.i.: **she** ⁓ed **away in disgust** она́ с отвраще́нием отверну́лась

□ ⁓ **back** v.t. (repel) от|сыла́ть, -осла́ть наза́д; **we were** ⁓ed **back at the frontier** нас верну́ли с грани́цы; (return to former position): **we cannot** ⁓ **the clock back** (fig.) мы не мо́жем поверну́ть вре́мя вспять
 ● v.i. пов|ора́чивать, -ерну́ть наза́д; пойти́ (pf.) обра́тно

□ ⁓ **down** v.t. (reduce by ⁓ing) уб|авля́ть, -а́вить; ⁓ **the volume down!** (TV, etc.) уба́вьте звук!; (reject) отв|ерга́ть, -е́ргнуть; отка́з|ываться, -а́ться от + g.; **my offer was** ⁓ed **down** моё предложе́ние бы́ло отве́ргнуто

□ ⁓ **in** v.t. (hand over) сда|ва́ть, -ть; **he** ⁓ed **himself in to the police** он сда́лся поли́ции

□ ⁓ **off** v.t. (e.g. light, engine) выключа́ть, вы́ключить; гаси́ть, по-; (tap) закр|ыва́ть, -ы́ть
 ● v.i. (make a diversion) св|ора́чивать, -ерну́ть

□ ⁓ **on** v.t. (e.g. light, engine, radio) включ|а́ть, -и́ть; (tap) откр|ыва́ть, -ы́ть; (fig.): **this music** ⁓s **me on** (infml) э́та му́зыка заво́дит меня́

□ ⁓ **out** v.t. (expel) прог|оня́ть, -на́ть; исключ|а́ть, -и́ть; (switch off) гаси́ть, по-; туши́ть, по-; (produce) выпуска́ть, вы́пустить; произв|оди́ть, -ести́; (empty) вывора́чивать, вы́вернуть
 ● v.i. (prove) ока́з|ываться, -а́ться; **let us see how things** ⁓ **out** посмо́трим, како́й оборо́т при́мут дела́; **he** ⁓ed **out to be a liar** он оказа́лся лжецо́м; **it** ⁓ed **out that he was right** получи́лось, что он был прав; (assemble) соб|ира́ться, -ра́ться

□ ⁓ **over** v.t. (overturn) перев|ора́чивать, -ерну́ть; опроки́|дывать, -нуть; (reverse position of): **I** ⁓ed **over the page** я переверну́л страни́цу; (hand over) перед|ава́ть, -а́ть; (have as a turnover, comm.) име́ть (impf.) оборо́т + g.
 ● v.i. (overturn) перев|ора́чиваться, -ерну́ться; (change position) перев|ора́чиваться, -ерну́ться; (revolve): **is the engine** ⁓ing **over?** дви́гатель враща́ется?

□ ⁓ **round** v.t. (change or reverse position of) перев|ора́чивать, -ерну́ть; **he** ⁓ed **his car round** он разверну́л маши́ну
 ● v.i. (change position): **he** ⁓ed **round to look** он оберну́лся, что́бы посмотре́ть; (revolve) враща́ться (impf.)

□ ⁓ **up** v.t. (increase flow of) приб|авля́ть, -а́вить; уси́ли|вать, -ть
 ● v.i. (arrive) появ|ля́ться, -и́ться; (be found; occur) ока́з|ываться, -а́ться; подв|ёртываться, -ерну́ться; (happen; become available) подверну́ться (pf.)

■ ⁓**around** n. (reversal of policy, opinion, etc.) поворо́т на 180 гра́дусов; ⁓-**off** n. поворо́т, бокова́я доро́га; (repulsive thing) что-н. отврати́тельное; ⁓**out** n. (assembly): **there was a very good** ⁓**out** собра́лось о́чень

мно́го наро́ду; ⁓**over** n. (in business) оборо́т (капита́ла); (of staff) теку́честь (ка́дров); ⁓**pike** n. (AmE, tolled highway) пла́тная автомагистра́ль; ⁓**stile** n. турнике́т; ⁓-**up** n. (BrE, of trouser) манже́та, отворо́т

turner /'tə:nə(r)/ n. то́карь (m.)

turning /'tə:nɪŋ/ n. поворо́т
■ ⁓ **point** n. (fig.) кри́зис, перело́м; **it was a** ⁓ **point in his career** э́то был поворо́тный моме́нт в его́ карье́ре

turnip /'tə:nɪp/ n. ре́па

turquoise /'tə:kwɔɪz/ n. бирюзо́вый цвет

turret /'tʌrɪt/ n. ба́шенка; (on a tank, warship, etc.) ба́шня

turtle /'tə:t(ə)l/ n. черепа́ха

tusk /tʌsk/ n. клык, би́вень (m.)

tussle /'tʌs(ə)l/ n. дра́ка

tutor /'tju:tə(r)/ n. (private teacher) репети́тор; (university teacher) преподава́тель (-ница (infml))

tutorial /tju:'tɔ:rɪəl/ n. ≈ семина́р

tutu /'tu:tu:/ n. па́чка (балерины)

tuxedo /tʌk'si:dəʊ/ n. (pl. ⁓s or ⁓es) (AmE) смо́кинг

 TV abbr. (of **television**) ТВ (телеви́дение); (set) телеви́зор, (infml) те́лик, я́щик

twang /twæŋ/ n. (of plucked string) звеня́щий звук натя́нутой струны́; (nasal voice) гнуса́вый го́лос

tweak /twi:k/ v.t. **1** (pull sharply) ущипну́ть (pf.) **2** (infml, adjust) соверше́нствовать, у-

tweed /twi:d/ n. твид; **a** ⁓ **jacket** тви́довый пиджа́к

tweet /twi:t/ n. **1** ще́бет, чири́канье **2** (comput., a message posted using Twitter®) твит
 ● v.i. **1** щебета́ть (impf.); чири́кать (impf.) **2** (comput., post a message using Twitter®) тви́тить (impf.)

tweezers /'twi:zəz/ n. pl. пинце́т

twelfth /twelfθ/ n. (date) двена́дцатое число́; (fraction) одна́ двена́дцатая
 ● adj. двена́дцатый

twelve /twelv/ n. двена́дцать
 ● adj. двена́дцать + g. pl.

twentieth /'twentɪəθ/ n. (date) двадца́тое число́; (fraction) одна́ двадца́тая
 ● adj. двадца́тый

twent|y /'twentɪ/ n. два́дцать; **she is still in her** ⁓**ies** ей ещё нет тридцати́; **the** ⁓**ies** (decade) двадца́тые го́ды
 ● adj. два́дцать + g. pl.

 twice /twaɪs/ adv. (two times) два́жды, два ра́за; (doubly) вдво́е, в два ра́за; ⁓ **a day** два́жды (or два ра́за) в день; **he is** ⁓ **my age** он вдво́е ста́рше меня́; ⁓ **as much** в два ра́за (or вдво́е) бо́льше

twiddl|e /'twɪd(ə)l/ v.t. верте́ть (impf.); крути́ть (impf.); **he sat there** ⁓ing **his thumbs** он бил баклу́ши; он безде́льничал

twig /twɪg/ n. (on tree) ве́тка; (when cut) прут

twilight /'twaɪlaɪt/ n. су́мер|ки (-ек)

t (margin tab)

twin /twɪn/ n. близне́ц; (in pl.) близнецы́, дво́йня (f. sg.)

● adj. одина́ковый; **they are ~ brothers** они́ (бра́тья-)близнецы́

● v.t. (**twinned**, **twinning**) (fig.) соедин|я́ть, -и́ть

■ **~ beds** n. pl. две односпа́льные крова́ти

twine /twaɪn/ n. бечёвка, шнуро́к

twinge /twɪndʒ/ n. при́ступ о́строй бо́ли; (fig.) му́ка; **~s of conscience** угрызе́ния со́вести

twinkle /'twɪŋk(ə)l/ v.i. мерца́ть (impf.); сверка́ть (impf.); **his eyes ~d with amusement** его́ глаза́ ве́село блесте́ли

twirl /twɜːl/ n. враще́ние

● v.t. & i. верте́ть(ся) (impf.); крути́ть(ся) (impf.)

twist /twɪst/ n. **1** (sharp turning motion) круче́ние **2** (sharp change of direction) изги́б, поворо́т; **a ~ in the plot** круто́й поворо́т сюже́та **3** (sth ~ed or spiral in shape) пе́тля; у́зел

● v.t. **1** (screw round) крути́ть (or скру́чивать), с-; **I ~ed my ankle** я подверну́л но́гу **2** (contort) искрив|ля́ть, -и́ть; (fig.) иска|жа́ть, -зи́ть **3** (wind) обв|ива́ть, -и́ть; обм|а́тывать, -ота́ть

● v.i. **1** (wriggle) ко́рчиться (impf.); извива́ться (impf.) **2** (twine) обв|ива́ться, -и́ться; **the tendrils ~ed round their support** побе́ги расте́ния вили́сь вокру́г жёрдочки

□ **~ off** v.t. откру́|чивать, -ти́ть

twisted /'twɪstɪd/ adj. (perverted) извращённый

twit /twɪt/ n. (BrE, infml) о́лух (infml)

twitch /twɪtʃ/ n. подёргивание, су́дорога

● v.t. **1** (jerk) дёргать (impf.) **2** (move spasmodically) подёргивать (impf.) + i.

● v.i. дёргаться (impf.), подёргиваться (impf.)

twitter /'twɪtə(r)/ n. **1** (chirping) щебет **2** (T~®) (service for micro-blogging) Тви́ттер **3** (chirp) щебета́ть (impf.)

⚔ **two** /tuː/ n. (число́/но́мер) два; (~ people) дво́е; **~ each, in ~s, at a time, ~ by ~** по́ два/дво́е; (cut, divide) **in ~** на́двое/попола́м; **the plate broke in ~** таре́лка разби́лась на две ча́сти; (figure, thing numbered 2) дво́йка; **I put ~ and ~ together** я сообрази́л, что к чему́; **that makes ~ of us** вот и я то́же

● adj. два + g. sg.; (for masculine nouns denoting people and pluralia tantum, also) дво́е + g. pl.; **~ students** два студе́нта, дво́е студе́нтов; **~ children** дво́е дете́й; два ребёнка; **~ watches** дво́е часо́в

■ **~-dimensional** adj. двухме́рный; **~-faced** adj. (fig.) двули́чный; **~-fold** adj. двойно́й

● adv. вдво́е; **~-seater** n. двухме́стный автомоби́ль/самолёт; **~-time** v.t. (infml) обма́н|ывать, -у́ть; измен|я́ть, -и́ть (жене́/му́жу); **~-way** adj. (e.g. traffic) двусторо́нний

tycoon /taɪˈkuːn/ n. (business magnate) магна́т

tying /'taɪɪŋ/ pres. part. of ▶ **tie**

tympani /'tɪmpənɪ/ n. = timpani

tympanist /'tɪmpənɪst/ n. = timpanist

⚔ **type** /taɪp/ n. **1** (class) тип, род **2** (letters for printing) шрифт

● v.t. (write with ~writer/computer) печа́тать, на- (на маши́нке/компью́тере)

● v.i. печа́тать (impf.) (на маши́нке/компью́тере)

■ **~cast** adj.: **he is ~cast as the butler** он всегда́ игра́ет роль дворе́цкого; **~face** n. шрифт; **~writer** n. пи́шущая маши́нка

typhoid /'taɪfɔɪd/ n. (also ~ **fever**) брюшно́й тиф

typhoon /taɪˈfuːn/ n. тайфу́н

⚔ **typical** /'tɪpɪk(ə)l/ adj. типи́чный; **that is ~ of him** э́то сво́йственно ему́

typify /'tɪpɪfaɪ/ v.t. быть типи́чным представи́телем + g.

typist /'taɪpɪst/ n. (female) машини́стка

typographic /taɪpəˈɡræfɪk/, **typographical** /taɪpəˈɡræfɪk(ə)l/ adjs. типогра́фский

typography /taɪˈpɒɡrəfɪ/ n. (art, process) полигра́фия; (of books) книгопеча́тание; (appearance of printed matter) оформле́ние (книги и т. п.)

tyrannical /tɪˈrænɪk(ə)l/ adj. тирани́ческий

tyrannize /'tɪrənaɪz/ v.t. & i. тира́нить (impf.)

tyranny /'tɪrənɪ/ n. тирани́я

tyrant /'taɪərənt/ n. тира́н

tyre /'taɪə(r)/ (AmE **tire**) n. ши́на

tzar /zɑː(r)/ n. = tsar

Uu

UAE *abbr.* (*of* **United Arab Emirates**) ОАЭ (Объединённые Ара́бские Эмира́ты)

ubiquitous /juːˈbɪkwɪtəs/ *adj.* вездесу́щий, повсеме́стный

ubiquity /juːˈbɪkwɪˈtɪ/ *n.* вездесу́щность

udder /ˈʌdə(r)/ *n.* вы́мя (*nt.*)

UEFA /juːˈeɪfə/ *abbr.* (*of* **Union of European Football Associations**) УЕФА́ (*m. & f. indecl.*)

UFO /juːefˈəʊ, ˈjuːfəʊ/ *n.* (*pl.* **UFOs**) (*of* **unidentified flying object**) НЛО (*m. indecl.*) (неопо́знанный лета́ющий объе́кт)

Uganda /juːˈɡændə/ *n.* Уга́нда

Ugandan /juːˈɡændən/ *n.* уганди́|ец (-йка)
● *adj.* уганди́йский

ugly /ˈʌɡlɪ/ *adj.* (**uglier, ugliest**) **1** (unsightly) уро́дливый, безобра́зный **2** (threatening) опа́сный
■ ~ **duckling** *n.* га́дкий утёнок

UK *abbr.* (*of* **United Kingdom**) Соединённое Короле́вство (*Великобрита́нии и Се́верной Ирла́ндии*)
● *adj.* (велико)брита́нский

Ukraine /juːˈkreɪn/ *n.* Украи́на; **in** ~ в Украи́не

Ukrainian /juːˈkreɪnɪən/ *n.* (person) украи́н|ец (-ка); (language) украи́нский язы́к
● *adj.* украи́нский

Ulan Bator /uːˈlɑːn ˈbɑːtə(r)/ *n.* Ула́н-Ба́тор

ulcer /ˈʌlsə(r)/ *n.* я́зва

ulcerated /ˈʌlsəreɪtɪd/ *adj.* изъязвлённый

Ulster /ˈʌlstə(r)/ *n.* О́льстер

ulterior /ʌlˈtɪərɪə(r)/ *adj.* скры́тый, невы́раженный
■ ~ **motive** *n.* скры́тый моти́в

ultimate /ˈʌltɪmət/ *adj.* после́дний, оконча́тельный

√ **ultimately** /ˈʌltɪmətlɪ/ *adv.* в конце́ концо́в

ultimatum /ʌltɪˈmeɪtəm/ *n.* ультима́тум

ultrasound /ˈʌltrəsaʊnd/ *n.* ультразву́к; ~ **scan** иссле́дование с по́мощью ультразвуково́го излуче́ния

ultraviolet /ʌltrəˈvaɪələt/ *adj.* ультрафиоле́товый

umbilical /ʌmˈbɪlɪk(ə)l/ *adj.*: ~ **cord** пупови́на

umbrage /ˈʌmbrɪdʒ/ *n.* оби́да; **take** ~ (**at**) об|ижа́ться, -и́деться (на + *a.*)

umbrella /ʌmˈbrelə/ *n.* зо́нтик, зонт

umpire /ˈʌmpaɪə(r)/ *n.* (arbitrator) посре́дник; (in games) судья́ (*m.*)

umpteenth /ʌmpˈtiːnθ/ *adj.* (infml) э́нный; **I have told you for the** ~ **time!** ско́лько раз я тебе́ говори́л!

UN *abbr.* (*of* **United Nations (Organization)**) ООН (*f. indecl.*) (Организа́ция Объединённых На́ций)

un- /ʌn/ *neg. pref.* (*often expressed by pref.*) не… (*e.g.* ▶ **unable**), *or* без…, бес… (*e.g.* ▶ **unashamed**)

√ **unable** /ʌnˈeɪb(ə)l/ *adj.* неспосо́бный; **he is** ~ **to swim** он не уме́ет пла́вать; **I am** ~ **to say** я не могу́ сказа́ть

unabridged /ʌnəˈbrɪdʒd/ *adj.* несокращённый, по́лный

unacceptable /ʌnəkˈseptəb(ə)l/ *adj.* неприе́млемый

unaccompanied /ʌnəˈkʌmpənɪd/ *adj.* нике́м не сопровожда́емый; (mus.) без аккомпанеме́нта

unaccountable /ʌnəˈkaʊntəb(ə)l/ *adj.* (inexplicable) необъясни́мый; (irrational) безотчётный; (not responsible): ~ **to** не несу́щий отве́тственности пе́ред + *i.*

unaccounted for /ʌnəˈkaʊntɪd/ *adj.* (missing): **two people were** ~ не досчита́лись двух челове́к

unaccustomed /ʌnəˈkʌstəmd/ *adj.* непривы́кший; ~ **as I am to public speaking** хотя́ я и не привы́к выступа́ть

unacknowledged /ʌnəkˈnɒlɪdʒd/ *adj.* непри́знанный

unadulterated /ʌnəˈdʌltəreɪtɪd/ *adj.* настоя́щий, неподде́льный; ~ **nonsense** чисте́йший/полне́йший вздор; **the** ~ **truth** чи́стая пра́вда

unaffected /ʌnəˈfektɪd/ *adj.* **1** (without affectation) непринуждённый **2** (not harmed or influenced): **our plans were** ~ **by the weather** пого́да не измени́ла на́ших пла́нов

unaided /ʌnˈeɪdɪd/ *adj.* без посторо́нней по́мощи

unalloyed /ʌnəˈlɔɪd/ *adj.* нелеги́рованный, чи́стый (*о мета́лле*); (fig.): ~ **pleasure** ниче́м не омрачённая ра́дость

unambiguous /ʌnæmˈbɪgjʊəs/ *adj.* недвусмы́сленный

unanimity /juːnəˈnɪmɪtɪ/ *n.* единоду́шие

unanimous /juːˈnænɪməs/ *adj.* единоду́шный, единогла́сный; **the resolution was passed** ~**ly** резолю́ция была́ при́нята единогла́сно

unannounced /ʌnəˈnaʊnst/ *adj.* (to arrive, enter) без докла́да

unanswered /ʌnˈɑːnsəd/ *adj.* оста́вшийся без отве́та

unapologetic /ʌnəpɒləˈdʒetɪk/ *adj.* не прибега́ющий к оправда́ниям

unappealing /ʌnəˈpiːlɪŋ/ *adj.* неприя́тный

u

unappreciative /ˌʌnəˈpriːʃ(ɪ)ətɪv/ adj.
неблагода́рный

unapproachable /ˌʌnəˈprəʊtʃəb(ə)l/ adj.
недосту́пный

unarmed /ʌnˈɑːmd/ adj. невооружённый
■ ~ **combat** n. самозащи́та без ору́жия

unashamed /ˌʌnəˈʃeɪmd/ adj. бессты́дный

unasked /ʌnˈɑːskt/ adj. непро́шеный

unassailable /ˌʌnəˈseɪləb(ə)l/ adj.: an ~
fortress непристу́пная кре́пость; an ~
argument неопроверж́ймый до́вод

unassuming /ˌʌnəˈsjuːmɪŋ/ adj.
непритяза́тельный

unattached /ˌʌnəˈtætʃt/ adj. не привя́занный/
прикреплённый (to: к + d.); she is ~ она́
одино́ка

unattainable /ˌʌnəˈteɪnəb(ə)l/ adj.
недосяга́емый

unattractive /ˌʌnəˈtræktɪv/ adj.
непривлека́тельный

unauthorized /ʌnˈɔːθəraɪzd/ adj.
неразрешённый; (person) посторо́нний

unavailable /ˌʌnəˈveɪləb(ə)l/ adj.
недосту́пный; he was ~ он был за́нят

unavoidabl|e /ˌʌnəˈvɔɪdəb(ə)l/ adj. (sure to
happen) неизбе́жный; I was ~y detained я не
мог освободи́ться (ра́ньше)

unaware /ˌʌnəˈweə(r)/ adj. незна́ющий; he
was ~ of my presence он не подозрева́л
о моём прису́тствии; I was ~ that he was
married я не знал, что он жена́т

unawares /ˌʌnəˈweəz/ adv. неча́янно; I was
taken ~ by his question его́ вопро́с засти́г
меня́ враспло́х

unbalanced /ʌnˈbælənst/ adj. (biased)
односторо́нний; (mentally disturbed)
неуравнове́шенный, неусто́йчивый

unbearable /ʌnˈbeərəb(ə)l/ adj.
невыноси́мый

unbeaten /ʌnˈbiːt(ə)n/ adj.
непревзойдённый

unbeknown /ˌʌnbɪˈnəʊn/ (infml
unbeknownst /-ˈnəʊnst/) adv.: he did it ~
to me он сде́лал э́то без моего́ ве́дома

unbelievable /ˌʌnbɪˈliːvəb(ə)l/ adj. (infml,
amazing) невероя́тный

unbiased, unbiassed /ʌnˈbaɪəst/ adj.
беспристра́стный

unblemished /ʌnˈblemɪʃt/ adj. чи́стый; (fig.)
незапя́тнанный

unblock /ʌnˈblɒk/ v.t.: the plumber ~ed the
drain водопрово́дчик прочи́стил водосто́к

unbolt /ʌnˈbəʊlt/ v.t. (door) отп|ира́ть, -ере́ть

unborn /ʌnˈbɔːn/ adj.: her ~ child её ещё не
роди́вшийся ребёнок

unbounded /ʌnˈbaʊndɪd/ adj. безме́рный

unbridled /ʌnˈbraɪd(ə)ld/ adj. (fig.)
необу́зданный

unbroken /ʌnˈbrəʊkən/ adj.: only one plate
was ~ то́лько одна́ таре́лка уцеле́ла; his
spirit remained ~ его́ дух не́ был сло́млен;

an ~ record непревзойдённый/непоби́тый
реко́рд; ~ sleep непреры́вный сон

unburden /ʌnˈbɜːd(ə)n/ v.t.: he ~ed his soul
(or himself) to me он изли́л мне ду́шу

unbutton /ʌnˈbʌt(ə)n/ v.t. расстёг|ивать,
-ну́ть

uncalled for /ʌnˈkɔːld fɔː(r)/ adj. неуме́стный

uncanny /ʌnˈkænɪ/ adj. (**uncannier,
uncanniest**) стра́нный

unceasing /ʌnˈsiːsɪŋ/ adj. беспреры́вный

unceremonious /ˌʌnserɪˈməʊnɪəs/ adj.
(abrupt, discourteous) бесцеремо́нный

uncertain /ʌnˈsɜːt(ə)n/ adj. **1** (hesitant,
in doubt) неуве́ренный; he was ~ what
to do он не знал, что де́лать **2** (not
clear) нея́сный; in no ~ terms весьма́
недвусмы́сленно **3** (changeable, unreliable): the
weather is ~ пого́да изме́нчива; my position
is ~ (shaky) моё положе́ние неопределённо

uncertainty /ʌnˈsɜːt(ə)ntɪ/ n. **1** (hesitation)
неуве́ренность **2** (unreliable nature)
изме́нчивость

unchanged /ʌnˈtʃeɪndʒd/ adj.
неизмени́вшийся; to remain ~ ост|ава́ться,
-а́ться без измене́ний

uncharitable /ʌnˈtʃærɪtəb(ə)l/ adj. жесто́кий

uncharted /ʌnˈtʃɑːtɪd/ adj. не отме́ченный
на ка́рте; (also fig.) неиссле́дованный,
неизве́данный

unchecked /ʌnˈtʃekt/ adj.: an ~ advance (mil.)
беспрепя́тственное продвиже́ние

uncivilized /ʌnˈsɪvɪlaɪzd/ adj.
нецивилизо́ванный

unclean /ʌnˈkliːn/ adj. нечи́стый

uncomfortable /ʌnˈkʌmftəb(ə)l/ adj. (lit.,
fig.) неудо́бный; (situation) нело́вкий

uncommon /ʌnˈkɒmən/ adj. ре́дкий

uncommunicative /ˌʌnkəˈmjuːnɪkətɪv/ adj.
неразгово́рчивый

uncomplimentary /ˌʌnkɒmplɪˈmentərɪ/ adj.
неле́стный

uncompromising /ʌnˈkɒmprəmaɪzɪŋ/ adj.
бескомпроми́ссный

unconcealed /ˌʌnkənˈsiːld/ adj.
нескрыва́емый

unconcern /ˌʌnkənˈsɜːn/ n. беззабо́тность,
беспе́чность; безразли́чие, равноду́шие

unconcerned /ˌʌnkənˈsɜːnd/ adj. (carefree)
беззабо́тный; (indifferent) безразли́чный

unconditional /ˌʌnkənˈdɪʃən(ə)l/ adj.
безусло́вный, безогово́рочный

unconfirmed /ˌʌnkənˈfɜːmd/ adj.
неподтверждённый

unconnected /ˌʌnkəˈnektɪd/ adj. не
свя́занный

unconscious /ʌnˈkɒnʃəs/ n.: the ~ (psych.)
подсозна́ние
● adj. **1** (senseless) потеря́вший созна́ние;
he was ~ он был без созна́ния/в
обмо́роке; he was knocked ~ он потеря́л
созна́ние от уда́ра **2** (unaware) не
сознаю́щий **3** (unintentional) нево́льный

u

unconsciousness /ʌn'kɒnʃəsnɪs/ *n.* (physical) бессозна́тельное/обморо́чное состоя́ние; (unawareness) отсу́тствие (о)созна́ния, неосо́знанность

unconstitutional /ʌnkɒnstɪ'tju:ʃən(ə)l/ *adj.* неконституцио́нный, противоре́чащий конститу́ции

uncontested /ʌnkən'testɪd/ *adj.* неоспори́мый

uncontrollable /ʌnkən'trəʊləb(ə)l/ *adj.*: an ~ temper неукроти́мый нрав; an ~ child неуправля́емый ребёнок

unconventional /ʌnkən'venʃən(ə)l/ *adj.* нетрадицио́нный; (person, behaviour) нешабло́нный

unconvincing /ʌnkən'vɪnsɪŋ/ *adj.* неубеди́тельный

uncooked /ʌn'kʊkt/ *adj.* сыро́й

uncooperative /ʌnkəʊ'ɒpərətɪv/ *adj.* равноду́шный

uncountable /ʌn'kaʊntəb(ə)l/ *adj.* (gram.) неисчисля́емый

uncouth /ʌn'ku:θ/ *adj.* грубый

uncover /ʌn'kʌvə(r)/ *v.t.* (take cover off) сн|има́ть, -ять покро́в с + g.; (fig.) раскр|ыва́ть, -ы́ть

unctuous /'ʌŋktʃʊəs/ *adj.* (ingratiating) еле́йный (liter.), чрезме́рно уго́дливый, слаща́во-любе́зный

uncultivated /ʌn'kʌltɪveɪtɪd/ *adj.* (of land) необрабо́танный; (of person) некульту́рный

uncut /ʌn'kʌt/ *adj.* (page, loop) неразре́занный; (grass) неподстри́женный; the film was shown ~ фильм показа́ли в по́лной ве́рсии

undamaged /ʌn'dæmɪdʒd/ *adj.* неповреждённый

undaunted /ʌn'dɔ:ntɪd/ *adj.* неустраши́мый

undecided /ʌndɪ'saɪdɪd/ *adj.* (not settled) нерешённый; (hesitating) нереши́тельный

undeniable /ʌndɪ'naɪəb(ə)l/ *adj.* неоспори́мый, я́вный

◆ **under** /'ʌndə(r)/ *adv.* вниз; the ship went ~ кора́бль затону́л
● *prep.* **1** под + *i.*; (of motion) под + *a.*; (out) from ~ из-под + *g.* **2** (less than) ме́ньше + *g.*; ни́же + *g.*; he earns ~ £400 a week он зараба́тывает ме́ньше четырёхсо́т фу́нтов в неде́лю; children ~ 14 де́ти моло́же (*or* в во́зрасте до) четы́рнадцати лет **3** (var. uses): you are ~ arrest вы аресто́ваны; ~ the circumstances при сложи́вшихся обстоя́тельствах; ~ discussion обсужда́емый; (in progress): the investigation is ~ way ведётся рассле́дование

underarm /'ʌndərɑ:m/ *adj.*: an ~ deodorant дезодора́нт для подмы́шек; an ~ throw бросо́к сни́зу; serve ~ под|ава́ть, -а́ть сни́зу

undercarriage /'ʌndəkærɪdʒ/ *n.* (of a plane) шасси́ (*nt. indecl.*)

undercharge /ʌndə'tʃɑ:dʒ/ *v.t.* брать, взять с кого́-н. недоста́точно

underclothes /'ʌndəkləʊðz/ *n. pl.* ни́жнее бельё

undercoat /'ʌndəkəʊt/ *n.* (of paint) грунто́вка

undercover /ʌndə'kʌvə(r)/ *adj.* та́йный

undercurrent /'ʌndəkʌrənt/ *n.* подво́дное тече́ние; (fig.) скры́тая тенде́нция

undercut /ʌndə'kʌt/ *v.t.*: he ~ his competitor он назна́чил це́ну ни́же, чем его́ конкуре́нт

underdeveloped /ʌndədɪ'veləpt/ *adj.* недора́звитый; ~ countries слабора́звитые стра́ны

underdog /'ʌndədɒg/ *n.* (sport) побеждённая сторона́; (downtrodden person) неуда́чник

underdone /ʌndə'dʌn/ *adj.* (of food) недожа́ренный

underestimate /ʌndər'estɪmeɪt/ *v.t.* недооце́н|ивать, -и́ть

underfed /ʌndə'fed/ *adj.* недоеда́ющий; (infant) недоко́рмленный

underfoot /ʌndə'fʊt/ *adv.* под нога́ми

underfunded /ʌndə'fʌndɪd/ *adj.*: the project was ~ прое́кт получи́л недоста́точное финанси́рование

undergo /ʌndə'gəʊ/ *v.t.* испы́т|ывать, -а́ть; he has to ~ an operation ему́ предстои́т опера́ция

undergraduate /ʌndə'grædjʊət/ *n.* студе́нт (-ка)

underground /'ʌndəgraʊnd/ *n.* **1** (BrE, ~ railway) метро́ (*indecl.*) **2** (~ movement) подпо́лье
● *adj.* подзе́мный; (fig., secret, subversive) подпо́льный
● *adv.* (position) под землёй; (direction) под зе́млю; (fig.) подпо́льно

undergrowth /'ʌndəgrəʊθ/ *n.* подле́сок

underhand /'ʌndəhænd/ *adj.* (secret, deceitful) закули́сный, та́йный

underlay /'ʌndəleɪ/ *n.* (fabric) подкла́дка, подсти́лка

underl|ie /ʌndə'laɪ/ *v.t.* (fig.): ~ying causes причи́ны, лежа́щие в осно́ве (*чего*)

underline /ʌndə'laɪn/ *v.t.* (lit., fig.) подч|ёркивать, -еркну́ть

underling /'ʌndəlɪŋ/ *n.* ме́лкий чино́вник

undermine /ʌndə'maɪn/ *v.t.* подк|а́пывать, -опа́ть; (fig.) разр|уша́ть, -у́шить; his authority is ~d его́ авторите́т подрыва́ют

underneath /ʌndə'ni:θ/ *adv.* внизу́, ни́же
● *prep.* под + *i.*; (of motion) под + *a.*

undernourished /ʌndə'nʌrɪʃt/ *adj.* недоеда́ющий; (infant) недоко́рмленный

underpants /'ʌndəpænts/ *n. pl.* (мужски́е) трус|ы́ (-о́в)

underpass /'ʌndəpɑ:s/ *n.* прое́зд под полотно́м желе́зной доро́ги

underpay /ʌndə'peɪ/ *v.t.* (worker) недопл|а́чивать, -ати́ть + *d.*

underpin /ʌndə'pɪn/ *v.t.* подв|оди́ть, -ести́ фунда́мент под + *a.*; (fig.) подде́рж|ивать, -а́ть

underprivileged /ʌndə'prɪvɪlɪdʒd/ *adj.* неиму́щий

underrate /ʌndə'reɪt/ *v.t.* недооце́н|ивать, -и́ть

u

underscore /ˌʌndəˈskɔː(r)/ *v.t.* подч|ёркивать, -еркну́ть

undersecretary /ˌʌndəˈsekrətəri/ *n.* замести́тель (*m.*) /помо́щник мини́стра

undersell /ˌʌndəˈsel/ *v.t.* (another seller) прод|ава́ть, -а́ть дешéвле (*кого*)

undershirt /ˈʌndəʃɜːt/ *n.* (AmE) ма́йка

underside /ˈʌndəsaɪd/ *n.* низ; ни́жняя часть; (fig., less favourable aspect) непригля́дная сторона́

understaffed /ˌʌndəˈstɑːft/ *adj.* неукомплекто́ванный

⚡ **understand** /ˌʌndəˈstænd/ *v.t.* **1** (comprehend) пон|има́ть, -я́ть; **he can make himself understood in English** он мо́жет объясни́ться по-англи́йски; **he ~s children** он уме́ет обраща́ться с детьми́ **2** (gather): **I ~ you are leaving** я слы́шал, что вы уезжа́ете

understandable /ˌʌndəˈstændəb(ə)l/ *adj.* поня́тный

⚡ **understanding** /ˌʌndəˈstændɪŋ/ *n.* **1** (intellect) ум **2** (comprehension) понима́ние **3** (sympathy) понима́ние **4** (agreement) соглаше́ние; **on the clear ~ that …** то́лько при усло́вии, что… ● *adj.* (sympathetic) отзы́вчивый, чу́ткий

understatement /ˈʌndəsteɪtmənt/ *n.* преуменьше́ние

understudy /ˈʌndəstʌdi/ *n.* дублёр

undertake /ˌʌndəˈteɪk/ *v.t.* **1** (take on) предприн|има́ть, -я́ть **2** (promise) обя́з|ываться, -а́ться

undertaker /ˈʌndəteɪkə(r)/ *n.* заве́дующий похоро́нным бюро́

undertaking /ˈʌndəteɪkɪŋ/ *n.* (enterprise) предприя́тие; (pledge) обяза́тельство

undertone /ˈʌndətəʊn/ *n.* полуто́н; **in an ~** вполго́лоса; (fig.) отте́нок

undervalue /ˌʌndəˈvælju:/ *v.t.* недооце́н|ивать, -и́ть

underwater /ˌʌndəˈwɔːtə(r)/ *adj.* подво́дный

underwear /ˈʌndəweə(r)/ *n.* (ни́жнее) бельё

underweight /ˌʌndəˈweɪt/ *adj.*: **she's ~** она́ сли́шком худа́я

underworld /ˈʌndəwɜːld/ *n.* (criminal society) престу́пный мир

underwriter /ˈʌndəraɪtə(r)/ *n.* (insurer) страхо́вщик; (guarantor) гара́нт

undeserved /ˌʌndɪˈzɜːvd/ *adj.* незаслу́женный

undesirable /ˌʌndɪˈzaɪərəb(ə)l/ *adj.* нежела́тельный

undetected /ˌʌndɪˈtektɪd/ *adj.* необнару́женный

undeveloped /ˌʌndɪˈveləpt/ *adj.* неразвито́й; **an ~ country** слаборазви́тая страна́; **~ land** необрабо́танная земля́

undignified /ʌnˈdɪɡnɪfaɪd/ *adj.* недосто́йный

undisciplined /ʌnˈdɪsɪplɪnd/ *adj.* недисциплини́рованный

undiscovered /ˌʌndɪˈskʌvəd/ *adj.* неоткры́тый

undiscriminating /ˌʌndɪˈskrɪmɪneɪtɪŋ/ *adj.* неразбо́рчивый

undisguised /ˌʌndɪsˈɡaɪzd/ *adj.* незамаскиро́ванный

undisputed /ˌʌndɪˈspju:tɪd/ *adj.* неоспори́мый

undisturbed /ˌʌndɪˈstɜːbd/ *adj.* (peaceful) споко́йный; (untouched) нетро́нутый; (indifferent) равноду́шный; **he was ~ by the news** но́вость (ничу́ть) не встрево́жила его́

undivided /ˌʌndɪˈvaɪdɪd/ *adj.*: **~ attention** неразде́льное внима́ние

undo /ʌnˈdu:/ *v.t.* **1** (unfasten) развя́з|ывать, -а́ть **2** (annul) уничт|ожа́ть, -о́жить; (treaty, agreement) аннули́ровать (*impf., pf.*)

undoubted /ʌnˈdaʊtɪd/ *adj.* несомне́нный; **you are ~ly right** вы, несомне́нно/ безусло́вно, пра́вы

undress /ʌnˈdres/ *v.t. & i.* разд|ева́ть(ся), -е́ть(ся)

undrinkable /ʌnˈdrɪŋkəb(ə)l/ *adj.* неприго́дный для питья́

undue /ʌnˈdju:/ *adj.* чрезме́рный

undulat|e /ˈʌndjʊleɪt/ *v.i.* волнова́ться (*impf.*); колыха́ться (*impf.*); **an ~ing landscape** холми́стый пейза́ж

undulating /ˈʌndjʊleɪtɪŋ/ *adj.*: холми́стый

unduly /ʌnˈdju:li/ *adv.* чрезме́рно

undying /ʌnˈdaɪɪŋ/ *adj.* бессме́ртный

unearned /ʌnˈɜːnd/ *adj.* незарабо́танный; **~ income** ре́нтный дохо́д, дохо́д от сбереже́ний, це́нных бума́г, недви́жимости

unearth /ʌnˈɜːθ/ *v.t.* выка́пывать, вы́копать; **the body was ~ed** те́ло вы́копали; (fig., discover) раск|а́пывать, -опа́ть

unearthly /ʌnˈɜːθli/ *adj.* **1** (supernatural) неземно́й **2** (ghostly) при́зрачный **3** (infml): **at this/that/some/an ~ hour** ни свет ни заря́; **don't call me again at that/this ~ hour!** не звони́ мне бо́льше в таку́ю рань!

unease /ʌnˈiːz/ *n.* нело́вкость, стеснённость; (distress) трево́га

uneasiness /ʌnˈiːzɪnɪs/ *n.* нело́вкость (*смуще́ние*)

uneasy /ʌnˈiːzi/ *adj.* **1** (anxious) беспоко́йный **2** (ill at ease) стеснённый

uneconomic /ˌʌniːkəˈnɒmɪk/ *adj.* неэконо́мный; нерента́бельный

uneconomical /ˌʌniːkəˈnɒmɪk(ə)l/ *adj.* неэконо́мный

uneducated /ʌnˈedjʊkeɪtɪd/ *adj.* необразо́ванный

unemployable /ˌʌnɪmˈplɔɪəb(ə)l/ *adj.* нетрудоспосо́бный

unemployed /ˌʌnɪmˈplɔɪd/ *adj.* безрабо́тный; (*as n.*) **the ~** безрабо́тные (*pl.*)

unemployment /ˌʌnɪmˈplɔɪmənt/ *n.* безрабо́тица
■ **~ benefit** *n.* посо́бие по безрабо́тице

unending /ʌnˈendɪŋ/ *adj.* несконча́емый, бесконе́чный

unenthusiastic /ˌʌnɪnθjuːziˈæstɪk/ *adj.* невосто́рженный

unenviable /ʌnˈenvɪəb(ə)l/ *adj.* незавидный
unequal /ʌnˈiːkw(ə)l/ *adj.* неравный
unequivocal /ʌnɪˈkwɪvək(ə)l/ *adj.* недвусмысленный; (support) определённый
unerring /ʌnˈəːrɪŋ/ *adj.* безошибочный
UNESCO /juːˈneskəʊ/ *n.* (*abbr. of* **United Nations Educational, Scientific, and Cultural Organization**) ЮНЕСКО (*f. indecl.*) (Организация Объединённых Наций по вопросам образования, науки и культуры)
unethical /ʌnˈeθɪk(ə)l/ *adj.* неэтичный
uneven /ʌnˈiːv(ə)n/ *adj.* неровный; неравномерный
uneventful /ʌnɪˈventfʊl/ *adj.* тихий
unexceptionable /ʌnɪkˈsepʃənəb(ə)l/ *adj.* безупречный
unexceptional /ʌnɪkˈsepʃ(ə)n(ə)l/ *adj.* неисключительный, заурядный
unexciting /ʌnɪkˈsaɪtɪŋ/ *adj.* скучный
unexpected /ʌnɪkˈspektɪd/ *adj.* неожиданный
unfailing /ʌnˈfeɪlɪŋ/ *adj.* (friend) верный; (support) неизменный
unfair /ʌnˈfeə(r)/ *adj.* несправедливый; ~ **advantage** незаконное преимущество
unfairness /ʌnˈfeənɪs/ *n.* несправедливость
unfaithful /ʌnˈfeɪθfʊl/ *adj.* неверный; **his wife was** ~ **to him** жена ему изменила
unfaithfulness /ʌnˈfeɪθfʊlnɪs/ *n.* неверность (**to**: + *d.*)
unfamiliar /ʌnfəˈmɪljə(r)/ *adj.* незнакомый; **I am** ~ **with the district** я не знаю этот район
unfashionable /ʌnˈfæʃənəb(ə)l/ *adj.* немодный
unfasten /ʌnˈfɑːs(ə)n/ *v.t.* откреп|лять, -ить; (untie) отвяз|ывать, -ать; (unbutton, unclasp) отстёг|ивать, -нуть; (open) откр|ывать, -ыть
unfavourable /ʌnˈfeɪvərəb(ə)l/ (*AmE* **unfavorable**) *adj.* неблагоприятный
unfeeling /ʌnˈfiːlɪŋ/ *adj.* бесчувственный; жестокий
unfinished /ʌnˈfɪnɪʃt/ *adj.* незаконченный
unfit /ʌnˈfɪt/ *adj.* неподходящий; **food** ~ **for (human) consumption** негодная к употреблению пища; ~ **to rule** неспособный править
unflattering /ʌnˈflætərɪŋ/ *adj.* нелестный
unfold /ʌnˈfəʊld/ *v.t.* развёр|тывать, -нуть; (fig.) раскр|ывать, -ыть
● *v.i.* развёр|тываться, -нуться; **as the story** ~**s** по ходу повествования
unforeseeable /ʌnfɔːˈsiːəb(ə)l/ *adj.* непредвиденный
unforeseen /ʌnfɔːˈsiːn/ *adj.* непредвиденный
unforgettable /ʌnfəˈgetəb(ə)l/ *adj.* незабываемый
unforgivable /ʌnfəˈgɪvəb(ə)l/ *adj.* непростительный
unforgiving /ʌnfəˈgɪvɪŋ/ *adj.* непрощающий
unfortunate /ʌnˈfɔːtʃənət/ *adj.* (person) несчастный; (remark) неудачный

✓ **unfortunately** /ʌnˈfɔːtʃənətlɪ/ *adv.* к сожалению; ~ **for him** к несчастью для него
unfounded /ʌnˈfaʊndɪd/ *adj.* необоснованный
unfriendly /ʌnˈfrendlɪ/ *adj.* недружелюбный
unfulfilled /ʌnfʊlˈfɪld/ *adj.* неудовлетворённый
unfurnished /ʌnˈfəːnɪʃt/ *adj.* немеблированный, необставленный
ungainly /ʌnˈgeɪnlɪ/ *adj.* неловкий, неуклюжий
ungodly /ʌnˈgɒdlɪ/ *adj.* (infml) = **unearthly 3**
ungovernable /ʌnˈgʌvənəb(ə)l/ *adj.* неуправляемый
ungracious /ʌnˈgreɪʃəs/ *adj.* невежливый
ungrammatical /ʌngrəˈmætɪk(ə)l/ *adj.* неграмотный (*о тексте*)
ungrateful /ʌnˈgreɪtfʊl/ *adj.* неблагодарный
unguarded /ʌnˈgɑːdɪd/ *adj.* (e.g. town) незащищённый; (e.g. prisoner) неохраняемый; (careless) неосторожный
unhappily /ʌnˈhæpɪlɪ/ *adv.* **1** (without happiness) несчастливо **2** (unfortunately) к несчастью
unhappiness /ʌnˈhæpɪnɪs/ *n.* несчастье, грусть
unhappy /ʌnˈhæpɪ/ *adj.* (sorrowful) несчастливый, несчастный, грустный; (unfortunate) неудачный
unharmed /ʌnˈhɑːmd/ *adj.* невредимый; (*pred.*) цел и невредим
unhealthy /ʌnˈhelθɪ/ *adj.* **1** (in or indicating ill health) нездоровый, болезненный **2** (infml, dangerous) вредный
unheard /ʌnˈhəːd ɒv/ *adj.* неслыханный, небывалый
unheeded /ʌnˈhiːdɪd/ *adj.* незамеченный; **his advice went** ~ к его совету не прислушивались
unhelpful /ʌnˈhelpfʊl/ *adj.* бесполезный; (person) неотзывчивый
unhinge /ʌnˈhɪndʒ/ *v.t.* (lit.) сн|имать, -ять с петель; (fig.) расстр|аивать, -оить; **the tragedy** ~**d his mind** от пережитой трагедии он помешался
unhook /ʌnˈhʊk/ *v.t.* расстёг|ивать, -нуть
unhurried /ʌnˈhʌrɪd/ *adj.* неторопливый
unhurt /ʌnˈhəːt/ *adj.* невредимый
unhygienic /ʌnhaɪˈdʒiːnɪk/ *adj.* негигиеничный
unicorn /ˈjuːnɪkɔːn/ *n.* единорог
unidentified /ʌnaɪˈdentɪfaɪd/ *adj.* неопознанный
unification /juːnɪfɪˈkeɪʃ(ə)n/ *n.* объединение
uniform /ˈjuːnɪfɔːm/ *n.* форма; (esp. mil.) мундир
● *adj.* однообразный; одинаковый; стандартный
uniformed /ˈjuːnɪfɔːmd/ *adj.* одетый в форму; в мундире
uniformity /juːnɪˈfɔːmɪtɪ/ *n.* единообразие
unify /ˈjuːnɪfaɪ/ *v.t.* объедин|ять, -ить

u

unilateral /ˌjuːnɪˈlætər(ə)l/ *adj.* односторо́нний

unimaginable /ˌʌnɪˈmædʒɪnəb(ə)l/ *adj.* невообрази́мый

unimaginative /ˌʌnɪˈmædʒɪnətɪv/ *adj.* прозаи́чный

unimpeachable /ˌʌnɪmˈpiːtʃəb(ə)l/ *adj.* безупре́чный, безукори́зненный

unimpeded /ˌʌnɪmˈpiːdɪd/ *adj.* беспрепя́тственный

unimportant /ˌʌnɪmˈpɔːt(ə)nt/ *adj.* нева́жный, незначи́тельный

unimpressed /ˌʌnɪmˈprest/ *adj.*: I was ~ by his threats его́ угро́зы не произвели́ на меня́ никако́го впечатле́ния

uninhabitable /ˌʌnɪnˈhæbɪtəb(ə)l/ *adj.* непригодный для жилья́

uninhabited /ˌʌnɪnˈhæbɪtɪd/ *adj.* необита́емый

uninhibited /ˌʌnɪnˈhɪbɪtɪd/ *adj.* откры́тый, нестесни́тельный

uninitiated /ˌʌnɪˈnɪʃɪeɪtɪd/ *adj.* непосвящённый

uninjured /ˌʌnˈɪndʒəd/ *adj.* непострада́вший; he was ~ by his fall при паде́нии он не пострада́л

unintelligible /ˌʌnɪnˈtelɪdʒɪb(ə)l/ *adj.* неразбо́рчивый

unintended /ˌʌnɪnˈtendɪd/ *adj.* ненаме́ренный; (unforeseen) непредусмотренный

unintentional /ˌʌnɪnˈtenʃən(ə)l/ *adj.* ненаме́ренный

uninterested /ˌʌnˈɪntrestɪd/ *adj.* безразли́чный (in: к + *d.*)

uninteresting /ˌʌnˈɪntrestɪŋ/ *adj.* неинтере́сный

uninvited /ˌʌnɪnˈvaɪtɪd/ *adj.* незва́ный

uninviting /ˌʌnɪnˈvaɪtɪŋ/ *adj.* непривлека́тельный; an ~ prospect неприя́тная перспекти́ва

◆ **union** /ˈjuːnjən/ *n.* **1** (joining, uniting) объедине́ние, сою́з **2** (association) сою́з; students' ~ студе́нческий сою́з; (building) студе́нческий клуб **3** (trade ~) профсою́з
■ U~ Jack *n.* госуда́рственный флаг Великобрита́нии

◆ **unique** /juːˈniːk/ *adj.* уника́льный, еди́нственный (в своём ро́де)

unisex /ˈjuːnɪseks/ *adj.*: ~ clothes оде́жда, подходя́щая для обо́их поло́в; ~ hairdresser's парикма́херская для мужчи́н и же́нщин

unison /ˈjuːnɪs(ə)n/ *n.* (fig.) гармо́ния; they acted in perfect ~ они́ де́йствовали в по́лном согла́сии

◆ **unit** /ˈjuːnɪt/ *n.* **1** (single entity) едини́ца; це́лое **2** (math., and of measurement) едини́ца; monetary ~ де́нежная едини́ца **3** (mil.) часть **4** (of furniture etc.) се́кция
■ ~ trust *n.* (BrE) довери́тельный паево́й фонд

◆ ключева́я ле́ксика

unite /juːˈnaɪt/ *v.t.* соедин|я́ть, -и́ть; the U~d Nations (organization) Организа́ция Объединённых На́ций; the U~d Kingdom Соединённое Короле́вство; the U~d States Соединённые Шта́ты
● *v.i.* соедин|я́ться, -и́ться; ~d front еди́ный фронт

unity /ˈjuːnɪtɪ/ *n.* **1** (oneness; coherence) еди́нство **2** (concord) согла́сие

universal /ˌjuːnɪˈvɜːs(ə)l/ *adj.* всео́бщий, универса́льный

universe /ˈjuːnɪvɜːs/ *n.* вселе́нная

◆ **university** /ˌjuːnɪˈvɜːsɪtɪ/ *n.* университе́т

unjust /ʌnˈdʒʌst/ *adj.* несправедли́вый

unjustified /ʌnˈdʒʌstɪfaɪd/ *adj.* неопра́вданный

unkempt /ʌnˈkempt/ *adj.* растрёпанный

unkind /ʌnˈkaɪnd/ *adj.* недо́брый, злой; (unpleasant) нелюбе́зный; be ~ to sb пло́хо обраща́ться (*impf.*) с кем-н.

unkindness /ʌnˈkaɪndnɪs/ *n.* злость; нелюбе́зность

unknown /ʌnˈnəʊn/ *n.* неизве́стное
● *adj.* неизве́стный

unlace /ʌnˈleɪs/ *v.t.* расшнуро́в|ывать, -а́ть

unlawful /ʌnˈlɔːfʊl/ *adj.* незако́нный

unleaded /ʌnˈledɪd/ *adj.*: ~ petrol неэтили́рованный бензи́н

unleash /ʌnˈliːʃ/ *v.t.* спус|ка́ть, -ти́ть с при́вязи; (fig.) да|ва́ть, -ть во́лю + *d.*

unleavened /ʌnˈlev(ə)nd/ *adj.* пре́сный (хлеб)

◆ **unless** /ʌnˈles/ *conj.* (if not) е́сли (то́лько) не; I shall go ~ it rains я пойду́, е́сли (то́лько) не бу́дет дождя́; (until) пока́ не; I won't continue ~ he apologizes я не бу́ду продолжа́ть, пока́ он не извини́тся; (except if) ра́зве (что/ то́лько); I don't know why he is late, ~ he has lost his way не зна́ю, почему́ он опа́здывает — ра́зве что заблуди́лся

◆ **unlike** /ʌnˈlaɪk/ *adj. & prep.* (different from) непохо́жий, ра́зный; he is ~ his sister он не похо́ж на свою́ сестру́; ~ the others, he works hard в отли́чие от други́х он рабо́тает усе́рдно

unlikelihood /ʌnˈlaɪklɪhʊd/ *n.* неправдоподо́бие; маловероя́тность; невероя́тность

◆ **unlikely** /ʌnˈlaɪklɪ/ *adj.* (tale) неправдоподо́бный; (not to be expected): it is ~ he will recover маловероя́тно, что он попра́вится

unlimited /ʌnˈlɪmɪtɪd/ *adj.* неограни́ченный; (expanse) безграни́чный

unlined /ʌnˈlaɪnd/ *adj.* **1** : ~ paper нелино́ванная бума́га **2** : an ~ coat пальто́ без подкла́дки

unload /ʌnˈləʊd/ *v.t.* выгружа́ть, вы́грузить; разгру|жа́ть, -зи́ть; (fig.): she ~ed her worries on to him она́ облегчи́ла ду́шу, подели́вшись с ним свои́ми забо́тами

unlock /ʌnˈlɒk/ *v.t.* отп|ира́ть, -ере́ть (ключо́м)

unluckily /ʌnˈlʌkɪlɪ/ *adv.* к несча́стью; ~ for him к несча́стью для него́

unlucky /ʌn'lʌkɪ/ *adj.* (having bad luck): **he is ~ at cards** ему́ не везёт в ка́ртах; (causing bad luck) несчастли́вый

unmanageable /ʌn'mænɪdʒəb(ə)l/ *adj.* неуправля́емый

unmarried /ʌn'mærɪd/ *adj.* (man) нежена́тый, холосто́й; (woman) незаму́жняя; **he is ~** он не жена́т; **she is ~** она́ не за́мужем

unmask /ʌn'mɑːsk/ *v.t.* (fig.) разоблач|а́ть, -и́ть

unmentionable /ʌn'menʃənəb(ə)l/ *adj.* неприли́чный, запре́тный

unmistakable /ʌnmɪ'steɪkəb(ə)l/ *adj.* ве́рный, я́сный, очеви́дный

unmitigated /ʌn'mɪtɪgeɪtɪd/ *adj.* по́лный

unmoved /ʌn'muːvd/ *adj.* бесчу́вственный

unnamed /ʌn'neɪmd/ *adj.* нена́званный; (unidentified) неизве́стный

unnatural /ʌn'nætʃər(ə)l/ *adj.* неесте́ственный

unnecessary /ʌn'nesəsərɪ/ *adj.* нену́жный; (excessive) изли́шний

unnerve /ʌn'nɜːv/ *v.t.* обесси́ли|вать, -ть

unnoticed /ʌn'nəʊtɪst/ *adj.* незаме́ченный

unobservant /ʌnəb'zɜːv(ə)nt/ *adj.* ненаблюда́тельный

unobstructed /ʌnəb'strʌktɪd/ *adj.* незагоро́женный

unobtainable /ʌnəb'teɪnəb(ə)l/ *adj.* недосту́пный

unobtrusive /ʌnəb'truːsɪv/ *adj.* скро́мный

unoccupied /ʌn'ɒkjʊpaɪd/ *adj.* неза́нятый, свобо́дный; **an ~ house** пусто́й дом

unofficial /ʌnə'fɪʃ(ə)l/ *adj.* неофициа́льный

unorthodox /ʌn'ɔːθədɒks/ *adj.* неортодокса́льный, сме́лый

unpack /ʌn'pæk/ *v.t. & i.* распако́в|ывать(ся), -а́ть(ся)

unpaid /ʌn'peɪd/ *adj.* **1** неопла́ченный; (of debt, bill, etc.) неупла́ченный **2** (of person, unsalaried) не получа́ющий пла́ту/жа́лованье

unpalatable /ʌn'pælətəb(ə)l/ *adj.* невку́сный; (fig.) неприя́тный; **an ~ truth** го́рькая пра́вда

unparalleled /ʌn'pærəleld/ *adj.* несравни́мый

unpatriotic /ʌnpætrɪ'ɒtɪk/ *adj.* (behaviour) непатриоти́ческий; (person) непатриоти́чный

unperturbed /ʌnpə'tɜːbd/ *adj.* невозмути́мый

unpick /ʌn'pɪk/ *v.t.* расп|а́рывать, -оро́ть (шов)

unplanned /ʌn'plænd/ *adj.* незаплани́рованный; (unexpected) неожи́данный

unpleasant /ʌn'plez(ə)nt/ *adj.* неприя́тный

unpleasantness /ʌn'plezəntnɪs/ *n.* неприя́тность

unplug /ʌn'plʌg/ *v.t.* отключ|а́ть, -и́ть

unpopular /ʌn'pɒpjʊlə(r)/ *adj.* непопуля́рный

unprecedented /ʌn'presɪdentɪd/ *adj.* беспрецеде́нтный

unpredictable /ʌnprɪ'dɪktəb(ə)l/ *adj.* непредсказу́емый

unpremeditated /ʌnprɪ'medɪteɪtɪd/ *adj.* непреднаме́ренный

unprepared /ʌnprɪ'peəd/ *adj.* неподгото́вленный; **his speech was ~** он произнёс свою́ речь экспро́мтом

unprepossessing /ʌnpriːpə'zesɪŋ/ *adj.* нераспола́гающий

unpretentious /ʌnprɪ'tenʃəs/ *adj.* непретенцио́зный

unprincipled /ʌn'prɪnsɪp(ə)ld/ *adj.* беспринци́пный

unprintable /ʌn'prɪntəb(ə)l/ *adj.* нецензу́рный

unproductive /ʌnprə'dʌktɪv/ *adj.* непродукти́вный

unprofessional /ʌnprə'feʃən(ə)l/ *adj.* непрофессиона́льный; **~ conduct** наруше́ние профессиона́льной э́тики

unprofitable /ʌn'prɒfɪtəb(ə)l/ *adj.* невы́годный

unprompted /ʌn'prɒmptɪd/ *adj.* неподска́занный, спонта́нный

unprotected /ʌnprə'tektɪd/ *adj.* незащищённый; **~ sex** незащищённый секс

unprovoked /ʌnprə'vəʊkt/ *adj.* неспровоци́рованный

unqualified /ʌn'kwɒlɪfaɪd/ *adj.* **1** (without reservations) безогово́рочный **2** (not competent) некомпете́нтный; **I am ~ to judge this** я недоста́точно компете́нтен, что́бы суди́ть об э́том

unquestionable /ʌn'kwestʃənəb(ə)l/ *adj.* (undoubted) несомне́нный; (indisputable) неоспори́мый

unravel /ʌn'ræv(ə)l/ *v.t.* (**unravelled**, **unravelling**, AmE **unraveled**, **unraveling**) распу́т|ывать, -ать; (fig.) разга́д|ывать, -а́ть

unreal /ʌn'rɪəl/ *adj.* (imaginary) нереа́льный; (strange) фантасти́ческий

unrealistic /ʌnrɪə'lɪstɪk/ *adj.* нереа́льный

unreasonable /ʌn'riːzənəb(ə)l/ *adj.* не(благо)разу́мный; (excessive) чрезме́рный

unrecognizable /ʌn'rekəgnaɪzəb(ə)l/ *adj.* неузнава́емый

unrelated /ʌnrɪ'leɪtɪd/ *adj.* **1** (not connected) несвя́занный (**to:** с + *i.*) **2** (not kin): **he is ~ to me** он мне не ро́дственник

unrelenting /ʌnrɪ'lentɪŋ/ *adj.* (implacable) неумоли́мый; (ceaseless) неослабева́ющий

unreliable /ʌnrɪ'laɪəb(ə)l/ *adj.* (person) ненадёжный; (information) недостове́рный

unremitting /ʌnrɪ'mɪtɪŋ/ *adj.* неосла́бный; (incessant) беспреста́нный

unrequited /ʌnrɪ'kwaɪtɪd/ *adj.*: **~ love** неразделённая/безотве́тная любо́вь

unreserved /ʌnrɪ'zɜːvd/ *adj.* (not set aside) незаброни́рованный; (open, frank) открове́нный; (wholehearted) по́лный; **I agree with you ~ly** я по́лностью с ва́ми согла́сен

unresolved /ʌnrɪ'zɒlvd/ *adj.* нереши́тельный

u

unrest /ʌn'rest/ *n.* (disquiet) беспокойство;
(social, political) волнéние (*nt. pl.*)

unrestricted /ʌnrɪ'strɪktɪd/ *adj.*
неограниченный

unrewarding /ʌnrɪ'wɔ:dɪŋ/ *adj.*
неблагодарный

unripe /ʌn'raɪp/ *adj.* неспéлый, незрéлый

unrivalled /ʌn'raɪv(ə)ld/ (AmE **unrivaled**)
adj. непревзойдённый

unroll /ʌn'rəʊl/ *v.t. & i.* развёр|тывать(ся),
-ну́ть(ся)

unruffled /ʌn'rʌf(ə)ld/ *adj.* (fig.)
невозмутимый

unruly /ʌn'ru:lɪ/ *adj.* (**unrulier, unruliest**)
непокорный

unsafe /ʌn'seɪf/ *adj.* небезопасный

unsaid /ʌn'sed/ *adj.*: **some things are better
left** ~ есть вéщи, о которых лу́чше
умолчать

unsatisfactory /ʌnsætɪs'fæktərɪ/ *adj.*
неудовлетворительный

unsatisfied /ʌn'sætɪsfaɪd/ *adj.*
неудовлетворённый

unsavoury /ʌn'seɪvərɪ/ (AmE **unsavory**) *adj.*
(fig.) сомнительный

unscathed /ʌn'skeɪðd/ *adj.* цел и невредим

unscheduled /ʌn'ʃedju:ld/ *adj.*
незапланированный; **an** ~ **flight** рейс вне
расписания

unscrew /ʌn'skru:/ *v.t. & i.* отвин|чивать(ся),
-ти́ть(ся)

unscrupulous /ʌn'skru:pjʊləs/ *adj.*
беспринципный

unseasonable /ʌn'si:zənəb(ə)l/ *adj.* не по
сезону; ~ **weather** погода не по сезону; (fig.,
untimely) несвоевременный

unseemly /ʌn'si:mlɪ/ *adj.* непристойный

unseen /ʌn'si:n/ *adj.* невидимый

unselfish /ʌn'selfɪʃ/ *adj.* бескорыстный

unsettled /ʌn'set(ə)ld/ *adj.* неустойчивый

unsettling /ʌn'setlɪŋ/ *adj.* тревожный

unshakeable /ʌn'ʃeɪkəb(ə)l/ *adj.*
непоколебимый

unshaken /ʌn'ʃeɪkən/ *adj.* (resolute)
непоколебимый, непоколéблимый

unshaven /ʌn'ʃeɪv(ə)n/ *adj.* небритый

unsightly /ʌn'saɪtlɪ/ *adj.* некрасивый,
непригля́дный

unskilled /ʌn'skɪld/ *adj.*
неквалифицированный; ~ **labourer**
разнорабочий

unsociable /ʌn'səʊʃəb(ə)l/ *adj.*
необщительный

unsocial /ʌn'səʊʃ(ə)l/ *adj.*
антиобщественный; **to work** ~ **hours**
работать во врéмя, отличáющееся от
общепринятого

unsolicited /ʌnsə'lɪsɪtɪd/ *adj.* (not asked
for) непрошеный; (given, done voluntarily)
добровольный

unsophisticated /ʌnsə'fɪstɪkeɪtɪd/ *adj.*
(person, approach) простой, простодушный;
(thing, work) безыскусный

unsound /ʌn'saʊnd/ *adj.* (bad, rotten)
испорченный, гнилой; (unwholesome)
нездоровый; (unstable) непрочный; ~ **views**
необоснованные взгля́ды; **of** ~ **mind**
душевнобольной; **a man of** ~ **judgement**
человéк, лишённый здрáвого смы́сла

unsparing /ʌn'speərɪŋ/ *adj.* (merciless)
беспощадный, безжалостный; (generous)
щéдрый; (diligent) усéрдный; ~ **in his efforts**
не щадя́щий сил

unspeakable /ʌn'spi:kəb(ə)l/ *adj.*
невыразимый

unspoiled /ʌn'spɔɪld/, **unspoilt**
/ʌn'spɔɪlt/ *adjs.* неиспорченный; (of person)
неизбалованный

unspoken /ʌn'spəʊkən/ *adj.* невысказанный

unstable /ʌn'steɪb(ə)l/ *adj.* неустойчивый,
нестабильный

unsteady /ʌn'stedɪ/ *adj.* нетвёрдый; **he was**
~ **on his legs** он нетвёрдо держа́лся на
ногáх

unstinting /ʌn'stɪntɪŋ/ *adj.* (generous) щéдрый

unstuck /ʌn'stʌk/ *adj.*: **the stamp came** ~
мáрка отклéилась; (fig., infml): **my schemes
came** ~ мои плáны ру́хнули

unsubstantiated /ʌnsəb'stænʃɪeɪtɪd/ *adj.*
недоказанный

unsuccessful /ʌnsək'sesfʊl/ *adj.*
безуспéшный, неудáчный; **he was** ~ **in the
exam** он не сдал экзáмен

unsuitable /ʌn'sju:təb(ə)l/ *adj.*
неподходящий

unsung /ʌn'sʌŋ/ *adj.* (not celebrated)
невоспéтый; **an** ~ **hero** невоспéтый герой

unsure /ʌn'ʃɔ:(r)/ *adj.* (not confident)
неувéренный; **he was** ~ **of his ground** он не
чу́вствовал себя́ достáточно компетéнтным;
~ **of oneself** не увéренный в себé

unsuspecting /ʌnsə'spektɪŋ/ *adj.*
неподозревáющий

unsweetened /ʌn'swi:t(ə)nd/ *adj.*
неподслащённый

unswerving /ʌn'swɜ:vɪŋ/ *adj.* (fig.)
непоколебимый

unsympathetic /ʌnsɪmpə'θetɪk/ *adj.*
чёрствый, несочувствующий

untangle /ʌn'tæŋɡ(ə)l/ *v.t.* распу́т|ывать, -ать

untaxed /ʌn'tækst/ *adj.* не облагáемый
налогом

untenable /ʌn'tenəb(ə)l/ *adj.*: ~ **arguments**
неубеди́тельные доводы; **an** ~ **position**
(mil.) позиция, непригодная для обороны;
невы́годная позиция

unthinkable /ʌn'θɪŋkəb(ə)l/ *adj.*
немы́слимый

unthinking /ʌn'θɪŋkɪŋ/ *adj.* (thoughtless)
бездумный; (inadvertent) нечáянный;
машинáльный

untidiness /ʌn'taɪdɪnɪs/ *n.* неопря́тность,
неаккурáтность

⚥ ключевая лексика

untidy /ʌnˈtaɪdɪ/ *adj.* неопря́тный, неаккура́тный

untie /ʌnˈtaɪ/ *v.t.* развя́з|ывать, -а́ть; отвя́з|ывать, -а́ть; расшнуро́в|ывать, -а́ть

✒ **until** /ənˈtɪl/ *prep. & conj.* = till²; unless and ∼ то́лько когда́/е́сли

untimely /ʌnˈtaɪmlɪ/ *adj.* (premature) преждевре́менный; (ill-timed) неуме́стный

untiring /ʌnˈtaɪərɪŋ/ *adj.* (person) неутоми́мый; (work, efforts) неуста́нный

unto /ˈʌntʊ/ *prep.* (archaic) = to

untold /ʌnˈtəʊld/ *adj.* **1** (suffering, delight) невырази́мый **2** (damage) неисчисли́мый; ∼ wealth несме́тные бога́тства

untouchable /ʌnˈtʌtʃəb(ə)l/ *n.* (member of lowest-caste Hindu group) неприкаса́емый ● *adj.* (unattainable) недосяга́емый, недосту́пный; (impossible to compete with) недосяга́емый

untoward /ʌntəˈwɔːd/ *adj.*: nothing ∼ happened ничего́ плохо́го не случи́лось

untrained /ʌnˈtreɪnd/ *adj.* необу́ченный

untranslatable /ʌntrænzˈleɪtəb(ə)l/ *adj.* непереводи́мый

untroubled /ʌnˈtrʌb(ə)ld/ *adj.* невозмути́мый

untrue /ʌnˈtruː/ *adj.* (inaccurate) неве́рный, ло́жный; (unfaithful) неве́рный

untrustworthy /ʌnˈtrʌstwɜːðɪ/ *adj.* ненадёжный

untruth /ʌnˈtruːθ/ *n.* непра́вда

untruthful /ʌnˈtruːθfʊl/ *adj.* (of thing) неве́рный, ло́жный; (of person or thing) лжи́вый

unused¹ /ʌnˈjuːzd/ *adj.* (not put to use) неиспо́льзованный; my ticket was ∼ я не испо́льзовал свой биле́т

unused² /ʌnˈjuːst/ *adj.* (unaccustomed) непривы́чный (to: к + *d.*); I am ∼ to this я к э́тому не привы́к

✒ **unusual** /ʌnˈjuːʒʊəl/ *adj.* необыкнове́нный, необы́чный; ∼ly осо́бенно, исключи́тельно

unutterable /ʌnˈʌtərəb(ə)l/ *adj.* невырази́мый, несказа́нный

unvarnished /ʌnˈvɑːnɪʃt/ *adj.* (fig.): the ∼ truth неприкра́шенная/го́лая пра́вда

unveil /ʌnˈveɪl/ *v.t.* (statue) откр|ыва́ть, -ы́ть; (plans) изл|ага́ть, -ожи́ть

unwanted /ʌnˈwɒntɪd/ *adj.* нежела́нный; they made me feel ∼ они́ да́ли мне поня́ть, что я ли́шний среди́ них

unwarranted /ʌnˈwɒrəntɪd/ *adj.* необосно́ванный

unwary /ʌnˈweərɪ/ *adj.* неосторо́жный

unwavering /ʌnˈweɪvərɪŋ/ *adj.* непоколеби́мый

unwelcome /ʌnˈwelkəm/ *adj.* неприя́тный

unwell /ʌnˈwel/ *adj.* нездоро́вый; I felt ∼ мне нездоро́вилось; I have been ∼ я был нездоро́в

unwieldy /ʌnˈwiːldɪ/ *adj.* (**unwieldier, unwieldiest**) громо́здкий

unwilling /ʌnˈwɪlɪŋ/ *adj.* нежела́ющий; he was ∼ to agree он не пожела́л согласи́ться

unwillingness /ʌnˈwɪlɪŋnɪs/ *n.* нежела́ние

unwind /ʌnˈwaɪnd/ *v.t. & i.* разма́тывать(ся), -ота́ть(ся); (fig.): the wine helped him to ∼ вино́ помогло́ ему́ рассла́биться

unwise /ʌnˈwaɪz/ *adj.* не(благо)разу́мный

unwitting /ʌnˈwɪtɪŋ/ *adj.* неча́янный

unworthy /ʌnˈwɜːðɪ/ *adj.* недосто́йный (*кого/чего*)

unwrap /ʌnˈræp/ *v.t.* разв|ора́чивать (*or* разв|ёртывать), -ерну́ть

unwritten /ʌnˈrɪt(ə)n/ *adj.*: an ∼ law непи́саный зако́н

unzip /ʌnˈzɪp/ *v.t.* (coat) расстёг|ивать, -ну́ть; (bag) раскр|ыва́ть, -ы́ть

✒ **up** /ʌp/ *n.*: ∼s and downs (of fortune) взлёты (*m. pl.*) и паде́ния (*nt. pl.*)
● *adv.* **1** (in a higher position) вверху́, наверху́; high ∼ in the sky высоко́ в не́бе; 'this side ∼!' «верх!»; the notice was ∼ on the board на доске́ висе́ло объявле́ние; prices are ∼ це́ны подняли́сь; (advanced): he is 20 points ∼ on his opponent он на два́дцать очко́в впереди́ проти́вника; he is well ∼ in his subject он прекра́сно зна́ет свой предме́т; (with greater intensity): sing ∼!/speak ∼! (по́йте)/(говори́те) гро́мче! **2** (into a higher position) вверх, наве́рх; she carried the suitcases ∼ она́ отнесла́ чемода́ны наве́рх; (∼wards) вы́ше, бо́льше; children from the age of twelve ∼ де́ти от двена́дцати (лет) и ста́рше **3** (out of bed; standing; active): he was already ∼ when I called когда́ я пришёл, он уже́ встал; she was soon ∼ and about again она́ вско́ре опра́вилась; I was ∼ late last night я вчера́ о́чень по́здно лёг **4** (expr. completion or expiry): time's ∼ вре́мя истекло́; the game is ∼! ка́рта би́та! **5** (infml, happening; amiss): what's ∼? в чём де́ло?; что тут происхо́дит?; there's something ∼ with the radio (ра́дио)приёмник барахли́т **6** ∼ against (in contact with): the table was (right) ∼ against the wall стол стоя́л (пря́мо) у стены́ (*or* вплотну́ю к стене́); (confronted by): you are ∼ against stiff opposition вы име́ете де́ло с упо́рным сопротивле́нием **7** ∼ to (equal to): I don't feel ∼ to it я не чу́вствую себя́ в си́лах сде́лать э́то; (as far as) до + *g.*; ∼ to now, ∼ till now до сих пор; I am ∼ to chapter 3 я дочита́л до тре́тьей главы́; (incumbent upon): it is ∼ to us to help э́то мы должны́ помо́чь; it's ∼ to you now тепе́рь э́то/всё зави́сит от вас; (occupied with): what is he ∼ to? чем он занима́ется?; he is ∼ to no good он замы́слил что́-то недо́брое
● *prep.*: they live ∼ the hill они́ живу́т на горе́/холме́; he ran ∼ the hill он взбежа́л на́ гору, на хо́лм; the cat was ∼ a tree кот взобра́лся на де́рево; he went ∼ the stairs он подня́лся по ле́стнице; they live ∼ the street (further along) они́ живу́т по/на э́той у́лице

up-and-coming /ʌpənˈkʌmɪŋ/ *adj.* многообеща́ющий

upbeat /ˈʌpbiːt/ *adj.* оптимисти́чный, бо́дрый

upbringing /ˈʌpbrɪŋɪŋ/ *n.* воспита́ние

u

♂ **update** /ʌp'deɪt/ v.t. (one's wardrobe) обнов|ля́ть, -и́ть; (equipment) модернизи́ровать (impf., pf.); (records) испр|авля́ть, -а́вить

upgrade n. /'ʌpɡreɪd/ (modernization) модерниза́ция; (comput., of software) обновле́ние, апгре́йд (infml); (comput., of hardware) модерниза́ция, апгре́йд (infml); (of travel class) перево́д в бо́лее высо́кий кла́сс обслу́живания
● v.t. /ʌp'ɡreɪd/ (modernize) модернизи́ровать (impf., pf.); (comput., software) обнов|ля́ть, -и́ть; (comput., hardware) модернизи́ровать (impf., pf.); (raise in rank) пов|ыша́ть, -ы́сить в до́лжности; (a traveller) перев|оди́ть, -ести́ в бо́лее высо́кий класс (обслу́живания); **we were ~d to business class** нас перевели́ в би́знес-класс

upheaval /ʌp'hiːv(ə)l/ n. (political) потрясе́ние (nt. pl.); (emotional) потрясе́ние

uphill /'ʌphɪl/ adj. иду́щий в го́ру; **an ~ task** тяжёлая зада́ча
● adv. в го́ру

uphold /ʌp'həʊld/ v.t. (support) (lit., fig.) подде́рж|ивать, -а́ть

upholster /ʌp'həʊlstə(r)/ v.t. об|ива́ть, -и́ть; подб|ива́ть, -и́ть; **an ~ed chair** кре́сло с мя́гкой оби́вкой

upholstery /ʌp'həʊlstərɪ/ n. оби́вка

upkeep /'ʌpkiːp/ n. содержа́ние

uplift[1] /'ʌplɪft/ n. (act of raising) подъём; (moral elevation) духо́вный подъём

uplift[2] /ʌp'lɪft/ v.t. подн|има́ть, -я́ть

upload /ʌp'ləʊd/ v.t. (comput.) загру|жа́ть, -зи́ть на друго́й (удалённый) компью́тер

upmarket /ʌp'mɑːkɪt/ adj. элита́рный, дорого́й

♂ **upon** /ə'pɒn/ prep. **1** see ▸ **on 2**: **once ~ a time** одна́жды; **once ~ a time there lived …** жи́л-бы́л… (fem. жила́-была́…); **~ my word, soul!** (expressing surprise etc.) Го́споди!; **~ my honour!** че́стное сло́во!; **the holidays are ~ us** приближа́ются кани́кулы; **the enemy is ~ us** враг уже́ бли́зок

♂ **upper** /'ʌpə(r)/ adj. ве́рхний; вы́сший; **he got the ~ hand** он одержа́л верх
■ **~ class** adj. относя́щийся к вы́сшему о́бществу; **U~ House** n. (in UK) пала́та ло́рдов; (in USA) сена́т; **~most** adj. са́мый ве́рхний, вы́сший; **it was ~most in my mind** э́то бо́льше всего́ занима́ло мои́ мы́сли

upright /'ʌpraɪt/ adj. (erect) вертика́льный; (honourable) че́стный
● adv.: **stand ~** стоя́ть (impf.) пря́мо

uprising /'ʌpraɪzɪŋ/ n. (rebellion) восста́ние

uproar /'ʌprɔː(r)/ n. (noise) шум; (confusion) возмуще́ние

uproarious /ʌp'rɔːrɪəs/ adj. (noisy) шу́мный, бу́рный, бу́йный; (funny) ужа́сно/невозмо́жно смешно́й

uproot /ʌp'ruːt/ v.t. вырыва́ть, вы́рвать с ко́рнем; (fig., displace) высел|я́ть, -ить

♂ ключевая лексика

upset[1] /'ʌpset/ n. **1** (physical) недомога́ние; **stomach ~** расстро́йство желу́дка **2** (emotional shock) огорче́ние

upset[2] /ʌp'set/ v.t. (knock over) опроки́|дывать, -нуть; (make unhappy) расстр|а́ивать, -о́ить; (food): **rich food ~s my stomach** от жи́рной пи́щи у меня́ расстра́ивается желу́док

upshot /'ʌpʃɒt/ n. развя́зка

upside down /ʌpsaɪd 'daʊn/ adv. вверх дном, вверх нога́ми

upstage /ʌp'steɪdʒ/ v.t. (fig., overshadow) затм|ева́ть, -и́ть

upstairs /ʌp'steəz/ adv. (position) наверху́; (direction) наве́рх; **he ran ~** он побежа́л наве́рх; (attr.) **the ~ rooms** ве́рхние ко́мнаты

upstanding /ʌp'stændɪŋ/ adj. **1** (honest) че́стный, прямо́й **2** (standing up) стоя́щий; **be ~!** вста́ньте!

upstart /'ʌpstɑːt/ n. вы́скочка (c.g.)

upstream /'ʌpstriːm/ adv. про́тив тече́ния; **~ of** вы́ше + g.

upsurge /'ʌpsɜːdʒ/ n. (of unrest, in production) подъём; (of feelings) наплы́в

uptake /'ʌpteɪk/ n.: **quick on the ~** (infml) сообрази́тельный, бы́стро сообража́ющий

uptight /ʌp'taɪt/ adj. (infml, tense, angry) напряжённый, нерво́зный

up-to-date /ʌptə'deɪt/ adj. совреме́нный, нове́йший, (са́мый) после́дний

upturn /'ʌptɜːn/ n. (fig.) сдвиг (к лу́чшему); улучше́ние

upward /'ʌpwəd/ adj. напра́вленный вверх; **an ~ trend in prices** тенде́нция к повыше́нию цен
● adv. (also ~s) вверх

Urals /'jʊər(ə)lz/ n. pl. (mountains) Ура́льские го́ры (f. pl.), Ура́л

uranium /jʊ'reɪnɪəm/ n. ура́н; (attr.) ура́новый

Uranus /'jʊərənəs/ n. Ура́н

♂ **urban** /'ɜːbən/ adj. городско́й

urbane /ə'beɪn/ adj. све́тский, учти́вый

urchin /'ɜːtʃɪn/ n. беспризо́рни|к (-ца)

Urdu /'ʊəduː/ n. (язы́к) урду́ (m. indecl.)

♂ **urge** /ɜːdʒ/ n. побужде́ние, стремле́ние
● v.t. **1** (impel) (also ~ **on**, ~ **forward**) гнать (impf.); под|гоня́ть, -огна́ть **2** (exhort) угова́ривать (impf.)

urgency /'ɜːdʒ(ə)nsɪ/ n. сро́чность, неотло́жность; **as a matter of ~** в сро́чном поря́дке

urgent /'ɜːdʒ(ə)nt/ adj. сро́чный, неотло́жный; **he is in ~ need of money** он кра́йне нужда́ется в деньга́х

urinal /jʊə'raɪn(ə)l/ n. писсуа́р

urinary /'jʊərɪnərɪ/ adj. мочево́й

urinate /'jʊərɪneɪt/ v.i. мочи́ться, по-

urine /'jʊərɪn/ n. моча́

URL abbr. (of **uniform/universal resource locator**) (comput.) URL-а́дрес

urn /ɜːn/ n. (vase for ashes etc.) у́рна, ва́за

Uruguay /'jʊərəɡwaɪ/ n. Уругва́й

Uruguayan /jʊərə'gwaɪən/ *n.* уругва́|ец (-йка)
● *adj.* уругва́йский

US, **USA** *abbr.* (*of* **United States of America**) США (*pl., indecl.*) (Соединённые Шта́ты Аме́рики)
● *adj.* америка́нский

◆ **us** /ʌs/ *obj. of* ▶ **we**

usable /'juːzəb(ə)l/ *adj.* примени́мый, (при)го́дный

usage /'juːsɪdʒ/ *n.* ■ (utilization) употребле́ние, испо́льзование; по́льзование (of: + *i.*) ■ (habitual process) у́зус, пра́ктика, обыкнове́ние; **in accordance with general ~** согла́сно общепри́нятой пра́ктике; **a guide to English ~** уче́бник англи́йского словоупотребле́ния

◆ **use¹** /juːs/ *n.* ■ (utilization) употребле́ние, испо́льзование; по́льзование (of: + *i.*); **make good ~ of your time!** испо́льзуйте ва́ше вре́мя как сле́дует!; **he put his talents to good ~** он пра́вильно испо́льзовал свои́ спосо́бности ■ (purpose) назначе́ние; **применение** ■ (value) по́льза, толк; **this machine is no longer (of) any ~** э́та маши́на бо́льше не годи́тся; **will this be of ~ to you?** вам э́то пригоди́тся?; **it's no ~ grumbling** что то́лку ворча́ть? ■ (power of using): **he lost the ~ of his legs** он утра́тил спосо́бность ходи́ть ■ (right to use): **I gave him the ~ of my car** я разреши́л ему́ по́льзоваться мое́й маши́ной

◆ **use²** /juːz/ *v.t.* ■ (employ) употребл|я́ть, -и́ть; по́льзоваться, вос- + *i.*; испо́льзовать (*impf., pf.*); **a ~d car** подержанная маши́на ■ (~ up: consume) расхо́довать, из-; тра́тить, по-; испо́льзовать (*impf., pf.*); **this car ~s a lot of fuel** э́та маши́на расхо́дует мно́го бензи́на ■ (treat) обраща́ться (*impf.*) с + *i.*; об|ходи́ться, -ойти́сь с + *i.* ■ (exploit): **I feel as if I have been ~d** я чу́вствую, что меня́ испо́льзовали в чьи́х-то це́лях

used¹ /juːst/ *pred. adj.* ■ (accustomed): **get ~ to** прив|ыка́ть, -ы́кнуть к + *d.*; **he is ~ to it** он к э́тому привы́к; **he is ~ to dining late** он привы́к обе́дать по́здно ■ (+ inf., of habitual situation in the past): **he ~ to be a teacher** он ра́ньше был учи́телем; **I ~ not to like him** пре́жде он мне не нра́вился

used² /juːzd/ *attr. adj.* ■ (already having been made use of): **a ~ envelope** ста́рый конве́рт ■ (AmE, second-hand) поде́ржанный

◆ **useful** /'juːsfʊl/ *adj.* поле́зный

useless /'juːslɪs/ *adj.* (worthless) неприго́дный; (futile) беспо́лезный; (infml, incompetent): **he is**

~ at tennis он никуды́шный тенниси́ст

◆ **user** /'juːzə(r)/ *n.* (one who uses) употребля́ющий; потреби́тель (*m.*); (comput.) по́льзователь (*m.*)
■ **~-friendly** *adj.* удо́бный в употребле́нии; (comput.) дру́жественный

usher /'ʌʃə(r)/ *v.t.* (*also* **~ in**) вв|оди́ть, -ести́

usherette /ʌʃə'ret/ *n.* билетёрша (infml)

USSR *abbr.* (*of* **Union of Soviet Socialist Republics**) (hist.) СССР (*m. indecl.*) (Сою́з Сове́тских Социалисти́ческих Респу́блик)

◆ **usual** /'juːʒʊəl/ *adj.* обы́чный, обыкнове́нный; **it is ~ to remove one's hat** шля́пу при́нято снима́ть; **he is late as ~** он, как всегда́, опа́здывает; **the bus was fuller than ~** автобус был перепо́лнен бо́льше обы́чного

◆ **usually** /'juːʒʊəlɪ/ *adv.* обы́чно

usurp /jʊ'zə:p/ *v.t.* узурпи́ровать (*impf., pf.*)

usury /'juːʒərɪ/ *n.* ростовщи́чество

utensil /juː'tens(ə)l/ *n.* инструме́нт; (*pl., collect.*) у́тварь

uterus /'juːtərəs/ *n.* (anat.) ма́тка

utilitarian /jʊtɪlɪ'teərɪən/ *n.* утилитари́ст (-ка)
● *adj.* утилита́рный

utility /juː'tɪlɪtɪ/ *n.* ■ (usefulness) поле́зность, практи́чность, вы́годность ■: **public ~ies** коммуна́льные услу́ги (*f. pl.*)
■ **~y room** *n.* кладова́я

utilization /juːtɪlaɪ'zeɪʃ(ə)n/ *n.* испо́льзование; утилиза́ция

utilize /'juːtɪlaɪz/ *v.t.* испо́льзовать (*impf., pf.*)

utmost /'ʌtməʊst/ *n.*: **he did his ~ to avoid defeat** он сде́лал всё возмо́жное, что́бы избежа́ть пораже́ния
● *adjs.* кра́йний

Utopia /juː'təʊpɪə/ *n.* уто́пия

Utopian /juː'təʊpɪən/ *adj.* утопи́ческий

utter¹ /'ʌtə(r)/ *adj.* по́лный, абсолю́тный, соверше́нный

utter² /'ʌtə(r)/ *v.t.* (sound, cry) изд|ава́ть, -а́ть; (words) произн|оси́ть, -ести́

utterance /'ʌtərəns/ *n.* ■ (action) произнесе́ние; **he gave ~ to his anger** он вы́разил свой гнев ■ (something said, pronouncement) выска́зывание

utterly /'ʌtəlɪ/ *adv.* соверше́нно

U-turn /'juːtə:n/ *n.* разворо́т; (fig.) ре́зкое измене́ние поли́тики

UV *abbr.* (*of* **ultraviolet**) ультрафиоле́товый

Uzbek /'ʊzbek/ *n.* (person) узбе́|к (-чка); (language) узбе́кский язы́к
● *adj.* узбе́кский

Uzbekistan /ʊzbekɪ'stɑːn/ *n.* Узбекиста́н

u

Vv

v. *abbr.* (*of* **versus**) про́тив + *g.*

vacanc|y /'veɪkənsɪ/ *n.* (job) вака́нсия; (place on course etc.) ме́сто; (room): **no ~ies** свобо́дных ко́мнат нет, «мест нет»

vacant /'veɪk(ə)nt/ *adj.* **1** (unoccupied) свобо́дный; **a ~ post** вака́нтная до́лжность, вака́нсия **2** (of mind, expression, etc.) отсу́тствующий

vacate /ver'keɪt/ *v.t.* освобо|жда́ть, -ди́ть; **he will ~ the post in May** он уйдёт с до́лжности в ма́е

vacation /və'keɪʃ(ə)n/ *n.* **1** (at university) кани́кул|ы (*pl., g.* —); **long ~** ле́тние кани́кулы **2** (holiday) о́тпуск, о́тдых; **on ~** в о́тпуске

vaccinate /'væksɪneɪt/ *v.t.* де́лать, с- приви́вку (+ *d.*) (**against:** + *g.*)

vaccination /væksɪ'neɪʃ(ə)n/ *n.* приви́вка

vaccine /'væksi:n/ *n.* вакци́на

vacillate /'væsɪleɪt/ *v.i.* колеба́ться (*impf.*)

vacuous /'vækjʊəs/ *adj.* пусто́й

vacuum /'vækjʊəm/ *n.* **1** (empty place) ва́куум **2** (infml) (*in full* **~ cleaner**) пылесо́с
● *v.t. & i.* (infml) (clean with ~ **cleaner**) пылесо́сить, про-
■ **~ flask** *n.* (BrE) те́рмос

vagabond /'vægəbɒnd/ *n.* (vagrant) бродя́га (*c.g.*), скита́лец

vagary /'veɪgərɪ/ *n.* причу́да, капри́з

vagina /və'dʒaɪnə/ *n.* влага́лище

vaginal /və'dʒaɪn(ə)l/ *adj.* влага́лищный, вагина́льный

vagrant /'veɪgrənt/ *n.* бродя́га (*c.g.*)

vague /veɪg/ *adj.* неопределённый, сму́тный, нея́сный; **he was rather ~ about his plans** он был весьма́ укло́нчив относи́тельно свои́х пла́нов

vagueness /'veɪgnɪs/ *n.* неопределённость, сму́тность, нея́сность

vain /veɪn/ *adj.* **1** (unavailing; fruitless) тще́тный, напра́сный; **they tried in ~ to get a seat** они́ безуспе́шно пыта́лись найти́ ме́сто **2** (conceited) тщесла́вный

valedictory /vælɪ'dɪktərɪ/ *adj.* проща́льный; (AmE, as *n.*) речь на шко́льном вы́пуске

valentine /'væləntaɪn/ *n.* (missive) валенти́нка, (анони́мное) любо́вное посла́ние в день свято́го Валенти́на

valet /'væleɪ/ *n.* камерди́нер, слуга́ (*m.*)

valiant /'væljənt/ *adj.* до́блестный; (of effort) геро́йческий

valid /'vælɪd/ *adj.* **1** (sound) ве́ский, обосно́ванный; **~ objections** убеди́тельные возраже́ния **2** (law) действи́тельный; **a ticket ~ for 3 months** биле́т, действи́тельный в тече́ние трёх ме́сяцев

validate /'vælɪdeɪt/ *v.t.* утвер|жда́ть, -ди́ть

validation /vælɪ'deɪʃ(ə)n/ *n.* утвержде́ние, подтвержде́ние

valley /'vælɪ/ *n.* (*pl.* **~s**) доли́на

valour /'vælə(r)/ (AmE **valor**) *n.* до́блесть

valuable /'væljʊəb(ə)l/ *n.* (*usu. in pl.*) це́нности (*f. pl.*)
● *adj.* це́нный, поле́зный, ва́жный

valuation /væljʊ'eɪʃ(ə)n/ *n.* оце́нка

✍ **value** /'vælju:/ *n.* **1** (worth) це́нность, ва́жность **2** (in money etc.) це́нность, сто́имость; **property is rising in ~** недви́жимое иму́щество поднима́ется в цене́; **the book is good ~ for money** (BrE) э́та кни́га — вы́годная поку́пка **3** (*in pl.*) (standards) (*духо́вные и т. п.*) це́нности (*f. pl.*)
● *v.t.* (**values, valued, valuing**) **1** (estimate ~ of) оце́н|ивать, -и́ть **2** (regard highly) цени́ть (*impf.*)

valuer /'væljʊə(r)/ *n.* (BrE) оце́нщик

valve /vælv/ *n.* кла́пан

vampire /'væmpaɪə(r)/ *n.* вампи́р

van /væn/ *n.* фурго́н

vandal /'vænd(ə)l/ *n.* ванда́л

vandalism /'vændəlɪz(ə)m/ *n.* вандали́зм

vandalize /'vændəlaɪz/ *v.t.* разр|уша́ть, -у́шить

vanguard /'vængɑːd/ *n.* аванга́рд

vanilla /və'nɪlə/ *n.* вани́ль; (*attr.*) вани́льный

vanish /'vænɪʃ/ *v.i.* исч|еза́ть, -е́знуть

vanity /'vænɪtɪ/ *n.* тщесла́вие

vanquish /'væŋkwɪʃ/ *v.t.* побе|жда́ть, -ди́ть; покор|я́ть, -и́ть

vantage /'vɑːntɪdʒ/ *n.*: **~ point** вы́годная пози́ция

vapour /'veɪpə(r)/ (AmE **vapor**) *n.* **1** (steam) пар **2** (gaseous manifestation): **~ trail** инверсио́нный след

variable /'veərɪəb(ə)l/ *n.* (math.) переме́нная (величина́)
● *adj.* изме́нчивый, непостоя́нный

variance /'veərɪəns/ *n.*: **this is at ~ with what we heard** э́то противоре́чит тому́, что мы слы́шали

variant /'veərɪənt/ *n.* вариа́нт

variation /veərɪ'eɪʃ(ə)n/ *n.* **1** (fluctuation) измене́ние; колеба́ние; **~s of temperature** колеба́ния (*nt. pl.*) температу́ры **2** (divergence) отклоне́ние

varicose /'værɪkəʊs/ *adj.* варико́зный
■ **~ veins** *n. pl.* варико́зные ве́ны

✍ ключева́я ле́ксика

varied /'veərɪd/ *adj.* разнообра́зный

variegated /'veərɪgeɪtɪd/ *adj.* разноцве́тный, пёстрый

variety /və'raɪətɪ/ *n.* **1** (diversity) разнообра́зие **2** (number of different things) ряд; мно́жество; **for a ~ of reasons** по це́лому ря́ду соображе́ний, по ря́ду причи́н **3**: **~ show** эстра́дное представле́ние **4** (type) разнови́дность, вид, сорт

varifocals /'veərɪfəʊk(ə)lz/ *n. pl.* (spectacles) очк|и́ (-о́в) с переме́нным фо́кусным расстоя́нием

various /'veərɪəs/ *adj.* **1** (diverse) разли́чный, ра́зный, разнообра́зный **2** (with pl.) (several) мно́гие (*pl.*); ра́зные (*pl.*)

varnish /'vɑːnɪʃ/ *n.* лак; (fig.) лоск
● *v.t.* покр|ыва́ть, -ы́ть ла́ком

var|y /'veərɪ/ *v.t.* меня́ть (*impf.*); измен|я́ть, -и́ть; разнообра́зить (*impf.*)
● *v.i.* **1** (change) меня́ться (*impf.*); **the menu never ~ies** меню́ никогда́ не меня́ется **2** (differ) ра|сходи́ться, -зойти́сь; отлича́ться, -и́ться; **opinions ~y** мне́ния расхо́дятся

vase /vɑːz/ *n.* ва́за

vasectomy /və'sektəmɪ/ *n.* (med.) вазэктоми́я

Vaseline® /'væsɪliːn/ *n.* вазели́н

vast /vɑːst/ *adj.* обши́рный; огро́мный; (grandiose) грандио́зный

vastness /'vɑːstnɪs/ *n.* ширь; огро́мность; грандио́зность

VAT /viːer'tiː, væt/ *n.* (BrE) (*abbr. of* **value added tax**) НДС (нало́г на доба́вленную сто́имость)

vat /væt/ *n.* бо́чка, чан

Vatican /'vætɪkən/ *n.* Ватика́н

vault¹ /vɔːlt/ *n.* **1** (arched roof) свод **2** (underground room) подва́л, по́греб; (of a bank) храни́лище

vault² /vɔːlt/ *v.t. & i.* перепры́г|ивать, -нуть

VCR *abbr.* (*of* **video cassette recorder**) видеомагнитофо́н

VD *abbr.* (*of* **venereal disease**) венери́ческая боле́знь

VDU (BrE) *abbr.* (*of* **visual display unit**) диспле́й

veal /viːl/ *n.* теля́тина

veer /vɪə(r)/ *v.i.* измен|я́ть, -и́ть направле́ние; пов|ора́чивать(ся), -ерну́ть(ся)

vegan /'viːgən/ *n.* стро́гий вегетариа́нец

vegetable /'vedʒtəb(ə)l/ *n.* о́вощ
● *adj.* овощно́й; **~ oils** расти́тельные масла́

vegetarian /vedʒɪ'teərɪən/ *n.* вегетариа́н|ец (-ка)
● *adj.* вегетариа́нский

vegetate /'vedʒɪteɪt/ *v.i.* (fig.) прозяба́ть (*impf.*)

vegetation /vedʒɪ'teɪʃ(ə)n/ *n.* (plant life) расти́тельность

veggie burger /'vedʒɪ bə:gə(r)/ *n.* вегетариа́нский га́мбургер

vehemence /'viːəməns/ *n.* си́ла, я́рость

vehement /'viːəmənt/ *adj.* си́льный, я́ростный

vehicle /'vɪək(ə)l/ *n.* тра́нспортное сре́дство

veil /veɪl/ *n.* вуа́ль
● *v.t.*: **a ~ed threat** скры́тая угро́за

vein /veɪn/ *n.* **1** (anat.) ве́на, жи́ла **2** (fissure in rock) жи́ла **3** (style): **in the same ~** в то́м же ду́хе/то́не/сти́ле

Velcro® /'velkrəʊ/ *n.*: **~ fastener** застёжка «велкро́», липу́чка

velocity /vɪ'lɒsɪtɪ/ *n.* ско́рость; быстрота́

velvet /'velvɪt/ *n.* ба́рхат; **a ~ dress** ба́рхатное пла́тье

velvety /'velvɪtɪ/ *adj.* ба́рхатный, бархати́стый

vendetta /ven'detə/ *n.* венде́тта

vending machine /'vendɪŋ/ *n.* (торго́вый) автома́т (*по продаже сигарет, напитков и т. п.*)

vendor /'vendə(r)/ *n.* продав|е́ц (-щи́ца)

veneer /vɪ'nɪə(r)/ *n.* шпон, фане́ра; (fig.) вне́шний лоск

venerable /'venərəb(ə)l/ *adj.* **1** (revered) почте́нный; **~ ruins** дре́вние/свяще́нные разва́лины **2**: **V~** (as title) преподо́бный

venerate /'venəreɪt/ *v.t.* чтить (*impf.*); почита́ть (*impf.*); благогове́ть (*impf.*) пе́ред + *i.*

veneration /venə'reɪʃ(ə)n/ *n.* почте́ние, благогове́ние

venereal /vɪ'nɪərɪəl/ *adj.*: **~ disease** венери́ческая боле́знь

Venetian /vɪ'niːʃ(ə)n/ *n.* венециа́н|ец (-ка)
● *adj.* венециа́нский
■ **~ blind** *n.* жалюзи́ (*pl. indecl.*)

Venezuela /venɪ'zweɪlə/ *n.* Венесуэ́ла

Venezuelan /venɪ'zweɪlən/ *n.* венесуэ́л|ец (-ка)
● *adj.* венесуэ́льский

vengeance /'vendʒ(ə)ns/ *n.* **1** месть; отмще́ние (liter.) **2**: **with a ~** (infml, in a high degree) во́всю, с лихво́й

vengeful /'vendʒfʊl/ *adj.* мсти́тельный

Venice /'venɪs/ *n.* Вене́ция

venison /'venɪs(ə)n/ *n.* олени́на

venom /'venəm/ *n.* яд; (fig.) яд, зло́ба

venomous /'venəməs/ *adj.* ядови́тый

vent /vent/ *n.* дымохо́д; **he gave ~ to his feelings** он дал во́лю свои́м чу́вствам
● *v.t.* (fig.) изл|ива́ть, -и́ть; да|ва́ть, -ть вы́ход + *d.*

ventilate /'ventɪleɪt/ *v.t.* прове́три|вать, -ть

ventilation /ventɪ'leɪʃ(ə)n/ *n.* вентиля́ция

ventilator /'ventɪleɪtə(r)/ *n.* (also med.) вентиля́тор

ventriloquist /ven'trɪləkwɪst/ *n.* чревовеща́тель (*m.*)

venture /'ventʃə(r)/ *n.* **1** (risky undertaking) риско́ванное предприя́тие **2** (business enterprise) (комме́рческое) предприя́тие
● *v.i.* (dare) осме́ли|ваться, -ться; **I ~ to suggest** осме́люсь предложи́ть; **~ out** риск|ова́ть, -ну́ть вы́сунуть нос на у́лицу
■ **~ capital** *n.* (fin.) ве́нчурный капита́л

V

venue /'venju:/ *n.* ме́сто (проведе́ния) (*конце́рта/соревнова́ний*)

veracity /vəˈræsɪtɪ/ *n.* правди́вость; достове́рность

veranda /vəˈrændə/ *n.* вера́нда

verb /vɜːb/ *n.* глаго́л

verbal /'vɜːb(ə)l/ *adj.* **1** (of or in words) слове́сный **2** (oral) у́стный

verbalize /'vɜːbəlaɪz/ *v.t.* (put into words) выража́ть, вы́разить слова́ми

verbatim /vɜːˈbeɪtɪm/ *adv.* досло́вно

verbiage /'vɜːbɪɪdʒ/ *n.* многосло́вие; пустосло́вие

verbose /vɜːˈbəʊs/ *adj.* многосло́вный

verbosity /vɜːˈbɒsɪtɪ/ *n.* многосло́вие

verdict /'vɜːdɪkt/ *n.* (law) верди́кт, пригово́р; **the jury brought in a ~ of guilty/not guilty** суд прися́жных вы́нес обвини́тельный/оправда́тельный пригово́р; (fig., judgement) заключе́ние, пригово́р; **what's the ~?** како́в пригово́р?

verge /vɜːdʒ/ *n.* край; (BrE, of road) обо́чина; (fig.): **on the ~ of destruction** на краю́ ги́бели; **on the ~ of tears** на гра́ни слёз; **he was on the ~ of betraying his secret** он чуть не вы́дал свою́ та́йну
   ● *v.i.*: **it ~s on madness** э́то грани́чит с безу́мием

verifiable /'verɪfaɪəb(ə)l/ *adj.* поддаю́щийся прове́рке

verification /ˌverɪfɪˈkeɪʃ(ə)n/ *n.* прове́рка; подтвержде́ние

verify /'verɪfaɪ/ *v.t.* (check accuracy of) прове|ря́ть, -е́рить; (confirm) подтвер|жда́ть, -ди́ть

veritable /'verɪtəb(ə)l/ *adj.* настоя́щий, су́щий

vermicelli /ˌvɜːmɪˈtʃelɪ/ *n.* вермише́ль

vermin /'vɜːmɪn/ *n.* **1** (rats, foxes, etc.) вреди́тели (*m. pl.*) **2** (parasitic insects) парази́ты (*m. pl.*)

vernacular /vəˈnækjʊlə(r)/ *n.* **1** (local language) иско́нный язы́к; **Latin gave place to the ~** латы́нь уступи́ла ме́сто иско́нным языка́м **2** (dialect) диале́кт; наре́чие **3** (jargon) жарго́н, арго́ (*nt. indecl.*) **4** (colloquial speech) просторе́чие
   ● *adj.* иско́нный, ме́стный; просторе́чный

versatile /'vɜːsətaɪl/ *adj.* (person) разносторо́нний; (device) универса́льный

versatility /ˌvɜːsəˈtɪlɪtɪ/ *n.* разносторо́нность; универса́льность

verse /vɜːs/ *n.* **1** (stanza of poem, song) строфа́; (in Bible) стих **2** (*sg. or pl.*) (poetry, poems) стихи́ (*m. pl.*); **he wrote in ~** он писа́л в стиха́х

 ✧ **version** /'vɜːʃ(ə)n/ *n.* **1** (individual account) ве́рсия, расска́з **2** (form or variant of text etc.) вариа́нт, текст

versus /'vɜːsəs/ *prep.* про́тив + *g.*

vertebra /'vɜːtɪbrə/ *n.* (*pl.* **vertebrae** /-briː/) позвоно́к

vertebrate /'vɜːtɪbrət/ *n.* позвоно́чное (живо́тное)

vertical /'vɜːtɪk(ə)l/ *adj.* вертика́льный; **a ~ cliff** отве́сный утёс

vertigo /'vɜːtɪɡəʊ/ *n.* головокруже́ние

verve /vɜːv/ *n.* жи́вость, эне́ргия

 ✧ **very** /'verɪ/ *adj.* **1** (exact; identical) тот са́мый; **this ~ day** сего́дня же **2** (extreme) са́мый; **at the ~ end** в са́мом конце́ **3** (in emphasis): **the ~ idea of it** одна́ мысль об э́том
   ● *adv.* **1** (exceedingly) о́чень; **I don't feel ~ well** я чу́вствую себя́ нева́жно; **I can't sing ~ well** я дово́льно пло́хо пою́ **2** (emph., with superl. etc.) са́мый; **the ~ best** са́мый лу́чший; наилу́чший; **the ~ next day** на сле́дующий же день; **you may keep it for your ~ own** мо́жете э́то взять (себе́) насовсе́м

vessel /'ves(ə)l/ *n.* **1** (receptacle) сосу́д **2** (ship) су́дно, кора́бль (*m.*) **3** (anat.) сосу́д; **blood ~** кровено́сный сосу́д

vest[1] /vest/ *n.* (BrE, undergarment) ма́йка; (AmE, waistcoat) жиле́т

vest[2] /vest/ *v.t.*: **~ed interest** ли́чная заинтересо́ванность

vestibule /'vestɪbjuːl/ *n.* вестибю́ль (*m.*)

vestige /'vestɪdʒ/ *n.* след

vestment /'vestmənt/ *n.* (eccl.) облаче́ние, ри́за

vestry /'vestrɪ/ *n.* (eccl., room) ри́зница

vet[1] /vet/ *n.* (veterinary surgeon) ветвра́ч, ветерина́р
   ● *v.t.* (**vetted, vetting**) (investigate) пров|еря́ть, -е́рить

vet[2] /vet/ *n.* (AmE, infml, veteran) ветера́н

veteran /'vetərən/ *n.* (lit., fig.) ветера́н
   ● *adj.* многоо́пытный, старе́йший

veterinarian /ˌvetərɪˈneərɪən/ *n.* (AmE) ветерина́р

veterinary /'vetərɪnərɪ/ *adj.*: **~ surgeon** (BrE) ветерина́рный врач

veto /'viːtəʊ/ *n.* (*pl.* **~es**) ве́то (*nt. indecl.*)
   ● *v.t.* (**vetoes, vetoed**) нал|ага́ть, -ожи́ть ве́то на + *a.*

vex /veks/ *v.t.* доса|жда́ть, -ди́ть; раздраж|а́ть, -и́ть; **a ~ed question** больно́й вопро́с

VHF *abbr.* (of **very high frequency**) ОВЧ (о́чень высо́кая частота́)

 ✧ **via** /'vaɪə/ *prep.* че́рез + *a.*

viable /'vaɪəb(ə)l/ *adj.* (able to survive) жизнеспосо́бный; (infml, feasible) осуществи́мый

viaduct /'vaɪədʌkt/ *n.* виаду́к, путепрово́д

vibes /vaɪbz/ *n. pl.* (infml) (atmosphere) флюи́ды (*m. pl.*); (mus., vibraphone) вибрафо́н

vibrancy /'vaɪbrənsɪ/ *n.* (liveliness) жи́вость; (of colours) я́ркость

vibrant /'vaɪbrənt/ *adj.* (lively) живо́й, по́лный жи́зни; (of colours) со́чный, я́ркий

vibraphone /'vaɪbrəfəʊn/ *n.* вибрафо́н

vibrate /vaɪˈbreɪt/ *v.i.* вибри́ровать, дрожа́ть (*both impf.*)

vibration /vaɪˈbreɪʃ(ə)n/ *n.* вибра́ция, дрожь

vibrato /vɪˈbrɑːtəʊ/ *n. & adv.* (mus.) вибра́то (*nt. indecl.*)

vicar /ˈvɪkə(r)/ *n.* свяще́нник

vicarage /ˈvɪkərɪdʒ/ *n.* дом свяще́нника

vicarious /vɪˈkeərɪəs/ *adj.* ко́свенный; **feel ~ pleasure** пережива́ть (*impf.*) чужу́ю ра́дость

vice¹ /vaɪs/ *n.* поро́к

vice² /vaɪs/ (AmE **vise**) *n.* (tool) тиск|и́ (-о́в)

vice³ /vaɪs/:
■ **~ chairman** *n.* замести́тель (*m.*) председа́теля; **~ chancellor** *n.* (BrE) ре́ктор; **~-president** *n.* ви́це-президе́нт

vice versa /vaɪs ˈvɜːsə/ *adv.* наоборо́т

vicinity /vɪˈsɪnɪti/ *n.* окру́га, окре́стность; **in the ~ of** в райо́не + *g.*

vicious /ˈvɪʃəs/ *adj.* **1** (spiteful) злой **2**: **a ~ circle** поро́чный круг

viciousness /ˈvɪʃəsnɪs/ *n.* зло́бность

vicissitude /vɪˈsɪsɪtjuːd/ *n.* превра́тность

✓ **victim** /ˈvɪktɪm/ *n.* же́ртва; (of accident) пострада́вший

victimization /vɪktɪmaɪˈzeɪʃ(ə)n/ *n.* пресле́дование

victimize /ˈvɪktɪmaɪz/ *v.t.* подв|ерга́ть, -е́ргнуть пресле́дованию

victor /ˈvɪktə(r)/ *n.* победи́тель (*m.*)

Victorian /vɪkˈtɔːrɪən/ *n.* виктори́ан|ец (-ка)
● *adj.* викториа́нский; (fig.) старомо́дный

victorious /vɪkˈtɔːrɪəs/ *adj.* победоно́сный, побе́дный

✓ **victory** /ˈvɪktəri/ *n.* побе́да (**over**: над + *i.*)

✓ **video** /ˈvɪdɪəʊ/ *n.* (*pl.* **~s**) (a **~ recorder** (BrE), film, cassette) ви́део (*indecl.*)
● *v.t.* (**videoes, videoed**) запи́с|ывать, -а́ть на ви́део
■ **~ camera** *n.* видеока́мера; **~ cassette** *n.* видеокассе́та; **~ (cassette) recorder** *n.* видеомагнитофо́н; **~ clip** *n.* (видео)кли́п; **~ conference** *n.* видеоконфере́нция; **~ game** *n.* видеоигра́; **~phone** *n.* видеотелефо́н; **~tape** *n.* видеоле́нта; видеоплёнка

vie /vaɪ/ *v.i.* (**vying**) состяза́ться (*impf.*); сопе́рничать (*impf.*); **they ~d with each other for first place** они́ состяза́лись за пе́рвое ме́сто

Vienna /vɪˈenə/ *n.* Ве́на

Vietnam /vjetˈnæm/ *n.* Вьетна́м

Vietnamese /vjetnəˈmiːz/ *n.* (*pl.* **~**) (person) вьетна́м|ец (-ка); (language) вьетна́мский язы́к
● *adj.* вьетна́мский

✓ **view** /vjuː/ *n.* **1** (scene, prospect) вид; пейза́ж; **you get a good ~ from here** отсю́да хоро́ший вид **2** (sight; field of vision) вид; **in full ~ of the audience** на виду́ у пу́блики **3** (fig.): **look at it from my point of ~** посмотри́те на э́то с мое́й то́чки зре́ния **4** (inspection) смотр, просмо́тр; **private ~(ing)** закры́тый просмо́тр **5** (mental attitude or opinion) взгляд, мне́ние; (*in pl.*) взгля́ды (*m. pl.*), убежде́ния (*nt. pl.*); **in my ~** по-мо́ему; по моему́ мне́нию **6** (intention) наме́рение; **I am saving with a ~ to buying a house** я коплю́ де́ньги, что́бы купи́ть дом **7** (consideration): **in ~ of**

ввиду́ + *g.*; **in ~ of recent developments** в све́те после́дних происше́ствий
● *v.t.* **1** (survey; gaze on) смотре́ть, по- на + *a.*; рассм|а́тривать, -отре́ть **2** (inspect) осм|а́тривать, -отре́ть **3** (fig., consider) рассм|а́тривать, -отре́ть; оцен|ива́ть, -и́ть
■ **~finder** *n.* видоиска́тель (*m.*); **~point** *n.* то́чка зре́ния

viewer /ˈvjuːə(r)/ *n.* (of TV) (теле)зри́тель (-ница)

vigil /ˈvɪdʒɪl/ *n.* бде́ние

vigilance /ˈvɪdʒɪləns/ *n.* бди́тельность

vigilant /ˈvɪdʒɪlənt/ *adj.* бди́тельный

vigilante /vɪdʒɪˈlænti/ *n.* ≈ дружи́нник

vigorous /ˈvɪɡərəs/ *adj.* энерги́чный, бо́дрый

vigour /ˈvɪɡə(r)/ (AmE **vigor**) *n.* эне́ргия, бо́дрость

Viking /ˈvaɪkɪŋ/ *n.* ви́кинг

vile /vaɪl/ *adj.* гну́сный, ни́зкий

vilify /ˈvɪlɪfaɪ/ *v.t.* поноси́ть (*impf.*); черни́ть, о-

villa /ˈvɪlə/ *n.* ви́лла

✓ **village** /ˈvɪlɪdʒ/ *n.* дере́вня; (larger) село́

villager /ˈvɪlɪdʒə(r)/ *n.* деревенск|ий/ се́льск|ий жи́тель (-ая -ница)

villain /ˈvɪlən/ *n.* злоде́й

Vilnius /ˈvɪlnɪəs/ *n.* Ви́льнюс

vinaigrette /vɪnɪˈɡret/ *n.* сала́тная запра́вка из у́ксуса, оли́вкового ма́сла и спе́ций

vindicate /ˈvɪndɪkeɪt/ *v.t.* опра́вд|ывать, -а́ть

vindication /vɪndɪˈkeɪʃ(ə)n/ *n.* оправда́ние

vindictive /vɪnˈdɪktɪv/ *adj.* мсти́тельный

vindictiveness /vɪnˈdɪktɪvnɪs/ *n.* мсти́тельность

vine /vaɪn/ *n.* (grape~) виногра́дная лоза́; (climbing or trailing plant) вью́щееся/ползу́чее расте́ние

vinegar /ˈvɪnɪɡə(r)/ *n.* у́ксус

vineyard /ˈvɪnjɑːd/ *n.* виногра́дник

vintage /ˈvɪntɪdʒ/ *n.* **1** (year of wine production): **the 1950 ~** вино́ урожа́я ты́сяча девятьсо́т пятидеся́того го́да; **this is a good ~** э́то хоро́ший год (*о вине*); **~ wine** ма́рочное вино́ **2** (fig.): **a ~ car** (BrE) автомоби́ль (*m.*) ста́рой ма́рки

vinyl /ˈvaɪnɪl/ *n.* вини́л; (*attr.*) вини́ловый

viola¹ /vɪˈəʊlə/ *n.* (musical instrument) альт

viola² /ˈvaɪələ/ *n.* (bot.) фиа́лка

violate /ˈvaɪəleɪt/ *v.t.* **1** (infringe, transgress) нар|уша́ть, -у́шить; преступ|а́ть, -и́ть **2** (profane) оскверн|я́ть, -и́ть

violation /vaɪəˈleɪʃ(ə)n/ *n.* наруше́ние; оскверне́ние

✓ **violence** /ˈvaɪələns/ *n.* си́ла, наси́лие; **he resorted to ~** он прибе́г(нул) к наси́лию

✓ **violent** /ˈvaɪələnt/ *adj.* **1** (strong, forceful) си́льный, нейстовый, я́ростный **2** (using or involving force): **he became ~** он на́чал буйствовать

violet /ˈvaɪələt/ *n.* (bot.) фиа́лка; (colour) фиоле́товый цвет
● *adj.* (of colour) фиоле́товый

violin /vaɪəˈlɪn/ *n.* скри́пка

v

violinist /vaɪə'lɪnɪst/ *n.* скрипа́ч (-ка)

VIP *abbr.* (*of* **very important person**) высокопоста́вленное лицо́, высо́кий гость, VIP-гость

viper /'vaɪpə(r)/ *n.* гадю́ка

viral /'vaɪər(ə)l/ *adj.* ви́русный

virgin /'vɜːdʒɪn/ *n.* (female) де́вственница; (male) де́вственник
■ ~ **forest** *n.* де́вственный лес

virginal /'vɜːdʒɪn(ə)l/ *adj.* де́вственный; непоро́чный

virginity /və'dʒɪnɪtɪ/ *n.* де́вственность, неви́нность, непоро́чность; **lose one's** ~ теря́ть, по- неви́нность, лиш|а́ться, -и́ться де́вственности

Virgo /'vɜːgəʊ/ *n.* (*pl.* ~**s**) Де́ва

virile /'vɪraɪl/ *adj.* му́жественный

virility /vɪ'rɪlɪtɪ/ *n.* (sexual potency) мужска́я си́ла, полова́я поте́нция; (manliness) му́жественность

virologist /vaɪ'rɒlədʒɪst/ *n.* вирусо́лог

virology /vaɪ'rɒlədʒɪ/ *n.* вирусоло́гия

virtual /'vɜːtʃʊəl/ *adj.* **1** факти́ческий; **we remained** ~ **strangers** факти́чески мы остава́лись соверше́нно незнако́мыми людьми́ **2** (comput., phys.) виртуа́льный
■ ~ **reality** *n.* (comput.) виртуа́льная реа́льность

✓ **virtually** /'vɜːtʃʊəlɪ/ *adv.* факти́чески, практи́чески; **the dress was** ~ **new** э́то бы́ло факти́чески/практи́чески но́вое пла́тье; **it's** ~ **impossible** э́то факти́чески/практи́чески невозмо́жно

virtue /'vɜːtʃuː/ *n.* **1** (moral excellence) доброде́тель **2** (good quality, advantage) досто́инство, преиму́щество **3** (consideration): **by** ~ **of his long service** на основа́нии его́ многоле́тней слу́жбы

virtuosity /vɜːtʃʊ'ɒsɪtɪ/ *n.* виртуо́зность

virtuoso /vɜːtʃʊ'əʊsəʊ/ *n.*: **a** ~ **performance** виртуо́зное исполне́ние

virtuous /'vɜːtʃʊəs/ *adj.* доброде́тельный

virulence /'vɪrʊləns/ *n.* (of poison) си́ла, смерте́льность; (of disease) тя́жесть; (of bacteria) вируле́нтность; (of temper, speech, etc.) зло́ба, я́рость

virulent /'vɪrʊlənt/ *adj.* (of poison) сильноде́йствующий; смерте́льный; (of disease) тяжёлый; (of bacteria) вируле́нтный; (of temper, words, etc.) зло́бный, я́ростный

virus /'vaɪərəs/ *n.* (also comput.) ви́рус

visa /'viːzə/ *n.* ви́за

viscount /'vaɪkaʊnt/ *n.* вико́нт

viscountess /'vaɪkaʊntɪs/ *n.* виконте́сса

viscous /'vɪskəs/ *adj.* вя́зкий, ли́пкий

vise /vaɪs/ *n.* (AmE) = **vice²**

visibility /vɪzɪ'bɪlɪtɪ/ *n.* ви́димость

visibl|e /'vɪzɪb(ə)l/ *adj.* **1** (perceptible by eye) ви́димый **2** (apparent; obvious) я́вный, очеви́дный; **she was** ~**y annoyed** она́ была́ заме́тно раздражена́

✓ **vision** /'vɪʒ(ə)n/ *n.* **1** (faculty of sight) зре́ние **2** (imaginative insight) проница́тельность **3** (apparition) при́зрак; привиде́ние **4** (sth imagined or dreamed of) мечта́

visionary /'vɪʒənərɪ/ *n.* прови́д|ец (-ица)
● *adj.* дальнови́дный, му́дрый

✓ **visit** /'vɪzɪt/ *n.* (call) визи́т, посеще́ние; (trip, stay) пое́здка, пребыва́ние; **make, pay a** ~ **to sb** посе|ща́ть, -ти́ть (*or* наве|ща́ть, -сти́ть) кого́-н.
● *v.t.* (**visited**, **visiting**) (place) посе|ща́ть, -ти́ть; (person) наве|ща́ть, -сти́ть; **he** ~**ed Europe** он побыва́л в Евро́пе; он съе́здил в Евро́пу; **I have never** ~**ed New York** я никогда́ не быва́л в Нью-Йо́рке
● *v.i.* (AmE): ~ **with** (go to see) посе|ща́ть, -ти́ть (*or* наве|ща́ть, -сти́ть) кого́-н.
■ ~**ing card** *n.* (BrE) визи́тная ка́рточка; ~**ing hours** *n. pl.* приёмные часы́; часы́ посеще́ния

✓ **visitor** /'vɪzɪtə(r)/ *n.* гость (*m.*), посети́тель (*m.*)

visor /'vaɪzə(r)/ *n.* (of helmet) щито́к; (of windscreen) солнцезащи́тный щито́к

vista /'vɪstə/ *n.* перспекти́ва, вид

visual /'vɪʒʊəl/ *adj.* зри́тельный; визуа́льный
■ ~ **aids** *n. pl.* нагля́дные посо́бия; ~ **arts** *n. pl.* изобрази́тельные иску́сства

visualize /'vɪʒʊəlaɪz/ *v.t.* предст|авля́ть, -а́вить себе́

✓ **vital** /'vaɪt(ə)l/ *adj.* **1** (concerned with life) жи́зненный; ~ **statistics** (joc., woman's measurements) объём груди́, та́лии и бёдер **2** (essential) насу́щный; **it is of** ~ **importance** э́то вопро́с/де́ло первостепе́нной ва́жности **3** (lively) живо́й

vitality /vaɪ'tælɪtɪ/ *n.* жи́вость

vitamin /'vɪtəmɪn/ *n.* витами́н
■ ~ **C** *n.* витами́н C (*pronounced* це)

viticulture /'vɪtɪkʌltʃə(r)/ *n.* виногра́дарство

vitriolic /vɪtrɪ'ɒlɪk/ *adj.* ядови́тый (*комментарий и т. п.*)

viva /'vaɪvə/ (BrE) у́стный экза́мен

vivacious /vɪ'veɪʃəs/ *adj.* живо́й, оживлённый

vivacity /vɪ'væsɪtɪ/ *n.* жи́вость, оживле́ние

vivid /'vɪvɪd/ *adj.* **1** (bright) я́ркий **2** (lively) живо́й, пы́лкий; **a** ~ **imagination** пы́лкое воображе́ние **3** (clear and distinct) чёткий, я́сный

vividness /'vɪvɪdnɪs/ *n.* я́ркость, жи́вость; чёткость

vivisection /vɪvɪ'sekʃ(ə)n/ *n.* вивисе́кция

vixen /'vɪks(ə)n/ *n.* лиси́ца(-са́мка)

viz. /vɪz/ *adv.* то есть, т. е., и и́менно

vocabulary /və'kæbjʊlərɪ/ *n.* (of an individual) слова́рный запа́с; (of a language) слова́рный соста́в

vocal /'vəʊk(ə)l/ *adj.* **1** (of or using the voice) голосово́й, речево́й **2** (eloquent) красноречи́вый
● *n.* (*usu. in pl.*) вока́льная па́ртия

vocalist /'vəʊkəlɪst/ *n.* вокали́ст (-ка)

vocation /və'keɪʃ(ə)n/ *n.* призва́ние

vocational /və'keɪʃən(ə)l/ *adj.* профессиона́льный

✓ ключева́я ле́ксика

vociferous /vəˈsɪfərəs/ *adj.* шýмный
vodka /ˈvɒdkə/ *n.* вóдка
vogue /vəʊg/ *n.* мóда; in ~ в мóде
✧ **voice** /vɔɪs/ *n.* гóлос; he shouted at the top of his ~ он кричáл во весь гóлос; I lost my ~ я потерял гóлос
　● *v.t.* выражáть, выразить
　■ ~ **mail** *n.* голосовáя пóчта; ~-**over** *n.* (TV etc.) гóлос за кáдром; кáдровый комментáрий
void /vɔɪd/ *n.* пустотá
　● *adj.* **1** (empty) пустóй; лишённый (чего) **2** (invalid) недействительный
volatile /ˈvɒlətaɪl/ *adj.* (of person) непостоянный, изменчивый
volcanic /vɒlˈkænɪk/ *adj.* вулканический
volcano /vɒlˈkeɪnəʊ/ *n.* (*pl.* ~**es**) вулкáн
Volga /ˈvɒlgə/ *n.* Вóлга
volley /ˈvɒlɪ/ *n.* (*pl.* ~**s**) **1** (simultaneous discharge) залп; (fig.): a ~ **of oaths** потóк брáни **2** (tennis etc.) удáр с лёта
　● *v.t.* (**volleys, volleyed**) удар|ять, -áрить с лёта
volleyball /ˈvɒlɪbɔːl/ *n.* волейбóл
volt /vəʊlt/ *n.* вольт
voltage /ˈvəʊltɪdʒ/ *n.* напряжéние, вольтáж
✧ **volume** /ˈvɒljuːm/ *n.* **1** (tome) том **2** (of sound) грóмкость
　■ ~ **control** *n.* регулятор грóмкости
voluminous /vəˈluːmɪnəs/ *adj.* огрóмный; ~ **folds** пышные склáдки; a ~ **work** объёмистое произведéние; a ~ **writer** плодовитый писáтель
voluntary /ˈvɒləntərɪ/ *adj.* добровóльный
　■ ~ **redundancy** *n.* добровóльный ухóд с рабóты; ~ **work** *n.* общественнная рабóта
volunteer /vɒlənˈtɪə(r)/ *n.* добровóльный помóщник; (in army) добровóлец
　● *v.t.* предл|агáть, -ожить; дéлать, с-добровóльно
　● *v.i.* вызывáться, вызваться сдéлать что-н.;

no one ~ed желáющих не нашлóсь
voluptuous /vəˈlʌptʃʊəs/ *adj.* чýвственный
vomit /ˈvɒmɪt/ *n.* рвóта
　● *v.i.* (**vomited, vomiting**): he ~ed егó вырвало
voracious /vəˈreɪʃəs/ *adj.* прожóрливый
✧ **vote** /vəʊt/ *n.* **1** (act of voting) голосовáние **2** (~ cast) гóлос **3** (affirmation) вóтум; a ~ **of confidence** вóтум довéрия **4** (right to ~) прáво гóлоса
　● *v.i.* голосовáть, про-; they are voting on the resolution они голосýют резолюцию
　● *with adv.*: they were ~d in by a large majority их избрáли большинствóм голосóв
✧ **voter** /ˈvəʊtə(r)/ *n.* избирáтель (*m.*)
voting /ˈvəʊtɪŋ/ *n.* голосовáние; учáстие в выборах (об избирателях)
vouch /vaʊtʃ/ *v.i.* ручáться, поручиться; I can ~ **for his honesty** я готóв поручиться за егó чéстность
voucher /ˈvaʊtʃə(r)/ *n.* талóн
vow /vaʊ/ *n.* обéт, клятва; he broke his marriage ~**s** он нарýшил брáчный обéт
　● *v.t.* кляcться, по-; he ~ed (sc. resolved) never to return он поклялся никогдá не возвращáться
vowel /ˈvaʊəl/ *n.* (ling.) глáсный (звук)
voyage /ˈvɔɪɪdʒ/ *n.* (by sea) (морскóе) путешéствие; плáвание
voyeur /vwaːˈjɜː(r)/ *n.* вуайерист
vs *abbr.* (of **versus**) прóтив + g.
V-sign /ˈviːsaɪn/ *n.* **1** (BrE, gesture of contempt) ≈ фига (жест) **2** (for victory) знак побéды
vulgar /ˈvʌlgə(r)/ *adj.* вульгáрный, пóшлый, грýбый
vulgarity /vʌlˈgærɪtɪ/ *n.* вульгáрность, пóшлость, грýбость
vulnerable /ˈvʌlnərəb(ə)l/ *adj.* уязвимый
vulture /ˈvʌltʃə(r)/ *n.* гриф (птица)
vulva /ˈvʌlvə/ *n.* (*pl.* ~**s**) (anat.) вýльва

Ww

wacky /ˈwækɪ/ *adj.* (**wackier, wackiest**) (infml) сумасшéдший, чóкнутый
wad /wɒd/ *n.* **1** (pad) комóк **2** (of papers, banknotes) пáчка
waddle /ˈwɒd(ə)l/ *v.i.* ходить (indet.) враздвáл(оч)ку (infml)
wade /weɪd/ *v.i.* проб|ирáться, -рáться; (fig.): I have ~d through all his novels я (с трудóм) одолéл все егó ромáны
wafer /ˈweɪfə(r)/ *n.* (cul.) вáфля

waffle¹ /ˈwɒf(ə)l/ *n.* (cul.) вáфля
waffle² /ˈwɒf(ə)l/ (infml) *n.* (BrE, verbiage) водá (в речи, в статьé)
　● *v.i.* (also ~ **on**) (BrE) занимáться (impf.) болтовнёй
waft /wɒft/ *v.t.* дон|осить, -ести
　● *v.i.* дон|оситься, -естись
wag /wæg/ *v.t.* (**wagged, wagging**) (one's tail) вил|ять, -ьнýть + i.
　● *v.i.* (**wagged, wagging**) (of dog's tail)

вил|я́ть, -ьну́ть; **this will set tongues ~ging** э́то даст по́вод к спле́тням

☞ **wage¹** /weɪdʒ/ n. (also **wages** pl.) зарабо́тная пла́та; зарпла́та; **a living ~** прожи́точный ми́нимум

■ **~ earner** n. наёмный рабо́чий; (breadwinner) корми́л|ец (-и́ца)

wage² /weɪdʒ/ v.t. (war) вести́ (impf.); (campaign) пров|оди́ть, -ести́

wager /'weɪdʒə(r)/ n. пари́ (nt. indecl.); **lay a ~** держа́ть (impf.) пари́

waggle /'wæg(ə)l/ v.t. & i. (ears, toes) шевели́ть, по- + i.

● v.i. (of ears, toes) шевели́ться, по-; (shake slightly) пока́чиваться (impf.)

wagon /'wægən/ n. ■ (horse-drawn) пово́зка; ■ (with cover) фурго́н ■ (BrE, on railway) ваго́н-платфо́рма ■: **he is on the ~** (fig., not drinking alcohol) он бро́сил пить

wail /weɪl/ n. (cry, howl) вопль (m.); (fig., of the wind, sirens) вой

● v.i. вопи́ть (impf.); выть (impf.)

waist /weɪst/ n. та́лия

■ **~coat** n. (BrE) жиле́т

☞ **wait** /weɪt/ n. ■ (act or time of ~ing) ожида́ние; **we had a long ~ for the bus** мы до́лго жда́ли авто́буса ■ (ambush): **the robbers lay in ~ for their victim** граби́тели подстерега́ли свою́ же́ртву

● v.t.: **you must ~ your turn** вы должны́ дожда́ться свое́й о́череди

● v.i. ■ (refrain from action) ждать (impf.), подожда́ть (pf.); **we must ~ and see what happens** подождём — посмо́трим, что бу́дет да́льше; **I could hardly ~ to … я сгора́л от нетерпе́ния (+ inf.); I ~ed for the rain to stop** я ждал, когда́ ко́нчится дождь ■ (act as servant): **she ~s on him hand and foot** она́ его́ по́лностью обслу́живает; **he ~ed at table** он прислу́живал за столо́м ■ **~ up: she ~ed up for him** она́ не ложи́лась (спать) до его́ прихо́да

■ **~ing list** n. спи́сок (кандида́тов, очереднико́в); о́чередь; **~ing room** n. (doctor's etc.) приёмная; (station) зал ожида́ния

waiter /'weɪtə(r)/ n. официа́нт

waitress /'weɪtrɪs/ n. официа́нтка

waive /weɪv/ v.t. (forgo) отка́з|ываться, -а́ться от + g.; (claims) возде́рж|иваться, -а́ться от + g.; (rules) не соблю|да́ть, -сти́ + g.

waiver /'weɪvə(r)/ n. отка́з (от + g.)

☞ **wake¹** /weɪk/ v.t. (past **woke**, p.p. **woken**) буди́ть, раз-

● v.i. (past **woke**, p.p. **woken**) (also **~ up**) прос|ыпа́ться, -ну́ться; **~ up!** (lit., fig.) просни́тесь!

wake² /weɪk/ n. (of vessel) кильва́тер; (fig.): **there was havoc in the ~ of the storm** бу́ря оста́вила по́сле себя́ многочи́сленные разруше́ния

wakeful /'weɪkfʊl/ adj. (person) бо́дрствующий; **we had a ~ night** мы провели́ бессо́нную ночь

☞ ключева́я ле́ксика

waken /'weɪkən/ v.t. буди́ть, раз-; (fig.) буди́ть, про-

Wales /weɪlz/ n. Уэ́льс

☞ **walk** /wɔːk/ n. ■ (action of ~ing) ходьба́; **a short ~ away** в не́скольких шага́х отсю́да/отту́да ■ (excursion) (пе́шая) прогу́лка; (long-distance) похо́д; **I'm going for a ~** я пойду́ прогуля́юсь/погуля́ю; **I went on a ten-mile ~** я был в десятими́льном похо́де ■ (~ing pace) шаг ■ (gait) похо́дка, по́ступь ■ (route for ~ing): **there are some pleasant ~s round here** здесь есть прия́тные места́ для прогу́лок ■ (path) тропа́ ■ (contest): **long-distance ~** (спорти́вная) ходьба́ на дли́нную диста́нцию

● v.t. (take for a ~) выгу́ливать, вы́гулять; гуля́ть, по- с (+ i.); (cause to ~): **he ~ed his horse up the hill** он пусти́л ло́шадь ша́гом в го́ру; (accompany) сопрово|жда́ть, -ди́ть; **he offered to ~ her home** он вы́звался проводи́ть её домо́й

● v.i. ■ (move on foot) ходи́ть (indet.), идти́ (det.); (stroll about) прогу́ливаться (impf.); **I ~ed ten miles** я прошёл де́сять миль; **I ~ed into a shop** я вошёл в магази́н; **they ~ed into an ambush** они́ попа́ли в заса́ду ■ (opp. ride) ходи́ть (indet.), идти́ (det.) пешко́м ■ (opp. run): **he ~ed the last 100 metres** после́дние сто ме́тров он прошёл ша́гом ■ (take exercise etc. on foot) ходи́ть (indet.) пешко́м; (stroll) гуля́ть (impf.); **I spent 2 weeks ~ing in Scotland** я броди́л две неде́ли по Шотла́ндии

□ **~ away** v.i. уходи́ть, уйти́; **he ~ed away with several prizes** он без труда́ завоева́л/получи́л не́сколько призо́в

□ **~ in** v.i. входи́ть, войти́

□ **~ off** v.t. (annul by ~ing): **he was ~ing off a heavy lunch** он соверша́л прогу́лку по́сле сы́тного обе́да

● v.i. уходи́ть, уйти́; **someone ~ed off with my hat** кто-то унёс мою́ шля́пу

□ **~ on** v.i. (continue ~ing) продолжа́ть (impf.) идти́

□ **~ out** v.i. выходи́ть, вы́йти; **the men are threatening to ~ out** (strike) рабо́чие грозя́т забасто́вкой

□ **~ up** v.i. (approach) под|ходи́ть, -ойти́; **I ~ed up to him** я подошёл к нему́

■ **~over** n. лёгкая побе́да; **~way** n. перехо́д (сооруже́ние)

walker /'wɔːkə(r)/ n. челове́к, соверша́ющий пе́шие/пешехо́дные прогу́лки; пе́ший тури́ст; **a popular route for ~s** популя́рный пешехо́дный маршру́т

walkie-talkie /wɔːkɪ'tɔːkɪ/ n. ра́ция

walking /'wɔːkɪŋ/ n. ходьба́

■ **~ shoes** n. pl. о́бувь для ходьбы́; **~ stick** n. трость

Walkman® /'wɔːkmən/ n. пле́ер

☞ **wall** /wɔːl/ n. (lit., fig.) стена́, сте́нка; (attr.) насте́нный

● v.t.: **~ed garden** обнесённый стено́й сад

■ **~paper** n. обо́|и (-ев) ● v.t. обкле́и|вать, -ть обо́ями

wallaby /'wɒləbɪ/ n. кенгуру́-валла́би (m. indecl.)

wallet /'wɒlɪt/ *n.* бума́жник

wallop /'wɒləp/ *v.t.* (**walloped, walloping**) (infml) дуба́сить, от-

wallow /'wɒləʊ/ *v.i.* (in mud, water) валя́ться (*impf.*); (fig.) купа́ться (*impf.*) (*в чём*); ~ **in grief** упива́ться (*impf.*) свои́м го́рем

walnut /'wɔːlnʌt/ *n.* гре́цкий оре́х; (wood) оре́х

walrus /'wɔːlrəs/ *n.* морж

waltz /wɔːls/ *n.* вальс
 • *v.i.* танцева́ть (*impf.*) вальс

wan /wɒn/ *adj.* (**wanner, wannest**) бле́дный, изнурённый; a ~ **light** сла́бый/ ту́склый свет; a ~ **smile** сла́бая улы́бка

wand /wɒnd/ *n.* волше́бная па́лочка

wander /'wɒndə(r)/ *v.t.* броди́ть, стра́нствовать, скита́ться (*all impf.*) по + *d.*
 • *v.i.* **1** (go aimlessly) броди́ть (*impf.*); **his mind was** ~**ing** (absent-mindedly) его́ мы́сли блужда́ли; (in delirium) он бре́дил **2** (stray) заблуди́ться (*pf.*); (lit., fig.) отклон|я́ться, -и́ться; **we** ~**ed from the track** мы сби́лись с пути́; **don't let your attention** ~ не отвлека́йтесь
 □ ~ **about** *v.i.* броди́ть (*impf.*)
 □ ~ **off** *v.i.* брести́, по- куда́-н.

wanderer /'wɒndərə(r)/ *n.* стра́нник, скита́лец

wane /weɪn/ *v.i.* (of the moon) убыва́ть (*impf.*); (fig., decline) ослабева́ть (*impf.*)

wangle /'wæŋɡ(ə)l/ *v.t.* заполучи́ть (*pf.*) хи́тростью; **he** ~**d £5 out of me** он вы́клянчил (infml) у меня́ 5 фу́нтов

wannabe /'wɒnəbɪ/ *n.* (sl.) челове́к, мечта́ющий стать (*кем-н.*)

want /wɒnt/ *n.* **1** (lack) недоста́ток, отсу́тствие; **for** ~ **of** за неиме́нием + *g.* **2** (need) нужда́
 • *v.t.* **1** (need; require) нужда́ться (*impf.*) в + *p.*; **I don't** ~ **any bread today** сего́дня мне хлеб не ну́жен; **he is** ~**ed by the police** его́ разы́скивает поли́ция; **you're** ~**ed on the telephone** вас (про́сят) к телефо́ну **2** (desire) хоте́ть (*impf.*) (+ *g. or a. or inf.*); жела́ть (*impf.*) (+ *g. or inf.*); **what do you** ~? что вы хоти́те?; что вам ну́жно?; **she** ~**s to go away** она́ хо́чет уе́хать/уйти́; **she** ~**s me to go away** она́ хо́чет, что́бы я уе́хал/ушёл

wanting /'wɒntɪŋ/ *adj.* недоста́точный; **he was tried and found** ~ он не вы́держал испыта́ния

wanton /'wɒnt(ə)n/ *adj.* (wilful) своенра́вный; ~ **cruelty** бессмы́сленная жесто́кость

war /wɔː(r)/ *n.* **1** война́; **make, wage** ~ **on** вести́ (*det.*) войну́ с + *i.* **2** (attr.) вое́нный
 ■ ~ **game** *n.* (in pl.) (military exercises) (вое́нные) уче́ния; (leisure activity) вое́нная игра́; ~**head** *n.* боеголо́вка; ~**like** *adj.* (martial) вои́нственный; ~**ship** *n.* вое́нный кора́бль; ~**time** *n.* вое́нное вре́мя

ward /wɔːd/ *n.* **1** (person under guardianship) подопе́чный **2** (urban division) о́круг **3** (in hospital etc.) пала́та
 • *v.t.*: ~ **off** (a blow) отра|жа́ть, -зи́ть; ~ **off danger** отвра|ща́ть, -ти́ть опа́сность

warden /'wɔːd(ə)n/ *n.* **1** (BrE, of hostel) комена́нт **2**: **traffic** ~ (BrE) инспе́ктор, контроли́рующий соблюде́ние пра́вил парко́вки и стоя́нки (*в черте города*)

warder /'wɔːdə(r)/ *n.* (BrE, in prison) надзира́тель (*m.*)

wardrobe /'wɔːdrəʊb/ *n.* **1** гардеро́б **2** (theatr.) костюме́рная

warehouse /'weəhaʊs/ *n.* (това́рный) склад

wares /weəz/ *n. pl.* това́ры (*m. pl.*)

warfare /'wɔːfeə(r)/ *n.* война́

warm /wɔːm/ *adj.* тёплый
 • *v.t.* греть (*impf.*); (food, water) подогр|ева́ть, -е́ть; нагр|ева́ть, -е́ть; ~ **oneself at the fire** гре́ться (*impf.*) у ками́на/огня́
 • *v.i.* гре́ться (*impf.*); (of objects) нагр|ева́ться, -е́ться; (of people, room) согр|ева́ться, -е́ться; (fig.): **he** ~**ed to the subject as he went on** по ме́ре расска́за он всё бо́льше воодушевля́лся; **I** ~**ed to(wards) him as I got to know him** чем лу́чше я его́ узнава́л, тем бо́льше располо́жения он вызыва́л у меня́
 □ ~ **up** *v.t.* разогр|ева́ть, -е́ть; согр|ева́ть, -е́ть; **a fire will** ~ **up the room** ками́н обогре́ет ко́мнату
 • *v.i.* согр|ева́ться, -е́ться; **it** (sc. the weather) **is** ~**ing up** тепле́ет; **he** ~**ed up before the race** он сде́лал разми́нку пе́ред нача́лом соревнова́ния
 ■ ~-**hearted** *adj.* серде́чный; ~-**up** *n.* разми́нка

warmth /wɔːmθ/ *n.* теплота́

warn /wɔːn/ *v.t.* (caution) предупре|жда́ть, -ди́ть; (of danger etc.) предостер|ега́ть, -е́чь

warning /'wɔːnɪŋ/ *n.* предупрежде́ние, предостереже́ние; **give** ~ **of** предупре|жда́ть, -ди́ть о + *p.*
 • *adj.* предупрежда́ющий; предостерега́ющий

warp /wɔːp/ *v.t.* **1** (distort) коро́бить, по-; искрив|ля́ть, -и́ть **2** (fig.) иска|жа́ть, -зи́ть; a ~**ed sense of humour** извращённое чу́вство ю́мора
 • *v.i.* коро́биться, по-

warrant /'wɒrənt/ *n.* о́рдер; суде́бное распоряже́ние
 • *v.t.* опра́вд|ывать, -а́ть

warranty /'wɒrəntɪ/ *n.* гара́нтия

warren /'wɒrən/ *n.* (rabbits') кро́личья нора́; (fig.) лабири́нт

warrior /'wɒrɪə(r)/ *n.* во́ин

Warsaw /'wɔːsɔː/ *n.* Варша́ва

wart /wɔːt/ *n.* борода́вка

wary /'weərɪ/ *adj.* (**warier, wariest**) осторо́жный; **be** ~ **of** остерега́ться (*impf.*) + *g.*

was /wɒz/ *1st and 3rd pers. sg. past of* ▶ **be**

wash /wɒʃ/ *n.* **1** (act of ~ing) мытьё; **I must have a** ~ мне на́до помы́ться/умы́ться; **she gave the floor a good** ~ она́ тща́тельно вы́мыла пол **2** (laundry) сти́рка **3** (motion of water etc.) прибо́й
 • *v.t.* (cleanse with water etc.) мыть, по-/вы́-; (hands, face, child) умы|ва́ть, -ть; (clothes) стира́ть, по-/вы́-; ~ **one's hands and face**

w

мыть, по-/вы- ру́ки и лицо́; ~ **dishes** мыть, по-/вы- посу́ду
● *v.i.* (~ oneself) мы́ться, по-/вы-
□ ~ **away** *v.t.* (carry off) смыва́ть, -ы́ть
□ ~ **out** *v.t.* (of colour): **you look ~ed out** у вас утомлённый вид
□ ~ **up** *v.t. & i.* (BrE, dishes) мыть, по-/вы- (посу́ду); (AmE, have a wash) мы́ться, по-/вы-; (on to shore) выбра́сывать, вы́бросить на бе́рег
■ ~**basin**, ~**bowl** *nn.* ра́ковина; ~**cloth** *n.* (AmE) махро́вая салфе́тка для лица́; ~**out** *n.* прова́л, неуда́ча

washable /ˈwɒʃəb(ə)l/ *adj.* мо́ющийся
washer /ˈwɒʃə(r)/ *n.* (tech.) прокла́дка
washing /ˈwɒʃɪŋ/ *n.* **1** (action) мытьё, умыва́ние, сти́рка **2** (clothes) бельё
■ ~ **machine** *n.* стира́льная маши́на; ~ **powder** *n.* (BrE) стира́льный порошо́к; ~-**up** *n.* (BrE): **do the ~-up** мыть, по-/вы- посу́ду; ~-**up liquid** *n.* (BrE) сре́дство для мытья́ посу́ды

Washington /ˈwɒʃɪŋt(ə)n/ *n.* Вашингто́н
wasp /wɒsp/ *n.* оса́
waspish /ˈwɒspɪʃ/ *adj.* язви́тельный, ко́лкий
wastage /ˈweɪstɪdʒ/ *n.* убы́ток, уте́чка
✍ **waste** /weɪst/ *n.* **1** (extravagant use): **it is a ~** (рас)тра́та, растра́чивание; ~ **of money** пуста́я тра́та де́нег; **go, run to ~** пропада́ть (*impf.*) да́ром **2** (refuse, superfluous material) отхо́ды (*m. pl.*), отбро́сы (*m. pl.*), му́сор
● *adj.* **1** (superfluous) ли́шний, нену́жный; (rejected) брако́ванный; ~ **products** отхо́ды (*m. pl.*) **2** (of land): ~ **ground** невозде́ланная земля́; ~**land** пусты́рь (*m.*), пу́стошь; **lay ~** опустоша́|ть, -и́ть
● *v.t.* **1** (make no use of, squander) тра́тить, ис-/по- да́ром/зря/впусту́ю; растра́|чивать, -тить; ~ **one's chance** упус|ка́ть, -ти́ть слу́чай **2** (wear away) изнур|я́ть, -и́ть
■ ~**basket** *n.* (AmE) му́сорная корзи́на; ~ **paper** *n.* макулату́ра; ~-**paper basket** *n.* (BrE) корзи́на для бума́г; ~ **pipe** *n.* сливна́я/водоотво́дная труба́

wasteful /ˈweɪstfʊl/ *adj.* расточи́тельный
waster /ˈweɪstə(r)/ *n.* (wasteful person) расточи́тель (*m.*); (infml, good-for-nothing) никуды́шный/никчёмный челове́к; безде́льник
✍ **watch¹** /wɒtʃ/ *n.* (alert state) надзо́р, присмо́тр, наблюде́ние; **keep ~** (guard) наблюда́ть (*impf.*) (on: за + *i.*); **the dog keeps ~ on, over the house** соба́ка карау́лит/сторожи́т дом
● *v.t.* **1** (look at) смотре́ть (*impf.*); **he was ~ing TV** он смотре́л телеви́зор; **I ~ed him draw** я смотре́л, как он рису́ет **2** (keep under observation) следи́ть (*impf.*) за + *i.*; смотре́ть (*impf.*) за + *i.*; (be careful of) следи́ть (*impf.*) за + *i.*; ~ **your step!** (fig.) (infml *also* ~ **it!**) бу́дьте осторо́жны! **3** (guard) сторожи́ть (*impf.*)
● *v.i.* **1** смотре́ть, наблюда́ть, следи́ть (*all impf.*); **he ~ed for the postman** он поджида́л почтальо́на; **he ~ed over her interests**

он стоя́л на стра́же её интере́сов **2** (be careful): ~ **how you cross the street!** бу́дьте осторо́жны (*or* смотри́те) при перехо́де у́лицы!
□ ~ **out** *v.i.* (beware) остерега́ться + *g.*
■ ~**dog** *n.* (lit.) сторожева́я соба́ка; (fig.) наблюда́тель (*m.*); ~**man** *n.* сто́рож; ~**word** *n.* деви́з

watch² /wɒtʃ/ *n.* (timepiece) час|ы́ (*pl., g.* -о́в)
■ ~**band** (AmE), ~ **strap** (BrE) *nn.* ремешо́к для часо́в
watchful /ˈwɒtʃfʊl/ *adj.* бди́тельный
✍ **water** /ˈwɔːtə(r)/ *n.* **1** вода́ **2** (*attr.*): ~ **sports** во́дные ви́ды спо́рта
● *v.t.* **1** (plants) пол|ива́ть, -и́ть водо́й **2** (animals) пои́ть, на-
● *v.i.* (of eyes) слези́ться (*impf.*); **his eyes were ~ing with the wind** от ве́тра у него́ слези́лись глаза́; **the sight of food made my mouth ~** при ви́де еды́ у меня́ потекли́ слю́нки
□ ~ **down** *v.t.* (lit.) разб|авля́ть, -а́вить; (fig.) смягч|а́ть, -и́ть
■ ~**colour** (AmE ~**color**) *n.* (paint) акваре́ль, акваре́льные кра́ски (*f. pl.*); (painting) акваре́ль, акваре́льный рису́нок; ~**course** *n.* ру́сло; ~**cress** *n.* кресс водяно́й; ~**fall** *n.* водопа́д; ~ **feature** *n.* (in gardening) элеме́нт аквадиза́йна (*искусственный пруд, фонтан*); ~ **level** *n.* у́ровень (*m.*) воды́; ~**lily** *n.* кувши́нка; ~**logged** *adj.* забело́ченный; ~ **main** *n.* водопрово́дная магистра́ль; ~**mark** *n.* водяно́й знак; ~**melon** *n.* арбу́з; ~**proof** *adj.* непромока́емый ● *n.* (BrE) непромока́емый плащ; ~**skiing** *n.* воднолы́жный спорт; ~**skis** *n. pl.* во́дные лы́жи (*f. pl.*); ~**tight** *adj.* (lit.) водонепроница́емый; (fig., of argument etc.) неопровержи́мый; ~**way** *n.* фарва́тер; ~**works** *n. pl.* водопрово́дная ста́нция
watering /ˈwɔːtərɪŋ/ *n.* поли́вка
■ ~ **can** *n.* ле́йка
watery /ˈwɔːtərɪ/ *adj.* водяни́стый, жи́дкий; ~ **eyes** слезя́щиеся глаза́
watt /wɒt/ *n.* ватт
wattage /ˈwɒtɪdʒ/ *n.* мо́щность в ва́ттах
✍ **wave** /weɪv/ *n.* **1** (ridge of water) волна́ **2** (fig., temporary increase) подъём, волна́; **crime ~** ре́зкий рост престу́пности **3** (phys.) волна́; **short/medium/long ~s** коро́ткие/сре́дние/дли́нные во́лны **4** (undulation): **her hair has a natural ~** у неё (от приро́ды) вью́щиеся во́лосы **5** (gesture) взмах
● *v.t.* **1** (move to and fro or up and down) маха́ть, по- + *i.*; разма́хивать (*impf.*) + *i.* **2** (express by hand-waving): ~ **goodbye** маха́ть, по- (руко́й) на проща́ние
● *v.i.* **1** (move to and fro or up and down) развева́ться (*impf.*); кача́ться (*impf.*) **2** (~ one's hand) маха́ть, по-; ~ **at sb** маха́ть, по- кому́-н.
■ ~**band** *n.* диапазо́н волн; ~**length** *n.* длина́ волны́; **he and I are on the same ~length** (fig.) мы с ним легко́ нахо́дим о́бщий язы́к

W

waver /'weɪvə(r)/ *v.i.* **1** (falter) дрожа́ть, за-; дро́гнуть (*pf.*) **2** (hesitate) колеба́ться (*impf.*)

wavy /'weɪvɪ/ *adj.* (**wavier, waviest**) волни́стый; ~ **hair** вью́щиеся во́лосы

wax¹ /wæks/ *n.* воск; (in the ears) се́ра
■ ~**work** *n.* (dummy) восковáя фигу́ра; ~**works** *n.* (museum) галере́я восковы́х фигу́р

wax² /wæks/ *v.i.* (of moon) прибывáть (*impf.*)

waxy /'wæksɪ/ *adj.* (**waxier, waxiest**) восковóй

⚡ **way** /weɪ/ *n.* **1** (road, path) доро́га, путь (*m.*); (track) тропá **2** (route, journey) путь (*m.*); **which is the best ~ to London?** как лу́чше прое́хать в Ло́ндон?; **we made our ~ to the dining room** мы прошли́ в столо́вую; (with preps.): **by ~ of London** че́рез Ло́ндон; **by the ~** (incidentally) кста́ти; ме́жду про́чим; **on the ~** по доро́ге; на/по пути́; **he was on his ~ to the bank** он шёл в банк; **he went out of his ~ to help me** он прояви́л немáлое усе́рдие, что́бы помо́чь мне; **out of the ~** (remote) в стороне́; далеко́; (with adv. indicating direction): ~ **back** обрáтная доро́га; ~ **in** вход; ~ **out** (lit., fig.) вы́ход **3** (direction) сторонá, направле́ние; **which ~ did they go?** в каку́ю сто́рону они́ пошли́?; **this ~ сюдá; you can't have it both ~s** ли́бо одно́, ли́бо друго́е; что́-нибудь одно́ **4** (of reversible things): **his hat is on the wrong ~ round** он наде́л шля́пу зáдом наперёд; **the picture is the wrong ~ up** карти́на пове́шена вверх ногáми; **is the flag the right ~ up?** флаг пове́шен прáвильно? **5** (distance, time) расстоя́ние; **a long ~ off** (away) далеко́; **it is only a little ~ to the shop** до магази́нов совсе́м недалеко́; **all the ~** всю доро́гу; (fig.) по́лностью **6** (a long ~) далеко́; ~ **back** (long ago) давны́м-давно́; ~ **ahead of the others** намно́го впереди́ остальны́х **7** (clear passage) прое́зд, прохо́д; **get in the ~** мешáть, по- (*кому́*); **get out of the ~!** (прочь) с доро́ги!; **make ~ for the President!** доро́гу президе́нту!; **you are standing in the ~** вы загорáживаете доро́гу; **give ~** (fail to resist) поддавáться, -áться; (collapse) провáл|иваться, -и́ться; разрывáться, -орвáться; ру́хнуть (*pf.*); **his legs gave ~** у него́ подкоси́лись но́ги; (make concessions) уступ|áть, -и́ть; (allow precedence) уступ|áть, -и́ть доро́гу **8** (means) сре́дство, ме́тод, приём **9** (manner) сре́дство, спо́соб, о́браз, ме́тод, приём; **in this ~** таки́м о́бразом; **one ~ or another** так и́ли инáче; **in the same ~** (то́чно) так же; **I love the ~ he smiles** мне о́чень нрáвится, как он улыбáется; **try to see it my ~** попытáйтесь встать на моё ме́сто; **let's put it this ~** скáжем так; **either ~** (in either fashion) любы́м из двух спо́собов; (in either case) в обо́их случáях, в любо́м слу́чае; **whichever ~ you look at it** с како́й стороны́ (на э́то) ни посмотре́ть; **by ~ of an apology** в кáчестве извине́ния; (preference): **have it your own ~!** будь/пусть бу́дет по-вáшему!; **have, get one's own ~** доб|ивáться, -и́ться своего́ **10** (custom) обы́чай, привы́чка; **~ of life** о́браз жи́зни; **he has a ~ of not**

paying his bills у него́ есть привы́чка не плати́ть по счетáм; **that's the ~ of the world** так уж заведено́/во́дится на све́те; **mend one's ~s** испр|авля́ться, -áвиться **11** (state) положе́ние, состоя́ние **12** (sense) смысл, отноше́ние; **in a ~** в не́котором смы́сле/ отноше́нии; **in some ~s** в не́которых отноше́ниях; **in no ~** ничу́ть, нико́им о́бразом; **were you involved in any ~?** бы́ли ли вы каки́м-нибудь о́бразом в э́том замéшаны? **13** (scale, degree): **in a big ~** в широ́ком/большо́м масштáбе
■ ~**lay** *v.t.* подстер|егáть, -éчь; ~**out** *adj.* (infml) замечáтельный, бесподо́бный; ~**side** *n.* обо́чина (доро́ги); (*attr.*) придоро́жный; **fall by the ~side** (fig.) выбывáть, вы́быть из стро́я

wayward /'weɪwəd/ *adj.* своенрáвный

waywardness /'weɪwədnɪs/ *n.* своенрáвие

WC (BrE) *abbr.* (*of* **water closet**) туале́т (убо́рная)

⚡ **we** /wiː/ *pers. pron.* (*obj.* **us**, *poss.* **our, ours**) мы; ~ **lawyers** мы, адвокáты

⚡ **weak** /wiːk/ *adj.* слáбый
■ ~**willed** *adj.* слабово́льный

weaken /'wiːkən/ *v.t.* осл|абля́ть, -áбить
● *v.i.* слабе́ть, о-

weakling /'wiːklɪŋ/ *n.* хи́лый челове́к

weakness /'wiːknɪs/ *n.* слáбость, хи́лость

wealth /welθ/ *n.* богáтство, состоя́ние; (fig., profusion) оби́лие; **a ~ of detail** мно́жество подро́бностей; **a ~ of experience** богате́йший о́пыт

wealthy /'welθɪ/ *adj.* (**wealthier, wealthiest**) богáтый, состоя́тельный

wean /wiːn/ *v.t.* отн|имáть, -я́ть от груди́; (fig.) отуч|áть, -и́ть (*от чего́*)

⚡ **weapon** /'wepən/ *n.* ору́жие; (piece of artillery) ору́дие
■ ~**s of mass destruction** *n. pl.* ору́жие мáссового пораже́ния/уничтоже́ния

weaponry /'wepənrɪ/ *n.* ору́жие

⚡ **wear** /weə(r)/ *n.* **1** (articles or type of clothing) оде́жда, плáтье; **beach ~** пля́жная оде́жда; (~ing of clothes): **a suit for everyday ~** бу́дничный/повседне́вный костю́м **2** (continued use) изно́с; **this material stands up to hard ~** э́тот материáл прекрáсно но́сится
● *v.t.* (*past* **wore**, *p.p.* **worn**) **1** (garments or accessories) носи́ть (*indet.*); (put on) над|евáть, -éть; **what shall I ~?** что мне надéть?; (of hair): ~ **one's hair long** носи́ть (*indet.*) дли́нные во́лосы; ~ **one's hair short** коро́тко стри́чься (*impf.*); (fig.): ~**ing a smile** с улы́бкой (на лице́); ~**ing a frown** нахму́рившись **2** (damage surface of) ст|ирáть, -ерéть; (damage by use) трепáть, ис-, изн|áшивать, -оси́ть; (clothing) прот|ирáть, -ерéть **3** (produce by friction): **you've worn a hole in your trousers** вы протёрли брю́ки до дыр
● *v.i.* (*past* **wore**, *p.p.* **worn**): ~ **thin** изн|áшиваться, -оси́ться; (fig.): **his patience wore thin** его́ терпе́ние бы́ло на исхо́де
□ ~ **away** *v.t. & i.* ст|ирáть(ся), -ерéть(ся);

weather had worn away the inscription ве́тры и дожди́ стёрли на́дпись; **the cliffs were worn away in places** ска́лы места́ми вы́ветрились

☐ **~ down** *v.t. & i.* изн|а́шивать(ся), -оси́ть(ся); (fig.): **they wore down the enemy's resistance** они́ сломи́ли сопротивле́ние проти́вника

☐ **~ off** *v.t. & i.* сти|ра́ть(ся), -ере́ть(ся); (fig.) (постепе́нно) проходи́ть (*impf.*); **the novelty soon wore off** вско́ре новизна́ прошла́

☐ **~ out** *v.t. & i.* изн|а́шивать(ся), -оси́ть(ся); (fig.) утом|ля́ть(ся), -и́ть(ся)

weariness /'wɪərɪnɪs/ *n.* утомле́ние; (boredom) ску́ка

wearing /'weərɪŋ/ *adj.* надое́дливый

weary /'wɪərɪ/ *adj.* (**wearier, weariest**) **1** (tired) уста́лый; **the journey made him ~** путеше́ствие его́ утоми́ло **2**: **~ of** (fed up with) уста́вший от *чего*
● *v.t. & i.* утом|ля́ть(ся), -и́ть(ся)

weasel /'wi:z(ə)l/ *n.* ла́ска (*хищное животное*); **~ words** (fig.) двусмы́сленные слова́, двусмы́сленности (*f. pl.*)
● *v.t.* (**weaselled, weaselling**, AmE **weaseled, weaseling**) (insinuate): **she ~led her way (or herself) into my confidence** она́ вкра́лась/втёрлась (infml) ко мне в дове́рие

☞ **weather** /'weðə(r)/ *n.* пого́да; **what's the ~ like?** кака́я сего́дня пого́да?; **be, feel under the ~** (fig.) нева́жно себя́ чу́вствовать (*impf.*)
● *v.t.* (survive) выде́рживать, вы́держать
■ **~-beaten** *adj.* обве́тренный; **~ forecast** *n.* прогно́з пого́ды; **~proof** *adj.* погодоусто́йчивый

weave (or **wove**) /wi:v/ *v.t.* (*past* **wove**, *p.p.* **woven** or **wove**) **1** (thread, flowers, etc.) плести́, с-; спле|та́ть, -сти́ **2** (make basket, etc. by weaving) плести́, с-; (cloth) ткать, со-
● *v.i.* (*past* **wove**, *p.p.* **woven** or **wove**) петля́ть (*impf.*), идти́ (*det.*) непрямы́м путём

weaver /'wi:və(r)/ *n.* ткач (-и́ха)

☞ **web** /web/ *n.* **1** (*also* **spider's ~**) паути́на; (fig.) сеть, паути́на, сплете́ние **2** (**the Web**, comput.) Всеми́рная паути́на, Сеть, Интерне́т
■ **~-footed** *adj.* перепо́нчатый; **~log** *n.* (comput.) сетево́й журна́л, блог; **~logger** *n.* (comput.) бло́ггер; **~ page** *n.* (comput.) веб-страни́ца, страни́ца в Интерне́те

webbed /webd/ *adj.* перепо́нчатый

website /'websaɪt/ *n.* (comput.) сайт, веб-са́йт

wedding /'wedɪŋ/ *n.* сва́дьба, бракосочета́ние; (in church) венча́ние
■ **~ anniversary** *n.* годовщи́на сва́дьбы; **~ day** *n.* день (*m.*) сва́дьбы; **~ dress** *n.* сва́дебное пла́тье; **~ ring** *n.* обруча́льное кольцо́

wedge /wedʒ/ *n.* клин; **it's the thin end of the ~** ≈ э́то ещё (то́лько) цвето́чки(, а я́годки (бу́дут) впереди́); **a ~ of cake** кусо́к то́рта
● *v.t.* закреп|ля́ть, -и́ть кли́ном; **~ in** вкли́н|ивать, -и́ть

☞ **Wednesday** /'wenzdeɪ/ *n.* среда́

weed /wi:d/ *n.* сорня́к; (in water) во́доросль
● *v.t.* (clear of ~s) поло́ть, вы́-

☐ **~ out** *v.t.* устран|я́ть, -и́ть
■ **~killer** *n.* гербици́д

weedy /'wi:dɪ/ *adj.* (**weedier, weediest**) (BrE, weak-looking) то́щий

☞ **week** /wi:k/ *n.* неде́ля; **the ~ before last** позапро́шлая неде́ля; **the ~ after next** че́рез одну́ неде́лю; **a ~ today** ро́вно че́рез неде́лю; **(on) Monday ~** (BrE) че́рез понеде́льник; **~ in, ~ out** (це́лыми) неде́лями; **three times a ~** три ра́за в неде́лю; **working ~** рабо́чая неде́ля
■ **~day** *n.* бу́дний/рабо́чий день

weekend /wi:k'end/ *n.* коне́ц неде́ли, уик-э́нд/уике́нд, суббо́та и воскресе́нье

weekly /'wi:klɪ/ *n.* еженеде́льник
● *adj.* еженеде́льный
● *adv.* еженеде́льно

weep /wi:p/ *v.i.* (*past and p.p.* **wept**) **1** (shed tears) пла́кать, за-; (profusely) рыда́ть (*impf.*) **2** (of a wound) мо́кнуть (*impf.*)

weigh /weɪ/ *v.t.* **1** (find or test weight of) взве́|шивать, -сить; **~ oneself** взве́|шиваться, -ситься; (fig., consider; compare) взве́|шивать, -сить **2** (of ~ed object: amount to) ве́сить (*impf.*); **what do you ~?** ско́лько вы ве́сите?; како́й у вас вес?
● *v.i.*: **~ on** (be depressing or burdensome to) тяготи́ть (*impf.*)

☐ **~ down** *v.t.* (burden) отяго|ща́ть, -ти́ть; **the branches were ~ed down with, by fruit** ве́тви гну́лись под тя́жестью плодо́в; (fig., be burdensome to) угнета́ть (*impf.*)

☐ **~ in** *v.i.* (be weighed before contest) взве́|шиваться, -ситься пе́ред соревнова́нием

☐ **~ out** *v.t.* отве́|шивать, -сить

☐ **~ up** *v.t.* (lit., fig.) взве́|шивать, -сить

☞ **weight** /weɪt/ *n.* **1** (heaviness) вес; **3 lbs in ~** ве́сом (в) три фу́нта; **gain, put on ~** приб|авля́ть, -а́вить в ве́се; **lose ~** теря́ть, по- в ве́се; **pull one's ~** (fig.) выполня́ть, вы́полнить свою́ до́лю рабо́ты; **throw one's ~ about** (fig.) распоряжа́ться (*impf.*), ва́жничать (*impf.*) **2** (load) тя́жесть, груз; (fig.) бре́мя (*nt.*); **it was a great ~ off my mind** сло́вно ка́мень с души́ свали́лся **3** (object for weighing or ~ing) ги́ря **4** (importance; influence) вес; влия́ние; авторите́т; **his opinion carries great ~** с его́ мне́нием о́чень счита́ются
● *v.t.* утяжел|я́ть, -и́ть
■ **~lifter** *n.* штанги́ст; **~lifting** *n.* подня́тие тя́жестей

weightlessness /'weɪtlɪsnɪs/ *n.* невесо́мость

weighty /'weɪtɪ/ *adj.* (**weightier, weightiest**) (heavy) тяжёлый; (important) ва́жный

weir /wɪə(r)/ *n.* плоти́на

weird /wɪəd/ *adj.* **1** (unearthly) таи́нственный **2** (strange) стра́нный

weirdness /'wɪədnɪs/ *n.* таи́нственность; стра́нность

☞ **welcome** /'welkəm/ *n.* приём; **they gave us a warm ~** они́ нас раду́шно при́няли
● *adj.* **1** (gladly received) жела́нный; **this is ~ news** э́то прия́тное изве́стие; **make sb**

W

(feel) ~ ока́з|ывать, -а́ть кому́-н. раду́шный приём **2** (*pred.*) (ungrudgingly permitted): **you are ~ to take it!** пожа́луйста, бери́те!; **you're ~ to try!** пожа́луйста, (по)про́буйте!; **you're ~!** (no thanks are required) пожа́луйста!; не́ за что!

• *v.t.* приве́тствовать (*impf.*); a **welcoming smile** приве́тливая улы́бка; **I would ~ the opportunity** я был бы рад (тако́му) слу́чаю

• *int.* добро́ пожа́ловать!

weld /weld/ *v.t. & i.* свар|ива́ть(ся), -и́ть(ся)

welder /'weldə(r)/ *n.* сва́рщик

welding /'weldɪŋ/ *n.* сва́рка

welfare /'welfeə(r)/ *n.* (well-being) благополу́чие; (organized provision for social needs) социа́льное обеспе́чение; (AmE, social security) посо́бие (по безрабо́тице *и т. n.*); **the W~ State** госуда́рство всео́бщего благосостоя́ния/благоде́нствия; ≈ социа́льное госуда́рство

well¹ /wel/ *n.* (for water) коло́дец; (for oil) нефтяна́я сква́жина

⚡ **well²** /wel/ *adj.* (**better, best**) (*usu. pred.*) **1** (in good health) здоро́вый; **I haven't been ~** мне нездоро́вилось, я был нездоро́в; **you don't look ~** вы пло́хо вы́глядите **2** (right, satisfactory): **all's ~** всё хорошо́/прекра́сно; **всё в поря́дке 3** (*as n.*): **leave ~** ((AmE) *also* ~ **enough) alone** от добра́ добра́ не и́щут **4** ((just) as) ~ (advisable): **it would be (just) as** ~ **to ask** не меша́ло бы спроси́ть

• *adv.* (**better, best**) **1** (satisfactorily) хорошо́; **I did not sleep ~** я пло́хо спал; ~ **done!** здо́рово!; молоде́ц! **2** (very, thoroughly; properly) о́чень, весьма́; **I am ~ aware of it** я э́то прекра́сно зна́ю; **the picture was ~ worth £2,000** э́та карти́на вполне́ сто́ила двух ты́сяч фу́нтов **3** (considerably, with advs. & preps.) гора́здо; далеко́: ~ **past 40** далеко́ за со́рок **4** (favourably): ~ **off** бога́тый; **I wish him ~** я жела́ю ему́ благополу́чия **5** (successfully) уда́чно, благополу́чно; **all went ~** всё прошло́ благополу́чно **6** (wisely) разу́мно, пра́вильно; **you would be ~ advised to stay** с ва́шей стороны́ бы́ло бы благоразу́мно оста́ться **7** (indeed): **it may ~ be true** (э́то) вполне́ возмо́жно **8**: **as ~** (in addition) то́же; та́кже; вдоба́вок; сверх того́; **there was meat as ~ as fish** там была́ не то́лько ры́ба, но и мя́со

• *int.* ну; ну а; (expr. surprise) ну!; вот те ра́з!; ~, ~! ну и ну!; (expr. expectation): ~ **then?** ну как?; (expr. impatient interrogation): ~, **what do you want?** ну, так чего́ вы хоти́те?; (expr. agreement): **very** ~, **I'll do it** хорошо́, я сде́лаю э́то; (expr. concession): ~, **you can come if you like** что ж(е), е́сли хоти́те, приходи́те; (expr. resignation): **oh** ~, **it can't be helped** (ну) что ж, ничего́ не поде́лаешь; (in summing up) ну вот; ~ **then** (ну) так вот

▪ ~**-balanced** *adj.* уравнове́шенный; a ~**-balanced diet** сбаланси́рованная дие́та; ~**-behaved** *adj.* (благо)воспи́танный; ~**-being** *n.* благополу́чие; ~**-disposed** *adj.* благожела́тельный; ~**-dressed** *adj.* хорошо́ оде́тый; ~**-educated** *adj.* хорошо́

образо́ванный; ~**-fed** *adj.* сы́тый; (of animals) отко́рмленный; ~**-heeled** *adj.* (infml) состоя́тельный; ~**-informed** *adj.* зна́ющий; ~**-kept** *adj.* содержа́щийся в поря́дке; ~**-known** *adj.* (of person) изве́стный; (of facts) (обще)изве́стный; ~**-made** *adj.* хорошо́ сде́ланный; ~**-mannered** *adj.* воспи́танный; ~**-meaning** *adj.* де́йствующий из лу́чших побужде́ний; ~**-off** *adj.* состоя́тельный; ~**-paid** *adj.* хорошо́ опла́чиваемый; ~**-read** *adj.* начи́танный; ~**-thought-out** *adj.* проду́манный; ~**-timed** *adj.* то́чно/хорошо́ рассчи́танный; (words/act) ска́занный/сде́ланный кста́ти; ~**-to-do** *adj.* состоя́тельный; ~**-wisher** *n.* доброжела́тель (-ница); ~**-worn** *adj.* (lit.) поно́шенный; (fig., trite) изби́тый

wellington /'welɪŋt(ə)n/ *n.* (*also* ~ **boot**) (BrE) рези́новый сапо́г

welly /'welɪ/ *n.* (BrE, infml) **1** = **wellington 2** (vigour) си́ла, эне́ргия

Welsh /welʃ/ *n.* **1**: **the** ~ (*as pl.*) (people) валли́йцы (*m. pl.*), уэ́льсцы (*m. pl.*) **2** (language) валли́йский язы́к

• *adj.* валли́йский, уэ́льский

wench /wentʃ/ *n.* (archaic or joc.) де́вка

wend /wend/ *v.t.*: ~ **one's way** держа́ть (*impf.*) путь

went /went/ *past of* ▸ **go**

wept /wept/ *past and p.p. of* ▸ **weep**

were /wə(r)/ *2nd pers. sg. past, pl. past, and past subj. of* ▸ **be**

weren't /wə:nt/ *neg. of* ▸ **were**

⚡ **west** /west/ *n.* за́пад; **to the ~ of** к за́паду от + *g.*; **the W~** (pol.) За́пад

• *adv.* на за́пад; к за́паду

• *adj.* за́падный

▪ **W~ Germany** *n.* (hist.) За́падная Герма́ния; **W~ Indian** *adj.* вест-и́ндский • *n.* жи́тель (*m.*) (-ница) стран(– острово́в) Кари́бского бассе́йна; **W~ Indies** *n. pl.* Вест-И́ндия

westerly /'westəlɪ/ (wind) за́падный ве́тер

• *adj.* за́падный

⚡ **western** /'west(ə)n/ *n.* ве́стерн

• *adj.* за́падный

westerner /'westənə(r)/ *n.* жи́тель (*m.*) (-ница) за́пада

westernize /'westənaɪz/ *v.t.* внедр|я́ть, -и́ть за́падный о́браз жи́зни в + *a.*, подв|ерга́ть, -е́ргнуть вестерниза́ции

westward /'westwəd/ *adj.* за́падный

• *adv.* (*also* **westwards**) на за́пад; к за́паду, в за́падном направле́нии

wet /wet/ *adj.* (**wetter, wettest**) **1** (soaked) мо́крый; ~ **through** промо́кший наскво́зь/до ни́тки; **get** ~ пром|ока́ть, -о́кнуть **2** (rainy) дождли́вый **3** (damp) сыро́й, вла́жный; ~ **paint** све́жая кра́ска **4** (BrE, infml, inept) вя́лый

• *v.t.* (**wetting**, *past and p.p.* ~ *or* **wetted**) (make ~) мочи́ть, на-; **the child** ~ **itself** ребёнок обмочи́лся/опи́сался (infml); **the child** ~ **its bed** ребёнок опи́сал посте́ль

▪ ~ **blanket** *n.* (fig., infml) зану́да (*c.g.*), ну́дный человéк; ~ **suit** *n.* гидрокостю́м

whack /wæk/ (infml) *n.* (blow) удáр
● *v.t.* (hit) бить, по-; **I feel ~ed** (BrE, exhausted) я чу́вствую себя́ вконéц разби́тым

whale /weɪl/ *n.* **1** кит **2**: **we had a ~ of a time** мы потрясáюще/здóрово провели́ врéмя

whaler /ˈweɪlə(r)/ *n.* (man) китобóй; (ship) китобóец, китобóйное су́дно

wharf /wɔːf/ *n.* (*pl.* **wharves** *or* **wharfs**) при́стань

⚡ **what** /wɒt/ *pron.* **1** (*interrog.*) что?; ~**'s that?** что э́то (такóе)?; ~ **(did you say)?** что (вы сказáли)?; что?; ~ **is it?**; ~**'s the matter?** в чём дéло?; ~ **is she like?** (in appearance) как онá вы́глядит?; (in character) какáя онá?; ~**'s the date?** какóе сегóдня числó?; ~ **is his name?** как егó зову́т?; ~ **do you think?** как вы ду́маете?; ~ **about money?** а дéньги?; ~ **about a walk?** не пройти́сь ли нам?; ~ **for?** зачéм?; ~ **are you talking about?** о чём вы говори́те?; ~ **if …?** а что, éсли…? **2** (*rel.*) (то), что; **and, ~ is more** … к тому́ же…; **he is sorry for ~ happened** он жалéет о случи́вшемся; **tell me ~ you remember** расскажи́те мне всё, что пóмните; **(do) you know ~?** знáете что?; **I'll tell you ~!** вот что я вам скажу́!; ~ **with one thing and another** то из-за одногó, то из-за другóго **3** (whatever): **I will do ~ I can** я сдéлаю (всё), что могу́
● *adj.* **1** (*interrog.*) какóй; какóв?; ~ **colour are his eyes?** какóго цвéта у негó глазá?; ~ **kind of (a)** какóй; ~ **time is it?** котóрый час?; ~**'s the use?** какóй смысл? **2** (*rel.*): ~ **little he published** то немнóгое, что он опубликовáл; **I gave him ~ money I had** я óтдал ему́ все дéньги, каки́е у меня́ бы́ли **3** (exclamatory): ~ **a fool he is!** какóй дурáк!; ~ **a pity/shame!** какáя жáлость/ досáда!; ~ **lovely soup!** какóй прекрáсный суп!
■ ~**-d'ye-call-it,** ~**'sit** *nn.* как егó; э́то сáмое…

⚡ **whatever** /wɒtˈevə(r)/ *pron.* **1** (anything that): **do ~ you like** дéлайте, что хоти́те **2** (no matter what): ~ **happens** что бы ни случи́лось **3** (in questions, expressing surprise, confusion, etc.): ~ **are you doing?** что вы там дéлаете?
● *adj.* **1** (any): **he took ~ food he could find** он забрáл всю еду́, каку́ю тóлько мог найти́ **2** (no matter what) какóй/какóв бы ни **3** (emphasizing neg. or interrog.): **there is no doubt ~ of his guilt** в егó винóвности нет ни малéйшего сомнéния

wheat /wiːt/ *n.* пшени́ца

wheedle /ˈwiːd(ə)l/ *v.t.*: ~ **sth out of sb** выпрáшивать, вы́просить что-н. у когó-н.

wheel /wiːl/ *n.* колесó; (steering ~) руль (*m.*); **he was at the ~** (*sc.* driving) **for 12 hours** он сидéл за рулём 12 часóв; (potter's ~) круг
● *v.t.* катáть, вози́ть (*both indet.*); кати́ть

(*det.*); везти́ (*det.*)
● *v.i.* кружи́ть(ся) (*impf.*); **he ~ed round to face me** он кру́то повернýлся ко мне
■ ~**barrow** *n.* тáчка; ~**chair** *n.* инвали́дная коля́ска

wheeler-dealer /wiːləˈdiːlə(r)/ *n.* (infml) махинáтор

wheeze /wiːz/ *v.i.* сопéть (*impf.*)

wheezy /ˈwiːzɪ/ *adj.* хри́плый

whelk /welk/ *n.* (mollusc) брюхонóгий моллю́ск

⚡ **when** /wen/ *adv.* **1** (*interrog.*) когдá; **say ~!** (to sb pouring a drink) скажи́те, когдá довóльно! **2** (*rel.*): **there have been occasions ~** бы́ли слу́чаи, когдá…; **the day ~ I met you** день, когдá я вас встрéтил
● *with preps.*: ~ **do you have to be there by?** к какóму чáсу вам нýжно там быть?; ~ **does it date from?** к какóму врéмени э́то отнóсится?; **since ~?** как давнó?; **till, until ~?** до каки́х пор?
● *conj.* когдá; как (тóлько); пóсле тогó как; тогдá, когдá; (by the time that) покá; ~ **she saw him, she …** когдá онá уви́дела егó, онá…; (and then) и тогдá; как (вдруг); да вдруг; (although) хотя́; **they won ~ everyone thought they would lose** они́ вы́играли, хотя́ все ду́мали, что они́ проигрáют

whence /wens/ *adv. & conj.* (liter.) (*also* **from ~**) откýда; (*interrog.*) ~ **this confusion?** отчегó такóе смятéние?; (*rel.*) **return it ~ it came** верни́те э́то по принадлéжности

whenever /wenˈevə(r)/ *adv. & conj.* **1** (at whatever time) когдá; **come ~ you like** приходи́те, когдá угóдно **2** (on every occasion when) кáждый/вся́кий раз, когдá

⚡ **where** /weə(r)/ *adv.* **1** (*interrog.*) где; (whither) кудá; ~ **did he hit you?** кудá он вас удáрил? **2** (*rel.*) где; **the hotel ~ we stopped** гости́ница, в котóрой мы останови́лись; (without antecedent) там, где; **that's ~ you're wrong** вот где вы ошибáетесь
● *with preps.*: ~ **from?** откýда?; ~ **does he come from?** откýда он (рóдом)?; ~ **to?** кудá?; **I've no idea ~ he can have got to** поня́тия не имéю, кудá он мог дéться

whereabouts /ˈweərəbaʊts/ *n. pl.* местонахождéние
● *adv.* где; ~ **did you find it?** где вы э́то нашли́?; (whither) кудá

whereas /weərˈæz/ *conj.* тогдá как; а

whereby /weəˈbaɪ/ *adv.* (liter., by means of which) посрéдством котóрого; (according to which): **there is a rule ~ …** существýет прáвило, соглáсно котóрому…

whereupon /weərəˈpɒn/ *adv.* (and then) пóсле чегó; вслéдствие чегó; тогдá

wherever /weərˈevə(r)/ *adj. & conj.* где; кудá; ~ **sit ~ you like** сади́тесь, кудá угóдно; ~ **he goes he makes friends** где бы он ни оказáлся, он приобретáет друзéй

whet /wet/ *v.t.* (**whetted, whetting**) (fig.) возбуж|дáть, -ди́ть

⚡ **whether** /ˈweðə(r)/ *conj.* **1** (introducing indirect question) ли; **I asked ~ he was coming with** us я спроси́л, пойдёт ли он с на́ми; **the question is ~ to go or stay** вопро́с в том — идти́ и́ли остава́ться **2** (introducing alternative hypotheses): **~ you like it or not, I shall go** нра́вится вам э́то и́ли нет, а я пойду́

◆ **which** /wɪtʃ/ *pron.* **1** (interrog.) како́й, кото́рый; (of person) кто; **~ is the right answer?** како́й отве́т пра́вильный?; **~ of these bags is the heavier?** кака́я из э́тих су́мок тяжеле́е?; **I cannot tell ~ is ~** (of persons) я ника́к не могу́ разобра́ться, кто из них кто **2** (rel.) кото́рый; **the book (~) I was reading has gone** кни́га, кото́рую я чита́л, пропа́ла

● *adj.* **1** (direct or indirect question) како́й; **~ shoes are yours?** каки́е (тут) ту́фли ва́ши?; **~ film do you mean?** како́й фильм вы име́ете в виду́? **2** (rel.) како́й; кото́рый; **ten years, during ~ time he spoke to nobody** де́сять лет, в тече́ние кото́рых он ни с кем не говори́л

whichever /wɪtʃˈevə(r)/ *pron. & adj.* како́й бы ни, како́й уго́дно; **take ~ book you like** бери́те каку́ю уго́дно кни́гу; **~ way you go, you'll have plenty of time** како́й бы доро́гой вы ни пошли́, вы вполне́ успе́ете; **~ way you look at it** с како́й стороны́ (на э́то) ни посмотре́ть

whiff /wɪf/ *n.* дунове́ние; (pleasant smell) лёгкий арома́т; (BrE, unpleasant smell) душо́к

◆ **while** /waɪl/ *n.* (како́е-то) вре́мя; **after a ~** че́рез не́которое вре́мя; **I am going away for a ~** я уезжа́ю на не́которое вре́мя; **a long, good ~ ago** давны́м-давно́; **a short ~ ago, back** неда́вно; **it may take some** (*or* quite a) **~** возмо́жно, что э́то бу́дет не ско́ро; **once in a ~** и́зредка; **it was well worth ~** э́то сто́ило затра́ченного вре́мени/труда́; **I will make it worth his ~** я постара́юсь, что́бы он не разочарова́лся

● *v.t.*: **~ away** корота́ть, с- (*время*)

● *conj.* (also **whilst**) **1** (during the time that) пока́; в то вре́мя, как; **be good ~ I'm away!** веди́ себя́ хорошо́, пока́ меня́ нет до́ма!; **~ asleep** во сне; **~ in Paris I visited the Louvre** во вре́мя (моего́) пребыва́ния в Пари́же, я посети́л Лувр **2** (whereas) а; тогда́ как

whilst /waɪlst/ *conj.* = **while** conj.

whim /wɪm/ *n.* при́хоть, капри́з

whimper /ˈwɪmpə(r)/ *n.* (of person) хны́канье; (of dog) поску́ливание

● *v.i.* (of person) хны́кать (*impf.*); (of dog) скули́ть (*impf.*)

whimsical /ˈwɪmzɪk(ə)l/ *adj.* (fanciful) причу́дливый; (capricious) капри́зный

whine /waɪn/ *v.i.* скули́ть (*impf.*) (also fig.)

whinge /wɪndʒ/ *v.i.* (**whingeing**) (BrE, infml) скули́ть (*impf.*) (*жа́ловаться*)

whinny /ˈwɪnɪ/ *n.* (gentle) ти́хое ржа́ние; (joyful) ра́достное ржа́ние

● *v.i.* (gently) ти́хо ржа́ть, за-; (joyfully) ра́достно ржа́ть, за-

whip /wɪp/ *n.* **1** (short) плеть, плётка; (long) кнут **2** (party official) секрета́рь (*m.*) парла́ментской фра́кции

● *v.t.* (**whipped, whipping**) **1** (flog)

поро́ть, вы-; хлеста́ть, от-; сечь, вы- **2** (beat into froth) взби́ва́ть, -и́ть; **~ped cream** взби́тые сли́вки **3** (infml, move rapidly): **as I entered he ~ped the papers into a drawer** когда́ я вошёл, он бы́стро су́нул бума́ги в я́щик (стола́)

□ **~ up** *v.t.* (beat into froth) взби́ва́ть, -и́ть; (fig., stimulate): **~ up enthusiasm** возбу|жда́ть, -ди́ть энтузиа́зм; (infml, improvise) де́лать, с- на ско́рую ру́ку

■ **~lash** *n.* (injury) тра́вма ше́и в результа́те ре́зкого движе́ния (*чаще всего в автоава́рии*); **~-round** *n.* (BrE, infml, collection) сбор де́нег (на благотвори́тельные це́ли)

whir /wɜː(r)/ *v.i.* = **whirr**

whirl /wɜːl/ *n.* **1** (revolving movement) круже́ние; (fig.) смяте́ние; **my head is in a ~** у меня́ голова́ идёт кру́гом **2** (bustling activity) водоворо́т, вихрь (*m.*)

● *v.t. & i.* верте́ть(ся) (*impf.*); кружи́ть(ся) (*impf.*)

■ **~pool** *n.* водоворо́т; **~wind** *n.* вихрь (*m.*)

whirr, whir /wɜː(r)/ *v.i.* (**whirred, whirring**) жужжа́ть (*impf.*)

whisk /wɪsk/ *n.* муто́вка

● *v.t.* взби́ва́ть, -и́ть

● *v.i.* (move briskly) мча́ться, по-

□ **~ away, ~ off** *vv.t.* (carry off quickly) бы́стро ун|оси́ть, -ести́; (lead off quickly) бы́стро ув|оди́ть, -ести́

whisker /ˈwɪskə(r)/ *n.* (in pl.) (facial hair) бакенба́рд|ы (*pl., g.* —); (of animal) усы́ (*m. pl.*)

whisky /ˈwɪskɪ/ (AmE **whiskey**) *n.* ви́ски (*nt. indecl.*)

whisper /ˈwɪspə(r)/ *n.* шёпот; **he spoke in a ~** он говори́л шёпотом

● *v.i.* шепта́ться (*impf.*)

● *v.t.* шепта́ть, про-

whistle /ˈwɪs(ə)l/ *n.* **1** (sound) свист **2** (instrument) свисто́к

● *v.t.* (tune) насви́стывать, -исте́ть

● *v.i.* свисте́ть, про-, сви́стнуть; **the train ~d as it entered the tunnel** при вхо́де в тунне́ль по́езд дал гудо́к

■ **~-blower** *n.* (reporter of wrongdoing) доно́счи|к (-ца)

Whit /wɪt/ *adj.*: **~ Monday** Ду́хов день; **~ Sunday** = Whitsun

◆ **white** /waɪt/ *n.* **1** (colour) бе́лый цвет; белизна́ **2** (of the eyes, an egg) бело́к **3** (racial type) белоко́жий, бе́лый

● *adj.* бе́лый; **grow ~** беле́ть, по-; **the W~ House** Бе́лый дом; **a ~ lie** ложь во спасе́ние

■ **~ coffee** *n.* (BrE) ко́фе с молоко́м; **~-collar** *adj.*: **~-collar worker** n. слу́жащий; **~ goods** *n. pl.* (domestic appliances) бытовы́е электроприбо́ры; **~wash** *n.* побе́лка; (fig.) обеле́ние, оправда́ние ● *v.t.* бели́ть, по-; (fig.) обел|я́ть, -и́ть; опра́вд|ывать, -а́ть; **~-water rafting** *n.* сплав вниз по го́рному пото́ку

whiten /ˈwaɪt(ə)n/ *v.t.* бели́ть, по-

Whitsun /ˈwɪts(ə)n/ *n.* (Whit Sunday) Тро́ицын день; Тро́ица; see also ▸ Whit

whittle /ˈwɪt(ə)l/ *v.t.* (wood) строга́ть, вы-

w

□ ~ **away** *v.t.* (fig.) ум|еньша́ть, -е́ньшить; his savings were ~d away его́ сбереже́ния постепе́нно исся́кли

whizz, whiz /wɪz/ *v.i.* (**whizzed**, **whizzing**) прон|оси́ться, -ести́сь со сви́стом

■ ~**-kid** *n.* (infml) ≈ восходя́щая звезда́ (*о молодо́м челове́ке*)

♂ **who** /huː/ *pron.* (*obj.* **whom** *or informally* **who**, *poss.* **whose**) **1** (*interrog.*) кто; ~ **is he?** кто он (тако́й)? **2** (*rel.*) кото́рый, како́й, кто; **people** ~ **live in the city** лю́ди, кото́рые живу́т в го́роде; **those** ~ те, кто/кото́рые; **anyone** ~ вся́кий, кто; **Mr X,** ~ **is my uncle** г-н X, мой дя́дя

♂ **whoever** /huːˈevə(r)/ *pron.* **1** (*rel.*) (anyone who) кто бы ни, кто уго́дно; ~ **comes will be welcome** кто бы ни пришёл, бу́дет жела́нным го́стем **2** (*interrog., used for emphasis*) (who) кто то́лько; ~ **would have thought it?** кто бы мог поду́мать?

♂ **whole** /həʊl/ *n.* (single entity) це́лое; (totality) все, всё; **taken as a** ~ в це́лом; **on the** ~ в о́бщем (и це́лом); в основно́м
● *adj.* **1** (intact; undamaged) це́лый, невреди́мый **2** (in one piece) целико́м **3** (complete) весь, це́лый, це́льный; **he ate a** ~ **chicken** он съел це́лого цыплёнка; **the** ~ **world** весь мир
■ ~**hearted** *adj.* беззаве́тный; ~**heartedly** *adv.* от всей души́; ~**sale** *n.* опто́вая торго́вля ● *adj.* опто́вый; (fig.) ма́ссовый ● *adv.* о́птом; (fig.) в ма́ссовом масшта́бе; ~**saler** *n.* оптови́к

wholesome /ˈhəʊlsəm/ *adj.* **1** (promoting health) поле́зный **2** (sound) здра́вый

wholly /ˈhəʊllɪ/ *adv.* по́лностью; целико́м

♂ **whom** /huːm/ *obj. of* ▸ **who**

whopper /ˈwɒpə(r)/ *n.* (infml) грома́дина

whopping /ˈwɒpɪŋ/ *adj.* (infml) (*also* ~ **great**) огро́мный,

whore /hɔː(r)/ *n.* (pej.) шлю́ха (infml)

♂ **whose** /huːz/ *pron.* (interrog.) чей; ~ **partner are you?** чей вы партнёр?; (*rel.*) кото́рого; **the people** ~ **house we bought** лю́ди, у кото́рых мы купи́ли дом

♂ **why** /waɪ/ *adv.* **1** (interrog.) (for what reason?) почему́; (for what purpose?) заче́м; ~ **do you ask?** почему́ вы спра́шиваете?; ~ **hurry?** заче́м спеши́ть?; ~ **not?** а почему́ бы нет? **2** (*rel.*): **I don't know** ~ **he's late** я не зна́ю, почему́ он опа́здывает; **the reasons** ~ … причи́ны, по кото́рым…

wick /wɪk/ *n.* фити́ль (*m.*)

wicked /ˈwɪkɪd/ *adj.* (depraved) гре́шный; (roguish) лука́вый

wicker /ˈwɪkə(r)/ *adj.*: ~ **chair** плетёное кре́сло
■ ~**work** *n.* плете́ние

wicket /ˈwɪkɪt/ *n.* **1** (*also* ~ **gate**) кали́тка **2** (at cricket) воро́т|ца (-ец)
■ ~**keeper** *n.* ловя́щий мяч за воро́тцами (*в кри́кете*)

♂ **wide** /waɪd/ *adj.* **1** широ́кий; (in measuring)

шириной в + *a.*; **the table is 3 feet** ~ ширина́ стола́ 3 фу́та **2** (extensive) широ́кий, обши́рный; ~ **interests** широ́кий круг интере́сов **3** (off target): **his answer was** ~ **of the mark** он попа́л па́льцем в не́бо
● *adv.* **1** (to full extent): **open the door** ~! откро́йте дверь на́стежь!; **he is** ~ **awake** у него́ сна ни в одно́м глазу́; **his mouth was** ~ **open** рот его́ был широко́ раскры́т **2** (off target) ми́мо це́ли
■ ~**-angle** *adj.*: ~**-angle lens** широкоуго́льный объекти́в; ~**-eyed** *adj.* (surprised) изумлённый; (naive) наи́вный; ~ **open** откры́тый; ~**-ranging** *adj.* (intellect etc.) разносторо́нний; ~**screen** *adj.*: ~**screen film** широкоэкра́нный фильм; ~**spread** *adj.* (широко́) распространённый

♂ **widely** /ˈwaɪdlɪ/ *adv.* **1** (to a large extent) широко́; ~ **differing opinions** ре́зко расходя́щиеся мне́ния **2** (over a large area) далеко́; ~ **scattered** разбро́санный; **it is** ~ **believed that …** мно́гие счита́ют, что…

widen /ˈwaɪd(ə)n/ *v.t. & i.* расш|иря́ть(ся), -и́рить(ся)

widow /ˈwɪdəʊ/ *n.* вдова́
● *v.t.* де́лать, с- вдово́й

widower /ˈwɪdəʊə(r)/ *n.* вдове́ц

width /wɪtθ/ *n.* ширина́

wield /wiːld/ *v.t.* (hold) держа́ть (*impf.*) в рука́х; ~ **authority** по́льзоваться (*impf.*) вла́стью

♂ **wife** /waɪf/ *n.* (*pl.* **wives**) жена́

Wi-Fi® /ˈwaɪfaɪ/ *n.* (comput.) (техноло́гия) вай-фа́й, Wi-Fi, беспроводно́й Интерне́т

wig /wɪg/ *n.* пари́к

wiggle /ˈwɪg(ə)l/ *v.t.* (ears, toes) шевели́ть, по- + *i.*; **she** ~**s her hips** она́ пока́чивает бёдрами

wiggly /ˈwɪglɪ/ *adj.* (**wigglier**, **wiggliest**): **a** ~ **line** волни́стая ли́ния; **a** ~ **tooth** шата́ющийся зуб

wigwam /ˈwɪgwæm/ *n.* вигва́м

wiki /ˈwɪkɪ/ *n.* (*pl.* ~**s**) ви́ки (*f. indecl.*) (*веб-сайт, содержа́ние кото́рого посети́тель мо́жет редакти́ровать*)

♂ **wild** /waɪld/ *n.* **1** (~ **state**): **this animal is not found in the** ~ э́то живо́тное не встреча́ется в ди́кой приро́де **2** (*in pl.*) (uncultivated tract) ди́кое ме́сто; **in the** ~**s of Africa** на ди́ких просто́рах А́фрики
● *adj.* **1** (not domesticated; not cultivated) ди́кий **2** (not civilized) ди́кий **3** (of scenery: desolate) ди́кий **4** (unrestrained, disorderly) необу́зданный, бу́рный; **she lets her children run** ~ она́ разреша́ет де́тям бе́гать без присмо́тра; **he let the garden run** ~ он запусти́л сад **5** (tempestuous) бу́рный, бу́йный **6** (excited, passionate) вне себя́; **they were** ~ **about him** они́ бы́ли в (ди́ком) восто́рге от него́ **7** (reckless; ill-considered) безу́мный; **a** ~ **scheme** безу́мная зате́я
■ ~ **boar** *n.* каба́н; ~ **card** *n.* (comput.) универса́льный си́мвол; ~**fire** *n.*: **the news spread like** ~**fire** но́вость распространи́лась с молниено́сной быстрото́й; ~ **flower** *n.* дикорасту́щий цвето́к; ~ **goose chase** *n.*

бессмы́сленное предприя́тие

wilderness /'wɪldənɪs/ *n.* ди́кая ме́стность; пусты́ня

wildlife /'waɪldlaɪf/ *n.* жива́я приро́да

■ ∼ **sanctuary** *n.* запове́дник

wiles /waɪlz/ *n. pl.* ухищре́ния (*nt. pl.*)

wilful /'wɪlfʊl/ (AmE **willful**) *adj.* **1** (of person) своенра́вный, своево́льный **2** (intentional) умы́шленный

wilfulness /'wɪlfʊlnɪs/ (AmE **willfulness**) *n.* своенра́вие, своево́лие; преднаме́ренность

will[1] /wɪl/ *n.* **1** (faculty; determination, desire) во́ля; free ∼ свобо́да во́ли; against my ∼ про́тив моего́ жела́ния; the ∼ to live во́ля к жи́зни **2** (document of bequeathal) завеща́ние
● *v.t.* **1** (compel) заст|авля́ть, -а́вить; he ∼ed himself to stay awake (уси́лием во́ли) он заста́вил себя́ бо́дрствовать **2**: God ∼ing е́сли на то бу́дет во́ля Бо́жья

■ ∼**power** *n.* си́ла во́ли

will[2] /wɪl/ *v.t. & i.* (3rd pers. sg. pres. **will**) (*see also* ▶ **would**) **1** (expr. future): he ∼ be president он бу́дет президе́нтом; he said he would be back by 3 он сказа́л, что вернётся к трём; I won't do it again я бо́льше не бу́ду **2** (expr. willingness): I ∼ come with you я пойду́ с ва́ми; he won't help me он не хо́чет мне помо́чь; the window won't open окно́ (ника́к) не открыва́ется; pass the salt, ∼ (*or* would) you? бу́дьте любе́зны, переда́йте соль **3** (expr. inevitability): boys ∼ be boys ма́льчики есть ма́льчики; accidents ∼ happen вся́кое быва́ет **4** (expr. habit): he would often come to see me он ча́сто заходи́л ко мне **5** (expr. surmise, probability): she would have been about 60 when she died ей бы́ло, должно́ быть, о́коло шести́десяти, когда́ она́ умерла́

willing /'wɪlɪŋ/ *adj.* **1** (readily disposed) скло́нный, располо́женный; I am ∼ to admit … я гото́в призна́ть… **2** (readily given or shown) доброво́льный

willingness /'wɪlɪŋnɪs/ *n.* гото́вность, жела́ние

willow /'wɪləʊ/ *n.* и́ва

willy /'wɪlɪ/ *n.* (BrE, infml) (мужско́й) член

willy-nilly /ˌwɪlɪ'nɪlɪ/ *adv.* во́лей-нево́лей

wilt /wɪlt/ *v.i.* (lit., fig.) ни́кнуть, по-

wily /'waɪlɪ/ *adj.* (**wilier, wiliest**) хи́трый

wimp /wɪmp/ *n.* (infml) слизня́к

win /wɪn/ *n.* (gain) вы́игрыш; (victory) побе́да
● *v.t.* (**winning**, *past and p.p.* **won**) **1** (be victorious in) вы́игрывать, вы́играть; the Allies won the war сою́зники вы́играли войну́; who won the election? кто победи́л на вы́борах?; ∼ a race побе́|жда́ть, -ди́ть в забе́ге **2** (gain) выи́грывать, вы́играть; he won £50 from me он вы́играл у меня́ 50 фу́нтов; ∼ a medal завоё|вывать, -а́ть меда́ль; ∼ sb's confidence заслу́ж|ивать, -и́ть чьё-н. дове́рие
● *v.i.* (**winning**, *past and p.p.* **won**): ∼ by 4 goals to 1 вы́играть (*pf.*) со счётом 4:1
□ ∼ **back** *v.t.* отьи́гр|ывать, -а́ть

wince /wɪns/ *v.i.* содрог|а́ться, -ну́ться

winch /wɪntʃ/ *n.* лебёдка
● *v.t.* подн|има́ть, -я́ть с по́мощью лебёдки

wind[1] /wɪnd/ *n.* **1** ве́тер **2** (breath) дыха́ние; get back one's ∼ отдыша́ться (*pf.*); knock the ∼ out of sb (fig.) ошеломл|я́ть, -и́ть кого́-н. **3** (BrE, in bowels etc.) га́зы (*m. pl.*) (в желу́дке/кише́чнике); break ∼ по́ртить, ис- во́здух **4** (∼ instruments) духовы́е (инструме́нты) (*m. pl.*)
● *v.t.* (deprive of breath): the blow ∼ed him от уда́ра у него́ дух перехвати́ло

■ ∼**fall** *n.* (of money) непредви́денный дохо́д; ∼ **farm** *n.* райо́н обслу́живания ветряны́х электроста́нций; ∼**mill** *n.* ветряна́я ме́льница; ∼**pipe** *n.* дыха́тельное го́рло; ∼**screen**, ∼**shield** (AmE) *nn.* лобово́е/ветрово́е стекло́; ∼**screen wiper** стеклоочисти́тель (*m.*), «дво́рник»; ∼**swept** *adj.* (of terrain) откры́тый ве́тру; (of hair etc.) растрёпанный

wind[2] /waɪnd/ *v.t.* (*past and p.p.* **wound**) **1** (cause to encircle, curve or curl): she wound the wool into a ball она́ смота́ла шерсть в клубо́к; a rope was wound round the pole на шест была́ намо́тана верёвка **2** (fold, wrap) уку́т|ывать, -ать **3** (rotate) верте́ть (*impf.*) **4**: ∼ a clock зав|оди́ть, -ести́ часы́
● *v.i.* (*past and p.p.* **wound**) (twist) ви́ться (*impf.*); извива́ться (*impf.*); the path ∼s up the hill доро́жка/тропи́нка змейко́й поднима́ется в го́ру; ∼ing staircase винтова́я ле́стница
□ ∼ **down** *v.t.* опус|ка́ть, -ти́ть
□ ∼ **up** *v.t.*: ∼ up a clock зав|оди́ть, -ести́ часы́; (BrE, tease) дразни́ть (*impf.*); (fig., settle) заверш|а́ть, -и́ть; I am ∼ing up my affairs я свора́чиваю свои́ дела́; (fig., terminate) зак|а́нчивать, -о́нчить

window /'wɪndəʊ/ *n.* **1** окно́; (dim., also cashier's etc.) око́шко; (of shop) витри́на; (in full ∼ of opportunity) ре́дкая возмо́жность **2** (comput.) окно́

■ ∼ **box** *n.* (нару́жный) я́щик для цвето́в; ∼ **cleaner** *n.* мо́йщик о́кон; ∼ **ledge** *n.* (нару́жный) подоко́нник; ∼**pane** *n.* око́нное стекло́; ∼ **seat** *n.* дива́н у окна́; ∼-**shopping** *n.* рассма́тривание/ разгля́дывание витри́н; ∼ **sill** *n.* подоко́нник

windsurfer /'wɪndsɜːfə(r)/ *n.* виндсёрфинги́ст (-ка)

windsurfing /'wɪndsɜːfɪŋ/ *n.* виндсёрфинг

windy /'wɪndɪ/ *adj.* (**windier, windiest**) **1** (characterized by wind) ве́треный **2** (exposed to wind) обдува́емый ве́тром

wine /waɪn/ *n.* (виногра́дное) вино́

■ ∼ **bar** *n.* ви́нный бар; ∼ **glass** *n.* бока́л, рю́мка; ∼**grower** *n.* виноде́л; ∼-**growing** *n.* виноде́лие ● *adj.* виноде́льческий; ∼ **list** *n.* ка́рта вин; ∼ **tasting** *n.* дегуста́ция вин

wing /wɪŋ/ *n.* **1** (of bird, building, organization, car) крыло́ **2** (in pl.) (of stage) кули́сы (*f. pl.*);

w

wait in the ~s (fig.) ждать (*impf.*) своего ча́са

winger /'wɪŋə(r)/ *n.* (player) кра́йний напада́ющий

wink /wɪŋk/ *n.* мига́ние; (as signal, joke) подми́гивание; **I didn't sleep a ~** я всю ночь не сомкну́л глаз
● *v.i.:* **~ at sb** подми́г|ивать, -ну́ть кому́-н.; (of star, light, etc.) мига́ть (*impf.*)

✎ **winner** /'wɪnə(r)/ *n.* победи́тель (-ница); (successful thing) ве́рное де́ло

winning /'wɪnɪŋ/ *adj.* **1** (victorious) вы́игравший **2** (bringing about a win) вы́игрышный **3** (attractive) привлека́тельный
■ **~ post** *n.* фи́нишный столб

winnings /'wɪnɪŋz/ *n. pl.* вы́игрыш (*де́ньги*)

✎ **winter** /'wɪntə(r)/ *n.* зима́; **in ~** зимо́й; (*attr.*) зи́мний
● *v.i.* зимова́ть, пере-
■ **~time** *n.* зима́

wintry /'wɪntri/ *adj.* (**wintrier, wintriest**) зи́мний, моро́зный; (fig.) холо́дный

wipe /waɪp/ *v.t.* **1** (rub clean or dry) вытира́ть, вы́тереть; (~ surface of) обт|ира́ть, -ере́ть; **~ sb's nose** вытира́ть, вы́тереть кому́-н. нос; **~ one's eyes** вытира́ть, вы́тереть слёзы; **~ your shoes on the mat!** вы́трите боти́нки о ко́врик! **2** (erase) ст|ира́ть, -ере́ть
□ **~ away** *v.t.* ст|ира́ть, -ере́ть; (tears) вытира́ть, вы́тереть
□ **~ down** *v.t.* прот|ира́ть, -ере́ть
□ **~ off** *v.t.* ст|ира́ть, -ере́ть
□ **~ out** *v.t.* (destroy) уничт|ожа́ть, -о́жить; **the disease ~d out the entire population** эпиде́мия по́лностью уничто́жила всё населе́ние
□ **~ up** *v.t.* подт|ира́ть, -ере́ть

wire /'waɪə(r)/ *n.* **1** про́волока **2** (elec.) про́вод **3** (infml, telegram) телегра́мма
● *v.t.* **1** (elec.): **they ~d the house** они́ сде́лали прово́дку в до́ме **2** (infml, send telegram to) телеграфи́ровать (*impf., pf.*) + *d.*

wiring /'waɪərɪŋ/ *n.* (elec.) (электро)прово́дка

wiry /'waɪəri/ *adj.* (**wirier, wiriest**) (of person) жи́листый; (of hair) жёсткий

wisdom /'wɪzdəm/ *n.* му́дрость; (prudence) благоразу́мие
■ **~ tooth** *n.* зуб му́дрости

wise /waɪz/ *adj.* **1** (sage) му́дрый **2** (sensible) благоразу́мный; **you were ~ not to attempt it** вы пра́вильно сде́лали, что не ста́ли про́бовать **3** (well informed) осведомлённый; **now that you've told me I am none the ~r** да́же по́сле ва́шего объясне́ния я ма́ло что понима́ю
■ **~ guy** *n.* (AmE, infml) у́мник

✎ **wish** /wɪʃ/ *n.* **1** (desire) жела́ние; (request) про́сьба; **make a ~!** загада́йте жела́ние!; **you acted against my ~es** вы поступи́ли про́тив мое́й во́ли **2** (on another's behalf) пожела́ние; **with best ~es!** с наилу́чшими пожела́ниями!
● *v.t.* **1** (want, require) жела́ть (*impf.*); хоте́ть (*impf.*) (*both + a. or g., inf., or чтобы*) **2** (expr. unfulfilled desire): **I ~ I knew everything**

е́сли бы (то́лько) я всё знал; **как бы я хоте́л всё знать; I ~ you'd be quiet** нельзя́ ли не шуме́ть (*or* поти́ше)?; **I ~ he hadn't left so soon** как жаль, что он ушёл так ра́но; **I ~ he were alive** е́сли бы то́лько он был жив **3** (with double object): **I ~ him well** я жела́ю ему́ добра́; **I ~ you many happy returns** поздравля́ю вас с днём рожде́ния
● *v.i.:* **~ for** мечта́ть о + *p.*

wishful /'wɪʃfʊl/ *adj.:* **~ thinking** самообольще́ние; приня́тие жела́емого за действи́тельное

wisp /wɪsp/ *n.:* **a ~ of hair** прядь воло́с; **a ~ of smoke** стру́йка ды́ма

wispy /'wɪspi/ *adj.* (**wispier, wispiest**): **~ hair** ре́дкие во́лосы

wistaria /wɪ'steəriə/, **wisteria** /wɪ'stɪəriə/ *n.* (bot.) глици́ния

wistful /'wɪstfʊl/ *adj.* тоскли́вый

wit /wɪt/ *n.* **1** (*also* ~s) (intelligence) ум, ра́зум **2** (wittiness) остроу́мие **3** (person) остря́|к (-чка (infml))

witch /wɪtʃ/ *n.* ве́дьма
■ **~craft** *n.* чёрная ма́гия; **~ doctor** *n.* зна́харь (*m.*); **~-hunt** *n.* (fig.) охо́та на ведьм

✎ **with** /wɪð/ *prep.* **1** (in the company of) *usu.* с + *i.*; **come ~ me!** пойдёмте со мной!; **he is ~ the manager** он у заве́дующего; **the boy was left ~ his aunt** ма́льчика оста́вили у тётки (*or* с тёткой); (denoting host) у + *g.*; **we stayed ~ our friends** мы жи́ли у друзе́й **2** (denoting means): **I am writing ~ a pen** я пишу́ ру́чкой; **he walks ~ a stick** он хо́дит с па́л(оч)кой **3** (expr. antagonism or separation): **don't argue ~ me** не спо́рьте со мной; **at war ~** в состоя́нии войны́ с + *i.* **4** (denoting cause) от + *g.*; **she was shaking ~ fright** она́ дрожа́ла от стра́ха **5** (denoting characteristic): **a girl ~ blue eyes** де́вушка с голубы́ми глаза́ми; **a suit ~ grey stripes** костю́м в се́рую поло́ску **6** (denoting manner etc.): **~ pleasure** с удово́льствием; **~ care** осторо́жно **7** (in the same direction or degree as; at the same time as): **one must move ~ the times** на́до идти́ в но́гу со вре́менем; **~ the approach of spring** с наступле́нием весны́ **8** (denoting attendant circumstance): **a holiday ~ all expenses paid** по́лностью опла́ченный о́тпуск; **~ your permission** с ва́шего разреше́ния

withdraw /wɪð'drɔː/ *v.t.* (*past* **withdrew**, *p.p.* **withdrawn**) отн|има́ть, -я́ть; **~ an offer** брать, взять обра́тно/наза́д предложе́ние; **~ money from the bank** сн|има́ть, -ять де́ньги со счёта (в ба́нке); **~ troops** выводи́ть, вы́вести войска́; **a ~n character** за́мкнутый челове́к
● *v.i.* (*past* **withdrew**, *p.p.* **withdrawn**) удал|я́ться, -и́ться; **~ into oneself** зам|ыка́ться, -кну́ться в себе́; (mil.) уходи́ть, уйти́

withdrawal /wɪð'drɔːəl/ *n.* (of a product from the market) изъя́тие; (of a person from an election) сня́тие; (of troops) вы́вод
■ **~ symptoms** *n. pl.* абстине́нтный синдро́м

withdrawn /wɪð'drɔːn/ *p.p. of* ▶ **withdraw**

w

withdrew /wɪð'druː/ *past of* ▸ **withdraw**
wither /'wɪðə(r)/ *v.t.* **1** иссуша́|ть, -и́ть
2 (fig.) губи́ть, по-; a ~ing glance
испепеля́ющий взгляд
● *v.i.* вя́нуть, за-
withhold /wɪð'həʊld/ *v.t.* (*past and p.p.*
withheld /-'held/) отка́з|ывать, -а́ть в чём;
~ one's consent не да|ва́ть, -ть согла́сия; ~
payment заде́рж|ивать, -а́ть опла́ту
within /wɪ'ðɪn/ *adv.* внутри́; from ~ изнутри́
● *prep.* **1** (inside) в + *p.*; внутри́ + *g.*;
these walls в э́тих стена́х **2** (not further than;
accessible to) в преде́лах + *g.*; the library is
~ walking distance до библиоте́ки мо́жно
дойти́ пешко́м **3** (of time) в тече́ние + *g.*; ~
three days в тече́ние трёх дней; I can finish
the job ~ a week я могу́ (за)ко́нчить э́ту
рабо́ту за неде́лю **4** (~ limits of) в преде́лах/
ра́мках + *g.*; live ~ one's income жить (*impf.*)
по сре́дствам
without /wɪ'ðaʊt/ *prep.* без + *g.*; ~ doubt
без сомне́ния; ~ fail непреме́нно; it goes ~
saying само́ собо́й разуме́ется; (with gerund):
~ thinking не поду́мав
withstand /wɪð'stænd/ *v.t.* (*past and p.p.*
withstood /-'stʊd/) устоя́ть (*pf.*) пе́ред + *i.*;
выде́рживать, вы́держать
witness /'wɪtnɪs/ *n.* свиде́тель (-ница); bear
~ свиде́тельствовать (*impf.*)
● *v.t.* **1** (event) быть свиде́телем + *g.*; no
one ~ed the accident никто́ не ви́дел,
как произошла́ катастро́фа **2** (signature)
заве́р|я́ть, -е́рить
■ ~ box, (AmE) stand *nn.* ме́сто для да́чи
свиде́тельских показа́ний
witticism /'wɪtɪsɪz(ə)m/ *n.* остро́та
witty /'wɪtɪ/ *adj.* (**wittier, wittiest**)
остроу́мный
wives /waɪvz/ *pl. of* ▸ **wife**
wizard /'wɪzəd/ *n.* волше́бник
WMD *abbr.* (*of* **weapons of mass
destruction**) ОМП (ору́жие ма́ссового
пораже́ния)
wobble /'wɒb(ə)l/ *v.t. & i.* (*also* ~ **about**)
шата́ть(ся) (*impf.*)
wobbly /'wɒblɪ/ *adj.* (**wobblier,
wobbliest**) ша́ткий, неусто́йчивый
woe /wəʊ/ *n.* **1** (grief) го́ре **2** (in pl.) (troubles)
бе́ды (*f. pl.*)
woeful /'wəʊfʊl/ *adj.* ско́рбный, го́рестный;
(deplorable) жа́лкий; a ~ countenance
ско́рбное лицо́; ~ ignorance вопию́щее
неве́жество
wok /wɒk/ *n.* сковорода́ (с вы́пуклым
дни́щем) (*в кита́йской ку́хне*)
woke /wəʊk/ *past of* ▸ **wake¹**
woken /'wəʊk(ə)n/ *p.p. of* ▸ **wake¹**
wolf /wʊlf/ *n.* (*pl.* **wolves**) (animal) волк; cry
~ (fig.) подн|има́ть, -я́ть ло́жную трево́гу
● *v.t.* (infml) (*also* ~ **down**) прогл|а́тывать,
-оти́ть с жа́дностью
■ ~ whistle *n.* (infml) свист при ви́де краси́вой
де́вушки
woman /'wʊmən/ *n.* (*pl.* **women**)

1 же́нщина **2** (*attr.*): ~ doctor же́нщина-
врач; ~ friend подру́га, прия́тельница
womanize /'wʊmənaɪz/ *v.i.* (infml, philander)
пу́таться (*impf.*) с ба́бами (infml); гоня́ться
(*impf.*) за ю́бками
womanizer /'wʊmənaɪzə(r)/ *n.* ба́бник (infml)
womanly /'wʊmənlɪ/ *adj.* (figure)
же́нственный; (virtues) же́нский
womb /wuːm/ *n.* ма́тка
women /'wɪmɪn/ *pl. of* ▸ **woman**
won /wʌn/ *past and p.p. of* ▸ **win**
wonder /'wʌndə(r)/ *n.* **1** (miracle, marvel) чу́до;
(surprising thing): it's a ~ that... удиви́тельно,
что...; no ~ he was angry! неудиви́тельно,
что он рассерди́лся! **2** (amazement)
изумле́ние, восхище́ние
● *v.i.* **1** (desire to know; deliberate) (*usu. with
clause*): I ~ who that was интере́сно/
любопы́тно, кто бы э́то мог быть; he ~ed
if she was coming он гада́л, придёт она́ или
нет; I was ~ing whether to invite him я не
мог реши́ть, приглаша́ть его́ или нет **2** (feel
curiosity) интересова́ться (*impf.*); I was ~ing
about that я и сам разду́мывал об э́том;
'Why do you ask?' — 'I just ~ed' «Почему́
вы спра́шиваете?» — «Про́сто так» **3** (feel
surprised, marvel (at)) удивл|я́ться, -и́ться (*чему́*);
пора|жа́ться, -зи́ться (*чему́*)
wonderful /'wʌndəfʊl/ *adj.* (pleasing)
чуде́сный, чу́дный; what ~ weather! кака́я
чу́дная пого́да!
wonky /'wɒŋkɪ/ *adj.* (**wonkier, wonkiest**)
(BrE, infml) (unstable) ша́ткий; (crooked) криво́й
wont /wəʊnt/ (archaic or liter.) *n.*: as is his ~ по
своему́ обыкнове́нию
● *adj.*: as he was ~ to say как он люби́л
говори́ть
won't /wəʊnt/ *neg. of* ▸ **will²**
woo /wuː/ *v.t.* (**woos, wooed**) (archaic)
уха́живать (*impf.*) за + *i.*
wood /wʊd/ *n.* **1** in sing. or pl. (forest) лес;
~ed country леси́стая ме́стность; (fig.): we're
not out of the ~ yet ещё не все опа́сности/
тру́дности позади́ **2** (substance) де́рево;
touch, (AmE) knock on ~! тьфу, тьфу! чтоб не
сгла́зить! **3** (as fuel) дрова́ (*pl., g. —*)
■ ~land *n.* леси́стая ме́стность; ~pecker
n. дя́тел; ~wind *n.* (*collect.*) деревя́нные
духовы́е инструме́нты (*m. pl.*); ~work
n. (BrE, carpentry) столя́рная рабо́та; (articles)
деревя́нные изде́лия; ~worm *n.* личи́нка
древото́чца
wooden /'wʊd(ə)n/ *adj.* (also fig.) деревя́нный
woody /'wʊdɪ/ *adj.* (**woodier, woodiest**)
(wooded) леси́стый; (of or like wood)
деревя́нный
woof /wʊf/ *n.* (dog's bark) га́вканье, лай; ~!
гав!
wool /wʊl/ *n.* шерсть; pull the ~ over sb's
eyes (fig.) пус|ка́ть, -ти́ть пыль в глаза́
кому́-н.
woollen /'wʊlən/ (AmE **woolen**) *adj.*
шерстяно́й

W

woolly /'wʊlɪ/ *adj.* (**woollier, woolliest**) **1** (bearing or covered with wool) шерсти́стый **2** (fig., lacking definition) нея́сный

♂ **word** /wɜːd/ *n.* **1** сло́во; **I couldn't get a ~ in (edgeways)** мне не удало́сь вста́вить ни сло́ва; **he never has a good ~ for anyone** он ни о ком до́брого сло́ва не ска́жет; **may I have a ~ with you?** мо́жно вас на па́ру слов?; **in a ~** (одни́м) сло́вом; **in other ~s** ина́че говоря́, други́ми слова́ми; **a man of few ~s** немногосло́вный челове́к; **put in a good ~ for sb** замо́лвить (*pf.*) слове́чко за кого́-н.; **~ for ~** сло́во в сло́во; **translate ~ for ~** переводи́ть, -ести́ досло́вно/ буква́льно **2** (*in pl.*) (quarrel): **they had ~s** они́ поссо́рились **3** (*in pl.*) (text set to music) текст, слова́ (*nt. pl.*) **4** (news) изве́стие, сообще́ние; **he sent ~ that he was not coming** он пе́редал, что не смо́жет прийти́; **the ~ got round that ...** ста́ло изве́стно, что... **5** (promise) сло́во, обеща́ние; **give one's ~** да|ва́ть, -ть сло́во; обеща́ть (*impf., pf.*); **keep one's ~** держа́ть, с- сло́во; **he was as good as his ~** он сдержа́л сло́во; **you must take my ~ for it** вам придётся пове́рить мне на́ слово **6** (command) сло́во, прика́з; **just say the ~!** то́лько скажи́те/прикажи́те!

● *v.t.* формули́ровать, с-

■ **~ processing** *n.* редакти́рование те́кста; **~ processor** *n.* те́кстовый реда́ктор

wording /'wɜːdɪŋ/ *n.* реда́кция (*те́кста, статьи́*)

wore /wɔː(r)/ *past of* ▶ wear

♂ **work** /wɜːk/ *n.* **1** (labour, task) рабо́та, труд; (official, professional) рабо́та, слу́жба; (school etc.) заня́тия (*nt. pl.*); **he is at ~** он сейча́с рабо́тает; **she is at ~ on a dictionary** она́ рабо́тает над словарём; **get to ~ on** нач|ина́ть, -а́ть рабо́ту над + *i.*; **get down to ~** прин|има́ться, -я́ться/бра́ться, взя́ться за рабо́ту/де́ло **2** (employment) рабо́та, слу́жба; **it is hard to find ~** тру́дно найти́ рабо́ту; **in ~** рабо́тающий; **out of ~** без рабо́ты **3** (literary or artistic composition) произведе́ние, сочине́ние; (publication) изда́ние; **the ~s of Chopin** произведе́ния Шопе́на; **a ~ of art** произведе́ние иску́сства **4** (*in pl.*) (parts of machine) механи́зм **5** (*in pl.*) (BrE, factory) заво́д, фа́брика, предприя́тие; **steel ~s** сталелите́йный заво́д

● *v.t.* (*past and p.p.* **worked**) **1** (cause to ~): **he ~s his men hard** он заставля́ет люде́й мно́го рабо́тать; **he ~ed himself to death** он изнёл себя́ рабо́той **2** (set in motion) прив|оди́ть, -ести́ в движе́ние/де́йствие; **how do you ~ this machine?** как управля́ть э́той маши́ной? **3** (effect): **~ wonders** твори́ть (*impf.*) чудеса́ **4** (achieve by ~ing): **he ~ed his way through university** все го́ды студе́нчества он сам зараба́тывал себе́ на жизнь; **he ~ed his way up to the rank of manager** он проби́лся в директора́ **5** (excite) возбу|жда́ть, -ди́ть; **he ~ed the crowd into a frenzy** он довёл толпу́ до неи́стовства

● *v.i.* **1** (be employed) рабо́тать (*над чем*), труди́ться, служи́ть (*all impf.*); **he ~ed for 6 hours** он рабо́тал 6 часо́в; **~ with sb** сотру́дничать (*impf.*) с кем-н. **2** (operate) рабо́тать (*impf.*); де́йствовать (*impf.*); **the brakes won't ~** тормоза́ отказа́ли **3** (produce desired effect): **the plan ~ed** план уда́лся; **the medicine ~ed** лека́рство помогло́/ поде́йствовало **4** (exert influence) рабо́тать, де́йствовать (*both impf.*); **~ against** меша́ть, по- + *d.* **5** (move gradually): **a screw ~ed loose** винт осла́б

□ **~ off** *v.t.*: **he ran round the house to ~ off some of his energy** он пробе́жался вокру́г до́ма, что́бы дать вы́ход свое́й эне́ргии; **I shall never be able to ~ off this debt** я никогда́ не смогу́ отрабо́тать э́тот долг

□ **~ out** *v.t.* (devise) разраб|а́тывать, -о́тать; (calculate) вычисл|я́ть, вы́числить; (solve) разреш|а́ть, -и́ть

● *v.i.* (turn out) ока́з|ываться, -а́ться; (turn out well) об|ходи́ться, -ойти́сь; **everything ~ed out** всё обошло́сь; (be calculated): **the expenses ~ out at £70** расхо́ды составля́ют 70 фу́нтов; (train, of an athlete) тренирова́ться (*impf.*)

□ **~ up** *v.t.* (develop): **I can't ~ up any interest in economics** я ника́к не могу́ пробуди́ть в себе́ интере́с к эконо́мике; (*pred.*) **I'm ~ed up** (excited) я взволно́ван; (worried) я расстро́ен

■ **~bench** *n.* верста́к; **~ experience** *n.* (BrE) произво́дственная пра́ктика (*для шко́льников*); **~force** *n.* рабо́чая си́ла; **~load** *n.* нагру́зка; **~man** *n.* рабо́тник; **~manship** *n.* мастерство́; **~out** *n.* трениро́вка; **~shop** *n.* (small) мастерска́я; (large) цех; **~station** *n.* (comput.) рабо́чая ста́нция; **~top** *n.* (BrE) ве́рхняя пане́ль; **~-to-rule** *n.* (BrE) ≈ италья́нская забасто́вка (*рабо́та стро́го по пра́вилам*)

workable /'wɜːkəb(ə)l/ *adj.* **1** (of mine etc.) рента́бельный **2** (feasible) выполни́мый

workaholic /wɜːkə'hɒlɪk/ *n.* трудого́лик

♂ **worker** /'wɜːkə(r)/ *n.* рабо́тник, трудя́щийся; **office ~** слу́жащий

♂ **working** /'wɜːkɪŋ/ *n.* **1** (*usu. in pl.*) (operation) рабо́та, де́йствие **2** (*attr.*) (pert. to work) рабо́чий; **in ~ order** в испра́вности

● *adj.* рабо́чий

■ **~ capital** *n.* оборо́тный капита́л; **~ class** *n.* рабо́чий класс; **~-class** *adj.* рабо́чий; **~-class families** се́мьи рабо́чих; **~ conditions** *n. pl.* усло́вия труда́

♂ **world** /wɜːld/ *n.* **1** (universe) мир; **out of this ~** (infml, stupendous) потряса́ющий; **in this ~** на э́том све́те **2** (fig. uses): **what in the ~ has happened?** что же, наконе́ц, случи́лось?; **why in the ~ didn't you tell me?** ну почему́ же вы мне не сказа́ли?; **I wouldn't hurt him for the ~** я его́ ни за что (на све́те) не стал бы обижа́ть; **the boss thinks the ~ of him** он у хозя́ина на о́чень высо́ком счету́; **I felt on top of the ~** я был на седьмо́м не́бе от сча́стья **3** (infinite amount) мно́го, у́йма (infml); **a ~ of difference** огро́мная ра́зница;

w

it will do him a ~ of good это пойдёт ему на пользу **4** (geog., the earth's countries and peoples) мир, свет; **(all)** over the ~ по всему све́ту; go round the ~ объе́зжа́ть, -е́хать весь свет; a ~ power вели́кая держа́ва **5** (human affairs) жизнь; go up in the ~ де́лать, с- карье́ру; go down in the ~ утра́|чивать, -тить было́е положе́ние **6** (domain) мир; сфе́ра; the ~ of nature ца́рство приро́ды

■ **W~ Bank** n. Всеми́рный банк; ~ **champion** n. чемпио́н ми́ра; **W~ Cup** n. Ку́бок ми́ра по футбо́лу; ~**-famous** adj. всеми́рно изве́стный; ~ **record** n. мирово́й реко́рд; ~ **view** n. мировоззре́ние; ~ **war** n. мирова́я война́; ~**wide** adj. всеми́рный, мирово́й ● adv. по всему́ све́ту/ми́ру; **W~ Wide Web** n. Всеми́рная паути́на, Интерне́т, Сеть

worldly /ˈwɜːldlɪ/ adj. (**worldlier**, **worldliest**) **1** (material) земно́й, материа́льный **2**: a ~ **person** о́пытный челове́к

■ ~**wise** adj. о́пытный

worm /wɜːm/ n. червь (m.)
● v.t. (extract) вытя́гивать, вы́тянуть

worn /wɔːn/ p.p. of ▶ wear

worried /ˈwʌrɪd/ adj. обеспоко́енный, озабо́ченный

worrier /ˈwʌrɪə(r)/ n.: he's a ~ он ве́чно беспоко́ится

worr|y /ˈwʌrɪ/ n. **1** (anxiety) трево́га, забо́та **2** (sth causing anxiety) неприя́тность, забо́та; he is a ~y to me он доставля́ет мне мно́го беспоко́йства/забо́т/хлопо́т; financial ~ies фина́нсовые пробле́мы (f. pl.)
● v.t. **1** (cause anxiety to) беспоко́ить (impf.); what is ~ying you? что вас беспоко́ит?; чем вы озабо́чены?; **I'm** ~ied about my son я беспоко́юсь о сы́не **2** (bother) надоеда́ть (impf.) + d.; the noise doesn't ~y me шум не меша́ет мне
● v.i. беспоко́иться, волнова́ться, расстра́иваться (all impf.); **don't** ~y! не беспоко́йтесь!; you are ~ying over nothing вы напра́сно расстра́иваетесь/волну́етесь

worse /wɜːs/ n. ху́дшее; there is ~ to come ху́дшее ещё впереди́; a change for the ~ переме́на к ху́дшему; things went from bad to ~ положе́ние станови́лось всё ху́же и ху́же
● adj. ху́дший; you will only make matters ~ вы то́лько уху́дшите положе́ние; ~ **luck!** к сожале́нию! (as pred.) ху́же; the patient is ~ **today** больно́му сего́дня ху́же; his work is getting ~ его́ рабо́та стано́вится ху́же; they are ~ off than we они́ в ху́дшем положе́нии, чем мы; (financially) они́ ме́нее состоя́тельны, чем мы
● adv. ху́же; we played ~ than ever мы игра́ли как никогда́ пло́хо; you might do ~ than accept мо́жет быть, и сто́ит приня́ть

worsen /ˈwɜːs(ə)n/ v.t. & i. ухудша́ть(ся), уху́дшить(ся)

worship /ˈwɜːʃɪp/ n. поклоне́ние
● v.t. & i. (**worshipped**, **worshipping**, AmE worshiped, worshiping) поклоня́ться (impf.) + d.; ~ **God** моли́ться (impf.) Бо́гу; (attend ~) моли́ться (impf.); (adore) боготвори́ть (impf.)

worshipper /ˈwɜːʃɪpə(r)/ (AmE **worshiper**) n. моля́щийся

worst /wɜːst/ n. наиху́дшее; са́мое плохо́е; the ~ is over ху́дшее позади́; the ~ of it is that ... ху́же всего́ то, что...; if the ~ comes to the ~ в са́мом ху́дшем слу́чае; you saw him at his ~ вы ви́дели его́ с наиху́дшей стороны́; at (the) ~ you may have to pay a fine в кра́йнем слу́чае вам придётся уплати́ть штраф
● adj. наиху́дший; са́мый плохо́й; you came at the ~ possible time вы пришли́ в са́мое неподходя́щее вре́мя
● adv. (of objects) ху́же всего́; (of people) ху́же всех

❖ **worth** /wɜːθ/ n. (value) це́нность; (merit) досто́инство; of great ~ значи́тельный; (quantity of specified value): give me a pound's ~ of sweets да́йте мне конфе́т на (оди́н) фунт
● pred. adj. **1** (of value equal to): it's ~ about £1 э́то сто́ит о́коло (одного́) фу́нта; what is your house ~? во ско́лько оце́нивается ваш дом?; it's ~ a lot to me для меня́ э́то о́чень це́нно/ва́жно **2** (deserving of) сто́ящий, заслу́живающий; it's not ~ the trouble of asking не сто́ит спра́шивать; it is ~ while сто́ит; it's hardly ~ mentioning об э́том вряд ли сто́ит упомина́ть; well ~ having о́чень сто́ящий/поле́зный **3** (possessed of): he is ~ 3 billion его́ ли́чное состоя́ние оце́нивается в 3 миллиа́рда; (fig.): he ran for all he was ~ он мча́лся во весь дух

■ ~**while** adj. це́нный, сто́ящий

worthless /ˈwɜːθlɪs/ adj. (goods) ничего́ не сто́ящий; (person, contribution) ничто́жный

worthy /ˈwɜːðɪ/ adj. (**worthier**, **worthiest**) **1** (deserving respect) досто́йный, почте́нный; a ~ **cause** досто́йное де́ло **2** (deserving) досто́йный, заслу́живающий + g.; ~ of **note** досто́йный внима́ния; ~ of a place in the team досто́йный быть чле́ном кома́нды **3** (appropriate) подоба́ющий + d.; ~ of the occasion подоба́ющий слу́чаю

❖ **would** /wʊd/ v. aux. (see also ▶ will²) **1** (conditional): he ~ be angry if he knew он бы рассерди́лся, е́сли (бы) узна́л **2** (expr. wish): **I** ~ **like to know** я хоте́л бы знать; **I** ~ **rather** я бы предпочёл **3** (of typical action etc.): you ~ do that! с тебя́ ста́нется!; of course he ~ say that ну коне́чно, он э́то ска́жет **4** (of habitual action) see ▶ will² 4

■ ~**-be** adj.: a ~**-be writer** начина́ющий писа́тель

wouldn't /ˈwʊd(ə)nt/ neg. of ▶ would

wound¹ /wuːnd/ n. ра́на, ране́ние
● v.t. ра́нить (impf., pf.); he was ~ed in the leg его́ ра́нило в но́гу; there were many ~ed бы́ло мно́го ра́неных

wound² /waʊnd/ past and p.p. of ▶ wind²

wove /wəʊv/ past of ▶ weave

woven /ˈwəʊv(ə)n/ p.p. of ▶ weave

wow /waʊ/ *int.* здóрово!; вот э́то да́!; ух!
• *v.t.* (sl.) прив|оди́ть, -ести́ в восто́рг
WPC (BrE) *abbr.* (*of* **woman police constable**) же́нщина-полице́йский
wrangle /ˈræŋɡ(ə)l/ *n.* ссóра
• *v.i.* ссóриться (*impf.*)
wrap /ræp/ *n.* **1** (lit., shawl) шаль, платóк; (rug) плед **2** (fig.): **under** ∼**s** (fig.) в тáйне
• *v.t.* (**wrapped, wrapping**) **1** (cover) зав|орáчивать, -ернýть; закýт|ывать, -ать; (parcel) об|орáчивать, -ернýть; **they were** ∼**ping presents** они́ завора́чивали подáрки; ∼ **oneself in a blanket** зав|орáчиваться, -ернýться в одея́ло **2** (wind as a covering) об|орáчивать, -ернýть; **we** ∼ **sacking round the pipes in winter** зимóй мы обора́чиваем трýбы мешкови́ной; **he** ∼**ped his arms around her** он заключи́л её в объя́тия; он óбнял её
□ ∼ **up** *v.t.* (cover up) зав|орáчивать, -ернýть; (conclude) свора́чивать, сверну́ть (infml); (summarize) крáтко сумми́ровать (*impf., pf.*); (*pass.*) (be engrossed) погру|жáться, -зи́ться (**in**: в + *a.*)
• *v.i.* (put on extra clothes) закýт|ываться, -аться
wrapper /ˈræpə(r)/ *n.* обёртка
wrapping /ˈræpɪŋ/ *n.* обёртка, упакóвка
■ ∼ **paper** *n.* обёрточная бумáга
wrath /rɒθ/ *n.* гнев
wrathful /ˈrɒθfʊl/ *adj.* гне́вный, я́ростный
wreak /riːk/ *v.t.*: ∼ **havoc (on)** нан|оси́ть, -ести́ ущéрб + *d.*
wreath /riːθ/ *n.* венóк
wreck /rek/ *n.* **1** (∼ed ship) затонýвший корáбль **2** (damaged vehicle, building, person, etc.) развáлина
• *v.t.* **1** (ship): **the ship was** ∼**ed** сýдно потерпéло крушéние; **the ship was** ∼**ed on the cliffs** корáбль разби́лся о скáлы **2** (car) разб|ивáть, -и́ть; (building) разр|ушáть, -ýшить; (equipment) ломáть, с- **3** (hope, life) разб|ивáть, -и́ть; (weekend) пóртить, ис-
wreckage /ˈrekɪdʒ/ *n.* (remains) облóмки (*m. pl.*) крушéния *и т. п.*
wren /ren/ *n.* крапи́вник (*птица*)
wrench /rentʃ/ *n.* **1** (fig.) тоскá, боль **2** (tool) гáечный ключ
• *v.t.*: **he** ∼**ed the door open** он рéзко рванýл дверь на себя́; **he** ∼**ed the paper out of my hand** он вы́рвал у меня́ бумáгу из рук
wrestle /ˈres(ə)l/ *v.i.* борóться (*impf.*); (fig.): ∼ **with a problem** би́ться (*impf.*) над задáчей; **he** ∼**d with his conscience** он борóлся со свое́й сóвестью
wrestler /ˈreslə(r)/ *n.* борéц
wrestling /ˈreslɪŋ/ *n.* борьбá
wretch /retʃ/ *n.* негодя́й
wretched /ˈretʃɪd/ *adj.* (**wretcheder, wretchedest**) (miserable) несчáстный; (unpleasant) сквéрный; (damned) прокля́тый
wriggle /ˈrɪɡ(ə)l/ *n.* изги́б, изви́в
• *v.t.* (*also* ∼ **about**): ∼ **one's toes** шевели́ть

(*impf.*) пáльцами ног; **he** ∼**d free** он вы́вернулся/вы́скользнул
• *v.i.* (*also* ∼ **about**) извивáться (*impf.*); **the baby** ∼**d out of my arms** ребёнок вы́скользнул у меня́ из рук; ∼ **out of a responsibility** уви́л|ивать, -ьнýть от отвéтственности

wring /rɪŋ/ *v.t.* (*past and p.p.* **wrung**) **1** (sb's hand) пож|имáть, -áть; **he wrung his hands in despair** он в отчáянии ломáл себé рýки; (squeeze out by twisting) выжимáть, вы́жать; ∼ **clothes dry** отж|имáть, -áть бельё дóсуха; (chicken's neck) свора́чивать, сверну́ть **2** (fig., extract by force) вырывáть, вы́рвать; **I wrung a promise from him** я вы́рвал у негó обещáние
□ ∼ **out** *v.t.* (clothes) отж|имáть, -жáть; (water) отж|имáть, -áть
wrinkle /ˈrɪŋk(ə)l/ *n.* (on skin) морщи́на
• *v.t.*: ∼ **one's nose** мóрщить, с- нос
• *v.i.* мя́ться, по-/из-
wrist /rɪst/ *n.* запя́стье
■ ∼**watch** *n.* нарýчные час|ы́ (-óв)
writ /rɪt/ *n.* (written injunction) судéбный прикáз; (summons) повéстка; **serve a** ∼ **on sb** вруч|áть, -и́ть комý-н. судéбный прикáз
write /raɪt/ *v.t.* (*past* **wrote**, *p.p.* **written**) **1** писáть, на- **2**: ∼ **a cheque** (BrE), **check** (AmE) выпи́сывать, вы́писать чек **3** (compose) писáть, на-; сочин|я́ть, -и́ть
• *v.i.* (*past* **wrote**, *p.p.* **written**) **1** писáть (*impf.*) **2** (compose) сочин|я́ть, -и́ть; писáть, на-
□ ∼ **away** *v.i.*: **he wrote away, off for a catalogue** он вы́писал каталóг
□ ∼ **back** *v.i.* отв|ечáть, -éтить (письмóм)
□ ∼ **down** *v.t.* (make a note of) запи́с|ывать, -áть
□ ∼ **off** *v.t.* (cancel): ∼ **off a debt** спи́с|ывать, -áть долг; (recognize loss of): ∼ **off £500 for depreciation** спи́с|ывать, -áть 500 фýнтов на амортизáцию; **the car had to be written off** маши́ну пришлóсь списáть
• *v.i.* = **write away**
□ ∼ **out** *v.t.* выпи́сывать, вы́писать
■ ∼**-off** *n.*: **the car was a** ∼**-off** маши́ну списáли; ∼**-up** *n.* (account) отчёт; (review) óтзыв, рецéнзия
writer /ˈraɪtə(r)/ *n.* **1** (person writing) áвтор **2** (author) писáтель (-ница)
■ ∼**'s block** *n.* отсýтствие вдохновéния
writhe /raɪð/ *v.i.* кóрчиться (*impf.*)
writing /ˈraɪtɪŋ/ *n.* **1** (ability, art) письмó, грáмота **2** (written words; inscription) нáдпись; **in** ∼ пи́сьменно; в пи́сьменной фóрме **3** (handwriting) пóчерк **4** (literary composition) произведéние
■ ∼ **pad** *n.* блокнóт; ∼ **paper** *n.* пи́счая бумáга
written /ˈrɪt(ə)n/ *p.p. of* ▸ **write**
wrong /rɒŋ/ *n.* **1** (evil) зло; (immoral action) дурнóй постýпок **2** (unjust action or its result) несправедли́вость, оби́да **3** (state of error): **you are in the** ∼ вы непрáвы/виновáты
• *adj.* **1** (sinful) грéшный; (reprehensible) дурнóй; **it is** ∼ **to steal** воровáть нехорошó **2** (mistaken) непрáвый; **you are** ∼ вы непрáвы/ошибáетесь; **he proved them** ∼ он

⚜ ключевáя лéксика

доказа́л, что они́ ошиба́лись **3** (incorrect) непра́вильный, неве́рный, оши́бочный; (unsuitable) неподходя́щий; **take the ~ turning** св|ора́чивать, -ерну́ть не туда́; **my food went down the ~ way** пи́ща попа́ла не в то го́рло; **that's the ~ way to go about it** э́то де́лается не так; **this shirt is the ~ size/colour** э́та руба́шка не того́ разме́ра/цве́та; **the clock is ~** часы́ иду́т непра́вильно; **you have the ~ number** вы не туда́ попа́ли (*по телефо́ну*) **4** (out of order; causing concern) нела́дный; **what's ~?** что случи́лось?; **what's ~ with you?** что с тобо́й?; **there's something ~ with my car** с мое́й маши́ной что́-то не в поря́дке; **to go ~** срыва́ться, сорва́ться; **our plans went ~** на́ши пла́ны спу́тались; **where did we go ~?** (make a mistake) в чём мы оши́блись? **5** (of health): **the doctor asked me what was ~** врач спроси́л, на что я жа́луюсь; **he found nothing ~ with me** он не нашёл у меня́ никаки́х боле́зней
● *adv.* (incorrectly) непра́вильно, не так; (reprehensibly) пло́хо; **you did ~ to shout at the child** ты пло́хо сде́лал, что накрича́л на ребёнка
● *v.t.* (treat unjustly) быть несправедли́вым к + *d.*
■ **~doer** *n.* (sinner) гре́шни|к (-ца); (offender) правонаруши́тель (-ница); **~foot** *v.t.* (BrE) заст|ига́ть, -и́гнуть враспло́х

wrongful /ˈrɒŋfʊl/ *adj.* несправедли́вый

wrongly /ˈrɒŋlɪ/ *adv.* (reprehensibly) ду́рно; (incorrectly) непра́вильно; (by mistake) по оши́бке

wrote /rəʊt/ *past of* ▸ write

wrought /rɔːt/ *adj.*: **~ iron** ко́ваное/сва́рочное желе́зо

wrung /rʌŋ/ *past and p.p. of* ▸ wring

wry /raɪ/ *adj.* криво́й

WWW *abbr.* (*of* **World Wide Web**) Всеми́рная паути́на, Интерне́т, Сеть

WYSIWYG /ˈwɪzɪwɪɡ/ *abbr.* (*of* **what you see is what you get**) (comput.) режи́м по́лного соотве́тствия (*печа́тного изображе́ния и изображе́ния на экра́не*)

Xx

X /eks/ *n.* (unknown quantity or person) X, икс; **~ marks the spot where the body was found** кресто́м обозна́чено ме́сто, где был на́йден труп; **an ~(-rated) film** фильм катего́рии X (*то́лько для взро́слых*)
■ **~-ray** *n.* (*in pl.*) рентге́новские лучи́ (*m. pl.*); (single image obtained) рентге́новский сни́мок; (procedure) рентге́н
● *v.t.* просве́|чивать, -ти́ть рентге́новскими луча́ми; де́лать, с- рентге́н (*чего́-н*)

xenophobia /zenəˈfəʊbɪə/ *n.* ксенофо́бия

xenophobic /zenəˈfəʊbɪk/ *adj.* отлича́ющийся ксенофо́бией, ксенофо́бский

Xmas /ˈeksməs/ *n.* = Christmas

xylophone /ˈzaɪləfəʊn/ *n.* (mus.) ксилофо́н

Yy

yacht /jɒt/ *n.* я́хта
■ **~sman** *n.* яхтсме́н; **~swoman** *n.* яхтсме́нка

yachting /ˈjɒtɪŋ/ *n.* па́русный спорт

Yank /jæŋk/ *n.* (infml) я́нки (*m. indecl.*)

yank /jæŋk/ *n.* рыво́к
● *v.t.* дёр|гать, -нуть
□ **~ off** *v.t.* срыва́ть, сорва́ть

yap /jæp/ *n.* тя́вканье
● *v.i.* (**yapped**, **yapping**) тя́вк|ать, -нуть

yard¹ /jɑːd/ *n.* (unit of measure) ярд (*0,9144 м*)
■ **~stick** *n.* (fig.) мери́ло, крите́рий

yard² /jɑːd/ *n.* **1** (BrE, of house) (*also* **court~**) двор **2** (AmE, garden) са́д(ик) **3** (for industrial purposes): **timber ~** склад пиломатериа́лов; **builder's ~** склад стройматериа́лов

yarn /jɑːn/ *n.* **1** (spun thread) пря́жа **2** (infml, story) расска́з

yawn /jɔːn/ *n.* зево́к

• *v.i.* зев|а́ть, -ну́ть; (fig., of chasm) зия́ть (*impf.*)

yay /jeɪ/ *int.* (infml, expressing triumph, approval, or encouragement) ура́!

yeah /jeə/ *adv.* (infml) да; ага́

♂ **year** /jɪə(r)/ *n.* **1** год; I have known him for ten ~s я его́ зна́ю уже́ де́сять лет; ~ in, ~ out из го́да в год; all the ~ round кру́глый год; he's in the third ~ (as school pupil) он в тре́тьем кла́ссе; he is in his third ~ (as college student) он на тре́тьем ку́рсе **2** (*in pl.*) (a long time): it is ~s since I saw him я его́ це́лую ве́чность не ви́дел **3** (*in pl.*) (age) лета́; he looks young for his ~s он мо́лодо вы́глядит для свои́х лет; he is getting on in ~s он (уже́) в возрасте

yearly /ˈjɪəlɪ/ *adj.* (happening once a year) ежего́дный; (pert. to a year): ~ income годово́й дохо́д
• *adv.* (once a year) раз в год; (every year) ка́ждый год

yearn /jəːn/ *v.i.* **1**: ~ for тоскова́ть (*impf.*) по + *d.*; жа́ждать (*impf.*) + *g.* **2**: ~ to жажда́ть (*impf.*) (+ *inf.*); мечта́ть (*impf.*) (+ *inf.*)

yearning /ˈjəːnɪŋ/ *n.* тоска́ (for: по + *d.*); жа́жда (for: + *g.*)

yeast /jiːst/ *n.* дрожж|и (-ей)

yell /jel/ *n.* (пронзи́тельный) крик
• *v.t.* выкри́кивать, вы́крикнуть
• *v.i.* вопи́ть, за-; кри́ча́ть, -и́кнуть

yellow /ˈjeləʊ/ *n.* желтизна́; жёлтый цвет
• *adj.* жёлтый; go, turn ~ желте́ть, по-
• *v.i.* желте́ть, по-
■ Y~ Pages® *n. pl.* «Жёлтые страни́цы»

yellowish /ˈjeləʊɪʃ/ *adj.* желтова́тый

yelp /jelp/ *n.* визг
• *v.i.* визжа́ть, взви́згнуть

Yemen /ˈjemən/ *n.* Йе́мен

Yemeni /ˈjemənɪ/ *n.* йе́мен|ец (-ка)
• *adj.* йе́менский

yen /jen/ *n.* (*pl.* ~) (currency) ие́на

♂ **yes** /jes/ *adv.* да; (in reply to neg. question) нет; Didn't you see him? — Yes, I did Ты не ви́дел его́? — Нет, ви́дел.; ~, please да, спаси́бо

♂ **yesterday** /ˈjestədeɪ/ *n.* вчера́ (*indecl.*); вчера́шний день; ~'s paper вчера́шняя газе́та; since ~ со вчера́шнего дня; the day before ~ позавчера́
• *adv.* вчера́; ~ morning/evening вчера́ у́тром/ве́чером

♂ **yet** /jet/ *adv.* **1** (so far, up to now) до сих пор; пока́ ещё; as ~ пока́; (with neg.) ещё; he has not read the book ~ он ещё не чита́л э́ту кни́гу; (with interrog.) уже́, ещё; has the post arrived ~? по́чта ещё не пришла́?; по́чта уже́ пришла́? **2** (some day; before all is over) ещё; he will win ~ он ещё победи́т **3** (still) ещё; he has ~ to learn of the disaster он ещё не зна́ет о катастро́фе **4** (so early) уже́; need you go ~? вам уже́ пора́ (идти́)?; Shall we go? — Not just ~ Пойдёмте? — Не сейча́с/ Чуть по́зже **5** (with comp.) (even) да́же, ещё; this book is ~ more interesting э́та кни́га

ещё интере́снее **6** (again, in addition) ещё; there is ~ another reason есть ещё и друга́я причи́на **7** (nevertheless) тем не ме́нее; всё-таки; всё же
• *conj.* одна́ко

yew /juː/ *n.* (tree, wood) тис

Yiddish /ˈjɪdɪʃ/ *n.* и́диш, евре́йский язы́к
• *adj.*: a ~ newspaper газе́та на и́дише

yield /jiːld/ *n.* **1** (crop) урожа́й **2** (return) дохо́д **3** (quantity produced) вы́ход
• *v.t.* **1** (bring in; produce) прин|оси́ть, -ести́; произв|оди́ть, -ести́; да|ва́ть, -ть **2** (give up) уступ|а́ть, -и́ть; ~ ground сда|ва́ть, -ть террито́рию; (fig.) сда|ва́ть, -ть (свои́) пози́ции
• *v.i.* уступ|а́ть, -и́ть; подд|ава́ться, -а́ться; he would not ~ to persuasion он не поддава́лся никаки́м угово́рам; (of a door) под|дава́ться, -а́ться

yob /jɒb/ *n.* (BrE, infml) хулига́н

yobbish /ˈjɒbɪʃ/ *adj.* (BrE, infml) хулига́нский

yoga /ˈjəʊgə/ *n.* йо́га

yogurt, yoghurt /ˈjɒgət/ *n.* йо́гурт

yoke /jəʊk/ *n.* (sense 3: *pl.* ~ or ~s) **1** (fitted to oxen etc.) ярмо́, хому́т **2** (fig.) и́го, ярмо́; the Tartar ~ (hist.) тата́рское и́го; shake off the ~ сбр|а́сывать, -о́сить и́го/ярмо́ **3**: ~ oxen (pair) упря́жка воло́в **4** (for carrying pails etc.) коромы́сло **5** (of dress) коке́тка (*верхняя (плечевая/набедренная) часть платья/юбки, к которой пришивается основная их часть*)
• *v.t.* (lit.) впря|га́ть, -чь в ярмо́; (fig., link) соедин|я́ть, -и́ть; сочета́ть (*impf., pf.*)

yokel /ˈjəʊk(ə)l/ *n.* деревёнщина (*c.g.*)

yolk /jəʊk/ *n.* желто́к

♂ **you** /juː/ *pers. pron.* (*obj.* you, *poss.* your, yours) **1** (*familiar sg.*) ты; (*pl. and polite sg.*) вы; ~ and I ты и я; мы с тобо́й/ва́ми; ~ and he ты/вы и он; вы с ним; this is for ~ э́то для тебя́/вас, э́то тебе́/вам **2** (one, anyone): ~ never can tell никогда́ не зна́ешь, кто его́ зна́ет(?)
■ ~-know-who *n.* (infml) сам зна́ешь, кто; э́тот са́мый

♂ **young** /jʌŋ/ *n.*: the ~ молодёжь; (~ animals) детёныши (*m. pl.*); (birds) птенцы́ (*m. pl.*)
• *adj.* (younger /ˈjʌŋgə(r)/, youngest /ˈjʌŋgɪst/) молодо́й, ю́ный; ~ children ма́ленькие де́ти; ~ people молодёжь; he is ~er than I он моло́же меня́

youngish /ˈjʌŋɪʃ/ *adj.* дово́льно молодо́й

youngster /ˈjʌŋstə(r)/ *n.* (boy) ма́льчик; (girl) де́вочка; (child) ребёнок

♂ **your** /jɔː(r)/ *adj.* (*familiar sg.*) твой; (*pl. and polite sg.*) ваш; (referring to subj. of clause) свой

yours /jɔːz/ *pron.* (*familiar sg.*) твой; (*pl. and polite sg.*) ваш; (referring to subj. of clause) свой; a friend of ~ оди́н из ва́ших прия́телей; my teacher and ~ (2 people) на́ши с ва́ми учителя́; (1 person) наш с ва́ми учи́тель; here is my hat — have you found ~? вот моя́ шля́па, а вы свою́ нашли́?

♂ **yourself** /jɔːˈself/ *pron.* **1** (refl.) себя́ (*d., p.* себе́, *i.* собо́й); -ся/-сь (*suff.*); don't

♂ ключева́я ле́ксика

deceive ∼! не обма́нывайте себя́!; не обма́нывайтесь!; **did you hurt** ∼? ты уши́бся/уши́блась? **2** (emph.) сам; **you wrote to him** ∼ вы са́ми ему́ писа́ли; **do it** ∼! сде́лай сам! **3** (after preps.): **why are you sitting by** ∼? почему́ вы сиди́те в одино́честве?; **did you do it all by** ∼? вы э́то сде́лали са́ми? **4**: **you don't look** ∼ **today** вы нева́жно вы́глядите сего́дня

⚡ **youth** /juːθ/ n. **1** (state or period) мо́лодость, ю́ность; **in my** ∼ в мо́лодости **2** (young man) ю́ноша (m.) **3** (young people) молодёжь
  ■ ∼ **club** n. молодёжный клуб; ∼ **hostel** n. молодёжная (тур)ба́за/гости́ница

youthful /ˈjuːθfʊl/ adj. ю́ный, ю́ношеский; (of face, person, etc.) молодо́й, ю́ный
youthfulness /ˈjuːθfʊlnɪs/ n. мо́лодость; (of appearance) моложа́вость
yuan /jʊˈɑːn/ n. (pl. ∼) юа́нь (m.)
yucca /ˈjʌkə/ n. ю́кка
Yugoslav /ˈjuːɡəslɑːv/, **Yugoslavian** /juːɡəˈslɑːvɪən/ adjs. (hist.) югосла́вский
Yugoslavia /juːɡəˈslɑːvɪə/ n. (hist.) Югосла́вия
Yule /juːl/ n. (archaic) Рождество́; Свя́т|ки (-ок)
yummy /ˈjʌmɪ/ adj. (**yummier, yummiest**) (infml) вку́сный
yuppie /ˈjʌpɪ/ n. (infml pej.) я́ппи (m. indecl.) (преуспевающий молодой человек)

Zz

Zagreb /ˈzɑːɡreb/ n. За́греб
Zambia /ˈzæmbɪə/ n. За́мбия
Zambian /ˈzæmbɪən/ n. замби́|ец (-йка)
  ● adj. замби́йский
zany /ˈzeɪnɪ/ adj. (**zanier, zaniest**) смешно́й
zap /zæp/ (sl.) v.t. (**zapped, zapping**) (kill, destroy) мочи́ть, за- (sl.); (comput., delete) стира́ть, стере́ть
  ● v.i. (**zapped, zapping**) (move quickly) мча́ться (impf.)
zeal /ziːl/ n. рве́ние
zealot /ˈzelət/ n. фана́т|ик (-и́чка)
zealous /ˈzeləs/ adj. ре́вностный
zebra /ˈzebrə/ n. зе́бра
  ■ ∼ **crossing** n. (BrE) «зе́бра» (пешеходный переход)
zenith /ˈzenɪθ/ n. (lit., fig.) зени́т
zero /ˈzɪərəʊ/ n. (pl. ∼s) ноль (m.), нуль (m.); **ten degrees below** ∼ ми́нус де́сять гра́дусов
  ■ ∼ **hour** n. час «Ч»
  ● v.i. (**zeroes, zeroed**): ∼ **in on a target** пристре́л|иваться, -я́ться
zest /zest/ n. пыл; энтузиа́зм; ∼ **for life** жизнера́достность
zigzag /ˈzɪɡzæɡ/ n. зигза́г
  ● adj. зигзагообра́зный
  ● v.i. (**zigzagged, zigzagging**) де́лать (impf.) зигза́ги
Zimbabwe /zɪmˈbɑːbwɪ/ n. Зимба́бве (nt. indecl.)
Zimbabwean /zɪmˈbɑːbwɪən/ n. зимбабви́|ец (-йка)

  ● adj. зимбабви́йский
zinc /zɪŋk/ n. цинк
Zionism /ˈzaɪənɪz(ə)m/ n. сиони́зм
Zionist /ˈzaɪənɪst/ n. сиони́ст (-ка)
zip /zɪp/ n. **1** (also **zipper**) (застёжка-)мо́лния **2** (infml, energy) пыл, эне́ргия **3**: **Z**∼ **code** (AmE) (почто́вый) и́ндекс
  ● v.t. (**zipped, zipping**) (usu. ∼ **up**) застёг|ивать, -ну́ть (на мо́лнию)
  ● v.i. (**zipped, zipping**) (rush) мча́ться (impf.)
zit /zɪt/ n. (AmE, infml, pimple) пры́щик
zodiac /ˈzəʊdɪæk/ n. зодиа́к
zombie /ˈzɒmbɪ/ n. (fig., infml) вя́лый/апати́чный челове́к
⚡ **zone** /zəʊn/ n. зо́на, по́яс
zoo /zuː/ n. зоопа́рк
zoological /zəʊəˈlɒdʒɪk(ə)l/ adj. зоологи́ческий
  ■ ∼ **gardens** n. pl. зоопа́рк, зоологи́ческий сад
zoologist /zəʊˈɒlədʒɪst/ n. зоо́лог
zoology /zəʊˈɒlədʒɪ/ n. зооло́гия
zoom /zuːm/ n. (attr.): ∼ **lens** объекти́в с переме́нным фо́кусным расстоя́нием
  ● v.i. **1** (move quickly): **cars** ∼**ed past** маши́ны проноси́лись ми́мо **2** (phot., cin.): ∼ **in on** да|ва́ть, -ть кру́пный план + g.
zucchini /zʊˈkiːnɪ/ n. (pl. ∼ or ∼**s**) (AmE) кабачо́к
Zumba® /ˈzʊmbə/ n. зу́мба-фи́тнес (программа фитнеса, основанная на танцах под латиноамериканскую музыку)
Zurich /ˈzjʊərɪk/ n. Цю́рих

y

z

Contents

Glossary of grammatical terms

NB: Items in **bold** type refer the user to a separate entry in the glossary.

Accusative: In Russian, the **case** used to express the **direct object** of a **transitive verb**; also, the case used after certain prepositions.

Active: In an active **clause**, the **subject** of the verb performs the action, e.g. '*Sam* (subject) *identified* (verb) *the suspect*' (as opposed to the passive construction 'the suspect was identified by Sam', where *the suspect* is the subject but is not doing the identifying). Cf. **Passive**.

Adjectival noun: An adjective that functions as a noun, e.g. 'the *empties*' (= empty bottles), '*mobile*' (= mobile phone), 'the *Greens*' (= environmentalists), Russian *столóвая* 'dining room', *морóженое* 'ice cream'.

Adjective: A word that describes a **noun** or **pronoun**, giving information about its shape, colour, size, etc., e.g. *triangular, red, large, beautiful* in 'a *triangular* sign', 'the *red* dress', 'it is *large*', 'they are *beautiful*'.

Adverb: A word expressing the manner, frequency, time, place, or extent of an action, e.g. *slowly* and *often* in 'Sue walked *slowly*', 'He *often* stumbled'. Adverbs can also **modify** **clauses**, e.g. 'Sue *probably* went home', **adjectives**, e.g. 'Sue is *very* tall', and other adverbs, e.g. 'Sue left *extremely* early'.

Affirmative: An affirmative **sentence** or **clause** is a positive statement that explicitly asserts a state of affairs, e.g. *The taxi is waiting*. Cf. **Negative**.

Agree: Words are said to agree when they are put in the correct form in

relation to another word. In Standard English and in Russian, a singular noun or pronoun has to have a singular verb, e.g. '*he goes*' (Russian *он идёт*), and a plural noun or pronoun has to have a plural verb, e.g. '*they go*' (Russian *они идут*). **Demonstratives** also agree in **number** with the **nouns** they modify, e.g. '*this table*' (Russian *этот стол*), '*these tables*' (Russian *эти столы*). In Russian, adjectives, pronouns, and most declined numerals are in the same **case** as the noun they modify, and adjectives, nouns, and verbs have the same **gender** and **number**.

Animate accusative rule: A convention in Russian, whereby in some contexts the form of the accusative is identical with that of the genitive case. This applies **(a)** to masculine singular animate nouns: *Я вúжу мáльчика* 'I see the boy', **(b)** to all plural animate nouns: *Я вúжу мáльчиков/дéвочек/живóтных* 'I see the boys/girls/animals', **(c)** to pronouns, adjectives, and participles that agree with the nouns listed under (a) and (b): *Я знáю э{}тих нóвых учителéй* 'I know these new teachers', and **(d)** to the numerals *одúн, два/две, три, четы́ре*, and to *óба/óбе* (also all the collective numerals): *Онá пригласúла трёх подрýг* 'She invited three friends', *Он смотрéл на обóих брáтьев* 'He was looking at both brothers'.

Animate noun: A noun denoting a living being, e.g. *captain, elephant* (Russian *капитáн, слон*).

Antecedent: An earlier word, phrase, or clause to which another word (especially a following **relative**

pronoun) refers back, e.g. '*The man (whom) I know*' (Russian *Челове́к, кото́рого я зна́ю*).

Article: see **Definite article, Indefinite article**.

Aspect: A grammatical category of the verb that expresses the nature of an action or process, viewing it either as continuous or habitual (imperfective aspect), or as completed (perfective aspect). Cf. **Submeanings of the aspects**.

Attributive adjective: An **adjective** placed in front of the noun it modifies, e.g. *empty* in 'the *empty* house' (Russian *пусто́й дом*). Cf. **Predicative adjective**.

Auxiliary verb: In English, a verb which functions together with another verb to form a particular **tense** of the other verb, or to form the **passive**, a question, a **negative**, or an **imperative**. In Russian, the future of the verb *быть* 'to be' combines, as an auxiliary verb, with the infinitive of imperfective verbs to form the future of those verbs, e.g. *Я бу́ду рабо́тать* 'I will work', while the past and future tenses and the conditional mood of *быть* combine with the short forms of perfective passive participles to express past, future, and conditional meanings, e.g. *он был назна́чен* 'he was appointed', *он бу́дет назна́чен* 'he will be appointed', *он был бы назна́чен* 'he would be/would have been appointed'.

Case: In Russian, the form of a noun, pronoun, adjective, or numeral that shows its function within the **clause** (e.g. whether it is the **subject** or **object**). Russian has six cases (**nominative, accusative, genitive, dative, instrumental**, and **prepositional**).

Clause: A sentence, or part of a sentence, consisting of a **subject** and a **verb**, e.g. *Mike snores*, or a structure containing **participles** or **infinitives** (with no subject), e.g. '*While waiting* for a bus, I fell asleep' or 'I asked her *to call a taxi*'.

Collective: A term applied to nouns that denote a group of beings or objects, e.g. *herd* (Russian *ста́до*), *clientele* (Russian *клиенту́ра*), *luggage* (Russian *бага́ж*). In Russian, there are also collective numerals (for the numbers from two to ten), which denote a group of individuals, e.g. *дво́е* ('two'), *тро́е* ('three'), *де́сятеро* ('ten'), or combine with **plural-only nouns**.

Comparative: The form of an **adjective** or **adverb** used when comparing one thing with another, to express a greater degree of a quality, e.g. *cheaper, more expensive, more accurately* in 'this book is *cheaper*', 'a *more expensive* holiday ', 'he described it *more accurately*'. Cf. **Superlative**.

Compound: A word or phrase created by putting two or more existing forms together. In English and Russian, compounds are sometimes written as one word, sometimes as two, and sometimes hyphenated, e.g. *motorway* (Russian *автостра́да*), *good-humoured* (Russian *доброду́шный*), *drawing board* (Russian *чертёжная доска́*), *bow tie* (Russian *га́лстук-ба́бочка*).

Conditional: A verb form which expresses what would happen, or would have happened, if something else (had) occurred. English normally uses *if* with a form of the **auxiliary verb** *would* to express this notion: *If I won the lottery I would buy a car / If I had won... I would have bought....* Russian uses the particle *бы*: *Я пое́хал бы, е́сли бы бы́ло вре́мя* 'I *would* have gone if there had been time'.

Conjugate: To list the different forms or **inflections** of a verb as they vary according to tense, number, person, or voice, e.g. the verb 'to read' is conjugated in the present tense as follows: (I) *read*, (you) *read*, (he/she/it) *reads*, (we) *read*, (you) *read*, (they) *read*. Cf. the equivalent Russian conjugation of *чита́ть*: (я) *чита́ю*, (ты) *чита́ешь*, (он/она́/оно́) *чита́ет*, (мы) *чита́ем*, (вы) *чита́ете*, (они́) *чита́ют*.

Conjugation: In inflected languages, a class to which a verb is assigned according to how it is **conjugated**. In Russian, *чита́ть* belongs to the first (or -e-) conjugation and *говори́ть* belongs to the second (or -и-) conjugation.

Conjunction: A word whose function is to join single words, **clauses**, or **phrases**. Coordinating conjunctions (notably *and* and *or*) join words, clauses, or phrases, e.g. 'John *and* Mary', 'I'll go to the cinema *or* meet my friend for dinner'. Subordinating conjunctions (e.g. *that, because, while*) join clauses, e.g. 'I think *that* he is wrong', 'They left *because* it was late', 'I'll push *while* you lift'. Correlative conjunctions consist of words corresponding to each other and regularly used together, e.g. *both ... and*, *either ... or*.

Consonant: A speech sound that is produced with some restriction on the flow of air, e.g. *b, ch, r*. It can be combined with a **vowel** to form a **syllable**.

Consonant mutation: The change in a consonant when it occurs adjacent to another sound.

Continuous: A verb form indicating that an action or process is or was ongoing, e.g. 'He *is waiting*', 'She *was laughing*'. Also known as *progressive*.

Dative: In Russian, the **case** used to express the **indirect object** of a **verb**; also, the case used after certain prepositions and certain verbs.

Declension: In inflected languages, the class to which a noun is assigned according to how it is **declined**. Russian has three declensions. The first affects masculine nouns (except for those ending in -*a* or -*я*) and neuter nouns, the second feminine nouns (except for those ending in a soft sign), and the third feminine soft-sign nouns.

Decline: To list the different forms or **inflections** of a noun, adjective, pronoun, or numeral as they vary according to **case**. In English, only pronouns can really be said to decline, e.g. *he, him*.

Definite article: In English, the word *the*, which introduces a noun phrase and implies that the thing mentioned has already been mentioned or is common knowledge, e.g. '*the* book on *the* table'. Russian has no definite article, but achieves the same effect through word order (with the thing which has already been mentioned in first position in the sentence, e.g. *Кни́га на столе́* '*The* book is on the table'), or by using words such as *э́тот* 'this'. Cf. **Indefinite article**.

Delimitation: A process by which the meaning of an adjective is limited to a particular sphere, e.g. *Страна́ бога́та ле́сом* 'The country is rich *in* forest'.

Demonstrative: A word indicating the person or thing referred to, e.g. *this, that, these, those* in '*this* book' (Russian *э́та* кни́га), '*that* house' (Russian *тот* дом), '*these* books' (Russian *э́ти* кни́ги), '*those* people' (Russian *те* лю́ди).

Direct object: A word or phrase **governed** by a verb, e.g. *dogs* in 'She loves *dogs*' (Russian Она́ лю́бит *соба́к*). In an **active** sentence, the person or thing affected by the action is the direct object. In Russian, the direct object is usually expressed by the accusative case. Cf. **Indirect object**.

Direct speech: In direct speech, the speaker's words or thoughts are presented unchanged, using quotation marks, e.g. '"*The shops are still open,*" said Jill'. Russian uses « » (known as guillemets) to show direct speech. Cf. **Indirect speech**.

Emphatic pronoun: The pronouns *myself, himself, themselves*, etc., used for emphasis or to personalize, e.g. 'I did it *myself*'. Russian uses *сам*: Я *сам* сде́лал э́то.

Ending: A letter or letters added to the stem of a word when it is declined or conjugated, e.g. (in English) dog*s*, laugh*ed*, (in Russian) вод*а́* 'water', на стол*е́* 'on the table', зелё*ными* (instrumental plural) 'green', пиш*у́* 'I write', писа́*ла* 'she was writing'.

Feminine: see **Gender**.

Finite: A verb form which has a specific **tense**, **number**, and **person**, e.g. *rings* in 'She *rings* the doctor' (Russian Она *звонит* врачу). Here, *rings/звонит* is the third-person singular present tense of the verb *to ring/звонить*. A **clause** with a finite verb is called a finite clause. Cf. **Non-finite**.

Fleeting vowel: A vowel (*e*, *ё*, or *o*) that appears in some forms of a Russian word, but not in others, e.g. *e* in *болен* (masculine short form of *больной* 'sick'), *ё* in *сестёр* (genitive plural of *сестра* 'sister'), *o* in *сон* 'sleep' (genitive singular of *сна*), *разобью* (first-person singular of *разбить* 'to smash').

Future: The future **tense** is used when the time of the event described has not yet happened. English uses the auxiliary verbs *shall* and *will*, the present continuous, and *going to*, to express this notion: '*I shall meet* you in the restaurant', '*They will be* pleased', '*We're leaving* at six', '*I'm going to buy* a new car'. To express **imperfective** future meaning, Russian uses the future tense of *быть* + imperfective infinitive, e.g. Я *буду работать*, 'I *shall work*' or 'I *shall be working*'. To express **perfective** future meaning, Russian uses conjugated forms of the perfective verb, e.g. Я *спрошу* 'I *shall ask*'. Cf. **Aspect**.

Gender: In some languages, nouns and pronouns are divided into grammatical classes called genders. The gender of a noun or pronoun can affect the form of words such as verbs or adjectives that accompany them and may need to **agree** with them in gender. Russian has three genders, **masculine**, **feminine**, and **neuter**. The gender of a Russian noun can usually be identified from its ending: nouns ending in a consonant or *-й* are masculine (e.g. *стул* 'chair', *край* 'edge'); most nouns ending in *-a* or *-я* are feminine (e.g. *яма* 'hole', *шея* 'neck'), and nouns ending in *-o* or *-e* are neuter (e.g. *окно* 'window', *море* 'sea'). Gender in Russian applies in the singular only. Plural nouns and pronouns do not exhibit gender.

Genitive: In Russian, the **case** used to express possession; also, the case used after most cardinal numerals and after **indefinite numerals**, certain prepositions, and certain verbs.

Gerund: In English, a verb form in *-ing* that functions like a noun, e.g. *running* in 'She loves *running*' (cf. the Russian use of the **infinitive** in this meaning: Она *любит бегать*). By contrast, the Russian gerund is a verbal adverb that replaces a clause. The imperfective gerund usually ends in *-я* (e.g. Он стоит, *куря* 'He stands, *smoking*'), the perfective in *-в* (e.g. *Поужинав*, он встал '*Having dined*, he got up').

Govern: A word requiring a noun or pronoun to be in a particular **case** is said to govern the noun or pronoun (e.g. the Russian verb *владеть* 'to own' governs the instrumental case, and the preposition *через* 'across' governs the accusative case).

Hard consonant: A consonant that appears at the end of a word (e.g. final *-m* in *нет* 'no'), or is followed by *a*, *ы*, *o*, *y*, or (rarely) *э* (e.g. *г* and *m* in *газета* 'newspaper', *н* in *чёрный* 'black', *л* and *в* in *слово* 'word', *д* and *м* in *дума* 'duma'). Exceptions are the consonants ч and щ which are always soft even if at the end of a word or followed by the above-listed vowels, and ж, ц, and ш which are always hard. Cf. **Soft consonant**.

Historic present: Use of the present tense in order to make the description of a past event more vivid, e.g. 'Suddenly he *breaks* into a run'.

Imperative: The form of the verb used to express a command, e.g. *come* in '*Come* here!'

Imperfective: see **Aspect**.

Impersonal construction: A construction in which an action or state does not involve a specific person or thing as the grammatical subject, e.g. *Стемнело* 'It grew dark', *Как тебя зовут?* 'What is your name?'

Inanimate noun: A noun denoting a non-living thing, e.g. *hall, happiness* (Russian *зал, счáстье*).

Indeclinable: A term applied to a noun, pronoun, or adjective that has no **inflections**. In English, the pronoun *you* is indeclinable (whereas *I, he, she*, and *they* change to *me, him, her*, and *them* in the object case, e.g. the dog bit *me/you/him/her/them*). In Russian, many **loanwords** are indeclinable (e.g. *таксú* 'taxi', *беж adj.* 'beige'), as are the possessive pronouns *егó*, 'his/its', *её* 'her(s)/its', *их* 'their(s)'.

Indefinite adverb: An adverb that does not refer to any place, time, manner, etc. in particular, e.g. *somewhere, sometime, somehow* (Russian *гдé-то, когдá-то, кáк-то*).

Indefinite article: In English, the word *a/an*, which introduces a noun phrase and implies that the thing mentioned is non-specific, e.g. 'she bought *a* book'. Russian has no indefinite article, but achieves the same effect through word order (with an object mentioned for the first time appearing at the end of the sentence, e.g. На столé лежúт *кáрта* 'A map is lying on the table'). Cf. **Definite article**.

Indefinite numeral: In Russian, a numeral that denotes an indefinite quantity, e.g. *мнóго* 'much, many', *нéсколько* 'several'.

Indefinite pronoun: A pronoun that does not refer to any person or thing in particular, e.g. *someone* (Russian *ктó-то*), *something* (Russian *чтó-то*), *anyone* (Russian *ктó-нибудь*), *anything* (Russian *чтó-нибудь*).

Indicative: The form of a verb used to express a simple statement of fact, when an event is considered to be definitely taking place or to have taken place, e.g. 'He *is asleep*' (Russian Он *спит*), 'He *fell asleep*' (Russian Он *заснýл*). Cf. **Subjunctive**.

Indirect object: A word or phrase referring to the person who receives the **direct object**, e.g. *the driver* in

the sentences 'She gave the ticket to *the driver*' or 'She gave *the driver* the ticket'. In Russian, the indirect object is usually expressed by the dative case, e.g. Онá подарúла часы́ *сы́ну* 'She gave the watch *to her son*'. Cf. **Direct object**.

Indirect speech: In indirect speech, the speaker's words or thoughts are reported in a subordinate clause using a reporting verb. In English a change of tense and person is needed, e.g. 'He said "*I want* a drink"' (direct speech) becomes 'He said *he wanted* a drink'. In Russian, only the person changes, not the tense, e.g. Он сказáл: «*Я гóлоден*» 'He said "I'm hungry"' becomes Он сказáл, что *он гóлоден* 'He said that *he was* hungry'.

Infinitive: The basic form of the verb, e.g. *laugh, damage, be*. It is not bound to a particular subject or tense and in English is often preceded by *to* or by another verb, e.g. 'I want *to see* her', 'She came *to see* me', 'Let me *see*'. Russian infinitives end in *-ть, -ти*, or *-чь* (e.g. *писáть* 'to write', *вестú* 'to lead', *мочь* 'to be able').

Inflection: A change in the form of a word (usually the ending), to express tense, gender, number, or case, etc., e.g. the English plural ending *-s* in 'cars' or the past tense inflection *-ed* in 'I visit*ed* my uncle'. Russian is a highly-inflected language in which nouns, pronouns, adjectives, and numerals decline, and verbs conjugate. Cf. **Case, Conjugate, Conjugation, Declension**, and **Decline**.

Instrumental: In Russian, the **case** used to express the means by which something is done; also, the case used after certain prepositions and certain verbs.

Interrogative adverb: An adverb used to ask questions, e.g. *how* in 'How are you?' (Russian *Как* (вы) поживáете?) or *when* in 'When will they arrive?' (Russian *Когдá* онú приéдут?).

Interrogative pronoun: A pronoun used to ask questions, e.g. *which* in 'Which do you want?' (Russian *Какóй* вы хотúте?).

Intonation: The use of the pitch of the voice to convey meaning, e.g. *Well? Did you ask her?* (rising intonation) and *Well! I've never been so insulted!* (falling intonation). Different languages have different intonation patterns.

Intransitive verb: A verb not taking a **direct object**, e.g. slept in 'He slept soundly' (Russian Он крéпко *спал*), and read in 'He can't read' (Russian Он не умéет *читáть*). Cf. **Transitive verb**.

Invariable: another term for **indeclinable** (when referring to nouns, adjectives, and pronouns). Adverbs and gerunds are also invariable in Russian.

Irregular verb: In English, a verb such as 'sing' whose **inflections** do not follow one of the usual **conjugation** patterns of the language (past sang by contrast with the usual past tense suffix -*ed*, e.g. walk*ed*). In Russian, the only truly irregular verbs are *бежáть* 'to run', *дать* 'to give', *есть* 'to eat', and *хотéть* 'to want'. Cf. **Regular verb**.

Loanword: A word borrowed from another language, e.g. Russian *кóфе* 'coffee'.

Locative case: A term used as an alternative to the prepositional case to describe prepositional phrases that denote location and are introduced by *в* 'in' or *на* 'on': *в дóме* 'in the house', *на столé* 'on the table'. Some nouns have special locative forms in stressed *у*, *ю*, or *и*: *в лесý* 'in the forest', *на краю́* 'on the edge', *на двери́* 'on the door'.

Main clause: In a **sentence** with more than one **clause**, the clause which is not **subordinate** to any of the others is known as the main clause, e.g. 'Peter stopped' in 'When it got too dark to see where he was going, Peter stopped'. A main clause can stand alone as a sentence. Cf. **Subordinate clause**.

Masculine: see **Gender**.

Mobile stress: A feature of some Russian words whereby the stressed syllable changes in one or more forms of the word's declension or conjugation, etc. Stress may move from the stem

onto the ending, e.g. *стол* 'table', genitive singular *столá*; *слóво* 'word', nominative plural *словá*; *печь* 'stove', locative singular *печи́*; masculine short form *дóрог* 'is dear', feminine *дорогá*; *пять* 'five', genitive *пяти́*. It may also move from the ending onto the stem, e.g. *рекá* 'river', accusative singular *рéку* (also *рекý*); *окнó* 'window', nominative plural *óкна*. In conjugation, stress shift occurs only from the ending onto the stem, e.g. *пишý* 'I write', *пи́шет* 'he writes'.

Modify: A word or phrase modifies another word or phrase when it provides additional information about it. Modifying expressions include **adjectives**, e.g. *slow* in 'A *slow* train', and **adverbs**, e.g. *slowly* in 'The train moved *slowly*'.

Negative: A negative **sentence** or **clause** asserts that something is not the case, using a negative **particle**, e.g. '*The taxi is not waiting*'. Similarly, a negative **adverb** (*nowhere, never*) or negative **pronoun** (*nobody, nothing*). Cf. **Affirmative**.

Neuter: see **Gender**.

Nominative: In Russian, the **case** used to express the **subject** of a clause.

Non-finite: A term applied to a verb form which has no specific **tense**, **number**, or **person**, e.g. *waiting* in 'While *waiting* for a bus, Peter read the paper'. Russian uses a **gerund** in such contexts, e.g. *Ожидáя* автóбус, Пи́тер читáл газéту. Cf. **Finite**.

Noun: A word that identifies a person, e.g. *milkman, girl, uncle*, a physical object, e.g. *cup, book, building*, or an abstract notion, e.g. *beauty, health, unpleasantness*.

Noun phrase: A group of words including a noun, which functions in a sentence as subject, object, or prepositional object.

Number: A grammatical classification whereby a word is either **singular** or **plural**.

Numeral: A word expressing a number. Members of the series of numbers *one, two,* etc. are referred to as cardinal numbers or cardinal numerals. Members of the series *first, second,* etc. are referred to as ordinal numbers or ordinal numerals. Russian also has a series of collective numerals, e.g. *двóе* in *двóе* детéй 'two children', *трóе* in *трóе* сáнок 'three sledges'.

Object: see **Direct object**, **Indirect object**.

Oblique cases: All **cases** other than the **nominative**.

Participle: In English, a word formed from a verb and used as an adjective or as a noun, or to form compound verb forms. The English present participle ends in *-ing*, e.g. '*Thinking* I was late, I hurried' (Russian uses a **gerund** in such contexts: *Дýмая,* что я опáздываю, я торопúлся), and the past participle ends in *-ed*, e.g. 'I have *finished*' (Russian uses a **finite verb** in such contexts: Я кóнчил). Russian has four participles, present active, past active, present passive, and past passive, which either replace **relative clauses**, e.g. Дéвочка, *читáющая/ читáвшая/прочитáвшая* кнúгу 'the girl *who is reading/who was reading/who has read* the book', мотóр, *провéренный* механиками 'an engine *which has been checked* by the mechanics', or (using the short form of the past passive participle) function as **predicates**, e.g. Дом *прóдан* 'The house *has been sold*'.

Particle: In Russian, a word or a part of a word that invests other words or phrases with expressive nuances of meaning, e.g. *Не* я ошúбся! 'I'm not the one who got it wrong!', *Ну* и проголодáлся же я! 'Am I hungry!'

Partitive genitive: The genitive case used to denote a part, as opposed to the whole, of a substance, e.g. мнóго *молокá* 'a lot of milk', кусóк *мя́са* 'a piece of meat'. Some nouns have special partitive genitive forms in *-у* or *-ю*: тарéлка сýп*у* 'a plate of soup', Хóчешь ча́*ю*? 'Would you like some tea?'

Part of speech: Any of the classes into which words are categorized for grammatical purposes. The main ones are **Noun**, **Adjective**, **Pronoun**, **Verb**, **Adverb**, **Preposition**, and **Conjunction**.

Passive: The form of the **clause** used when the individual referred to by the **subject** undergoes (rather than performs) the action, e.g. '*The soldier was nominated* for an award' (Russian Солдáт был представлен к нагрáде). Cf. **Active**.

Past: The past **tense** is used when the time of the event described precedes the time of utterance, e.g. 'Peter *lived* in London'. Cf. **Present**.

Perfect: A verb form indicating an action or process seen as completed, e.g. 'She *has paid* the bill'. In Russian this is rendered by a perfective past form of the verb, e.g. Онá *оплатúла* счёт.

Perfective: see **Aspect**.

Person: Person forms are the grammatical forms (especially **pronouns**) that refer to or agree with the speaker and other individuals addressed or mentioned, e.g. *I, we* (first-person pronouns, Russian я, мы), *you* (second-person pronoun, Russian ты, вы), *he, she, it, they* (third-person pronouns, Russian он, онá, онó, онú).

Personal pronoun: A **pronoun** that refers to a person or to people known to the speaker, e.g. *I, he, she, it, they* (Russian я, он, онá, онó, онú).

Phrase: A group of words that function together in a **clause**, e.g. *The courier* is a (noun) phrase within the clause '*The courier* will go there'.

Plural: A word or form referring to more than one person or object, e.g. *children, books, we, are*. Cf. **Singular**.

Plural-only noun: A noun that has the form of a plural but can refer to a singular object or a number of like objects, e.g. *сáнки* 'sledge, sledges'.

Possessive: A pronoun indicating possession, e.g. Russian *мой* 'my, mine', *твой* 'your, yours', *егó* 'his, its', *её* 'her, hers, its', *наш* 'our, ours', *ваш* 'your, yours', *их* 'their, theirs'. Possessives are used both adjectivally (e.g. *наш дом* 'our house') and pronominally (e.g. *Этот дом — наш* 'This house is ours').

Predicate: The part of a clause that states something about the **subject**, e.g. *closed the door softly* in 'Mary *closed the door softly*', or *went home* in 'We *went home*'. Cf. **Subject**.

Predicative adjective: An **adjective** that appears in a separate **phrase** from the noun it modifies, often following the verb 'to be', e.g. *empty* in 'The house was *empty*'. Russian often uses a short-form adjective in such contexts: Дом был *пуст*. Cf. **Attributive adjective**.

Predicative adverb: In Russian, an adverb that is used as a predicate, e.g. *Весело* 'It's fun', Ему *грустно* 'He feels sad'.

Prefix: An element that is added to the beginning of a word to change its meaning or grammatical form, e.g. *mis-* and *re-* in '*mis*understand', '*re*consider', Russian *при-* in *при*бáвить 'to add' and *от-* in *от*платúть 'to pay back'. Cf. **Suffix**.

Preposition: A word governing and usually preceding a noun or pronoun, expressing its relationship to another word in the sentence, e.g. 'She arrived *after* dinner', 'What did you do it *for*?' This relationship can be spatial, e.g. 'The book is *on* the table' (Russian Кнúга *на* столé), temporal, e.g. 'He arrived *in* March' (Russian Он приéхал *в* мáрте), causal, e.g. 'She blushed *with* shame' (Russian Онá покраснéла *от* стыдá), etc. A Russian preposition governs one of the **oblique cases**.

Prepositional: In Russian, the **case** used after certain prepositions, mainly to express location. See also **Locative case**.

Present: The present **tense** is used when the time of the event described includes the time of utterance, e.g. *lives* in 'Peter *lives* in London'. Cf. **Past**.

Progressive: another term for **Continuous**.

Pronoun: A word that substitutes for a noun or noun phrase, e.g. *them* in 'Children don't like *them*' (instead of 'Children don't like *vegetables*'). Cf. Russian Дéти не любят *их* (instead of *овощéй*).

Reflexive pronoun: A pronoun that is the object of the verb, but refers back to the subject of the clause in denoting the same individual, e.g. *herself* in: 'She blamed *herself*'. Russian uses the declinable reflexive pronoun *себя́* in such contexts, e.g. Он смóтрит на *себя́* 'He looks at *himself*', Он купúл *себé* мотоцúкл, 'He bought *himself* a motorcycle', Онá довóльна *собóй* 'She is pleased with *herself*'. Cf. also **Reflexive verb**.

Reflexive verb: In Russian, a verb that ends in the reflexive particle *-ся/-сь*, e.g. Он одевáется 'He dresses (*himself*)', Я мóюсь 'I wash (*myself*)'.

Regular verb: A verb such as *laugh* whose **inflections** follow one of the usual **conjugation** patterns. In English, this involves (among other things) forming the **past tense** by adding *-ed* to the infinitive, e.g. laugh*ed* in 'They *laughed* at me'. Cf. **Irregular verb**.

Relative clause: A clause that is introduced by a **relative pronoun**.

Relative pronoun: A pronoun (*who, whose, which,* or *that*) used to introduce a subordinate clause and referring back to a person or thing in the preceding clause, e.g. 'Peter lost the book *that/which* he bought', 'The man *who* is waiting is my brother', or 'Have you met the man *whose* sister got married?' Russian uses the relevant forms of *котóрый*.

Reported speech: another term for **Indirect speech**.

Sentence: A structure with at least one **finite** verb, and consisting of one or more **clauses**, e.g. '*John laughed*', '*John sat down and waited*', '*While waiting for the bus, John saw an accident*'.

Singular: A word or form referring to just one person or thing, e.g. *child*, *book*, *I*, *is*. Cf. **Plural**.

Soft consonant: In Russian, a consonant followed by a soft sign (e.g. *m* in *мать*), or by the vowels *я, е, и, ё*, or *ю* (e.g. *n* in *пять*, *н* in *нёбо*, *n* in *пиво*, *л* in *лёд*, *m* in *утюг*). The consonants *ч* and *щ* are always pronounced soft, while *ж, ц*, and *ш* are always pronounced hard. Cf. **Hard consonant**.

Spelling rules: In Russian, the following rules:

(a) *ы* is replaced by *и* after г, к, х, ж, ч, ш, and щ.

(b) unstressed *о* is replaced by *e* after ж, ч, ш, щ, and ц.

(c) *ю* and *я* are replaced by *у* and *а* after г, к, х, ж, ч, ш, and щ.

(d) the preposition *о* 'about, concerning' is spelt *об* before words beginning *a, э, и, о*, and *y*, and *обо* before *мне* and *всём/всех*: *обо мне* 'about me', *обо всём* 'about everything', *обо всех* 'about everyone'.

Stem: The base form or root of the word to which **endings**, **prefixes**, and **suffixes** may be added, e.g. *box* in *box*es, *consider* in 're*consider*' and *understand* in '*understand*ing'. Cf. Russian *книг-* in *книг*а 'book', *говор-* in *говор*и́ть 'to speak', and *-ход* in вос*хо́д* 'rising', *студе́нт-* in *студе́нт*ка 'female student'.

Stress: The **syllable** of a word receiving relatively greater force or emphasis than the other(s) is said to receive stress or to be the stressed syllable, e.g. *wín*dow, *ка́рта* 'map' (stressed on the first syllable), *dedúc*tion, *доро́га* 'road' (stressed medially), *suppóse*, *страна́* 'country' (stressed on the final syllable).

Subject: The part of the **clause** referring to the individual of whom or the object of which the **predicate** is asserted, e.g. *Anna* in: '*Anna* closed the door' or *The picture* in '*The picture* hangs on the wall'. In Russian, the subject usually appears in the nominative case, e.g. *А́нна закры́ла дверь*, *Карти́на виси́т на стене́*. Cf. **Predicate**.

Subjunctive: The form of the verb used in some languages when no claim is being made that the action or event actually takes (or took) place. The subjunctive is not often used in English, but can still be seen in expressions like *if I were you*. In Russian, the subjunctive is the structure used when an action is desired. It is formed using *чтобы* + past tense, e.g. *Она́ хо́чет, чтобы я ушёл* ('She wants me *to go away*'). Cf. **Indicative**.

Submeanings of the aspects: Aspectual meanings other than those that denote continuous or habitual action or process (imperfective), and those that denote completion (perfective). Submeanings describe intermittent action or process (imperfective *побаливает* 'hurts on and off'), inception (perfective *заплакать* 'to burst into tears'), and short duration (perfective *поспать* 'to have a nap'). Cf. **Aspect**.

Subordinate clause: A clause that cannot normally stand alone without a **main clause** and is usually introduced by a **conjunction**, e.g. *when it rang* in 'She answered the phone *when it rang*', or *because he is ill* in 'He is not at work *because he is ill*'. Cf. **Main clause**.

Suffix: An element that is added to the end of a word or **stem** to change its meaning or grammatical form, e.g. *-ing* and *-ness* in 'understand*ing*', 'kind*ness*', Russian *-ка* in *студе́нт*ка 'female student', *-ина́* in *глубина́* 'depth'. Cf. **Prefix**.

Superlative: The form of an **adjective** or **adverb** used when comparing one thing with another to express the greatest degree of a quality, e.g. *cheapest* (Russian *са́мый дешёвый*), *most beautiful* (Russian *са́мый краси́вый*), *least desirable* (Russian *наиме́нее жела́тельный*). Cf. **Comparative**.

Syllable: A unit of pronunciation that is normally less than a word but greater than a single sound, e.g. *abracadabra* has five syllables: *ab-ra-ca-dab-ra*, as does Russian *путеводи́тель* ('guide'): *пу-те-во-ди́-тель*.

Tense: The relationship between the time of utterance and the time of an event described in the clause is expressed by verb tense forms or **inflections**, e.g. 'Anna *waits*' (present tense, Russian А́нна *ждёт*), 'Anna *waited*' (past tense, Russian А́нна *ждала́*).

Transitive verb: A verb taking a **direct object**, e.g. *read* in 'She *was reading* a book' (Russian Она́ *чита́ла* кни́гу). Cf. **Intransitive verb**.

Verb: A word that expresses an action, process, or state of affairs, e.g. 'He closed the door' (Russian Он *закры́л* дверь), 'She laughs' (Russian Она́ *смеётся*), 'They were at home' (Russian Они́ *бы́ли* до́ма).

Verbal noun: In Russian, a noun derived from a verb stem and describing the action of the verb from which it derives, e.g. *разви́тие* 'development', *приготовле́ние* 'preparation', *обрабо́тка* 'processing'.

Verbs of motion: In Russian, a series of fourteen pairs of imperfective verbs that denote various types of motion, one in each pair (the 'unidirectional') describing movement in one direction (*Он идёт домо́й* 'He is on his way home'), the other (the 'multidirectional') describing movement in general (*Она́ хо́дит бы́стро* 'She walks fast'), movement in various directions (*Он хо́дит взад и вперёд* 'He is walking up and down'), or habitual movement (*Я ча́сто хожу́ в кино́* 'I often go to the cinema').

Vocative: In Russian, the form of a noun used in addressing someone. The nominative case usually fulfils this function: *Серге́й Па́влович!* 'Sergei Pavlovich!', but some truncated forms are used in colloquial Russian, e.g. *мам!* 'Mum!', *Вань!* 'Vanya!' *Бо́же* in *Бо́же мой!* 'My God!' is a relic of the former vocative case (the nominative form being *Бог*).

Voiced and voiceless consonants: Consonants pronounced, respectively, with and without vibration of the vocal cords. In Russian, the voiceless consonants are к, п, с, т, ф, х, ц, ч, ш, and щ. The other consonants are voiced.

Vowel: A basic speech sound that is produced by the unrestricted flow of air, e.g. *a* in h*a*t, *ee* in f*ee*t, or *ow* in h*ow*. A vowel forms the nucleus of a **syllable**. Cf. **Consonant**.

Russian declensions and conjugations

The following is a comprehensive but not exhaustive guide to Russian declension and conjugation.

The vertical line | shows the division between the stem and the ending of a word.

When using these tables, the reader should bear in mind the Spelling Rules (see below), e.g. the nominative plural of кни́га is кни́ги, and the Notes on the declension of nouns (after Table 17 below).

Spelling Rules

The following Spelling Rules are important because they affect the endings of many nouns, adjectives, and verbs.

1. Unstressed o does not follow ж, ц, ч, ш, or щ; instead, e is used, e.g. с му́жем, шесть, ме́сяцев, с касси́ршей, хоро́шее пальто́.

2. ю and я do not follow г, к, х, ц, ч, ш, or щ; they become у and a, e.g. держа́ть; я держу́, они́ де́ржат; слы́шать: я слы́шу, они́ слы́шат.

3. ы does not follow г, к, ж, х, ч, ш, or щ; it becomes и, e.g. две кни́ги, больши́е дома́.

Nouns

Masculine Nouns

TABLE		Singular	Plural
1	Nominative	авто́бус	авто́бус|ы
	Accusative	авто́бус	авто́бус|ы
	Genitive	авто́бус|а	авто́бус|ов
	Dative	авто́бус|у	авто́бус|ам
	Instrumental	авто́бус|ом	авто́бус|ами
	Prepositional	авто́бус|е	авто́бус|ах

This declension, comprising nouns ending in a hard consonant, is the most common declension for masculine nouns in Russian.

TABLE		Singular	Plural
2	Nominative	трамва́|й	трамва́|и
	Accusative	трамва́|й	трамва́|и
	Genitive	трамва́|я	трамва́|ев
	Dative	трамва́|ю	трамва́|ям
	Instrumental	трамва́|ем	трамва́|ями
	Prepositional	трамва́|е	трамва́|ях

This declension consists of nouns ending in -ай, -ей, -ой, or -уй.

Other common Russian words belonging to this declension are май, сара́й, слу́чай, урожа́й, чай; клей, руче́й, хокке́й, юбиле́й; бой, геро́й; поцелу́й.

TABLE 3		Singular	Plural
	Nominative	репорта́ж	репорта́ж|и
	Accusative	репорта́ж	репорта́ж|и
	Genitive	репорта́ж|а	репорта́ж|ей
	Dative	репорта́ж|у	репорта́ж|ам
	Instrumental	репорта́ж|ем	репорта́ж|ами
	Prepositional	репорта́ж|е	репорта́ж|ах

This declension consists of nouns ending in -ж, -ш, or -щ, which are stressed on the stem in oblique cases.

Other nouns of this declension are пейза́ж, пляж, фарш, о́вощ, and това́рищ.

TABLE 4		Singular	Plural
	Nominative	эта́ж	этаж|и́
	Accusative	эта́ж	этаж|и́
	Genitive	этаж|а́	этаж|е́й
	Dative	этаж|у́	этаж|а́м
	Instrumental	этаж|о́м	этаж|а́ми
	Prepositional	этаж|е́	этаж|а́х

These nouns differ from those in Table 3 by being stressed on the ending rather than on the stem in oblique cases; in the instrumental singular they end in -о́м instead of -ем.

Other such nouns are бага́ж, борщ, каранда́ш, нож, and плащ.

TABLE 5		Singular	Plural
	Nominative	сцена́ри|й	сцена́ри|и
	Accusative	сцена́ри|й	сцена́ри|и
	Genitive	сцена́ри|я	сцена́ри|ев
	Dative	сцена́ри|ю	сцена́ри|ям
	Instrumental	сцена́ри|ем	сцена́ри|ями
	Prepositional	сцена́ри|и	сцена́ри|ях

Nouns belonging to this declension tend to be obscure or technical terms. One fairly common word is ге́ний, meaning 'genius'.

TABLE 6		Singular	Plural
	Nominative	спекта́кл|ь	спекта́кл|и
	Accusative	спекта́кл|ь	спекта́кл|и
	Genitive	спекта́кл|я	спекта́кл|ей
	Dative	спекта́кл|ю	спекта́кл|ям
	Instrumental	спекта́кл|ем	спекта́кл|ями
	Prepositional	спекта́кл|е	спекта́кл|ях

Masculine nouns ending in a soft sign belong to this declension. Other common words belonging to this group are автомоби́ль, апре́ль (and other names of months), Кремль, портфе́ль, рубль, and слова́рь.

Feminine nouns

TABLE 7	Singular	Plural
Nominative	газе́т|а	газе́т|ы
Accusative	газе́т|у	газе́т|ы
Genitive	газе́т|ы	газе́т
Dative	газе́т|е	газе́т|ам
Instrumental	газе́т|ой	газе́т|ами
Prepositional	газе́т|е	газе́т|ах

This is the most common declension for feminine nouns in Russian. A few masculine nouns, e.g. де́душка, мужчи́на, and па́па, also belong to this declension.

Remember the Spelling Rules, whereby ы and unstressed o do not follow certain letters (see p. 838), e.g. кни́ги (*books*), афи́ши (*posters*), с учени́цей (*with the pupil*).

TABLE 8	Singular	Plural
Nominative	неде́л|я	неде́л|и
Accusative	неде́л|ю	неде́л|и
Genitive	неде́л|и	неде́л|ь
Dative	неде́л|е	неде́л|ям
Instrumental	неде́л|ей	неде́л|ями
Prepositional	неде́л|е	неде́л|ях

This declension is for feminine nouns ending in a consonant + -я. A few masculine nouns also belong to this declension, e.g. дя́дя, судья́. Other feminine nouns of this declension are ба́шня, дере́вня, пе́сня, спа́льня, and ту́фля. Some nouns of this declension have a genitive plural form ending in -ей, e.g. дя́дя, семья́, and тётя. This is indicated at the dictionary entries.

TABLE 9	Singular	Plural
Nominative	ста́нци|я	ста́нци|и
Accusative	ста́нци|ю	ста́нци|и
Genitive	ста́нци|и	ста́нци|й
Dative	ста́нци|и	ста́нци|ям
Instrumental	ста́нци|ей	ста́нци|ями
Prepositional	ста́нци|и	ста́нци|ях

This declension consists of feminine nouns ending in -ия. Other nouns of this declension are а́рмия, исто́рия, ли́ния, организа́ция, фами́лия, and the names of most countries.

TABLE 10	Singular	Plural
Nominative	галере́|я	галере́|и
Accusative	галере́|ю	галере́|и
Genitive	галере́|и	галере́|й
Dative	галере́|е	галере́|ям
Instrumental	галере́|ей	галере́|ями
Prepositional	галере́|е	галере́|ях

This declension consists of feminine nouns ending in -ея or -уя. Other such nouns are алле́я, батаре́я, иде́я, ше́я, and ста́туя.

TABLE		Singular	Plural
11	Nominative	бол|ь	бо́л|и
	Accusative	бол|ь	бо́л|и
	Genitive	бо́л|и	бо́л|ей
	Dative	бо́л|и	бо́л|ям
	Instrumental	бо́л|ью	бо́л|ями
	Prepositional	бо́л|и	бо́л|ях

This declension is for feminine nouns ending in -ь. Other such nouns are жизнь, крова́ть, ме́бель, пло́щадь, посте́ль, тетра́дь, and the numbers ending in -ь.

Neuter Nouns

TABLE		Singular	Plural
12	Nominative	чу́вств|о	чу́вств|а
	Accusative	чу́вств|о	чу́вств|а
	Genitive	чу́вств|а	чувств
	Dative	чу́вств|у	чу́вств|ам
	Instrumental	чу́вств|ом	чу́вств|ами
	Prepositional	чу́вств|е	чу́вств|ах

This declension is for neuter nouns ending in -o. Other such nouns are блю́до, ма́сло, молоко́, пи́во, and сло́во.

TABLE		Singular	Plural
13	Nominative	учи́лищ|е	учи́лищ|а
	Accusative	учи́лищ|е	учи́лищ|а
	Genitive	учи́лищ|а	учи́лищ
	Dative	учи́лищ|у	учи́лищ|ам
	Instrumental	учи́лищ|ем	учи́лищ|ами
	Prepositional	учи́лищ|е	учи́лищ|ах

This declension is for neuter nouns ending in -ще or -це. Other nouns of this declension are кла́дбище, полоте́нце, and со́лнце.

TABLE		Singular	Plural
14	Nominative	зда́ни|е	зда́ни|я
	Accusative	зда́ни|е	зда́ни|я
	Genitive	зда́ни|я	зда́ни|й
	Dative	зда́ни|ю	зда́ни|ям
	Instrumental	зда́ни|ем	зда́ни|ями
	Prepositional	зда́ни|и	зда́ни|ях

This declension is for neuter nouns ending in -ие. Other such nouns are внима́ние, путеше́ствие, and удивле́ние.

TABLE		Singular	Plural
15	Nominative	воскресе́н|ье	воскресе́н|ья
	Accusative	воскресе́н|ье	воскресе́н|ья
	Genitive	воскресе́н|ья	воскресе́н|ий
	Dative	воскресе́н|ью	воскресе́н|ьям
	Instrumental	воскресе́н|ьем	воскресе́н|ьями
	Prepositional	воскресе́н|ье	воскресе́н|ьях

This declension is for neuter nouns ending in -ье or -ьё. Other such nouns are варе́нье, сиде́нье, and сча́стье.

TABLE		Singular	Plural
16	Nominative	мóр|е	мор|я́
	Accusative	мóр|е	мор|я́
	Genitive	мóр|я	мор|éй
	Dative	мóр|ю	мор|я́м
	Instrumental	мóр|ем	мор|я́ми
	Prepositional	мóр|е	мор|я́х

This declension is for neuter nouns ending in a consonant + -e, but not -ще or -це.
In practice, the only other two nouns of this declension are гóре and пóле.

TABLE		Singular	Plural
17	Nominative	врéм|я	врем|ена́
	Accusative	врéм|я	врем|ена́
	Genitive	врéм|ени	врем|ён
	Dative	врéм|ени	врем|ена́м
	Instrumental	врéм|енем	врем|ена́ми
	Prepositional	врéм|ени	врем|ена́х

This declension is for a small number of neuter nouns ending in -мя. Others
belonging to this group are и́мя, пла́мя, and сéмя.

Notes on the declension of nouns

The accusative ending for masculine singular animate and all plural animate nouns
(those denoting living beings) coincides with the genitive ending, e.g.

он уви́дел большо́го чёрного во́лка (he saw a big black wolf)
мы попроси́ли свои́х друзéй помо́чь (we asked our friends to help)

Some masculine nouns take the ending -ý or -ю́ in the prepositional singular after
в and на, e.g. в лесý, на мостý; some feminine nouns ending in -ь take -и́, e.g. в тени́.
They are said to be in the locative case. Where this happens it is shown at the
dictionary entry.

Some masculine nouns have the ending -a in the nominative plural, e.g. па́спорт,
бéрег. Others have the ending -ья, e.g. брат, стул. Where this happens it is shown
at the dictionary entry.

Some nouns are indeclinable. They usually end in a vowel, are neuter, and have been
borrowed into Russian from another language. Examples are кафé, ра́дио, такси́.

Many nouns change their stress in declension. This is shown in the individual
dictionary entries.

Verbs

The -e- conjugation

чита́\|ть:

TABLE		Singular	Plural
18	1st person	чита́|ю	чита́|ем
	2nd person	чита́|ешь	чита́|ете
	3rd person	чита́|ет	чита́|ют

сия|ть:

TABLE		Singular	Plural
19	1st person	сия|ю	сия|ем
	2nd person	сия|ешь	сия|ете
	3rd person	сия|ет	сия|ют

Verbs of this type differ from those belonging to Table 18 only by having a я at the end of the stem, instead of an а.

про́б|овать:

TABLE		Singular	Plural
20	1st person	про́б|ую	про́б|уем
	2nd person	про́б|уешь	про́б|уете
	3rd person	про́б|ует	про́б|уют

The verbs of this conjugation are not stressed on the suffix -овать.

рис|ова́ть:

TABLE		Singular	Plural
21	1st person	рис|у́ю	рис|у́ем
	2nd person	рис|у́ешь	рис|у́ете
	3rd person	рис|у́ет	рис|у́ют

Verbs of this conjugation differ from those belonging to Table 20 only in having the stress on the suffix rather than on the stem.

Note: The conjugation of other -e- conjugation verbs (those ending in -ать, -еть, -нуть, and -ять) is given in the dictionary entries.

The -i- conjugation

говор|и́ть:

TABLE		Singular	Plural
22	1st person	говор|ю́	говор|и́м
	2nd person	говор|и́шь	говор|и́те
	3rd person	говор|и́т	говор|я́т

стро́|ить:

TABLE		Singular	Plural
23	1st person	стро́|ю	стро́|им
	2nd person	стро́|ишь	стро́|ите
	3rd person	стро́|ит	стро́|ят

Verbs of this conjugation differ from those belonging to Table 22 by ending in a vowel + -ить. Other examples are кле́ить, сто́ить.

Note: The conjugation of other -i- conjugation verbs (those ending in -ать, -еть, and -ять) is given in the dictionary entries.

In addition, where the stem of a verb ends in б, п, м, в, or ф, and an л is inserted before the ending of the first person singular, this is shown in the dictionary entries (e.g. люби́ть: я люблю́; спать: я сплю).

Also, where the consonant at the end of the stem changes in the first person singular, this is shown in the dictionary entries (e.g. ви́деть: я ви́жу; плати́ть: я плачу́; спроси́ть: я спрошу́).

Adjectives

TABLE 24a	Singular			Plural
	Masculine	**Feminine**	**Neuter**	
Nominative	краси́в|ый	краси́в|ая	краси́в|ое	краси́в|ые
Accusative	краси́в|ый	краси́в|ую	краси́в|ое	краси́в|ые
Genitive	краси́в|ого	краси́в|ой	краси́в|ого	краси́в|ых
Dative	краси́в|ому	краси́в|ой	краси́в|ому	краси́в|ым
Instrumental	краси́в|ым	краси́в|ой	краси́в|ым	краси́в|ыми
Prepositional	краси́в|ом	краси́в|ой	краси́в|ом	краси́в|ых

Note: The words кото́рый and како́й decline like краси́вый, as do the ordinal numbers пе́рвый, второ́й, etc. Note that тре́тий has 'soft' endings and inserts a soft sign (-тья, -тье, -тьи).

Soft Adjectives

TABLE 24b	Singular			Plural
	Masculine	**Feminine**	**Neuter**	
Nominative	си́н|ий	си́н|яя	си́н|ее	си́н|ие
Accusative	си́н|ий	си́н|юю	си́н|ее	си́н|ие
Genitive	си́н|его	си́н|ей	си́н|его	си́н|их
Dative	си́н|ему	си́н|ей	си́н|ему	си́н|им
Instrumental	си́н|им	си́н|ей	си́н|им	си́н|ими
Prepositional	си́н|ем	си́н|ей	си́н|ем	си́н|их

Determiners/pronouns

мой (and similarly твой, свой):

TABLE 25	Singular			Plural
	Masculine	**Feminine**	**Neuter**	
Nominative	мой	моя́	моё	мои́
Accusative	мой	мою́	моё	мои́
Genitive	моего́	мое́й	моего́	мои́х
Dative	моему́	мое́й	моему́	мои́м
Instrumental	мои́м	мое́й	мои́м	мои́ми
Prepositional	моём	мое́й	моём	мои́х

наш (and similarly ваш)

	Singular			Plural
	Masculine	**Feminine**	**Neuter**	
Nominative	наш	на́ша	на́ше	на́ши
Accusative	наш	на́шу	на́ше	на́ши
Genitive	на́шего	на́шей	на́шего	на́ших
Dative	на́шему	на́шей	на́шему	на́шим
Instrumental	на́шим	на́шей	на́шим	на́шими
Prepositional	на́шем	на́шей	на́шем	на́ших

The other possessive determiners, его́, её, and их, are indeclinable.

э́тот:

TABLE 26		Singular			Plural
		Masculine	Feminine	Neuter	
	Nominative	э́тот	э́та	э́то	э́ти
	Accusative	э́тот	э́ту	э́то	э́ти
	Genitive	э́того	э́той	э́того	э́тих
	Dative	э́тому	э́той	э́тому	э́тим
	Instrumental	э́тим	э́той	э́тим	э́тими
	Prepositional	э́том	э́той	э́том	э́тих

сам, the emphatic pronoun, declines like **э́тот** and is stressed on the final syllable.

тот:

	Singular			Plural
	Masculine	Feminine	Neuter	
Nominative	тот	та	то	те
Accusative	тот	ту	то	те
Genitive	того́	той	того́	тех
Dative	тому́	той	тому́	тем
Instrumental	тем	той	тем	те́ми
Prepositional	том	той	том	тех

весь:

TABLE 27		Singular			Plural
		Masculine	Feminine	Neuter	
	Nominative	весь	вся	всё	все
	Accusative	весь	всю	всё	все
	Genitive	всего́	всей	всего́	всех
	Dative	всему́	всей	всему́	всем
	Instrumental	всем	всей	всем	все́ми
	Prepositional	всём	всей	всём	всех

Numbers

Cardinal Numbers		Ordinal Numbers	
one	оди́н/одна́/одно́	first	пе́рвый
two	два/две	second	второ́й
three	три	third	тре́тий
four	четы́ре	fourth	четвёртый
five	пять	fifth	пя́тый
six	шесть	sixth	шесто́й
seven	семь	seventh	седьмо́й
eight	во́семь	eighth	восьмо́й
nine	де́вять	ninth	девя́тый
ten	де́сять	tenth	деся́тый
eleven	оди́ннадцать	eleventh	оди́ннадцатый
twelve	двена́дцать	twelfth	двена́дцатый
thirteen	трина́дцать	thirteenth	трина́дцатый
fourteen	четы́рнадцать	fourteenth	четы́рнадцатый
fifteen	пятна́дцать	fifteenth	пятна́дцатый
sixteen	шестна́дцать	sixteenth	шестна́дцатый
seventeen	семна́дцать	seventeenth	семна́дцатый
eighteen	восемна́дцать	eighteenth	восемна́дцатый
nineteen	девятна́дцать	nineteenth	девятна́дцатый
twenty	два́дцать	twentieth	двадца́тый
twenty-one	два́дцать оди́н/одна́/одно́	twenty-first	два́дцать пе́рвый
twenty-two	два́дцать два/две	twenty-second	два́дцать второ́й
twenty-three	два́дцать три	twenty-third	два́дцать тре́тий
thirty	три́дцать	thirtieth	тридца́тый
forty	со́рок	fortieth	сороково́й
fifty	пятьдеся́т	fiftieth	пятидеся́тый
sixty	шестьдеся́т	sixtieth	шестидеся́тый
seventy	се́мьдесят	seventieth	семидеся́тый
eighty	во́семьдесят	eightieth	восьмидеся́тый
ninety	девяно́сто	nintieth	девяно́стый
hundred	сто	hundredth	со́тый
hundred and one	сто оди́н/одна́/одно́	hundred-and-first	сто пе́рвый
two hundred	две́сти	two-hundredth	двухсо́тый
three hundred	три́ста	three-hundredth	трёхсо́тый
four hundred	четы́реста	four-hundredth	четырёхсо́тый
five hundred	пятьсо́т	five-hundredth	пятисо́тый
six hundred	шестьсо́т	six-hundredth	шестисо́тый
thousand	ты́сяча	thousandth	ты́сячный
million	миллио́н	millionth	миллио́нный

оди́н:

	Singular			Plural
	Masculine	Feminine	Neuter	
Nominative	оди́н	одна́	одно́	одни́
Accusative	оди́н	одну́	одно́	одни́
Genitive	одного́	одно́й	одного́	одни́х
Dative	одному́	одно́й	одному́	одни́м
Instrumental	одни́м	одно́й	одни́м	одни́ми
Prepositional	одно́м	одно́й	одно́м	одни́х

For the declension of other numbers, see the dictionary entries.

Russian verbs

(a) The verb list contains examples of:
- (i)   verbs in **-чь** (e.g. бере́чь)
- (ii) verbs in **-ти** (e.g. вести́)
- (iii) verbs in **-сть** (e.g. сесть)
- (iv) verbs in **-оть** (e.g. боро́ться)
- (v)   verbs in **-ереть** (e.g. запере́ть)
- (vi) verbs in **-овать** and **-евать** (e.g. бесе́довать, воева́ть)
- (vii) verbs (first conjugation) with consonant change (e.g. писа́ть)
- (viii) verbs (second conjugation) with consonant change (e.g. бро́сить)
- (ix) second-conjugation verbs in **-ать/-ять** (e.g. стуча́ть, стоя́ть)
- (x)   first- and second-conjugation verbs in **-еть** (e.g. име́ть, горе́ть)
- (xi) monosyllabic verbs (e.g. брать)
- (xii) irregular verbs (e.g. хоте́ть)

(b) Most verbs listed are non-derivative (e.g. дать). Compound verbs are not normally given when a root verb is available (дать 'to give' appears, but not прода́ть 'to sell' or зада́ть 'to ask [a question]'). Some compounds have no commonly-used root verb, in which case a hyphenated root is given (e.g. -каза́ть).

(c) Also listed are verbs that have no -л in the masculine past (e.g. везти́ 'to convey', masculine past вёз).

(d) The pattern of presentation is:
- (i) for all verbs: present or future conjugation, and meaning; the verb's other aspect (if available)
- (ii) for selected verbs: the past tense; the government of the verb; the imperative; short forms of the perfective passive participle.

Note: Absence of a first-person singular form indicates that none exists, or that none exists in the meaning given (see, for example, греме́ть 'to thunder').

бежа́ть/по- 'to run': бегу́ бежи́шь бежи́т бежи́м бежи́те бегу́т; беги́!

бере́чь/по- 'to take care of': берегу́ бережёт берегу́т; берёг берегла́; береги́!

бесе́довать 'to converse': бесе́дую бесе́дует бесе́дуют

бить/по- 'to strike': бью бьёт бьют; бей!

бледне́ть/по- 'to grow pale': бледне́ю бледне́ет бледне́ют

блесте́ть 'to shine': блещу́ блести́т блестя́т; *pf.* **блесну́ть**

боле́ть (+ *i.*) 'to be ill (with)': боле́ю боле́ет боле́ют

боле́ть 'to hurt' (*intrans.*): боли́т боля́т

боро́ться (за + *a.*) 'to struggle (for)': борю́сь бо́рется бо́рются; бори́сь!

боя́ться (+ *g.*) 'to fear': бою́сь бои́тся боя́тся; (не) бо́йся!

брать 'to take': беру́ берёт беру́т; брал брала́ бра́ло; бери́!; *pf.* **взять**

бри́ться/по- 'to shave' (*intrans.*): бре́юсь бре́ется бре́ются

бро́сить 'to throw': бро́шу бро́сит бро́сят; брось!; бро́шен; *impf.* **броса́ть**

буди́ть/раз- 'to awaken' (*trans.*): бужу́ бу́дит бу́дят; буди́!; разбу́жен

быть 'to be': бу́ду бу́дет бу́дут; был была́ бы́ло; будь!

везти́ 'to convey': везу́ везёт везу́т; вёз везла́

ве́сить 'to weigh': ве́шу ве́сит ве́сят

вести́ 'to lead': веду́ ведёт веду́т; вёл вела́

взять 'to take': возьму́ возьмёт возьму́т; взял взяла́ взя́ло; возьми́!; взят взята́ взя́то; *impf.* **брать**

ви́деть/у- 'to see': ви́жу ви́дит ви́дят

висе́ть 'to hang' (*intrans.*): вишу́ виси́т вися́т

владе́ть (+ *i.*) 'to own': владе́ю владе́ет владе́ют

влечь 'to attract': влеку́ влечёт влеку́т; влёк влекла́; -влечён -влечена́ (*in compounds*)

води́ть 'to lead': вожу́ во́дит во́дят

воева́ть 'to wage war': вою́ю вою́ет вою́ют

возврати́ться 'to return' (*intrans.*): возвращу́сь возврати́тся возвратя́тся; *impf.* **возвраща́ться**

вози́ть 'to convey': вожу́ во́зит во́зят

возни́кнуть 'to arise': возни́кну возни́кнет возни́кнут; возни́к возни́кла; *impf.* **возника́ть**

волнова́ться/вз- 'to be excited': волну́юсь волну́ется волну́ются; (не) волну́йся!

врать/на- *or* **со-** 'to tell lies': вру врёт врут; врал врала́ вра́ло; (не) ври!

встава́ть 'to get up, stand up': встаю́ встаёт встаю́т; встава́й!; *pf.* **встать**

встать 'to get up, stand up': вста́ну вста́нет вста́нут; встань!; *impf.* **встава́ть**

встре́тить 'to meet': встре́чу встре́тит встре́тят; *impf.* **встреча́ть**

вы́глядеть (+ *i.*) 'to look, appear': вы́гляжу вы́глядит вы́глядят

вы́разить 'to express': вы́ражу вы́разит вы́разят; вы́ражен; *impf.* **выража́ть**

вяза́ть/с- 'to tie': вяжу́ вя́жет вя́жут; -вя́зан (*in compounds*)

гаси́ть/за- *or* **по-** 'to extinguish': гашу́ га́сит га́сят; зага́шен/пога́шен

ги́бнуть/по- 'to perish': ги́бну ги́бнет ги́бнут; гиб/ги́бнул ги́бла

гла́дить/вы- *or* **по-** 'to iron': гла́жу гла́дит гла́дят; вы́глажен

гляде́ть (на + *a.*) 'to look (at)': гляжу́ гляди́т глядя́т; *pf.* **гля́нуть**

гна́ться (за + *i.*) 'to chase (after)': гоню́сь го́нится го́нятся; гна́лся гнала́сь

годи́ться (в + *a.*) 'to be fit (for)': гожу́сь годи́тся годя́тся

голосова́ть/про- (за + *a.*) 'to vote (for)': голосу́ю голосу́ет голосу́ют

горди́ться (+ *i.*) 'to be proud of': горжу́сь горди́тся гордя́тся; горди́сь!

горе́ть/с- 'to burn' (*intrans.*): гори́т горя́т

гото́вить/при- 'to prepare': гото́влю гото́вит гото́вят; гото́вь!; пригото́влен

греме́ть/про- 'to thunder': греми́т гремя́т

греть 'to heat': гре́ю гре́ет гре́ют; -грет (*in compounds*)

грози́ть/при- (+ *d.*) 'to threaten': грожу́ грози́т грозя́т

грузи́ть/по- 'to load': гружу́ гру́зит гру́зят; погру́жен

дава́ть 'to give': даю́ даёт даю́т; дава́й!; *pf.* **дать**

дави́ть (на + *a.*) 'to press (upon)': давлю́ да́вит да́вят; -давлен (*in compounds*)

дать 'to give': дам дашь даст дади́м дади́те даду́т; дал дала́ да́ло; дай!; дан дана́; *impf.* **дава́ть**

де́йствовать 'to act': де́йствую де́йствует де́йствуют; де́йствуй!

держа́ть 'to hold': держу́ де́ржит де́ржат; держи́!; -держан (*in compounds*)

доба́вить 'to add': доба́влю доба́вит доба́вят; доба́вь!; доба́влен; *impf.* **добавля́ть**

дости́гнуть (+ *g.*) 'to achieve': дости́гну дости́гнет дости́гнут; дости́г дости́гла; дости́гнут; *impf.* **достига́ть**

дрема́ть 'to doze': дремлю́ дре́млет дре́млют

дрожа́ть 'to tremble': дрожу́ дрожи́т дрожа́т; *pf.* **дро́гнуть**

дуть 'to blow': ду́ю ду́ет ду́ют; *pf.* **ду́нуть**

дыша́ть 'to breathe': дышу́ ды́шит ды́шат

е́здить 'to travel': е́зжу е́здит е́здят; е́зди!

есть/съ- 'to eat': ем ешь ест еди́м еди́те едя́т; ешь!; съе́ден

е́хать/по- 'to travel': е́ду е́дет е́дут; поезжа́й!

жале́ть/по- 'to pity': жале́ю жале́ет жале́ют

жа́ловаться/по- (на + *a.*) 'to complain (of, about)': жа́луюсь жа́луется жа́луются

жать 'to press, squeeze': жму жмёт жмут; жми!; -жат (*in compounds*)

ждать/подо- (+ *a./g.*) 'to wait (for)': жду ждёт ждут; ждал ждала́ жда́ло; жди!

жева́ть 'to chew': жую́ жуёт жую́т

же́ртвовать/по- (+ *i.*) 'to sacrifice': же́ртвую же́ртвует же́ртвуют

жечь/с- 'to burn' (*trans.*): жгу жжёт жгут; жёг жгла; жги!; -жжён -жжена́ (*in compounds*)

жить 'to live': живу́ живёт живу́т; жил жила́ жи́ло

забо́титься/по- (о + *p.*) 'to care about': забо́чусь забо́тится забо́тятся

забы́ть 'to forget': забу́ду забу́дет забу́дут; (не) забу́дь!; забы́т; *impf.* **забыва́ть**

заве́довать (+ *i.*) 'to be in charge of': заве́дую заве́дует заве́дуют

зави́довать/по- (+ *d.*) 'to envy': зави́дую зави́дует зави́дуют

зави́сеть (от + *g.*) 'to depend (on)': зави́шу зави́сит зави́сят

закры́ть 'to shut': закро́ю закро́ет закро́ют; закро́й!; закры́т; *impf.* **закрыва́ть**

замёрзнуть 'to freeze' (*intrans.*): замёрзну замёрзнет замёрзнут; замёрз замёрзла; *impf.* **замерза́ть**

заме́тить 'to notice': заме́чу заме́тит заме́тят; заме́чен; *impf.* **замеча́ть**

заня́ть 'to occupy': займу́ займёт займу́т; за́нял заняла́ за́няло; займи́!; за́нят занята́ за́нято; *impf.* **занима́ть**

запере́ть 'to lock': запру́ запрёт запру́т; за́пер заперла́ за́перло; запри́!; за́перт заперта́ за́перто; *impf.* **запира́ть**

запрети́ть 'to forbid': запрещу́ запрети́т запретя́т; запрещён запрещена́; *impf.* **запреща́ть**

заряди́ть 'to load, charge': заряжу́ заряди́т заря́дя́т; заряжён заряжена́; *impf.* **заряжа́ть**

захвати́ть 'to seize': захвачу́ захва́тит захва́тят; захва́чен; *impf.* **захва́тывать**

защити́ть (от + *g.*) 'to defend (from)': защищу́ защити́т защитя́т; защищён защищена́; *impf.* **защища́ть**

заяви́ть 'to declare': заявлю́ зая́вит зая́вят; зая́влен; *impf.* **заявля́ть**

звать/по- 'to call': зову́ зовёт зову́т; звал звала́ зва́ло; зови́!; -зван (*in compounds*)

звуча́ть 'to sound': звучи́т звуча́т

знако́миться/по- (с + *i.*) 'to become acquainted (with)': знако́млюсь знако́мится знако́мятся; знако́мься!

идти́ 'to go': иду́ идёт иду́т; шёл шла; иди́!

изобрести́ 'to invent': изобрету́ изобретёт изобрету́т; изобрёл изобрела́; изобретён изобретена́; *impf.* **изобрета́ть**

име́ть 'to have': име́ю име́ет име́ют

интересова́ться (+ *i.*) 'to be interested in': интересу́юсь интересу́ется интересу́ются

иска́ть (+ *a./g.*) 'to look for': ищу́ и́щет и́щут; ищи́!

испо́льзовать 'to use' (*impf. and pf.*): испо́льзую испо́льзует испо́льзуют; испо́льзуй!; испо́льзован

иссле́довать 'to investigate' (*impf. and pf.*): иссле́дую иссле́дует иссле́дуют; иссле́дован

исче́знуть 'to disappear': исче́зну исче́знет исче́знут; исче́з исче́зла; *impf.* **исчеза́ть**

-каза́ть (*only in compounds*): -кажу́ -ка́жет -ка́жут; -кажи́!; -ка́зан; *impf.* **-ка́зывать**

каза́ться/по- (+ *i.*) 'to seem': кажу́сь ка́жется ка́жутся

кати́ть 'to roll' (*trans.*): качу́ ка́тит ка́тят

ка́шлять 'to cough': ка́шляю ка́шляет ка́шляют; *pf.* **ка́шлянуть**

кипе́ть/вс- 'to boil' (*intrans.*): киплю́ (*in figurative sense only*) кипи́т кипя́т

класть 'to place': кладу́ кладёт кладу́т; клади́!; *pf.* **положи́ть**

колеба́ться/по- 'to hesitate': коле́блюсь коле́блется коле́блются

кома́ндовать (+ *i.*) 'to command': кома́ндую кома́ндует кома́ндуют

корми́ть/на- 'to feed': кормлю́ ко́рмит ко́рмят; нако́рмлен

кра́сить/вы́- *or* **по-** 'to paint': кра́шу кра́сит кра́сят; вы́крашен

красне́ть/по- 'to blush': красне́ю красне́ет красне́ют

красть/у- 'to steal': краду́ крадёт краду́т; укра́ден

кре́пнуть/о- 'to get stronger': кре́пну кре́пнет кре́пнут; креп кре́пла

крича́ть 'to shout': кричу́ кричи́т крича́т; кричи́!; *pf.* **кри́кнуть**

купи́ть 'to buy': куплю́ ку́пит ку́пят; купи́!; ку́плен; *impf.* **покупа́ть**

ла́зить 'to climb': ла́жу ла́зит ла́зят; (не) лазь!

лгать/со- *or* **на-** 'to tell lies': лгу лжёт лгут; лгал, лгала́, лга́ло; (не) лги!

лежа́ть 'to lie': лежу́ лежи́т лежа́т

лезть 'to climb': ле́зу ле́зет ле́зут; лез ле́зла; лезь!

лете́ть 'to fly': лечу́ лети́т летя́т

лечь 'to lie down': ля́гу ля́жет ля́гут; лёг легла́; ляг!; *impf.* **ложи́ться**

лиза́ть 'to lick': лижу́ ли́жет ли́жут; *pf.* **лизну́ть**

лить 'to pour': лью льёт льют; лил лила́ ли́ло; лей!; -лит (*in compounds*)

лови́ть 'to catch': ловлю́ ло́вит ло́вят; *pf.* **пойма́ть**

люби́ть 'to like, love': люблю́ лю́бит лю́бят

любова́ться/по- (+ *i. or* на + *a.*) 'to admire': любу́юсь любу́ется любу́ются

маха́ть (+ *i.*) 'to wave': машу́ ма́шет ма́шут; *pf.* **махну́ть**

мести́/под- 'to sweep': мету́ метёт мету́т; мёл мела́; подметён подметена́

молча́ть 'to be silent': молчу́ молчи́т молча́т; молчи́!

мочь/с- 'to be able': могу́ мо́жет мо́гут; мог могла́

мча́ться 'to race': мчусь мчи́тся мча́тся; мчись!

мы́ться/вы́- *or* **по-** 'to wash' (*intrans.*): мо́юсь мо́ется мо́ются; мо́йся!

награди́ть (за + *a.*) 'to reward (for)': награжу́ награди́т наградя́т; награждён награждена́; *impf.* **награжда́ть**

наде́ть 'to put on': наде́ну наде́нет наде́нут; наде́нь!; *impf.* **надева́ть**

наде́яться/по- (на + *a.*) 'to hope (for)': наде́юсь наде́ется наде́ются

назва́ть 'to name': назову́ назовёт назову́т; назва́л назвала́ назва́ло; на́зван; *impf.* **называ́ть**

найти́ 'to find': найду́ найдёт найду́т; нашёл нашла́; на́йден; *impf.* **находи́ть**

напа́сть (на + *a.*) 'to attack': нападу́ нападёт нападу́т; *impf.* **напада́ть**

находи́ть 'to find': нахожу́ нахо́дит нахо́дят; *pf.* **найти́**

находи́ться 'to be situated': нахожу́сь нахо́дится нахо́дятся

нача́ть 'to begin' (*trans.*): начну́ начнёт начну́т; на́чал начала́ на́чало; начни́!; на́чат начата́ на́чато; *impf.* **начина́ть**

нача́ться 'to begin' (*intrans.*): начнётся начну́тся; начался́ начала́сь; *impf.* **начина́ться**

ненави́деть 'to hate': ненави́жу ненави́дит ненави́дят

нести́ 'to carry': несу́ несёт несу́т; нёс несла́; неси́!

носи́ть 'to carry': ношу́ но́сит но́сят

ночева́ть/пере- 'to spend the night': ночу́ю ночу́ет ночу́ют

нра́виться/по- (+ *d.*) 'to please': нра́влюсь нра́вится нра́вятся

оби́деть 'to offend': оби́жу оби́дит оби́дят; оби́жен; *impf.* **обижа́ть**

обня́ть 'to embrace': обниму́ обни́мет обни́мут; о́бнял обняла́ о́бняло; обними́!; *impf.* **обнима́ть**

обогна́ть 'to overtake, outstrip': обгоню́ обго́нит обго́нят; обогна́л обогнала́ обогна́ло; *impf.* **обгоня́ть**

образова́ть 'to form' (*impf. and pf.*): образу́ю образу́ет образу́ют; образо́ван; *impf. also* **образо́вывать**

обрати́ться (к + *d.*) 'to turn (to)': обращу́сь обрати́тся обратя́тся; обрати́сь!; *impf.* **обраща́ться**

обсуди́ть 'to discuss': обсужу́ обсу́дит обсу́дят; обсуждён обсуждена́; *impf.* **обсужда́ть**

оде́ться 'to dress' (*intrans.*): оде́нусь оде́нется оде́нутся; оде́нься! *impf.* **одева́ться**

организова́ть 'to organize' (*impf. and pf.*): организу́ю организу́ет организу́ют; организо́ван

освети́ть 'to illuminate': освещу́ освети́т осветя́т; освещён освещена́; *impf.* **освеща́ть**

освободи́ть 'to free': освобожу́ освободи́т освободя́т; освобождён освобождена́; *impf.* **освобожда́ть**

остава́ться 'to remain': остаю́сь остаётся остаю́тся; остава́йся!; *pf.* **оста́ться**

останови́ться 'to stop' (*intrans.*): остановлю́сь остано́вится остано́вятся; останови́сь!; *impf.* **остана́вливаться**

оста́ться 'to remain': оста́нусь оста́нется оста́нутся; оста́нься! *impf.* **остава́ться**

отве́тить (на + *a.*) 'to answer': отве́чу отве́тит отве́тят; отве́ть!; *impf.* **отвеча́ть**

откры́ть 'to open' (*trans.*): откро́ю откро́ет откро́ют; откро́й!; откры́т; *impf.* **открыва́ть**

отня́ть 'to take away': отниму́ отни́мет отни́мут; о́тнял отняла́ о́тняло; отними́!; *impf.* **отнима́ть**

отпере́ть 'to unlock': отопру́ отопрёт отопру́т; отопри́!; о́тпер отперла́ о́тперло; о́тперт отперта́ о́тперто; *impf.* **отпира́ть**

ошиби́ться 'to make a mistake': ошибу́сь ошибётся ошибу́тся; оши́бся оши́блась; *impf.* **ошиба́ться**

па́хнуть (+ *i.*) 'to smell (of)': па́хнет па́хнут; пах па́хла

перестава́ть 'to stop' (*intrans.*): перестаю́ перестаёт перестаю́т; *pf.* **переста́ть**

переста́ть 'to stop' (*intrans.*): переста́ну переста́нешь переста́нут; переста́нь!; *impf.* **перестава́ть**

петь/с- 'to sing': пою́ поёт пою́т; пой!

печь/ис- 'to bake': пеку́ печёт пеку́т; пёк пекла́; испечён испечена́

писа́ть/на- 'to write': пишу́ пи́шет пи́шут; пиши́!; напи́сан

пить/вы́- 'to drink': пью пьёт пьют; пил, пила́, пи́ло; пей!; вы́пит

пла́кать 'to weep': пла́чу пла́чет пла́чут; (не) плачь!

плати́ть/за- (за + *a.*) 'to pay (for)': плачу́ пла́тит пла́тят; плати́!; запла́чен

плева́ть 'to spit': плюю́ плюёт плюю́т; *pf.* **плю́нуть**

плыть 'to swim': плыву́ плывёт плыву́т; плыл плыла́ плы́ло

победи́ть 'to win': победи́т победя́т; побеждён побеждена́; *impf.* **побежда́ть**

подве́ргнуть (+ *d.*) 'to subject (to)': подве́ргну подве́ргнет подве́ргнет; подве́рг подве́ргла; подве́ргнут; *impf.* **подверга́ть**

пове́сить 'to hang' (*trans.*): пове́шу пове́сит пове́сят; пове́сь!; пове́шен; *impf.* **ве́шать**

подня́ть 'to lift': подниму́ подни́мет подни́мут; по́днял подняла́ по́дняло; подними́!; по́днят поднята́ по́днято; *impf.* **поднима́ть**

подтверди́ть 'to confirm': подтвержу́ подтверди́т подтвердя́т; подтверждён подтверждена́; *impf.* **подтвержда́ть**

поздра́вить (с + *i.*) 'to congratulate (on)': поздра́влю поздра́вит поздра́вят; поздра́вь!; *impf.* **поздравля́ть**

покры́ть 'to cover': покро́ю покро́ет покро́ют; покро́й!; покры́т; *impf.* **покрыва́ть**

ползти́ 'to crawl': ползу́ ползёт ползу́т; полз ползла́

по́льзоваться/вос- (+ *i.*) 'to use': по́льзуюсь по́льзуется по́льзуются

помо́чь (+ *d.*) 'to help': помогу́ помо́жет помо́гут; помо́г помогла́; помоги́!; *impf.* **помога́ть**

пони́зить 'to lower': пони́жу пони́зит пони́зят; пони́жен; *impf.* **понижа́ть**

поня́ть 'to understand': пойму́ поймёт пойму́т; по́нял поняла́ по́няло; пойми́!; по́нят понята́ по́нято; *impf.* **понима́ть**

по́ртить/ис- 'to spoil': по́рчу по́ртит по́ртят; испо́рчен

посади́ть 'to plant, seat': посажу́ поса́дит поса́дят; поса́жен; *impf.* **сажа́ть**

посвяти́ть (+ *d.*) 'to dedicate (to)': посвящу́ посвяти́т посвятя́т; посвящён посвящена́; *impf.* **посвяща́ть**

посети́ть 'to visit': посещу́ посети́т посетя́т; посещён посещена́; *impf.* **посеща́ть**

пра́вить (+ *i.*) 'to rule, govern':
пра́влю пра́вит пра́вят

пра́здновать/от- 'to celebrate':
пра́здную пра́зднует пра́зднуют

преврати́ть (в + *a.*) 'to transform
(into)': превращу́ преврати́т превратя́т;
превращён превращена́; *impf.*
превраща́ть

предупреди́ть 'to warn':
предупрежу́ предупреди́т предупредя́т;
предупреждён предупреждена́; *impf.*
предупрежда́ть

прекрати́ть 'to stop, curtail':
прекращу́ прекрати́т прекратя́т;
прекрати́!; прекращён прекращена́;
impf. **прекраща́ть**

преодоле́ть 'to overcome':
преодоле́ю преодоле́ет преодоле́ют;
преодолён преодолена́; *impf.*
преодолева́ть

прибли́зиться (к + *d.*) 'to approach':
прибли́жусь прибли́зится прибли́зятся;
impf. **приближа́ться**

привы́кнуть (к + *d.*) 'to get used
(to)': привы́кну привы́кнет привы́кнут;
привы́к привы́кла; *impf.* **привыка́ть**

пригласи́ть 'to invite': приглашу́
пригласи́т приглася́т; пригласи́!;
приглашён приглашена́; *pf.*
приглаша́ть

признава́ться (в + *p.*) 'to confess
(to)': признаю́сь признаётся
признаю́тся; *pf.* **призна́ться**

приня́ть 'to accept': приму́ при́мет
при́мут; при́нял приняла́ при́няло;
прими́!; при́нят принята́ при́нято; *impf.*
принима́ть

про́бовать/по- 'to test, try': про́бую
про́бует про́буют; про́буй!

проси́ть/по- (+ *a./g.*) 'to request':
прошу́ про́сит про́сят; проси́!

прости́ть (за + *a.*) 'to forgive (for)':
прощу́ прости́т простя́т; прости́!;
прощён прощена́; *impf.* **проща́ть**

прости́ться (с + *i.*) 'to say goodbye
(to)': прощу́сь прости́тся простя́тся;
impf. **проща́ться**

простуди́ться 'to catch cold':
простужу́сь просту́дится просту́дятся;
impf. **простужа́ться**

пря́тать/с- 'to hide': пря́чу пря́чет
пря́чут; прячь!; спря́тан

пусти́ть 'to let go': пущу́ пу́стит
пу́стят; пу́щен; *impf.* **пуска́ть**

ра́доваться/об- (+ *d.*) 'to rejoice
(at)': ра́дуюсь ра́дуется ра́дуются

разби́ть 'to smash': разобью́ разобьёт
разобью́т; разбе́й! разби́т; *impf.*
разбива́ть

разви́ться 'to develop' (*intrans.*):
разовью́сь разовьётся разовью́тся;
разви́лся развила́сь; *impf.* **развива́ться**

разде́ться 'to get undressed':
разде́нусь разде́нется разде́нутся;
разде́нься!; *impf.* **раздева́ться**

расста́ться (с + *i.*) 'to part (with)':
расста́нусь расста́нется расста́нутся;
impf. **расстава́ться**

расти́/вы́- 'to grow' (*intrans.*): расту́
растёт расту́т; рос росла́

рвать 'to tear': рву рвёт рвут; рвал
рвала́ рва́ло

ре́зать/раз- 'to cut': ре́жу ре́жет
ре́жут; режь!; разре́зан

рисова́ть/на- 'to draw': рису́ю рису́ет
рису́ют; нарисо́ван

руби́ть 'to chop': рублю́ ру́бит ру́бят;
-рублен (*in compounds*)

руководи́ть (+ *i.*) 'to manage':
руковожу́ руководи́т руководя́т

сади́ться 'to sit down': сажу́сь
сади́тся садя́тся; сади́сь!; *pf.* **сесть**

свисте́ть 'to whistle': свищу́ свисти́т
свистя́т; *pf.* **сви́стнуть**

серди́ться/рас- 'to get angry':
сержу́сь се́рдится се́рдятся; (не)
серди́сь!

сесть 'to sit down': ся́ду ся́дет ся́дут;
сядь!; *impf.* **сади́ться**

се́ять/по- 'to sow': се́ю се́ет се́ют;
посе́ян

сиде́ть 'to sit': сижу́ сиди́т сидя́т; сиди́!

сказа́ть 'to say': скажу́ ска́жет ска́жут; скажи́!; ска́зан; *impf.* **говори́ть**

скрыть 'to conceal': скро́ю скро́ет скро́ют; скрой!; скрыт; *impf.* **скрыва́ть**

слать 'to send': шлю шлёт шлют; шли!

следи́ть (за + *i.*) 'to track': слежу́ следи́т следя́т

сле́довать/по- (за + *i.*) 'to follow': сле́дую сле́дует сле́дуют

слы́шать/у- 'to hear': слы́шу слы́шит слы́шат; услы́шан

сметь/по- 'to dare': сме́ю сме́ет сме́ют

смея́ться/по- (над + *i.*) 'to laugh (at)': смею́сь смеётся смею́тся; (не) сме́йся!

смотре́ть/по- (на + *a.*) 'to look (at)': смотрю́ смо́трит смо́трят; смотри́!

снять 'to take off': сниму́ сни́мет сни́мут; снял сняла́ сня́ло; сними́!; снят снята́ сня́то; *impf.* **снима́ть**

сове́товать/по- (+ *d.*) 'to advise': сове́тую сове́тует сове́туют

согласи́ться (на + *a.*/с + *i.*) 'to agree (to something/with someone)': соглашу́сь согласи́тся соглася́тся; *impf.* **соглаша́ться**

спасти́ 'to save': спасу́ спасёт спасу́т; спас спасла́; спасён спасена́; *impf.* **спаса́ть**

спать 'to sleep': сплю спит спят; спал спала́ спа́ло; спи!

спроси́ть 'to ask': спрошу́ спро́сит спро́сят; спроси́!; *impf.* **спра́шивать**

ста́вить/по- 'to put, stand' (*trans.*): ста́влю ста́вит ста́вят; ставь!; поста́влен

стать 'to become': ста́ну ста́нет ста́нут; стань!; *impf.* **станови́ться**

стере́ть 'to erase': сотру́ сотрёт сотру́т; стёр стёрла; сотри́!; стёрт; *impf.* **стира́ть**

стоя́ть 'to stand' (*intrans.*): стою́ стои́т стоя́т; стой!

стричь/о- 'to cut (hair or nails)': стригу́ стрижёт стригу́т; стриг стри́гла; остри́жен

ступи́ть 'to step': ступлю́ сту́пит сту́пят; *impf.* **ступа́ть**

стуча́ть/по- (в + *a.*) 'to knock (at)': стучу́ стучи́т стуча́т

суди́ть 'to judge': сужу́ су́дит су́дят

танцева́ть/с- 'to dance': танцу́ю танцу́ет танцу́ют

та́ять/рас- 'to melt' (*intrans.*): та́ет та́ют

темне́ть/по- 'to grow dark': темне́ет темне́ют

тере́ть 'to rub': тру трёт трут; тёр тёрла; три!

терпе́ть 'to bear, tolerate': терплю́ те́рпит те́рпят

течь 'to flow': течёт теку́т; тёк текла́

топи́ть 'to heat': топлю́ то́пит то́пят; -топлен (*in compounds*)

торгова́ть (+ *i.*) 'to trade (in)': торгу́ю торгу́ет торгу́ют

торопи́ться/по- 'to hurry': тороплю́сь торо́пится торо́пятся; торопи́сь!

тра́тить/ис- (на + *a.*) 'to expend (on)': тра́чу тра́тит тра́тят; трать!; истра́чен

тре́бовать/по- (+ *g./a.*) 'to demand': тре́бую тре́бует тре́буют

труди́ться 'to labour': тружу́сь тру́дится тру́дятся; труди́сь!

трясти́ 'to shake' (*trans.*): трясу́ трясёт трясу́т; тряс трясла́; *pf.* **тряхну́ть**

убеди́ть 'to convince': убеди́т убедя́т; убеждён убеждена́; *impf.* **убежда́ть**

удиви́ться (+ *d.*) 'to be surprised (at)': удивлю́сь удиви́тся удивя́тся; *impf.* **удивля́ться**

укрепи́ть 'to strengthen': укреплю́ укрепи́т укрепя́т; укреплён укреплена́; *impf.* **укрепля́ть**

умере́ть 'to die': умру́ умрёт умру́т; у́мер умерла́ у́мерло; *impf.* **умира́ть**

уме́ть 'to know how': уме́ю уме́ет уме́ют

упа́сть 'to fall': упаду́ упадёт упаду́т; *impf.* **па́дать**

употреби́ть 'to use': употреблю́ употреби́т употребя́т; употреблён употреблена́; *impf.* **употребля́ть**

успе́ть 'to have time': успе́ю успе́ет успе́ют; *impf.* **успева́ть**

установи́ть 'to establish': установлю́ устано́вит устано́вят; устано́влен; *impf.* **устана́вливать**

уча́ствовать (в + *p.*) 'to participate in': уча́ствую уча́ствует уча́ствуют

уче́сть 'to take account of': учту́ учтёт учту́т; учёл учла́; учти́!; учтён учтена́; *impf.* **учи́тывать**

ходи́ть 'to go': хожу́ хо́дит хо́дят; ходи́!

хоте́ть/за- 'to want': хочу́ хо́чешь хо́чет хоти́м хоти́те хотя́т

худе́ть/по- 'to lose weight': худе́ю худе́ет худе́ют

цвести́ 'to flower': цветёт цвету́т; цвёл цвела́

чеса́ть/по- 'to scratch': чешу́ че́шет че́шут

чи́стить/вы́- *or* **по-** 'to clean': чи́щу чи́стит чи́стят; вы́чищен/почи́щен

чу́вствовать 'to feel': чу́вствую чу́вствует чу́вствуют

шепта́ть 'to whisper': шепчу́ ше́пчет ше́пчут; *pf.* **шепну́ть**

шить/с- 'to sew': шью шьёт шьют; шей!

шуме́ть 'to make a noise': шуми́т шумя́т

шути́ть/по- 'to joke': шучу́ шу́тит шу́тят

эконо́мить/с- 'to economize': эконо́млю эконо́мит эконо́мят; сэконо́млен

яви́ться (+ *i.*) 'to be': явлю́сь я́вится я́вятся; *impf.* **явля́ться**

Заметки об английской грамматике

Существительные

Артикли

Неопределённый артикль

Неопределённый артикль **a** стоит перед словами, начинающимися на согласный или на сочетания, содержащие звук /j/:

a ball	мяч
a girl	девочка
a union	союз

Перед гласным или перед непроизносимым /h/ неопределённый артикль принимает форму **an**:

an apple	яблоко
an hour	час

Неопределённый артикль обычно употребляется с исчисляемыми существительными. Рассмотрим следующие случаи употребления:

- с названиями профессий:

She is a doctor	Она врач
He is an engineer	Он инженер

- после предлогов:

She works as a tour guide	Она работает гидом/экскурсоводом
Anna has gone without an umbrella	Анна ушла без зонта

- в обобщающих высказываниях:

A whale is larger than a frog	Кит больше лягушки

Определённый артикль

Определённый артикль **the** употребляется с существительными единственного и множественного числа:

the cat	кошка
the owls	совы

Определённый артикль не употребляется с существительными, обозначающими:

- учреждения:

I don't go to church	Я не хожу в церковь
He's starting school next week	Он пойдёт в школу на следующей неделе

Но когда определённый артикль обозначает здания, а не учреждения, он употребляется:

Turn right at the school	У школы поверните направо

- время еды:

  | **Breakfast is at 8.30** | Завтрак в 8:30 |
  | **Dinner is ready** | Обед готов |

- время суток, после предлогов (за исключением **in** и **during**):

  | **I am never out at night** | Вечером я всегда дома |
  | **They left in the morning** | Они уехали утром |

- абстрактные понятия:

  | **Hatred is a destructive force** | Ненависть — разрушительная сила |
  | **The book is on English grammar** | Это книга об английской грамматике |

- болезни:

  | **She's got tonsillitis** | У неё ангина |

- времена года:

  | **Spring is here!** | Наступила весна |
  | **It's like winter today** | Сегодня совсем зима |

- страны:

  | **Russia** | Россия |
  | **England** | Англия |

- улицы, парки и т. д.:

  | **a concert in Hyde Park** | концерт в Гайд-парке |
  | **I work on Baker Street** | Я работаю на Бейкер-стрит |

Определённый артикль, однако, употребляется в предложениях, в которых рассматриваются конкретные примеры:

| **The breakfast he served was awful** | Завтрак, который он подал, был ужасным |
| **The winter of 2011 was very mild** | Зима 2011 года была очень мягкая |

Следующие классы существительных всегда употребляются с определённым артиклем:

- географические названия во множественном числе:

the Netherlands	Нидерланды
the United States	Соединённые Штаты
the Alps	Альпы

- названия рек, морей и океанов:

the Thames	Темза
the Black Sea	Чёрное море
the Pacific	Тихий океан

- названия гостиниц, пабов, театров, музеев и проч.:

the Hilton	Хилтон
the Fox and Hounds	Лиса и гончие
the New Theatre	Новый театр
the British Museum	Британский музей

Множественное число

Множественное число существительных обычно образуется прибавлением к слову окончания **-s**:

| **dog — dogs** | **tape — tapes** |

К словам, оканчивающимся на **-s**, **-ss**, **-sh**, **-ch**, **-x**, **-zz**, следует добавлять окончание **-es**:

| **dress — dresses** | **box — boxes** |

Такое же окончание появляется в словах, оканчивающихся на *согласный* + **y**.

Причём конечный **-y** становится **-i-**:

baby — babies

Подобного не происходит у существительных, оканчивающихся на сочетание *гласный* + **y**:

valley — valleys

Существительные, оканчивающиеся на **-o**, получают во множественном числе или **-s**, или **-es**:

potato — potatoes	**tomato — tomatoes**
solo — solos	**zero — zeros**

У существительных, оканчивающихся на **-f(e)**, возможны три варианта окончания множественного числа:

life — lives	**dwarf — dwarfs/dwarves**
roof — roofs	

Ниже приводится список наиболее часто встречающихся нерегулярных форм множественного числа:

child — children	**foot — feet**
man — men	**mouse — mice**
tooth — teeth	**woman — women**

Субстантивные словосочетания

Данные сочетания строятся по следующим образцам:

существительное + существительное:

summer dress	летнее платье
tennis shoes	теннисные туфли
record collection	коллекция пластинок

существительное + герундий:

disco dancing	танцы на дискотеке
dressmaking	швейное дело

герундий + существительное:

parking meter	паркинговый автомат
writing course	писательские курсы
boarding card	посадочный талон

Множественное число таких сочетаний образуется прибавлением окончания множественного числа только к основному в смысловом отношении слову:

a record collection — record collections

a photo album — photo albums

Женский род

Категория рода у неодушевлённых существительных отсутствует в английском языке. Так, существительные **cousin**, **friend**, **doctor** могут называть лиц и мужского, и женского пола. Поэтому, если при обозначении профессии или степени родства, требуется указать на род, то используются описательные конструкции типа **a male student**, **a woman doctor**.

Родительный (притяжательный) падеж

Родительный (притяжательный) падеж оформляется сочетанием **s** с апострофом, который стоит или перед **s** или после него (**'s/s'**).

's добавляется к существительным единственного числа:

the boy's book   книга мальчика

Апостроф без **s** добавляется к существительным, оканчивающимся во множественном числе на **-s**:

the boys' room   комната мальчиков
the boys' books   книги мальчиков

Если существительное относится к нерегулярной группе, и его множественное число не оканчивается на **-s**, то в родительном (притяжательном) падеже множественного числа употребляется **-'s**:

the children's toys   игрушки детей

В родительном (притяжательном) падеже имён собственных, оканчивающихся на **-s**, может встречаться и **'s**, и **s'** (вариант с **s'** более употребительный): **Keats's poetry** или **Keats' poetry** (поэзия Китса). С греческими и римскими именами, оканчивающимися на **-s**, как правило, употребляется только апостроф: **Socrates' death** (смерть Сократа), **Catullus' poetry** (поэзия Катулла).

Родительный (притяжательный) падеж употребляется с существительными, обозначающими людей, животных (в особенности домашних), а также с названиями стран:

Andrew's house   дом Эндрю
the lion's den   логово льва
America's foreign policy   внешняя политика Америки

Родительный (притяжательный) падеж может выражать следующие отношения:

We are going to Anne's   Мы идём к Анне (домой)
We are going to Peter and Anne's   Мы идём к Питеру и Анне (домой)
(форма **Peter's and Anne's** неупотребительна, если **Peter** и **Anne** рассматриваются как смысловая пара)

Jane Austen's and George Orwell's   Романы Джейн Остин и Джорджа
novels   Оруэлла
(Джейн Остин и Джордж Оруэлл рассматриваются здесь по отдельности)

I got it at the baker's/chemist's   Я купил это в булочной/аптеке
(дословно: **at the baker's shop/at the chemist's shop**)

В разговорном языке довольно часто встречается форма двойного родительного падежа:

He is a friend of my brother's   Он друг моего брата
It was an idea of Anne's   Это было идеей Анны/Это была идея Анны

Прилагательные

Прилагательные в английском языке имеют только одну форму. Они не согласуются с существительным ни в роде, ни в числе, ни в падеже:

an old man   пожилой мужчина
five old women   пять пожилых женщин

Положение прилагательных в предложении

Прилагательные могут стоять перед определяемым существительным: **a long story** (**длинная история**), или после него: **This story is long** (**Эта история длинная**). Однако некоторые прилагательные употребляются только после существительных: **The girl is upset** (**Девочка расстроена**). Нельзя сказать **the upset girl**.

Сравнительная и превосходительная форма

Существует три степени сравнения: положительная, сравнительная и превосходная.

Односложные прилагательные образуют сравнительную и превосходную степени добавлением **-(e)r** и **-(e)st** соответственно:

dull	скучный
duller	скучнее
dullest	скучнейший

big	большой
bigger	больше
biggest	самый большой

(Обратите внимание на удвоение конечного согласного.)

nice	хороший
nicer	лучше
nicest	самый лучший

Многосложные прилагательные образуют сравнительную и превосходную степень при помощи вспомогательных слов **more** и **most**:

generous	щедрый
more generous	более щедрый, щедрее
most generous	самый щедрый, щедрейший

По такому же образцу образуются сравнительная и превосходная степени некоторых двусложных прилагательных, например, **useful** (**полезный**).

Однако в большинстве своём двусложные прилагательные не подчиняются одному определённому правилу. С большой долей вероятности можно только утверждать, что прилагательные, оканчивающиеся на **-y, -le, -ow, -er**, образуют сравнительную и превосходную степени при помощи окончаний **-er/-est**. Например:

pretty (**-y** меняется на **-i-**)	милый
prettier	милее, более милый
prettiest	милейший, самый милый

narrow	узкий
narrower	уже, более узкий
narrowest	самый узкий

curious	любопытный
more curious	любопытнее, более любопытный
most curious	любопытнейший, самый любопытный

Сравнительная и превосходная степень прилагательных, образованных от действительных и страдательных причастий, образуется при помощи вспомогательных слов **more** и **most**:

boring	скучный
more boring	скучнее, более скучный
most boring	скучнейший, самый скучный

Most также употребляется в значении «чрезвычайно», «очень»:

That was a most interesting story   Это была очень интересная/интереснейшая
                                        история

Ниже приводится список наиболее употребительных нерегулярных прилагательных:

bad	плохой
worse	хуже, более плохой
worst	самый плохой/наихудший
good	хороший
better	лучше, более хороший
best	лучший, самый лучший
little	маленький
less	меньше, меньший
least	меньше всего
many/much	много
more	больше
most	больше всего
far	далёкий
farther	более далёкий
farthest	самый далёкий (только о расстоянии)
old	старший
elder	старше
eldest	самый старший

При этом регулярные формы (**old, older, oldest — старый, старее, самый старый**) описывают и людей, и предметы.

Отрицательная форма сравнительной степени образуется при помощи слов **less/least**:

far	далёкий
less far	менее далёкий
least far	наименее далёкий

Прилагательные могут употребляться в функции существительных, особенно, когда они обозначают группу людей:

the young	молодые, молодёжь
the old	старые, старики
the unemployed	безработные

Притяжательные прилагательные

К притяжательным прилагательным относятся:

my	мой
our	наш
your	твой
your	ваш
his, her, its	его (м. р.), её (ж. р.), его (ср. р.)
their	их

Род этих прилагательных зависит от рода обладателя предмета, а не от рода самого предмета:

his mother	его мать
her mother	её мать
their mother	их мать

Притяжательные прилагательные не согласуются с определяемым существительным в числе:

my cat	моя кошка
my cats	мои кошки

Наречия

Наречия определяют:

■ прилагательные:

The job was extremely dangerous	Работа была чрезвычайно опасной

■ глаголы:

He finished quickly	Он быстро закончил

■ другие наречия:

very quickly	очень быстро

Extremely, quickly, very являются наречиями.

Большинство наречий образуется прибавлением **-ly** к прилагательному:

sad — sadly	(печальный — печально)
brave — bravely	(храбрый — храбро)
beautiful — beautifully	(красивый — красиво)

При образовании наречий по такой модели возможны некоторые изменения в орфографии:

true — truly	(верный — верно)
due — duly	(должный — должно)
whole — wholly	(цельный — целиком)

Другие важные орфографические изменения:

конечный **-y** меняется на **-i-**:	**ready — readily**
конечное **-le** на **-ly**:	**gentle — gently**

Некоторые наречия совпадают по форме с соответствующими им прилагательными:

back (задний, назад), **early** (ранний, рано), **far** (далеко, далёкий), **fast** (быстрый, быстро), **left** (левый, налево), **little** (маленький, мало), **long** (длинный, длинно), **only** (единственный, только), **right** (правый, направо), **still** (спокойный, спокойно), **straight** (прямой, прямо), **well** (хороший, хорошо), **wrong** (неправильный, неправильно):

a wrong answer	неправильный ответ
He did it wrong	Он сделал это неправильно
an early summer	раннее лето
Summer arrived early	Лето наступило рано
a straight road	прямая дорога
He came straight to the point	Он перешёл прямо к делу

Местоимения

Личные местоимения

Именительный падеж		Косвенный падеж	
I	(я)	me	(меня, мне, мной)
you	(ты)	you	(тебя, тебе, тобой)
he	(он)	him	(его, ему, им)
she	(она)	her	(её, ей, ею)
it	(оно)	it	(его, ему, им)
we	(мы)	us	(нас, нам, нами)
you	(вы)	you	(вас, вам, вами)
they	(они)	them	(их, им, ими)

В английском языке глагольные формы не выражают лица. Поэтому русская глагольная форма **иду** должна переводиться на английский язык сочетанием **I go**, а не отдельной формой **go**.

Местоимения в косвенных падежах являются в предложении:

■ прямыми дополнениями:

    Mary loves him   Мэри любит его

■ косвенными дополнениями без предлога:

    John gave me a lift   Джон подвёз меня

■ косвенными дополнениями с предлогом:

    The book is from her   Книга от неё

Другие функции личных местоимений

he, she

Эти местоимения иногда обозначают животных, особенно домашних:

    Poor Whiskers, we had to take   Бедный Уискерс. Нам пришлось отнести его к
    him to the vet's   ветеринару

it употребляется:

■ в безличных конструкциях:

    It's sunny   Солнечно
    It's hard to know what to do   Трудно понять, что надо делать
    It looks as though they were right   Кажется, они были правы

в конструкциях, выражающих время и пространство:

    It's five o'clock   Сейчас 5 часов
    It's January the sixth   Сегодня 6 января
    How far is it to Edinburgh?   Как далеко до Эдинбурга?

It's является сокращённой формой конструкции **it is**. Её не следует путать с притяжательным местоимением **its**.

you

Данное местоимение не имеет вежливой формы.

You употребляется в обобщённом значении, для обозначения людей вообще.

    You never know; it might be sunny   Как знать. Может быть, на этой неделе
    this week   будет солнечно
    You can't buy cars like that any more   Таких машин уже не купить

they

- употребляется в обобщённом значении для обозначения неопределённой группы людей, особенно, если они обладают какой-либо властью, силой или умением:

They don't make cars like that any more	Таких машин уже не делают
They will have to find the murderer first	Вначале им надо будет найти убийцу
You'll have to get them to repair the car	Тебе надо будет заставить их отремонтировать машину

- употребляется вместо **he** или **she** (**он, она**):

The person appointed will be answerable to the director. They will be responsible for...	Человек, назначенный на эту должность, будет подчиняться директору. Он будет отвечать за...
A personal secretary will assist them (= him/her)	Им будет помогать персональный секретарь

- соотносится с неопределёнными местоимениями **somebody, someone** (**кто-то**); **anybody, anyone** (**кто-нибудь**); **everybody, everyone** (**всякий, все**); **nobody, no one** (**никто**):

If anyone has seen my pen, will they please tell me?	Если кто-нибудь видел мою ручку, пусть он мне скажет

one

One, так же, как **you**, употребляется в обобщённом значении, но является более литературным:

One needs to get a clear picture of what one wants.	Человек должен точно знать, что он хочет

Следует избегать чрезмерного употребления в речи **one**.

Возвратные местоимения

myself (себя, сам)		**ourselves** (себя, сами)
yourself (себя, сам, сама)		**yourselves** (себя, сами)
himself, herself, itself (себя, сам, сама, само)		**themselves** (себя, сами)

примеры употребления:

I always buy myself a Christmas present (косвенное дополнение)	Я всегда покупаю себе рождественский подарок
She talks to herself (предложное дополнение)	Она разговаривает сама с собой
Do it yourself (эмфатическая конструкция)	Сделай это сам
He burned himself badly (прямое дополнение)	Он сильно обжёгся

Притяжательные местоименные существительные

mine	мой
yours	твой
his, hers	его, её
ours	наш
yours	ваш
theirs	их

Род этих слов зависит от рода их обладателя, а не от рода самого предмета:

Whose book is it? — It's hers	Чья эта книга?—Её
Whose shoes are these? — They are hers	Чьи эти туфли?—Её
Whose car is that? — It's theirs	Чья та машина?—Их

Вопросительные местоимения и прилагательные

who   кто
whom   кому
whose чей
which который, какой
what   что

Who употребляется для обозначения одушевлённого подлежащего:

Who is it?   Кто это?

Whom употребляется для обозначения одушевлённого дополнения:

To whom did you send the letter?   Кому ты послал письмо?
Whom did you see?   Кого ты видел?

Whom является литературной формой и часто заменяется местоимением who:

Who did you send the letter to?   Кому ты послал письмо?
Who did you see?   Кого ты видел?

Whose является родительным падежом **who**:

Whose are these?   Это чьи?
Whose socks are these?   Чьи это носки?

Which может относиться и к одушевлённым, и к неодушевлённым предметам, а также обозначать подлежащее:

Which of you are going?   Кто из вас идёт?
Which is bigger?   Какой/который больше?
Which box is bigger?   Какой из ящиков больше?

Дополнение:

Which of the singers do you prefer?   Какого певца ты предпочитаешь?
Which of the pictures do you prefer?   Какую картину ты предпочитаешь?

What относится только к неодушевлённым предметам и может обозначать подлежащее:

What is this?   Что это?
What type of bird is that? Какой это вид птиц?

дополнение:

What are you going to do?   Что ты собираешься делать?
What sort of books do you like? Какие книги тебе нравятся?

What используется в более широких и менее определённых толкованиях, нежели **which**.

Относительные местоимения

who, whom   который, которого, которому
that   который
which   который
whose   чей, который

Относительные местоимения обычно отсылают к предмету, который уже упоминался в речи (антецедент). Так, в предложении **She phoned the man who had contacted her earlier (Она позвонила мужчине, который обращался к ней ранее)** относительное местоимение **who** относится к слову **the man**.

антецедент	подлежащее	дополнение
люди	who/that	whom/who/that
предметы	which/that	which/that

люди: подлежащее

В данной функции употребляется относительное местоимение **who**, хотя возможно и употребление **that**:

There is a prize for the student who/that gets the highest mark
Студент, который наберёт самый высокий балл, получит приз

Whom является более литературной формой и часто заменяется местоимением **who** или **that**.

Относительное местоимение может опускаться:

The man she met last night was a spy
Мужчина, которого она вчера встретила, был шпионом

предметы: подлежащее

The book which is on the table was a present
Книга, которая лежит на столе, была мне подарена

John gave me the book which/that is on the table
Джон подарил мне книгу, которая лежит на столе

предметы: дополнение

The film, which we went to see last week, was excellent
Фильм, который мы смотрели на прошлой неделе, был прекрасным

В последнем примере относительное местоимение может опускаться:

The film we went to see last week was excellent

Whose является формой родительного падежа:

This is the boy whose dog has been killed Это мальчик, чью собаку убили

Форма **of which** употребляется в литературной или специальной речи и относится к неодушевлённым предметам:

Water, the boiling point of which is 100˚C, is a colourless liquid
Вода является бесцветной жидкостью, точка кипения которой — 100 ˚C

Запомните, что сочетание **who's** является сокращённой формой сочетания **who is**. Его не следует путать с относительным местоимением **whose** (**чей**).

Неопределённые местоимения и прилагательные

some/any	немного

Как прилагательные эти слова употребляются с существительными во множественном числе и с неисчисляемыми существительными:

Take some apples	Возьми немного яблок
Take some jam	Возьми немного варенья
Have you got any apples?	У вас есть яблоки?
Have you any jam?	У вас есть варенье?

Эти местоимения могут заменять существительные во множественном числе и неисчисляемые существительные:

I'd like some jam. — We haven't got any   Мне хочется варенья. — У нас его нет

Some (как прилагательное и как местоимение) употребляется:

■ в утвердительных высказываниях:

He bought some	Он купил немного
He bought some jam	Он купил немного варенья
He bought some apples	Он купил немного яблок

■ в вопросах, которые предполагают положительный ответ:

Can you lend me some money?	Ты можешь одолжить мне немного денег?

■ в предложениях и в просьбах:

Would you like some?	Хотите немного?
Could you buy some onions for me?	Купите мне, пожалуйста, немного лука

Any (как прилагательное и как местоимение) употребляется:

■ в высказываниях с отрицанием:

I haven't got any brothers or sisters	У меня нет ни братьев, ни сестёр

■ в вопросах:

Have you got any bananas?	У вас есть бананы?

Слова, производные от **some** и **any**, употребляются аналогичным образом:

I saw something really strange today	Сегодня я видел нечто очень странное
Did you meet anyone you know?	Ты видел каких-нибудь (своих) знакомых?
We didn't see anything interesting	Мы не видели ничего интересного

Глаголы

Инфинитив является основной формой глагола. Полная форма инфинитива включает частицу **to**:

to live (жить), **to die** (умереть) и т. д.

Список неправильных глаголов приводится на стр. 877.

Правильные глаголы спрягаются по следующему образцу:

инфинитив

want	**love (1)**	**stop (2)**	**prefer (3)**

настоящее время

wants	**loves**	**stops**	**prefers**

причастие настоящего времени/герундий

wanting	**loving**	**stopping**	**preferring**

простое прошедшее время/причастие прошедшего времени

wanted	**loved**	**stopped**	**preferred**

в таблице показаны следующие типы глаголов:

(1) инфинитив оканчивается на **-e**;

(2) односложный инфинитив оканчивается сочетанием *гласный + согласный*;

(3) инфинитив оканчивается сочетанием *ударный гласный + согласный*.

Герундий может употребляться как существительное:

I do not like dancing	Мне не нравится танцевать
Dancing is fun	Танцевать — весело

Времена

Настоящее время

to be (быть)	to have (иметь)
I am	I have
you are	you have
he/she/it is	he/she/it has
we are	we have
you are	you have
they are	they have

У остальных глаголов форма инфинитива и настоящего времени совпадает во всех лицах, за исключением 3 лица единственного числа, где к глаголу присоединяется окончание **-s**:

to want (хотеть)	I want, you want, he/she/it wants, we want, you want, they want
to love (любить)	I love, you love, he/she/it loves, we love, you love, they love

У глаголов, оканчивающихся в инфинитиве на **-s, -ss, -sh, -ch, -x, -zz**, в 3 лице единственного числа прибавляется окончание **-es**:

to watch (смотреть)	he/she/it watches
to kiss (целовать)	he/she/it kisses

Настоящее время выражает:

■ повторяющиеся действия, общепринятые истины, фактические утверждения:

He takes the 8 o'clock train to work	Он едет на работу 8-часовым поездом
The Earth rotates around the Sun	Земля вращается вокруг Солнца
I work in publishing	Я работаю в издательстве

■ вкусы и мнения:

I hate Mondays	Я ненавижу понедельник
He doesn't believe in God	Он не верит в Бога

■ чувственные восприятия:

The pie smells delicious	Пирог вкусно пахнет

Простое прошедшее время

Простое прошедшее время правильных глаголов образуется прибавлением окончания **-ed** к основе глагола:

I/you/he/she/it/we/you/they wanted

Неправильные глаголы имеют особые формы, которые следует заучивать. Таблица неправильных глаголов приводится на стр. 877.

Данное время служит для выражения законченных в прошлом действий или событий:

He flew to America last week   На прошлой неделе он улетел в Америку

Настоящее совершённое время

Данное время образуется при помощи вспомогательного глагола **to have** в форме настоящего времени и причастия прошедшего времени:

I/you have loved
he/she/it has loved
we/you/they have loved

Данное время служит для выражения действий, законченных в прошлом, но имеющих какую-либо связь с настоящим.

Разница между настоящим совершённым временем и простым прошедшим временем обнаруживается при сравнении следующих примеров:

Have you seen Peter this morning?   Ты видел Питера утром?
                                         (действие происходит утром)
Did you see Peter this morning?   Ты видел Питера сегодня утром?
                                         (действие происходит днём или вечером)

Прошедшее совершённое время

Данное время образуется при помощи вспомогательного глагола **to have** в форме прошедшего времени и причастия прошедшего времени:

I/you/he/she/it/we/you/they had wanted

Данное время служит для выражения действий, которые предшествовали другим действиям в прошлом:

She had already left home when I arrived   Когда я пришёл, она уже ушла из дома

Длительные времена

Данная группа времён образуется при помощи вспомогательного глагола **to be** и причастия настоящего времени.

Настоящее длительное время

I am singing   я пою
you are singing   ты поёшь
he is singing   он поёт
                      и т. д.

Настоящее длительное время описывает события, происходящие в момент речи, при этом любые действия рассматриваются, прежде всего, как процесс:

What are you doing? — I am trying to fix   Что ты делаешь? — Я пытаюсь починить
the television   телевизор
He always interrupts when I am reading   Он всегда мне мешает, когда я читаю
to the children   детям

Прошедшее длительное время

I was singing   я пел
you were singing ты пел
he was singing   он пел
                      и т. д.

Прошедшее длительное время описывает события, которые происходили одновременно с другими событиями в прошлом.

He rushed into my office while I was   Он ворвался в мой офис, когда я
talking to the director   разговаривал с директором

Настоящее совершённое и прошедшее совершённое могут употребляться в длительной форме: I have been writing (я писал), I had been writing (я писал), I will be writing (я буду писать).

Будущее время

В английском языке существует несколько способов выражения будущего времени:

■ вспомогательный глагол **will/shall** сочетается с инфинитивом.

Will употребляется для всех лиц в единственном и множественном числе.
Shall употребляется только в 1-м лице единственного и множественного числа:

I will/shall go	я пойду
we will/shall go	мы пойдём
you will go	ты пойдёшь
you will go	вы пойдёте
he/she/it will go	он/она/оно пойдёт
they will go	они пойдут

Will и отрицательные формы **will not** и **shall not** могут употребляться в сокращённой форме:

| You'll be angry | Ты будешь сердиться |
| We won't/shan't stay long | Мы останемся там ненадолго |

■ конструкция **going to**

Данная конструкция чаще всего употребляется для выражения намерения или предположения:

| I am going to go to London tomorrow | Завтра я еду в Лондон |
| The boss is going to be furious when he hears | Босс будет в ярости, когда услышит об этом |

Конструкцию **going to** в большинстве случаев можно заменить сочетанием с **will**:

| The boss will be furious when he hears | Босс будет в ярости, когда услышит об этом |
| I wonder whether the car is going to/will start | Интересно, машина заведётся? |

■ настоящее время в значении будущего

Настоящее время может употребляться в значении будущего, если событие должно произойти в определённый момент в будущем. Например, когда речь идет о событиях, предусмотренных расписанием или планом:

| When does term finish? | Когда заканчивается семестр? |
| The train for London leaves at 10 o'clock | Поезд на Лондон отходит в 10 часов |

■ настоящее длительное время

Подобно конструкции с **going to**, данное время может выражать намерение:

| I am spending Christmas in Paris | Рождество я проведу в Париже |
| Where are you going for your holidays? | Куда вы поедете в отпуск? |

Повелительное наклонение

Для выражения приказов и просьб употребляется основная форма глагола (инфинитив):

| Go home! | Иди домой! |
| Shut the door! | Закрой дверь! |

Отрицательная форма повелительного наклонения образуется при помощи вспомогательного глагола **do not** или, чаще, его сокращённой формы **don't**:

| Don't forget to phone Alan! | Не забудь позвонить Алану! |

Конструкция **let's** употребляется в 1-м лице множественного числа для выражения побуждений, предложений:

Let's go!	Давайте пойдём!/Идёмте!
Don't let's go!	Давайте не пойдём!
Let's not go!	Давайте не пойдём!

Вопросительная форма

Для образования настоящего и прошедшего времени данной формы используется вспомогательный глагол **do**, который согласуется с подлежащим в лице и числе:

Do you live here?	Ты здесь живёшь?
Did you live here?	Ты здесь жил?

Если предложение содержит вспомогательный глагол (**to have, to be**) или модальный глагол, то вопросительная форма образуется посредством изменения порядка слов, и сказуемое ставится перед подлежащим:

Are they going to get married?	Они собираются пожениться?
Have they seen us?	Они видели нас?
Can John come at eight?	Джон может прийти в восемь?

Если предложение содержит вопросительное местоимение, то вопросительные формы имеют следующий вид:

Who came?	Кто пришёл?
Who fed the cat?	Кто кормил кошку?
What have they done to you?	Что они с тобой сделали?
What shall we write about?	О чём мы будем писать?

В отрицательных предложениях частица **not**, если она употребляется в полной форме, ставится после подлежащего:

Did they not say they would come?/ **Didn't they say they would come?**	Разве они не сказали, что они придут?
Will the director not be there?/ **Won't the director be there?**	Разве директора там не будет?

В разговорной речи порядок слов в вопросительном предложении может быть таким же, как и в утвердительном, а сам вопрос обозначается повышением голоса (восходящей интонацией):

He told you to leave?	Он велел тебе уйти?
He left without saying a word?	Он ушёл, не сказав ни слова?

Присоединённые вопросы

В английском языке присоединёнными вопросами называются особые конструкции, употребляемые в конце предложения и побуждающие собеседника к подтверждению сказанного.

Положительное утверждение обычно сопровождается отрицательным присоединённым вопросом:

You smoke, don't you?	Ты куришь, не правда ли?/не так ли?

Вспомогательный глагол **don't** заменяет в присоединённом вопросе глагол smoke.

Отрицательное утверждение обычно сопровождается положительным присоединённым вопросом:

You don't smoke, do you?	Ты не куришь, не правда ли?

Если в (главном) предложении содержится вспомогательный или модальный глагол, то он повторяется и в присоединённом вопросе:

You aren't going, are you?	Ты не идёшь, не правда ли?
You will come, won't you?	Ты придёшь, не правда ли?
You shouldn't say that, should you?	Ты не должен так говорить, не правда ли?

Обратите внимание на форму глагола в присоединённом вопросе в случаях, когда в главном предложении употреблено сказуемое **am**:

I am lucky, aren't I?   Мне везёт, не правда ли?

Сказуемое в присоединённом вопросе употребляется в том же времени, что и сказуемое в главном предложении:

You wanted to go home, didn't you?   Ты хотел пойти домой, не правда ли?

Неполные предложения

Давая положительные или отрицательные ответы на вопросы, не обязательно повторять полную форму глагола. Достаточно употребить соответствующий вспомогательный глагол (**to be, to have, to do**) или модальный глагол, фигурирующий в вопросе:

Is it raining? — Yes, it is/No, it isn't   Дождь идёт? — Да, идёт/Нет, не идёт

Do you like fish? — Yes, I do/No, I don't   Ты любишь рыбу? — Да, люблю/Нет, не люблю

Can you drive? — Yes, I can/No, I can't   Ты умеешь водить машину? — Да, умею/Нет, не умею

Отрицательные предложения

Отрицательные предложения образуются при помощи вспомогательного глагола **do**, согласованного с подлежащим, и отрицательной частицы **not**. Сокращённые формы данной конструкции в настоящем времени выглядят следующим образом: **do + not = don't, does + not = doesn't, did + not = didn't**. Например:

They do not/don't understand English   Они не понимают по-английски

They did not/didn't go anywhere yesterday   Вчера они никуда не ходили

В эмфатических предложениях сказуемое употребляется в полной форме:

I do not approve!   Я (э)того не одобряю!

Модальные глаголы

can, could; may, might; shall, should; will, would; must; ought to

Модальные глаголы не изменяются по лицам и числам:

I can, you can, he can

Вопросительные формы образуются посредством изменения порядка слов, при этом сказуемое ставится перед подлежащим:

Can I go now?   Мне можно идти?

Модальные глаголы часто употребляются в сокращённой форме:

will и **shall** сокращаются до формы **'ll: I'll be going** (Я пойду)

would сокращается до формы **'d: I'd like a cup of tea** (Мне хочется чаю)

Отрицательная форма модальных глаголов образуется при помощи частицы **not** (**would not, might not** и т. д.). Отрицательная форма глагола **can — cannot** (в британском варианте английского языка пишется как одно слово).

Сокращённые формы отрицательных конструкций с модальными глаголами выглядят так: **can't, couldn't, mightn't, shan't, shouldn't, won't, wouldn't, mustn't, oughtn't.** (Форма **mayn't** малоупотребительна.)

can выражает:

- разрешение:

Can I leave the table, please?	Можно мне встать из-за стола?
I can have another sweet: daddy said so	Мне можно съесть ещё одну конфету: папа разрешил

- способность:

He can count to a hundred	Он умеет считать до ста
Can he drive?	Он умеет водить машину?

- возможность:

Accidents can happen	Неприятности случаются

- просьбу:

Can you help me, please?	Вы можете мне помочь?

could

Could является прошедшим временем **can**. В число его значений входят:

- разрешение, способность, возможность, просьба, относящиеся к прошлому:

Daddy said I could have another sweet	Папа сказал, что я могу съесть ещё одну конфету
By the time he was three, he could count to a hundred	К трём годам, он уже умел считать до ста
She asked if he could help her	Она спросила, может ли он ей помочь

- вежливые, официальные просьбы:

Could I leave a message, please?	Могу ли я оставить записку?

- возможность:

I don't know where John is; I suppose he could be at Anne's	Я не знаю, где Джон; возможно, (что) он у Анны

- возмущение:

You could have warned me!	Ты мог бы меня предупредить!

may

- разрешение и вежливая просьба:

May I use your phone, please?	Могу ли я воспользоваться вашим телефоном?
You may not leave the examination hall until I give the sign	Вы не можете покинуть экзаменационный зал, пока я не дам вам разрешения

- возможность:

We may get an extra day's holiday	У нас может быть дополнительный выходной (день)
They may have left	Возможно, (что) они уехали

might

- возможность:

Might, в отличие от **may**, предполагает, что указанная возможность маловероятна:

We might get a pay rise	Может быть нам повысят зарплату (= маловероятно, что это произойдёт)

Данная форма используется и в прошедшем времени:

He was afraid he might have arrived late	Он боялся, вдруг он опоздал

Might может также выражать:

- разрешение или вежливую просьбу:

Do you think I might have another whisky?	Вы позволите мне ещё одно виски?

- возмущение:

You might have phoned!	Мог бы и позвонить!

shall

Об употреблении **shall** в будущем времени см. стр. 910. **Shall** употребляется также для выражения:

- вопросов, которые предполагают получение совета или рекомендации:

Where shall we put the shopping?	Куда нам положить покупки?
What time shall I set the alarm for?	На какое время мне поставить будильник?

- предложения:

Shall I make you a cup of tea?	Сделать тебе чаю?
Shall we meet outside the station?	Давайте встретимся у вокзала

should

Should является прошедшим временем **shall**. Помимо этого **should** обозначает:

- правила и условности:

You shouldn't tell lies	Лгать нельзя
What do you think we should do?	Как, по-твоему, нам следует поступить?

- вероятность:

Once this job is finished, we should have more spare time	Когда мы закончим эту работу, у нас должно быть больше (свободного) времени
They should be here by now	Они должны были уже приехать
The key should be in that drawer	Ключ должен быть в этом ящике
That's where I left them	Я их там оставил

will

Об употреблении **will** в будущем времени см. стр. 910. Об употреблении **will** в условных предложениях см. стр. 916.

Кроме того, **will** выражает:

- свойства и внутренние характеристики:

Hot air will rise	Тёплый воздух поднимается
The stadium will seat 4,000 people	Стадион вмещает 4000 человек

- намерение, желание, одобрение:

Will you see to the post for me?	Вы займётесь почтой?
I'll do what I can to help him	Я помогу ему всем, чем могу

- предложение:

Will you have another slice of cake?	Не хотите ли ещё пирога?

- высокую степень вероятности:

There's someone at the door. That will be Anne	Кто-то стучит в дверь. Это должно быть Анна

- приказ:

You will go and wash your hands immediately	Немедленно/сейчас же идите и вымойте руки

would

Would является прошедшим временем **will**. Об употреблении **would** в условных предложениях см. стр. 916. Кроме того, **would** выражает:

- будущее прошедшее время:

| **He told me he would do it soon** | Он сказал мне, что сделает это скоро |
| **They said they wouldn't wait for me** | Они сказали мне, что не будут ждать меня |

- повторяющиеся действия в прошлом:

| **He would always get up at 6 a.m.** | Он всегда вставал в 6 утра |

must

- обязанность:

| **You must make sure you lock up** | Вы обязательно должны запереть дверь |
| **I must check whether my neighbour is all right** | Я должен проверить, всё ли в порядке у соседа |

Запомните, что **mustn't** выражает запрет:

| **You mustn't park there** | Там нельзя парковаться (= это запрещено) |

Если вы хотите сказать, что в совершении каких-либо действий нет необходимости, вы можете употребить конструкции **don't have to, needn't, don't need to**:

| **You don't have to eat that/You needn't eat that/You don't need to eat that** | Вам не надо это есть |

- возможность:

| **They must be there by now** | Они, наверное, уже там |
| **You must have been annoyed by the decision** | Должно быть, это решение рассердило вас |

ought

- обязанность:

| **You ought to be leaving** | Вам надо уходить |
| **They ought to kick him out** | Они должны выдворить его |

- вероятность, предположение:

| **They ought to be there by now** | Они должны быть уже там |
| **Two kilos of potatoes. That ought to be enough** | Два килограмма картофеля. Этого должно хватить |

Условные предложения с *if*

Существует три основных типа условных предложений с *if*:

if + настоящее время, главное предложение с **will** (для выражения реально осуществимых предположений):

If we hurry, we'll catch the train/We'll catch the train if we hurry
Если мы поторопимся, мы успеем на поезд

if + простое прошедшее, главное предложение с **would** (для выражения маловероятных предположений):

If I won the lottery, I would buy a new house/I would buy a new house if I won the lottery
Если бы я выиграл в лотерее, я бы купил новый дом

if + прошедшее совершённое, главное предложение с **would have** (для выражения невыполнимых предположений, относящихся к прошлому):

> **If Mike hadn't lost the tickets, we would have arrived on time/**
> **We would have arrived on time if Mike hadn't lost the tickets**
> Мы бы приехали вовремя, если бы Майк не потерял билеты

Глагольные сочетания

В английском языке многие глаголы образуют устойчивые сочетания с предлогами (т. н. фразовые глаголы), в которых присоединяемый предлог — аналогично глагольным приставкам в русском языке — меняет значение глагола:

to take (брать)

> **John took a book**   Джон взял книгу

to take off (**1.** снять **2.** взлететь)

> **He took off his boots/**   Он снял ботинки
> **He took his boots off**
>
> **The plane took off**   Самолёт взлетел

to take after (походить на, быть похожим на)

> **He takes after his mother**   Он походит/похож на свою мать

Обратите внимание на то, что дополнение может появляться в двух позициях: после предлога или между предлогом и глаголом (см. вышеприведённые примеры с глаголом **take off**).

Однако если в качестве дополнения выступает местоимение, то оно может стоять только между глаголом и предлогом:

> **He looked it up in the dictionary**   Он посмотрел это в словаре
> **They have put it off**   Они это отложили

Английские неправильные глаголы

Вариантные формы глаголов даются через запятую, например формы простого прошедшего времени глагола forbid: forbade, forbad.

* звёздочкой обозначаются вариантные формы, которые используются только в определённом значении (значениях) глагола, подробнее о них см. словарные статьи к соответствующим глаголам, например: *cost, costed.

Инфинитив	Простое прошедшее время	Причастие прошедшего времени	Инфинитив	Простое прошедшее время	Причастие прошедшего времени
arise	arose	arisen	come	came	come
awake	awoke	awoken	cost	*cost, costed	*cost, costed
be	was *sg.*, were *pl.*	been	creep	crept	crept
			cut	cut	cut
bear	bore	borne, born	deal	dealt	dealt
beat	beat	beaten	dig	dug	dug
become	became	become	dive	dived, (AmE) dove	dived, (AmE) dove
befall	befell	befallen			
beget	begot, (archaic) begat	begotten	do	did	done
			draw	drew	drawn
begin	began	begun	dream	dreamt, dreamed	dreamt, dreamed
behold	beheld	beheld			
bend	bent	bent	drink	drank	drunk
beseech	besought, beseeched	besought, beseeched	drive	drove	driven
			dwell	dwelled, dwelt	dwelled, dwelt
beset	beset	beset			
bet	bet, betted	bet, betted	eat	ate	eaten
bid	bid	bid	fall	fell	fallen
bind	bound	bound	feed	fed	fed
bite	bit	bitten	feel	felt	felt
bleed	bled	bled	fight	fought	fought
blow	blew	blown	find	found	found
break	broke	broken	flee	fled	fled
breed	bred	bred	fling	flung	flung
bring	brought	brought	floodlight	floodlit	floodlit
broadcast	broadcast	broadcast	fly	flew	flown
build	built	built	forbid	forbade, forbad	forbidden
burn	burnt, burned	burnt, burned	forecast	forecast, forecasted	forecast, forecasted
burst	burst	burst			
bust	bust, busted	bust, busted	for(e)go	for(e)went	for(e)gone
buy	bought	bought	foresee	foresaw	foreseen
cast	cast	cast	forget	forgot	forgotten, (AmE) forgot
catch	caught	caught			
choose	chose	chosen	forgive	forgave	forgiven
cling	clung	clung	forsake	forsook	forsaken
			freeze	froze	frozen

Инфинитив	Простое прошедшее время	Причастие прошедшего времени
get	got	got, (AmE) gotten
give	gave	given
go	went	gone
grind	ground	ground
grow	grew	grown
hang	*hung, hanged	*hung, hanged
have	had	had
hear	heard	heard
heave	heaved, (naut.) hove	heaved, (naut.) hove
hide	hid	hidden
hit	hit	hit
hold	held	held
hurt	hurt	hurt
inlay	inlaid	inlaid
keep	kept	kept
kneel	knelt, (esp. AmE) kneeled	knelt, (esp. AmE) kneeled
knit	knitted, knit	knitted, knit
know	knew	known
lay²	laid	laid
lead²	led	led
lean	leaned, (esp. BrE) leant	leaned, (esp. BrE) leant
leap	leapt, leaped	leapt, leaped
learn	learnt (esp. BrE), learned	learnt (esp. BrE), learned
leave	left	left
lend	lent	lent
let²	let	let
lie²	lay	lain
light¹	*lit, lighted	*lit, lighted
lose	lost	lost
make	made	made
mean	meant	meant
meet	met	met
mislay	mislaid	mislaid
mislead	misled	misled
mistake	mistook	mistaken
mow	mowed	mown, mowed
offset	offset	offset
OK	OK'd	OK'd
pay	paid	paid
prove	proved	proved, proven
put	put	put

Инфинитив	Простое прошедшее время	Причастие прошедшего времени
quit	quitted, quit	quitted, quit
read	read	read
rid	rid	rid
ride	rode	ridden
ring²	rang	rung
rise	rose	risen
run	ran	run
saw	sawed	sawn, sawed
say	said	said
see	saw	seen
seek	sought	sought
sell	sold	sold
send	sent	sent
set	set	set
sew	sewed	sewn, sewed
shake	shook	shaken
shave	shaved	*shaved, shaven
shear	sheared	shorn, sheared
shed	shed	shed
shine	*shone, shined	*shone, shined
shoe	shod	shod
shoot	shot	shot
show	showed	shown, showed
shrink	shrank	*shrunk, shrunken
shut	shut	shut
sing	sang	sung
sink	sank, sunk	*sunk, sunken
sit	sat	sat
slay	slew	slain
sleep	slept	slept
slide	slid	slid
sling	slung	slung
slink	slunk	slunk
slit	slit	slit
smell	smelt, smelled	smelt, smelled
sneak	sneaked, (AmE infml) snuck	sneaked, (AmE infml) snuck
sow	sowed	sown, sowed
speak	spoke	spoken
speed	*sped, speeded	*sped, speeded
spell	spelled, (esp. BrE) spelt	spelled, (esp. BrE) spelt
spend	spent	spent

Инфинитив	Простое прошедшее время	Причастие прошедшего времени	Инфинитив	Простое прошедшее время	Причастие прошедшего времени
spill	spilt, spilled	spilt, spilled	**swell**	swelled	swollen, swelled
spin	spun, span	spun	**swim**	swam	swum
spit²	spat, spit	spat, spit	**swing**	swung	swung
split	split	split	**take**	took	taken
spoil	spoiled, (esp. BrE) spoilt	spoiled, (esp. BrE) spoilt	**teach**	taught	taught
spread	spread	spread	**tear²**	tore	torn
spring²	sprang, (AmE) sprung	sprung	**tell**	told	told
stand	stood	stood	**think**	thought	thought
steal	stole	stolen	**throw**	threw	thrown
stick²	stuck	stuck	**thrust**	thrust	thrust
sting	stung	stung	**tread**	trod	trodden, trod
stink	stank, stunk	stunk			
strew	strewed	strewed, strewn	**understand**	understood	understood
stride	strode	stridden	**undo**	undid	undone
strike	struck	struck, (archaic) stricken	**unwind**	unwound	unwound
			upset²	upset	upset
string	strung	strung	**wake**	woke	woken
strive	strove, strived	striven, strived	**wear**	wore	worn
sublet	sublet	sublet	**weave**	wove	woven, wove
subpoena	subpoenaed, subpoena'd	subpoenaed, subpoena'd	**weep**	wept	wept
swear	swore	sworn	**wet**	wet, wetted	wet, wetted
sweat	sweated, (AmE) sweat	sweated, (AmE) sweat	**win²**	won	won
			wind²	wound	wound
sweep	swept	swept	**withdraw**	withdrew	withdrawn
			withhold	withheld	withheld
			withstand	withstood	withstood
			wring	wrung	wrung
			write	wrote	written

The Russian alphabet

Capital letters	Lower-case letters	Letter names	Capital letters	Lower-case letters	Letter names
А	а	а	Р	р	эр
Б	б	бэ	С	с	эс
В	в	вэ	Т	т	тэ
Г	г	гэ	У	у	у
Д	д	дэ	Ф	ф	эф
Е	е	е	Х	х	ха
Ё	ё	ё	Ц	ц	цэ
Ж	ж	жэ	Ч	ч	че
З	з	зэ	Ш	ш	ша
И	и	и	Щ	щ	ща
Й	й	и краткое	Ъ	ъ	твёрдый знак
К	к	ка	Ы	ы	ы
Л	л	эль	Ь	ь	мягкий знак
М	м	эм	Э	э	э
Н	н	эн	Ю	ю	ю
О	о	о	Я	я	я
П	п	пэ			

Английский алфавит

Прописные буквы	Строчные буквы	Названия букв	Прописные буквы	Строчные буквы	Названия букв
A	a	/eɪ/	N	n	/en/
B	b	/biː/	O	o	/əʊ/
C	c	/siː/	P	p	/piː/
D	d	/diː/	Q	q	/kjuː/
E	e	/iː/	R	r	/ɑː(r)/
F	f	/ef/	S	s	/es/
G	g	/dʒiː/	T	t	/tiː/
H	h	/eɪtʃ/	U	u	/juː/
I	i	/aɪ/	V	v	/viː/
J	j	/dʒeɪ/	W	w	/ˈdʌb(ə)ljuː/
K	k	/keɪ/	X	x	/eks/
L	l	/el/	Y	y	/waɪ/
M	m	/em/	Z	z	/zed/